Published in 1980 by the United
Nations Educational, Scientific
and Cultural Organization
7 place de Fontenoy, 75700 Paris
Photocomposition by
Computaprint Ltd. London.
Printed by Index Printers,
Dunstable.

Publié en 1980 par l'Organisation des
Nations Unies pour l'éducation,
la science et la culture,
7, place de Fontenoy, 75700 Paris
Photocomposition effectuée par
Computaprint Ltd. London.
Imprimé par Index Printers,
Dunstable.

Publicado en 1980 por la
Organización de las Naciones Unidas
para la Educación, la Ciencia
y la Cultura,
7, place de Fontenoy, 75700 Paris
Fotocomposición efectuada por
Computaprint Ltd. London
Impreso por Index Printers,
Dunstable.

unesco

statistical yearbook
annuaire statistique
anuario estadístico

1980

Reference tables
Education
Science and technology
Libraries
Book production
Newspapers and other periodicals
Cultural paper
Film and cinema
Radio broadcasting
Television

Cuadros de referencia
Educación
Ciencia y tecnología
Bibliotecas
Edición de libros
Periódicos y otras publicaciones periódicas
Papel cultural
Películas y cines
Radiodifusión sonora
Televisión

Tableaux de référence
Éducation
Science et technologie
Bibliothèques
Édition de livres
Journaux et autres périodiques
Papier culturel
Film et cinéma
Radiodiffusion sonore
Télévision

Contents

Table des matières

Indice

Culture and communication

Culture et communication

Cultura y comunicación

Introduction

This issue of the *Unesco Statistical Yearbook* has been prepared by the Office of Statistics with the co-operation of the National Commissions for Unesco and national statistical services, and with the help of the Statistical Office and the Population Division of the United Nations.

Each Member State is requested to report periodically to the Organization on its laws, regulations and statistics relating to its educational, scientific and cultural life and activities in accordance with Article VIII of the Constitution of Unesco. Data are gathered mainly from official replies to Unesco questionnaires and special surveys but also from official reports and publications, supplemented by information available to the Secretariat from other national and international sources. Where available data differ from the recommendations adopted or other concepts and definitions employed by Unesco, the statistical practice used in the country is followed, with a footnote where possible.

Some 200 countries and territories reply within the limits of their capabilities to Unesco questionnaires directly and the data they have kindly provided are incorporated in this *Yearbook*. The improvements in the tables and the additional information provided are referred to in the introduction to each subject chapter. The summary tables relating to culture and communication, previously given in the introduction to each of the corresponding chapters, have been grouped together and are now shown in chapter 6. As in the past the aim of the 1980 edition of the *Yearbook* has been to present figures for the latest year for which data are available; however by using the present *Yearbook* in combination with the earlier editions, a meaningful time series can be developed for most areas.

As in the previous edition the introductory texts to the tables are included with the relative chapters at the beginning of each subject and are presented in English, French and Spanish.

A number of other Unesco publications present statistical data. A list of these publications will be found at the end of this volume. All questions and comments, as well as any suggestions for further improvements in subsequent editions of the *Yearbook*, will be received gratefully by the Office of Statistics, Unesco, 7 Place de Fontenoy, 75700 Paris (France).

Explanatory note

The data presented in this publication relate in general to territorial units within *de facto* boundaries as at October 1979, depending in part on the availability of official statistics relating to such territories.

Table 1.1 on population is the most comprehensive in terms of geographic description; it constitutes the reference table of the *Yearbook* in respect of country nomenclature of geographic and administrative units. Changes in name, administration and status which occurred during 1978 and 1979 are given in the footnotes to Table 1.1.

The designations employed and the presentation of the material in this publication do not imply the expression of any opinion whatsoever on the part of the Unesco Secretariat concerning the legal status of any country or territory, or of its authorities, or concerning the delimitations of the frontiers of any country or territory.

The data which relate to the Federal Republic of Germany and the German Democratic Republic include the relevant data relating to Berlin for which separate data have not been supplied. This is without prejudice to any question of status which may be involved.

Beginning in 1975 the data shown for the Socialist Republic of Viet-Nam refer to the country as a whole. For the years preceding 1975 data are presented separately for North Viet-Nam (Democratic Republic of Viet-Nam) and South Viet-Nam (Republic of South Viet-Nam). Separate data for England and Wales, Northern Ireland and Scotland have been eliminated and data now shown refer to the United Kingdom.

The figures presented for the Byelorussian S.S.R. and the Ukrainian S.S.R. are already included with those of the U.S.S.R.

In some tables, the designation 'developed' and 'developing' countries is intended for statistical convenience and does not, necessarily, express a judgement about the stage reached by a particular country or area in the development process.

Data presented in this edition of the *Yearbook* which differ from the corresponding data for the same year given in earlier editions should be taken to reflect revisions made as a result of the receipt of further information.

Owing to the rounding of figures, the totals and sub-totals shown in the tables do not always correspond exactly to the sums of their component items. When data relating to a geographical unit are already included in the corresponding total, this is indicated by a footnote.

In order to simplify the graphic presentation of the tables and the explanatory notes referring to selected figures, a number of changes have been introduced in comparison with previous editions of the *Yearbook*. All footnote indicators are now shown against the name of the relevant countries or teritories, and are indicated by the symbol ‡ instead of by a number. The corresponding texts will be found at the end of each table; each note is composed of the name of the country or territory (in English), followed by the required explanation, for which the English text is preceded by the symbol E≫, the French text by FR≫, and the Spanish text by ESP≫. For a certain number of tables, there is also a general note which precedes the notes for individual countries; the reader's attention is drawn to these general notes for the explanatory material which they contain.

The following symbols are used:

— Magnitude nil

0 or 0.0 Magnitude less than half of unit employed

... Data not available

. Category not applicable

* Provisional or estimated data

./. Data included elsewhere with another category

≫ The figure immediately to the left of the arrow includes data relative to the columns where this symbol is indicated.

A break in the continuity of a time series is indicated by a vertical or horizontal line.

Introduction

Cette édition de l'*Annuaire statistique de l'Unesco* a été établie par l'Office des statistiques, avec la coopération des commissions nationales pour l'Unesco et des services nationaux de statistique, et avec le concours du Bureau de statistique et de la Division de la Population de l'Organisation des Nations Unies.

En vertu de l'article VIII de l'Acte constitutif de l'Unesco, chaque Etat membre est tenu d'adresser à l'Organisation un rapport périodique sur les lois, règlements et statistiques relatifs à sès institutions et à son activité dans les domaines de l'éducation, de la science et de la culture. Les données sont recueillies par le Secrétariat, principalement au moyen de questionnaires et d'enquêtes spéciales, mais aussi dans les publications et rapports officiels, le tout étant complété par des renseignements provenant d'autres sources nationales et internationales. Lorsque les données disponibles ne sont pas conformes aux recommandations adoptées ou aux autres concepts et définitions utilisés par l'Unesco, on a suivi la pratique adoptée par les pays, si possible avec une note explicative en bas de page.

Quelque 200 pays et territoires répondent dans la mesure de leurs possibilités aux questionnaires de l'Unesco, et les données qu'ils ont bien voulu fournir sont incorporées dans cet *Annuaire*. Les améliorations apportées à la présentation des tableaux, ainsi que les données supplémentaires qui y sont contenues, sont précisées dans l'introduction de chaque chapitre. Les tableaux récapitulatifs relatifs à la culture et la communication qui figuraient précédemment dans les textes d'introduction des chapitres correspondants, sont réunis à présent dans le chapitre 6. Comme par le passé, le but de l'édition de 1980 a été de présenter des chiffres concernant les dernières années pour lesquelles on dispose de statistiques. Toutefois, l'ensemble constitué par le présent *Annuaire* et les éditions précédentes offre aux utilisateurs une série chronologique valable pour la plupart des domaines.

Comme dans la précédente édition de l'*Annuaire*, les textes d'introduction aux différents chapitres et aux tableaux correspondants sont groupés au début de chaque chapitre et présentés successivement en anglais, en français et en espagnol.

Un certain nombre d'autres publications de l'Unesco contiennent également des renseignements statistiques; on en trouvera la liste à la fin de ce volume. Prière d'adresser toutes questions ou observations concernant le présent *Annuaire*, ainsi que toutes suggestions en vue d'améliorer les éditions ultérieures, à l'Office des statistiques de l'Unesco, 7, place de Fontenoy, 75700 Paris (France).

Notice explicative

Les données présentées dans cette publication se rapportent, en général, aux territoires tels qu'ils étaient délimités en octobre 1979 par les frontières de fait; elles proviennent en partie des statistiques officielles relatives à ces territoires.

Le tableau 1.1 (population) est le plus complet du point de vue géographique; il constitue le tableau de référence de l'*Annuaire* pour ce qui est de la nomenclature des pays, ainsi que des unités géographiques et administratives. Les changements survenus entre 1978 et 1979 en matière de noms, d'administration et de statut juridique sont indiqués en note dans le tableau 1.1.

Les désignations employées et la présentation adoptée dans cette publication ne sauraient être interprétées comme exprimant une prise de position du Secrétariat de l'Unesco sur le statut juridique ou le régime d'un pays ou d'un territoire quelconque, non plus que sur le tracé de ses frontières.

Les données relatives à la République fédérale d'Allemagne et à la République démocratique allemande incluent les données pertinentes relatives à Berlin, pour lequel des données séparées n'ont pas été fournies. Cela sans préjudice des questions de statut qui peuvent se poser à cet égard.

A partir de 1975, les données relatives à la République socialiste du Viêt-Nam se réfèrent à l'ensemble du pays. Pour les années antérieures à 1975, les données sont présentées séparément sous les noms de Nord Viêt-Nam (République démocratique du Viêt-Nam) et Sud Viêt-Nam (République du Sud Viêt-Nam). En ce qui concerne le Royaume-Uni, toutes les données sont actuellement présentées sous cette dénomination, les données séparées relatives à l'Angleterre et au pays de Galles, à l'Ecosse et à l'Irlande du Nord ayant été supprimées.

Les chiffres séparés présentés pour la R.S.S. de Biélorussie et la R.S.S. d'Ukraine sont déjà inclus dans l'U.R.S.S.

Dans quelques tableaux, la désignation pays 'développés' et 'en développement' est donnée pour des convenances statistiques et n'implique pas nécessairement un jugement sur le niveau atteint par tel pays ou région, en particulier dans leur processus de développement.

Lorsque les données présentées dans cette édition de l'*Annuaire* diffèrent des données correspondant à la même année qui figuraient dans les éditions précédentes, on doit considérer qu'il s'agit de chiffres révisés à la suite de nouveaux renseignements reçus.

Les chiffres et pourcentages ayant été arrondis, les totaux et les sous-totaux figurant dans les tableaux ne correspondent pas toujours exactement à la somme des éléments qui les composent. Lorsque les données qui font partie d'une unité géographique déterminée sont déjà comprises dans le total correspondant, le fait est signalé par une note.

Afin de simplifier la présentation des tableaux et des notes explicatives qui concernent certaines chiffres, on a procédé à quelques changements par rapport aux précédentes éditions de l'*Annuaire*. Tous les appels de notes suivent immédiatement le nom des pays ou territoires auxquels ils s'appliquent et sont indiqués par le symbole ‡, à la place d'un chiffre. On trouvera les textes correspondants à la fin de chaque tableau; chaque note est composée du nom du pays ou du territoire (en anglais), suivie de l'explication nécessaire. Le texte anglais est précédé du symbole E→,le texte français de FR→et le texte espagnol de ESP>Il y a aussi, pour un certain nombre de tableaux, une note générale précédant les notes spécifiques aux pays. Ces notes générales doivent particulièrement retenir l'attention du lecteur par les explications essentielles qu'elles contiennent.

Les symboles utilisés sont les suivants:

— Chiffre nul

0 ou 0.0 Chiffre inférieur à la moitié de l'unité employée

... Données non disponibles

. Catégorie sans objet

* Chiffre provisoire ou estimé

./. Données comprises dans une autre rubrique

→ Le chiffre immédiatement à gauche de la flèche comprend les données relatives aux colonnes où figure ce symbole.

Une discontinuité dans l'homogénéité des séries est indiquée par un trait vertical ou horizontal.

Introducción

La presente edición del *Anuario estadístico de la Unesco* ha sido preparada por la Oficina de Estadística, con la cooperación de las comisiones nacionales para la Unesco y de los servicios nacionales de estadística y con la ayuda de la Oficina de Estadística y de la División de Población de las Naciones Unidas.

En virtud del artículo VIII de la Constitución de la Unesco cada Estado Miembro debe someter a la Organización un informe periódico sobre las leyes, reglamentos y estadísticas relativos a sus instituciones y actividades educativas, científicas y culturales. Esos datos los reúne la Secretaría principalmente por medio de cuestionarios y de encuestas especiales, pero también utilizando las publicaciones e informes oficiales, completándose el todo mediante información procedente de otras fuentes nacionales e internacionales. Cuando los datos disponibles difieren de las recomendaciones aprobadas o de los demás conceptos y definiciones utilizados por la Unesco, se ha seguido el procedimiento adoptado en el país considerado, dando la explicación correspondiente, cuando ello es posible, en una nota al pie de página.

Unos 200 países y territorios han respondido en la medida de sus posibilidades a los cuestionarios de la Unesco y los datos que han tenido a bien facilitar se incorporan en este *Anuario*. Las mejoras introducidas en la presentación de los cuadros, así como los datos suplementarios contenidos en los mismos, se indican en la introducción de cada capítulo. Los cuadros recapitulativos relativos a la cultura y la comunicación que figuraban anteriormente en los textos de introducción de los capítulos correspondientes, aparecen ahora agrupados en el capítulo 6. Como en el pasado, la finalidad de la edición de 1980 es la de presentar cifras relativas a los últimos años sobre los cuales se dispone de estadísticas.

No obstante, el conjunto que constituye el presente *Anuario* y las ediciones precedentes ofrece a los usuarios una serie cronológica válida para la mayor parte de los campos de actividades de que se trata.

Como en la precedente edición del *Anuario*, los textos de introducción a los diferentes capítulos y a los cuadros correspondientes se agrupan al comienzo de cada capítulo y se presentan sucesivamente en inglés, francés y español.

Un cierto número de otras publicaciones de la Unesco contienen también información estadística. La lista de las mismas figura al final de este volumen. Se ruega que toda cuestión u observación relativa al presente *Anuario*, así como todas las sugerencias destinadas a mejorar las ediciones ulteriores, se dirijan a la Oficina de Estadística de la Unesco, 7, place de Fontenoy, 75700 Paris (Francia).

Nota explicativa

Los datos que figuran en la presente publicación se refieren, en general, a los territorios tal como estaban delimitados en octubre 1979 por sus fronteras de hecho, y proceden en parte de las estadísticas oficiales relativas a esos mismos territorios.

El cuadro 1.1 (Población) es el más completo desde el punto de vista geográfico. Constituye el cuadro de referencia del *Anuario* por lo que se refiere a la nomenclatura de los países, así como de las unidades geográficas y administrativas. Los cambios habidos entre 1978 y 1979 en materia de nombres, de administración y de estatuto jurídico se indican mediante nota en el cuadro 1.1.

Las designaciones empleadas y la presentación utilizada en esta publicación no deben interpretarse en el sentido de que expresen una opinión de la Secretaría de la Unesco sobre el estatuto jurídico o el régimen de un país o de un territorio cualquiera, como tampoco sobre el trazado de sus fronteras.

Los datos de la República Federal de Alemania y de la República Democrática Alemana comprenden los datos pertinentes relativos a Berlín, que no nos han sido procurados separadamente, lo que no prejuzga las cuestiones de estatuto que puenden plantearse al respecto.

A partir de 1975, los datos relativos a la República Socialista del Viet Nam se refieren al conjunto del país. Para los años anteriores a 1975 los datos se presentan separadamente bajo los nombres de Viet Nam del Norte (República Democrática del Viet Nam) y Viet Nam del Sur (República del Sud Viet Nam). En lo que se refiere al Reino Unido, todos los datos se presentan actualmente bajo esa denominación, habiéndose suprimido los datos separados relativos a Inglaterra y País de Gales, Escocia e Irlanda del Norte

Los datos separados que se presentan para la R.S.S. de Bielorrusia y la R.S.S. de Ucrania ya están incluidos en los de la U.R.S.S.

En algunos cuadros, la denominación países 'desarrollados' y 'en desarrollo' se da por conveniencias estadísticas, y no supone en ningún caso una toma de posición sobre el nivel alcanzado por tal o cual país o región en particular, en su proceso de desarrollo.

Cuando los datos presentados en esta edición del *Anuario* difieren de los datos correspondientes al mismo año que figuraban en las ediciones anteriores, debe considerarse que se trata de cifras revisadas de acuerdo con las nuevas informaciones recibidas.

Como las cifras y porcentajes se han redondeado, los totales y los sub-totales que figuran en los cuadros no siempre corresponden exactamente a la suma de los elementos que los componen. Cuando los datos relativos a una unidad geográfica determinada ya están incluidos en el total correspondiente, la indicación se da en una nota.

Con vistas a simplificar la presentación de los cuadros y de las notas explicativas relativas a ciertas cifras, se ha procedido a algunos cambios en relación con las anteriores ediciones del *Anuario*. Todas las llamadas de notas figuran al lado del país o territorio a que se refieren y se indican con el símbolo ‡, en lugar de una cifra. Los textos correspondientes aparecen al final de cada cuadro; las notas se componen del nombre del país o territorio (en inglés), seguido de la debida explicación. Los textos en inglés, francés y español están precedidos respectivamente de los símbolos E→, FR→ y ESP>. En un determinado número de cuadros figura igualmente una nota general, que precede las notas correspondientes a los países. Estas notas generales deben retener particularmente la atención del lector, dadas las explicaciones esenciales que contienen.

Los signos convencionales utilizados son los siguientes:

— Cifra nula

0 ó 0.0 Cifra inferior a la mitad de la unidad empleada

... Datos no disponibles

. Categoría sin objeto

* Cifra provisional o estimada

./. Datos comprendidos en otra rúbrica

→ La cifra situada inmediatamente a la izquierda de la flecha comprende los datos relativos a las columnas donde figura dicho símbolo.

Una interrupción en la homogeneidad de las series se indica mediante un trazo vertical u horizontal.

List of countries and territories

To facilitate the presentation of the tables in the body of the publication, the names of countries and territories and the different groupings of countries have been given in English only. For purposes of cross-reference, lists of the names of countries and territories, grouped according to continent and arranged in alphabetical order in English, French and Spanish are given in the following pages. The names of countries in French and Spanish are preceded by a numerical reference (in parentheses). The equivalent name in English can thus be read off opposite the number indicated.

Liste des pays et territoires

En vue de faciliter la présentation des tableaux, les noms des pays, des territoires et des différents groupes de pays ont été donnés en anglais seulement. Il sera néanmoins aisé de trouver l'équivalent anglais des noms en français et en espagnol en se servant de la liste ci-après, où les pays ont été classés séparément en anglais, français et espagnol et groupés, par continents, dans l'ordre alphabétique de chaque langue. Les noms des pays en espagnol et en français sont précédés d'un numéro entre parenthèses qui les renvoie à leur équivalent en anglais.

Lista de países y territorios

Con vistas a facilitar la presentación de los cuadros, los nombres de los países y territorios sólo se indican en inglés. Sin embargo, se podrá encontrar fácilmente el equivalente inglés de los nombres en español y en francés sirviéndose de la lista que figura a continuación, en la que los países se han clasificado separadamente en inglés, español y francés, agrupados por continentes, de acuerdo con el orden alfabético propio a cada lengua. Al lado de los nombres de los países en español y en francés figura un número entre paréntesis que corresponde al equivalente del orden alfabético inglés.

Africa

1 Algeria
2 Angola
3 Benin
4 Botswana
5 Burundi
6 Cape Verde
7 Central African Republic
8 Chad
9 Comoro
10 Congo
11 Djibouti
12 Egypt
13 Equatorial Guinea
14 Ethiopia
15 Gabon
16 Gambia
17 Ghana
18 Guinea
19 Guinea-Bissau
20 Ivory Coast
21 Kenya
22 Lesotho
23 Liberia
24 Libyan Arab Jamahiriya
25 Madagascar
26 Malawi
27 Mali
28 Mauritania
29 Mauritius
30 Morocco
31 Mozambique
32 Namibia
33 Niger
34 Nigeria
35 Reunion
36 Rwanda
37 St Helena
38 Sao Tome and Principe
39 Senegal
40 Seychelles
41 Sierra Leone
42 Somalia
43 South Africa
44 Sudan
45 Swaziland
46 Togo
47 Tunisia
48 Uganda

Afrique

(43) Afrique du Sud
(1) Algérie
(2) Angola
(3) Bénin
(4) Botswana
(5) Burundi
(6) Cap-Vert
(7) République centrafricaine
(9) Comores
(10) Congo
(20) Côte-d'Ivoire
(11) Djibouti
(12) Égypte
(14) Éthiopie
(15) Gabon
(16) Gambie
(17) Ghana
(18) Guinée
(19) Guinée-Bissau
(13) Guinée equatoriale
(51) Haute-Volta
(24) Jamahiriya arabe libyenne
(21) Kenya
(22) Lesotho
(23) Liberia
(25) Madagascar
(26) Malawi
(27) Mali
(30) Maroc
(29) Maurice
(28) Mauritanie
(31) Mozambique
(32) Namibie
(33) Niger
(34) Nigéria
(48) Ouganda
(49) République unie du Cameroun
(35) Reunion
(36) Rwanda
(52) Sahara occidental
(37) Sainte-Hélène
(38) Sao Tome et Principe
(39) Sénégal
(40) Seychelles
(41) Sierra Leone

África

(51) Alto Volta
(2) Angola
(1) Argelia
(3) Benin
(4) Botswana
(5) Burundi
(6) Cabo Verde
(49) República Unida de Camerún
(7) República Centroafricana
(9) Comores
(10) Congo
(20) Costa de Marfil
(8) Chad
(12) Egipto
(14) Etiopía
(15) Gabón
(16) Gambia
(17) Ghana
(18) Guinea
(19) Guinea-Bissau
(13) Guinea Ecuatorial
(24) Jamahiriya Arabe Libia
(21) Kenia
(22) Lesotho
(23) Liberia
(25) Madagascar
(26) Malawi
(27) Malí
(30) Marruecos
(29) Mauricio
(28) Mauritania
(31) Mozambique
(32) Namibia
(33) Níger
(34) Nigeria
(35) Reunión
(36) Rwanda
(52) Sahara Occidental
(37) Santa Elena
(38) Santo Tomé y Principe
(39) Senegal
(40) Seychelles
(41) Sierra Leona
(42) Somalia
(43) Sudáfrica
(44) Sudán
(45) Swazilandia

49 United Republic of Cameroon	(42) Somalie	(50) República Unida de Tanzania
50 United Republic of Tanzania	(44) Soudan	(46) Togo
51 Upper Volta	(45) Swaziland	(47) Túnez
52 Western Sahara	(50) Republique—Unie de Tanzanie	(48) Uganda
53 Zaire	(8) Tchad	(11) Yibuti
54 Zambia	(46) Togo	(53) Zaire
55 Zimbabwe	(47) Tunisie	(54) Zambia
	(53) Zaïre	(55) Zimbabwe
	(54) Zambie	
	(55) Zimbabwe	

North America	Amerique du Nord	América del Norte
56 Antigua	(56) Antigua	(56) Antigua
57 Bahama	(79) Antilles néerlandaises	(79) Antillas Neerlandesas
58 Barbados	(57) Bahamas	(57) Bahamas
59 Belize	(58) Barbade	(58) Barbados
60 Bermuda	(59) Belize	(59) Belize
61 British Virgin Islands	(60) Bermudes	(60) Bermudas
62 Canada	(63) Iles Caimanes	(62) Canadá
63 Cayman Islands	(62) Canada	(63) Islas Caiman
64 Costa Rica	(64) Costa Rica	(64) Costa Rica
65 Cuba	(65) Cuba	(65) Cuba
66 Dominica	(67) République dominicaine	(66) Dominica
67 Dominican Republic	(66) Dominique	(67) República Dominicana
68 El Salvador	(68) El Salvador	(68) El Salvador
69 Greenland	(90) États—Unis d'Amérique	(90) Estados Unidos de América
70 Grenada	(70) Grenade	(70) Granada
71 Guadeloupe	(69) Groenland	(69) Groenlandia
72 Guatemala	(71) Guadeloupe	(71) Guadalupe
73 Haiti	(72) Guatemala	(72) Guatemala
74 Honduras	(73) Haïti	(73) Haití
75 Jamaica	(74) Honduras	(74) Honduras
76 Martinique	(75) Jamaïque	(75) Jamaica
77 Mexico	(76) Martinique	(76) Martinica
78 Montserrat	(77) Mexique	(77) México
79 Netherlands Antilles	(78) Montserrat	(78) Montserrat
80 Nicaragua	(80) Nicaragua	(80) Nicaragua
81 Panama	(81) Panama	(81) Panamá
82 Former Canal Zone	(82) Ancienne Zone du Canal	(82) Antigua Zona del Canal
83 Puerto Rico	(83) Porto Rico	(83) Puerto Rico
84 St Kitts—Nevis and Anguilla	(84) Saint—Christophe—Nevis et Anguilla	(84) San Cristóbal—Nieves—Anguila
85 St Lucia	(85) Sainte—Lucie	(85) Santa Lucía
86 St Pierre and Miquelon	(86) Saint—Pierre—et—Miquelon	(86) San Pedro y Miquelón
87 St Vincent and the Grenadines	(87) Saint—Vincent—et—Grenadines	(87) San Vicente y Granadinas
88 Trinidad and Tobago	(88) Trinite—et—Tobago	(88) Trinidad y Tabago
89 Turks and Caicos Islands	(89) Iles Turques et Caiques	(89) Islas Turcas y Caicos
90 United States of America	(61) Iles Vierges britanniques	(61) Islas Vírgenes Británicas
91 United States Virgin Islands	(91) Iles Vierges des États—Unis	(91) Islas Vírgenes de Estados Unidos

South America	Amérique du Sud	América del Sur
92 Argentina	(92) Argentine	(92) Argentina
93 Bolivia	(93) Bolivie	(93) Bolivia
94 Brazil	(94) Bresil	(94) Brasil
95 Chile	(95) Chili	(96) Colombia
96 Colombia	(96) Colombie	(95) Chile
97 Ecuador	(97) Équateur	(97) Ecuador
98 Falkland Islands (Malvinas)	(98) Iles Falkland (Malvinas)	(98) Islas Falkland (Malvinas)
99 French Guiana	(100) Guyane	(100) Guyana
100 Guyana	(99) Guyane francaise	(99) Guyana Francesa
101 Paraguay	(101) Paraguay	(101) Paraguay
102 Peru	(102) Pérou	(102) Peru
103 Suriname	(103) Suriname	(103) Suriname
104 Uruguay	(104) Uruguay	(104) Uruguay
105 Venezuela	(105) Venezuela	(105) Venezuela

Asia

106 Afghanistan
107 Bahrain
108 Bangladesh
109 Bhutan
110 Brunei
111 Burma
112 China
113 Cyprus
114 Democratic Kampuchea
115 East Timor
116 Hong Kong
117 India
118 Indonesia
119 Iran
120 Iraq
121 Israel
122 Japan
123 Jordan
124 Korea, Democratic People's
   Republic of
125 Korea, Republic of
126 Kuwait
127 Lao People's Democratic
   Republic
128 Lebanon
129 Macau
130 Malaysia
131 Peninsular Malaysia
132 Sabah
133 Sarawak
134 Maldives
135 Mongolia
136 Nepal
137 Oman
138 Pakistan
139 Philippines
140 Qatar
141 Saudi Arabia
142 Singapore
143 Sri Lanka
144 Syrian Arab Republic
145 Thailand
146 Turkey
147 United Arab Emirates
148 Viet Nam
149 Yemen
150 Yemen, Democratic

Europe

151 Albania
152 Andorra
153 Austria
154 Belgium
155 Bulgaria
156 Czechoslovakia
157 Denmark
158 Faeroe Islands
159 Finland
160 France
161 German Democratic
   Republic
162 Germany, Federal
   Republic of
163 Gibraltar
164 Greece
165 Holy See
166 Hungary
167 Iceland
168 Ireland
169 Italy

Asie

(106) Afghanistan
(141) Arabie saoudite
(107) Bahrein
(108) Bangladesh
(109) Bhoutan
(111) Birmanie
(110) Brunéi
(112) Chine
(113) Chypre
(125) République de Corée
(147) Emirats arabes unis
(116) Hong-kong
(117) Inde
(118) Indonesie
(120) Irak
(119) Iran
(121) Israël
(122) Japon
(123) Jordanie
(114) Kampuchéa démocratique
(126) Koweït
(127) République populaire
   démocratique lao
(128) Liban
(129) Macao
(130) Malaisie
(131) Malaisie peninsulaire
(132) Sabah
(133) Sarawak
(134) Maldives
(135) Mongolie
(136) Nepal
(137) Oman
(138) Pakistan
(139) Philippines
(140) Qatar
(124) République populaire
   démocratique de Coree
(142) Singapour
(143) Sri Lanka
(144) République arabe
   syrienne
(145) Thaïlande
(115) Timor oriental
(146) Turquie
(148) Viet-nam
(149) Yemen
(150) Yemen democratique

Europe

(151) Albanie
(162) République fédérale
   d'Allemagne
(152) Andorre
(153) Autriche
(154) Belgique
(155) Bulgarie
(157) Danemark
(180) Espagne
(158) Iles Feroé
(159) Finlande
(160) France
(163) Gibraltar
(164) Grèce
(166) Hongrie
(168) Irlande
(167) Islande
(169) Italie
(170) Liechtenstein
(171) Luxembourg
(172) Malte

Asia

(106) Afganistán
(141) Arabia Saudita
(107) Bahrein
(108) Bangladesh
(111) Birmania
(110) Brunei
(109) Bután
(125) República de Corea
(124) República Popular
   Democratica
   de Corea
(112) China
(113) Chipre
(147) Emiratos Árabes Unidos
(139) Filipinas
(116) Hong-Kong
(117) India
(118) Indonesia
(119) Irán
(120) Irak
(121) Israel
(122) Japón
(123) Jordania
(114) Kampuchea Democratica
(126) Kuweit
(127) República Popular
   Democratica Lao
(128) Líbano
(129) Macao
(130) Malasia
(131) Malasia peninsular
(132) Sabah
(133) Sarawak
(134) Maldivas
(135) Mongolia
(136) Nepal
(137) Oman
(138) Paquistán
(140) Qatar
(142) Singapur
(144) República Árabe Siria
(143) Sri Lanka
(145) Tailandia
(115) Timor Oriental
(146) Turquia
(148) Viet Nam
(149) Yemen
(150) Yemen Democratico

Europa

(151) Albania
(162) República Federal de
   Alemania
(152) Andorra
(153) Austria
(154) Bélgica
(155) Bulgaria
(156) Checoslovaquia
(157) Dinamarca
(180) España
(158) Islas Feroé
(159) Finlandia
(160) Francia
(163) Gibraltar
(164) Grecia
(166) Hungria
(168) Irlanda
(167) Islandia
(169) Italia
(170) Liechtenstein
(171) Luxemburgo

170 Liechtenstein	(173) Monaco	(172) Malta
171 Luxembourg	(175) Norvège	(173) Mónaco
172 Malta	(174) Pays-Bas	(175) Noruega
173 Monaco	(176) Pologne	(174) Países Bajos
174 Netherlands	(177) Portugal	(176) Polonia
175 Norway	(161) République démocratique allemande	(177) Portugal
176 Poland		(183) Reino Unido
177 Portugal	(178) Roumanie	(161) República Democrática Alemana
178 Romania	(183) Royaume-Uni	
179 San Marino	(179) Saint-Marin	(178) Rumania
180 Spain	(165) Saint-Siege	(179) San Marino
181 Sweden	(181) Suède	(165) Santa Sede
182 Switzerland	(182) Suisse	(181) Suecia
183 United Kingdom	(156) Tchécoslovaquie	(182) Suiza
184 Yugoslavia	(184) Yougoslavie	(184) Yugoslavia

Oceania	Océanie	Oceanía
185 American Samoa	(186) Australie	(186) Australia
186 Australia	(187) Iles Cook	(187) Islas Cook
187 Cook Islands	(188) Fidji	(190) Guam
188 Fiji	(190) Guam	(191) Kiribati
189 French Polynesia	(191) Kiribati	(192) Nauru
190 Guam	(192) Nauru	(196) Niue
191 Kiribati	(196) Nioue	(197) Isla Norfolk
192 Nauru	(197) Ile Norfolk	(193) Nueva Caledonia
193 New Caledonia	(193) Nouvelle-Caledonie	(194) Nuevas Hébridas
194 New Hebrides	(195) Nouvelle-Zélande	(195) Nueva Zelandia
195 New Zealand	(194) Nouvelles-Hébrides	(198) Islas del Pacífico
196 Niue	(198) Iles du Pacifique	(199) Papua Nueva Guinea
197 Norfolk Island	(199) Papouasie - Nouvelle-Guinée	(189) Polinesia Francesa
198 Pacific Islands		(201) Islas Salomón
199 Papua New Guinea	(189) Polynésie française	(200) Samoa
200 Samoa	(201) Iles Salomon	(185) Samoa Americanas
201 Solomon Islands	(200) Samoa	(202) Islas Tokelau
202 Tokelau Islands	(185) Samoa americaines	(203) Tonga
203 Tonga	(202) Iles Tokelaou	(188) Viti
	(203) Tonga	

U.S.S.R.	URSS	URSS
204 U.S.S.R.	(204) URSS	(204) URSS
205 Byelorussian S.S.R.	(205) RSS de Biélorussie	(205) RSS de Bielorrusia
206 Ukrainian S.S.R.	(206) RSS d'Ukraine	(206) RSS de Ucrania

Continents, major areas and groups of countries	Continents, grandes régions et groupes de pays	Continentes, grandes regiones y grupos de países
World	Monde	Mundo
Africa	Afrique	África
America	Amérique	América
Asia	Asie	Asia
Europe	Europe	Europa
Oceania	Océanie	Oceania
U.S.S.R.	URSS	URSS
Developed countries	Pays développes	Países desarrollados
Developing countries	Pays en développement	Países en desarrollo
Africa (without Arab States)	Afrique (sans les Etats arabes)	África (sin los Estados árabes)
Northern America	Amérique septentrionale	América septentrional
Latin America	Amerique latine	América Latina
Asia (without Arab States)	Asie (sans les Etats arabes)	Asia (sin los Estados árabes)
Arab States	Etats arabes	Estados árabes

Reference tables 1
Tableaux de référence
Cuadros de referencia

1 Reference tables

Tableaux de référence

Cuadros de referencia

The first part of the *Yearbook* consists of two tables on population, one on illiteracy and one on educational attainment. They provide reference material for all the other tables presented in the *Yearbook* which are concerned with educational institutions, science, culture and mass media.

The size and density of a country's population directly affect the development of its educational institutions and facilities. The age structure of the population, particularly the younger age groups, in part determines a country's educational policy and forms the basis of national educational planning. Estimates of the population aged 5-24, in suitably combined age groups, are necessary for evaluating the progress of school enrolment.

Data on illiteracy and educational attainment provide an educational profile of the adult population which can serve as a complement to statistics on school and university enrolments.

TABLE 1.1

Table 1.1 contains data on total population, area and density for the world, for each continent, and for 206 countries and territories. It is the most comprehensive table in the *Yearbook* in the sense that practically all countries and territories of the world are included. The population data given are official mid-year estimates for the years 1970, 1975, 1976, 1977 and 1978. Area figures, unless otherwise noted, include inland waters. Population density figures (inhabitants per square kilometre) are not given for areas of less than 1,000 square kilometres. Readers interested in more detailed information on area, population and age structure are referred to the various editions of the *Demographic Yearbook* and the *Statistical Yearbook* of the United Nations.

In most cases the figures presented in this table are mid-year estimates published by the United Nations in their *Demographic Yearbook, Population and Vital Statistics Report* or *Monthly Bulletin of Statistics*. For detailed explanations of the source of these estimates, etc., please refer to Tables 1, 3 and 5 of the *United Nations Demographic Yearbook 1977* and the other publications mentioned.

TABLE 1.2

Table 1.2 presents estimates and projections of the total population and the population below age 25, for the world, by continents, major areas and groups of countries, for the years 1970, 1975, 1980, 1985, 1990 and 2000. Separate estimates are given for age-groups 0-4, 5-9, 10-14, 15-19 and 20-24 years, covering the ages of most relevance for education. The source of the data in Table 1.2 is the Population Division of the United Nations. The figures presented in this table correspond to the medium variant of the projections which were prepared by the United Nations Population Division in 1978.

The table is broken down into the six major areas of the world, and then into various other groupings which are described, where necessary, in footnote 1 at the end of the table.

Figure 1 shows the differences of population growth by each continent. Over the thirty years from 1970 to 2000, Europe's population will rise by only 13.2% and that of Northern America by 27.9%, whereas Latin America will rise by 115.1%, Africa by 134.0% and Asia by 72.7%. The population of Asia will continue to constitute over half the world's total during these thirty years.

Figure 2 shows graphically the world population pyramid for the period 1970-2000. The steps of the pyramid represent a continuing increase in live births for each five-year period. When the world total is analysed by major areas, the developing countries, and the Arab States in particular show the highest rates of increase.

TABLE 1.3

Table 1.3 presents data on the illiterate population and percentage illiteracy, based on censuses or surveys. The data are broken down by sex and wherever possible refer to the population aged fifteen years and over. A break-down by urban and rural areas is also shown wherever the data are available.

The purpose of this table is to present the most recent data on illiteracy received by the Unesco Office of Statistics. Readers interested in data for other years or for different age-groups are referred to the 1977 Unesco publication *Statistics of Educational Attainment and Illiteracy*.

Ability to both read and write is used as the criterion of literacy; hence all semi-literates - persons who can read but not write - are included with illiterates. Persons unspecified for literacy are excluded from calculations; hence the percentage of illiteracy for a given country is based on the number of reported illiterates, divided by the total number of reported literates and illiterates. (The same result is obtained by distributing the number of unspecified cases proportionately between the literates and illiterates).

TABLE 1.4

Table 1.4 shows the percentage distribution of the highest level of educational attainment of the adult population by sex, and wherever possible, by urban and rural areas. The data are derived from national censuses or sample surveys and were provided by the United Nations Statistical Office or were derived from regional or national publications. The purpose of this table is to present the most recent data on educational attainment received by the Unesco Office of Statistics for each country and territory. Readers interested in data for earlier years or in breakdowns by age are referred to the 1977 Unesco publication *Statistics of Educational Attainment and Illiteracy*.

The six levels of educational attainment, ranging from no schooling to post-secondary, are defined as follows:

No schooling. This term applies to those who have completed less than one year of schooling.

Incompleted first level. Since the duration of primary education may vary

1 Reference tables
Tableaux de référence
Cuadros de referencia

from four to eight years depending on the country, this category includes all those who completed at least one year of primary education but who did not complete the last year at the primary level. The structure in years of all countries' primary and secondary education can be found in Table 3.1.

Completed first level. Those who completed the final year of primary education but did not go on to secondary school are included in this group. In some cases (as indicated by a footnote) the data for the two final years of the primary level were combined, so that some individuals who reached only the penultimate year of study were counted in this group.

Entered second level, first cycle. This group comprises those whose level of educational attainment was limited to the lower stage of secondary school as defined in Table 3.1.

Entered second level, second cycle. This group consists of those who moved to the higher stage of secondary education from the lower stage, but did not proceed to post-secondary studies.

Post-secondary level. Anyone who undertook post-secondary studies, whether or not they completed the full course, would be counted in this group.

The number of people whose level of education was not stated has been subtracted from the total population. (Where the unknown category constituted more than 5 per cent of the population aged 25 or more, the actual numbers for each age group have been presented in the footnotes).

The proportion of the 15-24 age group with some post-secondary education is frequently less than that of the 25-34 age group, because a sizeable proportion of the 15-24 age group is too young to have reached the post-secondary entrance level. For this reason the total adult age range is taken as 25+ and not 15+ for the purposes of this table.

La première partie de l'*Annuaire statistique* se compose de deux tableaux sur la population, d'un sur l'analphabétisme et d'un autre sur le niveau d'instruction. Ces tableaux fournissent des données de référence pour tous les autres tableaux qui portent sur les établissements d'enseignement, la science, la culture et les moyens d'information.

Le nombre et la densité des habitants d'un pays influent directement sur le développement de ses établissements et de ses moyens d'enseignement. La structure par âge de la population, surtout en ce qui concerne les jeunes, détermine en partie la politique adoptée en matière d'enseignement et sert de base à la planification nationale de l'éducation. Pour prévoir la progression des effectifs scolaires, il faut disposer d'estimations de la population âgée de 5 à 24 ans, classée par groupes d'âge de façon appropriée.

Les données concernant l'analphabétisme et le niveau d'instruction présentent un profil éducatif de la population adulte et peuvent servir comme un complément aux statistiques sur les effectifs scolaires et universitaires.

TABLEAU 1.1

Le tableau 1.1 contient des données sur la population totale, la supercifie et la densité de peuplement de l'ensemble du monde, de chaque continent et de 206 pays et territoires. C'est le tableau le plus complet de l'*Annuaire*, en ce sens que presque tous les pays et territoires du monde y sont presque tous les pays et territoires du monde y figurent. Les chiffres relatifs à la population sont fondés sur les estimations officielles faites au milieu de l'année indiquée pour les années 1970, 1975, 1976, 1977 et 1978. Sauf indication contraire, les chiffres relatifs à la supercifie comprennent les eaux intérieures. La densité de la population (nombre d'habitants au kilomètre carré) n'est pas indiquée lorsque la superficie est inférieure à 1.000 km2. Les lecteurs désireux d'avoir des renseignements plus détaillés sur la superficie, la population et la structure par âge sont priés de se reporter aux diverses éditions de l'*Annuaire statistique* et de l'*Annuaire démographique* de l'Organisation des Nations Unies.

Les chiffres présentés dans ce tableau sont, en général, des 'estimations au milieu de l'année' publiées par l'Organisation des Nations Unies dans son *Annuaire démographique*, dans son périodique '*Population and Vital Statistics Report*' ou dans son *Bulletin Mensuel de Statistique*. Pour plus de détails sur l'origine de ces estimations, prière de se reporter aux tableaux 1, 3 et 5 de l'*Annuaire démographique de l'Organisation des Nations Unies 1977*, et aux autres publications indiquées.

TABLEAU 1.2

Dans le tableau 1.2 figurent les estimations et les projections pour les années 1970, 1975, 1980, 1985, 1990, et 2000 de la population totale et de la population de moins de 25 ans pour le monde entier, par continents, par grandes régions et par groupes de pays. Des estimations sont données séparément pour les groupes d'âge 0-4, 5-9, 10-14, 15-19 et 20-24 ans, qui sont ceux qui présentent le plus d'intérêt du point de vue de l'éducation.

Toutes ces données ont été préparées par la Division de la population de l'Organisation des Nations Unies en 1978. Elles correspondent à la variante moyenne des projections.

Le tableau présente les six grandes régions du monde, divisées elles-mêmes en divers autres groupes dont la composition, si nécessaire, est indiquée dans la note 1 qui figure au bas de ce tableau.

La figure 1 montre les différences d'accroissement de la population entre les continents. Au cours des trente années qui s'étendent de 1970 à 2000, la population européenne n'augmentera que de 13.2% et celle de l'Amérique septentrionale de 27.9%, alors que celle de l'Amérique latine augmentera de 115.1%, celle de l'Afrique de 134.0% et celle de l'Asie de 72.7%. Pendant ces trente années la population de l'Asie continuera de représenter plus de la moitié de la population mondiale.

La figure 2 représente la pyramide de la population mondiale pour la période 1970-2000. Les échelons de la pyramide correspondent à un accroissement continu des naissances vivantes pour chaque période de cinq années. Quand le total mondial est analysé par grandes régions, on constate que ce sont les pays en voie de développement, et en particulier les Etats arabes, qui ont le taux d'accroissement le plus élevé.

TABLEAU 1.3

Le tableau 1.3 présente des données sur la population analphabète et le pourcentage d'analphabètes, d'après des recensements ou enquêtes. Les données sont indiquées séparément par sexe et elles se rapportent, dans toute la mesure du possible, à la population de 15 ans et plus. Une répartition par zones urbaine et rurale est également présentée lorsque les données sont disponibles.

Le but de ce tableau est de présenter les données les plus récentes sur l'analphabétisme reçues à l'Office des Statistiques de l'Unesco.

Les lecteurs qui voudraient prendre connaissance des données relatives à d'autres années ou aux différents groupes d'âge doivent consulter la publication de l'Unesco *Statistiques sur le niveau d'instruction et l'analphabétisme*, parue en 1977.

Le critère d'alphabétisme est l'aptitude à lire et à écrire. Il s'ensuit que tous les semi-alphabètes —c'est-à-dire les personnes sachant lire mais non écrire— figurent parmi les analphabètes. Dans les calculs on n'a pas tenu compte des personnes pour lesquelles il n'est pas spécifié si elles sont alphabètes ou non. On a donc calculé le pourcentage d'analphabètes pour un pays donné en divisant le nombre des analphabètes connus par le total des alphabètes et analphabètes connus. (On arrive au même résultat en répartissant proportionnellement, entre la catégorie des alphabètes et celle des analphabètes, le nombre de personnes pour lesquelles il n'est pas spécifié si elles sont alphabètes ou non).

TABLEAU 1.4

Le tableau 1.4 présente la répartition en pourcentage de la population adulte d'après le plus haut degré d'instruction atteint, par sexe et, dans la mesure du possible, par zones urbaine et rurale. Les données sont tirées des recensements nationaux et des enquêtes par sondage, dont les résultats nous on été communiqués par l'Office des statistiques de l'Organisation des Nations Unies, ainsi que des publications régionales ou nationales.

Le but de ce tableau est de présenter les données les plus récentes sur le niveau d'instruction reçues à l'Office des Statistiques de l'Unesco pour chaque pays ou territoire. Les lecteurs qui voudraient prendre connaissance de la répartition par âge ou des données relatives aux années précédentes doivent consulter la publication de l'Unesco *Statistiques sur le niveau d'instruction et l'analphabétisme*.

Les six niveaux d'instruction présentés, qui s'étendent du groupe de personnes n'ayant reçu aucune éducation scolaire à celui des personnes ayant atteint le niveau postsecondaire, sont définis comme suit:

Personnes n'ayant reçu aucune éducation scolaire. Il s'agit des personnes qui ont fait moins d'une année de scolarité.

Personnes n'ayant pas terminé l'enseignement du premier degré. Etant donné que la durée de l'enseignement primaire peut varier selon les pays entre quatre et huit années, cette catégorie comprend toutes les personnes qui ont fait au moins une année d'enseignement primaire, mais qui n'ont pas terminé la dernière année de ce niveau. La structure en années d'études de l'enseignement du premier et du second degré figure pour tous les pays dans le tableau 3.1.

Personnes ayant terminé l'enseignement du premier degré. Comprend les personnes qui ont terminé la dernière année de l'enseignement primaire,

Reference tables 1
Tableaux de référence
Cuadros de referencia

mais qui n'ont pas accédé à l'enseignement secondaire. Dans quelques cas (indiqués par une note), les données correspondant aux deux dernières années de l'enseignement primaire ont été réunies, de sorte que les personnes n'ayant terminé que l'avant-dernière année sont comptées aussi dans ce groupe.

Personnes ayant accédé à l'enseignement du second degré, premier cycle. Ce groupe comprend toutes les personnes dont les études n'ont pas été au-delà du premier cycle de l'enseignement secondaire, tel qu'il est défini dans le tableau 3.1.

Personnes ayant accédé à l'enseignement du second degré, deuxième cycle. Ce groupe comprend les personnes qui sont passées du premier au deuxième cycle de l'enseignement secondaire, mais qui n'ont pas fait d'études postsecondaires.

Personnes ayant atteint le niveau postsecondaire. Toutes les personnes qui ont entrepris des études postsecondaires, qu'elles les aient ou non terminées, sont comptées dans ce groupe.

Le nombre des personnes dont le niveau d'instruction n'est pas connu a été soustrait du total de la population. (Lorsque la catégorie 'inconnu' représentait plus de 5 % de la population âgée de 25 ans ou plus, le chiffre absolu pour chaque groupe d'âge a été indiqué dans une note). En ce qui concerne le niveau postsecondaire, la proportion du groupe d'âge 15-24 ans est souvent inférieure à celle du groupe d'âge 25-34 ans, par le fait qu'une proportion notable du groupe d'âge 15-24 ans est encore trop jeune pour accéder au niveau postsecondaire. Pour cette raison, on a choisi comme total de la population adulte dans ce tableau le groupe d'âge 25 ans et plus et non 15 ans et plus.

La primera parte del *Anuario Estadístico* se compone de dos cuadros sobre la población, de un cuadro sobre el analfabetismo y de un cuadro sobre el nivel de instrucción. Estos cuadros proporcionan datos de referencia para todos los demás que se refieren a los establecimientos docentes, la ciencia, la cultura y los medios de comunicación.

El número y la densidad de habitantes de un país influyen directamente sobre el desarrollo de sus establecimientos y de sus posibilidades de enseñanza. La estructura por edades de la población, sobre todo en lo que atañe a los jóvenes, determina en parte la política adoptada en materia de educación y sirve de base a su planificación nacional. Para poder prever la evolución de la matrícula escolar, es preciso disponer de estimaciones de la población de 5 a 24 años de edad, clasificada adecuadamente por grupos de edad.

Los datos relativos al analfabetismo y al nivel de instrucción presentan un perfil educativo de la población adulta y pueden servir como complemento de las estadísticas sobre la matrícula escolar y universitaria.

CUADRO 1.1

El cuadro 1.1 contiene datos sobre la población total, la superficie y la densidad demográfica de todo el mundo, de cada continente y de 206 países y territorios. Se trata del cuadro más completo del Anuario, en el sentido de que figuran en él todos los países y territorios del globo. Las cifras relativas a la población se basan en las estimaciones oficiales efectuadas a mediados del año indicado (1970, 1975, 1976, 1977 y 1978). Cuando no se dice otra cosa, las cifras de superficie comprenden las aguas continentales. No se indica la densidad demográfica (número de habitantes por kilómetro cuadrado) cuando la superficie es de menos de 1.000 km2. Los lectores que deseen datos más detallados sobre la superficie, la población y la estructura por edades pueden consultar las diversas ediciones del *'Statistical Yearbook - Annuaire Statistique'* y *'Demographic Yearbook - Annuaire Demografique'* de las Naciones Unidas. En la mayoría de los casos, las cifras presentadas en este cuadro son las 'estimaciones a mediados de año' publicadas por las Naciones Unidas en su *'Demographic Yearbook - Annuaire Demographique'* o en sus publicaciones periódicas *'Population and Vital Statistics Report'* y *'Monthly Bulletin of Statistics'*. Pueden verse detalles complementarios sobre la fuente de las estimaciones, etc., en los cuadros 1, 3 y 5 del *Anuario* antes citado (edición de 1977) y en las otras publicaciones mencionadas.

CUADRO 1.2

En el cuadro 1.2 figuran las estimaciones y las proyecciones de la población total y de la población de menos de 25 años en todo el mundo, en los distintos continentes, grandes regiones y grupos de países, para los años 1970, 1975, 1980, 1985, 1990 y 2000. Se presentan por separado unas estimaciones relativas a los grupos de 0-4, 5-9, 10-14, 15-19, y 20-24 años de edad, que son los que ofrecen más interés desde el punto de vista de la educación. Todos estos datos han sido preparados en 1978 por la Division de población de las Naciones Unidas y corresponden a la variante media de las proyecciones. Se indican en el cuadro las seis regiones principales del mundo, subdivididas en otros varios grupos cuya composición, cuando procede, se indica en la nota 1.

En la figura 1 se indican las diferencias de crecimiento entre cada continente. En los 30 años que van de 1970 a 2000 la población europea sólo aumentará en un 13.2% y, en cambio, la de América septentrional en un 27.9%, la de América Latina en un 115.1%, la de Africa en un 134.0% y la de Asia en un 72.7%. Durante esos 30 años, la población de Asia seguirá representando a más de la mitad de la población mundial.

La figura 2 representa la pirámide de la población mundial para el periodo 1970-2000. Los escalones de esa pirámide corresponden a un crecimiento continuo de los nacimientos vivos en cada quinquenio. Cuando se analiza el total mundial por grandes regiones, se observa que los que tienen una tasa de crecimiento más alta son los países en vías de desarrollo, y en particular los Estados Arabes.

CUADRO 1.3

El cuadro 1.3 presenta datos sobre la población analfabeta y el porcentaje de analfabetos, de acuerdo con los censos o encuestas. Los datos se indican separadamente por sexo y se refieren, en la medida de lo posible, a la población de 15 años y más. Cuando se dispone de datos, tambien se presenta la repartición de las zonas urbana y rural.

La finalidad de este cuadro es la de presentar los datos más recientes sobre analfabetismo recibidos en la Oficina de Estadística de la Unesco. Los lectores que se interesen en los datos relativos a otros años o a los diferentes grupos de edad deben referirse a la publicación de la Unesco *Estadísticas sobre el nivel de instrucción y el analfabetismo,* aparecida en 1977.

El criterio de alfabetismo es la capacidad de leer y de escribir. De ahí se desprende que todos los semianalfabetos - esto es, las personas que saben leer pero no escribir - figuran entre los analfabetos. No se ha tenido en cuenta en los cálculos a las personas con respecto a las cuales no se especifica si son analfabetas o no. Se ha calculado, pues, el porcentaje de analfabetos de un país dado dividiendo el número de analfabetos conocidos por el total de los alfabetos y analfabetos conocidos. (Se llega al mismo resultado repartiendo proporcionalmente, entre la categoría de alfabetos y la de analfabetos el número de personas con respecto a las cuales no se especifica si son alfabetos o no).

CUADRO 1.4

El cuadro 1.4 presenta la distribución en porcentaje de la población adulta según el más alto nivel de instrucción alcanzado, por sexo y, cuando es posible, según las zonas urbana y rural. Los datos están tomados de censos nacionales y de sondeos cuyos resultados nos han sido comunicados por la Oficina de Estadística de las Naciones Unidas y de publicaciones regionales o nacionales. La finalidad de este cuadro es la de presentar los datos más recientes sobre nivel de instrucción recibidos en la Oficina de Estadística de la Unesco para cada país y territorio. Los lectores que se interesen en los datos relativos a los años anteriores o a la distribución por edad deben consultar la publicación de la Unesco *Estadísticas sobre el nivel de instrucción y el analfabetismo.* Los seis niveles de instrucción presentados, que van del grupo de personas sin ninguna escolaridad al de las personas que alcanzaron el nivel postsecundario, se definen como sigue:

Personas sin escolaridad: Se trata de las personas que no llegaron a completar un año de estudios.

Personas que no terminaron la enseñanza de primer grado. Como sea que la duración de la enseñanza primaria puede variar según los países entre cuatro y ocho años, esta categoría comprende todas las personas que terminaron como mínimo un año de enseñanza primaria, pero que no finalizaron el último año de este nivel. La estructura relativa a los años de estudio de las enseñanzas de primero y de segundo grado figura, para todos los países, en el cuadro 3.1.

Personas que terminaron la enseñanza de primer grado. Comprende las personas que terminaron el último año de enseñanza primaria, pero que no accedieron a la enseñanza secundaria. En algunos casos (indicados en una nota) se han reunido los datos correspondientes a los dos últimos años de enseñanza primaria, y las personas que sólo terminaron el penúltimo año se cuentan también en este grupo.

Personas que accedieron a la enseñanza de segundo grado, primer ciclo. Este grupo comprende todas las personas cuyos estudios no sobrepasaron el primer ciclo de la enseñanza secundaria, tal y como se define en el cuadro 3.1.

1 Reference tables
Tableaux de référence
Cuadros de referencia

Personas que accedieron a la enseñanza de segundo grado, segundo ciclo. Este grupo comprende las personas que pasaron del primero al segundo ciclo de la enseñanza secundaria, pero que no hicieron estudios postsecundarios.

Personas que alcanzaron el nivel postsecundario. Todas las personas que empezaron estudios postsecundario, que los hayan o no terminado, figuran en este grupo.

El número de personas sobre las cuales se desconoce el nivel de instrucción ha sido sustraído del total de la población. (Cuando la categoría 'desconocido' representaba más del 5 % de la población de 25 años o más, la cifra absoluta para cada grupo de edad se ha indicado en una nota).

En lo tocante a la enseñanza postsecundaria, la proporción del grupo de edad de 15 a 24 años es a menudo inferior a la del grupo de 25 a 34 años de edad, ya que una proporción notable de aquél es todavía demasiado joven para poder ingresar en ese grado de enseñanza. Por este motivo, se ha escogido como total de la población adulta en el cuadro el grupo de edad de 25 años y más, y no el de 15 años y más.

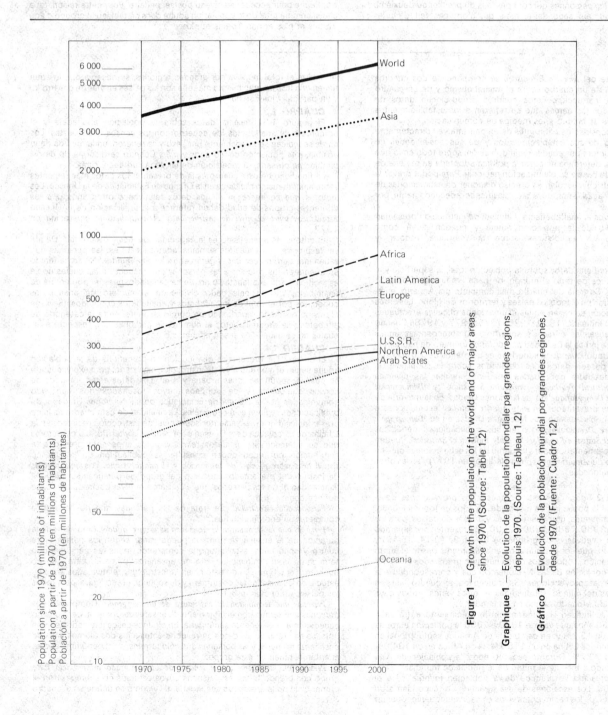

Population since 1970 (millions of inhabitants)
Population à partir de 1970 (en millions d'habitants)
Población a partir de 1970 (en millones de habitantes)

Figure 1 — Growth in the population of the world and of major areas since 1970. (Source: Table 1.2)

Graphique 1 — Evolution de la population mondiale par grandes regions, depuis 1970. (Source: Tableau 1.2)

Gráfico 1 — Evolución de la población mundial por grandes regiones, desde 1970. (Fuente: Cuadro 1.2)

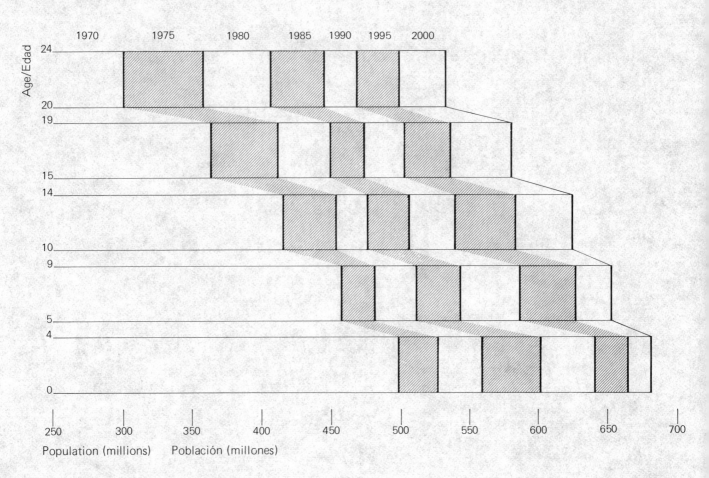

Figure 2 — World population aged 0-24, 1970-2000.
(Source; Table 1.2)

Graphique 2 — Population mondiale âgée de O à 24 ans, 1970-2000.
(Source: Tableau 1.2)

Gráfico 2 — Población mundial de O a 24 anos de edad, 1970-2000.
(Fuente: Cuadro 1.2)

Population, area and density, 1970-1978   1.1
Population, superficie et densité, 1970-1978
Población, superficie y densidad, 1970-1978

1.1 Population, area and density, 1970, 1975, 1977 and 1978

Population, superficie et densité, 1970, 1975, 1977 et 1978

Población, superficie y densidad, 1970, 1975, 1977 y 1978

| NUMBER OF COUNTRIES AND TERRITORIES PRESENTED IN THIS TABLE: 206 | NOMBRE DE PAYS ET DE TERRITOIRES PRESENTES DANS CE TABLEAU: 206 | NUMERO DE PAISES Y DE TERRITORIOS PRESENTADOS EN ESTE CUADRO: 206 |

CONTINENT AND COUNTRY	ESTIMATES OF MID-YEAR POPULATION (THOUSANDS)					AREA	INHABITANTS PER KM^2
CONTINENT ET PAYS	ESTIMATIONS DE LA POPULATION AU MILIEU DE L'ANNEE (MILLIERS)					SUPERFICIE	NOMBRE D'HABITANTS AU KM^2
CONTINENTE Y PAIS	ESTIMACIONES DE LA POBLACION A MEDIADOS DE AÑO (EN MILES)					SUPERFICIE	HABITANTES POR KM^2
	1970	1975	1976	1977	1978	(KM^2)	1978
	(1)	(2)	(3)	(4)	(5)	(6)	(7)
WORLD TOTAL	3 604 000	3 946 000	4 021 000	4 124 000	4 258 000	135 830 000	31
AFRICA	354 000	401 000	413 000	424 000	442 000	30 319 000	15
AMERICA, NORTH ‡	318 000	342 000	347 000	354 000	359 000	24 249 000	15
AMERICA, SOUTH	187 000	212 000	218 000	230 000	233 000	17 833 000	13
ASIA ‡	2 024 000	2 242 000	2 289 000	2 355 000	2 461 000	27 580 000	89
EUROPE ‡	459 000	474 000	476 000	478 000	480 000	4 937 000	97
OCEANIA ‡	19 300	21 000	21 400	22 000	22 000	8 510 000	3
U.S.S.R.	243 000	254 000	257 000	260 000	262 000	22 402 000	12
AFRICA							
ALGERIA	14 330	16 776	17 304	17 910	18 515	2 381 741	8
ANGOLA	5 590	6 260	6 410	6 570	6 732	1 246 700	5
BENIN	2 686	3 112	3 197	3 286	3 377	112 622	30
BOTSWANA	580	691	693	710	726	600 372	1
BURUNDI	3 620	3 930	4 030	4 140	4 256	27 834	153
CAPE VERDE	272	294	303	306	314	4 033	78
CENTRAL AFRICAN REPUBLIC ‡	...	...	...	...	...	622 984	...
CHAD	3 640	4 030	4 116	4 213	4 309	1 284 000	3
COMORO	271	306	314	320	320	2 171	147
CONGO	1 190	1 345	1 390	1 440	1 459	342 000	4
DJIBOUTI	95	106	108	111	113	22 000	5
EGYPT	33 329	37 233	37 870	38 741	39 636	1 001 449	40
EQUATORIAL GUINEA	290	310	316	322	346	28 051	12
ETHIOPIA	24 630	27 470	28 190	28 981	29 705	1 221 900	24
GABON	500	526	530	534	538	267 667	2

1.1 Population, area and density, 1970-1978
Population, superficie et densité, 1970-1978
Población, superficie y densidad, 1970-1978

CONTINENT AND COUNTRY	ESTIMATES OF MID—YEAR POPULATION (THOUSANDS)					AREA	INHABITANTS PER KM^2
CONTINENT ET PAYS	ESTIMATIONS DE LA POPULATION AU MILIEU DE L'ANNEE (MILLIERS)					SUPERFICIE	NOMBRE D'HABITANTS AU KM^2
CONTINENTE Y PAIS	ESTIMACIONES DE LA POBLACION A MEDIADOS DE AÑO (EN MILES)					SUPERFICIE	HABITANTES POR KM^2
	1970	1975	1976	1977	1978	(KM^2)	1978
	(1)	(2)	(3)	(4)	(5)	(6)	(7)
GAMBIA	460	524	538	553	569	11 295	50
GHANA	8 610	9 866	10 309	10 630	10 969	238 537	46
GUINEA	3 921	4 416	4 529	4 646	4 763	245 957	19
GUINEA—BISSAU	490	525	534	544	553	36 125	15
IVORY COAST	5 310	6 710	6 970	7 230	7 613	322 463	24
KENYA	11 230	13 399	13 847	14 337	14 856	582 646	26
LESOTHO	930	1 039	1 214	1 250	1 279	30 355	42
LIBERIA	1 340	1 570	1 630	1 680	1 742	111 369	16
LIBYAN ARAB JAMAHIRIYA	1 990	2 444	2 512	2 630	2 748	1 759 540	2
MADAGASCAR	6 800	7 680	7 870	8 080	8 289	587 041	14
MALAWI	4 440	5 044	5 175	5 526	5 669	118 484	48
MALI	5 050	5 810	5 960	6 210	6 290	1 240 000	5
MAURITANIA	1 250	1 420	1 460	1 500	1 544	1 030 700	2
MAURITIUS	830	899	895	909	924	2 045	452
MOROCCO	15 520	17 305	17 828	18 245	18 906	446 550	42
MOZAMBIQUE	8 230	9 239	9 444	9 678	9 935	783 030	13
NAMIBIA ‡	770	883	...	...	...	824 292	...
NIGER	4 016	4 600	4 727	4 859	4 994	1 267 000	4
NIGERIA ‡	56 350	65 660	67 760	69 940	72 217	923 768	78
REUNION	446	480	480	489	496	2 510	198
RWANDA	3 680	4 198	4 289	4 368	4 508	26 338	171
ST. HELENA	5	5	5	5	5	314	.
SAO TOME AND PRINCIPE	70	80	81	82	83	964	.
SENEGAL	3 925	4 136	5 115	5 250	5 381	196 192	27
SEYCHELLES	52	58	59	62	62	280	.
SIERRA LEONE	2 550	3 050	3 111	3 210	3 292	71 740	46
SOMALIA	2 789	3 170	3 261	3 354	3 443	637 657	5
SOUTH AFRICA	22 470	25 471	26 129	26 940	27 700	1 221 037	23
SUDAN	15 695	15 730	16 126	16 953	17 376	2 505 813	7
SWAZILAND	420	494	497	507	544	17 363	31
TOGO	1 960	2 222	2 283	2 348	2 409	56 000	43
TUNISIA	5 130	5 610	5 737	5 880	6 077	163 610	37
UGANDA	9 810	11 549	11 943	12 353	12 780	236 036	54
UNITED REPUBLIC OF CAMEROON	6 780	7 530	7 700	7 914	8 058	475 442	17
UNITED REPUBLIC OF TANZANIA	13 273	15 300	15 607	16 086	16 553	945 087	18
UPPER VOLTA	5 384	6 070	6 230	6 390	6 554	274 200	24
WESTERN SAHARA	80	117	128	139	152	266 000	1
ZAIRE	21 690	24 902	25 570	26 310	27 745	2 345 409	12
ZAMBIA	4 180	4 896	5 138	5 302	5 472	752 614	7
ZIMBABWE	5 310	6 310	6 530	6 740	6 930	390 580	18
AMERICA, NORTH							
ANTIGUA	70	70	71	72	74	442	.
BAHAMAS	170	204	211	220	225	13 935	16
BARBADOS	240	245	247	254	265	431	.
BELIZE	120	140	144	149	153	22 965	7
BERMUDA	54	56	57	57	58	53	.

Population, area and density, 1970-1978   1.1
Population, superficie et densité, 1970-1978
Población, superficie y densidad, 1970-1978

CONTINENT AND COUNTRY	ESTIMATES OF MID—YEAR POPULATION (THOUSANDS)					AREA	INHABITANTS PER KM²
CONTINENT ET PAYS	ESTIMATIONS DE LA POPULATION AU MILIEU DE L'ANNEE (MILLIERS)					SUPERFICIE	NOMBRE D'HABITANTS AU KM²
CONTINENTE Y PAIS	ESTIMACIONES DE LA POBLACION A MEDIADOS DE AÑO (EN MILES)					SUPERFICIE	HABITANTES POR KM²
	1970	1975	1976	1977	1978	(KM²)	1978
	(1)	(2)	(3)	(4)	(5)	(6)	(7)
BRITISH VIRGIN ISLANDS	10	11	12	12	12	153	.
CANADA	21 320	22 831	23 143	23 280	23 499	9 976 139	2
CAYMAN ISLANDS	10	11	11	11	12	259	.
COSTA RICA	1 730	1 968	2 018	2 071	2 111	50 700	42
CUBA	8 550	9 330	9 464	9 600	9 728	114 524	85
DOMINICA	74	75	76	80	81	751	.
DOMINICAN REPUBLIC	4 060	4 697	4 835	4 978	5 124	48 734	105
EL SALVADOR	3 534	4 007	4 123	4 255	4 354	21 041	207
GREENLAND	47	54	50	56	51	2 175 600	.
GRENADA	90	96	96	97	97	344	.
GUADELOUPE	327	330	330	330	330	1 779	186
GUATEMALA	5 270	6 080	6 256	6 436	6 621	108 889	61
HAITI	4 240	4 584	4 668	4 749	4 833	27 750	174
HONDURAS	2 640	3 090	3 200	3 320	3 439	112 088	31
JAMAICA	1 870	2 040	2 057	2 085	2 133	10 991	194
MARTINIQUE	338	330	320	320	325	1 102	295
MEXICO	50 690	60 145	62 329	64 594	66 944	1 972 547	34
MONTSERRAT	13	13	13	13	13	98	.
NETHERLANDS ANTILLES	222	242	241	245	246	961	.
NICARAGUA	1 830	2 155	2 233	2 312	2 395	133 000	18
PANAMA	1 430	1 668	1 719	1 771	1 826	75 650	24
FORMER CANAL ZONE ‡	44	44	44	38	45	1 432	31
PUERTO RICO ‡	2 720	3 120	3 213	3 303	3 317	8 897	373
ST. KITTS – NEVIS ANGUILLA	62	66	66	66	67	357	.
ST. LUCIA	101	108	110	112	113	616	.
ST. PIERRE AND MIQUELON	5	5	5	6	6	242	.
ST. VINCENT AND THE GRENADINES	93	90	90	90	96	388	.
TRINIDAD AND TOBAGO	1 030	1 080	1 100	1 120	1 133	5 130	221
TURKS AND CAICOS ISLANDS	6	6	6	6	6	430	.
UNITED STATES OF AMERICA ‡	204 880	213 611	215 118	216 817	218 059	9 363 123	23
U.S. VIRGIN ISLANDS ‡	59	92	96	...	104	344	.
AMERICA, SOUTH							
ARGENTINA	23 750	25 383	25 719	26 056	26 393	2 766 889	10
BOLIVIA	4 931	4 890	5 020	5 150	5 290	1 098 581	5
BRAZIL	92 520	106 230	109 181	112 239	115 397	8 511 965	14
CHILE ‡	9 370	10 253	10 454	10 656	10 857	756 945	14
COLOMBIA	20 530	23 542	24 372	25 048	25 645	1 138 914	23
ECUADOR	6 093	6 733	7 305	7 556	7 814	283 561	28
FALKLAND ISLANDS (MALVINAS)	2	2	2	2	2	12 173	.
FRENCH GUIANA	51	60	62	60	66	91 000	1
GUYANA	710	780	790	810	820	214 969	4
PARAGUAY	2 300	2 647	2 724	2 800	2 888	406 752	7
PERU ‡	13 450	15 470	15 910	16 358	16 819	1 285 216	13
SURINAME	370	360	370	370	374	163 265	2
URUGUAY	2 886	2 810	2 830	2 846	2 864	176 215	16
VENEZUELA	10 280	11 993	12 361	12 737	13 122	912 050	14

1.1 Population, area and density, 1970-1978
Population, superficie et densité, 1970-1978
Población, superficie y densidad, 1970-1978

CONTINENT AND COUNTRY CONTINENT ET PAYS CONTINENTE Y PAIS	ESTIMATES OF MID—YEAR POPULATION (THOUSANDS) ESTIMATIONS DE LA POPULATION AU MILIEU DE L'ANNEE (MILLIERS) ESTIMACIONES DE LA POBLACION A MEDIADOS DE AÑO (EN MILES)					AREA SUPERFICIE SUPERFICIE	INHABITANTS PER KM^2 NOMBRE D'HABITANTS AU KM^2 HABITANTES POR KM^2
	1970	1975	1976	1977	1978	(KM^2)	1978
	(1)	(2)	(3)	(4)	(5)	(6)	(7)
ASIA							
AFGHANISTAN	14 870	16 670	17 050	14 740	15 108	647 497	23
BAHRAIN	215	256	259	267	345	622	
BANGLADESH ‡	68 120	78 960	80 820	82 715	84 655	143 998	588
BHUTAN	1 055	1 173	1 202	1 232	1 240	47 000	26
BRUNEI	130	160	177	190	201	5 765	35
BURMA	27 180	30 340	31 000	31 512	32 205	676 552	48
CHINA	825 810	895 340	908 270	920 810	933 032	9 596 961	97
CYPRUS	600	620	610	610	616	9 251	67
DEMOCRATIC KAMPUCHEA	7 060	8 110	8 280	8 430	8 574	181 035	47
EAST TIMOR	602	658	688	704	720	14 925	48
HONG KONG ‡	3 960	4 367	4 383	4 514	4 606	1 045	4 408
INDIA ‡	539 080	598 097	610 077	625 818	638 388	3 287 590	194
INDONESIA	119 470	135 230	138 490	141 780	145 100	2 027 087	72
IRAN	28 662	33 019	33 590	34 274	35 213	1 648 000	21
IRAQ	9 440	11 124	11 505	11 907	12 327	434 924	28
ISRAEL	2 910	3 371	3 465	3 611	3 689	20 770	178
JAPAN	104 340	111 570	112 768	113 863	114 898	372 313	309
JORDAN ‡	2 300	2 702	2 779	2 890	2 984	97 740	31
KOREA, DEMOCRATIC PEOPLE'S REPUB. OF	13 892	15 852	16 260	16 660	17 072	120 538	142
KOREA, REPUBLIC OF ‡	32 240	35 280	35 860	36 436	37 019	98 484	376
KUWAIT	750	996	1 031	1 129	1 199	17 818	67
LAO PEOPLE'S DEMOCRATIC REPUBLIC ‡	2 962	3 303	3 383	3 464	3 546	236 800	15
LEBANON ‡	2 470	2 800	2 870	2 940	3 012	10 400	290
MACAU	250	271	275	279	276	16	.
MALAYSIA ‡	10 400	11 900	12 300	12 600	12 960	329 749	39
PENINSULAR MALAYSIA	8 770	...	...	...	...	131 588	.
SABAH	660	...	...	...	...	73 711	.
SARAWAK	970	...	...	...	...	124 450	...
MALDIVES	108	119	122	140	141	298	.
MONGOLIA	1 250	1 444	1 488	1 531	1 576	1 565 000	1
NEPAL	11 420	12 590	12 860	13 136	13 421	140 797	95
OMAN	660	766	791	817	839	212 457	4
PAKISTAN ‡	60 610	70 260	72 368	74 890	76 770	803 943	95
PHILIPPINES	36 850	42 513	43 751	45 028	46 351	300 000	155
QATAR	110	170	180	190	201	11 000	18
SAUDI ARABIA	6 200	7 180	7 400	7 630	7 866	2 149 690	4
SINGAPORE	2 070	2 250	2 278	2 308	2 334	581	.
SRI LANKA	12 514	13 510	13 730	13 971	14 346	65 610	219
SYRIAN ARAB REPUBLIC ‡	6 260	7 355	7 596	7 845	8 088	185 180	44
THAILAND ‡	36 215	41 869	42 960	44 039	45 100	514 000	88
TURKEY	34 850	40 350	41 090	42 134	43 210	780 576	55
UNITED ARAB EMIRATES	230	560	620	670	711	83 600	9
VIET—NAM	41 860	46 550	47 610	48 730	49 890	329 556	151
YEMEN	4 840	5 280	5 400	5 520	5 642	195 000	29
YEMEN, DEMOCRATIC	1 440	1 690	1 749	1 797	1 853	332 968	6

Population, area and density, 1970-1978   **1.1**
Population, superficie et densité, 1970-1978
Población, superficie y densidad, 1970-1978

CONTINENT AND COUNTRY	ESTIMATES OF MID—YEAR POPULATION (THOUSANDS)					AREA	INHABITANTS PER KM²
CONTINENT ET PAYS	ESTIMATIONS DE LA POPULATION AU MILIEU DE L'ANNEE (MILLIERS)					SUPERFICIE	NOMBRE D'HABITANTS AU KM²
CONTINENTE Y PAIS	ESTIMACIONES DE LA POBLACION A MEDIADOS DE AÑO (EN MILES)					SUPERFICIE	HABITANTES POR KM²
	1970	1975	1976	1977	1978	(KM²)	1978
	(1)	(2)	(3)	(4)	(5)	(6)	(7)
EUROPE							
ALBANIA	2 140	2 420	2 480	2 550	2 608	28 748	91
ANDORRA	15	27	29	29	30	453	.
AUSTRIA	7 430	7 523	7 514	7 518	7 508	83 849	90
BELGIUM	9 660	9 796	9 820	9 830	9 840	30 513	322
BULGARIA	8 490	8 722	8 761	8 804	8 814	110 912	79
CZECHOSLOVAKIA	14 330	14 802	14 918	15 031	15 138	127 869	118
DENMARK	4 930	5 059	5 073	5 088	5 104	43 069	119
FAEROE ISLANDS	38	42	40	40	40	1 399	29
FINLAND	4 610	4 707	4 727	4 737	4 752	337 009	14
FRANCE	50 775	52 790	52 890	53 079	53 278	547 026	97
GERMAN DEMOCRATIC REPUBLIC ‡	17 060	16 850	16 786	16 765	16 756	108 178	155
GERMANY, FEDERAL REPUBLIC OF ‡	60 710	61 832	61 513	61 396	61 310	248 577	247
GIBRALTAR	26	29	30	30	29	6	.
GREECE	8 790	9 046	9 165	9 270	9 360	131 944	71
HOLY SEE ‡	1	1	1	1	1	0	.
HUNGARY	10 340	10 540	10 600	10 648	10 685	93 030	115
ICELAND	200	218	220	222	224	103 000	2
IRELAND	2 950	3 127	3 162	3 192	3 236	70 283	46
ITALY	53 660	55 810	56 189	56 446	56 697	301 225	188
LIECHTENSTEIN	20	24	22	25	25	157	.
LUXEMBOURG	340	357	358	356	356	2 586	138
MALTA	326	330	330	332	340	316	.
MONACO	24	25	25	25	26	1	.
NETHERLANDS	13 030	13 653	13 770	13 853	13 986	40 844	342
NORWAY	3 879	4 007	4 026	4 042	4 059	324 219	13
POLAND ‡	32 530	34 020	34 362	34 698	35 010	312 677	112
PORTUGAL	9 040	9 430	9 660	9 730	9 798	92 082	106
ROMANIA	20 253	21 245	21 446	21 658	21 855	237 500	92
SAN MARINO	19	20	20	20	21	61	.
SPAIN	33 780	35 600	35 971	36 350	36 780	504 782	73
SWEDEN	8 046	8 195	8 222	8 255	8 278	449 964	18
SWITZERLAND	6 190	6 403	6 346	6 327	6 337	41 288	153
UNITED KINGDOM	55 410	55 962	55 928	55 852	55 822	244 046	229
YUGOSLAVIA	20 370	21 352	21 560	21 767	21 914	255 804	86
OCEANIA							
AMERICAN SAMOA ‡	29	29	31	34	30	197	.
AUSTRALIA ‡	12 510	13 770	13 920	14 074	14 249	7 686 848	2
COOK ISLANDS	24	25	18	18	26	236	.
FIJI	520	573	580	596	607	18 274	33
FRENCH POLYNESIA	109	128	132	136	146	4 000	37
GUAM ‡	90	104	102	104	113	549	.
KIRIBATI ‡	56	66	68	70	63	886	.
NAURU	7	8	8	8	8	21	.
NEW CALEDONIA	110	125	135	136	144	19 058	8
NEW HEBRIDES	84	95	97	99	104	14 763	7

1.1 Population, area and density, 1970-1978
Population, superficie et densité, 1970-1978
Población, superficie y densidad, 1970-1978

CONTINENT AND COUNTRY	ESTIMATES OF MID—YEAR POPULATION (THOUSANDS)					AREA	INHABITANTS PER KM^2
CONTINENT ET PAYS	ESTIMATIONS DE LA POPULATION AU MILIEU DE L'ANNEE (MILLIERS)					SUPERFICIE	NOMBRE D'HABITANTS AU KM^2
CONTINENTE Y PAIS	ESTIMACIONES DE LA POBLACION A MEDIADOS DE AÑO (EN MILES)					SUPERFICIE	HABITANTES POR KM^2
	1970	1975	1976	1977	1978	(KM^2)	1978
	(1)	(2)	(3)	(4)	(5)	(6)	(7)
NEW ZEALAND	2 816	3 070	3 090	3 105	3 107	268 676	12
NIUE	6	5	4	6	6	259	.
NORFOLK ISLAND	1	2	2	2	2	36	
PACIFIC ISLANDS ‡	102	120	123	126	134	1 779	75
PAPUA NEW GUINEA	2 490	2 756	2 829	2 905	3 000	461 691	7
SAMOA	143	152	151	153	154	2 842	54
SOLOMON ISLANDS	163	190	200	207	215	28 446	8
TOKELAU ISLANDS	2	2	2	2	2	10	.
TONGA	87	102	90	91	93	699	.
U.S.S.R.							
U.S.S.R. ‡	242 760	254 382	256 674	258 932	261 569	22 402 200	12
BYELORUSSIAN S.S.R. ‡	9 040	9 351	9 390	9 441	...	207 600	45
UKRAINIAN S.S.R.	47 310	48 900	49 100	49 389	49 478	603 700	82

GENERAL NOTE/REMARQUE GENERALE/NOTA GENERAL:
E—> AREA SHOWN INCLUDES LAND AREA AND INLAND WATERS, BUT EXCLUDES UNINHABITED POLAR REGIONS AND SOME UNINHABITED ISLANDS. POPULATION DENSITY IS NOT SHOWN FOR TERRITORIES LESS THAN 1,000 SQUARE KILOMETRES IN AREA.
FR—> LA SUPERFICIE INDIQUEE EST CELLE DES TERRES ET DES EAUX INTERIEURES, NON COMPRIS LES ZONES POLAIRES NI QUELQUES ILES INHABITEES. LA DENSITE N'EST PAS INDIQUEE LORSQUE LA SUPER—FICIE EST INFERIEURE A 1 000 KILOMETRES CARRES.
ESP> LA SUPERFICIE INCLUYE LAS TIERRAS Y LAS AGUAS CONTINENTALES, PERO NO LAS REGIONES POLARES Y CIERTAS ISLAS INHABITADAS. NO SE INDICA LA DEN—SIDAD DEMOGRAFICA EN EL CASO DE TERRITORIOS DE MENOS DE 1 000 KILOMETROS CUADRADOS DE SUPERFICIE.

AMERICA, NORTH:
E—> HAWAII, A STATE OF THE UNITED STATES OF AMERICA, IS INCLUDED IN NORTH AMERICA, RATHER THAN OCEANIA.
FR—> HAWAII, ETAT DES ETATS—UNIS D'AMERIQUE, EST COMPRIS DANS L'AMERIQUE DU NORD PLUTOT QUE DANS L'OCEANIE.
ESP> HAWAI, ESTADO DE LOS ESTADOS UNIDOS DE AMERICA, FIGURA EN "AMERICA DEL NORTE", Y NO EN "OCEANIA".

ASIA:
E—> EXCLUDING THE U.S.S.R., SHOWN SEPARATELY, BUT INCLUDING BOTH THE ASIAN AND THE EUROPEAN PORTIONS OF TURKEY.
FR—> NON COMPRIS L'U.R.S.S., QUI FAIT L'OBJET D'UNE RUBRIQUE DISTINCTE, MAIS Y COMPRIS LA PARTIE ASIATIQUE ET LA PARTIE EUROPEENNE DE LA TURQUIE.
ESP> QUEDA EXCLUIDA LA U.R.S.S. QUE SE INDICA POR SEPARADO, PERO SE INCLUYE LA TURQUIA EUROPEA Y LA ASIATICA.

EUROPE:
E—> EXCLUDING THE U.S.S.R., SHOWN SEPARATELY BELOW, AND THE EUROPEAN PORTION OF TURKEY, WHICH IS INCLUDED IN ASIA.
FR—> NON COMPRIS L'U.R.S.S., QUI FAIT L'OBJET D'UNE RUBRIQUE DISTINCTE, NI LA PARTIE EUROPEENNE DE LA TURQUIE, QUI EST COMPRISE DANS L'ASIE.
ESP> EXCLUIDA LA U.R.S.S. QUE SE INDICA MAS ADELANTE Y LA PARTE EUROPEA DE TURQUIA QUE QUEDA COMPRENDIDA EN "ASIA".

OCEANIA:
E—> HAWAII, A STATE OF THE UNITED STATES OF AMERICA, IS INCLUDED IN NORTH AMERICA, RATHER THAN IN OCEANIA.
FR—> HAWAII, ETATS DES ETATS—UNIS D'AMERIQUE, EST COMPRIS DANS L'AMERIQUE DU NORD PLUTOT QUE DANS L'OCEANIE.
ESP> HAWAI, ESTADO DE LOS ESTADOS UNIDOS DE AMERICA, FIGURA EN "AMERICA DEL NORTE", Y NO EN "OCEANIA".

CENTRAL AFRICAN REPUBLIC:
E—> ESTIMATES (IN MILLIONS) FOR 1965—1971, BASED ON RESULTS OF A SAMPLE SURVEY HELD IN 1959—1960, ARE: 1.43, 1.47, 1.50, 1.54, 1.58, 1.61, AND 1.64 RESPECTIVELY. ESTIMATES FOR 1965, 1967, 1968, 1970, AND 1974 BASED ON RESULTS OF THE 1968 "RECENSEMENT INSTANTANE", ARE 2.09, 2.20, 2.26, 2.37 AND 2.61 RESPECTIVELY.
FR—> LES ESTIMATIONS (EN MILLIONS) POUR 1965—1971, FONDEES SUR LES RESULTATS D'UNE EN—QUETE PAR SONDAGE EFFECTUEE EN 1959—1960 SONT: 1.43, 1.47, 1.50, 1.54, 1.58, 1.61 ET 1.64 RESPECTIVEMENT. LES ESTIMATIONS POUR 1965, 1967, 1968, 1970 ET 1974, FONDEES SUR LES RESULTATS DU RECENSEMENT INSTANTANE SONT: 2.09, 2.20, 2.26, 2.37 ET 2.61 RESPECTIVEMENT.

Population, area and density, 1970-1978 **1.1**
Population, superficie et densité, 1970-1978
Población, superficie y densidad, 1970-1978

CENTRAL AFRICAN REPUBLIC (CONT):
ESP> LAS ESTIMACIONES (EN MILLONES) PARA 1965—
1971, BASADAS EN LOS RESULTADOS DE UNA EN—
CUESTA POR SONDEO EFECTUADA EN 1959—1960 SON
LAS SIGUIENTES: 1.43, 1.47, 1.50, 1.54,
1.58, 1.61 Y 1.64 RESPECTIVAMENTE. LAS
ESTIMACIONES PARA 1965, 1967, 1968, 1970 Y 1974
FUNDADAS EN LOS RESULTADOS DE UN "RECENSEMENT
INSTANTANE" SON: 2.09, 2.20, 2.26, 2.37, Y
2.61 RESPECTIVAMENTE.

NAMIBIA:
E—> INHABITANTS PER SQUARE KILOMETRE REFER TO
1975.
FR—> LE NOMBRE D'HABITANTS AU KILOMETRE CARRE
SE REFERE A 1975.
ESP> EL NUMERO DE HABITANTES POR KILOMETRO
CUADRADO SE REFIERE A 1975.

NIGERIA:
E—> ESTIMATES BASED ON RESULTS OF CENSUS OF 5—8
NOVEMBER 1963, INCLUDING ADJUSTMENT FOR ESTI—
MATED OVER—ENUMERATION. OFFICIAL ESTIMATES
FOR 1968—1977 BASED ON THE UNADJUSTED CENSUS
RESULTS ARE: 62.99, 64.56, 66.17, 67.83, 69.52,
71.02, 72.83, 74.87, 76.74 AND 78.66.
FR—> ESTIMATIONS FONDEES SUR LES RESULTATS DU
RECENSEMENT DU 5—8 NOVEMBRE 1963, Y COMPRIS UN
AJUSTEMENT POUR COMPENSER L'ESTIMATION DU SUR—
DENOMBREMENT. LES ESTIMATIONS OFFICIELLES
POUR 1968—1977 FONDEES SUR LES RESULTATS NON—
AJUSTES DU RECENSEMENT SONT LES SUIVANTES:
62.99, 64.56, 66.17, 67.83, 69.52, 71.02,
72.83, 74.87, 76.74, ET 78.66.
ESP> ESTIMACIONES BASADAS EN LOS REULTADOS DEL
CENSO DEL 5—8 DE NOVIEMBRE DE 1963, INCLUIDO UN
REAJUSTE PARA COMPENSAR LA ESTIMACION DE LA
SOBREENUMERACION. LAS ESTIMACIONES OFICIALES
PARA 1968—1977, FUNDADAS EN LOS RESULTADOS
NO AJUSTADOS DEL CENSO SON LAS SIGUIENTES:
62.99, 64.56, 66.17, 67.83, 69.52, 71.02,
72.83, 74.87, 76.74 Y 78.66.

PANAMA (FORMER CANAL ZONE):
E—> "DE JURE" POPULATION, BUT INCLUDING ARMED
FORCES STATIONED IN THE AREA.
FR—> POPULATION DE DROIT, Y COMPRIS LES
MILITAIRES EN GARNISON SUR LE TERRITOIRE.
ESP> POBLACION DE JURE, INCLUIDOS LOS MILITARES
DESTACADOS EN LA ZONA.

PUERTO RICO:
E—> "DE JURE" POPULATION, BUT INCLUDING ARMED
FORCES STATIONED IN THE AREA.
FR—> POPULATION DE DROIT, Y COMPRIS LES
MILITAIRES EN GARNISON SUR LE TERRITOIRE.
ESP> POBLACION DE JURE, INCLUIDOS LOS MILITARES
DESTACADOS EN LA ZONA.

UNITED STATES OF AMERICA:
E—> "DE JURE" POPULATION, BUT EXCLUDING CIVI—
LIAN CITIZENS ABSENT FROM THE COUNTRY FOR AN
EXTENDED PERIOD OF TIME ESTIMATED AT 764,701
AT THE TIME OF THE 1960 CENSUS.
FR—> POPULATION DE DROIT, MAIS NON COMPRIS LES
CIVILS, ABSENTS DU PAYS POUR UNE DUREE INDETER—
MINEE DONT LE NOMBRE A ETE ESTIME A 764 701 LORS
DU RECENSEMENT DE 1960.
ESP> POBLACION DE JURE, PERO EXCLUIDOS LOS
CIVILES AUSENTES DEL PAIS DURANTE UN PLAZO
PROLONGADO, CUYO NUMERO SE ESTIMO EN 764 701 EN EL
CENSO DE 1960.

U.S. VIRGIN ISLANDS:
E—> "DE JURE" POPULATION, BUT INCLUDING ARMED

U.S. VIRGIN ISLANDS (CONT):
FORCES STATIONED IN THE AREA.
FR—> POPULATION DE DROIT, Y COMPRIS LES
MILITAIRES EN GARNISON SUR LE TERRITOIRE.
ESP> POBLACION DE JURE, INCLUIDOS LOS MILITARES
DESTACADOS EN LA ZONA.

CHILE:
E—> ESTIMATES INCLUDE ADJUSTMENT FOR UNDER—
ENUMERATION AT LATEST CENSUS.
FR—> LES ESTIMATIONS TIENNENT COMPTE D'UN AJUS—
TEMENT DESTINE A COMPENSER LES LACUNES DU
DENOMBREMENT LORS DU DERNIER RECENSEMENT.
ESP> LAS ESTIMACIONES TIENEN EN CUENTA UN AJUSTE
DESTINADO A COMPENSAR LAS LAGUNAS DE LA ENU—
MERACION CORRESPONDIENTES AL ULTIMO CENSO.

PERU:
E—> ESTIMATES INCLUDE ADJUSTMENT FOR UNDER—
ENUMERATION AT LATEST CENSUS.
FR—> LES ESTIMATIONS TIENNENT COMPTE D'UN AJUS—
TEMENT DESTINE A COMPENSER LES LACUNES DU
DENOMBREMENT LORS DU DERNIER RECENSEMENT.
ESP> LAS ESTIMACIONES TIENEN EN CUENTA UN AJUSTE
DESTINADO A COMPENSAR LAS LAGUNAS DE LA ENU—
MERACION CORRESPONDIENTES AL ULTIMO CENSO.

BANGLADESH:
E—> ESTIMATES INCLUDE ADJUSTMENT FOR UNDER—
ENUMERATION AT LATEST CENSUS.
FR—> LES ESTIMATIONS TIENNENT COMPTE D'UN AJUS—
TEMENT DESTINE A COMPENSER LES LACUNES DU
DENOMBREMENT LORS DU DERNIER RECENSEMENT.
ESP> LAS ESTIMACIONES TIENEN EN CUENTA UN AJUSTE
DESTINADO A COMPENSAR LAS LAGUNAS DE LA ENU—
MERACION CORRESPONDIENTES AL ULTIMO CENSO.

HONG KONG:
E—> ESTIMATES INCLUDE ADJUSTEMENT FOR UNDER—
ENUMERATION AT LATEST CENSUS. LAND AREA ONLY.
TOTAL INCLUDING OCEAN AREA WITHIN ADMINISTRATIVE
BOUNDARIES IS 2,916 SQUARE KILOMETRES.
FR—> LES ESTIMATIONS TIENNENT COMPTE D'UN AJUS—
TEMENT DESTINE A COMPENSER LES LACUNES DU DENOM—
BREMENT LORS DU DERNIER RECENSEMENT. SUPERFICIE
TERRESTRE SEULEMENT. LA SUPERFICIE TOTALE QUI
COMPREND LA ZONE MARITIME SE TROUVANT A L'INTE—
RIEUR DES LIMITES ADMINISTRATIVES, EST DE 2 916
KILOMETRES CARRES.
ESP> LAS ESTIMACIONES TIENEN EN CUENTA UN AJUSTE
DESTINADO A COMPENSAR LAS LAGUNAS DE LA ENUMERA—
CION CORRESPONDIENTES AL ULTIMO CENSO. SUPERFICIE
TERRESTRE SOLAMENTE. LA SUPERFICIE TOTAL, QUE
COMPRENDE LA ZONA MARITIMA SITUADA DENTRO DE LOS
LIMITES ADMINISTRATIVOS, ES DE 2 916 KILOMETROS
CUADRADOS.

INDIA:
E—> ESTIMATES INCLUDE ADJUSTMENT FOR UNDER—
ENUMERATION AT LATEST CENSUS. INCLUDING DATA FOR
THE INDIAN—HELD PART OF JAMMU AND KASHMIR, THE
FINAL STATUS OF WHICH HAS NOT YET BEEN DETERMINED.
FR—> LES ESTIMATIONS TIENNENT COMPTE D'UN AJUS—
TEMENT DESTINE A COMPENSER LES LACUNES DU DENOM—
BREMENT LORS DU DERNIER RECENSEMENT. Y COMPRIS LA
PARTIE DU JAMMU ET CACHEMIRE, OCCUPEE PAR L'INDE,
DONT LE STATUT DEFINITIF N'A PAS ENCORE ETE
DETERMINE.
ESP> LAS ESTIMACIONES TIENEN EN CUENTA UN AJUSTE
DESTINADO A COMPENSAR LAS LAGUNAS DE LA ENU—
MERACION CORRESPONDIENTE AL ULTIMO CENSO.
INCLUIDA LA PARTE DE JANMU Y DE CACHEMIRA
OCUPADA POR LA INDIA, Y CUYO REGIMEN DEFINITIVO
NO ESTA TODAVIA DETERMINADO.

1.1 Population, area and density, 1970-1978
Population, superficie et densité, 1970-1978
Población, superficie y densidad, 1970-1978

JORDAN:

E—> ESTIMATES EXCLUDE FOREIGN MILITARY AND
DIPLOMATIC PERSONNEL AND THEIR FAMILIES IN THE
COUNTRY. INCLUDING REGISTERED PALESTINIAN
REFUGEES NUMBERING 722,687 AT MIDYEAR 1967.

FR—> LES ESTIMATIONS NE COMPRENNENT PAS LES
MILITAIRES ET LE PERSONNEL DIPLOMATIQUE ETRANGERS
STATIONNES SUR LE TERRITOIRE ET LES MEMBRES DE
LEUR FAMILLE LES ACCOMPAGNANT. Y COMPRIS LES
REFUGIES IMMATRICULES DE PALESTINE, AU NOMBRE
DE 722 687 AU MILIEU DE L'ANNEE 1967.

ESP> LAS ESTIMACIONES NO COMPRENDEN LOS MILI-
TARES Y LOS MIEMBROS DE SUS FAMILIAS QUE VIVEN EN
LOCALES DEL EJERCITO Y LOS EXTRANJEROS. QUEDAN
INCLUIDOS LOS REFUGIADOS INSCRITOS EN PALESTINA
(722 687 A MEDIADOS DE 1967).

KOREA, REPUBLIC OF:

E—> EXCLUDING ALIEN ARMED FORCES, CIVILIAN
ALIENS EMPLOYED BY ARMED FORCES AND FOREIGN
DIPLOMATIC PERSONNEL AND THEIR DEPENDENTS.

FR—> NON COMPRIS LES MILITAIRES ETRANGERS ET LES
CIVILS ETRANGERS TRAVAILLANT DANS LES FORCES
ARMEES, LE PERSONNEL DIPLOMATIQUE ETRANGER ET
LES MEMBRES DE LEUR FAMILLE LES ACCOMPAGNANT.

ESP> EXCLUIDOS LOS MILITARES EXTRANJEROS, LOS
CIVILES EXTRANJEROS QUE TRABAJAN EN LAS FUERZAS
ARMADAS Y LOS DIPLOMATICOS EXTRANJEROS Y LOS
MIEMBROS DE SUS FAMILIAS QUE LES ACOMPANAN.

LAO PEOPLE'S DEMOCRATIC REPUBLIC:

E—> BASED ON RESULTS OF THE MAY 1958 ADMINIS-
TRATIVE COUNT WHICH WAS ADJUSTED UPWARDS BY 30%.

FR—> D'APRES LES RESULTATS DU DENOMBREMENT
ADMINISTRATIF DE MAI 1958, QUI ONT FAIT L'OBJET
D'UN AJUSTEMENT DE 30% POUR COMPENSER LES LACUNES.

ESP> SEGUN LOS RESULTADOS DE LA ENUMERACION
ADMINISTRATIVA DE MAYO DE 1958, QUE SE HAN AJUS-
TADO EN UN 30% PARA COMPENSAR LAS LAGUNAS.

LEBANON:

E—> LEBANESE NATIONALS ONLY, EXCLUDING REGIST-
ERED PALESTINIAN REFUGEES (200,000 ON 30 JUNE
1977).

FR—> RESSORTISSANTS LIBANAIS SEULEMENT; NON
COMPRIS LES REFUGIES IMMATRICULES DE PALESTINE,
AU NOMBRE DE 200 000 AU 30 JUIN 1977.

ESP> SUBDITOS LIBANESES SOLAMENTE; QUEDAN
EXCUIDOS LOS REFUGIADOS PALESTINOS INSCRITOS
(200 000, EL 30 DE JUNIO DE 1977).

MALAYSIA:

E—> THESE FIGURES INCLUDE PENINSULAR MALAYSIA,
SABAH AND SARAWAK.

FR—> CES DONNEES COMPRENNENT LA MALAISIE PENIN-
SULAIRE, SABAH ET SARAWAK.

ESP> ESTOS DATOS COMPRENDEN MALASIA PENINSULAR,
SABAH Y SARAWAK.

PAKISTAN:

E—> EXCLUDING DATA FOR THE PAKISTAN-HELD PART
OF KASHMIR AND JAMMU, THE FINAL STATUS OF WHICH
HAS NOT YET BEEN DETERMINED, AND JUNAGARDH,
MANAVADAR, GILGIT AND BALTISTAN.

FR—> NON COMPRIS LA PARTIE DU JAMMU ET CACHE-
MIRE OCCUPEE PAR LE PAKISTAN, DONT LA STATUT DEFI-
NITIF N'A PAS ENCORE ETE DETERMINE ET JANAGARDH,
LE MANAVADAR, LE GILGIT ET LE BALTISTAN.

ESP> EXCLUIDA LA PARTE DE JANMU Y DE CACHEMIRA
OCUPADA POR EL PAKISTAN, CUYO REGIMEN DEFINI-
TIVO NO ESTA TODAVIA DETERMINADO, Y INMAGARDH,
MANAVADAR, GILGIT Y BALTISTAN.

SYRIAN ARAB REPUBLIC:

E—> INCLUDING PALESTINIAN REFUGEES NUMBERING
193,000 ON 30 JUNE 1977.

FR—> Y COMPRIS LES REFUGIES PALESTINIENS, AU
NOMBRE DE 193 000 AU 30 JUIN 1977.

ESP> INCLUIDOS LOS REFUGIADOS PALESTINOS
(193 000 EL 30 DE JUNIO DE 1977).

THAILAND:

E—> ESTIMATES INCLUDE ADJUSTMENT FOR UNDER-
ENUMERATION AT LATEST CENSUS.

FR—> LES ESTIMATIONS TIENNENT COMPTE D'UN AJUS-
TEMENT DESTINE A COMPENSER LES LACUNES DU DENOM-
BREMENT LORS DU DERNIER RECENSEMENT.

ESP> LAS ESTIMACIONES TIENEN EN CUENTA UN AJUSTE
DESTINADO A COMPENSAR LAS LAGUNAS DE LA ENU-
MERACION CORRESPONDIENTES AL ULTIMO CENSO.

GERMAN DEMOCRATIC REPUBLIC:

E—> THE DATA WHICH RELATE TO THE FEDERAL REPU-
BLIC OF GERMANY AND THE GERMAN DEMOCRATIC REPU-
BLIC INCLUDE THE RELEVANT DATA RELATING TO BERLIN
FOR WHICH SEPARATE DATA HAVE NOT BEEN SUPLIED.
THIS IS WITHOUT PREJUDICE TO ANY QUESTION OF
STATUS WHICH MAY BE INVOLVED.

FR—> LES DONNEES SE RAPPORTANT A LA REPUBLIQUE
FEDERALE D'ALLEMAGNE ET A LA REPUBLIQUE
DEMOCRATIQUE ALLEMANDE INCLUENT LES DONNEES
RELATIVES A BERLIN POUR LEQUEL DES DONNEES
SEPAREES N'ONT PAS ETE FOURNIES. CELA SANS
PREJUDICE DES QUESTIONS DE STATUT QUI PEUVENT
SE POSER A CET EGARD.

ESP> LOS DATOS RELATIVOS A LA REPUBLICA FEDERAL
DE ALEMANIA Y A LA REPUBLICA DEMOCRATICA ALEMANA
COMPRENDEN LOS DATOS PERTINENTES CORRESPONDIENTES
A BERLIN, QUE NO NOS HAN SIDO PROCURADOS
SEPARADAMENTE, LO QUE NO PREJUZGA LAS
CUESTIONES DE ESTATUTO QUE PUEDEN PLANTEARSE
AL RESPECTO.

GERMANY, FEDERAL REPUBLIC OF:

E—> THE DATA WHICH RELATE TO THE FEDERAL REPU-
BLIC OF GERMANY AND THE GERMAN DEMOCRATIC REPUBLIC
INCLUDE THE RELEVANT DATA RELATING TO BERLIN
FOR WHICH SEPARATE DATA HAVE NOT BEEN SUP-
PLIED. THIS IS WITHOUT PREJUDICE TO ANY
QUESTION OF STATUS WHICH MAY BE INVOLVED.

FR—> LES DONNEES SE RAPPORTANT A LA REPUBLIQUE
FEDERALE D'ALLEMAGNE ET A LA REPUBLIQUE
DEMOCRATIQUE ALLEMANDE INCLUENT LES DONNEES
RELATIVES A BERLIN POUR LEQUEL DES DONNEES
SEPAREES N'ONT PAS ETE FOURNIES. CELA SANS
PREJUDICE DES QUESTIONS DE STATUT QUI PEUVENT
SE POSER A CET EGARD.

ESP> LOS DATOS RELATIVOS A LA REPUBLICA FEDERAL
DE ALEMANIA Y A LA REPUBLICA DEMOCRATICA ALEMANA
COMPRENDEN LOS DATOS PERTINENTES CORRESPONDIENTES
A BERLIN, QUE NO NOS HAN SIDO PROCURADOS
SEPARADAMENTE, LO QUE NO PREJUZGA LAS
CUESTIONES DE ESTATUTO QUE PUEDEN PLANTEARSE
AL RESPECTO.

HOLY SEE:

E—> AREA IS 0.44 SQUARE KILOMETRES.

FR—> SUPERCIFIE: 0,44 KILOMETRES CARRES.

ESP> SUPERFICIE: 0,44 KILOMETROS CUADRADOS.

POLAND:

E—> EXCLUDING CIVILIAN ALIENS WITHIN THE COUN-
TRY BUT INCLUDING CIVILIAN NATIONALS TEMPORARILY
OUTSIDE THE COUNTRY.

FR—> NON COMPRIS LES CIVILS ETRANGERS DANS LE
PAYS ET Y COMPRIS LES CIVILS NATIONAUX
TEMPORAIREMENT HORS DU PAYS.

ESP> EXCLUIDOS LOS CIVILES EXTRANJEROS
RESIDENTES EN EL PAIS, E INCLUIDOS LOS CIVILES
NACIONALES AUSENTES TEMPORALMENTE DEL PAIS.

Population, area and density, 1970-1978   1.1
Population, superficie et densité, 1970-1978
Población, superficie y densidad, 1970-1978

AMERICAN SAMOA:
  E—> "DE JURE" POPULATION, BUT INCLUDING ARMED FORCES STATIONED IN THE AREA.
  FR—> POPULATION DE DROIT, Y COMPRIS LES MILI-TAIRES EN GARNISON SUR LE TERRITOIRE.
  ESP> POPLACION DE JURE, INCLUIDOS LOS MILITARES DESTACADOS EN LA ZONA.

AUSTRALIA:
  E—> ESTIMATES INCLUDE ADJUSTMENT FOR UNDER-ENUMERATION AT LATEST CENSUS.
  FR—> CES ESTIMATIONS TIENNENT COMPTE D'UN AJUS-TEMENT DESTINE A COMPENSER LES LACUNES DU DENOM-BREMENT LORS DU DERNIER RECENSEMENT.
  ESP> LAS ESTIMACIONES TIENEN EN CUENTA UN AJUSTE DESTINADO A COMPENSAR LAS LAGUNAS DE LA ENU-MERACION CORRESPONDIENTES AL ULTIMO CENSO.

GUAM:
  E—> "DE JURE" POPULATION, BUT INCLUDING ARMED FORCES STATIONED IN THE AREA.
  FR—> POPULATION DE DROIT, Y COMPRIS LES MILI-TAIRES EN GARNISON SUR LE TERRITOIRE.
  ESP> POPLACION DE JURE, INCLUIDOS LOS MILITARES DESTACADOS EN LA ZONA.

KIRIBATI:
  E—> FORMERLY LISTED AS GILBERT ISLANDS. INCLUDING TUVALU.
  FR—> ANTERIEUREMENT PRESENTE SOUS LE NOM DE ILES GILBERT. Y COMPRIS TUVALU.
  ESP> ANTERIORMENTE CLASIFICADO CON EL NOMBRE DE ISLAS GILBERT. INCLUYE TUVALU.

PACIFIC ISLANDS:
  E—> AREA REFERS TO INHABITED DRY LAND ONLY.
  FR—> SUPERFICIE TERRESTRE HABITEE SEULEMENT.
  ESP> SUPERFICIE TERRESTRE SOLAMENTE.

U.S.S.R.:
  E—> THESE FIGURES INCLUDE DATA RELATIVE TO THE BYELORUSSIAN S.S.R. AND TO THE UKRAINIAN S.S.R.
  FR—> CES CHIFFRES COMPRENNENT LES DONNEES RELA-TIVES A LA R.S.S. DE BIELORUSSIE ET A LA R.S.S. D'UKRAINE.
  ESP> ESTAS CIFRAS INCLUYEN LOS DATOS RELATIVOS A LA R.S.S. DE BIELORRUSIA Y A LA R.S.S. DE UCRANIA.

BYELORUSSIAN S.S.R.:
  E—> INHABITANTS PER SQUARE KILOMETRE REFER TO 1977.
  FR—> LE NOMBRE D'HABITANTS AU KILOMETRE CARRE SE REFERE A 1977.
  ESP> EL NUMERO DE HABITANTES POR KILOMETRO CUADRADO SE REFIERE A 1977.

1.2 Estimated total population and population 0-24 years old, by continents, major areas and groups of countries, 1970-2000

Estimation de la population totale et de la population de 0 à 24 ans, par continents, grandes régions et groupes de pays, 1970-2000

Estimación de la población total y de la población de 0 a 24 años, por continentes, grandes regiones y grupos de países, 1970-2000

A = ALL AGES A = TOUS AGES A = TODAS LAS EDADES

CONTINENTS MAJOR AREAS AND GROUPS OF COUNTRIES / CONTINENTS GRANDES REGIONS ET GROUPES DE PAYS / CONTINENTES GRANDES REGIONES Y GRUPOS DE PAISES	AGE GROUP / GROUPE D'AGE / GRUPO DE EDAD	ESTIMATED POPULATION (THOUSANDS) / ESTIMATION DE LA POPULATION (EN MILLIERS) / POBLACION ESTIMADA (EN MILES)						ANNUAL AVERAGE INCREASE / ACCROISSEMENT MOYEN ANNUEL / CRECIMIENTO MEDIO ANNUAL		
		1970	1975	1980	1985	1990	2000	1970–75 (%)	1975–80 (%)	1980–2000 (%)
		(1)	(2)	(3)	(4)	(5)	(6)	(7)	(8)	(9)
WORLD TOTAL	A	3 676 756	4 033 308	4 415 013	4 830 204	5 275 744	6 199 360	1.9	1.8	1.7
	0–4	499 004	527 202	558 633	601 593	641 613	680 789	1.1	1.2	1.0
	5–9	457 507	481 498	510 596	542 970	587 019	652 221	1.0	1.0	1.2
	10–14	415 202	453 473	476 824	506 138	538 709	624 802	1.8	1.0	1.4
	15–19	362 668	411 117	449 470	472 971	502 452	579 698	2.5	1.8	1.3
	20–24	299 905	356 837	405 906	444 277	468 034	530 687	3.5	2.6	1.3
	0–24	2 034 286	2 230 127	2 401 429	2 567 948	2 737 827	3 068 197	1.9	1.5	1.2
AFRICA	A	353 826	405 845	469 359	544 545	630 378	828 050	2.8	3.0	2.9
	0–4	63 846	73 203	85 566	98 665	110 713	129 885	3.0	3.0	2.9
	5–9	51 310	58 589	67 944	80 185	93 302	116 637	2.7	3.0	2.7
	10–14	42 719	49 703	57 019	66 317	78 517	103 940	3.1	2.8	3.0
	15–19	35 831	41 765	48 727	55 987	65 231	90 448	3.1	3.1	3.1
	20–24	29 545	34 836	40 736	47 621	54 824	76 093	3.3	3.2	3.2
	0–24	223 250	258 095	299 992	348 775	402 587	517 003	2.9	3.1	2.8

		(1)	(2)	(3)	(4)	(5)	(6)	(7)	(8)	(9)
AMERICA	A	509 119	558 971	614 826	679 091	748 903	897 667	1.9	1.9	1.9
	0-4	64 705	68 120	74 836	84 697	91 810	101 311	1.0	1.9	1.5
	5-9	62 407	63 694	67 246	74 050	83 974	96 203	0.4	1.1	1.8
	10-14	57 785	62 561	63 814	67 381	74 190	91 354	1.6	0.4	1.8
	15-19	50 914	57 585	62 395	63 678	67 272	84 061	2.5	1.6	1.6
	20-24	42 744	50 312	57 059	61 889	63 250	73 721	3.3	2.5	1.3
	0-24	278 555	302 272	325 351	351 695	380 496	446 649	1.6	1.5	1.6
ASIA	A	2 091 159	2 318 768	2 557 851	2 810 126	3 077 447	3 611 942	2.1	2.0	1.7
	0-4	309 566	326 090	339 166	356 599	376 321	385 787	1.0	0.8	0.6
	5-9	278 934	298 127	315 971	330 003	348 449	376 631	1.3	1.2	0.9
	10-14	249 903	275 773	294 985	313 079	327 356	367 138	2.0	1.1	1.1
	15-19	215 101	246 954	272 963	292 325	310 612	343 998	2.8	2.0	1.2
	20-24	172 840	211 172	243 562	269 622	289 162	322 382	4.1	2.9	1.4
	0-24	1 226 343	1 358 116	1 466 646	1 561 628	1 651 900	1 795 936	2.1	1.5	1.0
EUROPE	A	459 456	474 171	483 538	492 405	501 178	520 232	0.6	0.4	0.4
	0-4	38 186	35 998	33 563	34 185	34 942	36 557	-1.2	-1.4	0.4
	5-9	38 638	38 472	35 836	33 427	34 044	35 748	-0.1	-0.9	-0.0
	10-14	37 639	38 746	38 443	35 813	33 394	34 780	0.6	-0.3	-0.5
	15-19	36 475	37 760	38 773	38 474	35 848	34 054	0.7	0.5	-0.6
	20-24	34 937	36 805	37 643	38 668	38 395	33 396	1.0	0.5	-0.6
	0-24	185 875	187 780	184 258	180 568	176 622	174 536	0.2	-0.4	-0.3
OCEANIA	A	19 323	21 158	22 774	24 479	26 201	29 652	1.8	1.5	1.3
	0-4	2 139	2 269	2 257	2 409	2 492	2 633	1.2	-0.1	0.8
	5-9	2 106	2 165	2 264	2 254	2 407	2 601	0.6	0.0	0.7
	10-14	1 972	2 139	2 176	2 276	2 267	2 508	1.0	0.3	0.7
	15-19	1 778	1 997	2 153	2 190	2 290	2 434	2.3	1.5	0.6
	20-24	1 648	1 792	2 010	2 166	2 203	2 293	1.7	2.3	0.7
	0-24	9 643	10 361	10 861	11 295	11 659	12 469	1.4	0.9	0.7
U.S.S.R.	A	243 873	254 393	266 666	279 559	291 637	311 817	0.8	0.9	0.8
	0-4	20 563	21 523	23 244	25 038	25 335	24 616	0.9	1.6	0.3
	5-9	24 112	20 452	21 335	23 052	24 842	24 402	-3.5	-3.6	0.7
	10-14	25 185	24 551	20 388	21 270	22 985	25 082	-0.5	-0.5	1.0
	15-19	22 569	25 057	24 459	20 316	21 200	24 703	2.1	-0.5	0.0
	20-24	18 191	21 920	24 896	24 311	20 200	22 801	3.8	2.6	-0.4
	0-24	110 620	113 503	114 322	113 987	114 563	121 604	0.5	0.1	0.3
DEVELOPED COUNTRIES	A	1 074 648	1 122 025	1 163 789	1 206 860	1 248 979	1 324 799	0.9	0.7	0.7
	0-4	92 154	91 206	89 896	94 880	97 148	98 145	-0.2	-0.3	0.4
	5-9	98 088	92 488	90 976	89 732	94 954	96 654	-1.2	-0.3	0.3
	10-14	98 286	99 224	90 857	91 348	90 080	97 056	0.1	-1.3	0.2
	15-19	93 491	98 567	99 376	93 040	91 537	95 521	1.1	0.2	0.2
	20-24	86 292	93 134	98 260	99 087	92 853	90 150	1.5	1.1	0.4
	0-24	468 311	474 618	471 365	468 087	466 572	477 525	0.3	-0.1	0.1

CONTINENTS MAJOR AREAS AND GROUPS OF COUNTRIES / GRANDES REGIONS ET GROUPES DE PAYS / GRANDES REGIONES Y GRUPOS DE PAISES	AGE GROUP / GROUPE D'AGE / GRUPO DE EDAD	ESTIMATED POPULATION (THOUSANDS) / ESTIMATION DE LA POPULATION (EN MILLIERS) / POBLACION ESTIMADA (EN MILES)						ANNUAL AVERAGE INCREASE / ACCROISSEMENT MOYEN ANNUEL / CRECIMIENTO MEDIO ANNUAL		
		1970 (1)	1975 (2)	1980 (3)	1985 (4)	1990 (5)	2000 (6)	1970-75 (%) (7)	1975-80 (%) (8)	1980-2000 (%) (9)
DEVELOPING COUNTRIES	A	2 602 108	2 911 283	3 251 224	3 623 344	4 026 766	4 874 560	2.3	2.2	2.0
	0-4	406 850	435 996	468 736	506 713	544 465	582 644	1.4	1.5	1.1
	5-9	359 419	389 010	419 620	453 238	492 065	555 568	1.6	1.5	1.4
	10-14	316 916	354 249	383 967	414 790	448 629	527 746	2.3	1.6	1.6
	15-19	269 177	312 550	350 094	379 931	410 916	484 177	3.0	2.3	1.6
	20-24	213 613	263 703	307 647	345 190	375 181	440 537	4.3	3.1	1.8
	0-24	1 565 975	1 755 508	1 930 064	2 099 861	2 271 255	2 590 672	2.3	1.9	1.5
AFRICA (EXCLUDING ARAB STATES)	A	271 297	311 774	360 628	419 065	486 395	644 384	2.8	3.0	2.9
	0-4	49 498	57 233	66 910	77 734	87 828	104 948	2.9	3.2	2.3
	5-9	39 071	45 203	52 783	62 330	73 123	93 064	3.0	3.1	2.9
	10-14	32 523	37 760	43 824	51 342	60 846	81 899	3.0	3.0	3.2
	15-19	27 399	31 795	36 929	42 932	50 392	70 580	3.0	3.0	3.3
	20-24	22 864	26 636	30 928	35 990	41 932	58 724	3.1	3.0	3.3
	0-24	171 356	198 627	231 373	270 328	314 121	409 214	3.0	3.1	2.9
NORTHERN AMERICA	A	226 389	236 379	246 350	258 494	270 469	289 546	0.9	0.8	0.8
	0-4	19 041	17 645	17 899	20 806	21 439	19 730	-1.5	0.3	0.5
	5-9	22 198	19 250	17 880	18 160	21 064	20 945	-2.8	-1.5	0.8
	10-14	23 112	22 326	19 743	18 367	18 634	22 193	-0.3	-2.8	0.6
	15-19	21 385	23 326	22 989	19 979	18 607	21 798	1.8	-0.3	-0.3
	20-24	19 057	21 321	23 310	22 970	20 008	18 928	2.3	1.8	-1.0
	0-24	104 793	104 302	101 819	100 281	99 752	103 595	-0.1	-0.5	0.1
LATIN AMERICA	A	282 730	322 593	368 476	420 596	478 433	608 122	2.7	2.7	2.5
	0-4	45 664	50 476	56 938	63 891	70 371	81 581	2.0	2.4	1.8
	5-9	40 209	44 443	49 367	55 890	62 910	75 257	2.0	2.1	2.1
	10-14	34 673	39 801	44 071	49 014	55 556	69 161	2.8	2.1	2.3
	15-19	29 529	34 259	39 407	43 699	48 665	62 263	3.0	2.8	2.3
	20-24	23 687	28 991	33 749	38 919	43 242	54 793	4.1	3.1	2.5
	0-24	173 762	197 970	223 532	251 413	280 743	343 055	2.6	2.5	2.2

	(1)	(2)	(3)	(4)	(5)	(6)	(7)	(8)	(9)
ASIA (EXCLUDING ARAB STATES)									
A	2 055 948	2 277 636	2 509 570	2 753 526	3 011 337	3 523 593	2.1	2.0	1.7
0-4	303 035	318 544	330 435	346 526	364 896	372 044	1.0	0.7	0.6
5-9	273 728	291 906	308 817	321 670	338 776	364 248	1.3	1.1	0.8
10-14	245 641	270 629	288 835	306 003	319 103	356 178	2.0	1.3	1.1
15-19	211 583	242 907	267 837	286 215	303 588	334 467	2.8	2.0	1.1
20-24	169 872	207 812	239 530	264 543	283 115	314 261	4.1	2.9	1.4
0-24	1 203 858	1 331 797	1 435 454	1 524 957	1 609 477	1 741 198	2.0	1.5	1.0
(ARAB STATES)									
A	117 740	135 204	157 012	182 080	210 093	272 015	2.8	3.0	2.8
0-4	20 878	23 515	27 386	31 003	34 308	38 677	2.4	3.1	1.7
5-9	17 444	19 607	22 313	26 187	29 851	35 954	2.4	2.6	2.4
10-14	14 457	17 087	19 344	22 051	25 925	33 001	3.4	2.5	2.8
15-19	11 951	14 017	16 924	19 166	21 862	29 399	3.2	3.8	2.8
20-24	9 648	11 560	13 841	16 711	18 939	25 490	3.7	3.7	3.1
0-24	74 378	85 786	99 809	115 117	130 886	162 522	2.9	3.1	2.5

GENERAL NOTE:
THE MAJOR AREAS AND GROUPS OF COUNTRIES SHOWN IN THIS TABLE ARE CONSTITUTED AS FOLLOWS:
DEVELOPED COUNTRIES:
ALL EUROPEAN COUNTRIES, U.S.S.R, UNITED STATES OF AMERICA, CANADA, JAPAN, ISRAEL, AUSTRALIA, NEW ZEALAND AND SOUTH AFRICA.
DEVELOPING COUNTRIES:
REST OF THE WORLD.
NORTHERN AMERICA:
BERMUDA, CANADA, GREENLAND, ST. PIERRE AND MIQUELON AND UNITED STATES OF AMERICA.
LATIN AMERICA:
REST OF AMERICA.
ARAB STATES:
ALGERIA, EGYPT, LIBYAN ARAB JAMAHIRIYA, MOROCCO, SUDAN, TUNISIA, BAHRAIN, IRAQ, JORDAN, KUWAIT, LEBANON, OMAN, QATAR, SAUDI ARABIA, SYRIAN ARAB REPUBLIC, UNITED ARAB EMIRATES, YEMEN, AND YEMEN, DEMOCRATIC.

NOTE GENERALE:
LES GRANDES REGIONS ET GROUPES DE PAYS QUI FIGURENT DANS CE TABLEAU COMPRENNENT LES PAYS ET TERRITOIRES SUIVANTS:
PAYS DEVELOPPES:
TOUS LES PAYS D'EUROPE, U.R.S.S., ETATS-UNIS D'AMERIQUE, CANADA, JAPON, ISRAEL, AUSTRALIE, NOUVELLE-ZELANDE ET AFRIQUE DU SUD.
PAYS EN VOIE DE DEVELOPPEMENT:
LE RESTE DU MONDE.
AMERIQUE SEPTENTRIONALE:
BERMUDES, CANADA, GROENLAND, SAINT-PIERRE-ET-MIQUELON ET ETATS-UNIS D'AMERIQUE.
AMERIQUE LATINE:
LE RESTE DE L'AMERIQUE.
ETATS ARABES:
ALGERIE, EGYPTE, JAMAHIRIYA ARABE LIBYENNE, MAROC, SOUDAN, TUNISIE, BAHREIN, IRAK, JORDANIE, KOWEIT, LIBAN, OMAN, QATAR, ARABIE SAOUDITE, REPUBLIQUE ARABE SYRIENNE, EMIRATS ARABES UNIS, YEMEN, ET YEMEN DEMOCRATIQUE.

NOTA GENERAL:
LAS REGIONES PRINCIPALES Y LOS GRUPOS DE PAISES QUE FIGURAN EN ESTE CUADRO COMPRENDEN LOS SIGUIENTES PAISES Y TERRITORIOS:
PAISES DESARROLLADOS:
TODOS LOS DE EUROPA, LA U.R.S.S., LOS ESTADOS UNIDOS DE AMERICA, EL CANADA, EL JAPON, ISRAEL, AUSTRALIA, NUEVA ZELANDIA Y SUDAFRICA.
PAISES EN VIAS DE DESARROLLO:
LOS DEMAS PAISES DEL MUNDO.
AMERICA SEPTENTRIONAL:
BERMUDAS, CANADA, GROENLANDIA, SAN PEDRO Y MIQUELON Y LOS ESTADOS UNIDOS DE AMERICA.
AMERICA LATINA:
LOS DEMAS PAISES DE AMERICA.
ESTADOS ARABES:
ARGELIA, EGIPTO, JAMAHIRIYA ARABE LIBIA, MARRUECOS, SUDAN, TUNEZ, BAHREIN, IRAK, JORDANIA, KUWEIT, LIBANO, OMAN, QATAR, ARABIA SAUDITA, REPUBLICA ARABE SIRIA, EMIRATOS ARABES UNIDOS, YEMEN, Y YEMEN DEMOCRATICO.

1.3 Illiterate population 15 years of age and over and percentage illiteracy, by sex

Population analphabète de 15 ans et plus et pourcentage d'analphabètes, par sexe

Población analfabeta de 15 años y más y porcentaje de analfabetos, por sexo

A = ALL AGES   A = TOUS AGES   A = TODAS LAS EDADES

NUMBER OF COUNTRIES AND TERRITORIES PRESENTED IN THIS TABLE: 158
NOMBRE DE PAYS ET DE TERRITOIRES PRESENTES DANS CE TABLEAU: 158
NUMERO DE PAISES Y DE TERRITORIOS PRESENTADOS EN ESTE CUADRO: 158

COUNTRY AND YEAR OF CENSUS OR SURVEY / PAYS ET ANNEE DU RECENSEMENT OU DE L'ENQUETE / PAIS Y AÑO DEL CENSO O DE LA ENCUESTA	AGE GROUP / GROUPE D'AGE / GRUPO DE EDAD	ILLITERATE POPULATION / POPULATION ANALPHABETE / POBLACION ANALFABETA			PERCENTAGE OF ILLITERATES / POURCENTAGE D'ANALPHABETES / PORCENTAJE DE ANALFABETOS		
		TOTAL TOTALE	MALE MASCULINE MASCULINA	FEMALE FEMININE FEMENINA	TOTAL	MALE MASCULIN MASCULINO	FEMALE FEMININ FEMENINO
	(1)	(2)	(3)	(4)	(5)	(6)	(7)
AFRICA							
ALGERIA 1971 TOTAL POPULATION	15+	4 656 715	1 735 230	2 921 485	73.6	58.2	87.4
URBAN POPULATION	15+	1 253 490	427 735	825 755	58.8	42.2	74.2
RURAL POPULATION	15+	3 403 225	1 307 495	2 095 730	81.1	66.5	94.0
ANGOLA ‡ 1950	A	4 019 834	1 946 327	2 073 507	97.0	95.7	98.2
BENIN ‡ 1962	15+	1 183 000	561 000	622 000	92.0	88.0	96.0
BOTSWANA 1964 RESIDENT POPULATION	15+	182 913	84 422	98 491	67.3	69.9	65.2
BURUNDI ‡ 1962	15+	1 256 000	569 000	687 000	86.1	79.0	93.0
CAPE VERDE 1970	14+	134 633	...	...	63.1	...	...
CENTRAL AFRICAN REPUBLIC ‡ 1962	15+	671 000	312 000	359 000	92.6	87.0	98.0
CHAD ‡ 1963 AFRICAN POPULATION	15+	1 296 550	525 230	771 320	94.4	87.9	99.4
COMORO ‡ 1966	15+	59 080	22 650	36 430	41.6	33.9	48.3
CONGO ‡ 1961	15+	389 000	151 000	238 000	84.4	70.0	97.0

		(1)	(2)	(3)	(4)	(5)	(6)	(7)
EGYPT	1976 TOTAL POPULATION	10+	15 611 162	6 201 496	9 409 666	56.5	43.2	71.0
	URBAN POPULATION	10+	4 981 655	1 867 155	3 114 500	39.7	28.5	51.8
	RURAL POPULATION	10+	10 629 507	4 334 341	6 295 166	70.6	55.5	86.9
ETHIOPIA ‡	1965	15+	11 670 000	5 665 000	6 005 000	94.0	92.0	96.0
GABON ‡	1960 AFRICAN POPULATION	15+	271 629	105 404	166 225	87.6	77.8	95.2
GAMBIA ‡	1962	15+	172 000	82 000	90 000	94.0	91.0	97.0
GHANA	1970	15+	3 293 320	1 285 320	2 008 000	69.8	56.9	81.6
GUINEA	1965	15+	1 665 000	724 000	941 000	91.4	86.0	96.0
GUINEA-BISSAU ‡	1962	15+	310 000	151 000	159 000	95.1	93.0	97.0
IVORY COAST ‡	1962	15+	1 855 000	891 000	964 000	95.0	92.0	98.0
KENYA ‡	1962	15+	3 758 000	1 559 000	2 199 000	80.5	70.0	90.0
LESOTHO ‡	1966	15+	197 849	101 690	96 159	41.4	56.0	32.4
LIBERIA	1962	15+	581 578	266 494	315 084	91.1	86.1	95.8
LIBYAN ARAB JAMAHIRIYA	1973 TOTAL POPULATION	10+	710 432	255 853	454 579	49.9	33.1	69.9
	LIBYAN POPULATION	10+	650 269	210 055	440 214	51.6	32.0	73.0
	NON-LIBYAN POPULATION	10+	60 163	45 798	14 365	36.7	39.2	30.7
MADAGASCAR ‡	1953 INDIGENOUS POPULATION	14+	...	...	...	66.5	59.2	73.0
MALAWI	1966 AFRICAN POPULATION	15+	1 755 287	680 580	1 074 707	77.9	66.3	87.7
MALI ‡	1962	15+	2 447 000	1 189 000	1 258 000	97.5	96.0	99.0
MAURITANIA	1977 TOTAL POPULATION	6+	895 877	...	...	82.6	...	...
	URBAN POPULATION	6+	158 375	...	...	63.1	...	...
	RURAL POPULATION	6+	737 502	...	...	88.5	...	...
MAURITIUS	1962	13+	163 192	59 316	103 876	39.2	28.5	50.0
MOROCCO	1971 TOTAL POPULATION	15+	6 407 137	2 654 041	3 753 096	78.6	66.4	90.2
	URBAN POPULATION	15+	1 824 363	653 049	1 171 314	61.3	45.6	75.8
	RURAL POPULATION	15+	4 582 774	2 000 992	2 581 782	88.5	78.1	98.7
MOZAMBIQUE ‡	1962	15+	3 543 000	1 676 000	1 867 000	88.6	85.0	92.0
NAMIBIA	1960 AFRICAN POPULATION	15+	154 044	69 488	84 556	61.6	54.8	68.7
NIGER ‡	1962	15+	1 702 000	801 000	901 000	98.6	98.0	99.0
NIGERIA ‡	1962	15+	17 980 000	7 887 000	10 093 000	84.6	75.0	94.0
REUNION ‡	1967	15+	81 379	42 504	38 875	37.1	40.3	34.1
RWANDA ‡	1962	15+	1 303 000	583 000	720 000	83.6	76.0	91.0
ST. HELENA	1976	16+	92	50	42	2.9	3.2	2.5

COUNTRY AND YEAR OF CENSUS OR SURVEY / PAYS ET ANNEE DU RECENSEMENT OU DE L'ENQUETE / PAIS Y AÑO DEL CENSO O DE LA ENCUESTA	AGE GROUP / GROUPE D'AGE / GRUPO DE EDAD (1)	ILLITERATE POPULATION POPULATION ANALPHABETE POBLACION ANALFABETA — TOTAL TOTALE (2)	MALE MASCULINE MASCULINA (3)	FEMALE FEMININE FEMENINA (4)	PERCENTAGE OF ILLITERATES POURCENTAGE D'ANALPHABETES PORCENTAJE DE ANALFABETOS — TOTAL (5)	MALE MASCULINO (6)	FEMALE FEMENINO (7)
SENEGAL ‡ 1961 AFRICAN POPULATION	15+	1 652 260	748 540	903 720	94.4	89.6	98.9
SEYCHELLES 1971	15+	12 494	6 465	6 029	42.3	44.4	40.2
SIERRA LEONE 1963	15+	1 287 728	607 700	680 028	93.3	90.4	96.1
SOMALIA ‡ 1962	15+	1 296 000	632 000	664 000	98.5	97.0	100.0
SOUTH AFRICA 1960 TOTAL POPULATION	15+	4 103 218	2 056 535	2 046 683	43.0	43.0	43.0
URBAN POPULATION	15+	1 173 091	769 659	403 432	...	...	...
RURAL POPULATION	15+	2 930 127	1 286 876	1 643 251	...	...	...
BANTU POPULATION	15+	3 742 561	1 891 405	1 851 156	59.0	58.0	59.0
WHITE POPULATION	15+	36 392	16 620	19 772	2.0	2.0	2.0
ASIATIC POPULATION	15+	68 851	17 309	51 542	26.0	13.0	40.0
COLOURED POPULATION	15+	255 414	131 201	124 213	31.0	33.0	30.0
SUDAN 1966	15+	6 089 000	2 720 000	3 369 000	85.3	74.7	96.3
SWAZILAND 1966	15+	...	...	...	...	68.7	72.5
TOGO 1970	15+	822 025	318 997	503 028	84.1	73.1	92.9
TUNISIA ‡ 1975 TOTAL POPULATION	15+	1 996 860	793 930	1 202 930	62.0	48.9	75.2
URBAN POPULATION	15+	816 130	301 160	514 960	49.5	36.9	62.1
RURAL POPULATION	15+	1 180 730	492 760	687 970	75.4	61.9	89.2
UGANDA ‡ 1962	15+	2 633 000	1 125 000	1 508 000	65.1	56.0	74.0
UNITED REPUBLIC OF CAMEROON ‡ 1962	15+	2 056 000	864 000	1 192 000	81.1	69.0	93.0
UNITED REPUBLIC OF TANZANIA 1967	15+	4 956 045	1 882 626	3 073 419	71.9	57.3	85.1
UPPER VOLTA ‡ 1962	15+	2 609 000	1 277 000	1 332 000	98.5	98.0	99.0
ZAIRE ‡ 1962	15+	5 881 000	2 159 000	3 722 000	68.7	51.0	86.0
ZAMBIA 1969	15+	1 129 444	403 601	725 843	52.7	39.0	65.5
ZIMBABWE ‡ 1962	15+	1 329 000	565 000	764 000	60.6	52.0	69.0
AMERICA, NORTH							
ANTIGUA 1960	15+	3 478	1 408	2 070	11.3	10.3	12.0
BAHAMAS 1963	15+	7 416	3 421	3 995	10.3	9.9	10.6
BARBADOS 1970	15+	1 234	...	...	0.8	...	...

		(1)	(2)	(3)	(4)	(5)	(6)	(7)
BELIZE	1960	15+	6 680	3 022	3 658	13.4	12.5	14.2
BERMUDA	1960	15+	561	385	176	2.1	2.7	1.2
BRITISH VIRGIN ISLANDS	1960	15+	292	168	124	7.2	8.5	5.9
CAYMAN ISLANDS	1960	15+	364	170	194	6.7	6.9	6.4
COSTA RICA	1973 TOTAL POPULATION	15+	121 312	59 084	62 228	11.6	11.4	11.8
	URBAN POPULATION	15+	23 177	8 522	14 655	4.9	4.0	5.7
	RURAL POPULATION	15+	98 135	50 562	47 573	17.0	16.6	17.5
CUBA	1953 TOTAL POPULATION	15+	820 337	459 775	360 562	22.1	24.2	20.0
	URBAN POPULATION	15+	255 709	122 687	133 022	11.1	11.0	11.2
	RURAL POPULATION	15+	564 628	337 088	227 540	40.0	42.6	36.7
DOMINICA	1970	10+	2 116	...	...	4.7	...	...
DOMINICAN REPUBLIC ‡	1970 TOTAL POPULATION	15+	678 910	319 825	359 085	32.8	31.2	34.3
	URBAN POPULATION	15+	165 841	...	...	19.0	...	...
	RURAL POPULATION	15+	517 796	...	...	43.4	...	...
EL SALVADOR	1975 TOTAL POPULATION	10+	1 064 159	...	...	37.9	...	...
GRENADA	1970	15+	1 086	...	...	2.2	...	...
GUADELOUPE	1967	15+	29 627	13 944	15 683	16.8	16.5	17.1
GUATEMALA	1973 TOTAL POPULATION	15+	1 526 600	647 440	879 160	53.9	46.1	61.5
	URBAN POPULATION	15+	291 380	97 460	193 920	28.2	20.0	35.5
	RURAL POPULATION	15+	1 235 220	549 980	685 240	68.6	59.9	77.6
HAITI	1971	15+	1 954 365	854 398	1 099 967	76.7	71.3	81.6
HONDURAS	1974 TOTAL POPULATION	15+	594 194	274 815	319 379	43.1	41.1	44.9
	URBAN POPULATION	15+	99 015	37 523	61 492	21.1	17.6	24.0
	RURAL POPULATION	15+	495 179	237 292	257 887	54.4	52.1	56.8
JAMAICA	1970	15+	44 397	...	...	4.6	...	...
MARTINIQUE	1967	15+	22 003	10 720	11 283	12.2	12.6	11.8
MEXICO	1970 TOTAL POPULATION	15+	6 693 706	2 772 999	3 920 707	25.8	21.8	29.6
	URBAN POPULATION	15+	2 621 751	979 296	1 642 455	16.7	13.1	20.0
	RURAL POPULATION	15+	4 071 955	1 793 703	2 278 252	39.7	34.3	45.3
MONTSERRAT	1960	15+	1 334	561	773	19.5	20.3	18.9
NETHERLANDS ANTILLES	1971	15+	8 699	4 083	4 616	7.5	7.4	7.6
NICARAGUA	1971 TOTAL POPULATION	15+	410 755	193 475	217 277	42.5	42.0	42.9
	URBAN POPULATION	15+	94 319	33 873	60 446	19.5	16.1	22.1
	RURAL POPULATION	15+	316 436	159 605	156 831	65.4	63.8	67.0
PANAMA	1970 TOTAL POPULATION	15+	175 152	86 388	88 764	21.7	21.0	22.2
	URBAN POPULATION	15+	26 221	10 985	15 236	6.3	5.6	7.0
	RURAL POPULATION	15+	149 162	75 687	73 475	38.1	35.5	41.1
PUERTO RICO ‡	1970 TOTAL POPULATION	15+	208 981	89 082	119 899	12.2	10.8	13.4
	URBAN POPULATION	15+	87 440	34 017	53 423	8.4	6.9	9.6
	RURAL POPULATION	15+	121 541	55 065	66 476	18.0	16.4	19.7

Illiterate population
Population analphabète
Población analfabeta

COUNTRY AND YEAR OF CENSUS OR SURVEY / PAYS ET ANNEE DU RECENSEMENT OU DE L'ENQUETE / PAIS Y AÑO DEL CENSO O DE LA ENCUESTA		AGE GROUP / GROUPE D'AGE / GRUPO DE EDAD (1)	ILLITERATE POPULATION / POPULATION ANALPHABETE / POBLACION ANALFABETA			PERCENTAGE OF ILLITERATES / POURCENTAGE D'ANALPHABETES / PORCENTAJE DE ANALFABETOS		
			TOTAL TOTALE (2)	MALE MASCULINE MASCULINA (3)	FEMALE FEMININE FEMENINA (4)	TOTAL (5)	MALE MASCULIN MASCULINO (6)	FEMALE FEMININ FEMENINO (7)
ST. KITTS - NEVIS ANGUILLA	1960	15+	3 605	1 492	2 113	11.8	11.2	12.2
ST. LUCIA	1970	10+	9 475	...	...	14.8	...	...
ST. PIERRE AND MIQUELON	1967	15+	39	6	33	1.1	0.3	1.9
ST. VINCENT AND THE GRENADINES	1946	15+	8 185	3 333	4 852	23.8	23.8	23.8
TRINIDAD AND TOBAGO	1970	15+	41 750	13 724	28 026	7.8	5.3	10.3
TURKS AND CAICOS ISLANDS	1960	15+	275	125	150	8.9	9.9	8.1
UNITED STATES OF AMERICA	1969	14+	1 435 000	708 000	727 000	1.0	1.1	1.0
AMERICA, SOUTH								
ARGENTINA	1970	15+	1 225 850	532 350	693 500	7.4	6.5	8.3
BOLIVIA 1976 TOTAL POPULATION		15+	1 012 212	324 622	687 590	37.3	24.8	49.0
URBAN POPULATION		15+	183 427	36 024	147 403	16.0	6.6	24.3
RURAL POPULATION		15+	828 785	288 598	540 187	53.0	37.7	67.8
BRAZIL 1976 TOTAL POPULATION		15+	15 644 700	6 916 600	8 728 100	24.3	22.0	26.5
URBAN POPULATION		10+	18 171 552	8 315 449	9 856 103	23.6	21.7	24.8
RURAL POPULATION		10+	7 427 313	2 972 258	4 455 055	14.4	12.0	16.6
RURAL POPULATION		10+	10 744 239	5 343 191	5 401 048	40.6	39.4	41.9
CHILE 1970 TOTAL POPULATION		15+	629 440	278 440	351 000	11.9	11.1	12.8
URBAN POPULATION		15+	309 980	119 760	190 220	7.6	6.4	8.6
RURAL POPULATION		15+	319 460	158 680	160 780	27.2	25.1	29.7
COLOMBIA 1973 TOTAL POPULATION		15+	2 110 850	933 027	1 177 823	19.2	18.0	20.2
URBAN POPULATION		15+	814 945	288 686	526 259	11.2	9.0	13.0
RURAL POPULATION		15+	1 295 905	644 341	651 564	34.7	32.8	36.8
ECUADOR 1974 TOTAL POPULATION		15+	932 723	390 435	542 288	25.8	21.8	29.6
URBAN POPULATION		15+	153 280	50 615	102 665	9.7	6.9	12.2
RURAL POPULATION		15+	779 443	339 820	439 623	38.2	32.3	44.4
FRENCH GUIANA	1967	15+	7 140	4 376	2 764	26.1	28.4	23.1
GUYANA ‡	1970	15+	32 008	...	...	8.7	...	...

48

			(1)	(2)	(3)	(4)	(5)	(6)	(7)
PARAGUAY	1972	TOTAL POPULATION	15+	256 690	93 150	163 540	19.9	14.9	24.5
		URBAN POPULATION	15+	61 570	18 240	43 330	11.4	7.4	14.7
		RURAL POPULATION	15+	195 120	74 910	120 210	25.9	19.7	32.3
PERU	1972	TOTAL POPULATION	15+	2 062 870	624 018	1 438 852	27.5	16.7	38.2
		URBAN POPULATION	15+	586 191	137 018	444 176	12.6	5.9	19.1
		RURAL POPULATION	15+	1 454 676	487 000	994 676	50.9	32.9	69.2
SURINAME	1964		15+	29 000	14 000	15 000	16.4	16.0	16.7
URUGUAY	1975	TOTAL POPULATION	15+	124 664	65 007	59 657	6.1	6.6	5.7
		URBAN POPULATION	15+	87 500	40 200	47 300	5.2	5.1	5.2
		RURAL POPULATION	15+	37 000	24 900	12 100	11.0	12.6	8.6
VENEZUELA	1971		15+	1 373 561	585 928	787 633	23.5	20.3	26.6
ASIA									
AFGHANISTAN	1975	TOTAL POPULATION	6+	...	...	...	87.8	80.8	96.3
		URBAN POPULATION	6+	...	...	...	73.2	63.8	84.3
		RURAL POPULATION	6+	...	...	...	90.5	83.8	98.4
BAHRAIN	1971	TOTAL POPULATION	15+	71 978	34 598	37 380	59.8	50.8	71.5
		URBAN POPULATION	15+	60 577	...	...	57.4	...	...
		RURAL POPULATION	15+	11 401	...	...	76.2	...	...
BANGLADESH	1974	TOTAL POPULATION	15+	27 531 843	12 228 895	15 302 948	74.2	62.7	86.8
		URBAN POPULATION	15+	1 846 447	906 854	939 593	51.9	42.1	66.8
		RURAL POPULATION	15+	25 685 396	11 322 041	14 363 355	76.5	65.3	88.5
BRUNEI	1971		15+	27 795	10 464	17 331	36.1	24.5	50.3
BURMA ‡	1962		15+	5 448 000	1 331 000	4 117 000	40.3	20.0	60.0
CYPRUS	1960		15+	87 405	20 501	66 904	24.1	11.8	35.6
DEMOCRATIC KAMPUCHEA	1962	URBAN POPULATION	15+	2 050 046	598 859	1 451 187	63.9	37.7	89.6
		POPULATION	15+	144 302	28 872	115 430	42.2	17.4	71.9
		POPULATION	15+	1 905 744	569 987	1 335 757	66.1	40.0	91.5
HONG KONG ‡	1971		15+	571 840	126 152	445 688	22.7	9.9	35.9
INDIA	1971	TOTAL POPULATION	15+	211 639 300	87 797 800	123 841 500	66.6	53.2	81.1
		URBAN POPULATION	15+	26 696 800	11 600 300	18 379 800	40.1	27.9	55.1
		RURAL POPULATION	15+	184 942 500	77 552 000	107 390 500	73.6	60.4	87.5
INDONESIA	1971	TOTAL POPULATION	15+	28 802 722	9 707 044	19 095 678	43.4	30.5	55.4
		URBAN POPULATION	15+	2 765 792	723 157	2 042 635	23.3	12.4	33.9
		RURAL POPULATION	15+	26 036 930	8 983 887	17 053 043	47.8	34.5	59.9
IRAN	1971	TOTAL POPULATION	6+	14 095 000	5 956 000	8 138 000	63.1	52.3	74.5
		URBAN POPULATION	6+	3 981 000	1 529 000	2 451 000	41.4	31.3	51.9
		RURAL POPULATION	6+	10 114 000	4 427 000	5 687 000	79.6	68.1	91.7
IRAQ ‡	1965		15+	3 089 546	1 320 836	1 768 710	75.8	64.5	87.2
ISRAEL	1971	TOTAL POPULATION	15+	238 296	73 074	165 222	12.1	7.4	16.7
		URBAN POPULATION	15+	181 175	55 125	126 050	10.6	6.5	14.7
		RURAL POPULATION	15+	57 121	17 949	39 172	21.4	13.1	30.3
JAPAN	1960	TOTAL POPULATION	15+	1 425 600	310 200	1 115 400	2.2	1.0	3.3
		URBAN POPULATION	15+	334 400	73 200	261 200	1.1	0.5	1.7
		RURAL POPULATION	15+	1 091 200	237 000	854 200	3.1	1.4	4.6

COUNTRY AND YEAR OF CENSUS OR SURVEY / PAYS ET ANNEE DU RECENSEMENT OU DE L'ENQUETE / PAIS Y AÑO DEL CENSO O DE LA ENCUESTA	AGE GROUP / GROUPE D'AGE / GRUPO DE EDAD (1)	ILLITERATE POPULATION / POPULATION ANALPHABETE / POBLACION ANALFABETA — TOTAL / TOTALE (2)	MALE / MASCULINE / MASCULINA (3)	FEMALE / FEMININE / FEMENINA (4)	PERCENTAGE OF ILLITERATES / POURCENTAGE D'ANALPHABETES / PORCENTAJE DE ANALFABETOS — TOTAL (5)	MALE / MASCULIN / MASCULINO (6)	FEMALE / FEMININ / FEMENINO (7)
JORDAN 1961	15+	630 023	228 851	401 172	67.6	49.9	84.8
KOREA, REPUBLIC OF ‡ 1970 TOTAL POPULATION	15+	2 263 783	500 196	1 763 587	12.4	5.6	19.3
URBAN POPULATION	15+	458 760	77 779	380 981	5.7	2.0	9.3
RURAL POPULATION	15+	1 805 023	422 417	1 382 606	17.8	8.5	26.6
KUWAIT 1975 TOTAL POPULATION	15+	223 970	102 192	121 778	40.4	32.0	52.0
KUWAITI POPULATION	15+	122 209	41 500	80 709	51.2	35.0	66.0
NON-KUWAITI POPULATION	15+	101 761	60 692	41 069	32.3	30.2	53.2
LAO PEOPLE'S DEMOCRATIC REPUBLIC ‡ 1962	15+	1 025 000	456 000	569 000	71.7	70.0	73.0
LEBANON 1970	10+	...	...	...	...	21.5	42.1
MACAU 1970 TOTAL POPULATION	15+	31 917	11 894	20 023	20.6	15.2	26.1
URBAN POPULATION	15+	31 010	11 491	19 519	20.6	15.1	26.2
RURAL POPULATION	15+	907	403	504	18.6	16.1	21.2
MALAYSIA							
PENINSULAR MALAYSIA 1970 TOTAL POPULATION	15+	2 013 097	672 769	1 340 328	41.5	27.8	54.9
URBAN POPULATION	15+	484 969	148 562	336 407	32.2	19.8	44.9
RURAL POPULATION	15+	1 528 128	524 207	1 003 921	45.6	31.5	59.6
SABAH 1970 TOTAL POPULATION	10+	236 578	99 539	137 039	55.7	44.8	67.6
URBAN POPULATION	10+	23 414	8 670	14 744	30.9	21.2	42.1
RURAL POPULATION	10+	213 164	90 869	122 295	61.1	50.1	73.0
SARAWAK 1970 TOTAL POPULATION	15+	312 983	127 372	185 611	65.1	53.4	76.6
URBAN POPULATION	15+	30 596	9 575	21 021	35.5	22.4	48.4
RURAL POPULATION	15+	282 387	117 797	164 590	71.5	60.1	82.8
MONGOLIA 1956	9–50	23 800	...	...	4.6	...	...
NEPAL 1975	15+	...	...	...	80.8	66.6	95.0
PAKISTAN 1972 TOTAL POPULATION	15+	28 976 600	13 859 100	15 117 500	79.3	70.4	89.7
URBAN POPULATION	15+	5 632 600	2 649 500	2 983 100	59.3	49.9	71.1
RURAL POPULATION	15+	23 344 000	11 209 600	12 134 400	86.3	78.0	95.8
PHILIPPINES 1970 TOTAL POPULATION	15+	3 646 423	1 595 768	2 050 655	17.4	15.7	19.1
URBAN POPULATION	10+	595 674	234 505	361 169	7.2	6.0	8.2
RURAL POPULATION	10+	3 581 878	1 661 753	1 920 125	21.3	19.8	22.8
SAUDI ARABIA ‡ 1962	15+	3 708 000	1 781 000	1 927 000	97.5	95.0	100.0
SINGAPORE 1970	15+	394 543	110 544	283 999	31.1	17.0	45.7

		(1)	(2)	(3)	(4)	(5)	(6)	(7)
SRI LANKA	1971 TOTAL POPULATION	15+	1 736 396	561 727	1 174 669	22.4	14.0	31.5
	URBAN POPULATION	15+	1 258 074	93 213	164 861	14.1	9.4	19.7
	RURAL POPULATION	15+	1 478 322	468 514	1 009 808	25.0	15.5	34.9
SYRIAN ARAB REPUBLIC	1970	15+	1 851 949	629 904	1 222 045	60.0	40.4	80.0
THAILAND	1970 TOTAL POPULATION	15+	4 039 468	1 187 461	2 852 007	21.4	12.8	29.7
	URBAN POPULATION	15+	342 322	85 050	257 272	12.3	6.3	18.1
	RURAL POPULATION	15+	3 697 146	1 102 411	2 594 735	22.9	13.9	31.6
TURKEY	1975	15+	9 550 432	2 763 057	6 787 375	39.7	22.8	56.9
UNITED ARAB EMIRATES	1975	10+	191 153	128 740	62 413	43.7	39.6	55.8
YEMEN ‡	1962	15+	2 841 000	1 366 000	1 475 000	97.5	95.0	100.0
YEMEN, DEMOCRATIC	1973 TOTAL POPULATION	10+	736 224	254 177	482 047	72.9	52.3	92.1
	URBAN POPULATION	10+	202 879	72 423	130 456	59.1	40.0	80.5
	RURAL POPULATION	10+	435 920	136 935	298 985	77.4	53.8	96.8
	NOMADS	10+	97 425	44 819	52 606	94.2	88.3	99.9
EUROPE								
ALBANIA	1955	9+	...	...	...	28.5	20.1	36.9
BELGIUM	1947	15+	222 391	104 727	117 664	3.3	3.2	3.4
BULGARIA	1965 TOTAL POPULATION	15+	586 148	140 592	445 556	9.4	4.5	14.1
	URBAN POPULATION	15+	147 283	35 774	111 509	5.0	2.4	7.5
	RURAL POPULATION	15+	438 865	104 818	334 047	13.2	6.4	19.9
FRANCE ‡	1946	14+	1 087 406	476 524	610 882	3.6	3.3	3.8
GIBRALTAR ‡	1951	5+	6 675	1 934	4 741	34.5	21.7	45.4
GREECE ‡	1971 TOTAL POPULATION	15+	1 030 040	217 480	812 560	15.6	6.7	23.7
	URBAN & SEMI-URBAN	15+	486 140	108 980	377 160	11.2	5.2	16.8
	RURAL POPULATION	15+	543 900	108 500	435 400	24.2	10.2	37.0
HUNGARY	1970 TOTAL POPULATION	15+	163 768	61 165	102 603	2.0	1.6	2.4
	URBAN POPULATION	15+	41 643	13 796	27 847	1.1	0.8	1.4
	RURAL POPULATION	15+	122 125	47 369	74 756	2.6	2.2	3.4
ITALY	1971	15+	2 487 142	928 403	1 558 739	6.1	4.7	7.4
MALTA ‡	1963	15+	66 000	30 000	36 000	33.5	31.0	36.0
POLAND	1970 TOTAL POPULATION	15+	537 149	144 767	392 382	2.2	1.3	3.1
	URBAN POPULATION	15+	156 581	34 445	122 136	1.2	0.6	1.8
	RURAL POPULATION	15+	380 568	110 322	270 246	3.5	2.1	4.8
PORTUGAL	1970	15+	1 786 170	636 530	1 149 640	29.0	22.4	34.7
ROMANIA	1956	15+	1 448 354	370 911	1 077 443	11.4	6.1	16.3
SPAIN	1970 TOTAL POPULATION	15+	2 413 209	671 470	1 741 739	9.8	5.7	13.6
	URBAN POPULATION	15+	1 005 499	244 910	760 589	7.5	3.9	10.7
	RURAL POPULATION	15+	1 407 710	426 560	981 150	12.5	7.7	17.2
YUGOSLAVIA	1971 TOTAL POPULATION	15+	2 478 207	590 215	1 887 992	16.5	8.1	24.3
	URBAN POPULATION	15+	461 816	98 904	362 912	7.7	3.4	11.6
	RURAL POPULATION	15+	2 016 391	491 311	1 525 080	22.3	11.2	32.8

COUNTRY AND YEAR OF CENSUS OR SURVEY / PAYS ET ANNEE DU RECENSEMENT OU DE L'ENQUETE / PAIS Y AÑO DEL CENSO O DE LA ENCUESTA	AGE GROUP / GROUPE D'AGE / GRUPO DE EDAD (1)	ILLITERATE POPULATION / POPULATION ANALPHABETE / POBLACION ANALFABETA			PERCENTAGE OF ILLITERATES / POURCENTAGE D'ANALPHABETES / PORCENTAJE DE ANALFABETOS		
		TOTAL / TOTALE (2)	MALE / MASCULINE / MASCULINA (3)	FEMALE / FEMININE / FEMENINA (4)	TOTAL (5)	MALE / MASCULIN / MASCULINO (6)	FEMALE / FEMININ / FEMENINO (7)
OCEANIA							
COOK ISLANDS ‡ 1951	15+	652	324	328	8.2	7.9	8.6
FIJI 1946	15+	50 129	22 288	27 841	35.6	29.2	43.0
FRENCH POLYNESIA 1962	15+	2 577	1 291	1 286	5.5	5.3	5.7
KIRIBATI ‡ 1947 INDIGENOUS POPULATION	10+	2 637	893	1 744	9.9	6.8	12.8
NEW CALEDONIA 1976	15+	7 133	3 370	3 763	8.7	7.8	9.7
NIUE ‡ 1951	15+	166	54	112	6.0	4.0	7.9
PAPUA NEW GUINEA 1971	10+	1 106 880	512 713	594 167	67.9	60.7	75.6
TOKELAU ISLANDS 1951 INDIGENOUS POPULATION	15+	25	11	14	2.8	2.6	2.9
TONGA 1976	15+	193	81	112	0.4	0.3	0.5
SAMOA 1971 TOTAL POPULATION	15+	1 581	819	762	2.2	2.2	2.1
URBAN POPULATION	15+	212	111	101	1.3	1.3	1.2
RURAL POPULATION	15+	1 369	708	661	2.5	2.5	2.4
U.S.S.R.							
U.S.S.R. 1979 TOTAL POPULATION	9-49	...	...	...	0.2	...	...
URBAN POPULATION	9-49	...	...	...	0.1	...	...
RURAL POPULATION	9-49	...	...	...	0.3	...	...
BYELORUSSIAN S.S.R. 1970 TOTAL POPULATION	9-49	...	...	...	0.2	0.2	0.2
URBAN POPULATION	9-49	...	...	...	0.1	0.1	0.1
RURAL POPULATION	9-49	...	...	...	0.3	0.3	0.4
UKRAINIAN S.S.R. 1970 TOTAL POPULATION	9-49	...	...	...	0.2	0.2	0.2
URBAN POPULATION	9-49	...	...	...	0.1	0.1	0.1
RURAL POPULATION	9-49	...	...	...	0.3	0.3	0.3

GENERAL NOTE / NOTE GENERALE / NOTA GENERAL
   E—> THE DATA FOR THOSE COUNTRIES WHICH ARE
REFERRED TO THIS GENERAL NOTE ARE ESTIMATES
PUBLISHED IN "STATISTICS ON ILLITERACY",
MINEDLIT 5, UNESCO, PARIS, 1965.
   FR-> LES DONNEES RELATIVES AUX PAYS OU IL EST
INDIQUE DE SE REFERER A CETTE NOTE, SONT DES
ESTIMATIONS PUBLIEES DANS "DONNEES STATISTIQUES
SUR L'ANALPHABETISME", MINEDLIT 5, UNESCO,
PARIS, 1965.
   ESP> LOS DATOS RELATIVOS A LOS PAISES DONDE SE
INDICA QUE DEBEN REFERIRSE A ESTA NOTA, SON
ESTIMACIONES PUBLICADAS EN "DATOS ESTADISTICOS
SOBRE ANALFABETISMO", MINEDLIT 5, UNESCO,
PARIS, 1965.

ANGOLA:
   E—> NOT INCLUDING SEMI-LITERATE PERSONS.
ILLITERACY DEFINED AS INABILITY TO EITHER READ
OR WRITE PORTUGUESE.
   FR-> NON COMPRIS LES SEMI-ALPHABETES. ANALPHA-
BETISME DEFINI COMME INAPTITUDE A LIRE OU ECRIRE
LE PORTUGAIS.
   ESP> EXCLUIDOS LOS SEMI-ALFABETOS. ANALFABE-
TISMO DEFINIDO COMO INCAPACIDAD DE LEER O DE
ESCRIBIR EN PORTUGUES.

BENIN:
   E—> SEE GENERAL NOTE.
   FR-> VOIR LA NOTE GENERALE.
   ESP> VEASE LA NOTA GENERAL.

BURUNDI:
   E—> SEE GENERAL NOTE.
   FR-> VOIR LA NOTE GENERALE.
   ESP> VEASE LA NOTA GENERAL.

CENTRAL AFRICAN REPUBLIC:
   E—> SEE GENERAL NOTE.
   FR-> VOIR LA NOTE GENERALE.
   ESP> VEASE LA NOTA GENERAL.

CHAD:
   E—> ESTIMATES FOR "DE JURE" POPULATION, BASED
ON RESULTS OF A SAMPLE SURVEY. ILLITERACY DEFINED
AS INABILITY TO EITHER READ OR WRITE FRENCH OR
ARABIC.
   FR-> ESTIMATION DE LA POPULATION DE DROIT,
FONDEE SUR LES RESULTATS D'UNE ENQUETE PAR
SONDAGE. ANALPHABETISME DEFINI COMME INAPTITUDE
A LIRE OU A ECRIRE LE FRANCAIS OU L'ARABE.
   ESP> LA ESTIMACION DE LA POBLACION DE DERECHO
SE FUNDA EN LOS RESULTADOS DE UNA ENCUESTA POR
SONDEO. ANALFABETISMO DEFINIDO COMO INCAPACIDAD
DE LEER O DE ESCRIBIR EN FRANCES O EN ARABE.

CONGO:
   E—> SEE GENERAL NOTE.
   FR-> VOIR LA NOTE GENERALE.
   ESP> VEASE LA NOTA GENERAL.

ETHIOPA:
   E—> SEE GENERAL NOTE.
   FR-> VOIR LA NOTE GENERALE.
   ESP> VEASE LA NOTA GENERAL.

GABON:
   E—> ILLITERACY DEFINED AS INABILITY TO EITHER
READ OR WRITE FRENCH.
   FR-> ANALPHABETISME DEFINI COMME INAPTITUDE A
LIRE OU A ECRIRE LE FRANCAIS.
   ESP> ANALFABETISMO DEFINIDO COMO INCAPACIDAD DE
LEER O DE ESCRIBIR EN FRANCES.

GAMBIA:
   E—> SEE GENERAL NOTE.
   FR-> VOIR LA NOTE GENERALE.
   ESP> VEASE LA NOTA GENERAL.

GUINEA-BISSAU:
   E—> SEE GENERAL NOTE.
   FR-> VOIR LA NOTE GENERALE.
   ESP> VEASE LA NOTA GENERAL.

IVORY COAST:
   E—> SEE GENERAL NOTE.
   FR-> VOIR LA NOTE GENERALE.
   ESP> VEASE LA NOTA GENERAL.

KENYA:
   E—> SEE GENERAL NOTE.
   FR-> VOIR LA NOTE GENERALE.
   ESP> VEASE LA NOTA GENERAL.

LESOTHO:
   E—> EXCLUDING ABSENTEE WORKERS AMOUNTING TO
12% OF TOTAL POPULATION AT TIME OF CENSUS.
   FR-> NON COMPRIS LES TRAVAILLEURS ABSENTS QUI
REPRESENTAIENT 12% DE LA POPULATION TOTALE AU
MOMENT DU RECENSEMENT.
   ESP> EXCLUIDOS LOS TRABAJADORES AUSENTES QUE
EQUIVALIAN AL 12% DE LA POBLACION TOTAL EN EL
MOMENTO DEL CENSO.

MADAGASCAR:
   E—> BASED ON A SAMPLE SURVEY. NOT INCLUDING
SEMI-LITERATE PERSONS.
   FR-> D'APRES UNE ENQUETE PAR SONDAGE. NON
COMPRIS LES SEMI-ALPHABETES.
   ESP> SEGUN UNA ENCUESTA POR SONDEO. EXCLUIDOS
LOS SEMI-ALFABETOS.

MALI:
   E—> SEE GENERAL NOTE.
   FR-> VOIR LA NOTE GENERALE.
   ESP> VEASE LA NOTA GENERAL.

MOZAMBIQUE:
   E—> SEE GENERAL NOTE.
   FR-> VOIR LA NOTE GENERALE.
   ESP> VEASE LA NOTA GENERAL.

DOMINICAN REPUBLIC:
E—> EXCLUDING POPULATION UNSPECIFIED FOR LITERACY (8%).
FR—> NON COMPRIS 8% DE LA POPULATION DONT L'APTITUDE A LIRE OU A ECRIRE EST INCONNUE.
ESP> EXCLUIDO EL 8% DE LA POBLACION CUYA CAPACIDAD PARA LEER O ESCRIBIR SE DESCONOCE.

PUERTO RICO:
E—> "DE JURE POPULATION BUT NOT INCLUDING ARMED FORCES STATIONED IN THE AREA.
FR—> POPULATION DE DROIT, MAIS NON COMPRIS LES MILITAIRES EN GARNISON SUR LE TERRITOIRE.
ESP> POBLACION DE DERECHO, PERO EXCLUIDOS LOS MILITARES RESIDENTES EN EL TERRITORIO.

GUYANA:
E—> PERSONS WITH NO SCHOOLING ARE DEFINED AS ILLITERATES.
FR—> LES PERSONNES SANS SCOLARITE ONT ETE CONSIDEREES COMME ETANT ANALPHABETES.
ESP> LAS PERSONAS SIN ESCOLARIDAD HAN SIDO CONSIDERADAS COMO ANALFABETOS.

BURMA:
E—> SEE GENERAL NOTE.
FR—> VOIR LA NOTE GENERALE.
ESP> VEASE LA NOTA GENERAL.

HONG KONG:
E—> PERSONS WITH NO SCHOOLING ARE DEFINED AS ILLITERATES.
FR—> LES PERSONNES SANS SCOLARITE ONT ETE CONSIDEREES COMME ETANT ANALPHABETES.
ESP> LAS PERSONAS SIN ESCOLARIDAD HAN SIDO CONSIDERADAS COMO ANALFABETOS.

IRAQ:
E—> EXCLUDING POPULATION UNSPECIFIED FOR LITERACY (10%).
FR—> NON COMPRIS 10% DE LA POPULATION DONT L'APTITUDE A LIRE OU A ECRIRE EST INCONNUE.
ESP> EXCLUIDO EL 10% DE LA POBLACION CUYA CAPACIDAD PARA LEER O ESCRIBIR SE DESCONOCE.

KOREA, REPUBLIC OF:
E—> BASED ON A SAMPLE SURVEY. EXCLUDING ALIEN ARMED FORCES, CIVILIAN ALIENS EMPLOYED BY ARMED FORCES AND FOREIGN DIPLOMATIC PERSONNEL AND THEIR DEPENDENTS.
FR—> D'APRES UNE ENQUETE PAR SONDAGE. NON COMPRIS LES MILITAIRES ETRANGERS, LES CIVILS ETRANGERS EMPLOYES PAR LES FORCES ARMEES NI LE PERSONNEL DIPLOMATIQUE ETRANGER ET LES MEMBRES DE LEUR FAMILLE LES ACCOMPAGNANT.
ESP> SEGUN UNA ENCUESTA POR SONDEO. EXCLUIDOS LOS MILITARES EXTRANJEROS, LOS CIVILES EXTRANJEROS EMPLEADOS POR LAS FUERZAS ARMADAS Y LOS DIPLO-MATICOS EXTRANJEROS Y LOS MIEMBROS DE SUS FAMILIAS QUE LES ACOMPANAN.

NIGER: SEE GENERAL NOTE.
E—>
FR—> VOIR LA NOTE GENERALE.
ESP> VEASE LA NOTA GENERAL.

NIGERIA: SEE GENERAL NOTE.
E—>
FR—> VOIR LA NOTE GENERALE.
ESP> VEASE LA NOTA GENERAL.

REUNION: EXCLUDING POPULATION UNSPECIFIED FOR LITERACY (3%).
E—>
FR—> NON COMPRIS 3% DE LA POPULATION DONT L'APTITUDE A LIRE OU A ECRIRE EST INCONNUE.
ESP> EXCLUIDO EL 3% DE LA POBLACION CUYA CAPACIDAD PARA LEER O ESCRIBIR SE DESCONOCE.

RWANDA: SEE GENERAL NOTE.
E—>
FR—> VOIR LA NOTE GENERALE.
ESP> VEASE LA NOTA GENERAL.

SENEGAL: BASED ON A SAMPLE SURVEY. ILLITERACY
E—> DEFINED AS INABILITY TO EITHER READ OR WRITE FRENCH.
FR—> D'APRES UNE ENQUETE PAR SONDAGE. ANAL-PHABETISME DEFINI COMME INAPTITUDE A LIRE OU A ECRIRE LE FRANCAIS.
ESP> SEGUN UNA ENCUESTA POR SONDEO. ANALFABE-TISMO DEFINIDO COMO INCAPACIDAD DE LEER O DE ESCRIBIR EN FRANCES.

SOMALIA: SEE GENERAL NOTE.
E—>
FR—> VOIR LA NOTE GENERALE.
ESP> VEASE LA NOTA GENERAL.

UGANDA: SEE GENERAL NOTE.
E—>
FR—> VOIR LA NOTE GENERALE.
ESP> VEASE LA NOTA GENERAL.

UNITED REPUBLIC OF CAMEROON:
E—> SEE GENERAL NOTE.
FR—> VOIR LA NOTE GENERALE.
ESP> VEASE LA NOTA GENERAL.

UPPER VOLTA: SEE GENERAL NOTE.
E—>
FR—> VOIR LA NOTE GENERALE.
ESP> VEASE LA NOTA GENERAL.

ZAIRE: SEE GENERAL NOTE.
E—>
FR—> VOIR LA NOTE GENERALE.
ESP> VEASE LA NOTA GENERAL.

ZIMBABWE: SEE GENERAL NOTE.
E—>
FR—> VOIR LA NOTE GENERALE.
ESP> VEASE LA NOTA GENERAL.

LAO PEOPLE'S DEMOCRATIC REPUBLIC:
E—> SEE GENERAL NOTE.
FR—> VOIR LA NOTE GENERALE.
ESP> VEASE LA NOTA GENERAL.

SAUDI ARABIA:
E—> SEE GENERAL NOTE.
FR—> VOIR LA NOTE GENERALE.
ESP> VEASE LA NOTA GENERAL.

YEMEN:
E—> SEE GENERAL NOTE.
FR—> VOIR LA NOTE GENERALE.
ESP> VEASE LA NOTA GENERAL.

FRANCE:
E—> EXCLUDING POPULATION UNSPECIFIED FOR
LITERACY (4%).
FR—> NON COMPRIS 4% DE LA POPULATION DONT
L'APTITUDE A LIRE OU A ECRIRE EST INCONNUE.
ESP> EXCLUIDO EL 4% DE LA POBLACION CUYA
CAPACIDAD PARA LEER O ESCRIBIR SE DESCONOCE.

GIBRALTAR:
E—> ILLITERACY DEFINED AS INABILITY TO EITHER
READ OR WRITE ENGLISH.
FR—> ANALPHABETISME DEFINI COMME INAPTITUDE A
LIRE OU A ECRIRE L'ANGLAIS.
ESP> ANALFABETISMO DEFINIDO COMO INCAPACIDAD DE
LEER O DE ESCRIBIR EN INGLES.

GREECE:
E—> BASED ON A SAMPLE SURVEY.
FR—> D'APRES UNE ENQUETE PAR SONDAGE.
ESP> SEGUN UNA ENCUESTA POR SONDEO.

MALTA:
E—> SEE GENERAL NOTE.
FR—> VOIR LA NOTE GENERALE.
ESP> VEASE LA NOTA GENERAL.

COOK ISLANDS:
E—> ILLITERACY DEFINED AS INABILITY TO EITHER
READ OR WRITE THE NATIVE LANGUAGE.
FR—> ANALPHABETISME DEFINI COMME INAPTITUDE A
LIRE OU A ECRIRE LA LANGUE INDIGENE.
ESP> ANALFABETISMO DEFINIDO COMO INCAPACIDAD DE
LEER O DE ESCRIBIR EN LA LENGUA INDIGENA.

KIRIBATI:
E—> ILLITERACY DEFINED AS INABILITY TO EITHER
READ OR WRITE THE NATIVE LANGUAGE.
FR—> ANALPHABETISME DEFINI COMME INAPTITUDE A
LIRE OU A ECRIRE LA LANGUE INDIGENE.
ESP> ANALFABETISMO DEFINIDO COMO INCAPACIDAD DE
LEER O DE ESCRIBIR EN LA LENGUA INDIGENA.

NIUE:
E—> ILLITERACY DEFINED AS INABILITY TO EITHER
READ OR WRITE THE NATIVE LANGUAGE.
FR—> ANALPHABETISME DEFINI COMME INAPTITUDE A
LIRE OU A ECRIRE LA LANGUE INDIGENE.
ESP> ANALFABETISMO DEFINIDO COMO INCAPACIDAD DE
LEER O DE ESCRIBIR EN LA LENGUA INDIGENA.

1.4 Educational attainment
Niveau d'instruction
Nivel de instrucción

1.4 Percentage distribution of population 25 years of age and over, by educational attainment and by sex

Répartition en pourcentage de la population de 25 ans et plus selon le niveau d'instruction, par sexe

Distribución en porcentaje de la población de 25 años y más según el nivel de instrucción, por sexo

C-1 = FIRST CYCLE
C-2 = SECOND CYCLE

C-1 = PREMIER CYCLE
C-2 = DEUXIEME CYCLE

C-1 = PRIMER CICLO
C-2 = SEGUNDO CICLO

A = ALL AGES

A = TOUS AGES

A = TODAS LAS EDADES

NUMBER OF COUNTRIES AND TERRITORIES PRESENTED IN THIS TABLE: 134

NOMBRE DE PAYS ET DE TERRITOIRES PRESENTES DANS CE TABLEAU: 134

NUMERO DE PAISES Y DE TERRITORIOS PRESENTADOS EN ESTE CUADRO: 134

COUNTRY / PAYS / PAIS	YEAR / ANNEE / AÑO	SEX / SEXE / SEXO	AGE GROUP / GROUPE D'AGE / GRUPO DE EDAD	TOTAL POPULATION / POPULATION TOTALE / POBLACION TOTAL	NO SCHOOLING / SANS SCOLARITE / SIN ESCOLARIDAD	FIRST LEVEL PREMIER DEGRE PRIMER GRADO INCOMPLETED / NON COMPLETE / INCOMPLETO	FIRST LEVEL PREMIER DEGRE PRIMER GRADO COMPLETED / COMPLETE / COMPLETO	ENTERED SECOND LEVEL ACCEDE AU SECOND DEGRE ACCEDIERON AL SEGUNDO GRADO C-1	C-2	POST-SECONDARY POST-SECONDAIRE POST-SECUNDARIA
				(1)	(2)	(3)	(4)	(5)	(6)	(7)
AFRICA										
ALGERIA	1971	MF	25+	4 173 435	84.4	13.0	→	2.2	→	0.3
TOTAL POPULATION		F	25+	2 256 695	95.9	3.3	→	0.7	→	0.1
URBAN POPULATION		MF	25+	1 410 185	73.5	20.5	→	5.2	→	0.8
		F	25+	741 965	89.5	8.3	→	2.0	→	0.2
RURAL POPULATION		MF	25+	2 763 250	89.9	9.2	→	0.6	→	0.1
		F	25+	1 514 730	99.0	0.9	→	0.1	→	0.0

HIGHEST LEVEL ATTAINED / NIVEAU D'INSTRUCTION ATTEINT NIVEL DE INSTRUCCION ALCANZADO

Educational attainment 1.4
Niveau d'instruction
Nivel de instrucción

				(1)	(2)	(3)	(4)	(5)	(6)	(7)
BOTSWANA	1971	MF	25+	198 681	70.5	24.3	2.1	1.8	0.6	0.6
		F	25+	111 419	67.9	28.5	1.5	1.3	0.4	0.4
GAMBIA	1973	MF	25+	203 986	94.9	0.8	0.5	3.6	→	0.2
		F	25+	97 345	97.1	0.5	0.2	2.0	→	0.1
GHANA	1960	MF	25+	2 602 580	86.2	12.1	→	1.1	→	0.7
		F	25+	1 258 670	94.1	5.3	→	0.3	→	0.3
KENYA‡ TOTAL POPULATION	1969	MF	25+	3 662 699	75.9	20.5	→	2.8	0.8	→
		F	25+	1 859 539	86.7	11.9	→	1.1	0.4	→
URBAN POPULATION		MF	25+	400 290	46.9	37.0	→	5.3	10.7	→
		F	25+	131 512	61.3	26.2	→	3.6	8.8	→
RURAL POPULATION		MF	25+	3 262 409	79.5	18.5	→	1.1	0.9	→
		F	25+	1 728 027	88.6	10.7	→	0.3	0.3	→
LESOTHO	1966	MF	25+	333 930	41.1	57.2	→	1.6	→	0.1
		F	25+	209 712	34.4	64.7	→	0.9	→	0.0
LIBERIA ‡	1962	MF	25+	471 049	92.3	2.1	2.9	1.7	→	1.0
		F	25+	235 420	96.5	0.8	1.4	0.8	→	0.5
LIBYAN ARAB JAMAHIRIYA ‡	1973	MF	10+	1 424 557	50.0	41.4	→	7.0	→	1.6
		F	10+	650 685	70.0	25.7	→	3.8	→	.5
MALAWI	1966	MF	25+	1 540 044	67.5	32.1	→	0.4	→	0.0
		F	25+	838 494	78.7	21.3	→	0.1	→	0.0
MAURITIUS	1972	MF	25+	311 824	36.0	32.6	18.3	11.9	→	1.2
		F	25+	157 317	48.0	30.3	12.3	9.0	→	0.5
NAMIBIA	1960	MF	25+	231 039	66.9	→	18.2	12.8	→	2.1
		F	25+	112 536	72.4	→	13.8	12.2	→	1.6
SENEGAL	1970	MF	6+	2 857 310	55.0	40.3	1.8	2.1	.7	.1
		M	6+	1 508 619	68.2	29.0	1.1	1.2	.4	.0
SEYCHELLES	1971	MF	25+	21 193	28.3	34.5	21.5	7.3	5.9	2.6
		F	25+	11 089	25.6	36.8	22.7	8.1	5.1	1.7
SIERRA LEONE	1963	MF	25+	994 789	94.4	0.4	2.9	1.1	0.9	0.3
		F	25+	480 976	96.5	0.2	1.9	0.6	0.7	0.1
SOUTH AFRICA ‡ TOTAL POPULATION	1970	MF	25+	8 685 224	42.1	21.4	5.3	20.7	6.7	3.7
		F	25+	4 448 424	43.7	20.8	5.6	20.9	6.0	3.1
URBAN POPULATION		MF	25+	4 749 910	23.6	21.9	7.1	31.2	10.6	5.6
		F	25+	2 159 486	19.9	21.2	8.0	35.1	10.7	5.1
RURAL POPULATION		MF	25+	3 935 314	64.6	20.8	3.3	8.1	1.9	1.3
		F	25+	2 288 938	66.1	20.3	3.4	7.5	1.5	1.2

1.4 Educational attainment
Niveau d'instruction
Nivel de instrucción

HIGHEST LEVEL ATTAINED / NIVEAU D'INSTRUCTION ATTEINT
NIVEL DE INSTRUCCION ALCANZADO

COUNTRY PAYS PAIS	YEAR ANNEE AÑO	SEX SEXE SEXO	AGE GROUP GROUPE D'AGE GRUPO DE EDAD	TOTAL POPULATION POPULATION TOTALE POBLACION TOTAL (1)	NO SCHOOLING SANS SCOLARITE SIN ESCOLARIDAD (2)	FIRST LEVEL / PREMIER DEGRE / PRIMER GRADO INCOMPLETE NON COMPLETE INCOMPLETO (3)	FIRST LEVEL / PREMIER DEGRE / PRIMER GRADO COMPLETED COMPLETE COMPLETO (4)	ENTERED SECOND LEVEL / ACCEDE AU SECOND DEGRE / ACCEDIERON AL SEGUNDO GRADO C-1 (5)	ENTERED SECOND LEVEL C-2 (6)	POST-SECONDARY POST-SECONDAIRE POST-SECUNDARIA (7)
SUDAN	1956	MF F	25+ 25+	3 552 000 1 749 000	91.2 98.9	6.1 0.6	1.9 0.3	0.5 0.1	0.3 0.1	→ →
SWAZILAND ‡	1966	MF F	25+ 25+	135 713 72 063	73.1 75.8	15.6 15.2	5.3 4.3	3.4 2.7	2.2 1.8	0.4 0.2
TOGO	1970	MF F	25+ 25+	710 152 394 826	89.8 96.5	5.8 2.1	3.3 1.0	0.7 0.3	0.2 0.1	0.1 0.0
TUNISIA TOTAL POPULATION	1975	MF F	25+ 25+	2 053 860 1 030 390	82.7 90.8	9.7 5.5	→ →	6.4 3.2	→ →	1.2 0.5
URBAN POPULATION		MF F	25+ 25+	1 214 890 529 500	75.4 83.6	13.3 9.6	→ →	9.3 5.9	→ →	2.0 1.0
RURAL POPULATION		MF F	25+ 25+	1 004 870 500 890	94.3 98.5	3.8 1.2	→ →	1.7 0.3	→ →	0.1 0.0
UGANDA AFRICAN POPULATION	1969	MF F	25+ 25+	3 540 142 1 722 312	71.8 86.3	23.5 12.5	3.0 0.9	1.7 0.3	0.1 0.0	0.1 0.0
ZAIRE	1955	MF F	25+ 25+	5 867 655 3 059 696	89.0 98.6	9.2 0.1	1.1 1.2	0.7 0.1	→ →	→ →
ZAMBIA ‡	1969	MF F	25+ 25+	1 476 584 744 933	63.9 79.0	25.4 16.8	6.5 2.2	2.0 0.5	1.7 1.2	0.6 0.3
ZIMBABWE	1969	MF F	25+ 25+	2 064 270 744 140	43.0 55.2	45.3 40.0	9.3 4.0	1.9 0.5	0.0 0.0	0.6 0.2
AMERICA, NORTH										
ANTIGUA ‡	1960	MF F	25+ 25+	21 007 12 049	4.3 4.3	13.2 13.0	74.5 75.6	7.4 6.8	→ →	0.6 0.3
BARBADOS	1970	MF F	25+ 25+	101 818 58 287	1.1 1.1	33.7 36.0	→ →	63.9 62.3	→ →	1.2 0.7

Educational attainment **1.4**
Niveau d'instruction
Nivel de instrucción

				(1)	(2)	(3)	(4)	(5)	(6)	(7)
BELIZE	1960	MF	25+	34 435	28.7	→	60.9	10.3	→	→
		F	25+	17 718	29.0	→	61.8	9.2	→	→
BERMUDA	1970	MF	A	51 847	10.2	41.5	→	43.8	→	4.5
		F	A	25 786	9.6	39.8	→	46.8	→	3.8
BRITISH VIRGIN ISLANDS	1970	MF	15+	9 456	15.1	66.7	→	15.8	→	2.4
		F	15+	4 446	15.9	65.1	→	17.6	→	1.4
CANADA TOTAL POPULATION	1976	MF	25+	12 618 015	1.8	18.5	12.2	36.6	→	30.9
		F	25+	6 449 805	1.9	18.2	12.0	39.4	→	28.5
URBAN POPULATION		MF	25+	9 719 770	1.6	17.1	10.9	37.0	→	33.3
		F	25+	5 055 130	1.8	17.5	11.1	39.6	→	30.0
RURAL POPULATION		MF	25+	2 898 255	2.4	23.3	16.3	35.0	→	22.9
		F	25+	1 394 695	2.2	21.1	15.1	38.3	→	23.4
CAYMAN ISLANDS	1960	MF	25+	4 044	4.8	12.7	74.8	7.8	→	→
		F	25+	2 284	4.2	12.7	75.7	7.4	→	→
COSTA RICA TOTAL POPULATION	1973	MF	25+	657 543	16.1	49.1	17.8	6.3	4.9	5.8
		F	25+	331 240	16.0	49.8	17.7	6.5	4.5	5.4
URBAN POPULATION		MF	25+	297 887	7.2	37.4	24.8	10.9	9.0	10.6
		F	25+	161 996	8.1	39.3	24.4	10.9	8.1	9.3
RURAL POPULATION		MF	25+	359 656	23.6	58.8	12.1	2.4	1.4	1.8
		F	25+	169 244	23.6	59.9	11.4	2.3	1.1	1.7
CUBA ‡	1953	MF	25+	2 629 574	24.3	41.3	28.8	3.9	→	1.7
		F	25+	1 259 573	22.8	42.3	29.8	3.9	→	1.1
DOMINICA	1960	MF	15+	32 894	14.1	53.4	25.5	6.4	→	0.5
		F	15+	18 390	13.1	52.2	28.3	6.2	→	0.2
DOMINICAN REPUBLIC TOTAL POPULATION	1970	MF	25+	1 145 090	40.1	41.6	4.3	9.6	2.5	1.9
		F	25+	563 150	42.8	40.9	3.9	8.7	2.4	1.3
URBAN POPULATION		MF	25+	487 675	22.9	42.1	7.4	18.3	5.2	4.1
RURAL POPULATION		MF	25+	657 415	52.8	41.2	2.0	3.2	0.5	0.3
EL SALVADOR	1971	MF	25+	1 240 245	54.7	38.3	→	6.1	→	0.9
GRENADA	1960	MF	15+	46 218	6.7	55.4	29.7	7.7	→	0.5
		F	15+	26 693	6.8	56.3	29.7	7.0	→	0.2

1.4 Educational attainment
Niveau d'instruction
Nivel de instrucción

HIGHEST LEVEL ATTAINED / NIVEAU D'INSTRUCTION ATTEINT
NIVEL DE INSTRUCCION ALCANZADO

COUNTRY / PAYS / PAIS	YEAR / ANNEE / AÑO	SEX / SEXE / SEXO	AGE GROUP / GROUPE D'AGE / GRUPO DE EDAD	TOTAL POPULATION / POPULATION TOTALE / POBLACION TOTAL (1)	NO SCHOOLING / SANS SCOLARITE / SIN ESCOLARIDAD (2)	FIRST LEVEL / PREMIER DEGRE / PRIMER GRADO INCOMPLETED / NON COMPLETE / INCOMPLETO (3)	COMPLETED / COMPLETE / COMPLETO (4)	ENTERED SECOND LEVEL / ACCEDE AU SECOND DEGRE / ACCEDIERON AL SEGUNDO GRADO C-1 (5)	C-2 (6)	ENTERED POST-SECONDARY / POST-SECONDAIRE / POST-SECUNDARIA (7)
GUATEMALA TOTAL POPULATION	1973	MF	25+	1 785 720	93.9	→	→	4.9	→	1.2
		F	25+	897 960	94.7	→	→	4.8	→	0.5
URBAN POPULATION		MF	25+	639 780	85.2	→	→	11.8	→	2.9
RURAL POPULATION		MF	25+	1 145 940	98.7	→	→	1.1	→	0.2
HAITI ‡	1971	MF	25+	1 726 128	83.5	8.5	4.0	2.0	1.8	0.3
		F	25+	915 644	88.0	5.9	3.2	1.6	1.1	0.2
HONDURAS TOTAL POPULATION	1974	MF	25+	858 459	53.1	34.5	6.0	1.5	3.8	1.0
		F	25+	440 453	56.3	32.1	6.0	1.4	3.8	0.4
URBAN POPULATION		MF	25+	279 554	29.5	41.1	12.5	3.9	10.0	3.0
		F	25+	152 135	33.7	40.2	12.0	3.5	9.5	1.1
RURAL POPULATION		MF	25+	578 905	64.5	31.4	2.9	0.4	0.8	0.1
		F	25+	288 318	68.3	27.8	2.8	0.3	0.8	0.0
JAMAICA	1960	MF	25+	677 628	18.8	75.3	→	5.5	→	0.5
		F	25+	362 010	16.4	77.8	→	5.6	→	0.2
MEXICO	1970	MF	20+	20 951 564	89.8	→	→	4.1	3.6	2.6
MONTSERRAT	1960	MF	25+	4 745	14.9	22.1	59.3	3.1	→	0.5
		F	25+	2 971	13.0	22.9	61.2	2.8	→	0.1
NETHERLANDS ANTILLES	1960	MF	25+	56 328	15.7	74.3	4.9	4.3	→	0.8
		F	25+	29 643	15.7	76.4	5.0	2.7	→	0.2
NICARAGUA	1971	MF	25+	593 100	53.9	19.3	22.5	→	4.4	→

Educational attainment 1.4
Niveau d'instruction
Nivel de instrucción

			(1)	(2)	(3)	(4)	(5)	(6)	(7)
PANAMA	1970	MF	25+	537 394	24.9	53.5	→	9.0	8.4	4.2
FORMER CANAL ZONE TOTAL POPULATION	1970	MF	25+	19 855	1.0	2.6	17.9	8.9	38.9	30.7
		F	25+	9 279	0.8	2.8	19.9	11.2	38.2	27.1
URBAN POPULATION		MF	25+	1 441	0.3	1.9	7.8	9.3	35.5	45.1
		F	25+	741	0.4	3.1	11.2	8.9	34.1	42.2
RURAL POPULATION		MF	25+	18 414	1.1	2.6	18.7	8.8	39.2	29.5
		F	25+	8 538	0.8	2.8	20.6	11.4	38.6	25.8
PUERTO RICO	1970	MF	25+	1 196 692	14.4	23.4	24.2	10.9	15.0	12.1
		F	25+	620 439	16.4	23.3	24.6	10.3	14.0	11.3
ST. KITTS - NEVIS ANGUILLA ‡	1960	MF	25+	22 117	5.0	18.2	72.1	4.2	→	0.6
		F	25+	12 756	4.9	17.8	73.0	3.9	→	0.4
ST. LUCIA	1960	MF	15+	47 764	26.3	45.1	24.9	3.4	→	0.3
		F	15+	26 472	25.0	44.9	26.8	3.2	→	0.1
ST. VINCENT AND THE GRENADINES	1960	MF	15+	40 429	7.9	64.5	21.4	5.9	→	0.3
		F	15+	22 922	7.7	65.4	21.8	5.1	→	0.1
TRINIDAD AND TOBAGO	1970	MF	25+	350 554	11.6	74.6	→	12.6	→	1.2
		F	25+	180 166	15.2	72.3	→	11.8	→	0.6
TURKS AND CAICOS ISLANDS	1970	MF	A	5 482	15.4	72.4	→	10.3	→	2.0
		F	A	2 884	14.6	72.6	→	11.5	→	1.3
UNITED STATES OF AMERICA	1971	MF	25+	109 632 000	7.0	→	20.0	50.7	→	22.3
		F	25+	58 275 000	6.4	→	19.3	55.5	→	18.8
U.S. VIRGIN ISLANDS TOTAL POPULATION	1970	MF	25+	28 891	1.6	7.0	39.3	34.5	→	17.6
		F	25+	14 449	1.6	6.6	40.1	35.7	→	16.0
URBAN POPULATION		MF	25+	7 308	1.3	6.1	48.6	33.9	→	10.2
		F	25+	3 834	1.4	5.7	49.0	33.9	→	10.0
RURAL POPULATION		MF	25+	21 583	1.7	7.3	36.2	34.7	→	20.1
		F	25+	10 615	1.7	6.9	36.9	36.3	→	18.1
AMERICA, SOUTH										
ARGENTINA	1970	MF	25+	12 366 850	8.3	41.8	30.6	7.8	7.5	4.0
		F	25+	6 304 250	9.5	41.8	31.5	6.1	8.5	2.5
BOLIVIA	1976	MF	20+	2 157 346	43.0	41.7	→	9.3	→	5.9
		F	20+	1 117 123	55.5	32.9	→	7.4	→	4.1
BRAZIL	1976	MF	25+	42 096 300	32.7	53.0	4.3	5.7	→	4.3
		F	25+	21 419 800	36.0	50.8	4.0	6.0	→	3.2

1.4 Educational attainment
Niveau d'instruction
Nivel de instrucción

HIGHEST LEVEL ATTAINED / NIVEAU D'INSTRUCTION ATTEINT
NIVEL DE INSTRUCCION ALCANZADO

COUNTRY / PAYS / PAIS	YEAR / ANNEE / AÑO	SEX / SEXE / SEXO	AGE GROUP / GROUPE D'AGE / GRUPO DE EDAD	TOTAL POPULATION / POPULATION TOTALE / POBLACION TOTAL	NO SCHOOLING / SANS SCOLARITE / SIN ESCOLARIDAD	FIRST LEVEL / PREMIER DEGRE / PRIMER GRADO		ENTERED SECOND LEVEL / ACCEDE AU SECOND DEGRE / ACCEDIERON AL SEGUNDO GRADO		POST-SECONDARY / POST-SECONDAIRE / POST-SECUNDARIA
						INCOMPLETED / NON COMPLETE / INCOMPLETO	COMPLETED / COMPLETE / COMPLETO	C-1	C-2	
				(1)	(2)	(3)	(4)	(5)	(6)	(7)
CHILE TOTAL POPULATION	1970	MF	25+	3 721 125	12.4	57.2	→	26.6	→	3.8
		F	25+	1 945 921	13.3	57.7	→	26.5	→	2.5
URBAN POPULATION		MF	25+	2 712 020	8.3	34.1	26.0	27.0	→	4.8
RURAL POPULATION		MF	25+	792 400	29.8	54.2	10.0	5.4	→	0.6
COLOMBIA TOTAL POPULATION	1973	MF	20+	8 478 100	22.4	55.9	→	18.4	→	3.3
		F	20+	4 483 086	23.7	56.0	→	18.5	→	1.8
URBAN POPULATION		MF	20+	5 593 002	14.2	54.8	→	26.1	→	4.9
		F	20+	3 108 408	16.1	56.2	→	25.1	→	2.6
RURAL POPULATION		MF	20+	2 885 098	38.4	58.0	→	3.5	→	0.2
		F	20+	1 374 677	40.8	55.6	→	3.5	→	0.1
ECUADOR TOTAL POPULATION	1974	MF	25+	2 296 282	31.9	53.7	→	5.9	5.3	3.2
		F	25+	1 160 896	36.8	49.8	→	6.0	5.8	1.7
URBAN POPULATION		MF	25+	958 110	13.0	56.7	→	12.1	11.2	7.0
		F	25+	508 630	16.4	56.3	→	11.9	11.9	3.5
RURAL POPULATION		MF	25+	1 338 172	45.4	51.5	→	1.5	1.1	0.4
		F	25+	652 265	52.8	44.7	→	1.3	1.1	0.2
GUYANA	1960	MF	15+	298 903	12.9	37.2	38.9	10.5	→	0.4
		F	15+	152 000	16.9	35.6	37.9	9.4	→	0.2
PARAGUAY TOTAL POPULATION	1972	MF	25+	842 223	19.6	57.7	10.3	5.9	4.6	2.0
		F	25+	438 419	25.4	53.8	10.6	5.1	4.0	1.2
URBAN POPULATION		MF	25+	346 870	11.3	46.8	16.5	11.0	9.8	4.6
		F	25+	192 086	15.4	47.0	17.5	9.5	8.0	2.5
RURAL POPULATION		MF	25+	495 353	25.5	65.3	5.9	2.2	0.9	0.2
		F	25+	246 333	33.2	59.1	5.1	1.6	0.8	0.1

Educational attainment 1.4
Niveau d'instruction
Nivel de instrucción

	Year		(1)	(2)	(3)	(4)	(5)	(6)	(7)
PERU ‡	1972	MF	5 008 980	35.0	47.1	→	13.4	→	4.5
		F	2 539 525	47.5	38.6	→	10.9	→	3.0
URBAN POPULATION		MF	7 073 800	23.7	31.1	17.6	12.8	10.1	4.8
		F	3 545 100	28.4	31.2	16.8	11.0	9.0	3.6
RURAL POPULATION		MF	4 689 400	57.7	32.8	6.3	2.0	0.9	0.3
		F	2 334 600	70.3	24.3	3.6	1.1	0.5	0.2
URUGUAY	1975	MF	1 590 200	9.9	36.7	29.6	17.4	→	6.3
		F	824 700	10.4	34.9	31.2	16.6	→	6.8
VENEZUELA ‡	1961	MF	2 360 041	49.1	28.4	15.7	3.1	2.2	1.5
		F	1 170 553	56.2	25.9	13.5	2.0	2.0	0.5
ASIA									
AFGHANISTAN TOTAL POPULATION	1975	MF	3 712 038	91.5	1.8	2.6	1.1	1.3	1.7
		F	1 671 245	98.1	0.2	0.2	0.3	0.3	0.8
URBAN POPULATION		MF	528 622	76.5	3.3	5.8	3.8	4.9	5.6
		F	235 684	91.3	1.3	1.4	1.7	2.1	2.1
RURAL POPULATION		MF	3 183 416	94.0	1.6	1.9	0.6	0.8	1.0
		F	1 435 561	99.3	0.1	0.1	0.0	0.0	1.0
BAHRAIN	1971	MF	81 520	77.4	5.5	4.2	9.2	→	3.8
		F	34 633	86.2	3.6	2.4	5.6	→	2.2
BANGLADESH	1974	MF	24 896 064	82.3	10.0	→	6.9	→	.9
		F	12 053 928	93.0	5.4	→	1.4	→	.1
BRUNEI	1971	MF	47 951	52.4	28.1	→	16.5	→	3.1
		F	21 062	72.6	16.1	→	9.7	→	1.7
BURMA URBAN POPULATION	1953	MF	1 317 108	67.0	17.2	→	15.0	→	0.7
		F	634 186	71.6	20.1	→	8.1	→	0.2
RURAL POPULATION	1954	MF	1 132 317	87.4	9.6	→	3.0	→	0.0
		F	581 032	91.3	7.6	→	1.1	→	0.0
CYPRUS	1960	MF	263 513	28.9	23.0	33.8	13.0	→	1.4
		F	137 897	42.4	23.7	24.4	9.0	→	0.5
HONG KONG	1976	MF	2 058 290	28.5	42.3	→	9.9	19.3	→
		F	1 014 150	44.7	34.8	→	6.7	13.8	→
INDIA TOTAL POPULATION	1971	MF	227 050 000	72.2	22.7	→	3.9	→	1.1
		F	108 813 000	86.6	11.7	→	1.3	→	0.3
URBAN POPULATION		MF	45 101 000	46.6	36.8	→	12.3	→	4.2
		F	20 122 000	64.2	28.7	→	5.5	→	1.7
RURAL POPULATION		MF	181 949 000	78.6	19.2	→	1.8	→	0.3
		F	88 692 000	91.7	7.9	→	0.4	→	0.0

1.4 Educational attainment
Niveau d'instruction
Nivel de instrucción

HIGHEST LEVEL ATTAINED / NIVEAU D'INSTRUCTION ATTEINT / NIVEL DE INSTRUCCION ALCANZADO

COUNTRY PAYS PAIS	YEAR ANNEE AÑO	SEX SEXE SEXO	AGE GROUP GROUPE D'AGE GRUPO DE EDAD	TOTAL POPULATION POPULATION TOTALE POBLACION TOTAL (1)	NO SCHOOLING SANS SCOLARITE SIN ESCOLARIDAD (2)	FIRST LEVEL / PREMIER DEGRE / PRIMER GRADO		ENTERED SECOND LEVEL / ACCEDE AU SECOND DEGRE / ACCEDIERON AL SEGUNDO GRADO		POST-SECONDARY POST-SECONDAIRE POST-SECUNDARIA (7)
						INCOMPLETED NON COMPLETE INCOMPLETO (3)	COMPLETED COMPLETE COMPLETO (4)	C-1 (5)	C-2 (6)	
INDONESIA TOTAL POPULATION	1971	MF F	25+ 25+	46 955 716 24 298 337	55.3 69.7	22.1 16.3	17.0 11.0	5.1 2.9	↗ ↗	0.5 0.2
URBAN POPULATION		MF F	10+ 10+	14 617 395 7 371 738	22.0 31.4	29.7 29.2	27.2 23.7	14.1 10.9	↗ ↗	7.0 4.8
RURAL POPULATION		MF F	10+ 10+	65 809 030 34 005 968	45.2 56.0	33.7 28.6	17.7 13.6	2.1 1.2	↗ ↗	1.3 0.7
IRAN	1966	MF F	25+ 25+	9 667 492 4 588 229	88.5 94.0	2.9 1.5	4.3 2.3	1.6 1.0	1.8 1.0	0.9 0.2
IRAQ	1965	MF F	25+ 25+	2 973 628 1 492 353	94.9 98.1	2.5 1.0	↗ ↗	1.7 0.6	↗ ↗	0.9 0.4
ISRAEL TOTAL POPULATION	1972	MF F	25+ 25+	1 369 627 696 062	17.0 22.3	37.0 35.7	↗ ↗	31.3 29.6	↗ ↗	14.8 12.4
JAPAN TOTAL POPULATION	1970	MF F	25+ 25+	58 859 800 30 670 300	0.9 1.4	60.6 63.1	↗ ↗	33.0 34.3	↗ ↗	5.5 1.3
URBAN POPULATION		MF F	25+ 25+	42 130 700 21 798 300	0.7 1.0	55.2 57.9	↗ ↗	37.3 39.5	↗ ↗	6.8 1.5
RURAL POPULATION		MF F	25+ 25+	16 729 200 8 871 900	1.5 2.2	74.1 75.8	↗ ↗	22.1 21.4	↗ ↗	2.3 0.6
JORDAN ‡	1961	MF F	25+ 25+	569 679 289 963	79.6 91.3	5.8 1.9	7.2 3.2	6.5 3.4	↗ ↗	0.8 0.3

Educational attainment 1.4
Niveau d'instruction
Nivel de instrucción

				(1)	(2)	(3)	(4)	(5)	(6)	(7)
KOREA, REPUBLIC OF‡										
TOTAL POPULATION	1970	MF	25+	12 582 515	72.6	↑↑	↑↑	21.8	↑↑	5.6
		F	25+	6 526 889	84.2	↑↑	↑↑	14.0	↑↑	1.8
URBAN POPULATION		MF	25+	5 147 871	53.0	↑↑	↑↑	36.0	↑↑	11.0
		F	25+	2 612 558	68.9	↑↑	↑↑	27.1	↑↑	4.0
RURAL POPULATION		MF	25+	7 434 384	86.2	↑↑	↑↑	12.0	↑↑	1.8
		F	25+	3 914 331	94.4	↑↑	↑↑	5.3	↑↑	0.3
KUWAIT	1975	MF	25+	203 267	37.5	16.8	↑↑	33.2	↑↑	12.5
		F	25+	58 271	30.7	17.9	↑↑	40.8	↑↑	10.7
MACAU ‡	1970	MF	25+	93 557	26.9	58.0	↑↑	13.7	↑↑	1.4
		F	25+	47 800	33.7	55.3	↑↑	10.2	↑↑	0.9
MALAYSIA										
PENINSULAR MALAYSIA										
TOTAL POPULATION	1970	MF	A	8 780 728	40.6	30.9	13.7	9.3	5.5	↑↑
		F	A	4 367 660	48.2	28.8	11.6	7.4	4.0	↑↑
URBAN POPULATION		MF	A	2 524 994	32.2	29.8	12.9	14.0	11.1	↑↑
		F	A	1 254 331	39.2	28.7	11.8	11.9	8.5	↑↑
RURAL POPULATION		MF	A	6 255 734	43.9	31.4	14.0	7.4	3.2	↑↑
		F	A	3 113 329	51.8	28.9	11.6	5.7	2.1	↑↑
SABAH										
TOTAL POPULATION	1970	MF	A	651 304	59.1	25.9	5.2	6.4	3.4	↑↑
		F	A	313 077	67.3	21.4	3.9	5.0	2.3	↑↑
URBAN POPULATION		MF	A	106 670	35.5	30.9	10.0	14.8	8.9	↑↑
		F	A	49 993	43.3	28.5	8.4	13.5	6.4	↑↑
RURAL POPULATION		MF	A	544 634	63.7	24.9	4.3	4.7	2.4	↑↑
		F	A	263 084	71.9	20.1	3.1	3.4	1.5	↑↑
SARAWAK										
TOTAL POPULATION	1970	MF	25+	320 523	72.2	14.6	5.5	4.7	2.0	0.9
		F	25+	158 963	84.2	8.1	3.3	2.8	1.1	0.5
URBAN POPULATION		MF	A	148 590	35.5	27.3	12.1	15.7	9.3	↑↑
		F	A	73 930	42.5	25.4	11.5	13.7	6.9	↑↑
RURAL POPULATION		MF	A	738 702	65.4	22.6	6.1	4.2	1.8	↑↑
		F	A	366 239	73.0	18.5	4.7	2.7	1.1	↑↑
MONGOLIA	1969	MF	12+	749 281	46.5	42.7	↑	7.7	↑	3.1
NEPAL	1971	MF	25+	4 864 271	99.6	0.1	↑↑	0.2	0.1	0.1
		F	25+	2 440 005	99.9	0.0	↑↑	0.0	0.0	0.0
PAKISTAN	1972	MF	25+	24 491 662	81.3	2.3	5.7	3.7	3.6	3.4
		F	25+	11 214 453	92.8	1.1	2.1	1.4	1.0	1.6

1.4 Educational attainment
Niveau d'instruction
Nivel de instrucción

HIGHEST LEVEL ATTAINED / NIVEAU D'INSTRUCTION ATTEINT / NIVEL DE INSTRUCCION ALCANZADO

COUNTRY / PAYS / PAIS	YEAR / ANNEE / AÑO	SEX / SEXE / SEXO	AGE GROUP / GROUPE D'AGE / GRUPO DE EDAD	TOTAL POPULATION / POPULATION TOTALE / POBLACION TOTAL (1)	NO SCHOOLING / SANS SCOLARITE / SIN ESCOLARIDAD (2)	FIRST LEVEL / PREMIER DEGRE / PRIMER GRADO — INCOMPLETED / NON COMPLETE / INCOMPLETO (3)	COMPLETED / COMPLETE / COMPLETO (4)	ENTERED SECOND LEVEL / ACCEDE AU SECOND DEGRE / ACCEDIERON AL SEGUNDO GRADO — C-1 (5)	C-2 (6)	POST-SECONDARY / POST-SECONDAIRE / POST-SECUNDARIA (7)
PHILIPPINES TOTAL POPULATION	1970	MF / F	25+ / 25+	12 696 808 / 6 469 367	19.7 / 22.1	38.1 / 38.5	18.0 / 18.2	7.6 / 6.7	6.5 / 5.0	9.6 / 9.4
URBAN POPULATION		MF / F	25+ / 25+	4 143 208 / 2 155 337	9.0 / 10.7	25.3 / 27.7	20.1 / 21.5	11.0 / 10.2	13.1 / 10.6	21.4 / 19.2
RURAL POPULATION		MF / F	25+ / 25+	8 553 600 / 4 314 030	24.9 / 27.8	44.3 / 43.9	17.0 / 16.6	6.0 / 4.9	3.3 / 2.3	4.6 / 4.6
SINGAPORE	1970	MF / F	25+ / 25+	78 790 / 39 086	47.6 / 65.8	29.6 / 19.4	→ / →	20.9 / 13.9	→ / →	2.0 / 1.0
SRI LANKA TOTAL POPULATION	1971	MF / F	25+ / 25+	5 114 600 / 991 991	29.5 / 40.9	23.5 / 20.5	35.4 / 28.2	→ / →	9.4 / 8.6	2.3 / 1.8
URBAN POPULATION		MF / F	25+ / 25+	1 206 933 / 549 530	20.6 / 27.4	16.3 / 16.2	42.5 / 38.7	→ / →	16.8 / 14.5	3.9 / 3.1
RURAL POPULATION		MF / F	25+ / 25+	3 907 627 / 1 875 203	32.3 / 44.9	25.7 / 21.8	33.2 / 25.1	→ / →	7.1 / 6.8	1.7 / 1.4
SYRIAN ARAB REPUBLIC	1970	MF / F	25+ / 25+	2 061 729 / 1 028 918	68.6 / 87.5	25.9 / 10.2	→ / →	4.3 / 2.0	→ / →	1.3 / 0.4
THAILAND ‡	1970	MF / F	25+ / 25+	12 086 148 / 6 218 946	34.1 / 43.3	60.5 / 53.6	→ / →	4.4 / 2.5	→ / →	1.1 / 0.7
TURKEY	1965	MF / F	20+ / 20+	15 328 982 / 7 750 286	58.0 / 76.8	11.6 / 5.3	23.6 / 14.4	5.7 / 3.2	→ / →	1.1 / 0.3
UNITED ARAB EMIRATES ‡	1975	MF / F	10+ / 10+	437 708 / 112 860	43.8 / 55.6	27.1 / 19.7	7.9 / 7.1	6.6 / 5.2	10.3 / 9.6	4.3 / 2.8

Educational attainment 1.4
Niveau d'instruction
Nivel de instrucción

			(1)	(2)	(3)	(4)	(5)	(6)	(7)
YEMEN, DEMOCRATIC TOTAL POPULATION	1973	MF	1 009 977	72.9	22.1	5.1	↑↑	↑↑	↑↑
		F	523 638	92.1	6.5	1.4	↑↑	↑↑	↑↑
URBAN POPULATION		MF 10+	343 126	59.1	30.2	10.7	↑↑	↑↑	↑↑
		F 10+	161 998	80.5	15.1	4.4	↑↑	↑↑	↑↑
RURAL POPULATION		MF 10+	666 851	80.0	17.9	2.1	↑↑	↑↑	↑↑
		F 10+	361 639	97.2	2.6	0.1	↑↑	↑↑	↑↑
EUROPE									
ALBANIA	1955	MF A	1 389 971	54.8	35.8	6.7	0.8	0.9	0.4
		F A	677 525	63.6	30.4	4.7	0.6	0.7	0.1
AUSTRIA	1971	MF 25+	4 593 727	61.7	↑↑	↑↑	35.8	↑↑	2.6
		F 25+	2 553 119	74.3	↑↑	↑↑	24.6	↑↑	1.1
BELGIUM	1970	MF 25+	5 927 487	5.5	↑↑	60.6	19.9	8.8	5.2
		F 25+	3 107 501	5.8	↑↑	64.0	19.4	7.7	3.2
BULGARIA TOTAL POPULATION	1965	MF 25+	4 380 919	49.0	↑↑	32.9	12.9	↑↑	5.2
		F 25+	2 026 263	55.3	↑↑	27.4	13.5	↑↑	3.8
URBAN POPULATION		MF 25+	2 022 838	29.6	↑↑	38.7	23.2	↑↑	8.5
		F 25+	978 326	34.4	↑↑	36.0	24.1	↑↑	5.5
RURAL POPULATION		MF 25+	2 335 286	66.3	↑↑	28.3	4.0	↑↑	1.3
		F 25+	1 075 873	72.9	↑↑	22.6	3.5	↑↑	1.0
CZECHOSLOVAKIA	1970	MF 25+	8 390 982	0.6	57.2	↑↑	38.2	↑↑	4.1
		F 25+	4 438 654	0.7	71.6	↑↑	25.6	↑↑	2.1
FINLAND	1970	MF 25+	2 610 744	69.9	↑↑	↑↑	17.8	6.2	6.1
		F 25+	1 407 176	69.3	↑↑	↑↑	20.2	5.3	5.3
GERMAN DEMOCRATIC REPUBLIC	1971	MF 25+	10 809 462	49.1	↑↑	↑↑	42.4	↑↑	8.5
		F 25+	6 150 022	64.4	↑↑	↑↑	31.0	↑↑	4.6
GERMANY, FEDERAL REPUBLIC OF	1970	MF 25+	38 558 900	77.7	↑↑	↑↑	↑↑	18.0	4.3
		F 25+	21 103 700	81.2	↑↑	↑↑	↑↑	16.9	1.9
GREECE TOTAL POPULATION	1971	MF 25+	5 242 196	42.7	↑↑	37.9	5.2	9.7	4.4
		F 25+	2 765 256	52.9	↑↑	32.7	3.6	8.6	2.3
URBAN POPULATION		MF 25+	3 395 184	34.6	↑↑	38.3	6.8	14.1	6.2
		F 25+	1 794 384	43.2	↑↑	35.7	5.1	12.8	3.2
RURAL POPULATION		MF 25+	1 847 012	57.7	↑↑	37.3	2.3	1.6	1.1
		F 25+	970 872	70.7	↑↑	27.1	0.8	.8	.6

1.4 Educational attainment
Niveau d'instruction
Nivel de instrucción

HIGHEST LEVEL ATTAINED / NIVEAU D'INSTRUCTION ATTEINT
NIVEL DE INSTRUCCION ALCANZADO

COUNTRY / PAYS / PAIS	YEAR ANNEE AÑO	SEX SEXE SEXO	AGE GROUP GROUPE D'AGE GRUPO DE EDAD	TOTAL POPULATION POPULATION TOTALE POBLACION TOTAL (1)	NO SCHOOLING SANS SCOLARITE SIN ESCOLARIDAD (2)	FIRST LEVEL — PREMIER DEGRE — PRIMER GRADO INCOMPLETED NON COMPLETE INCOMPLETO (3)	COMPLETED COMPLETE COMPLETO (4)	ENTERED SECOND LEVEL — ACCEDE AU SECOND DEGRE — ACCEDIERON AL SEGUNDO GRADO C-1 (5)	C-2 (6)	POST-SECONDARY POST-SECONDAIRE POST-SECUNDARIA (7)
HUNGARY	1975	MF	7+	9 441 000	2.0	45.4	52.6	→	→	→
		F	7+	4 893 000	2.3	48.2	49.5	→	→	→
ICELAND	1960	MF	25+	88 372	86.5	→	→	9.8	→	3.7
		F	25+	44 487	86.7	→	→	11.7	→	1.6
IRELAND	1971	MF	25+	1 562 091	67.9	→	→	27.4	→	4.6
		F	25+	790 413	65.8	→	→	30.6	→	3.6
ITALY ‡	1971	MF	25+	32 965 274	7.3	23.7	48.9	17.5	→	2.6
		F	25+	17 310 402	8.8	27.3	47.5	14.9	→	1.5
MALTA	1967	MF	25+	156 853	22.9	46.5	11.7	16.6	→	2.4
		F	25+	84 686	23.2	51.4	10.7	13.8	→	1.0
MONACO	1961	MF	A	22 297	4.5	60.9	→	27.9	→	6.8
NORWAY	1975	MF	16+	3 014 668	2.1	→	→	62.4	27.0	8.5
		F	16+	1 533 194	1.8	→	→	67.5	24.4	6.2
		F	16+	1 533 194	1.8	→	→	67.5	24.4	6.2
POLAND TOTAL POPULATION	1970	MF	25+	17 429 704	5.2	25.5	43.2	20.7	→	5.4
		F	25+	9 317 848	7.0	27.9	43.9	17.0	→	4.2
URBAN POPULATION	1970	MF	25+	9 339 337	2.9	12.9	44.0	31.3	→	8.9
		F	25+	5 064 976	4.2	15.3	47.2	26.7	→	6.6
RURAL POPULATION	1970	MF	25+	8 090 367	7.9	39.9	42.3	8.4	→	1.4
		F	25+	4 252 872	10.3	43.0	39.9	5.5	→	1.2
PORTUGAL	1960	MF	25+	4 845 008	45.1	28.8	21.6	3.5	→	1.1
		F	25+	2 612 841	52.5	27.8	16.7	2.6	→	0.4
SPAIN	1970	MF	25+	19 204 501	12.9	12.9	64.7	3.2	2.6	3.7
		F	25+	10 134 790	17.5	12.6	63.1	2.7	1.8	2.2
SWITZERLAND	1970	MF	25+	3 196 376	5.1	73.8	→	→	18.3	2.9
		F	25+	1 730 620	5.6	75.2	→	→	18.5	0.8

Educational attainment 1.4
Niveau d'instruction
Nivel de instrucción

				(1)	(2)	(3)	(4)	(5)	(6)	(7)
UNITED KINGDOM										
ENGLAND AND WALES OCCUPIED POPULATION ‡	1950	MF	25+	14 475 901	13.3	→	65.6	17.8	1.7	1.6
		F	25+	3 778 995	11.1	→	64.5	20.3	2.8	1.3
NORTHERN IRELAND	1961	MF	25+	765 333	6.6	→	67.1	22.2	2.3	1.8
		F	25+	405 176	6.8	→	64.8	24.5	2.8	1.1
SCOTLAND OCCUPIED POPULATION	1951	MF	25+	1 684 501	4.5	→	76.7	15.2	1.5	2.1
		F	25+	412 162	3.0	→	73.2	18.2	3.2	2.4
YUGOSLAVIA ‡	1971	MF	25+	11 160 871	23.9	38.4	18.5	15.3	→	3.9
		F	25+	5 874 912	33.8	36.2	19.2	8.8	→	2.1
OCEANIA										
AMERICAN SAMOA	1960	MF	25+	6 377	3.0	21.3	60.5	11.6	→	3.6
		F	25+	3 300	3.7	26.1	61.7	7.0	→	1.6
AUSTRALIA	1971	MF	25+	6 878 445	0.9	29.3	→	48.3	→	21.5
		F	25+	3 472 417	0.9	30.1	→	59.0	→	10.0
SOLOMON ISLANDS INDIGENOUS POPULAT.	1976	MF	25+	68 102	55.5	39.5	→	3.3	→	1.6
		F	25+	31 714	64.8	32.6	→	1.7	→	1.0
FIJI	1976	MF	25+	213 707	19.7	45.8	20.5	6.7	3.9	3.3
		F	25+	105 689	27.0	45.4	17.1	5.6	2.4	2.5
FRENCH POLYNESIA	1962	MF	20+	38 149	84.2	→	9.2	5.0	1.6	→
		F	20+	18 317	85.2	→	9.5	4.5	0.8	→
GUAM	1960	MF	25+	27 477	3.0	42.9	→	38.9	→	15.3
		F	25+	10 224	6.2	46.1	→	33.5	→	14.3
NEW CALEDONIA ‡	1976	MF	14+	76 774	9.4	75.6	→	13.1	→	2.0
		F	14+	36 291	10.5	75.9	→	12.2	→	1.4
NEW ZEALAND	1966	MF	25+	1 368 501	0.9	39.9	→	54.3	→	4.9
		F	25+	693 746	0.9	40.3	→	55.9	→	2.9
PACIFIC ISLANDS	1970	MF	25+	10 969	34.1	20.7	25.3	6.8	6.6	6.4
		F	25+	5 922	38.5	25.2	24.4	4.5	4.2	3.2
PAPUA NEW GUINEA INDIGENOUS POPULAT.	1971	MF	25+	917 993	85.7	12.0	→	2.3	→	→
		F	25+	452 973	89.5	9.7	→	0.8	→	→
SAMOA	1971	MF	25+	43 532	5.4	59.1	→	31.0	→	4.5
		F	25+	21 647	5.9	62.4	→	28.4	→	3.4

1.4 Educational attainment
Niveau d'instruction
Nivel de instrucción

COUNTRY	YEAR	SEX	AGE GROUP	TOTAL POPULATION	HIGHEST LEVEL ATTAINED / NIVEAU D'INSTRUCTION ATTEINT NIVEL DE INSTRUCCION ALCANZADO		FIRST LEVEL PREMIER DEGRE PRIMER GRADO		ENTERED SECOND LEVEL ACCEDE AU SECOND DEGRE ACCEDIERON AL SEGUNDO GRADO		POST-SECONDARY
PAYS	ANNEE	SEXE	GROUPE D'AGE	POPULATION TOTALE	NO SCHOOLING						POST-SECONDAIRE
PAIS	AÑO	SEXO	GRUPO DE EDAD	POBLACION TOTAL	SANS SCOLARITE	INCOMPLETED NON COMPLETE	COMPLETED COMPLETE	C-1	C-2	POST-SECUNDARIA
					SIN ESCOLARIDAD	INCOMPLETO	COMPLETO			
				(1)	(2)	(3)	(4)	(5)	(6)	(7)
U.S.S.R.										
U.S.S.R.	1970	MF	20+	149 478 148	48.4	→	→	44.4	→	7.2
	1970	F	20+	85 073 764	53.2	→	→	40.7	→	6.1
BYELORUSSIAN S.S.R.	1970	MF	20+	5 620 702	54.4	→	→	39.5	→	6.1
	1970	F	20+	3 212 486	59.4	→	→	35.4	→	5.2
UKRAINIAN S.S.R.	1970	MF	20+	31 482 631	48.8	→	→	44.7	→	6.5
	1970	F	20+	18 157 359	54.5	→	→	40.2	→	5.3

KENYA:
E—> THE CATEGORY "COMPLETED FIRST LEVEL" COM-
PRISES THE LAST TWO YEARS OF PRIMARY EDUCATION.
FR—> LA CATEGORIE "PREMIER DEGRE COMPLETE" COM-
PREND LES DEUX DERNIERES ANNEES DE L'ENSEIGNEMENT
DU PREMIER DEGRE.
ESP> LA CATEGORIA "PRIMER GRADO COMPLETO" COM-
PRENDE LOS DOS ULTIMOS AÑOS DE LA ENSEÑANZA DE
PRIMER GRADO.

LIBERIA:
E—>THE CATEGORY "COMPLETED FIRST LEVEL" COM-
SES THE LAST TWO YEARS OF PRIMARY EDUCATION.
FR—> LA CATEGORIE "PREMIER DEGRE COMPLETE". COM-
PREND LES DEUX DERNIERES ANNEES DE L'ENSEIGNEMENT
DU PREMIER DEGRE.
ESP> LA CATEGORIA "PRIMER GRADO COMPLETO" COM-
PRENDE LOS DOS ULTIMOS AÑOS DE LA ENSEÑANZA DE
PRIMER GRADO.

LIBYAN ARAB JAMAHIRIYA:
E—> THE CATEGORY "NO SCHOOLING" COMPRISES
ILLITERATES AND THOSE PERSONS WHO DID NOT STATE
THEIR LEVEL OF EDUCATION.
FR—> LA CATEGORIE "SANS SCOLARITE" COMPREND LES
ANALPHABETES ET LES PERSONNES DONT LE NIVEAU
D'INSTRUCTION EST INCONNU.
ESP> LA CATEGORIA "SIN ESCOLARIDAD" COMPRENDE
LOS ANALFABETOS Y LAS PERSONAS CUYO NIVEL DE
INSTRUCCION SE DESCONOCE.

SOUTH AFRICA:
E—> THOSE PERSONS WHO DID NOT STATE THEIR LEVEL
OF EDUCATION HAVE BEEN INCLUDED IN THE CATEGORY
"NO SCHOOLING".
FR—> LA CATEGORIE "SANS SCOLARITE" COMPREND LES
PERSONNES DONT LE NIVEAU D'INSTRUCTION EST
INCONNU.
ESP> LAS PERSONAS CUYO NIVEL DE INSTRUCCION SE
DESCONOCE FIGURAN EN LA CATEGORIA "SIN ESCOLA-
RIDA".

SWAZILAND:
E—> THE CATEGORY "COMPLETED FIRST LEVEL" COM-
PRISES THE LAST TWO YEARS OF PRIMARY EDUCATION.
FR—> LA CATEGORIE "PREMIER DEGRE COMPLETE" COM-
PREND LES DEUX DERNIERES ANNEES DE L'ENSEIGNEMENT
DU PREMIER DEGRE.
ESP> LA CATEGORIA "PRIMER GRADO COMPLETO" COM-
PRENDE LOS DOS ULTIMOS AÑOS DE LA ENSEÑANZA DE
PRIMER GRADO.

ZAMBIA:
E—> THE CATEGORY "COMPLETED FIRST LEVEL" COM-
PRISES THE LAST TWO YEARS OF PRIMARY EDUCATION.
FR—> LA CATEGORIE "PREMIER DEGRE COMPLETE" COM-
PREND LES DEUX DERNIERES ANNEES DE L'ENSEIGNEMENT
DU PREMIER DEGRE
ESP> LA CATEGORIA "PRIMER GRADO COMPLETO" COM-
PRENDE LOS DOS ULTIMOS AÑOS DE LA ENSEÑANZA DE
PRIMER GRADO.

Educational attainment 1.4
Niveau d'instruction
Nivel de instrucción

ANTIGUA:
E—> THE CATEGORY "COMPLETED FIRST LEVEL" COMPRISES THE LAST TWO YEARS OF PRIMARY EDUCATION.
FR—> LA CATEGORIE "PREMIER DEGRE COMPLETE" COMPREND LES DEUX DERNIERES ANNEES DE L'ENSEIGNEMENT DU PREMIER DEGRE.
ESP> LA CATEGORIA "PRIMER GRADO COMPLETO" COMPRENDE LOS DOS ULTIMOS AÑOS DE LA ENSEÑANZA DE PRIMER GRADO.

CUBA:
E—> THE CATEGORY "COMPLETED FIRST LEVEL" COMPRISES THE LAST TWO YEARS OF PRIMARY EDUCATION.
FR—> LA CATEGORIE "PREMIER DEGRE COMPLETE" COMPREND LES DEUX DERNIERES ANNEES DE L'ENSEIGNEMENT DU PREMIER DEGRE.
ESP> LA CATEGORIA "PRIMER GRADO COMPLETO" COMPRENDE LOS DOS ULTIMOS AÑOS DE LA ENSEÑANZA DE PRIMER GRADO.

HAITI:
E—> ILLITERACY DATA HAVE BEEN USED FOR THE CATEGORY "NO SCHOOLING".
FR—> LES DONNEES RELATIVES A L'ANALPHABETISME ONT ETE UTILISEES POUR LES PERSONNES SANS SCOLARITE.
ESP> SE HAN UTILIZADO LOS DATOS RELATIVOS AL ANALFABETISMO CON RESPECTO A LAS PERSONAS "SIN ESCOLARIDAD".

ST. KITTS-NEVIS-ANGUILLA:
E—> THE CATEGORY "COMPLETED FIRST LEVEL" COMPRISES THE LAST TWO YEARS OF PRIMARY EDUCATION.
FR—> LA CATEGORIE "PREMIER DEGRE COMPLETE" COMPREND LES DEUX DERNIERES ANNEES DE L'ENSEIGNEMENT DU PREMIER DEGRE.
ESP> LA CATEGORIA "PRIMER GRADO COMPLETO" COMPRENDE LOS DOS ULTIMOS AÑOS DE LA ENSEÑANZA DE PRIMER GRADO.

PERU:
E—> THOSE PERSONS WHO DID NOT STATE THEIR LEVEL OF EDUCATION HAVE BEEN INCLUDED IN THE CATEGORY "NO SCHOOLING".
FR—> LES PERSONNES DONT LE NIVEAU D'INSTRUCTION EST INCONNU SONT INCLUSES DANS LA CATEGORIE "SANS SCOLARITE".
ESP> LAS PERSONAS CUYO NIVEL DE INSTRUCCION SE DESCONOCE FIGURAN EN LA CATEGORIA "SIN ESCOLARIDAD".

VENEZUELA:
E—> THE NUMBER AND PERCENTAGE WITHIN THE TOTAL POPULATION OF PERSONS WHOSE EDUCATIONAL LEVEL IS UNKNOWN IS: MF 25+ 426,614 (15.3%); F 25+ 194,484 (14.2%).
FR—> PAR RAPPORT A LA POPULATION TOTALE, LE NOMBRE DE PERSONNES DONT LE NIVEAU D'INSTRUCTION EST INCONNU EST LE SUIVANT: MF 25+ 426 614 (15,3% F 25+ 194 484 (14,2%).
ESP> EN RELACION CON LA POBLACION TOTAL, EL NUMERO DE PERSONAS CUYO NIVEL DE INSTRUCCION SE DESCONOCE ES EL SIGUIENTE: MF 25+ 426 614 (15.3%); F 25+ 194 484 (14.2%).

JORDAN:
E—> THE CATEGORY "COMPLETED FIRST LEVEL" COMPRISES THE LAST TWO YEARS OF PRIMARY EDUCATION.
FR—> LA CATEGORIE "PREMIER DEGRE COMPLETE" COMPREND LES DEUX DERNIERES ANNEES DE L'ENSEIGNEMENT DU PREMIER DEGRE.
ESP> LA CATEGORIA "PRIMER GRADO COMPLETO" COMPRENDE LOS DOS ULTIMOS AÑOS DE LA ENSEÑANZA DE PRIMER GRADO.

KOREA, REPUBLIC OF:
E—> ILLITERACY DATA HAVE BEEN USED FOR THE CATEGORY "NO SCHOOLING".
FR—> LES DONNEES RELATIVES A L'ANALPHABETISME ONT ETE UTILISEES POUR LES PERSONNES SANS SCOLARITE.
ESP> SE HAN UTILIZADO LOS DATOS RELATIVOS AL ANALFABETISMO CON RESPECTO A LAS PERSONAS "SIN ESCOLARIDAD".

MACAU:
E—> ILLITERACY DATA HAVE BEEN USED FOR THE CATEGORY "NO SCHOOLING".
FR—> LES DONNEES RELATIVES A L'ANALPHABETISME ONT ETE UTILISEES POUR LES PERSONNES SANS SCOLARITE.
ESP> SE HAN UTILIZADO LOS DATOS RELATIVOS AL ANALFABETISMO CON RESPECTO A LAS PERSONAS "SIN ESCOLARIDAD".

THAILAND:
E—> ILLITERACY DATA HAVE BEEN USED FOR THE CATEGORY "NO SCHOOLING".
FR—> LES DONNEES RELATIVES A L'ANALPHABETISME ONT ETE UTILISEES POUR LES PERSONNES SANS SCOLARITE.
ESP> SE HAN UTILIZADO LOS DATOS RELATIVOS AL ANALFABETISMO CON RESPECTO A LAS PERSONAS "SIN ESCOLARIDAD".

UNITED ARAB EMIRATES:
E—> THE CATEGORY "NO SCHOOLING" COMPRISES ILLITERATES AND THOSE PERSONS WHO DID NOT STATE THEIR LEVEL OF EDUCATION.
FR—> LA CATEGORIE "SANS SCOLARITE" COMPREND LES ANALPHABETES ET LES PERSONNES DONT LE NIVEAU D'INSTRUCTION EST INCONNU.
ESP> LA CATEGORIA "SIN ESCOLARIDAD" COMPRENDE LOS ANALFABETOS Y LAS PERSONAS CUYO NIVEL DE INSTRUCCION SE DESCONOCE.

ITALY:
E—> ILLITERACY DATA HAVE BEEN USED FOR THE CATEGORY "NO SCHOOLING".
FR—> LES DONNEES RELATIVES A L'ANALPHABETISME ONT ETE UTILISEES POUR LES PERSONNES SANS SCOLARITE.
ESP> SE HAN UTILIZADO LOS DATOS RELATIVOS AL ANALFABETISMO CON RESPECTO A LAS PERSONAS "SIN ESCOLARIDAD".

1.4 Educational attainment
Niveau d'instruction
Nivel de instrucción

ENGLAND AND WALES:
E.—> THE NUMBER AND PERCENTAGE WITHIN THE TOTAL
POPULATION OF PERSONS WHOSE EDUCATIONAL LEVEL IS
UNKNOWN IS: MF 25+ 1,328,833 (8.4%); F 25+
434,022 (10.3%).
FR—> PAR RAPPORT A LA POPULATION TOTALE, LE
NOMBRE DE PERSONNES DONT LE NIVEAU D'INSTRUCTION
EST INCONNU EST LE SUIVANT: MF 25+ 1 328 833
(8.4%); F 25 + 434 022 (10.3%).
ESP> EN RELACION CON LA POBLACION TOTAL, EL
NUMERO DE PERSONAS CUYO NIVEL DE INSTRUCCION SE
DESCONOCE ES EL SIGUIENTE: MF 25+ 1 328 833
(8.4%); F 25+ 434 022 (10.3%).

YUGOSLAVIA:
E.—> THE CATEGORY "COMPLETED FIRST LEVEL" COM—
PRISES THE LAST TWO YEARS OF PRIMARY EDUCATION.
FR—> LA CATEGORIE "PREMIER DEGRE COMPLETE" COM—
PREND LES DEUX DERNIERES ANNEES DE L'ENSEIGNEMENT
DU PREMIER DEGRE.
ESP> LA CATEGORIA "PRIMER GRADO COMPLETO" COM—
PRENDE LOS DOS ULTIMOS AÑOS DE LA ENSEÑANZA DE
PRIMER GRADO.

NEW CALEDONIA:
E.—> THOSE PERSONS WHO DID NOT STATE THEIR LEVEL
OF EDUCATION HAVE BEEN INCLUDED IN THE CATEGORY
"NO SCHOOLING".
FR—> LA CATEGORIE "SANS SCOLARITE" COMPREND LES
PERSONNES DONT LE NIVEAU D'INSTRUCTION EST
INCONNU.
ESP> LAS PERSONAS CUYO NIVEL DE INSTRUCCION SE
DESCONOCE FIGURAN EN LA CATEGORIA "SIN
ESCOLARIDAD".

Education

Education

Educación

The following three chapters of the *Yearbook* assemble most of the basic statistical information collected and compiled by Unesco regarding public and private educational institutions at all levels. This collection of tables provides world-wide statistical data on such subjects as the number of schools; teachers, and pupils by sex and by level and type of education; students and graduates in higher education by sex, field of study and level of degree; foreign students in higher education by country of origin; students abroad; and expenditure on education, showing public expenditure by purpose, total expenditure as a percentage of gross national product and current expenditure by level and type of education, both public and private. As far as possible, data refer to the school year beginning in 1970, as well as the four most recent years.

For the purpose of these tables, the definitions and classifications set out in the revised Recommendation concerning the International Standardization of Educational Statistics, adopted by the General Conference of Unesco at its twentieth session (Paris, 1978), have been applied as far as possible. In accordance therewith education is classified by level as follows:

Education preceding the first level, which provides education for children who are not old enough to enter a school at the first level (e.g. at nursery school, kindergarten, infant school).

Education at the first level, of which the main function is to provide basic instruction in the tools of learning (e.g. at elementary school, primary school).

Education at the second level, based upon at least four years' previous instruction at first level, and providing general or specialized instruction, or both (e.g. at middle school, secondary school, high school, teacher-training school at this level, schools of a vocational or technical nature).

Education at the third level, which requires, as a minimum condition of admission, the successful completion of education at the second level, or evidence of the attainment of an equivalent level of knowledge (e.g. at university, teachers' college, higher professional school).

Special education, covering all types of education given to children who suffer from physical, mental, visual, social, hearing or speech handicaps, or from reading and writing difficulties.

The following definitions are also reproduced from the Recommendation:

A pupil (student) is a person enrolled in a school for systematic instruction at any level of education.

A teacher is a person directly engaged in instructing a group of pupils (students). Heads of educational institutions, supervisory and other personnel should be counted as teachers only when they have regular teaching functions.

A school (educational institution) is a group of pupils (students) of one or more grades organized to receive instruction of a given type and level under one teacher, or under more than one teacher and with an immediate head.

(a) *A public school* is a school operated by a public authority (national, federal, state or provincial, or local), whatever the origin of its financial resources.

(b) *A private school* is a school not operated by a public authority, whether or not it receives financial support from such authorities. Private schools may be defined as aided or non-aided, respectively, according as they derive or do not derive financial support from public authorities.

The enrolment data throughout these tables refer, in general, to the beginning of the school or academic year. In this connection, it should be pointed out that enrolment data may vary substantially according to the date at which the count is taken, i.e. at the beginning, in the middle, at the end of the school year, an average count, etc. The years stated indicate the calendar year in which the school or academic year begins. It is important to keep in mind that only in some forty countries does the school year begin in January, i.e. actually coincide with calendar year, whereas in the majority of countries and territories, it overlaps to a greater or lesser extent into the following calendar year. Appendix B gives information on the dates of commencement and end of the school and fiscal year in each country and territory.

Les trois chapitres de l'*Annuaire* qui suivent contiennent la plupart des données statistiques de base recueillies et élaborées par l'Unesco au sujet des établissements d'enseignement, publics et privés, de tous les degrés. La série de tableaux qui suit présente, pour l'ensemble du monde, des données statistiques sur : le nombre d'écoles; le nombre de maîtres et d'élèves par sexe et par degrés et types d'enseignement; le nombre

d'étudiants et de diplômés de l'enseignement supérieur, par sexe, par discipline et par niveau des grades ou diplômes; le nombre d'étudiants étrangers, par pays d'origine; le nombre d'étudiants inscrits à l'étranger; enfin, les dépenses afférentes à l'enseignement (dépenses publiques réparties selon leur destination, montant total des dépenses en pourcentage du produit national brut et dépenses ordinaires par degrés et types d'enseignement, public et privé). Dans la mesure du possible, les chiffres présentés se rapportent à l'année scolaire commençant en 1970, et aux quatre années les plus récentes.

Les définitions et classifications qui figurent dans la Recommandation révisée concernant la normalisation internationale des statistiques de l'éducation, adoptée par la Conférence générale de l'Unesco à sa vingtième session (Paris, 1978), ont été utilisées, autant qu'il a été possible, dans ces tableaux. Aux termes de cette Recommandation, l'enseignement est classé par degré, de la façon suivante:

Enseignement précédant le premier degré (dispensé, par exemple, dans les écoles maternelles, les écoles gardiennes ou les jardins d'enfants), qui assure l'éducation des enfants trop jeunes pour être admis à l'enseignement du premier degré.

Enseignement du premier degré (dispensé, par exemple, dans les écoles élémentaires ou les écoles primaires), qui a pour fonction principale de fournir les premiers éléments de l'instruction.

Enseignement du second degré (dispensé, par exemple dans les écoles moyennes, les lycées, les collèges, les gymnases, les athénés, les écoles complémentaires, ainsi que dans les écoles de ce degré destinées à la formation des maîtres et les écoles de caractère technique ou professionnel), qui implique quatre années au moins d'études préalables dans le premier degré et qui donne une formation générale ou spécialisée (ou les deux).

Enseignement du troisième degré (dispensé, par exemple, dans les universités, les diverses grandes écoles et instituts supérieurs, y compris les ecoles normales supérieures) qui exige comme condition minimale d'admission d'avoir suivi avec succès un enseignement complet du second degré ou de faire preuve de connaissances équivalentes.

Education spéciale, englobant tous les types d'enseignement destinés aux enfants déficients physiques, mentaux, visuels, auditifs, souffrant de difficultés de la parole ou de troubles de lecture et d'écriture et aux inadaptés sociaux.

Les définitions ci-après sont également tirées de la Recommandation:

Elève (étudiant): personne inscrite dans un établissement d'enseignement pour recevoir un enseignement systématique de n'importe quel degré.

Maître: personne assurant directement l'instruction d'un groupe d'élèves (étudiants); les chefs d'établissement, ainsi que les membres du personnel d'inspection, de surveillance et autres, ne devraient être rangés parmi les maîtres que s'ils exercent régulièrement des fonctions d'enseignement.

Établissement d'enseignement (école, institut, etc.): institution groupant des élèves (étudiants) d'une ou plusieurs années en vue de leur faire donner un enseignement d'un certain type et d'un certain degré par un ou plusieurs maîtres placés sous l'autorité directe d'un chef d'établissement.

(a) *Etablissement d'enseignement public*: établissement dont le fonctionnement est assuré par les pouvoirs publics (nationaux, fédéraux, d'etat ou provinciaux, ou locaux) quelle que soit l'origine de ses ressources financières.

(b) *Etablissement d'enseignement privé*: le fonctionnement n'est pas assuré par les pouvoirs publics qu'il reçoive ou non une aide financière de ceux-ci. Les établissements d'enseignement privé peuvent être classés en établissements subventionnés et établissements non subventionnés, selon qu'ils reçoivent ou non une aide financière des pouvoirs publics. Dans tous les tableaux, les donnés concernant les effectifs se rapportent d'ordinaire au début de l'année scolaire ou universitaire. A ce propos, il y a lieu de rappeler que les effectifs peuvent varier sensiblement, selon qu'il s'agit de chiffres relevés au début, au milieu ou à la fin de l'année scolaire ou encore de moyennes, etc...

Les années indiquées sont les années civiles pendant lesquelles commencent les années scolaires ou universitaires. Il ne faut pas oublier que l'année scolaire ne commence en janvier (c'est-à-dire coïncide avec l'année civile) que dans une quarantaine de pays du monde; dans la plupart des pays et territoires, elle empiète plus ou moins largement sur l'année civile qui suit. L'annexe B fournit des renseignements sur le commencement et la fin des années scolaires et budgétaires dans chaque pays et territoire.

Los tres capítulos siguientes del *Anuario* contienen la mayor parte de los datos estadísticos básicos solicitados por la Unesco en relación con los establecimientos docentes, públicos y privados, de todos los grados (niveles) de la enseñanza. En los cuadros que figuran a continuación se presentan datos estadísticos mundiales sobre el número de establecimientos docentes; el número de maestros y profesores y de alumnos por sexo, grado (niveles) y tipos de enseñanza; el número de estudiantes y diplomados de la enseñanza de tercer grado (superior), por sexo, ramas de estudio y por nivel de los títulos o diplomas; el número de estudiantes extranjeros, por país de origen y el número de estudiantes en el extranjero; por último, los gastos de educación (gastos públicos desglosados según su destino, porcentaje del Producto Nacional Bruto al que equivalen los gastos totales, y gastos ordinarios por grados y tipos de enseñanza, públicos y privados). En la medida de lo posible los datos se refieren al año escolar que empezó en 1970, y a los cuatro años más recientes.

En esos cuadros se han utilizado en lo posible las definiciones y clasificaciones que figuran en la Recomendación revisada sobre la normalización internacional de las estadísticas relativas a la educación aprobada por la Conferencia General de la Unesco en su 20a reunión (París, 1978). Con arreglo a esa Recomendación, la enseñanza queda clasificada por grados como sigue:

Enseñanza anterior al primer grado (por ejemplo, la que se da en guarderías infantiles, escuelas de párvulos o jardines de infancia): para los niños que no están aún en edad de ser admitidos en la enseñanza de primer grado.

Enseñanza de primer grado (por ejemplo, la que se da en escuelas elementales o en escuelas primarias), cuya función principal consiste en proporcionar los primeros elementos de la instrucción.

Enseñanza de segundo grado (por ejemplo, la que se da en escuelas de enseñanza media, secundarias, institutos, liceos, colegios, escuelas técnicas, escuelas normales de este grado), que implica cuatro años como mínimo de estudios previos en el primer grado y que da una formación general o especializada, o de ambas clases.

Enseñanza de tercer grado (por ejemplo, la que se da en las universidades, las escuelas técnicas superiores, las grandes escuelas especiales y las escuelas normales superiores), para la admisión a la cual se exige como condición mínima haber completado con éxito la enseñanza de segundo grado o demostrar la posesión de conocimientos equivalentes.

Educación especial: comprende toda la enseñanza general o profesional destinada a los deficientes físicos o mentales, visuales, auditivos, que sufren de dificultades de la palabra o de trastornos para la lectura y a los inadaptados sociales.

También están tomadas de la recomendación las siguientes definiciones:

Alumno (estudiante): la persona matriculada en un establecimiento docente para recibir una enseñanza sistemática de cualquier grado.

Maestro o profesor: La persona que se ocupa directamente de la instrucción de un grupo de alumnos (estudiantes). No debería incluirse entre los maestros o profesores a los directores de los establecimientos docentes, ni al personal de inspección, vigilancia, etc., más que cuando ejerzan regularmente funciones de enseñanza.

Establecimiento docente (escuela, instituto, etc.): grupo de alumnos (estudiantes) de uno o de varios años de estudios organizado para recibir una enseñanza de determinado tipo y determinado grado dada por uno o varios maestros o profesores, bajo la autoridad de un director de establecimiento.

(a) *Establecimiento docente público*: Establecimiento que depende de un órgano del poder público nacional, federal, provincial o local, cualquiera que sea el origen de sus recursos económicos.

(b) *Establecimiento docente privado*: establecimiento que no depende de un órgano del poder público, tanto si recibe una ayuda económica de éste como en caso contrario. Los establecimientos docentes privados pueden clasificarse en establecimientos subvencionados y establecimientos no subvencionados, según reciban o no una ayuda económica de los poderes públicos.

En todos los cuadros, los datos relativos a la matrícula se refieren habitualmente al principio del año escolar o universitario. Procede recordar a este respecto que la matrícula puede variar sensiblemente según se trate de cifras calculadas al principio, a mediados o al final del año escolar, de promedios, etc.

Los años indicados son los años civiles durante los cuales empiezan los años escolares universitarios. No hay que olvidar que el año escolar empieza en enero (es decir, coincide con el año civil) en sólo unos 40 países. En la mayoría de los países y territorios, está en forma más o menos pronunciada, a caballo del año civil subsiguiente. En el apéndice B se presentan datos sobre el comienzo y el final de los años escolares y de los ejercicios económicos en cada país y territorio.

2 Summary tables for all levels of education, by continents, major areas and groups of countries

Tableaux récapitulatifs pour tous les degrés d'enseignement, par continents, grandes régions et groupes de pays

Cuadros recapitulativos para todos los grados de enseñanza, por continentes, grandes regiones y grupos de países

This chapter, comprising 12 tables, provides a summary presentation of data for all levels of education. Together these tables convey a general picture of the quantitative development since 1965 and also of the present situation of education and expenditure on education in the whole world and in each major area and region.

Table 2.1
The data in this table provide for the latest year available a regional summary of the tabular and graphical information given in Table 3.1 of this *Yearbook*. The variations in the duration of compulsory education, the entrance ages to first level education and the duration of first level and second level general education are shown by continents, major areas and groups of countries.

Table 2.2 - 2.6
The definitions for each level of education are given in the introductory text to the 'Education' section. Data in the present edition are based mainly on the enrolment and the teachers figures shown for each individual country and territory in Tables 3.4, 3.7 and 3.11 of the *Yearbook*. It should be noted that the breakdown and percentage distribution by level of education are influenced by the length of schooling at each level, which, in turn depends on the criteria applied in the national definitions of levels (see Table 3.1). Since these criteria, particularly as concerns primary and secondary education, vary from country to country, caution should be exercised in making comparisons between areas and also in interpreting changes observed within a given area during the period under review.

Table 2.7
This table provides a frequency distribution of pupil-teacher ratios by level of education for 1965, 1970, 1975 and 1977. These ratios are calculated based on the figures shown in Tables 3.4, 3.7 and 3.11. Care should be exercised when making comparisons between areas and also when interpreting changes observed within a given period since the national definitions of the levels of education vary from country to country.

Table 2.8
The data in this table are based mainly on the enrolment and teachers' figures shown for each individual country and territory in Table 3.3 of the *Yearbook*. It should be noted that for this level of education only token efforts are evidenced in many countries and territories. Thus, caution should be exercised when making comparisons between areas and also in interpreting changes observed within a given area during the period under review.

Table 2.9
The data in this table are based mainly on the enrolment and teachers' figures shown for each individual country and territory in Table 3.7 of the *Yearbook*. Care should be exercised when making comparisons between areas and also in interpreting changes observed within a given area during the period under review because of the differences in the curricula and classifications used by countries and territories to define the role and function of teacher training and other education at the second level.

Table 2.10
This table has been prepared using the enrolment figures supplemented by estimates for foreign students by country or territory given in Table 3.14. It should be borne in mind that for certain major host countries, estimates have been also made, because of lack of recent data. A foreign student is defined as 'a person enrolled at an institution of higher education in a country or territory of which he is not a permanent resident'. However, the introductory text to Table 3.14 should be consulted for more precisions on this definition.

Table 2.11
This table presents gross enrolment ratios by level of education by continents, major areas and groups of countries for 1965, 1970, 1975 and 1977. These ratios are calculated by dividing the regional level enrolment using standardized age-groups (6-11, 12-17, 18-23, 6-23 years) and expressing the result as a percentage.
These gross enrolment ratios may be greater than 100 because of some countries having educational structures outside of the age-groups used for particular levels of education, entry age, rates of repetition, etc.

Table 2.12
The purpose of this table is to show the general trends in public expenditure on education, expressed in United States dollars at current market prices, between 1965-1977. The average annual growth rates of Gross National Product between 1965-1977 also are shown in order to provide a basis for comparison with the average annual growth rate of public expenditure on education. All growth rates are calculated using only the first and latest observations.
For most countries statistics for Gross National Product (GNP) and exchange rates have been obtained from the World Bank and the International Monetary Fund respectively. For countries with centrally planned economies, the Net Material Product (NMP) and educational expenditure are converted using the rates of exchange of the United Nations.
The data shown in this table should be considered as general approximate indications of the public resources allocated to education.

Ce chapitre, qui comprend 12 tableaux, présente des données récapitulatives pour tous les degrés d'enseignement. Ces tableaux donnent également une idée générale sur le développement quantitif à partir de 1965, ainsi que sur la situation actuelle de l'enseignement et des dépenses afférentes à l'enseignement dans l'ensemble du monde et dans chaque grande région et groupes de pays.

Tableau 2.1
Les données de ce tableau présentent pour la dernière année disponible, un resumé régional de l'information qui figure en forme de tableau et de graphique dans le tableau 3.1 de cet *Annuaire*. Les variations dans les durées de la scolarité obligatoire, les âges d'admission dans l'enseignement du premier degré et la durée des enseignements du premier degré et général du second degré sont présentées par continents, grandes régions et groupes de pays.

Tableaux 2.2 - 2.6
Pour la définition de chaque degré d'enseignement se reporter au texte introductif de la partie 'Education'. Les données de ce tableau sont basées, pour la plupart, sur les effectifs et le personnel enseignant indiquées pour chaque pays et territoire dans les tableaux 3.4, 3.7 et 3.11 de l'*Annuaire*. Il y a lieu de noter que la répartition, en chiffres absolus ou en pourcentage, entre les différents degrés d'enseignement dépend du nombre d'années d'études correspondant à chaque degré et, par suite, des critères appliqués dans chaque pays pour définir les degrés d'enseignement (voir tableau 3.1). Comme ces critères varient d'un pays à un autre, notamment en ce qui concerne le premier et le second degré, il convient de faire preuve de prudence lorsqu'on veut procéder à des comparaisons entre les régions ou interpréter les modifications constatées dans une région donnée pendant la période considérée.

Tableau 2.7
Ce tableau présente le nombre d'élèves par maître, par degrés d'enseignement, pour 1965, 1970, 1975 et 1977. Les calculs ont été effectués avec les données qui figurent dans les tableaux 3.4, 3.7 et 3.11. Il faut faire preuve de prudence lorsqu'on veut procéder à des comparaisons entre les régions ou interpréter les modifications constatées pendant la période considérée, les définitions nationales des degrés d'enseignement variant d'un pays à l'autre.

Tableau 2.8
Les données présentées dans ce tableau sont basées, pour la plupart, sur les effectifs et le personnel enseignant indiqués pour chaque pays et territoire dans le tableau 3.3 de l'*Annuaire*. Il y a lieu de noter que beaucoup de pays et territoires n'ont produit que des efforts insuffisants dans ce degré d'enseignement; il convient donc de faire preuve de prudence lorsqu'on veut procéder à des comparaisons entre les régions ou interpréter les modifications constatées dans une région donnée pendant la période considérée.

Tableau 2.9
Les données présentées dans ce tableau sont basées, pour la plupart, sur les effectifs et le personnel enseignant indiqués pour chaque pays et territoire dans le tableau 3.7 de l'*Annuaire*. Il convient de faire preuve de prudence lorsqu'on veut procéder à des comparaisons entre les régions ou interpréter les modifications constatées dans une région donnée pendant la période considérée, compte tenu des différences existant dans les programmes d'études et les classifications utilisées par les pays et territoires pour définir le rôle et la fonction de l'enseignement normal et de l'autre enseignement du second degré.

Tableau 2.10
Ce tableau a été préparé avec les données relatives aux effectifs des étudiants étrangers par pays ou territoire qui figurent dans le tableau 3.14. Il faut signaler que pour certains pays d'accueil importants, on a procédé à des estimations pour pallier le manque de donnés récentes. Un étudiant étranger se définit comme une 'personne inscrite dans un établissement d'enseignement supérieur d'un pays ou d'un territoire où elle n'a pas son domicile permanent'. Pour avoir plus de précisions sur cette définition, veuillez consulter le texte d'introduction du tableau 3.14.

Tableau 2.11
Ce tableau présente les taux d'inscription scolaire bruts par degrés d'enseignement, par continents, grandes régions et groupes de pays pour 1965, 1970, 1975 et 1977. Ces taux ont été calculés en divisant les effectifs régionaux établis par degrés d'enseignement par des groupes d'âge normalisés (6-11, 12-17, 18-23, 6-23), les résultats étant exprimés en pourcentages.

Les taux d'inscription scolaire bruts peuvent être supérieurs à 100, parce que quelques pays ont des structures d'enseignement en dehors des groupes d'âge utilisés pour chaque degré d'enseignement, âge d'admission, taux de redoublement, etc.

Tableau 2.12
Ce tableau a pour objet de montrer l'évolution des dépenses publiques d'enseignement exprimées en millions de dollars des Etats-Unis aux prix courants du marché entre les années 1965-1977. Pour comparer l'évolution des dépenses publiques d'enseignement par rapport à celle des Produits Nationaux Bruts, le tableau fait apparaître aussi les taux moyens d'accroissement annuel des PNB entre les années 1965-1977. Tous ces taux d'accroissement sont calculés en utilisant seulement les premières et les dernières observations.

Pour la majeure partie des pays, les données sur le produit national brut (PNB) et les taux de change sont fournis par la Banque Mondiale et le Fonds Monétaire International respectivement. Pour les pays dont l'économie est soumise à une planification centralisée, leur produit matériel net (PMN) et leurs dépenses d'enseignement sont convertis d'après les taux publiés par l'ONU.

Toutes les données doivent être considérées comme des indications générales et approximatives de l'ordre de grandeur des ressources publiques consacrées à l'enseignement.

Este capítulo, que comprende 12 cuadros, presenta datos recapitulativos para todos los grados de enseñanza. Estos cuadros dan igualmente una idea general del desarrollo cuantitativo a partir de 1965, así como de la situación actual de la enseñanza y de los gastos destinados a la educación en el conjunto del mundo y en cada una de las grandes regiones y grupos de países.

Cuadro 2.1
Los datos de este cuadro presentan para el último año disponible, un resumen regional de la información que figura en forma de cuadro y de gráfico en el cuadro 3.1 de este *Anuario*. Las variaciones en la duración de la escolaridad obligatoria, las edades de admisión en la enseñanza de primer grado y la duración de las enseñanza de primer grado y general de segundo grado, se presentan por continentes, grandes regiones y grupos de países.

Cuadros 2.2-2.6
Puede verse la definición de los distintos grados de enseñanza en la introducción del capítulo 'Educación'. La mayoría de los datos de este cuadro, se basan en las cifras de la matrícula y del personal docente indicadas en los cuadros 3.4, 3.7 y 3.11 del *Anuario* con respecto a cada país o territorio. Procede señalar que la distribución, en valor absoluto y en porcentajes, entre los distintos grados de enseñanza depende del número de años de estudio correspondiente a cada grado y, por ende, de los criterios aplicados en cada país para definir dichos grados (véase el cuadro 3.1). Como estos criterios varían según los paíse, en particular en el caso del primero y el segundo grado, habrá que tener presente estas circunstancias al hacer comparaciones entre las regiones o al interpretar las modificaciones obesrvadas en una región dada durante el período considerado.

Cuadro 2.7
Este cuadro presenta el número de alumnos por maestro, por grados de enseñanza, en 1965, 1970, 1975 y 1977. Los cálculos han sido efectuados con los datos que figuran en los cuadros 3.4, 3.7 y 3.11. Hay que mostrarse prudente cuando se desee proceder a comparaciones entre regiones o interpretar los cambios que se observen durante el periodo considerado, yo que las definiciones nacionales de los grados de enseñanz varían de un país a otro.

Cuadro 2.8
Los datos de este cuadro se basan principalmente en las cifras de matrícula escolar y de personal docente que figuran para cada país y territorio en el cuadro 3.3 del *Anuario*. Es de notar que para este grado de enseñanza, los esfuerzos realizados en la mayoría de los países han sido insuficientes. Es por ello que las comparaciones entre regiones deben efectuarse con mucha prudencia, al igual que la interpretación de los cambios que se observen en el interior de una misma región durante el periodo considerado.

Cuadro 2.9
Los datos presentados en este cuadro se basan principalmente en las cifras de matrícula escolar y de personal docente que figuran para cada país y territorio en el cuadro 3.7 del *Anuario*. Las comparaciones entre regiones deben efectuarse con mucha prudencia, al igual que la

interpretacion de los cambios que se observen en el interior de una misma región durante el periodo considerado, debido a las diferencias existentes en los programas de estudio y las clasificaciones utilizadas por los países y territorios para definir el papel y las funciones de la enseñanza normal y de la otra enseñanza de segundo grado.

Cuadro 2.10

Este cuadro ha sido preparado con los datos de matrícula relativos a los estudiantes extranjeros por país o territorio, que figuran en el cuadro 3.14. Hay que señalar que para ciertos países huéspedes importantes, se han efectuado estimaciones para cubrir la falta de datos recientes. Un estudiante extranjero se define como una 'persona matriculada en un establecimiento de enseñanza superior de un país o territorio en el que no tiene su domicilio fijo'. Para más precisiones sobre esta definición, debe consultarse el texto de introducción del cuadro 3.14.

Cuadro 2.11

Este cuadro presenta las tasas de escolarización brutas por grados de enseñanza, por continentes, grandes regiones y grupos de países para 1965, 1970, 1975 y 1977. Estas tasas se han calculado dividiendo las matrículas regionales establecidas por grados de enseñanza, por los grupos de edad normalizados (6-11, 12-17, 18-23, 6-23), los resultados expresándose en porcentaje.

Las tasas de escolarización brutas pueden ser superiores a 100, ya que algunos países tienen estructuras de enseñanza que se sitúan fuera de los grupos de edad utilizados para cada grado de enseñanza, edad de admisión, tasas de repetición, etc.

Cuadro 2.12

La finalidad de este cuadro consiste en exponer la evolución de los gastos públicos de educación, expresados a precios corrientes del mercado y en dólares de los Estados Unidos, entre los años 1965-1977.

Para comparar la evolución de los gastos públicos destinados a la educación en relación con la de los Productos Nacionales Brutos, el cuadro también pone de relieve las tasas medias de crecimiento anual de los PNB entre los años 1965-1977. Todas esas tasas de crecimiento han sido calculadas utilizando solamente las primeras y las últimas observaciones.

Para la mayoría de los países, los datos relativos al producto nacional bruto (PNB) y los tipos de cambio nos han sido procurados por el Banco Mundial y el Fondo Monetario Internacional respectivamente. Para los países cuya economía está sometida a una planificación centralizada, su producto material neto (PMN) y sus gastos de enseñanza han sido convertidos de acuerdo con los tipos de cambio publicados por las Naciones Unidas. Los datos del presente cuadro han de considerarse como una indicación general y aproximada del orden de magnitud de los recursos públicos dedicados al sector de la educación.

2.1 Education systems by regions
Systèmes d'enseignement par régions
Sistemas de enseñanza por regiones

2.1 Education systems by regions

Systèmes d'enseignement par régions

Sistemas de enseñanza por regiones

	WORLD	AFRICA	AMERICA	ASIA	EUROPE	OCEANIA	U.S.S.R.
	MONDE	AFRIQUE	AMERIQUE	ASIE	EUROPE	OCEANIE	U.R.S.S.
	MUNDO	AFRICA	AMERICA	ASIA	EUROPA	OCEANIA	U.R.S.S.

DURATION (IN YEARS) OF
COMPULSORY EDUCATION

DUREE DE LA SCOLARITE
OBLIGATOIRE (ANNEES)

DURACION DE LA ENSEÑANZA
OBLIGATORIA (ANOS)

5	9	3	1	5	–	–	–
6	35	12	10	11	2	–	–
7	10	5	4	1	–	–	–
8	34	6	7	4	13	4	–
9	31	5	8	6	10	2	–
10	29	5	12	–	5	4	3
11	6	1	2	1	1	1	–
12	5	–	3	–	–	2	–
13	1	1	–	–	–	–	–

NO COMPULSORY EDUCATION
PAS DE SCOLARITE OBLIGATOIRE

| ENSEÑANZA NO OBLIGATORIA | 36 | 16 | 2 | 12 | – | 6 | |

NOT SPECIFIED
NON SPECIFIE

| SIN ESPECIFICAR | 7 | 2 | – | 4 | 1 | – | – |

TOTAL COUNTRIES
NOMBRE TOTAL DE PAYS

| TOTAL DE PAISES | 203 | 56 | 49 | 44 | 32 | 19 | 3 |

ENTRANCE AGE, FIRST
LEVEL OF EDUCATION

AGE D'ENTREE DANS L'EN—
SEIGNEMENT DU 1ER DEGRE

EDAD DE INGRESO EN LA
ENSEÑANZA DE PRIMER GRADO

4	1	–	–	–	1	–	–
5	39	6	17	10	2	5	–
6	120	35	25	26	21	12	–
7	38	13	7	6	7	2	3
8	2	1	–	1	–	–	–

NOT SPECIFIED
NON SPECIFIE

| SIN ESPECIFICAR | 3 | 1 | – | 1 | 1 | – | – |

TOTAL COUNTRIES
NOMBRE TOTAL DE PAYS

| TOTAL DE PAISES | 203 | 56 | 49 | 44 | 32 | 19 | 3 |

Education systems by regions **2.1**
Systèmes d'enseignement par régions
Sistemas de enseñanza por regiones

DEVELOPED COUNTRIES	DEVELOPING COUNTRIES	AFRICA (WITHOUT ARAB STATES)	NORTHERN AMERICA	LATIN AMERICA	ASIA (WITHOUT ARAB STATES)	ARAB STATES
PAYS DEVELOPPES	PAYS EN DEVELOPPEMENT	AFRIQUE (SANS LES ETATS ARABES)	AMERIQUE SEPTEN- TRIONALE	AMERIQUE LATINE	ASIE (SANS LES ETATS ARABES)	ETATS ARABES
PAISES DESARROLLADOS	PAISES EN DESARROLLO	AFRICA (SIN LOS ESTADOS ARABES)	AMERICA SEPTEN- TRIONAL	AMERICA LATINA	ASIA (SIN LOS ESTADOS ARABES)	ESTADOS ARABES
—	9	3	—	1	5	—
2	33	9	—	10	8	6
—	10	5	1	3	1	—
13	21	5	—	7	3	2
13	18	4	—	8	4	3
11	18	5	2	10	—	—
2	4	1	—	2	1	—
—	5	—	1	2	—	—
—	1	1	—	—	—	—
—	36	16	—	2	7	5
1	6	1	—	—	3	2
42	161	50	4	45	32	18
1	—	—	—	—	—	—
4	36	6	2	14	8	2
26	93	31	2	24	18	13
10	28	11	—	7	4	3
—	2	1	—	—	1	—
1	2	1	—	—	1	—
42	161	50	4	45	32	18

2.1 Education systems by regions
Systèmes d'enseignement par régions
Sistemas de enseñanza por regiones

	WORLD	AFRICA	AMERICA	ASIA	EUROPE	OCEANIA	U.S.S.R.
	MONDE	AFRIQUE	AMERIQUE	ASIE	EUROPE	OCEANIE	U.R.S.S.
	MUNDO	AFRICA	AMERICA	ASIA	EUROPA	OCEANIA	U.R.S.S.

DURATION (IN YEARS) OF
1ST LEVEL EDUCATION

DUREE DE L'ENSEIGNEMENT
DU 1ER DEGRE (ANNEES)

DURACION DE LA ENSEÑANZA
DE PRIMER GRADO (ANOS)

	WORLD	AFRICA	AMERICA	ASIA	EUROPE	OCEANIA	U.S.S.R.
3	2	–	–	2	–	–	–
4	7	3	–	2	2	–	–
5	29	5	5	13	6	–	–
6	96	32	23	23	13	5	–
7	33	14	10	2	–	7	–
8	26	2	9	2	5	5	3
9	7	–	2	–	3	2	–
10	2	–	–	–	2	–	–
NOT SPECIFIED / NON SPECIFIE / SIN ESPECIFICAR	1	–	–	–	1	–	–
TOTAL COUNTRIES / NOMBRE TOTAL DE PAYS / TOTAL DE PAISES	203	56	49	44	32	19	3

DURATION (IN YEARS)
OF GENERAL EDUCATION
AT THE SECOND LEVEL

DUREE DE L'ENSEIGNEMENT
GENERAL DU 2ND DEGRE (ANNEES)

DURACION DE LA ENSEÑANZA
GENERAL DE 2NDO GRADO
(ANOS)

	WORLD	AFRICA	AMERICA	ASIA	EUROPE	OCEANIA	U.S.S.R.
1	1	–	–	–	–	1	–
2	1	–	–	–	1	–	–
3	3	–	2	–	1	–	–
4	22	2	2	3	5	7	3
5	25	9	9	4	2	1	–
6	70	17	19	20	8	5	–
7	71	28	16	16	7	5	–
8	7	–	1	1	5	–	–
9	2	–	1	1	2	–	–
NOT SPECIFIED / NON SPECIFIE / SIN ESPECIFICAR	1	–	–	–	1	–	–
TOTAL COUNTRIES / NOMBRE TOTAL DE PAYS / TOTAL DE PAISES	203	56	49	44	32	19	3

GENERAL NOTE / NOTE GENERALE / NOTA GENERAL:
 E—> FOR COMPOSITION OF THE MAJOR AREAS AND
GROUPS OF COUNTRIES, SEE THE GENERAL NOTE TO
TABLE 1.2.

Education systems by regions   2.1
Systèmes d'enseignement par régions
Sistemas de enseñanza por regiones

DEVELOPED COUNTRIES	DEVELOPING COUNTRIES	AFRICA (WITHOUT ARAB STATES)	NORTHERN AMERICA	LATIN AMERICA	ASIA (WITHOUT ARAB STATES)	ARAB STATES
PAYS DEVELOPPES	PAYS EN DEVELOPPEMENT	AFRIQUE (SANS LES ETATS ARABES)	AMERIQUE SEPTEN- TRIONALE	AMERIQUE LATINE	ASIE (SANS LES ETATS ARABES)	ETATS ARABES
PAISES DESARROLLADOS	PAISES EN DESARROLLO	AFRICA (SIN LOS ESTADOS ARABES)	AMERICA SEPTEN- TRIONAL	AMERICA LATINA	ASIA (SIN LOS ESTADOS ARABES)	ESTADOS ARABES

–	2	–	–	–	2	–
2	5	3	–	–	1	1
6	23	4	1	4	12	4
16	80	27	1	22	13	13
2	31	14	1	9	2	–
10	16	2	1	8	2	–
3	4	–	–	2	–	–
2	–	–	–	–	–	–
1	–	–	–	–	–	–
42	161	50	4	45	32	18

–	1	–	–	–	–	–
1	–	–	–	–	–	–
1	2	–	–	2	–	–
8	14	2	–	2	3	–
4	21	9	1	9	2	–
9	60	14	1	19	11	13
11	61	25	2	12	15	4
5	2	–	–	1	1	1
2	–	–	–	–	–	–
1	–	–	–	–	–	–
42	161	50	4	45	32	18

GENERAL NOTE/NOTE GENERALE/NOTA GENERAL (CONT.):
 FR-> POUR LA COMPOSITION DES GRANDES REGIONS
ET DES GROUPES DE PAYS, VOIR LA NOTE GENERALE
DU TABLEAU 1.2.
 ESP> PUEDE VERSE LA COMPOSICION DE LAS GRANDES
REGIONES Y GRUPOS DE PAISES EN LA NOTA GENERAL
DEL CUADRO 1.2.

2.2 School enrolment and teachers (total)
Effectifs scolaires et personnel enseignant (total)
Matrícula escolar y personal docente (total)

2.2 Estimated total enrolment and teachers by level of education

Estimation des effectifs et du personnel enseignant, par degrés d'enseignement

Estimación de la matrícula escolar y del personal docente, por grados de enseñanza

% 1965–70; 1970–77: ANNUAL AVERAGE INCREASE IN ENROLMENT AND TEACHERS FROM 1965 TO 1970 AND 1970 TO 1977, AS PERCENTAGE.

% 1965–70; 1970–77: ACCROISSEMENT MOYEN ANNUEL DES EFFECTIFS ET DU PERSONNEL ENSEIGNANT DE 1965 A 1970 ET DE 1970 A 1977, EN POURCENTAGE.

% 1965–70; 1970–77: CRECIMIENTO MEDIO ANUAL DE LA MATRICULA ESCOLAR Y DEL PERSONAL DOCENTE DE 1965 A 1970 Y DE 1970 A 1977, EN PORCENTAJE.

CONTINENTS, MAJOR AREAS AND GROUPS OF COUNTRIES / CONTINENTS, GRANDES REGIONS ET GROUPES DE PAYS / CONTINENTES, GRANDES REGIONES Y GRUPOS DE PAISES	YEAR / ANNEE / AÑO	NUMBER OF PUPILS ENROLLED (THOUSANDS) / NOMBRE D'ELEVES INSCRITS (MILLIERS) / NUMERO DE ALUMNOS MATRICULADOS (EN MILES)				NUMBER OF TEACHERS (THOUSANDS) / NOMBRE DE MAITRES (MILLIERS) / NUMERO DE MAESTROS Y PROFESORES (EN MILES)			
		TOTAL / TOTAL / TOTAL	1ST LEVEL / 1ER DEGRE / 1ER GRADO	2ND LEVEL / 2ND DEGRE / 2DO GRADO	3RD LEVEL / 3EME DEGRE / 3ER GRADO	TOTAL / TOTAL / TOTAL	1ST LEVEL / 1ER DEGRE / 1ER GRADO	2ND LEVEL / 2ND DEGRE / 2DO GRADO	3RD LEVEL / 3EME DEGRE / 3ER GRADO
		(1)	(2)	(3)	(4)	(5)	(6)	(7)	(8)
WORLD TOTAL ‡	1965	418 235	299 839	98 881	19 515	16 580	9 901	5 318	1 360
	1970	495 257	342 311	123 889	29 056	20 672	11 600	7 013	2 058
	1975	569 873	379 246	151 610	39 018	24 806	13 434	8 600	2 772
	1977	601 390	395 085	164 269	42 036	26 368	14 076	9 248	3 044
	% 1965–70	3.4	2.7	4.6	8.3	4.5	3.2	5.7	8.6
	% 1970–77	2.8	2.1	4.1	5.4	3.5	2.8	4.0	5.8
AFRICA	1965	29 896	26 539	3 047	311	835	660	154	20
	1970	39 251	33 852	4 920	478	1 090	830	225	35
	1975	54 893	45 280	8 718	894	1 593	1 160	372	61
	1977	63 292	51 748	10 449	1 095	1 875	1 353	448	74
	% 1965–70	5.6	5.0	10.1	9.0	5.5	4.7	7.9	11.8
	% 1970–77	7.1	6.3	11.4	12.6	8.1	7.2	10.3	11.3
AMERICA ‡	1965	99 340	67 386	25 149	6 805	4 216	2 272	1 401	543
	1970	120 008	76 969	32 260	10 779	5 416	2 725	1 916	775
	1975	136 877	85 669	35 546	15 662	6 657	3 482	2 113	1 063
	1977	141 076	87 057	37 415	16 604	7 021	3 551	2 281	1 189
	% 1965–70	3.9	2.7	5.1	9.6	5.1	3.7	6.5	7.4
	% 1970–77	2.3	1.8	2.1	6.4	3.8	3.9	2.5	6.3

School enrolment and teachers (total)   **2.2**
Effectifs scolaires et personnel enseignant (total)
Matrícula escolar y personal docente (total)

		(1)	(2)	(3)	(4)	(5)	(6)	(7)	(8)
ASIA ‡	1965	158 982	116 456	37 904	4 622	5 027	3 046	1 708	273
	1970	193 579	138 103	47 724	7 752	6 605	3 830	2 284	491
	1975	230 977	160 657	60 635	9 684	8 050	4 513	2 908	629
	1977	249 852	171 562	67 594	10 695	8 730	4 891	3 145	694
	% 1965–70	3.0	3.5	4.7	10.9	5.6	4.7	6.0	12.5
	% 1970–77	3.7	3.1	5.1	4.7	4.1	3.6	4.7	5.1
EUROPE	1965	75 820	48 841	23 222	3 756	3 764	1 923	1 528	313
	1970	84 174	50 451	28 483	5 240	4 556	2 113	1 978	464
	1975	91 012	49 073	34 374	7 565	5 363	2 274	2 413	677
	1977	92 574	47 984	36 378	8 212	5 583	2 246	2 605	732
	% 1965–70	2.1	0.7	4.2	6.9	3.9	1.9	5.3	8.2
	% 1970–77	1.4	-0.7	3.6	6.6	2.9	0.9	4.0	6.7
OCEANIA ‡	1965	3 583	2 335	1 088	161	152	87	54	10
	1970	4 191	2 614	1 350	226	183	96	72	15
	1975	4 561	2 605	1 597	359	236	112	98	26
	1977	4 724	2 680	1 651	393	253	119	107	28
	% 1965–70	3.2	2.3	4.4	7.0	3.8	2.0	5.9	8.4
	% 1970–77	1.7	0.4	2.9	8.2	4.7	3.1	5.8	9.3
U.S.S.R.	1965	50 614	38 284	8 470	3 861	2 586	. . .	. . .	201
	1970	54 054	40 321	9 152	4 581	2 822	. . .	. . .	278
	1975	51 553	35 961	10 738	4 854	2 907	. . .	. . .	317
	1977	49 872	34 053	10 782	5 037	2 907	. . .	. . .	327
	% 1965–70	1.3	1.0	1.6	3.5	1.8	. . .	. . .	6.7
	% 1970–77	-1.1	-2.4	2.4	1.4	0.4	. . .	. . .	2.3
DEVELOPED COUNTRIES	1965	212 344	135 325	62 076	14 943	10 062	5 548	3 444	1 070
	1970	230 610	139 800	69 669	21 140	11 780	6 030	4 210	1 539
	1975	238 667	132 182	79 279	27 206	13 236	6 273	5 008	1 955
	1977	238 893	128 587	81 527	28 383	13 551	6 269	5 202	2 079
	% 1965–70	1.7	0.7	2.3	7.2	3.2	1.7	4.1	7.5
	% 1970–77	0.5	-1.2	2.3	4.3	2.0	0.6	3.1	4.4
DEVELOPING COUNTRIES ‡	1965	205 891	164 514	36 805	4 572	6 518	4 353	1 874	290
	1970	264 647	202 511	54 220	7 916	8 892	5 570	2 803	519
	1975	331 206	247 064	72 331	11 812	11 570	7 161	3 592	817
	1977	362 893	266 498	82 742	13 653	12 817	7 807	4 046	965
	% 1965–70	5.1	4.2	8.1	11.6	6.4	5.1	8.4	12.3
	% 1970–77	4.6	4.0	6.2	8.1	5.4	4.9	5.4	9.3
AFRICA (EXCLUDING ARAB STATES)	1965	20 774	19 208	1 463	103	568	482	75	10
	1970	27 578	24 883	2 515	180	736	599	120	17
	1975	39 383	34 184	4 902	296	1 101	856	217	29
	1977	46 098	39 870	5 860	368	1 312	1 013	262	37
	% 1965–70	5.8	5.3	11.4	11.8	5.3	4.4	9.9	11.2
	% 1970–77	7.6	7.0	12.8	10.8	8.6	7.8	11.8	11.8
NORTHERN AMERICA	1965	57 143	32 923	18 330	5 890	2 523	1 200	892	432
	1970	63 611	32 919	21 552	9 140	3 098	1 361	1 121	615
	1975	64 436	29 294	23 140	12 003	3 442	1 460	1 260	722
	1977	62 938	27 949	22 877	12 112	3 473	1 430	1 280	763
	% 1965–70	2.2	-0.0	3.3	9.2	4.2	2.5	4.7	7.3
	% 1970–77	-0.2	-2.3	0.9	4.1	1.6	0.7	1.9	3.1

2.2 School enrolment and teachers (total)
Effectifs scolaires et personnel enseignant (total)
Matrícula escolar y personal docente (total)

CONTINENTS, MAJOR AREAS AND GROUPS OF COUNTRIES / CONTINENTS, GRANDES REGIONS ET GROUPES DE PAYS / CONTINENTES, GRANDES REGIONES Y GRUPOS DE PAISES	YEAR / ANNEE / AÑO	NUMBER OF PUPILS ENROLLED (THOUSANDS) / NOMBRE D'ELEVES INSCRITS (MILLIERS) / NUMERO DE ALUMNOS MATRICULADOS (EN MILES)				NUMBER OF TEACHERS (THOUSANDS) / NOMBRE DE MAITRES (MILLIERS) / NUMERO DE MAESTROS Y PROFESORES (EN MILES)			
		TOTAL	1ST LEVEL / 1ER DEGRE / 1ER GRADO	2ND LEVEL / 2ND DEGRE / 2DO GRADO	3RD LEVEL / 3EME DEGRE / 3ER GRADO	TOTAL	1ST LEVEL / 1ER DEGRE / 1ER GRADO	2ND LEVEL / 2ND DEGRE / 2DO GRADO	3RD LEVEL / 3EME DEGRE / 3ER GRADO
		(1)	(2)	(3)	(4)	(5)	(6)	(7)	(8)
LATIN AMERICA ‡	1965	42 197	34 463	6 819	915	1 693	1 072	509	111
	1970	56 397	44 050	10 709	1 639	2 319	1 364	795	160
	1975	72 441	56 376	12 407	3 659	3 216	2 022	853	341
	1977	78 139	59 108	14 539	4 492	3 548	2 121	1 001	426
	% 1965-70	6.0	5.0	9.4	12.4	6.5	4.9	9.3	7.6
	% 1970-77	4.8	4.3	4.5	15.5	6.3	6.5	3.3	15.0
ASIA (EXCLUDING ARAB STATES) ‡	1965	155 389	113 684	37 171	4 534	4 886	2 943	1 675	269
	1970	188 784	134 563	46 613	7 608	6 410	3 699	2 227	484
	1975	223 635	155 408	58 806	9 421	7 734	4 309	2 809	616
	1977	241 461	165 761	65 321	10 379	8 364	4 660	3 026	678
	% 1965-70	4.0	3.4	4.6	10.9	5.6	4.7	5.9	12.5
	% 1970-77	3.6	3.0	4.9	4.5	3.9	3.4	4.5	4.9
ARAB STATES	1965	12 715	10 102	2 317	295	408	281	113	14
	1970	16 469	12 510	3 517	443	549	363	161	25
	1975	22 852	16 345	5 646	861	808	509	255	45
	1977	25 585	17 679	6 863	1 043	929	571	306	53
	% 1965-70	5.3	4.4	8.7	8.5	6.1	5.3	7.3	12.3
	% 1970-77	6.5	5.1	10.0	13.0	7.8	6.7	9.6	11.3

School enrolment and teachers (total)   **2.2**
Effectifs scolaires et personnel enseignant (total)
Matrícula escolar y personal docente (total)

GENERAL NOTE / NOTE GENERALE / NOTA GENERAL:
E—> FOR COMPOSITION OF MAJOR AREAS AND GROUPS OF COUNTRIES, SEE GENERAL NOTE TO TABLE 1.2. THE SCHOOL YEAR BEGINS IN THE CALENDAR YEAR INDICATED. MORE INFORMATION ON THIS POINT IS GIVEN IN THE GENERAL INTRODUCTION TO THE "EDUCATION" CHAPTER. THE FIGURES IN THIS TABLE DO NOT INCLUDE DATA RELATING TO PRE-PRIMARY, SPECIAL AND ADULT EDUCATION.
FR—> POUR LA COMPOSITION DES GRANDES REGIONS ET DES GROUPES DE PAYS, VOIR LA NOTE GENERALE DU TABLEAU 1.2. L'ANNEE SCOLAIRE COMMENCE PENDANT L'ANNEE CIVILE INDIQUEE. POUR PLUS DE DETAILS, SE REPORTER A L'INTRODUCTION GENERALE DU CHAPITRE "EDUCATION". LES CHIFFRES DE CE TABLEAU NE COM-PRENNENT PAS L'ENSEIGNEMENT PREPRIMAIRE, L'EDUCATION SPECIALE ET L'EDUCATION DES ADULTES.
ESP> PUEDE VERSE LA COMPOSICION DE LAS GRANDES REGIONES Y GRUPOS DE PAISES EN LA NOTA GENERAL DEL CUADRO 1.2. EL AÑO ESCOLAR EMPIEZA DURANTE EL AÑO CIVIL INDICADO. PUEDEN VERSE MAS DETALLES A ESTE RESPECTO EN LA INTRODUCCION GENERAL DEL CAPITULO "EDUCACION". LAS CIFRAS DE ESTE CUADRO NO COMPRENDEN LA ENSEÑANZA PREPRIMARIA, LA EDUCACION ESPECIAL Y LA EDUCACION DE ADULTOS.

SECOND LEVEL / SECOND DEGRE / SEGUNDO GRADO:
E—> GENERAL, TEACHER TRAINING AND OTHER EDUCATION AT THE SECOND LEVEL OF A VOCATIONAL OR TECHNICAL NATURE.
FR—> GENERAL, NORMAL ET AUTRE ENSEIGNEMENT DU SECOND DEGRE DE CARACTERE TECHNIQUE OU PRO-FESSIONNEL.
ESP> GENERAL, NORMAL Y OTRA ENSEÑANZA DE SEGUNDO GRADO DE CARACTER TECNICO O PROFESIONAL.

THIRD LEVEL / TROISIEME DEGRE / TERCER GRADO:
E—> UNIVERSITIES AND OTHER INSTITUTIONS OF HIGHER EDUCATION.
FR—> UNIVERSITES ET AUTRES ETABLISSEMENTS D'ENSEIGNEMENT SUPERIEUR.
ESP> UNIVERSDADES Y OTROS ESTABLECIMIENTOS DE ENSEÑANZA SUPERIOR.

WORLD TOTAL:
E—> NOT INCLUDING CHINA AND THE DEMOCRATIC PEOPLE'S REPUBLIC OF KOREA. INCLUDING AN ALLOW-ANCE FOR TEACHERS IN THE U.S.S.R.
FR—> NON COMPRIS LA CHINE ET LA REPUBLIQUE DEMOCRATIQUE POPULAIRE DE COREE. Y COMPRIS UNE ESTIMATION DU PERSONNEL ENSEIGNANT DE L'U.R.S.S.
ESP> EXCLUIDAS CHINA Y LA REPUBLICA POPULAR DEMOCRATICA DE COREA. INCLUIDA UNA ESTIMACION DEL PERSONAL DOCENTE DE LA U.R.S.S.

AMERICA:
E—> BEGINNING 1971, THE DURATION OF PRIMARY SCHOOLING IN BRAZIL WAS INCREASED FROM 4 TO 8 YEARS AND THAT OF GENERAL EDUCATION AT THE SECOND LEVEL WAS REDUCED FROM 7 TO 3 YEARS.

AMERICA (CONT.):
FR—> A PARTIR DE 1971, LA DUREE DE L'ENSEIGNE-MENT DU PREMIER DEGRE A ETE PORTEE AU BRESIL DE 4 A 8 ANNEES, CELLE DE L'ENSEIGNEMENT GENERAL DU SECOND DEGRE AYANT ETE RAMENEE DE 7 A 3 ANNEES.
ESP> A PARTIR DE 1971, LA DURACION DE LA ENSEÑANZA DE PRIMER GRADO PASO EN EL BRASIL DE 4 A 8 AÑOS Y LA DE LA ENSEÑANZA GENERAL DE SEGUNDO GRADO DE 7 A 3 AÑOS.

ASIA:
E—> NOT INCLUDING CHINA AND THE DEMOCRATIC PEOPLE'S REPUBLIC OF KOREA.
FR—> NON COMPRIS LA CHINE ET LA REPUBLIQUE DEMOCRATIQUE POPULAIRE DE COREE.
ESP> EXCLUIDAS CHINA Y LA REPUBLICA POPULAR DEMOCRATICA DE COREA.

OCEANIA:
E—> BEGINNING 1973, OTHER SECONDARY EDUCATION OF A VOCATIONAL OR TECHNICAL NATURE IN AUSTRALIA IS PROVIDED IN THE THIRD LEVEL OF EDUCATION.
FR—> A PARTIR DE 1973, L'AUTRE ENSEIGNEMENT DU SECOND DEGRE DE CARACTERE TECHNIQUE OU PROFES-SIONNEL EST DISPENSE EN AUSTRALIE DANS L'ENSEIGNE-MENT DU TROISIEME DEGRE.
ESP> A PARTIR DE 1973, LA OTRA ENSEÑANZA DE SEGUNDO GRADO DE CARACTER TECNICO O PROFESIONAL SE IMPARTE EN AUSTRALIA EN LA ENSEÑANZA DE TERCER GRADO.

DEVELOPING COUNTRIES:
E—> NOT INCLUDING CHINA AND THE DEMOCRATIC PEOPLE'S REPUBLIC OF KOREA.
FR—> NON COMPRIS LA CHINE ET LA REPUBLIQUE DEMOCRATIQUE POPULAIRE DE COREE.
ESP> EXCLUIDAS CHINA Y LA REPUBLICA POPULAR DEMOCRATICA DE COREA.

LATIN AMERICA:
E—> BEGINNING 1971, THE DURATION OF PRIMARY SCHOOLING IN BRAZIL WAS INCREASED FROM 4 TO 8 YEARS AND THAT OF GENERAL EDUCATION AT THE SECOND LEVEL WAS REDUCED FROM 7 TO 3 YEARS.
FR—> A PARTIR DE 1971, LA DUREE DE L'ENSEIGNE-MENT DU PREMIER DEGRE A ETE PORTEE AU BRESIL DE 4 A 8 ANNEES, CELLE DE L'ENSEIGNEMENT GENERAL DU SECOND DEGRE AYANT ETE RAMENEE DE 7 A 3 ANNEES.
ESP> A PARTIR DE 1971, LA DURACION DE LA ENSEÑANZA DE PRIMER GRADO PASO EN EL BRASIL DE 4 A 8 AÑOS Y LA DE LA ENSEÑANZA GENERAL DE SEGUNDO GRADO DE 7 A 3 AÑOS.

ASIA (EXCLUDING ARAB STATES):
E—> NOT INCLUDING CHINA AND THE DEMOCRATIC PEOPLE'S REPUBLIC OF KOREA.
FR—> NON COMPRIS LA CHINE ET LA REPUBLIQUE DEMOCRATIQUE POPULAIRE DE COREE.
ESP> EXCLUIDAS CHINA Y LA REPUBLICA POPULAR DEMOCRATICA DE COREA.

Total enrolment and teachers: percentage distribution 2.3
Effectifs scolaires et personnel enseignant: répartition en pourcentage
Matrícula escolar y personal docente: distribución en porcentaje

2.3 Total enrolment and teachers: percentage distribution by level of education

Répartition en pourcentage des effectifs et du personnel enseignant, par degrés d'enseignement

Distribución en porcentaje de la matrícula escolar y del personal docente, por grados de enseñanza

(SEE NOTE CONCERNING TABLES 2.2 – 2.7)   (VOIR LA NOTE RELATIVE AUX TABLEAUX 2.2 – 2.7)   (VEASE LA NOTA RELATIVA A LOS CUADROS 2.2 – 2.7)

CONTINENTS, MAJOR AREAS AND GROUPS OF COUNTRIES / CONTINENTS, GRANDES REGIONS ET GROUPES DE PAYS / CONTINENTES, GRANDES REGIONES Y GRUPOS DE PAISES	YEAR ANNEE AÑO	PERCENTAGE DISTRIBUTION / REPARTITION EN POURCENTAGE / DISTRIBUCION PORCENTUAL							
		ENROLMENT EFFECTIFS MATRICULA				TEACHING STAFF PERSONNEL ENSEIGNANT PERSONAL DOCENTE			
		TOTAL TOTAL TOTAL	1ST LEVEL 1ER DEGRE 1ER GRADO	2ND LEVEL 2ND DEGRE 2DO GRADO	3RD LEVEL 3EME DEGRE 3ER GRADO	TOTAL TOTAL TOTAL	1ST LEVEL 1ER DEGRE 1ER GRADO	2ND LEVEL 2ND DEGRE 2DO GRADO	3RD LEVEL 3EME DEGRE 3ER GRADO
		(1)	(2)	(3)	(4)	(5)	(6)	(7)	(8)
WORLD TOTAL ‡	1965	100.0	71.7	23.6	4.7	100.0	59.7	32.1	8.2
	1970	100.0	69.1	25.0	5.9	100.0	56.1	33.9	10.0
	1975	100.0	66.5	26.6	6.8	100.0	54.2	34.7	11.2
	1977	100.0	65.7	27.3	7.0	100.0	53.4	35.1	11.5
AFRICA	1965	100.0	88.8	10.2	1.0	100.0	79.0	18.4	2.4
	1970	100.0	86.2	12.5	1.2	100.0	76.1	20.6	3.2
	1975	100.0	82.5	15.9	1.6	100.0	72.8	23.4	3.8
	1977	100.0	81.8	16.5	1.7	100.0	72.2	23.9	3.9
AMERICA ‡	1965	100.0	67.8	25.3	6.9	100.0	53.9	33.2	12.9
	1970	100.0	64.1	26.9	9.0	100.0	50.3	35.4	14.3
	1975	100.0	62.6	26.0	11.4	100.0	52.3	31.7	16.0
	1977	100.0	61.7	26.5	11.8	100.0	50.6	32.5	16.9
ASIA ‡	1965	100.0	73.3	23.8	2.9	100.0	60.6	34.0	5.4
	1970	100.0	71.3	24.7	4.0	100.0	58.0	34.6	7.4
	1975	100.0	69.6	26.3	4.2	100.0	56.1	36.1	7.8
	1977	100.0	68.7	27.1	4.3	100.0	56.0	36.0	7.9
EUROPE	1965	100.0	64.4	30.6	5.0	100.0	51.1	40.6	8.3
	1970	100.0	59.9	33.8	6.2	100.0	46.4	43.4	10.2
	1975	100.0	53.9	37.8	8.3	100.0	42.4	45.0	12.6
	1977	100.0	51.8	39.3	8.9	100.0	40.2	46.7	13.1
OCEANIA ‡	1965	100.0	65.2	30.4	4.5	100.0	57.2	35.5	6.6
	1970	100.0	62.4	32.2	5.4	100.0	52.5	39.3	8.2
	1975	100.0	57.1	35.0	7.9	100.0	47.5	41.5	11.0
	1977	100.0	56.7	34.9	8.3	100.0	47.0	42.3	11.1
U.S.S.R.	1965	100.0	75.6	16.7	7.6	100.0	...	...	7.8
	1970	100.0	74.6	16.9	8.5	100.0	...	...	9.9
	1975	100.0	69.8	20.8	9.4	100.0	...	...	10.9
	1977	100.0	68.3	21.6	10.1	100.0	...	...	11.2

2.3 Total enrolment and teachers: percentage distribution
Effectifs scolaires et personnel enseignant: répartition en pourcentage
Matrícula escolar y personal docente: distribución en porcentaje

CONTINENTS, MAJOR AREAS AND GROUPS OF COUNTRIES CONTINENTS, GRANDES REGIONS ET GROUPES DE PAYS CONTINENTES, GRANDES REGIONES Y GRUPOS DE PAISES	YEAR ANNEE AÑO	PERCENTAGE DISTRIBUTION REPARTITION EN POURCENTAGE DISTRIBUCION PORCENTUAL							
		ENROLMENT EFFECTIFS MATRICULA				TEACHING STAFF PERSONNEL ENSEIGNANT PERSONAL DOCENTE			
		TOTAL TOTAL TOTAL	1ST LEVEL 1ER DEGRE 1ER GRADO	2ND LEVEL 2ND DEGRE 2DO GRADO	3RD LEVEL 3EME DEGRE 3ER GRADO	TOTAL TOTAL TOTAL	1ST LEVEL 1ER DEGRE 1ER GRADO	2ND LEVEL 2ND DEGRE 2DO GRADO	3RD LEVEL 3EME DEGRE 3ER GRADO
		(1)	(2)	(3)	(4)	(5)	(6)	(7)	(8)
DEVELOPED COUNTRIES	1965	100.0	63.7	29.2	7.0	100.0	55.1	34.2	
	1970	100.0	60.6	30.2	9.2	100.0	51.2	35.7	10.6
	1975	100.0	55.4	33.2	11.4	100.0	47.4	37.8	13.1
	1977	100.0	53.9	34.2	11.9	100.0	46.3	38.4	14.8
									15.3
DEVELOPING COUNTRIES ‡	1965	100.0	79.9	17.9	2.2	100.0	66.8	28.8	4.4
	1970	100.0	76.5	20.5	3.0	100.0	62.6	31.5	5.8
	1975	100.0	74.6	21.8	3.6	100.0	61.9	31.0	7.1
	1977	100.0	73.4	22.8	3.8	100.0	60.9	31.6	7.5
AFRICA (EXCLUDING ARAB STATES)	1965	100.0	92.5	7.0	0.5	100.0	84.9	13.2	1.8
	1970	100.0	90.2	9.1	0.7	100.0	81.4	16.3	2.3
	1975	100.0	86.8	12.4	0.8	100.0	77.7	19.7	2.6
	1977	100.0	86.5	12.7	0.8	100.0	77.2	20.0	2.8
NORTHERN AMERICA	1965	100.0	57.6	32.1	10.3	100.0	47.6	35.4	17.1
	1970	100.0	51.8	33.9	14.4	100.0	43.9	36.2	19.9
	1975	100.0	45.5	35.9	18.6	100.0	42.4	36.6	21.0
	1977	100.0	44.4	36.3	19.2	100.0	41.2	36.9	22.0
LATIN AMERICA ‡	1965	100.0	81.7	16.2	2.2	100.0	63.3	30.1	6.6
	1970	100.0	78.1	19.0	2.9	100.0	58.8	34.3	6.9
	1975	100.0	77.8	17.1	5.1	100.0	62.9	26.5	10.6
	1977	100.0	75.6	18.6	5.7	100.0	59.8	28.2	12.0
ASIA (EXCLUDING ARAB STATES) ‡	1965	100.0	73.2	23.9	2.9	100.0	60.2	34.3	5.5
	1970	100.0	71.3	24.7	4.0	100.0	57.7	34.7	7.6
	1975	100.0	69.5	26.3	4.2	100.0	55.7	36.3	8.0
	1977	100.0	68.6	27.1	4.3	100.0	55.7	36.2	8.1
ARAB STATES	1965	100.0	79.4	18.2	2.3	100.0	68.9	27.7	3.4
	1970	100.0	76.0	21.4	2.7	100.0	66.1	29.3	4.6
	1975	100.0	71.5	24.7	3.8	100.0	63.0	31.6	5.6
	1977	100.0	69.1	26.8	4.1	100.0	61.5	32.9	5.7

Total enrolment and teachers: percentage distribution   **2.3**
Effectifs scolaires et personnel enseignant: répartition en pourcentage
Matrícula escolar y personal docente: distribución en porcentaje

GENERAL NOTE / NOTE GENERALE / NOTA GENERAL:
E—> FOR COMPOSITION OF MAJOR AREAS AND GROUPS
OF COUNTRIES, SEE GENERAL NOTE TO TABLE 1.2.   THE
SCHOOL YEAR BEGINS IN THE CALENDAR YEAR INDICATED.
MORE INFORMATION ON THIS POINT IS GIVEN IN THE
GENERAL INTRODUCTION TO THE "EDUCATION" CHAPTER.
THE FIGURES IN THIS TABLE DO NOT INCLUDE DATA
RELATING TO PRE—PRIMARY, SPECIAL AND ADULT
EDUCATION.
FR—> POUR LA COMPOSITION DES GRANDES REGIONS ET
DES GROUPES DE PAYS, VOIR LA NOTE GENERALE DU
TABLEAU 1.2.   L'ANNEE SCOLAIRE COMMENCE PENDANT
L'ANNEE CIVILE INDIQUEE.   POUR PLUS DE DETAILS,
SE REPORTER A L'INTRODUCTION GENERALE DU CHAPITRE
"EDUCATION".   LES CHIFFRES DE CE TABLEAU NE COM—
PRENNENT PAS L'ENSEIGNEMENT PREPRIMAIRE,
L'EDUCATION SPECIALE ET L'EDUCATION DES ADULTES.
ESP> PUEDE VERSE LA COMPOSICION DE LAS GRANDES
REGIONES Y GRUPOS DE PAISES EN LA NOTA GENERAL
DEL CUADRO 1.2.   EL AÑO ESCOLAR EMPIEZA DURANTE
EL AÑO CIVIL INDICADO.   PUEDEN VERSE MAS DETALLES
A ESTE RESPECTO EN LA INTRODUCCION GENERAL DEL
CAPITULO "EDUCACION".   LAS CIFRAS DE ESTE CUADRO
NO COMPRENDEN LA ENSEÑANZA PREPRIMARIA, LA
EDUCACION ESPECIAL Y LA EDUCACION DE ADULTOS.

SECOND LEVEL / SECOND DEGRE / SEGUNDO GRADO:
E—> GENERAL, TEACHER TRAINING AND OTHER
EDUCATION AT THE SECOND LEVEL OF A VOCATIONAL
OR TECHNICAL NATURE.
FR—> GENERAL, NORMAL ET AUTRE ENSEIGNEMENT DU
SECOND DEGRE DE CARACTERE TECHNIQUE OU PRO—
FESSIONNEL.
ESP> GENERAL, NORMAL Y OTRA ENSEÑANZA DE SEGUNDO
GRADO DE CARACTER TECNICO O PROFESIONAL.

THIRD LEVEL / TROISIEME DEGRE / TERCER GRADO:
E—> UNIVERSITIES AND OTHER INSTITUTIONS OF
HIGHER EDUCATION.
FR—> UNIVERSITES ET AUTRES ETABLISSEMENTS
D'ENSEIGNEMENT SUPERIEUR.
ESP> UNIVERSIDADES Y OTROS ESTABLECIMIENTOS DE
ENSEÑANZA SUPERIOR.

WORLD TOTAL:
E—> NOT INCLUDING CHINA AND THE DEMOCRATIC
PEOPLE'S REPUBLIC OF KOREA. INCLUDING AN ALLOW—
ANCE FOR TEACHERS IN THE U.S.S.R.
FR—> NON COMPRIS LA CHINE ET LA REPUBLIQUE
DEMOCRATIQUE POPULAIRE DE COREE. Y COMPRIS UNE
ESTIMATION DU PERSONNEL ENSEIGNANT DE L'U.R.S.S.
ESP> EXCLUIDAS CHINA Y LA REPUBLICA POPULAR
DEMOCRATICA DE COREA. INCLUIDA UNA ESTIMACION
DEL PERSONAL DOCENTE DE LA U.R.S.S.

AMERICA:
E—> BEGINNING 1971, THE DURATION OF PRIMARY
SCHOOLING IN BRAZIL WAS INCREASED FROM 4 TO 8
YEARS AND THAT OF GENERAL EDUCATION AT THE SECOND
LEVEL WAS REDUCED FROM 7 TO 3 YEARS.

AMERICA (CONT.):
FR—> A PARTIR DE 1971, LA DUREE DE L'ENSEIGNE—
MENT DU PREMIER DEGRE A ETE PORTEE AU BRESIL DE
4 A 8 ANNEES, CELLE DE L'ENSEIGNEMENT GENERAL DU
SECOND DEGRE AYANT ETE RAMENEE DE 7 A 3
ANNEES.
ESP> A PARTIR DE 1971, LA DURACION DE LA
ENSEÑANZA DE PRIMER GRADO PASO EN EL BRASIL DE
4 A 8 AÑOS Y LA DE LA ENSEÑANZA GENERAL DE SEGUNDO
GRADO DE 7 A 3 ANOS.

ASIA:
E—> NOT INCLUDING CHINA AND THE DEMOCRATIC
PEOPLE'S REPUBLIC OF KOREA.
FR—> NON COMPRIS LA CHINE ET LA REPUBLIQUE
DEMOCRATIQUE POPULAIRE DE COREE.
ESP> EXCLUIDAS CHINA Y LA REPUBLICA POPULAR
DEMOCRATICA DE COREA.

OCEANIA:
E—> BEGINNING 1973, OTHER SECONDARY EDUCATION
OF A VOCATIONAL OR TECHNICAL NATURE IN AUSTRALIA
IS PROVIDED IN THE THIRD LEVEL OF EDUCATION.
FR—> A PARTIR DE 1973, L'AUTRE ENSEIGNEMENT DU
SECOND DEGRE DE CARACTERE TECHNIQUE OU PROFES—
SIONNEL EST DISPENSE EN AUSTRALIE DANS L'ENSEIGNE—
MENT DU TROISIEME DEGRE.
ESP> A PARTIR DE 1973, LA OTRA ENSEÑANZA DE
SEGUNDO GRADO DE CARACTER TECNICO O PROFESIONAL
SE IMPARTE EN AUSTRALIA EN LA ENSEÑANZA DE TERCER
GRADO.

DEVELOPING COUNTRIES:
E—> NOT INCLUDING CHINA AND THE DEMOCRATIC
PEOPLE'S REPUBLIC OF KOREA.
FR—> NON COMPRIS LA CHINE ET LA REPUBLIQUE
DEMOCRATIQUE POPULAIRE DE COREE.
ESP> EXCLUIDAS CHINA Y LA REPUBLICA POPULAR
DEMOCRATICA DE COREA.

LATIN AMERICA:
E—> BEGINNING 1971, THE DURATION OF PRIMARY
SCHOOLING IN BRAZIL WAS INCREASED FROM 4 TO 8
YEARS AND THAT OF GENERAL EDUCATION AT THE SECOND
LEVEL WAS REDUCED FROM 7 TO 3 YEARS.
FR—> A PARTIR DE 1971, LA DUREE DE L'ENSEIGNE—
MENT DU PREMIER DEGRE A ETE PORTEE AU BRESIL DE
4 A 8 ANNEES, CELLE DE L'ENSEIGNEMENT GENERAL DU
SECOND DEGRE AYANT ETE RAMENEE DE 7 A 3
ANNEES.
ESP> A PARTIR DE 1971, LA DURACION DE LA
ENSEÑANZA DE PRIMER GRADO PASO EN EL BRASIL DE
4 A 8 AÑOS Y LA DE LA ENSEÑANZA GENERAL DE SEGUNDO
GRADO DE 7 A 3 ANOS.

ASIA (EXCLUDING ARAB STATES):
E—> NOT INCLUDING CHINA AND THE DEMOCRATIC
PEOPLE'S REPUBLIC OF KOREA.
FR—> NON COMPRIS LA CHINE ET LA REPUBLIQUE
DEMOCRATIQUE POPULAIRE DE COREE.
ESP> EXCLUIDAS CHINA Y LA REPUBLICA POPULAR
DEMOCRATICA DE COREA.

92

School enrolment (female) 2.4
Effectifs scolaires (féminins)
Matrícula escolar (femenina)

2.4 Estimated female enrolment by level of education
Estimation des effectifs féminins par degrés d'enseignement
Estimación de la matrícula escolar femenina por grados de enseñanza

(SEE NOTE CONCERNING TABLES 2.2 − 2.7)

% 1965−70; 1970−77: ANNUAL AVERAGE INCREASE IN ENROLMENT FROM 1965 TO 1970 AND 1970 TO 1977, AS PERCENTAGE.

(VOIR LA NOTE RELATIVE AUX TABLEAUX 2.2 − 2.7)

% 1965−70; 1970−77: ACCROISSEMENT MOYEN ANNUEL DES EFFECTIFS DE 1965 A 1970 ET DE 1970 A 1977, EN POURCENTAGE.

(VEASE LA NOTA RELATIVA A LOS CUADROS 2.2 − 2.7)

% 1965−70; 1970−77: CRECIMIENTO MEDIO ANUAL DE LA MATRICULA ESCOLAR DE 1965 A 1970 Y DE 1970 A 1977, EN PORCENTAJE.

CONTINENTS, MAJOR AREAS AND GROUPS OF COUNTRIES / CONTINENTS, GRANDES REGIONS ET GROUPES DE PAYS / CONTINENTES, GRANDES REGIONES Y GRUPOS DE PAISES	YEAR / ANNEE / AÑO	NUMBER OF GIRLS ENROLLED (THOUSANDS) / NOMBRE DE FILLES INSCRITES (MILLIERS) / NUMERO DE MUCHACHAS MATRICULADAS (EN MILES)				% OF GIRLS IN TOTAL (BOTH SEXES) ENROLMENT / % DE FILLES PAR RAPPORT AU TOTAL DES EFFECTIFS DES DEUX SEXES / % DE MUCHACHAS CON RESPECTO A LA MATRICULA TOTAL DE AMBOS SEXOS			
		TOTAL	1ST LEVEL / 1ER DEGRE / 1ER GRADO	2ND LEVEL / 2ND DEGRE / 2DO GRADO	3RD LEVEL / 3EME DEGRE / 3ER GRADO	TOTAL	1ST LEVEL / 1ER DEGRE / 1ER GRADO	2ND LEVEL / 2ND DEGRE / 2DO GRADO	3RD LEVEL / 3EME DEGRE / 3ER GRADO
		(1)	(2)	(3)	(4)	(5)	(6)	(7)	(8)
WORLD TOTAL ‡	1965	182 934	133 775	42 300	6 859	44	45	43	35
	1970	217 047	153 171	53 099	10 776	44	45	43	37
	1975	251 968	170 002	66 285	15 681	44	45	44	40
	1977	265 683	176 364	71 797	17 521	44	45	44	42
	% 1965−70	3.5	2.7	4.7	9.5				
	% 1970−77	2.9	2.0	4.4	7.2				
AFRICA	1965	11 210	10 259	890	61	37	39	29	20
	1970	15 155	13 504	1 542	109	39	40	31	23
	1975	22 056	18 807	3 025	224	40	42	35	25
	1977	25 720	21 646	3 797	277	41	42	36	25
	% 1965−70	6.2	5.7	11.6	12.3				
	% 1970−77	7.8	7.0	13.7	14.3				
AMERICA ‡	1965	47 843	32 838	12 415	2 590	48	49	49	38
	1970	57 853	37 585	15 922	4 346	48	49	49	40
	1975	66 281	41 883	17 508	6 890	48	49	49	44
	1977	69 066	42 650	18 585	7 830	49	49	50	47
	% 1965−70	3.9	2.7	5.1	10.9				
	% 1970−77	2.6	1.8	2.2	8.8				
ASIA ‡	1965	61 271	47 078	13 011	1 181	39	40	34	26
	1970	75 022	56 451	16 512	2 059	39	41	35	27
	1975	91 532	66 576	22 157	2 799	40	41	37	29
	1977	98 754	70 787	24 796	3 171	40	41	37	30
	% 1965−70	4.1	3.7	4.9	11.8				
	% 1970−77	4.0	3.3	6.0	6.4				
EUROPE	1965	35 877	23 726	10 890	1 262	47	49	47	34
	1970	40 032	24 629	13 466	1 937	48	49	47	37
	1975	43 953	23 875	16 900	3 177	48	49	49	42
	1977	44 757	23 319	17 902	3 537	48	49	49	43
	% 1965−70	2.2	0.7	4.3	8.9				
	% 1970−77	1.6	−0.8	4.2	9.0				

2.4   School enrolment (female)
       Effectifs scolaires (féminins)
       Matrícula escolar (femenina)

CONTINENTS, MAJOR AREAS AND GROUPS OF COUNTRIES / CONTINENTS, GRANDES REGIONS ET GROUPES DE PAYS / CONTINENTES, GRANDES REGIONES Y GRUPOS DE PAISES	YEAR / ANNEE / AÑO	NUMBER OF GIRLS ENROLLED (THOUSANDS) / NOMBRE DE FILLES INSCRITES (MILLIERS) / NUMERO DE MUCHACHAS MATRICULADAS (EN MILES)				% OF GIRLS IN TOTAL (BOTH SEXES) ENROLMENT / % DE FILLES PAR RAPPORT AU TOTAL DES EFFECTIFS DES DEUX SEXES / % DE MUCHACHAS CON RESPECTO A LA MATRICULA TOTAL DE AMBOS SEXOS			
		TOTAL / TOTAL / TOTAL	1ST LEVEL / 1ER DEGRE / 1ER GRADO	2ND LEVEL / 2ND DEGRE / 2DO GRADO	3RD LEVEL / 3EME DEGRE / 3ER GRADO	TOTAL / TOTAL / TOTAL	1ST LEVEL / 1ER DEGRE / 1ER GRADO	2ND LEVEL / 2ND DEGRE / 2DO GRADO	3RD LEVEL / 3EME DEGRE / 3ER GRADO
		(1)	(2)	(3)	(4)	(5)	(6)	(7)	(8)
OCEANIA ‡	1965	1 680	1 114	516	49	47	48	47	30
	1970	1 963	1 245	641	77	47	48	47	34
	1975	2 153	1 240	772	142	47	48	48	40
	1977	2 242	1 277	803	162	47	48	49	41
	% 1965–70	3.2	2.2	4.4	9.5				
	% 1970–77	1.9	0.4	3.3	11.2				
U.S.S.R.	1965	...	...	...	1 716	...	...	...	44
	1970	...	...	...	2 247	...	...	...	49
	1975	...	...	...	2 449	...	...	...	50
	1977	...	...	...	2 544	...	...	...	51
	% 1965–70	...	...	...	5.5				
	% 1970–77	...	...	...	1.8				
DEVELOPED COUNTRIES	1965	102 211	66 083	30 489	5 639	48	49	49	38
	1970	111 344	68 393	34 367	8 583	48	49	49	41
	1975	116 364	64 595	39 810	11 959	49	49	50	44
	1977	116 706	62 812	40 895	12 998	49	49	50	46
	% 1965–70	1.7	0.7	2.4	8.8				
	% 1970–77	0.7	−1.2	2.5	6.1				
DEVELOPING COUNTRIES ‡	1965	80 723	67 692	11 811	1 220	39	41	32	27
	1970	105 703	84 778	18 732	2 193	40	42	35	28
	1975	135 604	105 407	26 475	3 722	41	43	37	32
	1977	148 977	113 552	30 902	4 523	41	43	37	33
	% 1965–70	5.5	4.6	9.7	12.4				
	% 1970–77	5.0	4.3	7.4	10.9				
AFRICA (EXCLUDING ARAB STATES)	1965	8 055	7 578	456	21	39	39	31	20
	1970	11 017	10 159	823	36	40	41	33	20
	1975	16 329	14 534	1 737	58	41	43	35	20
	1977	19 170	16 949	2 148	73	42	43	37	20
	% 1965–70	6.5	6.0	12.5	11.4				
	% 1970–77	8.2	7.6	14.7	10.6				
NORTHERN AMERICA	1965	27 550	16 112	9 147	2 291	48	49	50	39
	1970	30 639	16 117	10 757	3 765	48	49	50	41
	1975	31 304	14 349	11 552	5 403	49	49	50	45
	1977	31 008	13 689	11 424	5 896	49	49	50	49
	% 1965–70	2.1	0.0	3.3	10.4				
	% 1970–77	0.2	−2.3	0.9	6.6				
LATIN AMERICA ‡	1965	20 292	16 726	3 268	298	48	49	48	33
	1970	27 215	21 467	5 166	581	48	49	48	35
	1975	34 977	27 535	5 956	1 487	48	49	48	41
	1977	38 058	28 961	7 162	1 935	49	49	49	43
	% 1965–70	6.0	5.1	9.6	14.3				
	% 1970–77	4.9	4.4	4.8	18.8				
ASIA (EXCLUDING ARAB STATES) ‡	1965	60 178	46 188	12 827	1 163	39	41	35	26
	1970	73 451	55 246	16 177	2 028	39	41	35	27
	1975	88 913	64 662	21 527	2 724	40	42	37	29
	1977	95 636	68 572	23 986	3 078	40	41	37	30
	% 1965–70	4.1	3.6	4.8	11.8				
	% 1970–77	3.8	3.1	5.8	6.1				

School enrolment (female) 2.4
Effectifs scolaires (féminins)
Matrícula escolar (femenina)

CONTINENTS, MAJOR AREAS AND GROUPS OF COUNTRIES CONTINENTS, GRANDES REGIONS ET GROUPES DE PAYS CONTINENTES, GRANDES REGIONES Y GRUPOS DE PAISES	YEAR ANNEE AÑO	NUMBER OF GIRLS ENROLLED (THOUSANDS) NOMBRE DE FILLES INSCRITES (MILLIERS) NUMERO DE MUCHACHAS MATRICULADAS (EN MILES)				% OF GIRLS IN TOTAL (BOTH SEXES) ENROLMENT % DE FILLES PAR RAPPORT AU TOTAL DES EFFECTIFS DES DEUX SEXES % DE MUCHACHAS CON RESPECTO A LA MATRICULA TOTAL DE AMBOS SEXOS			
		TOTAL TOTAL TOTAL	1ST LEVEL 1ER DEGRE 1ER GRADO	2ND LEVEL 2ND DEGRE 2DO GRADO	3RD LEVEL 3EME DEGRE 3ER GRADO	TOTAL TOTAL TOTAL	1ST LEVEL 1ER DEGRE 1ER GRADO	2ND LEVEL 2ND DEGRE 2DO GRADO	3RD LEVEL 3EME DEGRE 3ER GRADO
		(1)	(2)	(3)	(4)	(5)	(6)	(7)	(8)
ARAB STATES	1965	4 249	3 572	619	58	33	35	27	20
	1970	5 709	4 551	1 054	105	35	36	30	24
	1975	8 346	6 187	1 917	241	37	38	34	28
	1977	9 668	6 912	2 458	297	38	39	36	28
	% 1965–70	6.1	5.0	11.2	12.6				
	% 1970–77	7.8	6.2	12.9	16.0				

GENERAL NOTE / NOTE GENERALE / NOTA GENERAL:
E—> FOR COMPOSITION OF MAJOR AREAS AND GROUPS OF COUNTRIES, SEE GENERAL NOTE TO TABLE 1.2. THE SCHOOL YEAR BEGINS IN THE CALENDAR YEAR INDICATED. MORE INFORMATION ON THIS POINT IS GIVEN IN THE GENERAL INTRODUCTION TO THE "EDUCATION" CHAPTER. THE FIGURES IN THIS TABLE DO NOT INCLUDE DATA RELATING TO PRE–PRIMARY, SPECIAL AND ADULT EDUCATION.
FR–> POUR LA COMPOSITION DES GRANDES REGIONS ET DES GROUPES DE PAYS, VOIR LA NOTE GENERALE DU TABLEAU 1.2. L'ANNEE SCOLAIRE COMMENCE PENDANT L'ANNEE CIVILE INDIQUEE. POUR PLUS DE DETAILS, SE REPORTER A L'INTRODUCTION GENERALE DU CHAPITRE "EDUCATION". LES CHIFFRES DE CE TABLEAU NE COM–PRENNENT PAS L'ENSEIGNEMENT PREPRIMAIRE, L'EDUCATION SPECIALE ET L'EDUCATION DES ADULTES.
ESP> PUEDE VERSE LA COMPOSICION DE LAS GRANDES REGIONES Y GRUPOS DE PAISES EN LA NOTA GENERAL DEL CUADRO 1.2. EL AÑO ESCOLAR EMPIEZA DURANTE EL AÑO CIVIL INDICADO. PUEDEN VERSE MAS DETALLES A ESTE RESPECTO EN LA INTRODUCCION GENERAL DEL CAPITULO "EDUCACION". LAS CIFRAS DE ESTE CUADRO NO COMPRENDEN LA ENSEÑANZA PREPRIMARIA, LA EDUCACION ESPECIAL Y LA EDUCACION DE ADULTOS.

SECOND LEVEL / SECOND DEGRE / SEGUNDO GRADO:
E—> GENERAL, TEACHER TRAINING AND OTHER EDUCATION AT THE SECOND LEVEL OF A VOCATIONAL OR TECHNICAL NATURE.
FR–> GENERAL, NORMAL ET AUTRE ENSEIGNEMENT DU SECOND DEGRE DE CARACTERE TECHNIQUE OU PRO–FESSIONNEL.
ESP> GENERAL, NORMAL Y OTRA ENSEÑANZA DE SEGUNDO GRADO DE CARACTER TECNICO O PROFESIONAL.

THIRD LEVEL / TROISIEME DEGRE / TERCER GRADO:
E—> UNIVERSITIES AND OTHER INSTITUTIONS OF HIGHER EDUCATION.
FR–> UNIVERSITES ET AUTRES ETABLISSEMENTS D'ENSEIGNEMENT SUPERIEUR.
ESP> UNIVERSIDADES Y OTROS ESTABLECIMIENTOS DE ENSEÑANZA SUPERIOR.

WORLD TOTAL:
E—> NOT INCLUDING CHINA AND THE DEMOCRATIC PEOPLE'S REPUBLIC OF KOREA. INCLUDING AN ALLOW–ANCE FOR TEACHERS IN THE U.S.S.R.
FR–> NON COMPRIS LA CHINE ET LA REPUBLIQUE DEMOCRATIQUE POPULAIRE DE COREE. Y COMPRIS UNE ESTIMATION DU PERSONNEL ENSEIGNANT DE L'U.R.S.S.
ESP> EXCLUIDAS CHINA Y LA REPUBLICA POPULAR DEMOCRATICA DE COREA. INCLUIDA UNA ESTIMACION DEL PERSONAL DOCENTE DE LA U.R.S.S.

AMERICA:
E—> BEGINNING 1971, THE DURATION OF PRIMARY SCHOOLING IN BRAZIL WAS INCREASED FROM 4 TO 8 YEARS AND THAT OF GENERAL EDUCATION AT THE SECOND LEVEL WAS REDUCED FROM 7 TO 3 YEARS.
FR–> A PARTIR DE 1971, LA DUREE DE L'ENSEIGNE–MENT DU PREMIER DEGRE A ETE PORTEE AU BRESIL DE 4 A 8 ANNEES, CELLE DE L'ENSEIGNEMENT GENERAL DU SECOND DEGRE AYANT ETE RAMENEE DE 7 A 3 ANNEES.
ESP> A PARTIR DE 1971, LA DURACION DE LA ENSEÑANZA DE PRIMER GRADO PASO EN EL BRASIL DE 4 A 8 AÑOS Y LA DE LA ENSEÑANZA GENERAL DE SEGUNDO GRADO DE 7 A 3 ANOS.

ASIA:
E—> NOT INCLUDING CHINA AND THE DEMOCRATIC PEOPLE'S REPUBLIC OF KOREA.
FR–> NON COMPRIS LA CHINE ET LA REPUBLIQUE DEMOCRATIQUE POPULAIRE DE COREE.
ESP> EXCLUIDAS CHINA Y LA REPUBLICA POPULAR DEMOCRATICA DE COREA.

OCEANIA:
E—> BEGINNING 1973, OTHER SECONDARY EDUCATION OF A VOCATIONAL OR TECHNICAL NATURE IN AUSTRALIA IS PROVIDED IN THE THIRD LEVEL OF EDUCATION.
FR–> A PARTIR DE 1973, L'AUTRE ENSEIGNEMENT DU SECOND DEGRE DE CARACTERE TECHNIQUE OU PROFES–SIONNEL EST DISPENSE EN AUSTRALIE DANS L'ENSEIGNE–MENT DU TROISIEME DEGRE.
ESP> A PARTIR DE 1973, LA OTRA ENSEÑANZA DE SEGUNDO GRADO DE CARACTER TECNICO O PROFESIONAL SE IMPARTE EN AUSTRALIA EN LA ENSEÑANZA DE TERCER GRADO.

2.4 School enrolment (female)
Effectifs scolaires (féminins)
Matricula escolar (femenina)

DEVELOPING COUNTRIES:
E—> NOT INCLUDING CHINA AND THE DEMOCRATIC
PEOPLE'S REPUBLIC OF KOREA.
FR—> NON COMPRIS LA CHINE ET LA REPUBLIQUE
DEMOCRATIQUE POPULAIRE DE COREE.
ESP> EXCLUIDAS CHINA Y LA REPUBLICA POPULAR
DEMOCRATICA DE COREA.

LATIN AMERICA:
E—> BEGINNING 1971, THE DURATION OF PRIMARY
SCHOOLING IN BRAZIL WAS INCREASED FROM 4 TO 8
YEARS AND THAT OF GENERAL EDUCATION AT THE SECOND
LEVEL WAS REDUCED FROM 7 TO 3 YEARS.

LATIN AMERICA (CONT.):
FR—> A PARTIR DE 1971, LA DUREE DE L'ENSEIGNE—
MENT DU PREMIER DEGRE A ETE PORTEE AU BRESIL DE
4 A 8 ANNEES, CELLE DE L'ENSEIGNEMENT GENERAL DU
SECOND DEGRE AYANT ETE RAMENEE DE 7 A 3
ANNEES.
ESP> A PARTIR DE 1971, LA DURACION DE LA
ENSEÑANZA DE PRIMER GRADO PASO EN EL BRASIL DE
4 A 8 AÑOS Y LA DE LA ENSEÑANZA GENERAL DE SEGUNDO
GRADO DE 7 A 3 ANOS.

ASIA (EXCLUDING ARAB STATES):
E—> NOT INCLUDING CHINA AND THE DEMOCRATIC
PEOPLE'S REPUBLIC OF KOREA.
FR—> NON COMPRIS LA CHINE ET LA REPUBLIQUE
DEMOCRATIQUE POPULAIRE DE COREE.
ESP> EXCLUIDAS CHINA Y LA REPUBLICA POPULAR
DEMOCRATICA DE COREA.

Teachers (female) by level of education 2.5
Personnel enseignant (féminin) par degrés d'enseignement
Personal docente (femenino) por grados de enseñanza

2.5 Estimated female teachers by level of education (first and second levels only)

Estimation du personnel enseignant féminin, par degrés d'enseignement (premier et second degrés seulement)

Estimación del personal docente femenino, por grados de enseñanza (primer y segundo grado solamente)

(SEE NOTE CONCERNING TABLES 2.2 – 2.7) (VOIR LA NOTE RELATIVE AUX TABLEAUX 2.2 – 2.7) (VEASE LA NOTA RELATIVA A LOS CUADROS 2.2 – 2.7)		FIRST LEVEL/PREMIER DEGRE/PRIMER GRADO		SECOND LEVEL/SECOND DEGRE/SEGUNDO GRADO	
CONTINENTS, MAJOR AREAS AND GROUPS OF COUNTRIES CONTINENTS, GRANDES REGIONES ET GROUPES DE PAYS CONTINENTES, GRANDES REGIONES Y GRUPOS DE PAISES	YEAR ANNEE AÑO	TOTAL FEMALE TEACHERS TOTAL DU PERSONNEL ENSEIGNANT FEMININ TOTAL DEL PERSONAL DOCENTE FEMENINO (000)	AS % OF TOTAL TEACHERS (BOTH SEXES) EN % DU TOTAL DU PERSONNEL ENSEIGNANT (HOMMES ET FEMMES) EN % DEL TOTAL DE MAESTROS (AMBOS SEXOS) %	TOTAL FEMALE TEACHERS TOTAL DU PERSONNEL ENSEIGNANT FEMININ TOTAL DEL PERSONAL DOCENTE FEMENINO (000)	AS % OF TOTAL TEACHERS (BOTH SEXES) EN % DU TOTAL DU PERSONNEL ENSEIGNANT (HOMMES ET FEMMES) EN % DEL TOTAL DE MAESTROS (AMBOS SEXOS) %
		(1)	(2)	(3)	(4)
WORLD TOTAL ‡	1965	5 691	57	2 053	39
	1970	6 815	59	2 811	40
	1975	7 854	58	3 564	41
	1977	8 144	58	3 806	41
AFRICA	1965	188	28	39	25
	1970	255	31	72	32
	1975	371	32	119	32
	1977	433	32	148	33
AMERICA	1965	1 895	83	594	42
	1970	2 267	83	831	43
	1975	2 840	82	963	46
	1977	2 884	81	1 037	45
ASIA ‡	1965	970	32	405	24
	1970	1 366	36	611	27
	1975	1 647	36	850	29
	1977	1 814	37	919	29
EUROPE	1965	1 263	66	671	44
	1970	1 449	69	897	45
	1975	1 583	70	1 112	46
	1977	1 582	70	1 203	46
OCEANIA	1965	52	60	24	44
	1970	60	63	34	47
	1975	73	65	45	46
	1977	77	65	48	45
U.S.S.R.	1965	...	...	...	...
	1970	...	...	...	...
	1975	...	...	...	...
	1977	...	...	...	...

2.5 Teachers (female) by level of education
Personnel enseignant (féminin) par degrés d'enseignement
Personal docente (femenino) por grados de enseñanza

CONTINENTS, MAJOR AREAS AND GROUPS OF COUNTRIES	YEAR	FIRST LEVEL/PREMIER DEGRE/PRIMER GRADO		SECOND LEVEL/SECOND DEGRE/SEGUNDO GRADO	
		TOTAL FEMALE TEACHERS	AS % OF TOTAL TEACHERS (BOTH SEXES)	TOTAL FEMALE TEACHERS	AS % OF TOTAL TEACHERS (BOTH SEXES)
CONTINENTS, GRANDES REGIONS ET GROUPES DE PAYS	ANNEE	TOTAL DU PERSONNEL ENSEIGNANT FEMININ	EN % DU TOTAL DU PERSONNEL ENSEIGNANT (HOMMES ET FEMMES)	TOTAL DU PERSONNEL ENSEIGNANT FEMININ	EN % DU TOTAL DU PERSONNEL ENSEIGNANT (HOMMES ET FEMMES)
CONTINENTES, GRANDES REGIONES Y GRUPOS DE PAISES	AÑO	TOTAL DEL PERSONAL DOCENTE FEMENINO (000)	EN % DEL TOTAL DE MAESTROS (AMBOS SEXOS) %	TOTAL DEL PERSONAL DOCENTE FEMENINO (000)	EN % DEL TOTAL DE MAESTROS (AMBOS SEXOS) %
		(1)	(2)	(3)	(4)
DEVELOPED COUNTRIES	1965	3 883	70	1 487	43
	1970	4 333	72	1 883	45
	1975	4 549	73	2 350	47
	1977	4 559	73	2 433	47
DEVELOPING COUNTRIES ‡	1965	1 808	42	566	30
	1970	2 482	45	928	33
	1975	3 305	46	1 214	34
	1977	3 585	46	1 373	34
AFRICA (EXCLUDING ARAB STATES)	1965	129	27	22	29
	1970	170	28	46	38
	1975	266	31	76	35
	1977	316	31	94	36
NORTHERN AMERICA	1965	1 029	86	357	40
	1970	1 165	86	446	40
	1975	1 256	86	571	45
	1977	1 230	86	580	45
LATIN AMERICA	1965	866	81	237	47
	1970	1 102	81	385	48
	1975	1 584	78	392	46
	1977	1 655	78	457	46
ASIA (EXCLUDING ARAB STATES) ‡	1965	933	32	396	24
	1970	1 317	36	594	27
	1975	1 568	36	815	29
	1977	1 718	37	880	29
ARAB STATES	1965	95	34	26	23
	1970	134	37	44	27
	1975	184	36	77	30
	1977	213	37	93	30

GENERAL NOTE / NOTE GENERALE / NOTA GENERAL:

E—> FOR COMPOSITION OF MAJOR AREAS AND GROUPS OF COUNTRIES, SEE GENERAL NOTE TO TABLE 1.2. THE SCHOOL YEAR BEGINS IN THE CALENDAR YEAR INDICATED. MORE INFORMATION ON THIS POINT IS GIVEN IN THE GENERAL INTRODUCTION TO THE "EDUCATION" CHAPTER.

FR—> POUR LA COMPOSITION DES GRANDES REGIONS ET DES GROUPES DE PAYS, VOIR LA NOTE GENERALE DU TABLEAU 1.2. L'ANNEE SCOLAIRE COMMENCE PENDANT L'ANNEE CIVILE INDIQUEE. POUR PLUS DE DETAILS, SE REPORTER A L'INTRODUCTION GENERALE DU CHAPITRE "EDUCATION".

ESP> PUEDE VERSE LA COMPOSICION DE LAS GRANDES REGIONES Y GRUPOS DE PAISES EN LA NOTA GENERAL DEL CUADRO 1.2. EL AÑO ESCOLAR EMPIEZA DURANTE EL AÑO CIVIL INDICADO. PUEDEN VERSE MAS DETALLES A ESTE RESPECTO EN LA INTRODUCCION GENERAL DEL CAPITULO "EDUCACION".

SECOND LEVEL / SECOND DEGRE / SEGUNDO GRADO:

E—> GENERAL, TEACHER TRAINING AND OTHER EDUCATION AT THE SECOND LEVEL OF A VOCATIONAL OR TECHNICAL NATURE.

FR—> GENERAL, NORMAL ET AUTRE ENSEIGNEMENT DU SECOND DEGRE DE CARACTERE TECHNIQUE OU PRO—FESSIONNEL.

ESP> GENERAL, NORMAL Y OTRA ENSEÑANZA DE SEGUNDO GRADO DE CARACTER TECNICO O PROFESIONAL.

WORLD TOTAL:

E—> NOT INCLUDING CHINA AND THE DEMOCRATIC PEOPLE'S REPUBLIC OF KOREA. INCLUDING AN ALLOW—ANCE FOR TEACHERS IN THE U.S.S.R.

FR—> NON COMPRIS LA CHINE ET LA REPUBLIQUE DEMOCRATIQUE POPULAIRE DE COREE. Y COMPRIS UNE ESTIMATION DU PERSONNEL ENSEIGNANT DE L'U.R.S.S.

Teachers (female) by level of education   **2.5**
Personnel enseignant (féminin) par degrés d'enseignement
Personal docente (femenino) por grados de enseñanza

WORLD TOTAL (CONT.):
   ESP> EXCLUIDAS CHINA Y LA REPUBLICA POPULAR
DEMOCRATICA DE COREA. INCLUIDA UNA ESTIMACION
DEL PERSONAL DOCENTE DE LA U.R.S.S.

ASIA:
   E—> NOT INCLUDING CHINA AND THE DEMOCRATIC
PEOPLE'S REPUBLIC OF KOREA.
   FR—> NON COMPRIS LA CHINE ET LA REPUBLIQUE
DEMOCRATIQUE POPULAIRE DE COREE.
   ESP> EXCLUIDAS CHINA Y LA REPUBLICA POPULAR
DEMOCRATICA DE COREA.

DEVELOPING COUNTRIES:
   E—> NOT INCLUDING CHINA AND THE DEMOCRATIC
PEOPLE'S REPUBLIC OF KOREA.
   FR—> NON COMPRIS LA CHINE ET LA REPUBLIQUE
DEMOCRATIQUE POPULAIRE DE COREE.
   ESP> EXCLUIDAS CHINA Y LA REPUBLICA POPULAR
DEMOCRATICA DE COREA.

ASIA (EXCLUDING ARAB STATES):
   E—> NOT INCLUDING CHINA AND THE DEMOCRATIC
PEOPLE'S REPUBLIC OF KOREA.
   FR—> NON COMPRIS LA CHINE ET LA REPUBLIQUE
DEMOCRATIQUE POPULAIRE DE COREE.
   ESP> EXCLUIDAS CHINA Y LA REPUBLICA POPULAR
DEMOCRATICA DE COREA.

2.6 Index numbers of total and female enrolment and teachers by level of education (1965 = 100)

Indices: total des effectifs, effectifs féminins et personnel enseignant (1965 = 100)

Indices: total general, total de la matrícula escolar femenina y del personal docente, por grados de enseñanza (1965 = 100)

(SEE NOTE CONCERNING TABLES 2.2 – 2.7)
(VOIR LA NOTE RELATIVE AUX TABLEAUX 2.2 – 2.7)
(VEASE LA NOTA RELATIVA A LOS CUADROS 2.2 – 2.7)

CONTINENTS, MAJOR AREAS AND GROUPS OF COUNTRIES / CONTINENTS, GRANDES RÉGIONS ET GROUPES DE PAYS / CONTINENTES, GRANDES REGIONES Y GRUPOS DE PAISES	YEAR ANNEE AÑO	TOTAL ENROLMENT TOTAL DES EFFECTIFS MATRICULA TOTAL				FEMALE ENROLMENT EFFECTIFS FÉMININS MATRICULA FEMININA				TEACHING STAFF PERSONNEL ENSEIGNANT PERSONAL DOCENTE			
		TOTAL	1ST LEVEL 1ER DEGRE 1ER GRADO	2ND LEVEL 2ND DEGRE 2DO GRADO	3RD LEVEL 3EME DEGRE 3ER GRADO	TOTAL	1ST LEVEL 1ER DEGRE 1ER GRADO	2ND LEVEL 2ND DEGRE 2DO GRADO	3RD LEVEL 3EME DEGRE 3ER GRADO	TOTAL	1ST LEVEL 1ER DEGRE 1ER GRADO	2ND LEVEL 2ND DEGRE 2DO GRADO	3RD LEVEL 3EME DEGRE 3ER GRADO
		(1)	(2)	(3)	(4)	(5)	(6)	(7)	(8)	(9)	(10)	(11)	(12)
WORLD TOTAL ‡	1965	100	100	100	100	100	100	100	100	100	100	100	100
	1970	118	114	125	148	124	117	131	151	118	114	125	157
	1975	136	126	153	199	149	135	161	203	137	127	156	228
	1977	143	131	166	215	159	142	173	223	145	131	169	255
AFRICA	1965	100	100	100	100	100	100	100	100	100	100	100	100
	1970	131	127	161	153	130	125	146	175	135	131	173	178
	1975	183	170	286	287	190	175	241	305	196	183	339	367
	1977	211	194	342	352	224	205	290	370	229	210	426	454
AMERICA ‡	1965	100	100	100	100	100	100	100	100	100	100	100	100
	1970	120	114	128	158	128	119	136	142	120	114	128	167
	1975	137	127	141	230	157	153	150	195	138	127	141	266
	1977	142	129	148	243	166	156	162	218	144	129	149	302
ASIA ‡	1965	100	100	100	100	100	100	100	100	100	100	100	100
	1970	121	118	125	167	131	125	133	179	122	119	126	174
	1975	145	137	159	209	160	148	170	230	149	141	170	237
	1977	157	147	178	231	173	160	184	254	161	150	190	268
EUROPE	1965	100	100	100	100	100	100	100	100	100	100	100	100
	1970	111	103	122	139	121	109	129	148	111	103	123	153
	1975	120	100	148	201	142	118	157	216	122	100	155	251
	1977	122	98	156	218	148	116	170	233	124	98	164	280

2.6 Total and female enrolment and teachers: index numbers
Total des effectifs, effectifs féminins et personnel enseignant: indices
Matrícula escolar (total y femenina) y personal docente: indices

Total and female enrolment and teachers: index numbers   2.6
Total des effectifs, effectifs féminins et personnel enseignant: indices
Matrícula escolar (total y femenina) y personal docente: indices

Region	Year	(1)	(2)	(3)	(4)	(5)	(6)	(7)	(8)	(9)	(10)	(11)	(12)
OCEANIA ‡	1965	100	100	100	100	100	100	100	100	100	100	100	100
	1970	116	111	124	140	120	110	133	150	116	111	124	157
	1975	127	111	146	222	155	128	181	260	128	111	149	289
	1977	131	114	151	244	166	136	198	280	133	114	155	330
U.S.S.R.	1965	100	100	100	100	...	...	...	100	...	...	...	100
	1970	106	105	108	118	...	...	...	138	...	...	...	130
	1975	101	93	126	125	...	...	...	157	...	...	...	142
	1977	98	88	127	130	...	...	...	162	...	...	...	148
DEVELOPED COUNTRIES	1965	100	100	100	100	100	100	100	100	100	100	100	100
	1970	108	103	112	141	117	108	122	143	108	103	112	152
	1975	112	97	127	182	131	113	145	182	113	97	130	212
	1977	112	95	131	189	134	112	151	194	114	95	134	230
DEVELOPING COUNTRIES‡	1965	100	100	100	100	100	100	100	100	100	100	100	100
	1970	128	123	147	173	136	127	149	178	130	125	158	179
	1975	160	150	196	258	177	164	191	281	167	155	224	305
	1977	176	161	224	298	196	179	215	332	184	167	261	370
AFRICA (EXCLUDING ARAB STATES)	1965	100	100	100	100	100	100	100	100	100	100	100	100
	1970	132	129	171	174	129	124	160	170	136	134	180	171
	1975	189	177	335	287	193	177	289	290	202	191	380	276
	1977	221	207	400	357	230	210	349	370	237	223	471	347
NORTHERN AMERICA	1965	100	100	100	100	100	100	100	100	100	100	100	100
	1970	111	99	117	155	122	113	125	142	111	95	117	164
	1975	112	88	126	203	136	121	141	167	113	89	126	235
	1977	110	84	124	205	137	119	143	176	112	84	124	257
LATIN AMERICA ‡	1965	100	100	100	100	100	100	100	100	100	100	100	100
	1970	133	127	157	179	136	127	156	144	134	128	158	194
	1975	171	163	181	399	189	188	167	307	172	164	182	498
	1977	185	171	213	490	209	197	196	383	187	173	219	649
ASIA (EXCLUDING ARAB STATES) ‡	1965	100	100	100	100	100	100	100	100	100	100	100	100
	1970	121	118	151	167	131	125	132	179	122	119	126	174
	1975	143	136	243	207	158	146	167	228	147	139	167	234
	1977	155	145	296	228	171	158	180	252	158	148	186	264
ARAB STATES	1965	100	100	100	100	100	100	100	100	100	100	100	100
	1970	129	123	151	150	134	129	142	178	134	127	170	181
	1975	179	161	243	291	198	181	225	321	196	173	309	415
	1977	201	175	296	353	227	203	270	378	227	193	397	512

2.6 Total and female enrolment and teachers: index numbers
Total des effectifs, effectifs féminins et personnel enseignant: indices
Matrícula escolar (total y femenina) y personal docente: indices

GENERAL NOTE / NOTE GENERALE / NOTA GENERAL:

E—> FOR COMPOSITION OF MAJOR AREAS AND GROUPS OF COUNTRIES, SEE GENERAL NOTE TO TABLE 1.2. THE SCHOOL YEAR BEGINS IN THE CALENDAR YEAR INDICATED. MORE INFORMATION ON THIS POINT IS GIVEN IN THE GENERAL INTRODUCTION TO THE "EDUCATION" CHAPTER. THE FIGURES IN THIS TABLE DO NOT INCLUDE DATA RELATING TO PRE-PRIMARY, SPECIAL AND ADULT EDUCATION.

FR-> POUR LA COMPOSITION DES GRANDES REGIONS ET DES GROUPES DE PAYS, VOIR LA NOTE GENERALE DU TABLEAU 1.2. L'ANNEE SCOLAIRE COMMENCE PENDANT L'ANNEE CIVILE INDIQUEE. POUR PLUS DE DETAILS, SE REPORTER A L'INTRODUCTION GENERALE DU CHAPITRE "EDUCATION". LES CHIFFRES DE CE TABLEAU NE COM- PRENNENT PAS L'ENSEIGNEMENT PREPRIMAIRE, L'EDUCATION SPECIALE ET L'EDUCATION DES ADULTES.

ESP> PUEDE VERSE LA COMPOSICION DE LAS GRANDES REGIONES Y GRUPOS DE PAISES EN LA NOTA GENERAL DEL CUADRO 1.2. EL AÑO ESCOLAR EMPIEZA DURANTE EL AÑO CIVIL INDICADO. PUEDEN VERSE MAS DETALLES A ESTE RESPECTO EN LA INTRODUCCION GENERAL DEL CAPITULO "EDUCACION". LAS CIFRAS DE ESTE CUADRO NO COMPRENDEN LA ENSEÑANZA PREPRIMARIA, LA EDUCACION ESPECIAL Y LA EDUCACION DE ADULTOS.

SECOND LEVEL / SECOND DEGRE / SEGUNDO GRADO:

E—> GENERAL, TEACHER TRAINING AND OTHER EDUCATION AT THE SECOND LEVEL OF A VOCATIONAL OR TECHNICAL NATURE.

FR-> GENERAL, NORMAL ET AUTRE ENSEIGNEMENT DU SECOND DEGRE DE CARACTERE TECHNIQUE OU PRO- FESSIONNEL.

ESP> GENERAL, NORMAL Y OTRA ENSEÑANZA DE SEGUNDO GRADO DE CARACTER TECNICO O PROFESIONAL.

THIRD LEVEL / TROISIEME DEGRE / TERCER GRADO:

E—> UNIVERSITIES AND OTHER INSTITUTIONS OF HIGHER EDUCATION.

FR-> UNIVERSITES ET AUTRES ETABLISSEMENTS D'ENSEIGNEMENT SUPERIEUR.

ESP> UNIVERSIDADES Y OTROS ESTABLECIMIENTOS DE ENSEÑANZA SUPERIOR.

WORLD TOTAL:

E—> NOT INCLUDING CHINA AND THE DEMOCRATIC PEOPLE'S REPUBLIC OF KOREA. INCLUDING AN ALLOW- ANCE FOR TEACHERS IN THE U.S.S.R.

FR-> NON COMPRIS LA CHINE ET LA REPUBLIQUE DEMOCRATIQUE POPULAIRE DE COREE. Y COMPRIS UNE ESTIMATION DU PERSONNEL ENSEIGNANT DE L'U.R.S.S.

ESP> EXCLUIDAS CHINA Y LA REPUBLICA POPULAR DEMOCRATICA DE COREA. INCLUIDA UNA ESTIMACION DEL PERSONAL DOCENTE DE LA U.R.S.S.

AMERICA:

E—> BEGINNING 1971, THE DURATION OF PRIMARY SCHOOLING IN BRAZIL WAS INCREASED FROM 4 TO 8 YEARS AND THAT OF GENERAL EDUCATION AT THE SECOND LEVEL WAS REDUCED FROM 7 TO 3 YEARS.

AMERICA (CONT.):

FR-> A PARTIR DE 1971, LA DUREE DE L'ENSEIGNE- MENT DU PREMIER DEGRE A ETE PORTEE AU BRESIL DE 4 A 8 ANNEES, CELLE DE L'ENSEIGNEMENT GENERAL DU SECOND DEGRE AYANT ETE RAMENEE DE 7 A 3 ANNEES.

ESP> A PARTIR DE 1971, LA DURACION DE LA ENSEÑANZA DE PRIMER GRADO PASO EN EL BRASIL DE 4 A 8 AÑOS Y LA DE LA ENSEÑANZA GENERAL DE SEGUNDO GRADO DE 7 A 3 ANOS.

ASIA:

E—> NOT INCLUDING CHINA AND THE DEMOCRATIC PEOPLE'S REPUBLIC OF KOREA.

FR-> NON COMPRIS LA CHINE ET LA REPUBLIQUE DEMOCRATIQUE POPULAIRE DE COREE.

ESP> EXCLUIDAS CHINA Y LA REPUBLICA POPULAR DEMOCRATICA DE COREA.

OCEANIA:

E—> BEGINNING 1973, OTHER SECONDARY EDUCATION OF A VOCATIONAL OR TECHNICAL NATURE IN AUSTRALIA IS PROVIDED IN THE THIRD LEVEL OF EDUCATION.

FR-> A PARTIR DE 1973, L'AUTRE ENSEIGNEMENT DU SECOND DEGRE DE CARACTERE TECHNIQUE OU PROFES- SIONNEL EST DISPENSE EN AUSTRALIE DANS L'ENSEIGNE- MENT DU TROISIEME DEGRE.

ESP> A PARTIR DE 1973, LA OTRA ENSEÑANZA DE SEGUNDO GRADO DE CARACTER TECNICO O PROFESIONAL SE IMPARTE EN AUSTRALIA EN LA ENSEÑANZA DE TERCER GRADO.

DEVELOPING COUNTRIES:

E—> NOT INCLUDING CHINA AND THE DEMOCRATIC PEOPLE'S REPUBLIC OF KOREA.

FR-> NON COMPRIS LA CHINE ET LA REPUBLIQUE DEMOCRATIQUE POPULAIRE DE COREE.

ESP> EXCLUIDAS CHINA Y LA REPUBLICA POPULAR DEMOCRATICA DE COREA.

LATIN AMERICA:

E—> BEGINNING 1971, THE DURATION OF PRIMARY SCHOOLING IN BRAZIL WAS INCREASED FROM 4 TO 8 YEARS AND THAT OF GENERAL EDUCATION AT THE SECOND LEVEL WAS REDUCED FROM 7 TO 3 YEARS.

FR-> A PARTIR DE 1971, LA DUREE DE L'ENSEIGNE- MENT DU PREMIER DEGRE A ETE PORTEE AU BRESIL DE 4 A 8 ANNEES, CELLE DE L'ENSEIGNEMENT GENERAL DU SECOND DEGRE AYANT ETE RAMENEE DE 7 A 3 ANNEES.

ESP> A PARTIR DE 1971, LA DURACION DE LA ENSEÑANZA DE PRIMER GRADO PASO EN EL BRASIL DE 4 A 8 AÑOS Y LA DE LA ENSEÑANZA GENERAL DE SEGUNDO GRADO DE 7 A 3 ANOS.

ASIA (EXCLUDING ARAB STATES):

E—> NOT INCLUDING CHINA AND THE DEMOCRATIC PEOPLE'S REPUBLIC OF KOREA.

FR-> NON COMPRIS LA CHINE ET LA REPUBLIQUE DEMOCRATIQUE POPULAIRE DE COREE.

ESP> EXCLUIDAS CHINA Y LA REPUBLICA POPULAR DEMOCRATICA DE COREA.

Pupil-teacher ratios by level of education 2.7
Nombre d'élèves par maître, par degrés d'enseignement
Número de alumnos por maestro, por grados de enseñanza

2.7 Pupil-teacher ratios by level of education

Nombre d'élèves par maître, par degrés d'enseignement

Número de alumnos por maestro, por grados de enseñanza

A. EDUCATION AT THE FIRST LEVEL
   ENSEIGNEMENT DU PREMIER DEGRE
   ENSEÑANZA DE PRIMER GRADO

CONTINENTS, MAJOR AREAS AND GROUPS OF COUNTRIES	YEAR	FREQUENCY DISTRIBUTION ACCORDING TO THE PUPIL—TEACHER RATIO IN FIRST LEVEL EDUCATION					
CONTINENTS, GRANDES REGIONS ET GROUPES DE PAYS	ANNEE	DISTRIBUTION DE FREQUENCE SELON LE NOMBRE D'ELEVES PAR MAITRE DANS L'ENSEIGNEMENT DU PREMIER DEGRE					
CONTINENTES, GRANDES REGIONES Y GRUPOS DE PAISES	AÑO	DISTRIBUCION DE FRECUENCIA SEGUN EL NUMERO DE ALUMNOS POR MAESTRO EN LA ENSEÑANZA DE PRIMER GRADO					
		< 21	21–30	31–40	41–50	51–60	> 60
WORLD TOTAL	1965	18	65	63	29	10	6
	1970	23	76	53	28	7	6
	1975	37	68	53	22	10	5
	1977	33	78	47	25	8	4
AFRICA	1965	1	4	22	17	5	5
	1970	1	6	20	18	3	6
	1975	1	7	19	15	7	5
	1977	1	9	18	15	7	4
AMERICA	1965	3	19	18	6	2	—
	1970	4	20	18	4	2	—
	1975	6	20	17	5	—	—
	1977	6	23	14	5	—	—
ASIA	1965	3	12	12	6	3	1
	1970	4	18	9	6	2	—
	1975	8	15	12	2	3	—
	1977	8	15	11	5	1	—
EUROPE	1965	6	20	7	—	—	—
	1970	10	19	4	—	—	—
	1975	17	14	2	—	—	—
	1977	15	16	2	—	—	—
OCEANIA	1965	4	10	4	—	—	—
	1970	3	13	2	—	—	—
	1975	4	12	3	—	—	—
	1977	2	15	2	—	—	—
U.S.S.R.	1965	1					
	1970	1					
	1975	1					
	1977	1					

2.7 **Pupil-teacher ratios by level of education**
Nombre d'élèves par maître, par degrés d'enseignement
Número de alumnos por maestro, por grados de enseñanza

A. EDUCATION AT THE FIRST LEVEL (CONTINUATION)
    ENSEIGNEMENT DU PREMIER DEGRE (SUITE)
    ENSEÑANZA DE PRIMER GRADO (CONTINUACION)

CONTINENTS, MAJOR AREAS AND GROUPS OF COUNTRIES / CONTINENTS, GRANDES REGIONS ET GROUPES DE PAYS / CONTINENTES, GRANDES REGIONES Y GRUPOS DE PAISES	YEAR / ANNEE / AÑO	FREQUENCY DISTRIBUTION ACCORDING TO THE PUPIL–TEACHER RATIO IN FIRST LEVEL EDUCATION / DISTRIBUTION DE FREQUENCE SELON LE NOMBRE D'ELEVES PAR MAITRE DANS L'ENSEIGNEMENT DU PREMIER DEGRE / DISTRIBUCION DE FRECUENCIA SEGUN EL NUMERO DE ALUMNOS POR MAESTRO EN LA ENSEÑANZA DE PRIMER GRADO					
		< 21	21–30	31–40	41–50	51–60	> 60
DEVELOPED COUNTRIES	1965	8	24	7	1	–	–
	1970	12	24	3	1	–	–
	1975	20	18	1	1	–	–
	1977	18	20	1	1	–	–
DEVELOPING COUNTRIES	1965	10	41	56	28	10	6
	1970	11	52	50	27	7	6
	1975	17	50	52	21	10	5
	1977	15	58	46	24	8	4
AFRICA (EXCLUDING ARAB STATES)	1965	1	4	19	15	4	5
	1970	1	5	17	16	3	6
	1975	1	6	15	14	7	5
	1977	1	8	13	15	7	4
NORTHERN AMERICA	1965	1	3	–	–	–	–
	1970	–	4	–	–	–	–
	1975	1	3	–	–	–	–
	1977	2	2	–	–	–	–
LATIN AMERICA	1965	2	16	18	6	2	–
	1970	4	16	18	4	2	–
	1975	5	17	17	5	–	–
	1977	4	21	14	5	–	–
ASIA (EXCLUDING ARAB STATES)	1965	2	7	9	6	2	1
	1970	2	12	6	6	1	–
	1975	3	12	8	2	3	–
	1977	3	12	7	5	1	–
ARAB STATES	1965	1	5	6	2	2	–
	1970	2	7	6	2	1	–
	1975	5	4	8	1	–	–
	1977	5	4	9	–	–	–

Pupil-teacher ratios by level of education   2.7
Nombre d'élèves par maître, par degrés d'enseignement
Número de alumnos por maestro, por grados de enseñanza

B. EDUCATION AT THE SECOND LEVEL
    ENSEIGNEMENT DU SECOND DEGRE
    ENSEÑANZA DE SEGUNDO GRADO

CONTINENTS, MAJOR AREAS AND GROUPS OF COUNTRIES / CONTINENTS, GRANDES REGIONS ET GROUPES DE PAYS / CONTINENTES, GRANDES REGIONES Y GRUPOS DE PAISES	YEAR / ANNEE / AÑO	FREQUENCY DISTRIBUTION ACCORDING TO THE STUDENT-TEACHER RATIO IN SECOND LEVEL EDUCATION / DISTRIBUTION DE FREQUENCE SELON LE NOMBRE D'ETUDIANTS PAR PROFESSEUR DANS L'ENSEIGNEMENT DU SECOND DEGRE / DISTRIBUCION DE FRECUENCIA SEGUN EL NUMERO DE ESTUDIANTES POR PROFESOR EN LA ENSEÑANZA DE SEGUNDO GRADO				
		< 11	11–20	21–30	31–40	> 40
WORLD TOTAL	1965	9	108	62	9	1
	1970	8	112	65	6	—
	1975	9	109	64	10	1
	1977	11	108	63	9	2
AFRICA	1965	—	35	18	1	—
	1970	—	29	24	1	—
	1975	—	20	29	4	1
	1977	—	25	25	2	2
AMERICA	1965	5	22	17	2	1
	1970	4	26	17	1	—
	1975	2	30	13	3	—
	1977	2	32	11	3	—
ASIA	1965	2	16	15	4	—
	1970	1	20	13	4	—
	1975	3	20	14	3	—
	1977	2	16	18	4	—
EUROPE	1965	2	24	7	—	—
	1970	3	24	6	—	—
	1975	4	26	3	—	—
	1977	6	23	4	—	—
OCEANIA	1965	—	10	5	2	—
	1970	—	12	5	—	—
	1975	—	12	5	—	—
	1977	1	11	5	—	—
U.S.S.R.	1965		1			
	1970		1			
	1975		1			
	1977		1			
DEVELOPED COUNTRIES	1965	2	28	10	—	—
	1970	4	30	6	—	—
	1975	5	31	4	—	—
	1977	7	29	4	—	—
DEVELOPING COUNTRIES	1965	7	80	52	9	1
	1970	4	82	59	6	—
	1975	4	78	60	10	1
	1977	4	79	59	9	2

2.7 Pupil-teacher ratios by level of education
Nombre d'élèves par maître, par degrés d'enseignement
Número de alumnos por maestro, por grados de enseñanza

B. EDUCATION AT THE SECOND LEVEL (CONTINUATION)
   ENSEIGNEMENT DU SECOND DEGRE (SUITE)
   ENSEÑANZA DE SEGUNDO GRADO (CONTINUACION)

CONTINENTS, MAJOR AREAS AND GROUPS OF COUNTRIES / CONTINENTS, GRANDES REGIONS ET GROUPES DE PAYS / CONTINENTES, GRANDES REGIONES Y GRUPOS DE PAISES	YEAR ANNEE AÑO	FREQUENCY DISTRIBUTION ACCORDING TO THE STUDENT—TEACHER RATIO IN SECOND LEVEL EDUCATION / DISTRIBUTION DE FREQUENCE SELON LE NOMBRE D'ETUDIANTS PAR PROFESSEUR DANS L'ENSEIGNEMENT DU SECOND DEGRE / DISTRIBUCION DE FRECUENCIA SEGUN EL NUMERO DE ESTUDIANTES POR PROFESOR EN LA ENSEÑANZA DE SEGUNDO GRADO				
		< 11	11—20	21—30	31—40	> 40
AFRICA (EXCLUDING ARAB STATES)	1965	—	30	17	1	—
	1970	—	26	21	1	—
	1975	—	19	24	4	1
	1977	—	23	21	2	2
NORTHERN AMERICA	1965	1	2	1	—	—
	1970	1	3	—	—	—
	1975	—	4	—	—	—
	1977	—	4	—	—	—
LATIN AMERICA	1965	4	20	16	2	1
	1970	3	23	17	1	—
	1975	2	26	13	3	—
	1977	2	28	11	3	—
ASIA (EXCLUDING ARAB STATES)	1965	1	10	13	3	—
	1970	1	13	9	4	—
	1975	1	13	11	3	—
	1977	—	10	14	4	—
ARAB STATES	1965	1	11	3	1	—
	1970	—	10	7	—	—
	1975	2	8	8	—	—
	1977	2	8	8	—	—

Pupil-teacher ratios by level of education 2.7
Nombre d'élèves par maître, par degrés d'enseignement
Número de alumnos por maestro, por grados de enseñanza

C. EDUCATION AT THE THIRD LEVEL
    ENSEIGNEMENT DU TROISIEME DEGRE
    ENSEÑANZA DE TERCER GRADO

CONTINENTS, MAJOR AREAS AND GROUPS OF COUNTRIES	YEAR	FREQUENCY DISTRIBUTION ACCORDING TO THE STUDENT—TEACHER RATIO IN THIRD LEVEL EDUCATION					
CONTINENTS, GRANDES REGIONS ET GROUPES DE PAYS	ANNEE	DISTRIBUTION DE FREQUENCE SELON LE NOMBRE D'ETUDIANTS PAR PROFESSEUR DANS L'ENSEIGNEMENT DU TROISIEME DEGRE					
CONTINENTES, GRANDES REGIONES Y GRUPOS DE PAISES	AÑO	DISTRIBUCION DE FRECUENCIA SEGUN EL NUMERO DE ESTUDIANTES POR PROFESOR EN LA ENSEÑANZA DE TERCER GRADO					
		< 5	6—10	11—15	16—20	21—25	> 25
WORLD TOTAL	1965	18	49	30	21	7	3
	1970	8	52	42	29	4	3
	1975	10	58	41	24	6	5
	1977	13	57	45	21	10	3
AFRICA	1965	12	14	5	3	2	—
	1970	3	17	10	10	—	—
	1975	4	24	7	6	1	1
	1977	7	18	13	3	2	1
AMERICA	1965	4	15	5	6	—	—
	1970	—	12	11	6	—	1
	1975	1	9	13	5	—	2
	1977	1	11	8	8	2	—
ASIA	1965	—	7	9	6	2	3
	1970	2	6	13	7	2	1
	1975	2	7	12	9	2	1
	1977	2	9	14	6	3	1
EUROPE	1965	—	13	9	4	3	—
	1970	1	15	7	4	1	1
	1975	2	15	6	4	1	1
	1977	2	14	7	4	1	1
OCEANIA	1965	2	—	2	1	—	—
	1970	2	2	1	1	1	—
	1975	1	3	2	—	2	—
	1977	1	5	2	—	2	—
U.S.S.R.	1965				1		
	1970				1		
	1975			1			
	1977			1			
DEVELOPED COUNTRIES	1965	—	13	13	3	3	—
	1970	1	16	10	7	1	1
	1975	3	15	10	6	1	1
	1977	3	14	11	6	1	1
DEVELOPING COUNTRIES	1965	18	36	17	14	4	3
	1970	7	36	32	22	3	2
	1975	7	43	31	18	5	4
	1977	10	43	34	15	9	2

2.7 Pupil-teacher ratios by level of education
Nombre d'élèves par maître, par degrés d'enseignement
Número de alumnos por maestro, por grados de enseñanza

C. EDUCATION AT THE THIRD LEVEL (CONTINUATION)
   ENSEIGNEMENT DU TROISIEME DEGRE (SUITE)
   ENSEÑANZA DE TERCER GRADO (CONTINUACION)

CONTINENTS, MAJOR AREAS AND GROUPS OF COUNTRIES / CONTINENTS, GRANDES REGIONS ET GROUPES DE PAYS / CONTINENTES, GRANDES REGIONES Y GRUPOS DE PAISES	YEAR ANNEE AÑO	FREQUENCY DISTRIBUTION ACCORDING TO THE STUDENT—TEACHER RATIO IN THIRD LEVEL EDUCATION / DISTRIBUTION DE FREQUENCE SELON LE NOMBRE D'ETUDIANTS PAR PROFESSEUR DANS L'ENSEIGNEMENT DU TROISIEME DEGRE / DISTRIBUCION DE FRECUENCIA SEGUN EL NUMERO DE ESTUDIANTES POR PROFESOR EN LA ENSEÑANZA DE TERCER GRADO					
		< 5	6—10	11—15	16—20	21—25	> 25
AFRICA (EXCLUDING ARAB STATES)	1965	12	12	4	2	–	–
	1970	3	17	7	7	–	–
	1975	4	22	5	6	–	–
	1977	7	17	10	3	1	–
NORTHERN AMERICA	1965	–	–	1	1	–	–
	1970	–	–	1	1	–	–
	1975	–	–	–	2	–	–
	1977	–	–	–	2	–	–
LATIN AMERICA	1965	4	15	4	5	–	–
	1970	–	12	10	5	–	1
	1975	1	9	13	3	–	2
	1977	1	11	8	6	2	–
ASIA (EXCLUDING ARAB STATES)	1965	–	7	7	4	2	2
	1970	–	5	10	6	1	–
	1975	2	5	8	7	1	–
	1977	2	6	10	4	2	–
ARAB STATES	1965	–	2	3	3	2	1
	1970	2	1	6	4	1	1
	1975	–	4	6	2	2	2
	1977	–	4	7	2	2	2

GENERAL NOTE / NOTE GENERALE / NOTA GENERAL:
  E—> FOR COMPOSITION OF MAJOR AREAS AND GROUPS
OF COUNTRIES, SEE THE GENERAL NOTE TO TABLE 1.2.
  FR-> POUR LA COMPOSITION DES GRANDES REGIONS ET
DES GROUPES DE PAYS, VOIR LA NOTE GENERALE DU
TABLEAU 1.2.
  ESP> PUEDE VERSE LA COMPOSICION DE LAS GRANDES
REGIONES Y GRUPOS DE PAISES EN LA NOTA GENERAL
DEL CUADRO 1.2.

Education preceding the first level 2.8
Enseignement précédant le premier degré
Enseñanza anterior al primer grado

2.8 Estimated enrolment and teachers by sex for education preceding the first level

Estimation des effectifs et du personnel enseignant, par sexe, pour l'enseignement précédant le premier degré

Estimación de la matrícular escolar y del personal docente, por sexo, para la enseñanza anterior al primer grado

% 1965–70; 1970–77: ANNUAL AVERAGE INCREASE IN ENROLMENT AND TEACHERS FROM 1965 TO 1970 AND 1970 TO 1977, AS PERCENTAGE.

% 1965–70; 1970–77: ACCROISSEMENT MOYEN ANNUEL DES EFFECTIFS ET DU PERSONNEL ENSEIGNANT DE 1965 A 1970 ET DE 1970 A 1977, EN POURCENTAGE.

% 1965–70; 1970–77: CRECIMIENTO MEDIO ANUAL DE LA MATRICULA ESCOLAR Y DEL PERSONAL DOCENTE DE 1965 A 1970 Y DE 1970 A 1976, EN PORCENTAJE.

CONTINENTS, MAJOR AREAS AND GROUPS OF COUNTRIES CONTINENTS, GRANDES REGIONS ET GROUPES DE PAYS CONTINENTES, GRANDES REGIONES Y GRUPOS DE PAISES	YEAR ANNEE AÑO	TEACHING STAFF PERSONNEL ENSEIGNANT PERSONAL DOCENTE			PUPILS ENROLLED ELEVES INSCRITS MATRICULA ESCOLAR			
		TOTAL (000)	FEMALE FEMMES FEMENINO (000)	% F	TOTAL (000)	FEMALE FILLES FEMENINO (000)	% F	PRIVATE PRIVE PRIVADO %
		(1)	(2)		(3)	(4)		(5)
WORLD TOTAL ‡	1965	1 050	1 033	98	20 513	10 078	49	27
	1970	1 358	1 337	98	26 619	13 079	49	29
	1975	1 892	1 859	98	36 350	17 696	49	29
	1977	2 136	2 096	98	40 524	19 705	49	28
	% 1965–70	5.3	5.3		5.3	5.4		
	% 1970–77	6.7	6.6		6.2	6.0		
AFRICA	1965	4	4	100	141	70	50	82
	1970	6	5	83	194	93	48	74
	1975	29	23	79	673	242	36	82
	1977	33	27	82	778	260	33	86
	% 1965–70	8.4	4.6		6.6	5.8		
	% 1970–77	27.6	27.2		21.9	15.8		
AMERICA	1965	166	162	98	4 182	2 042	49	22
	1970	197	194	98	4 800	2 355	49	21
	1975	329	324	98	8 309	4 047	49	31
	1977	378	372	98	9 589	4 674	49	30
	% 1965–70	3.5	3.7		2.8	2.9		
	% 1970–77	9.8	9.7		10.4	10.3		
ASIA ‡	1965	89	79	89	2 428	1 183	49	58
	1970	134	121	90	3 736	1 816	49	60
	1975	179	164	92	5 094	2 494	49	57
	1977	230	213	93	6 431	3 134	49	51
	% 1965–70	8.5	8.9		9.0	8.9		
	% 1970–77	8.0	8.4		8.1	8.1		
EUROPE	1965	331	329	99	8 802	4 355	49	34
	1970	437	435	100	10 738	5 310	49	38
	1975	613	608	99	13 532	6 629	49	31
	1977	669	662	99	13 993	6 866	49	29
	% 1965–70	5.7	5.7		4.1	4.0		
	% 1970–77	6.3	6.2		3.9	3.7		
OCEANIA	1965	7	6	86	218	105	48	58
	1970	7	6	86	233	113	48	60
	1975	11	9	82	340	167	49	46
	1977	13	10	77	383	190	50	47
	% 1965–70	0.0	0.0		1.3	1.5		
	% 1970–77	9.2	7.6		7.4	7.7		

2.8 Education preceding the first level
Enseignement précédant le premier degré
Enseñanza anterior al primer grado

CONTINENTS, MAJOR AREAS AND GROUPS OF COUNTRIES CONTINENTS, GRANDES REGIONS ET GROUPES DE PAYS CONTINENTES, GRANDES REGIONES Y GRUPOS DE PAISES	YEAR ANNEE AÑO	TEACHING STAFF PERSONNEL ENSEIGNANT PERSONAL DOCENTE			PUPILS ENROLLED ELEVES INSCRITS MATRICULA ESCOLAR			PRIVATE PRIVE PRIVADO %
		TOTAL (000)	FEMALE FEMMES FEMENINO (000)	% F	TOTAL (000)	FEMALE FILLES FEMENINO (000)	% F	
		(1)	(2)		(3)	(4)		(5)
U.S.S.R.	1965	453	453	100	4 741	2 323	49	
	1970	576	576	100	6 919	3 390	49	
	1975	731	731	100	8 403	4 118	49	
	1977	813	813	100	9 350	4 582	49	
	% 1965—70	4.9	4.9		7.9	7.9		
	% 1970—77	5.0	5.0		4.4	4.4		
DEVELOPED COUNTRIES ‡	1965	966	953	99	17 827	8 753	49	25
	1970	1 232	1 216	99	22 749	11 174	49	26
	1975	1 686	1 663	99	30 254	14 768	49	26
	1977	1 860	1 831	98	32 459	15 854	49	24
	% 1965—70	5.0	5.0		5.0	5.0		
	% 1970—77	6.1	6.0		5.2	5.1		
DEVELOPING COUNTRIES ‡	1965	84	80	95	2 686	1 325	49	41
	1970	126	121	96	3 870	1 905	49	42
	1975	206	196	95	6 096	2 928	48	43
	1977	276	265	96	8 065	3 851	48	40
	% 1965—70	8.4	8.6		7.6	7.5		
	% 1970—77	11.9	11.9		11.1	10.6		
AFRICA (EXCLUDING ARAB STATES)	1965	3	2	67	91	46	51	75
	1970	4	3	75	124	59	48	61
	1975	6	6	100	206	100	49	52
	1977	6	6	100	206	100	49	59
	% 1965—70	5.9	8.4		6.4	5.1		
	% 1970—77	6.0	10.4		7.5	7.8		
NORTHERN AMERICA	1965	123	120	98	2 876	1 390	48	18
	1970	134	131	98	3 078	1 488	48	16
	1975	233	228	98	5 554	2 668	48	31
	1977	258	253	98	6 142	2 950	48	30
	% 1965—70	1.7	1.8		1.4	1.4		
	% 1970—77	9.8	9.9		10.4	10.3		
LATIN AMERICA	1965	43	42	98	1 306	652	50	30
	1970	63	63	100	1 722	867	50	28
	1975	96	95	99	2 755	1 379	50	31
	1977	120	119	99	3 446	1 724	50	30
	% 1965—70	7.9	8.4		5.7	5.9		
	% 1970—77	9.6	9.5		10.4	10.3		
ASIA (EXCLUDING ARAB STATES) ‡	1965	86	76	88	2 286	1 107	48	56
	1970	129	116	90	3 517	1 717	49	59
	1975	172	156	91	4 825	2 370	49	57
	1977	221	204	92	6 147	3 003	49	51
	% 1965—70	8.4	8.8		9.0	9.2		
	% 1970—77	8.0	8.4		8.3	8.3		
ARAB STATES	1965	4	4	100	192	100	52	83
	1970	7	7	100	289	134	46	81
	1975	30	25	83	736	265	36	85
	1977	36	30	83	855	292	34	85
	% 1965—70	11.8	11.8		8.5	6.0		
	% 1970—77	26.4	23.1		16.8	11.8		

Education preceding the first level 2.8
Enseignement précédant le premier degré
Enseñanza anterior al primer grado

GENERAL NOTE / NOTE GENERALE / NOTA GENERAL:
E—> FOR COMPOSITION OF MAJOR AREAS AND GROUPS OF COUNTRIES, SEE GENERAL NOTE TO TABLE 1.2. THE SCHOOL YEAR BEGINS IN THE CALENDAR YEAR INDICATED. MORE INFORMATION ON THIS POINT IS GIVEN IN THE GENERAL INTRODUCTION TO THE "EDUCATION" CHAPTER.
FR—> POUR LA COMPOSITION DES GRANDES REGIONS ET DES GROUPES DE PAYS, VOIR LA NOTE GENERALE DU TABLEAU 1.2. L'ANNEE SCOLAIRE COMMENCE PENDANT L'ANNEE CIVILE INDIQUEE. POUR PLUS DE DETAILS, SE REPORTER A L'INTRODUCTION GENERALE DU CHAPITRE "EDUCATION".
ESP> PUEDE VERSE LA COMPOSICION DE LAS GRANDES REGIONES Y GRUPOS DE PAISES EN LA NOTA GENERAL DEL CUADRO 1.2. EL AÑO ESCOLAR EMPIEZA DURANTE EL AÑO CIVIL INDICADO. PUEDEN VERSE MAS DETALLES A ESTE RESPECTO EN LA INTRODUCCION GENERAL DEL CAPITULO "EDUCACION".

WORLD TOTAL:
E—> NOT INCLUDING CHINA AND THE DEMOCRATIC PEOPLE'S REPUBLIC OF KOREA. INCLUDING AN ALLOW-ANCE FOR FEMALE ENROLMENT IN THE U.S.S.R.
FR—> NON COMPRIS LA CHINE ET LA REPUBLIQUE DEMOCRATIQUE POPULAIRE DE COREE. Y COMPRIS UNE ESTIMATION DES EFFECTIFS FEMININS DE L'U.R.S.S.
ESP> EXCLUIDAS CHINA Y LA REPUBLICA POPULAR DEMOCRATICA DE COREA. INCLUIDA UNA ESTIMACION DE LA MATRICULA ESCOLAR FEMENINA DE LA U.R.S.S.

ASIA:
E—> NOT INCLUDING CHINA AND THE DEMOCRATIC PEOPLE'S REPUBLIC OF KOREA.
FR—> NON COMPRIS LA CHINE ET LA REPUBLIQUE DEMOCRATIQUE POPULAIRE DE COREE.
ESP> EXCLUIDAS CHINA Y LA REPUBLICA POPULAR DEMOCRATICA DE COREA.

DEVELOPED COUNTRIES:
E—> INCLUDING AN ALLOWANCE FOR FEMALE ENROL-MENT IN THE U.S.S.R.
FR—> Y COMPRIS UNE ESTIMATION DES EFFECTIFS FEMININS DE L'U.R.S.S.
ESP> INCLUIDA UNA ESTIMACION DE LA MATRICULA ESCOLAR FEMENINA DE LA U.R.S.S.

DEVELOPING COUNTRIES:
E—> NOT INCLUDING CHINA AND THE DEMOCRATIC PEOPLE'S REPUBLIC OF KOREA.
FR—> NON COMPRIS LA CHINE ET LA REPUBLIQUE DEMOCRATIQUE POPULAIRE DE COREE.
ESP> EXCLUIDAS CHINA Y LA REPUBLICA POPULAR DEMOCRATICA DE COREA.

ASIA (EXCLUDING ARAB STATES):
E—> NOT INCLUDING CHINA AND THE DEMOCRATIC PEOPLE'S REPUBLIC OF KOREA.
FR—> NON COMPRIS LA CHINE ET LA REPUBLIQUE DEMOCRATIQUE POPULAIRE DE COREE.
ESP> EXCLUIDAS CHINA Y LA REPUBLICA POPULAR DEMOCRATICA DE COREA.

2.9 Percentage distribution of education at the second level by type and sex: enrolment and teachers

Répartition en pourcentage de l'enseignement du second degré par types et par sexe: effectifs et personnel enseignant

Repartición en porcentaje de la enseñanza de segundo grado, por tipos y por sexo: matrícula escolar y personal docente

2.9 Enrolment and teachers at the second level: % distribution
Effectifs et personnel enseignant du second degré: répartition en %
Matrícula escolar y personal docente de segundo grado: repartición en %

CONTINENTS MAJOR AREAS AND GROUPS OF COUNTRIES / CONTINENTS, GRANDES REGIONS ET GROUPES DE PAYS / CONTINENTES, REGIONES Y GRUPOS DE PAISES	YEAR ANNEE AÑO	PUPILS ENROLLED ELEVES INSCRITS MATRÍCULA ESCOLAR				TEACHING STAFF PERSONNEL ENSEIGNANT PERSONAL DOCENTE			
		TOTAL (%)	GENERAL EDUCATION ENSEIGNEMENT GENERAL ENSEÑANZA GENERAL (%)	TEACHER TRAINING ENSEIGNEMENT NORMAL ENSEÑANZA NORMAL (%)	OTHER SECOND LEVEL AUTRE ENSEIGNEMENT SECONDAIRE OTRA ENSEÑANZA SECUNDARIA (%)	TOTAL (%)	GENERAL EDUCATION ENSEIGNEMENT GENERAL ENSEÑANZA GENERAL (%)	TEACHER TRAINING ENSEIGNEMENT NORMAL ENSEÑANZA NORMAL (%)	OTHER SECOND LEVEL AUTRE ENSEIGNEMENT SECONDAIRE OTRA ENSEÑANZA SECUNDARIA (%)
		(1)	(2)	(3)	(4)	(5)	(6)	(7)	(8)
WORLD TOTAL ‡	1965	100.0	82.9	1.8	15.3	100.0	78.2	3.0	18.7
	1970	100.0	83.6	1.5	14.8	100.0	79.5	2.4	18.1
	1975	100.0	84.7	1.3	13.9	100.0	80.1	2.1	17.8
	1977	100.0	84.2	1.4	14.4	100.0	78.9	2.2	18.9
AFRICA	1965	100.0	80.1	6.0	13.9	100.0	72.1	9.1	18.8
	1970	100.0	82.9	4.3	12.8	100.0	76.4	6.2	16.9
	1975	100.0	85.4	4.2	10.3	100.0	77.7	7.5	15.1
	1977	100.0	85.4	4.6	10.0	100.0	77.5	7.8	14.7
AMERICA ‡	1965	100.0	91.2	2.4	6.4	100.0	84.6	4.6	10.8
	1970	100.0	91.0	1.7	7.4	100.0	85.8	3.0	11.2
	1975	100.0	89.9	1.6	8.5	100.0	85.3	2.7	12.1
	1977	100.0	88.7	1.7	9.7	100.0	84.1	2.6	13.2
ASIA ‡	1965	100.0	90.6	0.8	8.6	100.0	89.4	1.0	9.6
	1970	100.0	91.4	0.7	8.0	100.0	89.4	1.0	9.5
	1975	100.0	91.9	0.6	7.5	100.0	89.1	1.0	9.9
	1977	100.0	91.4	0.7	7.9	100.0	89.3	1.1	9.6

Enrolment and teachers at the second level: % distribution   2.9
Effectifs et personnel enseignant du second degré: répartition en %
Matrícula escolar y personal docente de segundo grado: repartición en %

		(1)	(2)	(3)	(4)	(5)	(6)	(7)	(8)
EUROPE	1965	100.0	70.4	2.1	27.7	100.0	62.1	2.4	35.5
	1970	100.0	71.6	1.5	26.3	100.0	65.3	1.8	32.9
	1975	100.0	74.3	1.0	24.6	100.0	67.6	1.3	31.2
	1977	100.0	73.3	1.0	25.6	100.0	64.6	1.4	34.1
OCEANIA	1965	100.0	....	....	....	100.0	....	....	....
	1970	100.0	....	....	....	100.0	....	....	....
	1975	100.0	....	....	....	100.0	....	....	....
	1977	100.0	....	....	....	100.0	....	....	....
U.S.S.R.	1965	100.0	57.5	2.8	39.7	100.0	71.6	5.1	23.3
	1970	100.0	52.1	3.7	44.2	100.0	66.0	6.3	27.7
	1975	100.0	57.9	3.7	38.5	100.0	68.6	5.7	25.8
	1977	100.0	56.8	3.8	39.4	100.0	65.9	6.2	27.9
DEVELOPED COUNTRIES ‡	1965	100.0	80.0	1.2	18.9	100.0	76.8	1.8	21.4
	1970	100.0	79.5	1.1	19.1	100.0	77.1	1.7	21.3
	1975	100.0	81.0	1.0	18.0	100.0	77.9	1.5	20.7
	1977	100.0	80.4	1.0	18.6	100.0	76.0	1.5	22.6
DEVELOPING COUNTRIES ‡	1965	100.0	87.9	2.9	9.2	100.0	80.9	5.2	13.8
	1970	100.0	88.8	1.9	9.3	100.0	83.2	3.4	13.4
	1975	100.0	88.2	1.8	9.5	100.0	83.2	3.1	13.8
	1977	100.0	88.0	1.9	10.1	100.0	82.8	3.1	14.1
AFRICA (EXCLUDING ARAB STATES)	1965	100.0	77.6	8.3	14.1	100.0	70.7	10.7	17.3
	1970	100.0	83.1	6.2	10.7	100.0	76.7	8.3	15.0
	1975	100.0	85.2	6.1	8.6	100.0	77.9	10.1	12.0
	1977	100.0	84.9	6.8	8.3	100.0	77.5	10.7	11.5
NORTHERN AMERICA	1965	100.0	....	—	....	100.0	....	—	....
	1970	100.0	....	—	....	100.0	....	—	....
	1975	100.0	....	—	....	100.0	....	—	....
	1977	100.0	....	—	....	100.0	....	—	....
LATIN AMERICA	1965	100.0	67.5	8.9	23.6	100.0	57.8	12.6	29.7
	1970	100.0	72.8	5.0	22.2	100.0	65.5	7.3	27.0
	1975	100.0	71.0	4.5	24.4	100.0	63.5	6.6	29.9
	1977	100.0	70.8	4.3	24.9	100.0	63.8	5.9	30.2
ASIA (EXCLUDING ARAB STATES) ‡	1965	100.0	90.5	0.7	8.7	100.0	89.3	1.1	9.6
	1970	100.0	91.3	0.6	8.1	100.0	89.4	0.9	9.6
	1975	100.0	91.8	0.6	7.7	100.0	89.0	0.9	10.0
	1977	100.0	91.3	0.6	8.0	100.0	89.2	1.0	9.7
ARAB STATES	1965	100.0	85.9	3.7	10.4	100.0	76.1	6.2	16.8
	1970	100.0	86.7	2.2	11.1	100.0	81.4	3.7	14.9
	1975	100.0	88.6	1.8	9.6	100.0	82.7	3.5	14.1
	1977	100.0	88.9	1.9	9.2	100.0	82.4	3.6	14.1

2.9 **Enrolment and teachers at the second level: % distribution**
Effectifs et personnel enseignant du second degré: répartition en %
Matrícula escolar y personal docente de segundo grado: repartición en %

GENERAL NOTE / NOTE GENERALE / NOTA GENERAL:
   E—> FOR COMPOSITION OF MAJOR AREAS AND GROUPS
OF COUNTRIES, SEE GENERAL NOTE TO TABLE 1.2.   THE
SCHOOL YEAR BEGINS IN THE CALENDAR YEAR INDICATED.
MORE INFORMATION ON THIS POINT IS GIVEN IN THE
GENERAL INTRODUCTION TO THE "EDUCATION" CHAPTER.
   FR-> POUR LA COMPOSITION DES GRANDES REGIONS ET
DES GROUPES DE PAYS, VOIR LA NOTE GENERALE DU
TABLEAU 1.2.   L'ANNEE SCOLAIRE COMMENCE PENDANT
L'ANNEE CIVILE INDIQUEE.   POUR PLUS DE DETAILS,
SE REPORTER A L'INTRODUCTION GENERALE DU CHAPITRE
"EDUCATION".
   ESP> PUEDE VERSE LA COMPOSICION DE LAS GRANDES
REGIONES Y GRUPOS DE PAISES EN LA NOTA GENERAL
DEL CUADRO 1.2.   EL AÑO ESCOLAR EMPIEZA DURANTE
EL AÑO CIVIL INDICADO.   PUEDEN VERSE MAS DETALLES
A ESTE RESPECTO EN LA INTRODUCCION GENERAL DEL
CAPITULO "EDUCACION".

WORLD TOTAL:
   E—> NOT INCLUDING NORTHERN AMERICA, CHINA,
DEMOCRATIC PEOPLE'S REPUBLIC OF KOREA, AUSTRALIA
AND NEW ZEALAND.
   FR-> NON COMPRIS L'AMERIQUE SEPTENTRIONALE, LA
CHINE, LA REPUBLIQUE POPULAIRE DEMOCRATIQUE DE
COREE, L'AUSTRALIE ET LA NOUVELLE-ZELANDE.
   ESP> EXCLUIDAS AMERICA SEPTENTRIONAL, CHINA,
LA REPUBLICA DEMOCRATICA POPULAR DE COREA,
AUSTRALIA Y NUEVA ZELANDIA.

AMERICA:
   E—> NOT INCLUDING NORTHERN AMERICA.
   FR-> NON COMPRIS L'AMERIQUE SEPTENTRIONALE.
   ESP> EXCLUIDA AMERICA SEPTENTRIONAL.

ASIA:
   E—> NOT INCLUDING CHINA AND THE DEMOCRATIC
PEOPLE'S REPUBLIC OF KOREA.
   FR-> NON COMPRIS LA CHINE ET LA REPUBLIQUE
POPULAIRE DEMOCRATIQUE DE COREE.
   ESP> EXCLUIDAS CHINA Y LA REPUBLICA POPULAR
DEMOCRATICA DE COREA.

DEVELOPED COUNTRIES:
   E—> NOT INCLUDING NORTHERN AMERICA, AUSTRALIA
AND NEW ZEALAND.
   FR-> NON COMPRIS L'AMERIQUE SEPTENTRIONALE,
L'AUSTRALIE ET LA NOUVELLE-ZELANDE.
   ESP> EXCLUIDAS AMERICA SEPTENTRIONAL, AUSTRALIA
Y NUEVA ZELANDIA.

DEVELOPING COUNTRIES:
   E—> NOT INCLUDING CHINA AND THE DEMOCRATIC
PEOPLE'S REPUBLIC OF KOREA.
   FR-> NON COMPRIS LA CHINE ET LA REPUBLIQUE
POPULAIRE DEMOCRATIQUE DE COREE.
   ESP> EXCLUIDAS CHINA Y LA REPUBLICA POPULAR
DEMOCRATICA DE COREA.

ASIA (EXCLUDING ARAB STATES):
   E—> NOT INCLUDING CHINA AND THE DEMOCRATIC
PEOPLE'S REPUBLIC OF KOREA.
   FR-> NON COMPRIS LA CHINE ET LA REPUBLIQUE
POPULAIRE DEMOCRATIQUE DE COREE.
   ESP> EXCLUIDAS CHINA Y LA REPUBLICA POPULAR
DEMOCRATICA DE COREA.

2.10 Estimated foreign-student enrolment at the third level of education

Estimation des effectifs d'étudiants étrangers dans l'enseignement du troisième degré

Estimación del número de estudiantes extranjeros en la enseñanza de tercer grado

CONTINENTS, MAJOR AREAS AND GROUPS OF COUNTRIES CONTINENTS, GRANDES REGIONS ET GROUPES DE PAYS CONTINENTES, GRANDES REGIONES Y GRUPOS DE PAISES	FOREIGN STUDENTS ENROLLED ETUDIANTS ETRANGERS INSCRITS ESTUDIANTES EXTRANJEROS MATRICULADOS					
	1965	1970	1974	1975	1976	1977
WORLD TOTAL ‡	354 959	508 811	674 961	764 782	848 757	928 020
AFRICA	27 059	28 659	36 195	39 304	40 435	42 730
AMERICA	112 766	191 857	243 400	289 296	317 246	362 493
ASIA	42 313	69 762	78 210	88 260	93 372	106 880
EUROPE	164 713	208 513	306 312	336 008	385 381	403 612
OCEANIA	8 108	10 020	10 844	11 914	12 323	12 305
DEVELOPED COUNTRIES	275 978	398 975	526 456	589 846	667 570	726 717
DEVELOPING COUNTRIES	78 981	109 836	148 505	174 936	181 187	201 303
AFRICA (EXCLUDING ARAB STATES)	6 474	10 739	9 050	9 390	9 642	9 361
NORTHERN AMERICA	93 993	166 971	195 580	227 405	255 157	295 627
LATIN AMERICA	18 773	24 886	47 820	61 891	62 089	66 866
ASIA (EXCLUDING ARAB STATES)	22 552	34 377	38 367	41 014	39 794	44 992
ARAB STATES	40 346	53 305	66 988	77 160	84 371	95 257

WORLD TOTAL:
E—> FOR COMPOSITION OF MAJOR AREAS AND GROUPS OF COUNTRIES, SEE GENERAL NOTE TO TABLE 1.2. NOT INCLUDING THE FOLLOWING 7 COUNTRIES FOR WHICH DATA ARE NOT AVAILABLE:
AFRICA: SOUTH AFRICA, ZIMBABWE.
AMERICA: PERU, VENEZUELA.
ASIA: CHINA, DEMOCRATIC PEOPLE'S REPUBLIC OF KOREA, MONGOLIA.
ESTIMATES FOR 1974, 1975 AND 1976 HAVE BEEN REVISED.
FR—> POUR LA COMPOSITION DES GRANDES REGIONS ET GROUPES DE PAYS, VOIR LA NOTE GENERALE DU TABLEAU 1.2. NON COMPRIS LES 7 PAYS CI—APRES POUR LESQUELS ON NE DISPOSE D'AUCUNE DONNEE:
AFRIQUE: AFRIQUE DU SUD, ZIMBABWE.

WORLD TOTAL (CONT.):
AMERIQUE: PEROU, VENEZUELA.
ASIE: CHINE, REPUBLIQUE POPULAIRE DEMOCRATIQUE DE COREE, MONGOLIE.
LES ESTIMATIONS POUR 1974, 1975 ET 1976 ONT ETE REVISEES.
ESP> VEASE EN LA NOTA GENERAL DEL CUADRO 1.2 LA COMPOSICION DE LAS GRANDES REGIONES Y GRUPOS DE PAISES. EXCLUIDOS LOS 7 PAISES SIGUIENTES, CON RESPECTO A LOS CUALES NO SE DISPONE DE DATOS:
AFRICA: SUDAFRICA, ZIMBABWE.
AMERICA: PERU, VENEZUELA.
ASIA: CHINA, REPUBLICA POPULAR DEMOCRATICA DE COREA, MONGOLIA.
LAS ESTIMACIONES PARA 1974, 1975 Y 1976 HAN SIDO REVISADAS.

Gross enrolment ratios 2.11
Taux d'inscription bruts
Tasas de escolarización brutas

2.11 Gross enrolment ratios by levels and by regions
Taux d'inscription bruts par degré d'enseignement et par régions
Tasas de escolarización brutas por grados de enseñanza y por regiones

CONTINENTS, MAJOR AREAS AND GROUPS OF COUNTRIES / CONTINENTS, GRANDES REGIONS ET GROUPES DE PAYS / CONTINENTES, GRANDES REGIONES Y GRUPOS DE PAISES	YEAR ANNEE AÑO	FIRST LEVEL PREMIER DEGRE PRIMER GRADO			SECOND LEVEL SECOND DEGRE SEGUNDO GRADO			THIRD LEVEL TROISIEME DEGRE TERCER GRADO			ALL LEVELS TOUS LES DEGRES TODOS LOS GRADOS		
		MF	M	F	MF	M	F	MF	M	F	MF	M	F
		(1)	(2)	(3)	(4)	(5)	(6)	(7)	(8)	(9)	(10)	(11)	(12)
WORLD TOTAL ‡	1965	82.3	89.6	74.8	32.2	36.3	27.9	7.7	9.9	5.5	45.2	50.2	40.1
	1970	84.1	91.2	76.7	35.3	39.7	30.8	9.9	12.4	7.5	47.2	52.1	42.0
	1975	86.3	93.3	78.9	38.3	42.3	34.2	11.6	13.7	9.5	48.7	53.3	43.8
	1977	87.3	94.8	79.6	40.0	44.2	35.6	11.9	13.6	10.1	49.4	54.1	44.5
AFRICA	1965	52.9	64.8	41.0	7.5	10.7	4.4	0.9	1.5	0.4	24.2	30.2	18.1
	1970	58.3	69.9	46.7	10.5	14.4	6.6	1.3	2.0	0.6	27.5	33.8	21.3
	1975	67.9	79.1	56.7	15.5	20.7	11.1	2.0	3.0	1.0	33.2	39.6	26.7
	1977	73.3	84.8	61.6	18.0	22.8	13.1	2.3	3.5	1.2	36.0	42.6	29.4
AMERICA	1965	100.5	101.7	99.3	44.4	44.5	44.3	15.1	18.6	11.5	58.9	60.4	57.3
	1970	104.8	105.6	103.9	49.3	49.3	49.3	19.9	23.6	16.1	62.1	63.6	60.6
	1975	112.9	113.8	112.0	49.0	49.1	49.0	24.8	27.5	22.0	64.7	65.9	63.4
	1977	113.0	113.7	112.3	50.2	49.9	50.6	25.0	26.2	23.8	64.7	65.3	64.1
ASIA ‡	1965	68.0	79.3	56.3	27.1	35.0	18.9	3.9	5.8	2.0	37.1	44.8	29.0
	1970	70.0	80.8	58.6	29.3	37.5	20.7	5.9	8.5	3.2	39.3	47.2	31.1
	1975	72.3	82.6	61.5	32.0	39.6	24.0	6.3	8.8	3.7	40.8	48.2	33.2
	1977	74.0	84.7	62.8	33.9	41.9	25.5	6.5	8.9	3.9	41.9	49.5	34.0
EUROPE	1965	109.2	109.8	108.6	53.3	55.5	51.1	9.7	12.7	6.6	59.8	61.8	57.7
	1970	109.5	109.3	109.9	64.1	66.2	61.9	12.2	15.2	9.2	63.1	64.9	61.3
	1975	105.6	105.9	105.4	74.8	74.3	75.3	17.0	19.4	14.5	66.5	67.3	65.6
	1977	104.6	104.9	104.2	78.4	77.8	79.0	18.3	20.4	16.1	67.5	68.2	66.7
OCEANIA	1965	104.1	106.1	101.9	53.7	55.0	52.4	9.6	12.9	6.0	60.2	62.3	58.1
	1970	105.1	107.2	102.9	60.1	61.6	58.6	11.1	14.2	7.8	61.9	64.0	59.7
	1975	100.5	102.5	98.4	63.9	64.3	63.5	16.2	19.2	13.1	62.4	64.2	60.5
	1977	102.5	104.6	100.3	64.5	64.5	64.5	16.9	19.4	14.3	63.0	64.5	61.4

2.11 Gross enrolment ratios
Taux d'inscription bruts
Tasas de escolarización brutas

CONTINENTS, MAJOR AREAS AND GROUPS OF COUNTRIES / CONTINENTS, GRANDES REGIONS ET GROUPES DE PAYS / CONTINENTES, GRANDES REGIONES Y GRUPOS DE PAISES	YEAR ANNEE AÑO	FIRST LEVEL PREMIER DEGRE PRIMER GRADO			SECOND LEVEL SECOND DEGRE SEGUNDO GRADO			THIRD LEVEL TROISIEME DEGRE TERCER GRADO			ALL LEVELS TOUS LES DEGRES TODOS LOS GRADOS		
		MF (1)	M (2)	F (3)	MF (4)	M (5)	F (6)	MF (7)	M (8)	F (9)	MF (10)	M (11)	F (12)
U.S.S.R.	1965	132.4	132.3	132.4	33.7	30.4	37.0	23.4	25.7	21.1	71.7	71.2	72.3
	1970	135.9	136.0	135.8	31.5	27.0	35.3	19.3	19.4	19.2	65.6	64.5	66.8
	1975	138.5	138.6	138.3	35.3	31.0	39.9	17.5	17.0	18.0	61.3	59.6	63.1
	1977	139.0	139.2	138.8	36.4	32.2	40.8	17.3	16.8	17.8	59.9	58.3	61.7
DEVELOPED COUNTRIES	1965	117.2	117.5	116.8	56.6	56.6	56.7	16.6	20.5	12.7	67.4	68.8	66.0
	1970	118.1	118.3	118.0	60.4	60.0	60.7	19.7	23.1	16.2	67.6	68.8	66.5
	1975	116.6	116.7	116.5	66.3	64.7	68.0	23.8	26.3	21.3	68.8	69.2	68.4
	1977	115.8	115.9	115.6	68.4	66.7	70.1	24.4	26.0	22.7	68.8	68.9	68.6
DEVELOPING COUNTRIES ‡	1965	66.1	76.6	55.4	18.6	25.0	12.1	2.8	4.1	1.5	33.8	40.6	26.8
	1970	70.1	80.1	59.8	23.0	29.7	16.2	4.3	6.1	2.4	37.3	44.1	30.3
	1975	75.7	85.2	65.9	26.2	32.6	19.5	5.3	7.2	3.4	40.2	46.6	33.5
	1977	78.1	87.9	67.9	28.4	34.9	21.6	5.7	7.5	3.9	41.7	48.2	34.9
AFRICA (EXCLUDING ARAB STATES)	1965	50.3	61.3	39.5	4.8	6.6	2.9	0.4	0.6	0.2	22.0	27.1	17.0
	1970	56.4	66.9	45.9	7.0	9.5	4.6	0.6	1.0	0.2	25.4	30.6	20.2
	1975	66.9	76.9	56.9	11.8	15.3	8.3	0.9	1.4	0.3	31.2	36.6	25.8
	1977	73.2	84.1	62.3	13.3	16.9	9.7	1.0	1.7	0.4	34.3	40.2	28.5
NORTHERN AMERICA	1965	123.0	123.4	122.6	76.1	75.0	77.3	30.2	36.6	23.7	81.2	82.9	79.5
	1970	120.9	121.0	120.7	80.1	78.8	81.5	38.3	44.7	31.9	81.6	83.2	79.9
	1975	120.9	121.0	120.0	82.7	81.3	84.2	45.3	49.3	41.1	81.8	82.8	80.8
	1977	120.0	120.0	120.0	82.9	81.5	84.3	44.0	44.8	43.3	80.3	80.2	80.4
LATIN AMERICA	1965	85.5	87.1	83.9	21.0	21.7	20.2	3.6	4.8	2.3	42.9	44.2	41.5
	1970	95.3	96.5	94.0	27.9	28.7	27.1	5.4	6.9	3.8	48.9	50.2	47.5
	1975	109.1	110.4	107.9	27.9	28.7	27.1	10.0	11.8	8.2	54.5	55.8	53.2
	1977	110.0	110.9	109.0	31.0	31.1	30.9	11.5	13.0	10.0	56.0	56.8	55.1
ASIA (EXCLUDING ARAB STATES) ‡	1965	68.5	79.5	56.9	27.4	35.3	19.2	4.0	5.8	2.0	37.3	45.0	29.4
	1970	70.3	80.9	59.1	29.5	37.7	20.9	5.9	8.6	3.2	39.5	47.3	31.4
	1975	72.3	82.3	61.7	32.0	39.5	24.0	6.3	8.8	3.7	40.8	47.9	33.2
	1977	73.9	84.4	62.9	33.7	41.7	25.4	6.5	8.9	3.9	41.8	49.2	34.0
(ARAB STATES)	1965	59.1	74.6	42.9	17.0	24.4	9.3	2.7	4.3	1.1	30.5	39.8	20.8
	1970	63.2	78.7	47.5	22.2	30.5	13.6	3.6	5.4	1.7	34.4	44.1	24.3
	1975	72.3	88.2	55.8	30.2	39.0	21.0	5.9	8.3	3.9	40.8	50.8	30.4
	1977	74.5	89.0	59.4	34.2	43.0	25.1	6.6	9.2	3.9	43.0	52.4	33.2

Gross enrolment ratios 2.11
Taux d'inscription bruts
Tasas de escolarización brutas

GENERAL NOTE / NOTE GENERALE / NOTA GENERAL:
E—> FOR COMPOSITION OF MAJOR AREAS AND GROUPS OF COUNTRIES, SEE GENERAL NOTE TO TABLE 1.2
FR—> POUR LA COMPOSITION DES GRANDES REGIONS ET GROUPES DE PAYS, VOIR LA NOTE GENERALE DU TABLEAU 1.2.
ESP> VEASE EN LA NOTA GENERAL DEL CUADRO 1.2 LA COMPOSICION DE LAS GRANDES REGIONES Y GRUPOS DE PAISES.

WORLD TOTAL:
E—> NOT INCLUDING CHINA, DEMOCRATIC PEOPLE'S REPUBLIC OF KOREA AND THE SOCIALIST REPUBLIC OF VIET-NAM.
FR—> NON COMPRIS LA CHINE, LA REPUBLIQUE POPULAIRE DEMOCRATIQUE DE COREE ET LA REPUBLIQUE SOCIALISTE DU VIET-NAM.
ESP> EXCLUIDAS CHINA, LA REPUBLICA POPULAR DEMOCRATICA DE COREA Y LA REPUBLICA SOCIALISTA DEL VIET-NAM.

ASIA:
E—> NOT INCLUDING CHINA, DEMOCRATIC PEOPLE'S REPUBLIC OF KOREA AND THE SOCIALIST REPUBLIC OF VIET-NAM.
FR—> NON COMPRIS LA CHINE, LA REPUBLIQUE POPULAIRE DEMOCRATIQUE DE COREE ET LA REPUBLIQUE SOCIALISTE DU VIET-NAM.

ASIA (CONT.):
ESP> EXCLUIDAS CHINA, LA REPUBLICA POPULAR DEMOCRATICA DE COREA Y LA REPUBLICA SOCIALISTA DEL VIET-NAM.

DEVELOPING COUNTRIES:
E—> NOT INCLUDING CHINA, DEMOCRATIC PEOPLE'S REPUBLIC OF KOREA AND THE SOCIALIST REPUBLIC OF VIET-NAM.
FR—> NON COMPRIS LA CHINE, LA REPUBLIQUE POPULAIRE DEMOCRATIQUE DE COREE ET LA REPUBLIQUE SOCIALISTE DU VIET-NAM.
ESP> EXCLUIDAS CHINA, LA REPUBLICA POPULAR DEMOCRATICA DE COREA Y LA REPUBLICA SOCIALISTA DEL VIET-NAM.

ASIA (EXCLUDING ARAB STATES):
E—> NOT INCLUDING CHINA, DEMOCRATIC PEOPLE'S REPUBLIC OF KOREA AND THE SOCIALIST REPUBLIC OF VIET-NAM.
FR—> NON COMPRIS LA CHINE, LA REPUBLIQUE POPULAIRE DEMOCRATIQUE DE COREE ET LA REPUBLIQUE SOCIALISTE DU VIET-NAM.
ESP> EXCLUIDAS CHINA, LA REPUBLICA POPULAR DEMOCRATICA DE COREA Y LA REPUBLICA SOCIALISTA DEL VIET-NAM.

Expenditure on education 2.12
Dépenses afférentes à l'enseignement
Gastos destinados a la educación

2.12 Estimated public expenditure on education, in United States dollars
Estimation des dépenses publiques afférentes à l'enseignement, en dollars des Etats-Unis
Estimación de los gastos destinados a la educación, en dólares de los Estados Unidos

A = PUBLIC EXPENDITURE ON EDUCATION
A = DEPENSES PUBLIQUES AFFERENTES À L'ENSEIGNEMENT
A = GASTOS PUBLICOS DESTINADOS A LA EDUCACION
B = GROSS NATIONAL PRODUCT
B = PRODUIT NATIONAL BRUT
B = PRODUCTO NACIONAL BRUTO

CONTINENTS, MAJOR AREAS AND GROUPS OF COUNTRIES / CONTINENTS, GRANDES REGIONS ET GROUPES DE PAYS / CONTINENTES, GRANDES REGIONES Y GRUPOS DE PAISES	PUBLIC EXPENDITURE ON EDUCATION (IN MILLIONS OF DOLLARS) / DEPENSES PUBLIQUES AFFERENTES A L'ENSEIGNEMENT (EN MILLIONS DE DOLLARS) / GASTOS PUBLICOS DESTINADOS A LA EDUCACION (EN MILLIONES DE DOLARES)				AVERAGE ANNUAL INCREASE / ACCROISSEMENT MOYEN ANNUEL / CRECIMIENTO MEDIO ANUAL 1965–1977		PUBLIC EXPENDITURE ON EDUCATION AS % OF GNP / DEPENSES PUBLIQUES AFFERENTES A L'ENSEIGNEMENT EN % DU PNB / GASTOS PUBLICOS DESTINADOS A LA EDUCACION EN % DEL PNB				PUBLIC EXPENDITURE ON EDUCATION PER INHABITANT ($) / DEPENSES PUBLIQUES AFFERENTES A L'ENSEIGNEMENT, PAR HABITANT ($) / GASTOS PUBLICOS DESTINADOS A LA EDUCACION POR HABITANTE ($)			
	1965	1970	1975	1977	A	B	1965	1970	1975	1977	1965	1970	1975	1977
WORLD TOTAL ‡	95 705	158 246	329 638	397 870	12.6	11.1	4.9	5.3	5.7	5.7	38	57	109	126
AFRICA ‡	1 347	2 343	6 934	9 759	17.9	13.8	3.4	4.1	5.2	5.2	5	7	18	24
AMERICA	43 436	76 869	127 354	153 814	11.1	9.4	5.1	6.2	5.9	6.1	94	151	228	265
ASIA ‡	7 228	12 921	44 209	61 825	19.6	16.3	3.5	3.6	4.8	4.9	7	11	33	44
EUROPE	27 033	42 093	107 009	124 957	13.6	11.7	4.3	4.6	5.3	5.3	61	92	226	261
OCEANIA	1 071	1 984	6 952	7 441	17.5	12.5	3.7	4.5	6.4	6.2	63	104	331	338
U.S.S.R.	15 591	22 036	37 181	40 074	8.2	8.0	7.3	6.8	7.6	7.4	67	90	146	155
DEVELOPED COUNTRIES ‡	87 783	145 849	292 381	348 202	12.2	10.8	5.1	5.6	6.0	6.0	87	139	267	314
DEVELOPING COUNTRIES ‡	7 922	12 397	37 257	49 668	16.5	13.2	3.0	3.3	4.1	4.3	5	7	19	24
AFRICA (EXCLUDING ARAB STATES) ‡	716	1 160	3 568	4 890	17.4	13.8	3.0	3.4	4.6	4.4	3	5	13	16
NORTHERN AMERICA	40 049	71 529	113 191	136 446	10.8	8.9	5.4	6.6	6.4	6.5	187	317	480	566
LATIN AMERICA	3 386	5 340	14 163	17 368	14.6	12.4	3.1	3.3	3.7	3.9	14	19	44	51
ASIA (EXCLUDING ARAB STATES) ‡	6 853	12 339	38 987	55 089	19.0	15.8	3.5	3.5	4.7	4.8	7	11	30	40
ARAB STATES	1 006	1 764	8 587	11 604	22.6	18.3	4.0	4.7	6.0	6.2	10	15	64	81

2.12 Expenditure on education
Dépenses afférentes à l'enseignement
Gastos destinados a la educación

GENERAL NOTE / NOTE GENERALE / NOTA GENERAL:
E—> FOR COMPOSITION OF MAJOR AREAS AND GROUPS
OF COUNTRIES, SEE GENERAL NOTE TO TABLE 1.2.
FR—> POUR LA COMPOSITION DES GRANDES REGIONS
ET GROUPES DE PAYS, VOIR LA NOTE GENERALE DU
TABLEAU 1.2.
ESP> VEASE LA NOTA GENERAL DEL CUADRO 1.2 PARA
LA COMPOSICION DE LAS GRANDES REGIONES Y GRUPOS
DE PAISES.

WORLD TOTAL:
E—> NOT INCLUDING SOUTH AFRICA, CHINA, DEMO-
CRATIC KAMPUCHEA, DEMOCRATIC PEOPLE'S REPUBLIC
OF KOREA, LAO PEOPLE'S DEMOCRATIC REPUBLIC AND
THE SOCIALIST REPUBLIC OF VIET-NAM.
FR—> NON COMPRIS L'AFRIQUE DU SUD, LA CHINE,
LE KAMPUCHEA DEMOCRATIQUE, LA REPUBLIQUE POPU-
LAIRE DEMOCRATIQUE DE COREE, LA REPUBLIQUE
POPULAIRE DEMOCRATIQUE LAO ET LA REPUBLIQUE
SOCIALISTE DU VIET-NAM.
ESP> EXCLUIDAS SUDAFRICA, CHINA, LA KAMPUCHEA
DEMOCRATICA, LA REPUBLICA POPULAR DEMOCRATICA DE
COREA, LA REPUBLICA POPULAR DEMOCRATICA LAO Y LA
REPUBLICA SOCIALISTA DEL VIET-NAM.

AFRICA:
E—> NOT INCLUDING SOUTH AFRICA.
FR—> NON COMPRIS L'AFRIQUE DU SUD.
ESP> EXCLUIDA SUDAFRICA.

ASIA:
E—> NOT INCLUDING CHINA, DEMOCRATIC KAMPUCHEA,
DEMOCRATIC PEOPLE'S REPUBLIC OF KOREA, LAO
PEOPLE'S DEMOCRATIC REPUBLIC AND THE SOCIALIST
REPUBLIC OF VIET-NAM.
FR—> NON COMPRIS LA CHINE, LE KAMPUCHEA DEMO-
CRATIQUE, LA REPUBLIQUE POPULAIRE DEMOCRATIQUE
DE COREE, LA REPUBLIQUE POPULAIRE DEMOCRATIQUE
LAO ET LA REPUBLIQUE SOCIALISTE DU VIET-NAM.

ASIA (CONT.):
ESP> EXCLUIDAS CHINA, LA KAMPUCHEA DEMOCRATICA,
LA REPUBLICA POPULAR DEMOCRATICA DE COREA, LA
REPUBLICA POPULAR DEMOCRATICA LAO Y LA REPUBLICA
SOCIALISTA DEL VIET-NAM.

DEVELOPED COUNTRIES:
E—> NOT INCLUDING SOUTH AFRICA.
FR—> NON COMPRIS L'AFRIQUE DU SUD.
ESP> EXCLUIDA SUDAFRICA.

DEVELOPING COUNTRIES:
E—> NOT INCLUDING CHINA, DEMOCRATIC KAMPUCHEA,
DEMOCRATIC PEOPLE'S REPUBLIC OF KOREA, LAO
PEOPLE'S DEMOCRATIC REPUBLIC AND THE SOCIALIST
REPUBLIC OF VIET-NAM.
FR—> NON COMPRIS LA CHINE, LE KAMPUCHEA DEMO-
CRATIQUE, LA REPUBLIQUE POPULAIRE DEMOCRATIQUE
DE COREE, LA REPUBLIQUE POPULAIRE DEMOCRATIQUE
LAO ET LA REPUBLIQUE SOCIALISTE DU VIET-NAM.
ESP> EXCLUIDAS CHINA, LA KAMPUCHEA DEMOCRATICA,
LA REPUBLICA POPULAR DEMOCRATICA DE COREA, LA
REPUBLICA POPULAR DEMOCRATICA LAO Y LA REPUBLICA
SOCIALISTA DEL VIET-NAM.

AFRICA (EXCLUDING ARAB STATES):
E—> NOT INCLUDING SOUTH AFRICA.
FR—> NON COMPRIS L'AFRIQUE DU SUD.
ESP> EXCLUIDA SUDAFRICA.

ASIA (EXCLUDING ARAB STATES):
E—> NOT INCLUDING CHINA, DEMOCRATIC KAMPUCHEA,
DEMOCRATIC PEOPLE'S REPUBLIC OF KOREA, LAO
PEOPLE'S DEMOCRATIC REPUBLIC AND THE SOCIALIST
REPUBLIC OF VIET-NAM.
FR—> NON COMPRIS LA CHINE, LE KAMPUCHEA DEMO-
CRATIQUE, LA REPUBLIQUE POPULAIRE DEMOCRATIQUE
DE COREE, LA REPUBLIQUE POPULAIRE DEMOCRATIQUE
LAO ET LA REPUBLIQUE SOCIALISTE DU VIET-NAM.
ESP> EXCLUIDAS CHINA, LA KAMPUCHEA DEMOCRATICA,
LA REPUBLICA POPULAR DEMOCRATICA DE COREA, LA
REPUBLICA POPULAR DEMOCRATICA LAO Y LA REPUBLICA
SOCIALISTA DEL VIET-NAM.

3 Education

Education

Educación

This chapter provides statistics on education preceding the first level, as well as on that at the first, second, and third levels of education. Data are also provided on education structures and on enrolment ratios for the different levels. Data on the number of students and teachers are provided for all levels of education; data on number of institutions are provided for education preceding the first level and for education at the first level; data on enrolment and graduates at the third level are also provided according to different types of disaggregation.

The text which follows is subdivided into three sections according to the type of data included in the tables of this chapter.

Section 1.

This section provides information by country on the entrance age, duration, compulsory education and enrolment ratios by level of education.

Table 3.1

This table provides a summary presentation of selected elements of the educational systems actually in force in 202 countries and territories. The information given here facilitates the correct interpretation of the figures shown in the educational tables in the *Yearbook*.

The first and the second columns provide data on compulsory education regulations. The first column shows lower and upper age limits. Thus 6-14, for example, means that children are subject to compulsory education laws, unless otherwise exempted, from their sixth birthday to their fourteenth birthday. The second column shows the number of years of compulsory school attendance. For example, regulations may stipulate that the duration of compulsory education shall be six years between the ages of 6 and 14. This means that a child would cease to be subject to the regulations either on his fourteenth birthday or on completion of six years' schooling (though he might then be only 12 or 13 years old).

However, in many countries and territories where the urgent problem is to provide sufficient schools for all children, the existence of compulsory school laws may be only of academic interest since almost all such regulations exempt a child from attending if there is no suitable school within reasonable distance of his home.

The third column gives the age at which children are accepted for education preceding the first level. For most countries education preceding the first level is still provided on a limited basis, often restricted to urban areas where only a small proportion of children within the ages shown is actually receiving pre-school education. The diagrams for all countries and territories which follow these three columns provide a pictorial representation of the duration and age of admission into first level and second level general education according to the education system presently in force. Information on teacher training and other second level education are not presented. the letters 'A' show the duration of first level education, the letters 'B' that for the first cycle of second level general education and the letters 'C' the duration of the second cycle of second level general education. It should be noted that for some countries and territories no distinction is made between the two cycles of second level general education. In these cases the duration of this level of education is shown simply by letters 'B'. Further, for a certain number of countries, the entrance age and duration of education at these two levels may vary depending on the area or type of school. For these countries the most common system is shown in the diagram. A footnote at the end of this figure indicates the other existing possibilities.

Table 3.2

This table presents school enrolment ratios for the years 1970, 1974,

1975, 1976 and 1977 where available. These enrolment ratios are shown for countries and territories whose population exceed 250,000. For countries whose population is less than 250,000, population data by single years of age are not available. Demographic data have been obtained from the Population Division of the United Nations and the enrolment data used to calculate the gross enrolment ratios appear in tables 3.4, 3.7 and 3.11 of this *Yearbook*. Where enrolment data by age for the primary and secondary levels are also available, a net enrolment ratio has been calculated.

All ratios are expressed as percentages. The gross enrolment ratio is the total enrolment of all ages divided by the population of the specific age groups which correspond to the age groups of primary and secondary schooling. The net enrolment ratio has been calculated by using only that part of the enrolment which corresponds to the age groups of primary and secondary schooling.

These ratios have been calculated taking into account the differing national systems of education and the duration of schooling at the first and second levels. At the third level the figures for the population aged 20-24 have been used throughout.

The age groups used to calculate enrolment ratios for the primary and secondary levels shown in the table, have been determined according to the following rules:

1. For countries which have a single school system at each level, the age group is defined in conformity with the normal entrance age and normal duration of general schooling at the first and second levels as given in table 3.1.
2. In the case of countries with several systems of the differing durations, the system followed by the majority of the pupils has been used.
3. When it has not been possible to identify one of several systems as being followed by a majority, then the most representative system has been used. Where it has been necessary to calculate an average of several systems and the calculation produced a fraction, the duration has been rounded up to the next highest year.
4. The durations used are those which were operative in that year. However, in the case of Malta and Spain, there used to be a grade overlap between the primary and secondary systems. This is no longer true and the enrolment ratios for these two countries have been calculated using the durations corresponding to the present structure of the educational system. For federal countries, e.g. Federal Republic of Germany, United States of America, the individual enrolment ratios for the first and second levels have been suppressed since they are distorted because of an overlap of durations for these two levels of education between states. The combined enrolment ratio, however, for these two levels of education does not suffer from this defect. It should be noted that for each of these two countries, the net enrolment ratio for first level education is estimated as 100.

The age group for the combined ratio for the first and second levels is defined by taking a whole range covered by two age groups defined for the first and second levels.

Enrolment ratios for the second level are based on the total enrolment including general education, teacher-training and other second level education. Table 3.7 should be consulted for more details on enrolment data. It should be emphasized that the gross enrolment ratio at the first and second levels includes pupils of all possible ages, whereas the population is limited to the range of official school ages defined according to the above-mentionned rules. Therefore, for countries with almost universal education among the school-age population at the first level, the gross enrolment ratio will exceed 100 if the actual age distribution of pupils spreads over outside the official school ages.

Section 2.

This section consists of seven tables, 3.3 to 3.9 concerned with education preceding the first level, and first and second level education. In consulting the tables in this chapter, reference should be made to the information on duration of schooling, etc., contained in Table 3.1 and its annex.

In general, the data shown in these tables are for the years 1970, 1974, 1975, 1976 and 1977.

Table 3.3

The data refer to education preceding the first level, e.g. kindergartens, nursery schools as well as infant classes attached to schools at higher levels. Nursery play centres, etc. have been excluded whenever possible. Figures on teachers refer, in general, to both full-time and part-time teachers. Unless otherwise stated, data cover both public and private schools. The enrolment in private institutions (aided and unaided) as a percentage of the total number of children enrolled in education preceding the first level has also been shown. However, data in this table should be considered as a minimum indication of the amount of pre-primary education since complete data are not available in all cases. Table 3.1 should be consulted for complementary information.

Table 3.4

In general, data in this table cover both public and private schools at the first level of education, including primary classes attached to secondary schools but excluding schools and classes organized for adults or for handicapped children. In consulting this table, reference should be made to the information given on duration of schooling in Table 3.1. Figures on teachers refer, in general, to both full-time and part-time teachers, excluding other instructional personnel without teaching function (e.g. certain principals, librarians, guidance personnel, etc.). However, it has not been possible to ascertain for which countries such other instructional personnel are included.

Table 3.5

The percentage distribution by grade appearing in this table is presented for the first level only and refers to total enrolment (MF) and female enrolment. These percentages are presented for 1970 and following years as available.

In most cases the data appearing in this table have been calculated on the basis of the duration of education at the first level as shown for each country in Table 3.1.

Table 3.6

The total number of repeaters as well as the percentage repeaters by grade appearing in this table have been calculated from figures taken from questionnaire replies and/or national publications. The total and percentages shown are for the first level only and refer to total and female repeaters for 1970 and following years as available.

The percentages presented in this table have been calculated by dividing the number of repeaters by the enrolment for the same year.

To maintain a consistent and coherent series on repetition as well as to facilitate the comparison of these data with those for enrolment by grade presented in Table 3.5, estimates have been made when the number of repeaters in private institutions was not available. In no case did the missing data constitute more than 5% of the total enrolment. The identification of these estimates is facilitated by the introduction of an asterisk which precedes the total number of repeaters.

The method of estimation used takes into account all available information. For example, the proportion of repeaters in private schools for previous years was used if available; when no other information was available, the data on repeaters were adjusted to reflect the incidence of private enrolment.

Table 3.7

This table gives the number of teachers and full-time pupils by sex enrolled in each of the three types of education at the second level, i.e. general, teacher-training and other second level as well as for all three types combined. Unless otherwise stated, data cover public and private schools. However, due to a lack of data on teachers, certain years have been omitted in this table although enrolment data are shown for these years.

In most cases, data include part-time teachers and their proportion is particularly substantial in 'other second level education'. Generally, it can be stated that, whenever the number of teachers seems disproportionately high in relation to the number of pupils enrolled, this is due to the fact that the figures include not only full-time teachers, but also various categories of part-time teachers. Instructional personnel without teaching functions (e.g. librarians, guidance personnel, certain principals, etc.) have been excluded whenever possible.

Second level, General: The term 'second level, general' refers to education in 'secondary schools' that provide general or specialized instruction based upon at least four years previous instruction at the first level, and which do not aim at preparing the pupils directly for a given trade or occupation. Such schools may be called high schools, middle schools, lyceums, gymnasiums, etc., and offer courses of study whose completion is a minimum condition for admission to university. In many countries, because of the desire to provide other types of training for students not proceeding to university, there has been a development of schools with the aim of providing both academic and vocational training. These 'composite' secondary schools are considered as equivalent to the academic type of secondary school and are classified as 'second level, general'.

Second level, Teacher-training: The term 'second level, teacher- training' refers to education in schools whose purpose is the training of students for the teaching profession, and which do not require as a prerequisite the completion of secondary school.

Second level, Other: The term 'second level, other' is here used to cover education of a vocational or technical nature provided in those 'secondary schools' which aim at preparing the pupils directly for a trade or occupation other than teaching. Such schools have many different names and vary greatly as to type and duration of training. Part-time courses and short courses abound and are excluded wherever possible.

For international comparisons, this table should be consulted in conjunction with Table 3.1.

Table 3.8

The percentage distribution by grade appearing in this table is presented for second level general education only and refers to total enrolment (MF) and female enrolment. These percentages are presented for 1970 and following years as available.

In most cases the data appearing in this table have been calculated on the basis of the duration of general education at the second level as shown for each country in Table 3.1.

Table 3.9

The total number of repeaters as well as the percentage repeaters by grade appearing in this table have been calculated from figures taken from questionnaire replies and/or national publications. The total and percentages shown are for second level general education only and refer to total and female repeaters for 1970 and following years as available.

The percentages presented in this table have been calculated by dividing the number of repeaters by the enrolment for the same year.

To maintain a consistent and coherent series on repetition as well as to facilitate the comparison of these data with those for enrolment by grade presented in Table 3.8, estimates have been made when the number of repeaters in private institutions was not available. In no case did the missing data constitute more than 5% of the total enrolment. The identification of these estimates is facilitated by the introduction of an asterisk which precedes the total number of repeaters.

The method of estimation used takes into account all available information. For example, the proportion of repeaters in private schools for previous years was used if available; when no other information was available, the data on repeaters were adjusted to reflect the incidence of private enrolment.

Section 3.

This section consists of six tables on the development of third-level education in the world.

According to the definition adopted by Unesco, education at the third level requires, as a minimum condition of entry, the successful completion of education at the second level or proof of equivalent knowledge or experience. It can be given in different types of institutions, such as universities, teacher-training institutes, technical institutes, etc.

The categories of data contained in this chapter are as follows:

Students: (I) Number of students enrolled per 100,000 inhabitants (Table 3.10). (II) Total by type of institution (Table 3.11) and by level of programme and field of study (Table 3.12). The latter table is compiled according to the definitions of the International Standard Classification of Education (ISCED).

Teachers: Total and by type of institution (Table 3.11).

Graduates: Breakdown by level of degree or diploma obtained and by field of study (Table 3.13).

Foreign students: Total and by country of origin (Tables 3.14 and 3.15).

Table 3.10 shows the number of students per 100,000 inhabitants.

Table 3.11 is where data on enrolment and teachers by institutions are shown. Table 3.12 presents the distribution of third level enrolment by level of programme and field of study. Table 3.13 contains data on graduates in higher education.

Figure 3 below shows the increase or decrease in the number of students per 100,000 inhabitants in the different continents, regions and groups of countries. In 1977, the ratio was four times higher in developed countries than in the developing countries. The difference between these 2 groups continues to increase. Thus in 1977, the number of students per 100,000 inhabitants in developing countries (66) was just slightly less than half the number of those for the developed countries in 1965. Other notable differences can be seen between the regions which make up this last group of countries when comparing the figures of Northern America (Canada and the United States of America) with those of Europe and the U.S.S.R.

Figure 4 shows the increase of female students in relation to total students. At the world level, female enrolment was around 42% in 1977 compared with 35% in 1965. Europe and the U.S.S.R. (46%) and Northern America (49%) actually show the highest percentages, followed by Latin America (43%). The proportion of female enrolment in Africa and Arab States is still less than 30% in spite of the good progress made during the years under consideration. As regards Asia, the increase was small with 26% in 1965 and 30% in 1977.

Table 3.10

This table shows, as a ratio, the number of students enrolled at the third level of education per 100,000 inhabitants. The ratios are provided for the years 1970, 1974, 1975, 1976 and 1977 and have been calculated using the enrolment data shown in Table 3.11 and the population figures provided by the Population Division of the United Nations.

Table 3.11

The data in this table refer in principle to teaching staff and students enrolled in all institutions, both public and private, at the third level for 1970, 1974, 1975, 1976 and 1977. For most countries and territories data are shown separately by type of institution: (a) universities and equivalent institutions (degree-granting); (b) teacher-training at the third level in non-university institutions (teacher-training colleges, etc.); (c) other education at the third level in non-university institutions (technical colleges, etc.).

It should be noted, however, that the criteria applied for determining the three types of institutions may not be exactly the same in each of the countries and territories covered. Moreover, following reforms in the educational system, a number of non-university institutions in a given country may be attached to universities or recognized as equivalent institutions from one year to the next. This will tend to impair international comparability and the breakdown by type of institution must therefore be used with caution.

As far as possible, the figures include both full-time and part-time teachers and students. Although as a general rule these figures do not cover correspondence courses, they do include them in certain well-defined cases (indicated by a note) in which such courses provide recognized third-level education leading to the same diplomas as intra-mural studies. Figures referring to teaching staff include, in principle, auxiliary teachers (assistants, demonstrators, etc.) but exclude staff with no teaching duties (administrators, laboratory technicians, etc.).

Table 3.12

This table, intended to supplement the information provided in Table 3.11, gives the breakdown by sex; field of study and level of programme of enrolment in higher education. The definitions used are based on the International Standard Classification of Education (ISCED).

The coverage of this table may sometimes be less complete than that of Table 3.11 as the distribution by field of study is not always available for the total number of students.

The different levels, indicated here by their ISCED codes (5, 6 and 7) may be defined as follows:

Level 5: Programmes leading to an award not equivalent to a first university degree. Programmes of this type are usually 'practical' in orientation in that they are designed to prepare students for particular vocational fields in which they can qualify as high-level technicians, teachers, nurses, production supervisors, etc.

Level 6: Programmes leading to a first university degree or equivalent qualification. Programmes of this type comprise those leading to typical first university degrees such as a 'Bachelors degree', a 'Licence', etc., as well as those which lead to first professional degrees such as 'Doctorates' awarded after completion of studies in medicine, engineering, law, etc.

Level 7: Programmes leading to a post-graduate university degree or equivalent qualification. Programmes of this type generally require a first university degree or equivalent qualification for admission. These are programmes of post-graduate study which tend to reflect specialization within a given subject area. Two types of programmes exist: i.e., those that are in extension of programmes leading to a first university degree and consisting primarily of course work, and those that consist primarily of independent research work. 'Field of Study' should be taken to mean the student's main area of specialization. The subjects falling within each of the major fields according to the ISCED classification are:

LEVELS	FIELDS OF STUDY		
5, 6, 7	14	EDUCATION SCIENCE AND TEACHER TRAINING	General teacher training, teacher training programmes with specialization in vocational subjects, education science.
5, 6, 7	22, 26	HUMANITIES, RELIGION AND THEOLOGY	Languages and literature, linguistics, comparative literature, programmes for interpreters and translators, history, archaeology, philosophy. Religion and theology.
5, 6, 7	18	FINE AND APPLIED ARTS	Art studies, drawing and painting, sculpturing, handicrafts, music, drama, photography and cinematography, interior design, history and philosophy of art.
5, 6, 7	38	LAW	Law, programmes for "notaires", local magistrates, jurisprudence.
5, 6, 7	30	SOCIAL AND BEHAVIOURAL SCIENCE	Social and behavioural science, economics, demography, political science, sociology, anthropology, psychology, geography, studies of regional cultures.
5, 6, 7	34	COMMERCIAL AND BUSINESS ADMINISTRATION	Business administration and commercial programmes, accountancy, secretarial programmes, business machine operation and electronic data processing, financial management, public administration, institutional administration.
5, 6, 7	84	MASS COMMUNICATION AND DOCUMENTATION	Journalism, programmes in radio and television broadcasting, public relations, communications arts, library science, programmes for technicians in museums and similar repositories, documentation techniques.
5, 6, 7	66	HOME ECONOMICS (domestic science)	Household arts, consumer food research and nutrition.
5	78	SERVICE TRADES	Cooking (restaurant and hotel-type), retailing, tourist trades, other service trades programmes.
5, 6, 7	42	NATURAL SCIENCE	Biological science, chemistry, geological science, physics, astronomy, meteorology, oceanography.

5, 6, 7	46	MATHEMATICS AND COMPUTER SCIENCE	General programmes in mathematics, statistics, actuarial science, computer science.
5, 6, 7	50	MEDICAL SCIENCE AND HEALTH-RELATED	Medicine, surgery and medical specialities, hygiene and public health, physiotherapy and occupational therapy; nursing, midwifery, medical X-ray techniques and other programmes in medical diagnostic and treatment techniques; medical technology, dentistry, stomatology and odontology, dental techniques, pharmacy, optometry.
5, 6, 7	54	ENGINEERING	Chemical engineering and materials techniques, civil engineering, electrical and electronics engineering, surveying, industrial engineering, metallurgical engineering, mining engineering, mechanical engineering, agricultural and forestry engineering techniques, fishery engineering techniques.
5, 6, 7	58	ARCHITECTURE AND TOWN PLANNING	Architecture, town planning, landscape architecture.
5	52	TRADE, CRAFT AND INDUSTRIAL PROGRAMMES	Food processing; electrical and electronics trades, metal trades, mechanical trades, air-conditioning trades; textile techniques, graphic arts, laboratory technicians, optical lens making.
5	70	TRANSPORT AND COMMUNICATIONS	Air crew and ships' officer programmes, railway operating trades, road motor vehicle operation programmes, postal service programmes.
5, 6, 7	62	AGRICULTURE, FORESTRY AND FISHERY	General programmes in agriculture, animal husbandry, horticulture, crop husbandry, agricultural economics, food sciences and technology, soil and water sciences, veterinary medicine, forestry, forest products technology, fishery science and technology.
6	01		General programmes.
5, 6, 7	89	OTHER PROGRAMMES	Criminology, civil security and military programme, social welfare, vocational counselling, physical education, environmental studies, nautical science. Other programmes.

Table 3.13

This table shows the number of students who have successfully completed their studies by level of degree or diploma obtained and by field of study.

In general, these degrees and diplomas were awarded at the end of the academic year which began during the calendar year indicated. For example, where the academic year does not coincide with the calendar year the data shown as 1977 refer to degrees awarded at the end of the academic year 1977/1978. More information on this point is given in the general introduction to the 'Education' chapter.

The three levels, represented here as 5, 6 and 7 are defined as follows:

Level 5: Diplomas and certificates not equivalent to a first university degree. These correspond to higher studies of reduced duration (generally less than three years). They include, for instance, certificates awarded to certain types of technicians, nursing diplomas, land-surveying diplomas, associate degrees, certificates of competence in law, etc.

Level 6: First university degrees or equivalent qualifications. These represent higher studies of normal duration (generally three to five years and, in certain cases, seven years). These are the most numerous. They include typical first degrees such as the Bachelor's degree, the 'Licence' etc., as well as in certain countries first professional degrees such as 'Doctorates' awarded after completion of studies in medicine, engineering, law, etc.

Level 7: Post-graduate university degrees or equivalent qualifications. These are those which persons who already possess a first university degree (or equivalent qualification) can obtain by continuing their studies. For example, the various diplomas obtained after completion of a first university degree (post-graduate diploma), the Master's degree, the various types of Doctorates, etc.

In certain countries, the studies leading to a first degree are divided into two cycles, the first of which lasts two years and serves to provide the students with basic training, resulting sometimes in a diploma. In general, these diplomas are excluded and only in the case of certain countries have

they been presented as level 5. The classification according to level is intended to establish a distinction between the different degrees and diplomas and to facilitate international comparability on third-level qualifications. It should be noted that the classification by level in no way implies an equivalence of the degrees and diplomas either within a country or between countries and that any comparative studies should be made with caution.

With regard to the subjects included in the various fields of study, see the introductory note to Table 3.12.

Table 3.14

A foreign student is defined as 'a person enrolled at an institution of higher education in a country or territory of which he is not a permanent resident'. It should, however, be noted that most of the countries have established their statistics concerning foreign students on the basis of nationality. The differences resulting from the application of these two criteria can, in certain countries, be quite appreciable; for example, those immigrants who have not taken the nationality of the host country but who are permanent residents.

Table 3.15

This table indicates the country or territory of origin of foreign students enrolled in institutions at the third level in fifty selected host countries.

The choice of these fifty countries was governed by the number of foreign students enrolled; the last year for which their distribution by country of origin was available (1977 for most countries) was taken as a basis. The following countries whilst host to many foreign students, have not been listed in the 50 selected countries as either a distribution by country of origin was not communicated or more recent data were not available: Brazil (25,642 students in 1974), Lebanon (20,857 students in 1969), U.S.S.R. (30,563 students in 1971), and India (7,804 students in 1970).

It should be noted that for a few countries, foreign students have been distributed by continent of origin instead of country of origin.

Foreign students enrolled in these fifty countries represent about 90 per cent of the known world total.

See also introductory note to Table 3.14.

A special study on students abroad (*Statistics of Students Abroad, 1969-1973*) has been published by Unesco as No. 21 in the series *Statistical Reports and Studies*.

Ce chapitre présente des statistiques relatives à l'enseignement précédant le premier degré, ainsi qu'aux enseignements du premier, du second et du troisième degré. Des données sont présentées sur les systèmes nationaux d'enseignement et les taux d'inscription scolaire ainsi que sur le personnel enseignant et les effectifs scolaires pour tous les niveaux d'enseignement; le nombre d'écoles est également indiqué pour les enseignements précédant le premier degré et le premier degré; les chiffres sur les effectifs et les diplômés du troisième degré sont présentés sous diverses formes.

Le texte qui suit est subdivisé en trois sections, en accord avec le type de données qui figurent dans les tableaux de ce chapitre.

Section 1.

Cette section procure des informations par pays sur l'âge d'admission, la durée et les taux d'inscription, pour les différents degrés d'enseignement.

Tableau 3.1

Ce tableau présente des données sommaires sélectionnées sur les systèmes d'enseignement actuellement en vigueur dans 202 pays et territoires. L'information ainsi présentée doit aider à interpréter correctement les chiffres qui figurent dans les tableaux de l'*Annuaire* consacrés à l'éducation.

Les première et deuxième colonnes présentent les données relatives à l'obligation scolaire. Dans la première colonne sont précisées les limites d'âge inférieure et supérieure. C'est ainsi que les deux chiffres 6-14 signifient que les lois instituant la scolarité obligatoire s'appliquent, sauf exception, aux enfants de 6 à 14 ans. La deuxième colonne indique le nombre d'années pendant lesquelles les enfants sont tenus de fréquenter l'école. Les règlements peuvent stipuler, par exemple, que la durée de l'enseignement obligatoire est de six années (entre 6 et 14 ans). En d'autres termes, l'enfant cesse d'être soumis à l'obligation scolaire soit lorsqu'il a atteint l'âge de 14 ans, soit lorsqu'il a terminé sa sixième année d'études (même s'il n'a alors que 12 ou 13 ans).

Néanmoins, dans beaucoup de pays et territoires, le problème le plus urgent consiste à disposer d'un nombre suffisant d'écoles pour tous les enfants, l'existence d'une loi sur la scolarité obligatoire n'ayant qu'un intérêt théorique, puisque la plupart de ces règlementations dispensent un enfant de fréquentation scolaire s'il n'existe pas une école à une distance raisonnable de son domicile.

La troisième colonne indique l'âge d'admission des enfants dans l'enseignement précédant le premier degré. Pour la plupart des pays, l'enseignement précédant le premier degré n'est encore dispensé que d'une façon limitée généralement aux zones urbaines, où une faible proportion seulement des enfants compris dans l'âge indiqué peuvent en bénéficier. Le diagramme qui suit et qui comprend les trois colonnes présente pour tous les pays et territoires une représentation graphique de la durée et de l'âge d'admission dans l'enseignement du premier degré et l'enseignement général du second degré, en accord avec les systèmes d'enseignement actuellement en vigueur. Les renseignements concernant l'enseignement normal et l'autre enseignement du second degré ne sont pas présentés. Les lettres 'A' montrent la durée de l'enseignement du premier degré, les lettres 'B' celle du premier cycle de l'enseignement général du second degré et les lettres 'C' la durée du deuxième cycle de l'enseignement général du second degré. Il faut noter que pour quelques pays et territoires il n'est pas fait de distinction entre les deux cycles de l'enseignement général du second degré. Dans ces cas, la durée de l'enseignement est montrée simplement dans les lettres 'B'. De plus, pour un certain nombre de pays, l'âge d'admission et la durée de l'enseignement dans ces deux degrés peut varier selon la zone ou le type d'école. Pour ces pays, le système le plus courant a été porté sur le diagramme. Une note à la fin du diagramme indique les autres possibilités existantes.

Finalement, une annexe à ce tableau précise les changements qui se sont produits dans le système d'enseignement d'un certain nombre de pays. Cette annexe doit être consultée lorsque l'on se réfère aux effectifs scolaires qui figurent dans les tableaux 3.3 à 3.9.

Tableau 3.2

Ce tableau présente, lorsqu'ils sont disponibles, les taux d'inscription pour les années 1970, 1974, 1975, 1976 et 1977 pour les pays et territoires dont la population est supérieure à 250.000 habitants. Pour les pays dont la population est inférieure à 250.000 habitants, les données de population par années d'âge simple ne sont pas disponibles. Les données démographiques nous ont été fournies par la division de la population de l'Organisation des Nations Unies et les effectifs qui ont servi pour calculer les taux d'inscription bruts sont ceux qui figurent dans les tableaux 3.4, 3.7 et 3.11 de cet *Annuaire*. Lorsqu'on disposait des effectifs par âge des enseignements du premier et du second degré, on a calculé un taux d'inscription net. Tous les taux d'inscription sont exprimés en

pourcentages. Le taux d'inscription brut pour les enseignements du premier et du second degré est le rapport entre les effectifs scolaires, quel que soit l'âge des élèves, et la population d'un groupe d'âge déterminé d'après la durée de la scolarité à chacun de ces niveaux. Le calcul du taux d'inscription net est basé seulement sur la partie des effectifs dont les groupes d'âge correspondent à la durée de la scolarité du premier et du second degré. Les taux ont été calculés en tenant compte de la diversité des systèmes nationaux d'enseignement et de la durée des études du premier et du second degré. Pour l'enseignement du troisième degré, on a pris en considération le groupe d'âge 20-24. Les groupes d'âge utilisés pour calculer les taux d'inscription relatifs aux enseignements du premier et du second degré, qui figurent dans le tableau ont été déterminés en accord avec les normes suivantes:

1. Pour les pays qui ont un type d'enseignement unique à tous les degrés, le groupe d'âge est déterminé conformément à l'âge normal d'admission et à la durée normale des études générales primaires et secondaires qui figurent dans le tableau 3.1.

2. Dans le cas des pays qui ont plusieurs types d'enseignement de durée différente, on a choisi le système qui s'applique à la majorité des élèves.

3. Lorsqu'il n'a pas été possible de déterminer, dans le cadre des différents types d'enseignement, celui qui s'appliquait à la majorité des élèves, on a pris comme base le type le plus représentatif. Quand il a été nécessaire de calculer une moyenne des différents systèmes et que le résultat donnait une fraction, la durée a été arrondie à l'année immédiatement supérieure.

4. Les durées d'enseignement considérées sont celles qui étaient en vigueur pour chaque année. Néanmoins, dans les cas de Malte et de l'Espagne, il y avait un chevauchement entre les enseignements primaire et secondaire. Ceci n'étant plus exact, les taux d'inscription pour les deux pays ont été calculés sur la base des durées d'enseignement qui correspondent à la structure actuelle du système scolaire. Pour des pays fédérés tels que la République Fédérale d'Allemagne ou les Etats Unis d'Amérique, les taux d'inscription scolaire séparés pour les enseignements du premier et du second degré ont été supprimés, car ils se trouvaient faussés. En effet, il peut y avoir, d'une part un chevauchement entre les enseignements du premier et du second degré et d'autre part, la durée de l'enseignement de chacun de ces degrés peut varier d'un état à l'autre. Néanmoins, le taux combiné d'inscription du premier et du second degré n'est pas affecté par ces différences. Il faut souligner que pour ces deux pays, le taux net d'inscription dans l'enseignement du premier degré est estimé à 100.

Le groupe d'âge considéré pour le calcul du taux concernant la totalité du premier et du second degré est déterminé par les limites extrêmes de l'ensemble des deux groupes d'âge définis pour le premier et le second degré.

Les taux d'inscription pour le second degré sont fondés sur les effectifs globaux des trois types d'enseignement du second degré (général, normal et autre enseignement du second degré). On trouvera des renseignements plus détaillés sur ces effectifs dans le tableau 3.7. Il convient de noter que le taux d'inscription brut dans le premier et le second degré comprend les élèves de tous les âges possibles alors que la population considérée est limitée aux groupes d'âge officiels déterminés selon les règles susmentionnées. Par conséquent, dans les pays où, pour le premier degré, la population d'âge scolaire est presque entièrement scolarisée, le taux d'inscription brut dépassera 100 si la répartition réelle des élèves par âge déborde les limites d'âge officielles.

Section 2.

Cette section comprend sept tableaux, 3.3 à 3.9, qui se réfèrent à l'enseignement précédant le premier degré et aux enseignements du premier et du second degré. En consultant les tableaux de ce chapitre, il faut se référer aux renseignements sur la durée de la scolarité, etc. contenus dans le tableau 3.1 et son annexe.

En général, les données présentées dans ces tableaux correspondent aux années 1970, 1974, 1975, 1976 et 1977.

Tableau 3.3

Les données se rapportent à l'enseignement qui précède le premier degré (jardins d'enfants, écoles maternelles et classes enfantines ouvertes dans des écoles de niveau plus élevé). Les garderies, crèches, etc. ont été, dans la mesure du possible, exclues. Les chiffres relatifs au personnel enseignant englobent, en général, le personnel à plein temps et le personnel à temps partiel. Sauf indication contraire, les données se rapportent à la fois aux établissements publics et aux établissements privés. Le pourcentage des effectifs inscrits dans les établissements privés (subventionnés et non subventionnés) par rapport au total des effectifs de l'enseignement précédant le premier degré a été indiqué. Il convient cependant de considérer les données de ce tableau comme une indication minimale de l'importance de l'enseignement précédant le premier degré, car on ne dispose pas de données complètes dans tous les cas. Pour des renseignements complémentaires, veuillez consulter le tableau 3.1.

Tableau 3.4

En général, les données de ce tableau se rapportent aux établissements d'enseignement du premier degré, publics et privés, y compris les classes primaires rattachées aux établissements du second degré, mais non compris les écoles et les classes destinées aux adultes et aux enfants déficients. Il convient, en consultant ce tableau, de se reporter aux renseignements donnés sur la durée de la scolarité au tableau 3.1. Les chiffres relatifs au personnel enseignant représentent, en général, le nombre total de maîtres à plein temps et à temps partiel, à l'exclusion du personnel qui n'est pas chargé d'enseignement (proviseurs, bibliothécaires, conseillers d'orientation professionnelle, etc.). Il n'a pas été possible de vérifier si cette règle a été suivie par tous les pays.

Tableau 3.5

La répartition en pourcentage par années d'études qui figure dans ce tableau est présentée pour l'enseignement du premier degré seulement et se réfère au total des effectifs (MF) et aux effectifs féminins. Ces pourcentages sont présentés pour l'année 1970 et les années suivantes, lorsque les données pour ces années sont disponibles.

En général, les données présentées dans ce tableau ont été calculées en fonction de la durée de l'enseignement du premier degré, telle qu'elle figure pour chaque pays et territoire dans le tableau 3.1.

Tableau 3.6

Le nombre total et le pourcentage de redoublants par années d'études qui figurent dans ce tableau ont été calculés avec les données qui ont été tirées des réponses aux questionnaires et/ou des publications nationales. Les totaux et pourcentages ne concernent que l'enseignement du premier degré et se réfèrent, lorsque les données étaient disponibles, aux redoublants (Total et filles) pour l'année 1970 et les années suivantes.

Les pourcentages présentés dans ce tableau ont été calculés en divisant le nombre de redoublants par les effectifs de la même année.

Afin d'assurer une série cohérente et consistante sur les redoublants et de faciliter la comparabilité de ces données avec celles des effectifs par années d'études présentés dans le tableau 3.5, des estimations ont été faites sur le nombre de redoublants dans les écoles privées, lorsque ces chiffres n'étaient pas disponibles. Les données manquantes ne représentent en aucun cas plus de 5% du total des effectifs. L'identification de ces estimations est facilitée par l'introduction d'un astérisque qui précède le nombre de redoublants.

La méthode d'estimation utilisée prend en considération toutes les informations disponibles, par exemple, la proportion des redoublants dans les écoles privées au cours des années antérieures est utilisée, lorsque ces chiffres sont connus. Si l'on ne dispose pas d'autres informations, les données sur les redoublants sont ajustées en accord avec l'importance des effectifs de l'enseignement privé.

Tableau 3.7

Ce tableau indique le nombre et la répartition par sexe du personnel enseignant et des élèves inscrits dans chacun des trois types d'enseignement du second degré: général, normal et autre enseignement du second degré, ainsi que l'effectif global. Sauf indication contraire, les données comprennent le personnel enseignant et les élèves des écoles publiques et des écoles privées. Toutefois, le manque de données concernant les enseignants, explique que pour certaines années, il n'ait pas été possible d'indiquer leur nombre. Les effectifs scolaires relatifs à ces années sont néanmoins présentés dans ce tableau.

Dans la plupart des cas, les chiffres comprennent les maîtres à temps partiel, qui sont particulièrement nombreux dans l'autre enseignement du second degré. D'une manière générale, on peut affirmer que, lorsque l'effectif des enseignants paraît anormalement élevé par rapport à celui des élèves, c'est dû au fait que les chiffres relatifs au personnel enseignant comprennent, non seulement le personnel à plein temps, mais aussi diverses catégories de personnel à temps partiel. Dans toute la mesure du possible, est exclu le personnel qui n'exerce pas de fonctions d'enseignement (par exemple les bibliothécaires, les orienteurs, certains chefs d'établissements, etc.).

Second degré, enseignement général: La formule 'second degré, enseignement général' désigne l'enseignement, général ou spécialisé, dispensé dans les 'écoles secondaires' à des enfants ayant déjà fait au moins quatre années d'études dans le premier degré, et qui ne vise pas à préparer directement les élèves à une profession ou à un emploi. Les écoles de ce type s'appellent collèges, lycées, gymnases, etc., et elles dispensent

un enseignement qu'il faut obligatoirement avoir terminé pour pouvoir être admis à l'université. Dans de nombreux pays, où l'on souhaite dispenser d'autres types de formation aux élèves qui ne se destinent pas aux études supérieures, on assiste au développement d'écoles qui offrent une formation tant générale que professionnelle. On considère que ces écoles secondaires 'composites' sont d'un niveau équivalent à celui des écoles secondaires traditionnelles: elles sont de ce fait classées dans la catégorie 'second degré, enseignement général'.

Second degré, enseignement normal: La formule 'second degré, enseignement normal' désigne l'enseignement dispensé dans les écoles dont le but est de préparer à la profession enseignante et dont l'accès n'est pas réservé aux jeunes gens qui ont fait des études secondaires complètes.

Autre enseignement du second degré: La formule 'autre enseignement du second degré' désigne ici l'enseignement de caractère technique ou professionnel dispensé dans des 'écoles secondaires' qui visent à préparer directement leurs élèves à un emploi ou une profession autre que l'enseignement. Ces écoles peuvent porter divers noms et la formation qu'elles dispensent varie largement quant à sa nature et à sa durée. Ce type d'enseignement comporte fréquemment des cours à mi-temps ou des cours de brève durée, qui ont été exclus dans toute la mesure du possible.

Pour effectuer des comparaisons internationales, ce tableau doit être consulté conjointement avec le tableau 3.1.

Tableau 3.8

La répartition en pourcentage par années d'études qui figure dans ce tableau est présentée pour l'enseignement général du second degré seulement et se réfère au total des effectifs (MF) et aux effectifs féminins. Ces pourcentages sont présentés pour l'année 1970 et les années suivantes, lorsque les données pour ces années sont disponibles.

En général, les données présentées dans ce tableau ont été calculées en fonction de la durée de l'enseignement du premier degré, telle qu'elle figure pour chaque pays et territoire dans le tableau 3.1.

Tableau 3.9

Le nombre total et le pourcentage de redoublants par années d'études qui figurent dans ce tableau ont été calculés avec les données qui ont été tirées des réponses aux questionnaires et/ou des publications nationales. Les totaux et les pourcentages ne concernent que l'enseignement général du second degré et se réfèrent, lorsque les données sont disponibles, aux redoublants (Total et filles) pour l'année 1970 et les années suivantes.

Les pourcentages présentés dans ce tableau ont été calculés en divisant le nombre de redoublants par les effectifs de la même année.

Afin d'assurer une série cohérente et consistante sur les redoublants et de faciliter la comparabilité de ces données avec celles des effectifs par années d'études présentés dans le tableau 3.8, des estimations ont été faites sur le nombre de redoublants dans les écoles privées, lorsque ces chiffres n'étaient pas disponibles. Les données manquantes ne représentent en aucun cas plus de 5% du total des effectifs. L'identification de ces estimations est facilitée par l'introduction d'un astérisque qui précède le nombre de redoublants.

La méthode d'estimation utilisée prend en considération toutes les informations disponibles, par exemple, la proportion des redoublants dans les écoles privées au cours des années antérieures est utilisée, lorsque ces chiffres sont connus. Si l'on ne dispose pas d'autres informations, les données sur les redoublants sont ajustées en accord avec l'importance des effectifs de l'enseignement privé.

Section 3.

La présente section comprend six tableaux statistiques sur le développement de l'enseignement du troisième degré dans les différents pays du monde.

L'enseignement du troisième degré, d'après la définition adoptée par l'Unesco, est celui qui exige comme condition minimale d'admission d'avoir suivi avec succès un enseignement complet du second degré ou de faire preuve de connaissances équivalentes. Il peut être dispensé dans différents types d'établissements tels que les universités, les écoles normales supérieures, les écoles techniques supérieures, etc.

Les catégories de données présentées dans ce chapitre sont les suivantes:

Etudiants: (i) nombre d'étudiants inscrits par 100.000 habitants (tableau 3.10) (ii) nombre total par type d'établissement (tableau 3.11) et par niveau de programme et disciplines (tableau 3.12). Ce dernier tableau est représenté selon les critères de la Classification Internationale Type de l'Education (CITE).

Personnel enseignant: nombre total et par type d'établissement (tableau 3.11).

Diplômés: répartition par disciplines et par niveau du grade ou diplôme obtenu (tableau 3.13).

Etudiants étrangers: nombre total et par pays d'origine (tableau 3.14 et

3.15).

Le tableau 3.10 présente le nombre d'étudiants par 100.000 habitants. Le tableau 3.11 donne le nombre des étudiants et du personnel enseignant par type d'établissement. Le tableau 3.12 présente la répartition des étudiants du troisième degré par niveau de programme et disciplines. Le tableau 3.13 contient des données sur les diplômés de l'enseignement supérieur.

La figure 3 ci-après montre l'accroissement ou la diminution du nombre d'étudiants par 100.000 habitants dans les différents continents, régions ou groupes de pays. En 1977, ce rapport était quatre fois plus élevé dans les pays développés que dans les pays en voie de développement. L'écart entre ces deux groupes de pays n'a cessé d'augmenter. Ainsi, en 1977 le nombre d'étudiants par 100.000 habitants dans les pays en voie de développement (66) était un peu moins que la moitié du nombre observé dans les pays développés en 1965. On constate aussi des différences notables entre les régions qui composent ce dernier groupe de pays en comparant les chiffres de l'Amérique septentrionale (Canada et Etats-Unis d'Amérique) et de l'Europe et l'U.R.S.S.

La figure 4 montre l'évolution de la part des effectifs du sexe féminin dans le nombre total d'étudiants. Au niveau mondial, la participation féminine était d'environ 42% en 1977 contre 35% en 1965. L'Europe et l'U.R.S.S. (46%) et l'Amérique septentrionale (49%) enregistrent actuellement les pourcentages les plus élevés, suivies par l'Amérique Latine (43%). Malgré une progression très forte au cours des deux années considérées, cette proportion reste inférieure à 30% en Afrique et dans les Etats Arabes. Dans le cas de l'Asie, la progression a été très faible: 26% en 1965 et 30% en 1977.

Tableau 3.10

Ce tableau présente, comme un taux, le nombre d'étudiants inscrits dans l'enseignement du troisième degré par 100.000 habitants. Les taux se réfèrent aux années 1970, 1974, 1975, 1976 et 1977 et ont été calculés en utilisant les effectifs indiqués dans le tableau 3.11 et les chiffres de population qui nous ont été fournis par la Division de la Population des Nations Unies.

Tableau 3.11

Ces données se rapportent en principe au personnel enseignant et aux étudiants inscrits dans tous les établissements, publics et privés, d'enseignement du troisième degré pour 1970, 1974, 1975, 1976 et 1977. Pour la plupart des pays et territoires, les données sont présentées séparément par type d'établissement: (a) universités et établissements équivalents (conférant des grades universitaires); (b) enseignement normal du troisième degré dans des établissements non universitaires (écoles normales supérieures, etc.); (c) autres formes d'enseignement du troisième degré dans des établissements non universitaires (écoles techniques supérieures, etc.)

Il faut cependant souligner que le critère appliqué pour déterminer les trois types d'établissements peut ne pas être exactement le même dans chacun des pays et territoires concernés. De plus, il se peut que dans un même pays, à la suite des réformes du système d'enseignement, plusieurs établissements non universitaires soient, d'une année à l'autre, rattachés aux universités ou considérés comme des établissements équivalents. Cela

rend difficile la comparabilité internationale et c'est pourquoi cette répartition par type d'établissement doit être utilisée avec précaution.

Dans la mesure du possible, ces statistiques couvrent aussi bien les professeurs et étudiants à plein temps que ceux à temps partiel. Bien que d'une manière générale, les statistiques ne couvrent pas les cours par correspondance, elles en tiennent compte dans certains cas bien déterminés (indiqués par une note) où ces cours dispensent un enseignement reconnu comme étant du troisième degré et sanctionné par les mêmes diplômes que l'enseignement intra-muros. Les chiffres relatifs au personnel enseignant incluent en principe le personnel auxiliaire (assistants, chefs de travaux, etc.) mais non le personnel qui n'exerce pas de fonctions d'enseignement (administrateurs, techniciens de laboratoire, etc.).

Tableau 3.12

Ce tableau, qui complète le tableau 3.11, donne la répartition, par sexe et par discipline, des étudiants inscrits dans des établissements d'enseignement du troisième degré. Les définitions utilisées correspondent aux critères de la Classification Internationale Type de l'Education (CITE).

Il arrive parfois que les renseignements fournis soient moins complets dans le présent tableau que dans le tableau 3.11, la répartition par discipline n'étant pas toujours disponible pour l'ensemble des étudiants.

Ces différents niveaux, qui sont ici désignés par leurs codes (5,6 et 7) dans la CITE, peuvent être définis comme suit:

Niveau 5: programmes conduisant à un diplôme n'équivalant pas à un premier grade universitaire. Ces programmes ont généralement un caractère 'pratique' en ce sens qu'ils ont pour objectif la formation professionnelle des étudiants dans des domaines précis où ils pourront se qualifier, par exemple, comme techniciens, enseignants, infirmiers, contrôleurs de la production, etc.

Niveau 6: programmes conduisant à un premier grade universitaire ou à un diplôme équivalent. Sont également compris ici les programmes qui conduisent aux titres de caractère professionnel, tels que les 'doctorats' décernés à la fin des études de médecine, de sciences de l'ingénieur, de droit, etc.

Niveau 7: programmes conduisant à un grade universitaire supérieur ou à un grade équivalent. Ces programmes s'adressent en général aux personnes déjà titulaires d'un premier grade universitaire ou d'un diplôme équivalent. IL s'agit de programmes d'études post-universitaires qui prévoient habituellement une spécialisation à l'intérieur même de la discipline choisie. En outre, les programmes sont de deux types principaux: ceux qui font suite aux programmes conduisant au premier grade universitaire, et qui comprennent surtout des études imposées, et ceux qui consistent essentiellement en travaux personnels de recherche. Par 'discipline' il faut entendre le domaine principal de spécialisation de l'étudiant. Les sujets compris dans chacune des disciplines principales en accord avec la classification de la CITE sont les suivants:

Niveaux	Domaines d'études		
5, 6, 7	14	SCIENCES DE L'EDUCATION ET FORMATION D'ENSEIGNANTS	Formation de personnel enseignant, préparation générale à l'enseignement, préparation à l'enseignement avec spécialisation dans des disciplines à caractère professionnel, sciences de l'éducation.
5, 6, 7	22, 26	LETTRES, RELIGION ET THEOLOGIE	Langues et littératures, linguistique, littérature comparée, formation d'interprètes et de traducteurs, histoire, archéologie, philosophie. Religion et théologie.
5, 6, 7	18	BEAUX-ARTS ET ARTS APPLIQUES	Etudes artistiques, dessin et peinture, sculpture, arts artisanaux, musique, arts du spectacle, photographie et cinématographie, décoration, histoire et philosophie de l'art.
5, 6, 7	38	DROIT	Droit, notariat, formation de magistrats locaux, jurisprudence.
5, 6, 7	30	SCIENCES SOCIALES ET SCIENCES DU COMPORTEMENT	Sciences sociales et sciences du comportement, sciences économiques, science politique, démographie, sociologie, anthropologie, psychologie, géographie, études des cultures régionales.
5, 6, 7	34	FORMATION AU COMMERCE ET A L'ADMINISTRATION DES ENTREPRISES	Administration des entreprises et enseignement commercial, comptabilité, secrétariat, mécanographie et traitement électronique de l'information, gestion financière, administration publique, administration d'établissements et de collectivités.
5, 6, 7	84	INFORMATION ET DOCUMENTATION	Journalisme, formations pour la radio et la télévision, relations avec le public, techniques de l'information, bibliothéconomie, formation des techniciens pour les musées et établissements analogues, techniques de la documentation.

5, 6, 7	66	ENSEIGNEMENT MENAGER	Arts ménagers, alimentation familiale, diététique et nutrition.
5	78	FORMATION POUR LE SECTEUR TERTIAIRE	Hôtellerie et restauration, commerce de détail, services de tourisme, autres formations pour le secteur tertiaire.
5, 6, 7	42	SCIENCES EXACTES ET NATURELLES	Sciences biologiques, chimie, sciences géologiques, physique, astronomie, météorologie, océanographie.
5, 6, 7	46	MATHEMATIQUES ET INFORMATIQUE	Mathématiques générales, statistique, science actuarielle, informatique.
5, 6, 7	50	SCIENCES MEDICALES, SANTE ET HYGIENE	Médecine, chirurgie et spécialisations médicales, hygiène et santé publique, physiothérapie et ergothérapie; formation d'infirmiers, de sages-femmes, de radiologues et autres formations aux techniques du diagnostic et du traitement des maladies, technologie médicale, art dentaire, stomatologie et odontologie, technologie dentaire, pharmacie, optométrie.
5, 6, 7	54	SCIENCES DE L'INGENIEUR	Génie chimique et technologie des matériaux, génie civil, électrotechnique et éloctronique, topographie, organisation industrielle, métallurgie, techniques minières, mécanique, technologie agricole et forestière, techniques de la pêche.
5, 6, 7	58	ARCHITECTURE ET URBANISME	Architecture, urbanisme, formation d'architectes paysagistes.
5	52	METIERS DE LA PRODUCTION INDUSTRIELLE	Traitement des denrées alimentaires; formation en électricité, en électronique, au travail des métaux, à la mécanique, aux techniques du conditionnement d'air; technologie des textiles, arts graphiques, techniciens de laboratoire, fabrication de verres optiques.
5	70	TRANSPORTS ET TELECOMMUNICATIONS	Formation de personnel des transports aériens, maritimes, ferroviaires, routiers et des services postaux.
5, 6, 7	62	AGRICULTURE, SYLVICULTURE ET HALIEUTIQUE	Enseignement agricole, zootechnie, horticulture, culture de plein champ, économie agricole, science et technologie de l'alimentation, pédologie et hydrologie, médecine vétérinaire, sylviculture, technologie des produits forestiers, halieutique (science et technologie de la pêche).
6	01		Programmes d'enseignement général.
5, 6, 7	89	AUTRES PROGRAMMES	Criminologie, formation militaire et pour la sécurité civile, formation de personnel des services sociaux, formation des conseillers d'orientation professionnelle, éducation physique, programmes relatifs à l'environnement, sciences nautique. Autres programmes.

Tableau 3.13

Ce tableau présente le nombre des étudiants qui ont terminé leurs études avec succès, selon le niveau du grade ou diplôme obtenu et par disciplines.

En principe, ces grades et diplômes ont été décernés à la fin de l'année universitaire commencée pendant l'année civile indiquée. Par exemple, dans le cas où l'année universitaire ne coïncide pas avec l'année civile, les données indiquées pour 1977 se réfèrent aux diplômes décernés à la fin de l'année universitaire 1977/1978. Pour plus de détails, se reporter à l'introduction générale de la partie 'Education'.

Les trois niveaux indiqués ici sous les numéros 5, 6 et 7 sont définis comme suit:

Niveau 5. Les diplômes et certificats non équivalents à un premier grade universitaire sont ceux décernés à la fin d'études supérieures de durée réduite (en général, moins de trois ans). Ils comprennent, par exemple, les certificats délivrés à certains types de techniciens, les diplômes d'infirmière, d'arpenteur, les grades d'associés, les certificats de capacité en droit, etc.

Niveau 6. Les premiers grades universitaires ou diplômes équivalents sont ceux qui sanctionnent des études supérieures de durée normale (en général, trois à cinq ans et parfois sept ans). Ce sont les plus nombreux. Ils comprennent non seulement les grades bien connus tels que la licence, le 'Bachelor's degree', etc., mais aussi les titres de caractère professionnel tels que les doctorats décernés dans certains pays à la fin des études de médecine, sciences de l'ingénieur, droit, etc.

Niveau 7. Les grades universitaires supérieurs ou diplômes équivalents sont ceux que peuvent obtenir, en poursuivant leurs études, les personnes déjà titulaires d'un premier grade universitaire (ou d'un diplôme équivalent). Par exemple les divers diplômes obtenus après la préparation d'un premier grade universitaire (diplôme de post-graduate), la maîtrise (master's degree), les divers types de doctorats, etc. Dans certains pays, les études conduisant au premier grade universitaire se divisent en deux cycles, dont le premier s'étend sur deux années et assure aux étudiants une formation de base, sanctionnée quelquefois par un diplôme. D'une manière générale, les statistiques ne tiennent pas compte de ces diplômes et dans les quelques cas où des pays les ont pris en considération, ils ont été classés dans le niveau 5. Le classement selon le niveau a été effectué afin d'établir une distinction entre les différents grades et diplômes et dans l'espoir de faciliter la comparabilité internationale des statistiques sur les diplômes de l'enseignement du troisième degré. Il faut néanmoins souligner qu'il n'est

pas souhaitable de procéder à des comparaisons approfondies, étant donné que le classement par niveau n'implique en aucune manière une équivalence des grades et diplômes, que ce soit à l'intérieur du pays considéré ou par rapport à d'autres pays.

En ce qui concerne les sujets inclus dans les diverses disciplines, voir la note d'introduction au tableau 3.12.

Tableau 3.14

Un étudiant étranger se définit comme une 'personne inscrite dans un établissement d'enseignement supérieur d'un pays ou d'un territoire où elle n'a pas son domicile permanent'. Il faut signaler cependant que la plupart des pays ont établi leurs statistiques concernant les étudiants étrangers d'après le concept de nationalité. Les différences résultant de l'application de ce concept peuvent être importantes dans certains pays où les statistiques tiennent compte, par exemple, des immigrants qui, n'ayant pas acquis la nationalité du pays hôte, Y résident cependant de façon permanente.

Tableau 3.15

Ce tableau présente, pour cinquante pays d'accueil sélectionés, le nombre d'étudiants étrangers inscrits dans les établissements d'enseignement du troisième degré avec l'indication du pays ou territoire d'origine.

Ces cinquante pays ont été choisis en fonction de l'importance du nombre d'étudiants étrangers inscrits et sur la base de la dernière année pour laquelle la distribution par pays d'origine était disponible (pour la majorité des pays, l'année 1977). Les pays indiqués ci-après auraient dû figurer parmi les cinquante pays sélectionnés, mais il n'a pas été possible d'en tenir compte soit parce que la répartition des étudiants étrangers par pays d'origine n'avait pas été communiquée, soit parce que des données plus récentes n'étaient pas disponibles. Il s'agit du Brésil (25 642 étudiants en 1974), du Liban (20 857 étudiants en 1969), de l'U.R.S.S. (30 563 étudiants en 1971) et de l'Inde (7 804 étudiants en 1970).

Il convient de noter que pour quelques pays, les étudiants étrangers sont répartis par continent d'origine et non pas par pays d'origine.

Les étudiants étrangers inscrits dans ces cinquante pays représentent environ 90 % du total mondial connu.

Voir aussi la note d'introduction au tableau 3.14.

Une étude spéciale portant sur les étudiants à l'étranger (*Statistiques des étudiants à l'étranger, 1969-1973*) a été publiée dans le numéro 21 de la collection *Rapports et études statistiques* de l'Unesco.

Este Capítulo facilita datos estadísticos sobre la enseñanza anterior al primer grado, como también sobre las enseñanzas de primero, segundo y tercer grado. También se presentan datos relativos a los sistemas de enseñanza y las tasas de escolarización, al igual que sobre el personal docente y los efectivos, para todos los grados de enseñanza. Se indican asimismo el número de escuelas en las enseñanzas anterior al primer grado y de primer grado, y las cifras relativas a los efectivos y los diplomados de la enseñanza de tercer grado se presentan bajo distintas formas.

El texto que sigue se subdivide en tres secciones, de acuerdo con los tipos de datos que figuran en este Capítulo.

Sección 1.

Esta sección facilita la información, por países, sobre la edad de admisión, la duración y las tasas de escolarización, para los diferentes grados de enseñanza.

Cuadro 3.1

Este cuadro presenta un resumen de datos seleccionados sobre los sistemas de enseñanza actualmente en vigor en 202 países y territorios. La información así procurada debe facilitar una interpretación correcta de las cifras que figuran en los cuadros del *Anuario* correspondientes a la educación.

En las columnas primera y segunda figuran datos relativos a la escolaridad obligatoria. En la primera se precisan los límites de edad inferior y superior. Así, por ejemplo, las cifras 6-14 significan que la ley que instituye la escolaridad obligatoria se aplica sin excepción a los niños de 6 a 14 años de edad. En la segunda columna puede verse el número de años durante los cuales los niños han de asistir a la escuela. Se puede estipular, por ejemplo, que la duración de la enseñanza obligatoria es de 6 años, entre los 6 y los 14 años de edad. En otras palabras, el niño deja de estar sometido a la obligación escolar o bien al cumplir los 14 años o bien cuando termina su sexto año de estudios (aunque sólo tenga entonces 12 ó 13 años).

Ahora bien, en muchos países y territorios el problema más urgente consiste en disponer de un número suficiente de escuelas para todos los niños; la existencia de una ley sobre la escolaridad obligatoria no tiene sino un interés teórico, dado que la mayoría de esas disposiciones eximen a los niños de la asistencia escolar si no existe una escuela a distancia razonable de su domicilio.

La tercera columna indica la edad de admisión de los niños en la enseñanza anterior al primer grado. Para la mayoría de los países, la enseñanza anterior al primer grado sigue dispensándose todavía de un modo limitado generalmente a las zonas urbanas, donde sólo puede beneficiarse de ella una pequeña proporción de los niños de la edad indicada. El diagrama siguiente que comprende las tres columnas muestra para todos los países y territorios una representación gráfica sobre la duración y la edad de admisión en la enseñanza de primer grado y en la enseñanza general de segundo grado, de acuerdo con los sistemas de educación actualmente en vigor. Las informaciones relativas a la enseñanza normal y a la otra enseñanza de segundo grado no se presentan. Las letras 'A' indican la duración del primer grado de enseñanza, las letras 'B' la duración del primer ciclo de la enseñanza general de segundo grado y las letras 'C' la duración del segundo ciclo de la enseñanza general de segundo grado. Es de notar que para algunos países y territorios no existe ninguna distinción entre los dos ciclos de enseñanza general de segundo grado. En tales casos, la duración de este grado de enseñanza se muestra simplemente en las letras 'B'. Además, para un cierto número de países, la edad de admisión y la duración de la enseñanza en estos dos grados pueden variar según la zona o el tipo de escuela. Para estos países, en el diagrama se ha indicado el sistema más corriente. Una nota al final del diagrama señala las otras posibilidades existentes.
nota al final del diagrama señala las otras posibilidades existentes.

Finalmente, en un anexo a este cuadro se precisan los cambios que se han producido en el sistema de enseñanza de un determinado número de países. Este anexo debe consultarse al referirse a los efectivos escolares que figuran en los cuadros 3.3 a 3.9.

Cuadro 3.2

Este cuadro presenta las tasas de escolarización para los años 1970, 1974, 1975, 1976 y 1977 para los países y territorios cuyos datos son disponibles y de una población superior a 250.000 habitantes. Para los países cuya población es inferior a 250.000 habitantes, no se dispone de los datos de población por años de edad simple. Los datos demográficos nos han sido procurados por la División de la Población de la Organización de las Naciones Unidas y la matrícula escolar que ha permitido el cálculo de las tasas de escolarización que figura en los cuadros 3.4, 3.7 y 3.11 del presente *Anuario*. Cuando se disponía de la matrícula por edad relativa a las enseñanzas de primer y de segundo grado, se ha calculado una tasa de escolarización neta. Todas las tasas de escolarización se expresan en porcentaje. La tasa de ecolarización bruta para las enseñanzas de primer y

de segundo grado es la relación entre la matrícula escolar, cualesquiera que sea la edad de los alumnos, y la población de un grupo de edad determinado según la duración de los estudios en cada uno de dichos niveles. El cálculo de la tasa de escolarización neta se basa únicamente en los efectivos cuyos grupos de edad corresponden a la duración de los estudios de primer y de segundo grado. Las tasas se han calculado teniendo en cuenta la diversidad de los sistemas de enseñanza y de la duración de los estudios de primer y de segundo grado. Para la enseñanza de tercer grado, se tomó en consideración el grupo de edad 20-24. Los grupos de edad utilizados para calcular las tasas de escolarización relativas a las enseñanzas de primer y de segundo grado que figuran en el cuadro han sido determinados como sigue:

1. Para los países que tienen un solo sistema de enseñanza para cada grado, el grupo de edad ha sido determinado de acuerdo con la edad normal de admisión y la duración normal de los estudios generales primario y secundario, tal como figuran en el cuadro 3.1.

2. En el caso de los países que tienen varios sistemas de enseñanza de diferente duración, se ha escogido el sistema que se aplica a la mayoría de los alumnos.

3. Cuando no pudo determinarse, en función de los diferentes sistemas de enseñanza, el que se aplicaba a la mayoría de los alumnos, se ha tomado como base el sistema más representativo. Siempre que ha sido necesario calcular un promedio de los diferentes sistemas y que el resultado daba una fracción, la duración se ha redondeado al año inmediatamente superior.

4. Las duraciones de escolaridad consideradas son las que estaban en vigor en los años correspondientes. Sin embargo, en los casos de Malta y de España había una imbricación entre las enseñanzas primaria y secundaria. Como tal imbricación ya ha desaparecido, las tasas de escolarización para los dos países se han calculado de acuerdo con la duración de los estudios que corresponde a la actual estructura del sistema de enseñanza. Para los países federales tales como la República Federal de Alemania y los Estados Unidos de América, las tasas separadas de escolarización para las enseñanzas de primer y de segundo grado han sido suprimidas, ya que son deformadas. En efecto, puede haber imbricación entre las enseñanzas de primer y de segundo grado y existir diferencias de un Estado a otro en lo que se refiere a la duración de los estudios de estos dos grados de enseñanza. Sin embargo, la tasa combinada de enseñanza de escolarización para las enseñanzas de primer y de segundo grado no se ve afectada por estas diferencias. Con respecto a estos dos países, es necesario indicar que la tasa neta de escolarización para la enseñanza de primer grado se estima a 100.

El grupo de edad considerado para el cálculo de la tasa combinada relativa al total de las enseñanzas de primer y de segundo grado queda determinado por los límites extremos del conjunto de los dos grupos de edad, definidos para ambos grados.

Las tasas de escolarización para el segundo grado se fundan en la matrícula global de los tres tipos de enseñanza (general, normal y otra enseñanza de segundo grado). Si se desean más detalles relativos a tales efectivos, puede consultarse el cuadro 3.7. Conviene señalar que la tasa de escolarización bruta comprende los alumnos de todas las edades para las enseñanzas de primer y de segundo grado, mientras que la población considerada se limita a los grupos de edad oficiales, determinados según las normas antes mencionadas. Por consiguiente, en los países donde, para el primer grado, la población de edad escolar está prácticamente escolarizada, la tasa de escolarización bruta sobrepasará 100 si la distribución de los alumnos por edad desborda los límites de edad oficiales.

Sección 2.

Esta sección comprende siete cuadros, 3.3 a 3.9, que se refieren a la enseñanza anterior al primer grado y a las enseñanzas de primero y de segundo grado. Al consultar los cuadros de este capítulo, hay que referirse a las informaciones sobre la duración de la escolaridad, etc. que figuran en el cuadro 3.1 y en su Anexo.

En general, los datos presentados en estos cuadros corresponden a los años 1970, 1974, 1975, 1976 y 1977.

Cuadro 3.3

Los datos se refieren a la enseñanza anterior al primer grado (jardines de la infancia, escuelas maternales y clases de párvulos adscritas a establecimientos docentes de grado superior). En la medida de lo posible, se han excluido las guarderías, centros de juego, etc. Las cifras relativas al personal docente abarcan, en general, el personal que trabaja en régimen de jornada completa y el de jornada parcial. Cuando no se indica otra cosa, los datos comprenden a la vez los establecimientos públicos y los privados. Se indica el porcentaje de la matrícula correspondiente a los establecimientos privados (subvencionados y no subvencionados) con respecto a la matrícula total de la enseñanza anterior al primer grado. Procede, sin embargo, considerar los datos de este cuadro como una indicación mínima de la importancia de la enseñanza anterior al primer grado, ya que no se dispone de datos completos en todos los casos. Para toda información complementaria debe consultarse el cuadro 3.1.

Cuadro 3.4

En general, los datos de este cuadro se refieren a los establecimientos de enseñanza de primer grado, públicos y privados, incluídos los adscritos a establecimientos de segundo grado; quedan excluídas, en cambio, las escuelas y las clases destinadas a los adultos y a los niños deficientes. Al consultar este cuadro, habrá que tener presentes los datos sobre la duración de la escolaridad que figuran en el cuadro 3.1. Las cifras relativas al personal docente, representan, en general, el número total de maestros de jornada completa y de jornada parcial, excluído el personal que no se dedica a la enseñanza (por ejemplo, ciertos directores, los bibliotecarios, los consejeros de orientación profesional, etc.). No ha sido posible comprobar si esta regla se aplica en todos los países.

Cuadro 3.5

La repartición en porcentaje por años de estudio que figura en este cuadro se presenta para la enseñanza de primer grado solamente y se refiere a la matrícula escolar total (MF) y femenina. Siempre que se ha dispuesto de datos, los porcentajes se refieren al año 1970 y siguientes.

En general, los datos de este cuadro se han calculado en función de la duración de la enseñanza de primer grado tal como figura, en relación con cada país y territorio, en el cuadro 3.1.

Cuadro 3.6

El número total y los porcentajes por años de estudio que figuran en este cuadro se han calculado con los datos que nos han facilitado por los países y territorios. Sólo conciernen la enseñanza de primer grado y los repetidores (MF, F) corresponden, cuando se ha dispuesto de datos, al año 1970 y siguientes.

El cálculo de los porcentajes se ha efectuado dividiendo el número de repetidores por la matrícula escolar relativa al mismo año.

Con el fin de asegurar una serie coherente y consistente sobre los repetidores y de facilitar la comparabilidad de estos datos con los de los efectivos por años de estudio presentados en el cuadro 3.5, se han efectuado estimaciones relativas al número de repetidores en las escuelas privadas cuando no se disponía de tales datos. En estos casos, la cantidad que faltaba nunca era superior al 5 % del efectivo total. La identificación de estas estimaciones se ve facilitada con la introducción de un asterisco que figura delante del número de repetidores.

El método de estimación utilizado toma en consideración todas las informaciones disponibles. Por ejemplo, la proporción de los repetidores en las escuelas privadas para los años anteriores se ha utilizado, cuando se dispone de tales datos. Si no se dispone de otra información, los datos relativos a los repetidores se ajustan de acuerdo con la importancia de los efectivos de la enseñanza privada.

Cuadro 3.7

En este cuadro se indican el número y la distribución por sexo del personal docente y de los alumnos matriculados de jornada completa en cada uno de los tres tipos de enseñanza de segundo grado (general, normal y otra enseñanza de segundo grado), al igual que los totales correspondientes. Salvo indicación contraria, los datos comprenden a la vez el personal docente y los alumnos de las escuelas públicas y privadas. Sin embargo, la falta de datos sobre el personal docente explica que para ciertos años no haya sido posible presentar los datos que les conciernen. La matrícula correspondiente a esos mismos años figura no obstante en el presente cuadro.

En la mayoría de los casos, las cifras engloban a los profesores de jornada parcial, cuyo número es particularmente importante en la otra enseñanza de segundo grado. Cabe decir que, en general, cuando el número de profesores parece desproporcionadamente alto comparado con el de los alumnos matriculados, se debe a que las cifras referentes al personal docente comprenden no solamente el personal de jornada completa sino también diversas categorías de personal de jornada parcial. En la medida de lo posible, ha quedado excluido el personal que no ejerce funciones docentes (por ejemplo, bibliotecarios, el personal de orientación, ciertos directores de establecimientos de enseñanza, etc.).

Segundo grado, enseñanza general: En la categoría de 'enseñanza general de segundo grado' se han incluido las 'escuelas de segundo grado' (es decir, las que dan una enseñanza general o especializada que implica cuatro años como mínimo de estudios previos en el primer grado) cuya finalidad no

consiste en preparar directamente a los alumnos para un oficio o una profesión determinada. Esas escuelas, que pueden llamarse escuelas secundarias, escuelas medias, liceos, gimnasios, etc., tienen un plan de estudios que conduce a la obtención de un diploma que es condición indispensable para el ingreso en la enseñanza superior. Bastantes países, para ofrecer otros tipos de formación a los alumnos que no aspiran a cursar estudios superiores, han creado escuelas donde se da una instrucción a la vez general y técnica. Esas escuelas secundarias de carácter mixto se consideran casi siempre como equivalentes a las escuelas secundarias de tipo general y deben ser agrupadas bajo la rúbrica 'enseñanza general de segundo grado'.

Segundo grado, enseñanza normal (formación de personal docente): La expresión 'segundo grado, formación de personal docente', se refiere a la enseñanza en escuelas destinadas a preparar para la profesión docente y cuyo acceso no requiere estudios secundarios completos.

Segundo grado, otra enseñanza: La expresión 'segundo grado, otra enseñanza' se utiliza para designar las 'escuelas de segundo grado' que tienen como finalidad preparar directamente a los alumnos para un oficio o una profesión determinada que no sea la docente. El nombre y el tipo de esas escuelas, varían considerablemente. Son frecuentes los ciclos de estudios de horario parcial y los de breve duración, que en la medida de lo posible han sido excluidos.

Para efectuar comparaciones internacionales, este cuadro debe consultarse conjuntamente con el cuadro 3.1.

Cuadro 3.8

La repartición en porcentaje por años de estudio que figura en este cuadro se presenta para la enseñanza general de segundo grado solamente y se refiere a la matrícula escolar total (MF) y femenina. Siempre que se ha dispuesto de datos, los porcentajes se refieren al año 1970 y siguientes.

En general, los datos de este cuadro se han calculado en función de la duración de la enseñanza general de segundo grado tal como figura, en relación con cada país y territorio, en el cuadro 3.1.

Cuadro 3.9

El número total y los porcentajes por años de estudio que figuran en este cuadro se han calculado con los datos que nos han sido facilitados por los países y territorios. Sólo conciernen la enseñanza general de segundo grado y los repetidores (MF, F) corresponden, cuando se ha dispuesto de datos, al año 1970 y siguientes.

El cáculo de los porcentajes se ha efectuado dividiendo el número de repetidores por la matrícula escolar relativa al mismo año.

Con el fin de asegurar una serie coherente y consistente sobre los repetidores y de facilitar la comparabilidad de estos datos con los de los efectivos por años de estudio presentados en el cuadro 3.8, se han efectuado estimaciones relativas al número de repetidores en las escuelas privadas cuando no se disponía de tales datos. En estos casos, la cantidad que faltaba nunca era superior al 5 % del efectivo total. La identificación de estas estimaciones se ve facilitada con la introducción de un asterisco que figura delante del número de repetidores.

El método de estimación utilizado toma en consideración todas las informaciones disponibles. Por ejemplo, la proporción de los repetidores en las escuelas privadas para los años anteriores se ha utilizado, cuando se dispone de tales datos. Si no se dispone de otra información, los datos relativos a los repetidores se ajustan de acuerdo con la importancia de los efectivos de la enseñanza privada.

Sección 3.

Esta sección comprende seis cuadros estadísticos sobre el desarrollo de la enseñanza de tercer grado en los distintos países del mundo.

Según la definición adoptada por la Unesco, la enseñanza de tercer grado es aquella en la que se exige, como condición mínima de admisión, haber terminado con éxito la enseñanza de segundo grado o demostrar la posesión de conocimientos equivalentes. Puede dispensarse en distintos tipos de establecimientos docentes tales como las universidades, las escuelas normales superiores, las escuelas técnicas superiores, etc.

Los datos presentados en este capítulo corresponden a las siguientes categorías:

Estudiantes: (i) número de estudiantes inscritos por 100.000 habitantes (cuadro 3.10); (ii) número total por tipo de establecimiento (cuadro 3.11) y por nivel de programa y ramas de estudio (cuadro 3.12). Este último cuadro se presenta según los criterios de la clasificación internacional normalizada de la educación (CINE).

Personal docente: número total y por tipo de establecimiento (cuadro 3.11).

Diplomados: distribución por ramas de estudio y según el nivel de los títulos y diplomas obtenidos (cuadro 3.13).

Estudiantes extranjeros: número total y por países de origen (cuadros 3.14 y 3.15).

El cuadro 3.10 presenta el número de estudiantes por 100.000 habitantes. El cuadro 3.11 da el número de los estudiantes y del personal docente por tipo de establecimiento. El cuadro 3.12 presenta la distribución de los estudiantes de la enseñanza de tercer grado por nivel de programa y ramas de estudio. El cuadro 3.13 contiene datos sobre los diplomados de la enseñanza superior.

En la figura 3 que aparece al final del texto puede verse el aumento o la disminución del numero de estudiantes por 100.000 habitantes en los diferentes continentes, regiones o grupos de países. En 1977, esta relación era cuatro veces más elevada en los países desarrollados que en los países en vías de desarrollo. La diferencia entre estos dos grupos de países aumenta sin cese. Por ello, en 1977, el número de estudiantes por 100. 000 habitantes en los países en vías de desarrollo (66) sólo era algo menos de la mitad del número observado en los países desarrollados en 1965. Se constatan igualmente notables diferencias entre las regiones que componen este último grupo de países, comparando las cifras de América septentrional (Canadá y Estados Unidos de América) y de Europa y la U.R.S.S.

La figura 4 muestra la evolución de la parte de los efectivos de sexo femenino en el número total de estudiantes. A nivel mundial, la participación femenina era aproximadamente del 42% en 1977 contra el 35% en 1965. Europa y la U.R.S.S. (46%) y América septentrional (49%) registran actualmente los porcentajes más elevados, seguidos por América Latina (43%). Pese a una marcada progresión en el curso de los dos años considerados, esta proporción sigue siendo inferior al 30% en Africa y en los Estados Arabes. En cuanto a Asia, la progresión ha sido muy débil: 26% en 1965 y 30% en 1977.

Cuadro 3.10

Este cuadro presenta, como una tasa, el número de estudiantes inscritos en la enseñanza de tercer grado por 100 000 habitantes. Las tasas se facilitan para los años 1970, 1974, 1975, 1976 y 1977 y han sido calculadas utilizando los efectivos que figuran en el cuadro 3.11 y las cifras de población que nos han sido comunicadas por la División de la Población de las Naciones Unidas.

Cuadro 3.11

En principio, los datos de este cuadro se refieren al personal docente y a los estudiantes inscritos en todos los establecimientos, públicos y privados, de la enseñanza de tercer grado, para 1970, 1974, 1975, 1976 y 1977. Para la mayoría de los países y territorios, los datos se presentan separadamente por tipos de establecimiento: a) universidades e instituciones equivalentes (que conceden títulos universitarios); b) enseñanza normal (formación de personal docente) de tercer grado, dispensada en establecimientos no universitarios (escuelas normales superiores, etc.); c) otras modalidades de enseñanza de tercer grado, dispensada en centros no universitarios (escuelas técnicas superiores, etc.)

Procede señalar, sin embargo, que los criterios aplicados para determinar los tres tipos de establecimiento puenden no ser exactamente los mismos en cada uno de los países y territorios. Es posible que, en un mismo país, debido a una reforma del sistema de enseñanza, ciertos establecimientos no universitarios queden, de un año para otro,

adscritos a unas universidades o considerados como establecimientos docentes equivalentes. Por todo ello, resulta difícil la comparabilidad internacional, y convendría utilizar con precaución esta distribución por tipo de establecimientos de enseñanza.

En la medida de lo posible, estas estadísticas abarcan a la vez a los profesores y estudiantes de jornada completa y de jornada parcial. Aunque, en general, las estadísticas no comprenden la enseñanza por correspondencia, se la tiene en cuenta en ciertos casos muy precisos (indicados en una nota), a saber, cuando se trata de una enseñanza reconocida como de tercer grado y que desemboca en la obtención de los mismos diplomas que los estudios intramuros. Las cifras relativas al personal docente comprenden, en principio, el personal auxiliar (adjuntos, encargados de prácticas, etc.) pero no el personal que no ejerce funciones docentes (administradores, técnicos de laboratorio, etc.).

Cuadro 3.12

Este cuadro que completa el 3.11, indica el número y la distribución, por sexo y por ramas de estudio, de los estudiantes matriculados en establecimientos de enseñanza superior. Las definiciones utilizadas corresponden a los criterios de la Clasificación Internacional Normalizada de la Educación (CINE).

Ocurre a veces que los datos facilitados son menos completos en el presente cuadro que en el 3.11, ya que no siempre se dispone de la distribución de los estudiantes por ramas de estudio.

Estos diferentes niveles, que se designan aquí según codificación (5, 6 y 7) en la CINE, pueden definirse como sigue:

Nivel 5: Programas que conducen a un diploma que no equivale a un primer grado universitario. Los programas de este tipo suelen ser de orientación 'práctica', y están destinados a preparar a los estudiantes para determinadas ramas profesionales en las que podrán calificarse, como por ejemplo técnicos, maestros, enfermeros, supervisores de producción, etc.

Nivel 6: Programas que conducen a un primer grado universitario o a un diploma equivalente. Figuran igualmente aquí los programas que conducen a los títulos de carácter profesional, tales como el de 'doctor' obtenido al terminar los estudios de medicina, ingeniería, derecho, etc.

Nivel 7: Programas que conducen a un grado universitario superior o a un diploma equivalente. Estos programas se destinan en general a las personas titulares de un primer grado universitario o calificación equivalente. Se trata de programas de estudio postuniversitarios que tienden a la especialización dentro del sector de estudio. Existen dos tipos principales de programas, es decir, los que constituyen una prolongación de programas que desembocan en la obtención de un primer título universitario y que entrañan sobre todo unos cursos, y los que consisten principalmente en la realización de un trabajo original de investigación. Por 'ramas de estudio' se comprende el campo principal de especialización del estudiante. las materias que figuran en cada una de las ramas principales de acuerdo con la clasificación de la CINE son las siguientes:

Grados	Sectores de estudios		
5, 6, 7	14	CIENCIAS DE LA EDUCACION Y FORMACION DE PERSONAL DOCENTE	Programas generales de formación de personal docente, formación de personal docente con especialización en materias profesionales o técnicas, ciencias de la educación.
5, 6, 7	22, 26	HUMANIDADES, RELIGION Y TEOLOGIA	Lenguas y literatura, lingüística, literatura comparada, formación de traductores e intérpretes, historia, arqueología, filosofía. Religión y teología.
5, 6, 7	18	BELLAS ARTES Y ARTES APLICADAS	Estudios artísticos, dibujo y pintura, escultura, artesanía, música, arte dramático, fotografía y cinematografía, decoración, historia y filosofía del arte.
5, 6, 7	38	DERECHO	Derecho, formación de notarios, formación de magistrados locales, jurisprudencia.
5, 6, 7	30	CIENCIAS SOCIALES Y DEL COMPORTAMIENTO	Ciencias sociales y del comportamiento, economía, ciencias políticas, demografía, sociología, antropología, psicología, geografía, estudio de las culturas regionales.
5, 6, 7	34	ENSEÑANZA COMERCIAL Y DE ADMINISTRACION DE EMPRESAS	Administración de empresas y enseñanza comercial, contabilidad, programas de secretaría, manejo de máquinas de oficina y tratamiento electrónico de datos, gestión financiera, administración pública, administración de instituciones.
5, 6, 7	84	DOCUMENTACION Y COMUNICACION SOCIAL	Periodismo, formación de personal de radio y televisión, relaciones públicas, comunicación, bibliotecología, formación de personal técnico de museos y establecimientos análogos, técnicas de la documentación.

5, 6, 7	66	ECONOMIA DOMESTICA (ENSEÑANZA DEL HOGAR)	Artes del hogar, nutrición e investigación sobre el consumo de alimentos y la alimentación familiar.
5	78	FORMACION PARA EL SECTOR DE LOS SERVICIOS	Arte culinario (hotelería y restaurantes), venta al detalle, turismo, otros programas relativos al sector de los servicios.
5, 6, 7	42	CIENCIAS NATURALES	Ciencias biológicas, química, ciencias geológicas, física, astronomía, meteorología, oceanografía.
5, 6, 7	46	MATEMATICAS E INFORMATICA	Programas generales de matemáticas, estadística, ciencia actuarial, informática.
5, 6, 7	50	CIENCIAS MEDICAS, SANIDAD E HIGIENE	Medicina, cirugía y especialidades médicas, higiene y sanidad pública, fisioterapia y ergoterapia; formación de enfermeros y de comadronas, tecnología médica de los rayos X y otras tecnologías del diagnóstico y tratamiento médicos, tecnología médica; odontología y estomatología, tecnología dentaria, farmacia, optometría.
5, 6, 7	54	INGENIERIA Y TECNOLOGIA	Ingeniería química y tecnología de materiales, ingeniería civil, ingeniería eléctrica y electrónica, topografía, organización industrial, ingeniería metalúrgica, ingeniería de minas, ingeniería mecánica, ingeniería agronómica, ingeniería forestal (de montes).
5, 6, 7	58	ARQUITECTURA Y URBANISMO	Arquitectura, urbanismo, arquitectura paisajística.
5	52	ARTES Y OFICIOS INDUSTRIALES	Tratamiento y elaboración de alimentos; oficios de la electricidad, de la electrónica, del metal, oficios relativos a la mecánica, al acondicionamiento de aire; técnicas textiles, artes gráficas, técnicos de laboratorio, fabricación de cristales y lentes ópticos.
5	70	TRANSPORTES Y COMUNICACIONES	Formación de personal para los transportes aéreos, marítimos, por ferrocarril y por carretera; programas relativos a los servicios postales.
5, 6, 7	62	ENSEÑANZA AGRONOMICA, DASONOMICA Y PESQUERA	Agronomía, zootecnía, horticultura, agricultura, economía agraria, tecnología y ciencias de la alimentación, hidrología y edafología, veterinaria, dasonomía, tecnología de los produtos forestales, ciencia y tecnología pesquera (haliéutica).
6	01		Enseñanza general.
5, 6, 7	89	OTROS PROGRAMAS	Criminología, enseñanza militar y programas relativos a la seguridad civil, asistencia social, orientación profesional, educación física, estudios mesológicos, ciencia náutica. Otros programas.

Cuadro 3.13

Este cuadro presenta el número de estudiantes que terminaron sus estudios con éxito, según el nivel del título o diploma obtenido y por ramas de estudio.

En principio, estos títulos y diplomas han sido concedidos al finalizar el año universitario empezado durante el año civil indicado. Por ejemplo, cuando el año universitario no coincide con el año civil, los datos que se indican para 1977 se refieren a los diplomas concedidos al finalizar el año universitario 1977/1978. Para más detalles, sírvanse referirse a la introducción general del capítulo 'Educación'.

Los tres niveles que aquí se indican con los números 5, 6 y 7 se definen como sigue:

Nivel 5. Diplomas y certificados no equivalentes a un primer título universitario concedidos al final de unos estudios superiores de breve duración (en general, menos de tres años). Comprenden, por ejemplo, los certificados concedidos a ciertos tipos de técnicos, los diplomas de enfermera o enfermero, los 'associate degrees', los certificados de competencia jurídica, etc.

Nivel 6. Primeros títulos universitarios o diplomas equivalentes, que sancionan unos estudios superiores de duración normal (en general de 3 a 5 años, y a veces 7). Son los más frecuentes. Comprenden no solamente títulos tan conocidos como la licenciatura, el 'Bachelor's degree', etc., sino también títulos de carácter profesional, como ciertos doctorados que se pueden obtener en algunos países al final de los estudios de medicina, ingeniería, derecho, etc.

Nivel 7. Títulos universitarios superiores o diplomas equivalentes, que pueden obtener, continuando sus estudios, quienes tienen ya un primer título universitario (o un diploma equivalente). Por ejemplo, los diversos diplomas obtenidos después de la preparación de un primer título universitario (diploma de postgraduado), la 'maîtrise' (master's degree), los diversos tipos de doctorado, etc.

En ciertos países, los estudios que desembocan en la obtención de un primer título universitario se dividen en dos ciclos, el primero de los cuales dura 2 años y da a los estudiantes una formación básica, sancionada algunas veces por un diploma.

En general, las estadísticas no toman en cuenta estos diplomas y en los pocos casos en que los países los han considerado han sido clasificados en el nivel 5.

La clasificación según el nivel se ha efectuado con vistas a establecer una distinción entre los diferentes títulos y diplomas y con la esperanza de facilitar la comparabilidad internacional de las estadísticas relativas a los diplomados de la enseñanza de tercer grado. Sin embargo, conviene subrayar que no es indicado proceder a comparaciones excesivas, ya que la clasificación por nivel no implica necesariamente una equivalencia de los títulos o diplomas, ya sea en el propio país o con respecto a otros países.

En lo que se refiere a las materias incluidas en las diversas disciplinas, véase la nota de introducción al cuadro 3.12.

Cuadro 3.14

Se define el estudiante extranjero como una 'persona matriculada en un establecimiento de enseñanza superior de un país o territorio en el que no tiene su domicilio fijo'. Sin embargo, es necesario señalar que la mayoría de países han establecido sus estadísticas sobre los estudiantes extranjeros ateniéndose al concepto de nacionalidad. Las diferencias motivadas por la aplicación de este concepto pueden ser importantes en ciertos países donde las estadísticas toman en consideración, por ejemplo, los inmigrantes que no habiendo adquirido la nacionalidad del país huesped residen sin embargo en el mismo de manera permanente.

Cuadro 3.15

Este cuadro presenta, para cincuenta países huéspedes seleccionados, el número de estudiantes extranjeros matriculados en establecimientos de enseñanza de tercer grado, señalando los países o territorios de origen.

Esos 50 países fueron escogidos en función de la importancia del número de estudiantes extranjeros matriculados y tomando como base el último año para el que se disponía de la distribución por países de origen (en el caso de la mayoría de ellos, se trata de 1977). Los países que se indican a continuación deberían haber figurado entre esos 50 países, pero no fue posible tomarlos en consideración por no conocerse la distribución de los estudiantes extranjeros por países de origen. Se trata de Brasil (25 642 estudiantes en 1974), Líbano (20 857 estudiantes en 1969), URSS (30 563 estudiantes en 1971), y la India (7 804 estudiantes en 1970).

Conviene señalar que para algunos países, los estudiantes extranjeros son repartidos por continente de origen y no por país de origen.

Los estudiantes extranjeros matriculados en esos 50 países equivalen aproximadamente al 90% del total mundial conocido.

Véase también la nota de introducción al cuadro 3.14. Un estudio especial relativo a los estudiantes en el extranjero *Statistiques des étudiants à l'étranger, 1969-1973* ha sido publicado en inglés y en francés en el número 21 de la colección *Informes y estudios estadísticos* de la Unesco.

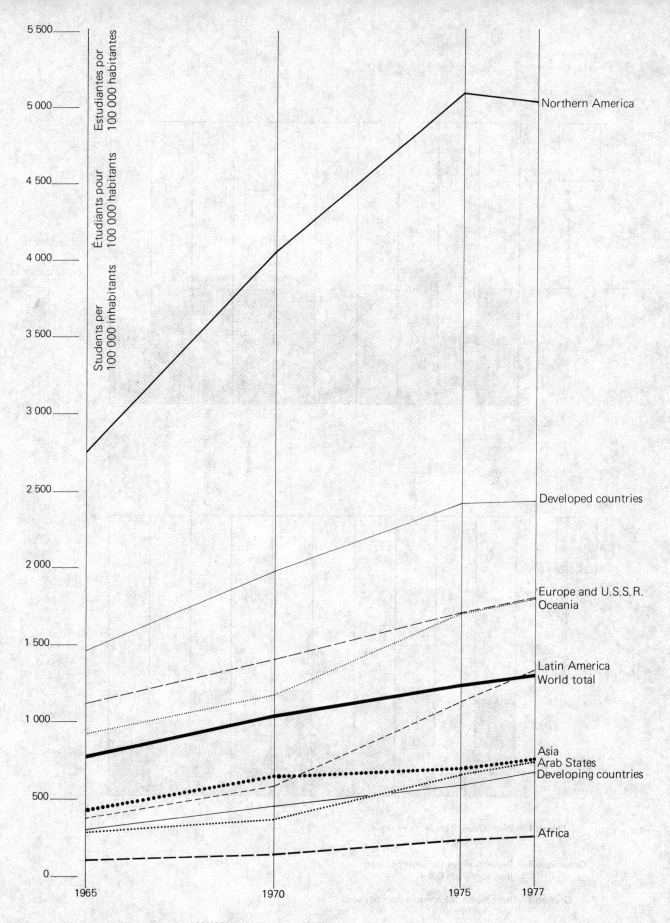

Figure 3 — Number of students per 100,000 inhabitants.
(not including China)

Graphique 3 — Nombre d'étudiants pour 100,000 habitants.
(non compris la Chine)

Gráfico 3 — Número de estudiantes por 100 000 habitantes.
(excluida China)

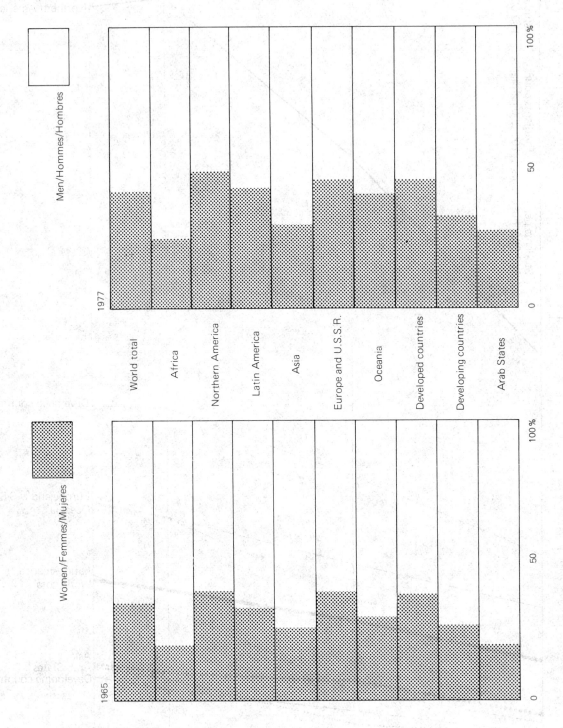

Men/Hommes/Hombres

Women/Femmes/Mujeres

1977

1965

World total

Africa

Northern America

Latin America

Asia

Europe and U.S.S.R.

Oceania

Developed countries

Developing countries

Arab States

100 %

50

0

Figure 4 — Distribution of students by sex.
(not including China)

Graphique 4 — Répartition des étudiants par sexe.
(non compris la Chine)

Gráfico 4 — Repartición de los estudiantes por sexo.
(excluida China)

National education systems **3.1**
Systèmes nationaux d'enseignement
Sistemas nacionales de enseñanza

3.1 National education systems
Systèmes nationaux d'enseignement
Sistemas nacionales de enseñanza

ENTRANCE AGE: FIRST AND SECOND LEVEL GENERAL EDUCATION
AGE D'ADMISSION: ENSEIGNEMENT DU PREMIER DEGRE ET GENERAL DU SECOND DEGRE
EDAD DE ADMISION: ENSEÑANZA DE PRIMER GRADO Y GENERAL DE SEGUNDO GRADO

Legend:
- A—A : FIRST LEVEL / PREMIER DEGRE / PRIMER GRADO
- B—B : SECOND LEVEL / SECOND DEGRE / SEGUNDO GRADO
- C—C : SUB-DIVISION / SOUSDIVISION / SUBDIVISION

COUNTRY / PAYS / PAIS	COMPULSORY EDUCATION — AGE LIMITS / LIMITES D'AGE / LIMITES DE EDAD	DURATION (YEARS) / DUREE (ANNEES) / DURACION (AÑOS)	ENTRANCE AGE TO EDUCATION PRECEDING THE FIRST LEVEL / AGE D'ADMISSION DANS L'ENSEIGNEMENT PRECEDANT LE PREMIER DEGRE / EDAD DE ADMISION EN LA ENSEÑANZA ANTERIOR AL PRIMER GRADO	General education structure (ages 4–20)
AFRICA				4 5 6 7 8 9 10 11 12 13 14 15 16 17 18 19 20
ALGERIA	6–14	8	—	A(6)–A–A–A–A–A B(12)–B–B C(15)–C–C(17)
ANGOLA	6–14	5	3	A(6)–A–A–A–A B(11)–B C(13)–C–C(15)
BENIN	5–12	7	—	A(5)–A–A–A–A–A–A B(12)–B C(14)–C–C(16)
BOTSWANA	—	—	—	A(6)–A–A–A–A–A–A B(13)–B–B C(16)–C(17)
BURUNDI	—	—	4	A(6)–A–A–A–A–A B(12)–B C(14)–C–C–C(17)
CAPE VERDE	6–12	5	4	A(6)–A–A–A–A–A B(12)–B C(14)–C(15)
CENTRAL AFRICAN REPUBLIC	6–14	8	4	A(6)–A–A–A–A–A B(12)–B–B–B C(16)–C(17)
CHAD	8–14	6	4	A(6)–A–A–A–A–A B(12)–B–B–B C(16)–C(17)
COMORO	6–15	9	⋯	A(6)–A–A–A–A–A B(12)–B–B–B C(16)–C(17)

3.1 National education systems
Systèmes nationaux d'enseignement
Sistemas nacionales de enseñanza

ENTRANCE AGE: FIRST AND SECOND LEVEL GENERAL EDUCATION
AGE D'ADMISSION: ENSEIGNEMENT DU PREMIER DEGRE ET GENERAL DU SECOND DEGRE
EDAD DE ADMISION: ENSEÑANZA DE PRIMER GRADO Y GENERAL DE SEGUNDO GRADO

COUNTRY / PAYS / PAIS	Compulsory education / Scolarité obligatoire / Escolaridad obligatoria — Age limits / Limites d'âge / Limites de edad	Duration (years) / Durée (années) / Duración (años)	Entrance age to education preceding the first level / Âge d'admission dans l'enseignement précédant le premier degré / Edad de admisión en la enseñanza anterior al primer grado	Entrance age chart (First level A—A; Second level B—B, C—C; Sub‑division)
CONGO	6–16	10	3	A(6)–A–A–A–A–A–B(12)–B–B–B–C(16)–C–C(18)
DJIBOUTI	—	—	—	A(6)–A–A–A–A–A–A–B(13)–B–B–C(16)–C–C(18)
EGYPT	6–12	6	—	A(6)–A–A–A–A–A–B(12)–B–B–C(15)–C–C(17)
EQUATORIAL GUINEA	6–14	8	2	A(6)–A–A–A–A–A–B(12)–B–C(14)–C–C(16)
ETHIOPIA	—	—	4	A(7)–A–A–A–A–A–B(13)–B–C(15)–C–C(17)
GABON	6–16	10	3	A(6)–A–A–A–A–A–B(12)–B–B–B–C(16)–C–C(18)
GAMBIA	—	—	2	A(7)–A–A–A–A–A–A–B(14)–B–B–C(17)–C(18)
GHANA	6–16	10	—	A(6)–A–A–A–A–A–B(12)–B–C(14)–C–C–C(17)
GUINEA	7–15	8	—	A(7)–A–A–A–A–A–B(13)–B–B–C(16)–C–C(18)
GUINEA–BISSAU	7–12	6	—	A(7)–A–A–A–A–A–B(13)–B–B–C(16)–C(17)
IVORY COAST	—	—	4	A(6)–A–A–A–A–A–B(12)–B–B–B–C(16)–C–C(18)
KENYA	—	—	—	A(6)–A–A–A–A–A–A–B(13)–B–B–C(16)–C(17)
LESOTHO	—	—	…	A(6)–A–A–A–A–A–A–B(13)–B–B–C(16)–C–C(18)
LIBERIA	6–16	11	4	A(6)–A–A–A–A–A–B(12)–B–B–C(15)–C–C(17)
LIBYAN ARAB JAMAHIRIYA	6–15	9	4	A(6)–A–A–A–A–A–B(12)–B–B–C(15)–C–C(17)
MADAGASCAR	6–13	6	3	A(6)–A–A–A–A–A–B(12)–B–B–C(15)–C–C(17)
MALAWI	—	—	—	A(6)–A–A–A–A–A–A–A–B(14)–B–C(16)–C–C(18)
MALI	6–15	9	3	A(7)–A–A–A–A–A–B(13)–B–B–C(16)–C–C(18)
MAURITANIA	6–12	6	—	A(6)–A–A–A–A–A–B(12)–B–B–C(15)–C–C(17)
MAURITIUS	5–12	7	3	A(5)–A–A–A–A–A–A–B(12)–B–B–C(15)–C–C(17)
MOROCCO	…	…	…	A(7)–A–A–A–A–B(12)–B–C(14)–C–C–C(17)
MOZAMBIQUE	6–14	7	3	A(6)–A–A–A–A–B(11)–B–C(13)–C(14)–…–C(17)
NAMIBIA	7–16	9	…	A(7)–A–A–A–A–A–B(13)–B–B–B–B–B–B(20)

National education systems 3.1
Systèmes nationaux d'enseignement
Sistemas nacionales de enseñanza

ENTRANCE AGE: FIRST AND SECOND LEVEL GENERAL EDUCATION
AGE D'ADMISSION: ENSEIGNEMENT DU PREMIER DEGRE ET GENERAL DU SECOND DEGRE
EDAD DE ADMISION: ENSEÑANZA DE PRIMER GRADO Y GENERAL DE SEGUNDO GRADO

COUNTRY / PAYS / PAIS	COMPULSORY EDUCATION — AGE LIMITS / LIMITES D'AGE / LIMITES DE EDAD	COMPULSORY EDUCATION — DURATION (YEARS) / DUREE (ANNEES) / DURACION (AÑOS)	ENTRANCE AGE TO EDUCATION PRECEDING THE FIRST LEVEL / AGE D'ADMISSION DANS L'ENSEIGNEMENT PRECEDANT LE PREMIER DEGRE / EDAD DE ADMISION EN LA ENSEÑANZA ANTERIOR AL PRIMER GRADO	FIRST LEVEL (A—A) ages	SECOND LEVEL (B—B) ages	SUB-DIVISION (C—C) ages
NIGER	7-15	8	4	6–12	13–16	17–18
NIGERIA	6-11	6	2	6–11	12–16	17
REUNION	6-16	10	2	6–10	11–12	13–17
RWANDA	7-13	6	—	7–12	13–15	16–17
ST. HELENA	5-15	10	3	5–11	12–15	16–17
SAO TOME AND PRINCIPE	6-12	6	5	6–11	12–15	16
SENEGAL	6-12	5	...	6–11	12–13	14–18
SEYCHELLES	—	—	4	5–9	10–12	13–15
SIERRA LEONE	—	—	3	5–11	12–14	15–16
SOMALIA	...	...	4	6–9	10–13	14–16
SOUTH AFRICA	7-14	7,9	3	7–11	12–15	16–17
SUDAN	7-12	6	5	7–12	13–14	15–17
SWAZILAND	—	—	—	6–12	13–15	16–17
TOGO	6-12	6	3	6–11	12–15	16–17
TUNISIA	6-15	6	3	6–11	12–14	15–17
UGANDA	—	—	...	6–12	13–14	15–16
UNITED REPUBLIC OF CAMEROON — EASTERN	6-11	6	4	6–11	12–15	16–17
UNITED REPUBLIC OF CAMEROON — WESTERN	—	—	3	6–12	13–16	17–18
UNITED REPUBLIC OF TANZANIA	7-14	7	3	7–13	14–17	
UPPER VOLTA	7-13	7	3	7–12	13–15	16–17
WESTERN SAHARA	6-16	8	4	6–11	12–15	16–17

3.1 National education systems
Systèmes nationaux d'enseignement
Sistemas nacionales de enseñanza

ENTRANCE AGE: FIRST AND SECOND LEVEL GENERAL EDUCATION
AGE D'ADMISSION: ENSEIGNEMENT DU PREMIER DEGRE ET GENERAL DU SECOND DEGRE
EDAD DE ADMISION: ENSEÑANZA DE PRIMER GRADO Y GENERAL DE SEGUNDO GRADO

Legend:
A—A : First level / Premier degré / Primer grado
B—B : Second level / Second degré / Segundo grado
B—B C—C : Sub-division / Sousdivision / Subdivisión

COUNTRY / PAYS / PAIS	COMPULSORY EDUCATION — AGE LIMITS / LIMITES D'AGE / LIMITES DE EDAD	DURATION (YEARS) / DUREE (ANNEES) / DURACION (AÑOS)	ENTRANCE AGE TO EDUCATION PRECEDING THE FIRST LEVEL / AGE D'ADMISSION DANS L'ENSEIGNEMENT PRECEDANT LE PREMIER DEGRE / EDAD DE ADMISION EN LA ENSEÑANZA ANTERIOR AL PRIMER GRADO	Chart (ages 4–20)
ZAIRE	6–11	6	3	A 6-11; B 12-13; C 15-17
ZAMBIA	–	–	3	A 7-13; B 14-16; C 17-18
ZIMBABWE	7–15	8	5	A 7-14; B 15-16; C 17-18
AMERICA, NORTH				
ANTIGUA	5–16	11	–	A 5-15; C 16-17
BAHAMAS	5–14	10	...	A 5-14; B 15-16; C 17
BARBADOS	5–14	9	3	A 5-13; B 14-16; C 17
BELIZE	6–14	8	3	A 6-13; B 14-16; C 17
BERMUDA	5–16	11,12	4	A 5-15; B 16-17; C 18-20
BRITISH VIRGIN ISLANDS	5–15	10	–	A 5-14; B 15-16
CANADA	6–15	8–10	5	A 6-15; B 16-17
CAYMAN ISLANDS	6–14	8	–	A 6-13; B 14-16
COSTA RICA	6–14	9	5	A 6-14; B 15-16; C 17
CUBA	6–14	6	4	A 6-11; B 12-14; C 15-16
DOMINICA	5–15	10	3	A 5-14; B 15-16; C 17
DOMINICAN REPUBLIC	7–14	7	4	A 6-13; B 14-16; C 17
EL SALVADOR	6–18	9	4	A 6-14; B 15-16; B 17-18
GRENADA	5–14	8	3	A 5-13; B 14-16; C 17
GUADELOUPE	6–16	10	2	A 6-15; B 16-17; C 18
GUATEMALA	7–14	6	4	A 6-12; B 13-15; C 16-17
HAITI	6–14	6	2	A 6-12; B 13-15; C 16-18
HONDURAS	6–13	6	4	A 6-12; B 13-15; C 16-18
JAMAICA	6–17	11	4	A 6-12; B 13-15; C 16-18

National education systems 3.1
Systèmes nationaux d'enseignement
Sistemas nacionales de enseñanza

ENTRANCE AGE: FIRST AND SECOND LEVEL GENERAL EDUCATION
AGE D'ADMISSION: ENSEIGNEMENT DU PREMIER DEGRE ET GENERAL DU SECOND DEGRE
EDAD DE ADMISION: ENSEÑANZA DE PRIMER GRADO Y GENERAL DE SEGUNDO GRADO

COUNTRY / PAYS / PAIS	COMPULSORY EDUCATION – AGE LIMITS / LIMITES D'AGE / LIMITES DE EDAD	DURATION (YEARS) / DUREE (ANNEES) / DURACION (AÑOS)	ENTRANCE AGE TO EDUCATION PRECEDING THE FIRST LEVEL / EDAD DE ADMISION EN LA ENSEÑANZA ANTERIOR AL PRIMER GRADO	FIRST LEVEL (A—A) / SECOND LEVEL (B—B) / SUB-DIVISION (B—B C—C) — ages 4–20
MARTINIQUE	6-16	10	2	A(6)–A–A–A–A(10) B(11)–B–B–B–B(15) C(16)–C(17)
MEXICO	6-14	6	3	A(6)–A–A–A–A(10) B(11)–B–B–B(14) C(15)–C–C(17)
MONTSERRAT	5-14	9	3	A(5)–A–A–A–A–A(10) B(11)–B–B–B–B(15) C(16)–C–C(18)
NETHERLANDS ANTILLES	–	–	3	A(6)–A–A–A–A–A(11) B(12)–B–B–B–B(16)
NICARAGUA	7-12	6	5	A(7)–A–A–A–A–A(12) B(13)–B–B(15) C(16)–C–C(18)
PANAMA	6-15	9	4	A(6)–A–A–A–A–A(11) B(12)–B–B(14) C(15)–B–B(17)
FORMER CANAL ZONE	6-14	–	5	A(6)–A–A–A–A–A(11) B(12)–B–B(14) C(15)–B–B(17)
PUERTO RICO	6-18	12	...	A(6)–A–A–A–A–A(11) B(12)–B(13) C(14)–C–C(18)
ST. KITTS-NEVIS-ANGUILLA	5-14	9	3	A(5)–A–A–A–A–A(11) B(12)–B–B–B(15) C(16)–C(17)
ST. LUCIA	5-15	10	–	A(5)–A–A–A–A–A(11) B(12)–B–B(14) C(15)–C(16)
ST. PIERRE AND MIQUELON	7-14	7	2	A(6)–A–A–A–A(10) B(11)–B–B–B(14) C(15)–C–C(17)
ST. VINCENT AND THE GRENADINES	5-15	10	3	A(5)–A–A–A–A–A(11) B(12)–B–B–B(15) C(16)–C(17)
TRINIDAD AND TOBAGO	6-12	7	–	A(6)–A–A–A–A–A(11) B(12)–B–B(14) C(15)–C(16)
TURKS AND CAICOS ISLANDS	4-14	9	...	A(4)–A–A–A–A–A–A–A(11) B(12)–B–B–B–B(16) C(17)–C(18)
UNITED STATES OF AMERICA	7-16	10	3	A(6)–A–A–A–A–A(11) B(12)–B–B(14) C(15)–C–C(17)
U.S. VIRGIN ISLANDS	6-18	12	4	A(6)–A–A–A–A–A(11) B(12)–B–B–B(15) C(16)–C(17)
AMERICA, SOUTH				
ARGENTINA	6-14	7	3	A(6)–A–A–A–A–A(11) B(12)–B–B(14) C(15)–C–C(17)
BOLIVIA	6-14	8	4	A(6)–A–A–A–A(10) B(11)–B–B(13) C(14)–B–B(16)
BRAZIL	7-14	8	4	A(7)–A–A–A–A(11) B(12)–B–B(14) C(15)–B–B(17)

3.1 National education systems
Systèmes nationaux d'enseignement
Sistemas nacionales de enseñanza

ENTRANCE AGE: FIRST AND SECOND LEVEL GENERAL EDUCATION
AGE D'ADMISSION: ENSEIGNEMENT DU PREMIER DEGRE ET GENERAL DU SECOND DEGRE
EDAD DE ADMISION: ENSEÑANZA DE PRIMER GRADO Y GENERAL DE SEGUNDO GRADO

COUNTRY / PAYS / PAIS	Compulsory education AGE LIMITS (LIMITES D'AGE / LIMITES DE EDAD)	DURATION (YEARS / ANNEES / AÑOS)	Entrance age to education preceding the first level	4	5	6	7	8	9	10	11	12	13	14	15	16	17	18	19	20
CHILE	6–15	8	2			A	A	A	A	A	A	A	A	B	B	B	B			
COLOMBIA	7–11	5	5				A	A	A	A	A	B	B	B	C	C				
ECUADOR	6–14	6	4			A	A	A	A	A	A	B	B	B	C	C	C			
FALKLAND ISLANDS (MALVINAS)	5–15	10	–		A	A	A	A	A	A	A	B	B	B	B	B				
FRENCH GUIANA	6–16	10	2			A	A	A	A	A	A	B	B	B	B	C	C			
GUYANA	6–15	8	3			A	A	A	A	A	A	B	B	B	B	B				
PARAGUAY	7–14	6	5				A	A	A	A	A	A	B	B	B	C	C			
PERU	6–14	9	4			A	A	A	A	A	A	B	B	B	B	B	C			
SURINAME	6–12	6	4			A	A	A	A	A	A	B	B	B	C	C				
URUGUAY	6–14	9	3			A	A	A	A	A	A	B	B	B	B	B	B			
VENEZUELA	7–13	6	4				A	A	A	A	A	A	B	B	B	C	C	C		
ASIA																				
AFGHANISTAN	7–15	9	2				A	A	A	A	A	A	B	B	B	B	B			
BAHRAIN	6–14	9	4			A	A	A	A	A	A	B	B	B	C	C	C			
BANGLADESH	–	–	4		A	A	A	A	B	B	B	B	B	C						
BHUTAN	–	–	3			A	A	A	B	B	B	B	B	C						
BRUNEI	5–16	9	...		A	A	A	A	A	B	B	B	B	C	C					
BURMA	–	–	4		A	A	A	A	A	A	B	B	B	B	B					
CHINA	...	...	3			A	A	A	A	A	B	B	B	B						
CYPRUS ‡	5–12	6	3		A	A	A	A	A	A	A	B	B	B	C	C				
DEMOCRATIC KAMPUCHEA	6–11	6	5			A	A	A	A	A	A	B	B	B	C	C	C			
EAST TIMOR	...	...	...			A	A	A	A	A	B	B	B	C	C					
HONG KONG	6–11	6	4			A	A	A	A	A	A	B	B	B	B	C	C			

National education systems 3.1
Systèmes nationaux d'enseignement
Sistemas nacionales de enseñanza

ENTRANCE AGE: FIRST AND SECOND LEVEL GENERAL EDUCATION
AGE D'ADMISSION: ENSEIGNEMENT DU PREMIER DEGRE ET GENERAL DU SECOND DEGRE
EDAD DE ADMISION: ENSEÑANZA DE PRIMER GRADO Y GENERAL DE SEGUNDO GRADO

Legend:
- A—A : FIRST LEVEL / PREMIER DEGRE / PRIMER GRADO
- B—B : SECOND LEVEL / SECOND DEGRE / SEGUNDO GRADO
- C—C : SUB-DIVISION / SOUSDIVISION / SUBDIVISION

Column groups:
- COMPULSORY EDUCATION / SCOLARITE OBLIGATOIRE / ESCOLARIDAD OBLIGATORIA
  - AGE LIMITS / LIMITES D'AGE / LIMITES DE EDAD
  - DURATION (YEARS) / DUREE (ANNEES) / DURACION (AÑOS)
- ENTRANCE AGE TO EDUCATION PRECEDING THE FIRST LEVEL / AGE D'ADMISSION DANS L'ENSEIGNEMENT PRECEDANT LE PREMIER DEGRE / EDAD DE ADMISION EN LA ENSEÑANZA ANTERIOR AL PRIMER GRADO

COUNTRY / PAYS / PAIS	AGE LIMITS	DURATION (YEARS)	ENTRANCE AGE PRECEDING FIRST LEVEL	4	5	6	7	8	9	10	11	12	13	14	15	16	17	18	19	20
INDIA ‡	6-11	5	...			A	A	A	A	A	B	B	B	C	C					
INDONESIA	7-12	6	5			A	A	A	A	A	A	B	B	B	C	C	C			
IRAN	6-14	8	4			A	A	A	A	A	B	B	B	C	C	C	C			
IRAQ	6-11	6	4			A	A	A	A	A	A	B	B	B	C	C	C			
ISRAEL	5-15	11	5			A	A	A	A	A	A	B	B	B	C	C	C			
JAPAN	6-15	9	3			A	A	A	A	A	A	B	B	B	C	C	C			
JORDAN	6-14	9	3			A	A	A	A	A	A	B	B	B	C	C				
KOREA, DEMOCRATIC PEOPLE'S REPUBLIC OF	7-15	8	4			A	A	A	A	B	B	B	B	C	C					
KOREA, REPUBLIC OF	6-12	6	5			A	A	A	A	A	A	B	B	B	C	C	C			
KUWAIT	6-14	8	4			A	A	A	A	B	B	B	B	C	C	C	C			
LAO PEOPLE'S DEMOCRATIC REPUBLIC	7-11	5	3			A	A	A	A	A	B	B	B	C	C	C				
LEBANON	-	-	3			A	A	A	A	A	B	B	B	C	C	C				
MACAU	6-12	5	4			A	A	A	A	A	A	B	B	B	C	C	C			
MALAYSIA																				
PENINSULAR MALAYSIA	-	-	4			A	A	A	A	A	A	B	B	B	C	C	C			
SABAH	6-13	6	4			A	A	A	A	A	A	B	B	B	C	C	C			
SARAWAK	6-12	6	4			A	A	A	A	A	A	B	B	B	C	C	C			
MALDIVES	-	-	3			A	A	A	A	A	B	B	B	C	C	C				
MONGOLIA	8-16	8	3			A	A	A	A	B	B	B	B	C	C	C				
NEPAL ‡	6-10	5	3			A	A	B	B	B	B	B	C	C	C					
OMAN	-	-	5			A	A	A	A	A	A	B	B	B	C	C	C			
PAKISTAN	-	-	3			A	A	A	A	A	B	B	B	C	C	C				
PHILIPPINES	7-12	6	3			A	A	A	A	A	A	A	B	B	C	C				

3.1 National education systems
Systèmes nationaux d'enseignement
Sistemas nacionales de enseñanza

ENTRANCE AGE: FIRST AND SECOND LEVEL GENERAL EDUCATION
AGE D'ADMISSION: ENSEIGNEMENT DU PREMIER DEGRE ET GENERAL DU SECOND DEGRE
EDAD DE ADMISION: ENSEÑANZA DE PRIMER GRADO Y GENERAL DE SEGUNDO GRADO

Legend:
- A—A = FIRST LEVEL / PREMIER DEGRE / PRIMER GRADO
- B—B = SECOND LEVEL / SECOND DEGRE / SEGUNDO GRADO
- B—C = SECOND LEVEL SECOND GRADE / SECOND DEGRE SEGUNDO GRADO
- C—C = SUB-DIVISION / SOUSDIVISION / SUBDIVISION

COUNTRY / PAYS / PAIS	COMPULSORY EDUCATION — AGE LIMITS (LIMITES D'AGE / LIMITES DE EDAD)	COMPULSORY EDUCATION — DURATION (YEARS) (DUREE ANNEES / DURACION AÑOS)	ENTRANCE AGE TO EDUCATION PRECEDING THE FIRST LEVEL	4	5	6	7	8	9	10	11	12	13	14	15	16	17	18	19	20
QATAR	–	–	...																	
SAUDI ARABIA	–	–	4			A	A	A	A	A	A	B	B	B	C	C				
SINGAPORE	–	–	4			A	A	A	A	A	A	B	B	B	B	C				
SRI LANKA	5–15	10	4		A	A	A	A	A	A	B	B	B	B	C	C	C			
SYRIAN ARAB REPUBLIC	6–12	6	5			A	A	A	A	A	A	B	B	B	C	C				
THAILAND	7–15	7	4			A	A	A	A	A	B	B	B	C	C	C	C			
TURKEY	6–14	5	3			A	A	A	A	A	B	B	B	C						
UNITED ARAB EMIRATES	6–12	6	4			A	A	A	A	A	A	B	B	B	C	C	C			
VIET-NAM	...	...	3			A	A	A	A	A	B	B	B	C	C	C				
YEMEN	...	...	3			A	A	A	A	A	A	B	B	B	C	C	C			
YEMEN, DEMOCRATIC	–	–	–			A	A	A	A	A	A	B	B	B	C	C	C			
EUROPE																				
ALBANIA	7–15	8	3			A	A	A	A	A	B	B	B	B	C					
ANDORRA FRENCH SCHOOLS	6–16	10	3			A	A	A	A	A	A	B	B	C	C	C				
SPANISH SCHOOLS	6–15	10	2			A	A	A	A	A	B	B	B	C						
AUSTRIA	6–15	9	3			A	A	A	A	B	B	B	B	C	C					
BELGIUM	6–14	8	3			A	A	A	A	A	A	B	B	C						
BULGARIA	7–14	8	3			A	A	A	A	A	A	B	B	B	C					
CZECHOSLOVAKIA	6–15	9	3			A	A	A	A	A	A	A	B	B	C					
DENMARK	7–16	9	5			A	A	A	A	A	A	B	B	B	B	B	C			
FINLAND	7–16	9	3			A	A	A	A	A	A	B	B	B	C	C				
FRANCE	6–16	10	3			A	A	A	A	A	B	B	B	B	C	C	C			

National education systems   3.1
Systèmes nationaux d'enseignement
Sistemas nacionales de enseñanza

ENTRANCE AGE: FIRST AND SECOND LEVEL GENERAL EDUCATION
AGE D'ADMISSION: ENSEIGNEMENT DU PREMIER DEGRE ET GENERAL DU SECOND DEGRE
EDAD DE ADMISION: ENSEÑANZA DE PRIMER GRADO Y GENERAL DE SEGUNDO GRADO

Column key:
- COMPULSORY EDUCATION / SCOLARITE OBLIGATOIRE / ESCOLARIDAD OBLIGATORIA — AGE LIMITS (LIMITES D'AGE / LIMITES DE EDAD); DURATION (YEARS) / DUREE (ANNEES) / DURACION (AÑOS)
- ENTRANCE AGE TO EDUCATION PRECEDING THE FIRST LEVEL / AGE D'ADMISSION DANS L'ENSEIGNEMENT PRECEDANT LE PREMIER DEGRE / EDAD DE ADMISION EN LA ENSEÑANZA ANTERIOR AL PRIMER GRADO
- FIRST LEVEL / PREMIER DEGRE / PRIMER GRADO = A
- SECOND LEVEL / SECOND DEGRE / SEGUNDO GRADO = B (first degree), C (second degree)
- SUB-DIVISION / SOUS-DIVISION / SUBDIVISION

Country (Pays / Pais)	Age limits	Duration (years)	Entrance age preceding first level	4	5	6	7	8	9	10	11	12	13	14	15	16	17	18	19	20
GERMAN DEMOCRATIC REPUBLIC	6–16	10	3			A	A	A	A	A	A	A	A	A	A		C	C		
GERMANY, FEDERAL REPUBLIC OF ‡	6–15	9	3			A	A	A	A	B	B	B	B	B	B	C	C	C		
GIBRALTAR	4–15	10	3		A	A	A	A	A	A	B	B	B	B	B	C	C			
GREECE	6–12	6	3			A	A	A	A	A	A	B	B	B	C	C	C			
HUNGARY	6–16	10	3			A	A	A	A	A	A	A	A	B	B	B	B			
ICELAND	7–15	8	6				A	A	A	A	A	A	B	B	B	C	C	C		
IRELAND	6–15	9	4			A	A	A	A	A	A	A	B	B	B	C	C			
ITALY	6–14	8	3			A	A	A	A	A	B	B	B	C	C	C	C			
LIECHTENSTEIN	6–14	8	4			A	A	A	A	A	B	B	B	C	C	C				
LUXEMBOURG	6–15	9	4			A	A	A	A	A	A	B	B	B	C	C	C			
MALTA	5–16	8	3		A	A	A	A	A	A	B	B	B	C	C	C				
MONACO	6–16	10	3			A	A	A	A	A	B	B	B	B	C	C	C			
NETHERLANDS	6–16	10	4			A	A	A	A	A	A	B	B	B	C	C	C			
NORWAY	7–16	9	5				A	A	A	A	A	A	B	B	C	C	C			
POLAND	7–15	8	3				A	A	A	A	A	A	A	B	B	B	B	B		
PORTUGAL	6–12	6	3			A	A	A	A	A	A	B	B	B	B	B				
ROMANIA	6–16	10	3			A	A	A	A	A	A	A	A	B	B	C	C			
SAN MARINO	6–14	8	3			A	A	A	A	A	B	B	B	C	C	C	C			
SPAIN	6–15	10	2			A	A	A	A	A	A	A	A	B	B	B	C			
SWEDEN	7–16	9	3				A	A	A	A	A	A	B	B	B	C	C			
SWITZERLAND	6–15	9	4			A	A	A	A	A	B	B	B	B	B	B	C	C		
UNITED KINGDOM	5–16	11	3		A	A	A	A	A	A	B	B	B	B	B	B	B			
YUGOSLAVIA	7–15	8	3				A	A	A	A	A	A	A	B	B	B	C			

3.1 National education systems
Systèmes nationaux d'enseignement
Sistemas nacionales de enseñanza

ENTRANCE AGE: FIRST AND SECOND LEVEL GENERAL EDUCATION
AGE D'ADMISSION: ENSEIGNEMENT DU PREMIER DEGRE ET GENERAL DU SECOND DEGRE
EDAD DE ADMISION: ENSEÑANZA DE PRIMER GRADO Y GENERAL DE SEGUNDO GRADO

COUNTRY / PAYS / PAIS	COMPULSORY EDUCATION — AGE LIMITS / LIMITES D'AGE / LIMITES DE EDAD	COMPULSORY EDUCATION — DURATION (YEARS) / DUREE (ANNEES) / DURACION (AÑOS)	ENTRANCE AGE TO EDUCATION PRECEDING THE FIRST LEVEL / AGE D'ADMISSION DANS L'ENSEIGNEMENT PRECEDANT LE PREMIER DEGRE / EDAD DE ADMISION ANTERIOR AL PRIMER GRADO	Entrance age diagram (ages 4–20)
OCEANIA				
AMERICAN SAMOA	6–18	12	3	A—A—A—A—A—A—B—B—C—C
AUSTRALIA	6–15	9,10	4	A—A—A—A—A—A—A—B—B—C
COOK ISLANDS	6–15	10	3	A—A—A—A—A—A—B—B—C
FIJI	–	–	4	A—A—A—A—A—A—B—B—C
FRENCH POLYNESIA	6–14	8	5	A—A—A—A—A—A—B—B—C—C
GUAM	6–18	12	4	A—A—A—A—A—A—B—B—C—C
KIRIBATI	–	–	4	A—A—A—A—A—A—B—B—C—C
NAURU	6–16	10	4	A—A—A—A—A—A—B—B—C
NEW CALEDONIA	6–14	8	3	A—A—A—A—A—A—B—B—B—C—C
NEW HEBRIDES FRENCH SCHOOLS	–	–	4	A—A—A—A—A—A—B—B—C—C
ENGLISH SCHOOLS	–	–	3	A—A—A—A—A—A—B—B—C
NEW ZEALAND	6–15	9	3	A—A—A—A—A—A—A—B—B—B
NIUE	5–14	8	2	A—A—A—A—A—A—A—A—B—B
NORFOLK ISLAND	5–15	11	–	A—A—A—A—A—A—A—B—B—B
PACIFIC ISLANDS	6–14	8	4	A—A—A—A—A—A—B—B—B—C—C
PAPUA NEW GUINEA	–	–	3	A—A—A—A—A—A—B—B—B—C—C
SAMOA	–	–	3	A—A—A—A—A—A—B—B—C—C
SOLOMON ISLANDS	–	–	3	A—A—A—A—A—A—A—A—B
TOKELAU ISLANDS	5–15	10	2	A—A—A—A—A—A—A—A—B
TONGA	6–14	9	3	A—A—A—A—A—A—B—B—C—C—C

Diagram legend — age axis: 4 5 6 7 8 9 10 11 12 13 14 15 16 17 18 19 20
A—A: FIRST LEVEL / PREMIER DEGRE / PRIMER GRADO
B—B: SECOND LEVEL / SECOND DEGRE / SEGUNDO GRADO
C—C: SUB-DIVISION / SOUSDIVISION / SUBDIVISION

National education systems 3.1
Systèmes nationaux d'enseignement
Sistemas nacionales de enseñanza

COUNTRY / PAYS / PAIS	COMPULSORY EDUCATION / SCOLARITE OBLIGATOIRE / ESCOLARIDAD OBLIGATORIA — AGE LIMITS / LIMITES D'AGE / LIMITES DE EDAD	DURATION (YEARS) / DUREE (ANNEES) / DURACION (AÑOS)	ENTRANCE AGE TO EDUCATION PRECEDING THE FIRST LEVEL / AGE D'ADMISSION DANS L'ENSEIGNEMENT PRECEDANT LE PREMIER DEGRE / EDAD DE ADMISION EN LA ENSEÑANZA ANTERIOR AL PRIMER GRADO	ENTRANCE AGE: FIRST AND SECOND LEVEL GENERAL EDUCATION — 4	5	6	7	8	9	10	11	12	13	14	15	16	17	18	19	20
U.S.S.R.																				
U.S.S.R.	7-17	10	3				A	A	A	A	A	A	A	A	B	B	C			
BYELORUSSIAN S.S.R.	7-17	10	3				A	A	A	A	A	A	A	A	B	B	B			
UKRAINIAN S.S.R.	7-17	10	3				A	A	A	A	A	A	A	A	B	B	B			

FIRST LEVEL / PREMIER DEGRE / PRIMER GRADO: A—A
SECOND LEVEL / SECOND DEGRE / SEGUNDO GRADO: B—B
SUB-DIVISION / SOUSDIVISION / SUBDIVISION: B—C

GENERAL NOTE / NOTE GENERALE / NOTA GENERAL:
E—> FOR CERTAIN COUNTRIES THE EDUCATIONAL STRUCTURE
ALLOWS FOR OTHER ALTERNATIVES: (SEE FOLLOWING TABLE).
FR—> POUR CERTAINS PAYS IL EXISTE D'AUTRES ALTERNATIVES
EN CE QUI CONCERNE LA STRUCTURE DE L'ENSEIGNEMENT: (VOIR
TABLEAU SUIVANT).
ESP> PARA CIERTOS PAISES EXISTEN OTRAS ALTERNATIVAS EN
LO QUE SE REFIERE A LA ESTRUCTURA DE LA ENSEÑANZA: (VEASE
EL CUADRO A CONTINUACION).

CYPRUS:
E—> GREEK EDUCATION ONLY.
FR—> ENSEIGNEMENT GREC SEULEMENT.
ESP> ENSEÑANZA GRIEGA SOLAMENTE.

INDIA:
E—> THIS INFORMATION PERTAINS TO THE MAJORITY OF
STATES.

INDIA (CONT.):
FR—> TOUTES CES INFORMATIONS CONCERNENT LA MAJORITE DES
ETATS.
ESP> TODOS ESTOS DATOS SE REFIEREN A LA MAYORIA DE LOS
ESTADOS.

NEPAL:
E—> ENGLISH SCHOOL SYSTEM.
FR—> SYSTEME D'ENSEIGNEMENT ANGLAIS.
ESP> SISTEMA INGLES DE ENSEÑANZA.

GERMANY, FEDERAL REPUBLIC OF:
E—> NOT INCLUDING 3 YEARS OF COMPULSORY PART-TIME
VOCATIONAL EDUCATION.
FR—> COMPTE NON TENU DE TROIS ANNEES OBLIGATOIRES
D'ENSEIGNEMENT TECHNIQUE A TEMPS PARTIEL.
ESP> EXCLUIDOS TRES AÑOS OBLIGATORIOS DE ENSEÑANZA
TECNICA EN REGIMEN DE JORNADA PARCIAL.

3.1 **National education systems**
Systèmes nationaux d'enseignement
Sistemas nacionales de enseñanza

COUNTRY / PAYS / PAIS	AGE LIMITS FOR COMPULSORY EDUCATION / LIMITES D'AGE SCOLARITE OBLIGATOIRE / LIMITES DE EDAD ESCOLARIDAD OBLIGATORIA	ENTRANCE AGE / AGE D'ADMISSION / EDAD DE ADMISION		DURATION (YEARS) / DUREE (ANNEES) / DURACION (AÑOS)	
		1ST LEVEL / 1ER DEGRE / 1ER GRADO	2ND LEVEL (GENERAL) / 2EME DEGRE (GENERAL) / 2NDO GRADO (GENERAL)	1ST LEVEL / 1ER DEGRE / 1ER GRADO	2ND LEVEL (GENERAL) / 2EME DEGRE (GENERAL) / 2NDO GRADO (GENERAL)
AFRICA					
CONGO	6–17				
DJIBOUTI			12		
EQUATORIAL GUINEA				8	
MADAGASCAR	7–14	7			
NIGERIA				7	
SAO TOME AND PRINCIPE			10,12		
SOUTH AFRICA	7–15 7–16				
UNITED REPUBLIC OF CAMEROON (EASTERN/ORIENTAL)				7	
AMERICA, NORTH					
ANTIGUA				7	
BELIZE					4+4
BRITISH VIRGIN ISLANDS				8	
CANADA	6–16 7–14 7–15 7–16				3+4
HONDURAS					3+2
PUERTO RICO			13	8	2+4
ST. KITTS–NEVIS– ANGUILLA					5+2
UNITED STATES OF AMERICA			13	8	4
U.S. VIRGIN ISLANDS			14	8	2+4
AMERICA, SOUTH					
ARGENTINA					3+3 3+4
SURINAME					2+3
ASIA					
CHINA				5	
CYPRUS				7	
HONG KONG					3+2
ISRAEL			14	8	3+3
JAPAN					3+4

National education systems 3.1
Systèmes nationaux d'enseignement
Sistemas nacionales de enseñanza

COUNTRY	AGE LIMITS FOR COMPULSORY EDUCATION	ENTRANCE AGE AGE D'ADMISSION EDAD DE ADMISION		DURATION (YEARS) DUREE (ANNEES) DURACION (AÑOS)	
		1ST LEVEL	2ND LEVEL (GENERAL)	1ST LEVEL	2ND LEVEL (GENERAL)
PAYS	LIMITES D'AGE SCOLARITE OBLIGATOIRE	1ER DEGRE	2EME DEGRE (GENERAL)	1ER DEGRE	2EME DEGRE (GENERAL)
PAIS	LIMITES DE EDAD ESCOLARIDAD OBLIGATORIA	1ER GRADO	2NDO GRADO (GENERAL)	1ER GRADO	2NDO GRADO (GENERAL)
MALDIVES					3+2
VIET-NAM					4+3
EUROPE					
ANDORRA (SPANISH SCHOOLS) (ECOLES ESPAGNOLES) (ESCUELAS ESPAÑOLAS)					4+4
AUSTRIA					4+5
GERMANY, FEDERAL REPUBLIC OF				4–9	4–6+3
GREECE					3+4
LIECHTENSTEIN					5+3
NETHERLANDS					4+2
SPAIN					4+4
SWEDEN					3+2
SWITZERLAND				4–6	4+4
					3+5
UNITED KINGDOM SCOTLAND			12	7	4–6
YUGOSLAVIA					4+2
OCEANIA					
AUSTRALIA	6–16	5		7	4+2
GUAM					2+4
KIRIBATI				6–9	
NEW HEBRIDES (FRENCH SCHOOLS) (ECOLES FRANCAISES) (ESCUELAS FRANCESAS)				7	
U.S.S.R.					
U.S.S.R.		14			2
BYELORUSSIAN S.S.R.		14			2
UKRAINIAN S.S.R.		14			2

3.1 National education systems
Systèmes nationaux d'enseignement
Sistemas nacionales de enseñanza

ANNEX   : STRUCTURAL CHANGES IN EDUCATIONAL SYSTEMS SINCE 1960
ANNEXE : CHANGEMENTS DE STRUCTURE DANS LES SYSTEMES D'ENSEIGNEMENT DEPUIS 1960
ANEXO   : CAMBIOS DE ESTRUCTURA EN LOS SISTEMAS DE ENSEÑANZA DESDE 1960

COUNTRY	YEAR OF CHANGE	FIRST LEVEL OF EDUCATION ENSEIGNEMENT DU PREMIER DEGRE ENSEÑANZA DE PRIMER GRADO		GENERAL EDUCATION AT THE SECOND LEVEL ENSEIGNEMENT GENERAL DU SECOND DEGRE ENSEÑANZA GENERAL DE SEGUND GRADO	
PAYS	ANNEE DU CHANGEMENT	DURATION (YEARS) DUREE (ANNEES) DURACIÓN (AÑOS)		DURATION (YEARS) DUREE (ANNEES) DURACIÓN (AÑOS)	
PAIS	AÑO DEL CAMBIO	FROM DE	TO A	FROM DE	TO A
AFRICA					
BURUNDI	1973	7	6	3+3	3+3
GUINEA	1964	4	6	5+3	3+3
LESOTHO	1971	8	7	3+2	3+2
MALAWI	1963	5	8	4+2	4+2
	1975	5	8	4+2	2+2
MALI	1962	6	5	3+3	4+3
	1969	5	6	4+3	3+3
MAURITANIA	1968	6	7	4+3	4+3
RWANDA	1969	7	6	6	4+3
SOMALIA	1976	4	6	4+4	4
SUDAN	1970	4	6	8	3+3
UGANDA	1963	6	6	2+4	2+3
	1968	6	7	2+3	4+2
UNITED REPUBLIC OF TANZANIA	1967	8	7	4+2	4+2
ZAMBIA	1966	8	7	4	3+2
AMERICA, NORTH					
EL SALVADOR	1971	6	9	5	2
	1973	6	9	2	3
PANAMA ‡	1975	6	9	3+3	3
AMERICA, SOUTH					
BOLIVIA	1969	6	8	6	4
BRAZIL	1971	4	8	7	3
CHILE	1967	6	8	3+3	4
ASIA					
AFGHANISTAN ‡	1975	6	8	6	4
BAHRAIN ‡	1977	6	6	2+3	3+3
IRAN	1972	6	5	3+3	3+3
	1977	5	5	3+3	3+4

National education systems 3.1
Systèmes nationaux d'enseignement
Sistemas nacionales de enseñanza

COUNTRY	YEAR OF CHANGE	FIRST LEVEL OF EDUCATION ENSEIGNEMENT DU PREMIER DEGRE ENSEÑANZA DE PRIMER GRADO		GENERAL EDUCATION AT THE SECOND LEVEL ENSEIGNEMENT GENERAL DU SECOND DEGRE ENSEÑANZA GENERAL DE SEGUND GRADO	
PAYS	ANNEE DU CHANGEMENT	DURATION (YEARS) DUREE (ANNEES) DURACIÓN (AÑOS)		DURATION (YEARS) DUREE (ANNEES) DURACIÓN (AÑOS)	
PAIS	AÑO DEL CAMBIO	FROM DE	TO A	FROM DE	TO A
LAO PEOPLE'S DEMOCRATIC REP	1976	6	5	4+3	3+3
MONGOLIA	1972	4	3	6	5+2
NEPAL	1971	5	3	5	4+3
SRI LANKA	1970	8	5	3	4+2
	1978	5	6	4+2	5+2
YEMEN, DEMOCRATIC	1968	4	6	7	3+3
EUROPE					
ALBANIA	1966	7	8	5	4
MALTA	1970	6,9	6	5+2	5+2
NORWAY	1972	7	6	3+3	3+3
POLAND	1966	7	8	4	4
SPAIN	1972	5,8	5	3+4	3+4

PANAMA:
  E—> STRUCTURAL CHANGES ARE BEING GRADUALLY
APPLIED.
  FR—> LES CHANGEMENTS DE STRUCTURE SONT MIS
GRADUELLEMENT EN APPLICATION.
  ESP> LOS CAMBIOS DE ESTRUCTURA SE PONEN
PAULATINAMENTE EN APLICACION.

AFGHANISTAN:
  E—> STRUCTURAL CHANGES ARE BEING GRADUALLY
APPLIED.
  FR—> LES CHANGEMENTS DE STRUCTURE SONT MIS
GRADUELLEMENT EN APPLICATION.
  ESP> LOS CAMBIOS DE ESTRUCTURA SE PONEN
PAULATINAMENTE EN APLICACION.

BAHRAIN:
  E—> STRUCTURAL CHANGES ARE BEING GRADUALLY
APPLIED.
  FR—> LES CHANGEMENTS DE STRUCTURE SONT MIS
GRADUELLEMENT EN APPLICATION.
  ESP> LOS CAMBIOS DE ESTRUCTURA SE PONEN
PAULATINAMENTE EN APLICACION.

School enrolment ratios 3.2
Taux d'inscription scolaire
Tasas de escolarización

3.2 Enrolment ratios for the first, second and third levels of education

Taux d'inscription dans les enseignements du premier, du second et du troisième degré

Tasas de escolarización para las enseñanzas de primero, segundo y tercer grado

NUMBER OF COUNTRIES AND
TERRITORIES PRESENTED IN
THIS TABLE: 146

NOMBRE DE PAYS ET DE
TERRITOIRES PRESENTES DANS
CE TABLEAU: 146

NUMERO DE PAISES Y DE
TERRITORIOS PRESENTADOS
EN ESTE CUADRO: 146

			ENROLMENT RATIOS / TAUX D'INSCRIPTION / TASAS DE ESCOLARIZACION					
COUNTRY	YEAR	SEX	FIRST LEVEL		SECOND LEVEL		1ST + 2ND LEVELS	3RD LEVEL
PAYS	ANNEE	SEXE	PREMIER DEGRE		SECOND DEGRE		1ER + 2ND DEGRE	3EME DEGRE
PAIS	AÑO	SEXO	PRIMER GRADO		SEGUNDO GRADO		1ER + 2DO GRADO	3ER GRADO
			GROSS BRUT BRUTA	NET NET NETA	GROSS BRUT BRUTA	NET NET NETA	GROSS BRUT BRUTA	GROSS BRUT BRUTA

AFRICA

ALGERIA	1970		(6–11)		(12–18)		(6–18)	(20–24)
		MF	79	...	12	11	48	2.07
		M	97	...	16	15	59	3.41
		F	61	...	7	6	35	0.84
	1974							
		MF	93	77	18	...	57	2.84
		M	111	91	23	...	69	4.36
		F	74	63	12	...	45	1.31
	1975							
		MF	96	79	20	...	59	3.07
		M	114	93	26	...	71	4.66
		F	77	65	14	...	47	1.44
	1976							
		MF	98	81	23	...	61	3.68
		M	116	94	29	...	73	5.54
		F	80	68	16	...	49	1.74
	1977							
		MF	99	82	27	23	64	4.20
		M	116	94	34	29	76	6.33
		F	82	70	19	17	51	1.95
	1978							
		MF	99	82	29	...	64	...
		M	114	93	36	...	76	...
		F	82	70	22	...	53	...
ANGOLA	1970		(6– 9)		(10–14)		(6–14)	(20–24)
		MF	73	...	9	...	40	0.49
		M	94	...	11	...	51	0.60
		F	51	...	7	...	29	0.39

3.2 School enrolment ratios
Taux d'inscription scolaire
Tasas de escolarización

COUNTRY	YEAR	SEX	ENROLMENT RATIOS / TAUX D'INSCRIPTION / TASAS DE ESCOLARIZACION				1ST + 2ND LEVELS	3RD LEVEL
			FIRST LEVEL		SECOND LEVEL			
PAYS	ANNEE	SEXE	PREMIER DEGRE		SECOND DEGRE		1ER + 2ND DEGRE	3EME DEGRE
PAIS	AÑO	SEXO	PRIMER GRADO		SEGUNDO GRADO		1ER + 2DO GRADO	3ER GRADO
			GROSS BRUT BRUTA	NET NET NETA	GROSS BRUT BRUTA	NET NET NETA	GROSS BRUT BRUTA	GROSS BRUT BRUTA
ANGOLA (CONT.)	1972							
		MF	82	...	12	...	45	0.61
		M	104	...	13	...	57	0.69
		F	59	...	10	...	34	0.52
BENIN	1970		(6–11)		(12–18)		(6–18)	(20–24)
		MF	40	...	5	...	23	0.14
		M	55	...	8	...	32	0.26
		F	25	...	3	...	14	0.02
	1974		(5–10)		(11–17)		(5–17)	(20–24)
		MF	51	...	9	...	31	0.76
		M	70	...	13	...	43	1.31
		F	32	...	5	...	19	0.23
	1975							
		MF	53	...	10	...	32	0.82
		M	74	...	14	...	45	1.41
		F	33	...	5	...	20	0.24
	1976							
		MF	...	...	...	...	...	0.88
		M	...	...	...	...	...	1.51
		F	...	...	...	...	...	0.26
	1977							
		MF	52	...	11	...	32	1.02
		M	71	...	15	...	45	1.73
		F	33	...	6	...	20	0.32
	1978							
		MF	59	...	11	...	36	1.16
		M	80	...	16	...	50	1.93
		F	37	...	6	...	22	0.41
	1979							
		MF	60	...	12	...	37	...
		M	78	...	18	...	49	...
		F	42	...	7	...	25	...
BOTSWANA	1970		(7–13)		(14–18)		(7–18)	(20–24)
		MF	66	...	7	...	45	–
		M	62	...	8	...	43	–
		F	70	...	6	...	47	–
	1974		(6–12)		(13–17)		(6–17)	(20–24)
		MF	71	55	15	10	51	0.48
		M	65	50	14	9	47	0.69
		F	78	60	15	11	55	0.29
	1975							
		MF	78	63	16	12	55	0.75
		M	70	57	16	10	50	1.09
		F	85	69	17	13	60	0.45
	1976							
		MF	82	68	18	13	58	0.82
		M	73	61	17	11	53	1.15
		F	90	74	19	15	64	0.53

School enrolment ratios 3.2
Taux d'inscription scolaire
Tasas de escolarización

COUNTRY	YEAR	SEX	ENROLMENT RATIOS / TAUX D'INSCRIPTION / TASAS DE ESCOLARIZACION					
			FIRST LEVEL		SECOND LEVEL		1ST + 2ND LEVELS	3RD LEVEL
PAYS	ANNEE	SEXE	PREMIER DEGRE		SECOND DEGRE		1ER + 2ND DEGRE	3EME DEGRE
PAIS	AÑO	SEXO	PRIMER GRADO		SEGUNDO GRADO		1ER + 2DO GRADO	3ER GRADO
			GROSS BRUT BRUTA	NET NET NETA	GROSS BRUT BRUTA	NET NET NETA	GROSS BRUT BRUTA	GROSS BRUT BRUTA
BOTSWANA (CONT.)	1977							
		MF	87	73	20	14	62	1.13
		M	78	66	18	12	56	1.59
		F	95	80	21	16	68	0.74
	1978							
		MF	89	75	20	14	64	...
		M	80	68	19	12	58	...
		F	98	82	21	16	70	...
BURUNDI	1970		(6–12)		(13–18)		(6–18)	(20–24)
		MF	27	...	2	...	17	0.15
		M	37	...	3	...	23	0.30
		F	18	...	1	...	11	0.02
	1974		(6–11)		(12–17)		(6–17)	(20–24)
		MF	21	...	3	...	13	0.24
		M	26	...	4	...	16	0.44
		F	16	...	2	...	9	0.05
	1975							
		MF	20	...	3	2	12	0.29
		M	25	...	4	2	16	Q.53
		F	16	...	2	1	9	0.07
	1976							
		MF	20	...	2	...	12	...
		M	24	...	3	...	15	...
		F	16	...	2	...	9	...
	1977							
		MF	21	...	3	...	13	...
		M	26	...	3	...	16	...
		F	17	...	2	...	10	...
	1978							
		MF	21	...	3	...	13	...
		M	26	...	4	...	16	...
		F	17	...	2	...	10	...
CENTRAL AFRICAN REPUBLIC	1970		(5–10)		(11–17)		(5–17)	(20–24)
		MF	65	45	4	4	35	0.06
		M	88	59	7	6	49	0.11
		F	42	32	2	1	22	0.00
	1974		(6–11)		(12–18)		(6–18)	(20–24)
		MF	75	...	7	...	42	0.20
		M	100	...	12	...	57	0.38
		F	51	...	2	...	27	0.02
	1975							
		MF	75	...	8	...	42	0.38
		M	97	...	13	...	56	0.73
		F	54	...	3	...	29	0.04
	1976							
		MF	78	54	9	...	44	0.37
		M	101	70	14	...	58	0.69
		F	55	39	3	...	29	0.05

3.2 School enrolment ratios
Taux d'inscription scolaire
Tasas de escolarización

			ENROLMENT RATIOS / TAUX D'INSCRIPTION / TASAS DE ESCOLARIZACION					
COUNTRY	YEAR	SEX	FIRST LEVEL		SECOND LEVEL		1ST + 2ND LEVELS	3RD LEVEL
PAYS	ANNEE	SEXE	PREMIER DEGRE		SECOND DEGRE		1ER + 2ND DEGRE	3EME DEGRE
PAIS	AÑO	SEXO	PRIMER GRADO		SEGUNDO GRADO		1ER + 2DO GRADO	3ER GRADO
			GROSS BRUT BRUTA	NET NET NETA	GROSS BRUT BRUTA	NET NET NETA	GROSS BRUT BRUTA	GROSS BRUT BRUTA
CENTRAL AFRICA REPUBLIC (CONT.)	1977							
		MF	78	...	...	...	...	0.56
		M	101	...	...	...	...	1.06
		F	55	...	...	...	...	0.08
CHAD	1970		(6–11)		(12–18)		(6–18)	(20–24)
		MF	35	...	2		19	—
		M	52	...	4	...	28	—
		F	17	...	0.30	...	9	—
	1974							
		MF	33	25	2	...	18	0.15
		M	49	36	4	...	27	0.28
		F	18	14	0.46	...	9	0.01
	1975							
		MF	35	...	3	...	19	0.16
		M	51	...	5	...	28	0.30
		F	18	...	1	...	9	0.02
	1976							
		MF	35	25	3	...	19	0.21
		M	51	37	6	...	29	0.41
		F	19	14	1	...	10	0.02
COMORO	1970		(6–11)		(12–18)		(6–18)	(20–24)
		MF	33	...	3	...	19	—
		M	46	...	4	...	26	—
		F	21	...	1	...	11	—
	1973							
		MF	48	...	7	...	28	—
		M	66	...	11	...	39	—
		F	30	...	3	...	17	—
CONGO	1970		(6–11)		(12–18)		(6–18)	(20–24)
		MF	130	...	20	...	77	1.75
		M	147	...	28	...	89	3.38
		F	114	...	12	...	64	0.17
	1974							
		MF	149	...	45	...	99	2.73
		M	162	...	59	...	112	5.08
		F	137	...	32	...	86	0.45
	1975							
		MF	151	100	51	43	103	2.87
		M	162	100	66	54	115	5.25
		F	140	100	37	31	90	0.56
	1976							
		MF	152		59		107	...
		M	162	...	75	...	120	...
		F	142	...	44	...	94	...
	1977							
		MF	154	100	65	...	111	...
		M	162	100	81	...	123	...
		F	146	100	49	...	99	...

School enrolment ratios   3.2
Taux d'inscription scolaire
Tasas de escolarización

			ENROLMENT RATIOS / TAUX D'INSCRIPTION / TASAS DE ESCOLARIZACION					
COUNTRY	YEAR	SEX	FIRST LEVEL		SECOND LEVEL		1ST + 2ND LEVELS	3RD LEVEL
PAYS	ANNEE	SEXE	PREMIER DEGRE		SECOND DEGRE		1ER + 2ND DEGRE	3EME DEGRE
PAIS	AÑO	SEXO	PRIMER GRADO		SEGUNDO GRADO		1ER + 2DO GRADO	3ER GRADO
			GROSS BRUT BRUTA	NET NET NETA	GROSS BRUT BRUTA	NET NET NETA	GROSS BRUT BRUTA	GROSS BRUT BRUTA
CONGO (CONT.)	1978							
		MF	156	100	69	...	114	...
		M	163	100	85	...	125	...
		F	148	100	53	...	102	...
EGYPT	1970		(5–10)		(11–16)		(5–16)	(20–24)
		MF	70	58	33	24	53	8.05
		M	85	70	44	32	67	11.63
		F	54	45	21	15	39	4.34
	1974		(6–11)		(12–17)		(6–17)	(20–24)
		MF	73	...	40	...	58	12.67
		M	88	...	53	...	72	17.63
		F	56	...	28	...	43	7.52
	1975							
		MF	73	...	43	...	59	13.72
		M	89	...	55	...	73	18.84
		F	57	...	30	...	44	8.40
	1976							
		MF	73	...	45	...	60	14.47
		M	89	...	57	...	74	19.80
		F	57	...	32	...	45	8.92
	1977							
		MF	73	...	46	...	60	...
		M	88	...	58	...	74	...
		F	57	...	34	...	46	...
	1978							
		MF	74	...	47	...	61	...
		M	88	...	60	...	74	...
		F	58	...	35	...	47	...
EQUATORIAL GUINEA	1970		(6–12)		(13–18)		(6–18)	(20–24)
		MF	63	...	16	...	43	—
		M	71	...	25	...	52	—
		F	55	...	8	...	35	—
	1973							
		MF	67	...	...	...	...	—
		M	74	...	...	...	...	—
		F	60	...	...	...	...	—
	1975							
		MF	...	...	11	...	...	—
		M	...	...	19	...	...	—
		F	...	...	4	...	...	—
ETHIOPIA	1970		(7–12)		(13–18)		(7–18)	(20–24)
		MF	16	...	4	...	11	0.21
		M	23	...	6	...	15	0.39
		F	10	...	2	...	7	0.03
	1974							
		MF	22	...	6	...	15	0.29
		M	30	...	9	...	20	0.53
		F	14	...	3	...	9	0.05

3.2 School enrolment ratios
Taux d'inscription scolaire
Tasas de escolarización

			ENROLMENT RATIOS / TAUX D'INSCRIPTION / TASAS DE ESCOLARIZACION					
COUNTRY	YEAR	SEX	FIRST LEVEL		SECOND LEVEL		1ST + 2ND LEVELS	3RD LEVEL
PAYS	ANNEE	SEXE	PREMIER DEGRE		SECOND DEGRE		1ER + 2ND DEGRE	3EME DEGRE
PAIS	AÑO	SEXO	PRIMER GRADO		SEGUNDO GRADO		1ER + 2DO GRADO	3ER GRADO
			GROSS BRUT BRUTA	NET NET NETA	GROSS BRUT BRUTA	NET NET NETA	GROSS BRUT BRUTA	GROSS BRUT BRUTA
ETHIOPIA (CONT.)	1975							
		MF	...	...	...	...	...	0.30
		M	...	...	...	...	...	0.55
		F	...	...	...	...	...	0.06
	1976							
		MF	...	...	...	...	...	0.31
		M	...	...	...	...	...	0.57
		F	...	...	...	...	...	0.06
	1977							
		MF	...	...	...	...	...	0.41
		M	...	...	...	...	...	0.76
		F	...	...	...	...	...	0.08
GABON	1970		(6—11)		(12—18)		(6—18)	(20—24)
		MF	164	...	15	...	88	0.41
		M	172	...	21	...	95	0.71
		F	156	...	9	...	80	0.12
	1974							
		MF	192	100	31	...	109	2.28
		M	198	100	40	...	116	4.07
		F	186	100	23	...	102	0.52
	1975							
		MF	202	...	33	...	115	2.33
		M	208	...	44	...	123	3.72
		F	197	...	23	...	107	0.95
	1976							
		MF	202	...	34	...	116	2.83
		M	207	...	44	...	123	4.68
		F	198	...	25	...	109	1.01
GAMBIA	1970		(6—11)		(12—18)		(6—18)	(20—24)
		MF	24	20	7	7	16	—
		M	33	28	11	11	23	—
		F	14	12	4	4	9	—
	1974		(8—13)		(14—19)		(8—19)	(20—24)
		MF	29	19	10	...	20	—
		M	39	26	14	...	28	—
		F	19	12	5	...	13	—
	1975							
		MF	31	20	10	7	22	—
		M	42	27	15	10	30	—
		F	21	13	5	3	14	—
	1976							
		MF	31	26	11	7	22	—
		M	43	36	16	11	30	—
		F	20	16	6	4	14	—
	1977							
		MF	33	31	11	7	23	—
		M	44	42	15	10	31	—
		F	21	20	7	5	15	—

School enrolment ratios 3.2
Taux d'inscription scolaire
Tasas de escolarización

COUNTRY	YEAR	SEX	ENROLMENT RATIOS / TAUX D'INSCRIPTION / TASAS DE ESCOLARIZACION				1ST + 2ND LEVELS	3RD LEVEL
			FIRST LEVEL		SECOND LEVEL		1ER + 2ND DEGRE	3EME DEGRE
PAYS	ANNEE	SEXE	PREMIER DEGRE		SECOND DEGRE		1ER + 2DO GRADO	3ER GRADO
PAIS	AÑO	SEXO	PRIMER GRADO		SEGUNDO GRADO			
			GROSS BRUT BRUTA	NET NET NETA	GROSS BRUT BRUTA	NET NET NETA	GROSS BRUT BRUTA	GROSS BRUT BRUTA
GAMBIA (CONT.)	1978							
		MF	37	36	12	...	26	–
		M	50	48	17	...	35	–
		F	24	23	7	...	16	–
GHANA	1970		(6–15)		(16–19)		(6–19)	(20–24)
		MF	64	...	14	...	52	0.76
		M	73	...	21	...	61	1.31
		F	54	...	8	...	43	0.21
	1974		(6–11)		(12–19)		(6–19)	(20–24)
		MF	66	...	32	...	49	0.98
		M	74	...	39	...	57	1.57
		F	57	...	25	...	41	0.40
	1975							
		MF	70	...	32	...	51	1.07
		M	80	...	40	...	60	1.82
		F	61	...	24	...	42	0.34
	1976							
		MF	71	...	32	...	51	...
		M	81	...	40	...	60	...
		F	62	...	24	...	43	...
	1977							
		MF	71	...	32	...	51	...
		M	80	...	39	...	59	...
		F	61	...	24	...	43	...
GUINEA	1970		(7–12)		(13–18)		(7–18)	(20–24)
		MF	33	...	13	...	24	0.58
		M	45	...	21	...	34	1.07
		F	21	...	5	...	14	0.09
	1971							
		MF	28	...	14	...	22	0.57
		M	39	...	21	...	31	1.06
		F	18	...	6	...	13	0.09
GUINEA–BISSAU	1970		(6–11)		(12–16)		(6–16)	(20–24)
		MF	44	...	9	...	29	–
		M	61	...	11	...	39	–
		F	27	...	6	...	18	–
	1974							
		MF	73	...	5	...	44	–
		M	96	...	7	...	59	–
		F	49	...	3	...	30	–
	1975							
		MF	75	45	4	4	46	–
		M	103	58	6	6	62	–
		F	48	32	3	3	29	–

3.2 School enrolment ratios
Taux d'inscription scolaire
Tasas de escolarización

			ENROLMENT RATIOS / TAUX D'INSCRIPTION / TASAS DE ESCOLARIZACION					
COUNTRY	YEAR	SEX	FIRST LEVEL		SECOND LEVEL		1ST + 2ND LEVELS	3RD LEVEL
PAYS	ANNEE	SEXE	PREMIER DEGRE		SECOND DEGRE		1ER + 2ND DEGRE	3EME DEGRE
PAIS	AÑO	SEXO	PRIMER GRADO		SEGUNDO GRADO		1ER + 2DO GRADO	3ER GRADO
			GROSS BRUT BRUTA	NET NET NETA	GROSS BRUT BRUTA	NET NET NETA	GROSS BRUT BRUTA	GROSS BRUT BRUTA
GUINEA–BISSAU (CONT.)	1976							
		MF	113	67	6	2	69	—
		M	152	86	9	2	93	—
		F	74	49	3	1	45	—
	1977							
		MF	112	66	10	10	71	—
		M	152	83	16	15	97	—
		F	72	48	4	4	45	—
IVORY COAST	1970		(6–11)		(12–18)		(6–18)	(20–24)
		MF	63	...	9	8	36	0.87
		M	81	...	14	12	47	1.38
		F	46	...	4	3	25	0.27
	1974	MF	65		11		39	1.12
		M	82	...	17	...	51	1.74
		F	48	...	6	...	28	0.40
	1975							
		MF	65	...	13	...	40	1.18
		M	82	...	19	...	51	1.83
		F	49	...	6	...	28	0.43
	1976							
		MF	68	50	13	...	42	1.40
		M	84	61	20	...	54	2.15
		F	51	38	6	...	30	0.53
	1977							
		MF	71		14	...	44	1.51
		M	88	...	21	...	56	2.34
		F	54	...	7	...	32	0.57
	1978							
		MF	...	...	15	...	...	1.79
		M	...	...	...	...	...	2.77
		F	...	...	...	...	...	0.68
KENYA	1970		(5–11)		(12–17)		(5–17)	(20–24)
		MF	60	...	8	...	39	0.88
		M	70	...	12	...	47	1.51
		F	49	...	5	...	32	0.25
	1974							
		MF	98	...	11	...	63	1.01
		M	107	...	15	...	71	1.71
		F	88	...	8	...	56	0.31
	1975							
		MF	100	76	13	8	65	1.08
		M	108	80	16	10	72	1.84
		F	92	71	9	7	59	0.33
	1976							
		MF	97	72	15	10	64	1.13
		M	104	75	19	12	70	1.92
		F	90	69	11	9	58	0.35

School enrolment ratios   3.2
Taux d'inscription scolaire
Tasas de escolarización

COUNTRY	YEAR	SEX	ENROLMENT RATIOS / TAUX D'INSCRIPTION / TASAS DE ESCOLARIZACION				1ST + 2ND LEVELS	3RD LEVEL
			FIRST LEVEL		SECOND LEVEL			
PAYS	ANNEE	SEXE	PREMIER DEGRE		SECOND DEGRE		1ER + 2ND DEGRE	3EME DEGRE
PAIS	AÑO	SEXO	PRIMER GRADO		SEGUNDO GRADO		1ER + 2DO GRADO	3ER GRADO
			GROSS BRUT BRUTA	NET NET NETA	GROSS BRUT BRUTA	NET NET NETA	GROSS BRUT BRUTA	GROSS BRUT BRUTA
KENYA (CONT.)	1977							
		MF	95	71	16	12	64	...
		M	101	74	20	13	69	...
		F	89	68	12	10	59	...
	1978							
		MF	99	...	18	...	67	...
		M	105	...	22	...	73	...
		F	94	...	14	...	62	...
LESOTHO	1970		(6—13)		(14—18)		(6—18)	(20—24)
		MF	89	68	7	5	61	0.47
		M	71	52	6	4	49	0.62
		F	108	83	7	6	73	0.32
	1974		(6—12)		(13—17)		(6—17)	(20—24)
		MF	109	...	13	...	73	0.58
		M	87	...	12	...	59	0.68
		F	131	...	14	...	87	0.48
	1975							
		MF	108	...	13	...	72	...
		M	88	...	12	...	59	...
		F	129	...	15	...	86	...
	1976							
		MF	105	71	14	10	71	...
		M	86	57	12	8	58	...
		F	125	86	16	13	84	...
LIBERIA	1970		(6—11)		(12—17)		(6—17)	(20—24)
		MF	53	...	9	...	34	0.98
		M	71	...	15	...	46	1.56
		F	35	...	4	...	21	0.42
	1974							
		MF	57	...	14	...	38	1.66
		M	74	...	21	...	50	2.53
		F	41	...	7	...	26	0.80
	1975							
		MF	59	...	16	...	40	1.91
		M	75	...	24	...	53	2.91
		F	42	...	8	...	27	0.92
	1976							
		MF	54	...	14	...	36	...
		M	70	...	21	...	48	...
		F	38	...	7	...	24	...
	1978							
		MF	64	...	20	...	45	...
		M	80	...	29	...	57	...
		F	48	...	11	...	32	...
LIBYAN ARAB JAMAHIRIYA	1970		(6—11)		(12—17)		(6—17)	(20—24)
		MF	111	86	21	13	70	3.03
		M	136	100	33	20	90	5.08
		F	84	71	8	6	50	0.70

3.2 School enrolment ratios
Taux d'inscription scolaire
Tasas de escolarización

			ENROLMENT RATIOS / TAUX D'INSCRIPTION / TASAS DE ESCOLARIZACION					
COUNTRY	YEAR	SEX	FIRST LEVEL		SECOND LEVEL		1ST + 2ND LEVELS	3RD LEVEL
PAYS	ANNEE	SEXE	PREMIER DEGRE		SECOND DEGRE		1ER + 2ND DEGRE	3EME DEGRE
PAIS	AÑO	SEXO	PRIMER GRADO		SEGUNDO GRADO		1ER + 2DO GRADO	3ER GRADO
			GROSS BRUT BRUTA	NET NET NETA	GROSS BRUT BRUTA	NET NET NETA	GROSS BRUT BRUTA	GROSS BRUT BRUTA
LIBYAN ARAB JAMAHIRIYA (CONT.)	1974							
		MF	137	100	44	35	97	5.81
		M	146	100	59	46	108	9.26
		F	128	100	28	23	84	1.94
	1975							
		MF	138	100	55	45	102	6.26
		M	145	100	71	56	113	9.78
		F	131	100	38	33	91	2.33
	1976							
		MF	134	100	64	51	104	6.19
		M	139	100	80	63	114	9.49
		F	128	100	47	38	94	2.53
	1977							
		MF	127	100	69	...	103	6.57
		M	131	100	82	...	111	10.10
		F	123	100	55	...	94	2.68
	1978							
		MF	123	...	67	...	100	...
		M	128	...	80	...	108	...
		F	119	...	54	...	92	...
MADAGASCAR	1970		(6–11)		(12–18)		(6–18)	(20–24)
		MF	88	...	11	...	50	1.03
		M	95	...	13	...	55	1.42
		F	81	...	9	...	45	0.64
	1974							
		MF	88	...	12	...	51	1.46
		M	95	...	14	...	55	2.01
		F	81	...	10	...	46	0.93
	1975							
		MF	94	...	12	...	54	1.53
		M	100	...	14	...	58	2.10
		F	87	...	10	...	50	0.97
	1976							
		MF	...	...	...	...	...	1.72
		M	...	...	...	...	...	2.24
		F	...	...	...	...	...	1.22
	1977							
		MF	...	...	...	...	...	2.25
		M	...	...	...	...	...	2.91
		F	...	...	...	...	...	1.60
	1978							
		MF	100	...	...	...	...	...
MALAWI	1970		(5–12)		(13–18)		(5–18)	(20–24)
		MF	35	...	2	...	23	0.26
		M	45	...	3	...	30	0.43
		F	26	...	1	...	17	0.09

School enrolment ratios 3.2
Taux d'inscription scolaire
Tasas de escolarización

			ENROLMENT RATIOS / TAUX D'INSCRIPTION / TASAS DE ESCOLARIZACION					
COUNTRY	YEAR	SEX	FIRST LEVEL		SECOND LEVEL		1ST + 2ND LEVELS	3RD LEVEL
PAYS	ANNEE	SEXE	PREMIER DEGRE		SECOND DEGRE		1ER + 2ND DEGRE	3EME DEGRE
PAIS	AÑO	SEXO	PRIMER GRADO		SEGUNDO GRADO		1ER + 2DO GRADO	3ER GRADO
			GROSS BRUT BRUTA	NET NET NETA	GROSS BRUT BRUTA	NET NET NETA	GROSS BRUT BRUTA	GROSS BRUT BRUTA
MALAWI (CONT.)	1974							
		MF	53	...	3	...	34	0.27
		M	64	...	4	...	42	0.47
		F	41	...	1	...	26	0.07
	1975		(5-12)		(13-16)		(5-16)	(20-24)
		MF	53	...	4	...	39	0.26
		M	65	...	5	...	48	0.46
		F	42	...	2	...	31	0.06
	1976							
		MF	53	...	4	...	39	0.26
		M	64	...	5	...	48	0.45
		F	43	...	2	...	31	0.06
	1977							
		MF	53	35	4	...	39	0.24
		M	63	40	5	...	47	...
		F	42	30	2	...	31	...
MALI	1970		(6-11)		(12-17)		(6-17)	(20-24)
		MF	24	15	5	3	16	0.17
		M	31	19	8	5	21	0.30
		F	17	11	2	2	10	0.04
	1974							
		MF	26	...	6	...	17	0.51
		M	33	...	10	...	23	0.93
		F	19	...	3	...	12	0.09
	1975							
		MF	27	...	7	...	18	0.59
		M	34	...	11	...	24	1.08
		F	19	...	4	...	12	0.12
	1976							
		MF	27	19	8	...	18	0.70
		M	35	...	12	...	24	1.27
		F	20	...	4	...	13	0.15
	1977							
		MF	28	...	9	...	19	0.80
		M	36	...	13	...	26	1.44
		F	20	...	5	...	13	0.19
	1978							
		MF	28	...	...	...	...	...
		M	36	...	...	...	...	...
		F	20	...	...	...	0..	...
MAURITANIA	1970		(6-12)		(13-19)		(6-19)	(20-24)
		MF	14	...	2	...	8	—
		M	20	...	3	...	13	—
		F	8	...	0.42	...	4	—
	1974							
		MF	17	...	3	...	11	—
		M	25	...	6	...	16	—
		F	9	...	1	...	6	—

3.2 School enrolment ratios
Taux d'inscription scolaire
Tasas de escolarización

			ENROLMENT RATIOS / TAUX D'INSCRIPTION / TASAS DE ESCOLARIZACION					
COUNTRY	YEAR	SEX	FIRST LEVEL		SECOND LEVEL		1ST + 2ND LEVELS	3RD LEVEL
PAYS	ANNEE	SEXE	PREMIER DEGRE		SECOND DEGRE		1ER + 2ND DEGRE	3EME DEGRE
PAIS	AÑO	SEXO	PRIMER GRADO		SEGUNDO GRADO		1ER + 2DO GRADO	3ER GRADO
			GROSS BRUT BRUTA	NET NET NETA	GROSS BRUT BRUTA	NET NET NETA	GROSS BRUT BRUTA	GROSS BRUT BRUTA
MAURITANIA (CONT.)	1975							
		MF	19	...	4	...	12	–
		M	24	...	7	...	16	–
		F	13	...	1	...	8	–
	1976							
		MF	23	...	4	...	15	–
		M	32	...	7	...	21	–
		F	15	...	1	...	9	–
	1977							
		MF	26	...	5	...	16	0.37
		M	34	...	9	...	23	0.67
		F	17	...	1	...	10	0.07
MAURITIUS	1970		(5–10)		(11–17)		(5–17)	(20–24)
		MF	106	...	31	...	68	2.64
		M	108	...	37	...	72	5.01
		F	105	...	25	...	64	0.25
	1974							
		MF	110	85	39	35	72	1.51
		M	110	85	44	38	75	2.54
		F	109	85	35	32	69	0.47
	1975							
		MF	109	84	41	36	72	1.21
		M	110	84	45	39	75	2.08
		F	109	83	37	33	70	0.33
	1976							
		MF	106	82	43	39	72	1.49
		M	107	82	47	41	74	2.46
		F	105	82	39	36	70	0.51
	1977							
		MF	105	86	50	44	75	1.56
		M	106	86	53	47	77	2.33
		F	104	85	46	42	72	0.78
	1978							
		MF	104	81	51	...	75	...
		M	105	81	53	...	77	...
		F	103	81	49	...	73	...
MOROCCO	1970		(7–11)		(12–18)		(7–18)	(20–24)
		MF	52	40	13	...	32	1.52
		M	67	...	18	...	42	2.67
		F	36	...	7	...	22	0.48
	1974							
		MF	57	44	14	...	34	2.59
		M	73	55	18	...	43	4.25
		F	41	32	10	...	25	0.95
	1975							
		MF	62	47	16	14	37	3.22
		M	78	58	21	17	47	5.19
		F	45	35	12	10	27	1.21

School enrolment ratios 3.2
Taux d'inscription scolaire
Tasas de escolarización

			ENROLMENT RATIOS / TAUX D'INSCRIPTION / TASAS DE ESCOLARIZACION					
COUNTRY	YEAR	SEX	FIRST LEVEL		SECOND LEVEL		1ST + 2ND LEVELS	3RD LEVEL
PAYS	ANNEE	SEXE	PREMIER DEGRE		SECOND DEGRE		1ER + 2ND DEGRE	3EME DEGRE
PAIS	AÑO	SEXO	PRIMER GRADO		SEGUNDO GRADO		1ER + 2DO GRADO	3ER GRADO
			GROSS BRUT BRUTA	NET NET NETA	GROSS BRUT BRUTA	NET NET NETA	GROSS BRUT BRUTA	GROSS BRUT BRUTA
MOROCCO (CONT.)	1976							
		MF	66	50	17	14	39	...
		M	83	62	22	18	49	...
		F	48	37	13	11	29	...
	1977							
		MF	69	53	19	15	41	4.24
		M	87	66	23	19	52	6.51
		F	51	39	14	12	31	1.81
	1978							
		MF	72	54	20	16	44	...
		M	90	67	25	20	54	...
		F	54	41	15	13	33	...
MOZAMBIQUE	1970		(6—10)		(11—15)		(6—15)	(20—24)
		MF	47	...	5	...	28	0.29
		M	62	...	6	...	37	0.32
		F	31	...	4	...	19	0.25
	1972							
		MF	51	40	6	3	30	0.37
		M	67	52	7	3	40	0.41
		F	34	28	5	3	21	0.33
	1976							
		MF	...	...	...	...	...	0.12
		M	...	...	...	...	...	0.17
		F	...	...	...	...	...	0.08
NIGER	1970		(7—12)		(13—19)		(7—19)	(20—24)
		MF	14	...	1	...	8	—
		M	18	...	2	...	10	—
		F	9	...	1	...	5	—
	1974							
		MF	16	...	2	...	9	0.09
		M	21	...	3	...	12	0.17
		F	12	...	1	...	7	0.02
	1975							
		MF	19	...	2	2	11	0.14
		M	25	...	3	3	14	0.25
		F	13	...	1	1	7	0.03
	1976							
		MF	21	18	3	2	12	0.19
		M	27	...	4	3	16	0.33
		F	15	...	1	1	8	0.05
	1977							
		MF	22	19	3	...	13	0.19
		M	29	...	4	...	17	0.32
		F	16	...	2	...	9	0.06
	1978							
		MF	23	...	...	...	...	...
		M	29	...	...	...	...	...
		F	17	...	...	...	...	...

3.2 School enrolment ratios
Taux d'inscription scolaire
Tasas de escolarización

			ENROLMENT RATIOS / TAUX D'INSCRIPTION / TASAS DE ESCOLARIZACION					
COUNTRY	YEAR	SEX	FIRST LEVEL		SECOND LEVEL		1ST + 2ND LEVELS	3RD LEVEL
PAYS	ANNEE	SEXE	PREMIER DEGRE		SECOND DEGRE		1ER + 2ND DEGRE	3EME DEGRE
PAIS	AÑO	SEXO	PRIMER GRADO		SEGUNDO GRADO		1ER + 2DO GRADO	3ER GRADO
			GROSS BRUT BRUTA	NET NET NETA	GROSS BRUT BRUTA	NET NET NETA	GROSS BRUT BRUTA	GROSS BRUT BRUTA
NIGERIA	1970		(6–12)		(13–17)		(6–17)	(20–24)
		MF	32	...	6	...	23	0.46
		M	41	...	8	...	29	0.79
		F	24	...	4	...	17	0.13
	1974							
		MF	...	...	...	...	...	0.75
		M	...	...	...	...	...	1.28
		F	...	...	...	...	...	0.22
	1975							
		MF	47	...	...	...	...	0.82
		M	...	...	...	...	...	1.41
		F	...	...	...	...	...	0.25
	1976							
		MF	62	...	13	...	44	1.04
		M	...	...	...	...	...	1.79
		F	...	...	...	...	...	0.32
	1977							
		MF	69	...	...	...	...	1.17
REUNION	1970		(6–10)		(11–17)		(6–17)	(20–24)
		MF	151	...	41	...	92	—
		M	153	...	35	...	90	—
		F	149	...	46	...	94	—
	1974							
		MF	143	...	54	...	93	—
		M	144	...	48	...	91	—
		F	141	...	60	...	96	—
	1975							
		MF	141	...	57	54	94	—
		M	144	...	51	...	92	—
		F	139	...	64	...	96	—
	1976							
		MF	140	...	62	57	95	—
		M	142	...	55	51	92	—
		F	138	...	68	63	98	—
	1977							
		MF	138	...	...	...	...	...
	1978							
		MF	138	...	66	61	95	...
		M	...	...	60	55	...	...
		F	...	...	72	67	...	...
RWANDA	1970		(7–12)		(13–18)		(7–18)	(20–24)
		MF	73	...	2	...	41	0.20
		M	83	...	3	...	47	0.36
		F	64	...	1	...	36	0.04
	1974							
		MF	60	...	2	...	34	0.30
		M	66	...	3	...	38	0.53
		F	54	...	1	...	31	0.07

School enrolment ratios 3.2
Taux d'inscription scolaire
Tasas de escolarización

			ENROLMENT RATIOS / TAUX D'INSCRIPTION / TASAS DE ESCOLARIZACION					
COUNTRY	YEAR	SEX	FIRST LEVEL		SECOND LEVEL		1ST + 2ND LEVELS	3RD LEVEL
PAYS	ANNEE	SEXE	PREMIER DEGRE		SECOND DEGRE		1ER + 2ND DEGRE	3EME DEGRE
PAIS	AÑO	SEXO	PRIMER GRADO		SEGUNDO GRADO		1ER + 2DO GRADO	3ER GRADO
			GROSS BRUT BRUTA	NET NET NETA	GROSS BRUT BRUTA	NET NET NETA	GROSS BRUT BRUTA	GROSS BRUT BRUTA
RWANDA (CONT.)	1975							
		MF	61	...	2	...	35	0.31
		M	66	...	3	...	38	0.55
		F	56	...	1	...	31	0.08
	1976							
		MF	64	58	2	2	36	0.30
		M	68	61	3	3	39	0.56
		F	59	54	1	1	33	0.05
SENEGAL	1970		(6–11)		(12–18)		(6–18)	(20–24)
		MF	38	...	9	...	24	1.37
		M	47	...	13	...	31	2.26
		F	30	...	5	...	18	0.46
	1974							
		MF	39	...	10	...	25	1.83
		M	48	...	14	...	32	3.06
		F	31	...	6	...	19	0.62
	1975							
		MF	39	...	10	...	25	1.94
		M	47	...	14	...	31	3.25
		F	30	...	6	...	18	0.67
	1976							
		MF	...	...	...	...	...	2.04
		M	...	...	...	...	...	3.33
		F	...	...	...	...	...	0.78
	1977							
		MF	41	31	...	...	...	2.10
		M	50	37	...	...	...	3.46
		F	32	25	...	...	...	0.78
SIERRA LEONE	1970		(5–11)		(12–18)		(5–18)	(20–24)
		MF	33	...	9	...	22	0.52
		M	40	...	12	...	28	0.89
		F	26	...	5	...	17	0.17
	1974							
		MF	34	...	11	...	24	0.65
		M	42	...	15	...	30	1.08
		F	27	...	7	...	18	0.23
	1975							
		MF	36	...	11	...	25	0.63
		M	43	...	15	...	31	1.07
		F	28	...	7	...	19	0.20
	1976							
		MF	37	...	12	...	26	0.59
		M	...	...	16	...	...	...
		F	...	...	7	...	...	...
	1977							
		MF	37	...	12	...	26	0.58
		M	45	...	16	...	32	...
		F	30	...	8	...	20	...

3.2 School enrolment ratios
Taux d'inscription scolaire
Tasas de escolarización

			ENROLMENT RATIOS / TAUX D'INSCRIPTION / TASAS DE ESCOLARIZACION					
COUNTRY	YEAR	SEX	FIRST LEVEL		SECOND LEVEL		1ST + 2ND LEVELS	3RD LEVEL
PAYS	ANNEE	SEXE	PREMIER DEGRE		SECOND DEGRE		1ER + 2ND DEGRE	3EME DEGRE
PAIS	AÑO	SEXO	PRIMER GRADO		SEGUNDO GRADO		1ER + 2DO GRADO	3ER GRADO
			GROSS BRUT BRUTA	NET NET NETA	GROSS BRUT BRUTA	NET NET NETA	GROSS BRUT BRUTA	GROSS BRUT BRUTA
SWAZILAND	1970		(6–12)		(13–17)		(6–17)	(20–24)
		MF	86	62	18	12	61	0.58
		M	89	61	21	12	64	0.72
		F	84	62	16	12	59	0.44
	1974							
		MF	97	70	29	19	72	1.46
		M	100	69	32	18	75	1.99
		F	95	71	26	19	70	0.94
	1975							
		MF	99	74	32	21	74	2.45
		M	101	72	35	20	77	3.35
		F	97	75	29	22	72	1.57
	1976							
		MF	99	75	33	23	75	2.41
		M	101	74	36	21	77	3.29
		F	97	76	31	24	73	1.55
	1977							
		MF	100	77	36	25	77	2.97
		M	102	76	39	23	79	3.73
		F	99	78	34	26	75	2.24
	1978							
		MF	101	78	37	...	78	...
		M	102	77	39	...	79	...
		F	100	79	35	...	77	...
TOGO	1970		(6–11)		(12–18)		(6–18)	(20–24)
		MF	69	53	7	6	39	0.52
		M	95	73	11	10	55	0.94
		F	42	33	3	3	24	0.12
	1974							
		MF	88	68	14	...	52	0.84
		M	117	90	22	...	71	1.49
		F	59	46	6	...	34	0.22
	1975							
		MF	94	...	18	...	58	1.19
		M	123	...	28	...	77	2.08
		F	65	...	9	...	38	0.32
	1976							
		MF	99	75	22	...	62	1.36
		M	128	96	34	...	83	2.32
		F	70	54	10	...	41	0.43
	1977							
		MF	102	72	25	...	65	...
		M	129	89	39	...	86	...
		F	75	55	12	...	45	...
	1978							
		MF	...	...	29	...	...	...
		M	...	...	45	...	...	...
		F	...	...	14			

School enrolment ratios 3.2
Taux d'inscription scolaire
Tasas de escolarización

			ENROLMENT RATIOS / TAUX D'INSCRIPTION / TASAS DE ESCOLARIZACION					
COUNTRY	YEAR	SEX	FIRST LEVEL		SECOND LEVEL		1ST + 2ND LEVELS	3RD LEVEL
PAYS	ANNEE	SEXE	PREMIER DEGRE		SECOND DEGRE		1ER + 2ND DEGRE	3EME DEGRE
PAIS	AÑO	SEXO	PRIMER GRADO		SEGUNDO GRADO		1ER + 2DO GRADO	3ER GRADO
			GROSS BRUT BRUTA	NET NET NETA	GROSS BRUT BRUTA	NET NET NETA	GROSS BRUT BRUTA	GROSS BRUT BRUTA
SOMALIA	1970		(6– 9)		(10–17)		(6–17)	(20–24)
		MF	9	...	4	...	6	0.38
		M	14	...	7	...	10	0.67
		F	5	...	2	...	3	0.10
	1975							
		MF	58	22	5	...	23	0.69
		M	76	25	7	...	31	1.24
		F	41	18	2	...	16	0.15
	1976		(6–11)		(12–15)		(6–15)	(20–24)
		MF	45	24	4	...	28	...
		M	58	28	6	...	37	...
		F	32	19	2	...	20	...
	1977							
		MF	44	22	4	...	28	...
		M	57	26	6	...	36	...
		F	32	18	2	...	20	...
SOUTH AFRICA	1970		(6–12)		(13–17)		(6–17)	(20–24)
		MF	99	67	18	...	69	4.51
		M	100	67	18	...	69	6.81
		F	99	68	17	...	68	2.26
	1972							
		MF	105	...	20	...	73	4.72
		M	105	...	20	...	73	7.10
		F	105	...	19	...	73	2.37
SUDAN	1970		(7–12)		(13–18)		(7–18)	(20–24)
		MF	38	...	7	...	24	1.16
		M	46	...	10	...	30	1.97
		F	29	...	4	...	18	0.31
	1974							
		MF	47	...	14	...	32	1.62
		M	61	...	19	...	42	2.63
		F	31	...	8	...	21	0.57
	1975							
		MF	47	...	14	...	32	1.52
		M	59	...	18	...	41	2.50
		F	34	...	9	...	23	0.49
	1976							
		MF	48	...	14	...	33	1.50
		M	59	...	19	...	41	2.36
		F	36	...	9	...	24	0.60
	1977							
		MF	49	...	15	...	34	1.63
		M	57	...	19	...	40	2.52
		F	42	...	10	...	27	0.70
	1978							
		MF	50	...	16	...	35	...
		M	58	...	20	...	41	...
		F	42	...	11	...	28	...

3.2 School enrolment ratios
Taux d'inscription scolaire
Tasas de escolarización

			ENROLMENT RATIOS / TAUX D'INSCRIPTION / TASAS DE ESCOLARIZACION					
COUNTRY	YEAR	SEX	FIRST LEVEL		SECOND LEVEL		1ST + 2ND LEVELS	3RD LEVEL
PAYS	ANNEE	SEXE	PREMIER DEGRE		SECOND DEGRE		1ER + 2ND DEGRE	3EME DEGRE
PAIS	AÑO	SEXO	PRIMER GRADO		SEGUNDO GRADO		1ER + 2DO GRADO	3ER GRADO
			GROSS BRUT BRUTA	NET NET NETA	GROSS BRUT BRUTA	NET NET NETA	GROSS BRUT BRUTA	GROSS BRUT BRUTA
TUNISIA	1970		(6–11)		(12–18)		(6–18)	(20–24)
		MF	100	76	23	...	63	2.87
		M	121	89	33	...	79	4.64
		F	80	62	13	...	47	1.16
	1974							
		MF	96	76	21	...	59	3.03
		M	115	90	28	...	72	4.65
		F	76	62	14	...	45	1.47
	1975							
		MF	97	...	21	17	60	4.23
		M	116	...	28	21	72	6.37
		F	78	...	15	12	47	2.14
	1976							
		MF	99	...	22	...	60	4.52
		M	118	...	28	...	73	6.70
		F	80	...	15	...	48	2.36
	1977							
		MF	100	77	23	20	61	4.96
		M	118	89	29	25	73	7.26
		F	82	65	17	15	49	2.66
	1978							
		MF	100	79	24	22	62	5.05
		M	117	90	30	27	73	7.17
		F	83	67	18	16	50	2.89
UGANDA ‡	1970		(6–12)		(13–18)		(6–18)	(20–24)
		MF	39	...	4	...	25	0.52
		M	48	...	6	...	31	0.86
		F	31	...	2	...	19	0.18
	1974							
		MF	43	...	4	...	27	0.60
		M	52	...	6	...	33	0.98
		F	35	...	2	...	21	0.23
	1975							
		MF	44	...	4	...	28	0.57
		M	51	...	6	...	33	0.94
		F	36	...	2	...	22	0.20
	1976							
		MF	47	...	4	...	30	0.52
		M	55	...	6	...	35	0.83
		F	39	...	2	...	24	0.20
	1977							
		MF	50	...	5	...	32	0.61
		M	58	...	7	...	37	0.92
		F	41	...	2	...	26	0.31
UNITED REPUBLIC OF CAMEROON	1970		(6–11)		(12–18)		(6–18)	(20–24)
		MF	91	63	8	6	50	0.51
		M	105	72	11	9	58	0.95
		F	77	55	4	4	41	0.08

School enrolment ratios   3.2
Taux d'inscription scolaire
Tasas de escolarización

			ENROLMENT RATIOS / TAUX D'INSCRIPTION / TASAS DE ESCOLARIZACION					
COUNTRY	YEAR	SEX	FIRST LEVEL		SECOND LEVEL		1ST + 2ND LEVELS	3RD LEVEL
PAYS	ANNEE	SEXE	PREMIER DEGRE		SECOND DEGRE		1ER + 2ND DEGRE	3EME DEGRE
PAIS	AÑO	SEXO	PRIMER GRADO		SEGUNDO GRADO		1ER + 2DO GRADO	3ER GRADO
			GROSS BRUT BRUTA	NET NET NETA	GROSS BRUT BRUTA	NET NET NETA	GROSS BRUT BRUTA	GROSS BRUT BRUTA
UNITED REPUBLIC OF CAMEROON (CONT.)	1974							
		MF	97	69	12	10	55	0.98
		M	109	76	16	13	63	1.75
		F	86	62	7	6	47	0.23
	1975							
		MF	100	71	13	11	57	1.10
		M	111	78	18	14	65	1.90
		F	88	64	8	7	49	0.33
	1976							
		MF	99	70	15	12	57	1.22
		M	109	77	19	16	65	2.10
		F	88	64	10	8	50	0.36
	1977							
		MF	101	72	16	13	59	1.32
		M	112	79	21	17	67	2.27
		F	91	66	11	9	51	0.39
UNITED REPUBLIC OF TANZANIA	1970		(7–13)		(14–19)		(7–19)	(20–24)
		MF	39	...	3	...	24	0.18
		M	47	...	4	...	30	0.31
		F	31	...	2	...	19	0.06
	1974							
		MF	58	...	3	...	36	0.28
		M	68	...	5	...	43	0.47
		F	49	...	2	...	30	0.08
	1975							
		MF	69	53	3	...	43	0.30
		M	79	...	5	...	49	0.51
		F	60	...	2	...	37	0.09
	1976							
		MF	70	...	4	...	43	0.24
		M	...	...	5	...	...	0.44
		F	...	...	2	...	...	0.04
	1977							
		MF	...	...	...	...	...	0.19
		M	...	...	...	...	...	0.34
		F	...	...	...	...	...	0.03
UPPER VOLTA	1970		(6–11)		(12–18)		(6–18)	(20–24)
		MF	12	9	1	1	7	0.04
		M	16	12	2	2	9	0.07
		F	9	7	1	1	5	0.01
	1974							
		MF	14	...	2	...	8	0.15
		M	18	...	2	...	10	0.24
		F	10	...	1	...	6	0.07
	1975		(7–12)		(13–19)		(7–19)	(20–24)
		MF	15	...	2	...	9	0.21
		M	19	...	3	...	11	0.34
		F	11	...	1	...	6	0.08

3.2 School enrolment ratios
Taux d'inscription scolaire
Tasas de escolarización

			ENROLMENT RATIOS / TAUX D'INSCRIPTION / TASAS DE ESCOLARIZACION					
COUNTRY	YEAR	SEX	FIRST LEVEL		SECOND LEVEL		1ST + 2ND LEVELS	3RD LEVEL
PAYS	ANNEE	SEXE	PREMIER DEGRE		SECOND DEGRE		1ER + 2ND DEGRE	3EME DEGRE
PAIS	AÑO	SEXO	PRIMER GRADO		SEGUNDO GRADO		1ER + 2DO GRADO	3ER GRADO
			GROSS BRUT BRUTA	NET NET NETA	GROSS BRUT BRUTA	NET NET NETA	GROSS BRUT BRUTA	GROSS BRUT BRUTA
UPPER VOLTA (CONT.)	1976							
		MF	15	13	2	...	9	0.26
		M	19	16	3	...	11	0.43
		F	11	9	1	...	6	0.10
	1977							
		MF	16	13	2	...	9	0.23
		M	20	17	3	...	12	0.36
		F	12	10	1	...	7	0.10
	1978							
		MF	17	14	2	...	10	...
		M	21	17	3	...	12	...
		F	12	10	1	...	7	...
ZAIRE	1970		(6–11)		(12–17)		(6–17)	(20–24)
		MF	88	63	9	...	52	0.65
		M	110	76	13	...	67	1.26
		F	65	50	4	...	37	0.07
	1974							
		MF	88	...	14	...	55	1.00
		M	105	...	20	...	67	1.83
		F	71	...	7	...	42	0.19
	1975							
		MF	89	...	15	...	55	...
		M	104	...	21	...	67	...
		F	73	...	8	...	43	...
	1976							
		MF	89	...	17	...	57	...
		M	103	...	22	...	67	...
		F	74	...	11	...	46	...
	1977							
		MF	90	...	19	...	58	...
		M	103	...	23	...	67	...
		F	77	...	14	...	48	...
ZAMBIA	1970		(7–13)		(14–18)		(7–18)	(20–24)
		MF	91	...	13	...	62	0.41
		M	101	...	18	...	71	0.69
		F	80	...	8	...	54	0.12
	1974							
		MF	99	...	14	...	68	1.19
		M	108	...	19	...	76	1.83
		F	89	...	9	...	60	0.56
	1975							
		MF	97	...	15	...	67	2.07
		M	106	...	20	...	75	3.60
		F	88	...	10	...	60	0.57
	1976							
		MF	98	85	16	...	68	2.09
		M	106	90	21	...	76	...
		F	89	80	11	...	61	...

School enrolment ratios 3.2
Taux d'inscription scolaire
Tasas de escolarización

			ENROLMENT RATIOS / TAUX D'INSCRIPTION / TASAS DE ESCOLARIZACION					
COUNTRY	YEAR	SEX	FIRST LEVEL		SECOND LEVEL		1ST + 2ND LEVELS	3RD LEVEL
PAYS	ANNEE	SEXE	PREMIER DEGRE		SECOND DEGRE		1ER + 2ND DEGRE	3EME DEGRE
PAIS	AÑO	SEXO	PRIMER GRADO		SEGUNDO GRADO		1ER + 2DO GRADO	3ER GRADO
			GROSS BRUT BRUTA	NET NET NETA	GROSS BRUT BRUTA	NET NET NETA	GROSS BRUT BRUTA	GROSS BRUT BRUTA
ZAMBIA (CONT.)	1977							
		MF	...	...	16	...	...	2.12
		M	...	...	22	...	...	...
		F	...	...	11	...	...	...
ZIMBABWE	1970		(7–11)		(12–17)		(7–17)	(20–24)
		MF	100	...	8	...	54	0.22
		M	114	...	10	...	62	0.34
		F	86	...	6	...	46	0.10
	1974							
		MF	99	...	9	...	54	...
		M	107	...	11	...	59	...
		F	91	...	7	...	50	...
	1975							
		MF	99	...	9	...	54	...
		M	107	...	11	...	59	...
		F	91	...	7	...	50	...
	1976							
		MF	97	...	9	...	54	...
		M	105	...	11	...	59	...
		F	90	...	7	...	49	...
AMERICA, NORTH								
BARBADOS	1970		(5–10)		(11–17)		(5–17)	(20–24)
		MF	102	86	68	...	85	3.85
		M	104	87	67	...	85	4.10
		F	101	86	69	...	85	3.60
	1974							
		MF	100	...	68	...	83	6.90
		M	106	...	68	...	85	7.76
		F	95	...	69	...	80	6.03
	1975		(5–10)		(11–16)		(5–16)	(20–24)
		MF	101	92	77	72	88	7.41
		M	99	92	75	69	86	8.35
		F	102	93	80	75	90	6.48
	1976							
		MF	109	98	77	73	91	7.94
		M	107	97	74	70	89	8.96
		F	111	99	80	76	94	6.93
	1977							
		MF	116	100	82	78	97	...
		M	115	100	79	75	95	...
		F	116	100	85	80	99	...
CANADA	1970		(6–13)		(14–19)		(6–19)	(20–24)
		MF	101	93	65	...	86	34.59
		M	101	92	65	...	87	41.22
		F	100	93	65	...	86	27.90

3.2 School enrolment ratios
Taux d'inscription scolaire
Tasas de escolarización

			ENROLMENT RATIOS / TAUX D'INSCRIPTION / TASAS DE ESCOLARIZACION					
COUNTRY	YEAR	SEX	FIRST LEVEL		SECOND LEVEL		1ST + 2ND LEVELS	3RD LEVEL
PAYS	ANNEE	SEXE	PREMIER DEGRE		SECOND DEGRE		1ER + 2ND DEGRE	3EME DEGRE
PAIS	AÑO	SEXO	PRIMER GRADO		SEGUNDO GRADO		1ER + 2DO GRADO	3ER GRADO
			GROSS BRUT BRUTA	NET NET NETA	GROSS BRUT BRUTA	NET NET NETA	GROSS BRUT BRUTA	GROSS BRUT BRUTA
CANADA (CONT.)	1974		(6–11)		(12–17)		(6–17)	(20–24)
		MF	98	...	92	...	95	34.47
		M	99	...	92	...	95	38.72
		F	98	...	93	...	95	30.19
	1975							
		MF	99	...	91	...	95	39.31
		M	99	...	90	...	94	43.31
		F	99	...	92	...	95	35.30
	1976							
		MF	100	...	91	...	95	38.65
		M	101	...	90	...	95	40.66
		F	100	...	92	...	96	36.64
	1977							
		MF	101	...	89	...	94	37.66
		M	101	...	88	...	94	38.79
		F	100	...	90	...	95	36.52
COSTA RICA	1970		(6–11)		(12–16)		(6–16)	(20–24)
		MF	110	89	28	22	76	10.55
		M	110	89	27	21	76	11.78
		F	109	88	29	23	76	9.30
	1974							
		MF	109	...	42	35	80	15.89
		M	117	...	40	...	84	17.60
		F	101	...	44	...	76	14.14
	1975							
		MF	107	92	43	...	79	18.27
		M	107	92	40	...	78	20.23
		F	106	92	45	...	79	16.26
	1976							
		MF	108	94	43	36	79	18.28
		M	109	93	41	34	79	20.19
		F	108	94	46	38	80	16.31
	1977							
		MF	109	...	44	...	80	18.53
		M	110	...	41	...	79	20.48
		F	108	...	47	...	81	16.52
	1978							
		MF	107	92	46	...	79	...
		M	108	91	43	...	78	...
		F	107	92	49	...	80	...
CUBA	1970		(6–11)		(12–18)		(6–18)	(20–24)
		MF	121	...	22	...	76	3.66
		M	121	...	21	...	75	4.36
		F	121	...	23	...	76	2.93
	1974							
		MF	124	...	36	...	84	9.07
		M	125	...	37	...	85	11.45
		F	122	...	36	...	83	6.61

School enrolment ratios 3.2
Taux d'inscription scolaire
Tasas de escolarización

			ENROLMENT RATIOS / TAUX D'INSCRIPTION / TASAS DE ESCOLARIZACION					
COUNTRY	YEAR	SEX	FIRST LEVEL		SECOND LEVEL		1ST + 2ND LEVELS	3RD LEVEL
PAYS	ANNEE	SEXE	PREMIER DEGRE		SECOND DEGRE		1ER + 2ND DEGRE	3EME DEGRE
PAIS	AÑO	SEXO	PRIMER GRADO		SEGUNDO GRADO		1ER + 2DO GRADO	3ER GRADO
			GROSS BRUT BRUTA	NET NET NETA	GROSS BRUT BRUTA	NET NET NETA	GROSS BRUT BRUTA	GROSS BRUT BRUTA
CUBA (CONT.)	1975							
		MF	124	...	42	...	85	10.97
		M	126	...	42	...	86	13.84
		F	122	...	42	...	84	...
	1976							
		MF	122	...	51	...	87	14.17
		M	125	...	50	...	88	16.59
		F	119	...	51	...	85	11.68
	1977							
		MF	...	...	...	...	...	16.34
	1978							
		MF	...	...	...	...	...	17.41
DOMINICAN REPUBLIC	1970		(7-12)		(13-18)		(7-18)	(20-24)
		MF	95	...	18	...	62	6.29
		M	95	...	18	...	61	7.08
		F	96	...	18	...	62	5.48
	1974							
		MF	94	...	26	...	64	9.27
		M	94	...	27	...	64	9.81
		F	95	...	26	...	65	8.71
	1975							
		MF	96	...	28	...	65	9.55
		M	95	...	...	...	...	10.60
		F	96	...	...	...	...	8.48
	1976							
		MF	...	...	...	...	...	9.89
		M	...	...	...	...	...	10.99
		F	...	...	...	...	...	8.77
	1977							
		MF	...	...	...	...	...	10.11
		M	...	...	...	...	...	11.16
		F	...	...	...	...	...	9.04
EL SALVADOR	1970		(7-12)		(13-17)		(7-17)	(20-24)
		MF	89	66	22	14	62	3.25
		M	92	67	23	14	64	4.73
		F	85	66	21	14	59	1.73
	1974		(7-15)		(16-18)		(7-18)	(20-24)
		MF	75	...	17	...	63	7.58
		M	77	...	19	...	65	10.46
		F	73	...	15	...	61	4.61
	1975							
		MF	77	...	19	...	65	7.90
		M	79	...	21	...	66	10.36
		F	75	...	17	...	63	5.37
	1976							
		MF	79	...	21	...	66	8.04
		M	80	...	23	...	67	10.47
		F	77	...	19	...	65	5.55

3.2 School enrolment ratios
     Taux d'inscription scolaire
     Tasas de escolarización

			ENROLMENT RATIOS / TAUX D'INSCRIPTION / TASAS DE ESCOLARIZACION					
COUNTRY	YEAR	SEX	FIRST LEVEL		SECOND LEVEL		1ST + 2ND LEVELS	3RD LEVEL
PAYS	ANNEE	SEXE	PREMIER DEGRE		SECOND DEGRE		1ER + 2ND DEGRE	3EME DEGRE
PAIS	AÑO	SEXO	PRIMER GRADO		SEGUNDO GRADO		1ER + 2DO GRADO	3ER GRADO
			GROSS BRUT BRUTA	NET NET NETA	GROSS BRUT BRUTA	NET NET NETA	GROSS BRUT BRUTA	GROSS BRUT BRUTA
EL SALVADOR (CONT.)	1977							
		MF	79	...	23	...	67	7.81
		M	80	...	25	...	68	...
		F	77	...	21	...	65	...
GUADELOUPE	1970		(6–10)		(11–17)		(6–17)	(20–24)
		MF	151	100	51	45	96	...
		M	152	100	44	...	93	...
		F	150	100	58	...	99	...
	1974							
		MF	136	...	68	...	96	...
		M	131	...	64	...	91	...
		F	141	...	74	...	102	...
	1975							
		MF	152	...	69	63	101	...
		M	154	...	64	57	99	...
		F	150	...	73	69	104	...
	1976							
		MF	164	...	71	65	106	...
		M	166	...	67	62	104	...
		F	161	...	75	69	108	...
	1977							
		MF	152	...	...	...	...	...
	1978							
		MF	156	...	77	70	106	...
		M	...	...	71	65	...	...
		F	...	...	84	75	...	...
GUATEMALA	1970		(7–12)		(13–18)		(7–18)	(20–24)
		MF	57	48	10	9	36	3.38
		M	62	52	12	...	40	5.42
		F	51	44	9	...	32	1.28
	1974							
		MF	60	50	14	9	39	3.67
		M	65	54	16	9	43	5.66
		F	55	46	12	8	35	1.61
	1975							
		MF	61	...	15	...	40	4.03
		M	67	...	17	...	44	6.10
		F	56	...	13	...	36	1.89
	1976							
		MF	...	...	...	...	...	4.43
		M	...	...	...	...	...	6.58
		F	...	...	...	...	...	2.21
	1977							
		MF	64	...	15	...	41	4.84
		M	68	...	17	...	45	7.09
		F	58	...	13	...	38	2.50

School enrolment ratios 3.2
Taux d'inscription scolaire
Tasas de escolarización

			ENROLMENT RATIOS / TAUX D'INSCRIPTION / TASAS DE ESCOLARIZACION					
COUNTRY	YEAR	SEX	FIRST LEVEL		SECOND LEVEL		1ST + 2ND LEVELS	3RD LEVEL
PAYS	ANNEE	SEXE	PREMIER DEGRE		SECOND DEGRE		1ER + 2ND DEGRE	3EME DEGRE
PAIS	AÑO	SEXO	PRIMER GRADO		SEGUNDO GRADO		1ER + 2DO GRADO	3ER GRADO
			GROSS BRUT BRUTA	NET NET NETA	GROSS BRUT BRUTA	NET NET NETA	GROSS BRUT BRUTA	GROSS BRUT BRUTA
HAITI	1970		(7–12)		(13–19)		(7–19)	(20–24)
		MF	51	...	6	...	29	0.44
		M	57	...	8	...	33	0.80
		F	46	...	4	...	25	0.10
	1974		(6–11)		(12–16)		(6–16)	(20–24)
		MF	55	...	...	...	...	0.52
		M	...	...	...	...	...	0.92
		F	...	...	...	...	...	0.12
	1975							
		MF	58	...	9	...	38	0.66
		M	...	...	12	...	...	1.00
		F	...	...	5	...	...	0.31
	1976							
		MF	59	...	9	...	38	0.73
		M	...	...	13	...	...	1.03
		F	...	...	6	...	...	0.44
	1977							
		MF	58	...	...	...	...	0.80
		M	...	...	...	...	...	1.12
		F	...	...	...	...	...	0.49
HONDURAS	1970		(7–12)		(13–18)		(7–18)	(20–24)
		MF	87	...	12	...	54	2.29
		M	87	...	12	...	54	3.39
		F	88	...	11	...	54	1.19
	1974		(6–11)		(12–17)		(6–17)	(20–24)
		MF	83	...	13	...	53	4.18
		M	83	...	14	...	53	5.57
		F	84	...	11	...	52	2.77
	1975							
		MF	84	...	12	...	53	4.62
		M	85	...	12	...	53	6.03
		F	83	...	12	...	52	3.18
	1976							
		MF	85	...	13	...	53	5.77
		M	85	...	13	...	53	7.71
		F	84	...	13	...	53	3.80
	1977							
		MF	...	...	...	...	...	7.25
		M	...	...	...	...	...	9.09
		F	...	...	...	...	...	5.37
JAMAICA	1970		(6–10)		(11–17)		(6–17)	(20–24)
		MF	119	...	46	...	82	5.47
		M	119	...	46	...	82	6.24
		F	119	...	45	...	82	4.78
	1974		(6–11)		(12–18)		(6–18)	(20–24)
		MF	98	92	55	54	77	6.75
		M	98	92	51	50	75	8.21
		F	98	93	59	59	79	5.42

3.2 School enrolment ratios
Taux d'inscription scolaire
Tasas de escolarización

			ENROLMENT RATIOS / TAUX D'INSCRIPTION / TASAS DE ESCOLARIZACION					
COUNTRY	YEAR	SEX	FIRST LEVEL		SECOND LEVEL		1ST + 2ND LEVELS	3RD LEVEL
PAYS	ANNEE	SEXE	PREMIER DEGRE		SECOND DEGRE		1ER + 2ND DEGRE	3EME DEGRE
PAIS	AÑO	SEXO	PRIMER GRADO		SEGUNDO GRADO		1ER + 2DO GRADO	3ER GRADO
			GROSS BRUT BRUTA	NET NET NETA	GROSS BRUT BRUTA	NET NET NETA	GROSS BRUT BRUTA	GROSS BRUT BRUTA
JAMAICA (CONT.)	1975							
		MF	98	90	57	56	77	...
		M	97	89	53	52	75	...
		F	98	90	62	61	80	...
	1976							
		MF	97	89	58	56	77	...
		M	96	88	55	53	75	...
		F	97	90	61	59	79	...
	1977							
		MF	98	...	58	...	77	...
		M	97	...	55	...	75	...
		F	98	...	61	...	79	...
MARTINIQUE	1970		(6–10)		(11–17)		(6–17)	(20–24)
		MF	152	100	58	53	100	...
		M	155	...	51	...	99	...
		F	148	...	64	...	102	...
	1974							
		MF	137	...	76	...	101	...
		M	137	...	69	...	97	...
		F	136	...	82	...	104	...
	1975							
		MF	142	...	71	65	99	...
		M	143	...	64	58	95	...
		F	140	...	78	72	103	...
	1976							
		MF	150	...	72	66	102	...
		M	152	...	65	60	98	...
		F	149	...	80	73	106	...
	1977							
		MF	147	...	...	...	...	...
	1978							
		MF	150	...	78	71	104	...
		M	...	...	70	65	...	...
		F	...	...	86	77	...	...
MEXICO	1970		(6–11)		(12–17)		(6–17)	(20–24)
		MF	104	81	22	16	68	6.07
		M	107	81	27	...	71	9.67
		F	102	82	17	...	64	2.45
	1974							
		MF	111	...	31	...	75	9.87
		M	114	...	36	...	79	...
		F	107	...	26	...	70	...
	1975							
		MF	112	...	35	...	77	10.61
		M	116	...	41	...	82	...
		F	109	...	28	...	72	...
	1976							
		MF	116	91	37	...	80	10.31
		M	117	...	41	...	83	14.78
		F	114	...	33	...	77	5.69

School enrolment ratios 3.2
Taux d'inscription scolaire
Tasas de escolarización

			ENROLMENT RATIOS / TAUX D'INSCRIPTION / TASAS DE ESCOLARIZACION				1ST + 2ND LEVELS	3RD LEVEL
COUNTRY	YEAR	SEX	FIRST LEVEL		SECOND LEVEL		1ER + 2ND DEGRE	3EME DEGRE
PAYS	ANNEE	SEXE	PREMIER DEGRE		SECOND DEGRE		1ER + 2DO GRADO	3ER GRADO
PAIS	AÑO	SEXO	PRIMER GRADO		SEGUNDO GRADO			
			GROSS BRUT BRUTA	NET NET NETA	GROSS BRUT BRUTA	NET NET NETA	GROSS BRUT BRUTA	GROSS BRUT BRUTA
MEXICO (CONT.)	1977							
		MF	116	...	39	...	81	11.43
		M	119	...	42	...	84	16.01
		F	114	...	36	...	78	6.68
	1978							
		MF	122	...	42	...	86	...
NICARAGUA	1970		(7–12)		(13–18)		(7–18)	(20–24)
		MF	83	65	18		54	5.68
		M	82	...	19	...	54	7.74
		F	84	...	17	...	54	3.62
	1974							
		MF	83	65	22	...	56	8.50
		M	81	...	22	...	55	11.18
		F	86	...	23	...	58	5.82
	1975							
		MF	85	...	25	...	58	9.28
		M	84	...	...	...	...	12.16
		F	87	...	...	...	...	6.40
	1976							
		MF	88	...	24	...	59	10.07
		M	85	...	23	...	57	13.15
		F	90	...	26	...	61	6.98
	1977							
		MF	86	...	28	...	60	10.86
		M	84	...	28	...	59	14.19
		F	89	...	29	...	62	7.52
	1978							
		MF	85	...	26	...	59	...
		M	83	...	25	...	57	...
		F	88	...	28	...	61	...
PANAMA	1970		(6–11)		(12–17)		(6–17)	(20–24)
		MF	105	79	39	28	75	6.56
		M	108	78	36	26	75	6.87
		F	103	79	41	31	75	6.23
	1974							
		MF	123	...	54	...	92	16.41
		M	125	...	51	...	91	15.63
		F	121	...	58	...	92	17.22
	1975		(6–14)		(15–17)		(6–17)	(20–24)
		MF	87	...	113	47	93	17.16
		M	88	...	106	43	92	16.79
		F	85	...	121	52	93	17.55
	1976							
		MF	88	83	113	...	93	19.21
		M	89	84	106	...	93	18.31
		F	86	82	122	...	94	20.17

3.2 School enrolment ratios
Taux d'inscription scolaire
Tasas de escolarización

			ENROLMENT RATIOS / TAUX D'INSCRIPTION / TASAS DE ESCOLARIZACION					
			FIRST LEVEL		SECOND LEVEL		1ST + 2ND LEVELS	3RD LEVEL
COUNTRY	YEAR	SEX	PREMIER DEGRE		SECOND DEGRE		1ER + 2ND DEGRE	3EME DEGRE
PAYS	ANNEE	SEXE	PRIMER GRADO		SEGUNDO GRADO		1ER + 2DO GRADO	3ER GRADO
PAIS	AÑO	SEXO	GROSS BRUT BRUTA	NET NET NETA	GROSS BRUT BRUTA	NET NET NETA	GROSS BRUT BRUTA	GROSS BRUT BRUTA
PANAMA (CONT.)	1977							
		MF	87	...	117	47	93	21.24
		M	89	...	108	42	93	20.06
		F	85	...	126	52	94	22.47
	1978							
		MF	88	83	116	49	94	20.68
		M	89	84	106	44	93	...
		F	86	82	125	53	95	...
PUERTO RICO	1970		(5–10)		(11–16)		(5–16)	(20–24)
		MF	117	...	71	...	94	27.10
		M	118	...	69	...	94	27.60
		F	116	...	73	...	95	26.67
	1974							
		MF	106	...	73	...	89	30.83
		M	107	...	70	...	88	29.03
		F	105	...	75	...	90	32.49
	1975							
		MF	103	...	75	...	89	31.63
		M	103	...	73	...	88	30.23
		F	102	...	78	...	90	32.96
	1976							
		MF	105	...	70	...	87	31.46
		M	...	...	...	...	...	28.83
		F	...	...	...	...	...	33.99
	1977							
		MF	...	...	...	...	...	36.09
		M	...	...	...	...	...	32.17
		F	...	...	...	...	...	39.93
TRINIDAD AND TOBAGO	1970		(5–11)		(12–16)		(5–16)	(20–24)
		MF	106	87	42	33	83	2.79
		M	106	85	40	30	81	3.49
		F	107	88	44	35	84	2.06
	1974							
		MF	99	82	39	...	75	3.01
		M	98	80	37	...	73	3.46
		F	100	83	42	...	77	2.51
	1975							
		MF	99	82	39	...	74	4.34
		M	98	80	36	...	72	...
		F	101	84	41	...	76	...
UNITED STATES OF AMERICA	1970		(6–12)		(13–17)		(6–17)	(20–24)
		MF	...	...	...	...	101	49.43
		M	...	...	...	...	100	57.71
		F	...	...	...	...	101	41.05
	1974							
		MF	...	...	...	...	99	54.53
		M	...	...	...	...	98	59.64
		F	...	...	...	...	99	49.35

School enrolment ratios 3.2
Taux d'inscription scolaire
Tasas de escolarización

			ENROLMENT RATIOS / TAUX D'INSCRIPTION / TASAS DE ESCOLARIZACION					
COUNTRY	YEAR	SEX	FIRST LEVEL		SECOND LEVEL		1ST + 2ND LEVELS	3RD LEVEL
PAYS	ANNEE	SEXE	PREMIER DEGRE		SECOND DEGRE		1ER + 2ND DEGRE	3EME DEGRE
PAIS	AÑO	SEXO	PRIMER GRADO		SEGUNDO GRADO		1ER + 2DO GRADO	3ER GRADO
			GROSS BRUT BRUTA	NET NET NETA	GROSS BRUT BRUTA	NET NET NETA	GROSS BRUT BRUTA	GROSS BRUT BRUTA
UNITED STATES OF AMERICA (CONT.)	1975							
		MF	...	...	...	...	101	58.17
		M	...	...	...	...	100	63.53
		F	...	...	...	...	102	52.73
	1976							
		MF	...	...	...	...	100	56.07
		M	...	...	...	...	99	58.81
		F	...	...	...	...	101	53.30
	1977							
		MF	...	...	...	...	100	56.03
		M	...	...	...	...	100	57.15
		F	...	...	...	...	101	54.90
AMERICA, SOUTH								
ARGENTINA	1970		(6—12)		(13—19)		(6—19)	(20—24)
		MF	106	96	32	28	70	14.23
		M	106	94	30	27	69	16.05
		F	107	97	35	30	72	12.36
	1974							
		MF	109	99	38	33	74	23.80
		M	109	98	36	32	73	25.65
		F	109	100	41	35	76	21.88
	1975							
		MF	109	...	40	...	75	28.12
		M	109	...	37	...	74	28.97
		F	110	...	42	...	77	27.23
	1976							
		MF	109	...	41	...	76	28.00
		M	109	...	38	...	74	28.73
		F	109	...	44	...	77	27.24
	1977							
		MF	110	...	41	...	76	28.60
		M	110	...	38	...	75	29.24
		F	111	...	44	...	78	27.93
	1978							
		MF	...	...	41	...	...	...
		M	...	...	37	...	...	...
		F	...	...	44	...	...	...
BOLIVIA	1970		(6—13)		(14—17)		(6—17)	(20—24)
		MF	76	...	25	...	62	9.75
		M	90	...	30	...	73	14.07
		F	62	...	21	...	50	5.49
	1974							
		MF	80	...	32	...	66	11.62
		M	89	...	37	...	74	16.73
		F	71	...	27	...	58	6.65

3.2 School enrolment ratios
Taux d'inscription scolaire
Tasas de escolarización

			ENROLMENT RATIOS / TAUX D'INSCRIPTION / TASAS DE ESCOLARIZACION					
COUNTRY	YEAR	SEX	FIRST LEVEL		SECOND LEVEL		1ST + 2ND LEVELS	3RD LEVEL
PAYS	ANNEE	SEXE	PREMIER DEGRE		SECOND DEGRE		1ER + 2ND DEGRE	3EME DEGRE
PAIS	AÑO	SEXO	PRIMER GRADO		SEGUNDO GRADO		1ER + 2DO GRADO	3ER GRADO
			GROSS BRUT BRUTA	NET NET NETA	GROSS BRUT BRUTA	NET NET NETA	GROSS BRUT BRUTA	GROSS BRUT BRUTA
BOLIVIA (CONT.)	1975							
		MF	84	73	31	21	69	12.57
		M	94	...	35	...	77	17.42
		F	75	...	26	...	61	7.86
	1976							
		MF	86	...	29		70	12.61
		M	96	...	34	...	78	17.50
		F	76	...	25	...	62	7.86
	1977							
		MF	...	...	...	...	...	12.58
		M	...	...	...	...	...	17.43
		F	...	...	...	...	...	7.85
BRAZIL	1970		(7—10)		(11—17)		(7—17)	(20—24)
		MF	125	73	26	18	65	5.26
		M	125	...	26	...	65	6.61
		F	125	...	26	...	65	3.94
	1974		(7—14)		(15—17)		(7—17)	(20—24)
		MF	90	73	24	8	74	9.79
		M	89	73	22	7	73	10.38
		F	90	73	26	9	74	9.22
	1975							
		MF	89		...	...		10.78
	1976							
		MF	88	...	...	...	...	12.62
CHILE	1970		(6—13)		(14—17)		(6—17)	(20—24)
		MF	107	93	39	29	87	9.40
		M	107	...	36	...	86	11.58
		F	108	...	42	...	88	7.22
	1974							
		MF	120	...	50	...	97	16.45
		M	120	...	46	...	96	...
		F	119	...	53	...	98	...
	1975							
		MF	118	99	48	34	95	16.52
		M	119	98	45	31	95	18.00
		F	118	100	52	36	96	15.01
	1976							
		MF	116	...	49	...	94	14.30
		M	116	...	45	...	93	16.30
		F	116	...	53	...	95	12.26
	1977							
		MF	117	...	50	...	95	13.46
		M	118	...	47	...	94	15.48
		F	117	...	54	...	96	11.40
	1978							
		MF	118	...	52	...	95	12.79
		M	118	...	49	...	95	14.71
		F	117	...	55	...	96	10.83

School enrolment ratios 3.2
Taux d'inscription scolaire
Tasas de escolarización

			ENROLMENT RATIOS / TAUX D'INSCRIPTION / TASAS DE ESCOLARIZACION						
COUNTRY	YEAR	SEX	FIRST LEVEL		SECOND LEVEL		1ST + 2ND LEVELS	3RD LEVEL	
PAYS	ANNEE	SEXE	PREMIER DEGRE		SECOND DEGRE		1ER + 2ND DEGRE	3EME DEGRE	
PAIS	AÑO	SEXO	PRIMER GRADO		SEGUNDO GRADO		1ER + 2DO GRADO	3ER GRADO	
			GROSS BRUT BRUTA	NET NET NETA	GROSS BRUT BRUTA	NET NET NETA	GROSS BRUT BRUTA	GROSS BRUT BRUTA	
COLOMBIA	1970		(7–11)		(12–17)		(7–17)	(20–24)	
		MF	103	...	24	...	64	4.66	
		M	101	...	24	...	63	6.83	
		F	105	...	24	...	65	2.50	
	1974								
		MF	111	...	36	...	72	6.76	
		M	108	...	35	...	71	...	
		F	113	...	36	...	74	...	
	1975								
		MF	114	...	37	...	74	8.14	
		M	111	...	36	...	72	11.72	
		F	116	...	37	...	75	4.46	
	1976		(6–10)		(11–16)		(6–16)	(20–24)	
		MF	117	...	38	...	75	...	
		M	115	...	38	...	74	...	
		F	120	...	39	...	77	...	
	1977								
		MF	121	...	41	...	78	9.60	
		M	118	...	40	...	76	11.54	
		F	123	...	41	...	79	7.60	
	1978								
		MF	124	...	43	...	81	10.73	
		M	122	...	43	...	79	...	
		F	127	...	44	...	82	...	
ECUADOR	1970		(6–11)		(12–17)		(6–17)	(20–24)	
		MF	100	80	26	...	67	7.86	
		M	103	82	28	...	69	10.91	
		F	97	79	24	...	64	4.76	
	1974								
		MF	105	81	36	26	74	23.26	
		M	108	82	37	26	76	...	
		F	103	80	34	25	72	...	
	1975								
		MF	107	82	40	28	77	27.84	
		M	110	82	41	28	79	...	
		F	104	81	38	27	74	...	
	1976								
		MF	110	...	43	...	79	28.51	
		M	113	...	46	...	82	...	
		F	107	...	41	...	77	...	
	1977								
		MF	108	...	46	...	80	...	
		M	110	...	48	...	82	...	
		F	106	...	43	...	78	...	
GUYANA	1970		(6–11)		(12–17)		(6–17)	(20–24)	
		MF	98	86	55	48	79	1.94	
		M	100	87	55	48	80	3.18	
		F	96	86	56	49	78	0.75	

3.2 School enrolment ratios
Taux d'inscription scolaire
Tasas de escolarización

			ENROLMENT RATIOS / TAUX D'INSCRIPTION / TASAS DE ESCOLARIZACION					
COUNTRY	YEAR	SEX	FIRST LEVEL		SECOND LEVEL		1ST + 2ND LEVELS	3RD LEVEL
PAYS	ANNEE	SEXE	PREMIER DEGRE		SECOND DEGRE		1ER + 2ND DEGRE	3EME DEGRE
PAIS	AÑO	SEXO	PRIMER GRADO		SEGUNDO GRADO		1ER + 2DO GRADO	3ER GRADO
			GROSS BRUT BRUTA	NET NET NETA	GROSS BRUT BRUTA	NET NET NETA	GROSS BRUT BRUTA	GROSS BRUT BRUTA
GUYANA (CONT.)	1975							
		MF	93	82	55	...	75	3.76
		M	93	82	55	...	75	4.84
		F	92	82	56	...	75	2.68
	1976							
		MF	99	88	60	...	80	...
		M	100	88	59	...	81	...
		F	98	88	60	...	80	...
PARAGUAY	1970		(7–12)		(13–18)		(7–18)	(20–24)
		MF	109	88	17	...	67	4.32
		M	115	91	17	...	70	5.00
		F	103	86	17	...	64	3.63
	1974							
		MF	106	...	20	...	66	5.96
		M	110	...	20	...	69	...
		F	101	...	20	...	64	...
	1975							
		MF	102	85	22	17	66	7.09
		M	106	87	23	17	68	...
		F	98	84	21	17	63	...
	1976							
		MF	103	86	23	18	66	6.98
		M	107	87	24	18	69	7.87
		F	99	84	22	18	64	6.09
	1977							
		MF	102	85	25	20	67	7.72
		M	106	87	26	20	70	8.83
		F	98	84	25	19	65	6.60
	1978							
		MF	...	...	...	...	...	7.69
		M	...	...	...	...	...	8.70
		F	...	...	...	...	...	6.69
PERU	1970		(6–11)		(12–17)		(6–17)	(20–24)
		MF	103	71	30	21	70	11.05
		M	111	75	34	23	76	14.42
		F	96	67	26	19	64	7.64
	1974		(6–11)		(12–16)		(6–16)	(20–24)
		MF	108	...	42	...	81	13.61
		M	113	...	46	...	86	18.22
		F	103	...	37	...	76	8.97
	1975							
		MF	110	...	44	...	82	14.19
		M	114	...	49	...	87	19.18
		F	105	...	39	...	78	9.16
	1976							
		MF	112	...	47	...	85	15.02
		M	116	...	52	...	90	20.31
		F	107	...	42	...	80	9.68

School enrolment ratios 3.2
Taux d'inscription scolaire
Tasas de escolarización

			ENROLMENT RATIOS / TAUX D'INSCRIPTION / TASAS DE ESCOLARIZACION					
COUNTRY	YEAR	SEX	FIRST LEVEL		SECOND LEVEL		1ST + 2ND LEVELS	3RD LEVEL
PAYS	ANNEE	SEXE	PREMIER DEGRE		SECOND DEGRE		1ER + 2ND DEGRE	3EME DEGRE
PAIS	AÑO	SEXO	PRIMER GRADO		SEGUNDO GRADO		1ER + 2DO GRADO	3ER GRADO
			GROSS BRUT BRUTA	NET NET NETA	GROSS BRUT BRUTA	NET NET NETA	GROSS BRUT BRUTA	GROSS BRUT BRUTA
PERU (CONT.)	1977							
		MF	112	...	50	...	86	15.79
		M	116	...	53	...	90	...
		F	106	...	46	...	81	...
	1978							
		MF	113	...	54	...	89	...
SURINAME	1970		(6—11)		(12—17)		(6—17)	(20—24)
		MF	127	...	42	...	90	1.19
		M	131	...	38	...	91	2.05
		F	123	...	46	...	90	0.39
	1974							
		MF	116	...	48	...	86	1.85
		M	123	...	42	...	88	3.58
		F	108	...	53	...	84	0.31
	1975							
		MF	99	...	47	...	76	2.14
		M	103	...	42	...	76	4.03
		F	96	...	52	...	76	0.47
	1976							
		MF	106	80	49	...	80	3.21
		M	110	81	47	...	82	4.79
		F	102	80	51	...	79	1.79
	1977							
		MF	103	78	50	...	79	3.40
		M	107	79	47	...	80	4.59
		F	100	77	53	...	78	2.28
	1978							
		MF	103	...	49	...	78	...
		M	107	...	46	...	79	...
		F	100	...	51	...	77	...
URUGUAY	1970		(6—11)		(12—17)		(6—17)	(20—24)
		MF	112	...	59	...	86	10.00
		M	115	...	53	...	85	11.50
		F	109	...	65	...	88	8.51
	1974							
		MF	107	...	65	...	86	12.09
		M	108	...	60	...	84	13.12
		F	105	...	70	...	88	11.04
	1975							
		MF	105	...	62	...	84	15.01
		M	...	...	...	...	...	16.66
		F	...	...	...	...	...	13.31
	1976							
		MF	99	...	63	...	81	16.41
		M	...	...	58	...	...	18.18
		F	...	...	67	...	...	14.59

3.2 School enrolment ratios
Taux d'inscription scolaire
Tasas de escolarización

			ENROLMENT RATIOS / TAUX D'INSCRIPTION / TASAS DE ESCOLARIZACION					
COUNTRY	YEAR	SEX	FIRST LEVEL		SECOND LEVEL		1ST + 2ND LEVELS	3RD LEVEL
PAYS	ANNEE	SEXE	PREMIER DEGRE		SECOND DEGRE		1ER + 2ND DEGRE	3EME DEGRE
PAIS	AÑO	SEXO	PRIMER GRADO		SEGUNDO GRADO		1ER + 2DO GRADO	3ER GRADO
			GROSS BRUT BRUTA	NET NET NETA	GROSS BRUT BRUTA	NET NET NETA	GROSS BRUT BRUTA	GROSS BRUT BRUTA
URUGUAY (CONT.)	1977							
		MF	106	...	63	...	84	17.81
		M	109	...	59	...	84	18.49
		F	102	...	67	...	85	17.11
	1978							
		MF	105	...	64	...	85	...
		M	103	...	61	...	82	...
		F	108	...	68	...	88	...
VENEZUELA	1970		(7—12)		(13—17)		(7—17)	(20—24)
		MF	94	78	34	26	70	11.64
		M	94	...	33	25	69	13.64
		F	95	...	35	27	71	9.60
	1974							
		MF	95	78	42	33	73	17.03
		M	95	...	40	31	72	18.61
		F	95	...	45	35	74	15.43
	1975							
		MF	99	81	43	34	76	18.32
		M	99	...	41	32	75	...
		F	99	...	46	36	77	...
	1976		(7—12)		(13—18)		(7—18)	(20—24)
		MF	103	83	38	32	72	20.21
		M	103	...	35	...	71	...
		F	102	...	40	...	73	...
	1977							
		MF	106	85	38	32	74	20.74
		M	106	...	35	30	73	...
		F	106	...	41	34	75	...
	1978							
		MF	108	...	...		...	...
ASIA								
AFGHANISTAN	1970		(7—12)		(13—18)		(7—18)	(20—24)
		MF	21	...	5	...	14	0.49
		M	35	...	9	...	23	0.81
		F	6	...	1	...	4	0.15
	1974							
		MF	23	18	7	6	16	0.67
		M	38	30	13	9	26	1.12
		F	7	6	2	2	5	0.19
	1975		(6—13)		(14—17)		(6—17)	(20—24)
		MF	20	...	6	...	16	0.74
		M	32	...	10	...	26	1.23
		F	6	...	1	...	5	0.21
	1976							
		MF	20	...	6	...	16	0.83
		M	33	...	10	...	27	1.39
		F	6	...	1	...	5	0.24

School enrolment ratios 3.2
Taux d'inscription scolaire
Tasas de escolarización

			ENROLMENT RATIOS / TAUX D'INSCRIPTION / TASAS DE ESCOLARIZACION					
COUNTRY	YEAR	SEX	FIRST LEVEL		SECOND LEVEL		1ST + 2ND LEVELS	3RD LEVEL
PAYS	ANNEE	SEXE	PREMIER DEGRE		SECOND DEGRE		1ER + 2ND DEGRE	3EME DEGRE
PAIS	AÑO	SEXO	PRIMER GRADO		SEGUNDO GRADO		1ER + 2DO GRADO	3ER GRADO
			GROSS BRUT BRUTA	NET NET NETA	GROSS BRUT BRUTA	NET NET NETA	GROSS BRUT BRUTA	GROSS BRUT BRUTA
AFGHANISTAN (CONT.)	1977							
		MF	20	17	7	...	16	0.93
		M	33	27	11	...	27	1.32
		F	6	6	2	...	5	0.51
BANGLADESH	1970		(5- 9)		(10-14)		(5-14)	(20-24)
		MF	52	...	19	...	37	2.10
		M	68	...	29	...	50	3.60
		F	34	...	8	...	22	0.43
	1974							
		MF	68	...	25	...	48	2.87
		M	88	...	38	...	65	4.98
		F	46	...	11	...	30	0.61
	1975							
		MF	71	...	25	...	50	2.57
		M	91	...	38	...	67	4.48
		F	50	...	11	...	32	0.54
	1976							
		MF	79	77	21	19	53	2.31
		M	100	98	31	28	68	3.92
		F	57	54	11	9	36	0.59
	1977							
		MF	72	70	22	17	49	2.54
		M	103	100	32	24	70	4.26
		F	40	38	11	9	27	0.72
	1978							
		MF	67	...	...	...	...	...
		M	87	...	...	...	...	...
		F	46	...	...	...	...	...
BHUTAN	1970		(6-10)		(11-16)		(6-16)	(20-24)
		MF	7	...	1	...	4	—
		M	12	...	1	...	6	—
		F	1	...	0.04	...	...	—
	1974							
		MF	8	...	1	...	5	—
		M	12	...	2	...	7	—
		F	4	...	0.23	...	2	—
	1976							
		MF	11	...	1	...	6	—
		M	15	...	1	...	8	—
		F	6	...	0.22	...	3	—
	1977							
		MF	12	...	1	...	6	—
		M	16	...	2	...	9	—
		F	7	...	0.30	...	3	—
	1978							
		MF	12	7	1	...	6	0.13
		M	16	10	2	...	9	0.19
		F	7	5	0.41	...	4	0.06

3.2 School enrolment ratios
Taux d'inscription scolaire
Tasas de escolarización

			ENROLMENT RATIOS / TAUX D'INSCRIPTION / TASAS DE ESCOLARIZACION					
COUNTRY	YEAR	SEX	FIRST LEVEL		SECOND LEVEL		1ST + 2ND LEVELS	3RD LEVEL
PAYS	ANNEE	SEXE	PREMIER DEGRE		SECOND DEGRE		1ER + 2ND DEGRE	3EME DEGRE
PAIS	AÑO	SEXO	PRIMER GRADO		SEGUNDO GRADO		1ER + 2DO GRADO	3ER GRADO
			GROSS BRUT BRUTA	NET NET NETA	GROSS BRUT BRUTA	NET NET NETA	GROSS BRUT BRUTA	GROSS BRUT BRUTA
BURMA	1970		(5– 9)		(10–15)		(5–15)	(20–24)
		MF	87	63	21	15	54	2.17
		M	92	65	26	18	59	2.68
		F	83	61	17	12	49	1.65
	1974							
		MF	83	...	22	...	53	2.10
		M	86	...	25	...	56	...
		F	80	...	19	...	49	...
	1975							
		MF	83	...	22	...	52	2.11
		M	86	...	24	...	55	...
		F	80	...	19	...	50	...
	1976							
		MF	83	...	20	...	51	2.24
		M	86	...	22	...	54	2.33
		F	79	...	18	...	49	2.16
	1977							
		MF	84	65	20	16	52	...
		M	87	67	22	18	54	...
		F	81	64	18	15	49	...
CHINA	1977		(7–12)		(13–16)		(7–16)	(20–24)
		MF	112	...	72	...	96	0.64
		M	111	...	86	...	101	0.88
		F	114	...	59	...	92	0.39
	1978							
		MF	118	...	79	...	102	...
		M	...	...	92	...	...	...
		F	...	...	65	...	...	...
CYPRUS ‡	1970		(5–10)		(11–16)		(5–16)	(20–24)
		MF	88	70	54	46	71	1.37
		M	87	70	57	47	73	1.56
		F	88	71	52	44	70	1.19
	1974							
		MF	78	65	58	49	68	1.10
		M	78	65	60	49	69	1.37
		F	78	65	57	48	67	0.84
	1975							
		MF	80	68	62	52	71	1.05
		M	80	67	63	52	71	1.25
		F	81	69	61	52	70	0.84
	1976							
		MF	81	70	65	55	73	1.33
		M	81	70	66	55	73	1.51
		F	82	71	64	54	72	1.15
	1977							
		MF	83	72	65	54	74	1.82
		M	83	71	65	54	73	1.65
		F	84	72	65	54	74	2.00

School enrolment ratios 3.2
Taux d'inscription scolaire
Tasas de escolarización

			ENROLMENT RATIOS / TAUX D'INSCRIPTION / TASAS DE ESCOLARIZACION					
COUNTRY	YEAR	SEX	FIRST LEVEL		SECOND LEVEL		1ST + 2ND LEVELS	3RD LEVEL
PAYS	ANNEE	SEXE	PREMIER DEGRE		SECOND DEGRE		1ER + 2ND DEGRE	3EME DEGRE
PAIS	AÑO	SEXO	PRIMER GRADO		SEGUNDO GRADO		1ER + 2DO GRADO	3ER GRADO
			GROSS BRUT BRUTA	NET NET NETA	GROSS BRUT BRUTA	NET NET NETA	GROSS BRUT BRUTA	GROSS BRUT BRUTA
CYPRUS (CONT.) ‡	1978							
		MF	84	73	66	56	75	...
		M	83	72	66	55	74	...
		F	85	74	66	57	75	...
DEMOCRATIC KAMPUCHEA	1970		(6–11)		(12–18)		(6–18)	(20–24)
		MF	28	...	8	...	18	1.54
		M	32	...	11	...	22	2.36
		F	24	...	5	...	15	0.70
	1972							
		MF	38	...	9	...	24	1.53
		M	44	...	12	...	28	2.44
		F	32	...	5	...	19	0.61
EAST TIMOR	1970		(6– 9)		(10–16)		(6–16)	(20–24)
		MF	50	...	1	...	21	–
		M	74	...	2	...	31	–
		F	26	...	1	...	11	...
	1973							
		MF	134	...	1	...	54	–
		M	177	...	2	...	72	–
		F	88	...	1	...	36	–
HONG KONG	1970		(5–10)		(11–17)		(5–17)	(20–24)
		MF	117	72	35	29	75	7.33
		M	119	72	39	32	78	9.75
		F	115	71	30	25	72	4.63
	1974							
		MF	122	75	45	39	78	9.26
		M	123	75	48	41	80	12.86
		F	120	74	42	36	75	5.23
	1975							
		MF	121	75	48	41	78	10.23
		M	123	75	50	43	80	14.50
		F	119	74	46	40	76	5.45
	1976							
		MF	119	75	52	45	79	9.68
		M	120	75	54	46	81	13.44
		F	117	75	50	43	77	5.51
	1977							
		MF	115	75	57	49	80	...
		M	116	75	59	50	82	...
		F	114	75	55	48	78	...
INDIA	1970		(5– 9)		(10–15)		(5–15)	(20–24)
		MF	73	57	26	21	50	8.19
		M	90	69	36	29	63	12.49
		F	56	45	15	12	36	3.65
	1974							
		MF	77	...	26	...	51	8.85
		M	92	...	35	...	63	13.25
		F	60	...	16	...	38	4.17

3.2 School enrolment ratios
Taux d'inscription scolaire
Tasas de escolarización

			ENROLMENT RATIOS / TAUX D'INSCRIPTION / TASAS DE ESCOLARIZACION					
COUNTRY	YEAR	SEX	FIRST LEVEL		SECOND LEVEL		1ST + 2ND LEVELS	3RD LEVEL
PAYS	ANNEE	SEXE	PREMIER DEGRE		SECOND DEGRE		1ER + 2ND DEGRE	3EME DEGRE
PAIS	AÑO	SEXO	PRIMER GRADO		SEGUNDO GRADO		1ER + 2DO GRADO	3ER GRADO
			GROSS BRUT BRUTA	NET NET NETA	GROSS BRUT BRUTA	NET NET NETA	GROSS BRUT BRUTA	GROSS BRUT BRUTA
INDIA (CONT.)	1975							
		MF	76	...	26	...	51	8.72
		M	92	...	35	...	63	13.00
		F	60	...	16	...	38	4.17
	1976							
		MF	79	...	26	...	52	8.56
		M	94	...	36	...	64	12.76
		F	62	...	17	...	39	4.09
	1977							
		MF	79	...	28	...	53	8.40
		M	94	...	37	...	65	12.52
		F	63	...	18	...	40	4.02
INDONESIA	1970		(7–12)		(13–18)		(7–18)	(20–24)
		MF	78	...	16	...	50	2.83
		M	83	...	21	...	56	4.74
		F	73	...	11	...	45	1.29
	1974							
		MF	79	66	18	16	52	2.43
		M	87	72	22	19	58	...
		F	71	59	14	12	45	...
	1975							
		MF	81	68	20	17	53	2.42
		M	87	72	24	20	58	...
		F	75	64	15	13	48	...
	1976							
		MF	84	71	20	18	55	2.46
		M	89	75	25	22	59	3.58
		F	79	67	16	14	50	1.37
	1977							
		MF	86	70	21	18	57	...
		M	91	74	25	22	61	...
		F	81	67	17	15	52	...
	1978							
		MF	94	80	22	20	61	...
		M	100	84	27	23	66	...
		F	89	76	18	16	56	...
IRAN	1970		(7–12)		(13–18)		(7–18)	(20–24)
		MF	73	60	27	...	52	3.08
		M	93	...	36	...	67	4.53
		F	52	...	18	...	37	1.59
	1974		(6–10)		(11–16)		(6–16)	(20–24)
		MF	90	...	43	...	66	4.65
		M	112	...	55	...	83	6.56
		F	67	...	31	...	49	2.69
	1975							
		MF	95	...	46	...	70	5.03
		M	116	...	58	...	87	6.94
		F	73	...	33	...	53	3.07

School enrolment ratios   3.2
Taux d'inscription scolaire
Tasas de escolarización

			ENROLMENT RATIOS / TAUX D'INSCRIPTION / TASAS DE ESCOLARIZACION					
COUNTRY	YEAR	SEX	FIRST LEVEL		SECOND LEVEL		1ST + 2ND LEVELS	3RD LEVEL
PAYS	ANNEE	SEXE	PREMIER DEGRE		SECOND DEGRE		1ER + 2ND DEGRE	3EME DEGRE
PAIS	AÑO	SEXO	PRIMER GRADO		SEGUNDO GRADO		1ER + 2DO GRADO	3ER GRADO
			GROSS BRUT BRUTA	NET NET NETA	GROSS BRUT BRUTA	NET NET NETA	GROSS BRUT BRUTA	GROSS BRUT BRUTA
IRAN (CONT.)	1976							
		MF	98	...	48	...	73	4.95
		M	119	...	61	...	90	6.85
		F	77	...	35	...	56	2.99
	1977		(6–10)		(11–17)		(6–17)	(20–24)
		MF	101	...	44	...	70	5.38
		M	121	...	55	...	85	...
		F	80	...	32	...	54	...
IRAQ	1970		(6–11)		(12–17)		(6–17)	(20–24)
		MF	69	55	24	19	49	5.20
		M	95	76	34	27	68	7.91
		F	41	34	14	12	29	2.37
	1974							
		MF	83	69	33	24	61	8.49
		M	110	89	46	33	81	11.75
		F	55	47	19	15	39	5.08
	1975							
		MF	94	79	35	25	67	8.98
		M	122	100	48	34	89	11.80
		F	64	55	21	16	45	6.03
	1976							
		MF	99	82	38	28	72	9.22
		M	125	100	52	38	92	12.27
		F	72	61	23	18	50	6.03
	1977							
		MF	100	84	44	34	75	8.96
		M	123	100	60	47	95	...
		F	77	65	27	21	55	...
	1978							
		MF	117	100	50	40	87	9.07
		M	130	100	68	55	103	...
		F	103	90	31	25	71	...
ISRAEL	1970		(6–13)		(14–17)		(6–17)	(20–24)
		MF	96	...	57	...	83	19.92
		M	97	...	54	...	82	21.54
		F	95	...	60	...	83	18.20
	1974							
		MF	97	...	66	...	87	23.21
		M	96	...	61	...	85	24.75
		F	97	...	72	...	89	21.62
	1975							
		MF	97	...	67	...	87	23.40
		M	96	...	61	...	85	25.00
		F	97	...	73	...	89	21.76
	1976							
		MF	96	...	67	...	87	25.29
		M	96	...	62	...	85	26.76
		F	97	...	73	...	90	23.77

3.2 School enrolment ratios
Taux d'inscription scolaire
Tasas de escolarización

COUNTRY	YEAR	SEX	ENROLMENT RATIOS / TAUX D'INSCRIPTION / TASAS DE ESCOLARIZACION				1ST + 2ND LEVELS	3RD LEVEL
PAYS	ANNEE	SEXE	FIRST LEVEL		SECOND LEVEL		1ER + 2ND DEGRE	3EME DEGRE
PAIS	AÑO	SEXO	PREMIER DEGRE		SECOND DEGRE		1ER + 2DO GRADO	3ER GRADO
			PRIMER GRADO		SEGUNDO GRADO			
			GROSS BRUT BRUTA	NET NET NETA	GROSS BRUT BRUTA	NET NET NETA	GROSS BRUT BRUTA	GROSS BRUT BRUTA
ISRAEL (CONT.)	1977							
		MF	97	...	68	...	88	24.73
		M	96	...	63	...	86	25.82
		F	97	...	73	...	90	23.59
JAPAN	1970		(6–11)		(12–17)		(6–17)	(20–24)
		MF	99	99	86	85	92	17.01
		M	99	99	86	85	93	24.52
		F	99	99	86	85	92	9.56
	1974							
		MF	98	...	91	...	94	22.65
		M	97	...	90	...	94	30.97
		F	98	...	91	...	94	14.27
	1975							
		MF	99	...	91	...	95	24.56
		M	99	...	91	...	95	33.05
		F	99	...	92	...	95	15.98
	1976							
		MF	99	99	92	...	96	26.06
		M	99	99	92	...	96	34.57
		F	99	99	93	...	96	17.42
	1977							
		MF	99	99	93	...	96	28.55
		M	99	99	92	...	96	38.18
		F	99	99	93	...	96	18.76
	1978							
		MF	98	98	93	...	96	32.48
		M	98	98	92	...	95	40.10
		F	98	98	94	...	96	24.68
JORDAN ‡	1970		(6–11)		(12–17)		(6–17)	(20–24)
		MF	72	...	33	...	55	2.19
		M	79	...	41	...	62	2.87
		F	65	...	23	...	47	1.41
	1974							
		MF	82	75	41	38	65	4.21
		M	87	80	48	44	70	5.31
		F	77	69	34	32	59	2.98
	1975							
		MF	83	75	45	42	66	5.26
		M	87	80	52	49	72	6.69
		F	78	70	38	35	61	3.69
	1976							
		MF	83	76	49	46	68	7.10
		M	87	80	56	52	73	8.85
		F	79	71	42	39	63	5.19
	1977							
		MF	83	76	53	49	70	7.25
		M	86	79	60	55	75	8.75
		F	79	72	46	42	64	5.61

School enrolment ratios 3.2
Taux d'inscription scolaire
Tasas de escolarización

COUNTRY	YEAR	SEX	ENROLMENT RATIOS / TAUX D'INSCRIPTION / TASAS DE ESCOLARIZACION					
			FIRST LEVEL		SECOND LEVEL		1ST + 2ND LEVELS	3RD LEVEL
PAYS	ANNEE	SEXE	PREMIER DEGRE		SECOND DEGRE		1ER + 2ND DEGRE	3EME DEGRE
PAIS	AÑO	SEXO	PRIMER GRADO		SEGUNDO GRADO		1ER + 2DO GRADO	3ER GRADO
			GROSS BRUT BRUTA	NET NET NETA	GROSS BRUT BRUTA	NET NET NETA	GROSS BRUT BRUTA	GROSS BRUT BRUTA
JORDAN (CONT.) ‡	1978							
		MF	83	77	56	52	71	...
		M	86	80	63	57	76	...
		F	80	73	49	46	66	...
KOREA, DEMOCRATIC PEOPLE'S REPUB. OF	1976		(5– 9)		(10–15)		(5–15)	(20–24)
		MF	113	...	...	...	...	...
		M	115	...	...	...	...	...
		F	112	...	...	...	...	...
KOREA, REPUBLIC OF	1970		(6–11)		(12–17)		(6–17)	(20–24)
		MF	105	96	43	38	77	8.02
		M	106	97	52	46	82	11.80
		F	105	95	34	31	72	4.01
	1974							
		MF	108	100	55	49	81	9.60
		M	107	100	63	56	85	13.76
		F	108	100	46	42	76	5.30
	1975							
		MF	109	100	57	53	82	9.80
		M	108	100	66	60	86	13.99
		F	109	100	49	45	78	5.45
	1976							
		MF	108	100	61	56	84	9.98
		M	108	100	70	63	88	14.36
		F	109	100	53	49	80	5.42
	1977							
		MF	109	100	65	60	86	10.31
		M	109	100	73	66	90	15.00
		F	109	100	57	53	82	5.39
	1978							
		MF	111	100	70	64	90	10.92
		M	111	100	77	69	93	15.94
		F	111	100	62	58	86	5.60
	1979							
		MF	111	100	74	68	93	...
		M	112	100	81	73	96	...
		F	111	100	67	62	89	...
KUWAIT	1970		(6– 9)		(10–17)		(6–17)	(20–24)
		MF	88	61	63	53	74	3.67
		M	100	67	70	57	83	3.32
		F	76	54	57	48	65	4.13
	1974							
		MF	91	67	64	55	75	6.74
		M	98	72	69	58	81	4.90
		F	83	63	59	51	70	8.94
	1975							
		MF	93	69	67	58	78	9.08
		M	100	73	71	61	83	7.19
		F	86	65	62	54	72	11.32

3.2 School enrolment ratios
Taux d'inscription scolaire
Tasas de escolarización

			ENROLMENT RATIOS / TAUX D'INSCRIPTION / TASAS DE ESCOLARIZACION					
COUNTRY	YEAR	SEX	FIRST LEVEL		SECOND LEVEL		1ST + 2ND LEVELS	3RD LEVEL
PAYS	ANNEE	SEXE	PREMIER DEGRE		SECOND DEGRE		1ER + 2ND DEGRE	3EME DEGRE
PAIS	AÑO	SEXO	PRIMER GRADO		SEGUNDO GRADO		1ER + 2DO GRADO	3ER GRADO
			GROSS BRUT BRUTA	NET NET NETA	GROSS BRUT BRUTA	NET NET NETA	GROSS BRUT BRUTA	GROSS BRUT BRUTA
KUWAIT (CONT.)	1976							
		MF	97	73	74	65	84	10.69
		M	103	75	79	69	89	8.87
		F	92	70	69	60	78	12.86
	1977							
		MF	100	82	74	66	85	12.87
		M	106	88	79	71	90	11.13
		F	94	76	68	61	79	14.88
	1978							
		MF	104	68	74	...	86	...
		M	110	74	79	...	92	...
		F	98	62	69	...	80	...
LAO PEOPLE'S DEMOCRATIC REPUBLIC	1970		(6—11)		(12—18)		(6—18)	(20—24)
		MF	54	...	3	...	29	0.16
		M	67	...	5	...	36	0.26
		F	40	...	2	...	21	0.06
	1974							
		MF	58	...	...	...	...	0.29
		M	67	...	...	...	...	0.42
		F	47	...	...	...	...	0.16
	1976		(6—10)		(11—16)		(6—16)	(20—24)
		MF	92	...	11	...	51	...
		M	106	...	14	...	60	...
		F	77	...	7	...	42	...
	1977							
		MF	92	...	14	...	52	...
		M	99	...	18	...	58	...
		F	85	...	9	...	47	...
LEBANON	1970		(5— 9)		(10—16)		(5—16)	(20—24)
		MF	118	...	40	...	76	23.55
		M	127	...	47	...	84	35.30
		F	109	...	32	...	68	11.30
	1977							
		MF	96	...	46	...	68	...
	1978							
		MF	...	...	...	...	...	27.77
MALAYSIA	1970		(6—11)		(12—18)		(6—18)	(20—24)
		MF	91	90	35	34	64	1.99
		M	95	94	40	39	68	2.77
		F	87	87	29	28	59	1.19
	1974							
		MF	92	...	43	...	67	3.21
		M	94	...	47	...	71	4.15
		F	90	...	38	...	64	2.25
	1975							
		MF	94	...	45	...	69	3.32
		M	95	...	50	...	72	4.28
		F	92	...	40	...	66	2.33

School enrolment ratios 3.2
Taux d'inscription scolaire
Tasas de escolarización

			ENROLMENT RATIOS / TAUX D'INSCRIPTION / TASAS DE ESCOLARIZACION					
COUNTRY	YEAR	SEX	FIRST LEVEL		SECOND LEVEL		1ST + 2ND LEVELS	3RD LEVEL
PAYS	ANNEE	SEXE	PREMIER DEGRE		SECOND DEGRE		1ER + 2ND DEGRE	3EME DEGRE
PAIS	AÑO	SEXO	PRIMER GRADO		SEGUNDO GRADO		1ER + 2DO GRADO	3ER GRADO
			GROSS BRUT BRUTA	NET NET NETA	GROSS BRUT BRUTA	NET NET NETA	GROSS BRUT BRUTA	GROSS BRUT BRUTA
MALAYSIA (CONT.)	1976							
		MF	94	...	48	...	71	3.42
		M	95	...	52	...	73	4.42
		F	92	...	44	...	68	2.39
	1977							
		MF	93	...	51	...	72	3.79
		M	94	...	...	...	...	4.74
		F	92	...	...	...	...	2.81
	1978							
		MF	92	...	55	...	73	...
MONGOLIA	1970		(8—11)		(12—15)		(8—15)	(20—24)
		MF	113	...	87	...	101	6.39
		M	113	...	87	...	101	6.67
		F	113	...	88	...	101	6.11
	1974		(8—10)		(11—17)		(8—17)	(20—24)
		MF	111	...	78	...	90	8.30
		M	111	...	75	...	87	8.19
		F	111	...	82	...	92	8.41
	1975							
		MF	108	...	81	...	90	8.38
		M	111	...	77	...	89	8.16
		F	105	...	84	...	92	8.60
NEPAL	1970		(6—10)		(11—15)		(6—15)	(20—24)
		MF	26	...	10	...	18	1.88
		M	43	...	16	...	30	3.06
		F	8	...	3	...	6	0.69
	1974		(6— 8)		(9—15)		(6—15)	(20—24)
		MF	45	...	13	...	23	2.17
		M	76	...	21	...	39	3.25
		F	14	...	4	...	7	0.87
	1975							
		MF	51	...	13	...	26	2.28
		M	84	...	22	...	43	3.40
		F	16	...	4	...	8	0.92
	1976							
		MF	59	...	12	...	28	1.83
		M	92	...	19	...	44	2.66
		F	24	...	4	...	11	0.82
	1977							
		MF	69	...	14	...	32	2.29
		M	104	...	22	...	50	3.31
		F	31	...	5	...	14	1.09
OMAN	1970		(6—11)		(12—18)		(6—18)	(20—24)
		MF	3	...	...	...	...	—
		M	6	...	...	...	...	—
		F	1	...	...	...	...	—

3.2 School enrolment ratios
Taux d'inscription scolaire
Tasas de escolarización

COUNTRY	YEAR	SEX	ENROLMENT RATIOS / TAUX D'INSCRIPTION / TASAS DE ESCOLARIZACION				1ST + 2ND LEVELS	3RD LEVEL
			FIRST LEVEL		SECOND LEVEL		1ER + 2ND DEGRE	3EME DEGRE
PAYS	ANNEE	SEXE	PREMIER DEGRE		SECOND DEGRE		1ER + 2DO GRADO	3ER GRADO
PAIS	AÑO	SEXO	PRIMER GRADO		SEGUNDO GRADO			
			GROSS BRUT BRUTA	NET NET NETA	GROSS BRUT BRUTA	NET NET NETA	GROSS BRUT BRUTA	GROSS BRUT BRUTA
OMAN (CONT.)	1974							
		MF	41	31	1	1	21	—
		M	60	44	1	1	31	—
		F	21	17	0.28	0.26	11	—
	1975							
		MF	44	32	1	1	23	—
		M	63	44	2	2	34	—
		F	24	20	0.40	0.36	13	—
	1976							
		MF	49	...	2	...	26	—
		M	68	...	3	...	37	—
		F	28	...	1	...	15	—
	1977							
		MF	53	41	5	4	30	—
		M	73	55	7	7	41	—
		F	33	27	2	2	18	—
	1978							
		MF	57	45	7	6	33	—
		M	76	59	11	10	45	—
		F	37	31	3	3	21	—
PAKISTAN	1970		(5– 9)		(10–16)		(5–16)	(20–24)
		MF	44	...	14	...	28	2.50
		M	62	...	22	...	40	3.79
		F	24	...	6	...	14	1.11
	1974							
		MF	49	...	16	...	31	1.90
		M	67	...	24	...	44	2.76
		F	29	...	8	...	18	0.97
	1975							
		MF	50	...	17	...	32	2.01
		M	68	...	25	...	45	2.96
		F	31	...	8	...	19	0.98
	1976							
		MF	51	...	...	...	...	2.01
		M	69	...	...	...	...	2.88
		F	32	...	...	...	...	1.07
PHILIPPINES	1970		(7–12)		(13–16)		(7–16)	(20–24)
		MF	114	...	50	...	91	19.94
		M	115	...	59	...	95	17.11
		F	113	...	42	...	88	22.97
	1974							
		MF	107	...	56	...	89	19.50
		M	104	...	65	...	90	...
		F	109	...	47	...	87	...
	1975							
		MF	105	93	56	...	87	20.13
		M	102	91	65	...	89	...
		F	107	95	47	...	86	...

School enrolment ratios   3.2
Taux d'inscription scolaire
Tasas de escolarización

			ENROLMENT RATIOS / TAUX D'INSCRIPTION / TASAS DE ESCOLARIZACION					
COUNTRY	YEAR	SEX	FIRST LEVEL		SECOND LEVEL		1ST + 2ND LEVELS	3RD LEVEL
PAYS	ANNEE	SEXE	PREMIER DEGRE		SECOND DEGRE		1ER + 2ND DEGRE	3EME DEGRE
PAIS	AÑO	SEXO	PRIMER GRADO		SEGUNDO GRADO		1ER + 2DO GRADO	3ER GRADO
			GROSS BRUT BRUTA	NET NET NETA	GROSS BRUT BRUTA	NET NET NETA	GROSS BRUT BRUTA	GROSS BRUT BRUTA
PHILIPPINES (CONT.)	1976							
		MF	103	...	59	...	88	20.61
	1977							
		MF	102	...	66	...	89	23.69
SAUDI ARABIA	1970		(6–11)		(12–17)		(6–17)	(20–24)
		MF	43	31	11	8	28	1.57
		M	58	41	17	13	39	2.83
		F	27	20	4	3	17	0.26
	1974							
		MF	56	41	20	12	39	3.29
		M	70	55	27	16	51	5.50
		F	40	28	12	8	28	0.99
	1975							
		MF	58	43	22	13	42	4.28
		M	73	55	29	17	53	6.72
		F	43	30	14	9	30	1.75
	1976							
		MF	59	44	24	15	44	5.16
		M	74	57	32	19	55	7.93
		F	44	30	17	11	32	2.29
	1977							
		MF	59	44	26	17	45	6.74
		M	74	57	33	21	56	10.46
		F	44	31	19	13	33	2.87
SINGAPORE	1970		(6–11)		(12–17)		(6–17)	(20–24)
		MF	105	94	46	44	77	6.76
		M	110	96	47	43	79	9.32
		F	101	92	45	44	74	4.14
	1974							
		MF	109	100	51	49	79	7.65
		M	112	100	51	47	80	10.23
		F	106	100	52	51	77	4.95
	1975							
		MF	111	100	53	49	79	9.22
		M	114	100	52	47	80	10.90
		F	107	100	53	52	78	7.46
	1976							
		MF	111	100	54	51	80	9.04
		M	114	100	54	48	81	11.13
		F	108	100	55	54	79	6.84
	1977							
		MF	110	100	55	55	80	9.12
		M	113	100	55	54	81	11.05
		F	107	100	56	56	79	7.08
	1978							
		MF	109	99	57	56	80	...
		M	111	99	56	55	81	...
		F	107	99	58	58	80	...

3.2 School enrolment ratios
Taux d'inscription scolaire
Tasas de escolarización

			ENROLMENT RATIOS / TAUX D'INSCRIPTION / TASAS DE ESCOLARIZACION					
COUNTRY	YEAR	SEX	FIRST LEVEL		SECOND LEVEL		1ST + 2ND LEVELS	3RD LEVEL
PAYS	ANNEE	SEXE	PREMIER DEGRE		SECOND DEGRE		1ER + 2ND DEGRE	3EME DEGRE
PAIS	AÑO	SEXO	PRIMER GRADO		SEGUNDO GRADO		1ER + 2DO GRADO	3ER GRADO
			GROSS BRUT BRUTA	NET NET NETA	GROSS BRUT BRUTA	NET NET NETA	GROSS BRUT BRUTA	GROSS BRUT BRUTA
SRI LANKA	1970		(6—10)		(11—17)		(6—17)	(20—24)
		MF	99	...	47	...	71	1.17
		M	104	...	46	...	72	1.33
		F	94	...	48	...	69	1.02
	1974							
		MF	81	...	50	...	64	1.31
		M	82	...	48	...	63	1.63
		F	81	...	51	...	64	0.99
	1975							
		MF	79	...	48	...	61	1.34
		M	82	...	47	...	62	1.71
		F	75	...	49	...	61	0.96
	1976							
		MF	79	...	48	...	61	1.34
		M	82	...	47	...	62	1.71
		F	75	...	48	...	60	0.97
	1977							
		MF	85	77	42	...	61	...
		M	89	...	42	...	63	...
		F	81	...	42	...	59	...
	1978		(5—10)		(11—17)		(5—17)	(20—24)
		MF	94	...	52	...	72	...
		M	98	...	63	...	80	...
		F	90	...	40	...	64	...
	1979							
		MF	98	...	53	...	74	...
SYRIAN ARAB REPUBLIC	1970		(6—11)		(12—17)		(6—17)	(20—24)
		MF	84	75	38	28	63	8.88
		M	102	91	54	40	81	14.10
		F	63	58	20	16	44	3.56
	1974							
		MF	91	83	47	39	73	12.69
		M	106	95	63	52	88	19.27
		F	75	68	30	26	56	5.93
	1975							
		MF	91	83	48	41	73	13.59
		M	105	95	64	54	88	20.01
		F	75	69	32	28	57	6.98
	1976							
		MF	90	83	48	43	72	14.14
		M	104	94	62	54	86	20.76
		F	75	70	33	30	57	7.29
	1977							
		MF	90	82	48	42	72	...
		M	104	93	61	53	85	...
		F	76	70	34	31	58	...

School enrolment ratios 3.2
Taux d'inscription scolaire
Tasas de escolarización

			ENROLMENT RATIOS / TAUX D'INSCRIPTION / TASAS DE ESCOLARIZACION					
COUNTRY	YEAR	SEX	FIRST LEVEL		SECOND LEVEL		1ST + 2ND LEVELS	3RD LEVEL
PAYS	ANNEE	SEXE	PREMIER DEGRE		SECOND DEGRE		1ER + 2ND DEGRE	3EME DEGRE
PAIS	AÑO	SEXO	PRIMER GRADO		SEGUNDO GRADO		1ER + 2DO GRADO	3ER GRADO
			GROSS BRUT BRUTA	NET NET NETA	GROSS BRUT BRUTA	NET NET NETA	GROSS BRUT BRUTA	GROSS BRUT BRUTA
SYRIAN ARAB REPUBLIC (CONT.)	1978							
		MF	92	83	48	43	73	...
		M	105	94	60	53	85	...
		F	78	72	35	32	60	...
THAILAND	1970		(7—13)		(14—18)		(7—18)	(20—24)
		MF	81	...	17	...	58	2.02
		M	85	...	20	...	62	2.39
		F	77	...	14	...	54	1.67
	1974							
		MF	84	...	24	...	62	3.86
		M	88	...	27	...	65	4.75
		F	81	...	20	...	58	3.02
	1975							
		MF	84	...	25	...	62	3.51
		M	87	...	28	...	65	4.29
		F	80	...	22	...	58	2.75
	1976							
		MF	83	...	27	...	62	4.48
		M	86	...	28	...	65	5.04
		F	79	...	26	...	59	3.93
	1977							
		MF	82	...	28	...	62	5.30
		M	85	...	29	...	64	6.13
		F	78	...	27	...	59	4.49
TURKEY	1970		(7—11)		(12—17)		(7—17)	(20—24)
		MF	110	...	27	...	67	6.02
		M	124	...	38	...	80	9.24
		F	94	...	15	...	53	2.41
	1974		(6—10)		(11—16)		(6—16)	(20—24)
		MF	106	...	27	...	64	6.44
		M	117	...	37	...	75	9.77
		F	95	...	17	...	54	2.84
	1976							
		MF	107	...	40	...	71	7.75
		M	118	...	55	...	84	11.43
		F	97	...	24	...	58	3.76
	1977							
		MF	105	...	41	...	71	8.00
		M	115	...	57	...	84	11.69
		F	95	...	26	...	58	4.04
VIET—NAM	1975		(6—10)		(11—16)		(6—16)	(20—24)
		MF	121	...	47	...	83	2.03
		M	121	...	46	...	83	2.44
		F	121	...	48	...	84	1.62
	1976							
		MF	123	100	49	43	86	2.46
		M	122	...	50	...	85	3.26
		F	124	...	49	...	86	1.64

3.2 School enrolment ratios
Taux d'inscription scolaire
Tasas de escolarización

COUNTRY PAYS PAIS	YEAR ANNEE AÑO	SEX SEXE SEXO	ENROLMENT RATIOS / TAUX D'INSCRIPTION / TASAS DE ESCOLARIZACION				1ST + 2ND LEVELS 1ER + 2ND DEGRE 1ER + 2DO GRADO	3RD LEVEL 3EME DEGRE 3ER GRADO
			FIRST LEVEL PREMIER DEGRE PRIMER GRADO		SECOND LEVEL SECOND DEGRE SEGUNDO GRADO			
			GROSS BRUT BRUTA	NET NET NETA	GROSS BRUT BRUTA	NET NET NETA	GROSS BRUT BRUTA	GROSS BRUT BRUTA
VIET—NAM (CONT.)	1977							
		MF	122	...	51	...	86	2.87
		M	128	...	56	...	91	3.91
		F	116	...	47	...	81	1.80
YEMEN	1970		(7—12)		(13—18)		(7—18)	(20—24)
		MF	12	...	1	...	7	0.02
		M	23	...	2	...	14	0.03
		F	2	...	0.10	...	1	0.00
	1974							
		MF	27	...	3	...	18	0.56
		M	48	...	6	...	32	1.22
		F	5	...	1	...	3	0.11
	1975							
		MF	29	22	4	3	19	0.68
		M	50	38	8	6	34	1.55
		F	7	5	1	1	4	0.11
	1976							
		MF	...	...	...	...	...	0.65
		M	...	...	...	...	...	1.48
		F	...	...	...	...	...	0.12
	1977							
		MF	...	...	...	...	...	1.14
		M	...	...	...	...	...	2.56
		F	...	...	...	...	...	0.22
YEMEN, DEMOCRATIC	1970		(7—12)		(13—18)		(7—18)	(20—24)
		MF	57	...	10	...	36	0.07
		M	91	...	16	...	58	0.11
		F	23	...	4	...	14	0.04
	1974							
		MF	71	...	20	...	50	0.75
		M	98	...	33	...	71	1.29
		F	44	...	8	...	29	0.26
	1975							
		MF	81	...	23	...	56	1.03
		M	110	...	35	...	79	1.55
		F	51	...	10	...	34	0.56
	1976							
		MF	81	...	26	...	57	1.55
		M	108	...	40	...	79	2.35
		F	53	...	13	...	35	0.85
	1977							
		MF	72	...	28	...	53	1.97
		M	92	...	42	...	70	2.92
		F	51	...	15	...	35	1.12

School enrolment ratios   3.2
Taux d'inscription scolaire
Tasas de escolarización

COUNTRY	YEAR	SEX	ENROLMENT RATIOS / TAUX D'INSCRIPTION / TASAS DE ESCOLARIZACION					
			FIRST LEVEL		SECOND LEVEL		1ST + 2ND LEVELS	3RD LEVEL
PAYS	ANNEE	SEXE	PREMIER DEGRE		SECOND DEGRE		1ER + 2ND DEGRE	3EME DEGRE
PAIS	AÑO	SEXO	PRIMER GRADO		SEGUNDO GRADO		1ER + 2DO GRADO	3ER GRADO
			GROSS BRUT BRUTA	NET NET NETA	GROSS BRUT BRUTA	NET NET NETA	GROSS BRUT BRUTA	GROSS BRUT BRUTA

EUROPE

ALBANIA	1970		(6–13)		(14–17)		(6–17)	(20–24)
		MF	104	...	38	...	85	15.16
		M	107	...	44	...	90	20.20
		F	101	...	31	...	81	9.98
	1971							
		MF	107	...	43	...	88	16.44
		M	110	...	50	...	93	22.03
		F	103	...	37	...	84	10.75
AUSTRIA	1970		(6– 9)		(10–17)		(6–17)	(20–24)
		MF	104	91	72	68	84	11.76
		M	104	...	71	...	83	16.34
		F	103	...	73	...	84	7.02
	1974							
		MF	102	89	75	71	84	16.66
		M	102	...	74	...	84	20.89
		F	101	...	76	...	85	12.33
	1975							
		MF	102	89	76	71	84	18.90
		M	102	...	75	...	84	23.28
		F	101	...	77	...	85	14.43
	1976							
		MF	102	89	75	73	84	20.11
		M	103	89	73	...	83	24.45
		F	102	90	76	...	85	15.67
	1977							
		MF	100	...	72	...	81	20.92
		M	101	...	71	...	80	24.86
		F	100	...	73	...	81	16.88
	1978							
		MF	100	...	72	...	80	...
		M	100	...	71	...	80	...
		F	99	...	73	...	81	...
BELGIUM	1970		(6–11)		(12–17)		(6–17)	(20–24)
		MF	106	...	81	...	94	17.49
		M	107	...	82	...	95	21.88
		F	105	...	80	...	93	12.93
	1974							
		MF	101	...	84	...	92	20.52
		M	102	...	83	...	92	23.65
		F	101	...	84	...	92	17.24
	1975							
		MF	102	...	85	...	93	21.32
		M	102	...	84	...	93	24.34
		F	101	...	86	...	93	18.13

3.2 School enrolment ratios
Taux d'inscription scolaire
Tasas de escolarización

COUNTRY PAYS PAIS	YEAR ANNEE AÑO	SEX SEXE SEXO	ENROLMENT RATIOS / TAUX D'INSCRIPTION / TASAS DE ESCOLARIZACION					
			FIRST LEVEL PREMIER DEGRE PRIMER GRADO		SECOND LEVEL SECOND DEGRE SEGUNDO GRADO		1ST + 2ND LEVELS 1ER + 2ND DEGRE 1ER + 2DO GRADO	3RD LEVEL 3EME DEGRE 3ER GRADO
			GROSS BRUT BRUTA	NET NET NETA	GROSS BRUT BRUTA	NET NET NETA	GROSS BRUT BRUTA	GROSS BRUT BRUTA
BELGIUM (CONT.)	1976							
		MF	102	96	88	81	95	22.40
		M	102	96	89	79	95	25.09
		F	101	96	88	82	94	19.58
	1977							
		MF	102	...	86	...	94	23.08
		M	101	...	86	...	93	25.48
		F	102	...	87	...	94	20.54
BULGARIA	1970		(7—14)		(15—17)		(7—17)	(20—24)
		MF	101	96	79	55	94	14.43
		M	101	96	79	52	95	14.04
		F	100	96	78	59	94	14.84
	1974							
		MF	98	...	88	...	95	18.79
		M	98	...	88	...	95	16.02
		F	98	...	88	...	95	21.63
	1975							
		MF	99	96	89	68	96	19.16
		M	99	96	89	...	96	16.14
		F	99	97	89	...	96	22.25
	1976							
		MF	99	97	90	65	96	19.43
		M	99	...	91	...	97	16.06
		F	99	...	88	...	96	22.88
	1977							
		MF	99	97	90	69	96	21.55
		M	99	97	94	...	97	15.79
		F	98	97	86	...	95	27.47
	1978							
		MF	96	...	90	...	94	...
		M	96	...	94	...	95	...
		F	95	...	86	...	93	...
CZECHOSLOVAKIA	1970		(6—14)		(15—18)		(6—18)	(20—24)
		MF	98	...	31	...	75	10.42
		M	98	...	24	...	73	12.74
		F	98	...	39	...	78	8.03
	1974							
		MF	96	...	34	...	76	11.15
		M	96	...	26	...	73	13.08
		F	97	...	43	...	79	9.15
	1975							
		MF	96	...	35	...	77	12.07
		M	96	...	27	...	74	14.11
		F	97	...	44	...	80	9.94
	1976							
		MF	97	...	36	...	78	13.31
		M	96	...	28	...	75	15.38
		F	97	...	46	...	81	11.15

School enrolment ratios 3.2
Taux d'inscription scolaire
Tasas de escolarización

COUNTRY	YEAR	SEX	ENROLMENT RATIOS / TAUX D'INSCRIPTION / TASAS DE ESCOLARIZACION				1ST + 2ND LEVELS	3RD LEVEL
			FIRST LEVEL		SECOND LEVEL		1ER + 2ND DEGRE	3EME DEGRE
PAYS	ANNEE	SEXE	PREMIER DEGRE		SECOND DEGRE		1ER + 2DO GRADO	3ER GRADO
PAIS	AÑO	SEXO	PRIMER GRADO		SEGUNDO GRADO		GROSS BRUT BRUTA	GROSS BRUT BRUTA
			GROSS BRUT BRUTA	NET NET NETA	GROSS BRUT BRUTA	NET NET NETA		
CZECHOSLOVAKIA (CONT.)	1977							
		MF	96	...	38	...	78	14.50
		M	96	...	28	...	75	16.79
		F	96	...	48	...	81	12.12
	1978							
		MF	94	...	40	...	78	15.25
		M	94	...	30	...	74	17.74
		F	95	...	50	...	81	12.64
DENMARK	1970		(6—11)		(12—17)		(6—17)	(20—24)
		MF	96	...	93	...	94	18.28
		M	95	...	103	...	99	22.49
		F	97	...	82	...	90	13.82
	1974							
		MF	103	...	74	...	89	27.58
		M	102	...	74	...	88	30.13
		F	104	...	74	...	89	24.90
	1975							
		MF	104	...	80	...	92	29.41
		M	103	...	82	...	93	31.98
		F	105	...	78	...	92	26.72
	1976							
		MF	103	...	80	...	91	29.94
		M	102	...	82	...	92	31.05
		F	104	...	78	...	91	28.77
	1977							
		MF	100	...	83	...	91	32.10
		M	...	...	84	...	91	33.57
		F	...	...	82	...	91	30.56
FINLAND	1970		(7—12)		(13—18)		(7—18)	(20—24)
		MF	82	...	102	71	92	13.34
		M	84	...	98	...	91	13.41
		F	79	...	106	...	93	13.26
	1974							
		MF	90	...	106	...	98	16.74
		M	92	...	100	...	96	16.31
		F	88	...	113	...	101	17.19
	1975							
		MF	89	...	81	...	85	18.36
		M	90	...	77	...	83	18.01
		F	88	...	86	...	87	18.74
	1976							
		MF	87	...	84	...	86	19.30
		M	88	...	80	...	84	18.88
		F	87	...	89	...	88	19.74
	1977							
		MF	86	...	86	...	86	20.42
		M	87	...	82	...	84	19.98
		F	86	...	91	...	88	20.87

3.2 School enrolment ratios
Taux d'inscription scolaire
Tasas de escolarización

COUNTRY PAYS PAIS	YEAR ANNEE AÑO	SEX SEXE SEXO	ENROLMENT RATIOS / TAUX D'INSCRIPTION / TASAS DE ESCOLARIZACION					
			FIRST LEVEL PREMIER DEGRE PRIMER GRADO		SECOND LEVEL SECOND DEGRE SEGUNDO GRADO		1ST + 2ND LEVELS 1ER + 2ND DEGRE 1ER + 2DO GRADO	3RD LEVEL 3EME DEGRE 3ER GRADO
			GROSS BRUT BRUTA	NET NET NETA	GROSS BRUT BRUTA	NET NET NETA	GROSS BRUT BRUTA	GROSS BRUT BRUTA
FINLAND (CONT.)	1978							
		MF	85	...	89	...	87	...
		M	86	...	85	...	85	...
		F	85	...	94	...	90	...
FRANCE	1970		(6—10)		(11—17)		(6—17)	(20—24)
		MF	117	98	74	67	92	19.50
		M	118	98	71	64	90	22.79
		F	117	98	77	70	93	16.03
	1974							
		MF	110	...	83	...	95	23.25
		M	111	...	81	...	93	24.08
		F	110	...	86	...	96	22.39
	1975							
		MF	109	98	84	76	95	24.45
		M	110	...	81	...	93	25.10
		F	109	...	87	...	96	23.78
	1976							
		MF	109	98	83	77	94	24.64
		M	110	98	79	74	92	24.50
		F	109	98	86	80	95	24.79
	1977							
		MF	111	...	83	...	94	25.73
		M	111	...	79	...	92	25.52
		F	110	...	87	...	96	25.96
	1978							
		MF	112	100	83	78	95	...
		M	113	100	79	74	93	...
		F	111	100	87	82	97	...
GERMAN DEMOCRATIC REPUBLIC	1970		(7—16)		(17—18)		(7—18)	(20—24)
		MF	93	...	92	...	93	32.77
		M	92	...	94	...	92	36.55
		F	94	...	88	...	93	28.82
	1974							
		MF	94	...	89	...	94	24.61
		M	93	...	92	...	93	22.83
		F	96	...	86	...	94	26.48
	1975							
		MF	94	...	89	...	93	29.45
		M	93	...	92	...	93	...
		F	96	...	86	...	94	...
	1976							
		MF	94	...	92	...	93	28.40
		M	92	...	95	...	93	...
		F	95	...	89	...	94	...
	1977							
		MF	93	...	93	...	93	28.51
	1978		(6—15)		(16—17)		(6—17)	(20—24)
		MF	97	...	89	...	96	...

School enrolment ratios 3.2
Taux d'inscription scolaire
Tasas de escolarización

			ENROLMENT RATIOS / TAUX D'INSCRIPTION / TASAS DE ESCOLARIZACION						
COUNTRY	YEAR	SEX	FIRST LEVEL		SECOND LEVEL		1ST + 2ND LEVELS	3RD LEVEL
PAYS	ANNEE	SEXE	PREMIER DEGRE		SECOND DEGRE		1ER + 2ND DEGRE	3EME DEGRE
PAIS	AÑO	SEXO	PRIMER GRADO		SEGUNDO GRADO		1ER + 2DO GRADO	3ER GRADO
			GROSS BRUT BRUTA	NET NET NETA	GROSS BRUT BRUTA	NET NET NETA	GROSS BRUT BRUTA	GROSS BRUT BRUTA
GERMANY, FEDERAL REPUBLIC OF	1970		(6– 9)		(10–18)		(6–18)	(20–24)
		MF	...	...	...	...	78	13.41
		M	...	...	...	...	78	19.18
		F	...	...	...	...	78	7.37
	1974							
		MF	...	...	...	...	81	19.07
		M	...	...	...	...	80	25.12
		F	...	...	...	...	82	12.87
	1975							
		MF	...	...	...	...	80	24.45
		M	...	...	...	...	77	29.76
		F	...	...	...	...	82	19.03
	1976							
		MF	...	...	...	...	80	24.39
		M	...	...	...	...	79	29.62
		F	...	...	...	...	81	19.05
	1977							
		MF	...	...	...	...	79	24.70
		M	...	...	...	...	78	29.46
		F	...	...	...	...	80	19.80
	1978							
		MF	...	...	...	...	77	...
GREECE	1970		(6–11)		(12–17)		(6–17)	(20–24)
		MF	107	97	63	52	85	13.52
		M	108	97	70	56	89	17.92
		F	106	97	55	48	81	8.81
	1974		(5–10)		(11–16)		(5–16)	(20–24)
		MF	104	88	75	56	90	17.66
		M	105	88	84	60	94	22.01
		F	103	88	65	52	85	12.98
	1975							
		MF	103	88	78	58	91	18.36
		M	104	88	88	63	96	22.21
		F	103	88	67	53	85	14.17
	1976							
		MF	104	88	79	60	92	18.99
		M	104	88	89	64	97	22.66
		F	103	88	69	56	87	14.98
HUNGARY	1970		(6–13)		(14–17)		(6–17)	(20–24)
		MF	97	94	63	31	84	10.08
		M	98	94	71	25	88	11.36
		F	97	93	55	37	80	8.76
	1974							
		MF	99	...	62	...	85	11.31
		M	99	...	66	...	87	11.68
		F	99	...	57	...	83	10.92

3.2 School enrolment ratios
Taux d'inscription scolaire
Tasas de escolarización

			ENROLMENT RATIOS / TAUX D'INSCRIPTION / TASAS DE ESCOLARIZACION					
COUNTRY	YEAR	SEX	FIRST LEVEL		SECOND LEVEL		1ST + 2ND LEVELS	3RD LEVEL
PAYS	ANNEE	SEXE	PREMIER DEGRE		SECOND DEGRE		1ER + 2ND DEGRE	3EME DEGRE
PAIS	AÑO	SEXO	PRIMER GRADO		SEGUNDO GRADO		1ER + 2DO GRADO	3ER GRADO
			GROSS BRUT BRUTA	NET NET NETA	GROSS BRUT BRUTA	NET NET NETA	GROSS BRUT BRUTA	GROSS BRUT BRUTA
HUNGARY (CONT.)	1975							
		MF	99	...	63	...	86	11.66
		M	99	...	67	...	87	11.79
		F	99	...	58	...	84	11.53
	1976							
		MF	99	96	65	32	87	12.07
		M	98	95	69	24	88	11.82
		F	99	96	62	41	86	12.33
	1977							
		MF	98	95	68	33	88	12.14
		M	98	94	70	24	89	11.73
		F	98	95	65	42	87	12.58
	1978							
		MF	97	94	69	65	88	...
		M	96	93	72	68	89	...
		F	97	94	65	63	87	...
ICELAND	1970		(7–12)		(13–19)		(7–19)	(20–24)
		MF	98	...	80	...	89	9.86
		M	97	...	84	...	91	14.11
		F	100	...	75	...	87	5.15
	1974							
		MF	100	...	80	...	89	14.11
		M	100	...	87	...	93	18.04
		F	100	...	73	...	86	9.88
	1975							
		MF	99	...	82	...	90	15.15
		M	99	...	89	...	94	18.57
		F	99	...	75	...	86	11.52
	1976							
		MF	99	99	83	72	90	19.98
		M	99	...	89	...	93	...
		F	100	...	77	...	88	...
IRELAND	1970		(6–11)		(12–16)		(6–16)	(20–24)
		MF	106	92	79	63	94	13.49
		M	107	92	78	62	94	17.39
		F	105	92	79	65	94	9.43
	1974							
		MF	106	94	90	74	99	16.33
		M	106	94	90	72	99	20.42
		F	106	95	91	76	99	12.06
	1975							
		MF	106	94	88	76	98	19.30
		M	106	94	85	74	97	24.80
		F	106	94	92	78	100	13.55
	1976							
		MF	106	94	91	78	99	19.09
		M	106	94	87	76	97	23.28
		F	105	94	95	80	101	14.73

School enrolment ratios 3.2
Taux d'inscription scolaire
Tasas de escolarización

			ENROLMENT RATIOS / TAUX D'INSCRIPTION / TASAS DE ESCOLARIZACION					
COUNTRY	YEAR	SEX	FIRST LEVEL		SECOND LEVEL		1ST + 2ND LEVELS	3RD LEVEL
PAYS	ANNEE	SEXE	PREMIER DEGRE		SECOND DEGRE		1ER + 2ND DEGRE	3EME DEGRE
PAIS	AÑO	SEXO	PRIMER GRADO		SEGUNDO GRADO		1ER + 2DO GRADO	3ER GRADO
			GROSS BRUT BRUTA	NET NET NETA	GROSS BRUT BRUTA	NET NET NETA	GROSS BRUT BRUTA	GROSS BRUT BRUTA
IRELAND (CONT.)	1977							
		MF	105	94	92	79	99	18.82
		M	105	93	87	77	97	22.92
		F	105	94	97	81	101	14.55
	1978							
		MF	104	93	92	80	99	...
		M	105	93	87	77	97	...
		F	104	94	97	82	101	...
ITALY	1970		(6–10)		(11–18)		(6–18)	(20–24)
		MF	110	...	61	...	81	16.69
		M	112	...	66	...	85	20.38
		F	109	...	55	...	77	12.85
	1974							
		MF	108	...	67	...	84	23.72
		M	108	...	71	...	86	28.34
		F	107	...	63	...	81	18.92
	1975							
		MF	106	98	70	66	84	25.07
		M	107	98	74	68	87	30.08
		F	106	99	66	64	82	19.87
	1976							
		MF	105	...	72	...	85	26.22
		M	105	...	75	...	87	31.16
		F	104	...	68	...	82	21.11
	1977							
		MF	103	...	73	...	85	26.83
		M	104	...	75	...	86	31.34
		F	103	...	70	...	83	22.15
	1978							
		MF	103	...	73	...	84	...
LUXEMBOURG	1970		(6–11)		(12–18)		(6–18)	(20–24)
		MF	112	...	48	45	78	1.56
		M	110	...	49	45	78	1.77
		F	113	...	46	44	78	1.33
	1974							
		MF	97	93	59	56	76	1.96
		M	97	93	59	55	76	2.10
		F	97	93	59	57	76	1.81
	1975							
		MF	97	92	60	57	77	1.74
		M	98	93	60	56	77	1.98
		F	96	92	61	58	77	1.50
	1976							
		MF	98	93	62	59	78	1.60
		M	98	93	62	57	77	1.84
		F	98	93	63	60	78	1.36

3.2 School enrolment ratios
Taux d'inscription scolaire
Tasas de escolarización

COUNTRY PAYS PAIS	YEAR ANNEE AÑO	SEX SEXE SEXO	ENROLMENT RATIOS / TAUX D'INSCRIPTION / TASAS DE ESCOLARIZACION					
			FIRST LEVEL PREMIER DEGRE PRIMER GRADO		SECOND LEVEL SECOND DEGRE SEGUNDO GRADO		1ST + 2ND LEVELS 1ER + 2ND DEGRE 1ER + 2DO GRADO	3RD LEVEL 3EME DEGRE 3ER GRADO
			GROSS BRUT BRUTA	NET NET NETA	GROSS BRUT BRUTA	NET NET NETA	GROSS BRUT BRUTA	GROSS BRUT BRUTA
LUXEMBOURG (CONT.)	1977							
		MF	98	93	64	61	79	1.08
		M	98	92	65	60	79	1.22
		F	99	94	64	61	79	0.93
	1978							
		MF	98	...	...	...	...	...
		M	97	...	...	...	...	...
		F	98	...	...	...	...	...
MALTA	1970		(5—10)		(11—17)		(5—17)	(20—24)
		MF	108	84	50	47	75	5.59
		M	109	84	52	49	77	7.78
		F	107	84	49	46	74	3.62
	1974							
		MF	100	87	71	66	83	6.87
		M	100	87	76	69	86	10.25
		F	100	88	65	63	79	3.66
	1975							
		MF	102	91	75	71	85	4.63
		M	102	90	80	74	89	6.83
		F	102	91	69	67	82	2.54
	1976							
		MF	108	94	72	69	86	5.64
		M	106	92	78	73	89	8.38
		F	110	95	66	65	83	3.03
	1977							
		MF	110	96	71	68	87	5.47
		M	109	96	77	71	90	8.32
		F	111	97	66	65	84	2.73
NETHERLANDS	1970		(6—11)		(12—17)		(6—17)	(20—24)
		MF	102	93	75	69	89	19.51
		M	101	92	81	72	91	27.47
		F	102	94	69	65	86	11.11
	1974							
		MF	98	91	85	77	92	23.19
		M	98	90	89	78	94	31.27
		F	99	92	80	76	90	14.72
	1975							
		MF	99	92	89	80	94	25.47
		M	99	91	92	81	95	33.60
		F	100	93	85	80	92	16.99
	1976							
		MF	100	92	91	82	95	27.01
		M	99	91	94	82	97	35.08
		F	100	93	87	81	94	18.60
	1977							
		MF	100	93	92	82	96	28.15
		M	99	91	95	82	97	35.97
		F	101	94	89	82	95	19.98

School enrolment ratios 3.2
Taux d'inscription scolaire
Tasas de escolarización

			ENROLMENT RATIOS / TAUX D'INSCRIPTION / TASAS DE ESCOLARIZACION					
COUNTRY	YEAR	SEX	FIRST LEVEL		SECOND LEVEL		1ST + 2ND LEVELS	3RD LEVEL
PAYS	ANNEE	SEXE	PREMIER DEGRE		SECOND DEGRE		1ER + 2ND DEGRE	3EME DEGRE
PAIS	AÑO	SEXO	PRIMER GRADO		SEGUNDO GRADO		1ER + 2DO GRADO	3ER GRADO
			GROSS BRUT BRUTA	NET NET NETA	GROSS BRUT BRUTA	NET NET NETA	GROSS BRUT BRUTA	GROSS BRUT BRUTA
NETHERLANDS (CONT.)	1978							
		MF	101	93	92	82	96	...
		M	100	92	95	82	97	...
		F	102	95	89	82	95	...
NORWAY	1970		(7—13)		(14—19)		(7—19)	(20—24)
		MF	89	88	83	65	87	15.91
		M	85	...	84	...	84	21.52
		F	93	...	83	...	89	9.94
	1974		(7—12)		(13—18)		(7—18)	(20—24)
		MF	101	...	89	...	95	21.20
		M	101	...	89	...	95	26.42
		F	101	...	90	...	96	15.69
	1975							
		MF	101	100	88	79	95	22.06
		M	101	99	88	79	94	26.82
		F	101	100	88	80	95	17.06
	1976							
		MF	101	100	89	80	95	24.33
		M	101	100	88	80	95	27.14
		F	101	100	89	81	95	21.38
	1977							
		MF	100	99	90	81	95	24.12
		M	100	99	89	81	95	26.40
		F	100	99	91	82	96	21.74
POLAND	1970		(7—14)		(15—18)		(7—18)	(20—24)
		MF	101	95	49	38	83	14.05
		M	103	95	41	33	81	14.61
		F	99	95	57	44	84	13.47
	1974							
		MF	100	...	53	...	82	15.59
		M	102	...	46	...	80	14.38
		F	99	...	60	...	84	16.85
	1975							
		MF	100	...	53	...	82	16.81
		M	102	...	46	...	80	15.15
		F	99	...	60	...	84	18.53
	1976							
		MF	100	...	55	...	83	17.66
		M	102	...	48	...	81	15.55
		F	99	...	62	...	85	19.85
	1977							
		MF	100	...	67	...	88	17.77
		M	...	...	60	...	...	15.68
		F	...	...	75	...	...	19.93
	1978							
		MF	100	...	...	...	...	...

3.2 School enrolment ratios
Taux d'inscription scolaire
Tasas de escolarización

			ENROLMENT RATIOS / TAUX D'INSCRIPTION / TASAS DE ESCOLARIZACION					
COUNTRY	YEAR	SEX	FIRST LEVEL		SECOND LEVEL		1ST + 2ND LEVELS	3RD LEVEL
PAYS	ANNEE	SEXE	PREMIER DEGRE		SECOND DEGRE		1ER + 2ND DEGRE	3EME DEGRE
PAIS	AÑO	SEXO	PRIMER GRADO		SEGUNDO GRADO		1ER + 2DO GRADO	3ER GRADO
			GROSS BRUT BRUTA	NET NET NETA	GROSS BRUT BRUTA	NET NET NETA	GROSS BRUT BRUTA	GROSS BRUT BRUTA
PORTUGAL	1970		(6–11)		(12–16)		(6–16)	(20–24)
		MF	98	83	57	31	80	7.97
		M	99	83	63	34	84	9.31
		F	96	82	51	28	77	6.76
	1974							
		MF	110	...	49	...	83	8.92
		M	111	...	50	...	84	10.29
		F	110	...	47	...	82	7.62
	1975							
		MF	113	88	53	28	86	10.46
		M	114	87	53	27	87	11.66
		F	112	88	52	29	85	9.28
	1976							
		MF	114	89	54	30	87	12.29
		M	116	89	53	...	87	14.06
		F	112	89	54	...	86	10.55
	1977							
		MF	117	92	55	30	88	10.77
		M	119	92	54	29	89	12.40
		F	115	93	56	31	88	9.14
ROMANIA	1970		(6–13)		(14–17)		(6–17)	(20–24)
		MF	112	...	44	...	87	10.05
		M	111	...	51	...	89	11.24
		F	113	...	38	...	85	8.82
	1974							
		MF	110	...	57	...	91	8.71
		M	110	...	59	...	92	9.65
		F	109	...	55	...	89	7.74
	1975							
		MF	109	...	62	...	93	9.17
		M	110	...	65	...	95	9.94
		F	108	...	59	...	92	8.37
	1976							
		MF	106	...	69	...	95	9.59
		M	106	...	73	...	96	10.50
		F	105	...	66	...	93	8.66
	1977							
		MF	101	...	79	...	95	9.90
		M	102	...	84	...	97	10.84
		F	101	...	73	...	93	8.92
	1978							
		MF	106	...	84	...	100	10.33
		M	109	...	90	...	104	11.58
		F	103	...	77	...	96	9.03
SPAIN	1970		(6–10)		(11–16)		(6–16)	(20–24)
		MF	123	94	56	40	88	8.91
		M	121	93	64	45	91	12.87
		F	125	95	48	35	85	4.83

School enrolment ratios 3.2
Taux d'inscription scolaire
Tasas de escolarización

			ENROLMENT RATIOS / TAUX D'INSCRIPTION / TASAS DE ESCOLARIZACION					
COUNTRY	YEAR	SEX	FIRST LEVEL		SECOND LEVEL		1ST + 2ND LEVELS	3RD LEVEL
PAYS	ANNEE	SEXE	PREMIER DEGRE		SECOND DEGRE		1ER + 2ND DEGRE	3EME DEGRE
PAIS	AÑO	SEXO	PRIMER GRADO		SEGUNDO GRADO		1ER + 2DO GRADO	3ER GRADO
			GROSS BRUT BRUTA	NET NET NETA	GROSS BRUT BRUTA	NET NET NETA	GROSS BRUT BRUTA	GROSS BRUT BRUTA
SPAIN (CONT.)	1974							
		MF	113	100	78	64	94	17.39
		M	112	100	80	66	95	22.99
		F	113	100	76	62	93	11.82
	1975		(6–10)		(11–17)		(6–17)	(20–24)
		MF	111	100	73	63	89	20.36
		M	111	100	74	65	90	26.17
		F	111	100	71	61	89	14.64
	1976							
		MF	110	98	76	66	91	21.54
		M	110	98	77	67	91	26.75
		F	110	99	75	64	90	16.39
SWEDEN	1970		(7–12)		(13–19)		(7–19)	(20–24)
		MF	94	...	73	...	82	21.34
		M	93	...	73	...	83	24.04
		F	95	...	72	...	82	18.51
	1974							
		MF	100	...	71	...	85	22.08
		M	100	...	71	...	85	23.45
		F	101	...	71	...	85	20.65
	1975							
		MF	101	100	67	...	83	28.80
		M	101	100	64	...	82	33.72
		F	102	100	70	...	85	23.68
	1976							
		MF	100	...	67	...	83	30.97
		M	100	...	64	...	81	35.25
		F	101	...	70	...	84	26.52
	1977							
		MF	99	...	69	...	83	34.82
		M	99	...	66	...	81	38.11
		F	99	...	72	...	85	31.37
	1978							
		MF	99	...	73	...	85	...
		M	99	...	70	...	83	...
		F	99	...	76	...	86	...
SWITZERLAND	1970		(6–11)		(12–19)		(6–19)	(20–24)
		MF	78	...	48	...	61	9.98
		M	77	...	49	...	62	14.87
		F	78	...	47	...	61	4.88
	1974							
		MF	85	...	51	...	66	13.02
		M	84	...	55	...	68	18.63
		F	86	...	47	...	64	7.46
	1975							
		MF	85	...	52	...	67	13.60
		M	85	...	56	...	69	19.42
		F	86	...	48	...	64	7.95

3.2 School enrolment ratios
Taux d'inscription scolaire
Tasas de escolarización

COUNTRY	YEAR	SEX	ENROLMENT RATIOS / TAUX D'INSCRIPTION / TASAS DE ESCOLARIZACION				1ST + 2ND LEVELS	3RD LEVEL
PAYS	ANNEE	SEXE	FIRST LEVEL PREMIER DEGRE		SECOND LEVEL SECOND DEGRE		1ER + 2ND DEGRE	3EME DEGRE
PAIS	AÑO	SEXO	PRIMER GRADO		SEGUNDO GRADO		1ER + 2DO GRADO	3ER GRADO
			GROSS BRUT BRUTA	NET NET NETA	GROSS BRUT BRUTA	NET NET NETA	GROSS BRUT BRUTA	GROSS BRUT BRUTA
SWITZERLAND (CONT.)	1976							
		MF	85	72	57	51	69	14.19
		M	84	71	58	50	69	20.21
		F	85	73	55	52	68	8.34
	1977							
		MF	87	73	54	52	68	16.00
		M	86	72	55	51	68	23.32
		F	87	74	54	52	68	8.80
	1978							
		MF	86	73	55	50	68	...
		M	86	71	52	48	66	...
		F	87	74	57	53	70	...
UNITED KINGDOM	1970		(5—10)		(11—17)		(5—17)	(20—24)
		MF	104	98	73	73	88	14.07
		M	104	98	74	74	89	18.55
		F	104	98	73	73	88	9.48
	1974							
		MF	105	98	81	81	93	16.55
		M	105	98	81	81	92	20.85
		F	105	98	82	82	93	12.08
	1975							
		MF	105	98	83	82	93	18.90
		M	105	98	82	82	93	23.65
		F	106	98	83	83	94	13.94
	1976							
		MF	106	98	83	...	93	...
		M	105	...	82	...	93	...
		F	106	...	84	...	94	...
YUGOSLAVIA	1970		(7—10)		(11—18)		(7—18)	(20—24)
		MF	106	78	69	58	81	15.93
		M	108	79	78	62	88	18.85
		F	103	77	58	54	73	12.87
	1974							
		MF	103	...	73	...	82	18.61
		M	104	...	77	...	86	21.50
		F	101	...	68	...	79	15.58
	1975							
		MF	103	79	76	70	84	19.98
		M	104	...	79	...	87	23.51
		F	101	...	72	...	82	16.29
	1976							
		MF	101	...	78	...	85	20.42
		M	102	...	81	...	88	24.16
		F	99	...	74	...	82	16.51
	1977							
		MF	99	...	79	...	86	21.49
		M	100	...	83	...	89	25.56
		F	98	...	75	...	83	17.25

School enrolment ratios 3.2
Taux d'inscription scolaire
Tasas de escolarización

			ENROLMENT RATIOS / TAUX D'INSCRIPTION / TASAS DE ESCOLARIZACION						
COUNTRY	YEAR	SEX	FIRST LEVEL		SECOND LEVEL		1ST + 2ND LEVELS	3RD LEVEL
PAYS	ANNEE	SEXE	PREMIER DEGRE		SECOND DEGRE		1ER + 2ND DEGRE	3EME DEGRE
PAIS	AÑO	SEXO	PRIMER GRADO		SEGUNDO GRADO		1ER + 2DO GRADO	3ER GRADO
			GROSS BRUT BRUTA	NET NET NETA	GROSS BRUT BRUTA	NET NET NETA	GROSS BRUT BRUTA	GROSS BRUT BRUTA
YUGOSLAVIA (CONT.)	1978							
		MF	99	...	82	...	87	22.52
		M	100	...	86	...	90	26.69
		F	98	...	78	...	84	18.18
OCEANIA								
AUSTRALIA	1970		(5—11)		(12—17)		(5—17)	(20—24)
		MF	98	...	69	...	85	16.62
		M	98	...	70	...	86	21.70
		F	98	...	67	...	85	11.21
	1974							
		MF	91	85	71	70	82	22.24
		M	92	84	71	70	82	26.69
		F	91	85	71	70	82	17.62
	1975							
		MF	92	85	73	71	83	23.96
		M	92	85	73	71	83	27.98
		F	92	86	73	72	83	19.80
	1976							
		MF	92	86	73	72	83	24.91
		M	92	85	73	71	83	28.18
		F	92	86	74	72	83	21.52
	1977							
		MF	94	88	73	72	84	25.31
		M	94	87	72	71	84	28.43
		F	93	88	74	72	84	22.09
	1978							
		MF	...	...	...	...	...	25.60
		M	...	...	...	...	...	28.22
		F	...	...	...	...	...	22.88
FIJI	1970		(6—13)		(14—17)		(6—17)	(20—24)
		MF	99	...	34	...	80	0.91
		M	101	...	39	...	83	1.32
		F	98	...	29	...	77	0.50
	1974							
		MF	111	100	49	39	91	1.99
		M	111	100	50	39	91	2.75
		F	110	100	47	38	90	1.24
	1975							
		MF	111		51	...	91	2.04
		M	112	...	51	...	92	2.83
		F	111		51	...	91	1.26
	1976							
		MF	112	...	55	...	93	...
		M	112		54	...	93	...
		F	111		56	...	93	...

3.2 School enrolment ratios
Taux d'inscription scolaire
Tasas de escolarización

			ENROLMENT RATIOS / TAUX D'INSCRIPTION / TASAS DE ESCOLARIZACION					
COUNTRY	YEAR	SEX	FIRST LEVEL		SECOND LEVEL		1ST + 2ND LEVELS	3RD LEVEL
PAYS	ANNEE	SEXE	PREMIER DEGRE		SECOND DEGRE		1ER + 2ND DEGRE	3EME DEGRE
PAIS	AÑO	SEXO	PRIMER GRADO		SEGUNDO GRADO		1ER + 2DO GRADO	3ER GRADO
			GROSS BRUT BRUTA	NET NET NETA	GROSS BRUT BRUTA	NET NET NETA	GROSS BRUT BRUTA	GROSS BRUT BRUTA
FIJI (CONT.)	1977							
		MF	111	100	58	46	93	...
		M	111	100	58	46	94	...
		F	111	100	59	47	93	...
NEW ZEALAND	1970		(5–10)		(11–17)		(5–17)	(20–24)
		MF	110	100	77	76	93	18.40
		M	111	100	77	76	94	21.82
		F	109	100	76	75	92	14.82
	1974							
		MF	105	100	79	78	91	26.58
		M	106	99	79	78	92	32.71
		F	104	100	80	79	91	20.13
	1975							
		MF	107	100	81	79	93	27.81
		M	108	100	80	79	93	33.82
		F	106	100	81	80	93	21.49
	1976							
		MF	108	100	82	80	94	28.25
		M	109	100	81	80	94	34.06
		F	108	100	82	81	94	22.12
	1977							
		MF	...	...	...		...	28.20
PAPUA NEW GUINEA	1970		(7–12)		(13–18)		(7–18)	(20–24)
		MF	52	...	8	...	32	0.51
		M	64	...	11	...	40	0.82
		F	39	...	4	...	24	0.17
	1974							
		MF	56	...	10	...	35	2.66
		M	69	...	13	...	44	4.28
		F	41	...	7	...	26	0.89
	1975							
		MF	57	...	12	...	36	...
		M	69	...	16	...	45	...
		F	44	...	7	...	27	...
	1976							
		MF	58	...	12	...	37	...
		M	71	...	16	...	46	...
		F	45	...	7	...	28	...
	1977							
		MF	59	...	12	...	37	...
		M	70	...	17	...	46	...
		F	47	...	7	...	28	...
	1978							
		MF	60	60	13	...	38	...
		M	70	70	18	...	46	...
		F	49	49	8	...	30	...

School enrolment ratios   **3.2**
Taux d'inscription scolaire
Tasas de escolarización

			ENROLMENT RATIOS / TAUX D'INSCRIPTION / TASAS DE ESCOLARIZACION					
COUNTRY	YEAR	SEX	FIRST LEVEL		SECOND LEVEL		1ST + 2ND LEVELS	3RD LEVEL
PAYS	ANNEE	SEXE	PREMIER DEGRE		SECOND DEGRE		1ER + 2ND DEGRE	3EME DEGRE
PAIS	AÑO	SEXO	PRIMER GRADO		SEGUNDO GRADO		1ER + 2DO GRADO	3ER GRADO
			GROSS BRUT BRUTA	NET NET NETA	GROSS BRUT BRUTA	NET NET NETA	GROSS BRUT BRUTA	GROSS BRUT BRUTA

U.S.S.R.

Country	Year	Sex	First Gross	First Net	Second Gross	Second Net	1+2 Gross	3rd Gross
U.S.S.R.	1970		(7–14)		(15–17)		(7–17)	(20–24)
		MF	101	...	65	...	92	25.18
		M	101	...	58	...	90	25.43
		F	101	...	73	...	94	24.92
	1974							
		MF	98	...	69	...	89	22.35
		M	97	...	61	...	87	21.93
		F	98	...	77	...	92	22.79
	1975							
		MF	97	...	70	...	89	22.14
		M	97	...	62	...	87	21.52
		F	97	...	79	...	92	22.79
	1976							
		MF	97	...	72	...	89	21.84
		M	97	...	63	...	87	...
		F	97	...	81	...	92	...
	1977							
		MF	98	...	71	...	90	21.58
	1978							
		MF	99	...	69	...	90	...

GENERAL NOTE/NOTE GENERALE/NOTA GENERAL
  E—> THE POPULATION DATA USED TO CALCULATE
THESE ENROLMENT RATIOS HAVE BEEN REVISED BY THE
UNITED NATIONS POPULATION DIVISION. SOME RATIOS
VARY SIGNIFICANTLY FROM THOSE PUBLISHED PREVIOUSLY
AS A RESULT OF THESE NEW POPULATION DATA.
  FR—> LES DONNEES RELATIVES A LA POPULATION UTILI-
SEES POUR LE CALCUL DES TAUX D'INSCRIPTION SCOLAIRE
ONT ETE REVISEES PAR LA DIVISION DE LA POPULATION
DE L'ORGANISATION DES NATIONS UNIES. LES QUELQUES
CHANGEMENTS SIGNIFICATIFS QUI SE MANIFESTENT DANS
LES TAUX D'INSCRIPTION PAR RAPPORT A CEUX QUI
AVAIENT ETE PUBLIES PRECEDEMMENT, S'EXPLIQUENT PAR
L'EMPLOI DES NOUVELLES DONNEES SUR LA POPULATION.
  ESP> LOS DATOS RELATIVOS A LA POBLACION UTILIZADOS
PARA EL CALCULO DE LAS TASAS DE ESCOLARIZACION, HAN
SIDO REVISADOS POR LA DIVISION DE POBLACION DE LAS
NACIONES UNIDAS. LOS CAMBIOS SIGNIFICATIVOS QUE SE
MANIFIESTAN EN ALGUNAS TASAS DE ESCOLARIZACION EN
RELACION CON LAS QUE SE HABIAN PUBLICADO ANTERIOR-
MENTE, SE EXPLICAN POR EL EMPLEO DE LOS NUEVOS
DATOS DE POBLACION.

UGANDA:
  E—> GOVERNMENT-MAINTAINED AND AIDED SCHOOLS
ONLY.
  FR-> ECOLES PUBLIQUES ET SUBVENTIONNEES SEULE-
MENT.
  ESP> ESCUELAS PUBLICAS Y SUBVENCIONADAS SOLA-
MENTE.

CYPRUS:
  E—> ENROLMENT DATA EXCLUDE TURKISH SCHOOLS.
  FR-> LES DONNEES NE TIENNENT PAS COMPTE DE
L'ENSEIGNEMENT TURC.
  ESP> LOS DATOS EXCLUYEN LA ENSEÑANZA TURCA.

JORDAN:
  E—> ENROLMENT DATA REFER TO THE EAST BANK ONLY.
  FR-> LES DONNEES SE REFERENT A LA RIVE ORIENTALE
SEULEMENT.
  ESP> LOS DATOS SE REFIEREN A LA ORILLA ORIENTAL
SOLAMENTE.

216

Education preceding the first level 3.3
Enseignement précédant le premier degré
Enseñanza anterior al primer grado

3.3 Education preceding the first level: institutions, teachers and pupils

Enseignement précédant le premier degré: établissements, personnel enseignant et élèves

Enseñanza anterior al primer grado: establecimientos, personal docente y alumnos

NUMBER OF COUNTRIES AND TERRITORIES PRESENTED IN THIS TABLE: 157	NOMBRE DE PAYS ET DE TERRITOIRES PRESENTES DANS CE TABLEAU: 157	NUMERO DE PAISES Y DE TERRITORIOS PRESENTADOS EN ESTE CUADRO: 157

| COUNTRY | YEAR | SCHOOLS | TEACHING STAFF PERSONNEL ENSEIGNANT PERSONAL DOCENTE | | | PUPILS ENROLLED ELEVES INSCRITS ALUMNOS MATRICULADOS | | | |
| PAYS | ANNEE | ECOLES | | | | | | | |
PAIS	AÑO	ESCUELAS	TOTAL	FEMALE FEMININ FEMENINO	% F	TOTAL	FEMALE FEMININ FEMENINO	% F	% PRIVATE PRIVE PRIVADA
		(1)	(2)	(3)	(4)	(5)	(6)	(7)	(8)
AFRICA									
ANGOLA	1970	46	78	...	...	2 567	1 332	52	...
	1972	62	111	...	...	3 464	...	...	...
BURUNDI ‡	1970	...	18	18	100	916	419	46	72
	1974	...	...	...	...	530	257	48	...
	1975	...	...	...	...	594	292	49	...
	1976	...	13	11	85	493	215	44	...
	1978	...	...	...	...	446	222	50	...
CENTRAL AFRICAN REPUBLIC ‡	1970	107	180	...	...	7 779	3 558	46	—
	1974	...	213	213	100	*8 496	*4 037	*48	*9
	1975	...	213	213	100	10 673	4 932	50	8
CHAD	1971	14	50	50	100	1 152	...	...	...
COMORO	1970	1	1	1	100	55	24	44	100
	1971	1	2	2	100	82	56	68	100
CONGO	1970	1	10	10	100	355	153	43	—
	1977	32	268	268	100	3 221	1 557	48	—
	1978	32	352	352	100	2 859	...	...	—
DJIBOUTI	1970	1	4	4	100	*200	...	...	*100
	1974	1	2	2	100	156	84	54	100
	1975	1	2	2	100	159	91	57	100
	1978	1	8	8	100	273	...	...	100
EGYPT	1970	35	632	607	96	24 558	12 469	51	100
	1974	...	...	...	...	35 897	17 973	50	100
	1975	...	...	...	...	41 948	20 719	49	100
	1976	...	...	...	...	47 252	23 000	49	100
	1977	363	1 399	1 385	99	73 546	26 237	36	100
	1978	373	1 343	1 333	99	59 050	29 518	50	97
GHANA	1970	...	...	...	...	18 841	9 508	50	100
	1974	...	...	...	...	*26 125	...	...	...
GUINEA—BISSAU	1970	3	12	...	...	217	161	74	100
	1975	...	...	...	...	26 733	11 376	43	...

3.3 Education preceding the first level
Enseignement précédant le premier degré
Enseñanza anterior al primer grado

COUNTRY PAYS PAIS	YEAR ANNEE AÑO	SCHOOLS ECOLES ESCUELAS	TEACHING STAFF PERSONNEL ENSEIGNANT PERSONAL DOCENTE			PUPILS ENROLLED ELEVES INSCRITS ALUMNOS MATRICULADOS			
			TOTAL	FEMALE FEMININ FEMENINO	% F	TOTAL	FEMALE FEMININ FEMENINO	% F	% PRIVATE PRIVE PRIVADA
		(1)	(2)	(3)	(4)	(5)	(6)	(7)	(8)
IVORY COAST	1970	...	...	...	...	4 110	2 120	52	57
	1975	...	108	...	...	4 656	2 260	49	60
	1976	...	108	...	...	4 669	2 229	48	60
	1977	12	...	...	...	5 059	2 334	46	63
	1978	...	...	...	...	5 563	2 565	46	...
LIBYAN ARAB JAMAHIRIYA	1970	15	55	51	93	1 365	616	45	43
	1974	61	340	340	100	6 087	2 677	44	37
	1975	62	364	364	100	7 727	3 346	43	38
	1976	68	414	412	100	8 236	3 533	43	39
	1977	...	297		...	5 240	...	...	—
	1978	36	116	116	100	3 242	1 380	43	—
MAURITIUS	1970	...	400	394	99	10 504	5 104	49	100
	1974	272	333	327	98	8 667	4 095	47	100
	1975	283	358	356	99	9 233	4 498	49	100
	1976	234	282	281	100	8 024	3 883	48	100
	1977	214	304	302	99	7 914	3 893	49	100
	1978	351	453	448	99	11 680	5 724	49	100
MOROCCO ‡	1970	...	...	...	...	9 552	4 448	47	100
	1974	...	...	...	...	323 105	67 738	21	...
	1975	...	...	...	...	375 567	...	...	...
	1976	...	...	...	...	425 581	110 997	26	...
	1977	...	...	...	...	445 732	109 679	25	...
	1978	23 484	25 521	...	...	478 570	116 114	24	...
MOZAMBIQUE	1970	10	31	29	94	1 059	627	59	100
	1972	14	50	50	100	1 336	709	53	100
NIGER	1974	6	19	19	100	770	391	51	100
	1975	6	19	19	100	874	424	49	100
	1976	7	25	25	100	1 239	642	52	100
	1977	12	43	42	98	1 489	726	49	80
	1978	16	42	42	100	1 671	808	48	77
REUNION ‡	1970	28	298	...	...	13 125	...	...	16
	1975	...	514	...	...	26 700	...	...	10
	1976	...	...	...	...	27 879	...	...	10
	1978	119	733	730	100	34 354	15 522	45	17
ST. HELENA	1970	...	6	6	100	75	50	67	—
	1974	3	12	12	100	102	50	49	—
	1976	3	10	10	100	85	46	54	—
	1977	3	10	10	100	84	45	54	—
SAO TOME AND PRINCIPE	1970	2	5	...	...	224	120	54	100
	1976	...	...	...	...	1 627	760	47	—
	1977	...	...	...	...	1 318	651	49	—
SEYCHELLES	1970	33	*40	*40	*100	*390	*250	*64	*100
	1974	39	41	41	100	1 560	865	55	94
	1976	41	...	...	...	1 787	909	51	96
	1978	36	77	77	100	2 130	1 109	52	31
	1979	37	79	79	100	1 805	900	50	24
SIERRA LEONE	1970	...	...	...	...	1 717	...	...	100
	1972	26	104	104	100	1 968	979	50	100
SOMALIA	1970	8	15	12	80	595	273	46	100
	1975	9	68	61	90	1 080	499	46	—
	1976	10	88	85	97	1 206	588	49	—
	1977	17	104	98	94	1 645	767	47	—

Education preceding the first level 3.3
Enseignement précédant le premier degré
Enseñanza anterior al primer grado

COUNTRY PAYS PAIS	YEAR ANNEE AÑO	SCHOOLS ECOLES ESCUELAS	TEACHING STAFF PERSONNEL ENSEIGNANT PERSONAL DOCENTE			PUPILS ENROLLED ELEVES INSCRITS ALUMNOS MATRICULADOS			
			TOTAL	FEMALE FEMININ FEMENINO	% F	TOTAL	FEMALE FEMININ FEMENINO	% F	% PRIVATE PRIVE PRIVADA
		(1)	(2)	(3)	(4)	(5)	(6)	(7)	(8)
SUDAN	1970	...	323	323	100	16 508	7 819	47	100
	1971	...	334	334	100	16 879	7 999	47	100
SWAZILAND	1969	4	8	8	100	120	70	58	100
	1976	39	67	67	100	1 605	850	53	30
	1978	50	32	32	100	1 880	...	...	—
TOGO	1970	114	152	97	64	9 414	3 983	42	71
	1974	92	134	108	81	6 242	2 876	46	61
	1975	94	133	119	89	6 723	3 270	49	64
	1976	89	128	120	94	5 458	2 585	47	57
	1977	103	144	141	98	6 124	2 873	47	58
	1978	126	195	195	100	8 142	3 864	47	52
UNITED REPUBLIC OF CAMEROON	1970	14	...	...	...	12 557	6 136	49	69
	1976	276	747	747	100	23 594	11 452	49	42
	1977	290	915	915	100	25 354	12 472	49	40
UPPER VOLTA	1970	3	...	...	...	355	169	48	28
	1974	8	9	9	100	478	227	47	84
	1975	...	19	19	100	497	239	48	87
	1976	...	...	...	...	729	356	49	91
	1977	...	...	...	...	580	256	44	88
	1978	...	...	...	...	785	358	46	91
WESTERN SAHARA	1970	1	8	8	100	244	85	35	—
ZAIRE	1969	...	308	...	...	13 715	6 463	47	80
	1970	...	...	...	...	18 315	...	...	...
	1972	211	466	...	...	19 671	9 426	48	100
AMERICA, NORTH									
ANTIGUA	1974	15	21	21	100	595	321	54	100
	1975	26	43	43	100	985	502	51	100
BAHAMAS	1970	*40	*70	...	...	*1 500	...	...	*100
BARBADOS ‡	1969	1	3	3	100	40	20	50	...
	1975	*114	86	...	...	*2 661	*1 400	*53	*7
	1976	*111	*118	*109	*92	*3 156	*1 669	*53	*6
	1977	117	137	111	95	3 131	1 658	53	10
BELIZE	1970	3	...	...	...	*135	...	...	*100
	1975	25	...	...	...	1 084	...	...	100
BERMUDA ‡	1970	30	27	27	100	1 205	578	48	74
	1974	10	31	31	100	398	189	47	...
	1975	10	...	...	...	396	192	48	...
	1976	29	70	70	100	1 009	497	49	61
	1977	10	32	32	100	400	185	46	...
CANADA	1970	...	18 400	...	...	350 242	170 219	49	3
	1974	...	*19 800	...	...	384 919	187 022	49	3
	1975	...	*18 100	...	...	398 476	193 620	49	2
	1976	...	*18 000	...	...	393 147	190 852	49	3
	1977	...	...	...	...	377 841	183 334	49	2
COSTA RICA	1970	106	256	251	98	7 483	3 879	52	17
	1974	340	529	...	...	15 578	7 510	48	14
	1975	318	500	500	100	15 608	7 789	50	11
	1976	316	564	560	99	18 074	9 138	51	10
	1977	416	598	...	...	18 971	8 504	45	10
	1978	...	...	...	...	*19 726	...	...	...

3.3 Education preceding the first level
Enseignement précédant le premier degré
Enseñanza anterior al primer grado

COUNTRY PAYS PAIS	YEAR ANNEE AÑO	SCHOOLS ECOLES ESCUELAS	TEACHING STAFF PERSONNEL ENSEIGNANT PERSONAL DOCENTE			PUPILS ENROLLED ELEVES INSCRITS ALUMNOS MATRICULADOS			
			TOTAL	FEMALE FEMININ FEMENINO	% F	TOTAL	FEMALE FEMININ FEMENINO	% F	% PRIVATE PRIVE PRIVADA
		(1)	(2)	(3)	(4)	(5)	(6)	(7)	(8)
CUBA	1970	...	4 037	...	...	134 258	66 377	49	—
	1974	...	4 214	4 214	100	122 099	60 206	49	—
	1975	...	4 358	...	...	126 565	61 951	49	—
	1976	...	4 775	...	...	151 294	73 997	49	—
DOMINICA	1969	34	46	41	89	2 084	1 169	56	100
	1974	49	67	65	97	2 383	1 276	54	100
	1975	52	60	58	97	2 300	1 269	55	100
	1976	52	65	53	82	2 400	1 373	57	100
	1977	58	65	65	100	2 280	1 176	52	100
DOMINICAN REPUBLIC	1970	249	...	...	...	9 213	4 733	51	91
	1973	...	...	...	...	*12 800	...	...	...
EL SALVADOR ‡	1970	235	737	712	97	24 211	12 793	53	15
	1974	266	550	550	100	37 939	20 086	53	11
	1975	320	592	592	100	42 227	22 101	52	13
	1976	...	...	...	...	*53 109	*27 926	*53	*12
GRENADA	1970	85	117	117	100	2 101	1 135	54	100
	1976	71	94	94	100	2 487	1 293	52	100
	1977	73	100	100	100	2 867	1 548	54	100
GUADELOUPE ‡	1970	8	93	93	100	5 763	...	...	22
	1975	...	300	...	...	11 313	...	...	15
	1976	...	...	...	...	13 840	...	...	13
	1978	50	488	476	98	16 335	8 077	49	12
GUATEMALA	1970	257	678	639	94	21 463	10 718	50	32
	1974	333	973	894	92	27 620	13 854	50	37
	1975	342	999	927	93	30 254	14 877	49	36
	1977	414	1 193	1 075	90	37 105	18 724	50	41
HONDURAS	1970	123	217	217	100	9 720	4 981	51	*25
	1974	187	332	332	100	13 253	6 819	51	18
	1975	234	406	406	100	16 136	8 073	50	16
	1976	278	497	497	100	20 205	10 512	52	15
JAMAICA ‡	1970	26	353	...	...	9 621	*4 759	*49	...
	1974	1 589	2 681	...	...	97 773	50 611	52	84
	1975	1 705	3 163	...	...	126 217	67 771	54	83
	1976	1 837	3 454	3 451	100	128 413	66 495	52	87
MARTINIQUE ‡	1970	41	405	405	100	18 044	...	...	5
	1975	...	574	...	...	21 459	...	...	2
	1976	...	...	...	...	22 323	...	...	3
	1978	66	631	627	99	20 423	10 146	50	3
MEXICO	1970	3 237	11 968	11 968	100	422 682	213 529	51	7
	1974	3 641	13 153	*13 153	*100	490 380	...	...	9
	1975	4 156	14 073	*14 073	*100	537 090	265 705	49	8
	1976	4 727	16 089	16 089	100	627 880	314 188	50	8
	1977	4 994	17 142	17 142	100	659 023	329 548	50	9
	1978	*5 397	*20 299	*20 299	*100	*693 494	...	...	*9
MONTSERRAT ‡	1969	8	14	14	100	300	...	...	100
	1976	10	23	23	100	444	...	...	...
	1977	10	23	23	100	400	...	...	...
NICARAGUA	1970	...	...	...	...	10 148	5 335	53	68
	1974	6	...	...	...	9 084	...	...	70
	1978	...	...	...	...	9 074	4 792	53	89

Education preceding the first level 3.3
Enseignement précédant le premier degré
Enseñanza anterior al primer grado

COUNTRY PAYS PAIS	YEAR ANNEE AÑO	SCHOOLS ECOLES ESCUELAS	TEACHING STAFF PERSONNEL ENSEIGNANT PERSONAL DOCENTE			PUPILS ENROLLED ELEVES INSCRITS ALUMNOS MATRICULADOS			% PRIVATE PRIVE PRIVADA
			TOTAL	FEMALE FEMININ FEMENINO	% F	TOTAL	FEMALE FEMININ FEMENINO	% F	
		(1)	(2)	(3)	(4)	(5)	(6)	(7)	(8)
PANAMA	1970	130	229	227	99	6 921	3 532	51	58
	1974	216	428	427	100	11 374	5 727	50	39
	1975	224	457	457	100	12 398	6 297	51	40
	1976	223	428	422	99	12 554	6 458	51	43
	1977	220	460	456	99	13 177	6 499	49	41
	1978	301	651	627	96	15 702	7 882	50	35
FORMER CANAL ZONE ‡	1970	...	...	...	...	1 003	...	...	...
	1977	...	...	...	...	796	...	...	...
PUERTO RICO	1970	...	...	...	...	17 596	...	...	...
	1972	...	...	...	...	18 545	...	...	...
ST. PIERRE AND MIQUELON	1970	4	12	12	100	365	176	48	67
	1973	3	11	11	100	423	229	54	65
TURKS AND CAICOS ISLANDS	1975	2	6	5	83	95	...	...	100
UNITED STATES OF AMERICA ‡	1970	...	...	...	...	2 726 000	...	...	...
	1974	...	...	...	...	*4 858 000	...	...	*35
	1976	...	...	...	...	*5 450 000	...	...	*32
	1977	...	...	...	...	2 783 717	...	...	...
U.S. VIRGIN ISLANDS ‡	1971	...	...	...	...	1 258	...	...	...
	1977	...	...	...	...	1 950	...	...	...
AMERICA, SOUTH									
ARGENTINA	1970	3 808	11 639	11 558	99	223 251	112 949	51	31
	1974	4 890	16 084	16 010	100	317 793	159 983	50	32
	1975	5 694	18 991	18 928	100	369 082	185 743	50	30
	1976	6 208	20 632	20 591	100	402 702	203 015	50	29
	1977	6 435	22 060	21 997	100	430 916	216 510	50	30
BOLIVIA ‡	1970	323	806	...	...	62 044	*29 098	*47	7
	1974	...	1 434	...	...	74 031	...	...	6
	1975	373	1 472	...	...	40 242	22 148	55	11
BRAZIL	1970	6 616	16 996	16 801	99	374 267	188 307	50	41
	1974	8 636	26 355	25 919	98	529 845	264 921	50	48
	1975	9 158	26 393	26 086	99	566 008	281 283	50	49
	1976	9 271	30 686	...	...	667 159	...	...	...
CHILE	1970	1 092	...	...	...	60 360	31 483	52	28
	1974	1 852	*2 512	...	...	109 584	...	...	27
	1975	1 761	2 512	2 504	100	124 697	...	...	21
	1976	1 856	3 144	3 097	99	131 608	66 813	51	17
	1977	2 051	3 205	3 187	99	148 181	75 259	51	19
	1978	*2 336	*3 672	*3 505	*95	*166 900	*84 785	*51	*19
COLOMBIA	1974	1 708	4 170	...	...	84 705	...	...	77
	1975	2 013	3 887	...	...	95 908	...	...	70
	1976	2 130	4 143	...	...	107 553	...	...	68
	1977	2 199	4 259	...	...	116 569	...	...	67
	1978	2 473	5 030	...	...	*126 341	...	...	*66
ECUADOR	1970	175	417	388	93	13 755	6 989	51	24
	1974	231	643	603	94	21 215	10 723	51	33
	1975	277	732	699	95	24 672	12 507	51	36
	1976	288	760	730	96	26 654	13 696	51	36
	1977	339	910	858	94	28 504	14 227	50	41

3.3 Education preceding the first level
Enseignement précédant le premier degré
Enseñanza anterior al primer grado

COUNTRY / PAYS / PAIS	YEAR / ANNEE / AÑO	SCHOOLS / ECOLES / ESCUELAS	TEACHING STAFF / PERSONNEL ENSEIGNANT / PERSONAL DOCENTE			PUPILS ENROLLED / ELEVES INSCRITS / ALUMNOS MATRICULADOS			
			TOTAL	FEMALE FEMININ FEMENINO	% F	TOTAL	FEMALE FEMININ FEMENINO	% F	% PRIVATE PRIVE PRIVADA
		(1)	(2)	(3)	(4)	(5)	(6)	(7)	(8)
FRENCH GUIANA ‡	1970	4	37	...	...	2 370	1 288	54	32
	1975	8	56	...	...	3 359	...	...	...
	1976	...	...	...	...	3 401	...	...	14
	1978	13	96	96	100	3 572	1 793	50	11
GUYANA	1976	356	1 662	1 643	99	25 784	12 910	50	–
PARAGUAY	1970	...	257	257	100	7 564	3 864	51	49
	1974	...	...	...	...	*7 600	...	...	...
	1977	...	...	...	...	8 280	4 260	51	61
PERU	1970	639	2 016	...	...	74 318	38 557	52	28
	1974	1 739	4 164	...	...	138 045	69 629	50	26
	1975	2 098	4 459	4 390	98	172 051	85 062	49	27
	1976	2 345	5 009	4 959	99	191 123	93 650	49	27
	1977	2 553	5 374	...	...	195 895	*97 870	*50	26
	1978	...	5 552	...	...	286 600	...	...	25
SURINAME	1970	239	736	736	100	19 942	10 170	51	68
	1974	258	653	653	100	20 307	10 357	51	59
	1975	309	589	589	100	17 581	8 722	50	59
	1976	264	620	607	98	20 384	9 982	49	61
	1977	282	701	699	100	20 979	10 435	50	64
	1978	291	687	683	99	19 782	9 825	50	60
URUGUAY ‡	1970	...	650	...	...	20 131	9 796	49	...
	1974	511	880	...	...	39 019	19 478	50	35
	1975	...	...	...	...	40 239	...	...	32
	1978	...	988	...	...	44 413	22 132	50	30
VENEZUELA	1970	754	1 444	1 437	100	50 159	24 687	49	49
	1974	1 282	4 238	4 219	100	152 266	75 782	50	29
	1975	1 338	6 246	...	...	224 600	...	...	21
	1976	1 556	7 901	...	...	284 957	...	...	19
	1977	1 719	8 949	...	...	329 019	...	...	19
ASIA									
AFGHANISTAN ‡	1970	6	42	42	100	979	451	46	–
	1974	6	74	74	100	1 473	...	...	–
	1975	8	95	95	100	1 891	919	49	–
	1976	27	164	164	100	2 891	*1 211	*42	–
	1977	26	220	220	100	3 733	1 637	44	–
BAHRAIN	1970	...	...	...	...	1 097	...	...	100
	1974	...	...	...	...	1 408	664	47	100
	1976	...	...	...	...	2 658	1 306	49	100
	1977	...	73	73	100	2 403	1 164	48	100
	1978	...	81	80	99	2 621	1 268	48	100
BANGLADESH	1973	25	195	120	62	8 215	5 050	61	100
BRUNEI	1970	13	31	30	97	1 214	545	45	100
	1974	13	41	41	100	1 373	620	45	100
	1975	14	39	39	100	1 496	688	46	100
	1976	17	58	58	100	1 850	879	48	100
	1977	19	63	62	98	2 172	1 048	48	100
	1978	27	106	102	96	2 661	1 283	48	100
CHINA	1978	*164 000	...	...	...	*7 870 000	...	...	...
CYPRUS ‡	1970	109	236	231	98	4 325	2 087	48	88
	1974	80	173	172	99	3 221	1 551	48	83
	1975	96	222	218	98	4 229	2 067	49	74
	1976	105	259	256	99	5 394	2 664	49	78
	1977	117	294	290	99	5 824	2 859	49	78
	1978	135	350	347	99	6 802	3 320	49	78

Education preceding the first level 3.3
Enseignement précédant le premier degré
Enseñanza anterior al primer grado

COUNTRY PAYS PAIS	YEAR ANNEE AÑO	SCHOOLS ECOLES ESCUELAS	TEACHING STAFF PERSONNEL ENSEIGNANT PERSONAL DOCENTE			PUPILS ENROLLED ELEVES INSCRITS ALUMNOS MATRICULADOS			
			TOTAL	FEMALE FEMININ FEMENINO	% F	TOTAL	FEMALE FEMININ FEMENINO	% F	% PRIVATE PRIVE PRIVADA
		(1)	(2)	(3)	(4)	(5)	(6)	(7)	(8)
DEMOCRATIC KAMPUCHEA‡	1969	35	48	...	...	1 478	...	...	46
	1972	...	76	...	...	2 325	...	...	...
EAST TIMOR ‡	1971	1	2	...	...	18	6	33	100
HONG KONG	1970	875	3 674	3 499	95	140 960	67 214	48	100
	1974	832	4 006	3 870	97	151 456	72 581	48	100
	1975	839	4 168	4 025	97	160 184	76 755	48	100
	1976	806	4 395	4 262	97	172 410	82 573	48	100
	1977	805	4 728	4 573	97	186 225	89 561	48	100
INDIA	1970	3 895	8 338	7 339	88	357 749	167 538	47	...
	1974	5 077	9 678	...	...	521 456	234 160	45	...
	1977	6 513	...	...	...	690 352	309 750	45	...
INDONESIA	1970	9 220	15 030	...	...	394 100	191 800	49	88
	1974	12 427	21 153	21 098	100	511 829	283 315	55	...
	1976	12 935	24 503	24 400	100	579 876	320 889	55	95
	1977	14 840	27 223	...	...	674 292	...	...	...
	1978	16 026	29 356	29 277	100	754 497	416 408	55	100
IRAN	1970	349	954	924	97	19 308	8 706	45	83
	1974	981	3 059	3 026	99	88 854	40 574	46	34
	1975	1 804	6 985	6 952	100	175 424	79 978	46	26
	1976	2 342	9 123	9 101	100	211 869	97 434	46	20
	1977	2 918	9 791	9 783	100	235 136	108 298	46	18
IRAQ	1970	123	614	609	99	13 686	5 955	44	33
	1974	203	1 391	1 391	100	35 367	16 567	47	—
	1975	245	1 913	1 913	100	44 413	20 578	46	—
	1976	276	2 291	2 291	100	51 840	24 223	47	—
	1977	306	2 603	2 603	100	56 347	26 488	47	—
	1978	333	2 862	2 862	100	67 275	31 717	47	—
ISRAEL	1970	3 568	4 155	...	...	121 858	...	...	—
	1974	4 503	5 142	5 138	100	152 246	74 584	49	—
	1975	4 789	5 522	5 518	100	161 710	79 233	49	—
	1976	4 993	5 693	5 687	100	164 722	80 837	49	—
	1977	5 215	5 838	5 830	100	168 257	82 990	49	—
JAPAN	1970	10 920	73 913	64 223	87	1 690 404	827 000	49	75
	1974	12 686	90 328	78 959	87	2 233 470	1 092 738	49	76
	1975	13 108	93 853	82 255	88	2 292 591	1 121 244	49	75
	1976	13 492	98 072	86 216	88	2 371 422	1 160 313	49	74
	1977	13 854	102 587	88 459	86	2 453 687	1 199 419	49	74
	1978	14 229	106 332	93 732	88	2 497 895	1 221 337	49	74
JORDAN ‡	1970	35	298	284	95	10 674	4 674	44	100
	1974	160	442	439	99	15 107	6 369	42	99
	1975	158	453	451	100	14 952	6 343	42	99
	1976	147	435	434	100	14 299	6 300	44	99
	1977	153	440	439	100	14 045	5 931	42	100
	1978	167	520	518	100	15 241	6 650	44	99
KOREA, REPUBLIC OF	1970	484	1 660	1 239	75	22 271	9 837	44	100
	1974	588	2 013	1 540	77	27 774	12 177	44	100
	1975	611	2 153	1 689	78	32 032	14 150	44	100
	1976	635	2 288	1 854	81	37 197	16 421	44	99
	1977	665	2 415	2 011	83	41 866	18 346	44	99
	1978	721	2 561	2 158	84	47 571	21 203	45	99
	1979	794	2 896	2 467	85	57 430	25 647	45	97

3.3 Education preceding the first level
Enseignement précédant le premier degré
Enseñanza anterior al primer grado

COUNTRY PAYS PAIS	YEAR ANNEE AÑO	SCHOOLS ECOLES ESCUELAS	TEACHING STAFF PERSONNEL ENSEIGNANT PERSONAL DOCENTE			PUPILS ENROLLED ELEVES INSCRITS ALUMNOS MATRICULADOS			
			TOTAL	FEMALE FEMININ FEMENINO	% F	TOTAL	FEMALE FEMININ FEMENINO	% F	% PRIVATE PRIVE PRIVADA
		(1)	(2)	(3)	(4)	(5)	(6)	(7)	(8)
KUWAIT ‡	1970	44	1 022	1 022	100	19 273	9 001	47	33
	1974	103	1 280	1 280	100	21 334	9 905	46	41
	1975	101	1 299	1 299	100	24 097	11 223	47	40
	1976	103	1 442	1 442	100	25 519	11 859	46	42
	1977	103	1 501	1 501	100	25 964	12 073	46	41
	1978	57	1 167	1 167	100	16 199	7 850	48	...
LAO PEOPLE'S DEMOCRATIC REPUBLIC‡	1970	6	11	11	100	314	182	58	...
	1977	40	85	85	100	2 358	989	42	...
LEBANON	1970	...	...	...	...	137 744	64 160	47	81
	1977	...	...	...	...	117 397	...	...	76
MACAU	1969	68	193	...	...	7 650	3 420	45	...
	1970	68	176	...	...	7 063	3 307	47	...
	1971	60	176	...	...	6 259	3 038	49	...
MALAYSIA PENINSULAR MALAYSIA	1970	367	841	763	91	25 065	11 225	45	100
	1974	490	1 328	1 280	96	43 936	19 969	45	100
	1976	530	1 366	1 344	98	50 752	23 352	46	100
	1977	593	1 833	1 814	99	60 475	28 266	47	100
	1978	632	2 056	2 029	99	66 419	31 341	47	100
SABAH	1971	50	107	106	99	3 851	1 811	47	100
	1974	47	124	123	99	4 564	2 160	47	100
	1975	...	...	...	...	5 293	2 572	49	...
	1976	49	163	163	100	6 004	2 913	49	...
SARAWAK	1970	68	151	147	97	4 907	2 282	47	100
	1974	80	189	187	99	7 124	3 307	46	100
MALDIVES ‡	1970	3	30	30	100	857	386	45	...
	1977	2	27	27	100	1 258	437	35	32
	1978	...	32	32	100	1 257	...	...	32
MONGOLIA	1970	...	...	...	...	32 000	...	...	—
	1974	534	2 458	1 924	78	35 961	18 951	53	—
	1975	542	1 367	1 367	100	36 974	19 497	53	—
NEPAL	1970	...	...	...	...	89 608	...	...	...
	1971	—	—	—	—	—	—	—	—
	1977	—	—	—	—	—	—	—	—
OMAN	1974	1	2	2	100	42	21	50	100
	1975	1	4	4	100	160	68	43	100
	1976	...	...	...	...	54	...	...	100
	1977	1	...	...	...	46	17	37	100
	1978	...	...	...	...	226	110	49	100
PHILIPPINES	1970	...	*1 500	*1 500	*100	51 857	*25 000	*48	97
	1974	2 137	...	...	...	79 865	...	...	86
QATAR	1970	11	47	47	100	686	310	45	100
	1974	11	40	40	100	1 236	543	44	100
	1975	12	38	38	100	1 434	635	44	100
	1976	16	88	88	100	2 098	967	46	100
	1977	16	66	66	100	1 750	768	44	100
	1978	18	73	72	99	1 971	861	44	100
SAUDI ARABIA	1970	43	191	190	99	6 058	2 332	38	80
	1974	88	392	383	98	13 903	5 573	40	92
	1975	92	439	425	97	15 485	6 528	42	91
	1976	103	463	453	98	16 007	6 863	43	92
	1977	123	610	592	97	18 024	7 725	43	94

Education preceding the first level 3.3
Enseignement précédant le premier degré
Enseñanza anterior al primer grado

COUNTRY PAYS PAIS	YEAR ANNEE AÑO	SCHOOLS ECOLES ESCUELAS	TEACHING STAFF PERSONNEL ENSEIGNANT PERSONAL DOCENTE TOTAL	FEMALE FEMININ FEMENINO	% F	PUPILS ENROLLED ELEVES INSCRITS ALUMNOS MATRICULADOS TOTAL	FEMALE FEMININ FEMENINO	% F	% PRIVATE PRIVE PRIVADA
		(1)	(2)	(3)	(4)	(5)	(6)	(7)	(8)
SINGAPORE	1970	48	200	199	100	4 822	2 259	47	100
	1974	53	264	262	99	5 142	2 464	48	100
	1975	52	278	276	99	4 883	2 320	48	100
	1976	50	254	254	100	5 015	2 401	48	100
	1977	50	270	270	100	5 674	2 704	48	100
	1978	50	274	274	100	6 274	2 954	47	100
SYRIAN ARAB REPUBLIC	1970	259	723	696	96	26 438	11 550	44	100
	1974	318	982	951	97	32 948	14 460	44	100
	1975	323	1 012	980	97	33 477	14 940	45	100
	1976	349	1 097	1 061	97	36 679	16 175	44	100
	1977	340	1 038	1 007	97	32 633	14 739	45	100
	1978	354	1 073	1 040	97	33 429	14 822	44	100
THAILAND	1970	395	2 857	...	...	134 355	64 499	48	56
	1974	2 286	...	...	...	188 767	90 515	48	57
	1975	2 864	...	...	...	214 620	103 582	48	58
	1976	...	...	...	...	243 041	117 703	48	58
	1977	...	...	...	...	262 184	126 918	48	57
TURKEY	1970	112	185	176	95	4 201	1 902	45	96
	1974	147	234	226	97	4 943	2 205	45	82
	1977	128	264	254	96	4 855	2 227	46	80
UNITED ARAB EMIRATES ‡	1970	2	47	...	...	1 114	...	...	...
	1974	16	235	...	...	4 415	1 389	*48	...
	1975	...	186	186	100	7 603	3 895	51	51
	1976	...	241	241	100	8 252	3 957	48	53
	1977	13	224	224	100	9 424	4 346	46	65
	1978	15	237	237	100	9 250	4 229	46	63
VIET-NAM	1976	...	27 133	24 459	90	907 239	438 338	48	...
	1977	3 924	39 197	*38 805	*99	1 102 363	...	...	...
YEMEN	1975	2	4	4	100	322	157	49	100
YEMEN, DEMOCRATIC	1970	8	28	25	89	991	...	...	81
	1974	6	68	68	100	1 535	699	46	...
	1975	11	145	145	100	2 820	1 262	45	...
	1976	17	176	176	100	3 891	1 758	45	...
	1977	18	191	188	98	4 743	2 219	47	...
EUROPE									
ALBANIA	1970	...	2 460	2 460	100	47 524	...	...	—
	1971	...	2 713	2 713	100	52 727	...	...	—
ANDORRA	1969	...	19	19	100	907	475	52	...
	1974	...	...	...	...	1 594	754	47	...
AUSTRIA	1970	2 079	4 423	4 423	100	120 359	58 924	49	36
	1974	2 647	5 083	5 031	99	148 221	72 501	49	34
	1975	2 882	5 578	5 522	99	154 318	75 551	49	33
	1976	3 034	5 989	5 939	99	156 278	76 472	49	32
	1977	3 209	6 497	...	...	160 081	78 391	49	31
	1978	3 360	6 860	6 817	99	161 711	79 096	49	...
BELGIUM ‡	1970	...	17 916	17 916	100	458 702	224 709	49	59
	1974	...	...	...	...	442 032	216 143	49	57
	1975	5 226	17 460	17 460	100	437 838	214 159	49	57
	1976	4 788	17 306	17 306	100	427 370	208 798	49	57
	1977	4 513	16 833	16 833	100	404 229	197 227	49	58

3.3 Education preceding the first level
Enseignement précédant le premier degré
Enseñanza anterior al primer grado

COUNTRY / PAYS / PAIS	YEAR / ANNEE / AÑO	SCHOOLS / ECOLES / ESCUELAS	TEACHING STAFF / PERSONNEL ENSEIGNANT / PERSONAL DOCENTE			PUPILS ENROLLED / ELEVES INSCRITS / ALUMNOS MATRICULADOS			
			TOTAL	FEMALE FEMININ FEMENINO	% F	TOTAL	FEMALE FEMININ FEMENINO	% F	% PRIVATE PRIVE PRIVADA
		(1)	(2)	(3)	(4)	(5)	(6)	(7)	(8)
BULGARIA	1970	8 037	18 185	18 185	100	331 960	164 847	50	—
	1974	7 515	22 265	22 265	100	379 629	186 171	49	—
	1975	7 550	24 137	24 137	100	392 625	191 806	49	—
	1976	7 263	25 900	25 900	100	394 878	192 581	49	—
	1977	6 807	26 408	26 408	100	396 925	193 770	49	—
	1978	6 602	27 479	27 479	100	404 001	193 770	48	—
CZECHOSLOVAKIA	1970	8 227	28 562	28 562	100	377 593	...	...	—
	1974	8 871	32 551	32 551	100	440 022	...	...	—
	1975	9 226	34 755	34 755	100	475 004	...	...	—
	1976	9 554	36 715	36 715	100	522 066	...	...	—
	1977	10 010	39 650	39 650	100	579 526	...	...	—
	1978	10 443	42 501	42 501	100	629 203	...	...	—
DENMARK	1970	...	...	...	...	20 874	10 109	48	...
	1974	...	1 679	1 629	97	42 919	20 834	49	7
	1975	...	...	...	...	44 859	21 776	49	7
	1976	...	1 868	1 806	97	48 834	...	...	7
	1977	...	2 043	1 927	94	54 930	...	...	7
FINLAND ‡	1970	395	1 191	1 191	100	25 464	12 740	50	
	1974	...	1 355	1 355	100	45 095	22 096	49	...
	1975	...	1 639	1 639	100	59 526	...	...	20
	1976	...	2 753	2 753	100	57 048	...	...	16
	1977	...	3 404	...	...	61 857	...	...	13
	1978	...	...	...	...	66 656	...	...	...
FRANCE ‡	1970	9 617	43 237	43 220	100	2 213 346	1 083 050	49	15
	1974	12 208	53 670	53 599	100	2 540 469	1 214 842	48	14
	1975	13 051	57 658	57 514	100	2 591 142	...	...	14
	1976	13 952	62 270	62 046	100	2 598 669	1 268 592	49	14
	1977	*14 746	*64 676	...	...	*2 575 972	*1 259 683	*49	*13
	1978	15 297	75 890	65 750	99	2 502 843	1 389 626	56	13
GERMAN DEMOCRATIC REPUBLIC	1970	11 087	41 874	41 874	100	620 158	...	...	—
	1974	11 542	50 421	50 421	100	694 492	...	...	—
	1975	11 648	51 998	*51 998	*100	693 163	...	...	—
	1976	11 714	52 956	52 956	100	671 281	...	...	—
	1977	11 754	53 503	53 503	100	638 767	...	...	—
	1978	11 807	53 784	53 784	100	606 827	...	...	—
GERMANY, FEDERAL REPUBLIC OF ‡	1970	18 618	...	...	...	1 191 434	...	...	78
	1974	24 872	109 559	107 931	99	1 653 583	800 209	48	...
	1975	26 305	...	...	...	1 655 825	801 640	48	...
	1976	26 558	...	...	...	1 759 422	851 896	48	...
	1977	25 662	...	...	...	1 626 343	777 984	48	...
GIBRALTAR ‡	1971	1	1	1	100	20	11	55	...
	1974	1	1	1	100	14	5	36	...
	1975	1	1	1	100	13	6	46	...
	1976	1	1	1	100	17	8	47	...
	1977	1	1	1	100	17	8	47	...
GREECE	1970	2 402	2 747	2 747	100	87 087	42 239	49	15
	1974	3 258	4 025	4 025	100	109 643	53 311	49	15
	1975	3 279	4 137	4 137	100	108 357	52 459	48	15
	1976	3 481	4 504	4 504	100	118 120	57 365	49	15
HUNGARY	1970	3 457	12 481	12 481	100	227 279	109 368	48	—
	1974	3 945	18 410	18 410	100	315 644	153 659	49	—
	1975	4 077	20 512	20 512	100	329 408	159 052	48	—
	1976	4 198	22 445	22 445	100	349 209	167 562	48	—
	1977	4 286	24 063	24 063	100	384 367	184 357	48	—
	1978	4 317	25 710	25 710	100	422 476	204 814	48	—

Education preceding the first level 3.3
Enseignement précédant le premier degré
Enseñanza anterior al primer grado

COUNTRY PAYS PAIS	YEAR ANNEE AÑO	SCHOOLS ECOLES ESCUELAS	TEACHING STAFF PERSONNEL ENSEIGNANT PERSONAL DOCENTE			PUPILS ENROLLED ELEVES INSCRITS ALUMNOS MATRICULADOS			
			TOTAL	FEMALE FEMININ FEMENINO	% F	TOTAL	FEMALE FEMININ FEMENINO	% F	% PRIVATE PRIVE PRIVADA
		(1)	(2)	(3)	(4)	(5)	(6)	(7)	(8)
ICELAND	1971	34	...	...	...	2 560	...	...	...
	1974	58	...	...	...	3 419	...	...	9
	1975	...	...	...	...	3 592	...	...	8
	1976	...	...	...	...	3 656	...	...	...
IRELAND	1974	...	4 186	...	...	131 731	64 320	49	100
	1975	...	4 408	3 218	73	135 783	66 179	49	100
	1976	...	4 570	3 311	72	141 392	68 878	49	100
	1977	...	4 588	3 341	73	141 454	68 919	49	100
	1978	...	4 645	3 392	73	139 278	67 736	49	100
ITALY	1970	23 922	47 967	47 967	100	1 586 785	777 874	49	94
	1974	26 557	58 626	58 626	100	1 767 612	866 077	49	68
	1975	27 485	63 523	63 523	100	1 822 527	892 143	49	65
	1976	29 803	74 874	74 874	100	1 866 104	915 865	49	69
	1977	30 244	79 363	79 363	100	1 894 238	928 822	49	66
	1978	*29 762	...	...	...	*1 854 219	...	...	*63
LUXEMBOURG	1970	...	317	317	100	7 814	3 891	50	1
	1974	...	377	377	100	8 487	4 181	49	1
	1975	...	394	394	100	8 625	4 230	49	
	1976	...	395	391	99	8 372	4 013	48	
	1977	...	393	392	100	7 057	3 384	48	
	1978	...	388	...	...	6 928	3 355	48	
MALTA	1970	21	...	...	...	2 640	1 232	47	100
	1974	35	*182	*123	*68	3 434	1 627	47	100
	1975	43	406	347	85	6 237	2 940	47	60
	1976	45	409	344	84	7 093	3 474	49	57
	1977	...	...	...	...	6 949	3 411	49	56
MONACO ‡	1971	8	23	23	100	634	308	49	32
	1976	...	...	...	...	352	...	...	...
	1977	8	...	...	...	573	173	47	36
NETHERLANDS	1970	6 379	15 954	15 954	100	491 732	239 680	49	75
	1974	7 325	18 549	18 549	100	513 606	250 905	49	72
	1975	7 568	20 565	20 565	100	518 890	252 806	49	71
	1976	7 730	20 989	20 989	100	498 831	243 250	49	71
	1977	7 834	20 895	20 895	100	465 992	227 684	49	71
	1978	7 897	20 854	20 854	100	438 175	213 451	49	70
NORWAY	1971	733	2 504	...	...	12 991	...	...	...
	1974	...	...	...	...	25 529	...	...	...
	1975	...	5 516	...	...	30 479	...	...	...
	1976	1 069	7 068	...	...	36 535	...	...	...
	1977	1 472	9 875	...	...	49 796	*24 401	*49	41
POLAND	1970	19 600	37 807	...	...	744 968	...	...	—
	1974	31 688	41 271	40 223	97	1 094 344	...	...	—
	1975	31 176	44 542	43 957	99	1 107 648	...	...	—
	1976	31 400	48 499	47 597	98	1 174 897	...	...	—
	1977	32 454	51 719	50 513	98	1 235 585	...	...	—
	1978	31 668	52 766	52 136	99	1 275 741	...	...	—
PORTUGAL	1970	317	692	692	100	17 135	8 285	48	100
	1974	685	1 830	1 789	98	42 490	19 877	47	91
	1975	679	1 903	1 842	97	44 832	21 354	48	91
	1976	936	2 910	2 837	97	61 868	29 356	47	89
	1977	993	3 243	3 158	97	64 739	30 845	48	46
ROMANIA	1970	10 336	18 887	18 887	100	448 244	224 483	50	—
	1974	13 289	31 743	31 743	100	770 016	385 569	50	—
	1975	13 537	33 789	33 789	100	812 420	404 766	50	—
	1976	13 600	35 001	35 001	100	825 028	408 190	49	—
	1977	13 429	35 068	35 068	100	837 884	412 982	49	—
	1978	13 520	36 659	36 659	100	872 374	429 508	49	—

3.3 Education preceding the first level
Enseignement précédant le premier degré
Enseñanza anterior al primer grado

COUNTRY PAYS PAIS	YEAR ANNEE AÑO	SCHOOLS ECOLES ESCUELAS	TEACHING STAFF PERSONNEL ENSEIGNANT PERSONAL DOCENTE			PUPILS ENROLLED ELEVES INSCRITS ALUMNOS MATRICULADOS			
			TOTAL	FEMALE FEMININ FEMENINO	% F	TOTAL	FEMALE FEMININ FEMENINO	% F	% PRIVATE PRIVE PRIVADA
		(1)	(2)	(3)	(4)	(5)	(6)	(7)	(8)
SAN MARINO	1970	14	30	30	100	684	313	46	5¡
	1974	16	34	34	100	704	320	45	31
	1975	16	68	68	100	735	356	48	31
	1976	16	69	69	100	731	363	50	29
	1977	16	73	73	100	760	387	51	25
	1978	17	74	74	100	732	356	49	...
SPAIN	1970	...	20 745	*20 745	*100	819 914	419 583	51	56
	1974	...	23 104	22 767	99	853 322	437 180	51	62
	1975	...	24 621	24 287	99	920 336	471 437	51	62
	1976	...	26 988	25 880	96	956 184	489 290	51	59
	1977	...	...	...	...	1 008 796	511 947	51	55
SWEDEN	1971	...	10 100	...	...	*113 400	...	...	...
	1974	5 194	...	...	...	158 994	...	...	...
	1975	5 913	...	...	...	206 726	...	...	...
	1976	6 207	...	...	...	224 878	...	...	...
	1977	6 912	...	...	...	250 651	...	...	...
SWITZERLAND	1976	...	...	...	...	130 116	60 417	46	12
	1977	...	...	...	...	127 869	61 929	48	19
	1978	...	...	...	...	124 807	60 478	48	19
UNITED KINGDOM	1970	...	...	...	...	383 096	186 656	49	9
	1974	...	...	...	...	527 630	258 399	49	6
	1975	...	...	...	...	571 545	278 910	49	5
YUGOSLAVIA	1970	1 616	9 738	9 196	94	115 507	55 989	48	—
	1974	2 168	16 140	14 947	93	171 217	81 500	48	—
	1975	2 308	17 794	16 889	95	188 526	90 792	48	—
	1976	2 474	20 408	19 145	94	210 724	101 321	48	—
	1977	2 640	22 239	20 901	94	228 309	108 676	48	—
	1978	2 794	24 753	23 320	94	248 059	118 894	48	—
OCEANIA									
AMERICAN SAMOA ‡	1970	—	—	—	—	—	—	—	—
	1974	...	...	...	...	*2 000	...	...	...
	1977	...	...	...	...	1 716	...	...	...
AUSTRALIA ‡	1970	*1 440	*1 715	*1 715	*100	77 508	...	...	100
	1974	...	...	...	...	182 545	88 972	49	...
	1975	...	...	...	...	186 652	90 903	49	...
	1976	...	...	...	...	203 146	99 529	49	...
	1977	...	...	...	...	203 114	99 166	49	...
FIJI	1974	108	324	324	100	3 256	1 562	48	100
	1975	117	256	256	100	3 339	1 603	48	100
	1977	130	163	163	100	3 581	1 633	46	100
FRENCH POLYNESIA	1970	...	...	...	...	6 512	3 232	50	...
	1974	8	244	244	100	7 939	3 767	47	25
	1975	9	265	265	100	8 117	3 949	49	26
	1976	13	289	...	...	8 265	...	...	25
GUAM	1970	...	...	...	...	2 175	...	...	...
	1973	...	...	...	...	2 279	...	...	...
NEW CALEDONIA	1970	...	149	149	100	3 044	1 527	50	52
	1974	...	...	...	...	4 911	1 454	30	38
	1975	...	...	...	...	6 195	...	...	—
	1976	...	...	...	...	5 577	2 790	50	39
	1977	...	...	...	...	6 451	3 171	49	36

Education preceding the first level 3.3
Enseignement précédant le premier degré
Enseñanza anterior al primer grado

COUNTRY	YEAR	SCHOOLS	TEACHING STAFF PERSONNEL ENSEIGNANT PERSONAL DOCENTE			PUPILS ENROLLED ELEVES INSCRITS ALUMNOS MATRICULADOS			
PAYS	ANNEE	ECOLES							
PAIS	AÑO	ESCUELAS	TOTAL	FEMALE FEMININ FEMENINO	% F	TOTAL	FEMALE FEMININ FEMENINO	% F	% PRIVATE PRIVE PRIVADA
		(1)	(2)	(3)	(4)	(5)	(6)	(7)	(8)
NEW HEBRIDES	1970	...	23	12	52	336	222	66	51
	1974	12	23	23	100	577	290	50	51
	1976	26	41	41	100	1 076	522	49	53
	1977	35	52	52	100	1 273	609	48	49
NEW ZEALAND ‡	1970	847	619	619	100	24 336	12 053	50	100
	1974	1 041	742	742	100	30 171	...	...	100
	1975	...	836	835	100	32 357	...	...	...
	1976	1 121	2 254	2 250	100	58 140	28 559	49	...
NIUE	1970	1	2	2	100	30	...	...	—
	1974	10	40	40	100	302	136	45	—
	1975	13	45	45	100	352	171	49	—
PACIFIC ISLANDS	1970	*25	*30	...	...	466	243	52	...
	1974	...	...	...	...	695	335	48	32
	1975	...	...	...	...	691	367	53	52
PAPUA NEW GUINEA	1975	...	...	...	...	51	21	41	...
	1976	...	...	...	...	76	32	42	...
	1978	...	...	...	...	1 530	...	...	54
SAMOA	1970	1	5	5	100	80	39	49	100
	1974	19	75	69	92	1 830	925	51	100
	1975	21	80	68	85	1 926	982	51	100
	1976	26	96	83	86	2 113	1 085	51	100
	1977	*40	123	98	80	*2 200	*1 284	*58	*100
SOLOMON ISLANDS	1970	2	7	7	100	50	22	44	100
	1972	2	4	4	100	*65	*32	*49	*100
TOKELAU ISLANDS	1978	3	3	3	100	70	36	51	—
	1979	3	3	3	100	75	38	51	—
TONGA	1975	11	25	25	100	..8	337	59	100
U.S.S.R.									
U.S.S.R. ‡	1970	83 134	576 276	576 276	100	6 701 748	...	...	—
	1974	96 257	701 484	701 484	100	7 944 759	...	...	—
	1975	99 392	730 723	730 723	100	8 403 162	...	...	—
	1976	117 584	...	...	...	8 864 000	...	...	—
	1977	120 131	...	...	...	11 695 000	...	...	—
	1978	122 255	...	...	...	11 301 000	...	...	—
BYELORUSSIAN S.S.R.	1970	2 062	...	...	...	220 191	...	...	—
	1974	2 531	...	...	...	327 283	...	...	—
	1976	...	...	...	...	371 601	...	...	—
	1977	...	...	...	...	396 186	...	...	—
	1978	...	...	...	...	416 900	...	...	—
UKRAINIAN S.S.R.	1970	13 257	113 600	...	...	1 208 200	...	...	—
	1974	16 918	...	...	...	1 778 000	...	...	—
	1975	17 707	...	...	...	1 886 000	...	...	—
	1976	18 627	...	...	...	2 023 100	...	...	—
	1977	21 271	...	...	...	2 224 200	...	...	—
	1978	21 659	...	...	...	2 301 600	...	...	—

3.3   **Education preceding the first level**
      Enseignement précédant le premier degré
      Enseñanza anterior al primer grado

BURUNDI:
   E—> FOR 1976 AND 1978, DATA REFER TO PUBLIC
EDUCATION ONLY.
   FR—> POUR LES ANNEES 1976 ET 1978, LES DONNEES
SE REFERENT A L'ENSEIGNEMENT PUBLIC SEULEMENT.
   ESP> EN 1976 Y 1978 LOS DATOS SE REFIEREN A LA
ENSEÑANZA PUBLICA SOLAMENTE.

CENTRAL AFRICAN REPUBLIC:
   E—> THE FIGURES SHOWN IN COLUMNS 6 AND 7 FOR
1975 REFER TO PUBLIC EDUCATION ONLY.
   FR—> EN 1975 LES DONNEES DES COLONNES 6 ET 7
SE REFERENT A L'ENSEIGNEMENT PUBLIC SEULEMENT.
   ESP> EN 1975 LOS DATOS DE LAS COLUMNAS 6 Y 7
SE REFIEREN A LA ENSEÑANZA PUBLICA SOLAMENTE.

MOROCCO:
   E—> FOR 1970, DATA REFER TO PRIVATE
KINDERGARTENS ONLY. FROM 1974, DATA ONLY
COVER KORANIC SCHOOLS.
   FR—> EN 1970 LES DONNEES SE REFERENT AUX JARDINS
D'ENFANTS PRIVES SEULEMENT. A PARTIR DE 1974, LES
DONNEES NE SE REFERENT QU'AUX ECOLES CORANIQUES.
   ESP> EN 1970 LOS DATOS SE REFIEREN A LOS
JARDINES DE LA INFANCIA PRIVADOS SOLAMENTE.
A PARTIR DE 1974, LOS DATOS SE REFIEREN
EXCLUSIVAMENTE A LAS ESCUELAS CORANICAS.

REUNION:
   E—> THE FIGURES SHOWN IN COLUMNS 1 AND 2 FOR
1970; 2 FOR 1975 REFER TO PUBLIC EDUCATION ONLY.
   FR—> LES CHIFFRES DES COLONNES 1 ET 2 POUR 1970,
ET 2 POUR 1975, SE REFERENT A L'ENSEIGNEMENT
PUBLIC SEULEMENT.
   ESP> LAS CHIFRAS DE LAS COLUMNAS 1 Y 2 EN 1970
Y DE LA COLUMNA 2 EN 1975 SE REFIEREN A LA
ENSEÑANZA PUBLICA SOLAMENTE.

BARBADOS:
   E—> THE FIGURES SHOWN IN COLUMNS 2 FOR 1975;
2, 3 AND 4 FOR 1976; 3 AND 4 FOR 1977 REFER TO
PUBLIC EDUCATION ONLY.
   FR—> LES CHIFFRES DES COLONNES 2 POUR 1975;
2, 3 ET 4 POUR 1976; 3 ET 4 POUR 1977 SE REFERENT
A L'ENSEIGNEMENT PUBLIC SEULEMENT.
   ESP> LAS CIFRAS DE LAS COLUMNAS 2 PARA 1975;
2, 3 Y 4 PARA 1976 Y 3 Y 4 PARA 1977 SE REFIEREN
A LA ENSEÑANZA PUBLICA SOLAMENTE.

BERMUDA:
   E—> THE FIGURES SHOWN IN COLUMNS 2, 3 AND 4
FOR 1970 AND ALL DATA FOR 1974, 1975 AND 1977
REFER TO PUBLIC EDUCATION ONLY.
   FR—> LES DONNEES DES COLONNES 2, 3 ET 4 EN
1970, ET TOUTES LES DONNEES DES ANNEES 1974,
1975 ET 1977 SE REFERENT A L'ENSEIGNEMENT
PUBLIC SEULEMENT.
   ESP> LOS DATOS DE LAS COLUMNAS 2, 3 Y 4 EN 1970
Y TODOS LOS DATOS RELATIVOS A 1974, 1975 Y 1977
SE REFIEREN A LA ENSEÑANZA PUBLICA SOLAMENTE.

EL SALVADOR:
   E—> FOR 1975, THE FIGURES SHOWN IN COLUMNS
2, 3 AND 4 REFER TO PUBLIC EDUCATION ONLY.
   FR—> POUR 1975 LES DONNEES DES COLONNES 2, 3 ET
4 SE REFERENT A L'ENSEIGNEMENT PUBLIC SEULEMENT.
   ESP> EN 1975 LOS DATOS DE LAS COLUMNAS 2, 3 Y 4
SE REFIEREN A LA ENSEÑANZA PUBLICA SOLAMENTE.

GUADELOUPE:
   E—> THE FIGURES SHOWN IN COLUMNS 1, 2, 3 AND 4
FOR 1970; 2 FOR 1975 REFER TO PUBLIC EDUCATION
ONLY.
   FR—> LES CHIFFRES DES COLONNES 1, 2, 3 ET 4 EN
1970; 2 EN 1975 SE REFERENT A L'ENSEIGNEMENT
PUBLIC SEULEMENT.

GUADELOUPE (CONT.):
   ESP> LAS CIFRAS DE LAS COLUMNAS 1, 2, 3 Y 4 EN
1970, Y DE LA COLUMNA 2 EN 1975 SE REFIEREN A LA
ENSEÑANZA PUBLICA SOLAMENTE.

JAMAICA:
   E—> FROM 1974, DATA INCLUDE BASIC SCHOOLS FOR
WHICH DATA ARE NOT AVAILABLE FOR EARLIER YEARS.
   FR—> A PARTIR DE 1974, LES DONNEES INCLUENT LES
"BASIC SCHOOLS" POUR LESQUELLES ON NE DISPOSE PAS
DE DONNEES POUR LES ANNEES ANTERIEURES.
   ESP> A PARTIR DE 1974, LOS DATOS INCLUYEN LAS
"BASIC SCHOOLS" PARA LAS QUE NO SE DISPONE DE
DATOS RELATIVOS A LOS AÑOS ANTERIORES.

MARTINIQUE:
   E—> THE FIGURES SHOWN IN COLUMNS 2, 3 AND 4 FOR
1970; 2 FOR 1975 REFER TO PUBLIC EDUCATION ONLY.
   FR—> LES CHIFFRES DES COLONNES 2, 3 ET 4 EN
1970; 2 EN 1975 SE REFERENT A L'ENSEIGNEMENT
PUBLIC SEULEMENT.
   ESP> LAS CIFRAS DE LAS COLUMNAS 2, 3 Y 4 EN 1970
Y DE LA COLUMNA 2 EN 1975 SE REFIEREN A LA
ENSEÑANZA PUBLICA SOLAMENTE.

MONTSERRAT:
   E—> FOR 1976 AND 1977 DATA REFER TO PUBLIC
EDUCATION ONLY.
   FR—> EN 1976 ET 1977 LES DONNEES SE REFERENT A
L'ENSEIGNEMENT PUBLIC SEULEMENT.
   ESP> EN 1976 Y 1977 LOS DATOS SE REFIEREN A
LA ENSEÑANZA PUBLICA SOLAMENTE.

PANAMA (FORMER CANAL ZONE):
   E—> DATA REFER TO PUBLIC EDUCATION ONLY.
   FR—> LES DONNEES SE REFERENT A L'ENSEIGNEMENT
PUBLIC SEULEMENT.
   ESP> LOS DATOS SE REFIEREN A LA ENSEÑANZA
PUBLICA SOLAMENTE.

UNITED STATES OF AMERICA:
   E—> FOR 1976 DATA INCLUDE SPECIAL EDUCATION.
FOR 1977 DATA REFER TO PUBLIC EDUCATION ONLY.
   FR—> EN 1976, LES DONNEES INCLUENT L'EDUCATION
SPECIALE. EN 1977 LES DONNEES SE REFERENT A
L'ENSEIGNEMENT PUBLIC SEULEMENT.
   ESP> EN 1976, LOS DATOS INCLUYEN LA EDUCACION
ESPECIAL. EN 1977 LOS DATOS SE REFIEREN A LA
ENSEÑANZA PUBLICA SOLAMENTE.

U.S. VIRGIN ISLANDS:
   E—> FOR 1977 DATA REFER TO PUBLIC EDUCATION
ONLY.
   FR—> EN 1977 LES DONNEES SE REFERENT A
L'ENSEIGNEMENT PUBLIC SEULEMENT.
   ESP> EN 1977 LOS DATOS SE REFIEREN A LA
ENSEÑANZA PUBLICA SOLAMENTE.

BOLIVIA:
   E—> THE FIGURES SHOWN IN COLUMNS 2 FOR 1970;
5, 6 AND 7 FOR 1975 DO NOT INCLUDE DATA ON
PUBLIC RURAL SCHOOLS.
   FR—> LES CHIFFRES DES COLONNES 2 EN 1970;
5, 6 ET 7 EN 1975 N'INCLUENT PAS LES ECOLES
PUBLIQUES RURALES.
   ESP> LAS CIFRAS DE LA COLUMNA 2 EN 1970 Y DE
LAS COLUMNAS 5, 6 Y 7 EN 1975 NO INCLUYEN LAS
ESCUELAS PUBLICAS RURALES.

FRENCH GUIANA:
   E—> THE FIGURES SHOWN IN COLUMNS 1 AND 2 FOR
1970; 2 FOR 1975 REFER TO PUBLIC EDUCATION ONLY.
   FR—> LES CHIFFRES DES COLONNES 1 ET 2 POUR 1970;
2 POUR 1975 SE REFERENT A L'ENSEIGNEMENT PUBLIC
SEULEMENT.

Education preceding the first level 3.3
Enseignement précédant le premier degré
Enseñanza anterior al primer grado

FRENCH GUIANA (CONT.):
   ESP> LAS CIFRAS DE LAS COLUMNAS 1 Y 2 EN 1970
Y DE LA COLUMNA 2 EN 1975 SE REFIEREN A LA
ENSEÑANZA PUBLICA SOLAMENTE.

URUGUAY:
   E—> THE FIGURES SHOWN IN COLUMNS 2, 5, 6 AND
7 FOR 1970; 1 AND 2 FOR 1974; 2 FOR 1978 REFER
TO PUBLIC EDUCATION ONLY.
   FR-> LES CHIFFRES DES COLONNES 2, 5, 6 ET 7
EN 1970; 1 ET 2 EN 1974; 2 EN 1978 SE REFERENT
A L'ENSEIGNEMENT PUBLIC SEULEMENT.
   ESP> LAS CIFRAS DE LAS COLUMNAS 2, 5, 6 Y 7
EN 1970; DE LAS COLUMNAS 1 Y 2 EN 1974 Y DE LA
COLUMNA 2 EN 1978 SE REFIEREN A LA ENSEÑANZA
PUBLICA SOLAMENTE.

AFGHANISTAN:
   E—> THE FIGURES FOR 1970, 1974 AND 1975 REFER
TO KABUL ONLY.
   FR-> LES DONNEES DES ANNEES 1970, 1974 ET 1975
SE REFERENT A KABOUL SEULEMENT.
   ESP> LOS DATOS PARA 1970, 1974 Y 1975 SE
REFIEREN A KABUL SOLAMENTE.

CYPRUS:
   E—> NOT INCLUDING TURKISH SCHOOLS.
   FR-> NON COMPRIS LES ECOLES TURQUES.
   ESP> EXCLUIDAS LAS ESCUELAS TURCAS.

DEMOCRATIC KAMPUCHEA:
   E—> FOR 1972 THE FIGURES REFER TO PUBLIC
EDUCATION ONLY.
   FR-> EN 1972 LES DONNEES SE REFERENT A
L'ENSEIGNEMENT PUBLIC SEULEMENT.
   ESP> EN 1972 LOS DATOS SE REFIEREN A LA
ENSEÑANZA PUBLICA SOLAMENTE.

EAST TIMOR:
   E—> NOT INCLUDING MISSION SCHOOLS.
   FR-> NON COMPRIS LES ECOLES DE MISSION.
   ESP> EXCLUIDAS LAS ESCUELAS DE LAS MISIONES.

JORDAN:
   E—> DATA REFER TO THE EAST BANK ONLY.
   FR-> LES DONNEES SE REFERENT A LA RIVE
ORIENTALE SEULEMENT.
   ESP> LOS DATOS SE REFIEREN A LA ORILLA ORIENTAL
SOLAMENTE.

KUWAIT:
   E—> THE FIGURES SHOWN IN COLUMN 1 FOR 1970 AND
ALL DATA FOR 1978 REFER TO PUBLIC EDUCATION ONLY.
   FR-> LES CHIFFRES DE LA COLONNE 1 EN 1970 ET
LES DONNEES DE L'ANNEE 1978 SE REFERENT A
L'ENSEIGNEMENT PUBLIC SEULEMENT
   ESP> LAS CIFRAS DE LA COLUMNA 1 EN 1970 Y LOS
DATOS RELATIVOS A 1978 SE REFIEREN A LA ENSEÑANZA
PUBLICA SOLAMENTE.

LAO PEOPLE'S DEMOCRATIC REPUBLIC:
   E—> FOR 1970 THE DATA REFER TO PUBLIC
EDUCATION ONLY.
   FR-> EN 1970 LES DONNEES SE REFERENT A
L'ENSEIGNEMENT PUBLIC SEULEMENT.
   ESP> EN 1970 LOS DATOS SE REFIEREN A LA
ENSEÑANZA PUBLICA SOLAMENTE.

MALDIVES:
   E—> FOR 1977 AND 1978 THE FIGURES SHOWN IN
COLUMNS 2, 3 AND 4 REFER TO PUBLIC EDUCATION ONLY.
   FR-> EN 1977 ET 1978 LES DONNEES DES COLONNES
2, 3 ET 4 SE REFERENT A L'ENSEIGNEMENT PUBLIC
SEULEMENT.
   ESP> EN 1977 Y 1978 LOS DATOS DE LAS COLUMNAS
2, 3 Y 4 SE REFIEREN A LA ENSEÑANZA PUBLICA
SOLAMENTE.

UNITED ARAB EMIRATES:
   E—> THE FIGURES SHOWN IN COLUMNS 5 FOR 1970,
6 AND 7 FOR 1974; 2, 3 AND 4 FOR 1975 AND 1976;
1, 2, 3 AND 4 FOR 1977 AND 1978 REFER TO PUBLIC
EDUCATION ONLY.
   FR-> LES CHIFFRES DES COLONNES 5 EN 1970, 6 ET
7 EN 1974; 2, 3 ET 4 EN 1975 ET 1976; 1, 2, 3 ET
4 EN 1977 ET 1978 SE REFERENT A L'ENSEIGNEMENT
PUBLIC SEULEMENT.
   ESP> LAS CIFRAS DE LAS COLUMNAS 5 EN 1970,
6 Y 7 EN 1974, 2, 3 Y 4 EN 1975 Y 1976
Y 1, 2, 3 Y 4 EN 1977 Y 1978 SE REFIEREN A LA
ENSEÑANZA PUBLICA SOLAMENTE.

BELGIUM:
   E—> WITH THE EXCEPTION OF 1977, THE FIGURES
SHOWN IN COLUMNS 5, 6 AND 7 INCLUDE SPECIAL
EDUCATION.
   FR-> LES DONNEES DES COLONNES 5, 6 ET 7
INCLUENT L'EDUCATION SPECIALE, EXCEPTE POUR
L'ANNEE 1977.
   ESP> SALVO PARA 1977, LOS DATOS DE LAS COLUMNAS
5, 6 Y 7 INCLUYEN LA EDUCACION ESPECIAL.

FINLAND:
   E—> FOR 1974 AND 1975 THE FIGURES SHOWN IN
COLUMNS 2, 3 AND 4 REFER TO PUBLIC EDUCATION ONLY.
THE FIGURES SHOWN IN COLUMNS 5 AND 8 FOR 1975 AND
ALL DATA FOR 1976, 1977 AND 1978 INCLUDE SPECIAL
EDUCATION.
   FR-> EN 1974 ET 1975 LES DONNEES DES COLONNES
2, 3 ET 4 SE REFERENT A L'ENSEIGNEMENT PUBLIC
SEULEMENT. LES CHIFFRES DES COLONNES 5 ET 8 EN
1975; TOUTES LES DONNEES EN 1976, 1977 ET 1978
INCLUENT L'EDUCATION SPECIALE.
   ESP> EN 1974 Y 1975 LOS DATOS DE LAS COLUMNAS
2, 3 Y 4 SE REFIEREN A LA ENSEÑANZA PUBLICA
SOLAMENTE. LAS CIFRAS DE LAS COLUMNAS 5 Y 8 EN
1975 Y TODOS LOS DATOS EN 1976, 1977 Y 1978
INCLUYEN LA EDUCACION ESPECIAL.

FRANCE:
   E—> THE FIGURES SHOWN IN COLUMNS 2, 3 AND 4 FOR
1970, 1974, 1975 AND 1976; 2 FOR 1977; 3 AND 4
FOR 1978 REFER TO PUBLIC EDUCATION ONLY.
   FR-> LES CHIFFRES DES COLONNES 2, 3 ET 4 EN
1970, 1974, 1975 ET 1976; 2 EN 1977; 3 ET 4 EN
1978 SE REFERENT A L'ENSEIGNEMENT PUBLIC
SEULEMENT.
   ESP> LAS CIFRAS DE LAS COLUMNAS 2, 3 Y 4 EN
1970, 1974, 1975 Y 1976; DE LA COLUMNA 2 EN 1977
Y DE LAS COLUMNAS 3 Y 4 EN 1978 SE REFIEREN A LA
ENSEÑANZA PUBLICA SOLAMENTE.

GERMANY, FEDERAL REPUBLIC OF:
   E—> FOR 1974, THE FIGURES SHOWN IN COLUMNS
5, 6 AND 7 INCLUDE SPECIAL EDUCATION.
   FR-> POUR 1974, LES CHIFFRES DES COLONNES
5, 6 ET 7 INCLUENT L'EDUCATION SPECIALE.
   ESP> EN 1974, LAS CIFRAS DE LAS COLUMNAS 5, 6 Y
7 INCLUYEN LA EDUCACION ESPECIAL.

GIBRALTAR:
   E—> DATA REFER TO PUBLIC EDUCATION ONLY.
   FR-> LES DONNEES SE REFERENT A L'ENSEIGNEMENT
PUBLIC SEULEMENT.
   ESP> LOS DATOS SE REFIEREN A LA ENSEÑANZA
PUBLICA SOLAMENTE.

MONACO:
   E—> THE FIGURES SHOWN IN COLUMNS 2, 3 AND 4
FOR 1974; 5 FOR 1976; 6 AND 7 FOR 1977 REFER TO
PUBLIC EDUCATION ONLY.
   FR-> LES CHIFFRES DES COLONNES 2, 3 ET 4 EN
1974; 5 EN 1976; 6 ET 7 EN 1977 SE REFERENT A
L'ENSEIGNEMENT PUBLIC. SEULEMENT.

3.3 **Education preceding the first level**
Enseignement précédant le premier degré
Enseñanza anterior al primer grado

MONACO (CONT.):
  ESP> LAS CIFRAS DE LAS COLUMNAS 2, 3 Y 4 EN
1974, DE LA COLUMNA 5 EN 1976 Y DE LAS COLUMNAS
6 Y 7 EN 1977 SE REFIEREN A LA ENSEÑANZA PUBLICA
SOLAMENTE.

AMERICAN SAMOA:
  E—> FOR 1977 THE FIGURES REFER TO PUBLIC
EDUCATION ONLY.
  FR—> EN 1977 LES DONNEES SE REFERENT A
L'ENSEIGNEMENT PUBLIC SEULEMENT.
  ESP> EN 1977 LOS DATOS SE REFIEREN A LA
ENSEÑANZA PUBLICA SOLAMENTE.

AUSTRALIA:
  E—> FOR 1970, DATA DO NOT INCLUDE PREPRIMARY
CLASSES IN PRIMARY SCHOOLS. FROM 1974 TO 1977
THE DATA DO NOT INCLUDE KINDERGARDENS CLASSES.
  FR—> EN 1970, LES DONNEES NE COMPRENNENT PAS
LES CLASSES MATERNELLES RATTACHEES AUX ECOLES
PRIMAIRES. DE 1974 A 1977 LES DONNEES NE
TIENNENT PAS COMPTE DES JARDINS D'ENFANTS.

AUSTRALIA (CONT.):
  ESP> EN 1970 LOS DATOS EXCLUYEN LAS CLASES
MATERNALES ADSCRITAS A LAS ESCUELAS PRIMARIAS.
DE 1974 A 1977 LOS DATOS EXCLUYEN LOS JARDINES
DE LA INFANCIA.

NEW ZEALAND:
  E—> FOR 1976 DATA INCLUDE PLAY CENTRES.
  FR—> POUR 1976 LES DONNEES INCLUENT LES
GARDERIES D'ENFANTS.
  ESP> PARA 1976 LOS DATOS INCLUYEN LAS
GUARDERIAS.

U.S.S.R.:
  E—> THE FIGURES SHOWN IN COLUMN 1 FOR 1976 AND
ALL DATA FOR 1977 AND 1978 INCLUDE PLAY CENTRES
  FR—> LES CHIFFRES DE LA COLONNE 1 POUR 1976 ET
TOUTES LES DONNEES POUR 1977 ET 1978 INCLUENT
LES GARDERIES D'ENFANTS.
  ESP> LAS CIFRAS DE LA COLUMNA 1 EN 1976 Y TODOS
LOS DATOS RELATIVOS A 1977 Y 1978 INCLUYEN LAS
GUARDERIAS.

Education at the first level 3.4
Enseignement du premier degré
Enseñanza de primer grado

3.4 Education at the first level: institutions, teachers and pupils

Enseignement du premier degré: établissements, personnel enseignant et élèves

Enseñanza de primer grado: establecimientos, personal docente y alumnos

NUMBER OF COUNTRIES AND TERRITORIES PRESENTED IN THIS TABLE: 199	NOMBRE DE PAYS ET DE TERRITOIRES PRESENTES DANS CE TABLEAU: 199	NUMERO DE PAISES Y DE TERRITORIOS PRESENTADOS EN ESTE CUADRO: 199

COUNTRY PAYS PAIS	YEAR ANNEE AÑO	SCHOOLS ECOLES ESCUELAS	TEACHING STAFF PERSONNEL ENSEIGNANT PERSONAL DOCENTE			PUPILS ENROLLED ELEVES INSCRITS ALUMNOS MATRICULADOS			PUPIL/TEACHER RATIO NOMBRE D'ELEVES PAR MAITRE NUMERO DE ALUMNOS POR MAESTRO
			TOTAL	FEMALE FEMININ FEMENINO	% F	TOTAL	FEMALE FEMININ FEMENINO	% F	
		(1)	(2)	(3)	(4)	(5)	(6)	(7)	(8)
AFRICA									
ALGERIA ‡	1970	6 109	*47 178	*12 266	*26	*1 887 148	*707 933	*38	*40
	1974	...	60 179	...	...	2 525 365	999 746	40	42
	1975	7 798	65 043	...	...	2 663 248	1 064 576	40	41
	1976	8 182	70 498	...	...	2 785 264	1 129 643	41	40
	1977	8 377	77 009	...	...	2 897 500	1 183 208	41	38
	1978	8 653	80 853	...	...	2 975 861	1 230 573	41	37
ANGOLA	1970	4 418	9 786	...	...	434 370	154 932	36	44
	1972	5 208	12 622	...	...	516 131	...	...	41
BENIN ‡	1970	969	3 929	1 114	28	173 897	54 484	31	44
	1974	1 325	4 864	...	...	259 880	81 623	31	53
	1975	1 497	5 786	1 369	24	279 673	86 897	31	48
	1977	...	6 326	1 481	23	293 648	93 423	32	46
	1978	2 072	6 048	1 476	24	339 899	108 230	32	56
	1979	2 258	6 547	1 542	24	357 348	120 197	35	55
BOTSWANA	1970	282	2 275	1 231	54	83 002	44 053	53	36
	1974	316	3 047	1 941	64	103 711	56 613	55	34
	1975	323	3 509	2 333	66	116 293	63 949	55	33
	1976	335	3 921	2 651	68	125 588	69 205	55	32
	1977	349	4 495	3 134	70	137 290	75 655	55	31
	1978	376	4 641	3 284	71	145 459	80 248	55	31
BURUNDI ‡	1970	970	4 955	1 267	26	181 758	59 843	33	37
	1974	...	*4 159	*1 755	*42	129 518	48 869	38	*31
	1975	...	*4 209	*1 814	*43	129 597	50 045	39	*31
	1976	...	4 224	1 824	43	130 739	51 234	39	31
	1977	...	4 379	1 997	46	142 234	55 530	39	32
	1978	...	4 445	...	...	145 782	57 399	39	33
CAPE VERDE	1970	354	730	...	...	45 103	19 953	44	62
	1972	...	...	...	...	70 905	32 702	46	...
CENTRAL AFRICAN REPUBLIC	1970	754	2 768	466	17	176 300	57 669	33	64
	1974	717	3 159	563	18	215 887	73 381	34	68
	1975	732	3 329	592	18	221 412	79 554	36	67
	1976	...	3 505	647	18	234 482	83 131	35	67
	1977	...	...	...	...	241 201	85 403	35	...

3.4 Education at the first level
Enseignement du premier degré
Enseñanza de primer grado

COUNTRY PAYS PAIS	YEAR ANNEE AÑO	SCHOOLS ECOLES ESCUELAS	TEACHING STAFF PERSONNEL ENSEIGNANT PERSONAL DOCENTE			PUPILS ENROLLED ELEVES INSCRITS ALUMNOS MATRICULADOS			PUPIL/ TEACHER RATIO NOMBRE D'ELEVES PAR MAITRE
			TOTAL	FEMALE FEMININ FEMENINO	% F	TOTAL	FEMALE FEMININ FEMENINO	% F	NUMERO DE ALUMNOS POR MAESTRO
		(1)	(2)	(3)	(4)	(5)	(6)	(7)	(8)
CHAD ‡	1970	...	*2 824	*142	*5	183 250	46 191	25	*65
	1974	...	*2 820	*186	*7	192 725	51 173	27	77
	1975	...	*2 512	*133	*5	*212 983	*55 963	*26	77
	1976	783	2 610	142	5	210 882	56 319	27	77
COMORO	1970	100	361	41	11	15 047	4 749	32	42
	1973	130	554	*67	*12	23 194	7 239	31	42
CONGO	1970	892	3 898	*590	*15	241 101	105 890	44	62
	1974	1 033	5 053	781	15	307 194	141 431	46	61
	1975	1 033	5 434	945	17	319 101	148 445	47	59
	1976	...	...	...	...	330 456	154 931	47	...
	1977	1 230	6 675	1 551	23	345 736	164 656	48	52
	1978	1 273	6 832	1 685	25	358 761	171 601	48	53
DJIBOUTI	1970	31	180	58	32	6 422	1 926	30	36
	1974	...	251	83	33	9 306	3 432	37	37
	1975	...	268	95	35	9 764	3 464	35	36
	1978	41	358	...	...	14 121	...	...	39
EGYPT ‡	1970	8 606	*99 918	*52 991	*53	3 794 911	1 433 270	38	*38
	1974	10 140	*103 600	*53 113	*51	4 145 454	*1 574 272	*38	*40
	1975	10 346	118 251	56 323	48	4 120 936	1 585 273	38	35
	1976	10 569	126 397	59 151	47	4 151 956	1 610 451	39	33
	1977	10 818	124 263	57 277	46	4 211 345	1 651 215	39	34
	1978	11 051	127 021	58 074	46	4 287 124	1 697 509	40	34
EQUATORIAL GUINEA	1970	...	...	...	...	31 600	13 891	44	...
	1973	559	630	165	26	35 977	16 091	45	57
ETHIOPIA	1970	2 297	13 514	1 679	12	655 427	205 676	31	48
	1974	...	...	...	...	959 272	307 379	32	...
GABON	1970	676	2 211	327	15	100 625	47 890	48	46
	1974	734	2 412	507	21	121 407	58 995	49	50
	1975	746	2 664	535	20	128 552	62 736	49	48
	1976	766	2 746	608	22	130 398	63 689	49	47
GAMBIA	1970	95	624	207	33	17 140	5 251	31	27
	1974	101	864	*289	*33	22 424	7 424	33	26
	1975	103	948	...	...	24 617	8 169	33	26
	1976	99	940	286	30	25 513	8 235	32	27
	1977	111	1 094	...	...	27 560	8 931	32	25
	1978	122	1 241	413	33	32 196	10 480	33	26
GHANA ‡	1970	10 759	47 957	12 720	27	1 419 838	610 016	43	30
	1974	6 886	35 334	11 534	33	1 050 500	458 778	44	30
	1975	6 966	38 381	12 674	33	1 156 758	502 479	43	30
	1976	7 248	41 407	14 458	35	1 212 728	527 403	43	29
	1977	7 229	45 119	17 126	38	1 245 853	543 532	44	28
GUINEA	1970	1 984	5 304	...	...	191 287	60 644	32	36
	1971	...	*4 698	...	...	169 132	54 447	32	*36
GUINEA-BISSAU ‡	1970	261	616	...	...	27 974	8 428	30	45
	1974	...	...	...	...	75 634	...	...	...
	1975	536	2 163	...	...	53 844	17 168	32	*34
	1976	625	2 493	...	...	83 781	27 442	33	34
	1977	636	2 599	...	...	85 575	27 629	32	33
IVORY COAST	1970	2 252	11 170	1 492	13	502 865	182 950	36	45
	1974	2 700	14 403	1 735	12	641 369	238 996	37	45
	1975	2 904	15 358	1 906	12	672 707	253 582	38	44
	1976	3 195	17 044	2 255	13	735 511	277 846	38	43
	1977	3 591	18 704	...	...	810 244	310 617	38	43

Education at the first level 3.4
Enseignement du premier degré
Enseñanza de primer grado

COUNTRY PAYS PAIS	YEAR ANNEE AÑO	SCHOOLS ECOLES ESCUELAS	TEACHING STAFF PERSONNEL ENSEIGNANT PERSONAL DOCENTE			PUPILS ENROLLED ELEVES INSCRITS ALUMNOS MATRICULADOS			PUPIL/ TEACHER RATIO NOMBRE D'ELEVES PAR MAITRE
			TOTAL	FEMALE FEMININ FEMENINO	% F	TOTAL	FEMALE FEMININ FEMENINO	% F	NUMERO DE ALUMNOS POR MAESTRO
		(1)	(2)	(3)	(4)	(5)	(6)	(7)	(8)
KENYA	1970	6 123	41 479	11 344	27	1 427 589	591 282	41	34
	1974	7 668	78 340	...	...	2 705 878	1 214 347	45	35
	1975	8 161	86 107	24 594	29	2 881 155	1 319 654	46	33
	1976	8 544	89 074	25 401	29	2 894 617	1 340 493	46	32
	1977	8 896	89 773	25 787	29	2 974 849	1 387 429	47	33
	1978	9 349	...	...	...	*3 232 000	...	...	...
LESOTHO ‡	1970	1 350	3 964	2 373	60	183 395	109 954	60	46
	1974	...	...	...	...	218 038	129 981	60	...
	1975	1 079	4 226	2 939	70	221 922	131 014	59	53
	1976	1 075	4 233	2 981	70	222 004	130 843	59	52
LIBERIA ‡	1970	889	3 384	939	28	120 245	39 565	33	36
	1974	1 059	*3 795	...	...	149 687	...	...	*39
	1975	...	*3 832	*1 140	*30	157 821	56 750	36	*41
	1976	879	3 709	1 039	28	150 046	52 753	35	40
	1978	1 142	4 567	1 194	26	192 185	72 261	38	42
LIBYAN ARAB JAMAHIRIYA	1970	1 324	12 304	2 978	24	350 225	129 595	37	28
	1974	1 940	22 842	6 473	28	522 473	237 088	45	23
	1975	2 042	24 331	7 086	29	556 169	256 065	46	23
	1976	2 394	28 627	8 400	29	571 723	267 682	47	20
	1977	2 150	26 182	9 079	35	574 770	270 820	47	22
	1978	2 187	26 715	9 521	36	587 067	276 416	47	22
MADAGASCAR	1970	5 845	14 424	4 117	29	938 015	433 105	46	65
	1974	...	...	...	...	1 037 714	...	...	...
	1975	7 355	18 688	7 089	38	1 133 013	531 081	47	61
	1978	8 002	23 937	...	...	1 311 000	...	...	55
MALAWI ‡	1970	1 990	8 382	1 987	24	362 561	134 763	37	43
	1974	2 091	10 524	...	...	611 678	238 392	39	58
	1975	2 140	10 588	...	...	641 709	253 563	40	61
	1976	2 371	9 305	...	...	663 940	265 379	40	71
	1977	2 294	11 115	2 817	27	675 740	271 913	40	61
MALI	1970	...	5 086	977	19	203 703	72 658	36	40
	1974	...	...	...	...	240 521	87 107	36	...
	1975	1, 063	6 213	1 148	18	252 393	90 033	36	41
	1976	...	...	...	...	265 496	96 087	36	...
	1977	...	...	...	...	280 459	100 796	36	...
	1978	1 116	6 877	1 266	18	293 227	106 333	36	43
MAURITANIA	1970	...	*1 331	*71	*5	31 945	*8 881	*28	*24
	1974	...	...	...	...	44 786	...	...	...
	1975	...	1 439	...	...	50 465	18 106	36	35
	1976	...	1 668	...	...	64 611	21 213	33	39
	1977	...	1 765	125	7	72 954	24 982	34	41
MAURITIUS ‡	1970	347	4 731	*1 956	*41	150 402	73 042	49	32
	1974	...	5 568	2 262	41	152 417	74 741	49	27
	1975	...	5 791	...	...	150 573	73 711	49	26
	1976	...	5 848	2 462	42	139 439	68 362	49	24
	1977	236	6 088	2 604	43	136 019	66 594	49	22
	1978	244	6 352	2 758	43	133 432	64 976	49	21
MOROCCO ‡	1970	1 532	34 277	6 262	18	1 175 277	397 959	34	34
	1974	1 705	38 486	7 953	21	1 413 993	504 658	36	37
	1975	1 928	37 226	7 725	21	1 547 647	555 589	36	40
	1976	1 964	40 197	8 614	21	1 667 773	600 010	36	40
	1977	...	43 484	9 977	23	1 793 772	649 792	36	40
	1978	2 248	47 722	11 641	24	1 925 187	702 231	36	39

3.4 Education at the first level
Enseignement du premier degré
Enseñanza de primer grado

COUNTRY PAYS PAIS	YEAR ANNEE AÑO	SCHOOLS ECOLES ESCUELAS	TEACHING STAFF PERSONNEL ENSEIGNANT PERSONAL DOCENTE			PUPILS ENROLLED ELEVES INSCRITS ALUMNOS MATRICULADOS			PUPIL/ TEACHER RATIO NOMBRE D'ELEVES PAR MAITRE NUMERO DE ALUMNOS POR MAESTRO
			TOTAL	FEMALE FEMININ FEMENINO	% F	TOTAL	FEMALE FEMININ FEMENINO	% F	
		(1)	(2)	(3)	(4)	(5)	(6)	(7)	(8)
MOZAMBIQUE	1970	4 088	7 220	...	...	496 910	...		69
	1972	3 947	8 345	2 735	33	577 997	196 787	34	69
NIGER	1970	699	2 275	*476	*21	88 594	30 563	34	39
	1974	990	2 974	960	32	120 984	43 024	36	41
	1975	1 249	3 617	1 124	31	142 182	50 029	35	39
	1976	1 297	4 019	1 261	31	159 515	56 324	35	40
	1977	1 385	4 298	1 382	32	176 297	62 226	35	41
	1978	...	...	...	...	187 251	68 948	37	...
NIGERIA	1970	14 902	103 152	24 409	24	3 515 827	1 299 598	37	34
	1975	...	...	...	...	*6 081 000	...	...	...
	1976	...	...	...	...	*8 268 800	...	...	...
	1977	...	...	...	...	*9 485 300	...	...	...
REUNION ‡	1970	368	3 114	...	...	99 565	...	...	30
	1974			...	...	97 326	...	...	...
	1975	371	3 661	...	...	95 810	...	...	26
	1976	367		...	...	94 239	...	...	...
	1977	...	...	...	...	91 290	...	...	...
	1978	364	3 216	2 302	72	89 494	...	...	28
RWANDA	1970	2 022	7 025	1 627	23	419 059	184 877	44	60
	1974	1 824	7 854	2 141	27	386 719	175 690	45	49
	1975	1 668	8 022	2 355	29	401 521	184 814	46	50
	1976	1 606	8 161	2 529	31	434 150	202 381	47	53
ST. HELENA	1970	8	40	39	98	780	420	54	20
	1974	8	37	36	97	729	354	49	20
	1975	8	...	...	...	755	365	48	...
	1976	8	41	40	98	774	380	49	19
	1977	8	42	41	98	789	392	50	19
SAO TOME AND PRINCIPE	1970	44	271	...	...	9 018	3 980	44	33
	1976	...	...	...	...	12 663	6 010	47	...
	1977	...	527	280	53	14 162	6 663	47	27
SENEGAL ‡	1970	...	*5 843	...	...	262 928	101 734	39	*45
	1974	...	...	...	...	306 698	...	...	...
	1975	...	5 562	...	...	*311 800	...	...	49
	1977	1 420	8 186	1 685	21	346 585	137 276	40	42
SEYCHELLES	1970	35	381	343	90	9 224	4 629	50	24
	1974	35	416	403	97	10 355	5 269	51	25
	1975	36	428	406	95	10 232	5 268	51	24
	1976	35	435	...	...	9 950	4 996	50	23
	1977	...	...	...	...	10 001	5 054	51	...
	1978	28	427	...	...	10 123	5 086	50	24
	1979	28	405	397	98	9 978	4 943	50	25
SIERRA LEONE	1970	1 023	5 142	...	...	166 107	66 741	40	32
	1974	1 132	5 993	1 459	24	191 692	75 313	39	32
	1975	1 074	6 373	1 530	24	205 910	81 470	40	32
	1976	...	...	...	...	218 376	...	...	...
	1977	1 118	7 088	1 793	25	227 815	90 832	40	32
SOMALIA ‡	1970	204	981	139	14	32 610	8 071	25	33
	1975	730	3 481	565	16	197 706	70 122	35	57
	1976	1 002	6 540	1 263	19	229 030	81 119	35	35
	1977	1 085	8 392	2 051	24	228 544	83 109	36	27
SOUTH AFRICA ‡	1970			...	...	3 738 696	1 854 405	50	
	1972	15 615	120 284	...	...	4 653 452	...	...	*41

Education at the first level 3.4
Enseignement du premier degré
Enseñanza de primer grado

COUNTRY	YEAR	SCHOOLS	TEACHING STAFF PERSONNEL ENSEIGNANT PERSONAL DOCENTE			PUPILS ENROLLED ELEVES INSCRITS ALUMNOS MATRICULADOS			PUPIL/ TEACHER RATIO NOMBRE D'ELEVES PAR MAITRE
PAYS	ANNEE	ECOLES							
PAIS	AÑO	ESCUELAS	TOTAL	FEMALE FEMININ FEMENINO	% F	TOTAL	FEMALE FEMININ FEMENINO	% F	NUMERO DE ALUMNOS POR MAESTRO
		(1)	(2)	(3)	(4)	(5)	(6)	(7)	(8)
SUDAN ‡	1970	4 061	17 740	6 788	38	825 620	311 864	38	47
	1974	4 088	28 689	9 238	32	1 130 856	372 045	33	39
	1975	4 719	31 695	9 990	32	1 169 279	416 156	36	37
	1976	4 832	33 783	*10 499	*31	1 217 510	450 474	37	36
	1977	4 945	34 988	10 933	31	1 302 040	536 181	41	37
	1978	5 468	38 881	12 605	32	1 358 193	551 657	41	35
SWAZILAND	1970	351	1 706	*1 041	*61	69 055	33 484	48	40
	1974	403	2 220	1 642	74	86 110	42 162	49	39
	1975	412	2 363	1 805	76	89 528	43 984	49	38
	1976	420	2 513	...	...	92 721	45 719	49	37
	1977	436	2 672	2 093	78	96 835	47 937	50	36
	1978	436	2 853	2 253	79	100 700	50 095	50	35
TOGO	1970	916	3 909	758	19	228 505	70 850	31	58
	1974	1 199	5 627	1 127	20	329 443	110 878	34	59
	1975	1 362	6 080	1 224	20	362 895	126 041	35	60
	1976	1 640	6 528	1 281	20	395 381	141 373	36	61
	1977	1 814	7 251	1 512	21	421 436	155 586	37	58
TUNISIA	1970	2 208	*19 712	...	...	935 738	364 867	39	*47
	1974	...	22 225	*4 950	*22	910 532	351 391	39	41
	1975	2 319	23 320	*5 597	*24	932 787	364 370	39	40
	1976	2 440	23 983	6 004	25	968 436	*379 903	*39	40
	1977	2 460	25 149	6 582	26	991 908	*394 083	*40	39
	1978	2 522	25 593	6 872	27	1 004 144	406 066	40	39
UGANDA ‡	1970	2 755	21 471	...	...	720 127	282 928	39	34
	1974	3 184	26 339	...	...	901 674	360 909	40	34
	1975	3 472	28 681	8 216	29	973 604	390 461	40	34
	1976	3 563	29 765	8 661	29	1 036 920	426 781	41	35
	1977	3 854	32 554	9 655	30	1 139 413	471 299	41	35
UNITED REPUBLIC OF CAMEROON	1970	...	*19 359	...	...	923 234	392 788	43	*48
	1974	4 349	20 803	2 641	13	1 074 021	474 091	44	52
	1975	4 506	22 209	3 055	14	1 122 900	500 049	45	51
	1976	4 584	23 029	3 365	15	1 146 437	513 667	45	50
	1977	4 711	24 046	3 777	16	1 202 841	540 410	45	50
UNITED REPUBLIC OF TANZANIA ‡	1970	4 222	20 094	5 439	27	922 083	363 678	39	46
	1974	5 804	29 735	9 709	33	1 592 396	668 112	42	54
	1975	8 152	39 245	13 675	35	1 954 443	844 248	43	50
	1976	5 804	38 199	13 372	35	1 956 320	...	...	51
UPPER VOLTA	1970	603	*2 370	*386	*16	105 351	38 322	36	*44
	1974	688	2 813	488	17	133 614	49 986	37	47
	1975	712	2 997	544	18	141 177	52 275	37	47
	1976	726	3 124	574	18	149 270	54 959	37	48
	1977	765	3 204	603	19	159 948	58 840	37	50
	1978	810	3 263	655	20	170 721	62 938	37	52
WESTERN SAHARA	1970	...	94	27	29	3 040	956	31	32
	1973	...	204	...	...	5 505	...	...	27
ZAIRE	1970	4 756	*72 546	...	...	3 088 011	1 135 556	37	*43
	1974	...	...	...	...	3 429 076	1 347 705	39	...
	1975	...	...	...	...	*3 551 936	*1 418 749	*40	...
	1976	...	...	...	...	*3 681 684	*1 496 362	*41	...
	1977	7 909	...	...	...	*3 818 934	*1 590 113	*42	...

3.4 Education at the first level
Enseignement du premier degré
Enseñanza de primer grado

COUNTRY PAYS PAIS	YEAR ANNEE AÑO	SCHOOLS ECOLES ESCUELAS	TEACHING STAFF PERSONNEL ENSEIGNANT PERSONAL DOCENTE			PUPILS ENROLLED ELEVES INSCRITS ALUMNOS MATRICULADOS			PUPIL/ TEACHER RATIO NOMBRE D'ELEVES PAR MAITRE
			TOTAL	FEMALE FEMININ FEMENINO	% F	TOTAL	FEMALE FEMININ FEMENINO	% F	NUMERO DE ALUMNOS POR MAESTRO
		(1)	(2)	(3)	(4)	(5)	(6)	(7)	(8)
ZAMBIA	1970	2 564	14 852	4 990	34	694 670	308 994	44	47
	1974	2 669	17 881	6 488	36	858 191	388 000	45	48
	1975	2 710	18 096	6 735	37	872 392	396 384	45	48
	1976	2 743	19 089	7 244	38	907 867	414 968	46	48
ZIMBABWE	1970	3 848	...	...	...	736 508	...	...	...
	1974	3 708	20 540	...	...	835 721	...	...	41
	1975	3 623	21 202	...	...	862 877	...	...	41
	1976	3 666	21 792	...	...	883 059	406 228	46	41
AMERICA, NORTH									
ANTIGUA ‡	1970	40	538	448	83	12 575	5 950	47	23
	1974	57	460	379	82	10 939	5 362	49	*24
	1975	59	524	443	85	11 340	5 507	49	*22
BAHAMAS ‡	1970	*192	*707	*487	*92	32 142	...	...	*45
	1974	...	...	...	...	31 727	...	...	...
	1975	...	...	...	...	31 707	15 915	50	...
	1976	...	...	...	...	31 928	16 097	50	...
	1977	...	...	...	...	32 315	16 373	51	...
	1978	...	...	...	...	32 123	16 255	51	...
BARBADOS ‡	1970	...	...	...	...	37 866	18 539	49	...
	1974	...	...	...	...	31 020	15 224	49	...
	1975	...	...	...	...	*32 884	*16 426	*50	...
	1976	...	...	...	...	*33 989	*16 975	*50	...
	1977	130	1 227	...	...	*34 324	*17 112	*50	*28
BELIZE ‡	1970	181	*1 150	*800	*70	31 629	*15 511	*49	*28
	1975	194	1 207	871	72	33 444	16 057	48	*27
	1976	...	...	...	...	32 986	16 266	49	...
BERMUDA	1970	28	341	290	85	7 986	4 006	50	23
	1974	22	325	278	86	6 919	3 321	48	21
	1975	22	...	...	...	6 808	3 288	48	...
	1976	22	374	301	80	6 614	3 197	48	18
	1977	22	319	276	87	6 466	3 151	49	20
BRITISH VIRGIN ISLANDS	1970	20	94	77	82	2 156	976	45	23
	1974	28	108	96	89	2 181	1 090	50	20
	1975	28	123	112	91	2 251	1 109	49	18
	1978	25	109	95	87	2 251	1 090	48	21
CANADA ‡	1970	...	159 900	...	...	3 736 450	1 817 268	49	23
	1974	...	257 300	...	...	2 534 137	1 229 011	48	*20
	1975	...	256 200	...	...	2 440 016	1 190 489	49	*20
	1976	...	255 900	...	...	2 372 784	1 156 234	49	*19
	1977	...	...	...	...	2 289 568	1 115 793	49	...
CAYMAN ISLANDS ‡	1969	13	39	30	77	1 673	573	34	43
	1971	...	...	...	...	1 623	853	53	...
	1974	9	51	40	78	1 897	964	51	23
	1975	16	55	46	84	1 933	948	49	23
	1976	15	88	75	85	2 234	1 129	51	25
COSTA RICA ‡	1970	2 523	11 720	8 735	75	349 378	170 892	49	30
	1974	2 712	12 643	...	...	367 901	167 409	46	29
	1975	2 770	12 429	...	...	361 303	176 792	49	29
	1976	2 790	12 973	9 623	77	365 957	178 696	49	28
	1977	2 865	12 500	...	...	367 026	179 126	49	29
	1978	...	...	...	...	347 649	169 035	49	...

Education at the first level 3.4
Enseignement du premier degré
Enseñanza de primer grado

COUNTRY PAYS PAIS	YEAR ANNEE AÑO	SCHOOLS ECOLES ESCUELAS	TEACHING STAFF PERSONNEL ENSEIGNANT PERSONAL DOCENTE			PUPILS ENROLLED ELEVES INSCRITS ALUMNOS MATRICULADOS			PUPIL/ TEACHER RATIO NOMBRE D'ELEVES PAR MAITRE NUMERO DE ALUMNOS POR MAESTRO
			TOTAL	FEMALE FEMININ FEMENINO	% F	TOTAL	FEMALE FEMININ FEMENINO	% F	
		(1)	(2)	(3)	(4)	(5)	(6)	(7)	(8)
CUBA	1970	15 190	56 555	...	...	1 530 376	748 676	49	27
	1974	15 547	74 237	47 600	64	1 799 857	867 867	48	24
	1975	14 886	77 472	55 543	72	1 795 752	862 687	48	23
	1976	14 312	80 845	...	...	1 747 738	835 976	48	22
DOMINICA ‡	1970	...	...	...	...	17 808	8 479	48	...
	1974	57	672	448	67	17 675	8 481	48	*38
	1975	...	674	477	71	17 166	8 276	48	*38
	1976	57	680	480	71	17 570	8 669	49	*38
	1977					17 402	8 569	49	...
	1978	62	887	614	69	16 540	8 127	49	*27
DOMINICAN REPUBLIC ‡	1970	5 214	13 796	10 205	70	764 085	380 086	50	55
	1974	5 376	16 824	...	...	867 592	...	...	52
	1975	5 487	17 932	...	...	903 440	392 199	49	50
EL SALVADOR ‡	1970	2 787	14 193	9 971	70	531 309	251 857	47	37
	1974	3 018	15 346	...	...	704 246	342 204	49	43
	1975	3 103	14 256	9 677	68	759 460	366 612	48	50
	1976	3 099	16 563	11 004	66	796 250	386 948	49	48
	1977	...	...	...	...	*823 030	*398 013	*48	...
GRENADA ‡	1970	58	800	466	58	30 355	14 990	49	38
	1974	...	...	...	...	22 072	10 648	48	...
	1975	63	...	...	...	21 195	10 125	48	...
	1976	63	633	410	65	20 259	9 707	48	32
	1977	62	610	406	67	19 618	9 378	48	32
GUADELOUPE	1970	335	*2 058	...	...	70 288	34 241	49	*34
	1974	...	...	...	...	59 392	...	...	31
	1975	257	2 018	...	...	62 813	...	...	31
	1976	...	...	...	...	63 934	...	...	...
	1977	...	...	...	...	56 567	...	...	...
	1978	243	2 139	1 471	69	55 202	...	...	26
GUATEMALA	1970	5 240	14 137	9 070	64	505 691	223 636	44	36
	1974	5 927	17 213	10 646	62	601 189	268 785	45	35
	1975	6 122	18 129	11 162	62	627 126	280 719	45	35
	1977	6 301	19 707	12 124	62	681 503	307 460	45	35
HAITI	1971	2 083	7 472	4 282	57	391 220	...	...	52
	1974	2 730	11 320	...	...	451 040	...	...	40
	1975	2 788	11 816	...	...	487 135	...	...	41
	1976	2 798	12 953	...	...	510 716	...	...	39
	1977	2 841	12 554	6 381	51	517 723	...	...	41
HONDURAS	1970	4 098	10 816	...	...	381 685	189 761	50	35
	1974	4 422	12 302	...	...	442 668	220 813	50	36
	1975	4 602	13 045	...	...	460 744	225 965	49	35
	1976	4 698	13 649	9 483	69	483 210	239 617	50	35
JAMAICA ‡	1970	748	8 053	...	...	376 075	*187 661	*50	47
	1974	981	9 417	...	...	372 260	185 803	50	40
	1975	923	11 531	...	...	371 876	185 568	50	32
	1976	915	9 889	8 070	88	367 625	183 202	50	37
	1977	...	7 092	5 737	81	350 816	173 978	50	49
MARTINIQUE	1970	246	*2 425	...	...	68 785	33 694	49	*28
	1974	...	...	...	...	59 528	...	...	26
	1975	238	2 273	...	...	58 747	...	...	26
	1976	238	...	...	...	58 749	...	...	...
	1977	...	...	...	...	54 720	...	...	...
	1978	231	2 156	1 545	72	53 029	...	...	25

3.4 Education at the first level
Enseignement du premier degré
Enseñanza de primer grado

COUNTRY / PAYS / PAIS	YEAR / ANNEE / AÑO	SCHOOLS / ECOLES / ESCUELAS	TEACHING STAFF PERSONNEL ENSEIGNANT PERSONAL DOCENTE			PUPILS ENROLLED ELEVES INSCRITS ALUMNOS MATRICULADOS			PUPIL/ TEACHER RATIO NOMBRE D'ELEVES PAR MAITRE NUMERO DE ALUMNOS POR MAESTRO
			TOTAL	FEMALE FEMININ FEMENINO	% F	TOTAL	FEMALE FEMININ FEMENINO	% F	
		(1)	(2)	(3)	(4)	(5)	(6)	(7)	(8)
MEXICO	1970	46 010	201 453	122 123	61	9 248 290	4 433 507	48	46
	1974	48 848	242 029	...	...	10 999 713	5 230 438	48	45
	1975	55 618	255 939	*159 055	*62	11 461 415	5 450 446	48	45
	1976	53 571	274 717	170 562	62	12 148 221	5 872 822	48	44
	1977	54 642	286 156	...	...	12 560 035	6 031 156	48	44
	1978	*68 704	*334 146	...	...	*13 604 476	...	...	*41
MONTSERRAT	1969	15	100	82	82	2 641	1 263	48	26
	1975	16	106	91	86	2 635	1 261	48	25
	1976	16	95	84	88	2 356	1 143	49	25
NICARAGUA ‡	1970	2 068	7 645	6 047	79	285 285	143 394	50	*39
	1974	2 241	8 494	6 913	81	324 579	...	...	*39
	1975	2 298	8 817	...	...	341 500	*171 500	*50	39
	1976	2 367	9 255	...	...	362 103	183 996	51	39
	1977	*2 439	*9 714	...	...	368 289	187 583	51	*38
	1978	2 402	10 122	8 339	82	375 259	190 817	51	37
PANAMA ‡	1970	1 784	9 431	7 539	80	255 287	122 472	48	27
	1974	2 168	12 133	9 713	80	328 460	158 064	48	27
	1975	2 171	12 459	10 053	81	342 043	163 828	48	27
	1976	2 178	11 943	9 366	78	353 646	169 883	48	30
	1977	2 193	12 509	9 681	77	357 753	171 568	48	29
	1978	2 260	13 032	10 068	77	368 738	176 927	48	28
FORMER CANAL ZONE ‡	1970	21	*298	...	...	7 110	...	...	*30
	1974	...	...	...	...	5 714	...	...	...
	1975	...	*235	...	...	*5 449	...	...	*23
	1976	...	*200	...	...	4 581	...	...	*23
	1977	...	...	...	...	4 308	...	...	...
PUERTO RICO ‡	1970	1 938	*15 930	...	...	472 742	...	...	*31
	1974	...	27 870	...	...	438 800	...	...	*24
	1975	...	17 270	...	...	385 903	...	...	22
	1976	...	*16 570	...	...	395 563	...	...	*24
ST. KITTS — NEVIS ANGUILLA	1969	37	392	290	74	12 786	6 305	49	33
	1970	39	*313	*229	*73	12 724	6 263	49	*41
ST. LUCIA	1970	...	...	...	...	23 484	12 092	51	...
	1974	...	...	...	...	29 090	14 088	48	...
	1975	75	...	...	...	29 791	14 518	49	...
	1976	76	939	709	76	29 858	14 576	49	32
ST. PIERRE AND MIQUELON	1970	5	40	31	78	930	547	59	23
	1973	6	34	21	62	874	404	46	26
ST. VINCENT AND THE GRENADINES ‡	1970	60	880	417	47	28 225	13 944	49	*27
	1974	...	...	...	...	20 724	10 188	49	...
	1975	61	1 210	518	43	21 854	10 605	49	18
TRINIDAD AND TOBAGO ‡	1970	469	6 548	3 873	59	225 689	111 242	49	*34
	1974	472	6 566	4 114	63	202 943	100 474	50	*31
	1975	476	6 471	4 022	62	199 033	98 990	50	*31
TURKS AND CAICOS ISLANDS ‡	1970	14	106	88	83	1 615	...	...	15
	1974	16	94	*82	*87	1 676	...	...	18
	1975	17	83	75	90	1 764	...	...	21
	1976	16	83	75	90	1 800	...	...	22
	1977	14	80	71	89	1 692	802	47	21

Education at the first level   3.4
Enseignement du premier degré
Enseñanza de primer grado

COUNTRY	YEAR	SCHOOLS	TEACHING STAFF PERSONNEL ENSEIGNANT PERSONAL DOCENTE			PUPILS ENROLLED ELEVES INSCRITS ALUMNOS MATRICULADOS			PUPIL/ TEACHER RATIO
				FEMALE FEMININ	%		FEMALE FEMININ	%	NOMBRE D'ELEVES PAR MAITRE
PAYS	ANNEE	ECOLES							NUMERO DE ALUMNOS
PAIS	AÑO	ESCUELAS	TOTAL	FEMENINO	F	TOTAL	FEMENINO	F	POR MAESTRO
		(1)	(2)	(3)	(4)	(5)	(6)	(7)	(8)
UNITED STATES OF AMERICA ‡	1970	81 849	*1 316 000	...	...	*31 900 000	...	...	*24
	1974	*79 070	*1 331 000	...	...	*27 141 000	...	...	*20
	1975	*77 619	*1 354 000	...	...	*26 846 000	...	...	*20
	1976	*76 970	*1 293 000	...	...	*25 928 000	...	...	*20
	1977	...	*1 330 000	...	...	*25 652 000	...	...	*19
U.S. VIRGIN ISLANDS ‡	1970	*36	*490	...	...	*12 800	...	...	*26
	1974	...	1 541	...	...	*16 379	...	...	*16
	1975	*42	*1 111	...	...	*17 997	...	...	*16
	1976	*43	*1 117	...	...	*17 668	...	...	*15
	1977	...	...	...	...	13 770	...	...	...
AMERICA, SOUTH									
ARGENTINA	1970	19 847	175 929	161 401	92	3 385 790	1 672 717	49	19
	1974	20 488	185 566	171 736	93	3 544 591	1 744 713	49	19
	1975	20 646	195 997	181 141	92	3 579 304	1 764 223	49	18
	1976	20 590	199 256	184 376	93	3 601 243	1 769 842	49	18
	1977	20 590	199 384	184 522	93	3 680 185	1 810 975	49	18
BOLIVIA	1970	...	25 509	...	...	679 123	276 556	41	27
	1974	...	35 302	...	...	809 579	358 328	44	23
	1975	4 893	38 737	...	...	879 826	390 720	44	23
	1976	...	...	...	...	*922 850	...	...	...
BRAZIL ‡	1970	146 136	457 406	433 542	95	12 812 029	6 368 913	50	28
	1974	180 915	887 424	754 855	85	19 286 611	9 610 291	50	22
	1975	188 260	896 652	...	...	19 549 249	...	...	22
CHILE ‡	1970	7 387	40 823	28 132	69	2 040 071	1 010 613	50	39
	1974	8 238	67 963	...	...	2 332 659	1 149 545	49	34
	1975	8 461	65 817	48 615	74	2 298 998	1 130 358	49	35
	1976	8 156	57 164	41 417	72	2 243 274	1 104 325	49	39
	1977	8 304	70 561	50 363	71	2 242 111	1 101 891	49	32
	1978	8 210	71 846	51 960	72	2 232 990	1 096 617	49	31
COLOMBIA	1970	27 094	86 005	66 370	77	3 286 052	1 652 884	50	38
	1974	32 230	115 310	...	...	3 791 543	1 917 425	51	33
	1975	33 202	121 957	...	...	3 911 244	1 974 005	50	32
	1976	33 940	125 830	...	...	4 058 044	2 044 037	50	32
	1977	34 240	128 494	...	...	4 160 527	2 091 913	50	32
	1978	35 203	131 214	...	...	*4 265 598	*2 144 935	*50	*33
ECUADOR ‡	1970	7 692	26 609	16 899	64	1 016 483	490 379	48	38
	1974	8 978	31 054	*20 185	*65	1 164 223	566 685	49	37
	1975	9 608	31 360	20 439	65	1 228 589	596 282	49	39
	1976	9 696	33 567	21 824	65	1 278 402	620 438	49	38
	1977	10 179	37 161	24 648	66	1 298 450	652 842	49	*36
FALKLAND ISLANDS (MALVINAS) ‡	1970	42	37	15	41	383	198	52	10
	1974	...	...	...	...	181	91	50	...
	1975	18	23	11	48	206	99	48	9
	1976	...	*23	*11	*48	206	99	48	*9
	1977	...	*23	*11	*48	206	99	48	*9
	1978	...	29	9	31	219	104	47	8
FRENCH GUIANA ‡	1970	51	343	...	...	8 322	4 137	50	*31
	1974	...	...	...	...	6 465	...	...	...
	1975	46	259	...	...	7 594	...	...	29
	1976	48	...	...	...	7 861	...	...	...
	1977	...	...	...	...	8 125	...	...	...
	1978	46	279	203	73	8 508	...	...	30

3.4 Education at the first level
Enseignement du premier degré
Enseñanza de primer grado

COUNTRY PAYS PAIS	YEAR ANNEE AÑO	SCHOOLS ECOLES ESCUELAS	TEACHING STAFF PERSONNEL ENSEIGNANT PERSONAL DOCENTE			PUPILS ENROLLED ELEVES INSCRITS ALUMNOS MATRICULADOS			PUPIL/ TEACHER RATIO NOMBRE D'ELEVES PAR MAITRE
			TOTAL	FEMALE FEMININ FEMENINO	% F	TOTAL	FEMALE FEMININ FEMENINO	% F	NUMERO DE ALUMNOS POR MAESTRO
		(1)	(2)	(3)	(4)	(5)	(6)	(7)	(8)
GUYANA ‡	1970	388	4 485	2 460	55	130 484	63 914	49	29
	1975	...	4 052	2 791	69	130 240	64 015	49	32
	1976	435	4 335	2 896	67	140 394	68 996	49	32
PARAGUAY ‡	1970	3 045	13 135	...	...	424 179	199 480	47	32
	1974	...	16 401	...	...	454 986	215 728	47	*32
	1975	...	...	...	...	452 249	214 459	47	...
	1976	...	...	...	...	467 552	221 543	47	...
	1977	...	...	...	...	478 584	227 044	47	...
PERU	1970	18 439	65 965	...	...	2 341 068	1 074 300	46	35
	1974	19 780	72 993	...	...	2 741 060	...	...	38
	1975	19 701	72 641	...	...	2 840 625	...	...	39
	1976	*19 701	73 849	...	...	2 961 252	...	...	40
	1977	19 420	75 491	...	...	3 019 624	*1 426 772	*47	40
	1978	...	*77 844	...	...	*3 126 000	...	...	*40
SURINAME	1970	270	2 487	1 542	62	91 834	44 080	48	37
	1974	284	3 005	1 923	64	91 769	42 214	46	31
	1975	309	2 552	1 659	65	80 171	38 248	48	31
	1976	313	3 016	2 011	67	86 958	41 324	48	29
	1977	313	3 077	2 304	75	85 250	40 713	48	28
	1978	324	3 068	2 342	76	85 060	40 565	48	28
URUGUAY ‡	1970	2 312	12 009	...	...	354 096	169 175	48	29
	1974	2 324	14 434	...	...	331 047	161 346	49	23
	1975	2 308	13 572	...	...	322 602	...	...	24
	1976	2 317	13 788	...	...	345 739	...	...	*22
	1977	...	...	...	...	269 779	129 088	48	...
	1978	2 316	13 821	...	...	325 888	164 875	51	24
VENEZUELA ‡	1970	10 509	50 822	43 617	86	1 769 680	878 860	50	35
	1974	11 098	63 198	53 808	85	1 990 123	984 529	49	31
	1975	11 859	69 466	...	...	2 108 413	1 041 196	49	30
	1976	12 375	74 895	...	...	2 204 074	1 086 627	49	29
	1977	12 838	79 899	...	...	2 309 173	1 139 486	49	29
	1978	9 613	92 428	...	...	2 374 339	...	...	*28
ASIA									
AFGHANISTAN ‡	1970	3 020	13 116	2 183	17	540 685	76 143	14	41
	1974	3 371	17 579	3 215	18	654 209	94 511	14	37
	1975	3 371	18 558	3 353	18	784 568	115 795	15	*37
	1976	3 339	20 406	3 495	17	841 046	127 915	15	*37
	1977	3 371	23 571	3 593	15	872 322	134 590	15	37
BAHRAIN ‡	1970	81	...	...	...	38 711	*16 313	*42	...
	1974	...	1 916	855	45	43 965	19 113	43	*21
	1975	...	2 044	946	46	41 751	18 219	44	*21
	1976	...	2 010	940	47	45 640	20 160	44	*21
	1977	...	2 235	1 056	41	46 326	20 550	44	*21
	1978	...	2 345	1 107	47	47 825	21 447	45	*21
BANGLADESH	1970	...	...	...	...	5 283 787	1 693 057	32	...
	1974	...	...	...	...	7 747 559	2 561 459	33	...
	1975	...	...	...	...	8 349 834	2 839 021	34	...
	1976	40 313	172 448	8 758	5	9 483 090	3 319 703	35	55
	1977	...	...	...	...	8 822 533	2 356 134	27	...
	1978	43 830	187 078	9 597	5	8 312 011	2 753 541	33	44
BHUTAN ‡	1970	...	436	60	14	9 039	456	5	*22
	1974	...	538	98	18	12 810	3 039	24	*27
	1976	...	...	...	...	16 671	4 481	27	...
	1977	...	1 054	...	...	18 821	5 209	28	*20
	1978	...	1 146	...	...	19 595	5 435	28	*20

Education at the first level 3.4
Enseignement du premier degré
Enseñanza de primer grado

COUNTRY PAYS PAIS	YEAR ANNEE AÑO	SCHOOLS ECOLES ESCUELAS	TEACHING STAFF PERSONNEL ENSEIGNANT PERSONAL DOCENTE			PUPILS ENROLLED ELEVES INSCRITS ALUMNOS MATRICULADOS			PUPIL/ TEACHER RATIO NOMBRE D'ELEVES PAR MAITRE
			TOTAL	FEMALE FEMININ FEMENINO	% F	TOTAL	FEMALE FEMININ FEMENINO	% F	NUMERO DE ALUMNOS POR MAESTRO
		(1)	(2)	(3)	(4)	(5)	(6)	(7)	(8)
BRUNEI	1970	128	1 190	481	40	27 941	13 356	48	23
	1974	136	1 584	681	43	30 747	14 655	48	19
	1975	139	1 582	684	43	30 109	14 324	48	19
	1976	146	1 679	744	44	30 824	14 718	48	18
	1977	153	1 761	787	45	32 188	15 490	48	18
	1978	157	1 996	922	46	33 053	15 884	48	17
BURMA	1970	17 399	68 156	28 919	42	3 177 739	1 492 027	47	47
	1974	*17 619	*65 079	*36 328	*56	*3 404 071	*1 623 497	*48	*52
	1975	18 670	...	...	...	3 475 749	1 658 078	48	...
	1976	...	...	...	...	3 564 473	1 689 480	47	...
	1977	19 919	68 251	32 491	48	3 711 464	1 763 881	48	54
CHINA	1977	...	...	...	...	*140000 000	*70 000 000	*50	...
	1978	*949 000	...	...	...	*146240 000	...	...	...
CYPRUS ‡	1970	565	2 280	914	40	69 160	33 472	48	30
	1974	394	2 078	880	42	56 649	27 312	48	27
	1975	402	2 101	916	44	56 602	27 388	48	27
	1976	436	2 163	970	45	55 366	26 878	49	26
	1977	433	2 320	1 062	46	55 166	26 862	49	24
	1978	439	2 263	1 014	45	54 309	26 504	49	24
DEMOCRATIC KAMPUCHEA‡	1970	1 490	20 046	2 945	17	337 729	138 884	43	17
	1972	1 534	20 374	3 346	16	479 616	198 303	41	24
EAST TIMOR	1970	328	699	...	...	32 873	8 369	25	47
	1973	...	...	...	...	92 697	29 866	32	...
HONG KONG	1970	1 547	22 383	14 610	65	739 619	350 450	47	33
	1974	1 185	21 641	14 723	68	677 421	324 787	48	31
	1975	1 126	20 666	14 172	69	642 611	308 075	48	31
	1976	965	19 695	13 735	70	606 860	290 354	48	31
	1977	914	19 073	13 448	71	574 822	275 131	48	30
INDIA ‡	1970	408 378	1 376 176	334 852	24	57 045 441	21 306 280	37	41
	1974	443 461	1 546 696	378 323	24	64 855 638	24 589 098	38	42
	1975	453 530	1 559 137	387 122	25	65 660 022	25 010 985	38	42
	1976	466 332	...	...	...	69 060 730	26 370 820	38	...
	1977	477 037	1 354 460	326 006	24	70 149 960	26 953 273	38	*41
INDONESIA ‡	1970	64 040	514 007	*163 454	*32	14 870 220	*6 780 820	*46	29
	1974	66 944	573 061	*194 268	*34	16 892 010	7 446 014	44	29
	1975	72 760	603 327	...	...	17 776 617	8 088 266	45	29
	1976	80 261	618 818	225 860	36	18 779 943	8 679 236	46	30
	1977	83 539	549 519	198 575	36	17 265 291	7 977 034	46	31
	1978	112 145	592 439	216 566	37	22 024 819	10 176 976	46	30
IRAN ‡	1970	25 758	105 295	47 576	45	3 415 650	1 206 720	35	32
	1974	35 796	135 021	66 776	49	4 119 157	1 508 387	37	31
	1975	36 738	152 106	79 492	52	4 468 299	1 685 364	38	29
	1976	38 369	167 457	90 054	54	4 768 588	1 828 788	38	28
	1977	24 814	154 577	99 635	64	5 020 686	1 952 472	39	32
IRAQ	1970	5 616	49 822	16 957	34	1 098 865	318 509	29	22
	1974	6 194	57 621	21 509	37	1 523 955	493 408	32	26
	1975	7 595	69 812	25 557	37	1 776 095	591 613	33	25
	1976	8 165	70 663	29 132	41	1 949 718	691 545	35	28
	1977	8 387	78 060	31 856	41	2 048 566	765 072	37	26
	1978	10 560	87 148	37 748	43	2 459 870	1 058 695	43	28

3.4 Education at the first level
Enseignement du premier degré
Enseñanza de primer grado

COUNTRY PAYS PAIS	YEAR ANNEE AÑO	SCHOOLS ECOLES ESCUELAS	TEACHING STAFF PERSONNEL ENSEIGNANT PERSONAL DOCENTE			PUPILS ENROLLED ELEVES INSCRITS ALUMNOS MATRICULADOS			PUPIL/ TEACHER RATIO NOMBRE D'ELEVES PAR MAITRE NUMERO DE ALUMNOS POR MAESTRO
			TOTAL	FEMALE FEMININ FEMENINO	% F	TOTAL	FEMALE FEMININ FEMENINO	% F	
		(1)	(2)	(3)	(4)	(5)	(6)	(7)	(8)
ISRAEL	1970	1 587	*27 780	...	...	478 951	*229 917	*48	*17
	1974	1 500	29 195	...	...	523 184	255 229	49	18
	1975	1 503	32 657	...	...	535 320	261 338	49	16
	1976	1 507	34 579	26 144	76	549 413	268 529	49	16
	1977	1 529	35 838	27 474	77	567 915	277 578	49	16
JAPAN ‡	1970	25 034	364 906	191 872	51	9 558 139	4 706 222	49	26
	1974	24 606	406 347	219 663	54	10 006 496	4 925 143	49	*25
	1975	24 650	402 553	228 728	55	10 280 642	5 056 696	49	26
	1976	24 717	411 379	236 312	55	10 525 494	5 174 672	49	26
	1977	24 777	419 953	243 341	55	10 735 927	5 274 487	49	26
	1978	24 828	448 269	252 677	56	11 146 874	5 431 877	49	25
JORDAN ‡	1970	865	7 150	3 278	46	277 619	122 087	44	39
	1974	1 132	10 418	5 270	51	371 631	171 179	46	36
	1975	1 165	11 136	5 719	51	386 012	179 394	46	35
	1976	1 123	11 661	6 307	54	402 401	187 831	47	35
	1977	1 109	12 757	7 218	57	414 490	194 074	47	32
	1978	1 076	13 374	7 653	57	431 107	203 323	47	32
KOREA, DEMOCRATIC PEOPLE'S REPUB. OF	1976	4 700	...	...	...	2 561 674	1 242 980	49	...
KOREA, REPUBLIC OF	1970	5 961	101 095	29 428	29	5 749 301	2 754 648	48	57
	1974	6 315	107 436	36 112	34	5 618 768	2 715 586	48	52
	1975	6 367	108 126	36 440	34	5 599 074	2 709 133	48	52
	1976	6 405	109 530	37 409	34	5 503 737	2 666 904	48	50
	1977	6 408	112 997	39 599	35	5 514 417	2 672 527	48	49
	1978	6 426	115 245	41 040	36	5 604 365	2 719 650	49	49
	1979	6 450	117 290	42 276	36	5 640 712	2 738 454	49	48
KUWAIT ‡	1970	83	3 555	1 967	55	75 513	31 797	42	21
	1974	171	5 729	3 119	54	101 876	46 333	45	18
	1975	177	6 360	3 471	55	111 820	51 099	46	18
	1976	195	7 269	4 004	55	125 120	57 979	46	17
	1977	203	7 920	4 534	57	135 479	62 534	46	17
	1978	154	6 918	3 724	54	116 721	54 418	47	17
LAO PEOPLE'S DEMOCRATIC REPUBLIC‡	1970	3 264	6 796	1 966	29	244 803	90 546	37	36
	1974	...	7 248	1 882	26	278 755	...	...	38
	1976	...	...	...	...	414 423	172 640	42	...
	1977	5 893	14 218	4 046	28	424 330	193 690	46	30
LEBANON ‡	1970	1 772	34 735	17 000	49	435 066	197 157	45	*23
	1977	...	...	...	...	380 695	...	...	...
MACAU ‡	1970	88	886	...	...	25 052	11 769	47	28
	1972	...	...	...	...	23 095	10 900	47	...
MALAYSIA									
PENINSULAR MALAYSIA ‡	1970	4 443	45 307	16 912	37	1 429 649	676 361	47	32
	1974	4 383	48 844	20 280	42	1 543 805	746 511	48	32
	1975	4 369	49 225	20 864	42	1 593 804	772 521	48	32
	1976	4 375	49 941	21 426	43	1 608 101	780 278	49	32
	1977	4 328	50 531	...	...	1 609 335	...	...	32
	1978	4 341	52 492	...	...	1 637 143	...	...	31
SABAH	1970	695	4 655	...	...	110 607	48 040	43	24
	1974	775	4 764	1 682	35	123 419	55 018	45	26
	1975	780	5 012	...	...	125 592	56 593	45	25
	1976	803	4 944	1 888	38	127 271	57 739	45	26
	1977	807	5 032	...	...	127 555	...	...	25

Education at the first level   3.4
Enseignement du premier degré
Enseñanza de primer grado

COUNTRY PAYS PAIS	YEAR ANNEE AÑO	SCHOOLS ECOLES ESCUELAS	TEACHING STAFF PERSONNEL ENSEIGNANT PERSONAL DOCENTE			PUPILS ENROLLED ELEVES INSCRITS ALUMNOS MATRICULADOS			PUPIL/ TEACHER RATIO NOMBRE D'ELEVES PAR MAITRE
			TOTAL	FEMALE FEMININ FEMENINO	% F	TOTAL	FEMALE FEMININ FEMENINO	% F	NUMERO DE ALUMNOS POR MAESTRO
		(1)	(2)	(3)	(4)	(5)	(6)	(7)	(8)
SARAWAK	1970	1 220	4 404	1 306	30	144 007	64 327	45	33
	1974	1 216	4 561	1 320	29	165 484	75 274	45	36
	1975	1 238	5 106	...	...	173 927	79 603	46	34
	1976	1 249	5 307	1 674	32	189 347	87 268	46	36
	1977	1 260	5 704	1 867	33	193 024	89 722	46	34
MALDIVES ‡	1970	2	29	24	83	648	336	52	22
	1974	...	...	...	...	1 425	708	50	...
	1975	...	...	...	...	1 472	728	49	...
	1976	...	...	...	...	1 597	755	47	...
	1977	4	29	17	59	2 747	1 230	45	46
	1978	...	...	...	...	1 541	731	47	...
MONGOLIA ‡	1970	...	4 800	...	...	146 014	...	...	30
	1974	163	4 144	2 256	54	127 986	63 738	50	31
	1975	...	...	...	...	129 802	63 420	49	...
NEPAL ‡	1970	...	17 988	...	...	389 825	58 093	15	22
	1974	...	17 526	...	...	470 365	69 331	15	27
	1975	8 314	18 874	...	...	542 524	84 008	15	29
	1976	8 768	20 775	1 706	8	643 835	129 276	20	31
	1977	9 067	23 395	1 860	8	769 049	169 640	22	33
OMAN ‡	1970	16	196	30	15	3 478	470	14	18
	1974	163	2 008	437	22	48 649	12 266	25	24
	1975	181	2 055	550	27	54 611	14 901	27	27
	1976	...	...	...	...	62 630	17 962	29	...
	1977	238	2 932	835	28	70 751	21 414	30	*24
	1978	260	3 464	1 021	29	78 136	25 027	32	*23
PAKISTAN	1970	43 710	96 288	27 183	28	3 992 834	1 061 664	27	41
	1974	51 568	123 361	37 127	30	4 988 873	1 430 116	29	40
	1975	54 384	131 400	44 900	34	5 293 504	1 570 000	30	40
	1976	*56 831	*140 000	*47 000	*34	*5 610 000	*1 720 000	*31	*40
PHILIPPINES ‡	1970	...	243 833	196 680	81	6 968 978	...	...	29
	1974	29 118	259 833	...	...	7 525 169	3 800 549	51	29
	1975	30 839	261 817	...	...	7 665 396	3 540 857	49	29
	1976	...	252 862	...	...	7 864 415	...	...	31
	1977	...	256 370	...	...	7 992 406	...	...	31
QATAR	1970	89	772	355	46	15 025	6 727	45	19
	1974	92	1 100	593	54	22 287	10 664	48	20
	1975	100	1 252	678	54	23 615	11 246	48	19
	1976	91	1 377	769	56	25 266	11 977	47	18
	1977	93	1 577	904	57	26 065	12 500	48	17
	1978	97	1 813	1 084	60	27 031	13 115	49	15
SAUDI ARABIA ‡	1970	1 877	17 435	4 716	27	422 744	132 277	31	24
	1974	3 028	29 989	8 860	30	625 773	223 255	36	21
	1975	3 460	34 481	10 568	31	677 803	246 559	36	20
	1976	3 878	38 435	11 911	31	726 063	266 425	37	*19
	1977	4 444	40 779	13 060	32	752 977	278 338	37	*18
SINGAPORE	1970	427	12 259	8 094	66	363 518	169 693	47	30
	1974	396	10 985	7 367	67	337 816	159 354	47	31
	1975	391	10 777	7 223	67	328 401	154 995	47	30
	1976	379	10 597	7 100	67	316 265	149 587	47	30
	1977	376	10 345	6 927	67	306 349	144 694	47	30
	1978	364	10 347	6 888	67	297 102	141 120	47	29

3.4 Education at the first level
Enseignement du premier degré
Enseñanza de primer grado

COUNTRY PAYS PAIS	YEAR ANNEE AÑO	SCHOOLS ECOLES ESCUELAS	TEACHING STAFF PERSONNEL ENSEIGNANT PERSONAL DOCENTE			PUPILS ENROLLED ELEVES INSCRITS ALUMNOS MATRICULADOS			PUPIL/ TEACHER RATIO NOMBRE D'ELEVES PAR MAITRE
			TOTAL	FEMALE FEMININ FEMENINO	% F	TOTAL	FEMALE FEMININ FEMENINO	% F	NUMERO DE ALUMNOS POR MAESTRO
		(1)	(2)	(3)	(4)	(5)	(6)	(7)	(8)
SRI LANKA ‡	1970	...	...	...	...	1 671 428	786 963	47	...
	1974		100 910	...	...	1 387 701	...	...	*30
	1975	...	99 067	51 526	52	1 367 860	646 171	47	*30
	1976	8 649	48 096	...	...	1 385 001	655 556	47	29
	1977	...	50 665	...	...	1 492 141	706 268	47	29
	1978	8 712	60 835	36 501	60	1 957 137	...	...	32
	1979	...	...	...	...	1 975 749	...	...	...
SYRIAN ARAB REPUBLIC ‡	1970	5 500	25 134	9 949	40	924 969	335 940	36	37
	1974	6 760	34 995	14 858	42	1 211 570	475 092	39	35
	1975	7 018	37 621	17 035	45	1 273 944	504 939	40	34
	1976	7 228	40 218	19 935	50	1 316 152	528 109	40	33
	1977	7 265	42 387	20 906	49	1 356 428	550 445	41	32
	1978	7 531	46 132	23 449	51	1 407 223	578 416	41	31
THAILAND ‡	1970	...	162 512	...	...	5 634 782	2 637 599	47	35
	1974	41 521	217 015	...	...	6 543 164	3 088 050	47	30
	1975	42 179	239 128	...	...	6 686 477	3 161 807	47	28
	1976	...	225 387	100 974	45	6 810 747	3 231 400	47	*28
	1977	...	240 844	110 600	46	6 955 623	3 306 786	48	*28
TURKEY	1970	38 227	132 577	45 186	34	5 011 926	2 120 332	42	38
	1974	41 191	160 271	60 362	38	5 377 708	2 384 532	44	34
	1976	...	...	...	...	*5 499 456	*2 460 692	*45	...
	1977	43 249	184 123	75 845	41	*5 454 356	*2 453 687	*45	*30
UNITED ARAB EMIRATES ‡	1970	...	806	...	...	22 009	8 300	38	27
	1974	...	2 727	1 321	48	40 229	17 628	44	15
	1975	...	3 191	1 563	49	46 513	21 039	45	15
	1976	145	3 876	1 937	50	60 742	28 296	47	14
	1977	...	4 179	2 172	52	67 058	31 565	47	14
	1978	119	4 474	2 367	53	72 627	34 515	48	14
VIET-NAM	1975	15 170	204 998	114 331	56	7 403 715	3 650 762	49	36
	1976	11 337	217 064	140 363	65	7 722 524	3 838 769	50	36
	1977	...	227 984	115 644	51	7 784 587	3 643 871	47	34
VIET-NAM, (FORMER NORTH)	1970	...	115 544	65 547	57	4 374 385	2 059 756	47	38
	1974	...	116 564	81 409	70	4 096 341	1 983 188	48	35
VIET-NAM, (FORMER SOUTH)	1970	7 978	52 194	34 266	66	2 718 036	1 245 465	46	52
	1973	9 117	64 254	45 239	70	3 020 000	1 372 105	45	47
YEMEN ‡	1970	821	1 726	...	...	88 217	8 263	9	51
	1974	1 952	5 773	...	...	232 784	22 788	10	40
	1975	2 139	6 604	562	9	255 301	28 201	11	38
YEMEN, DEMOCRATIC ‡	1970	872	4 316	887	21	134 522	26 597	20	31
	1974	963	6 467	1 582	24	196 466	59 611	30	30
	1975	962	6 659	1 743	26	228 544	71 004	31	34
	1976	976	9 018	2 420	27	233 930	75 083	32	*34
	1977	927	10 078	2 770	27	212 795	74 219	35	*34
EUROPE									
ALBANIA ‡	1970	1 374	18 944	9 094	48	496 523	235 429	47	26
	1971	1 429	20 555	10 234	50	518 002	245 448	47	25
ANDORRA ‡	1970	...	...	...	...	3 334	1 695	51	...
	1974	...	142	107	75	2 185	1 088	50	*20
	1975	...	...	...	...	3 802	1 802	47	...

Education at the first level 3.4
Enseignement du premier degré
Enseñanza de primer grado

COUNTRY PAYS PAIS	YEAR ANNEE AÑO	SCHOOLS ECOLES ESCUELAS	TEACHING STAFF PERSONNEL ENSEIGNANT PERSONAL DOCENTE TOTAL	FEMALE FEMININ FEMENINO	% F	PUPILS ENROLLED ELEVES INSCRITS ALUMNOS MATRICULADOS TOTAL	FEMALE FEMININ FEMENINO	% F	PUPIL/ TEACHER RATIO NOMBRE D'ELEVES PAR MAITRE NUMERO DE ALUMNOS POR MAESTRO
		(1)	(2)	(3)	(4)	(5)	(6)	(7)	(8)
AUSTRIA ‡	1970	3 973	24 815	15 709	63	531 934	258 631	49	21
	1974	3 644	25 308	...	...	513 027	250 055	49	20
	1975	3 590	26 374	18 608	71	501 843	244 462	49	19
	1976	3 548	...	...	...	492 723	240 124	49	...
	1977	3 508	28 492	20 515	72	466 933	227 431	49	16
	1978	3 494	26 049	19 271	74	445 103	216 939	49	17
BELGIUM ‡	1970	...	51 692	29 053	56	1 021 511	495 752	49	*20
	1974	...	...	...	...	955 255	465 140	49	...
	1975	7 773	48 625	27 777	57	940 961	458 069	49	*19
	1976	5 995	48 041	27 796	58	923 677	449 134	49	*19
	1977	5 265	46 484	26 788	58	878 514	429 694	49	19
BULGARIA ‡	1970	3 933	47 798	32 973	69	1 049 829	510 001	49	22
	1974	3 444	47 688	33 320	70	976 848	473 331	48	20
	1975	3 419	48 445	34 159	71	980 318	475 402	48	20
	1976	3 371	49 345	34 639	70	980 857	475 186	48	20
	1977	3 334	49 470	34 840	70	984 194	476 707	48	20
	1978	3 296	49 958	35 240	71	973 007	470 488	48	*19
CZECHOSLOVAKIA	1970	10 831	97 712	70 969	73	1 966 448	962 237	49	20
	1974	9 840	96 124	72 467	75	1 884 332	923 392	49	20
	1975	9 285	95 634	73 210	77	1 881 414	921 541	49	20
	1976	8 550	93 192	71 777	77	1 882 371	920 627	49	20
	1977	7 910	92 636	71 530	77	1 883 709	921 917	49	20
	1978	7 398	91 876	71 614	78	1 877 773	920 043	49	20
DENMARK ‡	1970	2 403	47 314	24 044	51	443 031	218 569	49	*16
	1974	2 225	58 425	30 927	53	487 329	...	...	*16
	1975	...	58 012	...	...	490 891	...	...	*16
	1976	...	58 954	...	...	480 810	...	...	*16
	1977	2 234	58 957	30 906	52	461 838	...	...	*16
FINLAND ‡	1970	4 507	17 360	*10 390	*60	386 230	*183 459	*47	22
	1974	4 383	23 235	...	...	406 058	194 659	48	17
	1975	...	24 494	14 990	61	453 737	219 795	48	19
	1976	4 324	27 414	...	...	438 804	213 615	49	*19
	1977	4 299	25 096	...	...	422 638	206 202	49	17
	1978	...	...	...	...	406 921	198 804	49	...
FRANCE ‡	1970	63 520	184 326	...	...	4 939 683	2 412 399	49	23
	1974	57 084	224 145	152 945	68	4 670 406	2 279 233	49	19
	1975	55 886	256 781	167 285	65	4 601 550	...	...	18
	1976	55 093	221 343	149 292	67	4 568 134	2 218 667	49	18
	1977	*54 044	*221 574	...	...	4 618 436	2 249 039	49	*21
	1978	53 192	230 634	137 040	67	4 647 552	2 251 326	48	20
GERMAN DEMOCRATIC REPUBLIC ‡	1970	6 035	137 963	...	...	2 534 077	...	...	18
	1974	5 063	155 932	...	...	2 602 027	...	...	17
	1975	5 067	158 543	...	...	2 578 782	...	...	16
	1976	5 037	161 477	...	...	2 532 924	...	...	16
	1977	5 053	165 755	...	...	2 480 952	...	...	15
	1978	5 064	167 424	...	...	2 420 494	...	...	14
GERMANY, FEDERAL REPUBLIC OF	1970	21 501	248 499	137 912	55	6 344 774	3 111 690	49	26
	1974	18 094	275 830	161 420	59	6 481 775	3 141 266	48	23
	1975	18 107	273 041	164 202	60	6 425 217	3 106 972	48	24
	1976	18 237	269 043	163 895	61	6 277 564	3 028 269	48	23
	1977	17 848	274 576	169 113	62	6 019 128	2 896 491	48	22
	1978	*17 797	...	...	...	*5 718 124	...	...	...

3.4 Education at the first level
Enseignement du premier degré
Enseñanza de primer grado

COUNTRY PAYS PAIS	YEAR ANNEE AÑO	SCHOOLS ECOLES ESCUELAS	TEACHING STAFF PERSONNEL ENSEIGNANT PERSONAL DOCENTE			PUPILS ENROLLED ELEVES INSCRITS ALUMNOS MATRICULADOS			PUPIL/ TEACHER RATIO NOMBRE D'ELEVES PAR MAITRE NUMERO DE ALUMNOS POR MAESTRO
			TOTAL	FEMALE FEMININ FEMENINO	% F	TOTAL	FEMALE FEMININ FEMENINO	% F	
		(1)	(2)	(3)	(4)	(5)	(6)	(7)	(8)
GIBRALTAR	1970	...	...	...	...	3 382	1 658	49	...
	1974	14	150	134	89	2 759	1 354	49	18
	1975	14	158	139	88	2 808	1 390	50	18
	1976	13	150	134	89	2 677	1 321	49	18
	1977	13	161	140	87	2 778	1 412	51	17
GREECE ‡	1970	9 513	29 336	13 898	47	907 446	435 422	48	31
	1974	9 640	30 458	14 424	47	927 848	446 245	48	30
	1975	9 633	30 953	14 565	47	935 730	450 506	48	30
	1976	9 743	32 665	15 593	48	938 597	452 284	48	29
HUNGARY ‡	1970	5 480	63 125	46 046	73	1 115 993	538 310	48	18
	1974	...	65 687	...	...	1 039 586	504 606	49	16
	1975	5 502	66 861	...	...	1 051 095	510 180	49	16
	1976	...	68 425	57 123	78	1 072 423	521 288	49	16
	1977	4 856	70 007	59 088	78	1 090 062	529 184	49	16
	1978	4 567	76 750	61 025	80	1 106 744	537 907	49	*16
ICELAND ‡	1970	187	1 383	694	50	27 066	13 157	49	20
	1974	124	1 379	751	54	26 922	13 216	49	*21
	1975	183	1 380	751	54	26 418	12 912	49	*21
	1976	...	1 732	...	...	25 924	12 716	49	*21
IRELAND ‡	1970	4 090	16 981	...	...	520 122	253 558	49	31
	1974	3 659	13 397	...	...	402 219	196 744	49	30
	1975	3 558	13 060	8 472	65	404 818	197 491	49	31
	1976	3 508	13 076	9 461	72	406 432	197 984	49	31
	1977	3 463	13 242	9 634	73	410 402	200 066	49	31
	1978	3 433	13 803	10 075	73	414 624	201 936	49	30
ITALY	1970	37 095	224 646	173 312	77	4 856 953	2 351 309	48	22
	1974	34 411	250 523	...	...	4 933 657	2 399 434	49	20
	1975	33 233	255 267	211 337	83	4 833 415	2 348 516	49	19
	1976	32 625	271 307	227 309	84	4 735 301	2 300 628	49	17
	1977	31 995	271 747	230 546	85	4 648 504	2 258 465	49	17
	1978	*31 524	...	...	...	*4 584 300	...	...	...
LUXEMBOURG ‡	1970	1 605	1 750	930	53	34 530	16 973	49	20
	1974	...	1 484	799	54	29 749	14 604	49	20
	1975	...	1 521	810	53	29 430	14 468	49	19
	1976	...	...	...	...	29 032	14 354	49	...
	1977	...	1 437	...	...	28 465	14 027	49	20
	1978	...	1 449	...	...	27 510	13 472	49	19
MALTA ‡	1970	109	1 391	1 007	72	40 021	19 317	48	29
	1974	144	*1 495	*1 015	*68	30 322	14 798	49	*20
	1975	134	*1 421	*974	*69	29 834	14 465	48	*21
	1976	135	1 529	1 001	65	30 863	15 241	49	20
	1977	148	1 931	1 296	67	31 363	15 275	49	*21
MONACO ‡	1970	8	48	32	67	1 486	761	51	23
	1976	...	...	...	...	1 145	...	...	...
	1977	7	...	...	...	1 558	510	42	...
NETHERLANDS ‡	1970	8 225	49 243	24 353	49	1 462 376	717 218	49	*30
	1974	8 486	52 503	24 298	46	1 448 177	710 863	49	*28
	1975	8 568	52 700	24 216	46	1 453 467	714 053	49	*28
	1976	8 616	52 718	23 928	45	1 448 084	711 833	49	*27
	1977	8 658	53 720	24 123	45	1 434 705	705 748	49	*27
	1978	8 690	55 362	25 093	45	1 413 277	696 244	49	26

Education at the first level 3.4
Enseignement du premier degré
Enseñanza de primer grado

COUNTRY PAYS PAIS	YEAR ANNEE AÑO	SCHOOLS ECOLES ESCUELAS	TEACHING STAFF PERSONNEL ENSEIGNANT PERSONAL DOCENTE			PUPILS ENROLLED ELEVES INSCRITS ALUMNOS MATRICULADOS			PUPIL/ TEACHER RATIO NOMBRE D'ELEVES PAR MAITRE
			TOTAL	FEMALE FEMININ FEMENINO	% F	TOTAL	FEMALE FEMININ FEMENINO	% F	NUMERO DE ALUMNOS POR MAESTRO
		(1)	(2)	(3)	(4)	(5)	(6)	(7)	(8)
NORWAY ‡	1970	3 060	19 713	*11 941	*61	385 628	*197 323	*51	20
	1974	...	45 217	22 841	51	386 559	188 348	49	*17
	1975	...	46 901	23 818	51	390 129	190 060	49	*17
	1976	3 442	41 893	22 592	54	396 194	192 731	49	*17
	1977	3 350	43 971	24 023	55	396 672	193 115	49	*17
POLAND	1970	26 126	228 743	182 301	80	5 256 970	2 530 233	48	23
	1974	16 106	212 900	170 327	80	4 453 433	2 149 777	48	21
	1975	14 738	208 173	167 976	81	4 309 823	2 081 313	48	21
	1976	13 731	202 031	160 805	80	4 198 667	...	...	21
	1977	13 082	198 987	158 759	80	4 137 242	...	...	21
	1978	12 590	199 982	164 659	82	4 105 450	...	...	21
PORTUGAL ‡	1970	17 018	29 554	26 274	89	992 446	482 955	49	34
	1974	16 147	55 046	45 105	82	1 179 200	571 926	49	21
	1975	13 111	59 485	48 074	81	1 204 567	581 147	48	20
	1976	12 405	62 647	50 161	80	1 207 902	578 541	48	19
	1977	12 455	63 808	51 953	81	1 220 123	584 315	48	19
ROMANIA ‡	1970	14 927	135 615	87 111	64	2 878 693	1 417 540	49	21
	1974	14 761	139 790	93 579	67	2 889 946	1 390 552	48	*21
	1975	14 695	144 978	97 201	67	3 019 776	1 448 732	48	*21
	1976	14 591	147 582	100 450	68	3 125 584	1 502 301	48	*21
	1977	14 608	148 922	102 129	69	3 153 016	1 520 803	48	*21
	1978	14 587	150 415	103 793	69	3 423 135	1 614 288	47	*23
SAN MARINO	1970	17	89	72	81	1 639	751	46	18
	1974	16	107	91	85	1 698	803	47	16
	1975	15	116	100	86	1 692	789	47	15
	1976	15	117	99	85	1 663	770	46	14
	1977	14	132	113	86	1 623	740	46	12
	1978	14	132	114	86	1 588	751	47	12
SPAIN ‡	1970	...	115 607	67 143	58	3 929 569	1 959 526	50	34
	1974	30 720	169 149	98 042	58	3 692 600	1 808 109	49	*29
	1975	...	172 122	100 477	58	3 653 320	1 786 175	49	*29
	1976	...	197 706	113 559	57	3 624 136	1 766 516	49	*29
SWEDEN	1970	...	*30 800	*25 600	*83	615 331	302 153	49	*20
	1974	4 819	42 958	34 446	80	688 806	337 178	49	16
	1975	...	34 185	27 575	81	698 677	341 764	49	20
	1976	...	37 740	30 056	81	698 017	341 147	49	18
	1977	...	38 689	31 305	81	689 839	336 640	49	18
	1978	...	...	...	...	686 811	334 285	49	...
SWITZERLAND ‡	1970	...	...	...	...	500 492	247 094	49	...
	1974	...	...	...	...	561 645	276 865	49	...
	1975	...	...	...	...	556 885	274 382	49	...
	1976	...	...	...	...	503 153	247 591	49	...
	1977	...	...	...	...	502 337	246 829	49	...
	1978	...	...	...	...	524 724	253 831	48	...
UNITED KINGDOM ‡	1970	29 504	248 908	192 409	77	5 806 349	2 833 864	49	*25
	1974	...	282 793	222 336	79	5 811 517	2 835 750	49	*22
	1975	...	285 786	230 659	81	5 725 167	2 793 625	49	*22
	1976	...	280 315	219 163	78	5 636 473	2 749 889	49	*22
YUGOSLAVIA ‡	1970	13 995	58 353	38 830	67	1 579 064	753 729	48	27
	1974	13 540	58 955	40 152	68	1 503 582	724 329	48	26
	1975	13 442	60 904	40 766	67	1 494 825	725 255	48	25
	1976	13 333	60 653	41 819	69	1 461 191	712 182	48	24
	1977	13 287	58 386	40 325	69	1 434 342	693 356	48	25
	1978	13 119	57 335	45 333	79	1 427 769	689 371	48	25

3.4 Education at the first level
Enseignement du premier degré
Enseñanza de primer grado

COUNTRY PAYS PAIS	YEAR ANNEE AÑO	SCHOOLS ECOLES ESCUELAS	TEACHING STAFF PERSONNEL ENSEIGNANT PERSONAL DOCENTE			PUPILS ENROLLED ELEVES INSCRITS ALUMNOS MATRICULADOS			PUPIL/ TEACHER RATIO NOMBRE D'ELEVES PAR MAITRE NUMERO DE ALUMNOS POR MAESTRO
			TOTAL	FEMALE FEMININ FEMENINO	% F	TOTAL	FEMALE FEMININ FEMENINO	% F	
		(1)	(2)	(3)	(4)	(5)	(6)	(7)	(8)
OCEANIA									
AMERICAN SAMOA ‡	1970	*32	*350	...	...	*8 100	...	...	*23
	1974	...	...	...	...	*7 013	...	...	...
	1975	...	*270	...	...	6 052	...	...	*22
	1976	...	*300	...	...	5 778	...	...	*19
	1977	...	...	...	...	5 307	...	...	...
AUSTRALIA ‡	1970	8 354	64 670	*45 300	*70	1 812 000	878 600	48	28
	1974	8 076	73 745	52 258	71	1 596 281	776 739	49	*23
	1975	8 009	78 390	56 185	72	1 603 408	780 896	49	*22
	1976	8 007	81 747	58 498	72	1 611 213	785 099	49	*21
	1977	7 989	85 855	61 390	72	1 642 976	801 643	49	*21
COOK ISLANDS	1970	33	291	170	58	5 902	*3 000	*51	20
	1973	...	...	...	...	5 987	3 006	50	...
FIJI	1970	616	3 773	1 879	50	121 374	58 419	48	32
	1974	636	4 229	2 268	54	135 092	66 051	49	32
	1975	641	4 274	2 281	53	134 971	66 131	49	32
	1976	...	...	...	...	133 627	65 510	49	...
	1977	644	4 209	2 365	56	132 440	65 056	49	31
FRENCH POLYNESIA	1970	*159	*771	530	*69	24 148	11 723	49	*31
	1974	166	1 149	866	75	27 780	13 491	49	24
	1975	167	1 213	950	78	28 533	13 853	49	24
	1976	167	1 295	...	...	28 883	13 868	48	22
GUAM ‡	1970	*31	*713	...	...	*17 927	...	...	*25
	1974	...	1 496	...	...	*17 811	...	...	*22
	1975	39	*919	...	...	*20 215	...	...	*22
	1976	...	*770	...	...	*16 945	...	...	*22
KIRIBATI ‡	1970	*218	*546	...	...	*14 570	...	...	*27
	1974	*111	*271	...	...	*13 056	...	...	*48
	1977	81	435	171	39	13 679	6 673	49	31
	1978	84	429	189	44	13 481	6 565	49	31
NAURU	1971	10	65	40	62	1 118	548	49	17
	1974	...	...	...	...	1 392	648	47	...
NEW CALEDONIA ‡	1970	251	940	442	47	21 632	10 694	49	23
	1974	237	1 307	...	...	24 844	12 171	49	*22
	1975	235	1 431	...	...	24 943	12 207	49	*20
	1976	234	1 383	...	...	25 691	12 570	49	*21
	1977	240	1 462	...	...	26 215	12 922	49	*21
NEW HEBRIDES ‡	1970	275	778	229	29	18 250	7 983	44	23
	1974	...	814	257	32	19 834	8 888	45	24
	1975	...	...	...	...	20 095	9 029	45	...
	1976	264	595	...	...	20 639	9 235	45	25
	1977	276	839	108	32	21 161	9 448	45	25
NEW ZEALAND ‡	1970	2 596	18 791	11 989	64	400 445	193 825	48	21
	1974	2 554	20 086	12 602	63	388 996	188 513	48	19
	1975	2 544	21 187	13 517	64	393 448	190 984	49	19
	1976	2 595	21 339	13 564	64	395 789	192 338	49	19
NIUE ‡	1970	8	71	31	44	1 299	630	48	18
	1974	8	*65	*27	*42	1 216	574	47	*19
	1975	8	65	27	42	1 122	543	48	17
	1976	...	...	...	...	1 038	467	45	...

Education at the first level 3.4
Enseignement du premier degré
Enseñanza de primer grado

COUNTRY PAYS PAIS	YEAR ANNEE AÑO	SCHOOLS ECOLES ESCUELAS	TEACHING STAFF PERSONNEL ENSEIGNANT PERSONAL DOCENTE			PUPILS ENROLLED ELEVES INSCRITS ALUMNOS MATRICULADOS			PUPIL/ TEACHER RATIO NOMBRE D'ELEVES PAR MAITRE NUMERO DE ALUMNOS POR MAESTRO
			TOTAL	FEMALE FEMININ FEMENINO	% F	TOTAL	FEMALE FEMININ FEMENINO	% F	
		(1)	(2)	(3)	(4)	(5)	(6)	(7)	(8)
NORFOLK ISLAND	1975	1	7	4	57	210	94	45	30
	1976	1	7	5	71	211	96	45	30
	1977	1	7	5	71	204	92	45	29
	1978	1	7	4	57	204	98	48	29
PACIFIC ISLANDS	1970	225	1 267	*350	*28	28 906	13 713	47	23
	1974	247	1 264	379	30	30 939	14 836	48	24
	1975	248	1 526	499	33	30 285	14 544	48	20
	1976	256	1 482	...	...	31 274	15 036	48	21
PAPUA NEW GUINEA	1970	1 620	6 439	...	...	191 083	69 739	36	30
	1974	1 687	7 545	1 815	24	229 527	82 310	36	30
	1975	1 762	7 544	1 721	23	238 267	88 994	37	32
	1976	1 818	8 067	1 861	23	250 715	93 744	37	31
	1977	...	...	...	...	259 380	99 355	38	...
	1978	2 101	8 805	2 094	24	268 147	*106 152	*40	30
SAMOA	1970	173	1 051	...	...	29 405	14 254	48	28
	1974	...	*1 130	*791	*70	31 401	14 882	47	*28
	1975	152	*1 216	*773	*64	32 642	16 713	51	*27
	1976	150	*1 322	*853	*65	32 872	15 895	48	*25
	1977	151	*1 346	*906	*67	33 382	16 015	48	*25
	1978	152	*1 471	*1 006	*68	33 349	15 983	48	*23
SOLOMON ISLANDS	1970	418	885	194	22	21 270	7 743	36	24
	1974	323	974	276	28	26 088	10 181	39	27
	1975	344	1 071	312	29	28 219	10 743	38	26
TOKELAU ISLANDS	1976	...	...	...	...	386	201	52	...
	1977	...	...	...	...	421	208	49	...
	1978	...	27	13	48	458	229	50	17
	1979	...	27	13	48	461	249	54	17
TONGA	1970	128	658	288	44	17 865	8 548	48	27
	1974	126	668	304	46	16 932	8 062	48	25
	1975	...	688	368	53	19 260	9 176	48	28
	1976	...	...	...	...	19 474	9 255	48	...
	1977	...	...	...	...	19 416	9 224	48	...
	1978	112	761	412	54	19 730	9 415	48	26
	1979	...	...	...	...	19 815	9 446	48	
U.S.S.R.									
U.S.S.R. ‡	1970	172 555	2 360 878	1 668 697	71	40 321 483	...	...	17
	1974	152 449	2 415 008	1 705 582	71	37 155 807	...	...	15
	1975	147 083	2 399 299	1 692 153	71	35 960 941	...	...	15
	1976	142 200	2 374 000	1 673 000	70	34 778 000	...	...	15
	1977	138 000	2 354 000	1 660 000	71	34 053 000	...	...	14
	1978	134 600	2 335 000	1 653 000	71	33 640 000	...	...	14
BYELORUSSIAN S.S.R. ‡	1970	10 650	105 600	...	...	1 516 382	...	...	14
	1974	8 911	108 211	...	...	1 370 145	...	...	13
	1975	8 408	106 893	...	...	1 319 025	...	...	12
	1976	7 969	104 863	...	...	1 266 001	...	...	12
	1977	7 568	102 379	...	...	1 227 820	...	...	12
	1978	7 180	100 500	...	...	1 201 500	...	...	12
UKRAINIAN S.S.R. ‡	1970	27 185	445 300	...	...	6 668 000	*3 270 000	*49	15
	1974	24 317	450 000	...	...	6 155 300	...	...	14
	1975	23 435	445 400	...	...	5 970 000	...	...	13
	1976	22 708	438 800	...	...	5 803 200	...	...	13
	1977	22 039	432 700	...	...	5 703 700	...	...	13
	1978	21 572	428 100	...	...	5 642 800	...	...	13

3.4 Education at the first level
Enseignement du premier degré
Enseñanza de primer grado

ALGERIA:
E—> BEGINNING 1974, DATA ON TEACHING STAFF DO NOT INCLUDE TEACHERS IN "OUCFA" SCHOOLS. IN 1978 ENROLMENT IN "OUCFA" SCHOOLS WAS 3,619 PUPILS (F. 2,641).
FR—> A PARTIR DE 1974, LE PERSONNEL ENSEIGNANT N'INCLUT PAS CELUI DE L'OUCFA. LES ECOLES DE L'OUCFA COMPTAIENT 3,619 ELEVES (DONT 2,641 FILLES) EN 1978.
ESP> A PARTIR DE 1974, LOS DATOS RELATIVOS AL PERSONAL DOCENTE NO INCLUYEN LOS DE LAS ESCUELAS DE LA "OUCFA". LAS ESCUELAS DE LA "OUCFA" TENIAN 3619 ALUMNOS (F 2641) EN 1978.

BENIN:
E—> FOR 1979 THE FIGURES SHOWN IN COLUMNS 6 AND 7 REFER TO PUBLIC EDUCATION ONLY.
FR—> POUR 1979 LES DONNEES DES COLONNES 6 ET 7 SE REFERENT A L'ENSEIGNEMENT PUBLIC SEULEMENT.
ESP> EN 1979 LOS DATOS DE LAS COLUMNAS 6 Y 7 SE REFIEREN A LA ENSEÑANZA PUBLICA SOLAMENTE.

BURUNDI:
E—> SEE ANNEX TO TABLE 3.1.
FR—> VOIR L'ANNEXE DU TABLEAU 3.1.
ESP> VEASE EL ANEXO DEL CUADRO 3.1.

CHAD:
E—> FROM 1974 TO 1976 THE FIGURES SHOWN IN COLUMNS 2, 3 AND 4 REFER TO PUBLIC EDUCATION ONLY. FOR 1976, THE FIGURES SHOWN IN COLUMNS 5, 6 AND 7 DO NOT INCLUDE MOSLEM PRIVATE EDUCATION (9,453 PUPILS IN 1975).
FR—> DE 1974 A 1976 LES CHIFFRES DES COLONNES 2, 3 ET 4 SE REFERENT A L'ENSEIGNEMENT PUBLIC SEULEMENT. EN 1976, LES CHIFFRES DES COLONNES 5, 6 ET 7 N'INCLUENT PAS L'ENSEIGNEMENT PRIVE MUSULMAN (9 453 ELEVES EN 1975).
ESP> DE 1974 A 1976 LAS CIFRAS DE LAS COLUMNAS 2, 3 Y 4 SE REFIEREN A LA ENSEÑANZA PUBLICA SOLAMENTE. EN 1976, LAS CIFRAS DE LAS COLUMNAS 5, 6 Y 7 NO INCLUYEN LA ENSEÑANZA PRIVADA MULSULMANA (9453 ALUMNOS EN 1975).

EGYPT:
E—> BEGINNING 1975, DATA FOR AL AZHAR UNIVERSITY ARE NOT INCLUDED.
FR—> A PARTIR DE 1975, NON COMPRIS LES DONNEES RELATIVES A L'UNIVERSITE AL AZHAR.
ESP> A PARTIR DE 1975, EXCLUIDOS LOS DATOS RELATIVOS A LA UNIVERSIDAD AL-AZHAR.

GHANA:
E—> BEGINNING 1974, DATA REFER TO GRADES I–VI; PREVIOUSLY TO GRADES I–X. BEGINNING 1974, DATA REFER TO PUBLIC EDUCATION ONLY.
FR—> A PARTIR DE 1974, LES DONNEES SE REFERENT AUX CLASSES ALLANT DE LA PREMIERE A LA SIXIEME ANNEE D'ETUDES; POUR LES ANNEES ANTERIEURES DE LA PREMIERE A LA DIXIEME ANNEE. DE 1974 A 1977, LES DONNEES SE REFERENT A L'ENSEIGNEMENT PUBLIC SEULEMENT.
ESP> A PARTIR DE 1974, LOS DATOS SE REFIEREN A LAS CLASES I–VI; PARA LOS AÑOS ANTERIORES A LAS CLASES I–X. DE 1974 A 1977, LOS DATOS SE REFIEREN A LA ENSEÑANZA PUBLICA SOLAMENTE.

GUINEA BISSAU:
E—> FOR 1974, DATA ON PUPILS INCLUDE EDUCATION PRECEDING THE FIRST LEVEL AND ADULT EDUCATION. FOR 1975, THE FIGURE SHOWN IN COLUMN 2 INCLUDES EDUCATION PRECEDING THE FIRST LEVEL.
FR—> POUR 1974, LES EFFECTIFS INCLUENT L'ENSEIGNEMENT PRECEDANT LE PREMIER DEGRE ET L'EDUCATION DES ADULTES. POUR 1975, LE CHIFFRE DE LA COLONNE 2 INCLUT L'ENSEIGNEMENT PRECEDANT LE PREMIER DEGRE.

GUINEA–BISSAU (CONT.):
ESP> EN 1974, LOS ALUMNOS INCLUYEN LA ENSEÑANZA ANTERIOR AL PRIMER GRADO Y LA EDUCACION DE ADULTOS. EN 1975, LA CIFRA DE LA COLUMNA 2 INCLUYE LA ENSEÑANZA ANTERIOR AL PRIMER GRADO.

LESOTHO:
E—> SEE ANNEX TO TABLE 3.1.
FR—> VOIR L'ANNEXE DU TABLEAU 3.1.
ESP> VEASE EL ANEXO DEL CUADRO 3.1.

LIBERIA:
E—> DATA INCLUDE EDUCATION PRECEDING THE FIRST LEVEL.
FR—> LES DONNEES INCLUENT L'ENSEIGNEMENT PRECEDANT LE PREMIER DEGRE.
ESP> LOS DATOS INCLUYEN LA ENSEÑANZA ANTERIOR AL PRIMER GRADO.

MALAWI:
E—> FOR 1977, THE FIGURES SHOWN IN COLUMNS 3 AND 4 REFER TO PUBLIC EDUCATION ONLY.
FR—> POUR 1977, LES DONNEES DES COLONNES 3 ET 4 SE REFERENT A L'ENSEIGNEMENT PUBLIC SEULEMENT.
ESP> PARA 1977, LOS DATOS DE LAS COLUMNAS 3 Y 4 SE REFIEREN A LA ENSEÑANZA PUBLICA SOLAMENTE.

MAURITIUS:
E—> FROM 1976, DATA DO NOT INCLUDE RODRIGUEZ.
FR—> A PARTIR DE 1976, LES DONNEES N'INCLUENT PAS RODRIGUEZ.
ESP> A PARTIR DE 1976, LOS DATOS NO INCLUYEN RODRIGUEZ.

MOROCCO:
E—> FROM 1975, THE FIGURES SHOWN IN COLUMNS 2, 3, 4 AND 8 REFER TO PUBLIC EDUCATION ONLY.
FR—> A PARTIR DE 1975, LES DONNEES DES COLONNES 2, 3, 4 ET 8 SE REFERENT A L'ENSEIGNEMENT PUBLIC SEULEMENT.
ESP> A PARTIR DE 1975, LOS DATOS DE LAS COLUMNAS 2, 3, 4 Y 8 SE REFIEREN A LA ENSEÑANZA PUBLICA SOLAMENTE.

REUNION:
E—> FOR 1970, THE FIGURES SHOWN IN COLUMNS 2 AND 8 REFER TO PUBLIC EDUCATION ONLY.
FR—> EN 1970, LES DONNEES DES COLONNES 2 ET 8 SE REFERENT A L'ENSEIGNEMENT PUBLIC SEULEMENT.
ESP> EN 1970, LOS DATOS DE LAS COLUMNAS 2 Y 8 SE REFIEREN A LA ENSEÑANZA PUBLICA SOLAMENTE.

SENEGAL:
E—> FOR 1975, THE FIGURES SHOWN IN COLUMNS 2 AND 8 REFER TO PUBLIC EDUCATION ONLY.
FR—> EN 1975, LES DONNEES DES COLONNES 2 ET 8 SE REFERENT A L'ENSEIGNEMENT PUBLIC SEULEMENT.
ESP> EN 1975, LOS DATOS DE LAS COLUMNAS 2 Y 8 SE REFIEREN A LA ENSEÑANZA PUBLICA SOLAMENTE.

SOMALIA:
E—> SEE ANNEX TO TABLE 3.1. FOR 1976 AND 1977 DATA INCLUDE INTERMEDIATE EDUCATION.
FR—> VOIR L'ANNEXE DU TABLEAU 3.1. LES ANNEES 1976 ET 1977 INCLUENT L'ENSEIGNEMENT INTERMEDIAIRE.
ESP> VEASE EL ANEXO DEL CUADRO 3.1. LOS AÑOS 1976 Y 1977 INCLUYEN LA ENSEÑANZA INTERMEDIA.

SOUTH AFRICA:
E—> FOR 1975, DATA INCLUDE ALL EDUCATION AT THE SECOND LEVEL.
FR—> EN 1975, LES DONNEES INCLUENT TOUT L'ENSEIGNEMENT DU SECOND DEGRE.
ESP> EN 1975, LOS DATOS INCLUYEN TODA LA ENSEÑANZA DE SEGUNDO GRADO.

Education at the first level 3.4
Enseignement du premier degré
Enseñanza de primer grado

SUDAN:
   E—> SEE ANNEX TO TABLE 3.1.
   FR-> VOIR L'ANNEXE DU TABLEAU 3.1.
   ESP> VEASE EL ANEXO DEL CUADRO 3.1.

UGANDA:
   E—> DATA REFER TO GOVERNMENT—MAINTAINED AND
AIDED SCHOOLS ONLY.
   FR-> LES DONNEES SE REFERENT AUX ECOLES
PUBLIQUES ET SUBVENTIONNEES SEULEMENT.
   ESP> LOS DATOS SE REFIEREN A LAS ESCUELAS
PUBLICAS Y SUBVENCIONADAS SOLAMENTE.

UNITED REPUBLIC OF TANZANIA:
   E—> FOR 1970 AND 1974, DATA REFER TO TANZANIA
MAINLAND ONLY. FOR 1976, DATA REFER TO GOVERNMENT—
MAINTAINED AND AIDED SCHOOLS ONLY.
   FR-> EN 1970 ET 1974, LES DONNEES SE REFERENT A
LA TANZANIE CONTINENTALE SEULEMENT. EN 1976, LES
DONNEES SE REFERENT AUX ECOLES PUBLIQUES ET
SUBVENTIONNEES SEULEMENT.
   ESP> EN 1970 Y 1974, LOS DATOS SE REFIEREN A
TANZANIA CONTINENTAL SOLAMENTE. EN 1976, LOS
DATOS SE REFIEREN A LAS ESCUELAS PUBLICAS Y
SUBVENCIONADAS SOLAMENTE.

ANTIGUA:
   E—> FOR 1974 AND 1975 THE FIGURES SHOWN IN
COLUMNS 2, 3 AND 4 INCLUDE SECONDARY CLASSES
ATTACHED TO PRIMARY SCHOOLS.
   FR-> EN 1974 ET 1975 LES DONNEES DES COLONNES
2, 3 ET 4 INCLUENT LES CLASSES SECONDAIRES
RATTACHEES AUX ECOLES PRIMAIRES.
   ESP> EN 1974 Y 1975 LOS DATOS DE LAS COLUMNAS
2, 3 Y 4 INCLUYEN LAS CLASES SECUNDARIAS
ADSCRITAS A LAS ESCUELAS PRIMARIAS.

BAHAMAS:
   E—> FOR 1970, THE FIGURES SHOWN IN COLUMNS 3
AND 4 REFER TO PUBLIC EDUCATION ONLY. FOR 1970
AND 1974 THE FIGURE SHOWN IN COLUMN 5 INCLUDES
SPECIAL EDUCATION.
   FR-> EN 1970, LES DONNEES DES COLONNES 3 ET 4 SE
REFERENT A L'ENSEIGNEMENT PUBLIC SEULEMENT. EN
1970 ET 1974, LA COLONNE 5 INCLUT L'EDUCATION
SPECIALE.
   ESP> EN 1970, LOS DATOS DE LAS COLUMNAS 3 Y 4 SE
REFIEREN A LA ENSEÑANZA PUBLICA SOLAMENTE. EN
1970 Y 1974, LA COLUMNA 5 INCLUYE LA EDUCACION
ESPECIAL.

BARBADOS:
   E—> FOR 1970 AND 1974 DATA REFER TO GOVERNMENT—
MAINTAINED AND AIDED SCHOOLS ONLY.
   FR-> POUR 1970 ET 1974 LES DONNEES SE REFERENT
AUX ECOLES PUBLIQUES ET SUBVENTIONNEES SEULEMENT.
   ESP> EN 1970 Y 1974 LOS DATOS SE REFIEREN A LAS
ESCUELAS PUBLICAS Y SUBVENCIONADAS SOLAMENTE.

BELIZE:
   E—> FOR 1975, THE FIGURES SHOWN IN COLUMNS 2,
3, 4, 6 AND 7 AND DATA FOR 1976 REFER TO
GOVERNMENT—MAINTAINED AND AIDED SHOOLS ONLY.
   FR-> EN 1975, LES DONNEES DES COLONNES 2, 3,
4, 6 ET 7 ET TOUS LES CHIFFRES POUR 1976, SE
REFERENT AUX ECOLES PUBLIQUES ET SUBVENTIONNEES
SEULEMENT.
   ESP> EN 1975, LOS DATOS DE LAS COLUMNAS 2, 3,
4, 6 Y 7 Y TODAS LAS CIFRAS DE 1976, SE REFIEREN
A LAS ESCUELAS PUBLICAS Y SUBVENCIONADAS
SOLAMENTE.

CANADA:
   E—> BEGINNING 1974, DATA REFER TO GRADES I—VI;
PREVIOUSLY TO GRADES I—VIII. FROM 1974 TO 1976,
TEACHING STAFF INCLUDES GENERAL EDUCATION AT THE
SECOND LEVEL.

CANADA (CONT.):
   FR-> A PARTIR DE 1974, LES DONNEES SE REFERENT
AUX CLASSES ALLANT DE LA PREMIERE A LA SIXIEME
ANNEE; ANTERIEUREMENT DE LA PREMIERE A LA
HUITIEME ANNEE. DE 1974 A 1976 LE PERSONNEL
ENSEIGNANT INCLUT L'ENSEIGNEMENT GENERAL DU
SECOND DEGRE.
   ESP> A PARTIR DE 1974, LOS DATOS SE REFIEREN
A LAS CLASES I—VI; EN LOS AÑOS PRECEDENTES, A
LAS CLASES I—VIII. DE 1974 A 1976, EL PERSONAL
DOCENTE INCLUYE LA ENSEÑANZA GENERAL DE SEGUNDO
GRADO.

CAYMAN ISLANDS:
   E—> THE FIGURES SHOWN IN COLUMNS 1, 2, 3, 4
AND 8 FOR 1974; 2, 3, 4 AND 8 FOR 1975 REFER TO
PUBLIC EDUCATION ONLY.
   FR-> LES CHIFFRES DES COLONNES 1, 2, 3, 4 ET 8
POUR 1974; 2, 3, 4 ET 8 POUR 1975 SE REFERENT A
L'ENSEIGNEMENT PUBLIC SEULEMENT.
   ESP> LAS CIFRAS DE LAS COLUMNAS 1, 2, 3, 4 Y 8
PARA 1974 Y DE LAS COLUMNAS 2, 3, 4 Y 8 PARA
1975, SE REFIEREN A LA ENSEÑANZA PUBLICA SOLAMENTE.

COSTA RICA:
   E—> THE FIGURES SHOWN IN COLUMNS 3 AND 4 FOR
1976; 2 AND 8 FOR 1977; 5, 6 AND 7 FOR 1978 REFER
TO PUBLIC EDUCATION ONLY.
   FR-> LES CHIFFRES DES COLONNES 3 ET 4 EN 1976;
2 ET 8 EN 1977 ET 5, 6 ET 7 EN 1978 SE REFERENT
A L'ENSEIGNEMENT PUBLIC SEULEMENT.
   ESP> LAS CIFRAS DE LAS COLUMNAS 3 Y 4 EN 1976,
DE LAS COLUMNAS 2 Y 8 EN 1977 Y DE LAS COLUMNAS
5, 6 Y 7 EN 1978 SE REFIEREN A LA ENSEÑANZA
PUBLICA SOLAMENTE.

DOMINICA:
   E—> BEGINNING 1974, THE FIGURES SHOWN IN
COLUMNS 2, 3, 4 AND 8 INCLUDE GENERAL EDUCATION
AT THE SECOND LEVEL.
   FR-> A PARTIR DE 1974, LES DONNEES DES COLONNES
2, 3, 4 ET 8 INCLUENT L'ENSEIGNEMENT GENERAL DU
SECOND DEGRE.
   ESP> A PARTIR DE 1974, LOS DATOS DE LAS COLUMNAS
2, 3, 4 Y 8 INCLUYEN LA ENSEÑANZA GENERAL DE
SEGUNDO GRADO.

DOMINICAN REPUBLIC:
   E—> THE FIGURES SHOWN IN COLUMNS 3 AND 4 FOR
1970; 6 AND 7 FOR 1975 REFER TO PUBLIC EDUCATION
ONLY.
   FR-> LES CHIFFRES DES COLONNES 3 ET 4 EN 1970;
6 ET 7 EN 1975 SE REFERENT A L'ENSEIGNEMENT
PUBLIC SEULEMENT.
   ESP> LAS CIFRAS DE LAS COLUMNAS 3 Y 4 EN 1970
Y DE LAS COLUMNAS 6 Y 7 EN 1975 SE REFIEREN A LA
ENSEÑANZA PUBLICA SOLAMENTE.

EL SALVADOR:
   E—> SEE ANNEX TO TABLE 3.1. DATA FOR 1970,
1975, 1976, 1977 AND THE FIGURE SHOWN IN COLUMN
2 FOR 1974 INCLUDE EVENING SCHOOLS. THE FIGURES
SHOWN IN COLUMNS 2 AND 8 FOR 1974; 2, 3, 4 AND 8
FOR 1975 REFER TO PUBLIC EDUCATION ONLY.
   FR-> VOIR L'ANNEXE DU TABLEAU 3.1. LES DONNEES
EN 1970, 1975, 1976, 1977 ET LE CHIFFRE DE LA
COLONNE 2 EN 1974 COMPRENNENT LES ECOLES DU SOIR.
LES CHIFFRES DES COLONNES 2 ET 8 EN 1974; 2, 3,
4 ET 8 EN 1975 SE REFERENT A L'ENSEIGNEMENT
PUBLIC SEULEMENT.
   ESP> VEASE EL ANEXO DEL CUADRO 3.1. LOS DATOS
RELATIVOS A 1970, 1975, 1976 Y 1977 Y LA CIFRA DE
LA COLUMNA 2 EN 1974 COMPRENDEN LAS ESCUELAS
NOCTURNAS. LAS CIFRAS DE LAS COLUMNAS 2 Y 8 EN
1974 Y DE LAS COLUMNAS 2, 3, 4 Y 8 EN 1975 SE
REFIEREN A LA ENSEÑANZA PUBLICA SOLAMENTE.

3.4 Education at the first level
Enseignement du premier degré
Enseñanza de primer grado

GRENADA:
E—> BEGINNING 1974, FORMS I, II AND III
PREVIOUSLY CLASSIFIED AS EDUCATION AT THE FIRST
LEVEL ARE NOW INCLUDED IN GENERAL EDUCATION AT
THE SECOND LEVEL.
FR-> A PARTIR DE 1974 LES "FORMS I, II ET III"
CLASSEES ANTERIEUREMENT DANS L'ENSEIGNEMENT DU
PREMIER DEGRE ONT ETE INCLUSES DANS L'ENSEIGNEMENT
GENERAL DU SECOND DEGRE.
ESP> A PARTIR DE 1974 LAS "FORMS I, II Y III"
CLASIFICADAS ANTERIORMENTE EN LA ENSEÑANZA DE
PRIMER GRADO, HAN SIDO INCLUIDAS EN LA ENSEÑANZA
GENERAL DE SEGUNDO GRADO.

JAMAICA:
E—> DATA FOR 1970, 1977 AND THE FIGURES SHOWN
IN COLUMNS 3 AND 4 FOR 1976 REFER TO PUBLIC
EDUCATION ONLY.
FR-> LES DONNEES EN 1970, 1977 ET CELLES DES
COLONNES 3 ET 4 EN 1976 SE REFERENT A
L'ENSEIGNEMENT PUBLIC SEULEMENT.
ESP> LOS DATOS CORRESPONDIENTES A 1970 Y 1977
Y LAS CIFRAS DE LAS COLUMNAS 3 Y 4 EN 1976 SE
REFIEREN A LA ENSEÑANZA PUBLICA SOLAMENTE.

NICARAGUA:
E—> FOR 1970 AND 1974 THE FIGURES SHOWN IN
COLUMNS 2, 3 AND 4 INCLUDE EDUCATION PRECEDING
THE FIRST LEVEL.
FR-> EN 1970 ET 1974 LES DONNEES DES COLONNES
2, 3 ET 4 INCLUENT L'ENSEIGNEMENT PRECEDANT LE
PREMIER DEGRE.
ESP> EN 1970 Y 1974 LOS DATOS DE LAS COLUMNAS
2, 3 Y 4 INCLUYEN LA ENSEÑANZA ANTERIOR AL PRIMER
GRADO.

PANAMA:
E—> SEE ANNEX TO TABLE 3.1.
FR-> VOIR L'ANNEXE DU TABLEAU 3.1.
ESP> VEASE EL ANEXO DEL CUADRO 3.1.

FORMER CANAL ZONE:
E—> FOR 1970, THE FIGURE SHOWN IN COLUMN 2
INCLUDES EDUCATION PRECEDING THE FIRST LEVEL,
WHILST THAT IN COLUMN 5 INCLUDES SPECIAL EDUCATION.
FOR 1976 AND 1977 DATA REFER TO PUBLIC EDUCATION
ONLY.
FR-> EN 1970, LE CHIFFRE DE LA COLONNE 2 INCLUT
L'ENSEIGNEMENT PRECEDANT LE PREMIER DEGRE ET CELUI
DE LA COLONNE 5 INCLUT L'EDUCATION SPECIALE. EN
1976 ET 1977 LES DONNEES SE REFERENT A
L'ENSEIGNEMENT PUBLIC SEULEMENT.
ESP> EN 1970, LA CIFRA DE LA COLUMNA 2 INCLUYE
LA ENSEÑANZA ANTERIOR AL PRIMER GRADO Y LA DE LA
COLUMNA 5 LA EDUCACION ESPECIAL. EN 1976 Y 1977
LOS DATOS SE REFIEREN A LA ENSEÑANZA PUBLICA
SOLAMENTE.

PUERTO RICO:
E—> FOR 1970 THE FIGURE SHOWN IN COLUMN 2
INCLUDES EDUCATION PRECEDING THE FIRST LEVEL.
FOR 1974 THE FIGURE SHOWN IN COLUMN 2 INCLUDES
GENERAL EDUCATION AT THE SECOND LEVEL. FOR
1975 AND 1976 THE FIGURES REFER TO PUBLIC
EDUCATION.
FR-> EN 1970 LE CHIFFRE DE LA COLONNE 2 INCLUT
L'ENSEIGNEMENT PRECEDA T LE PREMIER DEGRE. EN
1974 LE CHIFFRE DE LA COLONNE 2 INCLUT
L'ENSEIGNEMENT GENERAL DU SECOND DEGRE. EN 1975
ET 1976 LES DONNEES SE REFERENT A L'ENSEIGNEMENT
PUBLIC SEULEMENT.
ESP> EN 1970 LA CIFRA DE LA COLUMNA 2 INCLUYE
LA ENSEÑANZA ANTERIOR AL PRIMER GRADO. EN 1974
LA CIFRA DE LA COLUMNA 2 COMPRENDE LA ENSEÑANZA
GENERAL DE SEGUNDA GRADO. EN 1975 Y 1976 LOS
DATOS SE REFIEREN A LA ENSEÑANZA PUBLICA SOLAMENTE.

ST. VINCENT AND THE GRENADINES:
E—> FOR 1970 THE FIGURES SHOWN IN COLUMNS 5, 6
AND 7 INCLUDE SECONDARY CLASSES ATTACHED TO
PRIMARY SCHOOLS.
FR-> EN 1970 LES CHIFFRES DES COLONNES 5, 6 ET
7 INCLUENT LES CLASSES SECONDAIRES RATTACHEES AUX
ECOLES PRIMAIRES.
ESP> EN 1970 LAS CIFRAS DE LAS COLUMNAS 5, 6 Y
7 INCLUYEN LAS CLASES SECUNDARIAS ADSCRITAS A LAS
ESCUELAS PRIMARIAS.

TRINIDAD AND TOBAGO:
E—> THE DATA REFER TO GOVERNMENT-MAINTAINED AND
AIDED SCHOOLS ONLY. THE FIGURES SHOWN IN COLUMNS
1, 2, 3 AND 4 INCLUDE INTERMEDIATE DEPARTMENTS OF
SECONDARY SCHOOLS.
FR-> LES DONNEES SE REFERENT AUX ECOLES
PUBLIQUES ET SUBVENTIONNEES SEULEMENT. LES
DONNEES DES COLONNES 1, 2, 3 ET 4 INCLUENT LES
SECTIONS INTERMEDIAIRES DES ECOLES SECONDAIRES.
ESP> LOS DATOS SE REFIEREN A LAS ESCUELAS
PUBLICAS Y SUBVENCIONADAS SOLAMENTE. LOS DATOS
DE LAS COLUMNAS 1, 2, 3 Y 4 INCLUYEN LAS SECCIONES
INTERMEDIAS DE LAS ESCUELAS SECUNDARIAS.

TURKS AND CAICOS ISLANDS:
E—> FOR 1977, DATA REFER TO PUBLIC EDUCATION
ONLY.
FR-> EN 1977, LES DONNEES SE REFERENT A
L'ENSEIGNEMENT PUBLIC SEULEMENT.
ESP> EN 1977, LOS DATOS SE REFIEREN A LA
ENSEÑANZA PUBLICA SOLAMENTE.

UNITED STATES OF AMERICA:
E—> FOR 1970 DATA INCLUDE EDUCATION PRECEDING
THE FIRST LEVEL. BEGINNING 1975, THE FIGURE SHOWN
IN COLUMN 5 INCLUDES SPECIAL EDUCATION.
FR-> EN 1970, LES DONNEES INCLUENT L'ENSEIGNEMENT
PRECEDANT LE PREMIER DEGRE. A PARTIR DE 1975, LE
CHIFFRE DE LA COLONNE 5 INCLUT L'EDUCATION SPECIALE.
ESP> EN 1970, LOS DATOS INCLUYEN LA ENSEÑANZA
ANTERIOR AL PRIMER GRADO. A PARTIR DE 1975, LA
CIFRA DE LA COLUMNA 5 INCLUYE LA EDUCACION ESPECIAL.

U.S. VIRGIN ISLANDS:
E—> FOR 1970, DATA INCLUDE EDUCATION PRECEDING
THE FIRST LEVEL. FOR 1974, THE FIGURE SHOWN IN
COLUMN 2 INCLUDES GENERAL EDUCATION AT THE SECOND
LEVEL. FOR 1976, THE FIGURE SHOWN IN COLUMN 5
INCLUDES SPECIAL EDUCATION. FOR 1977 DATA REFER
TO PUBLIC EDUCATION ONLY.
FR-> EN 1970, LES DONNEES INCLUENT L'ENSEIGNEMENT
PRECEDANT LE PREMIER DEGRE. EN 1974, LE CHIFFRE
DE LA COLONNE 2 COMPREND L'ENSEIGNEMENT GENERAL DU
SECOND DEGRE. EN 1976, LE CHIFFRE DE LA COLONNE 5
INCLUT L'EDUCATION SPECIALE. EN 1977, LES DONNEES
SE REFERENT A L'ENSEIGNEMENT PUBLIC SEULEMENT.
ESP> EN 1970, LOS DATOS INCLUYEN LA ENSEÑANZA
ANTERIOR AL PRIMER GRADO. EN 1974, LA CIFRA DE LA
COLUMNA 2 COMPRENDE LA ENSEÑANZA GENERAL DE
SEGUNDO GRADO. EN 1976, LA CIFRA DE LA COLUMNA 5
INCLUYE LA EDUCACION ESPECIAL Y EN 1977, LOS DATOS
SE REFIEREN A LA ENSEÑANZA PUBLICA SOLAMENTE.

BRAZIL:
E—> SEE ANNEX TO TABLE 3.1.
FR-> VOIR L'ANNEXE DU TABLEAU 3.1.
ESP> VEASE EL ANEXO DEL CUADRO 3.1.

CHILE:
E—> FOR 1970, THE FIGURES SHOWN IN COLUMNS 2,
3, 4 AND 8 REFER TO PUBLIC EDUCATION ONLY.
FR-> EN 1970, LES DONNEES DES COLONNES 2, 3, 4
ET 8 SE REFERENT A L'ENSEIGNEMENT PUBLIC
SEULEMENT.
ESP> EN 1970, LOS DATOS DE LAS COLUMNAS 2, 3,
4 Y 8 SE REFIEREN A LA ENSEÑANZA PUBLICA
SOLAMENTE.

Education at the first level 3.4
Enseignement du premier degré
Enseñanza de primer grado

ECUADOR:
E—> DATA FOR 1970 AND 1977 (EXCEPT FOR COLUMN 5 FOR 1977) INCLUDE EVENING SCHOOLS.
FR—> TOUTES LES DONNEES EN 1970 ET CELLES DE 1977 (A L'EXCEPTION DE LA COLONNE 5), INCLUENT LES ECOLES DU SOIR.
ESP> TODOS LOS DATOS EN 1970 Y LOS DE 1977 (EXCEPTO LA COLUMNA 5), INCLUYEN LAS ESCUELAS NOCTURNAS.

FALKLAND ISLANDS (MALVINAS):
E—> FOR 1970, DATA INCLUDE GENERAL EDUCATION AT THE SECOND LEVEL.
FR—> EN 1970, LES DONNEES INCLUENT L'ENSEIGNEMENT GENERAL DU SECOND DEGRE.
ESP> EN 1970, LOS DATOS INCLUYEN LA ENSEÑANZA GENERAL DE SEGUNDO GRADO.

FRENCH GUIANA:
E—> FOR 1970, THE FIGURE SHOWN IN COLUMN 2 INCLUDES EDUCATION PRECEDING THE FIRST LEVEL.
FR—> EN 1970, LE CHIFFRE DE LA COLONNE 2 INCLUT L'ENSEIGNEMENT PRECEDANT LE PREMIER DEGRE.
ESP> EN 1970, LA CIFRA DE LA COLUMNA 2 INCLUYE LA ENSEÑANZA ANTERIOR AL PRIMER GRADO.

GUYANA:
E—> FOR 1970, DATA REFER TO PUBLIC EDUCATION ONLY.
FR—> EN 1970, LES DONNEES SE REFERENT A L'ENSEIGNEMENT PUBLIC SEULEMENT.
ESP> EN 1970, LOS DATOS SE REFIEREN A LA ENSEÑANZA PUBLICA SOLAMENTE.

PARAGUAY:
E—> DATA INCLUDE EVENING SCHOOLS. FOR 1974, THE FIGURE SHOWN IN COLUMN 2 INCLUDES EDUCATION PRECEDING THE FIRST LEVEL.
FR—> LES DONNEES INCLUENT LES ECOLES DU SOIR. EN 1974, LE CHIFFRE DE LA COLONNE 2 COMPREND L'ENSEIGNEMENT PRECEDANT LE PREMIER DEGRE.
ESP> LOS DATOS INCLUYEN LAS ESCUELAS NOCTURNAS. EN 1974, LA CIFRA DE LA COLUMNA 2 COMPRENDE LA ENSEÑANZA ANTERIOR AL PRIMER GRADO.

URUGUAY:
E—> FOR 1976, THE FIGURE SHOWN IN COLUMN 5 INCLUDES EDUCATION PRECEDING THE FIRST LEVEL. FOR 1977, DATA REFER TO PUBLIC EDUCATION ONLY.
FR—> EN 1976, LE CHIFFRE DE LA COLONNE 5 INCLUT L'ENSEIGNEMENT PRECEDANT LE PREMIER DEGRE. EN 1977, LES DONNEES NE SE REFERENT QU'A L'ENSEIGNEMENT PUBLIC.
ESP> EN 1976, LA CIFRA DE LA COLUMNA 5 INCLUYE LA ENSEÑANZA ANTERIOR AL PRIMER GRADO. EN 1977, LOS DATOS SOLO SE REFIEREN A LA ENSEÑANZA PUBLICA.

VENEZUELA:
E—> FOR 1978, THE FIGURE SHOWN IN COLUMN 2 INCLUDES EDUCATION PRECEDING THE FIRST LEVEL.
FR—> EN 1978, LE CHIFFRE DE LA COLONNE 2 INCLUT L'ENSEIGNEMENT PRECEDANT LE PREMIER DEGRE.
ESP> EN 1978, LA CIFRA DE LA COLUMNA 2 INCLUYE LA ENSEÑANZA ANTERIOR AL PRIMER GRADO.

AFGHANISTAN:
E—> SEE ANNEX TO TABLE 3.1. FOR 1975 AND 1976, THE FIGURES SHOWN IN COLUMNS 2, 3 AND 4 DO NOT INCLUDE PRIMARY CLASSES ATTACHED TO MIDDLE AND SECONDARY SCHOOLS.
FR—> VOIR L'ANNEXE DU TABLEAU 3.1. EN 1975 ET 1976, LES COLONNES 2, 3 ET 4 NE COMPRENNENT PAS LES CLASSES PRIMAIRES RATTACHEES AUX ECOLES MOYENNES ET SECONDAIRES.
ESP> VEASE EL ANEXO DEL CUADRO 3.1. EN 1975 Y 1976, LAS COLUMNAS 2, 3 Y 4 NO INCLUYEN LAS CLASES PRIMARIAS ADSCRITAS A LAS ESCUELAS MEDIAS Y SECUNDARIAS.

BAHRAIN:
E—> BEGINNING 1974, THE FIGURES SHOWN IN COLUMNS 2, 3 AND 4 INCLUDE PART OF INTERMEDIATE EDUCATION. THE FIGURES SHOWN IN COLUMNS 5, 6 AND 7 FOR 1975; 2, 3 AND 4 FOR 1976, 1977 AND 1978 REFER TO PUBLIC EDUCATION ONLY.
FR—> A PARTIR DE 1974, LES CHIFFRES DES COLONNES 2, 3 ET 4 COMPRENNENT UNE PARTIE DE L'ENSEIGNEMENT INTERMEDIAIRE. LES DONNEES DES COLONNES 5, 6 ET 7 EN 1975; 2, 3 ET 4 EN 1976, 1977 ET 1978 SE REFERENT A L'ENSEIGNEMENT PUBLIC SEULEMENT.
ESP> A PARTIR DE 1974, LAS CIFRAS DE LAS COLUMNAS 2, 3 Y 4 COMPRENDEN UNA PARTE DE LA ENSEÑANZA INTERMEDIA. LOS DATOS DE LAS COLUMNAS 5, 6 Y 7 EN 1975 Y 2, 3 Y 4 EN 1976, 1977 Y 1978 SE REFIEREN A LA ENSEÑANZA PUBLICA SOLAMENTE.

BHUTAN:
E—> DATA ON TEACHING STAFF INCLUDE GENERAL EDUCATION AT THE SECOND LEVEL.
FR—> LE PERSONNEL ENSEIGNANT COMPREND L'ENSEIGNEMENT GENERAL DU SECOND DEGRE.
ESP> EL PERSONAL DOCENTE INCLUYE EL DE LA ENSEÑANZA GENERAL DE SEGUNDO GRADO.

CYPRUS:
E—> NOT INCLUDING TURKISH SCHOOLS.
FR—> NON COMPRIS LES ECOLES TURQUES.
ESP> EXCLUIDAS LAS ESCUELAS TURCAS.

DEMOCRATIC KAMPUCHEA:
E—> FOR 1970, THE FIGURES SHOWN IN COLUMNS 3, 4, 6 AND 7 REFER TO PUBLIC EDUCATION ONLY.
FR—> EN 1970, LES DONNEES DES COLONNES 3, 4, 6 ET 7 SE REFERENT A L'ENSEIGNEMENT PUBLIC SEULEMENT.
ESP> EN 1970, LOS DATOS DE LAS COLUMNAS 3, 4, 6 Y 7 SE REFIEREN A LA ENSEÑANZA PUBLICA SOLAMENTE.

INDIA:
E—> FOR 1977, THE FIGURES SHOWN IN COLUMNS 2, 3 AND 4 DO NOT INCLUDE TEACHERS IN PRIMARY CLASSES ATTACHED TO SECONDARY SCHOOLS.
FR—> EN 1977, LES DONNEES DES COLONNES 2, 3 ET 4 NE COMPRENNENT PAS LE PERSONNEL ENSEIGNANT DES CLASSES PRIMAIRES RATTACHEES AUX ECOLES SECONDAIRES.
ESP> EN 1977, LOS DATOS DE LAS COLUMNAS 2, 3 Y 4 NO INCLUYEN EL PERSONAL DOCENTE DE LAS CLASES PRIMARIAS ADSCRITAS A LAS ESCUELAS SECUNDARIAS.

INDONESIA:
E—> DATA FOR 1977 AND THE FIGURES SHOWN IN COLUMNS 2, 3, 4 AND 8 FOR 1978 DO NOT INCLUDE RELIGIOUS SCHOOLS.
FR—> LES DONNEES EN 1977 ET CELLES DES COLONNES 2, 3, 4 ET 8 EN 1978 N'INCLUENT PAS LES ECOLES RELIGIEUSES.
ESP> TODOS LOS DATOS EN 1977 Y LOS DE LAS COLUMNAS 2, 3, 4 Y 8 EN 1978 EXCLUYEN LAS ESCUELAS RELIGIOSAS.

IRAN:
E—> SEE ANNEX TO TABLE 3.1.
FR—> VOIR L'ANNEXE DU TABLEAU 3.1.
ESP> VEASE EL ANEXO DEL CUADRO 3.1.

JAPAN:
E—> THE FIGURES SHOWN IN COLUMNS 3, 4, 6 AND 7 FOR 1970, 1975, 1976 AND 1977; 2, 3, 4, 6 AND 7 FOR 1974 AND ALL DATA FOR 1978 INCLUDE SPECIAL EDUCATION.
FR—> LES CHIFFRES DES COLONNES 3, 4, 6 ET 7 POUR 1970, 1975, 1976 ET 1977; 2, 3, 4, 6 ET 7 EN 1974 ET TOUTES LES DONNEES DE L'ANNEE 1978, INCLUENT L'EDUCATION SPECIALE.

3.4 Education at the first level
Enseignement du premier degré
Enseñanza de primer grado

JAPAN (CONT.):
   ESP> LAS CIFRAS DE LAS COLUMNAS 3, 4, 6 Y 7 PARA
1970, 1975, 1976 Y 1977; 2, 3, 4, 6 Y 7 EN 1974 Y
TODOS LOS DATOS DEL AÑO 1978, INCLUYEN LA EDUCACION
ESPECIAL.

JORDAN:
   E—> DATA REFER TO THE EAST BANK ONLY. INCLUDING
UNRWA SCHOOLS WITH 2,187 (F. 1,083) TEACHERS AND
92,727 (F. 44,582) PUPILS IN 1978.
   FR—> LES DONNEES SE REFERENT A LA RIVE ORIENTALE
SEULEMENT. Y COMPRIS LES ECOLES DE L'UNRWA QUI
COMPTAIENT 2 187 MAITRES (DONT 1 083 DU SEXE
FEMININ) ET 92 727 ELEVES (DONT 44 582 FILLES) EN
1978.
   ESP> LOS DATOS SE REFIEREN A LA ORILLA ORIENTAL
SOLAMENTE. INCLUIDAS LAS ESCUELAS DEL O.O.P.S.P.
(ORGANIZACION DE OBRAS PUBLICAS Y SOCORRO PARA LOS
REFUGIADOS DE PALESTINA) QUE TENIAN 2 187 MAESTROS
(F 1 083) Y 92 727 ALUMNOS (F 44 582) EN 1978.

KUWAIT:
   E—> FOR 1978 DATA REFER TO PUBLIC EDUCATION ONLY.
   FR—> EN 1978, LES DONNEES SE REFERENT A
L'ENSEIGNEMENT PUBLIC SEULEMENT.
   ESP> EN 1978, LOS DATOS SE REFIEREN A LA ENSEÑANZA
PUBLICA SOLAMENTE.

LAO PEOPLE'S DEMOCRATIC REPUBLIC:
   E—> SEE ANNEX TO TABLE 3.1. FOR 1974 DATA REFER
TO PUBLIC EDUCATION ONLY.
   FR—> VOIR L'ANNEXE DU TABLEAU 3.1. EN 1974 LES
DONNEES SE REFERENT A L'ENSEIGNEMENT PUBLIC
SEULEMENT.
   ESP> VEASE EL ANEXO DEL CUADRO 3.1. EN 1974,
LOS DATOS SE REFIEREN A LA ENSEÑANZA PUBLICA
SOLAMENTE.

LEBANON:
   E—> FOR 1970 THE FIGURES SHOWN IN COLUMNS 2, 3
AND 4 INCLUDE GENERAL EDUCATION AT THE SECOND
LEVEL. INCLUDING UNRWA SCHOOLS WITH 721 TEACHERS
(F. ...) AND 26,686 (F. 12,513) PUPILS IN 1970.
   FR—> EN 1970 LES CHIFFRES DES COLONNES 2, 3, ET
4 INCLUENT L'ENSEIGNEMENT GENERAL DU SECOND DEGRE.
Y COMPRIS LES ECOLES DE L'UNRWA QUI COMPTAIENT
721 MAITRES (DE SEXE FEMININ ...) ET 26 686
ELEVES (DONT 12 513 FILLES) EN 1970.
   ESP> EN 1970 LAS CIFRAS DE LAS COLUMNAS 2, 3 Y
4 INCLUYEN LA ENSEÑANZA GENERAL DE SEGUNDO GRADO.
INCLUIDAS LAS ESCUELAS DEL O.O.P.S.R.P. QUE TENIAN
721 MAESTROS (F ...) Y 26 686 ALUMNOS (F 12 513)
EN 1970.

MACAU:
   E—> FROM 1970, MISSION SCHOOLS ARE NOT INCLUDED.
   FR—> A PARTIR DE 1970, NON COMPRIS LES ECOLES DE
MISSION.
   ESP> A PARTIR DE 1970, EXCLUIDAS LAS ESCUELAS DE
LAS MISIONES.

MALAYSIA
PENINSULAR MALAYSIA:
   E—> FOR 1977 AND 1978 DATA REFER TO GOVERNMENT-
MAINTAINED AND AIDED SCHOOLS ONLY.
   FR—> EN 1977 ET 1978 LES DONNEES SE REFERENT AUX
ECOLES PUBLIQUES ET SUBVENTIONNEES SEULEMENT.
   ESP> EN 1977 Y 1978 LOS DATOS SE REFIEREN A LAS
ESCUELAS PUBLICAS Y SUBVENCIONADAS SOLAMENTE.

MALDIVES:
   E—> THE FIGURES SHOWN IN COLUMNS 2, 3, 4 AND 8
FOR 1977; 5, 6 AND 7 FOR 1978 REFER TO PUBLIC
EDUCATION ONLY.
   FR—> LES CHIFFRES DES COLONNES 2, 3, 4, ET 8
POUR 1977; 5, 6 ET 7 POUR 1978 SE REFERENT A
L'ENSEIGNEMENT PUBLIC SEULEMENT.

MALDIVES (CONT.):
   ESP> LAS CIFRAS DE LAS COLUMNAS 2, 3, 4, Y 8
PARA 1977 Y DE LAS COLUMNAS 5, 6 Y 7 PARA 1978
SE REFIEREN A LA ENSEÑANZA PUBLICA SOLAMENTE.

MONGOLIA:
   E—> SEE ANNEX TO TABLE 3.1.
   FR—> VOIR L'ANNEXE DU TABLEAU 3.1.
   ESP> VEASE EL ANEXO DEL CUADRO 3.1.

NEPAL:
   E—> SEE ANNEX TO TABLE 3.1.
   FR—> VOIR L'ANNEXE DU TABLEAU 3.1.
   ESP> VEASE EL ANEXO DEL CUADRO 3.1.

OMAN:
   E—> FOR 1977 AND 1978 THE FIGURES SHOWN IN
COLUMNS 2, 3 AND 4 INCLUDE EDUCATION PRECEDING
THE FIRST LEVEL.
   FR—> EN 1977 ET 1978 LES DONNEES DES COLONNES
2, 3 ET 4 INCLUENT L'ENSEIGNEMENT PRECEDANT LE
PREMIER DEGRE.
   ESP> EN 1977 Y 1978 LOS DATOS DE LAS COLUMNAS
2, 3 Y 4 INCLUYEN LA ENSEÑANZA ANTERIOR AL PRIMER
GRADO.

PHILIPPINES:
   E—> FOR 1975 THE FIGURES SHOWN IN COLUMNS 6
AND 7 REFER TO PUBLIC EDUCATION ONLY.
   FR—> EN 1975 LES DONNEES DES COLONNES 6 ET 7
SE REFERENT A L'ENSEIGNEMENT PUBLIC SEULEMENT.
   ESP> EN 1975 LOS DATOS DE LAS COLUMNAS 6 Y 7
SE REFIEREN A LA ENSEÑANZA PUBLICA SOLAMENTE.

SAUDI ARABIA:
   E—> FOR 1976 AND 1977 THE FIGURES SHOWN IN
COLUMNS 5, 6 AND 7 INCLUDE EVENING SCHOOLS.
   FR—> EN 1976 ET 1977 LES DONNEES DES COLONNES
5, 6 ET 7 INCLUENT LES ECOLES DU SOIR.
   ESP> EN 1976 Y 1977 LOS DATOS DE LAS COLUMNAS
5, 6 Y 7 INCLUYEN LAS ESCUELAS NOCTURNAS.

SRI LANKA:
   E—> SEE ANNEX TO TABLE 3.1. FOR 1974 AND 1975,
TEACHING STAFF INCLUDES GENERAL EDUCATION AT THE
SECOND LEVEL. DATA ON PUPILS FOR 1974 AND 1975,
AS WELL AS ALL DATA BEGINNING 1976 REFER TO PUBLIC
EDUCATION ONLY.
   FR—> VOIR L'ANNEXE DU TABLEAU 3.1. EN 1974 ET
1975, LE PERSONNEL ENSEIGNANT INCLUT L'ENSEIGNEMENT
GENERAL DU SECOND DEGRE. EN 1974 ET 1975, LES
ELEVES, ET A PARTIR DE 1976 TOUTES LES DONNEES,
SE REFERENT A L'ENSEIGNEMENT PUBLIC SEULEMENT.
   ESP> VEASE EL ANEXO DEL CUADRO 3.1. EN 1974 Y
1975, EL PERSONAL DOCENTE INCLUYE LA ENSEÑANZA
GENERAL DE SEGUNDO GRADO. EN 1974 Y 1975, LOS
ALUMNOS, Y A PARTIR DE 1976 TODOS LOS DATOS, SE
REFIEREN A LA ENSEÑANZA PUBLICA SOLAMENTE.

SYRIAN ARAB REPUBLIC:
   E—> INCLUDING UNRWA SCHOOLS WITH 769 (F. 394)
TEACHERS AND 28,143 (F. 13,063) PUPILS IN 1975.
   FR—> Y COMPRIS LES ECOLES DE L'UNRWA QUI
COMPTAIENT 769 MAITRES (DONT 394 DE SEXE FEMININ)
ET 28 143 ELEVES (DONT 13 063 FILLES) EN 1975.
   ESP> INCLUIDAS LAS ESCUELAS DEL O.O.P.S.R.P.
QUE TENIAN 769 MAESTROS (F 394) Y 28 143 ALUMNOS
(F 13 036) EN 1975.

THAILAND:
   E—> FOR 1976 AND 1977, THE FIGURES SHOWN IN
COLUMNS 2, 3 AND 4 REFER TO PUBLIC EDUCATION ONLY.
   FR—> EN 1976 ET 1977, LES DONNEES DES COLONNES
2, 3 ET 4 SE REFERENT A L'ENSEIGNEMENT PUBLIC
SEULEMENT.
   ESP> EN 1976 Y 1977 LOS DATOS DE LAS COLUMNAS
2, 3 Y 4 SE REFIEREN A LA ENSEÑANZA PUBLICA
SOLAMENTE.

Education at the first level 3.4
Enseignement du premier degré
Enseñanza de primer grado

UNITED ARAB EMIRATES:
   E—> THE FIGURES FOR 1970, 1974 AND 1975 AS WELL
AS DATA IN COLUMNS 2, 3, 4 AND 8 FOR 1976 AND 1977;
COLUMNS 1, 2, 3, 4 AND 8 FOR 1978 REFER TO PUBLIC
EDUCATION ONLY.
   FR-> LES CHIFFRES DES ANNEES 1970, 1974 ET 1975;
DES COLONNES 2, 3, 4 ET 8 EN 1976 ET 1977; DES
COLONNES 1, 2, 3, 4 ET 8 EN 1978 SE REFERENT A
L'ENSEIGNEMENT PUBLIC SEULEMENT.
   ESP> LAS CIFRAS DE LOS AÑOS 1970, 1974 Y 1975;
DE LAS COLUMNAS 2, 3, 4 EN 1976 Y 1977 Y DE
LAS COLUMNAS 1, 2, 3, 4 Y 8 EN 1978, SE REFIEREN
A LA ENSEÑANZA PUBLICA SOLAMENTE.

YEMEN:
   E—> DATA FOR 1974 AS WELL AS THE FIGURES SHOWN
IN COLUMNS 2, 3, 4 AND 8 FOR 1975 REFER TO PUBLIC
EDUCATION ONLY.
   FR-> LES DONNEES DE 1974 ET CELLES DES COLONNES
2, 3, 4 ET 8 EN 1975 SE REFERENT A L'ENSEIGNEMENT
PUBLIC SEULEMENT.
   ESP> LOS DATOS DE 1974 Y LOS DE LAS COLUMNAS 2,
3, 4 Y 8 EN 1975 SE REFIEREN A LA ENSEÑANZA
PUBLICA SOLAMENTE.

YEMEN DEMOCRATIC:
   E—> THE FIGURES SHOWN IN COLUMNS 2, 3 AND 4 FOR
1976 AND 1977 INCLUDE DATA FOR THE FIRST CYCLE OF
GENERAL EDUCATION AT THE SECOND LEVEL.
   FR-> LES CHIFFRES DES COLONNES 2, 3 ET 4 EN 1976
ET 1977 COMPRENNENT LES DONNEES RELATIVES AU
PREMIER CYCLE DE L'ENSEIGNEMENT GENERAL DU SECOND
DEGRE.
   ESP> LAS CIFRAS DE LAS COLUMNAS 2, 3 Y 4 EN 1976
Y 1977 INCLUYEN LOS DATOS RELATIVOS AL PRIMER CICLO
DE LA ENSEÑANZA GENERAL DE SEGUNDO GRADO.

ALBANIA:
   E—> INCLUDING EVENING AND CORRESPONDENCE
COURSES.
   FR-> Y COMPRIS LES COURS DU SOIR ET PAR
CORRESPONDANCE.
   ESP> INCLUIDOS LOS CURSOS NOCTURNOS Y POR
CORRESPONDENCIA.

ANDORRA:
   E—> DATA FOR 1970 AND 1975 AND THE FIGURES SHOWN
IN COLUMNS 2, 3 AND 4 FOR 1974 INCLUDE EDUCATION
PRECEDING THE FIRST LEVEL.
   FR-> LES DONNEES EN 1970 ET 1975 ET CELLES DES
COLONNES 2, 3 ET 4 EN 1974 INCLUENT L'ENSEIGNEMENT
PRECEDANT LE PREMIER DEGRE.
   ESP> TODOS LOS DATOS EN 1970 Y 1975 Y LOS DE LAS
COLUMNAS 2, 3 Y 4 EN 1974 INCLUYEN LA ENSEÑANZA
ANTERIOR AL PRIMER GRADO.

AUSTRIA:
   E—> FOR 1970, 1974 AND 1975 DATA ON TEACHING
STAFF INCLUDE GRADES V-VIII OF THE "VOLKSSCHULEN"
CLASSIFIED UNDER EDUCATION AT THE SECOND LEVEL.
   FR-> EN 1970, 1974 ET 1975 LES DONNEES RELATIVES
AU PERSONNEL ENSEIGNANT COMPRENNENT LES CLASSES
ALLANT DE LA CINQUIEME A LA HUITIEME ANNEE DES
"VOLKSSCHULEN" QUI FONT PARTIE DE L'ENSEIGNEMENT
DU SECOND DEGRE.
   ESP> EN 1970, 1974 Y 1975 LOS DATOS RELATIVOS AL
PERSONAL DOCENTE COMPRENDEN LAS CLASES QUE VAN DEL
QUINTO AL OCTAVO AÑO DE LAS "VOLKSSCHULEN" QUE
ACTUALMENTE SE CLASIFICAN EN LA ENSEÑANZA DE
SEGUNDO GRADO.

BELGIUM:
   E—> WITH THE EXCEPTION OF 1977, DATA ON PUPILS
INCLUDE SPECIAL EDUCATION.
   FR-> EXCEPTE POUR L'ANNEE 1977, LES DONNEES SE
REFERANT AUX ELEVES INCLUENT L'EDUCATION SPECIALE.
   ESP> EXCEPTO PARA 1977, LOS DATOS RELATIVOS A
LOS ALUMNOS INCLUYEN LA EDUCACION ESPECIAL.

BULGARIA:
   E—> FOR 1978, THE FIGURES SHOWN IN COLUMNS 5,
6 AND 7 INCLUDE EVENING SCHOOLS.
   FR-> EN 1978, LES DONNEES DES COLONNES 5, 6 ET
7 INCLUENT LES ECOLES DU SOIR.
   ESP> EN 1978, LOS DATOS DE LAS COLUMNAS 5, 6 Y 7
INCLUYEN LAS ESCUELAS NOCTURNAS.

DENMARK:
   E—> SERIES REVISED. DATA ON TEACHING STAFF
INCLUDE GENERAL EDUCATION AT THE SECOND LEVEL.
   FR-> DONNEES REVISEES. LES DONNEES RELATIVES
AU PERSONNEL ENSEIGNANT INCLUENT L'ENSEIGNEMENT
GENERAL DU SECOND DEGRE.
   ESP> DATOS REVISADOS. LOS DATOS RELATIVOS AL
PERSONAL DOCENTE INCLUYEN LA ENSEÑANZA GENERAL
DE SEGUNDO GRADO.

FINLAND:
   E—> BEGINNING 1975, THE FIGURES INCLUDE
SPECIAL EDUCATION. FOR 1976, THE FIGURE SHOWN IN
COLUMN 2 DOES NOT INCLUDE TEACHERS IN PRIMARY
CLASSES ATTACHED TO SECONDARY SCHOOLS.
   FR-> A PARTIR DE 1975, LES DONNEES INCLUENT
L'EDUCATION SPECIALE. EN 1976, LE CHIFFRE DE LA
COLONNE 2 NE COMPREND PAS LE PERSONNEL ENSEIGNANT
DES ECOLES PRIMAIRES RATTACHEES AUX ECOLES
SECONDAIRES.
   ESP> A PARTIR DE 1975, LOS DATOS INCLUYEN LA
EDUCACION ESPECIAL. EN 1976, LA CIFRA DE LA
COLUMNA 2 NO INCLUYE EL PERSONAL DOCENTE DE LAS
ESCUELAS PRIMARIAS ADSCRITAS A LAS ESCUELAS
SECUNDARIAS.

FRANCE:
   E—> THE FIGURES SHOWN IN COLUMNS 2, 3, 4 AND 8
FOR 1970, 1974, 1976; 3, 4 AND 8 FOR 1978 REFER TO
PUBLIC EDUCATION ONLY.
   FR-> LES CHIFFRES DES COLONNES 2, 3, 4 ET 8 EN
1970, 1974, 1976; 3, 4 ET 8 EN 1978 SE REFERENT A
L'ENSEIGNEMENT PUBLIC SEULEMENT.
   ESP> LAS CIFRAS DE LAS COLUMNAS 2, 3, 4 Y 8 EN
1970, 1974 Y 1976 Y DE LAS COLUMNAS 3, 4 Y 8 EN
1978 SE REFIEREN A LA ENSEÑANZA PUBLICA SOLAMENTE.

GERMAN DEMOCRATIC REPUBLIC:
   E—> DATA ON TEACHING STAFF INCLUDE GENERAL
EDUCATION AT THE SECOND LEVEL AND SPECIAL EDUCATION.
   FR-> LES DONNEES RELATIVES AU PERSONNEL ENSEIGNANT
INCLUENT L'ENSEIGNEMENT GENERAL DU SECOND DEGRE ET
L'EDUCATION SPECIALE.
   ESP> LOS DATOS RELATIVOS AL PERSONAL DOCENTE
INCLUYEN LA ENSEÑANZA GENERAL DE SEGUNDO GRADO Y
LA EDUCACION ESPECIAL.

GREECE:
   E—> FOR 1976 DATA INCLUDE EVENING SCHOOLS.
   FR-> EN 1976 LES DONNEES INCLUENT LES ECOLES DU
SOIR.
   ESP> EN 1976 LOS DATOS INCLUYEN LAS ESCUELAS
NOCTURNAS.

HUNGARY:
   E—> THE FIGURES SHOWN IN COLUMNS 3 AND 4 FOR
1976 AND 1977; 2, 3 AND 4 FOR 1978 INCLUDE
SPECIAL EDUCATION.
   FR-> LES CHIFFRES DES COLONNES 3 ET 4 EN 1976
ET 1977; 2, 3 ET 4 EN 1978 INCLUENT L'EDUCATION
SPECIALE.
   ESP> LAS CIFRAS DE LAS COLUMNAS 3 Y 4 EN 1976
Y 1977 Y DE LAS COLUMNAS 2, 3 Y 4 EN 1978,
INCLUYEN LA EDUCACION ESPECIAL.

ICELAND:
   E—> FOR 1974, 1975 AND 1976 TEACHING STAFF
INCLUDES EDUCATION PRECEDING THE FIRST LEVEL.

3.4　**Education at the first level**
Enseignement du premier degré
Enseñanza de primer grado

ICELAND (CONT.):
　FR—> EN 1974, 1975 ET 1976 LE PERSONNEL
ENSEIGNANT INCLUT L'ENSEIGNEMENT PRECEDANT LE
PREMIER DEGRE.
　ESP> EN 1974, 1975 Y 1976 EL PERSONAL DOCENTE
INCLUYE LA ENSEÑANZA ANTERIOR AL PRIMER GRADO.

IRELAND:
　E—> FOR 1970 DATA INCLUDE EDUCATION PRECEDING
THE FIRST LEVEL.
　FR—> EN 1970 LES DONNEES INCLUENT L'ENSEIGNEMENT
PRECEDANT LE PREMIER DEGRE.
　ESP> EN 1970 LOS DATOS INCLUYEN LA ENSEÑANZA
ANTERIOR AL PRIMER GRADO.

LUXEMBOURG:
　E—> BEGINNING 1974, DATA PREVIOUSLY CLASSIFIED
AS EDUCATION AT THE FIRST LEVEL ARE NOW INCLUDED
IN THE FIRST CYCLE OF GENERAL EDUCATION AT THE
SECOND LEVEL.
　FR—> A PARTIR DE 1974, LES DONNEES ANTERIEUREMENT
CLASSEES DANS L'ENSEIGNEMENT DU PREMIER DEGRE ONT
ETE INCLUSES DANS LE PREMIER CYCLE DE
L'ENSEIGNEMENT GENERAL DU SECOND DEGRE.
　ESP> A PARTIR DE 1974, CIERTOS DATOS
ANTERIORMENTE CLASIFICADOS EN LA ENSEÑANZA DE
PRIMER GRADO HAN SIDO INCLUIDOS EN EL PRIMER
CICLO DE LA ENSEÑANZA GENERAL DE SEGUNDO GRADO.

MALTA:
　E—> SEE ANNEX TO TABLE 3.1. FOR 1977 TEACHING
STAFF INCLUDES EDUCATION PRECEDING THE FIRST LEVEL.
　FR—> VOIR L'ANNEXE DU TABLEAU 3.1. EN 1977 LE
PERSONNEL ENSEIGNANT INCLUT L'ENSEIGNEMENT
PRECEDANT LE PREMIER DEGRE.
　ESP> VEASE EL ANEXO DEL CUADRO 3.1. EN 1977
EL PERSONAL DOCENTE INCLUYE LA ENSEÑANZA ANTERIOR
AL PRIMER GRADO.

MONACO:
　E—> THE FIGURES SHOWN IN COLUMNS 2, 3, 4 AND 8
FOR 1970; 5 FOR 1976; 6 AND 7 FOR 1977 REFER TO
PUBLIC EDUCATION ONLY.
　FR—> LES CHIFFRES DES COLONNES 2, 3, 4 ET 8
POUR 1970; 5 POUR 1976; 6 ET 7 POUR 1977 SE
REFERENT A L'ENSEIGNEMENT PUBLIC SEULEMENT.
　ESP> LAS CIFRAS DE LAS COLUMNAS 2, 3, 4 Y 8 EN
1970; DE LA COLUMNA 5 EN 1976 Y DE LAS COLUMNAS
6 Y 7 EN 1977, SE REFIEREN A LA ENSEÑANZA
PUBLICA SOLAMENTE.

NETHERLANDS:
　E—> APART FROM 1978, THE FIGURES SHOWN IN
COLUMNS 2, 3 AND 4 REFER TO FULL-TIME TEACHING
STAFF ONLY.
　FR—> EXCEPTE POUR 1978, LES CHIFFRES DES
COLONNES 2, 3 ET 4 SE REFERENT AU PERSONNEL
ENSEIGNANT A PLEIN TEMPS SEULEMENT.
　ESP> EXCEPTO PARA 1978, LAS CIFRAS DE LAS
COLUMNAS 2, 3 Y 4 SE REFIEREN AL PERSONAL DOCENTE
DE JORNADA COMPLETA SOLAMENTE.

NORWAY:
　E—> SEE ANNEX TO TABLE 3.1. APART FROM 1970,
DATA ON TEACHING STAFF INCLUDE GENERAL EDUCATION
AT THE SECOND LEVEL.
　FR—> VOIR L'ANNEXE DU TABLEAU 3.1. EXCEPTE POUR
L'ANNEE 1970, LES DONNEES SE REFERANT AU PERSONNEL
ENSEIGNANT INCLUENT L'ENSEIGNEMENT GENERAL DU
SECOND DEGRE.
　ESP> VEASE EL ANEXO DEL CUADRO 3.1. EXCEPTO
PARA 1970, LOS DATOS RELATIVOS AL PERSONAL DOCENTE
INCLUYEN LA ENSEÑANZA GENERAL DE SEGUNDO GRADO.

PORTUGAL:
　E—> BEGINNING 1974, DATA ON PREPARATORY
EDUCATION PREVIOUSLY CLASSIFIED AT THE SECOND
LEVEL ARE SHOWN AT THE FIRST LEVEL OF EDUCATION.

PORTUGAL (CONT.):
　FR—> A PARTIR DE 1974, LES DONNEES RELATIVES
AUX COURS PREPARATOIRES ANTERIEUREMENT CLASSEES
DANS L'ENSEIGNEMENT DU SECOND DEGRE ONT ETE
INCLUSES DANS L'ENSEIGNEMENT DU PREMIER DEGRE.
　ESP> A PARTIR DE 1974, LOS DATOS RELATIVOS A
LOS CURSOS PREPARATORIOS ANTERIORMENTE CLASIFICADOS
EN LA ENSEÑANZA DE SEGUNDO GRADO, HAN SIDO
INCLUIDOS EN LA ENSEÑANZA DE PRIMER GRADO.

ROMANIA:
　E—> APART FROM 1970, DATA ON PUPILS INCLUDE
EVENING COURSES FOR ADULTS.
　FR—> EXCEPTE POUR 1970, LES DONNEES CONCERNANT
LES EFFECTIFS INCLUENT LES COURS DU SOIR POUR
ADULTES.
　ESP> EXCEPTO PARA 1970, LOS DATOS RELATIVOS A LOS
ALUMNOS INCLUYEN LOS CURSOS NOCTURNOS PARA ADULTOS.

SPAIN:
　E—> SEE ANNEX TO TABLE 3.1. BEGINNING 1974 DATA
ON TEACHING STAFF INCLUDE FIGURES FOR THE FIRST CYCLE
OF GENERAL EDUCATION AT THE SECOND LEVEL.
　FR—> VOIR L'ANNEXE DU TABLEAU 3.1. A PARTIR DE
1974, LE PERSONNEL ENSEIGNANT INCLUT LES DONNEES
RELATIVES AU PREMIER CYCLE DE L'ENSEIGNEMENT
GENERAL DU SECOND DEGRE.
　ESP> VEASE EL ANEXO DEL CUADRO 3.1. A PARTIR
DE 1974, EL PERSONAL DOCENTE INCLUYE LOS DATOS
RELATIVOS AL PRIMER CICLO DE LA ENSEÑANZA GENERAL
DE SEGUNDO GRADO.

SWITZERLAND:
　E—> FOR 1970, 1974, 1975 THE FIGURES SHOWN IN
COLUMNS 5, 6 AND 7 REFER TO PUBLIC EDUCATION ONLY
AND INCLUDE SPECIAL EDUCATION. FOR 1978 DATA
INCLUDE SPECIAL EDUCATION.
　FR—> EN 1970, 1974, 1975 LES DONNEES DES
COLONNES 5, 6 ET 7 SE REFERENT A L'ENSEIGNEMENT
PUBLIC SEULEMENT ET INCLUENT L'EDUCATION SPECIALE.
EN 1978 LES DONNEES INCLUENT L'EDUCATION SPECIALE.
　ESP> EN 1970, 1974 Y 1975 LOS DATOS DE LAS
COLUMNAS 5, 6 Y 7 SE REFIEREN A LA ENSEÑANZA
PUBLICA SOLAMENTE E INCLUYEN LA EDUCACION ESPECIAL.
EN 1978 LOS DATOS INCLUYEN IGUALMENTE LA EDUCACION
ESPECIAL.

UNITED KINGDOM:
　E—> DATA ON TEACHING STAFF INCLUDE EDUCATION
PRECEDING THE FIRST LEVEL.
　FR—> LE PERSONNEL ENSEIGNANT INCLUT L'ENSEIGNEMENT
PRECEDANT LE PREMIER DEGRE.
　ESP> EL PERSONAL DOCENTE INCLUYE LA ENSEÑANZA
ANTERIOR AL PRIMER GRADO.

YUGOSLAVIA:
　E—> FOR 1975 AND 1976 THE FIGURES SHOWN IN
COLUMNS 6 AND 7 INCLUDE SPECIAL EDUCATION AND
REFER TO BEGINNING OF SCHOOL YEAR; FOR OTHER
YEARS TO THE END OF SCHOOL YEAR.
　FR—> EN 1975 ET 1976 LES DONNEES DES COLONNES
6 ET 7 INCLUENT L'EDUCATION SPECIALE ET SE REFERENT
AU DEBUT DE L'ANNEE SCOLAIRE; POUR LES AUTRES
ANNEES, A LA FIN DE L'ANNEE.
　ESP> EN 1975 Y 1976 LOS DATOS DE LAS COLUMNAS
6 Y 7 INCLUYEN LA EDUCACION ESPECIAL Y SE REFIEREN
AL COMIENZO DEL AÑO ESCOLAR. PARA LOS OTROS ANOS,
AL FINAL DEL ANO.

AMERICAN SAMOA:
　E—> FOR 1970 DATA INCLUDE EDUCATION PRECEDING
THE FIRST LEVEL. FOR 1975, 1976 AND 1977 DATA
REFER TO PUBLIC EDUCATION ONLY.
　FR—> EN 1970 LES DONNEES INCLUENT L'ENSEIGNEMENT
PRECEDANT LE PREMIER DEGRE. EN 1975, 1976 ET 1977
LES DONNEES SE REFERENT A L'ENSEIGNEMENT PUBLIC
SEULEMENT.

Education at the first level **3.4**
Enseignement du premier degré
Enseñanza de primer grado

AMERICAN SAMOA (CONT.):
   ESP> EN 1970, LOS DATOS INCLUYEN LA ENSEÑANZA
ANTERIOR AL PRIMER GRADO. EN 1975, 1976 Y 1977,
LOS DATOS SE REFIEREN A LA ENSEÑANZA PUBLICA
SOLAMENTE.

AUSTRALIA:
   E—> ALL DATA FOR 1970 AND THE FIGURES SHOWN IN
COLUMNS 2, 3 AND 4 FOR 1974 TO 1977 INCLUDE PRE-
PRIMARY CLASSES, SPECIAL EDUCATION, UPGRADED AND
CORRESPONDENCE COURSES.
   FR—> TOUTES LES DONNEES DE L'ANNEE 1970 ET POUR
LES COLONNES 2, 3 ET 4 DES ANNEES 1974 A 1977 LES
DONNEES COMPRENNENT LES CLASSES PREPRIMAIRES,
L'EDUCATION SPECIALE, LES "UPGRADED COURSES" ET
LES COURS PAR CORRESPONDANCE.
   ESP> TODOS LOS DATOS DEL AÑO 1970 Y LOS DE LAS
COLUMNAS 2, 3 Y 4 PARA LOS AÑOS 1974 A 1977,
COMPRENDEN LAS CLASES PREPRIMARIAS, LA EDUCACION
ESPECIAL, LAS "UPGRADED COURSES" Y LOS CURSOS POR
CORRESPONDENCIA.

GUAM:
   E—> FOR 1970 THE FIGURE SHOWN IN COLUMN 2
INCLUDES EDUCATION PRECEDING THE FIRST LEVEL. FOR
1974 THE FIGURE SHOWN IN COLUMN 2 INCLUDES GENERAL
EDUCATION AT THE FIRST LEVEL. FOR 1976 DATA REFER
TO PUBLIC EDUCATION ONLY.
   FR—> EN 1970 LE CHIFFRE DE LA COLONNE 2 INCLUT
L'ENSEIGNEMENT PRECEDANT LE PREMIER DEGRE. EN
1974 LE CHIFFRE DE LA COLONNE 2 INCLUT
L'ENSEIGNEMENT GENERAL DU SECOND DEGRE. EN 1976
LES DONNEES SE REFERENT A L'ENSEIGNEMENT PUBLIC
SEULEMENT.
   ESP> EN 1970, LA CIFRA DE LA COLUMNA 2 INCLUYE
LA ENSEÑANZA ANTERIOR AL PRIMER GRADO. EN 1977,
LA CIFRA DE LA COLUMNA 2 INCLUYE LA ENSEÑANZA
GENERAL DE SEGUNDO GRADO. EN 1976, LOS DATOS SE
REFIEREN A LA ENSEÑANZA PUBLICA SOLAMENTE.

KIRIBATI:
   E—> FOR 1970 DATA INCLUDE SECONDARY CLASSES
ATTACHED TO PRIMARY SCHOOLS.
   FR—> EN 1970 LES DONNEES COMPRENNENT LES CLASSES
RATTACHEES AUX ECOLES PRIMAIRES.
   ESP> EN 1970, LOS DATOS INCLUYEN LAS CLASES
SECUNDARIAS ADSCRITAS A LAS ESCUELAS PRIMARIAS.

NEW CALEDONIA:
   E—> BEGINNING 1974 THE FIGURES SHOWN IN COLUMN
2 INCLUDE EDUCATION PRECEDING THE FIRST LEVEL.
   FR—> A PARTIR DE 1974 LES CHIFFRES DE LA COLONNE
2 INCLUENT L'ENSEIGNEMENT PRECEDANT LE PREMIER
DEGRE.
   ESP> A PARTIR DE 1974, LAS CIFRAS DE LA COLUMNA
2 INCLUYEN LA ENSEÑANZA ANTERIOR AL PRIMER GRADO.

NEW HEBRIDES:
   E—> FOR 1976 THE FIGURES SHOWN IN COLUMNS 2
AND 8 REFER TO PUBLIC EDUCATION ONLY. FOR 1977
THE FIGURES SHOWN IN COLUMNS 3 AND 4 REFER TO
ENGLISH EDUCATION ONLY.

NEW HEBRIDES (CONT.):
   FR—> EN 1976 LES DONNEES DES COLONNES 2 ET 8
SE REFERENT A L'ENSEIGNEMENT PUBLIC SEULEMENT.
EN 1977 LES DONNEES DES COLONNES 3 ET 4 SE
REFERENT A L'ENSEIGNEMENT ANGLOPHONE SEULEMENT.
   ESP> EN 1976 LOS DATOS DE LAS COLUMNAS 2 Y 8
SE REFIEREN A LA ENSEÑANZA PUBLICA SOLAMENTE.
EN 1977 LOS DATOS DE LAS COLUMNAS 3 Y 4 SE
REFIEREN AL SISTEMA INGLES DE ENSEÑANZA
SOLAMENTE.

NEW ZEALAND:
   E—> DATA INCLUDE SPECIAL EDUCATION AND THE
TEACHING STAFF INCLUDES DATA FOR FORMS I AND II
(EDUCATION AT THE SECOND LEVEL).
   FR—> LES DONNEES INCLUENT L'ÉDUCATION SPECIALE,
ET LE PERSONNEL ENSEIGNANT INCLUT LES "FORMS I ET
II" (ENSEIGNEMENT DU SECOND DEGRE).
   ESP> LOS DATOS INCLUYEN LA EDUCACION ESPECIAL.
EL PERSONAL DOCENTE COMPRENDE LAS "FORMS I Y II"
(ENSEÑANZA DE SEGUNDO GRADO).

NIUE:
   E—> FOR 1970 DATA REFER TO GRADES I—VII; FOR
1974, 1975 AND 1976 TO GRADES I—VIII.
   FR—> POUR 1970 LES DONNEES SE RAPPORTENT AUX
CLASSES ALLANT DE LA PREMIERE A LA SEPTIEME ANNEE;
POUR 1974, 1975 ET 1976 AUX CLASSES ALLANT DE LA
PREMIERE A LA HUITIEME ANNEE.
   ESP> EN 1970 LOS DATOS SE REFIEREN A LAS CLASES
I—VII; EN 1974, 1975 Y 1976 A LAS CLASES I—VIII.

U.S.S.R.:
   E—> FIGURES ON SCHOOLS AND TEACHING STAFF COVER
GENERAL EDUCATION AT THE FIRST AND SECOND LEVELS.
   FR—> LES DONNEES RELATIVES AU NOMBRE D'ECOLES
ET AU PERSONNEL ENSEIGNANT SE RAPPORTENT A
L'ENSEIGNEMENT GENERAL DU PREMIER ET DU SECOND
DEGRE.
   ESP> LOS DATOS RELATIVOS AL NUMERO DE ESCUELAS
Y AL PERSONAL DOCENTE SE REFIEREN A LA ENSEÑANZA
GENERAL DE PRIMERO Y DE SEGUNDO GRADO.

BYELORUSSIAN S.S.R.:
   E—> DATA ON TEACHING STAFF INCLUDE GENERAL
EDUCATION AT THE SECOND LEVEL.
   FR—> LES DONNEES RELATIVES AU PERSONNEL
ENSEIGNANT INCLUENT L'ENSEIGNEMENT GENERAL DU
SECOND DEGRE.
   ESP> LOS DATOS RELATIVOS AL PERSONAL DOCENTE
INCLUYEN LA ENSEÑANZA GENERAL DE SEGUNDO GRADO.

UKRAINIAN S.S.R.:
   E—> DATA ON TEACHING STAFF INCLUDE GENERAL
EDUCATION AT THE SECOND LEVEL.
   FR—> LES DONNEES RELATIVES AU PERSONNEL
ENSEIGNANT INCLUENT L'ENSEIGNEMENT GENERAL DU
SECOND DEGRE.
   ESP> LOS DATOS RELATIVOS AL PERSONAL DOCENTE
INCLUYEN LA ENSEÑANZA GENERAL DE SEGUNDO GRADO.

Percentage distribution (first level) by grade 3.5
Répartition en pourcentage (premier degré) par années d'études
Distribución en porcentaje (primer grado) por años de estudio

3.5 Education at the first level: percentage distribution of enrolment by grade

Enseignement du premier degré: répartition en pourcentage des effectifs par années d'études

Enseñanza de primer grado: distribución en porcentaje de la matrícula escolar por años de estudio

NUMBER OF COUNTRIES AND TERRITORIES PRESENTED IN THIS TABLE: 177	NOMBRE DE PAYS ET DE TERRITOIRES PRESENTES DANS CE TABLEAU: 177	NUMERO DE PAISES Y DE TERRITORIOS PRESENTADOS EN ESTE CUADRO: 177

COUNTRY PAYS PAIS	YEAR ANNEE AÑO	SEX SEXE SEXO	GRADE / ANNEES D'ETUDES / AÑOS DE ESTUDIO									
			I	II	III	IV	V	VI	VII	VIII	IX	X
AFRICA												
ALGERIA ‡	1975	MF	19	17	17	16	14	12	5			
		F	20	17	17	16	14	12	4			
	1977	MF	18	17	17	15	14	13	5			
		F	19	18	17	15	14	12	4			
	1978	MF	18	17	17	15	14	13	5			
		F	19	18	18	15	14	12	4			
ANGOLA	1969	MF	37	31	16	10	6	0	0			
		F	39	30	15	9	7	0	0			
	1971	MF	34	32	17	10	7	0	0			
		F	37	31	16	9	7	0	0			
BENIN ‡	1970	MF	27	19	15	13	13	13				
		F	28	19	15	13	12	12				
	1975	MF	28	18	17	13	12	12				
		F	28	19	17	13	12	12				
	1978	MF	31	18	16	12	12	12				
		F	31	19	16	12	11	12				
	1979	MF	25	23	16	12	11	13				
		F	25	24	16	12	11	12				
BOTSWANA	1970	MF	15	17	19	16	14	11	8			
		F	15	17	19	16	14	11	8			
	1975	MF	22	18	17	12	9	9	12			
		F	21	17	18	12	9	9	13			
	1977	MF	19	17	18	14	13	9	9			
		F	18	17	18	14	14	10	10			
	1978	MF	17	17	16	16	13	12	10			
		F	16	16	16	16	13	12	11			
BURUNDI	1970	MF	26	20	18	14	11	8	3			
		F	29	21	18	13	10	7	3			
	1975	MF	22	17	17	15	15	13				
		F	23	18	17	16	14	12				

3.5 Percentage distribution (first level) by grade
Répartition en pourcentage (premier degré) par années d'études
Distribución en porcentaje (primer grado) por años de estudio

COUNTRY PAYS PAIS	YEAR ANNEE AÑO	SEX SEXE SEXO	GRADE / ANNEES D'ETUDES / AÑOS DE ESTUDIO									
			I	II	III	IV	V	VI	VII	VIII	IX	X
BURUNDI (CONT.)	1977	MF	24	17	15	15	16	12				
		F	24	18	16	15	15	12				
	1978	MF	23	18	16	15	15	13				
		F	24	18	16	15	15	12				
CENTRAL AFRICAN REPUBLIC	1970	MF	33	21	16	11	10	10				
		F	37	23	16	10	8	6				
	1975	MF	27	21	17	12	10	12				
		F	29	23	17	12	9	10				
	1976	MF	27	20	16	13	11	13				
		F	30	21	17	12	10	10				
	1977	MF	26	21	17	13	11	13				
		F	28	22	17	12	10	10				
CHAD ‡	1970	MF	39	18	14	10	9	12				
	1975	MF	35	19	15	10	9	12				
		F	39	21	16	9	8	8				
	1976	MF	36	19	15	10	9	12				
		F	40	20	15	9	7	8				
CONGO	1970	MF	24	19	17	13	12	15				
	1975	MF	23	19	19	15	13	12				
		F	24	19	19	15	12	11				
	1977	MF	22	17	20	16	13	11				
		F	23	18	20	16	13	11				
	1978	MF	21	17	20	16	13	12				
		F	22	17	20	16	13	12				
DJIBOUTI	1970	MF	17	21	18	19	14	11				
		F	16	22	20	19	12	10				
	1975	MF	20	21	15	14	13	16				
		F	18	20	20	15	15	13				
	1978	MF	13	27	20	13	14	13				
EGYPT ‡	1970	MF	20	19	17	18	13	14				
		F	21	19	17	18	12	13				
	1975	MF	18	20	14	17	15	16				
		F	19	20	14	17	14	15				
	1977	MF	19	20	17	18	13	14				
		F	19	20	17	17	14	12				
	1978	MF	18	20	17	18	15	12				
		F	19	20	17	18	14	12				
ETHIOPIA	1970	MF	31	18	16	13	11	10				
		F	32	18	15	13	10	11				
	1973	MF	31	18	15	14	11	10				
		F	30	18	16	14	11	12				
GABON	1970	MF	35	17	14	11	10	12				
		F	37	18	15	11	10	9				
	1975	MF	34	18	15	11	10	11				
		F	35	18	15	11	10	10				

Percentage distribution (first level) by grade　3.5
Répartition en pourcentage (premier degré) par années d'études
Distribución en porcentaje (primer grado) por años de estudio

COUNTRY PAYS PAIS	YEAR ANNEE AÑO	SEX SEXE SEXO	GRADE / ANNEES D'ETUDES / AÑOS DE ESTUDIO									
			I	II	III	IV	V	VI	VII	VIII	IX	X
GABON (CONT.)	1976	MF	34	18	15	11	10	11				
		F	35	18	15	11	10	10				
GAMBIA	1970	MF	17	16	16	15	16	20				
		F	19	19	16	14	14	18				
	1975	MF	21	17	17	15	13	18				
		F	21	19	17	15	12	16				
	1977	MF	20	18	17	15	14	17				
		F	21	17	18	15	13	16				
	1978	MF	23	18	15	14	13	16				
		F	25	19	14	14	13	15				
GHANA ‡	1970	MF	15	12	11	10	10	10	9	9	8	6
		F	16	12	11	10	10	10	9	8	7	5
	1975	MF	23	18	17	16	14	13				
		F	23	18	17	15	14	12				
	1976	MF	22	19	17	15	14	13				
		F	23	19	17	15	14	12				
	1977	MF	22	19	17	15	14	13				
		F	23	19	17	15	14	13				
GUINEA–BISSAU	1975	MF	51	22	13	9	4	2				
		F	61	19	9	6	3	2				
	1976	MF	54	18	10	7	7	4				
		F	64	17	7	4	5	3				
	1977	MF	45	22	13	9	7	4				
		F	55	21	10	6	5	3				
IVORY COAST	1970	MF	23	18	16	14	13	15				
		F	25	20	17	14	13	12				
	1975	MF	20	17	16	14	14	18				
		F	22	18	17	14	14	15				
	1976	MF	20	18	16	14	14	19				
		F	22	19	16	14	13	16				
	1977	MF	21	17	16	14	13	19				
		F	23	18	17	14	12	16				
KENYA	1970	MF	21	17	15	13	11	11	11			
		F	22	18	16	14	11	10	9			
	1975	MF	23	25	15	12	9	8	8			
		F	24	26	15	12	9	8	7			
	1976	MF	20	19	21	13	10	9	8			
		F	20	19	21	13	10	8	7			
	1977	MF	20	16	17	17	11	9	8			
		F	20	17	18	18	11	9	7			
LESOTHO	1970	MF	23	18	16	13	12	9	4	4		
		F	21	17	16	13	13	10	5	4		
	1975	MF	23	20	17	13	11	9	8			
		F	20	19	16	14	12	10	9			
	1976	MF	23	19	17	14	11	9	8			
		F	20	18	17	14	12	10	9			

3.5 Percentage distribution (first level) by grade
Répartition en pourcentage (premier degré) par années d'études
Distribución en porcentaje (primer grado) por años de estudio

COUNTRY PAYS PAIS	YEAR ANNEE AÑO	SEX SEXE SEXO	I	II	III	IV	V	VI	VII	VIII	IX	X
LIBERIA ‡	1970	MF	12	21	18	14	11	10	8	7		
		F	15	24	19	13	11	8	6	4		
	1975	MF	34	——>	18	13	11	9	8	7		
		F	38	——>	18	13	10	8	7	5		
	1976	MF	33	——>	18	14	11	10	8	6		
		F	38	——>	18	13	11	9	7	5		
	1978	MF	32	——>	18	14	11	10	8	7		
		F	36	——>	19	13	11	9	7	6		
LIBYAN ARAB JAMAHIRIYA	1970	MF	29	20	17	14	12	8				
		F	35	22	17	12	9	5				
	1975	MF	19	16	16	18	17	15				
		F	20	16	17	18	17	12				
	1976	MF	20	17	15	16	17	15				
		F	21	17	16	16	17	13				
	1977	MF	20	17	16	16	15	16				
		F	21	18	16	16	15	14				
MADAGASCAR	1970	MF	36	22	16	12	7	7				
		F	36	21	17	12	7	6				
	1974	MF	38	20	15	12	8	7				
	1975	MF	37	20	16	12	8	7				
		F	37	20	16	12	8	7				
MALAWI	1970	MF	27	18	15	11	9	6	6	8		
	1975	MF	29	20	15	11	8	6	4	6		
		F	33	21	16	11	7	5	4	4		
	1976	MF	27	18	15	11	9	7	5	7		
		F	31	20	16	11	8	6	4	5		
	1977	MF	27	18	15	11	9	7	5	8		
		F	30	19	16	11	8	6	4	5		
MALI	1970	MF	28	21	16	12	11	11				
		F	30	22	17	12	10	9				
	1975	MF	26	20	18	14	13	9				
		F	27	20	19	14	12	9				
	1977	MF	25	20	18	14	12	10				
		F	26	20	18	14	12	9				
	1978	MF	23	22	18	15	12	10				
		F	24	22	18	15	12	10				
MAURITANIA	1970	MF	19	20	19	11	6	11	14			
	1975	MF	26	12	15	17	11	10	10			
		F	26	16	15	17	11	9	8			
	1976	MF	24	21	14	12	12	9	8			
		F	27	23	14	12	11	7	6			
	1977	MF	21	21	18	12	9	10	8			
		F	24	22	19	12	8	9	7			
MAURITIUS ‡	1970	MF	17	17	15	15	13	22				
		F	17	17	16	15	13	21				

Percentage distribution (first level) by grade 3.5
Répartition en pourcentage (premier degré) par années d'études
Distribución en porcentaje (primer grado) por años de estudio

COUNTRY PAYS PAIS	YEAR ANNEE AÑO	SEX SEXE SEXO	GRADE / ANNEES D'ETUDES / AÑOS DE ESTUDIO									
			I	II	III	IV	V	VI	VII	VIII	IX	X
MAURITIUS (CONT.) ‡	1975	MF	14	15	14	16	15	26				
		F	14	15	14	16	15	26				
	1977	MF	14	15	15	16	15	26				
		F	14	15	14	16	15	26				
	1978	MF	14	14	15	15	15	27				
		F	14	14	15	15	15	26				
MOROCCO	1970	MF	25	19	19	17	20					
		F	25	20	19	17	19					
	1975	MF	25	20	19	17	19					
		F	25	20	19	17	18					
	1977	MF	25	20	19	17	19					
		F	25	20	19	17	19					
	1978	MF	24	20	19	17	20					
		F	25	20	19	17	20					
MOZAMBIQUE	1972	MF	55	21	12	7	5					
		F	59	20	10	6	4					
NIGER	1970	MF	25	21	17	14	12	11				
		F	26	22	18	14	11	9				
	1975	MF	29	22	16	13	10	11				
		F	28	22	16	13	10	10				
	1976	MF	24	24	18	12	11	11				
		F	24	23	19	12	11	11				
	1977	MF	22	22	20	15	11	12				
		F	22	22	20	15	11	11				
NIGERIA	1970	MF	29	20	17	13	10	9	2			
		F	31	21	17	13	10	8	1			
	1973	MF	24	20	19	15	12	9	1			
		F	26	21	19	15	11	8	1			
REUNION	1975	MF	22	20	20	20	18					
	1977	MF	21	19	19	21	20					
	1978	MF	20	19	19	21	21					
RWANDA	1970	MF	29	21	17	14	10	8				
		F	30	22	18	14	10	7				
	1975	MF	28	18	16	14	12	11				
		F	29	18	17	14	12	10				
	1976	MF	30	20	15	14	11	10				
		F	31	20	15	14	10	9				
SAO TOME AND PRINCIPE	1976	MF	42	23	18	17						
		F	44	22	17	17						
	1977	MF	45	23	17	16						
		F	45	23	16	16						
SENEGAL	1970	MF	20	18	17	15	14	17				
		F	21	19	17	15	14	15				
	1977	MF	21	18	17	15	15	15				
		F	21	18	17	15	14	15				

3.5 Percentage distribution (first level) by grade
Répartition en pourcentage (premier degré) par années d'études
Distribución en porcentaje (primer grado) por años de estudio

COUNTRY PAYS PAIS	YEAR ANNEE AÑO	SEX SEXE SEXO	GRADE / ANNEES D'ETUDES / AÑOS DE ESTUDIO									
			I	II	III	IV	V	VI	VII	VIII	IX	X
SEYCHELLES	1970	MF	19	18	17	17	15	13				
		F	19	19	16	17	15	13				
	1975	MF	17	17	17	16	17	16				
		F	16	17	17	16	16	17				
	1977	MF	16	16	17	18	18	16				
		F	15	16	17	18	18	17				
	1978	MF	17	16	16	17	17	17				
		F	16	15	17	17	17	18				
	1979	MF	17	18	16	16	17	17				
		F	17	17	15	16	17	17				
SIERRA LEONE	1970	MF	23	16	15	14	12	10	10			
		F	25	17	15	14	12	9	8			
	1975	MF	26	18	15	13	11	9	8			
		F	27	18	15	13	11	8	7			
	1977	MF	26	17	15	13	11	9	8			
		F	27	18	15	13	11	9	8			
SOMALIA ‡	1970	MF	31	23	24	22						
		F	33	23	23	21						
	1975	MF	68	19	8	5						
		F	73	17	6	4						
	1976	MF	30	38	18	6	5	–	–	3		
		F	34	39	15	5	4	–	–	2		
	1977	MF	18	23	32	17	6	5	–	0		
		F	20	25	33	14	5	4	–	–		
SUDAN	1970	MF	23	22	19	17	14	5				
	1975	MF	22	19	16	15	14	14				
		F	22	19	16	15	14	14				
	1977	MF	22	19	17	15	14	13				
		F	23	19	16	15	13	14				
	1978	MF	22	19	17	15	14	13				
		F	22	19	17	15	14	13				
SWAZILAND	1970	MF	21	18	17	15	12	9	9			
		F	20	18	17	15	11	10	9			
	1975	MF	20	16	16	14	13	11	10			
		F	19	16	16	14	13	11	11			
	1977	MF	20	17	16	14	12	11	10			
		F	20	17	16	14	13	11	10			
	1978	MF	20	17	16	14	12	11	10			
		F	20	17	15	14	12	11	10			
TOGO	1970	MF	32	18	16	12	11	11				
		F	35	19	16	11	10	9				
	1975	MF	29	19	17	12	11	11				
		F	33	20	17	12	10	8				
	1976	MF	29	19	17	13	12	11				
		F	31	20	17	12	10	8				
	1977	MF	27	20	17	13	11	11				
		F	30	21	17	13	10	9				

Percentage distribution (first level) by grade **3.5**
Répartition en pourcentage (premier degré) par années d'études
Distribución en porcentaje (primer grado) por años de estudio

COUNTRY PAYS PAIS	YEAR ANNEE AÑO	SEX SEXE SEXO	I	II	III	IV	V	VI	VII	VIII	IX	X
			_	_	GRADE / ANNEES D'ETUDES / AÑOS DE ESTUDIO _	_	_	_	_	_	_	_
TUNISIA ‡	1970	MF	20	19	17	15	14	14				
	1975	MF	17	16	16	16	16	19				
		F	18	17	16	16	16	17				
	1977	MF	18	16	15	15	15	19	2			
		F	19	17	15	15	15	18	1			
	1978	MF	19	16	15	15	15	17	2			
		F	20	17	16	14	15	15	2			
UGANDA ‡	1975	MF	20	17	15	13	12	12	11			
		F	22	18	16	13	12	11	9			
	1976	MF	20	17	16	13	11	12	11			
		F	22	18	16	13	12	11	9			
	1977	MF	21	17	15	13	11	11	11			
		F	22	18	16	13	11	11	9			
UNITED REPUBLIC OF CAMEROON	1970	MF	28	19	16	13	11	11	1			
		F	29	19	17	13	11	10	1			
	1975	MF	27	18	17	13	12	12	1			
		F	27	18	17	13	12	11	1			
	1976	MF	26	18	17	13	12	13	1			
		F	27	18	17	13	12	12	1			
	1977	MF	26	18	17	13	12	13	2			
		F	26	18	17	13	12	12	1			
UNITED REPUBLIC OF TANZANIA ‡	1970	MF	21	19	17	15	11	9	8			
		F	22	19	17	16	11	9	7			
	1974	MF	29	16	14	12	10	10	9			
		F	31	17	14	12	10	9	8			
	1975	MF	28	23	13	11	9	8	8			
		F	30	24	13	10	9	8	7			
UPPER VOLTA	1970	MF	24	20	16	15	12	13				
		F	24	20	17	15	12	12				
	1975	MF	24	20	18	14	12	13				
		F	24	20	18	14	12	12				
	1977	MF	24	19	17	14	12	14				
		F	24	19	17	14	12	13				
	1978	MF	24	20	16	14	12	14				
		F	24	21	16	14	12	14				
ZAIRE	1970	MF	30	22	17	13	10	8				
		F	35	23	17	12	8	5				
	1975	MF	26	20	18	14	12	10				
		F	28	20	19	14	11	8				
	1976	MF	25	19	18	15	12	11				
		F	27	20	19	15	11	9				
	1977	MF	24	19	18	15	12	11				
		F	25	19	19	16	12	10				
ZAMBIA	1970	MF	18	18	17	16	11	10	10			
		F	20	19	18	16	10	9	8			

3.5 Percentage distribution (first level) by grade
Répartition en pourcentage (premier degré) par années d'études
Distribución en porcentaje (primer grado) por años de estudio

COUNTRY / PAYS / PAIS	YEAR / ANNEE / AÑO	SEX / SEXE / SEXO	GRADE / ANNEES D'ETUDES / AÑOS DE ESTUDIO									
			I	II	III	IV	V	VI	VII	VIII	IX	X
ZAMBIA (CONT.)	1975	MF	17	16	16	16	12	11	11			
		F	18	17	17	16	12	10	10			
	1976	MF	17	16	16	16	12	12	11			
		F	18	17	16	16	12	11	10			
AMERICA, NORTH												
ANTIGUA	1970	MF	13	16	16	14	15	14	12			
		F	14	14	16	14	16	15	11			
	1974	MF	16	13	14	15	14	14	13			
		F	16	13	14	15	14	14	13			
	1975	MF	18	13	13	15	14	14	13			
		F	17	13	14	15	15	13	13			
BARBADOS ‡	1970	MF	23	15	15	15	15	16				
		F	24	15	15	15	16	15				
	1975	MF	18	16	17	17	17	16				
		F	17	16	17	17	16	17				
	1976	MF	19	15	16	16	17	17				
		F	19	15	16	17	17	17				
	1977	MF	18	16	16	16	16	17				
		F	19	17	16	16	16	17				
BELIZE ‡	1970	MF	19	14	13	13	11	11	9	10		
		F	19	14	14	12	11	11	9	10		
	1975	MF	19	13	13	13	12	11	9	9		
		F	19	13	13	12	13	11	9	10		
BERMUDA	1974	MF	12	14	14	15	15	15	16			
		F	12	14	14	14	14	15	17			
	1975	MF	13	14	14	14	15	16	15			
		F	13	13	13	14	14	17	16			
	1976	MF	14	14	14	14	14	15	15			
		F	14	14	14	14	14	14	15			
	1977	MF	14	15	14	14	14	15	15			
		F	14	15	14	14	14	15	15			
BRITISH VIRGIN ISLANDS	1975	MF	21	12	13	12	13	11	14	4		
		F	22	12	13	12	12	11	15	4		
	1978	MF	22	12	12	13	12	12	13	4		
		F	23	10	14	14	12	11	12	5		
CANADA	1970	MF	13	13	12	13	13	13	11	12		
		F	13	13	12	13	13	13	11	13		
	1975	MF	16	15	15	16	18	19				
		F	16	15	16	16	18	19				
	1976	MF	17	16	16	16	17	18				
		F	17	16	16	16	17	19				
	1977	MF	17	17	16	16	16	18				
		F	17	17	16	16	17	18				
CAYMAN ISLANDS	1971	MF	16	15	17	19	17	16				
		F	13	15	18	18	17	19				

Percentage distribution (first level) by grade 3.5
Répartition en pourcentage (premier degré) par années d'études
Distribución en porcentaje (primer grado) por años de estudio

COUNTRY PAYS PAIS	YEAR ANNEE AÑO	SEX SEXE SEXO	GRADE / ANNEES D'ETUDES / AÑOS DE ESTUDIO									
			I	II	III	IV	V	VI	VII	VIII	IX	X
CAYMAN ISLANDS (CONT.)	1974	MF	17	17	15	16	19	16				
		F	17	17	14	16	18	18				
	1975	MF	18	18	14	15	18	18				
		F	17	18	14	15	18	17				
COSTA RICA ‡	1970	MF	22	19	18	16	13	11				
		F	22	19	18	17	13	11				
	1975	MF	18	17	19	16	15	14				
		F	18	17	19	17	15	15				
	1976	MF	19	19	17	15	17	13				
		F	19	19	17	15	17	14				
	1977	MF	19	20	17	14	16	14				
		F	18	19	17	14	16	15				
	1978	MF	17	20	18	15	15	14				
		F	17	20	18	15	16	15				
CUBA	1970	MF	30	19	16	16	11	8				
		F	28	19	16	16	12	9				
	1975	MF	17	17	17	18	16	13				
		F	17	17	17	18	17	14				
	1976	MF	14	18	17	17	18	16				
		F	14	17	17	17	18	17				
DOMINICA	1970	MF	34	⟶	15	14	13	12	11			
		F	34	⟶	14	14	13	12	14			
	1975	MF	16	13	15	14	15	14	12			
		F	15	14	15	14	15	14	12			
	1977	MF	16	15	13	14	14	14	14			
		F	16	16	14	13	14	13	14			
	1978	MF	16	14	15	14	15	13	14			
		F	14	15	14	14	14	14	14			
DOMINICAN REPUBLIC	1970	MF	39	19	16	11	8	6				
		F	38	19	16	12	9	6				
	1974	MF	35	19	16	12	10	8				
EL SALVADOR ‡	1970	MF	33	20	16	13	10	9				
		F	33	20	16	12	10	8				
	1975	MF	28	18	13	10	8	7	6	5	4	
		F	28	18	13	10	8	7	6	5	4	
	1976	MF	27	17	13	10	8	7	6	5	4	
		F	27	18	14	11	8	7	6	5	4	
	1977	MF	27	17	13	11	8	7	6	5	5	
		F	27	17	14	11	9	7	6	5	4	
GRENADA	1975	MF	16	13	13	14	15	15	14			
		F	16	13	13	14	15	15	14			
	1976	MF	17	14	13	14	14	15	14			
		F	16	14	13	14	14	14	15			
	1977	MF	18	14	13	13	14	14	13			
		F	17	13	13	14	14	15	14			
GUADELOUPE ‡	1970	MF	25	20	19	17	12	3	4			
		F	23	20	19	17	14	3	4			

3.5 Percentage distribution (first level) by grade
Répartition en pourcentage (premier degré) par années d'études
Distribución en porcentaje (primer grado) por años de estudio

COUNTRY PAYS PAIS	YEAR ANNEE AÑO	SEX SEXE SEXO	GRADE / ANNEES D'ETUDES / AÑOS DE ESTUDIO								
			I	II	III	IV	V	VI	VII	VIII	IX
GUADELOUPE (CONT.) ‡	1975	MF	23	20	20	20	17				
	1977	MF	22	19	19	21	19				
	1978	MF	22	20	19	20	19				
GUATEMALA	1970	MF	38	22	16	10	8	6			
		F	38	21	16	10	8	6			
	1975	MF	37	20	16	11	9	7			
		F	37	20	15	11	9	7			
	1977	MF	37	20	16	11	9	7			
		F	37	20	16	11	9	8			
HAITI ‡	1975	MF	17	22	19	15	12	9	7		
		F	14	22	19	16	13	9	7		
	1976	MF	16	22	18	16	12	9	7		
		F	14	22	18	16	13	9	7		
	1977	MF	16	22	18	15	12	9	8		
		F	13	22	18	16	13	10	8		
HONDURAS	1970	MF	35	21	16	12	9	7			
		F	34	21	16	12	9	7			
	1975	MF	36	21	16	12	9	7			
		F	35	21	16	12	9	7			
	1976	MF	36	21	16	12	9	7			
JAMAICA ‡	1975	MF	17	17	18	17	16	14			
		F	17	17	18	17	16	15			
	1976	MF	17	17	17	18	16	14			
		F	17	17	17	18	16	15			
	1977	MF	17	17	17	17	16	15			
		F	17	17	17	17	16	16			
MARTINIQUE ‡	1970	MF	22	18	18	18	15	4	4		
		F	22	18	18	18	16	4	3		
	1975	MF	21	21	20	20	18				
	1977	MF	21	19	19	20	21				
	1978	MF	20	19	19	20	21				
MEXICO	1970	MF	29	20	17	14	11	9			
	1975	MF	27	20	17	14	12	10			
		F	27	20	17	14	12	10			
	1977	MF	26	20	17	15	12	10			
		F	26	20	17	14	12	10			
	1978	MF	27	19	17	14	12	10			
MONTSERRAT ‡	1975	MF	14	9	13	11	14	12	12	6	8
		F	13	9	12	10	14	13	14	5	9
	1976	MF	16	9	12	14	14	14	13	4	5
		F	16	9	11	13	12	14	14	4	6
	1977	MF	14	14	13	12	15	14	13	2	3
		F	14	14	13	11	15	13	16	2	3

Percentage distribution (first level) by grade   3.5
Répartition en pourcentage (premier degré) par années d'études
Distribución en porcentaje (primer grado) por años de estudio

COUNTRY PAYS PAIS	YEAR ANNEE AÑO	SEX SEXE SEXO	GRADE / ANNEES D'ETUDES / AÑOS DE ESTUDIO									
			I	II	III	IV	V	VI	VII	VIII	IX	X
NICARAGUA	1970	MF	39	20	16	11	8	6				
		F	37	20	16	11	8	6				
	1974	MF	38	20	15	12	9	7				
	1977	MF	36	20	16	12	9	7				
		F	34	20	16	12	10	8				
	1978	MF	36	19	15	13	9	8				
		F	35	19	16	13	10	8				
PANAMA	1970	MF	25	20	17	14	12	10				
		F	25	20	18	15	13	11				
	1975	MF	21	18	17	16	15	12	1	1	0	
		F	20	18	17	16	15	12	1	1	0	
	1977	MF	20	17	16	15	14	13	2	2	1	
		F	20	17	16	15	14	13	2	1	1	
	1978	MF	20	17	16	15	14	12	4	2	1	
		F	20	17	16	15	14	13	4	2	1	
FORMER CANAL ZONE ‡	1970	MF	17	17	17	17	17	16				
	1975	MF	19	16	15	15	18	17				
	1976	MF	20	18	15	15	15	17				
	1977	MF	20	19	17	15	15	14				
PUERTO RICO ‡	1970	MF	18	17	17	17	16	14				
	1975	MF	17	16	17	17	17	16				
	1976	MF	17	16	17	17	17	16				
ST. LUCIA ‡	1975	MF	11	12	12	13	12	13	12	8	8	
		F	11	12	12	13	12	13	12	8	8	
	1976	MF	11	11	12	12	12	12	13	7	9	
		F	11	11	11	13	12	12	13	7	9	
ST. VINCENT AND THE GRENADINES ‡	1970	MF	15	14	11	11	10	10	12	7	6	5
		F	15	14	10	10	10	11	11	7	6	5
	1974	MF	16	14	14	14	15	14	12			
		F	16	13	14	15	15	14	13			
	1975	MF	20	14	13	14	14	13	12			
		F	19	14	12	14	14	14	13			
TRINIDAD AND TOBAGO ‡	1970	MF	14	12	12	12	11	10	15	8	5	
		F	14	12	12	11	11	10	16	8	5	
	1974	MF	12	11	12	12	12	11	18	8	5	
		F	12	11	12	12	12	11	18	7	5	
	1975	MF	12	11	12	12	12	11	18	8	5	
		F	12	11	12	12	12	11	19	8	5	
TURKS AND CAICOS ISLANDS ‡	1974	MF	17	12	12	16	15	13	8	7		
	1977	MF	14	13	14	16	13	12	11	8		
		F	16	12	13	17	15	11	10	6		
UNITED STATES OF AMERICA ‡	1970	MF	13	12	13	13	12	12	13	12		

271

3.5 Percentage distribution (first level) by grade
Répartition en pourcentage (premier degré) par années d'études
Distribución en porcentaje (primer grado) por años de estudio

COUNTRY PAYS PAIS	YEAR ANNEE AÑO	SEX SEXE SEXO	GRADE / ANNEES D'ETUDES / AÑOS DE ESTUDIO									
			I	II	III	IV	V	VI	VII	VIII	IX	X
UNITED STATES OF AMERICA (CONT.) ‡	1975	MF	15	14	14	14	15	16	6	6		
	1976	MF	16	14	14	14	15	15	6	6		
	1977	MF	16	15	15	14	14	15	6	6		
U.S. VIRGIN ISLANDS ‡	1975	MF	18	16	17	17	16	15				
	1976	MF	19	16	16	16	17	15				
	1977	MF	18	18	17	16	16	16				
AMERICA, SOUTH												
ARGENTINA ‡	1970	MF	21	17	15	14	12	11	9			
		F	21	17	15	14	12	11	10			
	1975	MF	20	17	15	14	13	12	10			
		F	19	16	15	14	13	12	11			
	1976	MF	20	17	15	14	12	12	10			
		F	19	16	15	14	13	12	11			
	1977	MF	20	16	15	14	12	11	10			
		F	20	16	15	14	13	11	11			
BOLIVIA	1970	MF	27	19	15	11	9	7	6	5		
		F	30	20	15	11	8	6	5	5		
	1974	MF	25	19	15	12	10	8	7	6		
		F	27	20	15	11	9	7	6	5		
	1975	MF	27	18	15	11	10	7	7	5		
BRAZIL	1970	MF	45	22	16	17						
	1974	MF	32	16	13	11	9	7	6	5		
		F	31	16	13	11	9	8	6	5		
	1975	MF	31	16	13	11	10	8	6	5		
CHILE	1970	MF	19	17	15	14	12	10	8	6		
		F	19	16	15	14	12	10	8	6		
	1975	MF	16	15	14	13	13	11	10	8		
		F	16	15	14	13	13	11	10	8		
	1977	MF	16	14	14	14	13	12	10	8		
		F	16	14	13	14	13	12	11	9		
	1978	MF	16	14	13	13	13	12	10	9		
		F	16	14	13	13	13	12	11	9		
COLOMBIA	1970	MF	38	24	17	12	9					
		F	38	25	19	13	7					
	1974	MF	36	23	18	13	11					
		F	34	23	18	13	11					
	1975	MF	35	23	18	13	11					
		F	34	23	18	13	11					
	1977	MF	35	23	18	13	11					
		F	34	23	18	13	11					
	1978	MF	*35	*23	*18	*13	*11					
		F	*34	*23	*18	*13	*11					

Percentage distribution (first level) by grade 3.5
Répartition en pourcentage (premier degré) par années d'études
Distribución en porcentaje (primer grado) por años de estudio

COUNTRY PAYS PAIS	YEAR ANNEE AÑO	SEX SEXE SEXO	GRADE / ANNEES D'ETUDES / AÑOS DE ESTUDIO									
			I	II	III	IV	V	VI	VII	VIII	IX	X
•ECUADOR ‡	1970	MF	29	19	17	14	11	10				
		F	29	20	17	14	11	9				
	1975	MF	26	19	17	14	12	11				
		F	27	19	17	15	12	11				
	1976	MF	26	20	16	14	12	11				
		F	26	19	16	15	12	11				
	1977	MF	26	19	16	14	13	12				
		F	26	19	16	14	13	12				
FALKLAND ISLANDS (MALVINAS)	1971	MF	10	12	17	9	13	15	11	13		
		F	13	13	20	9	8	16	10	12		
	1975	MF	17	22	10	18	16	18				
		F	13	19	13	18	16	20				
	1977	MF	17	22	10	18	16	18				
		F	13	19	13	18	16	20				
	1978	MF	16	19	18	15	14	19				
		F	13	18	21	16	13	18				
FRENCH GUIANA ‡	1970	MF	25	22	18	19	10	3	4			
		F	24	23	18	18	10	3	4			
	1975	MF	27	22	20	17	14					
	1977	MF	25	22	19	18	16					
	1978	MF	24	21	20	18	17					
GUYANA ‡	1970	MF	18	15	16	17	17	18				
		F	18	15	16	17	17	18				
	1975	MF	18	17	17	17	15	16				
		F	17	17	17	18	15	16				
	1976	MF	20	16	16	17	16	16				
		F	19	16	16	17	16	16				
PARAGUAY ‡	1970	MF	29	23	18	13	10	7				
		F	30	23	18	13	10	7				
	1975	MF	27	22	18	14	11	8				
		F	27	22	18	14	11	8				
	1976	MF	27	22	18	14	11	8				
		F	27	21	18	14	11	9				
	1977	MF	27	22	17	14	11	9				
		F	27	22	18	14	11	9				
PERU	1970	MF	28	20	16	14	12	10				
		F	28	20	16	14	12	10				
	1975	MF	24	20	17	15	12	10				
	1977	MF	22	19	18	16	14	12				
		F	*22	*19	*18	*16	*13	*11				
	1978	MF	21	19	17	16	15	12				
SURINAME	1975	MF	21	18	17	17	15	13				
		F	20	17	17	17	16	14				
	1977	MF	21	18	16	17	15	13				
		F	20	17	16	17	16	14				

Percentage distribution (first level) by grade
Répartition en pourcentage (premier degré) par années d'études
Distribución en porcentaje (primer grado) por años de estudio

COUNTRY PAYS PAIS	YEAR ANNEE AÑO	SEX SEXE SEXO	GRADE / ANNEES D'ETUDES / AÑOS DE ESTUDIO									
			I	II	III	IV	V	VI	VII	VIII	IX	X
SURINAME (CONT.)	1978	MF	21	18	17	16	15	13				
		F	20	17	17	16	16	14				
URUGUAY ‡	1970	MF	20	18	18	16	15	13				
	1975	MF	19	17	17	16	16	14				
	1977	MF	21	18	17	16	15	14				
		F	20	18	16	16	15	14				
	1978	MF	20	18	17	16	15	13				
		F	20	18	17	16	15	14				
VENEZUELA	1970	MF	22	21	18	16	13	10				
		F	21	20	18	16	14	11				
	1975	MF	23	19	17	16	14	11				
		F	22	19	17	16	14	12				
	1977	MF	23	20	18	16	13	11				
		F	22	19	18	16	13	12				
	1978	MF	22	19	18	16	13	11				
ASIA												
AFGHANISTAN	1970	MF	24	20	18	16	12	9				
		F	27	20	18	15	12	9				
	1974	MF	26	19	18	15	12	10				
		F	27	21	19	14	11	9				
	1975	MF	22	18	17	13	11	8	7	5		
		F	23	19	17	13	10	8	6	4		
	1976	MF	21	17	16	14	11	8	8	5		
		F	22	18	16	14	10	8	8	4		
	1977	MF	22	16	16	14	11	9	7	5		
		F	23	18	17	15	10	8	5	3		
BAHRAIN ‡	1970	MF	*18	*16	*16	*20	*15	*14				
		F	*18	*17	*18	*18	*14	*15				
	1975	MF	*18	*18	*18	*18	*15	*13				
		F	*18	*18	*18	*18	*15	*13				
	1977	MF	17	16	17	18	17	15				
		F	18	17	17	17	16	15				
	1978	MF	18	17	16	17	16	16				
		F	19	17	16	16	16	16				
BANGLADESH	1969	MF	37	22	17	14	11					
		F	41	22	16	12	9					
	1977	MF	39	20	16	12	12					
		F	41	20	16	11	11					
	1978	MF	39	21	16	12	12					
		F	41	20	16	11	11					
BHUTAN ‡	1977	MF	51	17	13	9	6	4				
		F	55	17	12	8	5	4				
	1978	MF	50	17	13	9	6	4				
		F	52	17	12	8	6	4				

Percentage distribution (first level) by grade 3.5
Répartition en pourcentage (premier degré) par années d'études
Distribución en porcentaje (primer grado) por años de estudio

COUNTRY PAYS PAIS	YEAR ANNEE AÑO	SEX SEXE SEXO	GRADE / ANNEES D'ETUDES / AÑOS DE ESTUDIO									
			I	II	III	IV	V	VI	VII	VIII	IX	X
BRUNEI	1974	MF	15	14	14	23	14	19				
		F	15	15	14	23	14	19				
	1975	MF	15	15	14	22	16	17				
		F	15	15	15	22	16	17				
	1977	MF	16	14	14	14	16	25				
		F	16	14	14	14	16	25				
	1978	MF	16	15	14	14	16	26				
		F	16	15	14	14	16	26				
BURMA ‡	1970	MF	37	22	17	14	10					
		F	39	23	17	13	9					
	1975	MF	37	21	17	14	10					
		F	38	22	17	14	9					
	1976	MF	37	21	18	14	10					
		F	38	22	17	14	10					
	1977	MF	37	21	17	14	10					
		F	38	21	17	14	10					
CYPRUS ‡	1970	MF	17	16	16	16	17	17	1	0		
		F	16	16	16	16	17	18	1	0		
	1975	MF	19	15	17	16	15	17	0	0		
		F	19	15	17	16	15	17	0	0		
	1977	MF	16	16	18	15	18	17	0	—		
		F	16	16	18	15	18	17	0	—		
	1978	MF	16	16	16	19	16	18	0			
		F	15	16	16	19	16	18	0			
DEMOCRATIC KAMPUCHEA	1970	MF	34	20	16	12	9	8				
		F	35	20	17	12	9	7				
	1972	MF	36	22	15	11	9	7				
		F	37	22	15	11	8	7				
HONG KONG	1970	MF	18	17	18	18	16	13				
		F	18	17	18	18	16	13				
	1975	MF	15	15	17	18	18	17				
		F	15	15	17	18	18	17				
	1976	MF	15	15	16	17	19	18				
		F	15	15	16	17	18	18				
	1977	MF	16	15	16	17	18	18				
		F	16	15	16	17	18	19				
INDIA	1970	MF	36	22	17	14	11					
		F	37	22	17	13	10					
	1975	MF	33	22	18	14	12					
		F	35	22	18	14	11					
	1976	MF	33	23	18	15	12					
		F	35	23	18	14	11					
INDONESIA ‡	1971	MF	23	21	19	16	12	9				
	1975	MF	27	21	17	14	11	9				
		F	28	21	17	14	11	8				
	1977	MF	25	22	18	15	11	9				
		F	25	22	18	15	11	9				

3.5 Percentage distribution (first level) by grade
Répartition en pourcentage (premier degré) par années d'études
Distribución en porcentaje (primer grado) por años de estudio

COUNTRY PAYS PAIS	YEAR ANNEE AÑO	SEX SEXE SEXO	GRADE / ANNEES D'ETUDES / AÑOS DE ESTUDIO									
			I	II	III	IV	V	VI	VII	VIII	IX	X
INDONESIA (CONT.) ‡	1978	MF	26	21	18	15	12	9				
		F	26	21	18	14	11	9				
IRAN	1970	MF	23	20	17	15	13	12				
		F	24	20	17	15	13	11				
	1975	MF	27	23	18	16	16					
		F	30	23	17	15	14					
	1976	MF	26	22	19	16	16					
		F	28	23	19	15	14					
	1977	MF	26	22	19	17	17					
		F	27	22	19	17	15					
IRAQ	1970	MF	25	18	15	15	16	11				
		F	26	19	15	15	15	9				
	1975	MF	25	19	15	15	15	10				
		F	29	20	15	14	13	8				
	1977	MF	19	20	18	16	15	12				
		F	22	22	18	15	13	9				
	1978	MF	27	16	16	16	14	10				
		F	35	16	16	14	11	8				
ISRAEL	1974	MF	14	13	13	13	12	12	12	11		
		F	14	13	13	13	12	12	12	11		
	1975	MF	14	13	13	13	13	12	11	11		
		F	14	13	13	13	13	12	11	11		
	1976	MF	15	14	13	12	12	12	11	11		
		F	15	14	13	12	12	12	11	11		
	1977	MF	15	14	13	12	12	12	12	11		
		F	15	14	13	12	12	12	11	11		
JAPAN ‡	1970	MF	17	17	16	16	16	17				
		F	17	17	16	16	16	17				
	1975	MF	18	18	15	16	17	16				
		F	18	18	15	16	17	16				
	1977	MF	18	17	17	17	14	16				
		F	18	17	17	17	14	16				
	1978	MF	18	17	17	17	17	14				
		F	18	17	17	17	17	14				
JORDAN ‡	1970	MF	21	20	17	16	14	12				
		F	22	21	17	16	13	11				
	1975	MF	18	17	18	17	16	14				
		F	19	17	18	17	16	13				
	1977	MF	18	17	17	17	16	15				
		F	19	17	17	17	16	14				
	1978	MF	19	17	16	17	16	15				
		F	19	17	16	17	16	14				
KOREA, REPUBLIC OF	1970	MF	18	17	17	17	16	15				
		F	18	17	17	17	15	15				
	1975	MF	18	16	17	16	16	17				
		F	17	16	17	16	16	17				

Percentage distribution (first level) by grade 3.5
Répartition en pourcentage (premier degré) par années d'études
Distribución en porcentaje (primer grado) por años de estudio

COUNTRY PAYS PAIS	YEAR ANNEE AÑO	SEX SEXE SEXO	I	II	III	IV	V	VI	VII	VIII	IX	X
KOREA, REPUBLIC OF (CONT.)	1978	MF	18	17	16	17	16	16				
		F	18	17	16	17	16	16				
	1979	MF	17	18	17	16	17	16				
		F	17	18	17	16	17	16				
KUWAIT ‡	1970	MF	25	25	26	24						
		F	26	25	26	23						
	1975	MF	29	26	23	21						
		F	29	26	23	21						
	1977	MF	28	28	24	21						
		F	28	28	23	21						
	1978	MF	26	27	26	21						
		F	26	27	26	20						
LAO PEOPLE'S DEMOCRATIC REPUBLIC	1970	MF	41	20	15	10	7	7				
		F	44	21	15	9	6	5				
	1976	MF	49	20	13	10	9					
		F	52	20	12	9	7					
	1977	MF	45	23	14	10	8					
		F	46	23	14	10	8					
MALAYSIA												
PENINSULAR MALAYSIA ‡	1970	MF	18	18	18	16	15	14				
		F	19	18	18	16	15	13				
	1975	MF	18	17	17	16	16	15				
		F	18	17	17	16	16	15				
	1977	MF	17	17	17	17	16	16				
	1978	MF	18	17	16	17	16	16				
SABAH	1970	MF	19	17	16	15	15	17				
		F	20	17	16	15	15	16				
	1975	MF	20	17	17	16	15	16				
		F	20	17	17	16	15	15				
	1976	MF	19	18	17	16	15	15				
		F	20	18	17	16	15	15				
	1977	MF	18	18	17	16	15	16				
SARAWAK	1970	MF	20	18	18	15	16	13				
		F	20	18	18	15	16	12				
	1975	MF	20	20	17	17	14	13				
		F	20	20	17	17	14	12				
	1976	MF	20	18	18	16	15	13				
		F	20	18	18	16	15	13				
MONGOLIA	1970	MF	28	25	24	22						
	1975	MF	35	34	31							
		F	35	34	32							
NEPAL	1975	MF	57	24	19							
		F	58	24	18							
	1976	MF	61	22	17							
		F	66	20	15							

3.5 Percentage distribution (first level) by grade
Répartition en pourcentage (premier degré) par années d'études
Distribución en porcentaje (primer grado) por años de estudio

COUNTRY PAYS PAIS	YEAR ANNEE AÑO	SEX SEXE SEXO	GRADE / ANNEES D'ETUDES / AÑOS DE ESTUDIO									
			I	II	III	IV	V	VI	VII	VIII	IX	X
NEPAL (CONT.)	1977	MF	59	24	17							
		F	65	21	14							
OMAN	1970	MF	66	17	9	4	3	1				
		F	63	18	10	9	–	–				
	1975	MF	23	29	20	15	9	3				
		F	30	31	21	11	5	2				
	1977	MF	26	20	17	19	12	7				
		F	29	21	17	18	10	5				
	1978	MF	24	21	16	16	14	8				
		F	28	23	16	14	12	7				
PAKISTAN	1970	MF	32	22	18	15	12					
		F	36	22	17	14	11					
	1974	MF	32	21	18	15	13					
		F	35	21	17	15	12					
	1975	MF	32	22	18	16	13					
		F	35	21	17	15	12					
PHILIPPINES ‡	1970	MF	23	19	17	15	14	12				
	1975	MF	22	19	17	16	14	12				
		F	21	18	17	16	15	13				
	1976	MF	21	18	17	16	15	13				
QATAR ‡	1970	MF	22	20	18	17	14	9				
		F	23	20	18	17	14	7				
	1975	MF	20	19	17	17	15	12				
		F	21	19	18	17	15	11				
	1977	MF	19	19	17	16	15	13				
		F	19	18	17	17	16	13				
	1978	MF	20	18	17	17	15	13				
		F	20	17	17	17	16	13				
SAUDI ARABIA ‡	1970	MF	24	19	18	17	12	9				
		F	25	22	19	16	11	7				
	1975	MF	24	19	17	17	13	10				
		F	24	20	17	16	13	9				
	1976	MF	22	20	17	16	14	11				
		F	22	20	18	16	13	11				
	1977	MF	22	19	18	16	14	11				
		F	22	19	18	17	14	11				
SINGAPORE	1970	MF	15	15	16	16	17	21				
		F	16	16	16	17	17	19				
	1975	MF	14	14	16	16	17	22				
		F	14	15	16	17	18	21				
	1977	MF	15	15	16	17	17	20				
		F	16	15	16	17	18	20				
	1978	MF	16	16	16	17	17	19				
		F	16	16	16	17	17	19				
SRI LANKA ‡	1970	MF	25	22	21	18	15					
		F	25	22	20	18	15					

Percentage distribution (first level) by grade 3.5
Répartition en pourcentage (premier degré) par années d'études
Distribución en porcentaje (primer grado) por años de estudio

COUNTRY PAYS PAIS	YEAR ANNEE AÑO	SEX SEXE SEXO	GRADE / ANNEES D'ETUDES / AÑOS DE ESTUDIO									
			I	II	III	IV	V	VI	VII	VIII	IX	X
SRI LANKA (CONT.) ‡	1975	MF F	25 25	23 23	19 20	14 13	19 20					
	1978	MF	14	22	19	17	15	13				
	1979	MF	*16	*17	*20	*18	*1	*14				
SYRIAN ARAB REPUBLIC ‡	1970	MF F	23 26	20 21	17 17	15 14	13 12	11 10				
	1975	MF F	20 21	18 19	17 18	17 17	15 14	13 11				
	1977	MF F	21 22	18 19	17 17	16 16	14 14	13 12				
	1978	MF F	21 22	19 19	17 18	16 16	14 14	13 11				
THAILAND	1970	MF F	26 27	21 22	20 20	17 17	7 6	5 4	4 4			
	1975	MF F	23 24	19 19	19 19	17 17	9 9	7 7	6 6			
	1976	MF F	23 23	19 19	18 19	16 17	10 9	8 7	6 6			
	1977	MF F	22 22	19 19	18 18	16 16	10 10	8 8	7 6			
TURKEY	1970	MF F	25 26	20 21	19 19	19 18	16 15					
	1976	MF F	23 23	21 21	20 20	18 18	19 18					
	1977	MF F	23 23	21 21	20 20	19 19	17 17					
UNITED ARAB EMIRATES ‡	1974	MF F	24 25	21 21	18 18	16 14	13 13	9 8				
	1975	MF F	22 24	21 22	18 18	16 15	13 13	9 8				
	1977	MF F	19 20	19 20	19 20	17 17	14 13	11 10				
	1978	MF F	18 18	19 19	19 19	18 18	15 14	12 11				
VIET-NAM	1976	MF F	28 28	22 22	19 19	17 17	14 14					
YEMEN	1970	MF	39	25	17	10	6	4				
	1972	MF F	42 49	25 23	16 12	8 8	5 5	4 3				
	1973	MF F	40 41	24 24	17 16	9 9	6 6	4 4				
YEMEN, DEMOCRATIC	1970	MF F	32 34	22 21	17 16	12 11	9 10	7 7				
	1975	MF F	23 26	21 23	19 20	14 13	12 10	11 8				

3.5 Percentage distribution (first level) by grade
Répartition en pourcentage (premier degré) par années d'études
Distribución en porcentaje (primer grado) por años de estudio

COUNTRY PAYS PAIS	YEAR ANNEE AÑO	SEX SEXE SEXO	GRADE / ANNEES D'ETUDES / AÑOS DE ESTUDIO									
			I	II	III	IV	V	VI	VII	VIII	IX	X
YEMEN, DEMOCRATIC (CONT.)	1976	MF	21	19	19	18	13	11				
		F	23	21	21	18	11	8				
	1977	MF	20	16	18	18	17	12				
		F	22	17	19	18	15	10				
EUROPE												
AUSTRIA	1970	MF	26	25	25	24						
		F	26	25	25	24						
	1975	MF	25	25	25	25						
		F	25	25	25	25						
	1977	MF	24	24	26	26						
		F	24	24	26	26						
	1978	MF	24	24	25	27						
		F	23	24	25	27						
BELGIUM ‡	1970	MF	19	17	16	16	16	15				
		F	19	17	16	16	16	16				
	1975	MF	17	16	16	17	17	17				
		F	18	16	16	17	17	17				
	1976	MF	17	16	16	17	17	17				
		F	17	16	16	16	17	17				
	1977	MF	17	16	16	16	17	17				
		F	17	16	16	16	17	17				
BULGARIA ‡	1970	MF	14	13	13	13	13	12	12	11		
		F	14	13	13	13	13	12	12	11		
	1975	MF	14	12	12	12	12	13	12	12		
		F	14	12	12	12	12	13	12	12		
	1977	MF	14	14	13	12	12	12	12	12		
		F	14	14	14	12	12	12	12	12		
	1978	MF	14	13	14	13	12	12	12	11		
		F	14	13	14	14	12	11	11	11		
CZECHOSLOVAKIA	1970	MF	12	11	11	11	11	11	12	11	10	
		F	12	11	11	11	11	11	12	11	11	
	1975	MF	11	11	11	11	12	12	11	10	9	
		F	11	11	11	11	12	12	11	11	9	
	1977	MF	12	11	11	11	11	11	12	12	9	
		F	12	11	11	11	11	11	12	12	9	
	1978	MF	13	12	11	11	11	11	11	11	9	
		F	13	12	11	11	11	11	11	11	9	
DENMARK	1970	MF	18	17	16	16	16	16				
		F	18	17	16	16	16	16				
	1975	MF	15	16	18	18	17	16				
	1976	MF	15	15	17	18	18	17				
	1977	MF	15	15	16	17	19	19				
FINLAND ‡	1970	MF	20	20	20	20	11	9	0			
	1975	MF	16	16	16	16	18	18				

Percentage distribution (first level) by grade 3.5
Répartition en pourcentage (premier degré) par années d'études
Distribución en porcentaje (primer grado) por años de estudio

COUNTRY PAYS PAIS	YEAR ANNEE AÑO	SEX SEXE SEXO	GRADE / ANNEES D'ETUDES / AÑOS DE ESTUDIO									
			I	II	III	IV	V	VI	VII	VIII	IX	X
FINLAND (CONT.) ‡	1977	MF	15	15	17	17	18	18				
		F	15	15	17	17	18	18				
	1978	MF	15	16	16	17	18	18				
		F	15	16	16	17	18	18				
FRANCE ‡	1970	MF	22	19	18	19	19	3				
		F	22	19	19	19	19	3				
	1975	MF	22	19	19	20	20	—				
	1977	MF	22	20	19	19	20	—				
		F	22	20	19	19	20	—				
	1978	MF	22	20	19	19	19	—				
		F	21	20	19	19	20	—				
GERMANY, FEDERAL REPUBLIC OF ‡	1970	MF	27	26	25	21						
		F	27	26	25	21						
	1975	MF	24	25	25	25						
		F	24	25	25	25						
	1976	MF	23	25	26	26						
		F	23	25	26	26						
	1977	MF	23	24	26	27						
		F	23	24	26	27						
GIBRALTAR	1971	MF	6	13	13	15	10	13	13	16		
		F	6	13	13	15	11	14	12	16		
	1975	MF	11	12	12	12	13	13	14	14		
		F	11	11	13	12	12	13	14	14		
	1976	MF	10	13	12	13	12	13	14	14		
		F	10	12	13	13	13	12	14	13		
	1977	MF	10	11	13	11	13	12	12	18		
		F	9	12	13	11	15	12	11	17		
GREECE ‡	1970	MF	18	17	16	16	17	16				
		F	18	17	16	16	16	16				
	1975	MF	17	17	17	17	16	15				
		F	17	17	17	17	16	15				
	1976	MF	17	17	17	17	17	16				
		F	17	17	17	17	17	16				
HUNGARY	1970	MF	12	11	11	12	13	13	13	14		
		F	12	11	11	12	13	13	13	14		
	1975	MF	15	14	13	12	12	12	11	11		
		F	15	14	13	12	12	12	11	11		
	1977	MF	14	14	13	13	12	12	11	11		
		F	14	14	13	13	12	12	11	11		
	1978	MF	14	13	13	13	13	12	11	11		
		F	14	13	13	13	13	12	11	·11		
ICELAND	1970	MF	17	17	16	17	17	16				
		F	17	17	16	17	17	16				
	1975	MF	15	16	17	17	17	18				
		F	15	16	17	17	18	17				

3.5 Percentage distribution (first level) by grade
Répartition en pourcentage (premier degré) par années d'études
Distribución en porcentaje (primer grado) por años de estudio

COUNTRY PAYS PAIS	YEAR ANNEE AÑO	SEX SEXE SEXO	GRADE / ANNEES D'ETUDES / AÑOS DE ESTUDIO									
			I	II	III	IV	V	VI	VII	VIII	IX	X
ICELAND (CONT.)	1976	MF	16	16	16	17	18	18				
		F	16	15	16	17	17	18				
IRELAND	1975	MF	17	17	17	17	17	16				
		F	17	17	17	17	17	16				
	1977	MF	17	17	17	16	16	17				
		F	17	17	17	16	16	17				
	1978	MF	17	17	17	16	16	16				
		F	17	17	17	16	16	16				
ITALY	1970	MF	22	21	20	19	18					
		F	22	21	20	19	18					
	1975	MF	19	20	20	21	21					
		F	19	20	20	21	21					
	1976	MF	18	20	20	20	21					
		F	18	20	20	20	21					
	1977	MF	19	20	20	20	20					
		F	19	20	21	20	20					
LUXEMBOURG	1970	MF	17	15	15	15	14	14	5	3	1	
		F	17	15	15	15	14	14	5	4	2	
	1975	MF	18	16	17	17	17	15				
		F	17	16	17	17	17	16				
	1977	MF	18	16	17	17	16	16				
		F	18	16	17	16	17	17				
	1978	MF	17	16	17	17	17	16				
		F	16	16	17	17	17	17				
MALTA ‡	1970	MF	13	14	18	18	18	18	1	1		
		F	12	14	18	17	18	18	1	1		
	1975	MF	20	16	17	15	17	14	0	0		
		F	20	16	17	16	17	14	0	0		
	1976	MF	17	19	16	16	16	17				
		F	17	19	15	16	16	17				
	1977	MF	17	17	19	16	16	15				
		F	17	17	19	15	16	16				
NETHERLANDS	1970	MF	18	17	17	16	16	16				
		F	18	17	17	17	16	16				
	1975	MF	18	17	16	16	17	16				
		F	17	17	16	16	17	17				
	1977	MF	17	17	17	16	16	16				
		F	17	17	17	16	16	16				
	1978	MF	16	17	17	17	16	16				
		F	16	17	17	17	17	16				
NORWAY	1970	MF	16	16	16	16	16	16	5			
		F	16	16	16	16	16	16	5			
	1975	MF	17	17	17	17	16	16				
		F	17	17	17	17	16	16				
	1976	MF	17	17	17	17	17	16				
		F	17	17	17	17	17	16				

Percentage distribution (first level) by grade   3.5
Répartition en pourcentage (premier degré) par années d'études
Distribución en porcentaje (primer grado) por años de estudio

COUNTRY PAYS PAIS	YEAR ANNEE AÑO	SEX SEXE SEXO	GRADE / ANNEES D'ETUDES / AÑOS DE ESTUDIO									
			I	II	III	IV	V	VI	VII	VIII	IX	X
NORWAY (CONT.)	1977	MF	16	17	17	17	17	17				
		F	16	17	17	17	17	16				
POLAND	1970	MF	11	11	12	12	14	14	14	13		
	1975	MF	12	11	12	12	13	13	13	13		
	1976	MF	12	12	12	12	13	13	13	13		
	1977	MF	13	12	12	12	13	13	13	13		
PORTUGAL ‡	1970	MF	28	24	22	20	4	2				
		F	28	23	22	21	4	2				
	1975	MF	16	25	18	17	13	11				
		F	16	24	18	17	13	11				
	1976	MF	39	——>	35	——>	13	12				
		F	39	——>	36	——>	13	12				
	1977	MF	42	——>	34	——>	13	11				
		F	41	——>	35	——>	13	11				
ROMANIA	1970	MF	13	12	12	12	12	12	12	12	2	1
		F	12	12	12	11	12	12	12	12	3	2
	1972	MF	11	11	12	13	13	12	12	12	2	1
		F	11	11	12	12	13	12	12	12	4	2
	1973	MF	15	10	11	12	13	13	12	11	2	1
		F	15	10	11	12	13	13	12	11	3	1
SAN MARINO	1970	MF	21	20	20	20	19					
		F	20	23	19	19	18					
	1975	MF	19	21	19	20	20					
		F	18	21	21	20	21					
	1977	MF	19	18	20	22	21					
		F	17	19	19	23	22					
	1978	MF	19	19	19	21	22					
		F	21	17	19	20	23					
SPAIN	1970	MF	26	19	19	18	9	5	3	2		
		F	25	19	19	18	9	5	3	2		
	1975	MF	21	20	20	20	20					
		F	21	20	20	20	20					
	1976	MF	21	20	20	20	20					
		F	21	20	20	20	20					
SWEDEN	1970	MF	18	17	16	16	16	16				
		F	18	17	16	16	16	16				
	1975	MF	16	17	17	17	17	16				
		F	16	17	17	17	17	16				
	1977	MF	16	16	16	17	17	17				
		F	16	15	16	17	17	17				
	1978	MF	17	16	16	17	18	18				
		F	17	16	16	17	18	18				
SWITZERLAND ‡	1975	MF	17	17	18	18	16	13				
		F	17	17	18	18	16	13				
	1977	MF	18	18	19	19	15	11				
		F	17	18	19	19	15	11				

3.5 **Percentage distribution (first level) by grade**
Répartition en pourcentage (premier degré) par années d'études
Distribución en porcentaje (primer grado) por años de estudio

COUNTRY PAYS PAIS	YEAR ANNEE AÑO	SEX SEXE SEXO	GRADE / ANNEES D'ETUDES / AÑOS DE ESTUDIO									
			I	II	III	IV	V	VI	VII	VIII	IX	X
SWITZERLAND (CONT.) ‡	1978	MF	17	18	19	19	15	11				
		F	17	18	19	20	15	11				
YUGOSLAVIA ‡	1970	MF	26	25	25	24						
		F	26	25	25	24						
	1975	MF	25	25	25	25						
		F	25	25	25	25						
	1977	MF	25	25	25	25						
		F	25	25	25	25						
	1978	MF	26	25	25	25						
		F	26	25	25	25						
OCEANIA												
AMERICAN SAMOA ‡	1971	MF	15	14	14	15	13	12	9	7		
	1975	MF	13	14	12	12	12	13	12	12		
	1976	MF	12	13	13	11	12	13	13	12		
	1977	MF	13	12	13	13	12	12	13	12		
AUSTRALIA	1971	MF	19	15	15	15	15	15	5			
		F	19	15	15	15	15	15	5			
	1975	MF	17	16	15	15	15	16	5			
		F	17	16	15	15	15	16	5			
	1976	MF	17	16	15	15	15	15	5			
		F	17	16	16	15	15	15	5			
	1977	MF	18	16	16	15	15	15	5			
		F	18	16	16	15	15	15	5			
COOK ISLANDS	1971	MF	13	13	13	16	12	11	11	11		
		F	13	12	12	16	13	12	11	11		
	1973	MF	13	12	12	12	12	15	11	13		
		F	13	12	13	11	12	15	11	13		
FIJI	1970	MF	15	14	14	13	12	11	11	9		
		F	15	14	15	13	12	11	11	9		
	1974	MF	13	14	13	13	13	12	11	10		
		F	13	14	13	13	13	12	11	11		
	1975	MF	13	13	14	13	13	13	11	11		
		F	13	13	14	13	13	13	11	11		
	1976	MF	13	13	13	14	13	13	12	11		
		F	13	12	13	14	13	13	12	11		
	1977	MF	13	13	13	13	13	13	12	11		
		F	13	12	12	13	13	13	12	11		
FRENCH POLYNESIA	1971	MF	22	21	20	17	12	8				
		F	22	20	19	17	13	9				
	1974	MF	22	20	19	17	12	9				
		F	22	20	18	18	14	9				
	1975	MF	21	20	19	17	13	10				
		F	20	20	19	17	14	10				

Percentage distribution (first level) by grade   3.5
Répartition en pourcentage (premier degré) par années d'études
Distribución en porcentaje (primer grado) por años de estudio

COUNTRY PAYS PAIS	YEAR ANNEE AÑO	SEX SEXE SEXO	GRADE / ANNEES D'ETUDES / AÑOS DE ESTUDIO									
			I	II	III	IV	V	VI	VII	VIII	IX	X
FRENCH POLYNESIA (CONT.)	1976	MF	20	20	19	18	12	11				
		F	20	19	19	19	14	10				
GUAM ‡	1970	MF	17	18	22	15	15	14				
		F	17	18	22	14	15	14				
	1975	MF	51	——>	——>	16	17	16				
	1976	MF	51	——>	——>	16	17	16				
KIRIBATI	1977	MF	13	13	13	13	13	14	9	8	5	
		F	14	13	13	13	13	14	9	7	5	
	1978	MF	11	13	14	13	13	14	10	7	5	
		F	11	13	14	13	13	14	10	7	5	
NAURU	1973	MF	20	15	18	12	11	14	10			
		F	21	15	17	12	11	14	11			
	1974	MF	15	20	14	11	17	11	12			
		F	14	22	14	11	16	12	12			
NEW CALEDONIA	1970	MF	24	19	17	17	13	11				
		F	23	18	17	17	13	12				
	1975	MF	21	17	17	18	15	11				
		F	21	17	17	18	16	11				
	1976	MF	23	17	17	17	15	11				
		F	22	18	16	17	16	11				
NEW HEBRIDES	1970	MF	24	21	17	16	9	6	6			
		F	24	22	18	17	8	6	6			
	1975	MF	20	20	17	16	13	12	3			
		F	20	20	17	16	12	12	3			
	1976	MF	19	20	17	16	13	13	3			
		F	20	20	17	16	12	12	3			
	1977	MF	20	19	17	16	13	13	3			
		F	20	19	17	16	13	12	3			
NEW ZEALAND ‡	1970	MF	36	——>	16	16	16	15				
		F	36	——>	16	17	16	15				
	1975	MF	36	——>	16	16	16	16				
		F	36	——>	16	16	16	16				
	1976	MF	37	——>	16	16	16	16				
		F	37	——>	16	16	16	16				
NIUE	1970	MF	17	15	14	14	13	12	14			
		F	17	17	14	14	13	13	12			
	1975	MF	13	9	11	10	18	13	15	12		
		F	12	8	10	11	16	14	16	12		
	1976	MF	15	12	13	11	13	12	14	11		
		F	16	10	12	12	15	11	11	14		
NORFOLK ISLAND	1975	MF	16	15	14	13	12	13	16			
		F	14	11	16	17	10	15	18			
	1977	MF	17	18	16	15	13	9	12			
		F	18	14	14	20	16	4	13			
	1978	MF	15	16	18	17	15	12	8			
		F	14	18	15	13	19	15	4			

3.5 Percentage distribution (first level) by grade
Répartition en pourcentage (premier degré) par années d'études
Distribución en porcentaje (primer grado) por años de estudio

COUNTRY PAYS PAIS	YEAR ANNEE AÑO	SEX SEXE SEXO	I	II	III	IV	V	VI	VII	VIII	IX	X
						GRADE / ANNEES D'ETUDES / AÑOS DE ESTUDIO						
PACIFIC ISLANDS	1970	MF	14	13	13	14	12	12	11	11		
		F	15	13	13	14	12	11	11	10		
	1975	MF	15	13	13	13	12	12	11	12		
		F	14	13	13	13	12	12	12	11		
	1976	MF	16	13	13	12	12	12	11	11		
		F	15	13	13	12	12	12	11	12		
PAPUA NEW GUINEA	1974	MF	20	20	16	16	15	13				
		F	21	20	16	16	15	12				
	1975	MF	22	17	18	15	15	14				
		F	22	18	18	14	15	13				
	1977	MF	23	18	18	14	14	12				
		F	25	19	18	14	14	11				
	1978	MF	21	20	17	16	13	13				
		F	22	21	17	16	12	12				
SAMOA	1970	MF	15	15	14	13	13	13	17			
		F	16	15	14	13	12	13	17			
	1975	MF	14	18	13	14	14	13	13			
		F	14	15	13	20	13	13	13			
	1977	MF	15	15	15	15	14	14	13			
		F	15	15	15	15	14	14	13			
	1978	MF	15	15	15	15	15	14	13			
		F	15	14	14	15	14	14	14			
SOLOMON ISLANDS	1971	MF	21	20	17	16	10	8	8			
	1974	MF	20	19	17	16	11	9	8			
		F	22	21	17	15	10	8	7			
	1975	MF	21	16	17	15	14	9	8			
		F	23	17	18	14	13	8	7			
TOKELAU ISLANDS	1976	MF	16	15	13	14	10	11	11	10		
		F	13	16	13	13	11	12	10	11		
	1977	MF	13	15	14	13	14	10	11	10		
		F	12	14	15	13	14	10	11	12		
	1978	MF	20	13	13	12	12	12	9	10		
		F	24	11	13	13	11	11	7	9		
	1979	MF	20	12	13	12	12	11	10	9		
		F	22	11	13	11	12	10	10	10		
TONGA	1975	MF	18	22	16	14	11	19				
		F	18	23	16	14	11	18				
	1978	MF	14	14	16	21	15	19				
		F	14	14	17	22	15	19				
	1979	MF	14	13	14	16	21	21				
		F	14	13	14	17	21	21				
U.S.S.R.												
U.S.S.R.	1970	MF	13	12	13	13	13	13	12	11		
	1975	MF	12	11	12	12	13	13	13	14		

Percentage distribution (first level) by grade 3.5
Répartition en pourcentage (premier degré) par années d'études
Distribución en porcentaje (primer grado) por años de estudio

COUNTRY PAYS PAIS	YEAR ANNEE AÑO	SEX SEXE SEXO	GRADE / ANNEES D'ETUDES / AÑOS DE ESTUDIO									
			I	II	III	IV	V	VI	VII	VIII	IX	X
U.S.S.R. (CONT.)	1977	MF	13	12	12	12	12	12	13	14		
BYELORUSSIAN S.S.R.	1970	MF	12	12	13	13	13	13	12	12		
	1975	MF	11	11	12	12	13	13	14	15		
	1977	MF	12	11	12	12	13	13	14	14		
	1978	MF	13	12	12	12	12	13	13	14		
UKRAINIAN S.S.R.	1970	MF	12	12	13	13	13	13	12			
	1975	MF	12	12	12	12	13	13	13	14		
	1976	MF	12	12	12	12	12	13	14	14		
	1977	MF	13	12	12	12	12	12	13	14		

ALGERIA:
E—> ENROLMENT IN GRADE VII REFERS TO "FIN
D'ETUDES" CLASSES.
FR—> LES EFFECTIFS DE LA 7 EME ANNEE D'ETUDES
SE REFERENT AUX CLASSES DE FIN D'ETUDES.
ESP> LOS EFECTIVOS DEL SEPTIMO AÑO DE ESTUDIOS
SE REFIEREN A LAS CLASES DE "FIN D'ETUDES".

BENIN:
E—> FOR 1979, FEMALE ENROLMENT REFERS TO
PUBLIC EDUCATION ONLY.
FR—> POUR 1979, LES EFFECTIFS FEMININS SE
REFERENT A L'ENSEIGNEMENT PUBLIC SEULEMENT.
ESP> EN 1979, LA MATRICULA FEMENINA SE REFIERE
A LA ENSEÑANZA PUBLICA SOLAMENTE.

CHAD:
E—> FOR 1976, DATA DO NOT INCLUDE MOSLEM PRIVATE
EDUCATION (9,453 PUPILS IN 1975).
FR—> POUR 1976, LES DONNEES N'INCLUENT PAS
L'ENSEIGNEMENT PRIVE MUSULMAN (9 453 ELEVES EN 1975).
ESP> EN 1976, LOS DATOS NO INCLUYEN LA ENSEÑANZA
PRIVADA MUSULMANA (9 453 ALUMNOS EN 1975).

EGYPT:
E—> BEGINNING 1975, DATA DO NOT INCLUDE FIGURES
FOR AL AZHAR UNIVERSITY.
FR—> A PARTIR DE 1975, LES CHIFFRES N'INCLUENT PAS
LES DONNEES RELATIVES A L'UNIVERSITE AL AZHAR.
ESP> A PARTIR DE 1975, EXCLUIDOS LOS DATOS
RELATIVOS A LA UNIVERSIDAD AL AZHAR.

GHANA:
E—> BEGINNING 1975 DATA REFER TO PUBLIC
EDUCATION ONLY.
FR—> A PARTIR DE 1975 LES DONNEES SE REFERENT
A L'ENSEIGNEMENT PUBLIC SEULEMENT.
ESP> A PARTIR DE 1975 LOS DATOS SE REFIEREN A
LA ENSEÑANZA PUBLICA SOLAMENTE.

LIBERIA:
E—> DATA INCLUDE EDUCATION PRECEDING THE FIRST
LEVEL.
FR—> LES DONNEES INCLUENT L'EDUCATION PRECEDANT
LE PREMIER DEGRE.
ESP> LOS DATOS INCLUYEN LA ENSEÑANZA ANTERIOR
AL PRIMER GRADO.

MAURITIUS:
E—> DATA FOR 1977 AND 1978 DO NOT INCLUDE
RODRIGUEZ.
FR—> POUR 1977 ET 1978 LES DONNEES N'INCLUENT
PAS RODRIGUEZ.
ESP> EN 1977 Y 1978 LOS DATOS NO INCLUYEN
RODRIGUEZ.

SOMALIA:
E—> FOR 1976 AND 1977 DATA INCLUDE INTERMEDIATE
EDUCATION.
FR—> POUR 1976 ET 1977 LES DONNEES INCLUENT
L'ENSEIGNEMENT INTERMEDIAIRE.
ESP> EN 1976 Y 1977 LOS DATOS NO INCLUYEN LA
ENSEÑANZA INTERMEDIA.

TUNISIA:
E—> BEGINNING 1977, GRADE VII HAS BEEN
INTRODUCED EXPERIMENTALLY.
FR—> A PARTIR DE 1977, UNE SEPTIEME ANNEE
D'ETUDES A ETE CREEE A TITRE EXPERIMENTAL.
ESP> A PARTIR DE 1977, SE HA CREADO UN SEPTIMO
AÑO DE ESTUDIOS A TITULO EXPERIMENTAL.

UGANDA:
E—> DATA REFER TO GOVERNMENT—MAINTAINED AND
AIDED SCHOOLS ONLY.
FR—> LES DONNEES SE REFERENT AUX ECOLES
PUBLIQUES ET SUBVENTIONNEES SEULEMENT.
ESP> LOS DATOS SE REFIEREN A LAS ESCUELAS
PUBLICAS Y SUBVENCIONADAS SOLAMENTE.

UNITED REPUBLIC OF TANZANIA:
E—> FOR 1970 AND 1974 DATA REFER TO TANZANIA
MAINLAND ONLY.
FR—> POUR 1970 ET 1974 LES DONNEES SE REFERENT
A LA TANZANIE CONTINENTALE SEULEMENT.
ESP> EN 1970 Y 1974 LOS DATOS SE REFIEREN A
TANZANIA CONTINENTAL SOLAMENTE.

BARBADOS:
E—> FOR 1970 DATA REFER TO GOVERNMENT—
MAINTAINED AND AIDED SCHOOLS ONLY.
FR—> POUR 1970 LES DONNEES SE REFERENT AUX
ECOLES PUBLIQUES ET SUBVENTIONNEES SEULEMENT.
ESP> EN 1970 LOS DATOS SE REFIEREN A LAS
ESCUELAS PUBLICAS Y SUBVENCIONADAS SOLAMENTE.

3.5 Percentage distribution (first level) by grade
Répartition en pourcentage (premier degré) par années d'études
Distribución en porcentaje (primer grado) por años de estudio

BELIZE:
E—> DATA REFER TO GOVERNMENT—MAINTAINED AND AIDED SCHOOLS ONLY.
FR—> LES DONNEES SE REFERENT AUX ECOLES PUBLIQUES ET SUBVENTIONNEES SEULEMENT.
ESP> LOS DATOS SE REFIEREN A LAS ESCUELAS PUBLICAS Y SUBVENCIONADAS SOLAMENTE.

COSTA RICA:
E—> FOR 1978 DATA REFER TO PUBLIC EDUCATION ONLY.
FR—> POUR 1978 LES DONNEES SE REFERENT A L'ENSEIGNEMENT PUBLIC SEULEMENT.
ESP> EN 1978, LOS DATOS SE REFIEREN A LA ENSEÑANZA PUBLICA SOLAMENTE.

EL SALVADOR:
E—> DATA INCLUDE EVENING SCHOOLS.
FR—> LES DONNEES INCLUENT LES ECOLES DU SOIR.
ESP> LOS DATOS INCLUYEN LAS ESCUELAS NOCTURNAS.

GUADELOUPE:
E—> IN 1970, ENROLMENT IN GRADES VI AND VII REFERS TO "FIN D'ETUDES" CLASSES.
FR—> EN 1970, LES EFFECTIFS DES SIXIEME ET SEPTIEME ANNEES D'ETUDES SE REFERENT AUX CLASSES DE FIN D'ETUDES.
ESP> EN 1970, LOS EFECTIVOS PARA EL SEXTO Y SEPTIMO AÑO DE ESTUDIOS SE REFIEREN A LAS CLASES DE "FIN D'ETUDES".

HAITI:
E—> NOT INCLUDING PRIVATE RURAL SCHOOLS.
FR—> NON COMPRIS LES ECOLES PRIVEES RURALES.
ESP> LOS DATOS NO TOMAN EN CONSIDERACION LAS ESCUELAS PRIVADAS RURALES.

JAMAICA:
E—> FOR 1977 DATA REFER TO PUBLIC EDUCATION ONLY.
FR—> EN 1977 LES DONNEES SE REFERENT A L'ENSEIGNEMENT PUBLIC SEULEMENT.
ESP> EN 1977, LOS DATOS SE REFIEREN A LA ENSEÑANZA PUBLICA SOLAMENTE.

MARTINIQUE:
E—> IN 1970, ENROLMENT IN GRADES VI AND VII REFERS TO "FIN D'ETUDES" CLASSES.
FR—> EN 1970, LES EFFECTIFS DES SIXIEME ET SEPTIEME ANNEES D'ETUDES SE REFERENT AUX CLASSES DE FIN D'ETUDES.
ESP> EN 1970, LOS EFECTIVOS PARA EL SEXTO Y SEPTIMO AÑO DE ESTUDIOS SE REFIEREN A LAS CLASES DE "FIN D'ETUDES".

MONTSERRAT:
E—> ENROLMENT IN GRADES VIII AND IX REFERS TO "FIN D'ETUDES" CLASSES.
FR—> LES EFFECTIFS DES HUITIEME ET NEUVIEME ANNEES D'ETUDES SE REFERENT AUX CLASSES DE FIN D'ETUDES.
ESP> LOS EFECTIVOS PARA EL OCTAVO Y NOVENO AÑO DE ESTUDIOS SE REFIEREN A LAS CLASES DE "FIN D'ETUDES".

PANAMA (FORMER CANAL ZONE):
E—> ALL DATA REFER TO PUBLIC EDUCATION ONLY. FOR 1970 DATA INCLUDE SPECIAL EDUCATION.
FR—> TOUTES LES DONNEES SE REFERENT A L'ENSEIGNEMENT PUBLIC SEULEMENT. EN 1970 LES DONNEES INCLUENT L'EDUCATION SPECIALE.
ESP> TODOS LOS DATOS SE REFIEREN A LA ENSEÑANZA PUBLICA SOLAMENTE. EN 1970, LOS DATOS INCLUYEN LA EDUCACION ESPECIAL.

PUERTO RICO:
E—> ALL DATA REFER TO PUBLIC EDUCATION ONLY. DATA REFER TO ENROLMENT IN THE FIRST SIX GRADES OF FIRST LEVEL EDUCATION ONLY.
FR—> TOUTES LES DONNEES SE REFERENT A L'ENSEIGNEMENT PUBLIC SEULEMENT. LES DONNEES SE REFERENT AUX EFFECTIFS DES SIX PREMIERES ANNEES D'ETUDES DE L'ENSEIGNEMENT DU PREMIER DEGRE.
ESP> TODOS LOS DATOS SE REFIEREN A LA ENSEÑANZA PUBLICA SOLAMENTE. LOS DATOS CORRESPONDEN A LOS EFECTIVOS DE LOS SEIS PRIMEROS AÑOS DE ESTUDIO DE LA ENSEÑANZA DE PRIMER GRADO.

ST. LUCIA:
E—> ENROLMENT IN GRADES VIII AND IX REFERS TO "FIN D'ETUDES" CLASSES.
FR—> LES EFFECTIFS DES HUITIEME ET NEUVIEME ANNEES D'ETUDES SE REFERENT AUX CLASSES DE FIN D'ETUDES.
ESP> LOS EFECTIVOS PARA EL OCTAVO Y NOVENO AÑO DE ESTUDIOS SE REFIEREN A LAS CLASES DE "FIN D'ETUDES".

ST. VINCENT AND THE GRENADINES:
E—> IN 1970 DATA INCLUDE SECONDARY CLASSES ATTACHED TO PRIMARY SCHOOLS.
FR—> EN 1970 LES DONNEES INCLUENT LES CLASSES SECONDAIRES RATTACHEES AUX ECOLES PRIMAIRES.
ESP> EN 1970 LOS DATOS INCLUYEN LAS CLASES SECUNDARIAS ADSCRITAS A LAS ESCUELAS PRIMARIAS.

TRINIDAD AND TOBAGO:
E—> ENROLMENT IN GRADES VIII AND IX REFERS TO "FIN D'ETUDES" CLASSES. DATA REFER TO GOVERNMENT—MAINTAINED AND AIDED SCHOOLS ONLY.
FR—> LES EFFECTIFS DES HUITIEME ET NEUVIEME ANNEES D'ETUDES SE REFERENT AUX CLASSES DE FIN D'ETUDES. LES DONNEES SE REFERENT AUX ECOLES PUBLIQUES ET SUBVENTIONNEES SEULEMENT.
ESP> LOS EFECTIVOS PARA EL OCTAVO Y NOVENO AÑO DE ESTUDIOS SE REFIEREN A LAS CLASES DE "FIN D'ETUDES". LOS DATOS SE REFIEREN A LAS ESCUELAS PUBLICAS Y SUBVENCIONADAS SOLAMENTE.

TURKS AND CAICOS ISLANDS:
E—> DATA REFER TO PUBLIC EDUCATION ONLY.
FR—> LES DONNEES SE REFERENT A L'ENSEIGNEMENT PUBLIC SEULEMENT.
ESP> LOS DATOS SE REFIEREN A LA ENSEÑANZA PUBLICA SOLAMENTE.

UNITED STATES OF AMERICA:
E—> FOR 1976 AND 1977 FIGURES FOR GRADES VII AND VIII ONLY INCLUDE ENROLMENT IN SCHOOLS ORGANISED AS ELEMENTARY SCHOOLS. BEGINNING 1975, DATA INCLUDE SPECIAL EDUCATION.
FR—> POUR 1976 ET 1977, LES CHIFFRES POUR LES SEPTIEME ET HUITIEME ANNEES D'ETUDES SE REFERENT SEULEMENT AUX EFFECTIFS DES ECOLES QUI NE PROCURENT QUE L'ENSEIGNEMENT DU PREMIER DEGRE. A PARTIR DE 1975 LES DONNEES INCLUENT L'EDUCATION SPECIALE.
ESP> EN 1976 Y 1977, LAS CIFRAS PARA EL SEPTIMO Y OCTAVO AÑO DE ESTUDIOS SE REFIEREN UNICAMENTE A LAS ESCUELAS QUE SOLO OTORGAN ENSEÑANZA DE PRIMER GRADO. A PARTIR DE 1975, LOS DATOS INCLUYEN LA EDUCACION ESPECIAL.

U.S. VIRGIN ISLANDS:
E—> ENROLMENT IN THE FIRST SIX GRADES OF FIRST LEVEL EDUCATION ONLY. DATA REFER TO PUBLIC EDUCATION ONLY. FOR 1976, DATA REFER TO SPECIAL EDUCATION.
FR—> EFFECTIFS DES SIX PREMIERES ANNEES D'ETUDES DE L'ENSEIGNEMENT DU PREMIER DEGRE SEULEMENT. LES DONNEES SE REFERENT A L'ENSEIGNEMENT PUBLIC SEULEMENT. EN 1976, LES DONNEES INCLUENT L'EDUCATION SPECIALE.

Percentage distribution (first level) by grade 3.5
Répartition en pourcentage (premier degré) par années d'études
Distribución en porcentaje (primer grado) por años de estudio

U.S. VIRGIN ISLANDS (CONT.):
  ESP> EFECTIVOS DE LOS SEIS PRIMEROS AÑOS DE
ESTUDIO DE LA ENSEÑANZA DE PRIMER GRADO SOLAMENTE.
LOS DATOS SE REFIEREN A LA ENSEÑANZA PUBLICA
SOLAMENTE. EN 1976, LOS DATOS INCLUYEN LA
EDUCACION ESPECIAL.

ARGENTINA:
  E—> DATA INCLUDE SPECIAL EDUCATION.
  FR—> LES DONNEES INCLUENT L'EDUCATION SPECIALE.
  ESP> LOS DATOS INCLUYEN LA EDUCACION ESPECIAL.

ECUADOR:
  E—> DATA INCLUDE EVENING SCHOOLS.
  FR—> LES DONNEES INCLUENT LES ECOLES DU SOIR.
  ESP> LOS DATOS INCLUYEN LAS ESCUELAS NOCTURNAS.

FRENCH GUIANA:
  E—> IN 1970, ENROLMENT IN GRADES VI AND VII
REFERS TO "FIN D'ETUDES" CLASSES.
  FR—> EN 1970, LES EFFECTIFS DES SIXIEME ET
SEPTIEME ANNEES D'ETUDES SE REFERENT AUX CLASSES
DE FIN D'ETUDES.
  ESP> EN 1970, LOS EFECTIVOS PARA EL SEXTO Y
SEPTIMO AÑO DE ESTUDIOS SE REFIEREN A LAS CLASES
DE "FIN D'ETUDES".

GUYANA:
  E—> FOR 1970 DATA REFER TO PUBLIC EDUCATION
ONLY.
  FR—> POUR 1970 LES DONNEES SE REFERENT A
L'ENSEIGNEMENT PUBLIC SEULEMENT.
  ESP> EN 1970, LOS DATOS SE REFIEREN A LA ENSEÑANZA
PUBLICA SOLAMENTE.

PARAGUAY:
  E—> ALL DATA INCLUDE EVENING SCHOOLS.
  FR—> TOUTES LES DONNEES INCLUENT LES ECOLES DU
SOIR.
  ESP> TODOS LOS DATOS INCLUYEN LAS ESCUELAS
NOCTURNAS.

URUGUAY:
  E—> DATA REFER TO PUBLIC EDUCATION ONLY.
  FR—> LES DONNEES SE REFERENT A L'ENSEIGNEMENT
PUBLIC SEULEMENT.
  ESP> LOS DATOS SE REFIEREN A LA ENSEÑANZA
PUBLICA SOLAMENTE.

BAHRAIN:
  E—> FOR 1975 DATA REFER TO PUBLIC EDUCATION
ONLY.
  FR—> EN 1975 LES DONNEES SE REFERENT A
L'ENSEIGNEMENT PUBLIC SEULEMENT.
  ESP> EN 1975, LOS DATOS SE REFIEREN A LA ENSEÑANZA
PUBLICA SOLAMENTE.

BHUTAN:
  E—> ENROLMENT IN GRADE 1 REFERS TO INFANT
CLASSES.
  FR—> LES EFFECTIFS DE LA PREMIERE ANNEE D'ETUDES
SE REFERENT AUX CLASSES ENFANTINES.
  ESP> LOS EFECTIVOS DEL PRIMER AÑO DE ESTUDIOS SE
REFIEREN A LAS CLASES DE PARVULOS.

BURMA:
  E—> GRADE 1 REFERS TO KINDERGARTENS.
  FR—> LA PREMIERE ANNEE D'ETUDES SE REFERE AUX
JARDINS D'ENFANTS.
  ESP> EL PRIMER AÑO DE ESTUDIOS SE REFIERE A LOS
JARDINES DE LA INFANCIA.

CYPRUS:
  E—> NOT INCLUDING TURKISH SCHOOLS. ENROLMENT
IN GRADES VII AND VIII EXISTS ONLY IN PRIVATE
SCHOOLS.

CYPRUS (CONT.):
  FR—> NON COMPRIS LES ECOLES TURQUES. LES
EFFECTIFS DES SEPTIEME ET HUITIEME ANNEES D'ETUDES
SE REFERENT SEULEMENT AUX ECOLES PRIVEES.
  ESP> EXCLUIDAS LAS ESCUELAS TURCAS. LOS
EFECTIVOS PARA EL SEPTIMO Y EL OCTAVO AÑO DE
ESTUDIOS SE REFIEREN SOLAMENTE A LAS ESCUELAS
PRIVADAS.

INDONESIA:
  E—> FOR 1977 DATA DO NOT INCLUDE RELIGIOUS
SCHOOLS.
  FR—> EN 1977, LES DONNEES N'INCLUENT PAS LES
ECOLES RELIGIEUSES.
  ESP> EN 1977, LOS DATOS NO INCLUYEN LAS ESCUELAS
RELIGIOSAS.

JAPAN:
  E—> DATA INCLUDE SPECIAL EDUCATION.
  FR—> LES DONNEES INCLUENT L'EDUCATION SPECIALE.
  ESP> LOS DATOS INCLUYEN LA EDUCACION ESPECIAL.

JORDAN:
  E—> DATA REFER TO THE EAST BANK ONLY.
INCLUDING UNRWA SCHOOLS WITH 92,727 (F 44,582)
PUPILS IN 1978.
  FR—> LES DONNEES SE RAPPORTENT A LA RIVE
ORIENTALE SEULEMENT. Y COMPRIS LES ECOLES DE
L'UNRWA QUI COMPTAIENT 92 727 ELEVES (DONT 44 582
FILLES) EN 1978.
  ESP> LOS DATOS SE REFIEREN A LA ORILLA ORIENTAL
SOLAMENTE. INCLUIDAS LAS ESCUELAS DEL O.O.P.S.R.P.
QUE TENIAN 92 727 ALUMNOS (F 44 582) EN 1978.

KUWAIT:
  E—> ALL DATA REFER TO PUBLIC EDUCATION ONLY.
  FR—> TOUTES LES DONNEES SE REFERENT A
L'ENSEIGNEMENT PUBLIC SEULEMENT.
  ESP> TODOS LOS DATOS SE REFIEREN A LA ENSEÑANZA
PUBLICA SOLAMENTE.

MALAYSIA
PENINSULAR MALAYSIA:
  E—> FOR 1977 AND 1978 DATA REFER TO GOVERNMENT-
MAINTAINED AND AIDED SCHOOLS ONLY.
  FR—> EN 1977 ET 1978 LES DONNEES SE REFERENT AUX
ECOLES PUBLIQUES ET SUBVENTIONNEES SEULEMENT.
  ESP> EN 1977 Y 1978 LOS DATOS SE REFIEREN A LAS
ESCUELAS PUBLICAS Y SUBVENCIONADAS SOLAMENTE.

PHILIPPINES:
  E—> FOR 1975 DATA FOR FEMALE ENROLMENT REFER
TO PUBLIC EDUCATION ONLY.
  FR—> LES EFFECTIFS FEMININS DE L'ANNEE 1975 SE
REFERENT A L'ENSEIGNEMENT PUBLIC SEULEMENT.
  ESP> EN 1975, LOS EFECTIVOS FEMENINOS SE REFIEREN
A LA ENSEÑANZA PUBLICA SOLAMENTE.

QATAR:
  E—> ALL DATA REFER TO PUBLIC EDUCATION ONLY.
  FR—> TOUTES LES DONNEES SE REFERENT A
L'ENSEIGNEMENT PUBLIC SEULEMENT.
  ESP> TODOS LOS DATOS SE REFIEREN A LA ENSEÑANZA
PUBLICA SOLAMENTE.

SAUDI ARABIA:
  E—> FOR 1976 AND 1977 DATA INCLUDE EVENING
SCHOOLS.
  FR—> EN 1976 ET 1977 LES DONNEES INCLUENT LES
ECOLES DU SOIR.
  ESP> EN 1976 Y 1977 LOS DATOS INCLUYEN LAS
ESCUELAS NOCTURNAS.

3.5 **Percentage distribution (first level) by grade**
Répartition en pourcentage (premier degré) par années d'études
Distribución en porcentaje (primer grado) por años de estudio

SRI LANKA:
E—> FOR 1975, 1978 AND 1979 DATA REFER TO PUBLIC
EDUCATION ONLY.
FR-> EN 1975, 1978 ET 1979 LES DONNEES SE REFERENT
A L'ENSEIGNEMENT PUBLIC SEULEMENT.
ESP> EN 1975, 1978 Y 1979 LOS DATOS SE REFIEREN
A LA ENSEÑANZA PUBLICA SOLAMENTE.

SYRIAN ARAB REPUBLIC:
E—> INCLUDING UNRWA SCHOOLS WITH 28,143
(F. 13,063) PUPILS IN 1975.
FR-> Y COMPRIS LES ECOLES DE L'UNRWA QUI
COMPTAIENT 28 143 (DONT 13 063 FILLES) ELEVES
EN 1975.
ESP> INCLUIDAS LAS ESCUELAS DEL O.O.P.S.R.P.
QUE TENIAN 28 143 ALUMNOS (F 13 063) EN 1975.

UNITED ARAB EMIRATES:
E—> DATA REFER TO PUBLIC EDUCATION ONLY.
FR-> LES DONNEES SE REFERENT A L'ENSEIGNEMENT
PUBLIC SEULEMENT.
ESP> LOS DATOS SE REFIEREN A LA ENSEÑANZA
PUBLICA SOLAMENTE.

BELGIUM:
E—> ALL DATA INCLUDE SPECIAL EDUCATION.
FR-> LES DONNEES INCLUENT L'EDUCATION SPECIALE.
ESP> LOS DATOS INCLUYEN LA EDUCACION ESPECIAL.

BULGARIA:
E—> ALL DATA INCLUDE EVENING SCHOOLS.
FR-> LES DONNEES INCLUENT LES ECOLES DU SOIR.
ESP> LOS DATOS INCLUYEN LAS ESCUELAS NOCTURNAS.

FINLAND:
E—> FOR 1975, 1977 AND 1978 DATA INCLUDE
SPECIAL EDUCATION.
FR-> EN 1975, 1977 ET 1978 LES DONNEES INCLUENT
L'EDUCATION SPECIALE.
ESP> EN 1975, 1977 Y 1978 LOS DATOS INCLUYEN
LA EDUCACION ESPECIAL.

FRANCE:
E—> GRADE VI REFERS TO "FIN D'ETUDES" CLASSES.
FR—> LA SIXIEME ANNEE D'ETUDES SE REFERE A LA
CLASSE DE FIN D'ETUDES.
ESP> EL SEXTO AÑO DE ESTUDIOS SE REFIERE A LA
CLASE DE "FIN D'ETUDES".

GERMANY, FEDERAL REPUBLIC OF:
E—> DATA REFER TO THE FIRST 4 GRADES OF FIRST
LEVEL EDUCATION.
FR-> LES DONNEES SE REFERENT AUX QUATRE PREMIERES
ANNEES DE L'ENSEIGNEMENT DU PREMIER DEGRE.
ESP> LOS DATOS SE REFIEREN A LOS CUATRO PRIMEROS
AÑOS DE LA ENSEÑANZA DE PRIMER GRADO.

GREECE:
E—> ALL DATA INCLUDE EVENING SCHOOLS.
FR-> LES DONNEES INCLUENT LES ECOLES DU SOIR.
ESP> LOS DATOS INCLUYEN LAS ESCUELAS NOCTURNAS.

MALTA:
E—> ENROLMENT IN GRADES VII AND VIII EXISTS
ONLY IN PRIVATE SCHOOLS.
FR-> LES EFFECTIFS DES SEPTIEME ET HUITIEME
ANNEES D'ETUDES SE REFERENT SEULEMENT AUX
ECOLES PRIVEES.
ESP> LOS EFECTIVOS DEL SEPTIMO Y OCTAVO AÑO
DE ESTUDIOS SE REFIEREN SOLAMENTE A LAS
ESCUELAS PRIVADAS.

PORTUGAL:
E—> BEGINNING 1974, DATA ON PREPARATORY
EDUCATION PREVIOUSLY CLASSIFIED AT THE SECOND
LEVEL ARE SHOWN AT THE FIRST LEVEL EDUCATION.
FR-> A PARTIR DE 1974, LES DONNEES RELATIVES
AUX COURS PREPARATOIRES ANTERIEUREMENT CLASSEES
DANS L'ENSEIGNEMENT DU SECOND DEGRE ONT ETE
INCLUSES DANS L'ENSEIGNEMENT DU PREMIER DEGRE.
ESP> A PARTIR DE 1974, LOS DATOS RELATIVOS A
LOS CURSOS PREPARATORIOS ANTERIORMENTE CLASIFICADOS
EN LA ENSEÑANZA DE SEGUNDO GRADO, HAN SIDO
INCLUIDOS EN LA ENSEÑANZA DE PRIMER GRADO.

SWITZERLAND:
E—> DATA INCLUDE SPECIAL EDUCATION.
FR-> LES DONNEES INCLUENT L'EDUCATION SPECIALE.
ESP> LOS DATOS INCLUYEN LA EDUCACION ESPECIAL.

YUGOSLAVIA:
E—> IN 1975, DATA FOR FEMALE ENROLMENT INCLUDE
SPECIAL EDUCATION.
FR-> EN 1975, LES EFFECTIFS FEMININS INCLUENT
L'EDUCATION SPECIALE.
ESP> EN 1975, LOS EFECTIVOS FEMENINOS INCLUYEN
LA EDUCACION ESPECIAL.

AMERICAN SAMOA:
E—> DATA REFER TO PUBLIC EDUCATION ONLY.
FR-> LES DONNEES SE REFERENT A L'ENSEIGNEMENT
PUBLIC SEULEMENT.
ESP> LOS DATOS SE REFIEREN A LA ENSEÑANZA
PUBLICA SOLAMENTE.

GUAM:
E—> DATA REFER TO PUBLIC EDUCATION ONLY.
FR-> LES DONNEES SE REFERENT A L'ENSEIGNEMENT
PUBLIC SEULEMENT.
ESP> LOS DATOS SE REFIEREN A LA ENSEÑANZA
PUBLICA SOLAMENTE.

NEW ZEALAND:
E—> ALL DATA INCLUDE SPECIAL EDUCATION.
FR-> LES DONNEES INCLUENT L'EDUCATION SPECIALE.
ESP> LOS DATOS INCLUYEN LA EDUCACION ESPECIAL.

Percentage repeaters by grade (first level) 3.6
Pourcentage de redoublants par années d'études (premier degré)
Porcentaje de repetidores por años de estudio (primer grado)

3.6 Education at the first level: percentage repeaters by grade

Enseignement du premier degré: pourcentage de redoublants par années d'études

Enseñanza de primer grado: porcentaje de repetidores por años de estudio

NUMBER OF COUNTRIES AND
TERRITORIES PRESENTED IN
THIS TABLE: 119

NOMBRE DE PAYS ET DE
TERRITOIRES PRESENTES DANS
CE TABLEAU: 119

NUMERO DE PAISES Y DE
TERRITORIOS PRESENTADOS
EN ESTE CUADRO: 119

COUNTRY PAYS PAIS	YEAR ANNEE AÑO	SEX SEXE SEXO	PERCENTAGE REPEATERS BY GRADE POURCENTAGE DE REDOUBLANTS PAR ANNEES D'ETUDES PORCENTAJE DE REPETIDORES POR AÑOS DE ESTUDIO									
			TOTAL	I	II	III	IV	V	VI	VII	VIII	IX
AFRICA												
ALGERIA ‡	1975	MF	*333 877	7	9	13	12	13	21	22		
		F	*128 261	7	9	13	12	13	21	20		
	1977	MF	*377 905	9	9	12	12	13	21	25		
		F	*145 880	8	9	12	12	13	21	23		
	1978	MF	*387 390	8	10	12	12	13	22	26		
		F	*151 037	9	9	11	11	13	21	23		
BENIN	1970	MF	30 321	12	13	16	17	22	34			
		F	10 135	12	15	17	18	25	36			
	1975	MF	60 673	15	18	19	21	26	41			
		F	20 281	16	19	21	23	30	44			
	1978	MF	60 000	13	15	18	17	21	37			
		F	20 841	12	16	20	19	23	39			
	1979	MF	82 980	20	18	24	20	28	39			
		F	28 317	19	16	25	22	29	35			
BOTSWANA	1970	MF	276	0	0	0	0	0	0	3		
		F	160	0	0	0	0	0	–	3		
	1975	MF	3 361	0	0	0	0	0	0	21		
	1977	MF	3 099	0	0	0	0	0	0	22		
	1978	MF	2 909	0	0	0	0	0	1	17		
BURUNDI	1970	MF	39 720	25	21	20	18	20	27	20		
		F	12 349	24	20	19	16	18	25	16		
	1975	MF	33 171	19	18	25	27	32	40			
		F	12 028	18	17	24	26	29	38			
	1977	MF	36 879	22	19	21	25	35	40			
		F	14 003	22	18	20	25	35	39			
	1978	MF	39 591	25	18	21	27	36	42			
		F	15 301	24	18	21	26	36	42			

3.6   Percentage repeaters by grade (first level)
       Pourcentage de redoublants par années d'études (premier degré)
       Porcentaje de repetidores por años de estudio (primer grado)

COUNTRY PAYS PAIS	YEAR ANNEE AÑO	SEX SEXE SEXO	PERCENTAGE REPEATERS BY GRADE POURCENTAGE DE REDOUBLANTS PAR ANNEES D'ETUDES PORCENTAJE DE REPETIDORES POR AÑOS DE ESTUDIO								
			TOTAL	I	II	III	IV	V	VI	VII	VIII	IX
CENTRAL AFRICAN REPUBLIC	1970	MF	49 614	32	29	23	22	21	36			
		F	17 054	34	30	25	23	24	33			
	1975	MF	78 173	41	31	32	29	29	46			
		F	27 310	40	30	32	29	30	43			
	1976	MF	74 670	33	30	29	26	27	47			
CHAD ‡	1970	MF	49 578	29	33	18	16	18	37			
	1975	MF	74 299	40	33	31	27	30	54			
		F	18 784	39	34	32	27	26	44			
	1976	MF	79 342	40	32	34	26	31	58			
		F	20 233	37	34	35	27	31	50			
CONGO	1970	MF	78 633	34	28	32	25	26	49			
	1975	MF	83 438	31	23	29	22	21	28			
		F	37 940	30	22	28	23	21	27			
	1977	MF	85 116	28	19	29	24	23	23			
		F	40 093	27	18	29	24	23	22			
	1978	MF	88 706	28	18	29	26	21	23			
		F	42 166	28	18	29	26	21	23			
DJIBOUTI	1970	MF	*685	5	*11	*10	*10	*10	*20			
		F	*183	3	*9	*10	*9	*9	*21			
	1975	MF	1 843	3	20	23	19	21	32			
		F	549	4	18	17	17	16	25			
EGYPT	1970	MF	170 316	—	—	—	16	—	11			
		F	82 277	—	—	—	26	—	9			
	1975	MF	*279 831	—	12	—	15	—	11			
		F	*109 907	—	13	—	16	—	10			
	1977	MF	*293 489	—	16	—	12	—	11			
		F	*138 624	—	20	—	19	—	9			
	1978	MF	*370 401	—	12	—	12	—	31			
		F	*194 070	—	17	—	17	—	42			
GABON	1974	MF	42 088	50	33	29	21	21	23			
		F	20 144	50	33	29	21	20	18			
	1975	MF	43 752	49	33	30	21	22	20			
		F	21 576	49	32	31	22	22	20			
	1976	MF	44 000	48	33	29	19	20	24			
		F	21 448	47	33	29	19	21	25			
GAMBIA	1970	MF	2 310	9	7	7	7	9	36			
		F	575	6	5	6	6	4	37			
	1975	MF	2 568	7	4	4	5	6	35			
		F	798	6	4	3	3	6	37			
	1977	MF	5 089	15	15	14	15	15	36			
		F	1 638	16	17	14	14	16	32			
	1978	MF	5 014	12	9	12	11	12	38			
		F	1 642	12	10	14	11	11	39			

Percentage repeaters by grade (first level)   3.6
Pourcentage de redoublants par années d'études (premier degré)
Porcentaje de repetidores por años de estudio (primer grado)

COUNTRY / PAYS / PAIS	YEAR ANNEE AÑO	SEX SEXE SEXO	TOTAL	I	II	III	IV	V	VI	VII	VIII	IX
GHANA	1970	MF	*42 681	6	3	3	2	2	3	3	2	3
		F	*20 273	6	3	3	3	3	3	3	3	4
	1975	MF	*26 854	5	2	2	2	1	1			
		F	*12 353	5	2	2	2	1	1			
	1976	MF	*28 677	5	2	2	1	1	1			
		F	*13 306	5	2	2	1	1	1			
	1977	MF	*28 191	5	2	2	1	1	1			
		F	*13 138	5	2	2	1	1	1			
GUINEA–BISSAU	1975	MF	11 217	21	25	19	19	17	15			
	1976	MF	15 187	19	16	15	16	20	24			
IVORY COAST	1975	MF	140 548	17	15	16	15	21	41			
		F	52 207	18	16	17	16	21	38			
	1976	MF	140 734	13	12	15	13	19	42			
		F	52 537	14	13	16	15	20	39			
	1977	MF	144 160	12	11	10	12	16	44			
		F	54 182	13	12	11	14	17	41			
KENYA	1970	MF	73 333	3	3	4	4	4	6	16		
		F	28 560	3	3	4	4	4	6	16		
	1975	MF	150 919	5	3	4	5	4	7	16		
	1976	MF	175 053	6	5	4	5	5	6	15		
	1977	MF	176 913	6	6	6	5	5	7	10		
LESOTHO	1975	MF	13 385	9	4	4	3	3	3	18		
		F	8 030	9	4	4	3	3	3	19		
	1976	MF	17 398	10	7	6	5	5	5	18		
		F	10 181	10	8	6	4	5	5	19		
LIBERIA ‡	1978	MF	22 033	12	——>	13	12	11	10	9	8	
		F	8 985	13	——>	14	13	13	12	10	10	
LIBYAN ARAB JAMAHIRIYA	1970	MF	90 175	32	20	24	22	27	25			
		F	32 332	30	19	24	22	27	23			
	1975	MF	*91 358	10	11	13	28	15	21			
		F	*40 591	10	11	13	28	16	19			
	1976	MF	*83 650	13	9	12	19	19	16			
		F	*36 728	12	9	12	18	18	12			
	1977	MF	84 683	13	10	11	19	19	18			
		F	36 808	13	9	11	18	19	14			
MADAGASCAR	1970	MF	271 965	37	26	24	25	18	29			
		F	121 884	36	25	22	25	18	29			
	1974	MF	184 283	24	15	14	15	9	16			
	1975	MF	276 203	30	21	21	21	16	26			
		F	125 637	29	20	20	21	15	26			

3.6 Percentage repeaters by grade (first level)
Pourcentage de redoublants par années d'études (premier degré)
Porcentaje de repetidores por años de estudio (primer grado)

COUNTRY PAYS PAIS	YEAR ANNEE AÑO	SEX SEXE SEXO	PERCENTAGE REPEATERS BY GRADE POURCENTAGE DE REDOUBLANTS PAR ANNEES D'ETUDES PORCENTAJE DE REPETIDORES POR AÑOS DE ESTUDIO								
			TOTAL	I	II	III	IV	V	VI	VII	VIII	IX
MALAWI	1975	MF	105 732	19	16	15	11	8	10	13	37	
		F	42 846	19	16	16	13	9	11	15	37	
	1976	MF	117 501	20	18	17	14	10	11	13	36	
		F	48 307	20	18	18	15	11	13	15	35	
	1977	MF	108 125	17	16	15	12	8	10	11	38	
		F	43 818	17	17	16	13	9	11	14	38	
MALI	1970	MF	53 619	25	23	27	23	29	37			
	1975	MF	57 843	22	23	23	21	23	28			
	1977	MF	74 417	25	27	27	26	27	28			
	1978	MF	78 368	28	24	28	24	29	29			
		F	29 511	28	25	30	26	30	30			
MAURITANIA	1975	MF	7 460	8	16	14	14	16	19	29		
		F	3 175	10	14	17	20	20	26	34		
	1976	MF	8 685	10	9	15	14	12	17	31		
		F	3 308	12	11	18	17	17	21	33		
	1977	MF	10 582	14	11	11	17	11	16	30		
		F	4 242	16	14	14	23	13	17	34		
MOROCCO	1970	MF	*350 085	23	21	26	30	49				
	1975	MF	*434 392	23	20	26	30	44				
	1977	MF	*499 773	24	20	25	27	45				
		F	*174 611	24	18	24	26	43				
	1978	MF	*542 138	24	20	24	27	45				
		F	*188 968	24	19	23	26	43				
MOZAMBIQUE	1972	MF	161 740	30	27	25	22	22				
		F	53 468	29	26	23	20	20				
NIGER	1970	MF	17 034	15	17	18	16	22	36			
		F	6 052	15	18	21	16	22	36			
	1975	MF	18 580	6	10	14	12	18	33			
		F	6 638	7	10	14	13	19	33			
	1976	MF	20 263	5	10	12	14	16	34			
		F	7 385	5	10	12	15	16	34			
	1977	MF	21 742	4	12	11	10	15	31			
		F	8 095	4	12	12	11	15	32			
REUNION	1975	MF	20 949	31	21	18	19	19				
	1977	MF	17 488	24	17	15	19	19				
RWANDA	1970	MF	124 104	37	25	24	26	26	36			
		F	53 579	37	25	24	25	26	31			
	1976	MF	73 336	21	13	14	14	13	24			
		F	33 191	20	12	14	14	13	23			
SAO TOME AND PRINCIPE	1976	MF	5 900	51	42	44	46					
		F	2 403	40	40	40	40					

Percentage repeaters by grade (first level)   3.6
Pourcentage de redoublants par années d'études (premier degré)
Porcentaje de repetidores por años de estudio (primer grado)

COUNTRY PAYS PAIS	YEAR ANNEE AÑO	SEX SEXE SEXO	PERCENTAGE REPEATERS BY GRADE POURCENTAGE DE REDOUBLANTS PAR ANNEES D'ETUDES PORCENTAJE DE REPETIDORES POR AÑOS DE ESTUDIO									
			TOTAL	I	II	III	IV	V	VI	VII	VIII	IX
SENEGAL	1970	MF	52 136	15	16	16	16	20	37			
		F	20 516	16	17	18	17	21	36			
	1977	MF	51 745	11	12	13	14	14	27			
		F	20 915	12	13	14	15	15	26			
SEYCHELLES	1970	MF	57	1	0	1	1	0	1			
		F	37	1	0	1	1	0	1			
	1975	MF	117	0	0	0	1	1	4			
		F	70	0	0	0	2	1	4			
	1977	MF	55	1	0	0	0	1	1			
		F	15	1	0	0	0	0	1			
	1978	MF	82	0	0	0	1	1	2			
		F	43	0	1	1	2	1	1			
SUDAN	1970	MF	19 872	–	–	4	4	4	9			
SWAZILAND	1970	MF	7 275	10	7	8	10	13	12	22		
		F	3 272	9	5	7	9	12	12	22		
	1975	MF	9 084	9	6	8	11	11	11	18		
		F	4 001	8	5	7	8	10	11	18		
	1977	MF	10 187	10	8	10	10	11	11	16		
		F	4 443	9	7	8	8	9	11	16		
	1978	MF	10 775	11	8	10	10	12	11	17		
		F	4 665	10	6	8	8	10	10	16		
TOGO	1970	MF	77 455	39	26	30	24	33	48			
		F	24 563	39	29	32	26	35	46			
	1975	MF	104 553	37	24	26	20	25	34			
		F	37 759	36	25	28	22	27	34			
	1976	MF	111 167	37	25	26	18	22	31			
		F	41 188	37	26	28	19	24	31			
	1977	MF	117 159	36	25	25	21	22	31			
		F	44 718	35	25	27	23	25	33			
TUNISIA ‡	1970	MF	*273 498	29	26	26	26	29	42			
	1975	MF	*180 346	11	13	14	14	19	41			
		F	*65 990	11	12	13	13	18	41			
	1977	MF	*214 438	16	14	16	17	23	42	–		
		F	*79 156	16	13	14	16	21	41	–		
	1978	MF	*222 228	16	16	17	18	27	43	–		
		F	*83 765	16	15	15	16	25	42	–		
UGANDA ‡	1975	MF	99 358	12	11	11	11	11	12	2		
	1976	MF	117 499	12	12	12	12	13	14	3		
UNITED REPUBLIC OF CAMEROON	1975	MF	281 517	30	22	23	18	21	33	4		
		F	122 450	30	22	23	18	21	32	4		
	1976	MF	297 114	32	23	25	19	21	33	6		
		F	129 807	31	22	24	19	21	31	5		
	1977	MF	220 382	24	16	18	13	15	21	5		
		F	95 135	22	15	18	13	15	19	5		

3.6 **Percentage repeaters by grade (first level)**
Pourcentage de redoublants par années d'études (premier degré)
Porcentaje de repetidores por años de estudio (primer grado)

| COUNTRY
PAYS
PAIS | YEAR
ANNEE
AÑO | SEX
SEXE
SEXO | PERCENTAGE REPEATERS BY GRADE
POURCENTAGE DE REDOUBLANTS PAR ANNEES D'ETUDES
PORCENTAJE DE REPETIDORES POR AÑOS DE ESTUDIO | | | | | | | | |
			TOTAL	I	II	III	IV	V	VI	VII	VIII	IX
UNITED REPUBLIC OF TANZANIA ‡	1970	MF	14 520	1	1	1	3	0	0	6		
	1974	MF	7 763	0	0	0	0	0	0	3		
	1975	MF	8 001	0	0	0	0	0	0	2		
		F	2 862	0	0	0	0	0	0	2		
UPPER VOLTA	1970	MF	17 011	12	14	15	14	16	31			
		F	6 545	13	15	16	15	18	31			
	1975	MF	24 638	15	14	14	14	14	37			
		F	9 754	17	15	16	16	16	38			
	1977	MF	30 002	14	15	17	16	17	38			
		F	11 489	16	15	17	18	18	38			
	1978	MF	30 655	14	13	15	15	17	37			
		F	11 853	15	13	17	17	19	37			
ZAIRE	1970	MF	706 657	28	22	23	19	18	17			
		F	265 374	28	22	23	20	19	17			
	1975	MF	748 274	24	23	22	19	17	15			
		F	305 160	24	23	22	20	17	15			
	1976	MF	758 244	24	22	22	19	16	15			
		F	315 144	24	22	22	20	17	15			
	1977	MF	768 988	23	22	22	19	16	14			
		F	326 124	23	22	22	19	17	14			
ZAMBIA	1975	MF	17 922	0	1	1	3	1	1	8		
		F	6 955	0	1	1	3	1	1	7		
	1976	MF	15 662	0	0	1	3	1	1	8		
		F	6 073	0	0	1	2	1	1	7		
AMERICA, NORTH												
ANTIGUA	1974	MF	136	3	0	1	1	2	0	1		
		F	55	3	1	0	1	1	0	1		
	1975	MF	216	4	1	1	1	2	1	4		
		F	97	4	1	1	0	1	0	5		
BERMUDA ‡	1974	MF	512	3	3	7	11	12	13	10		
		F	197	2	3	7	10	9	10	8		
COSTA RICA	1970	MF	36 119	18	13	10	7	4	1			
		F	15 582	17	11	9	7	4	1			
	1975	MF	23 394	—	13	14	—	8	3			
		F	9 428	—	11	12	—	6	2			
	1976	MF	22 926	—	11	15	—	7	3			
		F	9 239	—	10	12	—	6	2			
CUBA	1970	MF	330 673	34	19	15	20	15	9			
		F	143 707	31	16	14	18	14	9			
	1975	MF	145 897	20	10	6	6	3	2			
	1976	MF	48 214	0	6	4	4	1	1			
DOMINICAN REPUBLIC	1970	MF	170 381	33	21	18	13	10	6			
		F	79 017	31	19	17	13	10	6			

Percentage repeaters by grade (first level) 3.6
Pourcentage de redoublants par années d'études (premier degré)
Porcentaje de repetidores por años de estudio (primer grado)

COUNTRY PAYS PAIS	YEAR ANNEE AÑO	SEX SEXE SEXO	PERCENTAGE REPEATERS BY GRADE POURCENTAGE DE REDOUBLANTS PAR ANNEES D'ETUDES PORCENTAJE DE REPETIDORES POR AÑOS DE ESTUDIO								
			TOTAL	I	II	III	IV	V	VI	VII	VIII	IX
EL SALVADOR ‡	1975	MF	55 428	15	8	6	4	3	2	1	0	0
	1976	MF	59 558	15	9	6	5	3	3	1	1	1
		F	27 755	14	8	6	5	3	2	1	1	1
GRENADA	1975	MF	1 288	9	5	4	5	7	5	7		
	1976	MF	1 426	10	6	7	5	6	6	9		
	1977	MF	2 225	17	10	10	6	7	12	14		
		F	922	17	10	8	4	4	10	14		
GUADELOUPE ‡	1970	MF	17 510	31	24	22	22	22	18	28		
		F	7 535	26	22	21	20	20	13	24		
	1975	MF	12 508	27	17	17	19	19				
	1977	MF	9 667	21	14	17	18	14				
GUATEMALA	1970	MF	79 909	26	13	11	7	5	2			
	1975	MF	93 022	26	12	11	7	5	2			
HAITI ‡	1975	MF	43 466	—	14	14	15	14	13	7		
		F	21 464	—	14	15	16	16	14	7		
	1976	MF	31 105	—	9	10	11	10	10	3		
		F	16 428	—	9	12	12	11	15	3		
	1977	MF	46 054	—	12	14	17	16	13	6		
		F	23 329	—	13	14	18	18	14	6		
JAMAICA	1975	MF	13 431	7	3	2	2	2	6			
		F	5 909	6	2	1	2	2	7			
	1976	MF	16 127	8	3	3	3	3	8			
		F	7 132	6	3	2	2	2	9			
MARTINIQUE ‡	1970	MF	15 796	27	20	19	19	22	36	43		
		F	6 919	23	17	17	18	19	37	39		
	1975	MF	10 364	22	15	14	16	21				
	1977	MF	9 196	21	14	15	16	17				
MEXICO	1975	MF	1 266 286	17	12	10	9	7	2			
		F	569 828	16	11	10	9	7	2			
	1977	MF	1 209 646	18	10	8	6	4	2			
NICARAGUA	1970	MF	36 423	16	13	11	10	8	5			
		F	17 696	16	13	11	9	8	5			
	1974	MF	44 470	18	13	12	11	9	5			
	1977	MF	49 131	19	13	11	10	7	4			
		F	23 275	18	12	11	9	6	4			
	1978	MF	52 165	20	14	11	10	8	4			
		F	25 080	19	14	11	9	8	4			

3.6 Percentage repeaters by grade (first level)
Pourcentage de redoublants par années d'études (premier degré)
Porcentaje de repetidores por años de estudio (primer grado)

COUNTRY PAYS PAIS	YEAR ANNEE AÑO	SEX SEXE SEXO	TOTAL	I	II	III	IV	V	VI	VII	VIII	IX
						PERCENTAGE REPEATERS BY GRADE POURCENTAGE DE REDOUBLANTS PAR ANNEES D'ETUDES PORCENTAJE DE REPETIDORES POR AÑOS DE ESTUDIO							
PANAMA	1970	MF	39 323	24	17	16	12	10	3			
		F	16 827	22	15	14	11	9	3			
	1975	MF	42 250	21	17	14	10	6	2	1	1	1
		F	17 319	19	14	12	8	5	2	0	1	2
	1977	MF	39 156	18	14	12	10	7	2	7	4	6
		F	15 780	16	12	10	8	6	2	5	2	5
	1978	MF	40 689	18	14	12	10	7	3	7	5	5
		F	16 192	16	12	10	8	6	2	5	4	5
AMERICA, SOUTH												
ARGENTINA ‡	1970	MF	385 468	23	13	11	9	6	4	1		
		F	167 535	22	12	10	7	5	3	1		
	1975	MF	340 089	21	12	10	6	5	3	1		
	1976	MF	360 858	21	12	10	7	5	4	1		
BRAZIL	1970	MF	2 465 124	28	16	12	8					
	1974	MF	2 984 149	24	17	11	10	12	11	9	6	
		F	1 358 696	22	15	10	9	10	9	8	5	
CHILE	1970	MF	212 598	17	13	12	10	8	5	4	3	
		F	95 275	16	12	11	9	7	5	2	2	
	1975	MF	287 170	20	15	13	11	10	8	10	6	
		F	124 968	19	13	11	10	9	7	8	5	
	1977	MF	281 700	18	15	13	12	13	11	9	5	
		F	137 778	18	15	13	12	13	11	9	5	
COLOMBIA	1970	MF	545 876	22	16	13	10	8				
		F	263 991	21	15	12	9	10				
	1974	MF	*582 292	20	16	13	11	8				
		F	*272 157	18	15	12	10	7				
ECUADOR ‡	1970	MF	125 895	18	12	11	10	8	6			
		F	58 618	18	12	10	10	8	6			
	1975	MF	143 014	17	13	10	9	7	6			
		F	66 822	16	12	10	9	7	5			
FRENCH GUIANA ‡	1970	MF	2 061	31	26	19	25	17	12	29		
		F	871	25	22	19	20	18	16	23		
	1975	MF	1 274	23	15	15	14	15				
	1977	MF	1 212	21	13	15	14	10				
GUYANA ‡	1970	MF	12 040	13	6	9	7	8	12			
		F	5 441	11	6	8	6	7	12			
	1975	MF	10 880	16	5	6	5	5	14			
		F	4 969	15	4	5	4	4	15			
	1976	MF	10 225	13	4	5	3	4	13			
		F	4 769	12	4	4	3	3	14			

Percentage repeaters by grade (first level) 3.6
Pourcentage de redoublants par années d'études (premier degré)
Porcentaje de repetidores por años de estudio (primer grado)

COUNTRY PAYS PAIS	YEAR ANNEE AÑO	SEX SEXE SEXO	PERCENTAGE REPEATERS BY GRADE POURCENTAGE DE REDOUBLANTS PAR ANNEES D'ETUDES PORCENTAJE DE REPETIDORES POR AÑOS DE ESTUDIO									
			TOTAL	I	II	III	IV	V	VI	VII	VIII	IX
PARAGUAY ‡	1970	MF	74 943	25	22	16	11	7	4			
		F	30 597	23	19	14	9	5	3			
	1975	MF	69 378	24	19	15	10	6	3			
		F	29 582	22	17	13	8	4	2			
	1976	MF	68 606	22	18	14	9	5	3			
		F	28 962	20	16	13	8	4	2			
	1977	MF	67 570	22	17	14	9	5	2			
		F	28 703	20	15	12	8	4	2			
PERU	1970	MF	398 615	26	19	14	13	11	6			
		F	176 208	26	19	13	12	9	5			
	1975	MF	289 700	16	12	9	8	7	4			
	1977	MF	283 171	12	12	10	9	7	3			
SURINAME	1975	MF	19 157	27	25	21	26	23	20			
		F	8 178	25	21	16	23	21	21			
	1977	MF	21 626	28	25	23	27	24	23			
		F	9 159	24	20	19	24	23	26			
	1978	MF	21 938	30	26	23	26	26	22			
		F	9 496	27	21	19	24	25	24			
URUGUAY ‡	1970	MF	50 973	30	19	17	14	12	7			
	1977	MF	41 986	27	16	14	13	11	7			
		F	17 382	25	14	11	11	9	6			
	1978	MF	41 973	26	16	14	13	12	9			
		F	17 348	24	14	11	11	10	7			
VENEZUELA	1970	MF	38 050	–	–	–	8	6	–			
	1975	MF	57 389	–	–	–	10	8	–			
	1977	MF	175 012	10	8	8	8	6	2			
ASIA												
AFGHANISTAN	1974	MF	176 040	30	22	23	32	30	22			
		F	24 484	30	21	22	32	28	20			
	1977	MF	261 494	36	29	27	33	29	24	32	17	
		F	26 687	13	16	18	32	27	22	22	7	
BHUTAN ‡	1977	MF	3 973	18	30	25	19	19	26			
	1978	MF	683	1	4	3	9	9	8			
		F	249	–	9	9	13	11	6			
BRUNEI	1974	MF	2 809	5	5	5	4	4	29			
		F	1 111	3	3	3	3	4	26			
	1975	MF	2 492	5	3	4	5	3	28			
		F	1 068	4	3	3	5	3	27			
	1977	MF	2 864	5	4	4	9	3	20			
		F	1 119	4	3	3	6	2	18			
	1978	MF	3 258	6	5	5	10	4	22			
		F	1 267	4	3	4	6	3	19			

3.6 **Percentage repeaters by grade (first level)**
Pourcentage de redoublants par années d'études (premier degré)
Porcentaje de repetidores por años de estudio (primer grado)

| COUNTRY PAYS PAIS | YEAR ANNEE AÑO | SEX SEXE SEXO | PERCENTAGE REPEATERS BY GRADE POURCENTAGE DE REDOUBLANTS PAR ANNEES D'ETUDES PORCENTAJE DE REPETIDORES POR AÑOS DE ESTUDIO | | | | | | | | |
			TOTAL	I	II	III	IV	V	VI	VII	VIII	IX
BURMA ‡	1970	MF	665 187	25	17	21	18	21				
		F	353 383	24	28	24	17	21				
	1973	MF	608 979	25	20	19	18	15				
		F	221 793	25	20	18	19	14				
CYPRUS ‡	1970	MF	1 569	9	4	0	0	0	0	−	−	
		F	670	8	3	0	0	0	0	−	−	
	1975	MF	552	4	1	0	0	0	0	−	−	
		F	225	3	1	0	0	0	0	−	−	
	1977	MF	444	4	1	0	−	−	0	−	−	
		F	164	3	1	−	−	−	−	−	−	
	1978	MF	366	4	1	0	−	−	0	−	−	
		F	146	3	0	0	−	−	−	−		
INDIA	1970	MF	11 883 950	26	20	18	17	16				
		F	4 552 495	26	20	19	18	17				
INDONESIA	1975	MF	1 906 099	15	12	11	9	7	2			
	1977	MF	*2 172 800	17	13	11	8	7	2			
	1978	MF	*2 646 758	17	15	12	9	7	3			
IRAN	1970	MF	310 686	11	11	8	7	7	9			
		F	78 882	7	8	6	6	6	5			
IRAQ	1970	MF	226 554	17	16	15	22	32	25			
		F	68 812	18	17	16	25	35	22			
	1975	MF	262 313	14	13	11	14	25	11			
		F	84 038	14	12	11	15	26	7			
	1977	MF	276 683	17	13	9	11	22	8			
		F	92 905	17	11	8	11	19	4			
	1978	MF	231 891	5	12	9	9	18	6			
		F	79 594	4	11	8	8	15	4			
JAPAN ‡			−	−	−	−	−	−	−			
JORDAN ‡	1975	MF	15 892	0	0	6	8	6	5			
		F	7 713	0	0	6	9	6	5			
	1977	MF	16 276	0	0	5	7	8	5			
		F	8 106	0	0	5	7	8	5			
	1978	MF	11 692	0	0	0	4	7	6			
		F	5 688	0	0	0	4	7	6			
KOREA, REPUBLIC OF ‡	1970	MF	4 375	0	0	0	0	0	0			
		F	1 860	0	0	0	0	0	0			
	1979	MF	−	−	−	−	−	−	−			
		F	−	−	−	−	−	−	−			

Percentage repeaters by grade (first level) 3.6
Pourcentage de redoublants par années d'études (premier degré)
Porcentaje de repetidores por años de estudio (primer grado)

COUNTRY PAYS PAIS	YEAR ANNEE AÑO	SEX SEXE SEXO	PERCENTAGE REPEATERS BY GRADE POURCENTAGE DE REDOUBLANTS PAR ANNEES D'ETUDES PORCENTAJE DE REPETIDORES POR AÑOS DE ESTUDIO									
			TOTAL	I	II	III	IV	V	VI	VII	VIII	IX
KUWAIT ‡	1970	MF	8 961	13	14	20	15					
		F	3 868	14	14	19	14					
	1975	MF	12 105	13	13	16	11					
		F	5 632	14	13	16	10					
	1977	MF	10 747	11	10	10	6					
		F	4 793	11	10	10	5					
	1978	MF	11 887	15	12	8	4					
		F	4 156	9	10	7	3					
MALAYSIA PENINSULAR MALAYSIA ‡			—	—	—	—	—	—	—			
SABAH ‡			—	—	—	—	—	—	—			
SARAWAK ‡			—	—	—	—	—	—	—			
OMAN	1975	MF	5 097	11	7	12	11	4	8			
		F	1 352	9	8	9	16	5	5			
	1977	MF	10 668	13	12	12	22	18	13			
		F	2 999	12	12	12	20	18	11			
	1978	MF	9 587	11	10	9	20	15	11			
		F	2 840	10	10	10	16	14	12			
PHILIPPINES ‡	1976	MF	115 114	2	2	2	1	1	1			
		F	46 486	...	...	...	...	...	...			
QATAR ‡	1970	MF	3 438	26	24	25	28	26	5			
		F	1 546	25	21	26	30	26	2			
	1975	MF	4 692	23	22	21	24	25	14			
		F	2 165	22	20	20	22	28	11			
	1977	MF	3 704	22	17	15	19	15	5			
		F	1 727	21	17	14	18	16	3			
	1978	MF	3 546	20	18	14	15	13	6			
		F	1 572	20	15	12	14	13	4			
SAUDI ARABIA ‡	1975	MF	103 091	17	14	14	21	14	9			
		F	28 922	13	11	11	16	11	6			
	1976	MF	85 980	14	11	13	18	9	2			
		F	28 938	13	10	16	14	7	3			
	1977	MF	92 137	15	14	13	15	11	2			
		F	27 830	13	11	11	13	9	1			
SINGAPORE	1975	MF	25 758	0	0	2	3	4	28			
		F	8 633	0	0	2	2	3	21			
	1977	MF	63 959	8	12	18	23	24	35			
		F	23 704	6	10	14	18	19	27			
	1978	MF	37 375	6	6	11	14	14	22			
		F	13 584	5	5	8	11	10	17			

3.6 Percentage repeaters by grade (first level)
Pourcentage de redoublants par années d'études (premier degré)
Porcentaje de repetidores por años de estudio (primer grado)

COUNTRY PAYS PAIS	YEAR ANNEE AÑO	SEX SEXE SEXO	PERCENTAGE REPEATERS BY GRADE POURCENTAGE DE REDOUBLANTS PAR ANNEES D'ETUDES PORCENTAJE DE REPETIDORES POR AÑOS DE ESTUDIO								
			TOTAL	I	II	III	IV	V	VI	VII	VIII	IX
SRI LANKA	1970	MF	371 141	29	22	21	19	18				
		F	154 773	26	19	18	16	16				
	1975	MF	*224 919	15	12	15	25	13				
	1978	MF	*188 113	–	11	11	12	11	8			
	1979	MF	*251 831	5	18	12	14	141	10			
SYRIAN ARAB REPUBLIC ‡	1970	MF	100 728	13	11	10	10	9	10			
		F	32 818	11	11	10	10	8	5			
	1975	MF	129 136	12	11	11	9	7	9			
		F	49 965	12	11	11	9	7	5			
	1977	MF	119 440	10	10	9	8	7	6			
		F	45 029	10	10	9	8	6	4			
	1978	MF	124 358	11	9	9	8	7	7			
		F	46 398	11	9	9	8	6	4			
THAILAND	1975	MF	688 053	19	12	11	4	7	4	2		
		F	295 924	18	10	10	3	7	3	1		
	1976	MF	688 154	19	11	11	4	8	4	1		
		F	296 270	17	10	9	3	7	3	1		
	1977	MF	706 423	18	11	11	4	9	4	2		
		F	306 413	17	10	9	4	8	4	2		
UNITED ARAB EMIRATES ‡	1974	MF	7 462	12	15	17	24	31	19			
		F	3 126	13	17	16	22	31	13			
	1975	MF	7 072	12	16	16	20	18	8			
		F	3 177	13	16	15	20	17	7			
	1977	MF	6 163	8	9	12	14	12	9			
		F	2 762	9	10	11	13	10	7			
EUROPE												
AUSTRIA	1970	MF	30 612	6	6	5	5					
		F	11 714	5	5	4	4					
	1977	MF	18 399	3	5	4	3					
	1978	MF	13 768	2	4	3	3					
BELGIUM ‡	1975	MF	225 439	14	20	25	26	31	28			
		F	104 927	14	20	24	25	28	27			
	1976	MF	216 462	14	20	25	26	28	28			
		F	101 132	14	20	24	25	27	27			
	1977	MF	206 836	13	20	24	26	28	28			
		F	96 003	13	19	22	24	27	27			
BULGARIA ‡	1970	MF	63 014	8	6	4	4	10	7	5	3	
	1975	MF	20 173	3	2	1	2	4	2	2	1	
	1977	MF	19 165	3	2	1	2	3	2	1	1	
	1978	MF	17 511	3	2	1	2	2	2	1	1	

Percentage repeaters by grade (first level) 3.6
Pourcentage de redoublants par années d'études (premier degré)
Porcentaje de repetidores por años de estudio (primer grado)

COUNTRY PAYS PAIS	YEAR ANNEE AÑO	SEX SEXE SEXO	PERCENTAGE REPEATERS BY GRADE POURCENTAGE DE REDOUBLANTS PAR ANNEES D'ETUDES PORCENTAJE DE REPETIDORES POR AÑOS DE ESTUDIO								
			TOTAL	I	II	III	IV	V	VI	VII	VIII	IX
CZECHOSLOVAKIA	1970	MF	76 008	4	4	4	4	4	7	5	3	0
	1975	MF	15 664	0	2	1	1	1	1	1	0	0
		F	5 940	0	2	1	1	1	1	0	0	0
	1977	MF	16 664	1	1	1	1	1	1	1	0	0
		F	6 192	1	1	1	1	1	1	1	0	0
	1978	MF	16 692	2	1	0	1	1	1	1	0	0
		F	6 191	1	1	0	1	1	1	1	0	0
FRANCE ‡	1970	MF	651 139	17	11	10	11	15	12			
		F	290 291	16	10	9	11	14	12			
	1975	MF	424 459	14	7	6	7	11	–			
	1977	MF	410 323	12	6	6	8	11	–			
	1978	MF	428 303	12	7	7	8	11	–			
GERMANY, FEDERAL REPUBLIC OF ‡	1970	MF	140 129	4	4	2	3					
		F	58 689	4	3	2	2					
	1975	MF	126 768	5	4	2	2					
		F	52 931	4	3	2	2					
	1976	MF	113 681	4	4	2	2					
		F	47 603	4	3	2	2					
	1977	MF	94 604	3	3	2	2					
		F	39 111	3	3	2	2					
GREECE ‡	1970	MF	47 321	11	6	6	4	3	1			
		F	18 772	10	5	5	3	2	0			
	1975	MF	26 860	7	3	3	1	1	0			
		F	10 592	6	3	2	1	1	0			
	1976	MF	21 776	6	3	2	1	1	0			
		F	8 671	5	3	2	1	1	0			
HUNGARY	1970	MF	42 226	7	5	4	3	5	4	3	0	
	1975	MF	28 457	5	3	2	2	4	3	2	0	
		F	10 700	5	2	2	1	3	2	1	0	
	1977	MF	21 556	5	2	2	1	2	2	1	0	
		F	7 807	4	2	1	1	2	1	1	0	
	1978	MF	20 710	4	2	2	1	2	2	1	0	
		F	7 566	4	2	1	1	2	1	1	0	
ITALY	1970	MF	350 037	9	8	7	6	5				
		F	146 481	8	7	6	5	4				
	1975	MF	143 873	5	4	3	2	2				
		F	56 497	4	3	2	2	1				
	1976	MF	118 698	4	3	2	2	1				
		F	46 834	3	2	2	2	1				
	1977	MF	102 431	3	3	2	2	1				
		F	39 289	3	2	1	1	1				

3.6 Percentage repeaters by grade (first level)
   Pourcentage de redoublants par années d'études (premier degré)
   Porcentaje de repetidores por años de estudio (primer grado)

COUNTRY PAYS PAIS	YEAR ANNEE AÑO	SEX SEXE SEXO	PERCENTAGE REPEATERS BY GRADE POURCENTAGE DE REDOUBLANTS PAR ANNEES D'ETUDES PORCENTAJE DE REPETIDORES POR AÑOS DE ESTUDIO								
			TOTAL	I	II	III	IV	V	VI	VII	VIII	IX
LUXEMBOURG	1975	MF	1 809	12	7	7	5	3	3			
		F	792	11	5	7	4	2	3			
	1977	MF	1 604	11	6	7	5	2	2			
		F	696	11	5	6	4	2	2			
	1978	MF	1 688	12	7	8	5	3	2			
		F	700	11	6	6	3	3	2			
MALTA ‡	1970	MF	660	6	3	1	0	0	1	1	0	
		F	271	5	2	1	0	0	2	0	1	
	1975	MF	310	0	1	1	2	1	1	2	—	
		F	169	0	1	1	3	1	1	3	—	
	1976	MF	295	1	1	1	1	1	1			
		F	138	1	0	1	1	1	1			
	1977	MF	1 281	2	2	4	6	6	6			
		F	601	1	1	5	7	5	5			
NETHERLANDS	1970	MF	45 790	7	4	3	2	2	1			
		F	18 983	5	3	2	2	2	1			
	1975	MF	35 673	5	3	2	2	1	1			
		F	14 546	4	3	2	2	1	1			
	1977	MF	39 670	6	4	2	2	1	1			
		F	15 257	4	3	2	2	1	1			
	1978	MF	38 845	6	4	2	2	1	1			
		F	14 095	4	3	2	1	1	1			
POLAND	1970	MF	272 623	4	4	4	5	8	7	6	2	
	1975	MF	107 828	2	1	1	1	5	4	4	1	
	1976	MF	108 775	2	1	1	2	5	4	3	1	
	1977	MF	108 442	2	2	1	2	5	4	3	1	
PORTUGAL ‡	1970	MF	255 208	36	24	20	24	14	6			
		F	117 468	34	23	18	24	13	5			
	1975	MF	136 656	3	16	10	14	10	15			
		F	56 808	2	14	8	13	8	12			
	1976	MF	158 276	21	——→	6	——→	10	12			
		F	66 326	19	——→	6	——→	8	10			
	1977	MF	202 989	22	——→	11	——→	14	15			
		F	86 165	20	——→	10	——→	11	13			
SAN MARINO	1970	MF	72	4	7	2	2	7				
SWITZERLAND ‡	1977	MF	11 522	2	2	2	2	2	2			
		F	5 027	2	2	2	2	2	2			
	1978	MF	10 843	2	2	2	2	2	2			
		F	4 713	2	2	2	2	2	2			
YUGOSLAVIA	1970	MF	120 849	10	8	7	5					
	1975	MF	55 334	6	4	3	2					
	1977	MF	36 378	5	2	2	1					
	1978	MF	29 521	4	2	1	1					

Percentage repeaters by grade (first level)   3.6
Pourcentage de redoublants par années d'études (premier degré)
Porcentaje de repetidores por años de estudio (primer grado)

| COUNTRY
PAYS
PAIS | YEAR
ANNEE
AÑO | SEX
SEXE
SEXO | PERCENTAGE REPEATERS BY GRADE
POURCENTAGE DE REDOUBLANTS PAR ANNEES D'ETUDES
PORCENTAJE DE REPETIDORES POR AÑOS DE ESTUDIO | | | | | | | | |
			TOTAL	I	II	III	IV	V	VI	VII	VIII	IX
OCEANIA												
FIJI	1974	MF	*9 575	5	4	5	5	6	9	12	13	
FRENCH POLYNESIA	1974	MF	5 165	23	18	19	20	23	–			
		F	2 261	18	14	15	20	25	–			
KIRIBATI	1977	MF	660	5	2	2	4	2	10	6	8	9
		F	296	5	1	1	4	2	10	5	7	9
	1978	MF	720	8	3	5	6	4	7	5	5	7
		F	339	7	3	5	6	4	6	4	5	8
NEW CALEDONIA	1970	MF	2 083	10	10	10	10	10	9			
		F	1 003	9	9	9	9	9	10			
NORFOLK ISLAND	1978	MF	6	3	6	6	3	–	–	–		
		F	2	–	6	7	–	–	–	–		
SOLOMON ISLANDS	1975	MF	1 541	8	5	6	5	3	2	9		
		F	603	7	5	6	7	4	2	8		
TONGA	1977	MF	1 014	–	–	–	–	–	31			
		F	429	–	–	–	–	–	29			
	1978	MF	1 140	–	–	–	–	–	30			
		F	489	–	–	–	–	–	27			
U.S.S.R.												
U.S.S.R.	1970	MF	765 000	2	1	1	2	2	3	2	2	
	1975	MF	183 000	1	0	0	1	0	1	1	0	
	1977	MF	146 000	1	0	0	0	0	0	0	0	
BYELORUSSIAN S.S.R.	1970	MF	19 400	1	1	1	1	1	2	1	1	
	1975	MF	5 689	1	0	0	0	0	0	0	0	
	1977	MF	5 363	0	0	0	0	0	0	0	0	
	1978	MF	5 200	1	0	0	0	0	0	0	0	
UKRAINIAN S.S.R.	1970	MF	41 300	1	0	0	1	1	1	1	0	
	1975	MF	11 100	0	0	0	0	0	0	0	0	
	1976	MF	12 100	1	0	0	0	0	0	0	0	
	1977	MF	11 200	1	0	0	0	0	0	0	0	

ALGERIA:
  E—> ENROLMENT IN GRADE VII REFERS TO "FIN D'ETUDES" CLASSES.
  FR–> LES EFFECTIFS DE LA SEPTIEME ANNEE D'ETUDES SE REFERENT AUX CLASSES DE FIN D'ETUDES.
  ESP> LOS EFECTIVOS DEL SEPTIMO AÑO DE ESTUDIOS SE REFIEREN A LAS CLASES DE "FIN D'ETUDES".

CHAD:
  E—> DATA DO NOT INCLUDE MOSLEM PRIVATE EDUCATION.
  FR–> LES DONNEES NE TIENNENT PAS COMPTE DE L'ENSEIGNEMENT PRIVE MUSULMAN.
  ESP> LOS DATOS NO INCLUYEN LA ENSEÑANZA PRIVADA MUSULMANA.

3.6 **Percentage repeaters by grade (first level)**
Pourcentage de redoublants par années d'études (premier degré)
Porcentaje de repetidores por años de estudio (primer grado)

LIBERIA:
E—> DATA INCLUDE EDUCATION PRECEDING THE
FIRST LEVEL.
FR-> LES DONNEES INCLUENT L'ENSEIGNEMENT
PRECEDANT LE PREMIER DEGRE.
ESP> LOS DATOS INCLUYEN LA ENSEÑANZA ANTERIOR
AL PRIMER GRADO.

TUNISIA:
E—> BEGINNING 1977, GRADE VII HAS BEEN
INTRODUCED EXPERIMENTALLY.
FR-> A PARTIR DE 1977, UNE SEPTIEME ANNEE
D'ETUDES A ETE CREEE A TITRE EXPERIMENTAL.
ESP> A PARTIR DE 1977, SE HA INTRODUCIDO UN
SEPTIMO AÑO DE ESTUDIOS A TITULO EXPERIMENTAL.

UGANDA:
E—> GOVERNMENT—MAINTAINED AND AIDED SCHOOLS
ONLY.
FR-> ECOLES PUBLIQUES ET SUBVENTIONNEES
SEULEMENT.
ESP> ESCUELAS PUBLICAS Y SUBVENCIONADAS
SOLAMENTE.

UNITED REPUBLIC OF TANZANIA:
E—> FOR 1970 AND 1974 DATA REFER TO TANZANIA
MAINLAND ONLY.
FR-> POUR 1970 ET 1974 LES DONNEES SE REFERENT
A LA TANZANIE CONTINENTALE SEULEMENT.
ESP> EN 1970 Y 1974 LOS DATOS SE REFIEREN A
TANZANIA CONTINENTAL SOLAMENTE.

BERMUDA:
E—> DATA REFER TO PUBLIC EDUCATION ONLY.
FR-> LES DONNEES SE REFERENT A L'ENSEIGNEMENT
PUBLIC SEULEMENT.
ESP> LOS DATOS SE REFIEREN A LA ENSEÑANZA
PUBLICA SOLAMENTE.

EL SALVADOR:
E—> DATA INCLUDE EVENING SCHOOLS.
FR-> LES DONNEES INCLUENT LES ECOLES DU SOIR.
ESP> LOS DATOS INCLUYEN LAS ESCUELAS NOCTURNAS.

GUADELOUPE:
E—> IN 1970, ENROLMENT IN GRADES VI AND VII
REFERS TO "FIN D'ETUDES" CLASSES.
FR-> EN 1970, LES EFFECTIFS DES SIXIEME ET
SEPTIEME ANNEES D'ETUDES SE REFERENT AUX CLASSES
DE FIN D'ETUDES.
ESP> EN 1970, LOS EFECTIVOS DEL SEXTO Y SEPTIMO
AÑO DE ESTUDIOS SE REFIEREN A LAS CLASES DE "FIN
D'ETUDES".

HAITI:
E—> NOT INCLUDING PRIVATE RURAL SCHOOLS.
FR-> LES DONNEES N'INCLUENT PAS LES ECOLES
PRIVEES RURALES.
ESP> EXCLUIDAS LAS ESCUELAS RURALES PRIVADAS.

MARTINIQUE:
E—> IN 1970, ENROLMENT IN GRADES VI AND VII
REFERS TO "FIN D'ETUDES" CLASSES.
FR-> EN 1970, LES EFFECTIFS DES SIXIEME ET
SEPTIEME ANNEES D'ETUDES SE REFERENT AUX CLASSES
DE FIN D'ETUDES.
ESP> EN 1970, LOS EFECTIVOS DEL SEXTO Y SEPTIMO
AÑO DE ESTUDIOS SE REFIEREN A LAS CLASES DE "FIN
D'ETUDES".

ARGENTINA:
E—> DATA INCLUDE SPECIAL EDUCATION.
FR-> LES DONNEES INCLUENT L'EDUCATION SPECIALE.
ESP> LOS DATOS INCLUYEN LA EDUCACION ESPECIAL.

ECUADOR:
E—> DATA INCLUDE EVENING SCHOOLS.
FR-> LES DONNEES INCLUENT LES ECOLES DU SOIR.
ESP> LOS DATOS INCLUYEN LAS ESCUELAS NOCTURNAS.

FRENCH GUIANA:
E—> IN 1970, ENROLMENT IN GRADES VI AND VII
REFERS TO "FIN D'ETUDES" CLASSES.
FR-> EN 1970, LES EFFECTIFS DES SIXIEME ET
SEPTIEME ANNEES D'ETUDES SE REFERENT AUX CLASSES
DE FIN D'ETUDES.
ESP> EN 1970, LOS EFECTIVOS DEL SEXTO Y SEPTIMO
AÑO DE ESTUDIOS SE REFIEREN A LAS CLASES DE "FIN
D'ETUDES".

GUYANA:
E—> IN 1970, DATA REFER TO PUBLIC EDUCATION
ONLY.
FR-> EN 1970, LES DONNEES SE REFERENT A
L'ENSEIGNEMENT PUBLIC SEULEMENT.
ESP> EN 1970, LOS DATOS SE REFIEREN A LA
ENSEÑANZA PUBLICA SOLAMENTE.

PARAGUAY:
E—> DATA INCLUDE EVENING SCHOOLS.
FR-> LES DONNEES INCLUENT LES ECOLES DU SOIR.
ESP> LOS DATOS INCLUYEN LAS ESCUELAS NOCTURNAS.

URUGUAY:
E—> DATA REFER TO PUBLIC EDUCATION ONLY.
FR-> LES DONNEES SE REFERENT A L'ENSEIGNEMENT
PUBLIC SEULEMENT.
ESP> LOS DATOS SE REFIEREN A LA ENSEÑANZA
PUBLICA SOLAMENTE.

BHUTAN:
E—> ENROLMENT IN GRADE 1 REFERS TO INFANT
CLASSES.
FR-> LES EFFECTIFS DE LA PREMIERE ANNEE
D'ETUDES SE REFERENT AUX CLASSES ENFANTINES.
ESP> LOS EFECTIVOS DEL PRIMER AÑO DE ESTUDIOS
SE REFIEREN A LAS CLASES DE PARVULOS.

BURMA:
E—> GRADE 1 REFERS TO KINDERGARTENS.
FR-> LA PREMIERE ANNEE D'ETUDES SE REFERE AUX
JARDINS D'ENFANTS.
ESP> EL PRIMER AÑO DE ESTUDIOS SE REFIERE A LOS
JARDINES DE LA INFANCIA.

CYPRUS:
E—> NOT INCLUDING TURKISH SCHOOLS. ENROLMENT
IN GRADES VII AND VIII EXISTS ONLY IN PRIVATE
SCHOOLS.
FR-> NON COMPRIS LES ECOLES TURQUES. LES
EFFECTIFS DES SEPTIEME ET HUITIEME ANNEES
D'ETUDES SE REFERENT SEULEMENT AUX ECOLES PRIVEES.
ESP> EXCLUIDAS LAS ESCUELAS TURCAS. LOS
EFECTIVOS PARA EL SEPTIMO Y OCTAVO AÑO DE ESTUDIOS
SE REFIEREN A LAS ESCUELAS PRIVADAS SOLAMENTE.

JAPAN:
E—> POLICY OF AUTOMATIC PROMOTION IN FIRST
LEVEL EDUCATION PRACTICED.
FR-> UNE POLITIQUE DE PROMOTION AUTOMATIQUE POUR
L'ENSEIGNEMENT DU PREMIER DEGRE EST APPLIQUEE.
ESP> SE APLICA UNA POLITICA DE PROMOCION
AUTOMATICA PARA LA ENSEÑANZA DE PRIMER GRADO.

JORDAN:
E—> DATA REFER TO THE EAST BANK ONLY.
INCLUDING UNRWA SCHOOLS WITH 92,727 (F. 44,582)
PUPILS IN 1978.
FR-> LES DONNEES SE RAPPORTENT A LA RIVE
ORIENTALE SEULEMENT. Y COMPRIS LES ECOLES DE
L'UNRWA QUI COMPTAIENT 92 727 ELEVES (DONT 44 582
FILLES) EN 1978.
ESP> LOS DATOS SE REFIEREN A LA ORILLA ORIENTAL
SOLAMENTE. INCLUIDAS LAS ESCUELAS DEL
"O.O.P.S.R.P."QUE TENIAN 92 727 ALUMNOS
(F. 44 582) EN 1978.

Percentage repeaters by grade (first level) 3.6
Pourcentage de redoublants par années d'études (premier degré)
Porcentaje de repetidores por años de estudio (primer grado)

KOREA, REPUBLIC OF:
E—> BEGINNING 1972, COUNTRY PRACTICES POLICY OF AUTOMATIC PROMOTION IN PRIMARY EDUCATION.
FR-> A PARTIR DE 1972, LE PAYS PRATIQUE UNE POLITIQUE DE PROMOTION AUTOMATIQUE POUR L'ENSEIGNEMENT DU PREMIER DEGRE.
ESP> A PARTIR DE 1972, EL PAIS APLICA UNA POLITICA DE PROMOCION AUTOMATICA PARA LA ENSEÑANZA DE PRIMER GRADO.

KUWAIT:
E—> DATA REFER TO PUBLIC EDUCATION ONLY.
FR-> LES DONNEES SE REFERENT A L'ENSEIGNEMENT PUBLIC SEULEMENT.
ESP> LOS DATOS SE REFIEREN A LA ENSEÑANZA PUBLICA SOLAMENTE.

MALAYSIA:
PENINSULAR MALAYSIA:
E—> POLICY OF AUTOMATIC PROMOTION IN FIRST LEVEL EDUCATION PRACTICED.
FR-> UNE POLITIQUE DE PROMOTION AUTOMATIQUE POUR L'ENSEIGNEMENT DU PREMIER DEGRE EST APPLIQUEE.
ESP> SE APLICA UNA POLITICA DE PROMOCION AUTOMATICA PARA LA ENSEÑANZA DE PRIMER GRADO.

SABAH:
E—> POLICY OF AUTOMATIC PROMOTION IN FIRST LEVEL EDUCATION PRACTICED.
FR-> UNE POLITIQUE DE PROMOTION AUTOMATIQUE POUR L'ENSEIGNEMENT DU PREMIER DEGRE EST APPLIQUEE.
ESP> SE APLICA UNA POLITICA DE PROMOCION AUTOMATICA PARA LA ENSEÑANZA DE PRIMER GRADO.

SARAWAK:
E—> POLICY OF AUTOMATIC PROMOTION IN FIRST LEVEL EDUCATION PRACTICED.
FR-> UNE POLITIQUE DE PROMOTION AUTOMATIQUE POUR L'ENSEIGNEMENT DU PREMIER DEGRE EST APPLIQUEE.
ESP> SE APLICA UNA POLITICA DE PROMOCION AUTOMATICA PARA LA ENSEÑANZA DE PRIMER GRADO.

PHILIPPINES:
E—> FOR 1976, DATA REFER TO PUBLIC EDUCATION ONLY, AND FEMALE ENROLMENT BY GRADE IS NOT AVAILABLE TO CALCULATE THE PERCENTAGE REPEATERS FOR FEMALES BY GRADE.
FR-> POUR 1976 LES DONNEES SE REFERENT A L'ENSEIGNEMENT PUBLIC, ET LES EFFECTIFS FEMININS PAR ANNEES D'ETUDES NE SONT PAS DISPONIBLES POUR CALCULER LE POURCENTAGE DES REDOUBLANTS POUR LES FILLES PAR ANNEES D'ETUDES.
ESP> EN 1976 LOS DATOS SE REFIEREN A LA ENSEÑANZA PUBLICA SOLAMENTE Y NO SE DISPONE DE LA MATRICULA FEMENINA POR AÑO DE ESTUDIOS PARA CALCULAR EL PORCENTAJE FEMENINO DE REPETIDORES.

QATAR:
E—> DATA REFER TO PUBLIC EDUCATION ONLY.
FR-> LES DONNEES SE REFERENT A L'ENSEIGNEMENT PUBLIC SEULEMENT.
ESP> LOS DATOS SE REFIEREN A LA ENSEÑANZA PUBLICA SOLAMENTE.

SAUDI ARABIA:
E—> FOR 1976 AND 1977 DATA INCLUDE EVENING SCHOOLS.
FR-> POUR 1976 ET 1977 LES DONNEES INCLUENT LES ECOLES DU SOIR.
ESP> EN 1976 Y 1977 LOS DATOS INCLUYEN LAS ESCUELAS NOCTURNAS.

SYRIAN ARAB REPUBLIC:
E—> INCLUDING UNRWA SCHOOLS WITH 28,143 (F. 13,063) PUPILS IN 1975.
FR-> Y COMPRIS LES ECOLES DE L'UNRWA QUI COMPTAIENT 28 143 ELEVES (DONT 13 063 FILLES) EN 1975.
ESP> INCLUIDAS LAS ESCUELAS DEL O.O.P.S.R.P. QUE TENIAN 28 143 ALUMNOS (F. 13 063) EN 1975.

UNITED ARAB EMIRATES:
E—> DATA REFER TO PUBLIC EDUCATION ONLY.
FR-> LES DONNEES SE REFERENT A L'ENSEIGNEMENT PUBLIC SEULEMENT.
ESP> LOS DATOS SE REFIEREN A LA ENSEÑANZA PUBLICA SOLAMENTE.

BELGIUM:
E—> DATA INCLUDE SPECIAL EDUCATION.
FR-> LES DONNEES INCLUENT L'EDUCATION SPECIALE.
ESP> LOS DATOS INCLUYEN LA EDUCACION ESPECIAL.

BULGARIA:
E—> DATA INCLUDE EVENING SCHOOLS.
FR-> LES DONNEES INCLUENT LES ECOLES DU SOIR.
ESP> LOS DATOS INCLUYEN LAS ESCUELAS NOCTURNAS.

FRANCE:
E—> GRADE VI REFERS TO "FIN D'ETUDES" CLASS.
FR-> LA SIXIEME ANNEE D'ETUDES SE REFERE A LA CLASSE DE FIN D'ETUDES.
ESP> EL SEXTO AÑO DE ESTUDIOS SE REFIERE A LA CLASE DE "FIN D'ETUDES".

GERMANY, FEDERAL REPUBLIC OF:
E—> DATA REFER TO THE FIRST 4 GRADES OF FIRST LEVEL EDUCATION.
FR-> LES DONNEES SE REFERENT AUX QUATRE PREMIERES ANNEES DE L'ENSEIGNEMENT DU PREMIER DEGRE.
ESP> LOS DATOS SE REFIEREN A LOS CUATRO PRIMEROS AÑOS DE LA ENSEÑANZA DE PRIMER GRADO.

GREECE:
E—> DATA INCLUDE EVENING SCHOOLS.
FR-> LES DONNEES INCLUENT LES ECOLES DU SOIR.
ESP> LOS DATOS INCLUYEN LAS ESCUELAS NOCTURNAS.

MALTA:
E—> ENROLMENT IN GRADES VII AND VIII EXISTS ONLY IN PRIVATE SCHOOLS.
FR-> LES EFFECTIFS DES SEPTIEME ET HUITIEME ANNEES D'ETUDES SE REFERENT SEULEMENT AUX ECOLES PRIVEES.
ESP> LOS EFECTIVOS PARA EL SEPTIMO Y OCTAVO AÑO DE ESTUDIOS SE REFIEREN A LAS ESCUELAS PRIVADAS SOLAMENTE.

PORTUGAL:
E—> BEGINNING 1974, DATA ON PREPARATORY EDUCATION PREVIOUSLY CLASSIFIED AT THE SECOND LEVEL ARE SHOWN AT THE FIRST LEVEL.
F-> A PARTIR DE 1974, LES DONNEES RELATIVES AUX COURS PREPARATOIRES ANTERIEUREMENT CLASSEES DANS L'ENSEIGNEMENT DU SECOND DEGRE ONT ETE INCLUSES DANS L'ENSEIGNEMENT DU PREMIER DEGRE.
ESP> A PARTIR DE 1974, LOS DATOS RELATIVOS A LOS CURSOS PREPARATORIOS ANTERIORMENTE CLASIFICADOS EN LA ENSEÑANZA DE SEGUNDO GRADO, HAN SIDO INCLUIDOS EN LA ENSEÑANZA DE PRIMER GRADO.

SWITZERLAND:
E—> DATA INCLUDE SPECIAL EDUCATION.
FR-> LES DONNEES INCLUENT L'EDUCATION SPECIALE.
ESP> LOS DATOS INCLUYEN LA EDUCACION ESPECIAL.

3.7 Education at the second level: teachers and pupils
Enseignement du second degré: personnel enseignant et élèves
Enseñanza de segundo grado: personal docente y alumnos

3.7 Education at the second level (general, teacher-training and other second level): teachers and students

Enseignement du second degré (général, normal et autre enseignement du second degré): personnel enseignant et élèves

Enseñanza de segundo grado (general, normal y otra enseñanza de segundo grado): personal docente y alumnos

TEACHERS : PERSONNEL ENSEIGNANT/PERSONAL DOCENTE
STUDENTS : ELEVES/ALUMNOS

NUMBER OF COUNTRIES AND TERRITORIES PRESENTED IN THIS TABLE: 198

NOMBRE DE PAYS ET DE TERRITOIRES PRESENTES DANS CE TABLEAU: 198

COUNTRY PAYS PAIS	YEAR ANNEE AÑO	TOTAL SECOND LEVEL TOTAL DU SECOND DEGRE TOTAL DEL SEGUNDO GRADO			GENERAL EDUCATION ENSEIGNEMENT GENERAL ENSEÑANZA GENERAL		
		TOTAL	FEMALE FEMININ FEMENINO	% F	TOTAL	FEMALE FEMININ FEMENINO	% F
		(1)	(2)	(3)	(4)	(5)	(6)
AFRICA							
ALGERIA ‡	TEACHERS 1970	11 487	*4 866	*42	*7 837	*3 021	*39
	1974	16 656	...	...	15 340	...	...
	1975	19 764	...	...	18 269	...	...
	1976	22 605	...	...	20 861	...	...
	1977	27 764	...	...	25 882	...	...
	1978	32 621	...	...	30 614	...	...
	STUDENTS 1970	242 335	68 562	28	186 261	53 480	29
	1974	429 684	141 896	33	406 565	135 081	33
	1975	512 428	172 769	34	490 818	167 200	34
	1976	615 267	210 603	34	592 265	204 349	35
	1977	745 838	266 040	36	721 999	259 056	36
	1978	851 784	314 977	37	828 661	308 157	37
ANGOLA	TEACHERS 1970	3 814	...	...	2 669	...	...
	1972	4 723	...	...	3 110	...	...
	STUDENTS 1970	57 829	24 131	42	43 966	19 132	44
	1972	79 055	...	...	58 932	...	...
BENIN	TEACHERS 1970	*869	*136	*16	786	*116	*15
	1974	...	...	...	1 092	...	...
	1975	1 509	...	...	1 349	259	19
	1977	...	...	...	1 198	...	...
	1978	...	...	...	1 215	...	...
	STUDENTS 1970	22 132	*6 500	*29	21 049	6 322	30
	1974	43 123	...	...	41 802	12 261	29
	1975	47 428	...	...	45 572	12 926	28
	1977	55 075	15 733	29	51 664	14 590	28
	1978	...	...	...	55 434	14 940	27
	1979	...	...	...	64 275	17 299	27
BOTSWANA ‡	TEACHERS 1970	353	102	29	197	56	28
	1974	727	*246	*34	492	*176	*36
	1975	860	256	30	570	167	29
	1976	920	286	31	653	207	32
	1977	928	292	31	649	208	32
	1978	1 126	351	31	731	256	35

308

Education at the second level: teachers and pupils   3.7
Enseignement du second degré: personnel enseignant et élèves
Enseñanza de segundo grado: personal docente y alumnos

NUMERO DE PAISES Y DE TERRITORIOS PRESENTADOS EN
ESTE CUADRO: 198

TEACHER TRAINING ENSEIGNEMENT NORMAL ENSEÑANZA NORMAL			OTHER SECOND LEVEL AUTRE ENSEIGNEMENT DU SECOND DEGRE OTRA ENSEÑANZA DE SEGUNDO GRADO			YEAR ANNEE	COUNTRY PAYS
TOTAL	FEMALE FEMININ FEMENINO	% F	TOTAL	FEMALE FEMININ FEMENINO	% F	AÑO	PAIS
(7)	(8)	(9)	(10)	(11)	(12)		
							AFRICA
484	*97	*20	3 166	*1 748	*55	1970	ALGERIA ‡
727	...	...	589	...	...	1974	
792	...	...	*703	...	...	1975	
901	...	...	843	...	...	1976	
1 059	...	...	823	...	...	1977	
986	...	...	1 021	...	...	1978	
8 333	2 926	35	47 741	12 156	25	1970	
7 955	2 607	33	15 164	4 208	28	1974	
8 809	2 891	33	12 801	2 678	21	1975	
11 196	3 796	34	11 806	2 458	21	1976	
12 041	4 325	36	11 798	2 659	23	1977	
11 219	4 125	37	11 904	2 695	23	1978	
154	...	...	991	...	...	1970	ANGOLA
330	...	...	1 283	...	...	1972	
1 696	1 133	67	12 167	3 866	32	1970	
3 388	...	...	16 735	...	...	1972	
10	2	20	*73	*18	*25	1970	BENIN
10	5	50	150	...	...	1974	
10	5	50	150	...	...	1975	
...	...	...	...	...	...	1977	
...	...	...	...	...	...	1978	
171	24	14	912	*154	*17	1970	
170	29	17	1 151	...	...	1974	
169	29	17	1 687	...	...	1975	
172	43	25	3 239	1 100	34	1977	
...	...	...	...	...	...	1978	
...	...	...	...	...	...	1979	
32	7	22	124	39	31	1970	BOTSWANA ‡
46	22	48	189	48	25	1974	
48	20	42	242	69	29	1975	
51	15	29	216	64	30	1976	
46	15	33	233	69	30	1977	
55	20	36	340	75	22	1978	

3.7 Education at the second level: teachers and pupils
Enseignement du second degré: personnel enseignant et élèves
Enseñanza de segundo grado: personal docente y alumnos

COUNTRY PAYS PAIS	YEAR ANNEE AÑO	TOTAL SECOND LEVEL TOTAL DU SECOND DEGRE TOTAL DEL SEGUNDO GRADO			GENERAL EDUCATION ENSEIGNEMENT GENERAL ENSEÑANZA GENERAL		
		TOTAL	FEMALE FEMININ FEMENINO	% F	TOTAL	FEMALE FEMININ FEMENINO	% F
		(1)	(2)	(3)	(4)	(5)	(6)
BOTSWANA (CONT.) ‡	STUDENTS 1970	5 197	2 364	45	3 905	1 831	47
	1974	12 245	6 274	51	10 308	5 346	52
	1975	14 286	7 418	52	12 098	6 392	53
	1976	16 275	8 676	53	13 991	7 549	54
	1977	17 896	9 751	54	15 496	8 521	55
	1978	18 977	10 101	53	16 086	8 981	56
BURUNDI ‡	TEACHERS 1970	824	192	23	324	52	16
	1974	...	...	...	283	...	...
	1975	916	...	...	326	71	22
	1976	...	...	...	404	71	18
	1977	...	...	...	425	79	19
	1978	...	...	...	...	...	...
	STUDENTS 1970	9 244	2 452	27	3 969	566	14
	1974	13 667	4 633	34	6 295	1 772	28
	1975	15 395	4 946	32	7 143	1 934	27
	1976	13 453	...	...	6 416	1 578	25
	1977	14 215	...	...	6 663	1 820	27
	1978	...	...	...	7 864	1 917	24
CAPE VERDE	TEACHERS 1970	...	...	...	...	...	...
	STUDENTS 1970	...	...	...	...	...	...
	1972	...	...	...	...	...	...
CENTRAL AFRICAN REPUBLIC	TEACHERS 1970	524	...	...	363	...	...
	1974	...	...	...	345	...	...
	1975	...	...	...	515	134	26
	1977	...	...	...	...	...	...
	STUDENTS 1970	11 288	2 143	19	9 691	1 606	17
	1974	*20 116	*3 513	*17	*17 907	*2 883	*16
	1975	*22 923	*4 121	*18	*20 635	*3 495	*17
	1976	...	...	...	*22 426	*3 946	*18
	1977	...	...	...	...	...	...
CHAD ‡	TEACHERS 1970	...	...	...	*386	*75	*19
	1974	...	...	...	*371	...	...
	1976	...	...	...	590	73	12
	STUDENTS 1970	10 556	802	8	9 105	738	8
	1974	...	...	...	12 885	...	...
	1975	16 391	...	...	15 128	...	...
	1976	19 580	...	...	18 382	...	...
COMORO	TEACHERS 1970	63	20	32	61	20	33
	1973	128	*52	*41	125	*52	*42
	STUDENTS 1970	1 273	322	25	1 249	316	25
	1973	3 197	...	...	3 175	...	...
CONGO	TEACHERS 1970	1 037	226	22	693	128	18
	1974	2 143	275	13	1 703	162	10
	1975	2 413	266	11	2 042	182	9
	1977	3 344	311	9	2 883	230	8
	1978	3 706	326	9	3 099	217	7
	STUDENTS 1970	34 267	10 298	30	30 371	9 065	30
	1974	87 968	31 198	35	81 541	28 932	35
	1975	102 110	36 782	36	94 276	33 720	36
	1976	122 006	45 296	37	114 341	41 844	37
	1977	136 642	52 133	38	127 210	47 593	37
	1978	149 386	57 695	39	138 525	52 577	38

Education at the second level: teachers and pupils 3.7
Enseignement du second degré: personnel enseignant et élèves
Enseñanza de segundo grado: personal docente y alumnos

TEACHER TRAINING ENSEIGNEMENT NORMAL ENSEÑANZA NORMAL			OTHER SECOND LEVEL AUTRE ENSEIGNEMENT DU SECOND DEGRE OTRA ENSEÑANZA DE SEGUNDO GRADO			YEAR ANNEE AÑO	COUNTRY PAYS PAIS
TOTAL	FEMALE FEMININ FEMENINO	% F	TOTAL	FEMALE FEMININ FEMENINO	% F		
(7)	(8)	(9)	(10)	(11)	(12)		
283	151	53	1 009	382	38	1970	BOTSWANA
409	306	75	1 528	622	41	1974	(CONT.) ‡
489	373	76	1 699	653	38	1975	
562	428	76	1 722	699	41	1976	
646	496	77	1 754	734	42	1977	
669	537	80	2 222	583	26	1978	
210	78	37	290	62	21	1970	BURUNDI ‡
311	...	...	...	...	...	1974	
398	...	...	192	...	...	1975	
316	96	30	...	...	...	1976	
209	60	29	...	...	...	1977	
355	106	30	...	...	...	1978	
3 085	1 065	35	2 190	821	37	1970	
5 078	1 945	38	2 294	916	40	1974	
5 381	2 245	42	2 871	767	27	1975	
5 538	2 719	49	1 499	...	...	1976	
5 858	2 601	44	1 694	...	...	1977	
6 320	2 779	44	...	...	...	1978	
15	...	...	36	...	...	1970	CAPE VERDE
21	20	95	557	138	25	1970	CENTRAL AFRICAN
329	180	55	556	176	32	1972	REPUBLIC
31	*14	*45	130	*33	*25	1970	CENTRAL AFRICAN REPUBLIC
47	12	26	...	...	...	1974	
47	12	26	...	...	...	1975	
...	...	...	128	...	...	1977	
234	106	45	1 363	431	32	1970	
442	186	42	1 767	444	25	1974	
517	194	38	1 771	432	24	1975	
522	232	44	...	...	...	1976	
...	...	...	2 523	779	31	1977	
*29	*12	*41	...	...	...	1970	CHAD ‡
...	...	...	...	...	...	1974	
...	...	...	...	...	...	1976	
423	21	5	1 028	43	4	1970	
447	...	...	...	...	...	1974	
549	...	...	714	...	...	1975	
549	...	...	649	84	13	1976	
2	–	–	–	–	–	1970	COMORO
3	–	–	–	–	–	1973	
24	6	25	–	–	–	1970	
22	...	...	–	–	–	1973	
28	7	25	316	91	29	1970	CONGO
50	12	24	390	101	26	1974	
34	8	24	337	76	23	1975	
61	3	5	400	78	20	1977	
102	10	10	505	99	20	1978	
548	130	24	3 348	1 103	33	1970	
901	231	26	5 526	2 035	37	1974	
705	185	26	7 129	2 877	40	1975	
704	211	30	6 961	3 241	47	1976	
898	229	26	8 534	4 311	51	1977	
1 228	229	19	9 633	4 889	51	1978	

3.7 Education at the second level: teachers and pupils
Enseignement du second degré: personnel enseignant et élèves
Enseñanza de segundo grado: personal docente y alumnos

COUNTRY PAYS PAIS	YEAR ANNEE AÑO	TOTAL SECOND LEVEL TOTAL DU SECOND DEGRE TOTAL DEL SEGUNDO GRADO			GENERAL EDUCATION ENSEIGNEMENT GENERAL ENSEÑANZA GENERAL		
		TOTAL	FEMALE FEMININ FEMENINO	% F	TOTAL	FEMALE FEMININ FEMENINO	% F
		(1)	(2)	(3)	(4)	(5)	(6)
DJIBOUTI	TEACHERS 1970	...	...	...	61	30	49
	1974	141	61	43	80	45	56
	1975	148	57	39	85	41	48
	1978	...	...	...	...	...	...
	STUDENTS 1970	1 385	376	27	758	248	33
	1974	2 158	595	28	1 554	509	33
	1975	1 994	531	27	1 398	443	32
	1978	3 123	...	...	2 551	...	...
EGYPT ‡	TEACHERS 1970	57 986	13 687	24	41 947	10 989	26
	1974	69 470	19 403	28	46 080	14 979	33
	1975	78 789	20 962	27	51 740	16 105	31
	1976	80 745	22 986	28	52 700	17 533	33
	1977	91 083	25 926	28	59 766	19 838	33
	1978	100 288	28 338	28	67 562	21 720	32
	STUDENTS 1970	1 448 242	465 901	32	1 147 366	370 128	32
	1974	1 982 752	658 202	33	1 601 171	527 071	33
	1975	2 107 891	733 132	35	1 697 382	591 753	35
	1976	2 282 454	813 838	36	1 828 390	646 109	35
	1977	2 408 247	869 612	36	1 935 088	696 813	36
	1978	2 523 642	929 629	37	1 990 383	727 617	37
EQUATORIAL GUINEA	TEACHERS 1970	*175	...	...	...	...	...
	1975	165	18	11	115	14	12
	STUDENTS 1970	6 014	1 556	26	5 198	1 490	29
	1975	4 523	751	17	3 984	709	18
ETHIOPIA	TEACHERS 1970	4 876	785	16	4 115	598	15
	1973	6 929	968	14	6 181	820	13
	STUDENTS 1970	*135 163	33 681	*25	126 341	30 604	24
	1973	191 703	52 434	27	183 044	49 775	27
GABON	TEACHERS 1970	512	145	28	369	116	31
	1974	...	...	...	616	392	64
	1975	1 016	...	...	812	248	31
	1976	1 121	331	30	894	289	32
	STUDENTS 1970	9 983	2 851	29	8 244	2 488	30
	1974	20 999	*7 650	*36	17 575	7 019	40
	1975	22 542	7 870	35	19 721	7 174	36
	1976	23 460	8 616	37	20 367	7 832	38
GAMBIA	TEACHERS 1970	254	67	26	224	61	27
	1974	348	78	22	304	71	23
	1975	347	89	26	304	78	26
	1976	437	102	23	391	92	24
	1977	436	...	...	387	...	...
	1978	...	...	...	416	118	28
	STUDENTS 1970	5 042	1 223	24	4 712	1 175	25
	1974	6 162	1 637	27	5 791	1 564	27
	1975	6 618	*1 785	*27	6 178	1 690	27
	1976	7 456	2 194	29	6 834	2 059	30
	1977	7 588	2 454	32	6 994	2 314	33
	1978	...	...	...	7 464	2 278	31
GHANA ‡	TEACHERS 1970	5 842	1 009	17	3 388	633	19
	1974	22 759	4 988	22	21 099	4 715	22
	1975	25 142	5 443	22	23 181	5 139	22
	1976	27 054	6 626	24	25 081	6 315	25
	1977	28 666	6 276	22	27 464	6 135	22

Education at the second level: teachers and pupils   3.7
Enseignement du second degré: personnel enseignant et élèves
Enseñanza de segundo grado: personal docente y alumnos

TEACHER TRAINING ENSEIGNEMENT NORMAL ENSEÑANZA NORMAL			OTHER SECOND LEVEL AUTRE ENSEIGNEMENT DU SECOND DEGRE OTRA ENSEÑANZA DE SEGUNDO GRADO			YEAR ANNEE AÑO	COUNTRY PAYS PAIS
TOTAL	FEMALE FEMININ FEMENINO	% F	TOTAL	FEMALE FEMININ FEMENINO	% F		
(7)	(8)	(9)	(10)	(11)	(12)		
1	1	100	...	...	...	1970	DJIBOUTI
3	1	33	58	15	26	1974	
4	1	25	59	15	25	1975	
5	2	40	...	...	...	1978	
17	1	6	610	127	21	1970	
15	7	47	589	79	13	1974	
36	7	19	560	81	14	1975	
63	10	16	509	...	...	1978	
2 351	835	36	13 688	1 863	14	1970	EGYPT ‡
2 673	1 070	40	20 717	3 354	16	1974	
2 755	1 048	38	24 294	3 809	16	1975	
2 830	1 078	38	25 215	4 375	17	1976	
3 080	1 208	39	28 237	4 880	17	1977	
3 373	1 311	39	29 353	5 307	18	1978	
25 595	11 583	45	275 281	84 190	31	1970	
33 275	14 410	43	348 306	116 721	34	1974	
33 014	14 509	44	377 495	126 870	34	1975	
32 744	14 460	44	421 320	153 269	36	1976	
36 522	16 623	46	436 637	156 176	36	1977	
40 595	19 278	47	492 664	182 734	37	1978	
...	...	...	...	...		1970	EQUATORIAL GUINEA
21	4	19	29	−	−	1975	
213	66	31	603	−	−	1970	
169	42	25	370	−	−	1975	
158	28	18	603	159	26	1970	ETHIOPIA
194	19	10	554	129	23	1973	
2 802	483	17	*6 020	2 594	*43	1970	
3 126	617	20	5 533	2 042	37	1973	
22	5	23	121	24	20	1970	GABON
34	*7	*21	...	...	...	1974	
36	...	...	168	38	23	1975	
38	9	24	189	33	17	1976	
131	29	22	1 608	334	21	1970	
382	*87	*23	3 042	544	18	1974	
371	124	33	2 450	572	23	1975	
548	199	36	2 545	585	23	1976	
12	4	33	18	2	11	1970	GAMBIA
19	5	26	25	*2	*8	1974	
13	5	38	30	6	20	1975	
15	3	20	31	7	23	1976	
15	...	...	34	...	...	1977	
27	7	26	...	...	...	1978	
149	31	21	181	17	9	1970	
99	31	31	272	42	15	1974	
111	45	41	329	*50	*15	1975	
195	62	32	427	73	17	1976	
193	45	23	401	95	24	1977	
231	48	21	...	...	...	1978	
1 324	234	18	1 130	142	13	1970	GHANA ‡
757	182	24	903	91	10	1974	
939	201	21	1 022	103	10	1975	
909	199	22	1 064	112	11	1976	
212	45	21	990	96	10	1977	

3.7 Education at the second level: teachers and pupils
Enseignement du second degré: personnel enseignant et élèves
Enseñanza de segundo grado: personal docente y alumnos

COUNTRY	YEAR	TOTAL SECOND LEVEL TOTAL DU SECOND DEGRE TOTAL DEL SEGUNDO GRADO			GENERAL EDUCATION ENSEIGNEMENT GENERAL ENSEÑANZA GENERAL		
PAYS	ANNEE		FEMALE FEMININ	%		FEMALE FEMININ	%
PAIS	AÑO	TOTAL	FEMENINO	F	TOTAL	FEMENINO	F
		(1)	(2)	(3)	(4)	(5)	(6)
GHANA (CONT.) ‡	STUDENTS 1970	99 299	27 473	28	59 669	15 374	26
	1974	536 660	207 490	39	514 321	201 927	39
	1975	555 980	212 667	38	532 520	207 214	39
	1976	576 779	219 164	38	551 699	213 095	39
	1977	592 262	227 371	38	568 947	221 873	39
GUINEA	TEACHERS 1970	2 785	...	...	2 360	...	...
	STUDENTS 1970	63 409	13 064	21	59 918	12 430	21
	1971	...	...	...	65 210	14 926	23
GUINEA—BISSAU	TEACHERS 1970	233	...	...	141	...	...
	1975	182	...	...	130	...	...
	1976	...	...	...	192	...	...
	STUDENTS 1970	4 215	1 526	36	3 268	1 245	38
	1974	...	...	...	2 191	707	32
	1975	2 109	656	31	1 676	536	32
	1976	3 177	755	24	2 785	692	25
	1977	5 371	1 114	21	4 922	1 090	22
IVORY COAST ‡	TEACHERS 1970	*3 279	...	...	*2 579	...	...
	1974	...	...	...	3 959	...	...
	1975	...	...	...	3 247	...	...
	1976	...	...	...	3 423	...	...
	STUDENTS 1970	69 101	14 785	21	62 356	13 242	21
	1974	104 730	...	...	95 477	23 057	24
	1975	119 482	...	...	102 387	25 207	25
	1976	127 492	...	...	112 141	28 133	25
	1977	...	...	...	125 749	32 836	26
	1978	...	...	...	143 221	...	...
KENYA ‡	TEACHERS 1970	6 599	1 878	28	5 881	1 690	29
	1974	...	...	...	...	...	...
	1975	9 730	...	...	...	...	...
	1976	12 077	3 485	29	...	...	...
	1977	13 357	...	...	12 696	3 549	28
	STUDENTS 1970	136 030	40 183	30	126 855	37 528	30
	1974	207 970	70 460	34	195 832	67 111	34
	1975	240 969	84 782	35	...	...	...
	1976	288 537	106 756	37	...	...	...
	1977	328 737	125 734	38	...	...	...
	1978	...	...	...	367 248	...	...
LESOTHO	TEACHERS 1970	329	149	45	256	115	45
	1975	740	387	52	605	302	50
	1976	763	369	48	621	294	47
	STUDENTS 1970	7 342	3 970	54	6 028	3 168	53
	1974	...	...	...	14 908	7 955	53
	1975	16 462	9 154	56	15 611	8 552	55
	1976	17 939	10 194	57	16 726	9 393	56
LIBERIA ‡	TEACHERS 1970	1 016	*193	*19	918	176	19
	1974	...	...	...	*1 331	...	...
	1975	...	...	...	...	...	...
	1976	...	...	...	1 696	220	13
	1978	...	...	...	2 713	461	17
	STUDENTS 1970	16 771	3 860	23	15 494	3 617	23
	1974	...	...	...	*26 733	...	...
	1975	34 151	8 498	25	32 978	8 331	25
	1976	31 224	7 531	24	29 544	7 310	25
	1978	47 446	13 474	28	45 668	13 247	29

Education at the second level: teachers and pupils 3.7
Enseignement du second degré: personnel enseignant et élèves
Enseñanza de segundo grado: personal docente y alumnos

TEACHER TRAINING ENSEIGNEMENT NORMAL ENSEÑANZA NORMAL			OTHER SECOND LEVEL AUTRE ENSEIGNEMENT DU SECOND DEGRE OTRA ENSEÑANZA DE SEGUNDO GRADO			YEAR ANNEE	COUNTRY PAYS
TOTAL	FEMALE FEMININ FEMENINO	% F	TOTAL	FEMALE FEMININ FEMENINO	% F	AÑO	PAIS
(7)	(8)	(9)	(10)	(11)	(12)		
16 478	5 343	32	23 152	6 756	29	1970	GHANA (CONT.) ‡
6 399	2 569	40	15 940	2 994	19	1974	
4 541	1 932	43	18 919	3 521	19	1975	
3 876	1 868	48	21 204	4 201	20	1976	
3 631	1 794	49	19 684	3 704	19	1977	
275	...	...	150	...	...	1970	GUINEA
1 478	232	16	2 013	402	20	1970	
...	...	...	...	...	...	1971	
37	...	...	55	...	...	1970	GUINEA–BISSAU
12	...	...	40	5	13	1975	
...	...	...	23	4	17	1976	
390	143	37	557	138	25	1970	
132	78	59	...	...	...	1974	
90	43	48	343	77	22	1975	
202	29	14	190	34	18	1976	
373	17	5	76	7	9	1977	
87	16	18	613	144	23	1970	IVORY COAST ‡
...	...	...	620	*148	*24	1974	
...	...	...	...	...	...	1975	
...	...	...	...	...	...	1976	
1 622	475	29	5 123	1 068	21	1970	
1 088	...	...	8 165	*1 402	*17	1974	
1 337	368	28	15 758	...	...	1975	
1 390	...	...	13 961	...	...	1976	
1 994	...	...	...	...	...	1977	
...	...	...	...	...	...	1978	
575	188	33	143	–	–	1970	KENYA‡
671	...	...	...	...	...	1974	
541	170	31	...	...	...	1975	
639	150	23	...	...	...	1976	
661	...	...	...	...	...	1977	
6 749	2 655	39	2 426	–	–	1970	
8 479	3 349	39	3 659	–	–	1974	
8 666	3 253	38	5 468	–	–	1975	
8 149	3 091	38	...	...	...	1976	
8 427	2 896	34	...	...	...	1977	
*8 800	...	...	...	...	...	1978	
40	23	58	33	11	33	1970	LESOTHO
69	46	67	66	39	59	1975	
39	28	72	103	47	46	1976	
695	459	66	619	343	55	1970	
357	272	76	...	...	...	1974	
304	221	73	547	381	70	1975	
378	269	71	835	532	64	1976	
32	2	6	66	*15	*23	1970	LIBERIA ‡
...	...	...	...	...	...	1974	
53	12	23	...	...	...	1975	
40	3	8	63	5	8	1976	
38	3	8	...	...	...	1978	
390	65	17	887	178	20	1970	
...	...	...	...	...	...	1974	
322	55	17	851	112	13	1975	
444	89	20	1 236	132	11	1976	
597	83	14	1 181	144	12	1978	

3.7 **Education at the second level: teachers and pupils**
Enseignement du second degré: personnel enseignant et élèves
Enseñanza de segundo grado: personal docente y alumnos

COUNTRY PAYS PAIS	YEAR ANNEE AÑO	TOTAL SECOND LEVEL TOTAL DU SECOND DEGRE TOTAL DEL SEGUNDO GRADO			GENERAL EDUCATION ENSEIGNEMENT GENERAL ENSEÑANZA GENERAL		
		TOTAL	FEMALE FEMININ FEMENINO	% F	TOTAL	FEMALE FEMININ FEMENINO	% F
		(1)	(2)	(3)	(4)	(5)	(6)
LIBYAN ARAB JAMAHIRIYA	TEACHERS 1970	4 343	455	10	3 549	387	11
	1974	9 862	1 284	13	7 898	950	12
	1975	11 819	...	...	9 464	1 287	14
	1976	*14 691	...	...	12 316	1 958	16
	1977	15 135	2 719	18	12 792	2 223	17
	1978	...	...	...	12 915	2 291	18
	STUDENTS 1970	53 953	9 819	18	45 488	7 834	17
	1974	129 875	39 682	31	106 149	28 716	27
	1975	166 122	55 722	34	140 486	43 464	31
	1976	200 063	72 087	36	173 354	58 532	34
	1977	224 567	86 726	39	194 866	70 786	36
	1978	...	...	...	196 079	71 319	36
MADAGASCAR	TEACHERS 1970	5 709	...	...	4 757	*1 632	*34
	1975	...	...	...	5 088	...	...
	STUDENTS 1970	113 270	45 073	40	101 412	41 902	41
	1975	...	...	...	131 836	57 005	43
MALAWI ‡	TEACHERS 1970	*722	*236	*33	*578	*181	*31
	1974	873	...	...	694	...	...
	1975	931	...	...	748	...	...
	1976	...	...	...	725	...	...
	1977	...	...	...	707	289	41
	STUDENTS 1970	11 727	*3 216	*27	10 397	*2 776	*27
	1974	16 627	...	...	13 900	3 786	27
	1975	16 797	...	...	14 489	4 117	28
	1976	...	...	...	14 826	4 444	30
	1977	...	...	...	15 079	4 573	30
MALI	TEACHERS 1970	2 242	392	17	1 818	317	17
	1974	...	...	...	*2 303	...	...
	1975	...	...	...	2 567	452	18
	STUDENTS 1970	34 620	7 549	22	29 683	6 614	22
	1974	49 034	*12 177	*25	42 668	10 620	25
	1975	55 465	*14 311	*26	48 488	12 358	25
	1976	...	...	...	55 814	15 037	27
	1977	...	...	...	64 491	17 325	27
MAURITANIA	TEACHERS 1970	...	...	...	*148		
	1977	...	...	...	389	53	14
	STUDENTS 1970	...	...	...	3 408	382	11
	1974	...	...	...	5 493	...	...
	1975	...	...	...	6 571	...	...
	1976	...	...	...	7 995	...	...
	1977	...	...	...	9 728	...	...
MAURITIUS ‡	TEACHERS 1970	...	...	...	1 747	*570	*33
	1974	2 027	732	36	1 921	699	36
	1975	2 124	...	...	*2 012	...	...
	1976	2 236	821	37	2 123	788	37
	1977	2 555	953	37	2 439	919	38
	1978	2 884	1 146	40	2 769	1 112	40
	STUDENTS 1970	...	...	...	43 969	17 542	40
	1974	62 015	27 067	44	60 441	26 454	44
	1975	65 113	28 869	44	63 492	28 195	44
	1976	68 833	31 050	45	66 920	30 304	45
	1977	79 603	36 744	46	78 038	36 133	46
	1978	81 871	38 633	47	80 479	38 112	47

Education at the second level: teachers and pupils   3.7
Enseignement du second degré: personnel enseignant et élèves
Enseñanza de segundo grado: personal docente y alumnos

TEACHER TRAINING ENSEIGNEMENT NORMAL ENSEÑANZA NORMAL			OTHER SECOND LEVEL AUTRE ENSEIGNEMENT DU SECOND DEGRE OTRA ENSEÑANZA DE SEGUNDO GRADO			YEAR ANNEE AÑO	COUNTRY PAYS PAIS
TOTAL	FEMALE FEMININ FEMENINO	% F	TOTAL	FEMALE FEMININ FEMENINO	% F		
(7)	(8)	(9)	(10)	(11)	(12)		
							LIBYAN ARAB JAMAHIRIYA
463	68	15	331	—	—	1970	
1 514	292	19	450	42	9	1974	
1 832	437	24	523	...	...	1975	
2 006	477	24	*369	...	...	1976	
1 968	456	23	375	40	11	1977	
...	...	...	487	40	8	1978	
5 377	1 985	37	3 088	—	—	1970	
19 546	10 966	56	4 180	—	—	1974	
20 748	12 258	59	4 888	—	—	1975	
21 719	13 116	60	4 990	439	9	1976	
24 153	15 038	62	5 548	902	16	1977	
...	...	...	6 267	*812	*13	1978	
224	...	...	728	...	...	1970	MADAGASCAR
...	...	...	...	...	...	1975	
2 009	676	34	9 849	2 495	25	1970	
...	...	...	...	...	...	1975	
*110	*45	*41	*34	*10	*29	1970	MALAWI ‡
95	...	...	84	...	...	1974	
94	...	...	89	...	...	1975	
93	20	22	...	...	...	1976	
90	17	19	...	...	...	1977	
991	*353	*36	339	*87	*26	1970	
1 283	461	36	1 444	...	...	1974	
1 100	226	21	1 208	...	...	1975	
1 375	462	34	...	...	...	1976	
1 433	449	31	...	...	...	1977	
92	20	22	332	55	17	1970	MALI
126	...	...	...	...	...	1974	
...	...	...	...	...	...	1975	
1 551	269	17	3 386	666	20	1970	
1 843	306	17	*4 523	*1 251	*28	1974	
*1 969	*383	*19	*5 008	*1 570	*31	1975	
2 006	455	23	...	...	...	1976	
2 261	452	20	...	...	...	1977	
...	...	...	—	—	—	1970	MAURITANIA
...	...	...	...	...	...	1977	
...	...	...	—	—	—	1970	
...	...	...	...	...	...	1974	
...	...	...	...	...	...	1975	
297	...	...	...	...	...	1976	
430	...	...	...	...	...	1977	
...	...	...	...	...	...	1970	MAURITIUS ‡
23	10	43	83	23	28	1974	
19	8	42	93	26	28	1975	
20	9	45	93	24	26	1976	
23	11	48	93	23	25	1977	
24	10	42	91	24	26	1978	
...	...	...	538	245	46	1970	
645	247	38	929	366	39	1974	
589	245	42	1 032	429	42	1975	
700	294	42	1 213	452	37	1976	
424	164	39	1 141	447	39	1977	
341	154	45	1 051	367	35	1978	

3.7 Education at the second level: teachers and pupils
Enseignement du second degré: personnel enseignant et élèves
Enseñanza de segundo grado: personal docente y alumnos

COUNTRY PAYS PAIS	YEAR ANNEE AÑO	TOTAL SECOND LEVEL TOTAL DU SECOND DEGRE TOTAL DEL SEGUNDO GRADO			GENERAL EDUCATION ENSEIGNEMENT GENERAL ENSEÑANZA GENERAL		
		TOTAL	FEMALE FEMININ FEMENINO	% F	TOTAL	FEMALE FEMININ FEMENINO	% F
		(1)	(2)	(3)	(4)	(5)	(6)
MOROCCO ‡	TEACHERS 1970	14 680	4 378	30	13 988	4 196	30
	1974	...	...	...	16 716	4 657	28
	1975	...	...	...	19 613	5 381	27
	1976	...	...	...	22 273	6 151	28
	1977	...	...	...	24 686	6 501	26
	1978	...	...	...	28 385	7 373	26
	STUDENTS 1970	298 880	84 499	28	289 327	82 527	29
	1974	403 673	131 002	32	397 248	128 918	32
	1975	486 173	...	...	468 870	160 119	34
	1976	529 027	185 662	35	510 509	178 410	35
	1977	589 610	213 320	36	564 010	201 869	36
	1978	662 034	245 081	37	631 942	231 875	37
MOZAMBIQUE	TEACHERS 1970	2 561	...	...	1 431	...	...
	1972	2 788	1 543	55	1 682	1 081	64
	STUDENTS 1970	42 868	...	...	26 668	...	...
	1972	54 650	21 858	40	36 155	16 106	45
NIGER	TEACHERS 1970	346	75	22	268	64	24
	1974	586	112	19	508	104	20
	1975	637	146	23	571	137	24
	1976	787	158	20	713	148	21
	1977	...	...	...	803	127	16
	STUDENTS 1970	6 999	1 876	27	6 337	1 655	26
	1974	12 333	3 302	27	11 581	3 124	27
	1975	14 462	3 983	28	13 621	3 785	28
	1976	18 098	5 119	28	17 093	4 878	29
	1977	...	...	...	21 065	5 981	28
NIGERIA ‡	TEACHERS 1970	16 794	3 064	18	13 277	2 546	19
	1977	...	...	...	...	...	...
	STUDENTS 1970	356 565	114 272	32	293 498	96 798	33
	1976	998 609	...	...	826 926	...	...
	1977	...	...	...	...	...	...
REUNION	TEACHERS 1970	1 312	...	...	...	...	...
	1975	2 363	...	...	...	...	...
	1978	3 084	...	...	...	...	...
	STUDENTS 1970	30 853	...	...	28 086	16 192	58
	1974	46 389	25 670	55	...	...	...
	1975	50 467	27 954	55	...	...	...
	1976	55 127	30 397	55	...	...	...
	1978	61 068	33 334	55	45 743	26 220	57
RWANDA	TEACHERS 1970	770	...	...	...	...	...
	1974	707	169	24	...	...	...
	1975	752	194	26	...	...	...
	1976	820	216	26	...	...	...
	STUDENTS 1970	10 259	3 387	33	7 398	2 247	30
	1974	11 228	3 730	33	7 935	2 473	31
	1975	12 046	3 978	33	8 704	2 680	31
	1976	12 570	4 122	33	8 870	2 768	31
ST. HELENA	TEACHERS 1970	35	24	69	33	24	73
	1974	38	30	79	33	28	85
	1976	48	34	71	44	34	77
	1977	41	30	73	38	30	79

Education at the second level: teachers and pupils **3.7**
Enseignement du second degré: personnel enseignant et élèves
Enseñanza de segundo grado: personal docente y alumnos

TEACHER TRAINING ENSEIGNEMENT NORMAL ENSEÑANZA NORMAL			OTHER SECOND LEVEL AUTRE ENSEIGNEMENT DU SECOND DEGRE OTRA ENSEÑANZA DE SEGUNDO GRADO			YEAR ANNEE AÑO	COUNTRY PAYS PAIS
TOTAL	FEMALE FEMININ FEMENINO	% F	TOTAL	FEMALE FEMININ FEMENINO	% F		
(7)	(8)	(9)	(10)	(11)	(12)		
120	19	16	572	163	28	1970	MOROCCO ‡
364	...	...	...	...	...	1974	
*486	...	...	...	...	...	1975	
443	86	19	...	...	...	1976	
628	...	...	...	...	...	1977	
847	161	19	...	...	...	1978	
2 567	823	32	6 986	1 149	16	1970	
3 922	1 429	36	2 503	655	26	1974	
3 953	1 716	43	13 350			1975	
4 472	1 963	44	14 046	5 289	38	1976	
7 413	3 521	47	18 187	7 930	44	1977	
11 238	5 344	48	18 854	7 862	42	1978	
114	*56	*49	1 016	...	...	1970	MOZAMBIQUE
122	57	47	984	405	41	1972	
1 169	510	44	15 031	...	...	1970	
1 279	545	43	17 216	5 207	30	1972	
50	6	12	28	5	18	1970	NIGER
51	4	8	27	4	15	1974	
41	4	10	25	5	20	1975	
42	7	17	32	3	9	1976	
48	8	17	...	...	...	1977	
474	218	46	188	3	2	1970	
485	161	33	267	*17	*6	1974	
608	184	30	233	14	6	1975	
731	228	31	274	13	5	1976	
1 225	370	30	...	...	...	1977	
1 857	366	20	1 660	152	9	1970	NIGERIA ‡
...	...	...	1 861	...	...	1977	
32 866	9 160	28	30 201	8 314	28	1970	
144 503	...	...	27 180	...	...	1976	
...	...	...	34 665	...	...	1977	
*19	...	...	...	...	...	1970	REUNION
...	...	...	...	...	...	1975	
—	—	—	...	...	...	1978	
669	...	...	2 098	...	...	1970	
...	...	...	5 500	2 522	46	1974	
...	...	...	5 943	2 820	47	1975	
...	...	...	6 732	3 123	46	1976	
—	—	—	15 325	7 114	46	1978	
...	...	...	...	...	...	1970	RWANDA
...	...	...	...	...	...	1974	
...	...	...	...	...	...	1975	
...	...	...	...	...	...	1976	
1 606	595	37	1 255	545	43	1970	
1 571	632	40	1 722	625	36	1974	
1 552	665	43	1 790	633	35	1975	
1 603	650	41	2 097	704	34	1976	
2	—	—	—	—	—	1970	ST. HELENA
3	2	67	2	—	—	1974	
—	—	—	4	—	—	1976	
—	—	—	3	—	—	1977	

3.7 **Education at the second level: teachers and pupils**
Enseignement du second degré: personnel enseignant et élèves
Enseñanza de segundo grado: personal docente y alumnos

COUNTRY PAYS PAIS	YEAR ANNEE AÑO	TOTAL SECOND LEVEL TOTAL DU SECOND DEGRE TOTAL DEL SEGUNDO GRADO			GENERAL EDUCATION ENSEIGNEMENT GENERAL ENSEÑANZA GENERAL		
		TOTAL	FEMALE FEMININ FEMENINO	% F	TOTAL	FEMALE FEMININ FEMENINO	% F
		(1)	(2)	(3)	(4)	(5)	(6)
ST. HELENA (CONT.)	STUDENTS 1970	413	230	56	408	225	55
	1974	542	278	51	528	274	52
	1975	524	281	54	509	276	54
	1976	530	276	52	509	276	54
	1977	525	264	50	505	264	52
	1978	583	293	50	561	286	51
SAO TOME AND PRINCIPE	TEACHERS 1970	...	...	...	73	...	...
	STUDENTS 1970	...	...	...	1 463	643	44
	1976	...	...	...	3 674	1 691	46
	1977	...	...	...	3 145	1 469	47
SENEGAL ‡	TEACHERS 1970	...	...	...	*1 838	*471	*26
	STUDENTS 1970	59 401	16 925	28	53 298	14 942	28
	1974	...	...	...	...	...	...
	1975	...	...	...	53 552	...	...
SEYCHELLES ‡	TEACHERS 1970	120	74	62	106	64	60
	1974	173	99	57	141	85	60
	1975	177	102	58	145	90	62
	1976	...	...	...	58	17	29
	1977	...	...	...	...	...	...
	1978	242	...	...	200	...	...
	1979	288	184	64	215	155	72
	STUDENTS 1970	2 359	1 308	55	2 131	1 153	54
	1974	3 778	2 018	53	3 238	1 746	54
	1975	3 778	2 125	56	3 465	1 901	55
	1976	3 272	1 815	55	3 036	1 707	56
	1977	...	...	...	4 243	2 332	55
	1978	4 622	2 497	54	4 361	2 382	55
	1979	5 143	2 745	53	4 601	2 468	54
SIERRA LEONE ‡	TEACHERS 1970	1 699	480	28	1 495	438	29
	1974	1 629	587	36	1 395	532	38
	1975	2 596	901	35	2 378	854	36
	1977	...	...	...	2 507	678	27
	STUDENTS 1970	34 646	9 766	28	33 318	9 455	28
	1974	47 861	14 807	31	45 277	14 283	32
	1975	50 478	15 991	32	48 534	15 589	32
	1976	...	...	...	51 564	...	...
	1977	...	...	...	53 897	17 467	32
SOMALIA ‡	TEACHERS 1970	1 022	103	10	*937	*88	*9
	1974	—	—	—	—	—	—
	1975	1 529	130	9	1 161	102	9
	1976	959	115	12	522	48	9
	1977	916	92	10	528	62	12
	STUDENTS 1970	24 862	5 151	21	23 847	4 996	21
	1974	—	—	—	—	—	—
	1975	31 857	7 566	24	26 611	6 119	23
	1976	12 389	2 763	22	6 308	1 111	18
	1977	14 178	3 523	25	7 998	1 855	23
SOUTH AFRICA ‡	STUDENTS 1970	563 194	...	...	542 194	264 461	49
SUDAN ‡	TEACHERS 1970	8 006	1 459	18	7 435	1 401	19
	1974	11 802	...	...	10 946	2 073	19
	1975	13 166	...	...	12 097	2 528	21
	1976	...	...	...	*12 880	*2 534	*20
	1977	14 882	...	...	13 792	2 821	20
	1978	18 437	3 648	20	17 072	3 462	20

Education at the second level: teachers and pupils   3.7
Enseignement du second degré: personnel enseignant et élèves
Enseñanza de segundo grado: personal docente y alumnos

TEACHER TRAINING ENSEIGNEMENT NORMAL ENSEÑANZA NORMAL			OTHER SECOND LEVEL AUTRE ENSEIGNEMENT DU SECOND DEGRE OTRA ENSEÑANZA DE SEGUNDO GRADO			YEAR ANNEE AÑO	COUNTRY PAYS PAIS
TOTAL	FEMALE FEMININ FEMENINO	% F	TOTAL	FEMALE FEMININ FEMENINO	% F		
(7)	(8)	(9)	(10)	(11)	(12)		
5	5	100	—	—	—	1970	ST. HELENA (CONT.)
4	4	100	10	—	—	1974	
5	5	100	10	—	—	1975	
—	—	—	21	—	—	1976	
—	—	—	20	—	—	1977	
6	4	67	16	3	19	1978	
...	...	...	34	...	...	1970	SAO TOME AND PRINCIPE
...	...	...	206	50	24	1970	
...	...	...	...	...	...	1976	
...	...	...	...	...	...	1977	
...	...	...	...	...	...	1970	SENEGAL ‡
656	208	32	5 447	1 775	33	1970	
...	...	...	6 965	...	...	1974	
...	...	...	8 182	...	...	1975	
—	—	—	14	10	71	1970	SEYCHELLES ‡
—	—	—	32	14	44	1974	
—	—	—	32	12	38	1975	
—	—	—	...	...	...	1976	
—	—	—	...	...	...	1977	
—	—	—	42	10	24	1978	
—	—	—	73	29	40	1979	
—	—	—	228	155	68	1970	
—	—	—	540	272	50	1974	
—	—	—	313	224	72	1975	
—	—	—	236	108	46	1976	
—	—	—	...	...	...	1977	
—	—	—	261	115	44	1978	
—	—	—	542	277	51	1979	
141	37	26	63	5	8	1970	SIERRA LEONE ‡
148	45	30	86	10	12	1974	
120	34	28	98	13	13	1975	
...	...	...	...	...	...	1977	
792	219	28	536	92	17	1970	
1 407	424	30	1 177	100	8	1974	
1 145	355	31	799	47	6	1975	
...	...	...	...	...	...	1976	
...	...	...	...	...	...	1977	
13	9	69	*72	*6	*8	1970	SOMALIA ‡
—	—	—	—	—	—	1974	
181	—	—	187	28	15	1975	
207	22	11	230	45	20	1976	
148	5	3	240	25	10	1977	
237	36	15	*778	*119	*15	1970	
—	—	—	—	—	—	1974	
3 422	1 128	33	1 824	319	17	1975	
3 251	1 088	33	2 830	564	20	1976	
2 281	777	34	3 899	891	23	1977	
*21 000	...	...	...	...	...	1970	SOUTH AFRICA ‡
246	58	24	325	—	—	1970	SUDAN ‡
391	...	...	465	...	...	1974	
420	...	...	649	—	—	1975	
...	...	...	777	—	—	1976	
488	...	...	602	70	12	1977	
723	126	17	602	60	10	1978	

3.7 Education at the second level: teachers and pupils
Enseignement du second degré: personnel enseignant et élèves
Enseñanza de segundo grado: personal docente y alumnos

COUNTRY PAYS PAIS	YEAR ANNEE AÑO	TOTAL SECOND LEVEL TOTAL DU SECOND DEGRE TOTAL DEL SEGUNDO GRADO			GENERAL EDUCATION ENSEIGNEMENT GENERAL ENSEÑANZA GENERAL		
		TOTAL	FEMALE FEMININ FEMENINO	% F	TOTAL	FEMALE FEMININ FEMENINO	% F
		(1)	(2)	(3)	(4)	(5)	(6)
SUDAN (CONT.) ‡	STUDENTS 1970	132 626	37 416	28	128 379	36 514	28
	1974	272 553	*81 253	*30	261 223	78 556	30
	1975	281 839	86 806	31	268 120	*84 196	*31
	1976	306 913	96 221	31	293 055	93 380	32
	1977	326 250	109 031	33	313 093	106 047	34
	1978	351 984	118 347	34	335 322	114 464	34
SWAZILAND	TEACHERS 1970	...	...	...	432	*148	*34
	1974	...	...	...	611	223	36
	1975	...	...	...	739	291	39
	1976	...	...	...	885	372	42
	1977	1 073	445	41	978	419	43
	1978	...	...	...	1 073	457	43
	STUDENTS 1970	8 438	...	...	8 027	3 458	43
	1974	14 964	...	...	14 301	6 417	45
	1975	16 867	...	...	16 227	7 378	45
	1976	18 105	...	...	17 396	8 082	46
	1977	20 211	9 546	47	19 359	9 204	48
	1978	...	...	...	20 584	9 927	48
TOGO	TEACHERS 1970	880	218	25	663	157	24
	1974	*1 335	*238	*18	1 111	190	17
	1975	1 634	*268	*16	1 358	204	15
	1976	2 161	285	13	1 832	231	13
	1977	2 377	291	12	2 030	252	12
	1978	...	...	...	2 328	301	13
	STUDENTS 1970	22 003	4 926	22	19 746	4 099	21
	1974	48 415	11 242	23	44 306	10 025	23
	1975	64 590	15 345	24	59 162	13 760	23
	1976	81 374	18 582	23	74 567	17 008	23
	1977	96 276	22 190	23	88 409	20 168	23
	1978	114 971	27 405	24	105 770	24 751	23
TUNISIA ‡	TEACHERS 1970	6 883	...	...	...	...	...
	1974	8 575	*2 528	*29	...	...	...
	1975	8 769	...	...	...	...	...
	1976	9 776	2 795	29	...	...	...
	1977	11 874	3 019	29	...	...	...
	1978	12 262	3 559	29	...	...	...
	STUDENTS 1970	191 445	52 928	28	158 594	43 900	28
	1974	196 447	61 796	31	163 159	52 412	32
	1975	201 825	67 977	34	144 632	49 841	34
	1976	211 361	73 410	35	149 837	53 296	36
	1977	230 868	81 137	35	159 341	57 866	36
	1978	250 197	89 640	36	170 425	62 556	37
UGANDA ‡	TEACHERS 1970	2 435	...	...	1 816	...	...
	1974	2 418	433	18	1 894	366	19
	1975	2 599	...	...	1 994	392	20
	1976	3 233	624	19	2 626	540	21
	1977	2 770	672	24	2 126	592	28
	STUDENTS 1970	48 221	...	...	40 697	9 720	24
	1974	53 586	...	...	45 478	10 595	23
	1975	55 263	14 357	26	45 871	12 112	26
	1976	66 986	18 245	27	56 884	15 431	27
	1977	70 647	19 441	28	59 882	16 317	27
UNITED REPUBLIC OF CAMEROON	TEACHERS 1970	...	...	...	2 200	502	23
	1974	5 069	1 025	20	3 699	707	19
	1975	4 805	970	20	3 309	628	19
	1976	6 348	1 222	19	4 318	753	17
	1977	6 988	1 382	20	4 728	841	18

Education at the second level: teachers and pupils 3.7
Enseignement du second degré: personnel enseignant et élèves
Enseñanza de segundo grado: personal docente y alumnos

TEACHER TRAINING ENSEIGNEMENT NORMAL ENSEÑANZA NORMAL			OTHER SECOND LEVEL AUTRE ENSEIGNEMENT DU SECOND DEGRE OTRA ENSEÑANZA DE SEGUNDO GRADO			YEAR ANNEE	COUNTRY PAYS
TOTAL	FEMALE FEMININ FEMENINO	% F	TOTAL	FEMALE FEMININ FEMENINO	% F	AÑO	PAIS
(7)	(8)	(9)	(10)	(11)	(12)		
2 391	902	38	1 856	—	—	1970	SUDAN (CONT.) ‡
4 814	1 947	40	6 516	*750	*12	1974	
4 723	1 993	42	8 996	617	7	1975	
4 707	2 021	43	9 151	820	9	1976	
4 221	1 754	42	8 936	1 230	14	1977	
4 878	1 936	40	11 784	1 947	17	1978	
...	...	...	...	...	...	1970	SWAZILAND
...	...	...	...	...	...	1974	
...	...	...	...	...	...	1975	
...	...	...	...	...	...	1976	
49	22	45	46	4	9	1977	
41	16	39	...	...	...	1978	
215	169	79	196	*49	*25	1970	
198	159	80	465	...	...	1974	
196	159	81	444	...	...	1975	
229	171	75	480	...	...	1976	
364	247	68	488	95	19	1977	
239	171	72	...	...	...	1978	
16	2	13	201	59	29	1970	TOGO
*20	*3	*15	204	45	22	1974	
25	*5	*20	251	59	24	1975	
24	1	4	305	53	17	1976	
21	—	—	326	39	12	1977	
21	1	5	...	...	...	1978	
153	22	14	2 104	805	38	1970	
198	29	15	3 911	1 188	30	1974	
310	41	13	5 118	1 544	30	1975	
329	42	13	6 478	1 532	24	1976	
388	94	24	7 479	1 928	26	1977	
478	135	28	8 723	2 519	29	1978	
...	...	...	...	...	...	1970	TUNISIA ‡
133	15	11	...	...	...	1974	
			...	...	...	1975	
86	34	40	...	...	...	1976	
125	36	29	...	...	...	1977	
128	35	27	...	...	...	1978	
11 677	3 868	33	21 174	5 160	24	1970	
3 027	1 406	46	30 261	7 978	26	1974	
1 059	554	52	56 134	17 582	31	1975	
1 079	716	66	60 445	19 398	32	1976	
1 987	1 303	66	69 540	21 968	32	1977	
2 898	1 865	64	76 874	25 219	33	1978	
309	74	24	*310	...	...	1970	UGANDA ‡
288	66	23	236	1		1974	
330	...	...	275	*1		1975	
343	83	24	264	1		1976	
374	80	21	270	—	—	1977	
3 967	1 192	30	3 557	...	...	1970	
5 246	2 089	40	2 862	...	...	1974	
6 096	2 160	35	3 296	85	3	1975	
6 414	2 709	42	3 688	105	3	1976	
6 946	3 005	43	3 819	119	3	1977	
...	...	...	900	250	28	1970	UNITED REPUBLIC OF CAMEROON
130	34	26	1 240	284	23	1974	
132	22	17	1 364	320	23	1975	
162	41	25	1 868	428	23	1976	
144	32	22	2 116	509	24	1977	

3.7 Education at the second level: teachers and pupils
Enseignement du second degré: personnel enseignant et élèves
Enseñanza de segundo grado: personal docente y alumnos

COUNTRY PAYS PAIS		YEAR ANNEE AÑO	TOTAL SECOND LEVEL TOTAL DU SECOND DEGRE TOTAL DEL SEGUNDO GRADO			GENERAL EDUCATION ENSEIGNEMENT GENERAL ENSEÑANZA GENERAL		
			TOTAL	FEMALE FEMININ FEMENINO	% F	TOTAL	FEMALE FEMININ FEMENINO	% F
			(1)	(2)	(3)	(4)	(5)	(6)
UNITED REPUBLIC OF CAMEROON (CONT.)	STUDENTS	1970	76 461	21 896	29	56 031	14 817	26
		1974	126 654	40 072	32	93 934	28 579	30
		1975	143 812	46 813	33	106 266	33 398	31
		1976	163 810	55 213	34	121 054	38 974	32
		1977	183 179	62 881	34	135 518	44 414	33
UNITED REPUBLIC OF TANZANIA ‡	TEACHERS	1970	2 449	677	28			
		1974	2 967	...	...	2 440	705	29
		1975	3 218	...	...	2 606	740	28
		1976	3 731	...	...	2 930	796	27
	STUDENTS	1970	44 941	12 934	29			...
		1974	59 411	18 040	30	50 297	14 230	28
		1975	62 998	19 439	31	53 257	15 208	29
		1976	67 859	23 595	35	57 143	17 739	31
UPPER VOLTA ‡	TEACHERS	1970	474	...	...	296	...	...
		1974	757	...	...	555	...	...
		1975	818	...	...	580	...	...
		1978	...	...	...	401	...	...
	STUDENTS	1970	10 717	3 000	28	8 803	2 202	25
		1974	15 470	4 755	31	12 682	3 723	29
		1975	16 227	5 123	32	13 167	4 037	31
		1976	18 081	5 286	29	14 958	4 579	31
		1977	...	...	...	16 128	5 022	31
		1978	21 018	6 882	33	17 401	5 532	32
WESTERN SAHARA	TEACHERS	1970	54	27	50	54	27	50
	STUDENTS	1970	1 000	357	36	1 000	357	36
		1973	621	158	25	621	158	25
ZAIRE	STUDENTS	1970	248 318	53 350	21	185 370	38 615	21
		1974	446 067	118 788	27	300 339	73 370	24
		1975	...	...	...	*326 884	*86 642	*27
		1976	...	...	...	*397 408	*131 633	*33
		1977	*643 675	*240 845	*37	*458 776	*177 351	*39
ZAMBIA	TEACHERS	1970	...	...	...	2 465	824	33
		1974	...	...	...	3 038	1 009	33
		1975	...	...	...	3 202	1 042	33
		1976	...	...	...	3 478	1 137	33
		1977	...	...	...	3 539	1 108	31
	STUDENTS	1970	56 182	18 294	33	52 472	17 267	33
		1974	70 812	23 589	33	65 764	22 200	34
		1975	77 866	...	...	73 049	25 066	34
		1976	83 637	...	...	78 805	26 934	34
		1977	89 473	...	...	83 757	28 482	34
ZIMBABWE ‡	TEACHERS	1974	...	...	...	3 359	...	...
		1975	...	...	...	3 737	...	...
		1976	...	...	...	3 766	...	...
	PUPILS	1970	...	...	...	49 543	...	...
		1974	...	...	...	64 968	...	...
		1975	...	...	...	69 181	...	...
		1976	80 612	...	...	71 816	...	...

Education at the second level: teachers and pupils   3.7
Enseignement du second degré: personnel enseignant et élèves
Enseñanza de segundo grado: personal docente y alumnos

TEACHER TRAINING ENSEIGNEMENT NORMAL ENSEÑANZA NORMAL			OTHER SECOND LEVEL AUTRE ENSEIGNEMENT DU SECOND DEGRE OTRA ENSEÑANZA DE SEGUNDO GRADO			YEAR ANNEE AÑO	COUNTRY PAYS PAIS
TOTAL	FEMALE FEMININ FEMENINO	% F	TOTAL	FEMALE FEMININ FEMENINO	% F		
(7)	(8)	(9)	(10)	(11)	(12)		
3 030	703	23	17 400	6 376	37	1970	UNITED REPUBLIC OF
1 115	291	26	31 605	11 202	35	1974	CAMEROON (CONT.)
1 284	327	25	36 262	13 088	36	1975	
1 572	389	25	41 184	15 850	38	1976	
1 712	426	25	45 949	18 041	39	1977	
327	86	26	...	...	...	1970	UNITED REPUBLIC OF TANZANIA ‡
527	...	...	...	...	...	1974	
612	...	...	...	...	...	1975	
627	...	...	174	18	10	1976	
3 762	1 510	40	...	...	...	1970	
9 114	3 810	42	...	...	...	1974	
9 741	4 231	43	...	...	...	1975	
8 951	5 249	59	1 765	607	34	1976	
39	...	...	139	...	...	1970	UPPER VOLTA ‡
27	...	...	175	...	...	1974	
28	14	50	210	40	19	1975	
...	...	...	...	...	...	1978	
337	37	11	1 577	761	48	1970	
382	72	19	2 406	960	40	1974	
391	117	30	2 669	969	36	1975	
286	111	39	2 837	596	21	1976	
...	...	...	...	...	...	1977	
238	56	24	3 379	1 294	38	1978	
—	—	—	—	—	—	1970	WESTERN SAHARA
—	—	—	—	—	—	1970	
—	—	—	—	—	—	1973	
39 088	9 694	25	23 860	5 041	21	1970	ZAIRE
83 164	24 109	29	62 564	21 309	34	1974	
*88 142	*25 604	*29	...	...	...	1975	
*93 431	*27 193	*29	...	...	...	1976	
*99 904	*28 938	*29	*84 995	*34 556	*41	1977	
167	49	29	...	...	...	1970	ZAMBIA
205	51	25	...	...	...	1974	
220	49	22	...	...	...	1975	
229	43	19	...	...	...	1976	
268	55	21	...	...	...	1977	
1 934	710	37	1 776	*317	*18	1970	
2 187	973	44	2 861	...	...	1974	
2 246	1 022	46	2 571	...	...	1975	
2 486	1 138	46	2 346	...	...	1976	
3 046	1 346	44	2 670	...	...	1977	
...	...	...	...	...	...	1974	ZIMBABWE ‡
...	...	...	...	...	...	1975	
...	...	...	...	...	...	1976	
2 081	...	...	...	...	...	1970	
2 707	...	...	...	...	...	1974	
2 494	...	...	...	...	...	1975	
2 861	...	...	5 935	...	...	1976	

3.7 Education at the second level: teachers and pupils
Enseignement du second degré: personnel enseignant et élèves
Enseñanza de segundo grado: personal docente y alumnos

COUNTRY PAYS PAIS	YEAR ANNEE AÑO	TOTAL SECOND LEVEL TOTAL DU SECOND DEGRE TOTAL DEL SEGUNDO GRADO			GENERAL EDUCATION ENSEIGNEMENT GENERAL ENSEÑANZA GENERAL		
		TOTAL	FEMALE FEMININ FEMENINO	% F	TOTAL	FEMALE FEMININ FEMENINO	% F
		(1)	(2)	(3)	(4)	(5)	(6)
AMERICA, NORTH							
ANTIGUA ‡	TEACHERS 1970	...	138	57	*47	38	*81
	1974	242	197	63	205	125	61
	1975	313			280	181	65
	STUDENTS 1970	...		...	5 000	2 726	55
	1974	6 430	3 476	54	6 201	3 342	54
	1975	6 827	...	...	6 629	3 465	52
BAHAMAS ‡	TEACHERS 1970	641	*343	*54	548	*310	*57
	1974	...	...	...	...	...	...
	1975	...	...	...	...	...	...
	STUDENTS 1970	21 422	...	...	20 495	...	...
	1974	...	...	...	26 512	...	...
	1975	...	...	...	28 056	14 468	52
	1976	...	...	...	29 472	15 116	51
	1977	...	...	...	29 832	15 218	51
	1978	...	...	...	30 015	15 215	51
BARBADOS ‡	TEACHERS 1975	1 421	...	...	...	...	...
	1976	1 432	...	...	...	...	...
	1977	1 517	...	...	...	...	...
	STUDENTS 1970	...	...	...	19 007	8 912	47
	1974	22 341	10 686	48	...	...	...
	1975	29 025	14 963	52	...	...	...
	1976	28 677	14 695	51	...	...	...
	1977	30 021	15 255	51	...	...	...
BELIZE	TEACHERS 1970	...	...	...	269	155	58
	1976	349	166	48	343	160	47
	STUDENTS 1970	...	...	...	4 212	2 216	53
	1974	...	...	...	4 503	2 370	53
	1975	...	...	...	5 008	2 759	55
	1976	5 420	3 779	70	5 369	3 728	69
BERMUDA	TEACHERS 1970	*301	156	*52	261	151	58
	1974	...	...	...	325	174	54
	1976	...	...	...	466	...	...
	1977	...	...	...	404	207	51
	STUDENTS 1970	4 268	2 284	54	3 844	2 077	54
	1974	...	...	...	4 700	2 500	53
	1975	...	...	...	4 824	2 517	52
	1976	...	...	...	5 393	2 806	52
	1977	...	...	...	5 269	2 729	52
BRITISH VIRGIN ISLANDS	TEACHERS 1974	46	27	59	...	...	...
	1975	48	25	52	...	...	...
	STUDENTS 1970	865	475	55	...	...	...
	1974	796	430	54	...	...	...
	1975	821	456	56	...	...	...
	1978	814	479	59	...	...	...
CANADA ‡	TEACHERS 1970	...	...	...	97 000	...	...
	STUDENTS 1970	...	...	...	1 636 913	799 141	49
	1974	...	...	...	2 596 732	1 277 731	49
	1975	...	...	...	2 588 133	1 275 780	49
	1976	...	...	...	2 582 205	1 276 345	49
	1977	...	...	...	2 528 387	1 249 289	49

Education at the second level: teachers and pupils   3.7
Enseignement du second degré: personnel enseignant et élèves
Enseñanza de segundo grado: personal docente y alumnos

TEACHER TRAINING ENSEIGNEMENT NORMAL ENSEÑANZA NORMAL			OTHER SECOND LEVEL AUTRE ENSEIGNEMENT DU SECOND DEGRE OTRA ENSEÑANZA DE SEGUNDO GRADO			YEAR ANNEE AÑO	COUNTRY PAYS PAIS
TOTAL	FEMALE FEMININ FEMENINO	% F	TOTAL	FEMALE FEMININ FEMENINO	% F		
(7)	(8)	(9)	(10)	(11)	(12)		
							AMERICA, NORTH
*11	2	*18	...	...	...	1970	ANTIGUA ‡
10	8	80	27	5	19	1974	
13	11	85	20	5	25	1975	
95	*45	*47				1970	
104	89	86	125	45	36	1974	
96	77	80	102	...	...	1975	
32	19	59	61	14	23	1970	BAHAMAS ‡
58	...	...	91	...	...	1974	
21	...	...	92	...	...	1975	
500	...	...	427	...	...	1970	
627	...	...	2 299	...	...	1974	
731	...	...	1 823	...	...	1975	
...	...	...	...	...	...	1976	
...	...	...	...	...	...	1977	
...	...	...	...	...	...	1978	
—	—	—	...	...	...	1975	BARBADOS ‡
—	—	—	...	...	...	1976	
—	—	—	...	...	...	1977	
—	—	—	806	...	...	1970	
—	—	—	...	...	...	1974	
—	—	—	...	...	...	1975	
—	—	—	...	...	...	1976	
...	...	...	...	...	...	1977	
6	5	83	...	...	...	1970	BELIZE
—	—	—	6	6	100	1976	
75	53	71	...	...	...	1970	
—	—	—	...	...	...	1974	
—	—	—	...	...	...	1975	
—	—	—	51	51	100	1976	
—	—	—	*40	5	*13	1970	BERMUDA
—	—	—	...	...	...	1974	
—	—	—	...	...	...	1976	
—	—	—	...	...	...	1977	
—	—	—	424	207	49	1970	
—	—	—	...	...	...	1974	
—	—	—	...	...	...	1975	
—	—	—	...	...	...	1976	
—	—	—	...	...	...	1977	
—	—	—	...	...	...	1974	BRITISH VIRGIN ISLANDS
—	—	—	...	...	...	1975	
—	—	—	...	...	...	1970	
—	—	—	...	...	...	1974	
—	—	—	...	...	...	1975	
—	—	—	...	...	...	1978	
—			...	...	...	1970	CANADA ‡
—	—	—	...	...	...	1970	
—	—	—	...	...	...	1974	
—	—	—	...	...	...	1975	
—	—	—	...	...	...	1976	
—	—	—	...	...	...	1977	

3.7 Education at the second level: teachers and pupils
Enseignement du second degré: personnel enseignant et élèves
Enseñanza de segundo grado: personal docente y alumnos

COUNTRY	YEAR	TOTAL SECOND LEVEL TOTAL DU SECOND DEGRE TOTAL DEL SEGUNDO GRADO			GENERAL EDUCATION ENSEIGNEMENT GENERAL ENSEÑANZA GENERAL		
PAYS	ANNEE		FEMALE FEMININ	%		FEMALE FEMININ	%
PAIS	AÑO	TOTAL	FEMENINO	F	TOTAL	FEMENINO	F
		(1)	(2)	(3)	(4)	(5)	(6)
CAYMAN ISLANDS ‡	TEACHERS 1974	82	...	...	82	...	...
	1975	106	55	52	106	55	52
	1976	114	64	56	114	64	56
	STUDENTS 1974	1 556	800	51	1 556	800	51
	1975	1 495	794	53	1 495	794	53
	1976	1 558	776	50	1 558	776	50
COSTA RICA ‡	TEACHERS 1970	3 691	1 745	47	3 285	1 659	51
	1974	...	...	...	...	...	...
	1975	4 929	...	...	3 866	1 995	58
	1976	5 915	...	...	4 264	...	...
	STUDENTS 1970	61 068	31 119	51	55 079	28 990	53
	1974	106 511	55 011	52	88 953	47 232	53
	1975	111 538	57 763	52	91 227	48 736	53
	1976	116 037	60 725	52	93 862	50 548	54
	1977	121 202	63 814	53	...	...	...
	1978	147 547	74 978	51	...	...	...
CUBA	TEACHERS 1970	21 781	...	...	15 273	7 418	49
	1974	35 035	16 412	47	26 504	13 244	50
	1975	42 306	20 032	47	32 755	16 317	50
	1976	56 347	26 378	47	45 149	22 376	50
	STUDENTS 1970	235 241	...	...	186 667	100 864	54
	1974	449 041	218 611	49	337 524	179 018	53
	1975	554 365	273 106	49	420 315	224 804	53
	1976	715 807	352 979	49	535 109	285 256	53
DOMINICA	TEACHERS 1974	...	...	...	...	...	...
	1975	...	...	...	...	...	...
	1976	...	...	...	...	...	...
	1978	...	...	...	...	...	...
	STUDENTS 1974	6 379	3 997	63	5 434	3 117	57
	1975	6 487	3 826	59	5 896	3 282	56
	1976	6 516	3 931	60	5 900	3 432	58
	1977	6 342	3 768	59	5 996	3 500	58
	1978	6 779	4 012	59	6 343	3 649	58
DOMINICAN REPUBLIC	TEACHERS 1970	4 668	2 644	57	4 393	2 576	59
	STUDENTS 1970	119 653	...	...	107 008	53 987	50
	1974	191 402	...	...	171 199	...	...
	1975	206 985	...	...	186 276	...	...
EL SALVADOR ‡	TEACHERS 1970	3 531	1 145	32	...	...	...
	1975	2 869	...	...	...	...	...
	STUDENTS 1970	88 307	41 351	47	60 870	26 451	43
	1974	44 700	19 570	44	25 551	11 072	43
	1975	51 731	22 987	44	29 559	13 037	44
	1976	59 079	26 466	45	32 449	14 435	44
	1977	*64 842	*29 088	*45	*32 613	*14 026	*43
GRENADA ‡	TEACHERS 1970	161	70	43	129	54	42
	1976	...	...	...	377	138	37
	1977	...	...	...	403	164	41
	STUDENTS 1970	4 081	1 868	46	3 039	1 696	56
	1974	...	...	...	9 910	...	...
	1975	...	...	...	10 197	...	...
	1976	...	...	...	10 088	5 528	55
	1977	...	...	...	10 077	5 493	55
GUADELOUPE	TEACHERS 1975	2 147	...	...	...	...	...
	1978	2 602	...	...	...	...	...

Education at the second level: teachers and pupils 3.7
Enseignement du second degré: personnel enseignant et élèves
Enseñanza de segundo grado: personal docente y alumnos

TEACHER TRAINING ENSEIGNEMENT NORMAL ENSEÑANZA NORMAL			OTHER SECOND LEVEL AUTRE ENSEIGNEMENT DU SECOND DEGRE OTRA ENSEÑANZA DE SEGUNDO GRADO			YEAR ANNEE AÑO	COUNTRY PAYS PAIS
TOTAL	FEMALE FEMININ FEMENINO	% F	TOTAL	FEMALE FEMININ FEMENINO	% F		
(7)	(8)	(9)	(10)	(11)	(12)		
—	—	—	—	—	—	1974	CAYMAN ISLANDS ‡
—	—	—	—	—	—	1975	
—	—	—	—	—	—	1976	
—	—	—	—	—	—	1974	
—	—	—	—	—	—	1975	
—	—	—	—	—	—	1976	
—	—	—	406	86	21	1970	COSTA RICA ‡
—	—	—	892	...	...	1974	
—	—	—	1 063	...	...	1975	
—	—	—	1 651	...	...	1976	
—	—	—	5 989	2 129	36	1970	
—	—	—	17 558	7 779	44	1974	
—	—	—	20 311	9 027	44	1975	
—	—	—	22 175	10 177	46	1976	
—	—	—	...	...	...	1977	
—	—	—	...	...	...	1978	
1 863	1 209	65	4 645	...	...	1970	CUBA
2 409	1 430	59	6 122	1 738	28	1974	
2 640	1 512	57	6 911	2 203	32	1975	
2 604	1 466	56	8 594	2 536	30	1976	
21 008	...	...	27 566	5 448	20	1970	
31 346	20 708	66	80 171	18 885	24	1974	
34 076	23 494	69	99 974	24 808	25	1975	
35 493	25 129	71	145 205	42 594	29	1976	
13	6	46	...	...	...	1974	DOMINICA
13	8	62	...	...	...	1975	
16	11	69	27	12	44	1976	
14	2	14	25	12	48	1978	
55	41	75	890	839	94	1974	
43	32	74	548	512	93	1975	
49	35	71	567	464	82	1976	
49	37	76	297	231	78	1977	
50	36	72	386	327	85	1978	
45	35	78	230	33	14	1970	DOMINICAN REPUBLIC
600	419	70	12 045	...	...	1970	
1 103	...	...	19 100	...	...	1974	
1 389	...	...	19 320	...	...	1975	
—	—	—	...	...	...	1970	EL SALVADOR ‡
25	13	52	...	...	...	1975	
—	—	—	27 437	14 900	54	1970	
318	190	60	18 831	8 308	44	1974	
620	374	60	21 552	9 576	44	1975	
868	531	61	25 762	11 500	45	1976	
*1 069	*708	*66	*31 160	*14 354	*46	1977	
12	5	42	20	11	55	1970	GRENADA ‡
...	...	...	...	...	...	1976	
...	...	...	...	...	...	1977	
57	36	63	985	136	14	1970	
...	...	...	...	...	...	1974	
...	...	...	...	...	...	1975	
...	...	...	...	...	...	1976	
...	...	...	...	...	...	1977	
—	—	—	...	...	...	1975	GUADELOUPE
—	—	—	...	...	...	1978	

3.7 Education at the second level: teachers and pupils
Enseignement du second degré: personnel enseignant et élèves
Enseñanza de segundo grado: personal docente y alumnos

COUNTRY PAYS PAIS	YEAR ANNEE AÑO	TOTAL SECOND LEVEL TOTAL DU SECOND DEGRE TOTAL DEL SEGUNDO GRADO			GENERAL EDUCATION ENSEIGNEMENT GENERAL ENSEÑANZA GENERAL		
		TOTAL	FEMALE FEMININ FEMENINO	% F	TOTAL	FEMALE FEMININ FEMENINO	% F
		(1)	(2)	(3)	(4)	(5)	(6)
GUADELOUPE (CONT.) STUDENTS 1970		29 162	...	...	24 429	13 902	57
1974		42 667	22 531	53	...	...	...
1975		43 805	23 291	53	...	...	...
1976		45 611	23 976	53	...	...	...
1978		48 329	25 890	54	34 991	19 556	56
GUATEMALA ‡ TEACHERS 1970		5 473	1 739	32	...	...	...
1977		...	...	...	5 269	...	...
STUDENTS 1970		75 474	31 039	41	55 932	22 057	39
1974		86 046	39 388	46	62 271	27 209	44
1975		95 189	42 925	45	69 903	29 563	42
1977		111 813	53 007	47	79 201	35 219	44
HAITI TEACHERS 1975		...	...	...	3 388	311	9
1976		...	...	...	3 324	...	...
STUDENTS 1975		...	...	...	55 213	25 630	46
1976		...	...	...	55 816	...	...
HONDURAS ‡ TEACHERS 1975		*3 132	...	...	...	...	...
STUDENTS 1970		39 839	18 693	47	28 949	12 740	44
1974		...	...	...	49 416	...	...
1975		51 896	...	...	36 956	18 925	51
1976		...	...	...	43 769	23 470	54
JAMAICA ‡ TEACHERS 1970		2 782	...	...	2 553	...	...
1974		7 361	2 512	39	7 056	...	...
1975		6 473	...	...	6 181	...	...
1976		10 168	4 682	46	9 828	4 528	46
1977		...	...	...	...	...	...
STUDENTS 1970		73 360	...	...	69 331	35 102	51
1974		196 605	105 803	54	191 863	103 448	54
1975		216 248	115 784	54	211 309	113 379	54
1976		225 741	118 352	52	220 566	115 699	52
1977		...	...	...	206 016	106 429	52
MARTINIQUE TEACHERS 1970		...	...	...	1 691	...	...
1975		2 357	...	...	...	...	...
1978		3 040	...	...	...	...	...
STUDENTS 1970		31 884	...	...	29 454	...	...
1974		46 844	25 204	54	...	...	...
1975		45 260	24 576	54	...	...	...
1976		46 052	25 265	55	...	...	...
1978		48 600	26 469	54	34 156	19 540	57
MEXICO TEACHERS 1970		109 470	...	...	...	...	...
1974		139 001	...	...	...	...	...
1975		169 781	55 218	33	141 730	42 016	30
1976		200 491	...	...	167 404	...	...
1977		207 917	...	...	174 350	...	...
1978		*229 670	...	...	*193 448	...	...
STUDENTS 1970		1 584 342	609 669	38	1 107 906	...	...
1974		2 554 041	1 034 463	41	2 190 412	794 184	36
1975		2 938 972	1 159 319	39	2 506 014	853 580	34
1976		3 263 507	1 433 810	44	2 805 474	1 134 553	40
1977		3 502 830	1 584 030	45	3 024 000	1 261 984	42
1978		*3 899 878	...	...	*3 375 026	...	...
MONTSERRAT TEACHERS 1975		...	...	...	...	...	...
1976		37	24	65	30	21	70
STUDENTS 1975		539	...	...	482	...	...
1976		543	283	52	493	263	53

Education at the second level: teachers and pupils 3.7
Enseignement du second degré: personnel enseignant et élèves
Enseñanza de segundo grado: personal docente y alumnos

TEACHER TRAINING ENSEIGNEMENT NORMAL ENSEÑANZA NORMAL			OTHER SECOND LEVEL AUTRE ENSEIGNEMENT DU SECOND DEGRE OTRA ENSEÑANZA DE SEGUNDO GRADO			YEAR ANNEE AÑO	COUNTRY PAYS PAIS
TOTAL	FEMALE FEMININ FEMENINO	% F	TOTAL	FEMALE FEMININ FEMENINO	% F		
(7)	(8)	(9)	(10)	(11)	(12)		
334	...	...	4 399	2 417	55	1970	GUADELOUPE (CONT.)
...	...	...	6 655	3 359	50	1974	
...	...	...	6 796	3 344	49	1975	
...	...	...	7 554	3 620	48	1976	
—	—	—	13 338	6 334	47	1978	
			...	...	...	1970	GUATEMALA ‡
1 053	...	...	...	...	...	1977	
8 192	4 563	56	11 350	4 419	39	1970	
11 741	6 515	55	12 034	5 664	47	1974	
13 631	7 464	55	11 655	5 898	51	1975	
18 060	10 394	58	14 552	7 394	51	1977	
...	...	...	...	...	...	1975	HAITI
...	...	...	...	...	...	1976	
...	...	...	...	...	...	1975	
...	...	...	...	...	...	1976	
...	...	...	...	...	...	1975	HONDURAS ‡
3 801	2 610	69	7 089	3 343	47	1970	
2 279	...	...	...	...	...	1974	
2 004	1 415	71	*12 936	...	...	1975	
...	...	...	...	...	...	1976	
—	—	—	229	...	...	1970	JAMAICA ‡
—	—	—	305	...	...	1974	
—	—	—	292	...	...	1975	
—	—	—	340	154	45	1976	
—	—	—	...	...	...	1977	
—	—	—	4 029	1 740	43	1970	
—	—	—	4 742	2 355	50	1974	
—	—	—	4 939	2 405	49	1975	
—	—	—	5 175	2 653	51	1976	
—	—	—	...	...	...	1977	
...	...	...	...	...	...	1970	MARTINIQUE
...	...	...	...	...	...	1975	
—	—	—	...	...	...	1978	
419	...	...	2 011	...	...	1970	
...	...	...	6 240	3 611	58	1974	
...	...	...	6 026	3 499	58	1975	
...	...	...	6 486	3 742	58	1976	
—	—	—	14 444	6 929	48	1978	
5 131	2 232	44	...	...	...	1970	MEXICO
7 014	...	...	...	...	...	1974	
8 396	3 089	37	19 655	10 113	51	1975	
9 572	...	...	23 515	...	...	1976	
10 486	...	...	23 081	...	...	1977	
*11 280	...	...	*24 942	...	...	1978	
52 852	34 657	66	423 584	...	...	1970	
90 747	60 800	67	272 882	179 479	66	1974	
111 502	74 706	67	321 456	231 033	72	1975	
135 981	89 441	66	322 052	209 816	65	1976	
157 012	103 699	66	321 818	218 347	68	1977	
*177 238	...	...	*347 614	...	...	1978	
—	—	—	8	3	38	1975	MONTSERRAT
—	—	—	7	3	43	1976	
—	—	—	57	24	42	1975	
—	—	—	50	20	40	1976	

3.7 Education at the second level: teachers and pupils
Enseignement du second degré: personnel enseignant et élèves
Enseñanza de segundo grado: personal docente y alumnos

COUNTRY PAYS PAIS	YEAR ANNEE AÑO	TOTAL SECOND LEVEL TOTAL DU SECOND DEGRE TOTAL DEL SEGUNDO GRADO			GENERAL EDUCATION ENSEIGNEMENT GENERAL ENSEÑANZA GENERAL		
		TOTAL	FEMALE FEMININ FEMENINO	% F	TOTAL	FEMALE FEMININ FEMENINO	% F
		(1)	(2)	(3)	(4)	(5)	(6)
NICARAGUA	TEACHERS 1970	1 979	...	...	1 495	...	...
	1974	2 006	831	41	1 375	...	...
	1975	2 602	...	...	...	...	...
	1976	2 779	...	...	...	...	...
	1977	*3 145	...	...	...	...	...
	STUDENTS 1970	51 383	24 347	47	45 185	21 253	47
	1974	71 044	35 373	50	64 433	...	...
	1975	80 200	...	...	...	...	...
	1976	80 855	42 509	53	74 619	39 208	53
	1977	98 533	49 940	51	81 916	40 965	50
	1978	94 703	48 814	52	79 075	40 388	51
PANAMA ‡	TEACHERS 1970	3 784	2 127	56	2 561	1 465	57
	1974	5 780	3 145	54	3 572	1 969	55
	1975	5 666	3 101	55	3 472	1 939	56
	1976	5 701	3 125	55	3 448	1 924	56
	1977	5 882	3 194	54	3 563	1 988	56
	1978	5 952	3 378	57	3 712	2 089	56
	STUDENTS 1970	78 466	40 799	52	50 920	25 377	50
	1974	123 060	63 833	52	79 705	40 770	51
	1975	125 745	65 608	52	81 928	42 002	51
	1976	129 579	67 784	52	85 130	43 800	51
	1977	137 185	72 252	53	92 363	48 248	52
	1978	139 191	73 603	53	95 682	50 476	53
FORMER CANAL ZONE ‡	TEACHERS 1970	*239	...	...	...	...	...
	1975	*187	...	...	...	...	...
	1976	*172	...	...	...	...	...
	STUDENTS 1970	*5 733	...	...	...	...	...
	1974	*5 075	...	...	...	...	...
	1975	*5 038	...	...	...	...	...
	1976	*4 460	...	...	...	...	...
	1977	3 601	...	...	...	...	...
PUERTO RICO ‡	TEACHERS 1970	*10 432	...	...	...	...	...
	1975	*8 526	...	...	...	...	...
	1976	*8 191	...	...	...	...	...
	STUDENTS 1970	*274 139	...	...	...	...	...
	1974	301 199	...	...	...	...	...
	1975	292 847	...	...	...	...	...
	1976	273 077	...	...	...	...	...
ST. KITTS – NEVIS ANGUILLA	TEACHERS 1970	...	...	...	*141	*75	*53
	STUDENTS 1970	...	...	...	3 350	1 758	52
ST. LUCIA ‡	TEACHERS 1970	...	...	...	...	...	...
	1974	...	...	...	...	...	...
	1975	307	132	43	*241	*114	*47
	1976	276	...	...	231	...	...
	STUDENTS 1970	*1 942	*910	*47	1 699	835	49
	1974	4 579	...	...	4 181	2 424	58
	1975	4 464	...	...	4 078	2 375	58
	1976	4 528	2 548	56	4 191	2 400	57
ST. PIERRE AND MIQUELON	TEACHERS 1970	39	15	38	28	11	39
	1973	36	20	56	30	17	57
	STUDENTS 1970	377	191	51	302	159	53
	1973	504	278	55	409	231	56

Education at the second level: teachers and pupils 3.7
Enseignement du second degré: personnel enseignant et élèves
Enseñanza de segundo grado: personal docente y alumnos

TEACHER TRAINING ENSEIGNEMENT NORMAL ENSEÑANZA NORMAL			OTHER SECOND LEVEL AUTRE ENSEIGNEMENT DU SECOND DEGRE OTRA ENSEÑANZA DE SEGUNDO GRADO			YEAR ANNEE AÑO	COUNTRY PAYS PAIS
TOTAL	FEMALE FEMININ FEMENINO	% F	TOTAL	FEMALE FEMININ FEMENINO	% F		
(7)	(8)	(9)	(10)	(11)	(12)		
110	...	...	374	...	...	1970	NICARAGUA
55	...	...	576	...	...	1974	
...	...	...	...	...	...	1975	
...	...	...	...	...	...	1976	
...	...	...	...	...	...	1977	
1 757	1 350	77	4 441	1 744	39	1970	
1 024	...	...	5 587	...	...	1974	
...	...	...	...	...	...	1975	
1 309	939	72	4 927	2 362	48	1976	
1 688	1 317	78	14 929	7 658	51	1977	
2 053	1 568	76	13 575	6 858	51	1978	
94	51	54	1 129	611	54	1970	PANAMA ‡
271	165	61	1 937	1 011	52	1974	
244	141	58	1 950	1 021	52	1975	
181	107	59	2 072	1 094	53	1976	
113	64	57	2 206	1 142	52	1977	
73	42	58	2 167	1 247	58	1978	
2 194	1 727	79	25 352	13 695	54	1970	
7 186	5 193	72	36 169	17 870	49	1974	
5 850	4 300	74	37 967	19 306	51	1975	
3 308	2 506	76	41 141	21 478	52	1976	
1 317	1 043	79	43 505	22 961	53	1977	
849	643	76	42 660	22 484	53	1978	
–	–	–	...	...	...	1970	FORMER CANAL
–	–	–	...	...	...	1975	ZONE ‡
–	–	–	...	...	...	1976	
–	–	–	...	...	...	1970	
–	–	–	...	...	...	1974	
–	–	–	...	...	...	1975	
–	–	–	...	...	...	1976	
...	...	...	...	...	...	1977	
–	–	–	...	...	...	1970	PUERTO RICO ‡
–	–	–	...	...	...	1975	
–	–	–	...	...	...	1976	
–	–	–	...	...	...	1970	
–	–	–	...	...	...	1974	
–	–	–	...	...	...	1975	
–	–	–	...	...	...	1976	
–			...	...	...	1970	ST. KITTS – NEVIS ANGUILLA
–	–	–	...	...	...	1970	
*15	*7	*47	...	...	...	1970	ST. LUCIA ‡
15	10	67	28	3	11	1974	
25	13	52	41	5	12	1975	
13	7	54	32	6	19	1976	
*100	*62	*62	143	13	9	1970	
162	...	...	236	62	26	1974	
156	...	...	230	59	26	1975	
152	92	61	185	56	30	1976	
							ST. PIERRE AND MIQUELON
–	–	–	11	4	36	1970	
–	–	–	6	3	50	1973	
–	–	–	75	32	43	1970	
–	–	–	95	47	49	1973	

3.7 Education at the second level: teachers and pupils
Enseignement du second degré: personnel enseignant et élèves
Enseñanza de segundo grado: personal docente y alumnos

COUNTRY / PAYS / PAIS	YEAR / ANNEE / AÑO	TOTAL SECOND LEVEL / TOTAL DU SECOND DEGRE / TOTAL DEL SEGUNDO GRADO			GENERAL EDUCATION / ENSEIGNEMENT GENERAL / ENSEÑANZA GENERAL		
		TOTAL	FEMALE FEMININ FEMENINO	% F	TOTAL	FEMALE FEMININ FEMENINO	% F
		(1)	(2)	(3)	(4)	(5)	(6)
ST. VINCENT AND THE GRENADINES	TEACHERS 1970	...	...	...	...	...	...
	1975	243	104	43	217	94	43
	STUDENTS 1970	3 158	1 564	50	3 073	1 524	50
	1974	...	...	...	4 549	2 633	58
	1975	5 084	2 974	58	4 685	2 771	59
TRINIDAD AND TOBAGO ‡	TEACHERS 1970	1 996	885	44	1 894	866	46
	STUDENTS 1970	52 639	27 257	52	49 810	26 430	53
	1974	...	...	...	29 255	14 625	50
	1975	...	...	...	32 516	16 350	50
TURKS AND CAICOS ISLANDS	TEACHERS 1970	18	6	33	18	6	33
	1974	36	15	42	36	15	42
	1975	35	*13	*37	35	*13	*37
	1976	38	13	34	38	13	34
	1977	43	22	51	43	22	51
	STUDENTS 1970	227	...	...	227	...	...
	1974	639	*300	*47	639	*300	*47
	1975	671	...	...	671	...	...
	1976	671	...	...	671	...	...
	1977	711	383	54	711	383	54
UNITED STATES OF AMERICA ‡	TEACHERS 1970	*1 024 000	...	...	...	...	...
	1974	*1 083 000	...	...	...	...	...
	1975	*1 109 000	...	...	...	...	...
	1976	*1 116 000	...	...	...	...	...
	1977	1 130 000	...	...	...	...	...
	STUDENTS 1970	*19 910 000	...	...	...	...	...
	1974	*19 981 000	...	...	...	...	...
	1975	*20 546 000	...	...	...	...	...
	1976	*20 355 000	...	...	...	...	...
	1977	20 342 000	...	...	...	...	...
U.S. VIRGIN ISLANDS ‡	TEACHERS 1975	*592	...	...	...	...	...
	1976	*615	...	...	...	...	...
	STUDENTS 1974	*9 160	...	...	...	...	...
	1975	*10 590	...	...	...	...	...
	1976	*11 799	...	...	...	...	...
	1977	9 879	...	...	...	...	...
AMERICA, SOUTH							
ARGENTINA ‡	TEACHERS 1970	134 264	83 047	62	57 785	41 849	72
	1974	155 480	96 962	62	61 376	44 609	73
	1975	161 859	101 216	63	62 334	45 526	73
	1976	169 704	105 505	62	59 765	43 881	73
	1977	173 714	110 461	64	60 199	45 425	75
	1978	173 041	110 395	64	59 489	45 221	76
	STUDENTS 1970	976 979	512 830	52	405 435	246 911	61
	1974	1 197 729	622 900	52	440 304	265 458	60
	1975	1 243 058	650 902	52	454 194	275 784	61
	1976	1 283 056	673 354	52	445 397	274 644	62
	1977	1 288 107	680 316	53	441 907	277 277	63
	1978	1 293 073	685 030	53	442 117	278 341	63

Education at the second level: teachers and pupils 3.7
Enseignement du second degré: personnel enseignant et élèves
Enseñanza de segundo grado: personal docente y alumnos

TEACHER TRAINING ENSEIGNEMENT NORMAL ENSEÑANZA NORMAL			OTHER SECOND LEVEL AUTRE ENSEIGNEMENT DU SECOND DEGRE OTRA ENSEÑANZA DE SEGUNDO GRADO			YEAR ANNEE AÑO	COUNTRY PAYS PAIS
TOTAL	FEMALE FEMININ FEMENINO	% F	TOTAL	FEMALE FEMININ FEMENINO	% F		
(7)	(8)	(9)	(10)	(11)	(12)		
20	5	25	–	–	–	1970	ST. VINCENT AND THE GRENADINES
14	8	57	12	2	17	1975	
85	40	47	–	–	–	1970	
329	207	63				1974	
291	172	59	108	31	29	1975	
–	–	–	102	19	19	1970	TRINIDAD AND TOBAGO ‡
–	–	–	2 829	827	29	1970	
–	–	–	3 266	842	26	1974	
–	–	–	3 833	1 110	29	1975	
–	–	–				1970	TURKS AND CAICOS ISLANDS
–	–	–				1974	
–	–	–				1975	
–	–	–				1976	
–	–	–				1977	
–	–	–				1970	
–	–	–				1974	
–	–	–				1975	
–	–	–				1976	
–	–	–				1977	
–	–	–	...	...	...	1970	UNITED STATES OF AMERICA ‡
–	–	–	...	...	...	1974	
–	–	–	...	...	...	1975	
–	–	–	...	...	...	1976	
...	...	...	...	...	...	1977	
–	–	–	...	...	...	1970	
–	–	–	...	...	...	1974	
–	–	–	...	...	...	1975	
–	–	–	...	...	...	1976	
...	...	...	...	...	...	1977	
–	–	–	...	...	...	1975	U.S. VIRGIN ISLANDS ‡
–	–	–	...	...	...	1976	
–	–	–	...	...	...	1974	
–	–	–	...	...	...	1975	
–	–	–	...	...	...	1976	
–	–	–	...	...	...	1977	
							AMERICA, SOUTH
192	149	78	76 287	41 049	54	1970	ARGENTINA ‡
–	–	–	94 104	52 353	56	1974	
–	–	–	99 525	55 690	56	1975	
–	–	–	109 939	61 624	56	1976	
–	–	–	113 515	65 036	57	1977	
–	–	–	113 552	65 174	57	1978	
566	549	97	570 978	265 370	46	1970	
–	–	–	757 425	357 442	47	1974	
–	–	–	788 864	375 118	48	1975	
–	–	–	837 659	398 710	48	1976	
–	–	–	846 200	403 039	48	1977	
–	–	–	850 956	406 689	48	1978	

3.7 Education at the second level: teachers and pupils
Enseignement du second degré: personnel enseignant et élèves
Enseñanza de segundo grado: personal docente y alumnos

COUNTRY PAYS PAIS	YEAR ANNEE AÑO	TOTAL SECOND LEVEL TOTAL DU SECOND DEGRE TOTAL DEL SEGUNDO GRADO			GENERAL EDUCATION ENSEIGNEMENT GENERAL ENSEÑANZA GENERAL		
		TOTAL	FEMALE FEMININ FEMENINO	% F	TOTAL	FEMALE FEMININ FEMENINO	% F
		(1)	(2)	(3)	(4)	(5)	(6)
BOLIVIA	TEACHERS 1970	...	...	...	4 370	...	...
	1974	...	...	...	6 049	...	...
	1975	7 143	...	...	...	...	...
	STUDENTS 1970	...	...	...	75 146	29 462	39
	1974	...	...	...	112 204	45 789	41
	1975	130 029	...	...	...	...	...
	1976	128 081	...	...	...	...	...
BRAZIL ‡	TEACHERS 1970	308 552	164 457	53	208 312	114 244	55
	1974	156 174	80 897	52	...	...	
	STUDENTS 1970	4 086 073	2 062 069	50	3 055 652	1 516 877	50
	1974	1 681 728	902 113	54	628 178	322 917	51
CHILE	TEACHERS 1974	26 637	...	...	18 049	...	...
	1975	29 567	14 730	50	17 799	9 802	55
	1976	30 850	15 781	51	19 341	10 991	57
	1977	28 460	15 214	53	18 806	11 061	59
	1978	28 803	15 112	52	18 067	10 549	58
	STUDENTS 1970	302 064	160 305	53	202 506	114 613	57
	1974	453 116	240 872	53	291 068	169 982	58
	1975	448 911	238 533	53	285 806	166 363	58
	1976	465 935	250 951	54	307 946	179 346	58
	1977	487 264	258 092	53	318 441	180 823	57
	1978	510 471	268 215	53	324 379	182 941	56
COLOMBIA	TEACHERS 1970	43 695	...	...	33 637	...	...
	1974	66 334	...	...	49 931	...	...
	1975	70 451	...	...	50 480	...	...
	1976	75 468	...	...	53 465	...	...
	1977	79 742	...	...	56 402	...	...
	1978	84 258	...	...	...	...	...
	STUDENTS 1970	750 055	365 652	49	538 479	226 674	42
	1974	1 284 347	640 504	50	1 003 314	...	...
	1975	1 370 567	683 639	50	1 031 237	...	...
	1976	1 490 779	743 908	50	1 107 466	...	...
	1977	1 616 111	806 713	50	1 187 148	...	...
	1978	1 751 980	871 531	50	...	...	...
ECUADOR ‡	TEACHERS 1970	15 699	5 141	33	11 160	3 512	31
	1974	21 085	7 147	34	...	...	
	1975	23 446	8 315	35	18 335	6 514	36
	1976	*26 107	...	...	...	...	...
	1977	*29 006	...	...	...	...	...
	STUDENTS 1970	216 727	98 500	45	182 514	79 018	43
	1974	336 702	160 291	48	293 981	134 780	46
	1975	383 624	182 678	48	339 771	156 333	46
	1976	*431 315	...	...	...	...	...
	1977	472 949	...	...	...	...	...
FALKLAND ISLANDS (MALVINAS)	TEACHERS 1976	16	6	38	16	6	38
	1977	16	6	38	16	6	38
	1978	14	5	36	14	5	36
	STUDENTS 1974	114	47	41	114	47	41
	1975	126	55	44	126	55	44
	1976	110	48	44	110	48	44
	1977	110	48	44	110	48	44
	1978	96	47	49	96	47	49
FRENCH GUIANA	TEACHERS 1970	182	...	...	114	...	...
	1975	338	...	...	...	...	...
	1978	476	...	...	...	...	...

Education at the second level: teachers and pupils   3.7
Enseignement du second degré: personnel enseignant et élèves
Enseñanza de segundo grado: personal docente y alumnos

TEACHER TRAINING ENSEIGNEMENT NORMAL ENSEÑANZA NORMAL			OTHER SECOND LEVEL AUTRE ENSEIGNEMENT DU SECOND DEGRE OTRA ENSEÑANZA DE SEGUNDO GRADO			YEAR ANNEE AÑO	COUNTRY PAYS PAIS
TOTAL	FEMALE FEMININ FEMENINO	% F	TOTAL	FEMALE FEMININ FEMENINO	% F		
(7)	(8)	(9)	(10)	(11)	(12)		
344	...	...	...	...	...	1970	BOLIVIA
...	...	...	...	...	...	1974	
...	...	...	...	...	...	1975	
4 356	1 679	39	...	...	...	1970	
...	...	...	...	...	...	1974	
...	...	...	...	...	...	1975	
...	...	...	...	...	...	1976	
39 423	28 174	71	60 817	22 039	36	1970	BRAZIL ‡
...	...	...	...	...	...	1974	
347 873	289 055	83	682 548	256 137	38	1970	
270 723	241 658	89	782 827	337 538	43	1974	
—	—	—	8 588	...	...	1974	CHILE
—	—	—	11 768	4 928	42	1975	
—	—	—	11 509	4 790	42	1976	
—	—	—	9 654	4 153	43	1977	
—	—	—	10 736	4 563	43	1978	
—	—	—	99 558	45 692	46	1970	
—	—	—	162 048	70 890	44	1974	
—	—	—	163 105	72 170	44	1975	
—	—	—	157 989	71 605	45	1976	
—	—	—	168 823	77 269	46	1977	
—	—	—	186 092	85 274	46	1978	
						1970	COLOMBIA
3 919	...	...	12 484	...	...	1974	
4 897	...	...	15 074	...	...	1975	
5 071	...	...	16 932	...	...	1976	
5 024	...	...	18 316	...	...	1977	
...	...	...	...	...	...	1978	
59 990	46 192	77	151 586	92 786	61	1970	
64 638	...	...	216 395	...	...	1974	
82 843	...	...	256 487	...	...	1975	
83 597	...	...	299 716	...	...	1976	
80 373	...	...	348 590	...	...	1977	
...	...	...	...	...	...	1978	
1 052	457	43	3 487	1 172	34	1970	ECUADOR ‡
...	...	...	4 617	1 557	34	1974	
130	31	24	4 981	1 770	36	1975	
*153	...	...	...	...	...	1976	
*189	...	...	...	...	...	1977	
10 203	6 405	63	24 010	13 077	54	1970	
3 294	2 230	68	39 427	23 281	59	1974	
913	488	53	42 940	25 857	60	1975	
*2 191	...	...	...	...	...	1976	
*2 911	...	...	...	...	...	1977	
—	—	—	—	—	—	1976	FALKLAND ISLANDS (MALVINAS)
—	—	—	—	—	—	1977	
—	—	—	—	—	—	1978	
—	—	—	—	—	—	1974	
—	—	—	—	—	—	1975	
—	—	—	—	—	—	1976	
—	—	—	—	—	—	1977	
—	—	—	—	—	—	1978	
—	—	—	68	...	...	1970	FRENCH GUIANA
...	...	...	...	...	...	1975	
...	...	...	...	...	...	1978	

3.7　Education at the second level: teachers and pupils
Enseignement du second degré: personnel enseignant et élèves
Enseñanza de segundo grado: personal docente y alumnos

COUNTRY PAYS PAIS	YEAR ANNEE AÑO	TOTAL SECOND LEVEL TOTAL DU SECOND DEGRE TOTAL DEL SEGUNDO GRADO			GENERAL EDUCATION ENSEIGNEMENT GENERAL ENSEÑANZA GENERAL		
		TOTAL	FEMALE FEMININ FEMENINO	% F	TOTAL	FEMALE FEMININ FEMENINO	% F
		(1)	(2)	(3)	(4)	(5)	(6)
FRENCH GUIANA (CONT.)	STUDENTS 1970	3 099	*1 678	*54	2 213	*1 298	*59
	1974	5 251	2 771	53	...	...	...
	1975	5 534	2 867	52	...	...	...
	1976	5 916	3 031	51			
	1978	6 502	3 490	54	4 472	2 500	56
GUYANA	TEACHERS 1970	2 364	1 096	46	2 262	1 063	47
	1975	...	...	...	3 202	1 144	36
	1976				3 660	1 379	38
	STUDENTS 1970	60 412	30 536	51	57 093	28 958	51
	1975	71 327	36 021	51	66 326	33 530	51
	1976	...	...	...	73 285	37 063	51
PARAGUAY	TEACHERS 1970	5 938	3 455	58	4 170	2 366	57
	1974	7 013	...	...	...	...	...
	STUDENTS 1970	55 777	27 813	50	48 742	23 157	48
	1974	*71 600	...	...	*67 900	...	...
	1975	75 424	37 363	50	70 048	36 107	52
	1976	81 915	40 522	49	76 585	39 241	51
	1977	92 437	45 391	49	87 010	43 028	50
PERU	TEACHERS 1970	31 587	...	...	...	...	...
	1974	34 769	...	...	...	...	...
	1975	34 136	...	...	26 033	...	...
	1976	34 555	...	...	26 987	...	...
	1977	35 183	...	...	28 761	...	...
	1978	*37 383	...	...	...	...	...
	STUDENTS 1970	546 183	233 977	43	453 001	192 948	43
	1974	747 560	330 805	44	572 967	253 695	44
	1975	813 489	...	...	627 059	...	...
	1976	890 106	...	...	699 547	...	...
	1977	969 129	*443 528	*46	791 930	*362 070	*46
	1978	*1 090 200	...	...	...	...	...
SURINAME ‡	TEACHERS 1970	1 367	641	47	899	502	56
	1974	1 706	701	41	1 152	542	47
	1975	1 793	901	50	1 127	733	65
	1976	1 917	809	42	1 191	640	54
	1977	1 785	871	49	1 290	741	57
	1978	1 867	1 014	54	1 460	883	60
	STUDENTS 1970	23 504	12 784	54	20 926	11 541	55
	1974	29 562	16 470	56	25 524	14 807	58
	1975	30 603	16 726	55	26 442	14 850	56
	1976	32 247	16 678	52	25 872	14 109	55
	1977	34 121	17 897	52	27 775	15 291	55
	1978	34 372	17 927	52	28 636	15 852	55
URUGUAY ‡	STUDENTS 1970	174 300	...	...	132 125	74 366	56
	1974	193 146	...	...	151 675	...	...
	1975	186 192	...	...	144 497	...	...
	1976	...	...	...	141 731	80 360	57
	1977	...	...	...	153 739	82 692	54
	1978	...	...	...	151 962	80 050	53
VENEZUELA ‡	TEACHERS 1970	22 983	8 998	39	13 721	5 541	40
	1974	35 671	15 762	44	...	...	...
	1975	39 876	...	...	...	...	...
	1976	46 964	...	...	...	...	...
	1977	47 137	...	...	...	...	...

Education at the second level: teachers and pupils   3.7
Enseignement du second degré: personnel enseignant et élèves
Enseñanza de segundo grado: personal docente y alumnos

TEACHER TRAINING ENSEIGNEMENT NORMAL ENSEÑANZA NORMAL			OTHER SECOND LEVEL AUTRE ENSEIGNEMENT DU SECOND DEGRE OTRA ENSEÑANZA DE SEGUNDO GRADO			YEAR ANNEE AÑO	COUNTRY PAYS PAIS
TOTAL	FEMALE FEMININ FEMENINO	% F	TOTAL	FEMALE FEMININ FEMENINO	% F		
(7)	(8)	(9)	(10)	(11)	(12)		
–	–	–	886	*380	*43	1970	FRENCH GUIANA
...	...	...	1 356	616	45	1974	(CONT.)
...	...	...	1 536	701	46	1975	
...	...	...	1 663	754	45	1976	
–	–	–	2 030	990	49	1978	
30	17	57	72	16	22	1970	GUYANA
–	–	–	...	...	...	1975	
–	–	–	...	...	...	1976	
259	136	53	3 060	1 442	47	1970	
–	–	–	5 001	2 491	50	1975	
–	–	–	...	...	...	1976	
1 003	776	77	765	313	41	1970	PARAGUAY
–	–	–	...	...	...	1974	
3 545	3 170	89	3 490	1 486	43	1970	
–	–	–	*3 700	...	...	1974	
–	–	–	5 376	1 256	23	1975	
–	–	–	5 330	1 281	24	1976	
–	–	–	5 427	2 363	44	1977	
			...	...		1970	PERU
						1974	
–	–	–	8 103	...	...	1975	
–	–	–	7 568	...	...	1976	
–	–	–	6 422	...	...	1977	
–	–	–	...	...	...	1978	
–	–	–	93 182	41 029	44	1970	
–	–	–	174 593	77 110	44	1974	
–	–	–	186 430	...	...	1975	
–	–	–	190 559	...	...	1976	
–	–	–	177 199	*81 458	*46	1977	
–	–	–	...	...	...	1978	
372	119	32	96	20	21	1970	SURINAME ‡
386	124	32	168	35	21	1974	
399	124	31	267	44	16	1975	
346	104	30	380	65	17	1976	
174	59	34	321	71	22	1977	
158	63	40	249	68	27	1978	
1 228	946	77	1 350	297	22	1970	
1 424	1 120	79	2 584	543	21	1974	
1 894	1 454	77	2 267	422	19	1975	
1 998	1 575	79	4 377	994	23	1976	
1 874	1 461	78	4 472	1 145	26	1977	
1 342	1 040	77	4 394	1 035	24	1978	
6 217	...	...	35 958	14 786	41	1970	URUGUAY‡
4 773	4 295	90	36 698	13 192	36	1974	
3 997	3 638	91	37 698	14 439	38	1975	
...	...	...	42 271	...	...	1976	
...	...	...	...	...	...	1977	
...	...	...	...	...	...	1978	
1 199	608	51	8 063	2 849	35	1970	VENEZUELA ‡
...	...	...	...	...	...	1974	
...	...	...	...	...	...	1975	
...	...	...	...	...	...	1976	
...	...	...	...	...	...	1977	

3.7 Education at the second level: teachers and pupils
Enseignement du second degré: personnel enseignant et élèves
Enseñanza de segundo grado: personal docente y alumnos

COUNTRY PAYS PAIS	YEAR ANNEE AÑO	TOTAL SECOND LEVEL TOTAL DU SECOND DEGRE TOTAL DEL SEGUNDO GRADO			GENERAL EDUCATION ENSEIGNEMENT GENERAL ENSEÑANZA GENERAL		
		TOTAL	FEMALE FEMININ FEMENINO	% F	TOTAL	FEMALE FEMININ FEMENINO	% F
		(1)	(2)	(3)	(4)	(5)	(6)
VENEZUELA (CONT.) ‡	STUDENTS 1970	425 146	215 443	51	279 867	141 213	50
	1974	631 210	330 439	52	583 163	303 159	52
	1975	669 138	351 890	53	622 428	...	...
	1976	719 680	...	...	664 531	...	...
	1977	751 430	400 364	53	689 895	...	...
ASIA							
AFGHANISTAN ‡	TEACHERS 1970	5 021	618	12	4 248	572	13
	1974	7 866	963	12	7 176	907	13
	1975	7 939	1 090	14	7 425	1 049	14
	1976	6 850	...	...	6 294	976	16
	1977	5 437	935	17	4 753	890	19
	STUDENTS 1970	116 174	15 253	13	107 609	14 736	14
	1974	172 797	20 442	12	167 397	19 795	12
	1975	92 160	10 505	11	87 537	9 854	11
	1976	91 833	10 845	12	85 612	10 242	12
	1977	112 643	19 851	18	103 040	18 470	18
BAHRAIN ‡	TEACHERS 1974	...	...	...	646	323	50
	1975	...	...	...	704	346	49
	1976	776	363	47	...	...	...
	1977	844	383	45	...	...	...
	STUDENTS 1970	13 652	*5 569	*41	12 697	*5 531	*44
	1974	18 074	8 480	47	16 133	8 007	50
	1975	...	...	...	15 800	7 797	49
	1976	18 282	8 671	47	16 522	8 174	49
	1977	21 485	10 272	48	19 654	9 696	49
	1978	22 853	10 660	47	20 589	9 914	48
BANGLADESH ‡	TEACHERS 1976	...	...	...	98 965	6 365	6
	STUDENTS 1974	...	...	...	2 366 148	512 270	22
	1975	...	...	...	2 442 842	516 740	21
	1976	2 183 413	...	...	2 164 328	531 745	25
	1977	...	...	...	2 213 068	469 309	21
BHUTAN ‡	TEACHERS 1970	...	...	...	...	...	...
	1974	...	...	...	...	...	...
	STUDENTS 1970	714	24	3	393	10	3
	1974	1 788	173	10	1 054	164	16
	1976	...	...	...	817	164	20
	1977	1 536	...	...	1 169	226	19
	1978	...	...	...	1 610	308	19
BRUNEI	TEACHERS 1970	565	144	25	532	138	26
	1974	859	261	30	784	250	32
	1975	782	287	37	684	276	40
	1976	1 021	304	30	908	291	32
	1977	1 065	344	32	936	329	35
	1978	1 138	356	31	987	341	35
	STUDENTS 1970	10 974	4 911	45	10 421	4 721	45
	1974	13 704	6 473	47	12 906	6 197	48
	1975	14 614	6 946	48	13 687	6 666	49
	1976	15 946	7 711	48	15 077	7 411	49
	1977	16 005	7 813	49	15 204	7 524	49
	1978	16 410	8 088	49	15 571	7 751	50
BURMA	TEACHERS 1970	24 636	...	...	23 768	11 858	50
	1974	...	...	...	*23 186	*12 477	*54
	1977	23 853	13 710	57	23 548	13 561	58

Education at the second level: teachers and pupils   3.7
Enseignement du second degré: personnel enseignant et élèves
Enseñanza de segundo grado: personal docente y alumnos

TEACHER TRAINING ENSEIGNEMENT NORMAL ENSEÑANZA NORMAL			OTHER SECOND LEVEL AUTRE ENSEIGNEMENT DU SECOND DEGRE OTRA ENSEÑANZA DE SEGUNDO GRADO			YEAR ANNEE AÑO	COUNTRY PAYS PAIS
TOTAL	FEMALE FEMININ FEMENINO	% F	TOTAL	FEMALE FEMININ FEMENINO	% F		
(7)	(8)	(9)	(10)	(11)	(12)		
11 664	8 151	70	133 615	66 079	49	1970	VENEZUELA (CONT.)
13 807	12 335	89	34 240	14 945	44	1974	
16 445	14 708	89	30 265	...	...	1975	
21 391	...	...	33 758	...	...	1976	
24 785	...	...	36 750	...	...	1977	
							ASIA
341	14	4	432	32	7	1970	AFGHANISTAN ‡
226	*19	*8	464	37	8	1974	
—	—	—	514	*41	*8	1975	
—	—	—	556	...	...	1976	
—	—	—	684	45	7	1977	
3 597	40	1	4 968	477	10	1970	
950	87	9	4 450	560	13	1974	
—	—	—	4 623	651	14	1975	
—	—	—	6 221	603	10	1976	
—	—	—	9 603	1 381	14	1977	
—	—	—	...	...	...	1974	BAHRAIN ‡
—	—	—	...	...	...	1975	
—	—	—	...	...	...	1976	
—	—	—	...	...	...	1977	
—	—	—	955	38	4	1970	
—	—	—	1 941	473	24	1974	
—	—	—	1 655	458	28	1975	
—	—	—	1 760	497	28	1976	
—	—	—	1 831	576	31	1977	
—	—	—	2 264	746	33	1978	
...	...	...	...	...	...	1976	BANGLADESH ‡
...	...	...	...	...	...	1974	
...	...	...	...	...	...	1975	
7 610	1 368	18	11 475	...	...	1976	
9 070	2 017	22	...	...	...	1977	
7	1	14	18	—	—	1970	BHUTAN ‡
4	2	50	50	...	...	1974	
50	14	28	271	—	—	1970	
39	9	23	695	—	—	1974	
30	10	33	...	...	...	1976	
51	14	27	316	...	...	1977	
93	...	...	...	...	...	1978	
24	6	25	9	—	—	1970	BRUNEI
42	11	26	33	—	—	1974	
37	11	30	61	—	—	1975	
57	13	23	56	—	—	1976	
61	15	25	68	—	—	1977	
66	15	23	85	—	—	1978	
434	190	44	119	—	—	1970	
601	276	46	197	—	—	1974	
613	273	45	314	7	2	1975	
591	297	50	278	3	1	1976	
527	288	55	274	1		1977	
533	323	61	306	14	5	1978	
307	...	...	561	...	...	1970	BURMA
						1974	
257	128	50	48	21	44	1977	

3.7 Education at the second level: teachers and pupils
Enseignement du second degré: personnel enseignant et élèves
Enseñanza de segundo grado: personal docente y alumnos

COUNTRY PAYS PAIS	YEAR ANNEE AÑO	TOTAL SECOND LEVEL TOTAL DU SECOND DEGRE TOTAL DEL SEGUNDO GRADO			GENERAL EDUCATION ENSEIGNEMENT GENERAL ENSEÑANZA GENERAL		
		TOTAL	FEMALE FEMININ FEMENINO	% F	TOTAL	FEMALE FEMININ FEMENINO	% F
		(1)	(2)	(3)	(4)	(5)	(6)
BURMA (CONT.)	STUDENTS 1970	791 059	309 100	39	780 463	306 541	39
	1974	...	...	...	*890 137	*377 387	*42
	1975	923 432	409 280	44	917 896	406 237	44
	1976	887 176	392 956	44	881 983	390 163	44
	1977	885 621	397 648	45	880 355	394 654	45
CHINA	STUDENTS 1977	*60 000 000	*24 000 000	*40	...	...	...
	1978	*65 483 000	*26 848 000	*41	...	...	...
CYPRUS ‡	TEACHERS 1970	2 011	768	38	1 705	714	42
	1974	2 242	877	39	1 881	823	44
	1975	2 451	985	40	2 066	913	44
	1976	2 621	1 083	41	2 179	991	45
	1977	2 718	1 131	42	2 240	1 040	46
	1978	2 853	1 184	42	2 345	1 094	47
	STUDENTS 1970	42 305	19 590	46	37 866	19 025	50
	1974	46 800	21 981	47	41 037	21 600	53
	1975	49 373	23 435	47	43 261	23 049	53
	1976	50 633	23 963	47	44 059	23 499	53
	1977	49 358	23 522	48	42 635	22 817	54
	1978	48 886	23 488	48	42 441	22 777	54
DEMOCRATIC KAMPUCHEA ‡	TEACHERS 1970	3 937	...	...	3 629	...	...
	1972	...	...	...	2 544	502	20
	STUDENTS 1970	86 999	26 872	31	82 700	24 821	30
	1972	...	...	...	99 936	31 191	31
EAST TIMOR	TEACHERS 1970	...	...	...	20	...	...
	STUDENTS 1970	...	...	...	411	112	27
	1973	1 559	546	35	464	164	35
HONG KONG	TEACHERS 1970	10 542	3 799	36	...	...	...
	1974	13 687	5 371	39	...	...	...
	1975	15 149	6 198	41	...	...	...
	1976	13 077	5 950	45	...	...	...
	1977	14 079	6 626	47	...	...	...
	STUDENTS 1970	230 894	96 588	42	216 790	91 868	42
	1974	338 400	154 543	46	317 799	148 460	47
	1975	368 655	172 405	47	347 146	166 083	48
	1976	395 621	184 415	47	372 100	177 519	48
	1977	424 538	200 237	47	398 033	192 447	48
INDIA ‡	TEACHERS 1970	964 445	222 280	23	948 887	218 246	23
	1974	1 133 161	286 378	25	1 117 932	282 417	25
	1975	...	...	...	1 180 233	303 644	26
	1977	...	...	...	1 505 565	415 610	28
	STUDENTS 1970	20 114 304	5 679 985	28	19 895 111	5 597 550	28
	1974	22 977 254	6 949 966	30	22 795 523	6 876 423	30
	1975	23 638 666	7 195 555	30	23 447 697	7 116 654	30
	1976	...	...	...	24 325 788	7 480 309	31
	1977	...	...	...	26 343 780	8 201 999	31
INDONESIA ‡	TEACHERS 1970	187 776	*50 668	*27	130 826	*35 453	*27
	1974	222 002	47 956	22	151 260	34 474	23
	1975	...	...	...	...	...	...
	1976	...	...	...	168 068	38 544	23
	1977	...	...	...	140 472	32 005	23
	1978	...	...	...	156 811	36 864	24

Education at the second level: teachers and pupils 3.7
Enseignement du second degré: personnel enseignant et élèves
Enseñanza de segundo grado: personal docente y alumnos

TEACHER TRAINING ENSEIGNEMENT NORMAL ENSEÑANZA NORMAL			OTHER SECOND LEVEL AUTRE ENSEIGNEMENT DU SECOND DEGRE OTRA ENSEÑANZA DE SEGUNDO GRADO			YEAR ANNEE AÑO	COUNTRY PAYS PAIS
TOTAL	FEMALE FEMININ FEMENINO	% F	TOTAL	FEMALE FEMININ FEMENINO	% F		
(7)	(8)	(9)	(10)	(11)	(12)		
4 498	2 344	52	6 098	215	4	1970	BURMA (CONT.)
...	...	...	...	...	...	1974	
4 890	2 827	58	646	216	33	1975	
4 529	2 586	57	664	207	31	1976	
4 603	2 803	61	663	191	29	1977	
...	...	...	*680 000	...	...	1977	CHINA
...	...	...	*889 000	...	...	1978	
–	–	–	306	54	18	1970	CYPRUS ‡
–	–	–	361	54	15	1974	
–	–	–	385	72	19	1975	
–	–	–	442	92	21	1976	
–	–	–	478	91	19	1977	
–	–	–	508	90	18	1978	
–	–	–	4 439	565	13	1970	
–	–	–	5 763	381	7	1974	
–	–	–	6 112	386	6	1975	
–	–	–	6 574	464	7	1976	
–	–	–	6 723	705	10	1977	
–	–	–	6 445	711	11	1978	
28	12	43	280	...	...	1970	DEMOCRATIC KAMPUCHEA ‡
...	...	...	309	37	16	1972	
1 260	352	28	3 039	1 699	56	1970	
...	...	...	3 483	217	25	1972	
...	...	...	*34	...	...	1970	EAST TIMOR
...	...	...	*666	230	*35	1970	
248	116	47	847	266	31	1973	
			...	...		1970	HONG KONG
			...	...		1974	
			...	...		1975	
			...	...		1976	
			...	...		1977	
–	–	–	14 104	4 720	33	1970	
–	–	–	20 601	6 083	30	1974	
–	–	–	21 509	6 322	29	1975	
–	–	–	23 521	6 896	29	1976	
–	–	–	26 505	7 790	29	1977	
1 534	420	27	14 024	3 614	26	1970	INDIA ‡
...	...	...	...	...	...	1974	
...	...	...	...	...	...	1975	
...	...	...	...	...	...	1977	
18 974	6 705	35	200 219	75 730	38	1970	
18 102	8 253	46	163 629	65 290	40	1974	
19 379	8 704	45	171 590	70 197	41	1975	
13 596	6 676	49	...	...	...	1976	
...	...	...	...	...	...	1977	
8 170	1 580	19	48 780	13 635	28	1970	INDONESIA ‡
7 607	1 566	21	*63 135	*11 916	*19	1974	
8 311	1 830	22	...	...	...	1975	
8 882	1 948	22	...	...	...	1976	
11 975	2 626	22	...	...	...	1977	
14 006	3 169	23	...	...	...	1978	

3.7 Education at the second level: teachers and pupils
Enseignement du second degré: personnel enseignant et élèves
Enseñanza de segundo grado: personal docente y alumnos

COUNTRY PAYS PAIS	YEAR ANNEE AÑO	TOTAL SECOND LEVEL TOTAL DU SECOND DEGRE TOTAL DEL SEGUNDO GRADO			GENERAL EDUCATION ENSEIGNEMENT GENERAL ENSEÑANZA GENERAL		
		TOTAL	FEMALE FEMININ FEMENINO	% F	TOTAL	FEMALE FEMININ FEMENINO	% F
		(1)	(2)	(3)	(4)	(5)	(6)
INDONESIA (CONT.)	STUDENTS 1970	2 459 875	840 534	34	1 815 645	*673 604	*37
	1974	3 189 469	1 170 508	37	2 400 044	*936 017	*39
	1975	3 570 080	1 366 151	38	2 709 953	1 088 838	40
	1976	3 833 129	1 475 413	38	2 881 499	1 166 922	40
	1977	4 084 307	1 579 093	39	3 088 243	1 264 246	41
	1978	4 467 512	1 747 874	39	3 371 231	1 391 891	41
IRAN ‡	TEACHERS 1970	30 886	8 122	26	28 244	7 574	27
	1974	69 414	26 779	39	62 936	25 527	41
	1975	81 855	32 306	39	73 056	30 560	42
	1976	96 395	37 855	39	84 092	35 429	42
	1977	...	...	...	91 960	38 683	42
	STUDENTS 1970	1 056 787	349 078	33	1 012 920	334 757	33
	1974	1 989 567	705 651	35	1 818 323	658 675	36
	1975	2 183 137	778 875	36	1 988 670	727 458	37
	1976	2 356 878	848 668	36	2 109 381	786 891	37
	1977	...	...	...	2 202 863	840 826	38
IRAQ	TEACHERS 1970	13 276	4 364	33	12 309	4 124	34
	1974	18 437	7 234	39	16 862	6 808	40
	1975	21 454	8 542	40	19 397	8 008	41
	1976	21 967	8 841	40	19 471	8 145	42
	1977	24 255	9 424	39	21 256	8 547	40
	1978	29 209	11 120	38	25 254	10 054	40
	STUDENTS 1970	313 972	90 830	29	304 240	88 595	29
	1974	479 885	137 743	29	457 763	131 879	29
	1975	525 255	152 487	29	493 384	141 497	29
	1976	593 928	179 690	30	552 042	164 442	30
	1977	716 822	216 664	30	664 297	196 133	30
	1978	845 992	255 739	30	781 766	231 743	30
ISRAEL	TEACHERS 1970	*14 031	...	...	...	...	...
	STUDENTS 1970	142 521	*73 073	*51	76 264	*43 203	*57
	1974	...	...	...	94 832	54 139	57
	1975	...	...	...	96 625	55 509	57
	1976	...	...	...	99 148	56 943	57
	1977	...	...	...	102 209	58 541	57
JAPAN ‡	TEACHERS 1970	470 533	124 533	26	...	...	...
	1974	503 608	120 265	24	...	...	...
	1975	502 946	124 792	25	...	...	...
	1976	510 604	128 999	25	...	...	...
	1977	507 306	134 115	26	...	...	...
	1978	537 474	138 499	26	...	...	...
	STUDENTS 1970	8 666 937	4 281 261	49	7 040 472	3 565 298	51
	1974	8 682 029	4 306 797	50	7 163 740	3 596 301	50
	1975	8 795 346	4 362 848	50	7 290 314	3 655 221	50
	1976	8 993 333	4 432 518	49	7 511 229	3 734 113	50
	1977	9 111 661	4 452 199	49	7 676 315	3 774 782	49
	1978	9 492 113	4 651 640	49	7 973 963	3 960 208	50
JORDAN ‡	TEACHERS 1970	4 252	1 455	34	4 093	1 427	35
	1974	6 666	2 490	37	6 334	2 414	38
	1975	7 768	3 027	39	7 410	2 945	40
	1976	8 779	3 526	40	8 300	3 419	41
	1977	9 962	3 970	40	9 394	3 825	41
	1978	11 223	4 694	42	10 613	4 522	43
	STUDENTS 1970	97 612	33 280	34	94 659	32 601	34
	1974	143 326	57 068	40	137 832	55 448	40
	1975	164 186	66 856	41	157 745	64 963	41
	1976	185 700	77 077	42	178 153	74 960	42
	1977	209 742	88 310	42	200 916	85 479	43
	1978	231 088	99 895	43	221 822	96 833	44

Education at the second level: teachers and pupils   3.7
Enseignement du second degré: personnel enseignant et élèves
Enseñanza de segundo grado: personal docente y alumnos

TEACHER TRAINING ENSEIGNEMENT NORMAL ENSEÑANZA NORMAL			OTHER SECOND LEVEL AUTRE ENSEIGNEMENT DU SECOND DEGRE OTRA ENSEÑANZA DE SEGUNDO GRADO			YEAR ANNEE AÑO	COUNTRY PAYS PAIS
TOTAL	FEMALE FEMININ FEMENINO	% F	TOTAL	FEMALE FEMININ FEMENINO	% F		
(7)	(8)	(9)	(10)	(11)	(12)		
99 400	46 700	47	544 830	120 230	22	1970	INDONESIA
76 095	39 895	52	713 330	194 596	27	1974	(CONT.) ‡
102 847	59 865	58	757 280	217 448	29	1975	
133 756	78 453	59	817 874	230 038	28	1976	
180 574	104 777	58	815 490	210 070	26	1977	
212 331	121 880	57	883 950	234 103	26	1978	
461	157	34	2 181	391	18	1970	IRAN ‡
1 248	308	25	5 230	944	18	1974	
1 733	485	28	7 066	1 261	18	1975	
2 262	608	27	10 041	1 818	18	1976	
2 988	749	25	...	...	...	1977	
13 288	8 060	61	30 579	6 261	20	1970	
37 799	20 363	54	133 445	26 613	20	1974	
43 958	22 352	51	150 509	29 065	19	1975	
46 025	22 425	49	201 472	39 352	20	1976	
54 435	24 532	45	...	...	...	1977	
–	–	–	967	240	25	1970	IRAQ
67	33	49	1 508	393	26	1974	
403	262	65	1 654	272	16	1975	
590	398	67	1 906	298	16	1976	
666	465	70	2 333	412	18	1977	
682	467	68	3 273	599	18	1978	
–	–	–	9 732	2 235	23	1970	
1 089	639	59	21 033	5 225	25	1974	
8 096	5 485	68	23 775	5 505	23	1975	
13 521	9 481	70	28 365	5 767	20	1976	
17 337	12 685	73	35 188	7 846	22	1977	
16 040	11 823	74	48 186	12 173	25	1978	
...	...	...	...	...	...	1970	ISRAEL
3 507	2 870	82	62 750	*27 000	*43	1970	
...	...	...	72 854	33 196	46	1974	
...	...	...	73 543	33 720	46	1975	
...	...	...	74 040	33 321	45	1976	
...	...	...	74 677	33 148	44	1977	
–	–	–	...	...	...	1970	JAPAN ‡
–	–	–	...	...	...	1974	
–	–	–	...	...	...	1975	
–	–	–	...	...	...	1976	
–	–	–	...	...	...	1977	
–	–	–	...	...	...	1978	
–	–	–	1 626 465	715 963	44	1970	
–	–	–	1 518 289	710 496	47	1974	
–	–	–	1 505 032	707 627	47	1975	
–	–	–	1 482 104	698 405	47	1976	
–	–	–	1 435 346	677 417	47	1977	
–	–	–	1 518 150	691 432	46	1978	
–	–	–	159	28	18	1970	JORDAN ‡
–	–	–	332	76	23	1974	
–	–	–	358	82	23	1975	
–	–	–	479	107	22	1976	
–	–	–	568	145	26	1977	
–	–	–	610	172	28	1978	
–	–	–	2 953	679	23	1970	
–	–	–	5 494	1 620	29	1974	
–	–	–	6 441	1 893	29	1975	
–	–	–	7 547	2 117	28	1976	
–	–	–	8 826	2 831	32	1977	
–	–	–	9 266	3 062	33	1978	

3.7 Education at the second level: teachers and pupils
Enseignement du second degré: personnel enseignant et élèves
Enseñanza de segundo grado: personal docente y alumnos

COUNTRY / PAYS / PAIS	YEAR / ANNEE / AÑO	TOTAL SECOND LEVEL TOTAL DU SECOND DEGRE TOTAL DEL SEGUNDO GRADO			GENERAL EDUCATION ENSEIGNEMENT GENERAL ENSEÑANZA GENERAL		
		TOTAL	FEMALE FEMININ FEMENINO	% F	TOTAL	FEMALE FEMININ FEMENINO	% F
		(1)	(2)	(3)	(4)	(5)	(6)
KOREA, REPUBLIC OF ‡	TEACHERS 1970	52 232	7 953	15	41 052	7 001	17
	1974	77 389	14 232	18	62 318	12 693	20
	1975	83 811	16 596	20	67 332	14 659	22
	1976	88 230	17 606	20	70 606	15 441	22
	1977	92 103	19 633	21	73 342	17 216	23
	1978	101 159	23 242	23	76 208	18 775	25
	1979	104 796	25 900	25	79 296	20 997	26
	STUDENTS 1970	1 906 918	723 568	38	1 634 175	644 820	39
	1974	2 879 948	1 161 095	40	2 460 152	1 018 011	41
	1975	3 111 510	1 268 430	41	2 674 972	1 126 247	42
	1976	3 322 010	1 371 734	41	2 862 881	1 220 236	43
	1977	3 492 091	1 465 977	42	2 990 877	1 293 065	43
	1978	3 692 809	1 582 482	43	3 137 727	1 383 450	44
	1979	4 087 460	1 822 224	45	3 282 151	1 479 563	45
KUWAIT ‡	TEACHERS 1970	5 476	2 435	44	4 794	2 188	46
	1974	8 703	4 108	47	8 227	4 011	49
	1975	9 168	4 549	50	8 805	4 483	51
	1976	11 198	5 433	49	10 868	5 385	50
	1977	12 187	5 890	48	11 914	5 850	49
	1978	11 506	5 615	49	11 339	5 602	49
	STUDENTS 1970	70 734	30 185	43	67 038	28 423	42
	1974	97 689	44 042	45	95 870	43 558	45
	1975	108 219	49 127	45	106 891	48 928	46
	1976	131 589	59 656	45	130 405	59 536	46
	1977	143 392	65 128	45	142 521	65 054	46
	1978	129 402	59 384	46	128 697	59 358	46
LAO PEOPLE'S DEMOCRATIC REPUBLIC ‡	TEACHERS 1970	915	226	25	436	103	24
	1977	3 085	781	25	2 494	630	25
	STUDENTS 1970	15 453	4 101	27	10 026	2 659	27
	1976	48 669	15 930	33	42 049	12 928	31
	1977	64 108	21 760	34	56 294	19 132	34
LEBANON ‡	TEACHERS 1970	...	...	...	...	...	...
	STUDENTS 1970	165 854	...	...	159 871	64 141	40
	1977	...	...	...	232 255	...	...
MACAU	TEACHERS 1970	725	...	...	556	...	...
	STUDENTS 1970	10 007	4 491	45	8 960	4 183	47
	1972	10 279	5 987	58	7 391	3 970	54
MALAYSIA							
PENINSULAR MALAYSIA ‡	TEACHERS 1970	20 822	8 227	40	20 347	8 098	40
	1974	27 576	11 801	43	26 595	11 531	43
	1975	...	...	...	28 255	12 300	44
	1976	30 814	13 346	43	29 924	13 148	44
	1977	31 353	...	...	30 310	...	...
	1978		...	...	32 149	...	...
	STUDENTS 1970	538 865	222 071	41	521 840	213 686	41
	1974	759 676	332 934	44	735 492	321 220	44
	1975	...	...	...	780 454	346 597	44
	1976	851 947	384 665	45	838 968	381 391	45
	1977	853 347	...	...	839 309	...	...
	1978	893 362	...	...	877 815	...	...

Education at the second level: teachers and pupils   3.7
Enseignement du second degré: personnel enseignant et élèves
Enseñanza de segundo grado: personal docente y alumnos

TEACHER TRAINING ENSEIGNEMENT NORMAL ENSEÑANZA NORMAL			OTHER SECOND LEVEL AUTRE ENSEIGNEMENT DU SECOND DEGRE OTRA ENSEÑANZA DE SEGUNDO GRADO			YEAR ANNEE AÑO	COUNTRY PAYS PAIS
TOTAL	FEMALE FEMININ FEMENINO	% F	TOTAL	FEMALE FEMININ FEMENINO	% F		
(7)	(8)	(9)	(10)	(11)	(12)		
–	–	–	11 180	952	9	1970	KOREA, REPUBLIC OF ‡
–	–	–	15 071	1 539	10	1974	
–	–	–	16 479	1 937	12	1975	
–	–	–	17 624	2 165	12	1976	
–	–	–	18 761	2 417	13	1977	
–	–	–	24 951	4 467	18	1978	
–	–	–	25 500	4 903	19	1979	
–	–	–	272 743	78 748	29	1970	
–	–	–	419 796	143 084	34	1974	
–	–	–	436 538	142 183	33	1975	
–	–	–	459 129	151 498	33	1976	
–	–	–	501 214	172 912	34	1977	
–	–	–	555 082	199 032	36	1978	
–	–	–	805 309	342 661	43	1979	
293	175	60	389	72	19	1970	KUWAIT ‡
–	–	–	476	97	20	1974	
–	–	–	363	66	18	1975	
–	–	–	330	48	15	1976	
–	–	–	273	40	15	1977	
–	–	–	167	13	8	1978	
1 642	1 095	67	2 054	667	32	1970	
–	–	–	1 819	484	27	1974	
–	–	–	1 328	199	15	1975	
–	–	–	1 184	120	10	1976	
–	–	–	871	74	8	1977	
–	–	–	705	26	4	1978	
218	46	21	261	77	30	1970	LAO PEOPLE'S DEMOCRATIC REPUBLIC ‡
386	110	28	205	41	20	1977	
3 283	901	27	2 144	541	25	1970	
5 726	2 767	48	894	235	26	1976	
6 191	2 156	35	1 623	472	29	1977	
466	168	36	...	...	...	1970	LEBANON ‡
3 393	1 644	48	2 590	...	...	1970	
...	...	...	...	...	...	1977	
16	...	...	153	...	...	1970	MACAU
65	64	98	982	244	25	1970	
61	58	95	2 827	1 959	69	1972	
							MALAYSIA
–	–	–	475	129	27	1970	PENINSULAR MALAYSIA ‡
–	–	–	981	270	28	1974	
...	...	...	...	...	...	1975	
–	–	–	890	198	22	1976	
–	–	–	1 043	...	...	1977	
–	–	–	...	...	...	1978	
–	–	–	17 025	8 385	49	1970	
–	–	–	24 184	11 714	48	1974	
...	...	...	...	...	...	1975	
–	–	–	12 979	3 274	25	1976	
–	–	–	14 038	...	...	1977	
–	–	–	15 547	...	...	1978	

3.7 Education at the second level: teachers and pupils
Enseignement du second degré: personnel enseignant et élèves
Enseñanza de segundo grado: personal docente y alumnos

COUNTRY PAYS PAIS	YEAR ANNEE AÑO	TOTAL SECOND LEVEL TOTAL DU SECOND DEGRE TOTAL DEL SEGUNDO GRADO			GENERAL EDUCATION ENSEIGNEMENT GENERAL ENSEÑANZA GENERAL		
		TOTAL	FEMALE FEMININ FEMENINO	% F	TOTAL	FEMALE FEMININ FEMENINO	% F
		(1)	(2)	(3)	(4)	(5)	(6)
SABAH	TEACHERS 1970	1 141	...	...	1 071		
	1974	1 799	...	...	1 702	695	41
	1975	...	...	...	1 823		
	1976	2 013	...	...	1 978	760	38
	1977	...	...	...	2 104	...	...
	STUDENTS 1970	31 513	12 412	39	30 603	12 072	39
	1974	44 223	...	...	43 257	18 096	42
	1975	46 931	...	...	45 873	19 412	42
	1976	52 453	...	...	52 153	22 492	43
	1977	...	...	...	57 029	...	...
SARAWAK	TEACHERS 1970	1 507	520	35	1 424	498	35
	1974	1 851	697	38	1 823	689	38
	1976	...	...	...	2 413	925	38
	1977	...	...	...	2 810	1 053	37
	STUDENTS 1970	36 071	13 938	39	35 459	13 730	39
	1974	50 621	21 352	42	50 315	21 246	42
	1975	...	...	...	61 342	25 964	42
	1976	...	...	...	70 167	30 078	43
	1977	...	...	...	77 438	33 732	44
MALDIVES	TEACHERS 1970	26	10	38	26	10	38
	STUDENTS 1970	327	119	36	327	119	36
	1974	...	...	...	446	242	54
	1975	...	...	...	459	255	56
	1976	...	...	...	525	264	50
	1977	...	...	...	712	587	82
MONGOLIA ‡	TEACHERS 1970	...	...	...	4 000	...	...
	1974	7 423	3 854	52	6 511	3 405	52
	1975	...	...	...	...	...	...
	STUDENTS 1970	96 543	...	...	84 343	...	...
	1974	173 111	89 499	52	161 309	82 108	51
	1975	184 688	95 719	52	172 134	87 715	51
NEPAL ‡	TEACHERS 1970	...	...	...	5 484	...	...
	1974	8 739	...	...	...	...	...
	1975	9 947	...	...	...	...	...
	1976	11 295	*1 055	*9	10 609	...	...
	1977	12 439	1 126	9	11 630	...	...
	STUDENTS 1970	...	...	...	115 614	15 824	14
	1974	258 365	36 782	14	243 463	...	...
	1975	281 816	40 459	14	...	...	...
	1976	262 748	45 932	17	243 231	...	...
	1977	308 797	55 386	18	285 154	...	...
OMAN	TEACHERS 1974	138	27	20	116	27	23
	1975	208	33	16	188	33	18
	1977	704	131	19	629	128	20
	1978	934	214	23	841	206	24
	STUDENTS 1974	723	153	21	653	153	23
	1975	1 379	227	16	1 295	227	18
	1976	2 579	503	20	2 345	503	21
	1977	5 647	1 022	18	5 216	1 000	19
	1978	8 534	1 710	20	7 963	1 672	21
PAKISTAN	TEACHERS 1970	73 846	19 343	26	70 621	18 811	27
	1974	96 947	27 312	28	94 032	26 649	28
	1975	108 524	31 942	29	105 189	31 195	30

Education at the second level: teachers and pupils 3.7
Enseignement du second degré: personnel enseignant et élèves
Enseñanza de segundo grado: personal docente y alumnos

TEACHER TRAINING ENSEIGNEMENT NORMAL ENSEÑANZA NORMAL			OTHER SECOND LEVEL AUTRE ENSEIGNEMENT DU SECOND DEGRE OTRA ENSEÑANZA DE SEGUNDO GRADO			YEAR ANNEE	COUNTRY PAYS
TOTAL	FEMALE FEMININ FEMENINO	% F	TOTAL	FEMALE FEMININ FEMENINO	% F	AÑO	PAIS
(7)	(8)	(9)	(10)	(11)	(12)		
50	...	...	20	–	–	1970	SABAH
67	...	...	30	...	...	1974	
72	...	...	...	...	...	1975	
–	–	–	35	...	...	1976	
–	–	–	...	...	...	1977	
730	340	47	180	–	–	1970	
676	...	...	290	...	...	1974	
744	...	...	314	...	...	1975	
–	–	–	300	...	...	1976	
–	–	–	...	...	...	1977	
55	14	25	28	8	29	1970	SARAWAK
–	–	–	28	8	29	1974	
–	–	–	...	...	...	1976	
–	–	–	...	...	...	1977	
269	45	17	343	163	48	1970	
			306	106	35	1974	
...	...	...	...	...	...	1975	
–	–	–	...	...	...	1976	
–	–	–	...	...	...	1977	
–	–	–	–	–	–	1970	MALDIVES
–	–	–	–	–	–	1970	
–	–	–	...	...	...	1974	
–	–	–	...	...	...	1975	
–	–	–	...	...	...	1976	
–	–	–	...	...	...	1977	
...	...	...	...	...	...	1970	MONGOLIA ‡
157	63	40	755	386	51	1974	
137	63	46	...	...	...	1975	
1 600	...	...	10 600	...	...	1970	
1 359	1 006	74	10 443	6 475	62	1974	
1 618	1 343	83	10 936	6 661	61	1975	
...	...	...	...	...	...	1970	NEPAL ‡
290	...	...	...	...	...	1974	
...	...	...	...	...	...	1975	
173	...	...	513	...	...	1976	
215	...	...	594	...	...	1977	
	...	...	...	...	...	1970	
3 843	...	...	11 059	...	...	1974	
...	...	...	...	...	...	1975	
2 702	...	...	16 815	...	...	1976	
2 768	...	...	20 875	...	...	1977	
–	–	–	22	–	–	1974	OMAN
–	–	–	20	–	–	1975	
8	3	38	67	–	–	1977	
16	8	50	77	–	–	1978	
–	–	–	70	–	–	1974	
–	–	–	84	–	–	1975	
25	–	–	209	–	–	1976	
64	22	34	367	–	–	1977	
115	38	33	456	–	–	1978	
922	210	23	2 303	322	14	1970	PAKISTAN
754	209	28	2 161	454	21	1974	
808	227	28	2 527	520	21	1975	

3.7 Education at the second level: teachers and pupils
Enseignement du second degré: personnel enseignant et élèves
Enseñanza de segundo grado: personal docente y alumnos

COUNTRY PAYS PAIS	YEAR ANNEE AÑO	TOTAL SECOND LEVEL TOTAL DU SECOND DEGRE TOTAL DEL SEGUNDO GRADO			GENERAL EDUCATION ENSEIGNEMENT GENERAL ENSEÑANZA GENERAL		
		TOTAL	FEMALE FEMININ FEMENINO	% F	TOTAL	FEMALE FEMININ FEMENINO	% F
		(1)	(2)	(3)	(4)	(5)	(6)
PAKISTAN (CONT.)	STUDENTS 1970	1 462 644	291 101	20	1 428 194	281 104	20
	1974	1 879 538	442 996	24	1 835 805	428 009	23
	1975	2 031 799	488 854	24	1 984 689	472 354	24
PHILIPPINES ‡	TEACHERS 1970	51 979	...	...	...	...	...
	1974	70 947	...	...	...	...	...
	1975	72 778	...	...	...	...	...
	1976	...	...	...	...	...	...
	1977	80 192	...	...	...	...	...
	STUDENTS 1970	1 714 875	...	...	...	...	...
	1974	2 188 031	...	...	...	...	...
	1975	2 254 543	...	...	1 591 594	...	...
	1976	2 435 877	...	...	...	...	...
	1977	2 857 421	...	...	1 887 469	...	...
QATAR	TEACHERS 1970	324	103	32	250	96	38
	1974	630	263	42	513	237	46
	1975	829	372	45	698	335	48
	1976	925	428	46	791	388	49
	1977	1 039	488	47	912	450	49
	1978	1 212	589	49	1 104	562	51
	STUDENTS 1970	4 095	1 314	32	3 649	1 200	33
	1974	7 811	3 334	43	7 139	3 091	43
	1975	10 109	4 829	48	9 416	4 560	48
	1976	10 347	4 759	46	9 716	4 542	47
	1977	11 469	5 384	47	10 915	5 190	48
	1978	12 911	6 106	47	12 445	5 990	48
SAUDI ARABIA ‡	TEACHERS 1970	5 064	786	16	3 993	369	9
	1974	12 551	2 543	20	10 964	2 220	20
	1975	13 971	3 360	24	12 154	3 038	25
	1976	18 431	4 477	24	16 458	3 989	24
	1977	22 291	5 332	24	20 046	4 697	23
	STUDENTS 1970	89 226	17 497	20	74 691	10 501	14
	1974	179 187	53 322	30	159 938	48 750	30
	1975	203 000	65 996	33	184 404	61 673	33
	1976	234 647	78 832	34	214 841	73 011	34
	1977	287 418	94 018	33	265 256	84 556	32
SINGAPORE ‡	TEACHERS 1970	7 513	3 061	41	6 358	2 853	45
	1974	7 894	3 421	43	5 947	3 092	52
	1975	7 951	...	...	5 812	3 240	56
	1976	7 993	3 560	45	5 879	3 345	57
	1977	8 025	3 686	46	...	...	...
	1978	8 050	3 822	47	...	...	...
	STUDENTS 1970	149 143	71 005	48	136 782	69 521	51
	1974	178 673	87 877	49	154 606	81 104	52
	1975	183 364	89 980	49	153 029	81 638	53
	1976	189 743	92 053	49	152 713	82 008	54
	1977	187 034	92 497	49	153 055	82 220	54
	1978	187 713	93 443	50	154 494	83 019	54
SRI LANKA ‡	TEACHERS 1974	...	...	...	...	...	...
	1976	...	...	...	57 854	...	...
	1977	...	...	...	62 714	...	...
	1978	...	...	...	58 755	28 077	48
	STUDENTS 1970	941 322	...	...	930 897	467 982	50
	1974	1 132 951	...	...	1 118 178	...	...
	1975	...	...	...	1 063 766	535 785	50
	1976	1 088 089	554 442	51	1 076 502	548 898	51
	1977	...	...	...	970 000	477 489	49
	1978	...	...	...	1 243 245	479 516	39
	1979	...	...	...	1 159 967	...	...

Education at the second level: teachers and pupils　3.7
Enseignement du second degré: personnel enseignant et élèves
Enseñanza de segundo grado: personal docente y alumnos

TEACHER TRAINING ENSEIGNEMENT NORMAL ENSEÑANZA NORMAL			OTHER SECOND LEVEL AUTRE ENSEIGNEMENT DU SECOND DEGRE OTRA ENSEÑANZA DE SEGUNDO GRADO			YEAR ANNEE AÑO	COUNTRY PAYS PAIS
TOTAL	FEMALE FEMININ FEMENINO	% F	TOTAL	FEMALE FEMININ FEMENINO	% F		
(7)	(8)	(9)	(10)	(11)	(12)		
12 877	3 030	24	21 573	6 967	32	1970	PAKISTAN (CONT.)
16 883	7 665	45	26 850	7 322	27	1974	
17 876	8 824	49	29 234	7 676	26	1975	
—	—	—	5 290	...	...	1970	PHILIPPINES ‡
—	—	—	6 046	...	...	1974	
—	—	—	...	...	...	1975	
—	—	—	30 717	...	...	1976	
—	—	—	...	...	...	1977	
—	—	—	...	...	...	1970	
—	—	—	...	...	...	1974	
—	—	—	662 949	...	...	1975	
—	—	—	...	...	...	1976	
—	—	—	969 952	...	...	1977	
30	7	23	44	—	—	1970	QATAR
47	26	55	70	—	—	1974	
56	37	66	75	—	—	1975	
59	40	68	75	—	—	1976	
56	38	68	71	—	—	1977	
40	27	68	68	—	—	1978	
237	114	48	209	—	—	1970	
307	243	79	365	—	—	1974	
324	269	83	369	—	—	1975	
256	217	85	375	—	—	1976	
231	194	84	323	—	—	1977	
136	116	85	330	—	—	1978	
762	359	47	309	58	19	1970	SAUDI ARABIA ‡
1 037	252	24	550	71	13	1974	
1 156	288	25	661	34	5	1975	
1 191	431	36	782	57	7	1976	
1 442	635	44	803	—	—	1977	
12 827	6 286	49	1 708	710	42	1970	
14 099	3 840	27	5 150	732	14	1974	
14 015	4 064	29	4 581	259	6	1975	
14 751	5 618	38	5 055	203	4	1976	
17 707	9 341	53	4 455	121	3	1977	
—	—	—	1 155	208	18	1970	SINGAPORE ‡
—	—	—	1 947	329	17	1974	
—	—	—	2 139	...	...	1975	
—	—	—	2 114	215	10	1976	
—	—	—	...	...	...	1977	
—	—	—	...	...	...	1978	
—	—	—	12 361	1 484	12	1970	
—	—	—	24 067	6 773	28	1974	
—	—	—	30 335	8 342	27	1975	
—	—	—	37 030	10 045	27	1976	
—	—	—	33 979	10 277	30	1977	
—	—	—	33 219	10 424	31	1978	
606	...	...	...	...	...	1974	SRI LANKA ‡
...	...	...	1 239	72	6	1976	
...	...	...	...	...	...	1977	
...	...	...	...	...	...	1978	
6 294	...	...	4 131	...	...	1970	
10 026	7 273	73	4 747	...	...	1974	
8 855	5 852	66	...	...	...	1975	
6 809	3 946	58	4 778	1 598	33	1976	
4 767	...	...	...	...	...	1977	
5 170	...	...	...	...	...	1978	
...	...	...	...	...	...	1979	

3.7 Education at the second level: teachers and pupils
Enseignement du second degré: personnel enseignant et élèves
Enseñanza de segundo grado: personal docente y alumnos

COUNTRY PAYS PAIS	YEAR ANNEE AÑO	TOTAL SECOND LEVEL TOTAL DU SECOND DEGRE TOTAL DEL SEGUNDO GRADO			GENERAL EDUCATION ENSEIGNEMENT GENERAL ENSEÑANZA GENERAL		
		TOTAL	FEMALE FEMININ FEMENINO	% F	TOTAL	FEMALE FEMININ FEMENINO	% F
		(1)	(2)	(3)	(4)	(5)	(6)
SYRIAN ARAB REPUBLIC ‡	TEACHERS 1970	15 045	3 374	22	13 483	3 219	24
	1974	23 289	7 033	30	20 479	6 494	32
	1975	24 895	7 506	30	22 704	7 062	31
	1976	23 743	...	...	21 493	...	...
	1977	24 347	5 710	23	21 795	5 129	24
	1978	28 145	7 010	25	25 214	6 253	25
	STUDENTS 1970	327 639	85 206	26	315 803	84 170	27
	1974	458 327	138 461	30	434 281	133 624	31
	1975	488 409	152 060	31	463 348	146 925	32
	1976	512 187	166 343	32	485 873	160 367	33
	1977	545 468	182 363	33	520 044	176 461	34
	1978	579 739	200 208	35	552 677	193 419	35
THAILAND ‡	TEACHERS 1970	*44 756	*10 623	*24	35 641	6 631	54
	1974	...	...	...	...	...	...
	1975	43 830	...	...	29 527	...	...
	1976	49 229	26 190	53	34 782	19 864	57
	1977	...	...	...	42 290	23 886	56
	STUDENTS 1970	695 023	290 207	42	511 929	209 795	41
	1974	1 066 486	455 530	43	858 924	364 343	42
	1975	1 193 741	523 203	44	956 427	414 461	43
	1976	1 324 539	619 998	47	1 053 625	466 201	44
	1977	...	...	...	1 112 554	501 542	45
TURKEY	TEACHERS 1970	47 452	17 368	37	32 413	12 111	37
	1974	...	...	...	...	...	...
	1977	...	...	...	...	...	...
	STUDENTS 1970	1 308 779	373 167	29	1 064 635	290 351	27
	1974	...	...	...	...	...	...
	1975	2 120 876	665 603	31	1 746 160	549 551	31
	1976	2 374 353	719 877	30	1 938 545	600 225	31
	1977	2 497 047	766 611	31	2 028 476	638 872	31
UNITED ARAB EMIRATES ‡	TEACHERS 1970	...	...	...	302		
	1974	845	...	...	914	317	35
	1975	...	...	...	1 389	564	41
	1976	...	...	...	1 748	728	42
	1977	...	...	...	...	...	...
	1978	...	...	...	...	...	...
	STUDENTS 1970	4 622	...	...	4 008	746	19
	1974	9 211	3 040	33	8 791	2 919	33
	1975	11 597	4 215	36	11 183	4 123	37
	1976	16 244	6 327	39	15 927	6 254	39
	1977	18 905	7 989	42	18 610	7 963	43
	1978	22 668	9 681	43	22 384	9 681	43
VIET—NAM	TEACHERS 1975	115 348	65 954	57	108 454	64 209	59
	1976	127 635	73 389	57	119 388	71 230	60
	1977	...	...	...	129 183	67 514	52
	STUDENTS 1975	2 987 997	1 503 076	50	2 915 753	1 462 826	50
	1976	3 200 912	1 563 012	49	3 108 629	1 522 217	49
	1977	...	...	...	3 301 145	1 497 530	45
VIET—NAM, (FORMER NORTH)	TEACHERS 1970	58 123	20 415	35	...	...	...
	1974	81 906	43 072	53	...	...	...
	STUDENTS 1970	1 471 626	636 300	43	...	...	...
	1974	2 011 754	967 768	48	1 946 103	935 639	48
VIET—NAM, (FORMER SOUTH)	TEACHERS 1970	22 427	5 423	24	21 205	5 188	24
	1973	...	...	...	32 131	9 156	28

Education at the second level: teachers and pupils 3.7
Enseignement du second degré: personnel enseignant et élèves
Enseñanza de segundo grado: personal docente y alumnos

TEACHER TRAINING ENSEIGNEMENT NORMAL ENSEÑANZA NORMAL			OTHER SECOND LEVEL AUTRE ENSEIGNEMENT DU SECOND DEGRE OTRA ENSEÑANZA DE SEGUNDO GRADO			YEAR ANNEE	COUNTRY PAYS
TOTAL	FEMALE FEMININ FEMENINO	% F	TOTAL	FEMALE FEMININ FEMENINO	% F	AÑO	PAIS
(7)	(8)	(9)	(10)	(11)	(12)		
250	93	37	1 312	62	5	1970	SYRIAN ARAB
506	243	48	2 304	*296	*13	1974	REPUBLIC ‡
514	253	49	1 677	191	11	1975	
567	217	38	1 683	241	14	1976	
642	338	53	1 910	243	13	1977	
792	451	57	2 139	306	14	1978	
653	357	55	11 183	679	6	1970	
2 835	1 318	46	21 211	*3 519	*17	1974	
3 015	1 371	45	22 046	3 764	17	1975	
2 615	1 295	50	23 699	4 681	20	1976	
1 570	788	50	23 854	5 114	21	1977	
1 117	606	54	25 945	6 183	24	1978	
3 105	1 621	52	*6 010	*2 371	*39	1970	THAILAND ‡
4 087	2 090	51	*8 498	*3 455	*41	1974	
4 588	2 343	51	*9 715	*3 991	*41	1975	
4 688	2 342	50	*9 759	*3 984	*41	1976	
4 790	2 496	52	...	...	...	1977	
28 253	14 409	51	154 841	66 003	43	1970	
42 871	20 532	48	164 691	70 655	43	1974	
46 248	22 944	50	191 066	85 798	45	1975	
44 406	23 157	52	226 508	130 640	58	1976	
34 922	19 924	57	...	...	...	1977	
2 644	814	31	12 395	4 443	36	1970	TURKEY
3 281	...	...	15 692	...	...	1974	
2 001	525	26	...	...	...	1977	
65 145	30 544	47	178 999	52 272	29	1970	
58 948	28 136	48	252 850	78 307	31	1974	
53 445	25 181	47	*321 271	*90 871	*28	1975	
40 775	17 670	43	*395 033	*101 982	*26	1976	
32 102	13 362	42	*436 469	114 377	*26	1977	
18	...	...	43	–	–	1970	UNITED ARAB
4	...	...	81	–	–	1974	EMIRATES ‡
...	...	...	90	1	1	1975	
...	...	...	101	2	2	1976	
...	...	...	103	2	2	1977	
–	–	–	100	1	1	1978	
156	...	...	458	–	–	1970	
170	121	71	250	–	–	1974	
118	92	78	296	–	–	1975	
89	73	82	228	–	–	1976	
34	26	76	261	–	–	1977	
–	–	–	284	–	–	1978	
				...	...	1975	VIET–NAM
2 336	607	26	5 911	1 552	26	1976	
...	...	...	...	...	...	1977	
						1975	
25 730	17 803	69	66 553	22 992	35	1976	
42 583	22 144	52	...	...	...	1977	
							VIET–NAM,
...	...	...	...	...	...	1970	(FORMER NORTH)
...	...	...	...	...	...	1974	
						1970	
21 850	10 092	46	43 801	22 037	50	1974	
							VIET–NAM,
104	20	19	1 118	215	19	1970	(FORMER SOUTH)
385	66	17	...	...	...	1973	

3.7 Education at the second level: teachers and pupils
Enseignement du second degré: personnel enseignant et élèves
Enseñanza de segundo grado: personal docente y alumnos

COUNTRY PAYS PAIS	YEAR ANNEE AÑO	TOTAL SECOND LEVEL TOTAL DU SECOND DEGRE TOTAL DEL SEGUNDO GRADO			GENERAL EDUCATION ENSEIGNEMENT GENERAL ENSEÑANZA GENERAL		
		TOTAL	FEMALE FEMININ FEMENINO	% F	TOTAL	FEMALE FEMININ FEMENINO	% F
		(1)	(2)	(3)	(4)	(5)	(6)
VIET—NAM, (FORMER SOUTH, CONT.)	STUDENTS 1970 1973	734 122 1 097 412	300 454 ...	41 ...	711 240 1 064 311	293 392 438 127	41 41
YEMEN	TEACHERS 1970 1974 1975	... 1 019 *1 345	— ... *59	— ... *4	207 835 *1 172	— ... *21	— ... *2
	STUDENTS 1970 1974 1975	5 716 17 985 24 822	290 1 630 2 854	5 9 11	5 176 16 513 22 368	150 1 124 2 211	3 7 10
YEMEN, DEMOCRATIC	TEACHERS 1970 1974 1975 1976 1977	900 1 769 2 194	166 401 447	18 23 20	769 1 656 2 071	162 383 431	21 23 21 ... ...
	STUDENTS 1970 1974 1975 1976 1977	17 590 39 709 46 341 57 883 66 681	3 552 8 280 10 270 13 866 17 281	20 21 22 24 26	16 631 38 389 44 829 55 762 64 388	3 343 7 988 9 924 13 324 16 606	20 21 22 24 26
EUROPE							
ALBANIA	TEACHERS 1970 1971	2 362 3 030	666 986	28 33	1 157 1 318	333 466	29 35
	STUDENTS 1970 1971	40 407 48 473	18 252 22 641	45 47	20 514 23 229	9 832 11 489	48 49
ANDORRA	STUDENTS 1970 1974 1975	724 1 339 1 753	317 637 1 092	44 48 62	724 1 339 1 753	317 637 1 092	44 48 62
AUSTRIA ‡	TEACHERS 1970 1974 1977 1978	35 212 46 531 56 151 56 927	15 948 ... 27 591 29 156	45 ... 49 51	26 739 36 450 42 630 42 868	12 540 ... 22 196 23 141	47 ... 52 54
	STUDENTS 1970 1974 1975 1976 1977 1978	630 254 734 316 755 670 770 575 727 657 729 621	312 099 363 452 374 266 382 261 360 902 361 472	50 49 50 50 50 50	541 718 618 298 629 852 638 869 590 588 585 347	264 399 301 808 307 616 312 186 287 335 283 778	49 49 49 49 49 48
BELGIUM	STUDENTS 1970 1974 1975 1976 1977	723 703 788 773 809 071 849 937 832 621	350 036 387 450 ... 413 035 410 980	48 49 ... 49 49	334 891 391 978 402 393 442 275 412 644	156 258 190 820 196 689 212 613 203 870	47 49 49 48 49
BULGARIA ‡	TEACHERS 1970 1974 1975 1976 1977 1978	23 053 25 968 27 045 27 236 26 972 26 730	11 206 13 118 14 079 15 555 13 890 13 941	49 51 52 57 51 52	6 270 7 530 7 637 7 830 7 626 7 585	3 801 4 699 4 822 5 046 4 833 4 771	61 62 63 64 63 63
	STUDENTS 1970 1974 1975 1976 1977 1978	318 725 344 034 344 015 340 992 337 389 ...	... ...	... ...	84 036 98 824 101 206 101 194 98 853 102 872	... ... 69 843	 68

Education at the second level: teachers and pupils   3.7
Enseignement du second degré: personnel enseignant et élèves
Enseñanza de segundo grado: personal docente y alumnos

TEACHER TRAINING ENSEIGNEMENT NORMAL ENSEÑANZA NORMAL			OTHER SECOND LEVEL AUTRE ENSEIGNEMENT DU SECOND DEGRE OTRA ENSEÑANZA DE SEGUNDO GRADO			YEAR ANNEE AÑO	COUNTRY PAYS PAIS
TOTAL	FEMALE FEMININ FEMENINO	% F	TOTAL	FEMALE FEMININ FEMENINO	% F		
(7)	(8)	(9)	(10)	(11)	(12)		
4 943	2 869	58	17 939	4 193	23	1970	VIET-NAM (FORMER
8 015	4 003	50	25 086	...	...	1973	SOUTH, CONT.)
...	—	—	12	—	—	1970	YEMEN
130	...	...	54	—	—	1974	
113	38	34	60	—	—	1975	
412	140	34	128	—	—	1970	
920	506	55	552	—	—	1974	
1 306	643	49	1 148	—	—	1975	
32	3	9	99	1	1	1970	YEMEN, DEMOCRATIC
47	10	21	66	8	12	1974	
62	8	13	61	8	13	1975	
72	8	11	68	5	7	1976	
57	5	9	...	...	...	1977	
386	122	32	573	87	15	1970	
631	169	27	689	123	18	1974	
794	231	29	718	115	16	1975	
1 083	324	30	1 038	218	21	1976	
1 070	370	35	1 223	305	25	1977	
							EUROPE
...	...	...	...	...	...	1970	ALBANIA
...	...	...	...	...	...	1971	
...	...	...	...	...	...	1970	
...	...	...	...	...	...	1971	
—	—	—	—	—	—	1970	ANDORRA
—	—	—	—	—	—	1974	
—	—	—	—	—	—	1975	
612	464	76	7 861	2 944	37	1970	AUSTRIA ‡
581	449	77	9 500	3 533	37	1974	
685	540	79	12 836	4 855	38	1977	
710	564	79	13 349	5 451	41	1978	
4 135	4 109	99	84 401	43 591	52	1970	
6 069	6 026	99	109 949	55 618	51	1974	
6 283	6 247	99	119 535	60 403	51	1975	
6 254	6 227	100	125 452	63 848	51	1976	
6 050	6 019	99	131 019	67 548	52	1977	
5 866	5 828	99	138 408	71 866	52	1978	
16 014	11 344	71	372 798	182 434	49	1970	BELGIUM
—	—	—	396 795	196 630	50	1974	
—	—	—	406 678	...	...	1975	
—	—	—	407 662	200 422	49	1976	
—	—	—	419 977	207 110	49	1977	
...	...	...	...	...	...	1970	BULGARIA ‡
—	—	—	18 438	8 419	46	1974	
—	—	—	19 408	9 257	48	1975	
—	—	—	19 406	10 509	54	1976	
—	—	—	19 346	9 057	47	1977	
—	—	—	19 145	9 170	48	1978	
65	65	100	234 624	98 680	42	1970	
—	—	—	245 210	103 765	42	1974	
—	—	—	242 809	101 406	42	1975	
—	—	—	239 798	97 402	41	1976	
—	—	—	238 536	93 815	39	1977	
—	—	—	244 890	95 108	39	1978	

3.7 Education at the second level: teachers and pupils
Enseignement du second degré: personnel enseignant et élèves
Enseñanza de segundo grado: personal docente y alumnos

COUNTRY / PAYS / PAIS	YEAR / ANNEE / AÑO		TOTAL SECOND LEVEL / TOTAL DU SECOND DEGRE / TOTAL DEL SEGUNDO GRADO			GENERAL EDUCATION / ENSEIGNEMENT GENERAL / ENSEÑANZA GENERAL		
			TOTAL	FEMALE FEMININ FEMENINO	% F	TOTAL	FEMALE FEMININ FEMENINO	% F
			(1)	(2)	(3)	(4)	(5)	(6)
CZECHOSLOVAKIA	TEACHERS	1970	22 504	9 646	43	6 332	3 419	54
		1974	24 559	11 706	48	8 059	4 611	57
		1975	24 880	12 160	49	8 236	4 814	58
		1976	25 009	12 379	49	8 384	4 951	59
		1977	25 003	12 506	50	8 326	4 956	60
		1978	25 481	12 841	50	8 481	5 078	60
	STUDENTS	1970	320 629	194 166	61	101 729	65 740	65
		1974	317 917	194 552	61	119 998	77 287	64
		1975	320 531	196 646	61	121 283	77 136	64
		1976	328 544	201 367	61	123 823	77 972	63
		1977	337 488	207 884	62	126 492	78 828	62
		1978	355 314	219 035	62	133 067	81 798	61
DENMARK ‡	TEACHERS	1974	...	...	...	...	...	...
	STUDENTS	1970	407 103	...	...	283 464	143 253	51
		1974	334 597	...	...	313 204	...	...
		1975	365 561	...	...	327 588	...	...
		1976	371 291	...	...	332 689	...	...
		1977	...	...	...	349 939	178 169	51
FINLAND ‡	TEACHERS	1970	32 247	17 091	53	22 099	13 491	61
		1974	...	...	...	24 291	...	...
		1975	...	...	...	23 139	...	...
		1976	30 799	...	...	21 399	...	...
		1977	28 595	...	...	19 430	...	...
		1978	32 651	...	...	19 549	...	...
	STUDENTS	1970	509 691	259 281	51	407 978	215 680	53
		1974	...	...	...	391 905	210 463	54
		1975	419 808	218 933	52	337 575	180 566	53
		1976	431 090	222 903	52	341 421	181 393	53
		1977	437 675	225 963	52	343 759	182 429	53
		1978	446 041	230 112	52	345 603	183 532	53
FRANCE ‡	TEACHERS	1970	270 949	109 683	54	...	...	...
		1974	...	...	...	317 144	...	...
		1975	316 341	...	...	...	...	...
		1976	319 246	...	...	...	...	...
		1977	*331 669	...	...	...	...	...
		1978	358 916	...	...	300 145	...	...
	STUDENTS	1970	4 281 446	2 189 968	51	3 460 577	1 785 173	52
		1974	4 957 483	...	...	4 117 725	2 120 445	51
		1975	5 035 153	2 558 971	51	4 009 721	...	...
		1976	4 961 775	2 532 587	51	3 915 908	2 039 467	52
		1977	4 948 694	2 537 381	51	3 888 963	2 044 167	53
		1978	4 976 489	2 555 736	51	3 900 006	2 053 334	53
GERMAN DEMOCRATIC REPUBLIC	STUDENTS	1970	485 588	...	...	54 654	...	...
		1974	468 080	...	...	49 206	...	...
		1975	460 639	...	...	47 854	...	...
		1976	481 162	...	...	47 562	...	...
		1977	499 653	...	...	46 836	...	...
		1978	509 132	...	...	46 024	...	...
GERMANY, FEDERAL REPUBLIC OF ‡	TEACHERS	1970	219 112	75 591	34	151 985	54 060	36
		1974	*248 528	*91 279	*37	202 815	76 831	38
		1975	...	...	...	210 891	81 694	39
		1976	256 021	100 901	39	204 637	83 096	41
		1977	265 696	106 830	40	215 340	88 695	41

Education at the second level: teachers and pupils 3.7
Enseignement du second degré: personnel enseignant et élèves
Enseñanza de segundo grado: personal docente y alumnos

TEACHER TRAINING ENSEIGNEMENT NORMAL ENSEÑANZA NORMAL			OTHER SECOND LEVEL AUTRE ENSEIGNEMENT DU SECOND DEGRE OTRA ENSEÑANZA DE SEGUNDO GRADO			YEAR ANNEE AÑO	COUNTRY PAYS PAIS
TOTAL	FEMALE FEMININ FEMENINO	% F	TOTAL	FEMALE FEMININ FEMENINO	% F		
(7)	(8)	(9)	(10)	(11)	(12)		
442	226	51	15 730	6 001	38	1970	CZECHOSLOVAKIA
528	313	59	15 972	6 782	42	1974	
616	366	59	16 028	6 980	44	1975	
698	422	60	15 927	7 006	44	1976	
745	463	62	15 932	7 087	44	1977	
825	529	64	16 175	7 234	45	1978	
6 742	6 519	97	212 158	121 907	57	1970	
7 533	7 362	98	190 386	109 903	58	1974	
8 786	8 615	98	190 462	110 895	58	1975	
10 256	10 072	98	194 465	113 323	58	1976	
11 111	10 934	98	199 885	118 122	59	1977	
12 387	12 196	98	209 860	125 041	60	1978	
—	—	—	5 290	...	...	1974	DENMARK ‡
—	—	—	123 639	...	...	1970	
—	—	—	21 393	...	...	1974	
—	—	—	37 973	...	...	1975	
—	—	—	38 602	...	...	1976	
—	—	—	...	...	...	1977	
392	267	68	9 756	3 333	34	1970	FINLAND ‡
...	...	...	*11 500	...	...	1974	
						1975	
108	52	48	9 292	3 678	40	1976	
71	31	44	9 094	3 626	40	1977	
71	33	46	13 031	5 397	41	1978	
1 521	1 130	74	100 192	42 471	42	1970	
...	...	...	*115 000	*53 000	*46	1974	
703	470	67	81 530	37 897	46	1975	
898	628	70	88 771	40 882	46	1976	
690	443	64	93 226	43 091	46	1977	
745	506	68	99 693	46 074	46	1978	
2 349	1 245	53	...	...	...	1970	FRANCE ‡
2 691	1 278	47	...	...	...	1974	
...	...	...	...	...	...	1975	
...	...	...	...	...	...	1976	
—	—	—	...	...	...	1977	
—	—	—	58 771	...	...	1978	
27 429	15 078	55	793 440	389 717	49	1970	
26 317	...	...	813 441	382 877	47	1974	
16 000	...	...	1 009 432	...	...	1975	
16 050	9 655	60	1 029 817	483 465	47	1976	
—	—	—	1 059 731	493 214	47	1977	
—	—	—	1 076 483	502 402	47	1978	
—	—	—	430 934	...	...	1970	GERMAN DEMOCRATIC REPUBLIC
—	—	—	418 874	...	...	1974	
—	—	—	412 785	...	...	1975	
—	—	—	433 600	...	...	1976	
—	—	—	452 817	...	...	1977	
—	—	—	463 108	...	...	1978	
—	—	—	67 127	21 531	32	1970	GERMANY, FEDERAL REPUBLIC OF ‡
—	—	—	*45 713	*14 448	*32	1974	
—	—	—	...	...	...	1975	
—	—	—	51 384	17 805	35	1976	
—	—	—	50 356	18 135	36	1977	

3.7 Education at the second level: teachers and pupils
Enseignement du second degré: personnel enseignant et élèves
Enseñanza de segundo grado: personal docente y alumnos

COUNTRY PAYS PAIS		YEAR ANNEE AÑO	TOTAL SECOND LEVEL TOTAL DU SECOND DEGRE TOTAL DEL SEGUNDO GRADO			GENERAL EDUCATION ENSEIGNEMENT GENERAL ENSEÑANZA GENERAL		
			TOTAL	FEMALE FEMININ FEMENINO	% F	TOTAL	FEMALE FEMININ FEMENINO	% F
			(1)	(2)	(3)	(4)	(5)	(6)
GERMANY, FEDERAL RE- PUBLIC OF (CONT.) ‡	STUDENTS	1970	2 704 796	1 308 829	48	2 245 694	1 064 281	47
		1974	3 642 429	1 845 736	51	3 013 888	1 502 376	50
		1975	3 638 200	1 961 574	54	3 176 508	1 593 215	50
		1976	3 810 911	1 951 249	51	3 349 488	1 693 803	51
		1977	3 966 376	2 044 950	52	3 486 612	1 772 365	51
		1978	...	...	...	*3 399 629	...	...
GIBRALTAR	TEACHERS	1974	146	59	40	126	59	47
		1975	132	53	40	114	53	46
		1976	131	52	40	113	52	46
		1977	139	53	38	120	53	44
	STUDENTS	1970	1 794	898	50	...	...	...
		1974	1 605	791	49	1 561	791	51
		1975	1 629	824	51	1 587	823	52
		1976	1 777	1 001	56	1 718	992	58
		1977	1 769	853	48	1 719	852	50
GREECE ‡	TEACHERS	1970	...	...	...	12 958	6 315	49
		1974	...	...	...	17 624	9 330	53
		1975	...	...	...	18 719	9 952	53
		1976	...	...	...	21 797	11 688	54
	STUDENTS	1970	520 323	222 953	43	422 022	209 064	50
		1974	635 140	270 293	43	501 023	252 273	50
		1975	661 796	283 855	43	529 205	266 493	50
		1976	694 216	295 558	43	562 695	276 682	49
HUNGARY	TEACHERS	1970	22 442	...	...	7 196	...	...
		1974	22 324	...	...	6 700	...	...
		1975	22 781	...	...	6 663	...	...
		1976	23 404	...	...	6 740	3 963	59
		1977	23 873	11 372	48	6 659	3 986	60
		1978	24 235	11 609	48	6 675	4 005	60
	STUDENTS	1970	465 324	198 219	43	122 988	82 308	67
		1974	384 548	172 779	45	102 079	66 819	65
		1975	371 898	168 126	45	99 656	64 905	65
		1976	366 362	169 484	46	95 042	61 558	65
		1977	353 026	161 077	46	90 413	58 795	65
		1978	350 957	161 026	46	88 417	57 552	65
ICELAND	TEACHERS	1970	2 207	618	28	1 453	465	32
		1974	2 413	707	29	1 547	498	32
		1975	2 387	699	29	1 538	506	33
		1976	...	...	...	1 631	...	...
	STUDENTS	1970	*23 144	*10 176	*44	18 074	8 547	47
		1974	25 028	11 155	45	19 829	9 778	49
		1975	*25 853	11 566	*45	20 292	10 089	50
		1976	26 506	12 160	46	20 764	10 338	50
IRELAND ‡	TEACHERS	1970		...	...	10 426	5 981	57
		1974	20 856	...	...	...	...	...
		1975	18 913	9 537	50	...	...	...
		1976	19 146	...	...	...	...	...
		1977	19 260	...	...	...	...	...
		1978	19 430	...	...	...	...	...
	STUDENTS	1970	208 705	106 360	51	154 575	85 541	55
		1974	256 652	131 704	51	247 609	124 028	50
		1975	270 956	138 851	51	260 999	130 601	50
		1976	281 121	144 393	51	270 106	135 221	50
		1977	288 110	148 486	52	274 188	138 039	50
		1978	292 658	151 179	52	277 929	140 634	51

358

Education at the second level: teachers and pupils   3.7
Enseignement du second degré: personnel enseignant et élèves
Enseñanza de segundo grado: personal docente y alumnos

TEACHER TRAINING ENSEIGNEMENT NORMAL ENSEÑANZA NORMAL			OTHER SECOND LEVEL AUTRE ENSEIGNEMENT DU SECOND DEGRE OTRA ENSEÑANZA DE SEGUNDO GRADO			YEAR ANNEE AÑO	COUNTRY PAYS PAIS
TOTAL	FEMALE FEMININ FEMENINO	% F	TOTAL	FEMALE FEMININ FEMENINO	% F		
(7)	(8)	(9)	(10)	(11)	(12)		
—	—	—	459 102	244 548	53	1970	GERMANY, FEDERAL
—	—	—	628 541	343 360	55	1974	REPUBLIC OF
—	—	—	461 692	368 359	80	1975	(CONT.) ‡
—	—	—	461 423	257 446	56	1976	
—	—	—	479 764	272 585	57	1977	
...	...	...	...	...	...	1978	
—	—	—	20	—	—	1974	GIBRALTAR
—	—	—	18	—	—	1975	
—	—	—	18	—	—	1976	
—	—	—	19	—	—	1977	
—	—	—	...	...	...	1970	
—	—	—	44	...	...	1974	
—	—	—	42	1	2	1975	
—	—	—	59	9	15	1976	
—	—	—	50	1	2	1977	
—	—	—	...	...	...	1970	GREECE ‡
—	—	—	...	...	...	1974	
—	—	—	...	...	...	1975	
—	—	—	...	...	...	1976	
—	—	—	98 301	13 889	14	1970	
—	—	—	134 117	18 020	13	1974	
—	—	—	132 591	17 362	13	1975	
—	—	—	131 521	18 876	14	1976	
—	—	—	15 246	...	...	1970	HUNGARY
...	...	...	...	...	...	1974	
...	...	...	...	...	...	1975	
...	...	...	...	...	...	1976	
...	...	...	...	...	...	1977	
...	...	...	...	...	...	1978	
—	—	—	342 336	115 911	34	1970	
3 552	3 552	100	278 917	102 408	37	1974	
4 913	4 913	100	267 329	98 308	37	1975	
5 744	5 744	100	265 576	102 182	38	1976	
6 442	6 442	100	256 171	95 840	37	1977	
6 677	6 677	100	255 863	96 797	38	1978	
96	28	29	658	125	19	1970	ICELAND
56	30	54	810	179	22	1974	
30	17	57	819	176	21	1975	
...	...	...	685	...	...	1976	
836	551	66	*4 234	*1 078	*25	1970	
222	182	82	4 977	1 195	24	1974	
210	172	82	*5 351	*1 305	*24	1975	
266	227	85	5 476	1 595	29	1976	
—	—	—	...	...	...	1970	IRELAND ‡
—	—	—	...	...	...	1974	
—	—	—	...	...	...	1975	
—	—	—	...	...	...	1976	
—	—	—	...	...	...	1977	
—	—	—	...	...	...	1978	
—	—	—	54 130	20 819	38	1970	
—	—	—	9 043	7 676	85	1974	
—	—	—	9 957	8 250	83	1975	
—	—	—	11 015	9 172	83	1976	
—	—	—	13 922	10 447	75	1977	
—	—	—	14 729	10 545	72	1978	

3.7 Education at the second level: teachers and pupils
Enseignement du second degré: personnel enseignant et élèves
Enseñanza de segundo grado: personal docente y alumnos

COUNTRY PAYS PAIS	YEAR ANNEE AÑO		TOTAL SECOND LEVEL TOTAL DU SECOND DEGRE TOTAL DEL SEGUNDO GRADO			GENERAL EDUCATION ENSEIGNEMENT GENERAL ENSEÑANZA GENERAL	
			TOTAL	FEMALE FEMININ FEMENINO	% F	TOTAL	FEMALE FEMININ FEMENINO	% F
			(1)	(2)	(3)	(4)	(5)	(6)
ITALY	TEACHERS	1970	332 106	...	...	229 554	...	...
		1974	...	...	...	...	...	...
		1975	432 867	...	...	...	...	...
		1976	462 617	259 782	56	294 619	184 385	63
		1977	481 698	271 360	56	304 707	191 134	63
	STUDENTS	1970	3 823 556	1 701 137	44	2 625 667	1 210 448	46
		1974	4 582 780	2 104 115	46	3 162 331	1 498 191	47
		1975	4 875 179	2 251 250	46	3 343 085	1 587 955	47
		1976	5 067 343	2 356 247	46	3 445 104	1 642 297	48
		1977	5 208 725	2 446 900	47	3 515 850	1 685 221	48
		1978	*5 267 381	...	...	*3 521 647	...	...
LUXEMBOURG ‡	TEACHERS	1970	1 451	367	25	661	184	28
		1975	...	...	...	959	...	...
	STUDENTS	1970	16 430	7 764	47	8 924	3 992	45
		1974	21 934	10 750	49	15 013	7 424	49
		1975	22 652	11 038	49	15 191	7 573	50
		1976	23 314	11 434	49	15 905	8 202	52
		1977	24 056	11 677	49	16 590	8 301	50
MALTA	TEACHERS	1970	1 662	...	...	1 432	543	38
		1974	2 435	908	37	2 095	886	42
		1975	2 498	934	37	*2 089	*897	*43
		1976	2 467	928	38	2 016	862	43
		1977	*2 511	*879	*35	*1 872	*791	*42
	STUDENTS	1970	24 388	...	...	21 938	11 134	51
		1974	31 736	14 505	46	28 073	14 111	50
		1975	32 409	14 927	46	28 022	14 196	51
		1976	30 285	13 719	45	25 953	12 893	50
		1977	28 921	13 052	45	24 524	12 112	49
MONACO ‡	TEACHERS	1970	144	...	...	116	...	...
	STUDENTS	1970	2 445	...	...	2 033	...	...
		1976	1 993	...	...	1 395	...	...
		1977	2 825	...	...	2 027	673	33
NETHERLANDS	TEACHERS	1970	...	...	...	38 849	8 677	22
		1974	...	...	...	45 790	10 919	24
		1975	...	...	...	48 193	11 859	25
	STUDENTS	1970	1 006 327	450 746	45	591 311	281 282	48
		1974	1 210 259	560 299	46	740 280	364 473	49
		1975	1 283 585	600 323	47	766 391	380 114	50
		1976	1 330 981	623 499	47	794 745	397 263	50
		1977	1 361 333	641 257	47	811 998	408 249	50
		1978	1 367 340	647 675	47	811 090	412 454	51
NORWAY	TEACHERS	1970	31 459	10 351	33	20 618	7 427	36
		1974	...	...	...	...	...	...
		1975	...	...	...	...	...	...
	STUDENTS	1970	302 792	147 053	49	243 714	120 046	49
		1974	331 149	162 892	49	264 925	*132 018	*50
		1975	326 640	159 629	49	263 941	131 998	50
		1976	329 817	161 707	49	264 020	132 808	50
		1977	336 408	166 118	49	267 869	135 203	50
POLAND ‡	TEACHERS	1970	164 353	64 819	39	22 358	13 146	59
		1974	170 764	77 833	46	34 152	21 852	64
		1975	171 610	...	...	34 114	21 899	64
		1976	...	...	...	31 753	21 016	66
		1977	...	...	...	30 282	20 274	67

Education at the second level: teachers and pupils　3.7
Enseignement du second degré: personnel enseignant et élèves
Enseñanza de segundo grado: personal docente y alumnos

TEACHER TRAINING ENSEIGNEMENT NORMAL ENSEÑANZA NORMAL			OTHER SECOND LEVEL AUTRE ENSEIGNEMENT DU SECOND DEGRE OTRA ENSEÑANZA DE SEGUNDO GRADO			YEAR ANNEE AÑO	COUNTRY PAYS PAIS
TOTAL	FEMALE FEMININ FEMENINO	% F	TOTAL	FEMALE FEMININ FEMENINO	% F		
(7)	(8)	(9)	(10)	(11)	(12)		
17 996	...	...	84 556	...	...	1970	ITALY
19 233	...	...	...	...	...	1974	
18 899	...	...	119 646	...	...	1975	
19 298	13 174	68	148 700	62 223	42	1976	
19 921	13 354	67	157 070	66 872	43	1977	
221 623	197 546	89	976 266	293 143	30	1970	
195 817	178 934	91	1 224 632	426 990	35	1974	
198 426	183 161	92	1 333 668	480 134	36	1975	
201 465	187 412	93	1 420 774	526 538	37	1976	
206 299	193 034	94	1 486 576	568 645	38	1977	
*217 962	...	...	*1 527 772	...		1978	
—	—	—	790	183	23	1970	LUXEMBOURG ‡
—	—	—	...	...	...	1975	
—	—	—	7 506	3 772	50	1970	
—	—	—	6 921	3 326	48	1974	
—	—	—	7 461	3 465	46	1975	
—	—	—	7 409	3 232	44	1976	
—	—	—	7 466	3 376	45	1977	
—	—	—	*230	...	...	1970	MALTA
—	—	—	340	22	6	1974	
—	—	—	409	37	9	1975	
—	—	—	451	66	15	1976	
—	—	—	639	88	14	1977	
—	—	—	2 450	...	...	1970	
—	—	—	3 663	394	11	1974	
—	—	—	4 387	731	17	1975	
—	—	—	4 332	826	19	1976	
—	—	—	4 397	940	21	1977	
—	—	—	28	...	...	1970	MONACO ‡
—	—	—	412	...	...	1970	
—	—	—	598	...	...	1976	
—	—	—	798	...	...	1977	
...	...	...	...	...	...	1970	NETHERLANDS
...	...	...	...	...	...	1974	
...	...	...	...	...	...	1975	
7 429	7 429	100	407 587	162 035	40	1970	
10 849	10 820	100	459 130	185 006	40	1974	
10 830	10 789	100	506 364	209 420	41	1975	
10 700	10 643	99	525 536	215 593	41	1976	
10 097	10 031	99	539 238	222 977	41	1977	
8 877	8 816	99	547 373	226 405	41	1978	
—	—	—	10 841	2 924	27	1970	NORWAY
—	—	—	10 318	3 293	32	1974	
—	—	—	10 332	3 387	33	1975	
—	—	—	59 078	27 007	46	1970	
—	—	—	66 224	*30 874	*47	1974	
—	—	—	62 699	27 631	44	1975	
—	—	—	65 797	28 899	44	1976	
—	—	—	68 539	30 915	45	1977	
3 742	1 619	43	138 253	50 054	36	1970	POLAND ‡
...	...	...	136 612	55 981	41	1974	
...	...	...	137 496	...	...	1975	
...	...	...	...	...	...	1976	
...	...	...	...	...	...	1977	

3.7 Education at the second level: teachers and pupils
Enseignement du second degré: personnel enseignant et élèves
Enseñanza de segundo grado: personal docente y alumnos

COUNTRY PAYS PAIS	YEAR ANNEE AÑO	TOTAL SECOND LEVEL TOTAL DU SECOND DEGRE TOTAL DEL SEGUNDO GRADO			GENERAL EDUCATION ENSEIGNEMENT GENERAL ENSEÑANZA GENERAL		
		TOTAL	FEMALE FEMININ FEMENINO	% F	TOTAL	FEMALE FEMININ FEMENINO	% F
		(1)	(2)	(3)	(4)	(5)	(6)
POLAND (CONT.) ‡	STUDENTS 1970	1 361 343	776 845	57	401 306	286 837	71
	1974	1 473 747	814 394	55	482 699	343 924	71
	1975	1 440 796	799 249	55	471 594	334 944	71
	1976	1 428 465	791 481	55	452 246	320 269	71
	1977	1 677 044	917 456	55	420 973	298 058	71
PORTUGAL ‡	TEACHERS 1970	26 782	*14 298	*53	17 018	9 972	59
	1974	27 312	15 183	56	13 605	8 154	60
	1975	29 714	16 586	56	14 903	8 816	59
	1976	30 572	16 408	54	15 651	8 515	54
	1977	21 847	12 305	56	12 363	7 343	59
	STUDENTS 1970	445 574	201 850	45	290 969	143 644	49
	1974	415 648	199 928	48	245 160	130 348	53
	1975	466 491	226 858	49	330 008	171 949	52
	1976	482 593	238 713	49	369 236	193 656	52
	1977	499 557	249 699	50	409 045	213 292	52
ROMANIA ‡	TEACHERS 1970	36 604	15 455	42	13 831	7 407	54
	1974	42 862	18 727	44	13 204	7 093	54
	1975	48 655	21 621	44	14 539	8 007	55
	1976	53 196	23 052	43	15 261	8 569	56
	1977	55 452	22 306	40	8 420	4 158	49
	1978	55 294	21 974	40	8 226	3 978	48
	STUDENTS 1970	659 715	275 189	42	255 667	153 929	60
	1974	801 531	378 160	47	221 358	145 881	66
	1975	1 091 154	505 156	46	361 062	202 790	56
	1976	1 171 466	534 819	46	371 201	202 765	55
	1977	1 192 439	531 121	45	196 206	98 422	50
	1978	1 219 287	539 811	44	180 259	91 251	51
SAN MARINO	TEACHERS 1970	75	41	55	75	41	55
	1974	93	51	55	93	51	55
	1975	108	62	57	108	62	57
	STUDENTS 1970	901	422	47	901	422	47
	1974	1 140	541	47	1 140	541	47
	1975	1 211	575	47	1 211	575	47
	1976	1 221	577	47	1 221	577	47
	1977	1 209	556	46	1 209	556	46
	1978	1 197	563	47	1 197	563	47
SPAIN ‡	TEACHERS 1970	90 770	...	...	62 269	...	...
	1974	...	...	...	...	...	...
	1975	...	...	...	...	...	...
	1976	...	...	...	...	...	...
	STUDENTS 1970	1 950 496	814 673	42	1 521 858	695 036	46
	1974	2 918 126	1 390 994	48	2 461 310	1 204 867	49
	1975	3 188 619	1 530 843	48	2 638 551	1 295 197	49
	1976	3 381 677	1 638 709	48	2 764 761	1 368 494	49
SWEDEN ‡	TEACHERS 1970	*54 970	*24 101	*44	...	...	...
	1974	54 656	24 792	45	54 656	24 792	45
	1975	54 200	24 303	45	...	...	...
	1976	56 725	26 387	47	36 049	17 607	49
	1977	61 759	29 237	47	39 942	19 900	50
	STUDENTS 1970	554 480	267 532	48	416 001	198 781	48
	1974	531 594	259 146	49	531 594	259 146	49
	1975	507 642	258 556	51	369 012	189 047	51
	1976	513 287	260 146	51	377 044	192 372	51
	1977	536 287	273 174	51	397 184	203 021	51
	1978	575 190	291 834	51	424 300	216 452	51

Education at the second level: teachers and pupils 3.7
Enseignement du second degré: personnel enseignant et élèves
Enseñanza de segundo grado: personal docente y alumnos

TEACHER TRAINING ENSEIGNEMENT NORMAL ENSEÑANZA NORMAL			OTHER SECOND LEVEL AUTRE ENSEIGNEMENT DU SECOND DEGRE OTRA ENSEÑANZA DE SEGUNDO GRADO			YEAR ANNEE AÑO	COUNTRY PAYS PAIS
TOTAL	FEMALE FEMININ FEMENINO	% F	TOTAL	FEMALE FEMININ FEMENINO	% F		
(7)	(8)	(9)	(10)	(11)	(12)		
26 585	21 442	81	933 452	468 566	50	1970	POLAND (CONT.) ‡
19 087	15 681	82	971 961	454 789	47	1974	
20 089	16 776	84	949 113	447 529	47	1975	
...	...	...	...	...	...	1976	
...	...	...	...	...	...	1977	
342	175	51	9 422	*4 151	*44	1970	PORTUGAL ‡
614	346	56	13 093	6 683	51	1974	
826	501	61	13 985	7 269	52	1975	
702	395	56	14 219	7 498	53	1976	
761	429	56	8 723	4 533	52	1977	
5 313	4 845	91	149 292	53 361	36	1970	
8 765	8 108	93	161 723	61 472	38	1974	
9 166	7 841	86	127 317	47 068	37	1975	
6 913	5 501	80	106 444	39 556	37	1976	
8 128	6 459	79	82 384	29 948	36	1977	
1 280	735	57	21 493	7 313	34	1970	ROMANIA ‡
1 291	788	61	28 367	10 846	38	1974	
1 248	728	58	32 868	12 886	39	1975	
1 361	...	...	36 574	...	...	1976	
1 587	990	62	45 445	17 158	38	1977	
1 400	849	61	45 668	17 147	38	1978	
23 732	20 229	85	380 316	101 031	27	1970	
19 461	16 794	86	560 712	215 485	38	1974	
18 898	16 958	90	711 194	285 408	40	1975	
19 842	18 228	92	780 423	313 826	40	1976	
18 442	17 193	93	977 791	415 506	42	1977	
10 874	10 260	94	1 028 154	438 300	43	1978	
—	—	—	—	—	—	1970	SAN MARINO
—	—	—	—	—	—	1974	
—	—	—	—	—	—	1975	
—	—	—	—	—	—	1970	
—	—	—	—	—	—	1974	
—	—	—	—	—	—	1975	
—	—	—	—	—	—	1976	
—	—	—	—	—	—	1977	
—	—	—	—	—	—	1978	
2 179	1 236	57	26 322	...	...	1970	SPAIN ‡
—	—	—	29 739	6 974	23	1974	
—	—	—	37 744	10 283	27	1975	
—	—	—	40 588	9 833	24	1976	
47 541	26 876	57	381 097	92 761	24	1970	
—	—	—	456 816	186 127	41	1974	
—	—	—	550 068	235 646	43	1975	
—	—	—	616 916	270 215	44	1976	
—	—	—	...	...	...	1970	SWEDEN ‡
—	—	—	—	—	—	1974	
...	...	...	...	...	...	1975	
...	...	...	...	...	...	1976	
...	...	...	...	...	...	1977	
—	—	—	138 479	68 751	50	1970	
—	—	—	—	—	—	1974	
1 078	759	70	137 552	68 750	50	1975	
1 116	781	70	135 127	66 993	50	1976	
724	504	70	138 379	69 649	50	1977	
184	109	59	150 706	75 273	50	1978	

3.7 Education at the second level: teachers and pupils
Enseignement du second degré: personnel enseignant et élèves
Enseñanza de segundo grado: personal docente y alumnos

COUNTRY PAYS PAIS	YEAR ANNEE AÑO	TOTAL SECOND LEVEL TOTAL DU SECOND DEGRE TOTAL DEL SEGUNDO GRADO			GENERAL EDUCATION ENSEIGNEMENT GENERAL ENSEÑANZA GENERAL		
		TOTAL	FEMALE FEMININ FEMENINO	% F	TOTAL	FEMALE FEMININ FEMENINO	% F
		(1)	(2)	(3)	(4)	(5)	(6)
SWITZERLAND ‡	STUDENTS 1970	345 786	164 563	48	316 337	152 223	48
	1974	359 354	177 404	49	323 743	158 260	49
	1975	371 978	184 124	49	334 629	163 961	49
	1976	446 452	...	...	410 640	201 530	49
	1977	431 178	...	...	400 834	203 078	49
	1978	...	...	...	421 394	208 031	49
UNITED KINGDOM	TEACHERS 1970	...	...	...	252 512	121 192	48
	1974	...	...	...	299 006	143 501	48
	1975	...	...	...	308 827	147 810	48
	1976	...	...	...	315 732	150 250	48
	STUDENTS 1970	4 149 067	2 009 046	48	4 006 527	1 943 944	49
	1974	4 990 440	2 441 276	49	4 815 483	2 349 688	49
	1975	5 154 371	2 525 945	49	4 945 770	2 413 008	49
	1976	5 285 143	2 594 937	49	5 055 642	2 469 468	49
YUGOSLAVIA ‡	TEACHERS 1970	88 493	41 257	47	71 581	34 610	48
	1974	92 139	46 487	50	78 920	40 065	51
	1975	...	...	...	...	...	...
	1976	...	...	...	...	...	...
	1977	125 753	60 450	48	...	...	...
	1978	127 906	63 287	49	...	...	...
	STUDENTS 1970	1 982 018	892 631	45	1 441 815	668 453	46
	1974	2 191 083	1 005 475	46	1 580 559	740 904	47
	1975	2 264 101	1 061 877	47	1 693 749	814 509	48
	1976	2 311 746	1 079 248	47	1 806 474	855 864	47
	1977	2 356 321	1 090 573	46	1 881 214	884 881	47
	1978	2 413 788	1 118 171	46	1 912 231	901 743	47
OCEANIA							
AMERICAN SAMOA ‡	TEACHERS 1970	*120	...	...	...	...	...
	1975	*70	...	...	...	...	...
	1976	78	...	...	...	...	...
	STUDENTS 1970	*2 300	...	...	...	...	...
	1974	*2 373	...	...	...	...	...
	1975	*2 097	...	...	...	...	...
	1976	*2 602	...	...	...	...	...
	1977	2 269	...	...	...	...	...
AUSTRALIA	TEACHERS 1970	...	...	...	54 668	*25 700	*47
	1974	68 623	32 083	47	68 623	32 083	47
	1975	74 041	34 463	47	74 041	34 463	47
	1976	77 638	35 895	46	77 638	35 895	46
	1977	80 980	37 311	46	80 980	37 311	46
	STUDENTS 1970	1 136 960	...	...	956 210	456 788	48
	1974	1 059 180	515 494	49	1 059 180	515 494	49
	1975	1 095 691	534 215	49	1 095 691	534 215	49
	1976	1 114 250	544 744	49	1 114 250	544 744	49
	1977	1 116 347	549 534	49	1 116 347	549 534	49
COOK ISLANDS	TEACHERS 1970	76	20	26	67	18	27
	1971	75	21	28	65	18	28
	STUDENTS 1970	1 120	533	48	1 070	513	48
	1971	1 213	588	48	1 138	548	48
FIJI	TEACHERS 1970	724	233	32	598	213	36
	1974	1 327	473	36	1 103	387	35
	1975	...	...	...	1 184	430	36
	1977	...	...	...	1 662	630	38

Education at the second level: teachers and pupils 3.7
Enseignement du second degré: personnel enseignant et élèves
Enseñanza de segundo grado: personal docente y alumnos

TEACHER TRAINING ENSEIGNEMENT NORMAL ENSEÑANZA NORMAL			OTHER SECOND LEVEL AUTRE ENSEIGNEMENT DU SECOND DEGRE OTRA ENSEÑANZA DE SEGUNDO GRADO			YEAR ANNEE AÑO	COUNTRY PAYS PAIS
TOTAL	FEMALE FEMININ FEMENINO	% F	TOTAL	FEMALE FEMININ FEMENINO	% F		
(7)	(8)	(9)	(10)	(11)	(12)		
10 271	6 340	62	19 178	6 000	31	1970	SWITZERLAND ‡
11 251	7 594	67	24 360	11 550	47	1974	
11 070	7 564	68	26 279	12 599	48	1975	
15 485	11 111	72	20 327	...	...	1976	
13 966	10 221	73	16 378	...	...	1977	
11 308	8 456	75	...	...	...	1978	
—	—	—	...	...	...	1970	UNITED KINGDOM
—	—	—	...	...	...	1974	
—	—	—	...	...	...	1975	
—	—	—	...	...	...	1976	
—	—	—	142 540	65 102	46	1970	
—	—	—	174 957	91 588	52	1974	
—	—	—	208 601	112 937	54	1975	
—	—	—	229 501	125 469	55	1976	
1 117	397	36	15 795	6 250	40	1970	YUGOSLAVIA ‡
768	323	42	12 451	6 099	49	1974	
849	325	38	18 867	9 674	51	1975	
796	315	40	...	...	...	1976	
...	...	...	...	...	...	1977	
...	...	...	...	...	...	1978	
16 873	10 774	64	523 330	213 404	41	1970	
9 039	6 474	72	601 485	258 097	43	1974	
9 133	6 762	74	561 219	240 606	43	1975	
9 828	6 885	70	495 444	216 499	44	1976	
8 111	5 951	73	466 996	199 741	43	1977	
6 122	4 519	74	495 435	211 909	43	1978	
							OCEANIA
—	—	—	...	...	...	1970	AMERICAN SAMOA ‡
—	—	—	...	...	...	1975	
—	—	—	...	...	...	1976	
—	—	—	...	...	...	1970	
—	—	—	...	...	...	1974	
—	—	—	...	...	...	1975	
—	—	—	...	...	...	1976	
—	—	—	...	...	...	1977	
—	—	—	...	...	...	1970	AUSTRALIA
—	—	—	—	—	—	1974	
—	—	—	—	—	—	1975	
—	—	—	—	—	—	1976	
—	—	—	—	—	—	1977	
—	—	—	180 750	...	—	1970	
—	—	—	—	—	—	1974	
—	—	—	—	—	—	1975	
—	—	—	—	—	—	1976	
—	—	—	—	—	—	1977	
9	2	22	—	—	—	1970	COOK ISLANDS
10	3	30	—	—	—	1971	
50	20	40	—	—	—	1970	
75	40	53	—	—	—	1971	
34	11	32	92	9	10	1970	FIJI
50	21	42	174	65	37	1974	
...	...	...	...	...	...	1975	
...	...	...	...	...	...	1977	

3.7 Education at the second level: teachers and pupils
Enseignement du second degré: personnel enseignant et élèves
Enseñanza de segundo grado: personal docente y alumnos

COUNTRY PAYS PAIS	YEAR ANNEE AÑO	TOTAL SECOND LEVEL TOTAL DU SECOND DEGRE TOTAL DEL SEGUNDO GRADO			GENERAL EDUCATION ENSEIGNEMENT GENERAL ENSEÑANZA GENERAL		
		TOTAL	FEMALE FEMININ FEMENINO	% F	TOTAL	FEMALE FEMININ FEMENINO	% F
		(1)	(2)	(3)	(4)	(5)	(6)
FIJI (CONT.)	STUDENTS 1970	17 509	7 364	42	16 207	7 129	44
	1974	28 423	13 735	48	26 202	12 738	49
	1975	30 545	15 056	49	28 072	13 826	49
	1976	33 062	16 649	50	30 758	15 259	50
	1977	35 416	17 649	50	32 995	16 358	50
FRENCH POLYNESIA	TEACHERS 1970	417	182	44	341	150	44
	1974	567	245	43	406	183	45
	1975	569	253	44	434	190	44
	1976	661	280	42	478	214	45
	STUDENTS 1970	6 492	3 613	56	5 383	3 030	56
	1974	8 868	4 895	55	7 046	3 981	57
	1975	9 035	5 074	56	7 280	4 164	57
	1976	9 668	5 452	56	7 727	4 431	57
GUAM ‡	TEACHERS 1970	*495	...	...	...	...	...
	1974	...	...	...	...	...	...
	1975	*595	...	...	...	...	...
	1976	*520	...	...	...	...	...
	STUDENTS 1970	*10 055	...	...	...	...	...
	1974	*12 629	...	...	...	...	...
	1975	*13 242	...	...	...	...	...
	1976	11 625	...	...	...	...	...
KIRIBATI ‡	TEACHERS 1970	76	25	33	44	16	36
	1974	...	...	...	63	29	46
	1977	117	33	28	74	25	34
	1978	...	...	...	92	37	40
	STUDENTS 1970	1 071	325	30	622	264	42
	1974	...	...	...	854	377	44
	1975	...	...	...	795	378	48
	1976	...	...	...	739	358	48
	1977	1 256	535	43	1 000	486	49
	1978	1 694	724	43	1 400	667	48
NAURU	STUDENTS 1973	...	...	...	443	238	54
NEW CALEDONIA ‡	TEACHERS 1970	404	175	43	251	128	51
	1974	561	...	...	330	...	...
	1975	...	...	...	379	217	57
	1976	657	298	45	406	212	52
	1977	...	...	...	467	258	55
	STUDENTS 1970	5 132	2 345	46	3 745	1 858	50
	1974	7 240	3 572	49	5 012	2 665	53
	1975	7 960	3 995	50	5 604	3 016	54
	1976	8 862	4 456	50	6 406	3 433	54
	1977	...	...	...	7 268	3 909	54
NEW HEBRIDES	TEACHERS 1970	71	28	39	50	17	34
	1974	96	32	33	67	24	36
	1976	125	...	...	96	...	...
	1977	198	...	...	...	...	...
	STUDENTS 1970	784	331	42	541	204	38
	1974	1 295	500	39	1 016	413	41
	1975	1 505	636	42	1 263	555	44
	1976	1 788	738	41	1 480	628	42
	1977	2 679	1 067	40	1 791	774	43
NEW ZEALAND ‡	TEACHERS 1970	...	...	...	9 932	4 290	43
	1974	...	...	...	10 980	4 185	38
	1975	...	...	...	12 107	4 784	40
	1976	...	...	...	12 367	4 787	39

Education at the second level: teachers and pupils 3.7
Enseignement du second degré: personnel enseignant et élèves
Enseñanza de segundo grado: personal docente y alumnos

TEACHER TRAINING ENSEIGNEMENT NORMAL ENSEÑANZA NORMAL			OTHER SECOND LEVEL AUTRE ENSEIGNEMENT DU SECOND DEGRE OTRA ENSEÑANZA DE SEGUNDO GRADO			YEAR ANNEE AÑO	COUNTRY PAYS PAIS
TOTAL	FEMALE FEMININ FEMENINO	% F	TOTAL	FEMALE FEMININ FEMENINO	% F		
(7)	(8)	(9)	(10)	(11)	(12)		
313	140	45	989	95	10	1970	FIJI (CONT.)
506	264	52	1 715	733	43	1974	
535	297	56	1 938	933	48	1975	
604	342	57	1 700	1 048	62	1976	
743	422	57	1 678	869	52	1977	
5	2	40	71	30	42	1970	FRENCH POLYNESIA
6	—	—	155	62	40	1974	
6	3	50	129	60	47	1975	
6	3	50	177	63	36	1976	
76	54	71	1 033	529	51	1970	
103	80	78	1 719	834	49	1974	
111	85	77	1 644	825	50	1975	
120	88	73	1 821	933	51	1976	
—	—	—	...	...	...	1970	GUAM ‡
—	—	—	...	...	...	1974	
—	—	—	...	...	...	1975	
—	—	—	...	...	...	1976	
—	—	—	...	...	...	1970	
—	—	—	...	...	...	1974	
—	—	—	...	...	...	1975	
—	—	—	...	...	...	1976	
16	6	38	16	3	19	1970	KIRIBATI ‡
17	10	59	...	...	...	1974	
15	5	33	28	3	11	1977	
15	5	33	...	...	...	1978	
112	33	29	337	28	8	1970	
95	46	48	...	...	...	1974	
...	...	...	...	...	...	1975	
						1976	
73	43	59	183	6	3	1977	
94	51	54	200	6	3	1978	
...	...	...	...	...	...	1973	NAURU
26	8	31	127	39	31	1970	NEW CALEDONIA ‡
26	11	42	205	68	33	1974	
30	6	35	...	...	...	1975	
23	11	48	228	75	33	1976	
...	...	...	252	81	32	1977	
41	30	73	1 346	457	34	1970	
133	90	68	2 095	817	39	1974	
135	85	63	2 221	894	40	1975	
140	90	64	2 316	933	40	1976	
...	...	...	2 575	1 111	43	1977	
9	4	44	12	7	58	1970	NEW HEBRIDES
11	3	27	18	5	28	1974	
12	4	33	17	3	18	1976	
...	...	...	50	...	...	1977	
100	33	33	143	94	66	1970	
112	51	46	167	36	22	1974	
103	50	49	139	31	22	1975	
137	71	52	171	39	23	1976	
113	57	50	775	236	30	1977	
—	—	—	...	...	...	1970	NEW ZEALAND ‡
—	—	—	...	...	...	1974	
—	—	—	...	...	...	1975	
—	—	—	...	...	...	1976	

3.7 Education at the second level: teachers and pupils
Enseignement du second degré: personnel enseignant et élèves
Enseñanza de segundo grado: personal docente y alumnos

COUNTRY PAYS PAIS	YEAR ANNEE AÑO	TOTAL SECOND LEVEL TOTAL DU SECOND DEGRE TOTAL DEL SEGUNDO GRADO			GENERAL EDUCATION ENSEIGNEMENT GENERAL ENSEÑANZA GENERAL		
		TOTAL	FEMALE FEMININ FEMENINO	% F	TOTAL	FEMALE FEMININ FEMENINO	% F
		(1)	(2)	(3)	(4)	(5)	(6)
NEW ZEALAND (CONT.) ‡	STUDENTS 1970	...	...	...	303 835	147 235	48
	1974	...	...	...	341 506	167 507	49
	1975	354 107	174 178	49	351 720	172 313	49
	1976	362 430	178 407	49	359 564	176 196	49
NIUE ‡	TEACHERS 1970	24	10	42	24	10	42
	1974	19	8	42	19	8	42
	1975	22	9	41	22	9	41
	STUDENTS 1970	462	204	44	462	204	44
	1974	243	133	55	243	133	55
	1975	271	133	49	271	133	49
	1976	286	144	50	286	144	50
NORFOLK ISLAND	TEACHERS 1975	7	2	29	7	2	29
	1977	7	2	29	7	2	29
	1978	7	1	14	7	1	14
	STUDENTS 1975	100	53	53	100	53	53
	1976	98	47	48	98	47	48
	1977	100	53	53	100	53	53
	1978	88	48	55	88	48	55
PACIFIC ISLANDS	TEACHERS 1970	...	...	...	251	98	39
	1974	...	...	...	497	168	34
	1975	...	...	...	528	156	30
	1976	...	...	...	468	...	...
	STUDENTS 1970	6 005	...	...	5 596	2 163	39
	1974	...	...	...	7 970	3 434	43
	1975	...	...	...	7 951	3 500	44
	1976	...	...	...	8 022	3 419	43
PAPUA NEW GUINEA	TEACHERS 1970	...	...	...	807	...	...
	1974	1 906	679	36	1 226	494	40
	1975	2 034	700	34	1 282	482	38
	1976	1 880	602	32	1 242	409	33
	1978	...	...	...	1 503	123	8
	STUDENTS 1970	24 365	6 472	27	17 785	4 849	27
	1974	34 094	...	...	27 046	8 601	32
	1975	41 391	*11 731	*28	29 762	9 379	32
	1976	43 004	*12 118	*28	31 455	9 621	31
	1977	...	...	...	*32 339	*9 694	*30
	1978	...	...	...	36 749	11 233	31
SAMOA	TEACHERS 1970	460	...	...	419	...	...
	1974	...	...	...	...	...	...
	1975	...	...	...	...	...	...
	1976	...	...	...	...	...	...
	1977	...	...	...	...	...	...
	1978	...	...	...	...	...	...
	STUDENTS 1970	10 147	5 261	52	9 717	5 097	52
	1974	11 868	*5 876	*50	11 115	5 627	51
	1975	15 943	*8 062	*51	15 098	7 712	51
	1976	16 571	8 275	50	15 876	7 997	50
	1977	17 643	9 161	52	16 985	8 875	52
	1978	18 068	9 036	50	17 404	8 755	50
SOLOMON ISLANDS	TEACHERS 1970	98	33	34	64	19	30
	1974	...	...	...	93	24	26
	1975	131	37	28	87	28	32
	STUDENTS 1970	1 400	358	26	1 042	251	24
	1974	...	...	...	1 625	407	25
	1975	2 005	503	25	1 555	412	26

Education at the second level: teachers and pupils   3.7
Enseignement du second degré: personnel enseignant et élèves
Enseñanza de segundo grado: personal docente y alumnos

TEACHER TRAINING ENSEIGNEMENT NORMAL ENSEÑANZA NORMAL			OTHER SECOND LEVEL AUTRE ENSEIGNEMENT DU SECOND DEGRE OTRA ENSEÑANZA DE SEGUNDO GRADO			YEAR ANNEE AÑO	COUNTRY PAYS PAIS
TOTAL	FEMALE FEMININ FEMENINO	% F	TOTAL	FEMALE FEMININ FEMENINO	% F		
(7)	(8)	(9)	(10)	(11)	(12)		
–	–	–	...	...	...	1970	NEW ZEALAND
–	–	–	...	...	...	1974	(CONT.) ‡
–	–	–	2 387	1 865	78	1975	
–	–	–	2 866	2 211	77	1976	
–	–	–	–	–	–	1970	NIUE ‡
–	–	–	–	–	–	1974	
–	–	–	–	–	–	1975	
–	–	–	–	–	–	1970	
–	–	–	–	–	–	1974	
–	–	–	–	–	–	1975	
–	–	–	–	–	–	1976	
–	–	–	–	–	–	1975	NORFOLK ISLAND
–	–	–	–	–	–	1977	
–	–	–	–	–	–	1978	
–	–	–	–	–	–	1975	
–	–	–	–	–	–	1976	
–	–	–	–	–	–	1977	
–	–	–	–	–	–	1978	
...	...	...	16	*1	*6	1970	PACIFIC ISLANDS
–	–	–	...	...	...	1974	
–	–	–	...	...	...	1975	
...	...	...	...	...	...	1976	
239	...	...	170	5	3	1970	
–	–	–	...	...	...	1974	
–	–	–	...	...	...	1975	
...	...	...	...	...	...	1976	
...	...	...	...	...	...	1970	PAPUA NEW GUINEA
200	77	39	480	108	23	1974	
166	76	46	586	142	24	1975	
143	67	47	495	126	25	1976	
185	67	36	...	...	...	1978	
1 865	559	30	4 715	1 064	23	1970	
1 904	...	...	5 144	...	...	1974	
1 990	715	36	9 639	*1 637	*17	1975	
1 974	767	39	9 575	*1 730	*18	1976	
...	...	...	...	...	...	1977	
2 658	847	32	...	...	...	1978	
22	13	59	19	–	–	1970	SAMOA
36	20	56	45	3	7	1974	
30	15	50	*48	*3	*6	1975	
20	10	50	57	11	19	1976	
20	10	50	48	13	27	1977	
23	12	52	37	12	32	1978	
303	164	54	127	–	–	1970	
439	*214	*49	314	*35	*11	1974	
490	263	54	355	*87	*25	1975	
411	227	55	284	51	18	1976	
427	237	56	231	49	21	1977	
430	215	50	234	66	28	1978	
11	6	55	23	8	35	1970	SOLOMON ISLANDS
						1974	
18	5	28	26	4	15	1975	
110	31	28	248	76	31	1970	
110	45	41	...	...	...	1974	
137	46	34	313	45	14	1975	

3.7 Education at the second level: teachers and pupils
Enseignement du second degré: personnel enseignant et élèves
Enseñanza de segundo grado: personal docente y alumnos

COUNTRY PAYS PAIS	YEAR ANNEE AÑO	TOTAL SECOND LEVEL TOTAL DU SECOND DEGRE TOTAL DEL SEGUNDO GRADO			GENERAL EDUCATION ENSEIGNEMENT GENERAL ENSEÑANZA GENERAL		
		TOTAL	FEMALE FEMININ FEMENINO	% F	TOTAL	FEMALE FEMININ FEMENINO	% F
		(1)	(2)	(3)	(4)	(5)	(6)
TOKELAU ISLANDS	TEACHERS 1978	...	...	...	6	3	50
	1979	...	...	...	6	3	50
	STUDENTS 1978	...	...	...	80	43	54
	1979	...	...	...	80	43	54
TONGA	TEACHERS 1970	428	182	43	417	176	42
	1974	...	...		474	196	41
	1975	338	221	65	304	210	69
	STUDENTS 1970	10 159	4 870	48	10 057	4 816	48
	1974				10 420	5 063	49
	1975	11 351	5 482	48	10 685	5 229	49
	1976	...	...	...	11 713	5 769	49
	1977	...	...	...	12 157	6 028	50
	1978	...	...	...	12 368	6 108	49
U.S.S.R.							
U.S.S.R. ‡	TEACHERS 1970	...	...	...	...	...	...
	1974	...	...	...	...	...	...
	1975	...	...	...	...	...	...
	1976	...	...	...	...	...	...
	1977	...	...	...	...	...	...
	1978	...	...	...	...	...	...
	STUDENTS 1970	9 151 655	...	...	4 763 655	...	...
	1974	10 414 122	...	...	5 936 322	...	...
	1975	10 738 197	...	...	6 213 397	...	...
	1976	10 950 800	...	...	6 328 000	...	...
	1977	10 782 200	...	...	6 120 000	...	...
	1978	10 484 900	...	...	5 813 000	...	...
BYELORUSSIAN S.S.R. ‡	TEACHERS 1974	...	...	...	...	...	...
	1975	...	...	...	...	...	...
	1976	...	...	...	...	...	...
	1977	...	...	...	...	...	...
	1978	...	...	...	...	...	...
	STUDENTS 1970	346 023	*194 060	*56	199 891	*114 000	*57
	1974	404 648	...	...	251 931	...	...
	1975	406 201	...	...	251 516	...	...
	1976	409 489	...	...	250 281	...	...
	1977	403 018	...	...	240 831	...	...
	1978	392 100	...	...	228 800	...	...
UKRAINIAN S.S.R. ‡	TEACHERS 1974	...	...	...	...	...	...
	1975	...	...	...	...	...	...
	1976	...	...	...	...	...	...
	1977	...	...	...	...	...	...
	1978	...	...	...	...	...	...
	STUDENTS 1970	1 627 700	877 000	54	829 800	464 700	56
	1974	1 785 600	...	...	1 005 700	...	...
	1975	1 821 900	...	...	1 038 100	...	...
	1976	1 842 100	...	...	1 036 500	...	...
	1977	1 791 800	...	...	984 700	...	...
	1978	1 736 200	...	...	930 700	...	...

Education at the second level: teachers and pupils   3.7
Enseignement du second degré: personnel enseignant et élèves
Enseñanza de segundo grado: personal docente y alumnos

TEACHER TRAINING ENSEIGNEMENT NORMAL ENSEÑANZA NORMAL			OTHER SECOND LEVEL AUTRE ENSEIGNEMENT DU SECOND DEGRE OTRA ENSEÑANZA DE SEGUNDO GRADO			YEAR ANNEE AÑO	COUNTRY PAYS PAIS
TOTAL	FEMALE FEMININ FEMENINO	% F	TOTAL	FEMALE FEMININ FEMENINO	% F		
(7)	(8)	(9)	(10)	(11)	(12)		
...	...	...	12	6	50	1978	TOKELAU ISLANDS
...	...	...	12	6	50	1979	
...	...	...	197	86	44	1978	
...	...	...	197	86	44	1979	
11	6	55	–	–	–	1970	TONGA
	...					1974	
11	7	64	23	4	17	1975	
102	54	53	–	–	–	1970	
	...		522	201	39	1974	
117	71	61	549	182	33	1975	
140	78	56	...	...	...	1976	
141	78	55	...	...	...	1977	
146	79	54	...	...	...	1978	
							U.S.S.R.
...	...	...	182 816	91 408	50	1970	U.S.S.R. ‡
...	...	...	212 428	106 214	50	1974	
...	...	...	218 428	109 214	50	1975	
...	...	...	224 000	...	...	1976	
...	...	...	226 900	...	...	1977	
...	...	...	229 700	...	...	1978	
340 100	311 870	92	4 047 900	2 037 210	50	1970	
372 300	341 300	92	4 105 500	2 031 900	49	1974	
395 000	*363 400	*92	4 129 800	2 079 990	50	1975	
402 900	...	...	4 219 900	...	...	1976	
410 300	...	...	4 251 900	...	...	1977	
415 000	...	...	4 256 900	...	...	1978	
...	...	...	8 048	...	...	1974	BYELORUSSIAN S.S.R. ‡
...	...	...	8 210	...	...	1975	
...	...	...	8 471	...	...	1976	
...	...	...	8 541	...	...	1977	
...	...	...	8 600	...	...	1978	
9 212	...	...	136 920	...	...	1970	
	...	...		...	...	1974	
11 651	...	...	143 034	...	...	1975	
11 673	...	...	147 535	...	...	1976	
11 443	...	...	150 744	...	...	1977	
11 600	...	...	151 700	...	...	1978	
...	...	...	39 600	...	...	1974	UKRAINIAN S.S.R. ‡
...	...	...	40 400	...	...	1975	
...	...	...	41 300	...	...	1976	
...	...	...	41 800	...	...	1977	
...	...	...	41 700	...	...	1978	
45 700	*36 800	*81	752 200	*375 500	*50	1970	
...	...	...	...	...	...	1974	
...	...	...	...	...	...	1975	
64 300	...	...	741 300	...	...	1976	
65 300	...	...	741 800	...	...	1977	
63 100	...	...	742 400	...	...	1978	

3.7 Education at the second level: teachers and pupils
Enseignement du second degré: personnel enseignant et élèves
Enseñanza de segundo grado: personal docente y alumnos

ALGERIA:
  E—> TEACHERS AND STUDENTS: FROM 1974, CERTAIN
FIELDS OF STUDY PREVIOUSLY CLASSIFIED UNDER OTHER
SECOND LEVEL EDUCATION OF A VOCATIONAL OR TECH-
NICAL NATURE ARE NOW REPORTED UNDER GENERAL
EDUCATION.
      TEACHERS: FROM 1975, DATA SHOWN IN COLUMN 4
DO NOT INCLUDE TEACHERS IN "OUCFA" SCHOOLS. IN
1978, ENROLMENT IN "OUCFA" SCHOOLS WAS 7,493
PUPILS (F. 2,092).
  FR—> PERSONNEL ENSEIGNANT ET ELEVES: A PARTIR DE
1974, CERTAINES BRANCHES D'ETUDES ANTERIEUREMENT
CLASSEES DANS L'AUTRE ENSEIGNEMENT DU SECOND DEGRE
DE CARACTERE TECHNIQUE OU PROFESSIONNEL SONT
MAINTENANT COMPTEES AVEC L'ENSEIGNEMENT GENERAL.
      PERSONNEL ENSEIGNANT: A PARTIR DE 1975, LES
DONNEES DE LA COLONNE 4 NE COMPRENNENT PAS LES
MAITRES DES ECOLES DE L'OUCFA; LES EFFECTIFS DE
CES ECOLES ETAIENT EN 1978, DE 7 493 ELEVES
(F. 2 092).
  ESP> PERSONAL DOCENTE Y ALUMNOS: A PARTIR DE
1974, CIERTAS RAMAS DE ESTUDIO ANTERIORMENTE CLA-
SIFICADAS EN LA ENSEÑANZA DE SEGUNDO GRADO DE
CARACTER TECNICO O PROFESIONAL FIGURAN EN LA
ENSEÑANZA GENERAL.
      PERSONAL DOCENTE: A PARTIR DE 1975, LOS
DATOS DE LA COLUMNA 4 NO INCLUYEN EL PERSONAL
DOCENTE DE LAS ESCUELAS DEL "OUCFA". EN 1978, LOS
EFECTIVOS DE ESTAS ESCUELAS ERAN DE 7 493 ALUMNOS
(F. 2 902).

BOTSWANA:
  E—> TEACHERS AND STUDENTS: FOR 1970, THE
FIGURES SHOWN IN COLUMNS 4, 5 AND 6 REFER TO
GOVERNMENT-MAINTAINED AND AIDED SCHOOLS ONLY.
  FR—> PERSONNEL ENSEIGNANT ET ELEVES: POUR 1970,
LES CHIFFRES DES COLONNES 4, 5 ET 6 SE REFERENT
AUX ECOLES PUBLIQUES ET SUBVENTIONNEES SEULEMENT.
  ESP> PERSONAL DOCENTE Y ALUMNOS: EN 1970, LAS
CIFRAS DE LAS COLUMNAS 4, 5 Y 6 SE REFIEREN A LAS
ESCUELAS PUBLICAS Y SUBVENCIONADAS SOLAMENTE.

BURUNDI:
  E—> TEACHERS AND STUDENTS: FROM 1976, THE
FIGURES SHOWN IN COLUMNS 4, 5 AND 6 REFER TO
PUBLIC EDUCATION ONLY.
  FR—> PERSONNEL ENSEIGNANT ET ELEVES: A PARTIR
DE 1976, LES CHIFFRES DES COLONNES 4, 5 ET 6 SE
REFERENT A L'ENSEIGNEMENT PUBLIC SEULEMENT.
  ESP> PERSONAL DOCENTE Y ALUMNOS: A PARTIR DE
1976, LAS CIFRAS DE LAS COLUMNAS 4, 5 Y 6 SE
REFIEREN A LA ENSEÑANZA PUBLICA SOLAMENTE.

CHAD:
  E—> TEACHERS: IN 1974 (COLUMN 4) AND IN 1976
(COLUMNS 4, 5 AND 6) FIGURES REFER TO PUBLIC
EDUCATION ONLY.
  FR—> PERSONNEL ENSEIGNANT: POUR 1974, LES
CHIFFRES DE LA COLONNE 4 ET EN 1976, CEUX DES
COLONNES 4, 5 ET 6 SE REFERENT A L'ENSEIGNEMENT
PUBLIC SEULEMENT.
  ESP> PERSONAL DOCENTE: EN 1974, LAS CIFRAS DE
LA COLUMNA 4 Y EN 1976 LAS DE LAS COLUMNAS 4, 5 Y
6 SE REFIEREN A LA ENSEÑANZA PUBLICA SOLAMENTE.

EGYPT:
  E—> TEACHERS AND STUDENTS: EXCEPT FOR 1970, THE
FIGURES SHOWN IN COLUMNS 1 TO 6 DO NOT INCLUDE
SECONDARY GENERAL CLASSES AT AL AZHAR UNIVERSITY
AND FOREIGN SCHOOLS. FOR 1970, THE FIGURES SHOWN
IN COLUMNS 4, 5 AND 6 DO NOT INCLUDE GENERAL
EDUCATION AT AL AZHAR UNIVERSITY.
      STUDENTS: BEGINNING 1975, THE FIGURES SHOWN
IN COLUMNS 4, 5 AND 6 INCLUDE PART-TIME PUPILS.
  FR—> PERSONNEL ENSEIGNANT ET ELEVES: A L'EXCEP-
TION DE 1970, LES CHIFFRES DES COLONNES 1 A 6 NE
COMPRENNENT NI LES CLASSES SECONDAIRES D'ENSEIGNE-
MENT GENERAL RATTACHEES A L'UNIVERSITE AL AZHAR,

EGYPT (CONT.):
NI LES ECOLES ETRANGERES. POUR 1970, LES DONNEES
DES COLONNES 4, 5 ET 6 N'INCLUENT PAS L'ENSEIGNE-
MENT GENERAL DU SECOND DEGRE DE L' UNIVERSITE
AL AZHAR.
      ELEVES: A PARTIR DE 1975, LES CHIFFRES DES
COLONNES 4, 5 ET 6 COMPRENNENT LES ELEVES A TEMPS
PARTIEL.
  ESP> PERSONAL DOCENTE Y ALUMNOS: SALVO PARA
1970, LAS CIFRAS DE LAS COLUMNAS 1 A 6 NO INCLUYEN
NI LAS CLASES SECUNDARIAS DE ENSEÑANZA GENERAL AD-
SCRITAS A LA UNIVERSIDAD AL AZHAR, NI LAS ESCUELAS
EXTRANJERAS. EN 1970, LOS DATOS DE LAS COLUMNAS
4, 5 Y 6 NO INCLUYEN LA ENSEÑANZA GENERAL DE
SEGUNDO GRADO DE LA UNIVERSIDAD AL AZHAR.
      ALUMNOS: A PARTIR DE 1975, LAS CIFRAS DE
LAS COLUMNAS 4, 5 Y 6 INCLUYEN LOS ALUMNOS DE
JORNADA PARCIAL.

GHANA:
  E—> TEACHERS AND STUDENTS: BEGINNING 1974, THE
FIGURES SHOWN IN COLUMNS 4, 5 AND 6 REFER TO PUB-
LIC EDUCATION ONLY AND RELATE TO GRADES VII – XV;
FOR PREVIOUS YEARS TO GRADES XI – XV.
      TEACHERS: FOR 1975 AND 1976, THE FIGURES
SHOWN IN COLUMNS 7, 8 AND 9 INCLUDE TEACHER TRAIN-
ING AT THE THIRD LEVEL.
  FR—> PERSONNEL ENSEIGNANT ET ELEVES: A PARTIR DE
1974, LES CHIFFRES DES COLONNES 4, 5 ET 6 SE
REFERENT A L'ENSEIGNEMENT PUBLIC SEULEMENT ET SE
RAPPORTENT AUX CLASSES ALLANT DE LA SEPTIEME A LA
QUINZIEME ANNEE D'ETUDES; POUR LES ANNEES
ANTERIEURES, DE LA ONZIEME A LA QUINZIEME ANNEE.
      PERSONNEL ENSEIGNANT: POUR 1975 ET 1976,
LES CHIFFRES DES COLONNES 7, 8 ET 9 INCLUENT
L'ENSEIGNEMENT NORMAL DU TROISIEME DEGRE.
  ESP> PERSONAL DOCENTE Y ALUMNOS: A PARTIR DE
1974, LAS CIFRAS DE LAS COLUMNAS 4. 5 Y 6 SE
REFIEREN A LA ENSEÑANZA PUBLICA SOLAMENTE Y A LAS
CLASES INCLUIDAS ENTRE EL SEPTIMO EL QUINCEAVO AÑO
DE ESTUDIOS; PARA LOS AÑOS ANTERIORES, DEL ONCEAVO
AL QUINCEAVO AÑO DE ESTUDIOS.

IVORY COAST:
  E—> TEACHERS: FOR 1975 AND 1976, THE FIGURES
SHOWN IN COLUMN 4 REFER TO PUBLIC EDUCATION ONLY.
  FR—> PERSONNEL ENSEIGNANT: POUR LES ANNEES 1975
ET 1976, LES CHIFFRES DE LA COLONNE 4 SE REFERENT
A L'ENSEIGNEMENT PUBLIC SEULEMENT.
  ESP> PERSONAL DOCENTE: EN 1975 Y 1976, LAS
CIFRAS DE LA COLUMNA 4 SE REFIEREN A LA ENSEÑANZA
PUBLICA SOLAMENTE.

KENYA:
  E—> TEACHERS: FOR 1977, THE FIGURES SHOWN IN
COLUMNS 4, 5 AND 6 INCLUDE DATA ON OTHER SECOND
LEVEL EDUCATION OF A VOCATIONAL OR TECHNICAL
NATURE.
  FR—> PERSONNEL ENSEIGNANT: POUR 1977, LES
CHIFFRES DES COLONNES 4, 5 ET 6 COMPRENNENT LES
DONNEES RELATIVES A L'AUTRE ENSEIGNEMENT DU
SECOND DEGRE DE CARACTERE TECHNIQUE OU
PROFESSIONNEL.
  ESP> PERSONAL DOCENTE: EN 1977, LAS CIFRAS DE
LAS COLUMNAS 4, 5 Y 6 INCLUYEN LOS DATOS RELATIVOS
A LA OTRA ENSEÑANZA DE SEGUNDO GRADO DE CARACTER
TECNICO O PROFESIONAL.

LIBERIA:
  E—> TEACHERS: FOR 1976, THE FIGURES SHOWN IN
COLUMNS 10, 11 AND 12 REFER TO PUBLIC EDUCATION
ONLY.
      STUDENTS: FOR 1978, THE FIGURES SHOWN IN
COLUMNS 10, 11 AND 12 REFER TO PUBLIC EDUCATION
ONLY.
  FR—> PERSONNEL ENSEIGNANT: POUR 1976, LES
CHIFFRES DES COLONNES 10, 11 ET 12 SE REFERENT A
L'ENSEIGNEMENT PUBLIC SEULEMENT.

Education at the second level: teachers and pupils 3.7
Enseignement du second degré: personnel enseignant et élèves
Enseñanza de segundo grado: personal docente y alumnos

LIBERIA (CONT.):
ELEVES: POUR 1978, LES CHIFFRES DES
COLONNES 10, 11 ET 12 SE REFERENT A L'ENSEIGNEMENT
PUBLIC SEULEMENT.
ESP> PERSONAL DOCENTE: EN 1976, LAS CIFRAS DE
LAS COLUMNAS 10, 11 Y 12 SE REFIEREN A LA
ENSEÑANZA PUBLICA SOLAMENTE.
ALUMNOS: EN 1978, LAS CIFRAS DE LAS COLUM-
NAS 10, 11 Y 12 SE REFIEREN A LA ENSEÑANZA PUBLICA
SOLAMENTE.

MALAWI:
E—> SEE ANNEX TO TABLE 3.1.
FR—> VOIR L'ANNEXE DU TABLEAU 3.1.
ESP> VEASE EL ANEXO DEL CUADRO 3.1.

MAURITIUS:
E—> TEACHERS AND STUDENTS: FROM 1976, THE
FIGURES DO NOT INCLUDE RODRIGUEZ.
FR—> PERSONNEL ENSEIGNANT ET ELEVES: A PARTIR DE
1976, LES CHIFFRES NE COMPRENNENT PAS RODRIGUEZ.
ESP> PERSONAL DOCENTE Y ALUMNOS: A PARTIR DE
1976, NO INCLUYEN LOS DATOS RELATIVOS A RODRIGUEZ.

MOROCCO:
E—> TEACHERS: BEGINNING 1974, THE FIGURES SHOWN
IN COLUMNS 4, 5 AND 6 REFER TO PUBLIC EDUCATION
ONLY. FOR 1975, 1976, 1977 AND 1978, THE FIGURES
SHOWN IN COLUMNS 4, 5 AND 6 INCLUDE DATA ON OTHER
SECOND LEVEL EDUCATION OF A VOCATIONAL OR
TECHNICAL NATURE.
FR—> PERSONNEL ENSEIGNANT: A PARTIR DE 1974, LES
CHIFFRES DES COLONNES 4, 5 ET 6 SE REFERENT A
L'ENSEIGNEMENT PUBLIC SEULEMENT. POUR LES ANNEES
1975, 1976, 1977 ET 1978 LES CHIFFRES DES COLONNES
4, 5 ET 6 COMPRENNENT L'AUTRE ENSEIGNEMENT DU
SECOND DEGRE DE CARACTERE TECHNIQUE OU PROFES-
SIONNEL.
ESP> PERSONAL DOCENTE: A PARTIR DE 1974, LAS
CIFRAS DE LAS COLUMNAS 4, 5 Y 6 SE REFIEREN A LA
ENSEÑANZA PUBLICA SOLAMENTE. EN 1975, 1976, 1977
Y 1978 LOS DATOS DE LAS COLUMNAS 4, 5 Y 6,
INCLUYEN LA OTRA ENSEÑANZA DE SEGUNDO GRADO DE
CARACTER TECNICO O PROFESIONAL.

NIGERIA:
E—> TEACHERS: FOR 1977, THE FIGURES SHOWN IN
COLUMN 10 EXCLUDE ONE TECHNICAL SCHOOL IN LAGOS
STATE.
STUDENTS: FOR 1976, THE FIGURES SHOWN IN
COLUMN 4 INCLUDE CERTAIN FIELDS OF STUDY
PREVIOUSLY CLASSIFIED UNDER OTHER SECOND LEVEL
EDUCATION OF A VOCATIONAL OR TECHNICAL NATURE.
FOR 1977, THE FIGURES SHOWN IN COLUMN 10 EXCLUDE
ONE TECHNICAL SCHOOL IN LAGOS STATE.
FR—> PERSONNEL ENSEIGNANT: POUR 1977, LES
CHIFFRES DE LA COLONNE 10 EXCLUENT UNE ECOLE
TECHNIQUE DE LAGOS.
ELEVES: POUR 1976, LES CHIFFRES DE LA
COLONNE 4 COMPRENNENT CERTAINES BRANCHES
D'ETUDES ANTERIEUREMENT CLASSEES DAND L'AUTRE
ENSEIGNEMENT DU SECOND DEGRE DE CARACTERE
TECHNIQUE OU PROFESSIONNEL. POUR 1977, LES
CHIFFRES DE LA COLONNE 10 EXCLUENT UNE ECOLE
TECHNIQUE DE LAGOS.
ESP> PERSONAL DOCENTE: EN 1977, LAS CIFRAS DE LA
COLUMNA 10 NO INCLUYEN UNA ESCUELA TECNICA DE
LAGOS.
ALUMNOS: EN 1976, LAS CIFRAS DE LA COLUMNA
4 COMPRENDEN CIERTAS RAMAS DE ESTUDIO ANTERIOR-
MENTE CLASIFICADAS EN LA OTRA ENSEÑANZA DE SEGUNDO
GRADO DE CARACTER TECNICO O PROFESIONAL. EN 1977,
LAS CIFRAS DE LA COLUMNA 10 NO INCLUYEN UNA
ESCUELA TECNICA DE LAGOS.

SENEGAL:
E—> STUDENTS: FOR 1975, THE FIGURES SHOWN IN
COLUMN 4 DO NOT INCLUDE PRIVATE LAIC SCHOOLS

SENEGAL (CONT.):
(10 321 PUPILS IN 1973).
FR—> ELEVES: POUR 1975, LES CHIFFRES DE LA
COLONNE 4 NE COMPRENNENT PAS LES ECOLES LAIQUES
PRIVEES (10 321 ELEVES EN 1973).
ESP> ALUMNOS: EN 1975, LAS CIFRAS DE LA COLUMNA
4 NO INCLUYEN LAS ESCUELAS LAICAS PRIVADAS (10 321
ALUMNOS EN 1973).

SEYCHELLES:
E—> TEACHERS: FOR 1976, THE FIGURES SHOWN IN
COLUMNS 4, 5 AND 6 REFER TO PUBLIC EDUCATION ONLY.
FR—> PERSONNEL ENSEIGNANT: POUR 1976, LES
CHIFFRES DES COLONNES 4, 5 ET 6 SE REFERENT A
L'ENSEIGNEMENT PUBLIC SEULEMENT.
ESP> PERSONAL DOCENTE: EN 1976, LAS CIFRAS DE
LAS COLUMNAS 4, 5 Y 6 SE REFIEREN A LA ENSEÑANZA
PUBLICA SOLAMENTE.

SIERRA LEONE:
E—> TEACHERS: FOR 1970, THE FIGURES SHOWN IN
COLUMNS 7, 8 AND 9 INCLUDE TEACHER TRAINING AT
THE THIRD LEVEL.
FR—> PERSONNEL ENSEIGNANT: POUR 1970, LES
CHIFFRES DES COLONNES 7, 8 ET 9 INCLUENT
L' ENSEIGNEMENT NORMAL DU TROISIEME DEGRE.
ESP> PERSONAL DOCENTE: EN 1970, LAS CIFRAS DE
LAS COLUMNAS 7, 8 Y 9. INCLUYEN LA ENSEÑANZA
NORMAL DE TERCER GRADO.

SOMALIA:
E—> SEE ANNEX TO TABLE 3.1
TEACHERS AND STUDENTS: FOR 1976 AND 1977,
THE FIGURES SHOWN IN COLUMNS 1 TO 6 DO NOT
INCLUDE INTERMEDIATE EDUCATION.
FR—> VOIR L'ANNEXE DU TABLEAU 3.1
PERSONNEL ENSEIGNANT ET ELEVES: POUR 1976,
ET 1977, LES CHIFFRES DES COLONNES 1 A 6 NE
COMPRENNENT PAS L'ENSEIGNEMENT INTERMEDIAIRE.
ESP> VEASE EL ANEXO DEL CUADRO 3.1.
PERSONAL DOCENTE Y ALUMNOS: EN 1976 Y 1977,
LAS CIFRAS DE LAS COLUMNAS 1 A 6 NO INCLUYEN LA
ENSEÑANZA INTERMEDIA.

SOUTH AFRICA:
E—> STUDENTS: FOR 1970, THE FIGURE SHOWN IN
COLUMN 7 INCLUDES TEACHER TRAINING AT THE THIRD
LEVEL.
FR—> ELEVES: POUR 1970, LE CHIFFRE DE LA
COLONNE 7 INCLUT L'ENSEIGNEMENT NORMAL DU
TROISIEME DEGRE.
ESP> ALUMNOS: EN 1970, LA CIFRA DE LA COLUMNA
7 INCLUYE LA ENSEÑANZA NORMAL DE TERCER GRADO.

SUDAN:
E—> SEE ANNEX TO TABLE 3.1.
FR—> VOIR L'ANNEXE DU TABLEAU 3.1.
ESP> VEASE EL ANEXO DEL CUADRO 3.1.

TUNISIA:
E—> TEACHERS: FOR 1970, 1974, 1975 AND 1976
(COLUMNS 1, 2 AND 3) AND FOR 1977 (COLUMNS 2 AND
3) FIGURES REFER TO PUBLIC EDUCATION ONLY.
STUDENTS: FOR 1970 AND 1974, DATA IN
COLUMNS 4, 5 AND 6 CONCERNING PRIVATE EDUCATION
OF A VOCATIONAL ON TECHNICAL NATURE ARE INCLUDED
WITH GENERAL EDUCATION AND DATA IN COLUMNS 10, 11
AND 12 REFER TO PUBLIC EDUCATION ONLY.
FR—> PERSONNEL ENSEIGNANT: POUR 1970, 1974, 1975
ET 1976, LES CHIFFRES DES COLONNES 1, 2 ET 3 SE
REFERENT A L'ENSEIGNEMENT PUBLIC SEULEMENT, AINSI
QUE LES CHIFFRES DES COLONNES 2 ET 3 EN 1977.
ELEVES: POUR 1970 ET 1974, LES DONNEES DES
COLONNES 4, 5 ET 6 CONCERNANT L'ENSEIGNEMENT PRIVE
DE L'AUTRE ENSEIGNEMENT DE CARACTERE TECHNIQUE OU
PROFESSIONNEL SONT INCLUSES AVEC L'ENSEIGNEMENT
GENERAL, POUR LES COLONNES 10, 11 ET 12, LES
DONNEES SE REFERENT A L'ENSEIGNEMENT PUBLIC

3.7 **Education at the second level: teachers and pupils**
Enseignement du second degré: personnel enseignant et élèves
Enseñanza de segundo grado: personal docente y alumnos

TUNISIA (CONT.):
SEULEMENT.
   ESP> PERSONAL DOCENTE: EN 1970, 1974, 1975 Y
1976 LAS CIFRAS DE LAS COLUMNAS 1, 2 Y 3 Y EN
1977 LAS DE LAS COLUMNAS 2 Y 3, SE REFIEREN A LA
ENSEÑANZA PUBLICA SOLAMENTE.
      ALUMNOS: EN 1970 Y 1974, LOS DATOS DE LAS
COLUMNAS 4, 5 Y 6 RELATIVOS A LA ENSEÑANZA PRIVADA
DE LA OTRA ENSEÑANZA DE CARACTER TECNICO O
PROFESIONAL QUEDAN INCLUIDOS CON LA ENSEÑANZA
GENERAL; PARA LAS COLUMNAS 10, 11 Y 12, LOS DATOS
SE REFIEREN A LA ENSEÑANZA PUBLICA SOLAMENTE.

UGANDA:
   E—> TEACHERS AND STUDENTS: THE FIGURES REFER
TO GOVERNMENT-MAINTAINED AND AIDED SCHOOLS ONLY.
   FR—> PERSONNEL ENSEIGNANT ET ELEVES: LES
CHIFFRES SE RAPPORTENT AUX ECOLES PUBLIQUES ET
SUBVENTIONNEES SEULEMENT.
   ESP> PERSONAL DOCENTE Y ALUMNOS: LAS CIFRAS
SE REFIEREN A LAS ESCUELAS PUBLICAS Y SUBVENCIO-
NADAS SOLAMENTE.

UNITED REPUBLIC OF TANZANIA:
   E—> TEACHERS AND STUDENTS: FOR 1974 AND 1975,
THE FIGURES SHOWN IN COLUMNS 4, 5 AND 6 INCLUDE
DATA ON OTHER SECOND LEVEL EDUCATION OF A
VOCATIONAL OR TECHNICAL NATURE AND FOR 1976, THE
FIGURES COVER ONLY A PART OF OTHER SECOND LEVEL
EDUCATION OF A VOCATIONAL OR TECHNICAL NATURE.
   FR—> PERSONNEL ENSEIGNANT ET ELEVES: POUR 1974
ET 1975, LES CHIFFRES DES COLONNES 4, 5 ET 6
COMPRENNENT LES DONNEES RELATIVES A L'AUTRE
ENSEIGNEMENT DU SECOND DEGRE DE CARACTERE
TECHNIQUE OU PROFESSIONNEL ET POUR 1976, LES
CHIFFRES NE COMPRENNENT QU'UNE PARTIE DE L'AUTRE
ENSEIGNEMENT DU SECOND DEGRE DE CARACTERE
TECHNIQUE OU PROFESSIONNEL.
   ESP> PERSONAL DOCENTE Y ALUMNOS: EN 1974 Y 1975,
LAS CIFRAS DE LAS COLUMNAS 4, 5 Y 6 INCLUYEN LOS
DATOS RELATIVOS A LA OTRA ENSEÑANZA DE SEGUNDO
GRADO DE CARACTER TECNICO O PROFESIONAL; EN 1976,
LAS CIFRAS SOLO COMPRENDEN UNA PARTE DE LA OTRA
ENSEÑANZA DE SEGUNDO GRADO DE CARACTER TECNICO O
PROFESIONAL.

UPPER VOLTA:
   E—> TEACHERS: FOR 1978, THE FIGURES SHOWN IN
COLUMN 4 REFER TO PUBLIC EDUCATION ONLY.
   FR—> PERSONNEL ENSEIGNANT: POUR 1978, LES
CHIFFRES DE LA COLONNE 4 NE REPRESENTENT QUE
L'ENSEIGNEMENT PUBLIC.
   ESP> PERSONAL DOCENTE: EN 1978, LAS CIFRAS DE LA
COLUMNA 4 SE REFIEREN A LA ENSEÑANZA PUBLICA
SOLAMENTE.

ZIMBABWE:
   E—> STUDENTS: FOR 1970, 1974 AND 1975, THE
FIGURES SHOWN IN COLUMN 7 REFER TO AFRICAN
EDUCATION ONLY.
   FR—> ELEVES: POUR 1970, 1974 ET 1975 LES CHIF-
FRES DE LA COLONNE 7 SE RAPPORTENT A L'ENSEI-
GNEMENT AFRICAIN SEULEMENT.
   ESP> ALUMNOS: EN 1970, 1974 Y 1975 LAS CIFRAS
DE LA COLUMNA 7 SE REFIEREN A LA ENSEÑANZA
AFRICANA SOLAMENTE.

ANTIGUA:
   E—> TEACHERS: IN 1970, THE FIGURES SHOWN IN
COLUMNS 4, 5 AND 6 REFER TO PUBLIC EDUCATION
ONLY AND IN 1974 AND 1975, FIGURES DO NOT INCLUDE
POST-PRIMARY CLASSES.
   FR—> PERSONNEL ENSEIGNANT: POUR LES COLONNES
4, 5 ET 6 DE L'ANNEE 1970, LES CHIFFRES SE
REFERENT A L'ENSEIGNEMENT PUBLIC SEULEMENT ET POUR
1974 ET 1975, ILS NE COMPRENNENT PAS LES CLASSES
SECONDAIRES RATTACHEES AUX ECOLES PRIMAIRES.

ANTIGUA (CONT.):
   ESP> PERSONAL DOCENTE: PARA LAS COLUMNAS 4, 5 Y
6 DEL AÑO 1970 LAS CIFRAS SE REFIEREN A LA
ENSEÑANZA PUBLICA SOLAMENTE; EN 1974 Y 1975, NO SE
INCLUYEN LAS CLASES SECUNDARIAS ADSCRITAS A LAS
ESCUELAS PRIMARIAS.

BAHAMAS:
   E—> TEACHERS: FOR 1970, THE FIGURES SHOWN IN
COLUMNS 7, 8 AND 9 INCLUDE TEACHER TRAINING AT THE
THIRD LEVEL.
      STUDENTS: FOR 1970, 1974 AND 1975, THE
FIGURES SHOWN IN COLUMN 7 INCLUDE TEACHER TRAINING
AT THE THIRD LEVEL. FOR 1974 AND 1975 THE FIGURES
SHOWN IN COLUMN 10 INCLUDE PART-TIME EDUCATION.
   FR—> PERSONNEL ENSEIGNANT: POUR 1970, LES CHIF-
FRES DES COLONNES 7, 8 ET 9 INCLUENT L'ENSEI-
GNEMENT NORMAL DU TROISIEME DEGRE.
      ELEVES: POUR 1970, 1974 ET 1975, LES CHIF-
FRES DE LA COLONNE 7 INCLUENT L'ENSEIGNEMENT
NORMAL DU TROISIEME DEGRE. POUR 1974 ET 1975, LES
CHIFFRES DE LA COLONNE 10 COMPRENNENT LES ELEVES A
TEMPS PARTIEL.
   ESP> PERSONAL DOCENTE: EN 1970, LAS CIFRAS DE
LAS COLUMNAS 7, 8 Y 9 INCLUYEN LA ENSEÑANZA NORMAL
DE TERCER GRADO.
      ALUMNOS: EN 1970, 1974 Y 1975, LAS CIFRAS
DE LA COLUMNA 7 INCLUYEN LA ENSEÑANZA NORMAL DE
TERCER GRADO. EN 1974 Y 1975, LAS CIFRAS DE LA
COLUMNA 10 COMPRENDEN LOS ALUMNOS DE JORNADA
PARCIAL.

BARBADOS:
   E—> STUDENTS: THE FIGURES SHOWN IN COLUMNS
4, 5 AND 6 IN 1970 AND COLUMNS 1, 2 AND 3 IN
1974 REFER TO PUBLIC EDUCATION ONLY.
   FR—> ELEVES: POUR 1970, LES CHIFFRES DES
COLONNES 4, 5 ET 6, AINSI QUE CEUX DES COLONNES
1, 2 ET 3 POUR 1974, SE REFERENT A L'ENSEIGNEMENT
PUBLIC SEULEMENT.
   ESP> ALUMNOS: EN 1970, LAS CIFRAS DE LAS
COLUMNAS 4, 5 Y 6 SE REFIEREN A LA ENSEÑANZA
PUBLICA SOLAMENTE. EN 1974, SON LAS COLUMNAS 1,2
Y 3 QUE SOLO SE REFIEREN A LA ENSEÑANZA PUBLICA.

CANADA:
   E—> STUDENTS: FIGURES EXCLUDE UNCLASSIFIED
PUPILS.
   FR—> ELEVES: LES CHIFFRES EXCLUENT LES ELEVES
NON REPARTIS PAR ANNEES D'ETUDES.
   ESP> ALUMNOS: LAS CIFRAS NO INCLUYEN LOS
ALUMNOS QUE NO PUDIERON REPARTIRSE POR AÑOS DE
ESTUDIO.

CAYMAN ISLANDS:
   E—> TEACHERS: FOR 1975, DATA REFER TO PUBLIC
EDUCATION ONLY.
   FR—> PERSONNEL ENSEIGNANT: POUR 1975, LES
DONNEES SE REFERENT A L'ENSEIGNEMENT PUBLIC
SEULEMENT.
   ESP> PERSONAL DOCENTE: EN 1975, LOS DATOS SE
REFIEREN A LA ENSEÑANZA PUBLICA SOLAMENTE.

COSTA RICA:
   E—> TEACHERS: IN 1975, FIGURES SHOWN IN
COLUMNS 5 AND 6 REFER TO PUBLIC EDUCATION ONLY.
      STUDENTS: FOR 1978, DATA REFER TO PUBLIC
EDUCATION AND INCLUDE EVENING SCHOOLS.
   FR—> PERSONNEL ENSEIGNANT: POUR LES COLONNES
5 ET 6 DE L'ANNEE 1975, LES CHIFFRES SE REFERENT
A L'ENSEIGNEMENT PUBLIC SEULEMENT.
      ELEVES: POUR 1978, LES DONNEES SE REFERENT
A L'ENSEIGNEMENT PUBLIC ET COMPRENNENT LES ECOLES
DU SOIR.
   ESP> PERSONAL DOCENTE: EN 1975, LOS DATOS DE LAS
COLUMNAS 5 Y 6 SE REFIEREN A LA ENSEÑANZA PUBLICA
SOLAMENTE.

Education at the second level: teachers and pupils   3.7
Enseignement du second degré: personnel enseignant et élèves
Enseñanza de segundo grado: personal docente y alumnos

COSTA RICA (CONT.):
     ALUMNOS: EN 1978, LOS DATOS SE REFIEREN A
LA ENSEÑANZA PUBLICA, INCLUYENDO LAS ESCUELAS
NOCTURNAS.

EL SALVADOR:
    E—> SEE ANNEX TO TABLE 3.1.
    FR—> VOIR L'ANNEXE DU TABLEAU 3.1.
    ESP: VEASE EL ANEXO DEL CUADRO 3.1.

GRENADA:
    E—> TEACHERS AND STUDENTS: BEGINNING 1974,
REVISED SERIES.
     STUDENTS: FROM 1974, FORMS I, II AND III,
PREVIOUSLY CLASSIFIED AS FIRST LEVEL OF EDUCATION
ARE NOW INCLUDED WITH GENERAL EDUCATION AT THE
SECOND LEVEL.
    FR—> PERSONNEL ENSEIGNANT ET ELEVES: SERIE
REVISEE A PARTIR DE 1974.
     ELEVES: A PARTIR DE 1974, LES "FORMS I,
II ET III" ANTERIEUREMENT CLASSEES DANS
L'ENSEIGNEMENT DU PREMIER DEGRE SONT MAINTENANT
INCLUSES DANS L'ENSEIGNEMENT GENERAL DU SECOND
SECOND DEGRE.
    ESP> PERSONAL DOCENTE Y ALUMNOS: SERIE REVISADA
A PARTIR DE 1974.
     ALUMNOS: A PARTIR DE 1974, LAS "FORMS I, II
Y III" ANTERIORMENTE CLASIFICADAS EN LA ENSEÑANZA
DE PRIMER GRADO, QUEDAN INCLUIDAS EN LA ENSEÑANZA
GENERAL DE SEGUNDO GRADO.

GUATEMALA:
    E—> TEACHERS AND STUDENTS: FOR 1970, ALL DATA
INCLUDE EVENING SCHOOLS AND FROM 1973, EXCLUDE
ARTISTIC EDUCATION WHICH, IN 1972, INCLUDED 56
TEACHERS (F.4) AND 1,023 PUPILS (F. 357).
    FR—>PERSONNEL ENSEIGNANT ET ELEVES: POUR 1970,
TOUTES LES DONNEES COMPRENNENT LES ECOLES DU SOIR
ET A PARTIR DE 1973, COMPTE NON TENU DE L'ENSEI—
GNEMENT ARTISTIQUE; EN 1972, CET ENSEIGNEMENT
COMPRENAIT 56 PROFESSEURS (F.4) ET 1 023 ELEVES
(F.357).
    ESP> PERSONAL DOCENTE Y ALUMNOS: EN 1970, TODOS
LOS DATOS INCLUYEN LAS ESCUELAS NOCTURNAS, Y A
PARTIR DE 1973, EXCLUIDA LA ENSEÑANZA ARTISTICA;
EN 1972, LA ENSEÑANZA ARTISTICA TENIA 56 PRO—
FESORES (F 4) Y 1 023 ALUMNOS (F 357).

HONDURAS:
    E—> STUDENTS: FOR 1970 AND 1974, THE FIGURES
SHOWN IN COLUMNS 4, 5 AND 6 INCLUDE DATA FOR
PART—TIME EDUCATION AND FOR 1976 FIGURES INCLUDE
TEACHER TRAINING.
    FR—> ELEVES: POUR 1970 ET 1974, LES CHIFFRES DES
COLONNES 4, 5 ET 6 COMPRENNENT LES ELEVES A TEMPS
PARTIEL ET POUR 1976, ILS INCLUENT L'ENSEIGNEMENT
NORMAL.
    ESP> ALUMNOS: EN 1970 Y 1974, LAS CIFRAS DE LAS
COLUMNAS 4, 5 Y 6 INCLUYEN LOS ALUMNOS DE JORNADA
PARCIAL. EN 1976, INCLUYEN LA ENSEÑANZA NORMAL.

JAMAICA:
    E—> TEACHERS: FOR 1970 (COLUMN 4) AND 1974
(COLUMNS 2 AND 3), THE FIGURES REFER TO PUBLIC
EDUCATION ONLY. FOR 1975, THE FIGURES SHOWN IN
COLUMNS 1 AND 4 DO NOT INCLUDE SENIOR DEPARTMENTS
OF ALL—AGE SCHOOLS.
     STUDENTS: FOR 1970 AND 1977, FIGURES SHOWN
IN COLUMNS 1 TO 6 REFER TO PUBLIC EDUCATION; FOR
1970, THE FIGURES DO NOT INCLUDE SENIOR DEPART—
MENTS OF ALL—AGE SCHOOLS.
    FR—> PERSONNEL ENSEIGNANT: POUR 1970 COLONNE 4,
1974 COLONNES 2 ET 3 LES CHIFFRES SE REFERENT A
L'ENSEIGNEMENT PUBLIC SEULEMENT. POUR 1975, LES
COLONNES 1 ET 4, NE COMPRENNENT PAS LES SECTIONS
SUPERIEURES DES "ECOLES COMPLETES".
     ELEVES: POUR 1970 ET 1977, LES CHIFFRES
DES COLONNES DE 1 A 6 SE REFERENT A L'ENSEIGNEMENT

JAMAICA (CONT.):
PUBLIC SEULEMENT. POUR 1970, ILS NE COMPRENNENT
PAS LES SECTIONS SUPERIEURES DES "ECOLES
COMPLETES".
    ESP> PERSONAL DOCENTE: LA COLUMNA 4 EN 1970
Y LAS COLUMNAS 2 Y 3 EN 1974, SE REFIEREN A LA
ENSEÑANZA PUBLICA SOLAMENTE. EN 1975, LAS CO—
LUMNAS 1 Y 4 NO INCLUYEN LAS SECCIONES SUPERIORES
DE LAS "ESCUELAS COMPLETAS".
     ALUMNOS: EN 1970 Y 1977, LAS CIFRAS DE
LAS COLUMNAS 1 A 6 SE REFIEREN A LA ENSEÑANZA
PUBLICA SOLAMENTE. EN 1970, DICHAS CIFRAS NO
COMPRENDEN LAS SECCIONES SUPERIORES DE LAS
"ESCUELAS COMPLETAS".

PANAMA:
    E—> SEE ANNEX TO TABLE 3.1.
    FR—> VOIR L'ANNEXE DU TABLEAU 3.1.
    ESP> VEASE EL ANEXO DEL CUADRO 3.1.

FORMER CANAL ZONE:
    E—> TEACHERS AND STUDENTS: FOR 1976, DATA
REFER TO PUBLIC EDUCATION ONLY.
     STUDENTS: FOR 1977, DATA REFER TO PUBLIC
EDUCATION ONLY.
    FR—> PERSONNEL ENSEIGNANT ET ELEVES: POUR 1976,
LES DONNEES SE REFERENT A L'ENSEIGNEMENT PUBLIC
SEULEMENT.
     ELEVES: POUR 1977, LES DONNEES SE REFERENT
A L'ENSEIGNEMENT PUBLIC SEULEMENT.
    ESP> PERSONAL DOCENTE Y ALUMNOS: EN 1976, LOS
DATOS SE REFIEREN A LA ENSEÑANZA PUBLICA SOLAMENTE.
     ALUMNOS: EN 1977, LOS DATOS SE REFIEREN A
LA ENSEÑANZA PUBLICA SOLAMENTE.

PUERTO RICO:
    E—> TEACHERS AND STUDENTS: FOR 1975 AND 1976,
THE FIGURES SHOWN IN COLUMN 1 REFER TO PUBLIC
EDUCATION ONLY.
     STUDENTS: FOR 1974, THE FIGURES SHOWN IN
COLUMN 1 DO NOT INCLUDE FEDERALLY OPERATED
SCHOOLS.
    FR—> PERSONNEL ENSEIGNANT ET ELEVES: POUR 1975
ET 1976, LES CHIFFRES DE LA COLONNE 1 SE REFERENT
A L'ENSEIGNEMENT PUBLIC SEULEMENT.
     ELEVES: POUR 1974, LES CHIFFRES DE LA
COLONNE 1 NE COMPRENNENT PAS LES ECOLES QUI
DEPENDENT DES AUTORITES FEDERALES.
    ESP> PERSONAL DOCENTE Y ALUMNOS: EN 1975 Y
1976, LAS CIFRAS DE LA COLUMNA 1 SE REFIEREN
A LA ENSEÑANZA PUBLICA SOLAMENTE.
     ALUMNOS: EN 1974, LAS CIFRAS DE LA
COLUMNA 1 NO INCLUYEN LAS ESCUELAS QUE DEPENDEN
DE LAS AUTORIDADES FEDERALES.

ST LUCIA:
    E—> STUDENTS: FOR 1970 THE FIGURES SHOWN IN
COLUMNS 4, 5 AND 6 DO NOT INCLUDE SENIOR DEPART—
MENTS OF ALL—AGE SCHOOLS.
    FR—> ELEVES: POUR 1970, LES CHIFFRES DES
COLONNES 4, 5 ET 6 NE COMPRENNENT PAS LES SECTIONS
SUPERIEURES DES "ECOLES COMPLETES".
    ESP> ALUMNOS: EN 1970, LAS CIFRAS DE LAS CO—
LUMNAS 4, 5 Y 6 NO INCLUYEN LAS SECCIONES SUPERIO—
RES DE LAS "ESCUELAS COMPLETAS".

TRINIDAD & TOBAGO:
    E—> TEACHERS: FOR 1970 THE FIGURES SHOWN IN
COLUMNS 10,11 AND 12 REFER TO FULL—TIME ONLY.
     STUDENTS: FOR 1974 AND 1975 THE FIGURES
SHOWN IN COLUMNS 4, 5 AND 6 REFER TO PUBLIC AND
AIDED SCHOOLS ONLY.
    FR—> PERSONNEL ENSEIGNANT: POUR 1970, LES
CHIFFRES DES COLONNES 10,11 ET 12 SE REFERENT
AU PERSONNEL A PLEIN TEMPS SEULEMENT.
     ELEVES: POUR 1974 ET 1975, LES CHIFFRES
DES COLONNES 4, 5 ET 6 SE REFERENT AUX ECOLES
PUBLIQUES ET SUBVENTIONNEES SEULEMENT.

3.7 Education at the second level: teachers and pupils
Enseignement du second degré: personnel enseignant et élèves
Enseñanza de segundo grado: personal docente y alumnos

TRINIDAD AND TOBAGO (CONT.):
ESP> PERSONAL DOCENTE: EN 1970, LAS CIFRAS
DE LAS COLUMNAS 10,11 Y 12 SE REFIEREN AL PERSO-
NAL DE JORNADA COMPLETA SOLAMENTE.
ALUMNOS: EN 1974 Y 1975, LAS CIFRAS DE LAS
COLUMNAS 4, 5 Y 6 SE REFIEREN A LAS ESCUELAS
PUBLICAS Y SUBVENCIONADAS SOLAMENTE.

UNITED STATES OF AMERICA:
E—> TEACHERS AND STUDENTS: FOR 1976 THE
FIGURES SHOWN IN COLUMN 1 INCLUDE SPECIAL
EDUCATION.
FR—> PERSONNEL ENSEIGNANT ET ELEVES: POUR
1976, LES CHIFFRES DE LA COLONNE 1 COMPRENNENT
L'EDUCATION SPECIALE.
ESP> PERSONAL DOCENTE Y ALUMNOS: EN 1976, LAS
CIFRAS DE LA COLUMNA 1 INCLUYEN LA EDUCACION
ESPECIAL.

U.S. VIRGIN ISLANDS:
E—> STUDENTS: FOR 1977 THE FIGURES SHOWN IN
COLUMN 1 REFER TO PUBLIC EDUCATION ONLY.
FR—> ELEVES: POUR 1977, LES CHIFFRES DE LA
COLONNE 1 SE REFERENT A L'ENSEIGNEMENT PUBLIC
SEULEMENT.
ESP> ALUMNOS: EN 1977, LAS CIFRAS DE LA CO-
LUMNA 1 SE REFIEREN A LA ENSEÑANZA PUBLICA
SOLAMENTE.

ARGENTINA:
E—> STUDENTS: FOR 1978, DATA INCLUDE PART-
TIME EDUCATION.
FR—> ELEVES: POUR 1978, LES DONNEES
COMPRENNENT LES ELEVES A TEMPS PARTIEL.
ESP> ALUMNOS: EN 1978, LOS DATOS INCLUYEN LOS
ALUMNOS DE JORNADA PARCIAL.

BRAZIL:
E—> SEE ANNEX TO TABLE 3.1.
FR—> VOIR L'ANNEXE DU TABLEAU 3.1.
ESP> VEASE EL ANEXO DEL CUADRO 3.1.

ECUADOR:
E—> TEACHERS AND STUDENTS: THE FIGURES SHOWN
IN COLUMNS 1 TO 6 INCLUDE EVENING SCHOOLS.
FR—> PERSONNEL ENSEIGNANT ET ELEVES: LES
CHIFFRES DES COLONNES 1 A 6 COMPRENNENT LES
ECOLES DU SOIR.
ESP> PERSONAL DOCENTE Y ALUMNOS: LAS CIFRAS
DE LAS COLUMNAS 1 A 6 INCLUYEN LAS ESCUELAS
NOCTURNAS.

SURINAME:
E—> TEACHERS: FOR 1977, FIGURES SHOWN IN
COLUMNS 7, 8 AND 9 REFER TO FULL-TIME ONLY.
FR—> PERSONNEL ENSEIGNANT: POUR 1977, LES
CHIFFRES DES COLONNES 7, 8 ET 9 SE RAPPORTENT
AU PERSONNEL A PLEIN TEMPS SEULEMENT.
ESP> PERSONAL DOCENTE: EN 1977, LAS CIFRAS DE
LAS COLUMNAS 7, 8 Y 9 SE REFIEREN AL PERSONAL DE
JORNADA COMPLETA SOLAMENTE.

URUGUAY:
E—> STUDENTS: FOR 1977 AND 1978 THE FIGURES
SHOWN IN COLUMNS 4, 5 AND 6 INCLUDE DATA ON OTHER
SECOND LEVEL EDUCATION OF A VOCATIONAL OR
TECHNICAL NATURE.
FR—> ELEVES: POUR 1977 ET 1978, LES CHIFFRES
DES COLONNES 4, 5 ET 6 COMPRENNENT L'AUTRE
ENSEIGNEMENT DE SECOND DEGRE DE CARACTERE
TECHNIQUE OU PROFESSIONNEL.
ESP> ALUMNOS: EN 1977 Y 1978, LAS CIFRAS DE
LAS COLUMNAS 4, 5 Y 6 INCLUYEN LA OTRA ENSE-
ÑANZA DE SEGUNDO GRADO DE CARACTER TECNICO O
PROFESIONAL.

VENEZUELA:
E—> STUDENTS: BEGINNING 1974, FOLLOWING THE
REORGANIZATION OF THE EDUCATIONAL SYSTEM, DATA
REPORTED FOR GENERAL EDUCATION INCLUDE THOSE
FOR THE FIRST CYCLE OF TEACHER TRAINING AND
OTHER SECOND LEVEL EDUCATION OF A VOCATIONAL
OR TECHNICAL NATURE.
FR—> ELEVES: A PARTIR DE 1974, SUIVANT LA
REORGANIZATION DU SYSTEME SCOLAIRE, LES DONNEES
RELATIVES A L'ENSEIGNEMENT GENERAL INCLUENT LE
PREMIER CYCLE DE L'ENSEIGNEMENT NORMAL ET DE
L'AUTRE ENSEIGNEMENT DU SECOND DEGRE DE CARACTERE
TECHNIQUE OU PROFESSIONNEL.
ESP> ALUMNOS: A PARTIR DE 1974, DE ACUERDO CON
LA REORGANIZACION DEL SISTEMA ESCOLAR, LOS DATOS
RELATIVOS A LA ENSEÑANZA GENERAL INCLUYEN EL
PRIMER CICLO DE LA ENSEÑANZA NORMAL Y DE LA OTRA
ENSEÑANZA DE SEGUNDO GRADO DE CARACTER TECNICO
O PROFESIONAL.

AFGHANISTAN:
E—> TEACHERS: FOR 1970 AND 1974 THE FIGURES
SHOWN IN COLUMNS 7, 8 AND 9 INCLUDE TEACHER
TRAINING AT THE THIRD LEVEL. FOR 1975 AND 1976
THE FIGURES SHOWN IN COLUMNS 4, 5 AND 6 INCLUDE
PRIMARY CLASSES ATTACHED TO MIDDLE AND SECONDARY
SCHOOLS.
STUDENTS: SEE ANNEX TO TABLE 3.1.
FR—> PERSONNEL ENSEIGNANT: POUR 1970 ET 1974,
LES CHIFFRES DES COLONNES 7, 8 ET 9 INCLUENT
L'ENSEIGNEMENT NORMAL DU TROISIEME DEGRE. POUR
1975 ET 1976, LES CHIFFRES DES COLONNES 4, 5 ET
6 COMPRENNENT LES CLASSES PRIMAIRES RATTACHEES
AUX ECOLES MOYENNES ET SECONDAIRES.
ELEVES: VOIR L'ANNEXE DU TABLEAU 3.1.
ESP> PERSONAL DOCENTE: EN 1970 Y 1974, LAS
CIFRAS DE LAS COLUMNAS 7, 8 Y 9 INCLUYEN LA ENSE-
ÑANZA NORMAL DE TERCER GRADO. EN 1975 Y 1976,
LAS CIFRAS DE LAS COLUMNAS 4, 5 Y 6 INCLUYEN LAS
CLASES PRIMARIAS ADSCRITAS A LAS ESCUELAS MEDIAS
Y SECUNDARIAS.
ALUMNOS: VEASE EL ANEXO DEL CUADRO 3.1.

BAHRAIN:
E—> TEACHERS: FOR 1974, 1975, 1976 AND 1977
THE FIGURES SHOWN IN COLUMNS 1 TO 6 DO NOT
INCLUDE A PART OF INTERMEDIATE EDUCATION.
STUDENTS: SEE ANNEX TO TABLE 3.1. FOR
1975 AND 1976 THE FIGURES SHOWN IN COLUMNS 4, 5
AND 6 REFER TO PUBLIC EDUCATION ONLY.
FR—> PERSONNEL ENSEIGNANT: POUR 1974, 1975,
1976 ET 1977, LES CHIFFRES DES COLONNES 1 A 6
NE COMPRENNENT PAS UNE PARTIE DE L'ENSEIGNEMENT
INTERMEDIAIRE.
ELEVES: VOIR L'ANNEXE DU TABLEAU 3.1.
POUR 1975 ET 1976, LES CHIFFRES DES COLONNES 4, 5
ET 6 SE REFERENT A L'ENSEIGNEMENT PUBLIC SEULEMENT.
ESP> PERSONAL DOCENTE: EN 1974, 1975, 1976 Y
1977, LAS CIFRAS DE LAS COLUMNAS 1 A 6 NO INCLU-
YEN UNA PARTE DE LA ENSEÑANZA INTERMEDIA.
ALUMNOS: VEASE EL ANEXO DEL CUADRO 3.1.
EN 1975 Y 1976 LAS CIFRAS DE LAS COLUMNAS 4, 5 Y 6
SE REFIEREN A LA ENSEÑANZA PUBLICA SOLAMENTE.

BANGLADESH:
E—> STUDENTS: FOR 1977 THE FIGURES SHOWN IN
COLUMNS 4, 5 AND 6 REFER TO PUBLIC EDUCATION
ONLY.
FR—> ELEVES: POUR 1977, LES CHIFFRES DES
COLONNES 4, 5 ET 6 SE REFERENT A L'ENSEIGNEMENT
PUBLIC SEULEMENT.
ESP> ALUMNOS: EN 1977, LOS DATOS DE LAS
COLUMNAS 4, 5 Y 6 SE REFIEREN A LA ENSEÑANZA
PUBLICA SOLAMENTE.

Education at the second level: teachers and pupils   3.7
Enseignement du second degré: personnel enseignant et élèves
Enseñanza de segundo grado: personal docente y alumnos

BHUTAN:
E—> TEACHERS: FOR 1970 AND 1974, DATA FOR
GENERAL EDUCATION ARE INCLUDED WITH EDUCATION
AT THE FIRST LEVEL.
FR-> PERSONNEL ENSEIGNANT: POUR 1970 ET 1974,
LES DONNEES RELATIVES A L'ENSEIGNEMENT GENERAL
SONT INCLUSES AVEC L'ENSEIGNEMENT DU PREMIER
DEGRE.
ESP> PERSONAL DOCENTE: EN 1970 Y 1974, LOS
DATOS RELATIVOS A LA ENSEÑANZA GENERAL QUEDAN
INCLUIDOS CON LA ENSEÑANZA DE PRIMER GRADO.

CYPRUS:
E—> TEACHERS AND STUDENTS: NOT INCLUDING
TURKISH SCHOOLS.
FR-> PERSONNEL ENSEIGNANT ET ELEVES: COMPTE
NON TENU DES ECOLES TURQUES.
ESP> PERSONAL DOCENTE Y ALUMNOS: EXCLUIDOS LOS
DATOS RELATIVOS A LAS ESCUELAS TURCAS.

DEMOCRATIC KAMPUCHEA:
E—> TEACHERS AND STUDENTS: FOR 1972 THE
FIGURES SHOWN IN COLUMNS 11 AND 12 REFER TO
PUBLIC EDUCATION ONLY.
FR-> PERSONNEL ENSEIGNANT ET ELEVES: POUR
1972, LES CHIFFRES DES COLONNES 11 ET 12 SE
REFERENT A L'ENSEIGNEMENT PUBLIC SEULEMENT.
ESP> PERSONAL DOCENTE Y ALUMNOS: EN 1972,
LAS CIFRAS DE LAS COLUMNAS 11 Y 12 SE REFIEREN
A LA ENSEÑANZA PUBLICA SOLAMENTE.

INDIA:
E—> TEACHERS: FOR 1977 THE FIGURES SHOWN IN
COLUMNS 4, 5 AND 6 INCLUDE TEACHERS IN PRIMARY
CLASSES ATTACHED TO SECONDARY SCHOOLS AND DO NOT
INCLUDE DATA FOR INTERMEDIATE AND PRE-UNIVERSITY
COURSES.
FR-> PERSONNEL ENSEIGNANT: POUR 1977, LES
CHIFFRES DES COLONNES 4, 5 ET 6 COMPRENNENT LE
PERSONNEL ENSEIGNANT DES CLASSES PRIMAIRES
RATTACHEES AUX ECOLES SECONDAIRES; COMPTE NON
TENU DES DONNEES RELATIVES AUX COURS INTER-
MEDIAIRES ET PREUNIVERSITAIRES.
ESP> PERSONAL DOCENTE: EN 1977, LAS CIFRAS DE
LAS COLUMNAS 4, 5 Y 6 INCLUYEN EL PERSONAL DOCENTE
DE LAS CLASES PRIMARIAS ADSCRITAS A LAS ESCUELAS
SECUNDARIAS; NO SE INCLUYEN LOS DATOS RELATI-
VOS A LOS CURSOS INTERMEDIOS Y PREUNIVERSITARIOS.

INDONESIA:
E—> TEACHERS: FOR 1977 AND 1978 THE FIGURES
SHOWN IN COLUMNS 4, 5 AND 6 DO NOT INCLUDE
TEACHERS IN RELIGIOUS SCHOOLS.
FR-> PERSONNEL ENSEIGNANT: POUR 1977 ET 1978,
LES CHIFFRES DES COLONNES 4, 5 ET 6 NE COMPRENNENT
PAS LES PROFESSEURS DES ECOLES RELIGIEUSES.
ESP> PERSONAL DOCENTE: EN 1977 Y 1978, LAS
CIFRAS DE LAS COLUMNAS 4, 5 Y 6 NO INCLUYEN LOS
PROFESORES DE LAS ESCUELAS RELIGIOSAS.

IRAN:
E—> SEE ANNEX TO TABLE 3.1.
FR-> VOIR L'ANNEXE DU TABLEAU 3.1.
ESP> VEASE EL ANEXO DEL CUADRO 3.1.

JAPAN:
E—> TEACHERS: FOR 1974 AND 1978 THE FIGURES
INCLUDE SPECIAL EDUCATION WHEREAS FOR 1970, 1975,
1976 AND 1977 THIS APPLIES TO COLUMNS 2 AND 3 ONLY.
STUDENTS: FROM 1970 TO 1977 THE FIGURES
SHOWN IN COLUMNS 2, 3, 5 AND 6 INCLUDE SPECIAL
EDUCATION. FOR 1978 THE FIGURES INCLUDE SPECIAL
EDUCATION AND PART-TIME PUPILS.
FR-> PERSONNEL ENSEIGNANT: POUR 1974 ET 1978,
LES CHIFFRES INCLUENT L'EDUCATION SPECIALE
AINSI QUE POUR 1970, 1975, 1976 ET 1977, COLONNES
2 ET 3 SEULEMENT.

JAPAN (CONT.):
ELEVES: DE 1970 A 1977, LES CHIFFRES DES
COLONNES 2, 3, 5 ET 6 INCLUENT L'EDUCATION
SPECIALE. POUR 1978, LES CHIFFRES COMPRENNENT
L'EDUCATION SPECIALE ET LES ELEVES A TEMPS PARTIEL.
ESP> PERSONAL DOCENTE: EN 1974 Y 1978, LAS
CIFRAS COMPRENDEN LA EDUCACION ESPECIAL. EN 1970,
1975, 1976 Y 1977, LA EDUCACION ESPECIAL QUEDA
INCLUIDA EN LAS CIFRAS DE LAS COLUMNAS 2 Y 3.
ALUMNOS: DE 1970 A 1977, LAS CIFRAS DE
LAS COLUMNAS 2, 3, 5 Y 6 COMPRENDEN LA EDUCACION
ESPECIAL. EN 1978, LAS CIFRAS INCLUYEN LA
EDUCACION ESPECIAL Y LOS ALUMNOS DE JORNADA
PARCIAL.

JORDAN:
E—> TEACHERS AND STUDENTS: DATA REFER TO THE
EAST BANK ONLY. INCLUDING UNRWA SCHOOLS WITH
1,111 (F.420) TEACHERS AND 34,317 (F.15,892)
PUPILS IN GENERAL EDUCATION IN 1978.
FR-> PERSONNEL ENSEIGNANT ET ELEVES: LES
DONNEES SE REFERENT A LA RIVE ORIENTALE SEULEMENT.
Y COMPRIS LES ECOLES DE L'"UNRWA" QUI COMPTAIENT
1 111 MAITRES (F.420) ET 34 317 ELEVES (F.15 892)
DANS L'ENSEIGNEMENT GENERAL EN 1978.
ESP> PERSONAL DOCENTE Y ALUMNOS: LOS DATOS SE
REFIEREN A LA ORILLA ORIENTAL SOLAMENTE. IN-
CLUIDAS LAS ESCUELAS DEL O.O.P.S.R.P. QUE TENIAN
1 111 PROFESORES (F. 420) Y 34 317 ALUMNOS
(F. 15 892) EN LA ENSEÑANZA GENERAL, EN 1978.

KOREA, REPUBLIC OF:
E—> STUDENTS: FOR 1979 THE FIGURES SHOWN IN
COLUMNS 1, 2, 3, 10, 11 AND 12 DO NOT INCLUDE
PROFESSIONAL TRADE SCHOOLS AND IN ADDITION FOR
COLUMNS 10,11 AND 12, THE FIGURES INCLUDE PART-
TIME EDUCATION.
FR-> ELEVES: POUR 1979, LES CHIFFRES DES
COLONNES 1, 2, 3, 10, 11 ET 12 NE COMPRENNENT PAS
LES ECOLES PROFESSIONNELLES "TRADE SCHOOLS" ET
POUR LES COLONNES 10, 11 ET 12, CES MEMES
CHIFFRES INCLUENT L'ENSEIGNEMENT A TEMPS PARTIEL.
ESP> ALUMNOS: EN 1979, LAS CIFRAS DE LAS CO-
LUMNAS 1, 2, 3, 10, 11 Y 12 NO COMPRENDEN LAS
ESCUELAS PROFESIONALES ("TRADE SCHOOLS"). EN LAS
COLUMNAS 10,11 Y 12 SE INCLUYE LA ENSEÑANZA DE
JORNADA PARCIAL.

KUWAIT:
E—> TEACHERS AND STUDENTS: FOR 1978, ALL
FIGURES REFER TO PUBLIC EDUCATION ONLY.
FR-> PERSONNEL ENSEIGNANT ET ELEVES: POUR
1978, LES DONNEES SE REFERENT A L'ENSEIGNEMENT
PUBLIC SEULEMENT.
ESP> PERSONAL DOCENTE Y ALUMNOS: EN 1978, LOS
DATOS SE REFIEREN A LA ENSEÑANZA PUBLICA SOLA-
MENTE.

LAO PEOPLE'S DEMOCRATIC REPUBLIC:
E—> SEE ANNEX TO TABLE 3.1.
FR-> VOIR L'ANNEXE DU TABLEAU 3.1.
ESP> VEASE EL ANEXO DEL CUADRO 3.1.

LEBANON:
E—> STUDENTS: INCLUDING UNRWA SCHOOLS WITH
7 577 (F.3,244) PUPILS ENROLLED IN GENERAL
EDUCATION AND 58 (F.—) PUPILS IN TEACHER
TRAINING IN 1970.
FR-> ELEVES: Y COMPRIS LES ECOLES DE L'"UNRWA"
QUI COMPTAIENT 7 577 ELEVES (F. 3 244) DANS
L'ENSEIGNEMENT GENERAL ET 58 ELEVES (F. —) DANS
L'ENSEIGNEMENT NORMAL EN 1970.
ESP> ALUMNOS: INCLUIDAS LAS ESCUELAS DEL
O.O.P.S.R.P. QUE EN 1970 TENIAN 7 577 ALUMNOS
(F. 3 244) EN LA ENSEÑANZA GENERAL Y 58 ALUMNOS
(F. —) EN LA ENSEÑANZA NORMAL.

3.7 Education at the second level: teachers and pupils
Enseignement du second degré: personnel enseignant et élèves
Enseñanza de segundo grado: personal docente y alumnos

MALAYSIA:
  PENINSULAR MALAYSIA:
  E—> TEACHERS AND STUDENTS: FOR 1976,
(COLUMNS 1, 2, 3, 10, 11 AND 12) FOR 1977 AND
1978, THE FIGURES REFER TO PUBLIC EDUCATION ONLY.
  FR—> PERSONNEL ENSEIGNANT ET ELEVES: POUR 1976
(COLONNES 1, 2, 3, 10, 11 ET 12) ET POUR 1977 ET
1978, LES CHIFFRES SE REFERENT A L'ENSEIGNEMENT
PUBLIC SEULEMENT.
  ESP> PERSONAL DOCENTE Y ALUMNOS: EN 1976
(COLUMNAS 1, 2, 3, 10, 11 Y 12) Y EN 1977 Y 1978
LOS DATOS SE REFIEREN A LA ENSEÑANZA PUBLICA
SOLAMENTE.

MONGOLIA:
  E—> SEE ANNEX TO TABLE 3.1.
  FR—> VOIR L'ANNEXE DU TABLEAU 3.1.
  ESP> VEASE EL ANEXO DEL CUADRO 3.1.

NEPAL:
  E—> SEE ANNEX TO TABLE 3.1.
  FR—> VOIR L'ANNEXE DU TABLEAU 3.1.
  ESP> VEASE EL ANEXO DEL CUADRO 3.1.

PHILIPPINES:
  E—> TEACHERS: FOR 1970 AND 1974 THE FIGURES
SHOWN IN COLUMN 10 REFER TO PUBLIC EDUCATION
ONLY.
  FR—> PERSONNEL ENSEIGNANT: POUR 1970 ET 1974,
LES CHIFFRES DE LA COLONNE 10 SE REFERENT A
L'ENSEIGNEMENT PUBLIC SEULEMENT.
  ESP> PERSONAL DOCENTE Y ALUMNOS: EN 1970 Y
1974, LAS CIFRAS DE LA COLUMNA 10 SE REFIEREN
A LA ENSEÑANZA PUBLICA SOLAMENTE.

SAUDI ARABIA:
  E—> TEACHERS: FOR 1977, THE FIGURES SHOWN IN
COLUMN 10 INCLUDE TECHNICAL COMMERCIAL AND INDUS-
TRIAL EDUCATION ONLY.
    STUDENTS: IN 1977, DATA SHOWN IN COLUMNS
4, 5 AND 6 INCLUDE EVENING SCHOOLS AND THOSE SHOWN
IN COLUMNS 10, 11 AND 12 INCLUDE TECHNICAL,
COMMERCIAL AND INDUSTRIAL EDUCATION ONLY.
  FR—> PERSONNEL ENSEIGNANT: POUR 1977, LES
CHIFFRES DE LA COLONNE 10 NE COMPRENNENT QUE
L'ENSEIGNEMENT TECHNIQUE, COMMERCIAL ET INDUSTRIEL.
    ELEVES: EN 1977, LES DONNEES DES COLONNES
4, 5 ET 6 INCLUENT LES ECOLES DU SOIR ET CELLES
DES COLONNES 10,11 ET 12 NE COMPRENNENT QUE
L'ENSEIGNEMENT TECHNIQUE, COMMERCIAL ET INDUSTRIEL.
  ESP> PERSONAL DOCENTE: EN 1977, LAS CIFRAS DE
LA COLUMNA 10 SOLO COMPRENDEN LA ENSEÑANZA TECNICA,
COMERCIAL E INDUSTRIAL.
    ALUMNOS: EN 1977, LOS DATOS DE LAS
COLUMNAS 4, 5 Y 6 INCLUYEN LAS ESCUELAS NOCTURNAS
Y LOS DE LAS COLUMNAS 10,11 Y 12 SOLO COMPRENDEN
LA ENSEÑANZA TECNICA, COMERCIAL E INDUSTRIAL.

SINGAPORE:
  E—> STUDENTS: FOR 1976 THE FIGURES SHOWN IN
COLUMNS 10,11 AND 12 INCLUDE SOME PART-TIME
PUPILS.
  FR—> ELEVES: POUR 1976, LES CHIFFRES DES
COLONNES 10,11 ET 12 COMPRENNENT QUELQUES ELEVES
A TEMPS PARTIEL.
  ESP> ALUMNOS: EN 1976, LAS CIFRAS DE LAS
COLUMNAS 10,11 Y 12 INCLUYEN ALGUNOS ALUMNOS DE
JORNADA PARCIAL.

SRI LANKA:
  E—> TEACHERS AND STUDENTS: DATA ON OTHER
SECOND LEVEL EDUCATION OF A VOCATIONAL OR
TECHNICAL NATURE REFER TO TECHNICAL INSTITUTES
ATTACHED TO THE MINISTRY OF EDUCATION ONLY.
    TEACHERS: FOR 1976 AND 1977 THE FIGURES
SHOWN IN COLUMN 4 REFER TO PUBLIC EDUCATION ONLY.
    STUDENTS: SEE ANNEX TO TABLE 3.1. FOR
1975, 1976, 1977 AND 1979 THE FIGURES SHOWN IN

SRI LANKA (CONT.):
COLUMNS 1 TO 6 REFER TO PUBLIC EDUCATION ONLY.
  FR—> PERSONNEL ENSEIGNANT ET ELEVES: LES
DONNEES RELATIVES A L'AUTRE ENSEIGNEMENT DU
SECOND DEGRE DE CARACTERE TECHNIQUE OU PROFES-
SIONNEL SE REFERENT AUX INSTITUTS TECHNIQUES
RATTACHES AU MINISTERE DE L'EDUCATION SEULEMENT.
    PERSONNEL ENSEIGNANT: POUR 1976 ET 1977
LES CHIFFRES DE LA COLONNE 4 SE REFERENT A
L'ENSEIGNEMENT PUBLIC SEULEMENT.
    ELEVES: VOIR L'ANNEXE DU TABLEAU 3.1.
POUR 1975, 1976, 1977 ET 1979, LES CHIFFRES DES
COLONNES 1 A 6 SE REFERENT A L'ENSEIGNEMENT
PUBLIC SEULEMENT.
  ESP> PERSONAL DOCENTE Y ALUMNOS: LOS DATOS
RELATIVOS A LA OTRA ENSEÑANZA DE SEGUNDO GRADO
DE CARACTER TECNICO O PROFESIONAL SE REFIEREN
A LOS INSTITUTOS TECNICOS DEPENDIENTES DEL
MINISTERIO DE EDUCACION SOLAMENTE.
    PERSONAL DOCENTE: EN 1976 Y 1977 LAS
CIFRAS DE LA COLUMNA 4 SE REFIEREN A LA ENSE-
ÑANZA PUBLICA SOLAMENTE.
    ALUMNOS: VEASE EL ANEXO DEL CUADRO 3.1.
EN 1975, 1976, 1977 Y 1979, LAS CIFRAS DE LAS
COLUMNAS 1 A 6 SE REFIEREN A LA ENSEÑANZA
PUBLICA SOLAMENTE.

SYRIAN ARAB REPUBLIC:
  E—> TEACHERS: THE FIGURES SHOWN IN COLUMNS
7, 8 AND 9 INCLUDE TEACHER TRAINING AT THE THIRD
LEVEL.
    STUDENTS: INCLUDING UNRWA SCHOOLS WITH
23,036 (F.10,379) PUPILS IN GENERAL EDUCATION
IN 1978.
  FR—> PERSONNEL ENSEIGNANT: LES CHIFFRES DES
COLONNES 7, 8 ET 9 INCLUENT L'ENSEIGNEMENT NORMAL
DU TROISIEME DEGRE.
    ELEVES: Y COMPRIS LES ECOLES DE L'"UNRWA"
QUI COMPTAIENT 23 036 ELEVES (F.10 379) DANS
L'ENSEIGNEMENT GENERAL EN 1978.
  ESP> PERSONAL DOCENTE: LAS CIFRAS DE LAS
COLUMNAS 7, 8 Y 9 INCLUYEN LA ENSEÑANZA NORMAL DE
TERCER GRADO.
    ALUMNOS: INCLUIDAS LAS ESCUELAS DEL
O.O.P.S.R.P. QUE EN 1978 TENIAN 23 036 ALUMNOS
(F. 10 379) EN LA ENSEÑANZA GENERAL.

THAILAND:
  E—> TEACHERS: FOR 1970 (COLUMNS 5 AND 6), 1975
(COLUMN 4), 1976 AND 1977 (COLUMNS 4, 5 AND 6) THE
FIGURES REFER TO PUBLIC EDUCATION ONLY. IN
ADDITION FOR ALL YEARS, FIGURES SHOWN IN COLUMNS
7, 8 AND 9 INCLUDE TEACHER TRAINING AT THE THIRD
LEVEL.
  FR—> PERSONNEL ENSEIGNANT: POUR 1970,
(COLONNES 5 ET 6), 1975 (COLONNE 4), 1976 ET 1977
(COLONNE 4, 5 ET 6) LES CHIFFRES SE REFERENT A
L'ENSEIGNEMENT PUBLIC SEULEMENT. DE PLUS, ET
POUR TOUTES LES ANNEES, LES CHIFFRES DES COLONNES
7, 8 ET 9 COMPRENNENT L'ENSEIGNEMENT NORMAL DU
TROISIEME DEGRE.
  ESP> PERSONAL DOCENTE: EN 1970 (COLUMNAS 5 Y
6), 1975 (COLUMNA 4), 1976 Y 1977 (COLUMNAS 4, 5
Y 6), LAS CIFRAS SE REFIEREN A LA ENSEÑANZA
PUBLICA SOLAMENTE. ADEMAS, PARA TODOS LOS ANOS,
LAS CIFRAS DE LAS COLUMNAS 7, 8 Y 9 COMPRENDEN
LA ENSEÑANZA NORMAL DE TERCER GRADO.

UNITED ARAB EMIRATES:
  E—> TEACHERS AND STUDENTS: FOR 1970, 1974
AND 1975 THE FIGURES SHOWN IN COLUMNS 4, 5 AND 6
REFER TO PUBLIC EDUCATION ONLY.
  FR—> PERSONNEL ENSEIGNANT ET ELEVES: POUR 1970,
1974 ET 1975, LES CHIFFRES DES COLONNES 4, 5 ET 6
SE REFERENT A L'ENSEIGNEMENT PUBLIC SEULEMENT.
  ESP> PERSONAL DOCENTE Y ALUMNOS: EN 1970, 1974
Y 1975, LAS CIFRAS DE LAS COLUMNAS 4, 5 Y 6 SE
REFIEREN A LA ENSEÑANZA PUBLICA SOLAMENTE.

Education at the second level: teachers and pupils 3.7
Enseignement du second degré: personnel enseignant et élèves
Enseñanza de segundo grado: personal docente y alumnos

AUSTRIA:
E—> TEACHERS: FOR 1970 AND 1974 THE FIGURES
SHOWN IN COLUMNS 4, 5 AND 6 DO NOT INCLUDE GRADES
V–VIII OF THE "VOLKSSCHULEN" WHICH ARE INCLUDED
IN THE FIRST LEVEL.
STUDENTS: FOR 1974, 1975 AND 1976 THE
FIGURES SHOWN IN COLUMNS 4, 5 AND 6 INCLUDE
SPECIAL EDUCATION.
FR—> PERSONNEL ENSEIGNANT: POUR 1970 ET 1974,
LES CHIFFRES RELATIFS AUX CLASSES V–VIII DES
"VOLKSSCHULEN" QUI DEVRAIENT FIGURER DANS LES
COLONNES 4, 5 ET 6 SONT COMPTEES DANS
L'ENSEIGNEMENT DU PREMIER DEGRE.
ELEVES: POUR 1974, 1975 ET 1976, LES
CHIFFRES DES COLONNES 4, 5 ET 6 COMPRENNENT
L'EDUCATION SPECIALE.
ESP> PERSONAL DOCENTE: EN 1970 Y 1974, LAS
CIFRAS RELATIVAS A LAS CLASES V–VIII DE LAS
"VOLKSSCHULEN", QUE DEBERIAN FIGURAR EN LAS
COLUMNAS 4, 5 Y 6 QUEDAN INCLUIDAS EN LA
ENSEÑANZA DE PRIMER GRADO.
ALUMNOS: EN 1974, 1975 Y 1976, LAS CIFRAS
DE LAS COLUMNAS 4, 5 Y 6 INCLUYEN LA EDUCACION
ESPECIAL.

BULGARIA:
E—> STUDENTS: FOR 1978 THE FIGURES SHOWN IN
COLUMNS 4, 5 AND 6 INCLUDE EVENING AND
CORRESPONDENCE COURSES; THE FIGURES SHOWN IN
COLUMNS 10, 11 AND 12 EXCLUDE VOCATIONAL SCHOOLS
WITH A DURATION OF 2 YEARS.
FR—> ELEVES: POUR 1978, LES CHIFFRES DES
COLONNES 4, 5 ET 6 COMPRENNENT LES COURS DU SOIR
ET PAR CORRESPONDANCE ET LES CHIFFRES DES
COLONNES 10, 11 ET 12 EXCLUENT LES ECOLES
PROFESSIONNELLES D'UN DUREE DE 2 ANNEES.
ESP> ALUMNOS: EN 1978, LAS CIFRAS DE LAS
COLUMNAS 4, 5 Y 6 INCLUYEN LOS CURSOS NOCTURNOS
Y POR CORRESPONDENCIA Y LAS CIFRAS DE LAS COLUM–
NAS 10, 11 Y 12 EXCLUYEN LAS ESCUELAS PROFESIONA–
LES DE UNA DURACION DE 2 ANOS.

DENMARK:
E—> TEACHERS: FOR 1974, DATA ON GENERAL
EDUCATION ARE INCLUDED WITH EDUCATION AT THE
FIRST LEVEL.
STUDENTS: DATA REVISED.
FR—> PERSONNEL ENSEIGNANT: POUR 1974, LES
DONNEES RELATIVES A L'ENSEIGNEMENT GENERAL SONT
INCLUSES AVEC L'ENSEIGNEMENT DU PREMIER DEGRE.
ELEVES: DONNEES REVISEES.
ESP> PERSONAL DOCENTE: EN 1974, LOS DATOS
RELATIVOS A LA ENSEÑANZA GENERAL QUEDAN INCLUIDOS
EN LA ENSEÑANZA DE PRIMER GRADO.
ALUMNOS: DATOS REVISADOS.

FINLAND:
E—> TEACHERS: FOR 1975, 1976 AND 1977 THE
FIGURES SHOWN IN COLUMNS 1 AND 4, INCLUDE TEACHERS
IN PRIMARY CLASSES ATTACHED TO SECONDARY SCHOOLS.
STUDENTS: FOR 1975, 1976, 1977 AND 1978
THE FIGURES SHOWN IN COLUMNS 1 TO 6 INCLUDE
SPECIAL EDUCATION AND FROM 1975 (COLUMNS 4, 5, AND
6), DUE TO A CHANGE IN CLASSIFICATION THE DATA
SERIES ARE NOT COMPARABLE WITH THE PREVIOUS YEARS.
FR—> PERSONNEL ENSEIGNANT: POUR 1975, 1976 ET
1977 LES CHIFFRES DES COLONNES 1 ET 4 COMPRENNENT
LE PERSONNEL ENSEIGNANT DES CLASSES PRIMAIRES
RATTACHEES AUX ECOLES SECONDAIRES.
ELEVES: POUR 1975, 1976, 1977 ET 1978,
LES CHIFFRES DES COLONNES 1 A 6 INCLUENT
L'ENSEIGNEMENT SPECIAL ET A PARTIR DE 1975
(COLONNES 4, 5, ET 6) LA SERIE N'EST PAS COMPARABLE
AVEC LES ANNEES PRECEDENTES, A LA SUITE D'UN
CHANGEMENT DE CLASSIFICATION.
ESP> PERSONAL DOCENTE: EN 1975, 1976 Y 1977,
LAS CIFRAS DE LAS COLUMNAS 1 Y 4 COMPRENDEN EL
PERSONAL DOCENTE DE LAS CLASES PRIMARIAS ADSCRITAS

FINLAND (CONT.):
A LAS ESCUELAS SECUNDARIAS.
ALUMNOS: DE 1975 A 1978, LAS CIFRAS DE
LAS COLUMNAS 1 A 6 INCLUYEN LA EDUCACION ESPECIAL,
Y, A PARTIR DE 1975 (COLUMNAS 4, 5 Y 6), LA SERIE
NO ES COMPARABLE CON LA DE LOS AÑOS ANTERIORES
DEBIDO A UN CAMBIO DE CLASIFICACION.

FRANCE:
E—> TEACHERS: FOR 1970 (COLUMNS 2 AND 3) AND
1974 (COLUMN 4) REFER TO PUBLIC EDUCATION ONLY.
IN ADDITION THE FIGURES FOR 1974 INCLUDE DATA ON
OTHER SECOND LEVEL EDUCATION OF A VOCATIONAL OR
TECHNICAL NATURE.
FR—> PERSONNEL ENSEIGNANT: POUR 1970, LES
CHIFFRES DES COLONNES 2 ET 3 SE REFERENT A
L'ENSEIGNEMENT PUBLIC SEULEMENT AINSI QUE CEUX
DE 1974 (COLONNE 4). DE PLUS CES MEMES CHIFFRES
EN 1974 COMPRENNENT L'AUTRE ENSEIGNEMENT DU SECOND
DEGRE DE CARACTERE TECHNIQUE AU PROFESSIONNEL.
ESP> PERSONAL DOCENTE: EN 1970, LAS CIFRAS DE
LAS COLUMNAS 2 Y 3 Y EN 1974 LAS DE LA COLUMNA
4, SE REFIEREN A LA ENSEÑANZA PUBLICA SOLAMENTE.
ADEMAS, LAS MISMAS CIFRAS COMPRENDEN EN 1974 LA
OTRA ENSEÑANZA DE SEGUNDO GRADO DE CARACTER
TECNICO O PROFESIONAL.

GERMANY, FEDERAL REPUBLIC OF:
E—> STUDENTS: BEGINNING 1971 (COLUMNS 10, 11
AND 12), CERTAIN TECHNICAL SCHOOLS PREVIOUSLY
SHOWN AS SECOND LEVEL EDUCATION ARE NOW
CLASSIFIED AT THE THIRD LEVEL OF EDUCATION.
FR—> ELEVES: A PARTIR DE 1971, (COLONNES 10,
11 ET 12) CERTAINES ECOLES TECHNIQUES ANTERIEURE–
MENT CLASSEES DANS L'ENSEIGNEMENT DU SECOND
DEGRE SONT COMPTEES DANS L'ENSEIGNEMENT DU
TROISIEME DEGRE.
ESP> ALUMNOS: A PARTIR DE 1971 (COLUMNAS 10,
11 Y 12) ALGUNAS ESCUELAS TECNICAS ANTERIORMENTE
CLASIFICADAS EN LA ENSEÑANZA DE SEGUNDO GRADO,
FIGURAN EN LA ENSEÑANZA DE TERCER GRADO.

GREECE:
E—> STUDENTS: FOR 1976 THE FIGURES SHOWN IN
COLUMNS 1 TO 6 INCLUDE EVENING SCHOOLS.
FR—> ELEVES: POUR 1976, LES CHIFFRES DES
COLONNES 1 A 6 COMPRENNENT LES ECOLES DU SOIR.
ESP> ALUMNOS: EN 1976, LAS CIFRAS DE LAS
COLUMNAS 1 A 6 INCLUYEN LAS ESCUELAS NOCTURNAS.

IRELAND:
E—> TEACHERS: BEGINNING 1975, THE NUMBER OF
TEACHERS ARE EXPRESSED IN FULL–TIME EQUIVALENT.
STUDENTS: FOR 1974 THE FIGURES SHOWN IN
COLUMNS 4, 5 AND 6 INCLUDE CERTAIN FIELDS OF STUDY
PREVIOUSLY CLASSIFIED UNDER OTHER SECOND LEVEL
EDUCATION OF A VOCATIONAL OR TECHNICAL NATURE.
FR—> PERSONNEL ENSEIGNANT: A PARTIR DE 1975,
LE NOMBRE DE PROFESSEURS EST COMPTE EN EQUIVA–
LENT PLEIN TEMPS.
ELEVES: POUR 1974, LES CHIFFRES DES
COLONNES 4, 5 ET 6 COMPRENNENT CERTAINES
BRANCHES D'ETUDES ANTERIEUREMENT CLASSEES DANS
L'AUTRE ENSEIGNEMENT DU SECOND DEGRE DE CARAC–
TERE TECHNIQUE OU PROFESSIONNEL.
ESP> PERSONAL DOCENTE: A PARTIR DE 1975, EL
NUMERO DE PROFESORES SE PRESENTA EN EQUIVALENCIA
DE JORNADA COMPLETA.
ALUMNOS: EN 1977, LAS CIFRAS DE LAS
COLUMNAS 4, 5 Y 6 INCLUYEN ALGUNAS RAMAS DE
ESTUDIO ANTERIORMENTE CLASIFICADAS EN LA OTRA
ENSEÑANZA DE SEGUNDO GRADO DE CARACTER TECNICO
O PROFESIONAL.

3.7   Education at the second level: teachers and pupils
Enseignement du second degré: personnel enseignant et élèves
Enseñanza de segundo grado: personal docente y alumnos

LUXEMBOURG:
   E—> STUDENTS: BEGINNING 1974, (COLUMNS 1 TO 6)
DATA PREVIOUSLY CLASSIFIED AS PRIMARY EDUCATION
ARE INCLUDED IN THE FIRST CYCLE OF SECOND LEVEL
GENERAL EDUCATION.
   FR-> ELEVES: A PARTIR DE 1974 (COLONNES 1 A 6)
CERTAINES DONNEES ANTERIEUREMENT COMPRISES DANS
L'ENSEIGNEMENT DU PREMIER DEGRE SONT INCLUSES
DANS LE PREMIER CYCLE DE L'ENSEIGNEMENT GENERAL
DU SECOND DEGRE.
   ESP> ALUMNOS: A PARTIR DE 1974 (COLUMNAS
1 A 6) CIERTOS DATOS ANTERIORMENTE COMPRENDIDOS
EN LA ENSEÑANZA DE PRIMER GRADO SE INCLUYEN EN
EL PRIMER CICLO DE LA ENSEÑANZA GENERAL DE SEGUNDO
GRADO.

MONACO:
   E—> STUDENTS: FOR 1976, DATA REFER TO PUBLIC
EDUCATION ONLY.
   FR-> ELEVES: POUR 1976, LES DONNEES SE REFERENT
A L'ENSEIGNEMENT PUBLIC SEULEMENT.
   ESP> ALUMNOS: EN 1976, LOS DATOS SE REFIEREN A
LA ENSEÑANZA PUBLICA SOLAMENTE.

POLAND:
   E—> TEACHERS: FOR 1970, THE FIGURES SHOWN IN
COLUMNS 10, 11 AND 12 INCLUDE EVENING AND
CORRESPONDENCE COURSES. FOR 1974 AND 1975, THE
FIGURES SHOWN IN COLUMNS 10, 11 AND 12 INCLUDE
TEACHER TRAINING, EVENING AND CORRESPONDENCE
COURSES.
   FR-> PERSONNEL ENSEIGNANT: POUR 1970, LES
CHIFFRES DES COLONNES 10, 11 ET 12 COMPRENNENT LES
COURS DU SOIR ET PAR CORRESPONDANCE. POUR 1974
ET 1975, LES CHIFFRES DES COLONNES 10, 11 ET 12
INCLUENT L'ENSEIGNEMENT NORMAL, LES COURS DU
SOIR ET PAR CORRESPONDANCE.
   ESP> PERSONAL DOCENTE: EN 1970, LAS CIFRAS
DE LAS COLUMNAS 10, 11 Y 12 COMPRENDEN LOS CURSOS
NOCTURNOS Y POR CORRESPONDENCIA. EN 1974 Y 1975,
LAS CIFRAS DE LAS COLUMNAS 10, 11 Y 12 INCLUYEN
LA ENSEÑANZA NORMAL, LOS CURSOS NOCTURNOS Y
LOS CURSOS POR CORRESPONDENCIA.

PORTUGAL:
   E—> TEACHERS AND STUDENTS: BEGINNING 1973,
THE PREPARATORY CYCLE OF EDUCATION HAS BEEN
CLASSIFIED AS EDUCATION AT THE FIRST LEVEL.
   FR-> PERSONNEL ENSEIGNANT ET ELEVES: A PARTIR
DE 1973, LE CYCLE D'ENSEIGNEMENT PREPARATOIRE
EST INCLUS DANS L'ENSEIGNEMENT DU PREMIER DEGRE.
   ESP> PERSONAL DOCENTE Y ALUMNOS: A PARTIR DE
1973, EL CICLO DE ENSEÑANZA PREPARATORIA SE
INCLUYE EN LA ENSEÑANZA DE PRIMER GRADO.

ROMANIA:
   E—> STUDENTS: BEGINNING 1975 THE FIGURES
SHOWN IN COLUMNS 1 TO 6 AND 10 TO 12 INCLUDE
PART-TIME AND ADULT PUPILS.
   FR-> ELEVES: A PARTIR DE 1975, LES CHIFFRES
DES COLONNES 1 A 6 ET DE 10 A 12 COMPRENNENT
LES ADULTES ET LES ELEVES A TEMPS PARTIEL.
   ESP> ALUMNOS: A PARTIR DE 1975, LAS CIFRAS
DE LAS COLUMNAS 1 A 6 Y 10 A 12 COMPRENDEN LOS
ADULTOS Y LOS ALUMNOS DE JORNADA PARCIAL.

SPAIN:
   E—> TEACHERS AND STUDENTS: FROM 1972, CERTAIN
TECHNICAL SCHOOLS ARE CLASSIFIED AT THE THIRD
LEVEL OF EDUCATION.
   FR-> PERSONNEL ENSEIGNANT ET ELEVES: A PARTIR
DE 1972, CERTAINES ECOLES TECHNIQUES ONT ETE
CLASSEES DANS L'ENSEIGNEMENT DU TROISIEME
DEGRE.
   ESP> PERSONAL DOCENTE Y ALUMNOS: A PARTIR
DE 1972, ALGUNAS ESCUELAS TECNICAS SE HAN CLA-
SIFICADO EN LA ENSEÑANZA DE TERCER GRADO.

SWEDEN:
   E—> STUDENTS: BEGINNING 1975, CERTAIN
COURSES PREVIOUSLY CLASSIFIED AS GENERAL EDUCA-
TION AT THE SECOND LEVEL (COLUMNS 1 TO 6) ARE
NOW CLASSIFIED AS THIRD LEVEL EDUCATION.
   FR-> ELEVES: A PARTIR DE 1975, CERTAINS COURS
ANTERIEUREMENT CLASSES DANS L'ENSEIGNEMENT
GENERAL DU SECOND DEGRE (COLONNES 1 A 6) SONT
INCLUS DANS L'ENSEIGNEMENT DU TROISIEME DEGRE.
   ESP> ALUMNOS: A PARTIR DE 1975, ALGUNOS CURSOS
ANTERIORMENTE CLASIFICADOS EN LA ENSEÑANZA GENERAL
DE SEGUNDO GRADO (COLUMNAS 1 A 6) FIGURAN INCLUI-
DOS EN LA ENSEÑANZA DE TERCER GRADO.

SWITZERLAND:
   E—> STUDENTS: FOR 1970, 1974 AND 1975, DATA
REFER TO PUBLIC EDUCATION ONLY. FOR 1976, 1977
(COLUMNS 5, 6, 8 AND 9) AND FOR 1978 (COLUMNS 4
TO 9) THE FIGURES INCLUDE PART-TIME AND ADULT
PUPILS.
   FR-> ELEVES: POUR 1970, 1974 ET 1975, LES
DONNEES SE REFERENT A L'ENSEIGNEMENT PUBLIC
SEULEMENT. POUR 1976, 1977 (COLONNES 5, 6, 8 ET 9)
ET 1978 (COLONNES 4 A 9) LES CHIFFRES COMPRENNENT
LES ADULTES ET LES ELEVES A TEMPS PARTIEL.
   ESP> ALUMNOS: EN 1970, 1974 Y 1975 LOS DATOS
SE REFIEREN A LA ENSEÑANZA PUBLICA SOLAMENTE.
EN 1976 Y 1977 (COLUMNAS 5, 6, 8 Y 9) Y 1978
(COLUMNAS 4 A 9), LAS CIFRAS COMPRENDEN LOS ADUL-
TOS Y LOS ALUMNOS DE JORNADA PARCIAL.

YUGOSLAVIA:
   E—> STUDENTS: FOR 1975 AND 1976 THE FIGURES
SHOWN IN COLUMNS 2, 3, 5 AND 6 INCLUDE SPECIAL
EDUCATION.
   FR-> ELEVES: POUR 1975 ET 1976, LES CHIFFRES
DES COLONNES 2, 3, 5 ET 6 INCLUENT L'EDUCATION
SPECIALE.
   ESP> ALUMNOS: EN 1975 Y 1976, LAS CIFRAS DE
LAS COLUMNAS 2, 3, 5 Y 6 INCLUYEN LA EDUCACION
ESPECIAL.

AMERICAN SAMOA:
   E—> TEACHERS: FOR 1975 AND 1976 THE FIGURES
SHOWN IN COLUMN 1 REFER TO PUBLIC EDUCATION
ONLY.
      STUDENTS: FOR 1975 AND 1977 THE FIGURES
SHOWN IN COLUMN 1 REFER TO PUBLIC EDUCATION ONLY.
   FR-> PERSONNEL ENSEIGNANT: POUR 1975 ET 1976,
LES CHIFFRES DE LA COLONNE 1 SE REFERENT A
L'ENSEIGNEMENT PUBLIC SEULEMENT.
      ELEVES: POUR 1975 ET 1977, LES CHIFFRES
DE LA COLONNE 1 SE REFERENT A L'ENSEIGNEMENT
PUBLIC SEULEMENT.
   ESP> PERSONAL DOCENTE: EN 1975 Y 1976, LAS
CIFRAS DE LA COLUMNA 1 SE REFIEREN A LA ENSEÑANZA
PUBLICA SOLAMENTE.
      ALUMNOS: EN 1975 Y 1977, LAS CIFRAS DE
LA COLUMNA 1 SE REFIEREN A LA ENSEÑANZA PUBLICA
SOLAMENTE.

GUAM:
   E—> TEACHERS AND STUDENTS: FOR 1976, THE
FIGURES SHOWN IN COLUMN 1 REFER TO PUBLIC
EDUCATION ONLY.
   FR-> PERSONNEL ENSEIGNANT ET ELEVES: POUR
1976, LES CHIFFRES DE LA COLONNE 1 SE REFERENT
A L'ENSEIGNEMENT PUBLIC SEULEMENT.
   ESP> PERSONAL DOCENTE Y ALUMNOS: EN 1976,
LAS CIFRAS DE LA COLUMNA 1 SE REFIEREN A LA EN-
SENANZA PUBLICA SOLAMENTE.

KIRIBATI:
   E—> TEACHERS AND STUDENTS: FOR 1970 THE
FIGURES SHOWN IN COLUMNS 4, 5 AND 6 DO NOT INCLUDE
SENIOR DEPARTMENTS OF ALL-AGE SCHOOLS.
   FR-> PERSONNEL ENSEIGNANT ET ELEVES: POUR
1970, LES CHIFFRES DES COLONNES 4, 5 ET 6 NE

Education at the second level: teachers and pupils   3.7
Enseignement du second degré: personnel enseignant et élèves
Enseñanza de segundo grado: personal docente y alumnos

KIRIBATI (CONT.):
COMPRENNENT PAS LES SECTIONS SUPERIEURES DES
"ECOLES COMPLETES".
   ESP> PERSONAL DOCENTE Y ALUMNOS: EN 1970, LAS
CIFRAS DE LAS COLUMNAS 4, 5 Y 6 NO INCLUYEN LAS
SECCIONES SUPERIORES DE LAS "ESCUELAS COMPLETAS".

NEW CALEDONIA:
   E—> TEACHERS: FOR 1975 THE FIGURES SHOWN IN
COLUMNS 8 AND 9 REFER TO PUBLIC EDUCATION ONLY.
   FR-> PERSONNEL ENSEIGNANT: POUR 1975, LES
CHIFFRES DES COLONNES 8 ET 9 SE REFERENT A
L'ENSEIGNEMENT PUBLIC SEULEMENT.
   ESP> PERSONAL DOCENTE: EN 1975, LAS CIFRAS DE
LAS COLUMNAS 8 Y 9 SE REFIEREN A LA ENSEÑANZA
PUBLICA SOLAMENTE.

NEW ZEALAND:
   E—> TEACHERS: THE FIGURES SHOWN IN COLUMNS
4, 5 AND 6 DO NOT INCLUDE TEACHERS OF FORM I AND
II, INCLUDED AT THE FIRST LEVEL.
      STUDENTS: FOR 1975 AND 1976 THE FIGURES
SHOWN IN COLUMNS 1 TO 6 INCLUDE SPECIAL EDUCATION.
   FR-> PERSONNEL ENSEIGNANT: LES CHIFFRES DES
COLONNES 4, 5 ET 6 NE COMPRENNENT PAS LE
PERSONNEL ENSEIGNANT DES "FORMS I ET II" INCLUS
DANS L'ENSEIGNEMENT DU PREMIER DEGRE.
      ELEVES: POUR 1975 ET 1976, LES CHIFFRES
DES COLONNES 1 A 6 INCLUENT L'EDUCATION SPECIALE.
   ESP> PERSONAL DOCENTE: LAS CIFRAS DE LAS CO-
LUMNAS 4, 5 Y 6 NO INCLUYEN EL PERSONAL DOCENTE
DE LAS "FORMS I Y II" QUE FIGURAN EN LA ENSE-
ÑANZA DE PRIMER GRADO.
      ALUMNOS: EN 1975 Y 1976, LAS CIFRAS DE
LAS COLUMNAS 1 A 6 INCLUYEN LA EDUCACION ESPECIAL.

NIUE:
   E—> STUDENTS: FOR 1974, 1975 AND 1976 THE
FIGURES SHOWN IN COLUMNS 4, 5 AND 6 REFER TO
GRADES IX-XII; FOR THE PREVIOUS YEARS TO GRADES
VIII-XII.
   FR-> ELEVES: POUR 1974, 1975 ET 1976, LES
CHIFFRES DES COLONNES 4, 5 ET 6 SE REFERENT AUX
CLASSES IX-XII, POUR LES ANNEES ANTERIEURES AUX
CLASSES VIII-XII.
   ESP> ALUMNOS: EN 1974, 1975 Y 1976, LAS CIFRAS
DE LAS COLUMNAS 4, 5 Y 6 SE REFIEREN A LAS CLASES
IX-XII; PARA LOS AÑOS ANTERIORES, A LAS CLASES
VIII-XII.

U.S.S.R.:
   E—> TEACHERS: FIGURES INCLUDE TEACHER TRAIN-
ING, EVENING AND CORRESPONDENCE COURSES; FOR ALL
YEARS, DATA REFERRING TO GENERAL EDUCATION ARE
INCLUDED WITH EDUCATION AT THE FIRST LEVEL.
      STUDENTS: DATA ON TEACHER TRAINING AND
OTHER SECOND LEVEL EDUCATION OF A VOCATIONAL OR
TECHNICAL NATURE INCLUDE EVENING AND
CORRESPONDENCE COURSES.
   FR-> PERSONNEL ENSEIGNANT: LES CHIFFRES
INCLUENT L'ENSEIGNEMENT NORMAL, LES COURS DU SOIR
ET PAR CORRESPONDANCE. LES DONNEES DES COLONNES
4, 5 ET 6 SE REFERANT A L'ENSEIGNEMENT GENERAL
SONT INCLUSES AVEC L'ENSEIGNEMENT DU PREMIER
DEGRE.
      ELEVES: LES DONNEES RELATIVES A
L'ENSEIGNEMENT NORMAL ET A L'AUTRE ENSEIGNEMENT
DU SECOND DEGRE DE CARACTERE TECHNIQUE OU
PROFESSIONNEL INCLUENT LES COURS DU SOIR ET PAR
CORRESPONDANCE.

U.S.S.R. (CONT.):
   ESP> PERSONAL DOCENTE: LAS CIFRAS INCLUYEN
LA ENSEÑANZA NORMAL Y LOS CURSOS NOCTURNOS Y POR
CORRESPONDENCIA. LOS DATOS DE LAS COLUMNAS 4, 5 Y
6 QUE SE REFIEREN A LA ENSEÑANZA GENERAL, FIGURAN
INCLUIDOS EN LA ENSEÑANZA DE PRIMER GRADO.
      ALUMNOS: LOS DATOS RELATIVOS A LA ENSE-
ÑANZA NORMAL Y A LA OTRA ENSEÑANZA DE SEGUNDO
GRADO DE CARACTER TECNICO O PROFESIONAL INCLUYEN
LOS CURSOS NOCTURNOS Y POR CORRESPONDENCIA.

BYELORUSSIAN S.S.R.:
   E—> TEACHERS: FIGURES INCLUDE TEACHER TRAIN-
ING, EVENING AND CORRESPONDENCE COURSES; FOR ALL
YEARS, DATA REFERRING TO GENERAL EDUCATION ARE
INCLUDED WITH EDUCATION AT THE FIRST LEVEL.
      STUDENTS: DATA ON TEACHER TRAINING AND
OTHER SECOND LEVEL EDUCATION OF A VOCATIONAL OR
TECHNICAL NATURE INCLUDE EVENING AND
CORRESPONDENCE COURSES.
   FR-> PERSONNEL ENSEIGNANT: LES CHIFFRES
INCLUENT L'ENSEIGNEMENT NORMAL, LES COURS DU SOIR
ET PAR CORRESPONDANCE. LES DONNEES DES COLONNES
4, 5 ET 6 SE REFERANT A L'ENSEIGNEMENT GENERAL
SONT INCLUSES AVEC L'ENSEIGNEMENT DU PREMIER
DEGRE.
      ELEVES: LES DONNEES RELATIVES A
L'ENSEIGNEMENT NORMAL ET A L'AUTRE ENSEIGNEMENT
DU SECOND DEGRE DE CARACTERE TECHNIQUE OU
PROFESSIONNEL INCLUENT LES COURS DU SOIR ET PAR
CORRESPONDANCE.
   ESP> PERSONAL DOCENTE: LAS CIFRAS INCLUYEN
LA ENSEÑANZA NORMAL Y LOS CURSOS NOCTURNOS Y POR
CORRESPONDENCIA. LOS DATOS DE LAS COLUMNAS 4, 5 Y
6 QUE SE REFIEREN A LA ENSEÑANZA GENERAL, FIGURAN
INCLUIDOS EN LA ENSEÑANZA DE PRIMER GRADO.
      ALUMNOS: LOS DATOS RELATIVOS A LA ENSE-
ÑANZA NORMAL Y A LA OTRA ENSEÑANZA DE SEGUNDO
GRADO DE CARACTER TECNICO O PROFESIONAL INCLUYEN
LOS CURSOS NOCTURNOS Y POR CORRESPONDENCIA.

UKRAINIAN S.S.R.:
   E—> TEACHERS: FIGURES INCLUDE TEACHER TRAIN-
ING, EVENING AND CORRESPONDENCE COURSES; FOR ALL
YEARS, DATA REFERRING TO GENERAL EDUCATION ARE
INCLUDED WITH EDUCATION AT THE FIRST LEVEL.
      STUDENTS: DATA ON TEACHER TRAINING AND
OTHER SECOND LEVEL EDUCATION OF A VOCATIONAL OR
TECHNICAL NATURE INCLUDE EVENING AND
CORRESPONDENCE COURSES.
   FR-> PERSONNEL ENSEIGNANT: LES CHIFFRES
INCLUENT L'ENSEIGNEMENT NORMAL, LES COURS DU SOIR
ET PAR CORRESPONDANCE. LES DONNEES DES COLONNES
4, 5 ET 6 SE REFERANT A L'ENSEIGNEMENT GENERAL
SONT INCLUSES AVEC L'ENSEIGNEMENT DU PREMIER
DEGRE.
      ELEVES: LES DONNEES RELATIVES A
L'ENSEIGNEMENT NORMAL ET A L'AUTRE ENSEIGNEMENT
DU SECOND DEGRE DE CARACTERE TECHNIQUE OU
PROFESSIONNEL INCLUENT LES COURS DU SOIR ET PAR
CORRESPONDANCE.
   ESP> PERSONAL DOCENTE: LAS CIFRAS INCLUYEN
LA ENSEÑANZA NORMAL Y LOS CURSOS NOCTURNOS Y POR
CORRESPONDENCIA. LOS DATOS DE LAS COLUMNAS 4, 5 Y
6 QUE SE REFIEREN A LA ENSEÑANZA GENERAL, FIGURAN
INCLUIDOS EN LA ENSEÑANZA DE PRIMER GRADO.
      ALUMNOS: LOS DATOS RELATIVOS A LA ENSE-
ÑANZA NORMAL Y A LA OTRA ENSEÑANZA DE SEGUNDO
GRADO DE CARACTER TECNICO O PROFESIONAL INCLUYEN
LOS CURSOS NOCTURNOS Y POR CORRESPONDENCIA.

Percentage distribution (second level general) by grade 3.8
Répartition en % (second degré général) par années d'études
Distribución en % (segundo grado general) por años de estudio

3.8 Education at the second level (general): percentage distribution of enrolment by grade

Enseignement du second degré (général): répartition en pourcentage des effectifs par années d'études

Enseñanza de segundo grado (general): distribución en porcentaje de la matrícula escolar por años de estudio

NUMBER OF COUNTRIES AND TERRITORIES PRESENTED IN THIS TABLE: 147	NOMBRE DE PAYS ET DE TERRITOIRES PRESENTES DANS CE TABLEAU: 147	NUMERO DE PAISES Y DE TERRITORIOS PRESENTADOS EN ESTE CUADRO: 147

COUNTRY PAYS PAIS	YEAR ANNEE AÑO	SEX SEXE SEXO	GRADE / ANNEES D'ETUDES / AÑOS DE ESTUDIO									
			I	II	III	IV	V	VI	VII	VIII	IX	X
AFRICA												
ALGERIA ‡	1970	MF	26	26	19	13	7	5	4			
		F	28	24	18	13	8	5	4			
	1975	MF	25	23	19	16	8	6	5			
		F	26	24	19	16	7	5	4			
	1977	MF	24	24	19	16	7	5	5			
		F	26	24	19	15	7	5	5			
	1978	MF	23	22	20	17	7	5	5			
		F	25	23	20	16	7	5	4			
BENIN	1970	MF	28	23	19	16	7	5	3			
		F	31	24	18	15	6	4	2			
	1975	MF	23	20	21	19	7	7	4			
		F	23	20	21	19	6	6	3			
	1978	MF	24	21	18	17	9	6	5			
		F	25	21	18	19	8	5	5			
	1979	MF	25	20	19	15	8	6	6			
		F	26	20	19	16	7	6	6			
BOTSWANA	1974	MF	37	28	23	7	5					
		F	41	28	21	5	4					
	1975	MF	36	30	21	8	6					
		F	38	33	20	5	4					
	1977	MF	33	30	24	8	6					
		F	35	31	24	6	4					
	1978	MF	31	29	25	8	7					
		F	33	31	25	6	5					
BURUNDI ‡	1970	MF	26	21	20	15	10	8				
		F	34	21	18	14	8	5				
	1975	MF	19	20	21	15	11	8	7			
		F	22	21	22	18	8	6	3			
	1976	MF	18	17	19	16	13	10	8			
		F	24	17	19	16	12	7	5			

3.8 Percentage distribution (second level general) by grade
Répartition en % (second degré général) par années d'études
Distribución en % (segundo grado general) por años de estudio

COUNTRY PAYS PAIS	YEAR ANNEE AÑO	SEX SEXE SEXO	GRADE / ANNEES D'ETUDES / AÑOS DE ESTUDIO									
			I	II	III	IV	V	VI	VII	VIII	IX	X
BURUNDI (CONT.) ‡	1977	MF	17	18	19	17	13	9	8			
		F	20	19	20	17	12	6	5			
CENTRAL AFRICAN REPUBLIC	1970	MF	38	23	15	13	6	2	2			
		F	50	23	11	9	4	1	1			
	1975	MF	28	23	19	17	8	4	2			
		F	38	26	18	10	4	2	2			
	1976	MF	26	23	18	16	9	5	3			
		F	37	25	17	13	4	2	1			
CHAD	1970	MF	29	24	20	14	7	3	2			
		F	34	23	16	13	6	4	4			
	1974	MF	26	22	21	19	6	4	3			
	1975	MF	28	22	18	18	6	4	4			
	1976	MF	26	23	19	19	6	4	4			
COMORO	1970	MF	23	19	19	16	10	7	6			
		F	28	19	21	14	7	7	4			
CONGO	1970	MF	29	27	18	15	6	3	2			
		F	36	31	17	11	3	1	1			
	1975	MF	31	23	18	13	7	4	3			
		F	36	25	19	13	4	2	1			
	1977	MF	29	22	19	16	6	4	4			
		F	34	24	18	14	5	3	2			
	1978	MF	27	21	19	19	6	4	4			
		F	32	24	19	17	4	2	2			
DJIBOUTI	1974	MF	28	23	15	14	9	6	6			
		F	22	24	15	15	10	7	7			
	1975	MF	24	26	17	12	10	6	5			
		F	22	20	14	13	15	10	7			
	1978	MF	37	26	14	10	7	4	2			
EGYPT ‡	1970	MF	*26	*22	*26	*8	*8	*10				
		F	26	22	26	8	8	10				
	1974	MF	26	23	28	7	7	8				
		F	*27	*24	*28	*7	*7	*8				
	1975	MF	*29	*23	*27	*7	*7	*7				
		F	*30	*23	*26	*7	*6	*7				
	1977	MF	25	24	30	7	6	8				
		F	26	24	29	7	6	8				
	1978	MF	25	23	29	7	7	9				
		F	26	24	29	7	7	5				
ETHIOPIA	1970	MF	32	26	18	12	8	5				
		F	33	30	17	11	6	3				
GABON	1970	MF	29	24	18	13	7	6	3			
		F	36	24	16	11	6	4	2			
	1975	MF	29	24	18	13	7	5	5			
		F	33	25	17	12	7	4	3			

Percentage distribution (second level general) by grade 3.8
Répartition en % (second degré général) par années d'études
Distribución en % (segundo grado general) por años de estudio

COUNTRY PAYS PAIS	YEAR ANNEE AÑO	SEX SEXE SEXO	GRADE / ANNEES D'ETUDES / AÑOS DE ESTUDIO									
			I	II	III	IV	V	VI	VII	VIII	IX	X
GABON (CONT.)	1976	MF	27	22	19	13	7	6	5			
		F	31	23	19	13	6	5	4			
GAMBIA	1970	MF	28	24	20	19	5	4	1			
		F	26	24	21	17	6	6	1			
	1975	MF	27	23	23	21	6	1				
		F	29	23	23	19	5	1				
	1977	MF	25	25	24	20	4	1				
		F	27	28	25	16	4	0				
	1978	MF	27	23	23	22	4	1				
		F	26	23	25	21	4	1				
GHANA ‡	1970	MF	23	21	18	17	15	3	3			
		F	27	21	18	16	14	2	2			
	1975	MF	28	25	23	20	2	1	0			
		F	29	26	23	19	2	0	0			
	1976	MF	29	26	23	19	2	1	1			
		F	30	26	23	19	2	0	0			
	1977	MF	28	26	23	19	2	1	1			
		F	30	26	23	18	2	0	0			
GUINEA	1971	MF	26	25	17	16	12	4				
		F	31	27	19	12	8	2				
GUINEA—BISSAU	1975	MF	41	28	16	9	6					
		F	45	29	14	6	6					
	1976	MF	41	29	12	14	4					
		F	42	30	12	13	3					
	1977	MF	47	23	16	9	5					
		F	49	24	18	7	3					
IVORY COAST	1970	MF	30	26	21	16	4	2	2			
		F	36	27	18	13	3	2	1			
	1975	MF	29	23	20	16	5	4	4			
		F	33	25	18	14	4	3	3			
	1976	MF	29	24	20	16	5	4	4			
		F	34	24	19	14	4	3	3			
	1977	MF	29	24	20	15	5	4	4			
		F	35	24	18	13	4	3	3			
	1978	MF	30	24	20	15	5	4	3			
KENYA ‡	1970	MF	32	29	19	15	2	2				
		F	36	30	18	13	2	1				
	1975	MF	32	28	20	16	2	2				
		F	35	29	19	13	2	1				
	1976	MF	34	27	20	16	2	2				
		F	37	27	19	14	1	1				
	1977	MF	33	28	19	16	2	2				
		F	36	29	18	14	1	1				
LESOTHO	1970	MF	38	29	22	7	4					
		F	39	30	21	6	4					
	1975	MF	32	29	23	7	8					
		F	34	29	22	7	7					

Percentage distribution (second level general) by grade
Répartition en % (second degré général) par années d'études
Distribución en % (segundo grado general) por años de estudio

COUNTRY PAYS PAIS	YEAR ANNEE AÑO	SEX SEXE SEXO	GRADE / ANNEES D'ETUDES / AÑOS DE ESTUDIO									
			I	II	III	IV	V	VI	VII	VIII	IX	X
LESOTHO (CONT.)	1976	MF	35	27	23	8	7					
		F	36	28	23	7	6					
LIBERIA	1970	MF	31	25	19	11	8	7				
		F	30	25	18	12	8	8				
	1975	MF	27	22	20	14	10	8				
		F	30	24	19	12	9	7				
	1976	MF	28	22	20	14	10	7				
		F	30	24	19	12	9	6				
	1977	MF	22	19	19	16	12	10				
		F	23	20	19	16	12	9				
LIBYAN ARAB JAMAHIRIYA	1970	MF	35	27	20	6	6	6				
		F	37	29	18	6	5	5				
	1975	MF	44	25	18	6	4	3				
		F	49	25	17	4	3	2				
	1976	MF	43	27	18	5	4	3				
		F	46	29	17	4	3	2				
	1977	MF	39	29	21	5	4	3				
		F	41	30	21	3	2	2				
MADAGASCAR	1970	MF	28	22	19	18	6	4	2			
		F	28	22	19	19	6	4	2			
	1975	MF	26	23	18	14	7	7	5			
		F	27	23	18	15	8	6	4			
MALAWI	1974	MF	30	31	20	20						
		F	34	35	15	16						
	1975	MF	30	30	20	19						
		F	34	34	17	15						
	1976	MF	30	29	20	21						
		F	33	32	18	16						
	1977	MF	31	30	20	19						
		F	34	32	17	17						
MALI	1970	MF	31	29	29	5	4	3				
		F	33	31	30	3	2	1				
	1975	MF	32	26	24	8	7	4				
		F	36	27	23	6	5	3				
	1976	MF	34	25	21	6	9	4				
		F	39	25	23	7	7	5				
	1977	MF	32	25	24	8	9	5				
		F	37	27	23	8	6	4				
MAURITANIA	1970	MF	24	22	17	19	10	5	3			
		F	27	26	18	16	7	3	3			
	1975	MF	30	21	17	13	9	6	4			
	1976	MF	31	23	15	13	9	5	5			
	1977	MF	33	23	20	—	15	5	4			
MAURITIUS ‡	1970	MF	22	20	16	17	21	2	2			
		F	24	20	17	17	18	2	2			

Percentage distribution (second level general) by grade 3.8
Répartition en % (second degré général) par années d'études
Distribución en % (segundo grado general) por años de estudio

COUNTRY PAYS PAIS	YEAR ANNEE AÑO	SEX SEXE SEXO	GRADE / ANNEES D'ETUDES / AÑOS DE ESTUDIO									
			I	II	III	IV	V	VI	VII	VIII	IX	X
MAURITIUS (CONT.) ‡	1975	MF	23	20	17	18	18	2	2			
		F	24	21	17	18	16	2	2			
	1977	MF	26	19	16	16	18	2	2			
		F	26	19	17	17	17	2	2			
	1978	MF	21	21	17	17	18	2	3			
		F	22	22	18	17	17	2	2			
MOROCCO	1970	MF	*23	*22	*19	*20	*7	*4	*4			
		F	*26	*23	*20	*18	*6	*4	*3			
	1975	MF	24	19	17	17	9	7	7			
		F	26	20	18	16	9	6	6			
	1977	MF	22	20	18	17	10	6	7			
		F	23	21	18	16	10	6	6			
	1978	MF	21	19	17	18	11	7	7			
		F	23	19	18	18	10	6	6			
NIGER	1970	MF	33	32	19	10	3	2	2			
		F	39	30	16	9	3	2	2			
	1975	MF	31	24	21	14	4	3	3			
		F	33	22	21	14	4	3	3			
	1976	MF	33	24	19	16	3	3	3			
		F	33	25	18	15	3	2	3			
NIGERIA ‡	1970	MF	31	23	19	14	11	1	1			
		F	33	24	19	13	10	1	1			
REUNION ‡	1970	MF	27	26	23	12	6	4	3			
		F	26	25	24	12	6	4	3			
	1974	MF	30	26	26	10	4	2	2			
		F	29	26	25	12	4	2	2			
	1975	MF	30	25	26	11	4	2	2			
		F	29	24	26	12	4	2	2			
	1976	MF	29	25	28	10	4	2	2			
		F	28	25	26	12	5	2	2			
	1978	MF	27	30	20	12	7	3	3			
		F	26	29	21	13	7	3	3			
RWANDA	1970	MF	36	27	20	7	5	5				
		F	35	32	26	3	3	1				
	1975	MF	36	25	22	6	5	5	2			
		F	39	29	25	3	3	2	—			
	1976	MF	33	27	21	5	6	5	2			
		F	37	31	25	3	2	2	0			
SAO TOME AND PRINCIPE	1976	MF	45	24	15	8	5	2	1			
		F	41	28	15	10	3	3	0			
SENEGAL	1970	MF	26	23	20	17	6	4	3			
		F	29	24	20	16	6	3	2			
SEYCHELLES ‡	1970	MF	44	41	6	4	4	2				
		F	45	41	7	3	3	0				
	1974	MF	44	36	11	4	3	1	1			
		F	43	37	12	5	3	0	1			

3.8 Percentage distribution (second level general) by grade
Répartition en % (second degré général) par années d'études
Distribución en % (segundo grado general) por años de estudio

COUNTRY PAYS PAIS	YEAR ANNEE AÑO	SEX SEXE SEXO	GRADE / ANNEES D'ETUDES / AÑOS DE ESTUDIO									
			I	II	III	IV	V	VI	VII	VIII	IX	X
SEYCHELLES (CONT.) ‡	1977	MF	38	34	14	8	5	1	0			
		F	35	34	15	9	6	0	0			
	1978	MF	36	33	17	7	6	1	1			
		F	34	32	19	8	6	0	0			
	1979	MF	36	32	18	7	5	1	1			
		F	36	31	18	8	6	0	0			
SIERRA LEONE	1970	MF	34	25	18	13	9	1	1			
		F	36	25	17	12	8	0	0			
	1974	MF	32	23	19	15	10	1	1			
		F	34	24	18	13	9	0	0			
	1977	MF	30	23	20	16	10	1	1			
		F	33	25	19	14	9	1	0			
SOMALIA	1970	MF	23	19	17	16	*9	*7	*5	*4		
		F	26	21	17	17	*7	*7	*3	*2		
	1975	MF	...	28	26	28	5	7	6			
		F	...	31	28	29	3	5	3			
	1976	MF	33	26	19	23						
		F	34	24	17	25						
	1977	MF	38	23	25	15						
		F	36	21	26	16						
SUDAN	1970	MF	28	26	20	10	8	7				
		F	30	26	19	10	9	6				
	1975	MF	29	24	25	*9	*7	*6				
		F	*32	*24	*25	*8	*6	*5				
	1977	MF	27	24	25	9	8	7				
		F	27	25	25	9	7	6				
	1978	MF	28	24	23	9	9	7				
		F	28	24	23	9	9	7				
SWAZILAND	1970	MF	39	29	21	6	4	0				
		F	43	29	20	5	3	0				
	1975	MF	35	27	20	10	7	0				
		F	38	28	19	9	7	0				
	1977	MF	33	27	21	10	8	0				
		F	35	29	21	9	7	0				
	1978	MF	31	27	22	11	8	0				
		F	33	28	22	9	7	1				
TOGO	1970	MF	32	22	19	15	6	3	2			
		F	36	23	18	14	5	2	2			
	1975	MF	37	24	16	13	5	4	2			
		F	42	24	15	11	4	3	1			
	1977	MF	32	25	19	14	5	4	2			
		F	36	26	18	13	3	3	1			
	1978	MF	32	22	20	16	4	3	3			
		F	38	22	19	14	3	2	2			
TUNISIA	1975	MF	24	19	17	11	10	9	10			
		F	24	20	17	11	10	9	8			

Percentage distribution (second level general) by grade 3.8
Répartition en % (second degré général) par années d'études
Distribución en % (segundo grado general) por años de estudio

COUNTRY PAYS PAIS	YEAR ANNEE AÑO	SEX SEXE SEXO	GRADE / ANNEES D'ETUDES / AÑOS DE ESTUDIO									
			I	II	III	IV	V	VI	VII	VIII	IX	X
TUNISIA (CONT.)	1977	MF	24	20	19	11	10	8	9			
		F	24	20	19	12	9	7	8			
	1978	MF	24	20	18	11	9	8	8			
		F	24	21	18	12	9	8	8			
UGANDA ‡	1970	MF	26	25	22	19	4	4				
		F	25	26	22	20	4	3				
	1975	MF	25	23	22	21	5	5				
		F	28	24	22	19	4	3				
	1976	MF	27	24	21	19	4	4				
		F	29	26	21	17	3	3				
	1977	MF	24	25	22	19	5	4				
		F	27	26	22	18	3	3				
UNITED REPUBLIC OF CAMEROON	1970	MF	29	23	18	15	7	5	3			
		F	34	25	18	14	5	3	2			
	1975	MF	28	21	17	16	7	7	4			
		F	31	23	18	16	6	4	2			
	1976	MF	28	21	18	16	7	6	4			
		F	31	22	18	16	5	4	3			
	1977	MF	27	21	18	16	7	6	4			
		F	31	23	17	15	6	4	3			
UNITED REPUBLIC OF TANZANIA ‡	1970	MF	25	24	22	21	4	3				
		F	28	25	22	21	3	2				
	1975	MF	26	25	22	20	4	4				
		F	28	27	22	19	2	2				
	1976	MF	25	24	23	21	3	3				
		F	28	25	23	21	2	2				
UPPER VOLTA	1970	MF	23	21	20	18	7	6	5			
		F	27	23	20	18	5	4	3			
	1975	MF	23	19	18	18	8	7	7			
		F	27	20	19	18	6	5	5			
	1977	MF	25	21	18	17	8	6	6			
		F	28	22	18	16	7	4	4			
	1978	MF	25	21	17	16	8	7	7			
		F	27	23	17	16	7	5	5			
ZAIRE	1970	MF	50	33	7	5	3	2				
		F	59	32	4	3	1	1				
	1975	MF	49	33	7	5	3	2				
		F	58	33	5	2	1	1				
	1976	MF	52	33	6	4	3	2				
		F	60	33	3	2	1	1				
	1977	MF	53	32	6	4	3	2				
		F	61	34	3	1	1	1				
ZAMBIA	1970	MF	29	29	16	15	10					
		F	34	33	13	12	8					
	1975	MF	29	26	23	11	10					
		F	32	27	24	10	7					

3.8　Percentage distribution (second level general) by grade
　　　Répartition en % (second degré général) par années d'études
　　　Distribución en % (segundo grado general) por años de estudio

COUNTRY PAYS PAIS	YEAR ANNEE AÑO	SEX SEXE SEXO	GRADE / ANNEES D'ETUDES / AÑOS DE ESTUDIO									
			I	II	III	IV	V	VI	VII	VIII	IX	X
ZAMBIA (CONT.)	1976	MF	28	27	24	11	10					
		F	30	28	25	9	8					
	1977	MF	27	25	25	11	10					
		F	29	27	27	9	8					
AMERICA, NORTH												
BARBADOS ‡	1970	MF	30	26	20	13	10	1	1			
		F	30	26	20	13	10	1	1			
	1975	MF	24	22	23	14	16	1				
		F	22	21	22	15	19	1				
	1976	MF	21	22	24	15	17	2				
		F	20	21	22	16	20	1				
	1977	MF	20	21	22	19	18	1				
		F	19	20	21	19	20	1				
CANADA	1970	MF	29	26	23	19	3					
		F	29	27	23	19	3					
	1975	MF	18	18	19	18	16	9	2			
		F	18	18	19	18	16	9	2			
	1976	MF	18	18	18	18	17	12	——>			
		F	18	18	18	18	17	12	——>			
	1977	MF	17	18	19	18	16	12				
		F	17	18	18	18	16	12				
COSTA RICA	1970	MF	37	24	17	11	10					
		F	36	25	18	12	10					
	1975	MF	29	24	25	14	9					
		F	28	24	25	14	8					
	1976	MF	29	28	19	14	9					
CUBA	1970	MF	43	24	14	11	4	4	0			
		F	41	23	15	12	5	4	0			
	1975	MF	37	29	16	10	4	3	2			
		F	37	29	16	10	4	3	2			
	1976	MF	37	27	17	10	4	3	2			
		F	36	27	18	10	5	3	2			
EL SALVADOR	1970	MF	33	26	22	11	8					
		F	34	27	22	9	7					
	1975	MF	43	33	24							
		F	43	33	24							
	1976	MF	42	32	26							
		F	42	32	26							
GRENADA	1970	MF	20	20	19	19	18	2	2			
		F	22	21	19	19	16	1	2			
	1976	MF	35	31	15	9	8	1	1			
		F	34	31	15	9	9	1	1			
	1977	MF	35	28	16	9	9	1	1			
		F	34	29	17	10	9	1	1			

Percentage distribution (second level general) by grade   3.8
Répartition en % (second degré général) par années d'études
Distribución en % (segundo grado general) por años de estudio

COUNTRY PAYS PAIS	YEAR ANNEE AÑO	SEX SEXE SEXO	GRADE / ANNEES D'ETUDES / AÑOS DE ESTUDIO									
			I	II	III	IV	V	VI	VII	VIII	IX	X
GUADELOUPE ‡	1976	MF	26	24	22	18	4	2	2			
		F	26	25	21	19	4	3	3			
	1978	MF	27	26	18	17	6	3	3			
		F	26	26	18	17	6	3	3			
GUATEMALA ‡	1970	MF	33	21	17	13	10	6	1			
		F	32	22	17	13	10	7	0			
	1975	MF	31	21	17	14	10	6	1			
		F	31	22	17	13	10	7	0			
HONDURAS ‡	1974	MF	42	27	21	5	4					
	1975	MF	42	27	21	6	4					
JAMAICA	1975	MF	27	23	22	13	11	4	1			
		F	26	23	22	13	12	4	1			
	1976	MF	27	24	22	14	11	1	0			
		F	25	24	23	15	12	1	0			
MARTINIQUE ‡	1976	MF	25	22	28	15	5	2	3			
		F	25	22	25	16	6	3	3			
	1978	MF	25	27	18	16	7	3	3			
		F	24	26	19	18	8	3	3			
MEXICO	1975	MF	31	24	20	12	8	4	0			
		F	36	28	23	7	5	3	0			
	1976	MF	31	25	20	11	8	5				
		F	34	27	22	8	6	3				
	1977	MF	31	25	21	11	8	5				
		F	33	27	22	8	6	4				
	1978	MF	31	25	20	11	8	5				
MONTSERRAT	1976	MF	51	2	28	11	9	1				
		F	48	2	27	13	9	1				
	1977	MF	32	22	29	9	7	2				
		F	32	23	27	8	8	1				
NICARAGUA	1970	MF	36	25	20	11	8	1				
PANAMA ‡	1970	MF	34	27	22	6	6	5				
	1975	MF	29	26	23	10	7	5				
		F	29	27	24	9	6	4				
	1977	MF	28	23	20	12	9	7				
		F	28	23	22	12	9	7				
	1978	MF	23	25	20	13	11	8				
		F	23	26	21	13	10	8				
PUERTO RICO ‡	1970	MF	23	20	18	16	13	10				
	1975	MF	21	20	18	17	13	11				
	1976	MF	22	20	18	16	13	10				
TRINIDAD AND TOBAGO ‡	1970	MF	21	20	18	17	21	4				
		F	21	20	18	17	20	3				
	1975	MF	16	17	16	26	17	8				
		F	16	16	16	26	17	8				

3.8 Percentage distribution (second level general) by grade
Répartition en % (second degré général) par années d'études
Distribución en % (segundo grado general) por años de estudio

COUNTRY PAYS PAIS	YEAR ANNEE AÑO	SEX SEXE SEXO	GRADE / ANNEES D'ETUDES / AÑOS DE ESTUDIO									
			I	II	III	IV	V	VI	VII	VIII	IX	X
TURKS AND CAICOS ISLANDS	1977	MF	23	22	20	16	19					
		F	19	21	25	16	19					
UNITED STATES OF AMERICA ‡	1975	MF	13	13	21	20	18	16				
	1976	MF	12	13	21	20	18	16				
	1977	MF	12	13	20	20	18	16				
AMERICA, SOUTH												
ARGENTINA ‡	1970	MF	25	21	19	18	16	1	0			
		F	24	20	20	18	16	0	0			
	1975	MF	25	22	19	18	15	1	0			
		F	25	22	20	18	15	1	0			
	1977	MF	24	22	20	18	16	1	0			
		F	25	22	19	18	16	1	0			
	1978	MF	25	21	20	18	15	1	0			
		F	25	21	20	18	15	1	0			
BOLIVIA ‡	1970	MF	40	27	19	15						
		F	40	27	18	14						
	1975	MF	36	28	20	16						
BRAZIL	1971	MF	49	31	20	0						
		F	49	31	20	0						
CHILE	1970	MF	36	28	22	14						
		F	35	28	23	14						
	1974	MF	34	27	21	17						
		F	33	28	22	17						
	1975	MF	34	27	23	16						
		F	33	27	24	16						
	1977	MF	34	26	23	17						
		F	33	26	23	17						
	1978	MF	34	27	24	16						
		F	33	26	24	17						
COLOMBIA ‡	1970	MF	35	22	16	12	9	7				
		F	36	22	16	11	8	7				
	1975	MF	24	27	17	14	10	8				
		F	24	26	18	15	11	7				
	1977	MF	23	19	16	18	13	11				
		F	23	20	16	16	13	12				
	1978	MF	26	20	16	13	13	11				
		F	24	20	17	14	13	12				
ECUADOR ‡	1970	MF	36	25	21	8	6	5				
		F	38	27	22	6	4	3				
	1974	MF	34	24	19	11	8	5				
		F	34	25	19	10	7	4				
	1975	MF	33	23	19	11	8	6				
		F	34	25	19	9	7	6				

Percentage distribution (second level general) by grade 3.8
Répartition en % (second degré général) par années d'études
Distribución en % (segundo grado general) por años de estudio

COUNTRY PAYS PAIS	YEAR ANNEE AÑO	SEX SEXE SEXO	GRADE / ANNEES D'ETUDES / AÑOS DE ESTUDIO									
			I	II	III	IV	V	VI	VII	VIII	IX	X
FALKLAND ISLANDS (MALVINAS)	1974	MF	22	25	23	17	14					
		F	19	23	26	19	13					
	1975	MF	20	22	14	28	16					
		F	16	20	18	27	18					
	1977	MF	25	16	24	17	17					
		F	31	13	25	19	13					
	1978	MF	24	24	22	17	14					
		F	21	28	21	17	13					
FRENCH GUIANA ‡	1976	MF	26	24	20	15	7	4	4			
		F	26	22	19	16	8	4	4			
	1978	MF	27	24	19	14	8	4	4			
		F	26	24	18	14	9	4	5			
GUYANA	1970	MF	35	28	21	7	8	1				
		F	35	28	22	7	7	1				
	1975	MF	30	26	25	9	9	1				
		F	30	26	25	9	9	1				
	1976	MF	30	25	25	9	10	1				
		F	30	25	25	9	10	1				
PARAGUAY	1970	MF	34	25	19	10	7	5				
		F	34	26	20	10	6	5				
	1975	MF	27	21	17	14	11	9				
		F	25	21	17	15	12	10				
	1976	MF	28	21	16	14	11	9				
		F	26	21	17	15	12	10				
	1977	MF	28	21	17	14	11	9				
		F	26	21	17	15	12	10				
PERU	1970	MF	29	22	19	16	13					
		F	29	22	20	16	13					
	1975	MF	30	24	18	15	13					
	1976	MF	29	24	20	15	12					
SURINAME	1975	MF	39	31	18	11	2	1				
		F	37	32	19	10	1	1				
	1976	MF	33	36	17	11	2	1				
		F	32	37	17	11	2	1				
	1977	MF	32	29	22	13	3	1				
		F	32	30	22	13	2	1				
URUGUAY ‡	1970	MF	25	21	18	15	13	9				
		F	25	20	18	15	13	9				
	1977	MF	27	22	17	14	11	9				
		F	24	21	18	14	12	11				
	1978	MF	27	23	19	13	11	7				
		F	25	22	18	15	12	8				
VENEZUELA ‡	1970	MF	35	24	19	13	10					
		F	35	24	19	12	10					
	1974	MF	36	25	21	11	8					
		F	35	25	21	11	7					

3.8 Percentage distribution (second level general) by grade
Répartition en % (second degré général) par années d'études
Distribución en % (segundo grado general) por años de estudio

COUNTRY PAYS PAIS	YEAR ANNEE AÑO	SEX SEXE SEXO	GRADE / ANNEES D'ETUDES / AÑOS DE ESTUDIO									
			I	II	III	IV	V	VI	VII	VIII	IX	X
VENEZUELA (CONT.) ‡	1975	MF	33	23	19	14	9	1				
		F	32	23	19	14	10	1				
	1976	MF	32	23	19	14	10	1				
		F	31	23	19	14	10	1				
	1977	MF	32	23	19	14	10	1				
		F	31	23	20	14	10	2				
ASIA												
AFGHANISTAN ‡	1970	MF	36	23	17	13	7	5				
		F	33	23	17	13	8	6				
	1974	MF	29	21	17	14	11	8				
		F	32	21	16	12	10	8				
	1975	MF	30	20	16	14	11	8				
		F	33	20	17	13	10	8				
	1976	MF	30	20	16	14	11	8				
		F	33	20	17	13	10	8				
BAHRAIN ‡	1970	MF	29	29	16	12	14					
		F	26	29	18	14	13					
	1975	MF	29	25	18	14	13					
		F	26	24	20	15	15					
	1977	MF	30	26	0	18	13	13				
		F	28	24	0	18	15	15				
	1978	MF	29	26	0	17	14	13				
		F	26	25	0	18	15	15				
BANGLADESH ‡	1976	MF	28	22	19	14	12	3	2			
		F	28	26	21	11	9	3	2			
	1977	MF	26	22	18	14	11	5	4			
		F	30	26	18	11	9	4	2			
BHUTAN	1974	MF	39	19	19	11	8	4				
		F	47	22	19	7	4	1				
	1976	MF	34	29	19	8	10					
		F	45	29	16	9	2					
	1977	MF	39	26	19	10	6					
		F	40	29	18	8	6					
	1978	MF	37	27	19	10	6					
		F	47	24	17	9	3					
BRUNEI	1970	MF	26	26	28	9	8	2	1			
		F	27	28	30	7	7	1	0			
	1975	MF	30	21	23	12	10	2	2			
		F	30	21	24	13	9	2	1			
	1977	MF	22	20	25	12	16	2	3			
		F	20	20	27	11	17	2	2			
	1978	MF	25	17	25	13	16	3	2			
		F	24	17	27	12	16	2	1			
BURMA	1970	MF	27	20	18	15	10	10				
		F	27	20	17	15	10	10				

Percentage distribution (second level general) by grade 3.8
Répartition en % (second degré général) par années d'études
Distribución en % (segundo grado general) por años de estudio

COUNTRY PAYS PAIS	YEAR ANNEE AÑO	SEX SEXE SEXO	GRADE / ANNEES D'ETUDES / AÑOS DE ESTUDIO									
			I	II	III	IV	V	VI	VII	VIII	IX	X
BURMA (CONT.)	1975	MF	26	20	18	15	12	10				
		F	25	20	17	15	12	11				
	1976	MF	27	20	17	18	7	11				
		F	25	19	17	19	7	13				
	1977	MF	27	21	17	16	9	9				
		F	25	20	17	17	9	10				
CYPRUS ‡	1970	MF	25	19	17	15	13	11	1			
		F	25	19	17	15	13	11	1			
	1975	MF	20	18	17	16	15	14	1			
		F	19	18	17	16	15	14	1			
	1977	MF	18	19	18	15	14	15	1			
		F	17	18	18	16	15	15	1			
	1978	MF	20	17	18	16	14	14	1			
		F	19	16	18	17	15	15	0			
HONG KONG	1970	MF	27	20	18	15	14	5	1			
		F	27	20	18	16	14	4	1			
	1975	MF	26	23	19	15	12	3	1			
		F	26	23	20	16	12	3	1			
	1976	MF	25	21	19	16	13	4	1			
		F	25	21	20	17	14	3	1			
	1977	MF	24	21	19	17	14	4	1			
		F	24	21	19	17	15	4	1			
INDIA	1974	MF	27	22	18	15	13	5	0			
		F	29	23	18	14	12	5	0			
	1975	MF	27	23	19	15	12	4	0			
		F	28	24	19	14	11	4	0			
	1976	MF	27	23	19	15	12	4	0			
		F	29	23	19	14	11	3	0			
INDONESIA ‡	1970	MF	30	26	22	8	7	7				
	1975	MF	34	26	21	7	6	5				
		F	36	26	21	7	5	5				
	1977	MF	34	25	22	8	6	5				
		F	35	26	22	7	6	4				
	1978	MF	31	26	22	9	7	5				
		F	33	27	22	8	6	4				
IRAN	1975	MF	38	27	17	2	9	8				
		F	38	27	17	2	9	7				
	1976	MF	26	21	18	12	11	12				
		F	25	21	17	13	12	12				
	1977	MF	26	22	18	12	10	7	6			
		F	25	21	17	13	11	7	6			
IRAQ	1970	MF	30	24	20	9	9	8				
		F	31	23	19	10	9	7				
	1975	MF	31	24	20	9	8	8				
		F	31	25	18	9	9	9				
	1977	MF	33	24	19	9	8	8				
		F	33	24	19	9	8	7				

3.8 Percentage distribution (second level general) by grade
Répartition en % (second degré général) par années d'études
Distribución en % (segundo grado general) por años de estudio

COUNTRY PAYS PAIS	YEAR ANNEE AÑO	SEX SEXE SEXO	GRADE / ANNEES D'ETUDES / AÑOS DE ESTUDIO									
			I	II	III	IV	V	VI	VII	VIII	IX	X
IRAQ (CONT.)	1978	MF	33	25	18	9	7	8				
		F	34	25	18	9	8	7				
ISRAEL	1974	MF	39	23	20	18	0					
		F	37	24	21	19	0					
	1975	MF	39	23	20	18	0					
		F	36	24	21	19	0					
	1976	MF	39	22	21	18	0					
		F	36	23	22	19	0					
	1977	MF	40	22	20	18	0					
		F	37	23	21	19	—					
JAPAN ‡	1970	MF	21	22	23	11	11	11	1			
	1975	MF	22	21	21	13	12	11	0			
	1977	MF	22	21	21	13	12	12	0			
		F	22	21	20	13	12	12	0			
	1978	MF	21	22	21	13	12	12	0			
		F	21	21	20	13	12	12	0			
JORDAN ‡	1970	MF	32	22	17	14	8	8				
		F	34	23	17	13	7	6				
	1974	MF	31	23	19	11	9	8				
		F	32	23	20	11	8	6				
	1975	MF	32	23	19	10	9	8				
		F	32	23	19	10	8	7				
	1977	MF	28	22	19	12	11	9				
		F	29	23	18	11	11	8				
	1978	MF	26	23	18	13	10	10				
		F	27	23	18	13	9	9				
KOREA, REPUBLIC OF	1970	MF	31	26	23	7	6	6				
		F	31	26	22	8	7	7				
	1975	MF	27	25	24	10	8	6				
		F	27	26	23	9	8	6				
	1978	MF	25	24	24	10	9	8				
		F	27	25	23	9	8	8				
	1979	MF	26	24	23	10	9	8				
		F	27	25	23	9	8	8				
KUWAIT ‡	1970	MF	23	20	17	14	9	7	5	4		
		F	23	20	18	14	10	7	5	4		
	1974	MF	22	17	15	13	10	9	7	6		
		F	21	17	15	13	11	10	8	6		
	1975	MF	24	17	15	12	12	9	7	6		
		F	22	16	14	12	13	9	8	6		
	1977	MF	21	18	15	12	13	9	7	5		
		F	20	18	15	12	13	9	7	6		
	1978	MF	22	18	15	12	11	9	7	6		
		F	21	17	15	12	12	10	7	6		
LAO PEOPLE'S DEMOCRATIC REPUBLIC ‡	1970	MF	39	19	15	13	6	4	3			
		F	38	21	16	11	7	4	3			

Percentage distribution (second level general) by grade 3.8
Répartition en % (second degré général) par années d'études
Distribución en % (segundo grado general) por años de estudio

COUNTRY PAYS PAIS	YEAR ANNEE AÑO	SEX SEXE SEXO	GRADE / ANNEES D'ETUDES / AÑOS DE ESTUDIO									
			I	II	III	IV	V	VI	VII	VIII	IX	X
LAO PEOPLE'S DEMOCRATIC REPUBLIC (CONT.) ‡	1976	MF F	49 50	29 29	15 15	4 3	2 2	2 1				
	1977	MF F	44 47	29 28	18 17	5 5	2 2	2 1				
MALAYSIA												
PENINSULAR MALAYSIA	1971	MF F	9 9	24 24	24 23	21 21	10 10	10 10	3 2			
	1975	MF F	7 7	25 26	22 22	21 21	12 12	11 10	2 1			
	1977	MF	8	24	22	21	12	10	3			
	1978	MF	8	24	23	20	11	11	3			
SABAH	1975	MF F	6 7	36 35	22 23	21 22	9 8	6 5	1 1			
	1976	MF F	6 6	29 29	29 29	21 21	8 8	7 7	1 1			
	1977	MF	6	27	24	27	8	7	0			
SARAWAK	1970	MF F	13 12	23 24	21 22	19 21	11 11	10 9	2 1			
	1975	MF F	16 15	25 25	22 22	17 17	10 10	8 8	3 2			
	1976	MF F	15 15	26 26	21 21	19 20	10 9	8 8	1 1			
	1977	MF F	14 14	25 25	22 22	19 19	11 11	8 8	1 1			
MONGOLIA	1974	MF F	25 24	22 21	17 17	18 18	12 12	3 4	3 3			
	1975	MF F	24 22	22 21	19 19	15 16	13 14	4 4	3 4			
NEPAL	1970	MF F	27 25	23 22	20 19	16 17	15 17					
	1976	MF	29	20	16	13	9	7	7			
	1977	MF	30	21	16	13	8	6	6			
OMAN	1974	MF F	49 47	21 16	17 24	9 12	3 —					
	1975	MF F	52 32	19 27	13 15	8 17	5 8	2 —				
	1977	MF F	60 54	18 23	11 9	4 6	3 4	3 4				
	1978	MF F	50 50	30 27	11 13	4 3	3 4	2 2				
PAKISTAN	1970	MF F	26 25	22 21	19 18	13 13	11 11	5 7	4 5			
	1975	MF F	*26 *26	*21 *22	*18 *18	*15 *14	*12 *11	*4 *5	*3 *4			
PHILIPPINES ‡	1970	MF	33	26	22	18						

3.8 Percentage distribution (second level general) by grade
Répartition en % (second degré général) par années d'études
Distribución en % (segundo grado general) por años de estudio

COUNTRY PAYS PAIS	YEAR ANNEE AÑO	SEX SEXE SEXO	GRADE / ANNEES D'ETUDES / AÑOS DE ESTUDIO									
			I	II	III	IV	V	VI	VII	VIII	IX	X
PHILIPPINES (CONT.) ‡	1975	MF	33	26	22	19						
	1976	MF	34	26	22	18						
QATAR ‡	1970	MF	31	23	19	11	8	7				
		F	33	24	19	11	7	6				
	1975	MF	25	22	19	14	11	9				
		F	26	23	21	14	9	8				
	1977	MF	26	21	17	15	12	10				
		F	23	22	18	16	11	9				
	1978	MF	27	20	18	14	11	10				
		F	25	19	19	14	13	10				
SAUDI ARABIA	1970	MF	37	24	17	11	7	4				
		F	48	19	15	9	6	3				
	1974	MF	35	24	17	11	7	5				
		F	36	26	17	11	6	4				
	1975	MF	33	25	19	10	8	6				
		F	33	26	19	10	8	5				
	1976	MF	31	25	20	10	7	7				
		F	30	25	21	10	7	7				
	1977	MF	31	23	20	12	8	6				
		F	31	24	21	10	8	6				
SINGAPORE	1970	MF	28	27	18	19	4	3				
		F	27	26	21	19	3	3				
	1975	MF	28	27	20	17	4	4				
		F	26	25	22	19	4	4				
	1977	MF	28	28	18	17	5	4				
		F	26	26	20	19	5	4				
	1978	MF	27	29	18	17	5	5				
		F	25	27	20	19	5	5				
SRI LANKA ‡	1970	MF	25	23	14	13	21	2	2			
		F	24	23	14	13	22	2	3			
	1975	MF	20	18	16	12	26	3	4			
		F	20	18	16	12	27	3	4			
	1977	MF	15	21	19	30	7	3	5			
		F	14	21	15	31	7	4	6			
	1978	MF	18	12	17	15	23	8	8			
	1979	MF	19	15	11	14	27	7	7			
SYRIAN ARAB REPUBLIC ‡	1970	MF	30	23	22	9	6	10				
		F	31	24	20	11	6	8				
	1975	MF	29	21	22	9	8	11				
		F	30	22	22	10	8	9				
	1977	MF	30	22	21	10	8	10				
		F	30	22	20	11	9	9				
	1978	MF	29	22	21	10	8	11				
		F	30	22	20	10	9	10				
THAILAND	1970	MF	35	29	24	8	4					
		F	35	29	24	8	5					

Percentage distribution (second level general) by grade   3.8
Répartition en % (second degré général) par années d'études
Distribución en % (segundo grado general) por años de estudio

COUNTRY PAYS PAIS	YEAR ANNEE AÑO	SEX SEXE SEXO	GRADE / ANNEES D'ETUDES / AÑOS DE ESTUDIO									
			I	II	III	IV	V	VI	VII	VIII	IX	X
THAILAND (CONT.)	1974	MF	35	30	25	7	4	0				
		F	34	29	24	7	4	0				
	1975	MF	34	29	25	7	4	0				
		F	33	29	25	8	5	0				
	1976	MF	32	29	25	8	6					
		F	31	28	24	10	8					
	1977	MF	30	28	25	16	——>					
		F	29	27	25	19	——>					
TURKEY	1970	MF	38	23	16	12	7	5	0			
		F	36	23	16	12	8	5	0			
UNITED ARAB EMIRATES ‡	1974	MF	34	24	14	12	8	7				
		F	36	24	16	12	7	6				
	1975	MF	33	25	17	12	8	6				
		F	35	25	16	12	7	5				
	1977	MF	32	23	18	12	9	7				
		F	31	23	17	13	9	7				
	1978	MF	32	22	19	11	9	7				
		F	32	21	19	12	9	7				
VIET—NAM	1976	MF	32	26	22	4	7	5	4			
		F	31	26	22	4	6	6	5			
YEMEN ‡	1970	MF	37	25	14	11	7	6				
	1975	MF	31	22	18	12	9	7				
		F	41	23	14	11	6	5				
YEMEN, DEMOCRATIC	1970	MF	38	24	20	9	5	4				
		F	42	19	19	10	5	5				
	1975	MF	33	27	18	9	6	6				
		F	33	28	17	10	6	6				
	1976	MF	35	25	19	9	7	5				
		F	38	23	20	8	8	4				
	1977	MF	33	27	19	9	6	6				
		F	32	28	18	10	6	6				
EUROPE												
AUSTRIA	1970	MF	24	22	20	18	9	3	2	2	0	
		F	24	22	20	19	8	3	2	2	1	
	1975	MF	22	21	21	19	9	3	3	2	0	
		F	22	21	21	20	8	3	3	3	0	
	1977	MF	21	21	21	20	9	2	2	2	0	
		F	21	21	22	21	8	3	2	2	0	
	1978	MF	21	21	21	21	9	3	2	2	0	
		F	21	21	21	21	8	3	2	2	0	
BELGIUM	1974	MF	25	22	19	14	11	9	0			
		F	25	22	20	13	11	9	0			
	1975	MF	25	21	19	14	11	9	0			
		F	25	22	20	13	11	9	0			

Percentage distribution (second level general) by grade
Répartition en % (second degré général) par années d'études
Distribución en % (segundo grado general) por años de estudio

COUNTRY PAYS PAIS	YEAR ANNEE AÑO	SEX SEXE SEXO	GRADE / ANNEES D'ETUDES / AÑOS DE ESTUDIO									
			I	II	III	IV	V	VI	VII	VIII	IX	X
BELGIUM (CONT.)	1976	MF	24	23	20	14	11	9	0			
		F	24	22	20	14	11	9	0			
	1977	MF	26	22	17	13	12	10	0			
		F	25	22	17	13	12	11	0			
BULGARIA ‡	1970	MF	40	30	30							
		F	40	31	29							
	1975	MF	37	31	31							
		F	38	31	31							
	1977	MF	36	32	32							
		F	36	32	32							
	1978	MF	37	31	33							
		F	37	30	33							
CZECHOSLOVAKIA	1970	MF	36	33	31	0						
		F	37	33	30	0						
	1975	MF	27	25	24	24						
		F	27	25	25	24						
	1977	MF	26	26	25	23						
		F	26	25	25	24						
	1978	MF	27	24	24	24						
		F	27	24	24	24						
DENMARK	1970	MF	25	24	22	18	6	5				
		F	24	24	22	19	6	5				
	1975	MF	23	22	22	20	7	6				
	1976	MF	23	22	22	20	7	6				
	1977	MF	23	22	20	23	6	6				
		F	22	21	20	23	7	6				
FINLAND	1975	MF	25	26	22	10	10	8				
	1977	MF	24	24	23	11	10	8				
		F	22	22	23	13	11	9				
	1978	MF	23	24	24	11	10	8				
		F	21	22	22	13	12	10				
FRANCE	1976	MF	23	23	19	17	8	5	6			
		F	22	21	19	17	9	6	6			
	1977	MF	22	23	20	17	8	5	5			
		F	21	21	19	17	9	6	6			
	1978	MF	22	21	20	17	8	5	6			
		F	21	20	20	17	10	6	6			
GERMANY, FEDERAL REPUBLIC OF ‡	1970	MF	16	20	19	17	15	6	3	2	2	
		F	16	20	19	17	15	6	2	2	2	
	1975	MF	18	18	18	17	14	6	3	3	2	
		F	18	18	18	17	14	7	3	3	2	
	1976	MF	17	17	18	17	15	7	3	3	2	
		F	17	17	18	17	16	8	2	3	2	
	1977	MF	17	17	17	17	16	8	3	2	3	
		F	17	16	17	17	16	9	3	2	2	

Percentage distribution (second level general) by grade 3.8
Répartition en % (second degré général) par années d'études
Distribución en % (segundo grado general) por años de estudio

COUNTRY PAYS PAIS	YEAR ANNEE AÑO	SEX SEXE SEXO	GRADE / ANNEES D'ETUDES / AÑOS DE ESTUDIO									
			I	II	III	IV	V	VI	VII	VIII	IX	X
GIBRALTAR	1974	MF	27	24	26	14	5	4				
		F	29	22	26	15	4	5				
	1975	MF	25	26	23	16	5	5				
		F	24	27	20	17	6	6				
	1976	MF	21	24	22	17	10	6				
		F	30	22	19	15	9	5				
	1977	MF	25	25	23	13	9	5				
		F	24	23	24	14	11	4				
GREECE ‡	1970	MF	25	19	17	15	13	10	1			
		F	25	19	17	15	13	11	0			
	1975	MF	21	19	17	16	14	13	0			
		F	21	19	17	16	14	13	0			
	1976	MF	22	19	17	16	14	12	0			
		F	21	19	17	16	14	13	0			
HUNGARY	1970	MF	25	27	26	22						
		F	26	27	25	22						
	1975	MF	25	25	25	24						
		F	26	25	25	24						
	1977	MF	24	24	26	26						
		F	25	24	26	25						
	1978	MF	27	24	24	25						
		F	27	24	24	25						
ICELAND	1974	MF	22	23	21	16	7	6	4			
		F	21	23	21	17	7	6	4			
	1975	MF	22	21	21	17	8	6	4			
		F	22	21	21	17	9	6	4			
	1976	MF	22	22	20	19	6	5	6			
		F	22	22	20	21	6	5	5			
ITALY	1970	MF	33	27	23	4	4	3	3	3		
		F	33	27	24	4	4	3	3	2		
	1975	MF	32	27	24	4	3	3	3	3		
		F	31	27	24	4	3	3	3	3		
	1976	MF	30	29	24	4	3	3	3	3		
		F	30	29	25	4	4	3	3	3		
	1977	MF	30	28	26	4	3	3	3	3		
		F	29	28	26	4	3	3	3	3		
LUXEMBOURG	1970	MF	23	19	19	12	10	8	9			
		F	24	21	18	12	9	7	8			
	1975	MF	34	20	16	12	6	5	6			
		F	34	21	17	12	6	5	6			
	1976	MF	32	24	20	7	6	6	6			
		F	31	27	19	7	6	5	5			
	1977	MF	32	26	19	6	6	5	6			
		F	31	26	20	7	6	5	5			
MALTA	1970	MF	56	14	12	11	6	1	1			
		F	55	13	11	11	7	1	1			

3.8 Percentage distribution (second level general) by grade
Répartition en % (second degré général) par années d'études
Distribución en % (segundo grado general) por años de estudio

COUNTRY PAYS PAIS	YEAR ANNEE AÑO	SEX SEXE SEXO	GRADE / ANNEES D'ETUDES / AÑOS DE ESTUDIO									
			I	II	III	IV	V	VI	VII	VIII	IX	X
MALTA (CONT.)	1975	MF	22	27	22	15	10	2	1			
		F	21	25	22	18	12	2	1			
	1976	MF	17	24	27	17	11	2	2			
		F	16	23	26	19	13	2	1			
	1977	MF	20	19	25	19	12	3	2			
		F	21	18	24	21	14	2	1			
NETHERLANDS	1970	MF	24	22	22	21	8	1				
		F	25	23	22	21	8	1				
	1975	MF	23	22	20	21	10	4				
		F	23	22	21	21	8	3				
	1977	MF	22	22	20	22	10	4				
		F	22	22	21	22	10	3				
	1978	MF	22	22	21	22	10	4				
		F	22	22	21	22	10	3				
POLAND	1970	MF	30	29	25	17						
		F	30	29	25	17						
	1975	MF	25	26	25	23						
		F	26	26	25	23						
	1976	MF	25	25	25	25						
	1977	MF	24	25	25	25						
PORTUGAL	1970	MF	27	26	12	9	14	4	8			
		F	26	26	13	9	14	4	7			
	1975	MF	33	17	26	9	16					
		F	31	18	27	9	15					
	1976	MF	26	27	22	10	16					
		F	25	27	23	10	15					
	1977	MF	26	22	28	9	15					
		F	24	21	29	10	16					
SAN MARINO	1970	MF	32	28	23	2	4	4	4	3		
		F	31	27	22	2	4	4	5	4		
	1975	MF	31	29	27	3	3	3	2	2		
		F	30	31	26	3	2	4	2	2		
	1977	MF	31	29	29	2	2	2	2	3		
		F	30	30	28	2	2	3	2	3		
	1978	MF	30	32	28	2	2	2	2	2		
		F	30	30	30	2	2	2	2	2		
SPAIN	1974	MF	27	23	23	11	9	7				
		F	27	23	24	11	9	6				
	1975	MF	29	22	21	11	11	7				
		F	28	22	21	11	10	7				
	1976	MF	27	23	19	11	11	9				
		F	27	23	19	11	11	9				
SWEDEN	1975	MF	28	27	27	7	6	4				
		F	27	26	26	8	8	4				
	1977	MF	30	28	26	7	6	3				
		F	29	27	25	8	7	4				

Percentage distribution (second level general) by grade   3.8
Répartition en % (second degré général) par années d'études
Distribución en % (segundo grado general) por años de estudio

COUNTRY PAYS PAIS	YEAR ANNEE AÑO	SEX SEXE SEXO	GRADE / ANNEES D'ETUDES / AÑOS DE ESTUDIO									
			I	II	III	IV	V	VI	VII	VIII	IX	X
SWEDEN (CONT.)	1978	MF	29	29	26	7	6	3				
		F	28	28	25	9	7	4				
YUGOSLAVIA ‡	1970	MF	26	23	20	17	4	3	3	3		
		F	25	22	20	17	5	4	4	3		
	1975	MF	22	21	20	19	8	4	3	3		
		F	23	20	19	18	9	4	4	3		
	1977	MF	20	19	18	17	12	7	2	3		
		F	20	19	18	17	12	8	2	3		
	1978	MF	19	19	19	17	12	10	2	2		
		F	19	19	19	17	12	10	2	2		
OCEANIA												
AUSTRALIA	1974	MF	16	24	22	19	11	7				
		F	16	24	22	19	11	7				
	1975	MF	15	24	23	19	11	7				
		F	15	24	23	20	11	7				
	1976	MF	15	23	22	20	12	8				
		F	15	23	22	20	12	8				
	1977	MF	15	23	22	20	12	8				
		F	14	22	24	20	12	8				
FIJI	1970	MF	35	35	24	6						
		F	37	36	23	4						
	1974	MF	36	38	22	5						
		F	36	39	22	4						
	1975	MF	35	36	24	5						
		F	36	37	24	4						
	1976	MF	35	35	24	6						
		F	35	36	24	4						
	1977	MF	33	36	24	6						
		F	33	37	24	5						
NEW ZEALAND	1974	MF	20	19	19	17	15	8	2			
		F	19	19	19	17	16	8	2			
	1975	MF	19	19	19	18	16	8	2			
		F	19	19	19	18	16	8	2			
	1976	MF	18	18	19	18	17	8	2			
		F	18	18	19	18	17	9	2			
NORFOLK ISLAND	1975	MF	32	29	22	17						
		F	28	34	23	15						
	1977	MF	32	29	22	17						
		F	28	34	23	15						
	1978	MF	25	31	25	19						
		F	25	25	31	19						
SAMOA	1975	MF	26	22	20	19	10	3	1			
		F	24	22	21	19	12	2	0			
	1977	MF	24	22	19	16	14	4	1			
		F	24	22	20	16	14	3	1			

3.8 Percentage distribution (second level general) by grade
Répartition en % (second degré général) par années d'études
Distribución en % (segundo grado general) por años de estudio

COUNTRY PAYS PAIS	YEAR ANNEE AÑO	SEX SEXE SEXO	GRADE / ANNEES D'ETUDES / AÑOS DE ESTUDIO									
			I	II	III	IV	V	VI	VII	VIII	IX	X
SAMOA (CONT.)	1978	MF	25	22	18	16	14	4	1			
		F	24	22	18	15	15	4	1			
TONGA	1975	MF	34	20	18	14	10	4	0			
		F	34	20	18	12	10	5	0			
	1977	MF	32	20	13	16	11	7	1			
		F	34	20	14	16	11	5	0			
	1978	MF	22	19	19	16	18	5	1			
		F	18	19	20	17	18	5	1			
U.S.S.R.												
U.S.S.R.	1970	MF	53	46	1							
	1975	MF	62	57	1							
	1977	MF	59	60	1							
BYELORUSSIAN S.S.R.	1970	MF	54	46	0							
	1975	MF	51	49	0							
	1977	MF	50	50	0							
	1978	MF	50	50	0							
UKRAINIAN S.S.R.	1970	MF	52	48	0							
	1975	MF	52	48	0							
	1976	MF	50	50	0							
	1977	MF	49	51	0							

ALGERIA:
E—> FOR 1975, 1977 AND 1978, POLYTECHNICAL
SECONDARY SCHOOLS ARE INCLUDED WITH GENERAL
EDUCATION.
FR—> POUR 1975, 1977 ET 1978, LES COLLEGES
D'ENSEIGNEMENT POLYTECHNIQUE SONT COMPTES AVEC
L'ENSEIGNEMENT GENERAL.
ESP> EN 1975, 1977 Y 1978, LOS COLEGIOS DE
ENSEÑANZA POLITECNICA FIGURAN INCLUIDOS CON LA
ENSEÑANZA GENERAL.

BURUNDI:
E—> FROM 1976, DATA REFER TO PUBLIC EDUCATION
ONLY.
FR—> A PARTIR DE 1976, LES DONNEES SE REFERENT A
L'ENSEIGNEMENT PUBLIC SEULEMENT.
ESP> A PARTIR DE 1976, LOS DATOS SE REFIEREN A
LA ENSEÑANZA PUBLICA SOLAMENTE.

EGYPT:
E—> NOT INCLUDING AL AZHAR UNIVERSITY.
FR—> LES DONNEES NE TIENNENT PAS COMPTE DE
L'UNIVERSITE AL AZHAR.
ESP> LOS DATOS NO INCLUYEN LA UNIVERSIDAD
AL AZHAR.

GHANA:
E—> DATA REFER TO PUBLIC EDUCATION ONLY.
FR—> LES DONNEES SE REFERENT A L'ENSEIGNEMENT
PUBLIC SEULEMENT.
ESP> LOS DATOS SE REFIEREN A LA ENSEÑANZA
PUBLICA SOLAMENTE.

KENYA:
E—> EXCEPTING 1970, FIGURES INCLUDE DATA ON
OTHER SECOND LEVEL EDUCATION OF A VOCATIONAL OR
TECHNICAL NATURE.
FR—> A L'EXCEPTION DE 1970, LES CHIFFRES
COMPRENNENT LES DONNEES RELATIVES A L'AUTRE ENSEI-
GNEMENT DU SECOND DEGRE DE CARACTERE TECHNIQUE OU
PROFESSIONNEL.
ESP> SALVO PARA 1970, LAS CIFRAS COMPRENDEN LOS
DATOS RELATIVOS A LA OTRA ENSEÑANZA DE SEGUNDO
GRADO DE CARACTER TECNICO O PROFESIONAL.

MAURITIUS:
E—> DATA DO NOT INCLUDE ENROLMENT FOR RODRIGUEZ.
FR—> LES DONNEES NE COMPRENNENT PAS LES EFFECTIFS
DE RODRIGUEZ.
ESP> LOS DATOS NO INCLUYEN LOS EFECTIVOS DE
RODRIGUEZ.

Percentage distribution (second level general) by grade 3.8
Répartition en % (second degré général) par années d'études
Distribución en % (segundo grado general) por años de estudio

NIGERIA:
   E—> DATA INCLUDE COMMERCIAL SCHOOLS.
   FR-> LES DONNEES COMPRENNENT LES ECOLES
COMMERCIALES.
   ESP> LOS DATOS INCLUYEN LAS ESCUELAS DE COMERCIO.

REUNION:
   E—> FOR 1974, 1975 AND 1976, FIGURES INCLUDE
TEACHER TRAINING.
   FR-> POUR 1974, 1975 ET 1976, LES CHIFFRES
INCLUENT L'ENSEIGNEMENT NORMAL.
   ESP> EN 1974, 1975 Y 1976, LAS CIFRAS INCLUYEN
LA ENSEÑANZA NORMAL.

SEYCHELLES:
   E—> FOR 1970, ENROLMENT FOR GRADE VII IS SHOWN
IN GRADE VI.
   FR-> POUR 1970, LES EFFECTIFS DE LA SEPTIEME
ANNEE D'ETUDES SONT INCLUS DANS LA SIXIEME.
   ESP> EN 1970, LOS EFECTIVOS DEL SEPTIMO AÑO DE
ESTUDIOS QUEDAN INCLUIDOS EN EL SEXTO.

UGANDA:
   E—> DATA REFER TO PUBLIC AND AIDED SCHOOLS
ONLY.
   FR-> LES DONNEES SE REFERENT AUX ECOLES PUBLIQUES
ET SUBVENTIONNEES SEULEMENT.
   ESP> LOS DATOS SE REFIEREN A LAS ESCUELAS PUBLICAS
Y SUBVENCIONADAS SOLAMENTE.

UNITED REPUBLIC OF TANZANIA:
   E—> FIGURES INCLUDE DATA ON OTHER SECOND LEVEL
EDUCATION OF A VOCATIONAL OR TECHNICAL NATURE.
   FR-> LES CHIFFRES COMPRENNENT LES DONNEES
RELATIVES A L'AUTRE ENSEIGNEMENT DU SECOND DEGRE
DE CARACTERE TECHNIQUE OU PROFESSIONNEL.
   ESP> LAS CIFRAS COMPRENDEN LOS DATOS RELATIVOS
A LA OTRA ENSEÑANZA DE SEGUNDO GRADO DE CARACTER
TECNICO O PROFESIONAL.

BARBADOS:
   E—> FOR 1975, 1976 AND 1977, FIGURES INCLUDE
DATA ON OTHER SECOND LEVEL EDUCATION OF A VOCATIONAL
OR TECHNICAL NATURE.
   FR-> POUR 1975, 1976 ET 1977, LES CHIFFRES
COMPRENNENT LES DONNEES RELATIVES A L'AUTRE ENSEI-
GNEMENT DU SECOND DEGRE DE CARACTERE TECHNIQUE OU
PROFESSIONNEL.
   ESP> EN 1975, 1976 Y 1977, SE INCLUYEN LOS DATOS
RELATIVOS A LA ENSEÑANZA DE SEGUNDO GRADO DE
CARACTER TECNICO O PROFESIONAL.

GUADELOUPE:
   E—> FOR 1976, FIGURES INCLUDE TEACHER TRAINING.
   FR-> POUR 1976, LES CHIFFRES INCLUENT L'ENSEI-
GNEMENT NORMAL.
   ESP> EN 1976, LOS DATOS COMPRENDEN LA ENSEÑANZA
NORMAL.

GUATEMALA:
   E—> DATA REFER TO ALL SECOND LEVEL, EXCLUDING
ARTISTIC EDUCATION (1,023; F. 357 PUPILS IN 1972)
AND INCLUDE EVENING SCHOOLS.
   FR-> LES DONNEES SE REFERENT AU TOTAL DE L'ENSEI-
GNEMENT DU SECOND DEGRE, COMPTE NON TENU DE L'ENSEI-
GNEMENT ARTISTIQUE (1 023, F. 357 ELEVES EN 1972)
ET Y COMPRIS LES ECOLES DU SOIR.
   ESP> LOS DATOS SE REFIEREN AL TOTAL DE LA
ENSEÑANZA DE SEGUNDO GRADO, EXCLUIDA LA ENSEÑANZA
ARTISTICA (1 023 ALUMNOS F 357, EN 1972), PERO
INCLUIDAS LAS ESCUELAS NOCTURNAS.

HONDURAS:
   E—> DATA INCLUDE PART-TIME STUDENTS.
   FR-> LES DONNEES COMPRENNENT LES ELEVES A TEMPS
PARTIEL.
   ESP> LOS DATOS COMPRENDEN LOS ALUMNOS DE JORNADA
PARCIAL.

MARTINIQUE:
   E—> FOR 1976, FIGURES INCLUDE TEACHER TRAINING.
   FR-> POUR 1976, LES CHIFFRES INCLUENT L'ENSEI-
GNEMENT NORMAL.
   ESP> EN 1976, LOS DATOS COMPRENDEN LA ENSEÑANZA
NORMAL.

PANAMA:
   E—> DATA REFER TO PUBLIC EDUCATION ONLY AND
FROM 1975, CHANGES IN THE EDUCATIONAL SYSTEM ARE
BEING GRADUALLY APPLIED.
   FR-> LES DONNEES SE REFERENT A L'ENSEIGNEMENT
PUBLIC SEULEMENT. A PARTIR DE 1975, UN CHANGEMENT
DE STRUCTURE EST MIS GRADUELLEMENT EN APPLICATION.
   ESP> LOS DATOS SE REFIEREN A LA ENSEÑANZA
PUBLICA SOLAMENTE Y A PARTIR DE 1975, UN CAMBIO
DE ESTRUCTURA SE PONE PAULATINAMENTE EN APLICACION.

PUERTO RICO:
   E—> DATA REFER TO PUBLIC EDUCATION ONLY.
   FR-> LES DONNEES SE REFERENT A L'ENSEIGNEMENT
PUBLIC SEULEMENT.
   ESP> LOS DATOS SE REFIEREN A LA ENSEÑANZA
PUBLICA SOLAMENTE.

TRINIDAD AND TOBAGO:
   E—> FOR 1975, FIGURES INCLUDE GOVERNMENT-
MAINTAINED AND AIDED SCHOOLS ONLY.
   FR-> POUR 1975, LES CHIFFRES NE COMPRENNENT QUE
LES ECOLES PUBLIQUES ET SUBVENTIONNEES.
   ESP> EN 1975, LOS DATOS SE REFIEREN A LAS
ESCUELAS PUBLICAS Y SUBVENCIONADAS SOLAMENTE.

UNITED STATES OF AMERICA:
   E—> DATA REFER TO HIGH SCHOOLS AND RELATE TO
PUBLIC EDUCATION ONLY.
   FR-> LES DONNEES SE REFERENT AUX ECOLES
D'ENSEIGNEMENT SECONDAIRE (HIGH SCHOOLS) ET SE
RAPPORTENT A L'ENSEIGNEMENT PUBLIC SEULEMENT.
   ESP> LOS DATOS SE REFIEREN A LAS ESCUELAS DE
ENSEÑANZA SECUNDARIA (HIGH SCHOOLS) Y A LA
ENSEÑANZA PUBLICA SOLAMENTE.

ARGENTINA:
   E—> FOR 1978, DATA INCLUDE PART-TIME EDUCATION.
   FR-> POUR 1978, LES DONNEES COMPRENNENT LES
ELEVES A TEMPS PARTIEL.
   ESP> EN 1978, LOS DATOS COMPRENDEN LOS ALUMNOS
DE JORNADA PARCIAL.

BOLIVIA:
   E—> FOR 1975, DATA REFER TO ALL SECOND LEVEL
EDUCATION.
   FR-> POUR 1975, LES DONNEES SE REFERENT A TOUT
L'ENSEIGNEMENT DU SECOND DEGRE.
   ESP> EN 1975, LOS DATOS SE REFIEREN A TODA LA
ENSEÑANZA DE SEGUNDO GRADO.

COLOMBIA:
   E—> DATA REFER TO ALL SECOND LEVEL EDUCATION.
   FR-> LES DONNEES SE REFERENT A TOUT L'ENSEI-
GNEMENT DU SECOND DEGRE.
   ESP> LOS DATOS SE REFIEREN A TODA LA ENSEÑANZA
DE SEGUNDO GRADO.

ECUADOR:
   E—> FIGURES INCLUDE EVENING SCHOOLS.
   FR-> Y COMPRIS LES ECOLES DU SOIR.
   ESP> INCLUIDAS LAS ESCUELAS NOCTURNAS.

FRENCH GUIANA:
   E—> FOR 1976, DATA INCLUDE TEACHER TRAINING.
   FR-> POUR 1976, LES DONNEES INCLUENT L'ENSEI-
GNEMENT NORMAL.
   ESP> EN 1976, LOS DATOS INCLUYEN LA ENSEÑANZA
NORMAL.

3.8 Percentage distribution (second level general) by grade
Répartition en % (second degré général) par années d'études
Distribución en % (segundo grado general) por años de estudio

URUGUAY:
E—> FOR 1977 AND 1978, DATA INCLUDE OTHER SECOND LEVEL EDUCATION OF A VOCATIONAL OR TECHNICAL NATURE.
FR-> POUR 1977 ET 1978, LES DONNEES COMPRENNENT L'AUTRE ENSEIGNEMENT DU SECOND DEGRE DE CARACTERE TECHNIQUE OU PROFESSIONNEL.
ESP> EN 1977 Y 1978, LOS DATOS INCLUYEN LA OTRA ENSEÑANZA DE SEGUNDO GRADO DE CARACTER TECNICO O PROFESIONAL.

VENEZUELA:
E—> BEGINNING 1974, DATA REFER TO ALL SECOND LEVEL EDUCATION AND DUE TO THE REORGANIZATION OF THE EDUCATIONAL SYSTEM DATA REPORTED FOR GENERAL EDUCATION INCLUDE THOSE FOR THE FIRST CYCLE OF TEACHER TRAINING AND OTHER SECOND LEVEL EDUCATION OF A VOCATIONAL OR TECHNICAL NATURE.
FR-> A PARTIR DE 1974, LES DONNEES SE REFERENT A TOUT L'ENSEIGNEMENT DU SECOND DEGRE ET SUIVENT LA REORGANISATION DU SYSTEME SCOLAIRE, C'EST A-DIRE QUE LES DONNEES RELATIVES A L'ENSEIGNEMENT GENERAL INCLUENT LE PREMIER CYCLE DE L'ENSEI-GNEMENT NORMAL ET DE L'AUTRE ENSEIGNEMENT DU SECOND DEGRE DE CARACTERE TECHNIQUE OU PROFESSIONNEL.
ESP> A PARTIR DE 1974, LOS DATOS SE REFIEREN A TODA LA ENSEÑANZA DE SEGUNDO GRADO Y SIGUEN LA REORGANIZACION DEL SISTEMA ESCOLAR, ES DECIR, QUE LOS DATOS RELATIVOS A LA ENSEÑANZA GENERAL INCLUYEN EL PRIMER CICLO DE LA ENSEÑANZA NORMAL Y DE LA OTRA ENSEÑANZA DE SEGUNDO GRADO DE CARACTER TECNICO O PROFESIONAL.

AFGHANISTAN:
E—> BEGINNING 1975, CHANGES IN THE EDUCATIONAL SYSTEM ARE BEING GRADUALLY APPLIED.
FR-> A PARTIR DE 1975, UN CHANGEMENT DE STUCTURE EST MIS GRADUELLEMENT EN APPLICATION.
ESP> A PARTIR DE 1975, UN CAMBIO DE ESTRUCTURA SE PONE PAULATINAMENTE EN APLICACION.

BAHRAIN:
E—> DATA REFER TO PUBLIC EDUCATION AND DO NOT INCLUDE RELIGIOUS SCHOOLS. IN ADDITION, FROM 1977, CHANGES IN THE EDUCATIONAL SYSTEM ARE BEING GRADUALLY APPLIED.
FR-> LES DONNEES SE REFERENT A L'ENSEIGNEMENT PUBLIC ET NE COMPRENNENT PAS LES ECOLES RELIGIEUSES. DE PLUS, A PARTIR DE 1977, LE CHANGEMENT DE STRUCTURE EST MIS GRADUELLEMENT EN APPLICATION.
ESP> LOS DATOS SE REFIEREN A LA ENSEÑANZA PUBLICA Y NO COMPRENDEN LAS ESCUELAS RELIGIOSAS. ADEMAS, A PARTIR DE 1977, UN CAMBIO DE ESTRUCTURA SE PONE PAULATINAMENTE EN APLICACION.

BANGLADESH:
E—> DATA REFER TO PUBLIC EDUCATION ONLY.
FR-> LES DONNEES SE REFERENT A L'ENSEIGNEMENT PUBLIC SEULEMENT.
ESP> LOS DATOS SE REFIEREN A LA ENSEÑANZA PUBLICA SOLAMENTE.

CYPRUS:
E—> THE DATA SHOWN DO NOT INCLUDE TURKISH SCHOOLS.
FR-> LES DONNEES NE COMPRENNENT PAS LES ECOLES TURQUES.
ESP> LOS DATOS NO COMPRENDEN LAS ESCUELAS TURCAS.

INDONESIA:
E—> DATA DO NOT INCLUDE RELIGIOUS SCHOOLS.
FR-> LES DONNEES NE COMPRENNENT PAS LES ECOLES RELIGIEUSES.
ESP> LOS DATOS NO COMPRENDEN LAS ESCUELAS RELIGIOSAS.

JAPAN:
E—> DATA INCLUDE SPECIAL EDUCATION AND PART-TIME STUDENTS.
FR-> LES DONNEES COMPRENNENT L'EDUCATION SPECIALE ET LES ELEVES A TEMPS PARTIEL.
ESP> LOS DATOS COMPRENDEN LA EDUCACION ESPECIAL Y LOS ALUMNOS DE JORNADA PARCIAL.

JORDAN:
E—> DATA REFER TO THE EAST BANK ONLY. INCLUDING UNRWA SCHOOLS WITH 34,317 (F. 15,892) PUPILS IN 1978.
FR-> LES DONNEES SE REFERENT A LA RIVE ORIENTALE SEULEMENT. Y COMPRIS LES ECOLES DE L'"UNRWA" QUI COMPTAIENT 34 317 ELEVES (F. 15 892) EN 1978.
ESP> LOS DATOS SE REFIEREN A LA ORILLA ORIENTAL SOLAMENTE. INCLUIDAS LA ESCUELAS DEL O.O.P.S.R.P. QUE TENIAN 34 317 ALUMNOS (F 15 892) IN 1978.

KUWAIT:
E—> DATA REFER TO PUBLIC EDUCATION ONLY.
FR-> LES DONNEES SE REFERENT A L'ENSEIGNEMENT PUBLIC SEULEMENT.
ESP> LOS DATOS SE REFIEREN A LA ENSEÑANZA PUBLICA SOLAMENTE.

LAO, PEOPLE'S DEMOCRATIC REPUBLIC:
E—> FOR 1970, DATA REFER TO PUBLIC EDUCATION ONLY.
FR-> POUR 1970, LES DONNEES SE REFERENT A L'ENSEIGNEMENT PUBLIC SEULEMENT.
ESP> EN 1970, LOS DATOS SE REFIEREN A LA ENSEÑANZA PUBLICA SOLAMENTE.

PHILIPPINES:
E—> DATA REFER TO ALL SECOND LEVEL EDUCATION.
FR-> LES DONNEES SE REFERENT A TOUT L'ENSEI-GNEMENT DU SECOND DEGRE.
ESP> LOS DATOS SE REFIEREN A TODA LA ENSEÑANZA DE SEGUNDO GRADO.

QATAR:
E—> DATA REFER TO PUBLIC EDUCATION ONLY.
FR-> LES DONNEES SE REFERENT A L'ENSEIGNEMENT PUBLIC SEULEMENT.
ESP> LOS DATOS SE REFIEREN A LA ENSEÑANZA PUBLICA SOLAMENTE.

SRI LANKA:
E—> DATA REFER TO PUBLIC EDUCATION ONLY.
FR-> LES DONNEES SE REFERENT A L'ENSEIGNEMENT PUBLIC SEULEMENT.
ESP> LOS DATOS SE REFIEREN A LA ENSEÑANZA PUBLICA SOLAMENTE.

SYRIAN ARAB REPUBLIC:
E—> DATA INCLUDE UNRWA SCHOOLS WITH 23,036 (F. 10,379) PUPILS IN 1978.
FR-> LES DONNEES COMPRENNNENT LES ECOLES DE L'"UNRWA" QUI COMPTAIENT 23 036 ELEVES (F. 10 379) EN 1978.
ESP> LOS DATOS INCLUYEN LAS ESCUELAS DEL OOPSRP QUE TENIAN 23 036 ALUMNOS (F 10 379) EN 1978.

UNITED ARAB EMIRATES:
E—> DATA REFER TO PUBLIC EDUCATION AND DO NOT INCLUDE RELIGIOUS SCHOOLS.
FR-> LES DONNEES SE REFERENT A L'ENSEIGNEMENT PUBLIC ET NE COMPRENNENT PAS LES ECOLES RELI-GIEUSES.
ESP> LOS DATOS SE REFIEREN A LA ENSEÑANZA PUBLICA Y NO INCLUYEN LAS ESCUELAS RELIGIOSAS.

YEMEN:
E—> DATA REFER TO PUBLIC EDUCATION ONLY.
FR-> LES DONNEES SE REFERENT A L'ENSEIGNEMENT PUBLIC SEULEMENT.

Percentage distribution (second level general) by grade 3.8
Répartition en % (second degré général) par années d'études
Distribución en % (segundo grado general) por años de estudio

YEMEN (CONT.):
 ESP> LOS DATOS SE REFIEREN A LA ENSEÑANZA
PUBLICA SOLAMENTE.

BULGARIA:
 E—> DATA INCLUDE EVENING AND CORRESPONDENCE
COURSES.
 FR—> Y COMPRIS LES COURS DU SOIR ET PAR
CORRESPONDANCE.
 ESP> INCLUIDOS LOS CURSOS NOCTURNOS Y POR
CORRESPONDENCIA.

GERMANY, FEDERAL REPUBLIC OF:
 E—> DATA CORRESPONDING TO THE ACTUAL STRUCTURE
OF THIS LEVEL OF EDUCATION ARE NOT AVAILABLE.
 FR—> LES DONNEES CORRESPONDANTES A LA STRUCTURE
ACTUELLE DE CE NIVEAU D'ENSEIGNEMENT NE SONT PAS
DISPONIBLES.
 ESP> NO SE DISPONE DE LOS DATOS CORRESPONDIENTES
A LA ESTRUCTURA ACTUAL DE ESTE GRADO DE ENSEÑANZA.

GREECE:
 E—> DATA INCLUDE EVENING SCHOOLS WHICH ARE OF
7 YEARS DURATION.
 FR-> LES DONNEES COMPRENNENT LES ECOLES DU SOIR
D'UNE DUREE DE 7 ANS.
 ESP> LOS DATOS COMPRENDEN LAS ESCUELAS NOCTURNAS
DE UNA DURACION DE 7 ANOS.

YUGOSLAVIA:
 E—> FOR 1975, DATA INCLUDE SPECIAL EDUCATION.
 FR-> POUR 1975, LES DONNEES INCLUENT L'EDUCATION
SPECIALE.
 ESP> EN 1975, LOS DATOS INCLUYEN LA EDUCACION
ESPECIAL.

Percentage repeaters by grade (second level general)   3.9
% des redoublants par années d'études (second degré général)
% de repetidores por años de estudio (segundo grado general)

3.9 Education at the second level (general): percentage repeaters by grade

Enseignement du second degré (général): pourcentage des redoublants par années d'études

Enseñanza de segundo grado (general): porcentaje de repetidores por años de estudio

NUMBER OF COUNTRIES AND TERRITORIES PRESENTED IN THIS TABLE: 100	NOMBRE DE PAYS ET DE TERRITOIRES PRESENTES DANS CE TABLEAU: 100	NUMERO DE PAISES Y DE TERRITORIOS PRESENTADOS EN ESTE CUADRO: 100

COUNTRY PAYS PAIS	YEAR ANNEE AÑO	SEX SEXE SEXO	PERCENTAGE REPEATERS BY GRADE POURCENTAGE DE REDOUBLANTS PAR ANNEES D'ETUDES PORCENTAJE DE REPETIDORES POR AÑOS DE ESTUDIO									
			TOTAL	I	II	III	IV	V	VI	VII	VIII	IX
AFRICA												
ALGERIA ‡	1970	MF	*12 924	6	8	7	9	5	4	9		
		F	*3 782	5	9	7	10	5	5	8		
	1975	MF	*26 431	4	5	4	10	4	3	13		
		F	*8 615	3	4	4	10	4	2	18		
	1977	MF	*41 082	5	4	4	11	4	3	13		
		F	*13 085	4	3	4	11	4	3	13		
	1978	MF	*52 275	5	5	5	10	5	5	15		
		F	*17 661	4	4	4	11	5	5	16		
BENIN	1970	MF	2 692	9	11	14	21	11	18	15		
		F	1 004	11	15	17	25	17	18	18		
	1975	MF	7 135	9	11	18	25	9	19	31		
		F	2 324	11	13	21	28	12	22	27		
	1978	MF	6 805	7	5	14	24	8	6	38		
	1979	MF	6 955	6	7	12	24	4	3	22		
BURUNDI ‡	1970	MF	190	3	5	5	7	8	2			
		F	23	3	6	6	5	2	—			
	1977	MF	585	9	9	9	9	9	9	8		
		F	214	11	12	13	13	11	14	5		
CENTRAL AFRICAN REPUBLIC	1970	MF	1 002	11	9	11	13	10	3	9		
		F	145	5	10	19	15	11	5	9		
CHAD	1970	MF	969	9	10	14	13	6	4	17		
	1974	MF	1 623	9	10	11	20	18	14	13		

3.9 Percentage repeaters by grade (second level general)
   % des redoublants par années d'études (second degré général)
   % de repetidores por años de estudio (segundo grado general)

COUNTRY PAYS PAIS	YEAR ANNEE AÑO	SEX SEXE SEXO	PERCENTAGE REPEATERS BY GRADE POURCENTAGE DE REDOUBLANTS PAR ANNEES D'ETUDES PORCENTAJE DE REPETIDORES POR AÑOS DE ESTUDIO									
			TOTAL	I	II	III	IV	V	VI	VII	VIII	IX
CONGO	1970	MF	5 082	13	17	20	24	12	11	5		
		F	1 751	15	20	24	31	12	8	4		
	1975	MF	16 429	19	18	17	20	9	16	14		
		F	7 107	22	20	20	26	10	22	10		
	1977	MF	28 193	23	20	19	28	21	12	31		
		F	12 235	25	24	22	31	30	18	55		
	1978	MF	35 989	26	22	23	36	21	20	28		
		F	14 884	28	24	26	39	19	26	42		
DJIBOUTI	1974	MF	141	9	5	7	9	13	13	23		
		F	45	11	4	5	8	12	13	19		
	1975	MF	92	5	4	7	10	7	11	12		
		F	31	6	3	10	9	6	12	7		
EGYPT	1974	MF	*249 456	6	5	34	5	4	31			
	1975	MF	*247 941	*5	*6	*32	*5	*4	*28			
	1977	MF	*305 035	6	6	29	5	5	35			
		F	*92 382	5	5	26	3	2	30			
	1978	MF	*338 596	7	7	32	5	5	37			
		F	*107 013	6	6	30	3	3	50			
GABON	1970	MF	784	11	8	10	9	11	7	10		
		F	225	11	6	13	9	7	—	5		
GAMBIA	1975	MF	85	0	0	1	2	9	3			
		F	24	0	1	1	2	14	0			
	1977	MF	421	6	5	6	8	1	3			
		F	148	7	7	6	7	1	—			
	1978	MF	143	1	1	3	4	—	1			
		F	43	1	1	4	3	—	3			
GHANA ‡	1970	MF	1 400	3	3	4	4	1	0	0		
		F	478	3	4	6	4	1	0	—		
	1975	MF	*7 796	*2	*2	*2	*0	*1	—	*0		
		F	*3 741	*2	*2	*3	*0	*0	—	*0		
	1976	MF	*7 796	*1	*2	*2	*0	*0	—	*0		
		F	*3 741	*2	*2	*3	*0	*0	—	*0		
GUINEA—BISSAU	1975	MF	251	13	17	21	12	8				
	1976	MF	378	21	12	4	—	18				
	1977	MF	882	15	27	14	21	8				
		F	306	22	48	18	32	21				
IVORY COAST	1970	MF	6 744	9	10	13	14	9	9	8		
		F	*1 621	14	10	14	14	*12	*5	*8		
	1975	MF	13 009	9	11	16	17	11	14	26		
		F	3 860	13	13	19	20	10	13	25		
	1976	MF	12 803	9	9	13	15	9	11	24		
		F	4 125	14	14	16	18	10	9	24		
LIBERIA	1977	MF	3 508	7	5	7	9	12	8			
		F	1 306	8	7	8	11	19	10			

Percentage repeaters by grade (second level general) 3.9
% des redoublants par années d'études (second degré général)
% de repetidores por años de estudio (segundo grado general)

COUNTRY PAYS PAIS	YEAR ANNEE AÑO	SEX SEXE SEXO	PERCENTAGE REPEATERS BY GRADE POURCENTAGE DE REDOUBLANTS PAR ANNEES D'ETUDES PORCENTAJE DE REPETIDORES POR AÑOS DE ESTUDIO									
			TOTAL	I	II	III	IV	V	VI	VII	VIII	IX
LIBYAN ARAB JAMAHIRIYA ‡	1970	MF	9 288	24	15	25	17	13	25			
		F	1 003	16	9	16	6	6	17			
	1975	MF	12 004	6	11	13	7	7	12			
		F	4 553	13	7	11	6	2	10			
	1976	MF	24 326	18	11	14	7	4	14			
		F	6 159	13	7	12	5	1	9			
	1977	MF	28 796	20	11	14	7	5	10			
		F	8 334	15	9	13	4	2	7			
MADAGASCAR	1970	MF	12 920	10	9	11	20	13	24	21		
		F	5 525	11	10	11	21	12	22	20		
	1975	MF	8 759	5	3	3	10	4	17	26		
		F	3 691	5	3	3	10	4	17	26		
MALI	1970	MF	8 164	28	18	40	2	37	18			
	1975	MF	10 701	20	21	28	3	33	20			
MAURITANIA	1970	MF	*374	*10	*9	*8	*18	*11	*7	*18		
MAURITIUS ‡	1975	MF	4 238	4	5	5	9	11	2	12		
		F	2 302	4	7	7	11	14	2	13		
	1977	MF	8 656	6	6	8	15	22	2	20		
		F	3 822	6	6	8	16	21	2	22		
	1978	MF	9 709	9	10	8	14	22	1	17		
		F	3 962	9	7	7	11	19	1	20		
MOROCCO	1970	MF	*50 116	*14	*15	*17	*29	*10	*5	*14		
	1975	MF	*72 937	9	11	14	28	12	10	33		
		F	*23 569	8	11	14	28	11	9	32		
	1977	MF	*78 398	9	10	9	24	14	8	34		
		F	*29 226	9	9	9	24	12	9	32		
	1978	MF	*84 315	8	9	10	23	12	8	33		
		F	*29 226	7	9	9	23	11	8	33		
NIGER	1970	MF	515	11	7	8	2	3	8	16		
		F	126	10	5	8	4	4	7	26		
	1975	MF	1 582	9	12	15	12	15	12	10		
		F	432	9	13	16	11	6	7	8		
	1976	MF	1 819	8	10	14	12	15	9	16		
		F	541	8	8	17	16	9	4	21		
REUNION ‡	1974	MF	5 057	15	10	12	13	9	9	18		
	1975	MF	5 327	13	11	12	12	7	9	20		
	1976	MF	5 681	15	12	8	13	16	10	11		
	1978	MF	5 361	13	10	12	9	14	13	26		

3.9   Percentage repeaters by grade (second level general)
   % des redoublants par années d'études (second degré général)
   % de repetidores por años de estudio (segundo grado general)

COUNTRY PAYS PAIS	YEAR ANNEE AÑO	SEX SEXE SEXO	PERCENTAGE REPEATERS BY GRADE POURCENTAGE DE REDOUBLANTS PAR ANNEES D'ETUDES PORCENTAJE DE REPETIDORES POR AÑOS DE ESTUDIO									
			TOTAL	I	II	III	IV	V	VI	VII	VIII	IX
RWANDA	1970	MF	203	2	5	2	2	2	0			
	1975	MF	499	6	8	4	3	5	3	1		
		F	222	8	12	6	4	3	2	–		
	1976	MF	433	7	7	3	4	5	3	2		
		F	177	9	10	1	6	9	2	–		
SAO TOME AND PRINCIPE	1976	MF	950	21	38	39	15	2	–	–		
		F	504	23	42	47	17	–	–	–		
SENEGAL	1970	MF	5 983	9	11	10	14	13	11	19		
SEYCHELLES	1970	MF	10	0	0	2	4	–	–			
		F	6	0	0	3	5	–	–			
	1974	MF	53	1	1	3	6	–	–	8		
		F	49	2	2	6	9	–	–			
	1977	MF	12	0	1	0	–	–	–			
		F	9	0	1	0	–	–	–			
	1978	MF	28	0	1	1	2	–	–	–		
		F	23	0	1	1	4	–	–			
SIERRA LEONE	1970	MF	3 297	9	10	10	12	10	1	1		
		F	1 296	13	13	13	16	19	–	–		
	1977	MF	8 675	17	16	17	18	11	2	2		
		F	3 066	19	16	18	20	14	4	4		
SUDAN	1970	MF	6 095	4	4	4	3	8	11			
		F	1 652	4	4	4	4	7	9			
SWAZILAND	1970	MF	826	13	14	3	4	4	–			
		F	383	12	16	4	3	5	–			
	1975	MF	712	4	6	4	4	3	–			
		F	329	4	6	4	5	2	–			
	1977	MF	662	4	5	3	3	1	2			
		F	338	4	5	3	3	0	–			
	1978	MF	634	4	4	3	2	0	–			
		F	324	4	3	4	2	0	–			
TOGO	1970	MF	3 839	16	17	21	28	18	19	24		
	1975	MF	9 067	14	10	16	27	12	25	15		
		F	2 542	17	14	19	32	12	28	19		
	1977	MF	17 671	22	16	17	24	15	35	20		
		F	4 594	27	19	19	26	15	31	17		
	1978	MF	21 106	18	18	18	30	15	23	22		
		F	5 329	19	21	20	31	17	23	23		

Percentage repeaters by grade (second level general) 3.9
% des redoublants par années d'études (second degré général)
% de repetidores por años de estudio (segundo grado general)

COUNTRY PAYS PAIS	YEAR ANNEE AÑO	SEX SEXE SEXO	PERCENTAGE REPEATERS BY GRADE POURCENTAGE DE REDOUBLANTS PAR ANNEES D'ETUDES PORCENTAJE DE REPETIDORES POR AÑOS DE ESTUDIO									
			TOTAL	I	II	III	IV	V	VI	VII	VIII	IX
TUNISIA	1975	MF	*18 442	13	12	12	9	12	10	23		
		F	*5 835	12	10	9	9	14	11	23		
	1977	MF	*19 048	12	10	11	8	10	9	27		
		F	*6 291	11	8	11	7	9	8	28		
	1978	MF	*20 510	11	9	13	9	10	10	28		
		F	*6 867	10	8	12	8	9	9	29		
UGANDA ‡	1976	MF	1 367	1	2	3	4	4	4			
	1977	MF	1 134	1	2	2	4	1	4			
UNITED REPUBLIC OF CAMEROON	1970	MF	6 116	8	8	11	17	9	16	24		
		F	1 688	8	9	12	18	10	22	27		
	1975	MF	11 385	8	7	9	18	8	17	21		
		F	3 918	9	8	11	20	10	19	24		
	1976	MF	14 097	8	9	10	20	8	20	20		
		F	4 770	9	10	11	21	8	21	20		
	1977	MF	15 668	9	8	10	18	8	21	22		
		F	5 376	10	10	11	20	8	20	23		
UPPER VOLTA	1970	MF	994	10	9	11	15	9	12	16		
		F	200	11	7	8	12	11	4	6		
	1975	MF	1 913	9	14	10	21	11	17	33		
		F	*524	*9	*9	*11	*23	*14	*16	*24		
	1978	MF	2 292	8	9	11	23	10	11	27		
		F	754	10	9	15	25	9	7	30		
ZAIRE	1970	MF	21 205	11	11	12	12	14	10			
		F	4 989	13	12	18	18	14	9			
ZAMBIA	1976	MF	617	0	0	3	0	0				
		F	329	0	0	5	0	0				
	1977	MF	731	0	0	3	0	0				
		F	406	0	0	5	0	0				
AMERICA, NORTH												
COSTA RICA	1970	MF	6 114	14	13	10	8	1				
		F	3 034	14	12	10	6	2				
CUBA	1970	MF	25 895	16	12	9	18	3	22	19		
		F	16 183	18	14	11	20	2	27	34		
	1975	MF	9 627	3	2	1	3	2	2	2		
	1976	MF	8 759	2	2	1	2	3	1	1		
EL SALVADOR	1970	MF	1 108	2	2	2	2	0				
		F	452	2	2	2	2	0				
	1975	MF	171	1	1	0						
		F	57	1	1	0						
	1976	MF	174	1	1	0						
		F	62	0	1	0						

3.9 Percentage repeaters by grade (second level general)
% des redoublants par années d'études (second degré général)
% de repetidores por años de estudio (segundo grado general)

COUNTRY PAYS PAIS	YEAR ANNEE AÑO	SEX SEXE SEXO	PERCENTAGE REPEATERS BY GRADE POURCENTAGE DE REDOUBLANTS PAR ANNEES D'ETUDES PORCENTAJE DE REPETIDORES POR AÑOS DE ESTUDIO									
			TOTAL	I	II	III	IV	V	VI	VII	VIII	IX
GUADELOUPE	1976	MF	4 538	9	12	12	13	18	17	23		
	1978	MF	3 738	8	10	10	13	14	18	25		
JAMAICA	1975	MF	*6 720	3	2	6	2	3	0	2		
		F	*3 175	2	2	6	2	3	0	2		
	1976	MF	7 408	3	2	6	2	5	0	2		
		F	3 667	2	2	6	2	5	–	2		
MARTINIQUE ‡	1976	MF	5 639	12	12	15	16	19	13	29		
	1978	MF	4 454	12	10	13	16	18	18	23		
MEXICO	1976	MF	51 700	1	1	1	6	5	3			
	1977	MF	41 417	1	1	1	4	4	2			
PANAMA ‡	1975	MF	4 356	8	6	5	5	7	2			
	1977	MF	6 018	10	8	6	6	8	5			
	1978	MF	6 309	10	8	6	7	8	6			
TRINIDAD AND TOBAGO ‡	1970	MF	1 107	0	0	0	0	9	3			
		F	505	0	0	0	0	8	4			
AMERICA, SOUTH												
ARGENTINA	1970	MF	27 192	11	8	7	5	1	0	0		
		F	14 282	10	7	6	4	0	0	1		
	1975	MF	27 895	9	7	6	5	1	0	2		
BOLIVIA	1970	MF	1 368	1	4	2	1					
BRAZIL	1971	MF	48 954	12	8	3	–					
		F	19 359	11	7	2	–					
CHILE	1974	MF	23 307	13	8	5	1					
		F	13 232	13	8	5	1					
	1975	MF	35 131	15	13	14	4					
		F	22 032	15	14	15	5					
	1977	MF	24 725	10	8	9	2					
		F	13 981	10	8	9	2					
ECUADOR ‡	1970	MF	16 506	11	9	9	9	5	2			
		F	5 938	9	8	7	6	3	1			
	1974	MF	23 381	9	8	7	10	6	2			
		F	8 891	8	7	5	8	3	1			
	1975	MF	26 867	9	8	7	11	7	2			
		F	10 776	8	7	6	8	6	1			
FRENCH GUIANA	1978	MF	264	2	6	3	7	14	12	18		
GUYANA	1970	MF	7 358	10	11	22	9	12	0			
		F	3 694	9	12	22	9	12	0			
	1975	MF	13 335	10	12	44	7	29	4			
		F	6 569	9	11	44	6	29	4			

Percentage repeaters by grade (second level general)   3.9
% des redoublants par années d'études (second degré général)
% de repetidores por años de estudio (segundo grado general)

COUNTRY PAYS PAIS	YEAR ANNEE AÑO	SEX SEXE SEXO	PERCENTAGE REPEATERS BY GRADE POURCENTAGE DE REDOUBLANTS PAR ANNEES D'ETUDES PORCENTAJE DE REPETIDORES POR AÑOS DE ESTUDIO								
			TOTAL	I	II	III	IV	V	VI	VII	VIII	IX
PERU	1970	MF	41 468	12	10	9	7	3				
		F	15 975	11	9	9	6	2				
	1975	MF	57 528	11	11	10	9	3				
	1976	MF	42 315	8	7	6	6	2				
SURINAME	1975	MF	3 806	19	14	9	9	—	—			
		F	1 983	18	14	7	8	—	—			
	1976	MF	2 098	9	7	8	13	—	—			
		F	1 106	9	6	12	11	—	—			
	1977	MF	3 593	14	14	12	13	—	—			
		F	1 901	13	14	11	15	—	—			
VENEZUELA ‡	1974	MF	56 919	12	11	14	—	—				
		F	28 716	11	10	14	—	—				
	1975	MF	72 000	12	11	13	9	4	2			
		F	36 389	11	10	14	8	4	1			
	1976	MF	78 847	13	11	13	9	3	2			
	1977	MF	87 105	13	12	15	9	4	1			
ASIA												
AFGHANISTAN	1974	MF	38 689	33	25	19	20	14	6			
		F	5 081	34	29	22	23	14	10			
BAHRAIN ‡	1970	MF	1 845	12	16	21	8	16				
		F	633	4	13	21	3	18				
	1975	MF	3 525	22	25	26	13	24				
		F	1 655	17	25	25	12	27				
	1977	MF	2 472	14	14	—	15	9	18			
		F	1 107	12	15	—	12	6	17			
	1978	MF	2 148	9	12	—	14	7	19			
		F	876	6	11	—	13	6	13			
BHUTAN	1976	MF	174	16	23	27	42	10				
	1977	MF	129	4	19	18	8	4				
	1978	MF	251	7	20	11	32	34				
		F	37	3	13	23	37	—				
BRUNEI	1975	MF	860	0	0	14	1	24	—	25		
		F	424	0	0	17	1	20	—	23		
	1977	MF	1 983	6	3	17	3	34	—	33		
		F	1 015	5	2	19	2	33	—	41		
	1978	MF	2 497	6	4	29	2	36	2	42		
		F	1 336	5	5	33	2	36	2	34		
BURMA	1970	MF	200 783	19	22	22	27	20	62			
		F	74 712	18	21	24	20	14	64			
CYPRUS ‡	1970	MF	1 672	5	5	5	5	3	1	—		
		F	686	5	4	4	4	2	2	—		
	1975	MF	586	2	2	1	1	1	0	—		
		F	162	1	1	1	1	0	0	—		

3.9 Percentage repeaters by grade (second level general)
% des redoublants par années d'études (second degré général)
% de repetidores por años de estudio (segundo grado general)

COUNTRY PAYS PAIS	YEAR ANNEE AÑO	SEX SEXE SEXO	PERCENTAGE REPEATERS BY GRADE POURCENTAGE DE REDOUBLANTS PAR ANNEES D'ETUDES PORCENTAJE DE REPETIDORES POR AÑOS DE ESTUDIO								
			TOTAL	I	II	III	IV	V	VI	VII	VIII	IX
CYPRUS (CONT.) ‡	1977	MF	884	4	3	2	2	1	0	–		
		F	356	3	2	2	1	1	0	–		
	1978	MF	931	3	3	2	2	2	0	0		
		F	351	2	2	2	2	1	0	–		
INDONESIA ‡	1975	MF	53 875	3	2	2	4	3	3			
	1977	MF	60 520	3	2	2	3	2	2			
	1978	MF	78 738	3	3	2	3	2	2			
IRAQ	1970	MF	92 531	32	32	38	11	14	41			
		F	24 085	33	29	28	13	15	30			
	1975	MF	98 833	18	21	25	8	11	33			
		F	24 600	20	19	16	9	10	22			
	1977	MF	136 548	17	24	24	10	11	35			
		F	31 443	15	21	14	8	8	25			
	1978	MF	159 593	21	21	23	8	11	32			
		F	38 777	19	19	14	8	10	23			
JAPAN ‡			–	–	–	–	–	–	–			
JORDAN ‡	1974	MF	11 571	10	7	13	4	1	10			
		F	4 629	9	8	14	3	1	7			
	1975	MF	12 901	10	8	12	4	1	6			
		F	5 266	10	8	12	4	2	4			
	1977	MF	9 716	7	5	2	3	1	12			
		F	4 014	7	5	2	3	1	11			
	1978	MF	9 263	6	4	2	3	2	7			
		F	3 429	6	4	2	2	1	4			
KOREA, REPUBLIC OF ‡	1970	MF	4 828	0	0	0	1	1	0			
		F	1 309	0	0	0	0	0	0			
KUWAIT ‡	1974	MF	17 362	32	23	23	20	14	15	11	9	
		F	6 515	29	19	19	15	11	14	8	6	
	1975	MF	17 130	28	22	20	12	15	17	10	10	
		F	6 003	24	17	16	7	9	13	8	7	
	1977	MF	17 831	23	17	15	6	14	15	9	7	
		F	7 067	18	13	11	5	17	15	8	8	
	1978	MF	16 955	19	15	13	7	18	11	5	5	
		F	6 406	15	12	11	5	16	9	4	4	
LAO PEOPLE'S DEMOCRATIC REPUBLIC ‡	1970	MF	445	5	5	8	6	9	11	9		
		F	123	6	7	10	6	9	5	7		
MALAYSIA PENINSULAR MALAYSIA ‡	1971	MF	12 081	–	–	0	5	1	10	0		
		F	4 956	–	–	–	6	0	9	0		
SABAH ‡			–	–	–	–	–	–	–			
SARAWAK ‡			–	–	–	–	–	–	–			

Percentage repeaters by grade (second level general) 3.9
% des redoublants par années d'études (second degré général)
% de repetidores por años de estudio (segundo grado general)

COUNTRY PAYS PAIS	YEAR ANNEE AÑO	SEX SEXE SEXO	PERCENTAGE REPEATERS BY GRADE POURCENTAGE DE REDOUBLANTS PAR ANNEES D'ETUDES PORCENTAJE DE REPETIDORES POR AÑOS DE ESTUDIO								
			TOTAL	I	II	III	IV	V	VI	VII	VIII	IX
MONGOLIA	1974	MF	7 330	11	5	3	1	0	1	0		
	1975	MF	5 834	7	5	3	1	0	1	0		
OMAN	1974	MF	12	2	1	2	2	0				
	1975	MF	16	1	2	2	1	—	—			
		F	8	3	2	11	3	—	—			
	1977	MF	369	9	3	8	2	1	14			
		F	61	8	3	11	—	—	10			
	1978	MF	610	10	4	13	2	0	3			
		F	101	6	7	8	8	2	—			
QATAR ‡	1970	MF	280	7	10	7	9	8	8			
		F	26	1	2	4	1	8	3			
	1975	MF	763	12	11	7	9	6	9			
		F	194	5	7	4	6	2	8			
	1977	MF	741	8	8	6 ·	11	3	4			
		F	311	6	5	5	14	3	4			
	1978	MF	1 074	11	8	9	12	6	6			
		F	337	5	6	8	7	2	6			
SAUDI ARABIA	1974	MF	14 346	12	9	7	9	4	4			
		F	2 643	6	6	5	5	1	2			
	1975	MF	16 546	13	8	8	7	3	3			
		F	3 186	7	5	4	6	1	2			
SINGAPORE	1970	MF	6 389	0	4	6	11	0	7			
		F	2 962	0	3	5	10	0	8			
	1975	MF	5 364	0	4	3	9	0	9			
		F	2 379	0	3	2	8	0	6			
	1977	MF	7 573	0	5	7	11	1	8			
		F	3 587	0	5	6	9	1	5			
	1978	MF	8 156	0	6	8	9	3	11			
		F	3 767	0	5	6	7	2	10			
SRI LANKA ‡	1970	MF	170 125	14	8	14	5	44	11	48		
		F	84 634	13	7	12	5	45	12	50		
	1975	MF	160 806	9	8	6	1	36	6	30		
	1977	MF	116 074	9	5	4	24	3	2	24		
	1979	MF	119 467	7	7	9	4	19	4	15		
SYRIAN ARAB REPUBLIC	1970	MF	53 209	16	9	29	4	7	29			
		F	10 661	13	9	20	4	3	21			
	1975	MF	*75 951	*15	*11	*29	*4	*3	*25			
		F	*19 177	*13	*9	*23	*4	*1	*22			
	1977	MF	71 077	14	10	22	4	2	21			
		F	20 078	12	9	18	4	1	20			
	1978	MF	75 914	15	10	21	5	3	21			
		F	21 676	13	7	18	4	2	19			

3.9 Percentage repeaters by grade (second level general)
% des redoublants par années d'études (second degré général)
% de repetidores por años de estudio (segundo grado general)

COUNTRY PAYS PAIS	YEAR ANNEE AÑO	SEX SEXE SEXO	TOTAL	I	II	III	IV	V	VI	VII	VIII	IX
							PERCENTAGE REPEATERS BY GRADE POURCENTAGE DE REDOUBLANTS PAR ANNEES D'ETUDES PORCENTAJE DE REPETIDORES POR AÑOS DE ESTUDIO					
THAILAND	1974	MF	36 494	4	4	2	12	5				
		F	12 367	3	3	1	11	5				
	1975	MF	44 165	4	4	3	11	10	—			
		F	15 669	3	3	2	10	11	—			
	1976	MF	38 361	4	4	2	2	7				
		F	12 713	3	3	2	1	7				
	1977	MF	35 257	4	4	2	1	——>				
		F	11 576	3	3	2	1	——>				
UNITED ARAB EMIRATES ‡	1974	MF	1 280	20	21	12	20	7	8			
		F	406	15	19	9	18	4	2			
	1975	MF	868	11	10	7	10	4	4			
		F	291	7	9	7	8	2	0			
	1977	MF	1 356	12	10	10	2	2	2			
		F	374	8	7	3	2	1	3			
EUROPE												
AUSTRIA ‡	1977	MF	27 666	3	4	4	5	8	14	13	3	1
	1978	MF	27 031	3	3	4	4	8	15	14	4	1
BELGIUM	1974	MF	101 774	22	25	29	32	25	25	34		
		F	47 624	22	25	28	31	22	22	28		
	1975	MF	103 775	21	25	29	32	25	25	28		
		F	49 267	21	24	29	32	23	22	18		
	1976	MF	104 453	20	22	26	29	23	22	73		
		F	50 399	21	23	27	29	22	21	88		
	1977	MF	103 131	24	25	26	28	24	23	22		
		F	48 550	24	24	26	26	20	21	17		
BULGARIA ‡	1970	MF	5 356	5	8	3						
	1975	MF	1 687	1	2	1						
	1977	MF	958	1	1	1						
	1978	MF	699	1	1	0						
CZECHOSLOVAKIA	1970	MF	686	1	1	0						
		F	377	1	1	0						
	1975	MF	417	0	1	0	0					
		F	216	0	0	0	0					
	1977	MF	273	0	0	0	0					
		F	149	0	0	0	0					
	1978	MF	280	0	0	0	0					
		F	158	0	0	0	0					
FRANCE	1976	MF	358 626	10	7	9	8	11	7	18		
	1977	MF	360 261	10	8	8	8	12	7	18		
	1978	MF	344 063	8	8	8	8	14	7	17		

Percentage repeaters by grade (second level general)   3.9
% des redoublants par années d'études (second degré général)
% de repetidores por años de estudio (segundo grado general)

COUNTRY PAYS PAIS	YEAR ANNEE AÑO	SEX SEXE SEXO	PERCENTAGE REPEATERS BY GRADE POURCENTAGE DE REDOUBLANTS PAR ANNEES D'ETUDES PORCENTAJE DE REPETIDORES POR AÑOS DE ESTUDIO									
			TOTAL	I	II	III	IV	V	VI	VII	VIII	IX
GERMANY, FEDERAL REPUBLIC OF ‡	1970	MF	238 442	4	4	5	5	5	7	11	8	3
		F	85 215	3	3	4	4	4	5	8	6	2
	1975	MF	263 841	2	4	6	5	5	7	7	5	3
		F	100 128	1	3	4	4	4	6	5	4	2
	1976	MF	248 587	2	4	5	5	5	5	7	5	3
		F	97 943	1	3	4	5	4	4	6	3	2
	1977	MF	247 597	1	3	5	6	5	5	4	4	3
		F	96 829	1	2	4	5	4	4	3	3	2
GREECE ‡	1970	MF	40 286	10	10	10	11	8	1	12		
		F	14 690	8	8	7	8	6	1	10		
	1975	MF	27 574	7	6	5	5	3	1	6		
		F	10 272	6	5	4	4	3	0	7		
	1976	MF	26 715	6	6	5	6	4	1	4		
		F	9 376	4	4	3	4	3	0	5		
HUNGARY	1970	MF	1 463	1	2	1	0					
ITALY	1970	MF	204 291	11	8	5	6	5	6	3	3	
		F	75 115	9	7	4	4	3	4	2	2	
	1975	MF	174 341	8	6	3	4	4	4	2	2	
		F	61 445	6	4	2	3	3	3	2	2	
	1976	MF	187 234	8	6	3	4	4	4	2	3	
		F	65 045	6	4	2	3	3	3	2	2	
	1977	MF	227 231	9	8	3	5	4	5	3	3	
		F	78 166	7	6	2	4	3	3	2	2	
LUXEMBOURG	1970	MF	1 013	13	12	17	5	6	3	17		
		F	321	9	8	12	4	6	3	10		
	1975	MF	1 172	7	10	8	4	7	7	10		
		F	479	6	8	7	5	7	5	7		
	1976	MF	1 734	11	12	11	9	6	8	19		
		F	770	9	10	9	8	4	7	19		
	1977	MF	1 555	10	11	8	9	7	4	13		
		F	687	9	9	8	8	6	2	11		
MALTA	1970	MF	348	1	4	2	2	0	−	−		
		F	128	1	2	1	1	0	−	−		
	1975	MF	145	1	0	1	1	0	0	0		
		F	53	1	0	0	0	0	−	−		
	1976	MF	756	1	6	3	2	2	1	2		
		F	453	2	7	4	2	1	0	1		
	1977	MF	1 322	4	8	8	3	3	1	6		
		F	565	5	7	6	3	2	1	8		
NETHERLANDS	1970	MF	54 756	8	11	8	10	11	9			
		F	21 684	6	9	7	10	9	7			
	1975	MF	87 071	10	13	12	11	11	10			
		F	37 986	8	12	11	9	11	10			

3.9 Percentage repeaters by grade (second level general)
% des redoublants par années d'études (second degré général)
% de repetidores por años de estudio (segundo grado general)

COUNTRY PAYS PAIS	YEAR ANNEE AÑO	SEX SEXE SEXO	PERCENTAGE REPEATERS BY GRADE POURCENTAGE DE REDOUBLANTS PAR ANNEES D'ETUDES PORCENTAJE DE REPETIDORES POR AÑOS DE ESTUDIO								
			TOTAL	I	II	III	IV	V	VI	VII	VIII	IX
NETHERLANDS (CONT.)	1977	MF	91 679	9	12	13	12	10	9			
		F	41 721	7	11	12	11	10	9			
	1978	MF	91 913	9	12	13	12	11	8			
		F	43 117	7	12	12	11	10	8			
POLAND	1975	MF	12 413	3	4	3	0					
	1976	MF	11 472	3	4	3	0					
	1977	MF	9 918	3	3	3	0					
PORTUGAL	1975	MF	41 488	0	15	25	4	20				
		F	21 646	0	14	25	3	20				
	1976	MF	47 216	—	6	27	6	29				
		F	24 830	—	6	27	7	28				
	1977	MF	81 915	15	21	24	6	30				
		F	42 002	14	20	24	5	29				
SAN MARINO	1970	MF	30	4	4	2	5	—	3	—	3	
	1975	MF	69	5	7	6	6	—	5	—	—	
YUGOSLAVIA	1970	MF	132 599	12	12	10	3	9	9	6	2	
	1975	MF	77 515	7	5	5	1	7	5	3	1	
	1977	MF	69 221	5	4	3	1	8	4	2	1	
	1978	MF	70 728	4	3	3	0	10	4	2	1	
OCEANIA												
FIJI	1974	MF	3 174	5	15	15	30					
U.S.S.R.												
U.S.S.R.	1970	MF	65 100	2	0	0						
	1975	MF	32 100	1	0	0						
	1977	MF	26 100	1	0	0						
BYELORUSSIAN S.S.R.	1970	MF	1 900	2	0	—						
	1975	MF	1 313	1	0	—						
	1977	MF	1 067	1	0	—						
	1978	MF	1 000	1	—	—						
UKRAINIAN S.S.R.	1970	MF	3 600	1	0	—						
	1975	MF	2 100	0	0	—						
	1976	MF	2 400	0	0	—						

Percentage repeaters by grade (second level general)   3.9
% des redoublants par années d'études (second degré général)
% de repetidores por años de estudio (segundo grado general)

ALGERIA:
E—> POLYTECHNICAL SECONDARY SCHOOLS HAVE BEEN INCLUDED IN GENERAL EDUCATION.
FR—> LES COLLEGES D'ENSEIGNEMENT POLYTECHNIQUE SONT COMPTES AVEC L'ENSEIGNEMENT GENERAL.
ESP> LOS GOLEGIOS DE ENSEÑANZA POLITECNICA FIGURAN INCLUIDOS CON LA ENSEÑANZA GENERAL.

BURUNDI:
E—> FOR 1977, DATA REFER TO PUBLIC EDUCATION ONLY.
FR—> POUR 1977, LES DONNEES SE REFERENT A L'ENSEIGNEMENT PUBLIC SEULEMENT.
ESP> EN 1977, LOS DATOS SE REFIEREN A LA ENSEÑANZA PUBLICA SOLAMENTE.

GHANA:
E—> DATA REFER TO PUBLIC EDUCATION ONLY.
FR—> LES DONNEES SE REFERENT A L'ENSEIGNEMENT PUBLIC SEULEMENT.
ESP> LOS DATOS SE REFIEREN A LA ENSEÑANZA PUBLICA SOLAMENTE.

LIBYAN ARAB JAMAHIRYA:
E—> FOR 1970, 1975 AND 1976, DATA REFER TO PUBLIC EDUCATION ONLY.
FR—> POUR 1970, 1975 ET 1976, LES DONNEES SE REFERENT A L'ENSEIGNEMENT PUBLIC SEULEMENT.
ESP> EN 1970, 1975 Y 1976, LOS DATOS SE REFIEREN A LA ENSEÑANZA PUBLICA SOLAMENTE.

MAURITIUS:
E—> DATA FOR RODRIGUEZ ARE NOT AVAILABLE.
FR—> LES DONNEES POUR RODRIGUEZ NE SONT PAS DISPONIBLES.
ESP> NO SE DISPONE DE LOS DATOS RELATIVOS A RODRIGUEZ.

REUNION:
E—> DATA INCLUDE TEACHER TRAINING.
FR—> LES DONNEES INCLUENT L'ENSEIGNEMENT NORMAL.
ESP> LOS DATOS INCLUYEN LA ENSEÑANZA NORMAL.

UGANDA:
E—> DATA REFER TO PUBLIC AND AIDED SCHOOLS ONLY.
FR—> LES DONNEES SE REFERENT AUX ECOLES PU- BLIQUES ET SUBVENTIONNEES SEULEMENT.
ESP> DATOS RELATIVOS A LAS ESCUELAS PUBLICAS Y SUBVENCIONADAS SOLAMENTE.

MARTINIQUE:
E—> FOR 1976, DATA INCLUDE TEACHER TRAINING.
FR—> POUR 1976, LES DONNEES INCLUENT L'ENSEI- GNEMENT NORMAL.
ESP> EN 1976, LOS DATOS INCLUYEN LA ENSEÑANZA NORMAL.

PANAMA:
E—> DATA REFER TO PUBLIC EDUCATION ONLY AND FROM 1975, CHANGES IN THE EDUCATIONEL SYSTEM ARE BEING GRADUALLY APPLIED.
FR—> LES DONNEES SE REFERENT A L'ENSEIGNEMENT PUBLIC SEULEMENT. A PARTIR DE 1975, UN CHANGEMENT DE STRUCTURE EST MIS GRADUELLEMENT EN APPLICATION.
ESP> LOS DATOS SE REFIEREN A LA ENSEÑANZA PUBLICA SOLAMENTE. A PARTIR DE 1975, UN CAMBIODE ESTRUCTURA SE PONE PAULATINAMENTE EN APLICACION.

TRINIDAD AND TOBAGO:
E—> DATA REFER TO GOVERNMENT- MAINTAINED AND AIDED SCHOOLS ONLY.
FR—> LES DONNEES SE REFERENT AUX ECOLES PUBLIQUES ET SUBVENTIONNEES SEULEMENT.
ESP> LOS DATOS SE REFIEREN A LAS ESCUELAS PUBLICAS Y SUBVENCIONADAS SOLAMENTE.

ECUADOR:
E—> DATA INCLUDE EVENING SCHOOLS.
FR—> Y COMPRIS LES ECOLES DU SOIR.
ESP> INCLUIDAS LAS ESCUELAS NOCTURNAS.

VENEZUELA:
E—> BEGINNING 1974, DATA REFER TO ALL SECOND LEVEL EDUCATION AND DUE TO THE REORGANIZATION OF THE EDUCATIONAL SYSTEM DATA REPORTED FOR GENERAL EDUCATION INCLUDE THOSE FOR THE FIRST CYCLE OF TEACHER TRAINING AND OTHER SECOND LEVEL EDUCATION OF A VOCATIONAL OR TECHNICAL NATURE.
FR—> A PARTIR DE 1974, LES DONNEES SE REFERENT A TOUT L'ENSEIGNEMENT DU SECOND DEGRE ET SUIVENT LA REORGANISATION DU SYSTEME SCOLAIRE, C'EST-A- DIRE, QUE LES DONNEES RELATIVES A L'ENSEIGNEMENT GENERAL INCLUENT LE PREMIER CYCLE DE L'ENSEI- GNEMENT NORMAL ET DE L'AUTRE ENSEIGNEMENT DU SECOND DEGRE DE CARACTERE TECHNIQUE OU PROFESSIONNEL.
ESP> A PARTIR DE 1974, LOS DATOS SE REFIEREN A TODA LA ENSEÑANZA DE SEGUNDO GRADO Y SIGUEN LA REORGANIZACION DEL SISTEMA ESCOLAR, ES DECIR, QUE LOS DATOS RELATIVOS A LA ENSEÑANZA GENERAL IN- CLUYEN EL PRIMER CICLO DE LA ENSEÑANZA NORMAL Y DE LA OTRA ENSEÑANZA DE SEGUNDO GRADO DE CARACTER TECNICO O PROFESIONAL.

BAHRAIN:
E—> DATA REFER TO PUBLIC EDUCATION AND DO NOT INCLUDE RELIGIOUS SCHOOLS. IN ADDITION, FROM 1977, CHANGES IN THE EDUCATIONAL SYSTEM ARE BEING GRADUALLY APPLIED.
FR—> LES DONNEES SE REFERENT A L'ENSEIGNEMENT PUBLIC ET NE COMPRENNENT PAS LES ECOLES RELIGIEUSES. DE PLUS, A PARTIR DE 1977, LE CHANGEMENT DE STRUCTURE EST MIS GRADUELLEMENT EN APPLICATION.
ESP> LOS DATOS SE REFIEREN A LA ENSEÑANZA PUBLICA Y NO COMPRENDEN LAS ESCUELAS RELIGIOSAS. ADEMAS, A PARTIR DE 1977, UN CAMBIO DE ESTRUCTURA SE PONE PAULATINAMENTE EN APLICACION.

CYPRUS:
E—> THE DATA SHOWN DO NOT INCLUDE TURKISH SCHOOLS.
FR—> NON COMPRIS LES ECOLES TURQUES.
ESP> EXCLUIDAS LAS ESCUELAS TURCAS.

INDONESIA:
E—> DATA DO NOT INCLUDE RELIGIOUS SCHOOLS.
FR—> LES DONNEES NE COMPRENNENT PAS LES ECOLES RELIGIEUSES.
ESP> LOS DATOS NO INCLUYEN LAS ESCUELAS RELIGIOSAS.

JAPAN:
E—> A POLICY OF AUTOMATIC PROMOTION IN SECOND LEVEL EDUCATION IS PRACTISED.
FR—> UNE POLITIQUE DE PROMOTION AUTOMATIQUE POUR L'ENSEIGNEMENT DU SECOND DEGRE EST APPLIQUEE.
ESP> SE APLICA UNA POLITICA DE PROMOCION AUTOMATICA PARA LA ENSEÑANZA DE SEGUNDO GRADO.

JORDAN:
E—> DATA REFER TO THE EAST BANK ONLY.
FR—> LES DONNEES SE REFERENT A LA RIVE ORIENTALE SEULEMENT.
ESP> LOS DATOS SE REFIEREN A LA ORILLA ORIENTAL SOLAMENTE.

3.9 Percentage repeaters by grade (second level general)
% des redoublants par années d'études (second degré général)
% de repetidores por años de estudio (segundo grado general)

KOREA, REPUBLIC OF:
  E—> BEGINNING 1973, A POLICY OF AUTOMATIC
PROMOTION IN SECOND LEVEL EDUCATION IS PRACTISED.
  FR—> A PARTIR DE 1973, UNE POLITIQUE DE
PROMOTION AUTOMATIQUE POUR L'ENSEIGNEMENT DU
SECOND DEGRE EST APPLIQUEE.
  ESP> A PARTIR DE 1973, SE APLICA UNA POLITICA
DE PROMOCION AUTOMATICA PARA LA ENSEÑANZA DE
SEGUNDO GRADO.

KUWAIT:
  E—> DATA REFER TO PUBLIC EDUCATION ONLY.
  FR—> LES DONNEES SE REFERENT A L'ENSEIGNEMENT
PUBLIC SEULEMENT.
  ESP> LOS DATOS SE REFIEREN A LA ENSEÑANZA
PUBLICA SOLAMENTE.

LAO PEOPLE'S DEMOCRATIC REPUBLIC:
  E—> DATA REFER TO PUBLIC EDUCATION ONLY.
  FR—> LES DONNEES SE REFERENT A L'ENSEIGNEMENT
PUBLIC SEULEMENT.
  ESP> LOS DATOS SE REFIEREN A LA ENSEÑANZA
PUBLICA SOLAMENTE.

MALAYSIA:
PENINSULAR MALAYSIA:
  E—> DATA REFER TO PUBLIC EDUCATION ONLY. IN
ADDITION FROM 1974, A POLICY OF AUTOMATIC PROMO-
TION IN SECOND LEVEL EDUCATION IS PRACTISED.
  FR—> LES DONNEES SE REFERENT A L'ENSEIGNEMENT
PUBLIC SEULEMENT; DE PLUS, DEPUIS 1974, LE PAYS
PRATIQUE UNE POLITIQUE DE PROMOTION AUTOMATIQUE
POUR L'ENSEIGNEMENT DU SECOND DEGRE.
  ESP> LOS DATOS SE REFIEREN A LA ENSEÑANZA
PUBLICA SOLAMENTE. A PARTIR DE 1974, SE APLICA
UNA POLITICA DE PROMOCION AUTOMATICA PARA LA
ENSEÑANZA DE SEGUNDO GRADO.

SABAH:
  E—> A POLICY OF AUTOMATIC PROMOTION IN SECOND
LEVEL EDUCATION IS PRACTISED.
  FR—> UNE POLITIQUE DE PROMOTION AUTOMATIQUE POU
L'ENSEIGNEMENT DU SECOND DEGRE EST APPLIQUEE.
  ESP> SE APLICA UNA POLITICA DE PROMOCION
AUTOMATICA PARA LA ENSEÑANZA DE SEGUNDO GRADO.

SARAWAK:
  E—> A POLICY OF AUTOMATIC PROMOTION IN SECOND
LEVEL EDUCATION IS PRACTISED.
  FR—> UNE POLITIQUE DE PROMOTION AUTOMATIQUE POU
L'ENSEIGNEMENT DU SECOND DEGRE EST APPLIQUEE.
  ESP> SE APLICA UNA POLITICA DE PROMOCION
AUTOMATICA PARA LA ENSEÑANZA DE SEGUNDO GRADO.

QATAR:
  E—> DATA REFER TO PUBLIC EDUCATION ONLY.
  FR—> LES DONNEES SE REFERENT A L'ENSEIGNEMENT
PUBLIC SEULEMENT.
  ESP> LOS DATOS SE REFIEREN A LA ENSEÑANZA
PUBLICA SOLAMENTE.
SRI LANKA:
  E—> DATA REFER TO PUBLIC EDUCATION ONLY.
  FR—> LES DONNEES SE REFERENT A L'ENSEIGNEMENT
PUBLIC SEULEMENT.
  ESP> LOS DATOS SE REFIEREN A LA ENSEÑANZA
PUBLICA SOLAMENTE.

UNITED ARAB EMIRATES:
  E—> DATA REFER TO PUBLIC EDUCATION AND DO NOT
INCLUDE RELIGIOUS SCHOOLS.
  FR—> LES DONNEES SE REFERENT A L'ENSEIGNEMENT
PUBLIC ET NE COMPRENNENT PAS LES ECOLES RELI-
GIEUSES.
  ESP> LOS DATOS SE REFIEREN A LA ENSEÑANZA
PUBLICA Y NO INCLUYEN LAS ESCUELAS RELIGIOSAS.

AUSTRIA:
  E—> DATA INCLUDE SPECIAL EDUCATION.
  FR—> Y COMPRIS L'EDUCATION SPECIALE.
  ESP> INCLUIDA LA EDUCACION ESPECIAL.

BULGARIA:
  E—> DATA INCLUDE EVENING AND CORRESPONDENCE
COURSES.
  FR—> LES DONNEES COMPRENNENT LES COURS DU SOIR
ET PAR CORRESPONDANCE.
  ESP> LOS DATOS INCLUYEN LOS CURSOS NOCTURNOS
Y POR CORRESPONDENCIA.

GERMANY, FEDERAL REPUBLIC OF:
  E—> DATA CORRESPONDING TO THE ACTUAL STRUCTURE
OF THIS LEVEL OF EDUCATION ARE NOT AVAILABLE.
  FR—> LES DONNEES CORRESPONDANTES A LA STRUCTURE
ACTUELLE DE CE NIVEAU D'ENSEIGNEMENT NE SONT PAS
DISPONIBLES.
  ESP> NO SE DISPONE DE LOS DATOS CORRESPONDIENTES
A LA ESTRUCTURA ACTUAL DE ESTE GRADO DE ENSEÑANZA.

GREECE:
  E—> DATA INCLUDE EVENING SCHOOLS WHICH ARE OF
7 YEARS DURATION.
  FR—> Y COMPRIS LES ECOLES DU SOIR D'UNE DUREE
DE 7 ANS.
  ESP> INCLUIDAS LAS ESCUELAS NOCTURNAS DE UNA
DURACION DE 7 ANOS.

Third level: enrolment per 100,000 inhabitants 3.10
Troisième degré: nombre d'étudiants par 100 000 habitants
Tercer grado: número de estudiantes por 100 000 habitantes

3.10 Education at the third level: enrolment per 100,000 inhabitants

Enseignement du troisième degré: nombre d'étudiants par 100 000 habitants

Enseñanza de tercer grado: número de estudiantes por 100 000 habitantes

NUMBER OF COUNTRIES AND TERRITORIES PRESENTED IN THIS TABLE: 134	NOMBRE DE PAYS ET DE TERRITOIRES PRESENTES DANS CE TABLEAU: 134	NUMERO DE PAISES Y DE TERRITORIOS PRESENTADOS EN ESTE CUADRO: 134

COUNTRY / PAYS / PAIS	SEX / SEXE / SEXO	NUMBER OF STUDENTS PER 100,000 INHABITANTS / NOMBRE D'ETUDIANTS PAR 100 000 HABITANTS / NUMERO DE ESTUDIANTES POR 100 000 HABITANTES					
		1970	1973	1974	1975	1976	1977
AFRICA							
ALGERIA	MF	147	206	237	267	323	368
	M	235	320	370	415	503	576
	F	62	95	108	122	148	165
ANGOLA	MF	42	55	59	62	65	68
	M	52	65	70	75	79	82
	F	33	46	48	50	52	55
BENIN	MF	12	66	64	70	75	87
	M	22	112	111	120	129	148
	F	2	23	19	21	22	27
BOTSWANA	MF	—	36	41	65	72	100
	M	—	56	60	96	102	142
	F	—	19	25	39	46	64
BURUNDI	MF	13	20	21	25	30	34
	M	25	32	38	46	54	61
	F	1	7	5	6	7	8
CENTRAL AFRICAN REPUBLIC	MF	5	15	16	31	30	47
	M	10	30	31	61	58	89
	F	...	2	2	3	4	7
CHAD	MF	—	16	12	14	18	23
	M	—	29	24	26	35	43
	F	—	2	1	1	2	2
CONGO	MF	149	200	228	240	252	267
	M	289	375	425	440	462	489
	F	14	31	37	47	50	53
EGYPT	MF	711	997	1 132	1 233	1 302	1 368
	M	1 037	1 410	1 590	1 710	1 800	1 891
	F	379	578	665	747	795	834
ETHIOPIA	MF	18	24	25	26	27	36
	M	34	44	46	48	50	66
	F	3	4	5	5	5	6
GABON	MF	34	129	191	195	236	282
	M	60	223	345	316	395	472
	F	10	38	43	78	83	99

3.10   Third level: enrolment per 100,000 inhabitants
        Troisième degré: nombre d'étudiants par 100 000 habitants
        Tercer grado: número de estudiantes por 100 000 habitantes

COUNTRY PAYS PAIS	SEX SEXE SEXO	NUMBER OF STUDENTS PER 100,000 INHABITANTS NOMBRE D'ETUDIANTS PAR 100 000 HABITANTS NUMERO DE ESTUDIANTES POR 100 000 HABITANTES					
		1970	1973	1974	1975	1976	1977
GHANA	MF	63	79	83	91	99	105
	M	109	135	133	155	168	179
	F	18	26	33	28	31	33
GUINEA	MF	50	59	65	68	71	73
	M	93	110	121	126	131	136
	F	8	9	10	11	11	12
IVORY COAST	MF	83	100	103	107	125	133
	M	138	163	166	171	198	212
	F	24	33	36	38	46	49
KENYA	MF	69	79	87	95	100	104
	M	119	135	148	161	169	176
	F	20	24	27	29	31	33
LESOTHO	MF	38	40	50	58	66	73
	M	50	53	58	68	76	84
	F	26	28	41	48	55	62
LIBERIA	MF	83	116	138	159	178	196
	M	132	178	211	243	272	299
	F	35	56	66	77	86	95
LIBYAN ARAB JAMAHIRIYA	MF	263	429	515	553	541	568
	M	448	695	819	860	823	865
	F	60	130	172	206	223	234
MADAGASCAR	MF	84	118	125	132	149	194
	M	118	162	173	182	194	253
	F	53	75	79	83	105	137
MALAWI	MF	22	22	23	22	22	21
	M	36	39	40	39	39	37
	F	8	6	6	5	5	5
MALI	MF	14	33	43	51	60	69
	M	26	61	79	92	108	122
	F	3	6	8	10	13	16
MAURITANIA	MF	–	–	–	–	–	32
	M	–	–	–	–	–	58
	F	–	–	–	–	–	6
MAURITIUS	MF	240	156	149	121	153	163
	M	456	261	251	209	253	245
	F	22	49	46	33	52	80
MOROCCO	MF	106	156	203	262	253	366
	M	177	257	331	427	404	580
	F	35	55	75	97	101	151
MOZAMBIQUE	MF	24	9	9	10	10	10
	M	28	10	10	13	14	14
	F	21	8	9	6	7	7
NIGER	MF	–	6	8	12	16	16
	M	–	12	14	21	28	28
	F	–	1	2	2	5	5
NIGERIA	MF	39	50	62	68	87	98
	M	68	90	107	117	149	167
	F	11	11	19	21	26	30
RWANDA	MF	16	19	26	27	26	27
	M	30	33	46	48	49	51
	F	3	6	6	7	5	5

Third level: enrolment per 100,000 inhabitants   3.10
Troisième degré: nombre d'étudiants par 100 000 habitants
Tercer grado: número de estudiantes por 100 000 habitantes

COUNTRY PAYS PAIS	SEX SEXE SEXO	NUMBER OF STUDENTS PER 100,000 INHABITANTS NOMBRE D'ETUDIANTS PAR 100 000 HABITANTS NUMERO DE ESTUDIANTES POR 100 000 HABITANTES					
		1970	1973	1974	1975	1976	1977
SENEGAL	MF	116	142	155	165	174	180
	M	195	240	260	275	283	295
	F	39	46	53	57	67	67
SIERRA LEONE ‡	MF	43	51	55	54	51	50
	M	74	88	93	92	88	85
	F	14	15	19	17	16	16
SOMALIA	MF	35	46	50	64	77	90
	M	61	84	90	116	139	162
	F	9	10	11	14	16	19
SOUTH AFRICA ‡	MF	370	408	423	437	449	461
	M	558	615	635	656	674	690
	F	186	205	215	222	229	235
SUDAN	MF	102	132	142	133	131	143
	M	175	217	232	221	208	222
	F	27	44	49	43	52	61
SWAZILAND ‡	MF	48	64	124	209	206	255
	M	60	87	170	287	282	320
	F	37	43	79	134	132	191
TOGO	MF	44	67	72	101	116	130
	M	79	119	126	178	198	221
	F	10	17	19	27	37	41
TUNISIA ‡	MF	202	228	254	366	403	454
	M	324	360	379	536	587	657
	F	82	96	127	190	214	246
UGANDA	MF	43	51	51	48	44	52
	M	72	84	84	80	71	79
	F	15	19	19	17	17	26
UNITED REPUBLIC OF CAMEROON	MF	40	77	84	96	106	115
	M	75	139	150	166	185	199
	F	6	17	20	28	31	34
UNITED REPUBLIC OF TANZANIA	MF	15	21	23	25	20	15
	M	26	35	39	43	36	28
	F	5	7	7	8	3	3
UPPER VOLTA	MF	3	8	13	18	22	19
	M	6	13	20	28	36	30
	F	1	3	6	7	9	8
ZAIRE	MF	57	79	88	97	107	115
	M	111	146	162	180	196	212
	F	6	14	16	18	20	22
ZAMBIA	MF	35	87	100	175	177	179
	M	59	140	154	303	307	314
	F	10	35	47	48	49	47
ZIMBABWE	MF	18	18	18	18	19	19
	M	29	27	27	27	27	27
	F	8	10	10	10	10	11
AMERICA, NORTH							
BARBADOS	MF	319	583	655	733	809	885
	M	368	693	781	868	952	1 040
	F	276	486	543	612	679	744

3.10 Third level: enrolment per 100,000 inhabitants
Troisième degré: nombre d'étudiants par 100 000 habitants
Tercer grado: número de estudiantes por 100 000 habitantes

COUNTRY PAYS PAIS	SEX SEXE SEXO	NUMBER OF STUDENTS PER 100,000 INHABITANTS NOMBRE D'ETUDIANTS PAR 100 000 HABITANTS NUMERO DE ESTUDIANTES POR 100 000 HABITANTES					
		1970	1973	1974	1975	1976	1977
CANADA ‡	MF	2 999	3 107	3 138	3 600	3 583	3 548
	M	3 582	3 546	3 543	3 980	3 790	3 686
	F	2 414	2 669	2 735	3 222	3 378	3 411
COSTA RICA	MF	893	1 208	1 491	1 761	1 803	1 869
	M	1 001	1 337	1 656	1 959	2 001	2 076
	F	784	1 076	1 323	1 560	1 600	1 658
CUBA	MF	307	613	740	885	1 128	1 275
	M	363	774	928	1 110	1 314	1 487
	F	248	444	543	650	934	1 055
DOMINICAN REPUBLIC	MF	520	760	813	851	893	924
	M	585	837	861	945	994	1 022
	F	454	680	764	754	790	824
EL SALVADOR	MF	266	512	647	682	702	691
	M	389	713	901	902	922	912
	F	140	308	390	460	480	466
GUATEMALA ‡	MF	292	372	331	367	404	441
	M	468	571	513	556	602	649
	F	110	168	145	171	200	227
HAITI	MF	37	45	44	56	63	69
	M	67	81	79	86	89	98
	F	8	10	10	26	37	42
HONDURAS	MF	184	296	346	385	484	609
	M	271	408	463	506	650	767
	F	95	184	228	263	317	449
JAMAICA	MF	369	427	449	470	492	...
	M	405	500	530	556	582	...
	F	334	357	371	388	406	...
MEXICO	MF	492	736	869	949	930	1 034
	M	782	1 145	1 352	1 476	1 347	1 465
	F	199	323	381	416	507	598
NICARAGUA	MF	476	690	779	861	938	1 008
	M	656	920	1 033	1 138	1 235	1 329
	F	299	464	529	589	645	692
PANAMA	MF	557	1 365	1 481	1 566	1 770	1 967
	M	588	1 331	1 415	1 539	1 691	1 867
	F	525	1 401	1 551	1 594	1 851	2 071
PUERTO RICO	MF	2 320	2 868	2 963	3 132	3 168	3 692
	M	2 227	2 723	2 747	2 981	2 915	3 331
	F	2 410	3 008	3 169	3 277	3 410	4 037
TRINIDAD AND TOBAGO	MF	231	267	277	413	421	430
	M	293	327	329	482	491	502
	F	169	205	222	340	347	354
UNITED STATES OF AMERICA	MF	4 148	4 559	4 819	5 238	5 111	5 197
	M	4 978	5 220	5 428	5 901	5 530	5 467
	F	3 352	3 927	4 238	4 606	4 713	4 939
AMERICA, SOUTH							
ARGENTINA ‡	MF	1 157	1 715	1 987	2 351	2 339	2 381
	M	1 318	1 865	2 174	2 463	2 442	2 479
	F	994	1 563	1 799	2 240	2 236	2 282

Third level: enrolment per 100,000 inhabitants 3.10
Troisième degré: nombre d'étudiants par 100 000 habitants
Tercer grado: número de estudiantes por 100 000 habitantes

COUNTRY PAYS PAIS	SEX SEXE SEXO	NUMBER OF STUDENTS PER 100,000 INHABITANTS NOMBRE D'ETUDIANTS PAR 100 000 HABITANTS NUMERO DE ESTUDIANTES POR 100 000 HABITANTES					
		1970	1973	1974	1975	1976	1977
BOLIVIA	MF	823	759	943	1 019	1 028	1 035
	M	1 198	1 094	1 360	1 413	1 427	1 436
	F	459	433	538	636	640	645
BRAZIL	MF	452	757	895	993	1 166	1 329
	M	564	824	944	1 006	1 168	1 329
	F	341	691	847	981	1 165	1 329
CHILE ‡	MF	837	1 482	1 444	1 467	1 293	1 249
	M	1 040	1 772	1 662	1 628	1 501	1 463
	F	638	1 198	1 230	1 310	1 088	1 038
COLOMBIA	MF	402	572	636	783	980	947
	M	591	836	930	1 143	1 427	1 155
	F	215	309	343	423	532	739
ECUADOR	MF	649	1 307	2 041	2 469	2 544	2 613
	M	909	1 752	2 678	3 174	3 271	3 357
	F	390	861	1 404	1 764	1 816	1 867
GUYANA	MF	157	304	336	361	383	404
	M	254	407	435	465	494	519
	F	61	203	237	256	272	290
PARAGUAY	MF	355	488	544	658	653	723
	M	413	562	632	765	738	829
	F	297	414	456	551	569	617
PERU	MF	935	1 096	1 199	1 263	1 346	1 425
	M	1 225	1 473	1 606	1 710	1 823	1 927
	F	643	717	789	814	866	919
SURINAME	MF	79	106	110	128	207	242
	M	132	198	205	232	301	325
	F	27	17	19	29	119	163
URUGUAY	MF	751	881	925	1 148	1 262	1 372
	M	869	982	1 026	1 306	1 436	1 464
	F	634	781	827	993	1 092	1 284
VENEZUELA	MF	942	1 359	1 532	1 688	1 891	1 963
	M	1 098	1 474	1 666	1 831	2 053	2 129
	F	781	1 240	1 395	1 541	1 726	1 795
ASIA							
AFGHANISTAN	MF	43	63	58	64	72	79
	M	72	104	99	107	121	114
	F	13	20	16	18	20	43
BANGLADESH	MF	172	192	246	222	201	224
	M	300	332	427	386	341	375
	F	35	43	52	47	52	63
BURMA	MF	166	174	176	180	192	204
	M	209	213	215	220	199	211
	F	125	136	138	140	186	198
CYPRUS	MF	114	135	96	94	122	170
	M	129	156	121	114	141	158
	F	99	115	73	75	103	183
DEMOCRATIC KAMPUCHEA	MF	131	137	133	136	139	143
	M	202	219	213	217	223	228
	F	60	55	53	54	56	57
HONG KONG ‡	MF	647	812	891	1 019	993	803
	M	894	1 169	1 272	1 479	1 407	1 154
	F	393	436	489	529	554	431

427

3.10 Third level: enrolment per 100,000 inhabitants
Troisième degré: nombre d'étudiants par 100 000 habitants
Tercer grado: número de estudiantes por 100 000 habitantes

COUNTRY PAYS PAIS	SEX SEXE SEXO	NUMBER OF STUDENTS PER 100,000 INHABITANTS NOMBRE D'ETUDIANTS PAR 100 000 HABITANTS NUMERO DE ESTUDIANTES POR 100 000 HABITANTES					
		1970	1973	1974	1975	1976	1977
INDIA ‡	MF	692	730	749	746	742	740
	M	1 048	1 094	1 117	1 107	1 101	1 098
	F	310	338	355	359	357	356
INDONESIA	MF	208	203	201	206	214	222
	M	316	295	291	298	311	322
	F	103	112	113	115	119	124
IRAN	MF	263	398	425	464	457	494
	M	389	556	601	640	633	685
	F	135	236	246	283	276	299
IRAQ	MF	454	635	739	781	801	778
	M	693	935	1 028	1 033	1 072	1 041
	F	205	323	440	522	521	507
ISRAEL	MF	1 866	2 239	2 244	2 249	2 394	2 293
	M	2 060	2 411	2 423	2 432	2 569	2 433
	F	1 668	2 065	2 064	2 065	2 219	2 153
JAPAN ‡	MF	1 744	1 899	1 959	2 017	2 045	2 150
	M	2 552	2 702	2 734	2 773	2 775	2 945
	F	965	1 124	1 209	1 284	1 337	1 379
JORDAN ‡	MF	197	323	356	439	588	597
	M	268	426	461	571	748	734
	F	121	215	245	301	421	452
KOREA, REPUBLIC OF	MF	642	751	804	857	922	1 015
	M	967	1 095	1 164	1 237	1 342	1 500
	F	313	401	440	472	495	522
KUWAIT	MF	361	585	608	809	920	1 080
	M	329	435	437	638	759	926
	F	403	770	817	1 015	1 111	1 261
LAO PEOPLE'S DEMOCRATIC REPUBLIC	MF	14	28	26	27	29	30
	M	23	44	37	39	41	44
	F	6	11	14	15	16	17
LEBANON	MF	1 725	1 801	1 830	1 858	1 881	1 902
	M	2 623	2 684	2 727	2 769	2 802	2 834
	F	815	907	921	935	947	958
MALAYSIA	MF	166	242	299	315	329	368
	M	231	328	387	407	427	463
	F	100	153	208	220	228	271
MONGOLIA	MF	551	676	679	683	686	689
	M	580	680	672	665	672	673
	F	522	671	685	700	699	705
NEPAL	MF	155	170	175	185	150	191
	M	251	274	281	297	234	293
	F	57	63	65	69	62	84
PAKISTAN ‡	MF	190	169	169	182	184	185
	M	289	250	246	270	265	267
	F	84	83	86	89	97	98
PHILIPPINES	MF	1 733	1 787	1 697	1 756	1 802	2 081
	M	1 527	1 591	1 513	1 558	1 599	3 893
	F	1 941	1 986	1 883	1 957	2 010	232
SAUDI ARABIA	MF	137	220	284	368	442	575
	M	249	378	478	582	684	900
	F	23	58	85	150	195	244

Third level: enrolment per 100,000 inhabitants 3.10
Troisième degré: nombre d'étudiants par 100 000 habitants
Tercer grado: número de estudiantes por 100 000 habitantes

COUNTRY PAYS PAIS	SEX SEXE SEXO	NUMBER OF STUDENTS PER 100,000 INHABITANTS NOMBRE D'ETUDIANTS PAR 100 000 HABITANTS NUMERO DE ESTUDIANTES POR 100 000 HABITANTES					
		1970	1973	1974	1975	1976	1977
SINGAPORE	MF	664	770	820	1 005	1 004	1 035
	M	904	1 068	1 097	1 191	1 241	1 261
	F	412	458	530	811	757	800
SRI LANKA ‡	MF	98	107	109	113	118	122
	M	107	128	132	141	147	153
	F	89	85	84	84	87	89
SYRIAN ARAB REPUBLIC	MF	682	861	949	1 002	1 055	1 097
	M	1 066	1 318	1 424	1 459	1 539	1 512
	F	278	381	449	520	547	661
THAILAND ‡	MF	155	283	339	317	412	494
	M	181	342	410	383	460	570
	F	129	224	269	251	364	419
TURKEY	MF	481	487	561	593	702	745
	M	770	766	870	907	1 059	1 108
	F	184	199	242	269	332	369
VIET—NAM	MF	...	...	...	173	210	246
	M	...	...	...	208	281	339
	F	...	...	...	137	139	153
YEMEN	MF	1	19	40	46	43	74
	M	2	35	73	86	80	137
	F	...	4	9	9	9	16
YEMEN, DEMOCRATIC	MF	6	24	58	85	112	145
	M	9	38	95	121	161	205
	F	3	11	21	49	64	85
EUROPE							
ALBANIA ‡	MF	1 174	1 509	1 602	1 692	1 773	1 848
	M	1 569	2 003	2 127	2 243	2 350	2 448
	F	771	1 003	1 066	1 127	1 182	1 233
AUSTRIA	MF	803	1 053	1 122	1 286	1 392	1 479
	M	1 209	1 457	1 510	1 699	1 813	1 884
	F	444	695	776	919	1 015	1 117
BELGIUM	MF	1 296	1 526	1 557	1 630	1 724	1 797
	M	1 689	1 871	1 877	1 949	2 020	2 076
	F	919	1 195	1 250	1 324	1 440	1 528
BULGARIA ‡	MF	1 170	1 412	1 468	1 474	1 479	1 620
	M	1 155	1 265	1 269	1 258	1 239	1 205
	F	1 185	1 559	1 667	1 690	1 717	2 032
CZECHOSLOVAKIA	MF	913	930	982	1 048	1 135	1 202
	M	1 163	1 158	1 205	1 283	1 373	1 457
	F	675	714	770	824	908	960
DENMARK ‡	MF	1 542	2 065	2 093	2 179	2 180	2 315
	M	1 968	2 351	2 368	2 453	2 341	2 508
	F	1 124	1 784	1 822	1 912	2 023	2 127
FINLAND	MF	1 298	1 453	1 523	1 639	1 683	1 750
	M	1 387	1 517	1 574	1 702	1 742	1 809
	F	1 214	1 393	1 476	1 579	1 628	1 694
FRANCE ‡	MF	1 581	1 805	1 892	1 970	1 971	2 050
	M	1 943	2 030	2 041	2 101	2 031	2 106
	F	1 236	1 590	1 749	1 845	1 913	1 996

3.10 Third level: enrolment per 100,000 inhabitants
Troisième degré: nombre d'étudiants par 100 000 habitants
Tercer grado: número de estudiantes por 100 000 habitantes

COUNTRY PAYS PAIS	SEX SEXE SEXO	NUMBER OF STUDENTS PER 100,000 INHABITANTS NOMBRE D'ETUDIANTS PAR 100 000 HABITANTS NUMERO DE ESTUDIANTES POR 100 000 HABITANTES					
		1970	1973	1974	1975	1976	1977
GERMAN DEMOCRATIC REPUBLIC ‡	MF	1 776	1 926	1 820	2 291	2 272	2 284
	M	2 201	2 153	1 869	2 348	2 324	2 331
	F	1 414	1 730	1 778	2 241	2 227	2 243
GERMANY, FEDERAL REPUBLIC OF	MF	830	1 192	1 279	1 684	1 707	1 745
	M	1 275	1 706	1 788	2 168	2 192	2 207
	F	425	723	815	1 241	1 263	1 322
GREECE	MF	975	1 090	1 241	1 296	1 351	1 344
	M	1 370	1 441	1 638	1 667	1 715	1 700
	F	599	753	860	940	1 001	1 001
HUNGARY ‡	MF	778	941	987	1 020	1 046	1 024
	M	919	1 042	1 074	1 087	1 079	1 043
	F	646	846	905	957	1 014	1 007
ICELAND	MF	836	1 143	1 253	1 363	1 831	2 240
	M	1 241	1 573	1 643	1 705	2 278	2 743
	F	419	703	854	1 014	1 375	1 724
IRELAND	MF	965	1 041	1 228	1 477	1 475	1 462
	M	1 262	1 325	1 562	1 934	1 831	1 812
	F	665	756	891	1 016	1 116	1 109
ITALY	MF	1 283	1 545	1 681	1 749	1 821	1 870
	M	1 637	1 922	2 091	2 184	2 251	2 274
	F	945	1 185	1 289	1 333	1 409	1 484
LUXEMBOURG ‡	MF	107	131	148	135	124	84
	M	127	146	162	157	145	97
	F	88	117	134	113	103	71
MALTA	MF	565	434	659	435	523	506
	M	779	670	1 004	655	796	792
	F	369	220	344	234	274	246
NETHERLANDS	MF	1 774	1 905	1 949	2 108	2 215	2 312
	M	2 569	2 678	2 699	2 851	2 950	3 033
	F	981	1 137	1 204	1 371	1 487	1 598
NORWAY	MF	1 291	1 613	1 621	1 663	1 822	1 807
	M	1 810	2 136	2 089	2 087	2 098	2 040
	F	777	1 096	1 160	1 244	1 549	1 578
POLAND ‡	MF	1 218	1 439	1 547	1 692	1 787	1 796
	M	1 318	1 435	1 489	1 593	1 644	1 655
	F	1 124	1 444	1 601	1 785	1 924	1 929
PORTUGAL ‡	MF	581	660	700	846	1 006	888
	M	681	712	832	984	1 208	1 078
	F	490	614	581	722	825	717
ROMANIA ‡	MF	746	693	728	775	816	842
	M	865	784	835	869	923	953
	F	631	605	625	683	712	734
SPAIN ‡	MF	666	1 166	1 287	1 518	1 616	1 713
	M	1 000	1 614	1 739	1 985	2 044	2 166
	F	347	739	857	1 073	1 209	1 281
SWEDEN ‡	MF	1 756	1 615	1 577	1 985	2 083	2 311
	M	2 026	1 776	1 717	2 381	2 433	2 602
	F	1 487	1 455	1 439	1 594	1 737	2 022
SWITZERLAND	MF	821	946	979	1 010	1 041	1 169
	M	1 255	1 385	1 423	1 457	1 501	1 734
	F	391	521	552	585	605	632

3.10 Third level: enrolment per 100,000 inhabitants
Troisième degré: nombre d'étudiants par 100 000 habitants
Tercer grado: número de estudiantes por 100 000 habitantes

COUNTRY PAYS PAIS	SEX SEXE SEXO	NUMBER OF STUDENTS PER 100,000 INHABITANTS NOMBRE D'ETUDIANTS PAR 100 000 HABITANTS NUMERO DE ESTUDIANTES POR 100 000 HABITANTES					
		1970	1973	1974	1975	1976	1977
UNITED KINGDOM ‡	MF	1 084	1 141	1 161	1 308	1 426	1 546
	M	1 488	1 511	1 532	1 716	1 868	2 024
	F	701	791	809	920	1 005	1 091
YUGOSLAVIA	MF	1 282	1 573	1 704	1 850	1 889	1 960
	M	1 582	1 866	2 046	2 260	2 318	2 417
	F	993	1 290	1 372	1 453	1 472	1 516
OCEANIA							
AUSTRALIA ‡	MF	1 431	1 693	1 884	2 016	2 097	2 145
	M	1 911	2 136	2 293	2 386	2 403	2 441
	F	944	1 244	1 470	1 644	1 789	1 847
FIJI	MF	85	188	194	202	219	238
	M	122	246	263	274	298	323
	F	47	129	124	128	139	151
NEW ZEALAND	MF	1 502	2 301	2 201	2 312	2 381	2 430
	M	1 823	3 040	2 775	2 880	2 942	3 052
	F	1 182	1 560	1 627	1 742	1 818	1 807
PAPUA NEW GUINEA	MF	43	214	226	239	251	263
	M	69	345	365	386	404	421
	F	14	72	76	81	86	91
U.S.S.R.							
U.S.S.R. ‡	MF	1 878	1 873	1 886	1 908	1 934	1 952
	M	2 078	2 022	2 031	2 037	2 059	2 076
	F	1 708	1 746	1 761	1 796	1 825	1 844

GENERAL NOTE/NOTE GENERALE/NOTA GENERAL:
   E—> FOR COUNTRIES MARKED WITH A ‡ SEE THE NOTES
TO TABLE 3.11.
   FR-> POUR LES PAYS SIGNALES PAR UN ‡ VOIR LES
NOTES DU TABLEAU 3.11.
   ESP> PARA LOS PAISES INDICADOS CON UN ‡ VEANSE
LAS NOTAS DEL CUADRO 3.11.

3.11 Third level: teachers and students by type of institution
Troisième degré: professeurs et étudiants par types d'établissement
Tercer grado: personal docente y estudiantes por tipos de establecimiento

3.11 Education at the third level: teachers and students by type of institution

Enseignement du troisième degré: personnel enseignant et étudiants par types d'établissement

Enseñanza de tercer grado: personal docente y estudiantes por tipos de establecimiento

TEACHERS = PERSONNEL ENSEIGNANT/PERSONAL DOCENTE
STUDENTS = ETUDIANTS/ESTUDIANTES

NUMBER OF COUNTRIES AND TERRITORIES PRESENTED IN THIS TABLE: 154

NOMBRE DE PAYS ET DE TERRITOIRES PRESENTES DANS CE TABLEAU: 154

COUNTRY / PAYS / PAIS		YEAR / ANNEE / AÑO	ALL INSTITUTIONS TOTAL DES ETABLISSEMENTS TODOS LOS ESTABLECIMIENTOS		UNIVERSITIES AND EQUIVALENT INSTITUTIONS UNIVERSITES ET ETABLISSEMENTS EQUIVALENTS UNIVERSIDADES Y ESTAB. EQUIVALENTES	
			TOTAL	FEMALE FEMININ FEMENINO	TOTAL	FEMALE FEMININ FEMENINO
AFRICA						
ALGERIA	TEACHERS	1971	1 718	...	1 718	...
		1976	5 366	...	5 366	...
		1977	5 856	...	5 856	...
	STUDENTS	1970	19 531	4 166	19 531	4 166
		1974	35 888	...	35 888	...
		1975	41 847	...	41 847	...
		1976	52 424	12 171	52 424	12 171
		1977	61 767	13 958	61 767	13 958
ANGOLA	TEACHERS	1970	273	...	225	...
	STUDENTS	1970	2 349	936	2 125	860
BENIN	TEACHERS	1970	33	4	33	4
		1974	143	...	143	...
		1975	153	...	148	...
		1978	...	...	159	...
	STUDENTS	1970	311	23	311	23
		1974	1 900	287	1 900	287
		1975	2 118	320	2 102	319
		1978	3 292	585	3 041	550
BOTSWANA	TEACHERS	1970	—	—	—	—
		1974	30	4	30	4
		1975	56	...	56	...
	STUDENTS	1970	—	—	—	—
		1974	289	96	289	96
		1975	469	152	469	152
		1976	527	182	527	182
		1977	755	262	755	262
BURUNDI	TEACHERS	1970	102	7	69	4
		1974	215	...	133	10
		1975	223	...	123	...

Third level: teachers and students by type of institution 3.11
Troisième degré: professeurs et étudiants par types d'établissement
Tercer grado: personal docente y estudiantes por tipos de establecimiento

NUMERO DE PAISES Y DE TERRITORIOS PRESENTADOS EN
ESTE CUADRO: 154

NON—UNIVERSITY TEACHER TRAINING ENSEIGNEMENT NORMAL NON—UNIVERSITAIRE ENSEÑANZA NORMAL NO UNIVERSITARIA		OTHER NON—UNIVERSITY INSTITUTIONS AUTRES ETABLISSEMENTS NON—UNIVERSITAIRES OTROS ESTABLECIMIENTOS NO UNIVERSITARIOS		YEAR ANNEE	COUNTRY PAYS
TOTAL	FEMALE FEMININ FEMENINO	TOTAL	FEMALE FEMININ FEMENINO	AÑO	PAIS
					AFRICA
–	–	–	–	1971	ALGERIA
–	–	–	–	1976	
–	–	–	–	1977	
–	–	–	–	1970	
–	–	–	–	1974	
–	–	–	–	1975	
–	–	–	–	1976	
–	–	–	–	1977	
–	–	48	...	1970	ANGOLA
–	–	224	76	1970	
–	–	–	–	1970	BENIN
–	–	–	–	1974	
5	...	–	–	1975	
...	...	19	...	1978	
–	–	–	–	1970	
–	–	–	–	1974	
16	1	–	–	1975	
190	19	61	16	1978	
–	–	–	–	1970	BOTSWANA
–	–	–	–	1974	
–	–	–	–	1975	
–	–	–	–	1970	
–	–	–	–	1974	
–	–	–	–	1975	
–	–	–	–	1976	
–	–	–	–	1977	
33	3	–	–	1970	BURUNDI
82	...	–	–	1974	
100	...	–	–	1975	

3.11 Third level: teachers and students by type of institution
Troisième degré: professeurs et étudiants par types d'établissement
Tercer grado: personal docente y estudiantes por tipos de establecimiento

COUNTRY PAYS PAIS		YEAR ANNEE AÑO	ALL INSTITUTIONS TOTAL DES ETABLISSEMENTS TODOS LOS ESTABLECIMIENTOS		UNIVERSITIES AND EQUIVALENT INSTITUTIONS UNIVERSITES ET ETABLISSEMENTS EQUIVALENTS UNIVERSIDADES Y ESTAB. EQUIVALENTES	
			TOTAL	FEMALE FEMININ FEMENINO	TOTAL	FEMALE FEMININ FEMENINO
BURUNDI (CONT.)	STUDENTS	1970	466	26	361	17
		1974	802	89	517	57
		1975	1 002	112	652	72
CENTRAL AFRICAN REPUBLIC	TEACHERS	1970	6	—	6	—
		1975	85	20	85	20
		1976	116	20	116	20
		1977	185	36	185	36
	STUDENTS	1970	88	3	88	3
		1974	318	20	318	20
		1975	625	31	625	31
		1976	616	41	616	41
		1977	972	70	972	70
CHAD	TEACHERS	1970	—	—	—	—
		1974	94	17	94	17
		1976	62	7	62	7
	STUDENTS	1970	—		—	
		1974	419	18	419	18
		1975	547	29	547	29
		1976	758	40	758	40
CONGO	TEACHERS	1970	117	24	71	13
		1974	225	19	206	15
		1975	165	25	165	25
	STUDENTS	1970	1 788	87	1 436	75
		1974	3 007	251	2 827	236
		1975	3 249	321	3 249	321
EGYPT	TEACHERS	1970	14 250	...	1 959	...
		1974	19 119	...	16 167	...
		1976	19 507	...	...	...
	STUDENTS	1970	233 304	61 790	213 404	55 840
		1974	408 235	118 853	367 734	107 143
		1975	*455 097	*136 577	411 097	123 847
		1976	*493 328	*149 077	445 328	135 277
ETHIOPIA	TEACHERS	1970	516	71	516	71
		1977	476	...	274	...
	STUDENTS	1970	4 543	354	4 543	354
		1977	10 824	...	8 539	...
GABON	STUDENTS	1970	172	26	172	26
		1974	986	...	511	...
		1975	1 014	207	651	148
		1976	1 245	224	780	168
GHANA	TEACHERS	1970	902	83	825	*65
		1975	1 103	...	963	...
	STUDENTS	1970	5 426	774	4 729	620
		1974	8 022	1 640	...	...
		1975	9 079	1 439	7 179	919
GUINEA	STUDENTS	1970	1 974	160	...	...
IVORY COAST	TEACHERS	1970	220	...	189	...

Third level: teachers and students by type of institution   3.11
Troisième degré: professeurs et étudiants par types d'établissement
Tercer grado: personal docente y estudiantes por tipos de establecimiento

NON—UNIVERSITY TEACHER TRAINING ENSEIGNEMENT NORMAL NON—UNIVERSITAIRE ENSEÑANZA NORMAL NO UNIVERSITARIA		OTHER NON—UNIVERSITY INSTITUTIONS AUTRES ETABLISSEMENTS NON—UNIVERSITAIRES OTROS ESTABLECIMIENTOS NO UNIVERSITARIOS		YEAR ANNEE	COUNTRY PAYS
TOTAL	FEMALE FEMININ FEMENINO	TOTAL	FEMALE FEMININ FEMENINO	AÑO	PAIS
105	9	—	—	1970	BURUNDI (CONT.)
285	32	—	—	1974	
350	40	—	—	1975	
					CENTRAL AFRICAN
—	—	—	—	1970	REPUBLIC
—	—	—	—	1975	
—	—	—	—	1976	
—	—	—	—	1977	
—	—	—	—	1970	
—	—	—	—	1974	
—	—	—	—	1975	
—	—	—	—	1976	
—	—	—	—	1977	
—	—	—	—	1970	CHAD
—	—	—	—	1974	
—	—	—	—	1976	
—	—	—	—	1970	
—	—	—	—	1974	
—	—	—	—	1975	
—	—	—	—	1976	
46	11	—	—	1970	CONGO
19	4	—	—	1974	
—	—	—	—	1975	
352	12	—	—	1970	
180	15	—	—	1974	
—	—	—	—	1975	
682	...	1 609	...	1970	EGYPT
940	...	2 012	...	1974	
...	...	...	...	1976	
4 874	2 061	15 026	3 889	1970	
13 283	4 324	27 218	7 386	1974	
*15 000	*4 870	*29 000	*7 860	1975	
*17 000	*5 500	*31 000	*8 300	1976	
—	—	—	—	1970	ETHIOPIA
72	...	130	...	1977	
—	—	—	—	1970	
1 035	...	1 250	...	1977	
—	—	—	—	1970	GABON
96	...	379	...	1974	
116	19	247	40	1975	
177	30	288	26	1976	
77	18	—	—	1970	GHANA
*140	...	—	—	1975	
697	154	—	—	1970	
...	...	—	—	1974	
*1 900	*520	—	—	1975	
...	...	...	...	1970	GUINEA
*31	...	—	—	1970	IVORY COAST

3.11 Third level: teachers and students by type of institution
Troisième degré: professeurs et étudiants par types d'établissement
Tercer grado: personal docente y estudiantes por tipos de establecimiento

| COUNTRY | | YEAR | ALL INSTITUTIONS TOTAL DES ETABLISSEMENTS TODOS LOS ESTABLECIMIENTOS | | UNIVERSITIES AND EQUIVALENT INSTITUTIONS UNIVERSITES ET ETABLISSEMENTS EQUIVALENTS UNIVERSIDADES Y ESTAB. EQUIVALENTES | |
| PAYS | | ANNEE | | | | |
PAIS		AÑO	TOTAL	FEMALE FEMININ FEMENINO	TOTAL	FEMALE FEMININ FEMENINO
IVORY COAST (CONT.)	STUDENTS	1970	4 381	615	4 001	590
		1975	7 174	1 218	6 274	1 123
		1976	8 701	1 543	7 551	1 418
		1977	*9 620	...	*8 353	...
		1978	*11 527	...	*9 651	...
KENYA	TEACHERS	1970	...	...	...	...
		1974	...	...	...	...
	STUDENTS	1970	7 795	...	2 786	...
		1974	11 351	...	6 548	...
		1975	...	...	6 327	...
		1976	...	...	6 361	...
LESOTHO	TEACHERS	1970	61	5	61	5
		1974	74	...	64	...
	STUDENTS	1970	402	138	402	138
		1974	577	240	536	223
LIBERIA	TEACHERS	1970	164	18	164	18
	STUDENTS	1970	1 109	238	1 109	238
		1975	2 404	536	2 404	536
LIBYAN ARAB JAMAHIRIYA	TEACHERS	1970	394	17	394	17
		1974	824	...	824	...
		1975	951	...	951	...
		1976	1 076	...	1 076	...
		1977	1 340	...	1 340	...
	STUDENTS	1970	5 222	561	5 222	561
		1974	11 997	1 892	11 997	1 892
		1975	13 427	2 358	13 427	2 358
		1976	13 723	2 661	13 723	2 661
		1977	15 018	2 909	15 018	2 909
MADAGASCAR	TEACHERS	1970	317	58	155	32
		1976	839	148	692	116
		1977	941	175	803	143
	STUDENTS	1970	5 738	1 825	4 025	1 275
		1974	9 354	...	9 354	...
		1975	8 385		8 385	
		1976	11 711	4 199	10 976	3 978
		1977	...	...	14 116	4 849
MALAWI	TEACHERS	1970	147	19	147	19
		1974	179	20	179	20
		1975	150	14	150	14
		1976	128	13	128	13
		1977	...	...	...	...
	STUDENTS	1970	980	173	980	173
		1974	1 153	146	1 153	146
		1975	1 148	138	1 148	138
		1976	1 179	146	1 179	146
		1977	1 153	...	1 153	...
MALI	TEACHERS	1970	151	10	—	—
		1974	327	...	—	—
		1975	...	...	—	—
		1976	349	...	—	—
		1977	450	...	—	—

Third level: teachers and students by type of institution 3.11
Troisième degré: professeurs et étudiants par types d'établissement
Tercer grado: personal docente y estudiantes por tipos de establecimiento

NON—UNIVERSITY TEACHER TRAINING ENSEIGNEMENT NORMAL NON—UNIVERSITAIRE ENSEÑANZA NORMAL NO UNIVERSITARIA		OTHER NON—UNIVERSITY INSTITUTIONS AUTRES ETABLISSEMENTS NON—UNIVERSITAIRES OTROS ESTABLECIMIENTOS NO UNIVERSITARIOS		YEAR ANNEE AÑO	COUNTRY PAYS PAIS
TOTAL	FEMALE FEMININ FEMENINO	TOTAL	FEMALE FEMININ FEMENINO		
380	25	—	—	1970	IVORY COAST (CONT.)
900	*95	—	—	1975	
1 150	*125	—	—	1976	
1 267	...	—	—	1977	
1 876	...	—	—	1978	
...	...	157	13	1970	KENYA
...	...	188	...	1974	
1 268	363	3 741	*200	1970	
484	122	4 319	350	1974	
488	124	...	...	1975	
519	...	...	...	1976	
—	—	—	—	1970	LESOTHO
10	8	—	—	1974	
—	—	—	—	1970	
41	17	—	—	1974	
—	—	—	—	1970	LIBERIA
—	—	—	—	1970	
—	—	—	—	1975	
—	—	—	—	1970	LIBYAN ARAB JAMAHIRIYA
—	—	—	—	1974	
—	—	—	—	1975	
—	—	—	—	1976	
—	—	—	—	1977	
—	—	—	—	1970	
—	—	—	—	1974	
—	—	—	—	1975	
—	—	—	—	1976	
—	—	—	—	1977	
42	15	120	11	1970	MADAGASCAR
84	21	63	11	1976	
78	22	60	10	1977	
216	166	1 497	384	1970	
—	—	—	—	1974	
—	—	—	—	1975	
620	177	115	44	1976	
...	...	...	...	1977	
—	—	—	—	1970	MALAWI
—	—	—	—	1974	
—	—	—	—	1975	
—	—	—	—	1976	
—	—	—	—	1977	
—	—	—	—	1970	
—	—	—	—	1974	
—	—	—	—	1975	
—	—	—	—	1976	
—	—	—	—	1977	
51	8	100	2	1970	MALI
84	...	243	...	1974	
101	...	...	...	1975	
122	...	227	...	1976	
217	...	243	...	1977	

3.11 Third level: teachers and students by type of institution
Troisième degré: professeurs et étudiants par types d'établissement
Tercer grado: personal docente y estudiantes por tipos de establecimiento

COUNTRY PAYS PAIS		YEAR ANNEE AÑO	ALL INSTITUTIONS TOTAL DES ETABLISSEMENTS TODOS LOS ESTABLECIMIENTOS		UNIVERSITIES AND EQUIVALENT INSTITUTIONS UNIVERSITES ET ETABLISSEMENTS EQUIVALENTS UNIVERSIDADES Y ESTAB. EQUIVALENTES	
			TOTAL	FEMALE FEMININ FEMENINO	TOTAL	FEMALE FEMININ FEMENINO
MALI (CONT.)	STUDENTS	1970	731	77	–	–
		1974	2 445	226	–	–
		1975	2 936	302	–	–
		1976	3 576	380	–	–
		1977	4 216	502	–	–
MAURITANIA	TEACHERS	1977	110	15	–	–
	STUDENTS	1977	477	46	–	–
MAURITIUS	TEACHERS	1971	192	7	192	7
		1974	171	10	171	10
		1975	155	9	155	9
		1976	231	14	182	6
		1977	240	35	147	12
	STUDENTS	1970	1 975	92	1 975	92
		1974	1 321	205	1 321	205
		1975	1 096	150	1 096	150
		1976	1 408	240	1 043	133
		1977	1 531	377	991	177
MOROCCO	TEACHERS	1970	620	73	503	67
		1974	1 921	194	883	65
		1975	1 642	...	937	160
		1977	...	...	1 912	317
		1978	...	...	2 067	354
	STUDENTS	1970	16 097	2 674	15 199	2 635
		1974	34 092	6 295	26 698	5 293
		1975	45 322	8 440	35 081	6 726
		1976	...	...	45 085	9 023
		1977	67 322	*13 889	53 400	11 613
		1978	...	...	62 107	15 411
MOZAMBIQUE	TEACHERS	1970	210	25	193	25
		1976	164	39	164	39
	STUDENTS	1970	1 982	875	1 887	875
		1976	906	304	906	304
NIGER	TEACHERS	1970	–	–	–	–
		1974	47	8	47	8
		1975	74	11	74	11
		1977	115	18	115	18
	STUDENTS	1970	–	–	–	–
		1974	357	38	357	38
		1975	541	56	541	56
		1976	765	110	765	110
		1977	784	120	784	120
NIGERIA	TEACHERS	1974	...	...	3 962	...
		1975	...	...	5 019	...
		1976	...	...	...	...
		1977	...	...	...	...
	STUDENTS	1970	15 560	2 286	14 510	2 066
		1974	39 562	...	30 297	5 231
		1975	44 964	...	32 971	5 114
		1976	58 953	...	41 499	...
		1977	68 382	...	48 928	...
REUNION	STUDENTS	1977	2 443	1 245	1 901	943
		1978	2 317	...	1 765	...

Third level: teachers and students by type of institution 3.11
Troisième degré: professeurs et étudiants par types d'établissement
Tercer grado: personal docente y estudiantes por tipos de establecimiento

NON–UNIVERSITY TEACHER TRAINING ENSEIGNEMENT NORMAL NON–UNIVERSITAIRE ENSEÑANZA NORMAL NO UNIVERSITARIA		OTHER NON–UNIVERSITY INSTITUTIONS AUTRES ETABLISSEMENTS NON–UNIVERSITAIRES OTROS ESTABLECIMIENTOS NO UNIVERSITARIOS		YEAR ANNEE AÑO	COUNTRY PAYS PAIS
TOTAL	FEMALE FEMININ FEMENINO	TOTAL	FEMALE FEMININ FEMENINO		
232	21	499	56	1970	MALI (CONT.)
1 055	88	1 390	138	1974	
1 248	142	1 688	160	1975	
1 731	184	1 845	196	1976	
1 290	154	2 926	348	1977	
55	7	55	8	1977	MAURITANIA
209	14	268	32	1977	
–	–	–	–	1971	MAURITIUS
–	–	–	–	1974	
–	–	–	–	1975	
49	8	–	–	1976	
93	23	–	–	1977	
–	–	–	–	1970	
–	–	–	–	1974	
–	–	–	–	1975	
365	107	–	–	1976	
540	200	–	–	1977	
–	–	117	6	1970	MOROCCO
293	84	745	45	1974	
388	...	317	...	1975	
...	...	...	...	1977	
...	...	...	...	1978	
–	–	898	39	1970	
3 130	616	4 264	386	1974	
5 415	1 150	4 826	564	1975	
...	...			1976	
8 819	*1 900	5 103	376	1977	
...	...	...	...	1978	
–	–	17	–	1970	MOZAMBIQUE
–	–	–	–	1976	
–	–	95	–	1970	
–	–	–	–	1976	
–	–	–	–	1970	NIGER
–	–	–	–	1974	
–	–	–	–	1975	
–	–	–	–	1977	
–	–	–	–	1970	
–	–	–	–	1974	
–	–	–	–	1975	
–	–	–	–	1976	
–	–	–	–	1977	
–	–	...	...	1974	NIGERIA
–	–	...	...	1975	
–	–	...	...	1976	
–	–	...	...	1977	
*1 050	*220	–	–	1970	
–	–	9 265	...	1974	
–	–	11 993	...	1975	
–	–	17 454	...	1976	
–	–	19 454	...	1977	
–	–	542	302	1977	REUNION
–	–	552	...	1978	

3.11 Third level: teachers and students by type of institution
Troisième degré: professeurs et étudiants par types d'établissement
Tercer grado: personal docente y estudiantes por tipos de establecimiento

COUNTRY / PAYS / PAIS		YEAR / ANNEE / AÑO	ALL INSTITUTIONS TOTAL DES ETABLISSEMENTS TODOS LOS ESTABLECIMIENTOS		UNIVERSITIES AND EQUIVALENT INSTITUTIONS UNIVERSITES ET ETABLISSEMENTS EQUIVALENTS UNIVERSIDADES Y ESTAB. EQUIVALENTES	
			TOTAL	FEMALE FEMININ FEMENINO	TOTAL	FEMALE FEMININ FEMENINO
RWANDA	TEACHERS	1970	96	10	66	5
		1974	148	17	89	10
		1975	175	...	89	...
		1976	215	30	119	17
	STUDENTS	1970	571	53	411	38
		1974	1 023	127	684	80
		1975	1 108	...	672	...
		1976	1 117	100	657	58
SENEGAL	TEACHERS	1974	374	...	374	...
		1975	412	...	412	...
		1976	...	...	...	...
		1977	900	...	900	...
	STUDENTS	1970	4 962	831	4 859	811
		1974	7 502	1 291	7 502	1 291
		1975	8 213	1 428	8 213	1 428
		1976	8 981	1 762	8 981	1 762
		1977	9 454	1 788	9 454	1 788
SEYCHELLES	TEACHERS	1970	7	3	—	—
		1974	8	7	—	—
		1976	16	9	—	—
		1977	24	9	—	—
		1978	26	14	—	—
	STUDENTS	1970	87	81	—	—
		1974	107	104	—	—
		1976	142	132	—	—
		1977	117	99	—	—
		1978	157	121	—	—
SIERRA LEONE ‡	TEACHERS	1974	322	16	322	16
		1975	289	38	289	38
		1976	...	...	...	...
		1977	...	...	...	...
	STUDENTS	1970	1 155	187	1 155	187
		1974	1 646	293	1 646	293
		1975	1 642	266	1 642	266
		1976	1 602	...	1 602	...
		1977	1 594	...	1 594	...
SOMALIA	TEACHERS	1970	58	—	58	—
		1974	128	...	128	...
		1975	324	...	286	...
	STUDENTS	1970	964	*125	964	*125
		1974	1 560	179	1 560	179
		1975	2 040	218	1 936	192
SOUTH AFRICA ‡	STUDENTS	1970	82 697	...	82 697	...
		1973	98 577	...	98 577	...
SUDAN	TEACHERS	1970	1 153	...	772	...
		1974	1 320	79	985	37
		1975	1 420	97	1 178	51
		1976	*1 963	*148	1 482	92
	STUDENTS	1970	14 308	1 852	12 057	1 491
		1974	22 204	3 800	20 367	3 375
		1975	21 342	3 408	19 208	2 973
		1976	21 590	4 220	19 362	3 742
		1977	24 109	5 089	21 572	4 467

Third level: teachers and students by type of institution   3.11
Troisième degré: professeurs et étudiants par types d'établissement
Tercer grado: personal docente y estudiantes por tipos de establecimiento

NON—UNIVERSITY TEACHER TRAINING ENSEIGNEMENT NORMAL NON—UNIVERSITAIRE ENSEÑANZA NORMAL NO UNIVERSITARIA		OTHER NON—UNIVERSITY INSTITUTIONS AUTRES ETABLISSEMENTS NON—UNIVERSITAIRES OTROS ESTABLECIMIENTOS NO UNIVERSITARIOS		YEAR ANNEE	COUNTRY PAYS
TOTAL	FEMALE FEMININ FEMENINO	TOTAL	FEMALE FEMININ FEMENINO	AÑO	PAIS
*30	*5	—	—	1970	RWANDA
45	6	14	1	1974	
73	...	13	...	1975	
62	11	34	2	1976	
*160	*15	—	—	1970	
256	47	83	—	1974	
326	...	110	...	1975	
196	33	264	9	1976	
—	—	—	—	1974	SENEGAL
—	—	—	—	1975	
—	—	—	—	1976	
—	—	—	—	1977	
103	20	—	—	1970	
—	—	—	—	1974	
—	—	—	—	1975	
—	—	—	—	1976	
—	—	—	—	1977	
7	3	—	—	1970	SEYCHELLES
8	7	—	—	1974	
16	9	—	—	1976	
24	9	—	—	1977	
26	14	—	—	1978	
87	81	—	—	1970	
107	104	—	—	1974	
142	132	—	—	1976	
117	99	—	—	1977	
157	121	—	—	1978	
—	—	—	—	1974	SIERRA LEONE ‡
—	—	—	—	1975	
—	—	—	—	1976	
—	—	—	—	1977	
—	—	—	—	1970	
—	—	—	—	1974	
—	—	—	—	1975	
—	—	—	—	1976	
—	—	—	—	1977	
—	—	—	—	1970	SOMALIA
—	—	—	—	1974	
—	—	38	...	1975	
—	—	—	—	1970	
—	—	—	—	1974	
—	—	104	26	1975	
—	—	—	—	1970	SOUTH AFRICA ‡
—	—	—	—	1973	
99	10	282	18	1970	SUDAN
61	5	274	37	1974	
11	1	231	45	1975	
*10	*1	471	55	1976	
709	144	1 542	217	1970	
206	29	1 631	396	1974	
179	18	1 955	417	1975	
174	15	2 054	463	1976	
201	8	2 336	614	1977	

3.11 Third level: teachers and students by type of institution
Troisième degré: professeurs et étudiants par types d'établissement
Tercer grado: personal docente y estudiantes por tipos de establecimiento

COUNTRY PAYS PAIS		YEAR ANNEE AÑO	ALL INSTITUTIONS TOTAL DES ETABLISSEMENTS TODOS LOS ESTABLECIMIENTOS		UNIVERSITIES AND EQUIVALENT INSTITUTIONS UNIVERSITES ET ETABLISSEMENTS EQUIVALENTS UNIVERSIDADES Y ESTAB. EQUIVALENTES	
			TOTAL	FEMALE FEMININ FEMENINO	TOTAL	FEMALE FEMININ FEMENINO
SWAZILAND ‡	TEACHERS	1974	106	30	75	20
		1975	136	25	86	12
		1976	146	26	86	12
		1977	104	28	48	10
	STUDENTS	1970	207	80	139	55
		1974	584	...	269	...
		1975	1 012	...	336	...
		1976	1 023	333	390	194
		1977	...	...	543	272
TOGO	TEACHERS	1970	48	12	48	12
		1974	186	35	186	35
		1975	236	39	236	39
	STUDENTS	1970	886	102	845	101
		1974	1 619	214	1 475	203
		1975	2 353	323	2 167	308
		1976	2 777	445	2 404	403
TUNISIA ‡	TEACHERS	1971	628		628	
		1974	1 350	192	1 350	192
		1975	1 427	217	1 427	217
		1976	3 089	...	3 089	...
		1977	3 471	...	3 471	...
		1978	3 600	...	3 600	...
	STUDENTS	1970	10 347	2 136	10 347	2 136
		1974	14 013	3 463	14 013	3 463
		1975	20 505	5 273	20 505	5 273
		1976	23 137	6 070	23 137	6 070
		1977	26 781	7 155	26 781	7 155
		1978	28 618	8 128	28 618	8 128
UGANDA	TEACHERS	1970	481	...	350	...
		1974	604	...	437	...
		1975	617	58	444	33
		1976	681	*59	489	*36
		1977	...	...	...	...
	STUDENTS	1970	4 232	744	2 953	518
		1974	5 618	1 065	3 955	643
		1975	5 474	988	3 914	619
		1976	5 148	1 018	3 461	555
		1977	6 312	1 607	3 406	581
UNITED REPUBLIC OF CAMEROON	TEACHERS	1970	220	21	158	14
	STUDENTS	1970	2 690	209	2 128	158
		1974	6 171	740	6 171	740
		1975	7 191	1 081	7 191	1 081
		1977	9 060	1 358	9 060	1 358
UNITED REPUBLIC OF TANZANIA	TEACHERS	1974	...	...	433	...
		1975	...	...	434	...
		1976	624	...	511	42
		1977	553	59	477	35
	STUDENTS	1970	2 027	335	1 823	294
		1974	3 424	530	2 763	328
		1975	3 064	420	2 644	270
		1976	3 096	235	2 206	231
		1977	2 534	237	2 304	195

Third level: teachers and students by type of institution   3.11
Troisième degré: professeurs et étudiants par types d'établissement
Tercer grado: personal docente y estudiantes por tipos de establecimiento

| NON—UNIVERSITY TEACHER TRAINING ENSEIGNEMENT NORMAL NON—UNIVERSITAIRE ENSEÑANZA NORMAL NO UNIVERSITARIA | | OTHER NON—UNIVERSITY INSTITUTIONS AUTRES ETABLISSEMENTS NON—UNIVERSITAIRES OTROS ESTABLECIMIENTOS NO UNIVERSITARIOS | | YEAR ANNEE | COUNTRY PAYS |
| | FEMALE FEMININ FEMENINO | | FEMALE FEMININ FEMENINO | | |
TOTAL	FEMENINO	TOTAL	FEMENINO	AÑO	PAIS
—	—	31	10	1974	SWAZILAND ‡
—	—	50	13	1975	
—	—	60	14	1976	
—	—	56	18	1977	
68	25	—	—	1970	
85	43	230	170	1974	
91	41	585	194	1975	
112	58	518	139	1976	
...	...	635	242	1977	
...	...	—	—	1970	TOGO
...	...	—	—	1974	
...	...	—	—	1975	
41	1	—	—	1970	
144	11	—	—	1974	
186	15	—	—	1975	
213	16	160	26	1976	
—	—	—	—	1971	TUNISIA ‡
—	—	—	—	1974	
—	—	—	—	1975	
—	—	—	—	1976	
—	—	—	—	1977	
—	—	—	—	1978	
—	—	—	—	1970	
—	—	—	—	1974	
—	—	—	—	1975	
—	—	—	—	1976	
—	—	—	—	1977	
—	—	—	—	1978	
48	9	83	8	1970	UGANDA
53	9	114	3	1974	
66	18	107	7	1975	
66	15	126	8	1976	
66	15	291	28	1977	
367	63	912	*163	1970	
471	128	1 192	294	1974	
471	124	1 089	245	1975	
446	116	1 241	347	1976	
402	111	2 504	915	1977	
					UNITED REPUBLIC OF
38	5	24	2	1970	CAMEROON
333	46	229	5	1970	
—	—	—	—	1974	
—	—	—	—	1975	
—	—	—	—	1977	
					UNITED REPUBLIC OF
...	...	—	—	1974	TANZANIA
...	...	—	—	1975	
—	—	113	...	1976	
—	—	76	24	1977	
204	41	—	—	1970	
661	202	—	—	1974	
420	150	—	—	1975	
—	—	890	4	1976	
—	—	230	42	1977	

3.11 Third level: teachers and students by type of institution
Troisième degré: professeurs et étudiants par types d'établissement
Tercer grado: personal docente y estudiantes por tipos de establecimiento

COUNTRY PAYS PAIS		YEAR ANNEE AÑO	ALL INSTITUTIONS TOTAL DES ETABLISSEMENTS TODOS LOS ESTABLECIMIENTOS		UNIVERSITIES AND EQUIVALENT INSTITUTIONS UNIVERSITES ET ETABLISSEMENTS EQUIVALENTS UNIVERSIDADES Y ESTAB. EQUIVALENTES	
			TOTAL	FEMALE FEMININ FEMENINO	TOTAL	FEMALE FEMININ FEMENINO
UPPER VOLTA	TEACHERS	1970	30	...	30	...
		1974	102	19	102	19
		1975	166	22	166	22
		1977	93	20	93	20
	STUDENTS	1970	183	27	183	27
		1974	756	170	756	170
		1975	1 067	212	1 067	212
		1977	1 233	268	1 233	268
ZAIRE	TEACHERS	1970	1 315	...	*695	...
	STUDENTS	1970	12 363	*675	7 565	*350
		1974	21 021	...	13 546	...
ZAMBIA	TEACHERS	1970	219	16	189	16
		1974	...	...	256	...
	STUDENTS	1970	1 433	214	1 231	182
		1974	4 681	*1 103	2 612	*440
		1975	8 403	*1 170	2 354	*395
		1976	8 783	...	2 569	...
		1977	9 192	...	3 111	...
AMERICA, NORTH						
BARBADOS	TEACHERS	1971	111	...	70	...
	STUDENTS	1970	763	349	459	179
		1974	...	...	991	...
		1975	...	...	1 065	...
		1976	...	...	1 140	...
BELIZE	TEACHERS	1970	15	8	—	—
		1974	23	15	—	—
	STUDENTS	1970	113	79	—	—
		1974	121	71	—	—
CANADA ‡	TEACHERS	1970	...	...	24 612	3 140
		1974	44 494	7 217	29 959	4 157
		1975	...	...	30 732	4 304
		1976	*49 533	...	31 533	4 533
		1977	52 114	...	32 167	4 781
	STUDENTS	1970	642 013	257 808	477 292	174 543
		1974	706 652	308 614	502 322	213 009
		1975	818 153	367 270	546 769	234 270
		1976	824 588	390 172	567 463	260 172
		1977	826 213	398 747	585 877	276 928
COSTA RICA	STUDENTS	1970	15 473	6 735	12 913	4 842
		1974	28 619	...	28 230	...
		1975	32 928	...	32 483	...
		1976	36 350	...	36 350	...
		1977	38 629	...	38 629	...
CUBA	TEACHERS	1970	4 129	...	4 129	...
		1974	5 725	...	5 725	...
		1975	5 380	...	5 380	...
		1976	6 263	...	6 263	...

Third level: teachers and students by type of institution   3.11
Troisième degré: professeurs et étudiants par types d'établissement
Tercer grado: personal docente y estudiantes por tipos de establecimiento

NON—UNIVERSITY TEACHER TRAINING ENSEIGNEMENT NORMAL NON—UNIVERSITAIRE ENSEÑANZA NORMAL NO UNIVERSITARIA		OTHER NON—UNIVERSITY INSTITUTIONS AUTRES ETABLISSEMENTS NON—UNIVERSITAIRES OTROS ESTABLECIMIENTOS NO UNIVERSITARIOS		YEAR ANNEE AÑO	COUNTRY PAYS PAIS
TOTAL	FEMALE FEMININ FEMENINO	TOTAL	FEMALE FEMININ FEMENINO		
–	–	–	–	1970	UPPER VOLTA
–	–	–	–	1974	
–	–	–	–	1975	
–	–	–	–	1977	
–	–	–	–	1970	
–	–	–	–	1974	
–	–	–	–	1975	
–	–	–	–	1977	
*330	...	*290	...	1970	ZAIRE
2 261	*280	2 537	*45	1970	
4 400	...	3 075	...	1974	
15	–	15	–	1970	ZAMBIA
48	6	...	...	1974	
98	32	104	–	1970	
594	150	1 475	513	1974	
778	161	5 271	614	1975	
645	...	5 569	...	1976	
658	...	5 423	...	1977	
					AMERICA, NORTH
38	20	3	–	1971	BARBADOS
*280	*170	24	–	1970	
...	...	...	...	1974	
...	...	...	...	1975	
...	...	...	...	1976	
15	8	–	–	1970	BELIZE
23	15	–	–	1974	
113	79	–	–	1970	
121	71	–	–	1974	
556	*210	...	...	1970	CANADA ‡
–	–	14 535	3 060	1974	
–	–	...	...	1975	
–	–	*18 000	...	1976	
75	...	19 872	...	1977	
10 601	7 921	154 120	75 344	1970	
–	–	204 330	95 605	1974	
–	–	271 384	133 000	1975	
–	–	257 125	130 000	1976	
517	238	239 819	121 581	1977	
2 360	1 693	*200	*200	1970	COSTA RICA
		389	...	1974	
		445	...	1975	
–	–	–	–	1976	
				1977	
–	–	–	–	1970	CUBA
–	–	–	–	1974	
–	–	–	–	1975	
–	–	–	–	1976	

3.11   Third level: teachers and students by type of institution
        Troisième degré: professeurs et étudiants par types d'établissement
        Tercer grado: personal docente y estudiantes por tipos de establecimiento

COUNTRY PAYS PAIS		YEAR ANNEE AÑO	ALL INSTITUTIONS TOTAL DES ETABLISSEMENTS TODOS LOS ESTABLECIMIENTOS		UNIVERSITIES AND EQUIVALENT INSTITUTIONS UNIVERSITES ET ETABLISSEMENTS EQUIVALENTS UNIVERSIDADES Y ESTAB. EQUIVALENTES	
			TOTAL	FEMALE FEMININ FEMENINO	TOTAL	FEMALE FEMININ FEMENINO
CUBA (CONT.)	STUDENTS	1970	26 342	10 366	26 342	10 366
		1974	68 051	24 409	68 051	24 409
		1975	82 688	...	82 688	...
		1976	106 850	43 301	106 850	43 301
		1977	122 456	...	122 456	...
		1978	130 100	...	130 100	...
DOMINICAN REPUBLIC	TEACHERS	1974	...	...	*2 000	...
		1975	...	...	1 435	...
		1976	...	...	...	...
	STUDENTS	1970	23 546	10 143	23 098	9 883
		1974	41 352	19 196	38 552	18 236
		1975	...	...	28 628	11 773
		1976	...	...	44 725	...
EL SALVADOR	TEACHERS	1970	751	126	680	107
		1974	1 951	481	1 602	377
		1975	2 137	485	1 880	379
		1977	1 809	562	1 557	407
	STUDENTS	1970	9 515	...	9 083	...
		1974	26 069	7 806	23 219	6 978
		1975	28 281	9 468	26 909	8 931
		1977	30 371	...	28 065	...
GUATEMALA ‡	TEACHERS	1970	1 314	...	1 314	...
		1974	1 354	...	1 354	...
		1975	1 411	...	1 411	...
		1976	1 934	...	1 934	...
	STUDENTS	1970	15 609	2 906	15 609	2 906
		1974	20 060	4 325	20 060	4 325
		1975	22 881	5 277	22 881	5 277
		1976	25 925	6 332	25 978	6 348
		1977	29 234	7 416	29 234	7 416
HAITI	TEACHERS	1975	408	48	366	47
		1976	448	68	366	45
		1977	...	...	384	...
	STUDENTS	1975	2 881	691	2 467	665
		1976	3 309	995	2 617	703
		1977	...	...	2 926	880
HONDURAS	TEACHERS	1974	642	...	549	...
		1975	817	...	648	116
		1976	886	...	710	153
		1977	1 136	...	964	251
	STUDENTS	1970	...	...	4 047	...
		1974	10 361	3 404	9 226	2 761
		1975	11 907	4 060	10 635	3 408
		1976	15 499	5 055	13 024	4 552
		1977	20 205	7 427	18 628	6 725
JAMAICA	TEACHERS	1970	567	...	291	...
	STUDENTS	1970	6 892	...	2 886	1 271
		1974	...	...	3 735	...
		1975	...	...	3 963	...
		1976	...	...	4 091	...
MEXICO	TEACHERS	1971	30 552	...	...	...
		1974	37 376	...	34 869	...
		1975	47 529	...	45 025	...
		1976	43 114	...	40 980	...
		1977	69 269	...	67 332	...

Third level: teachers and students by type of institution 3.11
Troisième degré: professeurs et étudiants par types d'établissement
Tercer grado: personal docente y estudiantes por tipos de establecimiento

NON—UNIVERSITY TEACHER TRAINING ENSEIGNEMENT NORMAL NON—UNIVERSITAIRE ENSEÑANZA NORMAL NO UNIVERSITARIA		OTHER NON—UNIVERSITY INSTITUTIONS AUTRES ETABLISSEMENTS NON—UNIVERSITAIRES OTROS ESTABLECIMIENTOS NO UNIVERSITARIOS		YEAR ANNEE AÑO	COUNTRY PAYS PAIS
TOTAL	FEMALE FEMININ FEMENINO	TOTAL	FEMALE FEMININ FEMENINO		
–	–	–	–	1970	CUBA (CONT.)
–	–	–	–	1974	
–	–	–	–	1975	
–	–	–	–	1976	
–	–	–	–	1977	
–	–	–	–	1978	
–	–	...	...	1974	DOMINICAN REPUBLIC
–	–	...	...	1975	
–	–	...	...	1976	
–	–	448	260	1970	
–	–	*2 800	*960	1974	
–	–	...	...	1975	
–	–	...	...	1976	
19	5	52	14	1970	EL SALVADOR
39	16	310	88	1974	
60	5	197	101	1975	
6	4	246	151	1977	
172	52	260	82	1970	
294	87	2 556	741	1974	
176	53	1 196	484	1975	
97	53	2 209	662	1977	
–	–	–	–	1970	GUATEMALA ‡
–	–	–	–	1974	
–	–	–	–	1975	
–	–	–	–	1976	
–	–	–	–	1970	
–	–	–	–	1974	
–	–	–	–	1975	
–	–	–	–	1976	
–	–	–	–	1977	
–	–	42	1	1975	HAITI
–	–	82	23	1976	
–	–	...	...	1977	
–	–	414	26	1975	
–	–	692	292	1976	
–	–	...	...	1977	
68	...	25	...	1974	HONDURAS
127	...	42	...	1975	
115	...	61	...	1976	
125	22	47	...	1977	
			...	1970	
928	643	207	–	1974	
969	651	303	1	1975	
2 146	1 401	329	2	1976	
1 074	702	503	–	1977	
151	...	*125	...	1970	JAMAICA
2 058	1 715	1 948	...	1970	
...	...	...	...	1974	
...	...	...	...	1975	
...	...	...	...	1976	
	...	...	...	1971	MEXICO
2 507	...	–	–	1974	
2 504	...	–	–	1975	
2 134	...	–	–	1976	
1 937	...	–	–	1977	

3.11 Third level: teachers and students by type of institution
Troisième degré: professeurs et étudiants par types d'établissement
Tercer grado: personal docente y estudiantes por tipos de establecimiento

COUNTRY PAYS PAIS		YEAR ANNEE AÑO	ALL INSTITUTIONS TOTAL DES ETABLISSEMENTS TODOS LOS ESTABLECIMIENTOS		UNIVERSITIES AND EQUIVALENT INSTITUTIONS UNIVERSITES ET ETABLISSEMENTS EQUIVALENTS UNIVERSIDADES Y ESTAB. EQUIVALENTES	
			TOTAL	FEMALE FEMININ FEMENINO	TOTAL	FEMALE FEMININ FEMENINO
MEXICO (CONT.)	STUDENTS	1970	247 637	49 844		...
		1974	498 361	...	453 015	...
		1975	562 056	...	520 194	...
		1976	569 266	154 398	525 035	132 732
		1977	654 959	188 252	622 072	171 573
NICARAGUA	TEACHERS	1970	604	...	492	...
	STUDENTS	1970	9 385	2 987	8 648	2 673
PANAMA	TEACHERS	1970	448	95	448	95
		1974	999	...	999	...
		1975	1 519	...	1 519	...
		1976	1 427	...	1 427	...
		1977	1 508	...	1 508	...
		1978	1 808	...	1 808	...
	STUDENTS	1970	8 947	3 800	8 947	3 800
		1974	24 292	12 400	24 292	12 400
		1975	26 289	*13 090	26 289	*13 090
		1976	30 473	15 608	30 473	15 608
		1977	34 720	17 907	34 720	17 907
		1978	34 780	...	34 780	...
FORMER CANAL ZONE	TEACHERS	1970	*70	...	*70	...
	STUDENTS	1970	1 244	629	1 244	629
		1974	1 675	794	1 675	794
		1975	1 590	796	1 590	796
		1976	1 333	648	1 333	648
		1977	1 378	737	1 378	737
PUERTO RICO	TEACHERS	1970	*4 000	...	...	...
	STUDENTS	1970	63 073	33 343	59 067	30 884
		1974	89 671	48 998	83 655	45 653
		1975	97 517	52 138	91 254	48 383
		1976	100 885	55 540	68 832	36 993
		1977	119 970	67 077	85 351	47 274
TRINIDAD AND TOBAGO	TEACHERS	1970	412	100	329	64
		1975	...	...	178	...
	STUDENTS	1970	2 375	857	1 671	464
		1974	2 962	1 164	2 202	754
		1975	4 940	...	2 229	702
		1976	...	...	2 310	828
		1977	...	...	2 477	890
UNITED STATES OF AMERICA	TEACHERS	1970	574 000	...	...	...
		1974	633 000	160 000	488 000	112 000
		1975	670 000	...	...	...
		1976	687 000	...	...	...
		1977	...	...	...	...
	STUDENTS	1970	8 498 117	3 507 163	6 288 196	2 609 357
		1974	10 223 729	4 601 300	6 912 182	3 072 195
		1975	11 184 859	5 035 862	7 223 037	3 235 908
		1976	11 012 137	5 201 309	7 128 816	3 298 132
		1977	11 285 787	5 496 763	7 242 845	3 418 610
U.S. VIRGIN ISLANDS	TEACHERS	1970	*40	...	*40	...

Third level: teachers and students by type of institution 3.11
Troisième degré: professeurs et étudiants par types d'établissement
Tercer grado: personal docente y estudiantes por tipos de establecimiento

NON—UNIVERSITY TEACHER TRAINING ENSEIGNEMENT NORMAL NON—UNIVERSITAIRE ENSEÑANZA NORMAL NO UNIVERSITARIA		OTHER NON—UNIVERSITY INSTITUTIONS AUTRES ETABLISSEMENTS NON—UNIVERSITAIRES OTROS ESTABLECIMIENTOS NO UNIVERSITARIOS		YEAR ANNEE AÑO	COUNTRY PAYS PAIS
TOTAL	FEMALE FEMININ FEMENINO	TOTAL	FEMALE FEMININ FEMENINO		
... 45 346	...	...	...	1970	MEXICO (CONT.)
41 862	...	—	—	1974	
42 762	20 793	1 469	873	1975	
31 475	16 032	1 412	647	1976	
				1977	
—	—	112	...	1970	NICARAGUA
—	—	737	314	1970	
—	—	—	—	1970	PANAMA
—	—	—	—	1974	
—	—	—	—	1975	
—	—	—	—	1976	
—	—	—	—	1977	
				1978	
—	—	—	—	1970	
—	—	—	—	1974	
—	—	—	—	1975	
—	—	—	—	1976	
—	—	—	—	1977	
				1978	
—	—	—	—	1970	FORMER CANAL ZONE
—	—	—	—	1970	
—	—	—	—	1974	
—	—	—	—	1975	
—	—	—	—	1976	
—	—	—	—	1977	
—	—	...	...	1970	PUERTO RICO
—	—	4 006	2 459	1970	
—	—	6 016	3 345	1974	
—	—	6 263	3 755	1975	
—	—	32 053	18 547	1976	
—	—	34 619	19 803	1977	
*83	*36	—	—	1970	TRINIDAD AND TOBAGO
157	77	...	...	1975	
704	393	—	—	1970	
*760	*410	—	—	1974	
1 287	876	1 424	...	1975	
1 274	905	...	...	1976	
...	...	...	...	1977	
—	—		...	1970	UNITED STATES OF AMERICA
—	—	145 000	48 000	1974	
—	—	...	...	1975	
—	—	...	...	1976	
—	—	...	...	1977	
—	—	2 209 921	897 806	1970	
—	—	3 311 547	1 529 105	1974	
—	—	3 961 822	1 799 954	1975	
—	—	883 321	1 903 177	1976	
—	—	4 042 942	2 078 361	1977	
—	—	—	—	1970	U.S. VIRGIN ISLANDS

3.11 Third level: teachers and students by type of institution
Troisième degré: professeurs et étudiants par types d'établissement
Tercer grado: personal docente y estudiantes por tipos de establecimiento

COUNTRY PAYS PAIS		YEAR ANNEE AÑO	ALL INSTITUTIONS TOTAL DES ETABLISSEMENTS TODOS LOS ESTABLECIMIENTOS		UNIVERSITIES AND EQUIVALENT INSTITUTIONS UNIVERSITES ET ETABLISSEMENTS EQUIVALENTS UNIVERSIDADES Y ESTAB. EQUIVALENTES	
			TOTAL	FEMALE FEMININ FEMENINO	TOTAL	FEMALE FEMININ FEMENINO
U.S. VIRGIN ISLANDS (CONT.)	STUDENTS	1970 1974 1975 1976 1977	1 445 1 918 2 069 2 122 2 119	830 1 270 1 301 1 350 1 435	1 445 1 918 2 069 2 122 2 119	830 1 270 1 301 1 350 1 435
AMERICA, SOUTH						
ARGENTINA ‡	TEACHERS	1970 1974 1975 1976 1977	22 477 41 968 45 204 39 007 39 970	6 889 15 715 17 665 15 605 16 090	16 004 30 613 33 176 25 863 26 400	3 186 8 198 9 770 6 837 7 200
	STUDENTS	1970 1974 1975 1976 1977	274 634 497 727 596 736 601 395 619 950	117 251 224 724 283 762 287 199 297 100	236 515 441 302 536 959 533 152 547 400	84 835 175 243 231 715 228 519 234 200
BOLIVIA	STUDENTS	1970 1974 1975 1976 1977	35 250 44 890 *49 850 *51 585 ...	... ...	28 662 31 201 34 350 34 585 41 408	... ...
BRAZIL	TEACHERS	1970 1974 1975	42 968 64 479 120 550	8 898 16 156 ...	42 968 64 479 120 550	8 898 16 156 ...
	STUDENTS	1970 1974 1975 1976	430 473 954 674 1 089 808 *1 316 640	162 176 452 260	430 473 954 674 1 089 808 *1 316 640	162 176 452 260 ... ...
CHILE ‡	TEACHERS	1974 1975	22 211 11 419	... ...	22 211 11 419	... ...
	STUDENTS	1970 1974 1975 1976 1977 1978	78 430 145 003 149 647 134 149 131 793 130 982	30 125 ... *67 400 56 996 55 293 55 016	78 430 145 003 149 647 134 149 131 793 130 982	30 125 ... *67 400 56 996 55 293 55 016
COLOMBIA	TEACHERS	1970 1974 1975 1976 1977 1978	10 295 17 655 21 153 ... 24 960 25 708	... ... 2 934 ... 4 469 ...	10 295 16 533 19 821 20 402 23 692 24 589	... ... 2 585 ... 4 158 ...
	STUDENTS	1970 1974 1975 1976 1977 1978	85 560 148 613 186 635 ... 237 477 274 893	22 936 ... ... 92 487 ...	85 560 141 782 179 762 202 437 229 475 263 697	22 936 ... ... 88 126 ...
ECUADOR	TEACHERS	1970	2 867	207	2 833	194
	STUDENTS	1970 1974 1975 1976	38 692 136 695 170 173 180 813	11 629	38 582 136 695 170 173 180 813	11 548 ... ...

Third level: teachers and students by type of institution   3.11
Troisième degré: professeurs et étudiants par types d'établissement
Tercer grado: personal docente y estudiantes por tipos de establecimiento

NON—UNIVERSITY TEACHER TRAINING ENSEIGNEMENT NORMAL NON—UNIVERSITAIRE ENSEÑANZA NORMAL NO UNIVERSITARIA		OTHER NON—UNIVERSITY INSTITUTIONS AUTRES ETABLISSEMENTS NON—UNIVERSITAIRES OTROS ESTABLECIMIENTOS NO UNIVERSITARIOS		YEAR ANNEE	COUNTRY PAYS
TOTAL	FEMALE FEMININ FEMENINO	TOTAL	FEMALE FEMININ FEMENINO	AÑO	PAIS
—	—	—	—	1970	U.S. VIRGIN ISLANDS
—	—	—	—	1974	(CONT.)
—	—	—	—	1975	
—	—	—	—	1976	
—	—	—	—	1977	
					AMERICA, SOUTH
6 473	3 703	./.	./.	1970	ARGENTINA ‡
11 355	7 517	./.	./.	1974	
12 028	7 895	./.	./.	1975	
13 144	8 768	./.	./.	1976	
13 570	8 890	./.	./.	1977	
31 107	27 024	7 012	5 392	1970	
47 671	42 847	8 754	6 634	1974	
51 306	45 861	8 471	6 186	1975	
58 254	51 962	9 989	6 718	1976	
60 430	55 010	12 120	7 890	1977	
6 598	...	—	—	1970	BOLIVIA
13 689	...	—	—	1974	
*15 500	...	—	—	1975	
*17 000	...	—	—	1976	
...	...	—	—	1977	
—	—	—	—	1970	BRAZIL
—	—	—	—	1974	
—	—	—	—	1975	
—	—	—	—	1970	
—	—	—	—	1974	
—	—	—	—	1975	
—	—	—	—	1976	
—	—	—	—	1974	CHILE ‡
—	—	—	—	1975	
—	—	—	—	1970	
—	—	—	—	1974	
—	—	—	—	1975	
—	—	—	—	1976	
—	—	—	—	1977	
—	—	—	—	1978	
—	—	—	—	1970	COLOMBIA
—	—	1 122	...	1974	
—	—	1 332	349	1975	
—	—	...	...	1976	
—	—	1 268	311	1977	
—	—	1 119	...	1978	
—	—	—	—	1970	
—	—	6 831	...	1974	
—	—	6 873	...	1975	
—	—	...	...	1976	
—	—	8 002	4 361	1977	
—	—	11 196	...	1978	
—	—	34	13	1970	ECUADOR
—	—	110	81	1970	
—	—	—	—	1974	
—	—	—	—	1975	
—	—	—	—	1976	

3.11   Third level: teachers and students by type of institution
       Troisième degré: professeurs et étudiants par types d'établissement
       Tercer grado: personal docente y estudiantes por tipos de establecimiento

COUNTRY PAYS PAIS		YEAR ANNEE AÑO	ALL INSTITUTIONS TOTAL DES ETABLISSEMENTS TODOS LOS ESTABLECIMIENTOS		UNIVERSITIES AND EQUIVALENT INSTITUTIONS UNIVERSITES ET ETABLISSEMENTS EQUIVALENTS UNIVERSIDADES Y ESTAB. EQUIVALENTES	
			TOTAL	FEMALE FEMININ FEMENINO	TOTAL	FEMALE FEMININ FEMENINO
FRENCH GUIANA	STUDENTS	1977	4 087	2 128	3 574	1 787
		1978	4 019	...	3 598	...
GUYANA	TEACHERS	1971	85	15	85	15
		1975	...	...	172	37
	STUDENTS	1970	1 112	218	1 112	218
		1975	2 852	1 012	1 749	486
PARAGUAY	TEACHERS	1970	956	...	923	...
		1976	...	...	1 767	381
		1977	...	...	1 756	369
		1978	...	...	1 945	441
	STUDENTS	1970	8 172	3 442	7 853	3 194
		1974	14 009	...	13 763	...
		1975	17 441	...	17 153	...
		1976	17 811	7 773	17 478	7 515
		1977	20 318	8 691	20 032	8 469
		1978	20 812	9 037	20 496	8 791
PERU	TEACHERS	1970	10 673	1 631	8 573	891
		1974	11 127	1 620	10 297	1 254
		1975	11 598	1 669	10 844	1 321
		1976	12 113	1 776	11 590	1 524
		1977	13 468	...	11 324	...
	STUDENTS	1970	126 234	43 349	108 535	32 973
		1974	180 699	59 273	170 448	52 860
		1975	195 641	62 850	186 511	59 684
		1976	190 635	62 124	183 233	59 459
		1977	233 420	...	192 686	...
SURINAME	TEACHERS	1976	106	3	106	3
		1977	118	4	118	4
	STUDENTS	1970	292	–	292	–
		1974	401	36	401	36
		1975	465	54	465	54
		1976	761	224	761	224
		1977	900	312	900	312
URUGUAY	TEACHERS	1974	2 315	525	2 315	525
		1975	2 332	530	2 332	530
		1977	3 263	...	3 263	...
	STUDENTS	1974	26 280	11 887	26 280	11 887
		1975	32 627	14 313	32 627	14 313
		1977	39 392	18 703	39 392	18 703
VENEZUELA	TEACHERS	1970	8 155	1 448	7 621	1 273
		1974	13 911	...	11 661	...
		1975	15 792	...	12 849	...
		1976	*19 787	...	15 391	...
		1977	21 534	...	16 621	...
	STUDENTS	1970	100 767	*41 150	94 831	*37 800
		1974	187 688	*84 580	165 238	*74 200
		1975	213 542	...	185 518	...
		1976	*247 518	...	202 422	...
		1977	265 671	...	218 392	...

Third level: teachers and students by type of institution   3.11
Troisième degré: professeurs et étudiants par types d'établissement
Tercer grado: personal docente y estudiantes por tipos de establecimiento

NON–UNIVERSITY TEACHER TRAINING ENSEIGNEMENT NORMAL NON–UNIVERSITAIRE ENSEÑANZA NORMAL NO UNIVERSITARIA		OTHER NON–UNIVERSITY INSTITUTIONS AUTRES ETABLISSEMENTS NON–UNIVERSITAIRES OTROS ESTABLECIMIENTOS NO UNIVERSITARIOS		YEAR ANNEE AÑO	COUNTRY PAYS PAIS
TOTAL	FEMALE FEMININ FEMENINO	TOTAL	FEMALE FEMININ FEMENINO		
–	–	513	341	1977	FRENCH GUIANA
–	–	421	...	1978	
–	–	–	–	1971	GUYANA
...	...	...	...	1975	
–	–	–	–	1970	
955	499	148	27	1975	
33	...	–	–	1970	PARAGUAY
...	...	–	–	1976	
...	...	–	–	1977	
...	...	–	–	1978	
319	248	–	–	1970	
246	...	–	–	1974	
288	...	–	–	1975	
333	258	–	–	1976	
286	222	–	–	1977	
316	246	–	–	1978	
2 100	740	–	–	1970	PERU
830	366	–	–	1974	
754	348	–	–	1975	
523	252	–	–	1976	
459	...	1 685	...	1977	
17 699	10 376	–	–	1970	
10 251	6 413	–	–	1974	
9 130	3 166	–	–	1975	
7 402	2 665	–	–	1976	
6 289	...	34 445	...	1977	
–	–	–	–	1976	SURINAME
–	–	–	–	1977	
–	–	–	–	1970	
–	–	–	–	1974	
–	–	–	–	1975	
–	–	–	–	1976	
–	–	–	–	1977	
–	–	–	–	1974	URUGUAY
–	–	–	–	1975	
–	–	–	–	1977	
–	–	–	–	1974	
–	–	–	–	1975	
–	–	–	–	1977	
464	160	*70	*15	1970	VENEZUELA
*1 000	...	*1 250	...	1974	
1 301	...	1 642	...	1975	
*1 573	...	*2 823	...	1976	
1 736	...	3 177	...	1977	
5 320	*3 200	616	*150	1970	
*12 500	*6 850	*9 950	*3 530	1974	
14 371	...	13 653	...	1975	
*21 327	...	*23 769	...	1976	
19 905	...	27 374	...	1977	

3.11 Third level: teachers and students by type of institution
Troisième degré: professeurs et étudiants par types d'établissement
Tercer grado: personal docente y estudiantes por tipos de establecimiento

COUNTRY PAYS PAIS		YEAR ANNEE AÑO	ALL INSTITUTIONS TOTAL DES ETABLISSEMENTS TODOS LOS ESTABLECIMIENTOS		UNIVERSITIES AND EQUIVALENT INSTITUTIONS UNIVERSITES ET ETABLISSEMENTS EQUIVALENTS UNIVERSIDADES Y ESTAB. EQUIVALENTES	
			TOTAL	FEMALE FEMININ FEMENINO	TOTAL	FEMALE FEMININ FEMENINO
ASIA						
AFGHANISTAN	TEACHERS	1970	793	44	724	41
		1974	982	64	737	42
		1975	...	...	...	...
		1976	...	...	825	37
		1977	...	...	737	36
	STUDENTS	1970	7 732	1 135	6 215	876
		1974	10 956	1 495	7 856	653
		1975	*12 256	*1 681	8 681	800
		1976	*14 214	*1 951	8 348	843
		1977	*16 147	*4 286	10 351	1 583
BAHRAIN	TEACHERS	1970	32	12	–	–
		1974	67	11	–	–
		1975	79	11	–	–
		1976	101	18	–	–
		1977	...	...	–	–
	STUDENTS	1970	289	151	–	–
		1974	669	334	–	–
		1975	703	371	–	–
		1976	1 226	645	–	–
		1977	1 207	516	–	–
BANGLADESH	TEACHERS	1970	7 201	581	1 138	69
		1976	13 503	1 370	2 103	175
		1977	13 110	1 309	2 153	176
	STUDENTS	1970	117 603	11 453	16 493	2 297
		1974	183 833	18 808	...	...
		1976	158 604	19 827	27 553	4 703
		1977	181 756	24 803	27 584	4 876
BHUTAN	TEACHERS	1978	26	–	10	–
	STUDENTS	1978	140	32	64	9
BRUNEI	TEACHERS	1977	48	13	–	–
	STUDENTS	1977	331	182	–	–
BURMA	TEACHERS	1970	3 509	...	...	...
		1974	3 297	...	...	...
		1976	...	...	2 606	858
	STUDENTS	1970	46 150	...	...	...
		1974	53 642	...	...	...
		1975	56 083	...	...	...
		1976	61 547	30 013	50 676	24 157
CHINA	STUDENTS	1977	*600 000	*180 000	...	...
CYPRUS	TEACHERS	1970	64	14	–	–
		1974	78	19	–	–
		1975	69	17	–	–
		1976	90	22	–	–
		1977	133	41	–	–
	STUDENTS	1970	698	306	–	–
		1974	611	233	–	–
		1975	602	241	–	–
		1976	782	334	–	–
		1977	1 097	595	–	–

Third level: teachers and students by type of institution 3.11
Troisième degré: professeurs et étudiants par types d'établissement
Tercer grado: personal docente y estudiantes por tipos de establecimiento

NON—UNIVERSITY TEACHER TRAINING ENSEIGNEMENT NORMAL NON—UNIVERSITAIRE ENSEÑANZA NORMAL NO UNIVERSITARIA		OTHER NON—UNIVERSITY INSTITUTIONS AUTRES ETABLISSEMENTS NON—UNIVERSITAIRES OTROS ESTABLECIMIENTOS NO UNIVERSITARIOS		YEAR ANNEE AÑO	COUNTRY PAYS PAIS
TOTAL	FEMALE FEMININ FEMENINO	TOTAL	FEMALE FEMININ FEMENINO		
					ASIA
55	2	14	1	1970	AFGHANISTAN
226	19	19	3	1974	
258	17	...	...	1975	
304	21	...	...	1976	
395	25	...	...	1977	
1 343	249	174	10	1970	
2 837	795	263	47	1974	
3 275	826	*300	*55	1975	
5 516	1 048	*350	*60	1976	
5 396	2 638	*400	*65	1977	
*32	*12	—	—	1970	BAHRAIN
39	11	28	—	1974	
43	11	36	—	1975	
53	13	48	5	1976	
43	15	...	...	1977	
289	151	—	—	1970	
337	260	332	74	1974	
281	239	422	132	1975	
329	279	471	162	1976	
403	310	804	206	1977	
122	29	5 941	483	1970	BANGLADESH
—	—	11 400	1 195	1976	
—	—	10 957	1 133	1977	
1 579	422	99 531	8 734	1970	
...	...			1974	
—	—	131 051	19 827	1976	
—	—	154 172	19 927	1977	
16	—	—	—	1978	BHUTAN
76	23	—	—	1978	
48	13	—	—	1977	BRUNEI
331	182	—	—	1977	
...	...	...	...	1970	BURMA
...	...	...	...	1974	
—	—	...	...	1976	
...	...	...	...	1970	
...	...	...	...	1974	
...	...	...	...	1975	
—	—	10 871	5 856	1976	
...	...	...	...	1977	CHINA
21	4	43	10	1970	CYPRUS
18	4	60	15	1974	
8	2	61	15	1975	
27	5	63	17	1976	
29	5	104	36	1977	
279	154	419	152	1970	
115	58	496	175	1974	
56	44	546	197	1975	
97	77	685	257	1976	
127	101	970	494	1977	

3.11 Third level: teachers and students by type of institution
Troisième degré: professeurs et étudiants par types d'établissement
Tercer grado: personal docente y estudiantes por tipos de establecimiento

COUNTRY / PAYS / PAIS		YEAR / ANNEE / AÑO	ALL INSTITUTIONS TOTAL DES ETABLISSEMENTS TODOS LOS ESTABLECIMIENTOS		UNIVERSITIES AND EQUIVALENT INSTITUTIONS UNIVERSITES ET ETABLISSEMENTS EQUIVALENTS UNIVERSIDADES Y ESTAB. EQUIVALENTES	
			TOTAL	FEMALE FEMININ FEMENINO	TOTAL	FEMALE FEMININ FEMENINO
DEMOCRATIC KAMPUCHEA	STUDENTS	1970	9 228	...	9 228	...
HONG KONG ‡	TEACHERS	1970	1 677	252	710	109
		1974	2 817	405	831	113
		1975	3 043	446	814	138
		1976	3 115	467	1 008	145
		1977	...	...	1 149	206
	STUDENTS	1970	25 516	7 608	5 610	1 842
		1974	38 265	10 189	7 701	2 305
		1975	44 482	11 194	8 264	2 435
		1976	44 210	11 939	8 988	2 784
		1977	...	...	9 708	3 083
INDIA ‡	TEACHERS	1971	*203 414	*32 096	...	...
		1974	*232 903	*37 984	...	...
		1975	235 822	39 272	...	...
	STUDENTS	1970	2 903 551	...	...	...
		1974	4 531 689	1 034 585	...	...
		1975	4 615 992	1 070 962	...	...
		1976	*3 198 550	*874 590	...	...
		1977	*3 216 350	*878 428	...	...
INDONESIA	TEACHERS	1970	20 018	...	...	...
		1974	43 720	...	...	...
		1976	46 668	...	29 128	...
	STUDENTS	1970	248 220	*62 400	...	...
		1974	264 433	...	...	...
		1975	278 200	...	...	...
		1976	296 326	83 158	173 537	45 542
IRAN ‡	TEACHERS	1970	6 474	797	3 828	424
		1974	12 310	1 682	6 046	746
		1975	13 392	1 831	6 253	893
		1976	13 952	2 058	7 091	1 119
	STUDENTS	1970	74 708	19 027	41 900	9 520
		1974	135 354	38 634	51 092	13 283
		1975	151 905	42 789	57 264	17 368
		1976	154 215	46 019	68 693	21 143
		1977	172 000	...	...	...
IRAQ ‡	TEACHERS	1970	1 822	155	1 822	155
		1974	3 270	568	2 721	421
		1975	3 801	748	2 965	383
		1976	3 014	549	2 277	345
		1977	3 777	540	3 536	454
		1978	5 464	...	3 711	513
	STUDENTS	1970	42 431	9 439	42 431	9 439
		1974	78 784	23 040	67 070	18 091
		1975	86 111	28 267	71 456	20 956
		1976	91 358	29 207	73 725	22 076
		1977	91 816	...	78 051	...
		1978	96 164	...	83 893	...
ISRAEL	TEACHERS	1970	*9 300	...	6 783	...
		1974	13 981	...	8 850	2 550
		1976	...	...	...	...
		1977	...	...	...	...
	STUDENTS	1970	55 486	*24 600	40 087	17 340
		1974	75 338	34 521	44 022	19 482
		1976	85 081	39 368	52 980	23 258
		1977	83 671	39 230	51 580	22 896

Third level: teachers and students by type of institution   3.11
Troisième degré: professeurs et étudiants par types d'établissement
Tercer grado: personal docente y estudiantes por tipos de establecimiento

NON—UNIVERSITY TEACHER TRAINING ENSEIGNEMENT NORMAL NON—UNIVERSITAIRE ENSEÑANZA NORMAL NO UNIVERSITARIA		OTHER NON—UNIVERSITY INSTITUTIONS AUTRES ETABLISSEMENTS NON—UNIVERSITAIRES OTROS ESTABLECIMIENTOS NO UNIVERSITARIOS		YEAR ANNEE AÑO	COUNTRY PAYS PAIS
TOTAL	FEMALE FEMININ FEMENINO	TOTAL	FEMALE FEMININ FEMENINO		
—	—	—	—	1970	DEMOCRATIC KAMPUCHEA
122	52	845	91	1970	HONG KONG ‡
211	92	1 775	200	1974	
209	86	2 020	222	1975	
197	80	1 910	242	1976	
...	...	1 204	57	1977	
1 870	1 287	18 036	4 479	1970	
3 759	2 501	26 805	5 383	1974	
3 818	2 501	32 400	6 258	1975	
2 650	1 685	32 572	7 470	1976	
...	...	23 740	4 488	1977	
...	...	...	...	1971	INDIA ‡
...	...	...	...	1974	
...	...	...	...	1975	
...	...	...	...	1970	
...	...	...	...	1974	
...	...	...	...	1975	
...	...	...	...	1976	
...	...	...	...	1977	
...	...	...	...	1970	INDONESIA
...	...	...	...	1974	
10 481	...	7 059	...	1976	
...	...	...	...	1970	
...	...	...	...	1974	
...	...	...	...	1975	
53 327	21 105	69 462	16 511	1976	
278	23	2 368	350	1970	IRAN ‡
444	110	5 820	826	1974	
637	86	6 502	852	1975	
./.	./.	6 861	939	1976	
6 516	1 308	26 292	8 199	1970	
7 369	614	76 893	24 737	1974	
8 108	1 569	86 533	23 852	1975	
./.	./.	85 522	24 876	1976	
...	...	...	...	1977	
—	—	—	—	1970	IRAQ ‡
239	77	310	70	1974	
405	263	431	102	1975	
247	82	490	122	1976	
241	6	./.	./.	1977	
257	...	1 496	262	1978	
—	—	—	—	1970	
7 449	3 721	4 265	1 228	1974	
8 238	5 627	6 417	1 684	1975	
7 665	4 245	9 968	2 886	1976	
6 252	...	7 513	...	1977	
4 448	...	7 823	...	1978	
1 145	...	*1 372	...	1970	ISRAEL
2 160	1 064	2 971	...	1974	
2 601	...	...	...	1976	
2 689	...	...	...	1977	
5 449	*4 660	9 950	*2 600	1970	
11 057	9 462	20 259	5 577	1974	
12 442	10 795	19 659	5 315	1976	
12 055	10 562	20 036	5 772	1977	

3.11 Third level: teachers and students by type of institution
Troisième degré: professeurs et étudiants par types d'établissement
Tercer grado: personal docente y estudiantes por tipos de establecimiento

COUNTRY PAYS PAIS		YEAR ANNEE AÑO	ALL INSTITUTIONS TOTAL DES ETABLISSEMENTS TODOS LOS ESTABLECIMIENTOS		UNIVERSITIES AND EQUIVALENT INSTITUTIONS UNIVERSITES ET ETABLISSEMENTS EQUIVALENTS UNIVERSIDADES Y ESTAB. EQUIVALENTES	
			TOTAL	FEMALE FEMININ FEMENINO	TOTAL	FEMALE FEMININ FEMENINO
JAPAN ‡	TEACHERS	1970	151 927	18 878	118 971	9 250
		1974	180 446	21 719	140 557	11 335
		1975	191 551	23 508	149 349	12 375
		1976	198 691	25 222	155 177	13 501
		1978	206 131	...	...	...
	STUDENTS	1970	1 819 323	512 759	1 503 286	287 823
		1974	2 155 893	676 467	1 762 040	383 738
		1975	2 248 903	727 256	1 840 708	412 072
		1976	2 299 344	763 162	1 896 859	435 466
		1977	2 436 862	793 255	1 996 128	453 960
		1978	2 693 972	1 011 983	...	...
JORDAN ‡	TEACHERS	1970	314	55	168	12
		1974	637	129	289	25
		1975	*797	*169	344	30
		1976	1 114	*217	539	*44
		1977	1 125	248	568	52
	STUDENTS	1970	4 518	1 349	2 913	859
		1974	9 302	3 120	4 805	1 405
		1975	11 873	3 969	5 307	1 694
		1976	16 420	5 726	7 524	2 600
		1977	17 219	6 366	8 358	2 970
KOREA, REPUBLIC OF	TEACHERS	1970	10 435	1 350	7 944	985
		1974	13 154	1 825	9 641	1 287
		1975	15 317	2 266	11 578	1 654
		1976	14 255	2 213	10 250	1 552
		1977	15 444	2 386	11 056	1 668
		1978	16 876	2 693	11 636	1 848
	STUDENTS	1970	201 436	48 863	153 054	33 448
		1974	273 479	74 235	204 597	52 355
		1975	297 219	81 228	222 856	57 717
		1976	325 460	86 655	245 101	62 390
		1977	365 107	93 168	268 549	66 005
		1978	418 875	104 515	296 933	71 258
KUWAIT	TEACHERS	1970	244	28	189	15
		1974	497	93	289	8
		1975	596	164	327	16
		1976	813	200	405	26
		1977	1 020	290	443	33
	STUDENTS	1970	2 686	1 300	2 225	1 078
		1974	5 800	3 506	4 658	2 724
		1975	8 104	4 608	6 246	3 499
		1976	9 934	5 466	7 733	4 228
		1977	12 391	6 638	9 728	5 189
LAO PEOPLE'S DEMOCRATIC REPUBLIC	TEACHERS	1970	...	...	—	—
		1974	152	13	152	13
	STUDENTS	1970	424	82	—	—
		1974	828	228	828	228
LEBANON	TEACHERS	1970	*2 300	...	*2 300	...
	STUDENTS	1970	42 578	*10 000	42 578	*10 000
		1978	78 628	...	78 628	...
MALAYSIA						
PENINSULAR MALAYSIA	TEACHERS	1970	1 213	225	561	69
		1974	2 624	600	1 347	227
		1976	5 007	1 109	2 753	495
		1977	4 506	1 065	2 740	550

Third level: teachers and students by type of institution   3.11
Troisième degré: professeurs et étudiants par types d'établissement
Tercer grado: personal docente y estudiantes por tipos de establecimiento

NON—UNIVERSITY TEACHER TRAINING ENSEIGNEMENT NORMAL NON—UNIVERSITAIRE ENSEÑANZA NORMAL NO UNIVERSITARIA		OTHER NON—UNIVERSITY INSTITUTIONS AUTRES ETABLISSEMENTS NON—UNIVERSITAIRES OTROS ESTABLECIMIENTOS NO UNIVERSITARIOS		YEAR ANNEE AÑO	COUNTRY PAYS PAIS
TOTAL	FEMALE FEMININ FEMENINO	TOTAL	FEMALE FEMININ FEMENINO		
–	–	32 956	9 628	1970	JAPAN ‡
–	–	39 889	10 384	1974	
–	–	42 202	11 133	1975	
–	–	43 514	11 721	1976	
–	–	...	...	1978	
–	–	316 037	224 936	1970	
–	–	393 853	292 729	1974	
–	–	408 195	315 184	1975	
–	–	404 585	328 917	1976	
–	–	440 734	339 295	1977	
–	–	...	...	1978	
76	22	70	21	1970	JORDAN ‡
166	69	182	35	1974	
228	87	*225	*52	1975	
335	122	240	51	1976	
357	145	200	51	1977	
1 282	317	323	173	1970	
3 314	1 264	1 183	451	1974	
5 104	1 870	1 462	405	1975	
7 006	2 723	1 890	403	1976	
6 543	3 020	2 318	376	1977	
660	41	1 831	324	1970	KOREA, REPUBLIC OF
809	51	2 704	487	1974	
791	50	2 948	562	1975	
766	49	3 239	612	1976	
725	49	3 663	669	1977	
526	38	4 714	807	1978	
12 190	6 619	36 192	8 796	1970	
11 176	5 980	57 706	15 900	1974	
8 504	4 933	65 859	18 578	1975	
5 813	3 579	74 546	20 686	1976	
3 876	2 430	92 682	24 733	1977	
4 308	2 962	117 634	30 295	1978	
55	13	–	–	1970	KUWAIT
175	70	33	15	1974	
175	97	94	51	1975	
186	106	222	68	1976	
317	161	260	96	1977	
461	222	–	–	1970	
990	630	152	152	1974	
984	605	874	504	1975	
875	508	1 326	730	1976	
1 037	635	1 626	814	1977	
					LAO PEOPLE'S
...	...	21	3	1970	DEMOCRATIC REPUBLIC
–	–	–	–	1974	
57	23	367	59	1970	
–	–	–	–	1974	
–	–	–	–	1970	LEBANON
–	–	–	–	1970	
–	–	–	–	1978	
					MALAYSIA
					PENINSULAR MALAYSIA
306	64	346	92	1970	
556	141	721	232	1974	
665	180	1 589	434	1976	
894	253	872	262	1977	

3.11 Third level: teachers and students by type of institution
Troisième degré: professeurs et étudiants par types d'établissement
Tercer grado: personal docente y estudiantes por tipos de establecimiento

COUNTRY PAYS PAIS		YEAR ANNEE AÑO	ALL INSTITUTIONS TOTAL DES ETABLISSEMENTS TODOS LOS ESTABLECIMIENTOS		UNIVERSITIES AND EQUIVALENT INSTITUTIONS UNIVERSITES ET ETABLISSEMENTS EQUIVALENTS UNIVERSIDADES Y ESTAB. EQUIVALENTES	
			TOTAL	FEMALE FEMININ FEMENINO	TOTAL	FEMALE FEMININ FEMENINO
PENINSULAR MALAYSIA (CONT.)	STUDENTS	1970	16 956	5 007	8 230	2 410
		1974	34 524	11 869	13 305	4 175
		1976	44 709	15 403	19 420	5 793
		1977	46 527	16 906	20 981	6 532
SARAWAK	TEACHERS	1974	62	12	—	—
	STUDENTS	1970	430	138	—	—
		1974	722	329	—	—
		1976	1 097	...	—	—
MONGOLIA	TEACHERS	1971	710	146	549	103
		1975	807	...	625	...
	STUDENTS	1970	6 874	...	5 176	....
		1975	9 861	5 054	7 677	3 777
NEPAL	TEACHERS	1974	1 800	...	1 800	...
		1975	1 516	...	1 516	...
		1976	1 756	...	1 756	...
		1977	1 980	...	1 980	...
	STUDENTS	1974	21 760	...	21 760	...
		1975	23 504	...	23 504	...
		1976	19 482	4 249	19 482	4 249
		1977	25 398	5 504	25 398	5 504
PAKISTAN ‡	TEACHERS	1970	3 439	372	3 439	372
		1974	3 772	476	3 772	476
		1975	5 327	750	5 327	750
		1976	5 583	803	5 583	803
	STUDENTS	1970	114 980	24 534	114 980	24 534
		1974	114 913	28 381	114 913	28 381
		1975	127 932	30 096	127 932	30 096
		1976	133 465	34 210	133 465	34 210
PHILIPPINES	TEACHERS	1970	28 977	*14 300	...	...
		1974	30 922	...	...	...
		1975	31 783	...	...	...
	STUDENTS	1970	651 514	362 221	...	...
		1974	721 398	...	...	...
		1975	769 749	...	...	...
		1976	814 889	...	...	...
		1977	969 952	...	...	...
QATAR	TEACHERS	1970	—	—	—	—
		1975	69	13	69	13
		1976	118	21	118	21
	STUDENTS	1970	—	—	—	—
		1975	779	447	779	447
		1976	910	528	910	528
SAUDI ARABIA	TEACHERS	1970	697	45	697	45
		1974	1 818	245	1 818	245
		1975	2 133	325	2 133	325
		1976	2 966	462	2 644	202
		1977	3 964	572	3 707	572
	STUDENTS	1970	8 492	691	8 492	691
		1974	19 773	2 922	19 773	2 922
		1975	26 437	5 310	26 437	5 310
		1976	32 729	7 118	30 710	5 691
		1977	43 897	9 187	41 616	9 187

Third level: teachers and students by type of institution 3.11
Troisième degré: professeurs et étudiants par types d'établissement
Tercer grado: personal docente y estudiantes por tipos de establecimiento

NON–UNIVERSITY TEACHER TRAINING ENSEIGNEMENT NORMAL NON–UNIVERSITAIRE ENSEÑANZA NORMAL NO UNIVERSITARIA		OTHER NON–UNIVERSITY INSTITUTIONS AUTRES ETABLISSEMENTS NON–UNIVERSITAIRES OTROS ESTABLECIMIENTOS NO UNIVERSITARIOS		YEAR ANNEE	COUNTRY PAYS
TOTAL	FEMALE FEMININ FEMENINO	TOTAL	FEMALE FEMININ FEMENINO	AÑO	PAIS
2 927	1 226	5 799	1 371	1970	PENINSULAR MALAYSIA
10 928	5 009	10 291	2 685	1974	(CONT.)
9 154	4 363	16 135	5 247	1976	
11 548	5 494	13 998	4 880	1977	
62	12	–	–	1974	SARAWAK
430	138	–	–	1970	
722	329	–	–	1974	
1 097	...	–	–	1976	
161	43	–	–	1971	MONGOLIA
182	...	–	–	1975	
1 698	...	–	–	1970	
2 184	1 277	–	–	1975	
–	–	–	–	1974	NEPAL
–	–	–	–	1975	
–	–	–	–	1976	
–	–	–	–	1977	
–	–	–	–	1974	
–	–	–	–	1975	
–	–	–	–	1976	
–	–	–	–	1977	
–	–	–	–	1970	PAKISTAN ‡
–	–	–	–	1974	
–	–	–	–	1975	
–	–	–	–	1976	
–	–	–	–	1970	
–	–	–	–	1974	
–	–	–	–	1975	
–	–	–	–	1976	
...	...	...	...	1970	PHILIPPINES
...	...	...	...	1974	
...	...	...	...	1975	
...	...	...	...	1970	
...	...	...	...	1974	
		...	...	1975	
...	...	...	...	1976	
...	...	...	...	1977	
–	–	–	–	1970	QATAR
–	–	–	–	1975	
–	–	–	–	1976	
–	–	–	–	1970	
–	–	–	–	1975	
–	–	–	–	1976	
–	–	–	–	1970	SAUDI ARABIA
–	–	–	–	1974	
–	–	–	–	1975	
59	–	263	260	1976	
166	–	91	–	1977	
–	–	–	–	1970	
–	–	–	–	1974	
–	–	–	–	1975	
592	–	1 427	1 427	1976	
1 769	–	512	–	1977	

3.11   Third level: teachers and students by type of institution
Troisième degré: professeurs et étudiants par types d'établissement
Tercer grado: personal docente y estudiantes por tipos de establecimiento

COUNTRY PAYS PAIS		YEAR ANNEE AÑO	ALL INSTITUTIONS TOTAL DES ETABLISSEMENTS TODOS LOS ESTABLECIMIENTOS		UNIVERSITIES AND EQUIVALENT INSTITUTIONS UNIVERSITES ET ETABLISSEMENTS EQUIVALENTS UNIVERSIDADES Y ESTAB. EQUIVALENTES	
			TOTAL	FEMALE FEMININ FEMENINO	TOTAL	FEMALE FEMININ FEMENINO
SINGAPORE	TEACHERS	1970	1 157	186	703	124
		1974	1 750	246	1 063	159
		1975	1 448	254	927	164
		1976	1 678	272	965	159
		1977	1 746	321	1 027	181
	STUDENTS	1970	13 771	4 167	6 889	2 398
		1974	18 195	5 757	8 142	3 637
		1975	22 607	8 933	8 539	3 768
		1976	22 969	8 483	8 875	4 004
		1977	24 053	9 103	8 772	3 852
SRI LANKA ‡	TEACHERS	1970	1 487	223	1 487	223
		1974	1 860	305	1 860	305
		1975	2 000	338	2 000	338
		1976	2 498	...	2 498	...
	STUDENTS	1970	12 325	5 334	12 325	5 334
		1974	14 568	5 438	14 568	5 438
		1975	15 426	5 506	15 426	5 506
		1976	13 154	5 234	13 154	5 234
SYRIAN ARAB REPUBLIC	TEACHERS	1970	...	...	1 037	70
		1974	...	...	939	65
		1975	...	...	1 332	106
		1976	...	...	...	...
	STUDENTS	1970	42 667	8 464	38 893	7 235
		1974	67 472	15 552	61 153	12 746
		1975	73 660	18 641	65 348	14 647
		1976	...	...	78 068	17 462
THAILAND ‡	TEACHERS	1970	7 506	2 866	6 532	2 458
		1974	10 010	4 483	10 010	4 483
		1975	9 070	5 121	9 070	5 121
		1976	14 050	6 693	12 979	6 269
		1977	12 986	5 997	11 930	5 549
	STUDENTS	1970	55 315	23 136	43 028	17 977
		1974	75 432	32 709	75 432	32 709
		1975	130 965	52 112	130 965	52 112
		1976	175 438	77 902	161 318	70 942
		1977	216 876	92 353	198 535	82 708
TURKEY	TEACHERS	1970	9 229	2 098	6 382	1 454
		1974	13 778	3 367	8 943	2 209
		1975	15 412	3 759	9 448	2 279
		1976	16 981	3 990	9 973	2 382
		1977	18 391	4 256	11 075	2 609
	STUDENTS	1970	169 793	32 034	76 739	16 079
		1974	218 934	46 430	87 685	18 625
		1975	237 604	52 954	93 541	21 160
		1976	287 499	66 836	98 976	23 318
		1977	312 871	76 251	108 216	27 111
UNITED ARAB EMIRATES	TEACHERS	1977	56	6	56	6
	STUDENTS	1977	519	205	519	205
VIET—NAM	TEACHERS	1975	9 642	1 705	823	90
		1976	10 475	1 836	1 031	113
		1977	13 428	2 389	...	...
	STUDENTS	1975	80 323	31 702	12 267	4 381
		1976	100 027	32 911	15 950	5 148
		1977	120 125	37 239	...	...

Third level: teachers and students by type of institution 3.11
Troisième degré: professeurs et étudiants par types d'établissement
Tercer grado: personal docente y estudiantes por tipos de establecimiento

NON—UNIVERSITY TEACHER TRAINING ENSEIGNEMENT NORMAL NON—UNIVERSITAIRE ENSEÑANZA NORMAL NO UNIVERSITARIA		OTHER NON—UNIVERSITY INSTITUTIONS AUTRES ETABLISSEMENTS NON—UNIVERSITAIRES OTROS ESTABLECIMIENTOS NO UNIVERSITARIOS		YEAR ANNEE AÑO	COUNTRY PAYS PAIS
TOTAL	FEMALE FEMININ FEMENINO	TOTAL	FEMALE FEMININ FEMENINO		
168	51	286	11	1970	SINGAPORE
104	33	583	54	1974	
104	33	417	57	1975	
139	50	574	63	1976	
152	61	567	79	1977	
2 097	1 356	4 785	413	1970	
887	549	9 166	1 571	1974	
4 643	3 393	9 425	1 772	1975	
3 513	2 430	10 581	2 049	1976	
4 646	3 206	10 635	2 045	1977	
—	—	—	—	1970	SRI LANKA ‡
—	—	—	—	1974	
—	—	—	—	1975	
—	—	—	—	1976	
—	—	—	—	1970	
—	—	—	—	1974	
—	—	—	—	1975	
—	—	—	—	1976	
...	...	155	1	1970	SYRIAN ARAB REPUBLIC
...	...	50	—	1974	
...	...	74	11	1975	
567	217	...	...	1976	
1 771	795	2 003	434	1970	
3 378	1 937	2 941	869	1974	
4 413	3 061	3 899	933	1975	
5 192	3 300	...	...	1976	
655	363	319	45	1970	THAILAND ‡
—	—	—	—	1974	
—	—			1975	
—	—	1 071	424	1976	
—	—	1 056	448	1977	
10 784	5 124	1 503	35	1970	
—	—	—	—	1974	
—	—			1975	
—	—	14 120	6 960	1976	
—	—	18 341	9 645	1977	
624	241	2 223	403	1970	TURKEY
1 860	572	2 975	596	1974	
2 573	805	3 391	675	1975	
3 146	843	3 862	765	1976	
3 063	815	4 253	832	1977	
8 781	3 316	84 273	12 639	1970	
29 893	10 804	101 356	17 001	1974	
41 113	14 930	102 950	16 864	1975	
70 663	23 217	117 860	20 301	1976	
93 437	29 673	111 218	19 467	1977	
—	—	—	—	1977	UNITED ARAB EMIRATES
—	—	—	—	1977	
1 948	337	6 871	1 278	1975	VIET—NAM
2 623	384	6 821	1 339	1976	
...	...	...	...	1977	
20 580	12 553	47 476	14 768	1975	
22 455	13 102	61 622	14 661	1976	
...	...	...	...	1977	

3.11 Third level: teachers and students by type of institution
Troisième degré: professeurs et étudiants par types d'établissement
Tercer grado: personal docente y estudiantes por tipos de establecimiento

COUNTRY PAYS PAIS		YEAR ANNEE AÑO	ALL INSTITUTIONS TOTAL DES ETABLISSEMENTS TODOS LOS ESTABLECIMIENTOS		UNIVERSITIES AND EQUIVALENT INSTITUTIONS UNIVERSITES ET ETABLISSEMENTS EQUIVALENTS UNIVERSIDADES Y ESTAB. EQUIVALENTES	
			TOTAL	FEMALE FEMININ FEMENINO	TOTAL	FEMALE FEMININ FEMENINO
VIET—NAM, (FORMER NORTH)	TEACHERS	1970 1974	7 807 8 658	1 062 1 450	... ...	... ...
	STUDENTS	1970 1974	69 912 55 701	17 686 17 206	... ...	... ...
VIET—NAM, (FORMER SOUTH)	STUDENTS	1970	57 657	...	...	...
YEMEN	TEACHERS	1970	15	—	15	—
	STUDENTS	1970 1974 1975 1976 1977	61 2 046 2 408 2 304 4 058	2 237 246 264 470	61 2 046 2 408 2 304 4 058	2 237 246 264 470
YEMEN, DEMOCRATIC	TEACHERS	1970 1974 1977	42 92 246	4 5 19	42 92 246	4 5 19
	STUDENTS	1970 1974 1977	91 934 2 517	25 170 751	91 934 2 517	25 170 751
EUROPE						
ALBANIA ‡	TEACHERS	1970	926	135	...	...
	STUDENTS	1970	25 469	8 275	16 402	4 633
AUSTRIA	TEACHERS	1970 1974 1975 1976 1977	6 980 10 487	832 1 409	6 671 9 580 10 001 10 624 10 996	743 1 080 1 282 1 410 1 439
	STUDENTS	1970 1974 1975 1976 1977	59 778 84 101 96 736 104 525 110 948	17 547 30 788 36 527 40 263 44 179	53 152 75 125 86 123 93 583 100 850	13 269 24 396 28 931 32 794 36 903
BELGIUM	STUDENTS	1970 1974 1975 1976 1977	124 857 152 129 159 660 169 649 177 145	45 231 62 329 66 167 72 181 76 675	75 106 80 980 83 360 86 782 89 349	21 483 26 404 27 773 29 649 31 209
BULGARIA ‡	TEACHERS	1970 1974 1975 1976 1977	7 680 10 805 12 230 13 944 14 657	2 006 3 378 3 937 4 329 5 047	7 125 9 924 11 248 11 619 12 135	1 752 2 942 3 411 3 081 3 716
	STUDENTS	1970 1974 1975 1976 1977	99 596 127 319 128 593 129 507 142 644	50 445 72 386 73 806 75 352 89 392	89 331 108 561 108 814 106 277 95 534	43 508 57 751 57 957 56 480 49 710

Third level: teachers and students by type of institution 3.11
Troisième degré: professeurs et étudiants par types d'établissement
Tercer grado: personal docente y estudiantes por tipos de establecimiento

NON–UNIVERSITY TEACHER TRAINING ENSEIGNEMENT NORMAL NON–UNIVERSITAIRE ENSEÑANZA NORMAL NO UNIVERSITARIA		OTHER NON–UNIVERSITY INSTITUTIONS AUTRES ETABLISSEMENTS NON–UNIVERSITAIRES OTROS ESTABLECIMIENTOS NO UNIVERSITARIOS		YEAR ANNEE AÑO	COUNTRY PAYS PAIS
TOTAL	FEMALE FEMININ FEMENINO	TOTAL	FEMALE FEMININ FEMENINO		
...	...	...	...	1970	VIET–NAM, (FORMER NORTH)
...	...	...	...	1974	
...	...	...	...	1970	
...	...	...	...	1974	
...	...	...	...	1970	VIET–NAM, (FORMER SOUTH)
–	–	–	–	1970	YEMEN
–	–	–	–	1970	
–	–	–	–	1974	
–	–	–	–	1975	
–	–	–	–	1976	
–	–	–	–	1977	
–	–	–	–	1970	YEMEN, DEMOCRATIC
–	–	–	–	1974	
–	–	–	–	1977	
–	–	–	–	1970	
–	–	–	–	1974	
–	–	–	–	1977	
					EUROPE
...	...	...	...	1970	ALBANIA ‡
6 179	1 877	2 888	1 765	1970	
309	89	...	...	1970	AUSTRIA
745	213	162	110	1974	
...	...	...	...	1975	
...	...	...	...	1976	
...	...	...	...	1977	
6 451	4 138	175	140	1970	
8 447	5 993	529	399	1974	
10 037	7 165	576	431	1975	
10 317	6 978	625	491	1976	
9 491	6 808	607	468	1977	
6 553	4 592	43 198	19 156	1970	BELGIUM
19 371	13 182	51 778	22 743	1974	
18 632	12 811	57 668	25 583	1975	
18 372	12 343	64 495	30 189	1976	
19 522	13 721	68 274	31 745	1977	
406	188	149	66	1970	BULGARIA ‡
613	311	268	125	1974	
709	384	273	142	1975	
828	440	1 497	808	1976	
837	439	1 685	892	1977	
6 921	4 771	3 344	2 166	1970	
14 728	12 165	4 030	2 470	1974	
15 046	12 670	4 733	3 179	1975	
13 760	11 265	9 470	7 607	1976	
12 808	9 964	34 302	29 718	1977	

3.11 Third level: teachers and students by type of institution
Troisième degré: professeurs et étudiants par types d'établissement
Tercer grado: personal docente y estudiantes por tipos de establecimiento

COUNTRY PAYS PAIS		YEAR ANNEE AÑO	ALL INSTITUTIONS TOTAL DES ETABLISSEMENTS TODOS LOS ESTABLECIMIENTOS		UNIVERSITIES AND EQUIVALENT INSTITUTIONS UNIVERSITES ET ETABLISSEMENTS EQUIVALENTS UNIVERSIDADES Y ESTAB. EQUIVALENTES	
			TOTAL	FEMALE FEMININ FEMENINO	TOTAL	FEMALE FEMININ FEMENINO
CZECHOSLOVAKIA	TEACHERS	1970	16 402	3 321	16 402	3 321
		1974	21 194	4 968	21 194	4 968
		1975	21 298	5 230	21 298	5 230
		1976	21 786	5 480	21 786	5 480
		1977	22 595	5 664	22 595	5 664
	STUDENTS	1970	131 099	49 678	131 099	49 678
		1974	144 325	58 043	144 325	58 043
		1975	155 059	62 514	155 059	62 514
		1976	168 677	69 131	168 677	69 131
		1977	179 780	73 535	179 780	73 535
		1978	184 011	74 718	184 011	74 718
DENMARK ‡	TEACHERS	1971	10 467	...	6 369	...
		1974	...	...	4 526	...
		1975	...	...	4 777	...
		1976	...	...	6 433	...
		1977	...	...	6 590	...
	STUDENTS	1970	76 024	27 895	43 944	14 330
		1974	105 414	*46 306	56 084	20 206
		1975	110 271	48 837	60 106	21 870
		1976	110 637	51 820	90 277	37 580
		1977	117 656	54 580	97 001	39 832
FINLAND	TEACHERS	1970	6 267	1 194	5 749	937
		1974	5 216	...	4 984	...
		1975	5 429	...	5 225	...
		1976	5 623	1 036	5 416	951
		1977	6 010	1 298	5 787	1 195
	STUDENTS	1970	59 769	28 916	57 739	27 391
		1974	71 526	35 797	69 925	34 341
		1975	77 206	38 437	75 765	37 151
		1976	79 689	39 786	78 176	38 418
		1977	83 165	41 577	81 903	40 447
FRANCE ‡	TEACHERS	1970	...	...	35 679	...
		1975	...	...	40 512	...
		1976	...	...	41 905	...
	STUDENTS	1970	801 156	...	661 156	...
		1974	989 439	*466 892	772 067	*362 000
		1975	1 038 576	*496 049	811 258	*386 000
		1976	1 042 738	*515 997	821 591	*391 900
		1977	1 086 938	*539 512	837 776	*399 000
GERMAN DEMOCRATIC REPUBLIC ‡	TEACHERS	1974	33 570	8 300	25 457	5 537
		1975	34 566	8 784	26 115	5 822
		1976	35 521	9 285	26 902	6 191
		1977	36 013	9 797	27 122	6 522
	STUDENTS	1970	303 141	130 254	138 541	49 354
		1974	306 783	160 747	151 330	69 059
		1975	386 000	...	142 567	66 899
		1976	382 204	...	135 207	62 892
		1977	384 158	...	134 826	62 551
GERMANY, FEDERAL REPUBLIC OF	TEACHERS	1970	...	...	...	...
		1974	99 385	...	82 364	...
		1975	144 834	...	103 578	...
		1976	153 232	...	106 754	...
		1977	...	...	...	...

Third level: teachers and students by type of institution 3.11
Troisième degré: professeurs et étudiants par types d'établissement
Tercer grado: personal docente y estudiantes por tipos de establecimiento

NON—UNIVERSITY TEACHER TRAINING ENSEIGNEMENT NORMAL NON—UNIVERSITAIRE ENSEÑANZA NORMAL NO UNIVERSITARIA		OTHER NON—UNIVERSITY INSTITUTIONS AUTRES ETABLISSEMENTS NON—UNIVERSITAIRES OTROS ESTABLECIMIENTOS NO UNIVERSITARIOS		YEAR ANNEE AÑO	COUNTRY PAYS PAIS
TOTAL	FEMALE FEMININ FEMENINO	TOTAL	FEMALE FEMININ FEMENINO		
–	–	–	–	1970	CZECHOSLOVAKIA
–	–	–	–	1974	
–	–	–	–	1975	
–	–	–	–	1976	
–	–	–	–	1977	
–	–	–	–	1970	
–	–	–	–	1974	
–	–	–	–	1975	
–	–	–	–	1976	
–	–	–	–	1977	
–	–	–	–	1978	
2 100	...	1 998	...	1971	DENMARK ‡
1 502	...	...	...	1974	
1 551	...	...	...	1975	
...	...	...	...	1976	
502	...	...	...	1977	
14 572	8 791	17 508	4 774	1970	FINLAND
22 952	*14 200	26 378	*11 900	1974	
22 744	13 837	27 421	13 130	1975	
9 515	7 618	10 845	6 622	1976	
9 065	7 307	11 590	7 441	1977	
403	199	115	58	1970	FINLAND
67	...	165	...	1974	
26	...	178	...	1975	
28	20	179	65	1976	
–	–	223	103	1977	
1 364	920	666	605	1970	
536	488	1 065	968	1974	
251	190	1 190	1 096	1975	
255	206	1 258	1 162	1976	
–	–	1 262	1 130	1977	
–	–	...	...	1970	FRANCE ‡
–	–	...	...	1975	
–	–	...	...	1976	
–	–	*140 000	...	1970	
–	–	217 372	104 892	1974	
–	–	227 318	110 049	1975	
–	–	221 147	*124 097	1976	
–	–	249 162	*140 512	1977	
1 888	845	6 225	1 918	1974	GERMAN DEMOCRATIC REPUBLIC ‡
1 904	859	6 547	2 103	1975	
1 992	929	6 627	2 165	1976	
2 105	995	6 786	2 280	1977	
./.	./.	164 600	80 900	1970	
24 269	21 409	131 184	70 279	1974	
25 208	22 183	218 225	...	1975	
22 577	19 512	224 420	...	1976	
22 844	19 601	226 488	...	1977	
4 190	1 011	8 581	179	1970	GERMANY, FEDERAL REPUBLIC OF
–	–	17 021	...	1974	
–	–	41 256	...	1975	
–	–	46 478	13 380	1976	
–	–	41 411	12 628	1977	

3.11 Third level: teachers and students by type of institution
Troisième degré: professeurs et étudiants par types d'établissement
Tercer grado: personal docente y estudiantes por tipos de establecimiento

COUNTRY PAYS PAIS		YEAR ANNEE AÑO	ALL INSTITUTIONS TOTAL DES ETABLISSEMENTS TODOS LOS ESTABLECIMIENTOS		UNIVERSITIES AND EQUIVALENT INSTITUTIONS UNIVERSITES ET ETABLISSEMENTS EQUIVALENTS UNIVERSIDADES Y ESTAB. EQUIVALENTES	
			TOTAL	FEMALE FEMININ FEMENINO	TOTAL	FEMALE FEMININ FEMENINO
GERMANY, FEDERAL REPUBLIC OF (CONT.)	STUDENTS	1970 1974 1975 1976 1977	503 819 786 711 1 041 225 1 054 289 1 073 733	135 317 261 886 400 986 407 432 424 604	352 131 641 243 836 002 871 909 905 645	89 092 226 505 282 113 293 038 311 778
GREECE	TEACHERS	1970 1974 1975 1976 1977	... ...	... ...	3 162 5 466 5 956 6 279 6 460	916 1 963 2 092 1 976 2 237
	STUDENTS	1970 1974 1975 1976 1977	85 776 111 441 117 246 122 833 117 892	26 976 39 415 43 361 46 391 44 202	72 269 92 920 95 385 95 017 96 650	22 382 32 685 35 701 36 696 37 423
HOLY SEE	TEACHERS	1970 1975 1976 1977	978 1 280 1 171 1 377	7 37 45 86	978 1 280 1 171 1 335	7 37 45 84
	STUDENTS	1970 1975 1976 1977	8 128 7 758 7 304 7 515	1 207 2 099 2 034 2 416	8 128 7 758 7 304 6 972	1 207 2 099 2 034 2 070
HUNGARY ‡	TEACHERS	1970 1974 1975 1976 1977	9 791 11 604 12 135 12 233 12 579	2 200 2 920 3 244 3 407 3 619	7 924 9 186 9 494 9 530 9 744	1 754 2 221 2 382 2 442 2 590
	STUDENTS	1970 1974 1975 1976 1977	80 536 103 390 107 555 110 528 108 649	34 432 48 831 51 952 55 161 54 929	54 627 65 234 67 983 69 619 67 896	23 957 31 688 33 081 34 201 32 938
ICELAND	TEACHERS	1970 1974 1975	237 447 575	20 48 68	237 403 527	20 34 54
	STUDENTS	1970 1974 1975 1976	1 706 2 695 2 970 4 035	422 909 1 094 ...	1 706 2 580 2 789 ...	422 835 965 ...
IRELAND	TEACHERS	1971 1974 1975 1976 1977	2 555 4 142 4 088 3 808 ...	... ...	2 142 2 424 2 261 1 934 1 726	... ...
	STUDENTS	1970 1974 1975 1976 1977	28 501 37 897 46 174 46 515 46 603	9 767 ... 15 842 17 735 17 631	22 225 24 581 24 976 25 764 27 140	7 543 ... 10 172 10 442 11 245
ITALY	TEACHERS	1970 1974 1975 1976 1977	44 171 42 639 41 824 43 277 43 120	... ...	44 171 42 639 41 824 43 277 43 120	... ...

Third level: teachers and students by type of institution 3.11
Troisième degré: professeurs et étudiants par types d'établissement
Tercer grado: personal docente y estudiantes por tipos de establecimiento

NON—UNIVERSITY TEACHER TRAINING ENSEIGNEMENT NORMAL NON—UNIVERSITAIRE ENSEÑANZA NORMAL NO UNIVERSITARIA		OTHER NON—UNIVERSITY INSTITUTIONS AUTRES ETABLISSEMENTS NON—UNIVERSITAIRES OTROS ESTABLECIMIENTOS NO UNIVERSITARIOS		YEAR ANNEE AÑO	COUNTRY PAYS PAIS
TOTAL	FEMALE FEMININ FEMENINO	TOTAL	FEMALE FEMININ FEMENINO		
63 387	40 332	88 301	5 893	1970	GERMANY, FEDERAL RE—
—	—	145 468	35 381	1974	PUBLIC OF (CONT.)
—	—	205 223	118 873	1975	
—	—	182 380	114 394	1976	
—	—	168 088	112 826	1977	
321	119	...	...	1970	GREECE
278	92	...	...	1974	
370	146	...	...	1975	
396	157	...	...	1976	
391	138	...	...	1977	
3 929	1 897	9 578	2 697	1970	
4 839	3 028	13 682	3 702	1974	
4 408	2 668	17 453	4 992	1975	
3 587	2 242	24 229	7 453	1976	
3 063	1 766	18 179	5 013	1977	
—	—	—	—	1970	HOLY SEE
—	—	—	—	1975	
—	—	—	—	1976	
—	—	2	2	1977	
—	—	—	—	1970	
—	—	—	—	1975	
—	—	—	—	1976	
189	28	354	318	1977	
343	115	1 524	331	1970	HUNGARY ‡
439	159	1 976	540	1974	
521	221	2 120	641	1975	
536	248	2 167	717	1976	
633	299	2 202	730	1977	
4 921	4 541	20 988	5 934	1970	
9 555	8 965	28 601	8 174	1974	
10 537	9 974	29 035	8 897	1975	
12 534	11 820	28 375	9 140	1976	
13 319	12 437	27 434	9 554	1977	
—	—	—	—	1970	ICELAND
44	14	—	—	1974	
48	14	—	—	1975	
—	—	—	—	1970	
115	74	—	—	1974	
181	129	—	—	1975	
...	...	—	—	1976	
142	...	271	...	1971	IRELAND
274	...	1 444	...	1974	
291	...	1 536	...	1975	
326	...	1 548	...	1976	
382	...	...	...	1977	
2 100	1 416	4 176	808	1970	
2 673	1 767	10 643	...	1974	
2 598	1 722	18 600	3 948	1975	
3 196	2 282	17 555	5 011	1976	
3 394	2 548	16 069	3 838	1977	
—	—	...	...	1970	ITALY
—	—	...	...	1974	
—	—	...	...	1975	
—	—	...	...	1976	
—	—	...	...	1977	

3.11 Third level: teachers and students by type of institution
Troisième degré: professeurs et étudiants par types d'établissement
Tercer grado: personal docente y estudiantes por tipos de establecimiento

COUNTRY PAYS PAIS		YEAR ANNEE AÑO	ALL INSTITUTIONS TOTAL DES ETABLISSEMENTS TODOS LOS ESTABLECIMIENTOS		UNIVERSITIES AND EQUIVALENT INSTITUTIONS UNIVERSITES ET ETABLISSEMENTS EQUIVALENTS UNIVERSIDADES Y ESTAB. EQUIVALENTES	
			TOTAL	FEMALE FEMININ FEMENINO	TOTAL	FEMALE FEMININ FEMENINO
ITALY (CONT.)	STUDENTS	1970	687 242	259 015	681 731	256 489
		1974	930 211	364 425	922 800	360 965
		1975	976 712	380 408	968 119	376 323
		1976	1 020 762	403 514	1 011 717	399 106
		1977	1 052 342	426 370	1 043 655	421 898
LUXEMBOURG ‡	TEACHERS	1970	*122	*13	–	–
		1974	137	11	–	–
		1975	137	11	–	–
		1976	163	...	–	–
		1977	172	19	–	–
	STUDENTS	1970	363	152	–	–
		1974	522	239	–	–
		1975	483	204	–	–
		1976	446	187	–	–
		1977	302	128	–	–
MALTA	TEACHERS	1970	320	35	178	*8
		1974	252	17	182	8
		1975	236	13	179	9
		1976	285	22	160	10
		1977	224	15	125	7
	STUDENTS	1970	1 839	626	1 103	316
		1974	2 158	590	1 042	302
		1975	1 425	401	844	256
		1976	1 720	472	1 257	342
		1977	1 674	426	1 123	315
NETHERLANDS	TEACHERS	1970	...	...	*11 500	*1 050
	STUDENTS	1970	231 167	64 070	103 382	20 338
		1974	264 297	81 916	112 528	26 020
		1975	288 026	94 021	120 134	29 995
		1976	305 150	102 855	129 196	33 811
		1977	320 501	111 224	137 426	37 522
NORWAY	TEACHERS	1970	5 118	847	2 673	298
		1975	6 650	1 071	3 757	446
		1976	6 697	1 103	3 845	470
		1977	6 679	1 170	3 851	485
	STUDENTS	1970	50 047	15 135	30 165	8 619
		1974	64 582	23 241	39 268	13 595
		1975	66 628	25 088	40 774	14 695
		1976	73 320	31 382	40 614	14 796
		1977	72 999	32 083	39 306	14 592
POLAND ‡	TEACHERS	1970	...	...	33 695	9 945
		1974	...	...	46 144	15 139
		1975	...	...	50 272	17 068
		1976	...	...	51 759	17 686
		1977	...	...	53 808	18 484
	STUDENTS	1970	397 897	188 734	330 789	139 835
		1974	521 899	277 502	426 701	206 144
		1975	575 499	311 867	468 129	230 503
		1976	613 842	339 036	491 030	245 423
		1977	622 631	343 009	491 367	243 710
PORTUGAL ‡	TEACHERS	1970	2 869	557	2 726	511
		1974	4 745	1 395	2 661	702
		1975	7 891	2 527	4 168	1 060
		1976	9 025	2 714	5 286	1 372
		1977	8 304	2 393	5 414	1 489

Third level: teachers and students by type of institution 3.11
Troisième degré: professeurs et étudiants par types d'établissement
Tercer grado: personal docente y estudiantes por tipos de establecimiento

NON–UNIVERSITY TEACHER TRAINING ENSEIGNEMENT NORMAL NON–UNIVERSITAIRE ENSEÑANZA NORMAL NO UNIVERSITARIA		OTHER NON–UNIVERSITY INSTITUTIONS AUTRES ETABLISSEMENTS NON–UNIVERSITAIRES OTROS ESTABLECIMIENTOS NO UNIVERSITARIOS		YEAR ANNEE	COUNTRY PAYS
TOTAL	FEMALE FEMININ FEMENINO	TOTAL	FEMALE FEMININ FEMENINO	AÑO	PAIS
–	–	5 511	2 526	1970	ITALY (CONT.)
–	–	7 411	3 460	1974	
–	–	8 593	4 085	1975	
–	–	9 045	4 408	1976	
–	–	8 687	4 472	1977	
*46	*8	76	*5	1970	LUXEMBOURG ‡
57	7	80	4	1974	
57	7	80	4	1975	
56	8	107	...	1976	
46	5	126	14	1977	
140	73	223	79	1970	
269	144	253	95	1974	
232	122	251	82	1975	
132	81	314	106	1976	
100	65	202	63	1977	
*42	*22	*100	*5	1970	MALTA
27	8	43	1	1974	
10	2	47	2	1975	
33	9	92	3	1976	
–	–	99	8	1977	
365	270	371	*40	1970	
112	53	1 004	235	1974	
179	81	402	64	1975	
249	113	214	17	1976	
172	70	379	41	1977	
...	...	...	...	1970	NETHERLANDS
68 223	27 685	59 562	16 047	1970	
78 325	34 477	73 444	21 419	1974	
80 971	35 643	86 921	28 383	1975	
82 524	37 387	93 430	31 657	1976	
83 112	38 793	99 963	34 909	1977	
1 007	345	1 438	204	1970	NORWAY
1 182	433	1 711	192	1975	
1 227	429	1 625	204	1976	
1 268	438	1 560	243	1977	
8 028	4 786	11 854	1 730	1970	
10 643	6 717	14 671	2 929	1974	
11 070	7 106	14 784	3 287	1975	
11 145	7 369	21 561	9 217	1976	
11 109	7 548	22 584	9 943	1977	
...	...	...	...	1970	POLAND ‡
...	...	...	...	1974	
...	...	...	...	1975	
...	...	...	...	1976	
...	...	...	...	1977	
./.	./.	67 108	48 899	1970	
./.	./.	95 198	71 358	1974	
./.	./.	107 370	81 364	1975	
./.	./.	122 812	93 613	1976	
./.	./.	131 264	99 299	1977	
143	46	./.	./.	1970	PORTUGAL‡
568	411	1 516	282	1974	
961	686	2 762	781	1975	
774	522	2 965	820	1976	
779	538	2 111	366	1977	

3.11 Third level: teachers and students by type of institution
Troisième degré: professeurs et étudiants par types d'établissement
Tercer grado: personal docente y estudiantes por tipos de establecimiento

COUNTRY PAYS PAIS		YEAR ANNEE AÑO	ALL INSTITUTIONS TOTAL DES ETABLISSEMENTS TODOS LOS ESTABLECIMIENTOS		UNIVERSITIES AND EQUIVALENT INSTITUTIONS UNIVERSITES ET ETABLISSEMENTS EQUIVALENTS UNIVERSIDADES Y ESTAB. EQUIVALENTES	
			TOTAL	FEMALE FEMININ FEMENINO	TOTAL	FEMALE FEMININ FEMENINO
PORTUGAL (CONT.) ‡	STUDENTS	1970	50 095	22 248	43 191	19 797
		1974	64 666	28 297	44 619	20 900
		1975	79 702	35 854	51 489	23 854
		1976	95 841	41 360	67 865	29 402
		1977	85 360	36 238	64 169	28 960
ROMANIA ‡	TEACHERS	1970	13 425	3 953	13 425	3 953
		1974	13 931	4 068	13 931	4 068
		1975	14 066	4 105	14 066	4 105
		1976	13 662	4 008	13 662	4 008
		1977	13 575	4 124	13 575	4 124
		1978	14 227	4 224	14 227	4 224
	STUDENTS	1970	151 885	65 353	151 885	65 353
		1974	152 728	66 555	152 728	66 555
		1975	164 567	73 690	164 567	73 690
		1976	174 888	77 419	174 888	77 419
		1977	182 337	80 619	182 337	80 619
		1978	190 560	81 736	190 560	81 736
SPAIN ‡	TEACHERS	1971	19 617	...	17 847	...
		1974	28 499	5 411	21 749	4 006
		1975	29 701	5 538	22 848	3 924
		1976	34 100	6 726	26 203	4 835
	STUDENTS	1970	224 904	60 051	213 159	56 307
		1974	453 389	154 484	330 969	112 503
		1975	540 238	195 616	405 869	144 699
		1976	581 064	222 500	430 055	159 435
SWEDEN ‡	STUDENTS	1970	141 218	59 855	124 765	46 473
		1974	128 879	59 044	106 447	41 335
		1975	162 640	65 626	113 348	41 529
		1976	171 181	71 788	118 940	48 830
		1977	190 105	83 689	...	...
SWITZERLAND	TEACHERS	1970	...	...	3 900	189
		1974	...	...	5 413	376
		1975	...	...	5 414	356
		1976	...	...	5 627	383
		1977	...	...	5 911	436
	STUDENTS	1970	51 426	...	42 178	9 499
		1974	62 584	...	50 663	13 245
		1975	64 720	...	52 623	14 088
		1976	72 375	19 801	54 198	15 123
		1977	74 730	20 732	55 898	16 272
UNITED KINGDOM ‡	STUDENTS	1970	601 300	199 800	258 700	73 900
		1974	703 645	252 714	332 415	110 303
		1975	732 947	264 254	346 066	117 682
YUGOSLAVIA	TEACHERS	1970	16 783	3 492	12 830	2 730
		1976	21 767	4 813	16 724	3 813
	STUDENTS	1970	261 203	103 011	180 129	69 225
		1974	359 651	147 145	251 551	100 822
		1975	394 992	157 514	271 517	109 450
		1976	406 542	160 830	287 324	114 709
		1977	425 485	167 070	305 925	120 900
		1978	439 608	173 558	324 969	129 019

Third level: teachers and students by type of institution   3.11
Troisième degré: professeurs et étudiants par types d'établissement
Tercer grado: personal docente y estudiantes por tipos de establecimiento

NON–UNIVERSITY TEACHER TRAINING ENSEIGNEMENT NORMAL NON–UNIVERSITAIRE ENSEÑANZA NORMAL NO UNIVERSITARIA		OTHER NON–UNIVERSITY INSTITUTIONS AUTRES ETABLISSEMENTS NON–UNIVERSITAIRES OTROS ESTABLECIMIENTOS NO UNIVERSITARIOS		YEAR ANNEE AÑO	COUNTRY PAYS PAIS
TOTAL	FEMALE FEMININ FEMENINO	TOTAL	FEMALE FEMININ FEMENINO		
634	284	6 270	2 167	1970	PORTUGAL (CONT.) ‡
2 031	1 537	18 016	5 860	1974	
3 139	2 198	25 074	9 802	1975	
2 930	1 874	25 046	10 084	1976	
2 956	2 017	18 235	5 261	1977	
–	–	–	–	1970	ROMANIA ‡
–	–	–	–	1974	
–	–	–	–	1975	
–	–	–	–	1976	
–	–	–	–	1977	
–	–	–	–	1978	
–	–	–	–	1970	
–	–	–	–	1974	
–	–	–	–	1975	
–	–	–	–	1976	
–	–	–	–	1977	
–	–	–	–	1978	
–	...	1 770	...	1971	SPAIN ‡
2 549	1 233	4 201	172	1974	
2 873	1 414	3 980	200	1975	
3 152	1 541	4 745	350	1976	
–	–	11 745	3 744	1970	
59 058	37 652	63 362	4 329	1974	
70 534	45 546	63 835	5 371	1975	
84 186	56 476	66 823	6 589	1976	
13 937	11 880	2 516	1 502	1970	SWEDEN ‡
13 119	10 583	9 313	7 126	1974	
14 476	11 331	34 816	12 766	1975	
13 734	11 293	38 507	11 665	1976	
...	...	...	...	1977	
...	...	...	...	1970	SWITZERLAND
...	...	...	...	1974	
...	...	...	...	1975	
...	...	...	...	1976	
...	...	...	...	1977	
1 737	1 131	7 511	...	1970	
4 927	3 001	6 994	...	1974	
5 211	3 151	6 886	...	1975	
–	–	18 177	4 678	1976	
3 354	–	18 832	4 460	1977	
123 800	89 400	218 800	36 500	1970	UNITED KINGDOM ‡
125 663	89 742	245 567	52 669	1974	
117 828	84 683	269 053	61 889	1975	
1 394	314	2 559	448	1970	YUGOSLAVIA
1 596	416	3 447	584	1976	
24 331	13 867	56 743	19 919	1970	
25 328	14 797	82 772	31 526	1974	
29 942	13 777	93 533	34 287	1975	
24 457	13 238	94 761	32 883	1976	
243 330	13 325	95 230	32 845	1977	
25 623	13 226	89 016	31 313	1978	

3.11 Third level: teachers and students by type of institution
Troisième degré: professeurs et étudiants par types d'établissement
Tercer grado: personal docente y estudiantes por tipos de establecimiento

COUNTRY PAYS PAIS		YEAR ANNEE AÑO	ALL INSTITUTIONS TOTAL DES ETABLISSEMENTS TODOS LOS ESTABLECIMIENTOS		UNIVERSITIES AND EQUIVALENT INSTITUTIONS UNIVERSITES ET ETABLISSEMENTS EQUIVALENTS UNIVERSIDADES Y ESTAB. EQUIVALENTES	
			TOTAL	FEMALE FEMININ FEMENINO	TOTAL	FEMALE FEMININ FEMENINO
OCEANIA						
AMERICAN SAMOA	TEACHERS	1970	—	—	—	—
	STUDENTS	1970	—	—	—	—
		1974	833	390	—	—
		1975	689	337	—	—
		1976	836	443	—	—
		1977	1 114	663	—	—
AUSTRALIA ‡	TEACHERS	1970	...	...	7 367	...
		1974	18 461	...	18 461	...
		1975	19 920	...	19 920	...
		1976	20 848	...	20 848	...
		1977	21 371	...	21 371	...
		1978	...	...	...	...
	STUDENTS	1970	179 664	58 771	116 778	34 931
		1974	252 972	98 269	252 972	98 269
		1975	274 738	111 596	274 738	111 596
		1976	289 701	123 098	289 701	123 098
		1977	300 030	128 667	300 030	128 667
		1978	309 783	135 896	309 783	135 896
FIJI	TEACHERS	1974	201	29	152	27
		1975	166	29	105	17
	STUDENTS	1970	442	119	442	119
		1974	1 089	342	816	282
		1975	1 810	478	1 386	385
GUAM	TEACHERS	1970	*125	...	*125	...
	STUDENTS	1970	2 719	1 298	2 719	1 298
		1974	3 558	1 698	3 558	1 698
		1975	3 800	1 616	3 800	1 616
		1976	3 710	1 827	3 710	1 827
		1977	4 343	2 123	4 343	2 123
NEW CALEDONIA	TEACHERS	1970	32	3	—	—
		1974	27	6	—	—
		1975	23	3	—	—
		1976	29	2	—	—
	STUDENTS	1970	101	...	—	—
		1974	188	83	—	—
		1975	178	62	—	—
		1976	366	100	—	—
NEW ZEALAND	TEACHERS	1970	...	...	2 907	360
		1974	...	...	3 787	432
		1975	...	...	4 108	454
		1976	...	...	4 247	485
	STUDENTS	1970	...	...	34 446	10 664
		1974	66 739	24 642	39 612	14 904
		1975	71 369	26 860	42 122	16 515
		1976	74 341	28 357	45 479	18 478
		1977	76 795	...	47 936	...
PACIFIC ISLANDS	TEACHERS	1977	55	...	18	8
	STUDENTS	1977	573	...	332	...

Third level: teachers and students by type of institution 3.11
Troisième degré: professeurs et étudiants par types d'établissement
Tercer grado: personal docente y estudiantes por tipos de establecimiento

NON—UNIVERSITY TEACHER TRAINING ENSEIGNEMENT NORMAL NON—UNIVERSITAIRE ENSEÑANZA NORMAL NO UNIVERSITARIA		OTHER NON—UNIVERSITY INSTITUTIONS AUTRES ETABLISSEMENTS NON—UNIVERSITAIRES OTROS ESTABLECIMIENTOS NO UNIVERSITARIOS		YEAR ANNEE AÑO	COUNTRY PAYS PAIS
TOTAL	FEMALE FEMININ FEMENINO	TOTAL	FEMALE FEMININ FEMENINO		
					OCEANIA
–	–	–	–	1970	AMERICAN SAMOA
–	–	–	–	1970	
–	–	833	390	1974	
–	–	689	337	1975	
–	–	836	443	1976	
–	–	1 114	663	1977	
...	...	...	...	1970	AUSTRALIA ‡
–	–	–	–	1974	
–	–	–	–	1975	
–	–	–	–	1976	
–	–	–	–	1977	
–	–	–	–	1978	
21 775	16 274	41 111	7 566	1970	
–	–	–	–	1974	
–	–	–	–	1975	
–	–	–	–	1976	
–	–	–	–	1977	
–	–	–	–	1978	
–	–	49	2	1974	FIJI
–	–	61	12	1975	
–	–	–	–	1970	
–	–	273	60	1974	
–	–	424	93	1975	
–	–	–	–	1970	GUAM
–	–	–	–	1970	
–	–	–	–	1974	
–	–	–	–	1975	
–	–	–	–	1976	
–	–	–	–	1977	
–	–	32	3	1970	NEW CALEDONIA
–	–	27	6	1974	
–	–	23	3	1975	
–	–	29	2	1976	
–	–	101	...	1970	
–	–	188	83	1974	
–	–	178	62	1975	
–	–	366	100	1976	
576	146	...	...	1970	NEW ZEALAND
637	130	...	...	1974	
610	142	...	...	1975	
624	165	...	...	1976	
7 908	6 010	...	...	1970	
8 565	6 407	18 562	3 331	1974	
7 779	5 702	21 369	4 643	1975	
7 521	5 569	21 341	4 310	1976	
6 837	...	22 022	...	1977	
–	–	37	...	1977	PACIFIC ISLANDS
–	–	241	...	1977	

3.11 Third level: teachers and students by type of institution
Troisième degré: professeurs et étudiants par types d'établissement
Tercer grado: personal docente y estudiantes por tipos de establecimiento

COUNTRY PAYS PAIS		YEAR ANNEE AÑO	ALL INSTITUTIONS TOTAL DES ETABLISSEMENTS TODOS LOS ESTABLECIMIENTOS		UNIVERSITIES AND EQUIVALENT INSTITUTIONS UNIVERSITES ET ETABLISSEMENTS EQUIVALENTS UNIVERSIDADES Y ESTAB. EQUIVALENTES	
			TOTAL	FEMALE FEMININ FEMENINO	TOTAL	FEMALE FEMININ FEMENINO
PAPUA NEW GUINEA	TEACHERS	1975	...	...	353	...
		1976	...	...	337	...
		1977	...	...	363	...
	STUDENTS	1970	...	...	1 032	165
		1975	...	...	2 869	338
		1976	...	...	3 602	318
		1977	...	...	2 983	321
SAMOA	TEACHERS	1970	24	1	—	—
		1975	*40	—	—	—
		1977	40	10	20	6
		1978	53	8	30	3
	STUDENTS	1970	114	1	—	—
		1975	249	*13	—	—
		1977	405	72	73	29
		1978	425	...	196	...
TONGA	TEACHERS	1970	...	...	—	—
		1977	22	7	11	1
	STUDENTS	1970	...	...	—	—
		1977	195	87	47	10
U.S.S.R.						
U.S.S.R. ‡	TEACHERS	1970	277 493	104 060	...	...
		1974	308 242	114 358	...	...
		1975	317 152	118 298	...	...
	STUDENTS	1970	4 580 642	2 246 970	...	...
		1974	4 751 000	2 388 828	...	...
		1975	4 853 958	2 448 551	...	...
		1976	4 950 000	...	...	...
		1977	5 037 200	...	...	...
BYELORUSSIAN S.S.R. ‡	STUDENTS	1970	140 034	72 568	...	...
		1974	153 022	...	...	...
		1975	159 903	...	...	...
		1976	164 598	...	...	...
		1977	167 812	89 711	...	...
UKRAINIAN S.S.R. ‡	STUDENTS	1970	806 600	*386 000	...	...
		1974	818 000	400 300	...	...
		1975	831 300	408 800	...	...
		1976	844 400	...	...	...
		1977	856 700	...	...	...

Third level: teachers and students by type of institution 3.11
Troisième degré: professeurs et étudiants par types d'établissement
Tercer grado: personal docente y estudiantes por tipos de establecimiento

NON–UNIVERSITY TEACHER TRAINING ENSEIGNEMENT NORMAL NON–UNIVERSITAIRE ENSEÑANZA NORMAL NO UNIVERSITARIA		OTHER NON–UNIVERSITY INSTITUTIONS AUTRES ETABLISSEMENTS NON–UNIVERSITAIRES OTROS ESTABLECIMIENTOS NO UNIVERSITARIOS		YEAR ANNEE	COUNTRY PAYS
TOTAL	FEMALE FEMININ FEMENINO	TOTAL	FEMALE FEMININ FEMENINO	AÑO	PAIS
...	...	...	...	1975	PAPUA NEW GUINEA
...	...	...	...	1976	
...	...	...	...	1977	
...	...	...	...	1970	
...	...	...	...	1975	
...	...	...	...	1976	
...	...	...	...	1977	
–	–	24	1	1970	SAMOA
–	–	*40		1975	
–	–	20	4	1977	
8	5	15	–	1978	
–	–	114	1	1970	
–	–	249	*13	1975	
–	–	332	43	1977	
11	2	218	43	1978	
–	–	–	–	1970	TONGA
11	6	–	–	1977	
–	–	–	–	1970	
148	77	–	–	1977	
					U.S.S.R.
...	...	...	...	1970	U.S.S.R. ‡
...	...	...	...	1974	
...	...	...	...	1975	
...	...	...	...	1970	
...	...	...	...	1974	
...	...	...	...	1975	
...	...	...	...	1976	
...	...	...	...	1977	
...	...	...	...	1970	BYELORUSSIAN S.S.R. ‡
...	...	...	...	1974	
...	...	...	...	1975	
...	...	...	...	1976	
...	...	...	...	1977	
...	...	...	...	1970	UKRAINIAN S.S.R. ‡
...	...	...	...	1974	
...	...	...	...	1975	
...	...	...	...	1976	
...	...	...	...	1977	

3.11 Third level: teachers and students by type of institution
Troisième degré: professeurs et étudiants par types d'établissement
Tercer grado: personal docente y estudiantes por tipos de establecimiento

SIERRA LEONE:
E—> DATA REFER TO THE UNIVERSITY OF SIERRA LEONE ONLY.
FR-> LES DONNEES SE REFERENT A L'UNIVERSITE DE SIERRA LEONE SEULEMENT.
ESP> LOS DATOS SE REFIEREN A LA UNIVERSIDAD DE SIERRA LEONE SOLAMENTE.

SOUTH AFRICA:
E—> INCLUDING CORRESPONDENCE COURSES.
FR-> Y COMPRIS LES COURS PAR CORRESPONDANCE.
ESP> INCLUIDOS LOS CURSOS POR CORRESPONDENCIA.

SWAZILAND:
E—> 1970, 1974, 1975 AND 1976 STUDENTS' DATA INCLUDE STUDENTS ABROAD.
FR-> POUR LES ANNEES 1970, 1974, 1975 ET 1976 LES ETUDIANTS A L'ETRANGER SONT INCLUS.
ESP> EN 1970, 1974, 1975 Y 1976 SE INCLUYEN LOS ESTUDIANTES EN EL EXTRANJERO.

TUNISIA:
E—> 1970 FOR STUDENTS, AND 1974 FOR BOTH TEACHERS AND STUDENTS, DATA REFER TO INSTITUTIONS ATTACHED TO THE MINISTRY OF EDUCATION.
FR-> EN 1970 POUR LES ETUDIANTS, ET EN 1974 POUR LES PROFESSEURS ET LES ETUDIANTS, LES DONNEES SE REFERENT AUX ETABLISSEMENTS RELEVANT DU MINISTERE DE L'EDUCATION SEULEMENT.
ESP> EN 1970 PARA LOS ESTUDIANTES Y EN 1974 PARA LOS PROFESORES Y LOS ESTUDIANTES, LOS DATOS SE REFIEREN SOLAMENTE A LOS ESTABLECIMIENTOS DEPENDIENTES DEL MINISTERIO DE EDUCACION.

CANADA:
E—> 1970 FOR STUDENTS, 1974 FOR BOTH TEACHERS AND STUDENTS AND 1976 AND 1977 FOR TEACHERS, DATA EXCLUDE ALL PART-TIME STUDENTS AND TEACHERS AT NON-UNIVERSITY INSTITUTIONS.
FR-> EN 1970 POUR LES ETUDIANTS, ET EN 1974 POUR LES PROFESSEURS ET LES ETUDIANTS, 1976 ET 1977 POUR LES PROFESSEURS LES DONNEES NE TIENNENT PAS COMPTE DES ETUDIANTS AINSI QUE DU PERSONNEL ENSEIGNANT A TEMPS PARTIEL DANS LES ETABLISSEMENTS DE TYPE NON-UNIVERSITAIRE.
ESP> EN 1970 PARA LOS ESTUDIANTES, EN 1974 PARA LOS PROFESORES Y LOS ESTUDIANTES Y EN 1976 Y 1977 PARA LOS PROFESORES, LOS DATOS NO TOMAN EN CONSIDERACION NI LOS ESTUDIANTES NI EL PERSONAL DOCENTE DE JORNADA PARCIAL DE LOS ESTABLECIMIENTOS NO UNIVERSITARIOS.

GUATEMALA:
E—> FOR ALL YEARS EXCEPT 1970, DATA REFER TO THE UNIVERSITY OF SAN CARLOS.
FR-> LES DONNEES SE RAPPORTENT A L'UNIVERSITE DE SAN CARLOS SEULEMENT, EXCEPTE POUR L'ANNEE 1970.
ESP> SALVO PARA 1970, LOS DATOS SE REFIEREN A LA UNIVERSIDAD DE SAN CARLOS SOLAMENTE.

ARGENTINA:
E—> THE TEACHING STAFF OF OTHER NON-UNIVERSITY INSTITUTIONS IS INCLUDED WITH THE STAFF OF NON-UNIVERSITY TEACHER TRAINING.
FR-> LES DONNEES RELATIVES AUX AUTRES ETABLIS-SEMENTS NON-UNIVERSITAIRES SONT INCLUSES AVEC L'ENSEIGNEMENT NORMAL NON-UNIVERSITAIRE.
ESP> LOS DATOS RELATIVOS A LOS OTROS ESTABLE-CIMIENTOS NO UNIVERSITARIOS QUEDAN INCLUIDOS EN LA ENSEÑANZA NORMAL NO UNIVERSITARIA.

CHILE:
E—> 1975 TEACHERS' DATA REFER TO FULL-TIME TEACHERS ONLY.
FR-> EN 1975, LES DONNEES SE REFERENT AUX PROFESSEURS A PLEIN TEMPS SEULEMENT.
ESP> EN 1975, LOS DATOS SE REFIEREN A LOS PROFESORES DE JORNADA COMPLETA SOLAMENTE.

HONG KONG:
E—> IN 1977 TECHNICAL INSTITUTES AS WELL AS POST-SECONDARY COLLEGES ARE NOT INCLUDED.
FR-> EN 1977 LES "TECHNICAL INSTITUTES" AINSI QUE LES "POST-SECONDARY COLLEGES" NE SONT PAS INCLUS.
ESP> EN 1977, NO SE INCLUYEN LOS "TECHNICAL INSTITUTES" NI LOS "POST-SECONDARY COLLEGES".

INDIA:
E—> STUDENTS' DATA INCLUDE INTERMEDIATE AND PRE-UNIVERSITY COURSES. IN 1975 THERE WERE 1,027,030 (F 274,110) STUDENTS.
FR-> LES DONNEES INCLUENT LES COURS INTERME-DIAIRES ET PRE-UNIVERSITAIRES. EN 1975 IL Y AVAIT 1 027 030 ETUDIANTS (F. 274 110).
ESP> LOS DATOS INCLUYEN LOS CURSOS INTERMEDIOS Y PREUNIVERSITARIOS. EN 1975, EL NUMERO DE ESTUDIANTES ERA DE 1 027 030 (F 274 110).

IRAN:
E—> 1976 DATA REFERRING TO NON-UNIVERSITY TEACHER TRAINING ARE INCLUDED IN UNIVERSITIES AND EQUIVALENT INSTITUTIONS.
FR-> EN 1976, LES DONNEES RELATIVES A L'ENSEI-GNEMENT NORMAL NON-UNIVERSITAIRE SONT INCLUSES AVEC CELLES DES UNIVERSITES ET ETABLISSEMENTS EQUIVALENTS.
ESP> EN 1976, LOS DATOS RELATIVOS A LA ENSEÑANZA NORMAL NO UNIVERSITARIA QUEDAN INCLUIDOS CON LOS DE LAS UNIVERSIDADES Y ESTABLECIMIENTOS EQUIVALENTES.

IRAQ:
E—> DATA FOR TEACHERS FOR 1977 REFERRING TO OTHER NON-UNIVERSITY INSTITUTIONS ARE INCLUDED IN UNIVERSITIES AND EQUIVALENT INSTITUTIONS.
FR-> POUR 1977, LES DONNEES RELATIVES AUX PROFESSEURS DES AUTRES ETABLISSEMENTS NON-UNIVERSITAIRES SONT INCLUSES AVEC CELLES DES UNIVERSITES ET ETABLISSEMENTS EQUIVALENTS.
ESP> EN 1977 LOS DATOS RELATIVOS A LOS PRO-FESORES DE LOS OTROS ESTABLECIMIENOS NO UNIVERSITARIOS QUEDAN INCLUIDOS CON LOS DE LAS UNIVERSIDADES Y ESTABLECIMIENTOS EQUIVALENTES.

JAPAN:
E—> INCLUDING CORRESPONDENCE COURSES.
FR-> Y COMPRIS LES COURS PAR CORRESPONDANCE.
ESP> INCLUIDOS LOS CURSOS POR CORRESPONDENCIA.

JORDAN:
E—> DATA REFER TO THE EAST BANK ONLY.
FR-> LES DONNEES SE RAPPORTENT A LA RIVE ORIENTALE SEULEMENT.
ESP> LOS DATOS SE REFIEREN A LA ORILLA ORIENTAL SOLAMENTE.

PAKISTAN:
E—> STUDENTS IN ARTS AND SCIENCES COLLEGES ARE CLASSIFIED PARTLY AT THE SECOND LEVEL (INTER-MEDIATE COURSES) AND PARTLY AT THE THIRD LEVEL (DEGREE COURSES), BUT A SIMILAR CLASSIFICATION FOR TEACHERS HAS NOT BEEN POSSIBLE AND, THEREFORE, HAVE BEEN INCLUDED AT THE SECOND LEVEL.
FR-> LES EFFECTIFS DES "ARTS AND SCIENCES COLLEGES" SONT CLASSES EN PARTIE AVEC L'ENSEI-GNEMENT DU SECOND DEGRE (INTERMEDIATE COURSE) ET EN PARTIE AVEC L'ENSEIGNEMENT DU TROISIEME DEGRE (DEGREE COURSE). CEPENDANT COMME IL N'ETAIT PAS POSSIBLE DE REPARTIR LE PERSONNEL ENSEIGNANT ENTRE LES DEUX DEGRES D'ENSEIGNEMENT, IL A ETE CLASSE DANS L'ENSEIGNEMENT DU SECOND DEGRE.
ESP> LOS EFECTIVOS DE LOS "ARTS AND SCIENCES COLLEGES" ESTAN CLASIFICADOS EN PARTE CON LA ENSEÑANZA DE SEGUNDO GRADO (INTERMEDIATE COURSE) Y EN PARTE CON LA ENSEÑANZA DE TERCER GRADO (DEGREE COURSE). SIN EMBARGO, COMO NO ERA

Third level: teachers and students by type of institution   3.11
Troisième degré: professeurs et étudiants par types d'établissement
Tercer grado: personal docente y estudiantes por tipos de establecimiento

PAKISTAN (CONT.)
POSIBLE REPARTIR EL PERSONAL DOCENTE ENTRE
LOS DOS GRADOS DE ENSEÑANZA, EL MISMO QUEDO
CLASIFICADO EN LA ENSEÑANZA DE SEGUNDO GRADO.

SRI LANKA:
   E—> 1976 DATA EXCLUDE STUDENTS PURSUING NON—
DEGREE COURSES.
   FR—> EN 1976, NON COMPRIS LES ETUDIANTS DONT
LES COURS NE SONT PAS SANCTIONNES PAR UN DIPLOME.
   ESP> EN 1976, EXCLUIDOS LOS ESTUDIANTES CUYOS
CURSOS NO SE VEN SANCIONADOS CON UN DIPLOMA.

THAILAND:
   E—> 1975, 1976 AND 1977 ENROLMENT INCLUDES
STUDENTS AT THE OPEN ADMISSION UNIVERSITY: 83,287
(F 37,410) STUDENTS IN 1976.
   FR—> POUR LES ANNEES 1975, 1976 ET 1977 LES
DONNEES INCLUENT L'"OPEN ADMISSION UNIVERSITY":
83 287 ETUDIANTS (F. 37 410) EN 1976.
   ESP> EN 1975, 1976 Y 1977 LOS DATOS INCLUYEN LA
"OPEN ADMISSION UNIVERSITY": 83 287 ESTUDIANTES,
(F. 37 410) EN 1976.

ALBANIA:
   E—> INCLUDING EVENING AND CORRESPONDENCE
COURSES.
   FR—> Y COMPRIS LES COURS DU SOIR ET PAR CORRES—
PONDANCE.
   ESP> INCLUIDOS LOS CURSOS NOCTURNOS Y POR
CORRESPONDENCIA.

BULGARIA:
   E—> INCLUDING EVENING AND CORRESPONDENCE COURSES.
THE SHARP RISE IN ENROLMENT IN 1977 FOR OTHER NON—
UNIVERSITY INSTITUTIONS WAS DUE TO THE INTRODUCTION
OF A NEW COURSE OF STUDY ORGANIZED IN POST—SECONDARY
MEDICAL SCIENCE INSTITUTIONS FOR MIDDLE—LEVEL
MEDICAL PROFESSIONALS.
   FR—> Y COMPRIS LES COURS DU SOIR ET PAR CORRES—
PONDANCE. EN 1977 L'IMPORTANTE AUGMENTATION DES
EFFECTIFS S'EXPLIQUE PAR LA CREATION DE NOUVEAUX
COURS A PLEIN TEMPS ET PAR CORRESPONDANCE,
ORGANISES DANS LES ETABLISSEMENTS D'ENSEIGNEMENT
POST—SECONDAIRE DES SCIENCES MEDICALES A
L'INTENTION DES CADRES MOYENS MEDICAUX (PERSONNEL
PARAMEDICAL).
   ESP> INCLUIDOS LOS CURSOS NOCTURNOS Y POR
CORRESPONDENCIA. EN 1977 EL IMPORTANTE AUMENTO
DE LOS EFECTIVOS SE EXPLICA POR LA CREACION DE
NUEVOS CURSOS DE JORNADA COMPLETA Y POR CORRES—
PONDANCIA, ORGANIZADOS EN LOS ESTABLECIMIENTOS
POST—SECUNDARIOS DE CIENCIAS MEDICAS Y DESTINADOS
A LOS CUADROS MEDIOS MEDICALES (PERSONAL PARA—
MEDICAL).

DENMARK:
   E—> 1974, 1975, 1976 AND 1977 DATA EXCLUDE
PART—TIME TEACHERS. 1976 AND 1977 STUDENTS'
DATA ARE NOT COMPARABLE WITH THOSE OF THE
PREVIOUS YEARS DUE TO CLASSIFICATION CHANGES.
   FR—> POUR LES ANNEES 1974, 1975, 1976 ET 1977
LES DONNEES EXCLUENT LES PROFESSEURS A TEMPS
PARTIEL. POUR 1976 ET 1977, LES DONNEES RELATIVES
AUX ETUDIANTS NE SONT PAS COMPARABLES AVEC CELLES
DES ANNEES ANTERIEURES A LA SUITE D'UN CHANGEMENT
DE CLASSIFICATION.
   ESP> EN 1974, 1975, 1976 Y 1977 LOS DATOS
RELATIVOS A LOS PROFESORES NO INCLUYEN EL PERSONAL
DE JORNADA PARCIAL. LOS DATOS SOBRE LOS ESTUDIAN—
TES PARA 1976 Y 1977, NO SON COMPARABLES CON LOS
DE LOS AÑOS ANTERIORES DEBIDO A UNO CAMBIO DE
CLASIFICACION.

FRANCE:
   E—> THE TOTAL NUMBER OF STUDENTS (ALL INSTITU—
TIONS) IS OVERESTIMATED DUE TO SOME STUDENTS
ENROLLED AT INSTITUTIONS, CONSIDERED HERE AS NON—
UNIVERSITY ("GRANDES ECOLES, CLASSES PREPARATOIRES
AUX GRANDES ECOLES" AND "SECTIONS DE TECHNICIENS
SUPERIEURS") BEING ENROLLED ALSO AT THE UNIVERSI—
TIES. THEIR NUMBER IS UNKNOWN.
   FR—> LE NOMBRE TOTAL D'ETUDIANTS (ENSEMBLE D'—
ETABLISSEMENTS) EST SURESTIME DU FAIT QUE CER—
TAINS ETUDIANTS INSCRITS DANS LES ETABLISSEMENTS
CONSIDERES ICI COMME NON—UNIVERSITAIRES (GRANDES
ECOLES ET SECTIONS DE TECHNICIENS SUPERIEURS) SONT
EGALEMENT INSCRITS DANS LES UNIVERSITES, SANS QUE
L'ON PUISSE EN INDIQUER LE NOMBRE EXACT.
   ESP> EL NUMERO TOTAL DE ESTUDIANTES (TODOS LOS
ESTABLECIMIENTOS) ESTA SOBRESTIMADO DEBIDO A QUE
CIERTOS ESTUDIANTES INSCRITOS EN LOS ESTABLECI—
MIENTOS CONSIDERADOS AQUI COMO NO UNIVERSITARIOS
(GRANDES ECOLES, CLASSES PREPARATOIRES A LAS
GRANDES ECOLES Y SECTIONS DE TECHNICIENS SUPE—
RIEURS) ESTAN INSCRITOS IGUALMENTE EN LAS UNIVER—
SIDADES, SIN QUE SEA POSIBLE PRECISAR SU NUMERO
CON EXACTITUD.

GERMAN, DEMOCRATIC REPUBLIC:
   E—> INCLUDING EVENING AND CORRESPONDENCE COURSES.
IN 1970, DATA FOR STUDENTS AT NON—UNIVERSITY TEACHER
TRAINING INSTITUTIONS ARE INCLUDED WITH OTHER NON—
UNIVERSITY INSTITUTIONS.
IN 1975, 1976 AND 1977, PREPARATORY
STUDIES FOR HIGHER EDUCATION, EXTENDED
SECONDARY SCHOOLS AND VOCATIONAL TRAINING
(INCLUDING UNIVERSITY ENTRANCE EXAMINATION) WERE
INCLUDED WITH EDUCATION AT THE THIRD LEVEL (NON—
UNIVERSITY) AS A RESULT OF THE APPLICATION OF
ISCED. THE CLASSIFICATION BY ISCED LEVELS 5, 6
AND 7 WAS ALSO CHANGED AND THEREFORE DATA FROM
1975 ARE NOT COMPARABLE WITH THE PREVIOUS CLASSI—
FICATION USED UNTIL 1974.
   FR—> Y COMPRIS LES COURS DU SOIR ET PAR CORRES—
PONDANCE. POUR LES ETUDIANTS, EN 1970, LES
DONNEES RELATIVES A L'ENSEIGNEMENT NORMAL NON—
UNIVERSITAIRE SONT INCLUSES AVEC CELLES DES AUTRES
ETABLISSEMENTS NON—UNIVERSITAIRES. EN 1975, 1976
ET 1977, LES ETUDES PREPARATOIRES A L'ENSEIGNEMENT
SUPERIEUR, LES ECOLES SECONDAIRES PROLONGEES ET
L'ENSEIGNEMENT TECHNIQUE (Y COMPRIS L'EXAMEN
D'ENTREE A L'UNIVERSITE) SONT COMPRIS DANS L'EN—
SEIGNEMENT DU TROISIEME DEGRE (NON—UNIVERSITAIRE),
A LA SUITE DE L'APPLICATION DE LA CITE. LA
CLASSIFICATION PAR NIVEAU CITE 5, 6 ET 7 A
ETE EGALEMENT MODIFIEE, ET LES DONNEES A PARTIR
DE 1975 NE SONT PLUS COMPARABLES AVEC LA
CLASSIFICATION UTILISEE JUSQU'EN 1974.
   ESP> INCLUIDOS LOS CURSOS NOCTURNOS Y POR
CORRESPONDENCIA. EN 1970, LOS DATOS RELATIVOS A
LA ENSEÑANZA NORMAL NO UNIVERSITARIA QUEDAN
INCLUIDOS CON LOS DE LOS OTROS ESTABLECIMIENTOS
NO UNIVERSITARIOS. EN 1975, 1976 Y 1977, LOS
ESTUDIOS PREPARATORIOS A LA ENSEÑANZA SUPERIOR,
LAS ESCUELAS SECUNDARIAS PROLONGADAS Y LA ENSE—
NANZA TECNICA (INCLUYENDO EL EXAMEN DE ENTRADA
A LA UNIVERSIDAD) ESTAN INCLUIDOS EN LA ENSEÑANZA
DE TERCER GRADO (NO UNIVERSITARIA) COMO RESULTADO
DE LA APLICACION DE LA CINE. LA CLASIFICACION
SEGUN LOS GRADOS CINE 5, 6 Y 7 TAMBIEN FUE
MODIFICADA Y LOS DATOS A PARTIR DE 1975 NO SON
COMPARABLES CON LA CLASIFICACION UTILIZADA HASTA
1974.

3.11 **Third level: teachers and students by type of institution**
Troisième degré: professeurs et étudiants par types d'établissement
Tercer grado: personal docente y estudiantes por tipos de establecimiento

HUNGARY:
E—> INCLUDING EVENING AND CORRESPONDENCE COURSES.
FR—> Y COMPRIS LES COURS DU SOIR ET PAR CORRES-PONDANCE.
ESP> INCLUIDOS LOS CURSOS NOCTURNOS Y POR CORRESPONDENCIA.

LUXEMBOURG:
E—> DATA REFER TO STUDENTS ENROLLED IN INSTI-TUTIONS LOCATED IN LUXEMBOURG. AT THIS LEVEL OF EDUCATION, THE MAJORITY OF STUDENTS PURSUE THEIR STUDIES ABROAD.
FR—> LES DONNEES SE REFERENT SEULEMENT AUX ETUDIANTS INSCRITS DANS LES INSTITUTIONS DU LUXEMBOURG. LA PLUS GRANDE PARTIE DES ETUDIANTS LUXEMBOURGEOIS POURSUIVENT LEURS ETUDES A CE NIVEAU D'ENSEIGNEMENT A L'ETRANGER.
ESP> LOS DATOS SE REFIEREN SOLAMENTE A LOS ESTUDIANTES MATRICULADOS EN LAS INSTITUCIONES EN LUXEMBURGO. LA MAYORIA DE LOS ESTUDIANTES DE LUXEMBURGO CURSAN SUS ESTUDIOS DE ESTE GRADO EN EL EXTRANJERO.

POLAND:
E—> DATA REFERRING TO NON—UNIVERSITY TEACHER TRAINING ARE INCLUDED WITH OTHER NON—UNIVERSITY INSTITUTIONS. DATA ALSO INCLUDE EVENING AND CORRESPONDENCE COURSES.
FR—> Y COMPRIS LES COURS DU SOIR ET PAR CORRES-PONDANCE. POUR LES ETUDIANTS, LES DONNEES RELATIVES A L'ENSEIGNEMENT NORMAL NON—UNIVERSI-TAIRE SONT INCLUSES AVEC CELLES DES AUTRES ETABLISSEMENTS NON—UNIVERSITAIRES.
ESP> INCLUIDOS LOS CURSOS NOCTURNOS Y POR CORRESPONDENCIA. PARA LOS ESTUDIANTES, LOS DATOS RELATIVOS A LA ENSEÑANZA NORMAL NO UNIVERSITARIA QUEDAN INCLUIDOS CON LOS OTROS ESTABLECIMIENTOS NO UNIVERSITARIOS.

PORTUGAL:
E—> 1970 DATA ON TEACHERS AT OTHER NON—UNIVER-SITY INSTITUTIONS ARE INCLUDED WITH UNIVERSITIES AND EQUIVALENT INSTITUTIONS.
FR—> EN 1970, POUR LES PROFESSEURS, LES DONNEES RELATIVES AUX AUTRES ETABLISSEMENTS NON—UNIVERSI-TAIRES SONT COMPRISES AVEC CELLES DES UNIVERSITES ET ETABLISSEMENTS EQUIVALENTS.
ESP> EN 1970, LOS DATOS RELATIVOS A LOS PROFE-SORES DE LOS OTROS ESTABLECIMIENTOS NO UNIVERSI-TARIOS QUEDAN ENGLOBADOS CON LOS CORRESPONDIENTES A LAS UNIVERSIDADES Y ESTABLECIMIENTOS EQUIVA-LENTES.

ROMANIA:
E—> INCLUDING EVENING AND CORRESPONDENCE COURSES.
FR—> Y COMPRIS LES COURS DU SOIR ET PAR CORRES-PONDANCE.
ESP> INCLUIDOS LOS CURSOS NOCTURNOS Y POR CORRESPONDENCIA.

SPAIN:
E—> 1975 AND 1976 STUDENTS' DATA INCLUDE "UNI-VERSIDAD DE EDUCACION A DISTANCIA" AT WHICH 24,506 (F. 6,383) AND 25,571 (F. 5,233) STUDENTS WERE ENROLLED IN 1975 AND 1976 RESPECTIVELY.

SPAIN (CONT.):
FR—> EN 1975 ET 1976 L'"UNIVERSIDAD DE EDUCACION A DISTANCIA" EST INCLUSE, AVEC 24 506 ETUDIANTS (F. 6 383) EN 1975 ET 25 571 ETUDIANTS (F. 5 233) INCRITS EN 1976.
ESP> EN 1975 Y 1976 SE INCLUYE LA UNIVERSIDAD DE EDUCACION A DISTANCIA: 24 506 ESTUDIANTES (F. 6 383) EN 1975 Y 25 571 ESTUDIANTES (F. 5 233) EN 1976.

SWEDEN:
E—> DATA ON STUDENTS IN 1975 AND 1976 INCLUDE FOR THE FIRST TIME SOME SCHOOLS (WITH NEARLY 26,000 STUDENTS) WHICH WERE PREVIOUSLY CLASSIFIED AT THE SECOND LEVEL
FR—> EN 1975 ET 1976 LES CHIFFRES DES ETUDIANTS TIENNENT COMPTE DE CERTAINES ECOLES, AVEC ENVIRON 26 000 ETUDIANTS, QUI AUPARAVANT ETAIENT CLASSEES DANS LEUR PRESQUE TOTALITE DANS L'ENSEIGNEMENT DU SECOND DEGRE.
ESP> EN 1975 Y 1976 LAS CIFRAS INCLUYEN POR PRIMERA VEZ CIERTAS ESCUELAS CON UNOS 26 000 ESTUDIANTES, QUE ANTERIORMENTE ESTABAN CLASIFI-CADAS EN SU CASI TOTALIDAD EN LA ENSEÑANZA DE SEGUNDO GRADO.

UNITED KINGDOM:
E—> BEGINNING 1974, INCLUDING STUDENTS AT THE OPEN UNIVERSITY: 51,035 (F 20,005) STUDENTS IN 1975.
FR—> A PARTIR DE 1974 LES EFFECTIFS DE L'"OPEN UNIVERSITY" SONT INCLUS: 51 035 ETUDIANTS (F. 20 005) EN 1975.
ESP> A PARTIR DE 1974, SE INCLUYE LA "OPEN UNIVERSITY": 51 035 ESTUDIANTES (F. 20 005) EN 1975.

AUSTRALIA:
E—> EXCLUDING PART—TIME TEACHERS.
FR—> LES PROFESSEURS A TEMPS PARTIEL SONT EXCLUS.
ESP> EXCLUIDOS LOS PROFESORES DE JORNADA PARCIAL.

U.S.S.R.
E—> INCLUDING EVENING AND CORRESPONDENCE COURSES.
FR—> Y COMPRIS LES COURS DU SOIR ET PAR CORRES-PONDANCE.
ESP> INCLUIDOS LOS CURSOS NOCTURNOS Y POR CORRES-PONDENCIA.

BYELORUSSIAN S.S.R.:
E—> INCLUDING EVENING AND CORRESPONDENCE COURSES.
FR—> Y COMPRIS LES COURS DU SOIR ET PAR CORRES-PONDANCE.
ESP> INCLUIDOS LOS CURSOS NOCTURNOS Y POR CORRES-PONDENCIA.

UKRAINIAN S.S.R.:
E—> INCLUDING EVENING AND CORRESPONDENCE COURSES.
FR—> Y COMPRIS LES COURS DU SOIR ET PAR CORRES-PONDANCE.
ESP> INCLUIDOS LOS CURSOS NOCTURNOS Y POR CORRES-PONDENCIA.

Third level: students by levels and fields 3.12
Troisième degré: étudiants par types de programmes et domaines d'études
Tercer grado: estudiantes por tipos de programas y sectores de estudio

3.12 Education at the third level: enrolment by ISCED levels and fields

Enseignement du troisième degré: nombre d'étudiants d'après les types de programmes et les domaines d'études de la CITE

Enseñanza de tercer grado: número de estudiantes según los tipos de programas y los sectores de estudio de la CINE

LEVEL 5: PROGRAMMES LEADING TO AN AWARD NOT EQUIVALENT TO A FIRST UNIVERSITY DEGREE

NIVEAU 5: PROGRAMMES CONDUISANT A UN DIPLOME N'EQUIVALANT PAS A UN PREMIER GRADE UNIVERSITAIRE

GRADO 5: PROGRAMAS QUE CONDUCEN A UN DIPLOMA QUE NO EQUIVALE A UN PRIMER GRADO UNIVERSITARIO

LEVEL 6: PROGRAMMES LEADING TO A FIRST UNIVERSITY DEGREE OR EQUIVALENT QUALIFICATION

NIVEAU 6: PROGRAMMES CONDUISANT A UN PREMIER GRADE UNIVERSITAIRE OU A UN DIPLOME EQUIVALENT

GRADO 6: PROGRAMAS QUE CONDUCEN A UN PRIMER GRADO UNIVERSITARIO O A UN DIPLOMA EQUIVALENTE

LEVEL 7: PROGRAMMES LEADING TO A POST-GRADUATE UNIVERSITY DEGREE OR EQUIVALENT QUALIFICATION

NIVEAU 7: PROGRAMMES CONDUISANT A UN GRADE UNIVERSITAIRE SUPE-RIEUR OU A UN DIPLOME EQUIVALENT

GRADO 7: PROGRAMAS QUE CONDUCEN A UN GRADO UNIVERSITARIO SUPERIOR O A UN DIPLOMA EQUIVALENTE

NUMBER OF COUNTRIES AND TERRITORIES PRESENTED IN THIS TABLE: 132

NOMBRE DE PAYS ET DE TERRITOIRES PRESENTES DANS CE TABLEAU: 132

NUMERO DE PAISES Y DE TERRITORIOS PRESENTADOS EN ESTE CUADRO: 132

3.12 Third level: students by levels and fields
Troisième degré: étudiants par types de programmes et domaines d'études
Tercer grado: estudiantes por tipos de programas y sectores de estudio

INTERNATIONAL STANDARD CLASSIFICATION OF EDUCATION BY LEVEL
CLASSIFICATION INTERNATIONALE TYPE DE L'EDUCATION PAR NIVEAUX
CLASIFICACION INTERNACIONAL NORMALIZADA DE LA EDUCACION POR GRADOS

COUNTRY / PAYS / PAIS	YEAR / ANNEE / AÑO	FIELD OF STUDY / BRANCHE D'ETUDES / RAMAS DE ESTUDIO	ALL LEVELS TOUS NIVEAUX TODOS LOS GRADOS MF	F	LEVEL 5 NIVEAU 5 GRADO 5 MF	F	LEVEL 6 NIVEAU 6 GRADO 6 MF	F	LEVEL 7 NIVEAU 7 GRADO 7 MF	F
AFRICA										
ALGERIA	1977	TOTAL	61 767	13 958	7 130	1 074	51 983	12 138	2 654	746
		EDUCATION SCIENCE & TCHR TRNG.	1 490	342	—	—	1 469	340	21	2
		HUMANITIES,RELIGION & THEOLOG.	5 541	2 110	—	—	5 002	1 925	539	185
		FINE AND APPLIED ARTS	—	—	—	—	—	—	—	—
		LAW	12 896	2 082	4 160	508	8 567	1 538	169	36
		SOCIAL AND BEHAVIOURAL SCIENCE	11 967	2 322	—	—	11 366	2 174	601	148
		COMMERCIAL & BUS. ADMINISTR.	426	87	—	—	426	87	—	—
		MASS COMMUNICATION & DOCUMENT.	294	88	—	—	294	88	—	—
		HOME ECONOMICS & DOMESTIC SC.	—	—	—	—	—	—	—	—
		SERVICE TRADES	—	—	—	—	—	—	—	—
		NATURAL SCIENCE	14 659	3 416	2 970	566	11 530	2 802	159	44
		MATHEMATICS & COMPUTER SCIENCE	1 206	218	—	—	1 206	218	—	—
		MEDICAL AND HEALTH-RELATED SC.	7 958	2 848	—	—	6 848	2 528	1 110	320
		ENGINEERING	2 727	141	—	—	2 727	141	—	—
		ARCHITECTURE & TOWN PLANNING	1 073	159	—	—	1 073	159	—	—
		TRADE, CRAFT & INDUSTR. PGMS.	—	—	—	—	—	—	—	—
		TRANSPORT AND COMMUNICATIONS	654	4	—	—	654	4	—	—
		AGRICULTURE,FORESTRY & FISH'G.	876	145	—	—	821	134	55	11
		OTHER AND NOT SPECIFIED	—	—	—	—	—	—	—	—
BENIN	1978	TOTAL	3 292	585	—	—	2 487	459	805	126
		EDUCATION SCIENCE & TCHR TRNG.	190	19	—	—	—	—	190	19
		HUMANITIES,RELIGION & THEOLOG.	249	59	—	—	217	50	32	9
		FINE AND APPLIED ARTS	—	—	—	—	—	—	—	—
		LAW	681	164	—	—	548	136	133	28
		SOCIAL AND BEHAVIOURAL SCIENCE	1 051	163	—	—	880	138	171	25
		COMMERCIAL & BUS. ADMINISTR.	163	61	—	—	106	46	57	15
		MASS COMMUNICATION & DOCUMENT.	—	—	—	—	—	—	—	—
		HOME ECONOMICS & DOMESTIC SC.	—	—	—	—	—	—	—	—
		SERVICE TRADES	—	—	—	—	—	—	—	—
		NATURAL SCIENCE	486	61	—	—	462	58	24	3
		MATHEMATICS & COMPUTER SCIENCE	—	—	—	—	—	—	—	—
		MEDICAL AND HEALTH-RELATED SC.	190	41	—	—	53	16	137	25
		ENGINEERING	221	15	—	—	221	15	—	—
		ARCHITECTURE & TOWN PLANNING	—	—	—	—	—	—	—	—
		TRADE, CRAFT & INDUSTR. PGMS.	—	—	—	—	—	—	—	—
		TRANSPORT AND COMMUNICATIONS	—	—	—	—	—	—	—	—
		AGRICULTURE,FORESTRY & FISH'G.	61	2	—	—	—	—	61	2
		OTHER AND NOT SPECIFIED	—	—	—	—	—	—	—	—

Third level: students by levels and fields   3.12
Troisième degré: étudiants par types de programmes et domaines d'études
Tercer grado: estudiantes por tipos de programas y sectores de estudio

COUNTRY / PAYS / PAIS: **BOTSWANA**

INTERNATIONAL STANDARD CLASSIFICATION OF EDUCATION BY LEVEL
CLASSIFICATION INTERNATIONALE TYPE DE L'EDUCATION PAR NIVEAUX
CLASIFICACION INTERNACIONAL NORMALIZADA DE LA EDUCACION POR GRADOS

YEAR / ANNEE / AÑO	FIELD OF STUDY / BRANCHE D'ETUDES / RAMAS DE ESTUDIO	ALL LEVELS TOUS NIVEAUX TODOS LOS GRADOS		LEVEL 5 NIVEAU 5 GRADO 5		LEVEL 6 NIVEAU 6 GRADO 6		LEVEL 7 NIVEAU 7 GRADO 7	
		MF	F	MF	F	MF	F	MF	F
1976	TOTAL	527	182	97	40	430	142	—	—
	EDUCATION SCIENCE & TCHR TRNG.	234	96	86	39	148	57	—	—
	HUMANITIES,RELIGION & THEOLOG.	7	1	—	—	7	1	—	—
	FINE AND APPLIED ARTS	—	—	—	—	—	—	—	—
	LAW	—	—	—	—	—	—	—	—
	SOCIAL AND BEHAVIOURAL SCIENCE	98	35	—	—	98	35	—	—
	COMMERCIAL & BUS. ADMINISTR.	83	33	—	—	83	33	—	—
	MASS COMMUNICATION & DOCUMENT.	1	—	—	—	1	—	—	—
	HOME ECONOMICS & DOMESTIC SC.	—	—	—	—	—	—	—	—
	SERVICE TRADES	—	—	—	—	—	—	—	—
	NATURAL SCIENCE	81	16	—	—	81	16	—	—
	MATHEMATICS & COMPUTER SCIENCE	11	1	11	1	—	—	—	—
	MEDICAL AND HEALTH-RELATED SC.	—	—	—	—	—	—	—	—
	ENGINEERING	—	—	—	—	—	—	—	—
	ARCHITECTURE & TOWN PLANNING	—	—	—	—	—	—	—	—
	TRADE, CRAFT & INDUSTR. PGMS.	—	—	—	—	—	—	—	—
	TRANSPORT AND COMMUNICATIONS	—	—	—	—	—	—	—	—
	AGRICULTURE,FORESTRY & FISH'G.	12	—	—	—	12	—	—	—
	OTHER AND NOT SPECIFIED	—	—	—	—	—	—	—	—
1977	TOTAL	755	262	163	68	592	194	—	—
	EDUCATION SCIENCE & TCHR TRNG.	148	66	148	66	—	—	—	—
	HUMANITIES,RELIGION & THEOLOG.	322	108	—	—	322	108	—	—
	FINE AND APPLIED ARTS	—	—	—	—	—	—	—	—
	LAW	—	—	—	—	—	—	—	—
	SOCIAL AND BEHAVIOURAL SCIENCE	176	47	—	—	176	47	—	—
	COMMERCIAL & BUS. ADMINISTR.	63	23	—	—	63	23	—	—
	MASS COMMUNICATION & DOCUMENT.	—	—	—	—	—	—	—	—
	HOME ECONOMICS & DOMESTIC SC.	—	—	—	—	—	—	—	—
	SERVICE TRADES	—	—	—	—	—	—	—	—
	NATURAL SCIENCE	15	2	15	2	—	—	—	—
	MATHEMATICS & COMPUTER SCIENCE	31	16	—	—	31	16	—	—
	MEDICAL AND HEALTH-RELATED SC.	—	—	—	—	—	—	—	—
	ENGINEERING	—	—	—	—	—	—	—	—
	ARCHITECTURE & TOWN PLANNING	—	—	—	—	—	—	—	—
	TRADE, CRAFT & INDUSTR. PGMS.	—	—	—	—	—	—	—	—
	TRANSPORT AND COMMUNICATIONS	—	—	—	—	—	—	—	—
	AGRICULTURE,FORESTRY & FISH'G.	—	—	—	—	—	—	—	—
	OTHER AND NOT SPECIFIED	—	—	—	—	—	—	—	—

3.12 Third level: students by levels and fields
Troisième degré: étudiants par types de programmes et domaines d'études
Tercer grado: estudiantes por tipos de programas y sectores de estudio

COUNTRY / PAYS / PAIS	YEAR / ANNEE / AÑO	FIELD OF STUDY / BRANCHE D'ETUDES / RAMAS DE ESTUDIO	INTERNATIONAL STANDARD CLASSIFICATION OF EDUCATION BY LEVEL — CLASSIFICATION INTERNATIONALE TYPE DE L'EDUCATION PAR NIVEAUX — CLASIFICACION INTERNACIONAL NORMALIZADA DE LA EDUCACION POR GRADOS							
			ALL LEVELS / TOUS NIVEAUX / TODOS LOS GRADOS		LEVEL 5 / NIVEAU 5 / GRADO 5		LEVEL 6 / NIVEAU 6 / GRADO 6		LEVEL 7 / NIVEAU 7 / GRADO 7	
			MF	F	MF	F	MF	F	MF	F
CENTRAL AFRICAN REPUBLIC	1977	TOTAL	972	–	375	17	533	45	64	8
		EDUCATION SCIENCE & TCHR	196	11	196	11	–	–	–	–
		HUMANITIES,RELIGION & TH	257	22	–	–	257	22	–	–
		FINE AND APPLIED ARTS	117	9	–	–	117	9	–	–
		LAW	–	–	–	–	–	–	–	–
		SOCIAL AND BEHAVIOURAL SCI	–	–	–	–	–	–	–	–
		COMMERCIAL & BUS. ADMINISTR	–	–	–	–	–	–	–	–
		MASS COMMUNICATION & DOCUMENT	–	–	–	–	–	–	–	–
		HOME ECONOMICS & DOMESTIC SC.	–	–	–	–	–	–	–	–
		SERVICE TRADES	–	–	–	–	–	–	–	–
		NATURAL SCIENCE	31	1	31	1	–	–	–	–
		MATHEMATICS & COMPUTER SCIENCE	40	3	34	2	5	1	1	–
		MEDICAL AND HEALTH-RELATED SC.	150	11	–	–	87	3	63	8
		ENGINEERING	58	–	58	–	–	–	–	–
		ARCHITECTURE & TOWN PLANNING	–	–	–	–	–	–	–	–
		TRADE, CRAFT & INDUSTR. PGMS.	–	–	–	–	–	–	–	–
		TRANSPORT AND COMMUNICATIONS	–	–	–	–	–	–	–	–
		AGRICULTURE,FORESTRY & FISH'G.	56	3	56	3	–	–	–	–
		OTHER AND NOT SPECIFIED	67	10	–	–	67	10	–	–
CHAD	1976	TOTAL	758	40	441	24	224	8	90	6
		EDUCATION SCIENCE & TCHR TRNG.	267	19	123	7	77	6	67	6
		HUMANITIES,RELIGION & THEOLOG.	276	13	193	12	83	1	–	–
		FINE AND APPLIED ARTS	–	–	–	–	–	–	–	–
		LAW	141	4	76	4	46	–	19	2
		SOCIAL AND BEHAVIOURAL SCIENCE	–	–	–	–	–	–	–	–
		COMMERCIAL & BUS. ADMINISTR.	–	–	–	–	–	–	–	–
		MASS COMMUNICATION & DOCUMENT.	–	–	–	–	–	–	–	–
		HOME ECONOMICS & DOMESTIC SC.	–	–	–	–	–	–	–	–
		SERVICE TRADES	–	–	–	–	–	–	–	–
		NATURAL SCIENCE	46	4	37	3	9	1	–	–
		MATHEMATICS & COMPUTER SCIENCE	15	–	15	–	–	–	–	–
		MEDICAL AND HEALTH-RELATED SC.	–	–	–	–	–	–	–	–
		ENGINEERING	13	–	–	–	9	–	4	–
		ARCHITECTURE & TOWN PLANNING	–	–	–	–	–	–	–	–
		TRADE, CRAFT & INDUSTR. PGMS.	–	–	–	–	–	–	–	–
		TRANSPORT AND COMMUNICATIONS	–	–	–	–	–	–	–	–
		AGRICULTURE,FORESTRY & FISH'G.	–	–	–	–	–	–	–	–
		OTHER AND NOT SPECIFIED	–	–	–	–	–	–	–	–

Third level: students by levels and fields   3.12
Troisième degré: étudiants par types de programmes et domaines d'études
Tercer grado: estudiantes por tipos de programas y sectores de estudio

INTERNATIONAL STANDARD CLASSIFICATION OF EDUCATION BY LEVEL
CLASSIFICATION INTERNATIONALE TYPE DE L'EDUCATION PAR NIVEAUX
CLASIFICACION INTERNACIONAL NORMALIZADA DE LA EDUCACION POR GRADOS

COUNTRY / PAYS / PAIS	YEAR / ANNEE / AÑO	FIELD OF STUDY / BRANCHE D'ETUDES / RAMAS DE ESTUDIO	ALL LEVELS / TOUS NIVEAUX / TODOS LOS GRADOS		LEVEL 5 / NIVEAU 5 / GRADO 5		LEVEL 6 / NIVEAU 6 / GRADO 6		LEVEL 7 / NIVEAU 7 / GRADO 7	
			MF	F	MF	F	MF	F	MF	F
EGYPT ‡	1976	TOTAL	462 328	140 777	—	—	410 633	126 801	34 695	8 476
		EDUCATION SCIENCE & TCHR TRNG.	55 269	19 311	—	—	35 843	13 026	2 426	785
		HUMANITIES,RELIGION & THEOLOG.	55 265	26 112	—	—	50 194	24 034	5 071	2 078
		FINE AND APPLIED ARTS	7 757	3 016	—	—	7 391	2 914	366	102
		LAW	45 479	9 637	—	—	41 226	9 278	4 253	359
		SOCIAL AND BEHAVIOURAL SCIENCE	7 935	3 654	—	—	6 520	3 194	1 415	460
		COMMERCIAL & BUS. ADMINISTR.	102 851	29 916	—	—	99 266	29 403	3 585	513
		MASS COMMUNICATION & DOCUMENT.	4 626	1 986	—	—	3 397	1 519	1 229	467
		HOME ECONOMICS & DOMESTIC SC.	2 025	2 025	—	—	1 986	1 986	39	39
		SERVICE TRADES	356	166	—	—	356	166	—	—
		NATURAL SCIENCE	16 687	5 913	—	—	14 577	5 222	2 110	691
		MATHEMATICS & COMPUTER SCIENCE	650	79	—	—	650	79	650	79
		MEDICAL AND HEALTH-RELATED SC.	52 193	15 992	—	—	47 085	14 495	5 108	1 497
		ENGINEERING	58 293	9 410	—	—	54 305	8 992	3 988	418
		ARCHITECTURE & TOWN PLANNING	—	—	—	—	—	—	—	—
		TRADE, CRAFT & INDUSTR. PGMS.	—	—	—	—	—	—	—	—
		TRANSPORT AND COMMUNICATIONS	—	—	—	—	—	—	—	—
		AGRICULTURE,FORESTRY & FISH'G.	46 596	10 802	—	—	42 513	9 981	4 083	821
		OTHER AND NOT SPECIFIED	6 346	2 758	—	—	5 974	2 591	372	167
ETHIOPIA ‡	1977	TOTAL	10 824	...	—	—	...	...	...	...
		EDUCATION SCIENCE & TCHR TRNG.	1 865	...	—	—	—	—	...	...
		HUMANITIES,RELIGION & THEOLOG.	—	...	—	—	—	—	—	—
		FINE AND APPLIED ARTS		...	—	—	—	—	—	—
		LAW	173	...	—	—	—	—	...	...
		SOCIAL AND BEHAVIOURAL SCIENCE	1 165	...	—	—	—	—	...	...
		COMMERCIAL & BUS. ADMINISTR.	1 309	...	—	—	—	—	...	...
		MASS COMMUNICATION & DOCUMENT.	—	...	—	—	—	—	—	—
		HOME ECONOMICS & DOMESTIC SC.		...	—	—	—	—	—	—
		SERVICE TRADES		...	—	—	—	—	—	—
		NATURAL SCIENCE	449	...	—	—	—	—	...	...
		MATHEMATICS & COMPUTER SCIENCE		...	—	—	—	—	—	—
		MEDICAL AND HEALTH-RELATED SC.	440	...	—	—	—	—	...	...
		ENGINEERING	551	...	—	—	—	—	...	...
		ARCHITECTURE & TOWN PLANNING	277	...	—	—	—	—	...	...
		TRADE, CRAFT & INDUSTR. PGMS.	158	...	—	—	—	—	...	...
		TRANSPORT AND COMMUNICATIONS		...	—	—	—	—	—	—
		AGRICULTURE,FORESTRY & FISH'G.	1 221	...	—	—	—	—	...	...
		OTHER AND NOT SPECIFIED	3 216	...	—	—	—	—	...	...

3.12 Third level: students by levels and fields
Troisième degré: étudiants par types de programmes et domaines d'études
Tercer grado: estudiantes por tipos de programas y sectores de estudio

COUNTRY / PAYS / PAIS	YEAR / ANNEE / AÑO	FIELD OF STUDY / BRANCHE D'ETUDES / RAMAS DE ESTUDIO	INTERNATIONAL STANDARD CLASSIFICATION OF EDUCATION BY LEVEL / CLASSIFICATION INTERNATIONALE TYPE DE L'EDUCATION PAR NIVEAUX / CLASIFICACION INTERNACIONAL NORMALIZADA DE LA EDUCACION POR GRADOS							
			ALL LEVELS / TOUS NIVEAUX / TODOS LOS GRADOS		LEVEL 5 / NIVEAU 5 / GRADO 5		LEVEL 6 / NIVEAU 6 / GRADO 6		LEVEL 7 / NIVEAU 7 / GRADO 7	
			MF	F	MF	F	MF	F	MF	F
GABON	1976	TOTAL	1 245	224						
		EDUCATION SCIENCE & TCHR TRNG.	177	30						
		HUMANITIES,RELIGION & THEOLOG.	314	78						
		FINE AND APPLIED ARTS	—	—						
		LAW	197	40						
		SOCIAL AND BEHAVIOURAL SCIENCE	162	22						
		COMMERCIAL & BUS. ADMINISTR.	50	6						
		MASS COMMUNICATION & DOCUMENT.	—	—						
		HOME ECONOMICS & DOMESTIC SC.	—	—						
		SERVICE TRADES	—	—						
		NATURAL SCIENCE	69	14						
		MATHEMATICS & COMPUTER SCIENCE	108	8						
		MEDICAL AND HEALTH-RELATED SC.	82	23						
		ENGINEERING	86	3						
		ARCHITECTURE & TOWN PLANNING	—	—						
		TRADE, CRAFT & INDUSTR. PGMS.	—	—						
		TRANSPORT AND COMMUNICATIONS	—	—						
		AGRICULTURE,FORESTRY & FISH'G.	—	—						
		OTHER AND NOT SPECIFIED	—	—						
IVORY COAST	1976	TOTAL	8 701	1 543						
		EDUCATION SCIENCE & TCHR TRNG.	1 150	125						
		HUMANITIES,RELIGION & THEOLOG.	2 374	641						
		FINE AND APPLIED ARTS	—	—						
		LAW	1 725	317						
		SOCIAL SCIENCES, TOTAL	1 165	125						
		NATURAL SCIENCES, TOTAL	1 124	111						
		MEDICAL AND HEALTH-RELATED SC.	861	186						
		ENGINEERING	—	—						
		ARCHITECTURE & TOWN PLANNING	—	—						
		TRADE, CRAFT & INDUSTR. PGMS.	—	—						
		TRANSPORT AND COMMUNICATIONS	—	—						
		AGRICULTURE,FORESTRY & FISH'G.	—	—						
		OTHER AND NOT SPECIFIED	302	38						

Third level: students by levels and fields   3.12
Troisième degré: étudiants par types de programmes et domaines d'études
Tercer grado: estudiantes por tipos de programas y sectores de estudio

INTERNATIONAL STANDARD CLASSIFICATION OF EDUCATION BY LEVEL
CLASSIFICATION INTERNATIONALE TYPE DE L'EDUCATION PAR NIVEAUX
CLASIFICACION INTERNACIONAL NORMALIZADA DE LA EDUCACION POR GRADOS

COUNTRY / PAYS / PAIS	YEAR / ANNEE / AÑO	FIELD OF STUDY / BRANCHE D'ETUDES / RAMAS DE ESTUDIO	ALL LEVELS / TOUS NIVEAUX / TODOS LOS GRADOS		LEVEL 5 / NIVEAU 5 / GRADO 5		LEVEL 6 / NIVEAU 6 / GRADO 6		LEVEL 7 / NIVEAU 7 / GRADO 7	
			MF	F	MF	F	MF	F	MF	F
KENYA ‡	1976	TOTAL	6 361	...						
		EDUCATION SCIENCE & TCHR TRNG.	1 780	...						
		HUMANITIES,RELIGION & THEOLOG.	—	...						
		FINE AND APPLIED ARTS	507	...						
		LAW	186	...						
		SOCIAL AND BEHAVIOURAL SCIENCE	458	...						
		COMMERCIAL & BUS. ADMINISTR.	9	...						
		MASS COMMUNICATION & DOCUMENT.	—	—						
		HOME ECONOMICS & DOMESTIC SC.	—	—						
		SERVICE TRADES	—	—						
		NATURAL SCIENCE	624	...						
		MATHEMATICS & COMPUTER SCIENCE	674	...						
		MEDICAL AND HEALTH-RELATED SC.	540	...						
		ENGINEERING	275	...						
		ARCHITECTURE & TOWN PLANNING	—	—						
		TRADE, CRAFT & INDUSTR. PGMS.	—	—						
		TRANSPORT AND COMMUNICATIONS	551	...						
		AGRICULTURE,FORESTRY & FISH'G.	757	...						
		OTHER AND NOT SPECIFIED	—	—						
LIBYAN ARAB JAMAHIRIYA	1975	TOTAL	13 427	2 358						
		EDUCATION SCIENCE & TCHR TRNG.	1 582	516						
		HUMANITIES,RELIGION & THEOLOG.	1 338	36						
		FINE AND APPLIED ARTS	2 485	775						
		LAW	1 874	106						
		SOCIAL AND BEHAVIOURAL SCIENCE	720	213						
		COMMERCIAL & BUS. ADMINISTR.	1 846	236						
		MASS COMMUNICATION & DOCUMENT.	—	—						
		HOME ECONOMICS & DOMESTIC SC.	—	—						
		SERVICE TRADES	—	—						
		NATURAL SCIENCE	189	73						
		MATHEMATICS & COMPUTER SCIENCE	—	—						
		MEDICAL AND HEALTH-RELATED SC.	900	188						
		ENGINEERING	1 648	127						
		ARCHITECTURE & TOWN PLANNING	—	—						
		TRADE, CRAFT & INDUSTR. PGMS.	—	—						
		TRANSPORT AND COMMUNICATIONS	—	—						
		AGRICULTURE,FORESTRY & FISH'G.	845	88						
		OTHER AND NOT SPECIFIED	—	—						

3.12 Third level: students by levels and fields
Troisième degré: étudiants par types de programmes et domaines d'études
Tercer grado: estudiantes por tipos de programas y sectores de estudio

INTERNATIONAL STANDARD CLASSIFICATION OF EDUCATION BY LEVEL
CLASSIFICATION INTERNATIONALE TYPE DE L'EDUCATION PAR NIVEAUX
CLASIFICACION INTERNACIONAL NORMALIZADA DE LA EDUCACION POR GRADOS

COUNTRY / PAYS / PAIS	YEAR / ANNEE / AÑO	FIELD OF STUDY / BRANCHE D'ETUDES / RAMAS DE ESTUDIO	ALL LEVELS TOUS NIVEAUX TODOS LOS GRADOS MF	F	LEVEL 5 NIVEAU 5 GRADO 5 MF	F	LEVEL 6 NIVEAU 6 GRADO 6 MF	F	LEVEL 7 NIVEAU 7 GRADO 7 MF	F
MADAGASCAR ‡	1977	TOTAL	14 116	4 849						
		EDUCATION SCIENCE & TCHR TRNG.	2 036	1 227						
		HUMANITIES,RELIGION & THEOLOG.	—	—						
		FINE AND APPLIED ARTS	2 356	711						
		LAW	2 372	842						
		SOCIAL AND BEHAVIOURAL SCIENCE	1 494	407						
		COMMERCIAL & BUS. ADMINISTR.	—	—						
		MASS COMMUNICATION & DOCUMENT.	—	—						
		HOME ECONOMICS & DOMESTIC SC.	—	—						
		SERVICE TRADES	—	—						
		NATURAL SCIENCE	1 310	497						
		MATHEMATICS & COMPUTER SCIENCE	494	86						
		MEDICAL AND HEALTH—RELATED SC.	2 001	776						
		ENGINEERING	1 168	65						
		ARCHITECTURE & TOWN PLANNING	./.	./.						
		TRADE, CRAFT & INDUSTR. PGMS.	./.	./.						
		TRANSPORT AND COMMUNICATIONS	—	—						
		AGRICULTURE,FORESTRY & FISH'G.	308	74						
		OTHER AND NOT SPECIFIED	577	162						
MALAWI	1977	TOTAL	1 153	...	562	...	591	...	—	—
		EDUCATION SCIENCE & TCHR TRNG.	124	...	116	...	8	...	—	—
		HUMANITIES,RELIGION & THEOLOG.	—	—	—	—	—	—	—	—
		FINE AND APPLIED ARTS	16	—	16	—	—	—	—	—
		LAW	41	—	—	—	41	—	—	—
		SOCIAL AND BEHAVIOURAL SCIENCE	28	...	—	...	28	...	—	—
		COMMERCIAL & BUS. ADMINISTR.	110	...	94	...	16	...	—	—
		MASS COMMUNICATION & DOCUMENT.	—	—	—	—	—	—	—	—
		HOME ECONOMICS & DOMESTIC SC.	—	—	—	—	—	—	—	—
		SERVICE TRADES	—	—	—	—	—	—	—	—
		NATURAL SCIENCE	36	...	—	...	36	...	—	—
		MATHEMATICS & COMPUTER SCIENCE	—	—	—	—	—	—	—	—
		MEDICAL AND HEALTH—RELATED SC.	15	...	15	...	—	...	—	—
		ENGINEERING	274	—	274	—	—	—	—	—
		ARCHITECTURE & TOWN PLANNING	—	—	—	—	—	—	—	—
		TRADE, CRAFT & INDUSTR. PGMS.	—	—	—	—	—	—	—	—
		TRANSPORT AND COMMUNICATIONS	—	—	—	—	—	—	—	—
		AGRICULTURE,FORESTRY & FISH'G.	236	...	47	...	189	...	—	—
		OTHER AND NOT SPECIFIED	273	...	—	...	273	...	—	—

Third level: students by levels and fields 3.12
Troisième degré: étudiants par types de programmes et domaines d'études
Tercer grado: estudiantes por tipos de programas y sectores de estudio

INTERNATIONAL STANDARD CLASSIFICATION OF EDUCATION BY LEVEL
CLASSIFICATION INTERNATIONALE TYPE DE L'EDUCATION PAR NIVEAUX
CLASIFICACION INTERNACIONAL NORMALIZADA DE LA EDUCACION POR GRADOS

COUNTRY / PAYS / PAIS	YEAR / ANNEE / AÑO	FIELD OF STUDY / BRANCHE D'ETUDES / RAMAS DE ESTUDIO	ALL LEVELS / TOUS NIVEAUX / TODOS LOS GRADOS MF	F	LEVEL 5 / NIVEAU 5 / GRADO 5 MF	F	LEVEL 6 / NIVEAU 6 / GRADO 6 MF	F	LEVEL 7 / NIVEAU 7 / GRADO 7 MF	F
MALI	1977	TOTAL	4 216	505	366	96	3 833	409	17	—
		EDUCATION SCIENCE & TCHR TRNG.	1 877	211	—	—	1 860	211	17	—
		HUMANITIES,RELIGION & THEOLOG.	—	—	—	—	—	—	—	—
		FINE AND APPLIED ARTS	—	—	—	—	—	—	—	—
		LAW	227	21	—	—	227	21	—	—
		SOCIAL AND BEHAVIOURAL SCIENCE	339	53	—	—	339	53	—	—
		COMMERCIAL & BUS. ADMINISTR.	597	119	342	91	255	28	—	—
		MASS COMMUNICATION & DOCUMENT.	—	—	—	—	—	—	—	—
		HOME ECONOMICS & DOMESTIC SC.	—	—	—	—	—	—	—	—
		SERVICE TRADES	—	—	—	—	—	—	—	—
		NATURAL SCIENCE	240	35	—	—	240	35	—	—
		MATHEMATICS & COMPUTER SCIENCE	—	—	—	—	—	—	—	—
		MEDICAL AND HEALTH-RELATED SC.	419	3	—	—	419	3	—	—
		ENGINEERING	—	—	—	—	—	—	—	—
		ARCHITECTURE & TOWN PLANNING	—	—	—	—	—	—	—	—
		TRADE, CRAFT & INDUSTR. PGMS.	—	—	—	—	—	—	—	—
		TRANSPORT AND COMMUNICATIONS	24	5	24	5	—	—	—	—
		AGRICULTURE,FORESTRY & FISH'G.	493	58	—	—	493	58	—	—
		OTHER AND NOT SPECIFIED	—	—	—	—	—	—	—	—
MAURITIUS	1977	TOTAL	1 531	377	868	162	655	215	8	—
		EDUCATION SCIENCE & TCHR TRNG.	540	200	—	—	540	200	—	—
		HUMANITIES,RELIGION & THEOLOG.	—	—	—	—	—	—	—	—
		FINE AND APPLIED ARTS	—	—	—	—	—	—	—	—
		LAW	—	—	—	—	—	—	—	—
		SOCIAL AND BEHAVIOURAL SCIENCE	349	124	313	115	36	9	—	—
		COMMERCIAL & BUS. ADMINISTR.	72	15	72	15	—	—	—	—
		MASS COMMUNICATION & DOCUMENT.	—	—	—	—	—	—	—	—
		HOME ECONOMICS & DOMESTIC SC.	—	—	—	—	—	—	—	—
		SERVICE TRADES	—	—	—	—	—	—	—	—
		NATURAL SCIENCE	57	7	57	7	—	—	—	—
		MATHEMATICS & COMPUTER SCIENCE	317	3	268	2	47	1	2	—
		MEDICAL AND HEALTH-RELATED SC.	—	—	—	—	—	—	—	—
		ENGINEERING	—	—	—	—	—	—	—	—
		ARCHITECTURE & TOWN PLANNING	—	—	—	—	—	—	—	—
		TRADE, CRAFT & INDUSTR. PGMS.	—	—	—	—	—	—	—	—
		TRANSPORT AND COMMUNICATIONS	—	—	—	—	—	—	—	—
		AGRICULTURE,FORESTRY & FISH'G.	117	14	79	9	32	5	6	—
		OTHER AND NOT SPECIFIED	79	14	79	14	—	—	—	—

3.12 Third level: students by levels and fields
Troisième degré: étudiants par types de programmes et domaines d'études
Tercer grado: estudiantes por tipos de programas y sectores de estudio

INTERNATIONAL STANDARD CLASSIFICATION OF EDUCATION BY LEVEL
CLASSIFICATION INTERNATIONALE TYPE DE L'EDUCATION PAR NIVEAUX
CLASIFICACION INTERNACIONAL NORMALIZADA DE LA EDUCACION POR GRADOS

COUNTRY / PAYS / PAIS	YEAR / ANNEE / AÑO	FIELD OF STUDY / BRANCHE D'ETUDES / RAMAS DE ESTUDIO	ALL LEVELS / TOUS NIVEAUX / TODOS LOS GRADOS MF	F	LEVEL 5 / NIVEAU 5 / GRADO 5 MF	F	LEVEL 6 / NIVEAU 6 / GRADO 6 MF	F	LEVEL 7 / NIVEAU 7 / GRADO 7 MF	F
MOROCCO ‡	1976	TOTAL	45 085	9 023	—	—	40 886	8 374	4 199	649
		EDUCATION SCIENCE & TCHR TRNG.	222	63	—	—	—	—	222	63
		HUMANITIES,RELIGION & THEOLOG.	10 668	3 139	—	—	9 492	2 938	1 176	201
		FINE AND APPLIED ARTS	—	—	—	—	—	—	—	—
		LAW	23 856	3 747	—	—	21 104	3 374	2 752	373
		SOCIAL AND BEHAVIOURAL SCIENCE	—	—	—	—	—	—	—	—
		COMMERCIAL & BUS. ADMINISTR.	—	—	—	—	—	—	—	—
		MASS COMMUNICATION & DOCUMENT.	—	—	—	—	—	—	—	—
		HOME ECONOMICS & DOMESTIC SC.	—	—	—	—	—	—	—	—
		SERVICE TRADES	—	—	—	—	—	—	—	—
		NATURAL SCIENCE	4 092	613	—	—	4 043	601	49	12
		MATHEMATICS & COMPUTER SCIENCE	5 781	1 443	—	—	5 781	1 443	—	—
		MEDICAL AND HEALTH-RELATED SC.	466	18	—	—	466	18	—	—
		ENGINEERING	—	—	—	—	—	—	—	—
		ARCHITECTURE & TOWN PLANNING	—	—	—	—	—	—	—	—
		TRADE, CRAFT & INDUSTR. PGMS.	—	—	—	—	—	—	—	—
		TRANSPORT AND COMMUNICATIONS	—	—	—	—	—	—	—	—
		AGRICULTURE,FORESTRY & FISH'G.	—	—	—	—	—	—	—	—
		OTHER AND NOT SPECIFIED	—	—	—	—	—	—	—	—
	1978	TOTAL	62 107	15 407	—	—	—	—	—	—
		EDUCATION SCIENCE & TCHR TRNG.	335	249	—	—	—	—	—	—
		HUMANITIES,RELIGION & THEOLOG.	16 415	5 338	—	—	—	—	—	—
		FINE AND APPLIED ARTS	—	—	—	—	—	—	—	—
		LAW	30 203	6 257	—	—	—	—	—	—
		SOCIAL AND BEHAVIOURAL SCIENCE	./.	./.	—	—	—	—	—	—
		COMMERCIAL & BUS. ADMINISTR.	—	—	—	—	—	—	—	—
		MASS COMMUNICATION & DOCUMENT.	—	—	—	—	—	—	—	—
		HOME ECONOMICS & DOMESTIC SC.	—	—	—	—	—	—	—	—
		SERVICE TRADES	—	—	—	—	—	—	—	—
		NATURAL SCIENCE	7 926	1 615	—	—	—	—	—	—
		MATHEMATICS & COMPUTER SCIENCE	6 652	1 902	—	—	—	—	—	—
		MEDICAL AND HEALTH-RELATED SC.	576	46	—	—	—	—	—	—
		ENGINEERING	—	—	—	—	—	—	—	—
		ARCHITECTURE & TOWN PLANNING	—	—	—	—	—	—	—	—
		TRADE, CRAFT & INDUSTR. PGMS.	—	—	—	—	—	—	—	—
		TRANSPORT AND COMMUNICATIONS	—	—	—	—	—	—	—	—
		AGRICULTURE,FORESTRY & FISH'G.	—	—	—	—	—	—	—	—
		OTHER AND NOT SPECIFIED	—	—	—	—	—	—	—	—

Third level: students by levels and fields 3.12
Troisième degré: étudiants par types de programmes et domaines d'études
Tercer grado: estudiantes por tipos de programas y sectores de estudio

COUNTRY / PAYS / PAIS	YEAR / ANNEE / AÑO	FIELD OF STUDY / BRANCHE D'ETUDES / RAMAS DE ESTUDIO	ALL LEVELS TOUS NIVEAUX TODOS LOS GRADOS		LEVEL 5 NIVEAU 5 GRADO 5		LEVEL 6 NIVEAU 6 GRADO 6		LEVEL 7 NIVEAU 7 GRADO 7	
			MF	F	MF	F	MF	F	MF	F
MOZAMBIQUE	1976	TOTAL	906	...	—	—	906	...	—	—
		EDUCATION SCIENCE & TCHR TRNG.	20	...	—	—	20	...	—	—
		HUMANITIES,RELIGION & THEOLOG.	104	...	—	—	104	...	—	—
		FINE AND APPLIED ARTS	—	—	—	—	—	—	—	—
		LAW	198	...	—	—	198	...	—	—
		SOCIAL AND BEHAVIOURAL SCIENCE	3	...	—	—	3	...	—	—
		COMMERCIAL & BUS. ADMINISTR.	126	—	—	—	126	—	—	—
		MASS COMMUNICATION & DOCUMENT.	—	—	—	—	—	—	—	—
		HOME ECONOMICS & DOMESTIC SC.	—	—	—	—	—	—	—	—
		SERVICE TRADES	—	—	—	—	—	—	—	—
		NATURAL SCIENCE	29	...	—	—	29	...	—	—
		MATHEMATICS & COMPUTER SCIENCE	14	...	—	—	14	...	—	—
		MEDICAL AND HEALTH-RELATED SC.	209	...	—	—	209	...	—	—
		ENGINEERING	144	...	—	—	144	...	—	—
		ARCHITECTURE & TOWN PLANNING	—	—	—	—	—	—	—	—
		TRADE, CRAFT & INDUSTR. PGMS.	—	—	—	—	—	—	—	—
		TRANSPORT AND COMMUNICATIONS	—	—	—	—	—	—	—	—
		AGRICULTURE,FORESTRY & FISH'G.	59	...	—	—	59	...	—	—
		OTHER AND NOT SPECIFIED	—	—	—	—	—	—	—	—
NIGER	1977	TOTAL	784	120	452	74	206	34	126	12
		EDUCATION SCIENCE & TCHR TRNG.	139	34	...	...	...	...	...	...
		HUMANITIES,RELIGION & THEOLOG.	166	45	...	...	...	...	...	...
		FINE AND APPLIED ARTS	—	—	...	...	...	...	...	...
		LAW	—	—	...	...	...	...	...	...
		SOCIAL SCIENCES, TOTAL	151	13	...	...	...	...	...	...
		NATURAL SCIENCE	93	3	...	...	...	...	...	...
		MATHEMATICS & COMPUTER SCIENCE	108	21	...	...	...	...	...	...
		MEDICAL AND HEALTH-RELATED SC.	—	—	...	...	...	...	...	...
		ENGINEERING, TOTAL	127	4	...	...	...	...	...	...
		AGRICULTURE,FORESTRY & FISH'G.	—	—	...	...	...	...	...	...
		OTHER AND NOT SPECIFIED	—	—	...	...	...	...	...	...

Column heading: INTERNATIONAL STANDARD CLASSIFICATION OF EDUCATION BY LEVEL / CLASSIFICATION INTERNATIONALE TYPE DE L'EDUCATION PAR NIVEAUX / CLASIFICACION INTERNACIONAL NORMALIZADA DE LA EDUCACION POR GRADOS

3.12 Third level: students by levels and fields
Troisième degré: étudiants par types de programmes et domaines d'études
Tercer grado: estudiantes por tipos de programas y sectores de estudio

COUNTRY / PAYS / PAIS	YEAR / ANNEE / AÑO	FIELD OF STUDY / BRANCHE D'ETUDES / RAMAS DE ESTUDIO	INTERNATIONAL STANDARD CLASSIFICATION OF EDUCATION BY LEVEL / CLASSIFICATION INTERNATIONALE TYPE DE L'EDUCATION PAR NIVEAUX / CLASIFICACION INTERNACIONAL NORMALIZADA DE LA EDUCACION POR GRADOS								
			ALL LEVELS / TOUS NIVEAUX / TODOS LOS GRADOS		LEVEL 5 / NIVEAU 5 / GRADO 5		LEVEL 6 / NIVEAU 6 / GRADO 6		LEVEL 7 / NIVEAU 7 / GRADO 7	
			MF	F	MF	F	MF	F	MF	F
NIGERIA	1975	TOTAL	44 964	...						
		EDUCATION SCIENCE & TCHR TRNG.	6 752	...						
		HUMANITIES,RELIGION & THEOLOG.	5 043	...						
		FINE AND APPLIED ARTS	842	...						
		LAW	1 939	...						
		SOCIAL AND BEHAVIOURAL SCIENCE	4 767	...						
		COMMERCIAL & BUS. ADMINISTR.	4 133	...						
		MASS COMMUNICATION & DOCUMENT.	—	—						
		HOME ECONOMICS & DOMESTIC SC.	352	...						
		SERVICE TRADES	—	—						
		NATURAL SCIENCE	4 622	...						
		MATHEMATICS & COMPUTER SCIENCE	—	—						
		MEDICAL AND HEALTH-RELATED SC.	3 976	...						
		ENGINEERING	6 295	...						
		ARCHITECTURE & TOWN PLANNING	—	—						
		TRADE, CRAFT & INDUSTR. PGMS.	—	—						
		TRANSPORT AND COMMUNICATIONS	—	—						
		AGRICULTURE,FORESTRY & FISH'G.	2 743	...						
		OTHER AND NOT SPECIFIED	3 500	...						
	1976	TOTAL	58 953	...						
		EDUCATION SCIENCE & TCHR TRNG.	8 955	...						
		HUMANITIES,RELIGION & THEOLOG.	6 252	...						
		FINE AND APPLIED ARTS	435	...						
		LAW	1 781	...						
		SOCIAL AND BEHAVIOURAL SCIENCE	4 805	...						
		COMMERCIAL & BUS. ADMINISTR.	7 026	...						
		MASS COMMUNICATION & DOCUMENT.	—	—						
		HOME ECONOMICS & DOMESTIC SC.	—	—						
		SERVICE TRADES	502	...						
		NATURAL SCIENCE	5 088	...						
		MATHEMATICS & COMPUTER SCIENCE	—	—						
		MEDICAL AND HEALTH-RELATED SC.	5 377	...						
		ENGINEERING	9 130	...						
		ARCHITECTURE & TOWN PLANNING	—	—						
		TRADE, CRAFT & INDUSTR. PGMS.	—	—						
		TRANSPORT AND COMMUNICATIONS	—	—						
		AGRICULTURE,FORESTRY & FISH'G.	3 040	...						
		OTHER AND NOT SPECIFIED	6 562	...						

Third level: students by levels and fields 3.12
Troisième degré: étudiants par types de programmes et domaines d'études
Tercer grado: estudiantes por tipos de programas y sectores de estudio

INTERNATIONAL STANDARD CLASSIFICATION OF EDUCATION BY LEVEL
CLASSIFICATION INTERNATIONALE TYPE DE L'EDUCATION PAR NIVEAUX
CLASIFICACION INTERNACIONAL NORMALIZADA DE LA EDUCACION POR GRADOS

COUNTRY / PAYS / PAIS	YEAR / ANNEE / AÑO	FIELD OF STUDY / BRANCHE D'ETUDES / RAMAS DE ESTUDIO	ALL LEVELS TOUS NIVEAUX TODOS LOS GRADOS MF	F	LEVEL 5 NIVEAU 5 GRADO 5 MF	F	LEVEL 6 NIVEAU 6 GRADO 6 MF	F	LEVEL 7 NIVEAU 7 GRADO 7 MF	F
REUNION ‡	1977	TOTAL	2 443	1 245						
		EDUCATION SCIENCE & TCHR TRNG.	340	201						
		HUMANITIES,RELIGION & THEOLOG.	678	417						
		FINE AND APPLIED ARTS	—	—						
		LAW	897	414						
		SOCIAL AND BEHAVIOURAL SCIENCE	—	—						
		COMMERCIAL & BUS. ADMINISTR.	87	29						
		MASS COMMUNICATION & DOCUMENT.	—	—						
		HOME ECONOMICS & DOMESTIC SC.	—	—						
		SERVICE TRADES	110	84						
		NATURAL SCIENCE	239	83						
		MATHEMATICS & COMPUTER SCIENCE	./.	./.						
		MEDICAL AND HEALTH-RELATED SC.	—	—						
		ENGINEERING	—	—						
		ARCHITECTURE & TOWN PLANNING	92	17						
		TRADE, CRAFT & INDUSTR. PGMS.	—	—						
		TRANSPORT AND COMMUNICATIONS	—	—						
		AGRICULTURE,FORESTRY & FISH'G.	—	—						
		OTHER AND NOT SPECIFIED	—	—						
	1978	TOTAL	2 317	...						
		EDUCATION SCIENCE & TCHR TRNG.	296	...						
		HUMANITIES,RELIGION & THEOLOG.	637	...						
		FINE AND APPLIED ARTS	—	—						
		LAW	807	...						
		SOCIAL AND BEHAVIOURAL SCIENCE	—	—						
		COMMERCIAL & BUS. ADMINISTR.	117	...						
		MASS COMMUNICATION & DOCUMENT.	—	—						
		HOME ECONOMICS & DOMESTIC SC.	—	—						
		SERVICE TRADES	256	...						
		NATURAL SCIENCE	204	...						
		MATHEMATICS & COMPUTER SCIENCE	./.	./.						
		MEDICAL AND HEALTH-RELATED SC.	—	—						
		ENGINEERING	—	—						
		ARCHITECTURE & TOWN PLANNING	—	—						
		TRADE, CRAFT & INDUSTR. PGMS.	—	—						
		TRANSPORT AND COMMUNICATIONS	—	—						
		AGRICULTURE,FORESTRY & FISH'G.	—	—						
		OTHER AND NOT SPECIFIED	—	—						

3.12 Third level: students by levels and fields
Troisième degré: étudiants par types de programmes et domaines d'études
Tercer grado: estudiantes por tipos de programas y sectores de estudio

INTERNATIONAL STANDARD CLASSIFICATION OF EDUCATION BY LEVEL
CLASSIFICATION INTERNATIONALE TYPE DE L'EDUCATION PAR NIVEAUX
CLASIFICACION INTERNACIONAL NORMALIZADA DE LA EDUCACION POR GRADOS

COUNTRY / PAYS / PAIS	YEAR / ANNEE / AÑO	FIELD OF STUDY / BRANCHE D'ETUDES / RAMAS DE ESTUDIO	ALL LEVELS / TOUS NIVEAUX / TODOS LOS GRADOS MF	F	LEVEL 5 / NIVEAU 5 / GRADO 5 MF	F	LEVEL 6 / NIVEAU 6 / GRADO 6 MF	F	LEVEL 7 / NIVEAU 7 / GRADO 7 MF	F
RWANDA ‡	1976	TOTAL	1 117	100	48	—	826	89	243	11
		EDUCATION SCIENCE & TCHR TRNG.	56	4	—	—	41	4	15	4
		HUMANITIES,RELIGION & THEOLOG.	285	16	—	—	223	16	62	—
		FINE AND APPLIED ARTS	—	—	—	—	—	—	—	—
		LAW	63	4	—	—	—	—	63	4
		SOCIAL AND BEHAVIOURAL SCIENCE	176	23	—	—	154	22	22	1
		COMMERCIAL & BUS. ADMINISTR.	./.	./.	—	—	./.	./.	./.	./.
		MASS COMMUNICATION & DOCUMENT.	—	—	—	—	—	—	—	—
		HOME ECONOMICS & DOMESTIC SC.	13	13	—	—	13	13	—	—
		SERVICE TRADES	—	—	—	—	—	—	—	—
		NATURAL SCIENCES, TOTAL	202	16	—	—	195	15	7	1
		MEDICAL AND HEALTH-RELATED SC.	144	14	—	—	91	10	53	4
		ENGINEERING	—	—	—	—	—	—	—	—
		ARCHITECTURE & TOWN PLANNING	—	—	—	—	—	—	—	—
		TRADE, CRAFT & INDUSTR. PGMS.	—	—	—	—	—	—	—	—
		TRANSPORT AND COMMUNICATIONS	—	—	—	—	—	—	—	—
		AGRICULTURE,FORESTRY & FISH'G.	21	1	—	—	—	—	21	1
		OTHER AND NOT SPECIFIED	157	9	48	—	109	9	—	—
SENEGAL	1976	TOTAL	8 981	1 762						
		EDUCATION SCIENCE & TCHR TRNG.	230	39						
		HUMANITIES,RELIGION & THEOLOG.	2 260	534						
		FINE AND APPLIED ARTS	—	—						
		LAW	1 388	260						
		SOCIAL AND BEHAVIOURAL SCIENCE	1 033	261						
		COMMERCIAL & BUS. ADMINISTR.	135	25						
		MASS COMMUNICATION & DOCUMENT.	235	32						
		HOME ECONOMICS & DOMESTIC SC.	—	—						
		SERVICE TRADES	44	—						
		NATURAL SCIENCE	988	98						
		MATHEMATICS & COMPUTER SCIENCE	—	—						
		MEDICAL AND HEALTH-RELATED SC.	1 428	347						
		ENGINEERING	143	—						
		ARCHITECTURE & TOWN PLANNING	—	—						
		TRADE, CRAFT & INDUSTR. PGMS.	299	30						
		TRANSPORT AND COMMUNICATIONS	—	—						
		AGRICULTURE,FORESTRY & FISH'G.	—	—						
		OTHER AND NOT SPECIFIED	798	136						

Third level: students by levels and fields 3.12
Troisième degré: étudiants par types de programmes et domaines d'études
Tercer grado: estudiantes por tipos de programas y sectores de estudio

INTERNATIONAL STANDARD CLASSIFICATION OF EDUCATION BY LEVEL
CLASSIFICATION INTERNATIONALE TYPE DE L'EDUCATION PAR NIVEAUX
CLASIFICACION INTERNACIONAL NORMALIZADA DE LA EDUCACION POR GRADOS

COUNTRY / PAYS / PAIS — YEAR / ANNEE / AÑO — FIELD OF STUDY / BRANCHE D'ETUDES / RAMAS DE ESTUDIO	ALL LEVELS TOUS NIVEAUX TODOS LOS GRADOS MF	F	LEVEL 5 NIVEAU 5 GRADO 5 MF	F	LEVEL 6 NIVEAU 6 GRADO 6 MF	F	LEVEL 7 NIVEAU 7 GRADO 7 MF	F
SENEGAL (CONT.) 1977								
TOTAL	9 454	...	4 339	...	2 989	...	2 126	...
EDUCATION SCIENCE & TCHR TRNG.	159	...	15	...	15	...	129	...
HUMANITIES,RELIGION & THEOLOG.	2 458	...	1 119	...	666	...	673	...
FINE AND APPLIED ARTS	26	...	9	...	17	...	—	...
LAW	1 507	...	863	...	478	...	166	...
SOCIAL AND BEHAVIOURAL SCIENCE	153	...	24	...	129	...	—	...
COMMERCIAL & BUS. ADMINISTR.	1 130	...	629	...	352	...	149	...
MASS COMMUNICATION & DOCUMENT.	259	...	132	...	127	...	—	...
HOME ECONOMICS & DOMESTIC SC.	—	—	—	—	—	—	—	—
SERVICE TRADES	—	—	—	—	—	—	—	—
NATURAL SCIENCE	432	—	93	—	232	—	107	—
MATHEMATICS & COMPUTER SCIENCE	1 000	—	647	—	138	—	215	—
MEDICAL AND HEALTH-RELATED SC.	1 532	...	453	...	505	...	574	...
ENGINEERING	253	...	50	...	90	...	113	...
ARCHITECTURE & TOWN PLANNING	—	—	—	—	—	—	—	—
TRADE, CRAFT & INDUSTR. PGMS.	425	...	250	—	175	—	—	—
TRANSPORT AND COMMUNICATIONS	—	—	—	—	—	—	—	—
AGRICULTURE,FORESTRY & FISH'G.	105	...	55	—	50	—	—	—
OTHER AND NOT SPECIFIED	15	—	—	—	15	—	—	—
SEYCHELLES 1978								
TOTAL	157	121	157	121	—	—	—	—
EDUCATION SCIENCE & TCHR TRNG.	157	121	157	121	—	—	—	—
HUMANITIES,RELIGION & THEOLOG.	—	—	—	—	—	—	—	—
FINE AND APPLIED ARTS	—	—	—	—	—	—	—	—
LAW	—	—	—	—	—	—	—	—
SOCIAL AND BEHAVIOURAL SCIENCE	—	—	—	—	—	—	—	—
COMMERCIAL & BUS. ADMINISTR.	—	—	—	—	—	—	—	—
MASS COMMUNICATION & DOCUMENT.	—	—	—	—	—	—	—	—
HOME ECONOMICS & DOMESTIC SC.	—	—	—	—	—	—	—	—
SERVICE TRADES	—	—	—	—	—	—	—	—
NATURAL SCIENCE	—	—	—	—	—	—	—	—
MATHEMATICS & COMPUTER SCIENCE	—	—	—	—	—	—	—	—
MEDICAL AND HEALTH-RELATED SC.	—	—	—	—	—	—	—	—
ENGINEERING	—	—	—	—	—	—	—	—
ARCHITECTURE & TOWN PLANNING	—	—	—	—	—	—	—	—
TRADE, CRAFT & INDUSTR. PGMS.	—	—	—	—	—	—	—	—
TRANSPORT AND COMMUNICATIONS	—	—	—	—	—	—	—	—
AGRICULTURE,FORESTRY & FISH'G.	—	—	—	—	—	—	—	—
OTHER AND NOT SPECIFIED	—	—	—	—	—	—	—	—

3.12 Third level: students by levels and fields
Troisième degré: étudiants par types de programmes et domaines d'études
Tercer grado: estudiantes por tipos de programas y sectores de estudio

INTERNATIONAL STANDARD CLASSIFICATION OF EDUCATION BY LEVEL
CLASSIFICATION INTERNATIONALE TYPE DE L'EDUCATION PAR NIVEAUX
CLASIFICACION INTERNACIONAL NORMALIZADA DE LA EDUCACION POR GRADOS

COUNTRY / PAYS / PAIS	YEAR / ANNEE / AÑO	FIELD OF STUDY / BRANCHE D'ETUDES / RAMAS DE ESTUDIO	ALL LEVELS TOUS NIVEAUX TODOS LOS GRADOS MF	F	LEVEL 5 NIVEAU 5 GRADO 5 MF	F	LEVEL 6 NIVEAU 6 GRADO 6 MF	F	LEVEL 7 NIVEAU 7 GRADO 7 MF	F
SOMALIA	1975	TOTAL	2 040	...	104	...	1 936	...	-	-
		EDUCATION SCIENCE & TCHR TRNG.	417	...	-	-	417	...	-	-
		HUMANITIES,RELIGION & THEOLOG.	-	-	-	-	-	-	-	-
		FINE AND APPLIED ARTS	-	-	-	-	-	-	-	-
		LAW	399	...	-	-	399	...	-	-
		SOCIAL AND BEHAVIOURAL SCIENCE	449	...	30	...	419	...	-	-
		COMMERCIAL & BUS. ADMINISTR.	44	...	44	...	-	-	-	-
		MASS COMMUNICATION & DOCUMENT.	-	-	-	-	-	-	-	-
		HOME ECONOMICS & DOMESTIC SC.	-	-	-	-	-	-	-	-
		SERVICE TRADES	-	-	-	-	-	-	-	-
		NATURAL SCIENCE	127	...	-	-	127	...	-	-
		MATHEMATICS & COMPUTER SCIENCE	-	-	-	-	-	-	-	-
		MEDICAL AND HEALTH-RELATED SC.	239	...	30	...	209	...	-	-
		ENGINEERING	95	...	-	-	95	...	-	-
		ARCHITECTURE & TOWN PLANNING	-	-	-	-	-	-	-	-
		TRADE, CRAFT & INDUSTR. PGMS.	-	-	-	-	-	-	-	-
		TRANSPORT AND COMMUNICATIONS	-	-	-	-	-	-	-	-
		AGRICULTURE,FORESTRY & FISH'G.	270	...	-	-	270	...	-	-
		OTHER AND NOT SPECIFIED	-	-	-	-	-	-	-	-
SUDAN	1977	TOTAL	24 119	5 089	2 537	622	21 572	4 467	-	-
		EDUCATION SCIENCE & TCHR TRNG.	822	109	179	3	643	106	-	-
		HUMANITIES,RELIGION & THEOLOG.	6 347	1 829	-	-	6 347	1 829	-	-
		FINE AND APPLIED ARTS	293	54	293	54	-	-	-	-
		LAW	2 544	536	-	-	2 544	536	-	-
		SOCIAL AND BEHAVIOURAL SCIENCE	1 304	110	-	-	1 304	110	-	-
		COMMERCIAL & BUS. ADMINISTR.	5 877	1 256	440	87	5 437	1 169	-	-
		MASS COMMUNICATION & DOCUMENT.	-	-	-	-	-	-	-	-
		HOME ECONOMICS & DOMESTIC SC.	245	245	245	245	-	-	-	-
		SERVICE TRADES	-	-	-	-	-	-	-	-
		NATURAL SCIENCE	730	180	-	-	730	180	-	-
		MATHEMATICS & COMPUTER SCIENCE	-	-	-	-	-	-	-	-
		MEDICAL AND HEALTH-RELATED SC.	1 696	379	257	130	1 439	249	-	-
		ENGINEERING	1 606	45	481	15	1 125	30	-	-
		ARCHITECTURE & TOWN PLANNING	306	45	63	20	243	25	-	-
		TRADE, CRAFT & INDUSTR. PGMS.	110	16	110	16	-	-	-	-
		TRANSPORT AND COMMUNICATIONS	-	-	-	-	-	-	-	-
		AGRICULTURE,FORESTRY & FISH'G.	2 088	280	447	47	1 641	233	-	-
		OTHER AND NOT SPECIFIED	141	5	22	5	119	-	-	-

Third level: students by levels and fields 3.12
Troisième degré: étudiants par types de programmes et domaines d'études
Tercer grado: estudiantes por tipos de programas y sectores de estudio

COUNTRY / PAYS / PAIS	YEAR / ANNEE / AÑO	FIELD OF STUDY / BRANCHE D'ETUDES / RAMAS DE ESTUDIO	INTERNATIONAL STANDARD CLASSIFICATION OF EDUCATION BY LEVEL / CLASSIFICATION INTERNATIONALE TYPE DE L'EDUCATION PAR NIVEAUX / CLASIFICACION INTERNACIONAL NORMALIZADA DE LA EDUCACION POR GRADOS								
			ALL LEVELS TOUS NIVEAUX TODOS LOS GRADOS		LEVEL 5 NIVEAU 5 GRADO 5		LEVEL 6 NIVEAU 6 GRADO 6		LEVEL 7 NIVEAU 7 GRADO 7	
			MF	F	MF	F	MF	F	MF	F
TOGO	1976	TOTAL	2 777	445						
		EDUCATION SCIENCE & TCHR TRNG.	267	28						
		HUMANITIES,RELIGION & THEOLOG.	643	133						
		FINE AND APPLIED ARTS	—	—						
		LAW	451	100						
		SOCIAL AND BEHAVIOURAL SCIENCE	614	93						
		COMMERCIAL & BUS. ADMINISTR.	—	—						
		MASS COMMUNICATION & DOCUMENT.	—	—						
		HOME ECONOMICS & DOMESTIC SC.	—	—						
		SERVICE TRADES	248	29						
		NATURAL SCIENCE	—	—						
		MATHEMATICS & COMPUTER SCIENCE	—	—						
		MEDICAL AND HEALTH-RELATED SC.	361	55						
		ENGINEERING	64	1						
		ARCHITECTURE & TOWN PLANNING	40	—						
		TRADE, CRAFT & INDUSTR. PGMS.	—	—						
		TRANSPORT AND COMMUNICATIONS	—	—						
		AGRICULTURE,FORESTRY & FISH'G.	89	6						
		OTHER AND NOT SPECIFIED	—	—						
TUNISIA ‡	1977	TOTAL	26 781	7 155	4 878	1 437	21 903	5 718	./.	./.
		EDUCATION SCIENCE & TCHR TRNG.	1 459	345	—	—	1 459	345	./.	./.
		HUMANITIES,RELIGION & THEOLOG.	4 510	1 616	—	—	4 510	1 616	./.	./.
		FINE AND APPLIED ARTS	188	86	—	—	188	86	./.	./.
		LAW	2 953	756	—	—	2 953	756	./.	./.
		SOCIAL AND BEHAVIOURAL SCIENCE	117	28	117	28	—	—	./.	./.
		COMMERCIAL & BUS. ADMINISTR.	2 251	476	—	—	2 251	476	./.	./.
		MASS COMMUNICATION & DOCUMENT.	650	189	281	91	369	98	./.	./.
		HOME ECONOMICS & DOMESTIC SC.	151	25	151	25	—	—	./.	./.
		SERVICE TRADES	1 084	239	438	101	646	138	./.	./.
		NATURAL SCIENCE	4 027	1 118	—	—	4 027	1 118	./.	./.
		MATHEMATICS & COMPUTER SCIENCE	85	15	—	—	85	15	./.	./.
		MEDICAL AND HEALTH-RELATED SC.	5 211	1 834	1 900	1 017	3 311	817	./.	./.
		ENGINEERING	967	59	—	—	967	59	./.	./.
		ARCHITECTURE & TOWN PLANNING	724	64	421	21	303	43	./.	./.
		TRADE, CRAFT & INDUSTR. PGMS.	56	21	56	21	—	—	./.	./.
		TRANSPORT AND COMMUNICATIONS	421	15	179	13	242	2	./.	./.
		AGRICULTURE,FORESTRY & FISH'G.	820	88	533	69	287	19	./.	./.
		OTHER AND NOT SPECIFIED	1 107	181	802	51	305	130	./.	./.

3.12 Third level: students by levels and fields
Troisième degré: étudiants par types de programmes et domaines d'études
Tercer grado: estudiantes por tipos de programas y sectores de estudio

INTERNATIONAL STANDARD CLASSIFICATION OF EDUCATION BY LEVEL
CLASSIFICATION INTERNATIONALE TYPE DE L'EDUCATION PAR NIVEAUX
CLASIFICACION INTERNACIONAL NORMALIZADA DE LA EDUCACION POR GRADOS

COUNTRY / PAYS / PAIS	YEAR / ANNEE / AÑO	FIELD OF STUDY / BRANCHE D'ETUDES / RAMAS DE ESTUDIO	ALL LEVELS TOUS NIVEAUX TODOS LOS GRADOS MF	F	LEVEL 5 NIVEAU 5 GRADO 5 MF	F	LEVEL 6 NIVEAU 6 GRADO 6 MF	F	LEVEL 7 NIVEAU 7 GRADO 7 MF	F
UGANDA	1977	TOTAL	6 312	1 607	3 050	1 062	3 209	540	53	5
		EDUCATION SCIENCE & TCHR TRNG.	620	149	567	144	—	—	53	5
		HUMANITIES,RELIGION & THEOLOG.	787	203	—	—	787	203	—	—
		FINE AND APPLIED ARTS	72	18	15	2	57	16	—	—
		LAW	183	33	—	—	183	33	—	—
		SOCIAL AND BEHAVIOURAL SCIENCE	64	23	—	—	64	23	—	—
		COMMERCIAL & BUS. ADMINISTR.	1 950	884	1 722	853	228	31	—	—
		MASS COMMUNICATION & DOCUMENT.	44	15	44	15	—	—	—	—
		HOME ECONOMICS & DOMESTIC SC.	—	—	—	—	—	—	—	—
		SERVICE TRADES	32	20	32	20	—	—	—	—
		NATURAL SCIENCE	648	78	—	—	648	78	—	—
		MATHEMATICS & COMPUTER SCIENCE	69	4	—	—	69	4	—	—
		MEDICAL AND HEALTH-RELATED SC.	524	83	—	—	524	83	—	—
		ENGINEERING	713	11	482	4	231	7	—	—
		ARCHITECTURE & TOWN PLANNING	33	6	33	6	—	—	—	—
		TRADE, CRAFT & INDUSTR. PGMS.	155	18	155	18	—	—	—	—
		TRANSPORT AND COMMUNICATIONS	—	—	—	—	—	—	—	—
		AGRICULTURE,FORESTRY & FISH'G.	418	62	—	—	418	62	—	—
		OTHER AND NOT SPECIFIED	—	—	—	—	—	—	—	—
UNITED REPUBLIC OF CAMEROON ‡	1977	TOTAL	9 060	1 358	4 842	696	1 749	297	2 469	365
		EDUCATION SCIENCE & TCHR TRNG.	2 459	376	767	119	510	88	1 182	169
		HUMANITIES,RELIGION & THEOLOG.	./.	./.	./.	./.	./.	./.	./.	./.
		FINE AND APPLIED ARTS	./.	./.	./.	./.	./.	./.	./.	./.
		LAW	4 097	653	2 622	403	771	130	704	120
		SOCIAL AND BEHAVIOURAL SCIENCE	./.	./.	./.	./.	./.	./.	./.	./.
		COMMERCIAL & BUS. ADMINISTR.	./.	./.	./.	./.	./.	./.	./.	./.
		MASS COMMUNICATION & DOCUMENT.	./.	./.	./.	./.	./.	./.	./.	./.
		HOME ECONOMICS & DOMESTIC SC.	./.	./.	./.	./.	./.	./.	./.	./.
		SERVICE TRADES	./.	./.	./.	./.	./.	./.	./.	./.
		NATURAL SCIENCE	1 783	219	1 171	124	275	47	337	48
		MATHEMATICS & COMPUTER SCIENCE	512	104	205	49	137	31	170	24
		MEDICAL AND HEALTH-RELATED SC.	200	6	68	1	56	1	76	4
		ENGINEERING	./.	./.	./.	./.	./.	./.	./.	./.
		ARCHITECTURE & TOWN PLANNING	./.	./.	./.	./.	./.	./.	./.	./.
		TRADE, CRAFT & INDUSTR. PGMS.	./.	./.	./.	./.	./.	./.	./.	./.
		TRANSPORT AND COMMUNICATIONS	./.	./.	./.	./.	./.	./.	./.	./.
		AGRICULTURE,FORESTRY & FISH'G.	./.	./.	./.	./.	./.	./.	./.	./.
		OTHER AND NOT SPECIFIED	9	—	9	—	—	—	—	—

Third level: students by levels and fields 3.12
Troisième degré: étudiants par types de programmes et domaines d'études
Tercer grado: estudiantes por tipos de programas y sectores de estudio

INTERNATIONAL STANDARD CLASSIFICATION OF EDUCATION BY LEVEL
CLASSIFICATION INTERNATIONALE TYPE DE L'EDUCATION PAR NIVEAUX
CLASIFICACION INTERNACIONAL NORMALIZADA DE LA EDUCACION POR GRADOS

COUNTRY / PAYS / PAIS	YEAR / ANNEE / AÑO	FIELD OF STUDY / BRANCHE D'ETUDES / RAMAS DE ESTUDIO	ALL LEVELS / TOUS NIVEAUX / TODOS LOS GRADOS		LEVEL 5 / NIVEAU 5 / GRADO 5		LEVEL 6 / NIVEAU 6 / GRADO 6		LEVEL 7 / NIVEAU 7 / GRADO 7	
			MF	F	MF	F	MF	F	MF	F
UNITED REPUBLIC OF TANZANIA	1977	TOTAL	2 534	...						
		EDUCATION SCIENCE & TCHR TRNG.	686	...						
		HUMANITIES,RELIGION & THEOLOG.	155	...						
		FINE AND APPLIED ARTS	16	...						
		LAW	158	...						
		SOCIAL AND BEHAVIOURAL SCIENCE	195	...						
		COMMERCIAL & BUS. ADMINISTR.	233	...						
		MASS COMMUNICATION & DOCUMENT.	—	—						
		HOME ECONOMICS & DOMESTIC SC.	—	—						
		SERVICE TRADES	—	—						
		NATURAL SCIENCE	115	...						
		MATHEMATICS & COMPUTER SCIENCE	94	...						
		MEDICAL AND HEALTH-RELATED SC.	160	...						
		ENGINEERING	360	...						
		ARCHITECTURE & TOWN PLANNING	—	—						
		TRADE, CRAFT & INDUSTR. PGMS.	—	—						
		TRANSPORT AND COMMUNICATIONS	—	—						
		AGRICULTURE,FORESTRY & FISH'G.	150	...						
		OTHER AND NOT SPECIFIED	212	...						
UPPER VOLTA	1977	TOTAL	1 233	268	—	—	996	218	237	50
		EDUCATION SCIENCE & TCHR TRNG.	662	157	—	—	519	115	143	42
		HUMANITIES,RELIGION & THEOLOG.	39	11	—	—	39	11	—	—
		FINE AND APPLIED ARTS	—	—	—	—	—	—	—	—
		LAW	154	27	—	—	117	22	37	5
		SOCIAL AND BEHAVIOURAL SCIENCE	139	57	—	—	139	57	—	—
		COMMERCIAL & BUS. ADMINISTR.	—	—	—	—	—	—	—	—
		MASS COMMUNICATION & DOCUMENT.	—	—	—	—	—	—	—	—
		HOME ECONOMICS & DOMESTIC SC.	—	—	—	—	—	—	—	—
		SERVICE TRADES	—	—	—	—	—	—	—	—
		NATURAL SCIENCE	100	4	—	—	95	4	5	—
		MATHEMATICS & COMPUTER SCIENCE	—	—	—	—	—	—	—	—
		MEDICAL AND HEALTH-RELATED SC.	—	—	—	—	—	—	—	—
		ENGINEERING, TOTAL	—	—	—	—	—	—	—	—
		AGRICULTURE,FORESTRY & FISH'G.	128	6	—	—	76	3	52	3
		OTHER AND NOT SPECIFIED	11	6	—	—	11	6	—	—

3.12 Third level: students by levels and fields
Troisième degré: étudiants par types de programmes et domaines d'études
Tercer grado: estudiantes por tipos de programas y sectores de estudio

INTERNATIONAL STANDARD CLASSIFICATION OF EDUCATION BY LEVEL
CLASSIFICATION INTERNATIONALE TYPE DE L'EDUCATION PAR NIVEAUX
CLASIFICACION INTERNACIONAL NORMALIZADA DE LA EDUCACION POR GRADOS

COUNTRY / PAYS / PAIS	YEAR / ANNEE / AÑO	FIELD OF STUDY / BRANCHE D'ETUDES / RAMAS DE ESTUDIO	ALL LEVELS TOUS NIVEAUX TODOS LOS GRADOS MF	F	LEVEL 5 NIVEAU 5 GRADO 5 MF	F	LEVEL 6 NIVEAU 6 GRADO 6 MF	F	LEVEL 7 NIVEAU 7 GRADO 7 MF	F
ZAMBIA ‡	1977	TOTAL	9 192	...	...	...	9 192	...	...	...
		EDUCATION SCIENCE & TCHR TRNG.	1 918	...	...	...	1 918	...	...	...
		HUMANITIES,RELIGION & THEOLOG.	730	...	...	...	730	...	...	...
		FINE AND APPLIED ARTS	173	...	...	...	173	...	...	...
		LAW	221	...	...	...	221	...	...	...
		SOCIAL AND BEHAVIOURAL SCIENCE	20	...	...	...	20	...	...	...
		COMMERCIAL & BUS. ADMINISTR.	1 158	...	...	...	1 158	...	...	...
		MASS COMMUNICATION & DOCUMENT.	10	...	...	...	10	...	...	...
		HOME ECONOMICS & DOMESTIC SC.	—	—	—	—	—	—	—	—
		SERVICE TRADES	—	—	—	—	—	—	—	—
		NATURAL SCIENCE	565	...	...	...	565	...	...	...
		MATHEMATICS & COMPUTER SCIENCE	—	—	—	—	—	—	—	—
		MEDICAL AND HEALTH-RELATED SC.	609	...	...	...	609	...	...	...
		ENGINEERING	1 430	...	...	...	1 430	...	...	...
		ARCHITECTURE & TOWN PLANNING	—	—	—	—	—	—	—	—
		TRADE CRAFT & INDUSTR. PGMS.	1 803	...	...	...	1 803	...	...	...
		TRANSPORT AND COMMUNICATIONS	160	...	...	...	160	...	...	...
		AGRICULTURE FORESTRY & FISH'G.	59	...	...	...	59	...	...	...
		OTHER AND NOT SPECIFIED	336	...	...	...	336	...	...	...
AMERICA, NORTH										
BARBADOS ‡	1976	TOTAL	1 140	...	39	...	1 054	...	47	...
		EDUCATION SCIENCE & TCHR TRNG.	39	...	39	...	—	—	—	—
		HUMANITIES,RELIGION & THEOLOG.	422	...	—	—	416	...	6	...
		FINE AND APPLIED ARTS	—	—	—	—	—	—	—	—
		LAW	—	—	—	—	—	—	—	—
		SOCIAL SCIENCES, TOTAL	290	...	—	—	262	...	28	...
		NATURAL SCIENCES, TOTAL	104	...	—	—	96	...	8	...
		MEDICAL AND HEALTH-RELATED SC.	285	...	—	—	280	...	5	...
		AGRICULTURE,FORESTRY & FISH'G.	—	—	—	—	—	—	—	—
		OTHER AND NOT SPECIFIED	—	—	—	—	—	—	—	—

Third level: students by levels and fields 3.12
Troisième degré: étudiants par types de programmes et domaines d'études
Tercer grado: estudiantes por tipos de programas y sectores de estudio

INTERNATIONAL STANDARD CLASSIFICATION OF EDUCATION BY LEVEL
CLASSIFICATION INTERNATIONALE TYPE DE L'EDUCATION PAR NIVEAUX
CLASIFICACION INTERNACIONAL NORMALIZADA DE LA EDUCACION POR GRADOS

COUNTRY / PAYS / PAIS	YEAR / ANNEE / AÑO	FIELD OF STUDY / BRANCHE D'ETUDES / RAMAS DE ESTUDIO	ALL LEVELS / TOUS NIVEAUX / TODOS LOS GRADOS MF	F	LEVEL 5 / NIVEAU 5 / GRADO 5 MF	F	LEVEL 6 / NIVEAU 6 / GRADO 6 MF	F	LEVEL 7 / NIVEAU 7 / GRADO 7 MF	F
CANADA ‡	1977	TOTAL	826 213	398 747	245 981	124 687	515 050	252 170	65 182	21 890
		EDUCATION SCIENCE & TCHR TRNG.	72 057	47 484	2 176	1 400	57 948	40 580	11 933	5 504
		HUMANITIES,RELIGION & THEOLOG.	127 093	63 659	82 692	38 683	34 141	20 709	10 260	4 267
		FINE AND APPLIED ARTS	29 455	17 219	13 656	7 260	14 883	9 462	916	497
		LAW	10 342	3 290	—	—	9 736	3 136	606	154
		SOCIAL AND BEHAVIOURAL SCIENCE	79 956	40 974	14 178	9 144	54 863	28 143	10 915	3 687
		COMMERCIAL & BUS. ADMINSTR.	114 567	47 777	49 529	28 770	57 494	17 528	7 544	1 479
		MASS COMMUNICATION & DOCUMENT.	8 409	5 039	3 597	2 141	3 459	1 890	1 353	1 008
		HOME ECONOMICS & DOMESTIC SC.	4 287	4 171	—	—	4 122	4 026	165	145
		SERVICE TRADES	—	—	—	—	—	—	—	—
		NATURAL SCIENCE	27 571	8 786	53	1	21 705	7 612	5 813	1 173
		MATHEMATICS & COMPUTER SCIENCE	14 076	4 135	68	35	12 328	3 809	1 680	291
		MEDICAL AND HEALTH-RELATED SC.	64 736	46 604	31 640	28 344	30 584	17 025	2 512	1 235
		ENGINEERING	67 256	4 808	30 243	2 813	31 919	1 746	5 094	249
		ARCHITECTURE & TOWN PLANNING	6 240	1 290	2 465	433	3 309	747	466	110
		TRADE, CRAFT & INDUSTR. PGMS.	—	—	—	—	—	—	—	—
		TRANSPORT AND COMMUNICATIONS	1 210	65	1 210	65	—	—	—	—
		AGRICULTURE,FORESTRY & FISH'G.	16 695	4 231	8 458	1 779	7 163	2 249	1 074	203
		OTHER AND NOT SPECIFIED	182 263	99 215	6 016	3 819	171 396	93 508	4 851	1 888
COSTA RICA	1977	TOTAL	38 629	....	....	....	....	....	....	....
		EDUCATION SCIENCE & TCHR TRNG.	2 005	....	....	....	....	....	....	....
		HUMANITIES,RELIGION & THEOLOG.	3 246	....	....	....	....	....	....	....
		FINE AND APPLIED ARTS	585	....	....	....	....	....	....	....
		LAW	1 344	....	....	....	....	....	....	....
		SOCIAL SCIENCES, TOTAL	7 504	....	....	....	....	....	....	....
		NATURAL SCIENCES, TOTAL	2 216	....	....	....	....	....	....	....
		MEDICAL AND HEALTH-RELATED SC.	3 199	....	....	....	....	....	....	....
		ENGINEERING, TOTAL	3 689	....	....	....	....	....	....	....
		AGRICULTURE, FORESTRY & FISH'G.	2 291	....	....	....	....	....	....	....
		OTHER AND NOT SPECIFIED	12 550	....	....	....	....	....	....	....

3.12 Third level: students by levels and fields
Troisième degré: étudiants par types de programmes et domaines d'études
Tercer grado: estudiantes por tipos de programas y sectores de estudio

INTERNATIONAL STANDARD CLASSIFICATION OF EDUCATION BY LEVEL
CLASSIFICATION INTERNATIONALE TYPE DE L'EDUCATION PAR NIVEAUX
CLASIFICACION INTERNACIONAL NORMALIZADA DE LA EDUCACION POR GRADOS

COUNTRY / PAYS / PAIS	YEAR / ANNEE / AÑO	FIELD OF STUDY / BRANCHE D'ETUDES / RAMAS DE ESTUDIO	ALL LEVELS / TOUS NIVEAUX / TODOS LOS GRADOS		LEVEL 5 / NIVEAU 5 / GRADO 5		LEVEL 6 / NIVEAU 6 / GRADO 6		LEVEL 7 / NIVEAU 7 / GRADO 7	
			MF	F	MF	F	MF	F	MF	F
CUBA ‡	1976	TOTAL	106 850	...	817	...	106 033	...	—	—
		EDUCATION SCIENCE & TCHR TRNG.	37 630	...	648	—	36 982	...	—	—
		HUMANITIES,RELIGION & THEOLOG.	4 183	...	—	—	4 183	—	—	—
		FINE AND APPLIED ARTS	234	...	—	—	234	—	—	—
		LAW	4 137	...	—	—	4 137	—	—	—
		SOCIAL AND BEHAVIOURAL SCIENCE	1 116	...	—	—	1 116	—	—	—
		COMMERCIAL & BUS. ADMINISTR.	10 496	...	—	—	10 496	—	—	—
		MASS COMMUNICATION & DOCUMENT.	2 032	...	—	—	2 032	—	—	—
		HOME ECONOMICS & DOMESTIC SC.	—	...	—	—	—	—	—	—
		SERVICE TRADES		...						
		NATURAL SCIENCE	4 190	...	—	—	4 190	—	—	—
		MATHEMATICS & COMPUTER SCIENCE	676	...	—	—	676	—	—	—
		MEDICAL AND HEALTH-RELATED SC.	8 006	...	—	—	8 006	—	—	—
		ENGINEERING	6 846	...	169	...	6 677	—	—	—
		ARCHITECTURE & TOWN PLANNING	4 683	...	—	—	4 683	—	—	—
		TRADE, CRAFT & INDUSTR. PGMS.	9 539	...	—	—	9 539	—	—	—
		TRANSPORT AND COMMUNICATIONS	1 539	...	—	—	1 539	—	—	—
		AGRICULTURE,FORESTRY & FISH'G.	11 463	...	—	—	11 463	—	—	—
		OTHER AND NOT SPECIFIED	80	...	—	—	80	—	—	—
	1978	TOTAL	130 100	...					—	—
		EDUCATION SCIENCE & TCHR TRNG.	48 178	...					—	—
		HUMANITIES,RELIGION & THEOLOG.	11 046	...					—	—
		FINE AND APPLIED ARTS	503	...					—	—
		LAW	13 956	...					—	—
		SOCIAL AND BEHAVIOURAL SCIENCE	./.	...					—	—
		COMMERCIAL & BUS. ADMINISTR.	./.	...					—	—
		MASS COMMUNICATION & DOCUMENT.	—	...					—	—
		HOME ECONOMICS & DOMESTIC SC.							—	—
		SERVICE TRADES	6 147	...					—	—
		NATURAL SCIENCE	./.	...					—	—
		MATHEMATICS & COMPUTER SCIENCE	13 757	...					—	—
		MEDICAL AND HEALTH-RELATED SC.	9 584	...					—	—
		ENGINEERING	./.	...					—	—
		ARCHITECTURE & TOWN PLANNING	8 821	...					—	—
		TRADE, CRAFT & INDUSTR. PGMS.	4 950	...					—	—
		TRANSPORT AND COMMUNICATIONS	13 158	...					—	—
		AGRICULTURE,FORESTRY & FISH'G.	—	...					—	—
		OTHER AND NOT SPECIFIED							—	—

Third level: students by levels and fields 3.12
Troisième degré: étudiants par types de programmes et domaines d'études
Tercer grado: estudiantes por tipos de programas y sectores de estudio

INTERNATIONAL STANDARD CLASSIFICATION OF EDUCATION BY LEVEL
CLASSIFICATION INTERNATIONALE TYPE DE L'EDUCATION PAR NIVEAUX
CLASIFICACION INTERNACIONAL NORMALIZADA DE LA EDUCACION POR GRADOS

COUNTRY / PAYS / PAIS	YEAR / ANNEE / AÑO	FIELD OF STUDY / BRANCHE D'ETUDES / RAMAS DE ESTUDIO	ALL LEVELS TOUS NIVEAUX TODOS LOS GRADOS MF	F	LEVEL 5 NIVEAU 5 GRADO 5 MF	F	LEVEL 6 NIVEAU 6 GRADO 6 MF	F	LEVEL 7 NIVEAU 7 GRADO 7 MF	F
DOMINICAN REPUBLIC ‡	1977	TOTAL	44 725	...	...	...	...	...	—	—
		EDUCATION SCIENCE & TCHR TRNG.	4 592	...	...	...	...	...		
		HUMANITIES,RELIGION & THEOLOG.	247	...	...	...	...	...		
		FINE AND APPLIED ARTS	497	...	...	...	...	...		
		LAW	968	...	...	...	...	...		
		SOCIAL AND BEHAVIOURAL SCIENCE	2 004	...	...	...	...	...		
		COMMERCIAL & BUS. ADMINISTR.	6 764	...	...	...	...	...		
		MASS COMMUNICATION & DOCUMENT.	198	...	...	...	...	...		
		HOME ECONOMICS & DOMESTIC SC.	7	...	...	...	...	...		
		SERVICE TRADES	356	...	...	...	...	...		
		NATURAL SCIENCE	824	...	...	...	...	...		
		MATHEMATICS & COMPUTER SCIENCE	11	...	...	...	...	...		
		MEDICAL AND HEALTH-RELATED SC.	8 095	...	...	...	...	...		
		ENGINEERING	6 205	...	...	...	...	...		
		ARCHITECTURE & TOWN PLANNING	1 518	...	...	...	...	...		
		TRADE, CRAFT & INDUSTR. PGMS.	—	...	—	...	—	...		
		TRANSPORT AND COMMUNICATIONS	—	...	—	...	—	...		
		AGRICULTURE,FORESTRY & FISH'G.	1 142	...	...	...	...	...		
		OTHER AND NOT SPECIFIED	11 297	...	...	...	...	...		
EL SALVADOR	1977	TOTAL	30 371	...	3 895	...	26 476	...	—	—
		EDUCATION SCIENCE & TCHR TRNG.	746	...	510	...	236	...		
		HUMANITIES,RELIGION & THEOLOG.	930	...	—	—	930	...		
		FINE AND APPLIED ARTS	37	...	37	—	—	—		
		LAW	1 847	...	—	—	1 847	...		
		SOCIAL AND BEHAVIOURAL SCIENCE	3 717	...	92	...	3 625	...		
		COMMERCIAL & BUS. ADMINISTR.	5 177	...	217	...	4 960	...		
		MASS COMMUNICATION & DOCUMENT.	142	...	30	...	112	...		
		HOME ECONOMICS & DOMESTIC SC.	—	—	—	—	—	—		
		SERVICE TRADES	—	—	—	—	—	—		
		NATURAL SCIENCE	62	...	62	...	—	—		
		MATHEMATICS & COMPUTER SCIENCE	1 635	...	4	...	1 631	...		
		MEDICAL AND HEALTH-RELATED SC.	299	...	50	...	249	...		
		ENGINEERING	5 776	...	965	...	4 811	...		
		ARCHITECTURE & TOWN PLANNING	8 311	...	1 235	...	7 076	...		
		TRADE, CRAFT & INDUSTR. PGMS.	1 081	...	110	...	971	...		
		TRANSPORT AND COMMUNICATIONS	286	...	286	...	—	—		
		AGRICULTURE,FORESTRY & FISH'G.	285	...	257	...	28	...		
		OTHER AND NOT SPECIFIED	40	...	40	...	—	—		

3.12 Third level: students by levels and fields
Troisième degré: étudiants par types de programmes et domaines d'études
Tercer grado: estudiantes por tipos de programas y sectores de estudio

INTERNATIONAL STANDARD CLASSIFICATION OF EDUCATION BY LEVEL
CLASSIFICATION INTERNATIONALE TYPE DE L'EDUCATION PAR NIVEAUX
CLASIFICACION INTERNACIONAL NORMALIZADA DE LA EDUCACION POR GRADOS

COUNTRY / PAYS / PAIS	YEAR / ANNEE / AÑO	FIELD OF STUDY / BRANCHE D'ETUDES / RAMAS DE ESTUDIO	ALL LEVELS / TOUS NIVEAUX / TODOS LOS GRADOS MF	F	LEVEL 5 / NIVEAU 5 / GRADO 5 MF	F	LEVEL 6 / NIVEAU 6 / GRADO 6 MF	F	LEVEL 7 / NIVEAU 7 / GRADO 7 MF	F
GUATEMALA ‡	1977	TOTAL	29 234	7 416	—	—	29 234	7 416	—	—
		EDUCATION SCIENCE & TCHR TRNG.	1 274	743	—	—	1 274	743	—	—
		HUMANITIES,RELIGION & THEOLOG.	219	118	—	—	219	118	—	—
		FINE AND APPLIED ARTS	—	—	—	—	—	—	—	—
		LAW	4 768	1 201	—	—	4 768	1 201	—	—
		SOCIAL AND BEHAVIOURAL SCIENCE	2 636	1 311	—	—	2 636	1 311	—	—
		COMMERCIAL & BUS. ADMINISTR.	5 975	1 388	—	—	5 975	1 388	—	—
		MASS COMMUNICATION & DOCUMENT.	199	95	—	—	199	95	—	—
		HOME ECONOMICS & DOMESTIC SC.	—	—	—	—	—	—	—	—
		SERVICE TRADES	—	—	—	—	—	—	—	—
		NATURAL SCIENCE	561	330	—	—	561	330	—	—
		MATHEMATICS & COMPUTER SCIENCE	—	—	—	—	—	—	—	—
		MEDICAL AND HEALTH-RELATED SC.	6 274	1 617	—	—	6 274	1 617	—	—
		ENGINEERING	3 487	196	—	—	3 487	196	—	—
		ARCHITECTURE & TOWN PLANNING	1 338	278	—	—	1 338	278	—	—
		TRADE, CRAFT & INDUSTR. PGMS.	—	—	—	—	—	—	—	—
		TRANSPORT AND COMMUNICATIONS	—	—	—	—	—	—	—	—
		AGRICULTURE,FORESTRY & FISH'G.	2 503	139	—	—	2 503	139	—	—
		OTHER AND NOT SPECIFIED	—	—	—	—	—	—	—	—
HAITI	1976	TOTAL	3 309	995	836	422	2 473	573	—	—
		EDUCATION SCIENCE & TCHR TRNG.	—	—	—	—	—	—	—	—
		HUMANITIES,RELIGION & THEOLOG.	149	15	94	—	55	15	—	—
		FINE AND APPLIED ARTS	—	—	—	—	—	—	—	—
		LAW	136	45	—	—	136	45	—	—
		SOCIAL AND BEHAVIOURAL SCIENCE	420	112	10	4	410	108	—	—
		COMMERCIAL & BUS. ADMINISTR.	—	—	—	—	—	—	—	—
		MASS COMMUNICATION & DOCUMENT.	—	—	—	—	—	—	—	—
		HOME ECONOMICS & DOMESTIC SC.	—	—	—	—	—	—	—	—
		SERVICE TRADES	—	—	—	—	—	—	—	—
		NATURAL SCIENCE	73	11	—	—	73	11	—	—
		MATHEMATICS & COMPUTER SCIENCE	—	—	—	—	—	—	—	—
		MEDICAL AND HEALTH-RELATED SC.	1 307	601	270	270	1 037	331	—	—
		ENGINEERING	570	45	—	—	570	45	—	—
		ARCHITECTURE & TOWN PLANNING	—	—	—	—	—	—	—	—
		TRADE, CRAFT & INDUSTR. PGMS.	—	—	—	—	—	—	—	—
		TRANSPORT AND COMMUNICATIONS	192	18	—	—	192	18	—	—
		AGRICULTURE,FORESTRY & FISH'G.	462	148	462	148	—	—	—	—
		OTHER AND NOT SPECIFIED	—	—	—	—	—	—	—	—

Third level: students by levels and fields   3.12
Troisième degré: étudiants par types de programmes et domaines d'études
Tercer grado: estudiantes por tipos de programas y sectores de estudio

INTERNATIONAL STANDARD CLASSIFICATION OF EDUCATION BY LEVEL
CLASSIFICATION INTERNATIONALE TYPE DE L'EDUCATION PAR NIVEAUX
CLASIFICACION INTERNACIONAL NORMALIZADA DE LA EDUCACION POR GRADOS

COUNTRY / PAYS / PAIS	YEAR / ANNEE / AÑO	FIELD OF STUDY / BRANCHE D'ETUDES / RAMAS DE ESTUDIO	ALL LEVELS TOUS NIVEAUX TODOS LOS GRADOS MF	F	LEVEL 5 NIVEAU 5 GRADO 5 MF	F	LEVEL 6 NIVEAU 6 GRADO 6 MF	F	LEVEL 7 NIVEAU 7 GRADO 7 MF	F
HONDURAS ‡	1977	TOTAL	18 628	6 725	—	—	18 628	6 725	—	—
		EDUCATION SCIENCE & TCHR TRNG.	247	167	—	—	247	167	—	—
		HUMANITIES,RELIGION & THEOLOG.	84	44	—	—	84	44	—	—
		FINE AND APPLIED ARTS	—	—	—	—	—	—	—	—
		LAW	1 795	607	—	—	1 795	607	—	—
		SOCIAL AND BEHAVIOURAL SCIENCE	2 864	1 486	—	—	2 864	1 486	—	—
		COMMERCIAL & BUS. ADMINISTR.	4 833	1 869	—	—	4 833	1 869	—	—
		MASS COMMUNICATION & DOCUMENT.	118	44	—	—	118	44	—	—
		HOME ECONOMICS & DOMESTIC SC.	—	—	—	—	—	—	—	—
		SERVICE TRADES	—	—	—	—	—	—	—	—
		NATURAL SCIENCE	396	297	—	—	396	297	—	—
		MATHEMATICS & COMPUTER SCIENCE	76	31	—	—	76	31	—	—
		MEDICAL AND HEALTH-RELATED SC.	3 209	1 483	—	—	3 209	1 483	—	—
		ENGINEERING	4 903	697	—	—	4 903	697	—	—
		ARCHITECTURE & TOWN PLANNING	—	—	—	—	—	—	—	—
		TRADE,CRAFT & INDUSTR. PGMS.	—	—	—	—	—	—	—	—
		TRANSPORT AND COMMUNICATIONS	—	—	—	—	—	—	—	—
		AGRICULTURE,FORESTRY & FISH'G.	103	—	—	—	103	—	—	—
		OTHER AND NOT SPECIFIED	—	—	—	—	—	—	—	—
JAMAICA ‡	1976	TOTAL	4 091	...	631	...	3 078	...	382	...
		EDUCATION SCIENCE & TCHR TRNG.	295	...	165	...	57	...	73	...
		HUMANITIES,RELIGION & THEOLOG.	1 020	...	—	—	979	...	41	...
		FINE AND APPLIED ARTS	—	—	—	—	—	—	—	—
		LAW	31	...	—	—	31	...	—	—
		SOCIAL AND BEHAVIOURAL SCIENCE	783	...	237	...	426	...	120	...
		COMMERCIAL & BUS. ADMINISTR.	82	...	82	...	—	—	—	—
		MASS COMMUNICATION & DOCUMENT.	35	...	35	...	—	—	—	—
		HOME ECONOMICS & DOMESTIC SC.	—	—	—	—	—	—	—	—
		SERVICE TRADES	—	—	—	—	—	—	—	—
		NATURAL SCIENCE	1 097	...	—	—	1 030	...	67	...
		MATHEMATICS & COMPUTER SCIENCE	—	—	—	—	—	—	—	—
		MEDICAL AND HEALTH-RELATED SC.	723	...	87	...	555	...	81	...
		ENGINEERING	25	...	25	...	—	—	—	—
		ARCHITECTURE & TOWN PLANNING	—	—	—	—	—	—	—	—
		TRADE,CRAFT & INDUSTR. PGMS.	—	—	—	—	—	—	—	—
		TRANSPORT AND COMMUNICATIONS	—	—	—	—	—	—	—	—
		AGRICULTURE,FORESTRY & FISH'G.	—	—	—	—	—	—	—	—
		OTHER AND NOT SPECIFIED	—	—	—	—	—	—	—	—

3.12 Third level: students by levels and fields
Troisième degré: étudiants par types de programmes et domaines d'études
Tercer grado: estudiantes por tipos de programas y sectores de estudio

INTERNATIONAL STANDARD CLASSIFICATION OF EDUCATION BY LEVEL
CLASSIFICATION INTERNATIONALE TYPE DE L'EDUCATION PAR NIVEAUX
CLASIFICACION INTERNACIONAL NORMALIZADA DE LA EDUCACION POR GRADOS

COUNTRY / PAYS / PAIS	YEAR / ANNEE / AÑO	FIELD OF STUDY / BRANCHE D'ETUDES / RAMAS DE ESTUDIO	ALL LEVELS TOUS NIVEAUX TODOS LOS GRADOS		LEVEL 5 NIVEAU 5 GRADO 5		LEVEL 6 NIVEAU 6 GRADO 6		LEVEL 7 NIVEAU 7 GRADO 7	
			MF	F	MF	F	MF	F	MF	F
MEXICO	1977	TOTAL	622 072	171 573	...	...	622 072	171 573	...	...
		EDUCATION SCIENCE & TCHR TRNG.	4 975	3 239	...	...	4 975	3 239	...	...
		HUMANITIES,RELIGION & THEOLOG.	10 722	5 664	...	...	10 722	5 664	...	...
		FINE AND APPLIED ARTS	2 440	1 059	...	...	2 440	1 059	...	...
		LAW	53 161	14 796	...	...	53 161	14 796	...	...
		SOCIAL AND BEHAVIOURAL SCIENCE	46 403	21 428	...	...	46 403	21 428	...	...
		COMMERCIAL & BUS. ADMINISTR.	114 307	37 538	...	...	114 307	37 538	...	...
		MASS COMMUNICATION & DOCUMENT.	7 521	3 514	...	...	7 521	3 514	...	...
		HOME ECONOMICS & DOMESTIC SC.	737	572	...	...	737	572	...	...
		SERVICE TRADES	3 937	2 058	...	...	3 937	2 058	...	...
		NATURAL SCIENCE	34 035	16 000	...	...	34 035	16 000	...	...
		MATHEMATICS & COMPUTER SCIENCE	5 592	1 374	...	...	5 592	1 374	...	...
		MEDICAL AND HEALTH-RELATED SC.	122 612	46 802	...	...	122 612	46 802	...	...
		ENGINEERING	112 049	8 567	...	...	112 049	8 567	...	...
		ARCHITECTURE & TOWN PLANNING	21 254	3 557	...	...	21 254	3 557	...	...
		TRADE, CRAFT & INDUSTR. PGMS.	32 216	2 082	...	...	32 216	2 082	...	...
		TRANSPORT AND COMMUNICATIONS	1 231	24	...	...	1 231	24	...	...
		AGRICULTURE,FORESTRY & FISH'G.	48 327	3 220	...	...	48 327	3 220	...	...
		OTHER AND NOT SPECIFIED	553	79	...	...	553	79	...	...
PANAMA	1977	TOTAL	34 720	17 908	7 078	3 447	27 569	14 442	73	19
		EDUCATION SCIENCE & TCHR TRNG.	2 263	1 640	602	477	1 623	1 146	38	17
		HUMANITIES,RELIGION & THEOLOG.	1 374	1 017	112	73	1 262	944	—	—
		FINE AND APPLIED ARTS	371	167	179	44	192	123	—	—
		LAW	1 515	509	—	—	1 515	509	—	—
		SOCIAL AND BEHAVIOURAL SCIENCE	2 581	1 088	964	610	1 617	478	—	—
		COMMERCIAL & BUS. ADMINISTR.	10 077	5 547	6	1	10 071	5 546	—	—
		MASS COMMUNICATION & DOCUMENT.	783	576	—	—	783	576	—	—
		HOME ECONOMICS & DOMESTIC SC.	479	453	—	—	479	453	—	—
		SERVICE TRADES	218	139	218	139	—	—	—	—
		NATURAL SCIENCE	1 518	572	100	57	1 383	513	35	2
		MATHEMATICS & COMPUTER SCIENCE	386	203	8	7	378	196	—	—
		MEDICAL AND HEALTH-RELATED SC.	3 080	1 988	24	10	3 056	1 978	—	—
		ENGINEERING	4 600	688	2 450	346	2 150	342	—	—
		ARCHITECTURE & TOWN PLANNING	1 196	336	85	32	1 111	304	—	—
		TRADE, CRAFT & INDUSTR. PGMS.	132	20	—	—	132	20	—	—
		TRANSPORT AND COMMUNICATIONS	66	38	—	—	66	38	—	—
		AGRICULTURE,FORESTRY & FISH'G.	156	25	156	25	—	—	—	—
		OTHER AND NOT SPECIFIED	3 925	2 902	2 174	1 626	1 751	1 276	—	—
FORMER CANAL ZONE	1977	TOTAL	1 378	737	967	506	411	231	—	—

Third level: students by levels and fields 3.12
Troisième degré: étudiants par types de programmes et domaines d'études
Tercer grado: estudiants par tipos de programas y sectores de estudio

INTERNATIONAL STANDARD CLASSIFICATION OF EDUCATION BY LEVEL
CLASSIFICATION INTERNATIONALE TYPE DE L'EDUCATION PAR NIVEAUX
CLASIFICACION INTERNACIONAL NORMALIZADA DE LA EDUCACION POR GRADOS

COUNTRY / PAYS / PAIS	YEAR / ANNEE / AÑO	FIELD OF STUDY / BRANCHE D'ETUDES / RAMAS DE ESTUDIO	ALL LEVELS TOUS NIVEAUX TODOS LOS GRADOS MF	F	LEVEL 5 NIVEAU 5 GRADO 5 MF	F	LEVEL 6 NIVEAU 6 GRADO 6 MF	F	LEVEL 7 NIVEAU 7 GRADO 7 MF	F
PUERTO RICO	1977	TOTAL	119 970	67 077	4 596	2 568	111 059	62 150	4 315	2 359
TRINIDAD AND TOBAGO ‡	1977	TOTAL	2 477	890	68	18	2 019	761	390	111
		EDUCATION SCIENCE & TCHR TRNG.	86	44	—	—	—	—	86	44
		HUMANITIES,RELIGION & THEOLOG.	600	363	—	—	575	355	25	8
		FINE AND APPLIED ARTS	—	—	—	—	—	—	—	—
		LAW	29	15	—	—	29	15	—	—
		SOCIAL SCIENCES, TOTAL	490	157	66	18	286	112	138	27
		NATURAL SCIENCES, TOTAL	417	186	2	—	386	174	29	12
		MEDICAL AND HEALTH—RELATED SC.	—	—	—	—	—	—	—	—
		ENGINEERING, TOTAL	523	25	—	—	486	21	37	4
		AGRICULTURE,FORESTRY & FISH'G.	332	100	—	—	257	84	75	16
		OTHER AND NOT SPECIFIED	—	—	—	—	—	—	—	—
UNITED STATES OF AMERICA	1977	TOTAL	11 285 787	5 496 763	1 294 819	613 377	8 905 998	4 314 639	1 084 970	488 755
U.S. VIRGIN ISLANDS	1977	TOTAL	2 119	1 435	1 445	967	616	420	58	48
AMERICA, SOUTH										
ARGENTINA	1977	TOTAL	536 450	255 903						
		EDUCATION SCIENCE & TCHR TRNG.	68 391	60 914						
		HUMANITIES,RELIGION & THEOLOG.	33 455	25 241						
		FINE AND APPLIED ARTS	6 960	5 041						
		LAW	61 597	29 052						
		SOCIAL AND BEHAVIOURAL SCIENCE	7 329	5 433						
		COMMERCIAL & BUS. ADMINISTR.	102 851	32 245						
		MASS COMMUNICATION & DOCUMENT.	—							
		HOME ECONOMICS & DOMESTIC SC.	—							
		SERVICE TRADES	—							
		NATURAL SCIENCE	20 391	11 654						
		MATHEMATICS & COMPUTER SCIENCE	96 937	52 231						
		MEDICAL AND HEALTH—RELATED SC.	71 602	9 707						
		ENGINEERING	31 625	13 013						
		ARCHITECTURE & TOWN PLANNING	—							
		TRADE, CRAFT & INDUSTR. PGMS.	—							
		TRANSPORT AND COMMUNICATIONS	—							
		AGRICULTURE,FORESTRY & FISH'G.	28 287	6 313						
		OTHER AND NOT SPECIFIED	7 025	5 059						

3.12 Third level: students by levels and fields
Troisième degré: étudiants par types de programmes et domaines d'études
Tercer grado: estudiantes por tipos de programas y sectores de estudio

INTERNATIONAL STANDARD CLASSIFICATION OF EDUCATION BY LEVEL
CLASSIFICATION INTERNATIONALE TYPE DE L'EDUCATION PAR NIVEAUX
CLASIFICACION INTERNACIONAL NORMALIZADA DE LA EDUCACION POR GRADOS

COUNTRY / PAYS / PAIS — YEAR / ANNEE / AÑO — FIELD OF STUDY / BRANCHE D'ETUDES / RAMAS DE ESTUDIO	ALL LEVELS / TOUS NIVEAUX / TODOS LOS GRADOS MF	F	LEVEL 5 / NIVEAU 5 / GRADO 5 MF	F	LEVEL 6 / NIVEAU 6 / GRADO 6 MF	F	LEVEL 7 / NIVEAU 7 / GRADO 7 MF	F
BOLIVIA 1977								
TOTAL	41 408	...	...	...	41 408	...	...	...
EDUCATION SCIENCE & TCHR TRNG.	1 150	...	...	...	1 150	...	...	...
HUMANITIES,RELIGION & THEOLOG.	79	...	...	...	79	...	...	...
FINE AND APPLIED ARTS	—	...	...	...	—	...	...	...
LAW	3 537	...	...	...	3 537	...	...	...
SOCIAL AND BEHAVIOURAL SCIENCE	5 531	...	...	...	5 531	...	...	...
COMMERCIAL & BUS. ADMINISTR.	7 458	...	...	...	7 458	...	...	...
MASS COMMUNICATION & DOCUMENT.	302	...	...	...	302	...	...	...
HOME ECONOMICS & DOMESTIC SC.	198	...	...	...	198	...	...	...
SERVICE TRADES	6	...	...	...	6	...	...	...
NATURAL SCIENCE	965	...	...	...	965	...	...	...
MATHEMATICS & COMPUTER SCIENCE	318	...	...	...	318	...	...	...
MEDICAL AND HEALTH-RELATED SC.	8 905	...	...	...	8 905	...	...	...
ENGINEERING	8 852	...	...	...	8 852	...	...	...
ARCHITECTURE & TOWN PLANNING	2 452	...	...	...	2 452	...	...	...
TRADE, CRAFT & INDUSTR. PGMS.	—	—	...	...	—	—	...	...
TRANSPORT AND COMMUNICATIONS	—	—	...	...	—	—	...	...
AGRICULTURE,FORESTRY & FISH'G.	1 655	...	...	...	1 655	...	...	...
OTHER AND NOT SPECIFIED	—	—	...	...	—	—	...	...
BRAZIL ‡ 1975								
TOTAL	1 089 808	...	...	...	...	...	...	...
EDUCATION SCIENCE & TCHR TRNG.	69 901	...	...	...	...	...	...	...
HUMANITIES,RELIGION & THEOLOG.	88 599	...	...	...	...	...	...	...
FINE AND APPLIED ARTS	17 061	...	...	...	...	...	...	...
LAW	90 702	...	...	...	...	...	...	...
SOCIAL AND BEHAVIOURAL SCIENCE	101 248	...	...	...	...	...	...	...
COMMERCIAL & BUS. ADMINISTR.	111 429	...	...	...	...	...	...	...
MASS COMMUNICATION & DOCUMENT.	2 358	...	...	...	...	...	...	...
HOME ECONOMICS & DOMESTIC SC.	655	...	...	...	...	...	...	...
SERVICE TRADES	4 691	...	...	...	...	...	...	...
NATURAL SCIENCE	60 006	...	...	...	...	...	...	...
MATHEMATICS & COMPUTER SCIENCE	31 213	...	...	...	...	...	...	...
MEDICAL AND HEALTH-RELATED SC.	80 601	...	...	...	...	...	...	...
ENGINEERING	89 319	...	...	...	...	...	...	...
ARCHITECTURE & TOWN PLANNING	12 708	...	...	...	...	...	...	...
TRADE, CRAFT & INDUSTR. PGMS.	—	—	...	...	...	...	...	...
TRANSPORT AND COMMUNICATIONS	—	—	...	...	...	...	...	...
AGRICULTURE,FORESTRY & FISH'G.	18 885	...	...	...	...	...	...	...
OTHER AND NOT SPECIFIED	310 432	...	...	...	...	...	...	...

Third level: students by levels and fields 3.12
Troisième degré: étudiants par types de programmes et domaines d'études
Tercer grado: estudiantes por tipos de programas y sectores de estudio

INTERNATIONAL STANDARD CLASSIFICATION OF EDUCATION BY LEVEL
CLASSIFICATION INTERNATIONALE TYPE DE L'EDUCATION PAR NIVEAUX
CLASIFICACION INTERNACIONAL NORMALIZADA DE LA EDUCACION POR GRADOS

COUNTRY / PAYS / PAIS	YEAR / ANNEE / AÑO	FIELD OF STUDY / BRANCHE D'ETUDES / RAMAS DE ESTUDIO	ALL LEVELS / TOUS NIVEAUX / TODOS LOS GRADOS		LEVEL 5 / NIVEAU 5 / GRADO 5		LEVEL 6 / NIVEAU 6 / GRADO 6		LEVEL 7 / NIVEAU 7 / GRADO 7	
			MF	F	MF	F	MF	F	MF	F
CHILE ‡	1978	TOTAL	130 982	...	./.	...	130 208	...	774	...
		EDUCATION SCIENCE & TCHR TRNG.	...	...	./.	...	37 338	...	...	...
		HUMANITIES,RELIGION & THEOLOG.	...	...	./.	...	3 288	...	...	...
		FINE AND APPLIED ARTS	...	...	./.	...	4 882	...	...	...
		LAW	...	...	./.	...	3 093	...	...	...
		SOCIAL AND BEHAVIOURAL SCIENCE	...	...	./.	...	16 138	...	...	...
		COMMERCIAL & BUS. ADMINISTR.	...	...	./.	...	./.	...	...	...
		MASS COMMUNICATION & DOCUMENT.	...	...	./.	...	./.	...	...	...
		HOME ECONOMICS & DOMESTIC SC.	...	...	./.	...	./.	...	...	...
		SERVICE TRADES	...	...	./.	...	./.	...	...	...
		NATURAL SCIENCE	...	...	./.	...	4 911	...	...	...
		MATHEMATICS & COMPUTER SCIENCE	...	...	./.	...	./.	...	...	...
		MEDICAL AND HEALTH-RELATED SC.	...	...	./.	...	15 408	...	...	...
		ENGINEERING	...	...	./.	...	38 572	...	...	...
		ARCHITECTURE & TOWN PLANNING	...	...	./.	...	./.	...	...	...
		TRADE, CRAFT & INDUSTR. PGMS.	...	...	./.	...	./.	...	...	...
		TRANSPORT AND COMMUNICATIONS	...	...	./.	...	./.	...	...	...
		AGRICULTURE,FORESTRY & FISH'G.	...	...	./.	...	6 578	...	...	...
		OTHER AND NOT SPECIFIED	...	...	./.	...	./.	...	...	...
COLOMBIA ‡	1977	TOTAL	237 477	92 487	—	—	232 765	91 181	4 712	1 306
		EDUCATION SCIENCE & TCHR TRNG.	43 616	24 804	—	—	42 949	24 472	667	332
		HUMANITIES,RELIGION & THEOLOG.	2 933	1 430	—	—	2 860	1 393	73	37
		FINE AND APPLIED ARTS	11 078	4 134	—	—	11 070	4 134	8	—
		LAW	27 437	10 520	—	—	26 046	10 069	1 391	451
		SOCIAL AND BEHAVIOURAL SCIENCE	11 258	8 670	—	—	11 192	8 632	66	38
		COMMERCIAL & BUS. ADMINISTR.	64 910	21 614	—	—	64 073	21 462	837	152
		MASS COMMUNICATION & DOCUMENT.	./.	./.	—	—	./.	./.	./.	./.
		HOME ECONOMICS & DOMESTIC SC.	./.	./.	—	—	./.	./.	./.	./.
		SERVICE TRADES	./.	./.	—	—	./.	./.	./.	./.
		NATURAL SCIENCE	6 702	3 732	—	—	6 437	3 608	265	125
		MATHEMATICS & COMPUTER SCIENCE	./.	./.	—	—	./.	./.	./.	./.
		MEDICAL AND HEALTH-RELATED SC.	23 321	12 146	—	—	22 517	11 984	804	162
		ENGINEERING	36 291	4 360	—	—	35 761	4 356	530	4
		ARCHITECTURE & TOWN PLANNING	./.	./.	—	—	./.	./.	./.	./.
		TRADE, CRAFT & INDUSTR. PGMS.	./.	./.	—	—	./.	./.	./.	./.
		TRANSPORT AND COMMUNICATIONS	./.	./.	—	—	./.	./.	./.	./.
		AGRICULTURE,FORESTRY & FISH'G.	9 931	1 077	—	—	9 860	1 071	71	6
		OTHER AND NOT SPECIFIED	—	—	—	—	—	—	—	—

3.12 Third level: students by levels and fields
Troisième degré: étudiants par types de programmes et domaines d'études
Tercer grado: estudiantes por tipos de programas y sectores de estudio

INTERNATIONAL STANDARD CLASSIFICATION OF EDUCATION BY LEVEL
CLASSIFICATION INTERNATIONALE TYPE DE L'EDUCATION PAR NIVEAUX
CLASIFICACION INTERNACIONAL NORMALIZADA DE LA EDUCACION POR GRADOS

COUNTRY / PAYS / PAIS	YEAR / ANNEE / AÑO	FIELD OF STUDY / BRANCHE D'ETUDES / RAMAS DE ESTUDIO	ALL LEVELS TOUS NIVEAUX TODOS LOS GRADOS MF	F	LEVEL 5 NIVEAU 5 GRADO 5 MF	F	LEVEL 6 NIVEAU 6 GRADO 6 MF	F	LEVEL 7 NIVEAU 7 GRADO 7 MF	F
FRENCH GUIANA ‡	1977	TOTAL	4 087	2 128						
		EDUCATION SCIENCE & TCHR TRNG.	344	248						
		HUMANITIES,RELIGION & THEOLOG.	552	376						
		FINE AND APPLIED ARTS	—	—						
		LAW	2 259	1 131						
		SOCIAL AND BEHAVIOURAL SCIENCE	159	47						
		COMMERCIAL & BUS. ADMINISTR.	—	—						
		MASS COMMUNICATION & DOCUMENT.	—	—						
		HOME ECONOMICS & DOMESTIC SC.	118	93						
		SERVICE TRADES	249	88						
		NATURAL SCIENCE	./.	./.						
		MATHEMATICS & COMPUTER SCIENCE	—	—						
		MEDICAL AND HEALTH-RELATED SC.	—	—						
		ENGINEERING	51	—						
		ARCHITECTURE & TOWN PLANNING	—	—						
		TRADE, CRAFT & INDUSTR. PGMS.	—	—						
		TRANSPORT AND COMMUNICATIONS	—	—						
		AGRICULTURE,FORESTRY & FISH'G.	355	145						
		OTHER AND NOT SPECIFIED	—	—						
	1978	TOTAL	4 019	...						
		EDUCATION SCIENCE & TCHR TRNG.	238	...						
		HUMANITIES,RELIGION & THEOLOG.	601	...						
		FINE AND APPLIED ARTS	—	—						
		LAW	2 110	...						
		SOCIAL AND BEHAVIOURAL SCIENCE	487	...						
		COMMERCIAL & BUS. ADMINISTR.	—	—						
		MASS COMMUNICATION & DOCUMENT.	—	—						
		HOME ECONOMICS & DOMESTIC SC.	—	—						
		SERVICE TRADES	183	...						
		NATURAL SCIENCE	294	...						
		MATHEMATICS & COMPUTER SCIENCE	./.	./.						
		MEDICAL AND HEALTH-RELATED SC.	106	...						
		ENGINEERING	—	—						
		ARCHITECTURE & TOWN PLANNING	—	—						
		TRADE, CRAFT & INDUSTR. PGMS.	—	—						
		TRANSPORT AND COMMUNICATIONS	—	—						
		AGRICULTURE,FORESTRY & FISH'G.	—	—						
		OTHER AND NOT SPECIFIED	—	—						

Third level: students by levels and fields   3.12
Troisième degré: étudiants par types de programmes et domaines d'études
Tercer grado: estudiantes por tipos de programas y sectores de estudio

INTERNATIONAL STANDARD CLASSIFICATION OF EDUCATION BY LEVEL
CLASSIFICATION INTERNATIONALE TYPE DE L'EDUCATION PAR NIVEAUX
CLASIFICACION INTERNACIONAL NORMALIZADA DE LA EDUCACION POR GRADOS

COUNTRY / PAYS / PAIS	YEAR / ANNEE / AÑO	FIELD OF STUDY / BRANCHE D'ETUDES / RAMAS DE ESTUDIO	ALL LEVELS TOUS NIVEAUX TODOS LOS GRADOS		LEVEL 5 NIVEAU 5 GRADO 5		LEVEL 6 NIVEAU 6 GRADO 6		LEVEL 7 NIVEAU 7 GRADO 7	
			MF	F	MF	F	MF	F	MF	F
PARAGUAY ‡	1977	TOTAL	20 318	8 691						
		EDUCATION SCIENCE & TCHR TRNG.	410	331						
		HUMANITIES,RELIGION & THEOLOG.	447	245						
		FINE AND APPLIED ARTS	448	372						
		LAW	3 860	1 667						
		SOCIAL AND BEHAVIOURAL SCIENCE	621	302						
		COMMERCIAL & BUS. ADMINISTR.	1 969	802						
		MASS COMMUNICATION & DOCUMENT.	123	70						
		HOME ECONOMICS & DOMESTIC SC.	25	25						
		SERVICE TRADES	—	—						
		NATURAL SCIENCE	913	559						
		MATHEMATICS & COMPUTER SCIENCE	651	339						
		MEDICAL AND HEALTH-RELATED SC.	1 708	1 082						
		ENGINEERING	1 222	146						
		ARCHITECTURE & TOWN PLANNING	978	440						
		TRADE, CRAFT & INDUSTR. PGMS.	—	—						
		TRANSPORT AND COMMUNICATIONS	—	—						
		AGRICULTURE,FORESTRY & FISH'G.	1 003	185						
		OTHER AND NOT SPECIFIED	5 940	2 126						
	1978	TOTAL	20 812	9 037						
		EDUCATION SCIENCE & TCHR TRNG.	404	322						
		HUMANITIES,RELIGION & THEOLOG.	354	195						
		FINE AND APPLIED ARTS	311	227						
		LAW	3 208	1 350						
		SOCIAL AND BEHAVIOURAL SCIENCE	633	459						
		COMMERCIAL & BUS. ADMINISTR.	2 365	1 005						
		MASS COMMUNICATION & DOCUMENT.	116	69						
		HOME ECONOMICS & DOMESTIC SC.	35	34						
		SERVICE TRADES	—	—						
		NATURAL SCIENCE	938	583						
		MATHEMATICS & COMPUTER SCIENCE	674	420						
		MEDICAL AND HEALTH-RELATED SC.	1 915	978						
		ENGINEERING	1 593	203						
		ARCHITECTURE & TOWN PLANNING	1 190	486						
		TRADE, CRAFT & INDUSTR. PGMS.	—	—						
		TRANSPORT AND COMMUNICATIONS	—	—						
		AGRICULTURE,FORESTRY & FISH'G.	1 108	219						
		OTHER AND NOT SPECIFIED	5 968	2 487						

3.12 Third level: students by levels and fields
Troisième degré: étudiants par types de programmes et domaines d'études
Tercer grado: estudiantes por tipos de programas y sectores de estudio

INTERNATIONAL STANDARD CLASSIFICATION OF EDUCATION BY LEVEL
CLASSIFICATION INTERNATIONALE TYPE DE L'EDUCATION PAR NIVEAUX
CLASIFICACION INTERNACIONAL NORMALIZADA DE LA EDUCACION POR GRADOS

COUNTRY / PAYS / PAIS	YEAR / ANNEE / AÑO	FIELD OF STUDY / BRANCHE D'ETUDES / RAMAS DE ESTUDIO	ALL LEVELS / TOUS NIVEAUX / TODOS LOS GRADOS MF	F	LEVEL 5 / NIVEAU 5 / GRADO 5 MF	F	LEVEL 6 / NIVEAU 6 / GRADO 6 MF	F	LEVEL 7 / NIVEAU 7 / GRADO 7 MF	F
PERU ‡	1977	TOTAL	233 420	...	33 420	...	198 979	...	1 021	—
		EDUCATION SCIENCE & TCHR TRNG.	32 544	...	194	...	32 350	...	—	—
		HUMANITIES,RELIGION & THEOLOG.	2 513	...	26	...	2 487	...	—	—
		FINE AND APPLIED ARTS	544	...	101	...	443	...	—	—
		LAW	11 869	—	—	—	11 869	—	—	—
		SOCIAL AND BEHAVIOURAL SCIENCE	34 413	...	—	—	34 413	...	—	—
		COMMERCIAL & BUS. ADMINISTR.	46 033	...	18 113	—	27 920	...	—	—
		MASS COMMUNICATION & DOCUMENT.	3 564	...	1 215	—	2 349	...	—	—
		HOME ECONOMICS & DOMESTIC SC.	1 112	...	1 035	—	77	...	—	—
		SERVICE TRADES	395	...	195	—	200	...	—	—
		NATURAL SCIENCE	3 328	...	—	—	3 328	...	—	—
		MATHEMATICS & COMPUTER SCIENCE	1 583	...	216	—	1 367	...	—	—
		MEDICAL AND HEALTH-RELATED SC.	20 833	...	2 084	—	18 749	...	—	—
		ENGINEERING	50 205	...	6 895	—	43 310	...	—	—
		ARCHITECTURE & TOWN PLANNING	5 669	...	—	—	5 669	...	—	—
		TRADE, CRAFT & INDUSTR. PGMS.	1 083	—	1 083	—	—	—	—	—
		TRANSPORT AND COMMUNICATIONS	143	—	143	—	—	—	—	—
		AGRICULTURE,FORESTRY & FISH'G.	10 371	...	1 010	—	9 361	...	—	—
		OTHER AND NOT SPECIFIED	7 218	...	1 110	—	5 087	...	1 021	—
SURINAME	1976	TOTAL	761	224	—	—	761	224	—	—
		EDUCATION SCIENCE & TCHR TRNG.	—	—	—	—	—	—	—	—
		HUMANITIES,RELIGION & THEOLOG.	—	—	—	—	—	—	—	—
		FINE AND APPLIED ARTS	—	—	—	—	—	—	—	—
		LAW	467	130	—	—	467	130	—	—
		SOCIAL AND BEHAVIOURAL SCIENCE	79	31	—	—	79	31	—	—
		COMMERCIAL & BUS. ADMINISTR.	—	—	—	—	—	—	—	—
		MASS COMMUNICATION & DOCUMENT.	—	—	—	—	—	—	—	—
		HOME ECONOMICS & DOMESTIC SC.	—	—	—	—	—	—	—	—
		SERVICE TRADES	—	—	—	—	—	—	—	—
		NATURAL SCIENCE	34	4	—	—	34	4	—	—
		MATHEMATICS & COMPUTER SCIENCE	—	—	—	—	—	—	—	—
		MEDICAL AND HEALTH-RELATED SC.	181	59	—	—	181	59	—	—
		ENGINEERING	—	—	—	—	—	—	—	—
		ARCHITECTURE & TOWN PLANNING	—	—	—	—	—	—	—	—
		TRADE, CRAFT & INDUSTR. PGMS.	—	—	—	—	—	—	—	—
		TRANSPORT AND COMMUNICATIONS	—	—	—	—	—	—	—	—
		AGRICULTURE,FORESTRY & FISH'G.	—	—	—	—	—	—	—	—
		OTHER AND NOT SPECIFIED	—	—	—	—	—	—	—	—

Third level: students by levels and fields 3.12
Troisième degré: étudiants par types de programmes et domaines d'études
Tercer grado: estudiantes por tipos de programas y sectores de estudio

INTERNATIONAL STANDARD CLASSIFICATION OF EDUCATION BY LEVEL
CLASSIFICATION INTERNATIONALE TYPE DE L'EDUCATION PAR NIVEAUX
CLASIFICACION INTERNACIONAL NORMALIZADA DE LA EDUCACION POR GRADOS

COUNTRY PAYS PAIS	YEAR ANNEE AÑO	FIELD OF STUDY / BRANCHE D'ETUDES / RAMAS DE ESTUDIO	ALL LEVELS TOUS NIVEAUX TODOS LOS GRADOS		LEVEL 5 NIVEAU 5 GRADO 5		LEVEL 6 NIVEAU 6 GRADO 6		LEVEL 7 NIVEAU 7 GRADO 7	
			MF	F	MF	F	MF	F	MF	F
SURINAME (CONT.)	1977	TOTAL	900	312	-	-	900	312	-	-
		EDUCATION SCIENCE & TCHR TRNG.	-	-	-	-	-	-	-	-
		HUMANITIES,RELIGION & THEOLOG.	-	-	-	-	-	-	-	-
		FINE AND APPLIED ARTS	-	-	-	-	-	-	-	-
		LAW	510	168	-	-	510	168	-	-
		SOCIAL AND BEHAVIOURAL SCIENCE	-	-	-	-	-	-	-	-
		COMMERCIAL & BUS. ADMINISTR.	155	64	-	-	155	64	-	-
		MASS COMMUNICATION & DOCUMENT.	-	-	-	-	-	-	-	-
		HOME ECONOMICS & DOMESTIC SC.	-	-	-	-	-	-	-	-
		SERVICE TRADES	-	-	-	-	-	-	-	-
		NATURAL SCIENCE	42	16	-	-	42	16	-	-
		MATHEMATICS & COMPUTER SCIENCE	-	-	-	-	-	-	-	-
		MEDICAL AND HEALTH-RELATED SC.	193	64	-	-	193	64	-	-
		AGRICULTURE,FORESTRY & FISH'G.	-	-	-	-	-	-	-	-
		OTHER AND NOT SPECIFIED	-	-	-	-	-	-	-	-
URUGUAY	1977	TOTAL	39 392	18 703	3 605	2 715	35 757	15 961	30	27
		EDUCATION SCIENCE & TCHR TRNG.	837	595	98	60	739	535	-	-
		HUMANITIES,RELIGION & THEOLOG.	341	172	341	172	-	-	-	-
		FINE AND APPLIED ARTS	-	-	-	-	-	-	-	-
		LAW	12 894	6 177	-	-	12 894	6 177	-	-
		SOCIAL AND BEHAVIOURAL SCIENCE	259	180	41	35	218	145	-	-
		COMMERCIAL & BUS. ADMINISTR.	3 976	1 778	796	448	3 180	1 330	-	-
		MASS COMMUNICATION & DOCUMENT.	196	183	196	183	-	-	-	-
		HOME ECONOMICS & DOMESTIC SC.	113	109	113	109	-	-	-	-
		SERVICE TRADES	-	-	-	-	-	-	-	-
		NATURAL SCIENCE	703	438	-	-	703	438	-	-
		MATHEMATICS & COMPUTER SCIENCE	616	214	-	-	616	214	-	-
		MEDICAL AND HEALTH-RELATED SC.	11 963	6 591	1 476	1 292	10 457	5 272	30	27
		ENGINEERING	1 480	133	-	-	1 480	133	-	-
		ARCHITECTURE & TOWN PLANNING	1 645	647	-	-	1 645	647	-	-
		TRADE, CRAFT & INDUSTR. PGMS.	88	-	88	-	-	-	-	-
		TRANSPORT AND COMMUNICATIONS	-	-	-	-	-	-	-	-
		AGRICULTURE,FORESTRY & FISH'G.	3 825	1 070	-	-	3 825	1 070	-	-
		OTHER AND NOT SPECIFIED	456	416	456	416	-	-	-	-

3.12 Third level: students by levels and fields
Troisième degré: étudiants par types de programmes et domaines d'études
Tercer grado: estudiantes por tipos de programas y sectores de estudio

COUNTRY / PAYS / PAIS	YEAR / ANNEE / AÑO	FIELD OF STUDY / BRANCHE D'ETUDES / RAMAS DE ESTUDIO	ALL LEVELS / TOUS NIVEAUX / TODOS LOS GRADOS		LEVEL 5 / NIVEAU 5 / GRADO 5		LEVEL 6 / NIVEAU 6 / GRADO 6		LEVEL 7 / NIVEAU 7 / GRADO 7	
			MF	F	MF	F	MF	F	MF	F
VENEZUELA	1977	TOTAL	265 671	...						—
		EDUCATION SCIENCE & TCHR TRNG.	24 491	...						—
		HUMANITIES,RELIGION & THEOLOG.	8 986	...						—
		FINE AND APPLIED ARTS	412	...						—
		LAW	13 783	...						—
		SOCIAL AND BEHAVIOURAL SCIENCE	17 860	...						—
		COMMERCIAL & BUS. ADMINISTR.	26 073	...						—
		MASS COMMUNICATION & DOCUMENT.	3 279	...						—
		HOME ECONOMICS & DOMESTIC SC.	2 112	...						—
		SERVICE TRADES	696	...						—
		NATURAL SCIENCE	11 034	...						—
		MATHEMATICS & COMPUTER SCIENCE	4 997	...						—
		MEDICAL AND HEALTH-RELATED SC.	22 622	...						—
		ENGINEERING	37 566	...						—
		ARCHITECTURE & TOWN PLANNING	5 213	...						—
		TRADE, CRAFT & INDUSTR. PGMS.	322	...						—
		TRANSPORT AND COMMUNICATIONS	—	—						—
		AGRICULTURE,FORESTRY & FISH'G.	8 483	...						—
		OTHER AND NOT SPECIFIED	77 742	...						—
ASIA										
AFGHANISTAN	1976	TOTAL	*14 214	*1 951	5 866	1 108	8 348	843	—	—
		EDUCATION SCIENCE & TCHR TRNG.	5 516	1 048	5 516	1 048	—	—	—	—
		HUMANITIES,RELIGION & THEOLOG.	1 725	328	—	—	1 725	328	—	—
		FINE AND APPLIED ARTS	—	—	—	—	—	—	—	—
		LAW	479	14	—	—	479	14	—	—
		SOCIAL SCIENCES, TOTAL	990	113	*350	*60	640	53	—	—
		NATURAL SCIENCES, TOTAL	936	211	—	—	936	211	—	—
		MEDICAL AND HEALTH-RELATED SC.	1 797	127	—	—	1 795	127	—	—
		ENGINEERING, TOTAL	1 808	95	—	—	1 808	95	—	—
		AGRICULTURE,FORESTRY & FISH'G.	963	15	—	—	963	15	—	—
		OTHER AND NOT SPECIFIED	—	—	—	—	—	—	—	—
	1977	TOTAL	*16 147	*4 286	5 796	2 703	10 351	1 583	—	—
		EDUCATION SCIENCE & TCHR TRNG.	5 396	2 638	5 396	2 638	—	—	—	—
		HUMANITIES,RELIGION & THEOLOG.	1 945	841	—	—	1 945	841	—	—
		FINE AND APPLIED ARTS	—	—	—	—	—	—	—	—
		LAW	420	38	—	—	420	38	—	—
		SOCIAL SCIENCES, TOTAL	1 118	116	*400	*65	718	51	—	—
		NATURAL SCIENCES, TOTAL	1 138	262	—	—	1 138	262	—	—
		MEDICAL AND HEALTH-RELATED SC.	1 979	140	—	—	1 979	140	—	—
		ENGINEERING, TOTAL	3 043	224	—	—	3 043	224	—	—
		AGRICULTURE,FORESTRY & FISH'G.	1 108	27	—	—	1 108	27	—	—
		OTHER AND NOT SPECIFIED	—	—	—	—	—	—	—	—

Third level: students by levels and fields 3.12
Troisième degré: étudiants par types de programmes et domaines d'études
Tercer grado: estudiantes por tipos de programas y sectores de estudio

INTERNATIONAL STANDARD CLASSIFICATION OF EDUCATION BY LEVEL
CLASSIFICATION INTERNATIONALE TYPE DE L'EDUCATION PAR NIVEAUX
CLASIFICACION INTERNACIONAL NORMALIZADA DE LA EDUCACION POR GRADOS

COUNTRY / PAYS / PAIS	YEAR / ANNEE / AÑO	FIELD OF STUDY / BRANCHE D'ETUDES / RAMAS DE ESTUDIO	ALL LEVELS TOUS NIVEAUX TODOS LOS GRADOS MF	F	LEVEL 5 NIVEAU 5 GRADO 5 MF	F	LEVEL 6 NIVEAU 6 GRADO 6 MF	F	LEVEL 7 NIVEAU 7 GRADO 7 MF	F
BAHRAIN	1976	TOTAL	1 226	645	1 226	645	—	—	—	—
		EDUCATION SCIENCE & TCHR TRNG.	329	279	329	279	—	—	—	—
		HUMANITIES,RELIGION & THEOLOG.	30	30	30	30	—	—	—	—
		FINE AND APPLIED ARTS	—	—	—	—	—	—	—	—
		LAW	—	—	—	—	—	—	—	—
		SOCIAL AND BEHAVIOURAL SCIENCE	600	300	600	300	—	—	—	—
		COMMERCIAL & BUS. ADMINISTR.	—	—	—	—	—	—	—	—
		MASS COMMUNICATION & DOCUMENT.	—	—	—	—	—	—	—	—
		HOME ECONOMICS & DOMESTIC SC.	—	—	—	—	—	—	—	—
		SERVICE TRADES	—	—	—	—	—	—	—	—
		NATURAL SCIENCE	—	—	—	—	—	—	—	—
		MATHEMATICS & COMPUTER SCIENCE	—	—	—	—	—	—	—	—
		MEDICAL AND HEALTH-RELATED SC.	267	36	267	36	—	—	—	—
		ENGINEERING	—	—	—	—	—	—	—	—
		ARCHITECTURE & TOWN PLANNING	—	—	—	—	—	—	—	—
		TRADE, CRAFT & INDUSTR. PGMS.	—	—	—	—	—	—	—	—
		TRANSPORT AND COMMUNICATIONS	—	—	—	—	—	—	—	—
		AGRICULTURE,FORESTRY & FISH'G.	—	—	—	—	—	—	—	—
		OTHER AND NOT SPECIFIED	—	—	—	—	—	—	—	—
	1977	TOTAL	1 207	532	1 207	532	—	—	—	—
		EDUCATION SCIENCE & TCHR TRNG.	403	310	403	310	—	—	—	—
		HUMANITIES,RELIGION & THEOLOG.	—	—	—	—	—	—	—	—
		FINE AND APPLIED ARTS	—	—	—	—	—	—	—	—
		LAW	268	164	268	164	—	—	—	—
		SOCIAL AND BEHAVIOURAL SCIENCE	—	—	—	—	—	—	—	—
		COMMERCIAL & BUS. ADMINISTR.	—	—	—	—	—	—	—	—
		MASS COMMUNICATION & DOCUMENT.	—	—	—	—	—	—	—	—
		HOME ECONOMICS & DOMESTIC SC.	—	—	—	—	—	—	—	—
		SERVICE TRADES	—	—	—	—	—	—	—	—
		NATURAL SCIENCE	—	—	—	—	—	—	—	—
		MATHEMATICS & COMPUTER SCIENCE	—	—	—	—	—	—	—	—
		MEDICAL AND HEALTH-RELATED SC.	—	—	—	—	—	—	—	—
		ENGINEERING	159	37	159	37	—	—	—	—
		ARCHITECTURE & TOWN PLANNING	—	—	—	—	—	—	—	—
		TRADE, CRAFT & INDUSTR. PGMS.	377	21	377	21	—	—	—	—
		TRANSPORT AND COMMUNICATIONS	—	—	—	—	—	—	—	—
		AGRICULTURE,FORESTRY & FISH'G.	—	—	—	—	—	—	—	—
		OTHER AND NOT SPECIFIED	—	—	—	—	—	—	—	—

3.12   Third level: students by levels and fields
      Troisième degré: étudiants par types de programmes et domaines d'études
      Tercer grado: estudiantes por tipos de programas y sectores de estudio

INTERNATIONAL STANDARD CLASSIFICATION OF EDUCATION BY LEVEL
CLASSIFICATION INTERNATIONALE TYPE DE L'EDUCATION PAR NIVEAUX
CLASIFICACION INTERNACIONAL NORMALIZADA DE LA EDUCACION POR GRADOS

COUNTRY / PAYS / PAIS — YEAR / ANNEE / AÑO — FIELD OF STUDY / BRANCHE D'ETUDES / RAMAS DE ESTUDIO	ALL LEVELS TOUS NIVEAUX TODOS LOS GRADOS MF	F	LEVEL 5 NIVEAU 5 GRADO 5 MF	F	LEVEL 6 NIVEAU 6 GRADO 6 MF	F	LEVEL 7 NIVEAU 7 GRADO 7 MF	F
BANGLADESH 1977								
TOTAL	181 756	24 803	14 450	6	156 610	22 888	10 696	1 909
EDUCATION SCIENCE & TCHR TRNG.	3 262	725	170	—	2 965	715	127	10
HUMANITIES,RELIGION & THEOLOG.	64 429	9 564	—	—	61 980	8 798	2 449	766
FINE AND APPLIED ARTS	296	63	—	—	291	61	5	2
LAW	7 231	356	—	—	6 980	347	251	9
SOCIAL AND BEHAVIOURAL SCIENCE	8 834	1 932	—	—	6 670	1 509	2 164	423
COMMERCIAL & BUS. ADMINISTR.	31 549	4 187	—	—	30 287	4 103	1 262	84
MASS COMMUNICATION & DOCUMENT.	282	65	88	6	82	32	112	27
HOME ECONOMICS & DOMESTIC SC.	380	371	—	—	314	305	66	66
SERVICE TRADES	—	—	—	—	—	—	—	—
NATURAL SCIENCE	36 072	6 220	—	—	32 825	5 784	3 247	436
MATHEMATICS & COMPUTER SCIENCE	1 788	230	—	—	1 233	198	555	32
MEDICAL AND HEALTH-RELATED SC.	7 273	809	—	—	7 210	801	63	8
ENGINEERING	17 343	31	13 905	—	3 384	28	54	3
ARCHITECTURE & TOWN PLANNING	146	26	—	—	131	25	15	1
TRADE, CRAFT & INDUSTR. PGMS.	287	—	287	—	—	—	—	—
TRANSPORT AND COMMUNICATIONS	—	—	—	—	—	—	—	—
AGRICULTURE,FORESTRY & FISH'G.	1 954	31	—	—	1 779	31	175	—
OTHER AND NOT SPECIFIED	630	193	—	—	479	151	151	42
BRUNEI 1977								
TOTAL	331	182	331	182	—	—	—	—
EDUCATION SCIENCE & TCHR TRNG.	—	—	—	—	—	—	—	—
HUMANITIES,RELIGION & THEOLOG.	—	—	—	—	—	—	—	—
FINE AND APPLIED ARTS	—	—	—	—	—	—	—	—
LAW	331	182	331	182	—	—	—	—
SOCIAL AND BEHAVIOURAL SCIENCE	—	—	—	—	—	—	—	—
COMMERCIAL & BUS. ADMINISTR.	—	—	—	—	—	—	—	—
MASS COMMUNICATION & DOCUMENT.	—	—	—	—	—	—	—	—
HOME ECONOMICS & DOMESTIC SC.	—	—	—	—	—	—	—	—
SERVICE TRADES	—	—	—	—	—	—	—	—
NATURAL SCIENCE	—	—	—	—	—	—	—	—
MATHEMATICS & COMPUTER SCIENCE	—	—	—	—	—	—	—	—
MEDICAL AND HEALTH-RELATED SC.	—	—	—	—	—	—	—	—
ENGINEERING	—	—	—	—	—	—	—	—
ARCHITECTURE & TOWN PLANNING	—	—	—	—	—	—	—	—
TRADE, CRAFT & INDUSTR. PGMS.	—	—	—	—	—	—	—	—
TRANSPORT AND COMMUNICATIONS	—	—	—	—	—	—	—	—
AGRICULTURE,FORESTRY & FISH'G.	—	—	—	—	—	—	—	—
OTHER AND NOT SPECIFIED	—	—	—	—	—	—	—	—

Third level: students by levels and fields   3.12
Troisième degré: étudiants par types de programmes et domaines d'études
Tercer grado: estudiantes por tipos de programas y sectores de estudio

INTERNATIONAL STANDARD CLASSIFICATION OF EDUCATION BY LEVEL
CLASSIFICATION INTERNATIONALE TYPE DE L'EDUCATION PAR NIVEAUX
CLASSIFICACION INTERNACIONAL NORMALIZADA DE LA EDUCACION POR GRADOS

COUNTRY / PAYS / PAIS	YEAR / ANNEE / AÑO	FIELD OF STUDY / BRANCHE D'ETUDES / RAMAS DE ESTUDIO	ALL LEVELS TOUS NIVEAUX TODOS LOS GRADOS MF	F	LEVEL 5 NIVEAU 5 GRADO 5 MF	F	LEVEL 6 NIVEAU 6 GRADO 6 MF	F	LEVEL 7 NIVEAU 7 GRADO 7 MF	F
BURMA ‡	1976	TOTAL	50 676	24 157	—	—	47 806	22 646	2 870	1 511
		EDUCATION SCIENCE & TCHR TRNG.	2 458	1 759	—	—	1 894	1 445	564	314
		HUMANITIES,RELIGION & THEOLOG.	3 050	1 376	—	—	2 865	1 287	185	89
		FINE AND APPLIED ARTS	—	—	—	—	—	—	—	—
		LAW	1 099	590	—	—	1 064	574	35	16
		SOCIAL AND BEHAVIOURAL SCIENCE	5 318	2 757	—	—	5 029	2 579	289	178
		COMMERCIAL & BUS. ADMINISTR.	3 328	2 165	—	—	3 111	2 087	217	78
		MASS COMMUNICATION & DOCUMENT.	—	—	—	—	—	—	—	—
		HOME ECONOMICS & DOMESTIC SC.	—	—	—	—	—	—	—	—
		SERVICE TRADES	—	—	—	—	—	—	—	—
		NATURAL SCIENCE	21 624	10 717	—	—	20 343	10 025	1 281	692
		MATHEMATICS & COMPUTER SCIENCE	5 280	2 284	—	—	5 100	2 189	180	95
		MEDICAL AND HEALTH-RELATED SC.	4 581	1 813	—	—	4 477	1 768	104	45
		ENGINEERING	—	—	—	—	—	—	—	—
		ARCHITECTURE & TOWN PLANNING	—	—	—	—	—	—	—	—
		TRADE, CRAFT & INDUSTR. PGMS.	—	—	—	—	—	—	—	—
		TRANSPORT AND COMMUNICATIONS	—	—	—	—	—	—	—	—
		AGRICULTURE,FORESTRY & FISH'G.	928	192	—	—	928	192	—	—
		OTHER AND NOT SPECIFIED	—	—	—	—	—	—	—	—
CYPRUS	1977	TOTAL	1 097	595	1 097	595	—	—	—	—
		EDUCATION SCIENCE & TCHR TRNG.	127	101	127	101	—	—	—	—
		HUMANITIES,RELIGION & THEOLOG.	—	—	—	—	—	—	—	—
		FINE AND APPLIED ARTS	—	—	—	—	—	—	—	—
		LAW	—	—	—	—	—	—	—	—
		SOCIAL AND BEHAVIOURAL SCIENCE	210	210	210	210	—	—	—	—
		COMMERCIAL & BUS. ADMINISTR.	—	—	—	—	—	—	—	—
		MASS COMMUNICATION & DOCUMENT.	—	—	—	—	—	—	—	—
		HOME ECONOMICS & DOMESTIC SC.	—	—	—	—	—	—	—	—
		SERVICE TRADES	115	37	115	37	—	—	—	—
		MEDICAL AND HEALTH-RELATED SC.	276	202	276	202	—	—	—	—
		ENGINEERING, TOTAL	347	45	347	45	—	—	—	—
		AGRICULTURE,FORESTRY & FISH'G.	22	—	22	—	—	—	—	—
		OTHER AND NOT SPECIFIED	—	—	—	—	—	—	—	—

3.12   Third level: students by levels and fields
Troisième degré: étudiants par types de programmes et domaines d'études
Tercer grado: estudiantes por tipos de programas y sectores de estudio

INTERNATIONAL STANDARD CLASSIFICATION OF EDUCATION BY LEVEL
CLASSIFICATION INTERNATIONALE TYPE DE L'EDUCATION PAR NIVEAUX
CLASIFICACION INTERNACIONAL NORMALIZADA DE LA EDUCACION POR GRADOS

COUNTRY / PAYS / PAIS	YEAR / ANNEE / AÑO	FIELD OF STUDY / BRANCHE D'ETUDES / RAMAS DE ESTUDIO	ALL LEVELS / TOUS NIVEAUX / TODOS LOS GRADOS MF	F	LEVEL 5 / NIVEAU 5 / GRADO 5 MF	F	LEVEL 6 / NIVEAU 6 / GRADO 6 MF	F	LEVEL 7 / NIVEAU 7 / GRADO 7 MF	F
HONG KONG	1976	TOTAL	44 210	11 939	35 371	9 168	7 606	2 370	1 233	401
		EDUCATION SCIENCE & TCHR TRNG.	3 275	1 952	2 650	1 685	—	—	625	267
		HUMANITIES,RELIGION & THEOLOG.	3 436	1 821	1 576	829	1 681	952	179	40
		FINE AND APPLIED ARTS	773	327	667	266	106	61	—	—
		LAW	196	70	29	2	138	56	29	12
		SOCIAL AND BEHAVIOURAL SCIENCE	3 904	1 730	2 172	1 000	1 655	701	77	29
		COMMERCIAL & BUS. ADMINISTR.	10 484	4 269	9 691	4 081	739	185	54	3
		MASS COMMUNICATION & DOCUMENT.	687	292	616	263	71	29	—	—
		HOME ECONOMICS & DOMESTIC SC.	—	—	—	—	—	—	—	—
		SERVICE TRADES	—	—	—	—	—	—	—	—
		NATURAL SCIENCE	2 123	365	599	113	1 396	216	128	36
		MATHEMATICS & COMPUTER SCIENCE	1 068	192	885	170	173	22	10	—
		MEDICAL AND HEALTH-RELATED SC.	800	116	—	—	765	106	35	10
		ENGINEERING	11 013	202	10 236	193	686	7	91	2
		ARCHITECTURE & TOWN PLANNING	2 243	127	2 042	90	196	35	5	2
		TRADE, CRAFT & INDUSTR. PGMS.	3 466	354	3 466	354	—	—	—	—
		TRANSPORT AND COMMUNICATIONS	—	—	—	—	—	—	—	—
		AGRICULTURE,FORESTRY & FISH'G.	—	—	—	—	—	—	—	—
		OTHER AND NOT SPECIFIED	742	122	742	122	—	—	—	—
	1977	TOTAL	...	...	...	...	8 218	2 572	1 557	508
		EDUCATION SCIENCE & TCHR TRNG.	2 080	1 165	—	—	1 794	1 061	818	346
		HUMANITIES,RELIGION & THEOLOG.	699	279	390	164	102	59	207	56
		FINE AND APPLIED ARTS	180	68	33	15	147	53	—	—
		LAW	—	—	—	—	—	—	33	15
		SOCIAL AND BEHAVIOURAL SCIENCE	2 007	903	189	115	1 717	753	101	35
		COMMERCIAL & BUS. ADMINISTR.	9 032	3 521	8 105	3 298	824	210	103	13
		MASS COMMUNICATION & DOCUMENT.	87	37	—	—	83	36	4	1
		HOME ECONOMICS & DOMESTIC SC.	—	—	—	—	—	—	—	—
		SERVICE TRADES	—	—	—	—	—	—	—	—
		NATURAL SCIENCE	2 034	339	651	101	1 261	211	122	27
		MATHEMATICS & COMPUTER SCIENCE	1 019	259	771	223	240	36	8	—
		MEDICAL AND HEALTH-RELATED SC.	804	107	—	—	762	97	42	10
		ENGINEERING	12 829	234	11 676	217	1 039	14	114	3
		ARCHITECTURE & TOWN PLANNING	224	41	—	—	219	39	5	2
		TRADE, CRAFT & INDUSTR. PGMS.	1 372	264	1 342	261	30	3	—	—
		TRANSPORT AND COMMUNICATIONS	—	—	—	—	—	—	—	—
		AGRICULTURE,FORESTRY & FISH'G.	—	—	—	—	—	—	—	—
		OTHER AND NOT SPECIFIED	263	8	263	8	—	—	—	—

INTERNATIONAL STANDARD CLASSIFICATION OF EDUCATION BY LEVEL
CLASSIFICATION INTERNATIONALE TYPE DE L'EDUCATION PAR NIVEAUX
CLASIFICACION INTERNACIONAL NORMALIZADA DE LA EDUCACION POR GRADOS

COUNTRY PAYS PAIS	YEAR ANNEE AÑO	FIELD OF STUDY BRANCHE D'ETUDES RAMAS DE ESTUDIO	ALL LEVELS TOUS NIVEAUX TODOS LOS GRADOS		LEVEL 5 NIVEAU 5 GRADO 5		LEVEL 6 NIVEAU 6 GRADO 6		LEVEL 7 NIVEAU 7 GRADO 7	
			MF	F	MF	F	MF	F	MF	F
INDIA ‡	1975	TOTAL	4 615 992	1 070 962	2 095 556	464 826	2 239 345	538 904	281 091	67 232
		EDUCATION SCIENCE & TCHR TRNG.	185 772	67 298	105 614	36 821	74 475	28 549	5 683	1 928
		HUMANITIES,RELIGION & THEOLOG.	2 127 995	650 669	1 008 590	253 885	974 116	350 718	145 289	46 066
		FINE AND APPLIED ARTS	143 593	7 511	-	-	140 527	7 329	3 066	182
		LAW	./.	./.	./.	./.	./.	./.	./.	./.
		SOCIAL AND BEHAVIOURAL SCIENCE	616 983	55 803	208 295	29 831	377 296	24 758	31 392	1 214
		COMMERCIAL & BUS. ADMINISTR.	./.	./.	./.	./.	./.	./.	./.	./.
		MASS COMMUNICATION & DOCUMENT.	-	-	-	-	-	-	-	-
		HOME ECONOMICS & DOMESTIC SC.	12 388	12 387	2 216	2 216	9 074	9 074	1 098	1 097
		SERVICE TRADES	-	-	-	-	-	-	-	-
		NATURAL SCIENCE	1 013 002	215 939	519 304	110 215	441 078	94 464	52 620	11 260
		MATHEMATICS & COMPUTER SCIENCE	134 742	33 038	22 345	11 115	101 151	19 086	11 246	2 837
		MEDICAL AND HEALTH-RELATED SC.	302 023	15 083	202 234	13 355	85 821	1 280	13 968	448
		ENGINEERING	./.	./.	./.	./.	./.	./.	./.	./.
		ARCHITECTURE & TOWN PLANNING	./.	./.	./.	./.	./.	./.	./.	./.
		TRADE, CRAFT & INDUSTR. PGMS.	./.	./.	./.	./.	./.	./.	./.	./.
		TRANSPORT AND COMMUNICATIONS	./.	./.	./.	./.	./.	./.	./.	./.
		AGRICULTURE,FORESTRY & FISH'G.	40 087	772	7 492	205	24 972	331	7 623	236
		OTHER AND NOT SPECIFIED	39 407	12 462	19 466	7 183	10 835	3 315	9 106	1 964
INDONESIA	1976	TOTAL	296 326	83 158						
		EDUCATION SCIENCE & TCHR TRNG.	73 366	27 902						
		HUMANITIES,RELIGION & THEOLOG.	5 324	2 933						
		FINE AND APPLIED ARTS	2 826	62						
		LAW	27 535	7 557						
		SOCIAL AND BEHAVIOURAL SCIENCE	45 785	11 060						
		COMMERCIAL & BUS. ADMINISTR.	6 347	1 232						
		MASS COMMUNICATION & DOCUMENT.	2 295	786						
		HOME ECONOMICS & DOMESTIC SC.	949	377						
		SERVICE TRADES	110	30						
		NATURAL SCIENCE	6 490	2 563						
		MATHEMATICS & COMPUTER SCIENCE	922	250						
		MEDICAL AND HEALTH-RELATED SC.	14 588	5 798						
		ENGINEERING	22 014	2 296						
		ARCHITECTURE & TOWN PLANNING	3 008	562						
		TRADE, CRAFT & INDUSTR. PGMS.	7 538	808						
		TRANSPORT AND COMMUNICATIONS	526	9						
		AGRICULTURE,FORESTRY & FISH'G.	16 822	3 600						
		OTHER AND NOT SPECIFIED	59 881	15 333						

3.12   Third level: students by levels and fields
       Troisième degré: étudiants par types de programmes et domaines d'études
       Tercer grado: estudiantes por tipos de programas y sectores de estudio

INTERNATIONAL STANDARD CLASSIFICATION OF EDUCATION BY LEVEL
CLASSIFICATION INTERNATIONALE TYPE DE L'EDUCATION PAR NIVEAUX
CLASIFICACION INTERNACIONAL NORMALIZADA DE LA EDUCACION POR GRADOS

COUNTRY / PAYS / PAIS	YEAR / ANNEE / AÑO	FIELD OF STUDY / BRANCHE D'ETUDES / RAMAS DE ESTUDIO	ALL LEVELS / TOUS NIVEAUX / TODOS LOS GRADOS		LEVEL 5 / NIVEAU 5 / GRADO 5		LEVEL 6 / NIVEAU 6 / GRADO 6		LEVEL 7 / NIVEAU 7 / GRADO 7	
			MF	F	MF	F	MF	F	MF	F
IRAN	1976	TOTAL	154 215	46 019	48 249	13 149	89 295	28 921	16 671	3 949
		EDUCATION SCIENCE & TCHR TRNG.	5 342	2 765	726	123	4 287	2 488	329	154
		HUMANITIES,RELIGION & THEOLOG.	26 348	11 429	9 353	3 717	16 401	7 495	594	217
		FINE AND APPLIED ARTS	4 659	1 820	1 473	716	2 078	858	1 108	246
		LAW	2 973	676	—	—	2 893	668	80	8
		SOCIAL SCIENCES, TOTAL	27 093	8 568	3 133	935	22 753	7 350	1 207	283
		NATURAL SCIENCES, TOTAL	27 317	6 885	8 418	2 278	18 461	4 495	438	112
		MEDICAL AND HEALTH-RELATED SC.	19 235	9 812	4 402	3 382	5 254	3 847	9 579	2 583
		ENGINEERING, TOTAL	34 411	3 063	19 371	1 898	12 473	941	2 567	224
		AGRICULTURE,FORESTRY & FISH'G.	6 837	1 001	1 373	100	4 695	779	769	122
		OTHER AND NOT SPECIFIED	—	—	—	—	—	—	—	—
IRAQ	1976	TOTAL	91 358	29 207	19 249	7 662	70 376	21 256	1 763	289
		EDUCATION, SCIENCE & TCHR TRNG.	16 900	7 273	7 665	4 245	9 190	3 023	45	5
		HUMANITIES,RELIGION & THEOLOG.	6 901	2 560	—	—	6 825	2 540	76	20
		FINE AND APPLIED ARTS	1 007	352	135	102	872	250	—	—
		LAW	2 761	489	—	—	2 661	484	100	5
		SOCIAL AND BEHAVIOURAL SCIENCE	6 800	2 530	127	68	6 572	2 453	101	9
		COMMERCIAL & BUS. ADMINISTR.	10 182	3 692	3 287	1 407	6 667	2 267	228	18
		MASS COMMUNICATION & DOCUMENT.	347	101	148	72	173	20	26	9
		HOME ECONOMICS & DOMESTIC SC.	101	101	101	101	—	—	—	—
		SERVICE TRADES	532	205	532	205	—	—	—	—
		NATURAL SCIENCE	6 310	2 223	—	—	5 981	2 133	329	90
		MATHEMATICS & COMPUTER SCIENCE	5 713	2 255	287	155	5 359	2 083	67	17
		MEDICAL AND HEALTH-RELATED SC.	6 290	2 163	453	51	5 630	2 035	207	77
		ENGINEERING	17 544	3 339	4 820	963	12 427	2 359	297	17
		ARCHITECTURE & TOWN PLANNING	343	110	—	—	303	105	40	5
		TRADE, CRAFT & INDUSTR. PGMS.	322	99	—	—	287	93	35	6
		TRANSPORT AND COMMUNICATIONS	—	—	—	—	—	—	—	—
		AGRICULTURE,FORESTRY & FISH'G.	8 472	1 443	1 694	293	6 566	1 139	212	11
		OTHER AND NOT SPECIFIED	833	272	—	—	833	272	—	—

Third level: students by levels and fields 3.12
Troisième degré: étudiants par types de programmes et domaines d'études
Tercer grado: estudiantes por tipos de programas y sectores de estudio

INTERNATIONAL STANDARD CLASSIFICATION OF EDUCATION BY LEVEL
CLASSIFICATION INTERNATIONALE TYPE DE L'EDUCATION PAR NIVEAUX
CLASIFICACION INTERNACIONAL NORMALIZADA DE LA EDUCACION POR GRADOS

COUNTRY / PAYS / PAIS	YEAR / ANNEE / AÑO	FIELD OF STUDY / BRANCHE D'ETUDES / RAMAS DE ESTUDIO	ALL LEVELS / TOUS NIVEAUX / TODOS LOS GRADOS		LEVEL 5 / NIVEAU 5 / GRADO 5		LEVEL 6 / NIVEAU 6 / GRADO 6		LEVEL 7 / NIVEAU 7 / GRADO 7	
			MF	F	MF	F	MF	F	MF	F
ISRAEL ‡	1976	TOTAL	85 081	39 368	32 101	16 110	40 020	17 919	12 960	5 339
		EDUCATION SCIENCE & TCHR TRNG.	29 939	22 837	14 073	11 886	11 828	8 308	4 038	2 643
		HUMANITIES,RELIGION & THEOLOG.	./.	./.	./.	./.	./.	./.	./.	./.
		FINE AND APPLIED ARTS	./.	./.	./.	./.	./.	./.	./.	./.
		LAW	1 624	519	—	—	1 502	499	122	20
		SOCIAL AND BEHAVIOURAL SCIENCE	15 528	5 936	1 952	351	10 514	4 397	3 062	1 188
		COMMERCIAL & BUS. ADMINISTR.	./.	./.	./.	./.	./.	./.	./.	./.
		MASS COMMUNICATION & DOCUMENT.	./.	./.	./.	./.	./.	./.	./.	./.
		HOME ECONOMICS & DOMESTIC SC.	./.	./.	./.	./.	./.	./.	./.	./.
		SERVICE TRADES	./.	./.	./.	./.	./.	./.	./.	./.
		NATURAL SCIENCE	6 742	3 014	./.	./.	4 131	2 068	2 611	946
		MATHEMATICS & COMPUTER SCIENCE	4 761	2 931	2 155	1 960	1 727	719	879	252
		MEDICAL AND HEALTH-RELATED SC.	./.	./.	./.	./.	./.	./.	./.	./.
		ENGINEERING	14 161	1 596	5 104	709	7 022	657	2 035	230
		ARCHITECTURE & TOWN PLANNING	./.	./.	./.	./.	./.	./.	./.	./.
		TRADE, CRAFT & INDUSTR. PGMS.	./.	./.	./.	./.	./.	./.	./.	./.
		TRANSPORT AND COMMUNICATIONS	./.	./.	./.	./.	./.	./.	./.	./.
		AGRICULTURE,FORESTRY & FISH'G.	1 039	234	./.	./.	826	174	213	60
		OTHER AND NOT SPECIFIED	11 287	2 301	8 817	1 204	2 470	1 097	./.	./.
	1977	TOTAL	83 671	39 230	32 091	16 334	38 633	17 647	12 947	5 249
		EDUCATION SCIENCE & TCHR TRNG.	29 528	22 671	13 709	11 692	12 054	8 599	3 765	2 380
		HUMANITIES,RELIGION & THEOLOG.	./.	./.	./.	./.	./.	./.	./.	./.
		FINE AND APPLIED ARTS	./.	./.	./.	./.	./.	./.	./.	./.
		LAW	1 640	575	—	—	1 468	537	172	38
		SOCIAL AND BEHAVIOURAL SCIENCE	16 813	6 519	2 287	539	11 435	4 722	3 091	1 258
		COMMERCIAL & BUS. ADMINISTR.	./.	./.	./.	./.	./.	./.	./.	./.
		MASS COMMUNICATION & DOCUMENT.	./.	./.	./.	./.	./.	./.	./.	./.
		HOME ECONOMICS & DOMESTIC SC.	./.	./.	./.	./.	./.	./.	./.	./.
		SERVICE TRADES	./.	./.	./.	./.	./.	./.	./.	./.
		NATURAL SCIENCE	6 915	3 039	./.	./.	4 095	2 027	2 820	1 012
		MATHEMATICS & COMPUTER SCIENCE	5 207	3 268	2 388	2 156	1 893	848	926	264
		MEDICAL AND HEALTH-RELATED SC.	./.	./.	./.	./.	./.	./.	./.	./.
		ENGINEERING	13 443	1 627	4 799	734	6 761	672	1 883	221
		ARCHITECTURE & TOWN PLANNING	./.	./.	./.	./.	./.	./.	./.	./.
		TRADE, CRAFT & INDUSTR. PGMS.	./.	./.	./.	./.	./.	./.	./.	./.
		TRANSPORT AND COMMUNICATIONS	./.	./.	./.	./.	./.	./.	./.	./.
		AGRICULTURE,FORESTRY & FISH'G.	1 217	318	./.	./.	927	242	290	76
		OTHER AND NOT SPECIFIED	8 908	1 213	8 908	1 213	—	—	—	—

3.12 Third level: students by levels and fields
Troisième degré: étudiants par types de programmes et domaines d'études
Tercer grado: estudiantes por tipos de programas y sectores de estudio

INTERNATIONAL STANDARD CLASSIFICATION OF EDUCATION BY LEVEL
CLASSIFICATION INTERNATIONALE TYPE DE L'EDUCATION PAR NIVEAUX
CLASIFICACION INTERNACIONAL NORMALIZADA DE LA EDUCACION POR GRADOS

COUNTRY / PAYS / PAIS — YEAR / ANNEE / AÑO — FIELD OF STUDY / BRANCHE D'ETUDES / RAMAS DE ESTUDIO	ALL LEVELS TOUS NIVEAUX TODOS LOS GRADOS MF	F	LEVEL 5 NIVEAU 5 GRADO 5 MF	F	LEVEL 6 NIVEAU 6 GRADO 6 MF	F	LEVEL 7 NIVEAU 7 GRADO 7 MF	F
JAPAN ‡ — 1976								
TOTAL	2 299 344	763 162	455 965	342 276	1 791 523	416 080	51 856	4 806
EDUCATION SCIENCE & TCHR TRNG.	227 755	178 289	88 037	87 675	138 087	90 165	1 631	449
HUMANITIES,RELIGION & THEOLOG.	321 990	218 242	74 891	73 296	238 620	142 905	8 479	2 041
FINE AND APPLIED ARTS	63 330	42 993	21 680	18 530	40 588	24 085	1 062	378
LAW	795 347	85 082	46 522	22 400	741 943	62 146	6 882	536
SOCIAL AND BEHAVIOURAL SCIENCE	./.	./.	./.	./.	./.	./.	./.	./.
COMMERCIAL & BUS. ADMINISTR.	./.	./.	./.	./.	./.	./.	./.	./.
MASS COMMUNICATION & DOCUMENT.	./.	./.	./.	./.	./.	./.	./.	./.
HOME ECONOMICS & DOMESTIC SC.	134 957	134 624	99 211	99 024	35 499	35 372	247	228
SERVICE TRADES	-	-	-	-	-	-	-	-
NATURAL SCIENCE	43 757	5 252	-	-	38 455	4 918	5 302	334
MATHEMATICS & COMPUTER SCIENCE	14 042	2 857	160	152	13 088	2 645	794	60
MEDICAL AND HEALTH-RELATED SC.	115 131	42 602	11 614	10 549	98 253	31 619	5 264	434
ENGINEERING	402 255	4 563	38 978	1 307	345 105	3 138	18 172	118
ARCHITECTURE & TOWN PLANNING	./.	./.	./.	./.	./.	./.	./.	./.
TRADE, CRAFT & INDUSTR. PGMS.	./.	./.	./.	./.	./.	./.	./.	./.
TRANSPORT AND COMMUNICATIONS	3 775	-	1 846	-	1 882	-	47	-
AGRICULTURE,FORESTRY & FISH'G.	62 145	6 387	3 858	674	54 530	5 509	3 757	204
OTHER AND NOT SPECIFIED	114 860	42 271	69 168	28 669	45 473	13 578	219	24
JORDAN ‡ — 1977								
TOTAL	17 219	6 366	10 514	3 879	5 973	2 378	732	109
EDUCATION SCIENCE & TCHR TRNG.	7 599	3 373	6 543	3 020	478	267	578	86
HUMANITIES,RELIGION & THEOLOG.	2 839	1 223	50	-	2 705	1 207	84	16
FINE AND APPLIED ARTS	-	-	-	-	-	-	-	-
LAW	54	32	54	32	-	-	-	-
SOCIAL AND BEHAVIOURAL SCIENCE	2 517	654	2 517	654	-	-	-	-
COMMERCIAL & BUS. ADMINISTR.	-	-	-	-	-	-	-	-
MASS COMMUNICATION & DOCUMENT.	-	-	-	-	-	-	-	-
HOME ECONOMICS & DOMESTIC SC.	-	-	-	-	-	-	-	-
SERVICE TRADES	-	-	-	-	-	-	-	-
NATURAL SCIENCE	1 449	493	-	-	1 405	488	44	5
MATHEMATICS & COMPUTER SCIENCE	327	104	34	4	267	98	26	2
MEDICAL AND HEALTH-RELATED SC.	876	350	394	169	482	181	-	-
ENGINEERING	330	72	-	-	330	72	-	-
ARCHITECTURE & TOWN PLANNING	-	-	-	-	-	-	-	-
TRADE, CRAFT & INDUSTR. PGMS.	922	-	922	-	-	-	-	-
TRANSPORT AND COMMUNICATIONS	-	-	-	-	-	-	-	-
AGRICULTURE,FORESTRY & FISH'G.	306	65	-	-	306	65	-	-
OTHER AND NOT SPECIFIED	-	-	-	-	-	-	-	-

Third level: students by levels and fields 3.12
Troisième degré: étudiants par types de programmes et domaines d'études
Tercer grado: estudiantes por tipos de programas y sectores de estudio

INTERNATIONAL STANDARD CLASSIFICATION OF EDUCATION BY LEVEL
CLASSIFICATION INTERNATIONALE TYPE DE L'EDUCATION PAR NIVEAUX
CLASIFICACION INTERNACIONAL NORMALIZADA DE LA EDUCACION POR GRADOS

COUNTRY / PAYS / PAIS	YEAR / ANNEE / AÑO	FIELD OF STUDY / BRANCHE D'ETUDES / RAMAS DE ESTUDIO	ALL LEVELS / TOUS NIVEAUX / TODOS LOS GRADOS		LEVEL 5 / NIVEAU 5 / GRADO 5		LEVEL 6 / NIVEAU 6 / GRADO 6		LEVEL 7 / NIVEAU 7 / GRADO 7	
			MF	F	MF	F	MF	F	MF	F
KOREA, REPUBLIC OF	1978	TOTAL	418 875	104 515	121 942	33 257	277 783	68 160	19 150	3 098
		EDUCATION SCIENCE & TCHR TRNG.	51 707	26 221	5 026	3 060	43 928	22 383	2 753	778
		HUMANITIES,RELIGION & THEOLOG.	29 226	8 701	1 421	302	25 815	7 860	1 990	539
		FINE AND APPLIED ARTS	19 948	15 423	4 867	3 699	14 269	11 205	812	519
		LAW	6 675	198	-	-	6 051	182	624	16
		SOCIAL AND BEHAVIOURAL SCIENCE	37 309	2 923	2 962	817	31 331	1 943	3 016	163
		COMMERCIAL & BUS. ADMINISTR.	15 630	1 330	1 390	289	11 834	934	2 406	107
		MASS COMMUNICATION & DOCUMENT.	2 903	1 510	1 058	931	1 739	527	106	52
		HOME ECONOMICS & DOMESTIC SC.	4 718	4 704	350	337	4 192	4 192	176	175
		SERVICE TRADES	3 037	1 363	2 170	1 149	848	209	19	5
		NATURAL SCIENCE	14 784	6 093	457	436	13 418	5 437	909	220
		MATHEMATICS & COMPUTER SCIENCE	3 966	979	-	-	3 686	953	280	26
		MEDICAL AND HEALTH-RELATED SC.	37 401	17 518	15 505	10 542	19 195	6 566	2 701	410
		ENGINEERING	109 535	4 848	49 390	3 876	58 517	943	1 628	29
		ARCHITECTURE & TOWN PLANNING	24 033	249	11 971	140	11 177	89	885	20
		TRADE, CRAFT & INDUSTR. PGMS.	2 058	9	890	-	1 125	9	43	-
		TRANSPORT AND COMMUNICATIONS	3 946	62	3 477	61	469	1	-	-
		AGRICULTURE,FORESTRY & FISH'G.	34 054	3 014	11 871	1 095	21 381	1 880	802	39
		OTHER AND NOT SPECIFIED	17 945	9 370	9 137	6 523	8 808	2 847	-	-
KUWAIT	1977	TOTAL	12 391	6 638	2 663	1 449	9 318	5 045	410	144
		EDUCATION SCIENCE & TCHR TRNG.	2 341	1 725	1 037	635	1 304	1 090	-	-
		HUMANITIES,RELIGION & THEOLOG.	1 468	830	-	-	1 192	741	276	89
		FINE AND APPLIED ARTS	-	-	-	-	-	-	-	-
		LAW	535	202	-	-	535	202	-	-
		SOCIAL AND BEHAVIOURAL SCIENCE	2 186	1 360	-	-	2 186	1 360	-	-
		COMMERCIAL & BUS. ADMINISTR.	2 874	1 333	1 211	667	1 598	649	65	17
		MASS COMMUNICATION & DOCUMENT.	-	-	-	-	-	-	-	-
		HOME ECONOMICS & DOMESTIC SC.	-	-	-	-	-	-	-	-
		SERVICE TRADES	-	-	-	-	-	-	-	-
		NATURAL SCIENCE	1 121	540	-	-	1 052	502	69	38
		MATHEMATICS & COMPUTER SCIENCE	798	283	-	-	798	283	-	-
		MEDICAL AND HEALTH-RELATED SC.	249	196	147	147	102	49	-	-
		ENGINEERING	551	169	-	-	551	169	-	-
		ARCHITECTURE & TOWN PLANNING	-	-	-	-	-	-	-	-
		TRADE, CRAFT & INDUSTR. PGMS.	268	-	268	-	-	-	-	-
		TRANSPORT AND COMMUNICATIONS	-	-	-	-	-	-	-	-
		AGRICULTURE,FORESTRY & FISH'G.	-	-	-	-	-	-	-	-
		OTHER AND NOT SPECIFIED	-	-	-	-	-	-	-	-

3.12 Third level: students by levels and fields
Troisième degré: étudiants par types de programmes et domaines d'études
Tercer grado: estudiantes por tipos de programas y sectores de estudio

INTERNATIONAL STANDARD CLASSIFICATION OF EDUCATION BY LEVEL
CLASSIFICATION INTERNATIONALE TYPE DE L'EDUCATION PAR NIVEAUX
CLASIFICACION INTERNACIONAL NORMALIZADA DE LA EDUCACION POR GRADOS

COUNTRY / PAYS / PAIS	YEAR / ANNEE / AÑO	FIELD OF STUDY / BRANCHE D'ETUDES / RAMAS DE ESTUDIO	ALL LEVELS TOUS NIVEAUX TODOS LOS GRADOS MF	F	LEVEL 5 NIVEAU 5 GRADO 5 MF	F	LEVEL 6 NIVEAU 6 GRADO 6 MF	F	LEVEL 7 NIVEAU 7 GRADO 7 MF	F
MALAYSIA										
PENINSULAR MALAYSIA	1977	TOTAL	42 421	15 486	26 098	10 359	15 838	4 968	485	159
		EDUCATION SCIENCE & TCHR TRNG.	13 782	6 598	13 181	6 340	472	212	129	46
		HUMANITIES, RELIGION & THEOLOG.	1 473	567	13	5	1 340	522	120	40
		FINE AND APPLIED ARTS	257	107	257	107	—	—	—	—
		LAW	316	124	—	—	297	118	19	6
		SOCIAL AND BEHAVIOURAL SCIENCE	4 320	1 628	15	5	4 252	1 605	53	18
		COMMERCIAL & BUS. ADMINISTR.	5 929	2 605	4 531	2 143	1 398	462	—	—
		MASS COMMUNICATION & DOCUMENT.	224	149	224	149	—	—	—	—
		HOME ECONOMICS & DOMESTIC SC.	153	132	—	—	153	132	—	—
		SERVICE TRADES	342	191	342	191	—	—	—	—
		NATURAL SCIENCE	4 651	1 530	550	235	3 976	1 253	125	42
		MATHEMATICS & COMPUTER SCIENCE	257	123	257	123	—	—	—	—
		MEDICAL AND HEALTH-RELATED SC.	1 336	393	—	—	1 312	386	24	7
		ENGINEERING	6 056	652	4 614	585	1 433	67	9	7
		ARCHITECTURE & TOWN PLANNING	743	231	521	182	222	49	—	—
		TRADE CRAFT & INDUSTR PGMS	—	—	—	—	—	—	—	—
		TRANSPORT AND COMMUNICATIONS	106	25	106	25	—	—	—	—
		AGRICULTURE, FORESTRY & FISH'G.	2 476	431	1 487	269	983	162	6	—
		OTHER AND NOT SPECIFIED	—	—	—	—	—	—	—	—
SARAWAK	1976	TOTAL	≶ 1 097	...						
		EDUCATION SCIENCE & TCHR TRNG.	—	...						
		HUMANITIES, RELIGION & THEOLOG.	—	...						
		FINE AND APPLIED ARTS	—	—						
		LAW	—	—						
		SOCIAL SCIENCES, TOTAL	—	—						
		NATURAL SCIENCES, TOTAL	—	—						
		MEDICAL AND HEALTH-RELATED SC.	—	—						
		ENGINEERING, TOTAL	—	—						
		AGRICULTURE, FORESTRY & FISH'G.	—	—						
		OTHER AND NOT SPECIFIED	—	—						

Third level: students by levels and fields 3.12
Troisième degré: étudiants par types de programmes et domaines d'études
Tercer grado: estudiantes por tipos de programas y sectores de estudio

INTERNATIONAL STANDARD CLASSIFICATION OF EDUCATION BY LEVEL
CLASSIFICATION INTERNATIONALE TYPE DE L'EDUCATION PAR NIVEAUX
CLASIFICACION INTERNACIONAL NORMALIZADA DE LA EDUCACION POR GRADOS

COUNTRY / PAYS / PAIS	YEAR / ANNEE / AÑO	FIELD OF STUDY / BRANCHE D'ETUDES / RAMAS DE ESTUDIO	ALL LEVELS / TOUS NIVEAUX / TODOS LOS GRADOS MF	F	LEVEL 5 / NIVEAU 5 / GRADO 5 MF	F	LEVEL 6 / NIVEAU 6 / GRADO 6 MF	F	LEVEL 7 / NIVEAU 7 / GRADO 7 MF	F
NEPAL ‡	1977	TOTAL	25 398	5 504	3 577	759	20 680	4 538	1 141	207
		EDUCATION SCIENCE & TCHR TRNG.	4 884	1 043	964	148	3 904	888	16	7
		HUMANITIES,RELIGION & THEOLOG.	8 746	2 820	300	39	7 731	2 632	715	149
		FINE AND APPLIED ARTS	106	39	—	—	106	39	—	—
		LAW	1 250	104	—	—	1 250	104	—	—
		SOCIAL AND BEHAVIOURAL SCIENCE	3 977	365	—	—	3 704	344	273	21
		COMMERCIAL & BUS. ADMINISTR.	—	—	—	—	—	—	—	—
		MASS COMMUNICATION & DOCUMENT.	—	—	—	—	—	—	—	—
		HOME ECONOMICS & DOMESTIC SC.	—	—	—	—	—	—	—	—
		SERVICE TRADES	—	—	—	—	—	—	—	—
		NATURAL SCIENCE	2 136	314	—	—	1 999	284	137	30
		MATHEMATICS & COMPUTER SCIENCE	./.	./.	—	—	./.	./.	./.	./.
		MEDICAL AND HEALTH-RELATED SC.	1 869	819	698	572	1 171	247	—	—
		ENGINEERING	1 615	—	1 615	—	—	—	—	—
		ARCHITECTURE & TOWN PLANNING	—	—	—	—	—	—	—	—
		TRADE, CRAFT & INDUSTR. PGMS.	—	—	—	—	—	—	—	—
		TRANSPORT AND COMMUNICATIONS	—	—	—	—	—	—	—	—
		AGRICULTURE,FORESTRY & FISH'G.	815	—	—	—	815	—	—	—
		OTHER AND NOT SPECIFIED	—	—	—	—	—	—	—	—
PAKISTAN ‡	1975	TOTAL	127 932	30 096	15 905	1 728	98 802	24 578	13 225	3 790
		EDUCATION SCIENCE & TCHR TRNG.	4 861	2 461	770	182	3 586	2 155	505	124
		HUMANITIES,RELIGION & THEOLOG.	41 283	17 630	1 274	210	34 101	15 068	5 908	2 352
		FINE AND APPLIED ARTS	381	108	381	108	—	—	—	—
		LAW	12 632	211	—	—	12 632	211	—	—
		SOCIAL AND BEHAVIOURAL SCIENCE	12 070	494	2 597	202	8 110	213	1 363	79
		COMMERCIAL & BUS. ADMINISTR.	./.	./.	./.	./.	./.	./.	./.	./.
		MASS COMMUNICATION & DOCUMENT.	1 867	1 867	827	827	896	896	144	144
		HOME ECONOMICS & DOMESTIC SC.	./.	./.	./.	./.	./.	./.	./.	./.
		SERVICE TRADES	—	—	—	—	—	—	—	—
		NATURAL SCIENCE	18 294	3 496	208	28	14 202	2 473	3 884	995
		MATHEMATICS & COMPUTER SCIENCE	./.	./.	./.	./.	./.	./.	./.	./.
		MEDICAL AND HEALTH-RELATED SC.	16 919	3 664	1 954	171	14 955	3 491	10	2
		ENGINEERING	13 867	58	6 143	—	7 654	57	70	1
		ARCHITECTURE & TOWN PLANNING	./.	./.	./.	./.	./.	./.	./.	./.
		TRADE, CRAFT & INDUSTR. PGMS.	—	—	—	—	—	—	—	—
		TRANSPORT AND COMMUNICATIONS	—	—	—	—	—	—	—	—
		AGRICULTURE,FORESTRY & FISH'G.	5 675	71	1 751	—	2 666	14	1 258	57
		OTHER AND NOT SPECIFIED	83	36	—	—	—	—	83	36

3.12 Third level: students by levels and fields
Troisième degré: étudiants par types de programmes et domaines d'études
Tercer grado: estudiantes por tipos de programas y sectores de estudio

INTERNATIONAL STANDARD CLASSIFICATION OF EDUCATION BY LEVEL
CLASSIFICATION INTERNATIONALE TYPE DE L'EDUCATION PAR NIVEAUX
CLASIFICACION INTERNACIONAL NORMALIZADA DE LA EDUCACION POR GRADOS

COUNTRY / PAYS / PAIS	YEAR / ANNEE / AÑO	FIELD OF STUDY / BRANCHE D'ETUDES / RAMAS DE ESTUDIO	ALL LEVELS / TOUS NIVEAUX / TODOS LOS GRADOS		LEVEL 5 / NIVEAU 5 / GRADO 5		LEVEL 6 / NIVEAU 6 / GRADO 6		LEVEL 7 / NIVEAU 7 / GRADO 7	
			MF	F	MF	F	MF	F	MF	F
PAKISTAN (CONT.) ‡	1976	TOTAL	133 465	34 210	16 782	2 027	102 657	27 759	14 026	4 424
		EDUCATION SCIENCE & TCHR TRNG.	4 053	2 019	702	202	2 792	1 611	559	206
		HUMANITIES,RELIGION & THEOLOG.	44 134	20 205	1 384	318	36 411	17 196	6 339	2 691
		FINE AND APPLIED ARTS	422	121	422	121	-	-	-	-
		LAW	9 551	190	-	-	9 551	190	-	-
		SOCIAL AND BEHAVIOURAL SCIENCE	./.	./.	./.	./.	./.	./.	./.	./.
		COMMERCIAL & BUS. ADMINISTR.	12 459	582	2 536	241	8 334	252	1 589	89
		MASS COMMUNICATION & DOCUMENT.	./.	./.	./.	./.	./.	./.	./.	./.
		HOME ECONOMICS & DOMESTIC SC.	2 086	2 086	887	887	1 040	1 040	159	159
		SERVICE TRADES	./.	./.	./.	./.	./.	./.	./.	./.
		NATURAL SCIENCE	19 672	4 193	253	53	15 366	2 987	4 053	1 153
		MATHEMATICS & COMPUTER SCIENCE	./.	./.	./.	./.	./.	./.	./.	./.
		MEDICAL AND HEALTH-RELATED SC.	19 856	4 565	2 204	205	17 642	4 360	10	-
		ENGINEERING	14 639	89	6 322	-	8 214	87	103	2
		ARCHITECTURE & TOWN PLANNING	./.	./.	./.	./.	./.	./.	./.	./.
		TRADE,CRAFT & INDUSTR. PGMS.	./.	./.	./.	./.	./.	./.	./.	./.
		TRANSPORT AND COMMUNICATIONS	./.	./.	./.	./.	./.	./.	./.	./.
		AGRICULTURE,FORESTRY & FISH'G.	6 289	105	2 072	-	3 093	21	1 124	84
		OTHER AND NOT SPECIFIED	304	55	-	-	214	15	90	40
PHILIPPINES ‡	1976	TOTAL	814 889	...	-	-	768 764	...	46 125	-
		EDUCATION SCIENCE & TCHR TRNG.	42 282	...	-	-	42 282	...	-	-
		HUMANITIES,RELIGION & THEOLOG.	-	-	-	-	-	-	-	-
		FINE AND APPLIED ARTS	6 918	...	-	-	6 918	...	-	-
		LAW	12 300	...	-	-	12 300	...	-	-
		SOCIAL AND BEHAVIOURAL SCIENCE	125 309	...	-	-	125 309	...	-	-
		COMMERCIAL & BUS. ADMINISTR.	360 550	...	-	-	360 550	...	-	-
		MASS COMMUNICATION & DOCUMENT.	-	-	-	-	-	-	-	-
		HOME ECONOMICS & DOMESTIC SC.	6 919	...	-	-	6 919	...	-	-
		SERVICE TRADES	-	-	-	-	-	-	-	-
		NATURAL SCIENCE	4 613	...	-	-	4 613	...	-	-
		MATHEMATICS & COMPUTER SCIENCE	-	-	-	-	-	-	-	-
		MEDICAL AND HEALTH-RELATED SC.	42 282	...	-	-	42 282	...	-	-
		ENGINEERING	133 765	...	-	-	133 765	...	-	-
		ARCHITECTURE & TOWN PLANNING	-	-	-	-	-	-	-	-
		TRADE,CRAFT & INDUSTR. PGMS.	-	-	-	-	-	-	-	-
		TRANSPORT AND COMMUNICATIONS	9 994	...	-	-	9 994	...	-	-
		AGRICULTURE,FORESTRY & FISH'G.	23 832	...	-	-	23 832	...	-	-
		OTHER AND NOT SPECIFIED	46 125	...	-	-	-	...	46 125	-

Third level: students by levels and fields 3.12
Troisième degré: étudiants par types de programmes et domaines d'études
Tercer grado: estudiantes por tipos de programas y sectores de estudio

INTERNATIONAL STANDARD CLASSIFICATION OF EDUCATION BY LEVEL
CLASSIFICATION INTERNATIONALE TYPE DE L'EDUCATION PAR NIVEAUX
CLASIFICACION INTERNACIONAL NORMALIZADA DE LA EDUCACION POR GRADOS

COUNTRY PAYS PAIS	YEAR ANNEE AÑO	FIELD OF STUDY BRANCHE D'ETUDES RAMAS DE ESTUDIO	ALL LEVELS TOUS NIVEAUX TODOS LOS GRADOS MF	F	LEVEL 5 NIVEAU 5 GRADO 5 MF	F	LEVEL 6 NIVEAU 6 GRADO 6 MF	F	LEVEL 7 NIVEAU 7 GRADO 7 MF	F
QATAR	1976	TOTAL	910	*522	—	—	765	516	145	*6
		EDUCATION SCIENCE & TCHR TRNG.	910	*522	—	—	765	516	145	*6
		HUMANITIES,RELIGION & THEOLOG.	—	—	—	—	—	—	—	—
		FINE AND APPLIED ARTS	—	—	—	—	—	—	—	—
		LAW	—	—	—	—	—	—	—	—
		SOCIAL AND BEHAVIOURAL SCIENCE	—	—	—	—	—	—	—	—
		COMMERCIAL & BUS. ADMINISTR.	—	—	—	—	—	—	—	—
		MASS COMMUNICATION & DOCUMENT.	—	—	—	—	—	—	—	—
		HOME ECONOMICS & DOMESTIC SC.	—	—	—	—	—	—	—	—
		SERVICE TRADES	—	—	—	—	—	—	—	—
		NATURAL SCIENCE	—	—	—	—	—	—	—	—
		MATHEMATICS & COMPUTER SCIENCE	—	—	—	—	—	—	—	—
		MEDICAL AND HEALTH-RELATED SC.	—	—	—	—	—	—	—	—
		ENGINEERING	—	—	—	—	—	—	—	—
		ARCHITECTURE & TOWN PLANNING	—	—	—	—	—	—	—	—
		TRADE, CRAFT & INDUSTR. PGMS.	—	—	—	—	—	—	—	—
		TRANSPORT AND COMMUNICATIONS	—	—	—	—	—	—	—	—
		AGRICULTURE,FORESTRY & FISH'G.	—	—	—	—	—	—	—	—
		OTHER AND NOT SPECIFIED	—	—	—	—	—	—	—	—
SAUDI ARABIA ‡	1977	TOTAL	43 897	9 187	2 281	—	41 616	9 187	—	—
		EDUCATION SCIENCE & TCHR TRNG.	6 248	2 348	1 769	—	4 479	2 348	—	—
		HUMANITIES,RELIGION & THEOLOG.	19 200	4 453	—	—	19 200	4 453	—	—
		FINE AND APPLIED ARTS	—	—	—	—	—	—	—	—
		LAW	—	—	—	—	—	—	—	—
		SOCIAL AND BEHAVIOURAL SCIENCE	./.	./.	—	—	./.	./.	—	—
		COMMERCIAL & BUS. ADMINISTR.	110	110	—	—	110	110	—	—
		MASS COMMUNICATION & DOCUMENT.	9 341	1 455	229	—	9 112	1 455	—	—
		HOME ECONOMICS & DOMESTIC SC.	—	—	—	—	—	—	—	—
		SERVICE TRADES	—	—	—	—	—	—	—	—
		NATURAL SCIENCE	2 465	313	—	—	2 465	313	—	—
		MATHEMATICS & COMPUTER SCIENCE	1 487	./.	—	—	1 487	./.	—	—
		MEDICAL AND HEALTH-RELATED SC.	3 669	422	—	—	3 669	422	—	—
		ENGINEERING	—	—	—	—	—	—	—	—
		ARCHITECTURE & TOWN PLANNING	283	—	283	—	—	—	—	—
		TRADE, CRAFT & INDUSTR. PGMS.	—	—	—	—	—	—	—	—
		TRANSPORT AND COMMUNICATIONS	—	—	—	—	—	—	—	—
		AGRICULTURE,FORESTRY & FISH'G.	871	—	—	—	871	—	—	—
		OTHER AND NOT SPECIFIED	223	86	—	—	223	86	—	—

3.12 Third level: students by levels and fields
Troisième degré: étudiants par types de programmes et domaines d'études
Tercer grado: estudiantes por tipos de programas y sectores de estudio

COUNTRY / PAYS / PAIS	YEAR / ANNEE / AÑO	FIELD OF STUDY / BRANCHE D'ETUDES / RAMAS DE ESTUDIO	INTERNATIONAL STANDARD CLASSIFICATION OF EDUCATION BY LEVEL — CLASSIFICATION INTERNATIONALE TYPE DE L'EDUCATION PAR NIVEAUX — CLASIFICACION INTERNACIONAL NORMALIZADA DE LA EDUCACION POR GRADOS							
			ALL LEVELS / TOUS NIVEAUX / TODOS LOS GRADOS		LEVEL 5 / NIVEAU 5 / GRADO 5		LEVEL 6 / NIVEAU 6 / GRADO 6		LEVEL 7 / NIVEAU 7 / GRADO 7	
			MF	F	MF	F	MF	F	MF	F
SINGAPORE ‡	1977	TOTAL	24 053	9 103	11 853	3 000	11 102	5 535	1 098	568
		EDUCATION SCIENCE & TCHR TRNG.	4 659	3 208	1 218	955	2 772	1 745	669	508
		HUMANITIES,RELIGION & THEOLOG.	2 146	1 288	—	—	2 078	1 266	68	22
		FINE AND APPLIED ARTS	—	—	—	—	—	—	—	—
		LAW	457	266	—	—	448	262	9	4
		SOCIAL AND BEHAVIOURAL SCIENCE	./.	./.	—	—	./.	./.	./.	./.
		COMMERCIAL & BUS. ADMINISTR.	2 920	1 388	711	391	2 093	985	116	12
		MASS COMMUNICATION & DOCUMENT.	—	—	—	—	—	—	—	—
		HOME ECONOMICS & DOMESTIC SC.	—	—	—	—	—	—	—	—
		SERVICE TRADES	—	—	—	—	—	—	—	—
		NATURAL SCIENCE	1 399	648	—	—	1 358	638	41	10
		MATHEMATICS & COMPUTER SCIENCE	—	—	—	—	—	—	—	—
		MEDICAL AND HEALTH-RELATED SC.	841	361	—	—	814	356	27	5
		ENGINEERING	9 666	1 333	8 468	1 223	1 036	103	162	7
		ARCHITECTURE & TOWN PLANNING	1 780	611	1 271	431	503	180	6	—
		TRADE, CRAFT & INDUSTR. PGMS.	—	—	—	—	—	—	—	—
		TRANSPORT AND COMMUNICATIONS	185	—	185	—	—	—	—	—
		AGRICULTURE,FORESTRY & FISH'G.	—	—	—	—	—	—	—	—
		OTHER AND NOT SPECIFIED	—	—	—	—	—	—	—	—
SRI LANKA ‡	1976	TOTAL	13 154	...	—	—	13 154	—	—	—
		EDUCATION SCIENCE & TCHR TRNG.	794	...	—	—	794	—	—	—
		HUMANITIES,RELIGION & THEOLOG.	7 110	...	—	—	7 110	—	—	—
		FINE AND APPLIED ARTS	—	...	—	—	—	—	—	—
		LAW	152	...	—	—	152	—	—	—
		SOCIAL SCIENCES, TOTAL	./.	...	—	—	./.	—	—	—
		NATURAL SCIENCES, TOTAL	1 870	...	—	—	1 870	—	—	—
		MEDICAL AND HEALTH-RELATED SC.	1 444	...	—	—	1 444	—	—	—
		ENGINEERING, TOTAL	1 270	...	—	—	1 270	—	—	—
		AGRICULTURE,FORESTRY & FISH'G.	514	...	—	—	514	—	—	—
		OTHER AND NOT SPECIFIED	—	...	—	—	—	—	—	—

Third level: students by levels and fields 3.12
Troisième degré: étudiants par types de programmes et domaines d'études
Tercer grado: estudiantes por tipos de programas y sectores de estudio

INTERNATIONAL STANDARD CLASSIFICATION OF EDUCATION BY LEVEL
CLASSIFICATION INTERNATIONALE TYPE DE L'EDUCATION PAR NIVEAUX
CLASIFICACION INTERNACIONAL NORMALIZADA DE LA EDUCACION POR GRADOS

COUNTRY / PAYS / PAIS	YEAR / ANNEE / AÑO	FIELD OF STUDY / BRANCHE D'ETUDES / RAMAS DE ESTUDIO	ALL LEVELS TOUS NIVEAUX TODOS LOS GRADOS		LEVEL 5 NIVEAU 5 GRADO 5		LEVEL 6 NIVEAU 6 GRADO 6		LEVEL 7 NIVEAU 7 GRADO 7	
			MF	F	MF	F	MF	F	MF	F
SYRIAN ARAB REPUBLIC	1976	TOTAL	83 260	20 762						
		EDUCATION SCIENCE & TCHR TRNG.	6 181	3 606						
		HUMANITIES,RELIGION & THEOLOG.	22 975	7 458						
		FINE AND APPLIED ARTS	618	204						
		LAW	9 322	1 170						
		SOCIAL AND BEHAVIOURAL SCIENCE	440	116						
		COMMERCIAL & BUS. ADMINISTR.	5 590	1 439						
		MASS COMMUNICATION & DOCUMENT.	—	—						
		HOME ECONOMICS & DOMESTIC SC.	—	—						
		SERVICE TRADES	—	—						
		NATURAL SCIENCE	9 044	2 331						
		MATHEMATICS & COMPUTER SCIENCE	—	—						
		MEDICAL AND HEALTH-RELATED SC.	7 511	1 936						
		ENGINEERING	13 001	1 537						
		ARCHITECTURE & TOWN PLANNING	—	—						
		TRADE, CRAFT & INDUSTR. PGMS.	—	—						
		TRANSPORT AND COMMUNICATIONS	—	—						
		AGRICULTURE,FORESTRY & FISH'G.	8 578	965						
		OTHER AND NOT SPECIFIED	—	—						
THAILAND ‡	1976	TOTAL	175 438	77 902	5 308	1 497	162 067	72 796	8 063	3 609
		EDUCATION SCIENCE & TCHR TRNG.	36 802	19 341	—	—	35 298	18 594	1 504	747
		HUMANITIES,RELIGION & THEOLOG.	14 685	10 111	—	—	14 162	9 731	523	380
		FINE AND APPLIED ARTS	1 418	329	—	—	1 306	293	112	36
		LAW	31 274	4 079	—	—	30 829	3 969	445	110
		SOCIAL SCIENCES, TOTAL	57 378	32 773	113	72	53 869	31 193	3 396	1 508
		NATURAL SCIENCES, TOTAL	9 781	5 123	96	45	9 024	4 713	661	365
		MEDICAL AND HEALTH-RELATED SC.	9 144	4 594	1 106	1 086	7 683	309	355	199
		ENGINEERING, TOTAL	10 758	496	3 993	294	6 071	106	694	96
		AGRICULTURE,FORESTRY & FISH'G.	4 198	1 056	—	—	3 825	888	373	168
		OTHER AND NOT SPECIFIED	—	—	—	—	—	—	—	—

3.12 Third level: students by levels and fields
Troisième degré: étudiants par types de programmes et domaines d'études
Tercer grado: estudiantes por tipos de programas y sectores de estudio

INTERNATIONAL STANDARD CLASSIFICATION OF EDUCATION BY LEVEL
CLASSIFICATION INTERNATIONALE TYPE DE L'EDUCATION PAR NIVEAUX
CLASIFICACION INTERNACIONAL NORMALIZADA DE LA EDUCACION POR GRADOS

COUNTRY / PAYS / PAIS	YEAR / ANNEE / AÑO	FIELD OF STUDY / BRANCHE D'ETUDES / RAMAS DE ESTUDIO	ALL LEVELS / TOUS NIVEAUX / TODOS LOS GRADOS MF	F	LEVEL 5 / NIVEAU 5 / GRADO 5 MF	F	LEVEL 6 / NIVEAU 6 / GRADO 6 MF	F	LEVEL 7 / NIVEAU 7 / GRADO 7 MF	F
THAILAND (CONT.) ‡	1977	TOTAL	216 876	92 353	3 721	806	204 799	87 863	8 356	3 684
		EDUCATION SCIENCE & TCHR TRNG.	38 949	21 829	—	—	37 280	21 025	1 669	804
		HUMANITIES,RELIGION & THEOLOG.	11 234	9 661	—	—	10 705	9 283	529	378
		FINE AND APPLIED ARTS	1 550	385	—	—	1 367	322	183	63
		LAW	46 019	7 270	—	—	45 611	7 160	408	110
		SOCIAL AND BEHAVIOURAL SCIENCE	40 421	14 389	—	—	38 462	13 631	1 959	758
		COMMERCIAL & BUS. ADMINISTR.	41 236	26 547	913	595	39 380	25 504	943	448
		MASS COMMUNICATION & DOCUMENT.	2 004	1 430	—	—	2 004	1 430	—	—
		HOME ECONOMICS & DOMESTIC SC.	—	—	—	—	—	—	—	—
		SERVICE TRADES	460	200	—	—	460	200	—	—
		NATURAL SCIENCE	8 536	3 500	—	—	7 772	3 093	764	407
		MATHEMATICS & COMPUTER SCIENCE	1 853	825	—	—	1 664	728	189	97
		ENGINEERING, TOTAL	10 255	240	2 602	5	7 021	133	632	102
		MEDICAL AND HEALTH-RELATED SC.	9 749	4 894	206	206	8 891	4 356	652	332
		AGRICULTURE,FORESTRY & FISH'G.	4 610	1 183	—	—	4 182	998	428	185
		OTHER AND NOT SPECIFIED	—	—	—	—	—	—	—	—
TURKEY	1977	TOTAL	312 871	76 251	95 688	27 537	217 183	48 714	—	—
		EDUCATION SCIENCE & TCHR TRNG.	93 973	29 704	83 735	26 464	10 238	3 240	—	—
		HUMANITIES,RELIGION & THEOLOG.	15 667	3 819	—	—	15 667	3 819	—	—
		FINE AND APPLIED ARTS	4 135	1 655	—	—	4 135	1 655	—	—
		LAW	11 232	2 188	—	—	11 232	2 188	—	—
		SOCIAL AND BEHAVIOURAL SCIENCE	35 711	8 157	3 217	378	32 494	7 779	—	—
		COMMERCIAL & BUS. ADMINISTR.	31 683	5 673	1 399	172	30 284	5 501	—	—
		MASS COMMUNICATION & DOCUMENT.	5 718	1 682	—	—	5 718	1 682	—	—
		HOME ECONOMICS & DOMESTIC SC.	724	708	—	—	724	708	—	—
		SERVICE TRADES	344	79	120	30	224	49	—	—
		NATURAL SCIENCE	11 115	3 796	1 504	124	9 611	3 672	—	—
		MATHEMATICS & COMPUTER SCIENCE	4 238	1 192	140	59	4 098	1 133	—	—
		MEDICAL AND HEALTH-RELATED SC.	25 783	8 884	—	—	25 783	8 884	—	—
		ENGINEERING	65 379	7 387	5 573	310	59 806	7 077	—	—
		ARCHITECTURE & TOWN PLANNING	842	354	—	—	842	354	—	—
		TRADE, CRAFT & INDUSTR. PGMS.	—	—	—	—	—	—	—	—
		TRANSPORT AND COMMUNICATIONS	456	—	—	—	456	—	—	—
		AGRICULTURE,FORESTRY & FISH'G.	5 871	973	—	—	5 871	973	—	—
		OTHER AND NOT SPECIFIED	—	—	—	—	—	—	—	—

Third level: students by levels and fields 3.12
Troisième degré: étudiants par types de programmes et domaines d'études
Tercer grado: estudiantes por tipos de programas y sectores de estudio

INTERNATIONAL STANDARD CLASSIFICATION OF EDUCATION BY LEVEL
CLASSIFICATION INTERNATIONALE TYPE DE L'EDUCATION PAR NIVEAUX
CLASIFICACION INTERNACIONAL NORMALIZADA DE LA EDUCACION POR GRADOS

COUNTRY / PAYS / PAIS	YEAR / ANNEE / AÑO	FIELD OF STUDY / BRANCHE D'ETUDES / RAMAS DE ESTUDIO	ALL LEVELS / TOUS NIVEAUX / TODOS LOS GRADOS MF	F	LEVEL 5 / NIVEAU 5 / GRADO 5 MF	F	LEVEL 6 / NIVEAU 6 / GRADO 6 MF	F	LEVEL 7 / NIVEAU 7 / GRADO 7 MF	F
UNITED ARAB EMIRATES	1977	TOTAL	519	205						
		EDUCATION SCIENCE & TCHR TRNG.	119	70						
		HUMANITIES,RELIGION & THEOLOG.	175	67						
		FINE AND APPLIED ARTS	—	—						
		LAW	130	21						
		SOCIAL AND BEHAVIOURAL SCIENCE	—	—						
		COMMERCIAL & BUS. ADMINISTR.	—	—						
		MASS COMMUNICATION & DOCUMENT.	—	—						
		HOME ECONOMICS & DOMESTIC SC.	—	—						
		SERVICE TRADES	95	47						
		NATURAL SCIENCE	—	—						
		MATHEMATICS & COMPUTER SCIENCE	—	—						
		MEDICAL AND HEALTH-RELATED SC.	—	—						
		ENGINEERING	—	—						
		ARCHITECTURE & TOWN PLANNING	—	—						
		TRADE, CRAFT & INDUSTR. PGMS.	—	—						
		TRANSPORT AND COMMUNICATIONS	—	—						
		AGRICULTURE,FORESTRY & FISH'G.	—	—						
		OTHER AND NOT SPECIFIED	—	—						
VIET-NAM ‡	1976	TOTAL	100 027	32 911	—		100 027	32 911	—	—
		EDUCATION SCIENCE & TCHR TRNG.	22 455	13 102			22 455	13 102		
		HUMANITIES,RELIGION & THEOLOG.	2 250	630			2 250	630		
		FINE AND APPLIED ARTS	1 328	236			1 328	236		
		LAW	—	—			—	—		
		SOCIAL AND BEHAVIOURAL SCIENCE	15 306	2 468			15 306	2 468		
		COMMERCIAL & BUS. ADMINISTR.	./.	./.			./.	./.		
		MASS COMMUNICATION & DOCUMENT.	—	—			—	—		
		HOME ECONOMICS & DOMESTIC SC.	—	—			—	—		
		SERVICE TRADES	—	—			—	—		
		NATURAL SCIENCE	13 345	2 740			13 345	2 740		
		MATHEMATICS & COMPUTER SCIENCE	./.	./.			./.	./.		
		MEDICAL AND HEALTH-RELATED SC.	9 909	4 817			9 909	4 817		
		ENGINEERING	22 019	5 948			22 019	5 948		
		ARCHITECTURE & TOWN PLANNING	—	—			—	—		
		TRADE, CRAFT & INDUSTR. PGMS.	—	—			—	—		
		TRANSPORT AND COMMUNICATIONS	—	—			—	—		
		AGRICULTURE,FORESTRY & FISH'G.	13 415	2 970			13 415	2 970		
		OTHER AND NOT SPECIFIED	—	—			—	—		

3.12 Third level: students by levels and fields
Troisième degré: étudiants par types de programmes et domaines d'études
Tercer grado: estudiantes por tipos de programas y sectores de estudio

INTERNATIONAL STANDARD CLASSIFICATION OF EDUCATION BY LEVEL
CLASSIFICATION INTERNATIONALE TYPE DE L'EDUCATION PAR NIVEAUX
CLASIFICACION INTERNACIONAL NORMALIZADA DE LA EDUCACION POR GRADOS

COUNTRY / PAYS / PAIS	YEAR / ANNEE / AÑO	FIELD OF STUDY / BRANCHE D'ETUDES / RAMAS DE ESTUDIO	ALL LEVELS TOUS NIVEAUX TODOS LOS GRADOS MF	F	LEVEL 5 NIVEAU 5 GRADO 5 MF	F	LEVEL 6 NIVEAU 6 GRADO 6 MF	F	LEVEL 7 NIVEAU 7 GRADO 7 MF	F
VIET-NAM (CONT.) ‡	1977	TOTAL	120 125	...	—	—	—	—	—	—
		EDUCATION SCIENCE & TCHR TRNG.	46 886	...	—	—	—	—	—	—
		HUMANITIES,RELIGION & THEOLOG.	3 091	...	—	—	—	—	—	—
		FINE AND APPLIED ARTS	./.	./.	—	—	—	—	—	—
		LAW	344	...	—	—	—	—	—	—
		SOCIAL AND BEHAVIOURAL SCIENCE	2 711	...	—	—	—	—	—	—
		COMMERCIAL & BUS. ADMINISTR.	10 648	...	—	—	—	—	—	—
		MASS COMMUNICATION & DOCUMENT.	—	—	—	—	—	—	—	—
		HOME ECONOMICS & DOMESTIC SC.	—	—	—	—	—	—	—	—
		SERVICE TRADES	—	—	—	—	—	—	—	—
		NATURAL SCIENCE	2 131	...	—	—	—	—	—	—
		MATHEMATICS & COMPUTER SCIENCE	478	...	—	—	—	—	—	—
		MEDICAL AND HEALTH-RELATED SC.	11 837	...	—	—	—	—	—	—
		ENGINEERING	5 490	...	—	—	—	—	—	—
		ARCHITECTURE & TOWN PLANNING	257	...	—	—	—	—	—	—
		TRADE, CRAFT & INDUSTR. PGMS.	24 022	...	—	—	—	—	—	—
		TRANSPORT AND COMMUNICATIONS	508	...	—	—	—	—	—	—
		AGRICULTURE,FORESTRY & FISH'G.	11 722	...	—	—	—	—	—	—
		OTHER AND NOT SPECIFIED	—	—	—	—	—	—	—	—
YEMEN	1977	TOTAL	4 058	470	—	—	4 058	470	—	—
		EDUCATION SCIENCE & TCHR TRNG.	2 056	236	—	—	2 056	236	—	—
		HUMANITIES,RELIGION & THEOLOG.	360	104	—	—	360	104	—	—
		FINE AND APPLIED ARTS	—	—	—	—	—	—	—	—
		LAW	416	16	—	—	416	16	—	—
		SOCIAL AND BEHAVIOURAL SCIENCE	—	—	—	—	—	—	—	—
		COMMERCIAL & BUS. ADMINISTR.	1 126	98	—	—	1 126	98	—	—
		MASS COMMUNICATION & DOCUMENT.	—	—	—	—	—	—	—	—
		HOME ECONOMICS & DOMESTIC SC.	—	—	—	—	—	—	—	—
		SERVICE TRADES	—	—	—	—	—	—	—	—
		NATURAL SCIENCE	100	16	—	—	100	16	—	—
		MATHEMATICS & COMPUTER SCIENCE	—	—	—	—	—	—	—	—
		MEDICAL AND HEALTH-RELATED SC.	—	—	—	—	—	—	—	—
		ENGINEERING	—	—	—	—	—	—	—	—
		ARCHITECTURE & TOWN PLANNING	—	—	—	—	—	—	—	—
		TRADE, CRAFT & INDUSTR. PGMS.	—	—	—	—	—	—	—	—
		TRANSPORT AND COMMUNICATIONS	—	—	—	—	—	—	—	—
		AGRICULTURE,FORESTRY & FISH'G.	—	—	—	—	—	—	—	—
		OTHER AND NOT SPECIFIED	—	—	—	—	—	—	—	—

Third level: students by levels and fields 3.12
Troisième degré: étudiants par types de programmes et domaines d'études
Tercer grado: estudiantes por tipos de programas y sectores de estudio

INTERNATIONAL STANDARD CLASSIFICATION OF EDUCATION BY LEVEL
CLASSIFICATION INTERNATIONALE TYPE DE L'EDUCATION PAR NIVEAUX
CLASIFICACION INTERNACIONAL NORMALIZADA DE LA EDUCACION POR GRADOS

COUNTRY / PAYS / PAIS	YEAR / ANNEE / AÑO	FIELD OF STUDY / BRANCHE D'ETUDES / RAMAS DE ESTUDIO	ALL LEVELS / TOUS NIVEAUX / TODOS LOS GRADOS MF	F	LEVEL 5 / NIVEAU 5 / GRADO 5 MF	F	LEVEL 6 / NIVEAU 6 / GRADO 6 MF	F	LEVEL 7 / NIVEAU 7 / GRADO 7 MF	F
YEMEN, DEMOCRATIC	1977	TOTAL	2 517	751	1 020	300	1 497	451	—	—
		EDUCATION SCIENCE & TCHR TRNG.	438	114	163	55	275	59	—	—
		HUMANITIES,RELIGION & THEOLOG.	858	359	441	181	417	178	—	—
		FINE AND APPLIED ARTS	—	—	—	—	—	—	—	—
		LAW	30	2	—	—	30	2	—	—
		SOCIAL AND BEHAVIOURAL SCIENCE	—	—	—	—	—	—	—	—
		COMMERCIAL & BUS. ADMINISTR.	557	160	121	29	436	131	—	—
		MASS COMMUNICATION & DOCUMENT.	—	—	—	—	—	—	—	—
		HOME ECONOMICS & DOMESTIC SC.	—	—	—	—	—	—	—	—
		SERVICE TRADES	—	—	—	—	—	—	—	—
		NATURAL SCIENCE	—	—	—	—	—	—	—	—
		MATHEMATICS & COMPUTER SCIENCE	184	59	—	—	184	59	—	—
		MEDICAL AND HEALTH-RELATED SC.	295	35	295	35	—	—	—	—
		ENGINEERING	—	—	—	—	—	—	—	—
		ARCHITECTURE & TOWN PLANNING	—	—	—	—	—	—	—	—
		TRADE, CRAFT & INDUSTR. PGMS.	—	—	—	—	—	—	—	—
		TRANSPORT AND COMMUNICATIONS	—	—	—	—	—	—	—	—
		AGRICULTURE,FORESTRY & FISH'G.	155	22	—	—	155	22	—	—
		OTHER AND NOT SPECIFIED	—	—	—	—	—	—	—	—
EUROPE										
AUSTRIA ‡	1977	TOTAL	110 948	44 179	10 595	7 439	100 353	36 740	./.	./.
		EDUCATION SCIENCE & TCHR TRNG.	12 351	8 119	9 491	6 808	2 860	1 311	./.	./.
		HUMANITIES,RELIGION & THEOLOG.	20 162	11 834	—	—	20 162	11 834	./.	./.
		FINE AND APPLIED ARTS	6 258	3 186	—	—	6 258	3 186	./.	./.
		LAW	9 617	2 609	—	—	9 617	2 609	./.	./.
		SOCIAL AND BEHAVIOURAL SCIENCE	8 773	3 568	—	—	8 773	3 568	./.	./.
		COMMERCIAL & BUS. ADMINISTR.	10 019	2 781	1 104	631	8 915	2 150	./.	./.
		MASS COMMUNICATION & DOCUMENT.	951	401	—	—	951	401	./.	./.
		HOME ECONOMICS & DOMESTIC SC.	2	2	—	—	2	2	./.	./.
		SERVICE TRADES	—	—	—	—	—	—	./.	./.
		NATURAL SCIENCE	5 811	1 863	—	—	5 811	1 863	./.	./.
		MATHEMATICS & COMPUTER SCIENCE	4 278	1 249	—	—	4 278	1 249	./.	./.
		MEDICAL AND HEALTH-RELATED SC.	15 534	6 112	—	—	15 534	6 112	./.	./.
		ENGINEERING	8 172	440	—	—	8 172	440	./.	./.
		ARCHITECTURE & TOWN PLANNING	4 615	644	—	—	4 615	644	./.	./.
		TRADE, CRAFT & INDUSTR. PGMS.	—	—	—	—	—	—	./.	./.
		TRANSPORT AND COMMUNICATIONS	—	—	—	—	—	—	./.	./.
		AGRICULTURE,FORESTRY & FISH'G.	1 927	454	—	—	1 927	454	./.	./.
		OTHER AND NOT SPECIFIED	2 478	917	—	—	2 478	917	./.	./.

3.12 Third level: students by levels and fields
Troisième degré: étudiants par types de programmes et domaines d'études
Tercer grado: estudiantes por tipos de programas y sectores de estudio

INTERNATIONAL STANDARD CLASSIFICATION OF EDUCATION BY LEVEL
CLASSIFICATION INTERNATIONALE TYPE DE L'EDUCATION PAR NIVEAUX
CLASIFICACION INTERNACIONAL NORMALIZADA DE LA EDUCACION POR GRADOS

COUNTRY — PAYS — PAIS / YEAR — ANNEE — AÑO / FIELD OF STUDY — BRANCHE D'ETUDES — RAMAS DE ESTUDIO	ALL LEVELS / TOUS NIVEAUX / TODOS LOS GRADOS MF	F	LEVEL 5 / NIVEAU 5 / GRADO 5 MF	F	LEVEL 6 / NIVEAU 6 / GRADO 6 MF	F	LEVEL 7 / NIVEAU 7 / GRADO 7 MF	F
BELGIUM ‡ — 1977								
TOTAL	177 145	76 675	70 232	41 709	106 913	34 966	./.	./.
EDUCATION SCIENCE & TCHR TRNG.	24 531	16 533	19 522	13 721	5 009	2 812	./.	./.
HUMANITIES,RELIGION & THEOLOG.	15 701	8 692	68	1	15 633	8 691	./.	./.
FINE AND APPLIED ARTS	7 676	3 825	7 416	3 747	260	78	./.	./.
LAW	10 833	3 803	179	93	10 654	3 710	./.	./.
SOCIAL AND BEHAVIOURAL SCIENCE	12 563	5 508	5 147	3 399	7 416	2 109	./.	./.
COMMERCIAL & BUS. ADMINISTR.	18 910	7 401	8 783	4 896	10 127	2 505	./.	./.
MASS COMMUNICATION & DOCUMENT.	154	17	154	17	—	—	./.	./.
HOME ECONOMICS & DOMESTIC SC.	1 877	806	1 877	806	—	—	./.	./.
SERVICE TRADES	—	—	—	—	—	—	—	—
NATURAL SCIENCE	12 574	4 816	3 223	1 172	9 351	3 644	./.	./.
MATHEMATICS & COMPUTER SCIENCE	2 191	531	1 936	455	255	76	./.	./.
MEDICAL AND HEALTH-RELATED SC.	42 732	21 825	16 343	12 538	26 389	9 287	./.	./.
ENGINEERING	15 483	784	2 367	120	13 116	664	./.	./.
ARCHITECTURE & TOWN PLANNING	2 724	537	1 269	267	1 455	270	./.	./.
TRADE, CRAFT & INDUSTR. PGMS.	2 006	72	916	47	1 090	25	./.	./.
TRANSPORT AND COMMUNICATIONS	—	—	—	—	—	—	—	—
AGRICULTURE,FORESTRY & FISH'G.	6 078	1 074	433	84	5 645	990	./.	./.
OTHER AND NOT SPECIFIED	1 112	451	599	346	513	105	./.	./.
BULGARIA ‡ — 1977								
TOTAL	142 644	89 392	47 110	39 682	93 252	48 801	2 282	909
EDUCATION SCIENCE & TCHR TRNG.	15 267	10 742	12 808	9 964	2 459	778	—	—
HUMANITIES,RELIGION & THEOLOG.	12 783	9 742	530	524	12 253	9 218	—	—
FINE AND APPLIED ARTS	3 439	1 781	322	188	3 094	1 575	23	18
LAW	1 776	857	—	—	1 749	844	27	13
SOCIAL AND BEHAVIOURAL SCIENCE	764	464	—	—	385	241	379	223
COMMERCIAL & BUS. ADMINISTR.	14 693	9 033	—	—	14 693	9 033	—	—
MASS COMMUNICATION & DOCUMENT.	1 450	946	—	—	1 450	946	—	—
HOME ECONOMICS & DOMESTIC SC.	—	—	—	—	—	—	—	—
SERVICE TRADES	1 680	1 243	1 680	1 243	—	—	—	—
NATURAL SCIENCE	4 370	2 779	—	—	4 104	2 632	266	147
MATHEMATICS & COMPUTER SCIENCE	2 799	1 816	—	—	2 659	1 777	140	39
MEDICAL AND HEALTH-RELATED SC.	41 870	33 974	30 728	27 339	11 001	6 549	141	86
ENGINEERING	34 608	13 161	—	—	33 528	12 879	1 080	282
ARCHITECTURE & TOWN PLANNING	1 007	504	—	—	966	479	41	25
TRADE, CRAFT & INDUSTR. PGMS.	—	—	—	—	—	—	—	—
TRANSPORT AND COMMUNICATIONS	1 850	547	1 042	424	783	121	25	2
AGRICULTURE,FORESTRY & FISH'G.	4 280	1 799	—	—	4 128	1 729	152	70
OTHER AND NOT SPECIFIED	8	4	—	—	—	—	8	4

Third level: students by levels and fields 3.12
Troisième degré: étudiants par types de programmes et domaines d'études
Tercer grado: estudiantes por tipos de programas y sectores de estudio

INTERNATIONAL STANDARD CLASSIFICATION OF EDUCATION BY LEVEL
CLASSIFICATION INTERNATIONALE TYPE DE L'EDUCATION PAR NIVEAUX
CLASIFICACION INTERNACIONAL NORMALIZADA DE LA EDUCACION POR GRADOS

COUNTRY / PAYS / PAIS	YEAR / ANNEE / AÑO	FIELD OF STUDY / BRANCHE D'ETUDES / RAMAS DE ESTUDIO	ALL LEVELS TOUS NIVEAUX TODOS LOS GRADOS		LEVEL 5 NIVEAU 5 GRADO 5		LEVEL 6 NIVEAU 6 GRADO 6		LEVEL 7 NIVEAU 7 GRADO 7	
			MF	F	MF	F	MF	F	MF	F
CZECHOSLOVAKIA	1977	TOTAL	179 780	73 535	—	—	179 780	73 535	—	—
		EDUCATION SCIENCE & TCHR TRNG.	29 164	21 967	—	—	29 164	21 967	—	—
		HUMANITIES, RELIGION & THEOLOG.	2 094	1 256	—	—	2 094	1 256	—	—
		FINE AND APPLIED ARTS	2 966	1 340	—	—	2 966	1 340	—	—
		LAW	9 444	4 434	—	—	9 444	4 434	—	—
		SOCIAL AND BEHAVIOURAL SCIENCE	2 429	1 439	—	—	2 429	1 439	—	—
		COMMERCIAL & BUS. ADMINISTR.	22 401	11 277	—	—	22 401	11 277	—	—
		MASS COMMUNICATION & DOCUMENT.	1 615	1 054	—	—	1 615	1 054	—	—
		HOME ECONOMICS & DOMESTIC SC.	—	—	—	—	—	—	—	—
		SERVICE TRADES	—	—	—	—	—	—	—	—
		NATURAL SCIENCE	2 625	1 230	—	—	2 625	1 230	—	—
		MATHEMATICS & COMPUTER SCIENCE	2 805	970	—	—	2 805	970	—	—
		MEDICAL AND HEALTH-RELATED SC.	17 490	10 309	—	—	17 490	10 309	—	—
		ENGINEERING	62 594	11 587	—	—	62 594	11 587	—	—
		ARCHITECTURE & TOWN PLANNING	1 560	478	—	—	1 560	478	—	—
		TRADE, CRAFT & INDUSTR. PGMS.	—	—	—	—	—	—	—	—
		TRANSPORT AND COMMUNICATIONS	4 536	725	—	—	4 536	725	—	—
		AGRICULTURE, FORESTRY & FISH'G.	17 294	5 317	—	—	17 294	5 317	—	—
		OTHER AND NOT SPECIFIED	763	152	—	—	763	152	—	—
DENMARK ‡	1977	TOTAL	117 656	54 580	24 618	18 185	93 038	36 395	.	.
		EDUCATION SCIENCE & TCHR TRNG.	25 547	16 087	9 300	7 501	16 247	8 586	.	.
		HUMANITIES, RELIGION & THEOLOG.	15 900	8 642	—	—	15 900	8 642	.	.
		FINE AND APPLIED ARTS	2 757	1 332	646	405	2 111	927	.	.
		LAW	4 462	1 609	—	—	4 462	1 609	.	.
		SOCIAL AND BEHAVIOURAL SCIENCE	10 716	3 923	—	—	10 716	3 923	.	.
		COMMERCIAL & BUS. ADMINISTR.	12 798	4 881	3 653	3 224	9 145	1 657	.	.
		MASS COMMUNICATION & DOCUMENT.	1 795	1 061	36	23	1 759	1 038	.	.
		HOME ECONOMICS & DOMESTIC SC.	—	—	—	—	—	—	.	.
		SERVICE TRADES	467	457	467	457	—	—	.	.
		NATURAL SCIENCE	5 122	1 312	—	—	5 122	1 312	.	.
		MATHEMATICS & COMPUTER SCIENCE	2 394	379	—	—	2 394	379	.	.
		MEDICAL AND HEALTH-RELATED SC.	16 792	10 976	6 842	6 283	9 950	4 693	.	.
		ENGINEERING	8 489	539	1 080	105	7 409	434	.	.
		ARCHITECTURE & TOWN PLANNING	2 592	661	—	—	2 592	661	.	.
		TRADE, CRAFT & INDUSTR. PGMS.	1 088	158	1 088	158	—	—	.	.
		TRANSPORT AND COMMUNICATIONS	1 058	6	990	5	68	1	.	.
		AGRICULTURE, FORESTRY & FISH'G.	2 001	588	337	20	1 664	568	.	.
		OTHER AND NOT SPECIFIED	3 678	1 969	179	4	3 499	1 965	.	.

3.12 Third level: students by levels and fields
Troisième degré: étudiants par types de programmes et domaines d'études
Tercer grado: estudiantes por tipos de programas y sectores de estudio

INTERNATIONAL STANDARD CLASSIFICATION OF EDUCATION BY LEVEL
CLASSIFICATION INTERNATIONALE TYPE DE L'EDUCATION PAR NIVEAUX
CLASIFICACION INTERNACIONAL NORMALIZADA DE LA EDUCACION POR GRADOS

COUNTRY / PAYS / PAIS	YEAR / ANNEE / AÑO	FIELD OF STUDY / BRANCHE D'ETUDES / RAMAS DE ESTUDIO	ALL LEVELS / TOUS NIVEAUX / TODOS LOS GRADOS MF	F	LEVEL 5 / NIVEAU 5 / GRADO 5 MF	F	LEVEL 6 / NIVEAU 6 / GRADO 6 MF	F	LEVEL 7 / NIVEAU 7 / GRADO 7 MF	F
FINLAND ‡	1977	TOTAL	122 427	57 788	41 924	18 038	75 902	38 338	4 601	1 412
		EDUCATION SCIENCE & TCHR TRNG.	7 370	5 438	2 108	1 950	5 230	3 471	32	17
		HUMANITIES,RELIGION & THEOLOG.	15 821	11 381	—	—	15 049	10 902	772	479
		FINE AND APPLIED ARTS	1 076	525	256	134	801	390	19	1
		LAW	3 620	1 355	—	—	3 352	1 296	268	59
		SOCIAL AND BEHAVIOURAL SCIENCE	10 526	6 263	—	—	9 889	5 993	637	270
		COMMERCIAL & BUS. ADMINISTR.	21 117	11 731	10 197	6 659	10 511	4 979	409	93
		MASS COMMUNICATION & DOCUMENT.	303	182	226	113	77	69	—	—
		HOME ECONOMICS & DOMESTIC SC.	227	221	—	—	216	210	11	11
		SERVICE TRADES	453	326	453	326	—	—	—	—
		NATURAL SCIENCE	7 169	3 358	—	—	6 581	3 149	588	209
		MATHEMATICS & COMPUTER SCIENCE	5 948	2 274	—	—	5 630	2 191	318	83
		MEDICAL AND HEALTH-RELATED SC.	13 247	10 174	7 712	7 200	5 460	2 929	75	45
		ENGINEERING	31 005	2 815	20 073	1 447	9 710	1 304	1 222	64
		ARCHITECTURE & TOWN PLANNING	1 132	431	—	—	1 061	412	71	19
		TRADE, CRAFT & INDUSTR. PGMS	—	—	—	—	—	—	—	—
		TRANSPORT AND COMMUNICATIONS	222	1	222	1	—	—	—	—
		AGRICULTURE, FORESTRY & FISH'G.	2 571	910	519	86	1 891	766	161	58
		OTHER AND NOT SPECIFIED	620	403	158	122	444	277	18	4
FRANCE ‡	1977	TOTAL	837 776	...	68 540	...	621 120	...	148 116	...
		EDUCATION SCIENCE & TCHR TRNG.	—	—	—	—	—	—	—	—
		HUMANITIES,RELIGION & THEOLOG.	254 677	...	—	—	211 988	...	42 689	...
		FINE AND APPLIED ARTS	—	—	—	—	—	—	—	—
		LAW	131 659	...	21 142	...	92 469	...	18 048	...
		SOCIAL AND BEHAVIOURAL SCIENCE	68 050	...	—	—	54 256	...	13 794	...
		NATURAL SCIENCE	133 140	...	—	—	101 418	...	31 722	...
		MEDICAL AND HEALTH-RELATED SC.	195 801	...	—	—	153 938	...	41 863	...
		ENGINEERING	./.	...	./.	...	./.	...	./.	...
		AGRICULTURE, FORESTRY & FISH'G.	54 449	...	47 398	...	7 051	...	./.	—
		OTHER AND NOT SPECIFIED	—	—	—	—	—	—	—	—

Third level: students by levels and fields   3.12
Troisième degré: étudiants par types de programmes et domaines d'études
Tercer grado: estudiantes por tipos de programas y sectores de estudio

INTERNATIONAL STANDARD CLASSIFICATION OF EDUCATION BY LEVEL
CLASSIFICATION INTERNATIONALE TYPE DE L'EDUCATION PAR NIVEAUX
CLASIFICACION INTERNACIONAL NORMALIZADA DE LA EDUCACION POR GRADOS

COUNTRY / PAYS / PAIS	YEAR / ANNEE / AÑO	FIELD OF STUDY / BRANCHE D'ETUDES / RAMAS DE ESTUDIO	ALL LEVELS / TOUS NIVEAUX / TODOS LOS GRADOS MF	F	LEVEL 5 / NIVEAU 5 / GRADO 5 MF	F	LEVEL 6 / NIVEAU 6 / GRADO 6 MF	F	LEVEL 7 / NIVEAU 7 / GRADO 7 MF	F
GERMAN DEMOCRATIC REPUBLIC ‡	1976	TOTAL	382 204	...	86 225	...	160 772	110 551	135 207	62 892
		EDUCATION SCIENCE & TCHR TRNG.	54 564	42 268	-	...	24 056	20 428	30 508	21 840
		HUMANITIES, RELIGION & THEOLOG.	7 475	3 483	-	...	1 061	527	6 414	2 956
		FINE AND APPLIED ARTS	3 894	1 744	-	...	1 178	745	2 716	999
		LAW	3 595	1 366	-	...	-	-	3 595	1 366
		SOCIAL AND BEHAVIOURAL SCIENCE	20 515	12 843	-	...	10 272	8 748	10 243	4 095
		COMMERCIAL & BUS. ADMINISTR.	42 814	28 659	-	...	28 138	21 433	14 676	7 226
		MASS COMMUNICATION & DOCUMENT.	2 670	2 093	-	...	1 684	1 491	986	602
		HOME ECONOMICS & DOMESTIC SC.	-	-	-	...	-	-	-	-
		SERVICE TRADES	-	-	-	...	-	-	-	-
		NATURAL SCIENCE	6 768	2 336	-	...	-	-	6 768	2 336
		MATHEMATICS & COMPUTER SCIENCE	4 639	1 942	-	...	860	477	3 779	1 465
		MEDICAL AND HEALTH-RELATED SC.	51 641	46 866	-	...	40 796	40 038	10 845	6 828
		ENGINEERING	78 167	21 604	-	...	41 773	12 292	36 394	9 312
		ARCHITECTURE & TOWN PLANNING	935	527	-	...	-	-	935	527
		TRADE, CRAFT & INDUSTR. PGMS.	-	-	-	...	-	-	-	-
		TRANSPORT AND COMMUNICATIONS	-	-	-	...	-	-	-	-
		AGRICULTURE, FORESTRY & FISH'G.	18 302	7 712	-	...	10 954	4 372	7 348	3 340
		OTHER AND NOT SPECIFIED	86 225	...	86 225	...	-	-	-	-
	1977	TOTAL	384 158	...	86 021	...	163 311	113 791	134 826	62 551
		EDUCATION SCIENCE & TCHR TRNG.	...	...	...	...	24 037	20 445	29 607	21 040
		HUMANITIES, RELIGION & THEOLOG.	...	...	...	...	1 010	525	6 534	3 132
		FINE AND APPLIED ARTS	...	...	...	...	1 187	750	2 778	1 071
		LAW	...	...	...	...	-	-	3 520	1 280
		SOCIAL AND BEHAVIOURAL SCIENCE	...	...	...	...	10 301	8 902	10 866	4 512
		COMMERCIAL & BUS. ADMINISTR.	...	...	...	...	28 156	21 886	13 513	7 093
		MASS COMMUNICATION & DOCUMENT.	...	...	...	...	1 670	1 464	961	580
		HOME ECONOMICS & DOMESTIC SC.	...	...	...	...	-	-	-	-
		SERVICE TRADES	...	...	...	...	-	-	-	-
		NATURAL SCIENCE	...	...	...	...	-	-	6 161	2 057
		MATHEMATICS & COMPUTER SCIENCE	...	...	...	...	930	440	3 284	1 136
		MEDICAL AND HEALTH-RELATED SC.	...	...	...	...	43 483	42 629	12 567	7 730
		ENGINEERING	...	...	...	...	41 692	12 228	36 576	9 017
		ARCHITECTURE & TOWN PLANNING	...	...	...	...	-	-	1 106	609
		TRADE, CRAFT & INDUSTR. PGMS.	...	...	...	...	-	-	-	-
		TRANSPORT AND COMMUNICATIONS	...	...	...	...	-	-	-	-
		AGRICULTURE, FORESTRY & FISH'G.	...	...	...	...	10 845	4 522	7 353	3 294
		OTHER AND NOT SPECIFIED	...	...	...	...	-	-	-	-

3.12 Third level: students by levels and fields
Troisième degré: étudiants par types de programmes et domaines d'études
Tercer grado: estudiantes por tipos de programas y sectores de estudio

INTERNATIONAL STANDARD CLASSIFICATION OF EDUCATION BY LEVEL
CLASSIFICATION INTERNATIONALE TYPE DE L'EDUCATION PAR NIVEAUX
CLASIFICACION INTERNACIONAL NORMALIZADA DE LA EDUCACION POR GRADOS

COUNTRY / PAYS / PAIS	YEAR / ANNEE / AÑO	FIELD OF STUDY / BRANCHE D'ETUDES / RAMAS DE ESTUDIO	ALL LEVELS / TOUS NIVEAUX / TODOS LOS GRADOS		LEVEL 5 / NIVEAU 5 / GRADO 5		LEVEL 6 / NIVEAU 6 / GRADO 6		LEVEL 7 / NIVEAU 7 / GRADO 7	
			MF	F	MF	F	MF	F	MF	F
GERMANY, FEDERAL REPUBLIC OF	1976	TOTAL	1 054 289	407 432	182 380	114 394	862 208	290 435	9 701	2 603
		EDUCATION SCIENCE & TCHR TRNG.	292 944	164 470	24 996	21 765	266 125	142 043	1 823	662
		HUMANITIES,RELIGION & THEOLOG.	47 599	22 468	1 409	1 103	44 479	20 790	1 711	575
		FINE AND APPLIED ARTS	29 042	13 864	2 415	1 134	26 460	12 674	167	56
		LAW	55 997	14 612	—	—	55 524	14 553	473	59
		SOCIAL AND BEHAVIOURAL SCIENCE	146 468	44 105	—	—	143 659	43 562	2 809	543
		COMMERCIAL & BUS. ADMINISTR.	16 816	5 457	11 517	3 662	5 299	1 795	—	—
		MASS COMMUNICATION & DOCUMENT.	2 901	1 369	—	—	2 901	1 369	—	—
		HOME ECONOMICS & DOMESTIC SC.	10 032	9 384	6 634	6 629	3 326	2 707	72	48
		SERVICE TRADES	619	503	619	503	—	—	—	—
		NATURAL SCIENCE	51 222	10 532	—	—	50 335	10 164	887	368
		MATHEMATICS & COMPUTER SCIENCE	23 774	4 086	—	—	23 373	4 048	401	38
		MEDICAL AND HEALTH-RELATED SC.	153 700	96 213	90 626	76 005	62 466	20 051	608	157
		ENGINEERING	162 114	7 185	27 905	1 820	133 984	5 362	225	3
		ARCHITECTURE & TOWN PLANNING	24 739	6 527	—	—	24 638	6 508	101	19
		TRADE, CRAFT & INDUSTR. PGMS.	5 077	488	5 077	488	—	—	—	—
		TRANSPORT AND COMMUNICATIONS	—	—	—	—	—	—	—	—
		AGRICULTURE,FORESTRY & FISH'G.	26 912	4 835	8 671	101	17 889	4 668	352	66
		OTHER AND NOT SPECIFIED	4 333	1 334	2 511	1 184	1 750	141	72	9
	1977	TOTAL	1 073 733	424 604	168 088	114 826	895 276	306 847	10 369	2 931
		EDUCATION SCIENCE & TCHR TRNG.	278 297	159 311	24 215	21 144	252 015	137 321	2 067	846
		HUMANITIES,RELIGION & THEOLOG.	54 931	27 135	1 694	1 381	51 403	25 079	1 834	675
		FINE AND APPLIED ARTS	31 014	15 226	2 626	1 249	28 269	13 944	119	33
		LAW	59 332	16 801	—	—	58 905	16 748	427	53
		SOCIAL AND BEHAVIOURAL SCIENCE	153 761	48 753	—	—	150 711	48 188	3 050	565
		COMMERCIAL & BUS. ADMINISTR.	17 551	6 105	7 179	4 520	10 372	1 585	—	—
		MASS COMMUNICATION & DOCUMENT.	3 262	1 511	—	—	3 226	1 501	36	10
		HOME ECONOMICS & DOMESTIC SC.	11 333	10 581	7 500	7 440	3 779	3 096	54	45
		SERVICE TRADES	—	—	—	—	—	—	—	—
		NATURAL SCIENCE	55 049	12 325	—	—	54 087	11 911	962	414
		MATHEMATICS & COMPUTER SCIENCE	24 346	4 432	—	—	23 949	4 391	397	41
		MEDICAL AND HEALTH-RELATED SC.	160 301	99 438	89 800	76 012	69 949	23 283	552	143
		ENGINEERING	159 944	7 280	18 792	1 224	140 812	6 053	340	3
		ARCHITECTURE & TOWN PLANNING	24 502	7 038	—	—	24 353	7 010	149	28
		TRADE, CRAFT & INDUSTR. PGMS.	4 416	333	4 416	333	—	—	—	—
		TRANSPORT AND COMMUNICATIONS	—	—	—	—	—	—	—	—
		AGRICULTURE,FORESTRY & FISH'G.	29 787	5 908	9 297	217	20 213	5 636	277	55
		OTHER AND NOT SPECIFIED	5 907	2 427	2 569	1 306	3 233	1 101	105	20

Third level: students by levels and fields   3.12

Troisième degré: étudiants par types de programmes et domaines d'études
Tercer grado: estudiantes por tipos de programas y sectores de estudio

INTERNATIONAL STANDARD CLASSIFICATION OF EDUCATION BY LEVEL
CLASSIFICATION INTERNATIONALE TYPE DE L'EDUCATION PAR NIVEAUX
CLASIFICACION INTERNACIONAL NORMALIZADA DE LA EDUCACION POR GRADOS

COUNTRY / PAYS / PAIS	YEAR / ANNEE / AÑO	FIELD OF STUDY / BRANCHE D'ETUDES / RAMAS DE ESTUDIO	ALL LEVELS / TOUS NIVEAUX / TODOS LOS GRADOS		LEVEL 5 / NIVEAU 5 / GRADO 5		LEVEL 6 / NIVEAU 6 / GRADO 6		LEVEL 7 / NIVEAU 7 / GRADO 7	
			MF	F	MF	F	MF	F	MF	F
GREECE ‡	1977	TOTAL	117 892	44 202	21 242	6 779	96 650	37 423	...	...
		EDUCATION SCIENCE & TCHR TRNG.	2 962	1 665	2 962	1 665	—	—	...	...
		HUMANITIES,RELIGION & THEOLOG.	12 219	9 392	—	—	12 219	9 392	...	...
		FINE AND APPLIED ARTS	284	165	—	—	284	165	...	...
		LAW	12 954	5 304	—	—	12 954	5 304	...	...
		SOCIAL AND BEHAVIOURAL SCIENCE	26 317	11 165	285	245	26 032	10 920	...	...
		COMMERCIAL & BUS. ADMINISTR.	11 415	3 810	3 086	1 313	8 329	2 497	...	...
		MASS COMMUNICATION & DOCUMENT.	—	—	—	—	—	—	...	...
		HOME ECONOMICS & DOMESTIC SC.	101	101	101	101	—	—	...	...
		SERVICE TRADES	749	270	749	270	—	—	...	...
		NATURAL SCIENCE	6 828	1 912	—	—	6 828	1 912	...	...
		MATHEMATICS & COMPUTER SCIENCE	6 224	1 510	—	—	6 224	1 510	...	...
		MEDICAL AND HEALTH-RELATED SC.	12 581	4 527	1 640	1 110	10 941	3 417	...	...
		ENGINEERING	19 944	2 533	11 146	1 664	8 798	869	...	...
		ARCHITECTURE & TOWN PLANNING	1 472	743	—	—	1 472	743	...	...
		TRADE, CRAFT & INDUSTR. PGMS.	434	162	434	162	—	—	...	...
		TRANSPORT AND COMMUNICATIONS	—	—	—	—	—	—	...	...
		AGRICULTURE,FORESTRY & FISH'G.	3 408	943	839	249	2 569	694	...	...
		OTHER AND NOT SPECIFIED	—	—	—	—	—	—	...	...
HOLY SEE	1977	TOTAL	7 515	2 416	1 784	835	2 379	648	3 352	933
		EDUCATION SCIENCE & TCHR TRNG.	744	303	157	5	107	45	480	253
		HUMANITIES,RELIGION & THEOLOG.	6 062	1 993	1 511	814	2 078	553	2 473	626
		FINE AND APPLIED ARTS	93	34	—	—	—	—	93	34
		LAW	367	18	78	1	101	7	188	10
		SOCIAL AND BEHAVIOURAL SCIENCE	182	48	38	15	73	23	71	10
		COMMERCIAL & BUS. ADMINISTR.	—	—	—	—	—	—	—	—
		MASS COMMUNICATION & DOCUMENT.	—	—	—	—	—	—	—	—
		HOME ECONOMICS & DOMESTIC SC.	—	—	—	—	—	—	—	—
		SERVICE TRADES	—	—	—	—	—	—	—	—
		NATURAL SCIENCE	—	—	—	—	—	—	—	—
		MATHEMATICS & COMPUTER SCIENCE	—	—	—	—	—	—	—	—
		MEDICAL AND HEALTH-RELATED SC.	—	—	—	—	—	—	—	—
		ENGINEERING	47	—	—	—	—	—	47	—
		ARCHITECTURE & TOWN PLANNING	—	—	—	—	—	—	—	—
		TRADE, CRAFT & INDUSTR. PGMS.	—	—	—	—	—	—	—	—
		TRANSPORT AND COMMUNICATIONS	—	—	—	—	—	—	—	—
		AGRICULTURE,FORESTRY & FISH'G.	20	20	—	—	20	20	—	—
		OTHER AND NOT SPECIFIED	—	—	—	—	—	—	—	—

3.12 Third level: students by levels and fields
Troisième degré: étudiants par types de programmes et domaines d'études
Tercer grado: estudiantes por tipos de programas y sectores de estudio

INTERNATIONAL STANDARD CLASSIFICATION OF EDUCATION BY LEVEL
CLASSIFICATION INTERNATIONALE TYPE DE L'EDUCATION PAR NIVEAUX
CLASIFICACION INTERNACIONAL NORMALIZADA DE LA EDUCACION POR GRADOS

COUNTRY / PAYS / PAIS	YEAR / ANNEE / AÑO	FIELD OF STUDY / BRANCHE D'ETUDES / RAMAS DE ESTUDIO	ALL LEVELS / TOUS NIVEAUX / TODOS LOS GRADOS MF	F	LEVEL 5 / NIVEAU 5 / GRADO 5 MF	F	LEVEL 6 / NIVEAU 6 / GRADO 6 MF	F	LEVEL 7 / NIVEAU 7 / GRADO 7 MF	F
HUNGARY ‡	1977	TOTAL	108 649	54 929	44 593	23 595	16 790	12 014	47 266	19 320
		EDUCATION SCIENCE & TCHR TRNG.	38 580	29 469	15 121	12 913	16 139	11 882	7 320	4 674
		HUMANITIES,RELIGION & THEOLOG.	2 209	1 354	614	478	—	—	1 595	876
		FINE AND APPLIED ARTS	1 179	509	—	—	—	—	1 179	509
		LAW	5 266	2 511	—	—	—	—	5 266	2 511
		SOCIAL AND BEHAVIOURAL SCIENCE	3 299	1 732	—	—	—	—	3 299	1 732
		COMMERCIAL & BUS. ADMINISTR.	6 294	4 262	5 099	3 600	—	—	1 195	662
		MASS COMMUNICATION & DOCUMENT.	—	—	—	—	—	—	—	—
		HOME ECONOMICS & DOMESTIC SC.	—	—	—	—	—	—	—	—
		SERVICE TRADES	784	403	784	403	—	—	—	—
		NATURAL SCIENCE	1 246	468	—	—	—	—	1 246	468
		MATHEMATICS & COMPUTER SCIENCE	1 917	736	771	433	—	—	1 146	303
		MEDICAL AND HEALTH-RELATED SC.	9 411	5 738	1 311	1 116	—	—	8 100	4 622
		ENGINEERING	12 744	1 814	2 918	608	—	—	9 826	1 206
		ARCHITECTURE & TOWN PLANNING	5 824	1 776	3 240	840	—	—	2 584	936
		TRADE, CRAFT & INDUSTR. PGMS.	9 533	776	9 533	776	—	—	—	—
		TRANSPORT AND COMMUNICATIONS	1 566	336	1 221	297	—	—	345	39
		AGRICULTURE, FORESTRY & FISH'G.	8 146	2 211	3 981	1 131	—	—	4 165	1 080
		OTHER AND NOT SPECIFIED	651	132	—	—	651	132	—	—
ICELAND ‡	1976	TOTAL	4 035	...	...	...	...	...	...	...
		EDUCATION SCIENCE & TCHR TRNG.	501	...	...	...	...	...	...	...
		HUMANITIES,RELIGION & THEOLOG.	792	...	...	...	...	...	...	...
		FINE AND APPLIED ARTS	178	...	...	...	...	...	...	...
		LAW	268	...	...	...	...	...	...	...
		SOCIAL AND BEHAVIOURAL SCIENCE	374	...	...	...	...	...	...	...
		COMMERCIAL & BUS. ADMINISTR.	—	—	—	—	—	—	—	—
		MASS COMMUNICATION & DOCUMENT.	—	—	—	—	—	—	—	—
		HOME ECONOMICS & DOMESTIC SC.	—	—	—	—	—	—	—	—
		SERVICE TRADES	—	—	—	—	—	—	—	—
		NATURAL SCIENCE	361	...	...	...	...	...	...	...
		MATHEMATICS & COMPUTER SCIENCE	./.	...	...	...	...	...	...	...
		MEDICAL AND HEALTH-RELATED SC.	864	...	...	...	...	...	...	...
		ENGINEERING	242	...	...	...	...	...	...	...
		ARCHITECTURE & TOWN PLANNING	—	—	—	—	—	—	—	—
		TRADE, CRAFT & INDUSTR. PGMS.	72	...	...	...	...	...	...	...
		TRANSPORT AND COMMUNICATIONS	72	...	...	...	...	...	...	...
		AGRICULTURE, FORESTRY & FISH'G.	17	...	...	...	...	...	...	...
		OTHER AND NOT SPECIFIED	—	—	—	—	—	—	—	—

Third level: students by levels and fields 3.12
Troisième degré: étudiants par types de programmes et domaines d'études
Tercer grado: estudiantes por tipos de programas y sectores de estudio

INTERNATIONAL STANDARD CLASSIFICATION OF EDUCATION BY LEVEL
CLASSIFICATION INTERNATIONALE TYPE DE L'EDUCATION PAR NIVEAUX
CLASIFICACION INTERNACIONAL NORMALIZADA DE LA EDUCACION POR GRADOS

COUNTRY / PAYS / PAIS	YEAR / ANNEE / AÑO	FIELD OF STUDY / BRANCHE D'ETUDES / RAMAS DE ESTUDIO	ALL LEVELS / TOUS NIVEAUX / TODOS LOS GRADOS MF	F	LEVEL 5 / NIVEAU 5 / GRADO 5 MF	F	LEVEL 6 / NIVEAU 6 / GRADO 6 MF	F	LEVEL 7 / NIVEAU 7 / GRADO 7 MF	F
IRELAND ‡	1977	TOTAL	46 627	17 667	16 023	4 464	26 278	11 402	4 326	1 801
		EDUCATION SCIENCE & TCHR TRNG.	5 657	3 974	666	456	3 115	2 417	1 876	1 101
		HUMANITIES,RELIGION & THEOLOG.	9 892	5 242	1 662	538	7 479	4 411	751	293
		FINE AND APPLIED ARTS	1 854	1 098	1 486	871	368	227		
		LAW	1 165	359	136	51	895	267	134	41
		SOCIAL AND BEHAVIOURAL SCIENCE	1 360	656	15	2	1 146	582	199	72
		COMMERCIAL & BUS. ADMINISTR.	5 171	1 229	2 599	583	2 461	639	111	7
		MASS COMMUNICATION & DOCUMENT.	111	31	103	26	-	-	8	5
		HOME ECONOMICS & DOMESTIC SC.	56	56	56	56	-	-	-	-
		SERVICE TRADES								
		NATURAL SCIENCE	5 590	2 232	2 019	823	3 063	1 249	508	160
		MATHEMATICS & COMPUTER SCIENCE	464	78	168	35	140	22	156	21
		MEDICAL AND HEALTH-RELATED SC.	3 916	1 467	206	198	3 527	1 206	183	63
		ENGINEERING	7 221	268	4 237	132	2 727	130	257	6
		ARCHITECTURE & TOWN PLANNING	208	49	1	-	184	43	23	6
		TRADE,CRAFT & INDUSTR. PGMS.	107	54	107	54	-	-	-	-
		TRANSPORT AND COMMUNICATIONS								
		AGRICULTURE,FORESTRY & FISH'G.	1 015	148	152	35	779	107	84	6
		OTHER AND NOT SPECIFIED	2 840	726	2 410	604	394	102	36	20
ITALY	1977	TOTAL	1 052 342	426 370	26 937	14 365	977 912	397 361	47 493	14 644
		EDUCATION SCIENCE & TCHR TRNG.	48 111	39 604	4 725	3 788	43 386	35 816		
		HUMANITIES,RELIGION & THEOLOG.	151 225	112 420			145 320	107 811	5 905	4 609
		FINE AND APPLIED ARTS	11 555	5 657	8 832	4 540	2 723	1 117		
		LAW	127 274	45 239	-	-	125 468	44 543	1 806	696
		SOCIAL AND BEHAVIOURAL SCIENCE	83 710	37 019	-	-	83 710	37 019		
		COMMERCIAL & BUS. ADMINISTR.	77 486	20 884	-	-	75 405	19 431	2 081	1 453
		MASS COMMUNICATION & DOCUMENT.								
		HOME ECONOMICS & DOMESTIC SC.								
		SERVICE TRADES								
		NATURAL SCIENCE	68 672	39 394			68 672	39 394		
		MATHEMATICS & COMPUTER SCIENCE	37 827	17 324	1 355	471	34 799	15 967	1 673	886
		MEDICAL AND HEALTH-RELATED SC.	249 379	80 014			214 807	73 214	34 572	6 800
		ENGINEERING	95 067	2 648			94 459	2 611	608	37
		ARCHITECTURE & TOWN PLANNING	54 805	14 891			54 492	14 799	313	92
		TRADE,CRAFT & INDUSTR. PGMS.								
		TRANSPORT AND COMMUNICATIONS								
		AGRICULTURE,FORESTRY & FISH'G.	34 883	5 668			34 426	5 625	457	43
		OTHER AND NOT SPECIFIED	12 348	5 608	12 025	5 566	245	14	78	28

3.12 Third level: students by levels and fields
Troisième degré: étudiants par types de programmes et domaines d'études
Tercer grado: estudiantes por tipos de programas y sectores de estudio

COUNTRY / PAYS / PAIS	YEAR / ANNEE / AÑO	FIELD OF STUDY / BRANCHE D'ETUDES / RAMAS DE ESTUDIO	ALL LEVELS / TOUS NIVEAUX / TODOS LOS GRADOS		LEVEL 5 / NIVEAU 5 / GRADO 5		LEVEL 6 / NIVEAU 6 / GRADO 6		LEVEL 7 / NIVEAU 7 / GRADO 7	
			MF	F	MF	F	MF	F	MF	F
LUXEMBOURG ‡	1977	TOTAL	302	128	302	128	—	—	—	—
		EDUCATION SCIENCE & TCHR TRNG.	100	65	100	65	—	—	—	—
		HUMANITIES,RELIGION & THEOLOG.	24	11	24	11	—	—	—	—
		FINE AND APPLIED ARTS	18	5	18	5	—	—	—	—
		LAW	47	13	47	13	—	—	—	—
		SOCIAL AND BEHAVIOURAL SCIENCE	—	—	—	—	—	—	—	—
		COMMERCIAL & BUS. ADMINISTR.	—	—	—	—	—	—	—	—
		MASS COMMUNICATION & DOCUMENT.	—	—	—	—	—	—	—	—
		HOME ECONOMICS & DOMESTIC SC.	—	—	—	—	—	—	—	—
		SERVICE TRADES	—	—	—	—	—	—	—	—
		NATURAL SCIENCE	12	4	12	4	—	—	—	—
		MATHEMATICS & COMPUTER SCIENCE	—	—	—	—	—	—	—	—
		MEDICAL AND HEALTH-RELATED SC.	56	19	56	19	—	—	—	—
		ENGINEERING	4	1	4	1	—	—	—	—
		ARCHITECTURE & TOWN PLANNING	—	—	—	—	—	—	—	—
		TRADE, CRAFT & INDUSTR. PGMS.	—	—	—	—	—	—	—	—
		TRANSPORT AND COMMUNICATIONS	—	—	—	—	—	—	—	—
		AGRICULTURE,FORESTRY & FISH'G.	3	2	3	2	—	—	—	—
		OTHER AND NOT SPECIFIED	38	8	38	8	—	—	—	—
MALTA	1977	TOTAL	1 674	426	171	76	1 479	347	24	3
		EDUCATION SCIENCE & TCHR TRNG.	172	70	116	49	56	21	—	—
		HUMANITIES,RELIGION & THEOLOG.	675	226	34	22	617	201	24	3
		FINE AND APPLIED ARTS	—	—	—	—	—	—	—	—
		LAW	107	11	—	—	107	11	—	—
		SOCIAL AND BEHAVIOURAL SCIENCE	310	41	21	5	289	36	—	—
		COMMERCIAL & BUS. ADMINISTR.	—	—	—	—	—	—	—	—
		MASS COMMUNICATION & DOCUMENT.	—	—	—	—	—	—	—	—
		HOME ECONOMICS & DOMESTIC SC.	—	—	—	—	—	—	—	—
		SERVICE TRADES	—	—	—	—	—	—	—	—
		NATURAL SCIENCE	123	43	—	—	123	43	—	—
		MATHEMATICS & COMPUTER SCIENCE	—	—	—	—	—	—	—	—
		MEDICAL AND HEALTH-RELATED SC.	119	34	—	—	119	34	—	—
		ENGINEERING	129	—	—	—	129	—	—	—
		ARCHITECTURE & TOWN PLANNING	39	1	—	—	39	1	—	—
		TRADE, CRAFT & INDUSTR. PGMS.	—	—	—	—	—	—	—	—
		TRANSPORT AND COMMUNICATIONS	—	—	—	—	—	—	—	—
		AGRICULTURE,FORESTRY & FISH'G.	—	—	—	—	—	—	—	—
		OTHER AND NOT SPECIFIED	—	—	—	—	—	—	—	—

Third level: students by levels and fields 3.12
Troisième degré: étudiants par types de programmes et domaines d'études
Tercer grado: estudiantes por tipos de programas y sectores de estudio

INTERNATIONAL STANDARD CLASSIFICATION OF EDUCATION BY LEVEL
CLASSIFICATION INTERNATIONALE TYPE DE L'EDUCATION PAR NIVEAUX
CLASIFICACION INTERNACIONAL NORMALIZADA DE LA EDUCACION POR GRADOS

COUNTRY / PAYS / PAIS	YEAR / ANNEE / AÑO	FIELD OF STUDY / BRANCHE D'ETUDES / RAMAS DE ESTUDIO	ALL LEVELS TOUS NIVEAUX TODOS LOS GRADOS MF	F	LEVEL 5 NIVEAU 5 GRADO 5 MF	F	LEVEL 6 NIVEAU 6 GRADO 6 MF	F	LEVEL 7 NIVEAU 7 GRADO 7 MF	F
NETHERLANDS ‡	1977	TOTAL	320 501	111 224	133 123	53 539	49 952	20 163	137 426	37 522
		EDUCATION SCIENCE & TCHR TRNG.	33 160	18 630	33 160	18 630	—	—	—	—
		HUMANITIES,RELIGION & THEOLOG.	44 653	20 933	—	—	19 923	10 182	24 730	10 751
		FINE AND APPLIED ARTS	17 197	8 084	13 050	5 882	4 147	2 202	—	—
		LAW	17 307	4 622	—	—	—	—	17 307	4 622
		SOCIAL AND BEHAVIOURAL SCIENCE	52 017	16 765	18 427	8 918	2 103	258	31 487	7 589
		COMMERCIAL & BUS. ADMINISTR.	5 839	457	5 839	457	—	—	—	—
		MASS COMMUNICATION & DOCUMENT.	2 321	1 621	2 321	1 621	—	—	—	—
		HOME ECONOMICS & DOMESTIC SC.	5 886	5 592	4 367	4 122	1 519	1 470	—	—
		SERVICE TRADES	927	345	927	345	—	—	—	—
		NATURAL SCIENCE	13 783	2 383	—	—	1 674	265	12 109	2 118
		MATHEMATICS & COMPUTER SCIENCE	4 023	583	—	—	1 815	311	2 208	272
		MEDICAL AND HEALTH-RELATED SC.	31 110	13 035	13 296	8 310	—	—	17 814	4 725
		ENGINEERING	54 311	4 254	31 705	3 552	5 467	—	17 139	702
		ARCHITECTURE & TOWN PLANNING	/.	/.	/.	/.	/.	/.	/.	/.
		TRADE, CRAFT & INDUSTR. PGMS.	3 505	28	3 505	28	—	—	—	—
		TRANSPORT AND COMMUNICATIONS	—	—	—	—	—	—	—	—
		AGRICULTURE,FORESTRY & FISH'G.	9 822	1 998	3 876	515	281	29	5 665	1 454
		OTHER AND NOT SPECIFIED	24 640	11 894	2 650	1 159	13 023	5 446	8 967	5 289
NORWAY ‡	1977	TOTAL	72 999	32 083	29 524	16 139	18 127	8 966	25 348	6 978
		EDUCATION SCIENCE & TCHR TRNG.	13 041	8 477	3 690	2 861	9 101	5 499	250	117
		HUMANITIES,RELIGION & THEOLOG.	11 155	5 881	2 885	1 775	3 223	2 071	5 047	2 035
		FINE AND APPLIED ARTS	777	360	175	110	575	240	27	10
		LAW	3 968	1 179	—	—	—	—	3 968	1 179
		SOCIAL AND BEHAVIOURAL SCIENCE	6 504	2 819	2 266	1 252	875	402	3 363	1 165
		COMMERCIAL & BUS. ADMINISTR.	6 508	2 067	4 046	1 720	2 426	345	36	2
		MASS COMMUNICATION & DOCUMENT.	158	60	158	60	—	—	—	—
		HOME ECONOMICS & DOMESTIC SC.	43	36	—	—	43	36	—	—
		SERVICE TRADES	—	—	—	—	—	—	—	—
		NATURAL SCIENCE	5 193	1 152	541	218	1 052	327	3 600	607
		MATHEMATICS & COMPUTER SCIENCE	/.	/.	/.	/.	/.	/.	/.	/.
		MEDICAL AND HEALTH-RELATED SC.	9 073	6 074	5 930	5 050	—	—	3 143	1 024
		ENGINEERING	9 635	1 018	5 242	677	352	16	4 041	325
		ARCHITECTURE & TOWN PLANNING	561	158	48	3	—	—	513	155
		TRADE, CRAFT & INDUSTR. PGMS.	254	102	254	102	—	—	—	—
		TRANSPORT AND COMMUNICATIONS	661	64	661	64	—	—	—	—
		AGRICULTURE,FORESTRY & FISH'G.	1 083	265	32	2	60	3	991	260
		OTHER AND NOT SPECIFIED	4 385	2 371	3 596	2 245	420	27	369	99

3.12   Third level: students by levels and fields
      Troisième degré: étudiants par types de programmes et domaines d'études
      Tercer grado: estudiantes por tipos de programas y sectores de estudio

INTERNATIONAL STANDARD CLASSIFICATION OF EDUCATION BY LEVEL
CLASSIFICATION INTERNATIONALE TYPE DE L'EDUCATION PAR NIVEAUX
CLASIFICACION INTERNACIONAL NORMALIZADA DE LA EDUCACION POR GRADOS

COUNTRY / PAYS / PAIS	YEAR / ANNEE / AÑO	FIELD OF STUDY / BRANCHE D'ETUDES / RAMAS DE ESTUDIO	ALL LEVELS TOUS NIVEAUX TODOS LOS GRADOS		LEVEL 5 NIVEAU 5 GRADO 5		LEVEL 6 NIVEAU 6 GRADO 6		LEVEL 7 NIVEAU 7 GRADO 7	
			MF	F	MF	F	MF	F	MF	F
POLAND ‡	1977	TOTAL	622 631	343 009	131 264	99 299	91 732	29 672	399 635	214 038
		EDUCATION SCIENCE & TCHR TRNG.	77 594	60 264	14 087	13 675	1 799	1 723	61 708	44 866
		HUMANITIES,RELIGION & THEOLOG.	40 439	30 102	—	—	—	—	40 439	30 102
		FINE AND APPLIED ARTS	8 242	4 107	213	129	72	23	7 957	3 955
		LAW	16 253	7 441	—	—	—	—	16 253	7 441
		SOCIAL AND BEHAVIOURAL SCIENCE	14 244	8 747	—	—	444	120	13 800	8 627
		COMMERCIAL & BUS. ADMINISTR.	110 292	74 246	38 613	33 243	27 252	14 326	44 427	26 677
		MASS COMMUNICATION & DOCUMENT.	4 433	3 446	—	—	—	—	4 433	3 446
		HOME ECONOMICS & DOMESTIC SC.	—	—	—	—	—	—	—	—
		SERVICE TRADES	—	—	—	—	—	—	—	—
		NATURAL SCIENCE	19 074	12 685	—	—	—	—	19 074	12 685
		MATHEMATICS & COMPUTER SCIENCE	8 705	8 790	—	—	—	—	8 705	8 790
		MEDICAL AND HEALTH-RELATED SC.	65 886	51 400	32 162	29 802	—	—	33 724	21 598
		ENGINEERING	178 113	50 256	39 858	19 228	46 699	7 789	91 556	23 239
		ARCHITECTURE & TOWN PLANNING	3 978	2 040	—	—	—	—	3 978	2 040
		TRADE, CRAFT & INDUSTR. PGMS.	—	—	—	—	—	—	—	—
		TRANSPORT AND COMMUNICATIONS	5 260	677	—	—	2 256	193	3 004	484
		AGRICULTURE,FORESTRY & FISH'G.	54 943	25 721	6 331	3 222	13 210	5 498	35 402	17 001
		OTHER AND NOT SPECIFIED	15 175	6 087	—	—	—	—	15 175	6 087
PORTUGAL ‡	1977	TOTAL	85 360	36 238	—	—	84 938	36 156	422	82
		EDUCATION SCIENCE & TCHR TRNG.	4 199	2 354	—	—	4 199	2 354	—	—
		HUMANITIES,RELIGION & THEOLOG.	18 209	12 521	—	—	18 159	12 481	50	40
		FINE AND APPLIED ARTS	2 926	1 377	—	—	2 926	1 377	—	—
		LAW	7 348	1 897	—	—	7 240	1 878	108	19
		SOCIAL AND BEHAVIOURAL SCIENCE	15 109	5 374	—	—	15 109	5 374	—	—
		COMMERCIAL & BUS. ADMINISTR.	./.	./.	—	—	./.	./.	./.	./.
		MASS COMMUNICATION & DOCUMENT.	./.	./.	—	—	./.	./.	./.	./.
		HOME ECONOMICS & DOMESTIC SC.	./.	./.	—	—	./.	./.	./.	./.
		SERVICE TRADES	./.	./.	—	—	./.	./.	./.	./.
		NATURAL SCIENCE	3 065	2 113	—	—	3 050	2 108	15	5
		MATHEMATICS & COMPUTER SCIENCE	1 714	1 205	—	—	1 714	1 205	—	—
		MEDICAL AND HEALTH-RELATED SC.	12 934	6 683	—	—	12 934	6 683	—	—
		ENGINEERING	16 366	2 086	—	—	16 305	2 073	61	13
		ARCHITECTURE & TOWN PLANNING	./.	./.	—	—	./.	./.	./.	./.
		TRADE, CRAFT & INDUSTR. PGMS.	./.	./.	—	—	./.	./.	./.	./.
		TRANSPORT AND COMMUNICATIONS	./.	./.	—	—	./.	./.	./.	./.
		AGRICULTURE,FORESTRY & FISH'G.	2 524	618	—	—	2 513	613	11	5
		OTHER AND NOT SPECIFIED	966	10	—	—	789	10	177	—

Third level: students by levels and fields   3.12
Troisième degré: étudiants par types de programmes et domaines d'études
Tercer grado: estudiantes por tipos de programas y sectores de estudio

INTERNATIONAL STANDARD CLASSIFICATION OF EDUCATION BY LEVEL
CLASSIFICATION INTERNATIONALE TYPE DE L'EDUCATION PAR NIVEAUX
CLASIFICACION INTERNACIONAL NORMALIZADA DE LA EDUCACION POR GRADOS

COUNTRY / PAYS / PAIS	YEAR / ANNEE / AÑO	FIELD OF STUDY / BRANCHE D'ETUDES / RAMAS DE ESTUDIO	ALL LEVELS TOUS NIVEAUX TODOS LOS GRADOS		LEVEL 5 NIVEAU 5 GRADO 5		LEVEL 6 NIVEAU 6 GRADO 6		LEVEL 7 NIVEAU 7 GRADO 7	
			MF	F	MF	F	MF	F	MF	F
ROMANIA ‡	1977	TOTAL	182 337	…	–	–	182 337	…	–	–
		EDUCATION SCIENCE & TCHR TRNG.	/	/	–	–	/	/	–	–
		HUMANITIES,RELIGION & THEOLOG.	18 297	…	–	–	18 297	…	–	–
		FINE AND APPLIED ARTS	2 600	…	–	–	2 600	…	–	–
		LAW	7 025	…	–	–	7 025	…	–	–
		SOCIAL AND BEHAVIOURAL SCIENCE	22 725	…	–	–	22 725	…	–	–
		COMMERCIAL & BUS. ADMINISTR.	–	–	–	–	–	–	–	–
		MASS COMMUNICATION & DOCUMENT.	–	–	–	–	–	–	–	–
		HOME ECONOMICS & DOMESTIC SC.	–	–	–	–	–	–	–	–
		SERVICE TRADES	–	–	–	–	–	–	–	–
		NATURAL SCIENCE	8 676	…	–	–	8 676	…	–	–
		MATHEMATICS & COMPUTER SCIENCE	4 893	…	–	–	4 893	…	–	–
		MEDICAL AND HEALTH-RELATED SC.	20 859	…	–	–	20 859	…	–	–
		ENGINEERING	80 273	…	–	–	80 273	…	–	–
		ARCHITECTURE & TOWN PLANNING	1 163	…	–	–	1 163	…	–	–
		TRADE,CRAFT & INDUSTR. PGMS.	–	–	–	–	–	–	–	–
		TRANSPORT AND COMMUNICATIONS	1 469	…	–	–	1 469	…	–	–
		AGRICULTURE,FORESTRY & FISH'G.	13 950	…	–	–	13 950	…	–	–
		OTHER AND NOT SPECIFIED	407	…	–	–	407	…	–	–
SPAIN ‡	1976	TOTAL	581 064	222 500	158 066	64 616	422 998	157 884	…	…
		EDUCATION SCIENCE & TCHR TRNG.	105 694	68 094	84 186	56 476	21 508	11 618	…	…
		HUMANITIES,RELIGION & THEOLOG.	57 943	35 507	–	–	57 943	35 507	…	…
		FINE AND APPLIED ARTS	6 172	2 827	3 188	1 551	2 984	1 276	…	…
		LAW	61 331	20 355	–	–	61 331	20 355	…	…
		SOCIAL AND BEHAVIOURAL SCIENCE	60 689	18 321	–	–	60 689	18 321	…	…
		COMMERCIAL & BUS. ADMINISTR.	15 059	3 790	15 059	3 790	–	–	…	…
		MASS COMMUNICATION & DOCUMENT.	7 116	2 667	–	–	7 116	2 667	…	…
		HOME ECONOMICS & DOMESTIC SC.	–	–	–	–	–	–	…	…
		SERVICE TRADES	–	–	–	–	–	–	…	…
		NATURAL SCIENCE	51 331	19 477	–	–	51 331	19 477	…	…
		MATHEMATICS & COMPUTER SCIENCE	3 303	1 063	–	–	3 303	1 063	…	…
		MEDICAL AND HEALTH-RELATED SC.	102 104	43 947	–	–	102 104	43 947	…	…
		ENGINEERING	64 339	1 899	34 286	1 113	30 053	786	…	…
		ARCHITECTURE & TOWN PLANNING	25 487	2 686	11 860	924	13 627	1 762	…	…
		TRADE,CRAFT & INDUSTR. PGMS.	–	–	–	–	–	–	…	…
		TRANSPORT AND COMMUNICATIONS	–	–	–	–	–	–	…	…
		AGRICULTURE,FORESTRY & FISH'G.	13 423	1 867	5 618	762	7 805	1 105	…	…
		OTHER AND NOT SPECIFIED	7 073	–	3 869	–	3 204	–	…	…

3.12 Third level: students by levels and fields
Troisième degré: étudiants par types de programmes et domaines d'études
Tercer grado: estudiantes por tipos de programas y sectores de estudio

INTERNATIONAL STANDARD CLASSIFICATION OF EDUCATION BY LEVEL
CLASSIFICATION INTERNATIONALE TYPE DE L'EDUCATION PAR NIVEAUX
CLASIFICACION INTERNACIONAL NORMALIZADA DE LA EDUCACION POR GRADOS

COUNTRY / PAYS / PAIS	YEAR / ANNEE / AÑO	FIELD OF STUDY / BRANCHE D'ETUDES / RAMAS DE ESTUDIO	ALL LEVELS / TOUS NIVEAUX / TODOS LOS GRADOS MF	F	LEVEL 5 / NIVEAU 5 / GRADO 5 MF	F	LEVEL 6 / NIVEAU 6 / GRADO 6 MF	F	LEVEL 7 / NIVEAU 7 / GRADO 7 MF	F
SWEDEN ‡	1977	TOTAL	190 105	83 689	...	...	...	...	...	...
		EDUCATION SCIENCE & TCHR TRNG.	20 555	15 678	14 240	11 001	6 315	4 677	—	—
		HUMANITIES,RELIGION & THEOLOG.	2 991	1 325	33	28	489	250	2 469	1 047
		FINE AND APPLIED ARTS	2 639	1 265	1 620	777	1 019	488	—	—
		LAW	1 824	773	—	—	1 677	744	147	29
		SOCIAL AND BEHAVIOURAL SCIENCE	7 933	2 458	2 325	380	2 488	1 056	3 120	1 022
		COMMERCIAL & BUS. ADMINISTR.	1 653	623	450	201	1 120	411	83	11
		MASS COMMUNICATION & DOCUMENT.	1 069	175	—	—	1 069	175	—	—
		HOME ECONOMICS & DOMESTIC SC.	180	175	180	175	—	—	—	—
		SERVICE TRADES	—	—	—	—	—	—	—	—
		NATURAL SCIENCE	3 173	655	—	—	773	221	2 400	434
		MATHEMATICS & COMPUTER SCIENCE	/	/	/	/	/	/	/	/
		MEDICAL AND HEALTH-RELATED SC.	22 449	15 013	12 493	11 213	7 735	3 340	2 221	460
		ENGINEERING	41 818	3 888	25 300	2 237	14 566	1 488	1 952	163
		ARCHITECTURE & TOWN PLANNING	1 529	560	—	—	1 529	560	—	—
		TRADE, CRAFT & INDUSTR. PGMS.	296	3	296	3	—	—	—	—
		TRANSPORT AND COMMUNICATIONS	492	62	492	62	—	—	—	—
		AGRICULTURE,FORESTRY & FISH'G.	1 911	574	300	15	1 245	499	366	60
		OTHER AND NOT SPECIFIED	77 593	39 173	...	...	...	...	...	...
SWITZERLAND ‡	1977	TOTAL	74 730	20 732	19 533	4 855	55 197	15 877	./.	./.
		EDUCATION SCIENCE & TCHR TRNG.	6 786	3 129	3 659	2 089	3 127	1 040	./.	./.
		HUMANITIES,RELIGION & THEOLOG.	9 676	4 690	1 000	598	8 676	4 092	./.	./.
		FINE AND APPLIED ARTS	1 255	720	560	320	695	400	./.	./.
		LAW	6 861	1 671	—	—	6 861	1 671	./.	./.
		SOCIAL AND BEHAVIOURAL SCIENCE	12 191	3 996	198	127	11 993	3 869	./.	./.
		COMMERCIAL & BUS. ADMINISTR.	2 041	200	2 041	200	—	—	./.	./.
		MASS COMMUNICATION & DOCUMENT.	108	90	108	90	—	—	./.	./.
		HOME ECONOMICS & DOMESTIC SC.	377	101	377	101	—	—	./.	./.
		SERVICE TRADES	342	79	342	79	—	—	./.	./.
		NATURAL SCIENCE	6 813	1 249	13	—	6 800	1 249	./.	./.
		MATHEMATICS & COMPUTER SCIENCE	1 563	245	—	—	1 563	245	./.	./.
		MEDICAL AND HEALTH-RELATED SC.	9 444	2 914	178	145	9 266	2 769	./.	./.
		ENGINEERING	9 897	128	6 278	70	3 619	58	./.	./.
		ARCHITECTURE & TOWN PLANNING	2 083	258	952	54	1 131	204	./.	./.
		TRADE, CRAFT & INDUSTR. PGMS.	2 195	105	2 195	105	—	—	./.	./.
		TRANSPORT AND COMMUNICATIONS	88	—	88	—	—	—	./.	./.
		AGRICULTURE,FORESTRY & FISH'G.	1 698	287	232	7	1 466	280	./.	./.
		OTHER AND NOT SPECIFIED	1 312	870	1 312	870	—	—	./.	./.

Third level: students by levels and fields 3.12
Troisième degré: étudiants par types de programmes et domaines d'études
Tercer grado: estudiantes por tipos de programas y sectores de estudio

INTERNATIONAL STANDARD CLASSIFICATION OF EDUCATION BY LEVEL
CLASSIFICATION INTERNATIONALE TYPE DE L'EDUCATION PAR NIVEAUX
CLASSIFICACION INTERNACIONAL NORMALIZADA DE LA EDUCACION POR GRADOS

COUNTRY / PAYS / PAIS	YEAR / ANNEE / AÑO	FIELD OF STUDY / BRANCHE D'ETUDES / RAMAS DE ESTUDIO	ALL LEVELS TOUS NIVEAUX TODOS LOS GRADOS MF	F	LEVEL 5 NIVEAU 5 GRADO 5 MF	F	LEVEL 6 NIVEAU 6 GRADO 6 MF	F	LEVEL 7 NIVEAU 7 GRADO 7 MF	F
UNITED KINGDOM ‡	1975	TOTAL	732 947	264 254	300 960	122 965	345 901	120 637	86 086	20 652
		EDUCATION SCIENCE & TCHR TRNG.	138 357	93 517	120 240	85 295	3 446	2 248	14 671	5 974
		HUMANITIES,RELIGION & THEOLOG.	63 562	40 183	3 357	3 005	50 793	33 184	9 412	3 994
		FINE AND APPLIED ARTS	21 033	13 064	3 282	2 911	16 013	9 293	1 738	860
		LAW	17 440	4 714	2 283	587	14 114	3 926	1 043	201
		SOCIAL AND BEHAVIOURAL SCIENCE	63 251	44 097	6 178	18 351	47 444	21 193	9 629	4 553
		COMMERCIAL & BUS. ADMINISTR.	76 710	./.	55 461	./.	9 480	./.	11 769	./.
		MASS COMMUNICATION & DOCUMENT.	2 460	./.	1 072	./.	965	./.	423	./.
		HOME ECONOMICS & DOMESTIC SC.	1 560	./.	262	./.	1 252	./.	46	./.
		SERVICE TRADES	5 021	./.	5 021	./.	–	–	–	–
		NATURAL SCIENCE	71 363	23 399	9 173	3 085	48 320	17 504	13 870	2 810
		MATHEMATICS & COMPUTER SCIENCE	20 646	20 091	4 402	8 060	12 888	10 462	5 356	1 569
		MEDICAL AND HEALTH-RELATED SC.	47 038	3 020	13 546	971	28 170	1 611	5 322	438
		ENGINEERING	104 869	./.	49 556	./.	45 108	./.	10 205	./.
		ARCHITECTURE & TOWN PLANNING	14 417	./.	5 390	./.	6 927	./.	2 100	./.
		TRADE, CRAFT & INDUSTR. PGMS.	1 748	./.	1 748	./.	–	–	–	–
		TRANSPORT AND COMMUNICATIONS	1 359	./.	1 359	./.	–	–	–	–
		AGRICULTURE,FORESTRY & FISH'G.	7 080	1 638	1 485	212	4 124	1 176	1 471	250
		OTHER AND NOT SPECIFIED	75 033	20 531	17 145	488	56 857	20 040	1 031	3
YUGOSLAVIA ‡	1976	TOTAL	406 542	160 830	119 218	46 121	287 324	114 709	.	.
		EDUCATION SCIENCE & TCHR TRNG.	31 249	15 391	23 821	12 733	7 428	2 658	.	.
		HUMANITIES,RELIGION & THEOLOG.	31 153	17 441	–	–	31 153	17 441	.	.
		FINE AND APPLIED ARTS	3 446	1 416	3 446	1 416	–	–	.	.
		LAW	50 623	23 958	957	492	49 666	23 466	.	.
		SOCIAL AND BEHAVIOURAL SCIENCE	98 272	46 381	35 557	17 710	62 715	28 671	.	.
		COMMERCIAL & BUS. ADMINISTR.	16 955	5 070	4 608	770	12 347	4 300	.	.
		MASS COMMUNICATION & DOCUMENT.	91	43	91	43	–	–	.	.
		HOME ECONOMICS & DOMESTIC SC.	636	505	130	39	506	466	.	.
		SERVICE TRADES	–	–	–	–	–	–	.	.
		NATURAL SCIENCE	4 473	1 780	3 233	1 240	1 240	540	.	.
		MATHEMATICS & COMPUTER SCIENCE	17 341	7 813	588	240	16 753	7 573	.	.
		MEDICAL AND HEALTH-RELATED SC.	26 323	16 886	4 667	3 869	21 656	13 017	.	.
		ENGINEERING	83 858	12 039	21 928	2 020	61 930	10 019	.	.
		ARCHITECTURE & TOWN PLANNING	4 278	1 925	–	–	4 278	1 925	.	.
		TRADE, CRAFT & INDUSTR. PGMS.	4 082	1 875	2 207	991	1 875	884	.	.
		TRANSPORT AND COMMUNICATIONS	10 824	1 164	9 833	173	991	991	.	.
		AGRICULTURE,FORESTRY & FISH'G.	14 834	3 896	14 448	386	386	3 510	.	.
		OTHER AND NOT SPECIFIED	8 104	3 247	4 857	379	3 247	2 868	.	.

3.12 Third level: students by levels and fields
Troisième degré: étudiants par types de programmes et domaines d'études
Tercer grado: estudiantes por tipos de programas y sectores de estudio

COUNTRY / PAYS / PAIS	YEAR / ANNEE / AÑO	FIELD OF STUDY / BRANCHE D'ETUDES / RAMAS DE ESTUDIO	ALL LEVELS TOUS NIVEAUX TODOS LOS GRADOS MF	F	LEVEL 5 NIVEAU 5 GRADO 5 MF	F	LEVEL 6 NIVEAU 6 GRADO 6 MF	F	LEVEL 7 NIVEAU 7 GRADO 7 MF	F
YUGOSLAVIA (CONT.) ‡	1977	TOTAL	425 485	167 070	119 843	46 173	305 642	120 897	...	...
		EDUCATION SCIENCE & TCHR TRNG.	33 150	16 120	23 617	12 770	9 533	3 350	...	...
		HUMANITES,RELIGION & THEOLOG.	33 215	18 014	—	—	33 215	18 014	...	...
		FINE AND APPLIED ARTS	3 603	1 470	—	—	3 603	1 470	...	...
		LAW	53 745	25 764	1 000	469	52 745	25 295	...	...
		SOCIAL AND BEHAVIOURAL SCIENCE	100 571	47 608	34 845	17 087	65 726	30 521	...	...
		COMMERCIAL & BUS. ADMINISTR.	14 965	4 713	4 378	806	10 587	3 907	...	...
		MASS COMMUNICATION & DOCUMENT.	28	17	28	17	—	—	...	...
		HOME ECONOMICS & DOMESTIC SC.	713	555	713	555	—	—	...	...
		SERVICE TRADES	5 109	1 892	2 828	1 072	2 281	820	...	...
		NATURAL SCIENCE	17 460	7 875	769	293	16 691	7 582	...	...
		MATHEMATICS & COMPUTER SCIENCE	/	/	/	/	/	/	...	...
		MEDICAL AND HEALTH-RELATED SC.	27 859	17 764	4 926	4 120	22 933	13 644	...	...
		ENGINEERING	89 774	12 229	23 275	1 897	66 499	10 332	...	...
		ARCHITECTURE & TOWN PLANNING	3 879	1 776	—	—	3 879	1 776	...	...
		TRADE, CRAFT & INDUSTR. PGMS.	4 006	1 984	4 006	1 984	—	—	...	...
		TRANSPORT AND COMMUNICATIONS	11 122	1 129	7 996	824	3 126	305	...	...
		AGRICULTURE,FORESTRY & FISH'G.	17 199	4 381	2 375	500	14 824	3 881	...	...
		OTHER AND NOT SPECIFIED	9 087	3 779	9 087	3 779	—	—	...	...
OCEANIA										
AMERICAN SAMOA	1977	TOTAL	1 114	663	344	203	770	460	—	—

INTERNATIONAL STANDARD CLASSIFICATION OF EDUCATION BY LEVEL
CLASSIFICATION INTERNATIONALE TYPE DE L'EDUCATION PAR NIVEAUX
CLASIFICACION INTERNACIONAL NORMALIZADA DE LA EDUCACION POR GRADOS

COUNTRY PAYS PAIS	YEAR ANNEE AÑO	FIELD OF STUDY BRANCHE D'ETUDES RAMAS DE ESTUDIO	ALL LEVELS TOUS NIVEAUX TODOS LOS GRADOS MF	F	LEVEL 5 NIVEAU 5 GRADO 5 MF	F	LEVEL 6 NIVEAU 6 GRADO 6 MF	F	LEVEL 7 NIVEAU 7 GRADO 7 MF	F
AUSTRALIA ‡	1977	TOTAL	300 876	128 950	77 134	45 625	181 880	69 019	41 862	14 306
		EDUCATION SCIENCE & TCHR TRNG.	75 750	49 749	47 318	33 837	13 905	8 574	14 527	7 338
		HUMANITIES,RELIGION & THEOLOG.	46 233	27 432	2 243	1 369	40 640	24 447	3 350	1 616
		FINE AND APPLIED ARTS	6 349	3 711	4 681	2 735	1 365	821	303	155
		LAW	10 593	2 870	571	101	8 771	2 532	1 251	237
		SOCIAL AND BEHAVIOURAL SCIENCE	20 954	7 758	928	370	16 773	6 232	3 253	1 156
		COMMERCIAL & BUS. ADMINISTR.	35 751	6 202	6 821	1 146	24 175	4 395	4 755	661
		MASS COMMUNICATION & DOCUMENT.	3 802	2 725	925	681	1 827	1 257	1 050	787
		HOME ECONOMICS & DOMESTIC SC.	700	689	616	607	57	56	27	26
		SERVICE TRADES	160	39	37	5	123	34		
		NATURAL SCIENCE	28 267	8 297	1 457	458	22 804	7 136	4 006	703
		MATHEMATICS & COMPUTER SCIENCE	5 469	1 208	267	57	3 789	920	1 413	231
		MEDICAL AND HEALTH-RELATED SC.	21 144	10 438	3 634	2 620	15 982	7 276	1 528	542
		ENGINEERING	22 801	431	2 188	28	17 768	319	2 845	84
		ARCHITECTURE & TOWN PLANNING	6 925	1 007	1 578	110	3 801	643	1 546	254
		TRADE, CRAFT & INDUSTR. PGMS.	1 017	336	559	216	307	108	151	12
		TRANSPORT AND COMMUNICATIONS	8		7				1	
		AGRICULTURE, FORESTRY & FISH'G.	6 461	1 368	1 391	245	3 903	980	1 167	143
		OTHER AND NOT SPECIFIED	8 492	4 690	1 913	1 040	5 890	3 289	689	361
FIJI	1975	TOTAL	1 810	...	1 009	...	800	...	1	...
		EDUCATION SCIENCE & TCHR TRNG.	854	...	607	...	247	...		...
		HUMANITIES,RELIGION & THEOLOG.	28	...	6	...	22	...		...
		FINE AND APPLIED ARTS	—	—	—	—				
		LAW								
		SOCIAL SCIENCES, TOTAL	294	...			293	...	1	...
		NATURAL SCIENCES, TOTAL	52	...			52	...		...
		MEDICAL AND HEALTH-RELATED SC.	285	...	285	...				
		ENG. TOTAL								
		AGRICULTURE, FORESTRY & FISH'G.	116	...	111	...	5	...		...
		OTHER AND NOT SPECIFIED	181	...			181	...		...
GUAM	1977	TOTAL	4 343	2 123	—	—	3 223	1 588	1 120	535

3.12 Third level: students by levels and fields
Troisième degré: étudiants par types de programmes et domaines d'études
Tercer grado: estudiantes por tipos de programas y sectores de estudio

INTERNATIONAL STANDARD CLASSIFICATION OF EDUCATION BY LEVEL
CLASSIFICATION INTERNATIONALE TYPE DE L'EDUCATION PAR NIVEAUX
CLASIFICACION INTERNACIONAL NORMALIZADA DE LA EDUCACION POR GRADOS

COUNTRY / PAYS / PAIS	YEAR / ANNEE / AÑO	FIELD OF STUDY / BRANCHE D'ETUDES / RAMAS DE ESTUDIO	ALL LEVELS TOUS NIVEAUX TODOS LOS GRADOS MF	F	LEVEL 5 NIVEAU 5 GRADO 5 MF	F	LEVEL 6 NIVEAU 6 GRADO 6 MF	F	LEVEL 7 NIVEAU 7 GRADO 7 MF	F
NEW CALEDONIA	1976	TOTAL	366	...	105	...	108	...	153	...
		EDUCATION SCIENCE & TCHR TRNG.	-	-	-	-	-	-	-	-
		HUMANITIES,RELIGION & THEOLOG.	-	-	-	-	-	-	-	-
		FINE AND APPLIED ARTS	192	-	105	-	87	-	-	-
		LAW	21	-	-	-	21	-	-	-
		SOCIAL AND BEHAVIOURAL SCIENCE	-	-	-	-	-	-	-	-
		COMMERCIAL & BUS. ADMINISTR.	-	-	-	-	-	-	-	-
		MASS COMMUNICATION & DOCUMENT	-	-	-	-	-	-	-	-
		HOME ECONOMICS & DOMESTIC SC.	-	-	-	-	-	-	-	-
		SERVICE TRADES	-	-	-	-	-	-	-	-
		NATURAL SCIENCE	-	-	-	-	-	-	-	-
		MATHEMATICS & COMPUTER SCIENCE	-	-	-	-	-	-	-	-
		MEDICAL AND HEALTH-RELATED SC.	-	-	-	-	-	-	-	-
		ENGINEERING	153	-	-	-	-	-	153	-
		ARCHITECTURE & TOWN PLANNING	-	-	-	-	-	-	-	-
		TRADE, CRAFT & INDUSTR. PGMS.	-	-	-	-	-	-	-	-
		TRANSPORT AND COMMUNICATIONS	-	-	-	-	-	-	-	-
		AGRICULTURE,FORESTRY & FISH'G.	-	-	-	-	-	-	-	-
		OTHER AND NOT SPECIFIED	-	-	-	-	-	-	-	-
NEW ZEALAND ‡	1976	TOTAL	76 419	29 213	26 226	6 710	44 793	20 917	5 400	1 586
		EDUCATION SCIENCE & TCHR TRNG.	32 917	12 314	22 118	4 971	9 915	6 941	884	402
		HUMANITIES,RELIGION & THEOLOG.	15 252	9 357	201	167	13 573	8 576	1 478	614
		FINE AND APPLIED ARTS	692	384	237	131	425	240	30	13
		LAW	2 988	791	-	-	2 588	707	400	84
		SOCIAL AND BEHAVIOURAL SCIENCE	857	430	-	-	634	355	223	75
		COMMERCIAL & BUS. ADMINISTR.	5 520	1 076	20	5	5 121	1 011	379	60
		MASS COMMUNICATION & DOCUMENT	-	-	-	-	-	-	-	-
		HOME ECONOMICS & DOMESTIC SC.	18	10	-	-	-	-	18	10
		SERVICE TRADES	201	200	133	132	63	63	5	5
		NATURAL SCIENCE	6 071	1 688	-	-	4 905	1 473	1 166	215
		MATHEMATICS & COMPUTER SCIENCE	42	8	-	-	-	-	42	8
		MEDICAL AND HEALTH-RELATED SC.	2 614	994	411	328	2 110	652	93	14
		ENGINEERING	2 627	101	19	-	2 394	97	214	4
		ARCHITECTURE & TOWN PLANNING	966	171	162	17	655	125	149	29
		TRADE, CRAFT & INDUSTR. PGMS.	-	-	-	-	-	-	-	-
		TRANSPORT AND COMMUNICATIONS	-	-	-	-	-	-	-	-
		AGRICULTURE,FORESTRY & FISH'G.	2 648	457	720	91	1 666	339	262	27
		OTHER AND NOT SPECIFIED	3 006	1 232	2 205	868	744	338	57	26

INTERNATIONAL STANDARD CLASSIFICATION OF EDUCATION BY LEVEL

CLASSIFICATION INTERNATIONALE TYPE DE L'EDUCATION PAR NIVEAUX

CLASIFICACION INTERNACIONAL NORMALIZADA DE LA EDUCACION POR GRADOS

COUNTRY / PAYS / PAIS	YEAR / ANNEE / AÑO	FIELD OF STUDY / BRANCHE D'ETUDES / RAMAS DE ESTUDIO	ALL LEVELS TOUS NIVEAUX TODOS LOS GRADOS MF	F	LEVEL 5 NIVEAU 5 GRADO 5 MF	F	LEVEL 6 NIVEAU 6 GRADO 6 MF	F	LEVEL 7 NIVEAU 7 GRADO 7 MF	F
PACIFIC ISLANDS	1977	TOTAL	573	...	241	...	332	...	—	—
		EDUCATION SCIENCE & TCHR TRNG.	297	...	—	—	297	...	—	—
		HUMANITIES,RELIGION & THEOLOG.	—	—	—	—	—	—	—	—
		FINE AND APPLIED ARTS	—	—	—	—	—	—	—	—
		LAW	—	—	—	—	—	—	—	—
		SOCIAL AND BEHAVIOURAL SCIENCE	—	—	—	—	—	—	—	—
		COMMERCIAL & BUS. ADMINISTR.	—	—	—	—	—	—	—	—
		MASS COMMUNICATION & DOCUMENT.	—	—	—	—	—	—	—	—
		HOME ECONOMICS & DOMESTIC SC.	—	—	—	—	—	—	—	—
		SERVICE TRADES	—	—	—	—	—	—	—	—
		NATURAL SCIENCE	—	—	—	—	—	—	—	—
		MATHEMATICS & COMPUTER SCIENCE	—	—	—	—	—	—	—	—
		MEDICAL AND HEALTH-RELATED SC.	35	...	—	—	35	...	—	—
		ENGINEERING	—	—	—	—	—	—	—	—
		ARCHITECTURE & TOWN PLANNING	—	—	—	—	—	—	—	—
		TRADE, CRAFT & INDUSTR. PGMS.	241	...	241	...	—	—	—	—
		TRANSPORT AND COMMUNICATIONS	—	—	—	—	—	—	—	—
		AGRICULTURE,FORESTRY & FISH'G.	—	—	—	—	—	—	—	—
		OTHER AND NOT SPECIFIED	—	—	—	—	—	—	—	—
PAPUA NEW GUINEA ‡	1977	TOTAL	2 983	321	556	62	2 329	239	98	20
		EDUCATION SCIENCE & TCHR TRNG.	139	32	16	6	112	23	11	3
		HUMANITIES,RELIGION & THEOLOG.	584	106	—	—	530	91	54	15
		FINE AND APPLIED ARTS	—	—	—	—	—	—	—	—
		LAW	195	13	—	—	192	13	3	—
		SOCIAL AND BEHAVIOURAL SCIENCE	104	5	—	—	102	5	2	—
		COMMERCIAL & BUS. ADMINISTR.	312	41	50	7	261	34	1	—
		MASS COMMUNICATION & DOCUMENT.	19	9	19	9	—	—	—	—
		HOME ECONOMICS & DOMESTIC SC.	—	—	—	—	—	—	—	—
		SERVICE TRADES	—	—	—	—	—	—	—	—
		NATURAL SCIENCE	298	42	—	—	283	40	15	2
		MATHEMATICS & COMPUTER SCIENCE	—	—	—	—	—	—	—	—
		MEDICAL AND HEALTH-RELATED SC.	123	17	—	—	116	17	7	—
		ENGINEERING	769	18	227	8	542	10	—	—
		ARCHITECTURE & TOWN PLANNING	69	1	—	—	69	1	—	—
		TRADE, CRAFT & INDUSTR. PGMS.	—	—	—	—	—	—	—	—
		TRANSPORT AND COMMUNICATIONS	—	—	—	—	—	—	—	—
		AGRICULTURE,FORESTRY & FISH'G.	154	5	28	—	121	5	5	—
		OTHER AND NOT SPECIFIED	217	32	216	32	1	—	—	—

3.12 Third level: students by levels and fields
Troisième degré: étudiants par types de programmes et domaines d'études
Tercer grado: estudiantes por tipos de programas y sectores de estudio

			INTERNATIONAL STANDARD CLASSIFICATION OF EDUCATION BY LEVEL / CLASSIFICATION INTERNATIONALE TYPE DE L'EDUCATION PAR NIVEAUX / CLASIFICACION INTERNACIONAL NORMALIZADA DE LA EDUCACION POR GRADOS							
			ALL LEVELS / TOUS NIVEAUX / TODOS LOS GRADOS		LEVEL 5 / NIVEAU 5 / GRADO 5		LEVEL 6 / NIVEAU 6 / GRADO 6		LEVEL 7 / NIVEAU 7 / GRADO 7	
COUNTRY / PAYS / PAIS	YEAR / ANNEE / AÑO	FIELD OF STUDY / BRANCHE D'ETUDES / RAMAS DE ESTUDIO	MF	F	MF	F	MF	F	MF	F
SAMOA	1978	TOTAL	425	...	218	72	207	...	—	—
		EDUCATION SCIENCE & TCHR TRNG.	11	2	—	—	11	2	—	—
		HUMANITIES,RELIGION & THEOLOG.	196	...	—	—	196	...	—	—
		FINE AND APPLIED ARTS	—	—	—	—	—	—	—	—
		LAW	—	—	—	—	—	—	—	—
		SOCIAL AND BEHAVIOURAL SCIENCE	218	72	218	72	—	—	—	—
		COMMERCIAL & BUS. ADMINISTR.	—	—	—	—	—	—	—	—
		MASS COMMUNICATION & DOCUMENT.	—	—	—	—	—	—	—	—
		HOME ECONOMICS & DOMESTIC SC.	—	—	—	—	—	—	—	—
		SERVICE TRADES	—	—	—	—	—	—	—	—
		NATURAL SCIENCE	—	—	—	—	—	—	—	—
		MATHEMATICS & COMPUTER SCIENCE	—	—	—	—	—	—	—	—
		MEDICAL AND HEALTH-RELATED SC.	—	—	—	—	—	—	—	—
		ENGINEERING	—	—	—	—	—	—	—	—
		ARCHITECTURE & TOWN PLANNING	—	—	—	—	—	—	—	—
		TRADE, CRAFT & INDUSTR. PGMS.	—	—	—	—	—	—	—	—
		TRANSPORT AND COMMUNICATIONS	—	—	—	—	—	—	—	—
		AGRICULTURE,FORESTRY & FISH'G.	—	—	—	—	—	—	—	—
		OTHER AND NOT SPECIFIED	—	—	—	—	—	—	—	—
TONGA	1977	TOTAL	195	87	195	87	—	—	—	—
		EDUCATION SCIENCE & TCHR TRNG.	87	77	87	77	—	—	—	—
		HUMANITIES,RELIGION & THEOLOG.	5	—	5	—	—	—	—	—
		FINE AND APPLIED ARTS	—	—	—	—	—	—	—	—
		LAW	12	—	12	—	—	—	—	—
		SOCIAL AND BEHAVIOURAL SCIENCE	9	1	9	1	—	—	—	—
		COMMERCIAL & BUS. ADMINISTR.	10	2	10	2	—	—	—	—
		MASS COMMUNICATION & DOCUMENT.	—	—	—	—	—	—	—	—
		HOME ECONOMICS & DOMESTIC SC.	—	—	—	—	—	—	—	—
		SERVICE TRADES	—	—	—	—	—	—	—	—
		NATURAL SCIENCE	13	—	13	—	—	—	—	—
		MATHEMATICS & COMPUTER SCIENCE	17	—	17	—	—	—	—	—
		MEDICAL AND HEALTH-RELATED SC.	—	—	—	—	—	—	—	—
		ENGINEERING	—	—	—	—	—	—	—	—
		ARCHITECTURE & TOWN PLANNING	6	—	6	—	—	—	—	—
		TRADE, CRAFT & INDUSTR. PGMS.	—	—	—	—	—	—	—	—
		TRANSPORT AND COMMUNICATIONS	—	—	—	—	—	—	—	—
		AGRICULTURE,FORESTRY & FISH'G.	—	—	—	—	—	—	—	—
		OTHER AND NOT SPECIFIED	36	7	36	7	—	—	—	—

Third level: students by levels and fields   3.12
Troisième degré: étudiants par types de programmes et domaines d'études
Tercer grado: estudiantes por tipos de programas y sectores de estudio

INTERNATIONAL STANDARD CLASSIFICATION OF EDUCATION BY LEVEL
CLASSIFICATION INTERNATIONALE TYPE DE L'EDUCATION PAR NIVEAUX
CLASIFICACION INTERNACIONAL NORMALIZADA DE LA EDUCACION POR GRADOS

COUNTRY / PAYS / PAIS	YEAR / ANNEE / AÑO	FIELD OF STUDY / BRANCHE D'ETUDES / RAMAS DE ESTUDIO	ALL LEVELS / TOUS NIVEAUX / TODOS LOS GRADOS		LEVEL 5 / NIVEAU 5 / GRADO 5		LEVEL 6 / NIVEAU 6 / GRADO 6		LEVEL 7 / NIVEAU 7 / GRADO 7	
			MF	F	MF	F	MF	F	MF	F
U.S.S.R.										
U.S.S.R. ‡	1976	TOTAL	4 950 000	...						
		EDUCATION SCIENCE & TCHR TRNG.	1 439 000	...						
		FINE AND APPLIED ARTS	46 000	...						
		LAW	359 000	...						
		MEDICAL AND HEALTH-RELATED SC.	357 000	...						
		ENGINEERING	2 273 000	...						
		TRANSPORT AND COMMUNICATIONS	./.	./.						
		AGRICULTURE,FORESTRY & FISH'G.	476 000	...						
		OTHER AND NOT SPECIFIED	—	—						
	1977	TOTAL	5 037 200	...						
		EDUCATION SCIENCE & TCHR TRNG.	1 465 400	...						
		FINE AND APPLIED ARTS	46 200	...						
		LAW	362 300	...						
		MEDICAL AND HEALTH-RELATED SC.	362 600	...						
		ENGINEERING	2 309 600	...						
		TRANSPORT AND COMMUNICATIONS	./.	./.						
		AGRICULTURE,FORESTRY & FISH'G.	491 100	...						
		OTHER AND NOT SPECIFIED	—	—						
BYELORUSSIAN S.S.R. ‡	1976	TOTAL	164 598	...						
		EDUCATION SCIENCE & TCHR TRNG.	54 467	...						
		FINE AND APPLIED ARTS	1 620	...						
		LAW	12 478	...						
		MEDICAL AND HEALTH-RELATED SC.	11 270	...						
		ENGINEERING	62 617	...						
		TRANSPORT AND COMMUNICATIONS	./.	./.						
		AGRICULTURE,FORESTRY & FISH'G.	22 146	...						
		OTHER AND NOT SPECIFIED	—	—						
	1977	TOTAL	167 812	89 711						
		EDUCATION SCIENCE & TCHR TRNG.	54 730	39 457						
		FINE AND APPLIED ARTS	1 628	863						
		LAW	12 931	9 453						
		MEDICAL AND HEALTH-RELATED SC.	11 288	6 025						
		ENGINEERING	64 439	26 359						
		TRANSPORT AND COMMUNICATIONS	./.	./.						
		AGRICULTURE,FORESTRY & FISH'G.	22 796	7 554						
		OTHER AND NOT SPECIFIED	—	—						

3.12 Third level: students by levels and fields
Troisième degré: étudiants par types de programmes et domaines d'études
Tercer grado: estudiantes por tipos de programas y sectores de estudio

INTERNATIONAL STANDARD CLASSIFICATION OF EDUCATION BY LEVEL
CLASSIFICATION INTERNATIONALE TYPE DE L'EDUCATION PAR NIVEAUX
CLASIFICACION INTERNACIONAL NORMALIZADA DE LA EDUCACION POR GRADOS

COUNTRY / PAYS / PAIS	YEAR / ANNEE / AÑO	FIELD OF STUDY / BRANCHE D'ETUDES / RAMAS DE ESTUDIO	ALL LEVELS TOUS NIVEAUX TODOS LOS GRADOS		LEVEL 5 NIVEAU 5 GRADO 5		LEVEL 6 NIVEAU 6 GRADO 6		LEVEL 7 NIVEAU 7 GRADO 7	
			MF	F	MF	F	MF	F	MF	F
UKRAINIAN S.S.R. ‡	1976	TOTAL	844 400	...						
		EDUCATION SCIENCE & TCHR TRNG.	211 600	...						
		FINE AND APPLIED ARTS	6 700	...						
		LAW	66 700	...						
		MEDICAL AND HEALTH-RELATED SC.	58 600	...						
		ENGINEERING	425 600	...						
		TRANSPORT AND COMMUNICATIONS	./.	./.						
		AGRICULTURE, FORESTRY & FISH'G.	75 200	...						
		OTHER AND NOT SPECIFIED	-	-						
	1977	TOTAL	856 700	...						
		EDUCATION SCIENCE & TCHR TRNG.	215 200	...						
		FINE AND APPLIED ARTS	6 800	...						
		LAW	68 200	...						
		MEDICAL AND HEALTH-RELATED SC.	58 900	...						
		ENGINEERING	429 900	...						
		TRANSPORT AND COMMUNICATIONS	./.	./.						
		AGRICULTURE, FORESTRY & FISH'G.	77 700	...						
		OTHER AND NOT SPECIFIED	-	-						

EGYPT:
E—> EXCLUDING VOCATIONAL-TRAINING CENTRES
(OTHER NON-UNIVERSITY INSTITUTIONS).
FR—> COMPTE NON TENU DES CENTRES DE FORMATION
TECHNIQUE (AUTRES ETABLISSEMENTS NON UNIVERSI-
TAIRES).
ESP> EXCLUIDOS LOS CENTROS DE FORMACION TECNICA
(OTROS ESTABLECIMIENTOS NO UNIVERSITARIOS).

ETHIOPIA:
E—> THE FIGURE SHOWN UNDER "OTHER AND NOT
SPECIFIED" REFERS MAINLY TO STUDENTS ENROLLED
EITHER IN THE FIRST YEAR OR IN THE PREPARATORY
YEAR (GENERAL STUDIES).
FR—> LES CHIFFRES PORTES SOUS LA RUBRIQUE
"AUTRES ET NON SPECIFIE" SE REFERENT, POUR LA
PLUPART, AUX ETUDIANTS INSCRITS SOIT EN PREMIERE
ANNEE, SOIT EN ANNEE PREPARATOIRE (ETUDES
GENERALES).
ESP> LAS CIFRAS INSCRITAS EN LA RUBRICA "OTROS Y
SIN ESPECIFICAR" SE REFIEREN A LOS ESTUDIANTES
MATRICULADOS YA SEA EN EL PRIMER AÑO O BIEN EN EL
AÑO PREPARATORIO (ESTUDIOS GENERALES).

KENYA:
E—> UNIVERSITY OF NAIROBI AND KENYATTA UNIVER-
SITY COLLEGE ONLY.
FR—> LES DONNEES SE REFERENT A L'UNIVERSITE DE
NAIROBI ET AU "KENYATTA UNIVERSITY COLLEGE"
SEULEMENT.
ESP> LOS DATOS SE REFIEREN A LA UNIVERSIDAD DE
NAIROBI Y AL "KENYATTA UNIVERSITY COLLEGE"
SOLAMENTE.

MADAGASCAR:
E—> UNIVERSITIES AND EQUIVALENT INSTITUTIONS
ONLY. ENGINEERING ALSO INCLUDES ARCHITECTURE AND
TOWN PLANNING, TRADE, CRAFT AND INDUSTRIAL
PROGRAMMES AND TRANSPORT AND COMMUNICATIONS.
FR—> UNIVERSITES ET ETABLISSEMENTS EQUIVALENTS
SEULEMENT. LES SCIENCES DE L'INGENIEUR COMPREN-
NENT EGALEMENT L'ARCHITECTURE ET L'URBANISME, LES
METIERS DE LA PRODUCTION INDUSTRIELLE ET LES
TRANSPORTS ET LES TELECOMMUNICATIONS.
ESP> UNIVERSIDADES Y ESTABLECIMIENTOS
EQUIVALENTES SOLAMENTE. LA INGENIERIA Y TECNOLOGIA
COMPRENDE IGUALMENTE LA ARQUITECTURA Y URBANISMO,
LAS ARTES Y OFICIOS INDUSTRIALES Y LOS TRANSPORTES
Y COMUNICACIONES.

Third level: students by levels and fields 3.12
Troisième degré: étudiants par types de programmes et domaines d'études
Tercer grado: estudiantes por tipos de programas y sectores de estudio

UNITED REPUBLIC OF CAMEROON (CONT.):
LES SCIENCES SOCIALES ET SCIENCES DU COMPORTEMENT,
LA FORMATION AU COMMERCE ET A L'ADMINISTRATION DES
ENTREPRISES, L'INFORMATION ET LA DOCUMENTATION,
L'ENSEIGNEMENT MENAGER ET LA FORMATION POUR LE
SECTEUR TERTIAIRE. LES SCIENCES EXACTES ET
NATURELLES COMPRENNENT EGALEMENT LES MATHEMATIQUES
ET L'INFORMATIQUE. LES SCIENCES DE L'INGENIEUR
COMPRENNENT L'ARCHITECTURE ET L'URBANISME. LES
METIERS DE LA PRODUCTION INDUSTRIELLE ET LES
TRANSPORTS ET LES COMMUNICATIONS.
ESP> LA EDUCACION COMPRENDE IGUALMENTE LAS
HUMANIDADES, LA RELIGION Y LA TEOLOGIA. EL
DERECHO COMPRENDE LAS CIENCIAS SOCIALES Y DEL
COMPORTAMIENTO. LA ENSEÑANZA COMERCIAL Y DE
ADMINISTRACION DE EMPRESAS, LA DOCUMENTACION Y
COMUNICACION SOCIAL, LA ENSEÑANZA DOMESTICA Y LA
FORMACION PARA EL SECTOR DE LOS SERVICIOS. LAS
CIENCIAS NATURALES COMPRENDEN IGUALMENTE LAS
MATEMATICAS Y LA INFORMATICA. LA INGENIERIA
Y TECNOLOGIA INCLUYE LA ARQUITECTURA Y EL
URBANISMO, LAS ARTES Y OFICIOS INDUSTRIALES Y LOS
TRANSPORTES Y COMUNICACIONES.

ZAMBIA:
E—> CERTAIN OF THE SOCIAL SCIENCES ARE INCLUDED
WITH HUMANITIES, RELIGION AND THEOLOGY. "OTHER
AND NOT SPECIFIED" DATA REFER TO PRE-VOCATIONAL
TRAINING.
FR—> UNE PARTIE DES SCIENCES SOCIALES ET DES
SCIENCES DU COMPORTEMENT EST INCLUSE DANS LES
LETTRES, LA RELIGION ET LA THEOLOGIE. LES DONNEES
CLASSEES SOUS LA RUBRIQUE "AUTRES ET NON SPECI-
FIE" SE REFERENT A "PRE-VOCATIONAL TRAINING".
ESP> UNA PARTE DE LAS CIENCIAS SOCIALES Y DEL
COMPORTAMIENTO QUEDA INCLUIDA CON LAS HUMANIDAS
LA RELIGION Y LA TEOLOGIA. LOS DATOS CLASIFICADOS
BAJO LA RUBRICA "OTROS Y SIN ESPECIFICAR" SE
REFIEREN A "PRE-VOCATIONAL TRAINING".

BARBADOS:
E—> UNIVERSITY OF THE WEST INDIES ONLY.
FR—> UNIVERSITE DE "WEST INDIES" SEULEMENT.
ESP> UNIVERSIDAD DE "WEST INDIES" SOLAMENTE.

CANADA:
E—> STUDENTS IN ARTS AND SCIENCES COURSES ARE
SHOWN UNDER "OTHER AND NOT SPECIFIED".
FR—> LES ETUDIANTS EN "ARTS AND SCIENCES
COURSES" SONT CLASSES SOUS LA RUBRIQUE "AUTRES ET
NON SPECIFIE".
ESP> LOS ESTUDIANTES EN "ARTS AND SCIENCES
COURSES" SE CLASIFICAN BAJO LA RUBRICA "OTROS Y
SIN ESPECIFICAR".

CUBA:
E—> IN 1978, SOCIAL AND BEHAVIOURAL SCIENCES
INCLUDE COMMERCIAL AND BUSINESS ADMINISTRATION,
MASS COMMUNICATION AND DOCUMENTATION, NATURAL
SCIENCES INCLUDE MATHEMATICS AND COMPUTER SCIENCE.
ENGINEERING INCLUDES ARCHITECTURE AND TOWN
PLANNING.
FR—> EN 1978, LES SCIENCES SOCIALES ET SCIENCES
DU COMPORTEMENT COMPRENNENT EGALEMENT LA FORMATION

MOROCCO:
E—> UNIVERSITIES ONLY. IN 1978 HUMANITIES,
RELIGION AND THEOLOGY ALSO INCLUDE SOCIAL AND
BEHAVIOURAL SCIENCES, MASS COMMUNICATION AND
DOCUMENTATION AND SERVICE TRADES.
FR—> UNIVERSITES SEULEMENT. EN 1978, LES
LETTRES, LA RELIGION ET LA THEOLOGIE COMPRENNENT
EGALEMENT LES SCIENCES SOCIALES ET SCIENCES DU
COMPORTEMENT, L'INFORMATION ET LA DOCUMENTATION
ET LA FORMATION POUR LE SECTEUR TERTIAIRE.
ESP> UNIVERSIDADES SOLAMENTE. EN 1978, LAS
HUMANIDADES, LA RELIGION Y LA TEOLOGIA COMPRENDEN
IGUALMENTE LAS CIENCIAS SOCIALES Y DEL COMPORTA-
MIENTO, LA DOCUMENTACION Y COMUNICACION SOCIAL
Y LA FORMACION PARA EL SECTOR DE LOS SERVICIOS.

REUNION:
E—> NATURAL SCIENCES ALSO INCLUDE MATHEMATICS
AND COMPUTER SCIENCE.
FR—> LES SCIENCES EXACTES ET NATURELLES COMPREN-
NENT LES MATHEMATIQUES ET L'INFORMATIQUE.
ESP> LAS CIENCIAS EXACTAS Y NATURALES COMPRENDEN
IGUALMENTE LAS MATEMATICAS Y LA INFORMATICA.

RWANDA:
E—> SOCIAL AND BEHAVIOURAL SCIENCE ALSO INCLUDE
COMMERCIAL AND BUSINESS ADMINISTRATION. NATURAL
SCIENCES ALSO INCLUDE MATHEMATICS AND COMPUTER
SCIENCE.
FR—> LES SCIENCES SOCIALES ET SCIENCES DU COM-
PORTEMENT COMPRENNENT EGALEMENT LA FORMATION AU
COMMERCE ET A L'ADMINISTRATION DES ENTREPRISES.
LES SCIENCES EXACTES ET NATURELLES COMPRENNENT
LES MATHEMATIQUES ET L'INFORMATIQUE.
ESP> LAS CIENCIAS SOCIALES Y DEL COMPORTAMIENTO
COMPRENDEN IGUALMENTE LA ENSEÑANZA COMERCIAL Y DE
ADMINISTRACION DE EMPRESAS. LAS CIENCIAS
NATURALES COMPRENDEN LAS MATEMATICAS Y LA INFOR-
MATICA.

TUNISIA:
E—> LAW AND ECONOMICS ARE COMBINED. LEVELS
6 AND 7 ARE ALSO COMBINED.
FR—> LE DROIT ET LES SCIENCES ECONOMIQUES SONT
CLASSES ENSEMBLE. LES DONNEES RELATIVES AUX
PROGRAMMES DU NIVEAU 7 SONT COMPRISES DANS CELLES
DU NIVEAU 6.
ESP> EL DERECHO Y LA ECONOMIA QUEDAN CLASIFI-
CADOS BAJO LA MISMA RUBRICA. LOS DATOS RELATIVOS
A LOS PROGRAMAS DE GRADO 7 QUEDAN ENGLOBADOS CON
LOS DE GRADO 6.

UNITED REPUBLIC OF CAMEROON:
E—> EDUCATION INCLUDES HUMANITIES, RELIGION
AND THEOLOGY. LAW INCLUDES SOCIAL AND BEHAVIOURAL
SCIENCES, COMMERCIAL AND BUSINESS ADMINISTRATION,
MASS COMMUNICATION AND DOCUMENTATION HOME ECONO-
MICS AND SERVICE TRADES. NATURAL SCIENCE. ENGI-
NEERING INCLUDES ARCHITECTURE AND TOWN PLANNING,
TRADE, CRAFT AND INDUSTRIAL PROGRAMMES AND
TRANSPORT AND COMMUNICATIONS.
FR—> L'EDUCATION COMPREND EGALEMENT LES LETTRES,
LA RELIGION ET LA THEOLOGIE. LE DROIT COMPREND

3.12 Third level: students by levels and fields
Troisième degré: étudiants par types de programmes et domaines d'études
Tercer grado: estudiantes por tipos de programas y sectores de estudio

CUBA (CONT.):
AU COMMERCE ET A L'ADMINISTRATION DES ENTREPRISES ET L'INFORMATION ET LA DOCUMENTATION. LES SCIENCES EXACTES ET NATURELLES COMPRENNENT LES MATHEMATIQUES ET L'INFORMATIQUE. LES SCIENCES DE L'INGENIEUR COMPRENNENT L'ARCHITECTURE ET L'URBANISME.
ESP> EN 1978, LAS CIENCIAS SOCIALES Y DEL COMPORTAMIENTO COMPRENDEN IGUALMENTE LA ENSEÑANZA COMERCIAL Y DE ADMINISTRACION DE EMPRESAS Y LA DOCUMENTACION Y COMUNICACION SOCIAL. LAS CIENCIAS NATURALES COMPRENDEN LAS MATEMATICAS Y LA INFORMATICA. LA INGENIERIA Y TECNOLOGIA COMPRENDE IGUALMENTE LA ARQUITECTURA Y EL URBANISMO.

DOMINICAN REPUBLIC:
E—> DATA REFER TO UNIVERSITIES AND EQUIVALENT DEGREE GRANTING INSTITUTIONS. THE FIGURES SHOWN UNDER "OTHER AND NOT SPECIFIED" REFER, IN THE MAIN, TO STUDENTS ENROLLED EITHER IN THE FIRST YEAR OR IN THE PREPARATORY YEAR (GENERAL STUDIES).
FR—> UNIVERSITES ET ETABLISSEMENTS EQUIVALENTS SEULEMENT. LES CHIFFRES PORTES SOUS LA RUBRIQUE "AUTRES ET NON SPECIFIE" SE REFERENT, POUR LA PLUPART, AUX ETUDIANTS INSCRITS SOIT EN PREMIERE ANNEE, SOIT EN ANNEE PREPARATOIRE (ETUDES GENERALES).
ESP> UNIVERSIDADES Y ESTABLECIMIENTOS EQUI- VALENTES SOLAMENTE. LAS CIFRAS QUE FIGURAN BAJO LA RUBRICA "OTROS Y SIN ESPECIFICAR", SE REFIEREN, EN SU MAYOR PARTE, A LOS ESTUDIANTES INSCRITOS EN EL PRIMER AÑO DE ESTUDIOS O EN EL AÑO PREPARATORIO (ESTUDIOS GENERALES).

GUATEMALA:
E—> UNIVERSITY OF SAN CARLOS ONLY.
FR—> UNIVERSITE DE SAN CARLOS SEULEMENT.
ESP> UNIVERSIDAD DE SAN CARLOS SOLAMENTE.

HONDURAS:
E—> UNIVERSITY OF HONDURAS ONLY.
FR—> UNIVERSITE DU HONDURAS SEULEMENT.
ESP> UNIVERSIDAD DE HONDURAS SOLAMENTE.

JAMAICA:
E—> UNIVERSITY OF THE WEST INDIES ONLY.
FR—> UNIVERSITE DE "WEST INDIES" SEULEMENT.
ESP> UNIVERSIDAD DE "WEST INDIES" SOLAMENTE.

TRINIDAD AND TOBAGO:
E—> UNIVERSITY OF THE WEST INDIES ONLY. NATURAL SCIENCES INCLUDE MATHEMATICS AND COMPUTER SCIENCE. ENGINEERING INCLUDES ARCHITECTURE AND TOWN PLANNING, TRADE, CRAFT AND INDUSTRIAL PROGRAMMES AND TRANSPORT AND COMMUNICATIONS.
FR—> UNIVERSITE DE "WEST INDIES" SEULEMENT. LES SCIENCES EXACTES ET NATURELLES COMPRENNENT LES MATHEMATIQUES ET L'INFORMATIQUE. LES SCIENCES DE L'INGENIEUR COMPRENNENT EGALEMENT L'ARCHITECTURE ET L'URBANISME, LES METIERS DE LA PRODUCTION INDUSTRIELLE ET LES TRANSPORTS ET LES TELECOMMUNI- CATIONS.

TRINIDAD AND TOBAGO (CONT.):
ESP> UNIVERSIDAD DE "WEST INDIES" SOLAMENTE. LAS CIENCIAS NATURALES COMPRENDEN LAS MATEMATICAS Y LA INFORMATICA. LA INGENIERIA Y TECNOLOGIA COMPRENDE IGUALMENTE LA ARQUITECTURA Y EL URBA- NISMO, LAS ARTES Y OFICIO INDUSTRIALES Y LOS TRANSPORTES Y COMUNICACIONES.

BRAZIL:
E—> THE FIGURES SHOWN UNDER "OTHER AND NOT SPECIFIED" REFER MAINLY TO STUDENTS ENROLLED EITHER IN THE FIRST YEAR OR IN THE PREPARATORY YEAR (GENERAL STUDIES).
FR—> LES CHIFFRES PORTES SOUS LA RUBRIQUE "AUTRES ET NON SPECIFIE" SE REFERENT, POUR LA PLUPART, AUX ETUDIANTS INSCRITS SOIT EN PREMIERE ANNEE, SOIT EN ANNEE PREPARATOIRE (ETUDES GENERALES).
ESP> LAS CIFRAS QUE FIGURAN EN LA RUBRICA "OTROS Y SIN ESPECIFICAR", SE REFIEREN, EN SU MAYOR PARTE, A LOS ESTUDIANTES INSCRITOS EN EL PRIMER AÑO DE ESTUDIOS O EN EL AÑO PREPARATORIO (ESTUDIOS GENERALES).

CHILE:
E—> DATA REFERRING TO PROGRAMMES OF LEVEL 5 ARE INCLUDED WITH LEVEL 6. SOCIAL AND BEHAVIOURAL SCIENCES INCLUDE COMMERCIAL AND BUSINESS ADMINIS- TRATION, MASS COMMUNICATION AND DOCUMENTATION, HOME ECONOMICS AND SERVICE TRADES. NATURAL SCIENCES INCLUDE MATHEMATICS AND COMPUTER SCIENCE. ENGINEERING INCLUDES ARCHITECTURE AND TOWN PLAN- NING, TRADE, CRAFT AND INDUSTRIAL PROGRAMMES AND TRANSPORT AND COMMUNICATIONS.
FR—> LES DONNEES RELATIVES AUX PROGRAMMES DU NIVEAU 5 SONT COMPRISES AVEC CELLES DU NIVEAU 6. LES SCIENCES SOCIALES ET SCIENCES DU COMPORTEMENT COMPRENNENT EGALEMENT LA FORMATION AU COMMERCE ET A L'ADMINISTRATION DES ENTREPRISES, L'INFORMATION ET LA DOCUMENTATION, L'ENSEIGNEMENT MENAGER ET LA FORMATION POUR LE SECTEUR TERTIAIRE. LES SCIENCES EXACTES ET NATURELLES COMPRENNENT LES MATHEMATIQUES ET L'INFORMATIQUE. LES SCIENCES DE L'INGENIEUR COMPRENNENT L'ARCHITECTURE ET L'URBA- NISME, LES METIERS DE LA PRODUCTION INDUSTRIELLE ET LES TRANSPORTS ET LES TELECOMMUNICATIONS.
ESP> LOS DATOS RELATIVOS A LOS PROGRAMAS DE GRADO 5 QUEDAN COMPRENDIDOS CON LOS DE GRADO 6. LAS CIENCIAS SOCIALES Y DEL COMPORTAMIENTO COM- PRENDEN IGUALMENTE LA ENSEÑANZA COMERCIAL Y DE ADMINISTRACION DE EMPRESAS, LA DOCUMENTACION Y COMUNICACION SOCIAL, LA ECONOMIA DOMESTICA Y LA FORMACION PARA EL SECTOR DE LOS SERVICIOS. LAS CIENCIAS NATURALES COMPRENDEN LAS MATEMATICAS Y LA INFORMATICA. LA INGENIERIA Y TECNOLOGIA COM- PRENDE LA ARQUITECTURA Y EL URBANISMO, LAS ARTES Y OFICIOS INDUSTRIALES Y LOS TRANSPORTES Y COMUNICACIONES.

COLOMBIA:
E—> DATA REFER TO UNIVERSITIES AND EQUIVALENT INSTITUTIONS ONLY. FINE AND APPLIED ARTS AND ARCHITECTURE ARE COMBINED. COMMERCIAL AND BUSI-

COLOMBIA (CONT.): NESS ADMINISTRATION INCLUDE MASS COMMUNICATION AND DOCUMENTATION. HOME ECONOMICS AND SERVICE TRADES. NATURAL SCIENCES INCLUDE MATHEMATICS AND COMPUTER SCIENCE. ENGINEERING INCLUDES TRADE, CRAFT AND INDUSTRIAL PROGRAMMES, TRANSPORT AND COMMUNICATIONS.

FR—> UNIVERSITES ET ETABLISSEMENTS EQUIVALENTS SEULEMENT. LES BEAUX-ARTS ET LES ARTS APPLIQUES COMPRENNENT L'ARCHITECTURE ET L'URBANISME. LA FORMATION AU COMMERCE ET A L'ADMINISTRATION DES ENTREPRISES COMPREND EGALEMENT L'INFORMATION ET LA DOCUMENTATION, L'ENSEIGNEMENT MENAGER ET LA FORMATION POUR LE SECTEUR TERTIAIRE. LES SCIENCES EXACTES ET NATURELLES COMPRENNENT LES MATHEMATIQUES ET L'INFORMATIQUE. LES SCIENCES DE L'INGENIEUR COMPRENNENT EGALEMENT LES METIERS DE LA PRODUCTION INDUSTRIELLE ET LES TRANSPORTS ET LES TELECOMMUNICATIONS.

ESP> UNIVERSIDADES Y ESTABLECIMIENTOS EQUIVALENTES SOLAMENTE. LAS BELLAS ARTES Y LAS ARTES APLICADAS COMPRENDEN LA ARQUITECTURA Y EL URBANISMO. LA ENSEÑANZA COMERCIAL Y DE ADMINISTRACION DE EMPRESAS COMPRENDE IGUALMENTE LA DOCUMENTACION Y COMUNICACION SOCIAL, LA ECONOMIA DOMESTICA Y LA FORMACION PARA EL SECTOR DE LOS SERVICIOS. LAS CIENCIAS NATURALES COMPRENDEN LAS MATEMATICAS Y LA INFORMATICA. LA INGENIERIA Y LA TECNOLOGIA COMPRENDE IGUALMENTE LAS ARTES Y OFICIOS INDUSTRIALES Y LOS TRANSPORTES Y COMUNICACIONES.

FRENCH GUIANA: E—> NATURAL SCIENCES INCLUDE MATHEMATICS AND COMPUTER SCIENCE.

FR—> LES SCIENCES EXACTES ET NATURELLES COMPRENNENT LES MATHEMATIQUES ET L'INFORMATIQUE.

ESP> LAS CIENCIAS NATURALES COMPRENDEN LAS MATEMATICAS Y LA INFORMATICA.

PARAGUAY: E—> THE FIGURES SHOWN UNDER "OTHER AND NOT SPECIFIED" REFER MAINLY TO STUDENTS ENROLLED EITHER IN THE FIRST YEAR OR IN THE PREPARATORY YEAR (GENERAL STUDIES).

FR—> LES CHIFFRES PORTES SOUS LA RUBRIQUE "AUTRES ET NON SPECIFIE" SE REFERENT, POUR LA PLU-PART, AUX ETUDIANTS INSCRITS SOIT EN PREMIERE ANNEE, SOIT EN ANNEE PREPARATOIRE (ETUDES GENERALES).

ESP> LAS CIFRAS QUE FIGURAN BAJO LA RUBRICA "OTROS Y SIN ESPECIFICAR" SE REFIEREN, EN SU MAYOR PARTE, A LOS ESTUDIANTES INSCRITOS EN EL PRIMER AÑO DE ESTUDIOS O EN EL AÑO PREPARATORIO (ESTUDIOS GENERALES).

PERU: E—> THE FIGURES SHOWN UNDER "OTHER AND NOT SPECIFIED" REFER MAINLY TO STUDENTS ENROLLED EITHER IN THE FIRST YEAR OR IN THE PREPARATORY YEAR (GENERAL STUDIES).

FR—> LES CHIFFRES PORTES SOUS LA RUBRIQUE "AUTRES ET NON SPECIFIE" SE REFERENT, POUR LA PLU-PART, AUX ETUDIANTS INSCRITS SOIT EN PREMIERE

PERU (CONT.): ANNEE, SOIT EN ANNEE PREPARATOIRE (ETUDES GENERALES).

"OTROS Y SIN ESPECIFICAR" SE REFIEREN, EN SU MAYOR PARTE, A LOS ESTUDIANTES INSCRITOS EN EL PRIMER AÑO DE ESTUDIOS O EN EL AÑO PREPARATORIO (ESTUDIOS GENERALES).

BURMA: E—> UNIVERSITIES AND EQUIVALENT INSTITUTIONS ONLY.

FR—> UNIVERSITES ET ETABLISSEMENTS EQUIVALENTS SEULEMENT.

ESP> UNIVERSIDADES Y ESTABLECIMIENTOS EQUIVALENTES SOLAMENTE.

INDIA: E—> FINE ARTS ARE INCLUDED WITH HUMANITIES. COMMERCIAL AND BUSINESS ADMINISTRATION INCLUDE SOCIAL AND BEHAVIOURAL SCIENCES. NATURAL SCIENCES INCLUDE MATHEMATICS AND COMPUTER SCIENCE. ENGINEERING INCLUDES ARCHITECTURE AND TOWN PLANNING. TRADE, CRAFT AND INDUSTRIAL PROGRAMMES AND TRANSPORT AND COMMUNICATIONS.

FR—> LES LETTRES, LA RELIGION ET LA THEOLOGIE COMPRENNENT EGALEMENT LES BEAUX-ARTS ET LES ARTS APPLIQUES. LA FORMATION AU COMMERCE ET A L'ADMINISTRATION DES ENTREPRISES COMPRENNENT LES SCIENCES SOCIALES ET SCIENCES DU COMPORTEMENT. LES SCIENCES EXACTES ET NATURELLES COMPRENNENT EGALEMENT LES MATHEMATIQUES ET L'INFORMATIQUE. LES SCIENCES DE L'INGENIEUR COMPRENNENT L'ARCHITECTURE ET L'URBANISME. LES METIERS DE LA PRODUCTION INDUSTRI-ELLE ET LES TRANSPORTS ET LES TELECOMMUNICATIONS.

ESP> LAS HUMANIDADES, LA RELIGION Y LA TEOLOGIA COMPRENDEN IGUALMENTE LAS BELLAS ARTES Y LAS ARTES APLICADAS. LA ENSEÑANZA COMERCIAL Y DE ADMINIS-TRACION DE EMPRESAS COMPRENDE IGUALMENTE LAS CIENCIAS SOCIALES Y DEL COMPORTAMIENTO. LAS CIENCIAS NATURALES COMPRENDEN LAS MATEMATICAS Y LA INFORMATICA. LA INGENIERIA Y TECNOLOGIA COMPRENDE IGUALMENTE LA ARQUITECTURA Y EL URBANISMO. LAS ARTES Y OFICIOS INDUSTRIALES Y LOS TRANSPORTES Y COMUNICACIONES.

ISRAEL: E—> EDUCATION SCIENCE AND TEACHER TRAINING INCLUDE HUMANITIES, RELIGION AND THEOLOGY, FINE AND APPLIED ARTS. SOCIAL AND BEHAVIOURAL SCIENCES INCLUDE COMMERCIAL AND BUSINESS ADMINISTRATION, MASS COMMUNICATION AND DOCUMENTATION. HOME ECONOMICS AND SERVICE TRADES. NATURAL SCIENCES INCLUDE MATHEMATICS AND COMPUTER SCIENCE. ENGI-NEERING INCLUDES ARCHITECTURE AND TOWN PLANNING, TRADE, CRAFT AND INDUSTRIAL PROGRAMMES, TRANSPORT AND COMMUNICATIONS.

FR—> LES SCIENCES DE L'EDUCATION ET LA FORMATION D'ENSEIGNANTS COMPRENNENT EGALEMENT LES LETTRES, LA RELIGION ET LA THEOLOGIE ET LES BEAUX ARTS ET LES ARTS APPLIQUES. LES SCIENCES SOCIALES ET SCI-ENCES DU COMPORTEMENT COMPRENNENT LA FORMATION AU COMMERCE ET A L'ADMINISTRATION DES ENTREPRISES, L'INFORMATION ET LA DOCUMENTATION, L'ENSEIGNEMENT

3.12 Third level: students by levels and fields
Troisième degré: étudiants par types de programmes et domaines d'études
Tercer grado: estudiantes por tipos de programas y sectores de estudio

ISRAEL (CONT.):
MENAGER ET LA FORMATION POUR LE SECTEUR TERTIAIRE. LES SCIENCES EXACTES ET NATURELLES COMPRENNENT EGALEMENT LES MATHEMATIQUES ET L'INFORMATIQUE. LES SCIENCES DE L'INGENIEUR COMPRENNENT L'ARCHITECTURE ET L'URBANISME, LES METIERS DE LA PRODUCTION INDUSTRIELLE ET LES TRANSPORTS ET LES TELECOMMUNICATIONS.
ESP> LA EDUCACION Y FORMACION DE PERSONAL DOCENTE COMPRENDEN IGUALMENTE LAS HUMANIDADES, LA RELIGION Y LA TEOLOGIA Y LAS BELLAS ARTES Y LAS ARTES APLICADAS. LAS CIENCIAS SOCIALES Y DEL COMPORTAMIENTO COMPRENDEN LA ENSEÑANZA COMERCIAL Y DE ADMINISTRACION DE EMPRESAS, LA DOCUMENTACION Y COMUNICACION SOCIAL, LA ECONOMIA DOMESTICA Y LA FORMACION PARA EL SECTOR DE LOS SERVICIOS. LAS CIENCIAS NATURALES COMPRENDEN LAS MATEMATICAS Y LA INFORMATICA. LA INGENIERIA Y TECNOLOGIA COMPRENDE IGUALMENTE LA ARQUITECTURA Y EL URBANISMO, LAS ARTES Y OFICIOS INDUSTRIALES Y LOS TRANSPORTES Y COMUNICACIONES.

JAPAN:
E--> INCLUDING CORRESPONDENCE COURSES. HUMANITIES, RELIGION AND THEOLOGY INCLUDE MASS COMMUNICATION AND DOCUMENTATION. SOCIAL AND BEHAVIOURAL SCIENCES INCLUDE LAW, COMMERCIAL AND BUSINESS ADMINISTRATION. ENGINEERING INCLUDES ARCHITECTURE AND TOWN PLANNING, TRADE, CRAFT AND INDUSTRIAL PROGRAMMES.
FR-> Y COMPRIS LES COURS PAR CORRESPONDANCE. LES LETTRES, LA RELIGION ET LA THEOLOGIE COMPRENNENT EGALEMENT L'INFORMATION ET LA DOCUMENTATION. LES SCIENCES SOCIALES ET SCIENCES DU COMPORTEMENT COMPRENNENT LE DROIT ET LA FORMATION AU COMMERCE ET A L'ADMINISTRATION DES ENTREPRISES. LES SCIENCES DE L'INGENIEUR COMPRENNENT EGALEMENT L'ARCHITECTURE ET L'URBANISME ET LES METIERS DE LA PRODUCTION INDUSTRIELLE.
ESP> INCLUIDOS LOS CURSOS POR CORRESPONDENCIA. LAS HUMANIDADES, LA RELIGION Y LA TEOLOGIA COMPRENDEN IGUALMENTE LA DOCUMENTACION Y COMUNICACION SOCIAL. LAS CIENCIAS SOCIALES Y DEL COMPORTAMIENTO COMPRENDEN IGUALMENTE EL DERECHO Y LA ENSEÑANZA COMERCIAL Y DE ADMINISTRACION DE EMPRESAS. LA INGENIERIA Y TECNOLOGIA COMPRENDE LA ARQUITECTURA Y EL URBANISMO Y LAS ARTES Y OFICIOS INDUSTRIALES.

JORDAN:
E--> DATA REFER TO THE EAST BANK ONLY.
FR-> LES DONNEES SE REFERENT A LA RIVE ORIENTALE SEULEMENT.
ESP> LOS DATOS SE REFIEREN A LA ORILLA ORIENTAL SOLAMENTE.

NEPAL:
E--> NATURAL SCIENCES INCLUDE MATHEMATICS AND COMPUTER SCIENCE.
FR-> LES SCIENCES EXACTES ET NATURELLES COMPRENNENT LES MATHEMATIQUES ET L'INFORMATIQUE.
ESP> LAS CIENCIAS NATURALES COMPRENDEN LAS MATEMATICAS Y LA INFORMATICA.

PAKISTAN:
E--> HUMANITIES, RELIGION AND THEOLOGY INCLUDE SOCIAL AND BEHAVIOURAL SCIENCES, MASS COMMUNICATION AND DOCUMENTATION AND SERVICE TRADES. NATURAL SCIENCES INCLUDE MATHEMATICS AND COMPUTER SCIENCE. ENGINEERING INCLUDES ARCHITECTURE AND TOWN PLANNING.
FR-> LES LETTRES, LA RELIGION ET LA THEOLOGIE COMPRENNENT LES SCIENCES SOCIALES ET SCIENCES DU COMPORTEMENT, L'INFORMATION ET LA DOCUMENTATION ET LA FORMATION POUR LE SECTEUR TERTIAIRE. LES SCIENCES EXACTES ET NATURELLES COMPRENNENT EGALEMENT LES MATHEMATIQUES ET L'INFORMATIQUE. LES SCIENCES DE L'INGENIEUR COMPRENNENT L'ARCHITECTURE ET L'URBANISME.
ESP> LAS HUMANIDADES, LA RELIGION Y LA TEOLOGIA COMPRENDEN LAS CIENCIAS SOCIALES Y DEL COMPORTAMIENTO, LA DOCUMENTACION Y COMUNICACION SOCIAL Y LAS CIENCIAS NATURALES COMPRENDEN IGUALMENTE LAS MATEMATICAS Y LA INFORMATICA. EN LA INGENIERIA Y TECNOLOGIA FIGURAN LA ARQUITECTURA Y EL URBANISMO.

PHILIPPINES:
E--> UNIVERSITIES AND EQUIVALENT INSTITUTIONS ONLY.
FR-> UNIVERSITES ET ETABLISSEMENTS EQUIVALENTS SEULEMENT.
ESP> UNIVERSIDADES Y ESTABLECIMIENTOS EQUIVALENTES SOLAMENTE.

SAUDI ARABIA:
E--> ISLAMIC LAW IS INCLUDED WITH HUMANITIES, RELIGION AND THEOLOGY. NATURAL SCIENCES INCLUDE MATHEMATICS AND COMPUTER SCIENCE.
FR-> LES LETTRES, LA RELIGION ET LA THEOLOGIE COMPRENNENT LE DROIT ISLAMIQUE. LES SCIENCES EXACTES ET NATURELLES COMPRENNENT LES MATHEMATIQUES ET L'INFORMATIQUE.
ESP> LAS HUMANIDADES, LA RELIGION Y LA TEOLOGIA COMPRENDEN EL DERECHO ISLAMICO. LAS CIENCIAS NATURALES COMPRENDEN LAS MATEMATICAS Y LA INFORMATICA.

SINGAPORE:
E--> HUMANITIES, RELIGION AND THEOLOGY INCLUDE SOCIAL AND BEHAVIOURAL SCIENCES.
FR-> LES LETTRES, LA RELIGION ET LA THEOLOGIE COMPRENNENT LES SCIENCES SOCIALES ET SCIENCES DU COMPORTEMENT.
ESP> LAS HUMANIDADES, LA RELIGION Y LA TEOLOGIA COMPRENDEN LAS CIENCIAS SOCIALES Y DEL COMPORTAMIENTO.

SRI LANKA:
E--> UNIVERSITIES AND EQUIVALENT INSTITUTIONS ONLY. HUMANITIES, RELIGION AND THEOLOGY INCLUDE SOCIAL AND BEHAVIOURAL SCIENCES, COMMERCIAL AND BUSINESS ADMINISTRATION, MASS COMMUNICATION AND DOCUMENTATION, HOME ECONOMICS AND SERVICE TRADES. NATURAL SCIENCES INCLUDE MATHEMATICS AND COMPUTER SCIENCE. ENGINEERING INCLUDES ARCHITECTURE AND TOWN PLANNING, TRADE, CRAFT AND INDUSTRIAL

Third level: students by levels and fields 3.12
Troisième degré: étudiants par types de programmes et domaines d'études
Tercer grado: estudiantes por tipos de programas y sectores de estudio

AUSTRIA (CONT.):
FR—> LES DONNEES RELATIVES AUX PROGRAMMES DU NIVEAU 7 SONT COMPRISES DANS CELLES DU NIVEAU 6.
ESP> LOS DATOS RELATIVOS A LOS PROGRAMAS DE GRADO 7 QUEDAN INCLUIDOS CON LOS DE GRADO 6.

BELGIUM:
E—> PROGRAMMES OF LEVEL 7 ARE INCLUDED WITH LEVEL 6.
FR—> LES DONNEES RELATIVES AUX PROGRAMMES DU NIVEAU 7 SONT COMPRISES DANS CELLES DU NIVEAU 6.
ESP> LOS DATOS RELATIVOS A LOS PROGRAMAS DE GRADO 7 QUEDAN INCLUIDOS CON LOS DE GRADO 6.

BULGARIA:
E—> INCLUDING EVENING AND CORRESPONDENCE COURSES. THE SHARP RISE IN ENROLMENT IS DUE TO THE INTRODUCTION OF A NEW COURSE OF STUDY —FULL TIME AND BY CORRESPONDENCE— ORGANISED IN POST-SECONDARY MEDICAL SCIENCE INSTITUTIONS FOR MIDDLE-LEVEL MEDICAL PROFESSIONALS (PARAMEDICAL).
FR—> Y COMPRIS LES COURS DU SOIR ET PAR CORRES-PONDANCE. L'IMPORTANTE AUGMENTATION DES EFFECTIFS S'EXPLIQUE PAR LA CREATION DE NOUVEAUX COURS A PLEIN TEMPS ET PAR CORRESPONDANCE ORGANISES DANS LES ETABLISSEMENTS POSTSECONDAIRES DE SCIENCES MEDICALES A L'INTENTION DES CADRES MOYENS MEDICAUX (PERSONNEL PARAMEDICAL).
ESP> INCLUIDOS LOS CURSOS NOCTURNOS Y POR CORRES-PONDENCIA. EL IMPORTANTE AUMENTO DE LOS EFECTIVOS SE EXPLICA POR LA CREACION DE NUEVOS CURSOS DE JORNADA COMPLETA Y POR CORRESPONDENCIA ORGANIZADOS EN LOS ESTABLECIMIENTOS POSTSECUNDARIOS DE CIEN-CIAS MEDICAS Y DESTINADOS A LOS CUADROS MEDIOS MEDICALES (PERSONAL PARAMEDICAL).

DENMARK:
E—> PROGRAMMES OF LEVEL 7 ARE INCLUDED WITH LEVEL 6.
FR—> LES DONNEES RELATIVES AUX PROGRAMMES DU NIVEAU 7 SONT COMPRISES DANS CELLES DU NIVEAU 6.
ESP> LOS DATOS RELATIVOS A LOS PROGRAMAS DE GRADO 7 QUEDAN INCLUIDOS CON LOS DE GRADO 6.

FINLAND:
E—> BEGINNING 1975, ENROLMENT DATA BY FIELD OF STUDY ARE NOT COMPARABLE WITH THOSE BY INSTITU-TIONS (SEE TABLE 3.11). COVERAGE IN THIS TABLE INCLUDES HIGHER EDUCATION COURSES IN NON-HIGHER EDUCATION INSTITUTIONS.
FR—> A PARTIR DE 1975, LES DONNEES SUR LES EFFECTIFS PAR DISCIPLINES NE SONT PAS COMPARABLES AVEC CELLES DU TABLEAU 3.11 PAR TYPES D'ETABLIS-SEMENT. LES CHIFFRES DE CE TABLEAU COMPRENNENT LES COURS D'ENSEIGNEMENT SUPERIEUR ORGANISES DANS DES ETABLISSEMENTS AUTRES QUE CEUX DE L'ENSEIGNE-MENT DU TROISIEME DEGRE.
ESP> A PARTIR DE 1975, LOS DATOS RELATIVOS A LOS EFECTIVOS POR RAMAS DE ESTUDIO NO SON COMPARABLES CON LOS DEL CUADRO 3.11 POR TIPOS DE ESTABLECI-MIENTO. LAS CIFRAS DE ESTE CUADRO COMPRENDEN LOS CURSOS DE ENSEÑANZA SUPERIOR ORGANIZADOS EN ESTA-BLECIMIENTOS OTROS QUE LOS DE LA ENSEÑANZA DE TERCER GRADO.

SRI LANKA (CONT.):
PROGRAMMES, TRANSPORT AND COMMUNICATIONS.
FR—> UNIVERSITES ET ETABLISSEMENTS EQUIVALENTS SEULEMENT. LES LETTRES, LA RELIGION ET LA THEOLOGIE, COMPRENNENT EGALEMENT LES SCIENCES SOCIALES ET SCIENCES DU COMPORTEMENT, LA FORMATION AU COMMERCE ET A L'ADMINISTRATION DES ENTREPRISES, L'INFORMATION ET LA DOCUMENTATION. L'ENSEIGNEMENT MENAGER ET LA FORMATION POUR LE SECTEUR TERTIAIRE. LES SCIENCES EXACTES ET NATURELLES COMPRENNENT LES MATHEMATIQUES ET L'INFORMATIQUE. L'ARCHITECTURE ET L'INGENIEUR COMPRENNENT EGALEMENT L'URBANISME, LES METIERS DE LA PRODUCTION INDUSTRIELLE ET LES TRANSPORTS ET LES TELE-COMMUNICATIONS.
ESP> UNIVERSIDADES Y ESTABLECIMIENTOS EQUIVA-LENTES SOLAMENTE. LAS HUMANIDADES, LA RELIGION Y LA TEOLOGIA COMPRENDEN IGUALMENTE LAS CIENCIAS SOCIALES Y DEL COMPORTAMIENTO, LA ENSEÑANZA COMERCIAL Y DE ADMINISTRACION DE EMPRESAS, LA DOCUMENTACION Y COMUNICACION SOCIAL, LA ECONOMIA DOMESTICA Y LA FORMACION PARA EL SECTOR DE LOS SERVICIOS. LAS CIENCIAS NATURALES COMPRENDEN LAS MATEMATICAS Y LA INFORMATICA. LA INGENIERIA Y TECNOLOGIA COMPRENDE IGUALMENTE LA ARQUITECTURA Y EL URBANISMO, LAS ARTES Y OFICIOS INDUSTRIALES Y LOS TRANSPORTES Y COMUNICACIONES.

THAILAND:
E—> ENGINEERING INCLUDES ARCHITECTURE AND TOWN PLANNING, TRADE, CRAFT AND INDUSTRIAL PROGRAMMES AND TRANSPORT AND COMMUNICATION.
FR—> LES SCIENCES DE L'INGENIEUR COMPRENNENT L'ARCHITECTURE ET L'URBANISME, LES METIERS DE LA PRODUCTION INDUSTRIELLE ET LES TRANSPORTS ET LES TELECOMMUNICATIONS.
ESP> LA INGENIERIA Y TECNOLOGIA COMPRENDE LA ARQUITECTURA Y EL URBANISMO, LAS ARTES Y OFICIOS INDUSTRIALES Y LOS TRANSPORTES Y COMUNICACIONES.

VIET-NAM:
E—> IN 1976, SOCIAL AND BEHAVIOURAL SCIENCES INCLUDE COMMERCIAL AND BUSINESS ADMINISTRATION. NATURAL SCIENCES INCLUDE MATHEMATICS AND COMPUTER SCIENCE. IN 1977, HUMANITIES, RELIGION AND THEOLOGY INCLUDE FINE AND APPLIED ARTS.
FR—> EN 1976, LES SCIENCES SOCIALES ET SCIENCES DU COMPORTEMENT COMPRENNENT EGALEMENT LA FORMATION AU COMMERCE ET A L'ADMINISTRATION DES ENTREPRISES. LES SCIENCES EXACTES ET NATURELLES COMPRENNENT LES MATHEMATIQUES ET L'INFORMATIQUE. EN 1977, LES LETTRES, LA RELIGION ET LA THEOLOGIE COMPRENNENT EGALEMENT LES BEAUX ARTS ET LES ARTS APPLIQUES.
ESP> EN 1976, LAS CIENCIAS SOCIALES Y DEL COMPORTAMIENTO COMPRENDEN IGUALMENTE LA ENSEÑANZA COMERCIAL Y DE ADMINISTRACION DE EMPRESAS. LAS CIENCIAS NATURALES COMPRENDEN LAS MATEMATICAS Y LA INFORMATICA. EN 1977, LAS HUMANIDADES, LA RELIGION Y LA TEOLOGIA COMPRENDEN IGUALMENTE LAS BELLAS ARTES Y LAS ARTES APLICADAS.

AUSTRIA:
E—> PROGRAMMES OF LEVEL 7 ARE INCLUDED WITH LEVEL 6.

3.12 **Third level: students by levels and fields**
Troisième degré: étudiants par types de programmes et domaines d'études
Tercer grado: estudiantes por tipos de programas y sectores de estudio

HUNGARY:
E—> INCLUDING EVENING AND CORRESPONDENCE COURSES.
FR—> Y COMPRIS LES COURS DU SOIR ET PAR CORRESPONDANCE.
ESP> INCLUIDOS LOS CURSOS NOCTURNOS Y POR CORRESPONDENCIA.

ICELAND:
E—> NATURAL SCIENCES INCLUDE MATHEMATICS AND COMPUTER SCIENCE.
FR—> LES SCIENCES EXACTES ET NATURELLES COMPRENNENT LES MATHEMATIQUES ET L'INFORMATIQUE.
ESP> LAS CIENCIAS NATURALES COMPRENDEN LAS MATEMATICAS Y LA INFORMATICA.

IRELAND:
E—> INCLUDING MULTIPLE COUNTING OF STUDENTS ENROLLED IN MORE THAN ONE FIELD OF STUDY.
FR—> Y COMPRIS LES ETUDIANTS INSCRITS DANS PLUSIEURS DISCIPLINES.
ESP> INCLUIDOS LOS ESTUDIANTES INSCRITOS EN DIVERSAS DISCIPLINAS.

LUXEMBOURG:
E—> DATA REFER ONLY TO STUDENTS ENROLLED IN INSTITUTIONS LOCATED IN LUXEMBOURG. THE MAJORITY OF THE STUDENTS FROM LUXEMBOURG PURSUE THEIR STUDIES AT THIS LEVEL OF EDUCATION IN FOREIGN INSTITUTIONS.
FR—> LES DONNEES SE REFERENT SEULEMENT AUX ETUDIANTS INSCRITS DANS LES INSTITUTIONS DU LUXEMBOURG. LA PLUS GRANDE PARTIE DES ETUDIANTS LUXEMBOURGEOIS POURSUIVENT LEURS ETUDES A CE NIVEAU D'ENSEIGNEMENT A L'ETRANGER.
ESP> LOS DATOS SE REFIEREN SOLAMENTE A LOS ESTUDIANTES MATRICULADOS EN LAS INSTITUCIONES EN LUXEMBURGO. LA MAYORIA DE LOS ESTUDIANTES DE LUXEMBURGO CURSAN SUS ESTUDIOS DE ESTE GRADO EN EL EXTRANJERO.

NETHERLANDS:
E—> ENGINEERING INCLUDES TRADE, CRAFT AND INDUSTRIAL PROGRAMMES.
FR—> LES SCIENCES DE L'INGENIEUR COMPRENNENT LES METIERS DE LA PRODUCTION INDUSTRIELLE.
ESP> LA INGENIERIA Y TECNOLOGIA COMPRENDE LAS ARTES Y OFICIOS INDUSTRIALES.

NORWAY:
E—> NATURAL SCIENCES INCLUDE MATHEMATICS AND COMPUTER SCIENCE.
FR—> LES SCIENCES EXACTES ET NATURELLES COMPRENNENT LES MATHEMATIQUES ET L'INFORMATIQUE.
ESP> LAS CIENCIAS NATURALES COMPRENDEN LAS MATEMATICAS Y LA INFORMATICA.

POLAND:
E—> INCLUDING EVENING AND CORRESPONDENCE COURSES.
FR—> Y COMPRIS LES COURS DU SOIR ET PAR CORRESPONDANCE.
ESP> INCLUIDOS LOS CURSOS NOCTURNOS Y POR CORRESPONDENCIA.

FRANCE:
E—> UNIVERSITIES ONLY (SEE TABLE 3.11). THE HEADING "HUMANITIES, RELIGION AND THEOLOGY" REFERS TO "LETTRES ET SCIENCES HUMAINES" WHICH INCLUDES THE MAJORITY OF THE SOCIAL SCIENCES (EXCEPTING ECONOMICS); THE NATURAL SCIENCES CATEGORY REFERS TO SCIENCES WHICH ALSO INCLUDE CERTAIN FIELDS OF ENGINEERING. THE HEADING "OTHER AND NOT SPECIFIED" REFERS TO THE UNIVERSITY INSTITUTS OF TECHNOLOGY (I.U.T.).
FR—> UNIVERSITES SEULEMENT (VOIR TABLEAU 3.11). LA RUBRIQUE "LETTRES, RELIGION ET THEOLOGIE" COMPREND LES LETTRES, ET SCIENCES HUMAINES QUI INCLUENT LA MAJORITE DES SCIENCES SOCIALES, EXCEPTE LES SCIENCES ECONOMIQUES. LES SCIENCES EXACTES ET NATURELLES COMPRENNENT EGALEMENT CERTAINES DISCIPLINES DES SCIENCES DE L'INGENIEUR. LA RUBRIQUE "AUTRES ET NON SPECIFIE" SE REFERE AUX INSTITUTS UNIVERSITAIRES DE TECHNOLOGIE (I.U.T.).
ESP> UNIVERSIDADES SOLAMENTE (VEASE CUADRO 3.11). SE REFIERE AL GRUPO DE "HUMANIDADES, RELIGION Y TEOLOGIA" QUE COMPRENDE LAS DISCIPLINAS DEPENDIENTES DE LAS CIENCIAS SOCIALES, SALVO LAS CIENCIAS ECONOMICAS. LA RUBRICA "CIENCIAS NATURALES" INCLUYE ALGUNOS ESTUDIOS RELATIVOS A LA INGENIERIA. LA RUBRICA "OTROS Y SIN ESPECIFICAR" SE REFIERE A LOS INSTITUTOS UNIVERSITARIOS DE TECNOLOGIA (I.U.T.).

GERMAN DEMOCRATIC REPUBLIC:
E—> INCLUDING EVENING AND CORRESPONDENCE COURSES. IN 1975, PREPARATORY STUDIES FOR HIGHER EDUCATION, EXTENDED SECONDARY SCHOOLS AND VOCATIONAL TRAINING (INCLUDING UNIVERSITY ENTRANCE EXAMINATION) WERE INCLUDED WITH EDUCATION AT THE THIRD LEVEL (NON UNIVERSITY) AS A RESULT OF THE APPLICATION OF ISCED.
FR—> Y COMPRIS LES COURS DU SOIR ET PAR CORRESPONDANCE. EN 1975, LES ETUDES PREPARATOIRES A L'ENSEIGNEMENT SUPERIEUR, LES ECOLES SECONDAIRES PROLONGEES ET L'ENSEIGNEMENT TECHNIQUE (Y COMPRIS L'EXAMEN D'ENTREE A L'UNIVERSITE) SONT COMPRIS DANS L'ENSEIGNEMENT DU TROISIEME DEGRE (NON-UNIVERSITAIRE) A LA SUITE DE L'APPLICATION DE LA CITE.
ESP> INCLUIDOS LOS CURSOS NOCTURNOS Y POR CORRESPONDENCIA. EN 1975, LOS ESTUDIOS PREPARATORIOS A LA ENSEÑANZA SUPERIOR, LAS ESCUELAS SECUNDARIAS PROLONGADAS Y LA ENSEÑANZA TECNICA (INCLUYENDO EL EXAMEN DE ENTRADA EN LA UNIVERSIDAD) ESTAN INCLUIDOS EN LA ENSEÑANZA DE TERCER GRADO (NO UNIVERSITARIA) COMO RESULTADO DE LA APLICACION DE LA CINE.

GREECE:
E—> BEGINNING 1975, DATA INCLUDE THIRD LEVEL TECHNICAL EDUCATION INSTITUTIONS.
FR—> A PARTIR DE 1975, LES DONNEES COMPRENNENT LES INSTITUTIONS DE L'ENSEIGNEMENT TECHNIQUE DU TROISIEME DEGRE.
ESP> A PARTIR DE 1975, LOS DATOS INCLUYEN LAS INSTITUCIONES DE ENSEÑANZA TECNICA DE TERCER GRADO.

Third level: students by levels and fields   **3.12**
Troisième degré: étudiants par types de programmes et domaines d'études
Tercer grado: estudiantes por tipos de programas y sectores de estudio

PORTUGAL:
E—> SOCIAL AND BEHAVIOURAL SCIENCES INCLUDE COMMERCIAL AND BUSINESS ADMINISTRATION, MASS COMMUNICATION AND DOCUMENTATION, HOME ECONOMICS AND SERVICE TRADES. ENGINEERING INCLUDES ARCHI-TECTURE AND TOWN PLANNING, TRADE, CRAFT AND INDUSTRIAL PROGRAMMES AND TRANSPORT AND COMMU-NICATIONS.

FR—> LES SCIENCES SOCIALES ET SCIENCES DU COMPORTEMENT COMPRENNENT EGALEMENT LA FORMATION AU COMMERCE ET A L'ADMINISTRATION DES ENTREPRISES, L'INFORMATION ET LA DOCUMENTATION, L'ENSEIGNEMENT MENAGER ET LA FORMATION POUR LE SECTEUR TERTIAIRE. LES SCIENCES DE L'INGENIEUR COMPRENNENT L'ARCHI-TECTURE ET L'URBANISME, LES METIERS DE LA PRODUC-TION INDUSTRIELLE ET LES TRANSPORTS ET LES TELE-COMMUNICATIONS.

ESP> LAS CIENCIAS SOCIALES Y DEL COMPORTAMIENTO COMPRENDEN IGUALMENTE LA ENSEÑANZA COMERCIAL Y DE ADMINISTRACION DE EMPRESAS, LA ECONOMIA DOMESTICA Y COMUNICACION SOCIAL, LA ECONOMIA DOMESTICA Y LA FORMACION PARA EL SECTOR DE LOS SERVICIOS. LA INGENIERIA Y TECNOLOGIA COMPRENDE LA ARQUITECTURA Y EL URBANISMO, LAS ARTES Y OFICIOS INDUSTRIALES Y LOS TRANSPORTES Y COMUNICACIONES.

ROMANIA:
E—> INCLUDING EVENING AND CORRESPONDENCE COURSES. HUMANITIES, RELIGION AND THEOLOGY IN-CLUDE EDUCATION SCIENCE AND TEACHER TRAINING.

FR—> Y COMPRIS LES COURS DU SOIR ET PAR CORRES-PONDANCE. LES LETTRES, LA RELIGION ET LA THEOLO-GIE COMPRENNENT LES SCIENCES DE L'EDUCATION ET LA FORMATION D'ENSEIGNANTS.

ESP> INCLUIDOS LOS CURSOS NOCTURNOS Y POR CORESPONDENCIA. LAS HUMANIDADES, LA RELIGION Y LA TEOLOGIA COMPRENDEN LA EDUCACION Y FORMACION DE PERSONAL DOCENTE.

SPAIN:
E—> PROGRAMMES OF LEVEL 7 ARE INCLUDED WITH LEVEL 6, INCLUDING "UNIVERSIDAD DE EDUCACION A DISTANCIA," AT WHICH 25,571 STUDENTS (F. 5,233) IN 1976.

FR—> LES DONNEES RELATIVES AUX PROGRAMMES DU NIVEAU 7 SONT COMPRISES DANS CELLES DU NIVEAU 6, Y COMPRIS LA "UNIVERSIDAD DE EDUCACION A DIS-TANCIA", AVEC 25 571 (F. 5 233) ETUDIANTS INSCRITS EN 1976.

ESP> LOS DATOS RELATIVOS A LOS PROGRAMAS DE GRADO 7 QUEDAN INCLUIDOS CON LOS DE GRADO 6, INCLUIDA LA UNIVERSIDAD DE EDUCACION A DISTANCIA, EN LA QUE HABIA 25 571 (F 5 233) ESTUDIANTES INCRISTOS EN 1976.

SWEDEN:
E—> DATA FOR 1977 ARE NOT STRICLY COMPARABLE WITH THOSE FOR 1976 DUE TO THE FACT THAT A CERTAIN NUMBER OF STUDENTS PREVIOUSLY CLASSIFIED IN ISCED LEVEL 6 (HUMANITIES, RELIGION AND THEOLOGY, AND NATURAL SCIENCES), ARE NOW CONSIDERED AS "OTHER AND NOT SPECIFIED". NATURAL SCIENCES ALSO INCLUDE MATHEMATICS AND COMPUTER SCIENCE.

SWEDEN (CONT.):
FR—> LES DONNEES POUR 1977 NE SONT PAS RIGOUREU-SEMENT COMPARABLES A CELLES DE 1976 ETANT DONNE QU'UN CERTAIN NOMBRE D'ETUDIANTS, PRECEDEMMENT CLASSES AU NIVEAU 6 DE LA REPARTITION CITE (LETTRES, RELIGION, THEOLOGIE ET SCIENCES NATU-RELLES) SONT MAINTENANT CLASSES DANS LA RUBRIQUE "AUTRES ET NON SPECIFIE". LES SCIENCES EXACTES ET NATURELLES COMPRENNENT LES MATHEMATIQUES ET L'INFORMATIQUE.

ESP> LOS DATOS PARA 1977 NO SON ESTRICTAMENTE COMPARABLES CON LOS DE 1976 DEBIDO A QUE UN CIERTO NUMERO DE ESTUDIANTES, ANTERIORMENTE CLASIFICADOS EN EL GRADO 6 DE LA REPARTICION CINE (HUMANIDADES, RELIGION, TEOLOGIA Y CIENCIAS NATURALES) FIGURAN ACTUALMENTE CLASIFICADOS EN LA RUBRICA "OTROS Y SIN ESPECIFICAR". LAS CIENCIAS NATURALES COM-PRENDEN LAS MATEMATICAS Y LA INFORMATICA.

SWITZERLAND:
E—> PROGRAMMES OF LEVEL 7 ARE INCLUDED WITH LEVEL 6.
FR—> LES DONNEES RELATIVES AUX PROGRAMMES DU NIVEAU 7 SONT COMPRISES DANS CELLES DU NIVEAU 6.
ESP> LOS DATOS RELATIVOS A LOS PROGRAMAS DE GRADO 7 QUEDAN INCLUIDOS CON LOS DE GRADO 6.

UNITED KINGDOM:
E—> INCLUDES STUDENTS AT THE OPEN UNIVERSITY: 51,035 (F. 20,005) STUDENTS IN 1975. FIELDS OF STUDY ARE, HOWEVER, NOT SPECIFIED. SOCIAL AND BEHAVIOURAL SCIENCES INCLUDE COMMERCIAL AND BUSINESS ADMINISTRATION, MASS COMMUNICATION AND DOCUMENTATION, HOME ECONOMICS AND SERVICE TRADES. NATURAL SCIENCES INCLUDE MATHEMATICS AND COMPUTER SCIENCE. ENGINEERING INCLUDES ARCHITECTURE AND TOWN PLANNING, TRADE, CRAFT AND INDUSTRIAL PRO-GRAMMES AND TRANSPORT AND COMMUNICATIONS.

FR—> LES EFFECTIFS DE L'"OPEN UNIVERSITY" SONT INCLUS: 51 035 ETUDIANTS (F. 20 005) EN 1975. LES DISCIPLINES NE SONT PAS SPECIFIEES. LES SCIENCES SOCIALES ET SCIENCES DU COMPORTEMENT COMPRENNENT EGALEMENT LA FORMATION AU COMMERCE ET A L'ADMINISTRATION DES ENTREPRISES, L'INFORMATION ET LA DOCUMENTATION, L'ENSEIGNEMENT MENAGER ET LA FORMATION POUR LE SECTEUR TERTIAIRE. LES SCIENCES EXACTES ET NATURELLES COMPRENNENT LES MATHEMA-TIQUES ET L'INFORMATIQUE. LES SCIENCES DE L'INGE-NIEUR COMPRENNENT EGALEMENT L'ARCHITECTURE ET L'-URBANISME, LES METIERS DE LA PRODUCTION INDUSTRI-ELLES ET LES TRANSPORTS ET LES TELECOMMUNICATIONS.

ESP> LOS ESTUDIANTES DE LA "OPEN UNIVERSITY" ESTAN INCLUIDOS: 51 035 ESTUDIANTES (F 20 005) EN 1975. LAS RAMAS DE ESTUDIO NO ESTAN ESPECIFICADAS. LAS CIENCIAS SOCIALES Y DEL COMPORTAMIENTO COMPRENDEN IGUALMENTE LA ENSEÑANZA COMERCIAL Y DE ADMINISTRACION DE EMPRESAS, LA DOCUMENTACION Y COMUNICACION SOCIAL, LA ECONOMIA DOMESTICA Y LA FORMACION PARA EL SECTOR DE LOS SERVICIOS. LAS CIENCIAS NATURALES COMPRENDEN LAS MATEMATICAS Y LA INFORMATICA. LA INGENIERIA Y TECNOLOGIA COMPRENDE IGUALMENTE LA ARQUITECTURA Y EL URBANISMO, LAS ARTES Y OFICIOS INDUSTRIALES Y LOS TRANSPORTES Y COMUNICACIONES.

3.12 Third level: students by levels and fields
Troisième degré: étudiants par types de programmes et domaines d'études
Tercer grado: estudiantes por tipos de programas y sectores de estudio

YUGOSLAVIA:
E—> NATURAL SCIENCES INCLUDE MATHEMATICS AND COMPUTER SCIENCE.
FR—> LES SCIENCES EXACTES ET NATURELLES COMPRENNENT LES MATHEMATIQUES ET L'INFORMATIQUE.
ESP> LAS CIENCIAS NATURALES COMPRENDEN LAS MATEMATICAS Y LA INFORMATICA.

AUSTRALIA:
E—> INCLUDING MULTIPLE COUNTING OF STUDENTS ENROLLED IN MORE THAN ONE FIELD OF STUDY.
FR—> Y COMPRIS LES ETUDIANTS INSCRITS DANS PLUSIEURS DISCIPLINES.
ESP> INCLUIDOS LOS ESTUDIANTES INSCRITOS EN DIVERSAS DISCIPLINAS.

NEW ZEALAND:
E—> INCLUDING MULTIPLE COUNTING OF STUDENTS ENROLLED IN MORE THAN ONE FIELD OF STUDY.
FR—> Y COMPRIS LES ETUDIANTS INSCRITS DANS PLUSIEURS DISCIPLINES.
ESP> INCLUIDOS LOS ESTUDIANTES INSCRITOS EN DIVERSAS DISCIPLINAS.

PAPUA NEW GUINEA:
E—> UNIVERSITIES AND EQUIVALENT INSTITUTIONS ONLY (SEE TABLE 3.11)
FR—> UNIVERSITES ET ETABLISSEMENTS EQUIVALENTS SEULEMENT (VOIR TABLEAU 3.11)
ESP> UNIVERSIDADES Y ESTABLECIMIENTOS EQUIVA—LENTES SOLAMENTE (VEASE EL CUADRO 3.11).

U.S.S.R.:
E—> THE FIGURES HAVE BEEN PROVIDED BY THE U.S.S.R. ACCORDING TO THEIR OWN SYSTEMS OF CLASSIFICATION. LAW AND ECONOMICS ARE COMBINED. MEDICAL AND HEALTH—RELATED SCIENCES INCLUDE PHYSICAL CULTURE AND SPORT. ENGINEERING INCLUDES TRANSPORT AND COMMUNICATIONS.
FR—> CES CHIFFRES SONT FOURNIS PAR L'U.R.S.S. SELON SON PROPRE SYSTEME DE CLASSIFICATION. LE DROIT COMPREND EGALEMENT LES SCIENCES ECONOMIQUES. LES SCIENCES MEDICALES, LA SANTE ET L'HYGIENE COMPRENNENT LA CULTURE PHYSIQUE ET LE SPORT. LES SCIENCES DE L'INGENIEUR COMPRENNENT LES TRANSPORTS ET LES TELECOMMUNICATIONS.
ESP> ESTAS CIFRAS HAN SIDO FACILITADAS POR LA U.R.S.S. CON ARREGLO A SU PROPIO SISTEMA DE CLASIFICACION. EL DERECHO COMPRENDE IGUALMENTE

U.S.S.R. (CONT.):
LAS CIENCIAS ECONOMICAS. LAS CIENCIAS MEDICAS, LA SANIDAD Y LA HIGIENE INCLUYEN LA CULTURA FISICA Y EL DEPORTE. LA INGENIERIA Y TECNOLOGIA COMPRENDE LOS TRANSPORTES Y COMUNICACIONES.

BYELORUSSIAN S.S.R.:
E—> THE FIGURES HAVE BEEN PROVIDED BY THE BYE—LORUSSIAN S.S.R. ACCORDING TO THEIR OWN SYSTEMS OF CLASSIFICATION. LAW AND ECONOMICS ARE COMBINED. MEDICAL AND HEALTH—RELATED SCIENCES INCLUDE PHYSICAL CULTURE AND SPORT. ENGINEERING INCLUDES TRANSPORT AND COMMUNICATIONS.
FR—> CES CHIFFRES SONT FOURNIS PAR LA R.S.S. DE BIELORUSSIE SELON SON PROPRE SYSTEME DE CLASSIFI—CATION. LE DROIT COMPREND EGALEMENT LES SCIENCES ECONOMIQUES. LES SCIENCES MEDICALES, LA SANTE ET L'HYGIENE COMPRENNENT LA CULTURE PHYSIQUE ET LE SPORT. LES SCIENCES DE L'INGENIEUR COMPRENNENT LES TRANSPORTS ET LES TELECOMMUNICATIONS.
ESP> ESTAS CIFRAS HAN SIDO FACILITADAS POR LA R.S.S. DE BIELORRUSIA CON ARREGLO A SU PROPIO SISTEMA DE CLASIFICACION. EL DERECHO COMPRENDE IGUALMENTE LAS CIENCIAS ECONOMICAS. LAS CIENCIAS MEDICAS, LA SANIDAD Y LA HIGIENE INCLUYEN LA CUL—TURA FISICA Y EL DEPORTE. LA INGENIERIA Y TECNO—LOGIA COMPRENDE LOS TRANSPORTES Y COMUNICACIONES.

UKRAINIAN S.S.R.:
E—> THE FIGURES HAVE BEEN PROVIDED BY THE UKRAINIAN S.S.R. ACCORDING TO THEIR OWN SYSTEMS OF CLASSIFICATION. LAW AND ECONOMICS ARE COMBINED. MEDICAL AND HEALTH—RELATED SCIENCES INCLUDE PHYSICAL CULTURE AND SPORT. ENGINEERING INCLUDES TRANSPORT AND COMMUNICATIONS.
FR—> CES CHIFFRES SONT FOURNIS PAR LA R.S.S. D'UKRAINE SELON SON PROPRE SYSTEME DE CLASSIFI—CATION. LE DROIT COMPREND EGALEMENT LES SCIENCES ECONOMIQUES. LES SCIENCES MEDICALES, LA SANTE ET L'HYGIENE COMPRENNENT LA CULTURE PHYSIQUE ET LE SPORT. LES SCIENCES DE L'INGENIEUR COMPRENNENT LES TRANSPORTS ET LES TELECOMMUNICATIONS.
ESP> ESTAS CIFRAS HAN SIDO FACILITADAS POR LA R.S.S. DE UCRANIA CON ARREGLO A SU PROPIO SISTEMA DE CLASIFICACION. EL DERECHO COMPRENDE IGUALMENTE LAS CIENCIAS ECONOMICAS. LAS CIENCIAS MEDICAS, LA SANIDAD Y LA HIGIENE INCLUYEN LA CULTURA FISICA Y EL DEPORTE. LA INGENIERIA Y TECNOLOGIA COMPRENDE LOS TRANSPORTES Y COMUNICACIONES.

Third level: graduates by levels and fields 3.13
Troisième degré: diplômés par niveaux et domaines d'études
Tercer grado: diplomados por niveles y sectores de estudio

3.13 Education at the third level: graduates by ISCED levels and fields

Enseignement du troisième degré: nombre de diplômés d'après le niveau du grade ou diplôme et les domaines d'études de la CITE

Enseñanza de tercer grado: número de diplomados según el nivel del título o diploma y los sectores de estudios de la CINE

LEVEL 5: DIPLOMAS AND CERTIFICATES NOT EQUIVALENT TO A FIRST UNIVERSITY DEGRE

LEVEL 6: FIRST UNIVERSITY DEGREES OR EQUIVALENT QUALIFICATIONS

LEVEL 7: POST-GRADUATE UNIVERSITY DEGREES OR EQUIVALENT QUALIFICATIONS

NUMBER OF COUNTRIES AND TERRITORIES PRESENTED IN THIS TABLE: 106

NIVEAU 5: DIPLOMES ET CERTIFICATS NON EQUIVALENTS A UN PREMIER GRADE UNIVERSI-TAIRE

NIVEAU 6: PREMIERS GRADES UNIVERSI-TAIRES OU DIPLOMES EQUIVALENTS

NIVEAU 7: GRADES UNIVERSITAIRES SUPERIEURS OU DIPLOMES EQUIVALENTS

NOMBRE DE PAYS ET DE TERRITOIRES PRESENTES DANS CE TABLEAU: 106

GRADO 5: DIPLOMAS Y CERTIFICADOS NO EQUIVALENTES A UN PRIMER TITULO UNIVERSI-TARIO

GRADO 6: PRIMEROS TITULOS UNI-VERSITARIOS O DIPLOMAS EQUIVALENTES

GRADO 7: TITULOS UNIVERSITARIOS SUPERIORES O DIPLOMAS EQUIVALENTES

NUMERO DE PAISES Y DE TERRITORIOS PRESENTADOS EN ESTE CUADRO: 106

3.13 Third level: graduates by levels and fields
Troisième degré: diplômés par niveaux et domaines d'études
Tercer grado: diplomados por niveles y sectores de estudio

INTERNATIONAL STANDARD CLASSIFICATION OF EDUCATION BY LEVEL
CLASSIFICATION INTERNATIONALE TYPE DE L'EDUCATION PAR NIVEAUX
CLASIFICACION INTERNACIONAL NORMALIZADA DE LA EDUCACION POR GRADOS

COUNTRY / PAYS / PAIS	YEAR / ANNEE / AÑO	FIELD OF STUDY / BRANCHE D'ETUDES / RAMAS DE ESTUDIO	ALL LEVELS / TOUS NIVEAUX / TODOS LOS GRADOS MF	F	LEVEL 5 / NIVEAU 5 / GRADO 5 MF	F	LEVEL 6 / NIVEAU 6 / GRADO 6 MF	F	LEVEL 7 / NIVEAU 7 / GRADO 7 MF	F
AFRICA										
ALGERIA	1977	TOTAL	5 928	...	-	-	5 928	...	-	-
		EDUCATION SCIENCE & TCHR TRNG.	73	...	-	-	73	...	-	-
		HUMANITIES,RELIGION & THEOLOG.	377	...	-	-	377	...	-	-
		FINE AND APPLIED ARTS.	-	-	-	-	-	-	-	-
		LAW	1 308	...	-	-	1 308	...	-	-
		SOCIAL AND BEHAVIOURAL SCIENCE	1 532	...	-	-	1 532	...	-	-
		COMMERCIAL & BUS. ADMINISTR.	149	...	-	-	149	...	-	-
		MASS COMMUNICATION & DOCUMENT.	43	...	-	-	43	...	-	-
		HOME ECONOMICS & DOMESTIC SC.	-	-	-	-	-	-	-	-
		SERVICE TRADES	-	-	-	-	-	-	-	-
		NATURAL SCIENCE	353	...	-	-	353	...	-	-
		MATHEMATICS & COMPUTER SCIENCE	152	...	-	-	152	...	-	-
		MEDICAL AND HEALTH-RELATED SC.	1 072	...	-	-	1 072	...	-	-
		ENGINEERING	502	...	-	-	502	...	-	-
		ARCHITECTURE & TOWN PLANNING	115	...	-	-	115	...	-	-
		TRADE, CRAFT & INDUSTR. PGMS.	-	-	-	-	-	-	-	-
		TRANSPORT AND COMMUNICATIONS	181	...	-	-	181	...	-	-
		AGRICULTURE,FORESTRY & FISH'G.	71	...	-	-	71	...	-	-
		OTHER AND NOT SPECIFIED	-	-	-	-	-	-	-	-
BENIN	1978	TOTAL	724	...	-	-	500	...	224	...
		EDUCATION SCIENCE & TCHR TRNG.	24	...	-	-	-	-	24	...
		HUMANITIES,RELIGION & THEOLOG.	92	...	-	-	72	-	20	-
		FINE AND APPLIED ARTS.	-	-	-	-	-	-	-	-
		LAW	163	...	-	-	108	-	55	-
		SOCIAL AND BEHAVIOURAL SCIENCE	275	...	-	-	229	-	46	-
		COMMERCIAL & BUS. ADMINISTR.	45	-	-	-	-	-	45	-
		MASS COMMUNICATION & DOCUMENT.	-	-	-	-	-	-	-	-
		HOME ECONOMICS & DOMESTIC SC.	-	-	-	-	-	-	-	-
		SERVICE TRADES	-	-	-	-	-	-	-	-
		NATURAL SCIENCE	85	...	-	-	51	-	34	...
		MATHEMATICS & COMPUTER SCIENCE	-	-	-	-	-	-	-	-
		MEDICAL AND HEALTH-RELATED SC.	-	-	-	-	-	-	-	-
		ENGINEERING	-	-	-	-	-	-	-	-
		ARCHITECTURE & TOWN PLANNING	-	-	-	-	-	-	-	-
		TRADE, CRAFT & INDUSTR. PGMS.	-	-	-	-	-	-	-	-
		TRANSPORT AND COMMUNICATIONS	-	-	-	-	-	-	-	-
		AGRICULTURE,FORESTRY & FISH'G.	40	...	-	-	40	-	-	-
		OTHER AND NOT SPECIFIED	-	-	-	-	-	-	-	-

Third level: graduates by levels and fields 3.13
Troisième degré: diplômés par niveaux et domaines d'études
Tercer grado: diplomados por niveles y sectores de estudio

INTERNATIONAL STANDARD CLASSIFICATION OF EDUCATION BY LEVEL
CLASSIFICATION INTERNATIONALE TYPE DE L'EDUCATION PAR NIVEAUX
CLASIFICACION INTERNACIONAL NORMALIZADA DE LA EDUCACION POR GRADOS

COUNTRY / PAYS / PAIS	YEAR / ANNEE / AÑO	FIELD OF STUDY / BRANCHE D'ETUDES / RAMAS DE ESTUDIO	ALL LEVELS TOUS NIVEAUX TODOS LOS GRADOS		LEVEL 5 NIVEAU 5 GRADO 5		LEVEL 6 NIVEAU 6 GRADO 6		LEVEL 7 NIVEAU 7 GRADO 7	
			MF	F	MF	F	MF	F	MF	F
CENTRAL AFRICAN REPUBLIC	1977	TOTAL	90	3	78	3	12	-	-	-
		EDUCATION SCIENCE & TCHR TRNG.	33	2	33	2	-	-	-	-
		HUMANITIES,RELIGION & THEOLOG	26	-	16	-	10	-	-	-
		FINE AND APPLIED ARTS.	9	-	9	-	-	-	-	-
		LAW	-	-	-	-	-	-	-	-
		SOCIAL AND BEHAVIOURAL SCIENCE	-	-	-	-	-	-	-	-
		COMMERCIAL & BUS. ADMINISTR.	-	-	-	-	-	-	-	-
		MASS COMMUNICATION & DOCUMENT.	-	-	-	-	-	-	-	-
		HOME ECONOMICS & DOMESTIC SC.	-	-	-	-	-	-	-	-
		SERVICE TRADES	5	-	5	-	-	-	-	-
		NATURAL SCIENCE	6	1	4	1	2	-	-	-
		MATHEMATICS & COMPUTER SCIENCE	-	-	-	-	-	-	-	-
		MEDICAL AND HEALTH-RELATED SC.	4	-	4	-	-	-	-	-
		ENGINEERING	-	-	-	-	-	-	-	-
		ARCHITECTURE & TOWN PLANNING	-	-	-	-	-	-	-	-
		TRADE, CRAFT & INDUSTR. PGMS.	-	-	-	-	-	-	-	-
		TRANSPORT AND COMMUNICATIONS	-	-	-	-	-	-	-	-
		AGRICULTURE,FORESTRY & FISH'G.	7	-	7	-	-	-	-	-
		OTHER AND NOT SPECIFIED	-	-	-	-	-	-	-	-
CHAD	1976	TOTAL	205	...	3	...	138	-	64	...
		EDUCATION SCIENCE & TCHR TRNG.	58	...	-	...	41	-	17	...
		HUMANITIES,RELIGION & THEOLOG	39	...	-	...	14	-	25	...
		FINE AND APPLIED ARTS.	-	-	-	-	-	-	-	-
		LAW	41	...	3	...	38	-	-	-
		SOCIAL AND BEHAVIOURAL SCIENCE	48	...	-	-	31	-	17	...
		COMMERCIAL & BUS. ADMINISTR.	-	-	-	-	-	-	-	-
		MASS COMMUNICATION & DOCUMENT.	-	-	-	-	-	-	-	-
		HOME ECONOMICS & DOMESTIC SC.	-	-	-	-	-	-	-	-
		SERVICE TRADES	7	-	-	-	7	-	-	-
		NATURAL SCIENCE	-	-	-	-	-	-	-	-
		MATHEMATICS & COMPUTER SCIENCE	-	-	-	-	-	-	-	-
		MEDICAL AND HEALTH-RELATED SC.	12	-	-	-	7	-	5	-
		ENGINEERING	-	-	-	-	-	-	-	-
		ARCHITECTURE & TOWN PLANNING	-	-	-	-	-	-	-	-
		TRADE, CRAFT & INDUSTR. PGMS.	-	-	-	-	-	-	-	-
		TRANSPORT AND COMMUNICATIONS	-	-	-	-	-	-	-	-
		AGRICULTURE,FORESTRY & FISH'G.	-	-	-	-	-	-	-	-
		OTHER AND NOT SPECIFIED	-	-	-	-	-	-	-	-

3.13　Third level: graduates by levels and fields
Troisième degré: diplômés par niveaux et domaines d'études
Tercer grado: diplomados por niveles y sectores de estudio

INTERNATIONAL STANDARD CLASSIFICATION OF EDUCATION BY LEVEL
CLASSIFICATION INTERNATIONALE TYPE DE L'EDUCATION PAR NIVEAUX
CLASIFICACION INTERNACIONAL NORMALIZADA DE LA EDUCACION POR GRADOS

COUNTRY / PAYS / PAIS	YEAR / ANNEE / AÑO	FIELD OF STUDY / BRANCHE D'ETUDES / RAMAS DE ESTUDIO	ALL LEVELS / TOUS NIVEAUX / TODOS LOS GRADOS		LEVEL 5 / NIVEAU 5 / GRADO 5		LEVEL 6 / NIVEAU 6 / GRADO 6		LEVEL 7 / NIVEAU 7 / GRADO 7	
			MF	F	MF	F	MF	F	MF	F
EGYPT ‡	1976	TOTAL	59 832	20 222	—	—	57 568	19 697	2 264	525
		EDUCATION SCIENCE & TCHR TRNG.	6 115	2 457	—	—	6 074	2 441	41	16
		HUMANITIES,RELIGION & THEOLOG	7 786	4 255	—	—	7 509	4 171	277	84
		FINE AND APPLIED ARTS.	1 354	611	—	—	1 306	596	48	15
		LAW	5 004	971	—	—	4 693	945	311	26
		SOCIAL AND BEHAVIOURAL SCIENCE	1 029	477	—	—	997	471	32	6
		COMMERCIAL & BUS. ADMINISTR.	12 156	4 342	—	—	12 057	4 336	99	6
		MASS COMMUNICATION & DOCUMENT.	664	271	—	—	653	267	11	4
		HOME ECONOMICS & DOMESTIC SC.	467	467	—	—	447	447	20	20
		SERVICE TRADES	69	35	—	—	69	35	—	—
		NATURAL SCIENCE	2 516	1 040	—	—	2 171	942	345	98
		MATHEMATICS & COMPUTER SCIENCE	./.	./.	—	—	./.	./.	./.	./.
		MEDICAL AND HEALTH-RELATED SC.	6 022	1 821	—	—	5 738	1 718	284	103
		ENGINEERING	7 311	959	—	—	7 078	935	233	24
		ARCHITECTURE & TOWN PLANNING	—	—	—	—	—	—	—	—
		TRADE, CRAFT & INDUSTR. PGMS.	—	—	—	—	—	—	—	—
		TRANSPORT AND COMMUNICATIONS	—	—	—	—	—	—	—	—
		AGRICULTURE,FORESTRY & FISH'G.	7 850	1 870	—	—	7 392	1 779	478	91
		OTHER AND NOT SPECIFIED	1 469	646	—	—	1 384	614	85	32
ETHIOPIA	1977	TOTAL	1 998	...	1 492	...	506	...	—	—
		EDUCATION SCIENCE & TCHR TRNG.	717	...	605	...	112	...	—	—
		HUMANITIES,RELIGION & THEOLOG	—	—	—	—	—	—	—	—
		FINE AND APPLIED ARTS.	—	—	—	—	—	—	—	—
		LAW	36	...	—	—	36	...	—	—
		SOCIAL AND BEHAVIOURAL SCIENCE	333	...	181	...	152	...	—	—
		COMMERCIAL & BUS. ADMINISTR.	257	...	205	...	52	...	—	—
		MASS COMMUNICATION & DOCUMENT.	—	—	—	—	—	—	—	—
		HOME ECONOMICS & DOMESTIC SC.	—	—	—	—	—	—	—	—
		SERVICE TRADES	—	—	—	—	—	—	—	—
		NATURAL SCIENCE	40	...	2	...	38	...	—	—
		MATHEMATICS & COMPUTER SCIENCE	56	...	32	...	24	...	—	—
		MEDICAL AND HEALTH-RELATED SC.	34	...	—	—	34	...	—	—
		ENGINEERING	136	...	136	...	—	—	—	—
		ARCHITECTURE & TOWN PLANNING	—	—	—	—	—	—	—	—
		TRADE, CRAFT & INDUSTR. PGMS.	—	—	—	—	—	—	—	—
		TRANSPORT AND COMMUNICATIONS	—	—	—	—	—	—	—	—
		AGRICULTURE,FORESTRY & FISH'G.	389	...	331	...	58	...	—	—
		OTHER AND NOT SPECIFIED	—	—	—	—	—	—	—	—

Third level: graduates by levels and fields 3.13
Troisième degré: diplômés par niveaux et domaines d'études
Tercer grado: diplomados por niveles y sectores de estudio

INTERNATIONAL STANDARD CLASSIFICATION OF EDUCATION BY LEVEL
CLASSIFICATION INTERNATIONALE TYPE DE L'EDUCATION PAR NIVEAUX
CLASIFICACION INTERNACIONAL NORMALIZADA DE LA EDUCACION POR GRADOS

COUNTRY / PAYS / PAIS	YEAR / ANNEE / AÑO	FIELD OF STUDY / BRANCHE D'ETUDES / RAMAS DE ESTUDIO	ALL LEVELS / TOUS NIVEAUX / TODOS LOS GRADOS		LEVEL 5 / NIVEAU 5 / GRADO 5		LEVEL 6 / NIVEAU 6 / GRADO 6		LEVEL 7 / NIVEAU 7 / GRADO 7	
			MF	F	MF	F	MF	F	MF	F
IVORY COAST ‡	1976	TOTAL	1 815	...	-	-	1 477	...	338	...
		EDUCATION SCIENCE & TCHR TRNG.	-	-	-	-	-	-	-	-
		HUMANITIES,RELIGION & THEOLOG	561	...	-	-	545	...	16	-
		FINE AND APPLIED ARTS.	-	-	-	-	-	-	-	-
		LAW	536	...	-	-	434	...	102	-
		SOCIAL AND BEHAVIOURAL SCIENCE	-	-	-	-	-	-	-	-
		COMMERCIAL & BUS. ADMINISTR.	-	-	-	-	-	-	-	-
		MASS COMMUNICATION & DOCUMENT.	-	-	-	-	-	-	-	-
		HOME ECONOMICS & DOMESTIC SC.	-	-	-	-	-	-	-	-
		SERVICE TRADES	-	-	-	-	-	-	-	-
		NATURAL SCIENCE	254	...	-	-	199	...	55	-
		MATHEMATICS & COMPUTER SCIENCE	/	...	-	-	/	...	/	-
		MEDICAL AND HEALTH-RELATED SC.	23	...	-	-	-	-	23	-
		ENGINEERING	-	-	-	-	-	-	-	-
		ARCHITECTURE & TOWN PLANNING	-	-	-	-	-	-	-	-
		TRADE, CRAFT & INDUSTR. PGMS.	-	-	-	-	-	-	-	-
		TRANSPORT AND COMMUNICATIONS	-	-	-	-	-	-	-	-
		AGRICULTURE,FORESTRY & FISH'G.	441	...	-	-	299	...	142	-
		OTHER AND NOT SPECIFIED	...	...	-	-	-	-	-	-
KENYA	1977	TOTAL	8 649	...	2 638	...	5 363	...	648	...
		EDUCATION SCIENCE & TCHR TRNG.	1 808	...	206	...	1 501	...	101	...
		HUMANITIES,RELIGION & THEOLOG	50	-	-	-	50	-	-	-
		FINE AND APPLIED ARTS.	197	-	-	-	188	-	9	-
		LAW	697	...	-	-	571	...	126	-
		SOCIAL AND BEHAVIOURAL SCIENCE	990	...	448	...	500	...	42	-
		COMMERCIAL & BUS. ADMINISTR.	145	-	145	-	-	-	-	-
		MASS COMMUNICATION & DOCUMENT.	77	-	77	-	-	-	-	-
		HOME ECONOMICS & DOMESTIC SC.	-	-	-	-	-	-	-	-
		SERVICE TRADES	-	-	-	-	-	-	-	-
		NATURAL SCIENCE	628	...	-	-	507	...	121	-
		MATHEMATICS & COMPUTER SCIENCE	-	-	-	-	-	-	-	-
		MEDICAL AND HEALTH-RELATED SC.	1 038	...	289	...	697	...	52	-
		ENGINEERING	1 727	...	1 230	...	474	...	23	-
		ARCHITECTURE & TOWN PLANNING	269	-	-	-	219	-	50	-
		TRADE, CRAFT & INDUSTR. PGMS.	-	-	-	-	-	-	-	-
		TRANSPORT AND COMMUNICATIONS	-	-	-	-	-	-	-	-
		AGRICULTURE,FORESTRY & FISH'G.	780	...	-	-	656	...	124	-
		OTHER AND NOT SPECIFIED	243	-	243	-	-	-	-	-

3.13 Third level: graduates by levels and fields
Troisième degré: diplômés par niveaux et domaines d'études
Tercer grado: diplomados por niveles y sectores de estudio

INTERNATIONAL STANDARD CLASSIFICATION OF EDUCATION BY LEVEL
CLASSIFICATION INTERNATIONALE TYPE DE L'EDUCATION PAR NIVEAUX
CLASIFICACION INTERNACIONAL NORMALIZADA DE LA EDUCACION POR GRADOS

COUNTRY / PAYS / PAIS	YEAR / ANNEE / AÑO	FIELD OF STUDY / BRANCHE D'ETUDES / RAMAS DE ESTUDIO	ALL LEVELS TOUS NIVEAUX TODOS LOS GRADOS		LEVEL 5 NIVEAU 5 GRADO 5		LEVEL 6 NIVEAU 6 GRADO 6		LEVEL 7 NIVEAU 7 GRADO 7	
			MF	F	MF	F	MF	F	MF	F
MADAGASCAR	1976	TOTAL	1 361	575	806	338	259	128	296	109
		EDUCATION SCIENCE & TCHR TRNG.	401	238	222	137	179	101	—	—
		HUMANITIES,RELIGION & THEOLOG	—	—	—	—	—	—	—	—
		FINE AND APPLIED ARTS.	—	—	—	—	—	—	—	—
		LAW	208	87	139	49	—	—	69	38
		SOCIAL AND BEHAVIOURAL SCIENCE	109	46	109	46	—	—	—	—
		COMMERCIAL & BUS. ADMINISTR.	166	67	110	41	—	—	56	26
		MASS COMMUNICATION & DOCUMENT.	—	—	—	—	—	—	—	—
		HOME ECONOMICS & DOMESTIC SC.	112	38	99	29	—	—	13	9
		SERVICE TRADES	14	7	14	7	—	—	—	—
		NATURAL SCIENCE	175	69	81	29	59	26	35	14
		MATHEMATICS & COMPUTER SCIENCE	47	7	—	—	21	1	26	6
		MEDICAL AND HEALTH-RELATED SC.	58	13	—	—	—	—	58	13
		ENGINEERING	32	—	32	—	—	—	—	—
		ARCHITECTURE & TOWN PLANNING	—	—	—	—	—	—	—	—
		TRADE, CRAFT & INDUSTR. PGMS.	—	—	—	—	—	—	—	—
		TRANSPORT AND COMMUNICATIONS	—	—	—	—	—	—	—	—
		AGRICULTURE,FORESTRY & FISH'G.	39	3	—	—	—	—	39	3
		OTHER AND NOT SPECIFIED	—	—	—	—	—	—	—	—
MALI	1977	TOTAL	576	88	78	39	492	49	6	—
		EDUCATION SCIENCE & TCHR TRNG.	273	27	—	—	267	27	6	—
		HUMANITIES,RELIGION & THEOLOG	—	—	—	—	—	—	—	—
		FINE AND APPLIED ARTS.	—	—	—	—	—	—	—	—
		LAW	30	2	—	—	30	2	—	—
		SOCIAL AND BEHAVIOURAL SCIENCE	64	11	—	—	64	11	—	—
		COMMERCIAL & BUS. ADMINISTR.	82	40	62	36	20	4	—	—
		MASS COMMUNICATION & DOCUMENT.	—	—	—	—	—	—	—	—
		HOME ECONOMICS & DOMESTIC SC.	—	—	—	—	—	—	—	—
		SERVICE TRADES	—	—	—	—	—	—	—	—
		NATURAL SCIENCE	34	5	—	—	34	5	—	—
		MATHEMATICS & COMPUTER SCIENCE	58	—	—	—	58	—	—	—
		MEDICAL AND HEALTH-RELATED SC.	—	—	—	—	—	—	—	—
		ENGINEERING	—	—	—	—	—	—	—	—
		ARCHITECTURE & TOWN PLANNING	—	—	—	—	—	—	—	—
		TRADE, CRAFT & INDUSTR. PGMS.	—	—	—	—	—	—	—	—
		TRANSPORT AND COMMUNICATIONS	—	—	—	—	—	—	—	—
		AGRICULTURE,FORESTRY & FISH'G.	16	3	16	3	—	—	—	—
		OTHER AND NOT SPECIFIED	19	—	—	—	19	—	—	—

Third level: graduates by levels and fields 3.13
Troisième degré: diplômés par niveaux et domaines d'études
Tercer grado: diplomados por niveles y sectores de estudio

INTERNATIONAL STANDARD CLASSIFICATION OF EDUCATION BY LEVEL
CLASSIFICATION INTERNATIONALE TYPE DE L'EDUCATION PAR NIVEAUX
CLASIFICACION INTERNACIONAL NORMALIZADA DE LA EDUCACION POR GRADOS

COUNTRY / PAYS / PAIS	YEAR / ANNEE / AÑO	FIELD OF STUDY / BRANCHE D'ETUDES / RAMAS DE ESTUDIO	ALL LEVELS TOUS NIVEAUX TODOS LOS GRADOS MF	F	LEVEL 5 NIVEAU 5 GRADO 5 MF	F	LEVEL 6 NIVEAU 6 GRADO 6 MF	F	LEVEL 7 NIVEAU 7 GRADO 7 MF	F
MAURITIUS	1977	TOTAL	383	106	359	106	24	—	—	—
		EDUCATION SCIENCE & TCHR TRNG.	129	48	129	48	—	—	—	—
		HUMANITIES,RELIGION & THEOLOG	—	—	—	—	—	—	—	—
		FINE AND APPLIED ARTS.	12	6	12	6	—	—	—	—
		LAW	88	48	88	48	—	—	—	—
		SOCIAL AND BEHAVIOURAL SCIENCE	—	—	—	—	—	—	—	—
		COMMERCIAL & BUS. ADMINISTR.	—	—	—	—	—	—	—	—
		MASS COMMUNICATION & DOCUMENT.	—	—	—	—	—	—	—	—
		HOME ECONOMICS & DOMESTIC SC.	—	—	—	—	—	—	—	—
		SERVICE TRADES	—	—	—	—	—	—	—	—
		NATURAL SCIENCE	—	—	—	—	—	—	—	—
		MATHEMATICS & COMPUTER SCIENCE	12	1	12	1	—	—	—	—
		MEDICAL AND HEALTH-RELATED SC.	86	—	86	—	—	—	—	—
		ENGINEERING	—	—	—	—	—	—	—	—
		ARCHITECTURE & TOWN PLANNING	—	—	—	—	—	—	—	—
		TRADE, CRAFT & INDUSTR. PGMS.	—	—	—	—	—	—	—	—
		TRANSPORT AND COMMUNICATIONS.	—	—	—	—	—	—	—	—
		AGRICULTURE,FORESTRY & FISH'G.	56	3	32	3	24	—	—	—
		OTHER AND NOT SPECIFIED	—	—	—	—	—	—	—	—
MOROCCO ‡	1977	TOTAL	3 407	639	—	—	3 356	637	51	2
		EDUCATION SCIENCE & TCHR TRNG.	310	115	—	—	310	115	—	—
		HUMANITIES,RELIGION & THEOLOG	796	234	—	—	789	234	7	—
		FINE AND APPLIED ARTS.	—	—	—	—	—	—	—	—
		LAW	1 981	223	—	—	1 937	221	44	2
		NATURAL SCIENCES TOTAL	152	33	—	—	152	33	—	—
		MEDICAL AND HEALTH-RELATED SC.	103	31	—	—	103	31	—	—
		ENGINEERING, TOTAL	65	3	—	—	65	3	—	—
		AGRICULTURE,FORESTRY & FISH'G.	—	—	—	—	—	—	—	—
		OTHER AND NOT SPECIFIED	—	—	—	—	—	—	—	—
MOZAMBIQUE	1976	TOTAL	75	23	—	—	75	23	—	—
		EDUCATION SCIENCE & TCHR TRNG.	15	7	—	—	15	7	—	—
		HUMANITIES,RELIGION & THEOLOG	—	—	—	—	—	—	—	—
		FINE AND APPLIED ARTS.	—	—	—	—	—	—	—	—
		LAW	25	3	—	—	25	3	—	—
		SOCIAL SCIENCES, TOTAL	8	5	—	—	8	5	—	—
		NATURAL SCIENCES, TOTAL	9	7	—	—	9	7	—	—
		MEDICAL AND HEALTH-RELATED SC.	2	1	—	—	2	1	—	—
		ENGINEERING, TOTAL	15	1	—	—	15	1	—	—
		AGRICULTURE,FORESTRY & FISH'G.	1	—	—	—	1	—	—	—
		OTHER AND NOT SPECIFIED	—	—	—	—	—	—	—	—

3.13 Third level: graduates by levels and fields
Troisième degré: diplômés par niveaux et domaines d'études
Tercer grado: diplomados por niveles y sectores de estudio

INTERNATIONAL STANDARD CLASSIFICATION OF EDUCATION BY LEVEL
CLASSIFICATION INTERNATIONALE TYPE DE L'EDUCATION PAR NIVEAUX
CLASIFICACION INTERNACIONAL NORMALIZADA DE LA EDUCACION POR GRADOS

COUNTRY / PAYS / PAIS	YEAR / ANNEE / AÑO	FIELD OF STUDY / BRANCHE D'ETUDES / RAMAS DE ESTUDIO	ALL LEVELS TOUS NIVEAUX TODOS LOS GRADOS MF	F	LEVEL 5 NIVEAU 5 GRADO 5 MF	F	LEVEL 6 NIVEAU 6 GRADO 6 MF	F	LEVEL 7 NIVEAU 7 GRADO 7 MF	F
REUNION ‡	1976	TOTAL	296	123	196	73	67	36	33	14
		EDUCATION SCIENCE & TCHR TRNG.	94	48	68	28	22	18	4	2
		HUMANITIES,RELIGION & THEOLOG	131	56	57	26	45	18	29	12
		FINE AND APPLIED ARTS.	20	6	20	6	—	—	—	—
		LAW	—	—	—	—	—	—	—	—
		SOCIAL AND BEHAVIOURAL SCIENCE	—	—	—	—	—	—	—	—
		COMMERCIAL & BUS. ADMINISTR.	27	13	27	13	—	—	—	—
		MASS COMMUNICATION & DOCUMENT.	—	—	—	—	—	—	—	—
		HOME ECONOMICS & DOMESTIC SC.	—	—	—	—	—	—	—	—
		SERVICE TRADES	—	—	—	—	—	—	—	—
		NATURAL SCIENCE	./.	./.	./.	./.	—	—	—	—
		MATHEMATICS & COMPUTER SCIENCE	—	—	—	—	—	—	—	—
		MEDICAL AND HEALTH-RELATED SC.	—	—	—	—	—	—	—	—
		ENGINEERING	—	—	—	—	—	—	—	—
		ARCHITECTURE & TOWN PLANNING	—	—	—	—	—	—	—	—
		TRADE,CRAFT & INDUSTR. PGMS.	—	—	—	—	—	—	—	—
		TRANSPORT AND COMMUNICATIONS	—	—	—	—	—	—	—	—
		AGRICULTURE,FORESTRY & FISH'G.	24	—	24	—	—	—	—	—
		OTHER AND NOT SPECIFIED	—	—	—	—	—	—	—	—
RWANDA	1976	TOTAL	157	27	—	—	115	21	42	6
		EDUCATION SCIENCE & TCHR TRNG.	7	2	—	—	7	2	—	—
		HUMANITIES,RELIGION & THEOLOG	28	2	—	—	28	2	—	—
		FINE AND APPLIED ARTS.	—	—	—	—	—	—	—	—
		LAW	25	2	—	—	—	—	25	2
		SOCIAL AND BEHAVIOURAL SCIENCE	39	3	—	—	29	2	10	1
		COMMERCIAL & BUS. ADMINISTR.	—	—	—	—	—	—	—	—
		MASS COMMUNICATION & DOCUMENT.	—	—	—	—	—	—	—	—
		HOME ECONOMICS & DOMESTIC SC.	3	3	—	—	3	3	—	—
		SERVICE TRADES	—	—	—	—	—	—	—	—
		NATURAL SCIENCE	39	6	—	—	36	4	3	2
		MATHEMATICS & COMPUTER SCIENCE	—	—	—	—	—	—	—	—
		MEDICAL AND HEALTH-RELATED SC.	12	8	—	—	12	8	—	—
		ENGINEERING	—	—	—	—	—	—	—	—
		ARCHITECTURE & TOWN PLANNING	—	—	—	—	—	—	—	—
		TRADE,CRAFT & INDUSTR. PGMS.	—	—	—	—	—	—	—	—
		TRANSPORT AND COMMUNICATIONS	—	—	—	—	—	—	—	—
		AGRICULTURE,FORESTRY & FISH'G.	4	1	—	—	—	—	4	1
		OTHER AND NOT SPECIFIED	—	—	—	—	—	—	—	—

Third level: graduates by levels and fields   3.13
Troisième degré: diplômés par niveaux et domaines d'études
Tercer grado: diplomados por niveles y sectores de estudio

INTERNATIONAL STANDARD CLASSIFICATION OF EDUCATION BY LEVEL
CLASSIFICATION INTERNATIONALE TYPE DE L'EDUCATION PAR NIVEAUX
CLASIFICACION INTERNACIONAL NORMALIZADA DE LA EDUCACION POR GRADOS

COUNTRY / PAYS / PAIS	YEAR / ANNEE / AÑO	FIELD OF STUDY / BRANCHE D'ETUDES / RAMAS DE ESTUDIO	ALL LEVELS / TOUS NIVEAUX / TODOS LOS GRADOS MF	F	LEVEL 5 / NIVEAU 5 / GRADO 5 MF	F	LEVEL 6 / NIVEAU 6 / GRADO 6 MF	F	LEVEL 7 / NIVEAU 7 / GRADO 7 MF	F
SENEGAL	1976	TOTAL	1 319	...	516	...	723	...	80	...
		EDUCATION SCIENCE & TCHR TRNG.	135	...	135	...	—	...	—	...
		HUMANITIES,RELIGION & THEOLOG	447	...	—	—	447	—	—	—
		FINE AND APPLIED ARTS.	—		—		—		—	
		LAW	124		—		113		11	
		SOCIAL AND BEHAVIOURAL SCIENCE	40	...	40	...	—	...	—	...
		COMMERCIAL & BUS. ADMINISTR.	114	...	—	...	114	...	—	...
		MASS COMMUNICATION & DOCUMENT.	89		89		—		—	
		HOME ECONOMICS & DOMESTIC SC.	—		—		—		—	
		SERVICE TRADES	—		—		—		—	
		NATURAL SCIENCE	34		34		—		—	
		MATHEMATICS & COMPUTER SCIENCE	39	...	39	...	—	...	—	...
		MEDICAL AND HEALTH-RELATED SC.	24	...	24	...	—	...	—	...
		ENGINEERING	92		—		37		55	
		ARCHITECTURE & TOWN PLANNING	49		23		12		14	
		TRADE, CRAFT & INDUSTR. PGMS.	15		15		—		—	
		TRANSPORT AND COMMUNICATIONS	19		19		—		—	
		AGRICULTURE,FORESTRY & FISH'G.	17		17		—		—	
		OTHER AND NOT SPECIFIED	81		81		—		—	
	1977	TOTAL	2 788	...	2 131	...	616	...	41	...
		EDUCATION SCIENCE & TCHR TRNG.	180		146		34		—	
		HUMANITIES,RELIGION & THEOLOG	841	...	724	—	117	—	—	—
		FINE AND APPLIED ARTS.	4		4		—		—	
		LAW	376		266		110		—	
		SOCIAL AND BEHAVIOURAL SCIENCE	75	...	75	...	—	...	—	...
		COMMERCIAL & BUS. ADMINISTR.	422		336		86		—	
		MASS COMMUNICATION & DOCUMENT.	89		89		—		—	
		HOME ECONOMICS & DOMESTIC SC.	6		—		6		—	
		SERVICE TRADES	36		36		—		—	
		NATURAL SCIENCE	190		139		51		—	
		MATHEMATICS & COMPUTER SCIENCE	—		—		—		—	
		MEDICAL AND HEALTH-RELATED SC.	100	...	—	...	59	...	41	...
		ENGINEERING	15		15		—		—	
		ARCHITECTURE & TOWN PLANNING	154		86		68		—	
		TRADE, CRAFT & INDUSTR. PGMS.	—		—		—		—	
		TRANSPORT AND COMMUNICATIONS	—		—		—		—	
		AGRICULTURE,FORESTRY & FISH'G.	50	...	50	...	—	...	—	...
		OTHER AND NOT SPECIFIED	250		165		85		—	

3.13 Third level: graduates by levels and fields
Troisième degré: diplômés par niveaux et domaines d'études
Tercer grado: diplomados por niveles y sectores de estudio

INTERNATIONAL STANDARD CLASSIFICATION OF EDUCATION BY LEVEL
CLASSIFICATION INTERNATIONALE TYPE DE L'EDUCATION PAR NIVEAUX
CLASIFICACION INTERNACIONAL NORMALIZADA DE LA EDUCACION POR GRADOS

COUNTRY / PAYS / PAIS	YEAR / ANNEE / AÑO	FIELD OF STUDY / BRANCHE D'ETUDES / RAMAS DE ESTUDIO	ALL LEVELS TOUS NIVEAUX TODOS LOS GRADOS MF	F	LEVEL 5 NIVEAU 5 GRADO 5 MF	F	LEVEL 6 NIVEAU 6 GRADO 6 MF	F	LEVEL 7 NIVEAU 7 GRADO 7 MF	F
SEYCHELLES	1977	TOTAL	35	33	35	33	—	—	—	—
		EDUCATION SCIENCE & TCHR TRNG.	35	33	35	33	—	—	—	—
		HUMANITIES,RELIGION & THEOLOG	—	—	—	—	—	—	—	—
		FINE AND APPLIED ARTS.	—	—	—	—	—	—	—	—
		LAW	—	—	—	—	—	—	—	—
		SOCIAL AND BEHAVIOURAL SCIENCE	—	—	—	—	—	—	—	—
		COMMERCIAL & BUS. ADMINISTR.	—	—	—	—	—	—	—	—
		MASS COMMUNICATION & DOCUMENT.	—	—	—	—	—	—	—	—
		HOME ECONOMICS & DOMESTIC SC.	—	—	—	—	—	—	—	—
		SERVICE TRADES	—	—	—	—	—	—	—	—
		NATURAL SCIENCE	—	—	—	—	—	—	—	—
		MATHEMATICS & COMPUTER SCIENCE	—	—	—	—	—	—	—	—
		MEDICAL AND HEALTH-RELATED SC.	—	—	—	—	—	—	—	—
		ENGINEERING	—	—	—	—	—	—	—	—
		ARCHITECTURE & TOWN PLANNING	—	—	—	—	—	—	—	—
		TRADE, CRAFT & INDUSTR. PGMS.	—	—	—	—	—	—	—	—
		TRANSPORT AND COMMUNICATIONS	—	—	—	—	—	—	—	—
		AGRICULTURE,FORESTRY & FISH'G.	—	—	—	—	—	—	—	—
		OTHER AND NOT SPECIFIED	—	—	—	—	—	—	—	—
SUDAN	1977	TOTAL	...	...	585	103	2 419	475	...	...
		EDUCATION SCIENCE & TCHR TRNG.	...	...	31	2	110	18	...	...
		HUMANITIES,RELIGION & THEOLOG	...	...	53	10	630	172	...	...
		FINE AND APPLIED ARTS.	...	...	—	—	—	—	...	...
		LAW	...	...	—	—	102	13	...	...
		SOCIAL AND BEHAVIOURAL SCIENCE	...	...	54	10	258	16	...	...
		COMMERCIAL & BUS. ADMINISTR.	...	...	25	25	538	176	...	...
		MASS COMMUNICATION & DOCUMENT.	...	...	—	—	—	—	...	...
		HOME ECONOMICS & DOMESTIC SC.	...	...	—	—	—	—	...	...
		SERVICE TRADES	...	...	—	—	—	—	...	...
		NATURAL SCIENCE	...	...	—	—	102	18	...	...
		MATHEMATICS & COMPUTER SCIENCE	...	...	78	38	226	26	...	...
		MEDICAL AND HEALTH-RELATED SC.	...	...	91	6	160	3	...	...
		ENGINEERING	...	...	41	8	16	4	...	...
		ARCHITECTURE & TOWN PLANNING	...	...	31	—	—	—	...	...
		TRADE, CRAFT & INDUSTR. PGMS.	...	...	—	—	—	—	...	...
		TRANSPORT AND COMMUNICATIONS	...	...	—	—	—	—	...	...
		AGRICULTURE,FORESTRY & FISH'G.	...	...	181	4	277	29	...	...
		OTHER AND NOT SPECIFIED	...	...	—	—	—	—	...	...

Third level: graduates by levels and fields 3.13
Troisième degré: diplômés par niveaux et domaines d'études
Tercer grado: diplomados por niveles y sectores de estudio

INTERNATIONAL STANDARD CLASSIFICATION OF EDUCATION BY LEVEL
CLASSIFICATION INTERNATIONALE TYPE DE L'EDUCATION PAR NIVEAUX
CLASIFICACION INTERNACIONAL NORMALIZADA DE LA EDUCACION POR GRADOS

COUNTRY / PAYS / PAIS	YEAR / ANNEE / AÑO	FIELD OF STUDY / BRANCHE D'ETUDES / RAMAS DE ESTUDIO	ALL LEVELS / TOUS NIVEAUX / TODOS LOS GRADOS MF	F	LEVEL 5 / NIVEAU 5 / GRADO 5 MF	F	LEVEL 6 / NIVEAU 6 / GRADO 6 MF	F	LEVEL 7 / NIVEAU 7 / GRADO 7 MF	F
SWAZILAND	1976	TOTAL	332	...	219	...	113	...	—	—
		EDUCATION SCIENCE & TCHR TRNG.	67	...	45	...	22	...	—	—
		HUMANITIES,RELIGION & THEOLOG	24	...	—	...	24	...	—	—
		FINE AND APPLIED ARTS.	—	...	—	...	—	...	—	—
		LAW	2	...	—	...	2	...	—	—
		SOCIAL AND BEHAVIOURAL SCIENCE	18	...	—	...	18	...	—	—
		COMMERCIAL & BUS. ADMINISTR.	11	...	11	...	—	...	—	—
		MASS COMMUNICATION & DOCUMENT.	—	...	—	...	—	...	—	—
		HOME ECONOMICS & DOMESTIC SC.	17	...	17	...	—	...	—	—
		SERVICE TRADES	—	...	—	...	—	...	—	—
		NATURAL SCIENCE	6	...	—	...	6	...	—	—
		MATHEMATICS & COMPUTER SCIENCE	—	...	—	...	—	...	—	—
		MEDICAL AND HEALTH-RELATED SC.	39	...	—	...	39	...	—	—
		ENGINEERING	—	...	—	...	—	...	—	—
		ARCHITECTURE & TOWN PLANNING	—	...	—	...	—	...	—	—
		TRADE, CRAFT & INDUSTR. PGMS.	126	...	126	...	—	...	—	—
		TRANSPORT AND COMMUNICATIONS	—	...	—	...	—	...	—	—
		AGRICULTURE,FORESTRY & FISH'G.	22	...	20	...	2	...	—	—
		OTHER AND NOT SPECIFIED	—	...	—	...	—	...	—	—
TUNISIA ‡	1977	TOTAL	3 611	886						
		EDUCATION SCIENCE & TCHR TRNG.	222	59						
		HUMANITIES,RELIGION & THEOLOG	382	165						
		FINE AND APPLIED ARTS.	28	10						
		LAW	232	34						
		SOCIAL AND BEHAVIOURAL SCIENCE	60	19						
		COMMERCIAL & BUS. ADMINISTR.	535	127						
		MASS COMMUNICATION & DOCUMENT.	45	7						
		HOME ECONOMICS & DOMESTIC SC.	384	80						
		SERVICE TRADES	167	68						
		NATURAL SCIENCES, TOTAL	400	132						
		MEDICAL AND HEALTH-RELATED SC.	191	4						
		ENGINEERING	247	13						
		ARCHITECTURE & TOWN PLANNING	43	9						
		TRADE, CRAFT & INDUSTR. PGMS.	47	1						
		TRANSPORT AND COMMUNICATIONS	199	8						
		AGRICULTURE,FORESTRY & FISH'G.	429	150						
		OTHER AND NOT SPECIFIED								

3.13 Third level: graduates by levels and fields
Troisième degré: diplômés par niveaux et domaines d'études
Tercer grado: diplomados por niveles y sectores de estudio

INTERNATIONAL STANDARD CLASSIFICATION OF EDUCATION BY LEVEL
CLASSIFICATION INTERNATIONALE TYPE DE L'EDUCATION PAR NIVEAUX
CLASIFICACION INTERNACIONAL NORMALIZADA DE LA EDUCACION POR GRADOS

COUNTRY / PAYS / PAIS	YEAR / ANNEE / AÑO	FIELD OF STUDY / BRANCHE D'ETUDES / RAMAS DE ESTUDIO	ALL LEVELS / TOUS NIVEAUX / TODOS LOS GRADOS MF	F	LEVEL 5 / NIVEAU 5 / GRADO 5 MF	F	LEVEL 6 / NIVEAU 6 / GRADO 6 MF	F	LEVEL 7 / NIVEAU 7 / GRADO 7 MF	F
UGANDA ‡	1977	TOTAL	1 391	...	266	...	1 077	199	48	9
		EDUCATION SCIENCE & TCHR TRNG.	405	107	162	43	237	61	6	3
		HUMANITIES,RELIGION & THEOLOG.	250	58	—	—	243	58	7	—
		FINE AND APPLIED ARTS.	29	5	15	2	14	3	—	—
		LAW	57	10	—	—	57	10	—	—
		SOCIAL AND BEHAVIOURAL SCIENCE	21	8	—	—	21	8	—	—
		COMMERCIAL & BUS. ADMINISTR.	117	9	41	6	69	3	7	—
		MASS COMMUNICATION & DOCUMENT.	26	—	26	—	—	—	—	—
		HOME ECONOMICS & DOMESTIC SC.	—	—	—	—	—	—	—	—
		SERVICE TRADES	15	—	15	—	—	—	—	—
		NATURAL SCIENCE	169	26	7	—	162	22	—	4
		MATHEMATICS & COMPUTER SCIENCE	21	—	—	—	21	—	—	—
		MEDICAL AND HEALTH-RELATED SC.	126	16	—	—	103	14	23	2
		ENGINEERING	43	1	—	—	43	1	—	—
		ARCHITECTURE & TOWN PLANNING	—	—	—	—	—	—	—	—
		TRADE, CRAFT & INDUSTR. PGMS.	—	—	—	—	—	—	—	—
		TRANSPORT AND COMMUNICATIONS	—	—	—	—	—	—	—	—
		AGRICULTURE,FORESTRY & FISH'G.	112	19	—	—	107	19	5	—
		OTHER AND NOT SPECIFIED	—	—	—	—	—	—	—	—
UNITED REPUBLIC OF CAMEROON ‡	1976	TOTAL	2 132	...	709	...	579	...	844	...
		EDUCATION SCIENCE & TCHR TRNG.	1 403	...	417	...	451	...	535	...
		HUMANITIES,RELIGION & THEOLOG.	./.	...	./.	...	./.	...	./.	...
		FINE AND APPLIED ARTS.	./.	...	./.	...	./.	...	./.	...
		NATURAL SCIENCE	517	...	198	...	104	...	215	...
		MATHEMATICS & COMPUTER SCIENCE	./.	...	./.	...	./.	...	./.	...
		MEDICAL AND HEALTH-RELATED SC.	94	...	24	...	24	...	46	...
		ENGINEERING	118	...	70	...	—	...	48	...
		ARCHITECTURE & TOWN PLANNING	./.	...	./.	...	./.	...	./.	...
		TRADE, CRAFT & INDUSTR. PGMS.	./.	...	./.	...	./.	...	./.	...
		TRANSPORT AND COMMUNICATIONS	./.	...	./.	...	./.	...	./.	...
		AGRICULTURE,FORESTRY & FISH'G.	./.	...	./.	...	./.	...	./.	...
		OTHER AND NOT SPECIFIED	—	—	—	—	—	—	—	—

Third level: graduates by levels and fields   3.13
Troisième degré: diplômés par niveaux et domaines d'études
Tercer grado: diplomados por niveles y sectores de estudio

INTERNATIONAL STANDARD CLASSIFICATION OF EDUCATION BY LEVEL
CLASSIFICATION INTERNATIONALE TYPE DE L'EDUCATION PAR NIVEAUX
CLASIFICACION INTERNACIONAL NORMALIZADA DE LA EDUCACION POR GRADOS

COUNTRY / PAYS / PAIS	YEAR / ANNEE / AÑO	FIELD OF STUDY / BRANCHE D'ETUDES / RAMAS DE ESTUDIO	ALL LEVELS TOUS NIVEAUX TODOS LOS GRADOS		LEVEL 5 NIVEAU 5 GRADO 5		LEVEL 6 NIVEAU 6 GRADO 6		LEVEL 7 NIVEAU 7 GRADO 7	
			MF	F	MF	F	MF	F	MF	F
UNITED REPUBLIC OF TANZANIA ‡	1977	TOTAL	1 354	165	403	73	803	78	148	14
		EDUCATION SCIENCE & TCHR TRNG.	460	72	230	42	230	30	–	–
		HUMANITIES,RELIGION & THEOLOG	./.	./.	./.	./.	–	–	–	–
		FINE AND APPLIED ARTS.	–	–	–	–	–	–	–	–
		LAW	159	10	66	4	59	3	34	3
		SOCIAL AND BEHAVIOURAL SCIENCE	265	32	–	–	181	23	84	9
		COMMERCIAL & BUS. ADMINISTR.	–	–	–	–	–	–	–	–
		MASS COMMUNICATION & DOCUMENT.	–	–	–	–	–	–	–	–
		HOME ECONOMICS & DOMESTIC SC.	21	21	21	21	–	–	–	–
		SERVICE TRADES	–	–	–	–	–	–	–	–
		NATURAL SCIENCE	84	3	–	–	73	2	11	1
		MATHEMATICS & COMPUTER SCIENCE	–	–	–	–	–	–	–	–
		MEDICAL AND HEALTH-RELATED SC.	173	10	86	6	69	3	18	1
		ENGINEERING	53	–	–	–	53	–	–	–
		ARCHITECTURE & TOWN PLANNING	–	–	–	–	–	–	–	–
		TRADE, CRAFT & INDUSTR. PGMS.	–	–	–	–	–	–	–	–
		TRANSPORT AND COMMUNICATIONS	–	–	–	–	–	–	–	–
		AGRICULTURE,FORESTRY & FISH'G.	139	17	–	–	138	17	1	–
		OTHER AND NOT SPECIFIED	–	–	–	–	–	–	–	–
ZAMBIA ‡	1976	TOTAL	481	...	–	–	481	...	–	–
		EDUCATION SCIENCE & TCHR TRNG.	135	...	–	–	135	...	–	–
		HUMANITIES,RELIGION & THEOLOG	130	...	–	–	130	...	–	–
		FINE AND APPLIED ARTS.	–	...	–	–	–	...	–	–
		LAW	50	...	–	–	50	...	–	–
		SOCIAL SCIENCES, TOTAL	./.	...	–	–	./.	...	–	–
		NATURAL SCIENCES, TOTAL	41	...	–	–	41	...	–	–
		MEDICAL AND HEALTH-RELATED SC.	62	...	–	–	62	...	–	–
		ENGINEERING, TOTAL	38	...	–	–	38	...	–	–
		AGRICULTURE,FORESTRY & FISH'G.	25	...	–	–	25	...	–	–
		OTHER AND NOT SPECIFIED	–	...	–	–	–	...	–	–

3.13 Third level: graduates by levels and fields
Troisième degré: diplômés par niveaux et domaines d'études
Tercer grado: diplomados por niveles y sectores de estudio

INTERNATIONAL STANDARD CLASSIFICATION OF EDUCATION BY LEVEL
CLASSIFICATION INTERNATIONALE TYPE DE L'EDUCATION PAR NIVEAUX
CLASIFICACION INTERNACIONAL NORMALIZADA DE LA EDUCACION POR GRADOS

COUNTRY / PAYS / PAIS	YEAR / ANNEE / AÑO	FIELD OF STUDY / BRANCHE D'ETUDES / RAMAS DE ESTUDIO	ALL LEVELS TOUS NIVEAUX TODOS LOS GRADOS MF	F	LEVEL 5 NIVEAU 5 GRADO 5 MF	F	LEVEL 6 NIVEAU 6 GRADO 6 MF	F	LEVEL 7 NIVEAU 7 GRADO 7 MF	F
AMERICA, NORTH										
CANADA ‡	1977	TOTAL	151 469	74 862	39 505	23 635	96 617	46 577	15 347	4 650
		EDUCATION SCIENCE & TCHR TRNG.	24 753	14 911	500	230	21 136	13 436	3 117	1 245
		HUMANITIES,RELIGION & THEOLOG	12 175	6 668	—	—	10 301	5 959	1 874	709
		FINE AND APPLIED ARTS.	5 344	3 195	2 497	1 352	2 661	1 749	186	94
		LAW	3 123	837	—	—	2 856	791	267	46
		SOCIAL AND BEHAVIOURAL SCIENCE	20 136	9 946	3 462	2 307	14 424	6 909	2 250	730
		COMMERCIAL & BUS. ADMINISTR.	20 289	8 271	9 738	5 897	8 527	2 076	2 024	298
		MASS COMMUNICATION & DOCUMENT.	2 282	1 333	920	513	857	450	505	370
		HOME ECONOMICS & DOMESTIC SC.	1 163	1 117	—	—	1 110	1 077	53	40
		SERVICE TRADES	—	—	—	—	—	—	—	—
		NATURAL SCIENCE	7 258	2 081	—	—	5 847	1 844	1 411	237
		MATHEMATICS & COMPUTER SCIENCE	3 031	817	—	—	2 558	738	473	79
		MEDICAL AND HEALTH-RELATED SC.	20 037	16 001	12 324	11 316	6 990	4 354	723	331
		ENGINEERING	12 016	721	5 924	538	4 853	152	1 239	31
		ARCHITECTURE & TOWN PLANNING	1 226	166	537	74	619	84	70	8
		TRADE, CRAFT & INDUSTR. PGMS.	—	—	—	—	—	—	—	—
		TRANSPORT AND COMMUNICATIONS	189	12	189	12	—	—	—	—
		AGRICULTURE,FORESTRY & FISH'G.	3 818	715	1 955	336	1 554	328	309	51
		OTHER AND NOT SPECIFIED	14 629	8 071	1 459	1 060	12 324	6 630	846	381
COSTA RICA ‡	1976	TOTAL	2 307	...	501	...	1 033	...	773	...
		EDUCATION SCIENCE & TCHR TRNG.	591	...	350	...	215	...	26	...
		HUMANITIES,RELIGION & THEOLOG	176	...	—	—	134	...	42	...
		FINE AND APPLIED ARTS.	32	...	—	—	13	...	19	...
		LAW	138	...	—	—	—	—	138	...
		SOCIAL AND BEHAVIOURAL SCIENCE	394	...	20	...	310	...	64	...
		COMMERCIAL & BUS. ADMINISTR.	161	...	—	—	146	...	15	...
		MASS COMMUNICATION & DOCUMENT.	46	...	—	—	46	...	—	—
		HOME ECONOMICS & DOMESTIC SC.	—	—	—	—	—	—	—	—
		SERVICE TRADES	—	—	—	—	—	—	—	—
		NATURAL SCIENCE	57	...	—	—	42	...	15	...
		MATHEMATICS & COMPUTER SCIENCE	21	...	—	—	11	...	10	...
		MEDICAL AND HEALTH-RELATED SC.	413	...	105	...	47	...	261	...
		ENGINEERING	165	...	26	...	69	...	70	...
		ARCHITECTURE & TOWN PLANNING	—	—	—	—	—	—	—	—
		TRADE, CRAFT & INDUSTR. PGMS.	—	—	—	—	—	—	—	—
		TRANSPORT AND COMMUNICATIONS	—	—	—	—	—	—	—	—
		AGRICULTURE,FORESTRY & FISH'G.	113	...	—	—	—	—	113	...
		OTHER AND NOT SPECIFIED	—	—	—	—	—	—	—	—

Third level: graduates by levels and fields   3.13
Troisième degré: diplômés par niveaux et domaines d'études
Tercer grado: diplomados por niveles y sectores de estudio

INTERNATIONAL STANDARD CLASSIFICATION OF EDUCATION BY LEVEL
CLASSIFICATION INTERNATIONALE TYPE DE L'EDUCATION PAR NIVEAUX
CLASIFICACION INTERNACIONAL NORMALIZADA DE LA EDUCACION POR GRADOS

COUNTRY PAYS PAIS	YEAR ANNEE AÑO	FIELD OF STUDY BRANCHE D'ETUDES RAMAS DE ESTUDIO	ALL LEVELS TOUS NIVEAUX TODOS LOS GRADOS		LEVEL 5 NIVEAU 5 GRADO 5		LEVEL 6 NIVEAU 6 GRADO 6		LEVEL 7 NIVEAU 7 GRADO 7	
			MF	F	MF	F	MF	F	MF	F
CUBA	1976	TOTAL	9 233	2 883	—	—	9 233	2 883	—	—
		EDUCATION SCIENCE & TCHR TRNG.	2 464	1 010	—	—	2 464	1 010	—	—
		HUMANITIES,RELIGION & THEOLOG	519	238	—	—	519	238	—	—
		FINE AND APPLIED ARTS.	—	—	—	—	—	—	—	—
		LAW	906	193	—	—	906	193	—	—
		SOCIAL AND BEHAVIOURAL SCIENCE	118	42	—	—	118	42	—	—
		COMMERCIAL & BUS. ADMINISTR.	582	211	—	—	582	211	—	—
		MASS COMMUNICATION & DOCUMENT.	455	229	—	—	455	229	—	—
		HOME ECONOMICS & DOMESTIC SC.	—	—	—	—	—	—	—	—
		SERVICE TRADES	—	—	—	—	—	—	—	—
		NATURAL SCIENCE	362	223	—	—	362	223	—	—
		MATHEMATICS & COMPUTER SCIENCE	45	18	—	—	45	18	—	—
		MEDICAL AND HEALTH-RELATED SC.	1 515	224	—	—	1 515	224	—	—
		ENGINEERING	394	40	—	—	394	40	—	—
		ARCHITECTURE & TOWN PLANNING	374	120	—	—	374	120	—	—
		TRADE,CRAFT & INDUSTR.PGMS.	540	144	—	—	540	144	—	—
		TRANSPORT AND COMMUNICATIONS	57	1	—	—	57	1	—	—
		AGRICULTURE,FORESTRY & FISH'G.	902	190	—	—	902	190	—	—
		OTHER AND NOT SPECIFIED	—	—	—	—	—	—	—	—
DOMINICAN REPUBLIC ‡	1977	TOTAL	1 692	...	305	...	1 387	...	—	—
		EDUCATION SCIENCE & TCHR TRNG.	238	...	107	...	131	...	—	—
		HUMANITIES,RELIGION & THEOLOG	8	5	—	—	8	5	—	—
		FINE AND APPLIED ARTS.	15	8	15	8	—	—	—	—
		LAW	57	18	—	—	57	18	—	—
		SOCIAL AND BEHAVIOURAL SCIENCE	117	...	34	...	83	...	—	—
		COMMERCIAL & BUS. ADMINISTR.	192	...	3	...	189	...	—	—
		MASS COMMUNICATION & DOCUMENT.	11	5	7	4	4	1	—	—
		HOME ECONOMICS & DOMESTIC SC.	68	68	—	—	68	68	—	—
		SERVICE TRADES	—	—	—	—	—	—	—	—
		NATURAL SCIENCE	51	26	20	8	31	18	—	—
		MATHEMATICS & COMPUTER SCIENCE	4	...	—	—	4	...	—	—
		MEDICAL AND HEALTH-RELATED SC.	523	304	99	94	424	210	—	—
		ENGINEERING	276	31	20	5	256	26	—	—
		ARCHITECTURE & TOWN PLANNING	46	...	—	—	46	...	—	—
		TRADE,CRAFT & INDUSTR.PGMS.	—	—	—	—	—	—	—	—
		TRANSPORT AND COMMUNICATIONS	—	—	—	—	—	—	—	—
		AGRICULTURE,FORESTRY & FISH'G.	86	...	—	—	86	...	—	—
		OTHER AND NOT SPECIFIED	—	—	—	—	—	—	—	—

3.13 Third level: graduates by levels and fields
Troisième degré: diplômés par niveaux et domaines d'études
Tercer grado: diplomados por niveles y sectores de estudio

INTERNATIONAL STANDARD CLASSIFICATION OF EDUCATION BY LEVEL
CLASSIFICATION INTERNATIONALE TYPE DE L'EDUCATION PAR NIVEAUX
CLASIFICACION INTERNACIONAL NORMALIZADA DE LA EDUCACION POR GRADOS

COUNTRY / PAYS / PAIS	YEAR / ANNEE / AÑO	FIELD OF STUDY / BRANCHE D'ETUDES / RAMAS DE ESTUDIO	ALL LEVELS TOUS NIVEAUX TODOS LOS GRADOS		LEVEL 5 NIVEAU 5 GRADO 5		LEVEL 6 NIVEAU 6 GRADO 6		LEVEL 7 NIVEAU 7 GRADO 7	
			MF	F	MF	F	MF	F	MF	F
EL SALVADOR	1977	TOTAL	1 190	331	635	187	555	144	—	—
		EDUCATION SCIENCE & TCHR TRNG.	70	39	70	39	—	—	—	—
		HUMANITIES,RELIGION & THEOLOG	60	26	—	—	60	26	—	—
		FINE AND APPLIED ARTS.	67	10	—	—	67	10	—	—
		LAW	45	15	7	7	38	8	—	—
		SOCIAL AND BEHAVIOURAL SCIENCE	—	—	—	—	—	—	—	—
		COMMERCIAL & BUS. ADMINISTR.	—	—	—	—	—	—	—	—
		MASS COMMUNICATION & DOCUMENT.	—	—	—	—	—	—	—	—
		HOME ECONOMICS & DOMESTIC SC.	—	—	—	—	—	—	—	—
		SERVICE TRADES	12	5	12	5	—	—	—	—
		NATURAL SCIENCE	10	7	—	—	10	7	—	—
		MATHEMATICS & COMPUTER SCIENCE	350	162	86	86	264	76	—	—
		MEDICAL AND HEALTH-RELATED SC.	362	50	362	50	—	—	—	—
		ENGINEERING	112	17	—	—	112	17	—	—
		ARCHITECTURE & TOWN PLANNING	—	—	—	—	—	—	—	—
		TRADE, CRAFT & INDUSTR. PGMS.	—	—	—	—	—	—	—	—
		TRANSPORT AND COMMUNICATIONS	—	—	—	—	—	—	—	—
		AGRICULTURE,FORESTRY & FISH'G.	102	—	98	—	4	—	—	—
		OTHER AND NOT SPECIFIED	—	—	—	—	—	—	—	—
GUATEMALA ‡	1977	TOTAL	1 443	409	—	—	1 443	409	—	—
		EDUCATION SCIENCE & TCHR TRNG.	463	228	—	—	463	228	—	—
		HUMANITIES,RELIGION & THEOLOG	12	7	—	—	12	7	—	—
		FINE AND APPLIED ARTS.	—	—	—	—	—	—	—	—
		LAW	136	24	—	—	136	24	—	—
		SOCIAL AND BEHAVIOURAL SCIENCE	123	50	—	—	123	50	—	—
		COMMERCIAL & BUS. ADMINISTR.	68	11	—	—	68	11	—	—
		MASS COMMUNICATION & DOCUMENT.	11	9	—	—	11	9	—	—
		HOME ECONOMICS & DOMESTIC SC.	—	—	—	—	—	—	—	—
		SERVICE TRADES	—	—	—	—	—	—	—	—
		NATURAL SCIENCE	21	12	—	—	21	12	—	—
		MATHEMATICS & COMPUTER SCIENCE	—	—	—	—	—	—	—	—
		MEDICAL AND HEALTH-RELATED SC.	372	58	—	—	372	58	—	—
		ENGINEERING	142	1	—	—	142	1	—	—
		ARCHITECTURE & TOWN PLANNING	13	2	—	—	13	2	—	—
		TRADE, CRAFT & INDUSTR. PGMS.	—	—	—	—	—	—	—	—
		TRANSPORT AND COMMUNICATIONS	—	—	—	—	—	—	—	—
		AGRICULTURE,FORESTRY & FISH'G.	82	7	—	—	82	7	—	—
		OTHER AND NOT SPECIFIED	—	—	—	—	—	—	—	—

Third level: graduates by levels and fields 3.13
Troisième degré: diplômés par niveaux et domaines d'études
Tercer grado: diplomados por niveles y sectores de estudio

INTERNATIONAL STANDARD CLASSIFICATION OF EDUCATION BY LEVEL
CLASSIFICATION INTERNATIONALE TYPE DE L'EDUCATION PAR NIVEAUX
CLASIFICACION INTERNACIONAL NORMALIZADA DE LA EDUCACION POR GRADOS

COUNTRY / PAYS / PAIS	YEAR / ANNEE / AÑO	FIELD OF STUDY / BRANCHE D'ETUDES / RAMAS DE ESTUDIO	ALL LEVELS TOUS NIVEAUX TODOS LOS GRADOS		LEVEL 5 NIVEAU 5 GRADO 5		LEVEL 6 NIVEAU 6 GRADO 6		LEVEL 7 NIVEAU 7 GRADO 7	
			MF	F	MF	F	MF	F	MF	F
HAITI ‡	1976	TOTAL	265	74						
		EDUCATION SCIENCE & TCHR TRNG.	21	10						
		HUMANITIES,RELIGION & THEOLOG.	–	–						
		FINE AND APPLIED ARTS.	3	–						
		LAW	3	–						
		SOCIAL AND BEHAVIOURAL SCIENCE	2	–						
		COMMERCIAL & BUS. ADMINISTR.	–	–						
		MASS COMMUNICATION & DOCUMENT.	–	–						
		HOME ECONOMICS & DOMESTIC SC.	–	–						
		SERVICE TRADES	–	–						
		NATURAL SCIENCE	22	2						
		MATHEMATICS & COMPUTER SCIENCE	–	–						
		MEDICAL AND HEALTH-RELATED SC.	185	62						
		ENGINEERING	–	–						
		ARCHITECTURE & TOWN PLANNING	–	–						
		TRADE, CRAFT & INDUSTR. PGMS.	–	–						
		TRANSPORT AND COMMUNICATIONS	–	–						
		AGRICULTURE,FORESTRY & FISH'G.	29	–						
		OTHER AND NOT SPECIFIED	–	–						
HONDURAS ‡	1977	TOTAL	242	52	–	–	242	52	–	–
		EDUCATION SCIENCE & TCHR TRNG.	3	3	–	–	3	3	–	–
		HUMANITIES,RELIGION & THEOLOG.	–	–	–	–	–	–	–	–
		FINE AND APPLIED ARTS.	–	–	–	–	–	–	–	–
		LAW	76	13	–	–	76	13	–	–
		SOCIAL AND BEHAVIOURAL SCIENCE	10	1	–	–	10	1	–	–
		COMMERCIAL & BUS. ADMINISTR.	8	–	–	–	8	–	–	–
		MASS COMMUNICATION & DOCUMENT.	–	–	–	–	–	–	–	–
		HOME ECONOMICS & DOMESTIC SC.	–	–	–	–	–	–	–	–
		SERVICE TRADES	–	–	–	–	–	–	–	–
		NATURAL SCIENCE	10	7	–	–	10	7	–	–
		MATHEMATICS & COMPUTER SCIENCE	–	–	–	–	–	–	–	–
		MEDICAL AND HEALTH-RELATED SC.	68	22	–	–	68	22	–	–
		ENGINEERING	67	6	–	–	67	6	–	–
		ARCHITECTURE & TOWN PLANNING	–	–	–	–	–	–	–	–
		TRADE, CRAFT & INDUSTR. PGMS.	–	–	–	–	–	–	–	–
		TRANSPORT AND COMMUNICATIONS	–	–	–	–	–	–	–	–
		AGRICULTURE,FORESTRY & FISH'G.	–	–	–	–	–	–	–	–
		OTHER AND NOT SPECIFIED	–	–	–	–	–	–	–	–

3.13 Third level: graduates by levels and fields
Troisième degré: diplômés par niveaux et domaines d'études
Tercer grado: diplomados por niveles y sectores de estudio

INTERNATIONAL STANDARD CLASSIFICATION OF EDUCATION BY LEVEL
CLASSIFICATION INTERNATIONALE TYPE DE L'EDUCATION PAR NIVEAUX
CLASIFICACION INTERNACIONAL NORMALIZADA DE LA EDUCACION POR GRADOS

COUNTRY / PAYS / PAIS	YEAR / ANNEE / AÑO	FIELD OF STUDY / BRANCHE D'ETUDES / RAMAS DE ESTUDIO	ALL LEVELS TOUS NIVEAUX TODOS LOS GRADOS MF	F	LEVEL 5 NIVEAU 5 GRADO 5 MF	F	LEVEL 6 NIVEAU 6 GRADO 6 MF	F	LEVEL 7 NIVEAU 7 GRADO 7 MF	F
JAMAICA ‡	1976	TOTAL	1 275	...						
		EDUCATION SCIENCE & TCHR TRNG.	17	...						
		HUMANITIES,RELIGION & THEOLOG	438	...						
		FINE AND APPLIED ARTS.	–	–						
		LAW	112	...						
		SOCIAL SCIENCES, TOTAL	187	...						
		NATURAL SCIENCES, TOTAL	234	...						
		MEDICAL AND HEALTH–RELATED SC.	102	...						
		ENGINEERING, TOTAL	115	...						
		AGRICULTURE,FORESTRY & FISH'G.	70	...						
		OTHER AND NOT SPECIFIED	–	–						
	1977	TOTAL	1 281	...						
		EDUCATION SCIENCE & TCHR TRNG.	21	...						
		HUMANITIES,RELIGION & THEOLOG	430	...						
		FINE AND APPLIED ARTS.	–	–						
		LAW	98	...						
		SOCIAL SCIENCES, TOTAL	199	...						
		NATURAL SCIENCES, TOTAL	282	...						
		MEDICAL AND HEALTH–RELATED SC.	105	...						
		ENGINEERING, TOTAL	113	...						
		AGRICULTURE,FORESTRY & FISH'G.	33	...						
		OTHER AND NOT SPECIFIED	–	–						

Third level: graduates by levels and fields 3.13
Troisième degré: diplômés par niveaux et domaines d'études
Tercer grado: diplomados por niveles y sectores de estudio

INTERNATIONAL STANDARD CLASSIFICATION OF EDUCATION BY LEVEL
CLASSIFICATION INTERNATIONALE TYPE DE L'EDUCATION PAR NIVEAUX
CLASIFICACION INTERNACIONAL NORMALIZADA DE LA EDUCACION POR GRADOS

COUNTRY / PAYS / PAIS	YEAR / ANNEE / AÑO	FIELD OF STUDY / BRANCHE D'ETUDES / RAMAS DE ESTUDIO	ALL LEVELS TOUS NIVEAUX TODOS LOS GRADOS		LEVEL 5 NIVEAU 5 GRADO 5		LEVEL 6 NIVEAU 6 GRADO 6		LEVEL 7 NIVEAU 7 GRADO 7	
			MF	F	MF	F	MF	F	MF	F
MEXICO ‡	1976	TOTAL	48 674	...	...	...	48 674	...	...	...
		EDUCATION SCIENCE & TCHR TRNG.	229	...	...	...	229	...	...	...
		HUMANITIES,RELIGION & THEOLOG	1 803	...	...	...	1 803	...	...	...
		FINE AND APPLIED ARTS.	78	...	...	...	78	...	...	...
		LAW	5 192	...	...	...	5 192	...	...	...
		SOCIAL AND BEHAVIOURAL SCIENCE	2 874	...	...	...	2 874	...	...	...
		COMMERCIAL & BUS. ADMINISTR.	9 987	...	...	...	9 987	...	...	...
		MASS COMMUNICATION & DOCUMENT.	550	...	...	...	550	...	...	...
		HOME ECONOMICS & DOMESTIC SC.	39	...	...	...	39	...	...	...
		SERVICE TRADES	354	...	...	...	354	...	...	...
		NATURAL SCIENCE	1 985	...	...	...	1 985	...	...	...
		MATHEMATICS & COMPUTER SCIENCE	412	...	...	...	412	...	...	...
		MEDICAL AND HEALTH-RELATED SC.	9 582	...	...	...	9 582	...	...	...
		ENGINEERING	5 861	...	...	...	5 861	...	...	...
		ARCHITECTURE & TOWN PLANNING	2 972	...	...	...	2 972	...	...	...
		TRADE, CRAFT & INDUSTR. PGMS.	2 830	...	...	...	2 830	...	...	...
		TRANSPORT AND COMMUNICATIONS	1 405	...	...	...	1 405	...	...	...
		AGRICULTURE,FORESTRY & FISH'G.	2 487	...	...	...	2 487	...	...	...
		OTHER AND NOT SPECIFIED	34	...	...	...	34	...	...	...
	1977	TOTAL	55 858	...	...	...	55 858	...	...	...
		EDUCATION SCIENCE & TCHR TRNG.	336	...	...	...	336	...	...	...
		HUMANITIES,RELIGION & THEOLOG	416	...	...	...	416	...	...	...
		FINE AND APPLIED ARTS.	128	...	...	...	128	...	...	...
		LAW	5 273	...	...	...	5 273	...	...	...
		SOCIAL AND BEHAVIOURAL SCIENCE	3 799	...	...	...	3 799	...	...	...
		COMMERCIAL & BUS. ADMINISTR.	11 731	...	...	...	11 731	...	...	...
		MASS COMMUNICATION & DOCUMENT.	694	...	...	...	694	...	...	...
		HOME ECONOMICS & DOMESTIC SC.	45	...	...	...	45	...	...	...
		SERVICE TRADES	276	...	...	...	276	...	...	...
		NATURAL SCIENCE	2 086	...	...	...	2 086	...	...	...
		MATHEMATICS & COMPUTER SCIENCE	301	...	...	...	301	...	...	...
		MEDICAL AND HEALTH-RELATED SC.	12 416	...	...	...	12 416	...	...	...
		ENGINEERING	8 933	...	...	...	8 933	...	...	...
		ARCHITECTURE & TOWN PLANNING	1 603	...	...	...	1 603	...	...	...
		TRADE, CRAFT & INDUSTR. PGMS.	3 936	...	...	...	3 936	...	...	...
		TRANSPORT AND COMMUNICATIONS	185	...	...	...	185	...	...	...
		AGRICULTURE,FORESTRY & FISH'G.	3 683	...	...	...	3 683	...	...	...
		OTHER AND NOT SPECIFIED	17	...	...	...	17	...	...	...

3.13 Third level: graduates by levels and fields
Troisième degré: diplômés par niveaux et domaines d'études
Tercer grado: diplomados por niveles y sectores de estudio

INTERNATIONAL STANDARD CLASSIFICATION OF EDUCATION BY LEVEL
CLASSIFICATION INTERNATIONALE TYPE DE L'EDUCATION PAR NIVEAUX
CLASIFICACION INTERNACIONAL NORMALIZADA DE LA EDUCACION POR GRADOS

COUNTRY / PAYS / PAIS — YEAR / ANNEE / AÑO — FIELD OF STUDY / BRANCHE D'ETUDES / RAMAS DE ESTUDIO

PANAMA ‡ — 1977

FIELD OF STUDY	ALL LEVELS TOUS NIVEAUX TODOS LOS GRADOS		LEVEL 5 NIVEAU 5 GRADO 5		LEVEL 6 NIVEAU 6 GRADO 6		LEVEL 7 NIVEAU 7 GRADO 7	
	MF	F	MF	F	MF	F	MF	F
TOTAL	2 062	1 132	463	259	1 599	873	./.	./.
EDUCATION SCIENCE & TCHR TRNG.	388	291	173	151	215	140	./.	./.
HUMANITIES,RELIGION & THEOLOG	111	84	12	6	99	78	./.	./.
FINE AND APPLIED ARTS.	11	3	10	2	1	1	./.	./.
LAW	83	21	—	—	83	21	./.	./.
SOCIAL AND BEHAVIOURAL SCIENCE	162	89	—	—	162	89	./.	./.
COMMERCIAL & BUS. ADMINISTR.	158	88	5	4	153	84	./.	./.
MASS COMMUNICATION & DOCUMENT.	17	10	—	—	17	10	./.	./.
HOME ECONOMICS & DOMESTIC SC.	32	32	—	—	32	32	./.	./.
SERVICE TRADES	—	—	—	—	—	—	./.	./.
NATURAL SCIENCE	168	93	49	29	119	64	./.	./.
MATHEMATICS & COMPUTER SCIENCE	90	58	39	28	51	30	./.	./.
MEDICAL AND HEALTH-RELATED SC.	409	257	21	21	388	236	./.	./.
ENGINEERING	260	21	142	9	118	12	./.	./.
ARCHITECTURE & TOWN PLANNING	64	21	7	5	57	16	./.	./.
TRADE CRAFT & INDUSTR. PGMS.	1	—	—	—	1	—	./.	./.
TRANSPORT AND COMMUNICATIONS	1	—	1	—	—	—	./.	./.
AGRICULTURE,FORESTRY & FISH G.	4	4	4	4	—	—	./.	./.
OTHER AND NOT SPECIFIED	103	60	—	—	103	60	./.	./.

FORMER CANAL ZONE — 1976

FIELD OF STUDY	ALL LEVELS		LEVEL 5		LEVEL 6		LEVEL 7	
	MF	F	MF	F	MF	F	MF	F
TOTAL	130	88	119	79	11	9	—	—
EDUCATION SCIENCE & TCHR TRNG.	—	—	—	—	—	—	—	—
HUMANITIES,RELIGION & THEOLOG	—	—	—	—	—	—	—	—
FINE AND APPLIED ARTS.	—	—	—	—	—	—	—	—
LAW	—	—	—	—	—	—	—	—
SOCIAL AND BEHAVIOURAL SCIENCE	—	—	—	—	—	—	—	—
COMMERCIAL & BUS. ADMINISTR.	—	—	—	—	—	—	—	—
MASS COMMUNICATION & DOCUMENT.	—	—	—	—	—	—	—	—
HOME ECONOMICS & DOMESTIC SC.	—	—	—	—	—	—	—	—
SERVICE TRADES	—	—	—	—	—	—	—	—
NATURAL SCIENCE	—	—	—	—	—	—	—	—
MATHEMATICS & COMPUTER SCIENCE	11	9	—	—	11	9	—	—
MEDICAL AND HEALTH-RELATED SC.	—	—	—	—	—	—	—	—
ENGINEERING	—	—	—	—	—	—	—	—
ARCHITECTURE & TOWN PLANNING	—	—	—	—	—	—	—	—
TRADE CRAFT & INDUSTR. PGMS.	—	—	—	—	—	—	—	—
TRANSPORT AND COMMUNICATIONS	—	—	—	—	—	—	—	—
AGRICULTURE,FORESTRY & FISH G.	119	79	119	79	—	—	—	—
OTHER AND NOT SPECIFIED	—	—	—	—	—	—	—	—

Third level: graduates by levels and fields 3.13
Troisième degré: diplômés par niveaux et domaines d'études
Tercer grado: diplomados por niveles y sectores de estudio

INTERNATIONAL STANDARD CLASSIFICATION OF EDUCATION BY LEVEL
CLASSIFICATION INTERNATIONALE TYPE DE L'EDUCATION PAR NIVEAUX
CLASIFICACION INTERNACIONAL NORMALIZADA DE LA EDUCACION POR GRADOS

COUNTRY / PAYS / PAIS	YEAR / ANNEE / AÑO	FIELD OF STUDY / BRANCHE D'ETUDES / RAMAS DE ESTUDIO	ALL LEVELS TOUS NIVEAUX TODOS LOS GRADOS MF	F	LEVEL 5 NIVEAU 5 GRADO 5 MF	F	LEVEL 6 NIVEAU 6 GRADO 6 MF	F	LEVEL 7 NIVEAU 7 GRADO 7 MF	F
PUERTO RICO ‡	1976	TOTAL	13 093	7 813	3 244	2 136	8 820	5 063	1 029	614
		EDUCATION SCIENCE & TCHR TRNG.	1 809	1 321	—	—	1 499	1 125	310	196
		HUMANITIES,RELIGION & THEOLOG	1 083	819	—	—	991	756	92	63
		FINE AND APPLIED ARTS.	305	203	—	—	305	203	—	—
		LAW	259	88	—	—	259	88	—	—
		SOCIAL AND BEHAVIOURAL SCIENCE	1 177	685	—	—	1 150	674	27	11
		COMMERCIAL & BUS. ADMINISTR.	1 713	647	—	—	1 592	623	121	24
		MASS COMMUNICATION & DOCUMENT.	37	29	—	—	6	4	31	25
		HOME ECONOMICS & DOMESTIC SC.	134	134	—	—	128	128	6	6
		SERVICE TRADES	—	—	—	—	—	—	—	—
		NATURAL SCIENCE	755	403	—	—	697	376	58	27
		MATHEMATICS & COMPUTER SCIENCE	120	62	—	—	117	61	3	1
		MEDICAL AND HEALTH-RELATED SC.	782	547	—	—	671	463	111	84
		ENGINEERING	398	22	—	—	392	22	6	—
		ARCHITECTURE & TOWN PLANNING	36	10	—	—	30	9	6	1
		TRADE, CRAFT & INDUSTR. PGMS.	—	—	—	—	—	—	—	—
		TRANSPORT AND COMMUNICATIONS	—	—	—	—	—	—	—	—
		AGRICULTURE,FORESTRY & FISH'G.	75	4	—	—	64	4	11	—
		OTHER AND NOT SPECIFIED	4 410	2 839	3 244	2 136	919	527	247	176
TRINIDAD AND TOBAGO ‡	1975	TOTAL	403	...	103	...	288	...	12	...
		EDUCATION SCIENCE & TCHR TRNG.	91	...	91	...	—	—	—	—
		HUMANITIES,RELIGION & THEOLOG	115	...	—	—	113	...	2	...
		FINE AND APPLIED ARTS.	—	—	—	—	—	—	—	—
		LAW	—	—	—	—	—	—	—	—
		SOCIAL SCIENCES, TOTAL	73	...	7	...	64	...	2	...
		NATURAL SCIENCES, TOTAL	68	...	3	...	63	...	2	...
		MEDICAL AND HEALTH-RELATED SC.	—	—	—	—	—	—	—	—
		ENGINEERING, TOTAL	27	...	2	...	25	...	—	—
		AGRICULTURE,FORESTRY & FISH'G.	29	...	—	—	23	...	6	...
		OTHER AND NOT SPECIFIED	—	—	—	—	—	—	—	—
	1977	TOTAL	585	...	6	...	458	...	121	...
		EDUCATION SCIENCE & TCHR TRNG.	67	...	—	—	—	—	67	...
		HUMANITIES,RELIGION & THEOLOG	123	...	—	—	122	...	1	...
		FINE AND APPLIED ARTS.	—	—	—	—	—	—	—	—
		LAW	24	...	—	—	24	...	—	—
		SOCIAL SCIENCES, TOTAL	104	...	6	...	73	...	25	...
		NATURAL SCIENCES, TOTAL	74	...	—	—	69	...	5	...
		MEDICAL AND HEALTH-RELATED SC.	—	—	—	—	—	—	—	—
		ENGINEERING, TOTAL	124	...	—	—	111	...	13	...
		AGRICULTURE,FORESTRY & FISH'G.	69	...	—	—	59	...	10	...
		OTHER AND NOT SPECIFIED	—	—	—	—	—	—	—	—

3.13 Third level: graduates by levels and fields
Troisième degré: diplômés par niveaux et domaines d'études
Tercer grado: diplomados por niveles y sectores de estudio

INTERNATIONAL STANDARD CLASSIFICATION OF EDUCATION BY LEVEL
CLASSIFICATION INTERNATIONALE TYPE DE L'EDUCATION PAR NIVEAUX
CLASIFICACION INTERNACIONAL NORMALIZADA DE LA EDUCACION POR GRADOS

COUNTRY / PAYS / PAIS	YEAR / ANNEE / AÑO	FIELD OF STUDY / BRANCHE D'ETUDES / RAMAS DE ESTUDIO	ALL LEVELS TOUS NIVEAUX TODOS LOS GRADOS		LEVEL 5 NIVEAU 5 GRADO 5		LEVEL 6 NIVEAU 6 GRADO 6		LEVEL 7 NIVEAU 7 GRADO 7	
			MF	F	MF	F	MF	F	MF	F
UNITED STATES OF AMERICA ‡	1976	TOTAL	1 837 903	838 725	598 245	275	983 909	435 979	350 396	157 471
		EDUCATION SCIENCE & TCHR TRNG.	249 737	177 252	—	—	120 370	93 252	129 367	84 000
		HUMANITIES,RELIGION & THEOLOG	128 233	62 680	—	—	101 439	49 941	26 794	12 739
		FINE AND APPLIED ARTS.	51 990	31 056	—	—	42 678	26 408	9 312	4 648
		LAW	36 297	8 027	—	—	34 663	7 811	1 634	216
		SOCIAL AND BEHAVIOURAL SCIENCE	162 556	72 676	—	—	136 857	63 699	25 699	9 409
		COMMERCIAL & BUS. ADMINISTR.	201 542	42 980	—	—	152 756	35 786	48 786	7 077
		MASS COMMUNICATION & DOCUMENT.	35 509	19 012	—	—	24 598	11 533	10 911	7 479
		HOME ECONOMICS & DOMESTIC SC.	19 933	18 967	—	—	17 439	16 717	2 494	2 250
		SERVICE TRADES	—	—	—	—	—	—	—	—
		NATURAL SCIENCE	95 285	28 210	—	—	76 102	23 888	19 183	4 322
		MATHEMATICS & COMPUTER SCIENCE	28 135	9 317	—	—	20 603	7 424	7 532	1 893
		MEDICAL AND HEALTH-RELATED SC.	90 832	56 497	—	—	78 842	47 921	11 990	8 576
		ENGINEERING	68 115	3 011	—	—	49 284	2 218	18 831	793
		ARCHITECTURE & TOWN PLANNING	11 609	1 919	—	—	8 337	1 192	3 272	727
		TRADE, CRAFT & INDUSTR. PGMS.	—	—	—	—	—	—	—	—
		TRANSPORT AND COMMUNICATIONS	—	—	—	—	—	—	—	—
		AGRICULTURE,FORESTRY & FISH'G.	27 795	5 774	—	—	23 053	5 139	4 742	635
		OTHER AND NOT SPECIFIED	630 335	301 347	598 245	275	96 888	43 365	29 849	12 707
U.S. VIRGIN ISLANDS	1976	TOTAL	113	81	28	24	80	53	5	4
		EDUCATION SCIENCE & TCHR TRNG.	31	28	—	—	26	24	5	4
		HUMANITIES,RELIGION & THEOLOG	3	3	—	—	3	3	—	—
		FINE AND APPLIED ARTS.	—	—	—	—	—	—	—	—
		LAW	—	—	—	—	—	—	—	—
		SOCIAL AND BEHAVIOURAL SCIENCE	12	3	—	—	12	3	—	—
		COMMERCIAL & BUS. ADMINISTR.	27	18	—	—	27	18	—	—
		MASS COMMUNICATION & DOCUMENT.	—	—	—	—	—	—	—	—
		HOME ECONOMICS & DOMESTIC SC.	—	—	—	—	—	—	—	—
		SERVICE TRADES	—	—	—	—	—	—	—	—
		NATURAL SCIENCE	7	2	—	—	7	2	—	—
		MATHEMATICS & COMPUTER SCIENCE	—	—	—	—	—	—	—	—
		MEDICAL AND HEALTH-RELATED SC.	1	—	—	—	1	—	—	—
		ENGINEERING	—	—	—	—	—	—	—	—
		ARCHITECTURE & TOWN PLANNING	—	—	—	—	—	—	—	—
		TRADE, CRAFT & INDUSTR. PGMS.	—	—	—	—	—	—	—	—
		TRANSPORT AND COMMUNICATIONS	—	—	—	—	—	—	—	—
		AGRICULTURE,FORESTRY & FISH'G.	—	—	—	—	—	—	—	—
		OTHER AND NOT SPECIFIED	32	27	28	24	4	3	—	—

Third level: graduates by levels and fields   **3.13**
Troisième degré: diplômés par niveaux et domaines d'études
Tercer grado: diplomados por niveles y sectores de estudio

INTERNATIONAL STANDARD CLASSIFICATION OF EDUCATION BY LEVEL
CLASSIFICATION INTERNATIONALE TYPE DE L'EDUCATION PAR NIVEAUX
CLASIFICACION INTERNACIONAL NORMALIZADA DE LA EDUCACION POR GRADOS

COUNTRY / PAYS / PAIS	YEAR / ANNEE / AÑO	FIELD OF STUDY / BRANCHE D'ETUDES / RAMAS DE ESTUDIO	ALL LEVELS / TOUS NIVEAUX / TODOS LOS GRADOS MF	F	LEVEL 5 / NIVEAU 5 / GRADO 5 MF	F	LEVEL 6 / NIVEAU 6 / GRADO 6 MF	F	LEVEL 7 / NIVEAU 7 / GRADO 7 MF	F
AMERICA, SOUTH										
BOLIVIA ‡	1976	TOTAL	1 973	...	234	...	1 739	...	—	—
		EDUCATION SCIENCE & TCHR TRNG.	—	...	—	...	—	...	—	—
		HUMANITIES,RELIGION & THEOLOG.	30	...	—	...	30	...	—	—
		FINE AND APPLIED ARTS.	133	...	24	...	109	...	—	—
		LAW	157	...	—	...	157	...	—	—
		SOCIAL SCIENCES, TOTAL	604	...	160	...	444	...	—	—
		NATURAL SCIENCES, TOTAL	24	...	2	...	22	...	—	—
		MEDICAL AND HEALTH-RELATED SC.	638	...	—	...	638	...	—	—
		ENGINEERING, TOTAL	246	...	48	...	198	...	—	—
		AGRICULTURE,FORESTRY & FISH'G.	141	...	—	...	141	...	—	—
		OTHER AND NOT SPECIFIED	—	...	—	...	—	...	—	—
CHILE	1977	TOTAL	14 474	7 503	383	185	13 824	7 204	267	114
		EDUCATION SCIENCE & TCHR TRNG.	5 921	4 065	—	—	5 815	4 003	106	62
		HUMANITIES,RELIGION & THEOLOG.	98	56	—	—	87	49	11	7
		FINE AND APPLIED ARTS.	92	49	14	7	78	42	—	—
		LAW	328	102	16	7	312	95	—	—
		SOCIAL AND BEHAVIOURAL SCIENCE	865	624	223	89	624	531	18	4
		COMMERCIAL & BUS. ADMINISTR.	953	185	—	—	953	185	—	—
		MASS COMMUNICATION & DOCUMENT.	357	295	—	—	357	295	—	—
		HOME ECONOMICS & DOMESTIC SC.	147	146	41	41	106	105	—	—
		SERVICE TRADES	16	6	—	—	16	6	—	—
		NATURAL SCIENCE	279	117	44	26	153	72	82	19
		MATHEMATICS & COMPUTER SCIENCE	70	23	—	—	59	22	11	1
		MEDICAL AND HEALTH-RELATED SC.	2 070	1 473	19	9	2 032	1 449	19	15
		ENGINEERING	1 507	138	2	—	1 495	135	10	3
		ARCHITECTURE & TOWN PLANNING	312	31	3	1	309	30	—	—
		TRADE, CRAFT & INDUSTR. PGMS.	760	38	—	—	760	38	—	—
		TRANSPORT AND COMMUNICATIONS	—	—	—	—	—	—	—	—
		AGRICULTURE,FORESTRY & FISH'G.	699	155	21	5	668	147	10	3
		OTHER AND NOT SPECIFIED	—	—	—	—	—	—	—	—

3.13 Third level: graduates by levels and fields
Troisième degré: diplômés par niveaux et domaines d'études
Tercer grado: diplomados por niveles y sectores de estudio

INTERNATIONAL STANDARD CLASSIFICATION OF EDUCATION BY LEVEL
CLASSIFICATION INTERNATIONALE TYPE DE L'EDUCATION PAR NIVEAUX
CLASIFICACION INTERNACIONAL NORMALIZADA DE LA EDUCACION POR GRADOS

COUNTRY / PAYS / PAIS	YEAR / ANNEE / AÑO	FIELD OF STUDY / BRANCHE D'ETUDES / RAMAS DE ESTUDIO	ALL LEVELS / TOUS NIVEAUX / TODOS LOS GRADOS		LEVEL 5 / NIVEAU 5 / GRADO 5		LEVEL 6 / NIVEAU 6 / GRADO 6		LEVEL 7 / NIVEAU 7 / GRADO 7	
			MF	F	MF	F	MF	F	MF	F
COLOMBIA ‡	1977	TOTAL	18 780	7 922	—	—	18 780	7 922	—	—
		EDUCATION SCIENCE & TCHR TRNG.	4 310	2 530	—	—	4 310	2 530	—	—
		HUMANITIES,RELIGION & THEOLOG	256	114	—	—	256	114	—	—
		FINE AND APPLIED ARTS.	1 048	464	—	—	1 048	464	—	—
		LAW	1 871	713	—	—	1 871	713	—	—
		SOCIAL AND BEHAVIOURAL SCIENCE	698	585	—	—	698	585	—	—
		COMMERCIAL & BUS. ADMINISTR.	4 553	1 414	—	—	4 553	1 414	—	—
		MASS COMMUNICATION & DOCUMENT.	./.	./.	—	—	./.	./.	—	—
		HOME ECONOMICS & DOMESTIC SC.	./.	./.	—	—	./.	./.	—	—
		SERVICE TRADES	—	—	—	—	—	—	—	—
		NATURAL SCIENCES, TOTAL	656	432	—	—	656	432	—	—
		MEDICAL AND HEALTH-RELATED SC.	2 022	1 308	—	—	2 022	1 308	—	—
		ENGINEERING, TOTAL	2 544	311	—	—	2 544	311	—	—
		AGRICULTURE,FORESTRY & FISH'G.	822	51	—	—	822	51	—	—
		OTHER AND NOT SPECIFIED	—	—	—	—	—	—	—	—
FRENCH GUIANA ‡	1976	TOTAL	437	209	222	111	118	58	97	40
		EDUCATION SCIENCE & TCHR TRNG.	44	31	44	31	—	—	—	—
		HUMANITIES,RELIGION & THEOLOG	—	—	—	—	—	—	—	—
		FINE AND APPLIED ARTS.	—	—	—	—	—	—	—	—
		LAW	262	139	101	58	85	49	76	32
		SOCIAL AND BEHAVIOURAL SCIENCE	—	—	—	—	—	—	—	—
		COMMERCIAL & BUS. ADMINISTR.	96	27	42	10	33	9	21	8
		MASS COMMUNICATION & DOCUMENT.	—	—	—	—	—	—	—	—
		HOME ECONOMICS & DOMESTIC SC.	—	—	—	—	—	—	—	—
		SERVICE TRADES	—	—	—	—	—	—	—	—
		NATURAL SCIENCE	22	12	22	12	—	—	—	—
		MATHEMATICS & COMPUTER SCIENCE	./.	./.	./.	./.	—	—	—	—
		MEDICAL AND HEALTH-RELATED SC.	—	—	—	—	—	—	—	—
		ENGINEERING	—	—	—	—	—	—	—	—
		ARCHITECTURE & TOWN PLANNING	—	—	—	—	—	—	—	—
		TRADE, CRAFT & INDUSTR. PGMS.	—	—	—	—	—	—	—	—
		TRANSPORT AND COMMUNICATIONS	—	—	—	—	—	—	—	—
		AGRICULTURE,FORESTRY & FISH'G.	—	—	—	—	—	—	—	—
		OTHER AND NOT SPECIFIED	13	—	13	—	—	—	—	—

INTERNATIONAL STANDARD CLASSIFICATION OF EDUCATION BY LEVEL
CLASSIFICATION INTERNATIONALE TYPE DE L'EDUCATION PAR NIVEAUX
CLASIFICACION INTERNACIONAL NORMALIZADA DE LA EDUCACION POR GRADOS

COUNTRY / PAYS / PAIS	YEAR / ANNEE / AÑO	FIELD OF STUDY / BRANCHE D'ETUDES / RAMAS DE ESTUDIO	ALL LEVELS / TOUS NIVEAUX / TODOS LOS GRADOS		LEVEL 5 / NIVEAU 5 / GRADO 5		LEVEL 6 / NIVEAU 6 / GRADO 6		LEVEL 7 / NIVEAU 7 / GRADO 7	
			MF	F	MF	F	MF	F	MF	F
GUYANA	1975	TOTAL	834	274	—	—	—	—	—	—
		EDUCATION SCIENCE & TCHR TRNG.	479	210	—	—	—	—	—	—
		HUMANITIES,RELIGION & THEOLOG	—	—	—	—	—	—	—	—
		FINE AND APPLIED ARTS.	—	—	—	—	—	—	—	—
		LAW	75	9	—	—	—	—	—	—
		SOCIAL AND BEHAVIOURAL SCIENCE	49	11	—	—	—	—	—	—
		COMMERCIAL & BUS. ADMINISTR.	—	—	—	—	—	—	—	—
		MASS COMMUNICATION & DOCUMENT.	—	—	—	—	—	—	—	—
		HOME ECONOMICS & DOMESTIC SC.	—	—	—	—	—	—	—	—
		SERVICE TRADES	—	—	—	—	—	—	—	—
		NATURAL SCIENCE	46	11	—	—	—	—	—	—
		MATHEMATICS & COMPUTER SCIENCE	—	—	—	—	—	—	—	—
		MEDICAL AND HEALTH-RELATED SC.	19	6	—	—	—	—	—	—
		ENGINEERING	76	7	—	—	—	—	—	—
		ARCHITECTURE & TOWN PLANNING	5	—	—	—	—	—	—	—
		TRADE, CRAFT & INDUSTR. PGMS.	—	—	—	—	—	—	—	—
		TRANSPORT AND COMMUNICATIONS	14	7	—	—	—	—	—	—
		AGRICULTURE,FORESTRY & FISH'G.	52	8	—	—	—	—	—	—
		OTHER AND NOT SPECIFIED	19	5	—	—	—	—	—	—
PERU ‡	1977	TOTAL	5 450	...	3 015	...	2 435	...	—	—
		EDUCATION SCIENCE & TCHR TRNG.	2 363	...	—	—	2 363	...	—	—
		HUMANITIES,RELIGION & THEOLOG	22	...	22	...	—	—	—	—
		FINE AND APPLIED ARTS.	—	—	—	—	—	—	—	—
		LAW	—	—	—	—	—	—	—	—
		SOCIAL AND BEHAVIOURAL SCIENCE	1 062	...	1 062	...	—	—	—	—
		COMMERCIAL & BUS. ADMINISTR.	—	—	—	—	—	—	—	—
		MASS COMMUNICATION & DOCUMENT.	—	—	—	—	—	—	—	—
		HOME ECONOMICS & DOMESTIC SC.	—	—	—	—	—	—	—	—
		SERVICE TRADES	26	...	26	...	—	—	—	—
		NATURAL SCIENCE	—	—	—	—	—	—	—	—
		MATHEMATICS & COMPUTER SCIENCE	467	...	467	...	—	—	—	—
		MEDICAL AND HEALTH-RELATED SC.	1 346	...	1 274	...	72	—	—	—
		ENGINEERING	—	—	—	—	—	—	—	—
		ARCHITECTURE & TOWN PLANNING	—	—	—	—	—	—	—	—
		TRADE, CRAFT & INDUSTR. PGMS.	—	—	—	—	—	—	—	—
		TRANSPORT AND COMMUNICATIONS	—	—	—	—	—	—	—	—
		AGRICULTURE,FORESTRY & FISH'G.	164	...	164	...	—	—	—	—
		OTHER AND NOT SPECIFIED	—	—	—	—	—	—	—	—

3.13   Third level: graduates by levels and fields
      Troisième degré: diplômés par niveaux et domaines d'études
      Tercer grado: diplomados por niveles y sectores de estudio

COUNTRY / PAYS / PAIS	YEAR / ANNEE / AÑO	FIELD OF STUDY / BRANCHE D'ETUDES / RAMAS DE ESTUDIO	ALL LEVELS / TOUS NIVEAUX / TODOS LOS GRADOS MF	F	LEVEL 5 / NIVEAU 5 / GRADO 5 MF	F	LEVEL 6 / NIVEAU 6 / GRADO 6 MF	F	LEVEL 7 / NIVEAU 7 / GRADO 7 MF	F
URUGUAY	1975	TOTAL	2 049	...	337	...	1 690	...	22	...
		EDUCATION SCIENCE & TCHR TRNG.	58	...	—	—	58	...	—	—
		HUMANITIES,RELIGION & THEOLOG	48	...	—	—	48	...	—	—
		FINE AND APPLIED ARTS.	580	...	304	...	276	...	—	—
		LAW	130	...	—	—	130	...	—	—
		SOCIAL SCIENCES, TOTAL	47	...	23	...	24	...	—	—
		NATURAL SCIENCES, TOTAL	631	...	10	...	599	...	22	...
		MEDICAL AND HEALTH-RELATED SC.	58	...	—	—	58	...	—	—
		ENGINEERING, TOTAL	262	...	—	—	262	...	—	—
		AGRICULTURE,FORESTRY & FISH'G.	235	...	—	—	235	...	—	—
		OTHER AND NOT SPECIFIED	—	...	—	—	—	...	—	—
VENEZUELA ‡	1977	TOTAL	14 030	...	—	—	14 030	...	—	—
		EDUCATION SCIENCE & TCHR TRNG.	1 956	...	—	—	1 956	...	—	—
		HUMANITIES,RELIGION & THEOLOG	830	...	—	—	830	...	—	—
		FINE AND APPLIED ARTS.	45	...	—	—	45	...	—	—
		LAW	1 050	...	—	—	1 050	...	—	—
		SOCIAL AND BEHAVIOURAL SCIENCE	1 071	...	—	—	1 071	...	—	—
		COMMERCIAL & BUS. ADMINISTR.	1 860	...	—	—	1 860	...	—	—
		MASS COMMUNICATION & DOCUMENT.	233	...	—	—	233	...	—	—
		HOME ECONOMICS & DOMESTIC SC.	153	...	—	—	153	...	—	—
		SERVICE TRADES	133	...	—	—	133	...	—	—
		NATURAL SCIENCE	937	...	—	—	937	...	—	—
		MATHEMATICS & COMPUTER SCIENCE	317	...	—	—	317	...	—	—
		MEDICAL AND HEALTH-RELATED SC.	1 588	...	—	—	1 588	...	—	—
		ENGINEERING	2 308	...	—	—	2 308	...	—	—
		ARCHITECTURE & TOWN PLANNING	354	...	—	—	354	...	—	—
		TRADE, CRAFT & INDUSTR. PGMS.	62	...	—	—	62	...	—	—
		TRANSPORT AND COMMUNICATIONS	—	...	—	—	—	...	—	—
		AGRICULTURE,FORESTRY & FISH'G.	596	...	—	—	596	...	—	—
		OTHER AND NOT SPECIFIED	537	...	—	—	537	...	—	—
ASIA										
AFGHANISTAN ‡	1976	TOTAL	1 291	120	—	—	1 291	120	—	—
		EDUCATION SCIENCE & TCHR TRNG.	309	64	—	—	309	64	—	—
		HUMANITIES,RELIGION & THEOLOG	—	—	—	—	—	—	—	—
		FINE AND APPLIED ARTS.	—	—	—	—	—	—	—	—
		LAW	—	—	—	—	—	—	—	—
		SOCIAL SCIENCES, TOTAL	161	3	—	—	161	3	—	—
		NATURAL SCIENCES, TOTAL	91	2	—	—	91	2	—	—
		MEDICAL AND HEALTH-RELATED SC.	202	36	—	—	202	36	—	—
		ENGINEERING, TOTAL	149	9	—	—	149	9	—	—
		AGRICULTURE,FORESTRY & FISH'G.	251	5	—	—	251	5	—	—
		OTHER AND NOT SPECIFIED	128	1	—	—	128	1	—	—

INTERNATIONAL STANDARD CLASSIFICATION OF EDUCATION BY LEVEL
CLASSIFICATION INTERNATIONALE TYPE DE L'EDUCATION PAR NIVEAUX
CLASIFICACION INTERNACIONAL NORMALIZADA DE LA EDUCACION POR GRADOS

Third level: graduates by levels and fields **3.13**
Troisième degré: diplômés par niveaux et domaines d'études
Tercer grado: diplomados por niveles y sectores de estudio

INTERNATIONAL STANDARD CLASSIFICATION OF EDUCATION BY LEVEL
CLASSIFICATION INTERNATIONALE TYPE DE L'EDUCATION PAR NIVEAUX
CLASIFICACION INTERNACIONAL NORMALIZADA DE LA EDUCACION POR GRADOS

COUNTRY / PAYS / PAIS	YEAR / ANNEE / AÑO	FIELD OF STUDY / BRANCHE D'ETUDES / RAMAS DE ESTUDIO	ALL LEVELS / TOUS NIVEAUX / TODOS LOS GRADOS MF	F	LEVEL 5 / NIVEAU 5 / GRADO 5 MF	F	LEVEL 6 / NIVEAU 6 / GRADO 6 MF	F	LEVEL 7 / NIVEAU 7 / GRADO 7 MF	F
BAHRAIN	1977	TOTAL	282	177	282	177	—	—	—	—
		EDUCATION SCIENCE & TCHR TRNG.	188	162	188	162	—	—	—	—
		HUMANITIES,RELIGION & THEOLOG	—	—	—	—	—	—	—	—
		FINE AND APPLIED ARTS.	—	—	—	—	—	—	—	—
		LAW	—	—	—	—	—	—	—	—
		SOCIAL AND BEHAVIOURAL SCIENCE	7	5	7	5	—	—	—	—
		COMMERCIAL & BUS. ADMINISTR.	—	—	—	—	—	—	—	—
		MASS COMMUNICATION & DOCUMENT.	—	—	—	—	—	—	—	—
		HOME ECONOMICS & DOMESTIC SC.	—	—	—	—	—	—	—	—
		SERVICE TRADES	—	—	—	—	—	—	—	—
		NATURAL SCIENCE	—	—	—	—	—	—	—	—
		MATHEMATICS & COMPUTER SCIENCE	—	—	—	—	—	—	—	—
		MEDICAL AND HEALTH-RELATED SC.	—	—	—	—	—	—	—	—
		ENGINEERING	28	9	28	9	—	—	—	—
		ARCHITECTURE & TOWN PLANNING	—	—	—	—	—	—	—	—
		TRADE, CRAFT & INDUSTR. PGMS.	59	1	59	1	—	—	—	—
		TRANSPORT AND COMMUNICATIONS	—	—	—	—	—	—	—	—
		AGRICULTURE,FORESTRY & FISH'G.	—	—	—	—	—	—	—	—
		OTHER AND NOT SPECIFIED	—	—	—	—	—	—	—	—
BANGLADESH	1977	TOTAL	19 499	…	…	…	…	…	…	…
		EDUCATION SCIENCE & TCHR TRNG.	1 939	…	…	…	…	…	…	…
		HUMANITIES,RELIGION & THEOLOG	7 299	…	…	…	…	…	…	…
		FINE AND APPLIED ARTS.	12	…	…	…	…	…	…	…
		LAW	586	…	…	…	…	…	…	…
		SOCIAL AND BEHAVIOURAL SCIENCE	1 091	…	…	…	…	…	…	…
		COMMERCIAL & BUS. ADMINISTR.	2 565	…	…	…	…	…	…	…
		MASS COMMUNICATION & DOCUMENT.	74	…	…	…	…	…	…	…
		HOME ECONOMICS & DOMESTIC SC.	3 251	…	…	…	…	…	…	…
		NATURAL SCIENCE	135	…	…	…	…	…	…	…
		MATHEMATICS & COMPUTER SCIENCE	977	…	…	…	…	…	…	…
		MEDICAL AND HEALTH-RELATED SC.	932	…	…	…	…	…	…	…
		ENGINEERING	24	…	…	…	…	…	…	…
		ARCHITECTURE & TOWN PLANNING	38	…	…	…	…	…	…	…
		TRADE, CRAFT & INDUSTR. PGMS.	—	…	…	…	…	…	…	…
		TRANSPORT AND COMMUNICATIONS	512	…	…	…	…	…	…	…
		AGRICULTURE,FORESTRY & FISH'G.	64	—	…	…	…	…	…	…
		OTHER AND NOT SPECIFIED								

3.13   Third level: graduates by levels and fields
       Troisième degré: diplômés par niveaux et domaines d'études
       Tercer grado: diplomados por niveles y sectores de estudio

INTERNATIONAL STANDARD CLASSIFICATION OF EDUCATION BY LEVEL
CLASSIFICATION INTERNATIONALE TYPE DE L'EDUCATION PAR NIVEAUX
CLASIFICACION INTERNACIONAL NORMALIZADA DE LA EDUCACION POR GRADOS

COUNTRY / PAYS / PAIS	YEAR / ANNEE / AÑO	FIELD OF STUDY / BRANCHE D'ETUDES / RAMAS DE ESTUDIO	ALL LEVELS / TOUS NIVEAUX / TODOS LOS GRADOS		LEVEL 5 / NIVEAU 5 / GRADO 5		LEVEL 6 / NIVEAU 6 / GRADO 6		LEVEL 7 / NIVEAU 7 / GRADO 7	
			MF	F	MF	F	MF	F	MF	F
BURMA	1976	TOTAL	12 183	...	—	—	11 476	...	707	...
		EDUCATION SCIENCE & TCHR TRNG.	974	...	—	—	447	...	527	...
		HUMANITIES,RELIGION & THEOLOG	595	...	—	—	591	...	4	...
		FINE AND APPLIED ARTS.	—	—	—	—	—	—	—	—
		LAW	482	...	—	—	482	...	—	—
		SOCIAL AND BEHAVIOURAL SCIENCE	1 183	...	—	—	1 180	...	3	...
		COMMERCIAL & BUS. ADMINISTR.	1 139	...	—	—	1 080	...	59	...
		MASS COMMUNICATION & DOCUMENT.	—	—	—	—	—	—	—	—
		HOME ECONOMICS & DOMESTIC SC.	—	—	—	—	—	—	—	—
		SERVICE TRADES	—	—	—	—	—	—	—	—
		NATURAL SCIENCE	5 173	...	—	—	5 136	...	37	...
		MATHEMATICS & COMPUTER SCIENCE	1 092	...	—	—	1 077	...	15	...
		MEDICAL AND HEALTH-RELATED SC.	703	...	—	—	646	...	57	...
		ENGINEERING	602	...	—	—	597	...	5	...
		ARCHITECTURE & TOWN PLANNING	14	...	—	—	14	...	—	—
		TRADE, CRAFT & INDUSTR. PGMS.	—	—	—	—	—	—	—	—
		TRANSPORT AND COMMUNICATIONS	—	—	—	—	—	—	—	—
		AGRICULTURE,FORESTRY & FISH'G.	226	...	—	—	226	...	—	—
		OTHER AND NOT SPECIFIED	—	—	—	—	—	—	—	—
CYPRUS	1977	TOTAL	382	207	382	207	—	—	—	—
		EDUCATION SCIENCE & TCHR TRNG.	52	40	52	40	—	—	—	—
		HUMANITIES,RELIGION & THEOLOG	—	—	—	—	—	—	—	—
		FINE AND APPLIED ARTS.	—	—	—	—	—	—	—	—
		LAW	—	—	—	—	—	—	—	—
		SOCIAL AND BEHAVIOURAL SCIENCE	39	39	39	39	—	—	—	—
		COMMERCIAL & BUS. ADMINISTR.	—	—	—	—	—	—	—	—
		MASS COMMUNICATION & DOCUMENT.	—	—	—	—	—	—	—	—
		HOME ECONOMICS & DOMESTIC SC.	—	—	—	—	—	—	—	—
		SERVICE TRADES	—	—	—	—	—	—	—	—
		NATURAL SCIENCE	84	34	84	34	—	—	—	—
		MATHEMATICS & COMPUTER SCIENCE	114	87	114	87	—	—	—	—
		MEDICAL AND HEALTH-RELATED SC.	85	7	85	7	—	—	—	—
		ENGINEERING	8	—	8	—	—	—	—	—
		ARCHITECTURE & TOWN PLANNING	—	—	—	—	—	—	—	—
		TRADE, CRAFT & INDUSTR. PGMS.	—	—	—	—	—	—	—	—
		TRANSPORT AND COMMUNICATIONS	—	—	—	—	—	—	—	—
		AGRICULTURE,FORESTRY & FISH'G.	—	—	—	—	—	—	—	—
		OTHER AND NOT SPECIFIED	—	—	—	—	—	—	—	—

Third level: graduates by levels and fields 3.13
Troisième degré: diplômés par niveaux et domaines d'études
Tercer grado: diplomados por niveles y sectores de estudio

INTERNATIONAL STANDARD CLASSIFICATION OF EDUCATION BY LEVEL
CLASSIFICATION INTERNATIONALE TYPE DE L'EDUCATION PAR NIVEAUX
CLASIFICACION INTERNACIONAL NORMALIZADA DE LA EDUCACION POR GRADOS

COUNTRY / PAYS / PAIS	YEAR / ANNEE / AÑO	FIELD OF STUDY / BRANCHE D'ETUDES / RAMAS DE ESTUDIO	ALL LEVELS TOUS NIVEAUX TODOS LOS GRADOS MF	F	LEVEL 5 NIVEAU 5 GRADO 5 MF	F	LEVEL 6 NIVEAU 6 GRADO 6 MF	F	LEVEL 7 NIVEAU 7 GRADO 7 MF	F
HONG KONG	1977	TOTAL	...	...	...	...	2 069	617	722	270
		EDUCATION SCIENCE & TCHR TRNG.	979	...	11	...	460	246	508	219
		HUMANITIES,RELIGION & THEOLOG	221	...	144	3	30	16	47	12
		FINE AND APPLIED ARTS.	77	...	—	...	45	18	32	5
		LAW	604	...	123	...	452	188	29	15
		SOCIAL AND BEHAVIOURAL SCIENCE	1 611	...	1 388	...	195	47	28	7
		COMMERCIAL & BUS. ADMINISTR.	18	...	—	...	18	7	—	—
		MASS COMMUNICATION & DOCUMENT.	—	—	—	—	—	—	—	—
		HOME ECONOMICS & DOMESTIC SC.	—	—	—	—	—	—	—	—
		SERVICE TRADES	—	—	—	—	—	—	—	—
		NATURAL SCIENCE	491	...	149	...	307	55	35	6
		MATHEMATICS & COMPUTER SCIENCE	155	...	111	...	40	5	4	—
		MEDICAL AND HEALTH-RELATED SC.	178	...	—	...	160	17	18	6
		ENGINEERING	3 119	...	2 816	...	282	18	21	—
		ARCHITECTURE & TOWN PLANNING	78	...	—	...	78	—	—	—
		TRADE,CRAFT & INDUSTR. PGMS.	343	...	341	...	2	—	—	—
		TRANSPORT AND COMMUNICATIONS	—	—	—	—	—	—	—	—
		AGRICULTURE,FORESTRY & FISH'G.	—	—	—	—	—	—	—	—
		OTHER AND NOT SPECIFIED	20	...	20	...	—	—	—	—
INDIA ‡	1975	TOTAL	677 725	...	—	—	562 712	165 421	115 013	...
		EDUCATION SCIENCE & TCHR TRNG.	63 761	...	—	—	61 862	25 556	1 899	...
		HUMANITIES,RELIGION & THEOLOG	340 981	...	—	—	264 787	102 227	76 194	...
		FINE AND APPLIED ARTS.	519	218	—	—	273	141	246	77
		LAW	24 686	...	—	—	24 366	1 769	320	...
		SOCIAL AND BEHAVIOURAL SCIENCE	94 543	...	—	—	83 606	5 907	10 937	343
		COMMERCIAL & BUS. ADMINISTR.	1 533	...	—	—	1 315	484	218	...
		MASS COMMUNICATION & DOCUMENT.	2 198	2 198	—	—	1 857	1 857	341	341
		HOME ECONOMICS & DOMESTIC SC.	—	—	—	—	—	—	—	—
		SERVICE TRADES	—	—	—	—	—	—	—	—
		NATURAL SCIENCE	108 209	...	—	—	90 285	24 104	17 924	...
		MATHEMATICS & COMPUTER SCIENCE	16 765	...	—	—	14 267	2 981	2 498	...
		MEDICAL AND HEALTH-RELATED SC.	13 942	...	—	—	12 541	108	1 401	...
		ENGINEERING	885	37	—	—	346	37	539	...
		ARCHITECTURE & TOWN PLANNING	—	—	—	—	—	—	—	—
		TRADE,CRAFT & INDUSTR. PGMS.	—	—	—	—	—	—	—	—
		TRANSPORT AND COMMUNICATIONS	—	—	—	—	—	—	—	—
		AGRICULTURE,FORESTRY & FISH'G.	8 271	...	—	—	5 965	26	2 306	...
		OTHER AND NOT SPECIFIED	1 432	213	—	—	1 242	183	190	30

3.13 Third level: graduates by levels and fields
Troisième degré: diplômés par niveaux et domaines d'études
Tercer grado: diplomados por niveles y sectores de estudio

INTERNATIONAL STANDARD CLASSIFICATION OF EDUCATION BY LEVEL
CLASSIFICATION INTERNATIONALE TYPE DE L'EDUCATION PAR NIVEAUX
CLASIFICACION INTERNACIONAL NORMALIZADA DE LA EDUCACION POR GRADOS

COUNTRY / PAYS / PAIS	YEAR / ANNEE / AÑO	FIELD OF STUDY / BRANCHE D'ETUDES / RAMAS DE ESTUDIO	ALL LEVELS TOUS NIVEAUX TODOS LOS GRADOS		LEVEL 5 NIVEAU 5 GRADO 5		LEVEL 6 NIVEAU 6 GRADO 6		LEVEL 7 NIVEAU 7 GRADO 7	
			MF	F	MF	F	MF	F	MF	F
INDONESIA	1976	TOTAL	26 666	6 454	—	—	26 434	6 374	232	80
		EDUCATION SCIENCE & TCHR TRNG.	5 338	1 729	—	—	5 337	1 729	1	1
		HUMANITIES,RELIGION & THEOLOG	363	137	—	—	358	137	5	—
		FINE AND APPLIED ARTS.	—	—	—	—	—	—	—	—
		LAW	2 699	635	—	—	2 691	633	8	2
		SOCIAL AND BEHAVIOURAL SCIENCE	4 200	870	—	—	4 172	862	28	8
		COMMERCIAL & BUS. ADMINISTR.	—	—	—	—	—	—	—	—
		MASS COMMUNICATION & DOCUMENT.	1 560	219	—	—	1 560	219	—	—
		HOME ECONOMICS & DOMESTIC SC.	—	—	—	—	—	—	—	—
		SERVICE TRADES	—	—	—	—	—	—	—	—
		NATURAL SCIENCE	885	446	—	—	775	392	110	54
		MATHEMATICS & COMPUTER SCIENCE	—	—	—	—	—	—	—	—
		MEDICAL AND HEALTH-RELATED SC.	2 031	756	—	—	1 963	743	68	13
		ENGINEERING	3 033	379	—	—	3 024	376	9	3
		ARCHITECTURE & TOWN PLANNING	—	—	—	—	—	—	—	—
		TRADE, CRAFT & INDUSTR. PGMS.	—	—	—	—	—	—	—	—
		TRANSPORT AND COMMUNICATIONS	—	—	—	—	—	—	—	—
		AGRICULTURE,FORESTRY & FISH'G.	2 539	482	—	—	2 536	482	3	—
		OTHER AND NOT SPECIFIED	4 018	801	—	—	4 018	801	—	—
IRAQ	1976	TOTAL	17 422	5 619	4 130	1 275	12 622	4 243	670	101
		EDUCATION SCIENCE & TCHR TRNG.	886	311	—	—	886	311	—	—
		HUMANITIES,RELIGION & THEOLOG	2 092	837	—	—	2 064	829	28	8
		FINE AND APPLIED ARTS.	262	134	59	47	203	87	—	—
		LAW	596	120	—	—	579	120	17	—
		SOCIAL AND BEHAVIOURAL SCIENCE	1 592	719	40	23	1 505	695	47	1
		COMMERCIAL & BUS. ADMINISTR.	2 124	913	751	315	1 305	595	68	3
		MASS COMMUNICATION & DOCUMENT.	453	229	430	221	—	—	23	8
		HOME ECONOMICS & DOMESTIC SC.	—	—	—	—	—	—	—	—
		SERVICE TRADES	191	99	191	99	—	—	—	—
		NATURAL SCIENCE	1 334	495	—	—	1 238	462	96	33
		MATHEMATICS & COMPUTER SCIENCE	1 026	457	122	67	873	387	31	3
		MEDICAL AND HEALTH-RELATED SC.	1 061	285	149	23	788	225	124	37
		ENGINEERING	3 789	603	1 844	359	1 788	239	157	5
		ARCHITECTURE & TOWN PLANNING	73	20	—	—	43	17	30	3
		TRADE, CRAFT & INDUSTR. PGMS.	123	39	—	—	120	39	3	—
		TRANSPORT AND COMMUNICATIONS	—	—	—	—	—	—	—	—
		AGRICULTURE,FORESTRY & FISH'G.	1 644	265	544	121	1 054	144	46	—
		OTHER AND NOT SPECIFIED	176	93	—	—	176	93	—	—

Third level: graduates by levels and fields 3.13
Troisième degré: diplômés par niveaux et domaines d'études
Tercer grado: diplomados por niveles y sectores de estudio

INTERNATIONAL STANDARD CLASSIFICATION OF EDUCATION BY LEVEL
CLASSIFICATION INTERNATIONALE TYPE DE L'EDUCATION PAR NIVEAUX
CLASIFICACION INTERNACIONAL NORMALIZADA DE LA EDUCACION POR GRADOS

COUNTRY PAYS PAIS	YEAR ANNEE AÑO	FIELD OF STUDY BRANCHE D'ETUDES RAMAS DE ESTUDIO	ALL LEVELS TOUS NIVEAUX TODOS LOS GRADOS		LEVEL 5 NIVEAU 5 GRADO 5		LEVEL 6 NIVEAU 6 GRADO 6		LEVEL 7 NIVEAU 7 GRADO 7	
			MF	F	MF	F	MF	F	MF	F
ISRAEL ‡	1976	TOTAL	10 144	4 397	—	—	6 876	3 042	3 268	1 355
		EDUCATION SCIENCE & TCHR TRNG.	3 418	2 430	—	—	2 108	1 498	1 310	932
		HUMANITIES,RELIGION & THEOLOG	./.	./.	—	—	./.	./.	./.	./.
		FINE AND APPLIED ARTS.	./.	./.	—	—	./.	./.	./.	./.
		LAW	383	133	—	—	366	129	17	4
		SOCIAL AND BEHAVIOURAL SCIENCE	2 415	1 069	—	—	1 926	890	489	179
		COMMERCIAL & BUS. ADMINISTR.	./.	./.	—	—	./.	./.	./.	./.
		MASS COMMUNICATION & DOCUMENT.	./.	./.	—	—	./.	./.	./.	./.
		HOME ECONOMICS & DOMESTIC SC.	./.	./.	—	—	./.	./.	./.	./.
		SERVICE TRADES	./.	./.	—	—	./.	./.	./.	./.
		NATURAL SCIENCE	1 539	432	—	—	849	315	690	117
		MATHEMATICS & COMPUTER SCIENCE	./.	./.	—	—	./.	./.	./.	./.
		MEDICAL AND HEALTH–RELATED SC.	497	172	—	—	97	82	400	90
		ENGINEERING	1 644	118	—	—	1 352	97	292	21
		ARCHITECTURE & TOWN PLANNING	./.	./.	—	—	./.	./.	./.	./.
		TRADE, CRAFT & INDUSTR. PGMS.	./.	./.	—	—	./.	./.	./.	./.
		TRANSPORT AND COMMUNICATIONS	./.	./.	—	—	./.	./.	./.	./.
		AGRICULTURE,FORESTRY & FISH'G.	248	43	—	—	178	31	70	12
		OTHER AND NOT SPECIFIED	—	—	—	—	—	—	—	—
	1977	TOTAL	9 799	4 452	—	—	6 658	2 993	3 141	1 459
		EDUCATION SCIENCE & TCHR TRNG.	3 105	2 169	—	—	1 811	1 240	1 294	929
		HUMANITIES,RELIGION & THEOLOG	./.	./.	—	—	./.	./.	./.	./.
		FINE AND APPLIED ARTS.	./.	./.	—	—	./.	./.	./.	./.
		LAW	325	109	—	—	310	104	15	5
		SOCIAL AND BEHAVIOURAL SCIENCE	2 334	1 117	—	—	1 837	942	497	175
		COMMERCIAL & BUS. ADMINISTR.	./.	./.	—	—	./.	./.	./.	./.
		MASS COMMUNICATION & DOCUMENT.	./.	./.	—	—	./.	./.	./.	./.
		HOME ECONOMICS & DOMESTIC SC.	./.	./.	—	—	./.	./.	./.	./.
		SERVICE TRADES	./.	./.	—	—	./.	./.	./.	./.
		NATURAL SCIENCE	1 465	639	—	—	888	460	577	179
		MATHEMATICS & COMPUTER SCIENCE	./.	./.	—	—	./.	./.	./.	./.
		MEDICAL AND HEALTH–RELATED SC.	543	214	—	—	118	95	425	119
		ENGINEERING	1 788	161	—	—	1 518	125	270	36
		ARCHITECTURE & TOWN PLANNING	./.	./.	—	—	./.	./.	./.	./.
		TRADE, CRAFT & INDUSTR. PGMS.	./.	./.	—	—	./.	./.	./.	./.
		TRANSPORT AND COMMUNICATIONS	./.	./.	—	—	./.	./.	./.	./.
		AGRICULTURE,FORESTRY & FISH'G.	239	43	—	—	176	27	63	16
		OTHER AND NOT SPECIFIED	—	—	—	—	—	—	—	—

3.13 Third level: graduates by levels and fields
Troisième degré: diplômés par niveaux et domaines d'études
Tercer grado: diplomados por niveles y sectores de estudio

INTERNATIONAL STANDARD CLASSIFICATION OF EDUCATION BY LEVEL
CLASSIFICATION INTERNATIONALE TYPE DE L'EDUCATION PAR NIVEAUX
CLASIFICACION INTERNACIONAL NORMALIZADA DE LA EDUCACION POR GRADOS

COUNTRY / PAYS / PAIS	YEAR / ANNEE / AÑO	FIELD OF STUDY / BRANCHE D'ETUDES / RAMAS DE ESTUDIO	ALL LEVELS / TOUS NIVEAUX / TODOS LOS GRADOS		LEVEL 5 / NIVEAU 5 / GRADO 5		LEVEL 6 / NIVEAU 6 / GRADO 6		LEVEL 7 / NIVEAU 7 / GRADO 7	
			MF	F	MF	F	MF	F	MF	F
JAPAN ‡	1976	TOTAL	504 638	212 381	284 722	136 391	204 987	74 714	14 929	1 276
		EDUCATION SCIENCE & TCHR TRNG.	54 588	47 142	33 279	33 190	20 885	13 816	424	136
		HUMANITIES,RELIGION & THEOLOG.	80 179	61 593	33 825	33 303	44 363	27 811	1 991	479
		FINE AND APPLIED ARTS.	16 748	12 861	8 097	7 544	8 250	5 155	401	162
		LAW	./.	./.	./.	./.	./.	./.	./.	./.
		SOCIAL AND BEHAVIOURAL SCIENCE	154 844	19 690	138 100	8 978	14 971	10 593	1 773	119
		COMMERCIAL & BUS. ADMINISTR.	./.	./.	./.	./.	./.	./.	./.	./.
		MASS COMMUNICATION & DOCUMENT.	./.	./.	./.	./.	./.	./.	./.	./.
		HOME ECONOMICS & DOMESTIC SC.	51 381	51 263	44 956	44 871	6 349	6 320	76	72
		SERVICE TRADES	./.	./.	./.	./.	./.	./.	./.	./.
		NATURAL SCIENCE	8 996	1 112	—	—	7 483	1 017	1 513	95
		MATHEMATICS & COMPUTER SCIENCE	2 802	653	82	79	2 529	557	191	17
		MEDICAL AND HEALTH-RELATED SC.	18 384	8 801	3 217	2 960	14 063	5 742	1 104	99
		ENGINEERING	89 673	999	15 331	411	68 126	556	6 216	32
		ARCHITECTURE & TOWN PLANNING	./.	./.	./.	./.	./.	./.	./.	./.
		TRADE, CRAFT & INDUSTR. PGMS.	./.	./.	./.	./.	./.	./.	./.	./.
		TRANSPORT AND COMMUNICATIONS	963	—	629	—	308	—	26	—
		AGRICULTURE,FORESTRY & FISH'G.	13 706	1 445	1 447	270	11 123	1 118	1 136	57
		OTHER AND NOT SPECIFIED	12 374	6 822	5 759	4 785	6 537	2 029	78	8
JORDAN ‡	1977	TOTAL	5 400	2 032	3 881	1 566	881	365	638	101
		EDUCATION SCIENCE & TCHR TRNG.	3 876	1 586	3 326	1 483	66	25	484	78
		HUMANITIES,RELIGION & THEOLOG.	444	186	24	—	336	170	84	16
		FINE AND APPLIED ARTS.	—	—	—	—	—	—	—	—
		LAW	—	—	—	—	—	—	—	—
		SOCIAL AND BEHAVIOURAL SCIENCE	25	16	25	16	—	—	—	—
		COMMERCIAL & BUS. ADMINISTR.	453	74	246	9	207	65	—	—
		MASS COMMUNICATION & DOCUMENT.	—	—	—	—	—	—	—	—
		HOME ECONOMICS & DOMESTIC SC.	—	—	—	—	—	—	—	—
		SERVICE TRADES	—	—	—	—	—	—	—	—
		NATURAL SCIENCE	137	34	—	—	93	29	44	5
		MATHEMATICS & COMPUTER SCIENCE	111	34	13	2	72	30	26	2
		MEDICAL AND HEALTH-RELATED SC.	144	97	68	56	76	41	—	—
		ENGINEERING	179	—	179	—	—	—	—	—
		ARCHITECTURE & TOWN PLANNING	—	—	—	—	—	—	—	—
		TRADE, CRAFT & INDUSTR. PGMS.	—	—	—	—	—	—	—	—
		TRANSPORT AND COMMUNICATIONS	—	—	—	—	—	—	—	—
		AGRICULTURE,FORESTRY & FISH'G.	31	5	—	—	31	5	—	—
		OTHER AND NOT SPECIFIED	—	—	—	—	—	—	—	—

Third level: graduates by levels and fields 3.13
Troisième degré: diplômés par niveaux et domaines d'études
Tercer grado: diplomados por niveles y sectores de estudio

INTERNATIONAL STANDARD CLASSIFICATION OF EDUCATION BY LEVEL
CLASSIFICATION INTERNATIONALE TYPE DE L'EDUCATION PAR NIVEAUX
CLASIFICACION INTERNACIONAL NORMALIZADA DE LA EDUCACION POR GRADOS

COUNTRY / PAYS / PAIS	YEAR / ANNEE / AÑO	FIELD OF STUDY / BRANCHE D'ETUDES / RAMAS DE ESTUDIO	ALL LEVELS / TOUS NIVEAUX / TODOS LOS GRADOS MF	F	LEVEL 5 / NIVEAU 5 / GRADO 5 MF	F	LEVEL 6 / NIVEAU 6 / GRADO 6 MF	F	LEVEL 7 / NIVEAU 7 / GRADO 7 MF	F
KOREA, REPUBLIC OF	1976	TOTAL	68 811	22 146	26 715	9 230	37 375	12 160	4 721	756
		EDUCATION SCIENCE & TCHR TRNG.	11 403	6 316	3 584	2 220	6 709	3 849	1 110	247
		HUMANITIES,RELIGION & THEOLOG	5 237	2 160	129	26	4 576	2 028	532	106
		FINE AND APPLIED ARTS.	2 716	2 199	462	417	2 071	1 656	183	126
		LAW	1 379	87	—	—	1 308	77	71	10
		SOCIAL AND BEHAVIOURAL SCIENCE	4 334	535	88	62	3 621	447	625	26
		COMMERCIAL & BUS. ADMINISTR.	2 865	230	393	47	2 003	176	469	7
		MASS COMMUNICATION & DOCUMENT.	594	361	260	208	333	153	1	—
		HOME ECONOMICS & DOMESTIC SC.	1 512	1 509	529	526	927	927	56	56
		SERVICE TRADES	527	234	443	189	84	45	—	—
		NATURAL SCIENCE	2 345	1 116	153	153	1 962	926	230	37
		MATHEMATICS & COMPUTER SCIENCE	611	153	—	—	611	153	—	—
		MEDICAL AND HEALTH-RELATED SC.	7 150	4 312	3 488	2 892	2 929	1 293	733	127
		ENGINEERING	13 051	436	6 449	328	6 163	103	439	5
		ARCHITECTURE & TOWN PLANNING	568	62	2 147	41	1 406	21	15	—
		TRADE, CRAFT & INDUSTR. PGMS.	238	8	152	—	86	8	—	—
		TRANSPORT AND COMMUNICATIONS	461	4	461	4	—	—	—	—
		AGRICULTURE,FORESTRY & FISH'G.	7 198	583	4 355	276	2 586	298	257	307
		OTHER AND NOT SPECIFIED	3 622	1 841	3 622	1 841	—	—	—	—
	1977	TOTAL	68 811	22 146	26 715	9 230	37 375	12 160	4 721	756
		EDUCATION SCIENCE & TCHR TRNG.	11 403	6 316	3 584	2 220	6 709	3 849	1 110	247
		HUMANITIES,RELIGION & THEOLOG	5 237	2 160	129	26	4 576	2 028	532	106
		FINE AND APPLIED ARTS.	2 716	2 199	462	417	2 071	1 656	183	126
		LAW	1 379	87	—	—	1 308	77	71	10
		SOCIAL AND BEHAVIOURAL SCIENCE	4 334	535	88	62	3 621	447	625	26
		COMMERCIAL & BUS. ADMINISTR.	2 865	230	393	47	2 003	176	469	7
		MASS COMMUNICATION & DOCUMENT.	594	361	260	208	333	153	1	—
		HOME ECONOMICS & DOMESTIC SC.	1 512	1 509	529	526	927	927	56	56
		SERVICE TRADES	527	234	443	189	84	45	—	—
		NATURAL SCIENCE	2 345	1 116	153	153	1 962	926	230	37
		MATHEMATICS & COMPUTER SCIENCE	611	153	—	—	611	153	—	—
		MEDICAL AND HEALTH-RELATED SC.	7 150	4 312	3 488	2 892	2 929	1 293	733	127
		ENGINEERING	13 051	436	6 449	328	6 163	103	439	5
		ARCHITECTURE & TOWN PLANNING	568	62	2 147	41	1 406	21	15	—
		TRADE, CRAFT & INDUSTR. PGMS.	238	8	152	—	86	8	—	—
		TRANSPORT AND COMMUNICATIONS	461	4	461	4	—	—	—	—
		AGRICULTURE,FORESTRY & FISH'G.	7 198	583	4 355	276	2 586	298	257	307
		OTHER AND NOT SPECIFIED	3 622	1 841	3 622	1 841	—	—	—	—

3.13 Third level: graduates by levels and fields
Troisième degré: diplômés par niveaux et domaines d'études
Tercer grado: diplomados por niveles y sectores de estudio

INTERNATIONAL STANDARD CLASSIFICATION OF EDUCATION BY LEVEL
CLASSIFICATION INTERNATIONALE TYPE DE L'EDUCATION PAR NIVEAUX
CLASIFICACION INTERNACIONAL NORMALIZADA DE LA EDUCACION POR GRADOS

COUNTRY / PAYS / PAIS	YEAR / ANNEE / AÑO	FIELD OF STUDY / BRANCHE D'ETUDES / RAMAS DE ESTUDIO	ALL LEVELS / TOUS NIVEAUX / TODOS LOS GRADOS MF	F	LEVEL 5 / NIVEAU 5 / GRADO 5 MF	F	LEVEL 6 / NIVEAU 6 / GRADO 6 MF	F	LEVEL 7 / NIVEAU 7 / GRADO 7 MF	F
MALAYSIA										
PENINSULAR MALAYSIA	1977	TOTAL	12 690	5 059	8 905	3 902	3 688	1 124	97	33
		EDUCATION SCIENCE & TCHR TRNG.	5 795	2 897	5 779	2 892	-	-	16	5
		HUMANITIES,RELIGION & THEOLOG	1 301	529	90	49	1 190	470	21	10
		FINE AND APPLIED ARTS.	73	30	73	30	-	-	-	-
		LAW	217	100	156	71	57	27	4	2
		SOCIAL AND BEHAVIOURAL SCIENCE	694	192	-	-	684	188	10	4
		COMMERCIAL & BUS. ADMINISTR.	969	451	835	379	134	72	-	-
		MASS COMMUNICATION & DOCUMENT.	56	27	56	27	-	-	-	-
		HOME ECONOMICS & DOMESTIC SC.	28	28	28	28	-	-	-	-
		SERVICE TRADES	97	62	97	62	-	-	-	-
		NATURAL SCIENCE	1 003	351	327	112	651	229	25	10
		MATHEMATICS & COMPUTER SCIENCE	50	23	41	21	-	-	9	2
		MEDICAL AND HEALTH-RELATED SC.	197	56	9	2	188	54	-	-
		ENGINEERING	1 180	132	705	99	475	33	-	-
		ARCHITECTURE & TOWN PLANNING	352	86	291	72	61	14	-	-
		TRADE, CRAFT & INDUSTR. PGMS.	48	5	32	3	16	2	-	-
		TRANSPORT AND COMMUNICATIONS	55	-	33	-	22	-	-	-
		AGRICULTURE,FORESTRY & FISH'G.	575	90	353	55	210	35	12	-
		OTHER AND NOT SPECIFIED	-	-	-	-	-	-	-	-
NEPAL ‡	1977	TOTAL	9 488	...	6 256	...	2 685	...	547	...
		EDUCATION SCIENCE & TCHR TRNG.	3 395	...	2 534	...	857	...	4	...
		HUMANITIES,RELIGION & THEOLOG	2 714	...	1 601	...	848	...	265	...
		FINE AND APPLIED ARTS.	./.	...	./.	...	./.	...	./.	...
		LAW	311	-	172	-	139	-	-	-
		SOCIAL AND BEHAVIOURAL SCIENCE	942	-	498	-	336	-	108	-
		COMMERCIAL & BUS. ADMINISTR.	-	-	-	-	-	-	-	-
		MASS COMMUNICATION & DOCUMENT.	-	-	-	-	-	-	-	-
		HOME ECONOMICS & DOMESTIC SC.	-	-	-	-	-	-	-	-
		SERVICE TRADES	-	-	-	-	-	-	-	-
		NATURAL SCIENCE	634	-	289	-	175	-	170	-
		MATHEMATICS & COMPUTER SCIENCE	./.	-	./.	-	./.	-	./.	-
		MEDICAL AND HEALTH-RELATED SC.	668	-	373	-	295	-	-	-
		ENGINEERING	346	-	346	-	-	-	-	-
		ARCHITECTURE & TOWN PLANNING	-	-	-	-	-	-	-	-
		TRADE, CRAFT & INDUSTR. PGMS.	-	-	-	-	-	-	-	-
		TRANSPORT AND COMMUNICATIONS	-	-	-	-	-	-	-	-
		AGRICULTURE,FORESTRY & FISH'G.	478	-	443	-	35	-	-	-
		OTHER AND NOT SPECIFIED	-	-	-	-	-	-	-	-

Third level: graduates by levels and fields 3.13
Troisième degré: diplômés par niveaux et domaines d'études
Tercer grado: diplomados por niveaux et sectores de estudio

INTERNATIONAL STANDARD CLASSIFICATION OF EDUCATION BY LEVEL
CLASSIFICATION INTERNATIONALE TYPE DE L'EDUCATION PAR NIVEAUX
CLASIFICACION INTERNACIONAL NORMALIZADA DE LA EDUCACION POR GRADOS

COUNTRY / PAYS / PAIS	YEAR / ANNEE / AÑO	FIELD OF STUDY / BRANCHE D'ETUDES / RAMAS DE ESTUDIO	ALL LEVELS TOUS NIVEAUX TODOS LOS GRADOS		LEVEL 5 NIVEAU 5 GRADO 5		LEVEL 6 NIVEAU 6 GRADO 6		LEVEL 7 NIVEAU 7 GRADO 7	
			MF	F	MF	F	MF	F	MF	F
PAKISTAN ‡	1976	TOTAL	...	...	...	...	36 964	11 356	...	...
		EDUCATION SCIENCE & TCHR TRNG.	2 964	928	626	192	4 638	2 484	360	76
		HUMANITIES,RELIGION & THEOLOG	./.	./.	./.	./.	37	13	2 301	723
		FINE AND APPLIED ARTS.	1 727	57	—	—	./.	./.	./.	./.
		LAW	—	—	—	—	1 727	57	—	—
		SOCIAL AND BEHAVIOURAL SCIENCE	1 855	211	27	—	1 591	209	237	—
		COMMERCIAL & BUS. ADMINISTR.	—	—	—	—	221	221	—	2
		MASS COMMUNICATION & DOCUMENT.	...	...	...	—	—	—	—	—
		HOME ECONOMICS & DOMESTIC SC.	...	...	...	—	—	—	30	30
		SERVICE TRADES	...	...	...	—	—	—	—	—
		NATURAL SCIENCE	417	56	18	8	135	21	989	270
		MATHEMATICS & COMPUTER SCIENCE	1 364	327	—	8	47	13	352	35
		MEDICAL AND HEALTH-RELATED SC.	—	—	—	—	1 271	315	93	12
		ENGINEERING	24	1	—	—	1 161	1	...	—
		ARCHITECTURE & TOWN PLANNING	...	—	—	—	24	—	—	—
		TRADE,CRAFT & INDUSTR. PGMS.	...	—	—	—	—	—	—	—
		TRANSPORT AND COMMUNICATIONS	—	—	—	—	—	—	—	—
		AGRICULTURE,FORESTRY & FISH'G.	916	12	347	—	284	2	285	12
		OTHER AND NOT SPECIFIED	28 977	8 843	95	2	25 828	8 022	3 054	819
PHILIPPINES ‡	1976	TOTAL	137 047	—	—	—	137 047	—	—	—
		EDUCATION SCIENCE & TCHR TRNG.	7 666	—	—	—	7 666	—	—	—
		HUMANITIES,RELIGION & THEOLOG	2 235	—	—	—	2 235	—	—	—
		FINE AND APPLIED ARTS.	1 583	—	—	—	1 583	—	—	—
		LAW	17 681	—	—	—	17 681	—	—	—
		SOCIAL AND BEHAVIOURAL SCIENCE	75 968	—	—	—	75 968	—	—	—
		COMMERCIAL & BUS. ADMINISTR.	1 265	—	—	—	1 265	—	—	—
		MASS COMMUNICATION & DOCUMENT.	468	—	—	—	468	—	—	—
		HOME ECONOMICS & DOMESTIC SC.	—	—	—	—	—	—	—	—
		SERVICE TRADES	—	—	—	—	—	—	—	—
		NATURAL SCIENCE	6 528	—	—	—	6 528	—	—	—
		MATHEMATICS & COMPUTER SCIENCE	—	—	—	—	—	—	—	—
		MEDICAL AND HEALTH-RELATED SC.	13 983	—	—	—	13 983	—	—	—
		ENGINEERING	./.	—	—	—	./.	—	—	—
		ARCHITECTURE & TOWN PLANNING	./.	—	—	—	./.	—	—	—
		TRADE,CRAFT & INDUSTR. PGMS.	—	—	—	—	—	—	—	—
		TRANSPORT AND COMMUNICATIONS	—	—	—	—	—	—	—	—
		AGRICULTURE,FORESTRY & FISH'G.	4 642	—	—	—	4 642	—	—	—
		OTHER AND NOT SPECIFIED	5 028	—	—	—	5 028	—	—	—

3.13 Third level: graduates by levels and fields
Troisième degré: diplômés par niveaux et domaines d'études
Tercer grado: diplomados por niveles y sectores de estudio

INTERNATIONAL STANDARD CLASSIFICATION OF EDUCATION BY LEVEL
CLASSIFICATION INTERNATIONALE TYPE DE L'EDUCATION PAR NIVEAUX
CLASIFICACION INTERNACIONAL NORMALIZADA DE LA EDUCACION POR GRADOS

COUNTRY / PAYS / PAIS	YEAR / ANNEE / AÑO	FIELD OF STUDY / BRANCHE D'ETUDES / RAMAS DE ESTUDIO	ALL LEVELS / TOUS NIVEAUX / TODOS LOS GRADOS		LEVEL 5 / NIVEAU 5 / GRADO 5		LEVEL 6 / NIVEAU 6 / GRADO 6		LEVEL 7 / NIVEAU 7 / GRADO 7	
			MF	F	MF	F	MF	F	MF	F
QATAR	1976	TOTAL	196	103	—	—	117	79	79	24
		EDUCATION SCIENCE & TCHR TRNG.	196	103	—	—	117	79	79	24
		HUMANITIES,RELIGION & THEOLOG	—	—	—	—	—	—	—	—
		FINE AND APPLIED ARTS.	—	—	—	—	—	—	—	—
		LAW	—	—	—	—	—	—	—	—
		SOCIAL AND BEHAVIOURAL SCIENCE	—	—	—	—	—	—	—	—
		COMMERCIAL & BUS. ADMINISTR.	—	—	—	—	—	—	—	—
		MASS COMMUNICATION & DOCUMENT.	—	—	—	—	—	—	—	—
		HOME ECONOMICS & DOMESTIC SC.	—	—	—	—	—	—	—	—
		SERVICE TRADES	—	—	—	—	—	—	—	—
		NATURAL SCIENCE	—	—	—	—	—	—	—	—
		MATHEMATICS & COMPUTER SCIENCE	—	—	—	—	—	—	—	—
		MEDICAL AND HEALTH-RELATED SC.	—	—	—	—	—	—	—	—
		ENGINEERING	—	—	—	—	—	—	—	—
		ARCHITECTURE & TOWN PLANNING	—	—	—	—	—	—	—	—
		TRADE, CRAFT & INDUSTR. PGMS.	—	—	—	—	—	—	—	—
		TRANSPORT AND COMMUNICATIONS	—	—	—	—	—	—	—	—
		AGRICULTURE,FORESTRY & FISH'G.	—	—	—	—	—	—	—	—
		OTHER AND NOT SPECIFIED	—	—	—	—	—	—	—	—
SAUDI ARABIA ‡	1976	TOTAL	3 088	414	—	—	3 088	414	—	—
		EDUCATION SCIENCE & TCHR TRNG.	782	216	—	—	782	216	—	—
		HUMANITIES,RELIGION & THEOLOG	1 223	154	—	—	1 223	154	—	—
		FINE AND APPLIED ARTS.	—	—	—	—	—	—	—	—
		LAW	./.	./.	—	—	./.	./.	—	—
		SOCIAL AND BEHAVIOURAL SCIENCE	358	44	—	—	358	44	—	—
		COMMERCIAL & BUS. ADMINISTR.	—	—	—	—	—	—	—	—
		MASS COMMUNICATION & DOCUMENT.	—	—	—	—	—	—	—	—
		HOME ECONOMICS & DOMESTIC SC.	—	—	—	—	—	—	—	—
		SERVICE TRADES	—	—	—	—	—	—	—	—
		NATURAL SCIENCE	192	—	—	—	192	—	—	—
		MATHEMATICS & COMPUTER SCIENCE	—	—	—	—	—	—	—	—
		MEDICAL AND HEALTH-RELATED SC.	67	—	—	—	67	—	—	—
		ENGINEERING	374	—	—	—	374	—	—	—
		ARCHITECTURE & TOWN PLANNING	—	—	—	—	—	—	—	—
		TRADE, CRAFT & INDUSTR. PGMS.	—	—	—	—	—	—	—	—
		TRANSPORT AND COMMUNICATIONS	—	—	—	—	—	—	—	—
		AGRICULTURE,FORESTRY & FISH'G.	92	—	—	—	92	—	—	—
		OTHER AND NOT SPECIFIED	—	—	—	—	—	—	—	—

Third level: graduates by levels and fields   3.13
Troisième degré: diplômés par niveaux et domaines d'études
Tercer grado: diplomados por niveles y sectores de estudio

INTERNATIONAL STANDARD CLASSIFICATION OF EDUCATION BY LEVEL
CLASSIFICATION INTERNATIONALE TYPE DE L'EDUCATION PAR NIVEAUX
CLASIFICACION INTERNACIONAL NORMALIZADA DE LA EDUCACION POR GRADOS

COUNTRY / PAYS / PAIS	YEAR / ANNEE / AÑO	FIELD OF STUDY / BRANCHE D'ETUDES / RAMAS DE ESTUDIO	ALL LEVELS / TOUS NIVEAUX / TODOS LOS GRADOS MF	F	LEVEL 5 / NIVEAU 5 / GRADO 5 MF	F	LEVEL 6 / NIVEAU 6 / GRADO 6 MF	F	LEVEL 7 / NIVEAU 7 / GRADO 7 MF	F
SINGAPORE ‡	1977	TOTAL	5 461	1 795	3 001	658	2 252	1 061	208	76
		EDUCATION SCIENCE & TCHR TRNG.	331	258	250	202	—	—	81	56
		HUMANITIES,RELIGION & THEOLOG	741	463	—	—	721	457	20	6
		FINE AND APPLIED ARTS.	109	79	—	—	109	79	—	—
		LAW	./.	./.	./.	./.	./.	./.	./.	./.
		SOCIAL AND BEHAVIOURAL SCIENCE	802	348	155	61	647	287	—	—
		COMMERCIAL & BUS. ADMINISTR.	—	—	—	—	—	—	—	—
		MASS COMMUNICATION & DOCUMENT.	—	—	—	—	—	—	—	—
		HOME ECONOMICS & DOMESTIC SC.	—	—	—	—	—	—	—	—
		SERVICE TRADES	—	—	—	—	—	—	—	—
		NATURAL SCIENCE	318	132	—	—	310	130	8	2
		MATHEMATICS & COMPUTER SCIENCE	—	—	—	—	—	—	—	—
		MEDICAL AND HEALTH-RELATED SC.	243	88	—	—	189	77	54	11
		ENGINEERING	2 377	264	2 137	255	195	8	45	1
		ARCHITECTURE & TOWN PLANNING	402	163	321	140	81	23	—	—
		TRADE CRAFT & INDUSTR. PGMS.	—	—	—	—	—	—	—	—
		TRANSPORT AND COMMUNICATIONS	138	—	138	—	—	—	—	—
		AGRICULTURE FORESTRY & FISH'G.	—	—	—	—	—	—	—	—
		OTHER AND NOT SPECIFIED	—	—	—	—	—	—	—	—
SRI LANKA ‡	1975	TOTAL	4 079	1 374	492	86	3 263	1 210	324	78
		EDUCATION SCIENCE & TCHR TRNG.	252	79	—	—	80	36	172	43
		HUMANITIES,RELIGION & THEOLOG	2 396	969	102	48	2 164	890	130	31
		FINE AND APPLIED ARTS.	25	21	18	18	7	3	—	—
		LAW	94	28	—	—	94	28	—	—
		SOCIAL SCIENCES, TOTAL	./.	./.	./.	./.	./.	./.	./.	./.
		NATURAL SCIENCES, TOTAL	340	121	—	—	330	118	10	3
		MEDICAL AND HEALTH-RELATED SC.	268	110	—	—	257	109	11	1
		ENGINEERING, TOTAL	639	30	372	20	267	10	—	—
		AGRICULTURE,FORESTRY & FISH'G.	65	16	—	—	64	16	1	—
		OTHER AND NOT SPECIFIED	—	—	—	—	—	—	—	—

3.13 Third level: graduates by levels and fields
Troisième degré: diplômés par niveaux et domaines d'études
Tercer grado: diplomados por niveles y sectores de estudio

COUNTRY / PAYS / PAIS	YEAR / ANNEE / AÑO	FIELD OF STUDY / BRANCHE D'ETUDES / RAMAS DE ESTUDIO	INTERNATIONAL STANDARD CLASSIFICATION OF EDUCATION BY LEVEL / CLASSIFICATION INTERNATIONALE TYPE DE L'EDUCATION PAR NIVEAUX / CLASIFICACION INTERNACIONAL NORMALIZADA DE LA EDUCACION POR GRADOS							
			ALL LEVELS / TOUS NIVEAUX / TODOS LOS GRADOS		LEVEL 5 / NIVEAU 5 / GRADO 5		LEVEL 6 / NIVEAU 6 / GRADO 6		LEVEL 7 / NIVEAU 7 / GRADO 7	
			MF	F	MF	F	MF	F	MF	F
SYRIAN ARAB REPUBLIC	1976	TOTAL	6 211	1 280						
		EDUCATION SCIENCE & TCHR TRNG.	59	21						
		HUMANITIES,RELIGION & THEOLOG	2 029	570						
		FINE AND APPLIED ARTS.	77	21						
		LAW	321	28						
		SOCIAL AND BEHAVIOURAL SCIENCE	—	—						
		COMMERCIAL & BUS. ADMINISTR.	226	50						
		MASS COMMUNICATION & DOCUMENT.	—	—						
		HOME ECONOMICS & DOMESTIC SC.	—	—						
		SERVICE TRADES	—	—						
		NATURAL SCIENCE	883	229						
		MATHEMATICS & COMPUTER SCIENCE	—	—						
		MEDICAL AND HEALTH-RELATED SC.	737	167						
		ENGINEERING	1 321	145						
		ARCHITECTURE & TOWN PLANNING	—	—						
		TRADE CRAFT & INDUSTR. PGMS.	—	—						
		TRANSPORT AND COMMUNICATIONS	—	—						
		AGRICULTURE,FORESTRY & FISH'G.	558	49						
		OTHER AND NOT SPECIFIED	—	—						
THAILAND ‡	1976	TOTAL	27 778	12 084	3 052	751	23 141	10 607	1 585	726
		EDUCATION SCIENCE & TCHR TRNG.	10 335	5 237	72	7	9 879	5 055	384	175
		HUMANITIES,RELIGION & THEOLOG	1 437	1 281	1	1	1 336	1 203	100	77
		FINE AND APPLIED ARTS.	336	29	105	19	221	5	10	5
		LAW	2 608	287	814	80	1 792	207	2	—
		SOCIAL SCIENCES, TOTAL	5 976	3 041	159	93	5 361	2 766	456	182
		NATURAL SCIENCES, TOTAL	1 359	162	22	10	1 154	28	183	124
		MEDICAL AND HEALTH-RELATED SC.	2 750	1 469	536	531	1 879	809	335	129
		ENGINEERING, TOTAL	2 131	366	1 340	8	725	346	66	12
		AGRICULTURE,FORESTRY & FISH'G.	846	212	3	2	794	188	49	22
		OTHER AND NOT SPECIFIED	—	—	—	—	—	—	—	—

Third level: graduates by levels and fields   3.13
Troisième degré: diplômés par niveaux et domaines d'études
Tercer grado: diplomados por niveles y sectores de estudio

INTERNATIONAL STANDARD CLASSIFICATION OF EDUCATION BY LEVEL
CLASSIFICATION INTERNATIONALE TYPE DE L'EDUCATION PAR NIVEAUX
CLASIFICACION INTERNACIONAL NORMALIZADA DE LA EDUCACION POR GRADOS

COUNTRY / PAYS / PAIS	YEAR / ANNEE / AÑO	FIELD OF STUDY / BRANCHE D'ETUDES / RAMAS DE ESTUDIO	ALL LEVELS TOUS NIVEAUX TODOS LOS GRADOS		LEVEL 5 NIVEAU 5 GRADO 5		LEVEL 6 NIVEAU 6 GRADO 6		LEVEL 7 NIVEAU 7 GRADO 7	
			MF	F	MF	F	MF	F	MF	F
TURKEY	1976	TOTAL	42 274	10 186						
		EDUCATION SCIENCE & TCHR TRNG.	14 007	4 969						
		HUMANITIES,RELIGION & THEOLOG	1 219	331						
		FINE AND APPLIED ARTS.	573	189						
		LAW	1 025	225						
		SOCIAL AND BEHAVIOURAL SCIENCE	4 730	891						
		COMMERCIAL & BUS. ADMINISTR.	3 605	614						
		MASS COMMUNICATION & DOCUMENT.	474	144						
		HOME ECONOMICS & DOMESTIC SC.	101	101						
		SERVICE TRADES	135	14						
		NATURAL SCIENCE	1 587	322						
		MATHEMATICS & COMPUTER SCIENCE	508	123						
		MEDICAL AND HEALTH-RELATED SC.	3 751	1 369						
		ENGINEERING	9 743	799						
		ARCHITECTURE & TOWN PLANNING	101	30						
		TRADE, CRAFT & INDUSTR. PGMS.	—	—						
		TRANSPORT AND COMMUNICATIONS	98	—						
		AGRICULTURE,FORESTRY & FISH'G.	617	65						
		OTHER AND NOT SPECIFIED	—	—						
VIET-NAM	1976	TOTAL	17 799	6 965	—	—	17 799	6 965	—	—
		EDUCATION SCIENCE & TCHR TRNG.	3 917	1 928	—	—	3 917	1 928	—	—
		HUMANITIES,RELIGION & THEOLOG	788	187	—	—	788	187	—	—
		FINE AND APPLIED ARTS.	78	24	—	—	78	24	—	—
		LAW	—	—	—	—	—	—	—	—
		SOCIAL AND BEHAVIOURAL SCIENCE	2 310	820	—	—	2 310	820	—	—
		COMMERCIAL & BUS. ADMINISTR.	—	—	—	—	—	—	—	—
		MASS COMMUNICATION & DOCUMENT.	—	—	—	—	—	—	—	—
		HOME ECONOMICS & DOMESTIC SC.	—	—	—	—	—	—	—	—
		SERVICE TRADES	—	—	—	—	—	—	—	—
		NATURAL SCIENCE	1 896	564	—	—	1 896	564	—	—
		MATHEMATICS & COMPUTER SCIENCE	—	—	—	—	—	—	—	—
		MEDICAL AND HEALTH-RELATED SC.	1 627	832	—	—	1 627	832	—	—
		ENGINEERING	2 917	702	—	—	2 917	702	—	—
		ARCHITECTURE & TOWN PLANNING	—	—	—	—	—	—	—	—
		TRADE, CRAFT & INDUSTR. PGMS.	—	—	—	—	—	—	—	—
		TRANSPORT AND COMMUNICATIONS	—	—	—	—	—	—	—	—
		AGRICULTURE,FORESTRY & FISH'G.	1 518	621	—	—	1 518	621	—	—
		OTHER AND NOT SPECIFIED	2 748	1 287	—	—	2 748	1 287	—	—

3.13 Third level: graduates by levels and fields
Troisième degré: diplômés par niveaux et domaines d'études
Tercer grado: diplomados por niveles y sectores de estudio

INTERNATIONAL STANDARD CLASSIFICATION OF EDUCATION BY LEVEL
CLASSIFICATION INTERNATIONALE TYPE DE L'EDUCATION PAR NIVEAUX
CLASIFICACION INTERNACIONAL NORMALIZADA DE LA EDUCACION POR GRADOS

COUNTRY / PAYS / PAIS	YEAR / ANNEE / AÑO	FIELD OF STUDY / BRANCHE D'ETUDES / RAMAS DE ESTUDIO	ALL LEVELS / TOUS NIVEAUX / TODOS LOS GRADOS MF	F	LEVEL 5 / NIVEAU 5 / GRADO 5 MF	F	LEVEL 6 / NIVEAU 6 / GRADO 6 MF	F	LEVEL 7 / NIVEAU 7 / GRADO 7 MF	F
YEMEN, DEMOCRATIC	1977	TOTAL	478	159	222	104	256	55	—	—
		EDUCATION SCIENCE & TCHR TRNG.	139	32	54	18	85	14	—	—
		HUMANITIES,RELIGION & THEOLOG	233	110	168	86	65	24	—	—
		FINE AND APPLIED ARTS.	—	—	—	—	—	—	—	—
		LAW	—	—	—	—	—	—	—	—
		SOCIAL AND BEHAVIOURAL SCIENCE	88	14	—	—	88	14	—	—
		COMMERCIAL & BUS. ADMINISTR.	—	—	—	—	—	—	—	—
		MASS COMMUNICATION & DOCUMENT.	—	—	—	—	—	—	—	—
		HOME ECONOMICS & DOMESTIC SC.	—	—	—	—	—	—	—	—
		SERVICE TRADES	—	—	—	—	—	—	—	—
		NATURAL SCIENCE	—	—	—	—	—	—	—	—
		MATHEMATICS & COMPUTER SCIENCE	—	—	—	—	—	—	—	—
		MEDICAL AND HEALTH-RELATED SC.	—	—	—	—	—	—	—	—
		ENGINEERING	—	—	—	—	—	—	—	—
		ARCHITECTURE & TOWN PLANNING	—	—	—	—	—	—	—	—
		TRADE, CRAFT & INDUSTR. PGMS.	—	—	—	—	—	—	—	—
		TRANSPORT AND COMMUNICATIONS	—	—	—	—	—	—	—	—
		AGRICULTURE,FORESTRY & FISH'G.	18	3	—	—	18	3	—	—
		OTHER AND NOT SPECIFIED	—	—	—	—	—	—	—	—
EUROPE										
AUSTRIA ‡	1976	TOTAL	7 297	2 011	96	51	5 483	1 594	1 718	366
		EDUCATION SCIENCE & TCHR TRNG.	1 341	682	—	—	1 287	665	54	17
		HUMANITIES,RELIGION & THEOLOG	480	157	57	43	210	41	213	73
		FINE AND APPLIED ARTS.	638	320	—	—	585	295	53	25
		LAW	929	155	—	—	403	66	526	89
		SOCIAL AND BEHAVIOURAL SCIENCE	382	120	39	8	173	42	170	70
		COMMERCIAL & BUS. ADMINISTR.	788	99	—	—	601	84	187	15
		MASS COMMUNICATION & DOCUMENT.	28	15	—	—	—	—	28	15
		HOME ECONOMICS & DOMESTIC SC.	—	—	—	—	—	—	—	—
		SERVICE TRADES	—	—	—	—	—	—	—	—
		NATURAL SCIENCE	309	39	—	—	64	2	245	37
		MATHEMATICS & COMPUTER SCIENCE	154	16	—	—	111	10	43	6
		MEDICAL AND HEALTH-RELATED SC.	1 085	314	—	—	1 082	312	3	2
		ENGINEERING	599	19	—	—	513	16	86	3
		ARCHITECTURE & TOWN PLANNING	308	26	—	—	280	26	28	—
		TRADE, CRAFT & INDUSTR. PGMS.	—	—	—	—	—	—	—	—
		TRANSPORT AND COMMUNICATIONS	—	—	—	—	—	—	—	—
		AGRICULTURE,FORESTRY & FISH'G.	146	15	—	—	95	8	51	7
		OTHER AND NOT SPECIFIED	110	34	—	—	79	27	31	7

Third level: graduates by levels and fields 3.13
Troisième degré: diplômés par niveaux et domaines d'études
Tercer grado: diplomados por niveles y sectores de estudio

COUNTRY / PAYS / PAIS	YEAR / ANNEE / AÑO	FIELD OF STUDY / BRANCHE D'ETUDES / RAMAS DE ESTUDIO	INTERNATIONAL STANDARD CLASSIFICATION OF EDUCATION BY LEVEL / CLASSIFICATION INTERNATIONALE TYPE DE L'EDUCATION PAR NIVEAUX / CLASIFICACION INTERNACIONAL NORMALIZADA DE LA EDUCACION POR GRADOS							
			ALL LEVELS TOUS NIVEAUX TODOS LOS GRADOS		LEVEL 5 NIVEAU 5 GRADO 5		LEVEL 6 NIVEAU 6 GRADO 6		LEVEL 7 NIVEAU 7 GRADO 7	
			MF	F	MF	F	MF	F	MF	F
BELGIUM ‡	1977	TOTAL	36 228	17 611	19 119	11 396	17 109	6 215	./.	./.
		EDUCATION SCIENCE & TCHR TRNG.	6 905	4 815	6 165	4 395	740	420	./.	./.
		HUMANITIES,RELIGION & THEOLOG	3 203	1 867	19	18	3 184	1 849	./.	./.
		FINE AND APPLIED ARTS.	610	304	592	298	18	6	./.	./.
		LAW	1 797	592	24	10	1 773	582	./.	./.
		SOCIAL AND BEHAVIOURAL SCIENCE	2 609	1 314	1 446	959	1 163	355	./.	./.
		COMMERCIAL & BUS. ADMINISTR.	5 347	2 329	3 150	1 746	2 197	583	./.	./.
		MASS COMMUNICATION & DOCUMENT.	20	2	—	—	20	2	.	.
		HOME ECONOMICS & DOMESTIC SC.	—	—	—	—	—	—	—	—
		SERVICE TRADES	502	236	502	236	—	—	./.	./.
		NATURAL SCIENCE	2 653	977	424	65	2 229	912	./.	./.
		MATHEMATICS & COMPUTER SCIENCE	569	218	569	218	—	—	./.	./.
		MEDICAL AND HEALTH-RELATED SC.	7 676	4 570	4 288	3 321	3 388	1 249	./.	./.
		ENGINEERING	2 686	137	1 264	66	1 422	71	./.	./.
		ARCHITECTURE & TOWN PLANNING	337	87	57	14	280	73	./.	./.
		TRADE, CRAFT & INDUSTR. PGMS.	561	36	534	35	27	1	./.	./.
		TRANSPORT AND COMMUNICATIONS	—	—	—	—	—	—	—	—
		AGRICULTURE,FORESTRY & FISH'G.	653	96	85	15	568	81	./.	./.
		OTHER AND NOT SPECIFIED	100	31	—	—	100	31	./.	./.
BULGARIA ‡	1976	TOTAL	36 721	25 773	17 647	15 134	18 880	10 565	194	74
		EDUCATION SCIENCE & TCHR TRNG.	5 712	4 731	5 341	4 595	371	136	—	—
		HUMANITIES,RELIGION & THEOLOG	2 971	2 214	145	145	2 826	2 069	—	—
		FINE AND APPLIED ARTS.	770	378	119	64	651	314	—	—
		LAW	488	218	—	—	488	218	—	—
		SOCIAL AND BEHAVIOURAL SCIENCE	135	74	—	—	117	67	18	7
		COMMERCIAL & BUS. ADMINISTR.	3 152	1 983	—	—	3 152	1 983	—	—
		MASS COMMUNICATION & DOCUMENT.	486	334	—	—	486	334	—	—
		HOME ECONOMICS & DOMESTIC SC.	—	—	—	—	—	—	—	—
		SERVICE TRADES	593	396	593	396	—	—	—	—
		NATURAL SCIENCE	887	627	—	—	848	612	39	15
		MATHEMATICS & COMPUTER SCIENCE	692	483	—	—	692	483	—	—
		MEDICAL AND HEALTH-RELATED SC.	12 587	10 841	11 116	9 794	1 451	1 031	20	16
		ENGINEERING	6 724	2 809	—	—	6 642	2 797	82	12
		ARCHITECTURE & TOWN PLANNING	204	102	—	—	204	102	—	—
		TRADE, CRAFT & INDUSTR. PGMS.	—	—	—	—	—	—	—	—
		TRANSPORT AND COMMUNICATIONS	—	—	—	—	—	—	—	—
		AGRICULTURE,FORESTRY & FISH'G.	455	163	333	140	122	23	—	—
		OTHER AND NOT SPECIFIED	865	420	—	—	830	396	35	24

3.13 Third level: graduates by levels and fields
Troisième degré: diplômés par niveaux et domaines d'études
Tercer grado: diplomados por niveles y sectores de estudio

INTERNATIONAL STANDARD CLASSIFICATION OF EDUCATION BY LEVEL
CLASSIFICATION INTERNATIONALE TYPE DE L'EDUCATION PAR NIVEAUX
CLASIFICACION INTERNACIONAL NORMALIZADA DE LA EDUCACION POR GRADOS

COUNTRY / PAYS / PAIS	YEAR / ANNEE / AÑO	FIELD OF STUDY / BRANCHE D'ETUDES / RAMAS DE ESTUDIO	ALL LEVELS / TOUS NIVEAUX / TODOS LOS GRADOS		LEVEL 5 / NIVEAU 5 / GRADO 5		LEVEL 6 / NIVEAU 6 / GRADO 6		LEVEL 7 / NIVEAU 7 / GRADO 7	
			MF	F	MF	F	MF	F	MF	F
CZECHOSLOVAKIA	1976	TOTAL	23 216	9 794	—	—	23 216	9 794	—	—
		EDUCATION SCIENCE & TCHR TRNG.	5 148	3 929	—	—	5 148	3 929	—	—
		HUMANITIES,RELIGION & THEOLOG	303	162	—	—	303	162	—	—
		FINE AND APPLIED ARTS.	378	157	—	—	378	157	—	—
		LAW	1 417	657	—	—	1 417	657	—	—
		SOCIAL AND BEHAVIOURAL SCIENCE	319	187	—	—	319	187	—	—
		COMMERCIAL & BUS. ADMINISTR.	1 980	1 072	—	—	1 980	1 072	—	—
		MASS COMMUNICATION & DOCUMENT.	314	187	—	—	314	187	—	—
		HOME ECONOMICS & DOMESTIC SC.	—	—	—	—	—	—	—	—
		SERVICE TRADES	—	—	—	—	—	—	—	—
		NATURAL SCIENCE	322	135	—	—	322	135	—	—
		MATHEMATICS & COMPUTER SCIENCE	240	67	—	—	240	67	—	—
		MEDICAL AND HEALTH-RELATED SC.	2 636	1 497	—	—	2 636	1 497	—	—
		ENGINEERING	7 017	927	—	—	7 017	927	—	—
		ARCHITECTURE & TOWN PLANNING	226	60	—	—	226	60	—	—
		TRADE, CRAFT & INDUSTR. PGMS.	—	—	—	—	—	—	—	—
		TRANSPORT AND COMMUNICATIONS	519	78	—	—	519	78	—	—
		AGRICULTURE,FORESTRY & FISH'G.	2 328	666	—	—	2 328	666	—	—
		OTHER AND NOT SPECIFIED	69	13	—	—	69	13	—	—
DENMARK ‡	1977	TOTAL	17 884	9 422	7 540	5 168	10 344	4 254	./.	./.
		EDUCATION SCIENCE & TCHR TRNG.	6 814	4 530	3 273	2 618	3 541	1 912	./.	./.
		HUMANITIES,RELIGION & THEOLOG	315	145	—	—	315	145	./.	./.
		FINE AND APPLIED ARTS.	163	96	90	63	73	33	./.	./.
		LAW	425	127	—	—	425	127	./.	./.
		SOCIAL AND BEHAVIOURAL SCIENCE	465	126	—	—	465	126	./.	./.
		COMMERCIAL & BUS. ADMINISTR.	1 465	648	536	505	929	143	./.	./.
		MASS COMMUNICATION & DOCUMENT.	403	250	—	—	403	250	./.	./.
		HOME ECONOMICS & DOMESTIC SC.	—	—	—	—	—	—	./.	./.
		SERVICE TRADES	—	—	—	—	—	—	./.	./.
		NATURAL SCIENCE	296	206	181	177	115	29	./.	./.
		MATHEMATICS & COMPUTER SCIENCE	139	13	—	—	139	13	./.	./.
		MEDICAL AND HEALTH-RELATED SC.	3 357	2 632	1 817	1 709	1 540	923	./.	./.
		ENGINEERING	1 654	86	500	49	1 154	37	./.	./.
		ARCHITECTURE & TCWN PLANNING	347	71	12	2	335	69	./.	./.
		TRADE, CRAFT & INDUSTR. PGMS.	533	29	533	29	—	—	./.	./.
		TRANSPORT AND COMMUNICATIONS	518	2	369	2	149	—	./.	./.
		AGRICULTURE,FORESTRY & FISH'G.	287	49	145	10	142	39	./.	./.
		OTHER AND NOT SPECIFIED	703	412	84	4	619	408	./.	./.

Third level: graduates by levels and fields 3.13
Troisième degré: diplômés par niveaux et domaines d'études
Tercer grado: diplomados por niveles y sectores de estudio

INTERNATIONAL STANDARD CLASSIFICATION OF EDUCATION BY LEVEL
CLASSIFICATION INTERNATIONALE TYPE DE L'EDUCATION PAR NIVEAUX
CLASIFICACION INTERNACIONAL NORMALIZADA DE LA EDUCACION POR GRADOS

COUNTRY PAYS PAIS	YEAR ANNEE AÑO	FIELD OF STUDY BRANCHE D'ETUDES RAMAS DE ESTUDIO	ALL LEVELS TOUS NIVEAUX TODOS LOS GRADOS		LEVEL 5 NIVEAU 5 GRADO 5		LEVEL 6 NIVEAU 6 GRADO 6		LEVEL 7 NIVEAU 7 GRADO 7	
			MF	F	MF	F	MF	F	MF	F
FINLAND	1977	TOTAL	27 114	14 058	14 802	7 725	11 644	6 198	668	135
		EDUCATION SCIENCE & TCHR TRNG.	2 567	2 021	1 188	1 105	1 373	915	6	1
		HUMANITIES,RELIGION & THEOLOG	2 107	1 528	—	—	2 024	1 499	83	29
		FINE AND APPLIED ARTS.	269	149	78	33	188	116	3	—
		LAW	436	140	—	—	405	138	31	2
		SOCIAL AND BEHAVIOURAL SCIENCE	1 517	912	4 235	2 909	1 436	891	81	21
		COMMERCIAL & BUS. ADMINISTR.	5 727	3 698	41	20	1 475	789	17	—
		MASS COMMUNICATION & DOCUMENT.	61	38	—	—	20	18	—	1
		HOME ECONOMICS & DOMESTIC SC.	13	13	—	—	12	12	—	—
		SERVICE TRADES	124	76	124	76	—	—	1	1
		NATURAL SCIENCE	1 200	482	—	—	1 042	440	158	42
		MATHEMATICS & COMPUTER SCIENCE	748	250	—	—	711	248	37	2
		MEDICAL AND HEALTH-RELATED SC.	5 117	4 031	3 353	3 152	1 658	855	106	24
		ENGINEERING	6 308	419	5 319	310	872	102	117	7
		ARCHITECTURE & TOWN PLANNING	62	18	—	—	54	15	8	3
		TRADE, CRAFT & INDUSTR. PGMS.	—	—	—	—	—	—	—	—
		TRANSPORT AND COMMUNICATIONS	155	2	155	2	—	—	—	—
		AGRICULTURE,FORESTRY & FISH'G.	454	117	180	21	256	93	18	3
		OTHER AND NOT SPECIFIED	249	164	129	97	118	67	2	—
FRANCE ‡	1976	TOTAL	162 632	...	68 117	...	38 273	19 764	55 942	20 124
		EDUCATION SCIENCE & TCHR TRNG.	45 682	28 031	15 834	10 334	18 215	11 403	11 633	6 294
		HUMANITIES,RELIGION & THEOLOG	—	—	—	—	—	—	—	—
		FINE AND APPLIED ARTS.	—	—	—	—	—	—	—	—
		LAW	24 935	11 197	8 959	4 180	8 445	3 706	7 531	3 311
		SOCIAL AND BEHAVIOURAL SCIENCE	2 274	1 117	1 194	594	845	406	235	117
		COMMERCIAL & BUS. ADMINISTR.	11 947	4 050	4 468	1 586	3 557	1 182	3 922	1 282
		MASS COMMUNICATION & DOCUMENT.	—	—	—	—	—	—	—	—
		HOME ECONOMICS & DOMESTIC SC.	—	—	—	—	—	—	—	—
		SERVICE TRADES	15 696	—	15 696	—	—	—	—	—
		NATURAL SCIENCE	21 983	8 297	7 417	2 885	6 821	2 713	7 745	2 699
		MATHEMATICS & COMPUTER SCIENCE	308	139	231	112	58	22	19	5
		MEDICAL AND HEALTH-RELATED SC.	15 408	5 819	—	—	332	332	15 076	5 487
		ENGINEERING	9 781	929	—	—	—	—	9 781	929
		ARCHITECTURE & TOWN PLANNING	—	—	—	—	—	—	—	—
		TRADE, CRAFT & INDUSTR. PGMS.	14 618	4 323	14 618	4 323	—	—	—	—
		TRANSPORT AND COMMUNICATIONS	—	—	—	—	—	—	—	—
		AGRICULTURE,FORESTRY & FISH'G.	—	—	—	—	—	—	—	—
		OTHER AND NOT SPECIFIED	—	—	—	—	—	—	—	—

3.13 Third level: graduates by levels and fields
Troisième degré: diplômés par niveaux et domaines d'études
Tercer grado: diplomados por niveles y sectores de estudio

INTERNATIONAL STANDARD CLASSIFICATION OF EDUCATION BY LEVEL
CLASSIFICATION INTERNATIONALE TYPE DE L'EDUCATION PAR NIVEAUX
CLASIFICACION INTERNACIONAL NORMALIZADA DE LA EDUCACION POR GRADOS

COUNTRY / PAYS / PAIS — YEAR / ANNEE / AÑO — FIELD OF STUDY / BRANCHE D'ETUDES / RAMAS DE ESTUDIO	ALL LEVELS TOUS NIVEAUX TODOS LOS GRADOS MF	F	LEVEL 5 NIVEAU 5 GRADO 5 MF	F	LEVEL 6 NIVEAU 6 GRADO 6 MF	F	LEVEL 7 NIVEAU 7 GRADO 7 MF	F
GERMAN DEMOCRATIC REPUBLIC ‡ — 1976								
TOTAL	107 752	...	34 994	...	42 456	29 332	30 302	14 275
EDUCATION SCIENCE & TCHR TRNG.	...	...	...	...	6 190	5 309	7 418	5 397
HUMANITIES,RELIGION & THEOLOG	...	...	...	...	296	129	1 425	567
FINE AND APPLIED ARTS.	...	...	...	...	269	166	475	162
LAW	...	...	...	...	–	–	616	271
SOCIAL AND BEHAVIOURAL SCIENCE	...	...	...	...	2 184	1 835	2 306	912
COMMERCIAL & BUS. ADMINISTR.	...	...	...	...	6 556	4 999	4 503	1 975
MASS COMMUNICATION & DOCUMENT.	...	...	...	...	469	420	214	119
HOME ECONOMICS & DOMESTIC SC.	...	...	...	...	–	–	–	–
SERVICE TRADES	...	...	...	...	–	–	–	–
NATURAL SCIENCE	...	...	...	...	–	–	1 569	548
MATHEMATICS & COMPUTER SCIENCE	...	...	...	...	224	142	916	453
MEDICAL AND HEALTH-RELATED SC.	...	...	...	...	11 794	11 543	1 087	585
ENGINEERING	...	...	...	...	11 241	3 474	8 058	2 468
ARCHITECTURE & TOWN PLANNING	...	...	...	...	–	–	47	20
TRADE, CRAFT & INDUSTR. PGMS.	...	...	...	...	–	–	–	–
TRANSPORT AND COMMUNICATIONS	...	...	...	...	–	–	–	–
AGRICULTURE,FORESTRY & FISH'G.	...	...	...	...	3 233	1 315	1 668	798
OTHER AND NOT SPECIFIED	...	...	...	...	–	–	–	–
GERMANY, FEDERAL REPUBLIC OF — 1976								
TOTAL	207 719	84 499	119 667	53 665	76 666	29 170	11 386	1 664
EDUCATION SCIENCE & TCHR TRNG.	42 240	22 685	229	139	41 746	22 480	265	66
HUMANITIES,RELIGION & THEOLOG	3 228	1 034	334	212	1 770	591	1 124	231
FINE AND APPLIED ARTS.	2 573	1 031	1 452	653	993	331	128	47
LAW	4 259	807	–	–	3 771	769	488	38
SOCIAL AND BEHAVIOURAL SCIENCE	22 110	6 841	11 364	4 795	9 722	1 910	1 024	136
COMMERCIAL & BUS. ADMINISTR.	1 618	439	1 583	437	35	2	–	–
MASS COMMUNICATION & DOCUMENT.	422	294	330	265	74	24	18	5
HOME ECONOMICS & DOMESTIC SC.	469	395	145	127	306	256	18	12
SERVICE TRADES	–	–	–	–	–	–	–	–
NATURAL SCIENCE	5 811	709	106	22	3 421	492	2 284	195
MATHEMATICS & COMPUTER SCIENCE	2 106	208	175	30	1 637	167	294	11
MEDICAL AND HEALTH-RELATED SC.	41 821	28 576	31 760	26 182	5 946	1 569	4 115	825
ENGINEERING	19 357	670	13 906	614	4 463	53	988	3
ARCHITECTURE & TOWN PLANNING	3 940	894	2 627	700	1 261	192	52	2
TRADE, CRAFT & INDUSTR. PGMS.	–	–	–	–	–	–	–	–
TRANSPORT AND COMMUNICATIONS	–	–	–	–	–	–	–	–
AGRICULTURE,FORESTRY & FISH'G.	2 564	471	749	111	1 239	268	576	92
OTHER AND NOT SPECIFIED	55 201	19 445	54 907	19 378	282	66	12	1

Third level: graduates by levels and fields 3.13
Troisième degré: diplômés par niveaux et domaines d'études
Tercer grado: diplomados por niveles y sectores de estudio

INTERNATIONAL STANDARD CLASSIFICATION OF EDUCATION BY LEVEL
CLASSIFICATION INTERNATIONALE TYPE DE L'EDUCATION PAR NIVEAUX
CLASIFICACION INTERNACIONAL NORMALIZADA DE LA EDUCACION POR GRADOS

COUNTRY / PAYS / PAIS	YEAR / ANNEE / AÑO	FIELD OF STUDY / BRANCHE D'ETUDES / RAMAS DE ESTUDIO	ALL LEVELS / TOUS NIVEAUX / TODOS LOS GRADOS		LEVEL 5 / NIVEAU 5 / GRADO 5		LEVEL 6 / NIVEAU 6 / GRADO 6		LEVEL 7 / NIVEAU 7 / GRADO 7	
			MF	F	MF	F	MF	F	MF	F
GREECE	1977	TOTAL	15 507	6 357	3 530	1 535	11 534	4 739	443	83
		EDUCATION SCIENCE & TCHR TRNG.	1 354	840	1 354	840	—	—	—	—
		HUMANITIES,RELIGION & THEOLOG	2 129	1 604	—	—	2 099	1 598	30	6
		FINE AND APPLIED ARTS.	30	13	—	—	30	13	—	—
		LAW	1 405	652	—	—	1 371	644	34	8
		SOCIAL AND BEHAVIOURAL SCIENCE	1 957	755	—	—	1 950	755	7	—
		COMMERCIAL & BUS. ADMINISTR.	1 856	702	356	199	1 500	503	—	—
		MASS COMMUNICATION & DOCUMENT.	—	—	—	—	—	—	—	—
		HOME ECONOMICS & DOMESTIC SC.	91	91	91	91	—	—	—	—
		SERVICE TRADES	—	—	—	—	—	—	—	—
		NATURAL SCIENCE	797	230	—	—	734	221	63	9
		MATHEMATICS & COMPUTER SCIENCE	647	163	—	—	617	158	30	5
		MEDICAL AND HEALTH-RELATED SC.	2 341	895	357	239	1 757	614	227	42
		ENGINEERING	2 395	245	1 300	141	1 079	102	16	2
		ARCHITECTURE & TOWN PLANNING	222	108	—	—	216	106	6	2
		TRADE, CRAFT & INDUSTR. PGMS.	—	—	—	—	—	—	—	—
		TRANSPORT AND COMMUNICATIONS	—	—	—	—	—	—	—	—
		AGRICULTURE,FORESTRY & FISH'G.	283	59	72	25	181	25	30	9
		OTHER AND NOT SPECIFIED	—	—	—	—	—	—	—	—
HOLY SEE	1977	TOTAL	1 958	392	131	100	740	115	1 087	177
		EDUCATION SCIENCE & TCHR TRNG.	234	113	5	2	116	40	113	71
		HUMANITIES,RELIGION & THEOLOG	1 424	249	124	98	524	57	776	94
		FINE AND APPLIED ARTS.	45	14	2	—	29	13	14	1
		LAW	212	11	—	—	67	3	145	8
		SOCIAL AND BEHAVIOURAL SCIENCE	43	5	—	—	4	2	39	3
		COMMERCIAL & BUS. ADMINISTR.	—	—	—	—	—	—	—	—
		MASS COMMUNICATION & DOCUMENT.	—	—	—	—	—	—	—	—
		HOME ECONOMICS & DOMESTIC SC.	—	—	—	—	—	—	—	—
		SERVICE TRADES	—	—	—	—	—	—	—	—
		NATURAL SCIENCE	—	—	—	—	—	—	—	—
		MATHEMATICS & COMPUTER SCIENCE	—	—	—	—	—	—	—	—
		MEDICAL AND HEALTH-RELATED SC.	—	—	—	—	—	—	—	—
		ENGINEERING	—	—	—	—	—	—	—	—
		ARCHITECTURE & TOWN PLANNING	—	—	—	—	—	—	—	—
		TRADE, CRAFT & INDUSTR. PGMS.	—	—	—	—	—	—	—	—
		TRANSPORT AND COMMUNICATIONS	—	—	—	—	—	—	—	—
		AGRICULTURE,FORESTRY & FISH'G.	—	—	—	—	—	—	—	—
		OTHER AND NOT SPECIFIED	—	—	—	—	—	—	—	—

3.13 Third level: graduates by levels and fields
Troisième degré: diplômés par niveaux et domaines d'études
Tercer grado: diplomados por niveles y sectores de estudio

INTERNATIONAL STANDARD CLASSIFICATION OF EDUCATION BY LEVEL
CLASSIFICATION INTERNATIONALE TYPE DE L'EDUCATION PAR NIVEAUX
CLASIFICACION INTERNACIONAL NORMALIZADA DE LA EDUCACION POR GRADOS

COUNTRY / PAYS / PAIS — YEAR / ANNEE / AÑO — FIELD OF STUDY / BRANCHE D'ETUDES / RAMAS DE ESTUDIO	ALL LEVELS TOUS NIVEAUX TODOS LOS GRADOS MF	F	LEVEL 5 NIVEAU 5 GRADO 5 MF	F	LEVEL 6 NIVEAU 6 GRADO 6 MF	F	LEVEL 7 NIVEAU 7 GRADO 7 MF	F
HUNGARY 1976								
TOTAL	25 934	13 424	...	...	...	...	...	...
EDUCATION SCIENCE & TCHR TRNG.	10 290	8 046	...	...	...	...	...	...
HUMANITIES,RELIGION & THEOLOG	662	422	252	198	—	—	410	224
FINE AND APPLIED ARTS.	182	97	—	—	—	—	182	97
LAW	729	335	—	—	—	—	729	335
SOCIAL AND BEHAVIOURAL SCIENCE	512	279	—	—	—	—	512	279
COMMERCIAL & BUS. ADMINISTR.	1 457	1 009	1 148	829	—	—	309	180
MASS COMMUNICATION & DOCUMENT.	—	—	—	—	—	—	—	—
HOME ECONOMICS & DOMESTIC SC.	—	—	—	—	—	—	—	—
SERVICE TRADES	174	92	174	92	—	—	—	—
NATURAL SCIENCE	222	64	—	—	—	—	222	64
MATHEMATICS & COMPUTER SCIENCE	380	115	155	115	—	—	225	55
MEDICAL AND HEALTH-RELATED SC.	1 447	845	61	46	—	—	1 386	799
ENGINEERING	2 732	478	389	3	—	—	2 343	475
ARCHITECTURE & TOWN PLANNING	1 296	331	871	234	—	—	425	97
TRADE, CRAFT & INDUSTR. PGMS	2 966	599	2 966	599	—	—	—	—
TRANSPORT AND COMMUNICATIONS	356	60	301	55	—	—	55	5
AGRICULTURE, FORESTRY & FISH'G.	2 443	582	1 563	360	—	—	880	222
OTHER AND NOT SPECIFIED	86	15	—	—	86	15	—	—
IRELAND ‡ 1977								
TOTAL	8 315	3 908	448	308	5 382	2 345	2 485	1 255
EDUCATION SCIENCE & TCHR TRNG.	1 841	1 172	138	111	13	10	1 690	1 051
HUMANITIES,RELIGION & THEOLOG	2 812	1 593	26	7	2 602	1 513	184	73
FINE AND APPLIED ARTS.	94	62	51	28	43	34	—	—
LAW	265	85	2	2	238	79	27	6
SOCIAL AND BEHAVIOURAL SCIENCE	338	168	22	9	268	135	68	31
COMMERCIAL & BUS. ADMINISTR.	640	145	27	19	558	132	60	4
MASS COMMUNICATION & DOCUMENT.	33	23	—	—	—	—	6	4
HOME ECONOMICS & DOMESTIC SC.	—	—	—	—	—	—	—	—
SERVICE TRADES	—	—	—	—	—	—	—	—
NATURAL SCIENCE	609	234	—	—	507	203	102	31
MATHEMATICS & COMPUTER SCIENCE	14	1	—	—	14	1	—	—
MEDICAL AND HEALTH-RELATED SC.	812	351	114	110	556	202	142	39
ENGINEERING	561	49	47	21	361	13	153	15
ARCHITECTURE & TOWN PLANNING	45	10	—	—	28	9	17	1
TRADE, CRAFT & INDUSTR. PGMS	—	—	—	—	—	—	—	—
TRANSPORT AND COMMUNICATIONS	—	—	—	—	—	—	—	—
AGRICULTURE, FORESTRY & FISH'G.	251	15	21	1	194	14	36	—
OTHER AND NOT SPECIFIED	—	—	—	—	—	—	—	—

Third level: graduates by levels and fields 3.13
Troisième degré: diplômés par niveaux et domaines d'études
Tercer grado: diplomados por niveles y sectores de estudio

INTERNATIONAL STANDARD CLASSIFICATION OF EDUCATION BY LEVEL
CLASSIFICATION INTERNATIONALE TYPE DE L'EDUCATION PAR NIVEAUX
CLASIFICACION INTERNACIONAL NORMALIZADA DE LA EDUCACION POR GRADOS

COUNTRY / PAYS / PAIS	YEAR / ANNEE / AÑO	FIELD OF STUDY / BRANCHE D'ETUDES / RAMAS DE ESTUDIO	ALL LEVELS TOUS NIVEAUX TODOS LOS GRADOS		LEVEL 5 NIVEAU 5 GRADO 5		LEVEL 6 NIVEAU 6 GRADO 6		LEVEL 7 NIVEAU 7 GRADO 7	
			MF	F	MF	F	MF	F	MF	F
ITALY	1976	TOTAL	86 460	36 032	4 138	2 123	73 246	31 786	9 076	2 123
		EDUCATION SCIENCE & TCHR TRNG.	5 189	4 037	464	360	4 532	3 540	193	137
		HUMANITIES,RELIGION & THEOLOG	16 484	12 707	—	—	16 172	12 476	312	231
		FINE AND APPLIED ARTS.	1 490	734	1 369	684	121	50	—	—
		LAW	6 776	1 986	—	—	6 554	1 908	222	78
		SOCIAL AND BEHAVIOURAL SCIENCE	5 398	2 279	—	—	5 398	2 279	—	—
		COMMERCIAL & BUS. ADMINISTR.	3 552	900	—	—	3 163	632	389	268
		MASS COMMUNICATION & DOCUMENT.	—	—	—	—	—	—	—	—
		HOME ECONOMICS & DOMESTIC SC.	—	—	—	—	—	—	—	—
		SERVICE TRADES	—	—	—	—	—	—	—	—
		NATURAL SCIENCE	6 370	3 691	—	—	6 370	3 691	—	—
		MATHEMATICS & COMPUTER SCIENCE	3 842	2 086	89	44	3 543	1 904	210	138
		MEDICAL AND HEALTH-RELATED SC.	21 826	5 298	—	—	14 691	4 149	7 135	1 149
		ENGINEERING	7 549	203	—	—	7 107	97	442	106
		ARCHITECTURE & TOWN PLANNING	4 234	942	—	—	4 206	935	28	7
		TRADE, CRAFT & INDUSTR. PGMS.	—	—	—	—	—	—	—	—
		TRANSPORT AND COMMUNICATIONS	—	—	—	—	—	—	—	—
		AGRICULTURE,FORESTRY & FISH'G.	1 507	130	—	—	1 380	124	127	6
		OTHER AND NOT SPECIFIED	2 243	1 039	2 216	1 035	9	1	18	3
MALTA	1977	TOTAL	395	156	127	56	254	98	14	2
		EDUCATION SCIENCE & TCHR TRNG.	156	74	106	52	50	22	—	—
		HUMANITIES,RELIGION & THEOLOG	86	40	—	—	78	39	8	1
		FINE AND APPLIED ARTS.	21	4	21	4	—	—	—	—
		LAW	22	2	—	—	22	2	—	—
		SOCIAL AND BEHAVIOURAL SCIENCE	—	—	—	—	—	—	—	—
		COMMERCIAL & BUS. ADMINISTR.	—	—	—	—	—	—	—	—
		MASS COMMUNICATION & DOCUMENT.	—	—	—	—	—	—	—	—
		HOME ECONOMICS & DOMESTIC SC.	—	—	—	—	—	—	—	—
		SERVICE TRADES	—	—	—	—	—	—	—	—
		NATURAL SCIENCE	26	15	—	—	20	14	6	1
		MATHEMATICS & COMPUTER SCIENCE	—	—	—	—	—	—	—	—
		MEDICAL AND HEALTH-RELATED SC.	31	20	—	—	31	20	—	—
		ENGINEERING	34	1	—	—	34	1	—	—
		ARCHITECTURE & TOWN PLANNING	19	—	—	—	19	—	—	—
		TRADE, CRAFT & INDUSTR. PGMS.	—	—	—	—	—	—	—	—
		TRANSPORT AND COMMUNICATIONS	—	—	—	—	—	—	—	—
		AGRICULTURE,FORESTRY & FISH'G.	—	—	—	—	—	—	—	—
		OTHER AND NOT SPECIFIED	—	—	—	—	—	—	—	—

3.13 Third level: graduates by levels and fields
Troisième degré: diplômés par niveaux et domaines d'études
Tercer grado: diplomados por niveles y sectores de estudio

INTERNATIONAL STANDARD CLASSIFICATION OF EDUCATION BY LEVEL
CLASSIFICATION INTERNATIONALE TYPE DE L'EDUCATION PAR NIVEAUX
CLASIFICACION INTERNACIONAL NORMALIZADA DE LA EDUCACION POR GRADOS

COUNTRY — PAYS — PAIS	YEAR — ANNEE — AÑO	FIELD OF STUDY — BRANCHE D'ETUDES — RAMAS DE ESTUDIO	ALL LEVELS TOUS NIVEAUX TODOS LOS GRADOS		LEVEL 5 NIVEAU 5 GRADO 5		LEVEL 6 NIVEAU 6 GRADO 6		LEVEL 7 NIVEAU 7 GRADO 7	
			MF	F	MF	F	MF	F	MF	F
NETHERLANDS ‡	1976	TOTAL	40 077	14 178	25 445	10 614	3 596	1 466	11 036	2 098
		EDUCATION SCIENCE & TCHR TRNG.	7 050	3 771	7 050	3 771	—	—	—	—
		HUMANITIES,RELIGION & THEOLOG	962	342	—	—	—	—	962	342
		FINE AND APPLIED ARTS.	1 516	643	1 429	600	87	43	—	—
		LAW	1 503	330	—	—	—	—	1 503	330
		SOCIAL AND BEHAVIOURAL SCIENCE	6 062	2 154	3 671	1 711	—	—	2 391	443
		COMMERCIAL & BUS. ADMINISTR.	806	43	806	43	—	—	—	—
		MASS COMMUNICATION & DOCUMENT.	944	681	944	681	—	—	—	—
		HOME ECONOMICS & DOMESTIC SC.	1 894	1 846	482	456	1 412	1 390	—	—
		SERVICE TRADES	202	64	202	64	—	—	—	—
		NATURAL SCIENCE	1 279	176	—	—	—	—	1 279	176
		MATHEMATICS & COMPUTER SCIENCE	129	9	—	—	—	—	129	9
		MEDICAL AND HEALTH-RELATED SC.	4 926	2 460	3 063	2 081	—	—	1 863	379
		ENGINEERING	9 342	971	5 586	921	1 888	—	1 868	50
		ARCHITECTURE & TOWN PLANNING	./.	./.	./.	./.	./.	./.	./.	./.
		TRADE, CRAFT & INDUSTR. PGMS.	1 008	1	1 008	1	—	—	—	—
		TRANSPORT AND COMMUNICATIONS	1 181	183	500	55	209	33	472	95
		AGRICULTURE,FORESTRY & FISH'G.	1 273	504	704	230	—	—	569	274
		OTHER AND NOT SPECIFIED								
NORWAY ‡	1975	TOTAL	22 822	10 820	14 674	7 880	8 148	2 940	./.	./.
		EDUCATION SCIENCE & TCHR TRNG.	7 085	4 102	2 877	1 938	4 208	2 164	./.	./.
		HUMANITIES,RELIGION & THEOLOG	2 159	1 127	1 247	759	912	368	./.	./.
		FINE AND APPLIED ARTS.	195	106	127	78	68	28	./.	./.
		LAW	287	42	—	—	287	42	./.	./.
		SOCIAL AND BEHAVIOURAL SCIENCE	1 097	503	812	437	285	66	./.	./.
		COMMERCIAL & BUS. ADMINISTR.	2 814	1 133	2 223	1 081	591	52	./.	./.
		MASS COMMUNICATION & DOCUMENT.	51	19	36	6	15	13	./.	./.
		HOME ECONOMICS & DOMESTIC SC.	15	13	15	13	—	—	./.	./.
		SERVICE TRADES	—	—	—	—	—	—	./.	./.
		NATURAL SCIENCE	19	5	19	5	—	—	./.	./.
		MATHEMATICS & COMPUTER SCIENCE	41	17	36	16	5	1	./.	./.
		MEDICAL AND HEALTH-RELATED SC.	2 545	1 870	1 981	1 759	564	111	./.	./.
		ENGINEERING	2 875	299	2 116	256	759	43	./.	./.
		ARCHITECTURE & TOWN PLANNING	137	17	60	2	77	15	./.	./.
		TRADE, CRAFT & INDUSTR. PGMS.	32	8	32	8	—	—	./.	./.
		TRANSPORT AND COMMUNICATIONS	425	29	425	29	—	—	./.	./.
		AGRICULTURE,FORESTRY & FISH'G.	185	29	3	—	182	29	./.	./.
		OTHER AND NOT SPECIFIED	2 860	1 501	2 665	1 493	195	8	./.	./.

Third level: graduates by levels and fields 3.13
Troisième degré: diplômés par niveaux et domaines d'études
Tercer grado: diplomados por niveles y sectores de estudio

INTERNATIONAL STANDARD CLASSIFICATION OF EDUCATION BY LEVEL
CLASSIFICATION INTERNATIONALE TYPE DE L'EDUCATION PAR NIVEAUX
CLASIFICACION INTERNACIONAL NORMALIZADA DE LA EDUCACION POR GRADOS

COUNTRY / PAYS / PAIS	YEAR / ANNEE / AÑO	FIELD OF STUDY / BRANCHE D'ETUDES / RAMAS DE ESTUDIO	ALL LEVELS TOUS NIVEAUX TODOS LOS GRADOS		LEVEL 5 NIVEAU 5 GRADO 5		LEVEL 6 NIVEAU 6 GRADO 6		LEVEL 7 NIVEAU 7 GRADO 7	
			MF	F	MF	F	MF	F	MF	F
POLAND	1976	TOTAL	137 054	86 495	51 207	40 370	14 969	4 898	70 878	41 227
		EDUCATION SCIENCE & TCHR TRNG.	24 075	19 399	7 653	7 380	465	380	15 957	11 639
		HUMANITIES,RELIGION & THEOLOG	9 258	6 885	68	44	—	—	9 258	6 885
		FINE AND APPLIED ARTS.	1 206	643	—	—	23	6	1 115	593
		LAW	2 341	1 032	—	—	—	—	2 341	1 032
		SOCIAL AND BEHAVIOURAL SCIENCE	2 234	1 373	—	—	109	31	2 125	1 342
		COMMERCIAL & BUS. ADMINISTR.	28 954	21 032	15 101	13 030	5 179	2 642	8 674	5 360
		MASS COMMUNICATION & DOCUMENT.	284	244	—	—	—	—	284	244
		HOME ECONOMICS & DOMESTIC SC.	—	—	—	—	—	—	—	—
		SERVICE TRADES	—	—	—	—	—	—	—	—
		NATURAL SCIENCE	4 742	3 227	—	—	26	18	4 716	3 209
		MATHEMATICS & COMPUTER SCIENCE	2 037	1 252	—	—	—	—	2 037	1 252
		MEDICAL AND HEALTH-RELATED SC.	17 769	15 248	13 161	12 338	—	—	4 608	2 910
		ENGINEERING	32 863	11 267	14 165	7 182	7 263	1 064	11 435	3 021
		ARCHITECTURE & TOWN PLANNING	339	166	—	—	—	—	339	166
		TRADE, CRAFT & INDUSTR. PGMS.	—	—	—	—	—	—	—	—
		TRANSPORT AND COMMUNICATIONS	438	51	—	—	311	28	127	23
		AGRICULTURE,FORESTRY & FISH'G.	7 595	3 479	1 059	396	1 593	729	4 943	2 354
		OTHER AND NOT SPECIFIED	2 919	1 197	—	—	—	—	2 919	1 197
PORTUGAL ‡	1977	TOTAL	15 609	7 328	—	—	15 580	7 328	29	—
		EDUCATION SCIENCE & TCHR TRNG.	2 981	2 028	—	—	2 981	2 028	—	—
		HUMANITIES,RELIGION & THEOLOG	2 733	1 743	—	—	2 733	1 743	—	—
		FINE AND APPLIED ARTS.	396	219	—	—	396	219	—	—
		LAW	751	188	—	—	751	188	—	—
		SOCIAL AND BEHAVIOURAL SCIENCE	1 992	798	—	—	1 992	798	—	—
		COMMERCIAL & BUS. ADMINISTR.	./.	./.	—	—	./.	./.	—	—
		MASS COMMUNICATION & DOCUMENT.	./.	./.	—	—	./.	./.	—	—
		HOME ECONOMICS & DOMESTIC SC.	./.	./.	—	—	./.	./.	—	—
		SERVICE TRADES	./.	./.	—	—	./.	./.	—	—
		NATURAL SCIENCE	371	310	—	—	371	310	—	—
		MATHEMATICS & COMPUTER SCIENCE	286	243	—	—	286	243	—	—
		MEDICAL AND HEALTH-RELATED SC.	2 687	1 401	—	—	2 687	1 401	—	—
		ENGINEERING	2 622	312	—	—	2 622	312	—	—
		ARCHITECTURE & TOWN PLANNING	./.	./.	—	—	./.	./.	—	—
		TRADE, CRAFT & INDUSTR. PGMS.	./.	./.	—	—	./.	./.	—	—
		TRANSPORT AND COMMUNICATIONS	./.	./.	—	—	./.	./.	—	—
		AGRICULTURE,FORESTRY & FISH'G.	551	86	—	—	551	86	—	—
		OTHER AND NOT SPECIFIED	239	—	—	—	210	—	29	—

3.13 Third level: graduates by levels and fields
Troisième degré: diplômés par niveaux et domaines d'études
Tercer grado: diplomados por niveles y sectores de estudio

INTERNATIONAL STANDARD CLASSIFICATION OF EDUCATION BY LEVEL
CLASSIFICATION INTERNATIONALE TYPE DE L'EDUCATION PAR NIVEAUX
CLASIFICACION INTERNACIONAL NORMALIZADA DE LA EDUCACION POR GRADOS

COUNTRY / PAYS / PAIS	YEAR / ANNEE / AÑO	FIELD OF STUDY / BRANCHE D'ETUDES / RAMAS DE ESTUDIO	ALL LEVELS TOUS NIVEAUX TODOS LOS GRADOS		LEVEL 5 NIVEAU 5 GRADO 5		LEVEL 6 NIVEAU 6 GRADO 6		LEVEL 7 NIVEAU 7 GRADO 7	
			MF	F	MF	F	MF	F	MF	F
SPAIN ‡	1976	TOTAL	55 948	24 025	521	—	22 530	11 283	32 897	12 742
		EDUCATION SCIENCE & TCHR TRNG.	17 297	11 210	—	—	15 959	10 488	1 338	722
		HUMANITIES,RELIGION & THEOLOG	6 676	4 011	—	—	—	—	6 676	4 011
		FINE AND APPLIED ARTS.	987	492	—	—	462	272	525	220
		LAW	3 477	1 052	—	—	—	—	3 477	1 052
		SOCIAL AND BEHAVIOURAL SCIENCE	5 300	2 221	—	—	—	—	5 300	2 221
		COMMERCIAL & BUS. ADMINISTR.	1 223	306	—	—	1 223	306	—	—
		MASS COMMUNICATION & DOCUMENT.	629	186	—	—	—	—	629	186
		HOME ECONOMICS & DOMESTIC SC.	—	—	—	—	—	—	—	—
		SERVICE TRADES	—	—	—	—	—	—	—	—
		NATURAL SCIENCE	4 302	1 609	—	—	—	—	4 302	1 609
		MATHEMATICS & COMPUTER SCIENCE	269	90	—	—	—	—	269	90
		MEDICAL AND HEALTH-RELATED SC.	6 237	2 463	—	—	—	—	6 237	2 463
		ENGINEERING	4 780	118	—	—	3 146	99	1 634	19
		ARCHITECTURE & TOWN PLANNING	2 352	158	—	—	1 310	78	1 042	80
		TRADE, CRAFT & INDUSTR. PGMS.	—	—	—	—	—	—	—	—
		TRANSPORT AND COMMUNICATIONS	—	—	—	—	—	—	—	—
		AGRICULTURE,FORESTRY & FISH'G.	991	109	—	—	430	40	561	69
		OTHER AND NOT SPECIFIED	1 428	—	521	—	—	—	907	—
SWEDEN ‡	1976	TOTAL	35 837	18 111	17 398	9 529	17 618	8 371	821	211
		EDUCATION SCIENCE & TCHR TRNG.	9 623	7 189	5 010	3 929	4 613	3 260	—	—
		HUMANITIES,RELIGION & THEOLOG	1 406	811	107	88	1 200	699	99	24
		FINE AND APPLIED ARTS.	537	251	265	108	271	143	1	—
		LAW	747	188	—	—	743	186	4	2
		SOCIAL AND BEHAVIOURAL SCIENCE	4 151	1 349	666	38	3 233	1 200	252	111
		COMMERCIAL & BUS. ADMINISTR.	./.	./.	./.	./.	./.	./.	./.	./.
		MASS COMMUNICATION & DOCUMENT.	536	368	41	34	495	334	—	—
		HOME ECONOMICS & DOMESTIC SC.	80	75	80	75	—	—	—	—
		SERVICE TRADES	—	—	—	—	—	—	—	—
		NATURAL SCIENCE	884	280	—	—	686	239	198	41
		MATHEMATICS & COMPUTER SCIENCE	./.	./.	./.	./.	./.	./.	./.	./.
		MEDICAL AND HEALTH-RELATED SC.	8 511	6 175	5 593	5 011	2 720	1 135	198	29
		ENGINEERING	6 045	364	4 201	203	1 796	157	48	4
		ARCHITECTURE & TOWN PLANNING	166	50	—	—	156	50	10	—
		TRADE, CRAFT & INDUSTR. PGMS.	—	—	—	—	—	—	—	—
		TRANSPORT AND COMMUNICATIONS	280	11	280	11	—	—	—	—
		AGRICULTURE,FORESTRY & FISH'G.	521	89	298	16	212	73	11	—
		OTHER AND NOT SPECIFIED	2 350	911	857	16	1 493	895	—	—

Third level: graduates by levels and fields   3.13
Troisième degré: diplômés par niveaux et domaines d'études
Tercer grado: diplomados por niveles y sectores de estudio

INTERNATIONAL STANDARD CLASSIFICATION OF EDUCATION BY LEVEL
CLASSIFICATION INTERNATIONALE TYPE DE L'EDUCATION PAR NIVEAUX
CLASIFICACION INTERNACIONAL NORMALIZADA DE LA EDUCACION POR GRADOS

COUNTRY / PAYS / PAIS	YEAR / ANNEE / AÑO	FIELD OF STUDY / BRANCHE D'ETUDES / RAMAS DE ESTUDIO	ALL LEVELS TOUS NIVEAUX TODOS LOS GRADOS		LEVEL 5 NIVEAU 5 GRADO 5		LEVEL 6 NIVEAU 6 GRADO 6		LEVEL 7 NIVEAU 7 GRADO 7	
			MF	F	MF	F	MF	F	MF	F
SWITZERLAND ‡	1976	TOTAL	7 504	1 603	—	—	5 823	1 393	1 681	210
		EDUCATION SCIENCE & TCHR TRNG.	776	312	—	—	769	311	7	1
		HUMANITIES,RELIGION & THEOLOG	1 009	390	—	—	781	352	228	38
		FINE AND APPLIED ARTS.	160	22	—	—	154	22	6	—
		LAW	861	136	—	—	743	127	118	9
		SOCIAL AND BEHAVIOURAL SCIENCE	1 080	151	—	—	929	149	151	2
		NATURAL SCIENCE	1 147	210	—	—	767	170	380	40
		MEDICAL AND HEALTH-RELATED SC.	1 705	347	—	—	1 072	233	633	114
		ENGINEERING	540	17	—	—	427	16	113	1
		AGRICULTURE,FORESTRY & FISH'G.	226	18	—	—	181	13	45	5
		OTHER AND NOT SPECIFIED	—	—	—	—	—	—	—	—
YUGOSLAVIA ‡	1976	TOTAL	50 934	22 595	22 072	10 557	26 270	11 412	2 592	626
		EDUCATION SCIENCE & TCHR TRNG.	8 387	5 260	7 512	5 006	846	252	29	2
		HUMANITIES,RELIGION & THEOLOG	3 580	2 375	66	61	3 246	2 222	268	92
		FINE AND APPLIED ARTS.	690	285	73	33	560	229	57	23
		LAW	4 149	1 934	351	167	3 700	1 750	98	17
		SOCIAL AND BEHAVIOURAL SCIENCE	9 827	4 753	4 667	2 503	4 768	2 209	392	41
		COMMERCIAL & BUS. ADMINISTR.	2 143	568	1 376	308	759	260	8	—
		MASS COMMUNICATION & DOCUMENT.	—	—	—	—	—	—	—	—
		HOME ECONOMICS & DOMESTIC SC.	117	96	117	96	—	—	—	—
		SERVICE TRADES	515	245	409	189	106	56	—	—
		NATURAL SCIENCE	2 076	1 153	155	90	1 667	949	254	114
		MATHEMATICS & COMPUTER SCIENCE	.../.	.../.	.../.	.../.	—	—	.../.	.../.
		MEDICAL AND HEALTH-RELATED SC.	4 404	2 700	1 103	844	2 943	1 756	358	100
		ENGINEERING	8 870	1 462	2 759	319	5 498	1 031	613	112
		ARCHITECTURE & TOWN PLANNING	651	320	—	—	594	303	57	17
		TRADE, CRAFT & INDUSTR. PGMS.	552	231	552	231	—	—	—	—
		TRANSPORT AND COMMUNICATIONS	672	246	498	231	174	15	—	—
		AGRICULTURE,FORESTRY & FISH'G.	2 046	480	362	62	1 409	380	275	38
		OTHER AND NOT SPECIFIED	1 255	487	1 072	417	—	—	183	70

3.13 Third level: graduates by levels and fields
Troisième degré: diplômés par niveaux et domaines d'études
Tercer grado: diplomados por niveles y sectores de estudio

INTERNATIONAL STANDARD CLASSIFICATION OF EDUCATION BY LEVEL
CLASSIFICATION INTERNATIONALE TYPE DE L'EDUCATION PAR NIVEAUX
CLASIFICACION INTERNACIONAL NORMALIZADA DE LA EDUCACION POR GRADOS

COUNTRY / PAYS / PAIS	YEAR / ANNEE / AÑO	FIELD OF STUDY / BRANCHE D'ETUDES / RAMAS DE ESTUDIO	ALL LEVELS / TOUS NIVEAUX / TODOS LOS GRADOS MF	F	LEVEL 5 / NIVEAU 5 / GRADO 5 MF	F	LEVEL 6 / NIVEAU 6 / GRADO 6 MF	F	LEVEL 7 / NIVEAU 7 / GRADO 7 MF	F
OCEANIA										
AMERICAN SAMOA	1977	TOTAL	97	51	97	51	—	—	—	—
		EDUCATION SCIENCE & TCHR TRNG.	—	—	—	—	—	—	—	—
		HUMANITIES,RELIGION & THEOLOG	—	—	—	—	—	—	—	—
		FINE AND APPLIED ARTS.	—	—	—	—	—	—	—	—
		LAW	—	—	—	—	—	—	—	—
		SOCIAL AND BEHAVIOURAL SCIENCE	—	—	—	—	—	—	—	—
		COMMERCIAL & BUS. ADMINISTR.	—	—	—	—	—	—	—	—
		MASS COMMUNICATION & DOCUMENT.	—	—	—	—	—	—	—	—
		HOME ECONOMICS & DOMESTIC SC.	—	—	—	—	—	—	—	—
		SERVICE TRADES	—	—	—	—	—	—	—	—
		NATURAL SCIENCE	—	—	—	—	—	—	—	—
		MATHEMATICS & COMPUTER SCIENCE	—	—	—	—	—	—	—	—
		MEDICAL AND HEALTH-RELATED SC.	—	—	—	—	—	—	—	—
		ENGINEERING	—	—	—	—	—	—	—	—
		ARCHITECTURE & TOWN PLANNING	—	—	—	—	—	—	—	—
		TRADE, CRAFT & INDUSTR. PGMS.	—	—	—	—	—	—	—	—
		TRANSPORT AND COMMUNICATIONS	—	—	—	—	—	—	—	—
		AGRICULTURE,FORESTRY & FISH'G.	—	—	—	—	—	—	—	—
		OTHER AND NOT SPECIFIED	97	51	97	51	—	—	—	—
AUSTRALIA	1977	TOTAL	59 718	...	19 844	...	28 625	...	11 249	...
		EDUCATION SCIENCE & TCHR TRNG.	23 313	...	14 706	...	1 625	...	6 982	...
		HUMANITIES,RELIGION & THEOLOG	7 966	...	21	...	7 677	...	268	...
		FINE AND APPLIED ARTS.	940	...	762	...	127	...	51	...
		LAW	1 499	...	30	...	1 331	...	138	...
		SOCIAL AND BEHAVIOURAL SCIENCE	4 690	...	161	...	3 975	...	554	...
		COMMERCIAL & BUS. ADMINISTR.	2 972	...	1 125	...	1 235	...	612	...
		MASS COMMUNICATION & DOCUMENT.	465	...	54	...	—	...	411	...
		HOME ECONOMICS & DOMESTIC SC.	91	...	91	...	—	...	—	...
		SERVICE TRADES	16	...	16	...	—	...	—	...
		NATURAL SCIENCE	5 585	...	238	...	4 813	...	534	...
		MATHEMATICS & COMPUTER SCIENCE	870	...	59	...	559	...	252	...
		MEDICAL AND HEALTH-RELATED SC.	3 741	...	895	...	2 462	...	384	...
		ENGINEERING	3 919	...	812	...	2 685	...	422	...
		ARCHITECTURE & TOWN PLANNING	963	...	147	...	643	...	173	...
		TRADE, CRAFT & INDUSTR. PGMS.	157	...	130	...	13	...	14	...
		TRANSPORT AND COMMUNICATIONS	1	...	1	...	—	...	—	...
		AGRICULTURE,FORESTRY & FISH'G.	1 236	...	386	...	570	...	280	...
		OTHER AND NOT SPECIFIED	1 294	...	211	...	910	...	173	...

Third level: graduates by levels and fields   3.13
Troisième degré: diplômés par niveaux et domaines d'études
Tercer grado: diplomados por niveles y sectores de estudio

INTERNATIONAL STANDARD CLASSIFICATION OF EDUCATION BY LEVEL
CLASSIFICATION INTERNATIONALE TYPE DE L'EDUCATION PAR NIVEAUX
CLASIFICACION INTERNACIONAL NORMALIZADA DE LA EDUCACION POR GRADOS

COUNTRY / PAYS / PAIS	YEAR / ANNEE / AÑO	FIELD OF STUDY / BRANCHE D'ETUDES / RAMAS DE ESTUDIO	ALL LEVELS TOUS NIVEAUX TODOS LOS GRADOS		LEVEL 5 NIVEAU 5 GRADO 5		LEVEL 6 NIVEAU 6 GRADO 6		LEVEL 7 NIVEAU 7 GRADO 7	
			MF	F	MF	F	MF	F	MF	F
GUAM	1976	TOTAL	310	166	64	22	191	108	55	36
		EDUCATION SCIENCE & TCHR TRNG.	102	80	—	—	68	54	34	26
		HUMANITIES,RELIGION & THEOLOG	9	4	—	—	7	4	2	—
		FINE AND APPLIED ARTS.	6	1	—	—	4	1	2	—
		LAW	—	—	—	—	—	—	—	—
		SOCIAL AND BEHAVIOURAL SCIENCE	37	18	—	—	30	11	7	7
		COMMERCIAL & BUS. ADMINISTR.	59	29	—	—	55	28	4	1
		MASS COMMUNICATION & DOCUMENT.	1	—	—	—	1	—	—	—
		HOME ECONOMICS & DOMESTIC SC.	—	—	—	—	—	—	—	—
		SERVICE TRADES	—	—	—	—	—	—	—	—
		NATURAL SCIENCE	10	6	—	—	5	4	5	2
		MATHEMATICS & COMPUTER SCIENCE	9	3	—	—	9	3	—	—
		MEDICAL AND HEALTH-RELATED SC.	—	—	—	—	—	—	—	—
		ENGINEERING	—	—	—	—	—	—	—	—
		ARCHITECTURE & TOWN PLANNING	—	—	—	—	—	—	—	—
		TRADE, CRAFT & INDUSTR. PGMS.	—	—	—	—	—	—	—	—
		TRANSPORT AND COMMUNICATIONS	—	—	—	—	—	—	—	—
		AGRICULTURE,FORESTRY & FISH'G.	—	—	—	—	—	—	—	—
		OTHER AND NOT SPECIFIED	77	25	64	22	12	3	1	—
NEW ZEALAND ‡	1976	TOTAL	7 227	2 326	761	221	5 009	1 714	1 457	391
		EDUCATION SCIENCE & TCHR TRNG.	414	193	145	76	120	63	149	54
		HUMANITIES,RELIGION & THEOLOG	2 301	1 187	1	1	1 695	974	605	212
		FINE AND APPLIED ARTS.	122	63	58	26	55	31	9	6
		LAW	375	73	—	—	351	71	24	2
		SOCIAL AND BEHAVIOURAL SCIENCE	115	46	—	—	80	38	35	8
		COMMERCIAL & BUS. ADMINISTR.	647	93	—	—	586	87	61	6
		MASS COMMUNICATION & DOCUMENT.	13	4	—	—	—	—	13	4
		HOME ECONOMICS & DOMESTIC SC.	61	61	34	34	26	26	1	1
		SERVICE TRADES	—	—	—	—	—	—	—	—
		NATURAL SCIENCE	1 438	388	—	—	1 149	323	289	65
		MATHEMATICS & COMPUTER SCIENCE	7	2	4	1	—	—	3	1
		MEDICAL AND HEALTH-RELATED SC.	371	67	15	6	246	48	110	13
		ENGINEERING	517	19	33	1	440	18	44	—
		ARCHITECTURE & TOWN PLANNING	106	18	20	5	52	7	34	6
		TRADE, CRAFT & INDUSTR. PGMS.	—	—	—	—	—	—	—	—
		TRANSPORT AND COMMUNICATIONS	—	—	—	—	—	—	—	—
		AGRICULTURE,FORESTRY & FISH'G.	626	65	363	35	209	28	54	2
		OTHER AND NOT SPECIFIED	114	47	88	36	—	—	26	11

3.13 Third level: graduates by levels and fields
Troisième degré: diplômés par niveaux et domaines d'études
Tercer grado: diplomados por niveles y sectores de estudio

INTERNATIONAL STANDARD CLASSIFICATION OF EDUCATION BY LEVEL
CLASSIFICATION INTERNATIONALE TYPE DE L'EDUCATION PAR NIVEAUX
CLASIFICACION INTERNACIONAL NORMALIZADA DE LA EDUCACION POR GRADOS

COUNTRY / PAYS / PAIS	YEAR / ANNEE / AÑO	FIELD OF STUDY / BRANCHE D'ETUDES / RAMAS DE ESTUDIO	ALL LEVELS TOUS NIVEAUX TODOS LOS GRADOS MF	F	LEVEL 5 NIVEAU 5 GRADO 5 MF	F	LEVEL 6 NIVEAU 6 GRADO 6 MF	F	LEVEL 7 NIVEAU 7 GRADO 7 MF	F
PACIFIC ISLANDS	1977	TOTAL	248	...	101	...	147	...	—	—
		EDUCATION SCIENCE & TCHR TRNG.	112	...	—	—	112	...	—	—
		HUMANITIES,RELIGION & THEOLOG.	—	—	—	—	—	—	—	—
		FINE AND APPLIED ARTS.	—	—	—	—	—	—	—	—
		LAW	—	—	—	—	—	—	—	—
		SOCIAL AND BEHAVIOURAL SCIENCE	—	—	—	—	—	—	—	—
		COMMERCIAL & BUS. ADMINISTR.	—	—	—	—	—	—	—	—
		MASS COMMUNICATION & DOCUMENT.	—	—	—	—	—	—	—	—
		HOME ECONOMICS & DOMESTIC SC.	—	—	—	—	—	—	—	—
		SERVICE TRADES	—	—	—	—	—	—	—	—
		NATURAL SCIENCE	35	...	—	—	35	...	—	—
		MATHEMATICS & COMPUTER SCIENCE	—	—	—	—	—	—	—	—
		MEDICAL AND HEALTH-RELATED SC.	101	...	101	...	—	—	—	—
		ENGINEERING	—	—	—	—	—	—	—	—
		ARCHITECTURE & TOWN PLANNING	—	—	—	—	—	—	—	—
		TRADE, CRAFT & INDUSTR. PGMS.	—	—	—	—	—	—	—	—
		TRANSPORT AND COMMUNICATIONS	—	—	—	—	—	—	—	—
		AGRICULTURE,FORESTRY & FISH'G.	—	—	—	—	—	—	—	—
		OTHER AND NOT SPECIFIED	—	—	—	—	—	—	—	—
PAPUA NEW GUINEA	1977	TOTAL	414	...	106	...	303	...	5	...
		EDUCATION SCIENCE & TCHR TRNG.	52	...	35	...	17	...	—	—
		HUMANITIES,RELIGION & THEOLOG.	100	...	—	—	100	...	—	—
		FINE AND APPLIED ARTS.	—	—	—	—	—	—	—	—
		LAW	23	...	—	—	23	...	—	—
		SOCIAL AND BEHAVIOURAL SCIENCE	31	...	3	...	28	...	—	—
		COMMERCIAL & BUS. ADMINISTR.	58	...	9	...	49	...	—	—
		MASS COMMUNICATION & DOCUMENT.	17	...	17	...	—	—	—	—
		HOME ECONOMICS & DOMESTIC SC.	—	—	—	—	—	—	—	—
		SERVICE TRADES	—	—	—	—	—	—	—	—
		NATURAL SCIENCE	16	...	—	—	16	...	—	—
		MATHEMATICS & COMPUTER SCIENCE	—	—	—	—	—	—	—	—
		MEDICAL AND HEALTH-RELATED SC.	20	...	—	—	15	...	5	...
		ENGINEERING	41	...	17	...	24	...	—	—
		ARCHITECTURE & TOWN PLANNING	26	...	22	...	4	...	—	—
		TRADE, CRAFT & INDUSTR. PGMS.	—	—	—	—	—	—	—	—
		TRANSPORT AND COMMUNICATIONS	—	—	—	—	—	—	—	—
		AGRICULTURE,FORESTRY & FISH'G.	27	...	—	—	27	...	—	—
		OTHER AND NOT SPECIFIED	3	...	3	...	—	—	—	—

Third level: graduates by levels and fields 3.13
Troisième degré: diplômés par niveaux et domaines d'études
Tercer grado: diplomados por niveles y sectores de estudio

INTERNATIONAL STANDARD CLASSIFICATION OF EDUCATION BY LEVEL
CLASSIFICATION INTERNATIONALE TYPE DE L'EDUCATION PAR NIVEAUX
CLASIFICACION INTERNACIONAL NORMALIZADA DE LA EDUCACION POR GRADOS

COUNTRY / PAYS / PAIS	YEAR / ANNEE / AÑO	FIELD OF STUDY / BRANCHE D'ETUDES / RAMAS DE ESTUDIO	ALL LEVELS TOUS NIVEAUX TODOS LOS GRADOS MF	F	LEVEL 5 NIVEAU 5 GRADO 5 MF	F	LEVEL 6 NIVEAU 6 GRADO 6 MF	F	LEVEL 7 NIVEAU 7 GRADO 7 MF	F
U.S.S.R.										
U.S.S.R. ‡	1976	TOTAL	751 900	...		...		...		
		EDUCATION SCIENCE & TCHR TRNG.	243 100	...		...		...		
		FINE AND APPLIED ARTS.	8 100	...		...		...		
		LAW	61 100	...		...		...		
		MEDICAL AND HEALTH-RELATED SC.	56 000	...		...		...		
		ENGINEERING	316 500	...		...		...		
		TRANSPORT AND COMMUNICATIONS	./.	./.		./.		./.		
		AGRICULTURE,FORESTRY & FISH'G.	67 100	...		...		...		
		OTHER AND NOT SPECIFIED	—	—		—		—		
BYELORUSSIAN S.S.R. ‡	1976	TOTAL	26 783	...		...		...		
		EDUCATION SCIENCE & TCHR TRNG.	9 810	...		...		...		
		FINE AND APPLIED ARTS.	299	...		...		...		
		LAW	2 216	...		...		...		
		MEDICAL AND HEALTH-RELATED SC.	1 907	...		...		...		
		ENGINEERING	9 279	...		...		...		
		TRANSPORT AND COMMUNICATIONS	./.	./.		./.		./.		
		AGRICULTURE,FORESTRY & FISH'G.	3 272	...		...		...		
		OTHER AND NOT SPECIFIED	—	—		—		—		
UKRAINIAN S.S.R. ‡	1976	TOTAL	137 200	...		...		...		
		EDUCATION SCIENCE & TCHR TRNG.	37 900	...		...		...		
		FINE AND APPLIED ARTS.	1 200	...		...		...		
		LAW	11 600	...		...		...		
		MEDICAL AND HEALTH-RELATED SC.	9 500	...		...		...		
		ENGINEERING	65 300	...		...		...		
		TRANSPORT AND COMMUNICATIONS	./.	./.		./.		./.		
		AGRICULTURE,FORESTRY & FISH'G.	11 700	...		...		...		
		OTHER AND NOT SPECIFIED	—	—		—		—		

3.13 Third level: graduates by levels and fields
Troisième degré: diplômés par niveaux et domaines d'études
Tercer grado: diplomados por niveles y sectores de estudio

EGYPT:
E—> NATURAL SCIENCES INCLUDE MATHEMATICS AND
COMPUTER SCIENCE.
FR-> LES SCIENCES EXACTES ET NATURELLES COMPREN-
NENT LES MATHEMATIQUES ET L'INFORMATIQUE.
ESP> LAS CIENCIAS NATURALES COMPRENDEN LAS
MATEMATICAS Y LA INFORMATICA.

IVORY COAST:
E—> NATURAL SCIENCES INCLUDE MATHEMATICS AND
COMPUTER SCIENCE.
FR-> LES SCIENCES EXACTES ET NATURELLES COMPREN-
NENT LES MATHEMATIQUES ET L'INFORMATIQUE.
ESP> LAS CIENCIAS NATURALES COMPRENDEN LAS
MATEMATICAS Y LA INFORMATICA.

MOROCCO:
E—> UNIVERSITIES AND EQUIVALENT INSTITUTIONS
ONLY. NATURAL SCIENCES INCLUDE MATHEMATICS AND
COMPUTER SCIENCE.
FR-> UNIVERSITES ET ETABLISSEMENTS EQUIVALENTS
SEULEMENT. LES SCIENCES EXACTES ET NATURELLES
COMPRENNENT LES MATHEMATIQUES ET L'INFORMATIQUE.
ESP> UNIVERSIDADES Y ESTABLECIMIENTOS EQUIVALEN-
TES SOLAMENTE. LAS CIENCIAS NATURALES COMPRENDEN
LAS MATEMATICAS Y LA INFORMATICA.

REUNION:
E—> NATURAL SCIENCES INCLUDE MATHEMATICS AND
COMPUTER SCIENCE.
FR-> LES SCIENCES EXACTES ET NATURELLES COMPREN-
NENT LES MATHEMATIQUES ET L'INFORMATIQUE.
ESP> LAS CIENCIAS NATURALES COMPRENDEN LAS
MATEMATICAS Y LA INFORMATICA.

TUNISIA:
E—> NATURAL SCIENCES INCLUDE MATHEMATICS AND
COMPUTER SCIENCE.
FR-> LES SCIENCES EXACTES ET NATURELLES COMPREN-
NENT LES MATHEMATIQUES ET L'INFORMATIQUE.
ESP> LAS CIENCIAS NATURALES COMPRENDEN LAS
MATEMATICAS Y LA INFORMATICA.

UGANDA:
E—> UNIVERSITIES AND EQUIVALENT INSTITUTIONS
ONLY.
FR-> UNIVERSITES ET ETABLISSEMENTS EQUIVALENTS
SEULEMENT.
ESP> UNIVERSIDADES Y ESTABLECIMIENTOS EQUIVA-
LENTES SOLAMENTE.

UNITED REPUBLIC OF CAMEROON:
E—> EDUCATION INCLUDES HUMANITIES,
RELIGION AND THEOLOGY. NATURAL SCIENCES INCLUDE
MATHEMATICS AND COMPUTER SCIENCE. ENGINEERING
INCLUDES ARCHITECTURE AND TOWN PLANNING, TRADE,
CRAFT AND INDUSTRIAL PROGRAMMES AND TRANSPORT
AND COMMUNICATIONS.
FR-> L'EDUCATION COMPREND LES LETTRES, LA
RELIGION ET LA THEOLOGIE. LES SCIENCES EXACTES
ET NATURELLES COMPRENNENT EGALEMENT LES
MATHEMATIQUES ET L'INFORMATIQUE. LES SCIENCES
DE L'INGENIEUR COMPRENNENT L'ARCHITECTURE
ET L'URBANISME, LES METIERS DE LA PRODUCTION

UNITED REPUBLIC OF CAMEROON (CONT.):
INDUSTRIELLE ET LES TRANSPORTS ET LES TELECOMMUNI-
CATIONS.
ESP> LA EDUCACION COMPRENDE LAS HUMANIDADES,
LA RELIGION Y LA TEOLOGIA. LAS CIENCIAS
NATURALES COMPRENDEN LAS MATEMATICAS Y LA INFOR-
MATICA. LA INGENIERIA Y TECNOLOGIA COMPRENDE
LA ARQUITECTURA Y EL URBANISMO, LAS ARTES Y
OFICIOS INDUSTRIALES Y LOS TRANSPORTES Y
COMUNICACIONES.

UNITED REPUBLIC OF TANZANIA:
E—> SOCIAL AND BEHAVIOURAL SCIENCES INCLUDE
HUMANITIES, RELIGION AND THEOLOGY.
FR-> LES SCIENCES SOCIALES ET LES SCIENCES DU
COMPORTEMENT COMPRENNENT LES LETTRES, LA
RELIGION ET LA THEOLOGIE.
ESP> LAS CIENCIAS SOCIALES Y DEL COMPORTAMIENTO
COMPRENDEN LAS HUMANIDADES, LA RELIGION Y LA
TEOLOGIA.

ZAMBIA:
E—> UNIVERSITY OF ZAMBIA ONLY. HUMANITIES,
RELIGION AND THEOLOGY INCLUDE SOCIAL AND
BEHAVIOURAL SCIENCES.
FR-> UNIVERSITE DE ZAMBIE SEULEMENT. LES
LETTRES, LA RELIGION ET LA THEOLOGIE COMPRENNENT
LES SCIENCES SOCIALES ET LES SCIENCES DU
COMPORTEMENT.
ESP> UNIVERSIDAD DE ZAMBIA SOLAMENTE. LAS
HUMANIDADES, LA RELIGION Y LA TEOLOGIA COMPREN-
DEN LAS CIENCIAS SOCIALES Y DEL COMPORTAMIENTO.

CANADA:
E—> UNIVERSITIES AND EQUIVALENT INSTITUTIONS
ONLY.
FR-> UNIVERSITES ET ETABLISSEMENTS EQUIVALENTS
SEULEMENT.
ESP> UNIVERSIDADES Y ESTABLECIMIENTOS EQUIVA-
LENTES SOLAMENTE.

COSTA RICA:
E—> UNIVERSITY OF COSTA RICA ONLY.
FR-> UNIVERSITE DE COSTA RICA SEULEMENT.
ESP> UNIVERSIDAD DE COSTA RICA SOLAMENTE.

DOMINICAN REPUBLIC:
E—> UNIVERSITIES AND EQUIVALENT INSTITUTIONS
ONLY.
FR-> UNIVERSITES ET ETABLISSEMENTS EQUIVA-
LENTES SOLAMENTE.
ESP> UNIVERSIDADES Y ESTABLECIMIENTOS EQUIVA-
LENTES SOLAMENTE.

GUATEMALA:
E—> UNIVERSITY OF SAN CARLOS ONLY.
FR-> UNIVERSITE DE SAN CARLOS SEULEMENT.
ESP> UNIVERSIDAD DE SAN CARLOS SOLAMENTE.

HAITI:
E—> UNIVERSITIES ONLY.
FR-> UNIVERSITES SEULEMENT.
ESP> UNIVERSIDADES SOLAMENTE.

Third level: graduates by levels and fields 3.13
Troisième degré: diplômés par niveaux et domaines d'études
Tercer grado: diplomados por niveles y sectores de estudio

HONDURAS:
E—> UNIVERSITY OF HONDURAS ONLY.
FR—> UNIVERSITE DE HONDURAS SEULEMENT.
ESP> UNIVERSIDAD DE HONDURAS SOLAMENTE.

JAMAICA:
E—> UNIVERSITY OF THE WEST INDIES ONLY.
FR—> UNIVERSITE DE "WEST INDIES" SEULEMENT.
ESP> UNIVERSIDAD DE "WEST INDIES" SOLAMENTE.

MEXICO:
E—> UNIVERSITIES ONLY.
FR—> UNIVERSITES SEULEMENT.
ESP> UNIVERSIDADES SOLAMENTE.

PANAMA:
E—> PROGRAMMES OF LEVEL 7 ARE INCLUDED WITH LEVEL 6.
FR—> LES DONNEES RELATIVES AUX PROGRAMMES DU NIVEAU 7 SONT COMPRISES DANS CELLES DU NIVEAU 6.
ESP> LOS DATOS RELATIVOS A LOS PROGRAMAS DE GRADO 7 QUEDAN INCLUIDOS EN LOS DE GRADO 6.

PUERTO RICO:
E—> THE FIGURES UNDER "OTHER AND NOT SPECI-FIED" INCLUDE ASSOCIATE DEGREES FOR WHICH THE DISTRIBUTION BY FIELD OF STUDY IS NOT AVAIL-ABLE; THESE NUMBERED 3 244 (F. 2 136) IN 1976.
FR—> LES CHIFFRES PORTES SOUS LA RUBRIQUE "AUTRES ET NON SPECIFIE" COMPRENNENT DES GRADES D'ASSOCIES POUR LESQUELS LA REPARTITION PAR DISCIPLINE N'EST PAS DISPONIBLE ET DONT LE NOMBRE ETAIT DE 3 244 (F. 2 136) EN 1976.
ESP> LAS CIFRAS QUE FIGURAN EN LA RUBRICA "OTROS Y SIN ESPECIFICAR" COMPRENDEN LOS "ASSOCIATE DEGREES" CUYA REPARTICION POR RAMAS DE ESTUDIO SE DESCONOCE. EN 1976, EL NUMERO DE ALMUNOS ERA DE 3 244 (F. 2 136).

TRINIDAD AND TOBAGO:
E—> UNIVERSITY OF THE WEST INDIES ONLY.
FR—> UNIVERSITE DE "WEST INDIES" SEULEMENT.
ESP> UNIVERSIDAD DE "WEST INDIES" SOLAMENTE.

UNITED STATES OF AMERICA:
E—> THE FIGURES UNDER "OTHER AND NOT SPECI-FIED" INCLUDE ASSOCIATE DEGREES FOR WHICH THE DISTRIBUTION BY FIELD OF STUDY IS NOT AVAIL-ABLE: THESE NUMBERED 503,598 (F. 245,275) IN 1976.
FR—> LES CHIFFRES PORTES SOUS LA RUBRIQUE "AUTRES ET NON SPECIFIE" COMPRENNENT DES GRADES D'ASSOCIES POUR LESQUELS LA REPARTITION PAR DISCIPLINE N'EST PAS DISPONIBLE ET DONT LE NOMBRE ETAIT DE 503 598 (F. 245 275) EN 1976.
ESP> LAS CIFRAS QUE FIGURAN BAJO LA RUBRICA "OTROS Y SIN ESPECIFICAR" COMPRENDEN LOS "ASSOCIATE DEGREES" CUYA DISTRIBUCION POR RAMAS DE ESTUDIO SE DESCONOCE Y CUYO NUMERO ERA DE 503 598 (F. 245 275) EN 1976.

BOLIVIA:
E—> EXCLUDING HIGHER TEACHER TRAINING AT NON-UNIVERSITY INSTITUTIONS.
FR—> COMPTE NON TENU DE L'ENSEIGNEMENT NORMAL NON-UNIVERSITAIRE DU TROISIEME DEGRE.
ESP> NO INCLUYE LA ENSEÑANZA NORMAL NO UNIVER-SITARIA DE TERCER GRADO.

COLOMBIA:
E—> FINE AND APPLIED ARTS INCLUDE ARCHI-TECTURE AND TOWN PLANNING. COMMERCIAL AND BUSI-NESS ADMINISTRATION INCLUDE MASS COMMUNICATION AND DOCUMENTATION. HOME ECONOMICS AND SERVICE TRADES. NATURAL SCIENCES INCLUDE MATHEMATICS AND COMPUTER SCIENCE. ENGINEERING INCLUDES TRADE, CRAFT AND INDUSTRIAL PROGRAMMES, TRANS-PORT AND COMMUNICATIONS.
FR—> LES BEAUX-ARTS ET LES ARTS APPLIQUES COMPRENNENT L'ARCHITECTURE ET L'URBANISME. LA FORMATION AU COMMERCE ET A L'ADMINISTRATION DES ENTREPRISES COMPRENNENT EGALEMENT L'INFORMATION ET LA DOCUMENTATION, L'ENSEIGNE-MENT MENAGER ET LA FORMATION POUR LE SECTEUR TERTIAIRE. LES SCIENCES EXACTES ET NATURELLES COMPRENNENT EGALEMENT LES MATHEMATIQUES ET L'INFORMATIQUE. LES SCIENCES DE L'INGENIEUR COMPRENNENT LES METIERS DE LA PRODUCTION INDUSTRIELLE ET LES TRANSPORTS ET LES TELECOMMUNI-CATIONS.
ESP> LAS BELLAS ARTES Y LAS ARTES APLICADOS COMPRENDEN LA ARQUITECTURA Y EL URBANISMO. LA ENSEÑANZA COMERCIAL Y DE ADMINISTRACION DE EMPRESAS COMPRENDE IGUALMENTE LA DOCUMENTACION Y LA COMUNICACION SOCIAL. LA ECONOMICA DOMESTICA Y LA FORMACION PARA EL SECTOR DE LOS SERVICIOS. LAS CIENCIAS NATURALES INCLUYEN LAS MATEMATICAS Y LA INFORMATICA. LA INGENIERIA Y TECNOLOGIA COMPRENDE LAS ARTES Y OFICIOS INDUSTRIALES Y LOS TRANSPORTS Y COMUNICACIONES.

FRENCH GUIANA:
E—> NATURAL SCIENCES INCLUDE MATHEMATICS AND COMPUTER SCIENCE.
FR—> LES SCIENCES EXACTES ET NATURELLES COMPRENNENT LES MATHEMATIQUES ER L'INFORMATIQUE.
ESP> LAS CIENCIAS NATURALES COMPRENDEN LAS MATEMATICAS Y LA INFORMATICA.

PERU:
E—> EXCLUDING NON-UNIVERSITY TEACHER-TRAIN-ING AT THE THIRD LEVEL.
FR—> COMPTE NON TENU DE L'ENSEIGNEMENT NORMAL NON-UNIVERSITAIRE DU TROISIEME DEGRE.
ESP> NO INCLUYE LA ENSEÑANZA NORMAL NO UNIVERSITARIA DE TERCER GRADO.

VENEZUELA:
E—> UNIVERSITIES AND EQUIVALENT INSTITUTIONS ONLY.
FR—> UNIVERSITES ET ETABLISSEMENTS EQUIVALENTS SEULEMENT.

3.13 Third level: graduates by levels and fields
Troisième degré: diplômés par niveaux et domaines d'études
Tercer grado: diplomados por niveles y sectores de estudio

JAPAN:
E—> HUMANITIES, RELIGION AND THEOLOGY INCLUDE MASS COMMUNICATION AND DOCUMENTATION. SOCIAL AND BEHAVIOURAL SCIENCES INCLUDE LAW, COMMERCIAL AND BUSINESS ADMINISTRATION. ENGINEERING INCLUDES ARCHITECTURE AND TOWN PLANNING, TRADE, CRAFT AND INDUSTRIAL PROGRAMMES.
FR—> LES LETTRES, LA RELIGION ET LA THEOLOGIE COMPRENNENT L'INFORMATION ET LA DOCUMENTATION. LES SCIENCES SOCIALES ET LES SCIENCES DU COMPORTEMENT COMPRENNENT EGALEMENT LE DROIT, LA FORMATION AU COMMERCE ET A L'ADMINISTRATION DES ENTREPRISES. LES SCIENCES DE L'INGENIEUR COMPRENNENT L'ARCHITECTURE ET L'URBANISME ET LES METIERS DE LA PRODUCTION INDUSTRIELLE.
ESP> LAS HUMANIDADES, LA RELIGION Y LA TEOLOGIA COMPRENDEN LA DOCUMENTACION Y COMUNICACION SOCIAL. LAS CIENCIAS SOCIALES Y DEL COMPORTAMIENTO COMPRENDEN IGUALMENTE EL DERECHO, LA ENSEÑANZA COMERCIAL Y DE ADMINISTRACION DE EMPRESAS. LA INGENIERIA Y TECNOLOGIA COMPRENDE LA ARQUITECTURA Y EL URBANISME Y LAS ARTES Y ORICIOS INDUSTRIALES.

JORDAN:
E—> DATA REFER TO THE EAST BANK ONLY.
FR—> LES DONNEES SE REFERENT A LA RIVE ORIENTALE SEULEMENT.
ESP> LOS DATOS SE REFIEREN A LA ORILLA ORIENTAL SOLAMENTE.

NEPAL:
E—> HUMANITIES, RELIGION AND THEOLOGY INCLUDE FINE AND APPLIED ARTS. NATURAL SCIENCES INCLUDE MATHEMATICS AND COMPUTER SCIENCE.
FR—> LES LETTRES, LA RELIGION ET LA THEOLOGIE COMPRENNENT LES BEAUX-ARTS ET LES ARTS APPLIQUES. LES SCIENCES EXACTES ET NATURELLES COMPRENNENT LES MATHEMATIQUES ET L'INFORMATIQUE.
ESP> LAS HUMANIDADES, LA RELIGION Y LA TEOLOGIA COMPRENDEN LAS BELLAS ARTES Y LAS ARTES APLICADAS. LAS CIENCIAS NATURALES INCLUYEN LAS MATEMATICAS Y LA INFORMATICA.

PAKISTAN:
E—> HUMANITIES, RELIGION AND THEOLOGY INCLUDE FINE AND APPLIED ARTS.
FR—> LES LETTRES, LA RELIGION ET LA THEOLOGIE COMPRENNENT LES BEAUX-ARTS ET LES ARTS APPLIQUES.
ESP> LAS HUMANIDADES, LA RELIGION Y LA TEOLOGIA COMPRENDEN LAS BELLAS ARTES Y LAS ARTES APLICADAS.

PHILIPPINES:
E—> UNIVERSITIES AND EQUIVALENT INSTITUTIONS ONLY. ENGINEERING INCLUDES ARCHITECTURE AND TOWN PLANNING, TRADE, CRAFT AND INDUSTRIAL PROGRAMMES AND TRANSPORT AND COMMUNICATIONS.
FR—> UNIVERSITES ET ETABLISSEMENTS EQUIVALENTS SEULEMENT. LES SCIENCES DE L'INGENIEUR COMPRENNENT L'ARCHITECTURE ET L'URBANISME, LES METIERS DE LA PRODUCTION INDUSTRIELLE ET LES TRANSPORTS

VENEZUELA (CONT.):
ESP> UNIVERSIDADES Y ESTABLECIMIENTOS EQUIVALENTS SOLAMENTE.

AFGHANISTAN:
E—> UNIVERSITIES ONLY.
FR—> UNIVERSITES SEULEMENT.
ESP> UNIVERSIDADES SOLAMENTE.

INDIA:
E—> NATURAL SCIENCES INCLUDE MATHEMATICS AND COMPUTER SCIENCE.
FR—> LES SCIENCES EXACTES ET NATURELLES COMPRENNENT LES MATHEMATIQUES ET L'INFORMATIQUE.
ESP> LAS CIENCIAS NATURALES COMPRENDEN LAS MATEMATICAS Y LA INFORMATICA.

ISRAEL:
E—> UNIVERSITIES AND EQUIVALENT INSTITUTIONS ONLY. EDUCATION SCIENCE AND TEACHER TRAINING INCLUDE HUMANITIES, RELIGION AND THEOLOGY AND FINE AND APPLIED ARTS. SOCIAL AND BEHAVIOURAL SCIENCES INCLUDE COMMERCIAL AND BUSINESS ADMINISTRATION, MASS COMMUNICATION AND DOCUMENTATION, HOME ECONOMICS AND SERVICE TRADES. NATURAL SCIENCES INCLUDE MATHEMATICS AND COMPUTER SCIENCE. ENGINEERING INCLUDES ARCHITECTURE AND TOWN PLANNING, TRADE, CRAFT AND INDUSTRIAL PROGRAMMES, TRANSPORT AND COMMUNICATIONS.
FR—> UNIVERSITES ET ETABLISSEMENTS EQUIVALENTS SEULEMENT. LES SCIENCES DE L'EDUCATION ET LA FORMATION D'ENSEIGNANTS COMPRENNENT LES LETTRES, LA RELIGION, LA THEOLOGIE, LES BEAUX-ARTS ET LES ARTS APPLIQUES. LES SCIENCES SOCIALES ET LES SCIENCES DU COMPORTEMENT COMPRENNENT EGALEMENT LA FORMATION AU COMMERCE ET A L'ADMINISTRATION DES ENTREPRISES, L'INFORMATION ET LA DOCUMENTATION, L'ENSEIGNEMENT MENAGER ET LA FORMATION POUR LE SECTEUR TERTIAIRE. LES SCIENCES EXACTES ET NATURELLES COMPRENNENT LES MATHEMATIQUES ET L'INFORMATIQUE. LES SCIENCES DE L'INGENIEUR COMPRENNENT L'ARCHITECTURE ET L'URBANISME, LES METIERS DE LA PRODUCTION INDUSTRIELLE ET LES TRANSPORTS ET LES TELECOMMUNICATIONS.
ESP> UNIVERSIDADES Y ESTABLECIMIENTOS EQUIVALENTES SOLAMENTE. LA EDUCACION Y FORMACION DE PERSONAL DOCENTE COMPRENDE LAS HUMANIDADES, LA RELIGION Y LA TEOLOGIA Y LAS BELLAS ARTES Y LAS ARTES APLICADAS. LAS CIENCIAS SOCIALES Y DEL COMPORTAMIENTO COMPRENDEN IGUALMENTE LA ENSEÑANZA COMERCIAL Y DE ADMINISTRACION DE EMPRESAS, LA DOMESTICA Y COMUNICACION SOCIAL, LA ECONOMIA DOMESTICA Y LA FORMACION PARA EL SECTOR DE LOS SERVICIOS. LAS CIENCIAS NATURALES COMPRENDEN LAS MATEMATICAS Y LA INFORMATICA. LA INGENIERIA Y TECNOLOGIA COMPRENDE LA ARQUITECTURAY EL URBANIS—MO, LAS ARTES Y OFICIOS INDUSTRIALES Y LOS TRANSPORTES Y COMUNICACIONES.

Third level: graduates by levels and fields   **3.13**
Troisième degré: diplômés par niveaux et domaines d'études
Tercer grado: diplomados por niveles y sectores de estudio

THAILAND (CONT.):
LAS ARTES Y OFICIOS INDUSTRIALES Y LOS
TRANSPORTES Y COMUNICACIONES.

AUSTRIA:
E—> UNIVERSITIES AND EQUIVALENT INSTITUTIONS
ONLY.
FR-> UNIVERSITES ET ETABLISSEMENTS EQUIVALENTS
SEULEMENT.
ESP> UNIVERSIDADES Y ESTABLECIMIENTOS
EQUIVALENTES SOLAMENTE.

BELGIUM:
E—> PROGRAMMES OF LEVEL 7 ARE INCLUDED WITH
LEVEL 6.
FR—> LES DONNEES RELATIVES AUX PROGRAMMES DU
NIVEAU 7 SONT COMPRISES DANS CELLES DU NIVEAU 6.
ESP> LOS DATOS RELATIVOS A LOS PROGRAMAS DE
GRADO 7 QUEDAN INCLUIDOS CON LOS DE GRADO 6.

BULGARIA:
E—> THE SHARP RISE IN GRADUATES IS DUE TO THE
INTRODUCTION OF A NEW COURSE OF STUDY FULL-TIME
AND BY CORRESPONDENCE ORGANIZED IN POST-SECONDARY
MEDICAL SCIENCE INSTITUTIONS FOR MIDDLE-LEVEL
MEDICAL PROFESSIONALS (PARAMEDICAL).
FR—> L'IMPORTANTE AUGMENTATION DES DIPLOMES
S'EXPLIQUE PAR LA CREATION DE NOUVEAUX COURS A
PLEIN TEMPS ET PAR CORRESPONDANCE ORGANISES DANS
LES ETABLISSEMENTS POST-SECONDAIRES DE SCIENCES
MEDICALES A L'INTENTION DES CADRES MOYENS
MEDICAUX (PERSONNEL PARAMEDICAL).
ESP> EL IMPORTANTE AUMENTO DE LOS DIPLOMADOS
SE EXPLICA POR LA CREACION DE NUEVOS CURSOS DE
JORNADA COMPLETA Y POR CORRESPONDENCIA
ORGANIZADOS EN LOS ESTABLECIMIENTOS POSTSECUN-
DARIOS DE CIENCIAS MEDICAS Y DESTINADOS A LOS
CUADROS MEDIOS MEDICALES (PERSONAL PARAMEDICAL).

DENMARK:
E—> PROGRAMMES OF LEVEL 7 ARE INCLUDED WITH
LEVEL 6.
FR—> LES DONNEES RELATIVES AUX PROGRAMMES DU
NIVEAU 7 SONT COMPRISES DANS CELLES DU NIVEAU 6.
ESP> LOS DATOS RELATIVOS A LOS PROGRAMAS DE
GRADO 7 QUEDAN INCLUIDOS CON LOS DE GRADO 6.

FRANCE:
E—> DATA REFER ONLY TO THE PRINCIPAL DEGREES
AND DIPLOMAS AWARDED BY UNIVERSITIES AND THE
SCHOOLS OF ENGINEERS. INTERMEDIATE DIPLOMAS WHICH
CONSTITUTE THE FIRST CYCLE OF UNIVERSITY STUDIES
ARE EXCLUDED. THE HEADING "HUMANITIES, RELIGION
AND THEOLOGY" REFERS TO THE GROUP "LETTRES ET
SCIENCES HUMAINES" WHICH INCLUDES SOCIAL SCIENCES
WITH THE EXCEPTION OF ECONOMICS.
FR—> LES DONNEES SE REFERENT AUX PRINCIPAUX
GRADES ET DIPLOMES DELIVRES PAR LES UNIVERSITES
ET LES ECOLES D'INGENIEURS SEULEMENT. SONT
EXCLUS LES DIPLOMES INTERMEDIAIRES SANCTIONNANT
LE PREMIER CYCLE D'ETUDES UNIVERSITAIRES. LA
RUBRIQUE "LETTRES, RELIGION ET THEOLOGIE" SE
REFERE AU GROUPE DES "LETTRES ET SCIENCES
HUMAINES" QUI COMPREND LES DISCIPLINES RELEVANT

PHILIPPINES (CONT):
ET LES TELECOMMUNICATIONS.
ESP> UNIVERSIDADES Y ESTABLECIMIENTOS EQUIVA-
LENTES SOLAMENTE. LA INGENIERIA Y TECNOLOGIA
COMPRENDE LA ARQUITECTURA Y EL URBANISMO, LAS
ARTES Y OFICIOS INDUSTRIALES Y LOS TRANSPORTES
Y COMUNICACIONES.

SAUDI ARABIA:
E—>HUMANITIES, RELIGION AND THEOLOGY INCLUDE
ISLAMIC LAW.
FR—> LES LETTRES, LA RELIGION ET LA THEOLOGIE
COMPRENNENT LE DROIT ISLAMIQUE.
ESP> LAS HUMANIDADES, LA RELIGION Y LA TEOLOGIA
COMPRENDE EL DERECHO ISLAMICO.

SINGAPORE:
E—> HUMANITIES, RELIGION AND THEOLOGY INCLUDE
SOCIAL AND BEHAVIOURAL SCIENCES.
FR—> LES LETTRES, LA RELIGION ET LA THEOLOGIE
COMPRENNENT LES SCIENCES SOCIALES ET SCIENCES DU
COMPORTEMENT.
ESP> LAS HUMANIDADES, LA RELIGION Y LA TEOLOGIA
COMPRENDEN LAS CIENCIAS SOCIALES Y DEL COMPORTA-
MIENTO.

SRI LANKA:
E—> HUMANITIES, RELIGION AND THEOLOGY INCLUDE
SOCIAL AND BEHAVIOURAL SCIENCES.
FR—> LES LETTRES, LA RELIGION ET LA THEOLOGIE
COMPRENNENT EGALEMENT LES SCIENCES SOCIALES ET
LES SCIENCES DU COMPORTEMENT.
ESP> LAS HUMANIDADES, LA RELIGION Y LA TEOLOGIA
COMPRENDEN LAS CIENCIAS SOCIALES Y DEL COMPORTA-
MIENTO.

THAILAND:
E—> SOCIAL AND BEHAVIOURAL SCIENCES INCLUDE
COMMERCIAL AND BUSINESS ADMINISTRATION. MASS
COMMUNICATION AND DOCUMENTATION. HOME ECONOMICS
AND SERVICE TRADES. NATURAL SCIENCES INCLUDE
MATHEMATICS AND COMPUTER SCIENCES. ENGINEERING
INCLUDES ARCHITECTURE AND TOWN PLANNING, TRADE,
CRAFT AND INDUSTRIAL PROGRAMMES AND TRANSPORT AND
COMMUNICATIONS.
FR—> LES SCIENCES SOCIALES ET LES SCIENCES DU
COMPORTEMENT COMPRENNENT LA FORMATION AU
COMMERCE ET A L'ADMINISTRATION DES ENTREPRISES,
L'INFORMATION ET LA DOCUMENTATION, L'ENSEIGNEMENT
MENAGER ET LA FORMATION POUR LE SECTEUR TERTIAIRE.
LES SCIENCES EXACTES ET NATURELLES COMPRENNENT
LES MATHEMATIQUES ET L'INFORMATIQUE. LES
SCIENCES DE L'INGENIEUR COMPRENNENT
L'ARCHITECTURE ET L'URBANISME, LES METIERS
DE LA PRODUCTION INDUSTRIELLE ET LES TRANSPORTS
ET LES TELECOMMUNICATIONS.
ESP> LAS CIENCIAS SOCIALES Y DEL COMPORTAMIENTO
COMPRENDEN LA ENSEÑANZA COMERCIAL Y DE
ADMINISTRACION DE EMPRESAS, LA DOCUMENTACION Y
COMUNICACION SOCIAL, LA ECONOMIA DOMESTICA Y LA
FORMACION PARA EL SECTOR DE LOS SERVICIOS. LAS
CIENCIAS COMPRENDEN LAS MATEMATICAS Y LA
LA INFORMATICA. LA INGENIERIA Y TECNOLOGIA
COMPRENDEN LA ARQUITECTURA Y EL URBANISMO,

3.13 Third level: graduates by levels and fields
Troisième degré: diplômés par niveaux et domaines d'études
Tercer grado: diplomados por niveles y sectores de estudio

NORWAY:
E—> PROGRAMMES OF LEVEL 7 ARE INCLUDED WITH LEVEL 6.
FR—> LES DONNEES RELATIVES AUX PROGRAMMES DU NIVEAU 7 SONT COMPRISES DANS CELLES DU NIVEAU 6.
ESP> LOS DATOS RELATIVOS A LOS PROGRAMAS DE GRADO 7 QUEDAN INCLUIDOS CON LOS DE GRADO 6.

PORTUGAL:
E—> SOCIAL AND BEHAVIOURAL SCIENCES INCLUDE COMMERCIAL AND BUSINESS ADMINISTRATION, MASS COMMUNICATION AND DOCUMENTATION, HOME ECONOMICS AND SERVICE TRADES. ENGINEERING INCLUDES ARCHITECTURE AND TOWN PLANNING, TRADE, CRAFT AND INDUSTRIAL PROGRAMMES AND TRANSPORT AND COMMUNICATIONS.
FR—> LES SCIENCES SOCIALES ET LES SCIENCES DU COMPORTEMENT COMPRENNENT LA FORMATION AU COMMERCE ET A L'ADMINISTRATION DES ENTREPRISES; L'INFORMATION ET LA DOCUMENTATION, L'ENSEIGNEMENT MENAGER ET LA FORMATION POUR LE SECTEUR TERTIAIRE. LES SCIENCES DE L'INGENIEUR COMPRENNENT L'ARCHITECTURE ET L'URBANISME. LES METIERS DE LA PRODUCTION INDUSTRIELLE ET LES TRANSPORTS ET LES TELECOMMUNICATIONS.
ESP> LAS CIENCIAS SOCIALES Y DEL COMPORTAMIENTO COMPRENDEN LA ENSEÑANZA COMERCIAL Y DE ADMINISTRACION DE EMPRESAS, LA DOCUMENTACION Y COMUNICACION SOCIAL, LA ECONOMIA DOMESTICA Y LA FORMACION PARA EL SECTOR DE LOS SERVICIOS. LA INGENIERIA Y TECNOLOGIA COMPRENDE LA ARQUITECTURA Y EL URBANISMO. LAS ARTES Y OFICIOS INDUSTRIALES Y LOS TRANSPORTES Y COMUNICACIONES.

SPAIN:
E—> FOLLOWING IMPORTANT STRUCTURAL CHANGES IN THE EDUCATIONAL SYSTEM IN 1972 TEACHER-TRAINING AND CERTAIN TYPES OF VOCATIONAL EDUCATION PREVIOUSLY SHOWN AT THE SECOND LEVEL ARE NOW COUNTED AT THE THIRD LEVEL OF EDUCATION.
FR—> EN 1972 DES CHANGEMENTS STRUCTURELS IMPORTANTS ONT ETE INTRODUITS DANS L'ORGANISATION DE L'ENSEIGNEMENT. DE CE FAIT, A PARTIR DE CETTE DATE, L'ENSEIGNEMENT NORMAL ET CERTAINS TYPES D'ENSEIGNEMENT TECHNIQUE PRECEDEMMENT CLASSES DANS LE SECOND DEGRE FONT PARTIE DE L'ENSEIGNEMENT DU TROISIEME DEGRE.
ESP> EN 1972 SE HAN INTRODUCIDO IMPORTANTES CAMBIOS DE ESTRUCTURA. POR CONSIGUIENTE, A PARTIR DE DICHA FECHA, LA ENSEÑANZA NORMAL Y ALGUNOS TIPOS DE ENSEÑANZA TECNICA CLASIFICADOS ANTERIORMENTE EN EL SEGUNDO GRADO, FIGURAN EN EL TERCER GRADO.

SWEDEN:
E—> SOCIAL AND BEHAVIOURAL SCIENCES INCLUDE COMMERCIAL AND BUSINESS ADMINISTRATION. NATURAL SCIENCES INCLUDE MATHEMATICS AND COMPUTER SCIENCE.

FRANCE (CONT.):
DES SCIENCES SOCIALES, A L'EXCEPTION DES SCIENCES ECONOMIQUES.
ESP> SE TRATA EXCLUSIVAMENTE DE LOS PRINCIPALES TITULOS Y DIPLOMAS CONCEDIDOS POR LAS UNIVERSIDADES Y LAS ESCUELAS DE INGENIEROS. QUEDAN EXCLUIDOS LOS TITULOS Y DIPLOMAS DE NIVEL INTERMEDIO QUE SANCIONAN UN PRIMER CICLO DE ESTUDIOS UNIVERSITARIOS. LA RUBRICA "HUMANIDADES, RELIGION Y TEOLOGIA" SE REFIERE AL GRUPO DE HUMANIDADES Y CIENCIAS HUMANAS QUE COMPRENDE LAS DISCIPLINAS CLASIFICADAS EN LAS CIENCIAS SOCIALES, SALVO LAS CIENCIAS ECONOMICAS.

GERMAN DEMOCRATIC REPUBLIC:
E—> IN 1974, PREPARATORY STUDIES FOR HIGHER EDUCATION, EXTENDED SECONDARY SCHOOLS AND VOCATIONAL TRAINING (INCLUDING UNIVERSITY ENTRANCE EXAMINATION) WERE INCLUDED WITH EDUCATION AT THE THIRD LEVEL (NON UNIVERSITY) AS THE RESULT OF THE APPLICATION OF ISCED.
FR—> EN 1974, LES ETUDES PREPARATOIRES A L'ENSEIGNEMENT SUPERIEUR, LES ECOLES SECONDAIRES PROLONGEES ET L'ENSEIGNEMENT TECHNIQUE (Y COMPRIS L'EXAMEN D'ENTREE A L'UNIVERSITE) SONT COMPRIS DANS L'ENSEIGNEMENT DU TROISIEME DEGRE (NON-UNIVERSITAIRE) A LA SUITE DE L'APPLICATION DE LA CITE.
ESP> EN 1974, LOS ESTUDIOS PREPARATORIOS A LA ENSEÑANZA SUPERIOR, LAS ESCUELAS SECUNDARIAS PROLONGADAS Y LA ENSEÑANZA TECNICA (INCLUYENDO EL EXAMEN DE ENTRADA A LA UNIVERSIDAD) ESTAN INCLUIDOS EN LA ENSEÑANZA DE TERCER GRADO (NO UNIVERSITARIA) COMO RESULTADO DE LA APLICACION DE LA CINE.

IRELAND:
E—> UNIVERSITIES AND EQUIVALENT INSTITUTIONS ONLY.
FR—> UNIVERSITES ET ETABLISSEMENTS EQUIVALENTS SEULEMENT.
ESP> UNIVERSIDADES Y ESTABLECIMIENTOS EQUIVALENTES SOLAMENTE.

NETHERLANDS:
E—> EXCLUDING TEACHER-TRAINING GRADUATES FOR GENERAL SECONDARY SCHOOLS (ABOUT 3,000 GRADUATES IN 1971). ENGINEERING INCLUDES TRADE, CRAFT AND INDUSTRIAL PROGRAMMES.
FR—> NON COMPRIS LES DIPLOMES DE L'ENSEIGNEMENT NORMAL POUR LA FORMATION DE PROFESSEURS DES ECOLES D'ENSEIGNEMENT SECONDAIRE GENERAL (ENVIRON 3 000 EN 1971). LES SCIENCES DE L'INGENIEUR COMPRENNENT LES METIERS DE LA PRODUCTION INDUSTRIELLE.
ESP> EXCLUIDOS LOS DIPLOMADOS DE LA ENSEÑANZA NORMAL PARA LA FORMACION DE PROFESORES DE LAS ESCUELAS DE ENSEÑANZA SECUNDARIA GENERAL (APROXIMADAMENTE 3 000 EN 1971). LA INGENIERIA Y LA TECNOLOGIA COMPRENDE LAS ARTES Y OFICIOS INDUSTRIALES.

Third level: graduates by levels and fields 3.13
Troisième degré: diplômés par niveaux et domaines d'études
Tercer grado: diplomados por niveles y sectores de estudio

SWEDEN (CONT.):
FR-> LES SCIENCES SOCIALES ET LES SCIENCES DU COMPORTEMENT COMPRENNENT LA FORMATION AU COMMERCE ET A L'ADMINISTRATION DES ENTREPRISES. LES SCIENCES EXACTES ET NATURELLES COMPRENNENT LES MATHEMATIQUES ET L'INFORMATIQUE.
ESP> LAS CIENCIAS SOCIALES Y DEL COMPORTAMIENTO COMPRENDEN LA ENSEÑANZA COMERCIAL Y DE ADMINISTRACION DE EMPRESAS. LAS CIENCIAS NATURALES INCLUYEN LAS MATEMATICAS Y LA INFORMATICA.

SWITZERLAND:
E-> UNIVERSITIES AND EQUIVALENT INSTITUTIONS ONLY.
FR-> UNIVERSITES ET ETABLISSEMENTS EQUIVALENTS SEULEMENT.
ESP> UNIVERSIDADES Y ESTABLECIMIENTOS EQUIVALENTES SOLAMENTE.

YUGOSLAVIA:
E-> NATURAL SCIENCES INCLUDE MATHEMATICS AND COMPUTER SCIENCE.
FR-> LES SCIENCES EXACTES ET NATURELLES COMPRENNENT LES MATHEMATIQUES ET L'INFORMATIQUE.
ESP> LAS CIENCIAS NATURALES COMPRENDEN LAS MATEMATICAS Y LA INFORMATICA.

NEW ZEALAND:
E-> UNIVERSITIES ONLY.
FR-> UNIVERSITES SEULEMENT.
ESP> UNIVERSIDADES SOLAMENTE.

U.S.S.R.:
E->THESE FIGURES ARE PROVIDED BY THE U.S.S.R. ACCORDING TO THEIR OWN SYSTEMS OF CLASSIFICATION. LAW AND ECONOMICS ARE COMBINED. MEDICAL AND HEALTH RELATED SCIENCES INCLUDE PHYSICAL CULTURE AND SPORT. ENGINEERING INCLUDES TRANSPORT AND COMMUNICATIONS.
FR-> CES CHIFFRES SONT FOURNIS PAR L'URSS. SELON SON PROPRE SYSTEME DE CLASSIFICATION. LE DROIT COMPREND LES SCIENCES ECONOMIQUES. LES SCIENCES MEDICALES, LA SANTE ET L'HYGIENE COMPRENNENT LA CULTURE PHYSIQUE ET LE SPORT. LES SCIENCES DE L'INGENIEUR COMPRENNENT LES TRANSPORTS ET LES TELECOMMUNICATIONS.
ESP> ESTAS CIFRAS HAN SIDO FACILITADAS POR LA U.R.S.S. CON ARREGLO A SU PROPIO SISTEMA DE CLASIFICACION. EL DERECHO Y LA ECONOMIA FIGURAN CLASIFICADOS BAJO LA MISMA RUBRICA. LAS CIENCIAS

U.S.S.R. (CONT.):
MEDICAS, LA SANIDAD Y LA HIGIENE COMPRENDEN LA CULTURA FISICA Y EL DEPORTE. LA INGENIERIA Y TECNOLOGIA COMPRENDE LOS TRANSPORTES Y COMUNICACIONES.

BYELORUSSIAN S.S.R.:
E—->THESE FIGURES ARE PROVIDED BY THE BYELORUSSIAN S.S.R.ACCORDING TO THEIR OWN SYSTEMS OF CLASSIFICATION. LAW AND ECONOMICS ARE COMBINED. MEDICAL AND HEALTH RELATED SCIENCES INCLUDE PHYSICAL CULTURE AND SPORT. ENGINEERING INCLUDES TRANSPORT AND COMMUNICATIONS.
FR—> CES CHIFFRES SONT FOURNIS PAR LA R.S.S. DE BIELORUSSIE SELON SON PROPRE SYSTEME DE CLASSIFICATION. LE DROIT COMPREND LES SCIENCES ECONOMIQUES. LES SCIENCES MEDICALES, LA SANTE ET L'HYGIENE COMPRENNENT LA CULTURE PHYSIQUE ET LE SPORT. LES SCIENCES DE L'INGENIEUR COMPRENNENT LES TRANSPORTS ET LES TELECOMMUNICATIONS.
ESP> ESTAS CIFRAS HAN SIDO FACILITADAS POR LA R.S.S. DE BIELORRUSIA CON ARREGLO A SU PROPIO SISTEMA DE CLASIFICACION. EL DERECHO Y LA ECONOMIA FIGURAN CLASIFICADOS BAJO LA MISMA RUBRICA. LAS CIENCIAS MEDICAS, LA SANIDAD Y LA HIGIENE COMPRENDEN LA CULTURA FISICA Y EL DEPORTE. LA INGENIERA Y TECNOLOGIA COMPRENDE LOS TRANSPORTES Y COMUNICACIONES.

UKRAINIAN S.S.R.:
E—->THESE FIGURES ARE PROVIDED BY THE UKRAINIAN S.S.R. ACCORDING TO THEIR OWN SYSTEMS OF CLASSIFICATION. LAW AND ECONOMICS ARE COMBINED. MEDICAL AND HEALTH RELATED SCIENCES INCLUDE PHYSICAL CULTURE AND SPORT. ENGINEERING INCLUDES TRANSPORT AND COMMUNICATIONS.
FR—> CES CHIFFRES SONT FOURNIS PAR LA R.S.S. D'UKRAINE SELON SON PROPRE SYSTEME DE CLASSIFICATION. LE DROIT COMPREND LES SCIENCES ECONOMIQUES. LES SCIENCES MEDICALES, LA SANTE ET L'HYGIENE COMPRENNENT LA CULTURE PHYSIQUE ET LE SPORT. LES SCIENCES DE L'INGENIEUR COMPRENNENT LES TRANSPORTS ET LES TELECOMMUNICATIONS.
ESP> ESTAS CIFRAS HAN SIDO FACILITADAS POR LA R.S.S. DE UCRANIA CON ARREGLO A SU PROPIO SISTEMA DE CLASIFICACION. EL DERECHO Y LA ECONOMIA FIGURAN CLASIFICADOS BAJO LA MISMA RUBRICA. LAS CIENCIAS MEDICAS, LA SANIDAD Y LA HIGIENE COMPRENDEN LA CULTURA FISICA Y LA HIGIENE COMPRENDEN LA CULTURA FISICA Y EL DEPORTE. LA INGENIERIA Y TECNOLOGIA COMPRENDE LOS TRANSPORTES Y COMUNICACIONES.

Third level: foreign students 3.14
Troisième degré: étudiants étrangers
Tercer grado: estudiantes extranjeros

3.14 Education at the third level: number of foreign students enrolled

Enseignement du troisième degré: nombre d'étudiants étrangers inscrits

Enseñanza de tercer grado: número de estudiantes extranjeros matriculados

NUMBER OF COUNTRIES AND TERRITORIES PRESENTED IN THIS TABLE: 114
NOMBRE DE PAYS ET DE TERRITOIRES PRESENTES DANS CE TABLEAU: 114
NUMERO DE PAISES Y DE TERRITORIOS PRESENTADOS EN ESTE CUADRO: 114

HOST COUNTRY / PAYS D'ACCUEIL / PAIS HUESPED	FOREIGN STUDENTS ENROLLED (MF) / ETUDIANTS ETRANGERS INSCRITS (MF) / ESTUDIANTES EXTRANJEROS MATRICULADOS (MF)				
	1970	1974	1975	1976	1977
AFRICA					
ALGERIA	1 884	1 518	1 574	1 029	1 343
BENIN	72	20	26	32	...
BOTSWANA	...	42	121	...	...
BURUNDI	94	167	174	...	...
CENTRAL AFRICAN REPUBLIC	—	16	26	32	26
CHAD	—	46	57	45	...
CONGO	675	153	275	...	...
EGYPT	13 387	19 655	...	...	...
ETHIOPIA	87	99	...	228	...
GABON	—	...	...	...	...
GHANA	277	...	356	...	...
IVORY COAST	1 716	702	1 383	1 527	...
KENYA	998	213	483	...	...
LESOTHO	253	...	...	...	...
LIBYAN ARAB JAMAHIRIYA	1 007	1 002	1 262	956	890
MADAGASCAR	830	...	...	63	45
MALAWI	—	18	10	3	...
MALI	...	...	...	95	102
MAURITIUS	...	...	...	10	6
MOROCCO	596	929	1 804	1 778	...
MOZAMBIQUE	...	...	...	206	361
NIGER	268	146	247	332	...
NIGERIA	18	...	446	...	...
RWANDA	...	51	...	47	...
SENEGAL	2 061	2 099	2 118	2 150	2 224
SIERRA LEONE	241	416	354	669	984
SUDAN	638	3 772	1 828	686	...
TOGO	373	269	478	361	...
TUNISIA	408	...	446	222	...
UGANDA ‡	963	705	482	...	...
UNITED REPUBLIC OF CAMEROON	146	234	...	...	204
UNITED REPUBLIC OF TANZANIA ‡	360	239	134	184	...
UPPER VOLTA	8	136	...	...	89
ZAIRE	825	...	...	...	...
ZAMBIA	209	...	344	...	...

3.14 Third level: foreign students
Troisième degré: étudiants étrangers
Tercer grado: estudiantes extranjeros

FOREIGN STUDENTS ENROLLED (MF)
ETUDIANTS ETRANGERS INSCRITS (MF)
ESTUDIANTES EXTRANJEROS MATRICULADOS (MF)

HOST COUNTRY / PAYS D'ACCUEIL / PAIS HUESPED	1970	1974	1975	1976	1977
AMERICA, NORTH					
BARBADOS	193	...	...	...	...
CANADA ‡	22 263	...	*22 700	*24 500	*26 400
COSTA RICA ‡	...	...	...	1 190	...
CUBA	796	...	336	...	...
EL SALVADOR	...	...	...	...	...
GUATEMALA	434	985	1 038	1 228	...
HONDURAS	...	...	...	412	223
JAMAICA	961	...	...	...	852
MEXICO ‡	1 214	6 250	...	...	...
PANAMA	192	...	477	609	486
TRINIDAD AND TOBAGO	370	...	443	...	434
UNITED STATES OF AMERICA ‡	144 708	154 580	179 350	203 070	235 544
AMERICA, SOUTH					
ARGENTINA	8 862	16 615	...	...	...
BRAZIL	630	25 642	...	...	...
CHILE	...	1 043	940	940	703
COLOMBIA ‡	1 195	...	...	...	...
ECUADOR ‡	671	...	...	...	...
PARAGUAY	125	...	...	...	...
URUGUAY ‡	1 443	...	...	...	...
ASIA					
AFGHANISTAN	32	99	100	...	...
BAHRAIN	...	48	48	55	50
BANGLADESH	...	...	...	56	134
CYPRUS	9	15	20	17	9
HONG KONG	74	150	135	140	148
INDIA	7 804	...	8 880	...	...
IRAN	204	465	650	686	...
IRAQ	3 358	3 862	4 476	5 277	5 151
ISRAEL	2 952	...	...	...	...
JAPAN	10 471	13 564	14 485	14 737	...
JORDAN	39	113	197	308	326
KOREA, REPUBLIC OF	261	314	469	437	...
KUWAIT	658	2 401	2 871	3 660	4 280
LEBANON	22 184	...	...	...	...
MALAYSIA	43	...	...	...	...
PAKISTAN	...	1 297	1 582	1 690	...
PHILIPPINES	2 628	...	...	4 056	7 383
QATAR	—	...	...	380	380
SAUDI ARABIA	1 404	2 716	4 026	5 548	9 141
SINGAPORE	1 975	...	...	1 762	1 310
SRI LANKA	37	20	...	...	...
SYRIAN ARAB REPUBLIC	7 911	6 403	7 032	...	...
THAILAND	229	132	101	77	65
TURKEY	6 125	6 385	5 907	6 246	6 419
VIET-NAM, SOCIALIST REPUBLIC OF	...	...	140	220	...

Third level: foreign students 3.14
Troisième degré: étudiants étrangers
Tercer grado: estudiantes extranjeros

FOREIGN STUDENTS ENROLLED (MF)
ETUDIANTS ETRANGERS INSCRITS (MF)
ESTUDIANTES EXTRANJEROS MATRICULADOS (MF)

HOST COUNTRY / PAYS D'ACCUEIL / PAIS HUESPED	1970	1974	1975	1976	1977
EUROPE					
AUSTRIA	8 573	9 716	10 320	10 696	10 461
BELGIUM ‡	8 611	9 369	9 748	15 435	16 720
BULGARIA	2 325	2 484	2 533	2 526	2 503
CZECHOSLOVAKIA	3 619	3 400	3 370	3 438	3 383
DENMARK	1 644	...	1 958	3 227	4 106
FINLAND	250	461	529	573	571
FRANCE ‡	34 500	77 382	93 750	96 409	104 317
GERMAN DEMOCRATIC REPUBLIC	...	4 864	5 386	5 351	5 736
GERMANY, FEDERAL REPUBLIC OF	27 769	47 096	53 560	54 080	54 062
GREECE	5 796	9 929	10 049	9 448	9 354
HOLY SEE	8 128		5 740	7 304	7 515
HUNGARY	1 884	2 557	2 572	2 537	2 610
ICELAND	69	107	120	120	
IRELAND		1 464	1 513	1 263	1 991
ITALY	14 357	20 803	18 921	28 390	27 136
LUXEMBOURG	66	84	38	70	36
MALTA	32	33	16	27	35
NETHERLANDS	1 721	1 652			
NORWAY	420		931	926	...
POLAND	2 576	2 624	2 438	2 472	2 492
PORTUGAL	902		672	976	857
ROMANIA	1 766	3 833	4 971	6 677	...
SPAIN	10 575	8 417	8 909	7 814	...
SWEDEN ‡	*4 000		2 723	3 748	...
SWITZERLAND ‡	9 469	10 038	10 113	12 204	12 464
UNITED KINGDOM ‡	24 606	40 838	49 032	55 927	58 563
YUGOSLAVIA	3 239	2 324	2 358	2 491	2 822
OCEANIA					
AUSTRALIA	7 525	7 635	8 356	8 602	8 258
FIJI		177	233	...	...
NEW ZEALAND	2 495	2 688	2 965	3 193	...
PAPUA NEW GUINEA	...	344	360	...	327
SAMOA	...	...	...	28	...
TONGA	...	...	...	...	15
U.S.S.R.					
U.S.S.R.	27 918	...	...	...	...

UGANDA:
E—> UNIVERSITIES AND EQUIVALENT INSTITUTIONS
ONLY (SEE TABLE 3.11).
FR—> UNIVERSITES ET ETABLISSEMENTS EQUIVALENTS
SEULEMENT (VOIR TABLEAU 3.11).
ESP> UNIVERSIDADES Y ESTABLECIMIENTOS EQUIVA—
LENTES SOLAMENTE (VEASE EL CUADRO 3.11).

UNITED REPUBLIC OF TANZANIA:
E—> UNIVERSITIES AND EQUIVALENT INSTITUTIONS
ONLY (SEE TABLE 3.11).
FR—> UNIVERSITES ET ETABLISSEMENTS EQUIVALENTS
SEULEMENT (VOIR TABLEAU 3.11).
ESP> UNIVERSIDADES Y ESTABLECIMIENTOS EQUIVA—
LENTES SOLAMENTE (VEASE EL CUADRO 3.11).

3.14 Third level: foreign students
Troisième degré: étudiants étrangers
Tercer grado: estudiantes extranjeros

ECUADOR (CONT.):
FR—> EN 1970, LES DONNEES SE REFERENT A L'ANNEE ACADEMIQUE 1969/70.
ESP> EN 1970, LOS DATOS SE REFIEREN AL AÑO ACADEMICO 1969/70.

URUGUAY:
E—> DATA FOR 1970 REFER TO THE ACADEMIC YEAR 1969/70.
FR—> EN 1970, LES DONNEES SE REFERENT A L'ANNEE ACADEMIQUE 1969/70.
ESP> EN 1970, LOS DATOS SE REFIEREN AL AÑO ACADEMICO 1969/70.

BELGIUM:
E—> EXCEPT FOR 1976, DATA REFER TO UNIVERSITIES AND EQUIVALENT INSTITUTIONS ONLY.
FR—> A L'EXCEPTION DE 1976, LES DONNEES SE REFERENT AUX UNIVERSITES ET AUX ETABLISSEMENTS EQUIVALENTS SEULEMENT.
ESP> SALVO PARA 1976, LOS DATOS SE REFIEREN A LAS UNIVERSIDADES Y ESTABLECIMIENTOS EQUIVALENTES SOLAMENTE.

FRANCE:
E—> UNIVERSITIES ONLY. IN 1970 DATA DIFFER FROM THOSE FOR SUBSEQUENT YEARS DUE TO MORE COMPLETE INFORMATION BECOMING AVAILABLE.
FR—> UNIVERSITES SEULEMENT. EN 1970, LES DONNEES DIFFERENT SENSIBLEMENT DE CELLES DES ANNEES SUIVANTES, ETANT DONNE QUE DES INFORMATIONS PLUS COMPLETES NOUS ONT ETE FOURNIES.
ESP> UNIVERSIDADES SOLAMENTE. EN 1970, LAS CIFRAS DIFIEREN SENSIBLEMENTE DE LAS QUE SE PUBLICAN PARA LOS AÑOS SIGUIENTES, CUYOS DATOS ERAN MAS COMPLETOS.

SWEDEN:
E—> FOR 1975 AND 1976, FIRST YEAR UNIVERSITY STUDENTS ONLY.
FR—> EN 1975 ET 1976, LES DONNEES SE REFERENT AUX NOUVEAUX ENTRANTS DANS LES UNIVERSITES SEULEMENT (VOIR TABLEAU 3.11).
ESP> EN 1975 Y 1976, NUEVOS ENTRANTES EN LAS UNIVERSIDADES (VEASE EL CUADRO 3.11).

SWITZERLAND:
E—> UNIVERSITIES AND EQUIVALENT INSTITUTIONS ONLY (SEE TABLE 3.11).
FR—> UNIVERSITES ET ETABLISSEMENTS EQUIVALENTS SEULEMENT (VOIR TABLEAU 3.11).
ESP> UNIVERSIDADES Y ESTABLECIMIENTOS EQUIVALENTES SOLAMENTE (VEASE EL CUADRO 3.11).

UNITED KINGDOM:
E—> FOREIGN STUDENTS ENROLLED AT UNIVERSITIES (FOR FULL-TIME STUDY OR RESEARCH), TECHNICAL COLLEGES (ADVANCED COURSES) AND COLLEGES OF EDUCATION.
FR—> ETUDIANTS ETRANGERS INSCRITS DANS LES UNIVERSITES (POUR ETUDES OU RECHERCHES A PLEIN TEMPS), "TECHNICAL COLLEGES (ADVANCED COURSES)" ET "COLLEGES OF EDUCATION".
ESP> ESTUDIANTES EXTRANJEROS MATRICULADOS EN UNIVERSIDADES (PARA REALIZAR ESTUDIOS O INVESTIGACIONES EN REGIMEN DE JORNADA COMPLETA) EN LOS "TECHNICAL COLLEGES (ADVANCED COURSES)" Y EN LOS "COLLEGES OF EDUCATION".

CANADA:
E—> DATA FOR 1970 REFER TO FULL-TIME STUDENTS IN UNIVERSITIES. DATA FOR 1975, 1976 AND 1977 ARE ESTIMATES OF FULL-TIME AND PART-TIME STUDENTS IN UNIVERSITIES.
FR—> LES DONNEES RELATIVES A 1970 SE REFERENT AUX ETUDIANTS INSCRITS A PLEIN TEMPS DANS LES UNIVERSITES. EN 1975, 1976 ET 1977 IL S'AGIT D'UNE ESTIMATION DES ETUDIANTS INSCRITS A PLEIN TEMPS ET A TEMPS PARTIEL DANS LES UNIVERSITES.
ESP> LOS DATOS PARA 1970 SE REFIEREN A LOS ESTUDIANTES DE JORNADA COMPLETA INSCRITOS EN LAS UNIVERSIDADES. EN 1975, 1976 Y 1977 SE TRATA DE UNA ESTIMACION DE LOS ESTUDIANTES DE JORNADA COMPLETA Y DE JORNADA PARCIAL INSCRITOS EN LAS UNIVERSIDADES.

MEXICO:
E—> FOR 1977, DATA REFER TO THE "UNIVERSIDAD NACIONAL AUTONOMA" ONLY.
FR—> EN 1977 LES DONNEES SE REFERENT A L'"UNIVERSIDAD NACIONAL AUTONOMA" SEULEMENT.
ESP> EN 1977, UNIVERSIDAD NACIONAL AUTONOMA SOLAMENTE.

UNITED STATES OF AMERICA:
E—> THESE DATA RESULT FROM ENQUIRIES CONDUCTED ANNUALLY BY THE INSTITUTE OF INTERNATIONAL EDUCATION (NEW YORK), AND PUBLISHED REGULARLY IN A REPORT ENTITLED "OPEN DOORS". IT SHOULD BE NOTED THAT FOR THE 1975/76 SURVEY ON FOREIGN STUDENTS, A NEW METHOD WAS INTRODUCED BY THE INSTITUTE OF INTERNATIONAL EDUCATION. CONSEQUENTLY, DATA FROM 1975 REFER TO FOREIGN STUDENTS NOT POSSESSING AN IMMIGRANT'S VISA.
FR—> CES CHIFFRES PROVIENNENT DES ENQUETES ANNUELLES CONDUITES PAR L'"INSTITUTE OF INTERNATIONAL EDUCATION" (NEW YORK) ET DONT LES RESULTATS SONT PUBLIES REGULIEREMENT DANS LE RAPPORT INTITULE "OPEN DOORS". IL CONVIENT DE NOTER QUE POUR L'ENQUETE SUR LES ETUDIANTS EN 1975/76, UNE NOUVELLE METHODE A ETE UTILISEE PAR L'"INSTITUTE OF INTERNATIONAL EDUCATION". EN CONSEQUENCE, A PARTIR DE 1975, LES DONNEES SE REFERENT AUX ETUDIANTS ETRANGERS N'AYANT PAS UN VISA D'IMMIGRATION.
ESP> ESTAS CIFRAS PROCEDEN DE LAS ENCUESTAS ANUALES EFECTUADAS POR EL "INSTITUTE OF INTERNATIONAL EDUCATION" (NUEVA YORK), CUYOS RESULTADOS SE PUBLICAN REGULARMENTE EN EL INFORME TITULADO "OPEN DOORS". ES DE NOTAR QUE PARA LA ENCUESTA SOBRE LOS ESTUDIANTES EXTRANJEROS EFECTUADA EN 1975/76, EL "INSTITUTE OF INTERNATIONAL EDUCATION" HA UTILIZADO UN NUEVO METODO. EN CONSECUENCIA, A PARTIR DE 1975, LOS DATOS SE REFIEREN A LOS ESTUDIANTES EXTRANJEROS QUE NO POSEEN UN VISADO DE INMIGRACION.

COLOMBIA:
E—> DATA FOR 1970 REFER TO THE ACADEMIC YEAR 1969/70.
FR—> EN 1970, LES DONNEES SE REFERENT A L'ANNEE ACADEMIQUE 1969/70.
ESP> EN 1970, LOS DATOS SE REFIEREN AL AÑO ACADEMICO 1969/70.

ECUADOR:
E—> DATA FOR 1970 REFER TO THE ACADEMIC YEAR 1969/70.

Third level: foreign students by country of origin 3.15
Troisième degré: étudiants étrangers par pays d'origine
Tercer grado: estudiantes extranjeros por países de origen

3.15 Education at the third level: foreign students by country of origin, in 50 selected countries

Enseignement du troisième degré: étudiants étrangers répartis par pays d'origine, dans 50 pays choisis

Enseñanza de tercer grado: estudiantes extranjeros distribuidos por países de origen, en 50 países seleccionados

3.15 Third level: foreign students by country of origin
Troisième degré: étudiants étrangers par pays d'origine
Tercer grado: estudiantes extranjeros por países de origen

HOST COUNTRY ‡ PAYS D'ACCUEIL ‡ PAIS HUESPED ‡	YEAR ANNEE AÑO	TOTAL	AFRICA	ALGERIA	ANGOLA	BENIN	BOTSWANA	BURUNDI
UNITED STATES OF AMERICA ‡	1977	235 544	29 560	1 680	15	11	14	3
FRANCE	1977	104 317	52 096	8 549	6	1 333	1	107
UNITED KINGDOM	1977	58 563	12 624	940	1	2	58	5
GERMANY, FEDERAL REPUBLIC OF	1977	54 062	4 084	535	–	16	10	28
ITALY	1977	27 136	1 224	–	–	–	–	–
EGYPT	1974	19 655	1 201					
BELGIUM	1977	16 720	4 997	373	20	33	–	142
ARGENTINA	1974	16 615	12	2	–	–	–	–
JAPAN	1976	14 737	51	–	–	–	–	–
SWITZERLAND	1977	12 464	719	127	10	4	–	26
AUSTRIA	1977	10 461	308	22	1	–	–	–
GREECE	1977	9 354	634	4	–	–	–	12
INDIA	1975	8 880	2 201	–	7	–	1	–
AUSTRALIA	1977	8 258	299	1	–	–	1	–
SPAIN	1976	7 814	260	9	1	–	–	1
HOLY SEE	1977	7 515	444	9	11	4	–	7
PHILIPPINES	1977	7 383	152	–	–	–	–	–
SYRIAN ARAB REPUBLIC	1975	7 032	429	91	–	–	–	–
TURKEY	1976	6 246	18	–	–	–	–	–
GERMAN DEMOCRATIC REPUBLIC	1977	5 736	994					
SAUDI ARABIA	1976	5 548	1 342	16	–	–	–	–
IRAQ	1977	5 151	1 019	22	–	–	–	–
KUWAIT	1977	4 280	632	1	–	8	–	1
DENMARK	1977	4 106	145	11	–	–	–	4
ROMANIA	1974	3 833	1 162	28	10	7	–	8
SWEDEN ‡	1976	3 748	107	8	–	–	–	–
CZECHOSLOVAKIA	1977	3 383	336	56	–	1	–	2
YUGOSLAVIA	1977	2 822	521	5	9	–	–	–
HUNGARY	1977	2 610	452	30	–	6	–	–
BULGARIA	1976	2 526	145	53	–	–	–	–
POLAND	1977	2 492	330	67	–	2	–	–
SENEGAL	1977	2 224	1 679	3	1	166	–	14
IRELAND	1977	1 991	336	1	–	–	–	–
MOROCCO	1976	1 778	633	81	–	1	–	–
PAKISTAN	1976	1 690	176	2	–	–	–	–
NETHERLANDS	1974	1 652	80	1	–	–	1	–
IVORY COAST	1976	1 527	980	–	1	266	–	6
ALGERIA	1977	1 343	530		–	16	–	17
SINGAPORE	1977	1 310	–	–	–	–	–	–
GUATEMALA	1976	1 228	6	–	–	–	–	–
CUBA	1976	1 190	801	–	17	–	–	–
SUDAN	1977	984	861	–	–	–	–	–
LIBYAN ARAB JAMAHIRIYA	1977	890	568	3	–	–	–	–
PORTUGAL	1977	857	253	–	30	–	–	–
MEXICO ‡	1977	852	4	–	–	–	–	–
CHILE	1977	703	–	–	–	–	–	–
IRAN	1976	686	101	4	–	–	–	–
TOGO	1976	686	654	1	3	108	–	–
FINLAND	1977	571	86	3	–	–	–	1
PANAMA	1977	486	33	–	–	–	–	–
TOTAL (50 COUNTRIES) ‡		701 639	126 279	12 738	143	1 984	85	384

Third level: foreign students by country of origin 3.15
Troisième degré: étudiants étrangers par pays d'origine
Tercer grado: estudiantes extranjeros por países de origen

COUNTRY OF ORIGIN / PAYS D'ORIGINE / PAIS DE ORIGEN

HOST COUNTRY ‡ PAYS D'ACCUEIL ‡ PAIS HUESPED ‡	YEAR ANNEE AÑO	CENTRAL AFRICAN REPUBLIC	CHAD	CONGO	EGYPT	EQUATORIAL GUINEA	ETHIOPIA	GABON	GAMBIA
UNITED STATES OF AMERICA ‡	1977	7	10	2	1 500	—	1 570	4	140
FRANCE	1977	404	438	1 723	1 197	—	128	880	20
UNITED KINGDOM	1977	7	3	1	713	—	58	2	73
GERMANY, FEDERAL REPUBLIC OF	1977	7	10	10	845	—	106	11	1
ITALY	1977	—	—	—	99	—	156	—	—
EGYPT	1974								
BELGIUM	1977	40	17	30	42	14	9	15	—
ARGENTINA	1974	—	—	—	—	—	—	—	—
JAPAN	1976	—	—	—	27	—	3	—	—
SWITZERLAND	1977	9	2	3	119	3	7	—	—
AUSTRIA	1977	1	—	—	158	—	3	—	2
GREECE	1977	—	—	—	23	—	67	—	—
INDIA	1975	—	—	—	24	—	58	—	—
AUSTRALIA	1977	—	—	—	18	—	4	—	1
SPAIN	1976	—	—	—	4	15	—	—	1
HOLY SEE	1977	3	—	1	3	—	44	—	1
PHILIPPINES	1977	—	—	—	1	—	7	—	—
SYRIAN ARAB REPUBLIC	1975	—	3	—	88	—	—	—	2
TURKEY	1976	—	—	—	—	—	—	—	—
GERMAN DEMOCRATIC REPUBLIC	1977								
SAUDI ARABIA	1976	—	13	—	858	—	48	—	—
IRAQ	1977	—	37	1	265	—	3	—	—
KUWAIT	1977	—	2	—	459	—	2	—	—
DENMARK	1977	—	—	—	36	—	13	—	1
ROMANIA	1974	52	—	191	40	—	19	—	3
SWEDEN ‡	1976	—	—	—	22	—	18	—	—
CZECHOSLOVAKIA	1977	—	—	—	2	—	59	1	—
YUGOSLAVIA	1977	17	4	1	11	—	86	—	1
HUNGARY	1977	1	—	15	1	—	66	—	—
BULGARIA	1976	—	—	—	—	—	—	—	—
POLAND	1977	—	—	10	6	—	17	—	—
SENEGAL	1977	51	52	51	2	—	1	27	16
IRELAND	1977	—	—	—	4	—	2	—	—
MOROCCO	1976	5	7	1	96	—	—	28	—
PAKISTAN	1976	—	—	—	23	—	1	—	1
NETHERLANDS	1974	1	—		21	—	1	—	—
IVORY COAST	1976	41	—	8	1	—	1	15	1
ALGERIA	1977	—	5	99	7	—	—	5	1
SINGAPORE	1977	—	—	—	—	—	—	—	—
GUATEMALA	1976	—	—	—	1	—	—	—	—
CUBA	1976	—	—	170	—	16	—	—	—
SUDAN	1977	—	1	—	701	—	14	—	—
LIBYAN ARAB JAMAHIRIYA	1977	—	1	—	480	—	—	—	—
PORTUGAL	1977	1	—	1	—	1	—	—	—
MEXICO ‡	1977								
CHILE	1977	—	—	—	—	—	—	—	—
IRAN	1976	—	—	—	7	—	2	—	—
TOGO	1976	6	11	6	—	—	—	7	—
FINLAND	1977	—	—	—	5	—	15	—	—
PANAMA	1977	—	—	—	15	11	6	—	—
TOTAL (50 COUNTRIES) ‡		653	616	2 324	7 924	60	2 594	997	265

3.15 Third level: foreign students by country of origin
Troisième degré: étudiants étrangers par pays d'origine
Tercer grado: estudiantes extranjeros por países de origen

HOST COUNTRY ‡ / PAYS D'ACCUEIL ‡ / PAIS HUESPED ‡	YEAR / ANNEE / AÑO	COUNTRY OF ORIGIN / PAYS D'ORIGINE / PAIS DE ORIGEN							
		GHANA	GUINEA	IVORY COAST	KENYA	LESOTHO	LIBERIA	LIBYAN ARAB JAMAHIRIYA	MADAGASCAR
UNITED STATES OF AMERICA ‡	1977	1 650	11	250	1 430	25	750	2 090	25
FRANCE	1977	96	314	2 675	31	—	13	130	1 766
UNITED KINGDOM	1977	601	—	28	902	36	17	183	9
GERMANY, FEDERAL REPUBLIC OF	1977	262	12	23	35	2	14	54	34
ITALY	1977	—	—	—	—	—	159	—	—
EGYPT	1974								
BELGIUM	1977	9	9	111	—	—	2	6	21
ARGENTINA	1974	—	—	—	—	—	—	3	—
JAPAN	1976	2	—	1	1	—	1	—	1
SWITZERLAND	1977	7	2	10	2	—	1	3	31
AUSTRIA	1977	13	—	1	4	—	1	2	—
GREECE	1977	4	—	—	36	—	—	57	7
INDIA	1975	5	—	—	377	—	—	—	—
AUSTRALIA	1977	36	—	—	15	8	—	1	—
SPAIN	1976	—	—	—	1	—	1	1	—
HOLY SEE	1977	13	—	2	14	—	—	1	12
PHILIPPINES	1977	—	—	—	—	—	—	—	—
SYRIAN ARAB REPUBLIC	1975	1	—	—	—	—	—	8	—
TURKEY	1976	—	—	—	—	—	—	18	—
GERMAN DEMOCRATIC REPUBLIC	1977								
SAUDI ARABIA	1976	2	1	—	—	—	—	1	—
IRAQ	1977	—	—	—	28	—	—	—	—
KUWAIT	1977	2	—	2	10	—	—	—	—
DENMARK	1977	10	—	—	8	—	—	—	—
ROMANIA	1974	15	9	2	16	2	42	1	53
SWEDEN ‡	1976	—	—	—	—	—	—	—	1
CZECHOSLOVAKIA	1977	25	15	—	2	1	—	—	—
YUGOSLAVIA	1977	28	30	—	9	—	1	20	6
HUNGARY	1977	22	16	—	6	1	—	5	4
BULGARIA	1976	—	27	—	4	—	—	—	—
POLAND	1977	19	20	—	14	—	—	1	—
SENEGAL	1977	9	61	68	—	—	2	—	17
IRELAND	1977	6	—	—	9	—	—	7	—
MOROCCO	1976	—	5	3	—	—	—	55	—
PAKISTAN	1976	1	—	—	11	—	—	5	—
NETHERLANDS	1974	2	—	—	—	—	—	—	—
IVORY COAST	1976	36	73	—	—	—	21	—	—
ALGERIA	1977	—	30	—	—	—	—	—	48
SINGAPORE	1977	—	—	—	—	—	—	—	—
GUATEMALA	1976	—	—	—	—	—	—	—	—
CUBA	1976	—	417	—	—	—	—	—	28
SUDAN	1977	—	—	—	3	—	—	—	—
LIBYAN ARAB JAMAHIRIYA	1977	—	—	—	2	—	—	—	—
PORTUGAL	1977	—	1	—	—	—	—	—	—
MEXICO ‡	1977	—	—	—	—	—	—	—	—
CHILE	1977	—	—	—	—	—	—	—	—
IRAN	1976	2	—	—	15	—	—	—	—
TOGO	1976	25	20	17	—	—	—	—	—
FINLAND	1977	1	—	—	4	—	—	—	—
PANAMA	1977	—	—	—	—	—	—	—	—
TOTAL (50 COUNTRIES) ‡		2 904	1 073	3 193	2 989	75	1 025	2 652	2 063

Third level: foreign students by country of origin 3.15
Troisième degré: étudiants étrangers par pays d'origine
Tercer grado: estudiantes extranjeros por países de origen

HOST COUNTRY ‡ / PAYS D'ACCUEIL ‡ / PAIS HUESPED ‡	YEAR / ANNEE / AÑO	COUNTRY OF ORIGIN / PAYS D'ORIGINE / PAIS DE ORIGEN							
		MALAWI	MALI	MAURITANIA	MAURITIUS	MOROCCO	MOZAMBIQUE	NIGER	NIGERIA
UNITED STATES OF AMERICA ‡	1977	50	17	3	20	65	3	10	13 510
FRANCE	1977	10	895	201	713	11 728	1	309	164
UNITED KINGDOM	1977	191	8	13	609	30	13	13	4 312
GERMANY, FEDERAL REPUBLIC OF	1977	5	19	1	13	138	1	3	448
ITALY	1977	—	—	—	—	—	—	—	51
EGYPT	1974								
BELGIUM	1977	—	57	4	15	940	—	10	51
ARGENTINA	1974	—	—	—	—	3	—	—	—
JAPAN	1976	—	—	—	—	—	—	—	10
SWITZERLAND	1977	1	5	—	5	78	—	3	11
AUSTRIA	1977	—	—	—	—	2	—	3	53
GREECE	1977	—	—	—	—	—	—	—	55
INDIA	1975	15	—	—	766	1	9	—	69
AUSTRALIA	1977	6	—	18	—	1	—	—	50
SPAIN	1976	—	1	—	—	199	2	3	7
HOLY SEE	1977	1	1	2	3	—	7	10	112
PHILIPPINES	1977	—	—	—	—	—	—	—	138
SYRIAN ARAB REPUBLIC	1975	—	2	7	—	19	—	—	—
TURKEY	1976	—	—	—	—	—	—	—	—
GERMAN DEMOCRATIC REPUBLIC	1977								
SAUDI ARABIA	1976	—	11	—	—	40	—	—	40
IRAQ	1977	—	—	11	1	47	—	—	2
KUWAIT	1977	—	—	14	3	4	—	—	11
DENMARK	1977	—	—	1	—	9	—	—	15
ROMANIA	1974	—	8	11	11	13	3	—	83
SWEDEN ‡	1976	—	—	—	—	8	—	—	—
CZECHOSLOVAKIA	1977	—	—	—	3	5	1	—	48
YUGOSLAVIA	1977	—	24	—	—	5	3	—	23
HUNGARY	1977	—	11	—	1	4	—	—	85
BULGARIA	1976	—	—	—	—	—	—	—	—
POLAND	1977	—	1	4	—	8	—	—	41
SENEGAL	1977	—	228	86	6	23	—	85	30
IRELAND	1977	1	—	—	32	2	—	—	98
MOROCCO	1976	—	7	141	—	.	—	—	5
PAKISTAN	1976	1	—	21	8	—	—	—	1
NETHERLANDS	1974	—	1	—	—	5	—	—	7
IVORY COAST	1976	—	110	13	—	1	—	47	58
ALGERIA	1977	—	51	—	18	11	—	33	—
SINGAPORE	1977	—	—	—	—	—	—	—	—
GUATEMALA	1976	—	—	—	—	5	—	—	—
CUBA	1976	—	5	—	1	3	—	—	2
SUDAN	1977	—	1	—	13	—	—	—	2
LIBYAN ARAB JAMAHIRIYA	1977	—	—	—	—	4	—	1	1
PORTUGAL	1977	—	—	7	—	—	17	—	—
MEXICO ‡	1977	—	—	—	—	—	—	—	—
CHILE	1977	—	—	—	—	—	—	—	—
IRAN	1976	—	—	—	4	—	—	—	—
TOGO	1976	—	2	—	—	—	—	106	49
FINLAND	1977	1	—	—	1	2	—	—	32
PANAMA	1977	—	—	—	—	1	—	—	—
TOTAL (50 COUNTRIES) ‡		282	1 465	558	2 246	13 404	60	636	19 674

3.15 Third level: foreign students by country of origin
   Troisième degré: étudiants étrangers par pays d'origine
   Tercer grado: estudiantes extranjeros por países de origen

HOST COUNTRY ‡ / PAYS D'ACCUEIL ‡ / PAIS HUESPED ‡	YEAR ANNEE AÑO	COUNTRY OF ORIGIN / PAYS D'ORIGINE / PAIS DE ORIGEN							
		RWANDA	SENEGAL	SIERRA LEONE	SOMALIA	SOUTH AFRICA	SUDAN	SWAZILAND	TOGO
UNITED STATES OF AMERICA ‡	1977	4	24	790	42	860	340	30	17
FRANCE	1977	84	2 067	58	18	61	117	–	1 193
UNITED KINGDOM	1977	6	19	265	11	531	573	33	2
GERMANY, FEDERAL REPUBLIC OF	1977	26	44	44	34	108	82	–	78
ITALY	1977	26	–	–	204	22	–	–	–
EGYPT	1974								
BELGIUM	1977	134	75		3	17	7	1	25
ARGENTINA	1974	–	–	–	–	2	–	–	–
JAPAN	1976	–	–	–	–	1	3	–	–
SWITZERLAND	1977	47	8	1	1	7	5	–	8
AUSTRIA	1977	–	3	1	–	10	7	–	–
GREECE	1977	–	–	–	–	15	231	–	–
INDIA	1975	–	–	–	–	204	19	–	–
AUSTRALIA	1977	–	–	2	–	21	1	1	–
SPAIN	1976	2	2	–	–	1	3	–	–
HOLY SEE	1977	24	3	1	–	13	5	1	5
PHILIPPINES	1977	–	–	–	–	–	–	–	–
SYRIAN ARAB REPUBLIC	1975	–	1	–	3	–	135	–	–
TURKEY	1976	–	–	–	–	–	–	–	–
GERMAN DEMOCRATIC REPUBLIC	1977								
SAUDI ARABIA	1976	–	1	–	62	–	219	–	–
IRAQ	1977	–	1	–	61	–	253	–	–
KUWAIT	1977	–	5	–	43	2	18	–	–
DENMARK	1977	–	–	1	3	7	9	–	–
ROMANIA	1974	13	12	4	18	4	196	–	2
SWEDEN ‡	1976	–	–	–	–	2	–	–	–
CZECHOSLOVAKIA	1977	2	1	3	5	–	42	–	6
YUGOSLAVIA	1977	1	9	7	5	3	146	–	13
HUNGARY	1977	–	1	12	10	–	68	–	2
BULGARIA	1976	–	–	–	–	–	61	–	–
POLAND	1977	–	11	1	4	2	32	–	–
SENEGAL	1977	35	.	–	–	4	–	–	140
IRELAND	1977	–	–	9	1	134	10	2	–
MOROCCO	1976	–	33	1	–	–	70	–	1
PAKISTAN	1976	–	–	–	4	3	47	–	–
NETHERLANDS	1974	–	–	1	–	34	–	–	–
IVORY COAST	1976	–	48	7	–	–	2	–	60
ALGERIA	1977	–	21	–	–	–	8	–	38
SINGAPORE	1977	–	–	–	–	–	–	–	–
GUATEMALA	1976	–	–	–	–	–	–	–	–
CUBA	1976	–	5	–	23	–	1	–	–
SUDAN	1977	–	1	–	13	–	–	–	–
LIBYAN ARAB JAMAHIRIYA	1977	–	2	–	–	–	42	–	–
PORTUGAL	1977	–	–	–	–	2	–	–	–
MEXICO ‡	1977	–	–	–	–	–	–	–	–
CHILE	1977	–	–	–	–	–	–	–	–
IRAN	1976	–	1	–	1	–	8	–	–
TOGO	1976	1	5	–	–	–	1	–	–
FINLAND	1977	–	–	–	–	3	2	–	–
PANAMA	1977	–	–	–	–	–	–	–	–
TOTAL (50 COUNTRIES) ‡		405	2 403	1 208	569	2 073	2 763	68	1 590

Third level: foreign students by country of origin 3.15
Troisième degré: étudiants étrangers par pays d'origine
Tercer grado: estud:antes extranjeros por países de origen

HOST COUNTRY ‡ PAYS D'ACCUEIL ‡ PAIS HUESPED ‡	YEAR ANNEE AÑO	TUNISIA	UGANDA	UNITED REPUBLIC OF CAMEROON	UNITED REPUBLIC OF TANZANIA	UPPER VOLTA	ZAIRE	ZAMBIA	ZIMBABWE
COUNTRY OF ORIGIN / PAYS D'ORIGINE / PAIS DE ORIGEN									
UNITED STATES OF AMERICA ‡	1977	35	360	540	360	14	150	150	580
FRANCE	1977	9 510	20	3 149	10	930	994	17	5
UNITED KINGDOM	1977	21	147	100	411	4	15	575	1 001
GERMANY, FEDERAL REPUBLIC OF	1977	220	30	73	35	14	57	7	–
ITALY	1977	40	–	–	–	–	82	–	–
EGYPT	1974								
BELGIUM	1977	532	4	48	3	14	1 036	1	1
ARGENTINA	1974	2	–	–	–	–	–	–	–
JAPAN	1976	–	–	–	–	–	1	–	–
SWITZERLAND	1977	67	1	25	2	3	69	1	1
AUSTRIA	1977	4	2	2	5	–	7	–	1
GREECE	1977	–	28	11	14	–	19	–	14
INDIA	1975	–	142	–	364	–	–	87	41
AUSTRALIA	1977	1	23	–	28	–	–	9	17
SPAIN	1976	1	2	–	–	–	–	1	–
HOLY SEE	1977	5	43	9	25	2	39	1	1
PHILIPPINES	1977	–	1	–	4	–	–	–	1
SYRIAN ARAB REPUBLIC	1975	53	–	1	–	–	–	–	–
TURKEY	1976								
GERMAN DEMOCRATIC REPUBLIC	1977								
SAUDI ARABIA	1976	19	11	–	–	–	–	–	–
IRAQ	1977	200	31	–	–	–	–	–	–
KUWAIT	1977	1	10	–	9	–	–	1	–
DENMARK	1977	8	–	–	6	–	–	–	2
ROMANIA	1974	45	1	3	98	28	93	8	6
SWEDEN ‡	1976								
CZECHOSLOVAKIA	1977	23	10	–	5	3	–	1	10
YUGOSLAVIA	1977	9	7	3	10	2	8	9	2
HUNGARY	1977	18	3	–	43	12	2	2	1
BULGARIA	1976								
POLAND	1977	24	3	–	20	–	21	1	1
SENEGAL	1977	3	–	69	–	383	18		
IRELAND	1977	–	–	–	6	–	–	7	4
MOROCCO	1976	85	–	6	–	–	2	–	–
PAKISTAN	1976	–	1	–	23	–	–	–	–
NETHERLANDS	1974				3				
IVORY COAST	1976	1	1	25	–	131	5	–	–
ALGERIA	1977	53	–	17	–	20	–	–	–
SINGAPORE	1977	–	–	–	–	–	–	–	–
GUATEMALA	1976	–	–	–	–	–	–	–	–
CUBA	1976	8	1	2	67	–	2	–	–
SUDAN	1977	–	18	–	2	–	–	–	–
LIBYAN ARAB JAMAHIRIYA	1977	8	–	–	–	–	–	–	–
PORTUGAL	1977	–	–	–	–	–	11	1	3
MEXICO ‡	1977								
CHILE	1977	–	–	–	–	–	–	–	–
IRAN	1976	8	1	–	47	–	1	–	–
TOGO	1976	1	–	4	–	277	4	–	2
FINLAND	1977	–	4	–	6	–	–	–	–
PANAMA	1977	–	–	–	–	–	–	–	–
TOTAL (50 COUNTRIES) ‡		11 005	905	4 087	1 606	1 837	2 636	879	1 694

3.15 Third level: foreign students by country of origin
Troisième degré: étudiants étrangers par pays d'origine
Tercer grado: estudiantes extranjeros por países de origen

HOST COUNTRY ‡ PAYS D'ACCUEIL ‡ PAIS HUESPED ‡	YEAR ANNEE AÑO	AFRICA, OTHER AND NOT SPECIFIED	AMERICA, NORTH	ANTIGUA	BAHAMAS	BARBADOS	BELIZE	BERMUDA
UNITED STATES OF AMERICA ‡	1977	399	32 744	21	890	240	28	330
FRANCE	1977	31	5 989	–	–	4	–	–
UNITED KINGDOM	1977	82	5 226	12	45	119	18	40
GERMANY, FEDERAL REPUBLIC OF	1977	589	3 948	–	–	–	–	–
ITALY	1977	385	1 726	–	–	–	–	–
EGYPT	1974	1 201	–					
BELGIUM	1977	1 126	915	–	2	–	–	–
ARGENTINA	1974	–	402	–	–	–	–	–
JAPAN	1976	–	945	–	–	–	–	–
SWITZERLAND	1977	2	662	–	–	1	3	–
AUSTRIA	1977	–	479	–	–	–	–	–
GREECE	1977	37	351	–	–	–	–	–
INDIA	1975	13	121	–	–	–	–	–
AUSTRALIA	1977	36	307	–	–	–	–	1
SPAIN	1976	2	1 843	–	–	–	–	–
HOLY SEE	1977	6	919	–	1	–	–	–
PHILIPPINES	1977	–	1 968	–	–	–	–	–
SYRIAN ARAB REPUBLIC	1975	15	4	–	–	–	–	–
TURKEY	1976	–	–	–	–	–	–	–
GERMAN DEMOCRATIC REPUBLIC	1977	994	257					
SAUDI ARABIA	1976	–	–	–	–	–	–	–
IRAQ	1977	56	4	–	–	–	–	–
KUWAIT	1977	24	1	–	–	–	–	–
DENMARK	1977	1	314	–	–	–	–	–
ROMANIA	1974	4	209	–	–	–	–	–
SWEDEN ‡	1976	49	202	–	–	–	–	–
CZECHOSLOVAKIA	1977	3	58	–	–	–	–	–
YUGOSLAVIA	1977	4	70	–	–	–	–	–
HUNGARY	1977	4	95	–	–	–	–	–
BULGARIA	1976	–	127	–	–	–	–	–
POLAND	1977	–	354	–	–	–	–	–
SENEGAL	1977	28	5	–	–	–	–	–
IRELAND	1977	1	363	1	–	–	–	–
MOROCCO	1976	–	2	–	–	–	–	–
PAKISTAN	1976	23	5	–	–	–	–	–
NETHERLANDS	1974	2	146	–	–	–	–	–
IVORY COAST	1976	1	12	–	–	3	–	–
ALGERIA	1977	32	–	–	–	–	–	–
SINGAPORE	1977	–	1	–	–	–	–	–
GUATEMALA	1976	–	1 101	–	–	–	28	–
CUBA	1976	33	58	–	–	–	–	–
SUDAN	1977	92	1	–	–	–	–	–
LIBYAN ARAB JAMAHIRIYA	1977	24	–	–	–	–	–	–
PORTUGAL	1977	178	38	–	–	–	–	–
MEXICO ‡	1977	4	478	–	–	–	–	–
CHILE	1977	–	78	–	–	–	–	–
IRAN	1976	–	67	–	–	–	–	–
TOGO	1976	–	1	–	–	–	–	–
FINLAND	1977	4	77	–	–	–	–	–
PANAMA	1977	–	188	–	1	8	–	–
TOTAL (50 COUNTRIES) ‡		5 485	62 861	34	939	375	77	371

Third level: foreign students by country of origin 3.15
Troisième degré: étudiants étrangers par pays d'origine
Tercer grado: estudiantes extranjeros por países de origen

HOST COUNTRY ‡ PAYS D'ACCUEIL ‡ PAIS HUESPED ‡	YEAR ANNEE AÑO	CANADA	COSTA RICA	CUBA	DOMINICA	DOMINICAN REPUBLIC	EL SALVADOR	GRENADA	GUATEMALA
UNITED STATES OF AMERICA ‡	1977	12 600	590	3 530	—	540	810	57	420
FRANCE	1977	1 116	97	18	—	107	29	—	39
UNITED KINGDOM	1977	1 059	35	1	—	3	24	—	1
GERMANY, FEDERAL REPUBLIC OF	1977	308	40	4	—	14	33	3	35
ITALY	1977	108	9	—	—	—	—	—	—
EGYPT	1974								
BELGIUM	1977	71	9	6	—	4	17	—	5
ARGENTINA	1974	19	28	28	11	—	4	—	3
JAPAN	1976	40	2	—	—	2	8	—	2
SWITZERLAND	1977	109	6	1	—	1	10	—	1
AUSTRIA	1977	42	4	1	—	—	—	—	6
GREECE	1977	51	—	—	—	—	—	—	—
INDIA	1975	9	—	—	—	—	—	—	—
AUSTRALIA	1977	97	—	—	—	—	—	—	—
SPAIN	1976	19	52	278	—	44	5	—	13
HOLY SEE	1977	87	5	3	—	3	5	1	2
PHILIPPINES	1977	—	—	—	—	—	—	—	—
SYRIAN ARAB REPUBLIC	1975	2	—	—	—	—	—	—	—
TURKEY	1976	—	—	—	—	—	—	—	—
GERMAN DEMOCRATIC REPUBLIC	1977								
SAUDI ARABIA	1976	—	—	—	—	—	—	—	—
IRAQ	1977	—	—	—	—	—	—	—	—
KUWAIT	1977	—	1	—	—	—	—	—	—
DENMARK	1977	28	—	—	—	—	—	1	—
ROMANIA	1974	—	14	141	—	7	—	—	—
SWEDEN ‡	1976	12	—	—	—	—	—	—	—
CZECHOSLOVAKIA	1977	—	12	31	—	—	—	—	—
YUGOSLAVIA	1977	11	1	—	—	—	—	—	—
HUNGARY	1977	5	9	37	—	5	—	—	—
BULGARIA	1976	—	—	127	—	—	—	—	—
POLAND	1977	45	8	31	—	—	—	—	—
SENEGAL	1977	3	—	—	—	—	—	—	—
IRELAND	1977	55	—	—	—	—	—	2	—
MOROCCO	1976	1	—	—	—	—	—	—	—
PAKISTAN	1976	—	—	—	—	—	—	—	—
NETHERLANDS	1974	24	1	—	—	—	—	—	—
IVORY COAST	1976	2	—	—	—	—	—	—	—
ALGERIA	1977	—	—	—	—	—	—	—	—
SINGAPORE	1977	—	—	—	—	—	—	—	—
GUATEMALA	1976	1	59	43	—	—	376	—	.
CUBA	1976	—	2	.	—	6	8	—	1
SUDAN	1977	—	—	—	—	—	—	—	—
LIBYAN ARAB JAMAHIRIYA	1977	—	—	—	—	—	—	—	—
PORTUGAL	1977	3	—	1	—	—	—	—	—
MEXICO ‡	1977	5	43	9	—	36	24	—	17
CHILE	1977	—	6	1	—	1	6	—	3
IRAN	1976	3	—	—	—	—	—	—	—
TOGO	1976	1	—	—	—	—	—	—	—
FINLAND	1977	15	—	—	—	—	—	—	—
PANAMA	1977	—	31	17	—	3	33	—	5
TOTAL (50 COUNTRIES) ‡		15 951	1 064	4 308	11	780	1 393	63	553

637

3.15 Third level: foreign students by country of origin
Troisième degré: étudiants étrangers par pays d'origine
Tercer grado: estudiantes extranjeros por países de origen

HOST COUNTRY ‡ PAYS D'ACCUEIL ‡ PAIS HUESPED ‡	YEAR ANNEE AÑO	COUNTRY OF ORIGIN / PAYS D'ORIGINE / PAIS DE ORIGEN HAITI	HONDURAS	JAMAICA	MEXICO	NETHERLANDS ANTILLES	NICARAGUA	PANAMA	PUERTO RICO
UNITED STATES OF AMERICA ‡	1977	540	740	2 150	5 170	50	870	1 720	—
FRANCE	1977	310	21	17	578	—	77	89	—
UNITED KINGDOM	1977	1	4	189	343	15	12	18	7
GERMANY, FEDERAL REPUBLIC OF	1977	34	30	9	147	—	34	21	—
ITALY	1977	—	—	—	—	—	17	43	—
EGYPT	1974								
BELGIUM	1977	104	4	2	47	—	7	3	—
ARGENTINA	1974	7	20	—	15	—	19	81	3
JAPAN	1976	—	—	—	26	—	1	—	—
SWITZERLAND	1977	8	1	—	27	—	4	7	—
AUSTRIA	1977	1	—	1	14	—	1	1	—
GREECE	1977	—	—	—	5	—	—	1	—
INDIA	1975	—	—	—	—	—	—	—	—
AUSTRALIA	1977	—	—	2	3	—	—	—	—
SPAIN	1976	51	3	—	175	—	93	105	89
HOLY SEE	1977	5	2	—	278	—	3	3	4
PHILIPPINES	1977	—	—	—	—	—	—	—	—
SYRIAN ARAB REPUBLIC	1975	—	—	—	—	—	—	—	—
TURKEY	1976	—	—	—	—	—	—	—	—
GERMAN DEMOCRATIC REPUBLIC	1977								
SAUDI ARABIA	1976	—	—	—	—	—	—	—	—
IRAQ	1977	—	—	—	—	—	—	—	—
KUWAIT	1977	—	—	—	—	—	—	—	—
DENMARK	1977	—	—	3	4	—	—	—	—
ROMANIA	1974	—	1	—	4	—	1	6	—
SWEDEN ‡	1976	—	—	—	3	—	—	—	—
CZECHOSLOVAKIA	1977	—	1	—	2	—	2	7	—
YUGOSLAVIA	1977	—	—	—	3	—	—	7	1
HUNGARY	1977	—	—	3	—	—	—	6	—
BULGARIA	1976	—	—	—	—	—	—	—	—
POLAND	1977	—	1	—	3	—	—	10	—
SENEGAL	1977	1	—	—	—	—	—	—	—
IRELAND	1977	—	—	2	2	2	1	—	—
MOROCCO	1976	—	—	—	—	—	—	—	—
PAKISTAN	1976	—	—	—	—	—	—	—	—
NETHERLANDS	1974	1	—	—	—	—	—	—	—
IVORY COAST	1976	2	—	—	—	—	—	—	—
ALGERIA	1977	—	—	—	—	—	—	—	—
SINGAPORE	1977	—	—	—	—	—	—	—	—
GUATEMALA	1976	1	165	—	81	—	267	12	—
CUBA	1976	2	8	—	10	—	—	19	1
SUDAN	1977	—	—	—	—	—	—	—	—
LIBYAN ARAB JAMAHIRIYA	1977	—	—	—	—	—	—	—	—
PORTUGAL	1977	—	—	—	—	—	—	—	—
MEXICO ‡	1977	29	53	—	.	—	97	39	—
CHILE	1977	—	12	—	3	—	6	14	2
IRAN	1976	—	—	—	—	—	—	—	—
TOGO	1976	—	—	—	—	—	—	—	—
FINLAND	1977	—	—	—	1	—	—	—	—
PANAMA	1977	—	6	—	10	—	46	—	2
TOTAL (50 COUNTRIES) ‡		1 097	1 072	2 378	6 954	67	1 558	2 212	109

Third level: foreign students by country of origin 3.15
Troisième degré: étudiants étrangers par pays d'origine
Tercer grado: estudiantes extranjeros por países de origen

HOST COUNTRY ‡ PAYS D'ACCUEIL ‡ PAIS HUESPED ‡	YEAR ANNEE AÑO	COUNTRY OF ORIGIN / PAYS D'ORIGINE / PAIS DE ORIGEN					
		ST KITTS-NEVIS AND ANGUILLA	ST LUCIA	ST VINCENT AND THE GRENADINES	TRINIDAD AND TOBAGO	UNITED STATES OF AMERICA	AMERICA, NORTH OTHER AND NOT SPECIFIED
UNITED STATES OF AMERICA ‡	1977	—	—	—	1 020	.	428
FRANCE	1977	—	—	—	18	3 469	—
UNITED KINGDOM	1977	—	—	—	237	2 939	104
GERMANY, FEDERAL REPUBLIC OF	1977	—	—	—	3	3 233	—
ITALY	1977	—	—	—	—	1 549	—
EGYPT	1974						
BELGIUM	1977	—	—	—	—	634	—
ARGENTINA	1974	—	—	—	—	164	—
JAPAN	1976	—	—	—	1	863	—
SWITZERLAND	1977	—	—	—	3	480	—
AUSTRIA	1977	—	—	—	—	408	—
GREECE	1977	—	—	—	—	294	—
INDIA	1975	—	—	—	7	91	14
AUSTRALIA	1977	—	—	—	1	193	10
SPAIN	1976	—	—	—	—	916	—
HOLY SEE	1977	—	—	—	2	515	—
PHILIPPINES	1977	—	—	—	—	—	1 968
SYRIAN ARAB REPUBLIC	1975	—	—	—	—	2	—
TURKEY	1976	—	—	—	—	—	—
GERMAN DEMOCRATIC REPUBLIC	1977						257
SAUDI ARABIA	1976	—	—	—	—	—	—
IRAQ	1977	—	—	—	—	4	—
KUWAIT	1977	—	—	—	—	—	—
DENMARK	1977	—	—	—	3	275	—
ROMANIA	1974	—	—	—	—	35	—
SWEDEN ‡	1976	—	—	—	—	181	6
CZECHOSLOVAKIA	1977	—	—	—	—	3	—
YUGOSLAVIA	1977	—	—	—	—	47	—
HUNGARY	1977	—	—	—	—	30	—
BULGARIA	1976	—	—	—	—	—	—
POLAND	1977	—	—	—	—	256	—
SENEGAL	1977	—	—	—	—	1	—
IRELAND	1977	—	—	—	13	285	—
MOROCCO	1976	—	—	—	—	1	—
PAKISTAN	1976	—	—	—	—	5	—
NETHERLANDS	1974	—	—	—	1	119	—
IVORY COAST	1976	—	—	—	—	5	—
ALGERIA	1977	—	—	—	—	—	—
SINGAPORE	1977	—	—	—	—	1	—
GUATEMALA	1976	—	—	—	—	68	—
CUBA	1976	—	—	—	—	1	—
SUDAN	1977	—	—	—	—	1	—
LIBYAN ARAB JAMAHIRIYA	1977	—	—	—	—	—	—
PORTUGAL	1977	—	—	—	—	34	—
MEXICO ‡	1977	—	—	—	—	126	—
CHILE	1977	—	—	—	—	24	—
IRAN	1976	—	—	—	—	64	—
TOGO	1976	—	—	—	—	—	—
FINLAND	1977	—	—	—	—	61	—
PANAMA	1977	—	—	—	—	22	—
TOTAL (50 COUNTRIES) ‡		—	—	—	1 309	17 399	2 787

3.15 Third level: foreign students by country of origin
Troisième degré: étudiants étrangers par pays d'origine
Tercer grado: estudiantes extranjeros por países de origen

HOST COUNTRY ‡ / PAYS D'ACCUEIL ‡ / PAIS HUESPED ‡	YEAR / ANNEE / AÑO	COUNTRY OF ORIGIN / PAYS D'ORIGINE / PAIS DE ORIGEN							
		AMERICA, SOUTH	ARGENTINA	BOLIVIA	BRAZIL	CHILE	COLOMBIA	ECUADOR	GUYANA
UNITED STATES OF AMERICA ‡	1977	19 100	740	590	2 830	1 090	2 560	800	832
FRANCE	1977	5 705	674	160	1 520	860	731	148	7
UNITED KINGDOM	1977	1 972	76	11	397	317	132	27	225
GERMANY, FEDERAL REPUBLIC OF	1977	1 868	175	145	392	442	209	79	5
ITALY	1977	1 220	215	34	118	—	46	30	—
EGYPT	1974	16							
BELGIUM	1977	505	43	49	71	121	87	10	—
ARGENTINA	1974	11 050	.	2 909	563	795	183	65	—
JAPAN	1976	190	20	11	120	6	7	—	—
SWITZERLAND	1977	406	41	60	76	76	58	12	2
AUSTRIA	1977	164	20	2	37	22	28	1	—
GREECE	1977	26	1	—	11	4	3	—	—
INDIA	1975	29	—	—	—	—	—	—	29
AUSTRALIA	1977	15	2	—	2	1	2	—	—
SPAIN	1976	1 705	215	26	54	172	204	33	—
HOLY SEE	1977	479	72	5	175	24	104	18	—
PHILIPPINES	1977	—	—	—	—	—	—	—	—
SYRIAN ARAB REPUBLIC	1975	4	3	1	—	—	—	—	—
TURKEY	1976	—	—	—	—	—	—	—	—
GERMAN DEMOCRATIC REPUBLIC	1977	343							
SAUDI ARABIA	1976	13	—	—	—	—	—	—	—
IRAQ	1977	—	—	—	—	—	—	—	—
KUWAIT	1977	—	—	—	—	—	—	—	—
DENMARK	1977	89	12	—	12	59	1	—	1
ROMANIA	1974	468	2	19	1	250	29	71	—
SWEDEN ‡	1976	183	10	—	12	—	—	—	—
CZECHOSLOVAKIA	1977	48	—	13	1	5	6	11	1
YUGOSLAVIA	1977	39	10	8	1	14	—	—	1
HUNGARY	1977	117	4	21	2	27	5	26	1
BULGARIA	1976	—	—	—	—	—	—	—	—
POLAND	1977	157	4	19	35	7	18	29	—
SENEGAL	1977	1	—	—	1	—	—	—	—
IRELAND	1977	7	—	—	—	2	1	—	3
MOROCCO	1976	—	—	—	—	—	—	—	—
PAKISTAN	1976	—	—	—	—	—	—	—	—
NETHERLANDS	1974	30	2	4	10	4	3	—	—
IVORY COAST	1976	3	1	—	1	—	—	—	—
ALGERIA	1977	4	—	—	—	4	—	—	—
SINGAPORE	1977	—	—	—	—	—	—	—	—
GUATEMALA	1976	68	11	2	1	21	10	5	—
CUBA	1976	156	4	12	7	109	6	10	4
SUDAN	1977	—	—	—	—	—	—	—	—
LIBYAN ARAB JAMAHIRIYA	1977	—	—	—	—	—	—	—	—
PORTUGAL	1977	443	5	—	350	4	—	—	—
MEXICO ‡	1977	293	—	—	—	—	—	—	—
CHILE	1977	422	59	180	12	.	25	29	—
IRAN	1976	1	—	—	—	—	—	—	—
TOGO	1976	—	—	—	—	—	—	—	—
FINLAND	1977	31	2	5	3	16	1	1	—
PANAMA	1977	183	7	4	8	41	77	32	—
TOTAL (50 COUNTRIES) ‡		47 553	2 430	4 290	6 823	4 493	4 536	1 437	1 110

Third level: foreign students by country of origin 3.15
Troisième degré: étudiants étrangers par pays d'origine
Tercer grado: estudiantes extranjeros por países de origen

HOST COUNTRY ‡ PAYS D'ACCUEIL ‡ PAIS HUESPED ‡	YEAR ANNEE AÑO	COUNTRY OF ORIGIN / PAYS D'ORIGINE / PAIS DE ORIGEN						
		PARAGUAY	PERU	URUGUAY	VENEZUELA	AMERICA, SOUTH OTHER AND NOT SPECIFIED	ASIA	AFGHANISTAN
UNITED STATES OF AMERICA ‡	1977	26	1 950	200	7 420	62	130 970	450
FRANCE	1977	31	503	249	821	1	19 275	202
UNITED KINGDOM	1977	5	64	21	692	5	28 843	53
GERMANY, FEDERAL REPUBLIC OF	1977	24	212	31	154	–	21 299	453
ITALY	1977	–	67	–	506	204	4 799	–
EGYPT	1974					16	934	
BELGIUM	1977	5	80	21	18	–	2 439	1
ARGENTINA	1974	2 600	2 991	754	190	–	167	–
JAPAN	1976	1	20	–	5	–	13 036	14
SWITZERLAND	1977	3	31	20	27	–	1 196	11
AUSTRIA	1977	–	20	3	31	–	2 145	15
GREECE	1977	–	–	–	6	1	7 814	–
INDIA	1975	–	–	–	–	–	5 746	201
AUSTRALIA	1977	–	–	2	–	6	6 528	11
SPAIN	1976	7	290	43	661	–	1 302	–
HOLY SEE	1977	10	20	11	29	11	552	–
PHILIPPINES	1977	–	–	–	–	–	4 731	–
SYRIAN ARAB REPUBLIC	1975	–	–	–	–	–	6 568	–
TURKEY	1976	–	–	–	–	–	5 610	22
GERMAN DEMOCRATIC REPUBLIC	1977					343	1 917	
SAUDI ARABIA	1976	–	–	–	–	13	4 193	–
IRAQ	1977	–	–	–	–	–	4 075	13
KUWAIT	1977	–	–	–	–	–	3 402	2
DENMARK	1977	–	3	–	1	–	162	2
ROMANIA	1974	–	58	–	38	–	1 467	2
SWEDEN ‡	1976	–	–	–	–	161	378	–
CZECHOSLOVAKIA	1977	–	5	3	3	–	1 484	44
YUGOSLAVIA	1977	–	–	1	5	–	1 702	2
HUNGARY	1977	–	24	2	5	–	868	21
BULGARIA	1976	–	–	–	–	–	660	–
POLAND	1977	1	36	1	7	–	626	17
SENEGAL	1977	–	–	–	–	–	189	–
IRELAND	1977	–	–	–	1	–	276	–
MOROCCO	1976	–	–	–	–	–	1 061	–
PAKISTAN	1976	–	–	–	–	–	1 500	4
NETHERLANDS	1974	–	2	2	–	3	569	–
IVORY COAST	1976	–	1	–	–	–	77	–
ALGERIA	1977	–	–	–	–	–	806	–
SINGAPORE	1977	–	–	–	–	–	1 246	–
GUATEMALA	1976	–	7	–	11	–	8	–
CUBA	1976	–	–	2	2	–	134	–
SUDAN	1977	–	–	–	–	–	121	–
LIBYAN ARAB JAMAHIRIYA	1977	–	–	–	–	–	308	1
PORTUGAL	1977	–	–	1	83	–	6	–
MEXICO ‡	1977	–	–	–	–	293	16	–
CHILE	1977	6	81	16	14	–	23	–
IRAN	1976	–	–	–	1	–	479	115
TOGO	1976	–	–	–	–	–	3	–
FINLAND	1977	–	1	1	1	–	95	–
PANAMA	1977	1	13	–	–	–	23	–
TOTAL (50 COUNTRIES) ‡		2 720	6 479	1 384	10 732	1 119	291 828	1 656

3.15 Third level: foreign students by country of origin
Troisième degré: étudiants étrangers par pays d'origine
Tercer grado: estudiantes extranjeros por países de origen

HOST COUNTRY ‡ PAYS D'ACCUEIL ‡ PAIS HUESPED ‡	YEAR ANNEE AÑO	COUNTRY OF ORIGIN / PAYS D'ORIGINE / PAIS DE ORIGEN							
		BAHRAIN	BANGLADESH	BHUTAN	BRUNEI	BURMA	CHINA	CYPRUS	DEMOCRATIC KAMPUCHEA
UNITED STATES OF AMERICA ‡	1977	130	760	2	3	22	13 650	280	250
FRANCE	1977	6	15	3	—	6	770	633	889
UNITED KINGDOM	1977	185	384	5	404	21	156	1 044	5
GERMANY, FEDERAL REPUBLIC OF	1977	3	47	—	—	15	415	119	8
ITALY	1977	—	—	—	—	—	19	149	—
EGYPT	1974								
BELGIUM	1977	—	18	—	—	—	30	14	2
ARGENTINA	1974	—	—	—	—	—	3	—	—
JAPAN	1976	—	31	—	—	16	3 160	—	24
SWITZERLAND	1977	—	1	—	—	—	13	8	5
AUSTRIA	1977	—	—	—	—	—	82	14	1
GREECE	1977	—	—	—	—	—	—	5 798	—
INDIA	1975	55	133	107	—	13	2	—	1
AUSTRALIA	1977	—	66	4	13	29	46	9	9
SPAIN	1976	—	—	—	—	—	11	—	—
HOLY SEE	1977	—	5	—	—	—	21	4	—
PHILIPPINES	1977	—	—	—	—	—	358	—	—
SYRIAN ARAB REPUBLIC	1975	83	—	—	—	—	—	—	—
TURKEY	1976	—	—	—	—	—	—	1 952	—
GERMAN DEMOCRATIC REPUBLIC	1977								
SAUDI ARABIA	1976	193	—	—	—	6	4	—	—
IRAQ	1977	297	—	—	—	—	8	1	—
KUWAIT	1977	709	2	—	—	—	—	—	—
DENMARK	1977	—	1	—	—	—	1	1	—
ROMANIA	1974	—	5	—	—	—	16	32	10
SWEDEN ‡	1976	—	—	—	—	—	1	—	—
CZECHOSLOVAKIA	1977	—	11	—	—	—	—	105	1
YUGOSLAVIA	1977	—	—	—	—	2	2	27	—
HUNGARY	1977	—	10	—	—	1	—	24	—
BULGARIA	1976	—	—	—	—	—	—	62	—
POLAND	1977	—	41	—	—	—	1	14	—
SENEGAL	1977	—	—	—	—	—	—	—	—
IRELAND	1977	3	1	—	—	—	1	—	—
MOROCCO	1976	5	—	—	—	—	—	—	2
PAKISTAN	1976	12	—	—	—	4	35	—	—
NETHERLANDS	1974	—	1	—	—	—	11	—	—
IVORY COAST	1976	—	—	—	—	—	—	—	—
ALGERIA	1977	—	—	—	—	—	—	—	—
SINGAPORE	1977	—	—	3	2	2	15	—	—
GUATEMALA	1976	—	—	—	—	—	8	—	—
CUBA	1976	—	—	—	—	—	—	—	—
SUDAN	1977	—	—	—	—	—	—	—	—
LIBYAN ARAB JAMAHIRIYA	1977	2	—	—	—	—	3	—	—
PORTUGAL	1977	—	—	—	—	—	1	—	—
MEXICO ‡	1977	—	—	—	—	—	—	—	—
CHILE	1977	—	—	—	—	—	1	—	—
IRAN	1976	21	—	—	—	—	—	—	—
TOGO	1976	—	—	—	—	—	—	—	—
FINLAND	1977	—	4	—	—	—	4	2	—
PANAMA	1977	—	—	—	—	—	15	—	—
TOTAL (50 COUNTRIES) ‡		1 704	1 536	124	422	137	18 863	10 292	1 207

Third level: foreign students by country of origin 3.15
Troisième degré: étudiants étrangers par pays d'origine
Tercer grado: estudiantes extranjeros por países de origen

		COUNTRY OF ORIGIN / PAYS D'ORIGINE / PAIS DE ORIGEN							
HOST COUNTRY ‡ PAYS D'ACCUEIL ‡ PAIS HUESPED ‡	YEAR ANNEE AÑO	HONG KONG	INDIA	INDONESIA	IRAN	IRAQ	ISRAEL	JAPAN	JORDAN
UNITED STATES OF									
AMERICA ‡	1977	12 100	9 080	1 820	36 220	1 190	2 550	9 050	2 120
FRANCE	1977	39	375	166	3 225	442	446	1 216	288
UNITED KINGDOM	1977	2 244	1 080	364	4 303	1 513	268	330	537
GERMANY, FEDERAL									
REPUBLIC OF	1977	–	642	3 481	4 239	223	397	1 152	630
ITALY	1977	–	92	–	1 237	58	1 467	–	750
EGYPT	1974								
BELGIUM	1977	–	79	218	185	21	63	8	15
ARGENTINA	1974	–	–	2	5	–	17	63	12
JAPAN	1976	111	52	130	25	3	8	.	1
SWITZERLAND	1977	–	55	41	235	10	83	61	10
AUSTRIA	1977	3	51	50	785	54	57	261	62
GREECE	1977	–	–	3	16	52	35	6	1 016
INDIA	1975	–	.	18	1 101	45	–	28	207
AUSTRALIA	1977	619	165	564	26	1	10	130	9
SPAIN	1976	–	10	1	12	6	21	14	467
HOLY SEE	1977	2	–	252	19	6	6	22	9
PHILIPPINES	1977	–	–	292	1 183	–	–	425	–
SYRIAN ARAB REPUBLIC	1975	–	–	19	34	277	–	1	2 252
TURKEY	1976	–	–	–	1 860	681	–	–	666
GERMAN DEMOCRATIC REPUBLIC	1977								
SAUDI ARABIA	1976	–	57	118	15	147	–	–	659
IRAQ	1977	–	15	22	36	.	–	–	645
KUWAIT	1977	–	7	22	25	105	–	–	1 333
DENMARK	1977	–	23	2	22	3	24	30	9
ROMANIA	1974	–	–	2	10	69	51	5	266
SWEDEN ‡	1976	–	28	–	–	–	–	20	–
CZECHOSLOVAKIA	1977	–	31	–	20	92	58	2	113
YUGOSLAVIA	1977	–	3	5	12	336	–	3	752
HUNGARY	1977	–	–	–	3	22	24	1	51
BULGARIA	1976	–	–	–	–	34	–	–	–
POLAND	1977	–	15	–	9	33	–	3	40
SENEGAL	1977	–	–	–	7	1	–	–	–
IRELAND	1977	40	20	1	7	36	3	6	6
MOROCCO	1976	–	–	2	8	19	–	–	425
PAKISTAN	1976	–	–	4	275	18	–	2	518
NETHERLANDS	1974	–	20	421	16	3	43	3	11
IVORY COAST	1976	–	1	–	4	–	4	1	–
ALGERIA	1977	–	–	–	–	5	–	–	–
SINGAPORE	1977	9	–	124	–	–	–	–	–
GUATEMALA	1976	–	–	–	–	–	–	–	–
CUBA	1976	–	–	–	–	–	–	–	–
SUDAN	1977	–	4	2	–	2	–	–	5
LIBYAN ARAB JAMAHIRIYA	1977	–	–	–	–	6	–	–	51
PORTUGAL	1977	–	–	–	1	1	1	–	1
MEXICO ‡	1977	–	–	–	–	–	–	–	–
CHILE	1977	–	–	–	–	–	2	2	3
IRAN	1976	1	34	2	.	35	–	7	47
TOGO	1976	–	–	–	–	–	–	–	–
FINLAND	1977	–	27	–	2	2	2	22	2
PANAMA	1977	–	3	–	2	–	1	1	–
TOTAL (50 COUNTRIES) ‡		15 168	11 969	8 148	55 184	5 551	5 641	12 874	13 988

3.15 Third level: foreign students by country of origin
Troisième degré: étudiants étrangers par pays d'origine
Tercer grado: estudiantes extranjeros por países de origen

HOST COUNTRY ‡ PAYS D'ACCUEIL ‡ PAIS HUESPED ‡	YEAR ANNEE AÑO	KOREA, REPUBLIC OF	KOREA, DEMOCRATIC PEOPLE'S REPUBLIC OF	KOREA, NOT SPECIFIED	KUWAIT	LAO PEOPLE'S DEMOCRATIC REPUBLIC	LEBANON	MALAYSIA	MALDIVES
UNITED STATES OF AMERICA ‡	1977	4 220	–	–	1 810	69	3 370	3 250	–
FRANCE	1977	292	34	–	42	401	4 443	73	–
UNITED KINGDOM	1977	48	4	–	241	8	281	9 095	–
GERMANY, FEDERAL REPUBLIC OF	1977	697	24	–	6	5	220	48	–
ITALY	1977	–	–	–	–	–	243	–	–
EGYPT	1974								
BELGIUM	1977	21	2	–	–	–	475	73	–
ARGENTINA	1974	8	–	–	–	–	30	–	–
JAPAN	1976	...	...	8 321	6	10	4	129	–
SWITZERLAND	1977	15	3	–	5	–	100	3	–
AUSTRIA	1977	10	–	29	–	–	2	2	–
GREECE	1977	–	–	–	–	–	77	3	–
INDIA	1975	–	–	–	115	9	9	1 590	–
AUSTRALIA	1977	39	–	–	–	61	10	3 280	–
SPAIN	1976	2	–	–	2	–	143	–	–
HOLY SEE	1977	34	7	–	–	1	27	6	–
PHILIPPINES	1977	68	–	–	–	–	–	101	–
SYRIAN ARAB REPUBLIC	1975	–	1	–	6	–	362	–	–
TURKEY	1976	–	–	–	–	–	–	–	–
GERMAN DEMOCRATIC REPUBLIC	1977								
SAUDI ARABIA	1976	–	–	–	19	–	65	13	–
IRAQ	1977	–	1	–	29	–	308	29	–
KUWAIT	1977	–	–	–	.	–	147	8	–
DENMARK	1977	4	–	–	–	–	4	2	–
ROMANIA	1974	–	9	–	3	–	87	1	–
SWEDEN ‡	1976	–	–	–	–	–	–	–	–
CZECHOSLOVAKIA	1977	–	10	–	–	23	163	–	–
YUGOSLAVIA	1977	–	4	–	21	–	29	1	–
HUNGARY	1977	–	27	–	1	26	42	–	–
BULGARIA	1976	–	–	–	–	–	–	–	–
POLAND	1977	–	4	–	3	25	29	–	–
SENEGAL	1977	–	–	–	–	–	178	–	–
IRELAND	1977	–	–	–	22	–	4	92	–
MOROCCO	1976	1	–	–	–	–	98	–	–
PAKISTAN	1976	9	–	–	42	–	5	35	–
NETHERLANDS	1974	1	–	–	–	1	2	1	–
IVORY COAST	1976	–	–	–	–	–	65	–	–
ALGERIA	1977	–	–	–	–	–	130	–	–
SINGAPORE	1977	–	–	–	–	–	–	985	–
GUATEMALA	1976	–	–	–	–	–	–	–	–
CUBA	1976	–	9	–	–	8	3	–	–
SUDAN	1977	–	–	–	–	–	–	3	–
LIBYAN ARAB JAMAHIRIYA	1977	–	–	–	–	–	9	–	–
PORTUGAL	1977	–	–	–	–	–	1	–	–
MEXICO ‡	1977	–	–	–	–	–	–	–	–
CHILE	1977	–	–	–	–	–	–	–	–
IRAN	1976	1	4	–	4	–	65	1	–
TOGO	1976	–	–	–	–	–	3	–	–
FINLAND	1977	2	–	–	–	–	3	–	–
PANAMA	1977	–	–	–	–	–	1	–	–
TOTAL (50 COUNTRIES) ‡		5 472	143	8 350	2 377	647	11 237	18 824	–

Third level: foreign students by country of origin 3.15
Troisième degré: étudiants étrangers par pays d'origine
Tercer grado: estudiantes extranjeros por países de origen

HOST COUNTRY ‡ PAYS D'ACCUEIL ‡ PAIS HUESPED ‡	YEAR ANNEE AÑO	MONGOLIA	NEPAL	OMAN	PAKISTAN	PHILIPPINES	QATAR	SAUDI ARABIA	SINGAPORE
COUNTRY OF ORIGIN / PAYS D'ORIGINE / PAIS DE ORIGEN									
UNITED STATES OF AMERICA ‡	1977	–	69	140	2 740	2 070	180	6 560	610
FRANCE	1977	1	7	8	75	13	5	24	94
UNITED KINGDOM	1977	2	60	26	818	58	26	243	1 564
GERMANY, FEDERAL REPUBLIC OF	1977	2	17	–	258	34	2	27	40
ITALY	1977	–	–	–	–	–	–	15	–
EGYPT	1974								
BELGIUM	1977	–	1	–	25	23	–	–	–
ARGENTINA	1974	–	–	–	–	–	–	–	–
JAPAN	1976	1	55	–	23	77	–	10	55
SWITZERLAND	1977	–	2	1	6	5	–	4	–
AUSTRIA	1977	–	1	–	18	5	–	58	2
GREECE	1977	–	–	–	4	1	–	4	–
INDIA	1975	–	914	–	4	4	–	4	55
AUSTRALIA	1977	–	15	–	69	60	–	1	531
SPAIN	1976	–	–	–	1	28	–	–	–
HOLY SEE	1977	2	–	–	6	48	–	–	1
PHILIPPINES	1977	–	–	–	–	.	–	–	–
SYRIAN ARAB REPUBLIC	1975	–	–	27	2	–	3	55	–
TURKEY	1976	–	–	–	133	–	–	–	–
GERMAN DEMOCRATIC REPUBLIC	1977								
SAUDI ARABIA	1976	–	–	7	127	56	51		–
IRAQ	1977	–	–	28	32	–	3	66	–
KUWAIT	1977	–	–	27	11	17	13	178	–
DENMARK	1977	–	–	–	13	1	–	–	–
ROMANIA	1974	27	2	–	20	–	–	–	–
SWEDEN ‡	1976	–	–	–	13	–	–	–	–
CZECHOSLOVAKIA	1977	103	5	–	2	–	–	–	–
YUGOSLAVIA	1977	–	2	–	1	1	–	–	–
HUNGARY	1977	70	2	–	1	–	–	–	–
BULGARIA	1976	68	–	–	–	–	–	–	–
POLAND	1977	66	–	1	–	–	–	–	–
SENEGAL	1977	–	–	–	–	–	–	1	–
IRELAND	1977	–	–	–	9	3	2	6	2
MOROCCO	1976	–	–	–	3	–	–	1	–
PAKISTAN	1976	–	9	–	.	2	5	163	–
NETHERLANDS	1974	–	1	–	3	–	–	1	–
IVORY COAST	1976	–	–	–	–	–	–	–	–
ALGERIA	1977	–	–	–	–	–	–	–	–
SINGAPORE	1977	–	–	–	–	–	–	–	.
GUATEMALA	1976	–	–	–	–	–	–	–	–
CUBA	1976	1	–	–	–	–	–	1	2
SUDAN	1977	–	–	–	2	–	2	3	–
LIBYAN ARAB JAMAHIRIYA	1977	–	–	–	16	–	–	–	–
PORTUGAL	1977	–	–	–	–	–	–	–	–
MEXICO ‡	1977	–	–	–	–	–	–	–	–
CHILE	1977	–	–	–	–	–	–	–	–
IRAN	1976	–	–	–	82	1	–	3	–
TOGO	1976	–	–	–	–	–	–	–	–
FINLAND	1977	–	–	–	8	–	–	–	–
PANAMA	1977	–	–	–	–	–	–	–	–
TOTAL (50 COUNTRIES) ‡		343	1 162	265	4 525	2 507	292	7 428	2 956

3.15 Third level: foreign students by country of origin
Troisième degré: étudiants étrangers par pays d'origine
Tercer grado: estudiantes extranjeros por países de origen

		COUNTRY OF ORIGIN / PAYS D'ORIGINE / PAIS DE ORIGEN							
HOST COUNTRY ‡ / PAYS D'ACCUEIL ‡ / PAIS HUESPED ‡	YEAR / ANNEE / AÑO	SRI LANKA	SYRIAN ARAB REPUBLIC	THAILAND	TURKEY	UNITED ARAB EMIRATES	VIET-NAM	YEMEN	YEMEN DEMOCRATIC
UNITED STATES OF AMERICA ‡	1977	350	450	6 340	1 850	270	6 651	55	3
FRANCE	1977	43	1 312	347	1 296	21	1 813	81	126
UNITED KINGDOM	1977	1 602	149	334	1 241	53	33	36	8
GERMANY, FEDERAL REPUBLIC OF	1977	68	551	273	5 004	3	1 039	2	8
ITALY	1977	—	336	—	103	—	119	—	—
EGYPT	1974								
BELGIUM	1977	2	85	10	150	—	235	—	1
ARGENTINA	1974	—	10	—	7	10	—	—	—
JAPAN	1976	31	—	210	5	—	524	—	—
SWITZERLAND	1977	4	27	12	242	1	203	—	—
AUSTRIA	1977	1	82	19	436	—	44	1	—
GREECE	1977	—	202	3	576	—	—	—	—
INDIA	1975	412	4	632	—	—	6	24	—
AUSTRALIA	1977	137	1	352	3	—	228	—	—
SPAIN	1976	—	579	2	2	—	—	—	—
HOLY SEE	1977	22	19	4	—	—	25	—	—
PHILIPPINES	1977	—	—	2 304	—	—	—	—	—
SYRIAN ARAB REPUBLIC	1975	—	.	1	18	11	—	120	—
TURKEY	1976	—	296	—	.	—	—	—	—
GERMAN DEMOCRATIC REPUBLIC	1977								
SAUDI ARABIA	1976	—	178	57	20	18	—	568	468
IRAQ	1977	—	320	17	14	51	—	267	—
KUWAIT	1977	1	79	10	1	131	—	81	144
DENMARK	1977	1	3	2	8	—	4	2	—
ROMANIA	1974	3	124	—	—	—	614	—	109
SWEDEN ‡	1976	—	—	—	47	—	—	—	—
CZECHOSLOVAKIA	1977	2	234	—	1	—	363	—	99
YUGOSLAVIA	1977	4	351	—	14	—	—	28	10
HUNGARY	1977	3	98	—	—	—	322	42	69
BULGARIA	1976	—	137	—	—	—	359	—	—
POLAND	1977	—	63	—	—	—	199	23	—
SENEGAL	1977	—	1	—	1	—	—	—	—
IRELAND	1977	3	—	4	3	1	—	—	—
MOROCCO	1976	—	194	8	1	—	1	1	—
PAKISTAN	1976	15	38	63	10	15	—	—	—
NETHERLANDS	1974	1	2	2	24	—	1	—	—
IVORY COAST	1976	—	—	—	—	—	2	—	—
ALGERIA	1977	—	33	11	—	—	—	28	87
SINGAPORE	1977	—	—	9	—	—	—	—	—
GUATEMALA	1976								
CUBA	1976	—	18	—	—	—	56	15	—
SUDAN	1977	—	2	17	—	—	—	22	10
LIBYAN ARAB JAMAHIRIYA	1977	—	23	—	—	—	—	25	—
PORTUGAL	1977	—	—	—	—	—	—	—	—
MEXICO ‡	1977	—	—	—	—	—	—	—	—
CHILE	1977	—	2	—	—	10	—	—	—
IRAN	1976	1	2	1	27	—	1	24	—
TOGO	1976	—	—	—	—	—	—	—	—
FINLAND	1977	2	—	3	8	—	—	—	—
PANAMA	1977	—	—	—	1	—	—	—	—
TOTAL (50 COUNTRIES) ‡		2 708	6 005	11 047	11 113	595	12 842	1 445	1 142

Third level: foreign students by country of origin 3.15
Troisième degré: étudiants étrangers par pays d'origine
Tercer grado: estudiantes extranjeros por países de origen

HOST COUNTRY ‡ PAYS D'ACCUEIL ‡ PAIS HUESPED ‡	YEAR ANNEE AÑO	COUNTRY OF ORIGIN / PAYS D'ORIGINE / PAIS DE ORIGEN						
		PALESTINE (REFUGEES)	ASIA, OTHER AND NOT SPECIFIED	EUROPE	ALBANIA	ANDORRA	AUSTRIA	BELGIUM
UNITED STATES OF AMERICA ‡	1977	–	236	19 150	5	–	250	500
FRANCE	1977	–	3	18 535	16	60	210	688
UNITED KINGDOM	1977	–	17	6 861	3	–	39	117
GERMANY, FEDERAL REPUBLIC OF	1977	–	1 147	21 212	2	4	2 448	465
ITALY	1977	–	211	18 082	13	–	52	113
EGYPT	1974		934	222				
BELGIUM	1977	–	682	6 775	–	1	25	.
ARGENTINA	1974	–	–	4 955	–	–	55	19
JAPAN	1976	–	–	393	–	–	12	9
SWITZERLAND	1977	–	30	8 601	1	2	350	134
AUSTRIA	1977	–	–	7 168	–	–	.	19
GREECE	1977	–	18	390	195	–	2	1
INDIA	1975	–	53	260	–	–	2	–
AUSTRALIA	1977	–	30	415	–	–	4	4
SPAIN	1976	–	1	723	4	60	9	28
HOLY SEE	1977	–	4	5 072	–	–	36	37
PHILIPPINES	1977	–	–	–	–	–	–	–
SYRIAN ARAB REPUBLIC	1975	3 296	–	26	–	–	–	–
TURKEY	1976	–	–	–	–	–	–	–
GERMAN DEMOCRATIC REPUBLIC	1977		1 917	1 879				
SAUDI ARABIA	1976	1 081	266	–	–	–	–	–
IRAQ	1977	1 873	–	53	–	–	–	1
KUWAIT	1977	348	1	11	–	–	–	–
DENMARK	1977	–	–	2 389	–	–	20	9
ROMANIA	1974			489	11	–	7	1
SWEDEN ‡	1976	–	269	2 661	–	–	29	4
CZECHOSLOVAKIA	1977	2	–	1 311	–	1	–	–
YUGOSLAVIA	1977	92	–	440	4	–	9	–
HUNGARY	1977	8	–	974	–	–	1	–
BULGARIA	1976	–	–	281	–	–	–	–
POLAND	1977	–	40	923	–	–	2	2
SENEGAL	1977	–	–	349	–	–	–	3
IRELAND	1977	1	–	995	–	–	1	4
MOROCCO	1976	292	–	80	–	–	–	1
PAKISTAN	1976	217	–	8	–	–	–	–
NETHERLANDS	1974	–	–	734	–	1	27	132
IVORY COAST	1976	–	–	448	–	–	–	6
ALGERIA	1977	512	–	3	–	–	–	–
SINGAPORE	1977	–	97	1	–	–	–	–
GUATEMALA	1976	–	–	39	–	–	–	–
CUBA	1976	21	–	20	–	–	1	–
SUDAN	1977	47	–	1	–	–	–	–
LIBYAN ARAB JAMAHIRIYA	1977	170	2	14	–	–	–	–
PORTUGAL	1977	–	–	111	–	–	1	1
MEXICO ‡	1977	–	16	61	–	–	–	–
CHILE	1977	–	3	169	–	–	–	1
IRAN	1976	–	–	38	–	–	–	–
TOGO	1976	–	–	28	–	–	–	–
FINLAND	1977	–	2	260	–	–	5	–
PANAMA	1977	–	–	59	–	–	–	–
TOTAL (50 COUNTRIES) ‡		7 960	5 979	133 669	254	129	3 597	2 299

3.15 Third level: foreign students by country of origin
Troisième degré: étudiants étrangers par pays d'origine
Tercer grado: estudiantes extranjeros por países de origen

HOST COUNTRY ‡ / PAYS D'ACCUEIL ‡ / PAIS HUESPED ‡	YEAR / ANNEE / AÑO	BULGARIA	CZECHOSLOVAKIA	DENMARK	FINLAND	FRANCE	GERMAN DEMOCRATIC REPUBLIC	GERMANY, FEDERAL REPUBLIC OF	GERMANY, NOT SPECIFIED
UNITED STATES OF AMERICA ‡	1977	3	26	330	280	2 130	2	2 510	—
FRANCE	1977	89	84	142	119	.	91	2 337	—
UNITED KINGDOM	1977	9	11	92	68	366	7	776	—
GERMANY, FEDERAL REPUBLIC OF	1977	83	797	210	938	2 314	—	—	—
ITALY	1977	22	22	16	23	268	89	687	—
EGYPT	1974								
BELGIUM	1977	4	4	22	6	760	—	924	—
ARGENTINA	1974	4	9	4	3	558	87	20	—
JAPAN	1976	10	7	5	4	65	...	...	45
SWITZERLAND	1977	14	395	40	66	1 546	2	2 565	—
AUSTRIA	1977	31	35	18	138	90	—	2 613	—
GREECE	1977	6	1	6	4	26	—	19	—
INDIA	1975	—	—	—	—	33	—	6	—
AUSTRALIA	1977	2	2	3	1	18	20	—	—
SPAIN	1976	2	—	6	6	133	3	133	—
HOLY SEE	1977	—	19	1	—	141	1	117	—
PHILIPPINES	1977	—	—	—	—	—	—	—	—
SYRIAN ARAB REPUBLIC	1975	3	—	—	—	4	—	—	—
TURKEY	1976	—	—	—	—	—	—	—	—
GERMAN DEMOCRATIC REPUBLIC	1977								
SAUDI ARABIA	1976	—	—	—	—	—	—	—	—
IRAQ	1977	24	—	—	—	1	—	2	—
KUWAIT	1977	1	—	—	—	—	—	—	—
DENMARK	1977	6	15	.	60	123	—	300	—
ROMANIA	1974	93	32	1	1	5	91	47	—
SWEDEN ‡	1976	4	20	105	1 520	28	1	90	—
CZECHOSLOVAKIA	1977	380	.	—	2	3	355	1	—
YUGOSLAVIA	1977	45	17	1	—	3	10	23	—
HUNGARY	1977	93	185	—	2	2	205	7	—
BULGARIA	1976	.	—	—	—	—	228		—
POLAND	1977	185	184	1	9	12	308	15	—
SENEGAL	1977	2	—	—	1	325	—	3	—
IRELAND	1977	—	—	1	—	18	3	19	—
MOROCCO	1976	7	—	—	—	51	—	2	—
PAKISTAN	1976	—	—	—	—	—	—	—	—
NETHERLANDS	1974	3	54	17	9	44	—	164	—
IVORY COAST	1976	—	—	3	1	422	—	3	—
ALGERIA	1977	—	—	—	—	1	—	—	—
SINGAPORE	1977	—	—	—	—	—	—	—	—
GUATEMALA	1976	—	2	—	—	1	4	—	—
CUBA	1976	11	—	—	—	1	—	—	—
SUDAN	1977	—	—	—	—	—	—	—	—
LIBYAN ARAB JAMAHIRIYA	1977	8	—	—	—	—	—	—	—
PORTUGAL	1977	—	—	—	1	13	—	11	—
MEXICO ‡	1977	—	—	—	—	—	—	—	—
CHILE	1977	—	—	—	—	3	14	—	—
IRAN	1976	13	—	3	—	5	—	1	—
TOGO	1976	—	—	—	—	26	—	2	—
FINLAND	1977	7	2	12	.	18	1	47	—
PANAMA	1977	—	—	11	—	2	—	2	—
TOTAL (50 COUNTRIES) ‡		1 164	1 923	1 050	3 262	9 559	1 522	13 446	45

Third level: foreign students by country of origin 3.15
Troisième degré: étudiants étrangers par pays d'origine
Tercer grado: estudiantes extranjeros por países de origen

HOST COUNTRY ‡ PAYS D'ACCUEIL ‡ PAIS HUESPED ‡	YEAR ANNEE AÑO	GREECE	HUNGARY	ICELAND	IRELAND	ITALY	LIECHTENSTEIN	LUXEMBOURG	MALTA
UNITED STATES OF AMERICA ‡	1977	2 490	23	68	530	920	2	15	11
FRANCE	1977	4 039	89	53	146	1 343	5	812	15
UNITED KINGDOM	1977	2 461	15	130	540	259	–	49	93
GERMANY, FEDERAL REPUBLIC OF	1977	4 143	323	101	75	1 122	10	642	8
ITALY	1977	15 398	29	6	10	.	–	10	12
EGYPT	1974								
BELGIUM	1977	494	5	3	22	1 146	–	1 007	–
ARGENTINA	1974	14	19	–	9	1 827	–	–	–
JAPAN	1976	5	3	1	2	19	–	–	1
SWITZERLAND	1977	382	99	2	8	1 071	151	190	1
AUSTRIA	1977	812	65	20	12	1 929	55	223	2
GREECE	1977	.	1	–	–	21	–	–	–
INDIA	1975	–	4	–	–	–	–	–	–
AUSTRALIA	1977	33	1	–	9	24	–	2	5
SPAIN	1976	48	2	–	–	90	–	1	–
HOLY SEE	1977	35	6	–	209	3 368	–	4	33
PHILIPPINES	1977	–	–	–	–	–	–	–	–
SYRIAN ARAB REPUBLIC	1975	9	–	–	–	1	–	–	–
TURKEY	1976	–	–	–	–	–	–	–	–
GERMAN DEMOCRATIC REPUBLIC	1977								
SAUDI ARABIA	1976	–	–	–	–	–	–	–	–
IRAQ	1977	1	–	–	–	–	–	–	–
KUWAIT	1977	–	2	–	–	–	–	–	–
DENMARK	1977	15	5	347	16	31	–	–	1
ROMANIA	1974	30	27	1	–	4	–	–	–
SWEDEN ‡	1976	165	26	98	–	20	–	–	–
CZECHOSLOVAKIA	1977	93	95	–	–	3	–	–	–
YUGOSLAVIA	1977	208	25	6	–	45	–	–	–
HUNGARY	1977	7	.	–	–	–	–	–	–
BULGARIA	1976	–	53	–	–	–	–	–	–
POLAND	1977	16	117	–	–	2	1	–	–
SENEGAL	1977	1	–	–	–	1	–	–	–
IRELAND	1977	4	–	2	–	1	–	–	1
MOROCCO	1976	–	1	–	–	2	–	–	–
PAKISTAN	1976	–	–	–	–	–	–	–	–
NETHERLANDS	1974	36	5	1	5	22	–	6	–
IVORY COAST	1976	–	–	2	–	4	–	–	–
ALGERIA	1977	–	–	–	–	–	–	–	–
SINGAPORE	1977	–	–	–	–	–	–	–	–
GUATEMALA	1976	–	–	–	–	3	–	–	–
CUBA	1976								
SUDAN	1977	–	–	–	–	1	–	–	–
LIBYAN ARAB JAMAHIRIYA	1977	–	–	–	–	–	–	–	4
PORTUGAL	1977	–	2	–	–	8	–	–	–
MEXICO ‡	1977	–	–	–	–	–	–	–	–
CHILE	1977	1	1	–	–	10	–	–	3
IRAN	1976	–	–	–	2	3	–	–	1
TOGO	1976	–	–	–	–	–	–	–	–
FINLAND	1977	1	15	8	2	9	–	–	–
PANAMA	1977	4	–	–	–	3	–	–	–
TOTAL (50 COUNTRIES) ‡		30 945	1 058	849	1 597	13 312	224	2 961	191

3.15 Third level: foreign students by country of origin
Troisième degré: étudiants étrangers par pays d'origine
Tercer grado: estudiantes extranjeros por países de origen

HOST COUNTRY ‡ PAYS D'ACCUEIL ‡ PAIS HUESPED ‡	YEAR ANNEE AÑO	MONACO	NETHERLANDS	NORWAY	POLAND	PORTUGAL	ROMANIA	SAN MARINO	SPAIN
UNITED STATES OF AMERICA ‡	1977	3	980	880	280	340	40	—	740
FRANCE	1977	116	387	166	629	1 261	142	—	2 223
UNITED KINGDOM	1977	—	217	588	41	281	5	—	201
GERMANY, FEDERAL REPUBLIC OF	1977	—	1 432	705	242	171	154	—	723
ITALY	1977	—	41	40	52	31	61	175	73
EGYPT	1974								
BELGIUM	1977	—	1 404	58	55	264	12	—	322
ARGENTINA	1974	1	9	1	43	192	10	—	1 909
JAPAN	1976	—	13	5	9	20	3	—	13
SWITZERLAND	1977	1	234	207	78	120	27	—	345
AUSTRIA	1977	—	42	55	218	15	8	—	27
GREECE	1977	—	4	—	3	1	12	—	3
INDIA	1975	—	—	—	8	9	—	—	—
AUSTRALIA	1977	1	19	1	12	—	—	—	3
SPAIN	1976	2	19	17	10	8	5	—	.
HOLY SEE	1977	—	17	—	124	33	13	—	506
PHILIPPINES	1977	—	—	—	—	—	—	—	—
SYRIAN ARAB REPUBLIC	1975	—	—	—	2	—	1	—	1
TURKEY	1976	—	—	—	—	—	—	—	—
GERMAN DEMOCRATIC REPUBLIC	1977								
SAUDI ARABIA	1976	—	—	—	—	—	—	—	—
IRAQ	1977	—	—	—	5	—	2	—	—
KUWAIT	1977	—	—	—	—	—	—	—	—
DENMARK	1977	—	66	736	53	19	7	—	21
ROMANIA	1974	—	—	—	20	2	.	—	2
SWEDEN ‡	1976	—	32	251	80	6	5	—	23
CZECHOSLOVAKIA	1977	—	1	3	284	1	1	—	2
YUGOSLAVIA	1977	—	3	1	27	2	5	—	—
HUNGARY	1977	—	—	1	157	7	35	—	—
BULGARIA	1976	—	—	—	—	—	—	—	—
POLAND	1977	—	—	—	.	4	13	—	—
SENEGAL	1977	—	1	—	1	1	—	—	3
IRELAND	1977	—	8	79	1	2	—	—	6
MOROCCO	1976	—	—	—	5	2	2	—	5
PAKISTAN	1976	—	—	—	—	—	—	—	—
NETHERLANDS	1974	—	.	16	4	24	5	—	18
IVORY COAST	1976	—	—	—	—	—	—	—	1
ALGERIA	1977	—	—	—	—	—	2	—	—
SINGAPORE	1977	—	—	—	—	—	—	—	—
GUATEMALA	1976	—	—	—	—	—	—	—	27
CUBA	1976	—	—	—	2	—	—	—	5
SUDAN	1977	—	—	—	—	—	—	—	—
LIBYAN ARAB JAMAHIRIYA	1977	—	—	—	2	—	—	—	—
PORTUGAL	1977	—	2	—	2	.	—	—	65
MEXICO ‡	1977	—	—	—	—	—	—	—	—
CHILE	1977	—	1	—	—	1	—	—	52
IRAN	1976	—	1	—	4	1	—	—	—
TOGO	1976	—	—	—	—	—	—	—	—
FINLAND	1977	—	6	8	22	2	1	—	—
PANAMA	1977	—	—	—	—	2	—	—	35
TOTAL (50 COUNTRIES) ‡		124	4 939	3 818	2 475	2 820	571	175	7 354

Third level: foreign students by country of origin   3.15
Troisième degré: étudiants étrangers par pays d'origine
Tercer grado: estudiantes extranjeros por países de origen

HOST COUNTRY ‡ / PAYS D'ACCUEIL ‡ / PAIS HUESPED ‡	YEAR ANNEE AÑO	SWEDEN	SWITZERLAND	UNITED KINGDOM	YUGOSLAVIA	EUROPE, OTHER AND NOT SPECIFIED	OCEANIA	AUSTRALIA
UNITED STATES OF AMERICA ‡	1977	620	630	4 050	360	132	3 810	1 480
FRANCE	1977	250	566	2 127	326	4	158	126
UNITED KINGDOM	1977	71	220	.	54	148	1 044	756
GERMANY, FEDERAL REPUBLIC OF	1977	357	1 137	1 197	1 105	304	138	108
ITALY	1977	41	397	193	198	10	47	45
EGYPT	1974					222		
BELGIUM	1977	25	71	107	34	–	10	8
ARGENTINA	1974	11	16	30	105	–	13	13
JAPAN	1976	10	13	112	7	–	81	60
SWITZERLAND	1977	133	.	261	176	–	26	19
AUSTRIA	1977	71	190	113	367	–	23	20
GREECE	1977	5	3	63	12	2	59	56
INDIA	1975	–	–	194	4	–	371	2
AUSTRALIA	1977	1	11	196	6	37	660	.
SPAIN	1976	10	29	67	22	9	6	5
HOLY SEE	1977	2	34	169	160	7	42	28
PHILIPPINES	1977	–	–	–	–	–	–	–
SYRIAN ARAB REPUBLIC	1975	–	1	1	3	–	–	–
TURKEY	1976	–	–	–	–	–	–	–
GERMAN DEMOCRATIC REPUBLIC	1977					1 879	1	
SAUDI ARABIA	1976	–	–	–	–		–	–
IRAQ	1977	–	–	3	13	1	–	–
KUWAIT	1977	–	–	3	5	–	–	–
DENMARK	1977	264	51	211	13	–	7	5
ROMANIA	1974	–	1	3	110	–	–	–
SWEDEN ‡	1976	–	14	85	46	9	10	9
CZECHOSLOVAKIA	1977	–	2	–	84	–	–	–
YUGOSLAVIA	1977	–	2	4	.	–	8	8
HUNGARY	1977	1	–	–	271	–	1	1
BULGARIA	1976	–	–	–	–	–		
POLAND	1977	11	–	13	28	–	10	10
SENEGAL	1977	1	1	3	2	–	–	–
IRELAND	1977	3	5	836	–	1	11	10
MOROCCO	1976	–	–	–	2	–	–	–
PAKISTAN	1976	1	–	7	–	–	1	1
NETHERLANDS	1974	22	28	77	11	3	16	14
IVORY COAST	1976	1	2	3	–	–	–	–
ALGERIA	1977	–	–	1	–	–	–	–
SINGAPORE	1977	–	–	1	–	–	1	1
GUATEMALA	1976	–	–	2	–	–	–	–
CUBA	1976	–	–	–	–	–	–	–
SUDAN	1977	–	–	–	–	–	–	–
LIBYAN ARAB JAMAHIRIYA	1977	–	–	–	–	–	–	–
PORTUGAL	1977	–	2	3	–	–	1	1
MEXICO ‡	1977	–	–	–	–	61	–	–
CHILE	1977	–	1	1	3	77	1	–
IRAN	1976	–	–	4	–	–	–	–
TOGO	1976	–	–	–	–	–	–	–
FINLAND	1977	55	12	25	2	–	7	4
PANAMA	1977	–	–	2			–	–
TOTAL (50 COUNTRIES) ‡		1 966	3 439	10 166	3 529	2 906	6 563	2 790

3.15 Third level: foreign students by country of origin
Troisième degré: étudiants étrangers par pays d'origine
Tercer grado: estudiantes extranjeros por países de origen

		COUNTRY OF ORIGIN / PAYS D'ORIGINE / PAIS DE ORIGEN						
HOST COUNTRY ‡ PAYS D'ACCUEIL ‡ PAIS HUESPED ‡	YEAR ANNEE AÑO	FIJI	NEW ZEALAND	PACIFIC ISLANDS	PAPUA NEW GUINEA	SAMOA	TONGA	OCEANIA, OTHER AND NOT SPECIFIED
UNITED STATES OF								
AMERICA ‡	1977	30	410	1 795	16	13	13	53
FRANCE	1977	3	27	—	1	—	1	—
UNITED KINGDOM	1977	49	189	—	14	2	4	30
GERMANY, FEDERAL								
REPUBLIC OF	1977	—	28	—	—	—	1	1
ITALY	1977	—	2	—	—	—	—	—
EGYPT	1974							
BELGIUM	1977	—	2	—	—	—	—	—
ARGENTINA	1974	—	—	—	—	—	—	—
JAPAN	1976	—	20	—	1	—	—	—
SWITZERLAND	1977	1	6	—	—	—	—	—
AUSTRIA	1977	—	3	—	—	—	—	—
GREECE	1977	—	3	—	—	—	—	—
INDIA	1975	362	3	—	—	—	4	—
AUSTRALIA	1977	170	215	—	184	12	32	47
SPAIN	1976	—	1	—	—	—	—	—
HOLY SEE	1977	—	6	—	1	1	—	6
PHILIPPINES	1977	—	—	—	—	—	—	—
SYRIAN ARAB REPUBLIC	1975	—	—	—	—	—	—	—
TURKEY	1976	—	—	—	—	—	—	—
GERMAN DEMOCRATIC REPUBLIC	1977							1
SAUDI ARABIA	1976	—	—	—	—	—	—	—
IRAQ	1977	—	—	—	—	—	—	—
KUWAIT	1977	—	—	—	—	—	—	—
DENMARK	1977	—	2	—	—	—	—	—
ROMANIA	1974	—	—	—	—	—	—	—
SWEDEN ‡	1976	—	1	—	—	—	—	—
CZECHOSLOVAKIA	1977	—	—	—	—	—	—	—
YUGOSLAVIA	1977	—	—	—	—	—	—	—
HUNGARY	1977	—	—	—	—	—	—	—
BULGARIA	1976	—	—	—	—	—	—	—
POLAND	1977	—	—	—	—	—	—	—
SENEGAL	1977	—	—	—	—	—	—	—
IRELAND	1977	—	1	—	—	—	—	—
MOROCCO	1976	—	—	—	—	—	—	—
PAKISTAN	1976	—	—	—	—	—	—	—
NETHERLANDS	1974	—	2	—	—	—	—	—
IVORY COAST	1976	—	—	—	—	—	—	—
ALGERIA	1977	—	—	—	—	—	—	—
SINGAPORE	1977	—	—	—	—	—	—	—
GUATEMALA	1976	—	—	—	—	—	—	—
CUBA	1976	—	—	—	—	—	—	—
SUDAN	1977	—	—	—	—	—	—	—
LIBYAN ARAB JAMAHIRIYA	1977	—	—	—	—	—	—	—
PORTUGAL	1977	—	—	—	—	—	—	—
MEXICO ‡	1977	—	—	—	—	—	—	—
CHILE	1977	—	—	—	—	—	—	1
IRAN	1976	—	—	—	—	—	—	—
TOGO	1976	—	—	—	—	—	—	—
FINLAND	1977	—	3	—	—	—	—	—
PANAMA	1977	—	—	—	—	—	—	—
TOTAL (50 COUNTRIES) ‡		615	924	1 795	217	28	55	139

Third level: foreign students by country of origin   3.15
Troisième degré: étudiants étrangers par pays d'origine
Tercer grado: estudiantes extranjeros por países de origen

HOST COUNTRY ‡ / PAYS D'ACCUEIL ‡ / PAIS HUESPED ‡	YEAR / ANNEE / AÑO	COUNTRY OF ORIGIN / PAYS D'ORIGINE / PAIS DE ORIGEN			
		U.S.S.R.	ARAB STATES, NOT SPECIFIED	STATELESS	NOT SPECIFIED
UNITED STATES OF AMERICA ‡	1977	160	—	50	—
FRANCE	1977	104	—	198	2 257
UNITED KINGDOM	1977	20	—	7	1 966
GERMANY, FEDERAL REPUBLIC OF	1977	36	—	708	769
ITALY	1977	9	—	29	—
EGYPT	1974	—	17 264	—	18
BELGIUM	1977	3	—	198	878
ARGENTINA	1974	16	—	—	—
JAPAN	1976	5	—	36	—
SWITZERLAND	1977	7	187	—	660
AUSTRIA	1977	8	—	—	166
GREECE	1977	14	—	—	66
INDIA	1975	11	—	—	141
AUSTRALIA	1977	4	—	—	30
SPAIN	1976	3	—	—	1 972
HOLY SEE	1977	7	—	—	—
PHILIPPINES	1977	—	—	—	532
SYRIAN ARAB REPUBLIC	1975	1	—	—	—
TURKEY	1976	—	—	—	618
GERMAN DEMOCRATIC REPUBLIC	1977	344	—	1	—
SAUDI ARABIA	1976	—	—	—	—
IRAQ	1977	—	—	—	—
KUWAIT	1977	—	—	234	—
DENMARK	1977	3	95	—	902
ROMANIA	1974	38	—	—	—
SWEDEN ‡	1976	7	—	20	180
CZECHOSLOVAKIA	1977	125	—	—	21
YUGOSLAVIA	1977	16	—	1	25
HUNGARY	1977	103	—	—	—
BULGARIA	1976	134	—	—	1 179
POLAND	1977	92	—	—	—
SENEGAL	1977	—	—	1	—
IRELAND	1977	—	—	—	3
MOROCCO	1976	2	—	—	—
PAKISTAN	1976	—	—	—	—
NETHERLANDS	1974	—	—	77	—
IVORY COAST	1976	—	—	—	7
ALGERIA	1977	—	—	—	—
SINGAPORE	1977	—	—	—	61
GUATEMALA	1976	—	—	—	6
CUBA	1976	4	—	—	17
SUDAN	1977	—	—	—	—
LIBYAN ARAB JAMAHIRIYA	1977	—	—	—	—
PORTUGAL	1977	—	—	—	5
MEXICO ‡	1977	—	—	—	—
CHILE	1977	1	—	9	—
IRAN	1976	—	—	—	—
TOGO	1976	—	—	—	—
FINLAND	1977	15	—	—	—
PANAMA	1977	—	—	—	—
TOTAL (50 COUNTRIES) ‡	1977	1 292	17 546	1 569	12 479

3.15   Third level: foreign students by country of origin
Troisième degré: étudiants étrangers par pays d'origine
Tercer grado: estudiantes extranjeros por paises de origen

HOST COUNTRY / PAYS D'ACCUEIL / PAIS HUESPED:
E—> THE DATA PROVIDED IN THIS TABLE ARE TO BE
CONSIDERED AS INDICATIVE.   FOREIGN STUDENTS ENROL-
LED IN THESE 50 COUNTRIES REPRESENT APPROXIMATELY
90% OF THE KNOWN TOTAL.   THE FOLLOWING COUNTRIES,
WHILST HOST TO MANY FOREIGN STUDENTS, HAVE NOT
BEEN LISTED IN THE 50 SELECTED COUNTRIES EITHER
BECAUSE THE DISTRIBUTION BY COUNTRY OF ORIGIN WAS
NOT COMMUNICATED OR MORE RECENT DATA WERE NOT
AVAILABLE: CANADA (26,400 STUDENTS IN 1977);
BRAZIL (25,642 STUDENTS IN 1974); U.S.S.R (30,563
STUDENTS IN 1971); AND LEBANON (22,184 STUDENTS
IN 1970).
FR—> LES DONNEES PROCUREES DANS CE TABLEAU
DOIVENT ETRE CONSIDEREES A TITRE INDICATIF.   LES
ETUDIANTS INSCRITS DANS CES 50 PAYS REPRESENTENT
APPROXIMATIVEMENT 90% DU TOTAL CONNU.   LES PAYS
INDIQUES CI—APRES AURAIENT DU FIGURER PARMI LES
50 PAYS SELECTIONNES, MAIS IL N'A PAS ETE POSSIBLE
D'EN TENIR COMPTE, SOIT PARCE QUE LA REPARTITION
DES ETUDIANTS ETRANGERS PAR PAYS D'ORIGINE N'AVAIT
PAS ETE COMMUNIQUEE, SOIT PARCE QUE DES DONNEES
PLUS RECENTES N'ETAIENT PAS DISPONIBLES: CANADA
(26 400 ETUDIANTS EN 1977); BRESIL (25 642 ETU-
DIANTS EN 1974); U.R.S.S (30 563 ETUDIANTS EN
1971); ET LIBAN (22 184 ETUDIANTS EN 1970).
ESP> LOS DATOS PRESENTADOS EN ESTE CUADRO DEBEN
CONSIDERARSE COMO INDICATIVOS.   LOS ESTUDIANTES
EXTRANJEROS MATRICULADOS EN ESTOS 50 PAISES
REPRESENTAN 90% DEL TOTAL CONOCIDO.   LOS PAISES
INDICADOS A CONTINUACION DEBERIAN HABER FIGURADO
ENTRE LOS 50 PAISES SELECCIONADOS, PERO NO
PUDIERON TOMARSE EN CONSIDERACION DEBIDO A QUE LA
DISTRIBUCION POR PAIS DE ORIGEN NO FUE COMUNICADA
O QUE NO SE DISPONIA DE DATOS MAS RECIENTES:
CANADA (26 400 ESTUDIANTES EN 1977); BRASIL
(25 642 ESTUDIANTES EN 1974); U.R.S.S (30 563
ESTUDIANTES EN 1971); Y LIBANO (22 184 ESTUDIANTES
EN 1970).

UNITED STATES OF AMERICA:
E—> SOURCE: OPEN DOORS, 1978.   INSTITUTE OF
INTERNATIONAL EDUCATION (NEW YORK).   DATA REFER
TO FOREIGN STUDENTS NOT POSSESSING AN IMMIGRANT'S
VISA.
FR-> SOURCE: "OPEN DOORS, 1978.   INSTITUTE OF
INTERNATIONAL EDUCATION" (NEW YORK).   CES DONNEES
SE REFERENT AUX ETUDIANTS ETRANGERS N'AYANT PAS
UN VISA D'IMMIGRATION.
ESP> FUENTE: "OPEN DOORS, 1978.   INSTITUTE OF
INTERNATIONAL EDUCATION" (NUEVA YORK).   ESTOS
DATOS SE REFIEREN A LOS ESTUDIANTES EXTRANJEROS
QUE NO POSEEN UN VISADO DE INMIGRACION.

SWEDEN:
E—> FIRST YEAR STUDENTS AT UNIVERSITY ONLY.
FR-> NOUVEAUX ENTRANTS DANS LES UNIVERSITES
SEULEMENT.
ESP> ESTUDIANTES DE PRIMER AÑO EN LAS UNIVER-
SIDADES SOLAMENTE.

MEXICO:
E—> "UNIVERSIDAD NACIONAL AUTONOMA" ONLY.
FR-> "UNIVERSIDAD NACIONAL AUTONOMA" SEULEMENT.
ESP> UNIVERSIDAD NACIONAL AUTONOMA SOLAMENTE.

TOTAL (50 COUNTRIES):
E—> IT SHOULD BE NOTED THAT FOR A FEW COUN-
TRIES, FOREIGN STUDENTS HAVE BEEN DISTRIBUTED
BY CONTINENT OF ORIGIN INSTEAD OF COUNTRY OF
ORIGIN.
FR-> IL FAUT NOTER QUE POUR QUELQUES PAYS,
LA DISTRIBUTION DES ETUDIANTS ETRANGERS A ETE
FAITE PAR CONTINENT ET NON PAR PAYS D'ORIGINE.
ESP> DEBE NOTARSE QUE PARA ALGUNOS PAISES, LA
DISTRIBUCION DE ESTUDIANTES EXTRANJEROS FUE HECHA
POR CONTINENTE Y NO POR PAIS DE ORIGEN.

Educational expenditure 4
Dépenses de l'enseignement
Gastos de la educación

4 Educational expenditure
Dépenses de l'enseignement
Gastos de la educación

This chapter consists of four tables on educational expenditure. The expenditure is divided into two main categories.

Current expenditure includes expenditure on administration, emoluments of teachers and supporting teaching staff, school books and other teaching materials, scholarships, welfare services and all other expenditure for the maintenance of school buildings.

Capital expenditure refers to land, buildings, construction, equipment etc. This item also includes loan transactions.

The data presented in this chapter refer solely to *public expenditure on education* i.e. public expenditure on public education plus subsidies for private education. It has not been possible to show private expenditure on education due to lack of data for a great number of countries.

Public expenditure on education includes, unless otherwise indicated, educational expenditure at every level of administration according to the constitution of the States i.e. central or federal government, State government, provincial or regional authorities, local authorities.

It is not always possible to determine exactly whether or not the amount of foreign aid received has been included with total public expenditure on education. However, whenever information on the inclusion of foreign aid is available it is indicated in a footnote.

Data are expressed in national currency at current market prices. Exchange rates between national currencies and the United States dollar can be found in Appendix C.

Due to the receipt of further information recently received this edition of the *Yearbook* revises all earlier editions.

Table 4.1
This table presents total public expenditure on education distributed between current and capital.

Educational expenditure is also expressed as a percentage of the Gross National Product (GNP) and of total public expenditure, i.e. current and investment budgets of all government levels. For some countries use was made of the Gross Domestic Product (GDP) and, for countries with centrally-planned economies, the Net Material Product (NMP). It should be noted that, owing to the difference in the concepts of these aggregates, the percentages shown are not strictly comparable internationally. Where capital expenditure on education is missing the percentages refer to current educational expenditure in relation to Gross National Product on the one hand and to current national budget on the other.

Table 4.2
Public current expenditure on education in this table is divided into the following categories:

Administration: emoluments of administrative staff and other expenditure of the central and local administration.

Emoluments of teachers: salaries and all other additional benefits paid to teachers as well as to other auxiliary teaching staff.

Other direct instructional expenditure: expenditure directly related to instructional activities such as the purchase of textbooks, books and other scholastic supplies.

Scholarships and grants: scholarships and all other forms of financial aid granted to students for studies in the country or abroad.

Welfare services: boarding costs, school meals, transport, medical services, etc.

Not distributed: expenditure which cannot be distributed and other expenditure attached to the operation and maintenance of buildings and equipment.

Table 4.3
This table presents the percentage breakdown of public current expenditure by level of education.

The column 'other types' of education includes special, adult and other types of education which it has not been possible to classify by level.

The column 'not distributed' sometimes covers other than unspecified expenditure such as administrative expenditure for which there is no breakdown by level of education.

Table 4.4
This table, gives a cross classification of public current expenditure by level of education and by purpose for the latest year available. The categories used for the breakdown of expenditure by purpose are those defined in the note to Table 4.2. However, administrative expenditure is not shown separately but included with expenditure not distributed. As the breakdown received from the countries does not always correspond to all these categories the relative table entries have been omitted when necessary.

Ce chapitre contient quatre tableaux sur les dépenses de l'enseignement. Ces dépenses sont réparties selon deux grandes catégories:

Dépenses ordinaires: dépenses d'administration, emoluments du personnel enseignant et auxiliaire, manuels et fournitures scolaires, bourses d'études, services sociaux et toutes les autres dépenses de fonctionnement des établissements scolaires.

Dépenses en capital: dépenses relatives aux terrains, bâtiments,

4 Educational expenditure
Dépenses de l'enseignement
Gastos de la educación

constructions, équipements, etc. Cette rubrique comprend également les transactions afférentes aux prêts.

Les données présentées dans ce chapitre se réfèrent uniquement aux *dépenses publiques d'éducation*, c'est-à-dire, aux dépenses publiques pour l'enseignement public plus les subventions à l'enseignement privé. Faute de données pour la plupart des pays, il n'a pas été tenu compte des dépenses privées d'éducation.

Les dépenses publiques d'éducation comprennent, sauf indication contraire, toutes les dépenses effectuées à quelque échelon administratif que ce soit, en fonction de l'organisation politique des Etats: gouvernement central ou fédéral, gouvernements d'Etat, autorités de province ou régionales, autorités municipales et locales.

Il n'est pas toujours possible de déterminer d'une manière sûre si le montant des dépenses publiques d'éducation comprend aussi l'aide étrangère reçue. Cependant, une note signale tous les cas pour lesquels les informations disponibles indiquent expressément l'inclusion de l'aide étrangère.

Les données sont exprimées en monnaie nationale aux prix courants du marché. Les taux de change des monnaies nationales en dollars des Etats-Unis d'Amérique sont indiqués dans l'Annexe C.

A la suite des nouvelles informations qui nous sont récemment parvenues, les séries de chiffres parues dans les éditions précédentes ont été révisées dans cet *Annuaire*.

Tableau 4.1

Ce tableau présente le total des dépenses publiques d'éducation réparties entre dépenses ordinaires et en capital.

Le total des dépenses d'éducation est aussi exprimé en pourcentage du produit national brut (PNB) et de l'ensemble des dépenses publiques, c'est-à-dire, de la totalité des budgets ordinaires et d'investissement à tous les échelons du gouvernement.

Pour certains pays, pour le calcul des pourcentages, on a dû utiliser le produit intérieur brut (PIB) et, pour les pays dont l'économie est soumise à une planification centralisée, le produit matériel net.

Il convient de noter qu'en raison de la différence de conception de ces agrégats, les pourcentages présentés ne sont pas tout-à-fait comparables sur le plan international. Lorsque les dépenses en capital afférentes à l'enseignement ne sont pas disponibles, les pourcentages se réfèrent aux dépenses ordinaires d'éducation par rapport au PNB d'une part et au budget national de fonctionnement d'autre part.

Tableau 4.2

Les dépenses publiques ordinaires d'éducation sont réparties dans ce tableau selon les catégories suivantes:

Administration: émoluments du personnel administratif et autres dépenses de l'administration centrale et locale.

Emoluments du personnel enseignant: traitements et toutes sortes de primes additionnelles du personnel enseignant ainsi que du personnel auxiliaire apportant un concours direct à l'enseignement.

Autres dépenses directes d'enseignement: dépenses directement liées à l'enseignement telles que l'achat des manuels, livres et autres fournitures scolaires.

Bourses et allocations: bourses et toute autre forme d'aide financière accordée aux élèves pour étudier dans le pays et à l'étranger.

Services sociaux: frais d'internat, repas scolaires, transport scolaire, services médicaux, etc.

Non réparties: dépenses ne pouvant pas être réparties et autres dépenses liées au fonctionnement et à l'entretien des bâtiments et du matériel.

Tableau 4.3

Ce tableau présente la répartition en pourcentage des dépenses publiques ordinaires par degré d'enseignement.

La colonne intitulée 'autres types d'enseignement' regroupe l'éducation spéciale, l'éducation des adultes et autres types d'enseignement ne pouvant pas être classés par degrés.

La colonne intitulée 'non réparties' englobe souvent, outre les diverses dépenses non spécifiées, les dépenses d'administration quand celles-ci ne sont pas déjà réparties par degrés.

Tableau 4.4

Ce tableau indique la répartition croisée des dépenses publiques ordinaires par degré d'enseignement et selon leur destination. Seules sont publiées les données pour la dernière année disponible.

Les catégories utilisées pour la répartition des dépenses selon leur destination sont définies dans la note relative au tableau 4.2. Cependant, les dépenses relatives à l'administration ne sont pas indiquées séparément mais incluses avec les dépenses non réparties.

Comme les répartitions fournies par les pays n'utilisent pas nécessairement toutes ces catégories, les lignes correspondant aux catégories sans objet sont, le cas échéant, supprimées.

Este capítulo comprende cuatro cuadros relativos a los gastos destinados a la educación. Estos gastos se distribuyen según las dos categorías principales siguientes:

Gastos ordinarios: gastos de administración, emolumentos del personal docente y auxiliar, libros de texto y suministros escolares, becas de estudios, servicios sociales y todos los otros gastos de funcionamiento de los establecimientos escolares.

Gastos de capital: gastos relativos a los terrenos, edificios, construcciones, equipo, etc. Esta rúbrica comprende igualmente las operaciones de préstamos.

Los datos presentados en este capítulo se refieren únicamente a *los gastos públicos destinados a la educación*, es decir, a los gastos públicos para la enseñanza pública más las subvenciones para la enseñanza privada. Careciendo de datos para la mayoría de países, no se han tenido en cuenta los gastos privados destinados a la educación.

Los gastos públicos destinados a la educación comprenden, salvo indicación contraria, todos los gastos efectuados a cualquier nivel administrativo, en función de la organización política de los Estados: gobierno central o federal, gobiernos de Estado, autoridades de provincia o de región, autoridades municipales y locales.

No siempre es posible determinar con seguridad si el importe de los gastos públicos destinados a la educación también comprende la ayuda recibida del extranjero. Sin embargo, en una nota se señalan todos los casos para los que las informaciones disponibles indican expresamente la inclusión de la ayuda extranjera.

Los datos se presentan en moneda nacional a precios corrientes del mercado. Los tipos de cambio entre las monedas nacionales y el dólar de los Estados Unidos de América se indican en el Anexo C.

Para tener en cuenta los nuevos datos recientemente recibidos, las series de cifras publicadas en las precedentes ediciones han sido revisadas en este *Anuario*.

Cuadro 4.1

Este cuadro presenta el total de los gastos públicos destinados a la educación, distribuidos entre gastos ordinarios y gastos de capital.

El total de los gastos en educación también se expresa en porcentaje del Producto Nacional Bruto (PNB) y del total de los gastos públicos, es decir, de la totalidad de los presupuestos ordinarios y de inversión a todos los niveles de gobierno.

En ciertos países, para el cálculo de porcentajes ha debido utilizarse el Producto Interior Bruto (PIB) y para los países cuya economía está sometida a una planificación centralizada, el Producto Material Neto.

Es necesario señalar que en razón de la diferencia de concepción de esos agregados, los porcentajes presentados no son exactamente comparables en el plano internacional. Cuando no se dispone de los gastos de capital destinados a la educación, los porcentajes se refieren a los gastos ordinarios en relación con el PNB por un lado y con el presupuesto nacional de funcionamiento por el otro.

Cuadro 4.2

Los gastos públicos ordinarios destinados a la educación, se distribuyen en este cuadro de acuerdo con las siguientes categorías:

Administración: emolumentos del personal administrativo y otros gastos de la administración central y local.

Emolumentos del personal docente: sueldos y toda clase de primas adicionales del personal docente y del personal auxiliar que aporta una ayuda directa a la enseñanza.

Otros gastos directos de enseñanza: gastos directamente relacionados con la enseñanza, como la adquisición de libros de texto, libros y otros suministros escolares.

Becas y subvenciones: becas y toda otra forma de ayuda financiera concedida a los alumnos para estudiar en el país y en el extranjero.

Servicios sociales: gastos de internado, cantinas escolares, transportes escolares, servicios médicos, etc.

Sin distribución: gastos que no pueden ser distribuidos y otros gastos relacionados con el funcionamiento y la conservación de los edificios y del material.

Educational expenditure
Dépenses de l'enseignement
Gastos de la educación

4

Cuadro 4.3

Este cuadro presenta la distribución en porcentaje de los gastos públicos ordinarios por grados de enseñanza.

La columna titulada 'Otros tipos' de enseñanza agrupa la educación especial, la educación de adultos y los otros tipos de enseñanza que no pueden clasificarse por grados.

La columna titulada 'Sin distribución' comprende con frecuencia, además de los diversos gastos no especificados, los gastos de administración, cuando no han sido distribuidos por grados.

Cuadro 4.4

Este cuadro da la distribución cruzada de los gastos públicos ordinarios por grados de enseñanza y según su destino. Sólo se publican los datos relativos al último año disponible.

Las categorías utilizadas para la distribución de los gastos según su destino, se definen en la nota relativa al cuadro 4.2. Sin embargo, los gastos que corresponden a la administración no se indican por separado, figurando englobados con los gastos sin distribución.

Como las distribuciones efectuadas por los países no utilizan forzosamente todas estas categorías, las líneas correspondientes a las categorías sin objeto son, de ser necesario, suprimidas.

Public expenditure on education 4.1
Dépenses publiques afférentes à l'enseignement
Gastos públicos destinados a la educación

4.1 Public expenditure on education: total and as percentage of the GNP and of all public expenditure

Dépenses publiques afférentes à l'enseignement: total et pourcentage par rapport au PNB et à l'ensemble des dépenses publiques

Gastos públicos destinados a la educación: total y porcentaje en relación con el PNB y el conjunto de gastos públicos

NUMBER OF COUNTRIES AND TERRITORIES PRESENTED IN THIS TABLE: 191
NOMBRE DE PAYS ET DE TERRITOIRES PRESENTES DANS CE TABLEAU: 191
NUMERO DE PAISES Y DE TERRITORIOS PRESENTADOS EN ESTE CUADRO: 191

COUNTRY / PAYS / PAIS	YEAR / ANNEE / AÑO	CURRENCY / MONNAIE / MONEDA	TOTAL EXPENDITURE DEPENSES TOTALES GASTOS TOTALES (000)	CURRENT EXPENDITURE — DEPENSES ORDINAIRES — GASTOS ORDINARIOS AMOUNT / MONTANT / IMPORTE (000)	AS % OF TOTAL / EN % DU TOTAL / EN % DEL TOTAL (%)	CAPITAL EXPENDITURE DEPENSES EN CAPITAL GASTOS DE CAPITAL (000)	TOTAL AS % OF GROSS NATIONAL PRODUCT / EN % DU PRODUIT NATIONAL BRUT / EN % DEL PRODUCTO NACIONAL BRUTO (%)	TOTAL AS % OF ALL PUBLIC EXPENDITURE / EN % DE TOUTES DEPENSES PUBLIQUES / EN % DE TODOS LOS GASTOS PUBLICOS (%)
			(1)	(2)	(3)	(4)	(5)	(6)
AFRICA								
ALGERIA ‡	1970	DINAR	1 854 400	1 138 500	61.4	715 900	7.4	31.6
	1974		3 182 300	2 231 000	70.1	951 300	6.0	23.6
	1975		4 080 500	2 951 000	72.3	1 129 500	7.2	23.0
	1976		5 013 000	3 496 000	69.7	1 517 000	7.3	24.9
	1977		6 582 000	4 199 000	63.8	2 383 000	8.3	25.8
	1978		3 636 655	3 348 650	92.1	288 005	...	...
ANGOLA	1970	KWANZA	...	828 876	...	...	1.8	10.5
BENIN ‡	1970	FRANC C.F.A.	...	2 922 402	...	...	4.2	29.7
	1974		...	4 958 081	...	...	5.1	36.4
	1975		...	5 649 652	...	...	5.1	39.0
BOTSWANA	1970	PULA	3 025	2 559	84.6	466	5.2	12.3
	1974		11 748	6 155	52.4	5 593	5.7	12.2
	1975		15 927	8 688	54.5	7 239	7.2	13.9
	1976		17 470	12 025	68.8	5 445	6.1	16.0
	1977		22 633	15 920	70.3	6 713	7.7	15.6

4.1 Public expenditure on education
Dépenses publiques afférentes à l'enseignement
Gastos públicos destinados a la educación

COUNTRY / PAYS / PAIS	YEAR / ANNEE / AÑO	CURRENCY / MONNAIE / MONEDA	TOTAL EXPENDITURE / DEPENSES TOTALES / GASTOS TOTALES (000) (1)	CURRENT EXPENDITURE / DEPENSES ORDINAIRES / GASTOS ORDINARIOS — AMOUNT / MONTANT / IMPORTE (000) (2)	AS % OF TOTAL / EN % DU TOTAL / EN % DEL TOTAL (%) (3)	CAPITAL EXPENDITURE / DEPENSES EN CAPITAL / GASTOS DE CAPITAL (000) (4)	TOTAL AS % OF GROSS NATIONAL PRODUCT (%) (5)	TOTAL AS % OF ALL PUBLIC EXPENDITURE (%) (6)
BURUNDI	1970	FRANC	...	478 670	...	...	2.3	25.8
	1974		...	612 800	...	...	2.2	20.9
	1975		...	721 831	...	...	2.3	22.7
	1976		...	884 608	...	...	2.2	20.8
	1977		1 371 569	1 197 569	87.3	174 000	2.9	20.7
CAPE VERDE	1970	ESCUDO		22 871			*2.0	13.4
	1976			99 660				
	1977		145 387	108 387	74.6	37 000		10.2
	1978		205 455	125 245	61.0	80 210		10.6
CENTRAL AFRICAN REPUBLIC	1970	FRANC C.F.A.	3 905 000	1 859 200		512 000	3.8	16.1
	1975		4 142 000	3 393 000	86.9	217 000	5.0	...
	1976		4 547 000	3 925 000	94.8	158 000	4.6	...
	1977			4 389 000	96.5		4.4	...
CHAD ‡	1970	FRANC C.F.A.	...	1 943 114	...	...	2.6	13.0
	1974		...	1 983 533	...	...	2.2	10.0
	1975		...	2 297 200	...	...	2.2	11.9
	1976		...	2 787 000	...	...	2.4	17.2
COMORO	1971	FRANC	725 898	643 104	88.6	82 794	*8.7	...
CONGO ‡	1970	FRANC C.F.A.	4 373 238	4 223 345	96.6	149 893	6.0	23.7
	1974		7 889 829	7 329 829	92.9	560 000	6.0	19.1
	1975		12 752 237	10 537 237	82.6	2 215 000	8.3	18.2
	1976		14 694 408	13 850 859	94.3	843 549	9.0	27.6
DJIBOUTI	1970	FRANC	415 214	324 940	78.3	90 274	...	...
	1974		1 624 821	1 479 821	91.1	145 000	...	...
EGYPT	1970	POUND	145 030	134 423	92.7	10 607	4.8	15.8
	1974		217 317	204 041	93.9	13 276	5.3	...
	1975		262 328	226 668	86.4	35 660	5.6	...
	1976		305 661	283 742	93.0	21 289	5.4	...
	1977		405 661	330 427	81.5	75 234	5.9	...
ETHIOPIA ‡	1970	BIRR	122 180	60 539		16 441	2.8	19.4
	1974		140 941	113 253	80.4	27 688	2.6	...
	1975		127 990	112 859	88.2	15 131	2.3	...

Public expenditure on education 4.1
Dépenses publiques afférentes à l'enseignement
Gastos públicos destinados a la educación

Country	Currency	Year	(1)	(2)	(3)	(4)	(5)	(6)
GABON	FRANC C.F.A.	1970	2 758 603	2 636 103	95.6	122 500	3.2	16.2
		1974	6 009 322	5 530 602	92.0	478 720	2.5	*12.3
		1975	8 593 088	7 260 088	84.5	1 333 000	2.8	...
		1976	16 170 571	10 506 571	65.0	5 664 000	4.6	...
		1977	21 434 220	14 441 220	67.4	6 993 000	...	8.4
GAMBIA	DALASI	1970	2 558	2 415	94.4	143	3.2	...
		1974	5 204	3 783	72.7	1 421	3.4	...
		1975	7 007	5 471	78.1	1 536	4.1	...
		1976	8 353	7 356	88.1	997	3.9	9.2
		1978	12 561	9 043	72.0	3 518	...	...
GHANA ‡	CEDI	1970	95 430	83 813	87.8	11 617	4.3	19.6
		1974	228 076	194 114	85.1	33 962	4.9	19.6
		1975	309 024	240 682	77.9	68 342	5.3	21.5
		1976	380 038	293 102	77.1	86 936	4.0	...
GUINEA	SYLI	1970	...	593 000	...	...	6.4	28.3
GUINEA-BISSAU ‡	ESCUDO	1970		17 024				5.5
		1976	175 917					15.6
		1977	182 783	182 783	100.0	—		15.8
		1978	345 684	270 684	78.3	75 000	8.6	28.8
IVORY COAST ‡	FRANC C.F.A.	1970	26 077 402	21 318 402	81.8	4 759 000	6.7	24.1
		1974	42 052 000	38 331 000	91.2	3 721 000	6.1	33.9
		1975	56 627 000	48 123 000	85.0	8 504 000	7.4	35.3
		1976	71 988 000	61 888 000	86.0	10 100 000	6.9	...
		1977	...	70 354 000	...	...	...	...
KENYA ‡	SHILLING	1970	452 260	422 320	93.4	29 940	4.1	14.4
		1974	1 193 506	1 105 662	92.6	87 844	6.1	21.8
		1975	1 379 790	1 331 734	96.5	48 056	6.1	18.8
		1976	1 499 148	1 421 176	94.8	77 972	5.5	18.8
		1977	1 752 960	1 661 860	94.8	91 100	5.0	15.8
LESOTHO	RAND	1970	2 279	2 081	91.3	198	3.6	14.3
		1973	3 561	3 016	84.7	545	3.4	12.1
LIBERIA	DOLLAR	1970	7 900				2.7	...
		1974	11 300				2.2	...
		1975	13 866				2.4	...
		1976	16 817	14 298	85.0	2 519	2.6	...
		1977	24 726	20 732	83.8	3 994	3.5	...
		1978	31 387	26 917	85.8	4 470	...	...
LIBYAN ARAB JAMAHIRIYA ‡	DINAR	1970	56 163	35 821	63.8	20 342	4.6	13.3
		1974	130 227	91 109	70.0	39 118	3.7	10.5
		1975	224 908	122 485	54.5	102 423	6.4	14.5
		1976	262 133	154 402	58.9	107 731	5.8	14.7
		1977	282 663	183 160	64.8	99 503	5.5	14.4
		1978	323 400	201 500	62.3	121 900	...	13.0
MADAGASCAR ‡	FRANC	1970		8 637 345			3.6	14.8
		1974	12 340 776	10 668 873	86.5	1 671 903	3.4	18.5
		1975	12 313 747	11 726 747	95.2	587 903	3.3	18.5
		1976	16 970 015	16 149 414	95.2	820 601	4.3	
MALAWI	KWACHA	1970	10 804	7 958	73.7	2 846	4.1	13.2
		1974	11 857	10 690	90.2	1 167	2.4	12.5
		1975	13 052	11 992	91.9	1 060	2.2	9.6

4.1 Public expenditure on education
Dépenses publiques afférentes à l'enseignement
Gastos públicos destinados a la educación

COUNTRY / PAYS / PAIS	YEAR / ANNEE / AÑO	CURRENCY / MONNAIE / MONEDA	TOTAL EXPENDITURE / DEPENSES TOTALES / GASTOS TOTALES (000) (1)	CURRENT EXPENDITURE — DEPENSES ORDINAIRES — GASTOS ORDINARIOS: AMOUNT / MONTANT / IMPORTE (000) (2)	AS % OF TOTAL / EN % DU TOTAL / EN % DEL TOTAL (%) (3)	CAPITAL EXPENDITURE / DEPENSES EN CAPITAL / GASTOS DE CAPITAL (000) (4)	TOTAL AS % OF GROSS NATIONAL PRODUCT (%) (5)	TOTAL AS % OF ALL PUBLIC EXPENDITURE (%) (6)
MALI	1971	FRANC	...	6 498 257	...	...	4.0	30.6
	1975		...	11 670 222	...	...	4.7	29.3
	1977		16 548 631	16 312 518	98.6	236 113	5.1	...
MAURITANIA ‡	1970	OUGUIYA	362 000	344 000	95.0	18 000	4.0	21.9
	1975		...	723 100	...	...	4.7	14.7
	1976		847 400	836 800	98.7	10 600	4.5	14.3
	1977		1 087 000	1 082 000	99.5	5 000	5.8	13.7
MAURITIUS	1970	RUPEE	38 818	35 723	92.0	3 095	3.7	11.5
	1974		96 343	86 126	89.4	10 217	3.0	9.7
	1975		144 000	125 800	87.4	18 200	4.2	9.6
	1976		215 700	197 000	91.3	18 700	5.5	12.4
	1977		311 800	246 700	79.1	65 100	7.4	14.9
MOROCCO	1970	DIRHAM	712 045	649 357	91.2	62 688	3.7	16.8
	1975		1 846 709	1 591 988	86.2	254 721	4.8	14.3
	1976		2 472 914	1 801 546	72.9	671 368	5.7	15.6
	1977		3 139 903	2 222 766	80.8	917 137	6.5	...
	1978		3 411 432	2 682 184	78.6	729 248	...	...
MOZAMBIQUE	1970	ESCUDO	...	450 312	...	...	...	5.7
NIGER	1970	FRANC C.F.A.	2 044 129	1 917 650	93.8	126 479	2.0	19.9
	1974		3 042 700	2 751 200	90.4	291 500	2.6	...
	1975		5 249 700	4 566 400	87.0	683 300	4.1	21.6
	1977		9 358 900	6 557 300	70.1	2 801 600	4.9	21.6
NIGERIA	1970	NAIRA	*601 795	132 648	*54.2	*275 434	2.5	20.0
	1974		998 785	326 361	59.1	408 473	4.3	...
	1976		1 054 253	590 312	65.8	360 515	4.7	...
	1977		...	693 738	...	...	4.1	...
RWANDA	1970	FRANC	497 000	491 000	98.8	6 000	2.3	26.6
	1974		...	1 078 400	...	...	3.1	25.2
	1975		1 198 064	1 197 164	99.9	*900	2.5	20.7
	1976		1 254 492	1 239 492	98.8	15 000	2.1	20.2
	1977		1 550 570	1 504 570	97.0	46 000	2.3	19.5
	1978		1 800 090	1 651 190	91.7	148 900	...	...

Public expenditure on education 4.1
Dépenses publiques afférentes à l'enseignement
Gastos públicos destinados a la educación

Country	Currency	Year	(1)	(2)	(3)	(4)	(5)	(6)
ST. HELENA	POUND STERLING	1970	...	50	...	...	...	4.9
		1974	...	74	...	...	...	5.1
		1975	...	79	...	...	...	7.9
		1976	153	143	93.5	10	...	...
SAO TOME AND PRINCIPE	DOBRA	1970	...	13 305	...	...	...	11.3
SENEGAL ‡	FRANC C.F.A.	1970	9 000 000	8 800 000	...	200 000	3.8	...
		1974	9 531 375	8 998 056	97.8	533 319	...	21.3
		1976	...	15 643 100	94.4	...	3.5	19.8
		1977	...	19 098 200	...	...	4.1	21.5
SEYCHELLES	RUPEE	1970	4 289	3 855	89.9	434	*4.5	11.5
		1974	10 537	8 924	84.7	1 613	...	10.7
		1975	12 632	11 202	88.7	1 430	...	9.5
		1976	17 711	14 866	83.9	2 845	4.7	10.7
		1977	22 221	20 316	91.4	1 905	4.6	11.0
SIERRA LEONE	LEONE	1970	10 926	9 726	89.0	1 200	3.2	17.5
		1975	19 853	17 303	87.2	2 550	3.5	18.1
		1976	25 882	23 828	92.1	2 057	4.3	19.5
		1977	29 016	24 936	85.9	4 080	4.3	...
SOMALIA ‡	SHILLING	1970	23 664	23 664	100.0	—	1.8	7.6
		1974	63 600	45 800	72.0	17 800	3.5	9.7
		1975	92 400	77 300	83.7	15 100	4.2	12.5
		1976	118 071	90 314	76.5	27 757	4.6	13.4
		1977	147 379	121 831	82.7	25 548	5.4	13.9
		1978	144 273	116 773	80.9	27 500	...	10.6
SUDAN ‡	POUND	1970	27 102	25 309	93.4	1 793	2.9	12.6
		1974	68 257	61 157	89.6	7 100	5.5	14.8
SWAZILAND ‡	LILANGENI	1970	3 451	2 959	85.7	492	5.2	17.3
		1974	8 977	6 374	71.0	2 603	7.1	...
		1975	9 927	7 321	73.7	2 606	5.8	...
		1976	...	6 350	...	...	...	...
		1977	...	8 811	...	...	...	...
		1978	17 730	12 444	70.2	5 286	...	...
TOGO ‡	FRANC C.F.A.	1970	1 584 917	1 414 917	89.3	170 000	2.2	18.6
		1974	5 542 827	5 103 852	92.1	438 975	4.3	32.8
		1975	6 689 950	6 116 698	91.4	573 252	5.4	21.3
		1976	9 345 634	8 810 734	94.3	534 900	6.8	18.4
		1977	12 362 302	10 753 682	87.0	1 608 620	7.4	22.0
		1978	14 726 056	13 169 738	89.4	1 556 318	...	19.3
TUNISIA	DINAR	1970	51 429	43 383	84.4	8 046	7.0	23.2
		1974	76 043	66 691	87.0	9 352	5.0	17.7
		1975	87 533	76 139	87.0	11 394	5.0	16.4
		1976	98 805	87 235	88.3	11 570	5.2	17.0
		1977	142 621	112 733	79.0	29 888	6.8	19.5
		1978	...	118 300	...	...	...	...
UGANDA ‡	SHILLING	1970	361 646	298 015	82.4	63 631	3.9	17.8
		1974	474 170	438 751	92.5	35 419	3.0	...
		1975	603 323	529 014	...	39 624	3.2	18.0

4.1 Public expenditure on education
Dépenses publiques afférentes à l'enseignement
Gastos públicos destinados a la educación

COUNTRY / PAYS / PAIS	YEAR ANNEE AÑO	CURRENCY MONNAIE MONEDA	TOTAL EXPENDITURE DEPENSES TOTALES GASTOS TOTALES (000) (1)	CURRENT EXPENDITURE — DEPENSES ORDINAIRES — GASTOS ORDINARIOS AMOUNT MONTANT IMPORTE (000) (2)	AS % OF TOTAL EN % DU TOTAL EN % DEL TOTAL (%) (3)	CAPITAL EXPENDITURE DEPENSES EN CAPITAL GASTOS DE CAPITAL (000) (4)	TOTAL AS % OF GROSS NATIONAL PRODUCT (%) (5)	TOTAL AS % OF ALL PUBLIC EXPENDITURE (%) (6)
UNITED REPUBLIC OF CAMEROON	1970	FRANC C.F.A.	10 463 635	9 644 852	92.2	818 783	3.8	19.6
	1974		17 006 700	15 019 000	88.3	1 987 700	4.1	...
	1975		21 924 800	18 310 000	83.5	3 614 800	4.6	...
	1976		24 163 777	20 945 877	86.7	3 217 900	4.4	...
UNITED REPUBLIC OF TANZANIA	1970	SHILLING	407 900	337 600	82.8	70 300	4.5	16.0
	1975		799 532	600 789	75.1	198 743	4.2	13.0
	1976		982 000	727 900	74.1	254 100	4.3	15.5
	1977		1 324 042	1 090 090	82.3	233 952	4.7	14.1
UPPER VOLTA ‡	1970	FRANC C.F.A.	...	2 105 000	...	...	2.3	25.9
	1974		...	2 836 967	...	...	2.4	26.9
	1975		...	3 171 371	...	...	2.4	23.0
	1976		4 020 947	3 674 455	91.4	346 492	2.7	19.0
	1977		4 450 127	4 279 627	96.2	170 500	2.5	19.2
	1978		5 909 245	5 650 745	95.6	258 500	...	19.3
WESTERN SAHARA	1970	PESETA	56 322	44 322	78.7	12 000	...	...
	1973		103 032	86 332	83.8	16 700	...	...
ZAIRE	1970	ZAIRE	...	54 000	...	...	5.9	20.4
	1973		...	76 800	...	...	5.4	20.3
ZAMBIA	1970	KWACHA	56 063	44 391	79.2	11 672	4.5	10.9
	1974		91 370	69 670	76.3	21 700	5.0	14.4
	1975		98 020	75 420	76.9	22 600	6.3	11.9
	1976		115 880	94 140	81.2	21 740	6.3	...
	1977		113 076	95 461	84.4	17 615	6.1	...
	1978		114 560	101 230	88.4	13 330	...	...
ZIMBABWE	1970	DOLLAR	...	34 600	...	...	3.3	16.2
	1973		...	53 225	...	...	3.5	15.8

Public expenditure on education 4.1
Dépenses publiques afférentes à l'enseignement
Gastos públicos destinados a la educación

AMERICA, NORTH

Country / Currency	Year	(1)	(2)	(3)	(4)	(5)	(6)
ANTIGUA — E. CARIBBEAN DOLLAR	1970	2 248	2 233	99.3	15	3.0	10.4
	1974	5 134	4 654	90.7	480	4.3	12.5
	1975	6 346	5 681	89.5	665	4.9	14.4
	1976	7 675	6 742	87.8	933	5.9	13.8
	1977	7 823	7 013	89.6	810	...	11.5
BAHAMAS — DOLLAR	1970	22 802	18 079	79.3	4 723	*5.6	19.4
	1974	35 118	26 316	74.9	8 802	*7.2	25.0
	1975	32 495	29 938	92.1	2 557	*6.1	...
	1976	39 718	35 923	90.4	3 795	...	...
BARBADOS — DOLLAR	1970	20 969	19 784	94.3	1 185	6.3	21.2
	1975	48 827	42 256	86.5	6 571	6.6	...
	1976	*57 537	*47 397	*82.4	*10 140	*7.4	...
	1977	*75 615	*60 597	*80.1	*15 018	*8.5	...
BELIZE — DOLLAR	1970	3 257	3 211	98.6	46	4.1	...
	1974	5 209	4 733	90.9	476	3.6	...
BERMUDA — DOLLAR	1970	7 046	5 821	82.6	1 225	*3.7	18.8
	1974	11 192	9 735	87.0	1 457	...	18.0
	1975	10 877	10 417	95.8	460	...	...
	1976	10 142	9 512	93.8	630	...	...
BRITISH VIRGIN ISLANDS — UNITED STATES DOLLAR	1970	1 248	639	51.2	609	*4.9	13.1
	1974	887	821	92.6	66	4.7	...
	1975	1 002	967	96.5	35	4.8	13.2
	1976	1 115	907	81.3	208	4.3	12.4
	1977	...	1 026	...	...	...	...
CANADA — DOLLAR	1970	7 244 700	6 122 500	84.5	1 122 200	8.5	...
	1974	10 674 474	9 574 715	89.7	1 099 759	7.4	...
	1975	12 691 988	11 381 459	89.7	1 310 529	7.9	...
	1976	14 757 381	13 233 587	89.7	1 523 794	7.8	...
	1977	16 721 589	14 994 978	89.7	1 726 611	8.0	...
CAYMAN ISLANDS — JAMAICAN DOLLAR	1975	1 625	1 384	85.2	241		12.0
	1976	1 863	1 691	90.8	172		14.2
COSTA RICA — COLON	1970	331 500	318 500	96.1	13 000	5.2	*31.8
	1975	1 113 826	1 041 297	93.5	72 529	6.8	31.1
	1976	1 318 369	1 041 391	79.0	276 978	6.6	30.1
CUBA ‡ — PESO	1970	351 100	550 369	74.8	185 078	8.4	18.4
	1974	735 447				9.9	...
	1975	808 500				...	...
	1976	978 500				...	30.1
	1977	1 047 900				...	32.4
	1978	1 156 800				...	...
DOMINICAN REPUBLIC — PESO	1970	42 200	39 306	93.1	*2 894	2.9	15.9
	1976	75 977	62 595	82.4	13 382	2.0	13.3
	1977	79 237	67 783	85.5	11 454	1.9	12.6
EL SALVADOR — COLON	1970	74 315	69 621	93.7	4 694	2.9	27.6
	1975	150 893	138 364	91.7	12 529	3.4	22.2
	1976	196 896	182 715	92.8	14 181	3.6	23.3
	1977	238 266	213 536	89.6	24 730	3.7	26.0

4.1 Public expenditure on education
Dépenses publiques afférentes à l'enseignement
Gastos públicos destinados a la educación

COUNTRY / PAYS / PAIS	YEAR ANNEE AÑO	CURRENCY MONNAIE MONEDA	TOTAL EXPENDITURE DEPENSES TOTALES GASTOS TOTALES (000) (1)	CURRENT EXPENDITURE — DEPENSES ORDINAIRES — GASTOS ORDINARIOS — AMOUNT MONTANT IMPORTE (000) (2)	AS % OF TOTAL EN % DU TOTAL EN % DEL TOTAL (%) (3)	CAPITAL EXPENDITURE DEPENSES EN CAPITAL GASTOS DE CAPITAL (000) (4)	TOTAL AS % OF GROSS NATIONAL PRODUCT (%) (5)	TOTAL AS % OF ALL PUBLIC EXPENDITURE (%) (6)
GRENADA	1970	DOLLAR	5 263	3 665	69.6	1 598	9.3	*26.1
	1974		5 284	5 227	98.9	57	6.7	12.5
	1975		5 507	5 478	99.5	29	5.7	...
	1976		6 063	5 998	98.9	65	5.2	...
	1977		7 295	7 155	98.1	140	5.5	...
	1978		12 099	8 865	73.3	3 234	...	...
GUATEMALA	1970	QUETZAL	36 866	32 566	88.3	4 300	2.0	19.5
	1976		73 254	67 193	91.7	6 061	1.7	13.2
HAITI	1970	GOURDE	...	25 098	...	...	1.3	...
	1974		...	32 219	...	...	0.9	...
	1975		...	34 138	...	...	0.8	...
	1976		41 910	37 191	88.7	4 719	0.8	7.9
HONDURAS	1970	LEMPIRA	43 717	41 660	95.3	2 057	3.1	20.3
	1974		68 241	...	...	...	3.5	20.7
	1975		80 078	...	...	...	3.9	20.3
	1976		91 900	...	...	...	3.9	17.8
	1977		108 430	89 920	82.9	18 510	3.8	17.3
	1978		126 127	...	...	...	...	15.2
JAMAICA ‡	1970	DOLLAR	40 361	28 877	71.5	11 484	3.6	20.2
	1974		147 223	121 532	82.5	25 691	6.7	16.0
	1975		154 676	121 854	78.8	32 822	6.1	15.8
	1976		187 203	154 506	82.5	32 697	7.1	...
MEXICO ‡	1970	PESO	10 798 600	7 148 000	...	798 800	2.6	8.5
	1974		26 615 100	23 815 000	89.5	2 800 100	3.3	...
	1975		41 185 400	36 783 400	...	4 668 500	4.2	11.9
	1976		55 177 380	36 507 080	...	5 449 900	4.6	...
	1977		79 017 645	53 627 996	...	6 257 649	4.8	11.7
	1978		103 064 000	...	...	...	...	...
MONTSERRAT	1971	E. CARIBBEAN DOLLAR	1 148	624	54.4	524	...	...
NETHERLANDS ANTILLES	1971	GUILDER	15 786	15 664	99.2	122	...	...
	1977		123 400	104 900	85.0	18 500	...	...

Public expenditure on education 4.1
Dépenses publiques afférentes à l'enseignement
Gastos públicos destinados a la educación

Country / Currency	Year	(1)	(2)	(3)	(4)	(5)	(6)
NICARAGUA — CORDOBA	1970	122 541	120 901	98.7	1 640	2.3	18.1
	1974	254 500	...	...	...	2.5	15.6
	1975	282 400	...	...	...	2.6	...
	1976	346 200	...	...	...	2.8	...
	1978	407 150	323 058	79.3	84 092	...	12.8
PANAMA — BALBOA	1970	55 068	50 824	92.3	4 244	5.4	22.1
	1974	100 273	88 436	88.2	11 837	5.6	20.2
	1975	103 316	96 693	93.6	6 623	5.4	21.3
	1976	113 844	105 753	92.9	8 091	5.7	20.8
	1977	119 548	112 387	94.0	7 161	5.4	22.2
	1978	119 435	109 675	91.8	9 760	...	21.9
FORMER CANAL ZONE — UNITED STATES DOLLAR	1970	16 894	16 034	94.9	860	...	...
	1974	20 710	20 237	97.7	473	...	...
	1975	23 252	22 472	96.6	780	...	...
	1976	20 925	20 532	98.1	393	...	...
	1977	23 314	23 300	99.9	14	...	...
PUERTO RICO — UNITED STATES DOLLAR	1970	365 042	344 030	94.2	21 012	6.7	...
	1974	478 743	448 310	93.6	30 433	5.8	...
	1975	585 399	568 387	97.1	17 012	...	...
	1976	572 876	569 581	99.4	3 295	...	...
	1977	662 150	656 206	99.1	5 944	...	...
ST. KITTS - NEVIS ANGUILLA — E. CARIBBEAN DOLLAR	1970	1 381	...	...	...	4.7	9.7
	1974	2 325	...	...	...	3.4	6.9
	1975	2 541	...	...	...	3.3	7.3
	1976	3 759	...	...	...	4.5	...
	1977	3 944	...	...	...	...	...
	1978	4 354	...	...	...	...	...
ST. LUCIA — E. CARIBBEAN DOLLAR	1971	4 768	4 013	84.2	755	5.4	16.8
	1974	7 009	5 513	78.7	1 496	5.7	16.8
	1975	8 338	7 321	87.8	1 017	5.9	...
	1976	10 706	10 614	99.1	93	6.9	...
ST. PIERRE AND MIQUELON — FRANC C.F.A.	1971	111 928	108 328	96.8	3 600	...	12.3
	1974	374 409	...	...	...	...	...
ST. VINCENT AND THE GRENADINES — E. CARIBBEAN DOLLAR	1970	2 141	1 795	83.8	346	5.6	...
	1974	6 185	6 185	100.0	—	8.5	...
	1975	5 196	5 196	100.0	—	6.7	...
	1976	5 546	5 546	100.0	—	6.3	...
	1977	5 877	5 877	...	...	6.1	...
TRINIDAD AND TOBAGO — DOLLAR	1970	62 143	53 335	85.8	8 808	3.9	16.0
	1974	148 761	119 422	80.3	29 339	4.3	12.6
	1975	152 379	134 212	88.1	18 167	2.9	9.7
	1976	196 051	182 207	92.9	13 844	3.3	10.5
	1977	267 208	250 992	93.9	16 216	3.8	...
	1978	...	339 383	...	...	...	...
TURKS AND CAICOS ISLANDS — DOLLAR	1970	307	168	54.7	139	...	16.9
	1974	1 138	688	60.5	450	...	21.1
	1975	718	601	83.7	117	...	14.4
	1976	783	646	82.5	137	...	15.1

4.1   Public expenditure on education
      Dépenses publiques afférentes à l'enseignement
      Gastos públicos destinados a la educación

COUNTRY / PAYS / PAIS	YEAR / ANNEE / AÑO	CURRENCY / MONNAIE / MONEDA	TOTAL EXPENDITURE DEPENSES TOTALES GASTOS TOTALES (000)	CURRENT EXPENDITURE — DEPENSES ORDINAIRES — GASTOS ORDINARIOS AMOUNT / MONTANT / IMPORTE (000)	AS % OF TOTAL / EN % DU TOTAL / EN % DEL TOTAL (%)	CAPITAL EXPENDITURE DEPENSES EN CAPITAL GASTOS DE CAPITAL (000)	TOTAL AS % OF GROSS NATIONAL PRODUCT (%)	TOTAL AS % OF ALL PUBLIC EXPENDITURE (%)
			(1)	(2)	(3)	(4)	(5)	(6)
UNITED STATES OF AMERICA ‡	1970	DOLLAR	64 600	56 000	86.7	8 600	6.4	19.4
	1974		91 300	82 700	90.6	8 600	6.3	19.0
	1975		100 700	90 800	90.2	9 900	6.2	18.1
	1976		110 700	100 300	90.6	10 400	6.0	17.7
	1977		120 700	109 900	91.1	10 800	6.4	17.7
U.S. VIRGIN ISLANDS	1970	UNITED STATES DOLLAR	14 285	13 985	97.9	300	...	...
	1974		51 700	38 268	74.0	13 432	...	...
	1975		40 575	40 138	98.9	437	...	...
	1976		57 511	48 484	84.3	9 027	...	...
	1977		63 185	48 122	76.2	15 063	...	...
AMERICA, SOUTH								
ARGENTINA ‡	1971	PESO	4 330	...	...	...	3.3	16.0
	1974		13 181	12 195	92.5	986	2.7	9.5
	1975		35 773	33 562	93.8	2 211	...	...
	1976		119 293	105 086	88.1	14 207	...	...
	1977		495 497	426 417	86.1	69 080	2.4	10.7
BOLIVIA	1970	PESO	397 156	396 056	99.7	1 100	3.3	28.4
	1974		1 329 003	1 311 280	98.7	17 723	3.0	33.6
	1975		1 660 734	1 658 659	99.9	2 075	3.4	...
	1976		2 228 374	2 205 451	99.0	22 923	3.8	25.4
	1977		2 760 992	2 644 057	95.8	116 935	4.0	...
BRAZIL ‡	1970	CRUZEIRO	5 549 022	4 235 040	...	684 278	2.7	10.6
	1974		20 691 421	...	...	...	2.9	18.6
	1975		28 995 055	...	...	...	2.9	...
	1976		46 804 652	...	...	...	3.0	...
	1977		73 035 853	...	...	...	3.2	...
CHILE	1970	PESO	4 866	...	...	...	5.1	22.0
	1974		372 688	346 213	92.9	26 475	3.9	12.5
	1975		1 399 626	1 321 482	94.4	78 144	3.4	12.0
COLOMBIA ‡	1970	PESO	1 975 514	1 545 185	78.2	430 329	1.6	11.7
	1974		6 541 600	...	...	...	2.0	19.7
	1975		8 561 100	...	...	...	2.1	18.4
	1976		10 454 900	...	...	...	2.0	21.0

Public expenditure on education 4.1
Dépenses publiques afférentes à l'enseignement
Gastos públicos destinados a la educación

		(1)	(2)	(3)	(4)	(5)	(6)
ECUADOR	SUCRE						
	1970	1 445 003	1 133 523	78.4	311 480	4.3	23.2
	1974	2 631 100				3.0	23.2
	1975	3 386 500				3.1	25.9
	1976	4 487 000				3.5	28.3
	1977	6 703 875	5 756 300	85.9	947 575	4.5	
FALKLAND ISLANDS (MALVINAS)	POUND						
	1970	61	60		1		12.2
	1974	114	105		9		
	1975	137	128		9		13.5
GUYANA	DOLLAR						
	1970	23 209	19 089	82.2	4 120	4.7	13.2
	1974	55 165	42 810	77.6	12 355	6.1	15.4
	1975	57 064	47 944	84.0	9 120	4.9	9.8
	1976	75 795	63 490	83.8	12 305	7.0	9.5
	1977	80 607	71 796	89.1	8 811	7.6	13.8
	1978	97 517	86 030	88.2	11 487		
PARAGUAY	GUARANI						
	1970	1 600 956	1 421 834	88.8	179 122	2.2	15.3
	1974	2 409 000	1 904 100	79.0	504 900	1.4	17.5
	1975	2 710 000	2 292 300	84.6	417 700	1.4	
	1976	3 457 500	2 782 600	80.5	674 900	1.6	
	1977	3 998 200	3 325 700	83.2	672 500	1.5	
	1978	5 171 700	3 999 700	77.3	1 172 000		
PERU	SOL						
	1970	9 026 900	8 730 500	96.7	296 400	3.8	18.8
	1974	17 944 038	16 665 469	92.9	1 278 569	4.1	18.2
	1975	21 756 200	20 969 700	96.4	786 500	3.9	16.6
	1976	28 592 000	27 782 000	97.2	810 000	3.6	16.3
	1977	34 150 500	31 921 000	93.5	2 229 500	3.4	14.7
	1978	41 337 400	38 658 700	93.5	2 678 700		
SURINAME	GUILDER						
	1970	30 500	26 600	87.2	3 900	6.5	17.9
	1974	44 400	42 600	95.9	1 800	5.3	17.3
	1975	50 700	44 800	88.4	5 900	5.7	14.1
URUGUAY	PESO						
	1970	22 017				3.6	26.1
VENEZUELA	BOLIVAR						
	1970	2 355 222	2 220 651	94.3	134 571	4.8	22.9
	1974	4 710 316	4 529 180	96.2	181 136	3.8	
	1975	6 225 161	5 965 747	95.8	259 414	5.4	
	1976	7 129 700	6 864 100	96.3	265 600	5.3	
ASIA							
AFGHANISTAN ‡	AFGHANI						
	1970	913 202	817 276	89.5	95 926	1.2	
	1974	1 264 216	1 142 630	90.4	121 586	1.3	
	1977	1 788 029	1 636 529	91.5	151 500	1.3	
BAHRAIN	DINAR						
	1970	3 752	3 668	97.8	84	5.8	20.0
	1974	7 366	6 879	93.4	487	3.4	9.5
	1975	10 541	9 606	91.1	935	4.6	8.8
	1976	12 105	11 306	93.4	799		6.0
	1977	20 922	17 048	81.5	3 874		8.1
	1978	24 924	20 106	80.7	4 818		8.8
BANGLADESH	TAKA						
	1973	1 026 366	648 166	63.2	378 200	2.3	14.6
	1974	1 109 932	822 132	74.1	287 000	1.7	12.9
	1975	1 379 862	929 862	67.4	450 000	1.4	13.6
	1976	*1 493 002	*1 020 102	*68.3	*472 900	*1.5	

4.1 Public expenditure on education
Dépenses publiques afférentes à l'enseignement
Gastos públicos destinados a la educación

COUNTRY / PAYS / PAIS	YEAR / ANNEE / AÑO	CURRENCY / MONNAIE / MONEDA	TOTAL EXPENDITURE / DEPENSES TOTALES / GASTOS TOTALES (000) (1)	CURRENT EXPENDITURE — DEPENSES ORDINAIRES — GASTOS ORDINARIOS — AMOUNT / MONTANT / IMPORTE (000) (2)	AS % OF TOTAL / EN % DU TOTAL / EN % DEL TOTAL (%) (3)	CAPITAL EXPENDITURE / DEPENSES EN CAPITAL / GASTOS DE CAPITAL (000) (4)	TOTAL AS % OF GROSS NATIONAL PRODUCT / TOTAL EN % DU PRODUIT NATIONAL BRUT / TOTAL EN % DEL PRODUCTO NACIONAL BRUTO (%) (5)	TOTAL AS % OF ALL PUBLIC EXPENDITURE / TOTAL EN % DE TOUTES DEPENSES PUBLIQUES / TOTAL EN % DE TODOS LOS GASTOS PUBLICOS (%) (6)
BHUTAN ‡	1970	INDIAN RUPEE	8 781	4 982	56.7	3 799	...	...
	1974		23 275	12 853	55.2	10 422	...	...
	1977		21 470	14 975	69.7	6 495	...	13.9
BRUNEI	1970	DOLLAR	34 871	19 387	55.6	15 484	6.4	...
	1974		89 420	34 751	38.9	54 669	...	...
	1975		55 908	47 354	84.7	8 554	...	9.6
	1976		70 913	53 592	75.6	17 321	...	...
	1977		96 466	69 536	72.1	26 930	...	15.9
BURMA	1970	KYAT	317 072	295 265	93.1	21 807	3.1	19.4
	1974		384 540	365 050	94.9	19 490	2.0	16.0
	1975		405 257	385 990	95.2	19 267	1.7	15.3
	1976		449 203	432 658	96.3	16 546	1.7	14.4
	1977		486 818	470 430	96.6	16 388		12.2
CYPRUS ‡	1970	POUND	7 060	5 681	80.5	1 379	3.0	17.4
	1974		11 495	10 285	89.5	1 210	3.5	16.1
	1975		11 421	10 325	90.4	1 096	3.8	14.3
	1976		13 135	11 710	89.2	1 425	3.4	14.9
	1977		14 764	12 895	87.3	1 869	3.2	14.6
DEMOCRATIC KAMPUCHEA	1971	RIEL	2 656 878	2 654 061	99.9	2 817	3.8	14.2
EAST TIMOR	1970	PORTUGUESE- ESCUDO	...	7 394	...	...	...	5.1
HONG KONG	1970	DOLLAR	559 524	483 186	86.4	76 338	2.9	22.8
	1974		1 192 967	1 059 153	88.8	133 814	3.3	19.1
	1975		1 246 272	1 144 538	91.8	101 734	3.3	20.7
	1976		1 449 972	1 360 869	93.9	89 103	3.0	22.0
	1977		1 750 183	1 578 216	90.2	171 967	3.1	19.5
INDIA	1970	RUPEE	11 182 860	10 579 660	94.6	603 200	2.8	10.7
	1974		18 073 040	...	...	...	2.6	9.7
	1975		21 047 180	...	...	...	2.9	9.4
	1976		23 646 000	...	...	...	3.0	11.1
	1977		25 548 000	...	...	...	2.9	9.9
INDONESIA ‡	1970	RUPIAH	92 439	*83 000	*89.8	*9 439	2.8	...
	1974		226 670	170 949	75.4	55 721	2.2	...
	1975		364 390	277 076	76.0	87 314	3.0	...
	1976		249 513	112 422	45.1	137 091	1.7	8.9

Public expenditure on education   **4.1**
Dépenses publiques afférentes à l'enseignement
Gastos públicos destinados a la educación

Country	Currency	Year	(1)	(2)	(3)	(4)	(5)	(6)
IRAN	RIAL	1970	23 280 000	19 715 000	84.7	3 565 000	2.9	8.6
		1974	93 726 858	76 182 358	81.3	17 544 500	3.0	12.6
		1975		165 723 000			4.6	
		1976	259 995 564	230 748 564	88.8	29 247 000	5.6	14.1
		1977		301 661 000			5.1	
IRAQ	DINAR	1970		60 228			5.4	19.8
		1974		124 863			4.0	13.6
		1976	204 493	155 763	76.2	48 730	4.3	16.9
		1977		198 903			3.5	12.0
		1978		257 528				13.9
ISRAEL	POUND	1970	1 061 000				5.5	8.1
		1974	3 982 000	3 217 000	80.8	765 000	6.7	8.3
		1975	5 511 000	4 641 000	84.2	870 000	6.8	7.6
JAPAN ‡	YEN	1970	2 885 646	2 098 677	72.7	786 969	3.9	20.4
		1974	7 002 782	4 907 229		1 887 047	5.1	16.6
		1975	8 156 673	5 826 604		1 990 370	5.5	17.5
		1976	9 133 427	6 613 456		2 152 360	5.3	17.0
		1977	10 332 439	7 262 222		2 628 484	5.4	16.5
JORDAN ‡	DINAR	1970	8 706	7 239	83.1	1 467	3.9	9.3
		1974	13 755	11 624	84.5	2 131	3.7	8.3
		1975	16 698	13 900	83.2	2 798	4.2	7.7
		1976	20 222	16 957	83.9	3 265	3.5	7.7
		1977	25 652	22 598	88.1	3 054	3.5	6.9
KOREA, REPUBLIC OF ‡	WON	1970	95 691	73 809	77.1	21 882	3.7	21.4
		1975	220 282	163 800	74.4	56 482	2.4	13.9
		1976	399 462	350 315	87.7	49 147	3.3	
		1977	452 153	411 499	91.0	40 654	3.0	17.0
KUWAIT	DINAR	1970	35 832	34 630	96.6	1 202	4.2	11.8
		1974	84 628	74 273	87.8	10 355	2.7	14.7
		1975	112 024	90 069	80.4	21 954	3.2	13.6
		1976	132 447	113 750	85.9	18 697	3.3	7.3
		1977	168 768	129 183	76.5	39 585		7.4
LAO PEOPLE'S DEMOCRATIC REPUBLIC	KIP	1970		2 058 777			2.5	10.8
LEBANON ‡	POUND	1970	123 663	115 167	93.1	8 496	2.5	16.8
		1977	298 200	286 600	96.1	11 600		18.6
		1978		354 300				
MACAU	PATACA	1970		8 707				3.3
MALAYSIA	RINGGIT	1970	521 100	476 900	91.5	44 200	4.4	17.7
		1974	1 183 600	1 049 400	88.7	134 200	5.4	19.0
		1975	1 362 900	1 157 500	84.9	205 400	6.3	19.3
PENINSULAR MALAYSIA	RINGGIT	1970	484 267	442 039	91.3	42 228		
		1974	1 027 792	916 695	89.2	111 097		
		1975	1 158 845	992 192	85.6	166 653		
		1976	1 278 182	1 101 567	86.2	176 615		
		1977	1 742 489	1 571 180	90.2	171 309		
SABAH	RINGGIT	1970	27 125	24 287	89.5	2 838		
		1974	94 998	86 249	90.8	8 749		
		1975	105 848	89 559	84.6	16 289		
		1976	74 909	73 715	98.4	1 194		

4.1 Public expenditure on education
Dépenses publiques afférentes à l'enseignement
Gastos públicos destinados a la educación

COUNTRY / PAYS / PAIS	YEAR / ANNEE / AÑO	CURRENCY / MONNAIE / MONEDA	TOTAL EXPENDITURE / DEPENSES TOTALES / GASTOS TOTALES (000) (1)	CURRENT EXPENDITURE — DEPENSES ORDINAIRES — GASTOS ORDINARIOS: AMOUNT / MONTANT / IMPORTE (000) (2)	AS % OF TOTAL / EN % DU TOTAL / EN % DEL TOTAL (%) (3)	CAPITAL EXPENDITURE / DEPENSES EN CAPITAL / GASTOS DE CAPITAL (000) (4)	TOTAL AS % OF GROSS NATIONAL PRODUCT / TOTAL EN % DU PRODUIT NATIONAL BRUT / TOTAL EN % DEL PRODUCTO NACIONAL BRUTO (%) (5)	TOTAL AS % OF ALL PUBLIC EXPENDITURE / TOTAL EN % DE TOUTES DEPENSES PUBLIQUES / TOTAL EN % DE TODOS LOS GASTOS PUBLICOS (%) (6)
SARAWAK	1970	RINGGIT	32 976	28 988	87.9	3 988	...	...
	1974		77 721	63 562	81.8	14 159	...	...
	1975		97 747	74 491	76.2	23 256	...	...
	1976		108 484	85 347	78.7	23 137	...	...
	1977		133 285	100 861	75.7	32 424	...	...
MALDIVES	1970	RUPEE	1 774	...	...	...	...	...
	1975		...	1 115	...	...	...	...
	1976		...	1 017	...	58	...	...
	1978		1 279	1 221	95.5	...	*3.0	...
MONGOLIA	1970	TUGRIK	298 737	276 982	92.7	21 755	...	15.6
NEPAL	1970	RUPEE	51 689	...	...	...	0.6	6.7
	1974		158 848	...	...	...	1.2	9.1
	1975		229 463	201 776	87.9	27 687	1.5	10.7
	1976		257 874	...	...	...	1.6	10.9
	1977		277 671	...	...	...	1.7	9.0
	1978		322 705	...	...	...	...	8.6
OMAN	1971	RIAL	1 300	500	38.5	800	1.3	2.8
	1974		5 734	3 920	68.4	1 814	1.2	1.7
	1975		9 396	6 605	70.3	2 791	1.6	1.9
	1976		15 182	9 193	60.6	5 989	2.2	2.6
	1978		27 476	17 524	63.8	9 952	...	4.9
PAKISTAN	1970	RUPEE	789 907	480 370	60.8	309 537	1.7	4.2
	1974		1 744 491	1 221 103	70.0	523 388	2.0	4.9
	1975		2 488 206	1 731 089	69.6	757 117	2.2	5.2
	1976		2 802 610	2 020 279	72.1	782 331	2.1	5.1
	1977		3 300 718	2 445 697	74.1	855 021	2.2	5.2
	1978		3 875 900	2 808 900	72.5	1 067 000	...	...
PHILIPPINES ‡	1970	PESO	1 082 800	1 069 600	98.8	12 900	2.6	13.0
	1974		1 695 802	1 484 047	...	9 755	1.7	11.4
	1975		2 149 896	1 753 958	...	31 938	1.9	10.0
	1976		2 309 275	1 805 373	...	42 902	1.7	9.7
	1977		2 664 438	1 996 438	...	40 000	1.7	...
	1978		3 847 197	2 983 482	...	211 794	...	...

Public expenditure on education 4.1
Dépenses publiques afférentes à l'enseignement
Gastos públicos destinados a la educación

Country	Currency	Year	(1)	(2)	(3)	(4)	(5)	(6)
QATAR	RIYAL	1970	44 829	41 029	91.5	3 800	4.6	8.9
		1974	108 929	87 739	80.5	21 190	1.4	5.6
		1975	177 124	123 524	69.7	53 600	2.0	3.3
		1976	262 129	187 392	71.5	74 737	...	...
		1977	408 350	283 110	69.3	125 240	...	...
SAUDI ARABIA	RIYAL	1970	664 911	631 341	95.0	33 570	4.8	9.8
		1974	3 760 284	2 149 362	57.7	1 610 922	4.6	8.2
		1975	12 940 937	5 528 566	42.7	7 412 371	9.9	11.7
		1976	13 977 458	5 807 729	41.6	8 169 729	9.6	10.6
		1977	15 049 114	7 187 919	47.8	7 861 195	8.7	10.3
SINGAPORE	DOLLAR	1970	184 492	173 599	94.1	10 893	3.1	11.7
		1974	332 646	308 004	92.6	24 642	2.7	9.2
		1975	391 264	339 870	86.9	51 394	3.0	8.6
		1976	388 161	343 511	88.5	44 650	2.7	8.0
		1977	397 788	363 333	91.3	34 455	2.5	7.3
SRI LANKA	RUPEE	1970	544 382	506 392	93.0	37 990	4.3	13.6
		1974	625 017				2.9	10.8
		1975	729 590	682 680	93.6	46 910	3.1	10.1
		1976	814 223	760 581	93.4	53 642	3.1	9.8
		1977	854 919	827 870	96.8	27 049	2.7	*10.2
SYRIAN ARAB REPUBLIC ‡	POUND	1970	261 761	194 236	...	8 135	4.0	9.4
		1974	498 194	366 511	...	30 880	3.3	7.7
		1975	813 245	462 514	...	188 625	4.1	7.8
		1976	1 442 185	516 484	...	385 187	6.1	8.7
		1977	1 492 069					
THAILAND	BAHT	1970	4 732 588	3 461 635	73.1	1 270 953	3.5	16.7
		1974	7 301 797	5 503 093	75.4	1 798 704	2.7	18.4
		1975	10 605 251	7 775 347	73.3	2 829 904	3.6	20.7
		1976	13 175 524	8 732 955	66.3	4 442 569	4.0	20.8
		1977	14 841 200				4.0	
		1978	16 293 000	11 040 100	67.8	5 252 900		
TURKEY	LIRA	1970	4 269 835	3 032 807	71.0	1 237 028	2.9	13.7
		1977	46 942 432	37 961 875	80.9	8 980 557	5.4	...
UNITED ARAB EMIRATES	DIRHAM	1974	186 636	177 658	95.2	8 978	0.6	25.1
		1975	346 585	271 382	78.3	75 203	1.0	27.6
		1976	484 413	400 864	82.8	83 549	...	19.1
		1977	888 313	838 114	94.3	50 199	...	...
YEMEN	RIAL	1970	10 046	...	...	...	0.4	5.9
		1974	33 272	...	...	...	0.7	6.5
		1975	63 521	...	...	...	1.2	11.9
YEMEN, DEMOCRATIC	DINAR	1971	2 450	2 389	97.5	61	3.7	10.9
		1975	4 324				3.8	14.7
		1976	6 187	5 288	85.5	899		16.2
		1977	8 224	...	...	...	4.1	16.8

4.1 Public expenditure on education
Dépenses publiques afférentes à l'enseignement
Gastos públicos destinados a la educación

COUNTRY / PAYS / PAIS	YEAR / ANNEE / AÑO	CURRENCY / MONNAIE / MONEDA	TOTAL EXPENDITURE / DEPENSES TOTALES / GASTOS TOTALES (000) (1)	CURRENT EXPENDITURE – DEPENSES ORDINAIRES – GASTOS ORDINARIOS — AMOUNT / MONTANT / IMPORTE (000) (2)	— AS % OF TOTAL / EN % DU TOTAL / EN % DEL TOTAL (%) (3)	CAPITAL EXPENDITURE / DEPENSES EN CAPITAL / GASTOS DE CAPITAL (000) (4)	TOTAL AS % OF GROSS NATIONAL PRODUCT (%) (5)	TOTAL AS % OF ALL PUBLIC EXPENDITURE (%) (6)
EUROPE								
ALBANIA	1970	LEK	554 000	...	...	...	...	11.2
AUSTRIA	1970	SCHILLING	17 349 500	13 502 700	77.8	3 846 800	...	8.1
	1974		32 011 000	24 952 700	78.0	7 058 300	4.6	8.4
	1975		37 409 300	29 366 500	78.5	8 042 800	5.7	8.5
	1976		41 264 700	32 467 500	78.7	8 797 200	5.7	8.3
	1977		43 427 600	35 368 600	81.4	8 059 000	5.5	8.2
BELGIUM ‡	1970	FRANC	...	54 165 533	...	...	...	22.2
	1975		143 856 800	131 906 200	91.7	11 950 600	6.2	20.5
	1976		164 959 600	151 206 800	91.7	13 752 800	6.2	19.2
	1977		186 656 000	170 775 800	91.5	15 880 200	6.5	
BULGARIA ‡	1970	LEV	513 845	442 124	86.0	71 721	4.9	9.1
	1974		695 746	669 490	96.2	26 256	5.3	8.6
	1975		787 599	725 259	92.1	62 340	5.5	8.5
	1976		819 234	778 601	95.0	40 633	5.4	9.1
	1977		901 717	838 837	93.0	62 880	5.8	...
CZECHOSLOVAKIA ‡	1970	KORUNA	13 625 000	12 102 000	88.8	1 523 000	4.4	7.0
	1974		17 598 619	15 990 986	90.9	1 607 633	4.5	6.8
	1975		19 104 801	17 288 021	90.5	1 816 780	4.7	7.0
	1976		18 897 597	17 332 254	91.7	1 565 343	4.5	6.5
	1977		20 036 249	18 580 636	92.7	1 455 613	4.8	...
DENMARK ‡	1970	KRONE	8 137 000	6 294 000	77.4	1 843 000	6.8	16.9
	1975		14 643 000	12 036 000	82.2	2 607 000	7.5	16.7
	1976		16 801 000	14 600 000	86.9	2 201 000	7.8	15.2
	1977		18 441 000	16 202 000	87.9	2 239 000	6.7	...
FINLAND	1970	MARKKA	2 678 872	2 404 790	89.8	274 082	6.2	16.5
	1974		5 035 110	4 376 505	86.9	658 605	6.1	16.7
	1975		6 497 103	5 596 511	86.1	900 592	6.7	16.8
	1976		7 628 727	6 677 009	87.5	951 718	7.1	12.9
	1977		8 765 559	7 598 881	86.7	1 166 678	7.0	...
FRANCE ‡	1970	FRANC	38 386 800	24 598 921	...	4 221 868	4.7	...
	1975		80 475 045	46 844 110	...	4 292 035	5.7	...
	1976		96 693 858	54 455 190	...	4 434 268	5.8	...
	1977		108 150 500	62 738 600	...	3 975 400	5.8	...

Public expenditure on education   4.1
Dépenses publiques afférentes à l'enseignement
Gastos públicos destinados a la educación

Country	Currency	Year	(1)	(2)	(3)	(4)	(5)	(6)
GERMAN DEMOCRATIC REPUBLIC ‡	DDR MARK	1970	...	5 812 000	...	...	5.1	8.3
		1974	...	7 833 446	...	...	5.6	7.6
		1975	...	8 276 353	...	...	5.7	7.2
		1976	...	8 907 051	...	...	5.9	7.6
		1977	...	9 273 262	...	...	5.9	7.5
		1978	...	9 538 582	...	...	5.8	7.2
GERMANY, FEDERAL REPUBLIC OF ‡	DEUTSCHE MARK	1970	23 472 800	16 926 900	72.1	6 545 900	3.4	12.0
		1974	44 965 000	34 044 000	75.7	10 921 000	4.5	14.4
		1975	45 798 000	35 773 000	78.1	10 025 000	4.4	9.1
		1976	46 691 000	37 753 000	80.9	8 938 000	4.2	8.8
GIBRALTAR	POUND	1970	391	362	92.6	29	*3.1	...
		1974	811	709	87.4	102	...	...
		1975	997	909	91.2	88	...	...
		1976	1 604	1 443	90.0	161	...	...
		1977	1 745	1 699	97.4	46	...	...
GREECE ‡	DRACHMA	1970	6 239 900	5 090 900	81.6	1 149 000	2.0	9.6
		1974	10 291 047	9 347 600	90.8	943 447	1.8	8.0
HUNGARY ‡	FORINT	1970	12 208 066	10 641 431	87.2	1 566 635	4.4	...
		1974	17 411 071	15 226 971	87.5	2 184 100	4.6	...
		1975	19 325 492	16 719 792	86.5	2 605 700	4.8	...
		1976	20 080 583	17 579 883	87.5	2 500 700	4.6	...
		1977	22 518 611	19 385 911	86.1	3 132 700	4.7	...
ICELAND ‡	KRONA	1970	1 656 000	...	...	...	3.9	17.7
		1974	5 994 000	...	...	...	4.4	15.0
		1975	7 810 000	...	...	...	4.2	13.3
IRELAND	POUND	1970	82 185	68 980	83.9	13 205	4.9	10.8
		1974	157 105	135 000	85.9	22 105	5.4	...
		1975	230 483	198 856	86.3	31 627	6.5	10.8
		1976	276 836	245 669	88.7	31 167	6.2	11.0
		1977	335 543	287 433	85.7	48 110	6.2	11.2
ITALY ‡	LIRA	1970	2 500 061	2 429 439	97.2	70 622	4.3	13.8
		1974	5 085 647	4 575 617	90.0	510 030	5.2	11.7
		1975	5 675 784	5 060 156	89.2	615 628	5.0	9.3
		1976	7 346 892	6 467 905	88.0	878 987	5.1	...
LUXEMBOURG	FRANC	1970	2 244 400	1 664 900	74.2	579 500	4.4	14.8
		1975	5 023 200	3 903 300	77.7	1 119 900	5.0	15.0
		1976	6 197 500	4 619 800	74.5	1 577 700	5.2	16.0
		1977	6 520 200	5 225 200	80.1	1 295 000	5.2	14.1
MALTA	POUND	1970	6 436	5 913	91.9	523	6.3	13.0
		1974	6 509	6 163	94.7	346	4.5	10.2
		1975	7 105	6 881	96.8	224	3.9	7.6
		1976	8 856	8 733	98.6	123	4.0	9.2
		1977	9 063	8 938	98.6	125	3.5	9.7
MONACO	FRANC FRANCAIS	1970	35 282	17 118	58.2	14 744	...	10.4
		1974	...	20 538	...	...	...	...
		1977	...	28 716	...	...	...	...

4.1 Public expenditure on education
Dépenses publiques afférentes à l'enseignement
Gastos públicos destinados a la educación

COUNTRY / PAYS / PAIS	YEAR / ANNEE / AÑO	CURRENCY / MONNAIE / MONEDA	TOTAL EXPENDITURE / DEPENSES TOTALES / GASTOS TOTALES (000) (1)	CURRENT EXPENDITURE / DEPENSES ORDINAIRES / GASTOS ORDINARIOS — AMOUNT / MONTANT / IMPORTE (000) (2)	AS % OF TOTAL / EN % DU TOTAL / EN % DEL TOTAL (%) (3)	CAPITAL EXPENDITURE / DEPENSES EN CAPITAL / GASTOS DE CAPITAL (000) (4)	TOTAL AS % OF GROSS NATIONAL PRODUCT ... (%) (5)	TOTAL AS % OF ALL PUBLIC EXPENDITURE ... (%) (6)
NETHERLANDS	1970	GUILDER	8 874 000	7 069 000	79.7	1 805 000	7.7	29.4
	1974		15 436 000	12 720 000	82.4	2 716 000	8.2	28.5
	1975		18 096 000	14 881 000	82.2	3 215 000	8.7	23.7
	1976		20 322 000	17 021 000	83.8	3 301 000	8.5	25.4
	1977		21 968 000	18 666 000	85.0	3 302 000	8.4	25.4
NORWAY	1970	KRONE	4 771 600	3 696 100	77.5	1 075 500	5.9	15.5
	1974		8 923 000	7 206 000	80.8	1 717 000	7.0	15.1
	1975		10 456 000	8 427 000	80.6	2 029 000	7.7	14.7
	1976		12 865 000	10 608 000	82.5	2 257 000	7.7	15.1
	1977		14 186 000	11 484 000	81.0	2 702 000	7.6	14.4
POLAND ‡	1970	ZLOTY	...	28 506	...	...	3.8	8.7
	1974		...	44 306	...	...	3.7	9.0
	1975		...	50 449	...	...	3.7	8.7
	1976		...	56 114	...	...	3.5	8.4
	1977		...	59 175	...	...	3.4	7.7
	1978		...	64 117	...	...	3.1	7.3
PORTUGAL ‡	1970	ESCUDO	3 022 366	2 742 828	90.8	279 538	1.6	9.5
	1974		8 810 510	8 116 900	92.1	693 610	2.4	16.4
	1975		14 821 558	13 876 839	93.6	944 719	3.7	...
	1976		18 723 016	17 140 918	91.5	1 582 098	3.7	16.4
	1977		24 435 940	22 535 383	92.2	1 900 557	3.6	14.5
ROMANIA	1970	LEU	10 419 100	9 235 100	88.6	1 184 000	...	8.0
	1974		13 756 000	11 782 000	85.6	1 974 000	...	6.6
	1975		15 194 700	12 892 700	84.8	2 302 000	...	6.4
	1976		16 744 800	14 462 800	86.4	2 282 000	...	6.7
	1977		17 731 100	15 291 100	86.2	2 440 000	...	6.3
	1978		18 537 300	16 189 300	87.3	2 348 000	...	6.2
SAN MARINO	1970	LIRA	984 057	727 334	73.9	256 723	5.9	13.4
	1974		2 221 067	1 651 377	74.4	569 690	...	12.2
	1975		2 775 902	2 499 565	90.0	276 337	...	13.6
	1976		3 370 335	2 915 485	86.5	454 850	...	13.1
	1977		4 677 875	3 490 495	74.6	1 187 380	...	15.2
SPAIN ‡	1970	PESETA	53 156	35 420	66.6	17 736	2.1	15.2
	1974		83 090	71 688	86.3	11 402	1.7	11.0
	1976		154 003	134 391	87.3	19 612	2.2	16.8

Public expenditure on education 4.1
Dépenses publiques afférentes à l'enseignement
Gastos públicos destinados a la educación

Country	Year	(1)	(2)	(3)	(4)	(5)	(6)
SWEDEN — KRONA	1970	13 150 000	10 785 000	82.0	2 365 000	7.7	13.9
	1974	18 451 100	16 468 100	89.3	1 983 000	7.4	13.4
	1975	21 230 200	19 281 100	90.8	1 949 100	7.7	13.4
	1976	24 905 900	22 454 200	90.2	2 451 700	7.7	13.3
	1977	29 407 300	26 441 200	89.9	2 966 100	8.4	12.7
SWITZERLAND — FRANC	1970	3 726 000	2 765 600	74.2	960 400	4.2	18.4
	1974	6 999 300	5 560 800	79.4	1 438 500	4.8	19.5
	1975	7 392 300	5 978 800	80.9	1 413 500	5.1	19.4
	1976	7 657 200	6 350 400	82.9	1 306 800	5.2	18.6
	1977	7 903 800	6 734 300	85.2	1 169 500	5.2	18.9
UNITED KINGDOM ‡ — POUND STERLING	1970	2 740	2 334	85.2	406	5.2	14.1
	1974	5 528	4 892	88.5	636	6.4	14.1
	1975	7 020	6 292	89.6	728	6.4	14.0
	1976	7 849	7 132	90.9	717	6.2	14.3
YUGOSLAVIA — DINAR	1970	8 366 000	7 633 000	91.2	733 000	4.7	...
	1974	21 839 000	19 383 000	88.8	2 456 000	4.9	...
	1975	28 897 000	25 515 000	88.3	3 382 000	5.2	...
	1976	34 966 000	31 093 000	88.9	3 873 000	5.0	...
	1977	43 632 000	37 632 000	86.2	6 000 000	5.0	...
OCEANIA							
AMERICAN SAMOA — UNITED STATES DOLLAR	1970	5 072	5 072	100.0	—	...	...
	1974	9 990	9 890	99.0	100	...	...
	1975	9 642	7 962	82.6	1 680	...	...
	1976	8 550	8 550	100.0	—	...	...
	1977	8 626	8 626	100.0	—	...	...
AUSTRALIA — DOLLAR	1970	1 405 000	1 139 000	81.1	266 000	4.3	13.3
	1974	3 728 000	3 027 000	81.2	701 000	6.4	15.8
	1975	4 495 000	3 735 000	83.1	760 000	6.5	14.8
	1976	5 148 000	4 455 000	86.5	693 000	6.3	16.2
COOK ISLANDS — NEW ZEALAND DOLLAR	1970	900	813	90.3	87	...	...
FIJI — DOLLAR	1970	7 661	6 777	88.5	884	4.2	15.6
	1974	19 478	18 748	96.3	730	4.3	18.5
	1976	29 918	26 640	89.0	3 278	4.8	17.6
	1977	37 978	34 287	90.3	3 691	5.4	18.6
FRENCH POLYNESIA — FRANC C.F.P.	1970	1 256 103	1 150 442	91.6	105 661	...	...
	1974	3 625 225	2 635 885	72.7	989 340	...	...
	1975	3 740 422	3 268 311	87.4	472 111	...	...
GUAM — UNITED STATES DOLLAR	1970	23 594	22 434	95.1	1 160	...	...
	1974	52 050	51 848	99.6	202	...	...
	1975	52 874	52 723	99.7	151	...	...
	1976	44 428	44 428	100.0	—	...	...
	1977	44 867	44 867	100.0	—	...	...
KIRIBATI — AUSTRALIAN DOLLAR	1970	644	534	82.9	110	...	...
	1974	1 144	1 015	88.7	129	...	...
	1975	2 077	2 022	97.4	55	...	*9.0
	1977	2 157	2 100	97.4	57	...	*10.6
NAURU — AUSTRALIAN DOLLAR	1970	706	695	98.4	11	...	...
NEW CALEDONIA — FRANC C.F.P.	1970	1 532 908	1 371 269	89.5	161 639	...	14.1

4.1 Public expenditure on education
Dépenses publiques afférentes à l'enseignement
Gastos públicos destinados a la educación

COUNTRY / PAYS / PAIS	YEAR / ANNEE / AÑO	CURRENCY / MONNAIE / MONEDA	TOTAL EXPENDITURE / DEPENSES TOTALES / GASTOS TOTALES (000)	CURRENT EXPENDITURE / DEPENSES ORDINAIRES / GASTOS ORDINARIOS		CAPITAL EXPENDITURE / DEPENSES EN CAPITAL / GASTOS DE CAPITAL (000)	TOTAL AS % OF GROSS NATIONAL PRODUCT / TOTAL EN % DU PRODUIT NATIONAL BRUT / TOTAL EN % DEL PRODUCTO NACIONAL BRUTO (%)	TOTAL AS % OF ALL PUBLIC EXPENDITURE / TOTAL EN % DE TOUTES DEPENSES PUBLIQUES / TOTAL EN % DE TODOS LOS GASTOS PUBLICOS (%)
				AMOUNT / MONTANT / IMPORTE (000)	AS % OF TOTAL / EN % DU TOTAL / EN % DEL TOTAL (%)			
			(1)	(2)	(3)	(4)	(5)	(6)
NEW HEBRIDES	1970	AUSTRALIAN DOLLAR	1 064	682	64.1	382	...	...
	1974		1 833	1 520	82.9	313	...	...
	1975		1 888	1 444	76.5	444	...	...
NEW HEBRIDES	1970	FRANC FRANCAIS	10 393	10 377	99.8	16	...	...
	1975		42 681	38 288	89.7	4 393	...	...
	1977		76 545	73 868	96.5	2 677	...	...
NEW ZEALAND	1970	DOLLAR	267 616	212 525	79.4	55 091	4.9	14.3
	1974		529 800	434 558	82.0	95 242	5.3	13.5
	1975		631 751	503 643	79.7	128 108	5.5	...
	1976		704 678	575 566	81.7	129 112	5.1	...
	1977		813 887	675 222	83.0	138 665	5.4	...
NIUE	1970	NEW ZEALAND DOLLAR	331	310	93.7	21	...	...
	1974		465	465	100.0	—	...	...
	1975		631	595	94.3	36	...	...
NORFOLK ISLAND	1970	AUSTRALIAN DOLLAR	109	103	94.5	6	...	14.3
	1974		158	143	90.5	15	...	14.7
	1975		220	209	95.0	11	...	13.7
	1976		245	245	100.0	—	...	15.5
	1977		291	291	100.0	—	...	16.3
PACIFIC ISLANDS	1971	UNITED STATES DOLLAR	14 733	11 508	78.1	3 225	...	20.9
	1974		18 803	17 141	91.2	1 662	...	*24.3
	1975		23 469	21 501	91.6	1 968	...	17.8
	1976		22 285	20 205	90.7	2 080	...	...
	1977		23 029	22 642	98.3	387	...	...
PAPUA NEW GUINEA	1970	KINA	25 171	20 643	82.0	4 528	4.8	13.2
	1975		61 601	61 601	100.0	...	6.6	14.4
	1976		89 159	80 426	90.2	8 733	8.8	...
	1978		89 320	86 773	97.1	2 547	...	18.4
SAMOA	1970	TALA	1 366	1 193	87.3	173	6.3	...
	1974		1 525	...	...	...	5.4	...
	1975		1 939	1 939	100.0	...	6.0	...
	1976		2 206	2 206	100.0	—	...	...
	1977		2 263	2 240	99.0	23	...	...
SOLOMON ISLANDS	1970	AUSTRALIAN DOLLAR	1 084	784	72.3	300	3.8	11.7

Public expenditure on education   4.1
Dépenses publiques afférentes à l'enseignement
Gastos públicos destinados a la educación

Country	Currency	Year	Total	Current	Current %	Capital	% of GNP	% of total gov. exp.
... ISLANDS	NEW ZEALAND DOLLAR	1970	85	68	80.0	17	...	...
TONGA ‡	DOLLAR	1971	675	601	89.0	74	...	15.7
		1974	865	776	89.7	89	3.4	17.2
		1975	709	686	96.8	23	...	...
		1976	2 257	1 663	73.7	594	...	...
		1977	1 430	1 330	93.0	100	...	...
U.S.S.R.	ROUBLE	1970	19 834 000	16 528 000	83.3	3 306 000	6.8	12.8
		1974	26 938 800	22 870 500	84.9	4 068 300	7.6	13.6
		1975	27 747 100	23 415 900	84.4	4 331 200	7.6	12.9
		1976	28 849 400	24 169 900	83.8	4 679 500	7.5	12.7
		1977	29 906 300	24 956 900	83.4	4 950 000	7.4	12.3
		1978	31 304 700	26 219 900	83.8	5 084 800	7.4	12.0
BYELORUSSIAN S.S.R. ‡	ROUBLE	1970	655 418	540 408	82.5	115 010	...	...
		1974	1 027 800	855 700	83.3	172 100	...	18.7
		1975	1 040 600	859 300	82.6	181 300	...	...
		1976	1 066 300	883 500	82.9	182 800	...	...
		1977	1 100 800	909 700	82.6	191 100	...	...
UKRAINIAN S.S.R. ‡	ROUBLE	1970	3 757 900	3 135 800	83.4	622 100	6.9	28.1
		1974	4 886 900	4 214 300	86.2	672 600	7.5	...
		1975	5 014 000	4 312 200	86.0	701 800	7.6	...
		1976	5 213 600	4 467 400	85.7	746 200	7.5	27.4
		1977	5 350 000	4 545 300	85.0	804 700	...	27.7

ALGERIA:
E—> FOR 1978, EXPENDITURE OF THE MINISTRY OF PRIMARY AND SECONDARY EDUCATION ONLY.
FR—> EN 1978, DEPENSES DU MINISTERE DES ENSEIGNEMENTS PRIMAIRE ET SECONDAIRE SEULEMENT.
ESP> EN 1978, GASTOS DEL MINISTERIO DE LAS ENSEÑANZAS DE PRIMERO Y SEGUNDO GRADO SOLAMENTE.

BENIN:
E—> EXPENDITURE OF THE CENTRAL GOVERNMENT ONLY.
FR—> DEPENSES DU GOUVERNEMENT CENTRAL SEULEMENT.
ESP> GASTOS DEL GOBIERNO CENTRAL SOLAMENTE.

CHAD:
E—> EXPENDITURE OF THE CENTRAL GOVERNMENT ONLY.
FR—> DEPENSES DU GOUVERNEMENT CENTRAL SEULEMENT.
ESP> GASTOS DEL GOBIERNO CENTRAL SOLAMENTE.

CONGO:
E—> EXPENDITURE OF THE CENTRAL GOVERNMENT ONLY.
FR—> DEPENSES DU GOUVERNEMENT CENTRAL SEULEMENT.
ESP> GASTOS DEL GOBIERNO CENTRAL SOLAMENTE.

ETHIOPIA:
E—> DATA IN COLUMNS 2 (CURRENT EXPENDITURE) AND 4 (CAPITAL EXPENDITURE) IN 1970 AND IN ALL COLUMNS FOR THE OTHER YEARS DO NOT INCLUDE EXPENDITURE FOR UNIVERSITIES.
FR—> EN 1970, LES DONNEES DES COLONNES 2 (DEPENSES ORDINAIRES) ET 4 (DEPENSES EN CAPITAL) ET CELLES DE TOUTES LES COLONNES POUR LES AUTRES ANNEES NE COMPRENNENT PAS LES DEPENSES DES UNIVERSITES.

ETHIOPIA (CONT):
ESP> EN 1970, LOS GASTOS DE LAS COLUMNAS 2 (GASTOS ORDINARIOS) Y 4 (GASTOS DE CAPITAL) Y LOS DE TODAS LAS COLUMNAS PARA LOS OTROS AÑOS, NO INCLUYEN LOS GASTOS DE LAS UNIVERSIDADES.

GHANA:
E—> FOR 1976, EXPENDITURE ON UNIVERSITIES IS NOT INCLUDED.
FR—> EN 1976, LES DEPENSES DES UNIVERSITES NE SONT PAS INCLUSES.
ESP> EN 1976 NO SE INCLUYEN LOS GASTOS RELATIVOS A LAS UNIVERSIDADES.

GUINEA-BISSAU:
E—> FOR 1978, FOREIGN AID IS INCLUDED.
FR—> EN 1978, L'AIDE EXTERIEURE EST INCLUSE.
ESP> EN 1978, INCLUIDA LA AYUDA EXTERIOR.

IVORY COAST:
E—> FOREIGN AID IS INCLUDED.
FR—> L'AIDE EXTERIEURE EST INCLUSE.
ESP> INCLUIDA LA AYUDA EXTERIOR.

KENYA:
E—> EXPENDITURE OF THE MINISTRY OF EDUCATION ONLY.
FR—> DEPENSES DU MINISTERE DE L'EDUCATION SEULEMENT.
ESP> GASTOS DEL MINISTERIO DE EDUCACION SOLAMENTE.

4.1 **Public expenditure on education**
Dépenses publiques afférentes à l'enseignement
Gastos públicos destinados a la educación

UGANDA (CONT):
FR-> TOUTES LES DONNEES EN 1974 ET CELLES DES
COLONNES 2 ET 4 EN 1975, SE REFERENT AUX DEPENSES
DU MINISTERE DE L'EDUCATION SEULEMENT.
ESP> TODOS LOS DATOS EN 1974 Y LOS DE LAS
COLUMNAS 2 Y 4 EN 1974 NO SE INCLUYEN LOS DATOS
DE EDUCACION SOLAMENTE.

UPPER VOLTA:
E-> EXPENDITURE OF THE MINISTRY OF EDUCATION
ONLY.
FR-> DEPENSES DU MINISTERE DE L'EDUCATION
SEULEMENT.
ESP> GASTOS DEL MINISTERIO DE EDUCACION
SOLAMENTE.

CUBA:
E-> EXPENDITURE ON EDUCATION IS CALCULATED AS
PERCENTAGE OF GROSS MATERIAL PRODUCT.
FR-> LES DEPENSES D'ENSEIGNEMENT SONT CALCULEES
EN POURCENTAGE DU PRODUIT MATERIEL BRUT.
ESP> LOS GASTOS RELATIVOS A LA ENSEÑANZA SE CAL-
CULAN COMO PORCENTAJE DEL PRODUCTO MATERIAL BRUTO.

JAMAICA:
E-> FOR 1970 AND 1975, EXPENDITURE OF THE
MINISTRY OF EDUCATION ONLY.
FR-> EN 1970 ET 1975, DEPENSES DU MINISTERE
DE L'EDUCATION SEULEMENT.
ESP> EN 1970 Y 1975, GASTOS DEL MINISTERIO
DE EDUCACION SOLAMENTE.

MEXICO:
E-> FOR 1970, 1975, 1976 AND 1977, DATA IN
COLUMNS 2 AND 4 REFER TO EXPENDITURE OF THE
MINISTRY OF EDUCATION ONLY.
FR-> EN 1970, 1975, 1976 ET 1977, LES DONNEES
DES COLONNES 2 ET 4 SE REFERENT AUX DEPENSES
DU MINISTERE DE L'EDUCATION SEULEMENT.
ESP> EN 1970, 1975, 1976 Y 1977, LOS DATOS DE
LAS COLUMNAS 2 Y 4 SE REFIEREN AL MINISTERIO
DE EDUCACION SOLAMENTE.

UNITED STATES OF AMERICA:
E-> FIGURES IN COLUMNS 1, 2 AND 4 ARE IN
MILLIONS.
FR-> LES CHIFFRES DES COLONNES 1, 2 ET 4 SONT
EXPRIMES EN MILLIONS.
ESP> LAS CIFRAS DE LAS COLUMNAS 1, 2 Y 4 VIENEN
EXPRESADAS EN MILLONES.

ARGENTINA:
E-> FIGURES IN COLUMNS 1, 2 AND 4 ARE IN
MILLIONS. FOR 1974 AND 1976, EXPENDITURE OF
THE MINISTRY OF EDUCATION ONLY.
FR-> LES CHIFFRES DES COLONNES 1, 2 ET 4 SONT
EXPRIMES EN MILLIONS. EN 1974 ET 1976, DEPENSES
DU MINISTERE DE L'EDUCATION SEULEMENT.
ESP> LAS CIFRAS DE LAS COLUMNAS 1, 2 Y 4 VIENEN
EXPRESADAS EN MILLONES. EN 1974 Y 1976, GASTOS
DEL MINISTERIO DE EDUCACION SOLAMENTE.

LIBYAN ARAB JAMAHIRIYA:
E-> FOR 1970 AND 1974 EXPENDITURE ON UNIVER-
SITIES IS NOT INCLUDED.
FR-> EN 1970 ET 1974 LES DEPENSES DES UNIVER-
SITES NE SONT PAS INCLUSES.
ESP> EN 1970 Y 1974 NO SE INCLUYEN LOS DATOS
RELATIVOS A LAS UNIVERSIDADES.

MADAGASCAR:
E-> FOR 1970, FOREIGN AID FOR EDUCATION AT
THE THIRD LEVEL IS INCLUDED.
FR-> EN 1970, L'AIDE EXTERIEURE DESTINEE A
L'ENSEIGNEMENT DU TROISIEME DEGRE EST INCLUSE.
ESP> EN 1970, SE INCLUYE LA AYUDA EXTERIOR
DESTINADA A LA ENSEÑANZA DE TERCER GRADO.

MAURITANIA:
E-> EXPENDITURE OF THE CENTRAL GOVERNMENT ONLY.
FR-> DEPENSES DU GOUVERNEMENT CENTRAL SEULEMENT.
ESP> GASTOS DEL GOBIERNO CENTRAL SOLAMENTE.

SENEGAL:
E-> FOR 1974, EXPENDITURE OF THE MINISTRY OF
PRIMARY AND SECONDARY EDUCATION ONLY.
FR-> EN 1974, DEPENSES DU MINISTERE DES
ENSEIGNEMENTS PRIMAIRE ET SECONDAIRE SEULEMENT.
ESP> EN 1974, GASTOS DEL MINISTERIO DE LAS
ENSEÑANZAS DE PRIMERO Y DE SEGUNDO GRADO
SOLAMENTE.

SOMALIA:
E-> FOR 1978, NOT INCLUDING EXPENDITURE FOR
THIRD LEVEL EDUCATION.
FR-> EN 1978, LES DEPENSES DE L'ENSEIGNEMENT
DU TROISIEME DEGRE NE SONT PAS INCLUSES.
ESP> EN 1978, EXCLUIDOS LOS GASTOS RELATIVOS
A LA ENSEÑANZA DE TERCER GRADO.

SUDAN:
E-> FOR 1974, PRIVATE EXPENDITURE RELATING TO
PRIVATE EDUCATION IS INCLUDED.
FR-> EN 1974, LES DEPENSES PRIVEES AFFERENTES
A L'ENSEIGNEMENT PRIVE SONT INCLUSES.
ESP> EN 1974, INCLUIDOS LOS GASTOS PRIVADOS
CORRESPONDIENTES A LA ENSEÑANZA PRIVADA.

SWAZILAND:
E-> FOR 1976 AND 1977, EXPENDITURE OF THE
MINISTRY OF EDUCATION ONLY.
FR-> EN 1976 ET 1977, DEPENSES DU MINISTERE DE
L'EDUCATION SEULEMENT.
ESP> EN 1976 Y 1977, GASTOS DEL MINISTERIO DE
EDUCACION SOLAMENTE.

TOGO:
E-> FOREIGN AID IS INCLUDED.
FR-> L'AIDE EXTERIEURE EST INCLUSE.
ESP> INCLUIDA LA AYUDA EXTERIOR.

UGANDA:
E-> IN 1974, AND IN COLUMNS 2 AND 4 FOR 1975,
DATA REFER TO EXPENDITURE OF THE MINISTRY OF
EDUCATION ONLY.

Public expenditure on education **4.1**
Dépenses publiques afférentes à l'enseignement
Gastos públicos destinados a la educación

BRAZIL:
E—> REVISED SERIES. FOR 1970, EXPENDITURE OF MUNICIPALITIES ARE NOT INCLUDED IN COLUMNS 2 AND 4.
FR—> SERIE REVISEE. EN 1970, LES DEPENSES DES MUNICIPALITES NE SONT PAS INCLUSES DANS LES COLONNES 2 ET 4.
ESP> SERIES REVISADAS. EN 1970, EXCLUIDOS LOS GASTOS DE LOS MUNICIPIOS EN LAS COLUMNAS 2 Y 4.

COLOMBIA:
E—> EXPENDITURE OF THE MINISTRY OF EDUCATION ONLY.
FR—> DEPENSES DU MINISTERE DE L'EDUCATION SEULEMENT.
ESP> GASTOS DEL MINISTERIO DE EDUCACION SOLAMENTE.

AFGHANISTAN:
E—> FOR 1977, EXPENDITURE ON UNIVERSITIES IS NOT INCLUDED.
FR—> EN 1977, LES DEPENSES DES UNIVERSITES NE SONT PAS INCLUSES.
ESP> EN 1977 NO SE INCLUYEN LOS GASTOS RELATIVOS A LAS UNIVERSIDADES.

BHUTAN:
E—> FOR 1970, EXPENDITURE OF THE MINISTRY OF EDUCATION ONLY.
FR—> EN 1970, DEPENSES DU MINISTERE DE L'EDUCATION SEULEMENT.
ESP> EN 1970, GASTOS DEL MINISTERIO DE EDUCACION SOLAMENTE.

CYPRUS:
E—> EXPENDITURE BY THE OFFICE OF GREEK EDUCATION ONLY.
FR—> DEPENSES DU BUREAU GREC DE L'EDUCATION SEULEMENT.
ESP> GASTOS DEL SERVICIO GRIEGO DE EDUCACION SOLAMENTE.

INDONESIA:
E—> FIGURES IN COLUMNS 1, 2 AND 4 ARE IN MILLIONS. FOR 1970, PRIVATE EXPENDITURE RELATING TO PRIVATE EDUCATION IS INCLUDED. FOR 1976, EXPENDITURE OF THE CENTRAL GOVERNMENT ONLY.
FR—> LES CHIFFRES DES COLONNES 1, 2 ET 4 SONT EXPRIMES EN MILLIONS. EN 1970, LES DEPENSES PRIVEES AFFERENTES A L'ENSEIGNEMENT PRIVE SONT INCLUSES. EN 1976, DEPENSES DU GOUVERNEMENT CENTRAL SEULEMENT.
ESP> LAS CIFRAS DE LAS COLUMNAS 1, 2 Y 4 VIENEN EXPRESADAS EN MILLONES. EN 1970, SE INCLUYEN LOS GASTOS PRIVADOS CORRESPONDIENTES A LA ENSEÑANZA PRIVADA. EN 1976, GASTOS DEL GOBIERNO CENTRAL SOLAMENTE.

JAPAN:
E—> FIGURES IN COLUMNS 1, 2 AND 4 ARE IN MILLIONS. FROM 1974 TO 1977, DATA IN COLUMNS 2 AND 4 DO NOT INCLUDE PUBLIC SUBSIDIES TO PRIVATE EDUCATION.

JAPAN (CONT):
FR—> LES CHIFFRES DES COLONNES 1, 2 ET 4 SONT EXPRIMES EN MILLIONS. DE 1974 A 1977, LES DONNEES DES COLONNES 2 ET 4 NE COMPRENNENT PAS LES SUBVENTIONS PUBLIQUES A L'ENSEIGNEMENT PRIVE.
ESP> LAS CIFRAS DE LAS COLUMNAS 1, 2 Y 4 VIENEN EXPRESADAS EN MILLONES. DE 1974 A 1977, LOS DATOS DE LAS COLUMNAS 2 Y 4 NO INCLUYEN LAS SUBVENCIONES PUBLICAS A LA ENSEÑANZA PRIVADA.

JORDAN:
E—> DATA REFER TO THE EAST BANK ONLY. FROM 1974 TO 1977, EXPENDITURE ON UNIVERSITIES IS NOT INCLUDED.
FR—> LES DONNEES SE REFERENT A LA RIVE ORIENTALE SEULEMENT. DE 1974 A 1977, LES DEPENSES DES UNIVERSITES NE SONT PAS INCLUSES.
ESP> LOS DATOS SE REFIEREN A LA ORILLA ORIENTAL SOLAMENTE. DE 1974 A 1977, NO SE INCLUYEN LOS DATOS RELATIVOS A LAS UNIVERSIDADES.

KOREA, REPUBLIC OF:
E—> FIGURES IN COLUMNS 1, 2 AND 4 ARE IN MILLIONS.
FR—> LES CHIFFRES DES COLONNES 1, 2 ET 4 SONT EXPRIMES EN MILLIONS.
ESP> LAS CIFRAS DE LAS COLUMNAS 1, 2 Y 4 VIENEN EXPRESADAS EN MILLONES.

LEBANON:
E—> EXPENDITURE OF THE MINISTRY OF EDUCATION ONLY.
FR—> DEPENSES DU MINISTERE DE L'EDUCATION SEULEMENT.
ESP> GASTOS DEL MINISTERIO DE EDUCACION SOLAMENTE.

PHILIPPINES:
E—> FROM 1974 TO 1978, EXPENDITURE FOR STATE UNIVERSITIES AND COLLEGES IS NOT INCLUDED IN COLUMNS 2 AND 4.
FR—> DE 1974 A 1978, LES DEPENSES DES UNIVERSITES ET COLLEGES D'ETAT NE SONT PAS INCLUSES DANS LES COLONNES 2 ET 4.
ESP> DE 1974 A 1978, NO SE INCLUYEN EN LAS COLUMNAS 2 Y 4 LOS GASTOS RELATIVOS A LAS UNIVERSIDADES Y LOS COLEGIOS DE ESTADO.

SYRIAN ARAB REPUBLIC:
E—> EXPENDITURE ON EDUCATION AT THE THIRD LEVEL IS NOT INCLUDED IN COLUMNS 2 AND 4.
FR—> LES DEPENSES DE L'ENSEIGNEMENT DU TROISIEME DEGRE NE SONT PAS INCLUSES DANS LES COLONNES 2 ET 4.
ESP> EN LAS COLUMNAS 2 Y 4 NO SE INCLUYEN LOS GASTOS RELATIVOS A LA ENSEÑANZA DE TERCER GRADO.

BELGIUM:
E—> EXPENDITURE OF THE MINISTRY OF EDUCATION ONLY.
FR—> DEPENSES DU MINISTERE DE L'EDUCATION SEULEMENT.
ESP> GASTOS DEL MINISTERIO DE EDUCACION SOLAMENTE.

4.1 Public expenditure on education
Dépenses publiques afférentes à l'enseignement
Gastos públicos destinados a la educación

BULGARIA:
E—> EXPENDITURE ON EDUCATION IS CALCULATED AS PERCENTAGE OF NET MATERIAL PRODUCT.
FR-> LES DEPENSES D'ENSEIGNEMENT SONT CALCULEES EN POURCENTAGE DU PRODUIT MATERIEL NET.
ESP> LOS GASTOS RELATIVOS A LA ENSEÑANZA SE HAN CALCULADO COMO PORCENTAJE DEL PRODUCTO MATERIAL NETO.

CZECHOSLOVAKIA:
E—> EXPENDITURE ON EDUCATION IS CALCULATED AS PERCENTAGE OF NET MATERIAL PRODUCT.
FR-> LES DEPENSES D'ENSEIGNEMENT SONT CALCULEES EN POURCENTAGE DU PRODUIT MATERIEL NET.
ESP> LOS GASTOS RELATIVOS A LA ENSEÑANZA SE HAN CALCULADO COMO PORCENTAJE DEL PRODUCTO MATERIAL NETO.

DENMARK:
E—> EXPENDITURE ON EDUCATION IS CALCULATED AS PERCENTAGE OF GROSS DOMESTIC PRODUCT.
FR-> LES DEPENSES D'ENSEIGNEMENT SONT CALCULEES EN POURCENTAGE DU PRODUIT INTERIEUR BRUT.
ESP> LOS GASTOS RELATIVOS A LA ENSEÑANZA SE HAN CALCULADO COMO PORCENTAJE DEL PRODUCTO INTERIOR BRUTO.

FRANCE:
E—> DATA IN COLUMNS 2 AND 4 REFER TO EXPENDITURE OF THE MINISTRY OF EDUCATION AND MINISTRY OF THE UNIVERSITIES ONLY.
FR-> LES DONNEES DES COLONNES 2 ET 4 SE REFERENT AUX DEPENSES DU MINISTERE DE L'EDUCATION ET DU MINISTERE DES UNIVERSITES SEULEMENT.
ESP> LOS DATOS DE LAS COLUMNAS 2 Y 4 SE REFIEREN A LOS GASTOS DEL MINISTERIO DE EDUCACION Y DEL MINISTERIO DE LAS UNIVERSIDADES SOLAMENTE.

GERMAN DEMOCRATIC REPUBLIC:
E—> EXPENDITURE ON EDUCATION IS CALCULATED AS PERCENTAGE OF NET MATERIAL PRODUCT.
FR-> LES DEPENSES D'ENSEIGNEMENT SONT CALCULEES EN POURCENTAGE DU PRODUIT MATERIEL NET.
ESP> LOS GASTOS RELATIVOS A LA ENSEÑANZA SE HAN CALCULADO COMO PORCENTAJE DEL PRODUCTO MATERIAL NETO.

GERMANY, FEDERAL REPUBLIC OF:
E—> BEGINNING 1975 DATA ARE NOT COMPARABLE WITH THOSE FOR PREVIOUS YEARS. FOR 1970 AND 1974, FIGURES INCLUDE THE TOTALITY OF THE EXPENDITURE (INSTRUCTION AND RESEARCH) INCURRED BY ALL THIRD LEVEL INSTITUTIONS AND UNIVERSITY HOSPITALS; FROM 1975 ONWARDS, ONLY THE EXPENDITURE INCURRED FOR EDUCATIONAL PURPOSES IS TAKEN INTO ACCOUNT (RESEARCH IS THUS EXCLUDED).
FR-> A PARTIR DE 1975, LES DONNEES NE SONT PAS COMPARABLES A CELLES DES ANNEES PRECEDENTES. EN 1970 ET 1974, LES CHIFFRES INCLUENT LA TOTALITE DES DEPENSES (ENSEIGNEMENT ET RECHERCHE) EFFECTUEES PAR TOUS LES ETABLISSEMENTS DE L'EN-SEIGNEMENT DU TROISIEME DEGRE ET LES HOPITAUX UNIVERSITAIRES; DEPUIS 1975, SEULES LES DEPENSES

GERMANY, FED. REP. (CONT):
D'ENSEIGNEMENT SONT PRISES EN CONSIDERATION, CE QUI EXCLUT LA RECHERCHE.
ESP> A PARTIR DE 1975, LOS DATOS NE SON COM-A-RABLES CON LOS DE LOS AÑOS ANTERIORES. EN 1970 Y 1974 LAS CIFRAS INCLUYEN LA TOTALIDAD DE LOS GASTOS (ENSEÑANZA E INVESTIGACION) EFECTUADOS POR TODOS LOS ESTABLECIMIENTOS DE ENSEÑANZA DE TERCER GRADO Y LOS HOSPITALES UNIVERSITARIOS. DESDE 1975, SOLO SE TOMAN EN CONSIDERACION LOS GASTOS RELATIVOS A LA ENSEÑANZA, EXLUYENDOSE LA INVESTIGACION.

GREECE:
E—> FOR 1974, DATA DO NOT INCLUDE PUBLIC SUBSIDIES TO PRIVATE EDUCATION.
FR-> EN 1974, LES DONNEES NE COMPRENNENT PAS LES SUBVENTIONS PUBLIQUES A L'ENSEIGNEMENT PRIVE.
ESP> EN 1974, LOS DATOS NO INCLUYEN LAS SUBVEN-CIONES PUBLICAS A LA ENSEÑANZA PRIVADA.

HUNGARY:
E—> EXPENDITURE ON EDUCATION IS CALCULATED AS PERCENTAGE OF NET MATERIAL PRODUCT.
FR-> LES DEPENSES D'ENSEIGNEMENT SONT CALCULEES EN POURCENTAGE DU PRODUIT MATERIEL NET.
ESP> LOS DATOS RELATIVOS A LA ENSEÑANZA SE HAN CALCULADO COMO PORCENTAJE DEL PRODUCTO MATERIAL NETO.

ICELAND:
E—> EXPENDITURE OF THE CENTRAL GOVERNMENT ONLY.
FR-> DEPENSES DU GOUVERNEMENT CENTRAL SEULEMENT.
ESP> GASTOS DEL GOBIERNO CENTRAL SOLAMENTE.

ITALY:
E—> FIGURES IN COLUMNS 1, 2 AND 4 ARE IN MILLIONS.
FR-> LES CHIFFRES DES COLONNES 1, 2 ET 4 SONT EXPRIMES EN MILLIONS.
ESP> LAS CIFRAS DE LAS COLUMNAS 1, 2 Y 4 VIENEN EXPRESADAS EN MILLONES.

POLAND:
E—> FIGURES IN COLUMN 2 ARE IN MILLIONS. EXPENDITURE ON EDUCATION IS CALCULATED AS PER-CENTAGE OF NET MATERIAL PRODUCT.
FR-> LES CHIFFRES DE LA COLONNE 2 SONT EXPRIMES EN MILLIONS. LES DEPENSES D'ENSEIGNEMENT SONT CALCULEES EN POURCENTAGE DU PRODUIT MATERIEL NET.
ESP> LAS CIFRAS DE LA COLUMNA 2 VIENEN EXPRESADAS EN MILLONES. LOS GASTOS RELATIVOS A LA ENSEÑANZA SE HAN CALCULADO COMO PORCENTAJE DEL PRODUCTO MATERIAL NETO.

PORTUGAL:
E—> EXPENDITURE OF THE MINISTRY OF EDUCATION ONLY.
FR-> DEPENSES DU MINISTERE DE L'EDUCATION SEULEMENT.
ESP> GASTOS DEL MINISTERIO DE EDUCACION SOLAMENTE.

Public expenditure on education   **4.1**
Dépenses publiques afférentes à l'enseignement
Gastos públicos destinados a la educación

SPAIN:
E—> FIGURES IN COLUMNS 1, 2 AND 4 ARE IN MILLIONS.
FR—> LES CHIFFRES DES COLONNES 1, 2 ET 4 SONT EXPRIMES EN MILLIONS.
ESP> LAS CIFRAS DE LAS COLUMNAS 1, 2 Y 4 VIENEN EXPRESADAS EN MILLONES.

UNITED KINGDOM:
E—> FIGURES IN COLUMNS 1, 2 AND 4 ARE IN MILLIONS.
FR—> LES CHIFFRES DES COLONNES 1, 2 ET 4 SONT EXPRIMES EN MILLIONS.
ESP> LAS CIFRAS DE LAS COLUMNAS 1, 2 Y 4 VIENEN EXPRESADAS EN MILLONES.

TONGA:
E—> FOR 1975, EXPENDITURE OF THE MINISTRY OF EDUCATION ONLY.
FR—> EN 1975, DEPENSES DU MINISTERE DE L'EDUCATION SEULEMENT.
ESP> EN 1975, GASTOS DEL MINISTERIO DE EDUCACION SOLAMENTE.

U.S.S.R.:
E—> EXPENDITURE ON EDUCATION IS CALCULATED AS PERCENTAGE OF NET MATERIAL PRODUCT.
FR—> LES DEPENSES D'ENSEIGNEMENT SONT CALCULEES EN POURCENTAGE DU PRODUIT MATERIEL NET.
ESP> LOS GASTOS RELATIVOS A LA ENSEÑANZA SE HAN CALCULADO COMO PORCENTAJE DEL PRODUCTO MATERIAL NETO.

BYELORUSSIAN S.S.R.:
E—> EXPENDITURE ON EDUCATION IS CALCULATED AS PERCENTAGE OF NET MATERIAL PRODUCT.
FR—> LES DEPENSES D'ENSEIGNEMENT SONT CALCULEES EN POURCENTAGE DU PRODUIT MATERIEL NET.
ESP> LOS GASTOS RELATIVOS A LA ENSEÑANZA SE HAN CALCULADO COMO PORCENTAJE DEL PRODUCTO MATERIAL NETO.

UKRAINIAN S.S.R.:
E—> EXPENDITURE ON EDUCATION IS CALCULATED AS PERCENTAGE OF NET MATERIAL PRODUCT.
FR—> LES DEPENSES D'ENSEIGNEMENT SONT CALCULEES EN POURCENTAGE DU PRODUIT MATERIEL NET.
ESP> LOS GASTOS RELATIVOS A LA ENSEÑANZA SE HAN CALCULADO COMO PORCENTAJE DEL PRODUCTO MATERIAL NETO.

4.2 Public current expenditure by purpose
Dépenses publiques ordinaires selon leur destination
Gastos públicos ordinarios según su destino

4.2 Public current expenditure on education: distribution according to purpose

Dépenses publiques ordinaires afférentes à l'enseignement: répartition selon leur destination

Gastos públicos ordinarios destinados a la educación: distribución según su destino

NUMBER OF COUNTRIES AND TERRITORIES PRESENTED IN THIS TABLE: 138
NOMBRE DE PAYS ET DE TERRITOIRES PRESENTES DANS CE TABLEAU: 138
NUMERO DE PAISES Y DE TERRITORIOS PRESENTADOS EN ESTE CUADRO: 138

COUNTRY / PAYS / PAIS	YEAR ANNEE AÑO	CURRENCY MONNAIE MONEDA	TOTAL (000)	ADMINISTRATION ADMINISTRATION ADMINISTRACION %	EMOLUMENTS OF TEACHERS EMOLUMENTS DU PERSONNEL ENSEIGNANT SUELDOS DEL PERSONAL DOCENTE %	OTHER DIRECT INSTRUCTIONAL EXPENDITURE AUTRES DEPENSES DIRECTES D'ENSEIGNEMENT OTROS GASTOS DIRECTOS DE EDUCACION %	SCHOLARSHIPS AND GRANTS BOURSES ET ALLOCATIONS BECAS Y SUBVENCIONES %	WELFARE SERVICES SERVICES SOCIAUX SERVICIOS SOCIALES %	NOT DISTRIBUTED NON REPARTIES SIN DISTRIBUCION %
			(1)	(2)	(3)	(4)	(5)	(6)	(7)
AFRICA									
ALGERIA ‡	1974	DINAR	1 609 900	4.4	79.1	3.0	8.3	5.2	...
BENIN ‡	1970	FRANC C.F.A.	2 922 402	./.	66.1	3.3	18.3	0.6	11.7
	1975		5 649 652	./.	69.7	1.7	22.5	0.3	5.7
BOTSWANA ‡	1970	PULA	2 559	2.2	64.9	16.8	10.4	5.6	—
	1975		8 688	6.5	52.8	12.2	21.5	7.0	—
	1976		12 025	5.2	52.9	15.7	20.7	5.5	—
	1977		15 920	2.0	58.7	13.3	19.5	6.5	—
BURUNDI	1970	FRANC	478 670	0.9	72.4	7.4	5.9	13.4	—
	1975		721 831	0.7	71.9	10.9	4.1	11.8	0.6
	1976		884 608	0.5	72.9	10.5	4.6	10.3	1.3
CENTRAL AFRICAN REPUBLIC	1970	FRANC C.F.A.	1 859 200		84.3	4.6	11.1		
	1975		3 393 000	6.2	63.5	2.4	13.3	...	14.6
	1976		3 925 000	5.4	63.5	2.0	15.3	...	13.8
	1977		4 389 000	5.2	63.1	1.8	17.0	...	12.9

Public current expenditure by purpose   **4.2**
Dépenses publiques ordinaires selon leur destination
Gastos públicos ordinarios según su destino

Country	Currency	Year	(1)	(2)	(3)	(4)	(5)	(6)	(7)
CHAD ‡	FRANC C.F.A.	1970	1 943 114	...	61.5	18.1	20.4	...	./.
		1975	2 297 200	...	59.2	9.9	24.1	...	6.9
		1976	2 787 000	...	63.3	5.2	24.9	...	6.6
COMORO ‡	FRANC	1971	643 104	1.9	57.1	10.5	22.1	8.4	./.
CONGO ‡	FRANC C.F.A.	1970	4 223 345	4.8	74.0	6.5	14.7	↑	...
		1975	10 537 237	4.3	56.5	8.9	30.4	↑	...
		1976	13 850 859	3.8	63.4	7.1	25.7	↑	...
DJIBOUTI ‡	FRANC	1971	613 777	2.9	83.7	./.	5.1	1.4	6.9
		1974	1 479 821	1.1	89.9	./.	3.1	1.4	4.5
EGYPT ‡	POUND	1970	134 423	./.	84.4	...	...	...	15.6
		1975	226 668	./.	81.2	...	...	...	18.8
		1976	283 742	./.	78.8	...	...	...	21.2
		1977	330 427	./.	79.0	...	...	...	21.0
ETHIOPIA ‡	BIRR	1970	60 539	5.8	78.6	./.	1.1	1.1	13.4
		1975	112 859	...	84.9	5.3	4.8	↑	5.0
GABON ‡	FRANC C.F.A.	1970	2 636 103	...	31.3	...	34.0	...	...
		1975	7 260 088	...	47.2	...	25.8	...	...
		1976	10 506 571	...	43.9	./.	...	7.3	14.9
		1977	14 441 220	3.9	40.9	9.4	...	4.7	15.2
GAMBIA	DALASI	1970	2 415	5.1	74.2	4.4	9.4	3.1	3.8
		1975	5 471	4.4	69.1	3.5	10.0	6.9	6.1
		1976	7 356	5.6	62.5	3.4	7.8	5.7	15.0
		1978	9 043	13.8	76.8	4.9	...	...	4.5
GHANA ‡	CEDI	1970	83 813	10.7	78.5	./.	10.9	...	18.8
		1975	240 682	8.9	72.2	...	...	...	15.1
		1976	293 102	11.6	73.3	...	...	...	...
GUINEA-BISSAU ‡	ESCUDO	1978	270 684	6.3	55.4	2.6	33.6	1.8	0.3
IVORY COAST ‡	FRANC C.F.A.	1970	21 318 402	5.6	57.2	22.4	10.0	4.6	...
		1975	48 123 000	4.4	68.4	12.2	10.8	4.3	...
		1976	61 888 000	4.4	71.8	8.2	9.0	6.6	...
LIBYAN ARAB JAMAHIRIYA ‡	DINAR	1970	35 821	./.	79.9	./.	4.2	6.1	9.7
		1974	91 109	./.	87.2	./.	12.4	↑	0.3
		1977	154 660	1.5	91.5	1.5	...	2.6	4.4
MADAGASCAR	FRANC	1970	8 637 345	8.0	70.6	...	2.5	...	18.9
		1975	11 726 747	9.9	77.8	4.5	5.7	0.4	1.7
		1976	16 149 414	...	75.7	...	...	...	...
MALAWI ‡	KWACHA	1975	11 992	7.5	78.3	1.9	6.1	6.3	...
MALI ‡	FRANC	1975	11 670 222	./.	63.0	6.6	19.4	...	11.0
		1977	16 312 518	./.	61.0	3.5	29.1	...	6.4
MAURITIUS ‡	RUPEE	1970	35 723	3.7	81.7	2.7	0.6	...	14.0
		1974	86 126	4.5	84.2	...	3.3	2.5	2.8
		1976	197 000	3.0	75.0	1.3	3.5	4.5	12.8
		1977	246 700	3.9	79.3	0.2	3.6	3.0	10.1

4.2 Public current expenditure by purpose
Dépenses publiques ordinaires selon leur destination
Gastos públicos ordinarios según su destino

COUNTRY / PAYS / PAIS	YEAR ANNEE AÑO	CURRENCY MONNAIE MONEDA	TOTAL (000) (1)	ADMINISTRATION / AD-MINISTRATION / AD-MINISTRACION % (2)	EMOLUMENTS OF TEACHERS / EMOLUMENTS DU PERSONNEL ENSEIGNANT / SUELDOS DEL PERSONAL DOCENTE % (3)	OTHER DIRECT INSTRUCTIONAL EXPENDITURE / AUTRES DEPENSES DIRECTES D'ENSEIGNEMENT / OTROS GASTOS DIRECTOS DE EDUCACION % (4)	SCHOLARSHIPS AND GRANTS / BOURSES ET ALLOCATIONS / BECAS Y SUBVENCIONES % (5)	WELFARE SERVICES / SERVICES SOCIAUX / SERVICIOS SOCIALES % (6)	NOT DISTRIBUTED / NON REPARTIES / SIN DISTRIBUCION % (7)
MOROCCO ‡	1970	DIRHAM	649 357	./	84.9	...	...	...	2.5
	1976		1 561 014	13.8	78.2	1.0	4.2	0.2	6.6
	1977		1 887 883	./	93.4	...	...	...	6.6
	1978		2 280 860	./	94.5	...	...	...	5.5
NIGER	1970	FRANC C.F.A.	1 917 650	10.5	64.6	...	11.8	...	13.1
	1975		4 566 400	...	51.5	24.9	13.9	...	9.8
	1977		6 557 300	...	55.1	24.2	10.7	...	10.0
RWANDA ‡	1975	FRANC	1 197 164	3.6	80.2	2.9	5.0	6.8	1.5
	1976		1 239 492	2.4	84.3	2.4	3.1	6.8	1.0
	1977		1 504 570	2.7	80.5	2.8	6.2	5.7	2.1
	1978		1 651 190	2.7	82.0	2.8	5.3	6.0	1.2
ST. HELENA ‡	1970	POUND STERLING	50	8.0	54.0	./	2.0	12.0	24.0
	1975		79	16.5	49.4	17.7	2.5	10.1	3.8
	1976		143	11.9	46.2	7.7	21.7	8.4	4.2
SENEGAL ‡	1974	FRANC C.F.A.	8 998 056	12.6	68.1	2.5	3.7	6.1	7.0
SEYCHELLES	1970	RUPEE	3 855	5.5	70.3	...	1.9	4.6	17.7
	1975		11 202	6.3	77.7	5.7	2.1	3.4	4.7
	1976		14 866	9.7	73.7	5.2	3.8	2.1	5.5
	1977		20 316	10.4	81.7	3.8	2.8	1.1	0.2
SOMALIA	1970	SHILLING	23 664	7.7	68.1	24.2	...	...	...
	1976		90 314	...	62.2	18.4	...	10.2	9.2
	1977		121 831	...	67.3	16.5	...	7.7	8.5
SWAZILAND ‡	1970	LILANGENI	2 959	./	75.0	8.1	8.0	...	8.9
	1974		6 374	./	67.6	7.0	11.8	...	13.6
TOGO ‡	1970	FRANC C.F.A.	1 414 917	6.9	66.6	...	13.9	6.0	6.5
	1975		6 116 698	...	50.5	8.7	18.3	↑	22.4
	1977		10 753 682	...	47.9	10.6	17.4	↑	24.1
	1978		13 169 738	...	44.5	10.1	18.9	↑	26.5
UGANDA ‡	1970	SHILLING	244 431	4.3	72.0	...	11.7	...	12.1
	1975		529 014	3.4	60.8	26.0	4.8	5.1	-
UNITED REPUBLIC OF CAMEROON ‡	1970	FRANC C.F.A.	9 644 852	0.9	69.6	...	17.9	→	12.5
	1975		10 298 000	...	80.9	...	4.6	...	13.7
	1976		11 657 300	...	81.3	...	4.0	12.9	1.8

Public current expenditure by purpose **4.2**
Dépenses publiques ordinaires selon leur destination
Gastos públicos ordinarios según su destino

Country	Currency	Year	(1)	(2)	(3)	(4)	(5)	(6)	(7)
UNITED REPUBLIC OF TANZANIA ‡	SHILLING	1977	1 090 090	./.	49.3	27.7	7.3	8.8	6.9
UPPER VOLTA ‡	FRANC C.F.A.	1970	2 105 000	1.9	62.4	./.	7.1	8.3	20.3
		1975	3 171 371	2.2	59.7	1.6	29.6	6.1	0.8
		1977	4 279 627	2.6	59.2	1.4	29.0	5.8	2.1
WESTERN SAHARA	PESETA	1970	44 322	2.8	60.1	0.8	1.5	30.0	5.7
		1973	86 332	1.6	*81.4	...	1.5	14.7	...
ZAMBIA	KWACHA	1971	53 652	15.1	62.5	9.8	0.6	7.8	4.2
		1975	75 420	14.1	63.7	6.9	0.5	8.5	6.2
		1977	95 461	12.1	71.5	3.9	0.7	7.4	4.4
		1978	101 230	9.0	72.3	5.1	0.8	7.4	5.4
AMERICA, NORTH									
ANTIGUA ‡	E. CARIBBEAN DOLLAR	1971	2 509	7.3	73.2	3.1	2.2	1.1	13.2
		1975	5 681	6.1	58.9	3.8	16.7	2.0	12.4
		1976	6 742	5.1	56.8	3.2	21.8	1.7	11.3
		1977	7 013	4.5	54.5	3.8	21.3	6.7	9.2
BARBADOS ‡	DOLLAR	1970	19 784	3.3	77.1	4.2	1.2	10.5	3.6
		1973	32 984	2.6	72.1	4.9	1.2	10.4	8.9
BELIZE ‡	DOLLAR	1970	3 211	11.2	67.0	./.	8.6	3.0	10.2
		1974	4 733	5.7	64.7	2.4	24.9	2.3	—
BERMUDA ‡	DOLLAR	1970	5 821	3.0	71.9	./.	5.4	—	19.8
		1975	10 417	5.6	79.4	2.6	8.4	0.6	3.4
		1976	9 512	6.4	79.1	5.9	4.1	—	4.5
BRITISH VIRGIN ISLANDS ‡	UNITED STATES DOLLAR	1970	639	8.0	78.9	./.	2.8	2.3	8.0
		1975	967	4.0	74.0	3.1	6.3	2.6	9.9
		1976	907	4.4	79.8	2.8	9.2	2.1	1.8
		1977	1 026	4.5	79.3	2.7	8.3	2.4	2.7
CANADA	DOLLAR	1970	6 122 500	7.4	54.3	5.9	2.3		36.0
		1975	11 381 459	4.4	61.6	5.9	1.0	16.8	10.2
		1976	13 233 587	4.4	61.6	5.9	1.00	16.8	10.2
		1977	14 994 978	4.4	61.6	5.9	1.0	16.8	10.2
CAYMAN ISLANDS ‡	JAMAICAN DOLLAR	1975	1 384	6.4	76.3	5.6	3.3	8.1	0.4
		1976	1 691	./.	79.1	5.4	5.1	5.4	5.0
COSTA RICA	COLON	1970	318 500	11.9	92.6		1.9		...
		1975	1 041 297	4.3	82.6		2.1	0.8	3.6
		1976	1 041 391		85.5				7.3
DOMINICAN REPUBLIC ‡	PESO	1976	62 595	5.4	77.9	3.3	0.0	...	13.4
		1977	67 783	7.7	73.8	3.3			15.2
EL SALVADOR ‡	COLON	1970	69 621	7.0	87.3	./.	1.5	0.4	4.3
		1975	138 364	4.5	82.5	7.8	1.7		3.1
GRENADA	DOLLAR	1970	3 665	8.0	74.4	2.4		3.4	11.9
GUATEMALA ‡	QUETZAL	1970	32 566	4.3	82.6	./.	3.1	0.1	9.9
		1976	67 193	7.5	79.5	11.3	1.6	...	...

4.2　Public current expenditure by purpose
Dépenses publiques ordinaires selon leur destination
Gastos públicos ordinarios según su destino

COUNTRY / PAYS / PAIS	YEAR ANNEE AÑO	CURRENCY MONNAIE MONEDA	TOTAL (000) (1)	ADMINISTRATION AD-MINISTRATION AD-MINISTRACION % (2)	EMOLUMENTS OF TEACHERS EMOLUMENTS DU PERSONNEL ENSEIGNANT SUELDOS DEL PERSONAL DOCENTE % (3)	OTHER DIRECT INSTRUCTIONAL EXPENDITURE AUTRES DEPENSES DIRECTES D'ENSEIGNEMENT OTROS GASTOS DIRECTOS DE EDUCACION % (4)	SCHOLARSHIPS AND GRANTS BOURSES ET ALLOCATIONS BECAS Y SUBVENCIONES % (5)	WELFARE SERVICES SERVICES SOCIAUX SERVICIOS SOCIALES % (6)	NOT DISTRIBUTED NON RE-PARTIES SIN DISTRIBUCION % (7)
HAITI	1976	GOURDE	37 191	2.9	85.4	4.4	...	...	7.3
HONDURAS ‡	1970	LEMPIRA	41 660	3.4	79.8	1.7	3.7	...	11.4
	1977		89 920	./.	91.2	1.8	3.7	0.2	3.1
JAMAICA ‡	1976	DOLLAR	139 820	3.4	52.0	20.9	22.8	1.0	...
MEXICO ‡	1970	PESO	7 148 000	./.	72.0	./.	./.	8.4	19.6
	1975		26 783 400	./.	85.1	./.	0.4	0.8	13.7
	1976		36 507 080	./.	73.5	./.	0.3	0.2	25.9
	1977		53 627 996	4.2	66.4	4.7	0.4	9.3	14.9
NETHERLANDS ANTILLES	1971	GUILDER	15 664	6.8	78.6	14.5	5.1	2.2	...
	1977		104 900		71.4				...
NICARAGUA ‡	1970	CORDOBA	120 901	4.8	81.5	./.	1.7	3.3	8.7
PANAMA ‡	1970	BALBOA	50 824	12.7	66.5	...	9.5	...	11.3
	1975		96 693	4.1	83.7	...	3.9	...	8.3
	1977		112 387	5.5	84.1	...	3.1	...	7.3
	1978		109 675	12.7	81.6	...	3.6	...	2.1
ST. LUCIA ‡	1971	E. CARIBBEAN DOLLAR	4 013	./.	76.9	./.	6.3	0.1	16.7
	1975		7 321	4.8	69.3	3.9	2.9	2.3	16.9
	1976		10 614	4.2	67.6	3.3	1.9	2.8	20.2
TRINIDAD AND TOBAGO	1970	DOLLAR	53 335	4.2	77.3	...	12.1	...	6.4
TURKS AND CAICOS ISLANDS	1971	DOLLAR	243	4.1	75.7	...	5.8		14.4
	1975		601	11.8	74.0	4.2	9.7	0.3	
	1976		646	11.5	70.4	7.6	10.2	0.3	
AMERICA, SOUTH									
ARGENTINA ‡	1975	PESO	33 562	./.	93.3	...	0.7	...	6.0
	1977		426 417	./.	89.9	7.5	0.1	...	2.5
CHILE ‡	1975	PESO	1 321 482	5.8	73.2	0.9	...	...	20.1
COLOMBIA ‡	1973	PESO	3 294 665	4.6	73.6	...	1.7	2.5	17.5
ECUADOR ‡	1970	SUCRE	1 133 523	9.0	76.4	./.	2.0	1.5	11.0
	1977		5 756 300	4.2	83.9	2.7	0.5	0.9	7.8

Public current expenditure by purpose   4.2
Dépenses publiques ordinaires selon leur destination
Gastos públicos ordinarios según su destino

Country	Currency	Year	(1)	(2)	(3)	(4)	(5)	(6)	(7)
FALKLAND ISLANDS (MALVINAS) ‡	POUND	1970	60	...	58.3	·/·	16.7	20.0	5.0
		1974	105	...	57.1	3.8	15.2	23.8	—
GUYANA ‡	DOLLAR	1970	19 089	4.2	83.4	·/·	·/·	2.7	9.7
		1975	45 277	4.8	79.9	6.5	1.3	2.1	5.3
		1976	60 345	3.9	74.8	8.5	·/·	·/·	12.8
		1977	71 796	6.5	76.5	5.9	4.2	3.2	3.6
PARAGUAY ‡	GUARANI	1970	1 421 834	5.4	83.9	·/·	5.1	→	5.6
		1973	1 688 671	7.4	90.0	0.7	1.0	0.3	0.6
PERU ‡	SOL	1975	20 969 700	4.9	65.1	2.7	...	...	27.4
		1976	27 782 000	4.7	64.7	2.1	...	...	28.5
		1977	31 921 000	6.3	63.4	1.2	...	...	29.1
VENEZUELA ‡	BOLIVAR	1970	2 220 651	6.1	70.3	·/·	4.2	...	19.4
		1975	5 965 747	·/·	66.5	0.3	11.7	...	21.5
		1976	6 864 100	6.9	85.0	0.3	6.9	0.9	0.1
ASIA									
AFGHANISTAN ‡	AFGHANI	1970	817 276	...	67.6	21.2	3.6	...	7.6
		1974	940 630	...	86.6	7.9	1.4	...	4.1
		1977	1 636 529	10.8	57.1	11.0	0.7	2.1	18.4
BAHRAIN ‡	DINAR	1970	3 668	6.0	73.3	14.4	2.1	4.2	...
		1975	9 606	·/·	67.3	8.5	14.1	2.7	7.4
		1977	17 048	·/·	72.4	·/·	...	...	...
		1978	20 106	...	76.2	1.3	0.8	4.2	17.5
BHUTAN ‡	INDIAN RUPEE	1970	4 982	5.9	48.4	·/·	8.2	19.1	18.4
		1974	12 853	9.6	26.1	21.9	20.5	21.8	...
		1977	14 975	9.5	42.8	5.7	32.8	...	9.1
BRUNEI ‡	DOLLAR	1970	19 387	6.1	45.4	10.9	13.2	24.3	...
		1975	47 354	9.6	49.5	8.3	9.9	20.1	2.6
		1976	53 592	7.9	51.3	9.9	9.1	20.1	1.7
		1977	69 536	11.9	48.8	8.4	8.9	17.0	4.9
BURMA ‡	KYAT	1971	280 500	...	83.2	1.6	8.4	→	6.7
CYPRUS ‡	POUND	1970	5 681	5.6	72.0	·/·	1.2	3.4	17.8
		1975	10 325	6.5	79.1	3.3	1.7	2.5	6.7
		1976	11 710	6.6	77.9	3.6	1.7	2.9	7.3
		1977	12 895	6.9	78.9	3.0	1.5	2.9	6.7
HONG KONG ‡	DOLLAR	1970	483 186	6.1	81.2	·/·	2.4	3.0	7.4
		1975	1 144 538	4.8	79.4	1.4	4.4	1.9	8.2
		1976	1 360 869	4.8	78.9	1.3	4.6	1.8	8.5
		1977	1 578 216	5.2	78.8	1.5	4.6	1.8	8.2
INDIA ‡	RUPEE	1970	10 579 660	2.3	67.7	·/·	4.9	...	25.0
		1975	21 047 180	...	74.0	...	...	...	...
IRAN ‡	RIAL	1976	119 995 051	8.8	64.3	0.3	...	16.8	9.8
IRAQ ‡	DINAR	1970	60 228	5.9	86.9	·/·	1.7	...	5.5
		1976	155 763	15.8	65.3	9.4	1.1	...	8.4

4.2 Public current expenditure by purpose
Dépenses publiques ordinaires selon leur destination
Gastos públicos ordinarios según su destino

COUNTRY / PAYS / PAIS	YEAR / ANNEE / AÑO	CURRENCY / MONNAIE / MONEDA	TOTAL (000) (1)	ADMINISTRATION % (2)	EMOLUMENTS OF TEACHERS % (3)	OTHER DIRECT INSTRUCTIONAL EXPENDITURE % (4)	SCHOLARSHIPS AND GRANTS % (5)	WELFARE SERVICES % (6)	NOT DISTRIBUTED % (7)
ISRAEL	1975	POUND	4 641 000	3.9	45.7	...	...	...	50.4
JAPAN ‡	1970	YEN	2 098 677	6.5	55.1	/	0.8	4.3	33.4
	1975		5 826 604	4.8	67.7	8.0	0.9	5.0	13.6
	1976		6 613 456	7.2	66.4	6.5	0.9	4.9	14.2
	1977		7 262 222	6.6	66.4	6.5	0.9	5.0	14.7
JORDAN ‡	1970	DINAR	7 239	5.3	79.8	/	1.6	11.0	2.3
	1975		13 900	6.8	73.9	/	3.0	...	16.3
	1976		16 957	5.8	78.3	/	2.4	...	13.5
	1977		22 598	5.6	73.4	/	3.9	...	17.1
KOREA, REPUBLIC OF ‡	1970	WON	73 809	4.1	79.7	...	0.6	...	16.2
	1975		163 800	...	99.4	...	0.4	1.6	...
	1976		350 315	...	95.7	2.3	0.4	3.0	...
	1977		411 499	...	92.2	4.4	...	...	...
KUWAIT ‡	1970	DINAR	34 630	12.0	64.2	/	8.1	11.0	4.6
	1975		90 069	9.8	53.8	3.9	6.2	12.8	13.4
	1976		113 750	8.3	46.4	5.0	5.5	6.5	28.4
	1977		129 183	8.8	46.0	5.9	4.3	10.2	24.8
LAO PEOPLE'S DEMOCRATIC REPUBLIC	1970	KIP	2 058 777	5.6	73.9	...	16.3	...	4.2
MALAYSIA									
PENINSULAR MALAYSIA ‡	1970	RINGGIT	442 039	9.3	77.9	12.8	1.7	...	5.0
	1975		992 192	6.5	80.5	6.3	2.5	...	4.9
	1976		1 101 567	7.0	70.5	15.2	1.4	...	9.1
	1977		1 571 180	6.4	66.3	16.8	...	...	...
SABAH	1975	RINGGIT	89 559	3.7	81.3	9.1	5.4	0.0	0.5
	1976		73 715	8.0	75.8	9.5	6.7	0.0	...
SARAWAK	1975	RINGGIT	74 491	4.7	76.3	6.6	...	12.0	0.4
	1976		85 347	5.0	74.4	6.5	...	13.6	0.5
	1977		100 861	4.6	71.7	7.1	...	15.6	1.0
MONGOLIA	1970	TUGRIK	276 982	...	39.4	33.0	15.4	12.2	...
NEPAL	1975	RUPEE	201 776	13.2	52.5	5.2	5.1	2.0	22.0

Public current expenditure by purpose   **4.2**
Dépenses publiques ordinaires selon leur destination
Gastos públicos ordinarios según su destino

Country	Currency	Year	(1)	(2)	(3)	(4)	(5)	(6)	(7)
OMAN	RIAL	1975	6 605	15.8	67.2	2.6	10.0	3.2	1.2
		1976	9 193	19.1	65.6	0.9	11.0	2.3	1.1
		1978	17 524	12.3	65.0	5.2	10.3	5.7	1.5
PHILIPPINES ‡	PESO	1975	1 753 958	5.0	87.0	5.0	2.0	./.	1.0
QATAR ‡	RIYAL	1970	41 029	24.7	44.6	10.4	7.4	13.0	...
		1975	123 524	21.5	51.8	12.1	9.5	5.1	...
		1976	187 392	25.5	44.4	16.7	13.4	./.	...
		1977	283 110	18.9	58.9	5.1	10.8	4.4	1.8
SAUDI ARABIA	RIYAL	1970	631 341	...	68.7	20.7	...	...	27.2
		1975	5 528 566	...	52.2	23.2	...	...	28.9
		1976	5 807 729	...	48.0	14.7	...	...	24.6
		1977	7 187 919	...	60.6	...	...	...	...
SINGAPORE ‡	DOLLAR	1970	173 599	4.7	90.8	./.	0.6	0.3	3.6
		1975	339 870	2.9	90.5	...	1.1	0.0	5.5
		1976	343 511	3.7	90.7	...	1.8	0.1	3.7
		1977	363 333	3.8	91.3	...	2.0	0.0	2.8
SRI LANKA ‡	RUPEE	1970	506 392	2.9	85.0	1.6	0.0	...	12.1
		1975	682 680	4.5	78.2	...	...	2.3	13.4
		1977	827 870	...	93.7	...	...	...	...
SYRIAN ARAB REPUBLIC ‡	POUND	1975	462 514	4.8	77.0	5.9	2.5	3.9	5.9
		1976	516 484	7.0	76.5	5.7	6.1	1.3	3.4
THAILAND	BAHT	1970	3 461 635	11.9	65.4	...	...	...	22.6
		1975	7 775 347	3.8	77.2	3.7	3.3	6.7	5.3
		1976	8 732 955	3.4	76.0	4.2	1.8	4.6	10.0
TURKEY ‡	LIRA	1971	5 632 832	10.0	74.2	./.	0.6	4.5	10.7
		1977	37 961 875	./.	92.6	0.2	3.0	0.8	3.5
UNITED ARAB EMIRATES ‡	DIRHAM	1975	271 382	./.	66.4	3.7	10.0	9.8	10.1
		1976	400 864	...	69.1	4.9	10.1	9.2	6.6
		1977	838 114	...	66.6	...	...	...	...
YEMEN	RIAL	1974	26 632	23.5	53.8	15.6	7.1	...	...
YEMEN, DEMOCRATIC	DINAR	1971	2 389	6.2	77.2	...	1.8	4.0	...
		1976	5 288	7.1	84.4	3.5	0.9	4.1	10.7
EUROPE									
AUSTRIA ‡	SCHILLING	1970	13 502 700	34.9	51.3	./.	2.4	2.0	9.4
		1975	29 366 500	35.0	48.1	./.	3.2	2.3	11.4
		1976	32 467 500	35.7	49.3	./.	3.1	2.6	9.2
		1977	35 368 600	36.2	49.1	...	2.7	2.5	9.4
BELGIUM ‡	FRANC	1975	131 906 200	2.8	72.3	22.9	1.9	...	...
		1976	151 206 900	2.8	76.9	18.8	1.5	...	...
		1977	170 775 800	4.4	75.4	19.1	1.2	...	...
BULGARIA	LEV	1970	442 124	...	54.2	...	4.5	...	41.3
		1975	725 259	...	47.6	...	4.1	...	48.3
		1976	778 601	...	47.3	...	5.1	...	47.6
		1977	838 837	...	45.1	...	5.2	...	49.7

4.2 Public current expenditure by purpose
Dépenses publiques ordinaires selon leur destination
Gastos públicos ordinarios según su destino

COUNTRY / PAYS / PAIS	YEAR / ANNEE / AÑO	CURRENCY / MONNAIE / MONEDA	TOTAL (000) (1)	ADMINISTRATION / AD-MINIS-TRATION / AD-MINIS-TRACION % (2)	EMOLUMENTS OF TEACHERS / EMOLUMENTS DU PERSONNEL ENSEIGNANT / SUELDOS DEL PERSONAL DOCENTE % (3)	OTHER DIRECT INSTRUCTIONAL EXPENDITURE / AUTRES DEPENSES DIRECTES D'ENSEIGNEMENT / OTROS GASTOS DIRECTOS DE EDUCACION % (4)	SCHOLARSHIPS AND GRANTS / BOURSES ET ALLOCATIONS / BECAS Y SUBVENCIONES % (5)	WELFARE SERVICES / SERVICES SOCIAUX / SERVICIOS SOCIALES % (6)	NOT DISTRIBUTED / NON REPARTIES / SIN DISTRIBUCION % (7)
CZECHOSLOVAKIA ‡	1970	KORUNA	12 102 000	0.3	54.1	.	2.3	14.7	28.6
	1975		17 288 021	0.2	53.8	12.0	1.9	10.9	21.2
	1976		17 332 254	0.2	53.2	12.1	2.0	11.7	20.7
	1977		18 580 636	0.2	52.2	13.0	2.1	11.5	21.0
DENMARK	1977	KRONE	16 202 000	1.9	53.8	5.6	3.3	3.2	32.2
FINLAND ‡	1970	MARKKA	2 404 790	1.1	57.2	.	0.3	4.5	36.8
	1975		5 596 511	2.2	61.9	3.9	1.8	9.8	20.3
	1976		6 677 009	2.3	61.6	3.9	1.6	10.2	20.3
	1977		7 598 881	2.3	60.1	4.1	1.9	10.4	21.2
FRANCE ‡	1970	FRANC	24 598 921	2.9	78.5	./.	5.2	2.5	10.9
	1975		46 844 110	3.0	72.5	./.	4.0	3.6	16.8
	1976		54 455 190	2.9	74.1	./.	4.6	3.3	15.1
	1977		62 738 600	2.9	76.8	./.	4.4	3.6	12.2
GERMANY, FEDERAL REPUBLIC OF ‡	1970	DEUTSCHE MARK	16 926 900	1.3	72.8	./.	4.4	./.	21.4
	1975		35 773 000	1.5	68.6	9.9	8.1	2.7	9.2
	1976		37 753 000	1.3	69.7	9.7	6.9	2.6	9.7
GIBRALTAR ‡	1970	POUND	362	3.6	49.7	./.	13.8	./.	32.9
	1975		909	4.8	52.4	8.1	10.3	0.8	23.5
	1976		1 443	4.9	60.1	6.9	10.1	0.7	17.3
	1977		1 699	5.8	45.5	7.5	11.8	0.8	28.5
GREECE ‡	1970	DRACHMA	5 090 900	4.4	79.6	./.	3.2	> 2.8	12.8
	1974		9 347 600	3.9	79.6	./.	0.2	2.8	13.5
HUNGARY ‡	1970	FORINT	10 641 431	0.4	42.8	./.	3.4	14.4	39.0
	1975		16 719 792	0.2	44.4	./.	4.5	13.7	37.3
	1976		17 579 883	0.2	45.4	./.	4.4	15.1	34.9
	1977		19 385 911	0.2	46.4	./.	4.4	15.0	34.1
ICELAND ‡	1971	KRONA	1 471 234	3.3	80.7	./.	10.7	0.9	4.5
IRELAND	1970	POUND	68 980	3.5	62.1	2.3	1.4	7.6	25.4
	1975		198 856	3.8	70.7	.	7.4	4.1	11.8
	1976		245 669	3.6	72.7	2.0	7.7	3.8	10.1
	1977		287 433	3.6	68.4	0.5	7.1	4.1	16.2

Public current expenditure by purpose   **4.2**
Dépenses publiques ordinaires selon leur destination
Gastos públicos ordinarios según su destino

			(1)	(2)	(3)	(4)	(5)	(6)	(7)
ITALY ‡	LIRA	1970	2 429 439	16.5	62.2	...	3.6	...	21.3
		1975	5 060 156	...	73.4	...	3.6	3.4	19.6
		1976	6 467 905	...	74.3	...	2.5	3.3	19.9
LUXEMBOURG	FRANC	1975	3 903 300	...	80.8	...	1.6	...	17.6
		1976	4 619 800	...	81.5	...	1.5	...	17.0
		1977	5 225 200	...	81.7	...	1.5	...	16.8
MALTA ‡	POUND	1970	5 913	6.6	71.1	/	1.5	2.8	17.9
		1975	6 881	4.9	79.2	1.2	8.0	2.5	4.6
		1976	8 733	5.0	78.6	0.1	8.0	2.7	5.6
		1977	8 938	/	84.5	0.1	7.4	2.3	5.7
MONACO	FRANC FRANCAIS	1977	28 716	2.8	86.2	4.5	2.4	1.1	2.9
NETHERLANDS	GUILDER	1975	14 881 000	2.8	75.5	0.7	2.0	1.3	17.7
		1976	17 021 000	2.9	75.4	0.6	2.2	1.3	17.7
		1977	18 666 000	3.2	75.2	0.6	2.3	1.4	17.3
NORWAY ‡	KRONE	1970	3 696 100	/	74.8	...	6.3	...	18.8
		1975	8 427 000	2.0	71.3	...		...	19.4
		1976	10 608 000	2.2	65.4	...	6.6	...	25.7
		1977	11 484 000	2.1	67.9	...	6.7	...	23.2
PORTUGAL ‡	ESCUDO	1975	13 876 839	5.2	81.0	2.7	1.3	7.0	2.9
		1976	17 140 918	3.1	71.2	3.1	5.9	4.5	12.3
		1977	22 535 383	5.2	80.5	2.7	7.4	3.7	0.4
SAN MARINO	LIRA	1970	727 334	...	79.5	...	9.5	6.0	4.9
		1975	2 499 565	...	79.6	...	8.2	5.7	6.5
		1976	2 915 485	...	81.0	...	7.0	6.1	5.8
		1977	3 490 495	...	81.0	...	6.3	6.0	6.8
SPAIN ‡	PESETA	1970	35 420	4.0	69.3	6.2	20.4	>	—
		1974	71 688	4.8	78.4	6.2	10.1	0.6	—
		1976	134 391	3.8	83.8	4.5	7.8	0.1	—
SWEDEN	KRONA	1970	10 785 000	3.6	45.2	...	5.0	6.6	39.7
		1975	19 281 100	3.5	52.4	...	2.9	13.3	27.9
		1976	22 454 200	3.5	46.5	...	3.2	13.1	33.8
		1977	26 441 200	3.6	49.2	...	3.0	13.7	30.5
SWITZERLAND	FRANC	1970	2 765 600	1.4	60.7	...	2.3	0.9	34.6
		1975	5 978 800	13.0	61.5	...	2.4	...	23.1
		1976	6 350 400	12.9	63.3	...	2.6	...	21.2
		1977	6 734 300	12.9	61.4	...	2.4	...	23.3
YUGOSLAVIA	DINAR	1970	7 633 000	...	71.2	...		4.1	24.7
		1975	25 515 000	...	64.9	...	2.9	4.6	27.6
		1976	31 093 000	...	65.6	...	3.4	4.4	26.6
		1977	37 632 000	...	66.6	...	1.0	4.5	27.9
OCEANIA									
FIJI ‡	DOLLAR	1974	18 748	8.4	65.6	10.6	12.9	2.5	...
		1976	26 640	6.2	78.4	2.3	13.1	...	...
FRENCH POLYNESIA ‡	FRANC C.F.P.	1970	1 150 442	1.6	69.3	/	5.9	9.1	15.8
		1975	3 268 311		71.4	3.1	4.7	1.2	18.0
KIRIBATI	AUSTRALIAN DOLLAR	1970	534	10.7	46.1	...	15.9	...	
		1975	2 022	6.4	87.2	...	6.4	...	27.3

4.2 Public current expenditure by purpose
Dépenses publiques ordinaires selon leur destination
Gastos públicos ordinarios según su destino

COUNTRY / PAYS / PAIS	YEAR / ANNEE / AÑO	CURRENCY / MONNAIE / MONEDA	TOTAL (000)	ADMINISTRATION / ADMINISTRATION / ADMINISTRACION %	EMOLUMENTS OF TEACHERS / EMOLUMENTS DU PERSONNEL ENSEIGNANT / SUELDOS DEL PERSONAL DOCENTE %	OTHER DIRECT INSTRUCTIONAL EXPENDITURE / AUTRES DEPENSES DIRECTES D'ENSEIGNEMENT / OTROS GASTOS DIRECTOS DE EDUCACION %	SCHOLARSHIPS AND GRANTS / BOURSES ET ALLOCATIONS / BECAS Y SUBVENCIONES %	WELFARE SERVICES / SERVICES SOCIAUX / SERVICIOS SOCIALES %	NOT DISTRIBUTED / NON REPARTIES / SIN DISTRIBUCION %
			(1)	(2)	(3)	(4)	(5)	(6)	(7)
NAURU	1970	AUSTRALIAN DOLLAR	695	5.8	55.4	3.7	33.8	1.3	...
NEW HEBRIDES ‡	1970	AUSTRALIAN DOLLAR	682	15.0	54.3		5.3	11.0	14.5
	1975		1 444	15.6	54.7	13.0	14.5	2.1	...
NEW HEBRIDES ‡	1970	FRANC FRANCAIS	10 377	19.0	75.4	...	2.2	1.2	2.1
	1975		38 288	/.	82.5	/.	...	...	17.5
	1977		73 868	2.0	76.7	7.5	1.7	...	12.1
NEW ZEALAND ‡	1975	DOLLAR	503 643	5.9	58.0	2.1	8.7	2.7	22.6
	1976		575 566	4.7	66.6	1.9	4.8	2.1	19.8
	1977		675 222	4.7	65.9	1.8	4.3	2.2	21.1
NIUE ‡	1971	NEW ZEALAND DOLLAR	344	4.4	72.1	./	8.4	3.0	15.1
	1975		595	/.	87.2	9.7	...	...	...
NORFOLK ISLAND	1970	AUSTRALIAN DOLLAR	103	4.9	69.9	4.8	3.9	9.7	11.7
	1975		209	2.9	74.6	4.8	1.9	6.2	9.6
	1976		245	3.3	77.6	4.1	3.3	4.5	7.3
	1977		291	3.1	71.5	4.1	2.7	8.6	10.0
PACIFIC ISLANDS ‡	1970	UNITED STATES DOLLAR	10 297	7.9	52.6	/.	5.7	...	33.8
	1974		17 141	5.7	53.9	5.8	5.3	...	29.2
	1976		20 205	11.5	55.5	6.5	7.6	9.4	9.6
PAPUA NEW GUINEA	1971	KINA	27 783	8.3	53.4	5.9	9.3	0.1	28.9
	1976		80 426	4.6	81.6	5.9	6.7	1.1	...
	1978		86 773	14.2	68.8	4.2	5.7	5.8	1.3
SAMOA	1970	TALA	1 193	10.3	83.2	1.6	1.0	5.2	0.3
	1975		1 939	2.6	89.8	1.6	...	3.6	2.4
	1976		2 206	2.3	90.7	1.8	...	3.2	2.3
	1977		2 240	3.1	89.6	1.8	0.2	3.1	2.2
TONGA ‡	1971	DOLLAR	555	3.6	70.3	3.8	12.6	9.7	...
	1975		686	12.8	68.4	1.6	17.2	...	...
	1976		1 663	8.8	78.6	0.7	4.1	3.4	4.3
	1977		1 330	19.5	64.2	10.3	5.9	...	...

Public current expenditure by purpose   4.2
Dépenses publiques ordinaires selon leur destination
Gastos públicos ordinarios según su destino

ALGERIA:
E—> EXPENDITURE OF THE MINISTRY OF PRIMARY AND SECONDARY EDUCATION ONLY.
FR—> DEPENSES DU MINISTERE DES ENSEIGNEMENTS PRIMAIRE ET SECONDAIRE SEULEMENT.
ESP> GASTOS DEL MINISTERIO DE LAS ENSEÑANZAS DE PRIMERO Y SEGUNDO GRADO SOLAMENTE.

BENIN:
E—> EXPENDITURE OF THE CENTRAL GOVERNMENT ONLY. ADMINISTRATION IS INCLUDED PARTLY WITH EMOLUMENTS OF TEACHERS IN COLUMN 3 AND PARTLY IN COLUMN 7.
FR—> DEPENSES DU GOUVERNEMENT CENTRAL SEULEMENT. UNE PARTIE DE L'ADMINISTRATION EST INCLUSE AVEC LES EMOLUMENTS DU PERSONNEL ENSEIGNANT DANS LA COLONNE 3 ET L'AUTRE PARTIE DANS LA COLONNE 7.
ESP> GASTOS DEL GOBIERNO CENTRAL SOLAMENTE. LA ADMINISTRACION QUEDA REPARTIDA ENTRE LAS COLUMNAS 3 Y 7.

BOTSWANA:
E—> BETWEEN 1975 AND 1977, THE TOTALITY OF TRANSFERS TO UNIVERSITIES AND SUBSIDIES TO SECOND LEVEL SCHOOLS USED FOR ALL PURPOSES (SALARIES, ETC.) ARE INCLUDED IN COLUMN 5.
FR—> ENTRE 1975 ET 1977, LA TOTALITE DES TRANSFERTS AUX UNIVERSITES ET LES SUBVENTIONS AUX ECOLES DU SECOND DEGRE UTILISEES POUR DES DEPENSES DIVERSES (SALAIRES, ETC.) SONT INCLUSES DANS LA COLONNE 5.
ESP> ENTRE 1975 Y 1977 LA TOTALIDAD DE LAS TRANSFERENCIAS A LAS UNIVERSIDADES Y LAS SUBVENCIONES A LAS ESCUELAS DE SEGUNDO GRADO, UTILIZADAS PARA GASTOS DIVERSOS (SALARIOS, ETC.) QUEDAN INCLUIDAS EN LA COLUMNA 5.

CHAD:
E—> EXPENDITURE OF THE CENTRAL GOVERNMENT ONLY; FOR 1970, OTHER EXPENDITURE WHICH CANNOT BE DISTRIBUTED ACCORDING TO PURPOSE IS INCLUDED IN COLUMN 4.
FR—> DEPENSES DU GOUVERNEMENT CENTRAL SEULEMENT; EN 1970, LES AUTRES DEPENSES QUI NE PEUVENT ETRE REPARTIES SELON LEUR DESTINATION SONT INCLUSES DANS LA COLONNE 4.
ESP> GASTOS DEL GOBIERNO CENTRAL SOLAMENTE; EN 1970, LOS OTROS GASTOS QUE NO PUEDEN SER DISTRIBUIDOS SEGUN SU DESTINO QUEDAN INCLUIDOS EN LA COLUMNA 4.

COMORO:
E—> OTHER EXPENDITURE WHICH CANNOT BE DISTRIBUTED ACCORDING TO PURPOSE IS INCLUDED IN COLUMN 4.
FR—> LES AUTRES DEPENSES QUI NE PEUVENT ETRE REPARTIES SELON LEUR DESTINATION SONT INCLUSES DANS LA COLONNE 4.
ESP> LOS OTROS GASTOS QUE NO PUEDEN SER DISTRIBUIDOS SEGUN SU DESTINO QUEDAN INCLUIDOS EN LA COLUMNA 4.

CONGO:
E—> EXPENDITURE OF THE CENTRAL GOVERNMENT ONLY.
FR—> DEPENSES DU GOUVERNEMENT CENTRAL SEULEMENT.
ESP> GASTOS DEL GOBIERNO CENTRAL SOLAMENTE.

DJIBOUTI:
E—> OTHER DIRECT EXPENDITURE IS INCLUDED IN COLUMN 7.
FR—> LES AUTRES DEPENSES DIRECTES SONT INCLUSES DANS LA COLONNE 7.
ESP> LOS OTROS GASTOS DIRECTOS QUEDAN INCLUIDOS EN LA COLUMNA 7.

EGYPT:
E—> ADMINSTRATION IS INCLUDED IN COLUMN 3.
FR—> L'ADMINISTRATION EST INCLUSE DANS LA COLONNE 3.
ESP> LA ADMINISTRACION QUEDA INCLUIDA EN LA COLUMNA 3.

ETHIOPIA:
E—> EXPENDITURE FOR UNIVERSITIES IS NOT INCLUDED. FOR 1970, OTHER DIRECT EXPENDITURE IS INCLUDED IN COLUMN 7.
FR—> LES DEPENSES DES UNIVERSITES NE SONT PAS INCLUSES; EN 1970, LES AUTRES DEPENSES DIRECTES SONT INCLUSES DANS LA COLONNE 7.
ESP> NO SE INCLUYEN LOS GASTOS RELATIVOS A LAS UNIVERSIDADES. EN 1970, LOS OTROS GASTOS DIRECTOS QUEDAN INCLUIDOS EN LA COLUMNA 7.

GABON:
E—> FOR 1976, OTHER DIRECT EXPENDITURE IS INCLUDED IN COLUMN 5.
FR—> EN 1976, LES AUTRES DEPENSES DIRECTES SONT INCLUSES DANS LA COLONNE 5.
ESP> EN 1975, LOS OTROS GASTOS DIRECTOS QUEDAN INCLUIDOS EN LA COLUMNA 5.

GHANA:
E—> FOR 1976, EXPENDITURE ON UNIVERSITIES IS NOT INCLUDED.
FR—> EN 1976, LES DEPENSES DES UNIVERSITES NE SONT PAS INCLUSES.
ESP> EN 1976, NO SE INCLUYEN LOS GASTOS RELATIVOS A LAS UNIVERSIDADES.

GUINEA-BISSAU:
E—> FOREIGN AID IS INCLUDED.
FR—> L'AIDE EXTERIEURE EST INCLUSE.
ESP> INCLUIDA LA AYUDA EXTERIOR.

IVORY COAST:
E—> FOREIGN AID IS INCLUDED.
FR—> L'AIDE EXTERIEURE EST INCLUSE.
ESP> INCLUIDA LA AYUDA EXTERIOR.

4.2 **Public current expenditure by purpose**
Dépenses publiques ordinaires selon leur destination
Gastos públicos ordinarios según su destino

LIBYAN ARAB JAMAHIRIYA:
E—> EXPENDITURE ON UNIVERSITIES IS NOT IN-CLUDED; ADMINISTRATION IS INCLUDED IN COLUMN 3.
FR-> LES DEPENSES DES UNIVERSITES NE SONT PAS INCLUSES; L'ADMINISTRATION EST INCLUSE DANS LA COLONNE 3.
ESP> NO SE INCLUYEN LOS GASTOS RELATIVOS A LAS UNIVERSIDADES; LA ADMINISTRACION QUEDA INCLUIDA EN LA COLUMNA 3.

MALAWI:
E—> THE TOTALITY OF TRANSFERS TO UNIVERSITIES, USED FOR ALL PURPOSES (SALARIES, ETC.) IS IN-CLUDED IN COLUMN 3.
FR-> LA TOTALITE DES TRANSFERTS AUX UNIVERSITES UTILISEE POUR DES DEPENSES DIVERSES (SALAIRES, ETC.) EST INCLUSE DANS LA COLONNE 3.
ESP> LA TOTALIDAD DE LAS TRANSFERENCIAS A LAS UNIVERSIDADES UTILIZADAS PARA GASTOS DIVERSOS (SALARIOS, ETC.), QUEDA INCLUIDA EN LA COLUMNA 3.

MALI:
E—> ADMINISTRATION IS INCLUDED IN COLUMN 7.
FR-> L'ADMINISTRATION EST INCLUSE DANS LA COLONNE 7.
ESP> LA ADMINISTRACION QUEDA INCLUIDA EN LA COLUMNA 7.

MAURITIUS:
E—> TRANSFERS TO UNIVERSITIES AND OTHER THIRD LEVEL INSTITUTIONS, USED FOR ALL PURPOSES (SALARIES, ETC.) ARE INCLUDED IN COLUMN 3. FOR 1970, OTHER DIRECT EXPENDITURE IS INCLUDED IN COLUMN 7.
FR-> LES TRANSFERTS AUX UNIVERSITES ET AUTRES ETABLISSEMENTS D'ENSEIGNEMENT DU TROISIEME DEGRE, UTILISES POUR DES DEPENSES DIVERSES (SALAIRES, ETC.) SONT INCLUS DANS LA COLONNE 3. EN 1970, LES AUTRES DEPENSES DIRECTES SONT INCLUSES DANS LA COLONNE 7.
ESP> LAS TRANSFERENCIAS A LAS UNIVERSIDADES Y OTROS ESTABLECIMIENTOS DE ENSEÑANZA DE TERCER GRADO, UTILIZADAS PARA GASTOS DIVERSOS (SALARIOS, ETC.) QUEDAN INCLUIDAS EN LA COLUMNA 3. EN 1970, LOS OTROS GASTOS DIRECTOS SE INCLUYEN EN LA COLUMNA 7.

MOROCCO:
E—> FOR 1970, 1977 AND 1978, ADMINISTRATION IS INCLUDED IN COLUMN 3. FROM 1976 TO 1978, EX-PENDITURE OF THE MINISTRY OF PRIMARY AND SECONDARY EDUCATION ONLY.
FR-> EN 1970, 1977 ET 1978, L'ADMINISTRATION EST INCLUSE DANS LA COLONNE 3. DE 1976 A 1978, DEPENSES DU MINISTERE DES ENSEIGNEMENTS PRIMAIRE ET SECONDAIRE SEULEMENT.
ESP> EN 1970, 1977 Y 1978, LA ADMINISTRACION QUEDA INCLUIDA EN LA COLUMNA 3. DE 1976 A 1978, LOS GASTOS SE REFIEREN AL MINISTERIO DE LAS ENSEÑANZAS DE PRIMERO Y SEGUNDO GRADO SOLAMENTE.

RWANDA:
E—> WITH THE EXCEPTION OF SCHOLARSHIPS, TRANSFERS TO THIRD LEVEL INSTITUTIONS, USED FOR ALL PURPOSES (SALARIES, ETC.) ARE INCLUDED IN COLUMN 3.
FR-> A L'EXCEPTION DES BOURSES D'ETUDES, LES TRANSFERTS AUX ETABLISSEMENTS D'ENSEIGNEMENT DU TROISIEME DEGRE, UTILISES POUR DES DEPENSES DIVER-SES (SALAIRES, ETC.) SONT INCLUS DANS LA COLONNE 3.
ESP> SALVO LAS BECAS DE ESTUDIO, LAS TRANSFE-RENCIAS A LOS ESTABLECIMIENTOS DE ENSEÑANZA DE TERCER GRADO UTILIZADAS PARA GASTOS DIVERSOS (SALARIOS, ETC.) QUEDAN INCLUIDAS EN LA COLUMNA 3.

ST. HELENA:
E—> FOR 1970, OTHER DIRECT EXPENDITURE IS INCLUDED IN COLUMN 7.
FR-> EN 1970, LES AUTRES DEPENSES DIRECTES SONT INCLUSES DANS LA COLONNE 7.
ESP> EN 1970, LOS OTROS GASTOS DIRECTOS SE INCLUYEN EN LA COLUMNA 7.

SENEGAL:
E—> EXPENDITURE OF THE MINISTRY OF PRIMARY AND SECONDARY EDUCATION ONLY.
FR-> DEPENSES DU MINISTERE DES ENSEIGNEMENTS PRIMAIRE ET SECONDAIRE SEULEMENT.
ESP> GASTOS DEL MINISTERIO DE LAS ENSEÑANZAS DE PRIMERO Y DE SEGUNDO GRADO SOLAMENTE.

SWAZILAND:
E—> ADMINISTRATION IS INCLUDED IN COLUMN 3; TRANSFERS TO THE UNIVERSITY ARE SHOWN IN COLUMN 7.
FR-> L'ADMINISTRATION EST INCLUSE DANS LA COLONNE 3; LES TRANSFERTS A L'UNIVERSITE SONT PRESENTES DANS LA COLONNE 7.
ESP> LA ADMINISTRACION QUEDA INCLUIDA EN LA COLUMNA 3; LAS TRANSFERENCIAS A LA UNIVERSIDADES SE PRESENTAN EN LA COLUMNA 7.

TOGO:
E—> FOREIGN AID IS INCLUDED.
FR-> L'AIDE EXTERIEUR EST INCLUSE.
ESP> SE INCLUYE LA AYUDA EXTERIOR.

UGANDA:
E—> EXPENDITURE OF THE MINISTRY OF EDUCATION ONLY.
FR-> DEPENSES DU MINISTERE DE L'EDUCATION SEULEMENT.
ESP> GASTOS DEL MINISTERIO DE EDUCACION SOLAMENTE.

UNITED REPUBLIC OF CAMEROON:
E—> FOR 1975 AND 1976, EXPENDITURE OF THE MINISTRY OF EDUCATION ONLY.
FR-> EN 1975 ET 1976, DEPENSES DU MINISTERE DE L'EDUCATION SEULEMENT.
ESP> EN 1975 Y 1976, GASTOS DEL MINISTERIO DE EDUCACION SOLAMENTE.

Public current expenditure by purpose   4.2
Dépenses publiques ordinaires selon leur destination
Gastos públicos ordinarios según su destino

BRITISH VIRGIN ISLANDS:
E—> FOR 1970, OTHER DIRECT EXPENDITURE IS INCLUDED IN COLUMN 7.
FR—> EN 1970, LES AUTRES DEPENSES DIRECTES SONT INCLUSES DANS LA COLONNE 7.
ESP> EN 1970, LOS OTROS GASTOS DIRECTOS SE INCLUYEN EN LA COLUMNA 7.

CAYMAN ISLANDS:
E—> FOR 1976, ADMINISTRATION IS INCLUDED IN COLUMN 3.
FR—> EN 1976, L'ADMINISTRATION EST INCLUSE DANS LA COLONNE 3.
ESP> EN 1976, LA ADMINISTRACION SE INCLUYE EN LA COLUMNA 3.

DOMINICAN REPUBLIC:
E—> THE TOTALITY OF TRANSFERS TO UNIVERSITIES, USED FOR ALL PURPOSES (SALARIES, ETC.) IS INCLUDED IN COLUMN 3.
FR—> LA TOTALITE DES TRANSFERTS AUX UNIVERSITES, UTILISEE POUR DES DEPENSES DIVERSES (SALAIRES, ETC.) EST INCLUSE DANS LA COLONNE 3.
ESP> LA TOTALIDAD DE LAS TRANSFERENCIAS A LAS UNIVERSIDADES UTILIZADA PARA GASTOS DIVERSOS (SALARIOS, ETC.) QUEDA INCLUIDA EN LA COLUMNA 3.

EL SALVADOR:
E—> FOR 1970, THE TOTALITY OF TRANSFERS TO UNIVERSITIES, USED FOR ALL PURPOSES (SALARIES, ETC.) IS INCLUDED IN COLUMN 3.
FR—> EN 1970, LA TOTALITE DES TRANSFERTS. AUX UNIVERSITES, UTILISEE POUR DES DEPENSES DIVERSES (SALAIRES, ETC.) EST INCLUSE DANS LA COLONNE 3.
ESP> EN 1970, LA TOTALIDAD DE LAS TRANSFERENCIAS A LAS UNIVERSIDADES UTILIZADA PARA GASTOS DIVERSOS (SALARIOS, ETC.) QUEDA INCLUIDA EN LA COLUMNA 3.

GUATEMALA:
E—> FOR 1970, OTHER DIRECT EXPENDITURE IS INCLUDED IN COLUMN 7.
FR—> EN 1970, LES AUTRES DEPENSES DIRECTES SONT INCLUSES DANS LA COLONNE 7.
ESP> EN 1970, LOS OTROS GASTOS DIRECTOS SE INCLUYEN EN LA COLUMNA 7.

HONDURAS:
E—> FOR 1977, ADMINISTRATION AND THE TOTALITY OF TRANSFERS TO UNIVERSITIES, USED FOR ALL PURPOSES (SALARIES, ETC.) ARE INCLUDED IN COLUMN 3.
FR—> EN 1977, L'ADMINISTRATION ET LA TOTALITE DES TRANSFERTS AUX UNIVERSITES UTILISEES POUR DES DEPENSES DIVERSES (SALAIRES, ETC.) SONT INCLUSES DANS LA COLONNE 3.
ESP> EN 1977, LA ADMINISTRACION Y LA TOTALIDAD DE LAS TRANSFERENCIAS A LAS UNIVERSIDADES UTILIZADAS PARA GASTOS DIVERSOS (SALARIOS, ETC.) QUEDAN INCLUIDAS EN LA COLUMNA 3.

UNITED REPUBLIC OF TANZANIA:
E—> ADMINISTRATION IS INCLUDED IN COLUMN 3.
FR—> L'ADMINISTRATION EST INCLUSE DANS LA COLONNE 3.
ESP> LA ADMINISTRACION SE INCLUYE EN LA COLUMNA 3.

UPPER VOLTA:
E—> EXPENDITURE OF THE MINISTRY OF EDUCATION ONLY. FOR 1970, OTHER DIRECT EXPENDITURE AND SUBSIDIES TO PRIVATE EDUCATION ARE INCLUDED IN COLUMN 7.
FR—> DEPENSES DU MINISTERE DE L'EDUCATION SEULEMENT. EN 1970, L'AUTRES DEPENSES DIRECTES ET LES SUBVENTIONS A L'ENSEIGNEMENT PRIVE SONT INCLUSES DANS LA COLONNE 7.
ESP> GASTOS DEL MINISTERIO DE EDUCACION SOLA-MENTE. EN 1970, LOS OTROS GASTOS DIRECTOS Y LAS SUBVENCIONES A LA ENSEÑANZA PRIVADA FIGURAN INCLUIDOS EN LA COLUMNA 7.

ANTIGUA:
E—> CONTRIBUTIONS FOR THE UNIVERSITY OF THE WEST INDIES ARE INCLUDED IN COLUMN 5.
FR—> LES SUBVENTIONS A L'UNIVERSITE DES "WEST INDIES" SONT INCLUSES DANS LA COLONNE 5.
ESP> LAS SUBVENCIONES A LA UNIVERSIDAD DE "WEST INDIES" QUEDAN INCLUIDAS EN LA COLUMNA 5.

BARBADOS:
E—> THE TOTALITY OF TRANSFERS TO UNIVERSITIES AND SUBSIDIES TO SECOND LEVEL SCHOOLS, USED FOR ALL PURPOSES (SALARIES, ETC.) ARE INCLUDED IN COLUMN 3.
FR—> LA TOTALITE DES TRANSFERTS AUX UNIVERSITES ET LES SUBVENTIONS AUX ECOLES DU SECOND DEGRE, UTILISES POUR DES DEPENSES DIVERSES (SALAIRES, ETC.) SONT INCLUS DANS LA COLONNE 3.
ESP> LA TOTALIDAD DE LAS TRANSFERENCIAS A LAS UNIVERSIDADES Y LAS SUBVENCIONES A LAS ESCUELAS DE SEGUNDO GRADO UTILIZADAS PARA GASTOS DIVERSOS (SALARIOS, ETC.) QUEDAN INCLUIDAS EN LA COLUMNA 3.

BELIZE:
E—> FOR 1970, OTHER DIRECT EXPENDITURE IS INCLUDED IN COLUMN 7.
FR—> EN 1970, LES AUTRES DEPENSES DIRECTES SONT INCLUSES DANS LA COLONNE 7.
ESP> EN 1970, LOS OTROS GASTOS DIRECTOS SE INCLUYEN EN LA COLUMNA 7.

BERMUDA:
E—> FOR 1970, OTHER DIRECT EXPENDITURE IS INCLUDED IN COLUMN 7.
FR—> EN 1970, LES AUTRES DEPENSES DIRECTES SONT INCLUSES DANS LA COLONNE 7.
ESP> EN 1970, LOS OTROS GASTOS DIRECTOS SE INCLUYEN EN LA COLUMNA 7.

4.2 Public current expenditure by purpose
Dépenses publiques ordinaires selon leur destination
Gastos públicos ordinarios según su destino

JAMAICA:
E—> EXPENDITURE OF THE MINISTRY OF EDUCATION ONLY.
FR—> DEPENSES DU MINISTERE DE L'EDUCATION SEULEMENT.
ESP> GASTOS DEL MINISTERIO DE EDUCACION SOLAMENTE.

MEXICO:
E—> EXPENDITURE OF THE MINISTRY OF EDUCATION ONLY. FOR 1970, 1975 AND 1976, ADMINISTRATION AND OTHER DIRECT EXPENDITURE ARE INCLUDED IN COLUMN 7.
FR—> DEPENSES DU MINISTERE DE L'EDUCATION SEULEMENT. EN 1970, 1975 ET 1976, L'ADMINIS- TRATION ET LES AUTRES DEPENSES DIRECTES SONT INCLUSES DANS LA COLONNE 7.
ESP> GASTOS DEL MINISTERIO DE EDUCACION SOLAMENTE. EN 1970, 1975 Y 1976, LA ADMINISTRA- CION Y LOS OTROS GASTOS DIRECTOS QUEDAN INCLUIDOS EN LA COLUMNA 7.

NICARAGUA:
E—> OTHER DIRECT EXPENDITURE IS INCLUDED IN COLUMN 7.
FR—> LES AUTRES DEPENSES DIRECTES SONT INCLUSES DANS LA COLONNE 7.
ESP> LOS OTROS GASTOS DIRECTOS QUEDAN INCLUIDOS EN LA COLUMNA 7.

PANAMA:
E—> THE TOTALITY OF TRANSFERS TO UNIVERSITIES, USED FOR ALL PURPOSES (SALARIES, ETC.) IS INCLUDED IN COLUMN 3.
FR—> LA TOTALITE DES TRANSFERTS AUX UNIVERSITES, UTILISEE POUR DES DEPENSES DIVERSES (SALAIRES, ETC.) EST INCLUSE DANS LA COLONNE 3.
ESP> LA TOTALIDAD DE LAS TRANSFERENCIAS A LAS UNIVERSIDADES UTILIZADA PARA GASTOS DIVERSOS (SALARIOS, ETC.) QUEDA INCLUIDA EN LA COLUMNA 3.

ST. LUCIA:
E—> FOR 1971, ADMINISTRATION IS INCLUDED IN COLUMN 3 AND OTHER DIRECT EXPENDITURE IN COLUMN 7.
FR—> EN 1971, L'ADMINISTRATION EST INCLUSE DANS LA COLONNE 3 ET LES AUTRES DEPENSES DIRECTES SONT INCLUSES DANS LA COLONNE 7.
ESP> EN 1971, LA ADMINISTRACION QUEDA INCLUIDA EN LA COLUMNA 3 Y LOS OTROS GASTOS DIRECTOS EN LA COLUMNA 7.

ARGENTINA:
E—> FIGURES IN COLUMN 1 ARE IN MILLIONS. FOR 1975 AND 1977, ADMINISTRATION IS INCLUDED IN COLUMN 3.
FR—> LES CHIFFRES DE LA COLONNE 1 SONT EXPRIMES EN MILLIONS. EN 1975 ET 1977, L'ADMINISTRATION EST INCLUSE DANS LA COLONNE 3.
ESP> LAS CIFRAS DE LA COLUMNA 1 SE EXPRESAN EN MILLONES. EN 1975 Y 1977, LA ADMINISTRACION QUEDA INCLUIDA EN LA COLUMNA 3.

CHILE:
E—> THE TOTALITY OF TRANSFERS TO UNIVERSITIES, USED FOR ALL PURPOSES (SALARIES, ETC.) IS INCLUDED IN COLUMN 3.
FR—> LA TOTALITE DES TRANSFERTS AUX UNIVERSITES, UTILISEE POUR DES DEPENSES DIVERSES (SALAIRES, ETC.) EST INCLUSE DANS LA COLONNE 3.
ESP> LA TOTALIDAD DE LAS TRANSFERENCIAS A LAS UNIVERSIDADES, UTILIZADA PARA GASTOS DIVERSOS (SALARIOS, ETC.) QUEDA INCLUIDA EN LA COLUMNA 3.

COLOMBIA:
E—> EXPENDITURE OF THE MINISTRY OF EDUCATION ONLY; THE TOTALITY OF TRANSFERS TO UNIVERSITIES, USED FOR ALL PURPOSES (SALARIES, ETC.) IS INCLUDED IN COLUMN 3.
FR—> DEPENSES DU MINISTERE DE L'EDUCATION SEULEMENT; LA TOTALITE DES TRANSFERTS AUX UNIVERSITES, UTILISEE POUR LES DEPENSES DIVERSES (SALAIRES -ETC.) EST INCLUSE DANS LA COLONNE 3.
ESP> GASTOS DEL MINISTERIO DE EDUCACION SOLAMENTE; LA TOTALIDAD DE LAS TRANSFERENCIAS A LAS UNIVERSIDADES UTILIZADA PARA GASTOS DIVERSOS (SALARIOS, ETC.), QUEDA INCLUIDA EN LA COLUMNA 3.

ECUADOR:
E—> FOR 1970, OTHER DIRECT EXPENDITURE IS INCLUDED IN COLUMN 7.
FR—> EN 1970, LES AUTRES DEPENSES DIRECTES SONT INCLUSES DANS LA COLONNE 7.
ESP> EN 1970, LOS OTROS GASTOS DIRECTOS QUEDAN INCLUIDOS EN LA COLUMNA 7.

FALKLAND ISLANDS:
E—> FOR 1970, OTHER DIRECT EXPENDITURE IS INCLUDED IN COLUMN 7.
FR—> EN 1970, LES AUTRES DEPENSES DIRECTES SONT INCLUSES DANS LA COLONNE 7.
ESP> EN 1970, LOS OTROS GASTOS DIRECTOS QUEDAN INCLUIDOS EN LA COLUMNA 7.

GUYANA:
E—> THE TOTALITY OF TRANSFERS TO UNIVERSITIES, USED FOR ALL PURPOSES (SALARIES, ETC.) IS INCLUDED IN COLUMN 3. FOR 1970, OTHER DIRECT EXPENDITURE AND SCHOLARSHIPS ARE INCLUDED IN COLUMN 7. FOR 1976, WELFARE SERVICES AND SCHOLAR- SHIPS ARE INCLUDED IN COLUMN 7. FOR 1975 AND 1976, EXPENDITURE OF THE MINISTRY OF EDUCATION ONLY.
FR—> LA TOTALITE DES TRANSFERTS AUX UNIVERSITES UTILISEE POUR DES DEPENSES DIVERSES (SALAIRES, ETC.) EST INCLUSE DANS LA COLONNE 3. EN 1970, LES AUTRES DEPENSES DIRECTES ET LES BOURSES SONT INCLUSES DANS LA COLONNE 7. EN 1976, LES SERVICES SOCIAUX ET LES BOURSES SONT INCLUSES DANS LA COLONNE 7. EN 1975 ET 1976, DEPENSES DU MINISTERE DE L'EDUCATION SEULEMENT.

Public current expenditure by purpose   4.2
Dépenses publiques ordinaires selon leur destination
Gastos públicos ordinarios según su destino

AFGHANISTAN:
E—> FOR 1974 AND 1977, EXPENDITURE ON UNI-
VERSITIES IS NOT INCLUDED.
FR-> EN 1974 ET 1977, LES DEPENSES DES
UNIVERSITES NE SONT PAS INCLUSES.
ESP> EN 1974 Y 1977 NO SE INCLUYEN LOS GASTOS
RELATIVOS A LAS UNIVERSIDADES.

BAHRAIN:
E—> FROM 1975 TO 1978, ADMINISTRATION IS IN-
CLUDED IN COLUMN 3.
FR-> DE 1975 A 1978, L'ADMINISTRATION EST IN-
CLUSE DANS LA COLONNE 3.
ESP> DE 1975 A 1978, LA ADMINISTRACION QUEDA
INCLUIDA EN LA COLUMNA 3.

BHUTAN:
E—> FOR 1970, EXPENDITURE OF THE MINISTRY OF
EDUCATION ONLY; OTHER DIRECT EXPENDITURE IS IN-
CLUDED IN COLUMN 7.
FR-> EN 1970, DEPENSES DU MINISTERE DE
L'EDUCATION SEULEMENT; LES AUTRES DEPENSES DIRECTES
SONT INCLUSES DANS LA COLONNE 7.
ESP> EN 1970, GASTOS DEL MINISTERIO DE EDUCACION
SOLAMENTE; LOS OTROS GASTOS DIRECTOS QUEDAN
INCLUIDOS EN LA COLUMNA 7.

BRUNEI:
E—> FOR 1970, OTHER EXPENDITURE WHICH CANNOT
BE DISTRIBUTED ACCORDING TO PURPOSE IS INCLUDED
IN COLUMN 4.
FR-> EN 1970, LES AUTRES DEPENSES QUI NE PEUVENT
ETRE REPARTIES SELON LEUR DESTINATION SONT INCLUSES
DANS LA COLONNE 4.
ESP> EN 1970, LOS OTROS GASTOS QUE NO PUEDEN
REPARTIRSE SEGUN SU DESTINO, SE INCLUYEN EN LA
COLUMNA 4.

BURMA:
E—> EXPENDITURE OF THE MINISTRY OF EDUCATION
ONLY.
FR-> DEPENSES DU MINISTERE DE L'EDUCATION
SEULEMENT.
ESP> GASTOS DEL MINISTERIO DE EDUCACION
SOLAMENTE.

CYPRUS:
E—> EXPENDITURE OF THE OFFICE OF GREEK EDUCA-
TION ONLY; FOR 1970, OTHER DIRECT EXPENDITURE
IS INCLUDED IN COLUMN 7.
FR-> DEPENSES DU BUREAU GREC DE L'EDUCATION
SEULEMENT; EN 1970 LES AUTRES DEPENSES DIRECTES
SONT INCLUSES DANS LA COLONNE 7.
ESP> GASTOS DEL SERVICIO GRIEGO DE EDUCACION
SOLAMENTE; EN 1970, LOS OTROS GASTOS DIRECTOS SE
INCLUYEN EN LA COLUMNA 7.

HONG KONG:
E—> FOR 1970, OTHER DIRECT EXPENDITURE IS
INCLUDED IN COLUMN 7.
FR-> EN 1970, LES AUTRES DEPENSES DIRECTES SONT
INCLUSES DANS LA COLONNE 7.
ESP> EN 1970, LOS OTROS GASTOS DIRECTOS SE
INCLUYEN EN LA COLUMNA 7.

GUYANA (CONT):
ESP> LA TOTALIDAD DE LAS TRANSFERENCIAS A LAS
UNIVERSIDADES, UTILIZADA PARA GASTOS DIVERSOS
(SALARIOS, ETC.), QUEDA INCLUIDA EN LA COLUMNA 3.
EN 1970, LOS OTROS GASTOS DIRECTOS Y LAS BECAS,
SE INCLUYEN EN LA COLUMNA 7. EN 1976, LOS
SERVICIOS SOCIALES Y LAS BECAS FIGURAN EN LA
COLUMNA 7. EN 1975 Y 1976, LOS GASTOS SE REFIEREN
AL MINISTERIO DE EDUCACION SOLAMENTE.

PARAGUAY:
E—> THE TOTALITY OF TRANSFERS TO UNIVERSITIES,
USED FOR ALL PURPOSES (SALARIES, ETC.) IS
INCLUDED IN COLUMN 3. FOR 1970, OTHER DIRECT
EXPENDITURE IS INCLUDED IN COLUMN 7.
FR-> LA TOTALITE DES TRANSFERTS AUX UNIVERSITES,
UTILISEE POUR DES DEPENSES DIVERSES (SALAIRES,
ETC.) EST INCLUSE DANS LA COLONNE 3. EN 1970,
LES AUTRES DEPENSES DIRECTES SONT INCLUSES DANS
LA COLONNE 7.
ESP> LA TOTALIDAD DE LAS TRANSFERENCIAS A LAS
UNIVERSIDADES, UTILIZADA PARA GASTOS DIVERSOS
(SALARIOS, ETC.), QUEDA INCLUIDA EN LA COLUMNA 3.
EN 1970, LOS OTROS GASTOS DIRECTOS FIGURAN EN LA
COLUMNA 7.

PERU:
E—> TRANSFERS TO UNIVERSITIES AND SOME OTHER
INSTITUTIONS AS WELL AS VARIOUS TYPES OF PENSIONS
AND OTHER BENEFITS ARE SHOWN IN COLUMN 7.
FR-> LES TRANSFERTS AUX UNIVERSITES ET A
CERTAINS AUTRES ETABLISSEMENTS AINSI QUE
DIFFERENTS TYPES DE PENSIONS ET D'INDEMNITES SONT
PRESENTES DANS LA COLONNE 7.
ESP> LAS TRANSFERENCIAS A LAS UNIVERSIDADES Y A
ALGUNOS OTROS ESTABLECIMIENTOS Y LOS DIFERENTES
TIPOS DE PENSIONES E INDEMNIZACIONES QUEDAN
INCLUIDOS EN LA COLUMNA 7.

VENEZUELA:
E—> TRANSFERS TO UNIVERSITIES AND OTHER THIRD
LEVEL INSTITUTIONS, USED FOR ALL PURPOSES
(SALARIES, ETC.) ARE INCLUDED IN COLUMN 3. FOR
1970, OTHER DIRECT EXPENDITURE IS INCLUDED IN
COLUMN 7. FOR 1975, ADMINISTRATION IS INCLUDED
IN COLUMN 7.
FR-> LES TRANSFERTS AUX UNIVERSITES ET AUTRES
ETABLISSEMENTS D'ENSEIGNEMENT DU TROISIEME DEGRE,
UTILISES POUR DES DEPENSES DIVERSES (SALAIRES,
ETC.) SONT INCLUS DANS LA COLONNE 3. EN 1970,
LES AUTRES DEPENSES DIRECTES SONT INCLUSES DANS
LA COLONNE 7. EN 1975, L'ADMINISTRATION EST
INCLUSE DANS LA COLONNE 7.
ESP> LAS TRANSFERENCIAS A LAS UNIVERSIDADES Y
OTROS ESTABLECIMIENTOS DE ENSEÑANZA DE TERCER GRADO,
UTILIZADAS PARA GASTOS DIVERSOS (SALARIOS, ETC.), LOS
QUEDAN INCLUIDAS EN LA COLUMNA 3. EN 1970, LOS
OTROS GASTOS DIRECTOS FIGURAN EN LA COLUMNA 7 Y
EN 1975, LA ADMINISTRACION SE INCLUYE EN LA
COLUMNA 7.

4.2 Public current expenditure by purpose
Dépenses publiques ordinaires selon leur destination
Gastos públicos ordinarios según su destino

INDIA:
E—> FOR 1970, OTHER DIRECT EXPENDITURE IS INCLUDED IN COLUMN 7. FOR 1975, EMOLUMENTS OF TEACHERS ARE CALCULATED AS PERCENTAGE OF TOTAL CURRENT AND CAPITAL EXPENDITURE ON EDUCATION.
FR—> EN 1970, LES AUTRES DEPENSES DIRECTES SONT INCLUSES DANS LA COLONNE 7. EN 1975, LE POURCENTAGE DES EMOLUMENTS DU PERSONNEL ENSEIGNANT EST CALCULE SUR LE TOTAL DES DEPENSES ORDINAIRES ET EN CAPITAL.
ESP> EN 1970, LOS OTROS GASTOS DIRECTOS SE INCLUYEN EN LA COLUMNA 7. EN 1975, EL PORCENTAJE DE LOS EMOLUMENTOS DEL PERSONAL DOCENTE, SE CALCULA SOBRE EL TOTAL DE LOS GASTOS ORDINARIOS Y DE CAPITAL.

IRAN:
E—> EXPENDITURE OF THE MINISTRY OF EDUCATION ONLY; EXCLUDED ARE MAINLY THE MINISTRY OF HIGHER EDUCATION AND EXPENDITURE ON EDUCATION INCURRED BY OTHER MINISTRIES.
FR—> DEPENSES DU MINISTERE DE L'EDUCATION SEULEMENT; SONT EXCLUS LE MINISTERE DE L'ENSEIGNEMENT SUPERIEUR ET LES DEPENSES D'EDUCATION D'AUTRES MINISTERES.
ESP> GASTOS DEL MINISTERIO DE EDUCACION SOLAMENTE; QUEDAN EXCLUIDOS LOS GASTOS DEL MINISTERIO DE LA ENSEÑANZA SUPERIOR Y LOS QUE DESTINAN A LA ENSEÑANZA OTROS MINISTERIOS.

IRAQ:
E—> FOR 1970, OTHER DIRECT EXPENDITURE IS INCLUDED IN COLUMN 7.
FR—> EN 1970, LES AUTRES DEPENSES DIRECTES SONT INCLUSES DANS LA COLONNE 7.
ESP> EN 1970, LOS OTROS GASTOS DIRECTOS QUEDAN INCLUIDOS EN LA COLUMNA 7.

JAPAN:
E—> FIGURES IN COLUMN 1 ARE IN MILLIONS. FOR 1970, OTHER DIRECT EXPENDITURE IS INCLUDED IN COLUMN 7. FROM 1975 TO 1977, DATA DO NOT INCLUDE PUBLIC SUBSIDIES TO PRIVATE EDUCATION.
FR—> LES CHIFFRES DE LA COLONNE 1 SONT EXPRIMES EN MILLIONS. EN 1970, LES AUTRES DEPENSES DIRECTES SONT INCLUSES DANS LA COLONNE 7. DE 1975 A 1977, LES DONNEES NE COMPRENNENT PAS LES SUBVENTIONS PUBLIQUES A L'ENSEIGNEMENT PRIVE.
ESP> LAS CIFRAS DE LA COLUMNA 1 SE EXPRESAN EN MILLONES. EN 1970, LOS OTROS GASTOS DIRECTOS QUEDAN INCLUIDOS EN LA COLUMNA 7. DE 1975 A 1977, LOS DATOS NO COMPRENDEN LAS SUBVENCIONES PUBLICAS A LA ENSEÑANZA PRIVADA.

JORDAN:
E—> DATA REFER TO THE EAST BANK ONLY. OTHER DIRECT EXPENDITURE IS INCLUDED IN COLUMN 7. FROM 1975 TO 1977, EXPENDITURE ON UNIVERSITIES IS NOT INCLUDED.
FR—> LES DONNEES SE REFERENT A LA RIVE ORIENTALE SEULEMENT. LES AUTRES DEPENSES DIRECTES SONT INCLUSES DANS LA COLONNE 7. DE 1975 A 1977, LES DEPENSES DES UNIVERSITES NE SONT PAS INCLUSES.

JORDAN (CONT):
ESP> LOS DATOS SE REFIEREN A LA ORILLA ORIENTAL SOLAMENTE. LOS OTROS GASTOS DIRECTOS QUEDAN INCLUIDOS EN LA COLUMNA 7. DE 1975 A 1977, SE EXCLUYEN LOS GASTOS RELATIVOS A LAS UNIVERSIDADES.

KOREA, REPUBLIC OF:
E—> FIGURES IN COLUMN 1 ARE IN MILLIONS.
FR—> LES CHIFFRES DE LA COLONNE 1 SONT EXPRIMES EN MILLIONS.
ESP> LAS CIFRAS DE LA COLUMNA 1 SE EXPRESAN EN MILLONES.

KUWAIT:
E—> FOR 1970, OTHER DIRECT EXPENDITURE IS INCLUDED IN COLUMN 7.
FR—> EN 1970, LES AUTRES DEPENSES DIRECTES SONT INCLUSES DANS LA COLONNE 7.
ESP> EN 1970, LOS OTROS GASTOS DIRECTOS QUEDAN INCLUIDOS EN LA COLUMNA 7.

MALAYSIA:
PENINSULAR MALAYSIA:
E—> FOR 1975 AND 1977, TRANSFERS TO UNIVERSITIES AND OTHER THIRD LEVEL INSTITUTIONS, USED FOR ALL PURPOSES (SALARIES, ETC.) ARE INCLUDED IN COLUMN 3.
FR—> EN 1975 ET 1977 LES TRANSFERTS AUX UNIVERSITES ET AUTRES ETABLISSEMENTS D'ENSEIGNEMENT DU TROISIEME DEGRE UTILISES POUR DES DEPENSES DIVERSES (SALAIRES, ETC.) SONT INCLUS DANS LA COLONNE 3.
ESP> EN 1975 Y 1977, LAS TRANSFERENCIAS A LAS UNIVERSIDADES Y OTROS ESTABLECIMIENTOS DE ENSEÑANZA DE TERCER GRADO UTILIZADAS PARA GASTOS DIVERSOS (SALARIOS, ETC.) QUEDAN INCLUIDAS EN LA COLUMNA 3.

PHILIPPINES:
E—> EXPENDITURE FOR STATE UNIVERSITIES AND COLLEGES IS NOT INCLUDED. WELFARE SERVICES ARE INCLUDED IN COLUMN 7.
FR—> LES DEPENSES DES UNIVERSITES ET COLLEGES D'ETAT NE SONT PAS INCLUSES. LES SERVICES SOCIAUX SONT INCLUS DANS LA COLONNE 7.
ESP> NO ESTAN INCLUIDOS LOS GASTOS DE LAS UNIVERSIDADES Y LOS COLEGIOS DE ESTADO. LOS SERVICIOS SOCIALES FIGURAN EN LA COLUMNA 7.

QATAR:
E—> FOR 1976, WELFARE SERVICES ARE INCLUDED IN COLUMN 4.
FR—> EN 1976, LES SERVICES SOCIAUX SONT INCLUS DANS LA COLONNE 4.
ESP> EN 1976, LOS SERVICIOS SOCIALES QUEDAN INCLUIDOS EN LA COLUMNA 4.

SINGAPORE:
E—> TRANSFERS TO THIRD LEVEL INSTITUTIONS (NAMELY UNIVERSITIES), INDUSTRIAL TRAINING BOARD AND OTHER EDUCATIONAL ORGANIZATIONS (67,707,000 DOLLARS IN 1977), USED FOR ALL PURPOSES (SALARIES, ETC.) ARE INCLUDED IN COLUMN 3. FOR 1970, OTHER DIRECT EXPENDITURE IS INCLUDED IN COLUMN 7.

Public current expenditure by purpose 4.2
Dépenses publiques ordinaires selon leur destination
Gastos públicos ordinarios según su destino

BELGIUM:
E—> EXPENDITURE OF THE MINISTRY OF EDUCATION ONLY.
FR—> DEPENSES DU MINISTERE DE L'EDUCATION SEULEMENT.
ESP> GASTOS DEL MINISTERIO DE EDUCACION SOLAMENTE.

CZECHOSLOVAKIA:
E—> FOR 1970, OTHER DIRECT EXPENDITURE IS INCLUDED IN COLUMN 7.
FR—> EN 1970, LES AUTRES DEPENSES DIRECTES SONT INCLUSES DANS LA COLONNE 7.
ESP> EN 1970, LOS OTROS GASTOS DIRECTOS FIGURAN EN LA COLUMNA 7.

FINLAND:
E—> FOR 1970, OTHER DIRECT EXPENDITURE IS INCLUDED IN COLUMN 7.
FR—> EN 1970, LES AUTRES DEPENSES DIRECTES SONT INCLUSES DANS LA COLONNE 7.
ESP> EN 1970, LOS OTROS GASTOS DIRECTOS FIGURAN EN LA COLUMNA 7.

FRANCE:
E—> EXPENDITURE OF THE MINISTRY OF EDUCATION AND MINISTRY OF THE UNIVERSITIES ONLY. OTHER DIRECT EXPENDITURE IS INCLUDED IN COLUMN 7.
FR—> DEPENSES DU MINISTERE DE L'EDUCATION ET DU MINISTERE DES UNIVERSITES SEULEMENT. LES AUTRES DEPENSES DIRECTES SONT INCLUSES DANS LA COLONNE 7.
ESP> GASTOS DEL MINISTERIO DE EDUCACION Y DEL MINISTERIO DE LAS UNIVERSIDADES SOLAMENTE. LOS OTROS GASTOS DIRECTOS QUEDAN INCLUIDOS EN LA COLUMNA 7.

GERMANY, FEDERAL REPUBLIC OF:
E—> FOR 1970, OTHER DIRECT EXPENDITURE AND WELFARE SERVICES ARE INCLUDED IN COLUMN 7. BEGINNING 1975 DATA ARE NOT COMPARABLE WITH THOSE FOR 1970 AS FIGURES INCLUDE THE TOTALITY OF THE CURRENT EXPENDITURE (INSTRUCTION AND RESEARCH) INCURRED BY ALL THIRD LEVEL INSTITUTIONS; FROM 1975 ONWARD, ONLY THE EXPENDITURE INCURRED FOR EDUCATIONAL PURPOSES IS TAKEN INTO ACCOUNT (RESEARCH IS THUS EXCLUDED).
FR—> EN 1970, LES AUTRES DEPENSES DIRECTES ET LES SERVICES SOCIAUX SONT INCLUS DANS LA COLONNE 7. A PARTIR DE 1975, LES DONNEES NE SONT PAS COMPARABLES A CELLES DE 1970, OU LES CHIFFRES INCLUENT LA TOTALITE DES DEPENSES ORDINAIRES (ENSEIGNEMENT ET RECHERCHE) EFFECTUEES PAR TOUS LES ETABLISSEMENTS DE L'ENSEIGNEMENT DU TROISIEME DEGRE; DEPUIS 1975, SEULES LES DEPENSES D'ENSEIGNEMENT SONT PRISES EN CONSIDERATION, CE QUI EXCLUT LA RECHERCHE.
ESP> EN 1970, LOS OTROS GASTOS DIRECTOS Y LOS SERVICIOS SOCIALES QUEDAN INCLUIDOS EN LA COLUMNA 7. A PARTIR DE 1975, LOS DATOS NO SON COMPARABLES A LOS DE 1970, CUYAS CIFRAS INCLUYEN LA TOTALIDAD DE LOS GASTOS ORDINARIOS (ENSEÑANZA E INVESTIGACION) EFECTUADOS POR TODOS LOS ESTABLECIMIENTOS DE LA ENSEÑANZA DE TERCER GRADO. DESDE 1975, SOLO SE TOMAN EN CONSIDERACION LOS GASTOS RELATIVOS A LA ENSEÑANZA, LO QUE EXCLUYE LA INVESTIGACION.

SINGAPORE (CONT):
FR—> LES TRANSFERTS AUX ETABLISSEMENTS D'ENSEIGNEMENT DU TROISIEME DEGRE (NOTAMMENT LES UNIVERSITES), AU BUREAU DE L'ENSEIGNEMENT INDUSTRIEL ET A D'AUTRES ETABLISSEMENTS D'ENSEIGNEMENT (67 707 000 DOLLARS EN 1977) UTILISES POUR DES DEPENSES DIVERSES (SALAIRES, ETC.) SONT INCLUS DANS LA COLONNE 3. EN 1970, LES AUTRES DEPENSES DIRECTES SONT INCLUSES DANS LA COLONNE 7.
ESP> LAS TRANSFERENCIAS A LOS ESTABLECIMIENTOS DE ENSEÑANZA DE TERCER GRADO (EN PARTICULAR LAS UNIVERSIDADES), AL CONSEJO DE LA FORMACION INDUSTRIAL (INDUSTRIAL TRAINING BOARD) Y A OTROS ESTABLECIMIENTOS DE ENSEÑANZA (67 707 000 DOLARES EN 1977) UTILIZADAS PARA GASTOS DIVERSOS (SALARIOS, ETC.) QUEDAN INCLUIDAS EN LA COLUMNA 3. EN 1970, LOS OTROS GASTOS DIRECTOS FIGURAN EN LA COLUMNA 7.

SRI LANKA:
E—> FOR 1975, THE TOTALITY OF TRANSFERS TO UNIVERSITIES, USED FOR ALL PURPOSES (SALARIES, ETC.) IS INCLUDED IN COLUMN 3.
FR—> EN 1975, LA TOTALITE DES TRANSFERTS AUX UNIVERSITES, UTILISEE POUR DES DEPENSES DIVERSES (SALAIRES, ETC.) EST INCLUSE DANS LA COLONNE 3.
ESP> EN 1975, LA TOTALIDAD DE LAS TRANSFERENCIAS A LAS UNIVERSIDADES, UTILIZADA PARA GASTOS DIVERSOS (SALARIOS, ETC.), QUEDA INCLUIDA EN LA COLUMNA 3.

SYRIAN ARAB REPUBLIC:
E—> EXPENDITURE ON EDUCATION AT THE THIRD LEVEL IS NOT INCLUDED.
FR—> LES DEPENSES DE L'ENSEIGNEMENT DU TROISIEME DEGRE NE SONT PAS INCLUSES.
ESP> NO SE INCLUYEN LOS GASTOS RELATIVOS A LA ENSEÑANZA DE TERCER GRADO.

TURKEY:
E—> FOR 1971, OTHER DIRECT EXPENDITURE IS INCLUDED IN COLUMN 7. FOR 1977, ADMINISTRATION IS INCLUDED IN COLUMN 3.
FR—> EN 1971, LES AUTRES DEPENSES DIRECTES SONT INCLUSES DANS LA COLONNE 7. EN 1977, L'ADMINIS-TRATION EST INCLUSE DANS LA COLONNE 3.
ESP> EN 1971, LOS OTROS GASTOS DIRECTOS QUEDAN INCLUIDOS EN LA COLUMNA 7. EN 1977, LA ADMINIS-TRACION FIGURA EN LA COLUMNA 3.

UNITED ARAB EMIRATES:
E—> FOR 1975 AND 1976, ADMINISTRATION IS INCLUDED IN COLUMN 3.
FR—> EN 1975 ET 1976, L'ADMINISTRATION EST INCLUSE DANS LA COLONNE 3.
ESP> EN 1975 Y 1976, LA ADMINISTRACION QUEDA INCLUIDA EN LA COLUMNA 3.

AUSTRIA:
E—> OTHER DIRECT EXPENDITURE IS INCLUDED IN COLUMN 7.
FR—> LES AUTRES DEPENSES DIRECTES SONT INCLUSES DANS LA COLONNE 7.
ESP> LOS OTROS GASTOS DIRECTOS FIGURAN EN LA COLUMNA 7.

4.2 **Public current expenditure by purpose**
Dépenses publiques ordinaires selon leur destination
Gastos públicos ordinarios según su destino

GIBRALTAR:
E—> FOR 1970, OTHER DIRECT EXPENDITURE IS INCLUDED IN COLUMN 7.
FR—> EN 1970, LES AUTRES DEPENSES DIRECTES SONT INCLUSES DANS LA COLONNE 7.
ESP> EN 1970, LOS OTROS GASTOS DIRECTOS FIGURAN EN LA COLUMNA 7.

GREECE:
E—> OTHER DIRECT EXPENDITURE IS INCLUDED IN COLUMN 7.
FR—> LES AUTRES DEPENSES DIRECTES SONT INCLUSES DANS LA COLONNE 7.
ESP> LOS OTROS GASTOS DIRECTOS FIGURAN EN LA COLUMNA 7.

HUNGARY:
E—> OTHER DIRECT EXPENDITURE IS INCLUDED IN COLUMN 7.
FR—> LES AUTRES DEPENSES DIRECTES SONT INCLUSES DANS LA COLONNE 7.
ESP> LOS OTROS GASTOS DIRECTOS FIGURAN EN LA COLUMNA 7.

ICELAND:
E—> EXPENDITURE OF THE CENTRAL GOVERNMENT ONLY. OTHER DIRECT EXPENDITURE IS INCLUDED IN COLUMN 7.
FR—> DEPENSES DU GOUVERNEMENT CENTRAL SEULEMENT; LES AUTRES DEPENSES DIRECTES SONT INCLUSES DANS LA COLONNE 7.
ESP> GASTOS DEL GOBIERNO CENTRAL SOLAMENTE; LA COLUMNA 7 INCLUYE LOS OTROS GASTOS DIRECTOS.

ITALY:
E—> FIGURES IN COLUMN 1 ARE IN MILLIONS.
FR—> LES CHIFFRES DE LA COLONNE 1 SONT EXPRIMES EN MILLIONS.
ESP> LAS CIFRAS DE LA COLUMNA 1 SE EXPRESAN EN MILLONES.

MALTA:
E—> THE TOTALITY OF TRANSFERS TO THE UNIVERSITY, USED FOR ALL PURPOSES (SALARIES, ETC.) IS INCLUDED IN COLUMN 3. FOR 1970, OTHER DIRECT EXPENDITURE IS INCLUDED IN COLUMN 7. FOR 1977, ADMINISTRATION IS INCLUDED IN COLUMN 3.
FR—> LA TOTALITE DES TRANSFERTS A L'UNIVERSITE, UTILISEE POUR DES DEPENSES DIVERSES (SALAIRES, ETC.) EST INCLUSE DANS LA COLONNE 3. EN 1970, LES AUTRES DEPENSES DIRECTES SONT INCLUSES DANS LA COLONNE 7. EN 1977, L'ADMINISTRATION EST INCLUSE DANS LA COLONNE 3.
ESP> LA TOTALIDAD DE LAS TRANSFERENCIAS A LA UNIVERSIDAD, UTILIZADA PARA GASTOS DIVERSOS (SALARIOS, ETC.), QUEDA INCLUIDA EN LA COLUMNA 3. EN 1970, LOS OTROS GASTOS DIRECTOS FIGURAN EN LA COLUMNA 7, Y EN 1977, LA ADMINISTRACION SE INCLUYE EN LA COLUMNA 3.

NORWAY:
E—> FOR 1970, ADMINISTRATION IS INCLUDED IN COLUMN 3.
FR—> EN 1970, L'ADMINISTRATION EST INCLUSE DANS LA COLONNE 3.
ESP> EN 1970, LA ADMINISTRACION SE INCLUYE EN LA COLUMNA 3.

PORTUGAL:
E—> EXPENDITURE OF THE MINISTRY OF EDUCATION ONLY.
FR—> DEPENSES DU MINISTERE DE L'EDUCATION SEULEMENT.
ESP> GASTOS DEL MINISTERIO DE EDUCACION SOLAMENTE.

SPAIN:
E—> FIGURES IN COLUMN 1 ARE IN MILLIONS.
FR—> LES CHIFFRES DE LA COLONNE 1 SONT EXPRIMES EN MILLIONS.
ESP> LAS CIFRAS DE LA COLUMNA 1 SE EXPRESAN EN MILLONES.

FIJI:
E—> THE TOTALITY OF TRANSFERS TO THE UNIVERSITY, USED FOR ALL PURPOSES (SALARIES, ETC.) IS INCLUDED IN COLUMN 3.
FR—> LA TOTALITE DES TRANSFERTS A L'UNIVERSITE, UTILISEE POUR DES DEPENSES DIVERSES (SALAIRES, ETC.) EST INCLUSE DANS LA COLONNE 3.
ESP> LA TOTALIDAD DE LAS TRANSFERENCIAS A LA UNIVERSIDAD, UTILIZADA PARA GASTOS DIVERSOS (SALARIOS, ETC.), QUEDA INCLUIDA EN LA COLUMNA 3.

FRENCH POLYNESIA:
E—> FOR 1970, OTHER DIRECT EXPENDITURE IS INCLUDED IN COLUMN 7.
FR—> EN 1970, LES AUTRES DEPENSES DIRECTES SONT INCLUSES DANS LA COLONNE 7.
ESP> EN 1970, LOS OTROS GASTOS DIRECTOS QUEDAN INCLUIDOS EN LA COLUMNA 7.

NEW HEBRIDES (EXPENDITURE IN AUSTRALIAN DOLLARS – DEPENSES EN DOLLARS AUSTRALIENS – GASTOS EN DOLARES AUSTRALIANOS):
E—> FOR 1970, OTHER DIRECT EXPENDITURE IS INCLUDED IN COLUMN 7.
FR—> EN 1970, LES AUTRES DEPENSES DIRECTES SONT INCLUSES DANS LA COLONNE 7.
ESP> EN 1970, LOS OTROS GASTOS DIRECTOS QUEDAN INCLUIDOS EN LA COLUMNA 7.

NEW HEBRIDES (EXPENDITURE IN FRENCH FRANCS – DEPENSES EN FRANCS FRANCAIS – GASTOS EN FRANCOS FRANCESES):
E—> FOR 1975, ADMINISTRATION IS INCLUDED IN COLUMN 3.
FR—> EN 1975, L'ADMINISTRATION EST INCLUSE DANS LA COLONNE 3.
ESP> EN 1975, LA ADMINISTRACION FIGURA EN LA COLUMNA 3.

Public current expenditure by purpose   4.2
Dépenses publiques ordinaires selon leur destination
Gastos públicos ordinarios según su destino

NIUE:
E—> FOR 1971, OTHER DIRECT EXPENDITURE IS IN-
CLUDED IN COLUMN 7. FOR 1975, ADMINISTRATION IS
INCLUDED IN COLUMN 3.
FR—> EN 1971, LES AUTRES DEPENSES DIRECTES SONT
INCLUSES DANS LA COLONNE 7. EN 1975, L'ADMINIS-
TRATION EST INCLUSE DANS LA COLONNE 3.
ESP> EN 1971, LOS OTROS GASTOS DIRECTOS QUEDAN
INCLUIDOS EN LA COLUMNA 7. EN 1975, LA COLUMNA
3 INCLUYE LA ADMINISTRACION.

PACIFIC ISLANDS:
E—> FOR 1970, OTHER DIRECT EXPENDITURE IS IN-
CLUDED IN COLUMN 7.
FR—> EN 1970, LES AUTRES DEPENSES DIRECTES SONT
INCLUSES DANS LA COLONNE 7.
ESP> EN 1970, LOS OTROS GASTOS DIRECTOS QUEDAN
INCLUIDOS EN LA COLUMNA 7.

TONGA:
E—> FOR 1971 AND 1975, EXPENDITURE OF THE
MINISTRY OF EDUCATION ONLY.
FR—> EN 1971 ET 1975, DEPENSES DU MINISTERE DE
L'EDUCATION SEULEMENT.
ESP> EN 1971 Y 1975, GASTOS DEL MINISTERIO DE
EDUCACION SOLAMENTE.

NEW ZEALAND:
E—> FOR 1975, WITH THE EXCEPTION OF SCHOLAR-
SHIPS TO STUDENTS WHICH ARE SHOWN IN THE APPRO-
PRIATE COLUMN, GRANTS TO UNIVERSITIES (USED FOR
ALL PURPOSES, SALARIES, ETC.) ARE INCLUDED IN
COLUMN 7. FOR 1976 AND 1977, SCHOLARSHIPS, AS
WELL AS GRANTS TO UNIVERSITIES ARE INCLUDED IN
COLUMN 7.
FR—> EN 1975 A L'EXCEPTION DES BOURSES AUX
ETUDIANTS QUI FIGURENT DANS LA COLONNE APPROPRIEE,
LES ALLOCATIONS AUX UNIVERSITES (UTILISEES POUR
DES DEPENSES DIVERSES, SALAIRES, ETC.) SONT
INCLUSES DANS LA COLONNE 7. EN 1976 ET 1977, LES
BOURSES D'ETUDES AINSI QUE LES ALLOCATIONS AUX
UNIVERSITES SONT INCLUSES DANS LA COLONNE 7.
ESP> EN 1975, Y SALVO LAS BECAS A LOS ESTUDIANTES
QUE FIGURAN EN LA COLUMNA APROPIADA, LOS SUBSIDIOS
A LAS UNIVERSIDADES UTILIZADOS PARA GASTOS
DIVERSOS, (SALARIOS, ETC.), QUEDAN INCLUIDOS EN LA
COLUMNA 7. EN 1976 Y 1977, LAS BECAS DE ESTUDIO
Y LOS SUBSIDIOS A LAS UNIVERSIDADES FIGURAN EN LA
COLUMNA 7.

4.3 Public current expenditure by level of education
Dépenses publiques ordinaires par degrés d'enseignement
Gastos públicos ordinarios por grados de enseñanza

4.3 Public current expenditure on education: distribution by level of education

Dépenses publiques ordinaires afférentes à l'enseignement: répartition par degrés d'enseignement

Gastos públicos ordinarios destinados a la educación: distribución por grados de enseñanza

NUMBER OF COUNTRIES AND TERRITORIES PRESENTED IN THIS TABLE: 156
NOMBRE DE PAYS ET DE TERRITOIRES PRESENTES DANS CE TABLEAU: 156
NUMERO DE PAISES Y DE TERRITORIOS PRESENTADOS EN ESTE CUADRO: 156

COUNTRY / PAYS / PAIS	YEAR / ANNEE / AÑO	CURRENCY / MONNAIE / MONEDA	TOTAL (000)	PRE-PRIMARY / PRE-PRIMAIRE / PRE-PRIMARIA	1ST LEVEL / 1ER DEGRE / 1ER GRADO	SECOND LEVEL / SECOND DEGRE / SEGUNDO GRADO TOTAL	GENERAL / GENERAL / GENERAL	TEACHER-TRAINING / NORMAL / NORMAL	OTHER / AUTRE / OTRA	3RD LEVEL / 3EME DEGRE / 3ER GRADO	OTHER TYPES / AUTRES TYPES / OTROS TIPOS	NOT DISTRIBUTED / NON RE-PARTIES / SIN DISTRIBUCION
			(1)	(2)	(3)	(4)	(5)	(6)	(7)	(8)	(9)	(10)
AFRICA												
ALGERIA ‡	1974	DINAR	1 609 900	-	54.8	40.3	36.3	4.0	./.	...	0.5	4.4
BENIN ‡	1970	FRANC C.F.A.	2 922 402	-	50.0	33.8	23.7	2.3	7.7	4.9	0.9	10.4
	1975		5 649 652	-	37.3	36.8	27.1	1.1	8.6	11.4	1.4	13.1
BOTSWANA	1970	PULA	2 559	-	57.6	29.8	17.5	4.7	7.6	8.8	-	3.9
	1975		8 688	-	46.5	33.5	25.7	3.4	4.3	13.6	-	6.5
	1976		12 025	-	52.6	26.4	20.9	2.3	3.3	15.8	-	5.2
	1977		15 920	-	49.9	33.4	24.9	4.3	4.2	14.7	-	2.0
BURUNDI	1975	FRANC	721 831	-	45.0	33.3	13.0	12.4	7.9	19.5	0.9	1.2
	1976		884 608	-	42.9	34.3	14.3	12.6	7.3	19.5	1.6	1.8
CENTRAL AFRICAN REPUBLIC	1975	FRANC C.F.A.	3 393 000	-	54.5	14.5	...	...	...	9.9	1.1	20.1
	1976		3 925 000	-	54.2	14.8	...	...	...	11.4	0.9	18.6
	1977		4 389 000	-	53.8	14.9	...	...	...	12.9	0.8	17.6
COMORO	1971	FRANC	643 104	-	37.9	39.0	38.6	0.4	-	5.1	-	18.0

Public current expenditure by level of education   4.3
Dépenses publiques ordinaires par degrés d'enseignement
Gastos públicos ordinarios por grados de enseñanza

Country	Currency	Year	(1)	(2)	(3)	(4)	(5)	(6)	(7)	(8)	(9)	(10)
CONGO ‡	FRANC C.F.A.	1970	4 223 345	0.2	48.7	36.3	21.6	4.1	10.6	9.6	0.4	4.8
		1975	10 537 237	0.8	34.3	31.9	20.1	3.0	8.8	28.6	0.2	4.3
		1976	13 850 859	1.0	33.6	34.3	22.9	11.5	→	23.7	0.1	7.3
DJIBOUTI	FRANC	1970	324 920	—	48.3	50.9	...	...	...	—	—	0.8
		1974	1 479 821	—	47.5	43.3	...	...	...	—	—	9.2
EGYPT ‡	POUND	1970	134 423	./.	./.	79.6	...	...	...	20.4	—	—
		1975	226 668	./.	./.	70.0	...	...	...	30.0	—	—
		1976	283 742	./.	./.	72.2	...	...	...	27.8	—	—
		1977	330 427	./.	./.	67.2	...	...	...	32.8	—	—
ETHIOPIA ‡	BIRR	1970	60 539	—	55.4	35.6	25.4	4.7	5.6	...	0.4	8.5
		1975	112 859	—	47.9	50.7	42.8	4.1	3.8	...	1.4	—
GAMBIA ‡	DALASI	1970	2 415	—	43.3	26.0	20.9	3.6	1.6	25.1	—	30.6
		1975	5 471	—	44.0	21.3	16.9	1.7	2.7	16.8	—	34.6
		1976	7 356	—	42.9	19.7	16.0	1.6	2.0	2.1	—	43.0
GHANA ‡	CEDI	1970	83 813	—	39.2	27.8	14.7	10.6	2.4		0.5	7.9
		1975	240 682	—	24.5	37.0	28.7	5.6	2.7		0.7	21.3
		1976	293 102	—	31.9	46.0	36.8	5.7	3.5			19.3
GUINEA-BISSAU ‡	ESCUDO	1978	270 684	—	44.0	36.2	16.3	16.3	67.4	12.7	6.8	0.3
IVORY COAST ‡	FRANC C.F.A.	1970	21 318 402	—	28.7	35.7	26.5	1.4	7.8	13.8	11.6	10.2
		1975	48 123 000	—	37.0	38.6	36.4	2.1	—	18.7	—	5.7
		1976	61 888 000	—	39.9	37.5	35.9	1.6	—	17.0	—	5.6
		1977	70 354 000	—	39.9	37.0	34.7	2.2	—	17.9	—	5.3
KENYA ‡	SHILLING	1970	422 320	—	48.8	31.9	22.4	6.0	3.5	13.6	0.5	5.1
		1975	1 331 734	—	65.4	18.8	14.3	3.3	1.2	11.0	0.4	4.4
		1976	1 421 176	—	63.1	18.8	14.0	3.6	1.2	13.0	0.4	4.7
LESOTHO	RAND	1970	2 081	0.1	59.3	20.7	12.9	4.3	3.5	14.7	—	5.3
		1973	3 016	0.2	47.5	18.5	12.3	3.5	2.7	23.8	—	10.2
LIBERIA ‡	DOLLAR	1975	13 866	—	27.3	28.4	15.8	5.3	7.3	20.4	1.2	22.6
LIBYAN ARAB JAMAHIRIYA	DINAR	1977	183 160	—	47.4	30.5	24.7	4.8	1.1	15.6	4.8	1.7
MADAGASCAR ‡	FRANC	1970	8 637 345	—	48.5	19.3	11.5	3.5	4.2	25.0	1.6	5.7
		1975	11 726 747	—	42.9	30.5	19.1	4.2	7.2	13.9	—	12.7
		1976	16 149 414	—	42.2	29.0	17.6	3.9	7.5	16.5	—	12.2
MALAWI	KWACHA	1970	7 958	—	42.3	24.5	18.1	4.4	2.0	25.5	1.8	6.0
		1975	11 992	—	44.6	23.2	17.7	4.1	1.5	22.8	1.8	7.5
MALI ‡	FRANC	1975	11 670 222	0.1	39.7	25.5	17.7	4.4	3.5	22.9	0.9	11.0
		1977	16 312 518	0.2	46.0	26.4	13.8	4.5	8.0	20.1	0.8	6.4
MAURITANIA ‡	OUGUIYA	1975	723 100	—	45.3	39.5	25.7	6.0	7.7	14.6	0.3	0.3
		1976	836 800	—	39.9	42.9	26.1	9.1	7.7	16.5	0.3	0.4
		1977	1 082 000	—	36.5	48.8	33.0	8.2	7.5	14.1	0.2	0.3
MAURITIUS	RUPEE	1970	35 723	—	68.8	21.1	15.0	5.4	0.5	6.2	0.2	3.7
		1974	86 126	—	66.9	15.8	10.2	4.4	1.2	10.0	0.1	7.3
		1976	197 000	—	50.5	31.1	25.9	2.8	2.4	9.7	3.5	5.2
		1977	246 700	—	41.1	39.4	36.2	1.9	1.3	9.0	3.6	6.9

4.3 Public current expenditure by level of education
Dépenses publiques ordinaires par degrés d'enseignement
Gastos públicos ordinarios por grados de enseñanza

COUNTRY / PAYS / PAIS	YEAR ANNEE AÑO	CURRENCY MONNAIE MONEDA	TOTAL (000) (1)	PRE-PRIMARY PRE-PRIMAIRE PRE-PRIMARIA (2)	1ST LEVEL 1ER DEGRE 1ER GRADO (3)	SECOND LEVEL / SECOND DEGRE / SEGUNDO GRADO — TOTAL (4)	GENERAL GENE-RAL NORMAL (5)	TEACHER TRAINING GENE-RAL NORMAL (6)	OTHER AUTRE OTRA GRADO (7)	3RD LEVEL 3EME DEGRE 3ER GRADO (8)	OTHER TYPES AUTRES TYPES OTROS TIPOS (9)	NOT DISTRIBUTED NON RE-PARTIES SIN DISTRIBUCION (10)
MOROCCO	1970	DIRHAM	649 357	—	44.8	44.7	...	...	...	10.6	—	—
	1976		1 801 546	—	39.5	47.1	...	...	...	13.4	—	—
	1977		2 222 766	—	35.7	49.3	...	...	...	15.1	—	—
	1978		2 682 184	—	36.4	48.6	...	...	...	15.0	—	—
NIGER	1970	FRANC C.F.A.	1 917 650	—	60.5	25.2	23.7	——>	1.6	2.6	1.8	9.8
NIGERIA	1970	NAIRA	132 648	—	40.4	23.9	...	...	...	20.0	2.4	13.4
	1974		326 361	—	22.7	15.6	...	...	...	42.0	0.4	19.4
RWANDA	1970	FRANC	491 000	—	66.4	19.0	...	...	...	9.9	0.0	4.7
	1975		1 197 164	—	68.9	16.6	...	...	...	10.8	0.3	3.4
	1976		1 239 492	—	67.6	17.6	...	...	...	11.9	0.4	2.5
	1977		1 504 570	—	65.5	16.5	...	...	...	14.1	1.4	2.5
	1978		1 651 190	—	66.9	17.4	...	...	...	12.1	1.0	2.6
ST. HELENA ‡	1970	POUND STERLING	50	./.	14.0	52.0	40.0	6.0	6.0	2.0	8.0	24.0
	1975		79	1.3	./.	49.3	...	—	—	—	1.3	48.1
SENEGAL	1976	FRANC C.F.A.	15 643 100	—	49.8	21.1	13.3	——>	7.8	21.8	4.8	2.5
SEYCHELLES	1970	RUPEE	3 855	—	44.4	42.5	36.7	—	5.8	7.6	1.0	5.5
	1975		11 202	—	53.1	39.1	33.9	—	5.2	6.8	1.0	
	1976		14 866	—	33.8	33.1	27.0	—	6.1	10.2	1.8	21.0
SOMALIA	1970	SHILLING	23 664	1.2	62.5	26.9	23.6	3.3	—>	1.3	1.7	7.7
	1973		32 167		53.5	22.3	...	...	...	1.9	1.6	19.5
SUDAN	1970	POUND	25 309	0.2	40.1	22.4	16.9	2.8	2.7	17.8	3.4	16.2
SWAZILAND ‡	1975	LILANGENI	6 186	—	32.2	40.6	34.6	6.0	—	18.7	—	8.5
	1977		8 811	—	37.9	35.5	30.7	4.8	—	19.5	0.1	7.0
	1978		10 248	—	36.9	38.2	33.4	4.8	—	18.3	0.1	6.6
TOGO ‡	1970	FRANC C.F.A.	1 414 917	1.3	64.1	22.0	...	...	...	1.9	2.2	8.5
UGANDA ‡	1970	SHILLING	244 431	—	48.8	30.7	23.6	5.7	1.4	20.5	—	
	1975		529 014	—	41.1	33.4	25.4	5.9	2.1	21.9	—	3.6
UNITED REPUBLIC OF CAMEROON	1970	FRANC C.F.A.	9 644 852	—	40.7	28.4	15.0	4.3	9.1	15.8	6.9	8.2

Public current expenditure by level of education 4.3
Dépenses publiques ordinaires par degrés d'enseignement
Gastos públicos ordinarios por grados de enseñanza

Country	Currency	Year	(1)	(2)	(3)	(4)	(5)	(6)	(7)	(8)	(9)	(10)
UNITED REPUBLIC OF TANZANIA ‡	SHILLING	1970	337 600	—	41.5	22.5	17.2	5.3	./	12.0	16.8	7.2
		1976	727 900	—	50.5	25.5	17.6	8.0	./	12.6	4.8	6.5
		1977	1 090 090	—	56.8	23.4	16.6	5.6	1.2	15.0	4.9	—
UPPER VOLTA ‡	FRANC C.F.A.	1975	3 171 371	—	43.3	26.2	...	...	...	24.8	0.1	5.6
		1977	4 279 627	—	41.6	26.3	...	...	...	27.8	0.1	4.1
WESTERN SAHARA ‡	PESETA	1970	44 322	6.0	58.3	24.9	24.9	...	...	—	8.0	2.8
		1973	86 332	./.	65.8	28.5	28.5	...	...	—	5.8	—
ZAMBIA	KWACHA	1970	44 391	—	44.2	35.4	27.3	3.0	5.1	8.0	—	12.5
		1975	75 420	—	45.3	33.9	22.2	2.8	8.9	7.8	—	13.0
		1977	95 461	—	47.1	33.3	22.7	2.8	7.8	9.4	—	10.2
		1978	101 230	—	47.8	33.8	23.1	2.8	7.9	9.4	—	9.0
AMERICA, NORTH												
ANTIGUA	E. CARIBBEAN DOLLAR	1970	2 233	—	63.6	27.6	20.9	4.1	2.6	2.4	1.9	4.5
		1975	5 681	—	29.2	35.2	24.4	3.2	7.7	16.7	3.5	15.3
		1976	6 742	—	30.1	32.0	22.6	2.7	6.7	19.9	2.4	15.6
		1977	7 013	—	28.0	32.4	23.8	8.6	>	19.2	1.3	19.2
BARBADOS	DOLLAR	1970	19 784	—	34.7	34.0	31.2	—	2.8	13.0	2.6	15.7
		1975	42 256	—	27.3	29.7	27.7	—	2.0	18.5	1.3	23.2
		1976	*47 397	—	*27.0	*28.5	*26.6	—	*1.9	*19.5	*1.3	*23.7
BELIZE	DOLLAR	1970	3 211	—	57.0	17.0	9.9	—	7.1	13.3	—	12.7
BERMUDA	DOLLAR	1970	9 735	—								
		1974		3.3	36.1	37.4	...	...	...	11.7	4.7	6.9
BRITISH VIRGIN ISLANDS	UNITED STATES DOLLAR	1970	639	./.	48.0	39.0	...	...	...	2.8	3.1	7.0
		1975	967	./.	43.4	40.0	...	...	...	6.3	0.3	9.9
		1976	907	./.	45.5	34.3	...	...	...	9.2	1.1	9.9
		1977	1 026	./.	44.6	46.7	...	...	...	8.3	0.4	—
CANADA ‡	DOLLAR	1970	6 122 500	./.	./.	65.1	...	...	...	27.5	7.4	—
		1975	11 381 459	./.	./.	60.4	...	...	...	26.3	12.7	0.6
		1976	13 233 587	./.	./.	60.4	...	...	...	26.3	12.7	0.6
		1977	14 994 978	./.	./.	60.4	...	...	...	26.3	12.7	0.6
COSTA RICA ‡	COLON	1970	318 500	./.	51.2	18.9	...	...	...	10.5		19.4
		1975	1 041 297	./.	37.2	22.4	16.9	...	5.5	24.4	1.0	15.1
		1976	1 318 369	./.	33.7	22.3	16.6	...	5.7	28.2	4.6	11.2
DOMINICAN REPUBLIC	PESO	1970	39 306	—	41.1	18.3	...	...	...	20.7	7.6	12.5
		1976	62 595	—	37.5	20.4	15.1	1.7	3.5	19.6	3.8	18.6
		1977	67 783	—	34.9	19.9	14.7	1.9	3.3	18.8	3.6	22.8
EL SALVADOR	COLON	1970	69 621	—	57.9	11.8	9.3	1.1	0.3	21.4	2.5	6.4
		1975	138 364	—	57.5	6.6	6.3		0.3	23.7	1.3	10.9
		1976	182 715	—	56.1	5.3	4.8		0.5	22.1	1.7	14.8
		1977	213 536	—	54.6	5.3	4.9		0.4	22.8	2.0	15.4
GRENADA	DOLLAR	1970	3 665	—	91.5	>	...	...	...	8.5	—	—
		1975	5 478	—	53.5	19.9	...	...	...	19.3	—	7.3
		1977	7 155	—	49.1	20.0	...	...	...	15.6	—	15.3
		1978	8 865	—	52.0	20.5	...	...	...	14.1	—	13.4

4.3 Public current expenditure by level of education
Dépenses publiques ordinaires par degrés d'enseignement
Gastos públicos ordinarios por grados de enseñanza

COUNTRY / PAYS / PAIS	YEAR ANNEE AÑO	CURRENCY MONNAIE MONEDA	(1) TOTAL (000)	(2) PRE-PRIMARY	(3) 1ST LEVEL	(4) SECOND LEVEL TOTAL	(5) GENERAL	(6) TEACHER TRAINING	(7) OTHER	(8) 3RD LEVEL	(9) OTHER TYPES	(10) NOT DISTRIBUTED
GUATEMALA	1970	QUETZAL	32 566	2.8	55.2	16.9	6.8	3.5	6.7	13.1	4.5	7.4
	1976		67 193	2.5	51.3	15.5	8.9	2.9	3.6	19.9	3.3	7.5
HAITI ‡	1970	GOURDE	25 098	—	65.1	17.8	10.5	7.4	→	9.1	./.	8.0
	1975		34 138	—	63.0	17.5	11.1	6.5	→	11.4	./.	8.1
	1976		37 191	—	63.5	17.7	11.0	6.7	→	11.0	3.3	4.6
HONDURAS	1970	LEMPIRA	41 660	—	64.2	15.4	8.6	2.8	4.1	12.2	1.7	6.5
	1977		89 920	4.1	68.4	9.6	6.8	1.1	1.7	16.5	1.4	—
JAMAICA ‡	1970	DOLLAR	28 877	./.	44.7	35.6				8.8	1.0	9.8
	1975		121 854	2.2	33.5	32.3	28.9	—	3.5	19.8	1.9	10.3
	1976		139 820	3.0	30.3	35.3	31.2	0.9	3.2	21.1	0.7	9.6
MEXICO ‡	1970	PESO	7 148 400	3.1	47.7	27.2	19.7	1.7	5.7	10.4		11.5
	1975		26 783 000	2.3	42.9	31.1	...	...	...	12.6	0.8	10.3
	1976		36 507 080	2.4	41.4	18.2	11.1	0.4	6.8	22.4	4.2	11.3
	1977		53 627 996	2.3	40.4	19.5	10.7	—	8.7	28.8	4.5	4.5
NETHERLANDS ANTILLES	1971	GUILDER	15 664	3.7	77.2	→	...		...	7.1	6.5	5.5
	1977		104 900	4.4	29.6	23.8	...		...	1.8	23.2	17.2
NICARAGUA	1970	CORDOBA	120 901	—	57.9	17.6	11.1	3.0	3.6	10.0	9.7	4.8
	1978		323 058	—	49.5	28.5	15.5	2.1	10.9	12.5	9.5	—
PANAMA ‡	1970	BALBOA	50 824	—	38.9	18.7	14.3	3.1	6.1	10.8	18.4	13.2
	1975		96 693	—	39.1	23.5	11.2	2.7	7.2	12.6	./.	24.8
	1977		112 387	—	41.5	21.1	12.1	2.9	7.7	13.6	./.	23.9
	1978		109 675	—	45.9	22.7				15.4	./.	16.0
FORMER CANAL ZONE ‡	1970	UNITED STATES DOLLAR	16 034	./.	94.3	→				5.7	—	—
	1975		22 472	./.	93.9	→				6.1	—	—
	1976		20 532	./.	92.7	→				7.3	—	—
	1977		23 300	./.	93.7	→				6.3	—	—
PUERTO RICO ‡	1970	UNITED STATES DOLLAR	344 030	./.	75.2	→				24.8	—	—
	1975		568 387	./.	68.4	→				31.6	—	—
	1976		569 581	./.	69.9	→				30.1	—	—
	1977		656 206	./.	71.4	→				28.6	—	—
ST. KITTS – NEVIS ANGUILLA ‡	1970	E. CARIBBEAN DOLLAR	1 381	—	65.2	31.6	...		...	3.2	—	—
	1975		2 541	—	51.6	35.9	...		...	12.6	—	—
	1977		3 944	—	44.8	42.3	...		...	12.9	—	—
	1978		4 354	—	43.3	44.3	...		...	12.4	—	—

Public current expenditure by level of education **4.3**
Dépenses publiques ordinaires par degrés d'enseignement
Gastos públicos ordinarios por grados de enseñanza

Country	Currency	Year	(1)	(2)	(3)	(4)	(5)	(6)	(7)	(8)	(9)	(10)
ST. LUCIA	E. CARIBBEAN DOLLAR	1975	7 321	—	46.6	34.9	...	...	...	10.0	0.1	8.4
		1976	10 614	—	46.3	28.5	...	...	...	11.8	0.1	13.4
ST. VINCENT AND THE GRENADINES	E. CARIBBEAN DOLLAR	1970	1 795	—	75.6	20.1	15.9	3.1	1.0	—	0.8	3.6
		1975	5 196	—	52.6	19.9	13.7	1.9	4.3	—	1.4	26.1
		1976	5 546	—	52.7	20.0	14.0	1.9	4.2	—	1.7	25.6
		1977	5 877	—	53.6	20.2	14.4	1.8	4.1	—	1.7	24.5
TRINIDAD AND TOBAGO	DOLLAR	1970	53 335	—	52.5	24.0	21.3	—	2.7	13.9	1.0	8.5
		1976	182 207	—	42.8	20.0	18.6	—	1.4	21.0	0.3	15.9
TURKS AND CAICOS ISLANDS	DOLLAR	1975	601	—	52.2	22.8	22.6	0.2	...	—	—	25.1
		1976	646	—	46.0	41.3	...	...	...	—	—	12.7
UNITED STATES OF AMERICA ‡	DOLLAR	1970	56 000	./.	70.5	↑	...	...	...	29.5	—	—
		1975	90 300	./.	67.5	↑	...	...	...	32.5	—	—
		1976	100 900	./.	70.4	↑	...	...	...	29.6	—	—
		1977	109 900	./.	69.9	↑	...	...	...	30.1	—	—
U.S. VIRGIN ISLANDS ‡	UNITED STATES DOLLAR	1970	13 985	./.	75.6	↑	...	...	...	24.4	—	—
		1975	40 138	./.	84.6	↑	...	...	...	15.4	—	—
		1976	48 484	./.	85.1	↑	...	...	...	14.9	—	—
		1977	48 122	./.	85.7	↑	...	...	...	14.3	—	—
AMERICA, SOUTH												
ARGENTINA ‡	PESO	1970	1 620	1.4	29.0	30.3	17.9	3.0	9.4	21.0	2.2	16.2
		1975	33 562	./.	27.0	30.5	...	—	...	30.2	—	12.3
		1976	105 086	./.	27.3	33.1	22.9	—	10.1	27.3	—	12.3
		1977	426 417	./.	39.9	29.2	22.6	1.7	6.6	20.6	1.7	8.6
BOLIVIA	PESO	1970	396 056	1.9	60.2	12.8	11.0	...	1.8	10.9	2.0	12.0
		1975	1 658 659	2.1	60.4	7.3	...	...	...	15.0	2.3	13.0
		1976	2 205 451	2.1	60.5	6.5	...	...	...	18.4	2.4	10.1
		1977	2 644 057	2.4	67.2	6.4	...	...	...	15.6	2.7	5.6
BRAZIL ‡	CRUZEIRO	1975	25 194 300	./.	62.7	↑	...	...	...	26.1	2.3	8.9
		1976	39 355 200	./.	55.9	↑	...	...	...	27.5	1.6	15.0
		1977	61 296 200	./.	51.0	↑	...	...	...	29.8	1.7	17.5
CHILE ‡	PESO	1975	1 321 482	./.	34.9	13.5	7.7	—	5.8	25.2	4.1	22.4
COLOMBIA ‡	PESO	1970	1 545 185	0.1	36.5	16.9	6.8	4.0	6.2	23.9	1.4	21.2
		1973	3 294 665	0.3	43.8	22.0	7.2	3.2	11.6	10.5	0.8	22.6
ECUADOR	SUCRE	1970	1 133 523	—	45.9	41.0	22.0	7.9	11.1	9.9	1.1	2.0
		1977	5 756 300	—	40.4	29.5	22.2	—	7.3	24.0	0.7	5.3
GUYANA ‡	DOLLAR	1970	19 089	—	46.5	34.4	25.3	1.4	7.8	14.7	0.1	4.2
		1975	45 277	—	44.8	33.3	29.5	—	3.8	15.9	1.5	4.5
		1977	71 796	5.6	35.2	32.3	27.0	—	5.3	19.5	1.2	6.1
PARAGUAY	GUARANI	1970	1 421 834	—	64.8	17.1	12.0	2.2	2.8	16.5	1.7	9.2
		1973	1 688 671	—	56.5	15.1	8.9	1.3	4.8	17.9	1.3	
PERU ‡	SOL	1970	6 334 286	1.5	54.9	28.7	21.8	—	6.9	2.7	6.6	5.7
		1975	15 639 801	2.6	54.6	27.9	20.0	—	7.8	2.5	5.9	6.5
		1976	20 428 076	2.7	54.2	28.0	20.2	—	7.8	2.7	5.9	6.4
		1977	22 658 547	3.2	58.8	29.2	21.1	—	8.1	3.5	5.4	—

4.3 Public current expenditure by level of education
Dépenses publiques ordinaires par degrés d'enseignement
Gastos públicos ordinarios por grados de enseñanza

COUNTRY / PAYS / PAIS	YEAR / ANNEE / AÑO	CURRENCY / MONNAIE / MONEDA	TOTAL (000) (1)	PRE-PRIMARY / PRE-PRIMAIRE / PRE-PRIMARIA (2)	1ST LEVEL / 1ER DEGRE / 1ER GRADO (3)	SECOND LEVEL / SECOND DEGRE / SEGUNDO GRADO TOTAL (4)	GENERAL / GENERAL NORMAL (5)	TEACHER TRAINING / NORMAL (6)	OTHER / AUTRE / OTRA (7)	3RD LEVEL / 3EME DEGRE / 3ER GRADO (8)	OTHER TYPES / AUTRES TYPES / OTROS TIPOS (9)	NOT DISTRIBUTED / NON RE-PARTIES / SIN DISTRI-BUCION (10)
URUGUAY ‡	1970	PESO	22 017	./.	45.1	30.4	18.8	./.	11.6	19.0	–	5.5
VENEZUELA ‡	1970	BOLIVAR	2 220 651	./.	38.3	20.6	9.6	1.0	10.0	25.5	8.5	7.0
	1975		5 965 747	./.	22.1	18.4	11.4	0.5	6.5	37.0	1.4	21.0
ASIA												
AFGHANISTAN ‡	1970	AFGHANI	817 276	–	28.6	41.7	22.8	10.9	8.0	20.4	–	9.3
	1974		1 142 630	–	38.3	34.0	22.3	6.5	5.3	17.7	1.7	9.9
	1977		1 636 529	2.8	95.5	>						
BAHRAIN	1970	DINAR	3 668	–	48.7	40.6	34.9	–	5.7	4.7	–	6.0
BANGLADESH ‡	1973	TAKA	648 166	–	60.3	13.9	...	...	...	16.2	9.6	–
	1975		929 862	–	57.0	16.5	...	...	...	17.4	9.1	–
	1976		*1 020 102	–	*56.8	*15.2	...	...	...	*16.1	*12.0	–
BHUTAN ‡	1970	INDIAN RUPEE	4 982	–	22.0	70.0	58.9	3.0	8.1	–	1.7	6.3
	1974		12 853	–	13.6	23.9	13.0	0.9	10.1	52.8	–	9.6
	1977		14 975	1.9	18.2	23.6	14.2	2.6	6.8	45.8	–	10.5
BRUNEI	1970	DOLLAR	19 387	–	44.0	42.9	33.5	6.6	2.8	9.7	3.4	1.6
	1975		47 354	–	33.0	53.2	36.2	10.4	6.5	8.9	3.3	1.6
	1976		53 592	–	33.8	53.3	35.5	9.8	8.0	8.2	3.1	1.6
BURMA ‡	1971	KYAT	280 500	–	33.9	42.8	38.4	1.7	2.7	16.8	–	6.5
	1975		385 990	–	87.7	>	...	...	...	10.7	–	1.5
	1976		432 658	–	88.7	>	...	...	...	9.7	–	1.6
	1977		470 430	–	87.1	>	...	...	...	10.6	–	2.3
CYPRUS ‡	1970	POUND	5 681	0.5	46.5	40.2	32.0	–	8.1	6.9	3.5	2.4
	1975		10 325	0.5	42.7	48.8	40.3	–	8.5	3.4	2.7	1.9
	1976		11 710	0.9	41.0	49.6	41.2	–	8.4	3.3	3.3	2.0
	1977		12 895	0.8	39.1	50.6	41.9	–	8.8	3.8	3.4	2.2
HONG KONG	1970	DOLLAR	483 186	–	54.9	21.2	16.3	1.8	3.2	19.2	2.6	2.1
	1975		1 144 538	–	48.7	26.3	20.4	1.4	4.4	20.6	3.5	0.9
	1976		1 360 869	–	46.7	27.6	21.8	1.3	4.5	21.4	3.6	0.7
	1977		1 578 216	–	43.5	29.0	23.1	1.1	4.8	22.0	3.0	2.5
INDIA ‡	1970	RUPEE	10 579 660	0.2	22.2	42.5	41.7	0.1	0.7	24.6	1.4	9.2
	1975		21 047 180	0.2	21.2	40.3	39.7	0.1	0.6	22.0	1.5	14.8

Public current expenditure by level of education 4.3
Dépenses publiques ordinaires par degrés d'enseignement
Gastos públicos ordinarios por grados de enseñanza

Country	Currency	Year	(1)	(2)	(3)	(4)	(5)	(6)	(7)	(8)	(9)	(10)
IRAN	RIAL	1970	19 715 000	—	50.9	23.3	17.2	2.0	4.1	12.9	1.2	11.7
		1974	76 182 358	0.6	31.3	26.8	20.8	3.2	2.9	17.7	1.4	22.3
		1976	230 748 564	1.4	19.0	19.8	13.1	4.0	2.7	43.1	—	16.7
IRAQ ‡	DINAR	1970	60 228	./.	60.1	20.3	18.1	——→	2.2	17.0	—	2.7
		1976	155 763	./.	45.3	16.2	...	..	..	18.1	1.5	18.9
		1977	198 903	./.	43.5	18.4	...	..	..	25.3	1.3	11.4
ISRAEL ‡	POUND	1970	1 157 000	6.3	32.2	26.3	11.7	—	14.6	26.1	2.9	6.2
		1975	4 641 000	6.1	32.7	25.5	...	—	...	30.1	0.8	4.8
JAPAN ‡	YEN	1970	2 098 677	0.9	37.6	37.3	...	...	...	12.7	4.2	7.3
		1975	5 826 604	1.3	39.1	37.2	...	...	...	10.2	5.3	6.9
		1976	6 613 456	1.3	38.7	36.2	...	...	...	10.8	5.3	7.8
		1977	7 262 222	1.3	38.9	35.9	...	...	...	11.1	5.6	7.2
JORDAN ‡	DINAR	1970	7 239	—	./.	78.2	76.0	—	2.1	10.8	5.7	5.3
		1975	13 900	—	./.	78.4	74.3	—	4.1	4.6	0.4	17.1
		1976	16 957	—	./.	82.0	79.0	—	3.0	3.6	0.1	14.3
		1977	22 598	—	./.	78.5	74.7	—	3.8	3.8	0.3	17.4
KOREA, REPUBLIC OF ‡	WON	1970	73 809	—	64.3	23.1	...	—	...	8.3	0.3	4.1
		1975	163 800	—	62.4	25.5	...	—	...	12.2	—	—
		1976	350 315	—	68.3	23.4	...	—	...	8.1	0.2	—
		1977	411 499	—	60.7	31.8	...	—	...	7.3	0.2	—
KUWAIT	DINAR	1970	34 630	6.4	19.3	49.1	41.2	5.3	2.6	9.4	6.0	9.7
		1976	113 750	5.5	26.8	35.8	...	—	...	16.0	2.7	13.2
		1977	129 183	5.7	28.5	46.1	...	—	...	17.1	2.6	—
LAO PEOPLE'S DEMOCRATIC REPUBLIC	KIP	1970	2 058 777	—	62.5	23.6	7.5	12.0	4.1	7.0	1.4	5.6
MALAYSIA	RINGGIT	1971	536 200	—	44.9	29.7	26.7	2.4	0.6	10.3	0.4	14.8
PENINSULAR MALAYSIA	RINGGIT	1970	442 039	—	49.9	26.4	25.7	—	0.6	14.2	0.3	9.3
		1975	992 192	—	41.4	33.8	32.7	—	1.1	13.1	5.3	6.5
		1976	1 101 567	—	39.1	29.4	28.3	—	1.1	19.5	4.7	7.2
		1977	1 571 180	—	39.2	29.4	28.2	—	1.2	15.8	4.3	11.3
SABAH	RINGGIT	1975	89 559	—	49.1	45.6	39.3	5.1	1.1	...	—	5.3
		1976	73 715	—	51.4	40.1	33.5	5.4	1.2	...	—	8.5
SARAWAK	RINGGIT	1975	74 491	—	56.2	38.8	35.0	3.3	0.5	—	0.4	4.7
		1976	85 347	—	52.7	41.8	37.4	3.9	0.5	—	0.5	5.0
		1977	100 861	—	49.0	45.4	40.5	4.4	0.5	—	1.0	4.6
MONGOLIA ‡	TUGRIK	1970	276 982	11.5	./.	60.3	47.3	13.0	——→	13.9	11.7	2.5
NEPAL	RUPEE	1971	58 958	—	23.0	23.2	...	...	...	31.6	5.1	17.1
		1975	201 776	—	29.3	22.1	...	...	...	12.3	23.1	13.2
OMAN	RIAL	1974	3 920	—	88.2	3.9	1.5	—	2.3	8.1	—	19.1
		1976	9 193	—	64.1	5.8	...	—	...	11.0	—	—
PAKISTAN	RUPEE	1970	480 370	—	39.7	32.5	17.4	2.3	12.9	16.4	—	11.4
		1975	1 731 089	—	41.1	30.3	19.9	1.3	9.1	17.2	—	11.5
		1976	2 020 279	—	39.3	32.9	23.8	1.2	7.9	17.4	—	10.4
		1977	2 445 697	—	28.5	23.3	16.7	1.0	5.7	15.5	—	32.7

4.3 Public current expenditure by level of education
Dépenses publiques ordinaires par degrés d'enseignement
Gastos públicos ordinarios por grados de enseñanza

COUNTRY / PAYS / PAIS	YEAR ANNEE AÑO	CURRENCY MONNAIE MONEDA	TOTAL (000) (1)	PRE-PRIMARY PRE-PRIMAIRE PRE-PRIMARIA (2)	1ST LEVEL 1ER DEGRE 1ER GRADO (3)	SECOND LEVEL / SECOND DEGRE / SEGUNDO GRADO				3RD LEVEL 3EME DEGRE 3ER GRADO (8)	OTHER TYPES AUTRES TYPES OTROS TIPOS (9)	NOT DISTRI-BUTED NON RE-PARTIES SIN DISTRI-BUCION (10)
						TOTAL (4)	GENE-RAL GENE-RAL GENE-RAL (5)	TEACHER-TRAIN-ING NORMAL NORMAL (6)	OTHER AUTRE OTRA (7)			
PHILIPPINES ‡	1970	PESO	1 069 600	-	82.9	3.9	...	...	...	13.2	-	
	1976		2 266 373	-	65.7	6.7	...	...	...	22.4	-	5.3
	1977		2 624 438	-	61.4	7.1	...	...	...	25.9	-	5.7
	1978		3 635 403	-	57.9	6.7	...	...	...	19.9	-	15.5
QATAR	1970	RIYAL	41 029	0.1	40.7	23.2	14.8	3.6	4.8	7.2	4.2	24.7
	1975		123 524	0.2	32.8	32.5	24.2	3.7	4.6	9.4	3.7	21.5
	1976		187 392	0.2	32.6	25.4	20.8	2.2	2.4	13.2	3.0	25.5
	1977		283 110	0.1	37.9	28.2	23.7	2.1	2.4	10.7	3.8	19.3
SAUDI ARABIA ‡	1974	RIYAL	3 760 283	./.	43.3	15.9	2.4	10.1	3.3	39.8	1.0	—
SINGAPORE	1970	DOLLAR	173 599	-	44.2	33.5	23.6	-	9.9	14.7	1.0	6.6
	1975		339 870	-	38.1	34.3	26.2	-	8.0	17.6	6.4	3.7
	1976		343 511	-	38.8	36.0	27.7	-	8.3	15.3	6.0	3.9
	1977		363 333	-	38.5	36.4	28.4	-	8.0	14.8	6.4	4.0
SRI LANKA ‡	1970	RUPEE	506 392	-	60.9	25.0	81.9	1.5	1.1	7.1	2.7	4.4
	1975		682 680	-	./.	84.5	...	...	...	6.5	-	9.0
SYRIAN ARAB REPUBLIC ‡	1970	POUND	249 312	-	43.0	28.2	23.8	0.5	3.9	22.1		6.8
	1975		623 400	-	38.4	30.0	26.4	0.6	3.0	25.8	0.3	5.6
	1976		1 056 998	-	27.8	20.8	18.2	0.5	2.1	51.1	-	0.2
THAILAND	1970	BAHT	3 461 635	0.5	53.5	19.5	10.4	2.1	6.9	13.8	0.8	11.9
	1975		7 775 347	0.6	62.5	16.2	9.4	2.5	4.3	11.1	2.0	7.7
	1976		8 732 955	0.7	60.2	17.9	10.3	2.6	5.0	10.1	2.3	8.8
TURKEY	1977	LIRA	37 961 875	-	46.2	36.5	23.1	3.8	9.6	14.5	2.7	0.1
YEMEN, DEMOCRATIC ‡	1971	DINAR	2 389	-	87.6	} 4.7	3.6	0.4	0.7	3.0	3.2	6.2
	1976		5 288	1.3	68.3					2.5	0.6	22.7
EUROPE												
AUSTRIA	1970	SCHILLING	13 502 700	0.7	29.6	47.8	28.9	1.3	17.5	13.4	6.3	2.3
	1975		29 366 500	1.2	23.0	50.8	33.6	1.4	15.8	14.7	6.1	4.1
	1976		32 467 500	5.3	18.9	53.0	29.7	1.6	21.7	15.3	3.3	4.1
	1977		35 368 500	5.3	18.8	52.8	29.5	1.6	21.7	15.3	4.0	3.8
BELGIUM ‡	1970	FRANC	54 165 533	-	24.7	51.7	23.1	3.0	25.6	13.3	0.8	9.5
	1975		131 906 200	-	25.5	47.7	...	...	...	15.6	4.4	7.1
	1976		151 206 800	-	24.7	47.4	...	...	...	15.6	5.9	6.4
	1977		170 775 800	-	25.7	45.2	...	...	...	16.1	6.1	6.9

Dépenses publiques ordinaires par degrés d'enseignement
Gastos públicos ordinarios por grados de enseñanza

Country	Currency	Year	(1)	(2)	(3)	(4)	(5)	(6)	(7)	(8)	(9)	(10)
BULGARIA	LEV	1970	442 124	14.8	51.6	↑	...	...	...	14.5	19.2	—
		1975	725 259	18.5	45.4	↑	...	...	...	12.9	23.2	—
		1976	778 601	18.9	44.8	↑	...	...	...	13.2	23.1	—
		1977	838 837	18.8	42.3	↑	...	...	...	13.1	25.8	—
CZECHOSLOVAKIA	KORUNA	1970	12 102 000	8.3	36.4	15.6	2.7	12.9	↑	16.9	22.5	0.3
		1975	17 288 021	9.5	41.2	16.0	2.9	13.1	↑	19.1	14.0	0.2
		1976	17 332 254	10.8	42.9	14.9	3.1	11.8	↑	17.0	14.2	0.2
		1977	18 580 636	11.4	42.2	14.4	3.0	11.4	↑	16.5	15.2	0.2
DENMARK ‡	KRONE	1970	6 294 000	./.	./.	71.1	62.7	3.2	5.2	20.8	8.1	—
		1976	14 600 000	./.	./.	71.1	64.7	—	6.4	20.8	8.1	
		1977	16 200 000	./.	52.0	15.9		—		17.5	9.2	5.5
FINLAND	MARKKA	1970	2 404 790	—	35.8	49.5	30.8	0.6	18.1	9.8	3.9	1.1
		1975	5 596 511	—	46.1	31.3	13.5	0.1	17.7	12.8	7.6	2.3
		1976	6 677 009	—	47.8	29.1	10.8	0.1	18.1	12.6	8.2	2.3
		1977	7 598 881	—	49.8	27.5	7.8	0.1	19.6	12.7	7.7	2.3
FRANCE ‡	FRANC	1970	24 598 921	5.9	23.8	43.9	30.2	/	13.7	17.4	2.2	6.8
		1975	46 844 110	6.3	18.8	51.3	35.2	2.2	13.9	13.7	4.3	5.6
		1976	54 455 190	6.7	18.1	51.5	35.5	2.3	13.7	13.9	4.1	5.6
		1977	62 738 600	6.7	17.5	51.9	32.8	2.3	16.8	13.6	4.0	6.2
GERMAN DEMOCRATIC REPUBLIC ‡	DDR MARK	1971	6 369 366	7.8	./.	56.4	46.3	—	10.1	22.8	—	13.0
		1975	8 276 353	8.1	./.	57.4	49.0	—	8.4	20.8	—	13.7
		1977	9 273 262	7.6	./.	56.5	47.8	—	8.7	20.2	—	15.7
		1978	9 538 582	7.4	./.	55.6	46.5	—	9.1	20.2	—	16.8
GERMANY, FEDERAL REPUBLIC OF ‡	DEUTSCHE MARK	1970	16 926 900	./.	38.5	31.5	22.5	9.7	9.0	18.4	5.0	6.5
		1975	35 773 000	./.	19.1	50.7	41.6	—	9.1	15.0	6.9	8.3
		1976	37 753 000	./.	19.2	51.7	42.3	—	9.4	15.1	7.3	6.7
GIBRALTAR	POUND	1970	362	—	40.6	49.7	32.6	—	7.5	3.0	0.8	5.8
		1975	909	—	47.6	36.6	31.7	—	5.0	10.3	0.6	4.8
		1976	1 443	—	49.9	34.6	33.3	—	1.3	10.2	0.5	4.9
		1977	1 699	—	43.5	38.0	29.0	—	9.0	11.8	0.8	5.8
GREECE	DRACHMA	1970	5 090 900	2.2	48.8	28.3	24.1	—	4.2	15.5	1.4	3.7
		1974	9 347 600	3.5	40.6	29.9	25.1	—	4.8	22.0	0.1	3.9
HUNGARY	FORINT	1970	10 641 431	9.1	38.7	14.5	...	—	...	22.3	14.9	0.4
		1975	16 719 792	11.6	38.0	14.0	6.7	—	7.3	21.4	14.8	0.2
		1976	17 579 883	12.8	38.1	13.7	6.4	—	7.2	21.4	13.5	0.2
		1977	19 385 911	13.0	38.3	13.7	6.2	—	7.5	21.6	13.2	0.2
IRELAND ‡	POUND	1970	68 980	./.	42.8	40.9	24.8	—	16.1	13.9	...	2.4
		1975	199 666	./.	35.8	37.0	24.7	—	12.2	17.7	2.2	7.3
		1976	246 342	./.	35.4	37.6	25.4	—	12.2	17.8	2.2	7.1
		1977	288 043	./.	34.8	36.8	24.8	—	12.0	18.5	2.6	7.2
ITALY ‡	LIRA	1970	2 429 439	2.7	28.4	38.1	23.3	↑	14.8	8.8	4.6	17.4
		1975	5 060 156	4.8	30.0	42.4	29.0	↑	13.4	13.3	3.0	6.4
		1976	6 467 905	5.0	29.3	46.7		...		12.0	0.1	6.9
LUXEMBOURG ‡	FRANC	1970	1 356 500	./.	45.3	37.3	24.5	—	12.8	1.8	3.7	12.0
		1975	3 517 600	./.	41.9	40.1	26.6	—	13.4	2.3	4.2	11.5
		1976	3 995 200	./.	42.1	40.3	25.5	—	14.8	1.9	4.7	11.1
		1977	4 498 800	./.	41.5	41.1	25.9	—	15.2	1.8	4.8	10.8

4.3 Public current expenditure by level of education
Dépenses publiques ordinaires par degrés d'enseignement
Gastos públicos ordinarios por grados de enseñanza

COUNTRY / PAYS / PAIS	YEAR / ANNEE / AÑO	CURRENCY / MONNAIE / MONEDA	TOTAL (000) (1)	PRE-PRIMARY / PRE-PRIMAIRE / PRE-PRIMARIA (2)	1ST LEVEL / 1ER DEGRE / 1ER GRADO (3)	SECOND LEVEL — SECOND DEGRE — SEGUNDO GRADO TOTAL / TOTAL / TOTAL (4)	GENERAL / GENERAL / GENERAL (5)	TEACHER TRAINING / NORMAL / NORMAL (6)	OTHER / AUTRE / OTRA (7)	3RD LEVEL / 3EME DEGRE / 3ER GRADO (8)	OTHER TYPES / AUTRES TYPES / OTROS TIPOS (9)	NOT DISTRIBUTED / NON RE-PARTIES / SIN DISTRI-BUCION (10)
MALTA ‡	1970	POUND	5 913	./.	41.8	29.2	15.7	—	13.5	12.9	0.2	15.9
	1975		6 881	./.	25.4	49.1	37.8	—	11.2	13.5	1.6	10.5
	1976		8 733	./.	23.7	51.0	35.9	—	15.1	11.7	0.1	12.4
NETHERLANDS	1970	GUILDER	7 069 000	4.8	20.8	38.6	20.3	1.9	16.4	22.1	3.9	9.8
	1975		14 881 000	5.7	20.3	36.2	20.0	0.3	15.9	28.3	5.0	4.5
	1976		17 021 000	5.7	19.9	36.5	20.1	0.3	16.1	28.3	4.9	4.6
	1977		18 666 000	5.6	19.7	34.6	19.4	0.4	14.8	28.0	7.0	5.0
NORWAY ‡	1970	KRONE	4 771 600	—	47.5	23.4	12.6	—	10.8	12.2	6.1	10.7
	1975		8 427 000	—	48.8	24.7	11.6	—	13.1	13.3	10.9	2.3
	1976		10 608 000	—	46.4	24.1	10.7	—	13.4	12.7	7.3	9.5
	1977		11 484 000	—	48.5	26.7	...	...	...	14.1	8.6	2.1
POLAND ‡	1970	ZLOTY	28 506	6.6	34.1	25.8	4.1	1.0	20.7	18.0	14.6	0.9
	1975		50 449	7.0	27.6	23.4	4.3	0.3	18.7	25.4	15.8	0.9
	1977		59 175	7.2	26.7	22.3	5.0	...	17.3	26.6	16.4	0.8
	1978		64 117	7.1	27.4	22.1	4.9	...	17.2	25.8	16.8	0.8
PORTUGAL ‡	1975	ESCUDO	13 876 839	0.1	56.6	24.5	...	...	...	10.9	0.5	7.4
	1976		17 140 918	0.1	44.3	23.4	...	...	...	9.6	1.0	21.5
	1977		22 535 383	0.2	51.2	27.1	...	...	...	10.8	1.3	9.5
ROMANIA ‡	1970	LEU	9 235 100	6.3	./.	72.4	50.4	4.2 ›	17.8	14.6	6.7	—
	1974		11 782 000	10.0	./.	70.4	50.6	›	19.8	13.4	6.3	—
SAN MARINO ‡	1970	LIRA	727 334	./.	50.0	40.5	...	...	...	9.5	—	—
	1975		2 499 565	./.	52.0	25.1	...	...	...	8.2	—	6.5
	1976		2 915 485	./.	54.5	32.8	...	...	...	7.0	—	5.8
	1977		3 490 960	./.	59.0	34.7	...	...	...	6.3	—	—
SPAIN ‡	1970	PESETA	35 420	./.	52.3	23.4	14.5	—	8.9	18.2	1.3	4.7
	1976		134 391	./.	61.2	17.5	13.2	—	4.2	15.1	2.3	3.9
SWEDEN	1970	KRONA	10 785 000	—	42.7	17.7	...	...	...	14.5	3.7	21.4
	1975		19 281 100	—	38.3	13.3	...	...	...	12.3	6.6	29.6
	1976		22 454 200	—	39.1	12.8	...	...	...	11.9	6.7	29.5
	1977		26 441 200	—	37.7	12.3	...	...	...	11.0	7.6	31.4
SWITZERLAND ‡	1970	FRANC	2 765 600	1.8	33.2	40.2	16.0	11.0	13.2	17.5	0.6	6.6
	1975		5 978 800	3.2	./.	77.9	54.1	10.2	13.6	17.0	—	1.8
	1976		6 350 400	4.0	./.	78.2	51.2	11.1	16.0	15.9	—	1.9
	1977		6 734 300	3.1	./.	77.3	51.8	11.1	14.4	16.5	—	3.1

Public current expenditure by level of education 4.3
Dépenses publiques ordinaires par degrés d'enseignement
Gastos públicos ordinarios por grados de enseñanza

Country	Currency	Year	(1)	(2)	(3)	(4)	(5)	(6)	(7)	(8)	(9)	(10)
UNITED KINGDOM ‡	POUND STERLING	1970	2 334	./.	23.7	32.0	...	...	...	24.8	2.1	17.4
		1975	6 292	./.	24.8	36.5	...	...	...	21.1	3.0	14.6
		1976	7 132	./.	24.4	37.8	...	...	...	19.9	3.1	14.8
YUGOSLAVIA	DINAR	1970	7 633 000	—	51.5	26.8	5.1	2.0	19.8	14.8	1.7	5.2
		1975	25 515 000	—	48.9	25.5	4.2	1.1	20.1	15.2	1.7	8.7
		1976	31 093 000	—	50.6	24.4	...	...	...	15.8	1.4	7.8
		1977	37 632 000	—	50.9	24.7	...	...	...	17.2	1.8	5.4
OCEANIA												
AMERICAN SAMOA ‡	UNITED STATES DOLLAR	1975	7 962	./.	85.4	↑	...	...	...	14.6	—	—
		1976	8 550	./.	87.6	↑	...	...	...	12.4	—	—
		1977	8 626	./.	91.7	↑	...	...	...	8.3	—	—
COOK ISLANDS	NEW ZEALAND DOLLAR	1970	813	—	58.7	38.0	31.2	6.8	—	0.1	—	3.2
FIJI	DOLLAR	1970	6 777	—	65.2	29.5	19.2	4.4	5.9	7.7	2.1	5.3
		1976	26 640	—	50.3	33.7	...	...	...	8.9	0.3	6.2
		1977	34 287	—	49.9	36.5	...	...	...	...	...	4.4
FRENCH POLYNESIA ‡	FRANC C.F.P.	1970	1 150 442	—	58.7	40.9	39.5	1.4	./.	—	0.5	1.9
		1975	3 268 311	7.7	28.6	61.0	...	...	...	—	0.8	...
GUAM ‡	UNITED STATES DOLLAR	1970	22 434	./.	85.3	↑	...	...	...	14.7	—	—
		1975	52 723	./.	80.4	↑	...	...	...	19.6	—	—
		1976	44 428	./.	81.0	↑	...	...	...	19.0	—	—
		1977	44 867	./.	80.9	↑	...	...	...	19.1	—	—
KIRIBATI	AUSTRALIAN DOLLAR	1970	534	—	32.6	36.5	29.0	⎱ 8.6	7.5	14.6	5.6	10.7
		1974	1 015	—	48.3	35.2	23.3	⎰	3.3	10.6	—	5.9
		1977	2 100	—	36.2	46.5	12.9	7.1	26.4	3.8	—	13.6
NEW HEBRIDES	AUSTRALIAN DOLLAR	1970	682	—	55.7	29.3	12.9	11.1	5.3	3.7	0.6	14.4
		1975	1 444	0.4	40.0	39.6	19.4	9.3	10.9		0.7	15.6
NEW HEBRIDES ‡	FRANC FRANCAIS	1970	10 393	—	63.0	18.1	13.6	—	4.5	—	—	19.0
		1975	38 288	—	71.8	28.2	...	—	10.3	—	—	...
		1977	73 868	—	66.7	33.3	23.0	—	...	—	—	...
NEW ZEALAND ‡	DOLLAR	1970	212 525	./.	37.7	25.5	21.7	—	3.8	23.3	0.6	12.9
		1975	503 643	1.4	35.6	29.7	24.3	—	5.4	23.4	2.1	7.9
		1976	575 566	1.3	35.3	30.2	24.1	—	6.2	23.9	1.4	7.9
		1977	675 222		34.7	30.9	24.6	—	6.3	23.4	1.5	8.2
NIUE	NEW ZEALAND DOLLAR	1975	595	0.3	35.1	39.3	...	...	...	—	—	25.2
PACIFIC ISLANDS	UNITED STATES DOLLAR	1970	10 297	0.1	38.3	20.7	20.7	—	—	23.1	1.8	15.9
		1975	21 501	—	30.7	18.9	18.9	—	—	13.6	3.0	33.9
		1976	20 205	—	44.3	20.6	19.8	0.4	0.4	14.4	5.1	15.6
PAPUA NEW GUINEA ‡	KINA	1975	61 601	./.	39.6	22.6	12.3	4.1	6.1	31.0	1.2	5.6
		1976	80 426	./.	33.1	23.8	15.3	1.2	7.3	35.7	0.7	6.6
SAMOA	TALA	1975	1 939	—	65.2	18.8	13.7	2.7	2.4	—	3.5	12.6
		1976	2 206	—	58.3	21.8	14.4	2.4	5.0	—	3.0	16.9
		1977	2 240	—	59.6	23.0	14.7	2.7	5.6	—	3.1	14.3
TONGA ‡	DOLLAR	1971	555	—	51.2	30.3	20.2	7.9	2.2	1.1	—	17.5
		1974	692	—	50.0	35.1	23.6	7.4	4.2	1.3	—	13.6
		1977	1 330	—	46.6	25.5	17.5	6.8	1.2	5.3	—	22.6

4.3 Public current expenditure by level of education
Dépenses publiques ordinaires par degrés d'enseignement
Gastos públicos ordinarios por grados de enseñanza

COUNTRY / PAYS / PAIS	YEAR / ANNEE / AÑO	CURRENCY / MONNAIE / MONEDA	TOTAL (000) / TOTAL (000) / TOTAL (000)	PRE-PRIMARY / PRE-PRIMAIRE / PRE-PRIMARIA	1ST LEVEL / 1ER DEGRE / 1ER GRADO	SECOND LEVEL / SECOND DEGRE / SEGUNDO GRADO — TOTAL / TOTAL / TOTAL	GENE-RAL / GENE-RAL / GENE-RAL	TEACHER TRAIN-ING / NORMAL / NORMAL	OTHER / AUTRE / OTRA GRADO	3RD LEVEL / 3EME DEGRE / 3ER GRADO	OTHER TYPES / AUTRES TYPES / OTROS TIPOS	NOT DISTRI-BUTED / NON RE-PARTIES / SIN DISTRI-BUCION
			(1)	(2)	(3)	(4)	(5)	(6)	(7)	(8)	(9)	(10)
U.S.S.R.												
U.S.S.R. ‡	1970	ROUBLE	16 528 000	15.6	43.7	15.6	/	/	15.6	12.8	12.3	—
	1975		23 415 900	21.4	38.2	16.2	/	/	16.2	13.2	11.0	—
	1977		24 956 300	22.3	36.0	16.8	/	/	16.8	13.6	11.4	—
	1978		26 219 900	23.0	35.1	16.6	/	/	16.6	13.7	11.6	—
BYELORUSSIAN S.S.R. ‡	1970	ROUBLE	540 408	12.8	53.6	15.3	/	/	15.3	10.3	8.0	—
	1975		859 300	19.1	40.5	17.7	/	/	17.7	13.4	9.3	—
	1976		883 300	19.0	39.8	18.1	/	/	18.1	13.7	9.5	—
	1977		909 700	19.4	40.1	18.3	/	/	18.3	13.6	8.5	—
UKRAINIAN S.S.R. ‡	1970	ROUBLE	3 135 800	18.6	40.6	7.0	/	/	7.0	14.1	19.7	—
	1975		4 312 200	22.9	35.5	16.3	/	/	16.0	13.4	12.3	—
	1976		4 467 400	23.3	34.4	16.3	/	/	16.3	13.6	12.4	—
	1977		4 545 300	23.8	33.3	16.6	/	/	16.6	13.7	12.5	—

ALGERIA:
E—> EXPENDITURE OF THE MINISTRY OF PRIMARY AND SECONDARY EDUCATION ONLY. DATA FOR COLUMN 7 ARE INCLUDED IN COLUMN 5.
FR—> DEPENSES DU MINISTERE DES ENSEIGNEMENTS PRIMAIRE ET SECONDAIRE SEULEMENT. LES DONNEES DE LA COLONNE 7 SONT INCLUSES DANS LA COLONNE 5.
ESP> GASTOS DEL MINISTERIO DE LAS ENSEÑANZAS DE PRIMERO Y SECUNDO GRADO SOLAMENTE. LOS DATOS DE LA COLUMNA 7 QUEDAN INCLUIDOS EN LA COLUMNA 5.

BENIN:
E—> EXPENDITURE OF THE CENTRAL GOVERNMENT ONLY.
FR—> DEPENSES DU GOUVERNEMENT CENTRAL SEULEMENT.
ESP> GASTOS DEL GOBIERNO CENTRAL SOLAMENTE.

CONGO:
E—> EXPENDITURE OF THE CENTRAL GOVERNMENT ONLY.
FR—> DEPENSES DU GOUVERNEMENT CENTRAL SEULEMENT.
ESP> GASTOS DEL GOBIERNO CENTRAL SOLAMENTE.

EGYPT:
E—> EXPENDITURE ON PRE-PRIMARY AND FIRST LEVEL EDUCATION IS INCLUDED IN COLUMN 4.
FR—> LES DEPENSES DE L'ENSEIGNEMENT PREPRIMAIRE ET DU PREMIER DEGRE SONT INCLUSES DANS LA COLONNE 4.
ESP> LOS GASTOS DE LAS ENSEÑANZAS PREPRIMARIA Y DE PRIMER GRADO QUEDAN INCLUIDOS EN LA COLUMNA 4.

ETHIOPIA:
E—> EXPENDITURE ON UNIVERSITIES IS NOT INCLUDED.
FR—> LES DEPENSES DES UNIVERSITES NE SONT PAS INCLUSES.
ESP> NO SE INCLUYEN LOS GASTOS RELATIVOS A LAS UNIVERSIDADES.

GAMBIA:
E—> ONLY EMOLUMENTS OF TEACHERS ARE DISTRIBUTED BY LEVELS OF EDUCATION. ALL OTHER EXPENDITURE IS SHOWN IN COLUMN 10.

Public current expenditure by level of education 4.3
Dépenses publiques ordinaires par degrés d'enseignement
Gastos públicos ordinarios por grados de enseñanza

GAMBIA (CONT):
FR—> SEULS LES SALAIRES DU PERSONNEL ENSEIGNANT
SONT DISTRIBUES PAR DEGRE D'ENSEIGNEMENT. TOUTES
LES AUTRES DEPENSES SONT PRESENTEES DANS LA COLONNE
10.
ESP> SOLO SE DISTRIBUYEN POR GRADOS DE ENSEÑANZA
LOS SUELDOS DEL PERSONAL DOCENTE. TODOS LOS OTROS
GASTOS FIGURAN EN LA COLUMNA 10.

GHANA:
E—> FOR 1970, FIRST LEVEL REFERS TO GRADES I-X
(PRIMARY AND MIDDLE SCHOOLS). FROM 1975, MIDDLE
SCHOOLS (GRADES VII-X) ARE CLASSIFIED AT THE SECOND
LEVEL (GENERAL EDUCATION). FOR 1976, EXPENDITURE
ON UNIVERSITIES IS NOT INCLUDED.
FR—> EN 1970, L'ENSEIGNEMENT DU PREMIER DEGRE
CORRESPOND AUX DIX PREMIERES ANNEES D'ETUDES I A X
(ECOLES PRIMAIRES ET MOYENNES). A PARTIR DE 1975,
LES ECOLES MOYENNES (ANNEES D'ETUDES VII-X) SONT
CLASSEES DANS LE SECOND DEGRE (ENSEIGNEMENT
GENERAL). EN 1976, LES DEPENSES DES UNIVERSITES
NE SONT PAS INCLUSES.
ESP> EN 1970, LA ENSEÑANZA DE PRIMER GRADO
CORRESPONDE A LOS DIEZ PRIMEROS AÑOS DE ESTUDIO
I A X (ESCUELAS PRIMARIAS Y MEDIAS). A PARTIR DE
1975, LAS ESCUELAS MEDIAS (AÑOS DE ESTUDIO VII-
X) SE CLASIFICAN EN LA ENSEÑANZA GENERAL DE
SEGUNDO GRADO. EN 1976, NO SE INCLUYEN LOS DATOS
RELATIVOS A LAS UNIVERSIDADES.

GUINEA BISSAU:
E—> FOREIGN AID IS INCLUDED.
FR—> L'AIDE EXTERIEURE EST INCLUSE.
ESP> SE INCLUYE LA AYUDA EXTERIOR.

IVORY COAST:
E—> FOREIGN AID IS INCLUDED.
FR—> L'AIDE EXTERIEURE EST INCLUSE.
ESP> SE INCLUYE LA AYUDA EXTERIOR.

KENYA:
E—> EXPENDITURE OF THE MINISTRY OF EDUCATION
ONLY.
FR—> DEPENSES DU MINISTERE DE L'EDUCATION
SEULEMENT.
ESP> GASTOS DEL MINISTERIO DE EDUCACION
SOLAMENTE.

LIBERIA:
E—> CAPITAL EXPENDITURE IS INCLUDED.
FR—> LES DEPENSES EN CAPITAL SONT INCLUSES.
ESP> QUEDAN INCLUIDOS LOS GASTOS DE CAPITAL.

MADAGASCAR:
E—> FOR 1970, FOREIGN AID FOR EDUCATION AT THE
THIRD LEVEL IS INCLUDED.
FR—> EN 1970, L'AIDE EXTERIEURE DESTINEE A
L'ENSEIGNEMENT DU TROISIEME DEGRE EST INCLUSE.
ESP> EN 1970, QUEDA INCLUIDA LA AYUDA EXTERIOR
DESTINADA A LA ENSEÑANZA DE TERCER GRADO.

MALI:
E—> FIRST LEVEL EDUCATION REFERS TO
"ENSEIGNEMENT FONDAMENTAL" OF 9 YEARS (TWO CYCLES:
6 AND 3 YEARS). DURATION OF SECOND LEVEL
EDUCATION IS 3 YEARS.
FR—> L'ENSEIGNEMENT DU PREMIER DEGRE CORRESPOND
A L'ENSEIGNEMENT FONDAMENTAL DONT LA DUREE EST DE
9 ANS (DEUX CYCLES: 6 ET 3 ANS). L'ENSEIGNEMENT
DU SECOND DEGRE CORRESPOND A UN ENSEIGNEMENT
D'UNE DUREE DE 3 ANS.
ESP> LA ENSEÑANZA DE PRIMER GRADO CORRESPONDE
A LA ENSEÑANZA FUNDAMENTAL, CUYA DURACION ES DE 9
AÑOS (DOS CICLOS DE 6 Y 3 AÑOS). LA ENSEÑANZA DE
SEGUNDO GRADO TIENE UNA DURACIÓN DE 3 AÑOS.

MAURITANIA:
E—> EXPENDITURE OF THE CENTRAL GOVERNMENT ONLY.
FR—> DEPENSES DU GOUVERNEMENT CENTRAL SEULEMENT.
ESP> GASTOS DEL GOBIERNO CENTRAL SOLAMENTE.

ST. HELENA:
E—> FOR 1970, EXPENDITURE ON PRE-PRIMARY
EDUCATION IS INCLUDED IN COLUMN 3. FOR 1975,
EXPENDITURE ON FIRST LEVEL EDUCATION IS INCLUDED
IN COLUMN 4.
FR—> EN 1970, LES DEPENSES DE L'ENSEIGNEMENT
PREPRIMAIRE SONT INCLUSES DANS LA COLONNE 3. EN
1975, LES DEPENSES DE L'ENSEIGNEMENT DU PREMIER
DEGRE SONT INCLUSES DANS LA COLONNE 4.
ESP> EN 1970, LOS GASTOS DE LA ENSEÑANZA
PREPRIMARIA FIGURAN EN LA COLUMNA 3. EN 1975,
LOS GASTOS DE LA ENSEÑANZA DE PRIMER GRADO QUEDAN
INCLUIDOS EN LA COLUMNA 4.

SWAZILAND:
E—> EXPENDITURE OF THE MINISTRY OF EDUCATION
ONLY.
FR—> DEPENSES DU MINISTERE DE L'EDUCATION
SEULEMENT.
ESP> GASTOS DEL MINISTERIO DE EDUCACION
SOLAMENTE.

TOGO:
E—> FOREIGN AID IS INCLUDED.
FR—> L'AIDE EXTERIEURE EST INCLUSE.
ESP> SE INCLUYE LA AYUDA EXTERIOR.

UGANDA:
E—> EXPENDITURE OF THE MINISTRY OF EDUCATION
ONLY.
FR—> DEPENSES DU MINISTERE DE L'EDUCATION
SEULEMENT.
ESP> GASTOS DEL MINISTERIO DE EDUCACION
SOLAMENTE.

UNITED REPUBLIC OF TANZANIA:
E—> FOR 1970 AND 1976, DATA FOR COLUMN 7 ARE
INCLUDED IN COLUMN 5.
FR—> EN 1970 ET 1976, LES DONNEES DE LA COLONNE
7 SONT INCLUSES DANS LA COLONNE 5.
ESP> EN 1970 Y 1976, LOS DATOS DE LA COLUMNA 7
FIGURAN EN LA COLUMNA 5.

4.3 Public current expenditure by level of education
Dépenses publiques ordinaires par degrés d'enseignement
Gastos públicos ordinarios por grados de enseñanza

PANAMA:
E--> EXPENDITURE ON OTHER TYPES OF EDUCATION IS INCLUDED IN COLUMN 10.
FR-> LES DEPENSES AFFERENTES AUX AUTRES TYPES D'ENSEIGNEMENT SONT INCLUSES DANS LA COLONNE 10.
ESP> LOS GASTOS RELATIVOS A LOS OTROS TIPOS DE ENSEÑANZA QUEDAN INCLUIDOS EN LA COLUMNA 10.

FORMER CANAL ZONE:
E--> EXPENDITURE ON PRE-PRIMARY EDUCATION IS INCLUDED IN COLUMN 3.
FR-> LES DEPENSES DE L'ENSEIGNEMENT PREPRIMAIRE SONT INCLUSES DANS LA COLONNE 3.
ESP> LOS GASTOS DE LA ENSEÑANZA PREPRIMARIA FIGURAN EN LA COLUMNA 3.

PUERTO RICO:
E--> EXPENDITURE ON PRE-PRIMARY EDUCATION IS INCLUDED IN COLUMN 3.
FR-> LES DEPENSES DE L'ENSEIGNEMENT PREPRIMAIRE SONT INCLUSES DANS LA COLONNE 3.
ESP> LOS GASTOS DE LA ENSEÑANZA PREPRIMARIA FIGURAN EN LA COLUMNA 3.

ST. KITTS-NEVIS-ANGUILLA:
E--> CAPITAL EXPENDITURE IS INCLUDED.
FR-> LES DEPENSES EN CAPITAL SONT INCLUSES.
ESP> QUEDAN INCLUIDOS LOS GASTOS DE CAPITAL.

UNITED STATES OF AMERICA:
E--> FIGURES IN COLUMN 1 ARE IN MILLIONS. EXPENDITURE ON PRE-PRIMARY EDUCATION IS INCLUDED IN COLUMN 3.
FR-> LES CHIFFRES DE LA COLONNE 1 SONT EXPRIMES EN MILLIONS. LES DEPENSES DE L'ENSEIGNEMENT PREPRIMAIRE SONT INCLUSES DANS LA COLONNE 3.
ESP> LAS CIFRAS DE LA COLUMNA 1 SE EXPRESAN EN MILLONES. LOS GASTOS DE LA ENSEÑANZA PREPRIMARIA FIGURAN EN LA COLUMNA 3.

U.S. VIRGIN ISLANDS:
E--> EXPENDITURE ON PRE-PRIMARY EDUCATION IS INCLUDED IN COLUMN 3.
FR-> LES DEPENSES DE L'ENSEIGNEMENT PREPRIMAIRE SONT INCLUSES DANS LA COLONNE 3.
ESP> LOS GASTOS DE LA ENSEÑANZA PREPRIMARIA FIGURAN EN LA COLUMNA 3.

ARGENTINA:
E--> FIGURES IN COLUMN 1 ARE IN MILLIONS. FOR 1970 AND 1976, EXPENDITURE OF THE MINISTRY OF EDUCATION ONLY. FROM 1975 TO 1977, EXPENDITURE ON PRE-PRIMARY EDUCATION IS INCLUDED IN COLUMN 3.
FR-> LES CHIFFRES DE LA COLONNE 1 SONT EXPRIMES EN MILLIONS. EN 1970 ET 1976, DEPENSES DU MINISTERE DE L'EDUCATION SEULEMENT. DE 1975 A 1977, LES DEPENSES DE L'ENSEIGNEMENT PREPRIMAIRE SONT INCLUSES DANS LA COLONNE 3.
ESP> LAS CIFRAS DE LA COLUMNA 1 SE EXPRESAN EN MILLONES. EN 1970 Y 1976, GASTOS DEL MINISTERIO DE EDUCACION SOLAMENTE. DE 1975 A 1977, LOS GASTOS DE LA ENSEÑANZA PREPRIMARIA SE INCLUYEN EN LA COLUMNA 3.

UPPER VOLTA:
E--> EXPENDITURE OF THE MINISTRY OF EDUCATION ONLY.
FR-> DEPENSES DU MINISTERE DE L'EDUCATION SEULEMENT.
ESP> GASTOS DEL MINISTERIO DE EDUCACION SOLAMENTE.

WESTERN SAHARA:
E--> FOR 1973, EXPENDITURE ON PRE-PRIMARY EDUCATION IS INCLUDED IN COLUMN 3.
FR-> EN 1973, LES DEPENSES DE L'ENSEIGNEMENT PREPRIMAIRE SONT INCLUSES DANS LA COLONNE 3.
ESP> EN 1973, LOS GASTOS DE LA ENSEÑANZA PREPRIMARIA FIGURAN EN LA COLUMNA 3.

CANADA:
E--> EXPENDITURE ON PRE-PRIMARY AND FIRST LEVEL EDUCATION IS INCLUDED IN COLUMN 4.
FR-> LES DEPENSES DE L'ENSEIGNEMENT PREPRIMAIRE ET DU PREMIER DEGRE SONT INCLUSES DANS LA COLONNE 4.
ESP> LOS GASTOS DE LAS ENSEÑANZAS PREPRIMARIA Y DE PRIMER GRADO QUEDAN INCLUIDOS EN LA COLUMNA 4.

COSTA RICA:
E--> EXPENDITURE ON PRE-PRIMARY EDUCATION IS INCLUDED IN COLUMN 3. FOR 1976, CAPITAL EXPENDITURE IS INCLUDED.
FR-> LES DEPENSES DE L'ENSEIGNEMENT PREPRIMAIRE SONT INCLUSES DANS LA COLONNE 3. EN 1976, LES DEPENSES EN CAPITAL SONT INCLUSES.
ESP> LOS GASTOS DE LA ENSEÑANZA PREPRIMARIA FIGURAN EN LA COLUMNA 3. EN 1976, SE INCLUYEN LOS GASTOS DE CAPITAL.

HAITI:
E--> FOR 1970 AND 1975, EXPENDITURE ON OTHER TYPES OF EDUCATION IS INCLUDED IN COLUMN 10.
FR-> EN 1970 ET 1975, LES DEPENSES AFFERENTES AUX AUTRES TYPES D'ENSEIGNEMENT SONT INCLUSES DANS LA COLONNE 10.
ESP> EN 1970 Y 1976, LOS GASTOS RELATIVOS A LOS OTROS TIPOS DE ENSEÑANZA QUEDAN INCLUIDOS EN LA COLUMNA 10.

JAMAICA:
E--> EXPENDITURE OF THE MINISTRY OF EDUCATION ONLY. FOR 1970, EXPENDITURE ON PRE-PRIMARY EDUCATION IS INCLUDED IN COLUMN 3.
FR-> DEPENSES DU MINISTERE DE L'EDUCATION SEULEMENT. EN 1970, LES DEPENSES DE L'ENSEIGNEMENT PREPRIMAIRE SONT INCLUSES DANS LA COLONNE 3.
ESP> GASTOS DEL MINISTERIO DE EDUCACION SOLAMENTE. EN 1970, LOS GASTOS DE LA ENSEÑANZA PREPRIMARIA FIGURAN EN LA COLUMNA 3.

MEXICO:
E--> EXPENDITURE OF THE MINISTRY OF EDUCATION ONLY.
FR-> DEPENSES DU MINISTERE DE L'EDUCATION SEULEMENT.
ESP> GASTOS DEL MINISTERIO DE EDUCACION SOLAMENTE.

Public current expenditure by level of education 4.3
Dépenses publiques ordinaires par degrés d'enseignement
Gastos públicos ordinarios por grados de enseñanza

BRAZIL:
E—> DATA REFER TO CURRENT AND CAPITAL EXPENDITURE INCURRED BY THE FEDERAL GOVERNMENT AND BY THE FEDERAL STATES. EXPENDITURE OF MUNICIPALITIES IS NOT INCLUDED. COLUMN 3 REFERS TO PRE-PRIMARY, FIRST AND SECOND LEVELS OF EDUCATION AND ALSO INCLUDES SPECIAL EDUCATION AND "ENSINO SUPLETIVO".
FR—> LES DONNEES SE REFERENT AUX DEPENSES ORDINAIRES ET EN CAPITAL DU GOUVERNEMENT FEDERAL ET DES ETATS FEDERAUX. LES DEPENSES DES MUNICIPALITES NE SONT PAS INCLUSES. LA COLONNE 3 SE REFERE A L'ENSEIGNEMENT PREPRIMAIRE, DU PREMIER ET DU SECOND DEGRES ET INCLUT EGALEMENT L'EDUCATION SPECIALE ET L'"ENSINO SUPLETIVO".
ESP> LOS DATOS SE REFIEREN A LOS GASTOS ORDINARIOS Y DE CAPITAL DEL GOBIERNO FEDERAL Y DE LOS ESTADOS FEDERALES. NO SE INCLUYEN LOS GASTOS DE LAS MUNICIPALIDADES. LAS CIFRAS DE LA COLUMNA 3 SE REFIEREN A LAS ENSEÑANZAS PREPRIMARIA, DE PRIMERO Y DE SEGUNDO GRADO Y COMPRENDEN IGUALMENTE LA EDUCACION ESPECIAL Y EL "ENSINO SUPLETIVO".

CHILE:
E—> EXPENDITURE ON PRE-PRIMARY EDUCATION IS INCLUDED IN COLUMN 3.
FR—> LES DEPENSES DE L'ENSEIGNEMENT PREPRIMAIRE SONT INCLUSES DANS LA COLONNE 3.
ESP> LOS GASTOS DE LA ENSEÑANZA PREPRIMARIA FIGURAN EN LA COLUMNA 3.

COLOMBIA:
E—> EXPENDITURE OF THE MINISTRY OF EDUCATION ONLY.
FR—> DEPENSES DU MINISTERE DE L'EDUCATION SEULEMENT.
ESP> GASTOS DEL MINISTERIO DE EDUCACION SOLAMENTE.

GUYANA:
E—> FOR 1975, EXPENDITURE OF THE MINISTRY OF EDUCATION ONLY.
FR—> EN 1975, DEPENSES DU MINISTERE DE L'EDUCATION SEULEMENT.
ESP> EN 1975, GASTOS DEL MINISTERIO DE EDUCACION SOLAMENTE.

PERU:
E—> TRANFERS TO UNIVERSITIES AND SOME OTHER INSTITUTIONS AS WELL AS VARIOUS TYPES OF PENSIONS AND BENEFITS ARE NOT INCLUDED.
FR—> LES TRANSFERTS AUX UNIVERSITES ET A CERTAINS AUTRES ETABLISSEMENTS AINSI QUE DIFFERENTS TYPES DE PENSIONS ET D'INDEMNITES NE SONT PAS INCLUS.
ESP> NO SE INCLUYEN LAS TRANSFERENCIAS A LAS UNIVERSIDADES Y A ALGUNOS OTROS ESTABLECIMIENTOS, NI LOS DIFERENTES TIPOS DE PENSIONES Y DE INDEMNIZACIONES.

URUGUAY:
E—> CAPITAL EXPENDITURE IS INCLUDED. EXPENDITURE ON PRE-PRIMARY EDUCATION AND TEACHER TRAINING IS INCLUDED IN COLUMN 3.
FR—> LES DEPENSES EN CAPITAL SONT INCLUSES. LES DEPENSES DE L'ENSEIGNEMENT PREPRIMAIRE ET DE L'ENSEIGNEMENT NORMAL SONT INCLUSES DANS LA COLONNE 3.
ESP> SE INCLUYEN LOS GASTOS DE CAPITAL. LOS GASTOS RELATIVOS A LAS ENSEÑANZAS PREPRIMARIA Y NORMAL QUEDAN INCLUIDOS EN LA COLUMNA 3.

VENEZUELA:
E—> EXPENDITURE ON PRE-PRIMARY EDUCATION IS INCLUDED IN COLUMN 3.
FR—> LES DEPENSES DE L'ENSEIGNEMENT PREPRIMAIRE SONT INCLUSES DANS LA COLONNE 3.
ESP> LOS GASTOS DE LA ENSEÑANZA PREPRIMARIA FIGURAN EN LA COLUMNA 3.

AFGHANISTAN:
E—> FOR 1977, EXPENDITURE ON UNIVERSITIES IS NOT INCLUDED.
FR—> EN 1977, LES DEPENSES DES UNIVERSITES NE SONT PAS INCLUSES.
ESP> EN 1977, NO SE INCLUYEN LOS GASTOS RELATIVOS A LAS UNIVERSIDADES.

BANGLADESH:
E—> EXPENDITURE ON INTERMEDIATE COLLEGES AND INTERMEDIATE SECTIONS OF DEGREE COLLEGES (GRADES XI AND XII) IS INCLUDED WITH THIRD LEVEL EDUCATION.
FR—> LES DEPENSES DES "INTERMEDIATE COLLEGES" ET "INTERMEDIATE SECTIONS OF DEGREE COLLEGES" (XI EME ET XII EME ANNEES D'ETUDES) SONT CLASSEES AVEC L'ENSEIGNEMENT DU TROISIEME DEGRE.
ESP> LOS GASTOS DE LOS "INTERMEDIATE COLLEGES" Y DE LOS "INTERMEDIATE SECTIONS OF DEGREE COLLEGES" (XI Y XII AÑOS DE ESTUDIO) SE CLASIFICAN CON LOS DE LA ENSEÑANZA DE TERCER GRADO.

BHUTAN:
E—> FOR 1970, EXPENDITURE OF THE MINISTRY OF EDUCATION ONLY.
FR—> EN 1970, DEPENSES DU MINISTERE DE L'EDUCATION SEULEMENT.
ESP> EN 1970, GASTOS DEL MINISTERIO DE EDUCACION SOLAMENTE.

BURMA:
E—> FOR 1971, EXPENDITURE OF THE MINISTRY OF EDUCATION ONLY.
FR—> EN 1971, DEPENSES DU MINISTERE DE L'EDUCATION SEULEMENT.
ESP> EN 1971, GASTOS DEL MINISTERIO DE EDUCACION SOLAMENTE.

CYPRUS:
E—> EXPENDITURE BY THE OFFICE OF GREEK EDUCATION ONLY.
FR—> DEPENSES DU BUREAU GREC DE L'EDUCATION SEULEMENT.
ESP> GASTOS DEL SERVICIO GRIEGO DE EDUCACION SOLAMENTE.

4.3 Public current expenditure by level of education
Dépenses publiques ordinaires par degrés d'enseignement
Gastos públicos ordinarios por grados de enseñanza

MONGOLIA:
E—> EXPENDITURE ON FIRST LEVEL EDUCATION IS INCLUDED WITH EXPENDITURE ON GENERAL EDUCATION AT THE SECOND LEVEL AND SHOWN, THEREFORE, IN COLUMNS 4 AND 5.
FR—> LES DEPENSES DE L'ENSEIGNEMENT DU PREMIER DEGRE SONT INCLUSES DANS LES DEPENSES DE L'ENSEIGNEMENT GENERAL DU SECOND DEGRE ET SONT PRESENTEES EN CONSEQUENCE DANS LES COLONNES 4 ET 5.
ESP> LOS GASTOS DE LA ENSEÑANZA DE PRIMER GRADO QUEDAN INCLUIDOS EN LOS DE LA ENSEÑANZA GENERAL DE SEGUNDO GRADO, FIGURANDO POR CONSIGUIENTE EN LAS COLUMNAS 4 Y 5.

PHILIPPINES:
E—> FROM 1976 TO 1978, CAPITAL EXPENDITURE ON STATE UNIVERSITIES AND COLLEGES IS INCLUDED.
FR—> DE 1976 A 1978, LES DEPENSES EN CAPITAL DES UNIVERSITES ET COLLEGES D'ETAT SONT INCLUSES.
ESP> DE 1976 A 1978 SE INCLUYEN LOS GASTOS DE CAPITAL DE LAS UNIVERSIDADES Y LOS COLEGIOS DE ESTADO.

SAUDI ARABIA:
E—> CAPITAL EXPENDITURE IS INCLUDED; EXPENDITURE ON PRE-PRIMARY EDUCATION IS INCLUDED IN COLUMN 3.
FR—> LES DEPENSES EN CAPITAL SONT INCLUSES; LES DEPENSES DE L'ENSEIGNEMENT PREPRIMAIRE SONT INCLUSES DANS LA COLONNE 3.
ESP> SE INCLUYEN LOS GASTOS DE CAPITAL; LOS GASTOS RELATIVOS A LA ENSEÑANZA PREPRIMARIA FIGURAN EN LA COLUMNA 3.

SRI LANKA:
E—> FOR 1970, FIRST LEVEL EDUCATION REFERS TO GRADES I-VIII AND SECOND LEVEL TO GRADES IX-XII. FROM 1975, EXPENDITURE ON FIRST LEVEL EDUCATION (GRADES I-V) IS INCLUDED WITH EXPENDITURE ON GENERAL EDUCATION AT THE SECOND LEVEL (GRADE VI-XII) AND SHOWN, THEREFORE, IN COLUMNS 4 AND 5.
FR—> EN 1970, L'ENSEIGNEMENT DU PREMIER DEGRE CORRESPOND AUX ANNEES D'ETUDES I-VIII ET LE SECOND DEGRE AUX ANNEES D'ETUDES IX-XII. EN 1975, LES DEPENSES DE L'ENSEIGNEMENT DU PREMIER DEGRÉ (ANNEES D'ETUDES I-V) SONT INCLUSES DANS LES DEPENSES DE L'ENSEIGNEMENT GENERAL DU SECOND DEGRE (ANNEES D'ETUDES VI-XII) ET PRESENTEES EN CONSEQUENCE DANS LES COLONNES 4 ET 5.
ESP> EN 1970, LA ENSEÑANZA DE PRIMER GRADO CORRESPONDE A LOS AÑOS DE ESTUDIO I-VIII Y LA DE SEGUNDO GRADO A LOS AÑOS DE ESTUDIO IX-XII. EN 1975, LOS GASTOS DE LA ENSEÑANZA DE PRIMER GRADO (AÑOS I-V) SE INCLUYEN EN LOS DE LA ENSEÑANZA GENERAL DE SEGUNDO GRADO (AÑOS VI-XII), FIGURANDO POR CONSIGUIENTE EN LAS COLUMNAS 4 Y 5.

SYRIAN ARAB REPUBLIC:
E—> CAPITAL EXPENDITURE ON UNIVERSITIES IS INCLUDED.
FR—> LES DEPENSES EN CAPITAL DES UNIVERSITES SONT INCLUSES.
ESP> SE INCLUYEN LOS GASTOS DE CAPITAL RELATIVOS A LAS UNIVERSIDADES.

INDIA:
E—> FOR 1975, CAPITAL EXPENDITURE IS INCLUDED.
FR—> EN 1975, LES DEPENSES EN CAPITAL SONT INCLUSES.
ESP> EN 1975, SE INCLUYEN LOS GASTOS DE CAPITAL.

IRAQ:
E—> EXPENDITURE ON PRE-PRIMARY EDUCATION IS INCLUDED IN COLUMN 3.
FR—> LES DEPENSES DE L'ENSEIGNEMENT PREPRIMAIRE SONT INCLUSES DANS LA COLONNE 3.
ESP> LOS GASTOS DE LA ENSEÑANZA PREPRIMARIA SE INCLUYEN EN LA COLUMNA 3.

ISRAEL:
E—> FOR 1970, PRIVATE EXPENDITURE RELATING TO PRIVATE EDUCATION IS INCLUDED
FR—> EN 1970, LES DEPENSES PRIVEES AFFERENTES A L'ENSEIGNEMENT PRIVE SONT INCLUSES.
ESP> EN 1970, QUEDAN INCLUIDOS LOS GASTOS PRIVADOS DESTINADOS A LA ENSEÑANZA PRIVADA.

JAPAN:
E—> FIGURES IN COLUMN 1 ARE IN MILLIONS. FROM 1975 TO 1977, DATA DO NOT INCLUDE PUBLIC SUBSIDIES TO PRIVATE EDUCATION
FR—> LES CHIFFRES DE LA COLONNE 1 SONT EXPRIMES EN MILLIONS. DE 1975 A 1977, LES DONNEES NE COMPRENNENT PAS LES SUBVENTIONS PUBLIQUES A L'ENSEIGNEMENT PRIVE.
ESP> LAS CIFRAS DE LA COLUMNA 1 SE EXPRESAN EN MILLONES. DE 1975 A 1977, LOS DATOS NO COMPRENDEN LAS SUBVENCIONES PUBLICAS A LA ENSEÑANZA PRIVADA.

JORDAN:
E—> DATA REFER TO THE EAST BANK ONLY. EXPENDITURE ON FIRST LEVEL EDUCATION IS INCLUDED WITH EXPENDITURE ON GENERAL EDUCATION AT THE SECOND LEVEL AND SHOWN, THEREFORE, IN COLUMNS 4 AND 5. FROM 1975 TO 1977, EXPENDITURE ON UNIVERSITIES IS NOT INCLUDED.
FR—> LES DONNEES SE REFERENT A LA RIVE ORIENTALE SEULEMENT. LES DEPENSES DE L'ENSEIGNEMENT DU PREMIER DEGRE SONT INCLUSES DANS LES DEPENSES DE L'ENSEIGNEMENT GENERAL DU SECOND DEGRE ET SONT PRESENTEES EN CONSEQUENCE DANS LES COLONNES 4 ET 5. DE 1975 A 1977, LES DEPENSES DES UNIVERSITES NE SONT PAS INCLUSES.
ESP> LOS DATOS SE REFIEREN A LA ORILLA ORIENTAL SOLAMENTE. LOS GASTOS RELATIVOS A LA ENSEÑANZA DE PRIMER GRADO QUEDAN INCLUIDOS EN LOS DE LA ENSEÑANZA GENERAL DE SEGUNDO GRADO, FIGURANDO POR CONSIGUIENTE EN LAS COLUMNAS 4 Y 5. DE 1975 A 1977, NO SE INCLUYEN LOS GASTOS DE LAS UNIVERSIDADES.

KOREA REPUBLIC OF:
E—> FIGURES IN COLUMN 1 ARE IN MILLIONS.
FR—> LES CHIFFRES DE LA COLONNE 1 SONT EXPRIMES EN MILLIONS.
ESP> LAS CIFRAS DE LA COLUMNA 1 SE EXPRESAN EN MILLONES.

Public current expenditure by level of education 4.3
Dépenses publiques ordinaires par degrés d'enseignement
Gastos públicos ordinarios por grados de enseñanza

YEMEN, DEMOCRATIC:
E—> FOR 1976, EXPENDITURE ON SECOND LEVEL FIRST CYCLE (INTERMEDIATE EDUCATION) IS INCLUDED IN COLUMN 3.
FR—> EN 1976, LES DEPENSES DU PREMIER CYCLE DE L'ENSEIGNEMENT DU SECOND DEGRE (ENSEIGNEMENT INTERMEDIAIRE) SONT INCLUSES DANS LA COLONNE 3.
ESP> EN 1976, LOS GASTOS DEL PRIMER CICLO DE LA ENSEÑANZA DE SEGUNDO GRADO (ENSEÑANZA INTERMEDIA), SE INCLUYEN EN LA COLUMNA 3.

BELGIUM:
E—> EXPENDITURE OF THE MINISTRY OF EDUCATION ONLY.
FR—> DEPENSES DU MINISTERE DE L'EDUCATION SEULEMENT.
ESP> GASTOS DEL MINISTERIO DE EDUCACION SOLAMENTE.

DENMARK:
E—> FOR 1970 AND 1975, EXPENDITURE ON PRE-PRIMARY AND FIRST LEVEL EDUCATION IS INCLUDED WITH EXPENDITURE ON GENERAL EDUCATION AT THE SECOND LEVEL AND SHOWN, THEREFORE, IN COLUMNS 4 AND 5. FOR 1977, EXPENDITURE ON PRE-PRIMARY EDUCATION IS INCLUDED IN COLUMN 3.
FR—> EN 1970 ET 1975, LES DEPENSES DES ENSEIGNEMENTS PREPRIMAIRE ET DU PREMIER DEGRE SONT INCLUSES DANS LES DEPENSES DE L'ENSEIGNEMENT GENERAL DU SECOND DEGRE ET SONT PRESENTEES EN CONSEQUENCE DANS LES COLONNES 4 ET 5. EN 1977, LES DEPENSES DE L'ENSEIGNEMENT PREPRIMAIRE SONT INCLUSES DANS LA COLONNE 3.
ESP> EN 1970 Y 1975, LOS GASTOS DE LAS ENSEÑANZAS PREPRIMARIA Y DE PRIMER GRADO SE INCLUYEN EN LA ENSEÑANZA GENERAL DE SEGUNDO GRADO, FIGURANDO POR CONSIGUIENTE EN LAS COLUMNAS 4 Y 5. EN 1977, LOS GASTOS DE LA ENSEÑANZA PREPRIMARIA SE INCLUYEN EN LA COLUMNA 3.

FRANCE:
E—> EXPENDITURE OF THE MINISTRY OF EDUCATION AND MINISTRY OF THE UNIVERSITIES ONLY. FOR 1970, EXPENDITURE ON TEACHER TRAINING AT THE SECOND LEVEL IS INCLUDED IN COLUMN 8.
FR—> DEPENSES DU MINISTERE DE L'EDUCATION ET DU MINISTERE DES UNIVERSITES SEULEMENT. EN 1970, LES DEPENSES DE L'ENSEIGNEMENT NORMAL DU SECOND DEGRE SONT INCLUSES DANS LA COLONNE 8.
ESP> GASTOS DEL MINISTERIO DE EDUCACION Y DEL MINISTERIO DE LAS UNIVERSIDADES SOLAMENTE. EN 1970, LOS GASTOS DE LA ENSEÑANZA NORMAL DE SEGUNDO GRADO FIGURAN EN LA COLUMNA 8.

GERMAN DEMOCRATIC REPUBLIC:
E—> EXPENDITURE ON FIRST LEVEL EDUCATION IS INCLUDED WITH EXPENDITURE ON GENERAL EDUCATION AT THE SECOND LEVEL AND SHOWN, THEREFORE, IN COLUMNS 4 AND 5.
FR—> LES DEPENSES DE L'ENSEIGNEMENT DU PREMIER DEGRE SONT INCLUSES DANS LES DEPENSES DE L'ENSEIGNEMENT GENERAL DU SECOND DEGRE ET SONT PRESENTEES EN CONSEQUENCE, DANS LES COLONNES 4 ET 5.

FRANCE (CONT):
ESP> LOS GASTOS DE LA ENSEÑANZA DE PRIMER GRADO SE INCLUYEN EN LA ENSEÑANZA GENERAL DE SEGUNDO GRADO, FIGURANDO POR CONSIGUIENTE EN LAS COLUMNAS 4 Y 5.

GERMANY, FEDERAL REPUBLIC OF:
E—> EXPENDITURE ON PRE-PRIMARY EDUCATION IS INCLUDED IN COLUMN 3. FOR 1970, THE TOTALITY OF EXPENDITURE ON "GRUND-UND HAUPTSCHULEN" WAS CLASSIFIED WITH PRIMARY EDUCATION; FROM 1975 ONWARDS, IT IS DISTRIBUTED BETWEEN PRIMARY EDUCATION (56%) AND SECONDARY EDUCATION (44%). IT SHOULD BE NOTED THAT FOR 1970, EXPENDITURE FOR THIRD LEVEL EDUCATION INCLUDES EXPENDITURE FOR RESEARCH.
FR—> LES DEPENSES DE L'ENSEIGNEMENT PREPRIMAIRE SONT INCLUSES DANS LA COLONNE 3. EN 1970, LA TOTALITE DES DEPENSES RELATIVES AUX "GRUND-UND HAUPTSCHULEN" A ETE CLASSEE DANS L'ENSEIGNEMENT DU PREMIER DEGRE; A PARTIR DE 1975, CES DEPENSES SONT CLASSEES EN PARTIE AVEC L'ENSEIGNEMENT DU PREMIER DEGRE (56%) ET EN PARTIE AVEC L'ENSEIGNEMENT DU SECOND DEGRE (44%). IL FAUT AUSSI NOTER QU'EN 1970 LES DEPENSES DE L'ENSEIGNEMENT DU TROISIEME DEGRE INCLUENT LES DEPENSES POUR LA RECHERCHE.
ESP> LOS GASTOS DE LA ENSEÑANZA PREPRIMARIA SE INCLUYEN EN LA COLUMNA 3. EN 1970, LA TOTALIDAD DE LOS GASTOS RELATIVOS A LOS "GRUND-UND HAUPTSCHULEN" SE HA CLASIFICADO EN LA ENSEÑANZA DE PRIMER GRADO; A PARTIR DE 1975, ESTOS GASTOS SE HAN CLASIFICADO EN PARTE EN LA ENSEÑANZA DE PRIMER GRADO (56%) Y EN PARTE EN LA DEL SEGUNDO GRADO (44%). ES DE NOTAR QUE EN 1970 LOS GASTOS RELATIVOS A LA ENSEÑANZA DE TERCER GRADO INCLUYEN LOS GASTOS DESTINADOS A LA INVESTIGACION.

IRELAND:
E—> EXPENDITURE ON PRE-PRIMARY EDUCATION IS INCLUDED IN COLUMN 3. FROM 1975 TO 1977, EXPENDITURE RELATING TO DEBT SERVICE HAS BEEN INCLUDED WITH CURRENT EXPENDITURE.
FR—> LES DEPENSES DE L'ENSEIGNEMENT PREPRIMAIRE SONT INCLUSES DANS LA COLONNE 3. DE 1975 A 1977 LES DEPENSES RELATIVES AU SERVICE DE LA DETTE ONT ETE INCLUSES AVEC LES DEPENSES ORDINAIRES.
ESP> LOS GASTOS DE LA ENSEÑANZA PREPRIMARIA SE INCLUYEN EN LA COLUMNA 3. DE 1975 A 1977, LOS GASTOS RELATIVOS AL SERVICIO DE LA DEUDA, SE HAN INCLUIDO EN LOS GASTOS ORDINARIOS.

ITALY:
E—> FIGURES IN COLUMN 1 ARE IN MILLIONS.
FR—> LES CHIFFRES DE LA COLONNE 1 SONT EXPRIMES EN MILLIONS.
ESP> LAS CIFRAS DE LA COLUMNA 1 SE EXPRESAN EN MILLONES.

LUXEMBOURG:
E—> DATA REFER TO CENTRAL GOVERNMENT EXPENDITURE, INCLUDING REIMBURSEMENTS BY LOCAL AUTHORITIES OF STAFF EXPENDITURE. EXPENDITURE ON PRE-PRIMARY EDUCATION IS INCLUDED IN COLUMN 3.

4.3 Public current expenditure by level of education
Dépenses publiques ordinaires par degrés d'enseignement
Gastos públicos ordinarios por grados de enseñanza

LUXEMBOURG (CONT):
FR—> LES DONNEES SE REFERENT AUX DEPENSES DU GOUVERNEMENT CENTRAL, Y COMPRIS LES REMBOURSEMENTS PAR LES AUTORITES LOCALES DES DEPENSES DU PERSONNEL. LES DEPENSES DE L'ENSEIGNEMENT PREPRIMAIRE SONT INCLUSES DANS LA COLONNE 3.
ESP> LOS DATOS SE REFIEREN A LOS GASTOS DEL GOBIERNO CENTRAL, INCLUIDOS LOS REEMBOLSOS DE LOS GASTOS DE PERSONAL EFECTUADOS POR LAS AUTORIDADES LOCALES. LOS DATOS RELATIVOS A LA ENSEÑANZA PREPRIMARIA FIGURAN EN LA COLUMNA 3.

MALTA:
E—> EXPENDITURE ON PRE-PRIMARY EDUCATION IS INCLUDED IN COLUMN 3.
FR—> LES DEPENSES DE L'ENSEIGNEMENT PREPRIMAIRE SONT INCLUSES DANS LA COLONNE 3.
ESP> LOS GASTOS DE LA ENSEÑANZA PREPRIMARIA FIGURAN EN LA COLUMNA 3.

NORWAY:
E—> FOR 1970, CAPITAL EXPENDITURE IS INCLUDED.
FR—> EN 1970, LES DEPENSES EN CAPITAL SONT INCLUSES.
ESP> EN 1970, INCLUIDOS LOS GASTOS DE CAPITAL.

POLAND:
E—> FIGURES IN COLUMN 1 ARE IN MILLIONS.
FR—> LES CHIFFRES DE LA COLONNE 1 SONT EXPRIMES EN MILLIONS.
ESP> LAS CIFRAS DE LA COLUMNA 1 SE EXPRESAN EN MILLONES.

PORTUGAL:
E—> EXPENDITURE OF THE MINISTRY OF EDUCATION ONLY.
FR—> DEPENSES DU MINISTERE DE L'EDUCATION SEULEMENT.
ESP> GASTOS DEL MINISTERIO DE EDUCACION SOLAMENTE.

ROMANIA:
E—> EXPENDITURE ON FIRST LEVEL EDUCATION IS INCLUDED WITH EXPENDITURE ON GENERAL EDUCATION AT THE SECOND LEVEL AND IS SHOWN, THEREFORE, IN COLUMNS 4 AND 5.
FR—> LES DEPENSES DE L'ENSEIGNEMENT DU PREMIER DEGRE SONT INCLUSES DANS LES DEPENSES DE L'ENSEIGNEMENT GENERAL DU SECOND DEGRE ET SONT PRESENTEES EN CONSEQUENCE, DANS LES COLONNES 4 ET 5.
ESP> LOS GASTOS DE LA ENSEÑANZA DE PRIMER GRADO QUEDAN INCLUIDOS EN LOS DE LA ENSEÑANZA GENERAL DE SEGUNDO GRADO, FIGURANDO POR CONSIGUIENTE EN LAS COLUMNAS 4 Y 5.

SAN MARINO:
E—> EXPENDITURE IN PRE-PRIMARY EDUCATION IS INCLUDED IN COLUMN 3. DATA IN COLUMN 8 REFER TO SCHOLARSHIPS FOR THE STUDENTS AT THE SECOND AND THIRD LEVELS OF EDUCATION.

SAN MARINO (CONT):
FR—> LES DEPENSES DE L'ENSEIGNEMENT PREPRIMAIRE SONT INCLUSES DANS LA COLONNE 3. LES DONNEES DE LA COLONNE 8 SE REFERENT AUX BOURSES POUR LES ETUDIANTS DES ENSEIGNEMENTS DU SECOND ET DU TROISIEME DEGRE.
ESP> LOS GASTOS DE LA ENSEÑANZA PREPRIMARIA FIGURAN EN LA COLUMNA 3. LOS DATOS DE LA COLUMNA 8 SE REFIEREN A LAS BECAS PARA LOS ESTUDIANTES DE LAS ENSEÑANZAS DE SEGUNDO Y TERCER GRADO.

SPAIN:
E—> FIGURES IN COLUMN 1 ARE IN MILLIONS. EXPENDITURE ON PRE-PRIMARY EDUCATION IS INCLUDED IN COLUMN 3.
FR—> LES CHIFFRES DE LA COLONNE 1 SONT EXPRIMES EN MILLIONS. LES DEPENSES DE L'ENSEIGNEMENT PREPRIMAIRE SONT INCLUSES DANS LA COLONNE 3.
ESP> LAS CIFRAS DE LA COLUMNA 1 SE EXPRESAN EN MILLONES. LOS GASTOS DE LA ENSEÑANZA PREPRIMARIA FIGURAN EN LA COLUMNA 3.

SWITZERLAND:
E—> FROM 1975 TO 1977 EXPENDITURE ON FIRST LEVEL EDUCATION IS INCLUDED WITH EXPENDITURE ON GENERAL EDUCATION AT THE SECOND LEVEL AND IS SHOWN, THEREFORE, IN COLUMNS 4 AND 5.
FR—> DE 1975 A 1977 LES DEPENSES DE L'ENSEIGNEMENT DU PREMIER DEGRE SONT INCLUSES DANS LES DEPENSES DE L'ENSEIGNEMENT GENERAL DU SECOND DEGRE ET SONT PRESENTEES EN CONSEQUENCE, DANS LES COLONNES 4 ET 5.
ESP> DE 1975 A 1977 LOS GASTOS DE LA ENSEÑANZA DE PRIMER GRADO QUEDAN INCLUIDOS EN LOS DE LA ENSEÑANZA GENERAL DE SEGUNDO GRADO, FIGURANDO POR CONSIGUIENTE EN LAS COLUMNAS 4 Y 5.

UNITED KINGDOM:
E—> FIGURES IN COLUMN 1 ARE IN MILLIONS. EXPENDITURE ON PRE-PRIMARY EDUCATION IS INCLUDED IN COLUMN 3.
FR—> LES CHIFFRES DE LA COLONNE 1 SONT EXPRIMES EN MILLIONS. LES DEPENSES DE L'ENSEIGNEMENT PREPRIMAIRE SONT INCLUSES DANS LA COLONNE 3.
ESP> LAS CIFRAS DE LA COLUMNA 1 SE EXPRESAN EN MILLONES. LOS GASTOS DE LA ENSEÑANZA PREPRIMARIA FIGURAN EN LA COLUMNA 3.

AMERICAN SAMOA:
E—> EXPENDITURE ON PRE-PRIMARY EDUCATION IS INCLUDED IN COLUMN 3.
FR—> LES DEPENSES DE L'ENSEIGNEMENT PREPRIMAIRE SONT INCLUSES DANS LA COLONNE 3.
ESP> LOS GASTOS DE LA ENSEÑANZA PREPRIMARIA FIGURAN EN LA COLUMNA 3.

FRENCH POLYNESIA:
E—> FOR 1970, DATA FOR COLUMN 7 ARE INCLUDED IN COLUMN 5.
FR—> EN 1970, LES DONNEES DE LA COLONNE 7 SONT INCLUSES DANS LA COLONNE 5.
ESP> EN 1970, LOS DATOS DE LA COLUMNA 7 SE INCLUYEN EN LA COLUMNA 5.

Public current expenditure by level of education 4.3
Dépenses publiques ordinaires par degrés d'enseignement
Gastos públicos ordinarios por grados de enseñanza

U.S.S.R. (CONT):
PUES UNICAMENTE A LA ENSEÑANZA TECNICA Y PROFESIONAL
(COLUMNA 7) QUE COMPRENDE LA ENSEÑANZA NORMAL
(COLUMNA 6). LA EDUCACION ESPECIAL SE DISTRIBUYE
ENTRE LAS COLUMNAS 3 Y 7.

BYELORUSSIAN S.S.R.:
E—> EXPENDITURE ON PRE-PRIMARY EDUCATION
INCLUDES PLAYS CENTRES. GENERAL EDUCATION AT THE
SECOND LEVEL IS INCLUDED WITH FIRST LEVEL (COLUMN
3). TOTAL SECOND LEVEL (COLUMN 4) THEREFORE,
REFERS TO TECHNICAL AND VOCATIONAL EDUCATION ONLY
(COLUMN 7) WHICH INCLUDES TEACHER TRAINING (COLUMN
6). SPECIAL EDUCATION IS INCLUDED PARTLY IN
COLUMN 3 AND PARTLY IN COLUMN 7.
FR—> LES DEPENSES DE L'ENSEIGNEMENT PREPRIMAIRE
COMPRENNENT LES GARDERIES D'ENFANTS. L'ENSEIGNEMENT
GENERAL DU SECOND DEGRE EST INCLUS AVEC
L'ENSEIGNEMENT DU PREMIER DEGRE (COLONNE 3).
LE TOTAL DE L'ENSEIGNEMENT DU SECOND DEGRE (COLONNE
4) SE REFERE DONC UNIQUEMENT A L'ENSEIGNEMENT
TECHNIQUE ET PROFESSIONNEL (COLONNE 7) QUI
COMPREND L'ENSEIGNEMENT NORMAL (COLONNE 6).
L'ENSEIGNEMENT SPECIAL EST COMPRIS EN PARTIE DANS
LA COLONNE 3 ET EN PARTIE DANS LA COLONNE 7.
ESP> LOS GASTOS DE LA ENSEÑANZA PREPRIMARIA
COMPRENDEN LAS GUARDERIAS. LA ENSEÑANZA GENERAL
DE SEGUNDO GRADO SE INCLUYE EN LA ENSEÑANZA
DE PRIMER GRADO (COLUMNA 3). EL TOTAL DE LA
ENSEÑANZA DE SEGUNDO GRADO (COLUMNA 4) SE REFIERE
PUES UNICAMENTE A LA ENSEÑANZA TECNICA Y PROFESIONAL
(COLUMNA 7) QUE COMPRENDE LA ENSEÑANZA NORMAL
(COLUMNA 6). LA EDUCACION ESPECIAL SE DISTRIBUYE
ENTRE LAS COLUMNAS 3 Y 7.

UKRAINIAN S.S.R.:
E—> EXPENDITURE ON PRE-PRIMARY EDUCATION AT THE
INCLUDES PLAYS CENTRES. GENERAL EDUCATION AT THE
SECOND LEVEL IS INCLUDED WITH FIRST LEVEL (COLUMN
3). TOTAL SECOND LEVEL (COLUMN 4) THEREFORE,
REFERS TO TECHNICAL AND VOCATIONAL EDUCATION ONLY
(COLUMN 7) WHICH INCLUDES TEACHER TRAINING (COLUMN
6). SPECIAL EDUCATION IS INCLUDED PARTLY IN
COLUMN 3 AND PARTLY IN COLUMN 7.
FR—> LES DEPENSES DE L'ENSEIGNEMENT PREPRIMAIRE
COMPRENNENT LES GARDERIES D'ENFANTS. L'ENSEIGNEMENT
GENERAL DU SECOND DEGRE EST INCLUS AVEC
L'ENSEIGNEMENT DU PREMIER DEGRE (COLONNE 3).
LE TOTAL DE L'ENSEIGNEMENT DU SECOND DEGRE (COLONNE
4) SE REFERE DONC UNIQUEMENT A L'ENSEIGNEMENT
TECHNIQUE ET PROFESSIONNEL (COLONNE 7) QUI
COMPREND L'ENSEIGNEMENT NORMAL (COLONNE 6).
L'ENSEIGNEMENT SPECIAL EST COMPRIS EN PARTIE DANS
LA COLONNE 3 ET EN PARTIE DANS LA COLONNE 7.
ESP> LOS GASTOS DE LA ENSEÑANZA PREPRIMARIA
COMPRENDEN LAS GUARDERIAS. LA ENSEÑANZA GENERAL
DE SEGUNDO GRADO SE INCLUYE EN LA ENSEÑANZA
DE PRIMER GRADO (COLUMNA 3). EL TOTAL DE LA
ENSEÑANZA DE SEGUNDO GRADO (COLUMNA 4) SE REFIERE
PUES UNICAMENTE A LA ENSEÑANZA TECNICA Y PROFESIONAL
(COLUMNA 7) QUE COMPRENDE LA ENSEÑANZA NORMAL
(COLUMNA 6). LA EDUCACION ESPECIAL SE DISTRIBUYE
ENTRE LAS COLUMNAS 3 Y 7.

GUAM:
E—> EXPENDITURE ON PRE-PRIMARY EDUCATION IS
INCLUDED IN COLUMN 3.
FR—> LES DEPENSES DE L'ENSEIGNEMENT PREPRIMAIRE
SONT INCLUSES DANS LA COLONNE 3.
ESP> LOS GASTOS DE LA ENSEÑANZA PREPRIMARIA
FIGURAN EN LA COLUMNA 3.

NEW HEBRIDES (EXPENDITURE IN FRENCH FRANCS -
DEPENSES EN FRANCS FRANCAIS - GASTOS EN
FRANCOS FRANCESES):
E—> FOR 1970 CAPITAL EXPENDITURE IS INCLUDED.
FR—> EN 1970, LES DEPENSES EN CAPITAL SONT
INCLUSES.
ESP> EN 1970, INCLUIDOS LOS GASTOS DE CAPITAL.

NEW ZEALAND:
E—> FOR 1970, EXPENDITURE ON PRE-PRIMARY
EDUCATION IS INCLUDED IN COLUMN 3.
FR—> EN 1970, LES DEPENSES DE L'ENSEIGNEMENT
PREPRIMAIRE SONT INCLUSES DANS LA COLONNE 3.
ESP> EN 1970, LOS GASTOS DE LA ENSEÑANZA
PREPRIMARIA FIGURAN EN LA COLUMNA 3.

PAPUA NEW GUINEA:
E—> EXPENDITURE ON PRE-PRIMARY EDUCATION IS
INCLUDED IN COLUMN 3.
FR—> LES DEPENSES DE L'ENSEIGNEMENT PREPRIMAIRE
SONT INCLUSES DANS LA COLONNE 3.
ESP> LOS GASTOS DE LA ENSEÑANZA PREPRIMARIA
FIGURAN EN LA COLUMNA 3.

TONGA:
E—> FOR 1971 AND 1974, EXPENDITURE OF THE
MINISTRY OF EDUCATION ONLY.
FR—> EN 1971 ET 1974, DEPENSES DU MINISTERE DE
L'EDUCATION SEULEMENT.
ESP> EN 1971 Y 1974, GASTOS DEL MINISTERIO DE
EDUCACION SOLAMENTE.

U.S.S.R.:
E—> EXPENDITURE ON PRE-PRIMARY EDUCATION
INCLUDES PLAYS CENTRES. GENERAL EDUCATION AT THE
SECOND LEVEL IS INCLUDED WITH FIRST LEVEL (COLUMN
3). TOTAL SECOND LEVEL (COLUMN 4) THEREFORE,
REFERS TO TECHNICAL AND VOCATIONAL EDUCATION ONLY
(COLUMN 7) WHICH INCLUDES TEACHER TRAINING (COLUMN
6). SPECIAL EDUCATION IS INCLUDED PARTLY IN
COLUMN 3 AND PARTLY IN COLUMN 7.
FR—> LES DEPENSES DE L'ENSEIGNEMENT PREPRIMAIRE
COMPRENNENT LES GARDERIES D'ENFANTS. L'ENSEIGNEME
GENERAL DU SECOND DEGRE EST INCLUS AVEC
L'ENSEIGNEMENT DU PREMIER DEGRE (COLONNE 3).
LE TOTAL DE L'ENSEIGNEMENT DU SECOND DEGRE (COLONN
4) SE REFERE DONC UNIQUEMENT A L'ENSEIGNEMENT
TECHNIQUE ET PROFESSIONNEL (COLONNE 7) QUI
COMPREND L'ENSEIGNEMENT NORMAL (COLONNE 6).
L'ENSEIGNEMENT SPECIAL EST COMPRIS EN PARTIE DANS
LA COLONNE 3 ET EN PARTIE DANS LA COLONNE 7
ESP> LOS GASTOS DE LA ENSEÑANZA PREPRIMARIA
COMPRENDEN LAS GUARDERIAS. LA ENSEÑANZA GENERAL
DE SEGUNDO GRADO SE INCLUYE EN LA ENSEÑANZA
DE PRIMER GRADO (COLUMNA 3). EL TOTAL DE LA
ENSEÑANZA DE SEGUNDO GRADO (COLUMNA 4) SE REFIERE

4.4 Public current expenditure by level and by purpose
Dépenses publiques ordinaires par degré d'enseignement et destination
Gastos públicos ordinarios por grados de enseñanza y destino

4.4 Public current expenditure on education: distribution by level of education and by purpose
Dépenses publiques ordinaires afférentes à l'enseignement: répartition par degrés d'enseignement et selon leur destination
Gastos públicos ordinarios destinados a la educación: distribución por grados de enseñanza y según su destino

TOTAL CURRENT EXPENDITURE = TOTAL DES DEPENSES ORDINAIRES / TOTAL DE GASTOS ORDINARIOS
EMOLUMENTS OF TEACHERS = EMOLUMENTS DU PERSONNEL ENSEIGNANT / EMOLUMENTOS DEL PERSONAL DOCENTE
OTHER DIRECT INSTRUCTIONAL EXPENDITURE = AUTRES DEPENSES DIRECTES D'ENSEIGNEMENT / OTROS GASTOS DIRECTOS DE EDUCACION
SCHOLARSHIPS/GRANTS = BOURSES ET ALLOCATIONS / BECAS Y SUBVENCIONES
WELFARE SERVICES = SERVICES SOCIAUX / SERVICIOS SOCIALES
NOT DISTRIBUTED/ADMINISTRATION = NON REPARTIES/ADMINISTRATION / SIN DISTRIBUCION/ADMINISTRACION

NUMBER OF COUNTRIES AND TERRITORIES PRESENTED IN THIS TABLE: 81
NOMBRE DE PAYS ET DE TERRITOIRES PRESENTES DANS CE TABLEAU: 81
NUMERO DE PAISES Y DE TERRITORIOS PRESENTADOS EN ESTE CUADRO: 81

COUNTRY / PAYS / PAIS	YEAR / ANNEE / AÑO	PURPOSE / DESTINATION / DESTINO	TOTAL CURRENT EXPENDITURE (000) / TOTAL DES DEPENSES ORDINAIRES (000) / TOTAL DE GASTOS ORDINARIOS (000) (1)	PRE-PRIMARY / PRE-PRIMAIRE / PRE-PRIMARIA (2)	FIRST LEVEL / PREMIER DEGRE / PRIMER GRADO (3)	SECOND LEVEL / SECOND DEGRE / SEGUNDO GRADO (4)	THIRD LEVEL / TROISIEME DEGRE / TERCER GRADO (5)	OTHER TYPES AND NOT DISTRIBUTED / AUTRES TYPES ET NON REPARTIES / OTROS TIPOS Y SIN DISTRIBUCION (6)
AFRICA								
ALGERIA ‡ DINAR	1974	TOTAL CURRENT EXPENDITURE	1 609 900	—	882 165	649 133	...	78 602
		EMOLUMENTS OF TEACHERS	1 306 550	—	782 166	488 962	...	35 422
		OTHER DIRECT EXPENDITURE	86 125	—	10 750	32 195	...	43 180
		SCHOLARSHIPS/GRANTS	133 650	—	5 674	127 976	...	—
		WELFARE SERVICES	83 575	—	83 575	—	...	—

724

Public current expenditure by level and by purpose   4.4
Dépenses publiques ordinaires par degré d'enseignement et destination
Gastos públicos ordinarios por grados de enseñanza y destino

	(1)	(2)	(3)	(4)	(5)	(6)
BOTSWANA — PULA — 1977						
TOTAL CURRENT EXPENDITURE	15 920	—	7 938	5 318	2 342	322
EMOLUMENTS OF TEACHERS	9 347	—	6 630	2 717	—	—
OTHER DIRECT EXPENDITURE	2 111	—	1 046	1 065	—	—
SCHOLARSHIPS/GRANTS	3 099	—	26	731	2 342	—
WELFARE SERVICES	1 041	—	236	805	—	—
NOT DISTRIBUTED/ADMINISTRATION	322	—	—	—	—	322
BURUNDI — FRANC — 1976						
TOTAL CURRENT EXPENDITURE	884 608	—	379 375	303 211	172 783	29 239
EMOLUMENTS OF TEACHERS	644 637	—	374 094	184 404	72 418	13 721
OTHER DIRECT EXPENDITURE	92 629	—	5 281	28 097	59 251	—
SCHOLARSHIPS/GRANTS	41 114	—	—	—	41 114	—
WELFARE SERVICES	90 710	—	—	90 710	—	—
NOT DISTRIBUTED/ADMINISTRATION	15 518	—	—	—	—	15 518
CENTRAL AFRICAN REPUBLIC — FRANC C.F.A. — 1977						
TOTAL CURRENT EXPENDITURE	4 389 000	—	2 360 000	656 000	564 000	809 000
EMOLUMENTS OF TEACHERS	2 769 000	—	2 342 000	378 000	38 000	11 000
OTHER DIRECT EXPENDITURE	80 000	—	—	—	—	80 000
SCHOLARSHIPS/GRANTS	744 000	—	—	235 000	485 000	24 000
NOT DISTRIBUTED/ADMINISTRATION	796 000	—	18 000	43 000	41 000	694 000
CONGO ‡ — FRANC C.F.A. — 1976						
TOTAL CURRENT EXPENDITURE	13 850 859	135 709	4 655 968	4 756 134	3 281 583	1 021 465
EMOLUMENTS OF TEACHERS	8 784 967	112 644	4 553 743	3 217 902	461 477	439 201
OTHER DIRECT EXPENDITURE	979 668	23 065	102 225	247 217	552 971	54 190
SCHOLARSHIPS/GRANTS	3 558 150	—	—	1 291 015	2 267 135	—
NOT DISTRIBUTED/ADMINISTRATION	528 074	—	—	—	—	528 074
EGYPT ‡ — POUND — 1977						
TOTAL CURRENT EXPENDITURE	330 427	./.	./.	221 964	108 463	—
EMOLUMENTS OF TEACHERS	261 200	./.	./.	193 456	67 744	—
GHANA ‡ — CEDI — 1976						
TOTAL CURRENT EXPENDITURE	293 102	—	93 363	134 762	6 287	58 690
EMOLUMENTS OF TEACHERS	214 784	—	90 229	117 584	5 619	1 352
GUINEA-BISSAU ‡ — ESCUDO — 1978						
TOTAL CURRENT EXPENDITURE	270 684	—	119 000	98 000	34 500	19 184
EMOLUMENTS OF TEACHERS	150 000	—	109 000	22 000	7 000	12 000
OTHER DIRECT EXPENDITURE	7 000	—	2 000	—	—	2 000
SCHOLARSHIPS/GRANTS	91 000	—	—	66 000	25 000	—
WELFARE SERVICES	5 000	—	2 000	2 000	—	1 000
NOT DISTRIBUTED/ADMINISTRATION	17 684	—	6 000	6 000	1 500	4 184
IVORY COAST ‡ — FRANC C.F.A. — 1976						
TOTAL CURRENT EXPENDITURE	61 888	—	24 690	23 226	10 523	3 449
EMOLUMENTS OF TEACHERS	44 432	—	22 204	18 051	3 682	495
OTHER DIRECT EXPENDITURE	5 065	—	2 332	1 657	891	185
SCHOLARSHIPS/GRANTS	5 595	—	112	1 813	3 606	64
WELFARE SERVICES	3 922	—	42	1 530	2 344	6
NOT DISTRIBUTED/ADMINISTRATION	2 874	—	—	175	—	2 699
LIBYAN ARAB JAMAHIRIYA ‡ — DINAR — 1977						
TOTAL CURRENT EXPENDITURE	154 660	—	86 814	55 942	...	11 904
EMOLUMENTS OF TEACHERS	141 466	—	83 030	51 245	...	7 191
OTHER DIRECT EXPENDITURE	2 342	—	1 632	—	...	74
WELFARE SERVICES	4 051	—	918	2 594	...	539
NOT DISTRIBUTED/ADMINISTRATION	6 801	—	1 234	1 467	...	4 100
MADAGASCAR — FRANC — 1975						
TOTAL CURRENT EXPENDITURE	11 726 747	—	5 027 950	3 576 482	1 630 000	1 492 315
EMOLUMENTS OF TEACHERS	9 119 706	—	4 947 350	2 816 261	1 058 595	297 500
OTHER DIRECT EXPENDITURE	525 421	—	80 600	444 821	—	—
SCHOLARSHIPS/GRANTS	668 805	—	—	115 400	553 405	—
WELFARE SERVICES	52 000	—	—	—	18 000	34 000
NOT DISTRIBUTED/ADMINISTRATION	1 360 815	—	—	200 000	—	1 160 815

4.4 Public current expenditure by level and by purpose
Dépenses publiques ordinaires par degré d'enseignement et destination
Gastos públicos ordinarios por grados de enseñanza y destino

COUNTRY / PAYS / PAIS	YEAR / ANNEE / AÑO	PURPOSE / DESTINATION / DESTINO	TOTAL CURRENT EXPENDITURE (000) / TOTAL DES DEPENSES ORDINAIRES (000) / TOTAL DE GASTOS ORDINARIOS (000) (1)	PRE-PRIMARY / PRE-PRIMAIRE / PRE-PRIMARIA (2)	FIRST LEVEL / PREMIER DEGRE / PRIMER GRADO (3)	SECOND LEVEL / SECOND DEGRE / SEGUNDO GRADO (4)	THIRD LEVEL / TROISIEME DEGRE / TERCER GRADO (5)	OTHER TYPES AND NOT DISTRIBUTED / AUTRES TYPES ET NON REPARTIES / OTROS TIPOS Y SIN DISTRIBUCION (6)
MALAWI ‡ KWACHA	1975	TOTAL CURRENT EXPENDITURE	11 992	—	5 349	2 786	2 738	1 119
		EMOLUMENTS OF TEACHERS	9 387	—	5 302	1 281	2 738	66
		OTHER DIRECT EXPENDITURE	223	—	17	200	—	6
		SCHOLARSHIPS/GRANTS	734	—	—	710	—	24
		WELFARE SERVICES	750	—	30	595	—	125
		NOT DISTRIBUTED/ADMINISTRATION	898	—	—	—	—	898
MALI ‡ FRANC	1977	TOTAL CURRENT EXPENDITURE	16 312 518	40 106	7 510 445	4 306 782	3 270 954	1 184 231
		EMOLUMENTS OF TEACHERS	9 947 105	33 018	7 264 535	1 993 676	543 056	112 820
		OTHER DIRECT EXPENDITURE	570 516	7 088	245 910	235 030	58 988	23 500
		SCHOLARSHIPS/GRANTS	4 746 986	—	—	2 078 076	2 668 910	—
		WELFARE SERVICES	—	—	—	—	—	—
		NOT DISTRIBUTED/ADMINISTRATION	1 047 911	—	—	—	—	1 047 911
MAURITIUS RUPEE	1977	TOTAL CURRENT EXPENDITURE	246 700	—	101 500	97 100	22 200	25 900
		EMOLUMENTS OF TEACHERS	195 600	—	81 100	92 300	22 200	—
		OTHER DIRECT EXPENDITURE	500	—	100	200	—	—
		SCHOLARSHIPS/GRANTS	9 000	—	—	—	—	8 900
		WELFARE SERVICES	7 300	—	6 600	700	—	—
		NOT DISTRIBUTED/ADMINISTRATION	34 300	—	13 400	3 900	—	17 000
MOROCCO ‡ DIRHAM	1976	TOTAL CURRENT EXPENDITURE	1 561 014	—	711 474	848 940	...	600
		EMOLUMENTS OF TEACHERS	1 220 684	—	539 868	680 416	...	400
		OTHER DIRECT EXPENDITURE	65 715	—	14 720	50 995	...	—
		SCHOLARSHIPS/GRANTS	3 855	—	1 965	1 840	...	50
		WELFARE SERVICES	—	—	—	—	...	—
		NOT DISTRIBUTED/ADMINISTRATION	270 760	—	154 921	115 689	...	150
RWANDA ‡ FRANC	1977	TOTAL CURRENT EXPENDITURE	1 504 570	—	985 921	247 212	212 123	59 314
		EMOLUMENTS OF TEACHERS	1 210 530	—	942 576	149 830	118 124	—
		OTHER DIRECT EXPENDITURE	41 853	—	29 154	9 901	—	2 798
		SCHOLARSHIPS/GRANTS	93 999	—	—	—	93 999	—
		WELFARE SERVICES	84 999	—	—	84 999	—	—
		NOT DISTRIBUTED/ADMINISTRATION	73 189	—	14 191	2 482	—	56 516
SEYCHELLES RUPEE	1976	TOTAL CURRENT EXPENDITURE	14 866	—	5 024	4 923	1 521	3 398
		EMOLUMENTS OF TEACHERS	10 955	—	4 861	4 563	1 159	372
		OTHER DIRECT EXPENDITURE	769	—	—	—	—	769
		SCHOLARSHIPS/GRANTS	570	—	163	260	147	—
		WELFARE SERVICES	319	—	—	100	215	4
		NOT DISTRIBUTED/ADMINISTRATION	2 253	—	—	—	—	2 253

Public current expenditure by level and by purpose   4.4
Dépenses publiques ordinaires par degré d'enseignement et destination
Gastos públicos ordinarios por grados de enseñanza y destino

		(1)	(2)	(3)	(4)	(5)	(6)
UGANDA ‡ SHILLING	1975						
	TOTAL CURRENT EXPENDITURE	529 014	—	217 258	176 556	115 832	19 368
	EMOLUMENTS OF TEACHERS	321 578	—	211 837	56 518	53 183	40
	OTHER DIRECT EXPENDITURE	137 497	—	247	113 660	13 202	10 388
	SCHOLARSHIPS/GRANTS	25 265	—	—	726	24 539	—
	WELFARE SERVICES	26 836	—	363	2 521	23 803	149
	NOT DISTRIBUTED/ADMINISTRATION	17 838	—	4 811	3 131	1 105	8 791
UPPER VOLTA ‡ FRANC C.F.A.	1977						
	TOTAL CURRENT EXPENDITURE	4 279 627	—	1 779 354	1 125 812	1 191 803	182 658
	EMOLUMENTS OF TEACHERS	2 531 701	—	1 747 254	707 277	77 170	—
	OTHER DIRECT EXPENDITURE	60 568	—	32 100	26 098	2 370	—
	SCHOLARSHIPS/GRANTS	1 241 263	—	—	145 000	1 096 263	—
	WELFARE SERVICES	247 437	—	—	247 437	—	—
	NOT DISTRIBUTED/ADMINISTRATION	198 658	—	—	—	16 000	182 658
ZAMBIA KWACHA	1978						
	TOTAL CURRENT EXPENDITURE	101 230	—	48 400	34 170	9 540	9 120
	EMOLUMENTS OF TEACHERS	73 240	—	43 680	23 020	6 540	—
	OTHER DIRECT EXPENDITURE	5 150	—	3 170	1 650	330	—
	SCHOLARSHIPS/GRANTS	760	—	—	400	360	—
	WELFARE SERVICES	7 520	—	110	6 350	1 060	—
	NOT DISTRIBUTED/ADMINISTRATION	14 560	—	1 440	2 750	1 250	9 120
AMERICA, NORTH							
CANADA ‡ DOLLAR	1977						
	TOTAL CURRENT EXPENDITURE	14 875 416	./.	./.	8 999 627	3 941 985	1 933 804
	EMOLUMENTS OF TEACHERS	9 180 922	./.	./.	5 609 542	2 377 860	1 193 520
	OTHER DIRECT EXPENDITURE	879 908	./.	./.	537 625	227 896	114 387
	SCHOLARSHIPS/GRANTS	149 418	./.	./.	—	129 994	19 424
	WELFARE SERVICES	2 490 303	./.	./.	1 521 575	644 989	323 739
	NOT DISTRIBUTED/ADMINISTRATION	2 174 865	./.	./.	1 330 885	561 246	282 734
COSTA RICA ‡ COLON	1975						
	TOTAL CURRENT EXPENDITURE	1 041 297	./.	387 208	232 991	253 800	167 298
	EMOLUMENTS OF TEACHERS	860 168	./.	380 319	216 975	253 800	9 074
	OTHER DIRECT EXPENDITURE	20 173	./.	2 895	15 885	—	1 393
	SCHOLARSHIPS/GRANTS	—	./.	—	—	—	—
	WELFARE SERVICES	—	./.	—	131	—	—
	NOT DISTRIBUTED/ADMINISTRATION	160 956	./.	3 994	131	—	156 831
DOMINICAN REPUBLIC ‡ PESO	1977						
	TOTAL CURRENT EXPENDITURE	67 783	—	23 666	13 505	12 766	17 846
	EMOLUMENTS OF TEACHERS	50 024	—	22 884	12 807	12 766	1 567
	OTHER DIRECT EXPENDITURE	2 212	—	782	698	—	732
	SCHOLARSHIPS/GRANTS	10	—	—	—	—	10
	WELFARE SERVICES	—	—	—	—	—	—
	NOT DISTRIBUTED/ADMINISTRATION	15 537	—	—	—	—	15 537
EL SALVADOR COLON	1975						
	TOTAL CURRENT EXPENDITURE	138 364	—	79 576	9 126	32 821	16 841
	EMOLUMENTS OF TEACHERS	114 103	—	77 675	8 377	26 327	1 724
	OTHER DIRECT EXPENDITURE	10 858	—	1 901	494	4 647	3 816
	SCHOLARSHIPS/GRANTS	2 295	—	—	99	1 722	474
	WELFARE SERVICES	570	—	—	156	125	289
	NOT DISTRIBUTED/ADMINISTRATION	10 538	—	—	—	—	10 538
GUATEMALA ‡ QUETZAL	1976						
	TOTAL CURRENT EXPENDITURE	67 193	1 664	34 443	10 419	13 396	7 271
	EMOLUMENTS OF TEACHERS	53 445	1 519	33 401	8 114	9 845	566
	OTHER DIRECT EXPENDITURE	7 625	145	982	1 936	2 910	1 652
	SCHOLARSHIPS/GRANTS	1 070	—	60	369	641	—
	WELFARE SERVICES	—	—	—	—	—	—
	NOT DISTRIBUTED/ADMINISTRATION	5 053	—	—	—	—	5 053
HAITI GOURDE	1976						
	TOTAL CURRENT EXPENDITURE	37 191	—	23 608	6 585	4 085	2 913
	EMOLUMENTS OF TEACHERS	31 761	—	22 268	5 650	3 255	588
	OTHER DIRECT EXPENDITURE	1 628	—	455	758	415	—
	SCHOLARSHIPS/GRANTS	3 802	—	885	177	415	2 325
	WELFARE SERVICES	—	—	—	—	—	—
	NOT DISTRIBUTED/ADMINISTRATION	—	—	—	—	—	—

4.4 Public current expenditure by level and by purpose
Dépenses publiques ordinaires par degré d'enseignement et destination
Gastos públicos ordinarios por grados de enseñanza y destino

COUNTRY / PAYS / PAIS	YEAR / ANNEE / AÑO	PURPOSE / DESTINATION / DESTINO	TOTAL CURRENT EXPENDITURE (000) / TOTAL DES DEPENSES ORDINAIRES (000) / TOTAL DE GASTOS ORDINARIOS (000) (1)	PRE-PRIMARY / PRE-PRIMAIRE / PRE-PRIMARIA (2)	FIRST LEVEL / PREMIER DEGRE / PRIMER GRADO (3)	SECOND LEVEL / SECOND DEGRE / SEGUNDO GRADO (4)	THIRD LEVEL / TROISIEME DEGRE / TERCER GRADO (5)	OTHER TYPES AND NOT DISTRIBUTED / AUTRES TYPES ET NON REPARTIES / OTROS TIPOS Y SIN DISTRIBUCION (6)
HONDURAS ‡ LEMPIRA	1977	TOTAL CURRENT EXPENDITURE	89 920	3 725	61 506	8 642	14 793	1 254
		EMOLUMENTS OF TEACHERS	82 046	3 530	56 926	7 397	13 175	1 018
		OTHER DIRECT EXPENDITURE	1 605	93	1 200	118	93	101
		SCHOLARSHIPS/GRANTS	3 353	32	637	1 077	1 525	82
		WELFARE SERVICES	160	10	150	—	—	—
		NOT DISTRIBUTED/ADMINISTRATION	2 756	60	2 593	50	—	53
MEXICO ‡ PESO	1977	TOTAL CURRENT EXPENDITURE	53 627 996	1 253 725	21 684 995	10 441 292	15 419 962	4 828 022
		EMOLUMENTS OF TEACHERS	35 623 716	882 247	16 008 300	6 644 435	10 468 307	1 620 427
		OTHER DIRECT EXPENDITURE	2 543 646	101 187	355 805	1 201 900	583 364	301 390
		SCHOLARSHIPS/GRANTS	207 816	—	—	16 732	159 737	31 347
		WELFARE SERVICES	4 993 988	163 535	2 502 599	1 254 194	655 753	417 907
		NOT DISTRIBUTED/ADMINISTRATION	10 258 830	106 756	2 818 291	1 324 031	3 552 801	2 456 951
NETHERLANDS ANTILLES GUILDER	1977	TOTAL CURRENT EXPENDITURE	104 900	4 600	31 100	25 000	1 900	42 300
		EMOLUMENTS OF TEACHERS	74 900	4 000	27 600	21 800	1 300	20 200
		OTHER DIRECT EXPENDITURE	15 200	600	3 500	2 600	600	7 900
		SCHOLARSHIPS/GRANTS	5 400	—	—	600	—	4 800
		WELFARE SERVICES	2 300	—	—	—	—	2 300
		NOT DISTRIBUTED/ADMINISTRATION	7 100	—	—	—	—	7 100
PANAMA ‡ BALBOA	1978	TOTAL CURRENT EXPENDITURE	109 675	—	50 290	24 890	16 976	17 519
		EMOLUMENTS OF TEACHERS	89 419	—	48 847	21 225	16 976	2 371
		OTHER DIRECT EXPENDITURE	2 306	—	476	1 807	—	23
		SCHOLARSHIPS/GRANTS	4 002	—	—	—	—	4 002
		WELFARE SERVICES	—	—	—	—	—	—
		NOT DISTRIBUTED/ADMINISTRATION	13 948	—	967	1 858	—	11 123
AMERICA, SOUTH								
ARGENTINA ‡ PESO	1977	TOTAL CURRENT EXPENDITURE	426 417	./.	170 037	124 475	87 897	44 008
		EMOLUMENTS OF TEACHERS	383 246	./.	163 689	121 076	79 738	18 743
		OTHER DIRECT EXPENDITURE	32 177	—	6 348	3 272	7 557	15 000
		SCHOLARSHIPS/GRANTS	504	—	—	75	429	—
		WELFARE SERVICES	—	—	—	—	—	—
		NOT DISTRIBUTED/ADMINISTRATION	10 490	—	—	52	173	10 265
CHILE ‡ PESO	1975	TOTAL CURRENT EXPENDITURE	1 321 482	./.	460 976	177 795	333 004	349 707
		EMOLUMENTS OF TEACHERS	967 809	./.	411 931	159 648	333 004	63 226
ECUADOR SUCRE	1977	TOTAL CURRENT EXPENDITURE	5 756 300	—	2 326 714	1 700 800	1 382 614	346 172
		EMOLUMENTS OF TEACHERS	4 830 714	—	2 288 874	1 461 485	1 044 059	36 296
		OTHER DIRECT EXPENDITURE	153 982	—	3 910	144 852	5 220	—
		SCHOLARSHIPS/GRANTS	29 481	—	—	12 041	14 416	3 024
		WELFARE SERVICES	54 468	—	7 690	44 603	2 175	—
		NOT DISTRIBUTED/ADMINISTRATION	687 655	—	26 240	37 819	316 744	306 852

Public current expenditure by level and by purpose 4.4
Dépenses publiques ordinaires par degré d'enseignement et destination
Gastos públicos ordinarios por grados de enseñanza y destino

	(1)	(2)	(3)	(4)	(5)	(6)
GUYANA ‡ DOLLAR — 1977						
TOTAL CURRENT EXPENDITURE	71 796	4 049	25 274	23 222	14 027	5 224
EMOLUMENTS OF TEACHERS	54 946	3 340	22 803	17 342	11 334	1 177
OTHER DIRECT EXPENDITURE	4 244	140	245	2 550	132	127
SCHOLARSHIPS/GRANTS	3 000	100	215	368	1 890	427
WELFARE SERVICES	2 326	184	239	615	441	847
NOT DISTRIBUTED/ADMINISTRATION	7 280	285	1 772	2 347	230	2 646
PERU ‡ SOL — 1977						
TOTAL CURRENT EXPENDITURE	22 658 547	12 721 237	1 327 721	6 613 618	782 715	1 213 256
EMOLUMENTS OF TEACHERS	20 240 616	12 643 042	26 905	5 921 742	627 551	1 021 376
OTHER DIRECT EXPENDITURE	379 122	12 796	92 758	92 509	99 027	82 032
SCHOLARSHIPS/GRANTS						
WELFARE SERVICES						
NOT DISTRIBUTED/ADMINISTRATION	2 038 809	65 399	1 208 058	599 367	56 137	109 848
VENEZUELA ‡ BOLIVAR — 1975						
TOTAL CURRENT EXPENDITURE	5 965 747	—	1 319 000	1 098 544	2 209 837	1 338 366
EMOLUMENTS OF TEACHERS	3 967 995	—	1 154 774	854 076	1 897 674	61 471
OTHER DIRECT EXPENDITURE	17 719	—	4 473	4 306	—	8 940
SCHOLARSHIPS/GRANTS	697 343	—	53 652	52 492	312 163	279 036
WELFARE SERVICES	—	—	—	—	—	—
NOT DISTRIBUTED/ADMINISTRATION	1 282 690	—	106 101	187 670	—	988 919

ASIA

	(1)	(2)	(3)	(4)	(5)	(6)
AFGHANISTAN ‡ AFGHANI — 1977						
TOTAL CURRENT EXPENDITURE	1 636 529	45 511	1 563 309	↑	...	27 709
EMOLUMENTS OF TEACHERS	934 080	11 000	905 170	↑	...	17 830
OTHER DIRECT EXPENDITURE	179 280	—	179 280	↑	...	—
SCHOLARSHIPS/GRANTS	11 241	—	11 241	↑	...	—
WELFARE SERVICES	34 467	28 849	5 618	↑	...	—
NOT DISTRIBUTED/ADMINISTRATION	477 541	5 662	462 000	↑	...	9 879
BHUTAN INDIAN RUPEE — 1977						
TOTAL CURRENT EXPENDITURE	14 975	283	2 731	3 532	6 857	1 572
EMOLUMENTS OF TEACHERS	6 409	210	2 522	1 921	1 756	—
OTHER DIRECT EXPENDITURE	4 913	—	—	978	3 935	—
SCHOLARSHIPS/GRANTS						
WELFARE SERVICES						
NOT DISTRIBUTED/ADMINISTRATION	3 653	73	209	633	1 166	1 572
CYPRUS ‡ POUND — 1977						
TOTAL CURRENT EXPENDITURE	12 895	106	5 048	6 526	492	723
EMOLUMENTS OF TEACHERS	10 175	81	4 305	5 241	223	325
OTHER DIRECT EXPENDITURE	387	4	162	196	10	15
SCHOLARSHIPS/GRANTS	196	—	—	95	100	1
WELFARE SERVICES	376	5	75	232	27	37
NOT DISTRIBUTED/ADMINISTRATION	1 761	16	506	762	132	345
HONG KONG DOLLAR — 1977						
TOTAL CURRENT EXPENDITURE	1 578 216	—	685 978	457 733	346 838	87 667
EMOLUMENTS OF TEACHERS	1 242 954	—	655 428	370 887	180 595	36 044
OTHER DIRECT EXPENDITURE	23 034	—	415	4 375	17 009	1 235
SCHOLARSHIPS/GRANTS	72 658	—	3 295	58 638	10 226	499
WELFARE SERVICES	28 762	—	263	266	27 665	568
NOT DISTRIBUTED/ADMINISTRATION	210 808	—	26 577	23 567	111 343	49 321
INDIA ‡ RUPEE — 1975						
TOTAL CURRENT EXPENDITURE	21 047 180	33 020	4 463 150	8 479 540	4 638 390	3 433 080
EMOLUMENTS OF TEACHERS	15 584 020	27 440	4 312 780	7 788 090	3 329 410	126 300
OTHER DIRECT EXPENDITURE						
SCHOLARSHIPS/GRANTS						
WELFARE SERVICES						
NOT DISTRIBUTED/ADMINISTRATION						
IRAN ‡ RIAL — 1976						
TOTAL CURRENT EXPENDITURE	119 995 051	3 280 150	43 868 983	45 671 653	474 594	26 699 671
EMOLUMENTS OF TEACHERS	77 148 715	2 915 650	38 117 915	31 730 924	122 225	4 262 001
OTHER DIRECT EXPENDITURE	365 605	—	48 846	55 265	—	261 494
SCHOLARSHIPS/GRANTS						
WELFARE SERVICES	20 148 878	—	—	—	—	20 148 878
NOT DISTRIBUTED/ADMINISTRATION	22 331 853	364 500	5 702 222	13 885 464	352 369	2 027 298
IRAQ ‡ DINAR — 1976						
TOTAL CURRENT EXPENDITURE	155 763	...	70 524	25 267	28 260	31 712
EMOLUMENTS OF TEACHERS	101 685	...	66 867	19 846	12 871	2 101
OTHER DIRECT EXPENDITURE	16 497	...	3 180	3 505	9 410	402
SCHOLARSHIPS/GRANTS						
WELFARE SERVICES						
NOT DISTRIBUTED/ADMINISTRATION	37 581	...	477	1 916	5 979	29 209

4.4 Public current expenditure by level and by purpose
Dépenses publiques ordinaires par degré d'enseignement et destination
Gastos públicos ordinarios por grados de enseñanza y destino

COUNTRY / PAYS / PAIS	YEAR / ANNEE / AÑO	PURPOSE / DESTINATION / DESTINO	TOTAL CURRENT EXPENDITURE (000) / TOTAL DES DEPENSES ORDINAIRES (000) / TOTAL DE GASTOS ORDINARIOS (000) (1)	PRE-PRIMARY / PRE-PRIMAIRE / PRE-PRIMARIA (2)	FIRST LEVEL / PREMIER DEGRE / PRIMER GRADO (3)	SECOND LEVEL / SECOND DEGRE / SEGUNDO GRADO (4)	THIRD LEVEL / TROISIEME DEGRE / TERCER GRADO (5)	OTHER TYPES AND NOT DISTRIBUTED / AUTRES TYPES ET NON REPARTIES / OTROS TIPOS Y SIN DISTRIBUCION (6)
JAPAN ‡ YEN	1977	TOTAL CURRENT EXPENDITURE	7 262 222	93 702	2 823 531	2 608 971	803 095	932 923
		EMOLUMENTS OF TEACHERS	4 821 897	73 014	2 216 903	2 071 273	335 247	125 460
		OTHER DIRECT EXPENDITURE	471 210	4 553	135 054	236 188	80 940	14 475
		SCHOLARSHIPS/GRANTS	66 817	336	7 351	11 063	2	48 065
		WELFARE SERVICES	359 815	4 273	243 426	94 698	5 063	12 355
		NOT DISTRIBUTED/ADMINISTRATION	1 542 483	11 526	220 797	195 749	381 843	732 568
JORDAN ‡ DINAR	1977	TOTAL CURRENT EXPENDITURE	22 598	—	17 749	⟹	858	3 991
		EMOLUMENTS OF TEACHERS	16 581	—	16 298	⟹	254	29
KOREA, REPUBLIC OF ‡ WON	1977	TOTAL CURRENT EXPENDITURE	411 499	—	249 910	130 894	30 053	642
		EMOLUMENTS OF TEACHERS	379 322	—	238 023	119 146	21 838	315
		OTHER DIRECT EXPENDITURE	1 736	—	—	1 145	591	—
		NOT DISTRIBUTED/ADMINISTRATION	30 441	—	11 887	10 603	7 624	327
KUWAIT DINAR	1977	TOTAL CURRENT EXPENDITURE	129 183	7 300	36 800	59 600	22 083	3 400
		EMOLUMENTS OF TEACHERS	59 433	3 000	18 200	28 400	7 933	1 900
		OTHER DIRECT EXPENDITURE	7 572	—	400	1 200	5 972	—
		SCHOLARSHIPS/GRANTS	5 580	—	—	—	5 280	300
		WELFARE SERVICES	13 150	200	2 400	8 600	1 750	200
		NOT DISTRIBUTED/ADMINISTRATION	43 448	4 100	15 800	21 400	1 148	1 000
MALAYSIA								
PENINSULAR MALAYSIA ‡ RINGGIT	1977	TOTAL CURRENT EXPENDITURE	1 571 180	—	615 708	462 050	247 947	245 475
		EMOLUMENTS OF TEACHERS	1 042 126	—	441 169	351 126	247 947	1 884
		OTHER DIRECT EXPENDITURE	264 468	—	158 873	104 951	—	644
		SCHOLARSHIPS/GRANTS	21 639	—	15 666	5 973	—	—
		NOT DISTRIBUTED/ADMINISTRATION	242 947	—	—	—	—	242 947
SABAH RINGGIT	1976	TOTAL CURRENT EXPENDITURE	73 715	—	37 860	29 562	—	6 293
		EMOLUMENTS OF TEACHERS	55 892	—	37 190	18 518	—	184
		OTHER DIRECT EXPENDITURE	6 986	—	670	6 116	—	200
		SCHOLARSHIPS/GRANTS	4 926	—	—	4 926	—	—
		WELFARE SERVICES	2	—	—	2	—	—
		NOT DISTRIBUTED/ADMINISTRATION	5 909	—	—	—	—	5 909
SARAWAK RINGGIT	1977	TOTAL CURRENT EXPENDITURE	100 861	—	49 393	45 834	—	5 634
		EMOLUMENTS OF TEACHERS	72 288	—	45 310	26 978	—	—
		OTHER DIRECT EXPENDITURE	7 174	—	1 961	5 213	—	—
		SCHOLARSHIPS/GRANTS	15 765	—	2 122	13 643	—	—
		NOT DISTRIBUTED/ADMINISTRATION	5 634	—	—	—	—	5 634
NEPAL RUPEE	1975	TOTAL CURRENT EXPENDITURE	201 776	—	59 090	44 651	24 738	73 297
		EMOLUMENTS OF TEACHERS	105 999	—	51 903	37 540	16 556	—

Public current expenditure by level and by purpose 4.4
Dépenses publiques ordinaires par degré d'enseignement et destination
Gastos públicos ordinarios por grados de enseñanza y destino

Country / Currency / Year	Item	(1)	(2)	(3)	(4)	(5)	(6)
QATAR RIYAL — 1977	TOTAL CURRENT EXPENDITURE	283 110	400	107 389	79 813	30 268	65 240
	EMOLUMENTS OF TEACHERS	166 684	—	91 819	66 533	—	8 332
	OTHER DIRECT EXPENDITURE	14 500	—	6 900	6 300	—	1 300
	SCHOLARSHIPS/GRANTS	30 668	400	—	—	30 268	—
	WELFARE SERVICES	12 500	—	6 600	5 000	—	900
	NOT DISTRIBUTED/ADMINISTRATION	58 758	—	2 070	1 980	—	54 708
SINGAPORE ‡ DOLLAR — 1977	TOTAL CURRENT EXPENDITURE	363 333	—	139 736	132 325	53 611	37 661
	EMOLUMENTS OF TEACHERS	331 882	—	136 665	127 510	47 187	20 520
	OTHER DIRECT EXPENDITURE	7 365	—	—	941	6 424	—
	SCHOLARSHIPS/GRANTS	—	—	—	—	—	—
	WELFARE SERVICES	173	—	118	55	—	—
	NOT DISTRIBUTED/ADMINISTRATION	23 913	—	2 953	3 819	—	17 141
SYRIAN ARAB REPUBLIC ‡ POUND — 1976	TOTAL CURRENT EXPENDITURE	516 484	—	293 992	220 132	...	2 360
	EMOLUMENTS OF TEACHERS	395 103	—	225 611	168 825	...	667
	OTHER DIRECT EXPENDITURE	31 540	—	20 340	11 200	...	—
	SCHOLARSHIPS/GRANTS	—	—	—	—	...	—
	WELFARE SERVICES	6 736	—	4 515	2 221	...	—
	NOT DISTRIBUTED/ADMINISTRATION	83 105	—	43 526	37 886	...	1 693
THAILAND BAHT — 1976	TOTAL CURRENT EXPENDITURE	8 732 955	56 871	5 258 949	1 558 891	883 712	974 532
	EMOLUMENTS OF TEACHERS	6 634 808	48 152	4 751 318	1 034 044	576 565	224 729
	OTHER DIRECT EXPENDITURE	362 582	720	55 117	105 814	144 340	56 591
	SCHOLARSHIPS/GRANTS	156 018	—	6 568	12 844	13 241	123 365
	WELFARE SERVICES	404 257	350	170 820	101 570	42 758	88 759
	NOT DISTRIBUTED/ADMINISTRATION	1 175 290	7 649	275 126	304 619	106 808	481 088
TURKEY ‡ LIRA — 1977	TOTAL CURRENT EXPENDITURE	37 961 875	—	17 542 311	13 837 348	5 519 095	1 063 121
	EMOLUMENTS OF TEACHERS	35 138 635	—	17 089 166	12 839 867	4 289 011	920 591
	OTHER DIRECT EXPENDITURE	60 887	—	16 000	29 732	9 355	5 800
	SCHOLARSHIPS/GRANTS	1 141 468	—	70 000	184 891	884 427	2 150
	WELFARE SERVICES	288 315	—	2 000	6 520	233 945	45 850
	NOT DISTRIBUTED/ADMINISTRATION	1 332 570	—	365 145	776 338	102 357	88 730

EUROPE

Country / Currency / Year	Item	(1)	(2)	(3)	(4)	(5)	(6)
AUSTRIA ‡ SCHILLING — 1977	TOTAL CURRENT EXPENDITURE	35 368 500	1 876 500	6 664 100	18 681 000	5 402 300	2 744 600
	EMOLUMENTS OF TEACHERS	17 364 900	—	3 694 000	11 756 700	1 805 700	108 500
	SCHOLARSHIPS/GRANTS	972 000	42 400	12 800	145 100	314 600	457 100
	WELFARE SERVICES	895 200	93 400	3 000	182 500	515 100	101 200
	NOT DISTRIBUTED/ADMINISTRATION	16 136 400	1 740 700	2 954 300	6 596 700	2 766 900	2 077 800
BELGIUM ‡ FRANC — 1977	TOTAL CURRENT EXPENDITURE	170 775 800	—	43 966 300	77 183 200	27 504 900	22 121 400
	EMOLUMENTS OF TEACHERS	128 725 100	—	38 720 100	66 986 000	13 670 100	9 348 900
	OTHER DIRECT EXPENDITURE	32 581 000	—	5 246 200	10 197 200	13 834 800	3 302 800
	SCHOLARSHIPS/GRANTS	2 023 300	—	—	—	—	2 023 300
	NOT DISTRIBUTED/ADMINISTRATION	7 446 400	—	—	—	—	7 446 400
BULGARIA LEV — 1977	TOTAL CURRENT EXPENDITURE	838 837	157 342	355 036	→	110 282	216 177
	EMOLUMENTS OF TEACHERS	378 535	71 800	233 179	→	46 292	27 264
	SCHOLARSHIPS/GRANTS	43 570	—	13 237	→	30 333	—
	NOT DISTRIBUTED/ADMINISTRATION	416 732	85 542	108 620	→	33 657	188 913
CZECHOSLOVAKIA KORUNA — 1977	TOTAL CURRENT EXPENDITURE	18 580 636	2 114 815	7 847 460	2 683 454	3 061 975	2 872 932
	EMOLUMENTS OF TEACHERS	9 705 031	1 308 454	4 057 213	1 671 431	1 277 144	1 390 789
DENMARK ‡ KRONE — 1977	TOTAL CURRENT EXPENDITURE	16 202 000	...	8 430 000	2 569 000	2 840 000	2 379 000
	EMOLUMENTS OF TEACHERS	8 723 000	...	5 534 000	1 437 000	1 406 000	346 000
	OTHER DIRECT EXPENDITURE	909 000		437 000	205 000	160 000	107 000
	SCHOLARSHIPS/GRANTS	536 000		5 000	—	—	531 000
	WELFARE SERVICES	511 000		334 000	139 000	4 000	34 000
	NOT DISTRIBUTED/ADMINISTRATION	5 523 000		2 120 000	772 000	1 270 000	1 361 000

4.4 Public current expenditure by level and by purpose
Dépenses publiques ordinaires par degré d'enseignement et destination
Gastos públicos ordinarios por grados de enseñanza y destino

COUNTRY / PAYS / PAIS	YEAR / ANNEE / AÑO	PURPOSE / DESTINATION / DESTINO	TOTAL CURRENT EXPENDITURE / TOTAL DES DEPENSES ORDINAIRES / TOTAL DE GASTOS ORDINARIOS (000) (1)	PRE-PRIMARY / PRE-PRIMAIRE / PRE-PRIMARIA (2)	FIRST LEVEL / PREMIER DEGRE / PRIMER GRADO (3)	SECOND LEVEL / SECOND DEGRE / SEGUNDO GRADO (4)	THIRD LEVEL / TROISIEME DEGRE / TERCER GRADO (5)	OTHER TYPES AND NOT DISTRIBUTED / AUTRES TYPES ET NON REPARTIES / OTROS TIPOS Y SIN DISTRIBUCION (6)
FINLAND MARKKA	1977	TOTAL CURRENT EXPENDITURE	7 598 881	–	3 779 982	2 092 221	966 760	759 918
		EMOLUMENTS OF TEACHERS	4 564 257	–	2 322 639	1 293 107	586 147	362 364
		OTHER DIRECT EXPENDITURE	310 207	–	188 836	101 828	16 380	3 163
		SCHOLARSHIPS/GRANTS	141 089	–	9 087	45 741	85 792	469
		WELFARE SERVICES	789 649	–	538 424	145 662	102 909	2 654
		NOT DISTRIBUTED/ADMINISTRATION	1 793 679	–	720 996	505 883	175 532	391 268
FRANCE ‡ FRANC	1977	TOTAL CURRENT EXPENDITURE	62 738 600	4 207 400 [10]	12 980 700	32 552 400	6 561 600	6 436 500
		EMOLUMENTS OF TEACHERS	48 200 800	4 086 900 [10]	11 588 900	23 841 800	5 771 900	2 911 300
		SCHOLARSHIPS/GRANTS	2 735 600	–	1 011 100	1 521 600	175 300	27 600
		WELFARE SERVICES	2 272 600	23 700	162 600	2 013 000	32 700	40 600
		NOT DISTRIBUTED/ADMINISTRATION	9 529 400	96 800	217 900	5 176 000	581 700	3 457 000
GREECE ‡ DRACHMA	1974	TOTAL CURRENT EXPENDITURE	9 347 600	325 309	3 793 755	2 792 604	2 058 303	377 629
		EMOLUMENTS OF TEACHERS	7 437 774	292 070	3 556 325	2 454 595	1 130 290	4 494
		SCHOLARSHIPS/GRANTS	20 390	4	202	7 114	12 378	692
		WELFARE SERVICES	262 663	535	5 362	72 729	183 747	290
		NOT DISTRIBUTED/ADMINISTRATION	1 626 773	32 700	231 866	258 166	731 888	372 153
HUNGARY ‡ FORINT	1977	TOTAL CURRENT EXPENDITURE	19 385 911	2 526 687 [7]	7 424 936	2 654 512	4 185 776	2 594 000
		EMOLUMENTS OF TEACHERS	8 990 440	1 142 797 [3]	3 809 490	1 168 711	1 585 794	1 283 648
		SCHOLARSHIPS/GRANTS	856 989	–	–	52 216	804 773	–
		WELFARE SERVICES	2 901 332	–	150 339	676 177	1 795 209	279 607
		NOT DISTRIBUTED/ADMINISTRATION	6 637 150	1 383 890 [3]	3 465 107	757 408	–	1 030 745
IRELAND ‡ POUND	1977	TOTAL CURRENT EXPENDITURE	288 043	./.	100 217	106 048	53 347	28 431
		EMOLUMENTS OF TEACHERS	196 629	./.	95 456	75 572	22 464	3 137
		SCHOLARSHIPS/GRANTS	20 493	–	–	14 971	2 668	2 854
		WELFARE SERVICES	11 818	./.	–	5	–	11 813
		NOT DISTRIBUTED/ADMINISTRATION	59 103	–	4 761	15 500	28 215	10 627
ITALY ‡ LIRA	1976	TOTAL CURRENT EXPENDITURE	6 467 905	323 725	1 892 796	3 021 823	777 439	452 122
		EMOLUMENTS OF TEACHERS	4 804 106	187 176	1 597 852	2 430 033	392 107	196 938
		SCHOLARSHIPS/GRANTS	162 668	–	–	709	157 143	4 816
		WELFARE SERVICES	216 393	20 552	41 257	97 983	40 191	16 410
		NOT DISTRIBUTED/ADMINISTRATION	1 284 738	115 997	253 687	493 098	187 998	233 958
LUXEMBOURG ‡ FRANC	1977	TOTAL CURRENT EXPENDITURE	4 498 800	./.	1 867 000	1 847 600	80 200	704 000
		EMOLUMENTS OF TEACHERS	3 846 800	./.	1 794 600	1 600 300	39 700	412 200
		SCHOLARSHIPS/GRANTS	56 100	–	100	9 000	6 800	40 200
		WELFARE SERVICES	–	./.	–	–	–	–
		NOT DISTRIBUTED/ADMINISTRATION	595 900	–	72 300	238 300	33 700	251 600

Public current expenditure by level and by purpose   **4.4**
Dépenses publiques ordinaires par degré d'enseignement et destination
Gastos públicos ordinarios por grados de enseñanza y destino

Country / Currency	Year	Purpose	(1)	(2)	(3)	(4)	(5)	(6)
MALTA ‡ POUND	1976	TOTAL CURRENT EXPENDITURE	8 733	./.	2 066	4 453	1 019	1 195
		EMOLUMENTS OF TEACHERS	6 860	./.	1 875	3 959	942	84
		OTHER DIRECT EXPENDITURE	11	./.	4	7	—	—
		SCHOLARSHIPS/GRANTS	702	./.	154	402	77	69
		WELFARE SERVICES	234	./.	33	85	—	116
		NOT DISTRIBUTED/ADMINISTRATION	926	—	—	—	—	926
NETHERLANDS ‡ GUILDER	1977	TOTAL CURRENT EXPENDITURE	18 666	1 054	3 686	6 450	5 226	2 250
		EMOLUMENTS OF TEACHERS	14 032	859	2 968	5 478	3 532	1 195
		OTHER DIRECT EXPENDITURE	120	6	62	32	9	11
		SCHOLARSHIPS/GRANTS	436	—	—	143	266	27
		WELFARE SERVICES	254	1	10	—	86	157
		NOT DISTRIBUTED/ADMINISTRATION	3 824	188	646	797	1 333	860
NORWAY ‡ KRONE	1977	TOTAL CURRENT EXPENDITURE	11 484 000	—	5 567 000	3 071 000	1 619 000	1 227 000
		EMOLUMENTS OF TEACHERS	7 802 000	—	4 247 000	1 771 000	1 167 000	617 000
		NOT DISTRIBUTED/ADMINISTRATION	3 682 000	—	1 320 000	1 300 000	452 000	610 000
PORTUGAL ‡ ESCUDO	1977	TOTAL CURRENT EXPENDITURE	22 535 383	46 394	11 533 111	6 111 535	2 425 727	2 418 616
		EMOLUMENTS OF TEACHERS	18 141 177	13 738	10 614 602	5 349 193	1 656 384	507 260
		OTHER DIRECT EXPENDITURE	614 672	32 656	178 399	149 282	201 168	85 823
		SCHOLARSHIPS/GRANTS	1 672 812	—	451 322	563 315	58 703	566 816
		WELFARE SERVICES	840 883	—	281 626	45 225	508 108	5 924
		NOT DISTRIBUTED/ADMINISTRATION	1 265 839	—	7 162	4 520	1 364	1 252 793
SAN MARINO ‡ LIRA	1977	TOTAL CURRENT EXPENDITURE	3 490 495	./.	2 061 315	1 210 820	218 360	—
		EMOLUMENTS OF TEACHERS	2 826 627	./.	1 793 966	1 032 661	—	—
		SCHOLARSHIPS/GRANTS	218 360	./.	—	—	218 360	—
		WELFARE SERVICES	208 049	./.	99 498	108 551	—	—
		NOT DISTRIBUTED/ADMINISTRATION	237 459	./.	167 851	69 608	—	—
SPAIN ‡ PESETA	1976	TOTAL CURRENT EXPENDITURE	134 391	./.	82 257	23 458	20 298	8 378
		EMOLUMENTS OF TEACHERS	112 639	./.	75 605	20 015	14 243	2 776
		OTHER DIRECT EXPENDITURE	6 068	./.	1 759	760	3 296	253
		SCHOLARSHIPS/GRANTS	10 460	./.	4 893	2 683	2 759	125
		WELFARE SERVICES	137	./.	—	—	—	137
		NOT DISTRIBUTED/ADMINISTRATION	5 087	./.	—	—	—	5 087
SWEDEN ‡ KRONA	1977	TOTAL CURRENT EXPENDITURE	26 441 200	—	9 970 600	3 242 600	2 897 800	10 330 200
		EMOLUMENTS OF TEACHERS	13 020 300	—	8 752 600	2 430 100	1 837 600	—
		SCHOLARSHIPS/GRANTS	786 100	—	—	—	—	786 100
		WELFARE SERVICES	3 622 600	—	—	—	—	3 622 600
		NOT DISTRIBUTED/ADMINISTRATION	9 012 200	—	1 218 000	812 500	1 060 200	5 921 500
SWITZERLAND ‡ FRANC	1977	TOTAL CURRENT EXPENDITURE	6 734 300	207 500	5 207 100	>	1 109 000	210 700
		EMOLUMENTS OF TEACHERS	4 136 700	168 000	3 528 800	>	429 700	10 200
		SCHOLARSHIPS/GRANTS	159 600	—	91 200	>	61 800	6 600
		NOT DISTRIBUTED/ADMINISTRATION	2 438 000	39 500	1 587 100	>	617 500	193 900
YUGOSLAVIA ‡ DINAR	1977	TOTAL CURRENT EXPENDITURE	37 632 000	—	19 137 000	9 285 000	6 479 000	2 731 000
		EMOLUMENTS OF TEACHERS	25 071 000	—	14 325 000	6 464 000	3 933 000	349 000
		SCHOLARSHIPS/GRANTS	372 000	—	—	—	—	372 000
		WELFARE SERVICES	1 678 000	—	—	—	—	1 678 000
		NOT DISTRIBUTED/ADMINISTRATION	10 511 000	—	4 812 000	2 821 000	2 546 000	332 000

4.4 Public current expenditure by level and by purpose
Dépenses publiques ordinaires par degré d'enseignement et destination
Gastos públicos ordinarios por grados de enseñanza y destino

COUNTRY / PAYS / PAIS	YEAR ANNEE AÑO	PURPOSE DESTINATION DESTINO	TOTAL CURRENT EXPENDITURE (000) / TOTAL DES DEPENSES ORDINAIRES (000) / TOTAL DE GASTOS ORDINARIOS (000) (1)	PRE-PRIMARY / PRE-PRIMAIRE / PRE-PRIMARIA (2)	FIRST LEVEL / PREMIER DEGRE / PRIMER GRADO (3)	SECOND LEVEL / SECOND DEGRE / SEGUNDO GRADO (4)	THIRD LEVEL / TROISIEME DEGRE / TERCER GRADO (5)	OTHER TYPES AND NOT DISTRIBUTED / AUTRES TYPES ET NON REPARTIES / OTROS TIPOS Y SIN DISTRIBUCION (6)
OCEANIA								
NEW HEBRIDES AUSTRALIAN DOLLAR	1975	TOTAL CURRENT EXPENDITURE	1 444	6	578	572	53	235
		EMOLUMENTS OF TEACHERS	790	5	465	320	—	—
		OTHER DIRECT EXPENDITURE	188	1	106	81	53	—
		SCHOLARSHIPS/GRANTS	210	—	—	157	—	—
		WELFARE SERVICES	31	—	7	14	—	10
		NOT DISTRIBUTED/ADMINISTRATION	225	—	—	—	—	225
PACIFIC ISLANDS U.S. DOLLAR	1976	TOTAL CURRENT EXPENDITURE	20 205	—	8 956	4 158	2 909	4 182
		EMOLUMENTS OF TEACHERS	11 205	—	7 079	3 168	882	76
		OTHER DIRECT EXPENDITURE	1 311	—	565	248	498	—
		SCHOLARSHIPS/GRANTS	1 529	—	—	—	1 529	—
		WELFARE SERVICES	1 900	—	1 312	588	—	—
		NOT DISTRIBUTED/ADMINISTRATION	4 260	—	—	154	—	4 106
PAPUA NEW GUINEA ‡ KINA	1976	TOTAL CURRENT EXPENDITURE	80 426	./.	26 634	19 156	28 719	5 917
		EMOLUMENTS OF TEACHERS	65 637	./.	25 140	14 497	21 577	4 423
		OTHER DIRECT EXPENDITURE	8 489	./.	1 345	2 782	3 215	1 147
		SCHOLARSHIPS/GRANTS	5 382	./.	35	1 791	3 433	123
		WELFARE SERVICES	918		114	86	494	224
TONGA DOLLAR	1977	TOTAL CURRENT EXPENDITURE	1 330	—	620	339	71	300
		EMOLUMENTS OF TEACHERS	854	—	579	275	—	—
		OTHER DIRECT EXPENDITURE	137	—	41	46	—	50
		SCHOLARSHIPS/GRANTS	79	—	—	—	—	79
		NOT DISTRIBUTED/ADMINISTRATION	260	—	—	18	71	171

ALGERIA:
E—> EXPENDITURE OF THE MINISTRY OF PRIMARY AND SECONDARY EDUCATION ONLY.
FR—> DEPENSES DU MINISTERE DES ENSEIGNEMENTS PRIMAIRE ET SECONDAIRE SEULEMENT.
ESP> GASTOS DEL MINISTERIO DE LAS ENSEÑANZAS DE PRIMERO Y SEGUNDO GRADO SOLAMENTE.

CONGO:
E—> EXPENDITURE OF THE CENTRAL GOVERNMENT ONLY. SCHOLARSHIPS INCLUDE EXPENDITURE FOR WELFARE SERVICES.
FR—> DEPENSES DU GOUVERNEMENT CENTRAL SEULEMENT. LES BOURSES D'ETUDES COMPRENNENT AUSSI LES DEPENSES POUR LES SERVICES SOCIAUX.
ESP> GASTOS DEL GOBIERNO CENTRAL SOLAMENTE. LAS BECAS DE ESTUDIO TAMBIEN COMPRENDEN LOS GASTOS RELATIVOS A LOS SERVICIOS SOCIALES.

Public current expenditure by level and by purpose 4.4
Dépenses publiques ordinaires par degré d'enseignement et destination
Gastos públicos ordinarios por grados de enseñanza y destino

EGYPT:
E—> EXPENDITURE ON PRE-PRIMARY AND FIRST LEVEL EDUCATION IS INCLUDED IN COLUMN 4. EXPENDITURE ON ADMINISTRATION IS CLASSIFIED WITH EMOLUMENTS OF TEACHERS.
FR—> LES DEPENSES DES ENSEIGNEMENTS PREPRIMAIRE ET DU PREMIER DEGRE SONT INCLUSES DANS LA COLONNE 4. LES DEPENSES D'ADMINISTRATION SONT CLASSEES AVEC LES EMOLUMENTS DU PERSONNEL ENSEIGNANT
ESP> LOS GASTOS DE LAS ENSEÑANZAS PREPRIMARIA Y DE PRIMER GRADO QUEDAN INCLUIDOS EN LA COLUMNA 4. LOS GASTOS DE ADMINISTRACION SE CLASIFICAN CON LOS EMOLUMENTOS DEL PERSONAL DOCENTE.

GHANA:
E—> EXPENDITURE ON UNIVERSITIES IS NOT INCLUDED.
FR—> LES DEPENSES DES UNIVERSITES NE SONT PAS INCLUSES.
ESP> NO SE INCLUYEN LOS GASTOS RELATIVOS A LAS UNIVERSIDADES.

GUINEA BISSAU:
E—> FOREIGN AID IS INCLUDED.
FR—> L'AIDE EXTERIEURE EST INCLUSE.
ESP> SE INCLUYE LA AYUDA EXTERIOR.

IVORY COAST:
E—> FIGURES ARE IN MILLIONS. FOREIGN AID IS INCLUDED.
FR—> LES CHIFFRES SONT EXPRIMES EN MILLIONS. L'AIDE EXTERIEURE EST INCLUSE.
ESP> LAS CIFRAS SE EXPRESAN EN MILLONES. INCLUIDA LA AYUDA EXTERIOR.

LIBYAN ARAB JAMAHIRIYA:
E—> EXPENDITURE ON UNIVERSITIES IS NOT INCLUDED. EXPENDITURE ON ADMINISTRATION IS CLASSIFIED WITH EMOLUMENTS OF TEACHERS.
FR—> LES DEPENSES DES UNIVERSITES NE SONT PAS INCLUSES. LES DEPENSES D'ADMINISTRATION SONT CLASSEES AVEC LES EMOLUMENTS DU PERSONNEL ENSEIGNANT.
ESP> NO SE INCLUYEN LOS GASTOS RELATIVOS A LAS UNIVERSIDADES. LOS GASTOS DE ADMINISTRACION SE CLASIFICAN CON LOS EMOLUMENTOS DEL PERSONAL DOCENTE.

MALAWI:
E—> THE TOTALITY OF TRANSFERS TO UNIVERSITIES USED FOR ALL PURPOSES (SALARIES, ETC.), IS INCLUDED WITH EMOLUMENTS OF TEACHERS IN COLUMNS 1 AND 5.
FR—> LA TOTALITE DES TRANSFERTS AUX UNIVERSITES UTILISEE POUR DES DEPENSES DIVERSES (SALAIRES, ETC.) EST INCLUSE AVEC LES EMOLUMENTS DU PERSONNEL ENSEIGNANT DANS LES COLONNES 1 ET 5.
ESP> LA TOTALIDAD DE LAS TRANSFERENCIAS A LAS UNIVERSIDADES UTILIZADA PARA GASTOS DIVERSOS (SALARIOS, ETC.), QUEDA INCLUIDA EN LOS EMOLUMENTOS DEL PERSONAL DOCENTE, EN LAS COLUMNAS 1 Y 5.

MALI:
E—> FIRST LEVEL EDUCATION REFERS TO "ENSEIGNEMENT FONDAMENTAL" OF 9 YEARS (TWO CYCLES: 6 AND 3 YEARS). DURATION OF SECOND LEVEL EDUCATION IS 3 YEARS.
FR—> L'ENSEIGNEMENT DU PREMIER DEGRE CORRESPOND A L'ENSEIGNEMENT FONDAMENTAL DONT LA DUREE EST DE 9 ANS (DEUX CYCLES: 6 ET 3 ANS). L'ENSEIGNEMENT DU SECOND DEGRE CORRESPOND A UN ENSEIGNEMENT D'UNE DUREE DE 3 ANS.
ESP> LA ENSEÑANZA DE PRIMER GRADO CORRESPONDE A LA ENSEÑANZA FUNDAMENTAL CUYA DURACION ES DE 9 AÑOS (DOS CICLOS: 6 Y 3 AÑOS). LA ENSEÑANZA DE SEGUNDO GRADO TIENE UNA DURACION DE 3 AÑOS.

MOROCCO:
E—> EXPENDITURE OF THE MINISTRY OF PRIMARY AND SECONDARY EDUCATION ONLY. OTHER DIRECT INSTRUC-TIONAL EXPENDITURE IS INCLUDED WITH EXPENDITURE NOT DISTRIBUTED BY LEVEL.
FR—> DEPENSES DU MINISTERE DES ENSEIGNEMENTS PRIMAIRE ET SECONDAIRE SEULEMENT. LES AUTRES DEPENSES D'ENSEIGNEMENT SONT INCLUSES DANS LES DEPENSES NON REPARTIES.
ESP> GASTOS DEL MINISTERIO DE LAS ENSEÑANZAS DE PRIMERO Y SEGUNDO GRADO SOLAMENTE. LOS OTROS GASTOS DIRECTOS DE ENSEÑANZA SE INCLUYEN EN LOS GASTOS SIN DISTRIBUCION.

RWANDA:
E—> WITH THE EXCEPTION OF SCHOLARSHIPS, TRANSFERS TO INSTITUTIONS OF EDUCATION AT THE THIRD LEVEL, FOR ALL PURPOSES (SALARIES, ETC.), ARE INCLUDED WITH EMOLUMENTS OF TEACHERS.
FR—> A L'EXCEPTION DES BOURSES D'ETUDES, LES TRANSFERTS AUX ETABLISSEMENTS D'ENSEIGNEMENT DU TROISIEME DEGRE, UTILISES POUR DES DEPENSES DIVERSES (SALAIRES, ETC.) SONT INCLUS DANS LES EMOLUMENTS DU PERSONNEL ENSEIGNANT.
ESP> SALVO LAS BECAS DE ESTUDIO, LAS TRANS-FERENCIAS A LOS ESTABLECIMIENTOS DE ENSEÑANZA DE TERCER GRADO UTILIZADAS PARA GASTOS DIVERSOS (SALARIOS, ETC.), QUEDAN INCLUIDAS EN LOS EMOLUMENTOS DEL PERSONAL DOCENTE.

UGANDA:
E—> EXPENDITURE OF THE MINISTRY OF EDUCATION ONLY.
FR—> DEPENSES DU MINISTERE DE L'EDUCATION SEULEMENT
ESP> GASTOS DEL MINISTERIO DE EDUCACION SOLAMENTE.

UPPER VOLTA:
E—> EXPENDITURE OF THE MINISTRY OF EDUCATION ONLY.
FR—> DEPENSES DU MINISTERE DE L'EDUCATION SEULEMENT
ESP> GASTOS DEL MINISTERIO DE EDUCACION SOLAMENTE.

4.4 Public current expenditure by level and by purpose
Dépenses publiques ordinaires par degré d'enseignement et destination
Gastos públicos ordinarios por grados de enseñanza y destino

CANADA:
E—> DATA DO NOT INCLUDE PUBLIC SUBSIDIES TO PRIVATE EDUCATION. EXPENDITURE ON PRE-PRIMARY AND FIRST LEVEL EDUCATION IS INCLUDED IN COLUMN 4.
FR—> LES DONNEES NE COMPRENNENT PAS LES SUBVEN- TIONS PUBLIQUES A L'ENSEIGNEMENT PRIVE. LES DEPENSES DES ENSEIGNEMENTS PREPRIMAIRE ET DU PREMIER DEGRE SONT INCLUSES DANS LA COLONNE 4.
ESP> LOS DATOS NO COMPRENDEN LAS SUBVENCIONES PUBLICAS A LA ENSEÑANZA PRIVADA. LOS GASTOS DE LAS ENSEÑANZAS PREPRIMARIA Y DE PRIMER GRADO QUEDAN INCLUIDOS EN LA COLUMNA 4.

COSTA RICA:
E—> EXPENDITURE ON PRE-PRIMARY EDUCATION IS INCLUDED IN COLUMN 3. THE TOTALITY OF TRANSFERS TO UNIVERSITIES USED FOR ALL PURPOSES (SALARIES, ETC.) IS INCLUDED WITH EMOLUMENTS OF TEACHERS IN COLUMNS 1 AND 5.
FR—> LES DEPENSES DE L'ENSEIGNEMENT PREPRIMAIRE SONT INCLUSES DANS LA COLONNE 3. LA TOTALITE DES TRANSFERTS AUX UNIVERSITES UTILISEE POUR DES DEPENSES DIVERSES (SALAIRES, ETC.) EST INCLUSE AVEC LES EMOLUMENTS DU PERSONNEL ENSEIGNANT DANS LES COLONNES 1 ET 5.
ESP> LOS GASTOS DE LA ENSEÑANZA PREPRIMARIA QUEDAN INCLUIDOS EN LA COLUMNA 3. LA TOTALIDAD DE LAS TRANSFERENCIAS A LAS UNIVERSIDADES UTILIZADA PARA GASTOS DIVERSOS (SALARIOS, ETC.), SE INCLUYE CON LOS EMOLUMENTOS DEL PERSONAL DOCENTE, EN LAS COLUMNAS 1 Y 5.

DOMINICAN REPUBLIC:
E—> THE TOTALITY OF TRANSFERS TO UNIVERSITIES USED FOR ALL PURPOSES (SALARIES, ETC.) IS INCLUDED WITH EMOLUMENTS OF TEACHERS IN COLUMNS 1 AND 5.
FR—> LA TOTALITE DES TRANSFERTS AUX UNIVERSITES UTILISEE POUR DES DEPENSES DIVERSES (SALAIRES, ETC.) EST INCLUSE AVEC LES EMOLUMENTS DU PERSONNEL ENSEIGNANT DANS LES COLONNES 1 ET 5.
ESP> LA TOTALIDAD DE LAS TRANSFERENCIAS A LAS UNIVERSIDADES UTILIZADA PARA GASTOS DIVERSOS (SALARIOS, ETC),QUEDA INCLUIDA EN LOS EMOLUMENTOS DEL PERSONAL DOCENTE, EN LAS COLUMNAS 1 Y 5.

GUATEMALA:
E—> THE TOTALITY OF TRANSFERS TO UNIVERSITIES USED FOR ALL PURPOSES (SALARIES, ETC.) IS INCLUDED WITH EMOLUMENTS OF TEACHERS IN COLUMNS 1 AND 5.
FR—> LA TOTALITE DES TRANSFERTS AUX UNIVERSITES UTILISEE POUR DES DEPENSES DIVERSES (SALAIRES, ETC.) EST INCLUSE AVEC LES EMOLUMENTS DU PERSONNEL ENSEIGNANT DANS LES COLONNES 1 ET 5.
ESP> LA TOTALIDAD DE LAS TRANSFERENCIAS A LAS UNIVERSIDADES UTILIZADA PARA GASTOS DIVERSOS (SALARIOS, ETC), QUEDA INCLUIDA EN LOS EMOLUMENTOS DEL PERSONAL DOCENTE, EN LAS COLUMNAS 1 Y 5.

HONDURAS:
E—> THE TOTALITY OF TRANSFERS TO UNIVERSITIES USED FOR ALL PURPOSES (SALARIES, ETC.). IS INCLUDED WITH EMOLUMENTS OF TEACHERS IN COLUMNS 1 AND 5. EXPENDITURE ON ADMINISTRATION IS CLASSIFIED WITH EMOLUMENTS OF TEACHERS.
FR—> LA TOTALITE DES TRANSFERTS AUX UNIVERSITES UTILISEE POUR DES DEPENSES DIVERSES (SALAIRES, ETC.) EST INCLUSE AVEC LES EMOLUMENTS DU PERSONNEL ENSEIGNANT DANS LES COLONNES 1 ET 5. LES DEPENSES D'ADMINISTRATION SONT CLASSEES AVEC LES EMOLUMENTS DU PERSONNEL ENSEIGNANT.
ESP> LA TOTALIDAD DE LAS TRANSFERENCIAS A LAS UNIVERSIDADES UTILIZADA PARA GASTOS DIVERSOS (SALARIOS, ETC), QUEDA INCLUIDA EN LOS EMOLUMENTOS DEL PERSONAL DOCENTE, EN LAS COLUMNAS 1 Y 5. LOS GASTOS DE ADMINISTRACION SE CLASIFICAN CON LOS EMOLUMENTOS DEL PERSONAL DOCENTE.

MEXICO:
E—> EXPENDITURE OF THE MINISTRY OF EDUCATION ONLY. THE TOTALITY OF TRANSFERS TO UNIVERSITIES USED FOR ALL PURPOSES (SALARIES, ETC.) IS INCLUDED WITH EMOLUMENTS OF TEACHERS IN COLUMNS 1 AND 5.
FR—> DEPENSES DU MINISTERE DE L'EDUCATION SEULE- MENT. LA TOTALITE DES TRANSFERTS AUX UNIVERSITES UTILISEE POUR DES DEPENSES DIVERSES (SALAIRES, ETC.) EST INCLUSE AVEC LES EMOLUMENTS DU PERSONNEL ENSEIGNANT DANS LES COLONNES 1 ET 5.
ESP> GASTOS DEL MINISTERIO DE EDUCACION SOLA- MENTE. LA TOTALIDAD DE LAS TRANSFERENCIAS A LAS UNIVERSIDADES UTILIZADA PARA GASTOS DIVERSOS (SALARIOS, ETC), QUEDA INCLUIDA EN LOS EMOLUMENTOS DEL PERSONAL DOCENTE, EN LAS COLUMNAS 1 Y 5.

PANAMA:
E—> THE TOTALITY OF TRANSFERS TO UNIVERSITIES USED FOR ALL PURPOSES (SALARIES, ETC.). IS INCLUDED WITH EMOLUMENTS OF TEACHERS IN COLUMNS 1 AND 5.
FR—> LA TOTALITE DES TRANSFERTS AUX UNIVERSITES UTILISEE POUR DES DEPENSES DIVERSES (SALAIRES, ETC.) EST INCLUSE AVEC LES EMOLUMENTS DU PERSONNEL ENSEIGNANT DANS LES COLONNES 1 ET 5.
ESP> LA TOTALIDAD DE LAS TRANSFERENCIAS A LAS UNIVERSIDADES UTILIZADA PARA GASTOS DIVERSOS (SALARIOS, ETC), QUEDA INCLUIDA EN LOS EMOLUMENTOS DEL PERSONAL DOCENTE, EN LAS COLUMNAS 1 Y 5.

ARGENTINA:
E—> FIGURES ARE IN MILLIONS. EXPENDITURE ON ADMINISTRATION IS CLASSIFIED WITH EMOLUMENTS OF TEACHERS. EXPENDITURE ON PRE-PRIMARY EDUCATION IS INCLUDED IN COLUMN 3.
FR—> LES CHIFFRES SONT EXPRIMES EN MILLIONS. LES DEPENSES D'ADMINISTRATION SONT CLASSEES AVEC LES EMOLUMENTS DU PERSONNEL ENSEIGNANT. LES DEPENSES DE L'ENSEIGNEMENT PREPRIMAIRE SONT INCLUSES DANS LA COLONNE 3.
ESP> LAS CIFRAS SE EXPRESAN EN MILLONES. LOS GASTOS DE ADMINISTRACION SE CLASIFICAN CON LOS EMOLUMENTOS DEL PERSONAL DOCENTE, Y LOS DE LA ENSEÑANZA PREPRIMARIA FIGURAN EN LA COLUMNA 3.

Public current expenditure by level and by purpose **4.4**
Dépenses publiques ordinaires par degré d'enseignement et destination
Gastos públicos ordinarios por grados de enseñanza y destino

AFGHANISTAN:
E—> EXPENDITURE ON UNIVERSITIES IS NOT INCLUDED.
FR—> LES DEPENSES DES UNIVERSITES NE SONT PAS INCLUSES.
ESP> NO SE INCLUYEN LOS GASTOS RELATIVOS A LAS UNIVERSIDADES.

CYPRUS:
E—> EXPENDITURE OF THE OFFICE OF GREEK EDUCATION ONLY.
FR—> DEPENSES DU BUREAU GREC DE L'EDUCATION SEULEMENT.
ESP> GASTOS DEL SERVICIO GRIEGO DE EDUCACION SOLAMENTE.

INDIA:
E—> THE LINE RELATING TO TOTAL CURRENT EXPENDITURE INCLUDES CAPITAL EXPENDITURE.
FR—> LA LIGNE CORRESPONDANT AU TOTAL DES DEPENSES ORDINAIRES COMPREND AUSSI LES DEPENSES EN CAPITAL.
ESP> LA LINEA QUE CORRESPONDE AL TOTAL DE GASTOS ORDINARIOS, COMPRENDE IGUALMENTE LOS GASTOS DE CAPITAL.

IRAN:
E—> EXPENDITURE OF THE MINISTRY OF EDUCATION ONLY: EXCLUDED ARE MAINLY THE MINISTRY OF HIGHER EDUCATION AND EXPENDITURE ON EDUCATION INCURRED BY OTHER MINISTRIES.
FR—> DEPENSES DU MINISTERE DE L'EDUCATION SEULEMENT: SONT EXCLUS LE MINISTERE DE L'ENSEI-GNEMENT SUPERIEUR ET LES DEPENSES D'EDUCATION D'AUTRES MINISTERES.
ESP> GASTOS DEL MINISTERIO DE EDUCACION SOLAMENTE. QUEDAN EXCLUIDOS LOS GASTOS DEL MINISTERIO DE ENSEÑANZA SUPERIOR Y DE OTROS MINISTERIOS.

IRAQ:
E—> EXPENDITURE ON PRE-PRIMARY EDUCATION IS INCLUDED IN COLUMN 3. EXPENDITURE ON SCHOLARSHIPS IS CLASSIFIED WITH OTHER DIRECT EXPENDITURE.
FR—> LES DEPENSES DE L'ENSEIGNEMENT PREPRIMAIRE SONT INCLUSES DANS LA COLONNE 3. LES DEPENSES POUR LES BOURSES D'ETUDES SONT CLASSEES AVEC LES AUTRES DEPENSES DIRECTES.
ESP> LOS GASTOS DE LA ENSEÑANZA PREPRIMARIA QUEDAN INCLUIDOS EN LA COLUMNA 3. LAS BECAS DE ESTUDIO SE CLASIFICAN CON LOS OTROS GASTOS DIRECTOS.

JAPAN:
E—> FIGURES ARE IN MILLIONS. PUBLIC SUBSIDIES TO PRIVATE EDUCATION ARE NOT INCLUDED.
FR—> LES CHIFFRES SONT EXPRIMES EN MILLIONS. LES SUBVENTIONS PUBLIQUES A L'ENSEIGNEMENT PRIVE NE SONT PAS INCLUSES.
ESP> LAS CIFRAS SE EXPRESAN EN MILLONES. NO SE INCLUYEN LAS SUBVENCIONES PUBLICAS A LA ENSEÑANZA PRIVADA.

CHILE:
E—> THE TOTALITY OF TRANSFERS TO UNIVERSITIES USED FOR ALL PURPOSES (SALARIES, ETC.) IS INCLUDED WITH EMOLUMENTS OF TEACHERS IN COLUMNS 1 AND 5. EXPENDITURE ON PRE-PRIMARY EDUCATION IS INCLUDED IN COLUMN 3.
FR—> LA TOTALITE DES TRANSFERTS AUX UNIVERSITES UTILISEE POUR DES DEPENSES DIVERSES (SALAIRES, ETC.) EST INCLUSE AVEC LES EMOLUMENTS DU PERSONNEL ENSEIGNANT DANS LES COLONNES 1 ET 5. LES DEPENSES DE L'ENSEIGNEMENT PREPRIMAIRE SONT INCLUSES DANS LA COLONNE 3.
ESP> LA TOTALIDAD DE LAS TRANSFERENCIAS A LAS UNIVERSIDADES UTILIZADA PARA GASTOS DIVERSOS (SALARIOS, ETC) QUEDA INCLUIDA CON LOS EMOLUMENTOS DEL PERSONAL DOCENTE, EN LAS COLUMNAS 1 Y 5. LOS GASTOS DE LA ENSEÑANZA PREPRIMARIA SE INCLUYEN EN LA COLUMNA 3.

GUYANA:
E—> THE TOTALITY OF TRANSFERS TO UNIVERSITIES USED FOR ALL PURPOSES (SALARIES, ETC.) IS INCLUDED WITH EMOLUMENTS OF TEACHERS IN COLUMNS 1 AND 5.
FR—> LA TOTALITE DES TRANSFERTS AUX UNIVERSITES UTILISEE POUR DES DEPENSES DIVERSES (SALAIRES, ETC.) EST INCLUSE AVEC LES EMOLUMENTS DU PERSONNEL ENSEIGNANT DANS LES COLONNES 1 ET 5.
ESP> LA TOTALIDAD DE LAS TRANSFERENCIAS A LAS UNIVERSIDADES UTILIZADA PARA GASTOS DIVERSOS (SALARIOS, ETC) QUEDA INCLUIDA CON LOS EMOLUMENTOS DEL PERSONAL DOCENTE, EN LAS COLUMNAS 1 Y 5.

PERU:
E—> TRANSFERS TO UNIVERSITIES AND SOME OTHER INSTITUTIONS AS WELL AS VARIOUS TYPES OF PENSIONS AND BENEFITS ARE NOT INCLUDED.
FR—> LES TRANSFERTS AUX UNIVERSITES ET A CERTAINS AUTRES ETABLISSEMENTS AINSI QUE DIFFERENTS TYPES DE PENSIONS ET D'INDEMNITES NE SONT PAS INCLUS.
ESP> NO SE INCLUYEN LAS TRANSFERENCIAS A LAS UNIVERSIDADES Y A ALGUNOS OTROS ESTABLECIMIENTOS, NI LOS DIFERENTES TIPOS DE PENSIONES Y DE INDEMNIZACIONES.

VENEZUELA:
E—> TRANSFERS TO UNIVERSITIES AND OTHER THIRD LEVEL INSTITUTIONS, USED FOR ALL PURPOSES (SALARIES, ETC.) ARE INCLUDED WITH EMOLUMENTS OF TEACHERS IN COLUMNS 1 AND 5.
FR—> LES TRANSFERTS AUX UNIVERSITES ET AUTRES ETABLISSEMENTS D'ENSEIGNEMENT DU TROISIEME DEGRE, UTILISES POUR DES DEPENSES DIVERSES (SALAIRES, ETC.) SONT INCLUS AVEC LES EMOLUMENTS DU PERSONNEL ENSEIGNANT DANS LES COLONNES 1 ET 5.
ESP> LAS TRANSFERENCIAS A LAS UNIVERSIDADES Y OTROS ESTABLECIMIENTOS DE ENSEÑANZA DE TERCER GRADO, UTILIZADAS PARA GASTOS DIVERSOS (SALARIOS, ETC.), QUEDAN INCLUIDAS EN LOS EMOLUMENTOS DEL PERSONAL DOCENTE, EN LAS COLUMNAS 1 Y 5.

4.4 **Public current expenditure by level and by purpose**
Dépenses publiques ordinaires par degré d'enseignement et destination
Gastos públicos ordinarios por grados de enseñanza y destino

TURKEY:
E—> EXPENDITURE ON ADMINISTRATION IS CLASSIFIED WITH EMOLUMENTS OF TEACHERS.
FR—> LES DEPENSES D'ADMINISTRATION SONT CLASSEES AVEC LES EMOLUMENTS DU PERSONNEL ENSEIGNANT.
ESP> LOS GASTOS DE ADMINISTRACION SE CLASIFICAN CON LOS EMOLUMENTOS DEL PERSONAL DOCENTE.

AUSTRIA:
E—> OTHER DIRECT INSTRUCTIONAL EXPENDITURE IS INCLUDED WITH EXPENDITURE NOT DISTRIBUTED BY LEVEL.
FR—> LES AUTRES DEPENSES DIRECTES D'ENSEIGNEMENT SONT INCLUSES AVEC LES DEPENSES NON REPARTIES.
ESP> LOS OTROS GASTOS DIRECTOS DE ENSEÑANZA SE INCLUYEN CON LOS GASTOS SIN DISTRIBUCION.

BELGIUM:
E—> EXPENDITURE OF THE MINISTRY OF EDUCATION ONLY.
FR—> DEPENSES DU MINISTERE DE L'EDUCATION SEULEMENT.
ESP> GASTOS DEL MINISTERIO DE EDUCACION SOLAMENTE.

DENMARK:
E—> EXPENDITURE ON PRE-PRIMARY EDUCATION IS INCLUDED IN COLUMN 3.
FR—> LES DEPENSES DE L'ENSEIGNEMENT PREPRIMAIRE SONT INCLUSES DANS LA COLONNE 3.
ESP> LOS GASTOS DE LA ENSEÑANZA PREPRIMARIA SE INCLUYEN EN LA COLUMNA 3.

FRANCE:
E—> EXPENDITURE OF THE MINISTRY OF EDUCATION AND MINISTRY OF THE UNIVERSITIES ONLY. OTHER DIRECT INSTRUCTIONAL EXPENDITURE IS INCLUDED WITH EXPENDITURE NOT DISTRIBUTED BY LEVEL.
FR—> DEPENSES DU MINISTERE DE L'EDUCATION ET DU MINISTERE DES UNIVERSITES SEULEMENT. LES AUTRES DEPENSES DIRECTES D'ENSEIGNEMENT SONT INCLUSES AVEC LES DEPENSES NON REPARTIES.
ESP> GASTOS DEL MINISTERIO DE EDUCACION Y DEL MINISTERIO DE LAS UNIVERSIDADES SOLAMENTE. LOS OTROS GASTOS DIRECTOS DE ENSEÑANZA SE INCLUYEN CON LOS GASTOS SIN DISTRIBUCION.

GREECE:
E—> OTHER DIRECT INSTRUCTIONAL EXPENDITURE IS INCLUDED WITH EXPENDITURE NOT DISTRIBUTED BY LEVEL.
FR—> LES AUTRES DEPENSES DIRECTES D'ENSEIGNEMENT SONT INCLUSES AVEC LES DEPENSES NON REPARTIES.
ESP> LOS OTROS GASTOS DIRECTOS DE ENSEÑANZA SE INCLUYEN CON LOS GASTOS SIN DISTRIBUCION.

HUNGARY:
E—> OTHER DIRECT INSTRUCTIONAL EXPENDITURE IS INCLUDED WITH EXPENDITURE NOT DISTRIBUTED BY LEVEL.
FR—> LES AUTRES DEPENSES DIRECTES D'ENSEIGNEMENT SONT INCLUSES DANS LES DEPENSES NON REPARTIES.
ESP> LOS OTROS GASTOS DIRECTOS DE ENSEÑANZA SE INCLUYEN CON LOS GASTOS SIN DISTRIBUCION.

JORDAN:
E—> DATA REFER TO THE EAST BANK ONLY. EXPENDITURE ON UNIVERSITIES IS NOT INCLUDED.
FR—> LES DONNEES SE REFERENT A LA RIVE ORIENTALE SEULEMENT. LES DEPENSES DES UNIVERSITES NE SONT PAS INCLUSES.
ESP> LOS DATOS SE REFIEREN A LA ORILLA ORIENTAL SOLAMENTE. NO SE INCLUYEN LOS DATOS RELATIVOS A LAS UNIVERSIDADES.

KOREA, REPUBLIC OF:
E—, FIGURES ARE IN MILLIONS.
FR—> LES CHIFFRES SONT EXPRIMES EN MILLIONS.
ESP> LAS CIFRAS SE EXPRESAN EN MILLONES.

MALAYSIA:
PENINSULAR MALAYSIA:
E—> TRANSFERS TO UNIVERSITIES AND OTHER THIRD LEVEL INSTITUTIONS, USED FOR ALL PURPOSES (SALARIES, ETC.) ARE INCLUDED WITH EMOLUMENTS OF TEACHERS IN COLUMNS 1 AND 5.
FR—> LES TRANSFERTS AUX UNIVERSITES ET AUTRES ETABLISSEMENTS D'ENSEIGNEMENT DU TROISIEME DEGRE, UTILISES POUR DES DEPENSES DIVERSES (SALAIRES, ETC.) SONT INCLUS AVEC LES EMOLUMENTS DU PERSONNEL ENSEIGNANT DANS LES COLONNES 1 ET 5.
ESP> LAS TRANSFERENCIAS A LAS UNIVERSIDADES Y OTROS ESTABLECIMIENTOS DE ENSEÑANZA DE TERCER GRADO, UTILIZADAS PARA GASTOS DIVERSOS (SALARIOS, ETC.) QUEDAN INCLUIDAS CON LOS EMOLUMENTOS DEL PERSONAL DOCENTE, EN LAS COLUMNAS 1 Y 5.

SINGAPORE:
E—> TRANSFERS TO THIRD LEVEL INSTITUTIONS (NAMELY UNIVERSITIES) INDUSTRIAL TRAINING BOARD AND OTHER EDUCATIONAL ORGANIZATIONS (67 707 000 DOLLARS IN 1977) USED FOR ALL PURPOSES (SALARIES, ETC.) ARE INCLUDED WITH EMOLUMENTS OF TEACHERS.
FR—> LES TRANSFERTS AUX ETABLISSEMENTS DU TROISIEME DEGRE (NOTAMMENT LES UNIVERSITES), AU BUREAU DE L'ENSEIGNEMENT INDUSTRIEL, ET A D'AUTRES ETABLISSEMENTS D'ENSEIGNEMENT (67 707 000 DOLLARS EN 1977) UTILISES POUR DES DEPENSES DIVERSES (SALAIRES, ETC.) SONT INCLUS AVEC LES EMOLUMENTS DU PERSONNEL ENSEIGNANT.
ESP> LAS TRANSFERENCIAS A LOS ESTABLECIMIENTOS DE TERCER GRADO, (ESPECIALMENTE LAS UNIVERSIDADES) AL CONSEJO DE FORMACION INDUSTRIAL (INDUSTRIAL TRAINING BOARD) Y OTROS ESTABLECIMIENTOS DE ENSEÑANZA, POR UN TOTAL DE 67 707 000 DOLARES EN 1977, UTILIZADAS PARA GASTOS DIVERSOS (SALARIOS, ETC.) QUEDAN INCLUIDAS CON LOS EMOLUMENTOS DEL PERSONAL DOCENTE.

SYRIAN ARAB REPUBLIC:
E—> EXPENDITURE ON EDUCATION AT THE THIRD LEVEL IS NOT INCLUDED.
FR—> LES DEPENSES DE L'ENSEIGNEMENT DU TROISIEME DEGRE NE SONT PAS INCLUSES.
ESP> NO SE INCLUYEN LOS GASTOS RELATIVOS A LA ENSEÑANZA DE TERCER GRADO.

Public current expenditure by level and by purpose **4.4**
Dépenses publiques ordinaires par degré d'enseignement et destination
Gastos públicos ordinarios por grados de enseñanza y destino

IRELAND:
E—> EXPENDITURE RELATING TO DEBT SERVICE IS INCLUDED. EXPENDITURE ON PRE-PRIMARY EDUCATION IS INCLUDED IN COLUMN 3. OTHER DIRECT INSTRUC- TIONAL EXPENDITURE IS INCLUDED WITH EXPENDITURE NOT DISTRIBUTED BY LEVEL.
FR—> LES DEPENSES RELATIVES AU SERVICE DE LA DETTE SONT INCLUSES. LES DEPENSES DE L'ENSEI- GNEMENT PREPRIMAIRE SONT INCLUSES DANS LA COLONNE 3. LES AUTRES DEPENSES DIRECTES D'ENSEIGNEMENT SONT INCLUSES AVEC LES DEPENSES NON REPARTIES.
ESP> SE INCLUYEN LOS GASTOS RELATIVOS AL SERVICIO DE LA DEUDA. LOS GASTOS DE LA ENSEÑANZA PREPRIMARIA FIGURAN EN LA COLUMNA 3 Y LOS OTROS GASTOS DIRECTOS DE ENSEÑANZA QUEDAN INCLUIDOS CON LOS GASTOS SIN DISTRIBUCION.

ITALY:
E—> FIGURES ARE IN MILLIONS.
FR—> LES CHIFFRES SONT EXPRIMES EN MILLIONS.
ESP> LAS CIFRAS SE EXPRESAN EN MILLONES.

LUXEMBOURG:
E—> DATA REFER TO CENTRAL GOVERNMENT EXPENDITURE INCLUDING REIMBURSEMENTS BY LOCAL AUTHORITIES OF STAFF EXPENDITURE. EXPENDITURE ON PRE-PRIMARY EDUCATION IS INCLUDED IN COLUMN 3.
FR—> LES DONNEES SE REFERENT AUX DEPENSES DU GOUVERNEMENT CENTRAL, Y COMPRIS LES REMBOURSEMENTS PAR LES AUTORITES LOCALES DES DEPENSES DU PERSONNEL. LES DEPENSES DE L'ENSEIGNEMENT PREPRIMAIRE SONT INCLUSES DANS LA COLONNE 3.
ESP> LOS DATOS SE REFIEREN A LOS GASTOS DEL GOBIERNO CENTRAL, INCLUIDOS LOS REEMBOLSOS DE LOS GASTOS DE PERSONAL EFECTUADOS POR LAS AUTORIDADES LOCALES. LOS GASTOS DE LA ENSEÑANZA PREPRIMARIA FIGURAN EN LA COLUMNA 3.

MALTA:
E—> EXPENDITURE ON PRE-PRIMARY EDUCATION IS INCLUDED IN COLUMN 3.
FR—> LES DEPENSES DE L'ENSEIGNEMENT PREPRIMAIRE SONT INCLUSES DANS LA COLONNE 3.
ESP> LOS GASTOS DE LA ENSEÑANZA PREPRIMARIA SE INCLUYEN EN LA COLUMNA 3.

NETHERLANDS:
E—> FIGURES ARE IN MILLIONS.
FR—> LES CHIFFRES SONT EXPRIMES EN MILLIONS.
ESP> LAS CIFRAS SE EXPRESAN EN MILLONES.

NORWAY:
E—> EXPENDITURE ON SCHOLARSHIPS IS CLASSIFIED WITH EXPENDITURE NOT DISTRIBUTED BY LEVEL.
FR—> LES DEPENSES POUR LES BOURSES D'ETUDES SONT CLASSEES AVEC LES DEPENSES NON REPARTIES.
ESP> LOS GASTOS PARA LAS BECAS DE ESTUDIO SE CLASIFICAN CON LOS GASTOS SIN DISTRIBUCION.

PORTUGAL:
E—> EXPENDITURE OF THE MINISTRY OF EDUCATION ONLY.
FR—> DEPENSES DU MINISTERE DE L'EDUCATION SEULEMENT.
ESP> GASTOS DEL MINISTERIO DE EDUCACION SOLAMENTE.

SAN MARINO:
E—> EXPENDITURE ON PRE-PRIMARY EDUCATION IS INCLUDED IN COLUMN 3. DATA IN COLUMN 5 REFER TO SCHOLARSHIPS FOR SECOND AND THIRD LEVEL STUDENTS.
FR—> LES DEPENSES DE L'ENSEIGNEMENT PREPRIMAIRE SONT INCLUSES DANS LA COLONNE 3. LES DONNEES DE LA COLONNE 5 SE REFERENT AUX BOURSES POUR LES ETUDIANTS DES ENSEIGNEMENTS DES SECOND ET TROISIEME DEGRE.
ESP> LOS GASTOS DE LA ENSEÑANZA PREPRIMARIA SE INCLUYEN EN LA COLUMNA 3. LOS DATOS DE LA COLUMNA 5 SE REFIEREN A LAS BECAS PARA ESTUDIANTES DE LAS ENSEÑANZAS DE SEGUNDO Y TERCER GRADO.

SPAIN:
E—> FIGURES ARE IN MILLIONS. EXPENDITURE ON PRE-PRIMARY EDUCATION IS INCLUDED IN COLUMN 3.
FR—> LES CHIFFRES SONT EXPRIMES EN MILLIONS. LES DEPENSES DE L'ENSEIGNEMENT PREPRIMAIRE SONT INCLUSES DANS LA COLONNE 3.
ESP> LAS CIFRAS SE EXPRESAN EN MILLONES. LOS GASTOS DE LA ENSEÑANZA PREPRIMARIA FIGURAN EN LA COLUMNA 3.

PAPUA NEW GUINEA:
E—> EXPENDITURE ON PRE-PRIMARY EDUCATION IS INCLUDED IN COLUMN 3. EXPENDITURE ON ADMINIS- TRATION IS CLASSIFIED WITH OTHER DIRECT INSTRUC- TIONAL EXPENDITURE.
FR—> LES DEPENSES DE L'ENSEIGNEMENT PREPRIMAIRE SONT INCLUSES DANS LA COLONNE 3. LES DEPENSES D'ADMINISTRATION SONT CLASSEES AVEC LES AUTRES DEPENSES DIRECTES D'ENSEIGNEMENT.
ESP> LOS GASTOS DE LA ENSEÑANZA PREPRIMARIA SE INCLUYEN EN LA COLUMNA 3. LOS GASTOS DE ADMINIS- TRACION SE CLASIFICAN CON LOS OTROS GASTOS DIRECTOS DE ENSEÑANZA.

Science and technology 5
Science et technologie
Ciencia y tecnología

5 Science and technology
Science et technologie
Ciencia y tecnología

For more than two decades there has been an awareness of the need for statistics in the field of science and technology and their importance in the development of the various countries of the world. Nevertheless, this is a relatively new field of statistics still in its early stages and is only now becoming clearly defined. Despite the delayed start, Member States in increasing numbers are initiating and implementing formalized and continuing programmes of statistical data collection in science and technology.

In order to provide for the uniform collection and dissemination of such data on an international basis, Unesco is continuing to work with Member States and various expert bodies and individuals towards the development of an international standard in the field of statistics of science and technology, as already exists in various other fields of statistics. The most recent initiative of Unesco in this field was the organization of a Special Committee of Experts to prepare a draft recommendation on the international standardization of statistics on science and technology. The Recommendation was adopted by the General Conference at its twentieth session in November 1978.

This chapter presents selected results of the necessarily limited world-wide data collection effort by Unesco in the field of science and technology. Most of the data were obtained from replies to the statistical surveys of scientific and technological activities sent to the Member States of Unesco during 1978 and 1979. This material has been completed or supplemented by data collected in the previous annual or biennial surveys and from official reports and publications.

In utilizing these results the reader should keep in mind the factors which have an obvious bearing on the comparability and the degree of accuracy of the data. Science statistics have not reached the same stage of development in all countries. Whereas some countries have established systems of science data collection by means of regular surveys, others are just beginning to initiate systematic and comprehensive enquiries into their R&D activities and, of course, there are others which have yet to begin such an effort. Additionally, national statistical practices and concepts are not necessarily designed for the specific requirements of international comparisons. Consequently, most countries had to re-arrange their existing national data and often prepare estimates for the specific purposes of the Unesco enquiries. Very few countries were able to organize *ad hoc* surveys whose classifications and definitions conformed with those proposed in the Unesco questionnaire and which are listed below. It is to be hoped that with the gradual implementation of the Recommendation the quantity and quality of internationally comparable data will progressively improve.

As an example of the problem of comparability, the basic concept 'research and experimental development' is largely the same in all countries. However, the methods of measurement and the coverage of the data frequently differ, sometimes to an extent which renders international comparisons difficult. In most countries only those activities of research institutes, departments and similar research organizations which could be defined specifically as research or experimental development were included in the survey. However, in other countries, the total volume of activity of such research institutes and similar organizations is included, without making the necessary adjustments to exclude the so-called 'related' scientific and technological activities which are not classified as R&D.

Another example is the subject coverage where in earlier surveys some countries included R&D in social sciences and others omitted this significant segment of R&D, whilst for many European countries as well as countries of other continents, the coverage includes not only humanities, in some cases inseparable from social sciences, but other fields such as arts, pedagogy and law, disciplines which have been included in the surveys since 1971.

The following definitions were suggested for use in the *Statistical Survey of Scientific and Technological Activities* (doc. Unesco STS/Q/781).

These definitions are largely compatible with those used in previous surveys and comparability of the data obtained from the various surveys, though being limited for other reasons, is thus not seriously affected by the use of slightly different sets of definitions.

Type of personnel.

Scientist and engineer. Includes any person who has received scientific or technical training in the fields of science defined below as follows: completed education at the third level leading to an academic degree; or completed third level non-university education (or training) which does not lead to an academic degree but is nationally recognized as qualifying for a professional career; or training and professional experience which is nationally recognized (e.g. membership in professional societies, professional certificate or licence) as being equivalent to the formal education indicated above.

Technician. Includes any person who has received specialized vocational or technical training in any branch of knowledge or technology as follows: one to two years' training beyond completed education at the second level or three to four years' training beyond the first cycle of secondary education, whether or not leading to a degree or diploma; on-the-job training and professional experience which is nationally recognized as being equivalent to the level of education indicated.

Auxiliary personnel. The residual group includes skilled workers, such as machinists, sheet metal workers and other trade workers, operatives, etc., as well as unskilled workers; all clerical, administrative and other supporting personnel such as

5 Science and technology
Science et technologie
Ciencia y tecnología

secretarial personnel. Security, janitorial and maintenance personnel engaged in general 'housekeeping' activities are excluded.

Total stock of scientists, engineers and technicians.

The number of scientists, engineers and technicians as described above without regard to age, sex, economic activity or any other characteristic.

Number of economically active scientists, engineers and technicians.

This group includes all scientists, engineers and technicians of either sex, as specified above, who are engaged in, or actively seeking work in, some branch of the economy at the time of reference. For scientists and engineers only those who are employed at the professional level (i.e., one which normally requires a third level education or equivalent) should be included.

Full-and part-time personnel and full-time equivalent.

Personnel working full-time (FT). This includes all persons who devote substantially all of their working time exclusively to R&D activities, including administration of R&D.

Personnel working part-time(PT). This category includes all persons who divide their working time between R&D and other activities.

Full-time equivalent (FTE). This is an estimate of the amount of time devoted to R&D activities by the personnel in the above two groups. It includes all persons working full-time on R&D activities plus the proportion of working time devoted to R&D by part-time personnel.

Research and experimental development (R&D).

In general R&D is defined as any creative systematic activity undertaken to increase the stock of scientific and technical knowledge and to devise new applications. It includes fundamental research, applied research in such fields as agriculture, medicine, industrial chemistry, etc., and experimental development work leading to new devices, products or processes. It excludes scientific education, scientific and technical information, general-purpose data collection, routine testing, standardization and other technological activities related to production or use of established products or processes, as well as large-scale mineral and petroleum prospecting for exploitable deposits and not essentially for basic geological knowledge. In the social sciences, it includes activities of a research nature related to the solution of economic or social problems, but excludes routine activities such as censuses, market studies, etc. In the medical sciences, it excludes intensive medical care. In general, defence R&D is included. The criterion which distinguishes R&D from non-R&D activities is the presence or absence of an appreciable element of novelty or innovation.

Fundamental research. Any activity directed towards the increase of scientific knowledge or discovery of new fields of investigation, without any specific practical objective.

Applied research. Any activity directed towards the increase of scientific knowledge but with a specific practical aim in view.

Experimental development. Systematic use of the results of fundamental and applied research and of empirical knowledge directed towards the introduction of new materials, products, devices, processes and methods, or the improvement of existing ones, including the development of prototypes and pilot plants.

Sectors of performance.

The sectors of performance identify those areas of the economy in which R&D work is performed. The term 'sector of performance' distinguishes the execution or the performance of R&D activities from their financing. Three sectors of performance have been established for the purpose of the survey and defined, to the fullest extent possible, in accordance with the definitions of the United Nations 'System of National Accounts' (SNA) and those of the 'System of Balances of the National Economy of the Council for Mutual Economic Assistance' (Material Product System, MPS):

Productive sector:

(i) In general this sector includes:

(a) both domestic and foreign-owned industrial and trading establishments located in the country, which produce and distribute goods and services for sale, and organizations directly serving them, whatever their form of ownership, private, non-profit, or government. It also includes government monopolies and nationalized industries, particularly public utilities, transport undertakings, post offices, communications and broadcasting, and all other government establishments which function as productive units;

(b) also included are governmental or non-governmental organizations and private non-profit institutions mainly or exclusively serving industrial or trading establishments, except those institutes, experimental stations, etc., operating under the direct control of, or being associated with, institutions of higher education (see below). In socialist countries, R&D institutes of branch ministries are to be classified in this sector.

(ii) Integrated and non-integrated R&D.

Due to the different structure of the productive sector in countries with different socio-economic systems and in order to facilitate comparisons, the R&D effort should be measured on the following two 'levels':

(a) *Integrated R&D.* This includes all R&D activities integrated or directly associated with other economic activities of industrial and trading establishments, or groups of such establishments belonging to the same enterprise as defined in (i) (a) above.

(b) *Non-integrated R&D.* This includes all R&D activities not integrated or directly associated with other economic activities, executed by such governmental or non-governmental organizations or institutes defined in (i) (b) above which are serving a specific two- or three- digit group of the economy, defined in terms of the International Standard Industrial Classification of all economic activities (ISIC), even if they are partly or wholly financed by the State budget or, in the case of East European countries, by the Technical and Economic Progress Fund.

Higher education sector. This sector comprises all institutions of education at the third level which require, as a minimum condition of admission, the successful completion of education at the second level, or evidence of the attainment of an equivalent level of knowledge, i.e. all universities, colleges of technology, etc., whatever their source of finance, or their legal or economic status. It also includes experimental stations, clinics, and research institutes operating under the direct control of institutions of higher education, administered by or associated with them. It excludes national research councils which are classified in the General service sector.

General service sector. The General service sector includes all R&D activities not covered above and comprises mainly the remaining government R&D activities which are often important in volume and relevance. In general it includes all bodies, departments and establishments of government - central, state or provincial, district or county, municipal, town or village - which serve the community as a whole, and engage in a wide range of usual government services such as administration, defence and regulation of public order, health, cultural, recreational and other social services and promotion of economic growth and welfare and technological development. It includes laboratories of national research councils as well as academies of science, professional scientific organizations, State museums, scientific societies and other non-profit organizations which primarily serve government, even though they are not formally part of government. It excludes institutions of higher education, as well as government monopolies and nationalized industries which function as productive enterprises and government services and organizations which serve a specific two-or-three-digit group of the economy. These belong to the Productive sector or the Higher education sector, as defined above.

Field of science.

In its broadest sense the field of science is the area of the major subject of qualification although it could be extended to apply to occupation specialization. As further guidance to the classification groups show below, the principal corresponding two-digit codes of the broad fields of programme groups of courses of education as proposed by Unesco in the International Standard Classification of Education (ED/BIE/CONFINTE 35/Ref 8, Paris, July 1975) are indicated in brackets at the end of each field of science.

Natural sciences. Includes astronomy, bacteriology, biochemistry, biology, botany, chemistry, entomology, geology, geophysics, mathematics, meteorology, mineralogy, physics, zoology, and related subjects. (42, 46).

Engineering and technology. This category includes engineering proper, such as chemical, civil, electrical and

Science and technology 5
Science et technologie
Ciencia y tecnologia

mechanical engineering and specializations thereunder: applied sciences such as geodesy, industrial chemistry, and the like; architecture; specialized technologies or interdisciplinary fields such as industrial engineering, metallurgy, mining, systems engineering, textiles and similar subjects. (52, 54, 58, 70).

Medical sciences. Comprises anatomy, dentistry, medicine, midwifery, nursing, optometry, osteopathy, pharmacy, physiotherapy, public health and related subjects. (50).

Agriculture. Covers the disciplines of agronomy, dairying, fisheries, food processing, forestry and forest products, horticulture, rural science, veterinary medicine and related subjects. (62).

Social sciences and humanities (distributed when possible in two groups).

Group I - *Social sciences.* Includes anthropology (social and cultural) and ethnology, demography, economics, education and training, geography (human, economic, social), juridical sciences, linguistics (excluding studies of language carried out on given texts; these studies should be classified in group II under 'ancient and modern languages and literature'), management, political sciences, psychology, sociology, other social sciences and interdisciplinary, methodological and historical research related to the disciplines of this group. Note that psycho-physiology, physical anthropology and physical geography should in principal be classified with the Natural sciences. (14, 30, 34 38, 66, 84).

Group II - *Humanities.* Includes arts (history and critique of arts; excluding artistic 'research' of any kind), letters (ancient and modern languages and literature), philosophy and religion (history of sciences and techniques is included under philosophy), pre-history and history (auxiliary sciences of history, archeology, paleography, numismatics, etc.), other disciplines or research subjects belonging to this group and interdisciplinary, methodological, historical, etc. research related to the disciplines of this group. (18, 22, 26).

R&D expenditure.

To cover the full costs of R&D activities and to avoid double-counting, the measurement of expenditure should include all intra-mural current expenditure including overheads and intra-mural capital expenditure.

Current expenditure. This includes wages, salaries and all related elements of labour costs such as 'fringe benefits'. Also included are all expendable supplies and minor equipment and other supporting costs including share of overheads, for example: rent, maintenance and repair of buildings, replacement of office furniture, water, gas, electricity, administrative expenses, etc. Major items of equipment are included in the category of capital expenditure. Current expenditure is separated into total labour costs, minor equipment and other current costs.

Capital expenditure. Includes actual expenditure or investment in land, buildings and major equipment during year of reference. Any depreciation e.g. on major instruments, equipment and buildings, should be excluded. Capital expenditure is separated into major equipment and other capital expenditure.

Source of funds.

The sources of finance for expenditure on R&D are defined as follows:

Government funds. This includes all funds originating from the ordinary or extraordinary budget or from extra-budgetary sources of both the central government and the state and local governments such as provincial, district or county, municipal, town or village. It also includes the funds originating from those intermediary public and private organizations which are set up by government and whose financial means are exclusively provided by government.

Productive enterprise funds. This includes all those funds allocated to R&D which originate from the economic activities of establishments in the productive sector, that is, the R&D funds made available from the production of goods and services for sale on the market.

Special funds. This category of source of funds primarily provides for the structure of finance of R&D in East European countries. As far as these countries are concerned, special funds include, for the most part, the financial means originating

from the Technical and Economic Progress Fund and from similar funds.

Foreign funds. This category includes all funds received from abroad for R&D performed inside the reporting country by establishments, departments and institutions which are defined under 'Sectors of performance'. It covers funds received from international organizations (whether located inside or outside the country), foreign governments and private funds from abroad, including funds from parent or affiliated organizations or companies abroad.

Other funds. Includes all funds which cannot be classified in one of the preceding categories, such as endowments or gifts. This category also includes own funds of institutions of higher education.

Statistical unit.

In principle, the *unit of classification* used in the *Productive sector* is the establishment. Alternatively, the enterprise consisting of more than one establishment may be used as the unit of classification, particularly when the financial data cannot be ascertained for each individual establishment. In the case of a *market economy*, the statistical unit may also be a corporation, joint stock company, co-operative association, incorporated non-profit association, partnership, individual proprietorship or some other form of association. In the case of a *centrally-planned economy*, the enterprise may be a management and book-keeping unit and may consist of a number of establishments. It enters into contracts, has an independent plan of production, receives and disposes of income, maintains a separate bank account, and an independant, complete set of accounting records.

In the case of *non-integrated R&D* the typical unit of classification upd328/1may be a research association, a non-profit institute, a government institute which is serving a two-or-three digit group of the economy; in East European countries, it may be a research institute of a branch ministry.

The statistical unit used in the *General service sector* is a major organizational body, separately functioning or separately identifiable within a government department or instrumentality and not classified elsewhere. Such a unit may be a division, a laboratory or institute, a bureau, a central office, etc.

Major aims of national R&D.

The following scheme for classifying R&D expenditure in a functional rather than in an institutional or strictly sectorial way is an attempt by Unesco's Office of Statistics to obtain summary information on the broad pattern of national R&D efforts, on an internationally comparable basis. In some Member States similar statistics are already collected and expenditure is classified according to fields of application or objectives of national R&D. These terms having acquired quite varying connotations in such Member States, it seemed advisable that Unesco choose a term for its own nomenclature, which would avoid creating the impression that it reflects the stated objectives of governments. The classification of national R&D by major aims, which should be on ultimate purpose as suggested below, is thus rather an attempt to find a suitable common denominator which would allow a more systematic and analytical breakdown of R&D expenditure on an internationally comparable basis. The items listed under the twelve main aims are not to be considered exhaustive but as examples of the types of R&D which should be included in each main aim.

This continuing effort to classify R&D expenditure by major aims must of necessity still be considered experimental.

1. *Exploration and assessment of the earth, the seas, atmosphere and space.*

This heading covers R&D activities primarily related to the exploration and assessment of the earth's crust and mantle, seas, oceans, the atmosphere and space, and its administration, economics policy and planning. It does *not include* studies on soils for agricultural purposes, R&D on oceanography serving the fishing industry, R&D concerning the economic exploitation of sources of raw materials, fuel and energy, nor R&D concerning the use of satellite techniques for communication applications. The activities included in this group are undertaken with a view toward economic exploitation of results, thus *excluding* fundamental investigation in meteorology, geology, hydrography, etc. which is included under 'General advancement of knowledge'.

2. *Development of agriculture, forestry and fishing.*

This heading covers two categories of R&D activities, the first related to aspects of food, and the second concerned with non-food agricultural products and forestry. Under the first are included R&D on the production, storage and distribution of food e.g. livestock production and improvement of species, veterinary medicine, crop production and agronomy, R&D on agricultural machinery and agricultural chemicals, R&D on the processing of food and beverages, their storage and distribution, fisheries and their

5 Science and technology
Science et technologie
Ciencia y tecnología

related technologies, and the administration, economics, policy, and planning of agriculture and food production. The second category, development of non-food agricultural products and forestry, covers all R&D activities on non-food agricultural products such as wool, skins, tobacco, cotton, and other fibres, and on forestry and related technology.

3. *Promotion of industrial development.*

This major aim relates to all R&D activities contributing to the development and improvement of the manufacturing and mining industry. It includes R&D on the administration, economics, policy and planning of industrial development, on the production of textiles, wearing apparel and leather, wood and paper products, chemicals including petrochemicals, rubber and plastics, basic metals, fabricated metal products, machinery and equipment including transport vehicles, non-metallic products, mining other then fuels. It does *not include* industrial R&D performed in support of other objectives such as development of agriculture and food production, transport and communications, exploration of space, urban and rural planning, and defence.

4. *Production, conservation and distribution of energy.*

This heading covers all R&D activities relating to the production, supply, conservation and distribution of all forms of energy (including nuclear), and the administration, economics, policy and planning of energy; it includes the mining of solid fuels and related technology, petroleum and gas production as well as non-conventional energy sources (solar, wind) and small energy sources.

5. *Development of transport and communication.*

This group relates to the transportation systems and networks and systems of communication, covering land, air and water transport, radio and television, telephone and other communications including satellites as well as R&D on the administration, economics, policy and planning of transport and communication networks. It includes auxiliary services such as electronic traffic aids and radar stations but *excludes* engines, motors and means of transportation such as vehicles, ships and planes which are included in the aim 'Promotion of industrial development'.

6. *Development of education services.*

This major aim includes R&D activities concerning the administration, economics, policy and planning of education services at all levels. Formal education as well as out-of-school, in-service and other forms of adult education and training are included. R&D on both conventional and new technical devices and teaching methods such as programmed instruction, TV and other audio-visual techniques should also be considered in this group.

7. *Development of health services.*

This heading concerns all R&D activities directed to the protection and improvement of human health. It includes R&D on medical care (including surgery and obstetrics), disease prevention, nutrition and food hygiene, on the environmental impact on health, including labour medicine, on pharmaceutical products, vaccines and prosthetics as well as health administration, economics, policy and planning.

8. *Social development and other socio-economic services.*

This group relates to R&D activities concerning the administration, economics, policy and planning of social development and socio-economic services; it includes political organization, law and order, social security, culture, recreation and leisure, consumer protection, the improvement of working conditions, labour relations, manpower and migration, international relations including peace, international courts, treaties, and other social services. Also included are R&D activities on economic organization, money and banking, insurances, etc. This major aim also includes R&D activities concerning urban and rural planning such as domestic housing, sanitary services and other community services involved in the improvement of human settlements.

9. *Protection of the environment.*

This major aim covers all aspects of the 'protection' of the environment-the maintenance of the purity of the atmosphere, water and soil, the control of noise, environmental models and statistics and the regulation, economics, policy and planning relative to the environment. It *excludes* R&D on the environmental impact on health which should be included under 'Development of health services' and the environmental impact on human settlements which should be included under 8 above. Also *excluded* is R&D designed to prevent pollution by specific economic activities, which should be included with the relevant activities.

10. *General advancement of knowledge.*

This heading includes all R&D of very general orientation which cannot be classified in one of the other major aims but contributes to the general advancement of knowledge in the social as well as the natural sciences. It consists of fundamental and applied research which science councils, institutes of academies of sciences and universities undertake in the context of their broad vocation. It includes R&D on the administration, economics, policy and planning of R&D itself.

11. *Other aims.*

This item includes all other civil R&D undertaken with a specified aim which does not fall under any of the above headings. It would include for example, the improvment of information systems, computer science (hardware and software) but *exclude* expenditure on the gathering of data.

12. *Defence.*

This major aim includes nuclear, space and other R&D undertaken for military purposes. Sums spent on civil research by military institutions should, as far as possible, be distributed among the major civil objectives to which they may relate.

The tables provided in this chapter are presented in three sections. The first section consists of 5 tables relating to scientific and technical manpower. The stock of qualified manpower or their number economically active, i.e. those who possess the necessary qualifications to be classified as scientists, engineers and technicians, and the corresponding number of women is shown in table 5.1. Information relating to the concept of stock is usually obtained through the population census so that these data are not readily available every year. Where such information is lacking the number of economically active scientists, engineers and technicians is shown as an alternative.

Table 5.2 provides corresponding data for the scientists, engineers and technicians engaged in research and experimental development.

In table 5.3 only data for scientists and engineers engaged in research and experimental development are presented, distributed by the field of science of their qualification and according to whether they are occupied full-time or part-time. Their full-time equivalent is also shown and where possible separate data are given for women. It should be noted that in general the breakdown by field of science refers to the field of science of formal qualification but in some cases it has not always been possible to discern whether the breakdown refers to the field of study or the field of current specialization.

Table 5.4 presents all personnel engaged in R&D and the sector of performance, providing both the absolute numbers and the percentage distribution of total personnel according to their sector of performance and showing the type of personnel performing in these sectors.

The orientation of national R&D efforts can been seen from table 5.5 which presents, for a limited number of countries, scientists and engineers engaged in R&D according to their sector of performance and industry group or field of investigation to which their enterprise or institution belongs or their present field of investigation (this does not necessarily correspond to the original field of science of formal qualification of the personnel, the classification which is presented in table 5.3).

The second section, comprising 5 tables, provides a general picture of the cost of R&D activities measured on the basis of intramural expenditures for the performance of R&D. The data are given in national currencies.

In table 5.6 total expenditure for R&D is subdivided by type of expenditure - total, current and labour costs - and the relationship of current to total expenditure is provided.

In table 5.7 the absolute figures and the percentage distribution of current expenditure according to type of R&D activity - fundamental research, applied research or experimental development - are presented.

Table 5.8 shows the distribution of total and current expenditures by sector of performance, in absolute numbers and in percentages.

The structure of the financing of R&D can be seen in table 5.9 which gives the distribution of total and current expenditures by source of funds. The data are presented in national currencies and in percentages.

Table 5.10 presents the percentage distribution of government funds, or alternatively total national intramural expenditure, for R&D according to twelve major aims; this is an analytical breakdown of R&D expenditures classified 'functionally' (in table 5.8 the classification is 'institutional' or 'sectorial'), providing summary information on the broad pattern of national R&D efforts. This proposed classification should nevertheless still be considered as experimental.

The last section has been provided to convey a general picture of the development of R&D activities and to include additional indicators. The two tables providing historical data, tables 5.11 and 5.12 show for developing and developed countries the growth in human and financial resources devoted to R&D activities.

Table 5.11 presents the total personnel and scientists and engineers engaged in R&D for recent years, normally 1969 to 1978; the information for scientists and engineers is also expressed in index number on the base 1969=100.

Science and technology 5
Science et technologie
Ciencia y tecnología

In table 5.12 a time series of total and current expenditures devoted to R&D activities covers recent years, generally around 1969 to 1978. The relationship between current and total expenditures is also shown.

Table 5.13 provides selected indicators on science and technology. It shows the stock of qualified manpower, i.e. those who possess the necessary qualifications to be classified as scientists, engineers and technicians, and the scientists, engineers and technicians engaged in R&D, related to the total population; the relationship between all scientists and engineers and those engaged in R&D is also provided as well as the support ratios per scientist and engineer. These indicators are aligned with those concerning expenditure on R&D which is also related to the total population and number of R&D scientists and engineers and also given as a percentage of gross national product.

The reader will find in each table an indication of the number of countries and territories included. The total number of countries covered in the thirteen tables is 137. Because of obvious differences in definitions used and the incompleteness of the results, the data should be used with caution. In many instances, exceptions are indicated by footnotes. However, the absence of footnotes does not necessarily imply that the figures given agree with established definitions. It is for these reasons that the data have not been totalled by regions of the world and this practice should be discouraged until such time as statistics on science and technology may be collected with a higher degree of confidence. Research workers interested in obtaining further details or clarification pertaining to particular countries as regards national definitions, coverage or limitations of the data presented in the tables may address their enquiries to the Division of Statistics on Science and Technology of the Office of Statistics.

The absolute figures for R&D expenditure should not be compared country by country. Such comparisons would require the conversion of national currencies into a common currency by means of the official exchange rates, since special R&D exchange rates do not exist. Official exchange rates do not always reflect the real costs of R&D activities and comparisons based on such rates can result in misleading conclusions. However, they do have some limited value in indicating at least a gross order of magnitude of expenditure on R&D. For the rates of exchange between national currencies and the United States dollar, the reader is referred to Appendix C.

Cela fait plus de deux décennies qu'on a pris conscience de la nécessité des statistiques de la science et de la technologie et de leur importance pour le développement. Il s'agit toutefois d'un domaine relativement nouveau dont les éléments commencent seulement à se préciser plus clairement. Malgré cette mise en route tardive, de plus en plus nombreux sont les Etats membres qui déploient des efforts systématiques et soutenus pour rassembler des données statistiques sur la science et la technologie.

Soucieuse d'assurer l'uniformité des méthodes de rassemblement et de diffusion de ces données sur le plan international, l'Unesco ne cesse d'oeuvrer avec les Etats membres, divers organismes compétents et des spécialistes, afin de mettre au point des normes internationales pour les statistiques de la science et de la technologie, telles qu'il en existe déjà dans les autres branches de la statistique. L'initiative la plus récente de l'Unesco dans ce domaine à été l'organisation du Comité Spécial d'Experts afin de préparer un projet de recommandation concernant la normalisation internationale des statistiques relatives à la science et à la technologie. La Recommandation à été adoptée par la Conférence Générale à sa vingtième session, en novembre 1978.

Le lecteur trouvera consignés dans ce chapitre quelques résultats sélectionnés des efforts que l'Unesco a déployés pour rassembler à l'échelon mondial des données statistiques concernant la science et la technologie. Les données proviennent pour la plupart de réponses aux questionnaires sur les activités scientifiques et techniques que l'Unesco a adressés aux Etats membres en 1978 et 1979. Elles ont été complétées par des renseignements recueillis auparavant à l'aide des précédentes enquêtes annuelles et biennales et des rapports officiels et publications.

Pour interpréter les résultats ainsi obtenus, le lecteur doit tenir compte des divers facteurs qui influent manifestement sur la comparabilité et l'exactitude des données. Les statistiques de la science n'ont pas atteint dans tous les pays le même degré de développement. Alors que dans certains pays le rassemblement de ces statistiques est basé sur des enquêtes qui se succèdent à intervalles réguliers, il en est d'autres où les activités de R-D commencent seulement à faire l'objet d'une étude systématique, et d'autres encore où rien, jusqu'à présent, n'a été fait à cet égard. En outre, l'établissement des statistiques obéit, sur le plan national, à des concepts et à des méthodes qui ne sont pas nécessairement de nature à faciliter les comparaisons internationales. La plupart des pays ont donc dû, pour répondre aux questions de l'Unesco, remanier leurs données statistiques et recourir souvent à des estimations. Très rares sont ceux qui ont pu se livrer à des enquêtes spéciales reposant sur des classifications et définitions identiques à celles que proposait l'Unesco et qui sont énumérées ci-dessous. Nous espérons qu'avec l'application graduelle de la Recommandation, la quantité et la qualité des données comparables sur le plan international s'amélioreront progressivement.

Voici un exemple du problème que pose la comparabilité: le concept fondamental de 'recherche et développement expérimental' est à peu près le même dans tous les pays mais, pour ce qui est des méthodes de mesure et des éléments pris en considération, il y a souvent, d'un pays à l'autre, des différences qui rendent parfois difficiles toute comparaison internationale. On constate que, dans leurs réponses aux questionnaires, la plupart des pays ont uniquement retenu, parmi les tâches auxquelles se livrent les organismes de recherche (instituts, services gouvernementaux, etc.), celles qui pouvaient être expressément classées comme 'activités de R-D', alors que d'autres ont fait entrer en ligne de compte la totalité de ces tâches, sans en exclure, comme il aurait été nécessaire, les activités scientifiques et techniques 'connexes' qui ne sont pas, à proprement parler, des 'activités de R-D'.

Un autre exemple consiste dans la façon d'envisager la question de l'étendue des disciplines scientifiques dans les premières enquêtes où certains pays englobaient dans les activités de R-D celles qui concernaient les sciences sociales, alors que d'autres les en excluaient complètement; beaucoup de pays européens et certains pays d'autres continents y incluent non seulement celles qui ont trait aux sciences humaines, parfois inséparables de celles qui intéressent les sciences sociales, mais aussi celles qui ont trait à d'autres domaines, tels que les arts, la pédagogie et le droit, disciplines qui depuis 1971 sont incluses dans les enquêtes.

On trouvera ci-dessous la liste des définitions proposées pour être utilisées dans l'*Enquête statistique sur les activités scientifiques et techniques* (doc. Unesco STS/Q/781).

Ces définitions correspondent en grande partie à celles qui avaient été employées lors d'enquêtes antérieures et les légères modifications qu'elles ont subies ne nuisent guère à la comparabilité des données résultant des diverses enquêtes, comparabilité du reste limitée pour d'autres motifs.

Classification du personnel.

Scientifique et ingénieur. Toute personne ayant reçu une formation scientifique ou technique dans les disciplines scientifiques citées ci-dessous, ce qui implique: ou bien des études du troisième degré complètes jusqu'à l'obtention d'un grade universitaire; ou bien des études (ou une formation) non universitaire du troisième degré ne conduisant pas à l'obtention d'un grade universitaire, mais reconnues sur le plan national comme pouvant donner accès à une carrière de scientifique ou d'ingénieur; ou bien encore une formation ou expérience professionnelle reconnues équivalentes sur le plan national à l'un des deux types de formation précédents (par exemple, appartenance à une association professionnelle, obtention d'un certificat ou d'une licence professionnelle).

Technicien. Toute personne ayant reçu une formation professionnelle ou technique spécialisée dans n'importe quelle branche du savoir ou de la technologie, ce qui implique : soit une ou deux années d'études après achèvement du second cycle du second degré, ou trois ou quatre années d'études après achèvement du premier cycle du second degré (sanctionnées ou non par un diplôme), soit une formation sur le lieu de travail et une expérience professionnelle considérées comme équivalentes sur le plan national au niveau d'instruction indiqué.

Personnel auxiliaire. Le reste du personnel comprend les ouvriers qualifiés, tels que mécaniciens, tôliers, et autres gens de métier, les ouvriers semi-qualifiés et non qualifiés ainsi que le personnel de bureau, d'administration et tout autre personnel auxiliaire tel que le personnel de secrétariat. Il ne comprend pas le personnel de sécurité, de réception et d'entretien général.

5 Science and technology
Science et technologie
Ciencia y tecnología

Effectif total des scientifiques, ingénieurs et techniciens.
Nombre total des scientifiques, ingénieurs et techniciens répondant aux
définitions ci-dessus, indépendamment de l'âge, du sexe, de l'activité
économique ou de toutes autres caractéristiques.

Nombre des scientifiques, ingénieurs et techniciens économiquement actifs.
Ce groupe comprend tous les scientifiques, ingénieurs et techniciens
des deux sexes, définis ci-dessus, qui travaillent, ou cherchent activement
du travail, dans une branche de l'économie à la date de référence. En ce qui
concerne les scientifiques et les ingénieurs, ne doivent figurer dans ce
nombre que les personnes employées au niveau des 'cadres' (c'est-à-dire à
un niveau qui exige normalement des études du troisième degré ou
équivalentes).

Personnel à plein temps et à temps partiel et équivalent plein temps.
Personnel travaillant à plein temps (FT). Cette catégorie
comprend toutes les personnes qui consacrent pratiquement
tout leur temps de travail aux activités de R-D, y compris
l'administration de R-D.
Personnel travaillant à temps partiel (PT). A cette catégorie
appartiennent toutes les personnes qui partagent leur temps
de travail entre les activités de R-D et d'autres activités.
Equivalent plein temps (FTE). L'équivalent plein temps est
l'évaluation du temps consacré aux activités de R-D par le
personnel appartenant aux deux groupes ci-dessus. On
l'obtient en ajoutant au temps de travail des personnes
occupées à plein temps aux activités de R-D le temps que
consacre à ces activités le personnel à temps partiel.

Recherche et développement expérimental (R-D).
En général, l'expression 'recherche et développement expérimental'
enveloppe toutes les activités systématiquement créatrices visant à
accroître le stock de connaissances scientifiques et techniques et à en
imaginer de nouvelles applications. Elle comprend la recherche
fondamentale, la recherche appliquée dans les domaines tels que
l'agriculture, la médecine, la chimie industrielle, etc., et le développement
expérimental conduisant à la mise au point de nouveaux dispositifs ou
procédés. Elle ne comprend pas l'enseignement des sciences, la formation
scientifique et technique, le rassemblement de données de caractère
général, les essais de routine, les travaux de normalisation et les autres
activités techniques relatives à la production ou à l'emploi de produits
et procédés déjà connus, ni les grands travaux de prospections minière et
petrolière, lorsque ceux-ci visent à la découverte de gisements exploitables et
non pas essentiellement à l'accroissement des connaissances
géologiques fondamentales. Dans le domaine des sciences sociales, elle
comprend les activités de recherche portant sur la solution de problèmes
économiques ou sociaux, mais non les activités de routine telles que
recensements, études de marché, etc. Dans le domaine des sciences
médicales, ne pas tenir compte des soins médicaux. En général, les activités
de R-D relevant de la défense nationale doivent être incluses. Le critère qui
distingue les activités de R-D des autres activités est la présence ou
l'absence d'un degré appréciable de nouveauté ou d'innovation.

Recherche fondamentale. Toute activité visant à
l'accroissement des connaissances scientifiques ou à la
découverte de champs d'investigation nouveaux, sans but
pratique particulier.
Recherche appliquée. Toute activité visant à l'accroissement
des connaissances scientifiques en vue d'un but pratique
particulier.
Développement expérimental. Utilisation systématique des
résultats de la recherche fondamentale et appliquée ainsi que
des connaissances empiriques, en vue de mettre en usage de
nouveaux matériaux, produits, dispositifs, procédés et
méthodes, ou d'améliorer ceux qui existent déjà y compris la
mise au point de prototypes et d'installations pilotes.

Secteurs d'exécution.
Les secteurs d'exécution sont les secteurs de l'économie dans lesquels
s'exercent les activités de R-D. La notion de 'secteur d'exécution' permet
de distinguer entre l'exécution des activités de R-D et leur financement. Aux
fins de l'enquête, on a distingué trois secteurs d'exécution qui
correspondent, dans toute la mesure possible, aux définitions du 'système
de comptabilité nationale' (SCN) adopté par les Nations Unies et de
'l'Etablissement de la balance de l'économie nationale du conseil d'aide
économique mutuel' (comptabilité du produit matériel ou CPM):

Secteur de la production:
(i) En général, ce secteur comprend:
(a) Les entreprises industrielles et commerciales nationales
et étrangères situées dans le pays qui produisent et distribuent
des biens et des services contre rémunération ainsi que les
organisations desservant directement ces entreprises, quelles
que soient leurs formes de propriété (publique, privée ou à but
non lucratif). Il comprend aussi les monopoles d'Etat et les
industries nationalisées et en particulier les services publics,
entreprises de transport, postes, télécommunications et
radiodiffusion, et toutes les autres entreprises d'Etat qui
fonctionnent comme unités de production;
(b) Les organisations gouvernementales et non
gouvernementales et les institutions privées sans but lucratif
dont les activités consistent principalement ou exclusivement
à desservir les entreprises industrielles et commerciales, à
l'exception des instituts, stations expérimentales, etc., qui sont
placés sous le contrôle direct d'établissements
d'enseignement supérieur, ou qui leur sont associés (voir
ci-dessous). Dans les pays socialistes, les instituts de R-D
relevant des divers ministères sont à classer dans cette
catégorie.

(ii) Activités de R-D intégrées et non intégrées.
En raison des différences de structure du secteur de la
production dans les pays à systèmes socio-économiques
différents, et pour faciliter les comparaisons, il est proposé de
mesurer les efforts de R-D aux deux 'niveaux' suivants:
(a) *Activités de R-D intégrées:* comprennent toutes les activités de
R-D intégrées ou directement associées à d'autres activités
économiques d'établissements industriels et commerciaux
ou de groupes de ces établissements appartenant à la même
entreprise telle qu'elle est définie à l'alinéa (i) (a) ci-dessus.
(b) *Activités de R-D non intégrées:* comprennent toutes les activités
de R-D qui ne sont pas intégrées ou directement associées à
d'autres activités économiques exercées par les organisations
ou institutions gouvernementales ou non gouvernementales
définies à l'alinéa (i) (b) ci-dessus qui desservent un secteur de
l'économie désigné par deux ou trois chiffres dans la
Classification Internationale Type par Industrie, de toutes les
branches d'activités économiques (CITI), même si elles sont
partiellement ou entièrement financées par le budget de l'Etat
ou, dans le cas des pays de l'Europe de l'Est, par le Fonds de
développement technique et économique.

Secteur de l'enseignement supérieur. Ce secteur comprend tous
les établissements d'enseignement du troisième degré
exigeant comme condition minimale d'admission de l'étudiant
qu'il ait suivi avec succès un enseignement complet du second
degré ou fasse la preuve de connaissances équivalentes. Ce
seront donc toutes les universités, grandes écoles, etc., quels
que soient leur source de financement et leur statut juridique
ou économique. Ce secteur comprend aussi les stations
d'essais, dispensaires et instituts de recherche placés sous le
contrôle ou l'administration d'établissements
d'enseignement supérieur, ou qui leur sont associés. En
revanche, il ne comprend pas les conseils nationaux de
recherche qui sont classés dans le secteur de service
général.

Secteur de service général. Dans ce secteur se rangent toutes
les activités de R-D dont il n'a pas déjà été fait mention
ci-dessus; il n'englobe que le reste des activités de R-D de l'Etat
qui sont souvent importantes par leur volume et leur rôle. En
général, le secteur de l'Etat comprend donc tous les
organismes, ministères et établissements du gouvernement
central, des gouvernements des Etats ou provinces, de
l'administration des districts, villes et villages qui desservent
l'ensemble de la communauté et fournissent une large
gamme de services normalement assurés par l'Etat:
administration, défense et réglementation de l'ordre public,
santé publique, culture, organisation des loisirs et autres
services sociaux, développement de la croissance
économique, du bien-être et de la technologie, etc. Il
comprend également les laboratoires des conseils nationaux
de recherche ainsi que les académies des sciences, les
organisations scientifiques professionnelles, les musées d'Etat,
les sociétés scientifiques et autres organisations à but non
lucratif, qui sont avant tout au service de l'Etat, même si elles
ne font pas officiellement partie de l'administration. En sont
exclus les établissements d'enseignement supérieur, les
monopoles d'Etat et les industries nationalisées qui
fonctionnent comme des entreprises de production, ainsi que
les services et organisations de l'Etat qui appartiennent à un

Science and technology 5
Science et technologie
Ciencia y tecnología

secteur de l'économie désigné par deux ou trois chiffres. Toutes ces institutions sont à classer dans le secteur de la production ou celui de l'enseignement supérieur, conformément aux définitions ci-dessus.

Disciplines scientifiques.

D'une façon générale, la discipline scientifique correspond au domaine principal de la qualification, quoiqu'elle puisse être étendue de façon à s'appliquer à la spécialisation de l'emploi. A titre d'indication, en ce qui concerne les diverses disciplines comprises dans chaque groupe de la classification mentionnée ci-dessous, les principaux groupes de programmes représentés par des numeros de code à deux chiffres (correspondant aux domaines d'études) proposés par l'Unesco dans la Classification Internationale Type de l'Education (ED/BIE/Confinted 35/ Ref 8, Paris, juillet 1975) son indiqués entre parenthèses à la fin de chaque discipline scientifique.

Sciences exactes et naturelles. Ranger sous cette rubrique: Astronomie, bactériologie, biochimie, biologie, botanique, chimie, entomologie, géologie, géophysique, mathématiques, météorologie, minéralogie, physique, zoologie et disciplines connexes. (42,46).

Sciences de l'ingénieur. Ranger sous cette rubrique les sciences de l'ingénieur proprement dites, telles que le génie chimique, le génie civil, l'électrotechnique et la mécanique et leurs subdivisions spécialisées; les sciences appliquées telles que la géodésie, la chimie industrielle, etc.; l'architecture; les technologies specialisées ou domaines 'interdisciplinaires', par exemple analyse des systèmes, métallurgie, mines, organisation scientifique du travail, techniques textiles et disciplines connexes. (52, 54, 58, 70).

Sciences médicales. Ranger sous cette rubrique: anatomie, art dentaire, médecine, obstétrique, optométrie, ostéopathie, pharmacie, physiothérapie, santé publique, technique de l'infirmière et disciplines connexes. (50).

Agriculture. agronomie, horticulture, industrie laitière, médecine vétérinaire, pêche, science rurale, sylviculture et produits forestiers, traitements des produits alimentaires et disciplines connexes. (62).

Sciences sociales et humaines (à répartir en deux groupes autant que possible).

Groupe I - *Sciences sociales.* Anthropologie (sociale et culturelle) et ethnologie, démographie, économie, éducation et formation, géographie (humaine, économique et sociale), gestion, linguistique (à l'exclusion des études de langage effectuées sur des textes déterminés qui sont à classer dans le Groupe II 'langues et littératures anciennes et modernes'), psychologie, sciences juridiques, sciences politiques, sociologie, sciences sociales diverses et recherches interdisciplinaires, méthodologiques, historiques relatives aux disciplines de ce groupe. A noter que la psycho-physiologie, l'anthropologie physique et la géographie physique sont en principe à classer dans les sciences exactes et naturelles. (14, 30, 34, 38, 66, 84).

Groupe II - *Sciences humaines.* Arts (histoire et critique des arts) à l'exclusion des 'recherches' artistiques de toute sorte, humanités (langues et littératures anciennes et modernes), philosophie et religion (l'histoire des sciences et des techniques est à inclure dans la philosophie), préhistoire et histoire (sciences auxiliaires de l'histoire: archéologie, paléographie, numismatique, etc.), autres disciplines et sujets de recherche appartenant à ce groupe et recherches interdisciplinaires, méthodologiques, historiques, etc., relatives aux disciplines de ce groupe. (18, 22, 26).

Dépenses de R-D.

Afin d'inclure le coût total des activités de R-D tout en évitant une double comptabilisation, il convient de faire entrer dans le compte des dépenses toutes les dépenses courantes intra-muros, y compris les frais généraux et les dépenses en capital intra-muros.

Dépenses courantes. Ces dépenses comprennent les salaires, traitements, et tous frais connexes, y compris les 'avantages divers'. Elles comprennent aussi toutes les fournitures fongibles, le petit matériel et les autres frais accessoires, y compris une part des frais généraux, par exemple: loyer, entretien et réparation des bâtiments, remplacement du mobilier de bureau, eau, gaz, électricité, dépenses administratives, etc. L'achat du gros équipement est à porter sous 'dépenses en capital'. Les dépenses courantes doivent

être subdivisées en: (a) dépenses totales de personnel; (b) petit matériel; et (c) autres dépenses courantes.

Dépenses en capital. Comprennent les dépenses effectives d'investissement foncier ou immobilier et de gros équipement (pendant l'année considérée). L'amortissement du gros appareillage, de l'équipement et des bâtiments doit être exclu. Les dépenses en capital doivent être subdivisées en: (a) gros équipement et (b) autres dépenses en capital.

Sources de financement.

Les sources de financement des dépenses de R-D se définissent comme suit:

Fonds publics. Entrent dans cette catégorie tous les fonds provenant du budget ordinaire ou extraordinaire, ainsi que les fonds d'origine extra-budgétaire fournis par le gouvernement central ou celui des Etats, les autorités locales des provinces, districts ou comtés, ou les municipalités des villes et des villages; y entrent également les fonds provenant des organisations semi-publiques crées par le gouvernement et intégralement financées par lui.

Fonds provenant des entreprises de production. Entrent dans cette catégorie tous les fonds affectés à R-D et qui proviennent des activités économiques des établissements du secteur de la production, c'est-à-dire de la vente sur le marché des biens et des services qu'ils produisent.

Fonds spéciaux. Cette catégorie s'applique surtout aux structures de financement des activités de R-D dans les pays d'Europe orientale. Pour ces pays, on entendra, avant tout, par fonds spéciaux les moyens financiers provenant du 'fonds de développement technique et économique' et de fonds analogues.

Fonds étrangers. Entrent dans cette catégorie tous les fonds reçus de l'étranger pour des travaux de R-D exécutés à l'intérieur du pays par les établissements, départements et institutions qui appartiennent aux secteurs d'éxécution définis plus haut. Cette catégorie comprend notamment les fonds provenant d'organisations internationales (que celles-ci aient ou non leur siège dans le pays), ou de gouvernements étrangers ainsi que les fonds privés provenant de l'étranger (y compris les fonds envoyés par les organisations ou sociétés mères ou associées installées à l'étranger).

Fonds divers. Entrent dans cette catégorie tous les fonds qui ne peuvent être classés dans l'une des catégories précédentes, par exemple les dotations ou les dons. On y inclura aussi les fonds propres des établissements d'enseignement supérieur.

Unité statistique. En principe, l'*unité de classement* utilisée dans le *secteur de la production* est l'établissement. Une entreprise qui comprend plus d'un établissement peut être considérée aussi comme unité de classement tout particulièrement lorsqu'il n'est pas possible de déterminer les données financières relatives à chaque établissement. Dans le cas d'une *économie de marché* l'unité de classement peut être une société anonyme, une société par actions, une société coopérative, une association à but non lucratif, une société de personnes, une entreprise propriété d'une seule personne ou une forme quelconque de société ou d'association. Dans le cas d'une *économie centralisée*, l'entreprise peut être une unité de gestion et de comptabilité et peut comprendre un certain nombre d'établissements. Elle passe des contrats, à son propre plan de production, perçoit des revenus et en dispose, possède son propre compte bancaire et tient une comptabilité complète et indépendante.

Dans le cas des *activités de R-D non intégrées*, l'unité type de classement peut être une association de recherche, un établissement à but non lucratif, un institut d'Etat qui dessert un secteur de l'économie désignée par deux ou trois chiffres; dans les pays de l'Europe de l'Est, l'unité de classement peut être un institut de recherche rattaché au ministère compétent.

L'unité statistitique utilisée dans le *secteur de service général* est un organisme important, ayant un fonctionnement autonome ou constituant une entité distincte au sein d'un département ou d'un organisme gouvernemental, et non classé ailleurs. Cette unité peut être une division, un laboratoire ou un institut, un bureau, un office central, etc.

Finalités principales des activités de R-D.

Le système proposé ci-après, qui a pour objet de classer les dépenses de R-D selon le mode fonctionnel et non par institutions ou strictement par secteurs, est une initiative prise par l'Office des statistiques de l'Unesco pour obtenir, sur la structure générale des efforts nationaux de R-D, des renseignements sommaires comparables sur le plan international.

Certains Etats membres élaborent déjà des statistiques analogues où les dépenses sont classées selon les domaines d'application ou les objectifs

5 Science and technology
Science et technologie
Ciencia y tecnología

des activités nationales de R-D. Ces termes ayant pris des acceptions tout à fait différentes selon les Etats membres, il a paru souhaitable de choisir, pour la nomenclature de l'Unesco , un terme qui évite de donner l'impression qu'il s'agit des objectifs des gouvernements. Dans la classification des activités nationales de R-D selon leur finalité principale - qui est donnée ci-après - et qui doit être basée sur les objectifs, on a donc essayé de trouver un dénominateur commun approprié qui permette d'aboutir à une ventilation plus systématique et analytique des dépenses de R-D et d'obtenir ainsi des résultats comparables sur le plan international. Les rubriques qui figurent sous les douze catégories de finalités ne doivent pas être considérées comme exhaustives, mais plutôt comme exemples des types de R-D compris dans chaque finalité principale.

Cette tentative de classement des dépenses de R-D par finalités principales doit nécessairement être considérée comme une expérience.

1. *Exploration et évaluation de la terre, des mers, de l'atmosphère et de l'espace.*

Cette rubrique comprend les activités de R-D qui en premier lieu ont trait à l'exploration et à l'évaluation de la terre, des mers, des océans, de l'atmosphère et de l'espace ainsi qu'à leur administration, économie, politique et planification. Ne sont *pas comprises* les activités concernant les sols exercées à des fins agricoles, la R-D concernant l'océanographie utile à l'industrie de la pêche, la R-D concernant l'exploitation économique des matières premières, des combustibles et de l'énergie, la R-D concernant l'application de l'emploi des satellites pour les communications. Les activités rangées dans ce groupe sont entreprises en vue de l'exploitation économique des résultats et par conséquent on *exclut* la recherche fondamentale en météorologie, géologie, hydrologie, etc. qui est à classer dans la rubrique 'Promotion générale des connaissances'.

2. *Développement de l'agriculture, de la sylviculture et de la pêche.*

Ce chapitre couvre deux types d'activités de R-D, le premier relatif à l'aspect alimentaire et le second aux produits agricoles non alimentaires et à la sylviculture. Dans la première catégorie, on inclut la R-D sur la production, le stockage et la distribution des produits alimentaires comme par exemple l'élevage, l'amélioration des espèces, la médecine vétérinaire, la production et l'agronomie des récoltes, la R-D concernant le matériel agricole et les produits chimiques agricoles, la R-D sur le traitement des produits alimentaires et des boissons, leur stockage et leur distribution, l'industrie de la pêche et ses technologies, l'administration, l'économie, la politique et la planification de l'agriculture et de la production des denrées alimentaires. La seconde catégorie, qui englobe le développement des produits agricoles non alimentaires et de la sylviculture, comprend toutes les activités de R-D qui sont effectuées dans le domaine de la production de produits agricoles non alimentaires tels que la laine, les peaux, le tabac, le coton et d'autres fibres, ainsi qu'en matière de sylviculture et techniques connexes.

3. *Promotion du développement industriel.*

Cette finalité principale concerne toutes les activités de R-D qui contribuent au développement et au perfectionnement des industries minières et manufacturières. Elle comprend la R-D en matière d'administration, économie, politique et planification concernant la production textile, l'habillement et le cuir, les produits du bois et du papier, les produits chimiques (y compris la pétrochimie), le caoutchouc et le plastique dans l'industrie métallurgique de base et la fabrication d'ouvrages en métaux, de machines et de matériels (y compris les véhicules de transport) dans la fabrication des produits non métalliques, les minerais autres que les combustibles. Elle *ne comprend pas* la R-D industrielle destinée à soutenir d'autres fins telles que le développement de l'agriculture et de la production des denrées alimentaires, des transports et des communications, de l'exploration de l'espace, de la planification urbaine et rurale et de la défense.

4. *Production, conservation et distribution de l'énergie.*

Cette rubrique inclut toutes les activités de R-D relatives à la production, à l'approvisionnement, à la conservation et à la distribution de l'énergie sous toutes ses formes (y compris l'énergie nucléaire) et à l'administration, l'économie, la politique et la planification de l'énergie. Elle comprend l'exploitation minière des combustibles solides et les techniques connexes, la production du gaz et du pétrole ainsi que les sources d'énergie non conventionnelles (solaire, vent) et les petites sources d'énergie.

5. *Développement des transports et des communications.*

Ce groupe comprend les réseaux et systèmes de transports et communications terrestres, aériens, fluviaux et maritimes, la radio, la télévision, le téléphone et autres moyens de télécommunications y compris les satellites. Ce groupe inclut de même la R-D concernant l'administration, l'économie, la politique et la planification des transports et des réseaux de communication. Il inclut les services auxiliaires comme l'aide électronique à la circulation et les stations radar mais *exlut* les engins, moteurs et moyens

de transports tels que les véhicules, les bateaux et les aéronefs qui sont déjà compris sous la finalité 'promotion du développement industriel'.

6. *Développement des services d'enseignement.*

Sous cette finalité principale on range les activités de R-D concernant l'administration, l'économie, la politique et la planification des services d'enseignement à tous les niveaux. Elle comprend l'éducation scolaire et extrascolaire, la formation du personnel en service et toutes autres formes d'éducation et de formation des adultes. On doit aussi ranger dans ce groupe la R-D sur les techniques conventionnelles aussi bien que modernes et les méthodes d'enseignement telles que l'instruction programmée, la télévision et autres techniques audio-visuelles.

7. *Développement des services de santé.*

Cette rubrique comprend les activités de R-D ayant pour but la protection et l'amélioration de la santé humaine. Elle inclut la R-D sur les soins médicaux (y compris la chirurgie et l'obstétrique), la prévention des maladies, la nutrition et l'hygiène alimentaire, la R-D effectuée sur l'influence de l'environnement sur la santé y compris la médecine du travail et la R-D sur les produits pharmaceutiques, vaccins et prothèses; sont aussi incluses l'administration, l'économie, la politique et la planification de la santé.

8. *Développement social et autres services socio-économiques.*

Ce groupe comprend toutes les activités de R-D concernant l'administration, l'économie, la politique et la planification du développement social et des services socio-économiques. Y sont inclus l'organisation politique, la législation et l'ordre, la sécurité sociale, les activités culturelles et récréatives, la protection du consommateur, l'amélioration des conditions de travail, les rapports sociaux dans le travail, la main-d'oeuvre et l'émigration, les relations internationales y compris le maintien de la paix, les cours internationaux de justice, les traités et autres services sociaux. On range aussi dans ce groupe les programmes de R-D sur l'organisation économique, la monnaie et la banque, les assurances, etc. Cette finalité principale englobe enfin les activités de R-D concernant la planification rurale et urbaine telles que le logement des particuliers, les services sanitaires et autres services communautaires relatifs au bien-être de la population.

9. *Protection de l'environnement.*

Cette finalité principale couvre tous les aspects de la 'protection' de l'environnement: maintien de la pureté de l'atmosphère, des eaux et du sol, lutte contre le bruit, modèles et statistiques sur l'environnement, réglementation, économie, politique et planification relatives à l'environnement. Sont *exclues* les activités de R-D qui concernent l'influence de l'environnement sur la santé et qui doivent être comprises dans 'Développement des services de santé' et l'influence de l'environnement sur le bien-être humain (rubrique 8 ci-dessus). On *exclut* également la R-D destinée à lutter contre la pollution causée par certaines activités économiques, qui doit être classée avec les activités correspondantes.

10. *Promotion générale des connaissances.*

Sous cette rubrique, on classe toutes les activités de R-D qui du fait de leur orientation générale peuvent être rangées sous l'une ou l'autre des finalités principales, mais qui contribuent à la promotion générale des connaissances tant dans le domaine des sciences sociales que dans celui des sciences exactes et naturelles. Elle comprend la recherche fondamentale et appliquée effectuée par les conseils scientifiques, les instituts des académies des sciences et universités dans les domaines de leur compétence générale. Elle inclut également la R-D concernant l'administration, l'économie, la politique et la planification des activités de R-D.

11. *Autres finalités.*

Cette rubrique comprend toutes les autres activités civiles de R-D entreprises dans un but précis qui n'entre pas dans l'une des rubriques précédentes. Elle comprend par exemple la promotion des systèmes d'information, l'informatique (hardware et software) mais *exclut* les dépenses relatives au rassemblement des données.

12. *Défense.*

Cette finalité principale comprend les activités de R-D nucléaire, spatiale ou autre, entreprises à des fins militaires. Les sommes consacrées à la recherche civile par des institutions militaires devraient, dans toute la mesure du possible, être réparties entre les grandes catégories de fins civiles auxquelles elles peuvent être rattachées.

Les tableaux présentés dans ce chapitre sont classés en trois sections. La première section comprend 5 tableaux concernant le personnel scientifique et technique. L'effectif total ou le nombre économiquement actif du personnel qualifié, c'est à dire les personnes ayant les qualifications requises pour être classés comme scientifiques, ingénieurs et techniciens et le nombre correspondant de femmes figurent au tableau 5.1. L'information relative à l'effectif total (stock) est généralement obtenu lors

Science and technology 5
Science et technologie
Ciencia y tecnología

des recensements de population, ce qui fait que ces données ne sont pas disponibles tous les ans. Lorsque nous ne disposons pas de cette information, le nombre de scientifiques, ingénieurs et techniciens économiquement actifs est présenté comme une alternative.

Le tableau 5.2 donne des données correspondantes pour les scientifiques, ingénieurs et techniciens employés à des travaux de recherche et de développement expérimental.

Seules figurent au tableau 5.3 les données concernant les scientifiques et ingénieurs employés à des travaux de recherche et de développement expérimental classés selon la discipline scientifique correspondant à leur qualification et selon qu'ils sont employés à plein temps ou à temps partiel. On donne aussi leur équivalent plein temps et, si possible séparément, des données concernant les femmes. Il est à noter qu'en général, la répartition par discipline scientifique se réfère à la discipline scientifique correspondant au diplôme décerné, mais dans certains cas, il n'a pas été possible de déterminer si la distribution se rapportait au domaine d'étude ou au domaine scientifique auquel les personnes se consacrent actuellement.

Le tableau 5.4 concerne tout le personnel employé à des travaux de R-D et le secteur d'exécution. Il donne à la fois les chiffres absolus et la distribution en pourcentage du personnel total selon le secteur d'exécution et présente les catégories de personnel employées dans ces secteurs.

On peut voir l'orientation donnée aux efforts nationaux de R-D d'après le tableau 5.5 où figurent, pour un nombre limité de pays les scientifiques et ingénieurs occupés à des travaux de R-D selon le secteur d'exécution auquel ils appartiennent, la branche d'activité économique ou le domaine de recherche auquel appartient leur entreprise ou leur institution ou encore selon le domaine de recherche auquel ils se consacrent actuellement (ce qui n'est pas nécessairement la discipline scientifique initiale du personnel correspondant au diplôme décerné, dont la classification figure au tableau 5.3).

La deuxième section comprend 5 tableaux et donne un profil du coût des activités de R-D calculé sur la base des dépenses intra-muros engagées pour des travaux de R-D. Les données sont présentées en monnaie nationale.

Dans le tableau 5.6, la dépense totale de R-D est subdivisée par type de dépense (totale, courante, de main-d'oeuvre) et une relation entre dépenses totales et courantes est établie.

Le tableau 5.7 montre la distribution des dépenses courantes en chiffres absolus et en pourcentage par type d'activité de R-D - recherche fondamentale, recherche appliquée ou développement expérimental.

Le tableau 5.8 présente la distribution des dépenses totales et courantes par secteur d'exécution, en chiffres absolus et en pourcentages.

Quant à la structure du financement de la R-D, elle est présentée dans le tableau 5.9 où les dépenses courantes et en capital sont distribuées par source de financement. Les données sont présentées en monnaie nationale et en pourcentages.

Le tableau 5.10 donne la distribution des fonds publics, ou alternativement les dépenses totales nationales intra-muros, consacrés aux activités de R-D selon douze finalités principales; il s'agit là d'une ventilation analytique des dépenses de R-D d'après une classification 'fonctionnelle' (dans le tableau 5.8, la classification est 'institutionnelle ou sectorielle'); cette ventilation montre la structure générale des efforts nationaux de R-D. Néanmoins on doit toujours considérer cette tentative de classement

comme une expérience.

La dernière section donne une vue générale du développement des activités de R-D et comprend également des indicateurs supplémentaires. Les deux tableaux qui fournissent des données rétrospectives (5.11 et 5.12) montrent la croissance des ressources humaines et financières consacrées à la R-D dans les pays développés et en voie de développement.

Le tableau 5.11 présente l'effectif total du personnel scientifique et des ingénieurs employés à des travaux de R-D pendant les années récentes, en général de 1969 à 1978. Les informations concernant les scientifiques et ingénieurs sont traduites en nombres indexés sur la base 1969 = 100.

Le tableau 5.12 présente une série chronologique des dépenses totales et courantes consacrées aux activités de R-D pour les années récentes, en général de 1969 à 1978. On trouvera aussi le rapport entre les dépenses totales et courantes.

Le tableau 5.13 fournit des indicateurs sélectionnés sur la science et la technologie. On y présente l'effectif du personnel qualifié, c'est à dire les personnes ayant les qualifications requises pour être classées comme scientifiques, ingénieurs et techniciens ainsi que les scientifiques, ingénieurs et techniciens employés à des travaux de R-D par rapport à la population totale ainsi que le rapport entre le nombre total de scientifiques et ingénieurs et ceux employés à des travaux de R-D. On trouvera aussi le rapport entre le nombre de techniciens et celui des scientifiques et ingénieurs. Ces indicateurs sont alignés avec ceux qui concernent les dépenses de R-D rapportées, elles aussi, à la population totale et au nombre de scientifiques et ingénieurs employés à la R-D, et aussi exprimées en pourcentage du produit national brut.

Le lecteur trouvera le nombre des pays et territoires considérés indiqué en tête de chaque tableau. Pour les treize tableaux, le total des pays est de 137. Etant donné la diversité évidente des définitions appliquées et le caractère incomplet des résultats, il convient de n'utiliser les chiffres qu'avec prudence. Dans de nombreux cas, les exceptions sont indiquées dans les notes qui font suite aux tableaux; l'absence de notes n'implique cependant pas nécessairement que les chiffres cités sont conformes aux définitions du questionnaire. C'est pourquoi nous n'avons pas établi de totaux régionaux et nous estimons qu'il faut s'en abstenir jusqu'à ce qu'on puisse rassembler des données plus sûres en la matière. Les chercheurs qui souhaiteraient obtenir d'autres détails ou des éclaircissements sur un pays particulier en ce qui concerne les définitions nationales, la portée ou les limitations des données présentées dans les tableaux, peuvent adresser leur demande à l'Office des Statistiques, Division des Statistiques relatives à la Science et à la Technologie.

Il faut éviter de comparer, d'un pays à l'autre, les chiffres absolus qui concernent les dépenses de R-D. On ne pourrait procéder à de telles comparaisons qu'en convertissant en une même monnaie les sommes libellées en monnaie nationale et, comme il n'existe pas de taux de change qui soit spécialement applicable aux activités de R-D, il faudrait nécessairement se fonder, pour cela, sur les taux de change officiels. Or ces taux ne reflètent pas toujours le coût réel des activités de R-D et les comparaisons risquent alors d'être trompeuses. De telles comparaisons ne sont cependant pas totalement dénuées d'intérêt, car elles donnent au moins une idée de l'ordre de grandeur des dépenses de R-D. Le lecteur trouvera dans l'Annexe C les taux de change applicables à la conversion des monnaies nationales en dollars des Etats-Unis d'Amérique.

Hace ya más de dos decenios que se evidencia la necesidad de disponer de estadísticas relativas a la ciencia y a la tecnología, así como de su importancia para el desarrollo de los diversos países del mundo. Se trata, sin embargo, de un sector relativamente nuevo, cuyos elementos empiezan apenas a definirse con cierta claridad. A pesar de estos comienzos tardíos, cada vez es mayor el número de Estados Miembros que realizan esfuerzos sistemáticos y continuos para reunir datos estadísticos en materia de ciencia y tecnología.

La Unesco, deseosa de lograr la normalización de los métodos de compilación y difusión de dichos datos en el plano internacional, continúa colaborando con los Estados Miembros, diversos organismos competentes y los especialistas a fin de elaborar normas internacionales aplicables a las estadísticas de la ciencia y la tecnología, tales como las que ya existen en otras ramas de la estadística. La iniciativa más reciente de la Unesco a este respecto ha sido la organización del Comité Especial de Expertos encargado de preparar un proyecto de Recomendación sobre la normalización internacional de las estadísticas relativas a la ciencia y la tecnología, que fue adoptada por la Conferencia General en su vigésima

reunión, en noviembre de 1978.

El presente capítulo contiene una selección de los resultados alcanzados por la Unesco gracias al esfuerzo hecho, forzosamente a escala mundial, para reunir datos estadísticos relativos a la ciencia y la tecnología. Los datos proceden, en su mayor parte, de las respuestas al cuestionario sobre las actividades científicas y tecnológicas que la Unesco envió a los Estados Miembros en 1978 y 1979, habiendo sido completados con informaciones procedentes de las anteriores encuestas anuales o bienales y de informes oficiales y publicaciones.

Para interpretar estos resultados, el lector debe tener en cuenta diversos factores que influyen claramente sobre la comparabilidad y la exactitud de los datos. Las estadísticas de la ciencia no han alcanzado en todos los países el mismo grado de desarrollo. En algunos de ellos su compilación se basa en encuestas periódicas y regulares; en otros, en cambio, se está empezando apenas a estudiar de un modo sistemático las actividades de I y D, habiéndolos también en los que nada se ha hecho hasta ahora en tal sentido. Además, la compilación de estadísticas responde, en el plano nacional, a unos conceptos y métodos cuya índole no se presta

5 Science and technology
Science et technologie
Ciencia y tecnología

necesariamente a facilitar las comparaciones internacionales. En consecuencia, la mayor parte de los países se han visto obligados a reconsiderar la presentación de sus datos estadísticos, y con frecuencia han tenido que recurrir a estimaciones, para poder contestar a las preguntas de la Unesco. Son muy pocos los que han podido efectuar encuestas especiales basadas en unas clasificaciones y definiciones conformes a las que se proponen en el cuestionario de la Unesco y que se enumeran más adelante. Esperamos que con la aplicación gradual de la Recomendación, la cantidad y la calidad de los datos comparables en el plano internacional, mejorarán progresivamente.

Como ejemplo de los problemas que plantea la comparabilidad, cabe referirse al hecho de que, si el concepto fundamental de 'investigación y desarrollo experimental' es aproximadamente el mismo en todos los países, en lo que respecta a los métodos de medición y a los elementos que se toman en consideración, existen a menudo, de un país a otro, diferencias que a veces hacen difícil toda comparación internacional. Se observa que, en sus repuestas al cuestionario, la mayoría de los países sólo han considerado entre las tareas que desempeñan los organismos de investigación (institutos, servicios oficiales, etc.) las que pueden definirse específicamente como 'actividades de I y D', en tanto que otros se refieren a la totalidad de dichas tareas, sin excluir, como procedería, las actividades científicas y tecnológicas 'conexas' que no son verdaderamente 'actividades de I y D'.

Otro ejemplo se refiere a la manera de apreciar el alcance de las disciplinas científicas; en las primeras encuestas, ciertos países consideraban como actividades de I y D las relativas a las ciencias sociales, mientras que otros las excluían completamente. Muchos países europeos y algunos de otros continentes incluyen no sólo las actividades relativas a las humanidades, en algunos casos inseparables de las relativas a las ciencias sociales, sino también las vinculadas a otras disciplinas, tales como las artes, la pedagogía y el derecho, que a partir de 1971 figura en las encuestas.

Se presenta a continuación la lista de las definiciones propuestas para su empleo en la *Encuesta estadística sobre actividades científicas y tecnológicas* (doc. Unesco STS/Q/781).

Estas definiciones corresponden en gran parte a las utilizadas en encuestas anteriores y las leves modificaciones que se han introducido en ellas no afectan gran cosa a la comparabilidad de los datos procedentes de las diversas encuestas, comparabilidad que por lo demás queda limitada por otros motivos.

Tipo de personal.

Científico e ingeniero. Pertenece a este grupo toda persona que haya recibido formación científica o técnica en las ramas de la ciencia, lo que implica, o bien que haya terminado los estudios de enseñanza superior necesarios para la obtención de un título académico, o que haya terminado unos estudios de enseñanza (o una formación) superior no universitaria, que no confieren título universitario, pero que facultan para ejercer en el país correspondiente, una carrera profesional; o que posea experiencia profesional de una formación reconocida en el país (por ejemplo, pertenecer a asociaciones profesionales, tener un certificado o título profesional) que equivalga a la enseñanza de uno de los dos tipos precedentes.

Técnico. Pertenece a este grupo toda persona que haya recibido formación técnica o profesional especializada en cualquier rama del saber o de la tecnología, lo que implica: tener uno o dos años de formación tras haber terminado los estudios de enseñanza secundaria o de tres a cuatro años de formación posterior al primer ciclo de enseñanza secundaria (sancionada o no por un título o diploma) o bien tener experiencia profesional y formación en el empleo que se considere en el país como equivalente al nivel de instrucción indicado.

Personal auxiliar. Este grupo comprende los trabajadores especializados, tales como mecánicos, chapistas y obreros de otros oficios, operarios, etc., así como trabajadores semiespecializados y no especializados; todo el personal de oficina y administrativo y otro personal auxiliar, como el de secretaría. No comprende el personal de seguridad, de guardia y entretenimiento.

Número total de científicos, ingenieros y técnicos.

Se trata del número total de científicos ingenieros y técnicos tal como se describen en las anteriores definiciones, independientemente de su edad, sexo, actividad económica o cualquier otra característica.

Número de científicos, ingenieros y técnicos económicamente activos.

Este grupo comprende a todos los científicos, ingenieros y técnicos, de ambos sexos, tal como se describen en las anteriores definiciones, que trabajan o que buscan activamente trabajo en cualquier rama de la economía en la fecha de referencia. En lo que se refiere a los científicos e ingenieros, sólo deben figurar las personas empleadas en el nivel 'profesional', es decir, el que normalmente exige estudios de tercer grado o equivalentes.

Personal de jornada completa, de jornada parcial y equivalente de jornada completa.

Personal que trabaja a jornada completa (FT). Comprende todas las personas que dedican prácticamente todo su tiempo a actividades de I y D, inclusive la administración de la I y D.

Personal de jornada parcial (PT). Esta categoría comprende todas las personas que dividen su tiempo de trabajo entre actividades de I y D y de otra índole.

Equivalente de jornada completa (FTE). El equivalente de la jornada completa es la evaluación de la cantidad de tiempo dedicado a actividades de I y D por el personal perteneciente a los dos grupos antes mencionados. Corresponde al tiempo de trabajo de las personas que trabajan a jornada completa en actividades de I y D más la proporción de tiempo dedicado a I y D por el personal que trabaja a jornada parcial.

Investigación y desarrollo experimental (I y D).

Por I y D se entiende, en general, cualquier actividad creadora sistemática emprendida para aumentar la cantidad de conocimientos científicos y técnicos y para concebir nuevas aplicaciones. Comprende la investigación aplicada en ramas tales como la agricultura, la medicina, la química industrial, etc., y el desarrollo experimental que conduce a la creación de nuevos dispositivos o procedimientos. Queda excluida la educación científica, la información científica y técnica, el acopio de datos con fines generales, las pruebas y ensayos corrientes, la normalización y otras actividades tecnológicas relacionadas con la producción o el empleo de productos o de procedimientos ya conocidos, así como la prospección en gran escala de recursos minerales y petroleros, cuando su objetivo es la búsqueda de yacimientos explotables más bien que el aumento de conocimientos geológicos básicos. En las ciencias sociales, están comprendidas las actividades de investigación relacionadas con la solución de problemas económicos y sociales, pero no, en cambio, las actividades corrientes, tales como la realización de censos, estudios de mercado, etc. De las ciencias médicas, hay que excluir los servicios médicos. En general, se deberán incluir las actividades de I y D para la defensa nacional. El criterio para establecer la distinción entre las actividades de I y D y las que no lo son es la presencia o la ausencia de un cierto grado de novedades o de innovación.

Investigación fundamental. Es la que tiene por objeto aumentar los conocimientos científicos o el descubrimiento de nuevos campos de investigación, sin un objetivo práctico concreto.

Investigación aplicada. Es la que tiene por objeto aumentar los conocimientos científicos con una finalidad práctica concreta.

Desarrollo experimental. Empleo sistemático de los resultados de la investigación fundamental y aplicada, así como de los conocimientos empíricos con miras a introducir nuevos materiales, productos, dispositivos y métodos, a mejorar otros existentes, incluso el poner a punto prototipos e instalaciones experimentales.

Sectores de ejecución.

Los sectores de ejecución son aquellos sectores de la economía en los que se realizan actividades de I y D. El término 'sector de ejecución' distingue la realización o ejecución de actividades de I y D y su financiamiento. Para los fines de esta encuesta, se han establecido tres sectores de ejecución que se han definido, en la medida de lo posible, de conformidad con las definiciones del sector 'Sistema de Cuentas Nacionales' (SCN) de las Naciones Unidas y del 'Sistema de balances de la Economía Nacional' del Consejo de Ayuda Económica Mutua (CAEM).

Sector productivo:

i) En general, este sector engloba:

a) Las empresas nacionales y de propiedad extranjera, industriales y comerciales, situadas en el país, que producen y distribuyen productos y servicios para su venta, y las organizaciones que los sirven directamente, sea cual fuere su forma de propiedad (pública, privada o de carácter no lucrativo). Comprende asimismo los monopolios estatales y las industrias nacionalizadas, en particular los servicios públicos, empresas de transporte, correos, comunicaciones y radiodifusión, así como todos los otros establecimientos estatales que funcionan como unidades de producción.

Science and technology
Science et technologie
Ciencia y tecnología

5

b) Las organizaciones gubernamentales y no gubernamentales y las instituciones privadas de carácter no lucrativo que atienden principalmente o exclusivamente a los establecimientos industriales y comerciales, excepto aquellos institutos, estaciones experimentales, etc., que funcionan bajo el control directo o están asociados con instituciones de enseñanza superior (véase más abajo). En los países socialistas hay que clasificar en este sector los institutos de I y D que dependen de los diversos ministerios.

ii) Actividades de I y D integradas y no integradas.
Debido a la estructura diferente del sector productivo en los países que tienen sistemas socioeconómicos distintos y a fin de facilitar las comparaciones, se sugiere que los esfuerzos de I y D se midan en función de los dos 'niveles' siguientes:

a) *Actividades de I y D integradas*: comprenden todas las actividades de I y D integrada o asociadas directamente con otras actividades económicas de establecimientos industriales y comerciales, o grupos de dichos establecimientos que pertenecen a la misma empresa, tal como se define en i) a).

b) *Actividades de I y D no integradas*: comprenden todas las actividades de I y D no integradas o directamente asociadas con otras actividades económicas, llevadas a cabo por las organizaciones gubernamentales o no gubernamentales o por los institutos definidos en i) b)) que atienden a un sector concreto de la economía identificado por dos o tres cifras en la Clasificación Industrial Internacional Uniforme para todas las Actividades Económicas (C.I.I.U.), incluso si están parcial o totalmente financiadas por el presupuesto del Estado o, en el caso de los países de Europa oriental, por el Fondo de Progreso Técnico y Económico.

Sector de enseñanza superior. Este sector comprende todos los establecimientos de enseñanza de tercer grado, que exigen como condición mínima para el ingreso haber aprobado la enseñanza secundaria o demostrar que se posee un nivel equivalente de conocimientos, es decir, todas las universidades, colegios universitarios de tecnología etc., sea cual fuere su fuente de financiamiento o su situación jurídica o económica. También comprende las estaciones experimentales, dispensarios e institutos de investigación que funcionan bajo el control directo de instituciones de enseñanza superior, administrados por éstas o asociados con las mismas. No hay que hacer figurar en este sector a los consejos nacionales de investigación que se clasificarán en el sector de servicio general.

Sector de servicio general. Este sector abarca todas las actividades de I y D que no se han mencionado anteriormente, y sólo comprende el resto de las actividades estatales de I y D. En general, el sector estatal comprende pues, todos los organismos, departamentos y establecimientos del Gobierno central, de los Estados o condados, municipios, provincias, de la administración de los distritos, ciudades o aldeas, que atienden al conjunto de la comunidad y prestan gran cantidad de servicios que normalmente incumben al Estado, tales como la administración, defensa y reglamentación del orden público, servicios sanitarios, culturales, recreativos y otros de carácter social, y fomentan el crecimiento económico, la previsión social y el desarrollo tecnológico, etc. Comprende también los laboratorios de los consejos nacionales de investigación, así como las academias de ciencias, las organizaciones científicas profesionales, los museos del Estado, las sociedades científicas y otras organizaciones de carácter no lucrativo que prestan fundamentalmente servicios al Estado, incluso si oficialmente no forman parte de la administración. Deben excluirse las instituciones de enseñanza superior, los monopolios estatales y las industrias nacionalizadas que funcionen como empresas de producción, así como los servicios y organizaciones estatales que sirven a un sector concreto de la economía, identificado por dos o tres cifras. Todas esas instituciones pertenecen al sector productivo o al sector de enseñanza superior, de conformidad con las definiciones expuestas anteriormente.

Rama de la ciencia.
De una manera general, la rama científica corresponde al campo principal de la calificación, aunque también puede hacerse extensiva y aplicarse a la especialización del empleo. A título de indicación en lo que se refiere a las distintas disciplinas incluidas en cada uno de los grupos de

la clasificación más abajo mencionada, los principales grupos de programas presentados por una codificación de dos cifras correspondientes a los sectores de estudios propuestos por la Unesco en la clasificación Internacional Normalizada de la Educación (ED/BIE/CONFINTED:35 Ref. 8, París, julio de 1975) se indican entre paréntesis al final de cada rama de la ciencia.

Ciencias exactas y naturales. Este epígrafe comprende: astronomía, bacteriología, biología, bioquímica, botánica, entomología, física, geofísica, geología, matemáticas, meteorología, química, zoología y disciplinas conexas (42, 46).

Ingeniería y Tecnología. Esta categoría comprende: la ingeniería propiamente dicha, tal como la ingeniería civil, ingeniería mecánica, ingeniería eléctrica, ingeniería química con sus diversas especializaciones; ciencias aplicadas, como geodesia, química industrial, etc.; arquitectura; tecnologías especializadas o ramas interdisciplinarias, tales como la ingeniería industrial, ingeniería textil, metalurgia, minas, ingeniería de sistematización y disciplinas conexas (52, 54, 58, 70).

Ciencias médicas. Este epígrafe comprende: anatomía, estudios de enfermero y comadrona, fisioterapia, medicina, odontología, optometría, osteopatía, sanidad y disciplinas conexas (50).

Agricultura. Este epígrafe comprende: la agronomía, ciencia rural, fabricación de alimentos, horticultura, industrias lácteas, medicina veterinaria, pesquerías, silvicultura y productos forestales y disciplinas conexas (62).

Ciencias sociales y humanas (repartidas, a ser posible, en dos grupos).

Grupo I- *Ciencias sociales*: Antropología (social y y cultural) y etnología, ciencias jurídicas, ciencias políticas, demografía, economía, educación, capacitación, geografía (humana, económica, social), gestión, lingüística (excepto los estudios de lenguas efectuados sobre textos precisos que deben clasificarse en el grupo II, 'lenguas y literaturas antiguas y modernas'), psicología, sociología, ciencias sociales diversas e investigaciones interdisciplinarias, metodológicas o históricas, relativas a las disciplinas de este grupo. Adviértase que la psico-fisiología, la antropología física y la geografía física deben, en principio, clasificarse con las ciencias exactas y naturales (14, 30, 34, 38, 66, 84).

Grupo II - *Ciencias humanas*: Arte (historia y y crítica del arte) excepto las 'investigaciones' artísticas de cualquier tipo, humanidades (lenguas y literaturas antiguas y modernas), filosofía y religión (la historia de la ciencia y de la técnica se incluye con la filosofía), prehistoria e historia (ciencias auxiliares de la historia: arqueología, paleografía, numismática, etc.) otras disciplinas y temas de investigación pertencientes a este grupo, así como también las investigaciones interdisciplinarias, metodológicas, históricas, etc. relativas a las disciplinas de este grupo (18, 22, 26).

Gastos de I y D.
Para cubrir el costo total de las actividades de I y D y evitar la doble contabilización, el cálculo de los gastos deberá comprender todos los gastos ordinarios intramuros, incluidos los gastos generales y los gastos de capital intramuros.

Gastos ordinarios. Comprenden los sueldos y salarios y todos los elementos conexos, incluidos los 'beneficios adicionales'. Comprenden también todos los suministros fungibles y equipo secundario y otros costos auxiliares incluida la cuota de gastos generales, por ejemplo, el alquiler, el entretenimiento y reparación de edificios, la renovación de mobiliario de oficina, el agua, el gas, la electricidad, los gastos administrativos, etc. El equipo importante deberá figurar en la partida de 'gastos de capital'. Los gastos ordinarios se distribuirán en: a) gastos totales de personal, b) pequeño material y c) otros gastos ordinarios.

Gastos de capital. Comprenden los gastos reales o las inversiones en terrenos, edificios y equipo importante (durante el año de referencia). Debe excluirse la amortización de los instrumentos importantes, del equipo y de los edificios. Los gastos de capital deben subdividirse en: a) equipo importante y b) otros gastos de capital.

Origen de los fondos.
Las fuentes de financiamiento de los gastos de I y D se definen como sigue:

5   Science and technology
Science et technologie
Ciencia y tecnología

Fondos públicos. Comprenden todos los fondos procedentes del presupuesto ordinario y extraordinario o de fuentes extrapresupuestarias, tanto del gobierno central, como de los gobiernos de Estado, las autoridades locales, provinciales, de distrito o condado, municipales, de ciudad o aldea. También incluyen los fondos procedentes de aquellas organizaciones intermediarias, públicas o privadas, creadas por el gobierno y cuyos recursos económicos proporciona exclusivamente el Estado.

Fondos de las empresas de producción. Esta categoría comprende todos los fondos asignados a la I y D que tienen su origen en las actividades económicas de establecimientos del sector productivo, es decir, de la venta en el mercado de los bienes y servicios que producen.

Fondos especiales. Esta categoría se refiere sobre todo a las estructuras de financiamiento de las actividades de I y D en los países de Europa oriental. Por lo que se refiere a esos países, por fondos especiales se entenderá, sobre todo, los recursos económicos que tienen su origen en el 'Fondo de Progreso Técnico y Económico' y en fondos similares.

Fondos extranjeros. Esta categoría abarca todos los fondos recibidos del extranjero para las actividades de I y D realizadas en el país correspondiente, por establecimientos, departamentos e instituciones que pertenecen a los sectores de ejecución antes definidos. Esta categoría comprende en particular los fondos recibidos de organizaciones internacionales (sitas o no en el país), gobiernos extranjeros y fondos de origen privado procedentes del extranjero, incluidos los fondos de las organizaciones o sociedades centrales o afiliadas instaladas en el extranjero.

Otros fondos. Esta categoría comprende todos los fondos que no pueden clasificarse en una de las anteriores categorías, por ejemplo, las dotaciones o donaciones. Incluye asimismo los fondos propios de los establecimientos de enseñanza superior.

Unidad estadística.

En principio, la *unidad de clasificación* usada en el *Sector productivo* es el establecimiento. Una empresa que consiste en más de un establecimiento también puede ser considerada como una unidad de clasificación muy particularmente cuando no es posible determinar los datos financieros relativos a cada establecimiento. En el caso de una *economía de mercado*, la unidad de clasificación podría ser una sociedad de capital, una asociación cooperativista, una asociación sin fines de lucro, una sociedad de personas, una empresa particular o cualquier otra forma de asociación. En el caso de una *economía centralizada y planificada*, la empresa puede ser una unidad de gestión o de contabilidad y puede comprender un cierto número de establecimientos. Concierta contratos, tiene un plan de producción independiente, recibe y gasta los ingresos, mantiene un cuenta bancaria aparte y lleva una serie completa e independiente de libros de contabilidad.

En el caso de las actividades de *I y D no integradas*, la unidad típica de clasificación puede ser una asociación de investigación, un instituto de carácter no lucrativo, un instituto público o un sector de la economía identificado por dos o tres cifras; en los países de Europa oriental, puede ser un instituto de investigación que depende de un ministerio.

La unidad estadística usada en el *Sector de servicio general* es un organismo importante, que funcione de manera autónoma o que pueda identificarse por separado en un departamento o una institución oficial y que no estuviera clasificado en otra parte. Dicha unidad puede ser una división, un laboratorio o instituto, una oficina, una oficina central, etc.

Finalidades principales de las actividades nacionales de I y D.

El siguiente plan para clasificar los gastos de I y D en una forma funcional, en vez de hacerlo de manera institucional o estrictamente sectorial, constituye un intento de la Oficina de Estadística de la Unesco para obtener información sumaria sobre la distribución general de los enfuerzos nacionales de I y D, sobre una base comparable internacionalmente. En algunos Estados Miembros en los que ya se compilan estadísticas semejantes, los gastos se clasifican de conformidad con los sectores de aplicación o las finalidades de las actividades nacionales de I y D. Como esos términos han adquirido significados algo diferentes en esos Estados Miembros, pareció conveniente que la Unesco escogiera un término para su propia nomenclatura, lo que evitaría crear la impresión de que reflejaba los objetivos reales de los gobiernos. En la clasificación de las actividades nacionales de I y D por finalidades principales- según se indica a continuación - y que debe basarse en los

objetivos finales, se ha intentado encontrar un denominador común apropiado que permita realizar un desglose más sistemático y analítico de los gastos de I y D, como también obtener resultados comparables en el plan internacional. Los epígrafes que figuran en las dos categorías de finalidades no deben ser considerados como exhaustivos, sino más bien como ejemplo de los tipos de I y D comprendidos en cada finalidad principal.

Este esfuerzo para clasificar los gastos de I y D por finalidades principales tiene necesariamente carácter experimental.

1. *Exploración y evaluación de la tierra, los mares, la atmósfera y el espacio.*

Este epígrafe comprende las actividades de I y D que conciernen principalmente a la exploración y la evaluación de la corteza y la capa terrestres, los mares y océanos, la atmósfera y el espacio, así como la administración, economía, política y planeamiento de las mismas. *No se incluyen* los estudios de suelos para fines agrícolas, la I y D sobre oceanografía en beneficio de la industria pesquera, y la I y D referente a la explotación económica de fuentes de materias primas, combustibles y energía, así como tampoco la utilización de las técnicas de satélites para fines de comunicación. Las actividades incluidas en este grupo son emprendidas con miras a la explotación económica de los resultados y quedan *excluidas* por consiguiente la investigación fundamental en meteorología, geología, hidrología, etc. que debe clasificarse en 'adelanto general del saber'.

2. *Desarrollo de la agricultura, la silvicultura y la pesca.*

Este epígrafe comprende dos categorías de actividades de I y D, la primera referente a los aspectos de la alimentación y la segunda a los productos no alimenticios de la agricultura y la silvicultura. En la primera de estas dos categorías se incluye la I y D sobre producción, almacenamiento y distribución de alimentos, verbigracia la producción de ganado y la mejora de las razas, la medicina veterinaria, la producción y agronomía de las cosechas, la I y D sobre maquinaria agrícola o productos químicos agrícolas, la I y D sobre tratamiento de alimentos y bebidas, su almacenamiento y distribución, sobre pesquerías y tecnologías conexas, así como la administración, economía, política y planeamiento de la agricultura y de la producción de alimentos. La segunda categoría, o sea la del desarrollo de productos agrícolas no alimenticios y de la silvicultura, incluye las actividades de I y D sobre productos tales como lana, pieles, tabaco, algodón y otras fibras, y sobre la silvicultura y la tecnología relacionada.

3. *Fomento del desarrollo industrial.*

Esta finalidad principal se refiere a todas las actividades de I y D que contribuyen al desarrollo y mejoramiento de la industria manufacturera y minera. Se incluyen en ella la I y D sobre administración, economía, política y planeamiento del desarrollo industrial, sobre producción textil, vestidos y cuero, productos de la madera y el papel, substancias químicas incluyendo las petroquímicas, caucho y plásticos, metales básicos, productos metálicos manufacturados, maquinaria y equipo, incluidos vehículos para transportes, productos no metálicos, minería, excepto la de combustibles. *No se incluye* la I y D industrial realizada en apoyo de otros objetivos tales como desarrollo de la agricultura y de la producción alimenticia, transportes y comunicaciones, exploración del espacio, planificación urbana y rural, y defensa.

4. *Producción, conservación y distribución de la energía.*

Este epígrafe cubre las actividades de I y D referentes a la producción, al suministro, la conservación y la distribución de todo tipo de energía (comprendida la nuclear) y a la administración, economía, política y planeamiento de la energía; se incluyen la minería de combustibles sólidos y la tecnología relacionada, la producción de petróleo y gas, así como las fuentes no convencionales de energía (solar, viento) y las pequeñas fuentes de energía.

5. *Desarrollo de los transportes y las comunicaciones.*

Este grupo se refiere a los sistemas de transporte y a las redes y sistemas de comunicación, comprendiendo el transporte por tierra, aire y agua, la radio y la televisión, el teléfono y otras formas de telecomunicaciones incluidos los satélites, así como la I y D sobre administración, economía, política y planeamiento de las redes de transportes y comunicaciones. Se incluyen los servicios auxiliares tales como los dispositivos electrónicos para el tráfico y las estaciones de radar, pero *se excluye* la producción de máquinas, motores y medios de transporte como vehículos, barcos y aviones, que queda comprendida en la finalidad 'Fomento del desarrollo industrial'.

6. *Desarrollo de los servicios educativos.*

Esta finalidad principal comprende las actividades de I y D que se refieren a la administración, la economía, la política y el planeamiento de los servicios educativos a todos los niveles. Se incluyen la enseñanza escolar así como la extra-escolar, la formación en curso de empleo y otras formas de educación y capacitación de adultos. También se considera que

Science and technology
Science et technologie
Ciencia y tecnología

5

forma parte de este grupo la I y D sobre medios técnicos y métodos de enseñanza, tanto tradicionales como modernos, tales como enseñanza programada, TV y otras técnicas audiovisuales.

7. *Desarrollo de los servicios de sanidad.*

Este epígrafe comprende dos categorías de actividades de I y D, la primera referente a los aspectos de la salud humana. Abarca la I y D sobre asistencia facultativa (incluídas cirugía y obstetricia), prevención contra las enfermedades, higiene de la nutrición y de los alimentos, influencia del medio sobre la salud, incluída la medicina del trabajo, productos farmacéuticos, vacunas y prótesis, así como también la administración, economía, política y planeamiento referentes a la salud.

8. *Desarrollo social y otros servicios socio-económicos.*

Este grupo concierne las actividades de I y D relativas a la administración, economía, política y planeamiento del desarrollo social y de los servicios socio- económicos. Se incluye la organización política, la ley y el orden, la seguridad social, la cultura, las diversiones y el tiempo libre, la protección de los consumidores, el mejoramiento de las condiciones de trabajo, las relaciones laborales, la mano de obra y las migraciones, las relaciones internacionales, incluyendo la paz, los tribunales internacionales, los tratados y otros servicios sociales. También se incluyen las actividades de I y D acerca de la organización económica, dinero y banca, seguros etc. Se incluyen asimismo en esta finalidad principal las actividades de I y D referentes a la planificación urbana y rural, tales como viviendas, servicios sanitarios y otros servicios comunitarios relacionados con el bienestar de la población.

9. *Protección del medio ambiente.*

Esta finalidad principal cubre todos los aspectos de la 'protección' del medio tales como conservación de la pureza de la atmósfera, el agua y el suelo, control del ruído, modelos y estadísticas sobre el medio, así como la reglamentación, economía, política y planeamiento relativos al medio ambiente. Se excluye la I y D sobre la influencia del medio sobre la salud que debe incluirse en el epígrafe 'desarrollo de los servicios de sanidad', y la influencia del medio sobre el bienestar de la población que se incluye en el epígrafe 8. También *se excluye* la I y D dirigida a impedir la contaminación causada por ciertas actividades económicas, que debe incluirse con las actividades correspondientes.

10. *Adelanto general del saber.*

Este epígrafe abarca todas las actividades de I y D de una orientación muy general que no se pueden clasificar en ninguna de las otras finalidades principales, pero que contribuyen al adelanto general del saber en las ciencias sociales, así como en las exactas y naturales. Consiste en investigación fundamental y aplicada que los consejos científicos, institutos de academias de ciencias y universidades realizan en el amplio marco de sus funciones. Incluye la I y D referente a la administración, economía, política y planificación de la propia I y D.

11. *Otras finalidades.*

Este concepto incluye todas las demás actividades de I y D emprendidas con un objetivo específico que no corresponde a ninguno de los epígrafes anteriores. Incluirá por ejemplo el desarrollo de los sistemas de información, la ciencia de las computadoras (máquinas y programas), pero *se excluirán* los gastos relativos a la recolecta de datos.

12. *Defensa.*

Esta finalidad principal comprende la I y D sobre cuestiones nucleares, espaciales y de otro tipo ejecutadas para fines militares. Las sumas gastadas en investigaciones de carácter civil por las instituciones militares deben ser distribuídas, en la medida de lo posible, entre los principales objetivos civiles a los que correspondan.

Los cuadros que figuran en este capítulo se han clasificado en tres secciones. La primera sección comprende 5 cuadros que se refieren al personal científico y técnico. El número total o el número del personal calificado económicamente activo, es decir, las personas que poseen las calificaciones necesarias para ser clasificadas como científicos, ingenieros y técnicos, así como el número correspondiente de mujeres, figuran en el cuadro 5.1. La información relativa al número total (stock) se obtiene generalmente a través de los censos de población, no disponiéndose por consiguiente de este dato todos los años. Cuando carecemos de tal información, el número de científicos, ingenieros y técnicos económicamente activos se presenta como una alternativa.

El cuadro 5.2 indica los datos que se refieren a los científicos e ingenieros empleados en trabajos de investigación y de desarrollo experimental.

El cuadro 5.3 indica solamente los datos que se refieren a los científicos e ingenieros empleados en trabajos de investigación y de desarrollo experimental clasificados según la disciplina científica correspondiente a su calificación, y teniendo en cuenta su calidad de empleados de jornada completa o jornada parcial. Se da también su equivalente de jornada

completa y, en la medida de lo posible, datos separados relativos a las mujeres. Cabe destacar que, en general, la subdivisión por ramas de la ciencia se refiere a la disciplina científica que corresponde al título obtenido, pero que en algunos casos no ha sido posible determinar si se trata de la rama de estudio o de la rama de la ciencia a la que las personas se dedican actualmente.

El cuadro 5.4 se refiere a todo el personal empleado en trabajos de I y D y al sector de ejecución. Da a la vez las cifras absolutas y la repartición en porcentaje del conjunto del personal según el sector de ejecución, presentando igualmente las categorías de personal empleado en esos sectores.

Se puede notar la orientación dada a los esfuerzos nacionales de I y D en el cuadro 5.5 que presenta, para un número limitado de países, los científicos e ingenieros ocupados en trabajos de I y D según sus respectivos sectores de ejecución, la esfera de actividad económica, la disciplina de investigación a que pertenece su empresa o institución o bien según el campo de investigación al que se dedican en la actualidad. (Lo que no se ajusta necesariamente a la disciplina científica inicial del personal correspondiente al diploma concedido, cuya clasificación figura en el cuadro 5.3).

La segunda sección comprende 5 cuadros y da una idea del costo de las actividades de I y D, calculado sobre la base de los gastos intra-muros destinados a trabajos de I y D. Los datos se presentan en moneda nacional.

En el cuadro 5.6, los gastos totales de I y D se desglosan por tipo de gastos (total, ordinarios, de mano de obra), estableciéndose una relación entre los gastos totales y los gastos ordinarios.

El cuadro 5.7 muestra la repartición de los gastos ordinarios en cifras absolutas y en porcentaje por tipo de actividad de I y D - investigación fundamental, investigación aplicada o desarrollo experimental.

El cuadro 5.8 presenta la repartición de los gastos totales y ordinarios por sector de ejecución, en cifras absolutas y en porcentaje.

En cuanto a la estructura del financiamiento de la I y D, se indica en el cuadro 5.9, donde los gastos ordinarios y de capital se desglosan por fuente de financiamiento. Los datos se presentan en moneda nacional y en porcentaje.

El cuadro 5.10 da la repartición de los fondos públicos, o alternativamente de los gastos totales nacionales intra-muros destinados a las actividades de I y D de acuerdo con doce finalidades principales; se trata de una ventilación analítica de los gastos de I y D según una clasificación 'funcional' (en el cuadro 5.8, la clasificación es 'institucional o sectorial'); esta ventilación pone de relieve la estructura general de los esfuerzos nacionales de I y D. Sin embargo, este intento de clasificación debe seguir considerándose como una experiencia.

La última sección da una visión general del desarrollo de las actividades de I y D, y comprende igualmente indicadores adicionales. Los dos cuadros que procuran datos retrospectivos (5.11 y 5.12) muestran el crecimiento de los recursos humanos y financieros dedicados a la I y D en los países desarrollados y en vías de desarrollo.

El cuadro 5.11 presenta los efectivos totales del personal, de los científicos y de los ingenieros empleados en trabajos de I y D durante los últimos años, en general de 1969 a 1978. Las informaciones que se refieren a los científicos e ingenieros están traducidas en números índices sobre la base de 1969 = 100.

El cuadro 5.12 presenta una serie cronológica de los gastos totales y ordinarios dedicados a la I y D para los últimos años, en general de 1969 a 1978. También se indica la relación entre los gastos totales y ordinarios.

El cuadro 5.13 procura indicadores seleccionados sobre la ciencia y la tecnología. Presenta el efectivo del personal calificado, es decir, de las personas que poseen las calificaciones necesarias para ser clasificadas como científicos, ingenieros y técnicos, como también de los científicos, ingenieros y técnicos empleados en trabajos de I y D en relación con la población total, así como la relación entre el número total de científicos e ingenieros y los que están ocupados en trabajos de I y D. También se encontrará la relación entre el número de técnicos y el de científicos e ingenieros. Esos indicadores se ajustan con los que se refieren a los gastos de I y D, relacionados a su vez con la población total y con el número de científicos e ingenieros empleados en la I y D, y también expresados en porcentaje del producto nacional bruto.

El lector encontrará el número de países y de territorios considerados en el encabezamiento de cada cuadro. El número total de países cubiertos en los cuadros asciende a 137. Dada la evidente diversidad de las definiciones aplicadas y el carácter incompleto de los resultados, procede utilizar estas cifras con la mayor cautela. En muchos casos, se indican las excepciones en unas notas que complementan los cuadros. La ausencia de

5   Science and technology
Science et technologie
Ciencia y tecnología

notas no significa necesariamente que las cifras citadas se ajustan a las definiciones del cuestionario. Es la razón por la cual no se han calculado totales regionales, estimando que no deben efectuarse hasta que no se disponga de datos más seguros al respecto. Los investigadores que deseen obtener otros detalles o aclaraciones sobre un país en particular en lo que se refiere a las definiciones nacionales, el alcance o las limitaciones de los datos presentados en los cuadros, pueden dirigir su petición a la Oficina de Estadística, División de Estadísticas relativas a la Ciencia y la Tecnología.

Debe evitarse comparar, de un país a otro, las cifras absolutas referentes a los gastos de I y D. Sólo se podrían efectuar comparaciones semejantes convirtiendo en una misma moneda las sumas que figuran en moneda nacional, y como no existe un tipo de cambio especialmente aplicable a las actividades de I y D, sería necesario basarse para ello en los tipos de cambio oficiales. Como sea que tales tipos no siempre reflejan el costo real de las actividades de I y D, se corre el riesgo de que dichas comparaciones sean erróneas . Sin embargo, no carecen totalmente de interés ya que como mínimo dan una idea del orden de magnitud de los gastos de I y D. En el Anexo C pueden verse los tipos de cambio aplicables a la conversión de las monedas nacionales en dólares de los Estados Unidos de América.

Scientific and technical manpower   5.1
Personnel scientifique et technique
Personal científico y técnico

5.1 Number of scientists, engineers and technicians

Nombre de scientifiques, d'ingénieurs et de techniciens

Número de científicos, ingenieros y técnicos

PLEASE REFER TO INTRODUCTION FOR DEFINITIONS OF CATEGORIES IN THIS TABLE.	POUR LES DEFINITIONS DES CATEGORIES PRESENTEES DANS CE TABLEAU, SE REFERER A L'INTRODUCTION.	EN LA INTRODUCCION SE DAN LAS DEFINICIONES DE LAS CATE- GORIAS QUE FIGURAN EN ESTE CUADRO.
ST = STOCK OF SCIENTISTS, ENGINEERS AND TECHNICIANS	ST = EFFECTIF TOTAL DES SCIENTIFIQUES, DES INGE- NIEURS ET DES TECHNICIENS	ST = NUMERO TOTAL DE CIENTI- FICOS, INGENIEROS Y TECNICOS
EA = NUMBER OF ECONOMICALLY ACTIVE SCIENTISTS, ENGI- NEERS AND TECHNICIANS	EA = NOMBRE DES SCIENTIFIQUES, DES INGENIEURS ET DES TECHNICIENS ECONOMIQUEMENT ACTIFS	EA = NUMERO DE CIENTIFICOS, INGENIEROS Y TECNICOS ECONOMICAMENTE ACTIVOS
SET = SCIENTISTS, ENGINEERS AND TECHNICIANS	SET = SCIENTIFIQUES, INGENIEURS ET TECHNICIENS	SET = CIENTIFICOS, INGENIEROS Y TECNICOS
NUMBER OF COUNTRIES AND TERRITORIES PRESENTED IN THIS TABLE: 106	NOMBRE DE PAYS ET DE TERRITOIRES PRESENTES DANS CE TABLEAU: 106	NUMERO DE PAISES Y DE TERRITORIOS PRESENTADOS EN ESTE CUADRO: 106

COUNTRY / PAYS / PAIS	YEAR / ANNEE / AÑO	DEFINITION OF DATA / CODE / TIPO DE DATOS	TOTAL / TOTAL / TOTAL (SET)	SCIENTISTS AND ENGINEERS / SCIENTIFIQUES ET INGENIEURS / CIENTIFICOS E INGENIEROS — TOTAL	F	TECHNICIANS / TECHNICIENS / TECNICOS — TOTAL	F
			(1)	(2)	(3)	(4)	(5)
AFRICA							
BOTSWANA ‡	1972	ST	1 527	786	...	741	...
CONGO	1977	EA	...	...	...	3 461	...
DJIBOUTI	1973	ST	35	35	4	—	—
EGYPT	1973	ST	...	593 254	...	...	...
GAMBIA ‡	1973	ST	...	445	...	...	...
GHANA ‡	1970	EA	21 993	6 897	789	15 096	7 944
KENYA ‡	1975	EA	11 009	5 130	...	5 879	...
LIBYAN ARAB JAMAHIRIYA ‡	1973	EA	*18 921	*8 319	...	*10 602	...
MAURITIUS ‡	1972	ST	...	6 264	...	...	...
NIGERIA ‡	1970	ST	35 126	19 885	...	15 241	...
SEYCHELLES ‡	1973	ST	...	*300	...	...	...
SUDAN ‡	1971	ST	*16 431	*13 792	...	*2 639	...
SWAZILAND ‡	1977	EA	1 384	...	...	...	...
TOGO	1971	EA	672	461	...	211	...
TUNISIA ‡	1974	EA	11 135	3 421	...	7 714	...

5.1 Scientific and technical manpower
Personnel scientifique et technique
Personal científico y técnico

COUNTRY PAYS PAIS	YEAR ANNEE AÑO	DEFINITION OF DATA CODE TIPO DE DATOS	TOTAL TOTAL TOTAL (SET)	SCIENTISTS AND ENGINEERS SCIENTIFIQUES ET INGENIEURS CIENTIFICOS E INGENIEROS		TECHNICIANS TECHNICIENS TECNICOS	
				TOTAL	F	TOTAL	F
			(1)	(2)	(3)	(4)	(5)
UNITED REPUBLIC OF							
CAMEROON ‡	1970	ST	*3 500	...	...	...	...
ZAMBIA	1973	ST	37 000	11 000	...	26 000	...
AMERICA, NORTH							
ANTIGUA ‡	1970	ST	*780	*480	*410	*300	./.
BAHAMAS	1970	ST	*6 600	*3 000	*800	*3 600	*2 100
BELIZE ‡	1970	ST	728	201	96	527	271
BERMUDA	1970	EA	3 603	1 626	569	1 977	808
BRITISH VIRGIN							
ISLANDS ‡	1973	EA	*320	*120	*40	*200	*100
CANADA ‡	1971	ST	...	621 645	189 370	...	...
CAYMAN ISLANDS	1971	ST	550	200	20	350	35
CUBA	1977	ST	...	60 189	...	...	...
DOMINICAN REPUBLIC ‡	1970	ST	...	7 837	...	...	...
EL SALVADOR	1974	ST	7 262	5 489	...	1 773	...
GUATEMALA	1974	EA	12 656	5 551	...	7 105	...
HONDURAS	1974	EA	9 885	6 702	...	3 183	...
NETHERLANDS ANTILLES ‡	1971	ST	3 387	3 387	...	...	...
PANAMA	1976	ST	21 929	8 077	905	13 852	89
FORMER CANAL ZONE	1976	EA	1 437	1 268	678	169	47
PUERTO RICO ‡	1970	ST	...	72 998	...	...	...
TURKS AND CAICOS							
ISLANDS	1976	ST	*50	16	1	*34	*20
UNITED STATES OF							
AMERICA	1976	EA	3 410 000	2 452 000	212 000	958 000	...
AMERICA, SOUTH							
ARGENTINA	1976	ST	2 725 000	425 000	154 000	2 300 000	1 480 000
BOLIVIA	1974	ST	...	9 674	...	...	...
BRAZIL	1970	ST	1 718 822	541 328	138 496	1 177 494	793 750
CHILE ‡	1970	ST	...	69 946	20 496	...	...
ECUADOR	1974	ST	98 130	48 559	...	49 571	...
GUYANA ‡	1977	EA	1 579	611	85	968	123
PERU	1974	EA	*144 923	*84 923	...	60 000	...
URUGUAY	1970	ST	50 346	20 069	...	30 277	...
ASIA							
BANGLADESH ‡	1973	EA	*63 500	23 500	...	*40 000	...
BRUNEI	1971	EA	2 237	589	18	1 648	352
BURMA ‡	1975	EA	...	18 500	...	...	...
HONG KONG ‡	1976	ST	...	66 890	...	...	...
INDIA ‡	1977	ST	2 328 200	697 600	...	1 630 600	...
INDONESIA ‡	1976	ST	1 668 257	109 107	16 507	1 559 150	...
IRAN	1974	ST	217 632	161 183	...	56 449	...
IRAQ ‡	1972	EA	*68 334	*43 645	*10 901	*24 689	*2 950
ISRAEL	1974	ST	175 100	96 300	35 200	78 800	56 300
JAPAN	1975	EA	20 534 900	4 127 200	1 621 600	16 407 700	4 411 300
JORDAN ‡	1977	EA	17 232	11 575	1 623	5 657	704
KOREA, REPUBLIC OF	1977	ST	...	799 970	...	...	...
KUWAIT ‡	1975	ST	...	27 246	7 177	...	...
LEBANON ‡	1972	ST	...	*28 500	...	...	...

Scientific and technical manpower 5.1
Personnel scientifique et technique
Personal científico y técnico

COUNTRY PAYS PAIS	YEAR ANNEE AÑO	DEFINITION OF DATA CODE TIPO DE DATOS	TOTAL TOTAL TOTAL (SET)	SCIENTISTS AND ENGINEERS SCIENTIFIQUES ET INGENIEURS CIENTIFICOS E INGENIEROS		TECHNICIANS TECHNICIENS TECNICOS	
				TOTAL	F	TOTAL	F
			(1)	(2)	(3)	(4)	(5)
MALAYSIA							
PENINSULAR MALAYSIA	1970	ST	35 415	...		...	...
MONGOLIA	1972	ST	2 040	1 908	603	132	...
PAKISTAN ‡	1973	ST	...	*111 000	...	...	...
PHILIPPINES	1970	ST	...	1 083 742	603 145	...	...
QATAR ‡	1974	EA	1 929	1 352	...	577	...
SAUDI ARABIA ‡	1974	ST	...	*33 376	...	...	...
SINGAPORE ‡	1977	ST	...	12 616	...	...	...
SRI LANKA ‡	1971	ST	...	37 769	...	...	...
SYRIAN ARAB REPUBLIC	1970	ST	48 666	27 369	4 098	21 297	7 690
THAILAND ‡	1975	EA	67 632	20 288	...	47 344	...
YEMEN ‡	1974	ST	2 074	1 394	18	680	18
EUROPE							
AUSTRIA	1971	ST	...	118 294	27 870	...	...
BULGARIA	1977	EA	767 397	236 743	100 469	530 654	298 180
CZECHOSLOVAKIA	1973	EA	...	327 772	112 680	...	...
FINLAND	1977	ST	1 086 449	165 794	62 742	920 655	457 860
FRANCE	1975	ST	...	1 522 850	545 700	...	...
GERMAN DEMOCRATIC							
REPUBLIC ‡	1977	EA	1 253 900	444 700	147 100	809 200	...
GERMANY, FEDERAL							
REPUBLIC OF	1970	ST	1 189 000	1 083 000	193 000	106 000	42 000
GIBRALTAR	1970	ST	164	41	–	123	2
GREECE ‡	1971	ST	...	194 828	...	...	...
HOLY SEE ‡	1976	ST	544	535	11	9	3
HUNGARY ‡	1973	ST	819 485	336 143	113 224	483 342	230 163
ICELAND	1970	ST	...	3 169	...	...	...
IRELAND ‡	1971	ST	...	21 886	...	...	...
ITALY	1971	ST	4 242 466	884 813	271 674	3 357 653	1 548 666
NETHERLANDS	1971	ST	*742 000	*442 000	*144 000	*300 000	*208 000
NORWAY	1977	ST	...	86 100	13 250	...	...
POLAND	1974	ST	4 815 000	803 000	300 000	4 012 000	2 260 000
SAN MARINO	1976	ST	638	267	95	371	77
SWITZERLAND	1975	ST	...	254 000	25 400	...	...
YUGOSLAVIA	1976	ST	2 938 604	285 593	94 434	2 653 011	831 021
OCEANIA							
AMERICAN SAMOA	1973	EA	422	327	...	95	...
AUSTRALIA	1971	EA	595 133	147 758	30 431	447 375	169 713
COOK ISLANDS	1970	ST	305	164	78	141	34
FRENCH POLYNESIA	1973	EA	...	95	11	...	...
KIRIBATI	1971	EA	177	112	30	65	–
NEW CALEDONIA	1973	ST	145	69	...	76	...
NEW HEBRIDES	1972	ST	570	161	29	409	156
NEW ZEALAND	1971	ST	209 692	60 305	13 199	149 387	101 772
NIUE	1971	ST	6	2	–	4	–
NORFOLK ISLAND	1975	EA	24	22	7	2	–
PACIFIC ISLANDS	1973	ST	1 103	161	9	942	361
PAPUA NEW GUINEA ‡	1973	EA	12 798	2 646	...	10 152	...
SAMOA	1977	ST	514	350	140	164	36
SOLOMON ISLANDS ‡	1971	EA	894	129	...	765	...
TOKELAU ISLANDS	1971	ST	–	–	...	–	–

5.1 Scientific and technical manpower
Personnel scientifique et technique
Personal científico y técnico

COUNTRY PAYS PAIS	YEAR ANNEE AÑO	DEFINITION OF DATA CODE TIPO DE DATOS	TOTAL TOTAL TOTAL (SET)	SCIENTISTS AND ENGINEERS SCIENTIFIQUES ET INGENIEURS CIENTIFICOS E INGENIEROS		TECHNICIANS TECHNICIENS TECNICOS	
				TOTAL	F	TOTAL	F
			(1)	(2)	(3)	(4)	(5)
U.S.S.R.							
U.S.S.R. ‡	1977	EA	25 178 000	10 537 000	5 524 000	14 641 000	9 312 000
BYELORUSSIAN S.S.R. ‡	1977	EA	912 700	387 300	.	525 400	...
UKRAINIAN S.S.R. ‡	1977	EA	4 804 500	2 000 500	1 029 000	2 804 000	1 737 300

BOTSWANA:
E—> 557 OF THE SCIENTISTS AND ENGINEERS IN
COLUMN 2 AND 171 OF THE TECHNICIANS IN COLUMN 4
ARE FOREIGNERS.
FR—> 557 DES SCIENTIFIQUES ET INGENIEURS DE LA
COLONNE 2 ET 171 DES TECHNICIENS DE LA COLONNE 4
SONT RESSORTISSANTS ETRANGERS.
ESP> 557 CIENTIFICOS E INGENIEROS DE LA COLUMNA
2 Y 171 TECNICOS DE LA COLUMNA 4 SON EXTRANJEROS.

GAMBIA:
E—> DATA REFER TO PERSONS AGED 25 YEARS AND
OVER HAVING COMPLETED EDUCATION AT THE THIRD
LEVEL.
FR—> LES DONNEES SE REFERENT AUX PERSONNES AGEES
DE 25 ANS ET PLUS AYANT COMPLETE L'ENSEIGNEMENT DU
TROISIEME DEGRE.
ESP> LOS DATOS SE REFIEREN A LAS PERSONAS DE 25
AÑOS Y MAS QUE COMPLETARON LA ENSEÑANZA DE TERCER
GRADO.

GHANA:
E—> 1,761 OF THE SCIENTISTS AND ENGINEERS IN
COLUMN 2 AND 317 OF THE TECHNICIANS IN COLUMN 4
ARE FOREIGNERS. THE FIGURES IN COLUMNS 4 AND
5 DO NOT INCLUDE SOCIAL SCIENCES AND HUMANITIES.
FR—> 1 761 DES SCIENTIFIQUES ET INGENIEURS DE LA
COLONNE 2 ET 317 DES TECHNICIENS DE LA COLONNE 4
SONT RESSORTISSANTS ETRANGERS. LES CHIFFRES DES
COLONNES 4 ET 5 NE COMPRENNENT PAS LES SCIENCES
SOCIALES ET HUMAINES.
ESP> 1 761 CIENTIFICOS E INGENIEROS DE LA COLUM-
NA 2 Y 317 TECNICOS DE LA COLUMNA 4 SON EXTRAN-
JEROS. LAS CIFRAS DE LAS COLUMNAS 4 Y 5 EXCLUYEN
LAS CIENCIAS SOCIALES Y HUMANAS.

KENYA:
E—> DATA REFER TO PERSONS IN GAINFUL
EMPLOYMENT.
FR—> LES DONNEES SE REFERENT AUX PERSONNES QUI
OCCUPENT UN EMPLOI REMUNERE.
ESP> LOS DATOS SE REFIEREN A LAS PERSONAS QUE
OCUPAN UN EMPLEO REMUNERADO.

LIBYAN ARAB JAMAHIRIYA:
E—> APPROXIMATELY 79% OF THE SCIENTISTS AND
ENGINEERS IN COLUMN 2 AND 34% OF THE TECHNICIANS
IN COLUMN 4 ARE FOREIGNERS.
FR—> ENVIRON 79% DES SCIENTIFIQUES ET INGENIEURS
DE LA COLONNE 2 ET 34% DES TECHNICIENS DE LA
COLONNE 4 SONT RESSORTISSANTS ETRANGERS.
ESP> EL 79% APROXIMADAMENTE DE LOS CIENTIFICOS E
INGENIEROS DE LA COLUMNA 2 Y EL 34% DE LOS
TECNICOS DE LA COLUMNA 4 SON EXTRANJEROS.

MAURITIUS:
E—> DATA REFER TO PERSONS AGED 25 YEARS AND
OVER HAVING COMPLETED EDUCATION AT THE THIRD
LEVEL.
FR—> LES DONNEES SE REFERENT AUX PERSONNES AGEES
DE 25 ANS ET PLUS AYANT COMPLETE L'ENSEIGNEMENT DU
TROISIEME DEGRE.
ESP> LOS DATOS SE REFIEREN A LAS PERSONAS DE 25
AÑOS Y MAS QUE COMPLETARON LA ENSEÑANZA DE TERCER
GRADO.

NIGERIA:
E—> DATA RELATE TO THE YEAR 1970/71 AND DO NOT
INCLUDE SOCIAL SCIENCES AND HUMANITIES.
FR—> LES DONNEES SE REFERENT A L'ANNEE 1970/71
ET NE COMPRENNENT PAS LES SCIENCES SOCIALES ET
HUMAINES.
ESP> LOS DATOS SE REFIEREN AL AÑO 1970/71 Y
EXCLUYEN LOS DATOS RELATIVOS A LAS CIENCIAS
SOCIALES Y HUMANAS.

SEYCHELLES:
E—> APPROXIMATELY 150 OF THE SCIENTISTS AND
ENGINEERS IN COLUMN 2 ARE FOREIGNERS.
FR—> ENVIRON 150 DES SCIENTIFIQUES ET INGE-
NIEURS DE LA COLONNE 2 SONT RESSORTISSANTS
ETRANGERS.
ESP> UNOS 150 CIENTIFICOS E INGENIEROS DE LA
COLUMNA 2 SON EXTRANJEROS.

SUDAN:
E—> DATA RELATE TO THE YEAR 1971/72.
FR—> LES DONNEES SE REFERENT A L'ANNEE 1971/72.
ESP> LOS DATOS SE REFIEREN AL AÑO 1971/72.

SWAZILAND:
E—> DATA RELATE TO UNIVERSITY DEGREE-HOLDERS
OF WHICH 972 ARE FOREIGNERS.
FR—> LES DONNEES SE REFERENT AUX DIPLOMES DES
UNIVERSITES, DONT 972 SONT RESSORTISSANTS ETRAN-
GERS.
ESP> LOS DATOS SE REFIEREN A LOS DIPLOMADOS DE
LAS UNIVERSIDADES, DE LOS CUALES 972 SON EXTRAN-
JEROS.

TUNISIA:
E—> DATA ARE UNDER-ESTIMATED.
FR—> LES DONNEES SONT SOUS-ESTIMEES.
ESP> LOS DATOS SON SUBESTIMADOS.

UNITED REPUBLIC OF CAMEROON:
E—> APPROXIMATELY 1,000 OF THE TOTAL IN COLUMN
1 ARE FOREIGNERS.
FR—> ENVIRON 1000 PERSONNES DU TOTAL DE LA
COLONNE 1 SONT RESSORTISSANTS ETRANGERS.

Scientific and technical manpower **5.1**
Personnel scientifique et technique
Personal científico y técnico

UNITED REPUBLIC OF CAMEROON (CONT.):
ESP> APROXIMADAMENTE 1.000 PERSONAS DEL TOTAL DE LA COLUMNA 1 SON EXTRANJERAS.

ANTIGUA:
E—> DATA FOR FEMALE TECHNICIANS (COLUMN 5) ARE INCLUDED UNDER COLUMN 3.
FR—> LES DONNEES RELATIVES AUX TECHNICIENS DE LA COLONNE 5 SONT INCLUSES DANS LA COLONNE 3.
ESP> LOS DATOS RELATIVOS A LOS TECNICOS DE LA COLUMNA 5 ESTAN INCLUIDOS EN LA COLUMNA 3.

BELIZE:
E—> MOST OF THE 271 IN COLUMN 5 ARE NURSES.
FR—> LA PLUS GRANDE PARTIE DES DONNEES DE LA COLONNE 5 EST COMPOSEE D'INFIRMIERES.
ESP> LA MAYOR PARTE DE LOS DATOS QUE FIGURAN EN LA COLUMNA 5 SON ENFERMERAS.

BRITISH VIRGIN ISLANDS:
E—> 75 OF THE SCIENTISTS AND ENGINEERS IN COLUMN 2 AND 80 OF THE TECHNICIANS IN COLUMN 4 ARE FOREIGNERS.
FR—> 75 DES SCIENTIFIQUES ET INGENIEURS DE LA COLONNE 2 ET 80 DES TECHNICIENS DE LA COLONNE 4 SONT RESSORTISSANTS ETRANGERS.
ESP> 75 CIENTIFICOS E INGENIEROS DE LA COLUMNA 2 Y 80 TECNICOS DE LA COLUMNA 4 SON EXTRANJEROS.

CANADA:
E—> DATA FOR SCIENTISTS AND ENGINEERS REFER TO UNIVERSITY DEGREE—HOLDERS ONLY.
FR—> LES DONNEES RELATIVES AUX SCIENTIFIQUES ET INGENIEURS NE SE REFERENT QU'AUX DIPLOMES DES UNIVERSITES.
ESP> LOS DATOS RELATIVOS A LOS CIENTIFICOS E INGENIEROS SOLO SE REFIEREN A LAS PERSONAS QUE POSEEN UN TITULO UNIVERSITARIO.

DOMINICAN REPUBLIC:
E—> DATA REFER TO PERSONS AGED 25 YEARS AND OVER HAVING COMPLETED EDUCATION AT THE THIRD LEVEL.
FR—> LES DONNEES SE REFERENT AUX PERSONNES AGEES DE 25 ANS ET PLUS AYANT COMPLETE L'ENSEIGNEMENT DU TROISIEME DEGRE.
ESP> LOS DATOS SE REFIEREN A LAS PERSONAS DE 25 AÑOS Y MAS QUE COMPLETARON LA ENSEÑANZA DE TERCER GRADO.

NETHERLANDS ANTILLES:
E—> DATA REFER TO PERSONS AGED 25 YEARS AND OVER HAVING COMPLETED EDUCATION AT THE THIRD LEVEL.
FR—> LES DONNEES SE REFERENT AUX PERSONNES AGEES DE 25 ANS ET PLUS AYANT COMPLETE L'ENSEIGNEMENT DU TROISIEME DEGRE.
ESP> LOS DATOS SE REFIEREN A LAS PERSONAS DE 25 AÑOS Y MAS QUE COMPLETARON LA ENSEÑANZA DE TERCER GRADO.

PUERTO RICO:
E—> DATA REFER TO PERSONS AGED 25 YEARS AND OVER HAVING COMPLETED EDUCATION AT THE THIRD LEVEL.
FR—> LES DONNEES SE REFERENT AUX PERSONNES AGEES DE 25 ANS ET PLUS AYANT COMPLETE L'ENSEIGNEMENT DU TROISIEME DEGRE.
ESP> LOS DATOS SE REFIEREN A LAS PERSONAS DE 25 AÑOS Y MAS QUE COMPLETARON LA ENSEÑANZA DE TERCER GRADO.

CHILE:
E—> DATA REFER TO PERSONS WITH 5 TO 8 YEARS EDUCATION AT THE THIRD LEVEL.
FR—> LES DONNEES SE REFERENT AUX PERSONNES AYANT ACCOMPLI DE CINQ A HUIT ANNEES DANS L'ENSEIGNEMENT DU TROISIEME DEGRE.

CHILE (CONT.):
ESP> LOS DATOS SE REFIEREN A LAS PERSONAS QUE COMPLETARON DE CINCO A OCHO AÑOS EN LA ENSEÑANZA DE TERCER GRADO.

GUYANA:
E—> NOT INCLUDING DATA FOR SOCIAL SCIENCES AND HUMANITIES.
FR—> NON COMPRIS LES DONNEES POUR LES SCIENCES SOCIALES ET HUMAINES.
ESP> EXCLUIDOS LOS DATOS RELATIVOS A LAS CIENCIAS SOCIALES Y HUMANAS.

BANGLADESH:
E—> DATA RELATE TO THE YEAR 1973/74.
FR—> LES DONNEES SE REFERENT A L'ANNEE 1973/74.
ESP> LOS DATOS SE REFIEREN AL AÑO 1973/74.

BURMA:
E—> NOT INCLUDING DATA FOR SOCIAL SCIENCES AND HUMANITIES.
FR—> NON COMPRIS LES DONNEES POUR LES SCIENCES SOCIALES ET HUMAINES.
ESP> EXCLUIDOS LOS DATOS RELATIVOS A LAS CIENCIAS SOCIALES Y HUMANAS.

HONG KONG:
E—> DATA REFER TO PERSONS AGED 25 YEARS AND OVER HAVING COMPLETED EDUCATION AT THE THIRD LEVEL.
FR—> LES DONNEES SE REFERENT AUX PERSONNES AGEES DE 25 ANS ET PLUS AYANT COMPLETE L'ENSEIGNEMENT DU TROISIEME DEGRE.
ESP> LOS DATOS SE REFIEREN A LAS PERSONAS DE 25 AÑOS Y MAS QUE COMPLETARON LA ENSEÑANZA DE TERCER GRADO.

INDIA:
E—> DATA FOR SCIENTISTS AND ENGINEERS IN COLUMN 2 DO NOT INCLUDE SOCIAL SCIENCES AND HUMANITIES.
FR—> LES DONNEES RELATIVES AUX SCIENTIFIQUES ET INGENIEURS DE LA COLONNE 2 NE COMPRENNENT PAS LES SCIENCES SOCIALES ET HUMAINES.
ESP> LOS DATOS RELATIVOS A LOS TECNICOS E INGE- NIEROS DE LA COLUMNA 2 NO INCLUYEN LAS CIENCIAS SOCIALES Y HUMANAS.

INDONESIA:
E—> THE FIGURES IN COLUMNS 2 AND 3 REFER TO PERSONS WITH A UNIVERSITY EDUCATION; THOSE IN COLUMNS 4 AND 5 TO PERSONS WITH SENIOR VOCATIONAL (SECONDARY) AND NON—UNIVERSITY EDUCATION.
FR—> LES CHIFFRES DES COLONNES 2 ET 3 SE REFERENT AUX PERSONNES AYANT UNE FORMATION UNIVERSITAIRE; CEUX DES COLONNES 4 ET 5 AUX PERSONNES AYANT UNE FORMATION TECHNIQUE DE DEUXIEME CYCLE (SECONDAIRE) ET NON—UNIVERSITAIRE.
ESP> LAS CIFRAS DE LAS COLUMNAS 2 Y 3 SE REFIEREN A LAS PERSONAS QUE POSEEN UNA FORMACION UNIVERSITARIA; LAS DE LAS COLUMNAS 4 Y 5 A LAS PERSONAS QUE TIENEN UNA FORMACION TECNICA DE SEGUNDO CICLO (SECUNDARIA) Y NO UNIVERSITARIA.

IRAQ:
E—> DATA RELATE TO PERSONS EMPLOYED IN GOVERNMENT INSTITUTIONS ONLY.
FR—> LES DONNEES NE CONCERNENT QUE LES PERSONNES EMPLOYEES DANS LES INSTITUTIONS GOUVERNEMENTALES.
ESP> LOS DATOS SE REFIEREN A LAS PERSONAS EMPLEADAS EN LAS INSTITUCIONES GUBERNAMENTALES.

JORDAN:
E—> DATA REFER TO THE EAST BANK ONLY.
FR—> LES DONNEES SE REFERENT A LA RIVE ORIENTALE SEULEMENT.
ESP> LOS DATOS SE REFIEREN A LA ORILLA ORIENTAL SOLAMENTE.

5.1 Scientific and technical manpower
Personnel scientifique et technique
Personal científico y técnico

KUWAIT:
E—> DATA REFER TO UNIVERSITY GRADUATES OF WHOM
23,267 (F. 5,953) ARE FOREIGNERS.
FR–> LES DONNEES SE REFERENT AUX DIPLOMES DES
UNIVERSITES, DONT 23 267 (F. 5 953) SONT RESSOR–
TISSANTS ETRANGERS.
ESP> LOS DATOS SE REFIEREN A LOS DIPLOMADOS DE
LAS UNIVERSIDADES, DE LOS CUALES 23 267 (F. 5 953)
SON EXTRANJEROS.

LEBANON:
E—> DATA ARE BASED ON A SAMPLE SURVEY.
FR–> LES DONNEES SONT BASEES SUR UNE ENQUETE PAR
SONDAGE.
ESP> DATOS BASADOS EN UNA ENCUESTA POR SONDEO.

PAKISTAN:
E—> DATA RELATE TO THE YEAR 1973/74 AND DO
NOT INCLUDE SOCIAL SCIENCES AND HUMANITIES.
FR–> LES DONNEES SE REFERENT A L'ANNEE 1973/74
ET NE COMPRENNENT PAS LES SCIENCES SOCIALES ET
HUMAINES.
ESP> LOS DATOS SE REFIEREN AL AÑO 1973/74 Y
EXCLUYEN LAS CIENCIAS SOCIALES Y HUMANAS.

QATAR:
E—> DATA RELATE TO THE YEAR 1974/75; 90% OF
THE SCIENTISTS AND ENGINEERS IN COLUMN 2 AND 76%
OF THE TECHNICIANS IN COLUMN 4 ARE FOREIGNERS.
FR–> LES DONNEES SE REFERENT A L'ANNEE 1974/75;
90% DES SCIENTIFIQUES ET INGENIEURS DE LA COLONNE
2 ET 76% DES TECHNICIEN DE LA COLONNE 4 SONT
RESSORTISSANTS ETRANGERS.
ESP> LOS DATOS SE REFIEREN AL AÑO 1974/75; 90%
DE LOS CIENTIFICOS E INGENIEROS DE LA COLUMNA 2
Y 76% DE LOS TECNICOS DE LA COLUMNA 4 SON
EXTRANJEROS.

SAUDI ARABIA:
E—> THE FIGURES REFER TO SCIENTISTS AND
ENGINEERS WITH QUALIFICATIONS AT THE THIRD LEVEL
OF EDUCATION.
FR–> LES CHIFFRES SE REFERENT AUX SCIENTIFIQUES
ET INGENIEURS AVEC UNE FORMATION DE NIVEAU SUPE–
RIEUR.
ESP> LAS CIFRAS SE REFIEREN A LOS CIENTIFICOS E
INGENIEROS CON UNA FORMACION DE NIVEL SUPERIOR.

SINGAPORE:
E—> DATA DO NOT INCLUDE SOCIAL SCIENCES, HUMA–
NITIES AND AGRICULTURE.
FR–> NON COMPRIS LES SCIENCES SOCIALES ET
HUMAINES NI L'AGRICULTURE.
ESP> EXCLUIDAS LAS CIENCIAS SOCIALES Y HUMANAS
Y LA AGRICULTURA.

SRI LANKA:
E—> DATA REFER TO PERSONS AGED 25 YEARS AND
OVER HAVING COMPLETED EDUCATION AT THE THIRD
LEVEL.
FR–> LES DONNEES SE REFERENT AUX PERSONNES AGEES
DE 25 ANS ET PLUS AYANT COMPLETE L'ENSEIGNEMENT DU
TROISIEME DEGRE.
ESP> LOS DATOS SE REFIEREN A LAS PERSONAS DE 25
AÑOS Y MAS QUE COMPLETARON LA ENSEÑANZA DE TERCER
GRADO.

THAILAND:
E—> NOT INCLUDING DATA FOR SOCIAL SCIENCES AND
HUMANITIES.
FR–> NON COMPRIS LES DONNEES POUR LES SCIENCES
SOCIALES ET HUMAINES.
ESP> EXCLUIDOS LOS DATOS RELATIVOS A LAS
CIENCIAS SOCIALES Y HUMANAS.

YEMEN:
E—> DATA RELATE TO THE YEAR 1974/75.
FR–> LES DONNEES SE REFERENT A L'ANNEE
1974/75.
ESP> LOS DATOS SE REFIEREN AL AÑO 1974/75.

GERMAN DEMOCRATIC REPUBLIC:
E—> THE FIGURES IN COLUMNS 2 AND 3 REFER TO
UNIVERSITY GRADUATES; THE FIGURE IN COLUMN 4 TO
TECHNICAL COLLEGE GRADUATES.
FR–>LES CHIFFRES DES COLONNES 2 ET 3 SE REFERENT
AUX DIPLOMES DES UNIVERSITES; LE CHIFFRE DE LA
COLONNE 4 SE REFERE AUX DIPLOMES DES COLLEGES
TECHNIQUES.
ESP> LAS CIFRAS DE LAS COLUMNAS 2 Y 3 SE REFIE–
REN A LOS DIPLOMADOS DE LAS UNIVERSIDADES; LA
CIFRA DE LA COLUMNA 4 SE REFIERE A LOS DIPLOMADOS
DE LOS COLEGIOS TECNICOS.

GREECE:
E—> DATA REFER TO PERSONS AGED 25 YEARS AND
OVER HAVING COMPLETED EDUCATION AT THE THIRD
LEVEL.
FR–> LES DONNEES SE REFERENT AUX PERSONNES AGEES
DE 25 ANS ET PLUS AYANT COMPLETE L'ENSEIGNEMENT DU
TROISIEME DEGRE.
ESP> LOS DATOS SE REFIEREN A LAS PERSONAS DE 25
AÑOS Y MAS QUE COMPLETARON LA ENSEÑANZA DE TERCER
GRADO.

HOLY SEE:
E—> NOT INCLUDING DATA FOR MEDICAL SCIENCES.
FR–> NON COMPRIS LES DONNEES POUR LES SCIENCES
MEDICALES.
ESP> EXCLUIDOS LOS DATOS RELATIVOS A LAS
CIENCIAS MEDICAS.

HUNGARY:
E—> THE FIGURES IN COLUMN 2 AND 3 INCLUDE
TEACHING STAFF AT THE PRE–PRIMARY AND FIRST
LEVELS OF EDUCATION; THE FIGURES IN COLUMN 4 AND
5 REFER TO PERSONS WITH A FORMAL SECONDARY SCHOOL
EDUCATION.
FR–> LES CHIFFRES DES COLONNES 2 ET 3 COMPREN–
NENT LE PERSONNEL ENSEIGNANT DES ENSEIGNEMENTS
PRESCOLAIRE ET DU PREMIER DEGRE; LES CHIFFRES DES
COLONNES 4 ET 5 CONCERNENT LES PERSONNES AYANT UNE
QUALIFICATION RECONNUE DE NIVEAU SECONDAIRE.
ESP> LAS CIFRAS DE LAS COLUMNAS 2 Y 3 INCLUYEN
EL PERSONAL DOCENTE DE LAS ENSEÑANZAS PREPRIMERA–
RIA Y DE PRIMER GRADO; LAS DE LAS COLUMNAS 4 Y 5
SE REFIEREN A LAS PERSONAS QUE POSEEN UNA CALI–
FICACION RECONOCIDA DE NIVEL SECUNDARIO.

IRELAND:
E—> NOT INCLUDING DATA FOR SOCIAL SCIENCES AND
HUMANITIES.
FR–> NON COMPRIS LES DONNEES POUR LES SCIENCES
SOCIALES ET HUMAINES.
ESP> EXCLUIDOS LOS DATOS RELATIVOS A LAS
CIENCIAS SOCIALES Y HUMANAS.

PAPUA NEW GUINEA:
E—> 2,501 OF THE SCIENTISTS AND ENGINEERS IN
COLUMN 2 AND 7,213 OF THE TECHNICIANS IN COLUMN 4
ARE FOREIGNERS.
FR–> 2 501 SCIENTIFIQUES ET INGENIEURS DE LA
COLONNE 2 ET 7 213 TECHNICIENS DE LA COLONNE 4
SONT RESSORTISSANTS ETRANGERS.
ESP> 2 501 CIENTIFICOS E INGENIEROS DE LA
COLUMNA 2 Y 7 213 TECNICOS DE LA COLUMNA 4 SON
EXTRANJEROS.

Scientific and technical manpower   5.1
Personnel scientifique et technique
Personal científico y técnico

SOLOMON ISLANDS:
  E—> DATA RELATE TO THE YEAR 1971/72.
  FR—> LES DONNEES SE REFERENT A L'ANNEE 1971/72.
  ESP> LOS DATOS SE REFIEREN AL AÑO 1971/72.

U.S.S.R.:
  E—> REFERS TO SPECIALISTS IN THE NATIONAL
ECONOMY, I.E. PERSONS HAVING COMPLETED EDUCATION
AT THE THIRD LEVEL FOR SCIENTISTS AND ENGINEERS
AND SECONDARY SPECIALIZED EDUCATION FOR TECHNI-
CIANS.
  FR—> LES CHIFFRES SE REFERENT AUX SPECIALISTES
EMPLOYES DANS L'ECONOMIE NATIONALE, C.A.D., AUX
PERSONNES AYANT COMPLETE LES ETUDES DU TROISIEME
DEGRE POUR LES SCIENTIFIQUES ET INGENIEURS ET
L'EDUCATION SECONDAIRE SPECIALISEE POUR LES
TECHNICIENS.
  ESP> SE TRATA DE ESPECIALISTAS EMPLEADOS EN LA
ECONOMIA NACIONAL, ES DECIR, DE LAS PERSONAS QUE
COMPLETARON LOS ESTUDIOS DE TERCER GRADO PARA
LOS CIENTIFICOS E INGENIEROS Y LA ENSEÑANZA
SECUNDARIA ESPECIALIZADA PARA LOS TECNICOS.

BYELORUSSIAN S.S.R.:
  E—> REFERS TO SPECIALISTS IN THE NATIONAL
ECONOMY, I.E. PERSONS HAVING COMPLETED EDUCATION
AT THE THIRD LEVEL FOR SCIENTISTS AND ENGINEERS
AND SECONDARY SPECIALIZED EDUCATION FOR TECHNI-
CIANS.

BYELORUSSIAN S.S.R. (CONT.):
  FR—> LES CHIFFRES SE REFERENT AUX SPECIALISTES
EMPLOYES DANS L'ECONOMIE NATIONALE, C.A.D., AUX
PERSONNES AYANT COMPLETE LES ETUDES DU TROISIEME
DEGRE POUR LES SCIENTIFIQUES ET INGENIEURS ET
L'EDUCATION SECONDAIRE SPECIALISEE POUR LES
TECHNICIENS.
  ESP> SE TRATA DE ESPECIALISTAS EMPLEADOS EN LA
ECONOMIA NACIONAL, ES DECIR, DE LAS PERSONAS QUE
COMPLETARON LOS ESTUDIOS DE TERCER GRADO PARA
LOS CIENTIFICOS E INGENIEROS Y LA ENSEÑANZA
SECUNDARIA ESPECIALIZADA PARA LOS TECNICOS.

UKRAINIAN S.S.R.:
  E—> REFERS TO SPECIALISTS IN THE NATIONAL
ECONOMY, I.E. PERSONS HAVING COMPLETED EDUCATION
AT THE THIRD LEVEL FOR SCIENTISTS AND ENGINEERS
AND SECONDARY SPECIALIZED EDUCATION FOR TECHNI-
CIANS.
  FR—> LES CHIFFRES SE REFERENT AUX SPECIALISTES
EMPLOYES DANS L'ECONOMIE NATIONALE, C.A.D., AUX
PERSONNES AYANT COMPLETE LES ETUDES DU TROISIEME
DEGRE POUR LES SCIENTIFIQUES ET INGENIEURS ET
L'EDUCATION SECONDAIRE SPECIALISEE POUR LES
TECHNICIENS.
  ESP> SE TRATA DE ESPECIALISTAS EMPLEADOS EN LA
ECONOMIA NACIONAL, ES DECIR, DE LAS PERSONAS QUE
COMPLETARON LOS ESTUDIOS DE TERCER GRADO PARA
LOS CIENTIFICOS E INGENIEROS Y LA ENSEÑANZA
SECUNDARIA ESPECIALIZADA PARA LOS TECNICOS.

5.2   Scientific and technical personnel in R&D
       Personnel scientifique et technique dans la R-D
       Personal científico y técnico en I y D

5.2 Number of scientists, engineers and technicians engaged in research and experimental development

Nombre de scientifiques, d'ingénieurs et de techniciens employés à des travaux de recherche et de développement expérimental

Número de científicos, ingenieros y técnicos empleados en trabajos de investigación y de desarrollo experimental

PLEASE REFER TO INTRODUCTION FOR DEFINITIONS OF CATEGORIES IN THIS TABLE.	POUR LES DEFINITIONS DES CATE—GORIES PRESENTEES DANS CE TABLEAU, SE REFERER A L'INTRODUCTION.	EN LA INTRODUCCION SE DAN LAS DEFINICIONES DE LAS CATE—GORIAS QUE FIGURAN EN ESTE CUADRO.
SET = SCIENTISTS, ENGINEERS AND TECHNICIANS	SET = SCIENTIFIQUES, INGENIEURS ET TECHNICIENS	SET = CIENTIFICOS, INGENIEROS Y TECNICOS
FTE = FULL—TIME EQUIVALENT	FTE = EQUIVALENT PLEIN TEMPS	FTE = EQUIVALENTE DE JORNADA COMPLETA
NUMBER OF COUNTRIES AND TERRITORIES PRESENTED IN THIS TABLE: 118	NOMBRE DE PAYS ET DE TERRITOIRES PRESENTES DANS CE TABLEAU: 118	NUMERO DE PAISES Y DE TERRITORIOS PRESENTADOS EN ESTE CUADRO: 118

COUNTRY / PAYS / PAIS	YEAR / ANNEE / AÑO	TOTAL	SCIENTISTS AND ENGINEERS / SCIENTIFIQUES ET INGENIEURS / CIENTIFICOS E INGENIEROS (FTE)		TECHNICIANS / TECHNICIENS / TECNICOS	
		(SET)	TOTAL	F	TOTAL	F
		(1)	(2)	(3)	(4)	(5)
AFRICA						
ALGERIA ‡	1972	342	242	...	100	...
BOTSWANA	1973	42	24	–	18	–
CENTRAL AFRICAN REPUBLIC ‡	1975	79	76	8	3	–
CHAD ‡	1971	187	85	...	102	...
CONGO ‡	1977	...	284	...	...	...
EGYPT	1973	...	10 665	...	...	...
GABON ‡	1970	28	8	...	20	...
GHANA ‡	1976	9 819	4 084	...	5 735	...
IVORY COAST	1970	541	319	...	222	...
KENYA ‡	1975	544	361	...	183	...
LIBYAN ARAB JAMAHIRIYA ‡	1973	*192	*50	...	142	...
MADAGASCAR ‡	1971	298	201	19	97	...
MALAWI ‡	1977	431	189	7	242	4
MAURITIUS	1977	301	151	7	150	6
NIGER ‡	1976	94	93	18	1	–
NIGERIA ‡	1970	*2 816	2 083	...	*733	...
SENEGAL	1972	908	392	...	516	...
SEYCHELLES	1973	1	1	–	–	–
SUDAN	1978	6 537	3 266	...	3 271	...
TOGO ‡	1976	445	261	...	184	...

Scientific and technical personnel in R&D   5.2
Personnel scientifique et technique dans la R-D
Personal científico y técnico en I y D

COUNTRY / PAYS / PAIS	YEAR / ANNEE / AÑO	TOTAL / TOTAL / TOTAL	SCIENTISTS AND ENGINEERS / SCIENTIFIQUES ET INGENIEURS / CIENTIFICOS E INGENIEROS (FTE)		TECHNICIANS / TECHNICIENS / TECNICOS	
		(SET)	TOTAL	F	TOTAL	F
		(1)	(2)	(3)	(4)	(5)
TUNISIA ‡	1972	*1 370	*818	...	*552	...
UNITED REPUBLIC OF CAMEROON ‡	1970	...	329	...	...	...
ZAMBIA ‡	1976	400	250	24	150	9
AMERICA, NORTH						
BAHAMAS ‡	1970	*20	*19	—	*1	—
BELIZE	1970	19	15	—	4	—
BERMUDA ‡	1970	7	4	...	3	...
BRITISH VIRGIN ISLANDS	1973	—	—	—	—	—
CANADA	1977	40 553	24 590	...	15 963	...
CAYMAN ISLANDS	1971	6	3	—	3	1
CUBA	1978	11 049	4 972	...	6 077	...
EL SALVADOR ‡	1974	*1 321	802	...	*519	...
GUATEMALA	1978	981	549	...	432	...
HONDURAS ‡	1974	6	5	1	1	—
MEXICO	1974	...	5 896	1 247	...	...
PANAMA ‡	1975	505	204	67	301	*49
ST. PIERRE AND MIQUELON ‡	1972	11	7	—	4	1
TRINIDAD AND TOBAGO ‡	1970	572	380	...	192	...
TURKS AND CAICOS ISLANDS ‡	1976	2	2	1	—	—
UNITED STATES OF AMERICA ‡	1978	652 072	585 500	...	66 572	...
U.S. VIRGIN ISLANDS	1973	—	—	—	—	—
AMERICA, SOUTH						
ARGENTINA ‡	1978	*19 650	*8 250	...	*11 400	...
BRAZIL ‡	1978	...	24 015	...	34 559	...
CHILE	1975	...	5 948	...	...	...
COLOMBIA ‡	1971	...	1 140	...	...	...
ECUADOR ‡	1976	880	469	60	411	37
FALKLAND ISLANDS (MALVINAS)	1971	—	—	—	—	—
PARAGUAY	1971		134	...	...	...
PERU	1976	*6 167	*3 932	...	*2 235	...
URUGUAY ‡	1971	*2 237	*1 150	...	*1 087	...
VENEZUELA	1975	...	1 759	...	...	...
ASIA						
BANGLADESH ‡	1973	2 412	1 649	...	763	...
BRUNEI	1974	39	22	—	17	—
BURMA	1975	2 220	1 720	...	500	...
CYPRUS	1971	271	117	...	154	...
INDIA ‡	1976	54 105	28 233	...	25 872	...
INDONESIA ‡	1975	12 965	7 645	...	5 320	...
IRAN	1972	5 753	4 896	...	857	...
IRAQ ‡	1974	1 862	1 486	363	376	81
ISRAEL ‡	1978	...	14 722	...	...	...
JAPAN ‡	1978	492 082	407 708	...	84 374	...

5.2 Scientific and technical personnel in R&D
Personnel scientifique et technique dans la R-D
Personal científico y técnico en I y D

COUNTRY PAYS PAIS	YEAR ANNEE AÑO	TOTAL TOTAL TOTAL (SET)	SCIENTISTS AND ENGINEERS SCIENTIFIQUES ET INGENIEURS CIENTIFICOS E INGENIEROS (FTE) TOTAL	F	TECHNICIANS TECHNICIENS TECNICOS TOTAL	F
		(1)	(2)	(3)	(4)	(5)
JORDAN ‡	1977	...	452	21	...	...
KOREA, REPUBLIC OF ‡	1978	23 658	14 749	...	8 909	...
KUWAIT ‡	1977	767	606	96	161	21
LAO PEOPLE'S DEMOCRATIC REPUBLIC	1970	...	364	...	...	...
MONGOLIA ‡	1971	...	797	...	...	...
PAKISTAN ‡	1973	8 790	4 164	...	4 626	...
PHILIPPINES ‡	1976	6 055	3 647	...	2 408	...
SINGAPORE	1978	728	461	...	267	...
SRI LANKA ‡	1972	7 341	2 076	...	5 265	...
THAILAND ‡	1974	...	6 097	...	...	...
TURKEY ‡	1975	...	8 910	...	3 891	...
VIET—NAM ‡	1978	19 090	13 050	...	6 040	...
YEMEN ‡	1974	112	60	—	52	—
EUROPE						
AUSTRIA ‡	1972	4 660	1 870	...	2 790	...
BELGIUM	1977	21 579	13 883	...	7 696	...
BULGARIA ‡	1978	44 338	33 656	...	10 682	...
CZECHOSLOVAKIA ‡	1978	109 961	50 007	...	59 954	...
DENMARK ‡	1976	13 801	5 353	...	8 448	...
FINLAND ‡	1977	14 254	7 162	...	7 092	...
FRANCE ‡	1977	222 111	67 981	...	154 130	...
GERMAN DEMOCRATIC REPUBLIC ‡	1975	159 000	91 000	...	68 000	...
GERMANY, FEDERAL REPUBLIC OF	1977	215 372	110 972	...	104 400	...
GIBRALTAR	1971	—	—	—	—	—
GREECE	1976	4 328	2 569	...	1 759	...
HOLY SEE	1976	362	351	6	11	...
HUNGARY ‡	1978	51 192	25 308	...	25 884	...
ICELAND ‡	1975	547	229	...	318	...
IRELAND	1977	4 150	2 685	...	1 465	...
ITALY	1976	65 446	37 878	...	27 568	...
MALTA ‡	1973	61	39	...	22	...
NETHERLANDS ‡	1976	54 100	24 250	...	29 850	...
NORWAY ‡	1978	13 990	6 450	...	7 540	...
POLAND ‡	1978	153 700	91 600	...	62 100	...
PORTUGAL	1976	4 010	1 749	...	2 261	...
ROMANIA	1973	38 758	26 107	9 833	12 651	5 898
SAN MARINO	1977	—	—	—	—	—
SPAIN	1974	11 855	7 924	1 564	3 931	243
SWEDEN ‡	1977	36 283	14 102	...	22 181	...
SWITZERLAND ‡	1976	*26 586	*16 660	*1 700	*9 926	*3 500
UNITED KINGDOM ‡	1975	155 100	79 300	...	75 800	...
YUGOSLAVIA ‡	1978	33 828	22 048	...	11 780	...

Scientific and technical personnel in R&D 5.2
Personnel scientifique et technique dans la R-D
Personal científico y técnico en I y D

COUNTRY PAYS PAIS	YEAR ANNEE AÑO	TOTAL TOTAL TOTAL (SET)	SCIENTISTS AND ENGINEERS SCIENTIFIQUES ET INGENIEURS CIENTIFICOS E INGENIEROS (FTE)		TECHNICIANS TECHNICIENS TECNICOS	
			TOTAL	F	TOTAL	F
		(1)	(2)	(3)	(4)	(5)
OCEANIA						
AMERICAN SAMOA ‡	1971	5	3	—	2	—
AUSTRALIA ‡	1976	35 078	22 510	...	12 568	...
COOK ISLANDS	1970	9	9	...	—	...
FRENCH POLYNESIA ‡	1976	32	11	...	21	...
GUAM ‡	1978	*32	*12	...	*20	...
NAURU	1970	—	—	—	—	—
NEW CALEDONIA	1971	1	—	—	1	—
NEW HEBRIDES	1975	4	3	.5	1	—
NEW ZEALAND	1975	6 823	3 659	...	3 164	...
NORFOLK ISLAND	1973	—	—	—	—	—
PACIFIC ISLANDS	1978	16	5	...	11	...
PAPUA NEW GUINEA	1973	...	131	...	...	...
SAMOA ‡	1978	232	140	...	92	...
TOKELAU ISLANDS	1971	—	—	—	—	—
U.S.S.R.						
U.S.S.R. ‡	1978	...	1 314 000	522 600	...	...
BYELORUSSIAN S.S.R. ‡	1978	...	35 111	14 459	...	...
UKRAINIAN S.S.R. ‡	1978	...	185 134	67 930	...	...

ALGERIA:
E—> DATA RELATE TO THE HIGHER EDUCATION SECTOR ONLY.
FR-> LES DONNEES NE CONCERNENT QUE LE SECTEUR DE L'ENSEIGNEMENT SUPERIEUR.
ESP> LOS DATOS SE REFIEREN EXCLUSIVAMENTE AL SECTOR DE ENSEÑANZA SUPERIOR.

CENTRAL AFRICAN REPUBLIC:
E—> DATA RELATE TO THE HIGHER EDUCATION SECTOR ONLY.
FR-> LES DONNEES NE CONCERNENT QUE LE SECTEUR DE L'ENSEIGNEMENT SUPERIEUR.
ESP> LOS DATOS SE REFIEREN EXCLUSIVAMENTE AL SECTOR DE ENSEÑANZA SUPERIOR.

CHAD:
E—> DATA REFER TO 4 RESEARCH INSTITUTES ONLY.
FR-> LES DONNEES NE CONCERNENT QUE 4 INSTITUTS DE RECHERCHE.
ESP> LOS DATOS SE REFIEREN A 4 CENTROS DE INVESTIGACION SOLAMENTE.

CONGO:
E—> FULL-TIME PLUS PART-TIME SCIENTISTS AND ENGINEERS IN THE PRODUCTIVE SECTOR (NON-INTEGRATED R&D) AND THE HIGHER EDUCATION SECTOR ONLY.
FR-> SCIENTIFIQUES ET INGENIEURS A PLEIN TEMPS ET A TEMPS PARTIEL DANS LE SECTEUR DE LA PRODUCTION (ACTIVITES DE R-D NON-INTEGREES) ET LE SECTEUR DE L'ENSEIGNEMENT SUPERIEUR.
ESP> PARA LOS CIENTIFICOS E INGENIEROS DEL SECTOR PRODUCTIVO (ACTIVIDADES DE I Y D NO INTEGRADAS) Y DEL SECTOR DE ENSEÑANZA SUPERIOR, LOS DATOS SE REFIEREN A LOS EFECTIVOS DE JORNADA COMPLETA Y DE JORNADA PARCIAL.

GABON:
E—> DATA RELATE TO THE FRENCH "OFFICE DE LA RECHERCHE SCIENTIFIQUE ET TECHNIQUE OUTRE-MER" (ORSTOM) ONLY; THE SCIENTISTS AND ENGINEERS SHOWN IN COLUMN 2 ARE ALL FOREIGNERS.
FR-> LES DONNEES NE CONCERNENT QUE L'OFFICE FRANCAIS DE LA RECHERCHE SCIENTIFIQUE ET TECHNIQUE OUTRE-MER (ORSTOM). LES SCIENTIFIQUES ET INGENIEURS DE LA COLONNE 2 SONT TOUS RESSORTISSANTS ETRANGERS.
ESP> LOS DATOS SE REFIEREN AL "OFFICE(FRANCAIS) DE LA RECHERCHE SCIENTIFIQUE ET TECHNIQUE OUTRE-MER" (ORSTOM) SOLAMENTE. LOS CIENTIFICOS E INGENIEROS DE LA COLUMNA 2 SON TODOS EXTRANJEROS.

GHANA:
E—> DATA IN COLUMNS 1 AND 4 INCLUDE AUXILIARY PERSONNEL.
FR-> LES CHIFFRES DES COLONNES 1 ET 4 COMPRENNENT LE PERSONNEL AUXILIAIRE.
ESP> LAS CIFRAS DE LAS COLUMNAS 1 Y 4 INCLUYEN EL PERSONAL AUXILIAR.

KENYA:
E—> NOT INCLUDING DATA FOR HUMANITIES.
FR-> NON COMPRIS LES DONNEES POUR LES SCIENCES HUMAINES.
ESP> EXCLUIDOS LOS DATOS RELATIVOS A LAS CIENCIAS HUMANAS.

LIBYAN ARAB JAMAHIRIYA:
E—> APPROXIMATELY 80% OF THE SCIENTISTS AND ENGINEERS IN COLUMN 2 AND 40% OF THE TECHNICIANS IN COLUMN 4 ARE FOREIGNERS.

5.2   Scientific and technical personnel in R&D
Personnel scientifique et technique dans la R-D
Personal científico y técnico en I y D

LIBYAN ARAB JAMAHIRIYA (CONT.):
FR—> ENVIRON 80% DES SCIENTIFIQUES ET INGENIEURS
DE LA COLONNE 2 ET 40% DES TECHNICIENS DE LA
COLONNE 4 SONT RESSORTISSANTS ETRANGERS.
ESP> APROXIMADAMENTE EL 80% DE LOS CIENTIFICOS E
INGENIEROS DE LA COLUMNA 2 Y EL 40% DE LOS
TECNICOS DE LA COLUMNA 4 SON EXTRANJEROS.

MADAGASCAR:
E—> NOT INCLUDING DATA FOR THE PRODUCTIVE
SECTOR (INTEGRATED R&D).
FR—> NON COMPRIS LES DONNEES POUR LE SECTEUR DE
LA PRODUCTION (ACTIVITES DE R-D INTEGREES)
ESP> EXCLUIDOS LOS DATOS RELATIVOS AL SECTOR
PRODUCTIVO (ACTIVIDADES DE I Y D INTEGRADAS).

MALAWI:
E—> 115 OF THE SCIENTISTS AND ENGINEERS IN
COLUMN 2 AND 2 OF THE TECHNICIANS IN COLUMN 4
ARE FOREIGNERS.
FR—> 115 SCIENTIFIQUES ET INGENIEURS DE LA
COLONNE 2 ET 2 TECHNICIENS DE LA COLONNE 4 SONT
RESSORTISSANTS ETRANGERS.
ESP> 115 CIENTIFICOS E INGENIEROS DE LA COLUMNA
2 Y 2 TECNICOS DE LA COLUMNA 4 SON EXTRANJEROS.

NIGER:
E—> DATA REFER TO THE HIGHER EDUCATION SECTOR
ONLY. 59 (F. 18) OF THE SCIENTISTS AND ENGINEERS
IN COLUMNS 2 AND 3 ARE FOREIGNERS.
FR—> LES DONNEES NE CONCERNENT QUE LE SECTEUR DE
L'ENSEIGNEMENT SUPERIEUR. 59 (F. 18) SCIENTIFIQUES
ET INGENIEURS DES COLONNES 2 ET 3 SONT RESSOR-
TISSANTS ETRANGERS.
ESP> LOS DATOS SOLO INCLUYEN EL SECTOR DE
ENSEÑANZA SUPERIOR. 59 (F. 18) CIENTIFICOS E INGE-
NIEROS DE LAS COLUMNAS 2 Y 3 SON EXTRANJEROS.

NIGERIA:
E—> DATA RELATE TO THE YEAR 1970/71 AND DO NOT
INCLUDE DATA FOR SOCIAL SCIENCES AND HUMANITIES.
FR—> LES DONNEES SE REFERENT A L'ANNEE 1970/71
ET NE COMPRENNENT PAS LES DONNEES POUR LES SCIEN-
CES SOCIALES ET HUMAINES.
ESP> LOS DATOS SE REFIEREN AL AÑO 1970/71 Y NO
INCLUYEN LAS CIENCIAS SOCIALES Y HUMANAS.

TOGO:
E—> DATA REFERRING TO SCIENTISTS AND ENGINEERS
ARE FULL-TIME.
FR—> POUR LES SCIENTIFIQUES ET INGENIEURS, LES
DONNEES SE REFERENT AUX EFFECTIFS A PLEIN TEMPS.
ESP> PARA LOS CIENTIFICOS E INGENIEROS LOS DATOS
SE REFIEREN A LOS EFECTIVOS DE JORNADA COMPLETA.

TUNISIA:
E—> DATA RELATE TO THE NUMBER OF FULL-TIME PLUS
PART-TIME SCIENTISTS AND ENGINEERS.
FR—> LES DONNEES SE REFERENT AU NOMBRE DE SCIEN-
TIFIQUES ET INGENIEURS A PLEIN TEMPS ET A TEMPS
PARTIEL.
ESP> LOS DATOS SE REFIEREN AL NUMERO DE CIENTI-
FICOS E INGENIEROS DE JORNADA COMPLETA Y DE
JORNADA PARCIAL.

UNITED REPUBLIC OF CAMEROON:
E—> DATA RELATE TO THE YEAR 1970/71. APPROXI-
MATELY 204 OF THE SCIENTISTS AND ENGINEERS IN
COLUMN 2 ARE FOREIGNERS.
FR—> LES DONNEES SE REFERENT A L'ANNEE 1970/71.
ENVIRON 204 DES SCIENTIFIQUES ET INGENIEURS DE LA
COLONNE 2 SONT RESSORTISSANTS ETRANGERS.
ESP> LOS DATOS SE REFIEREN AL AÑO 1970/71.
APROXIMADAMENTE 204 CIENTIFICOS E INGENIEROS DE
LA COLUMNA 2 SON EXTRANJEROS.

ZAMBIA:
E—> PARTIAL DATA FOR 9 INSTITUTES ONLY. 222 OF
THE SCIENTISTS AND ENGINEERS IN COLUMN 2 ARE
FOREIGNERS.
FR—> DONNEES PARTIELLES POUR 9 INSTITUTS SEULE-
MENT. 222 SCIENTIFIQUES ET INGENIEURS DE LA COLON-
NE 2 SONT RESSORTISSANTS ETRANGERS.
ESP> DATOS PARCIALES PARA 9 INSTITUTOS
SOLAMENTE. 222 CIENTIFICOS E INGENIEROS DE LA
COLUMNA 2 SON EXTRANJEROS.

BAHAMAS:
E—> DATA REFER TO THE CENTRAL GOVERNMENT ONLY.
FR—> LES DONNEES NE CONCERNENT QUE LE GOUVERNE-
MENT CENTRAL.
ESP> LOS DATOS SOLO SE REFIEREN AL GOBIERNO
CENTRAL.

BERMUDA:
E—> NOT INCLUDING DATA FOR THE PRODUCTIVE
SECTOR AND EXCLUDING LAW, HUMANITIES AND EDUCA-
TION.
FR—> NON COMPRIS LES DONNEES POUR LE SECTEUR
DE LA PRODUCTION ET COMPTE NON TENU DES DONNEES
RELATIVES AU DROIT, AUX SCIENCES HUMAINES ET A
L'EDUCATION.
ESP> EXCLUIDOS LOS DATOS RELATIVOS AL SECTOR
PRODUCTIVO Y LOS QUE SE REFIEREN AL DERECHO, LAS
CIENCIAS HUMANAS Y LA EDUCACION.

EL SALVADOR:
E—> DATA CONCERN 28 INSTITUTES OUT OF A TOTAL
OF 41 WHICH PERFORM R&D.
FR—> LES DONNEES NE CONCERNENT QUE 28 INSTITUTS
SUR UN TOTAL DE 41 QUI EXECUTENT LES ACTIVITES DE
R-D.
ESP> LOS DATOS SOLO SE REFIEREN A 28 CENTROS
SOBRE UN TOTAL DE 41 QUE EJECUTAN ACTIVIDADES DE
I Y D.

HONDURAS:
E—> DATA RELATE TO ONE RESEARCH INSTITUTE ONLY.
SCIENTISTS AND ENGINEERS ARE FULL-TIME.
FR—> LES DONNEES NE CONCERNENT QU'UN INSTITUT DE
RECHERCHE. POUR LES SCIENTIFIQUES ET INGENIEURS,
LES DONNEES SE REFERENT AUX EFFECTIFS A PLEIN
TEMPS.
ESP> LOS DATOS SE REFIEREN A UN CENTRO DE INVES-
TIGACION SOLAMENTE. PARA LOS CIENTIFICOS E INGE-
NIEROS LOS DATOS SE REFIEREN A LOS EFECTIVOS DE
JORNADA COMPLETA.

PANAMA:
E—> THE TOTAL NUMBER OF TECHNICIANS INCLUDES 60
PERSONS FOR WHOM A DISTRIBUTION BY SEX IS NOT
AVAILABLE.
FR—> LE NOMBRE TOTAL DE TECHNICIENS COMPREND 60
PERSONNES POUR LESQUELLES LA REPARTITION PAR SEXE
N'EST PAS DISPONIBLE.
ESP> EL NUMERO TOTAL DE TECNICOS COMPRENDE 60
PERSONAS PARA LAS QUE SE DESCONOCE LA REPARTICION
POR SEXO.

ST PIERRE AND MIQUELON:
E—> DATA RELATE TO THE "INSTITUT SCIENTIFIQUE
ET TECHNIQUE DES PECHES MARITIMES" ONLY.
FR—> LES DONNEES NE CONCERNENT QUE L'INSTITUT
SCIENTIFIQUE ET TECHNIQUE DES PECHES MARITIMES.
ESP> LOS DATOS SOLO SE REFIEREN AL "INSTITUT
SCIENTIFIQUE ET TECHNIQUE DES PECHES MARITIMES".

TRINIDAD AND TOBAGO:
E—> DATA RELATE TO FULL-TIME PLUS PART-TIME
PERSONNEL AND DO NOT INCLUDE LAW, EDUCATION AND
ARTS.

Scientific and technical personnel in R&D 5.2
Personnel scientifique et technique dans la R-D
Personal científico y técnico en I y D

TRINIDAD AND TOBAGO (CONT.):
FR-> LES DONNEES SE REFERENT AU PERSONNEL A
PLEIN TEMPS ET A TEMPS PARTIEL ET NE COMPRENNENT
PAS LES DONNEES POUR LE DROIT, L'EDUCATION ET LES
ARTS.
ESP> LOS DATOS SE REFIEREN AL PERSONAL DE
JORNADA COMPLETA Y DE JORNADA PARCIAL Y EXCLUYEN
LOS DATOS RELATIVOS AL DERECHO, LA EDUCACION Y
LAS ARTES.

TURKS AND CAICOS:
E--> SCIENTISTS AND ENGINEERS ARE ALL
FOREIGNERS.
FR-> LES SCIENTIFIQUES ET INGENIEURS SONT TOUS
RESSORTISSANTS ETRANGERS.
ESP> TODOS LOS CIENTIFICOS E INGENIEROS SON
EXTRANJEROS.

UNITED STATES OF AMERICA:
E--> NOT INCLUDING DATA FOR LAW, HUMANITIES AND
EDUCATION. THE FIGURE IN COLUMN 4 CONCERNS TECH-
NICIANS IN HIGHER EDUCATION SECTOR ONLY.
FR-> NON COMPRIS LES DONNEES POUR LE DROIT, LES
SCIENCES HUMAINES ET L'EDUCATION. LE CHIFFRE DE
LA COLONNE 4 NE CONCERNE QUE LES TECHNICIENS DU
SECTEUR DE L'ENSEIGNEMENT SUPERIEUR.
ESP> EXCLUIDOS LOS DATOS RELATIVOS AL DERECHO,
LAS CIENCIAS HUMANAS Y LA EDUCACION. LA CIFRA DE
LA COLUMNA 4 SOLO SE REFIERE A LOS TECNICOS DEL
SECTOR DE ENSEÑANZA SUPERIOR.

ARGENTINA:
E--> DATA ARE IN NET MAN-YEARS.
FR-> LES DONNEES SONT EN ANNEES-HOMMES NETTES.
ESP> LOS DATOS SE INDICAN EN ANOS-HOMBRE NETOS.

BRAZIL:
E--> THE FIGURE IN COLUMN 2 DOES NOT INCLUDE
DATA FOR THE GENERAL SERVICE SECTOR WHILST THE
FIGURE IN COLUMN 4 REFERS TO THE PRODUCTIVE SECTOR
ONLY AND INCLUDES AUXILIARY PERSONNEL.
FR-> LE CHIFFRE DE LA COLONNE 2 NE TIENT PAS
COMPTE DES DONNEES RELATIVES AU SECTEUR DE SERVICE
GENERAL, TANDIS QUE LE CHIFFRE DE LA COLONNE 4 NE
SE REFERE QU'AU SECTEUR DE LA PRODUCTION ET NE
COMPREND PAS LE PERSONNEL AUXILIAIRE.
ESP> LA CIFRA DE LA COLUMNA 2 NO INCLUYE LOS
DATOS RELATIVOS AL SECTOR DE SEVICIO GENERAL,
MIENTRAS QUE LA CIFRA DE LA COLUMNA 4 SOLO SE
REFIERE AL SECTOR PRODUCTIVO Y NO COMPRENDE EL
PERSONAL AUXILIAR.

COLOMBIA:
E--> DATA RELATE TO THE NUMBER OF FULL-TIME
PLUS PART-TIME SCIENTISTS AND ENGINEERS AND DO NOT
INCLUDE LAW, HUMANITIES AND EDUCATION.
FR-> LES DONNEES SE REFERENT AU NOMBRE DE SCIEN-
TIFIQUES ET INGENIEURS A PLEIN TEMPS ET A TEMPS
PARTIEL ET NE COMPRENNENT PAS LE DROIT, LES SCIEN-
CES HUMAINES ET L'EDUCATION.
ESP> LOS DATOS SE REFIEREN AL NUMERO DE CIENTI-
FICOS E INGENIEROS DE JORNADA COMPLETA Y DE
JORNADA PARCIAL Y NO INCLUYEN EL DERECHO, LAS
CIENCIAS HUMANAS Y LA EDUCACION.

ECUADOR:
E--> DATA REFER TO R&D IN THE AGRICULTURAL
SCIENCES ONLY.
FR-> LES DONNEES SE REFERENT A LA R-D DANS LES
SCIENCES DE L'AGRICULTURE SEULEMENT.
ESP> LOS DATOS SE REFIEREN A LA I Y D DE LAS
CIENCIAS AGRICOLAS SOLAMENTE.

URUGUAY:
E--> DATA RELATE TO THE YEAR 1971/72.
FR-> LES DONNEES SE REFERENT A L'ANNEE 1971/72.
ESP> LOS DATOS SE REFIEREN AL AÑO 1971/72.

BANGLADESH:
E--> DATA RELATE TO THE YEAR 1973/74. THE
FIGURE IN COLUMN 2 REFERS TO FULL-TIME SCIENTISTS
AND ENGINEERS IN NATURAL SCIENCES AND ENGINEERING
ONLY.
FR->LES DONNEES SE REFERENT A L'ANNEE 1973/74.
LE CHIFFRE DE LA COLONNE 2 SE REFERE AUX SCIENTI-
FIQUES ET INGENIEURS A PLEIN TEMPS DANS LES
DOMAINES DES SCIENCES EXACTES ET NATURELLES ET DES
SCIENCES DE L'INGENIEUR.
ESP> LOS DATOS SE REFIEREN AL AÑO 1973/74. LA
CIFRA DE LA COLUMNA 2 SE REFIERE A LOS CIENTIFICOS
E INGENIEROS DE JORNADA COMPLETA, VINCULADOS CON
LAS CIENCIAS EXACTAS Y NATURALES Y LA INGENIERIA.

INDIA:
E--> NOT INCLUDING DATA FOR THE HIGHER EDUCATION
SECTOR. THE FIGURES IN COLUMNS 1 AND 4 INCLUDE
AUXILIARY PERSONNEL.
FR-> NON COMPRIS LES DONNEES POUR LE SECTEUR DE
L'ENSEIGNEMENT SUPERIEUR. LES CHIFFRES DES COLON-
NES 1 ET 4 COMPRENNENT LE PERSONNEL AUXILIAIRE.
ESP> EXCLUIDOS LOS DATOS RELATIVOS AL SECTOR DE
ENSEÑANZA SUPERIOR. LAS CIFRAS DE LAS COLUMNAS 1
Y 4 INCLUYEN EL PERSONAL AUXILIAR.

INDONESIA:
E--> DATA RELATE TO THE YEAR 1975/76.
FR-> LES DONNEES SE REFERENT A L'ANNEE 1975/76.
ESP> LOS DATOS SE REFIEREN AL AÑO 1975/76.

IRAQ:
E--> DATA REFER ONLY TO PERSONS WORKING IN
GOVERNMENT DEPARTMENTS CONCERNED WITH SCIENTIFIC
ACTIVITIES AND DO NOT INCLUDE THE PRODUCTIVE
SECTOR (INTEGRATED R&D); THE FIGURES IN COLUMNS 4
AND 5 ALSO EXCLUDE THE HIGHER EDUCATION SECTOR.
FR-> LES DONNEES NE SE REFERENT QU'AUX PERSONNES
EMPLOYEES DANS LES DEPARTEMENTS GOUVERNEMENTAUX
CONCERNES PAR LES ACTIVITES SCIENTIFIQUES ET NE
COMPRENNENT PAS LE SECTEUR DE LA PRODUCTION (ACTI-
VITES DE R-D INTEGREES); LES CHIFFRES DES COLONNES
4 ET 5 NE COMPRENNENT PAS LE SECTEUR DE L'ENSEI-
GNEMENT SUPERIEUR.
ESP> LOS DATOS SOLO SE REFIEREN A LAS PERSONAS
EMPLEADAS EN LOS SERVICIOS GUBERNAMENTALES QUE SE
OCUPAN DE ACTIVIDADES CIENTIFICAS Y NO INCLUYEN
EL SECTOR PRODUCTIVO (ACTIVIDADES DE I Y D INTE-
GRADAS); LAS CIFRAS DE LAS COLUMNAS 4 Y 5 NO
INCLUYEN EL SECTOR DE ENSEÑANZA SUPERIOR.

ISRAEL:
E--> DATA FOR SCIENTISTS AND ENGINEERS ARE FULL-
TIME AND INCLUDE SOME PART-TIME.
FR-> POUR LES SCIENTIFIQUES ET INGENIEURS LES
DONNEES SE REFERENT AUX EFFECTIFS A PLEIN TEMPS
ET COMPRENNENT UN CERTAIN NOMBRE A TEMPS PARTIEL.
ESP> PARA LOS CIENTIFICOS E INGENIEROS LOS DATOS
SE REFIEREN A LOS EFECTIVOS DE JORNADA COMPLETA,
INCLUYENDOSE UN CIERTO NUMERO DE JORNADA PARCIAL.

JAPAN:
E--> DATA FOR SCIENTISTS AND ENGINEERS
ARE FULL-TIME. NOT INCLUDING DATA FOR SOCIAL
SCIENCES AND HUMANITIES IN THE PRODUCTIVE SECTOR.
FR-> POUR LES SCIENTIFIQUES ET INGENIEURS, LES
DONNEES SE REFERENT AUX EFFECTIFS A PLEIN TEMPS.
NON COMPRIS LES DONNEES POUR LES SCIENCES SOCIALES
ET HUMAINES DANS LE SECTEUR DE LA PRODUCTION.
ESP> PARA LOS CIENTIFICOS E INGENIEROS LOS DATOS
SE REFIEREN A LOS EFECTIVOS DE JORNADA COMPLETA.
EXCLUIDOS LOS DATOS RELATIVOS A LAS CIENCIAS SO-
CIALES Y HUMANAS EN EL SECTOR PRODUCTIVO.

JORDAN:
E--> DATA RELATE TO THE EAST BANK ONLY. SCIEN-
TISTS AND ENGINEERS ARE FULL-TIME PLUS PART-TIME.

5.2 Scientific and technical personnel in R&D
Personnel scientifique et technique dans la R-D
Personal científico y técnico en I y D

JORDAN (CONT):
FR-> LES DONNEES SE REFERENT A LA RIVE ORIENTALE
SEULEMENT ET AU NOMBRE DE SCIENTIFIQUES ET INGE-
NIEURS A PLEIN TEMPS ET A TEMPS PARTIEL.
ESP> LOS DATOS SE REFIEREN A LA ORILLA ORIENTAL
SOLAMENTE Y AL NUMERO DE LOS CIENTIFICOS E INGE-
NIEROS DE JORNADA COMPLETA Y DE JORNADA PARCIAL.

KOREA, REPUBLIC OF:
E--> DATA RELATE TO THE NUMBER OF FULL-TIME PLUS
PART-TIME SCIENTISTS AND ENGINEERS AND DO NOT IN-
CLUDE LAW, HUMANITIES AND EDUCATION.
FR-> LES DONNEES SE REFERENT AU NOMBRE DE SCIEN-
TIFIQUES ET INGENIEURS A PLEIN TEMPS ET A TEMPS
ET NE COMPRENNENT PAS LE DROIT, LES SCIENCES
HUMAINES ET L'EDUCATION.
ESP> LOS DATOS SE REFIEREN AL NUMERO DE CIENTI-
FICOS E INGENIEROS DE JORNADA COMPLETA Y DE JOR-
NADA PARCIAL Y NO COMPRENDEN EL DERECHO, LAS
CIENCIAS HUMANAS Y LA EDUCACION.

KUWAIT:
E--> 422 (F. 45) OF THE SCIENTISTS AND ENGINEERS
IN COLUMNS 2 AND 3 AND 126 (F. 21) OF THE TECHNI-
CIANS IN COLUMNS 4 AND 5 ARE FOREIGNERS.
FR-> 422 (F. 45) SCIENTIFIQUES ET INGENIEURS DES
COLONNES 2 ET 3 ET 126 (F. 21) TECHNICIENS DES
COLONNES 4 ET 5 SONT RESSORTISSANTS ETRANGERS.
ESP> 422 (F. 45) CIENTIFICOS E INGENIEROS DE LAS
COLUMNAS 2 Y 3 Y 126 (F. 21) TECNICOS DE LAS
COLUMNAS 4 Y 5 SON EXTRANJEROS.

MONGOLIA:
E--> DATA RELATE TO THE ACADEMY OF SCIENCES
AND REFER TO SCIENTIFIC WORKERS.
FR-> LES DONNEES SE REFERENT AUX TRAVAILLEURS
SCIENTIFIQUES DE L'ACADEMIE DES SCIENCES SEULEMENT.
ESP> LOS DATOS SE REFIEREN A LOS TRABAJADORES
CIENTIFICOS DE LA ACADEMIA DE CIENCIAS SOLAMENTE.

PAKISTAN:
E--> DATA REFER TO THE YEAR 1973/74 AND RELATE
TO R&D ACTIVITIES CONCENTRATED MAINLY IN
GOVERNMENT-FINANCED RESEARCH ESTABLISHMENTS ONLY;
SOCIAL SCIENCES AND HUMANITIES IN THE HIGHER EDU-
CATION AND GENERAL SERVICE SECTORS ARE EXCLUDED.
FR-> LES DONNEES SE REFERENT A L'ANNEE 1973/74
ET CONCERNENT LES ACTIVITES DE R-D SE TROUVANT
POUR LA PLUPART DANS LES ETABLISSEMENTS DE RECHER-
CHE FINANCES PAR LE GOUVERNEMENT; LES SCIENCES
SOCIALES ET HUMAINES DES SECTEURS DE L'ENSEIGNE-
MENT SUPERIEUR ET DE SERVICE GENERAL SONT EXCLUES.
ESP> LOS DATOS SE REFIEREN AL AÑO 1973/74 Y
A LAS ACTIVIDADES DE I Y D CONCENTRADAS PRINCIPAL-
MENTE EN LOS ESTABLECIMIENTOS DE INVESTIGACION
SUBVENCIONADOS POR EL GOBIERNO; QUEDAN EXCLUIDAS
LAS CIENCIAS SOCIALES Y HUMANAS DE LOS SECTORES
DE ENSEÑANZA SUPERIOR Y DE SERVICIO GENERAL.

PHILIPPINES:
E--> DATA RELATE TO THE GENERAL SERVICE SECTOR
ONLY; SCIENTISTS AND ENGINEERS ARE FULL-TIME PLUS
PART-TIME.
FR-> LES DONNEES NE CONCERNENT QUE LE SECTEUR DE
SERVICE GENERAL; LES SCIENTIFIQUES ET INGENIEURS
SONT A PLEIN TEMPS ET A TEMPS PARTIEL.
ESP> LOS DATOS SOLO SE REFIEREN AL SECTOR DE
SERVICIO GENERAL; LOS CIENTIFICOS E INGENIEROS
ENGLOBAN LOS DE JORNADA COMPLETA Y DE JORNADA
PARCIAL.

SRI LANKA:
E--> NOT INCLUDING DATA FOR LAW, HUMANITIES AND
EDUCATION; DATA FOR THE PRODUCTIVE SECTOR (NON-
INTEGRATED R&D) ARE ALSO EXCLUDED. SCIENTISTS
AND ENGINEERS ARE FULL-TIME.

SRI LANKA (CONT.):
FR-> NON COMPRIS LES DONNEES POUR LE DROIT, LES
SCIENCES HUMAINES ET L'EDUCATION; COMPTE NON TENU
DES DONNEES RELATIVES AU SECTEUR DE LA PRODUCTION
(ACTIVITES DE R-D NON-INTEGREES). LES SCIENTIFI-
QUES ET INGENIEURS SONT A PLEIN TEMPS.
ESP> EXCLUIDOS LOS DATOS RELATIVOS AL DERECHO,
LAS CIENCIAS HUMANAS Y LA EDUCACION; NO SE
INCLUYEN LOS DATOS DEL SECTOR PRODUCTIVO (ACTIVI-
DADES DE I Y D NO-INTEGRADAS). LOS CIENTIFICOS E
INGENIEROS SON DE JORNADA COMPLETA.

THAILAND:
E--> DATA REFER TO THE YEAR 1974/75 AND RELATE
TO THE NATIONAL RESEARCH COUNCIL.
FR-> LES DONNEES SE REFERENT A L'ANNEE 1974/75
ET AU "NATIONAL RESEARCH COUNCIL".
ESP> LOS DATOS SE REFIEREN AL AÑO 1974/75 Y AL
"NATIONAL RESEARCH COUNCIL".

TURKEY:
E--> DATA REFER TO THE YEAR 1975/76. THE
FIGURE IN COLUMN 2 REFERS TO THE HIGHER EDUCATION
AND GENERAL SERVICE SECTORS WHILST THE FIGURE IN
COLUMN 4 REFERS TO THE GENERAL SERVICE SECTOR
ONLY. NOT INCLUDING DATA FOR SOCIAL SCIENCES AND
HUMANITIES.
FR-> LES DONNEES SE REFERENT A L'ANNEE 1975/76.
LE CHIFFRE DE LA COLONNE 2 SE REFERE AUX SECTEURS
DE L'ENSEIGNEMENT SUPERIEUR ET DE SERVICE GENERAL,
TANDIS QUE LE CHIFFRE DE LA COLONNE 4 NE SE REFERE
QU'AU SECTEUR DE SERVICE GENERAL. COMPTE NON TENU
DES SCIENCES SOCIALES ET HUMAINES.
ESP> LOS DATOS SE REFIEREN AL AÑO 1975/76. LA
CIFRA DE LA COLUMNA 2 SE REFIERE A LOS SECTORES DE
ENSEÑANZA SUPERIOR Y DE SERVICIO GENERAL, MIENTRAS
QUE LA CIFRA DE LA COLUMNA 4 SOLO SE REFIERE AL
SECTOR DE SERVICIO GENERAL. EXCLUIDAS LAS CIEN-
CIAS SOCIALES Y HUMANAS.

VIET-NAM:
E--> THE FIGURE IN COLUMN 4 DOES NOT INCLUDE
DATA FOR THE HIGHER EDUCATION SECTOR.
FR-> LE CHIFFRE DE LA COLONNE 4 NE COMPREND PAS
LES DONNEES RELATIVES AU SECTEUR DE L'ENSEIGNEMENT
SUPERIEUR.
ESP> LA CIFRA DE LA COLUMNA 4 NO INCLUYE LOS
DATOS RELATIVOS AL SECTOR DE ENSEÑANZA SUPERIOR.

YEMEN:
E--> DATA RELATE TO THE YEAR 1974/75.
FR-> LES DONNEES SE REFERENT A L'ANNEE
1974/75.
ESP> LOS DATOS SE REFIEREN AL AÑO 1974/75.

AUSTRIA:
E--> DATA RELATE TO THE PRODUCTIVE SECTOR ONLY.
FR-> LES DONNEES SE REFERENT AU SECTEUR DE LA
PRODUCTION SEULEMENT.
ESP> LOS DATOS SE REFIEREN AL SECTOR PRODUCTIVO
SOLAMENTE.

BULGARIA:
E--> THE FIGURE IN COLUMN 4 DOES NOT INCLUDE
DATA FOR THE HIGHER EDUCATION SECTOR.
FR-> LE CHIFFRE DE LA COLONNE 4 NE COMPREND PAS
LES DONNEES RELATIVES AU SECTEUR DE L'ENSEIGNEMENT
SUPERIEUR.
ESP> LA CIFRA DE LA COLUMNA 4 NO INCLUYE LOS
DATOS RELATIVOS AL SECTOR DE ENSEÑANZA SUPERIOR.

CZECHOSLOVAKIA:
E-->NOT INCLUDING SCIENTISTS AND ENGINEERS EN-
GAGED IN THE ADMINISTRATION OF R&D; OF MILITARY
R&D ONLY THAT PART CARRIED OUT IN CIVIL ESTA-
BLISHMENT IS INCLUDED.

Scientific and technical personnel in R&D   5.2
Personnel scientifique et technique dans la R-D
Personal científico y técnico en I y D

CZECHOSLOVAKIA (CONT.):
FR—> NON—COMPRIS LES SCIENTIFIQUES ET INGENIEURS EMPLOYES DANS LES SERVICES ADMINISTRATIFS DE R-D; POUR LA R—D DE CARACTERE MILITAIRE, SEULE LA PARTIE EFFECTUEE DANS LES ETABLISSEMENTS CIVILS A ETE CONSIDEREE.
ESP> EXCLUIDOS LOS CIENTIFICOS E INGENIEROS EM—PLEADOS EN LOS SERVICIOS ADMINISTRATIVOS DE I Y D; PARA LAS ACTIVIDADES DE I Y D DE CARACTER MILITAR SOLO SE HA CONSIDERADO LA PARTE CORRESPONDIENTE A LOS ESTABLECIMIENTOS CIVILES.

DENMARK:
E—> DATA RELATE TO THE YEAR 1976/77. THE FIGURES IN COLUMNS 1 AND 4 INCLUDE AUXILIARY PERSONNEL.
FR—> LES DONNEES SE REFERENT A L'ANNEE 1976/77. LES CHIFFRES DES COLONNES 1 ET 4 COMPRENNENT LE PERSONNEL AUXILIAIRE.
ESP> LOS DATOS SE REFIEREN AL AÑO 1976/77. LAS CIFRAS DE LAS COLUMNAS 1 Y 4 INCLUYEN EL PERSONAL AUXILIAR.

FINLAND:
E—> DATA IN COLUMNS 1 AND 4 INCLUDE AUXILIARY PERSONNEL.
FR—> LES CHIFFRES DES COLONNES 1 ET 4 COMPREN—NENT LE PERSONNEL AUXILIAIRE.
ESP> LAS CIFRAS DE LAS COLUMNAS 1 Y 4 INCLUYEN EL PERSONAL AUXILIAR.

FRANCE:
E—> DATA IN COLUMNS 1 AND 4 INCLUDE AUXILIARY PERSONNEL.
FR—> LES CHIFFRES DES COLONNES 1 ET 4 COMPREN—NENT LE PERSONNEL AUXILIAIRE.
ESP> LAS CIFRAS DE LAS COLUMNAS 1 Y 4 INCLUYEN EL PERSONAL AUXILIAR.

GERMAN DEMOCRATIC REPUBLIC:
E—> DATA IN COLUMNS 1 AND 4 INCLUDE AUXILIARY PERSONNEL.
FR—> LES CHIFFRES DES COLONNES 1 ET 4 COMPREN—NENT LE PERSONNEL AUXILIAIRE.
ESP> LAS CIFRAS DE LAS COLUMNAS 1 Y 4 INCLUYEN EL PERSONAL AUXILIAR.

HUNGARY:
E—> NOT INCLUDING SCIENTISTS AND ENGINEERS EN—GAGED IN THE ADMINISTRATION OF R&D; FIGURES IN COLUMNS 1 AND 4 INCLUDE SKILLED WORKERS.
FR—> NON COMPRIS LES SCIENTIFIQUES ET INGENIEURS EMPLOYES DANS LES SERVICES ADMINISTRATIFS DE R-D; LES CHIFFRES DES COLONNES 1 ET 4 COMPRENNENT LES OUVRIERS QUALIFIES.
ESP> NO INCLUYE LOS CIENTIFICOS E INGENIEROS EMPLEADOS EN LOS SERVICIOS ADMINISTRATIVOS DE I Y D. LAS CIFRAS DE LAS COLUMNAS 1 Y 4 COMPRENDEN LOS OBREROS CALIFICADOS.

ICELAND:
E—> NOT INCLUDING DATA FOR SOCIAL SCIENCES AND HUMANITIES.
FR—> COMPTE NON TENU DES SCIENCES SOCIALES ET HUMAINES.
ESP> EXCLUIDAS LAS CIENCIAS SOCIALES Y HUMANAS.

MALTA:
E—> DATA RELATE TO THE HIGHER EDUCATION SECTOR ONLY.
FR—> LES DONNEES NE CONCERNENT QUE LE SECTEUR DE L'ENSEIGNEMENT SUPERIEUR.
ESP> LOS DATOS SE REFIEREN EXCLUSIVAMENTE AL SECTOR DE ENSEÑANZA SUPERIOR.

NETHERLANDS:
E—> NOT INCLUDING DATA FOR SOCIAL SCIENCES AND HUMANITIES IN THE PRODUCTIVE SECTOR (INTEGRATED R&D). THE FIGURES IN COLUMNS 1 AND 4 INCLUDE AUXILIARY PERSONNEL.
FR—> NON COMPRIS LES SCIENCES SOCIALES ET HUMAI—NES DANS LES ACTIVITES DE R-D INTEGREES DU SECTEUR DE LA PRODUCTION. LES CHIFFRES DES COLONNES 1 ET 4 COMPRENNENT LE PERSONNEL AUXILIAIRE.
ESP> EXCLUIDAS LAS CIENCIAS SOCIALES Y HUMANAS EN LAS ACTIVIDADES DE I Y D INTEGRADAS DEL SECTOR PRODUCTIVO. LAS CIFRAS DE LAS COLUMNAS 1 Y 4 INCLUYEN EL PERSONAL AUXILIAR.

NORWAY:
E—> DATA IN COLUMNS 1 AND 4 INCLUDE AUXILIARY PERSONNEL.
FR—> LES CHIFFRES DES COLONNES 1 ET 4 COMPREN—NENT LE PERSONNEL AUXILIAIRE.
ESP> LAS CIFRAS DE LAS COLUMNAS 1 Y 4 INCLUYEN EL PERSONAL AUXILIAR.

POLAND:
E—> THE FIGURE IN COLUMN 4 REFERS TO PERSONS WITH A VOCATIONAL EDUCATION AT THE SECOND LEVEL; NOT INCLUDING TECHNICIANS IN THE HIGHER EDUCATION SECTOR.
FR—> LE CHIFFRE DE LA COLONNE 4 CONCERNE LES PERSONNES AYANT SUIVI UN ENSEIGNEMENT TECHNIQUE DU SECOND DEGRE; COMPTE NON TENU DES TECHNICIENS DANS LE SECTEUR DE L'ENSEIGNEMENT SUPERIEUR.
ESP> LA CIFRA DE LA COLUMNA 4 SE REFIERE A LAS PERSONAS QUE HAN RECIBIDO UNA FORMACION TECNICA DE SEGUNDO GRADO; EXCLUIDOS LOS TECNICOS DEL SECTOR DE ENSEÑANZA SUPERIOR.

SWEDEN:
E—> NOT INCLUDING DATA FOR SOCIAL SCIENCES AND HUMANITIES. THE FIGURES IN COLUMNS 1 AND 4 INCLUDE AUXILIARY PERSONNEL.
FR—> COMPTE NON TENU DES SCIENCES SOCIALES ET HUMAINES. LES CHIFFRES DES COLONNES 1 ET 4 COM—PRENNENT LE PERSONNEL AUXILIAIRE.
ESP> EXCLUIDAS LAS CIENCIAS SOCIALES Y HUMANAS. LAS CIFRAS DE LAS COLUMNAS 1 Y 4 INCLUYEN EL PERSONAL AUXILIAR.

SWITZERLAND:
E—> DATA IN COLUMNS 1,4 AND 5 INCLUDE AUXILIARY PERSONNEL.
FR—> LES CHIFFRES DES COLONNES 1,4 ET 5 COMPREN—NENT LE PERSONNEL AUXILIAIRE.
ESP> LAS CIFRAS DE LAS COLUMNAS 1,4 Y 5 INCLUYEN EL PERSONAL AUXILIAR.

UNITED KINGDOM:
E—> DATA RELATE TO THE YEAR 1975/76 AND DO NOT INCLUDE THE HIGHER EDUCATION SECTOR.
FR—> LES DONNEES SE REFERENT A L'ANNEE 1975/76 ET NE COMPRENNENT PAS LE SECTEUR DE L'ENSEIGNEMENT SUPERIEUR.
ESP> LOS DATOS SE REFIEREN AL AÑO 1975/76 Y NO COMPRENDEN EL SECTOR DE ENSEÑANZA SUPERIOR.

YUGOSLAVIA:
E—> NOT INCLUDING ACTIVITIES OF A MILITARY NATURE OR RELATING TO NATIONAL DEFENCE.
FR—> NON COMPRIS LES ACTIVITES DE CARACTERE MILITAIRE OU RELEVANT DE LA DEFENSE NATIONALE.
ESP> EXCLUIDAS LAS ACTIVIDADES DE CARACTER MILITAR O QUE CONCIERNEN LA DEFENSA NACIONAL.

AMERICAN SAMOA:
E—> DATA RELATE TO ONE RESEARCH INSTITUTE ONLY.

5.2 Scientific and technical personnel in R&D
Personnel scientifique et technique dans la R-D
Personal científico y técnico en I y D

AMERICAN SAMOA (CONT.):
FR—> LES DONNEES NE CONCERNENT QU'UN INSTITUT DE RECHERCHE.
ESP> LOS DATOS SE REFIEREN A UN CENTRO DE INVESTIGACION SOLAMENTE.

AUSTRALIA:
E—> DATA RELATE TO THE YEAR 1976/77.
FR—> LES DONNEES SE REFERENT A L'ANNEE 1976/77.
ESP> LOS DATOS SE REFIEREN AL AÑO 1976/77.

FRENCH POLYNESIA:
E—> DATA RELATE TO ONE RESEARCH INSTITUTE ONLY. SCIENTISTS AND ENGINEERS ARE FULL-TIME.
FR—> LES DONNEES NE CONCERNENT QU'UN INSTITUT DE RECHERCHE.POUR LES SCIENTIFIQUES ET INGENIEURS, LES DONNEES SE REFERENT AUX EFFECTIFS A PLEIN TEMPS.
ESP> LOS DATOS SE REFIEREN A UN CENTRO DE INVESTIGACION SOLAMENTE. PARA LOS CIENTIFICOS E INGENIEROS LOS DATOS SE REFIEREN A LOS EFECTIVOS DE JORNADA COMPLETA.

GUAM:
E—> DATA RELATE TO THE HIGHER EDUCATION SECTOR ONLY.
FR—> LES DONNEES NE CONCERNENT QUE LE SECTEUR DE L'ENSEIGNEMENT SUPERIEUR.
ESP> LOS DATOS SE REFIEREN EXCLUSIVAMENTE AL SECTOR DE ENSEÑANZA SUPERIOR.

SAMOA:
E—> DATA REFERRING TO SCIENTISTS AND ENGINEERS ARE FULL-TIME.
FR—> POUR LES SCIENTIFIQUES ET INGENIEURS, LES DONNEES SE REFERENT AUX EFFECTIFS A PLEIN TEMPS.
ESP> PARA LOS CIENTIFICOS E INGENIEROS LOS DATOS SE REFIEREN A LOS EFECTIVOS DE JORNADA COMPLETA.

U.S.S.R.:
E—> THE FIGURES IN COLUMNS 2 AND 3 REFER TO SCIENTIFIC WORKERS, I.E. ALL PERSONS WITH A HIGHER SCIENTIFIC DEGREE OR SCIENTIFIC TITLE, REGARDLESS OF THE NATURE OF THEIR WORK; PERSONS UNDERTAKING RESEARCH WORK IN SCIENTIFIC ESTABLISHMENTS AND SCIENTIFIC TEACHING STAFF IN INSTITUTIONS OF HIGHER EDUCATION; ALSO INCLUDES PERSONS UNDERTAKING SCIENTIFIC WORK IN INDUSTRIAL ENTERPRISES.
FR—> LES CHIFFRES DES COLONNES 2 ET 3 SE REFERENT AUX TRAVAILLEURS SCIENTIFIQUES, C'EST—A—DIRE, A TOUTES LES PERSONNES AYANT UN DIPLOME SCIENTIFIQUE SUPERIEUR OU UN TITRE SCIENTIFIQUE, SANS CONSIDERATION DE LA NATURE DE LEUR TRAVAIL; AUX PERSONNES QUI EFFECTUENT UN TRAVAIL DE RECHERCHE DANS DES INSTITUTIONS SCIENTIFIQUES ET AU PERSONNEL SCIENTIFIQUE ENSEIGNANT DANS DES ETABLISSEMENTS D'ENSEIGNEMENT SUPERIEUR; SONT INCLUSES AUSSI LES PERSONNES QUI EFFECTUENT DES TRAVAUX SCIENTIFIQUES DANS LES ENTREPRISES INDUSTRIELLES.
ESP> LAS CIFRAS DE LAS COLUMNAS 2 Y 3 SE REFIEREN A LOS TRABAJADORES CIENTIFICOS, ES DECIR, A TODAS LAS PERSONAS QUE POSEEN UN DIPLOMA CIENTIFICO SUPERIOR O UN TITULO CIENTIFICO, SIN TENER EN CUENTA LA NATURALEZA DE SU TRABAJO; A LAS PERSONAS QUE EFECTUAN UN TRABAJO DE INVESTIGACION EN LAS INSTITUCIONES CIENTIFICAS Y AL PERSONAL CIENTIFICO QUE EJERCE FUNCIONES DOCENTES EN LOS ESTABLECIMIENTOS DE ENSEÑANZA SUPERIOR; TAMBIEN SE INCLUYEN LAS PERSONAS QUE EFECTUAN TRABAJOS CIENTIFICOS EN LAS EMPRESAS INDUSTRIALES.

BYELORUSSIAN S.S.R.:
E—> THE FIGURES IN COLUMNS 2 AND 3 REFER TO SCIENTIFIC WORKERS, I.E. ALL PERSONS WITH A HIGHER SCIENTIFIC DEGREE OR SCIENTIFIC TITLE, REGARDLESS OF THE NATURE OF THEIR WORK; PERSONS UNDERTAKING RESEARCH WORK IN SCIENTIFIC ESTABLISHMENTS AND SCIENTIFIC TEACHING STAFF IN INSTITUTIONS OF HIGHER EDUCATION; ALSO INCLUDES PERSONS UNDERTAKING SCIENTIFIC WORK IN INDUSTRIAL ENTERPRISES.
FR—> LES CHIFFRES DES COLONNES 2 ET 3 SE REFERENT AUX TRAVAILLEURS SCIENTIFIQUES, C'EST—A—DIRE, A TOUTES LES PERSONNES AYANT UN DIPLOME SCIENTIFIQUE SUPERIEUR OU UN TITRE SCIENTIFIQUE, SANS CONSIDERATION DE LA NATURE DE LEUR TRAVAIL; AUX PERSONNES QUI EFFECTUENT UN TRAVAIL DE RECHERCHE DANS DES INSTITUTIONS SCIENTIFIQUES ET AU PERSONNEL SCIENTIFIQUE ENSEIGNANT DANS DES ETABLISSEMENTS D'ENSEIGNEMENT SUPERIEUR; SONT INCLUSES AUSSI LES PERSONNES QUI EFFECTUENT DES TRAVAUX SCIENTIFIQUES DANS LES ENTREPRISES INDUSTRIELLES.
ESP> LAS CIFRAS DE LAS COLUMNAS 2 Y 3 SE REFIEREN A LOS TRABAJADORES CIENTIFICOS, ES DECIR, A TODAS LAS PERSONAS QUE POSEEN UN DIPLOMA CIENTIFICO SUPERIOR O UN TITULO CIENTIFICO, SIN TENER EN CUENTA LA NATURALEZA DE SU TRABAJO; A LAS PERSONAS QUE EFECTUAN UN TRABAJO DE INVESTIGACION EN LAS INSTITUCIONES CIENTIFICAS Y AL PERSONAL CIENTIFICO QUE EJERCE FUNCIONES DOCENTES EN LOS ESTABLECIMIENTOS DE ENSEÑANZA SUPERIOR; TAMBIEN SE INCLUYEN LAS PERSONAS QUE EFECTUAN TRABAJOS CIENTIFICOS EN LAS EMPRESAS INDUSTRIALES.

UKRAINIAN S.S.R.:
E—> THE FIGURES IN COLUMNS 2 AND 3 REFER TO SCIENTIFIC WORKERS, I.E. ALL PERSONS WITH A HIGHER SCIENTIFIC DEGREE OR SCIENTIFIC TITLE, REGARDLESS OF THE NATURE OF THEIR WORK; PERSONS UNDERTAKING RESEARCH WORK IN SCIENTIFIC ESTABLISHMENTS AND SCIENTIFIC TEACHING STAFF IN INSTITUTIONS OF HIGHER EDUCATION; ALSO INCLUDES PERSONS UNDERTAKING SCIENTIFIC WORK IN INDUSTRIAL ENTERPRISES.
FR—> LES CHIFFRES DES COLONNES 2 ET 3 SE REFERENT AUX TRAVAILLEURS SCIENTIFIQUES, C'EST—A—DIRE, A TOUTES LES PERSONNES AYANT UN DIPLOME SCIENTIFIQUE SUPERIEUR OU UN TITRE SCIENTIFIQUE, SANS CONSIDERATION DE LA NATURE DE LEUR TRAVAIL; AUX PERSONNES QUI EFFECTUENT UN TRAVAIL DE RECHERCHE DANS DES INSTITUTIONS SCIENTIFIQUES ET AU PERSONNEL SCIENTIFIQUE ENSEIGNANT DANS DES ETABLISSEMENTS D'ENSEIGNEMENT SUPERIEUR; SONT INCLUSES AUSSI LES PERSONNES QUI EFFECTUENT DES TRAVAUX SCIENTIFIQUES DANS LES ENTREPRISES INDUSTRIELLES.
ESP> LAS CIFRAS DE LAS COLUMNAS 2 Y 3 SE REFIEREN A LOS TRABAJADORES CIENTIFICOS, ES DECIR, A TODAS LAS PERSONAS QUE POSEEN UN DIPLOMA CIENTIFICO SUPERIOR O UN TITULO CIENTIFICO, SIN TENER EN CUENTA LA NATURALEZA DE SU TRABAJO; A LAS PERSONAS QUE EFECTUAN UN TRABAJO DE INVESTIGACION EN LAS INSTITUCIONES CIENTIFICAS Y AL PERSONAL CIENTIFICO QUE EJERCE FUNCIONES DOCENTES EN LOS ESTABLECIMIENTOS DE ENSEÑANZA SUPERIOR; TAMBIEN SE INCLUYEN LAS PERSONAS QUE EFECTUAN TRABAJOS CIENTIFICOS EN LAS EMPRESAS INDUSTRIALES.

R&D scientists and engineers by field of science 5.3
Scientifiques et ingénieurs de R-D par discipline scientifique
Científicos e ingenieros de I y D por rama de la ciencia

5.3 Number of scientists and engineers engaged in research and experimental development by field of science

Nombre de scientifiques et d'ingénieurs employés à des travaux de recherche et de développement expérimental, par discipline scientifique

Número de científicos y de ingenieros empleados en trabajos de investigación y de desarrollo experimental, según la rama de la ciencia

PLEASE REFER TO INTRODUCTION FOR DEFINITIONS OF CATEGORIES IN THIS TABLE.	POUR LES DEFINITIONS DES CATE-GORIES PRESENTEES DANS CE TA-BLEAU, SE REFERER A L'INTRO-DUCTION.	EN LA INTRODUCCION SE DAN LAS DEFINICIONES DE LAS CATE-GORIAS QUE FIGURAN EN ESTE CUADRO.

FT = FULL TIME
PT = PART-TIME
FT+PT = FULL-TIME PLUS PART-TIME
FTE = FULL-TIME EQUIVALENT

FT = A PLEIN TEMPS
PT = A TEMPS PARTIEL
FT+PT = A PLEIN TEMPS ET A TEMPS PARTIEL ENSEMBLE
FTE = EQUIVALENT PLEIN TEMPS

FT = JORNADA COMPLETA
PT = JORNADA PARCIAL
FT+PT = JORNADA COMPLETA MAS JORNADA PARCIAL
FTE = EQUIVALENTE DE JOR-NADA COMPLETA

NUMBER OF COUNTRIES AND TERRITORIES PRESENTED IN THIS TABLE: 95

NOMBRE DE PAYS ET DE TERRITOIRES PRESENTES DANS CE TABLEAU: 95

NUMERO DE PAISES Y DE TERRITORIOS PRESENTADOS EN ESTE CUADRO: 95

COUNTRY / PAYS / PAIS	YEAR / ANNEE / AÑO	SEX / SEXE / SEXO	FT PT FTE	TOTAL (1)	NATURAL SCIENCES / SCIENCES EXACTES ET NATURELLES / CIENCIAS EXACTAS Y NATURALES (2)	ENGINEERING AND TECHNOLOGY / SCIENCES DE L'IN-GENIEUR / INGE-NIERIA Y TECNOLOGIA (3)	MEDICAL SCIENCES / SCIENCES MEDICALES / CIENCIAS MEDICAS (4)	AGRI-CULTURE / AGRI-CULTURE / AGRI-CULTURA (5)	SOCIAL SCIENCES AND HUMANITIES / SCIENCES SOCIALES ET HUMAINES / CIENCIAS SOCIALES Y HUMANAS (6)
AFRICA									
ALGERIA ‡	1972	MF	FT	–	–	–	–	–	—
		MF	PT	726	349	31	99	247	——>
		MF	FTE	242	117	9	33	83	——>
BOTSWANA	1973	MF	FT	16	–	–	–	16	–
		MF	PT	16	–	–	–	16	–
		MF	FTE	24	–	–	–	24	–
		F	FTE	–	–	–	–	–	–
CENTRAL AFRICAN REPUBLIC ‡	1975	MF	FT	62	35	5	–	4	18
		MF	PT	29	–	10	–	–	19
		MF	FTE	76	35	9	–	4	28
		F	FTE	8	1	3	–	–	4
CHAD ‡	1971	MF	FT	85	24	7	16	12	26
		MF	PT	–	–	–	–	–	–
		MF	FTE	85	24	7	16	12	26
CONGO ‡	1977	MF	FT	48	15	6	2	23	2
		MF	PT	236	73	17	8	12	126

5.3 R&D scientists and engineers by field of science
Scientifiques et ingénieurs de R-D par discipline scientifique
Científicos e ingenieros de I y D por rama de la ciencia

COUNTRY	YEAR	SEX	FT	TOTAL	FIELD OF SCIENCE / DISCIPLINE SCIENTIFIQUE / RAMA DE LA CIENCIA					
					NATURAL SCIENCES	ENGINEER- ING AND TECHNOLOGY	MEDICAL SCIENCES	AGRI- CULTURE	SOCIAL SCIENCES AND HUMANITIES
PAYS	ANNEE	SEXE	PT	TOTAL	SCIENCES EXACTES ET NATURELLES	SCIENCES DE L'IN- GENIEUR	SCIENCES MEDICALES	AGRI- CULTURE	SCIENCES SOCIALES ET HUMAINES
PAIS	AÑO	SEXO	FTE	TOTAL	CIENCIAS EXACTAS Y NATURALES	INGE- NIERIA Y TECNOLOGIA	CIENCIAS MEDICAS	AGRI- CULTURA	CIENCIAS SOCIALES Y HUMANAS
				(1)	(2)	(3)	(4)	(5)	(6)
EGYPT	1973	MF	FT	6 913	1 408	680	391	4 087	347
		MF	PT	11 256	2 301	1 944	2 889	2 082	2 040
		MF	FTE	10 665	2 175	1 328	1 354	4 781	1 027
GABON ‡	1970	MF	FT	8	4	—	—	—	4
		MF	PT	—	—	—	—	—	—
		MF	FTE	8	4	—	—	—	4
IVORY COAST	1970	MF	FT	319	84	—	14	173	48
		MF	PT	—	—	—	—	—	—
		MF	FTE	319	84	—	14	173	48
KENYA ‡	1975	MF	FTE	361	99	28	16	183	35
LIBYAN ARAB JAMAHIRIYA	1973	MF	FT	30	19	——→	—	11	—
		MF	PT	64	21	——→	15	3	25
		MF	FTE	*50	*25	——→	*5	*12	*8
MADAGASCAR ‡	1971	MF	FT	151	67	15	5	64	—
		MF	PT	151	66	—	8	9	68
		MF	FTE	201	89	15	8	67	22
		F	FTE	19	18	—	—	1	—
MALAWI	1977	MF	FT	118	35	1	—	63	19
		MF	PT	145	42	38	4	16	45
		MF	FTE	189	56	20	2	71	40
		F	FTE	7	2	—	—	—	5
MAURITIUS	1977	MF	FT	122	—	6	—	95	21
		MF	PT	77	15	20	—	37	5
		MF	FTE	151	5	10	—	113	23
		F	FTE	7	—	1	—	5	1
NIGER ‡	1976	MF	FT	93	46	—	4	9	34
		MF	PT	—	—	—	—	—	—
		MF	FTE	93	46	—	4	9	34
		F	FTE	18	9	—	—	—	9
NIGERIA ‡	1970	MF	FTE	2 083	548	409	582	544	...
SENEGAL	1972	MF	FT	232	45	36	8	121	22
		MF	PT	377	40	28	101	22	186
		MF	FTE	392	65	45	42	132	108
SEYCHELLES	1973	MF	FT	1	—	—	—	1	—
		MF	PT	—	—	—	—	—	—
		MF	FTE	1	—	—	—	1	—
		F	FTE	—	—	—	—	—	—
SUDAN ‡	1974	MF	FT	2 979	576	346	240	480	913
TOGO	1976	MF	FT	261	44	29	32	16	140
ZAMBIA ‡	1976	MF	FTE	250	83	112	10	21	24
		F	FTE	24	6	10	2	2	4

R&D scientists and engineers by field of science   5.3
Scientifiques et ingénieurs de R-D par discipline scientifique
Científicos e ingenieros de I y D por rama de la ciencia

					FIELD OF SCIENCE / DISCIPLINE SCIENTIFIQUE / RAMA DE LA CIENCIA				
COUNTRY	YEAR	SEX		TOTAL	NATURAL SCIENCES	ENGINEER- ING AND TECHNOLOGY	MEDICAL SCIENCES	AGRI- CULTURE	SOCIAL SCIENCES AND HUMANITIES
PAYS	ANNEE	SEXE	FT PT	TOTAL	SCIENCES EXACTES ET NATURELLES	SCIENCES DE L'IN- GENIEUR	SCIENCES MEDICALES	AGRI- CULTURE	SCIENCES SOCIALES ET HUMAINES
PAIS	AÑO	SEXO	FTE	TOTAL	CIENCIAS EXACTAS Y NATURALES	INGE- NIERIA Y TECNOLOGIA	CIENCIAS MEDICAS	AGRI- CULTURA	CIENCIAS SOCIALES Y HUMANAS
				(1)	(2)	(3)	(4)	(5)	(6)
AMERICA, NORTH									
BAHAMAS ‡	1970	MF	FTE	*19	*2	–	–	*10	*7
		F	FTE	–	–	–	–	–	–
BELIZE	1970	MF	FT	10	–	–	–	10	–
		MF	PT	10	–	–	–	10	–
		MF	FTE	15	–	–	–	15	–
		F	FTE	–	–	–	–	–	–
BERMUDA ‡	1970	MF	FT	–	–	–	–	–	...
		MF	PT	9	–	–	–	9	...
		MF	FTE	4	–	–	–	4	...
CAYMAN ISLANDS	1971	MF	FT	3	1	1	–	–	1
		MF	PT	–	–	–	–	–	–
		MF	FTE	3	1	1	–	–	1
		F	FTE	–	–	–	–	–	–
CUBA	1978	MF	FTE	4 972	668	1 441	1 112	1 257	494
EL SALVADOR ‡	1974	MF	FT	674	190	71	153	78	182
		MF	PT	255	–	98	60	14	83
		MF	FTE	802	190	120	183	85	224
GUATEMALA	1974	MF	FT	250	34	79	16	49	72
		MF	PT	134	18	42	9	27	38
		MF	FTE	310	43	98	20	61	88
HONDURAS ‡	1974	MF	FT	5	–	5	–	–	–
		F	FT	1	–	1	–	–	–
MEXICO ‡	1974	MF	FT	2 227	631	422	216	375	519
		MF	PT	6 219	1 379	1 232	919	594	1 772
		MF	FTE	5 896	1 523	1 170	648	765	1 535
		F	FTE	1 247	340	64	227	34	509
PANAMA ‡	1975	MF	FT	193	39	41	31	33	28
		MF	PT	34	1	2	21	–	–
		MF	FTE	204	39	41	40	33	28
		F	FTE	67	19	9	23	3	8
ST. PIERRE AND MIQUELON ‡	1972	MF	FT	7	7	–	–	–	–
		MF	PT	–	–	–	–	–	–
		MF	FTE	7	7	–	–	–	–
		F	FTE	–	–	–	–	–	–
TRINIDAD AND TOBAGO ‡	1970	MF	FT+PT	380	121	71	23	74	91
TURKS AND CAICOS ISLANDS	1976	MF	FT	2	2	–	–	–	–
		MF	PT	–	–	–	–	–	–
		MF	FTE	2	2	–	–	–	–
		F	FTE	1	1	–	–	–	–

5.3 R&D scientists and engineers by field of science
Scientifiques et ingénieurs de R-D par discipline scientifique
Científicos e ingenieros de I y D por rama de la ciencia

					FIELD OF SCIENCE / DISCIPLINE SCIENTIFIQUE / RAMA DE LA CIENCIA				
COUNTRY	YEAR	SEX	FT	TOTAL	NATURAL SCIENCES	ENGINEER- ING AND TECHNOLOGY	MEDICAL SCIENCES	AGRI- CULTURE	SOCIAL SCIENCES AND HUMANITIES
PAYS	ANNEE	SEXE	PT	TOTAL	SCIENCES EXACTES ET NATURELLES	SCIENCES DE L'IN- GENIEUR	SCIENCES MEDICALES	AGRI- CULTURE	SCIENCES SOCIALES ET HUMAINES
PAIS	AÑO	SEXO	FTE	TOTAL	CIENCIAS EXACTAS Y NATURALES	INGE- NIERIA Y TECNOLOGIA	CIENCIAS MEDICAS	AGRI- CULTURA	CIENCIAS SOCIALES Y HUMANAS
				(1)	(2)	(3)	(4)	(5)	(6)
AMERICA, SOUTH									
ARGENTINA ‡	1976	MF	FTE	*8 000	*2 960	*1 150	*1 750	*1 110	*1 030
		F	FTE	*1 975	*960	*70	*410	*120	*415
CHILE	1975	MF	FTE	5 948	1 885	1 367	1 562	411	723
COLOMBIA ‡	1971	MF	FT+PT	1 140	188	154	127	348	323
ECUADOR ‡	1976	MF	FT	378	88	33	—	242	15
		MF	PT	239	26	26	—	180	7
		MF	FTE	469	100	45	—	304	20
		F	FTE	60	38	9	—	9	4
PERU ‡	1970	MF	FT	1 522	445	76	267	494	151
		MF	PT	318	100	13	125	24	54
		MF	FTE	1 686	496	83	330	507	180
		F	FT+PT	197	83	6	56	28	13
URUGUAY ‡	1971	MF	FT+PT	*1 537	*184	*356	*359	*253	*160
		MF	FTE	*1 150	*142	*285	*239	*253	*109
VENEZUELA ‡	1975	MF	FTE	1 759	528	253	287	320	300
ASIA									
BANGLADESH ‡	1973	MF	FT	1 649	1 649	———>	...	...	...
BRUNEI	1971	MF	FT	7	2	—	—	5	—
		MF	PT	—	—	—	—	—	—
		MF	FTE	7	2	—	—	5	—
BURMA	1975	MF	FTE	1 720	900	300	120	100	300
CYPRUS	1971	MF	FT	117	15	—	10	35	57
		MF	PT	—	—	—	—	—	—
		MF	FTE	117	15	—	10	35	57
IRAN	1971	MF	FT	1 927	...	...	...	...	...
		MF	PT	4 972	...	...	...	...	...
		MF	FTE	3 584	509	279	703	1 294	799
IRAQ ‡	1974	MF	FT	1 209	374	133	6	355	341
		MF	PT	2 563	608	390	398	477	690
		MF	FTE	1 486	439	173	46	417	411
		F	FTE	363	185	12	7	31	128
ISRAEL	1974	MF	FT+PT	21 900	6 500	5 700	2 800	900	6 000
JAPAN ‡	1974	MF	FT	292 097	72 402	97 862	45 414	20 153	43 401
		F	FT	16 338	2 129	429	4 437	395	8 948
JORDAN ‡	1976	MF	FTE	208	37	42	7	43	79
KOREA, REPUBLIC OF ‡	1977	MF	FT+PT	12 771	2 001	5 635	1 558	2 880	697
KUWAIT	1977	MF	FTE	606	109	165	9	52	271
		F	FTE	96	30	13	—	15	38

R&D scientists and engineers by field of science 5.3
Scientifiques et ingénieurs de R-D par discipline scientifique
Científicos e ingenieros de I y D por rama de la ciencia

| | | | | FIELD OF SCIENCE / DISCIPLINE SCIENTIFIQUE / RAMA DE LA CIENCIA | | | | | |
COUNTRY PAYS PAIS	YEAR ANNEE AÑO	SEX SEXE SEXO	FT PT FTE	TOTAL TOTAL TOTAL	NATURAL SCIENCES SCIENCES EXACTES ET NATURELLES CIENCIAS EXACTAS Y NATURALES	ENGINEER- ING AND TECHNOLOGY SCIENCES DE L'IN- GENIEUR INGE- NIERIA Y TECNOLOGIA	MEDICAL SCIENCES SCIENCES MEDICALES CIENCIAS MEDICAS	AGRI- CULTURE AGRI- CULTURE AGRI- CULTURA	SOCIAL SCIENCES AND HUMANITIES SCIENCES SOCIALES ET HUMAINES CIENCIAS SOCIALES Y HUMANAS
				(1)	(2)	(3)	(4)	(5)	(6)
LAO PEOPLE'S DEMOCRATIC REPUBLIC	1970	MF	FTE	364	6	27	33	29	269
MONGOLIA ‡	1971	MF	FT	797	517	–	–	–	280
PAKISTAN ‡	1973	MF	FTE	4 164	113	1 431	194	1 809	617
PHILIPPINES ‡	1976	MF MF	FT PT	3 284 363	868 74	267 35	135 20	1 309 35	705 199
SRI LANKA ‡	1972	MF	FT	2 076	592	916	170	281	117
THAILAND ‡	1974	MF	FTE	6 097	547	724	853	764	3 209
TURKEY ‡	1975	MF	FTE	8 910	1 350	1 484	3 982	2 094	...
YEMEN ‡	1974	MF MF MF F	FT PT FTE FTE	60 – 60 –	23 – 23 –	– – – –	– – – –	30 – 30 –	7 – 7 –
EUROPE									
AUSTRIA ‡	1972	MF	FTE	1 870	75	1 779	1	11	4
BELGIUM ‡	1973	MF	FTE	7 347	2 399	1 486	748	571	2 120
BULGARIA ‡	1977	MF F	FTE FTE	19 216 6 681	3 427 1 310	6 251 1 524	3 579 1 459	1 956 451	4 003 1 737
CZECHOSLOVAKIA ‡	1970	MF	FTE	10 415	2 945	1 806	2 414	281	2 969
DENMARK	1973	MF	FTE	4 717	923	1 803	650	449	892
FINLAND ‡	1977	MF	FTE	7 162	1 703	2 875	516	450	1 575
FRANCE	1974	MF	FTE	65 069	51 476	——>	8 250	1 833	3 510
GERMANY, FEDERAL REPUBLIC OF ‡	1971	MF	FTE	22 499	7 677	3 313	5 828	1 345	4 336
HOLY SEE	1976	MF MF MF	FT PT FTE	235 281 351	7 2 8	1 – 1	– – –	– – –	227 279 342
HUNGARY ‡	1977	MF MF MF F	FT PT FTE FT+PT	14 036 22 767 24 316 9 175	2 501 2 289 3 228 1 124	6 250 12 083 13 698 3 728	986 2 539 1 539 1 162	1 805 1 227 2 194 719	2 494 4 629 3 657 2 442
ICELAND ‡	1970	MF	FTE	126	56	42	6	22	...
IRELAND	1975	MF	FTE	2 545	804	549	134	452	606
ITALY ‡	1972	MF MF MF	FT PT FTE	15 359 29 635 32 592	1 414 6 914 5 464	12 082 5 977 15 442	810 6 392 4 505	593 1 250 1 323	238 9 009 5 592
MALTA ‡	1973	MF	FTE	39	10	1	10	–	18

5.3 R&D scientists and engineers by field of science
Scientifiques et ingénieurs de R-D par discipline scientifique
Científicos e ingenieros de I y D por rama de la ciencia

COUNTRY PAYS PAIS	YEAR ANNEE AÑO	SEX SEXE SEXO	FT PT FTE	TOTAL TOTAL TOTAL	FIELD OF SCIENCE / DISCIPLINE SCIENTIFIQUE / RAMA DE LA CIENCIA				
					NATURAL SCIENCES SCIENCES EXACTES ET NATURELLES CIENCIAS EXACTAS Y NATURALES	ENGINEER- ING AND TECHNOLOGY SCIENCES DE L'IN- GENIEUR INGE- NIERIA Y TECNOLOGIA	MEDICAL SCIENCES SCIENCES MEDICALES CIENCIAS MEDICAS	AGRI- CULTURE AGRI- CULTURE AGRI- CULTURA	SOCIAL SCIENCES AND HUMANITIES SCIENCES SOCIALES ET HUMAINES CIENCIAS SOCIALES Y HUMANAS
				(1)	(2)	(3)	(4)	(5)	(6)
NETHERLANDS ‡	1973	MF	FTE	13 261	4 500	3 954	1 508	796	2 503
NORWAY ‡	1977	MF	FTE	6 317	*1 336	*2 661	*539	*450	*1 074
POLAND	1977	MF MF MF	FT PT FTE	83 600 55 200 100 100	5 300 13 300 9 200	66 800 22 400 73 500	2 600 8 800 5 300	3 700 6 100 5 500	5 200 4 600 6 600
PORTUGAL	1976	MF MF MF	FT PT FTE	934 2 198 1 749	 475	 455	 190	 358	 271
ROMANIA	1971	MF F	FTE FTE	22 888 7 611	4 838 2 616	10 575 2 722	2 539 894	2 632 697	2 304 682
SPAIN	1974	MF MF MF F	FT PT FTE FTE	7 219 2 307 7 924 1 564	1 295 368 1 423 478	3 575 658 3 829 380	904 657 1 078 300	593 111 632 149	852 513 962 257
SWITZERLAND	1976	MF	FTE	*16 660	*5 200	*8 500	*1 200	*300	*1 460
YUGOSLAVIA ‡	1977	MF	FTE	21 680	2 464	9 282	2 428	2 706	4 800
OCEANIA									
AMERICAN SAMOA ‡	1971	MF MF MF F	FT PT FTE FTE	3 — 3 —	3 — 3 —	— — — —	— — — —	— — — —	— — — —
AUSTRALIA ‡	1973	MF	FTE	25 746	6 737	8 706	1 587	2 844	5 872
COOK ISLANDS	1970	MF	FTE	9	1	2	1	4	1
FRENCH POLYNESIA ‡	1976	MF	FT	11	—	—	11	—	—
GUAM	1977	MF	FTE	213	50	120	15	10	18
NEW CALEDONIA	1971	MF MF MF F	FT PT FTE FTE	— 1 — —	— — — —	— — — —	— — — —	— 1 — —	— — — —
NEW HEBRIDES	1975	MF MF MF F	FT PT FTE FTE	2 2 3 0.5	— — — —	— — — —	— — — —	2 2 3 0.5	— — — —
NEW ZEALAND	1973	MF	FTE	*2 948	*2 057	*335	*66	*428	*62
PACIFIC ISLANDS	1973	MF MF MF F	FT PT FTE FTE	23 — 23 1	5 — 5 1	— — — —	1 — 1 —	17 — 17 —	— — — —
PAPUA NEW GUINEA	1973	MF	FTE	131	11	20	10	60	30

R&D scientists and engineers by field of science 5.3
Scientifiques et ingénieurs de R-D par discipline scientifique
Científicos e ingenieros de I y D por rama de la ciencia

COUNTRY / PAYS / PAIS	YEAR / ANNEE / AÑO	SEX / SEXE / SEXO	FT / PT / FTE	TOTAL / TOTAL / TOTAL	FIELD OF SCIENCE / DISCIPLINE SCIENTIFIQUE / RAMA DE LA CIENCIA				
					NATURAL SCIENCES / SCIENCES EXACTES ET NATURELLES / CIENCIAS EXACTAS Y NATURALES	ENGINEER-ING AND TECHNOLOGY / SCIENCES DE L'IN-GENIEUR / INGE-NIERIA Y TECNOLOGIA	MEDICAL SCIENCES / SCIENCES MEDICALES / CIENCIAS MEDICAS	AGRI-CULTURE / AGRI-CULTURE / AGRI-CULTURA	SOCIAL SCIENCES AND HUMANITIES / SCIENCES SOCIALES ET HUMAINES / CIENCIAS SOCIALES Y HUMANAS
				(1)	(2)	(3)	(4)	(5)	(6)
SAMOA	1977	MF	FT	140	33	60	34	5	8
		MF	PT	30	8	14	6	1	1
U.S.S.R.									
U.S.S.R. ‡	1974	MF	FT	1 169 700	240 600	548 000	59 000	41 700	240 900
		MF	PT	—	—	—	—	—	—
BYELORUSSIAN S.S.R. ‡	1974	MF	FT	29 285	7 065	10 058	1 221	1 716	8 749
		MF	PT	—	—	—	—	—	—
UKRAINIAN S.S.R. ‡	1974	MF	FT	162 116	32 236	77 103	9 674	5 908	33 016
		MF	PT	—	—	—	—	—	—

ALGERIA:
E—> DATA RELATE TO THE HIGHER EDUCATION SECTOR ONLY.
FR—> LES DONNEES NE CONCERNENT QUE LE SECTEUR DE L'ENSEIGNEMENT SUPERIEUR.
ESP> LOS DATOS SE REFIEREN AL SECTOR DE DE ENSEÑANZA SUPERIOR SOLAMENTE.

CENTRAL AFRICAN REPUBLIC:
E—> DATA RELATE TO THE HIGHER EDUCATION SECTOR ONLY.
FR—> LES DONNEES NE CONCERNENT QUE LE SECTEUR DE L'ENSEIGNEMENT SUPERIEUR.
ESP> LOS DATOS SE REFIEREN AL SECTOR DE ENSEÑANZA SUPERIOR SOLAMENTE.

CHAD:
E—> DATA RELATE TO 4 RESEARCH INSTITUTES ONLY.
FR—> LES DONNEES NE CONCERNENT QUE 4 INSTITUTS DE RECHERCHE.
ESP> LOS DATOS SE REFIEREN A 4 CENTROS DE INVESTIGACION SOLAMENTE.

CONGO:
E—> DATA RELATE TO THE PRODUCTIVE SECTOR (NON-INTEGRATED R&D) AND THE HIGHER EDUCATION SECTOR ONLY.
FR—> LES DONNEES SE REFERENT AU SECTEUR DE LA PRODUCTION (ACTIVITES DE R-D NON-INTEGREES) ET LE SECTEUR DE L'ENSEIGNEMENT SUPERIEUR SEULEMENT.
ESP> LOS DATOS SE REFIEREN AL SECTOR PRODUCTIVO (ACTIVIDADES DE I Y D NO INTEGRADAS) Y AL SECTOR DE ENSEÑANZA SUPERIOR SOLAMENTE.

GABON:
E—> DATA RELATE TO THE (FRENCH) "OFFICE DE LA RECHERCHE SCIENTIFIQUE ET TECHNIQUE OUTRE—MER" (ORSTOM) ONLY.
FR—> LES DONNEES NE CONCERNENT QUE L'OFFICE FRANCAIS DE LA RECHERCHE SCIENTIFIQUE ET TECH-NIQUE OUTRE—MER (ORSTOM).
ESP> DATOS RELATIVOS AL "OFFICE (FRANCAIS) DE LA RECHERCHE SCIENTIFIQUE ET TECHNIQUE OUTRE—MER" (ORSTOM) SOLAMENTE.

KENYA:
E—> NOT INCLUDING DATA FOR HUMANITIES.
FR—> NON COMPRIS LES DONNEES POUR LES SCIENCES HUMAINES.
ESP> EXCLUIDOS LOS DATOS RELATIVOS A LAS CIEN-CIAS HUMANAS.

MADAGASCAR:
E—> NOT INCLUDING DATA FOR THE PRODUCTIVE SECTOR (INTEGRATED R&D).
FR—> NON COMPRIS LES DONNEES POUR LE SECTEUR DE LA PRODUCTION (ACTIVITES DE R-D INTEGREES).
ESP> EXCLUIDOS LOS DATOS RELATIVOS AL SECTOR PRODUCTIVO (ACTIVIDADES DE I Y D INTEGRADAS).

NIGER:
E—> DATA RELATE TO THE HIGHER EDUCATION SECTOR ONLY.
FR—> LES DONNEES NE CONCERNENT QUE LE SECTEUR DE L'ENSEIGNEMENT SUPERIEUR.
ESP> LOS DATOS SE REFIEREN AL SECTOR DE ENSEÑANZA SUPERIOR SOLAMENTE.

NIGERIA:
E—> DATA REFER TO THE YEAR 1970/71 AND DO NOT INCLUDE SOCIAL SCIENCES AND HUMANITIES.
FR—> LES DONNEES SE REFERENT A L'ANNEE 1970/71 ET NE COMPRENNENT PAS LES SCIENCES SOCIALES ET HUMAINES.
ESP> LOS DATOS SE REFIEREN AL AÑO 1970/71 Y NO INCLUYEN LAS CIENCIAS SOCIALES Y HUMANAS.

SUDAN:
E—> DATA IN COLUMN 1 INCLUDE 424 SCIENTISTS AND ENGINEERS FOR WHOM A DISTRIBUTION BY FIELD OF SCIENCE IS UNKNOWN.
FR—> LES DONNEES DE LA COLONNE 1 COMPRENNENT 424 SCIENTIFIQUES ET INGENIEURS POUR LESQUELS UNE REPARTITION PAR DISCIPLINE SCIENTIFIQUE N'EST PAS CONNUE.
ESP> LOS DATOS DE LA COLUMNA 1 COMPRENDEN 424 CIENTIFICOS E INGENIEROS PARA LOS CUALES NO SE CONOCE LA DISTRIBUCION POR DISCIPLINA CIENTIFICA.

5.3   R&D scientists and engineers by field of science
    Scientifiques et ingénieurs de R-D par discipline scientifique
    Científicos e ingenieros de I y D por rama de la ciencia

ZAMBIA:
   E—> PARTIAL DATA FOR 9 INSTITUTES ONLY.
   FR—> DONNEES PARTIELLES POUR 9 INSTITUTS
SEULEMENT.
   ESP> DATOS PARCIALES PARA 9 INSTITUTOS
SOLAMENTE.

BAHAMAS:
   E—> DATA REFER TO THE CENTRAL GOVERNMENT ONLY.
   FR—> LES DONNEES NE CONCERNENT QUE LE GOUVERNE-
MENT CENTRAL.
   ESP> LOS DATOS SOLO SE REFIEREN AL GOBIERNO
CENTRAL.

BERMUDA:
   E—> NOT INCLUDING DATA FOR THE PRODUCTIVE
SECTOR AND EXCLUDING LAW, HUMANITIES AND EDUCA-
TION.
   FR—> NON COMPRIS LES DONNEES POUR LE SECTEUR
DE LA PRODUCTION ET COMPTE NON TENU DES DONNEES
RELATIVES AU DROIT, AUX SCIENCES HUMAINES ET A
L'EDUCATION.
   ESP> NO INCLUYE LOS DATOS PARA EL SECTOR
PRODUCTIVO NI LOS QUE SE REFIEREN AL DERECHO, LAS
CIENCIAS HUMANAS Y LA EDUCACION.

EL SALVADOR:
   E—> DATA CONCERN 28 INSTITUTES OUT OF A TOTAL
OF 41 WHICH PERFORM R&D.
   FR—> LES DONNEES NE CONCERNENT QUE 28 INSTITUTS
SUR UN TOTAL DE 41 QUI EXECUTENT LES ACTIVITES DE
R-D.
   ESP> LOS DATOS SOLO SE REFIEREN A 28 CENTROS
SOBRE UN TOTAL DE 41 QUE EJECUTAN ACTIVIDADES DE
I Y D.

HONDURAS:
   E—> DATA RELATE TO ONE RESEARCH INSTITUTE ONLY.
   FR—> LES DONNEES NE CONCERNENT QU'UN INSTITUT DE
RECHERCHE.
   ESP> LOS DATOS SE REFIEREN A UN CENTRO DE INVES-
TIGACION SOLAMENTE.

MEXICO:
   E—> DATA IN COLUMN 1 INCLUDE SCIENTISTS AND
ENGINEERS FOR WHOM A DISTRIBUTION BY FIELD OF
SCIENCE IS UNKNOWN.
   FR—> LES DONNEES DE LA COLONNE 1 COMPRENNENT LES
SCIENTIFIQUES ET INGENIEURS POUR LESQUELS UNE
REPARTITION PAR DISCIPLINE SCIENTIFIQUE N'EST PAS
CONNUE.
   ESP> LOS DATOS DE LA COLUMNA 1 COMPRENDEN LOS
CIENTIFICOS E INGENIEROS PARA LOS CUALES NO SE
CONOCE LA DISTRIBUCION POR DISCIPLINA CIENTIFICA.

PANAMA:
   E—> DATA IN COLUMN 1 INCLUDE SCIENTISTS AND
ENGINEERS FOR WHOM A DISTRIBUTION BY FIELD OF
SCIENCE IS UNKNOWN.
   FR—> LES DONNEES DE LA COLONNE 1 COMPRENNENT LES
SCIENTIFIQUES ET INGENIEURS POUR LESQUELS UNE
REPARTITION PAR DISCIPLINE SCIENTIFIQUE N'EST PAS
CONNUE.
   ESP> LOS DATOS DE LA COLUMNA 1 COMPRENDEN LOS
CIENTIFICOS E INGENIEROS PARA LOS CUALES NO SE
CONOCE LA DISTRIBUCION POR DISCIPLINA CIENTIFICA.

ST. PIERRE AND MIQUELON:
   E—> DATA RELATE TO THE "INSTITUT SCIENTIFIQUE
ET TECHNIQUE DES PECHES MARITIMES" ONLY.
   FR—> LES DONNEES NE CONCERNENT QUE L'INSTITUT
SCIENTIFIQUE ET TECHNIQUE DES PECHES MARITIMES.
   ESP> LOS DATOS SE REFIEREN AL "INSTITUT SCIEN-
TIFIQUE ET TECHNIQUE DES PECHES MARITIMES"
SOLAMENTE.

TRINIDAD AND TOBAGO:
   E—> NOT INCLUDING DATA FOR LAW, EDUCATION AND
ARTS.
   FR—> NON COMPRIS LES DONNEES POUR LE DROIT,
L'EDUCATION ET LES ARTS.
   ESP> EXCLUIDOS LOS DATOS RELATIVOS AL DERECHO,
LA EDUCACION Y LAS ARTES.

ARGENTINA:
   E—> DATA ARE IN NET MAN-YEARS.
   FR—> LES DONNEES SONT EN ANNEES-HOMME NETTES.
   ESP> LOS DATOS SE INDICAN EN ANOS-HOMBRE NETOS.

COLOMBIA:
   E—> NOT INCLUDING DATA FOR LAW, HUMANITIES AND
EDUCATION.
   FR—> NON COMPRIS LES DONNEES POUR LE DROIT,
LES SCIENCES HUMAINES ET L'EDUCATION.
   ESP> EXCLUIDOS LOS DATOS RELATIVOS AL DERECHO,
LAS CIENCIAS HUMANAS Y LA EDUCACION.

ECUADOR:
   E—> DATA REFER TO R&D IN THE AGRICULTURAL
SCIENCES ONLY.
   FR—> LES DONNEES SE REFERENT A LA R-D DANS LES
SCIENCES DE L'AGRICULTURE SEULEMENT.
   ESP> LOS DATOS SE REFIEREN A LA I Y D DE LAS
CIENCIAS AGRICOLAS SOLAMENTE.

PERU:
   E—> DATA IN COLUMN 1 INCLUDE SCIENTISTS AND
ENGINEERS FOR WHOM A DISTRIBUTION BY FIELD OF
SCIENCE IS UNKNOWN. NOT INCLUDING DATA FOR
HUMANITIES AND EDUCATION.
   FR—> LES DONNEES DE LA COLONNE 1 COMPRENNENT
LES SCIENTIFIQUES ET INGENIEURS POUR LESQUELS UNE
REPARTITION PAR DISCIPLINE SCIENTIFIQUE N'EST PAS
CONNUE. NON COMPRIS LES DONNEES POUR LES SCIENCES
HUMAINES ET L'EDUCATION.
   ESP> LOS DATOS DE LA COLUMNA 1 COMPRENDEN LOS
CIENTIFICOS E INGENIEROS PARA LOS CUALES NO SE
CONOCE LA DISTRIBUCION POR DISCIPLINA CIENTIFICA.
EXCLUIDOS LOS DATOS RELATIVOS A LAS CIENCIAS
HUMANAS Y LA EDUCACION.

URUGUAY:
   E—> DATA REFER TO THE YEAR 1971/72. THE
FIGURE IN COLUMN 1 INCLUDES SCIENTISTS AND
ENGINEERS FOR WHOM A DISTRIBUTION BY FIELD OF
SCIENCE IS UNKNOWN.
   FR—> LES DONNEES SE REFERENT A L'ANNEE 1971/72.
LES DONNEES DE LA COLONNE 1 COMPRENNENT LES SCIEN-
TIFIQUES ET INGENIEURS POUR LESQUELS UNE REPARTI-
TION PAR DISCIPLINE SCIENTIFIQUE N'EST PAS CONNUE.
   ESP> LOS DATOS SE REFIEREN AL AÑO 1971/72.
LOS DATOS DE LA COLUMNA 1 COMPRENDEN LOS CIEN-
TIFICOS E INGENIEROS PARA LOS CUALES NO SE CONOCE
LA DISTRIBUCION POR DISCIPLINA CIENTIFICA.

VENEZUELA:
   E—> DATA IN COLUMN 1 INCLUDE SCIENTISTS AND
ENGINEERS FOR WHOM A DISTRIBUTION BY FIELD OF
SCIENCE IS UNKNOWN.
   FR—> LES DONNEES DE LA COLONNE 1 COMPRENNENT
LES SCIENTIFIQUES ET INGENIEURS POUR LESQUELS UNE
REPARTITION PAR DISCIPLINE SCIENTIFIQUE N'EST PAS
CONNUE.
   ESP> LOS DATOS DE LA COLUMNA 1 COMPRENDEN LOS
CIENTIFICOS E INGENIEROS PARA LOS CUALES NO SE
CONOCE LA DISTRIBUCION POR DISCIPLINA CIENTIFICA.

BANGLADESH:
   E—> DATA REFER TO THE YEAR 1973/74.
   FR—>LES DONNEES SE REFERENT A L'ANNEE 1973/74.
   ESP> LOS DATOS SE REFIEREN AL AÑO 1973/74.

R&D scientists and engineers by field of science 5.3
Scientifiques et ingénieurs de R-D par discipline scientifique
Científicos e ingenieros de I y D por rama de la ciencia

IRAQ:
E—> DATA REFER ONLY TO THOSE WORKING IN GOVERN-
MENT DEPARTMENTS CONCERNED WITH SCIENTIFIC ACTIVI-
TIES AND DO NOT INCLUDE THE PRODUCTIVE SECTOR (IN-
TEGRATED R&D).
FR-> LES DONNEES NE SE REFERENT QU'AUX PERSONNES
EMPLOYEES DANS LES DEPARTEMENTS GOUVERNEMENTAUX
CONCERNES PAR LES ACTIVITES SCIENTIFIQUES ET NE
COMPRENNENT PAS LE SECTEUR DE LA PRODUCTION (ACTI-
VITES DE R-D INTEGREES).
ESP> LOS DATOS SOLO SE REFIEREN A LAS PERSONAS
EMPLEADAS EN LOS SERVICIOS GUBERNAMENTALES QUE SE
OCUPAN DE ACTIVIDADES CIENTIFICAS Y EXCLUYEN LOS
DATOS RELATIVOS AL SECTOR PRODUCTIVO (ACTIVIDADES
DE I Y D INTEGRADAS).

JAPAN:
E—> DATA IN COLUMN 1 INCLUDE 12,865 SCIENTISTS
AND ENGINEERS FOR WHOM A DISTRIBUTION BY FIELD OF
SCIENCE IS UNKNOWN. DATA RELATE TO REGULAR
RESEARCH WORKERS ONLY.
FR-> LES DONNEES DE LA COLONNE 1 COMPRENNENT
12 865 SCIENTIFIQUES ET INGENIEURS POUR LESQUELS
UNE REPARTITION PAR DISCIPLINE SCIENTIFIQUE N'EST
PAS CONNUE. LES DONNEES SE REFERENT AUX
CHERCHEURS REGULIERS SEULEMENT.
ESP> LOS DATOS DE LA COLUMNA 1 COMPRENDEN
12 865 CIENTIFICOS E INGENIEROS PARA LOS CUALES
NO SE CONOCE LA DISTRIBUCION POR DISCIPLINA
CIENTIFICA. LOS DATOS SOLO SE REFIEREN A LAS
PERSONAS QUE TRABAJAN REGULARMENTE EN ACTIVIDADES
DE INVESTIGACION.

JORDAN:
E—> DATA RELATE TO THE EAST BANK ONLY.
FR-> LES DONNEES SE REFERENT A LA RIVE ORIENTALE
SEULEMENT.
ESP> LOS DATOS SE REFIEREN A LA ORILLA ORIENTAL
SOLAMENTE.

KOREA, REPUBLIC OF:
E—> NOT INCLUDING DATA FOR LAW, HUMANITIES AND
EDUCATION.
FR-> NON COMPRIS LES DONNEES POUR LE DROIT, LES
SCIENCES HUMAINES ET L'EDUCATION.
ESP> EXCLUIDOS LOS DATOS RELATIVOS AL DERECHO,
LAS CIENCIAS HUMANAS Y LA EDUCACION.

MONGOLIA:
E—> DATA RELATE TO THE ACADEMY OF SCIENCES
AND REFER TO SCIENTIFIC WORKERS.
FR-> LES DONNEES NE CONCERNENT QUE L'ACADEMIE
DES SCIENCES ET SE REFERENT AUX TRAVAILLEURS
SCIENTIFIQUES.
ESP> LOS DATOS SE REFIEREN A LA ACADEMIA DE
CIENCIAS Y A LOS TRABAJADORES CIENTIFICOS.

PAKISTAN:
E—> DATA REFER TO THE YEAR 1973/74 AND RELATE
TO R&D ACTIVITIES CONCENTRATED MAINLY IN
GOVERNMENT-FINANCED RESEARCH ESTABLISHMENTS ;
EXCLUDING SOCIAL SCIENCES AND HUMANITIES IN THE
HIGHER EDUCATION AND GENERAL SERVICE SECTORS.
FR-> LES DONNEES SE REFERENT A L'ANNEE 1973/74
ET CONCERNENT LES ACTIVITES DE R-D SE TROUVANT
POUR LA PLUPART DANS LES ETABLISSEMENTS DE RECHER-
CHE FINANCES PAR LE GOUVERNEMENT; LES SCIENCES
SOCIALES ET HUMAINES DES SECTEURS DE L'ENSEIGNE-
MENT SUPERIEUR ET DE SERVICE GENERAL SONT EXCLUES.
ESP> LOS DATOS SE REFIEREN AL AÑO 1973/74 Y
A LAS ACTIVIDADES DE I Y D CONCENTRADAS PRINCIPAL-
MENTE EN LOS ESTABLECIMIENTOS DE INVESTIGACION
SUBVENCIONADOS POR EL GOBIERNO; QUEDAN EXCLUI-
DAS LAS CIENCIAS SOCIALES Y HUMANAS DE LOS SECTO-
RES DE ENSEÑANZA SUPERIOR Y DE SERVICIO GENERAL.

PHILIPPINES:
E—> DATA RELATE TO THE GENERAL SERVICE SECTOR
ONLY.
FR-> LES DONNEES NE CONCERNENT QUE LE SECTEUR DE
SERVICE GENERAL.
ESP> LOS DATOS SE REFIEREN AL SECTOR DE SERVICIO
GENERAL SOLAMENTE.

SRI LANKA:
E—> NOT INCLUDING DATA FOR EITHER THE PRODUC-
TIVE SECTOR (NON-INTEGRATED R&D) OR LAW, HUMANI-
TIES AND EDUCATION.
FR-> NON COMPRIS LES DONNEES RELATIVES AU
SECTEUR DE LA PRODUCTION (ACTIVITES DE R-D NON-
INTEGREES) NI LE DROIT, LES SCIENCES HUMAINES ET
L'EDUCATION.
ESP> NO INCLUYE LOS DATOS RELATIVOS AL SECTOR
PRODUCTIVO (ACTIVIDADES DE I Y D NO INTEGRADAS),
NI LOS QUE CONCIERNEN EL DERECHO, LAS CIENCIAS
HUMANAS Y LA EDUCACION.

THAILAND:
E—> DATA REFER TO THE YEAR 1974/75 AND RELATE
TO THE NATIONAL RESEARCH COUNCIL ONLY.
FR-> LES DONNEES SE REFERENT A L'ANNEE 1974/75
ET AU "NATIONAL RESEARCH COUNCIL" SEULEMENT.
ESP> LOS DATOS SE REFIEREN AL AÑO 1974/75 Y AL
"NATIONAL RESEARCH COUNCIL" SOLAMENTE.

TURKEY:
E—> DATA REFER TO THE YEAR 1975/76. NOT
INCLUDING DATA FOR EITHER THE PRODUCTIVE SECTOR
OR SOCIAL SCIENCES AND HUMANITIES.
FR-> LES DONNEES SE REFERENT A L'ANNEE 1975/76.
NON COMPRIS LES DONNEES RELATIVES AU SECTEUR DE LA
PRODUCTION NI LES SCIENCES SOCIALES ET HUMAINES.
ESP> LOS DATOS SE REFIEREN AL AÑO 1975/76. NO
SE INCLUYEN LOS DATOS RELATIVOS AL SECTOR PRODUC-
TIVO NI LAS CIENCIAS SOCIALES Y HUMANAS.

YEMEN:
E—> DATA REFER TO THE YEAR 1974/75.
FR-> LES DONNEES SE REFERENT A L'ANNEE 1974/75.
ESP> LOS DATOS SE REFIEREN AL AÑO 1974/75.

AUSTRIA:
E—> DATA REFER TO THE PRODUCTIVE SECTOR ONLY.
FR-> LES DONNEES SE REFERENT AU SECTEUR DE LA
PRODUCTION SEULEMENT.
ESP> LOS DATOS SE REFIEREN AL SECTOR PRODUCTIVO
SOLAMENTE.

BELGIUM:
E—> NOT INCLUDING DATA FOR THE PRODUCTIVE
SECTOR (INTEGRATED R&D). DATA IN COLUMN 1
INCLUDE SCIENTISTS AND ENGINEERS FOR WHOM A DIS-
TRIBUTION BY FIELD OF SCIENCE IS UNKNOWN.
FR-> NON COMPRIS LES DONNEES POUR LE SECTEUR
DE LA PRODUCTION (ACTIVITES DE R-D INTEGREES).
LES DONNEES DE LA COLONNE 1 COMPRENNENT LES
SCIENTIFIQUES ET INGENIEURS POUR LESQUELS UNE
REPARTITION PAR DISCIPLINE SCIENTIFIQUE N'EST PAS
CONNUE.
ESP> EXCLUIDOS LOS DATOS RELATIVOS AL SECTOR
PRODUCTIVO (ACTIVIDADES D I Y D INTEGRADAS).
LOS DATOS DE LA COLUMNA 1 COMPRENDEN LOS
CIENTIFICOS E INGENIEROS PARA LOS CUALES NO SE
CONOCE LA DISTRIBUCION POR DISCIPLINA CIENTIFICA.

BULGARIA:
E—> NOT INCLUDING 13,168 (F. 7,480) SCIENTISTS
AND ENGINEERS FOR WHOM A DISTRIBUTION BY FIELD OF
SCIENCE IS UNKNOWN. SCIENTISTS AND ENGINEERS
ENGAGED IN THE ADMINISTRATION OF R&D ARE
EXCLUDED.

5.3 R&D scientists and engineers by field of science
Scientifiques et ingénieurs de R-D par discipline scientifique
Científicos e ingenieros de I y D por rama de la ciencia

BULGARIA (CONT.):
FR—> COMPTE NON TENU DE 13 168 (F. 7 480)
SCIENTIFIQUES ET INGENIEURS POUR LESQUELS LA
REPARTITION PAR DISCIPLINE SCIENTIFIQUE N'EST PAS
DISPONIBLE. LES SCIENTIFIQUES ET INGENIEURS
EMPLOYES DANS LES SERVICES ADMINISTRATIFS SONT
EXCLUS.
ESP> NO SE INCLUYEN 13 168 (F. 7 480) CIEN-
TIFICOS E INGENIEROS PARA LOS CUALES NO SE
CONOCE LA DISTRIBUCION POR DISCIPLINA CIEN-
TIFICA. SE EXCLUYEN LOS CIENTIFICOS E INGE-
NIEROS EMPLEADOS EN LOS SERVICIOS ADMINISTA-
TIVOS.

CZECHOSLOVAKIA:
E—> OF MILITARY R&D ONLY THAT PART CARRIED
OUT IN CIVIL ESTABLISHMENTS IS INCLUDED. NOT IN-
CLUDING EITHER DATA FOR THE PRODUCTIVE SECTOR OR
SCIENTISTS AND ENGINEERS ENGAGED IN THE ADMINI-
STRATION OF R&D.
FR—> POUR LA R-D DE CARACTERE MILITAIRE, SEULE
LA PARTIE EFFECTUEE DANS LES ETABLISSEMENTS CIVILS
A ETE CONSIDEREE. NON COMPRIS LES DONNEES POUR LE
SECTEUR DE LA PRODUCTION, NI LES SCIENTIFIQUES ET
INGENIEURS EMPLOYES DANS LES TRAVAUX DE R-D.
ESP> PARA LAS ACTIVIDADES DE I Y D DE CARACTER
MILITAR SOLO SE HA CONSIDERADO LA PARTE CORRES-
PONDIENTE A LOS ESTABLECIMIENTOS CIVILES. NO SE
INCLUYEN LOS DATOS RELATIVOS AL SECTOR PRODUCTIVO
NI LOS CIENTIFICOS E INGENIEROS EMPLEADOS EN
TRABAJOS DE I Y D.

FINLAND:
E—> DATA IN COLUMN 1 INCLUDE SCIENTISTS AND
ENGINEERS FOR WHOM A DISTRIBUTION BY FIELD OF
SCIENCE IS UNKNOWN.
FR—> LES DONNES DE LA COLONNE 1 COMPRENNENT
LES SCIENTIFIQUES ET INGENIEURS POUR LESQUELS
UNE REPARTITION PAR DISCIPLINE SCIENTIFIQUE
N'EST PAS CONNUE.
ESP> LOS DATOS DE LA COLUMNA 1 COMPRENDEN LOS
CIENTIFICOS E INGENIEROS PARA LOS CUALES NO SE
CONOCE LA DISTRIBUCION POR DISCIPLINA CIENTIFICA.

GERMANY, FEDERAL REPUBLIC OF:
E—> NOT INCLUDING 56,589 SCIENTISTS AND ENGI-
NEERS IN THE PRODUCTIVE SECTOR, 10,827 IN THE
GENERAL SERVICE SECTOR AND A FURTHER 104 FOR WHOM
A DISTRIBUTION BY FIELD OF SCIENCE IS UNKNOWN.
FR—> COMPTE NON TENU DE 56 589 SCIENTIFIQUES ET
INGENIEURS DU SECTEUR DE LA PRODUCTION, 10 827 DU
SECTEUR DE SERVICE GENERAL ET 104 NON SPECIFIES,
DONT LA REPARTITION PAR DISCIPLINE SCIENTIFIQUE
N'EST PAS DISPONIBLE.
ESP> EXCLUIDOS 56 589 CIENTIFICOS E INGENIEROS
DEL SECTOR PRODUCTIVO, 10 827 DEL SECTOR DE
SERVICIO GENERAL Y 104 SIN ESPECIFICAR, PARA LOS
CUALES NO SE DISPONE DE REPARTICION POR DISCIPLI-
NA CIENTIFICA.

HUNGARY:
E—> NOT INCLUDING SCIENTISTS AND ENGINEERS EN-
GAGED IN THE ADMINISTRATION OF R&D.
FR—> NON COMPRIS LES SCIENTIFIQUES ET INGENIEURS
EMPLOYES DANS LES SERVICES ADMINISTRATIFS DE R-D.
ESP> NO INCLUYE LOS CIENTIFICOS E INGENIEROS
EMPLEADOS EN LOS SERVICIOS ADMINISTRATIVOS DE
I Y D.

ICELAND:
E—> NOT INCLUDING DATA FOR SOCIAL SCIENCES AND
HUMANITIES.
FR—> COMPTE NON TENU DES SCIENCES SOCIALES ET
HUMAINES.
ESP> EXCLUIDOS LOS DATOS RELATIVOS A LAS
CIENCIAS SOCIALES Y HUMANAS.

ITALY:
E—> DATA IN COLUMN 1 INCLUDE SCIENTISTS AND
ENGINEERS FOR WHOM A DISTRIBUTION BY FIELD OF
SCIENCE IS UNKNOWN.
FR—> LES DONNEES DE LA COLONNE 1 COMPRENNENT LES
SCIENTIFIQUES ET INGENIEURS POUR LESQUELS UNE
REPARTITION PAR DISCIPLINE SCIENTIFIQUE N'EST PAS
CONNUE.
ESP> LOS DATOS DE LA COLUMNA 1 COMPRENDEN LOS
CIENTIFICOS E INGENIEROS PARA LOS CUALES NO SE
CONOCE LA DISTRIBUCION POR DISCIPLINA CIENTIFICA.

MALTA:
E—> DATA RELATE TO THE HIGHER EDUCATION SECTOR
ONLY.
FR—> LES DONNEES NE CONCERNENT QUE LE SECTEUR
DE L'ENSEIGNEMENT SUPERIEUR.
ESP> LOS DATOS SE REFIEREN AL SECTOR DE
ENSEÑANZA SUPERIOR SOLAMENTE.

NETHERLANDS:
E—> NOT INCLUDING 9,293 SCIENTISTS AND ENGI-
NEERS FOR WHOM A DISTRIBUTION BY FIELD OF SCIENCE
IS UNKNOWN . SOCIAL SCIENCES AND HUMANITIES IN
THE PRODUCTIVE SECTOR (INTEGRATED R&D) ARE ALSO
EXCLUDED.
FR—> NON COMPRIS 9 293 SCIENTIFIQUES ET INGE-
NIEURS POUR LESQUELS LA REPARTITION PAR DISCIPLINE
SCIENTIFIQUE N'EST PAS DISPONIBLE. LES DONNEES
RELATIVES AUX SCIENCES SOCIALES ET HUMAINES DU
SECTEUR DE LA PRODUCTION (ACTIVITES DE R-D INTE-
GREES) SONT AUSSI EXCLUES.
ESP> EXCLUIDOS 9 293 CIENTIFICOS E INGENIEROS
PARA LOS CUALES NO SE DISPONE DE REPARTICION POR
DISCIPLINA CIENTIFICA. TAMBIEN SE EXCLUYEN LOS
DATOS RELATIVOS A LAS CIENCIAS SOCIALES Y HUMANAS
DEL SECTOR PRODUCTIVO (ACTIVIDADES DE I Y D INTE-
GRADAS).

NORWAY:
E—> DATA IN COLUMN 1 INCLUDE SCIENTISTS AND
ENGINEERS FOR WHOM A DISTRIBUTION BY FIELD OF
SCIENCE IS UNKNOWN.
FR—> LES DONNES DE LA COLONNE 1 COMPRENNENT
LES SCIENTIFIQUES ET INGENIEURS POUR LESQUELS
UNE REPARTITION PAR DISCIPLINE SCIENTIFIQUE N'EST
PAS CONNUE.
ESP> LOS DATOS DE LA COLUMNA 1 COMPRENDEN LOS
CIENTIFICOS E INGENIEROS PARA LOS CUALES NO SE
CONOCE LA DISTRIBUCION POR DISCIPLINA CIENTIFICA.

YUGOSLAVIA:
E—> NOT INCLUDING ACTIVITIES OF A MILITARY
NATURE OR RELATING TO NATIONAL DEFENCE.
FR—> NON COMPRIS LES ACTIVITES DE CARACTERE
MILITAIRE OU RELEVANT DE LA DEFENSE NATIONALE.
ESP> EXCLUIDAS LAS ACTIVIDADES DE CARACTER
MILITAR O QUE CONCIERNEN LA DEFENSA NACIONAL.

AMERICAN SAMOA:
E—> DATA RELATE TO ONE RESEARCH INSTITUTE ONLY.
FR—> LES DONNEES NE CONCERNENT QU'UN SEUL
INSTITUT DE RECHERCHE.
ESP> LOS DATOS SE REFIEREN A UN CENTRO DE INVES-
TIGACION SOLAMENTE.

AUSTRALIA:
E—> DATA REFER TO THE YEAR 1973/74.
FR—> LES DONNEES SE REFERENT A L'ANNEE 1973/74.
ESP> LOS DATOS SE REFIEREN AL AÑO 1973/74.

FRENCH POLYNESIA:
E—> DATA RELATE TO ONE RESEARCH INSTITUTE ONLY.
FR—> LES DONNEES NE CONCERNENT QU'UN SEUL
INSTITUT DE RECHERCHE.
ESP> LOS DATOS SE REFIEREN A UN CENTRO DE INVES-
TIGACION SOLAMENTE.

R&D scientists and engineers by field of science 5.3
Scientifiques et ingénieurs de R-D par discipline scientifique
Científicos e ingenieros de I y D por rama de la ciencia

U.S.S.R.:
E—> DATA IN COLUMN 1 INCLUDE SCIENTISTS AND
ENGINEERS FOR WHOM A DISTRIBUTION BY FIELD OF
SCIENCE IS UNKNOWN. FIGURES REFER TO SCIEN-
TIFIC WORKERS, I.E. ALL PERSONS WITH A HIGHER
SCIENTIFIC DEGREE OR SCIENTIFIC TITLE, REGARDLESS
OF THE NATURE OF THEIR WORK; PERSONS UNDERTAKING
RESEARCH WORK IN SCIENTIFIC ESTABLISHMENTS AND
SCIENTIFIC TEACHING STAFF IN INSTITUTIONS OF
HIGHER EDUCATION; ALSO INCLUDES PERSONS UNDER-
TAKING SCIENTIFIC WORK IN INDUSTRIAL ENTERPRISES.
FR—> LES DONNEES DE LA COLONNE 1 COMPRENNENT LES
SCIENTIFIQUES ET INGENIEURS POUR LESQUELS UNE RE-
PARTITION PAR BRANCHE DE SCIENCE N'EST PAS CONNUE.
LES CHIFFRES SE REFERENT AUX TRAVAILLEURS SCIENTI-
FIQUES, C.A.D., A TOUTES LES PERSONNES AYANT UN
DIPLOME SCIENTIFIQUE SUPERIEUR OU UN TITRE SCIEN-
TIFIQUE, SANS CONSIDERATION DE LA NATURE DE LEUR
TRAVAIL; AUX PERSONNES QUI EFFECTUENT UN TRAVAIL
DE RECHERCHE DANS DES INSTITUTIONS SCIENTIFIQUES
ET AU PERSONNEL SCIENTIFIQUE ENSEIGNANT DANS DES
ETABLISSEMENTS D'ENSEIGNEMENT SUPERIEUR; SONT
INCLUES AUSSI LES PERSONNES QUI EFFECTUENT DES
TRAVAUX SCIENTIFIQUES DANS LES ENTREPRISES
INDUSTRIELLES.
ESP> LOS DATOS DE LA COLUMNA 1 COMPRENDEN LOS
CIENTIFICOS E INGENIEROS PARA LOS CUALES NO SE
CONOCE LA DISTRIBUCION POR DISCIPLINA CIENTIFICA.
LOS DATOS SE REFIEREN A LOS TRABAJADORES CIENTI-
FICOS, ES DECIR, A TODAS LAS PERSONAS QUE POSEEN
UN DIPLOMA CIENTIFICO SUPERIOR O UN TITULO CIENTI-
FICO, SIN TENER EN CUENTA LA NATURALEZA DE SU
TRABAJO; A LAS PERSONAS QUE EFECTUAN UN TRABAJO DE
INVESTIGACION EN LAS INSTITUCIONES CIENTIFICAS Y
AL PERSONAL CIENTIFICO QUE EJERCE FUNCIONES
DOCENTES EN LOS ESTABLECIMIENTOS DE ENSEÑANZA
SUPERIOR; TAMBIEN SE INCLUYEN LAS PERSONAS QUE
EFECTUAN TRABAJOS CIENTIFICOS EN LAS EMPRESAS
INDUSTRIALES.

BYELORUSSIAN S.S.R.:
E—> DATA IN COLUMN 1 INCLUDE SCIENTISTS AND
ENGINEERS FOR WHOM A DISTRIBUTION BY FIELD OF
SCIENCE IS UNKNOWN. FIGURES REFER TO SCIEN-
TIFIC WORKERS, I.E. ALL PERSONS WITH A HIGHER
SCIENTIFIC DEGREE OR SCIENTIFIC TITLE, REGARDLESS
OF THE NATURE OF THEIR WORK; PERSONS UNDERTAKING
RESEARCH WORK IN SCIENTIFIC ESTABLISHMENTS AND
SCIENTIFIC TEACHING STAFF IN INSTITUTIONS OF
HIGHER EDUCATION; ALSO INCLUDES PERSONS UNDER-
TAKING SCIENTIFIC WORK IN INDUSTRIAL ENTERPRISES.
FR—> LES DONNEES DE LA COLONNE 1 COMPRENNENT LES
SCIENTIFIQUES ET INGENIEURS POUR LESQUELS UNE RE-
PARTITION PAR BRANCHE DE SCIENCE N'EST PAS CONNUE.
LES CHIFFRES SE REFERENT AUX TRAVAILLEURS SCIENTI-
FIQUES, C.A.D., A TOUTES LES PERSONNES AYANT UN
DIPLOME SCIENTIFIQUE SUPERIEUR OU UN TITRE SCIEN-
TIFIQUE, SANS CONSIDERATION DE LA NATURE DE LEUR
TRAVAIL; AUX PERSONNES QUI EFFECTUENT UN TRAVAIL
DE RECHERCHE DANS DES INSTITUTIONS SCIENTIFIQUES

BYELORUSSIAN S.S.R. (CONT.):
ET AU PERSONNEL SCIENTIFIQUE ENSEIGNANT DANS DES
ETABLISSEMENTS D'ENSEIGNEMENT SUPERIEUR; SONT
INCLUES AUSSI LES PERSONNES QUI EFFECTUENT DES
TRAVAUX SCIENTIFIQUES DANS LES ENTREPRISES
INDUSTRIELLES.
ESP> LOS DATOS DE LA COLUMNA 1 COMPRENDEN LOS
CIENTIFICOS E INGENIEROS PARA LOS CUALES NO SE
CONOCE LA DISTRIBUCION POR DISCIPLINA CIENTIFICA.
LOS DATOS SE REFIEREN A LOS TRABAJADORES CIENTI-
FICOS, ES DECIR, A TODAS LAS PERSONAS QUE POSEEN
UN DIPLOMA CIENTIFICO SUPERIOR O UN TITULO CIENTI-
FICO, SIN TENER EN CUENTA LA NATURALEZA DE SU
TRABAJO; A LAS PERSONAS QUE EFECTUAN UN TRABAJO DE
INVESTIGACION EN LAS INSTITUCIONES CIENTIFICAS Y
AL PERSONAL CIENTIFICO QUE EJERCE FUNCIONES
DOCENTES EN LOS ESTABLECIMIENTOS DE ENSEÑANZA
SUPERIOR; TAMBIEN SE INCLUYEN LAS PERSONAS QUE
EFECTUAN TRABAJOS CIENTIFICOS EN LAS EMPRESAS
INDUSTRIALES.

UKRAINIAN S.S.R.:
E—> DATA IN COLUMN 1 INCLUDE SCIENTISTS AND
ENGINEERS FOR WHOM A DISTRIBUTION BY FIELD OF
SCIENCE IS UNKNOWN. FIGURES REFER TO SCIEN-
TIFIC WORKERS, I.E. ALL PERSONS WITH A HIGHER
SCIENTIFIC DEGREE OR SCIENTIFIC TITLE, REGARDLESS
OF THE NATURE OF THEIR WORK; PERSONS UNDERTAKING
RESEARCH WORK IN SCIENTIFIC ESTABLISHMENTS AND
SCIENTIFIC TEACHING STAFF IN INSTITUTIONS OF
HIGHER EDUCATION; ALSO INCLUDES PERSONS UNDER-
TAKING SCIENTIFIC WORK IN INDUSTRIAL ENTERPRISES.
FR—> LES DONNEES DE LA COLONNE 1 COMPRENNENT LES
SCIENTIFIQUES ET INGENIEURS POUR LESQUELS UNE RE-
PARTITION PAR BRANCHE DE SCIENCE N'EST PAS CONNUE.
LES CHIFFRES SE REFERENT AUX TRAVAILLEURS SCIENTI-
FIQUES, C.A.D., A TOUTES LES PERSONNES AYANT UN
DIPLOME SCIENTIFIQUE SUPERIEUR OU UN TITRE SCIEN-
TIFIQUE, SANS CONSIDERATION DE LA NATURE DE LEUR
TRAVAIL; AUX PERSONNES QUI EFFECTUENT UN TRAVAIL
DE RECHERCHE DANS DES INSTITUTIONS SCIENTIFIQUES
ET AU PERSONNEL SCIENTIFIQUE ENSEIGNANT DANS DES
ETABLISSEMENTS D'ENSEIGNEMENT SUPERIEUR; SONT
INCLUES AUSSI LES PERSONNES QUI EFFECTUENT DES
TRAVAUX SCIENTIFIQUES DANS LES ENTREPRISES
INDUSTRIELLES.
ESP> LOS DATOS DE LA COLUMNA 1 COMPRENDEN LOS
CIENTIFICOS E INGENIEROS PARA LOS CUALES NO SE
CONOCE LA DISTRIBUCION POR DISCIPLINA CIENTIFICA.
LOS DATOS SE REFIEREN A LOS TRABAJADORES CIENTI-
FICOS, ES DECIR, A TODAS LAS PERSONAS QUE POSEEN
UN DIPLOMA CIENTIFICO SUPERIOR O UN TITULO CIENTI-
FICO, SIN TENER EN CUENTA LA NATURALEZA DE SU
TRABAJO; A LAS PERSONAS QUE EFECTUAN UN TRABAJO DE
INVESTIGACION EN LAS INSTITUCIONES CIENTIFICAS Y
AL PERSONAL CIENTIFICO QUE EJERCE FUNCIONES
DOCENTES EN LOS ESTABLECIMIENTOS DE ENSEÑANZA
SUPERIOR; TAMBIEN SE INCLUYEN LAS PERSONAS QUE
EFECTUAN TRABAJOS CIENTIFICOS EN LAS EMPRESAS
INDUSTRIALES.

R&D personnel by sector of performance 5.4
Personnel de R-D par secteur d'exécution
Personal de I y D por sector de ejecución

5.4 Total personnel engaged in research and experimental development by sector of performance and type of personnel

Total du personnel employé à des travaux de recherche et de développement expérimental, par secteur d'exécution et catégorie de personnel

Personal empleado en trabajos de investigación y de desarrollo experimental, por sector de ejecución y categoría de personal

PLEASE REFER TO INTRODUCTION FOR DEFINITIONS OF CATEGORIES IN-CLUDED IN THIS TABLE.

POUR LES DEFINITIONS DES CATEGORIES PRESENTEES DANS CE TABLEAU, SE REFERER A L'INTRODUCTION.

EN LA INTRODUCCION SE DAN LAS DEFINICIONES DE LAS CATEGORIAS QUE FIGURAN EN ESTE CUADRO.

SCIENTISTS AND ENGINEERS ENGAGED IN R & D ARE GIVEN IN FULL-TIME EQUIVALENT (FTE).

LE NOMBRE DE SCIENTIFIQUES ET D'INGENIEURS EMPLOYES A DES TRA-VAUX DE R-D EST EN EQUIVALENT PLEIN TEMPS (FTE).

EL NUMERO DE CIENTIFICOS Y DE INGENIEROS EMPLEADOS EN TRABAJOS DE I Y D SE DA EN EQUIVALENTE DE JORNADA COMPLETA (FTE).

NUMBER OF COUNTRIES AND TERRITORIES PRESENTED IN THIS TABLE: 98

NOMBRE DE PAYS ET DE TERRITOIRES PRESENTES DANS CE TABLEAU: 98

NUMERO DE PAISES Y DE TERRITORIOS PRESENTADOS EN ESTE CUADRO: 98

SECTOR OF PERFORMANCE / SECTEUR D'EXECUTION / SECTOR DE EJECUCION

COUNTRY / PAYS / PAIS	YEAR / ANNEE / AÑO	TYPE OF PERSONNEL / CATEGORIE DE PERSONNEL / CATEGORIA DE PERSONAL	ALL SECTORS / TOUS SECTEURS / TODOS LOS SECTORES	PRODUCTIVE SECTOR SECTEUR DE LA PRODUCTION SECTOR PRODUCTIVO		HIGHER EDUCATION / ENSEIGNEMENT SUPERIEUR / ENSEÑANZA SUPERIOR	GENERAL SERVICE / SERVICE GENERAL / SERVICIO GENERAL
				INTEGRATED R&D / ACTIVITES DE R-D INTEGREES / ACTIVIDADES DE I Y D INTEGRADAS	NON-INTEGRATED R&D / ACTIVITES DE R-D NON INTEGREES / ACTIVIDADES DE I Y D NO INTEGRADAS		
			(1)	(2)	(3)	(4)	(5)
AFRICA							
ALGERIA	1972	TOTAL IN R&D	...	...	...	342	...
		SCIENTISTS AND ENGINEERS	...	...	...	242	...
		TECHNICIANS	...	...	...	100	...
		AUXILIARY PERSONNEL	...	...	...	-	...
BOTSWANA ‡	1973	TOTAL IN R&D	42	-	-	42	
		% BY SECTOR				100.0	
		SCIENTISTS AND ENGINEERS	24	-	-	24	
		TECHNICIANS	18	-	-	18	

5.4 R&D personnel by sector of performance
Personnel de R-D par secteur d'exécution
Personal de I y D por sector de ejecución

SECTOR OF PERFORMANCE / SECTEUR D'EXECUTION / SECTOR DE EJECUCION

COUNTRY / PAYS / PAIS	YEAR / ANNEE / AÑO	TYPE OF PERSONNEL / CATEGORIE DE PERSONNEL / CATEGORIA DE PERSONAL	ALL SECTORS / TOUS SECTEURS / TODOS LOS SECTORES (1)	PRODUCTIVE SECTOR / SECTEUR DE LA PRODUCTION / SECTOR PRODUCTIVO — INTEGRATED R&D / ACTIVITES DE R-D INTEGREES / ACTIVIDADES DE I Y D INTEGRADAS (2)	PRODUCTIVE SECTOR — NON-INTEGRATED R&D / ACTIVITES DE R-D NON INTEGREES / ACTIVIDADES DE I Y D NO INTEGRADAS (3)	HIGHER EDUCATION / ENSEIGNEMENT SUPERIEUR / ENSEÑANZA SUPERIOR (4)	GENERAL SERVICE / SERVICE GENERAL / SERVICIO GENERAL (5)
CENTRAL AFRICAN REPUBLIC	1975	TOTAL IN R&D	...	...	...	85	...
		SCIENTISTS AND ENGINEERS	...	...	...	76	...
		TECHNICIANS	...	...	...	3	...
		AUXILIARY PERSONNEL	...	...	...	6	...
CONGO ‡	1977	SCIENTISTS AND ENGINEERS	284	...	48	236	...
		% BY SECTOR			16.9	83.1	...
EGYPT	1973	SCIENTISTS AND ENGINEERS	10 665	4 874	—>	3 752	2 039
		% BY SECTOR		45.7	—>	35.2	19.1
GABON ‡	1970	TOTAL IN R&D	86	—	—	—	86
		% BY SECTOR		—	—	—	100.0
		SCIENTISTS AND ENGINEERS	8	—	—	—	8
		TECHNICIANS	20	—	—	—	20
		AUXILIARY PERSONNEL	58	—	—	—	58
GHANA ‡	1972	TOTAL IN R&D	8 559	1 627	1 539	2 878	2 515
		% BY SECTOR		19.0	18.0	33.6	29.4
		SCIENTISTS AND ENGINEERS	3 559	700	759	1 200	900
		TECHNICIANS	5 000	927	780	1 678	1 615
		AUXILIARY PERSONNEL	./.	./.	./.	./.	./.
IVORY COAST ‡	1970	TOTAL IN R&D	541	—	393	148	—
		% BY SECTOR		—	72.6	27.4	—
		SCIENTISTS AND ENGINEERS	319	—	192	127	—
		TECHNICIANS	222	—	201	21	—
KENYA ‡	1975	TOTAL IN R&D	544	61	335	148	—
		% BY SECTOR		11.2	61.6	27.2	—
		SCIENTISTS AND ENGINEERS	361	29	210	122	—
		TECHNICIANS	183	32	125	26	—
LIBYAN ARAB JAMAHIRIYA	1973	TOTAL IN R&D	*295	295	—>	—	—
		% BY SECTOR		100.0	—>	—	—
		SCIENTISTS AND ENGINEERS	*50	*50	>	—	—
		TECHNICIANS	142	142	>	—	—
		AUXILIARY PERSONNEL	103	103	>	—	—

R&D personnel by sector of performance 5.4
Personnel de R-D par secteur d'exécution
Personal de I y D por sector de ejecución

			(1)	(2)	(3)	(4)	(5)
MADAGASCAR ‡	1971	TOTAL IN R & D	298	....	106	105	87
		% BY SECTOR	....	....	35.6	35.2	29.2
		SCIENTISTS AND ENGINEERS	201	....	84	50	67
		TECHNICIANS	97	....	22	55	20
		AUXILIARY PERSONNEL	....	....	....	....	....
MALAWI	1977	TOTAL IN R&D	1 909	752	874	217	66
		% BY SECTOR		39.4	45.8	11.4	3.4
		SCIENTISTS AND ENGINEERS	189	39	62	77	11
		TECHNICIANS	242	118	92	22	10
		AUXILIARY PERSONNEL	1 478	595	720	118	45
MAURITIUS	1977	TOTAL IN R&D	649	—	346	40	263
		% BY SECTOR		—	35.9	10.1	54.0
		SCIENTISTS AND ENGINEERS	151	—	44	24	83
		TECHNICIANS	150	—	59	14	77
		AUXILIARY PERSONNEL	348	—	243	2	103
NIGER	1976	TOTAL IN R&D	....	....		94	....
		% BY SECTOR		....			
		SCIENTISTS AND ENGINEERS	....	....		93	....
		TECHNICIANS	....	....		1	....
		AUXILIARY PERSONNEL	....	....			....
NIGERIA ‡	1970	TOTAL IN R&D	*2 816	—	—	*1 887	929
		% BY SECTOR		—	—	67.0	33.0
		SCIENTISTS AND ENGINEERS	2 083	—	—	1 711	372
		TECHNICIANS	*733	—	—	*176	557
		AUXILIARY PERSONNEL	...	—	—		...
SENEGAL ‡	1972	TOTAL IN R & D	908	47	498	281	82
		% BY SECTOR		5.2	54.8	31.0	9.0
		SCIENTISTS AND ENGINEERS	392	22	195	136	39
		TECHNICIANS	516	25	303	145	43
		AUXILIARY PERSONNEL		—	—	—	—
SEYCHELLES	1973	TOTAL IN R&D	1	—	1	—	—
		% BY SECTOR		—	100.0	—	—
		SCIENTISTS AND ENGINEERS	1	—	1	—	—
		TECHNICIANS	—	—	—	—	—
		AUXILIARY PERSONNEL	—	—	—	—	—
SUDAN	1978	TOTAL IN R&D	21 596	7 635	1 977	3 126	8 858
		% BY SECTOR		35.4	9.1	14.5	41.0
		SCIENTISTS AND ENGINEERS	3 266	621	239	1 065	1 341
		TECHNICIANS	3 271	1 174	204	351	1 542
		AUXILIARY PERSONNEL	15 059	5 840	1 534	1 710	5 975
TOGO ‡	1976	TOTAL IN R&D	445	./.	—	184	261
		% BY SECTOR		./.	—	41.3	58.7
		SCIENTISTS AND ENGINEERS	261	./.	—	160	101
		TECHNICIANS	184	./.	—	24	160
		AUXILIARY PERSONNEL			—		
ZAMBIA ‡	1976	TOTAL IN R&D	931	451	—	189	291
		% BY SECTOR		48.4	—	20.3	31.3
		SCIENTISTS AND ENGINEERS	250	112	—	54	84
		TECHNICIANS	150	21	—	74	55
		AUXILIARY PERSONNEL	531	318	—	61	152

5.4 R&D personnel by sector of performance
Personnel de R-D par secteur d'exécution
Personal de I y D por sector de ejecución

COUNTRY / PAYS / PAIS	YEAR ANNEE AÑO	TYPE OF PERSONNEL CATEGORIE DE PERSONNEL CATEGORIA DE PERSONAL	ALL SECTORS TOUS SECTEURS TODOS LOS SECTORES (1)	PRODUCTIVE SECTOR / SECTEUR DE LA PRODUCTION / SECTOR PRODUCTIVO		HIGHER EDUCATION ENSEIGNEMENT SUPERIEUR ENSEÑANZA SUPERIOR (4)	GENERAL SERVICE SERVICE GENERAL SERVICIO GENERAL (5)
				INTEGRATED R&D ACTIVITES DE R-D INTEGREES ACTIVIDADES DE I Y D INTEGRADAS (2)	NON-INTEGRATED R&D ACTIVITES DE R-D NON INTEGREES ACTIVIDADES DE I Y D NO INTEGRADAS (3)		
AMERICA, NORTH							
BELIZE	1970	TOTAL IN R&D	34	5	—	—	29
		% BY SECTOR		14.7	—	—	85.3
		SCIENTISTS AND ENGINEERS	15	2	—	—	13
		TECHNICIANS	4	2	—	—	2
		AUXILIARY PERSONNEL	15	1	—	—	14
BERMUDA ‡	1970	TOTAL IN R&D	10	...	...	—	10
		% BY SECTOR		...	...	—	100.0
		SCIENTISTS AND ENGINEERS	4	...	...	—	4
		TECHNICIANS	3	...	...	—	3
		AUXILIARY PERSONNEL	3	...	...	—	3
CANADA ‡	1977	TOTAL IN R&D	55 971	21 519	./.	13 830	20 622
		% BY SECTOR		38.5	./.	24.7	36.8
		SCIENTISTS AND ENGINEERS	24 590	9 685	./.	*7 350	7 555
		TECHNICIANS	15 963	7 198	./.	2 890	5 875
		AUXILIARY PERSONNEL	15 418	4 636	./.	3 590	7 192
CAYMAN ISLANDS	1971	TOTAL IN R&D	9	6	—	3	—
		% BY SECTOR		66.7	—	33.3	—
		SCIENTISTS AND ENGINEERS	3	2	—	1	—
		TECHNICIANS	3	2	—	1	—
		AUXILIARY PERSONNEL	3	2	—	1	—
CUBA	1977	TOTAL IN R&D	19 659	8 610	213	1 174	9 662
		% BY SECTOR		43.8	1.1	6.0	49.1
		SCIENTISTS AND ENGINEERS	4 959	1 720	120	590	2 529
		TECHNICIANS	6 075	2 276	69	319	3 411
		AUXILIARY PERSONNEL	8 625	4 614	24	265	3 722
GUATEMALA ‡	1974	TOTAL IN R&D	749	—	290	113	346
		% BY SECTOR		—	38.7	15.1	46.2
		SCIENTISTS AND ENGINEERS	310	—	166	43	101
		TECHNICIANS	439	—	124	70	245
HONDURAS ‡	1974	TOTAL IN R&D	7	—	—	—	7
		% BY SECTOR		—	—	—	100.0
		SCIENTISTS AND ENGINEERS	5	—	—	—	5
		TECHNICIANS	1	—	—	—	1
		AUXILIARY PERSONNEL	1	—	—	—	1

R&D personnel by sector of performance 5.4
Personnel de R-D par secteur d'exécution
Personal de I y D por sector de ejecución

Country / Year	Item	(1)	(2)	(3)	(4)	(5)
MEXICO 1974	SCIENTISTS AND ENGINEERS	5 896	701	1 272	1 968	1 955
	% BY SECTOR		11.9	21.6	33.4	33.1
PANAMA 1975	TOTAL IN R&D	982	—	600	249	133
	% BY SECTOR		—	61.1	25.4	13.5
	SCIENTISTS AND ENGINEERS	204	—	116	62	26
	TECHNICIANS	301	—	194	80	27
	AUXILIARY PERSONNEL	477	—	290	107	80
ST. PIERRE AND MIQUELON ‡ 1972	TOTAL IN R&D	37	37	—	—	—
	% BY SECTOR		100.0	—	—	—
	SCIENTISTS AND ENGINEERS	7	7	—	—	—
	TECHNICIANS	4	4	—	—	—
	AUXILIARY PERSONNEL	26	26	—	—	—
TRINIDAD AND TOBAGO ‡ 1970	TOTAL IN R&D	572	123	→	262	235
	SCIENTISTS AND ENGINEERS	380	82	→	187	130
	TECHNICIANS	192	41	→	75	105
TURKS AND CAICOS ISLANDS 1976	TOTAL IN R&D	2	—	2	—	—
	% BY SECTOR		—	100.0	—	—
	SCIENTISTS AND ENGINEERS	2	—	2	—	—
	TECHNICIANS	—	—	—	—	—
	AUXILIARY PERSONNEL	—	—			
UNITED STATES OF AMERICA ‡ 1978	TOTAL IN R & D	585 500	400 100	...	158 972	93 000
	SCIENTISTS AND ENGINEERS		...	→	92 400	...
	TECHNICIANS	66 572	...	...	66 572	...
AMERICA, SOUTH						
ARGENTINA ‡ 1978	TOTAL IN R&D	*27 500	*1 250	*500	*10 500	*15 250
	% BY SECTOR		*4.6	*1.8	*38.2	*55.4
	SCIENTISTS AND ENGINEERS	*8 250	*350	*150	*4 400	*3 350
	TECHNICIANS	*11 400	*500	*200	*4 000	*6 700
	AUXILIARY PERSONNEL	*7 850	*400	*150	*2 100	*5 200
BRAZIL ‡ 1978	TOTAL IN R&D	24 015	43 056	→	15 518	...
	SCIENTISTS AND ENGINEERS		8 497	→		...
	TECHNICIANS	5 392	5 392	→		...
	AUXILIARY PERSONNEL	29 167	29 167	→		...
CHILE 1975	SCIENTISTS AND ENGINEERS	5 948	627	→	4 975	346
	% BY SECTOR		10.5	→	83.6	5.8
COLOMBIA ‡ 1971	SCIENTISTS AND ENGINEERS	1 140	239	→	285	616
	% BY SECTOR		21.0	→	25.0	54.0
ECUADOR ‡ 1976	TOTAL IN R&D	1 038	4	787	247	—
	% BY SECTOR		0.4	75.8	23.8	—
	SCIENTISTS AND ENGINEERS	469	2	376	91	—
	TECHNICIANS	411	1	328	82	—
	AUXILIARY PERSONNEL	158	1	83	74	—
PARAGUAY 1971	SCIENTISTS AND ENGINEERS	134	38	→	49	47
	% BY SECTOR		28.3	→	36.6	35.1

5.4 R&D personnel by sector of performance
Personnel de R-D par secteur d'exécution
Personal de I y D por sector de ejecución

SECTOR OF PERFORMANCE / SECTEUR D'EXECUTION / SECTOR DE EJECUCION

COUNTRY / PAYS / PAIS	YEAR / ANNEE / AÑO	TYPE OF PERSONNEL / CATEGORIE DE PERSONNEL / CATEGORIA DE PERSONAL	ALL SECTORS / TOUS SECTEURS / TODOS LOS SECTORES (1)	PRODUCTIVE SECTOR — SECTEUR DE LA PRODUCTION — SECTOR PRODUCTIVO — INTEGRATED R&D / ACTIVITES DE R-D INTEGREES / ACTIVIDADES DE I Y D INTEGRADAS (2)	NON-INTEGRATED R&D / ACTIVITES DE R-D NON INTEGREES / ACTIVIDADES DE I Y D NO INTEGRADAS (3)	HIGHER EDUCATION / ENSEIGNEMENT SUPERIEUR / ENSEÑANZA SUPERIOR (4)	GENERAL SERVICE / SERVICE GENERAL / SERVICIO GENERAL (5)
PERU	1976	TOTAL IN R&D	*8 984	*992	*2 793	*1 609	*3 590
		% BY SECTOR		*11.0	*31.1	*17.9	*40.0
		SCIENTISTS AND ENGINEERS	*3 932	416	879	1 544	1 093
		TECHNICIANS	*2 235	*276	*587	*6	*1 366
		AUXILIARY PERSONNEL	*2 817	*300	*1 327	*59	*1 131
URUGUAY ‡	1971	TOTAL IN R&D	*3 033	*385	*758	*1 068	*822
		% BY SECTOR		*12.7	*25.0	*35.2	*27.1
		SCIENTISTS AND ENGINEERS	*1 150	*114	*280	*537	*219
		TECHNICIANS	*1 087	*138	*241	*336	*372
		AUXILIARY PERSONNEL	*796	*133	*237	*195	*231
VENEZUELA	1970	TOTAL IN R&D	4 608	27	—	2 785	1 796
		% BY SECTOR		0.6	—	60.4	39.0
		SCIENTISTS AND ENGINEERS	1 779	5	—	1 277	497
		TECHNICIANS	1 053	12	—	524	517
		AUXILIARY PERSONNEL	1 776	10	—	984	782
ASIA							
BRUNEI	1974	TOTAL IN R&D	407	357	—	—	50
		% BY SECTOR		87.7	—	—	12.3
		SCIENTISTS AND ENGINEERS	22	16	—	—	6
		TECHNICIANS	17	11	—	—	6
		AUXILIARY PERSONNEL	368	330	—	—	38
CYPRUS	1971	TOTAL IN R&D	511	—	88	—	423
		% BY SECTOR		—	17.2	—	82.8
		SCIENTISTS AND ENGINEERS	117	—	35	—	82
		TECHNICIANS	154	—	41	—	113
		AUXILIARY PERSONNEL	240	—	12	—	228
INDIA ‡	1976	SCIENTISTS AND ENGINEERS	28 233	3 634	——→	...	24 599
		% BY SECTOR		12.9			87.1
INDONESIA ‡	1975	TOTAL IN R&D	24 149	648	—	10 601	12 900
		% BY SECTOR		2.7	—	43.9	53.4
		SCIENTISTS AND ENGINEERS	7 645	107	—	4 693	2 845
		TECHNICIANS	5 320	238	—	1 794	3 288
		AUXILIARY PERSONNEL	11 184	303	—	4 114	6 767

R&D personnel by sector of performance 5.4
Personnel de R-D par secteur d'exécution
Personal de I y D por sector de ejecución

Country / Year		(1)	(2)	(3)	(4)	(5)
IRAN 1972	TOTAL IN R&D	9 865	2 946	→	5 372	1 547
	% BY SECTOR		29.9		54.4	15.7
	SCIENTISTS AND ENGINEERS	4 896	898	→	3 395	603
	TECHNICIANS	857	127	→	576	154
	AUXILIARY PERSONNEL	4 112	1 921	→	1 401	790
IRAQ ‡ 1974	TOTAL IN R & D	1 862	....	630	244	988
	% BY SECTOR			33.8	13.1	53.1
	SCIENTISTS AND ENGINEERS	1 486	....	489	244	753
	TECHNICIANS	376	....	141	...	235
ISRAEL ‡ 1974	SCIENTISTS AND ENGINEERS	21 900	6 500	./.	6 000	9 400
	% BY SECTOR		29.7	./.	27.4	42.9
JAPAN ‡ 1978	TOTAL IN R&D	564 915	305 742	→	197 831	61 342
	% BY SECTOR		54.1		35.0	10.9
	SCIENTISTS AND ENGINEERS	407 708	215 207	→	156 932	35 569
	TECHNICIANS	84 374	61 115	→	12 596	10 663
	AUXILIARY PERSONNEL	72 833	29 420	→	28 303	15 110
JORDAN ‡ 1976	TOTAL IN R&D	417	32	-	151	234
	% BY SECTOR		7.7	-	36.2	56.1
	SCIENTISTS AND ENGINEERS	208	16	-	75	117
	TECHNICIANS	146	11	-	53	82
	AUXILIARY PERSONNEL	63	5	-	23	35
KOREA, REPUBLIC OF ‡ 1978	TOTAL IN R&D	30 214	9 759	5 401	8 598	6 456
	% BY SECTOR		32.3	17.9	28.4	21.4
	SCIENTISTS AND ENGINEERS	14 749	4 304	2 066	5 721	2 658
	TECHNICIANS	8 909	4 055	1 508	1 592	1 754
	AUXILIARY PERSONNEL	6 556	1 400	1 827	1 285	2 044
KUWAIT ‡ 1977	TOTAL IN R&D	767	-	230	120	417
	% BY SECTOR			30.0	15.7	54.3
	SCIENTISTS AND ENGINEERS	606	-	183	111	312
	TECHNICIANS	161	-	47	9	105
LAO PEOPLE'S DEMOCRATIC REPUBLIC 1970	SCIENTISTS AND ENGINEERS	364			26	....
PAKISTAN ‡ 1973	TOTAL IN R&D	8 790	7 634	→	474	682
	% BY SECTOR		86.8		5.4	7.8
	SCIENTISTS AND ENGINEERS	4 164	3 304	→	362	498
	TECHNICIANS	4 626	*4 330	→	112	184
PHILIPPINES ‡ 1976	TOTAL IN R&D	....	....	....	....	*8 720
	SCIENTISTS AND ENGINEERS	....	....	....	....	*3 647
	TECHNICIANS	....	....	....	....	*2 408
	AUXILIARY PERSONNEL	....	....	....	....	*2 665
SINGAPORE 1978	TOTAL IN R&D	1 077	734	→	191	152
	% BY SECTOR		51.4		40.4	8.2
	SCIENTISTS AND ENGINEERS	461	328	→	91	42
	TECHNICIANS	267	169	→	54	44
	AUXILIARY PERSONNEL	349	237	→	46	66
SRI LANKA ‡ 1972	TOTAL IN R&D	37 288	11 074	....	781	25 433
	% BY SECTOR		29.7		2.1	68.2
	SCIENTISTS AND ENGINEERS	2 076	466	....	440	1 170
	TECHNICIANS	5 265	930	....	223	4 112
	AUXILIARY PERSONNEL	29 947	9 678	....	118	20 151

5.4 R&D personnel by sector of performance
Personnel de R-D par secteur d'exécution
Personal de I y D por sector de ejecución

SECTOR OF PERFORMANCE / SECTEUR D'EXECUTION / SECTOR DE EJECUCION

COUNTRY / PAYS / PAIS	YEAR / ANNEE / AÑO	TYPE OF PERSONNEL / CATEGORIE DE PERSONNEL / CATEGORIA DE PERSONAL	ALL SECTORS / TOUS SECTEURS / TODOS LOS SECTORES (1)	PRODUCTIVE SECTOR — INTEGRATED R&D / ACTIVITES DE R-D INTEGREES / ACTIVIDADES DE I Y D INTEGRADAS (2)	PRODUCTIVE SECTOR — NON-INTEGRATED R&D / ACTIVITES DE R-D NON INTEGREES / ACTIVIDADES DE I Y D NO INTEGRADAS (3)	HIGHER EDUCATION / ENSEIGNEMENT SUPERIEUR / ENSEÑANZA SUPERIOR (4)	GENERAL SERVICE / SERVICE GENERAL / SERVICIO GENERAL (5)
THAILAND ‡	1973	SCIENTISTS AND ENGINEERS	7 840	1 826		1 455	4 559
		% BY SECTOR		23.3		18.6	58.1
TURKEY ‡	1975	TOTAL IN R&D	8 910			7 239	11 693
		SCIENTISTS AND ENGINEERS	...			...	1 671
		TECHNICIANS	...			...	3 891
		AUXILIARY PERSONNEL					6 131
VIET-NAM ‡	1978 1976 1978	TOTAL IN R&D	25 050	8 100	7 650	3 830	5 470
		% BY SECTOR		32.3	30.6	15.3	21.8
		SCIENTISTS AND ENGINEERS	13 050	4 200	1 750	3 830	3 270
		TECHNICIANS	6 040	1 900	2 640		1 500
		AUXILIARY PERSONNEL	5 960	2 000	3 260		700
YEMEN ‡	1974	TOTAL IN R&D	112	—	58	—	54
		% BY SECTOR		—	51.8	—	48.2
		SCIENTISTS AND ENGINEERS	60	—	30	—	30
		TECHNICIANS	52	—	28	—	24
EUROPE							
AUSTRIA ‡	1972	TOTAL IN R&D	7 843	7 223	620	...	...
		% BY SECTOR		92.1	7.9	...	...
		SCIENTISTS AND ENGINEERS	1 870	1 703	167	...	...
		TECHNICIANS	2 790	2 537	253	...	...
		AUXILIARY PERSONNEL	3 183	2 982	200	...	...
BELGIUM	1977	TOTAL IN R&D	30 186	17 969	1 117	8 290	2 810
		% BY SECTOR		59.5	3.7	27.5	9.3
		SCIENTISTS AND ENGINEERS	13 883	6 302	413	5 862	1 306
		TECHNICIANS	7 696	4 834	302	1 742	818
		AUXILIARY PERSONNEL	8 607	6 833	402	686	686
BULGARIA ‡	1978	TOTAL IN R&D	65 992	44 149	>	9 846	11 997
		% BY SECTOR		66.9	>	14.9	18.2
		SCIENTISTS AND ENGINEERS	33 656	16 176	>	9 846	7 634
		TECHNICIANS	10 682	9 659	>		1 023
		AUXILIARY PERSONNEL	21 654	18 314	>		3 340
CZECHOSLOVAKIA ‡	1978	TOTAL IN R&D	165 695	70 299	66 071	4 913	24 412
		% BY SECTOR		42.4	39.9	3.0	14.7
		SCIENTISTS AND ENGINEERS	50 007	17 533	19 893	2 739	9 842
		TECHNICIANS	59 954	28 718	21 618	1 754	7 864
		AUXILIARY PERSONNEL	55 734	24 048	24 560	420	6 706

R&D personnel by sector of performance   5.4
Personnel de R-D par secteur d'exécution
Personal de I y D por sector de ejecución

		(1)	(2)	(3)	(4)	(5)
DENMARK ‡	1976					
TOTAL IN R&D		13 801	6 694	551	3 473	3 083
% BY SECTOR			48.5	4.0	25.2	22.3
SCIENTISTS AND ENGINEERS		5 353	1 483	214	2 190	1 466
TECHNICIANS		8 448	5 211	337	1 283	1 617
AUXILIARY PERSONNEL		./.	./.	./.	./.	./.
FINLAND ‡	1977					
TOTAL IN R&D		14 254	6 246	282	3 240	4 486
% BY SECTOR			43.8	2.0	22.7	31.5
SCIENTISTS AND ENGINEERS		7 162	2 625	139	2 454	1 944
TECHNICIANS		7 092	3 621	143	786	2 542
AUXILIARY PERSONNEL		./.	./.	./.		
FRANCE ‡	1977					
TOTAL IN R&D		222 111	118 715	6 068	43 930	53 398
% BY SECTOR			53.5	2.7	19.8	24.0
SCIENTISTS AND ENGINEERS		67 981	30 064	2 056	22 636	13 225
TECHNICIANS		154 130	53 538	2 403	21 294	40 173
AUXILIARY PERSONNEL			35 113	1 609		
GERMANY, FEDERAL REPUBLIC OF	1977					
TOTAL IN R&D		319 347	193 068	4 732	67 838	53 709
% BY SECTOR			60.5	1.5	21.2	16.8
SCIENTISTS AND ENGINEERS		110 972	64 484	1 739	27 085	17 664
TECHNICIANS		104 400	63 823	1 631	23 190	15 756
AUXILIARY PERSONNEL		103 975	64 761	1 362	17 563	20 289
GREECE	1976					
TOTAL IN R&D		5 345	1 758	→	1 181	2 406
% BY SECTOR			32.9	→	22.1	45.0
SCIENTISTS AND ENGINEERS		2 569	678	→	843	1 048
TECHNICIANS		1 759	684	→	220	855
AUXILIARY PERSONNEL		1 017	396	→	118	503
HOLY SEE	1976					
TOTAL IN R&D		424	—	—	424	—
% BY SECTOR			—	—	100.0	—
SCIENTISTS AND ENGINEERS		351	—	—	351	—
TECHNICIANS		11	—	—	11	—
AUXILIARY PERSONNEL		62	—	—	62	—
HUNGARY ‡	1978					
TOTAL IN R&D		63 263	17 462	24 512	7 969	13 320
% BY SECTOR			27.6	38.8	12.6	21.0
SCIENTISTS AND ENGINEERS		25 308	6 565	8 149	4 607	5 987
TECHNICIANS		25 884	10 897	8 346	2 629	4 012
AUXILIARY PERSONNEL		12 071	./.	8 017	733	3 321
ICELAND ‡	1970					
TOTAL IN R&D		256	7	—	40	209
% BY SECTOR			2.7	—	15.6	81.7
SCIENTISTS AND ENGINEERS		126	4	—	20	102
TECHNICIANS		130	3	—	20	107
IRELAND	1977					
TOTAL IN R&D		5 827	1 413	→	1 605	2 809
% BY SECTOR			24.3	→	27.5	48.2
SCIENTISTS AND ENGINEERS		2 685	525	→	1 277	883
TECHNICIANS		1 465	483	→	189	793
AUXILIARY PERSONNEL		1 677	405	→	139	1 133
ITALY	1976					
TOTAL IN R&D		95 675	39 434	→	38 023	18 218
% BY SECTOR			41.2	→	39.8	19.0
SCIENTISTS AND ENGINEERS		37 878	13 554	→	18 210	6 114
TECHNICIANS		27 568	13 615	→	7 780	6 173
AUXILIARY PERSONNEL		30 229	12 265	→	12 033	5 931

5.4 R&D personnel by sector of performance
Personnel de R-D par secteur d'exécution
Personal de I y D por sector de ejecución

SECTOR OF PERFORMANCE / SECTEUR D'EXECUTION / SECTOR DE EJECUCION

COUNTRY / PAYS / PAIS	YEAR / ANNEE / AÑO	TYPE OF PERSONNEL / CATEGORIE DE PERSONNEL / CATEGORIA DE PERSONAL	ALL SECTORS / TOUS SECTEURS / TODOS LOS SECTORES (1)	PRODUCTIVE SECTOR / SECTEUR DE LA PRODUCTION / SECTOR PRODUCTIVO — INTEGRATED R&D / ACTIVITES DE R-D INTEGREES / ACTIVIDADES DE I Y D INTEGRADAS (2)	NON-INTEGRATED R&D / ACTIVITES DE R-D NON INTEGREES / ACTIVIDADES DE I Y D NO INTEGRADAS (3)	HIGHER EDUCATION / ENSEIGNEMENT SUPERIEUR / ENSEÑANZA SUPERIOR (4)	GENERAL SERVICE / SERVICE GENERAL / SERVICIO GENERAL (5)
MALTA	1973	TOTAL IN R&D	...	...	...	73	...
		SCIENTISTS AND ENGINEERS	...	...	...	39	...
		TECHNICIANS	...	...	...	22	...
		AUXILIARY PERSONNEL	...	...	...	12	...
NETHERLANDS ‡	1976	TOTAL IN R&D	54 100	27 170	590	12 480	13 860
		% BY SECTOR		50.2	1.1	23.1	25.6
		SCIENTISTS AND ENGINEERS	24 250	11 310	270	5 750	6 920
		TECHNICIANS	29 850	5 740	100	6 730	2 210
		AUXILIARY PERSONNEL	./.	10 120	220	./.	4 730
NORWAY ‡	1978	TOTAL IN R&D	13 990	4 490	1 900	4 560	3 040
		% BY SECTOR		32.1	13.6	32.6	21.7
		SCIENTISTS AND ENGINEERS	6 450	1 370	1 070	2 620	1 390
		TECHNICIANS	7 540	3 120	830	1 940	1 650
		AUXILIARY PERSONNEL	./.	./.	./.	./.	./.
POLAND ‡	1978 1970 1978	TOTAL IN R&D	253 200	55 500	159 500	16 100	22 100
		% BY SECTOR		21.9	63.0	6.4	8.7
		SCIENTISTS AND ENGINEERS	91 600	16 400	48 900	16 100	10 200
		TECHNICIANS	62 100	21 000	37 200	...	3 900
		AUXILIARY PERSONNEL	99 500	18 100	73 400	...	8 000
PORTUGAL	1976	TOTAL IN R&D	6 721	1 080	→	1 554	4 087
		% BY SECTOR		16.1	→	23.1	60.8
		SCIENTISTS AND ENGINEERS	1 749	128	→	756	865
		TECHNICIANS	2 261	487	→	365	1 409
		AUXILIARY PERSONNEL	2 711	465	→	433	1 813
ROMANIA	1973	TOTAL IN R&D	62 918	4 570	42 992	5 942	9 414
		% BY SECTOR		7.3	68.3	9.4	15.0
		SCIENTISTS AND ENGINEERS	26 107	1 111	15 210	4 762	5 024
		TECHNICIANS	12 651	1 180	8 573	718	2 180
		AUXILIARY PERSONNEL	24 160	2 279	19 209	462	2 210
SPAIN ‡	1974	TOTAL IN R&D	23 182	11 108	./.	2 651	9 423
		% BY SECTOR		47.9	./.	11.4	40.7
		SCIENTISTS AND ENGINEERS	7 924	2 617	./.	2 316	2 991
		TECHNICIANS	3 931	3 043	./.	63	825
		AUXILIARY PERSONNEL	11 327	5 448	./.	272	5 607

R&D personnel by sector of performance 5.4
Personnel de R-D par secteur d'exécution
Personal de I y D por sector de ejecución

		(1)	(2)	(3)	(4)	(5)
SWEDEN ‡ 1977	TOTAL IN R&D	36 283	21 886	2 359	*8 500	3 538
	% BY SECTOR		60.3	6.5	23.4	9.8
	SCIENTISTS AND ENGINEERS	14 102	7 825	955	*3 500	1 822
	TECHNICIANS	22 181	14 061	1 404	*5 000	1 716
	AUXILIARY PERSONNEL	./.	./.	./.	./.	./.
SWITZERLAND ‡ 1975	TOTAL IN R&D	27 040	17 630	→	6 970	2 440
	% BY SECTOR		65.2	→	25.8	9.0
	SCIENTISTS AND ENGINEERS	16 230	10 590	→	4 670	970
	TECHNICIANS	10 810	7 040	→	2 300	1 470
	AUXILIARY PERSONNEL	./.	./.	→	./.	./.
UNITED KINGDOM ‡ 1975	TOTAL IN R&D	259 100	174 600	5 500	...	79 000
	% BY SECTOR		67.4	2.1	...	30.5
	SCIENTISTS AND ENGINEERS	79 300	57 600	2 000	...	19 700
	TECHNICIANS	75 800	63 300	1 700	...	10 800
	AUXILIARY PERSONNEL	104 000	53 700	1 800	...	48 500
YUGOSLAVIA ‡ 1977	TOTAL IN R&D	45 698	10 321	14 649	8 817	11 911
	% BY SECTOR		22.6	32.0	19.3	26.1
	SCIENTISTS AND ENGINEERS	21 680	3 347	5 340	7 023	5 970
	TECHNICIANS	10 366	3 572	3 825	675	2 294
	AUXILIARY PERSONNEL	13 652	3 402	5 484	1 119	3 647
OCEANIA						
AMERICAN SAMOA ‡ 1971	TOTAL IN R&D	15	15	—	—	—
	% BY SECTOR		100.0	—	—	—
	SCIENTISTS AND ENGINEERS	3	3	—	—	—
	TECHNICIANS	2	2	—	—	—
	AUXILIARY PERSONNEL	10	10	—	—	—
AUSTRALIA ‡ 1976	TOTAL IN R&D	43 574	9 129	5 732	15 290	13 423
	% BY SECTOR		21.0	13.1	35.1	30.8
	SCIENTISTS AND ENGINEERS	22 510	3 993	2 308	11 286	4 923
	TECHNICIANS	12 568	3 604	1 693	3 189	4 082
	AUXILIARY PERSONNEL	8 496	1 532	1 731	815	4 418
COOK ISLANDS 1970	TOTAL IN R&D	9	9	→	—	—
	% BY SECTOR		100.0	→	—	—
	SCIENTISTS AND ENGINEERS	9	9	→	—	—
	TECHNICIANS	—	—	—	—	—
	AUXILIARY PERSONNEL	—	—	—	—	—
FRENCH POLYNESIA ‡ 1976	TOTAL IN R&D	91	—	—	—	91
	% BY SECTOR		—	—	—	100.0
	SCIENTISTS AND ENGINEERS	11	—	—	—	11
	TECHNICIANS	21	—	—	—	21
	AUXILIARY PERSONNEL	59	—	—	—	59
GUAM 1977	TOTAL IN R&D	213	5	—	88	120
	% BY SECTOR		2.3	—	41.3	56.4
	SCIENTISTS AND ENGINEERS					
	TECHNICIANS					
	AUXILIARY PERSONNEL					
NEW CALEDONIA 1971	TOTAL IN R&D	1	—	—	—	1
	% BY SECTOR		—	—	—	100.0
	SCIENTISTS AND ENGINEERS	0	—	—	—	0
	TECHNICIANS	1	—	—	—	1
	AUXILIARY PERSONNEL	0	—	—	—	0

5.4 R&D personnel by sector of performance
Personnel de R-D par secteur d'exécution
Personal de I y D por sector de ejecución

			SECTOR OF PERFORMANCE / SECTEUR D'EXECUTION / SECTOR DE EJECUCION				
			ALL SECTORS	PRODUCTIVE SECTOR — SECTEUR DE LA PRODUCTION — SECTOR PRODUCTIVO		HIGHER EDUCATION	GENERAL SERVICE
				INTEGRATED R&D	NON-INTEGRATED R&D		
COUNTRY	YEAR	TYPE OF PERSONNEL	TOUS SECTEURS	ACTIVITES DE R-D INTEGREES	ACTIVITES DE R-D NON INTEGREES	ENSEIGNEMENT SUPERIEUR	SERVICE GENERAL
PAYS	ANNEE	CATEGORIE DE PERSONNEL					
PAIS	AÑO	CATEGORIA DE PERSONAL	TODOS LOS SECTORES	ACTIVIDADES DE I Y D INTEGRADAS	ACTIVIDADES DE I Y D NO INTEGRADAS	ENSEÑANZA SUPERIOR	SERVICIO GENERAL
			(1)	(2)	(3)	(4)	(5)
NEW HEBRIDES	1975	TOTAL IN R&D	39	—	39	—	—
		% BY SECTOR		—	100.0	—	—
		SCIENTISTS AND ENGINEERS	3	—	3	—	—
		TECHNICIANS	1	—	1	—	—
		AUXILIARY PERSONNEL	35	—	35	—	—
NEW ZEALAND ‡	1975	TOTAL IN R&D	8 003	1 896	3 254	1 256	1 597
		% BY SECTOR		23.7	40.6	15.7	20.0
		SCIENTISTS AND ENGINEERS	3 659	902	1 080	1 048	629
		TECHNICIANS	3 164	897	1 373	208	686
		AUXILIARY PERSONNEL	1 180	97	801	...	282
PACIFIC ISLANDS	1978	TOTAL IN R&D	22	—	16	—	6
		% BY SECTOR		—	72.7	—	27.3
		SCIENTISTS AND ENGINEERS	5	—	3	—	2
		TECHNICIANS	11	—	9	—	2
		AUXILIARY PERSONNEL	6	—	4	—	2
PAPUA NEW GUINEA	1973	SCIENTISTS AND ENGINEERS	131	105	—	26	—
		% BY SECTOR		80.2	—	19.8	—
SAMOA ‡	1978	TOTAL IN R&D	280	73	65	85	57
		% BY SECTOR		26.1	23.2	30.4	20.3
		SCIENTISTS AND ENGINEERS	140	30	25	60	25
		TECHNICIANS	92	18	25	21	25
		AUXILIARY PERSONNEL	48	25	15	4	4

BOTSWANA:
E—> NOT INCLUDING AUXILIARY PERSONNEL.
FR-> NON COMPRIS LE PERSONNEL AUXILIAIRE.
ESP> EXCLUIDO EL PERSONAL AUXILIAR.

CONGO:
E—> DATA REFERRING TO SCIENTISTS AND ENGINEERS ARE FULL-TIME PLUS PART-TIME.
FR-> POUR LES SCIENTIFIQUES ET INGENIEURS, LES DONNEES SE REFERENT AUX EFFECTIFS A PLEIN TEMPS ET A TEMPS PARTIEL.
ESP> PARA LOS CIENTIFICOS E INGENIEROS LOS DATOS SE REFIEREN A LOS EFECTIVOS DE JORNADA COMPLETA Y DE JORNADA PARCIAL.

GABON:
E—> DATA RELATE TO THE (FRENCH) "OFFICE DE LA RECHERCHE SCIENTIFIQUE ET TECHNIQUE OUTRE-MER" (ORSTOM) ONLY.
FR-> LES DONNEES NE CONCERNENT QUE L'OFFICE FRANCAIS DE LA RECHERCHE SCIENTIFIQUE ET TECHNIQUE OUTRE-MER (ORSTOM).
ESP> LOS DATOS SE REFIEREN AL "OFFICE (FRANCAIS) DE LA RECHERCHE SCIENTIFIQUE ET TECHNIQUE OUTRE-MER" (ORSTOM) SOLAMENTE.

GHANA:
E—> AUXILIARY PERSONNEL AND TECHNICIANS ARE COUNTED TOGETHER.

R&D personnel by sector of performance **5.4**
Personnel de R-D par secteur d'exécution
Personal de I y D por sector de ejecución

GHANA (CONT.):
FR—> LE PERSONNEL AUXILIAIRE ET LES TECHNICIENS SONT COMPTES ENSEMBLE.
ESP> EL PERSONAL AUXILIAR Y LOS TECNICOS SE CUENTAN CONJUNTAMENTE.

IVORY COAST
E—> NOT INCLUDING AUXILIARY PERSONNEL.
FR—> NON COMPRIS LE PERSONNEL AUXILIAIRE.
ESP> EXCLUIDO EL PERSONAL AUXILIAR.

KENYA:
E—> NOT INCLUDING AUXILIARY PERSONNEL. DATA FOR HUMANITIES ARE ALSO EXCLUDED.
FR—> NON COMPRIS LE PERSONNEL AUXILIAIRE. LES DONNEES RELATIVES AUX SCIENCES HUMAINES SONT EXCLUES.
ESP> NO INCLUYE EL PERSONAL AUXILIAR. SE EXCLUYEN LOS DATOS RELATIVOS A LAS CIENCIAS HUMANAS.

MADAGASCAR:
E—> NOT INCLUDING AUXILIARY PERSONNEL. DATA ALSO EXCLUDE THE PRODUCTIVE SECTOR (INTEGRATED R&D)
FR—> NON COMPRIS LE PERSONNEL AUXILIAIRE. LES DONNEES EXCLUENT EGALEMENT LE SECTEUR DE LA PRODUCTION (ACTIVITES DE R-D INTEGREES).
ESP> NO INCLUYE EL PERSONAL AUXILIAR. LOS DATOS EXCLUYEN IGUALMENTE EL SECTOR PRODUCTIVO (ACTIVIDADES DE I Y D INTEGRADAS).

NIGERIA:
E—> DATA RELATE TO THE YEAR 1970/71 AND DO NOT INCLUDE SOCIAL SCIENCES AND HUMANITIES.
FR—> LES DONNEES SE REFERENT A L'ANNEE 1970/71 ET NE COMPRENNENT PAS LES SCIENCES SOCIALES ET HUMAINES.
ESP> LOS DATOS SE REFIEREN AL AÑO 1970/71 Y NO INCLUYEN LAS CIENCIAS SOCIALES Y HUMANAS.

SENEGAL:
E—> NOT INCLUDING AUXILIARY PERSONNEL.
FR—> NON COMPRIS LE PERSONNEL AUXILIAIRE.
ESP> EXCLUIDO EL PERSONAL AUXILIAR.

TOGO:
E—> NOT INCLUDING AUXILIARY PERSONNEL. DATA REFERRING TO THE PRODUCTIVE SECTOR (INTEGRATED R&D) ARE INCLUDED WITH THE GENERAL SERVICE SECTOR. SCIENTISTS AND ENGINEERS ARE FULL-TIME.
FR—> NON COMPRIS LE PERSONNEL AUXILIAIRE. LES DONNEES RELATIVES AU SECTEUR DE LA PRODUCTION (ACTIVITES DE R-D INTEGREES) SONT COMPRISES AVEC CELLES DU SECTEUR DE SERVICE GENERAL. POUR LES SCIENTIFIQUES ET INGENIEURS, LES DONNEES SE REFERENT AUX EFFECTIFS A PLEIN TEMPS.
ESP> EXCLUIDO EL PERSONAL AUXILIAR. LOS DATOS CORRESPONDIENTES AL SECTOR PRODUCTIVO (ACTIVIDADES DE I Y D INTEGRADAS) FIGURAN EN EL SECTOR DE SERVICIO GENERAL. PARA LOS CIENTIFICOS E INGENIEROS LOS DATOS SE REFIEREN A LOS EFECTIVOS DE JORNADA COMPLETA.

ZAMBIA:
E—> PARTIAL DATA FOR 9 INSTITUTES ONLY.
FR—> DONNEES PARTIELLES POUR NEUF INSTITUTS SEULEMENT.
ESP> DATOS PARCIALES PARA NUEVE INSTITUTOS SOLAMENTE.

BERMUDA:
E—> NOT INCLUDING DATA FOR THE PRODUCTIVE SECTOR AND EXCLUDING LAW, HUMANITIES AND EDUCATION.
FR—> NON COMPRIS LES DONNEES POUR LE SECTEUR DE LA PRODUCTION ET COMPTE NON TENU DU DROIT, DES SCIENCES HUMAINES ET DE L'EDUCATION.
ESP> NO INCLUYE LOS DATOS RELATIVOS AL SECTOR PRODUCTIVO NI LOS QUE SE REFIEREN AL DERECHO, LAS CIENCIAS HUMANAS Y LA EDUCACION.

CANADA:
E—> DATA FOR THE PRODUCTIVE SECTOR (NON-INTEGRATED R&D) ARE INCLUDED WITH THE GENERAL SERVICE SECTOR.
FR—> LES DONNEES RELATIVES AU SECTEUR DE LA PRODUCTION (ACTIVITES DE R-D NON-INTEGREES) SONT COMPRISES AVEC CELLES DU SECTEUR DE SERVICE GENERAL.
ESP> LOS DATOS CORRESPONDIENTES AL SECTOR PRODUCTIVO (ACTIVIDADES DE I Y D NO INTEGRADAS) ESTAN INCLUIDOS EN EL SECTOR DE SERVICIO GENERAL.

GUATEMALA:
E—> NOT INCLUDING AUXILIARY PERSONNEL.
FR—> NON COMPRIS LE PERSONNEL AUXILIAIRE.
ESP> EXCLUIDO EL PERSONAL AUXILIAR.

HONDURAS:
E—> DATA RELATE TO ONE RESEARCH INSTITUTE ONLY. SCIENTISTS AND ENGINEERS ARE FULL-TIME.
FR—> LES DONNEES NE CONCERNENT QU'UN SEUL INSTITUT DE RECHERCHE. POUR LES SCIENTIFIQUES ET INGENIEURS, LES DONNEES SE REFERENT AUX EFFECTIFS A PLEIN TEMPS.
ESP> LOS DATOS SE REFIEREN A UN INSTITUTO DE INVESTIGACION SOLAMENTE. PARA LOS CIENTIFICOS E INGENIEROS LOS DATOS SE REFIEREN A LOS EFECTIVOS DE JORNADA COMPLETA.

ST. PIERRE AND MIQUELON:
E—> DATA RELATE TO THE "INSTITUT SCIENTIFIQUE ET TECHNIQUE DES PECHES MARITIMES" ONLY.
FR—> LES DONNEES NE CONCERNENT QUE L'INSTITUT SCIENTIFIQUE ET TECHNIQUE DES PECHES MARITIMES.
ESP> LOS DATOS SE REFIEREN AL "INSTITUT SCIENTIFIQUE ET TECHNIQUE DES PECHES MARITIMES" SOLAMENTE.

TRINIDAD AND TOBAGO:
E—> NOT INCLUDING AUXILIARY PERSONNEL. DATA REFERRING TO SCIENTISTS AND ENGINEERS ARE FULL-TIME PLUS PART-TIME. THE TOTALS IN COLUMN 1 ARE LESS THAN THE SUM OF THE COMPONENT PARTS DUE TO DOUBLE COUNTING IN THE DIFFERENT SECTORS. COLUMN 4 INCLUDES TECHNICAL SECONDARY SCHOOLS; COLUMN 5 REFERS TO OTHER GOVERNMENT SECTORS INCLUDING PRIVATE NON-PROFIT ORGANIZATIONS NOT PROVIDING

5.4 R&D personnel by sector of performance
Personnel de R-D par secteur d'exécution
Personal de I y D por sector de ejecución

BRAZIL:
E—> NOT INCLUDING DATA FOR THE GENERAL SERVICE SECTOR AND ALSO EXCLUDING TECHNICIANS AND AUXILI- ARY PERSONNEL IN THE HIGHER EDUCATION SECTOR.
FR—> NON COMPRIS LES DONNEES RELATIVES AU SECTEUR DE SERVICE GENERAL ET COMPTE NON TENU DES TECHNICIENS ET DU PERSONNEL AUXILIAIRE DU SECTEUR DE L'ENSEIGNEMENT SUPERIEUR.
ESP> NO INCLUYE LOS DATOS RELATIVOS AL SECTOR DE SERVICIO GENERAL, NI LOS QUE SE REFIEREN A LOS TECNICOS Y AL PERSONAL AUXILIAR DEL SECTOR DE ENSEÑANZA SUPERIOR.

COLOMBIA:
E—>DATA REFERRING TO SCIENTISTS AND ENGINEERS ARE FULL-TIME PLUS PART-TIME. NOT INCLUDING DATA FOR LAW, HUMANITIES AND EDUCATION.
FR—> POUR LES SCIENTIFIQUES ET INGENIEURS, LES DONNEES SE REFERENT AUX EFFECTIFS A PLEIN TEMPS ET A TEMPS PARTIEL. NON COMPRIS LES DONNEES POUR LE DROIT, LES SCIENCES HUMAINES ET L'EDUCATION.
ESP>PARA LOS CIENTIFICOS E INGENIEROS LOS DATOS SE REFIEREN A LOS EFECTIVOS DE JORNADA COMPLETA Y DE JORNADA PARCIAL. EXCLUIDOS LOS DATOS RELATIVOS AL DERECHO, LAS CIENCIAS HUMANAS Y LA EDUCACION.

ECUADOR:
E—> DATA REFER TO R&D IN THE AGRICULTURAL SCIENCES ONLY.
FR—> LES DONNEES SE REFERENT A LA R-D DANS LES SCIENCES DE L'AGRICULTURE SEULEMENT.
ESP> LOS DATOS SE REFIEREN A LA I Y D DE LAS CIENCIAS AGRICOLAS SOLAMENTE.

URUGUAY:
E—>DATA REFER TO THE YEAR 1971/72.
FR—> LES DONNEES SE REFERENT A L'ANNEE 1971/72.
ESP> LOS DATOS SE REFIEREN AL AÑO 1971/72.

INDIA:
E—> NOT INCLUDING DATA FOR THE HIGHER EDUCATION SECTOR. IN ADDITION, THERE ARE 25, 872 TECHNICIANS AND AUXILIARY PERSONNEL FOR WHOM A DISTRIBUTION BY SECTOR OF PERFORMANCE IS NOT AVAILABLE.
FR—> COMPTE NON TENU DU SECTEUR DE L'ENSEIGNE- MENT SUPERIEUR. EN OUTRE, IL Y A 25 872 TECHNI- CIENS ET MEMBRES DU PERSONNEL AUXILIAIRE POUR LESQUELS LA REPARTITION PAR SECTEUR D'EXECUTION N'EST PAS DISPONIBLE.
ESP> EXCLUIDOS LOS DATOS RELATIVOS AL SECTOR DE ENSEÑANZA SUPERIOR. EXISTEN ADEMAS 25 872 TECNICOS Y MIEMBROS DEL PERSONAL AUXILIAR CUYA REPARTICION POR SECTOR DE EJECUCION NO SE HA PRECISADO.

INDONESIA:
E—> DATA RELATE TO THE YEAR 1975/76.
FR—> LES DONNEES SE REFERENT A L'ANNEE 1975/76.
ESP> LOS DATOS SE REFIEREN AL AÑO 1975/76.

IRAQ:
E—> DATA REFER ONLY TO THOSE WORKING IN GOVERN- MENT DEPARTMENTS CONCERNED WITH SCIENTIFIC ACTIVI- TIES AND DO NOT INCLUDE THE PRODUCTIVE SECTOR (IN- TEGRATED R&D). TECHNICIANS IN THE HIGHER EDUCATION

TRINIDAD AND TOBAGO (CONT.): NOT INCLUDING SERVICES TO SPECIFIC ENTERPRISES. NOT INCLUDING DATA FOR LAW, EDUCATION AND ARTS.
FR—> NON COMPRIS LE PERSONNEL AUXILIAIRE. POUR LES SCIENTIFIQUES ET INGENIEURS, LES DONNEES SE REFERENT AUX EFFECTIFS A PLEIN TEMPS ET A TEMPS PARTIEL. LE TOTAL DE LA COLONNE 1 EST INFERIEUR A LA SOMME DES ELEMENTS QUI LE COMPOSENT EN RAISON D'UN DOUBLE COMPTE DANS LES DIFFERENTS SECTEURS. LE CHIFFRE DE LA COLONNE 4 COMPREND LES ECOLES TECHNIQUES DU SECOND DEGRE; LA COLONNE 5 SE REFERE AUX AUTRES SECTEURS GOUVERNEMENTAUX, Y COMPRIS LES ORGANISATIONS PRIVEES A BUT NON LUCRATIF QUI NE PROCURENT PAS DE SERVICE A DES GROUPES DETERMINES D'ENTREPRISES PRIVEES. NON COMPRIS LES DONNEES POUR LE DROIT, L'EDUCATION ET LES ARTS.
ESP> EXCLUIDO EL PERSONAL AUXILIAR. PARA LOS CIENTIFICOS E INGENIEROS LOS DATOS SE REFIEREN A LOS EFECTIVOS DE JORNADA COMPLETA Y DE JORNADA PARCIAL. EL TOTAL DE LA COLUMNA 1 ES INFERIOR AL TOTAL DE LOS ELEMENTOS QUE LA COMPONEN DEBIDO A QUE CIERTOS EFECTIVOS SE CONTABILIZAN A LA VEZ EN DIFERENTES SECTORES. LA CIFRA DE LA COLUMNA 4 INCLUYE LAS ESCUELAS TECNICAS DE SEGUNDO GRADO; LA COLUMNA 5 SE REFIERE A OTROS SECTORES OFICIALES, INCLUIDAS LAS ORGANIZACIONES PRIVADAS DE CARACTER NO LUCRATIVO, QUE NO PROCURAN SERVICIOS A DETERMI- NADOS GRUPOS DE EMPRESAS PRIVADAS. EXCLUIDO LOS DATOS RELATIVOS AL DERECHO, LA EDUCACION Y LAS ARTES.

UNITED STATES OF AMERICA:
E—> NOT INCLUDING AUXILIARY PERSONNEL. DATA FOR LAW, HUMANITIES AND EDUCATION ARE EXCLUDED. DATA REFERRING TO PRIVATE NON-PROFIT ORGANIZATIONS ARE INCLUDED WITH THE GENERAL SERVICE SECTOR.
FR—> NON COMPRIS LES DONNEES POUR LE DROIT, LES SCIENCES HUMAINES ET L'EDUCATION. LE SECTEUR DE SERVICE GENERAL COMPREND LES DONNEES RELATIVES AUX ORGANI- SATIONS PRIVEES A BUT NON LUCRATIF.
ESP> EXCLUIDO EL PERSONAL AUXILIAR. EXCLUIDOS LOS DATOS RELATIVOS AL DERECHO, LAS CIENCIAS HUMANAS Y LA EDUCACION. EL SECTOR DE SERVICIO GENERAL INCLUYE LOS DATOS CORRESPONDIENTES A LAS ORGANIZACIONES PRIVADAS DE CARACTER NO LUCRATIVO.

ARGENTINA:
E—> DATA ARE IN NET MAN-YEARS. THE FIGURES IN COLUMN 2 REFER TO PRIVATE ENTERPRISES, IN COLUMN 3 TO STATE AND MIXED ENTERPRISES AND COLUMN 5 INCLUDES PRIVATE AND NON-PROFIT ORGANIZATIONS.
FR—> LES DONNEES SONT EN ANNEES-HOMME NETTES. LE CHIFFRE DE LA COLONNE 2 SE REFERE AUX ENTRE- PRISES PRIVEES, LA COLONNE 3 AUX ENTREPRISES DE L'ETAT ET MIXTES, ET LA COLONNE 5 COMPREND AUSSI LES ORGANISATIONS PRIVEES A BUT NON LUCRATIF.
ESP> LOS DATOS SE INDICAN EN AÑOS-HOMBRE NETOS. LA CIFRA DE LA COLUMNA 2 SE REFIERE A LAS EMPRESAS PRIVADAS, LA DE LA COLUMNA 3 A LAS EMPRESAS ESTA- TALES Y MIXTAS Y LA DE LA COLUMNA 5 COMPRENDE IGUALMENTE LAS ORGANIZACIONES PRIVADAS DE CARACTER NO LUCRATIVO.

R&D personnel by sector of performance 5.4
Personnel de R-D par secteur d'exécution
Personal de I y D por sector de ejecución

IRAQ (CONT.):
SECTOR ARE ALSO EXCLUDED.
FR-> LES DONNEES NE SE REFERENT QU'AUX PERSONNES EMPLOYEES DANS LES DEPARTEMENTS GOUVERNEMENTAUX CONCERNES PAR LES ACTIVITES SCIENTIFIQUES ET NE COMPRENNENT PAS LE SECTEUR DE LA PRODUCTION (AC-TIVITES DE R-D NON-INTEGREES); LES TECHNICIENS DU SECTEUR DE L'ENSEIGNEMENT SUPERIEUR SONT AUSSI EXCLUS.
ESP> LOS DATOS SE REFIEREN UNICAMENTE A LAS PERSONAS EMPLEADAS EN LOS SERVICIOS GUBERNAMEN-TALES QUE SE OCUPAN DE ACTIVIDADES CIENTIFICAS Y NO COMPRENDEN EL SECTOR PRODUCTIVO (ACTIVIDADES DE I Y D INTEGRADAS); LOS TECNICOS DEL SECTOR DE ENSEÑANZA SUPERIOR TAMBIEN ESTAN EXCLUIDOS.

ISRAEL:
E-> DATA FOR THE PRODUCTIVE SECTOR (NON-INTE-GRATED R&D) ARE INCLUDED WITH THE GENERAL SERVICE SECTOR. SCIENTISTS AND ENGINEERS ARE FULL-TIME AND INCLUDE SOME PART-TIME.
FR-> LES DONNEES RELATIVES AU SECTEUR DE LA PRODUCTION SONT COMPRISES AVEC CELLES DU SECTEUR DE SERVICE GENERAL. POUR LES SCIENTIFIQUES ET INGENIEURS, LES DONNEES SE REFERENT AUX EFFECTIFS A PLEIN TEMPS ET COMPRENNENT UN CERTAIN NOMBRE A TEMPS PARTIEL.
ESP> LOS DATOS RELATIVOS AL SECTOR PRODUCTIVO QUEDAN INCLUIDOS CON LOS DEL SECTOR DE SERVICIO GENERAL. PARA LOS CIENTIFICOS E INGENIEROS, LOS DATOS SE REFIEREN A LOS EFECTIVOS DE JORNADA COM-PLETA, INCLUYENDOSE UN CIERTO NUMERO DE JORNADA PARCIAL.

JAPAN:
E-> DATA REFERRING TO SCIENTISTS AND ENGINEERS ARE FULL-TIME. NOT INCLUDING SOCIAL SCIENCES AND HUMANITIES IN THE PRODUCTIVE SECTOR.
FR-> POUR LES SCIENTIFIQUES ET LES INGENIEURS, LES DONNEES SE REFERENT AUX EFFECTIFS A PLEIN TEMPS. COMPTE NON TENU DES SCIENCES SOCIALES ET HUMAINES DANS LE SECTEUR DE LA PRODUCTION.
ESP> PARA LOS CIENTIFICOS E INGENIEROS LOS DATOS SE REFIEREN A LOS EFECTIVOS DE JORNADA COMPLETA. EXCLUIDAS LAS CIENCIAS SOCIALES Y HUMANAS DEL SECTOR PRODUCTIVO.

JORDAN:
E-> DATA REFER TO THE EAST BANK ONLY.
FR-> LES DONNEES SE REFERENT A LA RIVE ORIENTALE SEULEMENT.
ESP> LOS DATOS SE REFIEREN A LA ORILLA ORIENTAL SOLAMENTE.

KOREA, REPUBLIC OF:
E-> NOT INCLUDING DATA FOR LAW, HUMANITIES AND EDUCATION. SCIENTISTS AND ENGINEERS ARE FULL-TIME PLUS PART-TIME.
FR-> NON COMPRIS LES DONNEES POUR LE DROIT, LES SCIENCES SOCIALES ET L'EDUCATION. POUR LES SCIEN-TIFIQUES ET INGENIEURS, LES DONNEES SE REFERENT AUX EFFECTIFS A PLEIN TEMPS ET A TEMPS PARTIEL.

KOREA, REPUBLIC OF (CONT.):
ESP> EXCLUIDOS LOS DATOS RELATIVOS AL DERECHO, LAS CIENCIAS HUMANAS Y LA EDUCACION. PARA LOS CIENTIFICOS E INGENIEROS LOS DATOS SE REFIEREN A LOS EFECTIVOS DE JORNADA COMPLETA Y DE JORNADA PARCIAL.

KUWAIT:
E-> NOT INCLUDING AUXILIARY PERSONNEL.
FR-> NON COMPRIS LE PERSONNEL AUXILIAIRE.
ESP> EXCLUIDO EL PERSONAL AUXILIAR.

PAKISTAN:
E-> DATA RELATE TO THE YEAR 1973/74 AND REFER TO R&D ACTIVITIES CONCENTRATED MAINLY IN GOVERN-MENT-FINANCED RESEARCH ESTABLISHMENTS AND EXCLUDE SOCIAL SCIENCES AND HUMANITIES IN THE HIGHER EDUCATION AND GENERAL SERVICE SECTORS.
FR-> LES DONNEES SE REFERENT A L'ANNEE 1973/74 ET AUX ACTIVITES DE R-D SE TROUVANT POUR LA PLU-PART DANS LES ETABLISSEMENTS DE RECHERCHE FINANCES PAR LE GOUVERNEMENT; LES SCIENCES SOCIALES ET HUMAINES DES SECTEURS DE L'ENSEIGNEMENT SUPERIEUR ET DE SERVICE GENERAL SONT EXCLUES.
ESP> LOS DATOS SE REFIEREN AL AÑO 1973/74 Y A LAS ACTIVIDADES DE I Y D CONCENTRADAS PRINCIPAL-MENTE EN LOS ESTABLICIMIENTOS DE INVESTIGACION SUBVENCIONADOS POR EL GOBIERNO; EXCLUIDOS LOS DATOS RELATIVOS A LAS CIENCIAS SOCIALES Y HUMANAS DE LOS SECTORES DE ENSEÑANZA SUPERIOR Y DE SERVI-CIO GENERAL.

PHILIPPINES:
E-> DATA REFERRING TO SCIENTISTS AND ENGINEERS ARE FULL-TIME PLUS PART-TIME.
FR-> POUR LES SCIENTIFIQUES ET INGENIEURS, LES DONNEES SE REFERENT AUX EFFECTIFS A PLEIN TEMPS ET A TEMPS PARTIEL.
ESP> PARA LOS CIENTIFICOS E INGENIEROS LOS DATOS SE REFIEREN A LOS EFECTIVOS DE JORNADA COMPLETA Y DE JORNADA PARCIAL.

SRI LANKA:
E-> NOT INCLUDING DATA FOR EITHER THE PRODUC-TIVE SECTOR (NON-INTEGRATED R&D) OR LAW, HUMANI-TIES AND EDUCATION. DATA FOR SCIENTISTS AND ENGINEERS ARE FULL-TIME.
FR-> NON COMPRIS LES DONNEES RELATIVES AU SECTEUR DE LA PRODUCTION (ACTIVITES DE R-D NON-INTEGRES) NI LE DROIT, LES SCIENCES HUMAINES ET L'EDUCATION. POUR LES SCIENTIFIQUES ET INGENIEURS LES DONNEES SE REFERENT AUX EFFECTIFS A PLEIN TEMPS.
ESP> NO INCLUYE LOS DATOS RELATIVOS AL SECTOR PRODUCTIVO (ACTIVIDADES DE I Y D NO INTEGRADAS), NI EL DERECHO, LAS CIENCIAS HUMANAS Y LA EDUCA-CION. PARA LOS CIENTIFICOS E INGENIEROS, LOS DATOS SE REFIEREN A LOS EFECTIVOS DE JORNADA COMPLETA.

5.4 **R&D personnel by sector of performance**
Personnel de R-D par secteur d'exécution
Personal de I y D por sector de ejecución

THAILAND:
E—> NOT INCLUDING DATA FOR SOCIAL SCIENCES AND HUMANITIES. SCIENTISTS AND ENGINEERS ARE FULL-TIME.
FR—> NON COMPRIS LES DONNEES POUR LES SCIENCES SOCIALES ET HUMAINES. POUR LES SCIENTIFIQUES ET INGENIEURS, LES DONNEES SE REFERENT AUX EFFECTIFS A PLEIN TEMPS.
ESP> EXCLUIDAS LAS CIENCIAS SOCIALES Y HUMANAS. PARA LOS CIENTIFICOS E INGENIEROS, LOS DATOS SE REFIEREN A LOS EFECTIVOS DE JORNADA COMPLETA.

TURKEY:
E—> DATA REFER TO THE YEAR 1975/76. NOT INCLUD- ING DATA FOR EITHER THE PRODUCTIVE SECTOR OR SOCIAL SCIENCES AND HUMANITIES.
FR—> LES DONNEES SE REFERENT A L'ANNEE 1975/76. NON COMPRIS LES DONNEES POUR LE SECTEUR DE LA PRODUCTION NI POUR LES SCIENCES SOCIALES ET HUMAINES.
ESP> LOS DATOS SE REFIEREN AL AÑO 1975/76. NO INCLUYE LOS DATOS RELATIVOS AL SECTOR PRODUCTIVO, NI LAS CIENCIAS SOCIALES Y HUMANAS.

VIET-NAM:
E—> NOT INCLUDING DATA FOR TECHNICIANS AND AUXILIARY PERSONNEL IN THE HIGHER EDUCATION SECTOR.
FR—> NON COMPRIS LES DONNEES RELATIVES AUX TECHNICIENS ET AU PERSONNEL AUXILIAIRE DU SECTEUR DE L'ENSEIGNEMENT SUPERIEUR.
ESP> NO INCLUYE LOS DATOS RELATIVOS A LOS TECNI- COS Y AL PERSONAL AUXILIAR DEL SECTOR DE ENSEÑANZA SUPERIOR.

YEMEN:
E—> DATA REFER TO THE YEAR 1974/75.
FR—> LES DONNEES SE REFERENT A L'ANNEE 1974/75.
ESP> LOS DATOS SE REFIEREN AL AÑO 1974/75.

AUSTRIA:
E—> DATA REFER TO THE PRODUCTIVE SECTOR ONLY.
FR—> LES DONNEES SE REFERENT AU SECTEUR DE LA PRODUCTION SEULEMENT.
ESP> LOS DATOS SE REFIEREN AL SECTOR PRODUCTIVO SOLAMENTE.

BULGARIA:
E—> NOT INCLUDING DATA FOR TECHNICIANS AND AUXILIARY PERSONNEL IN THE HIGHER EDUCATION SECTOR.
FR—> NON COMPRIS LES DONNEES RELATIVES AUX TECHNICIENS ET AU PERSONNEL AUXILIAIRE DU SECTEUR DE L'ENSEIGNEMENT SUPERIEUR.
ESP> NO INCLUYE LOS DATOS RELATIVOS A LOS TECNI- COS Y AL PERSONAL AUXILIAR DEL SECTOR DE ENSEÑANZA SUPERIOR.

CZECHOSLOVAKIA:
E—> OF MILITARY R&D ONLY THAT PART CARRIED OUT IN CIVIL ESTABLISHMENTS IS INCLUDED; SCIENTISTS AND ENGINEERS ENGAGED IN THE ADMINISTRATION OF R&D ARE INCLUDED WITH AUXILIARY PERSONNEL.
FR—> POUR LA R-D DE CARACTERE MILITAIRE SEULE LA PARTIE EFFECTUEE DANS LES ETABLISSEMENTS CI- VILS A ETE CONSIDEREE. LES SCIENTIFIQUES ET INGE-

CZECHOSLOVAKIA (CONT.):
NIEURS EMPLOYES DANS LES SERVICES ADMINISTRATIFS DE R-D SONT COMPRIS AVEC LE PERSONNEL AUXILIAIRE.
ESP> PARA LA I Y D DE CARACTER MILITAR SOLO SE HA CONSIDERADO LA PARTE CORRESPONDIENTE A LOS ESTABLECIMIENTOS CIVILES. LOS CIENTIFICOS E INGE- NIEROS EMPLEADOS EN LOS SERVICIOS ADMINISTRATIVOS DE I Y D FIGURAN CON EL PERSONAL AUXILIAR.

DENMARK:
E—> AUXILIARY PERSONNEL AND TECHNICIANS ARE COUNTED TOGETHER.
FR—> LE PERSONNEL AUXILIAIRE ET LES TECHNICIENS SONT COMPTES ENSEMBLE.
ESP> EL PERSONAL AUXILIAR Y LOS TECNICOS SE CUENTAN CONJUNTAMENTE.

FINLAND:
E—> AUXILIARY PERSONNEL AND TECHNICIANS ARE COUNTED TOGETHER.
FR—> LE PERSONNEL AUXILIAIRE ET LES TECHNICIENS SONT COMPTES ENSEMBLE.
ESP> EL PERSONAL AUXILIAR Y LOS TECNICOS SE CUENTAN CONJUNTAMENTE.

FRANCE:
E—> AUXILIARY PERSONNEL AND TECHNICIANS IN COLUMNS 1,4 AND 5 ARE COUNTED TOGETHER.
FR—> LE PERSONNEL AUXILIAIRE ET LES TECHNICIENS DES COLONNES 1,4 ET 5 SONT COMPTES ENSEMBLE.
ESP> EL PERSONAL AUXILIAR Y LOS TECNICOS DE LAS COLUMNAS 1,4 Y 5 SE CUENTAN CONJUNTAMENTE.

HUNGARY:
E—> NOT INCLUDING PERSONNEL ENGAGED IN THE AD- MINISTRATION OF R&D. SKILLED WORKERS ARE INCLUDED WITH TECHNICIANS RATHER THAN WITH AUXILIARY PERSONNEL.
FR—> COMPTE NON TENU DU PERSONNEL EMPLOYE DANS LES SERVICES ADMINISTRATIFS DE R-D. LES OUVRIERS QUALIFIES SONT COMPRIS AVEC LES TECHNICIENS PLU- TOT QU'AVEC LE PERSONNEL AUXILIAIRE.
ESP> EXCLUIDO EL PERSONAL EMPLEADO EN LOS SER- VICIOS ADMINISTRATIVOS DE I Y D. LOS TRABAJADORES CALIFICADOS ESTAN MAS BIEN INCLUIDOS CON LOS TECNICOS QUE CON EL PERSONAL AUXILIAR.

ICELAND:
E—> NOT INCLUDING AUXILIARY PERSONNEL. DATA ALSO EXCLUDE SOCIAL SCIENCES AND HUMANITIES.
FR—> NON COMPRIS LE PERSONNEL AUXILIAIRE. LES DONNEES EXCLUENT EGALEMENT LES SCIENCES SOCIALES ET HUMAINES.
ESP> NO INCLUYE EL PERSONAL AUXILIAR. LOS DATOS EXCLUYEN IGUALMENTE LAS CIENCIAS SOCIALES Y HUMANAS.

NETHERLANDS:
E—> NOT INCLUDING SOCIAL SCIENCES AND HUMAN- ITIES IN THE PRODUCTIVE SECTOR (INTEGRATED R&D) . AUXILIARY PERSONNEL AND TECHNICIANS IN COLUMNS 1 AND 4 ARE COUNTED TOGETHER.

R&D personnel by sector of performance 5.4
Personnel de R-D par secteur d'exécution
Personal de I y D por sector de ejecución

NETHERLANDS (CONT.):
FR—> NON COMPRIS LES DONNEES POUR LES SCIENCES SOCIALES ET HUMAINES DU SECTEUR DE LA PRODUCTION (ACTIVITES DE R-D INTEGREES). LE PERSONNEL AUXILIAIRE ET LES TECHNICIENS DÉS COLONNES 1 ET 4 SONT COMPTES ENSEMBLE.
ESP> EXCLUIDOS LOS DATOS RELATIVOS A LAS CIENCIAS SOCIALES Y HUMANAS DEL SECTOR PRODUCTIVO (ACTIVIDADES DE I Y D INTEGRADAS). EL PERSONAL AUXILIAR Y LOS TECNICOS DE LAS COLUMNAS 1 Y 4 SE CUENTAN CONJUNTAMENTE.

NORWAY: AUXILIARY PERSONNEL AND TECHNICIANS ARE COUNTED TOGETHER.
FR—> LE PERSONNEL AUXILIAIRE ET LES TECHNICIENS SONT COMPTES ENSEMBLE.
ESP> EL PERSONAL AUXILIAR Y LOS TECNICOS SE CUENTAN CONJUNTAMENTE.

POLAND:
E—> NOT INCLUDING DATA FOR TECHNICIANS AND AUXILIARY PERSONNEL IN THE HIGHER EDUCATION SECTOR; DATA RELATING TO TECHNICIANS REFER ONLY TO THOSE PERSONS WITH A VOCATIONAL EDUCATION AT THE SECOND LEVEL.
FR—> NON COMPRIS LES DONNEES RELATIVES AUX TECHNICIENS ET AU PERSONNEL AUXILIAIRE DU SECTEUR DE L'ENSEIGNEMENT SUPERIEUR; LES TECHNICIENS NE COMPRENNENT QUE DES PERSONNES AYANT SUIVI UN ENSEIGNEMENT TECHNIQUE DU SECOND DEGRE.
ESP> EXCLUIDOS LOS DATOS RELATIVOS A LOS TECNICOS Y AL PERSONAL AUXILIAR DEL SECTOR DE ENSEÑANZA SUPERIOR; LOS TECNICOS SOLO COMPRENDEN LAS PERSONAS QUE HAN RECIBIDO UNA FORMACION TECNICA DE SEGUNDO GRADO.

SPAIN:
E—> DATA REFERRING TO THE PRODUCTIVE SECTOR (NON-INTEGRATED R&D) ARE INCLUDED WITH THE GENERAL SERVICE SECTOR.
FR—> LES DONNEES RELATIVES AU SECTEUR DE LA PRODUCTION (ACTIVITES DE R-D NON-INTEGREES) SONT COMPRISES AVEC CELLES DU SECTEUR DE SERVICE GENERAL.
ESP> LOS DATOS CORRESPONDIENTES AL SECTOR PRODUCTIVO (ACTIVIDADES DE I Y D NO INTEGRADAS) FIGURAN EN EL SECTOR DE SERVICIO GENERAL.

SWEDEN:
E—> NOT INCLUDING DATA FOR SOCIAL SCIENCES AND HUMANITIES. AUXILIARY PERSONNEL AND TECHNICIANS ARE COUNTED TOGETHER.
FR—> NON COMPRIS LES DONNEES POUR LES SCIENCES SOCIALES ET HUMAINES. LE PERSONNEL AUXILIAIRE ET LES TECHNICIENS SONT COMPTES ENSEMBLE.
ESP> EXCLUIDAS LAS CIENCIAS SOCIALES Y HUMANAS. EL PERSONAL AUXILIAR Y LOS TECNICOS SE CUENTAN CONJUNTAMENTE.

SWITZERLAND:
E—> AUXILIARY PERSONNEL AND TECHNICIANS ARE COUNTED TOGETHER.

SWITZERLAND (CONT.): LE PERSONNEL AUXILIAIRE ET LES TECHNICIENS SONT COMPTES ENSEMBLE.
ESP> EL PERSONAL AUXILIAR Y LOS TECNICOS SE CUENTAN CONJUNTAMENTE.

UNITED KINGDOM:
E—> DATA RELATE TO THE YEAR 1975/76 AND DO NOT INCLUDE THE HIGHER EDUCATION SECTOR.
FR—> LES DONNEES SE REFERENT A L'ANNEE 1975/76 ET NE COMPRENNENT PAS LE SECTEUR DE L'ENSEIGNEMENT SUPERIEUR.
ESP> LOS DATOS SE REFIEREN AL AÑO 1975/76 Y NO COMPRENDEN EL SECTOR DE ENSEÑANZA SUPERIOR.

YUGOSLAVIA:
E—> NOT INCLUDING ACTIVITIES OF A MILITARY NATURE OR RELATING TO NATIONAL DEFENCE.
FR—> NON COMPRIS LES ACTIVITES DE CARACTERE MILITAIRE OU RELEVANT DE LA DEFENSE NATIONALE.
ESP> EXCLUIDAS LAS ACTIVIDADES DE CARACTER MILITAR O QUE CONCIERNEN LA DEFENSA NACIONAL.

AMERICAN SAMOA:
E—> DATA RELATE TO ONE RESEARCH INSTITUTE ONLY.
FR—> LES DONNEES NE CONCERNENT QU'UN SEUL INSTITUT DE RECHERCHE.
ESP> LOS DATOS SE REFIEREN A UN CENTRO DE INVESTIGACION SOLAMENTE.

AUSTRALIA:
E—> DATA RELATE TO THE YEAR 1976/77.
FR—> LES DONNEES SE REFERENT A L'ANNEE 1976/77.
ESP> LOS DATOS SE REFIEREN AL AÑO 1976/77.

FRENCH POLYNESIA:
E—> DATA RELATE TO ONE RESEARCH INSTITUTE ONLY. SCIENTISTS AND ENGINEERS ARE FULL-TIME.
FR—> LES DONNEES NE CONCERNENT QU'UN SEUL INSTITUT DE RECHERCHE. POUR LES SCIENTIFIQUES ET LES INGENIEURS, LES EFFECTIFS SONT A PLEIN TEMPS.
ESP> LOS DATOS SE REFIEREN A UN CENTRO DE INVESTIGACION SOLAMENTE. PARA LOS CIENTIFICOS E INGENIEROS, LOS DATOS SE REFIEREN A LOS EFECTIVOS DE JORNADA COMPLETA.

NEW ZEALAND:
E—> NOT INCLUDING AUXILIARY PERSONNEL IN THE HIGHER EDUCATION SECTOR.
FR—> NON COMPRIS LE PERSONNEL AUXILIAIRE DANS LE SECTEUR DE L'ENSEIGNEMENT SUPERIEUR.
ESP> EXCLUIDO EL PERSONAL AUXILIAR DEL SECTOR DE ENSEÑANZA SUPERIOR.

SAMOA:
E—> DATA REFERRING TO SCIENTISTS AND ENGINEERS ARE FULL-TIME.
FR—> POUR LES SCIENTIFIQUES ET INGENIEURS, LES DONNEES SE REFERENT AUX EFFECTIFS A PLEIN TEMPS.
ESP> PARA LOS CIENTIFICOS E INGENIEROS, LOS DATOS SE REFIEREN A LOS EFECTIVOS DE JORNADA COMPLETA.

5.5   R&D scientists and engineers by fields of activity
       Scientifiques et ingénieurs de R-D par domaines d'activité
       Científicos e ingenieros de I y D por campos de actuación

5.5   Number of scientists and engineers engaged in research and experimental development by sector of performance and industry group or field of science

Nombre de scientifiques et d'ingénieurs employés à des travaux de recherche et de développement experimental, par secteur d'exécution et par branche d'activité économique ou discipline scientifique

Número de científicos e ingenieros empleados en trabajos de investigación y de desarrollo experimental, por sector de ejecución y por rama de actividad económica o rama de la ciencia

IT SHOULD BE NOTED THAT IN GENERAL THE BREAKDOWN BY INDUSTRY GROUP AND FIELD OF SCIENCE REFERS TO FIELD OF INVESTIGATION BUT FOR SECTIONS B AND C OF THE TABLE THE READER'S ATTENTION IS DRAWN TO THE GENERAL NOTE PRECEDING THE FOOTNOTES.

EN GENERAL, LA REPARTITION PAR BRANCHE D'ACTIVITE ECONOMIQUE ET DISCIPLINE SCIENTIFIQUE CORRESPOND AU DOMAINE DE RECHERCHE MAIS, POUR LES PARTIES B ET C DU TABLEAU, LE LECTEUR EST PRIE DE SE RAP-PORTER A LA REMARQUE GENERALE QUI PRECEDE LES NOTES QUI FIGURENT EN BAS DE PAGE.

PLEASE REFER TO INTRODUCTION FOR DEFINITIONS OF CATEGORIES INCLUDED IN THIS TABLE.

POUR LES DEFINITIONS DES CATEGORIES PRESENTEES DANS CE TABLEAU, SE REFERER A L'INTRODUCTION.

SCIENTISTS AND ENGINEERS ENGAGED IN R & D ARE GIVEN IN FULL-TIME EQUIVALENT (FTE).

LE NOMBRE DE SCIENTIFIQUES ET INGENIEURS EMPLOYES A DES TRAVAUX DE R-D EST EN EQUIVALENT PLEIN-TEMPS (FTE).

A.   PRODUCTIVE SECTOR

A.   SECTEUR DE LA PRODUCTION

NUMBER OF COUNTRIES AND TERRITORIES PRESENTED IN THIS TABLE: 46

NOMBRE DE PAYS ET DE TERRITOIRES PRESENTES DANS CE TABLEAU: 46

COUNTRY PAYS PAIS	YEAR ANNEE AÑO	TOTAL TOTAL TOTAL		INDUSTRY GROUP / AGRICULTURE, FORESTRY, HUNTING, AND FISHING AGRICULTURE, SYLVI-CULTURE, CHASSE ET PECHE AGRICULTURA, SILVI-CULTURA, CAZA Y PESCA		EXTRACTING INDUSTRIES INDUSTRIES EXTRACTIVES INDUSTRIAS EXTRACTIVAS	
		NUMBER NOMBRE NUMERO	%	NUMBER NOMBRE NUMERO	%	NUMBER NOMBRE NUMERO	%
		(1)	(2)	(3)	(4)	(5)	(6)
AFRICA							
EGYPT	1973	4 874	100	3 809	78.1	...	...
MALAWI	1977	99	100	99	100.0	—	—
ZAMBIA ‡	1976	112	100	10	8.9	102	91.1
AMERICA, NORTH							
CANADA ‡	1977	9 685	100	—	—	305	3.1
CUBA	1977	1 840	100	1 179	64.1	62	3.4
GUATEMALA	1974	166	100	88	53.0	65	39.2
MEXICO	1974	1 973	100	716	36.3	768	38.9
PANAMA	1975	116	100	7	6.0	8	6.9
TURKS AND CAICOS ISLANDS	1976	2	100	2	100.0	—	—

R&D scientists and engineers by fields of activity   **5.5**
Scientifiques et ingénieurs de R-D par domaines d'activité
Científicos e ingenieros de I y D por campos de actuación

EN GENERAL, LA REPARTICION POR SECTOR DE ACTIVIDAD
ECONOMICA Y DE DISCIPLINA CIENTIFICA CORRESPONDE
AL CAMPO DE LA INVESTIGACION, PERO PARA LAS PARTES
B Y C DEL CUADRO, EL LECTOR DEBE REFERIRSE A LA
NOTA GENERAL QUE PRECEDE LAS NOTAS QUE FIGURAN AL
PIE DE LA PAGINA.

EN LA INTRODUCCION SE DAN LAS DEFINICIONES DE
LAS CATEGORIAS QUE FIGURAN EN ESTE CUADRO.

EL NUMERO DE CIENTIFICOS E INGENIEROS EMPLEADOS
EN TRABAJOS DE I Y D SE DA EN EQUIVALENTE DE
JORNADA COMPLETA (FTE).

A.   SECTOR PRODUCTIVO

NUMERO DE PAISES Y DE TERRITORIOS PRESENTADOS EN
ESTE CUADRO: 46

BRANCHE D'ACTIVITE ECONOMIQUE / SECTOR DE ACTIVIDAD ECONOMICA							
MANUFACTURING INDUSTRIES		CONSTRUCTION, BUILDING AND PUBLIC WORKS		TRANSPORT AND COMMUNICATION		OTHER	
INDUSTRIES MANUFACTURIERES		CONSTRUCTION, BATIMENT ET TRAVAUX PUBLICS		TRANSPORTS ET COMMUNICATIONS		ACTIVITES DIVERSES	
INDUSTRIAS MANUFACTURERAS		CONSTRUCCION, EDIFICIOS Y OBRAS PUBLICAS		TRANSPORTES Y COMUNICACIONES		OTRAS ACTIVIDADES	
NUMBER NOMBRE NUMERO	%	NUMBER NOMBRE NUMERO	%	NUMBER NOMBRE NUMERO	%	NUMBER NOMBRE NUMERO	%
(7)	(8)	(9)	(10)	(11)	(12)	(13)	(14)
...	...	...	...	...	...	...	...
—	—	—	—	—	—	—	—
—	—	—	—	—	—	—	—
7 746	80.0	./.	./.	1 081	11.2	553	5.7
420	22.8	44	2.4	122	6.6	13	0.7
—	—	—	—	—	—	13	7.8
306	15.5	8	0.4	7	0.4	168	8.5
—	—	—	—	—	—	101	87.1
—	—	—	—	—	—	—	—

5.5   R&D scientists and engineers by fields of activity
Scientifiques et ingénieurs de R-D par domaines d'activité
Cientificos e ingenieros de I y D por campos de actuación

				INDUSTRY GROUP /		
COUNTRY	YEAR	TOTAL		AGRICULTURE, FORESTRY, HUNTING, AND FISHING	EXTRACTING INDUSTRIES	
PAYS	ANNEE	TOTAL		AGRICULTURE, SYLVI-CULTURE, CHASSE ET PECHE	INDUSTRIES EXTRACTIVES	
PAIS	AÑO	TOTAL		AGRICULTURA, SILVI-CULTURA, CAZA Y PESCA	INDUSTRIAS EXTRACTIVAS	
		NUMBER NOMBRE NUMERO	%	NUMBER NOMBRE NUMERO	%	NUMBER NOMBRE NUMERO	%
		(1)	(2)	(3)	(4)	(5)	(6)
AMERICA, SOUTH							
ARGENTINA ‡	1976	*450	100	*20	*4.4	*125	*27.8
CHILE	1975	627	100				
PARAGUAY	1971	38	100	15	39.5	4	10.5
PERU ‡	1970	106	100	16	15.1	./.	./.
URUGUAY ‡	1971	*394	100	*202	*51.3	*12	*3.0
ASIA							
BRUNEI	1974	16	100	16	100.0	–	–
IRAQ ‡	1974	489	100	385	78.7	104	21.3
JAPAN ‡	1977	213 433	100	392	0.2	874	0.4
KOREA, REPUBLIC OF ‡	1977	5 429	100	72	1.3	31	0.6
PAKISTAN ‡	1973	3 059	100	1 545	50.5	172	5.6
THAILAND ‡	1974	570	100	64	11.2	6	1.0
EUROPE							
AUSTRIA	1972	1 870	100	11	0.6	13	0.7
BELGIUM	1973	6 295	100	322	5.1	53	0.8
CZECHOSLOVAKIA ‡	1977	35 654	100	3 750	10.5	1 631	4.6
DENMARK ‡	1973	1 289	100	8	0.6		
FINLAND	1977	2 762	100	36	1.3	24	0.9
FRANCE	1977	32 120	100	264	0.8	309	1.0
GERMANY, FEDERAL REPUBLIC OF	1977	66 223	100	–	–	917	1.4
GREECE	1976	678	100	180	26.5	110	16.2
HUNGARY ‡	1977	14 160	100	1 529	10.8	412	2.9
IRELAND	1975	422	100	–	–	15	4.3
ITALY	1976	13 554	100	3	0.0	47	0.3
NETHERLANDS ‡	1976	11 580	100	130	1.1	–	–
NORWAY	1977	2 315	100	58	2.5	46	2.0
POLAND	1977	74 900	100	3 800	5.1	48 400	64.6
PORTUGAL	1976	128	100	–	–	–	–
ROMANIA	1970	11 340	100	1 689	14.9	913	8.0
SPAIN ‡	1974	2 617	100	22	0.8	125	4.8
SWEDEN ‡	1975	8 091	100	172	2.1	95	1.2
SWITZERLAND	1975	10 590	100	–	–	–	–
UNITED KINGDOM ‡	1975	59 700	100	–	–	1 000	1.7
YUGOSLAVIA ‡	1977	8 687	100	1 692	19.5	1 219	14.0
OCEANIA							
AUSTRALIA ‡	1973	4 108	100	2 528	61.5	501	12.2
GUAM	1977	5	100	5	100.0	–	–
NEW HEBRIDES	1975	3	100	3	100.0		
NEW ZEALAND	1975	1 982	100	793	40.0	69	3.5
SAMOA ‡	1977	60	100	22	36.7	3	5.0

R&D scientists and engineers by fields of activity   5.5
Scientifiques et ingénieurs de R-D par domaines d'activité
Científicos e ingenieros de I y D por campos de actuación

| BRANCHE D'ACTIVITE ECONOMIQUE / SECTOR DE ACTIVIDAD ECONOMICA | | | | | | | |
| MANUFACTURING INDUSTRIES / INDUSTRIES MANUFACTURIERES / INDUSTRIAS MANUFACTURERAS | | CONSTRUCTION, BUILDING AND PUBLIC WORKS / CONSTRUCTION, BATIMENT ET TRAVAUX PUBLICS / CONSTRUCCION, EDIFICIOS Y OBRAS PUBLICAS | | TRANSPORT AND COMMUNICATION / TRANSPORTS ET COMMUNICATIONS / TRANSPORTES Y COMUNICACIONES | | OTHER / ACTIVITES DIVERSES / OTRAS ACTIVIDADES | |
NUMBER NOMBRE NUMERO	%	NUMBER NOMBRE NUMERO	%	NUMBER NOMBRE NUMERO	%	NUMBER NOMBRE NUMERO	%
(7)	(8)	(9)	(10)	(11)	(12)	(13)	(14)
*245	*54.4	*5	*1.1	*40	*8.9	*15	*3.3
627	100.0	—	—	—	—	—	—
13	34.2	—	—	—	—	6	15.8
90	84.9	./.	./.	./.	./.	./.	./.
*65	*16.5	*21	*5.3	*13	*3.3	*81	*20.6
—	—	—	—	—	—	./.	./.
201 162	94.3	——>	——>	4 684	2.2	—	—
5 073	93.4	./.	./.	./.	./.	253	4.7
680	22.2	51	1.7	239	7.8	372	12.2
156	27.4	22	3.9	53	9.3	269	47.2
1 728	92.4	20	1.1	6	0.3	92	4.9
5 316	84.4	181	2.9	135	2.1	288	4.6
23 998	67.3	2 229	6.3	1 072	3.0	2 974	8.3
1 124	87.2	17	1.3	19	1.5	121	9.4
2 339	84.7	25	0.9	114	4.1	224	8.1
28 530	88.8	555	1.7	805	2.5	1 657	5.2
62 672	94.6	222	0.4	689	1.0	1 723	2.6
160	23.6	40	5.9	68	10.0	120	17.7
10 395	73.4	614	4.3	358	2.5	852	6.0
345	75.6	1	0.4	51	4.8	10	14.9
11 612	85.7	456	3.4	89	0.7	1 347	9.9
10 550	91.1	200	1.7	550	4.7	150	1.3
1 746	75.4	102	4.4	167	7.2	196	8.5
——>	——>	15 300	20.4	2 000	2.7	5 400	7.2
113	88.3	3	2.3	2	1.6	10	7.8
7 184	63.4	325	2.9	338	3.0	891	7.8
2 242	85.7	45	1.7	118	4.5	65	2.5
7 263	89.8	./.	./.	550	6.8	——>	——>
10 320	97.5	110	1.0	90	0.8	70	0.7
53 400	89.4	300	0.5	2 800	4.7	2 200	3.7
4 088	47.1	892	10.2	485	5.6	311	3.6
423	10.3	118	2.9	155	3.8	383	9.3
—	—	—	—	—	—	—	—
954	48.1	93	4.7	49	2.5	24	1.2
4	6.7	12	20.0	14	23.3	5	8.3

5.5 R&D scientists and engineers by fields of activity
Scientifiques et ingénieurs de R-D par domaines d'activité
Científicos e ingenieros de I y D por campos de actuación

B. HIGHER EDUCATION SECTOR

NUMBER OF COUNTRIES AND TERRITORIES PRESENTED IN
THIS TABLE: 52

B. SECTEUR DE L'ENSEIGNEMENT SUPERIEUR

NOMBRE DE PAYS ET DE TERRITOIRES PRESENTES DANS CE
TABLEAU: 52

COUNTRY PAYS PAIS	YEAR ANNEE AÑO	TOTAL TOTAL TOTAL		FIELD OF SCIENCE / NATURAL SCIENCES SCIENCES EXACTES ET NATURELLES CIENCIAS EXACTAS Y NATURALES	
		NUMBER NOMBRE NUMERO	%	NUMBER NOMBRE NUMERO	%
		(1)	(2)	(3)	(4)
AFRICA					
CENTRAL AFRICAN					
REPUBLIC	1975	76	100	35	46.1
EGYPT	1973	3 752	100	767	20.4
KENYA	1975	122	100	26	21.3
MALAWI	1977	77	100	21	27.3
NIGER	1976	93	100	46	49.4
TOGO ‡	1976	160	100	42	26.3
ZAMBIA ‡	1976	54	100	12	22.2
AMERICA, NORTH					
CANADA	1977	*7 350	100	*1 760	*24.0
CUBA	1977	590	100	22	3.7
GUATEMALA	1974	43	100	5	11.6
MEXICO	1974	1 968	100	719	36.5
PANAMA	1975	62	100	–	–
UNITED STATES OF					
AMERICA ‡	1977	*88 600	100	*40 200	*45.4
AMERICA, SOUTH					
ARGENTINA ‡	1976	*4 280	100	*1 690	*39.5
CHILE	1975	4 975	100	1 758	35.3
COLOMBIA ‡	1971	285	100	43	15.1
ECUADOR ‡	1976	91	100	18	19.8
PARAGUAY	1971	49	100	10	20.4
PERU ‡	1970	1 180	100	415	35.2
URUGUAY ‡	1971	*537	100	*89	*16.6
ASIA					
IRAQ ‡	1974	244	100	59	24.2
JAPAN ‡	1977	158 087	100	11 010	7.0
JORDAN ‡	1976	75	100	17	22.7
KOREA, REPUBLIC OF ‡	1977	4 836	100	760	15.7
PAKISTAN ‡	1973	362	100	113	31.2
THAILAND ‡	1974	900	100	206	22.9
TURKEY ‡	1975	7 239	100	1 264	17.5

R&D scientists and engineers by fields of activity   5.5
Scientifiques et ingénieurs de R-D par domaines d'activité
Científicos e ingenieros de I y D por campos de actuación

B. SECTOR DE ENSEÑANZA SUPERIOR

NUMERO DE PAISES Y DE TERRITORIOS PRESENTADOS EN
ESTE CUADRO: 52

DISCIPLINE SCIENTIFIQUE / RAMA DE LA CIENCIA							
ENGINEERING AND TECHNOLOGY SCIENCES DE L'INGENIEUR INGENIERA Y TECNOLOGIA		MEDICAL SCIENCES SCIENCES MEDICALES CIENCIAS MEDICAS		AGRICULTURE AGRICULTURE AGRICULTURA		SOCIAL SCIENCES AND HUMANITIES SCIENCES SOCIALES ET HUMAINES CIENCIAS SOCIALES Y HUMANAS	
NUMBER NOMBRE NUMERO	%	NUMBER NOMBRE NUMERO	%	NUMBER NOMBRE NUMERO	%	NUMBER NOMBRE NUMERO	%
(5)	(6)	(7)	(8)	(9)	(10)	(11)	(12)
9	11.8	–	–	4	5.3	28	36.8
648	17.3	963	25.7	694	18.5	680	18.1
23	18.9	16	13.1	24	19.7	33	27.0
19	24.7	2	2.6	6	7.8	29	37.6
–	–	4	4.3	9	9.7	34	36.6
–	–	23	14.4	8	5.0	87	54.4
6	11.1	10	18.5	6	11.1	20	37.0
*710	*9.6	*1 280	*17.4	*220	*3.0	*3 380	*46.0
288	48.8	72	12.2	170	28.8	38	6.4
6	14.0	10	23.3	3	7.0	19	44.2
250	12.7	214	10.9	183	9.3	602	30.6
16	25.8	14	22.6	32	51.6	–	–
*17 000	*19.2	*15 500	*17.5	*7 100	*8.0	*8 800	*9.9
*430	*10.0	*1 190	*27.8	*330	*7.7	*640	*15.0
808	16.2	1 493	30.0	211	4.2	705	14.2
60	21.1	32	11.2	25	8.8	125	43.8
28	30.8	–	–	45	49.4	–	–
–	–	17	34.7	19	38.8	3	6.1
83	7.0	216	18.3	324	27.4	142	12.0
*88	*16.4	*176	*32.8	*107	*19.9	*77	*14.3
36	14.7	40	16.4	42	17.2	67	27.5
29 856	18.9	52 092	33.0	7 218	4.6	57 911	36.6
1	1.3	4	5.3	7	9.3	46	61.3
1 692	35.0	1 176	24.3	1 098	22.7	110	2.3
61	16.9	61	16.9	127	35.1	...	...
88	9.8	433	48.1	173	19.2	...	...
1 265	17.5	3 917	54.1	793	11.0	...	...

5.5 R&D scientists and engineers by fields of activity
Scientifiques et ingénieurs de R-D par domaines d'activité
Científicos e ingenieros de I y D por campos de actuación

COUNTRY PAYS PAIS	YEAR ANNEE AÑO	TOTAL TOTAL TOTAL		FIELD OF SCIENCE / NATURAL SCIENCES SCIENCES EXACTES ET NATURELLES CIENCIAS EXACTAS Y NATURALES	
		NUMBER NOMBRE NUMERO	%	NUMBER NOMBRE NUMERO	%
		(1)	(2)	(3)	(4)
EUROPE					
BELGIUM	1973	5 784	100	2 584	44.7
BULGARIA	1977	9 112	100	1 510	16.6
CZECHOSLOVAKIA ‡	1977	2 656	100	361	13.6
DENMARK	1976	*2 143	100	*669	*31.2
FINLAND	1975	2 524	100	613	24.3
FRANCE	1977	22 636	100	14 725	65.0
GERMANY, FEDERAL REPUBLIC OF	1977	27 085	100	7 934	29.3
GREECE	1976	843	100	289	34.3
HUNGARY ‡	1977	4 324	100	1 150	26.6
IRELAND	1975	1 175	100	442	37.6
ITALY	1976	18 210	100	4 929	27.1
MALTA	1973	39	100	16	41.0
NETHERLANDS	1976	5 750	100	1 350	23.5
NORWAY	1977	2 600	100	725	27.9
POLAND	1977	15 500	100	3 900	25.2
PORTUGAL	1976	756	100	324	42.9
ROMANIA	1970	5 184	100	1 668	32.2
SPAIN	1974	2 316	100	817	35.3
SWEDEN	1975	*6 300	100	1 300	20.6
SWITZERLAND	1975	4 670	100	1 980	42.4
YUGOSLAVIA ‡	1977	7 023	100	489	7.0
OCEANIA					
AUSTRALIA ‡	1973	12 769	100	4 310	33.7
GUAM	1977	88	100	40	45.4
NEW ZEALAND	1975	1 048	100	270	25.8
SAMOA ‡	1977	58	100	25	43.1

C. GENERAL SERVICE SECTOR

NUMBER OF COUNTRIES AND TERRITORIES PRESENTED IN
THIS TABLE: 51

C. SECTEUR DE SERVICE GENERAL

NOMBRE DE PAYS ET DE TERRITOIRES PRESENTES DANS CE
TABLEAU: 51

COUNTRY PAYS PAIS	YEAR ANNEE AÑO	TOTAL TOTAL TOTAL		FIELD OF SCIENCE / NATURAL SCIENCES SCIENCES EXACTES ET NATURELLES CIENCIAS EXACTAS Y NATURALES	
		NUMBER NOMBRE NUMERO	%	NUMBER NOMBRE NUMERO	%
		(1)	(2)	(3)	(4)
AFRICA					
EGYPT	1973	2 039	100	771	37.8
GABON ‡	1970	8	100	4	50.0
MALAWI	1977	11	100	—	—
TOGO ‡	1976	101	100	2	2.0
ZAMBIA ‡	1976	84	100	70	83.3

R&D scientists and engineers by fields of activity 5.5
Scientifiques et ingénieurs de R-D par domaines d'activité
Científicos e ingenieros de I y D por campos de actuación

DISCIPLINE SCIENTIFIQUE / RAMA DE LA CIENCIA							
ENGINEERING AND TECHNOLOGY SCIENCES DE L'INGENIEUR INGENIERA Y TECNOLOGIA		MEDICAL SCIENCES SCIENCES MEDICALES CIENCIAS MEDICAS		AGRICULTURE AGRICULTURE AGRICULTURA		SOCIAL SCIENCES AND HUMANITIES SCIENCES SOCIALES ET HUMAINES CIENCIAS SOCIALES Y HUMANAS	
NUMBER NOMBRE NUMERO	%	NUMBER NOMBRE NUMERO	%	NUMBER NOMBRE NUMERO	%	NUMBER NOMBRE NUMERO	%
(5)	(6)	(7)	(8)	(9)	(10)	(11)	(12)
503	8.7	1 174	20.3	220	3.8	1 303	22.5
2 590	28.4	1 890	20.7	461	5.1	2 661	29.2
965	36.3	556	20.9	389	14.6	385	14.5
*270	*12.6	*296	*13.8	*120	*5.6	*788	*36.8
381	15.1	666	26.4	110	4.4	754	29.9
——>	——>	4 929	21.8	——>	——>	2 982	13.2
5 410	20.0	4 865	18.0	1 160	4.3	7 716	28.4
183	21.7	243	28.8	58	6.9	70	8.3
824	19.1	810	18.7	531	12.3	1 009	23.3
125	10.6	96	8.2	98	8.3	414	35.2
2 282	12.5	3 981	21.9	846	4.6	6 172	33.9
1	2.6	22	56.4	–	–	–	–
940	16.3	1 350	23.5	200	3.5	1 910	33.2
311	12.0	564	21.7	153	5.9	847	32.6
5 900	38.1	2 600	16.8	1 800	11.6	1 300	8.4
114	15.1	131	17.3	41	5.4	146	19.3
1 669	32.2	883	17.0	341	6.6	623	12.0
287	12.4	350	15.1	86	3.7	776	33.5
1 400	22.2	1 600	25.4	900	14.3	*1 100	*17.5
660	14.1	900	19.3	210	4.5	920	19.7
1 966	28.0	1 671	23.8	803	11.4	2 094	29.8
1 476	11.6	1 160	9.1	720	5.6	5 103	40.0
20	22.7	5	5.7	5	5.7	18	20.5
59	5.6	135	12.9	106	10.1	478	45.6
15	25.9	10	17.2	6	10.3	2	3.5

C. SECTOR DE SERVICIO GENERAL

NUMERO DE PAISES Y DE TERRITORIOS PRESENTADOS EN
ESTE CUADRO: 51

DISCIPLINE SCIENTIFIQUE / RAMA DE LA CIENCIA							
ENGINEERING AND TECHNOLOGY SCIENCES DE L'INGENIEUR INGENIERA Y TECNOLOGIA		MEDICAL SCIENCES SCIENCES MEDICALES CIENCIAS MEDICAS		AGRICULTURE AGRICULTURE AGRICULTURA		SOCIAL SCIENCES AND HUMANITIES SCIENCES SOCIALES ET HUMAINES CIENCIAS SOCIALES Y HUMANAS	
NUMBER NOMBRE NUMERO	%	NUMBER NOMBRE NUMERO	%	NUMBER NOMBRE NUMERO	%	NUMBER NOMBRE NUMERO	%
(5)	(6)	(7)	(8)	(9)	(10)	(11)	(12)
252	12.4	391	19.2	278	13.6	347	17.0
——>	——>	–	–	–	–	4	50.0
–	–	–	–	–	–	11	100.0
29	28.7	9	8.9	8	7.9	53	52.5
4	4.8	–	–	6	7.1	4	4.8

5.5   R&D scientists and engineers by fields of activity
      Scientifiques et ingénieurs de R-D par domaines d'activité
      Científicos e ingenieros de I y D por campos de actuación

COUNTRY PAYS PAIS	YEAR ANNEE AÑO	TOTAL TOTAL TOTAL		FIELD OF SCIENCE / NATURAL SCIENCES SCIENCES EXACTES ET NATURELLES CIENCIAS EXACTAS Y NATURALES	
		NUMBER NOMBRE NUMERO	%	NUMBER NOMBRE NUMERO	%
		(1)	(2)	(3)	(4)
AMERICA, NORTH					
BELIZE	1970	13	100	−	−
BERMUDA ‡	1970	4	100	−	−
CANADA ‡	1973	7 316	100	6 079	83.1
CUBA	1977	2 529	100	774	30.6
GUATEMALA	1974	101	100	17	16.8
MEXICO	1974	1 955	100	401	20.5
PANAMA	1975	26	100	−	−
AMERICA, SOUTH					
ARGENTINA ‡	1976	*3 270	100	*1 160	*35.5
CHILE	1975	346	100	127	36.7
COLOMBIA ‡	1971	616	100	147	23.9
PARAGUAY	1971	47	100	10	21.3
PERU ‡	1970	400	100	81	20.2
URUGUAY ‡	1971	*219	100	*33	*15.1
ASIA					
BRUNEI	1974	6	100	−	−
CYPRUS	1971	82	100	15	18.3
IRAQ ‡	1974	753	100	256	34.0
JAPAN ‡	1977	35 672	100	5 000	14.0
JORDAN ‡	1976	117	100	18	15.4
KOREA, REPUBLIC OF ‡	1977	2 506	100	27	1.1
PAKISTAN ‡	1973	498	100	228	45.8
PHILIPPINES	1976	3 647	100	942	25.8
THAILAND ‡	1974	1 418	100	249	17.6
TURKEY ‡	1975	1 671	100	86	5.1
EUROPE					
BELGIUM	1973	853	100	261	30.6
BULGARIA ‡	1977	10 104	100	1 917	19.0
CZECHOSLOVAKIA ‡	1977	9 456	100	2 807	29.7
DENMARK	1976	*1 462	100	*216	*14.8
FINLAND	1977	1 946	100	265	13.6
FRANCE	1975	13 256	100	7 810	58.9
GERMANY, FEDERAL REPUBLIC OF	1977	17 664	100	9 118	51.6
GREECE	1976	1 048	100	380	36.3
HUNGARY ‡	1977	5 832	100	1 906	32.7
IRELAND	1975	948	100	161	17.0
ITALY	1976	6 114	100	1 823	29.8
NORWAY	1977	1 402	100	296	21.1
POLAND	1977	9 700	100	5 300	54.6
PORTUGAL	1976	865	100	139	16.1
ROMANIA	1970	4 240	100	1 349	31.8
SPAIN ‡	1974	2 991	100	463	15.5
SWITZERLAND	1975	970	100	380	39.2
YUGOSLAVIA ‡	1977	5 970	100	1 732	29.0

R&D scientists and engineers by fields of activity   5.5
Scientifiques et ingénieurs de R-D par domaines d'activité
Científicos e ingenieros de I y D por campos de actuación

DISCIPLINE SCIENTIFIQUE / RAMA DE LA CIENCIA							
ENGINEERING AND TECHNOLOGY		MEDICAL SCIENCES		AGRICULTURE		SOCIAL SCIENCES AND HUMANITIES	
SCIENCES DE L'INGENIEUR		SCIENCES MEDICALES		AGRICULTURE		SCIENCES SOCIALES ET HUMAINES	
INGENIERA Y TECNOLOGIA		CIENCIAS MEDICAS		AGRICULTURA		CIENCIAS SOCIALES Y HUMANAS	
NUMBER NOMBRE NUMERO	%	NUMBER NOMBRE NUMERO	%	NUMBER NOMBRE NUMERO	%	NUMBER NOMBRE NUMERO	%
(5)	(6)	(7)	(8)	(9)	(10)	(11)	(12)
–	–	–	–	13	100.0	–	–
–	–	–	–	4	100.0	–	–
./.	./.	./.	./.	./.	./.	1 237	16.9
289	11.4	978	38.7	–	–	488	19.3
46	45.5	6	5.9	–	–	32	31.7
199	10.2	395	20.2	23	1.2	937	47.9
–	–	25	96.1	–	–	1	4.9
*445	*13.6	*525	*16.0	*750	*22.9	*390	*11.9
108	31.2	69	19.9	24	6.9	18	5.2
——>	——>	71	11.5	277	45.0	121	19.6
–	–	16	34.0	13	27.7	8	17.0
——>	——>	114	28.5	167	41.8	38	9.5
–	–	*89	*40.6	*8	*3.7	*89	*40.6
–	–	–	–	–	–	6	100.0
——>	——>	10	12.2	–	–	57	69.5
117	15.5	2	0.3	56	7.4	322	42.8
11 926	33.4	3 395	9.5	11 820	33.1	3 531	9.9
33	28.2	1	1.0	35	29.9	30	25.6
495	19.7	286	11.4	1 563	62.4	135	5.4
——>	——>	133	26.7	137	27.5	...	...
302	8.3	155	4.3	1 344	36.9	904	24.8
300	21.2	357	25.2	512	36.1	...	...
219	13.1	65	3.9	1 301	77.9	...	...
245	28.7	49	5.7	2	0.2	296	34.7
3 661	36.2	1 689	16.7	1 495	14.8	1 342	13.3
1 010	10.7	2 503	26.5	176	1.9	2 960	31.3
*225	*15.4	*450	*30.8	*279	*19.1	*292	*20.0
654	33.6	162	8.3	331	17.0	534	27.4
——>	——>	3 516	26.5	1 280	9.7	650	4.9
2 555	14.4	1 598	9.1	1 458	8.3	2 935	16.6
——>	——>	73	7.0	450	42.9	145	13.8
415	7.1	695	11.9	131	2.3	2 685	46.0
224	23.6	38	4.0	343	36.2	182	19.2
2 368	38.7	662	10.8	793	13.0	468	7.7
305	21.8	174	12.4	160	11.4	467	33.3
100	1.0	300	3.1	–	–	4 000	41.2
243	28.1	48	5.6	310	35.8	125	14.4
——>	——>	1 559	36.8	–	–	1 332	31.4
1 572	52.6	264	8.8	506	16.9	186	6.2
180	18.6	85	8.8	275	28.4	50	5.1
518	8.7	757	12.7	257	4.3	2 706	45.3

5.5 R&D scientists and engineers by fields of activity
Scientifiques et ingénieurs de R-D par domaines d'activité
Científicos e ingenieros de I y D por campos de actuación

COUNTRY	YEAR	TOTAL		FIELD OF SCIENCE / NATURAL SCIENCES	
PAYS	ANNEE	TOTAL		SCIENCES EXACTES ET NATURELLES	
PAIS	AÑO	TOTAL		CIENCIAS EXACTAS Y NATURALES	
		NUMBER NOMBRE NUMERO	%	NUMBER NOMBRE NUMERO	%
		(1)	(2)	(3)	(4)
OCEANIA					
AUSTRALIA ‡	1973	3 235	100	1 514	46.8
NEW CALEDONIA	1971	0.3	100	—	—
GUAM	1977	120	100	10	8.3
NEW ZEALAND ‡	1975	562	100	354	63.0
SAMOA ‡	1977	22	100	10	45.5

A: PRODUCTIVE SECTOR / SECTEUR DE LA PRODUCTION /
   SECTOR PRODUCTIVO.

ZAMBIA:
   E—> PARTIAL DATA.
   FR-> DONNEES PARTIELLES.
   ESP> DATOS PARCIALES.

CANADA:
   E—> DATA RELATIVE TO THE PRODUCTIVE SECTOR
(NON-INTEGRATED R&D) ARE INCLUDED WITH THE
GENERAL SERVICE SECTOR.
   FR-> LES DONNEES RELATIVES AU SECTEUR DE LA
PRODUCTION (ACTIVITES DE R-D NON-INTEGREES) SONT
COMPRISES AVEC LE SECTEUR DE SERVICE GENERAL.
   ESP> LOS DATOS CORRESPONDIENTES AL SECTOR PRO-
DUCTIVO (ACTIVIDADES DE I Y D NO INTEGRADAS)
ESTAN INCLUIDOS EN EL SECTOR DE SERVICIO GENERAL.

ARGENTINA:
   E—> DATA ARE IN NET MAN-YEARS AND RELATE TO
STATE AND PRIVATE ENTERPRISES.
   FR-> LES DONNEES SONT EN ANNEES-HOMME NETTES
ET SE REFERENT AUX ENTREPRISES DE L'ETAT ET AUX
ENTREPRISES PRIVEES.
   ESP> LOS DATOS SE INDICAN EN ANOS-HOMBRE NETOS
Y SE REFIEREN A LAS EMPRESAS ESTATALES Y A LAS
EMPRESAS PRIVADAS.

PERU:
   E—> NOT INCLUDING DATA FOR HUMANITIES AND
EDUCATION.
   FR-> NON COMPRIS LES DONNEES POUR LES SCIENCES
HUMAINES ET L'EDUCATION.
   ESP> EXCLUIDOS LOS DATOS RELATIVOS A LAS CIEN-
CIAS HUMANAS Y LA EDUCACION.

URUGUAY:
   E—> DATA RELATE TO THE YEAR 1971/72.
   FR-> LES DONNEES SE REFERENT A L'ANNEE 1971/72.
   ESP> LOS DATOS SE REFIEREN AL AÑO 1971/72.

IRAQ:
   E—> DATA RELATE TO NON-INTEGRATED R&D AND REFER
ONLY TO THOSE WORKING IN GOVERNMENT DEPARTMENTS
CONCERNED WITH SCIENTIFIC ACTIVITIES.
   FR-> LES DONNEES NE SE REFERENT QU'AUX ACTIVITES
DE R-D NON-INTEGREES ET SEULEMENT AUX PERSONNES
QUI SONT EMPLOYEES DANS LES DEPARTEMENTS GOUVERNE-
MENTAUX CONCERNES PAR LES ACTIVITES SCIENTIFIQUES.
   ESP> LOS DATOS SE REFIEREN UNICAMENTE A LAS
ACTIVIDADES DE I Y D NO INTEGRADAS Y A LAS PERSO-
NAS EMPLEADAS EN LOS SERVICIOS GUBERNAMENTALES
QUE SE OCUPAN DE ACTIVIDADES CIENTIFICAS.

JAPAN:
   E—> DATA RELATE TO FULL-TIME SCIENTISTS AND
ENGINEERS AND DO NOT INCLUDE SOCIAL SCIENCES AND
HUMANITIES.
   FR-> LES DONNEES SE REFERENT AUX SCIENTIFIQUES
ET INGENIEURS A PLEIN TEMPS ET NE COMPRENNENT
PAS LES SCIENCES SOCIALES ET HUMAINES.
   ESP> LOS DATOS SE REFIEREN A LOS CIENTIFICOS E
INGENIEROS DE JORNADA COMPLETA Y NO INCLUYEN LAS
CIENCIAS SOCIALES Y HUMANAS.

KOREA, REPUBLIC OF:
   E—> DATA RELATE TO FULL-TIME PLUS PART-TIME
SCIENTISTS AND ENGINEERS AND DO NOT INCLUDE LAW,
HUMANITIES AND EDUCATION.
   FR-> LES DONNEES SE REFERENT AUX SCIENTIFIQUES
ET INGENIEURS A PLEIN TEMPS ET A TEMPS PARTIEL ET
NE COMPRENNENT PAS LE DROIT, LES SCIENCES HUMAINES
ET L'EDUCATION.
   ESP> LOS DATOS SE REFIEREN A LOS CIENTIFICOS E
INGENIEROS DE JORNADA COMPLETA Y PARCIAL Y NO IN-
CLUYEN EL DERECHO, LAS CIENCIAS HUMANAS Y LA EDU-
CACION.

PAKISTAN:
   E—> DATA RELATE TO THE YEAR 1973/74 AND REFER
TO R&D ACTIVITIES CONCENTRATED MAINLY IN GOVERN-
MENT-FINANCED RESEARCH ESTABLISHMENTS. NOT INCLUD-
ING *245 SCIENTISTS AND ENGINEERS ENGAGED IN THE
PRODUCTIVE SECTOR (NON-INTEGRATED R&D) FOR WHOM A
DISTRIBUTION BY INDUSTRY IS NOT AVAILABLE.
   FR->LES DONNEES SE REFERENT A L'ANNEE 1973/74
ET AUX ACTIVITES DE R-D SE TROUVANT POUR LA PLU-
PART DANS LES ETABLISSEMENTS DE RECHERCHE FINANCES
PAR LE GOUVERNEMENT. NON COMPRIS *245 SCIENTIFI-
QUES ET INGENIEURS EMPLOYES DANS LE SECTEUR DE LA
PRODUCTION (ACTIVITES DE R-D NON INTEGREES) POUR
LESQUELS LA REPARTITION PAR BRANCHE D'ACTIVITE
ECONOMIQUE N'EST PAS DISPONIBLE.
   ESP> LOS DATOS SE REFIEREN AL AÑO 1973/74 Y A
LAS ACTIVIDADES DE I Y D CONCENTRADAS PRINCIPAL-
MENTE EN LOS ESTABLECIMIENTOS DE INVESTIGACION
SUBVENCIONADOS POR EL GOBIERNO. NO SE INCLUYE A
*245 CIENTIFICOS E INGENIEROS EMPLEADOS EN EL
SECTOR PRODUCTIVO (ACTIVIDADES DE I Y D NO INTE-
GRADAS) CUYA REPARTICION POR SECTOR DE ACTIVIDAD
ECONOMICA SE DESCONOCE.

THAILAND:
   E—> DATA RELATE TO THE YEAR 1974/75 AND DO NOT
INCLUDE A TOTAL OF 3,209 PERSONS ENGAGED IN SOCIAL
SCIENCES AND HUMANITIES FOR WHOM A BREAKDOWN BY
SECTOR IS NOT AVAILABLE.

R&D scientists and engineers by fields of activity   5.5
Scientifiques et ingénieurs de R-D par domaines d'activité
Científicos e ingenieros de I y D por campos de actuación

DISCIPLINE SCIENTIFIQUE / RAMA DE LA CIENCIA							
ENGINEERING AND TECHNOLOGY SCIENCES DE L'INGENIEUR INGENIERA Y TECNOLOGIA		MEDICAL SCIENCES SCIENCES MEDICALES CIENCIAS MEDICAS		AGRICULTURE AGRICULTURE AGRICULTURA		SOCIAL SCIENCES AND HUMANITIES SCIENCES SOCIALES ET HUMAINES CIENCIAS SOCIALES Y HUMANAS	
NUMBER NOMBRE NUMERO	%	NUMBER NOMBRE NUMERO	%	NUMBER NOMBRE NUMERO	%	NUMBER NOMBRE NUMERO	%
(5)	(6)	(7)	(8)	(9)	(10)	(11)	(12)
866	26.8	427	13.2	49	1.5	379	11.7
–	–	0.3	100.0	–	–	–	–
100	83.3	10	8.3	–	–	119	21.2
./.	./.	89	15.8	./.	./.		
8	36.4	2	9.1	1	4.5	1	4.5

THAILAND (CONT.):
   FR—> LES DONNEES SE REFERENT A L'ANNEE 1974/75
ET NE COMPRENNENT PAS 3 209 PERSONNES EMPLOYEES
DANS LES SCIENCES SOCIALES ET HUMAINES POUR LES-
QUELLES LA REPARTITION PAR SECTEUR N'EST PAS
DISPONIBLE.
   ESP> LOS DATOS SE REFIEREN AL AÑO 1974/75 Y NO
INCLUYEN 3 209 PERSONAS EMPLEADAS EN LAS CIENCIAS
SOCIALES Y HUMANAS PARA LAS QUE SE DESCONOCE LA
REPARTICION POR SECTOR.

CZECHOSLOVAKIA:
   E—> OF MILITARY R&D ONLY THAT PART CARRIED OUT-
IN CIVIL ESTABLISHMENTS IS INCLUDED. NOT INCLUDING
SCIENTISTS AND ENGINEERS ENGAGED IN THE ADMINIS-
TRATION OF R&D.
   FR—> POUR LA R–D DE CARACTERE MILITAIRE SEULE
LA PARTIE EFFECTUEE DANS LES ETABLISSEMENTS CI-
VILS A ETE CONSIDEREE. COMPTE NON TENU DES SCIEN-
TIFIQUES ET INGENIEURS EMPLOYES DANS LES SERVICES
ADMINISTRATIFS DE R–D.
   ESP> PARA LA I Y D DE CARACTER MILITAR SOLO SE
HA CONSIDERADO LA PARTE CORRESPONDIENTE A LOS
ESTABLECIMIENTOS CIVILES. EXCLUIDOS LOS CIENTIFI-
COS E INGENIEROS EMPLEADOS EN LOS SERVICIOS ADMI-
NISTRATIVOS DE I Y D.

DENMARK:
   E—> NOT INCLUDING 196 SCIENTISTS AND ENGINEERS
ENGAGED IN THE PRODUCTIVE SECTOR (NON–INTEGRATED
R&D) FOR WHOM A DISTRIBUTION BY INDUSTRY IS NOT
AVAILABLE.
   FR—> NON COMPRIS 196 SCIENTIFIQUES ET INGENIEURS
DU SECTEUR DE LA PRODUCTION (ACTIVITES DE R–D NON
INTEGREES) POUR LESQUELS LA REPARTITION PAR BRAN-
CHE D'ACTIVITE ECONOMIQUE N'EST PAS DISPONIBLE.
   ESP> EXCLUIDOS 196 CIENTIFICOS E INGENIEROS
EMPLEADOS EN EL SECTOR PRODUCTIVO (ACTIVIDADES DE
I Y D NO INTEGRADAS) CUYA REPARTICION POR SECTOR
DE ACTIVIDAD ECONOMICA SE DESCONOCE.

HUNGARY:
   E—> NOT INCLUDING SCIENTISTS AND ENGINEERS EN-
GAGED IN THE ADMINISTRATION OF R&D.
   FR—> COMPTE NON TENU DES SCIENTIFIQUES ET INGE-
NIEURS EMPLOYES DANS LES SERVICES ADMINISTRATIFS
DE R–D.
   ESP> EXCLUIDOS LOS CIENTIFICOS E INGENIEROS
EMPLEADOS EN LOS SERVICIOS ADMINISTRATIVOS DE
I Y D.

NETHERLANDS:
   E—> NOT INCLUDING SOCIAL SCIENCES AND HUMANI-
TIES IN THE PRODUCTIVE SECTOR (INTEGRATED R&D)
FOR WHICH A DISTRIBUTION BY INDUSTRY IS NOT AVAI-
LABLE.
   FR—> NON COMPRIS LES DONNEES POUR LES SCIENCES
SOCIALES ET HUMAINES DU SECTEUR DE LA PRODUCTION
(ACTIVITES DE R–D INTEGREES) POUR LESQUELLES LA
REPARTITION PAR BRANCHE D'ACTIVITE ECONOMIQUE
N'EST PAS DISPONIBLE.
   ESP> EXCLUIDOS LOS DATOS RELATIVOS A LAS CIEN-
CIAS SOCIALES Y HUMANAS DEL SECTOR PRODUCTIVO
(ACTIVIDADES DE I Y D INTEGRADAS) CUYA REPARTICION
POR SECTOR DE ACTIVIDAD ECONOMICA SE DESCONOCE.

SPAIN:
   E—> DATA RELATIVE TO THE PRODUCTIVE SECTOR
(NON–INTEGRATED R&D) ARE INCLUDED WITH THE
GENERAL SERVICE SECTOR.
   FR—> LES DONNEES RELATIVES AU SECTEUR DE LA
PRODUCTION (ACTIVITES DE R–D NON–INTEGREES) SONT
COMPRISES AVEC LE SECTEUR DE SERVICE GENERAL.
   ESP> LOS DATOS CORRESPONDIENTES AL SECTOR PRO-
DUCTIVO (ACTIVIDADES DE I Y D NO INTEGRADAS)
ESTAN INCLUIDOS EN EL SECTOR DE SERVICIO GENERAL.

SWEDEN:
   E—> NOT INCLUDING DATA FOR SOCIAL SCIENCES
AND HUMANITIES.
   FR—> NON COMPRIS LES DONNEES POUR LES SCIENCES
SOCIALES ET HUMAINES.
   ESP> EXCLUIDOS LOS DATOS CORRESPONDIENTES A
LAS CIENCIAS SOCIALES Y HUMANAS.

UNITED KINGDOM:
   E—> DATA RELATE TO THE YEAR 1975/76.
   FR—> LES DONNEES SE REFERENT A L'ANNEE 1975/76.
   ESP> LOS DATOS SE REFIEREN AL AÑO 1975/76.

YUGOSLAVIA:
   E—> NOT INCLUDING ACTIVITIES OF A MILITARY
NATURE OR RELATING TO NATIONAL DEFENCE.
   FR—> NON COMPRIS LES ACTIVITES DE CARACTERE
MILITAIRE OU RELEVANT DE LA DEFENSE NATIONALE.
   ESP> EXCLUIDAS LAS ACTIVIDADES DE CARACTER
MILITAR O QUE CONCIERNEN LA DEFENSA NACIONAL.

5.5 R&D scientists and engineers by fields of activity
Scientifiques et ingénieurs de R-D par domaines d'activité
Científicos e ingenieros de I y D por campos de actuación

AUSTRALIA:
E—> DATA RELATE TO THE YEAR 1973/74. NOT IN-
CLUDING 5,634 SCIENTISTS AND ENGINEERS ENGAGED
IN THE PRODUCTIVE SECTOR (INTEGRATED R&D) FOR
WHOM A DISTRIBUTION BY INDUSTRY IS NOT AVAILABLE.
FR—> LES DONNEES SE REFERENT A L'ANNEE 1973/74.
NON COMPRIS 5 634 SCIENTIFIQUES ET INGENIEURS DU
SECTEUR DE LA PRODUCTION (ACTIVITES DE R-D INTE-
GREES) POUR LESQUELS LA REPARTITION PAR BRANCHE
D'ACTIVITE ECONOMIQUE N'EST PAS DISPONIBLE.
ESP> LOS DATOS SE REFIEREN AL AÑO 1973/74.
EXCLUIDOS 5 634 CIENTIFICOS E INGENIEROS DEL
SECTOR PRODUCTIVO (ACTIVIDADES DE I Y D INTEGRA-
DAS) CUYA REPARTICION POR SECTOR DE ACTIVIDAD
ECONOMICA SE DESCONOCE.

SAMOA:
E—> DATA RELATE TO FULL-TIME SCIENTISTS AND
ENGINEERS.
FR—> LES DONNEES SE REFERENT AUX SCIENTIFIQUES
ET INGENIEURS A PLEIN TEMPS.
ESP> LOS DATOS SE REFIEREN A LOS CIENTIFICOS E
INGENIEROS DE JORNADA COMPLETA.

B: HIGHER EDUCATION SECTOR / SECTEUR DE L'ENSEI-
GNEMENT SUPERIEUR / SECTOR DE ENSEÑANZA
SUPERIOR.

GENERAL NOTE / NOTE GENERALE / NOTA GENERAL:

E—> IN SECTION B, FOR THE FOLLOWING COUNTRIES
DATA REFER TO FIELD OF QUALIFICATION:
AFRICA: CENTRAL AFRICAN REPUBLIC, KENYA, NIGER,
TOGO, ZAMBIA.
NORTH AMERICA: CUBA.
SOUTH AMERICA: COLOMBIA, ECUADOR.
ASIA: JORDAN, TURKEY.
EUROPE: SWITZERLAND.

FR—> DANS LA PARTIE B, LA REPARTITION CORRESPOND
AU DIPLOME DECERNE POUR LES PAYS SUIVANTS:
AFRIQUE: REPUBLIQUE CENTRAFRICAINE, KENYA,
NIGER, TOGO, ZAMBIE.
AMERIQUE DU NORD: CUBA.
AMERIQUE DU SUD: COLOMBIE, EQUATEUR.
ASIE: JORDANIE, TURQUIE.
EUROPE: SUISSE.

ESP> EN LA PARTE B, LA REPARTICION CORRESPONDE
AL DIPLOMA OTORGADO POR LOS PAISES SIGUIENTES:
AFRICA: REPUBLICA CENTROAFRICANA, KENIA, NIGER,
TOGO, ZAMBIA.
AMERICA DEL NORTE: CUBA.
AMERICA DEL SUR: COLOMBIA, ECUADOR.
ASIA: JORDANIA, TURQUIA.
EUROPA: SUIZA.

TOGO:
E—> DATA RELATE TO FULL-TIME SCIENTISTS AND
ENGINEERS.
FR—> LES DONNEES SE REFERENT AUX SCIENTIFIQUES
ET INGENIEURS A PLEIN TEMPS.
ESP> LOS DATOS SE REFIEREN A LOS CIENTIFICOS E
INGENIEROS DE JORNADA COMPLETA.

ZAMBIA:
E—> PARTIAL DATA.
FR—> DONNEES PARTIELLES.
ESP> DATOS PARCIALES.

UNITED STATES OF AMERICA:
E—> NOT INCLUDING DATA FOR LAW, HUMANITIES AND
EDUCATION.
FR—> NON COMPRIS LES DONNEES POUR LE DROIT, LES
SCIENCES HUMAINES ET L'EDUCATION.
ESP> EXCLUIDOS LOS DATOS RELATIVOS AL DERECHO,
LAS CIENCIAS HUMANAS Y LA EDUCACION.

ARGENTINA:
E—> DATA ARE IN NET MAN-YEARS.
FR—> LES DONNEES SONT EN ANNEES-HOMME NETTES.
ESP> LOS DATOS SE INDICAN EN ANOS-HOMBRE NETOS.

COLOMBIA:
E—> DATA RELATE TO FULL-TIME PLUS PART-TIME
SCIENTISTS AND ENGINEERS AND DO NOT INCLUDE LAW,
HUMANITIES AND EDUCATION.
FR—> LES DONNEES SE REFERENT AUX SCIENTIFIQUES
ET INGENIEURS A PLEIN TEMPS ET A TEMPS PARTIEL ET
NE COMPRENNENT PAS LE DROIT, LES SCIENCES HUMAINES
ET L'EDUCATION.
ESP> LOS DATOS SE REFIEREN A LOS CIENTIFICOS E
INGENIEROS DE JORNADA COMPLETA Y PARCIAL Y NO IN-
CLUYEN EL DERECHO, LAS CIENCIAS HUMANAS Y LA EDU-
CACION.

ECUADOR:
E—> DATA REFER TO R&D IN THE AGRICULTURAL
SCIENCES ONLY.
FR—> LES DONNEES SE REFERENT A LA R-D DANS LES
SCIENCES DE L'AGRICULTURE SEULEMENT.
ESP> LOS DATOS SE REFIEREN A LAS ACTIVIDADES DE
I Y D DE LAS CIENCIAS AGRICOLAS SOLAMENTE.

PERU:
E—> NOT INCLUDING DATA FOR HUMANITIES AND
EDUCATION.
FR—> NON COMPRIS LES DONNEES POUR LES SCIENCES
HUMAINES ET L'EDUCATION.
ESP> EXCLUIDOS LOS DATOS RELATIVOS A LAS CIEN-
CIAS HUMANAS Y LA EDUCACION.

URUGUAY:
E—> DATA RELATE TO THE YEAR 1971/72.
FR—> LES DONNEES SE REFERENT A L'ANNEE 1971/72.
ESP> LOS DATOS SE REFIEREN AL AÑO 1971/72.

IRAQ:
E—> DATA REFER ONLY TO THOSE WORKING IN GOVERN-
MENT DEPARTMENTS CONCERNED WITH SCIENTIFIC ACTIVI-
TIES.
FR—> LES DONNEES NE SE REFERENT QU'AUX PERSONNES
EMPLOYEES DANS LES DEPARTEMENTS GOUVERNEMENTAUX
CONCERNES PAR LES ACTIVITES SCIENTIFIQUES.
ESP> LOS DATOS SE REFIEREN UNICAMENTE A LAS
PERSONAS EMPLEADAS EN LOS SERVICIOS GUBERNAMENTA-
LES QUE SE OCUPAN DE ACTIVIDADES CIENTIFICAS.

JAPAN:
E—> DATA RELATE TO FULL-TIME SCIENTISTS AND
ENGINEERS.
FR—> LES DONNEES SE REFERENT AUX SCIENTIFIQUES
ET INGENIEURS A PLEIN TEMPS.
ESP> LOS DATOS SE REFIEREN A LOS CIENTIFICOS E
INGENIEROS DE JORNADA COMPLETA.

JORDAN:
E—> DATA RELATE TO THE EAST BANK ONLY.
FR—> LES DONNEES SE REFERENT A LA RIVE ORIENTALE
SEULEMENT.
ESP> LOS DATOS SE REFIEREN A LA ORILLA ORIENTAL
SOLAMENTE.

KOREA, REPUBLIC OF:
E—> DATA RELATE TO FULL-TIME PLUS PART-TIME
SCIENTISTS AND ENGINEERS AND DO NOT INCLUDE LAW,
HUMANITIES AND EDUCATION.
FR—> LES DONNEES SE REFERENT AUX SCIENTIFIQUES
ET INGENIEURS A PLEIN TEMPS ET A TEMPS PARTIEL ET
NE COMPRENNENT PAS LE DROIT, LES SCIENCES HUMAINES
ET L'EDUCATION.
ESP> LOS DATOS SE REFIEREN A LOS CIENTIFICOS E
INGENIEROS DE JORNADA COMPLETA Y PARCIAL Y NO IN-
CLUYEN EL DERECHO, LAS CIENCIAS HUMANAS Y LA EDU-
CACION.

R&D scientists and engineers by fields of activity   5.5
Scientifiques et ingénieurs de R-D par domaines d'activité
Científicos e ingenieros de I y D por campos de actuación

PAKISTAN:
  E—> DATA RELATE TO THE YEAR 1973/74 AND
REFER TO R&D ACTIVITIES CONCENTRATED MAINLY IN
GOVERNMENT—FINANCED RESEARCH ESTABLISHMENTS.
NOT INCLUDING SOCIAL SCIENCES AND HUMANITIES.
  FR-> LES DONNEES SE REFERENT A L'ANNEE 1973/74
ET AUX ACTIVITES DE R-D SE TROUVANT POUR LA
PLUPART DANS LES ETABLISSEMENTS DE RECHERCHE
FINANCES PAR LE GOUVERNEMENT. NON COMPRIS LES
DONNEES POUR LES SCIENCES SOCIALES ET HUMAINES.
  ESP> LOS DATOS SE REFIEREN AL AÑO 1973/74 Y A
LAS ACTIVIDADES DE I Y D CONCENTRADAS PRINCIPAL-
MENTE EN LOS ESTABLECIMIENTOS DE INVESTIGACION
SUBVENCIONADOS POR EL GOBIERNO. EXCLUIDOS LOS
DATOS CORRESPONDIENTES A LAS CIENCIAS SOCIALES Y
HUMANAS.

THAILAND:
  E—> DATA RELATE TO THE YEAR 1974/75 AND DO NOT
INCLUDE A TOTAL OF 3,209 PERSONS ENGAGED IN SOCIAL
SCIENCES AND HUMANITIES FOR WHOM A BREAKDOWN BY
SECTOR IS NOT AVAILABLE.
  FR-> LES DONNEES SE REFERENT A L'ANNEE 1974/75
ET NE COMPRENNENT PAS 3 209 PERSONNES EMPLOYEES
DANS LES SCIENCES SOCIALES ET HUMAINES POUR LES-
QUELLES LA REPARTITION PAR SECTEUR N'EST PAS
DISPONIBLE.
  ESP> LOS DATOS SE REFIEREN AL AÑO 1974/75 Y NO
INCLUYEN 3 209 PERSONAS EMPLEADAS EN LAS CIENCAS
SOCIALES Y HUMANAS PARA LAS QUE SE DESCONOCE LA
REPARTICION POR SECTOR.

TURKEY:
  E—> DATA RELATE TO THE YEAR 1975/76 AND DO NOT
INCLUDE SOCIAL SCIENCES AND HUMANITIES.
  FR-> LES DONNEES SE REFERENT A L'ANNEE 1975/76
ET NE COMPRENNENT PAS LES SCIENCES SOCIALES ET
HUMAINES.
  ESP> LOS DATOS SE REFIEREN AL AÑO 1975/76 Y NO
INCLUYEN LAS CIENCIAS SOCIALES Y HUMANAS.

CZECHOSLOVAKIA:
  E—> OF MILITARY R&D ONLY THAT PART CARRIED OUT
IN CIVIL ESTABLISHMENTS IS INCLUDED. NOT INCLUDING
SCIENTISTS AND ENGINEERS ENGAGED IN THE ADMINIS-
TRATION OF R&D.
  FR-> POUR LA R-D DE CARACTERE MILITAIRE SEULE
LA PARTIE EFFECTUEE DANS LES ETABLISSEMENTS CI-
VILS A ETE CONSIDEREE. COMPTE NON TENU DES SCIEN-
TIFIQUES ET INGENIEURS EMPLOYES DANS LES SERVICES
ADMINISTRATIFS DE LA R-D.
  ESP> PARA LA I Y D DE CARACTER MILITAR SOLO SE
HA CONSIDERADO LA PARTE CORRESPONDIENTE A LOS
ESTABLECIMIENTOS CIVILES. EXCLUIDOS LOS CIENTIFI-
COS E INGENIEROS EMPLEADOS EN LOS SERVICIOS ADMI-
NISTRATIVOS DE I Y D.

HUNGARY:
  E—> NOT INCLUDING SCIENTISTS AND ENGINEERS EN-
GAGED IN THE ADMINISTRATION OF R&D.
  FR-> COMPTE NON TENU DES SCIENTIFIQUES ET INGE-
NIEURS EMPLOYES DANS LES SERVICES ADMINISTRATIFS
DE R-D.
  ESP> EXCLUIDOS LOS CIENTIFICOS E INGENIEROS
EMPLEADOS EN LOS SERVICIOS ADMINISTRATIVOS DE
I Y D.

YUGOSLAVIA:
  E—> NOT INCLUDING ACTIVITIES OF A MILITARY
NATURE OR RELATING TO NATIONAL DEFENCE.
  FR-> NON COMPRIS LES ACTIVITES DE CARACTERE
MILITAIRE OU RELEVANT DE LA DEFENSE NATIONALE.
  ESP> EXCLUIDAS LAS ACTIVIDADES DE CARACTER
MILITAR O QUE CONCIERNEN LA DEFENSA NACIONAL.

AUSTRALIA:
  E—> DATA RELATE TO THE YEAR 1973/74.

AUSTRALIA (CONT.):
  FR-> LES DONNEES SE REFERENT A L'ANNEE 1973/74.
  ESP> LOS DATOS SE REFIEREN AL AÑO 1973/74.

SAMOA:
  E—> DATA RELATE TO FULL—TIME SCIENTISTS AND
ENGINEERS.
  FR-> LES DONNEES SE REFERENT AUX SCIENTIFIQUES
ET INGENIEURS A PLEIN TEMPS.
  ESP> LOS DATOS SE REFIEREN A LOS CIENTIFICOS E
INGENIEROS DE JORNADA COMPLETA.

C: GENERAL SERVICE SECTOR / SECTEUR DE SERVICE
   GENERAL / SECTOR DE SERVICIO GENERAL.

GENERAL NOTE / NOTE GENERALE / NOTA GENERAL:

  E—> IN SECTION C, FOR THE FOLLOWING COUNTRIES
DATA REFER TO FIELD OF QUALIFICATION:
  AFRICA: GABON, TOGO, ZAMBIA.
  NORTH AMERICA: BELIZE, BERMUDA, CUBA.
  SOUTH AMERICA: COLOMBIA.
  ASIA: CYPRUS, JORDAN, PHILIPPINES, TURKEY.
  EUROPE: SWITZERLAND.
  OCEANIA: NEW CALEDONIA.

  FR-> DANS LA PARTIE C, LA REPARTITION CORRESPOND
AU DIPLOME DECERNE POUR LES PAYS SUIVANTS:
  AFRIQUE: GABON, TOGO, ZAMBIE.
  AMERIQUE DU NORD: BELIZE, BERMUDES, CUBA.
  AMERIQUE DU SUD: COLOMBIE.
  ASIE: CHYPRE, JORDANIE, PHILIPPINES ET TURQUIE.
  EUROPE: SUISSE.
  OCEANIE: NOUVELLE CALEDONIE.

  ESP> EN LA PARTE C, LA REPARTICION CORRESPONDE
AL DIPLOMA OTORGADO POR LOS PAISES SIGUIENTES:
  AFRICA: GABON, TOGO, ZAMBIA.
  AMERICA DEL NORTE: BELIZE, BERMUDAS, CUBA.
  AMERICA DEL SUR: COLOMBIA.
  ASIA: CHIPRE, JORDANIA, FILIPINAS, TURQUIA.
  EUROPA: SUIZA.
  OCEANIA: NUEVA CALEDONIA.

GABON:
  E—> DATA RELATE TO THE (FRENCH) "OFFICE DE LA
RECHERCHE SCIENTIFIQUE ET TECHNIQUE OUTRE—MER"
(ORSTOM) ONLY.
  FR-> LES DONNEES NE CONCERNENT QUE L'OFFICE DE
LA RECHERCHE SCIENTIFIQUE ET TECHNIQUE OUTRE—MER
(ORSTOM) SEULEMENT.
  ESP> DATOS RELATIVOS AL "OFFICE(FRANCAIS) DE
LA RECHERCHE SCIENTIFIQUE ET TECHNIQUE OUTRE—MER"
(ORSTOM) SOLAMENTE.

TOGO:
  E—> DATA RELATIVE TO THE PRODUCTIVE SECTOR
(INTEGRATED R&D) ARE INCLUDED WITH THE GENERAL
SERVICE SECTOR. SCIENTISTS AND ENGINEERS ARE
FULL—TIME.
  FR-> LES DONNEES RELATIVES AU SECTEUR DE LA
PRODUCTION (ACTIVITES DE R-D INTEGREES) SONT
COMPRISES AVEC LE SECTEUR DE SERVICE GENERAL.
LES SCIENTIFIQUES ET INGENIEURS SONT A PLEIN
TEMPS.
  ESP> LOS DATOS CORRESPONDIENTES AL SECTOR PRO-
DUCTIVO (ACTIVIDADES I Y D INTEGRADAS) ESTAN IN-
CLUIDOS EN EL SECTOR DE SERVICIO GENERAL.LOS
DATOS SE REFIEREN A LOS CIENTIFICOS E INGENIEROS
DE JORNADA COMPLETA.

ZAMBIA:
  E—> PARTIAL DATA.
  FR-> DONNEES PARTIELLES.
  ESP> DATOS PARCIALES.

5.5 R&D scientists and engineers by fields of activity
Scientifiques et ingénieurs de R-D par domaines d'activité
Científicos e ingenieros de I y D por campos de actuación

BERMUDA:
E—> NOT INCLUDING DATA FOR LAW, HUMANITIES AND
EDUCATION.
FR—> NON COMPRIS LES DONNEES POUR LE DROIT, LES
SCIENCES HUMAINES ET L'EDUCATION.
ESP> EXCLUIDOS LOS DATOS RELATIVOS AL DERECHO,
LAS CIENCIAS HUMANAS Y LA EDUCACION.

CANADA:
E—>DATA RELATIVE TO THE PRODUCTIVE SECTOR (NON-
INTEGRATED R&D) ARE INCLUDED WITH THE GENERAL
SERVICE SECTOR. ENGINEERING AND TECHNOLOGY,
MEDICAL SCIENCES AND AGRICULTURE ARE INCLUDED
UNDER COLUMNS 3 AND 4.
FR—> LES DONNEES RELATIVES AU SECTEUR DE LA
PRODUCTION (ACTIVITES DE R-D NON INTEGREES) SONT
COMPRISES AVEC LE SECTEUR DE SERVICE GENERAL.
LES SCIENCES DE L'INGENIEUR ET DE LA TECHNOLOGIE,
LES SCIENCES MEDICALES ET L'AGRICULTURE SONT
COMPRISES AVEC CELLES QUI FIGURENT DANS LES
COLONNES 3 ET 4.
ESP> LOS DATOS CORRESPONDIENTES AL SECTOR
PRODUCTIVO (ACTIVIDADES DE I Y D NO INTEGRADAS)
ESTAN INCLUIDOS EN EL SECTOR DE SERVICIO GENERAL.
LOS DATOS RELATIVOS A LA INGENIERIA Y A LA TECNO-
LOGIA, A LAS CIENCIAS MEDICAS Y A LA AGRICULTURA,
QUEDAN ENGLOBADOS CON LOS QUE FIGURAN EN LAS
COLUMNAS 3 Y 4.

ARGENTINA:
E—> DATA ARE IN NET MAN-YEARS. INCLUDING PRI-
VATE NON-PROFIT ORGANIZATIONS.
FR—> LES DONNEES SONT EN ANNEES-HOMME NETTES.
Y COMPRIS LES ORGANISATIONS PRIVEES A BUT NON
LUCRATIF.
ESP > LOS DATOS SE INDICAN EN ANOS-HOMBRE NETOS.
INCLUIDAS LAS ORGANIZACIONES PRIVADAS DE CARACTER
NO LUCRATIVO.

COLOMBIA:
E—> DATA RELATE TO FULL-TIME PLUS PART-TIME
SCIENTISTS AND ENGINEERS AND DO NOT INCLUDE LAW,
HUMANITIES AND EDUCATION.
FR—> LES DONNEES SE REFERENT AUX SCIENTIFIQUES
ET INGENIEURS A PLEIN TEMPS ET A TEMPS PARTIEL ET
NE COMPRENNENT PAS LE DROIT, LES SCIENCES HUMAINES
ET L'EDUCATION.
ESP> LOS DATOS SE REFIEREN A LOS CIENTIFICOS E
INGENIEROS DE JORNADA COMPLETA Y PARCIAL Y NO IN-
CLUYEN EL DERECHO, LAS CIENCIAS HUMANAS Y LA EDU-
CACION.

PERU:
E—> NOT INCLUDING DATA FOR HUMANITIES AND
EDUCATION.
FR—> NON COMPRIS LES DONNEES POUR LES SCIENCES
HUMAINES ET L'EDUCATION.
ESP> EXCLUIDOS LOS DATOS RELATIVOS A LAS CIEN-
CIAS HUMANAS Y LA EDUCACION.

URUGUAY:
E—> DATA RELATE TO THE YEAR 1971/72.
FR—> LES DONNEES SE REFERENT A L'ANNEE 1971/72.
ESP> LOS DATOS SE REFIEREN AL AÑO 1971/72.

IRAQ:
E—> DATA REFER ONLY TO THOSE WORKING IN GOVERN-
MENT DEPARTMENTS CONCERNED WITH SCIENTIFIC ACTIVI-
TIES.
FR—> LES DONNEES NE SE REFERENT QU'AUX PERSONNES
SONT EMPLOYEES DANS LES DEPARTEMENTS GOUVERNEMEN-
TAUX CONCERNES PAR LES ACTIVITES SCIENTIFIQUES.
ESP> LOS DATOS SE REFIEREN UNICAMENTE A LAS PER-
SONAS EMPLEADAS EN LOS SERVICIOS GUBERNAMENTALES
QUE SE OCUPAN DE ACTIVIDADES CIENTIFICAS.

JAPAN:
E—> DATA RELATE TO FULL-TIME SCIENTISTS AND
ENGINEERS.
FR—> LES DONNEES SE REFERENT AUX SCIENTIFIQUES
ET INGENIEURS A PLEIN TEMPS.
ESP> LOS DATOS SE REFIEREN A LOS CIENTIFICOS E
INGENIEROS DE JORNADA COMPLETA.

JORDAN:
E—> DATA RELATE TO THE EAST BANK ONLY.
FR—> LES DONNEES SE REFERENT A LA RIVE ORIENTALE
SEULEMENT.
ESP> LOS DATOS SE REFIEREN A LA ORILLA ORIENTAL
SOLAMENTE.

KOREA, REPUBLIC OF:
E—> DATA RELATE TO FULL-TIME PLUS PART-TIME
SCIENTISTS AND ENGINEERS AND DO NOT INCLUDE LAW,
HUMANITIES AND EDUCATION.
FR—> LES DONNEES SE REFERENT AUX SCIENTIFIQUES
ET INGENIEURS A PLEIN TEMPS ET A TEMPS PARTIEL ET
NE COMPRENNENT PAS LE DROIT, LES SCIENCES HUMAINES
ET L'EDUCATION.
ESP> LOS DATOS SE REFIEREN A LOS CIENTIFICOS E
INGENIEROS DE JORNADA COMPLETA Y PARCIAL Y NO IN-
CLUYEN EL DERECHO, LAS CIENCIAS HUMANAS Y LA EDU-
CACION.

PAKISTAN:
E—> DATA RELATE TO THE YEAR 1973/74 AND
REFER TO R&D ACTIVITIES CONCENTRATED MAINLY IN
GOVERNMENT-FINANCED RESEARCH ESTABLISHMENTS.
NOT INCLUDING SOCIAL SCIENCES AND HUMANITIES.
FR—> LES DONNEES SE REFERENT A L'ANNEE 1973/74
ET AUX ACTIVITES DE R-D SE TROUVANT POUR LA
PLUPART DANS LES ETABLISSEMENTS DE RECHERCHE
FINANCES PAR LE GOUVERNEMENT. NON COMPRIS LES
DONNEES POUR LES SCIENCES SOCIALES ET HUMAINES.
ESP> LOS DATOS SE REFIEREN AL AÑO 1973/74 Y A
LAS ACTIVIDADES DE I Y D CONCENTRADAS PRINCIPAL-
MENTE EN LOS ESTABLECIMIENTOS DE INVESTIGACION
SUBVENCIONADOS POR EL GOBIERNO. EXCLUIDOS LOS
DATOS CORRESPONDIENTES A LAS CIENCIAS SOCIALES Y
HUMANAS.

THAILAND:
E—> DATA RELATE TO THE YEAR 1974/75 AND DO NOT
INCLUDE A TOTAL OF 3,209 PERSONS ENGAGED IN SOCIAL
SCIENCES AND HUMANITIES FOR WHOM A BREAKDOWN BY
SECTOR IS NOT AVAILABLE.
FR—> LES DONNEES SE REFERENT A L'ANNEE 1974/75
ET NE COMPRENNENT PAS 3 209 PERSONNES EMPLOYEES
DANS LES SCIENCES SOCIALES ET HUMAINES POUR LES-
QUELLES LA REPARTITION PAR SECTEUR N'EST PAS
DISPONIBLE.
ESP> LOS DATOS SE REFIEREN AL AÑO 1974/1975 Y
NO INCLUYEN 3 209 PERSONAS EMPLEADAS EN LAS CIEN-
CIAS SOCIALES Y HUMANAS PARA LAS QUE SE DESCONOCE
LA REPARTICION POR SECTOR.

TURKEY:
E—> NOT INCLUDING DATA FOR SOCIAL SCIENCES
AND HUMANITIES.
FR—> NON COMPRIS LES DONNEES POUR LES SCIENCES
SOCIALES ET HUMAINES.
ESP> EXCLUIDOS LOS DATOS CORRESPONDIENTES A
LAS CIENCIAS SOCIALES Y HUMANAS.

BULGARIA:
E—> INCLUDING DATA FOR THE PRODUCTIVE SECTOR
BUT EXCLUDING 13,168 SCIENTISTS AND ENGINEERS
FOR WHOM A DISTRIBUTION BY FIELD OF SCIENCE IS
NOT AVAILABLE.

R&D scientists and engineers by fields of activity 5.5
Scientifiques et ingénieurs de R-D par domaines d'activité
Científicos e ingenieros de I y D por campos de actuación

BULGARIA (CONT.):
FR—> Y COMPRIS LES DONNEES RELATIVES AU SECTEUR
DE LA PRODUCTION, MAIS NON COMPRIS 13 168 SCIEN-
TIFIQUES ET INGENIEURS POUR LESQUELS LA REPARTI-
TION PAR DISCIPLINE SCIENTIFIQUE N'EST PAS
DISPONIBLE.
ESP> INCLUYE LOS DATOS RELATIVOS AL SECTOR PRO-
DUCTIVO, PERO EXCLUYE 13 168 CIENTIFICOS E INGE-
NIEROS CUYA REPARTICION POR RAMA DE LA CIENCIA
SE DESCONOCE.

CZECHOSLOVAKIA:
E—> OF MILITARY R&D ONLY THAT PART CARRIED OUT—
IN CIVIL ESTABLISHMENTS IS INCLUDED. NOT INCLUDING
SCIENTISTS AND ENGINEERS ENGAGED IN THE ADMINIS-
TRATION OF R&D.
FR—> POUR LA R—D DE CARACTERE MILITAIRE SEULE
LA PARTIE EFFECTUEE DANS LES ETABLISSEMENTS CI-
VILS A ETE CONSIDEREE. COMPTE NON TENU DES SCIEN-
TIFIQUES ET INGENIEURS EMPLOYES DANS LES SERVICES
ADMINISTRATIFS DE R—D.
ESP> PARA LA I Y D DE CARACTER MILITAR SOLO SE
HA CONSIDERADO LA PARTE CORRESPONDIENTE A LOS
ESTABLECIMIENTOS CIVILES. EXCLUIDOS LOS CIENTIFI-
COS E INGENIEROS EMPLEADOS EN LOS SERVICIOS ADMI-
NISTRATIVOS DE I Y D.

HUNGARY:
E—> NOT INCLUDING SCIENTISTS AND ENGINEERS EN-
GAGED IN THE ADMINISTRATION OF R&D.
FR—> COMPTE NON TENU DES SCIENTIFIQUES ET INGE-
NIEURS EMPLOYES DANS LES SERVICES ADMINISTRATIFS
DE R—D.
ESP> EXCLUIDOS LOS CIENTIFICOS E INGENIEROS
EMPLEADOS EN LOS SERVICIOS ADMINISTRATIVOS DE
I Y D.

SPAIN:
E—> DATA RELATIVE TO THE PRODUCTIVE SECTOR
(NON—INTEGRATED R&D) ARE INCLUDED WITH THE
GENERAL SERVICE SECTOR.
FR—> LES DONNEES RELATIVES AU SECTEUR DE LA
PRODUCTION (ACTIVITES DE R—D NON—INTEGREES) SONT
COMPRISES AVEC LE SECTEUR DE SERVICE GENERAL.
ESP> LOS DATOS CORRESPONDIENTES AL SECTOR PRO-
DUCTIVO (ACTIVIDADES DE I Y D NO INTEGREADAS)
ESTAN INCLUIDOS EN EL SECTOR DE SERVICIO GENERAL.

YUGOSLAVIA:
E—> NOT INCLUDING ACTIVITIES OF A MILITARY
NATURE OR RELATING TO NATIONAL DEFENCE.
FR—> NON COMPRIS LES ACTIVITES DE CARACTERE
MILITAIRE OU RELEVANT DE LA DEFENSE NATIONALE.
ESP> EXCLUIDAS LAS ACTIVIDADES DE CARACTER
MILITAR O QUE CONCIERNEN LA DEFENSA NACIONAL.

AUSTRALIA:
E—> DATA RELATE TO THE YEAR 1973/74.
FR—> LES DONNEES SE REFERENT A L'ANNEE 1973/74.
ESP> LOS DATOS SE REFIEREN AL AÑO 1973/74.

NEW ZEALAND:
E—> NOT INCLUDING 67 SCIENTISTS AND ENGINEERS
FOR WHOM A DISTRIBUTION BY INDUSTRY IS NOT KNOWN.
FR—> COMPTE NON TENU DE 67 SCIENTIFIQUES ET IN-
GENIEURS POUR LESQUELS LA REPARTITION PAR BRANCHE
D'ACTIVITE ECONOMIQUE N'EST PAS DISPONIBLE.
ESP> EXCLUIDOS 67 CIENTIFICOS E INGENIEROS CUYA
REPARTICION POR SECTOR DE ACTIVIDAD ECONOMICA SE
DESCONOCE.

SAMOA:
E—> DATA RELATE TO FULL—TIME SCIENTISTS AND
ENGINEERS.
FR—> LES DONNEES SE REFERENT AUX SCIENTIFIQUES
ET INGENIEURS A PLEIN TEMPS.
ESP> LOS DATOS SE REFIEREN A LOS CIENTIFICOS E
INGENIEROS DE JORNADA COMPLETA.

5.6 Total expenditure for research and experimental development by type of expenditure

Dépenses totales consacrées à la recherche et au développement expérimental, par type de dépenses

Gastos totales dedicados a la investigación y al desarrollo experimental, por tipo de gastos

PLEASE REFER TO INTRODUCTION FOR DEFINITIONS OF CATEGORIES INCLUDED IN THIS TABLE.

POUR LES DEFINITIONS DES CATEGORIES PRESENTEES DANS CE TABLEAU, SE REFERER A L'INTRODUCTION.

EN LA INTRODUCCION SE DAN LAS DEFINICIONES DE LAS CATEGORIAS QUE FIGURAN EN ESTE CUADRO.

NUMBER OF COUNTRIES AND TERRITORIES PRESENTED IN THIS TABLE: 108

NOMBRE DE PAYS ET DE TERRITOIRES PRESENTES DANS CE TABLEAU: 108

NUMERO DE PAISES Y DE TERRITORIOS PRESENTADOS EN ESTE CUADRO: 108

COUNTRY / PAYS / PAIS	FISCAL YEAR BEGINNING / EXERCICE FINANCIER COMMENÇANT EN / COMIENZO DEL EJERCICIO ECONOMICO	CURRENCY / MONNAIE / MONEDA	TYPE OF EXPENDITURE / TYPE DE DEPENSES / TIPO DE GASTOS		CURRENT / COURANTES / ORDINARIOS			PERCENTAGE / POURCENTAGE / PORCENTAJE COL.(3)/COL.(1)
			TOTAL (000) (1)	CAPITAL (000) (2)	TOTAL (000) (3)	LABOUR COSTS / DEPENSES EN PERSONNEL / GASTOS DE PERSONAL (000) (4)	OTHER CURRENT COSTS / AUTRES DEPENSES COURANTES / OTROS GASTOS ORDINARIOS (000) (5)	(6)
AFRICA								
ALGERIA ‡	1972	DINAR	78 000	10 000	68 000	44 000	24 000	87.2
BOTSWANA	1973	PULA	220	187	33	...	...	15.0
CHAD ‡	1973	FRANC C.F.A.	255 220	...	...	...	...	...
CONGO ‡	1977	FRANC C.F.A.	634 241	-	634 241	...	...	-
EGYPT ‡	1973	POUND	29 940	4 950	22 000	16 870	5 130	81.6
GABON ‡	1970	FRANC C.F.A.	1 895	13	1 882	1 526	356	99.3
GHANA ‡	1971	CEDI	21 612	...	21 612	...	...	
IVORY COAST	1970	FRANC C.F.A.	1 401 124	16 000	1 385 124	865 908	519 216	98.9
KENYA ‡	1971	SHILLING	*102 940	*19 780	*83 160	...	...	*80.8
MADAGASCAR ‡	1971	FRANC	2 294 000	-	2 294 000	1 588 000	656 000	100.0
MALAWI	1977	KWACHA	1 290	282	1 008	...	...	78.1
MAURITIUS	1977	RUPEE	18 800	6 100	12 700	9 600	3 100	67.6
NIGER ‡	1976	FRANC C.F.A.	141 703	-	141 703	103 653	38 050	100.0
NIGERIA ‡	1970	NAIRA	23 800	...	*22 000	...	...	*92.4
SENEGAL ‡	1972	FRANC C.F.A.	...	...	2 176 000	785 000	1 391 000	...

R&D expenditure by type   5.6
Dépenses de R-D par type
Gastos de I y D por tipo

			(1)	(2)	(3)	(4)	(5)	(6)
SEYCHELLES	RUPEE	1973	402	112	290	225	65	72.1
SUDAN	POUND	1978	5 115	821	4 294	453	376	83.9
TOGO	FRANC C.F.A.	1971	...	...	1 070 829	486 453	584 376	...
UNITED REPUBLIC OF CAMEROON ‡	FRANC C.F.A.	1970	*1 765 000	...	...	...	...	...
UPPER VOLTA	FRANC C.F.A.	1970	*412 768	...	...	...	...	...
ZAMBIA	KWACHA	1972	6 261	1 535	4 726	2 423	2 303	75.5
AMERICA, NORTH								
BAHAMAS	DOLLAR	1970	*550	*20	...	...	...	...
BELIZE ‡	DOLLAR	1970	207	...	187	105	82	90.3
BERMUDA ‡	DOLLAR	1970	240	35	205	167	38	85.4
BRITISH VIRGIN ISLANDS	U.S. DOLLAR	1973	-	...	...	...	...	...
CANADA	DOLLAR	1977	2 241 700	211 100	2 030 600	-	-	90.6
CUBA	PESO	1978	83 163	14 755	68 408	41 002	27 406	82.3
EL SALVADOR ‡	COLON	1974	31 273	7 006	24 267	...	...	77.6
GUATEMALA	QUETZAL	1974	*5 139	*1 418	*3 721	*1 675	*2 046	*72.4
JAMAICA	DOLLAR	1971	...	...	1 095	...	...	...
MEXICO	PESO	1973	1 277 618	127 025	1 150 593	861 264	289 329	90.1
NICARAGUA ‡	CORDOBA	1971	7 847	...	...	...	...	...
PANAMA	BALBOA	1974	2 908	201	2 707	2 046	661	93.1
ST. PIERRE AND MIQUELON ‡	FRANC C.F.A.	1972	110 000	...	...	...	...	...
TRINIDAD AND TOBAGO ‡	DOLLAR	1970	5 171	800	4 371	3 012	1 359	84.5
TURKS AND CAICOS ISLANDS	U.S. DOLLAR	1974	8	...	...	...	...	...
UNITED STATES OF AMERICA ‡	DOLLAR	1978	...	...	47 295 000	...	...	...
AMERICA, SOUTH								
ARGENTINA	PESO	1976	*23 171 700	*2 664 500	*20 507 200	*13 679 100	*6 828 100	*88.5
BRAZIL ‡	CRUZEIRO	1978	20 781 000	...	...	...	...	...
COLOMBIA ‡	PESO	1971	210 614	5 205	205 409	...	...	97.5
ECUADOR ‡	SUCRE	1976	258 366	90 648	167 718	113 619	54 099	64.9
FALKLAND ISLANDS (MALVINAS)	POUND	1971	-	-	...	...	...	...
PARAGUAY	GUARANI	1971	*167 265	*43 306	123 959	...	...	74.1
PERU	SOL	1976	*2 314 754	*302 131	*2 012 623	...	...	86.9
URUGUAY ‡	PESO	1972	1 858	...	...	...	...	...
VENEZUELA ‡	BOLIVAR	1970	102 270	5 120	97 150	81 760	15 390	95.0
ASIA								
BANGLADESH ‡	TAKA	1974	113 530	61 370	52 160	...	...	45.9
BRUNEI	DOLLAR	1974	3 055	122	2 933	2 033	900	96.0
BURMA	KYAT	1973	11 960	3 787	8 173	...	...	68.3
CYPRUS	POUND	1971	1 088	102	986	408	578	90.6
INDIA	RUPEE	1976	4 022 500	...	...	...	...	...

5.6 R&D expenditure by type
Dépenses de R-D par type
Gastos de I y D por tipo

TYPE OF EXPENDITURE / TYPE DE DEPENSES / TIPO DE GASTOS

COUNTRY / PAYS / PAIS	CURRENCY / MONNAIE / MONEDA	FISCAL YEAR BEGINNING / EXERCICE FINANCIER COMMENÇANT EN / COMIENZO DEL EJERCICIO ECONOMICO	TOTAL (000) / TOTAL DE CAPITAL	CAPITAL (000) EN CAPITAL DE CAPITAL	CURRENT / COURANTES / ORDINARIOS			PERCENTAGE / POURCENTAGE / PORCENTAJE COL.(3)/COL.(1)
					TOTAL (000)	LABOUR COSTS / DEPENSES EN PERSONNEL / GASTOS DE PERSONAL (000)	OTHER CURRENT COSTS / AUTRES DEPENSES COURANTES / OTROS GASTOS ORDINARIOS (000)	
			(1)	(2)	(3)	(4)	(5)	(6)
INDONESIA ‡	RUPIAH	1975	*19 496 560	6 337 053	*13 159 507	...	...	67.5
IRAN ‡	RIAL	1972	3 531 807	1 285 018	2 246 789	...	...	63.6
IRAQ ‡	DINAR	1974	7 409	2 500	4 909	...	...	66.3
ISRAEL ‡	POUND	1978	6 154 300	211 300	5 943 000	...	...	96.6
JAPAN ‡	YEN	1977	3 651 319	553 476	3 097 843	...	...	84.8
JORDAN ‡	DINAR	1976	2 074	832	1 242	928	314	59.9
KOREA, REPUBLIC OF ‡	WON	1978	152 418 000	54 490 000	97 928 000	...	...	64.2
KUWAIT	DINAR	1977	6 284	1 419	4 865	2 962	1 903	77.4
MONGOLIA ‡	TUGRIK	1971	14 720	...	...	...	...	...
PAKISTAN ‡	RUPEE	1973	150 430	...	...	...	...	...
PHILIPPINES ‡	PESO	1973	218 106	...	...	...	...	...
SINGAPORE ‡	DOLLAR	1978	28 120	...	...	...	...	...
SRI LANKA ‡	RUPEE	1975	45 097	12 435	32 662	21 240	11 422	72.4
TURKEY ‡	LIRA	1978	7 601 531	...	...	...	...	...
VIET-NAM ‡	DONG	1979	108 300	39 500	68 800	...	...	63.5
YEMEN ‡	RIAL	1974	9 923	2 935	6 988	*5 960	*1 028	70.4
EUROPE								
AUSTRIA ‡	SCHILLING	1972	2 363 740	440 168	1 923 572	1 232 322	691 250	81.4
BELGIUM	FRANC	1977	38 894 080	3 976 863	34 917 217	...	...	89.8
BULGARIA	LEV	1977	334 900	49 900	285 000	...	...	85.1
CZECHOSLOVAKIA	KORUNA	1978	17 496 000	2 178 000	15 318 000	...	...	87.6
DENMARK ‡	KRONE	1973	1 654 000	165 000	1 489 000	984 000	505 000	90.0
FINLAND	MARKKA	1977	1 298 820	140 890	1 157 930	832 510	325 420	89.1
FRANCE	FRANC	1977	33 185 000	2 927 000	30 258 000	19 808 000	10 450 000	91.2
GERMANY, FEDERAL REPUBLIC OF ‡	DEUTSCHE MARK	1977	25 413 000	2 749 000	22 664 000	15 418 000	7 246 000	89.2
GIBRALTAR	POUND	1971	-	-	-	-	-	-
GREECE	DRACHNA	1976	1 739 220	...	...	...	...	...
HOLY SEE	LIRA	1976	1 677 989	268 844	1 409 145	1 103 482	305 663	84.0
HUNGARY	FORINT	1978	18 716 000	3 100 000	15 616 000	...	...	83.4
ICELAND	KRONA	1973	487 900	58 900	429 000	...	...	87.9
IRELAND	POUND	1977	43 209	6 059	37 150	...	...	86.0
ITALY ‡	LIRA	1976	1 352 565	143 189	1 209 376	819 252	390 124	89.4
MALTA ‡	POUND	1973	149	19	130	...	...	87.2
NETHERLANDS ‡	GUILDER	1976	4 964 000	483 000	4 481 000	3 153 000	1 328 000	90.3
NORWAY	KRONER	1977	2 675 000	332 900	2 342 300	1 530 300	812 000	87.6
POLAND	ZLOTY	1978	40 769 601	5 900 000	*34 900 000			*85.6
					1 146 353	894 529	251 824	89.6

R&D expenditure by type 5.6
Dépenses de R-D par type
Gastos de I y D por tipo

			(1)	(2)	(3)	(4)	(5)	(6)
ROMANIA	LEU	1973	3 354 196	723 035	2 631 161	1 240 001	1 391 160	78.4
SAN MARINO	LIRA	1976	—	—	—	—	—	
SPAIN	PESETA	1974	15 536 477	4 040 139	11 496 338	9 071 598	2 424 740	74.0
SWEDEN ‡	KRONA	1977	6 796 700	490 900	6 305 800	...	...	92.8
SWITZERLAND ‡	FRANC	1976	*3 363 000	*150 000	*3 212 000	*1 815 000	*1 397 000	95.5
UNITED KINGDOM ‡	POUND STERLING	1975	2 139 000	172 700	1 938 200	1 119 400	818 800	91.8
YUGOSLAVIA ‡	DINAR	1978	9 633 000	...	...	...	...	...
OCEANIA								
AMERICAN SAMOA ‡	U.S. DOLLAR	1971	120	20	100	70	30	83.3
AUSTRALIA	DOLLAR	1976	802 464	80 340	722 124	...	...	90.0
COOK ISLANDS	NEW ZEALAND DOLLAR	1970	112	...	...	...	...	...
FRENCH POLYNESIA ‡	FRANC C.F.P.	1976	140 240	4 750	135 430	106 126	29 304	96.6
GUAM ‡	U.S. DOLLAR	1973	579	249	330	187	143	57.0
NAURU	AUSTRALIAN DOLLAR	1970						
NEW CALEDONIA	FRANC C.F.P.	1971	1 440	200	1 240	940	300	86.1
NEW HEBRIDES	FRANC	1975	21 603	—	21 603	12 480	9 123	100.0
NEW ZEALAND	DOLLAR	1975	99 776	8 277	91 499	...	...	91.7
PACIFIC ISLANDS	U.S. DOLLAR	1978	185	—	185	...	...	100.0
TOKELAU ISLANDS	NEW ZEALAND DOLLAR	1971						
SAMOA	TALA	1978	2 500	2 000	500	—	—	20.0
U.S.S.R.								
U.S.S.R. ‡	ROUBLE	1977	18 300 000	...	...	...	...	...
BYELORUSSIAN S.S.R. ‡	ROUBLE	1970	46 399	13 019	33 380	...	...	71.9

ALGERIA:
E—> DATA RELATE TO THE HIGHER EDUCATION SECTOR ONLY.
FR—> LES DONNEES NE CONCERNENT QUE LE SECTEUR DE L'ENSEIGNEMENT SUPERIEUR.
ESP> LOS DATOS SE REFIEREN AL SECTOR DE ENSEÑANZA SUPERIOR SOLAMENTE.

CHAD:
E—> DATA RELATE TO 4 RESEARCH INSTITUTES ONLY.
FR—> LES DONNEES NE CONCERNENT QUE QUATRE INSTITUTS DE RECHERCHE.
ESP> LOS DATOS SE REFIEREN A CUATRO CENTROS DE INVESTIGACION SOLAMENTE.

CONGO:
E—> DATA RELATE TO THE PRODUCTIVE SECTOR (NON-INTEGRATED R&D) AND THE HIGHER EDUCATION SECTOR ONLY.
FR—> LES DONNEES SE REFERENT AUX SECTEURS DE LA PRODUCTION (ACTIVITES DE R-D NON-INTEGREES) ET DE L'ENSEIGNEMENT SUPERIEUR SEULEMENT.
ESP> LOS DATOS SE REFIEREN AL SECTOR PRODUCTIVO (ACTIVIDADES DE I Y D NO INTEGRADAS) Y AL SECTOR DE ENSEÑANZA SUPERIOR SOLAMENTE.

EGYPT:
E—> THE TOTAL IN COLUMN 1 INCLUDES 2 990 THOUSAND POUNDS FROM FOREIGN FUNDS FOR WHICH THE BREAKDOWN BETWEEN CAPITAL AND CURRENT EXPENDITURE IS NOT KNOWN; THIS FIGURE HAS BEEN EXCLUDED FROM THE PERCENTAGE CALCULATION IN COLUMN 6.
FR—> LE TOTAL DE LA COLONNE 1 COMPREND 2 990 MILLIERS DE LIVRES PROVENANT DES FONDS ETRANGERS, DONT LA REPARTITION ENTRE LES DEPENSES EN CAPITAL ET COURANTES N'A PAS ETE PRECISEE; ON N'A PAS TENU COMPTE DE CE CHIFFRE POUR CALCULER LE POURCENTAGE DE LA COLONNE 6.
ESP> EL TOTAL DE LA COLUMNA 1 INCLUYE 2 990 MILLARES DE LIBRAS PROCEDENTES DE FONDOS EXTRANJEROS, CUYA REPARTICION ENTRE GASTOS DE CAPITAL Y GASTOS ORDINARIOS NO SE HA PRECISADO; DICHA CIFRA NO SE HA TENIDO EN CUENTA PARA CALCULAR EL PORCENTAJE DE LA COLUMNA 6.

GABON:
E—> DATA RELATE TO THE (FRENCH) "OFFICE DE LA RECHERCHE SCIENTIFIQUE ET TECHNIQUE OUTRE-MER" (ORSTOM).
FR—> LES DONNEES NE CONCERNENT QUE L'OFFICE FRANCAIS DE LA RECHERCHE SCIENTIFIQUE ET TECHNIQUE OUTRE-MER (ORSTOM).

5.6 R&D expenditure by type
Dépenses de R-D par type
Gastos de I y D por tipo

NIGER:
E—> DATA RELATE TO THE HIGHER EDUCATION SECTOR ONLY.
FR—> LES DONNEES NE CONCERNENT QUE LE SECTEUR DE L'ENSEIGNEMENT SUPERIEUR.
ESP> LOS DATOS SE REFIEREN AL SECTOR DE ENSEÑANZA SUPERIOR SOLAMENTE.

NIGERIA:
E—> DATA REFER TO FEDERAL AND STATE GOVERNMENTS' BUDGETARY ESTIMATES FOR RESEARCH AND TECHNICAL DEVELOPMENT SERVICES AND UNIVERSITY EXPENDITURE ON RESEARCH AND EXPERIMENTAL DEVELOPMENT; NOT INCLUDING DATA FOR SOCIAL SCIENCES AND HUMANITIES.
FR—> LES DONNEES SE REFERENT A L'ESTIMATION BUDGETAIRE DU GOUVERNEMENT FEDERAL ET DES GOUVERNEMENTS DES ETATS POUR LA RECHERCHE ET LES SERVICES DE DEVELOPPEMENT TECHNIQUE ET LES DEPENSES DES UNIVERSITES DESTINEES A LA RECHERCHE ET AU DEVELOPPEMENT EXPERIMENTAL; NON COMPRIS LES DONNEES POUR LES SCIENCES SOCIALES ET HUMAINES.
ESP> LOS DATOS SE REFIEREN A LA ESTIMACION PRESUPUESTARIA DEL GOBIERNO FEDERAL Y DE LOS GOBIERNOS DE LOS ESTADOS PARA LAS ACTIVIDADES DE INVESTIGACION Y LOS SERVICIOS DE DESARROLLO TECNICO, ASI COMO LOS GASTOS DE LAS UNIVERSIDADES DESTINADOS A LA INVESTIGACION Y AL DESARROLLO EXPERIMENTAL, EXCLUIDOS LOS DATOS RELATIVOS A LAS CIENCIAS SOCIALES Y HUMANAS.

SENEGAL:
E—> DATA RELATE TO THE PRODUCTIVE SECTOR (NON-INTEGRATED R&D) AND THE HIGHER EDUCATION SECTOR.
FR—> LES DONNEES SE REFERENT AUX SECTEURS DE LA PRODUCTION (ACTIVITES DE R-D NON-INTEGREES) ET DE L'ENSEIGNEMENT SUPERIEUR.
ESP> LOS DATOS SE REFIEREN AL SECTOR PRODUCTIVO (ACTIVIDADES DE I Y D NO INTEGRADAS) Y AL SECTOR DE ENSEÑANZA SUPERIOR.

UNITED REPUBLIC OF CAMEROON:
E—> DATA RELATE TO THE YEAR 1970/71.
FR—> LES DONNEES SE REFERENT A L'ANNEE 1970/71.
ESP> LOS DATOS SE REFIEREN AL AÑO 1970/71.

BELIZE:
E—> DATA RELATE TO GOVERNMENT EXPENDITURE ONLY.
FR—> LES DONNEES NE CONCERNENT QUE LES DEPENSES DU GOUVERNEMENT.
ESP> LOS DATOS SE REFIEREN A LOS GASTOS DEL GOBIERNO SOLAMENTE.

BERMUDA:
E—> NOT INCLUDING DATA FOR THE PRODUCTIVE SECTOR AND EXCLUDING LAW, HUMANITIES AND EDUCATION
FR—> NON COMPRIS LES DONNEES POUR LE SECTEUR DE LA PRODUCTION ET COMPTE NON TENU DES DONNEES RELATIVES AU DROIT, AUX SCIENCES HUMAINES ET A L'EDUCATION.
ESP> EXCLUIDOS LOS DATOS RELATIVOS AL SECTOR PRODUCTIVO Y LOS QUE SE REFIEREN AL DERECHO, LAS CIENCIAS HUMANAS Y LA EDUCACION.

GABON (CONT.):
ESP> LOS DATOS SE REFIEREN AL "OFFICE (FRANCAIS) DE LA RECHERCHE SCIENTIFIQUE ET TECHNIQUE OUTRE—MER" (ORSTOM) SOLAMENTE.

GHANA:
E—> FIGURES ARE THE CURRENT NATIONAL SCIENTIFIC BUDGET ALLOCATED TO THE 3 UNIVERSITIES OF GHANA, THE COUNCIL OF SCIENTIFIC AND INDUSTRIAL RESEARCH, THE ATOMIC ENERGY COMMISSION AND THE FISHERIES RESEARCH UNIT.
FR—> CES CHIFFRES SE REFERENT AU CREDIT BUDGETAIRE NATIONAL ALLOUE AUX TROIS UNIVERSITES DU GHANA, LE "COUNCIL OF SCIENTIFIC AND INDUSTRIAL RESEARCH", L'"ATOMIC ENERGY COMMISSION" ET LA "FISHERIES RESEARCH UNIT" POUR LES DEPENSES COURANTES DESTINEES A LA SCIENCE.
ESP> ESTAS CIFRAS SE REFIEREN AL CREDITO CONSIGNADO EN EL PRESUPUESTO NACIONAL PARA LAS TRES UNIVERSIDADES DE GHANA, EL "COUNCIL OF SCIENTIFIC AND INDUSTRIAL RESEARCH" LA "ATOMIC ENERGY COMMISSION" Y LA "FISHERIES RESEARCH UNIT", A FIN DE CUBRIR LOS GASTOS ORDINARIOS DESTINADOS A LA CIENCIA.

KENYA:
E—> NOT INCLUDING DATA FOR HUMANITIES AND EDUCATION BUT INCLUDING SOME EDUCATIONAL RESEARCH; THE FIGURE IN COLUMN 2 DOES NOT INCLUDE DATA FOR THE PRODUCTIVE SECTOR (INTEGRATED R&D) AND THE HIGHER EDUCATION SECTOR.
FR—> COMPTE NON TENU DES DONNEES RELATIVES AUX SCIENCES HUMAINES ET A L'EDUCATION, A L'EXCEPTION D'UNE PARTIE DE LA RECHERCHE PEDAGOGIQUE; LE CHIFFRE DE LA COLONNE 2 NE COMPREND NI LES DONNEES POUR LE SECTEUR DE LA PRODUCTION (ACTIVITES DE R-D INTEGREES), NI CELLES RELATIVES A CELUI DE L'ENSEIGNEMENT SUPERIEUR.
ESP> NO SE INCLUYEN LOS DATOS RELATIVOS A LAS CIENCIAS HUMANAS Y A LA EDUCACION, PERO COMPRENDEN UNA PARTE DE LA INVESTIGACION PEDAGOGICA; EN LA CIFRA DE LA COLUMNA 2 NO SE INCLUYEN LOS DATOS RELATIVOS AL SECTOR PRODUCTIVO (ACTIVIDADES DE I Y D INTEGRADAS), Y AL SECTOR DE ENSEÑANZA SUPERIOR.

MADAGASCAR:
E—> NOT INCLUDING DATA FOR THE PRODUCTIVE SECTOR (INTEGRATED R&D); THE FIGURE IN COLUMN 3 INCLUDES 50 MILLION FRANCS FOR WHICH A DISTRIBUTION BETWEEN LABOUR COSTS AND OTHER CURRENT COSTS IS NOT AVAILABLE.
FR—> NON COMPRIS LES DONNEES POUR LE SECTEUR DE LA PRODUCTION (ACTIVITES DE R-D INTEGREES); LE CHIFFRE DE LA COLONNE 3 COMPREND 50 MILLIONS DE FRANCS DONT LA REPARTITION ENTRE LES DEPENSES EN PERSONNEL ET AUTRES DEPENSES COURANTES N'A PAS ETE PRECISEE.
ESP> EXCLUIDOS LOS DATOS RELATIVOS AL SECTOR PRODUCTIVO (ACTIVIDADES DE I Y D INTEGRADAS); EN LA CIFRA DE LA COLUMNA 3 ESTAN INCLUIDOS 50 MILLONES DE FRANCOS CUYA REPARTICION ENTRE GASTOS DE PERSONAL Y OTROS GASTOS ORDINARIOS SE DESCONOCE.

R&D expenditure by type 5.6
Dépenses de R-D par type
Gastos de I y D por tipo

ECUADOR:
E—> DATA REFER TO R&D IN THE AGRICULTURAL SCIENCES ONLY.
FR—> LES DONNEES SE REFERENT A LA R-D DANS LES SCIENCES DE L'AGRICULTURE SEULEMENT.
ESP> LOS DATOS SE REFIEREN A LA I Y D PARA LAS CIENCIAS AGRICOLAS SOLAMENTE.

VENEZUELA:
E—> IN 1975 TOTAL EXPENDITURE FOR R&D WAS 310,783 THOUSAND BOLIVARS FOR WHICH A BREAKDOWN IS NOT AVAILABLE.
FR—> EN 1975, LES DEPENSES TOTALES POUR LA R-D ETAIENT DE 310.783 MILLIERS DE BOLIVARS DONT LA REPARTITION N'EST PAS DISPONIBLE.
ESP> EN 1975, LOS GASTOS TOTALES PARA LA I Y D ASCENDIERON A 310.783 MILLARES DE BOLIVARES, CUYA REPARTICION SE DESCONOCE.

BANGLADESH:
E—> DATA DO NOT INCLUDE CURRENT EXPENDITURE IN THE HIGHER EDUCATION SECTOR.
FR—> COMPTE NON TENU DES DEPENSES COURANTES DU SECTEUR DE L'ENSEIGNEMENT SUPERIEUR.
ESP> EXCLUIDOS LOD GASTOS ORDINARIOS DEL SECTOR DE ENSEÑANZA SUPERIOR.

INDONESIA:
E—> DATA REFER TO THE DEVELOPMENT BUDGET AND DO NOT INCLUDE THE PRODUCTIVE SECTOR.
FR—> LES DONNEES SE REFERENT AU BUDGET DE DEVELOPPEMENT ET NE TIENNENT PAS COMPTE DU SECTEUR DE LA PRODUCTION.
ESP> LOS DATOS SE REFIEREN AL PRESUPUESTO DE DESARROLLO Y NO TOMAN EN CONSIDERACION EL SECTOR PRODUCTIVO.

IRAN:
E—> DATA RELATE TO GOVERNMENT EXPENDITURE ONLY.
FR—> LES DONNEES NE CONCERNENT QUE LES DEPENSES DU GOUVERNEMENT.
ESP> LOS DATOS SE REFIEREN A LOS GASTOS DEL GOBIERNO SOLAMENTE.

IRAQ:
E—> DATA REFER TO GOVERNMENT DEPARTMENTS CONCERNED ONLY WITH SCIENTIFIC ACTIVITIES.
FR—> LES DONNEES NE SE REFERENT Q'AUX DEPARTEMENTS GOUVERNEMENTAUX CONCERNES PAR LES ACTIVITES SCIENTIFIQUES.
ESP> LOS DATOS SE REFIEREN UNICAMENTE A LOS SERVICIOS GUBERNAMENTALES QUE SE OCUPAN DE LAS ACTIVIDADES CIENTIFICAS.

ISRAEL:
E—> DATA REFER TO EXPENDITURE IN THE FIELDS OF NATURAL SCIENCES AND ENGINEERING ONLY.
FR—> LES DONNEES SE REFERENT AUX DEPENSES DANS LES DOMAINES DES SCIENCES EXACTES ET NATURELLES ET DES SCIENCES DE L'INGENIEUR SEULEMENT.
ESP> LOS DATOS SOLO SE REFIEREN A LOS GASTOS RELATIVOS A LAS CIENCIAS EXACTAS Y NATURALES Y A LA INGENIERIA.

EL SALVADOR:
E—> DATA CONCERN 28 INSTITUTIONS OUT OF A TOTAL OF 41 WHICH PERFORM R&D.
FR—> LES DONNEES NE CONCERNENT QUE 28 INSTITUTS SUR UN TOTAL DE 41 QUI EXECUTENT LES ACTIVITES DE R-D.
ESP> LOS DATOS SOLO SE REFIEREN A 28 CENTROS SOBRE UN TOTAL DE 41 QUE EJERCEN ACTIVIDADES DE I Y D.

NICARAGUA:
E—> DATA RELATE TO 2 RESEARCH INSTITUTES ONLY.
FR—> LES DONNEES NE CONCERNENT QUE 2 INSTITUTS DE RECHERCHE.
ESP> LOS DATOS SE REFIEREN A DOS CENTROS DE INVESTIGACION SOLAMENTE.

ST. PIERRE AND MIQUELON:
E—> DATA CONCERN THE "INSTITUT SCIENTIFIQUE ET TECHNIQUE DES PECHES MARITIMES" ONLY.
FR—> LES DONNEES NE CONCERNENT QUE L'INSTITUT SCIENTIFIQUE ET TECHNIQUE DES PECHES MARITIMES.
ESP> LOS DATOS SE REFIEREN AL "INSTITUT SCIENTIFIQUE ET TECHNIQUE DES PECHES MARITIMES" SOLAMENTE.

TRINIDAD AND TOBAGO:
E—> NOT INCLUDING DATA FOR LAW, EDUCATION AND ARTS.
FR—> NON COMPRIS LES DONNEES POUR LE DROIT, L'EDUCATION ET LES ARTS.
ESP> EXCLUIDOS LOS DATOS RELATIVOS AL DERECHO, LA EDUCACION Y LAS ARTES.

UNITED STATES OF AMERICA:
E—> NOT INCLUDING DATA FOR LAW, HUMANITIES AND EDUCATION.
FR—> NON COMPRIS LES DONNEES POUR LE DROIT, LES SCIENCES HUMAINES ET L'EDUCATION.
ESP> EXCLUIDOS LOS DATOS RELATIVOS AL DERECHO, LAS CIENCIAS HUMANAS Y LA EDUCACION.

BRAZIL:
E—> NOT INCLUDING PRIVATE PRODUCTIVE ENTERPRISES.
FR—> COMPTE NON TENU DES ENTREPRISES PRIVEES DE PRODUCTION.
ESP> NO INCLUYE LAS EMPRESAS PRIVADAS DE PRODUCCION.

COLOMBIA:
E—> NOT INCLUDING DATA FOR LAW, HUMANITIES AND EDUCATION. IN 1978, GOVERNMENT EXPENDITURE AMOUNTED TO 699,272 THOUSAND PESOS.
FR—> NON COMPRIS LES DONNEES POUR LE DROIT, LES SCIENCES HUMAINES ET L'EDUCATION. EN 1978, LES DEPENSES DU GOUVERNEMEMT ETAIENT DE L'ORDRE DE 699.272 MILLIERS DE PESOS.
ESP> EXCLUIDOS LOS DATOS RELATIVOS AL DERECHO, LAS CIENCIAS HUMANAS Y LA EDUCACION. EN 1978, LOS GASTOS DEL GOBIERNO SE ELEVARON A 699.272 MILLARES DE PESOS.

5.6 R&D expenditure by type
Dépenses de R-D par type
Gastos de I y D por tipo

JAPAN:
E—> FIGURES IN MILLIONS. NOT INCLUDING DATA FOR SOCIAL SCIENCES AND HUMANITIES IN THE PRODUCTIVE SECTOR.
FR—> CHIFFRES EN MILLIONS. NON COMPRIS LES DONNEES POUR LES SCIENCES SOCIALES ET HUMAINES DANS LE SECTEUR DE LA PRODUCTION.
ESP> LAS CIFRAS VIENEN EXPRESADAS EN MILLONES. EXCLUIDOS LOS DATOS RELATIVOS A LAS CIENCIAS SOCIALES Y HUMANAS DEL SECTOR PRODUCTIVO.

JORDAN:
E—> DATA REFER TO THE EAST BANK ONLY.
FR—> LES DONNEES SE REFERENT A LA RIVE ORIENTALE SEULEMENT.
ESP> LOS DATOS SE REFIEREN A LA ORILLA ORIENTAL SOLAMENTE.

KOREA, REPUBLIC OF:
E—> NOT INCLUDING DATA FOR LAW, HUMANITIES AND EDUCATION.
FR—> NON COMPRIS LES DONNEES POUR LE DROIT, LES SCIENCES HUMAINES ET L'EDUCATION.
ESP> EXCLUIDOS LOS DATOS RELATIVOS AL DERECHO, LAS CIENCIAS HUMANAS Y LA EDUCACION.

MONGOLIA:
E—> DATA REFER TO THE BUDGET FOR THE ACADEMY OF SCIENCES ONLY.
FR—> LES DONNEES NE CONCERNENT QUE LE BUDGET DE L'ACADEMIE DES SCIENCES.
ESP> LOS DATOS SE REFIEREN AL PRESUPUESTO DE LA ACADEMIA DE CIENCIAS SOLAMENTE.

PAKISTAN:
E—> DATA RELATE TO THE YEAR 1973/74 AND REFER TO R&D ACTIVITIES WHICH ARE CONCENTRATED MAINLY IN GOVERNMENT-FINANCED RESEARCH ESTABLISHMENTS. SOCIAL SCIENCES AND HUMANITIES IN THE HIGHER EDUCATION AND GENERAL SERVICE SECTORS ARE NOT INCLUDED.
FR—> LES DONNEES SE REFERENT A L'ANNEE 1973/74 ET AUX ACTIVITES DE R-D SE TROUVANT POUR LA PLUPART DANS LES ETABLISSEMENTS DE RECHERCHE FINANCES PAR LE GOUVERNEMENT. LES SCIENCES SOCIALES ET HUMAINES DANS LES SECTEURS DE L'ENSEIGNEMENT SUPERIEUR ET DE SERVICE GENERAL SONT EXCLUES.
ESP> LOS DATOS SE REFIEREN AL AÑO 1973/74 Y A LAS ACTIVIDADES DE I Y D CONCENTRADAS PRINCIPAL-MENTE EN LOS ESTABLECIMIENTOS DE INVESTIGACION SUBVENCIONADOS POR EL GOBIERNO. NO SE INCLUYEN LOS DATOS RELATIVOS A LAS CIENCIAS SOCIALES Y HUMANAS EN LOS SECTORES DE ENSEÑANZA SUPERIOR Y DE SERVICIO GENERAL.

PHILIPPINES:
E—> DATA RELATE TO THE YEAR 1973/74.
FR—> LES DONNEES SE REFERENT A L'ANNEE 1973/74.
ESP> LOS DATOS SE REFIEREN AL AÑO 1973/74.

SRI LANKA:
E—> NOT INCLUDING CAPITAL EXPENDITURE IN THE HIGHER EDUCATION SECTOR.

SRI LANKA (CONT.):
FR—> COMPTE NON TENU DES DEPENSES EN CAPITAL DU SECTEUR DE L'ENSEIGNEMENT SUPERIEUR.
ESP> EXCLUIDOS LOS GASTOS DE CAPITAL DEL SECTOR DE ENSEÑANZA SUPERIOR.

TURKEY:
E—> DATA RELATE TO GOVERNMENT EXPENDITURE ONLY AND DO NOT INCLUDE THE PRODUCTIVE SECTOR. NOT INCLUDING DATA FOR SOCIAL SCIENCES AND HUMANITIES.
FR—> LES DONNEES NE CONCERNENT QUE LES DEPENSES DU GOUVERNEMENT ET NE COMPRENNENT PAS LE SECTEUR DE LA PRODUCTION. NON COMPRIS LES DONNEES POUR LES SCIENCES SOCIALES ET HUMAINES.
ESP> LOS DATOS SE REFIEREN A LOS GASTOS DEL GOBIERNO SOLAMENTE Y NO INCLUYEN EL SECTOR PRODUCTIVO. NO SE INCLUYEN LAS CIENCIAS SOCIALES Y HUMANAS.

YEMEN:
E—> DATA RELATE TO THE YEAR 1974/75.
FR—> LES DONNEES SE REFERENT A L'ANNEE 1974/75.
ESP> LOS DATOS SE REFIEREN AL AÑO 1974/75.

AUSTRIA:
E—> DATA RELATE TO THE PRODUCTIVE SECTOR.
FR—> LES DONNEES NE CONCERNENT QUE LE SECTEUR DE LA PRODUCTION.
ESP> LOS DATOS SE REFIEREN AL SECTOR PRODUCTIVO SOLAMENTE.

DENMARK:
E—> IN 1976 TOTAL EXPENDITURE FOR R&D AMOUNTED TO 2,662,800 THOUSAND KRONER.
FR—> EN 1976, LES DEPENSES TOTALES POUR LE R-D ETAIENT DE L'ORDRE DE 2 662 800 MILLIERS DE COURONNES.
ESP> EN 1976, LOS GASTOS TOTALES DEDICADOS A LA I Y D SE ELEVARON A 2 662 800 MILLARES DE CORONAS.

GERMANY, FEDERAL REPUBLIC OF:
E—> DATA IN COLUMN 1 INCLUDE 320 MILLION DEUTSCHE MARKS, FOR WHICH A DISTRIBUTION BY TYPE OF EXPENDITURE IS NOT AVAILABLE; THIS FIGURE HAS BEEN EXCLUDED FROM THE PERCENTAGE DISTRIBUTION IN COLUMN 6. NOT INCLUDING DATA FOR SOCIAL SCIENCES AND HUMANITIES IN THE PRODUCTIVE SECTOR.
FR—> LES DONNEES DE LA COLONNE 1 COMPRENNENT 320 MILLIONS DE DEUTSCHE MARKS DONT LA REPARTITION PAR TYPE DE DEPENSES N'EST PAS DISPONIBLE; ON N'A PAS TENU COMPTE DE CE CHIFFRE POUR CALCULER LE POURCENTAGE DE LA COLONNE 6. NON COMPRIS LES SCIENCES SOCIALES ET HUMAINES DANS LE SECTEUR DE LA PRODUCTION.
ESP> LOS DATOS DE LA COLUMNA 1 INCLUYEN 320 MILLONES DE MARCOS CUYA REPARTICION POR TIPO DE GASTOS SE DECONOCE; ESTA CIFRA NO SE HA TENIDO EN CUENTA PARA CALCULAR EL PORCENTAJE DE LA COLUMNA 6. NO SE INCLUYEN LAS CIENCIAS SOCIALES Y HUMANAS DEL SECTOR PRODUCTIVO.

R&D expenditure by type 5.6
Dépenses de R-D par type
Gastos de I y D por tipo

ITALY: FIGURES IN MILLIONS.
FR—> CHIFFRES EN MILLIONS.
ESP> CIFRAS EXPRESADAS EN MILLONES.

MALTA:
E—> DATA RELATE TO THE HIGHER EDUCATION SECTOR
ONLY.
FR—> LES DONNEES NE CONCERNENT QUE LE SECTEUR
DE L'ENSEIGNEMENT SUPERIEUR.
ESP> LOS DATOS SE REFIEREN AL SECTOR DE ENSEÑANZA
SUPERIOR SOLAMENTE.

NETHERLANDS:
E—> NOT INCLUDING SOCIAL SCIENCES AND HUMANITIES
IN THE PRODUCTIVE SECTOR (INTEGRATED R&D).
FR—> NON COMPRIS LES DONNEES POUR LES SCIENCES
SOCIALES ET HUMAINES DU SECTEUR DE LA PRODUCTION
(ACTIVITES DE R-D INTEGREES).
ESP> EXCLUIDOS LOS DATOS RELATIVOS A LAS CIENCIAS
SOCIALES Y HUMANAS DEL SECTOR PRODUCTIVO
(ACTIVIDADES DE I Y D INTEGRADAS).

SWEDEN:
E—> NOT INCLUDING DATA FOR SOCIAL SCIENCES AND
HUMANITIES.
FR—> NON COMPRIS LES DONNEES POUR LES SCIENCES
SOCIALES ET HUMAINES.
ESP> NO SE INCLUYEN LAS CIENCIAS SOCIALES Y
HUMANAS.

SWITZERLAND: NOT INCLUDING CAPITAL EXPENDITURE IN THE
PRODUCTIVE SECTOR.
FR—> COMPTE NON TENU DES DEPENSES EN CAPITAL DU
SECTEUR DE LA PRODUCTION.
ESP> EXCLUIDOS LOS GASTOS DE CAPITAL DEL SECTOR
PRODUCTIVO.

UNITED KINGDOM:
E—> DATA IN COLUMN 1 INCLUDE 28 MILLION POUNDS
STERLING FOR WHICH A DISTRIBUTION BY TYPE OF
EXPENDITURE IS NOT AVAILABLE; THIS FIGURE HAS
BEEN EXCLUDED FROM THE PERCENTAGE DISTRIBUTION
IN COLUMN 6. NOT INCLUDING DATA FOR SOCIAL
SCIENCES AND HUMANITIES IN THE PRODUCTIVE SECTOR.
FR—> LES DONNEES DE LA COLONNE 1 COMPRENNENT
28 MILLIONS DE LIVRES STERLING DONT LA REPARTITION
PAR TYPE DE DEPENSES N'EST PAS DISPONIBLE; ON N'A
PAS TENU COMPTE DE CE CHIFFRE POUR CALCULER LE
POURCENTAGE DE LA COLONNE 6. NON COMPRIS LES
SCIENCES SOCIALES ET HUMAINES DANS LE SECTEUR DE
LA PRODUCTION.
ESP> EL TOTAL DE LA COLUMNA 1 INCLUYE 28 MILLONES
DE LIBRAS ESTERLINAS, CUYA REPARTICION POR TIPOS
DE GASTOS SE DECONOCE, ESTA CIFRA NO SE HA TENIDO
EN CUENTA PARA EL CÁLCULO DEL PORCENTAJE DE LA
COLUMNA 6. NO INCLUYE LAS CIENCIAS SOCIALES Y
HUMANAS DEL SECTOR PRODUCTIVO.

YUGOSLAVIA:
E—> NOT INCLUDING ACTIVITIES OF A MILITARY
NATURE OR RELATING TO NATIONAL DEFENCE.
FR—> NON COMPRIS LES ACTIVITES DE CARACTERE
MILITAIRE OU RELEVANT DE LA DEFENSE NATIONALE.
ESP> EXCLUIDAS LAS ACTIVIDADES DE CARÁCTER
MILITAR O QUE CONCERNEN LA DEFENSA NACIONAL.

AMERICAN SAMOA:
E—> DATA RELATE TO ONE RESEARCH INSTITUTE ONLY.
FR—> LES DONNEES NE CONCERNENT QU'UN INSTITUT
DE RECHERCHE.
ESP> LOS DATOS SE REFIEREN A UN INSTITUTO DE
INVESTIGACION SOLAMENTE.

FRENCH POLYNESIA:
E—> DATA RELATE TO ONE RESEARCH INSTITUTE ONLY.
FR—> LES DONNEES NE CONCERNENT QU'UN INSTITUT
DE RECHERCHE.
ESP> LOS DATOS SE REFIEREN A UN INSTITUTO DE
INVESTIGACION SOLAMENTE.

GUAM:
E—> DATA RELATE TO THE HIGHER EDUCATION SECTOR
ONLY.
FR—> LES DONNEES NE CONCERNENT QUE LE SECTEUR
DE L'ENSEIGNEMENT SUPERIEUR.
ESP> LOS DATOS SE REFIEREN AL SECTOR DE ENSEÑANZA
SUPERIOR SOLAMENTE.

U.S.S.R.:
E—> "EXPENDITURE ON SCIENCE" FROM THE NATIONAL
BUDGET AND OTHER SOURCES.
FR—> MONTANT TOTAL DES SOMMES DEPENSEES POUR LA
SCIENCE D'APRES LE BUDGET NATIONAL ET AUTRES
SOURCES.
ESP> IMPORTE TOTAL DE LOS GASTOS EFECTUADOS PARA
LA CIENCIA, SEGUN EL PRESUPUESTO NACIONAL Y OTRAS
FUENTES.

BYELORUSSIAN S.S.R.:
E—> R&D EXPENDITURE RELATES TO RESEARCH
INSTITUTIONS ADMINISTERED BY THE COUNCIL OF
MINISTERS OF THE BYELORUSSIAN S.S.R.
FR—> LES DONNEES SE REFERENT AUX INSTITUTS DE
RECHERCHE ADMINISTRES PAR LE CONSEIL DES MINISTRES
DE R.S.S. DE BIELORUSSIE.
ESP> LOS DATOS SE REFIEREN A LOS INSTITUTOS DE
INVESTIGACION ADMINISTRADOS POR EL CONSEJO DE
MINISTROS DE LA R.S.S. DE BIELORRUSIA.

5.7 Current expenditure by type of R&D activity
Dépenses courantes par type d'activité de R-D
Gastos ordinarios por tipo de actividad de I y D

5.7 Current expenditure for research and experimental development by type of R&D activity

Dépenses courantes consacrées à la recherche et au développement expérimental, par type d'activité de R-D

Gastos ordinarios dedicados a la investigación y al desarrollo experimental, por tipo de actividad de I y D

PLEASE REFER TO INTRODUCTION FOR DEFINITIONS OF CATEGORIES INCLUDED IN THIS TABLE.

POUR LES DEFINITIONS DES CATEGORIES PRESENTEES DANS CE TABLEAU, SE REFERER A L'INTRODUCTION.

EN LA INTRODUCCION SE DAN LAS DEFINICIONES DE LAS CATEGORIAS QUE FIGURAN EN ESTE CUADRO.

NUMBER OF COUNTRIES AND TERRITORIES PRESENTED IN THIS TABLE: 67

NOMBRE DE PAYS ET DE TERRITOIRES PRESENTES DANS CE TABLEAU: 67

NUMERO DE PAISES Y DE TERRITORIOS PRESENTADOS EN ESTE CUADRO: 67

TYPE OF R&D ACTIVITY / TYPE D'ACTIVITE DE R-D / TIPO DE ACTIVIDAD DE I Y D

A=FUNDAMENTAL RESEARCH / RECHERCHE FONDAMENTALE / INVESTIGACION FUNDAMENTAL
B=APPLIED RESEARCH / RECHERCHE APPLIQUEE / INVESTIGACION APLICADA
C=EXPERIMENTAL DEVELOPMENT / DEVELOPPEMENT EXPERIMENTAL / DESARROLLO EXPERIMENTAL

COUNTRY / PAYS / PAIS	FISCAL YEAR BEGINNING / EXERCICE FINANCIER COMMENÇANT EN / COMIENZO DEL EJERCICIO ECONOMICO	CURRENCY / MONNAIE / MONEDA	AMOUNT OF CURRENT EXPENDITURE (000) / MONTANT DES DEPENSES COURANTES (000) / IMPORTE DE LOS GASTOS ORDINARIOS (000)				PERCENTAGE DISTRIBUTION / REPARTITION EN POURCENTAGE / DISTRIBUCION PORCENTUAL		
			TOTAL	A	B	C	A	B	C
			(1)	(2)	(3)	(4)	(5)	(6)	(7)
AFRICA									
BOTSWANA	1973	PULA	33	-	-	33	-	-	100.0
EGYPT ‡	1973	POUND	22 000	3 625	12 758	5 617	16.5	58.0	25.5
IVORY COAST ‡	1970	FRANC C.F.A.	1 401 124	481 883	719 241	200 000	34.4	51.3	14.3
KENYA ‡	1971	SHILLING	*102 940	*1 800	*101 140	---->	*1.7	*98.3	---->
MADAGASCAR ‡	1971	FRANC	2 294 000	600 000	1 694 000	-	26.2	73.8	-
MALAWI	1977	KWACHA	1 008	272	694	42	27.0	68.8	4.2
MAURITIUS	1977	RUPEE	12 700	-	11 200	1 500	-	88.2	11.8
NIGER ‡	1976	RUPEE	141 703	141 703	---->	---->	100.0	---->	---->
NIGERIA ‡	1970	NAIRA	*23 800	*4 200	*19 600	-	*17.6	*82.4	-
SEYCHELLES	1973	RUPEE	290	-	290	-	-	100.0	-
SUDAN ‡	1973	POUND	3 012	38	1 303	1 671	1.3	43.2	55.5

Current expenditure by type of R&D activity 5.7
Dépenses courantes par type d'activité de R-D
Gastos ordinarios por tipo de actividad de I y D

			(1)	(2)	(3)	(4)	(5)	(6)	(7)
AMERICA, NORTH									
BAHAMAS ‡	1970	DOLLAR	*550	*200	*290	*60	*36.4	*52.7	*10.9
BELIZE ‡	1970	DOLLAR	187	—	19	168	—	10.2	89.8
BERMUDA ‡	1970	DOLLAR	205	—	—	205	—	—	100.0
CANADA ‡	1972	DOLLAR	*1 035 000	*264 000	*380 000	*391 000	*25.5	*36.7	37.8
CUBA	1977	PESO	62 442	*625	*53 700	*8 117	1.0	86.0	13.0
EL SALVADOR ‡	1974	COLON	24 267	2 693	14 883	6 691	11.1	61.3	27.6
GUATEMALA ‡	1974	QUETZAL	*3 721	*337	*1 445	*1 939	*9.1	*38.8	*52.1
JAMAICA	1971	DOLLAR	1 094	992	>	102	90.7	>	9.3
MEXICO	1973	PESO	1 150 593	270 190	567 069	313 334	23.5	49.3	27.2
PANAMA	1974	BALBOA	2 707	1 341	170	1 196	49.5	6.3	44.2
ST. PIERRE AND MIQUELON ‡	1972	FRANC C.F.A.	110 000	—	110 000	—	—	100.0	—
TRINIDAD AND TOBAGO ‡	1970	DOLLAR	4 371	488	2 864	1 019	11.2	65.5	23.3
UNITED STATES OF AMERICA ‡	1977	DOLLAR	42 406 600	5 369 900	9 809 700	27 227 000	12.7	23.1	64.2
AMERICA, SOUTH									
ARGENTINA ‡	1976	PESO	*23 171 700	*6 107 100	*11 592 900	*5 471 700	*26.4	*50.0	*23.6
COLOMBIA ‡	1971	PESO	205 409	2 285	197 703	5 421	1.1	96.2	2.6
ECUADOR ‡	1976	SUCRE	167 718	25 372	93 912	48 434	15.1	56.0	28.9
PARAGUAY ‡	1971	GUARANI	123 959	7 245	62 194	54 520	5.8	50.2	44.0
URUGUAY ‡	1972	PESO	1 858	235	809	814	12.6	43.5	43.8
VENEZUELA ‡	1975	BOLIVAR	310 783	109 251	166 339	35 193	35.2	53.5	11.3
ASIA									
BRUNEI	1974	DOLLAR	2 933	626	1 497	810	21.3	51.0	27.6
CYPRUS ‡	1971	POUND	986	15	755	216	1.5	76.6	21.9
IRAQ ‡	1974	DINAR	4 909	1 335	1 787	1 786	27.2	36.4	36.4
ISRAEL ‡	1975	POUND	803 000	387 000	416 000	>	48.2	51.8	>
JAPAN ‡	1972	YEN	1 745 940	598 156	309 226	838 558	34.3	17.7	48.0
KOREA, REPUBLIC OF ‡	1973	WON	15 628 000	2 193 000	5 892 000	7 543 000	14.0	37.7	48.3
KUWAIT ‡	1977	DINAR	6 284	506	5 076	702	8.0	80.8	11.2
PHILIPPINES ‡	1976	PESO	153 736	25 528	98 360	29 848	16.6	64.0	19.4
SRI LANKA ‡	1975	RUPEE	32 662	1 231	25 316	6 115	3.8	77.5	18.7
YEMEN ‡	1974	RIAL	6 988	—	2 252	4 736	—	32.2	67.8
EUROPE									
BELGIUM	1973	FRANC	20 713 379	4 821 144	6 937 606	8 954 629	23.3	33.5	43.2
CZECHOSLOVAKIA	1977	KORUNA	14 493 000	1 490 000	13 003 000	>	10.3	89.7	>
DENMARK	1973	KRONER	1 489 000	363 000	405 000	721 000	24.4	27.2	48.4
FINLAND ‡	1971	MARKKA	354 840	71 217	118 637	164 986	20.1	33.4	46.5
FRANCE ‡	1977	FRANC	33 185 000	7 001 000	11 424 000	14 760 000	21.1	34.4	44.5
GERMANY, FEDERAL REPUBLIC OF ‡	1977	DEUTSCHE MARK	22 664 000	5 587 000	17 077 000	>	24.7	75.3	>
HOLY SEE	1976	LIRA	1 409 145	1 409 145	—	—	100.0	—	—
HUNGARY ‡	1977	FORINT	12 937 000	1 748 000	4 521 000	6 668 000	13.5	35.0	51.5
ICELAND ‡	1970	KRONER	*164 500	*33 800	*130 700	>	*20.6	*79.4	>
IRELAND	1975	POUND	27 252	4 291	10 926	12 035	15.7	40.1	44.2

5.7 Current expenditure by type of R&D activity
Dépenses courantes par type d'activité de R-D
Gastos ordinarios por tipo de actividad de I y D

TYPE OF R&D ACTIVITY / TYPE D'ACTIVITE DE R-D / TIPO DE ACTIVIDAD DE I Y D

A=FUNDAMENTAL RESEARCH / RECHERCHE FONDAMENTALE / INVESTIGACION FUNDAMENTAL
B=APPLIED RESEARCH / RECHERCHE APPLIQUEE / INVESTIGACION APLICADA
C=EXPERIMENTAL DEVELOPMENT / DEVELOPPEMENT EXPERIMENTAL / DESARROLLO EXPERIMENTAL

COUNTRY / PAYS / PAIS	FISCAL YEAR BEGINNING / EXERCICE FINANCIER COMMENÇANT EN / COMIENZO DEL EJERCICIO ECONOMICO	CURRENCY / MONNAIE / MONEDA	AMOUNT OF CURRENT EXPENDITURE (000) / MONTANT DES DEPENSES COURANTES (000) / IMPORTE DE LOS GASTOS ORDINARIOS (000)				PERCENTAGE DISTRIBUTION / REPARTITION EN POURCENTAGE / DISTRIBUCION PORCENTUAL		
			TOTAL (1)	A (2)	B (3)	C (4)	A (5)	B (6)	C (7)
ITALY ‡	1976	LIRA	1 209 376	253 477	504 699	451 200	21.0	41.7	37.3
MALTA ‡	1973	POUND	130	43	87	—	33.1	66.9	—
NORWAY	1977	KRONER	2 342 300	513 900	819 900	1 008 500	21.9	35.0	43.1
POLAND	1977	ZLOTY	33 204 500	5 022 800	8 841 900	19 339 800	15.1	26.6	58.2
PORTUGAL	1976	ESCUDO	1 146 353	156 142	487 556	502 655	13.6	42.5	43.9
ROMANIA	1973	LEU	2 631 161	357 696	2 273 465	⎱	13.6	86.4	⎱
SPAIN	1974	PESETA	11 496 338	2 057 995	4 108 594	5 329 749	17.9	35.7	46.4
SWEDEN ‡	1975	KRONA	4 754 200	905 400	833 700	3 015 100	19.0	17.5	63.4
SWITZERLAND	1975	FRANC	*3 212 000	*1 570 000	*1 549 000	*93 000	*48.9	*48.2	*2.9
UNITED KINGDOM ‡	1975	POUND STERLING	1 938 200	312 000	492 700	1 133 500	16.1	25.4	58.5
OCEANIA									
AMERICAN SAMOA ‡	1971	U.S. DOLLAR	100	—	100	—	—	100.0	—
COOK ISLANDS ‡	1970	NEW ZEALAND DOLLAR	112	—	112	—	—	100.0	—
FRENCH POLYNESIA ‡	1976	FRANC C.F.P.	140 240	—	50 420	89 820	—	36.0	64.0
GUAM ‡	1973	U.S. DOLLAR	579	127	452	—	21.9	78.1	—
NEW CALEDONIA	1971	FRANC C.F.P.	1 240	—	—	1 240	—	—	100.0
NEW HEBRIDES	1975	FRANC	21 603	—	21 603	—	—	100.0	—
SAMOA	1977	TALA	341	62	49	230	18.2	14.4	67.4

EGYPT:
E—> DATA DO NOT INCLUDE FOREIGN FUNDS.
FR—> NON COMPRIS LES FONDS ETRANGERS.
ESP> LOS DATOS NO INCLUYEN LOS FONDOS DE PROCE-
DENCIA EXTRANJERA.

IVORY COAST:
E—> DATA RELATE TO TOTAL EXPENDITURE.
FR—> LES DONNEES SE REFERENT AUX DEPENSES TOTALES.
ESP> LOS DATOS SE REFIEREN A LOS GASTOS TOTALES.

KENYA:
E—> NOT INCLUDING DATA FOR HUMANITIES AND EDU-
CATION, BUT INCLUDING SOME EDUCATIONAL RESEARCH.
THE TOTAL IN COLUMN 1 INCLUDES CAPITAL EXPENDITURE
BY THE PRODUCTIVE SECTOR.

FR—> NON COMPRIS LES DONNEES POUR LES SCIENCES
HUMAINES ET L'EDUCATION, A L'EXCEPTION D'UNE
PARTIE DE LA RECHERCHE PEDAGOGIQUE. LE TOTAL DE
LA COLONNE 1 COMPREND LES DEPENSES EN CAPITAL DU
SECTEUR DE LA PRODUCTION.
ESP> NO SE INCLUYEN LOS DATOS RELATIVOS A LAS
CIENCIAS HUMANAS Y LA EDUCACION, PERO COMPRENDEN
UNA PARTE DE LA INVESTIGACION PEDAGOGICA. EL
TOTAL DE LA COLUMNA 1 INCLUYE LOS GASTOS DE
CAPITAL DEL SECTOR PRODUCTIVO.

MADAGASCAR:
E—> NOT INCLUDING DATA FOR THE PRODUCTIVE
SECTOR (INTEGRATED R&D).
FR—> NON COMPRIS LES DONNEES POUR LE SECTEUR
DE LA PRODUCTION (ACTIVITES DE R-D INTEGREES).
ESP> EXCLUIDOS LOS DATOS RELATIVOS AL SECTOR
PRODUCTIVO (ACTIVIDADES DE I Y D INTEGRADAS).

Current expenditure by type of R&D activity 5.7
Dépenses courantes par type d'activité de R-D
Gastos ordinarios por tipo de actividad de I y D

NIGER:
E—> DATA RELATE TO THE HIGHER EDUCATION SECTOR ONLY.
FR—> LES DONNES SE REFERENT AU SECTEUR DE L'ENSEIGNEMENT SUPERIEUR SEULEMENT.
ESP> LOS DATOS SE REFIEREN AL SECTOR DE ENSENANZA SUPERIOR SOLAMENTE.

NIGERIA:
E—> DATA RELATE TO TOTAL EXPENDITURE DISTRIBUTED BY TYPE OF R&D ACTIVITY AND REFER TO FEDERAL AND STATE GOVERNMENTS' BUDGETARY ESTIMATES FOR RESEARCH AND TECHNICAL DEVELOPMENT SERVICES AND UNIVERSITY EXPENDITURE ON RESEARCH AND EXPERIMENTAL DEVELOPMENT; NOT INCLUDING DATA FOR SOCIAL SCIENCES AND HUMANITIES.
FR—> LES DONNEES CORRESPONDENT AUX DEPENSES TOTALES REPARTIES PAR TYPE D'ACTIVITE DE R-D ET SE REFERENT A L'ESTIMATION BUDGETAIRE DU GOUVERNEMENT FEDERAL ET DES GOUVERNEMENTS DES ETATS POUR LA RECHERCHE ET LES SERVICES DU DEVELOPPEMENT TECHNIQUE ET LES DEPENSES DES UNIVERSITES DESTINEES A LA RECHERCHE ET AU DEVELOPPEMENT EXPERIMENTAL. NON COMPRIS LES DONNEES POUR LES SCIENCES SOCIALES ET HUMAINES.
ESP> DATOS RELATIVOS A LOS GASTOS TOTALES REPARTIDOS POR TIPO DE ACTIVIDAD DE I Y D QUE SE REFIEREN A LA ESTIMACION PRESUPUESTARIA DEL GOBIERNO FEDERAL Y DE LOS GOBIERNOS DE LOS ESTADOS PARA LAS ACTIVIDADES DE INVESTIGACION Y LOS SERVICIOS DE DESAROLLO TECNICO, ASI COMO LOS GASTOS DE LAS UNIVERSIDADES DESTINADOS A LA INVESTIGACION Y AL DESAROLLO EXPERIMENTAL. EXCLUIDOS LOS DATOS RELATIVOS A LAS CIENCIAS SOCIALES Y HUMANAS.

SUDAN:
E—> DATA RELATE TO TOTAL EXPENDITURE.
FR—> LES DONNEES SE REFERENT AUX DEPENSES TOTALES.
ESP> LOS DATOS SE REFIEREN A LOS GASTOS TOTALES.

BAHAMAS:
E—> DATA RELATE TO TOTAL EXPENDITURE.
FR—> LES DONNEES SE REFERENT AUX DEPENSES TOTALES.
ESP> LOS DATOS SE REFIEREN A LOS GASTOS TOTALES.

BELIZE:
E—> DATA RELATE TO GOVERNMENT EXPENDITURE ONLY.
FR—> LES DONNEES NE CONCERNENT QUE LES DEPENSES PUBLIQUES.
ESP> LOS DATOS SE REFIEREN A LOS GASTOS PUBLICOS SOLAMENTE.

BERMUDA:
E—> NOT INCLUDING DATA FOR THE PRODUCTIVE SECTOR AND EXCLUDING DATA FOR LAW, HUMANITIES AND EDUCATION.
FR—> NON COMPRIS LES DONNEES POUR LE SECTEUR DE LA PRODUCTION ET COMPTE NON TENU DES DONNEES RELATIVES AU DROIT, AUX SCIENCES HUMAINES ET A L'EDUCATION.

BERMUDA (CONT.):
ESP> EXCLUIDOS LOS DATOS RELATIVOS AL SECTOR PRODUCTIVO Y LOS QUE SE REFIEREN AL DERECHO, LAS CIENCIAS HUMANAS Y LA EDUCACION.

CANADA:
E—> NOT INCLUDING DATA FOR SOCIAL SCIENCES AND HUMANITIES.
FR—> NON COMPRIS LES DONNEES POUR LES SCIENCES SOCIALES ET HUMAINES.
ESP> EXCLUIDOS LOS DATOS RELATIVOS A LAS CIENCIAS SOCIALES Y HUMANAS.

EL SALVADOR:
E—> DATA CONCERN 28 INSTITUTES OUT OF A TOTAL OF 41 WHICH PERFORM R&D.
FR—> LES DONNEES NE CONCERNENT QUE 28 INSTITUTS SUR UN TOTAL DE 41 QUI EXECUTENT LES ACTIVITES DE R-D.
ESP> LOS DATOS SOLO SE REFIEREN A 28 CENTROS SOBRE UN TOTAL DE 41 QUE EJERCEN ACTIVIDADES DE I Y D.

ST PIERRE AND MIQUELON:
E—> DATA RELATE TO THE "INSTITUT SCIENTIFIQUE ET TECHNIQUE DES PECHES MARITIMES" ONLY AND REFER TO TOTAL EXPENDITURE DISTRIBUTED BY TYPE OF R&D ACTIVITY.
FR—> LES DONNEES NE CONCERNENT QUE L'INSTITUT SCIENTIFIQUE ET TECHNIQUE DES PECHES MARITIMES ET CORRESPONDENT AUX DEPENSES TOTALES REPARTIES PAR TYPE D'ACTIVITE DE R-D.
ESP> LOS DATOS SE REFIEREN AL "INSTITUT SCIENTIFIQUE ET TECHNIQUE DES PECHES MARITIMES" SOLAMENTE Y CORRESPONDEN A LOS GASTOS TOTALES REPARTIDOS POR TIPO DE ACTIVIDAD DE I Y D.

TRINIDAD AND TOBAGO:
E—> NOT INCLUDING DATA FOR LAW, EDUCATION AND ARTS.
FR—> NON COMPRIS LES DONNEES POUR LE DROIT, L'EDUCATION ET LES ARTS.
ESP> EXCLUIDOS LOS DATOS RELATIVOS AL DERECHO, LA EDUCACION Y LAS ARTES.

UNITED STATES OF AMERICA:
E—> NOT INCLUDING DATA FOR LAW, HUMANITIES AND EDUCATION.
FR—> NON COMPRIS LES DONNEES POUR LE DROIT, LES SCIENCES HUMAINES ET L'EDUCATION.
ESP> EXCLUIDOS LOS DATOS RELATIVOS AL DERECHO, LAS CIENCIAS HUMANAS Y LA EDUCACION.

ARGENTINA:
E—> DATA RELATE TO TOTAL EXPENDITURE.
FR—> LES DONNEES SE REFERENT AUX DEPENSES TOTALES.
ESP> LOS DATOS SE REFIEREN A LOS GASTOS TOTALES.

COLOMBIA:
E—> NOT INCLUDING DATA FOR LAW, HUMANITIES AND EDUCATION.

5.7 Current expenditure by type of R&D activity
Dépenses courantes par type d'activité de R-D
Gastos ordinarios por tipo de actividad de I y D

COLOMBIA (CONT.):
FR-> NON COMPRIS LES DONNEES POUR LE DROIT, LES SCIENCES HUMAINES ET L'EDUCATION.
ESP> EXCLUIDOS LOS DATOS RELATIVOS AL DERECHO, LAS CIENCIAS HUMANAS Y LA EDUCACION.

ECUADOR:
E-> DATA REFER TO R&D IN THE AGRICULTURAL SCIENCES ONLY.
FR-> LES DONNEES SE REFERENT A LA R-D DANS LES SCIENCES DE L'AGRICULTURE SEULEMENT.
ESP> LOS DATOS SE REFIEREN A LA I Y D PARA LAS CIENCIAS AGRICOLAS SOLAMENTE.

URUGUAY:
E-> DATA RELATE TO TOTAL EXPENDITURE.
FR-> LES DONNEES SE REFERENT AUX DEPENSES TOTALES.
ESP> LOS DATOS SE REFIEREN A LOS GASTOS TOTALES.

VENEZUELA:
E-> DATA RELATE TO TOTAL EXPENDITURE BUT DO NOT INCLUDE THE PRODUCTIVE SECTOR (NON-INTEGRATED R&D).
FR-> LES DONNEES SE REFERENT AUX DEPENSES TOTALES MAIS NE COMPRENNENT PAS LE SECTEUR DE LA PRODUCTION (ACTIVITES DE R-D NON-INTEGREES).
ESP> LOS DATOS SE REFIEREN A LOS GASTOS TOTALES PERO NO INCLUYEN EL SECTOR PRODUCTIVO (ACTIVIDADES DE I Y D NO INTEGRADAS).

IRAQ:
E-> DATA REFER TO GOVERNMENT DEPARTMENTS CONCERNED ONLY WITH SCIENTIFIC ACTIVITIES.
FR-> LES DONNEES NE SE REFERENT QU'AUX DEPARTEMENTS GOUVERNEMENTAUX CONCERNES PAR LES ACTIVITES SCIENTIFIQUES.
ESP> LOS DATOS SE REFIEREN UNICAMENTE A LOS SERVICIOS GUBERNAMENTALES QUE SE OCUPAN DE LAS ACTIVIDADES CIENTIFICAS.

ISRAEL:
E-> DATA REFER TO THE CIVILIAN SECTOR ONLY AND DO NOT INCLUDE SOCIAL SCIENCES AND HUMANITIES.
FR-> LES DONNEES NE SE REFERENT QU'AU SECTEUR CIVIL ET NE COMPRENNENT PAS LES DONNEES POUR LES SCIENCES SOCIALES ET HUMAINES.
ESP> LOS DATOS SOLO SE REFIEREN AL SECTOR CIVIL Y NO INCLUYEN LAS CIENCIAS SOCIALES Y HUMANAS.

JAPAN:
E-> FIGURES IN MILLIONS. THE FIGURE IN COLUMN 1 REFERS TO TOTAL EXPENDITURE BY R&D ACTIVITIES AND DOES NOT INCLUDE 45 932 MILLION YEN FOR WHICH DISTRIBUTION BY TYPE OF R&D ACTIVITY IS NOT AVAILABLE.
FR-> CHIFFRES EN MILLIONS. LE CHIFFRE DE LA COLONNE 1 SE REFERE AUX DEPENSES TOTALES ET NE COMPREND PAS 45 932 MILLIONS DE YEN DONT LA REPARTITION PAR TYPE D'ACTIVITE DE R-D N'EST PAS DISPONIBLE.
ESP> CIFRAS EN MILLONES. LA CIFRA DE LA COLUMNA 1 SE REFIERE A LOS GASTOS TOTALES Y NO COMPRENDE 45 932 MILLONES DE YEN, CUYA REPARTICION POR TIPO DE ACTIVIDAD DE I Y D SE DESCONOCE.

KOREA, REPUBLIC OF:
E-> DATA RELATE TO TOTAL EXPENDITURE AND DO NOT INCLUDE LAW, HUMANITIES AND EDUCATION.
FR-> LES DONNEES SE REFERENT AUX DEPENSES TOTALES ET NE COMPRENNENT PAS LE DROIT, LES SCIENCES HUMAINES ET L'EDUCATION.
ESP> LOS DATOS SE REFIEREN A LOS GASTOS TOTALES EXCLUIDOS LOS DATOS RELATIVOS AL DERECHO, LAS CIENCIAS HUMANAS Y LA EDUCACION.

KUWAIT:
E-> DATA RELATE TO TOTAL EXPENDITURE.
FR-> LES DONNEES SE REFERENT AUX DEPENSES TOTALES.
ESP> LOS DATOS SE REFIEREN A LOS GASTOS TOTALES.

PHILIPPINES:
E-> DATA REFER TO TOTAL EXPENDITURE BY TYPE OF R&D ACTIVITY BY THE GENERAL SERVICE SECTOR.
FR-> LES DONNEES SE REFERENT AUX DEPENSES TOTALES REPARTIES PAR TYPE D'ACTIVITE DE R-D PAR LE SECTEUR DE SERVICE GENERAL.
ESP> LOS DATOS SE REFIEREN A LOS GASTOS TOTALES DEL SECTOR DE SERVICIO GENERAL REPARTIDOS POR TIPO DE ACTIVIDAD DE I Y D.

YEMEN:
E-> DATA RELATE TO THE YEAR 1974/75.
FR-> LES DONNEES SE REFERENT A L'ANNEE 1974/75.
ESP> LOS DATOS SE REFIEREN AL AÑO 1974/75.

FINLAND:
E-> DATA RELATE TO TOTAL EXPENDITURE.
FR-> LES DONNEES SE REFERENT AUX DEPENSES TOTALES.
ESP> LOS DATOS SE REFIEREN A LOS GASTOS TOTALES.

FRANCE:
E-> DATA RELATE TO TOTAL EXPENDITURE.
FR-> LES DONNEES SE REFERENT AUX DEPENSES TOTALES.
ESP> LOS DATOS SE REFIEREN A LOS GASTOS TOTALES.

GERMANY, FEDERAL REPUBLIC OF:
E-> THE TOTAL IN COLUMN 1 DOES NOT INCLUDE THE RELEVANT PORTION OF 320 MILLION DEUTSCHE MARKS FOR WHICH THE DISTRIBUTION BETWEEN CAPITAL AND CURRENT EXPENDITURE IS UNKNOWN. NOT INCLUDING DATA FOR SOCIAL SCIENCES AND HUMANITIES IN THE PRODUCTIVE SECTOR.
FR-> LE TOTAL DE LA COLONNE 1 NE COMPREND PAS LA PARTIE DE LA SOMME DE 320 MILLIONS DE DEUTSCHE MARKS DONT LA REPARTITION ENTRE LES DEPENSES COURANTES ET EN CAPITAL N'A PAS ETE PRECISEE. NON COMPRIS LES SCIENCES SOCIALES ET HUMAINES DANS LE SECTEUR DE LA PRODUCTION.
ESP> EL TOTAL DE LA COLUMNA 1 NO INCLUYE LA PARTE CORRESPONDIENTE DE LA SUMA DE 320 MILLONES DE MARCOS, CUYA REPARTICION ENTRE GASTOS ORDINARIOS Y GASTOS DE CAPITAL NO SE HA PRECISADO. EXCLUIDAS LAS CIENCIAS SOCIALES Y HUMANAS DEL SECTOR PRODUCTIVO.

Current expenditure by type of R&D activity 5
Dépenses courantes par type d'activité de R-D
Gastos ordinarios por tipo de actividad de I y D

UNITED KINGDOM:
E—> NOT INCLUDING THE RELEVANT PART OF
28 MILLION POUNDS STERLING FOR WHICH A BREAKDOWN
BETWEEN CURRENT AND CAPITAL EXPENDITURE IS NOT
KNOWN. DATA DO NOT INCLUDE SOCIAL SCIENCES AND
HUMANITIES.
FR—> NON COMPRIS LA PARTIE DE LA SOMME DE
28 MILLIONS DE LIVRES STERLING DONT LA VENTILATION
ENTRE DEPENSES COURANTES ET DEPENSES EN CAPITAL
N'A PAS ETE PRECISEE. NON COMPRIS LES DONNEES POUR
LES SCIENCES SOCIALES ET HUMAINES.
ESP> EXCLUIDA LA PARTE CORRESPONDIENTE DE LA
SUMA DE 28 MILLONES DE LIBRAS ESTERLINAS, CUYA
REPARTICION ENTRE GASTOS ORDINARIOS Y GASTOS DE
CAPITAL NO SE HA PRECISADO. EXCLUIDOS LOS DATOS
RELATIVOS A LAS CIENCIAS SOCIALES Y HUMANAS.

AMERICAN SAMOA:
E—> DATA RELATE TO ONE RESEARCH INSTITUTE ONLY.
FR—> LES DONNEES NE CONCERNENT QU'UN INSTITUT
DE RECHERCHE.
ESP> LOS DATOS SE REFIEREN A UN CENTRO DE
INVESTIGACION SOLAMENTE.

COOK ISLANDS:
E—> DATA RELATE TO TOTAL EXPENDITURE.
FR—> LES DONNEES SE REFERENT AUX DEPENSES
TOTALES.
ESP> LOS DATOS SE REFIEREN A LOS GASTOS TOTALES.

FRENCH POLYNESIA:
E—> DATA RELATE TO TOTAL EXPENDITURE AT ONE
RESEARCH INSTITUTE ONLY.
FR—> LES DONNEES SE REFERENT AUX DEPENSES
TOTALES ET NE CONCERNENT QU'UN INSTITUT DE
RECHERCHE.
ESP> LOS DATOS SE REFIEREN A LOS GASTOS TOTALES
Y SOLO CONCIERNEN UN INSTITUTO DE INVESTIGACION.

GUAM:
E—> DATA RELATE TO TOTAL EXPENDITURE BY THE
HIGHER EDUCATION SECTOR ONLY.
FR—> LES DONNEES SE REFERENT AUX DEPENSES
TOTALES DANS LE SECTEUR DE L'ENSEIGNEMENT
SUPERIEUR.
ESP> LOS DATOS SE REFIEREN A LOS GASTOS TOTALES
EN EL SECTOR DE ENSEÑANZA SUPERIOR.

HUNGARY:
E—> THE TOTAL IN COLUMN 1 DOES NOT INCLUDE
1,736 MILLION FORINTS FOR WHICH A BREAKDOWN BY
TYPE OF R&D ACTIVITY IS NOT AVAILABLE.
FR—> LE TOTAL DE LA COLONNE 1 NE COMPREND PAS
1 736 MILLIONS DE FORINTS DONT LA REPARTITION
PAR TYPE D'ACTIVITE N'EST PAS DISPONIBLE.
ESP> EL TOTAL DE LA COLUMNA 1 NO INCLUYE 1 736
MILLONES DE FORINTS, CUYA REPARTICION POR TIPO
DE ACTIVIDAD SE DESCONOCE.

ICELAND:
E—> DATA RELATE TO TOTAL EXPENDITURE AND DO NOT
INCLUDE SOCIAL SCIENCES AND HUMANITIES.
FR—> LES DONNEES SE REFERENT AUX DEPENSES
TOTALES ET NE COMPRENNENT PAS LES SCIENCES SOCIA—
LES ET HUMAINES.
ESP> LOS DATOS SE REFIEREN A LOS GASTOS TOTALES
Y EXCLUYEN LAS CIENCIAS SOCIALES Y HUMANAS.

ITALY:
E—> FIGURES IN MILLIONS.
FR—> CHIFFRES EN MILLIONS.
ESP> CIFRAS EN MILLONES.

MALTA:
E—> DATA RELATE TO THE HIGHER EDUCATION SECTOR
ONLY.
FR—> LES DONNEES SE REFERENT AU SECTEUR DE L'EN—
SEIGNEMENT SUPERIEUR SEULEMENT.
ESP> LOS DATOS SE REFIEREN AL SECTOR DE ENSENAN—
ZA SUPERIOR SOLAMENTE.

SWEDEN:
E—> NOT INCLUDING DATA FOR SOCIAL SCIENCES
AND HUMANITIES.
FR—> NON COMPRIS LES DONNEES POUR LES SCIENCES
SOCIALES ET HUMAINES.
ESP> EXCLUIDOS LOS DATOS RELATIVOS A LAS CIENCIAS
SOCIALES Y HUMANAS.

5.8 R&D expenditure by sector of performance
Dépenses de R-D par secteur d'exécution
Gastos de I y D por sector de ejecución

5.8 Total and current expenditure for research and experimental development by sector of performance

Dépenses totales et courantes consacrées à la recherche et au développement expérimental, par secteur d'exécution

Gastos totales y ordinarios dedicados a la investigación y al desarrollo experimental, por sector de ejecución

PLEASE REFER TO INTRODUCTION FOR DEFINITIONS OF CATEGORIES INCLUDED IN THIS TABLE.
POUR LES DEFINITIONS DES CATEGORIES PRESENTEES DANS CE TABLEAU, SE REFERER A L'INTRODUCTION.
EN LA INTRODUCCION SE DAN LAS DEFINICIONES DE LAS CATEGORIAS QUE FIGURAN EN ESTE CUADRO.

CURRENT EXPENDITURE = DEPENSES COURANTES
CURRENT EXPENDITURE = GASTOS ORDINARIOS

NUMBER OF COUNTRIES AND TERRITORIES PRESENTED IN THIS TABLE: 85
NOMBRE DE PAYS ET DE TERRITOIRES PRESENTES DANS CE TABLEAU: 85
NUMERO DE PAISES Y DE TERRITORIOS PRESENTADOS EN ESTE CUADRO: 85

COUNTRY / PAYS / PAIS	FISCAL YEAR BEGINNING / EXERCICE FINANCIER COMMENCANT EN / COMIENZO DEL EJERCICIO ECONOMICO	CURRENCY / MONNAIE / MONEDA	TYPE OF EXPENDITURE / TYPE DE DEPENSES / TIPO DE GASTOS	ALL SECTORS / TOUS SECTEURS / TODOS LOS SECTORES (000)	SECTEUR DE LA PRODUCTION / SECTOR PRODUCTIVO — INTEGRATED R&D / ACTIVITES DE R-D INTEGREES / ACTIVIDADES DE I Y D INTEGRADAS (000)	SECTEUR DE LA PRODUCTION / SECTOR PRODUCTIVO — NON-INTEGRATED R&D / ACTIVITES DE R-D NON-INTEGREES / ACTIVIDADES DE I Y D NO INTEGRADAS (000)	HIGHER EDUCATION / ENSEIGNEMENT SUPERIEUR / ENSEÑANZA SUPERIOR (000)	GENERAL SERVICE / SERVICE GENERAL / SERVICIO GENERAL (000)
				(1)	(2)	(3)	(4)	(5)
AFRICA								
BOTSWANA	1973	PULA	TOTAL	220	—	—	—	220
			%	100.0	—	—	—	100.0
			CURRENT	33	—	—	—	33
			%	100.0	—	—	—	100.0
CONGO ‡	1977	FRANC C.F.A.	TOTAL	634 241	...	610 487	23 754	...
			CURRENT	634 241	...	610 487	23 754	...
EGYPT ‡	1973	POUND	TOTAL	29 940	5 020	——>	18 520	6 400
			%	100.0	16.8	——>	61.8	21.4
			CURRENT	22 000	2 500	——>	14 500	5 000
			%	100.0	11.4	——>	65.9	22.7
IVORY COAST	1970	FRANC C.F.A.	TOTAL	1 401 124	—	1 067 241	333 883	—
			%	100.0	—	76.2	23.8	—
			CURRENT		—	1 051 241	333 883	—

R&D expenditure by sector of performance 5.8
Dépenses de R-D par secteur d'exécution
Gastos de I y D por sector de ejecución

	Year	Currency		(1)	(2)	(3)	(4)	(5)
KENYA ‡	1971	SHILLING	TOTAL	*102 940	*18 800	*74 840	*9 300	—
			%	100.0	*18.3	*72.7	*9.0	—
			CURRENT	*83 160	*18 800	*55 060	*9 300	—
			%	100.0	*22.6	*66.2	*11.2	—
MADAGASCAR ‡	1971	FRANC	TOTAL	2 294 000	...	1 544 000	50 000	700 000
			%	100.0	...	67.3	2.2	30.5
			CURRENT	2 294 000	...	1 544 000	50 000	700 000
			%	100.0	...	67.3	2.2	30.5
MALAWI	1977	KWACHA	TOTAL	1 290	366	898	13	13
			%	100.0	28.4	69.6	1.0	1.0
			CURRENT	1 008	360	635	5	8
			%	100.0	35.7	63.0	0.5	0.8
MAURITIUS	1977	RUPEE	TOTAL	18 800	—	12 100	400	6 300
			%	100.0	—	64.4	2.1	33.5
			CURRENT	12 700	—	9 500	400	2 800
			%	100.0	—	74.8	3.1	22.1
NIGERIA ‡	1970	NAIRA	TOTAL	23 800	—	—	4 200	19 600
			%	100.0	—	—	17.6	82.4
SENEGAL ‡	1972	FRANC C.F.A.	CURRENT	2 176 000	1 380 000	...	79 600	...
SEYCHELLES	1970	RUPEE	TOTAL	209	—	209	—	—
			%	100.0	—	100.0	—	—
			CURRENT	209	—	209	—	—
			%	100.0	—	100.0	—	—
SUDAN	1978	POUND	TOTAL	5 115	153	2 195	779	1 988
			%	100.0	3.0	42.9	15.2	38.9
TOGO	1971	FRANC C.F.A.	CURRENT	1 070 829	640 500	→	381 959	48 370
			%	100.0	59.8	→	35.7	4.5
ZAMBIA	1972	KWACHA	TOTAL	6 261	—	1 797	344	4 120
			%	100.0	—	28.7	5.5	65.8
			CURRENT	4 726	—	1 797	341	2 588
			%	100.0	—	38.0	7.2	54.8
AMERICA, NORTH								
BERMUDA ‡	1970	DOLLAR	TOTAL	240	...	...	—	240
			CURRENT	205	...	...	—	205
CANADA ‡	1977	DOLLAR	TOTAL	2 241 700	837 100	./.	*710 100	694 500
			%	100.0	37.3	./.	*31.7	31.0
			CURRENT	2 030 600	767 400	./.	*639 100	624 100
			%	100.0	37.8	./.	*31.5	30.7
CUBA	1977	PESO	TOTAL	74 258	35 324	1 275	4 243	33 416
			%	100.0	47.6	1.7	5.7	45.0
			CURRENT	62 442	26 341	1 275	4 243	30 594
			%	100.0	42.2	2.0	6.8	49.0
GUATEMALA	1974	QUETZAL	TOTAL	*5 139	*39	*1 136	*392	*3 572
			%	100.0	*0.8	*22.1	*7.6	*69.5
			CURRENT	*3 721	*37	*836	*356	*2 492
			%	100.0	*1.0	*22.4	*9.6	*67.0

5.8 R&D expenditure by sector of performance
Dépenses de R-D par secteur d'exécution
Gastos de I y D por sector de ejecución

COUNTRY / PAYS / PAIS	FISCAL YEAR BEGINNING / EXERCICE FINANCIER COMMENCANT EN / COMIENZO DEL EJERCICIO ECONOMICO	CURRENCY / MONNAIE / MONEDA	TYPE OF EXPENDITURE / TYPE DE DEPENSES / TIPO DE GASTOS	ALL SECTORS / TOUS SECTEURS / TODOS LOS SECTORES (000) (1)	PRODUCTIVE SECTOR · SECTEUR DE LA PRODUCTION · SECTOR PRODUCTIVO — INTEGRATED R&D / ACTIVITES DE R-D INTEGREES / ACTIVIDADES DE I Y D INTEGRADAS (000) (2)	NON-INTEGRATED R&D / ACTIVITES DE R-D NON-INTEGREES / ACTIVIDADES DE I Y D NO INTEGRADAS (000) (3)	HIGHER EDUCATION / ENSEIGNEMENT SUPERIEUR / ENSEÑANZA SUPERIOR (000) (4)	GENERAL SERVICE / SERVICE GENERAL / SERVICIO GENERAL (000) (5)
JAMAICA ‡	1971	DOLLAR	CURRENT	1 020	156	→	325	539
			%	100.0	15.3	→	31.9	52.8
MEXICO	1973	PESO	TOTAL	1 277 618	301 020	310 001	332 194	334 403
			%	100.0	23.5	24.3	26.0	26.2
			CURRENT	1 150 593	249 120	296 195	306 681	298 597
			%	100.0	21.6	25.7	26.7	26.0
PANAMA	1974	BALBOA	TOTAL	2 908	—	1 531	176	1 201
			%	100.0	—	52.6	6.1	41.3
			CURRENT	2 707	—	1 341	170	1 196
			%	100.0	—	49.5	6.3	44.2
ST. PIERRE AND MIQUELON ‡	1972	FRANC C.F.A.	TOTAL	110 000	110 000	—	—	—
			%	100.0	100.0	—	—	—
TRINIDAD AND TOBAGO ‡	1970	DOLLAR	TOTAL	5 171	1 772	→	1 371	2 028
			%	100.0	34.3	→	26.5	39.2
			CURRENT	4 371	1 447	→	1 003	1 920
			%	100.0	33.1	→	22.9	43.9
TURKS AND CAICOS ISLANDS	1974	U.S. DOLLAR	TOTAL	8	—	8	—	—
			%	100.0	—	100.0	—	—
UNITED STATES OF AMERICA ‡	1978	DOLLAR	CURRENT	47 295 000	33 250 000	→	5 960 000	8 085 000
			%	100.0	70.3	→	12.6	17.1
AMERICA, SOUTH								
ARGENTINA ‡	1976	PESO	TOTAL	*23 171 700	*741 500	*1 042 700	*7 299 100	*14 088 400
			%	100.0	*3.2	*4.5	*31.5	*60.8
			CURRENT	*20 507 200	*586 100	*728 400	*6 350 200	*12 842 500
			%	100.0	*2.8	*3.6	*31.0	*62.6
BRAZIL	1978	CRUZEIRO	TOTAL	20 781 000	4 178 000	2 264 000	5 548 000	8 791 000
			%	100.0	20.1	10.9	26.7	42.3
COLOMBIA ‡	1971	PESO	TOTAL	210 614	20 761	→	37 528	152 325
			%	100.0	9.8	→	17.8	72.3
			CURRENT	205 409	19 027	→	35 383	150 999
			%	100.0	9.3	→	17.2	73.5

R&D expenditure by sector of performance   5.8
Dépenses de R-D par secteur d'exécution
Gastos de I y D por sector de ejecución

				(1)	(2)	(3)	(4)	(5)
ECUADOR ‡	1976	SUCRE	TOTAL	258 366	1 230	217 278	39 858	—
			%	100.0	0.5	84.1	15.4	—
			CURRENT	167 718	380	141 759	25 579	—
			%	100.0	0.2	84.5	15.3	—
PARAGUAY	1971	GUARANI	CURRENT	123 959	18 560	→	19 984	85 415
			%	100.0	15.0	→	16.1	68.9
PERU	1976	SOL	TOTAL	*2 314 754	*126 087	*1 389 194	*169 366	*630 107
			%	100.0	*5.5	*60.0	*7.3	*27.2
URUGUAY	1972	PESO	TOTAL	1 858	264	913	362	319
			%	100.0	14.2	49.1	19.5	17.2
VENEZUELA ‡	1975	BOLIVAR	TOTAL	310 783	4 568	...	162 021	144 194
			%	100.0	1.5	...	52.1	46.4
ASIA								
BANGLADESH ‡	1974	TAKA	TOTAL	113 530	10 730	→	1 840	100 960
			%	100.0	9.4	→	1.6	88.9
			CURRENT	52 160	7 450	→	...	44 710
			%	100.0	14.3	→	...	85.7
BRUNEI	1974	DOLLAR	TOTAL	3 055	2 307	—	—	748
			%	100.0	75.5	—	...	24.5
			CURRENT	2 933	2 307	—	—	626
			%	100.0	78.7	—	—	21.3
CYPRUS	1971	POUND	TOTAL	1 088	—	235	—	853
			%	100.0	—	21.6	—	78.4
			CURRENT	986	—	216	—	770
			%	100.0	—	21.9	—	78.1
INDIA	1976	RUPEE	TOTAL	4 022 500	...	...	545 000	...
			%	100.0	...	...	13.5	...
INDONESIA ‡	1975	RUPIAH	TOTAL	*19 496 560	...	...	297 750	19 198 810
			%	100.0	...	...	1.5	98.5
			CURRENT	*13 159 507	...	...	79 435	13 080 072
			%	100.0	...	...	0.6	99.4
IRAN ‡	1972	RIAL	TOTAL	3 531 807	2 742 818	→	581 537	207 452
			%	100.0	77.7	→	16.5	5.9
			CURRENT	2 246 789	1 477 109	→	575 914	193 766
			%	100.0	65.7	→	25.6	8.6
IRAQ ‡	1974	DINAR	TOTAL	7 409	—	3 285	1 750	2 374
			%	100.0	—	44.3	23.6	32.0
			CURRENT	4 909	—	1 695	1 427	1 786
			%	100.0	—	34.5	29.1	36.4
ISRAEL ‡	1978	POUND	TOTAL	6 154 300	3 845 000	./.	1 839 700	469 700
			%	100.0	62.5	./.	29.9	7.6
JAPAN ‡	1977	YEN	TOTAL	3 651 319	2 109 500	→	1 012 297	529 522
			%	100.0	57.8	→	27.7	14.5
JORDAN ‡	1976	DINAR	TOTAL	2 074	140	→	614	1 320
			%	100.0	6.8	→	29.6	63.6
			CURRENT	1 242	137	→	510	595
			%	100.0	11.0	→	41.1	47.9

5.8 R&D expenditure by sector of performance
Dépenses de R-D par secteur d'exécution
Gastos de I y D por sector de ejecución

COUNTRY / PAYS / PAIS	FISCAL YEAR BEGINNING / EXERCICE FINANCIER COMMENCANT EN / COMIENZO DEL EJERCICIO ECONOMICO	CURRENCY / MONNAIE / MONEDA	TYPE OF EXPENDITURE / TYPE DE DEPENSES / TIPO DE GASTOS	ALL SECTORS / TOUS SECTEURS / TODOS LOS SECTORES (000) (1)	PRODUCTIVE SECTOR — SECTEUR DE LA PRODUCTION — SECTOR PRODUCTIVO: INTEGRATED R&D / ACTIVITES DE R-D INTEGREES / ACTIVIDADES DE I Y D INTEGRADAS (000) (2)	NON-INTEGRATED R&D / ACTIVITES DE R-D NON-INTEGREES / ACTIVIDADES DE I Y D NO INTEGRADAS (000) (3)	HIGHER EDUCATION / ENSEIGNEMENT SUPERIEUR / ENSEÑANZA SUPERIOR (000) (4)	GENERAL SERVICE / SERVICE GENERAL / SERVICIO GENERAL (000) (5)
KOREA, REPUBLIC OF ‡	1978	WON	TOTAL	152 418 000	53 802 000	42 627 000	20 543 000	35 446 000
			%	100.0	35.3	28.0	13.4	23.3
KUWAIT	1977	DINAR	TOTAL	6 284	—	1 501	617	4 166
			%	100.0	—	23.9	9.8	66.3
			CURRENT	4 865	—	1 056	589	3 220
			%	100.0	—	21.7	12.1	66.2
PAKISTAN ‡	1973	RUPEE	TOTAL	150 430	134 840	——>	7 940	7 650
			%	100.0	89.6	——>	5.3	5.1
PHILIPPINES ‡	1973	PESO	TOTAL	218 106	188	——>	62 571	155 347
			%	100.0	0.1	——>	28.7	71.2
SINGAPORE	1978	DOLLAR	TOTAL	28 120	17 363	——>	8 236	2 521
			%	100.0	61.7	——>	29.3	9.0
SRI LANKA ‡	1975	RUPEE	TOTAL	45 097	36 970	——>	1 382	6 745
			%	100.0	82.0	——>	3.0	15.0
			CURRENT	32 662	26 785	——>	1 382	4 495
			%	100.0	82.0	——>	4.2	13.8
TURKEY ‡	1977	LIRA	TOTAL	6 466 409	...	...	467 305	5 999 104
VIET-NAM	1979	DONG	TOTAL	108 300	76 500	——>	8 300	23 500
			%	100.0	70.6	——>	7.7	21.7
YEMEN ‡	1974	RIAL	TOTAL	9 923	—	5 906	—	4 017
			%	100.0	—	59.5	—	40.5
			CURRENT	6 988	—	4 736	—	2 252
			%	100.0	—	67.8	—	32.2
EUROPE								
AUSTRIA ‡	1972	SCHILLING	TOTAL	2 363 740	2 182 299	181 441	...	...
			CURRENT	1 923 572	1 777 027	146 545	...	...
BELGIUM	1977	FRANC	TOTAL	38 894 080	25 770 213	1 667 566	7 553 410	3 902 891
			%	100.0	66.3	4.3	19.4	10.0
BULGARIA	1977	LEV	TOTAL	334 900	200 700	——>	14 000	120 200
			%	100.0	59.9	——>	4.2	35.9

R&D expenditure by sector of performance   5.8
Dépenses de R-D par secteur d'exécution
Gastos de I y D por sector de ejecución

				(1)	(2)	(3)	(4)	(5)
CZECHOSLOVAKIA	1973	KORUNA	TOTAL	14 761 798	6 457 570	5 773 592	451 826	2 078 810
			%	100.0	43.7	39.1	3.1	14.1
			CURRENT	12 960 511	6 092 488	4 877 727	286 293	1 704 003
			%	100.0	47.0	37.6	2.2	13.1
DENMARK	1976	KRONE	TOTAL	2 662 800	1 196 900	111 400	761 100	593 400
	1977		%	100.0	44.9	4.2	28.6	22.3
FINLAND	1977	MARKKA	TOTAL	1 298 820	650 190	24 370	271 690	352 570
			%	100.0	50.1	1.9	20.9	27.1
			CURRENT	1 157 930	589 400	23 270	221 130	324 130
			%	100.0	50.9	2.0	19.1	28.0
FRANCE	1977	FRANC	TOTAL	33 185 000	19 704 000	928 000	5 176 000	7 377 000
			%	100.0	59.4	2.8	15.6	22.2
			CURRENT	30 258 000	18 405 000	834 000	4 636 000	6 383 000
			%	100.0	60.8	2.8	15.3	21.1
GERMANY, FEDERAL REPUBLIC OF ‡	1977	DEUTSCHE MARK	TOTAL	25 414 000	16 058 000	340 000	4 790 000	4 226 000
			%	100.0	63.2	1.3	18.9	16.6
			CURRENT	22 664 000	14 896 000	305 000	4 051 000	3 412 000
			%	100.0	65.7	1.3	17.9	15.1
GREECE	1976	DRACHMA	TOTAL	1 739 220	575 000	——>	114 450	1 049 770
			%	100.0	33.1	——>	6.6	60.3
HOLY SEE	1976	LIRA	TOTAL	1 677 989	—	—	1 677 989	—
			%	100.0	—	—	100.0	—
			CURRENT	1 409 145	—	—	1 409 145	—
			%	100.0	—	—	100.0	—
HUNGARY ‡	1978	FORINT	TOTAL	17 358 000	5 841 000	6 075 000	1 794 000	3 648 000
			%	100.0	33.7	35.0	10.3	21.0
ICELAND ‡	1970	KRONA	TOTAL	*164 500	*3 800	——>	*14 400	*146 300
			%	100.0	*2.3	——>	*8.8	*88.9
			CURRENT	*135 800	*3 800	——>	*14 400	*117 600
			%	100.0	*2.8	——>	*10.6	*86.6
IRELAND	1977	POUND	TOTAL	43 209	13 917	——>	7 277	22 015
			%	100.0	32.2	——>	16.8	51.0
ITALY ‡	1976	LIRA	TOTAL	1 352 565	740 298	——>	307 480	304 787
			%	100.0	54.7	——>	22.7	22.5
			CURRENT	1 209 376	678 939	——>	287 946	242 491
			%	100.0	56.1	——>	23.8	20.1
NETHERLANDS ‡	1976	GUILDER	TOTAL	4 964 000	2 565 000	57 000	1 196 000	1 146 000
			%	100.0	51.7	1.2	24.1	23.1
			CURRENT	4 481 000	2 340 000	54 000	1 075 000	1 012 000
			%	100.0	52.2	1.2	24.0	22.6
NORWAY	1977	KRONER	TOTAL	2 973 000	975 000	419 000	969 000	610 000
			%	100.0	32.8	14.1	32.6	20.5
POLAND	1978	ZLOTY	TOTAL	40 769 000	6 173 000	21 989 000	8 624 000	3 983 000
			%	100.0	15.1	53.9	21.1	9.8

5.8 R&D expenditure by sector of performance
Dépenses de R-D par secteur d'exécution
Gastos de I y D por sector de ejecución

COUNTRY / PAYS / PAIS	FISCAL YEAR BEGINNING / EXERCICE FINANCIER COMMENCANT EN / COMIENZO DEL EJERCICIO ECONOMICO	CURRENCY / MONNAIE / MONEDA	TYPE OF EXPENDITURE / TYPE DE DEPENSES / TIPO DE GASTOS	ALL SECTORS / TOUS SECTEURS / TODOS LOS SECTORES (000) (1)	PRODUCTIVE SECTOR — SECTEUR DE LA PRODUCTION — SECTOR PRODUCTIVO — INTEGRATED R&D / ACTIVITES DE R-D INTEGREES / ACTIVIDADES DE I Y D INTEGRADAS (000) (2)	NON-INTEGRATED R&D / ACTIVITES DE R-D NON-INTEGREES / ACTIVIDADES DE I Y D NO INTEGRADAS (000) (3)	HIGHER EDUCATION / ENSEIGNEMENT SUPERIEUR / ENSEÑANZA SUPERIOR (000) (4)	GENERAL SERVICE / SERVICE GENERAL / SERVICIO GENERAL (000) (5)
PORTUGAL ‡	1976	ESCUDO	TOTAL	1 279 591	269 608	→	224 085	785 898
			%	100.0	21.1	→	17.5	61.4
			CURRENT	1 146 353	251 052	→	194 282	701 019
			%	100.0	21.9	→	17.0	61.1
ROMANIA	1973	LEU	TOTAL	3 354 196	402 041	2 530 426	70 878	350 851
			%	100.0	12.0	75.4	2.1	10.5
			CURRENT	2 631 161	269 723	2 013 533	29 271	318 634
			%	100.0	10.3	76.5	1.1	12.1
SPAIN ‡	1974	PESETA	TOTAL	15 536 477	9 100 697	./.	825 600	5 610 180
			%	100.0	58.6	./.	5.3	36.1
			CURRENT	11 496 338	6 547 174	./.	711 600	4 237 564
			%	100.0	57.0	./.	6.2	36.9
SWEDEN ‡	1977	KRONA	TOTAL	6 796 700	4 284 000	538 700	1 392 000	58 200
			%	100.0	63.0	7.9	20.5	8.6
SWITZERLAND ‡	1976	FRANC	TOTAL	*3 363 000	*2 500 000	→	*630 000	*233 000
			%	100.0	*74.3	→	*18.7	*6.9
			CURRENT	*3 212 000	*2 500 000	→	*523 000	*189 000
			%	100.0	*77.8	→	*16.3	*5.9
UNITED KINGDOM ‡	1975	POUND STERLING	TOTAL	2 139 000	1 309 000	31 100	179 200	619 600
			%	100.0	61.2	1.4	8.4	29.0
			CURRENT	1 938 200	1 211 200	28 400	167 700	530 900
			%	100.0	62.5	1.5	8.6	27.4
YUGOSLAVIA ‡	1977	DINAR	TOTAL	6 226 000	1 526 000	2 580 000	420 000	1 700 000
			%	100.0	24.5	41.4	6.7	27.3
OCEANIA								
AMERICAN SAMOA ‡	1971	U.S. DOLLAR	TOTAL	120	120	—	—	—
			%	100.0	100.0	—	—	—
			CURRENT	100	100	—	—	—
			%	100.0	100.0	—	—	—
AUSTRALIA	1976	DOLLAR	TOTAL	802 464	198 871	138 853	184 322	280 418
			%	100.0	24.8	17.3	23.0	34.9
COOK ISLANDS	1970	NEW ZEALAND DOLLAR	TOTAL	112	112	→	—	—
			%	100.0	100.0	→	—	—

R&D expenditure by sector of performance 5.8
Dépenses de R-D par secteur d'exécution
Gastos de I y D por sector de ejecución

				(1)	(2)	(3)	(4)	(5)
FRENCH POLYNESIA ‡	1976	FRANC C.F.P.	TOTAL	140 240	—	—	—	140 240
			CURRENT	135 430	—	—	—	135 430
NEW CALEDONIA	1971	FRANC C.F.P.	TOTAL	1 440	—	—	—	1 440
			%	100.0	—	—	—	100.0
			CURRENT	1 240	—	—	—	1 240
			%	100.0	—	—	—	100.0
NEW HEBRIDES	1975	FRANC	TOTAL	21 603	—	21 603	—	—
			%	100.0	—	100.0	—	—
			CURRENT	21 603	—	21 603	—	—
			%	100.0	—	100.0	—	—
NEW ZEALAND	1975	DOLLAR	TOTAL	99 776	21 665	39 955	17 033	21 123
			%	100.0	21.7	40.0	17.1	21.2
			CURRENT	91 499	18 690	36 399	17 033	19 377
			%	100.0	20.4	39.8	18.6	21.2
PACIFIC ISLANDS	1978	U.S. DOLLAR	TOTAL	185	—	120	—	65
			%	100.0	—	64.9	—	35.1
SAMOA	1978	TALA	TOTAL	2 500	1 251	556	482	211
			%	100.0	50.0	22.2	19.3	8.4

CONGO:
E—> DATA REFER TO THE PRODUCTIVE SECTOR (NON—INTEGRATED R&D) AND TO THE HIGHER EDUCATION SECTOR ONLY.
FR—> LES DONNEES SE REFERENT AU SECTEUR DE LA PRODUCTION (ACTIVITES DE R-D NON-INTEGREES) ET AU SECTEUR DE L'ENSEIGNEMENT SUPERIEUR SEULEMENT.
ESP> LOS DATOS SE REFIEREN AL SECTOR PRODUCTIVO (ACTIVIDADES DE I Y D NO-INTEGRADAS) Y AL SECTOR DE ENSEÑANZA SUPERIOR SOLAMENTE.

EGYPT:
E—> TOTAL EXPENDITURE INCLUDES 2,990 THOUSAND POUNDS FROM FOREIGN FUNDS; THIS IS EXCLUDED FOR CURRENT EXPENDITURE AS A BREAKDOWN BY SECTOR OF PERFORMANCE IS NOT AVAILABLE
FR—> LES DEPENSES TOTALES COMPRENNENT 2 990 MILLIERS DE LIVRES PROVENANT DES FONDS ETRANGERS, DONT ON N'A PAS TENU COMPTE DANS LES DEPENSES COURANTES OU LA REPARTITION PAR SECTEUR D'EXECUTION N'EST PAS DISPONIBLE.
ESP> LOS GASTOS TOTALES INCLUYEN 2 900 000 LIBRAS PROCEDENTES DE FONDOS EXTRANJEROS; ESTA CIFRA ESTA EXCLUIDA DE LOS GASTOS ORDINARIOS PARA LOS QUE NO SE DISPONE DE UNA REPARTICION POR SECTOR DE EJECUCION

KENYA:
E—> NOT INCLUDING DATA FOR HUMANITIES AND EDUCATION BUT INCLUDING SOME EDUCATIONAL RESEARCH. THE TOTAL EXPENDITURES IN COLUMNS 2 AND 4 DO NOT INCLUDE CAPITAL EXPENDITURE; THESE AMOUNTS BEING EXCLUDED FROM THE TOTAL IN COLUMN 1.

KENYA (CONT.):
FR—> COMPTE NON TENU DES DONNEES RELATIVES AUX SCIENCES HUMAINES ET A L'EDUCATION, A L'EXCEPTION D'UNE PARTIE DE LA RECHERCHE PEDAGOGIQUE. LES DEPENSES TOTALES QUI FIGURENT DANS LES COLONNES 2 ET 4 NE COMPRENNENT PAS LES DEPENSES EN CAPITAL, CETTE SOMME ETANT EXCLUE DU TOTAL DE LA COLONNE 1.
ESP> EXCLUIDOS LOS DATOS RELATIVOS A LAS CIENCIAS HUMANAS Y A LA EDUCACION, SALVO UNA PARTE DE LA INVESTIGACION PEDAGOGICA. LOS GASTOS TOTALES QUE FIGURAN EN LAS COLUMNAS 2 Y 4 NO INCLUYEN LOS GASTOS DE CAPITAL, QUE QUEDAN EXCLUIDOS DE LA COLUMNA 1.

MADAGASCAR:
E—> NOT INCLUDING DATA FOR THE PRODUCTIVE SECTOR (INTEGRATED R&D)
FR—> COMPTE NON TENU DU SECTEUR DE LA PRODUCTION (ACTIVITES DE R-D INTEGREES)
ESP> EXCLUIDO EL SECTOR PRODUCTIVO (ACTIVIDADES DE I Y D INTEGRADAS).

NIGERIA:
E—> DATA RELATE TO FEDERAL AND STATE GOVERNMENTS' BUDGETARY ESTIMATES FOR RESEARCH AND TECHNICAL DEVELOPMENT SERVICES AND UNIVERSITY EXPENDITURE ON RESEARCH AND EXPERIMENTAL DEVELOPMENT. NOT INCLUDING DATA FOR SOCIAL SCIENCES AND HUMANITIES.
FR—> LES DONNEES SE REFERENT A L'ESTIMATION BUDGETAIRE DU GOUVERNEMENT FEDERAL ET DES GOUVERNEMENTS DES ETATS POUR LA RECHERCHE ET LES SCIENCES DU DEVELOPPEMENT TECHNIQUE ET LES DEPENSES DES DES UNIVERSITES DESTINEES A LA RECHERCHE ET AU DEVELOPPEMENT EXPERIMENTAL. NON COMPRIS LES DONNEES POUR LES SCIENCES SOCIALES ET HUMAINES.

5.8 R&D expenditure by sector of performance
Dépenses de R-D par secteur d'exécution
Gastos de I y D por sector de ejecución

ST. PIERRE AND MIQUELON:
E—> DATA REFER TO THE "INSTITUT SCIENTIFIQUE ET TECHNIQUE DES PECHES MARITIMES" ONLY.
FR—> LES DONNEES NE CONCERNENT QUE L'INSTITUT SCIENTIFIQUE ET TECHNIQUE DES PECHES MARITIMES.
ESP> LOS DATOS SE REFIEREN AL "INSTITUT SCIEN-TIFIQUE ET TECHNIQUE DES PECHES MARITIMES" SOLA-MENTE.

TRINIDAD AND TOBAGO:
E—> NOT INCLUDING DATA FOR LAW, EDUCATION AND ARTS; THE FIGURES IN COLUMN 4 INCLUDE DATA REFER-RING TO TECHNICAL SECONDARY SCHOOLS; FIGURES IN COLUMN 5 REFER TO OTHER GOVERNMENT SECTORS INCLUD-ING PRIVATE NON-PROFIT ORGANIZATIONS NOT PROVID-ING SERVICES TO SPECIFIC PRIVATE ENTERPRISES.
FR—> NON COMPRIS LES DONNEES POUR LE DROIT, L'EDUCATION ET LES ARTS; LES CHIFFRES DE LA COLONNE 4 COMPRENNENT LES DONNEES RELATIVES AUX ECOLES TECHNIQUES DU SECOND DEGRE; LES CHIFFRES DE LA COLONNE 5 SE REFERENT AUX AUTRES SECTEURS GOUVERNEMENTAUX, Y COMPRIS LES ORGANISATIONS PRIVES A BUT NON LUCRATIF QUI NE PROCURENT PAS DE SERVICES A DES GROUPES DETERMINES D'ENTREPRI-SES PRIVEES.
ESP> EXCLUIDOS LOS DATOS RELATIVOS AL DERECHO, LA EDUCACION Y LAS ARTES; LAS CIFRAS DE LA COLUMNA 4 INCLUYEN LOS DATOS RELATIVOS A LAS ESCUELAS TECNICAS DE SEGUNDO GRADO; LAS CIFRAS DE LA COLUM-NA 5 SE REFIEREN A LOS OTROS SECTORES OFICIALES INCLUIDAS LAS ORGANIZACIONES PRIVADAS DE CARACTER NO LUCRATIVO QUE NO PROCURAN SERVICIOS A GRUPOS DETERMINADOS DE EMPRESAS PRIVADAS.

UNITED STATES OF AMERICA:
E—> NOT INCLUDING DATA FOR LAW, HUMANITIES AND EDUCATION.
FR—> NON COMPRIS LES DONNEES POUR LE DROIT, LES SCIENCES HUMAINES ET L'EDUCATION.
ESP> EXCLUIDOS LOS DATOS RELATIVOS AL DERECHO, LAS CIENCIAS HUMANAS Y LA EDUCACION.

ARGENTINA:
E—> THE FIGURES IN COLUMN 2 REFER TO PRIVATE ENTERPRISES AND THOSE IN COLUMN 3 TO STATE AND MIXED ENTERPRISES WHILST COLUMN 5 INCLUDES PRIVATE NON-PROFIT INSTITUTIONS.
FR—> LE CHIFFRE DE LA COLONNE 2 SE REFERE AUX ENTREPRISES PRIVEES; CELUI DE LA COLONNE 3 AUX ENTREPRISES MIXTES ET D'ETAT ET CELUI DE LA COLON-NE 5 COMPREND AUSSI LES ORGANISATIONS PRIVEES A BUT NON LUCRATIF.
ESP> LA CIFRA DE LA COLUMNA 2 SE REFIERE A LAS EMPRESAS PRIVADAS, LA DE LA COLUMNA 3 A LAS EMPRESAS ESTATALES Y MIXTAS Y LA DE LA COLUMNA 5 COMPRENDE IGUALMENTE LAS ORGANIZACIONES PRIVADAS DE CARACTER NO LUCRATIVO.

COLOMBIA:
E—> NOT INCLUDING DATA FOR LAW, HUMANITIES AND EDUCATION.

NIGERIA (CONT.):
ESP> DATOS RELATIVOS A LA ESTIMACION PRESUPUES-TARIA DEL GOBIERNO FEDERAL Y DE LOS GOBIERNOS DE LOS ESTADOS PARA LAS ACTIVIDADES DE INVESTIGACION Y LOS SERVICIOS DE DESAROLLO TECNICO ASI COMO LOS GASTOS DE LAS UNIVERSIDADES DESTINADOS A LA INVES-TIGACION Y AL DESAROLLO EXPERIMENTAL EXCLUIDOS LOS DATOS RELATIVOS A LAS CIENCIAS SOCIALES Y HUMANAS.

SENEGAL:
E—> DATA REFER TO THE PRODUCTIVE SECTOR (INTE-GRATED R&D) AND TO THE HIGHER EDUCATION SECTOR ONLY.
FR—> LES DONNEES SE REFERENT AU SECTEUR DE LA PRODUCTION (ACTIVITES DE R-D INTEGREES) ET AU SECTEUR DE L'ENSEIGNEMENT SUPERIEUR SEULEMENT.
ESP> LOS DATOS SE REFIEREN AL SECTOR PRODUCTIVO (ACTIVIDADES DE I Y D INTEGRADAS) Y AL SECTOR DE ENSEÑANZA SUPERIOR SOLAMENTE.

BERMUDA:
E—> NOT INCLUDING DATA FOR THE PRODUCTIVE SECTOR AND EXCLUDING LAW, HUMANITIES AND EDUCATION.
FR—> COMPTE NON TENU DU SECTEUR DE LA PRODUCTION NI DES DONNEES RELATIVES AU DROIT, AUX SCIENCES HUMAINES ET A L'EDUCATION.
ESP> EXCLUIDO EL SECTOR PRODUCTIVO Y LOS DATOS RELATIVOS AL DERECHO, LAS CIENCIAS HUMANAS Y LA EDUCACION.

CANADA:
E—> DATA RELATING TO THE PRODUCTIVE SECTOR (NON-INTEGRATED R&D) ARE INCLUDED WITH THE GENERAL SERVICE SECTOR.
FR—> LES DONNEES RELATIVES AU SECTEUR DE LA PRODUCTION (ACTIVITES DE R-D NON-INTEGREES) SONT COMPRISES AVEC CELLES DU SECTEUR GENERAL.
ESP> LOS DATOS RELATIVOS AL SECTOR PRODUCTIVO (ACTIVIDADES DE I Y D NO-INTEGRADAS) SE INCLUYEN EN EL SECTOR DE SERVICIO GENERAL.

JAMAICA:
E—> THE TOTAL IN COLUMN 1 DOES NOT INCLUDE 74 000 DOLLARS FOR WHICH BREAKDOWN BY SECTOR OF PERFORMANCE IS NOT AVAILABLE; DATA IN COLUMNS 2 AND 3 RELATE TO PRIVATE ENTERPRISES AND IN COLUMN 5 TO THE GOVERNMENT SECTOR.
FR—> LE TOTAL DE LA COLONNE 1 NE COMPREND PAS 74 000 DOLLARS DONT LA REPARTITION PAR SECTEUR D'EXECUTION N'A PAS ETE PRECISEE. LES DONNEES QUI FIGURENT DANS LES COLONNES 2 ET 3 CONCERNENT LES ENTREPRISES PRIVEES ET CELLES DE LA COLONNE 5 LE SECTEUR DU GOUVERNEMENT.
ESP> EL TOTAL DE LA COLUMNA 1 NO INCLUYE 74 000 DOLARES CUYA REPARTICION POR SECTOR DE EJECUCION NO SE HA PRECISADO; LOS DATOS QUE FIGURAN EN LAS COLUMNAS 2 Y 3 SE REFIEREN A LAS EMPRESAS PRIVADAS Y LOS DE LA COLUMNA 5 AL SECTOR OFICIAL.

R&D expenditure by sector of performance 5.8
Dépenses de R-D par secteur d'exécution
Gastos de I y D por sector de ejecución

COLOMBIA (CONT.):
  FR—> NON COMPRIS LES DONNEES POUR LE DROIT, LES
  SCIENCES HUMAINES ET L'EDUCATION.
  ESP> EXCLUIDOS LOS DATOS RELATIVOS AL DERECHO,
  LAS CIENCIAS HUMANAS Y LA EDUCACION.

ECUADOR:
  E—> DATA REFER TO R&D IN THE AGRICULTURAL
  SCIENCES ONLY.
  FR—> LES DONNEES SE REFERENT A LA R-D DANS LES
  SCIENCES DE L'AGRICULTURE SEULEMENT.
  ESP> LOS DATOS SE REFIEREN A LA I Y D DE LAS
  CIENCIAS AGRICOLAS SOLAMENTE.

VENEZUELA:
  E—> NOT INCLUDING DATA FOR THE PRODUCTIVE
  SECTOR (NON-INTEGRATED R&D).
  FR—> COMPTE NON TENU DU SECTEUR DE LA PRODUCTION
  (ACTIVITES DE R-D NON-INTEGREES).
  ESP> EXCLUIDO EL SECTOR PRODUCTIVO (ACTIVIDADES
  DE I Y D NO INTEGRADAS).

BANGLADESH:
  E—> NOT INCLUDING CURRENT EXPENDITURE BY THE
  HIGHER EDUCATION SECTOR.
  FR—> NON COMPRIS LES DEPENSES COURANTES DU SEC-
  TEUR DE L'ENSEIGNEMENT SUPERIEUR.
  ESP> EXCLUIDOS LOS GASTOS ORDINARIOS DEL SECTOR
  DE ENSEÑANZA SUPERIOR.

INDONESIA:
  E—> DATA REFER TO THE DEVELOPMENT BUDGET ONLY
  AND DO NOT INCLUDE THE PRODUCTIVE SECTOR.
  FR—> LES DONNEES SE REFERENT AU BUDGET DE DEVE-
  LOPPEMENT ET NE TIENNENT PAS COMPTE DU SECTEUR DE
  LA PRODUCTION.
  ESP> LOS DATOS SE REFIEREN AL PRESUPUESTO DE
  DESAROLLO Y NO TOMAN EN CONSIDERACION EL SECTOR
  PRODUCTIVO.

IRAN:
  E—> DATA RELATE TO GOVERNMENT EXPENDITURE ONLY.
  FR—> LES DONNES SE REFERENT AUX DEPENSES PUBLI-
  QUES SEULEMENT.
  ESP> LOS DATOS SE REFIEREN A LOS GASTOS PUBLICOS
  SOLAMENTE.

IRAQ:
  E—> DATA REFER TO GOVERNMENT DEPARTMENTS CON-
  CERNED ONLY WITH SCIENTIFIC ACTIVITIES.
  FR—> LES DONNEES NE SE REFERENT QU'AUX DEPARTE-
  MENTS GOUVERNEMENTAUX CONCERNES PAR LES ACTIVITES
  SCIENTIFIQUES.
  ESP> LOS DATOS SE REFIEREN UNICAMENTE A LOS
  SERVICIOS GUBERNAMENTALES QUE SE OCUPAN DE LAS
  ACTIVIDADES CIENTIFICAS.

ISRAEL:
  E—> DATA RELATING TO THE PRODUCTIVE SECTOR
  (NON-INTEGRATED R&D) ARE INCLUDED WITH THE
  GENERAL SERVICE SECTOR.

ISRAEL (CONT.):
  FR—> LES DONNEES RELATIVES AU SECTEUR DE LA
  PRODUCTION (ACTIVITES DE R-D NON-INTEGREES) SONT
  COMPRISES AVEC CELLES DU SECTEUR DE SERVICE
  GENERAL.
  ESP> LOS DATOS RELATIVOS AL SECTOR PRODUCTIVO
  (ACTIVIDADES DE I Y D NO INTEGRADAS) SE INCLUYEN
  EN EL SECTOR DE SERVICIO GENERAL.

JAPAN:
  E—> FIGURES IN MILLIONS. NOT INCLUDING DATA FOR
  SOCIAL SCIENCES AND HUMANITIES IN THE PRODUCTIVE
  SECTOR.
  FR—> CHIFFRES EN MILLIONS. NON COMPRIS LES
  DONNEES POUR LES SCIENCES SOCIALES ET HUMAINES
  DANS LE SECTEUR DE LA PRODUCTION.
  ESP> LAS CIFRAS VIENEN EXPRESADAS EN MILLONES.
  EXCLUIDOS LOS DATOS RELATIVOS A LAS CIENCIAS
  SOCIALES Y HUMANAS DEL SECTOR PRODUCTIVO.

JORDAN:
  E—> DATA RELATE TO THE EAST BANK ONLY.
  FR—> LES DONNEES SE REFERENT A LA RIVE ORIENTA-
  LE SEULEMENT.
  ESP> LOS DATOS SE REFIEREN A LA ORILLA ORIENTAL
  SOLAMENTE.

KOREA, REPUBLIC OF:
  E—> NOT INCLUDING DATA FOR LAW, HUMANITIES AND
  EDUCATION.
  FR—> NON COMPRIS LES DONNEES POUR LE DROIT, LES
  SCIENCES HUMAINES ET L'EDUCATION.
  ESP> EXCLUIDOS LOS DATOS RELATIVOS AL DERECHO,
  LAS CIENCIAS HUMANAS Y LA EDUCACION.

PAKISTAN:
  E—> DATA RELATE TO THE YEAR 1973/74 AND REFER
  TO R&D ACTIVITIES WHICH ARE CONCENTRATED MAINLY IN
  GOVERNMENT-FINANCED RESEARCH ESTABLISHMENTS.
  SOCIAL SCIENCES AND HUMANITIES IN THE HIGHER EDU-
  CATION AND GENERAL SERVICE SECTORS ARE NOT
  INCLUDED.
  FR—> LES DONNEES SE REFERENT A L'ANNEE 1973/74
  ET AUX ACTIVITES DE R-D SE TROUVANT POUR LA PLU-
  PART DANS LES ETABLISSEMENTS DE RECHERCHE FINANCES
  PAR LE GOUVERNEMENT. LES SCIENCES SOCIALES ET
  HUMAINES NE SONT PAS COMPRISES DANS LES SECTEURS
  DE L'ENSEIGNEMENT SUPERIEUR ET DU SERVICE GENERAL.
  ESP> LOS DATOS SE REFIEREN AL AÑO 1973/74 Y A
  LAS ACTIVIDADES DE I Y D CONCENTRADAS PRINCIPAL-
  MENTE EN LOS ESTABLECIMIENTOS DE INVESTIGACION
  SUBVENCIONADOS POR EL GOBIERNO. NO SE INCLUYEN LOS
  DATOS RELATIVOS A LAS CIENCIAS SOCIALES Y HUMANAS,
  EN LOS SECTORES DE ENSEÑANZA SUPERIOR Y DE SERVI-
  CIO GENERAL.

PHILIPPINES:
  E—> DATA RELATE TO THE YEAR 1973/74.
  FR—> LES DONNEES SE REFERENT A L'ANNEE 1973/74.
  ESP> LOS DATOS SE REFIEREN AL AÑO 1973/74.

5.8 R&D expenditure by sector of performance
Dépenses de R-D par secteur d'exécution
Gastos de I y D por sector de ejecución

ICELAND:
E—>NOT INCLUDING DATA FOR SOCIAL SCIENCES AND HUMANITIES.
FR—>NON COMPRIS LES DONNEES POUR LES SCIENCES SOCIALES ET HUMAINES.
ESP>EXCLUIDOS LOS DATOS RELATIVOS A LAS CIENCIAS SOCIALES Y HUMANAS.

ITALY:
E—>FIGURES IN MILLIONS.
FR—>CHIFFRES EN MILLIONS.
ESP>LAS CIFRAS VIENEN EXPRESADAS EN MILLONES.

NETHERLANDS:
E—>NOT INCLUDING SOCIAL SCIENCES AND HUMANITIES IN THE PRODUCTIVE SECTOR (INTEGRATED R&D).
FR—>NON COMPRIS LES SCIENCES SOCIALES ET HUMAINES DU SECTEUR DE LA PRODUCTION (ACTIVITES DE R-D INTEGREES).
ESP>EXCLUIDAS LAS CIENCIAS SOCIALES Y HUMANAS DEL SECTOR PRODUCTIVO (ACTIVIDADES DE I Y D INTEGRADAS).

PORTUGAL:
E—>THE FIGURE IN COLUMN 5 INCLUDES 59,115 THOUSAND ESCUDOS FROM PRIVATE NON-PROFIT ORGANIZATIONS.
FR—>LE CHIFFRE DE LA COLONNE 5 COMPREND 59 115 MILLIERS D'ESCUDOS PROVENANT DES ORGANISATIONS PRIVEES A BUT NON LUCRATIF.
ESP>LOS DATOS DE LA COLUMNA 5 COMPRENDEN 59 115 MILLARES DE ESCUDOS PROCEDENTES DE ORGANIZACIONES PRIVADAS DE CARACTER NO LUCRATIVO.

SPAIN:
E—>DATA RELATING TO THE PRODUCTIVE SECTOR (NON-INTEGRATED R&D) ARE INCLUDED WITH THE GENERAL SERVICE SECTOR.
FR—>LES DONNEES RELATIVES AU SECTEUR DE LA PRODUCTION (ACTIVITES DE R-D NON-INTEGREES) SONT COMPRISES AVEC CELLES DU SECTEUR DE SERVICE GENERAL.
ESP>LOS DATOS RELATIVOS AL SECTOR PRODUCTIVO (ACTIVIDADES DE I Y D NO INTEGRADAS) SE INCLUYEN EN EL SECTOR DE SERVICIO GENERAL.

SWEDEN:
E—>NOT INCLUDING DATA FOR SOCIAL SCIENCES AND HUMANITIES.
FR—>NON COMPRIS LES DONNEES POUR LES SCIENCES SOCIALES ET HUMAINES.
ESP>EXCLUIDOS LOS DATOS RELATIVOS A LAS CIENCIAS SOCIALES Y HUMANAS.

SWITZERLAND:
E—>THE TOTALS IN COLUMNS 1 AND 2 DO NOT INCLUDE CAPITAL EXPENDITURE BY THE PRODUCTIVE SECTOR.
FR—>LE TOTAL DES COLONNES 1 ET 2 NE COMPREND PAS LES DEPENSES EN CAPITAL DU SECTEUR DE LA PRODUCTION
ESP>EXCLUIDOS LOS GASTOS DE CAPITAL DEL SECTOR PRODUCTIVO PARA EL TOTAL DE LAS COLUMNAS 1 Y 2.

SRI LANKA:
E—>THE TOTAL DOES NOT INCLUDE CAPITAL EXPENDITURE BY THE HIGHER EDUCATION SECTOR.
FR—>LE TOTAL NE COMPREND PAS LES DEPENSES EN CAPITAL DU SECTEUR DE L'ENSEIGNEMENT SUPERIEUR.
ESP>EXCLUIDOS LOS GASTOS DE CAPITAL DEL SECTOR DE ENSEÑANZA SUPERIOR.

TURKEY:
E—>DATA RELATE TO GOVERNMENT EXPENDITURE ONLY AND DO NOT INCLUDE THE PRODUCTIVE SECTOR; NOT INCLUDING DATA FOR SOCIAL SCIENCES AND HUMANITIES.
FR—>LES DONNEES SE REFERENT AUX DEPENSES PUBLIQUES SEULEMENT ET NE COMPRENNENT PAS LE SECTEUR DE LA PRODUCTION. NON COMPRIS LES SCIENCES SOCIALES ET HUMAINES.
ESP>LOS DATOS SE REFIEREN A LOS GASTOS PUBLICOS SOLAMENTE Y EXCLUYEN EL SECTOR PRODUCTIVO. EXCLUIDOS LOS DATOS RELATIVOS A LAS CIENCIAS SOCIALES Y HUMANAS.

YEMEN:
E—>DATA RELATE TO THE YEAR 1974/75.
FR—>LES DONNEES SE REFERENT A L'ANNEE 1974/75.
ESP>LOS DATOS SE REFIEREN AL AÑO 1974/75.

AUSTRIA:
E—>DATA RELATE TO THE PRODUCTIVE SECTOR ONLY.
FR—>LES DONNEES NE CONCERNENT QUE LE SECTEUR DE LA PRODUCTION.
ESP>LOS DATOS SE REFIEREN AL SECTOR PRODUCTIVO SOLAMENTE.

GERMANY, FEDERAL REPUBLIC OF:
E—>NOT INCLUDING 320 MILLION DEUTSCHE MARKS BY THE PRODUCTIVE SECTOR FOR WHICH A DISTRIBUTION BETWEEN CURRENT AND CAPITAL EXPENDITURE IN THE UNKNOWN. SOCIAL SCIENCES AND HUMANITIES IN THE PRODUCTIVE SECTOR ARE NOT INCLUDED.
FR—>NON COMPRIS 320 MILLIONS DE DEUTSCHE MARKS DANS LE SECTEUR DE LA PRODUCTION DONT LA REPARTITION ENTRE LES DEPENSES EN CAPITAL ET LES DEPENSES COURANTES N'A PAS ETE PRECISEE. NON COMPRIS LES SCIENCES SOCIALES ET HUMAINES DANS LE SECTEUR DE LA PRODUCTION.
ESP>EXCLUIDOS 320 MILLONES DE MARCOS DEL SECTOR PRODUCTIVO, CUYA REPARTICION ENTRE GASTOS ORDINARIOS Y GASTOS DE CAPITAL NO SE HA PRECISADO. NO INCLUYE LAS CIENCIAS SOCIALES Y HUMANAS DEL SECTOR PRODUCTIVO.

HUNGARY:
E—>NOT INCLUDING 1,358 MILLION FORINTS (ALL CURRENT EXPENDITURE) FOR WHICH A BREAKDOWN BY SECTOR IS NOT AVAILABLE.
FR—>COMPTE NON TENU DE 1 358 MILLIONS DE FORINTS (DEPENSES COURANTES) DONT LA REPARTITION PAR SECTEUR N'EST PAS DISPONIBLE.
ESP>EXCLUIDOS 1 358 MILLONES DE FORINTS (GASTOS ORDINARIOS), CUYA REPARTICION POR SECTOR SE DESCONOCE.

R&D expenditure by sector of performance 5.8
Dépenses de R-D par secteur d'exécution
Gastos de I y D por sector de ejecución

UNITED KINGDOM:
E—> CURRENT EXPENDITURE EXCLUDES THE RELEVANT PORTION OF 28 MILLION POUNDS STERLING FOR WHICH A DISTRIBUTION BETWEEN CURRENT AND CAPITAL EXPENDITURE IS UNKNOWN. NOT INCLUDING DATA FOR SOCIAL SCIENCES AND HUMANITIES.
FR—> LES DEPENSES COURANTES NE COMPRENNENT PAS LA SOMME DE 28 MILLIONS DE LIVRES STERLING DONT LA VENTILATION ENTRE LES DEPENSES COURANTES ET LES DEPENSES EN CAPITAL N'A PAS ETE PRECISEE. NON COMPRIS LES DONNEES POUR LES SCIENCES SOCIALES ET HUMAINES.
ESP> LOS GASTOS ORDINARIOS NO COMPRENDEN LA PARTE DE LA SUMA DE 28 MILLONES DE LIBRAS ESTERLINAS, CUYA REPARTICION ENTRE GASTOS ORDINARIOS Y GASTOS DE CAPITAL NO SE HA PRECISADO. EXCLUIDOS LOS DATOS RELATIVOS A LAS CIENCIAS SOCIALES Y HUMANAS.

YUGOSLAVIA:
E—> NOT INCLUDING ACTIVITIES OF A MILITARY NATURE OR RELATING TO NATIONAL DEFENCE.
FR—> NON COMPRIS LES ACTIVITES DE CARACTERE MILITAIRE OU RELEVANT DE LA DEFENSE NATIONALE.
ESP> EXCLUIDAS LAS ACTIVIDADES DE CARACTER MILITAR O QUE CONCIERNEN LA DEFENSA NACIONAL.

AMERICAN SAMOA:
E—> DATA REFER TO ONE RESEARCH INSTITUTE ONLY.
FR—> LES DONNEES NE CONCERNENT QU'UN INSTITUT DE RECHERCHE.
ESP> LOS DATOS SE REFIEREN A UN CENTRO DE INVESTIGACION SOLAMENTE.

FRENCH POLYNESIA:
E—> DATA REFER TO ONE RESEARCH INSTITUTE ONLY.
FR—>LES DONNEES NE CONCERNENT QU'UN INSTITUT DE RECHERCHE.
ESP> LOS DATOS SE REFIEREN A UN CENTRO DE INVESTIGACION SOLAMENTE.

5.9 R&D expenditure by source of funds
Dépenses de R-D selon la source de financement
Gastos de I y D según la fuente de financiamiento

5.9 Total and current expenditure for the performance of research and experimental development by source of funds

Dépenses totales et courantes consacrées à la recherche et au développement expérimental, selon la source de financement

Gastos totales y ordinarios dedicados a la investigación y al desarrollo experimental, según la fuente de financiamiento

5.9 TOTAL AND CURRENT EXPENDITURE FOR THE PERFORMANCE OF RESEARCH AND EXPERIMENTAL DEVELOPMENT BY SOURCE OF FUNDS
5.9 DEPENSES TOTALES ET COURANTES CONSACREES A LA RECHERCHE ET AU DEVELOPPEMENT EXPERIMENTAL, SELON LA SOURCE DE FINANCEMENT
5.9 GASTOS TOTALES Y ORDINARIOS DEDICADOS A LA INVESTIGACION Y AL DESARROLLO EXPERIMENTAL, SEGUN LA FUENTE DE FINANCIAMIENTO

PLEASE REFER TO INTRODUCTION FOR DEFINITIONS OF CATEGORIES INCLUDED IN THIS TABLE.
POUR LES DEFINITIONS DES CATEGORIES PRESENTES DANS CE TABLEAU, SE REFERER A L'INTRODUCTION.
EN LA INTRODUCCION SE DAN LAS DEFINICIONES DE LAS CATEGORIAS QUE FIGURAN EN ESTE CUADRO.

CURRENT EXPENDITURE = DEPENSES COURANTES
CURRENT EXPENDITURE = GASTOS ORDINARIOS

NUMBER OF COUNTRIES AND TERRITORIES PRESENTED IN THIS TABLE: 75
NOMBRE DE PAYS ET DE TERRITOIRES PRESENTES DANS CE TABLEAU: 75
NUMERO DE PAISES Y DE TERRITORIOS PRESENTADOS EN ESTE CUADRO: 75

COUNTRY / PAYS / PAIS	FISCAL YEAR BEGINNING / EXERCICE FINANCIER COMMENCANT EN / COMIENZO DEL EJERCICIO ECONOMICO	CURRENCY / MONNAIE / MONEDA	TYPE OF EXPENDITURE / TYPE DE DEPENSES / TIPO DE GASTOS	TOTAL (000)	SOURCE OF FUNDS / ORIGINE DES FONDS / ORIGEN DE LOS FONDOS				
					GOVERNMENT FUNDS / FONDS PUBLICS / FONDOS PUBLICOS (000)	SPECIAL FUNDS / FONDS SPECIAUX / FONDOS ESPECIALES (000)	PRODUCTIVE ENTERPRISE FUNDS / FONDS DES ENTREPRISES DE PRODUCTION / FONDOS DE LAS EMPRESAS DE PRODUCCION (000)	FOREIGN FUNDS / FONDS ETRANGERS / FONDOS EXTRANJEROS (000)	OTHER FUNDS / FONDS DIVERS / FONDOS DIVERSOS (000)
				(1)	(2)	(3)	(4)	(5)	(6)
AFRICA									
ALGERIA ‡	1972	DINAR	TOTAL	78 000	78 000	—	—	—	—
			%	100.0	100.0	—	—	—	—
			CURRENT	68 000	68 000	—	—	—	—
			%	100.0	100.0	—	—	—	—
BOTSWANA	1973	PULA	TOTAL	220	34	10	—	176	—
			%	100.0	15.4	4.5	—	80.0	—
			CURRENT	33	28	5	—		—
			%	100.0	84.8	15.2	—		—

R&D expenditure by source of funds 5.9
Dépenses de R-D selon la source de financement
Gastos de I y D según la fuente de financiamiento

Country	Year	Currency		(1)	(2)	(3)	(4)	(5)	(6)
EGYPT	1973	POUND	TOTAL	29 940	26 950	—	—	2 990	—
			%	100.0	90.0	—	—	10.0	—
IVORY COAST	1970	FRANC C.F.A.	TOTAL	1 401 124	425 621	200 000	—	775 503	—
			%	100.0	30.4	14.3	—	55.3	—
KENYA ‡	1971	SHILLING	TOTAL	*102 940	*84 140	—	*18 800	—	—
			%	100.0	*81.7	—	*18.3	—	—
			CURRENT	*83 160	*64 360	—	*18 800	—	—
			%	100.0	*77.4	—	*22.6	—	—
MADAGASCAR ‡	1971	FRANC	TOTAL	2 294 000	485 000	100 000	—	1 709 000	—
			%	100.0	21.1	4.4	—	74.5	—
MAURITIUS	1977	RUPEE	TOTAL	18 800	8 800	—	9 200	100	700
			%	100.0	46.8	—	48.9	0.5	3.7
			CURRENT	12 700	3 200	—	8 800	—	700
			%	100.0	25.2	—	69.3	—	5.5
NIGER ‡	1976	FRANC C.F.A.	TOTAL	141 703	141 703	—	—	—	—
			%	100.0	100.0	—	—	—	—
NIGERIA ‡	1970	NAIRA	TOTAL	23 822	23 026	—	—	*798	—
			%	100.0	96.7	—	—	*3.3	—
SENEGAL ‡	1971	FRANC C.F.A.	TOTAL	2 110 192	480 345	68 085	...	1 561 762	...
			%	100.0	22.8	3.2	...	74.0	...
SEYCHELLES	1973	RUPEE	TOTAL	402	290	—	—	112	—
			%	100.0	72.1	—	—	27.9	—
SUDAN	1975	POUND	TOTAL	5 115	4 809	—	30	35	241
			%	100.0	94.0	—	0.6	0.7	4.7
UPPER VOLTA	1970	FRANC C.F.A.	TOTAL	*412 768	*30 513	—	—	*323 377	*58 878
			%	100.0	*7.4	—	—	*78.3	*14.3
ZAMBIA	1972	KWACHA	TOTAL	6 261	3 701	—	45	1 800	715
			%	100.0	59.1	—	0.7	28.7	11.4
AMERICA, NORTH									
BERMUDA ‡	1970	DOLLAR	TOTAL	240	238	2	—	—	—
			%	100.0	99.2	0.8	—	—	—
CANADA	1977	DOLLAR	TOTAL	2 241 700	1 049 800	—	705 100	56 900	429 800
			%	100.0	46.8	—	31.5	2.5	19.2
CUBA	1978	PESO	TOTAL	83 163	77 053	—	—	6 110	—
			%	100.0	92.7	—	—	7.3	—
			CURRENT	68 408	65 924	—	—	2 484	—
			%	100.0	96.4	—	—	3.6	—
GUATEMALA	1974	QUETZAL	TOTAL	5 139	3 125	87	94	1 308	525
			%	100.0	60.8	1.7	1.8	25.5	10.2
			CURRENT	3 721	2 307	87	—	809	518
			%	100.0	62.0	2.3	—	21.7	13.9
MEXICO	1973	PESO	TOTAL	1 277 618	794 204	—	216 905	19 921	246 588
			%	100.0	62.1	—	17.0	1.6	19.3

5.9 R&D expenditure by source of funds
Dépenses de R-D selon la source de financement
Gastos de I y D según la fuente de financiamiento

COUNTRY / PAYS / PAIS	FISCAL YEAR BEGINNING / CURRENCY — EXERCICE FINANCIER COMMENCANT EN / MONNAIE — COMIENZO DEL EJERCICIO ECONOMICO / MONEDA	TYPE OF EXPENDITURE / TYPE DE DEPENSES / TIPO DE GASTOS	TOTAL (000) (1)	GOVERNMENT FUNDS / FONDS PUBLICS / FONDOS PUBLICOS (000) (2)	SPECIAL FUNDS / FONDS SPECIAUX / FONDOS ESPECIALES (000) (3)	PRODUCTIVE ENTERPRISE FUNDS / FONDS DES ENTREPRISES DE-PRODUCTION / FONDOS DE LAS EMPRESAS DE PRODUCCION (000) (4)	FOREIGN FUNDS / FONDS ETRANGERS / FONDOS EXTRANJEROS (000) (5)	OTHER FUNDS / FONDS DIVERS / FONDOS DIVERSOS (000) (6)
PANAMA	1975 BALBOA	TOTAL	3 296	1 764	—	330	942	260
		%	100.0	53.5	—	10.0	28.6	7.9
ST. PIERRE AND MIQUELON ‡	1972 FRANC C.F.A.	TOTAL	110 000	110 000	—	—	—	—
		%	100.0	100.0	—	—	—	—
UNITED STATES OF AMERICA ‡	1977 DOLLAR	CURRENT	42 406 600	21 472 500	—	19 413 600	—	1 520 600
		%	100.0	50.6	—	45.8	—	3.6
AMERICA, SOUTH								
ARGENTINA ‡	1976 PESO	TOTAL	*23 171 700	*20 152 900	—	*1 662 400	*702 300	*654 100
		%	100.0	*87.0	—	*7.2	*3.0	*2.8
BRAZIL ‡	1978 CRUZEIROS	TOTAL	20 781 000	6 436 000	./.	3 785 000	133 000	10 427 000
		%	100.0	31.0	./.	18.2	0.6	50.2
COLOMBIA ‡	1971 PESO	TOTAL	210 614	...	...	...	19 507	...
		%	100.0	...	...	...	9.3	...
ECUADOR ‡	1976 SUCRE	TOTAL	258 366	230 445	—	5 794	22 127	—
		%	100.0	89.2	—	2.2	8.6	—
		CURRENT	167 718	149 953	—	3 333	14 432	—
		%	100.0	89.4	—	2.0	8.6	—
PERU	1976 SOL	TOTAL	*2 314 754	*1 559 211	*466 345	⟩	*207 929	*81 269
		%	100.0	*67.4	*20.1	⟩	*9.0	*3.5
URUGUAY	1972 PESO	TOTAL	1 858	1 254	—	344	260	0.2
		%	100.0	67.5	—	18.5	14.0	0.0
ASIA								
BANGLADESH ‡	1974 TAKA	TOTAL	113 530	96 630	—	—	16 900	—
		%	100.0	85.1	—	—	14.9	—
BRUNEI	1974 DOLLAR	TOTAL	3 055	3 055	—	—	—	—
		%	100.0	100.0	—	—	—	—
		CURRENT	2 933	2 933	—	—	—	—
		%	100.0	100.0	—	—	—	—

R&D expenditure by source of funds 5.9
Dépenses de R-D selon la source de financement
Gastos de I y D según la fuente de financiamiento

Country	Year	Currency		(1)	(2)	(3)	(4)	(5)	(6)
CYPRUS	1971	POUND	TOTAL	1 088	1 062	19	—	7	—
			%	100.0	97.6	1.7	—	0.6	—
			CURRENT	986	965	19	—		—
			%	100.0	97.9	1.9	—	0.1	—
INDIA	1972	RUPEE	TOTAL	1 942 600	1 554 000	—	388 600	—	—
			%	100.0	80.0	—	20.0	—	—
IRAN	1971	RIAL	TOTAL	4 856 054	4 812 349	—	43 705	—	—
			%	100.0	99.1	—	0.9	—	—
			CURRENT	4 322 745	4 283 840	—	38 905	—	—
			%	100.0	99.1	—	0.9	—	—
ISRAEL ‡	1978	POUND	CURRENT	6 154 300	3 887 500	—	1 783 600	./.	483 300
			%	100.0	63.1	—	29.0	./.	7.9
JAPAN ‡	1976	YEN	TOTAL	3 320 685	976 486	—	2 341 456	2 743	—
			%	100.0	29.4	—	70.5	0.1	—
KOREA, REPUBLIC OF ‡	1978	WON	TOTAL	152 418 000	73 722 000	—	77 971 000	725 000	—
			%	100.0	48.4	—	51.1	0.5	—
PAKISTAN ‡	1973	RUPEE	TOTAL	150 430	150 430	—	—	—	—
			%	100.0	100.0	—	—	—	—
PHILIPPINES ‡	1973	PESO	TOTAL	218 106	187 555	28 751	—	1 800	—
			%	100.0	86.0	13.2	—	0.8	—
SINGAPORE ‡	1978	DOLLAR	TOTAL	28 120	10 626	./.	15 028	2 293	173
			%	100.0	37.8	./.	53.4	8.2	0.6
SRI LANKA ‡	1975	RUPEE	TOTAL	45 097	24 140	15 188	4 759	1 010	—
			%	100.0	53.5	33.7	10.6	2.2	—
VIET-NAM	1979	DONG	TOTAL	108 300	108 300	—	—	—	—
			%	100.0	100.0	—	—	—	—
YEMEN ‡	1974	RIAL	TOTAL	9 923	2 608	—	—	7 315	—
			%	100.0	26.3	—	—	73.7	—
EUROPE									
AUSTRIA ‡	1978	SCHILLING	TOTAL	10 685 100	5 655 100	—	4 950 000	—	80 000
			%	100.0	52.9	—	46.3	—	0.8
BELGIUM ‡	1977	FRANC	TOTAL	38 894 080	13 509 945	./.	24 405 896	345 634	632 605
			%	100.0	34.7	./.	62.8	0.9	1.6
BULGARIA ‡	1977	LEV	TOTAL	334 900	155 100	./.	179 800	—	—
			%	100.0	46.3	./.	53.7	—	—
CZECHOSLOVAKIA	1978	KORUNA	TOTAL	17 496 000	7 245 000	—	10 251 000	—	—
			%	100.0	41.4	—	58.6	—	—
DENMARK	1976	KRONE	TOTAL	2 662 800	1 415 500	—	1 158 500	31 400	57 400
			%	100.0	53.2	—	43.5	1.2	2.1
FINLAND	1977	MARKKA	TOTAL	1 298 820	608 200	—	666 020	8 730	15 870
			%	100.0	46.8	—	51.3	0.7	1.2
FRANCE	1977	FRANC	TOTAL	33 185 000	17 475 000	—	13 637 000	1 862 000	211 000
			%	100.0	52.7	—	41.1	5.6	0.6

5.9 R&D expenditure by source of funds
Dépenses de R-D selon la source de financement
Gastos de I y D según la fuente de financiamiento

COUNTRY / PAYS / PAIS	FISCAL YEAR BEGINNING / EXERCICE FINANCIER COMMENÇANT EN / COMIENZO DEL EJERCICIO ECONOMICO	CURRENCY / MONNAIE / MONEDA	TYPE OF EXPENDITURE / TYPE DE DEPENSES / TIPO DE GASTOS	TOTAL TOTAL TOTAL (000) (1)	GOVERNMENT FUNDS FONDS PUBLICS FONDOS PUBLICOS (000) (2)	SPECIAL FUNDS FONDS SPECIAUX FONDOS ESPECIALES (000) (3)	PRODUCTIVE ENTERPRISE FUNDS FONDS DES ENTREPRISES DE PRODUCTION FONDOS DE LAS EMPRESAS DE PRODUCCION (000) (4)	FOREIGN FUNDS FONDS ETRANGERS FONDOS EXTRANJEROS (000) (5)	OTHER FUNDS FONDS DIVERS FONDOS DIVERSOS (000) (6)
GERMANY, FEDERAL REPUBLIC OF ‡	1977	DEUTSCHE MARK	TOTAL %	25 733 000 100.0	11 143 000 43.3	– –	13 596 000 52.8	706 000 2.7	288 000 1.1
HUNGARY	1978	FORINT	TOTAL %	18 716 000 100.0	4 947 000 26.4	13 759 000 73.5	——> ——>	10 000 0.1	– –
IRELAND	1977	POUND	TOTAL %	43 209 100.0	21 659 50.1	– –	14 241 33.0	1 725 4.0	5 584 12.9
ITALY ‡	1976	LIRA	TOTAL %	1 352 565 100.0	588 648 43.5	25 089 1.9	670 395 49.6	21 554 1.6	46 879 3.5
MALTA ‡	1973	POUND	TOTAL	149	138	...	...	11	–
NETHERLANDS ‡	1976	GUILDER	TOTAL %	4 964 000 100.0	2 271 000 45.8	– –	2 425 000 48.9	228 000 4.6	40 000 0.8
NORWAY	1978	KRONER	TOTAL %	2 973 000 100.0	1 864 000 62.7	– –	980 000 33.0	37 000 1.2	92 000 3.1
POLAND	1973	ZLOTY	TOTAL % CURRENT %	29 000 000 100.0 24 000 000 100.0	12 200 000 42.1 12 000 000 50.0	13 900 000 47.9 10 000 000 41.7	2 900 000 10.0 2 000 000 8.3	– –	– –
PORTUGAL	1976	ESCUDO	TOTAL % CURRENT %	1 279 591 100.0 1 146 353 100.0	919 349 71.8 808 973 70.6	– –	264 803 20.7 246 187 21.5	14 231 1.1 13 050 1.1	81 220 6.3 78 143 6.8
ROMANIA	1973	LEU	TOTAL %	3 354 196 100.0	990 221 29.5	452 200 13.5	1 911 775 57.0	– –	– –
SPAIN	1974	PESETA	TOTAL %	15 536 477 100.0	6 290 396 40.5	– –	8 911 402 57.4	311 988 2.0	22 691 0.1
SWEDEN ‡	1977	KRONA	TOTAL %	6 796 700 100.0	2 576 600 37.9	– –	4 052 600 59.6	106 200 1.6	61 300 0.9
SWITZERLAND	1975	FRANC	CURRENT %	2 977 000 100.0	610 000 20.5	– –	2 332 000 78.3	– –	35 000 1.2

SOURCE OF FUNDS / ORIGINE DES FONDS / ORIGEN DE LOS FONDOS

R&D expenditure by source of funds 5.9
Dépenses de R-D selon la source de financement
Gastos de I y D según la fuente de financiamiento

				(1)	(2)	(3)	(4)	(5)	(6)
UNITED KINGDOM ‡	1975	POUND STERLING	TOTAL	2 139 000	1 106 800	-	872 800	105 000	54 300
			%	100.0	51.7	-	40.8	4.9	2.5
YUGOSLAVIA ‡	1977	DINAR	TOTAL	6 226 000	1 413 000	592 000	3 381 000	75 000	765 000
			%	100.0	22.7	9.5	54.3	1.2	12.3
OCEANIA									
AMERICAN SAMOA ‡	1971	U.S. DOLLAR	TOTAL	120	120	-	-	-	-
			%	100.0	100.0				
			CURRENT	100	100				
			%	100.0	100.0				
AUSTRALIA	1976	DOLLAR	TOTAL	802 464	584 252	-	193 850	14 206	10 156
			%	100.0	72.8	-	24.2	1.8	1.3
COOK ISLANDS	1970	NEW ZEALAND DOLLAR	TOTAL	112	112	-	-	-	-
			%	100.0	100.0				
FRENCH POLYNESIA ‡	1976	FRANC C.F.P.	TOTAL	140 240	140 240				
GUAM ‡	1975	U.S. DOLLAR	TOTAL	1 295	708	-	-	-	587
			%	100.0	54.7	-	-	-	45.3
NEW CALEDONIA	1971	FRANC C.F.P.	TOTAL	1 440	800	-	640	-	-
			%	100.0	55.6	-	44.4		
			CURRENT	1 240	800	-	440		
			%	100.0	64.5	-	35.5		
NEW HEBRIDES	1975	FRANC	TOTAL	21 603	19 941	1 662	-	-	-
			%	100.0	92.3	7.7	-	-	-
			CURRENT	21 603	19 941	1 662	-		
			%	100.0	92.3	7.7	-		
NEW ZEALAND	1975	DOLLAR	TOTAL	99 776	79 974	-	18 768	-	1 034
			%	100.0	80.2	-	18.8	-	1.0
PACIFIC ISLANDS	1978	U.S. DOLLAR	TOTAL	185	185	-	-	-	-
			%	100.0	100.0				
SAMOA ‡	1978	TALA	TOTAL	2 500	1 500	./.	500	200	300
			%	100.0	60.0	./.	20.0	8.0	12.0

KENYA:
E—> NOT INCLUDING DATA FOR HUMANITIES AND
EDUCATION BUT INCLUDING SOME EDUCATIONAL RESEARCH.
THE TOTAL EXPENDITURE IN COLUMN 1 DOES NOT INCLUDE
CAPITAL EXPENDITURE FOR THE PRODUCTIVE SECTOR
(INTEGRATED R&D) AND THE HIGHER EDUCATION SECTOR.
FR—> COMPTE NON TENU DES DONNEES RELATIVES AUX
SCIENCES HUMAINES ET A L'EDUCATION, A L'EXCEPTION
D'UNE PARTIE DE LA RECHERCHE PEDAGOGIQUE; LES
DEPENSES TOTALES DE LA COLONNE 1 NE COMPRENNENT
PAS LES DEPENSES EN CAPITAL DES SECTEURS DE LA
PRODUCTION (ACTIVITES DE R-D INTEGREES) ET DE
L'ENSEIGNEMENT SUPERIEUR.

ALGERIA:
E—> DATA RELATE TO THE HIGHER EDUCATION SECTOR
ONLY.
FR—> LES DONNEES NE CONCERNENT QUE LE SECTEUR
DE L'ENSEIGNEMENT SUPERIEUR.
ESP> LOS DATOS SE REFIEREN AL SECTOR DE ENSEÑANZA
SUPERIOR SOLAMENTE.

CHAD:
E—> DATA RELATE TO 4 RESEARCH INSTITUTES ONLY.
FR—> LES DONNEES NE CONCERNENT QUE QUATRE
INSTITUTS DE RECHERCHE.
ESP> LOS DATOS SE REFIEREN A CUATRO CENTROS DE
INVESTIGACION SOLAMENTE.

5.9 R&D expenditure by source of funds
Dépenses de R-D selon la source de financement
Gastos de I y D según la fuente de financiamiento

KENYA (CONT.):
ESP> EXCLUIDOS LOS DATOS RELATIVOS A LAS CIENCIAS HUMANAS Y A LA EDUCACION, SALVO UNA PARTE DE LA INVESTIGACION PEDAGOGICA; LOS GASTOS TOTALES DE LA COLUMNA 1 NO INCLUYEN LOS GASTOS DE CAPITAL DE LOS SECTORES PRODUCTIVO (ACTIVIDADES DE I Y D INTEGRADAS) Y DE ENSEÑANZA SUPERIOR.

MADAGASCAR:
E—> NOT INCLUDING DATA FOR THE PRODUCTIVE SECTOR (INTEGRATED R&D).
FR—> NON COMPRIS LES DONNEES POUR LE SECTEUR DE LA PRODUCTION (ACTIVITES DE R-D INTEGREES).
ESP> EXCLUIDOS LOS DATOS RELATIVOS AL SECTOR PRODUCTIVO (ACTIVIDADES DE I Y D INTEGRADAS).

NIGER:
E—> DATA RELATE TO THE HIGHER EDUCATION SECTOR ONLY.
FR—> LES DONNEES NE CONCERNENT QUE LE SECTEUR DE L'ENSEIGNEMENT SUPERIEUR.
ESP> LOS DATOS SE REFIEREN AL SECTOR DE ENSE-NANZA SUPERIOR SOLAMENTE.

NIGERIA:
E—> DATA RELATE TO FEDERAL AND STATE GOVERN-MENTS BUDGETARY ESTIMATES FOR RESEARCH AND TECHNICAL DEVELOPMENT SERVICES AND UNIVERSITY EXPENDITURE ON RESEARCH AND EXPERIMENTAL DEVELOPMENT; NOT INCLUDING SOCIAL SCIENCES AND HUMANITIES.
FR—> LES DONNEES SE REFERENT A L'ESTIMATION BUDGETAIRE DU GOUVERNEMENT FEDERAL ET DES GOUVERNEMENTS DES ETATS POUR LA RECHERCHE ET LES SERVICES DE DEVELOPPEMENT TECHNIQUE, ET AUX DEPENSES DES UNIVERSITES DESTINEES A LA RECHERCHE ET AU DEVELOPPEMENT EXPERIMENTAL; NON COMPRIS LES DONNEES POUR LES SCIENCES SOCIALES ET HUMAINES.
ESP> LOS DATOS SE REFIEREN A LA ESTIMACION PRESUPUESTARIA DEL GOBIERNO FEDERAL Y DE LOS GOBIERNOS DE LOS ESTADOS PARA LAS ACTIVIDADES DE INVESTIGACION Y LOS SERVICIOS DE DESARROLLO TECNICO, ASI COMO LOS GASTOS DE LAS UNIVERSIDADES DESTINADOS A LA INVESTIGACION Y AL DESARROLLO EXPERIMENTAL, EXCLUIDOS LOS DATOS RELATIVOS A LAS CIENCIAS SOCIALES Y HUMANAS.

SENEGAL:
E—> NOT INCLUDING PRODUCTIVE ENTERPRISE FUNDS AND OTHER FUNDS.
FR—> NON COMPRIS LES FONDS DES ENTREPRISES DE PRODUCTION ET LES FONDS DIVERS.
ESP> EXCLUIDOS LOS FONDOS DE LAS EMPRESAS DE PRODUCCION Y LOS FONDOS DIVERSOS.

BERMUDA:
E—> NOT INCLUDING DATA FOR THE PRODUCTIVE SECTOR AND EXCLUDING LAW, HUMANITIES AND EDUCATION.
FR—> NON COMPRIS LES DONNEES POUR LE SECTEUR DE LA PRODUCTION ET COMPTE NON TENU DES DONNEES RELATIVES AU DROIT, AUX SCIENCES HUMAINES ET A L'EDUCATION.

BERMUDA (CONT.):
ESP> EXCLUIDOS LOS DATOS RELATIVOS AL SECTOR PRODUCTIVO Y LOS QUE SE REFIEREN AL DERECHO, LAS CIENCIAS HUMANAS Y LA EDUCACION.

ST. PIERRE AND MIQUELON:
E—> DATA RELATE TO THE "INSTITUT SCIENTIFIQUE ET TECHNIQUE DES PECHES MARITIMES" ONLY.
FR—> LES DONNEES NE CONCERNENT QUE L'INSTITUT SCIENTIFIQUE ET TECHNIQUE DES PECHES MARITIMES.
ESP> LOS DATOS SE REFIEREN AL "INSTITUT SCIENTIFIQUE ET TECHNIQUE DES PECHES MARITIMES" SOLAMENTE.

UNITED STATES OF AMERICA:
E—> NOT INCLUDING DATA FOR LAW, HUMANITIES AND EDUCATION.
FR—> NON COMPRIS LES DONNEES POUR LE DROIT, LES SCIENCES HUMAINES ET L'EDUCATION.
ESP> EXCLUIDOS LOS DATOS RELATIVOS AL DERECHO, LAS CIENCIAS HUMANAS Y LA EDUCACION.

ARGENTINA:
E—> DATA IN COLUMN 4 RELATE TO FUNDS ORIGINATING FROM PRIVATE SOURCES.
FR—> LES DONNEES DE LA COLONNE 4 SE REFERENT AUX FONDS PROVENANT DES SOURCES PRIVEES.
ESP> LOS DATOS DE LA COLUMNA 4 SE REFIEREN A LOS FONDOS PROCEDENTES DE FUENTES PRIVADAS.

BRAZIL:
E—> DATA RELATING TO SPECIAL FUNDS (COLUMN 3) ARE INCLUDED WITH PRODUCTIVE ENTERPRISE FUNDS (COLUMN 4).
FR—> LES DONNEES RELATIVES AUX FONDS SPECIAUX (COLONNE 3) SONT COMPTEES AVEC CELLES DES ENTREPRISES DE LA PRODUCTION (COLONNE 4).
ESP> LOS DATOS RELATIVOS A LOS FONDOS ESPECIALES (COLUMNA 3) QUEDAN ENGLOBADOS EN LOS DE LAS EMPRESAS DE PRODUCCION (COLUMNA 4).

COLOMBIA:
E—> NOT INCLUDING DATA FOR LAW, HUMANITIES AND EDUCATION.
FR—> NON COMPRIS LES DONNEES POUR LE DROIT, LES SCIENCES HUMAINES ET L'EDUCATION.
ESP> EXCLUIDOS LOS DATOS RELATIVOS AL DERECHO, LAS CIENCIAS HUMANAS Y LA EDUCACION.

ECUADOR:
E—> DATA REFER TO R&D IN THE AGRICULTURAL SCIENCES ONLY.
FR—> LES DONNEES SE REFERENT A LA R-D DANS LES SCIENCES DE L'AGRICULTURE SEULEMENT.
ESP> LOS DATOS SE REFIEREN A LA I Y D PARA LAS CIENCIAS AGRICOLAS SOLAMENTE.

BANGLADESH:
E—> NOT INCLUDING CURRENT EXPENDITURE IN THE HIGHER EDUCATION SECTOR.
FR—> NON COMPRIS LES DEPENSES COURANTES DU SECTEUR DE L'ENSEIGNEMENT SUPERIEUR.

R&D expenditure by source of funds 5.9
Dépenses de R-D selon la source de financement
Gastos de I y D según la fuente de financiamiento

PHILIPPINES:
E—> DATA RELATE TO THE YEAR 1973/74.
FR—> LES DONNEES SE REFERENT A L'ANNEE 1973/74.
ESP> LOS DATOS SE REFIEREN AL AÑO 1973/74.

SINGAPORE:
E—> DATA RELATING TO SPECIAL FUNDS (COLUMN 3) ARE INCLUDED WITH PRODUCTIVE ENTERPRISE FUNDS (COLUMN 4).
FR—> LES DONNEES RELATIVES AUX FONDS SPECIAUX (COLONNE 3) SONT COMPTEES AVEC CELLES DES ENTRE- PRISES DE LA PRODUCTION (COLONNE 4).
ESP> LOS DATOS RELATIVOS A LOS FONDOS ESPECIALES (COLUMNA 3) QUEDAN ENGLOBADOS EN LOS DE LAS EMPRESAS DE PRODUCCION (COLUMNA 4).

SRI LANKA:
E—> NOT INCLUDING CAPITAL EXPENDITURE IN THE HIGHER EDUCATION SECTOR.
FR—> COMPTE NON TENU DES DEPENSES EN CAPITAL DU SECTEUR DE L'ENSEIGNEMENT SUPERIEUR.
ESP> EXCLUIDOS LOS GASTOS DE CAPITAL DEL SECTOR DE ENSEÑANZA SUPERIOR.

YEMEN:
E—> DATA RELATE TO THE YEAR 1974/75.
FR—> LES DONNEES SE REFERENT A L'ANNEE 1974/75.
ESP> LOS DATOS SE REFIEREN AL AÑO 1974/75.

AUSTRIA:
E—> DATA RELATE TO THE PRODUCTIVE SECTOR ONLY.
FR—> LES DONNEES NE CONCERNENT QUE LE SECTEUR DE LA PRODUCTION.
ESP> LOS DATOS SE REFIEREN AL SECTOR PRODUCTIVO SOLAMENTE.

BELGIUM:
E—> DATA RELATING TO SPECIAL FUNDS (COLUMN 3) ARE INCLUDED WITH PRODUCTIVE ENTERPRISE FUNDS (COLUMN 4).
FR—> LES DONNEES RELATIVES AUX FONDS SPECIAUX (COLONNE 3) SONT COMPTEES AVEC CELLES DES ENTRE- PRISES DE LA PRODUCTION (COLONNE 4).
ESP> LOS DATOS RELATIVOS A LOS FONDOS ESPECIALES (COLUMNA 3) QUEDAN ENGLOBADOS EN LOS DE LAS EMPRESAS DE PRODUCCION (COLUMNA 4).

BULGARIA:
E—> DATA RELATING TO SPECIAL FUNDS (COLUMN 3) ARE INCLUDED WITH PRODUCTIVE ENTERPRISE FUNDS (COLUMN 4).
FR—> LES DONNEES RELATIVES AUX FONDS SPECIAUX (COLONNE 3) SONT COMPTEES AVEC CELLES DES ENTRE- PRISES DE LA PRODUCTION (COLONNE 4).
ESP> LOS DATOS RELATIVOS A LOS FONDOS ESPECIALES (COLUMNA 3) QUEDAN ENGLOBADOS EN LOS DE LAS EMPRESAS DE PRODUCCION (COLUMNA 4).

GERMANY, FEDERAL REPUBLIC OF:
E—> SOCIAL SCIENCES AND HUMANITIES IN THE PRODUCTIVE SECTOR ARE NOT INCLUDED.

BANGLADESH (CONT.):
ESP> EXCLUIDOS LOS GASTOS ORDINARIOS DEL SECTOR DE ENSEÑANZA SUPERIOR.

ISRAEL:
E—> DATA REFER TO EXPENDITURE IN THE FIELDS OF NATURAL SCIENCES AND AGRICULTURE ONLY.
FR—> LES DONNEES SE REFERENT AUX DEPENSES DANS LES DOMAINES DES SCIENCES EXACTES ET NATURELLES ET AGRICULTURE SEULEMENT.
ESP> LOS DATOS SOLO SE REFIEREN A LOS GASTOS RELATIVOS A LAS CIENCIAS EXACTAS Y NATURALES Y A LA AGRICULTURA.

JAPAN:
E—> FIGURES IN MILLIONS. NOT INCLUDING DATA FOR THE SOCIAL SCIENCES AND HUMANITIES IN THE PRODUCTIVE SECTOR.
FR—> CHIFFRES EN MILLIONS. NON COMPRIS LES DONNEES POUR LES SCIENCES SOCIALES ET HUMAINES DANS LE SECTEUR DE LA PRODUCTION.
ESP> LAS CIFRAS VIENEN EXPRESADAS EN MILLONES. EXCLUIDOS LOS DATOS RELATIVOS A LAS CIENCIAS SOCIALES Y HUMANAS DEL SECTOR PRODUCTIVO.

KOREA, REPUBLIC OF:
E—> NOT INCLUDING DATA FOR LAW, HUMANITIES AND EDUCATION. DATA RELATING TO SPECIAL FUNDS (COLUMN 3) ARE INCLUDED WITH PRODUCTIVE ENTERPRISE FUNDS (COLUMN 4).
FR—> NON COMPRIS LES DONNEES POUR LE DROIT, LES SCIENCES HUMAINES ET L'EDUCATION. LES DONNEES RELATIVES AUX FONDS SPECIAUX (COLONNE 3) SONT COMPTEES AVEC CELLES DES ENTREPRISES DE LA PRODUCTION (COLONNE 4).
ESP> EXCLUIDOS LOS DATOS RELATIVOS AL DERECHO, LAS CIENCIAS HUMANAS Y LA EDUCACION. LOS DATOS RELATIVOS A LOS FONDOS ESPECIALES (COLUMNA 3) QUEDAN ENGLOBADOS EN LOS DE LAS EMPRESAS DE PRODUCCION (COLUMN 4).

PAKISTAN:
E—> DATA RELATE TO THE YEAR 1973/74 AND REFER TO R&D ACTIVITIES WHICH ARE CONCENTRED MAINLY IN GOVERNMENT-FINANCED RESEARCH ESTABLISHMENTS. SOCIAL SCIENCES AND HUMANITIES IN THE HIGHER EDUCATION AND GENERAL SERVICE SECTORS ARE NOT INCLUDED.
FR—> LES DONNEES SE REFERENT A L'ANNEE 1973/74 ET AUX ACTIVITES DE R-D SE TROUVANT POUR LA PLUPART DANS LES ETABLISSEMENTS DE RECHERCHE FINANCES PAR LE GOUVERNEMENT. LES SCIENCES SOCIALES ET HUMAINES SONT EXCLUES DANS LES SECTEURS DE L'ENSEIGNEMENT SUPERIEUR ET DE SERVICE GENERAL.
ESP> LOS DATOS SE REFIEREN AL AÑO 1973/74 Y A LAS ACTIVIDADES DE I Y D CONCENTRADAS PRINCIPAL- MENTE EN LOS ESTABLECIMIENTOS DE INVESTIGACION SUBVENCIONADOS POR EL GOBIERNO. NO SE INCLUYEN LOS DATOS RELATIVOS A LAS CIENCIAS SOCIALES Y HUMANAS, EN LOS SECTORES DE ENSEÑANZA SUPERIOR Y DE SERVICIO GENERAL.

5.9 R&D expenditure by source of funds
Dépenses de R-D selon la source de financement
Gastos de I y D según la fuente de financiamiento

GERMANY, FEDERAL REPUBLIC OF (CONT.):
FR—> NON COMPRIS LES SCIENCES SOCIALES ET HUMAINES DANS LE SECTEUR DE LA PRODUCTION.
ESP> NO INCLUYE LAS CIENCIAS SOCIALES Y HUMANAS DEL SECTOR PRODUCTIVO.

ITALY:
E—> FIGURES IN MILLIONS.
FR—> CHIFFRES EN MILLIONS.
ESP> CIFRAS EN MILLONES.

MALTA:
E—> DATA RELATE TO THE HIGHER EDUCATION SECTOR ONLY.
FR—> LES DONNEES NE CONCERNENT QUE LE SECTEUR DE L'ENSEIGNEMENT SUPERIEUR
ESP> LOS DATOS SE REFIEREN AL SECTOR DE ENSEÑANZA SUPERIOR SOLAMENTE.

NETHERLANDS:
E—> NOT INCLUDING SOCIAL SCIENCES AND HUMANITIES IN THE PRODUCTIVE SECTOR (INTEGRATED R&D).
FR—> NON COMPRIS LES DONNEES POUR LES SCIENCES SOCIALES ET HUMAINES DU SECTEUR DE LA PRODUCTION (ACTIVITES DE R-D INTEGREES).
ESP> EXCLUIDOS LOS DATOS RELATIVOS A LAS CIENCIAS SOCIALES Y HUMANAS DEL SECTOR PRODUCTIVO (ACTIVIDADES DE I Y D INTEGRADAS).

SWEDEN:
E—> NOT INCLUDING SOCIAL SCIENCES AND HUMANITIES.
FR—> NON COMPRIS LES SCIENCES SOCIALES ET HUMAINES.
ESP> EXCLUIDAS LAS CIENCIAS SOCIALES Y HUMANAS.

UNITED KINGDOM:
E—> NOT INCLUDING SOCIAL SCIENCES AND HUMANITIES. OF THE TOTAL IN COLUMN 6, 32,300 THOUSAND POUNDS STERLING REFER TO UNIVERSITIES' OWN FUNDS.
FR—> NON COMPRIS LES SCIENCES SOCIALES ET HUMAINES. DANS LE TOTAL DE LA COLONNE 6, IL Y A 32 300 000 LIVRES STERLING QUI SE REFERENT AUX FONDS PROPRES DES UNIVERSITES.

UNITED KINGDOM (CONT.):
ESP> EXCLUIDAS LAS CIENCIAS SOCIALES Y HUMANAS. EN EL TOTAL DE LA COLUMNA 6 HAY 32 300 000 LIBRAS ESTERLINAS QUE CORRESPONDEN A LOS FONDOS PROPIOS DE LAS UNIVERSIDADES.

YUGOSLAVIA:
E—> NOT INCLUDING ACTIVITIES OF A MILITARY NATURE OR RELATING TO NATIONAL DEFENCE.
FR—> NON COMPRIS LES ACTIVITES DE CARACTERE MILITAIRE OU RELEVANT DE LA DEFENSE NATIONALE.
ESP> EXCLUIDAS LAS ACTIVIDADES DE CARACTER MILITAR O QUE CONCIERNEN LA DEFENSA NACIONAL.

AMERICAN SAMOA:
E—> DATA RELATE TO ONE RESEARCH INSTITUTE ONLY.
FR—> LES DONNEES NE CONCERNENT QU'UN INSTITUT DE RECHERCHE.
ESP> LOS DATOS SE REFIEREN A UN INSTITUTO DE INVESTIGACION SOLAMENTE.

FRENCH POLYNESIA:
E—> DATA RELATE TO ONE RESEARCH INSTITUTE ONLY.
FR—> LES DONNEES NE CONCERNENT QU'UN INSTITUT DE RECHERCHE.
ESP> LOS DATOS SE REFIEREN A UN INSTITUTO DE INVESTIGACION SOLAMENTE.

GUAM:
E—> DATA RELATE TO THE HIGHER EDUCATION SECTOR ONLY.
FR—> LES DONNEES NE CONCERNENT QUE LE SECTEUR DE L'ENSEIGNEMENT SUPERIEUR.
ESP> LOS DATOS SE REFIEREN AL SECTOR DE ENSEÑANZA SUPERIOR SOLAMENTE.

SAMOA:
E—> DATA RELATING TO SPECIAL FUNDS (COLUMN 3) ARE INCLUDED WITH PRODUCTIVE ENTERPRISE FUNDS (COLUMN 4).
FR—> LES DONNEES RELATIVES AUX FONDS SPECIAUX (COLONNE 3) SONT COMPTEES AVEC CELLES DES ENTRE-PRISES DE LA PRODUCTION (COLONNE 4).
ESP> LOS DATOS RELATIVOS A LOS FONDOS ESPECIALES (COLUMNA 3) QUEDAN ENGLOBADOS EN LOS DE LAS EMPRESAS DE PRODUCCION (COLUMNA 4).

5.10 Intramural R&D expenditure by major aim
Dépenses de R-D intra-muros par finalités principales
Gastos de I y D intramuros por finalidades principales

5.10 Intramural expenditure for the performance of research and experimental development by major aim

Dépenses intra-muros afférentes aux activités de recherche et de développement expérimental, par finalités principales

PLEASE REFER TO INTRODUCTION FOR DEFINITIONS OF CATEGORIES INCLUDED IN THIS TABLE.

POUR LES DEFINITIONS DES CATEGORIES PRESENTEES DANS CE TABLEAU, SE REFERER A L'INTRODUCTION.

T = TOTAL EXPENDITURE
G = GOVERNMENT EXPENDITURE

T = DEPENSES TOTALES
G = DEPENSES PUBLIQUES

NUMBER OF COUNTRIES AND TERRITORIES PRESENTED IN THIS TABLE: 39

NOMBRE DE PAYS ET DE TERRITOIRES PRESENTES DANS CE TABLEAU: 39

					REPARTITION EN POURCENTAGE		
					EARTH AND SPACE LA TERRE ET L'ESPACE LA TIERRA Y EL ESPACIO I	AGRICULTURE AGRICULTURE AGRICULTURA II	INDUSTRIAL DEVELOPMENT DEVELOPPEMENT INDUSTRIEL DESARROLLO INDUSTRIAL III
COUNTRY / PAYS / PAIS	FISCAL YEAR BEGINNING / EXERCICE FINANCIER COMMENCANT EN / COMIENZO DEL EJERCICIO ECONOMICO	CURRENCY / MONNAIE / MONEDA	TYPE OF EXPENDITURE / TYPE DE DEPENSES / TIPO DE GASTOS	TOTAL (000)	%	%	%
				(1)	(2)	(3)	(4)
AFRICA							
SUDAN ‡	1973	POUND	T	3 012	./.	*63.4	*14.6
ZAMBIA	1972	KWACHA	T	6 261	28.9	30.9	8.3
AMERICA, NORTH							
CANADA ‡	1975	DOLLAR	G	1 000 500	5.0	20.7	16.8
CUBA	1977	PESO	T	62 442	–	32.9	15.9
GUATEMALA	1974	QUETZAL	T	*5 139	8.4	25.9	11.0
MEXICO ‡	1973	PESO	G	1 128 845	2.4	21.4	6.8
PANAMA	1975	BALBOA	G	1 765	13.6	9.9	14.4
UNITED STATES OF AMERICA ‡	1976	DOLLAR	G	23 929 100	14.8	1.9	1.5
AMERICA, SOUTH							
ARGENTINA	1976	PESO	T	*23 171 700	*2.5	*28.0	*11.5
BRAZIL	1977	CRUZEIRO	G	10 337 400	5.3	13.4	14.4
COLOMBIA	1977	PESO	G	644 442	2.8	43.9	6.3
VENEZUELA ‡	1973	BOLIVAR	T	235 257	...	25.8	18.6
ASIA							
BANGLADESH ‡	1974	TAKA	G	96 700	11.5	63.0	0.6
BRUNEI	1974	DOLLAR	G	3 055	75.5	–	–
INDIA ‡	1976	RUPEE	T	3 103 013	6.0	20.2	25.7
JAPAN ‡	1976	YEN	T	504 438 000	1.6	21.7	21.3
PAKISTAN ‡	1973	RUPEE	G	150 430	10.6	25.4	16.8
PHILIPPINES ‡	1976	PESO	T	176 930	3.5	46.2	12.3
SRI LANKA ‡	1975	RUPEE	G	24 140	–	48.8	10.8
THAILAND ‡	1975	BAHT	T	33 587 313	–	12.6	0.6

Intramural R&D expenditure by major aim   5.10
Dépenses de R-D intra-muros par finalités principales
Gastos de I y D intramuros por finalidades principales

Gastos intramuros destinados a las actividades de investigación y de desarrollo experimental, por finalidades principales

EN LA INTRODUCCION SE DAN LAS DEFINICIONES DE LAS
CATEGORIAS QUE FIGURAN EN ESTE CUADRO.

T = GASTOS TOTALES
G = GASTOS PUBLICOS

NUMERO DE PAISES Y DE TERRITORIOS PRESENTADOS EN
ESTE CUADRO: 39

PERCENTAGE DISTRIBUTION OF MAJOR AIMS /
DES FINALITES PRINCIPALES / REPARTICION EN PORCENTAJE DE LAS FINALIDADES PRINCIPALES

ENERGY ENERGIE ENERGIA IV % (5)	TRANSPORT AND COMMUNICATION TRANSPORTS ET COMMUNICATIONS TRANSPORTES Y COMUNICACIONES V % (6)	EDUCATION SERVICES SERVICES D'ENSEIGNEMENT SERVICIOS EDUCATIVOS VI % (7)	HEALTH SERVICES SERVICES DE SANTE SERVICIOS DE SANIDAD VII % (8)	SOCIO-ECONOMIC SERVICES SERVICES SOCIO-ECONOMIQUES SERVICIOS SOCIO-ECONOMICOS VIII % (9)	ENVIRONMENT ENVIRONNEMENT MEDIO AMBIENTE IX % (10)	ADVANCEMENT OF KNOWLEDGE PROMOTION DES CONNAISSANCES ADELANTO GENERAL DEL SABER X % (11)	OTHER AIMS AUTRES FINALITES OTRAS FINALIDADES XI % (12)	DEFENCE DEFENSE DEFENSA XII % (13)	COUNTRY PAYS PAIS
									AFRICA
*5.7	./.	./.	./.	./.	./.	*8.9	*0.6	./.	SUDAN ‡
–	–	0.8	3.9	–	–	27.3	–	–	ZAMBIA
									AMERICA, NORTH
8.5	4.2	./.	9.0	8.0	1.6	18.8	0.7	6.7	CANADA ‡
1.3	3.7	0.1	18.9	3.1	./.	12.9	11.2	–	CUBA
7.8	8.1	4.8	9.2	23.4	–	–	1.4	–	GUATEMALA
21.7	1.3	2.6	11.4	8.5	7.5	14.4	2.2	–	MEXICO ‡
18.6	–	–	0.6	40.7	–	–	2.2	–	PANAMA
9.6	2.9	0.5	12.4	1.1	1.3	3.8	0.6	49.6	UNITED STATES OF AMERICA ‡
									AMERICA, SOUTH
*4.5	*4.0	*2.5	*21.5	*2.5	*3.0	*10.0	*3.5	*6.5	ARGENTINA
22.3	5.7	1.6	0.6	3.8	0.8	26.9	5.2	./.	BRAZIL
4.6	8.4	2.2	9.9	3.6	2.1	15.7	0.5	–	COLOMBIA
0.5	1.5	5.4	26.1	1.5	0.8	12.3	7.4	...	VENEZUELA ‡
									ASIA
./.	0.5	1.9	1.2	./.	./.	./.	11.1	10.1	BANGLADESH ‡
–	–	–	–	–	–	–	24.5	–	BRUNEI
1.2	17.2	./.	6.2	0.3	./.	3.9	0.2	19.0	INDIA ‡
16.6	3.3	...	6.7	2.7	2.1	5.2	15.0	3.7	JAPAN ‡
24.7	7.8	5.8	4.6	./.	./.	./.	4.3	./.	PAKISTAN ‡
5.6	0.6	6.0	9.7	5.6	2.1	2.1	1.5	4.8	PHILIPPINES ‡
–	0.1	–	5.2	14.9	–	9.4	10.7	–	SRI LANKA ‡
0.9	15.9	29.8	4.5	11.1	–	–	–	24.6	THAILAND ‡

5.10 Intramural R&D expenditure by major aim
Dépenses de R-D intra-muros par finalités principales
Gastos de I y D intramuros por finalidades principales

COUNTRY / PAYS / PAIS	FISCAL YEAR BEGINNING / EXERCICE FINANCIER COMMENCANT EN / COMIENZO DEL EJERCICIO ECONOMICO	CURRENCY / MONNAIE / MONEDA	TYPE OF EXPENDITURE / TYPE DE DEPENSES / TIPO DE GASTOS	TOTAL (000)	REPARTITION EN POURCENTAGE		
					EARTH AND SPACE LA TERRE ET L'ESPACE LA TIERRA Y EL ESPACIO I %	AGRICULTURE AGRICULTURE AGRICULTURA II %	INDUSTRIAL DEVELOPMENT DEVELOPPEMENT INDUSTRIEL DESARROLLO INDUSTRIAL III %
				(1)	(2)	(3)	(4)
EUROPE							
DENMARK ‡	1976	KRONE	G	1 391 000	2.4	8.5	8.6
FINLAND ‡	1973	MARKKA	G	344 310	4.8	11.4	12.3
FRANCE ‡	1977	FRANC	G	19 933 000	8.4	4.0	11.4
GERMANY, FEDERAL REPUBLIC OF ‡	1977	DEUTSCHE MARK	G	12 702 500	6.8	2.1	6.2
HOLY SEE	1976	LIRA	T	1 677 989	–	–	–
HUNGARY ‡	1976	FORINT	T	9 030 000	./.	5.1	66.6
IRELAND ‡	1975	POUND	T	16 661	2.9	40.8	21.9
ITALY	1976	LIRA	G	582 807 000	10.5	3.1	10.4
NETHERLANDS	1976	GUILDER	T	4 964 000	0.6	4.7	54.3
NORWAY ‡	1977	KRONER	T	2 342 300	2.7	7.4	39.8
PORTUGAL ‡	1976	ESCUDO	T	726 783	8.0	42.8	8.8
SWEDEN ‡	1975	KRONOR	T	4 754 200	0.9	1.5	53.8
SWITZERLAND ‡	1975	FRANC	G	638 000	2.0	10.5	3.6
UNITED KINGDOM ‡	1975	POUND STERLING	G	1 381 700	0.7	4.4	10.3
OCEANIA							
AUSTRALIA	1973	DOLLAR	G	396 204	...	...	...
GUAM ‡	1973	U.S. DOLLAR	G	572	–	–	–
NEW HEBRIDES	1975	FRANC	G	19 941	–	100.0	–
NEW ZEALAND ‡	1975	DOLLAR	G	79 974	19.3	40.8	8.9
SAMOA	1975	TALA	G	217	–	8.9	8.7

SUDAN:
E—> DATA FOR COLUMNS 2, 6, 7, 8, 9, 10 AND 13 ARE NOT SEPARATELY AVAILABLE. FIGURES IN COLUMN 5 REFER TO "INFRASTRUCTURE AND SERVICES".
FR—> LA REPARTITION DES DONNEES RELATIVES AUX COLONNES 2, 6, 7, 8, 9, 10 ET 13 N'EST PAS DISPONIBLE. LES CHIFFRES DE LA COLONNE 5 CONCER-NENT L'"INFRAESTRUCTURE ET LES SERVICES".
ESP> NO SE DISPONE POR SEPARADO DE LOS DATOS CORRESPONDIENTES A LAS COLUMNAS 2, 6, 7, 8, 9, 10 Y 13. LAS CIFRAS DE LA COLUMNA 5 SE REFIEREN A "LA INFRAESTRUCTURA Y LOS SERVICIOS".

CANADA:
E—> DATA RELATE TO CURRENT EXPENDITURE ONLY.
FR—> LES DONNEES SE REFERENT AUX DEPENSES COURANTES SEULEMENT.
ESP> LOS DATOS SE REFIEREN A LOS GASTOS ORDI-NARIOS SOLAMENTE.

MEXICO:
E—> DATA REFER TO THE PUBLIC SECTOR EXPENDI-TURE, I.E., "GOBIERNO GENERAL", STATE PARTICI-PATION ENTERPRISES, AND PUBLIC CENTRES OF HIGHER EDUCATION.

MEXICO (CONT.):
FR—> LES DONNEES SE REFERENT AUX DEPENSES DU SECTEUR PUBLIC QUI COMPREND: LE "GOBIERNO GENERAL" LES ENTREPRISES AVEC PARTICIPATION DE L'ETAT ET LES CENTRES PUBLICS D'ENSEIGNEMENT SUPERIEUR.
ESP> LOS DATOS SE REFIEREN A LOS GASTOS DEL SECTOR PUBLICO QUE COMPRENDEN: EL GOBIERNO GENERAL LAS EMPRESAS A PARTICIPACION ESTATAL Y LOS CENTROS PUBLICOS DE ENSEÑANZA SUPERIOR.

UNITED STATES OF AMERICA:
E—> DATA ARE BASED ON FEDERAL OBLIGATIONS BY FUNCTION.
FR—> DONNEES BASEES SUR LES ENGAGEMENTS FEDE-RAUX DE R-D PAR FONCTION.
ESP> LOS DATOS SE BASAN EN LAS OBLIGACIONES FEDERALES DE I Y D POR FUNCIONES.

VENEZUELA:
E—> NOT INCLUDING DATA FOR COLUMNS 2 AND 13.
FR—> NON COMPRIS LES DONNEES RELATIVES AUX COLONNES 2 ET 13.
ESP> EXCLUIDOS LOS DATOS RELATIVOS A LAS COLUMNAS 2 Y 13.

Intramural R&D expenditure by major aim   5.10
Dépenses de R-D intra-muros par finalités principales
Gastos de I y D intramuros por finalidades principales

PERCENTAGE DISTRIBUTION OF MAJOR AIMS / DES FINALITES PRINCIPALES / REPARTICION EN PORCENTAJE DE LAS FINALIDADES PRINCIPALES

ENERGY ENERGIE ENERGIA IV %	TRANSPORT AND COMMUNICATION TRANSPORTS ET COMMUNICATIONS TRANSPORTES Y COMUNICACIONES V %	EDUCATION SERVICES SERVICES D'ENSEIGNEMENT SERVICIOS EDUCATIVOS VI %	HEALTH SERVICES SERVICES DE SANTE SERVICIOS DE SANIDAD VII %	SOCIO-ECONOMIC SERVICES SERVICES SOCIO-ECONOMIQUES SERVICIOS SOCIO-ECONOMICOS VIII %	ENVIRONMENT ENVIRONNEMENT MEDIO AMBIENTE IX %	ADVANCEMENT OF KNOWLEDGE PROMOTION DES CONNAISSANCES ADELANTO GENERAL DEL SABER X %	OTHER AIMS AUTRES FINALITES OTRAS FINALIDADES XI %	DEFENCE DEFENSE DEFENSA XII %	COUNTRY PAYS PAIS
(5)	(6)	(7)	(8)	(9)	(10)	(11)	(12)	(13)	
									EUROPE
2.2	0.4	0.5	6.1	5.0	0.9	60.5	4.2	0.8	DENMARK ‡
3.6	1.3	1.4	0.8	7.5	1.0	51.7	–	4.3	FINLAND ‡
8.4	3.2	./.	4.4	1.4	1.1	25.2	1.8	30.6	FRANCE ‡
12.3	1.6	./.	3.6	4.5	1.3	47.5	1.4	12.7	GERMANY, FEDERAL REPUBLIC OF ‡
–	–	100.0	–	–	–	–	–	–	HOLY SEE
⟶	1.5	1.1	⟶	./.	./.	15.8	9.8	...	HUNGARY ‡
0.7	2.0	1.8	7.0	4.9	5.6	12.5	–	–	IRELAND ‡
20.8	0.4	0.1	3.0	1.0	0.7	44.6	1.0	4.5	ITALY
1.9	0.9	0.3	2.4	1.3	1.2	29.2	1.8	1.3	NETHERLANDS
3.3	4.4	1.0	5.7	5.6	3.1	22.7	–	4.3	NORWAY ‡
⟶	17.8	./.	8.5	6.5	./.	1.8	5.8	–	PORTUGAL ‡
3.8	2.9	0.0	0.6	1.2	0.5	23.4	0.0	11.5	SWEDEN ‡
7.4	4.5	1.3	17.9	1.4	3.1	40.3	3.1	4.9	SWITZERLAND ‡
6.5	0.6	./.	2.1	0.9	2.4	21.4	2.3	48.4	UNITED KINGDOM ‡
									OCEANIA
...	...	0.3	1.8	2.2	2.6	...	...	12.4	AUSTRALIA
4.7	–	–	–	–	–	95.3	–	–	GUAM ‡
–	–	–	–	–	–	–	–	–	NEW HEBRIDES
–	1.2	./.	6.4	3.0	–	16.2	5.0	–	NEW ZEALAND‡
7.0	28.5	9.2	28.0	–	–	2.8	6.9	–	SAMOA

BANGLADESH:
   E—> DATA FOR COLUMNS 5, 9, 10, AND 11 ARE NOT AVAILABLE SEPARATELY.
   FR—> LA REPARTITION DES DONNEES RELATIVES AUX COLONNES 5, 9, 10 ET 11 N'EST PAS DISPONIBLE.
   ESP> NO SE DISPONE POR SEPARADO DE LOS DATOS CORRESPONDIENTES A LAS COLUMNAS 5, 9, 10 Y 11.

INDIA:
   E—> NOT INCLUDING 920, 000 THOUSAND RUPEES FOR WHICH DATA BY MAJOR AIM ARE NOT AVAILABLE.
   FR—> NON COMPRIS LA SOMME DE 920 000 MILLIERS DE ROUPIES POUR LAQUELLE LES DONNEES PAR FINALITES PRINCIPALES NE SONT PAS DISPONIBLES.
   ESP> NO INCLUYE LA SUMA DE 920 000 MILLARES DE RUPIAS, PARA LA QUE NO SE DISPONE DE DATOS POR FINALIDADES PRINCIPALES.

JAPAN:
   E—> DATA RELATE TO TOTAL EXPENDITURE IN THE GENERAL SERVICE SECTOR ONLY. DATA FOR COLUMN 7 ARE NOT AVAILABLE SEPARATELY.
   FR—> LES DONNEES SE REFERENT AUX DEPENSES TOTA-LES DU SECTEUR DE SERVICE GENERAL. LES DONNEES DE LA COLONNE 7 NE SONT PAS DISPONIBLES SEPAREMENT.
   ESP> LOS DATOS SE REFIEREN UNICAMENTE A LOS

JAPAN (CONT.):
GASTOS TOTALES DEL SECTOR DE SERVICIO GENERAL. NO SE DISPONE POR SEPARADO DE LOS DATOS CORRES-PONDIENTES A LA COLUMNA 7.

PAKISTAN:
   E—> NOT INCLUDING DATA FOR SOCIAL SCIENCES AND HUMANITIES IN THE HIGHER EDUCATION AND GENERAL SERVICE SECTORS.
   FR—> NON COMPRIS LES DONNEES POUR LES SCIENCES SOCIALES ET HUMAINES DANS LES SECTEURS DE L'ENSEI-GNEMENT SUPERIEUR ET DE SERVICE GENERAL.
   ESP> NO SE INCLUYEN LOS DATOS RELATIVOS A LAS CIENCIAS SOCIALES Y HUMANAS DE LOS SECTORES DE ENSEÑANZA SUPERIOR Y DE SERVICIO GENERAL.

PHILIPPINES:
   E—> DATA RELATE TO TOTAL EXPENDITURE IN THE GENERAL SERVICE SECTOR ONLY.
   FR—> LES DONNEES SE REFERENT AUX DEPENSES TOTALES DU SECTEUR DE SERVICE GENERAL SEULEMENT.
   ESP> LOS DATOS SE REFIEREN A LOS GASTOS TOTALES DEL SECTOR DE SERVICIO GENERAL SOLAMENTE.

5.10 Intramural R&D expenditure by major aim
Dépenses de R-D intra-muros par finalités principales
Gastos de I y D intramuros por finalidades principales

SRI LANKA:
E—> NOT INCLUDING CAPITAL EXPENDITURE FOR THE
HIGHER EDUCATION SECTOR.
FR—> NON COMPRIS LES DEPENSES EN CAPITAL DANS
LE SECTEUR DE L'ENSEIGNEMENT SUPERIEUR.
ESP> EXCLUIDOS LOS GASTOS DE CAPITAL DEL SECTOR
DE ENSEÑANZA SUPERIOR.

THAILAND:
E—> DATA ARE BASED ON THE PROVISIONAL BUDGET
FOR 1975.
FR—> LES DONNEES SONT FONDEES SUR LE BUDGET
PROVISOIRE POUR 1975.
ESP> LOS DATOS ESTAN BASADOS EN EL PRESUPUESTO
PROVISIONAL PARA 1975.

DENMARK:
E—> DATA ARE BASED ON A GOVERNMENT BUDGET ANA-
LYSIS. DATA RELATING TO "SPACE RESEARCH" ARE
INCLUDED IN COLUMN 12.
FR—> LES DONNEES SONT FONDEES SUR UNE ANALYSE
DU BUDGET. LES DONNEES CONCERNANT LA "RECHERCHE
SPATIALE" SONT COMPRISES DANS LA COLONNE 12.
ESP> LOS DATOS ESTAN BASADOS EN UN ANALISIS DEL
PRESUPUESTO. LOS DATOS RELATIVOS A LA "INVESTIGA-
CION ESPACIAL" ESTAN INCLUIDOS EN LA COLUMNA 12.

FINLAND:
E—> DATA ARE BASED ON A BUDGET ANALYSIS.
FR—> LES DONNEES SONT FONDEES SUR UNE ANALYSE
DU BUDGET.
ESP> LOS DATOS ESTAN BASADOS EN UN ANALISIS DEL
PRESUPUESTO.

FRANCE:
E—> DATA FOR COLUMN 7 ARE NOT AVAILABLE SEPARA-
TELY.
FR—> LES DONNEES RELATIVES A LA COLONNE 7 NE
SONT PAS DISPONIBLES SEPAREMENT.
ESP> NO SE DISPONE POR SEPARADO DE LOS DATOS
CORRESPONDIENTES A LA COLUMNA 7.

GERMANY, FEDERAL REPUBLIC OF:
E—> IN ADDITION, THE FIGURES INCLUDE FUNDS
GIVEN FOR FOREIGN AID. DATA FOR COLUMN 7 ARE IN-
CLUDED UNDER COLUMN 9. SOCIAL SCIENCES AND HUMA-
NITIES IN THE PRODUCTIVE SECTOR ARE NOT INCLUDED.
FR—> EN OUTRE, LES CHIFFRES COMPRENNENT DES
FONDS DESTINES A L'AIDE ETRANGERE. LES DONNEES
RELATIVES A LA COLONNE 7 SONT INCLUSES DANS LA
COLONNE 9. NON COMPRIS LES DONNEES POUR LES
SCIENCES SOCIALES ET HUMAINES DANS LE SECTEUR DE
LA PRODUCTION.
ESP> LA CIFRAS TAMBIEN COMPRENDEN LOS FONDOS
DESTINADOS A LA AYUDA EXTRANJERA. LOS DATOS
RELATIVOS A LA COLUMNA 7 QUEDAN INCLUIDOS EN LA
LA COLUMNA 9. NO INCLUYE LOS DATOS RELATIVOS A
LAS CIENCIAS SOCIALES Y HUMANAS DEL SECTOR PRO-
DUCTIVO.

HUNGARY:
E—> DATA REFER ONLY TO DIRECT EXPENDITURE ON
RESEARCH; DATA FOR COLUMNS 2, 9 AND 10 ARE INCLU-
DED UNDER COLUMN 12.
FR—> LES DONNEES CONCERNENT SEULEMENT LES
DEPENSES DIRECTES CONSACREES A LA RECHERCHE;
LES CHIFFRES RELATIFS AUX COLONNES 2, 9 ET 10
SONT COMPRIS DANS LA COLONNE 12.
ESP> LOS DATOS SE REFIEREN A LOS GASTOS
DIRECTOS CORRESPONDIENTES UNICAMENTE A LA INVES-
TIGACION; LOS DATOS RELATIVOS A LAS COLUMNAS 2,
9 Y 10 ESTAN INCLUIDOS EN LA COLUMNA 12.

IRELAND:
E—> DATA RELATE TO TOTAL EXPENDITURE IN THE
GENERAL SERVICE SECTOR ONLY.
FR—> LES DONNEES SE REFERENT AUX DEPENSES
TOTALES DU SECTEUR DE SERVICE GENERAL SEULEMENT.

IRELAND (CONT.):
ESP> LOS DATOS SE REFIEREN A LOS GASTOS TOTALES
DEL SECTOR DE SERVICIO GENERAL SOLAMENTE.

NORWAY:
E—>DATA RELATE TO CURRENT EXPENDITURE ONLY.
FR—> LES DONNEES SE REFERENT AUX DEPENSES
COURANTES SEULEMENT.
ESP> LOS DATOS SE REFIEREN A LOS GASTOS ORDINA-
RIOS SOLAMENTE.

PORTUGAL:
E—> DATA RELATE TO TOTAL EXPENDITURE IN THE
GENERAL SERVICE SECTOR ONLY, WITH THE EXCEPTION OF
59, 115 THOUSAND ESCUDOS FROM PRIVATE NON-PROFIT
ORGANIZATIONS. DATA FOR COLUMN 7 ARE INCLUDED UNDER
COLUMN 9 AND FOR COLUMN 10 UNDER COLUMN 6.
FR—> LES DONNEES SE REFERENT AUX DEPENSES DU
SECTEUR DE SERVICE GENERAL, A L'EXCEPTION DE 59 115
MILLIERS D'ESCUDOS PROVENANT DES ORGANISATIONS
PRIVEES A BUT NON LUCRATIF. LES DONNEES RELATIVES
A LA COLONNE 7 SONT COMPRISES DANS LA COLONNE 9 ET
CELLES DE LA COLONNE 10 DANS LA COLONNE 6.
ESP> LOS DATOS SE REFIEREN A LOS GASTOS TOTALES
DEL SECTOR DE SERVICIO GENERAL, EXCEPTUADA LA SUMA
DE 59 115 MILLARES DE ESCUDOS PROCEDENTE DE LAS
ORGANIZACIONES PRIVADAS DE CARACTER NO LUCRATIVO.
LOS DATOS CORRESPONDIENTES A LA COLUMNA 7 ESTAN
INCLUIDOS EN LA COLUMNA 9 Y LOS DE LA COLUMNA 10
EN LA COLUMNA 6.

SWEDEN:
E—> DATA RELATE TO CURRENT EXPENDITURE ONLY;
NOT INCLUDING DATA FOR SOCIAL SCIENCES AND HUMA-
NITIES.
FR—> LES DONNEES SE REFERENT AUX DEPENSES COU-
RANTES SEULEMENT; NON COMPRIS LES DONNEES POUR LES
SCIENCES SOCIALES ET HUMAINES.
ESP> LOS DATOS SE REFIEREN UNICAMENTE A LOS
GASTOS ORDINARIOS. EXCLUIDOS LOS DATOS RELATIVOS
A LAS CIENCIAS SOCIALES Y HUMANAS.

SWITZERLAND:
E—> DATA REFER TO THE FEDERAL ADMINISTRATION
AND "HAUTES ECOLES"; NOT INCLUDING CAPITAL EXPEN-
DITURE AMOUNTING TO 87 MILLION FRANCS FOR THE
"HAUTES ECOLES".
FR—> LES DONNEES SE REFERENT A L'ADMINISTRATION
FEDERALE ET AUX HAUTES ECOLES; COMPTE NON TENU DES
DEPENSES EN CAPITAL D'UN MONTANT DE 87 MILLIONS
DE FRANCS POUR LES HAUTES ECOLES.
ESP> LOS DATOS SE REFIEREN A LA ADMINISTRACION
FEDERAL Y A LAS "HAUTES ECOLES"; EXCLUIDOS LOS
GASTOS DE CAPITAL QUE ASCIENDEN A 87 MILLONES DE
FRANCOS PARA LAS "HAUTES ECOLES".

UNITED KINGDOM:
E—> DATA RELATE TO GOVERNMENT NET EXPENDITURE
(INTRAMURAL AND EXTRAMURAL); DATA FOR URBAN AND
RURAL PLANNING ARE INCLUDED UNDER COLUMN 6; DATA
FOR COLUMN 7 ARE INCLUDED UNDER COLUMNS 9 AND 11.
FR—> LES DONNEES SE REFERENT AUX DEPENSES NETTES
DU GOUVERNEMENT (INTRA-MUROS ET EXTRA-MUROS).
LES DONNEES POUR LA PLANIFICATION URBAINE ET RURA-
LE SONT INCLUSES DANS LA COLONNE 6. LES DONNEES
DE LA COLONNE 7 SONT COMPRISES DANS LES COLONNES
9 ET 11.
ESP> LOS DATOS SE REFIEREN A LOS GASTOS NETOS
DEL GOBIERNO (INTRA-MUROS Y EXTRA-MUROS). LOS
DATOS PARA LA PLANIFICACION URBANA Y RURAL ESTAN
INCLUIDOS EN LA COLUMNA 6 Y LOS DE LA COLUMNA 7
EN LAS COLUMNAS 9 Y 11.

GUAM:
E—> DATA REFER TO THE UNIVERSITY OF GUAM ONLY.
FR—> LES DONNEES SE REFERENT A L'UNIVERSITE DE
GUAM SEULEMENT.

Intramural R&D expenditure by major aim 5.10
Dépenses de R-D intra-muros par finalités principales
Gastos de I y D intramuros por finalidades principales

GUAM (CONT.):
  ESP> LOS DATOS SE REFIEREN A LA UNIVERSIDAD DE
GUAM SOLAMENTE.

NEW ZEALAND:
  E—> DATA FOR COLUMN 7 ARE INCLUDED UNDER
COLUMN 9.
  FR—> LES DONNEES RELATIVES A LA COLONNE 7
SONT INCLUSES DANS LA COLONNE 9.
  ESP> LOS DATOS RELATIVOS A LA COLUMNA 7 ESTAN
INCLUIDOS EN LA COLUMNA 9.

Historical data for R&D personnel   5.11
Données rétrospectives pour le personnel de R-D
Datos retrospectivos sobre el personal de I y D

5.11 Personnel engaged in research and experimental development: selected data for recent years

Personnel employé à des travaux de recherche et de développement expérimental: données sélectionnées pour des années récentes

Personal empleado en actividades de investigación y de desarrollo experimental: datos seleccionados sobre los últimos años

PLEASE REFER TO INTRODUCTION FOR DEFINITIONS OF CATEGORIES INCLUDED IN THIS TABLE.	POUR LES DEFINITIONS DES CATEGORIES PRESENTEES DANS CE TABLEAU, SE REFERER A L'INTRODUCTION.	EN LA INTRODUCCION SE DAN LAS DEFINICIONES DE LAS CATEGORIAS QUE FIGURAN EN ESTE CUADRO.
FTE = FULL—TIME EQUIVALENT	FTE = EQUIVALENT PLEIN TEMPS	FTE = EQUIVALENTE DE JORNADA COMPLETA
NUMBER OF COUNTRIES AND TERRITORIES PRESENTED IN THIS TABLE: 66	NOMBRE DE PAYS ET DE TERRITOIRES PRESENTES DANS CE TABLEAU: 66	NUMERO DE PAISES Y DE TERRITORIOS PRESENTADOS EN ESTE CUADRO: 66

			PERSONNEL ENGAGED IN R & D PERSONNEL EMPLOYE A DES TRAVAUX DE R—D PERSONAL DEDICADO A ACTIVIDADES DE I Y D	
			SCIENTISTS AND ENGINEERS SCIENTIFIQUES ET INGENIEURS CIENTIFICOS E INGENIEROS	
COUNTRY PAYS PAIS	YEAR ANNEE AÑO	TOTAL TOTAL TOTAL	NUMBER (FTE) NOMBRE (FTE) NUMERO (FTE)	INDEXES OF SCIENTISTS AND ENGINEERS (1969 = 100) INDICES DES SCIENTIFIQUES ET INGENIEURS (1969 = 100) INDICES DE LOS CIENTIFICOS E INGENIEROS (1969 = 100)
		(1)	(2)	(3)
DEVELOPING COUNTRIES				
AFRICA				
GABON ‡	1969 1970	84 86	6 8	100 133
GHANA ‡	1969 1970 1974 1975 1976	2 096 4 092 8 906 9 351 9 819	1 015 1 713 3 704 3 889 4 084	100 169 365 383 402
MADAGASCAR ‡	1970 1971	224 298	165 201	100 122
MAURITIUS	1969 1970 1975 1976 1977	*335 *364 605 521 649	61 78 135 138 151	100 128 221 226 248

5.11 Historical data for R&D personnel
Données rétrospectives pour le personnel de R-D
Datos retrospectivos sobre el personal de I y D

			PERSONNEL ENGAGED IN R & D PERSONNEL EMPLOYE A DES TRAVAUX DE R—D PERSONAL DEDICADO A ACTIVIDADES DE I Y D		
			SCIENTISTS AND ENGINEERS SCIENTIFIQUES ET INGENIEURS CIENTIFICOS E INGENIEROS		
COUNTRY	YEAR	TOTAL	NUMBER (FTE)	INDEXES OF SCIENTISTS AND ENGINEERS (1969 = 100)	
PAYS	ANNEE	TOTAL	NOMBRE (FTE)	INDICES DES SCIENTIFIQUES ET INGENIEURS (1969 = 100)	
PAIS	AÑO	TOTAL	NUMERO (FTE)	INDICES DE LOS CIENTIFICOS E INGENIEROS (1969 = 100)	
		(1)	(2)	(3)	
NIGER ‡	1972	...	28	100	
	1974	...	53	189	
	1975	...	79	282	
	1976	94	93	332	
SEYCHELLES	1969	...	1	100	
	1970	...	1	100	
	1971	2	2	200	
	1972	2	2	200	
	1973	1	1	100	
SUDAN ‡	1971	6 378	1 521	100	
	1974	16 598	3 324	218	
	1978	21 596	3 266	215	
ZAMBIA ‡	1969	*240	*60	100	
	1970	*285	*75	125	
	1973	1 060	260	433	
AMERICA, NORTH					
BERMUDA ‡	1969	10	4	100	
	1970	10	4	100	
CUBA	1969	12 361	1 850	100	
	1977	19 659	4 959	268	
	1978	19 868	4 972	269	
GUATEMALA ‡	1970	364	230	100	
	1972	*522	*267	116	
	1974	749	310	135	
	1978	981	549	239	
MEXICO ‡	1969	...	3 665	100	
	1970	12 456	3 743	102	
	1971	13 525	4 064	111	
	1974	...	8 446	230	
ST. PIERRE AND MIQUELON ‡	1969	6	5	100	
	1970	11	7	140	
	1972	11	7	140	
TURKS AND CAICOS ISLANDS ‡	1970	0.5	0.5	100	
	1972	3	2	400	
	1974	3	3	600	
	1975	3	3	600	
	1976	2	2	400	
AMERICA, SOUTH					
ARGENTINA ‡	1970	*21 250	*6 500	100	
	1975	*25 000	*7 500	115	
	1976	*26 500	*8 000	123	
	1977	*27 000	*8 100	123	
	1978	*27 500	*8 250	127	

Historical data for R&D personnel   5.11
Données rétrospectives pour le personnel de R-D
Datos retrospectivos sobre el personal de I y D

COUNTRY / PAYS / PAIS	YEAR / ANNEE / AÑO	PERSONNEL ENGAGED IN R & D / PERSONNEL EMPLOYE A DES TRAVAUX DE R—D / PERSONAL DEDICADO A ACTIVIDADES DE I Y D	SCIENTISTS AND ENGINEERS / SCIENTIFIQUES ET INGENIEURS / CIENTIFICOS E INGENIEROS	
		TOTAL / TOTAL / TOTAL	NUMBER (FTE) / NOMBRE (FTE) / NUMERO (FTE)	INDEXES OF SCIENTISTS AND ENGINEERS (1969 = 100) / INDICES DES SCIENTIFIQUES ET INGENIEURS (1969 = 100) / INDICES DE LOS CIENTIFICOS E INGENIEROS (1969 = 100)
		(1)	(2)	(3)
ECUADOR ‡	1970	1 103	595	100
	1973	761	544	91
FALKLAND ISLANDS (MALVINAS)	1969	6	5	100
	1970	—	—	—
	1971	—	—	—
VENEZUELA ‡	1970	4 608	1 779	100
	1973	5 109	2 720	153
	1975	...	1 759	99
ASIA				
BRUNEI ‡	1971	141	7	100
	1974	426	22	314
CYPRUS	1969	420	107	100
	1970	430	110	103
	1971	511	117	109
INDIA ‡	1973	40 497	...	...
	1974	59 239	...	...
	1976	54 105	...	...
IRAN ‡	1970	6 432	3 007	100
	1971	8 223	3 584	119
	1972	9 865	4 896	163
IRAQ ‡	1969	169	116	100
	1970	167	124	148
	1972	248	170	202
	1973	316	205	244
	1974	365	240	286
JORDAN ‡	1973	221	180	100
	1975	448	235	131
	1976	417	208	116
KOREA, REPUBLIC OF ‡	1969	12 145	5 337	100
	1970	12 922	5 628	105
	1976	27 051	11 661	218
	1977	30 867	12 771	239
	1978	30 214	14 749	276
PAKISTAN ‡	1971	7 231	3 655	100
	1973	8 790	4 164	114
VIET—NAM ‡	1972	15 630	7 780	100
	1974	16 490	9 160	117
	1976	24 560	11 230	144
	1978	25 050	13 050	168

5.11 Historical data for R&D personnel
Données rétrospectives pour le personnel de R-D
Datos retrospectivos sobre el personal de I y D

| | | | PERSONNEL ENGAGED IN R & D
PERSONNEL EMPLOYE A DES TRAVAUX DE R–D
PERSONAL DEDICADO A ACTIVIDADES DE I Y D | |
| | | | SCIENTISTS AND ENGINEERS
SCIENTIFIQUES ET INGENIEURS
CIENTIFICOS E INGENIEROS | |
COUNTRY PAYS PAIS	YEAR ANNEE AÑO	TOTAL TOTAL TOTAL	NUMBER (FTE) NOMBRE (FTE) NUMERO (FTE)	INDEXES OF SCIENTISTS AND ENGINEERS (1969 = 100) INDICES DES SCIENTIFIQUES ET INGENIEURS (1969 = 100) INDICES DE LOS CIENTIFICOS E INGENIEROS (1969 = 100)
		(1)	(2)	(3)
OCEANIA				
AMERICAN SAMOA ‡	1969	14	2	100
	1970	14	2	100
	1971	15	3	150
COOK ISLANDS	1969	12	12	100
	1970	9	9	75
FRENCH POLYNESIA ‡	1970	72	7	100
	1971	72	7	100
	1974	84	9	129
	1975	87	11	157
	1976	91	11	157
GUAM ‡	1973	16	10	100
	1975	*13	*4	*40
	1976	*20	*6	*60
	1977	*37	*10	*100
	1978	*46	*12	*120
NEW CALEDONIA	1969	1	0.2	100
	1970	1	0.2	100
	1971	1	0.2	100
NEW HEBRIDES	1969	26	1	100
	1970	25	3	300
	1973	28	2	200
	1974	39	4	400
	1975	39	3	300
PAPUA NEW GUINEA ‡	1971	...	110	100
	1972	...	115	105
	1973	...	131	119
SAMOA ‡	1975	698	234	100
	1976	254	135	58
	1977	266	140	60
	1978	280	140	60
DEVELOPED COUNTRIES				
AMERICA, NORTH				
CANADA ‡	1969	*53 200	*21 000	100
	1970	*52 225	*20 425	97
	1971	*52 618	*22 418	107
	1972	*52 964	*22 759	108
UNITED STATES OF AMERICA ‡	1969	...	559 200	100
	1970	...	549 500	98
	1976	...	550 200	98
	1977	...	571 800	102
	1978	...	585 500	105

Historical data for R&D personnel 5.11
Données rétrospectives pour le personnel de R-D
Datos retrospectivos sobre el personal de I y D

COUNTRY PAYS PAIS	YEAR ANNEE AÑO	PERSONNEL ENGAGED IN R & D PERSONNEL EMPLOYE A DES TRAVAUX DE R—D PERSONAL DEDICADO A ACTIVIDADES DE I Y D		
		TOTAL TOTAL TOTAL	SCIENTISTS AND ENGINEERS SCIENTIFIQUES ET INGENIEURS CIENTIFICOS E INGENIEROS	
			NUMBER (FTE) NOMBRE (FTE) NUMERO (FTE)	INDEXES OF SCIENTISTS AND ENGINEERS (1969 = 100) INDICES DES SCIENTIFIQUES ET INGENIEURS (1969 = 100) INDICES DE LOS CIENTIFICOS E INGENIEROS (1969 = 100)
		(1)	(2)	(3)
ASIA				
ISRAEL ‡	1970	...	2 800	100
	1971	...	2 960	106
	1972	...	2 900	104
	1973	...	3 100	111
	1974	...	3 350	120
JAPAN ‡	1969	427 950	275 686	100
	1970	459 274	298 814	108
	1976	566 222	399 842	145
	1977	570 180	407 192	148
	1978	564 915	407 708	148
EUROPE				
BELGIUM	1969	25 165	10 070	100
	1973	29 235	12 932	128
	1975	30 131	13 883	138
	1977	30 186	13 883	138
BULGARIA	1969	...	19 990	100
	1970	...	22 452	112
	1976	...	32 343	162
	1977	...	32 384	162
	1978	...	33 656	168
CZECHOSLOVAKIA ‡	1970	137 667	36 927	100
	1971	137 407	38 572	104
	1976	154 779	46 501	126
	1977	163 106	47 766	129
	1978	165 695	50 007	135
DENMARK ‡	1970	12 240	4 607	100
	1973	12 300	4 867	106
	1976	13 801	5 353	116
FINLAND ‡	1971	10 244	5 643	100
	1975	13 450	7 503	133
	1977	14 254	7 162	127
FRANCE	1969	201 100	57 200	100
	1970	202 869	59 004	100
	1974	216 029	64 619	113
	1975	219 700	65 300	114
	1977	222 100	68 000	119
GERMANY, FEDERAL REPUBLIC OF	1969	247 176	74 943	100
	1970	*270 000	*82 000	109
	1973	303 838	101 019	134
	1975	303 384	103 857	139
	1977	319 347	110 972	148
GREECE ‡	1969	2 470	1 032	100
	1976	5 345	2 569	249

5.11 Historical data for R&D personnel
Données rétrospectives pour le personnel de R-D
Datos retrospectivos sobre el personal de I y D

| | | | PERSONNEL ENGAGED IN R & D
PERSONNEL EMPLOYE A DES TRAVAUX DE R—D
PERSONAL DEDICADO A ACTIVIDADES DE I Y D | |
| | | | SCIENTISTS AND ENGINEERS
SCIENTIFIQUES ET INGENIEURS
CIENTIFICOS E INGENIEROS | |
COUNTRY PAYS PAIS	YEAR ANNEE AÑO	TOTAL TOTAL TOTAL	NUMBER (FTE) NOMBRE (FTE) NUMERO (FTE)	INDEXES OF SCIENTISTS AND ENGINEERS (1969 = 100) INDICES DES SCIENTIFIQUES ET INGENIEURS (1969 = 100) INDICES DE LOS CIENTIFICOS E INGENIEROS (1969 = 100)
		(1)	(2)	(3)
HUNGARY ‡	1969	48 800	15 304	100
	1970	50 749	16 282	106
	1976	61 254	23 573	154
	1977	61 595	24 316	159
	1978	63 263	25 308	165
ICELAND ‡	1969	243	116	100
	1970	256	126	109
	1971	233	134	116
	1973	314	156	134
	1975	547	229	197
IRELAND ‡	1969	3 847	1 549	100
	1971	4 475	1 857	120
	1974	4 946	2 065	133
	1975	5 498	2 580	167
	1977	5 827	2 685	173
ITALY	1969	70 009	25 363	100
	1970	75 376	27 618	109
	1974	86 655	34 308	135
	1975	94 686	37 925	150
	1976	95 675	37 878	149
NETHERLANDS ‡	1969	56 120	19 860	100
	1970	54 750	22 708	114
	1974	53 180	22 920	115
	1975	54 290	23 750	120
	1976	54 100	24 250	122
NORWAY	1969	9 268	4 058	100
	1970	9 730	4 280	106
	1976	13 390	6 080	150
	1977	13 687	6 317	156
	1978	13 990	6 450	159
POLAND ‡	1969	184 500	54 500	100
	1970	196 200	59 000	108
	1976	286 000	100 000	183
	1977	279 000	100 000	183
	1978	253 000	91 600	168
PORTUGAL ‡	1971	*7 156	*2 187	100
	1972	7 653	2 216	101
	1976	6 721	1 749	80
ROMANIA	1969	43 021	18 711	100
	1970	46 382	20 764	111
	1971	51 200	22 888	122
	1972	55 283	23 133	124
	1973	62 918	26 107	140
SPAIN	1969	14 522	5 135	100
	1970	16 187	5 842	114
	1972	23 501	8 945	174
	1973	21 220	7 163	139
	1974	23 182	7 924	154

COUNTRY / PAYS / PAIS	YEAR / ANNEE / AÑO	PERSONNEL ENGAGED IN R & D / PERSONNEL EMPLOYE A DES TRAVAUX DE R–D / PERSONAL DEDICADO A ACTIVIDADES DE I Y D — TOTAL	SCIENTISTS AND ENGINEERS / SCIENTIFIQUES ET INGENIEURS / CIENTIFICOS E INGENIEROS — NUMBER (FTE) / NOMBRE (FTE) / NUMERO (FTE)	INDEXES OF SCIENTISTS AND ENGINEERS (1969 = 100) / INDICES DES SCIENTIFIQUES ET INGENIEURS (1969 = 100) / INDICES DE LOS CIENTIFICOS E INGENIEROS (1969 = 100)
		(1)	(2)	(3)
SWEDEN ‡	1969	25 038	7 537	100
	1971	29 844	9 066	120
	1973	32 787	10 962	145
	1975	35 187	13 195	175
	1977	36 283	14 102	187
SWITZERLAND ‡	1969	*15 407	*12 001	100
	1970	*16 973	*13 294	111
	1975	27 040	16 230	135
	1976	*26 586	*16 660	139
UNITED KINGDOM ‡	1972	258 746	77 086	100
	1975	259 100	79 300	103
YUGOSLAVIA ‡	1969	36 294	14 453	100
	1970	36 467	15 118	105
	1976	44 644	20 918	145
	1977	45 698	21 680	150
	1978	51 018	22 048	153
OCEANIA				
AUSTRALIA ‡	1968	42 200	17 700	100
	1973	51 400	24 600	139
	1976	43 574	22 510	127
NEW ZEALAND ‡	1969	3 293	1 080	100
	1970	3 440	1 141	106
U.S.S.R.				
U.S.S.R. ‡	1969	...	883 420	100
	1970	...	927 709	105
	1976	...	1 253 500	142
	1977	...	1 279 600	145
	1978	...	1 314 000	149
BYELORUSSIAN S.S.R. ‡	1969	...	20 631	100
	1970	...	21 863	106
	1975	...	31 020	150
	1977	...	34 453	167
	1978	...	35 111	170
UKRAINIAN S.S.R. ‡	1969	...	122 754	100
	1970	...	129 781	106
	1976	...	173 730	142
	1977	...	179 515	146
	1978	...	185 134	151

5.11 Historical data for R&D personnel
Données rétrospectives pour le personnel de R-D
Datos retrospectivos sobre el personal de I y D

GABON:
E—> DATA RELATE TO THE (FRENCH) "OFFICE DE LA
RECHERCHE SCIENTIFIQUE ET TECHNIQUE OUTRE—MER"
(ORSTOM) ONLY; SCIENTISTS AND ENGINEERS IN
COLUMN 2 ARE ALL FOREIGNERS.
FR—> LES DONNEES NE CONCERNENT QUE L'OFFICE
FRANCAIS DE LA RECHERCHE SCIENTIFIQUE ET TECHNIQUE
OUTRE—MER (ORSTOM); LES CHIFFRES DE LA COLONNE 2
ONT TOUS TRAIT AUX RESSORTISSANTS ETRANGERS.
ESP> LOS DATOS SOLO SE REFIEREN AL "OFFICE
(FRANCAIS) DE LA RECHERCHE SCIENTIFIQUE ET
TECHNIQUE OUTRE—MER (ORSTOM); LOS DATOS DE LA
COLUMNA 2 SOLO CONCIERNEN LOS EXTRANJEROS.

GHANA:
E—> DATA FOR 1970 DO NOT INCLUDE AUXILIARY
PERSONNEL.
FR—> LES DONNEES POUR 1970 NE COMPRENNENT PAS
LE PERSONNEL AUXILIAIRE.
ESP> LOS DATOS PARA 1970 NO INCLUYEN EL PERSONAL
AUXILIAR.

MADAGASCAR:
E—> BASE YEAR: 1970=100. NOT INCLUDING DATA FOR
THE PRODUCTIVE SECTOR (INTEGRATED R&D); THE TOTALS
IN COLUMN 1 DO NOT INCLUDE AUXILIARY PERSONNEL.
FR—> ANNEE DE BASE: 1970=100. COMPTE NON TENU
DU SECTEUR DE LA PRODUCTION (ACTIVITES DE R—D
INTEGREES); LES TOTAUX DE LA COLONNE 1 NE TIENNENT
PAS COMPTE DU PERSONNEL AUXILIAIRE.
ESP> AÑO DE BASE: 1970=100. EXCLUIDO EL SECTOR
PRODUCTIVO (ACTIVIDADES DE I Y D INTEGRADAS). LOS
TOTALES DE LA COLUMNA 1 NO INCLUYEN EL PERSONAL
AUXILIAR.

NIGER:
E—> BASE YEAR: 1972=100. DATA RELATE TO THE
HIGHER EDUCATION SECTOR ONLY.
FR—> ANNEE DE BASE: 1972=100. LES DONNEES NE
CONCERNENT QUE LE SECTEUR DE L'ENSEIGNEMENT
SUPERIEUR.
ESP> AÑO DE BASE: 1972=100. LOS DATOS SOLO SE
REFIEREN AL SECTOR DE ENSEÑANZA SUPERIOR.

SUDAN:
E—> BASE YEAR: 1971=100. DATA FOR SCIENTISTS
AND ENGINEERS IN 1974 ARE FULL—TIME PLUS PART—TIME.
FR—> ANNEE DE BASE: 1971=100. LES DONNEES RELA—
TIVES AUX SCIENTIFIQUES ET INGENIEURS EN 1974 SONT
A PLEIN TEMPS ET A TEMPS PARTIEL.
ESP> AÑO DE BASE: 1971=100. EN 1974, LOS DATOS
RELATIVOS A LOS CIENTIFICOS E INGENIEROS SON DE
JORNADA COMPLETA Y DE JORNADA PARCIAL.

ZAMBIA:
E—> DATA FOR 1969 AND 1970 DO NOT INCLUDE
AUXILIARY PERSONNEL.
FR—> LES DONNEES POUR 1969 ET 1970 NE COMPREN—
NENT PAS LE PERSONNEL AUXILIAIRE.
ESP> LOS DATOS PARA 1969 Y 1970 NO INCLUYEN EL
PERSONAL AUXILIAR.

BERMUDA:
E—> NOT INCLUDING DATA FOR THE PRODUCTIVE SEC—
TOR AND EXCLUDING LAW, HUMANITIES AND EDUCATION.
FR—> NON COMPRIS LES DONNEES POUR LE SECTEUR
DE LA PRODUCTION ET COMPTE NON TENU DES DONNEES
RELATIVES AU DROIT, AUX SCIENCES HUMAINES ET A
L'EDUCATION.
ESP> EXCLUIDOS LOS DATOS RELATIVOS AL SECTOR
PRODUCTIVO Y LOS QUE SE REFIEREN AL DERECHO, LAS
CIENCIAS HUMANAS Y LA EDUCACION.

GUATEMALA:
E—> BASE YEAR 1970=100. THE TOTALS IN COLUMN 1
DO NOT INCLUDE AUXILIARY PERSONNEL.

GUATEMALA (CONT.):
FR—> ANNEE DE BASE: 1970=100. LES TOTAUX DE LA
COLONNE 1 NE COMPRENNENT PAS LE PERSONNEL AUXI—
LIAIRE.
ESP> AÑO DE BASE: 1970=100. LOS TOTALES DE LA
COLUMNA 1 NO INCLUYEN EL PERSONAL AUXILIAR.

MEXICO:
E—> DATA ARE FOR FULL—TIME PLUS PART—TIME PER—
SONNEL.
FR—> LES DONNEES SE REFERENT AU PERSONNEL A
PLEIN TEMPS ET A TEMPS PARTIEL.
ESP> LOS DATOS SE REFIEREN AL PERSONAL DE
JORNADA COMPLETA Y DE JORNADA PARCIAL.

ST PIERRE AND MIQUELON:
E—> DATA RELATE TO THE "INSTITUT SCIENTIFIQUE
ET TECHNIQUE DES PECHES MARITIMES"; THE TOTALS IN
COLUMN 1 DO NOT INCLUDE AUXILIARY PERSONNEL.
FR—> LES DONNEES NE CONCERNENT QUE L'INSTITUT
SCIENTIFIQUE ET TECHNIQUE DES PECHES MARITIMES;
LES TOTAUX DE LA COLONNE 1 NE TIENNENT PAS COMPTE
DU PERSONNEL AUXILIAIRE.
ESP> LOS DATOS SE REFIEREN SOLAMENTE AL"INSTITUT
SCIENTIFIQUE ET TECHNIQUE DES PECHES MARITIMES";
LOS TOTALES DE LA COLUMNA 1 NO INCLUYEN EL PERSO—
NAL AUXILIAR.

TURKS AND CAICOS ISLANDS:
E—> BASE YEAR: 1970=100.
FR—> ANNEE DE BASE: 1970=100.
ESP> AÑO DE BASE: 1970=100.

ARGENTINA:
E—> BASE YEAR: 1970=100. DATA ARE IN NET
MAN—YEARS.
FR—> ANNEE DE BASE: 1970=100. LES DONNEES SONT
EN ANNEES—HOMME NETTES.
ESP> AÑO DE BASE: 1970=100. LOS DATOS SE PRE—
SENTAN EN ANOS—HOMBRE NETOS.

ECUADOR:
E—> BASE YEAR 1970=100. THE TOTALS IN COLUMN 1
DO NOT INCLUDE AUXILIARY PERSONNEL.
FR—> ANNEE DE BASE: 1970=100. LES TOTAUX DE LA
COLONNE 1 NE COMPRENNENT PAS LE PERSONNEL AUXI—
LIAIRE.
ESP> AÑO DE BASE: 1970=100. LOS TOTALES DE LA
COLUMNA 1 NO INCLUYEN EL PERSONAL AUXILIAR.

VENEZUELA:
E—> BASE YEAR: 1970=100.
FR—> ANNEE DE BASE: 1970=100.
ESP> AÑO DE BASE: 1970=100.

BRUNEI:
E—> BASE YEAR: 1971=100.
FR—> ANNEE DE BASE: 1971=100.
ESP> AÑO DE BASE: 1971=100.

INDIA:
E—> REVISED SERIES. DATA RELATE TO THE YEAR
1973/74, 1974/75 AND 1976/77. NOT INCLUDING DATA
FOR THE HIGHER EDUCATION SECTOR IN 1976/77.
FR—> SERIE REVISEE. LES DONNEES SE REFERENT
AUX ANNEES 1973/74, 1974/75 ET 1976/77. COMPTE
NON TENU, EN 1976/77, DES DONNEES RELATIVES AU
SECTEUR DE L'ENSEIGNEMENT SUPERIEUR.
ESP> SERIES REVISADAS. LOS DATOS SE REFIEREN A
LOS AÑOS 1973/74, 1974/75 Y 1976/77. EN 1976/77
SE EXCLUYEN LOS DATOS RELATIVOS AL SECTOR DE
ENSEÑANZA SUPERIOR.

IRAN:
E—> BASE YEAR: 1970=100.
FR—> ANNEE DE BASE: 1970=100.
ESP> AÑO DE BASE: 1970=100.

Historical data for R&D personnel 5.11
Données rétrospectives pour le personnel de R-D
Datos retrospectivos sobre el personal de I y D

IRAQ:
E—> DATA RELATE TO THE FOUNDATION OF SCIENTIFIC RESEARCH ONLY. IN 1974 THERE WERE 1,862 PERSONS OF WHOM 1,486 ARE SCIENTISTS AND ENGINEERS WORKING IN GOVERNMENT DEPARTMENTS CONCERNED WITH SCIENTIFIC ACTIVITIES.
FR-> LES DONNEES NE CONCERNENT QUE LA"FOUNDATION OF SCIENTIFIC RESEARCH". IL Y AVAIT EN 1974, 1 862 PERSONNES, DONT 1 486 SCIENTIFIQUES ET INGENIEURS, EMPLOYEES DANS LES DEPARTEMENTS GOUVERNEMENTAUX CONCERNES PAR LES ACTIVITES SCIENTIFIQUES.
ESP> LOS DATOS SE REFIEREN A LA "FOUNDATION OF SCIENTIFIC RESEARCH". EN 1974 HABIA 1 862 PERSONAS DE LAS CUALES 1 486 ERAN CIENTIFICOS E INGENIEROS, EMPLEADAS EN LOS SERVICIOS GUBERNAMENTALES QUE SE OCUPAN DE LAS ACTIVIDADES CIENTIFICAS.

JORDAN:
E—> BASE YEAR: 1973=100. DATA RELATE TO THE EAST BANK ONLY. THE TOTALS IN COLUMN 1 DO NOT INCLUDE AUXILIARY PERSONNEL.
FR-> ANNEE DE BASE: 1973=100. LES DONNEES SE REFERENT A LA RIVE ORIENTALE SEULEMENT. LES TOTAUX DE LA COLONNE 1 NE TIENNENT PAS COMPTE DU PERSON-NEL AUXILIAIRE.
ESP> AÑO DE BASE: 1973=100. LOS DATOS SE REFIE-REN A LA ORILLA ORIENTAL SOLAMENTE. LOS TOTALES DE LA COLUMNA 1 NO INCLUYEN EL PERSONAL AUXILIAR.

KOREA, REPUBLIC OF:
E—> DATA REFERRING TO SCIENTISTS AND ENGINEERS ARE FULL-TIME PLUS PART-TIME; NOT INCLUDING LAW, HUMANITIES AND EDUCATION.
FR-> LES DONNEES RELATIVES AUX SCIENTIFIQUES ET INGENIEURS SONT A PLEIN TEMPS ET A TEMPS PARTIEL; LES DONNEES NE COMPRENNENT PAS LE DROIT, LES SCIENCES HUMAINES ET L'EDUCATION.
ESP> LOS DATOS RELATIVOS A LOS CIENTIFICOS E INGENIEROS SE REFIEREN AL PERSONAL DE JORNADA COMPLETA Y DE JORNADA PARCIAL, PERO NO INCLUYEN EL DERECHO, LAS CIENCIAS HUMANAS Y LA EDUCACION.

PAKISTAN:
E—> BASE YEAR 1971/72=100. DATA REFER RESPECTI-VELY TO THE YEARS 1971/72 AND 1973/74 AND RELATE TO R&D ACTIVITIES CONCENTRATED MAINLY IN GOVERN-MENT-FINANCED RESEARCH ESTABLISHMENTS ONLY; SOCIAL SCIENCES AND HUMANITIES IN THE HIGHER EDUCATION AND GENERAL SERVICE SECTORS ARE EXCLUDED. THE FIGURES IN COLUMN 1 DO NOT INCLUDE AUXILIARY PERSONAL.
FR-> ANNEE DE BASE: 1971/72=100. LES DONNEES SE REFERENT RESPECTIVEMENT AUX ANNEES 1971/72 ET 1973/74 ET AUX ACTIVITES DE R-D SE TROUVANT POUR LA PLUPART DANS LES ETABLISSEMENTS DE RECHERCHE FINANCES PAR LE GOUVERNEMENT. LES SCIENCES SO-CIALES ET HUMAINES DANS LES SECTEURS DE L'ENSEI-GNEMENT SUPERIEUR ET DE SERVICE GENERAL SONT EX-CLUES. LES TOTAUX DE LA COLONNE 1 NE TIENNENT PAS COMPTE DU PERSONNEL AUXILIAIRE.
ESP> AÑO DE BASE: 1971/72=100. LOS DATOS SE RE-FIEREN RESPECTIVAMENTE A LOS AÑOS 1971/72 Y 1973/74 Y A LAS ACTIVIDADES DE I Y D CONCENTRADAS PRINCI-PALMENTE EN ESTABLECIMIENTOS DE INVESTIGACION SUBVENCIONADOS POR EL GOBIERNO. SE EXCLUYEN LAS CIENCIAS SOCIALES Y HUMANAS DE LOS SECTORES DE ENSEÑANZA SUPERIOR Y DE SERVICIO GENERAL. LOS TOTALES DE LA COLUMNA 1 NO INCLUYEN EL PERSONAL AUXILIAR.

VIET-NAM:
E—> BASE YEAR: 1972=100. THE FIGURES IN COLUMN 1 DO NOT INCLUDE DATA FOR TECHNICIANS AND AUXILIARY PERSONAL IN THE HIGHER EDUCATION SECTOR.
FR-> ANNEE DE BASE: 1972=100. LES TOTAUX DE LA COLONNE 1 NE COMPRENNENT PAS LES TECHNICIENS NI LE PERSONNEL AUXILIAIRE DU SECTEUR DE L'ENSEIGNE-MENT SUPERIEUR.

VIET-NAM (CONT.):
ESP> AÑO DE BASE: 1972=100. LOS TOTALES DE LA COLUMNA 1 NO INCLUYEN EL PERSONAL AUXILIAR NI LOS TECNICOS DEL SECTOR DE ENSEÑANZA SUPERIOR.

AMERICAN SAMOA:
E—> DATA RELATE TO ONE RESEARCH INSTITUTE ONLY.
FR-> LES DONNEES NE CONCERNENT QU'UN INSTITUT DE RECHERCHE.
ESP> LOS DATOS SE REFIEREN A UN CENTRO DE INVES-TIGACION SOLAMENTE.

FRENCH POLYNESIA:
E—> BASE YEAR: 1970=100. DATA RELATE TO ONE RESEARCH INSTITUTE ONLY. SCIENTISTS AND ENGINEERS ARE FULL-TIME.
FR-> ANNEE DE BASE: 1970=100. LES DONNEES NE CONCERNENT QU'UN INSTITUT DE RECHERCHE. LES SCIEN-TIFIQUES ET INGENIEURS SONT A PLEIN TEMPS.
ESP> AÑO DE BASE: 1970=100. LOS DATOS SOLO SE REFIEREN A UN INSTITUTO DE INVESTIGACION. LOS CIEN-TIFICOS E INGENIEROS SON DE JORNADA COMPLETA.

GUAM:
E—> DATA RELATE TO THE HIGHER EDUCATION SECTOR ONLY.
FR-> LES DONNEES NE CONCERNENT QUE LE SECTEUR DE L'ENSEIGNEMENT SUPERIEUR.
ESP> LOS DATOS SOLO SE REFIEREN AL SECTOR DE ENSEÑANZA SUPERIOR SOLAMENTE.

PAPUA NEW GUINEA:
E—> BASE YEAR: 1971=100.
FR-> ANNEE DE BASE: 1971=100.
ESP> AÑO DE BASE: 1971=100.

SAMOA:
E—> BASE YEAR: 1975=100. DATA FOR 1975 DO NOT INCLUDE SOCIAL SCIENCES AND HUMANITIES. SCIENTISTS AND ENGINEERS ARE FULL-TIME.
FR-> ANNEE DE BASE: 1975=100. LES DONNEES POUR 1975 NE COMPRENNENT PAS LES SCIENCES SOCIALES ET HUMAINES ET SE REFERENT AUX SCIENTIFIQUES ET INGE-NIEURS A PLEIN TEMPS.
ESP> AÑO DE BASE: 1975=100. LOS DATOS PARA 1975 NO INCLUYEN LAS CIENCIAS SOCIALES Y HUMANAS Y SE REFIEREN A LOS CIENTIFICOS E INGENIEROS DE JORNADA COMPLETA.

CANADA:
E—> NOT INCLUDING DATA FOR SOCIAL SCIENCES AND HUMANITIES.
FR-> NON COMPRIS LES DONNEES POUR LES SCIENCES SOCIALES ET HUMAINES.
ESP> EXCLUIDOS LOS DATOS RELATIVOS A LAS CIEN-CIAS SOCIALES Y HUMANAS.

UNITED STATES OF AMERICA:
E—> NOT INCLUDING DATA FOR LAW, HUMANITIES AND EDUCATION.
FR-> NON COMPRIS LES DONNEES POUR LE DROIT, LES SCIENCES HUMAINES ET L'EDUCATION.
ESP> EXCLUIDOS LOS DATOS RELATIVOS AL DERECHO, LAS CIENCIAS HUMANAS Y LA EDUCACION.

ISRAEL:
E—> BASE YEAR: 1970=100. DATA REFER TO THE CIVILIAN SECTOR ONLY AND DO NOT INCLUDE SOCIAL SCIENCES AND HUMANITIES.
FR-> ANNEE DE BASE: 1970=100. LES DONNEES NE CONCERNENT QUE LE SECTEUR CIVIL ET NE COMPRENNENT PAS LES SCIENCES SOCIALES ET HUMAINES.
ESP> AÑO DE BASE: 1970=100. LOS DATOS SE REFIE-REN SOLAMENTE AL SECTOR CIVIL Y NO INCLUYEN LAS CIENCIAS SOCIALES Y HUMANAS.

5.11 **Historical data for R&D personnel**
Données rétrospectives pour le personnel de R-D
Datos retrospectivos sobre el personal de I y D

JAPAN:
E—> DATA FOR SCIENTISTS AND ENGINEERS ARE FULL-TIME. NOT INCLUDING DATA FOR SOCIAL SCIENCES AND HUMANITIES IN THE PRODUCTIVE SECTOR.
FR-> LES DONNEES SE REFERENT AUX SCIENTIFIQUES ET INGENIEURS A PLEIN TEMPS. NON COMPRIS LES DON-NEES RELATIVES AUX SCIENCES SOCIALES ET HUMAINES DANS LE SECTEUR DE LA PRODUCTION.
ESP> LOS DATOS SE REFIEREN A LOS CIENTIFICOS E INGENIEROS DE JORNADA COMPLETA. EXCLUIDOS LOS DATOS RELATIVOS A LAS CIENCIAS SOCIALES Y HUMANAS DEL SECTOR PRODUCTIVO.

CZECHOSLOVAKIA:
E—> BASE YEAR: 1970=100. SCIENTISTS AND ENGI-NEERS ENGAGED IN ADMINISTRATION ARE INCLUDED WITH AUXILIARY PERSONNEL; OF MILITARY R&D, ONLY THAT PART CARRIED OUT IN CIVIL ESTABLISHMENTS IS INCLUDED.
FR-> ANNEE DE BASE: 1970=100. LES SCIENTIFIQUES ET INGENIEURS EMPLOYES DANS LES SERVICES ADMINIS-TRATIFS DE R-D SONT COMPRIS AVEC LE PERSONNEL AUXILIAIRE; POUR LA R-D DE CARACTERE MILITAIRE, SEULE LA PARTIE EFFECTUEE DANS LES ETABLISSEMENTS CIVILS A ETE CONSIDEREE.
ESP> AÑO DE BASE: 1970=100. LOS CIENTIFICOS E INGENIEROS EMPLEADOS EN LOS SERVICIOS ADMINISTRA-TIVOS DE I Y D ESTAN INCLUIDOS CON EL PERSONAL AUXILIAR; PARA LA I Y D DE CARACTER MILITAR, SOLO SE HA CONSIDERADO LA PARTE CORRESPONDIENTE A LOS ESTABLECIMIENTOS CIVILES.

DENMARK:
E—> BASE YEAR: 1970=100.
FR-> ANNEE DE BASE: 1970=100.
ESP> AÑO DE BASE: 1970=100.

FINLAND:
E—> BASE YEAR: 1971=100.
FR-> ANNEE DE BASE: 1971=100.
ESP> AÑO DE BASE: 1971=100.

GREECE:
E—> DATA IN 1969 DO NOT INCLUDE SOCIAL SCIENCES AND HUMANITIES.
FR-> LES DONNEES POUR 1969 NE COMPRENNENT PAS LES SCIENCES SOCIALES ET HUMAINES.
ESP> LOS DATOS PARA 1969 NO INCLUYEN LAS CIEN-CIAS SOCIALES Y HUMANAS.

HUNGARY:
E—> NOT INCLUDING SCIENTISTS AND ENGINEERS ENGAGED IN THE ADMINISTRATION OF R&D.
FR-> NON COMPRIS LES SCIENTIFIQUES ET INGENIEURS EMPLOYES DANS LES SERVICES ADMINISTRATIFS DE R-D.
ESP> EXCLUIDOS LOS CIENTIFICOS E INGENIEROS EMPLEADOS EN LOS SERVICIOS ADMINISTRATIVOS DE I Y D.

ICELAND:
E—> THE TOTALS IN COLUMN 1 DO NOT INCLUDE AUXILIARY PERSONNEL. NOT INCLUDING DATA FOR SOCIAL SCIENCES AND HUMANITIES.
FR-> LES TOTAUX DE LA COLONNE 1 NE COMPRENNENT PAS LE PERSONNEL AUXILIAIRE. NON COMPRIS LES DONNEES POUR LES SCIENCES SOCIALES ET HUMAINES.
ESP> LOS TOTALES DE LA COLUMNA 1 NO INCLUYEN EL PERSONAL AUXILIAR. EXCLUIDOS LOS DATOS RELATIVOS A LAS CIENCIAS SOCIALES Y HUMANAS.

IRELAND:
E—> DATA FOR 1969 AND 1971 DO NOT INCLUDE HUMANITIES.
FR-> LES DONNEES POUR 1969 ET 1971 NE COMPREN-NENT PAS LES SCIENCES HUMAINES.
ESP> LOS DATOS RELATIVOS A 1969 Y 1971 NO INCLUYEN LAS CIENCIAS HUMANAS.

NETHERLANDS:
E—> NOT INCLUDING SOCIAL SCIENCES AND HUMANI-TIES IN THE PRODUCTIVE SECTOR (INTEGRATED R&D).
FR-> NON COMPRIS LES DONNEES POUR LES SCIENCES SOCIALES ET HUMAINES DANS LE SECTEUR DE LA PRO-DUCTION (ACTIVITES DE R-D INTEGREES).
ESP> EXCLUIDOS LOS DATOS RELATIVOS A LAS CIEN-CIAS SOCIALES Y HUMANAS DEL SECTOR PRODUCTIVO (ACTIVIDADES DE I Y D INTEGRADAS).

POLAND:
E—> DATA FOR 1976, 1977 AND 1978 DO NOT INCLUDE TECHNICIANS AND AUXILIARY PERSONNEL IN THE HIGHER EDUCATION SECTOR.
FR-> LES DONNEES POUR 1976, 1977 ET 1978 NE COMPRENNENT PAS LES TECHNICIENS NI LE PERSONNEL AUXILIAIRE DU SECTEUR DE L'ENSEIGNEMENT SUPERIEUR.
ESP> LOS DATOS PARA 1976, 1977 Y 1978 NO INCLU-YEN NI LOS TECNICOS NI EL PERSONAL AUXILIAR DEL SECTOR DE ENSEÑANZA SUPERIOR.

PORTUGAL:
E—> BASE YEAR: 1971=100.
FR-> ANNEE DE BASE: 1971=100.
ESP> AÑO DE BASE: 1971=100.

SWEDEN:
E—> NOT INCLUDING DATA FOR SOCIAL SCIENCES AND HUMANITIES.
FR-> NON COMPRIS LES DONNEES POUR LES SCIENCES SOCIALES ET HUMAINES.
ESP> EXCLUIDOS LOS DATOS RELATIVOS A LAS CIEN-CIAS SOCIALES Y HUMANAS.

SWITZERLAND:
E—> DATA FOR SCIENTISTS AND ENGINEERS IN 1969 AND 1970 ARE FULL-TIME PLUS PART-TIME.
FR-> LES DONNEES RELATIVES AUX SCIENTIFIQUES ET INGENIEURS EN 1969 ET 1970 SONT A PLEIN TEMPS ET A TEMPS PARTIEL.
ESP> LOS DATOS RELATIVOS A LOS CIENTIFICOS E IN-GENIEROS EN 1969 Y 1970 SE REFIEREN AL PERSONAL DE JORNADA COMPLETA Y DE JORNADA PARCIAL.

UNITED KINGDOM:
E—> DATA RELATE TO THE YEARS 1972/73 AND 1975/76 AND EXCLUDE THE HIGHER EDUCATION SECTOR.
FR-> LES DONNEES SE REFERENT AUX ANNEES 1972/73 ET 1975/76 ET NE COMPRENNENT PAS LE SECTEUR DE L'ENSEIGNEMENT SUPERIEUR.
ESP> LOS DATOS SE REFIEREN A LOS AÑOS 1972/73 Y 1975/76 Y NO INCLUYEN EL SECTOR DE ENSEÑANZA SUPERIOR.

YUGOSLAVIA:
E—> NOT INCLUDING ACTIVITIES OF A MILITARY NATURE OR RELATING TO NATIONAL DEFENCE.
FR-> NON COMPRIS LES ACTIVITES DE CARACTERE MILITAIRE OU RELEVANT DE LA DEFENSE NATIONALE.
ESP> EXCLUIDAS LAS ACTIVIDADES DE CARACTER MILITAR O QUE CONCIERNEN LA DEFENSA NACIONAL.

AUSTRALIA:
E—> BASE YEAR: 1968/69=100.
FR-> ANNEE DE BASE: 1968/69=100.
ESP> AÑO DE BASE: 1968/69=100.

NEW ZEALAND:
E—> DATA REFER TO SCIENTIFIC STAFF IN GOVERN-MENT DEPARTMENTS ONLY.
FR-> LES DONNEES SE REFERENT AU PERSONNEL QUI TRAVAILLE DANS LE DOMAINE DES SCIENCES DANS LES DEPARTEMENTS GOUVERNEMENTAUX.
ESP> LOS DATOS SE REFIEREN AL PERSONAL QUE TRA-BAJA EN LA ESFERA DE LA CIENCIA EN LAS ENTIDADES OFICIALES.

Historical data for R&D personnel   5.11
Données rétrospectives pour le personnel de R-D
Datos retrospectivos sobre el personal de I y D

U.S.S.R.:
E—> DATA REFER TO ALL PERSONS WITH A HIGHER
SCIENTIFIC DEGREE OR SCIENTIFIC TITLE, REGARDLESS
OF THE NATURE OF THEIR WORK; PERSONS UNDERTAKING
RESEARCH WORK IN SCIENTIFIC ESTABLISHMENTS AND
SCIENTIFIC TEACHING STAFF IN INSTITUTIONS OF
HIGHER EDUCATION; ALSO INCLUDES PERSONS UNDERTAK—
ING SCIENTIFIC WORK IN INDUSTRIAL ENTERPRISES.
FR—> LES DONNEES SE REFERENT AUX TRAVAILLEURS
SCIENTIFIQUES, C.A.D., A TOUTES LES PERSONNES
AYANT UN DIPLOME SCIENTIFIQUE SUPERIEUR OU UN
TITRE SCIENTIFIQUE, SANS CONSIDERATION DE LA
NATURE DE LEUR TRAVAIL; AUX PERSONNES QUI EFFEC—
TUENT UN TRAVAIL DE RECHERCHE DANS DES INSTITU—
TIONS SCIENTIFIQUES ET AU PERSONNEL SCIENTIFIQUE
ENSEIGNANT DANS DES ETABLISSEMENTS D'ENSEIGNEMENT
SUPERIEUR; SONT INCLUES AUSSI LES PERSONNES QUI
EFFECTUENT DES TRAVAUX SCIENTIFIQUES DANS LES
ENTREPRISES INDUSTRIELLES.
ESP> LOS DATOS SE REFIEREN A LOS TRABAJADORES
CIENTIFICOS, ES DECIR, A TODAS LAS PERSONAS QUE
POSEEN UN DIPLOMA CIENTIFICO SUPERIOR O UN TITULO
CIENTIFICO, SIN TENER EN CUENTA LA NATURALEZA DE
SU TRABAJO; A LAS PERSONAS QUE EFECTUAN UN
TRABAJO DE INVESTIGACION EN LAS INSTITUCIONES
CIENTIFICAS Y AL PERSONAL CIENTIFICO QUE EJERCE
FUNCIONES DOCENTES EN LOS ESTABLECIMIENTOS DE
ENSEÑANZA SUPERIOR; TAMBIEN SE INCLUYEN LAS PER—
SONAS QUE EFECTUAN TRABAJOS CIENTIFICOS EN LAS
EMPRESAS INDUSTRIALES.

BYELORUSSIAN S.S.R.:
E—> DATA REFER TO ALL PERSONS WITH A HIGHER
SCIENTIFIC DEGREE OR SCIENTIFIC TITLE, REGARDLESS
OF THE NATURE OF THEIR WORK; PERSONS UNDERTAKING
RESEARCH WORK IN SCIENTIFIC ESTABLISHMENTS AND
SCIENTIFIC TEACHING STAFF IN INSTITUTIONS OF
HIGHER EDUCATION; ALSO INCLUDES PERSONS UNDERTAK—
ING SCIENTIFIC WORK IN INDUSTRIAL ENTERPRISES.
FR—> LES DONNEES SE REFERENT AUX TRAVAILLEURS
SCIENTIFIQUES, C.A.D., A TOUTES LES PERSONNES
AYANT UN DIPLOME SCIENTIFIQUE SUPERIEUR OU UN
TITRE SCIENTIFIQUE, SANS CONSIDERATION DE LA
NATURE DE LEUR TRAVAIL; AUX PERSONNES QUI EFFEC—
TUENT UN TRAVAIL DE RECHERCHE DANS DES INSTITU—
TIONS SCIENTIFIQUES ET AU PERSONNEL SCIENTIFIQUE
ENSEIGNANT DANS DES ETABLISSEMENTS D'ENSEIGNEMENT

BYELORUSSIAN S.S.R. (CONT.):
SUPERIEUR; SONT INCLUES AUSSI LES PERSONNES QUI
EFFECTUENT DES TRAVAUX SCIENTIFIQUES DANS LES
ENTREPRISES INDUSTRIELLES.
ESP> LOS DATOS SE REFIEREN A LOS TRABAJADORES
CIENTIFICOS, ES DECIR, A TODAS LAS PERSONAS QUE
POSEEN UN DIPLOMA CIENTIFICO SUPERIOR O UN TITULO
CIENTIFICO, SIN TENER EN CUENTA LA NATURALEZA DE
SU TRABAJO; A LAS PERSONAS QUE EFECTUAN UN
TRABAJO DE INVESTIGACION EN LAS INSTITUCIONES
CIENTIFICAS Y AL PERSONAL CIENTIFICO QUE EJERCE
FUNCIONES DOCENTES EN LOS ESTABLECIMIENTOS DE
ENSEÑANZA SUPERIOR; TAMBIEN SE INCLUYEN LAS PER—
SONAS QUE EFECTUAN TRABAJOS CIENTIFICOS EN LAS
EMPRESAS INDUSTRIALES.

UKRAINIAN S.S.R.:
E—> DATA REFER TO ALL PERSONS WITH A HIGHER
SCIENTIFIC DEGREE OR SCIENTIFIC TITLE, REGARDLESS
OF THE NATURE OF THEIR WORK; PERSONS UNDERTAKING
RESEARCH WORK IN SCIENTIFIC ESTABLISHMENTS AND
SCIENTIFIC TEACHING STAFF IN INSTITUTIONS OF
HIGHER EDUCATION; ALSO INCLUDES PERSONS UNDERTAK—
ING SCIENTIFIC WORK IN INDUSTRIAL ENTERPRISES.
FR—> LES DONNEES SE REFERENT AUX TRAVAILLEURS
SCIENTIFIQUES, C.A.D., A TOUTES.LES PERSONNES
AYANT UN DIPLOME SCIENTIFIQUE SUPERIEUR OU UN
TITRE SCIENTIFIQUE, SANS CONSIDERATION DE LA
NATURE DE LEUR TRAVAIL; AUX PERSONNES QUI EFFEC—
TUENT UN TRAVAIL DE RECHERCHE DANS DES INSTITU—
TIONS SCIENTIFIQUES ET AU PERSONNEL SCIENTIFIQUE
ENSEIGNANT DANS DES ETABLISSEMENTS D'ENSEIGNEMENT
SUPERIEUR; SONT INCLUES AUSSI LES PERSONNES QUI
EFFECTUENT DES TRAVAUX SCIENTIFIQUES DANS LES
ENTREPRISES INDUSTRIELLES.
ESP> LOS DATOS SE REFIEREN A LOS TRABAJADORES
CIENTIFICOS, ES DECIR, A TODAS LAS PERSONAS QUE
POSEEN UN DIPLOMA CIENTIFICO SUPERIOR O UN TITULO
CIENTIFICO, SIN TENER EN CUENTA LA NATURALEZA DE
SU TRABAJO; A LAS PERSONAS QUE EFECTUAN UN
TRABAJO DE INVESTIGACION EN LAS INSTITUCIONES
CIENTIFICAS Y AL PERSONAL CIENTIFICO QUE EJERCE
FUNCIONES DOCENTES EN LOS ESTABLECIMIENTOS DE
ENSEÑANZA SUPERIOR; TAMBIEN SE INCLUYEN LAS PER—
SONAS QUE EFECTUAN TRABAJOS CIENTIFICOS EN LAS
EMPRESAS INDUSTRIALES.

Historical data on R&D expenditure 5.12
Données rétrospectives sur les dépenses de R-D
Datos retrospectivos sobre los gastos de I y D

5.12 Expenditure for research and experimental development: selected data for recent years

Dépenses consacrées à la recherche et au développement expérimental: données sélectionnées pour des années récentes

Gastos dedicados a la investigación y al desarrollo experimental: datos seleccionados sobre los últimos años

| PLEASE REFER TO INTRODUCTION FOR DEFINITIONS OF CATEGORIES INCLUDED IN THIS TABLE. | POUR LES DEFINITIONS DES CATEGORIES PRESENTEES DANS CE TABLEAU, SE REFERER A L'INTRODUCTION. | EN LA INTRODUCCION SE DAN LAS DEFINICIONES DE LAS CATEGORIAS QUE FIGURAN EN ESTE CUADRO. |

| NUMBER OF COUNTRIES AND TERRITORIES PRESENTED IN THIS TABLE: 71 | NOMBRE DE PAYS ET DE TERRITOIRES PRESENTES DANS CE TABLEAU: 71 | NUMERO DE PAISES Y DE TERRITORIOS PRESENTADOS EN ESTE CUADRO: 71 |

			EXPENDITURE FOR R & D DEPENSES CONSACREES A R—D GASTOS DEDICADOS A I Y D		
COUNTRY	FISCAL YEAR BEGINNING	CURRENCY	TOTAL	CURRENT EXPENDITURE DEPENSES COURANTES GASTOS ORDINARIOS	
PAYS	EXERCICE FINANCIER COMMENCANT EN	MONNAIE	TOTAL	AMOUNT	PERCENTAGE OF TOTAL
PAIS	COMIENZO DEL EJERCICIO ECONOMICO	MONEDA	TOTAL	MONTANT IMPORTE	POURCENTAGE DU TOTAL PORCENTAJE DEL TOTAL
			(000)	(000)	%
			(1)	(2)	(3)

DEVELOPING COUNTRIES

AFRICA

ALGERIA ‡	1971	DINAR	77 500	67 000	87.1
	1972		78 000	68 000	87.2
GABON ‡	1969	FRANC C.F.A.	1 647	1 603	97.3
	1970		1 895	1 882	99.3
MADAGASCAR ‡	1969	FRANC	1 480 000	1 438 000	97.2
	1970		2 043 000	2 015 000	98.6
	1971		2 294 000	2 294 000	100.0
MAURITIUS	1969	RUPEE	*4 187	*3 621	*86.5
	1970		*5 124	*4 290	*83.7
	1975		17 795	10 411	58.5
	1976		17 686	13 191	74.6
	1977		18 800	12 700	67.6

5.12 Historical data on R&D expenditure
Données rétrospectives sur les dépenses de R-D
Datos retrospectivos sobre los gastos de I y D

| | | | EXPENDITURE FOR R & D
DEPENSES CONSACREES A R—D
GASTOS DEDICADOS A I Y D | | |
COUNTRY PAYS PAIS	FISCAL YEAR BEGINNING EXERCICE FINANCIER COMMENCANT EN COMIENZO DEL EJERCICIO ECONOMICO	CURRENCY MONNAIE MONEDA	TOTAL TOTAL TOTAL (000)	CURRENT EXPENDITURE DEPENSES COURANTES GASTOS ORDINARIOS	
				AMOUNT MONTANT IMPORTE (000)	PERCENTAGE OF TOTAL POURCENTAGE DU TOTAL PORCENTAJE DEL TOTAL %
			(1)	(2)	(3)
NIGER ‡	1974	FRANC C.F.A.	40 140	40 140	100
	1975		92 794	92 794	100
	1976		141 703	141 703	100
SEYCHELLES	1969	RUPEE	161	...	...
	1970		209	209	100.0
	1971		206	155	75.2
	1972		272	212	77.9
	1973		402	290	72.1
SUDAN	1972	POUND	2 291	...	...
	1973		3 012	2 444	81.1
	1978		5 115	4 294	84.0
UNITED REPUBLIC OF CAMEROON ‡	1969	FRANC C.F.A.	*1 443 000	...	...
	1970		*1 765 000	...	...
ZAMBIA	1969	KWACHA	...	*1 500	...
	1970		...	*1 980	...
	1972		6 261	4 726	75.5
AMERICA, NORTH					
BERMUDA ‡	1969	DOLLAR	221	216	97.7
	1970		240	205	85.4
COSTA RICA ‡	1974	COLON	...	35 201	...
	1975		...	39 113	...
	1976		...	43 459	...
	1977		...	48 288	...
	1978		...	53 653	...
CUBA	1969	PESO	91 735	35 786	39.0
	1977		74 258	62 442	84.1
	1978		83 163	68 408	82.3
GUATEMALA	1970	QUETZAL	3 008	1 534	51.0
	1972		*3 932	*2 390	60.8
	1974		*5 139	*3 721	72.4
JAMAICA	1969	DOLLAR	...	833	...
	1970		...	1 060	...
	1971		...	1 095	...
MEXICO ‡	1969	PESO	...	519 134	...
	1970		*761 611	...	...
	1971		1 034 125	*570 172	55.1
	1973		1 277 618	1 150 593	90.1
PANAMA	1974	BALBOA	2 908	2 707	93.﹀
	1975		3 296	...	...
TRINIDAD AND TOBAGO ‡	1969	DOLLAR	4 180	3 923	93.8
	1970		5 171	4 371	84.5

Historical data on R&D expenditure   5.12
Données rétrospectives sur les dépenses de R-D
Datos retrospectivos sobre los gastos de I y D

COUNTRY PAYS PAIS	FISCAL YEAR BEGINNING EXERCICE FINANCIER COMMENCANT EN COMIENZO DEL EJERCICIO ECONOMICO	CURRENCY MONNAIE MONEDA	EXPENDITURE FOR R & D DEPENSES CONSACREES A R–D GASTOS DEDICADOS A I Y D		
			TOTAL TOTAL TOTAL (000) (1)	CURRENT EXPENDITURE DEPENSES COURANTES GASTOS ORDINARIOS	
				AMOUNT MONTANT IMPORTE (000) (2)	PERCENTAGE OF TOTAL POURCENTAGE DU TOTAL PORCENTAJE DEL TOTAL % (3)
TURKS AND CAICOS ISLANDS	1970 1971 1972 1973 1974	U.S. DOLLAR	25 25 40 51 8	... ...	... ...
AMERICA, SOUTH					
ARGENTINA	1970 1974 1976 1978	PESO	*207 500 1 630 600 *23 171 700 195 278 000	... 1 443 100 *20 507 200 136 550 000	... 88.5 *88.5 69.9
BRAZIL ‡	1975 1976 1977 1978	CRUZEIRO	8 020 000 10 346 500 10 599 000 20 781 000	... ...	... ...
ECUADOR	1970 1973	SUCRE	90 515 142 310	... ...	... ...
FALKLAND ISLANDS (MALVINAS)	1969 1970 1971	POUND	4 — —	... — —	... — —
VENEZUELA	1970 1973 1975	BOLIVAR	102 270 289 697 310 783	97 150	95.0 ... ...
ASIA					
BRUNEI	1971 1974	DOLLAR	... 3 055	2 425 2 933	... 96.0
CYPRUS	1969 1970 1971	POUND	922 909 1 088	806 810 986	87.4 89.1 90.6
INDIA ‡	1969 1970 1974 1975 1976	RUPEE	1 166 200 1 396 400 2 916 000 3 566 900 4 022 500	... ...	... ...
INDONESIA ‡	1972 1973 1974 1975 1976 1977	RUPIAH	*3 315 570 *4 773 947 *11 338 869 *19 496 580 *26 018 629 *32 471 711	*2 381 539 *3 317 431 *7 650 403 *13 159 507 *17 227 620 ...	71.8 69.5 67.5 67.5 66.2 ...
IRAN ‡	1970 1971 1972	RIAL	4 414 595 4 856 054 3 531 807	3 966 820 4 322 745 2 246 789	89.9 89.0 63.6

5.12 Historical data on R&D expenditure
Données rétrospectives sur les dépenses de R-D
Datos retrospectivos sobre los gastos de I y D

COUNTRY / PAYS / PAIS	FISCAL YEAR BEGINNING EXERCICE FINANCIER COMMENCANT EN COMIENZO DEL EJERCICIO ECONOMICO	CURRENCY MONNAIE MONEDA	EXPENDITURE FOR R & D DEPENSES CONSACREES A R—D GASTOS DEDICADOS A I Y D		
			TOTAL TOTAL TOTAL (000)	CURRENT EXPENDITURE DEPENSES COURANTES GASTOS ORDINARIOS	
				AMOUNT MONTANT IMPORTE (000)	PERCENTAGE OF TOTAL POURCENTAGE DU TOTAL PORCENTAJE DEL TOTAL %
			(1)	(2)	(3)
IRAQ ‡	1971	DINAR	1 839	1 448	78.7
	1972		2 361	1 794	76.0
	1973		2 310	1 791	77.5
	1974		3 471	2 743	79.0
JORDAN ‡	1975	DINAR	1 540	...	...
	1976		2 074	1 242	59.9
KOREA, REPUBLIC OF ‡	1969	WON	9 773 985	5 203 400	53.2
	1970		10 547 753	7 586 539	71.9
	1976		60 900 000	...	...
	1977		108 286 000	...	...
	1978		152 418 000	97 928 000	64.3
PAKISTAN ‡	1969	RUPEE	104 280	...	...
	1970		116 980	...	...
	1971		122 340	...	...
	1972		123 250	...	...
	1973		150 430	...	...
SRI LANKA ‡	1970	RUPEE	21 887	18 332	83.7
	1973		27 825	22 505	80.9
	1974		35 797	26 961	75.3
	1975		45 097	32 662	72.4
TURKEY ‡	1969	LIRA	434 700	...	...
	1970		492 000	...	...
	1971		554 400	...	...
	1977		6 466 409	...	...
	1978		7 601 531	...	...
VIET—NAM	1976	DONG	101 000	38 000	37.6
	1977		77 000	44 000	57.1
	1978		117 000	56 000	47.9
	1979		108 300	68 800	63.5
OCEANIA					
AMERICAN SAMOA ‡	1969	U.S. DOLLAR	80	70	87.5
	1970		100	80	80.0
	1971		120	100	83.3
COOK ISLANDS	1969	NEW ZEALAND DOLLAR	61	...	...
	1970		112	...	...
FRENCH POLYNESIA ‡	1970	FRANC C.F.P.	69 322	61 423	88.6
	1971		73 332	63 002	85.9
	1974		100 187	92 744	93.2
	1975		116 677	113 067	96.9
	1976		140 240	135 430	96.6
GUAM ‡	1973	U.S. DOLLAR	579	330	57.0
	1978		1 295	...	...
NEW CALEDONIA	1969	FRANC C.F.P.	1 440	1 240	86.1
	1970		1 440	1 240	86.1
	1971		1 440	1 240	86.1

Historical data on R&D expenditure 5.12
Données rétrospectives sur les dépenses de R-D
Datos retrospectivos sobre los gastos de I y D

COUNTRY PAYS PAIS	FISCAL YEAR BEGINNING EXERCICE FINANCIER COMMENCANT EN COMIENZO DEL EJERCICIO ECONOMICO	CURRENCY MONNAIE MONEDA	EXPENDITURE FOR R & D DEPENSES CONSACREES A R—D GASTOS DEDICADOS A I Y D		
			TOTAL TOTAL TOTAL (000) (1)	CURRENT EXPENDITURE DEPENSES COURANTES GASTOS ORDINARIOS	
				AMOUNT MONTANT IMPORTE (000) (2)	PERCENTAGE OF TOTAL POURCENTAGE DU TOTAL PORCENTAJE DEL TOTAL % (3)
NEW HEBRIDES	1969 1970 1973 1974 1975	FRANC	6 759 8 667 13 119 20 925 21 603	. . . . . . 13 119 20 925 21 603	. . . . . . 100 100 100
SAMOA	1975 1976 1977 1978	TALA	1 437 1 385 2 341 2 500	785 380 341 500	54.6 27.4 14.6 20.0
DEVELOPED COUNTRIES					
AMERICA, NORTH					
CANADA ‡	1969 1970 1973 1974 1975	DOLLAR	1 057 000 *1 103 000 1 345 000 1 562 000 1 729 000	841 000 *865 000 1 229 000 1 415 000 1 570 000	79.6 78.4 91.4 90.6 90.8
UNITED STATES OF AMERICA ‡	1969 1970 1976 1977 1978	DOLLAR	. . . .	26 169 000 26 545 000 38 816 000 42 902 000 47 295 000	. . . .
ASIA					
ISRAEL ‡	1969 1970 1973 1974 1975	POUND	. . . .	175 000 242 000 507 000 634 000 803 000	. . . .
JAPAN ‡	1969 1970 1975 1976 1977	YEN	1 064 653 1 355 505 2 974 573 3 320 685 3 651 319	839 784 1 058 154 2 490 844 2 816 147 3 097 843	78.9 78.1 83.7 84.8 84.8
EUROPE					
BELGIUM	1969 1973 1975 1977	FRANC	14 474 727 25 026 578 29 829 603 38 894 080	11 915 282 20 713 379 26 787 654 34 917 217	82.3 82.8 89.8 89.8
BULGARIA	1973 1974 1975 1976 1977	LEV	298 400 305 600 332 200 331 500 334 900	265 500 265 900 278 600 284 400 285 000	89.0 87.0 83.9 85.5 85.1

5.12 Historical data on R&D expenditure
Données rétrospectives sur les dépenses de R-D
Datos retrospectivos sobre los gastos de I y D

COUNTRY	FISCAL YEAR BEGINNING	CURRENCY	EXPENDITURE FOR R & D DEPENSES CONSACREES A R–D GASTOS DEDICADOS A I Y D		
			TOTAL	CURRENT EXPENDITURE DEPENSES COURANTES GASTOS ORDINARIOS	
PAYS	EXERCICE FINANCIER COMMENCANT EN	MONNAIE		AMOUNT	PERCENTAGE OF TOTAL
PAIS	COMIENZO DEL EJERCICIO ECONOMICO	MONEDA	TOTAL	MONTANT IMPORTE	POURCENTAGE DU TOTAL PORCENTAJE DEL TOTAL
			TOTAL (000)	(000)	%
			(1)	(2)	(3)
CZECHOSLOVAKIA	1970	KORUNA	11 391 000	9 524 000	83.6
	1971		11 789 000	10 104 000	85.7
	1976		16 670 000	14 111 000	84.6
	1977		16 875 000	14 493 000	85.9
	1978		17 496 000	15 318 000	87.6
DENMARK	1970	KRONE	1 174 300	1 026 600	87.4
	1973		1 667 200	1 503 400	90.0
	1976		2 662 800	2 376 300	89.2
FINLAND	1969	MARKKA	298 630	247 480	82.9
	1971		435 577	354 840	81.5
	1973		624 220	536 570	86.0
	1975		953 924	839 916	88.0
	1977		1 298 820	1 157 930	89.1
FRANCE	1969	FRANC	14 210 000	11 464 000	86.7
	1970		14 955 200	...	
	1975		26 203 100	23 486 600	89.6
	1976		29 774 000	26 954 000	90.5
	1977		23 185 000	30 258 000	91.2
GERMANY, FEDERAL REPUBLIC OF ‡	1969	DEUTSCHE MARK	10 866 900	8 940 200	82.3
	1970		*12 950 000	...	...
	1973		19 247 000	15 888 000	84.6
	1975		22 969 000	19 622 000	87.2
	1977		25 733 000	22 664 000	89.2
HUNGARY	1969	FORINT	6 308 500	5 076 100	80.5
	1970		7 525 000	5 862 000	77.9
	1976		14 489 000	11 870 000	81.9
	1977		17 446 000	14 673 000	84.1
	1978		18 716 000	15 616 000	83.4
ICELAND ‡	1969	KRONA	*159 700	*128 300	*80.3
	1970		*164 500	*135 800	*82.6
	1971		253 000	...	...
	1973		487 900	429 000	87.9
	1975		1 438 800	1 208 900	84.0
IRELAND ‡	1969	POUND	9 950	8 403	84.5
	1971		14 425	12 515	86.8
	1974		23 471	20 689	88.1
	1975		31 472	27 252	86.6
	1977		43 209	37 150	86.0
ITALY ‡	1969	LIRA	464 214	391 503	81.5
	1970		554 671	461 208	83.1
	1974		916 893	813 888	88.8
	1975		1 168 103	1 019 991	87.3
	1976		1 352 565	1 209 376	89.4
NETHERLANDS ‡	1969	GUILDER	2 227 000	1 884 000	84.6
	1970		2 441 000	2 075 000	85.0
	1974		3 892 000	3 490 000	89.7
	1975		4 440 000	4 008 000	90.3
	1976		4 964 000	4 481 000	90.3

Historical data on R&D expenditure 5.12
Données rétrospectives sur les dépenses de R-D
Datos retrospectivos sobre los gastos de I y D

COUNTRY / PAYS / PAIS	FISCAL YEAR BEGINNING / EXERCICE FINANCIER COMMENCANT EN / COMIENZO DEL EJERCICIO ECONOMICO	CURRENCY / MONNAIE / MONEDA	EXPENDITURE FOR R & D / DEPENSES CONSACREES A R–D / GASTOS DEDICADOS A I Y D		
			TOTAL / TOTAL / TOTAL (000)	CURRENT EXPENDITURE / DEPENSES COURANTES / GASTOS ORDINARIOS	
				AMOUNT / MONTANT / IMPORTE (000)	PERCENTAGE OF TOTAL / POURCENTAGE DU TOTAL / PORCENTAJE DEL TOTAL %
			(1)	(2)	(3)
NORWAY	1969	KRONE	764 500	652 000	85.3
	1970		873 000	786 000	90.0
	1976		2 358 000	2 102 000	89.1
	1977		2 675 200	2 342 300	87.6
	1978		2 973 000	...	...
POLAND	1969	ZLOTY	15 900 000	12 000 000	75.5
	1970		16 900 000	13 200 000	78.1
	1976		36 200 000	30 200 000	83.4
	1977		38 900 000	33 200 000	85.3
	1978		40 800 000	34 900 000	85.5
PORTUGAL	1971	ESCUDO	751 189	...	...
	1972		854 150	738 916	86.5
	1976		1 279 591	1 146 353	89.6
ROMANIA	1969	LEU	2 033 441	1 641 450	80.7
	1970		2 181 390	1 719 332	78.8
	1971		2 750 870	2 114 142	76.9
	1972		3 074 995	2 430 833	79.0
	1973		3 354 196	2 631 161	78.4
SPAIN	1969	PESETA	4 621 184	3 669 853	79.4
	1970		5 547 957	4 360 120	78.6
	1972		9 815 649	7 660 395	78.0
	1973		12 229 847	9 563 054	78.2
	1974		15 536 477	11 496 338	74.0
SWEDEN ‡	1969	KRONA	1 896 000	1 738 000	91.7
	1971		2 713 600	2 503 000	92.2
	1973		3 585 500	3 278 400	91.4
	1975		5 133 200	4 754 200	92.6
	1977		6 796 700	6 305 800	92.8
SWITZERLAND ‡	1969	FRANC	*1 531 100	...	...
	1970		*1 739 300	...	...
	1975		3 104 000	2 977 000	95.9
	1976		*3 363 000	*3 212 000	95.5
UNITED KINGDOM ‡	1969	POUND STERLING	1 045 362	923 032	88.8
	1972		1 310 134	1 172 475	90.7
	1975		2 139 000	1 938 200	91.8
YUGOSLAVIA ‡	1969	DINAR	1 316 300	...	...
	1970		1 646 000	...	...
	1976		4 907 000	...	...
	1977		6 226 000	...	...
	1978		9 633 000	...	...
OCEANIA					
AUSTRALIA	1973	DOLLAR	625 000	550 000	88.0
	1976		802 464	722 124	90.0
NEW ZEALAND ‡	1969	DOLLAR	21 010	...	...
	1970		24 270	...	...
	1971		29 317	...	...

5.12 Historical data on R&D expenditure
Données rétrospectives sur les dépenses de R-D
Datos retrospectivos sobre los gastos de I y D

COUNTRY	FISCAL YEAR BEGINNING	CURRENCY	EXPENDITURE FOR R & D DEPENSES CONSACREES A R–D GASTOS DEDICADOS A I Y D		
			TOTAL	CURRENT EXPENDITURE DEPENSES COURANTES GASTOS ORDINARIOS	
PAYS	EXERCICE FINANCIER COMMENCANT EN	MONNAIE	TOTAL	AMOUNT MONTANT	PERCENTAGE OF TOTAL POURCENTAGE DU TOTAL
PAIS	COMIENZO DEL EJERCICIO ECONOMICO	MONEDA	TOTAL (000)	IMPORTE (000)	PORCENTAJE DEL TOTAL %
			(1)	(2)	(3)
U.S.S.R.					
U.S.S.R. ‡	1969	ROUBLE	9 970 000	8 640 000	86.7
	1971		12 990 000	11 250 000	86.6
	1976		17 700 000	...	...
	1977		18 300 000	...	...
	1978		19 300 000	...	...
BYELORUSSIAN S.S.R. ‡	1969	ROUBLE	45 444	34 295	75.5
	1970		46 399	33 380	71.9

ALGERIA:
E—> DATA RELATE TO THE HIGHER EDUCATION SECTOR
ONLY.
FR-> LES DONNEES NE CONCERNENT QUE LE SECTEUR
DE L'ENSEIGNEMENT SUPERIEUR.
ESP> LOS DATOS SE REFIEREN AL SECTOR DE ENSEÑANZA
SUPERIOR SOLAMENTE.

GABON:
E—> DATA REFER TO THE (FRENCH) "OFFICE DE LA
RECHERCHE SCIENTIFIQUE ET TECHNIQUE OUTRE—MER"
(ORSTOM).
FR-> LES DONNEES NE CONCERNENT QUE L'OFFICE
FRANCAIS DE LA RECHERCHE SCIENTIFIQUE ET TECHNIQUE
OUTRE—MER (ORSTOM).
ESP> LOS DATOS SE REFIEREN AL "OFFICE (FRANCAIS)
DE LA RECHERCHE SCIENTIFIQUE ET TECHNIQUE OUTRE—
MER" (ORSTOM) SOLAMENTE.

MADAGASCAR:
E—> NOT INCLUDING DATA FOR HUMANITIES AND EDU-
CATION FOR 1969 AND 1970; NOT INCLUDING THE PRO-
DUCTIVE SECTOR FOR 1969; NOT INCLUDING THE PRODUC-
TIVE SECTOR (INTEGRATED R&D) FOR 1970 AND 1971.
FR-> NON COMPRIS LES DONNEES POUR LES SCIENCES
HUMAINES ET L'EDUCATION EN 1969 ET 1970; NON COM-
PRIS LES DONNEES POUR LE SECTEUR DE LA PRODUCTION
EN 1969; NON COMPRIS LES DONNEES POUR LE SECTEUR
DE LA PRODUCTION (ACTIVITES DE R-D INTEGREES) EN
1970 ET 1971.
ESP> PARA 1969 Y 1970 EXCLUIDOS LOS DATOS RELA-
TIVOS A LAS CIENCIAS HUMANAS Y A LA EDUCACION;
EN 1969, NO SE INCLUYE EL SECTOR PRODUCTIVO Y EN
1970 Y 1971 QUEDA EXCLUIDO EL SECTOR PRODUCTIVO
(ACTIVIDADES DE I Y D INTEGRADAS).

NIGER:
E—> DATA RELATE TO THE HIGHER EDUCATION SECTOR
ONLY.
FR-> LES DONNEES NE CONCERNENT QUE LE SECTEUR
DE L'ENSEIGNEMENT SUPERIEUR.
ESP> LOS DATOS SE REFIEREN AL SECTOR DE ENSEÑANZA
SUPERIOR SOLAMENTE.

UNITED REPUBLIC OF CAMEROON:
E—> DATA REFER RESPECTIVELY TO THE YEARS 1969/
70 AND 1970/71.
FR-> LES DONNEES SE REFERENT RESPECTIVEMENT AUX
ANNEES 1969/70 ET 1970/71.
ESP> LOS DATOS SE REFIEREN RESPECTIVAMENTE A LOS
AÑOS 1969/70 Y 1970/71.

BERMUDA:
E—> NOT INCLUDING DATA FOR THE PRODUCTIVE SECTOR
AND EXCLUDING LAW, HUMANITIES AND EDUCATION.
FR-> NON COMPRIS LES DONNEES POUR LE SECTEUR DE
LA PRODUCTION ET COMPTE NON TENU DES DONNEES
RELATIVES AU DROIT, AUX SCIENCES HUMAINES ET A
L'EDUCATION.
ESP> EXCLUIDOS LOS DATOS RELATIVOS AL SECTOR
PRODUCTIVO Y LOS QUE SE REFIEREN AL DERECHO, LAS
CIENCIAS HUMANAS Y LA EDUCACION.

COSTA RICA:
E—> DATA REFER TO GOVERNMENT EXPENDITURE ONLY
AND DO NOT INCLUDE THE PRODUCTIVE SECTOR.
FR-> LES DONNEES SE REFERENT AUX DEPENSES PUBLI-
QUES SEULEMENT ET NE COMPRENNENT PAS LE SECTEUR DE
LA PRODUCTION.
ESP> LOS DATOS SOLO SE REFIEREN A LOS GASTOS
PUBLICOS Y NO INCLUYEN EL SECTOR PRODUCTIVO.

MEXICO:
E—> DATA FOR CURRENT EXPENDITURE FOR 1969 (COL-
UMNS 2 AND 3) INCLUDE SOME CAPITAL EXPENDITURE AND
DO NOT INCLUDE LAW, HUMANITIES AND EDUCATION; FOR
1971 FIGURES IN COLUMNS 2 AND 3 REFER TO LABOUR
COSTS ONLY.
FR-> LES DONNEES RELATIVES AUX DEPENSES COURANTES
(COLONNES 2 ET 3) POUR 1969 COMPRENNENT DES DEPEN-
SES EN CAPITAL ET NE COMPRENNENT PAS LE DROIT, LES
SCIENCES HUMAINES ET L'EDUCATION; POUR 1971, LES
CHIFFRES DES COLONNES 2 ET 3 NE CONCERNENT QUE LES
DEPENSES DU PERSONNEL.
ESP> LOS DATOS RELATIVOS A LOS GASTOS ORDINARIOS
(COLUMNAS 2 Y 3) INCLUYEN EN 1969 CIERTOS GASTOS
DE CAPITAL Y NO COMPRENDEN EL DERECHO, LAS CIENCIAS

Historical data on R&D expenditure 5.12
Données rétrospectives sur les dépenses de R-D
Datos retrospectivos sobre los gastos de I y D

MEXICO (CONT.):
HUMANAS Y LA EDUCACION; EN 1971, LAS CIFRAS DE LAS
COLUMNAS 2 Y 3 SOLO CONCIERNEN LOS GASTOS DE
PERSONAL.

TRINIDAD AND TOBAGO:
   E—> NOT INCLUDING DATA FOR LAW, EDUCATION AND
ARTS.
   FR—> NON COMPRIS LES DONNEES POUR LE DROIT,
L'EDUCATION ET LES ARTS.
   ESP> EXCLUIDOS LOS DATOS RELATIVOS AL DERECHO,
LA EDUCACION Y LAS ARTES.

BRAZIL:
   E—> NOT INCLUDING PRIVATE PRODUCTIVE ENTERPRISES.
   FR—> COMPTE NON TENU DES ENTREPRISES PRIVEES DE
PRODUCTION.
   ESP> EXCLUIDAS LAS EMPRESAS PRIVADAS DE
PRODUCCION.

INDIA:
   E—> REVISED SERIES.
   FR—> SERIE REVISEE.
   ESP> SERIES REVISADAS.

INDONESIA:
   E—> DATA RELATE TO THE DEVELOPMENT BUDGET ONLY
AND DO NOT INCLUDE THE PRODUCTIVE SECTOR.
   FR—> LES DONNEES SE REFERENT AU BUDGET DE
DEVELOPPEMENT ET NE TIENNENT PAS COMPTE DU
SECTEUR DE LA PRODUCTION.
   ESP> LOS DATOS SE REFIEREN AL PRESUPUESTO DE
DESARROLLO Y NO TOMAN EN CONSIDERACION EL SECTOR
PRODUCTIVO.

IRAN:
   E—> DATA FOR 1972 REFER TO GOVERNMENT EXPENDI-
TURE ONLY.
   FR—> LES DONNEES POUR 1972 NE SE REFERENT Q'AUX
FONDS PUBLICS.
   ESP> LOS DATOS PARA 1972 SOLO SE REFIEREN A LOS
FONDOS PUBLICOS.

IRAQ:
   E—> PARTIAL DATA. IN 1974 EXPENDITURE FOR R&D
IN GOVERNMENT DEPARTMENTS CONCERNED ONLY WITH
SCIENTIFIC ACTIVITIES WAS 7,409 THOUSAND DINARS OF
WHICH 4,909 THOUSAND DINARS WERE CURRENT EXPEN-
DITURE.
   FR—> DONNEES PARTIELLES. EN 1974, LES DEPENSES
CONSACREES A LA R-D DANS LES DEPARTEMENTS GOUVER-
NEMENTAUX CONCERNES PAR LES ACTIVITES SCIENTIFI-
QUES S'ELEVAIENT A 7 409 000 DINARS DONT 4 909 000
CORRESPONDAIENT AUX DEPENSES COURANTES.
   ESP> DATOS PARCIALES. EN 1974 LOS GASTOS DESTI-
NADOS A LA I Y D EN LOS SERVICIOS GUBERNAMENTALES
QUE SE OCUPAN DE LAS ACTIVIDADES CIENTIFICAS
ALCANZARON LA SUMA DE 7 409 000 DINARES, DE LOS
CUALES 4 909 000 CORRESPONDIAN A LOS GASTOS
ORDINARIOS.

JORDAN:
   E—> DATA REFER TO THE EAST BANK ONLY.
   FR—> LES DONNEES SE REFERENT A LA RIVE ORIENTALE
SEULEMENT.
   ESP> LOS DATOS SE REFIEREN A LA ORILLA ORIENTAL
SOLAMENTE.

KOREA, REPUBLIC OF:
   E—> NOT INCLUDING DATA FOR LAW, HUMANITIES AND
EDUCATION.
   FR—> NON COMPRIS LES DONNEES POUR LE DROIT,
LES SCIENCES HUMAINES ET L'EDUCATION.
   ESP> EXCLUIDOS LOS DATOS RELATIVOS AL DERECHO,
LAS CIENCIAS HUMANAS Y LA EDUCACION.

PAKISTAN:
   E—> DATA REFER TO R&D ACTIVITIES WHICH ARE CON-

PAKISTAN (CONT.):
CENTRED MAINLY IN GOVERNMENT—FINANCED RESEARCH
ESTABLISHEMENTS. SOCIAL SCIENCES AND HUMANITIES
IN THE HIGHER EDUCATION AND GENERAL SERVICE SECTORS
ARE NOT INCLUDED.
   FR—> LES DONNEES SE REFERENT AUX ACTIVITES DE R-D
SE TROUVANT POUR LA PLUPART DANS LES ETABLISSEMENTS
DE RECHERCHE FINANCES PAR LE GOUVERNEMENT. LES
SCIENCES SOCIALES ET HUMAINES DANS LES SECTEURS
DE L'ENSEIGNEMENT SUPERIEUR ET DE SERVICE GENERAL
SONT EXCLUES.
   ESP> LOS DATOS SE REFIEREN A LAS ACTIVIDADES DE
I Y D CONCENTRADAS PRINCIPALMENTE EN LOS ESTABLE-
CIMIENTOS DE INVESTIGACION SUBVENCIONADOS POR EL
GOBIERNO. NO SE INCLUYEN LOS DATOS RELATIVOS A
LAS CIENCIAS SOCIALES Y HUMANAS, EN LOS SECTORES
DE ENSEÑANZA SUPERIOR Y DE SERVICIO GENERAL.

SRI LANKA:
   E—> NOT INCLUDING CAPITAL EXPENDITURE IN THE
HIGHER EDUCATION SECTOR.
   FR—> COMPTE NON TENU DES DEPENSES EN CAPITAL DU
SECTEUR DE L'ENSEIGNEMENT SUPERIEUR.
   ESP> EXCLUIDOS LOS GASTOS DE CAPITAL DEL SECTOR
DE ENSEÑANZA SUPERIOR.

TURKEY:
   E—> DATA RELATE TO GOVERNMENT EXPENDITURE ONLY
AND DO NOT INCLUDE THE PRODUCTIVE SECTOR. NOT
INCLUDING DATA FOR SOCIAL SCIENCES AND HUMANITIES.
   FR—> LES DONNEES NE CONCERNENT QUE LES DEPENSES
DU GOUVERNEMENT ET NE COMPRENNENT PAS LE SECTEUR
DE LA PRODUCTION. NON COMPRIS LES DONNEES POUR
LES SCIENCES SOCIALES ET HUMAINES.
   ESP> LOS DATOS SOLO SE REFIEREN A LOS GASTOS
DEL GOBIERNO Y NO INCLUYEN EL SECTOR PRODUCTIVO.
NO SE INCLUYEN LAS CIENCIAS SOCIALES Y HUMANAS.

AMERICAN SAMOA:
   E—> DATA RELATE TO ONE RESEARCH INSTITUTE ONLY.
   FR—> LES DONNEES NE CONCERNENT QU'UN INSTITUT
DE RECHERCHE.
   ESP> LOS DATOS SE REFIEREN A UN CENTRO DE INVES-
TIGACION SOLAMENTE.

FRENCH POLYNESIA:
   E—> DATA RELATE TO ONE RESEARCH INSTITUTE ONLY.
   FR—> LES DONNEES NE CONCERNENT QU'UN INSTITUT
DE RECHERCHE.
   ESP> LOS DATOS SE REFIEREN A UN CENTRO DE INVES-
TIGACION SOLAMENTE.

GUAM:
   E—> DATA RELATE TO THE HIGHER EDUCATION SECTOR
ONLY.
   FR—> LES DONNEES NE CONCERNENT QUE LE SECTEUR
DE L'ENSEIGNEMENT SUPERIEUR.
   ESP> LOS DATOS SE REFIEREN AL SECTOR DE ENSEÑANZA
SUPERIOR SOLAMENTE.

CANADA:
   E—> NOT INCLUDING DATA FOR SOCIAL SCIENCES AND
HUMANITIES.
   FR—> NON COMPRIS LES DONNEES POUR LES SCIENCES
SOCIALES ET HUMAINES.
   ESP> EXCLUIDOS LOS DATOS RELATIVOS A LAS CIENCIAS
SOCIALES Y HUMANAS.

UNITED STATES OF AMERICA:
   E—> NOT INCLUDING DATA FOR LAW, HUMANITIES AND
EDUCATION.
   FR—> NON COMPRIS LES DONNEES POUR LE DROIT,
LES SCIENCES HUMAINES ET L'EDUCATION.
   ESP> EXCLUIDOS LOS DATOS RELATIVOS AL DERECHO,
LAS CIENCIAS HUMANAS Y LA EDUCACION.

ISRAEL:
   E—> DATA REFER TO THE CIVILIAN SECTOR ONLY AND
DO NOT INCLUDE SOCIAL SCIENCES AND HUMANITIES.

5.12   Historical data on R&D expenditure
Données rétrospectives sur les dépenses de R-D
Datos retrospectivos sobre los gastos de I y D

ISRAEL (CONT.):
  FR–> LES DONNEES NE CONCERNENT QUE LE SECTEUR
CIVIL ET NE COMPRENNENT PAS LES SCIENCES SOCIALES
ET HUMAINES.
  ESP> LOS DATOS SE REFIEREN AL SECTOR CIVIL
SOLAMENTE Y NO COMPRENDEN LAS CIENCIAS SOCIALES
Y HUMANAS.

JAPAN:
  E–> FIGURES IN MILLIONS. NOT INCLUDING DATA
FOR SOCIAL SCIENCES AND HUMANITIES IN THE PRO-
DUCTIVE SECTOR.
  FR–> CHIFFRES EN MILLIONS. NON COMPRIS LES
DONNEES POUR LES SCIENCES SOCIALES ET HUMAINES
DANS LE SECTEUR DE LA PRODUCTION.
  ESP> CIFRAS EN MILLONES. EXCLUIDOS LOS DATOS
RELATIVOS A LAS CIENCIAS SOCIALES Y HUMANAS DEL
SECTOR PRODUCTIVO.

GERMANY, FEDERAL REPUBLIC OF:
  E–> FOR 1973, 1975 AND 1977, TOTAL EXPENDITURE
IN COLUMN 1 INCLUDES RESPECTIVELY 462,470 AND 320
MILLION DEUTSCHE MARKS FOR WHICH A DISTRIBUTION BY
CURRENT AND CAPITAL EXPENDITURE IS NOT AVAILABLE.
THESE FIGURES HAVE BEEN EXCLUDED FROM THE PERCEN-
TAGE CALCULATIONS SHOWN IN COLUMN 3.
  FR–> POUR 1973, 1975 ET 1977, LES DEPENSES
TOTALES DE LA COLONNE 1 COMPRENNENT RESPECTIVEMENT
462 470 ET 320 MILLIONS DE DEUTSCHE MARKS DONT LA
REPARTITION ENTRE DEPENSES COURANTES ET DEPENSES
EN CAPITAL N'A PAS ETE PRECISEE. ON N'A PAS TENU
COMPTE DE CES CHIFFRES POUR CALCULER LES POURCEN-
TAGES DE LA COLONNE 3.
  ESP> EN 1973, 1975 Y 1977 LOS GASTOS TOTALES
DE LA COLUMNA 1 INCLUYEN RESPECTIVAMENTE 462,470
Y 320 MILLONES DE MARCOS, CUYA REPARTICION ENTRE
GASTOS ORDINARIOS Y GASTOS DE CAPITAL NO SE HA
PRECISADO. DICHAS CIFRAS NO SE HAN TENIDO EN
CUENTA PARA CALCULAR LOS PORCENTAJES DE LA
COLUMNA 3.

ICELAND:
  E–> IN 1969 AND 1970 DATA DO NOT INCLUDE SOCIAL
SCIENCES AND HUMANITIES.
  FR–> LES DONNEES POUR 1969 ET 1970 NE COMPREN-
NENT PAS LES SCIENCES SOCIALES ET HUMAINES.
  ESP> LOS DATOS PARA 1969 Y 1970 NO COMPRENDEN
LAS CIENCIAS SOCIALES Y HUMANAS.

IRELAND:
  E–> DATA FOR 1969 AND 1971 DO NOT INCLUDE
HUMANITIES.
  FR–> LES DONNEES POUR 1969 ET 1971 NE COMPREN-
NENT PAS LES SCIENCES HUMAINES.
  ESP> LOS DATOS PARA 1969 Y 1971 NO INCLUYEN
LAS CIENCIAS HUMANAS.

ITALY:
  E–> FIGURES IN MILLIONS.
  FR–> CHIFFRES EN MILLIONS.
  ESP> CIFRAS EN MILLONES.

NETHERLANDS:
  E–> NOT INCLUDING SOCIAL SCIENCES AND HUMANITIES
IN THE PRODUCTIVE SECTOR (INTEGRATED R&D).
  FR–> NON COMPRIS LES DONNEES POUR LES SCIENCES
SOCIALES ET HUMAINES DU SECTEUR DE LA PRODUCTION
(ACTIVITES DE R–D INTEGREES).
  ESP> EXCLUIDOS LOS DATOS RELATIVOS A LAS CIENCIAS
SOCIALES Y HUMANAS DEL SECTOR PRODUCTIVO
(ACTIVIDADES DE I Y D INTEGRADAS).

SWEDEN:
  E–> NOT INCLUDING DATA FOR SOCIAL SCIENCES AND
HUMANITIES.
  FR–> NON COMPRIS LES DONNEES POUR LES SCIENCES
SOCIALES ET HUMAINES.

SWEDEN (CONT.):
  ESP> NO SE INCLUYEN LAS CIENCIAS SOCIALES Y
HUMANAS.

SWITZERLAND:
  E–> DATA FOR 1975 AND 1976 DO NOT INCLUDE
CAPITAL EXPENDITURE IN THE PRODUCTIVE SECTOR.
  FR–> LES DONNEES POUR 1975 ET 1976 NE COMPREN-
NENT PAS LES DEPENSES EN CAPITAL DU SECTEUR DE LA
PRODUCTION.
  ESP> LOS DATOS PARA 1975 Y 1976 EXCLUYEN LOS
GASTOS DE CAPITAL DEL SECTOR PRODUCTIVO.

UNITED KINGDOM:
  E–> FOR 1969, 1972 AND 1973, THE TOTAL EXPEN-
DITURE IN COLUMN 1 INCLUDES RESPECTIVELY 5,666;
17,788 AND 28,200 THOUSAND POUNDS STERLING FOR
WHICH A DISTRIBUTION BETWEEN CURRENT AND CAPITAL
EXPENDITURE IS NOT AVAILABLE; CURRENT EXPENDITURE
IN COLUMN 2 DOES NOT THEREFORE INCLUDE THE RELE-
VANT PORTIONS OF THESE SUMS. THESE FIGURES HAVE
BEEN EXCLUDED FROM THE PERCENTAGE CALCULATIONS
SHOWN IN COLUMN 3.
  FR–> LES DEPENSES TOTALES DE LA COLONNE 1 COM-
PRENNENT POUR 1969, 1972 ET 1973 RESPECTIVEMENT
5 666, 17 788 ET 28 200 MILLIERS DE LIVRES STER-
LING DONT LA REPARTITION ENTRE DEPENSES COURANTES
ET DEPENSES EN CAPITAL N'A PAS ETE PRECISEE; LES
DEPENSES COURANTES DE LA COLONNE 2 NE COMPRENNENT
DONC PAS UNE PARTIE DE CES SOMMES. ON N'A PAS
TENU COMPTE DE CES CHIFFRES POUR CALCULER LES
POURCENTAGES DE LA COLONNE 3.
  ESP> LOS GASTOS TOTALES DE LA COLUMNA 1 COM-
PRENDEN PARA 1969, 1972 Y 1973 RESPECTIVAMENTE
5 666, 17 788 Y 28 200 MILLARES DE LIBRAS ESTER-
LINAS, CUYA REPARTICION ENTRE GASTOS ORDINARIOS
Y GASTOS DE CAPITAL NO SE HA PRECISADO; LOS GASTOS
ORDINARIOS DE LA COLUMNA 2 NO INCLUYEN POR CONSI-
GUIENTE UNA PARTE DE DICHA SUMA. DICHAS CIFRAS
NO SE HAN TENIDO EN CUENTA PARA CALCULAR LOS
PORCENTAJES DE LA COLUMNA 3.

YUGOSLAVIA:
  E–> NOT INCLUDING ACTIVITIES OF A MILITARY
NATURE OR RELATING TO NATIONAL DEFENCE.
  FR–> NON COMPRIS LES ACTIVITES DE CARACTERE
MILITAIRE OU RELEVANT DE LA DEFENSE NATIONALE.
  ESP> EXCLUIDAS LAS ACTIVIDADES DE CARACTER
MILITAR O QUE CONCIERNEN LA DEFENSA NACIONAL.

NEW ZEALAND:
  E–> NOT INCLUDING FUNDS FROM OVERSEAS.
  FR–> NON COMPRIS LES FONDS EN PROVENANCE DE
L'ETRANGER.
  ESP> NO SE INCLUYEN LOS FONDOS PROCEDENTES DEL
EXTRANJERO.

U.S.S.R.:
  E–> "EXPENDITURE ON SCIENCE" FROM THE NATIONAL
BUDGET AND OTHER SOURCES.
  FR–> MONTANT TOTAL DES SOMMES DEPENSEES POUR LA
SCIENCE D'APRES LE BUDGET NATIONAL ET AUTRES
SOURCES.
  ESP> IMPORTE TOTAL DE LOS GASTOS DEDICADOS A
LA CIENCIA, SEGUN EL PRESUPUESTO NACIONAL Y OTRAS
FUENTES.

BYELORUSSIAN S.S.R.:
  E–> R&D EXPENDITURE RELATES TO RESEARCH
INSTITUTIONS ADMINISTERED BY THE COUNCIL OF
MINISTERS OF THE BYELORUSSIAN S.S.R.
  FR–> LES DONNEES SE REFERENT AUX INSTITUTS
DE RECHERCHE ADMINISTRES PAR LE CONSEIL DES
MINISTRES DE LA R.S.S. DE BIELORUSSIE.
  ESP> LOS DATOS SE REFIEREN A LOS CENTROS DE
INVESTIGACION ADMINISTRADOS POR EL CONSEJO DE
MINISTROS DE LA RSS DE BIELORRUSIA.

5.13 Human and financial resources for R&D (indicators)
Ressources humaines et financières pour la R-D (indicateurs)
Recursos humanos y financieros para la I y D (indicadores)

5.13 Selected indicators for scientific and technical manpower and expenditure for research and experimental development

Indicateurs sélectionnés pour le personnel scientifique et technique et les dépenses de recherche et de développement expérimental

Indicadores seleccionados para el personal científico y técnico y los gastos de investigación y de desarrollo experimental

PLEASE REFER TO INTRODUCTION FOR DEFINITIONS OF
CATEGORIES INCLUDED IN THIS TABLE.

  FTE = FULL—TIME EQUIVALENT
  SET = SCIENTISTS, ENGINEERS AND TECHNICIANS

NUMBER OF COUNTRIES AND TERRITORIES PRESENTED IN
THIS TABLE: 137

POUR LES DEFINITIONS DES CATEGORIES PRESENTEES
DANS CE TABLEAU, SE REFERER A L'INTRODUCTION.

  FTE = EQUIVALENT PLEIN TEMPS
  SET = SCIENTIFIQUES, INGENIEURS ET TECHNICIENS

NOMBRE DE PAYS ET DE TERRITOIRES PRESENTES DANS CE
TABLEAU: 137

COUNTRY / PAYS / PAIS	YEAR / ANNEE / AÑO	TOTAL STOCK / EFFECTIF TOTAL / NUMERO TOTAL — SCIENTISTS AND ENGINEERS PER MILLION POPULATION / SCIENTIFIQUES ET INGENIEURS PAR MILLION D'HABITANTS / CIENTIFICOS E INGENIEROS POR MILLON HABITANTES	TECHNICIANS PER MILLION POPULATION / TECHNICIENS PAR MILLION D'HABITANTS / TECNICOS POR MILLON HABITANTES	PERSONNEL ENGAGED IN R&D / PERSONNEL EMPLOYE A DES TRAVAUX R–D / PERSONAL DEDICADO A ACTIVIDADES DE I Y D — SCIENTISTS AND ENGINEERS (FTE) PER MILLION POPULATION / SCIENTIFIQUES ET INGENIEURS (FTE) PAR MILLION D'HABITANTS / CIENTIFICOS E INGENIEROS (FTE) POR MILLON HABITANTES	TECHNICIANS PER MILLION POPULATION / TECHNICIENS PAR MILLION D'HABITANTS / TECNICOS POR MILLON HABITANTES	NUMBER OF TECHNICIANS PER SCIENTIST AND ENGINEER / NOMBRE DE TECHNICIENS PAR SCIENTIFIQUE ET INGENIEUR / NUMERO DE TECNICOS POR CIENTIFICO E INGENIERO
		(1)	(2)	(3)	(4)	(5)
AFRICA						
ALGERIA ‡	1972	...	...	16	7	0.4
BOTSWANA ‡	1973	1 248	1 176	37	28	0.8
CENTRAL AFRICAN						
REPUBLIC	1975	...	...	*42	*2	0.04
CHAD ‡	1973	...	...	23	27	1.2
CONGO	1977	...	2 403	197	...	...
DJIBOUTI	1973	347	—	...	...	...
EGYPT	1973	16 656	...	299	...	...
GABON ‡	1970	...	...	16	40	2.5
GAMBIA	1973	903	...	...	...	...
GHANA ‡	1976	801	1 753	396	556	1.4
IVORY COAST	1970	...	...	60	42	0.7
KENYA ‡	1975	383	439	27	14	0.5
LIBYAN ARAB						
JAMAHIRIYA	1973	3 697	4 712	*22	*63	*2.8
MADAGASCAR ‡	1971	...	...	*29	*14	0.5
MALAWI	1977	...	...	34	44	1.3

Human and financial resources for R&D (indicators)   5.13
Ressources humaines et financières pour la R-D (indicateurs)
Recursos humanos y financieros para la I y D (indicadores)

EN LA INTRODUCCION SE DAN LAS DEFINICIONES DE LAS
CATEGORIAS QUE FIGURAN EN ESTE CUADRO.

FTE = EQUIVALENTE DE JORNADA COMPLETA
SET = CIENTIFICOS, INGENIEROS Y TECNICOS

NUMERO DE PAISES Y DE TERRITORIOS PRESENTADOS EN
ESTE CUADRO: 137

	EXPENDITURE FOR R&D DEPENSES CONSACREES A R—D GASTOS DEDICADOS A I Y D			
SET IN R&D AS % OF TOTAL STOCK	AS PERCENTAGE OF GROSS NATIONAL PRODUCT (%)	PER CAPITA (IN NATIONAL CURRENCY)	ANNUAL AVERAGE PER R&D SCIENTIST AND ENGINEER (IN NATIONAL CURRENCY)	CURRENCY
SET EN R—D EN % DE L'EFFECTIF TOTAL	EN POURCENTAGE DU PRODUIT NATIONAL BRUT (%)	PAR HABITANT (EN MONNAIE NATIONALE)	MOYENNE ANNUELLE PAR SCIENTIFIQUE ET INGENIEUR R-D (EN MONNAIE NATIONALE)	MONNAIE
SET EN I Y D EN % DEL NUMERO TOTAL	EN PORCENTAJE DEL PRODUCTO NACIONAL BRUTO (%)	POR PERSONA (EN MONEDA NACIONAL)	PROMEDIO ANUAL POR CIENTIFICO E INGE— NIERO DE I Y D (EN MONEDA NACIONAL)	MONEDA
(6)	(7)	(8)	(9)	
	0.3	5.1	322 300	DINAR
3.0	0.2	0.3	9 200	PULA
...	...			
...	0.4	*65.9	...	FRANC C.F.A
...	0.4	440.9	2 233 200	FRANC C.F.A
1.8	0.8	0.9	2 800	POUND
...	0.0	3.8	236 900	FRANC C.F.A
24.8	*0.9	2.4	7 000	CEDI
	*0.4	325.1	4 392 200	FRANC C.F.A
7.0	*0.8	*8.8	*180 900	SHILLING
*0.6				
...	*0.8	*339.9	*11 412 900	FRANC
	0.2	0.2	6 800	KWACHA

5.13 Human and financial resources for R&D (indicators)
Ressources humaines et financières pour la R-D (indicateurs)
Recursos humanos y financieros para la I y D (indicadores)

		TOTAL STOCK EFFECTIF TOTAL NUMERO TOTAL		PERSONNEL ENGAGED IN R&D PERSONNEL EMPLOYE A DES TRAVAUX R—D PERSONAL DEDICADO A ACTIVIDADES DE I Y D		
COUNTRY PAYS PAIS	YEAR ANNEE AÑO	SCIENTISTS AND ENGINEERS PER MILLION POPULATION SCIENTIFIQUES ET INGENIEURS PAR MILLION D'HABITANTS CIENTIFICOS E INGENIEROS POR MILLON HABITANTES	TECHNICIANS PER MILLION POPULATION TECHNICIENS PAR MILLION D'HABITANTS TECNICOS POR MILLON HABITANTES	SCIENTISTS AND ENGINEERS (FTE) PER MILLION POPULATION SCIENTIFIQUES ET INGENIEURS (FTE) PAR MILLION D'HABITANTS CIENTIFICOS E INGENIEROS (FTE) POR MILLON HABITANTES	TECHNICIANS PER MILLION POPULATION TECHNICIENS PAR MILLION D'HABITANTS TECNICOS POR MILLON HABITANTES	NUMBER OF TECHNICIANS PER SCIENTIST AND ENGINEER NOMBRE DE TECHNICIENS PAR SCIENTIFIQUE ET INGENIEUR NUMERO DE TECNICOS POR CIENTIFICO E INGENIERO
		(1)	(2)	(3)	(4)	(5)
MAURITIUS ‡	1977	7 361	...	166	165	1.0
NIGER	1976	...	...	20	...	0.01
NIGERIA ‡	1970	353	270	37	*13	*0.4
SENEGAL ‡	1972	...	...	95	125	1.3
SEYCHELLES ‡	1973	*5 357	...	18	—	—
SUDAN ‡	1978	*857	*164	188	188	1.0
SWAZILAND	1977	2 730	——>	...	...	...
TOGO ‡	1976	228	104	114	81	0.7
TUNISIA ‡	1974	606	1 367	*153	*104	*0.7
UNITED REPUBLIC OF CAMEROON ‡	1970	*516	——>	49	...	...
UPPER VOLTA	1970	...	...	...	...	...
ZAMBIA ‡	1976	2 373	5 609	49	29	0.6
AMERICA, NORTH						
ANTIGUA	1970	*6 857	*4 286	...	...	...
BAHAMAS	1970	*17 647	*21 176	*112	*6	*0.05
BELIZE	1970	1 675	4 392	125	33	0.3
BERMUDA	1970	30 111	36 611	74	56	0.8
BRITISH VIRGIN ISLANDS	1973	*12 000	*20 000	—	—	—
CANADA ‡	1977	28 780	...	1 056	686	0.7
CAYMAN ISLANDS	1971	20 000	35 000	300	300	1.0
CUBA ‡	1978	6 270	...	517	633	1.2
DOMINICAN REPUBLIC	1970	1 930	...	...	...	...
EL SALVADOR	1974	1 411	456	206	*133	*0.7
GUATEMALA	1974	*953	*1 220	*53	*75	1.4
HONDURAS	1974	2 501	1 188	2	...	0.2
JAMAICA	1971	...	...	...	...	...
MEXICO ‡	1974	*6 678	14 497	101	...	...
NETHERLANDS ANTILLES	1971	15 053	...	...	...	...
NICARAGUA	1971	...	...	...	...	...
PANAMA ‡	1976	4 699	8 058	122	180	1.5
PUERTO RICO	1970	26 838	...	...	...	...
ST. PIERRE AND MIQUELON	1972	...	...	1 167	667	0.6
TRINIDAD AND TOBAGO	1970	...	...	369	186	0.5
TURKS AND CAICOS ISLANDS	1976	2 667	*5 667	333	—	—
UNITED STATES OF AMERICA ‡	1978	11 398	4 453	2 685	305	0.1

Human and financial resources for R&D (indicators) 5.13
Ressources humaines et financières pour la R-D (indicateurs)
Recursos humanos y financieros para la I y D (indicadores)

EXPENDITURE FOR R&D
DEPENSES CONSACREES A R—D
GASTOS DEDICADOS A I Y D

SET IN R&D AS % OF TOTAL STOCK / SET EN R—D EN % DE L'EFFECTIF TOTAL / SET EN I Y D EN % DEL NUMERO TOTAL	AS PERCENTAGE OF GROSS NATIONAL PRODUCT (%) / EN POURCENTAGE DU PRODUIT NATIONAL BRUT (%) / EN PORCENTAJE DEL PRODUCTO NACIONAL BRUTO (%)	PER CAPITA (IN NATIONAL CURRENCY) / PAR HABITANT (EN MONNAIE NATIONALE) / POR PERSONA (EN MONEDA NACIONAL)	ANNUAL AVERAGE PER R&D SCIENTIST AND ENGINEER (IN NATIONAL CURRENCY) / MOYENNE ANNUELLE PAR SCIENTIFIQUE ET INGENIEUR R—D (EN MONNAIE NATIONALE) / PROMEDIO ANUAL POR CIENTIFICO E INGE-NIERO DE I Y D (EN MONEDA NACIONAL)	CURRENCY / MONNAIE / MONEDA
(6)	(7)	(8)	(9)	
1.6	0.5	20.7	124 500	RUPEE
...	*0.1	30.0	1 523 700	FRANC C.F.A
*10.5	*0.4	*0.4	*11 400	NAIRA
*0.3	0.8	*528.2	5 551 000	FRANC C.F.A
...	0.2	8.0	401 700	RUPEE
*1.8	*0.3	0.3	1 570	POUND
	...	...		
25.6	*1.5	530.1	9 074 800	FRANC C.F.A
...	...	...	...	.
...	*0.6	*302.4	*5 364 700	FRANC C.F.A
	*0.4	*76.7	...	FRANC C.F.A
2.4	0.6	14.2	*24 100	KWACHA
*0.6	...	*0.2	*28 900	DOLLAR
7.5	...	1.7	13 800	DOLLAR
0.3	...	4.8	60 000	DOLLAR
—	—	—	—	.
*3.6	1.1	96.3	91 200	DOLLAR
1.5	...	...	...	.
8.2	...	8.5	16 700	PESO
...	...	...		
*14.6	0.8	7.9	39 000	COLON
5.6	0.2	0.9	*16 600	QUETZAL
0.1	...	...	...	
...	*0.1	*0.6		DOLLAR
*1.1	0.2	22.7	*216 700	PESO
...	...	...	...	.
...	*0.1	*4.1		CORDOBA
*2.6	0.2	1.8	*14 300	BALBOA
...	...	...	...	.
...	...	18333.3	15 714 300	FRANC C.F.A
...	0.3	5.0	13 600	DOLLAR
12.5	...	1.3	*2 700	U.S. DOLLAR
20.0	*2.5	216.9	80 800	DOLLAR

5.13 Human and financial resources for R&D (indicators)
Ressources humaines et financières pour la R-D (indicateurs)
Recursos humanos y financieros para la I y D (indicadores)

COUNTRY / PAYS / PAIS	YEAR / ANNEE / AÑO	TOTAL STOCK — EFFECTIF TOTAL — NUMERO TOTAL		PERSONNEL ENGAGED IN R&D — PERSONNEL EMPLOYE A DES TRAVAUX R–D — PERSONAL DEDICADO A ACTIVIDADES DE I Y D		
		SCIENTISTS AND ENGINEERS PER MILLION POPULATION / SCIENTIFIQUES ET INGENIEURS PAR MILLION D'HABITANTS / CIENTIFICOS E INGENIEROS POR MILLON HABITANTES	TECHNICIANS PER MILLION POPULATION / TECHNICIENS PAR MILLION D'HABITANTS / TECNICOS POR MILLON HABITANTES	SCIENTISTS AND ENGINEERS (FTE) PER MILLION POPULATION / SCIENTIFIQUES ET INGENIEURS (FTE) PAR MILLION D'HABITANTS / CIENTIFICOS E INGENIEROS (FTE) POR MILLON HABITANTES	TECHNICIANS PER MILLION POPULATION / TECHNICIENS PAR MILLION D'HABITANTS / TECNICOS POR MILLON HABITANTES	NUMBER OF TECHNICIANS PER SCIENTIST AND ENGINEER / NOMBRE DE TECHNICIENS PAR SCIENTIFIQUE ET INGENIEUR / NUMERO DE TECNICOS POR CIENTIFICO E INGENIERO
		(1)	(2)	(3)	(4)	(5)
AMERICA, SOUTH						
ARGENTINA ‡	1978	16 525	89 428	*313	*432	*1.4
BOLIVIA	1974	1 769	...	...	...	...
BRAZIL ‡	1978	5 851	12 727	208	299	1.4
CHILE ‡	1975	7 465	...	580	...	...
COLOMBIA	1971	...	...	52	...	...
ECUADOR ‡	1976	6 986	7 131	64	56	0.9
FALKLAND ISLANDS (MALVINAS)	1971	...	...	—	—	—
GUYANA	1977	754	1 195	...	...	...
PARAGUAY	1971	...	...	54	...	...
PERU ‡	1976	*5 521	*3 900	135	136	1.0
URUGUAY ‡	1972	6 954	10 491	*394	*372	*0.9
VENEZUELA	1973	...	...	241	69	0.3
ASIA						
BANGLADESH ‡	1974	321	*546	23	10	0.5
BRUNEI ‡	1974	4 363	12 207	147	113	0.8
BURMA ‡	1975	610	...	57	16	0.3
CYPRUS ‡	1971	*7 381	*3 175	183	241	1.3
HONG KONG	1976	15 261	...	...	...	...
INDIA ‡	1977	1 115	2 606	46	42	0.9
INDONESIA ‡	1976	788	11 258	57	39	0.7
IRAN ‡	1974	5 015	1 756	160	28	0.2
IRAQ ‡	1974	*4 332	*2 451	138	35	0.3
ISRAEL ‡	1978	29 191	23 886	3 991	...	...
JAPAN ‡	1978	126 622	147 062	3 548	734	0.2
JORDAN ‡	1977	4 005	1 957	156	...	...
KOREA, REPUBLIC OF ‡	1978	21 956	...	398	241	0.6
KUWAIT ‡	1977	27 355	...	537	143	0.3
LAO PEOPLE'S DEMOCRATIC REPUBLIC	1970	...	...	123	...	...
LEBANON	1972	*9 629	...	...	...	...
MALAYSIA PENINSULAR MALAYSIA	1973	*3 125	...	...	...	...
MONGOLIA ‡	1972	1 451	100	621	...	...
PAKISTAN	1973	1 663	...	62	69	1.1
PHILIPPINES ‡	1976	29 410	...	83	55	0.7
QATAR	1974	15 191	6 483	...	...	...
SAUDI ARABIA	1974	*3 834	...	...	...	...
SINGAPORE ‡	1978	5 466	...	198	114	0.6
SRI LANKA ‡	1975	2960.0	...	159	404	2.5
SYRIAN ARAB REPUBLIC	1970	4 372	3 402	...	...	...
THAILAND ‡	1975	485	1 131	149	...	...
TURKEY ‡	1978	...	...	221	96	0.4
VIET–NAM ‡	1979	...	...	262	121	0.5
YEMEN ‡	1974	215	105	9	8	0.9

Human and financial resources for R&D (indicators) 5.13
Ressources humaines et financières pour la R-D (indicateurs)
Recursos humanos y financieros para la I y D (indicadores)

	EXPENDITURE FOR R&D DEPENSES CONSACREES A R–D GASTOS DEDICADOS A I Y D			
SET IN R&D AS % OF TOTAL STOCK SET EN R–D EN % DE L'EFFECTIF TOTAL SET EN I Y D EN % DEL NUMERO TOTAL	AS PERCENTAGE OF GROSS NATIONAL PRODUCT (%) EN POURCENTAGE DU PRODUIT NATIONAL BRUT (%) EN PORCENTAJE DEL PRODUCTO NACIONAL BRUTO (%)	PER CAPITA (IN NATIONAL CURRENCY) PAR HABITANT (EN MONNAIE NATIONALE) POR PERSONA (EN MONEDA NACIONAL)	ANNUAL AVERAGE PER R&D SCIENTIST AND ENGINEER (IN NATIONAL CURRENCY) MOYENNE ANNUELLE PAR SCIENTIFIQUE ET INGENIEUR R–D (EN MONNAIE NATIONALE) PROMEDIO ANUAL POR CIENTIFICO E INGE- NIERO DE I Y D (EN MONEDA NACIONAL)	CURRENCY MONNAIE MONEDA
(6)	(7)	(8)	(9)	
*1.9	*1.0	7398.9	*23 670 100	PESO
...	*0.9	180.1	865 300	CRUZEIRO
...	0.1	9.7	184 700	PESO
...	0.2	35.3	550 900	SUCRE
—	—	—	—	
...	0.2	70.6	1 248 200	GUARANI
*2.5	0.3	145.5	588 700	SOL
*5.7	0.2	0.6	*1 616	PESO
...	0.4	25.7	106 500	BOLIVAR
7.0	0.2	1.5	*68 800	TAKA
1.2	...	21.2	138 900	DOLLAR
9.3	0.1	0.4	...	KYAT
*2.3	0.4	1.7	9 300	POUND
...	...	...	...	
*4.1	0.5	6.6	...	RUPEE
*7.2	0.2	144.2	2 550 200	RUPIAH
3.8	0.3	115.6	721 400	RIAL
...	0.2	0.7	5 000	DINAR
3.5	*4.2	1668.3	418 000	POUND
2.8	1.9	31778.8	8 955 700	YEN
3.9	0.4	0.7	*4 590	DINAR
1.6	*1.0	4117.3	10 334 100	WON
...	0.1	5.6	10 400	DINAR
...	...	...	...	
...	...	...	...	
...	...	11.5	18 500	TUGRIK
3.8	0.2	2.3	25 300	RUPEE
...	0.3	5.4	...	PESO
...	...	...	...	
*3.6	*0.2	12.0	61 000	DOLLAR
...	0.2	*3.2	...	RUPEE
*30.7	...	...	...	
...	*0.9	175.9	...	LIRA
...	...	*2.2	*8 300	DONG
4.3	0.2	1.5	1 654 000	RIAL

5.13 Human and financial resources for R&D (indicators)
Ressources humaines et financières pour la R-D (indicateurs)
Recursos humanos y financieros para la I y D (indicadores)

		TOTAL STOCK EFFECTIF TOTAL NUMERO TOTAL		PERSONNEL ENGAGED IN R&D PERSONNEL EMPLOYE A DES TRAVAUX R–D PERSONAL DEDICADO A ACTIVIDADES DE I Y D		
COUNTRY PAYS PAIS	YEAR ANNEE AÑO	SCIENTISTS AND ENGINEERS PER MILLION POPULATION SCIENTIFIQUES ET INGENIEURS PAR MILLION D'HABITANTS CIENTIFICOS E INGENIEROS POR MILLON HABITANTES	TECHNICIANS PER MILLION POPULATION TECHNICIENS PAR MILLION D'HABITANTS TECNICOS POR MILLON HABITANTES	SCIENTISTS AND ENGINEERS (FTE) PER MILLION POPULATION SCIENTIFIQUES ET INGENIEURS (FTE) PAR MILLION D'HABITANTS CIENTIFICOS E INGENIEROS (FTE) POR MILLON HABITANTES	TECHNICIANS PER MILLION POPULATION TECHNICIENS PAR MILLION D'HABITANTS TECNICOS POR MILLON HABITANTES	NUMBER OF TECHNICIANS PER SCIENTIST AND ENGINEER NOMBRE DE TECHNICIENS PAR SCIENTIFIQUE ET INGENIEUR NUMERO DE TECNICOS POR CIENTIFICO E INGENIERO
		(1)	(2)	(3)	(4)	(5)
EUROPE						
AUSTRIA ‡	1972	15 866	...	250	373	1.5
BELGIUM	1977	25 651	...	1 412	783	0.6
BULGARIA ‡	1978	26 890	60 274	3 818	1 212	0.3
CZECHOSLOVAKIA ‡	1978	22 512	...	3 303	3 960	1.2
DENMARK ‡	1976	...	...	1 055	1 665	1.6
FINLAND	1977	35 000	194 354	1 512	1 497	1.0
FRANCE ‡	1977	28 847	...	1 281	2 904	2.3
GERMAN DEMOCRATIC REPUBLIC ‡	1977	26 525	48 267	5 401	4 036	0.8
GERMANY, FEDERAL REPUBLIC OF ‡	1977	17 839	1 746	1 807	1 700	0.9
GIBRALTAR	1970	1 577	4 731	–	–	–
GREECE ‡	1976	22 014	...	280	192	0.7
HUNGARY ‡	1978	32 228	46 342	2 369	2 422	1.0
ICELAND ‡	1975	15 845	...	1 050	1 459	1.4
IRELAND ‡	1977	7 367	...	841	459	0.6
ITALY ‡	1976	16 416	62 294	674	491	0.7
MALTA ‡	1973	5 421	...	121	68	0.6
NETHERLANDS ‡	1976	*33 500	*22 738	1 761	2 164	1.2
NORWAY ‡	1978	21 301	...	1 589	1 858	1.2
POLAND ‡	1978	23 834	119 082	2 616	1 774	0.7
PORTUGAL	1976	...	...	181	234	1.3
ROMANIA	1973	...	...	1 253	607	0.5
SAN MARINO	1976	13 350	18 550	–	–	–
SPAIN	1974	...	...	225	112	0.5
SWEDEN	1977	...	...	1 708	2 687	1.6
SWITZERLAND ‡	1976	39 669	...	*2 625	*1 564	*0.6
UNITED KINGDOM	1975	...	...	1 417	1 354	1.0
YUGOSLAVIA ‡	1978	13 246	123 052	1 006	538	0.5
OCEANIA						
AMERICAN SAMOA ‡	1973	10 219	2 969	103	69	0.7
AUSTRALIA ‡	1976	11 580	35 061	1 617	903	0.6
COOK ISLANDS ‡	1970	6 833	5 875	375	–	–
FIJI	1969	607	655	35		
FRENCH POLYNESIA ‡	1976	792	...	83	159	1.9
KIRIBATI	1971	1 965	1 140	...	...	...
GUAM ‡	1978	*4 760	...	*106	*177	*1.7
NAURU	1970	...	...	–	–	–
NEW CALEDONIA ‡	1973	580	639		9	0.0
NEW HEBRIDES ‡	1975	1 789	4 544	*30	*10	0.3
NEW ZEALAND ‡	1975	21 137	52 361	1 192	1 031	0.9
NIUE	1971	400	800	...	...	...
NORFOLK ISLAND ‡	1975	11 000	1 000	–	–	–
PACIFIC ISLANDS ‡	1978	1 464	8 564	37	82	2.2
PAPUA NEW GUINEA	1973	1 032	3 961	51	...	...

Human and financial resources for R&D (indicators) 5.13
Ressources humaines et financières pour la R-D (indicateurs)
Recursos humanos y financieros para la I y D (indicadores)

EXPENDITURE FOR R&D
DEPENSES CONSACREES A R-D
GASTOS DEDICADOS A I Y D

SET IN R&D AS % OF TOTAL STOCK / SET EN R-D EN % DE L'EFFECTIF TOTAL / SET EN I Y D EN % DEL NUMERO TOTAL	AS PERCENTAGE OF GROSS NATIONAL PRODUCT (%) / EN POURCENTAGE DU PRODUIT NATIONAL BRUT (%) / EN PORCENTAJE DEL PRODUCTO NACIONAL BRUTO (%)	PER CAPITA (IN NATIONAL CURRENCY) / PAR HABITANT (EN MONNAIE NATIONALE) / POR PERSONA (EN MONEDA NACIONAL)	ANNUAL AVERAGE PER R&D SCIENTIST AND ENGINEER (IN NATIONAL CURRENCY) / MOYENNE ANNUELLE PAR SCIENTIFIQUE ET INGENIEUR R-D (EN MONNAIE NATIONALE) / PROMEDIO ANUAL POR CIENTIFICO E INGENIERO DE I Y D (EN MONEDA NACIONAL)	CURRENCY / MONNAIE / MONEDA
(6)	(7)	(8)	(9)	
*1.6	0.4	315.6	1 264 000	SCHILLING
5.5	1.4	3956.7	2 801 600	FRANC
5.7	2.2	38.0	10 340	LEV
12.4	*4.2	1155.8	349 900	KORUNA
...	*1.1	*529.9	*518 400	KRONE
4.3	1.1	274.0	181 300	MARKKA
4.3	1.8	625.2	488 150	FRANC
22.8		...	...	.
*7.6	*2.3	419.1	231 900	DEUTSCHE MARK
—	—	—	—	.
...	0.2	189.7	401 900	DRACHMA
6.1	*3.9	1751.6	739 500	FORINT
4.0	0.5	2301.4	3 127 600	KRONA
8.6	0.8	13.5	16 100	POUND
3.5	0.8	23482.1	349 956 000	LIRA
1.3	0.1	0.5	3 800	POUND
*5.1	2.1	360.5	204 700	GUILDER
7.3	1.4	661.8	423 460	KRONE
12.5	1.9	1164.5	445 100	ZLOTY
...	*0.3	135.4	731 600	ESCUDO
...	...	161.0	128 500	LEU
—	—	—	—	.
...	0.3	440.7	1 960 700	PESETA
...	2.0	823.3	482 000	KRONA
*6.4	*2.3	*530.0	*207 200	FRANC
...	2.0	38.2	27 000	POUND STERLING
7.3	*1.1	439.6	436 900	DINAR
*1.0	...	4.0	40 000	U.S. DOLLAR
...	1.0	57.6	35 600	DOLLAR
5.5	1.3	5.6	12 400	NEW ZEALAND DOLLAR
...	...	1078.8	12 749 100	FRANC C.F.P.
*2.2	...	6.4	57 900	U.S. DOLLAR
—	—	—	—	.
0.0	0.0	13.1	5 760 000	FRANC C.F.P.
1.9	...	216.0	7 201 000	FRANC
...	0.9	32.5	27 300	DOLLAR
...	...	...	...	.
...	—	—	...	.
14.3	...	1.4	37 000	U.S.DOLLAR
5.0	...	...	...	.

5.13 Human and financial resources for R&D (indicators)
Ressources humaines et financières pour la R-D (indicateurs)
Recursos humanos y financieros para la I y D (indicadores)

COUNTRY / PAYS / PAIS	YEAR / ANNEE / AÑO	TOTAL STOCK / EFFECTIF TOTAL / NUMERO TOTAL		PERSONNEL ENGAGED IN R&D / PERSONNEL EMPLOYE A DES TRAVAUX R-D / PERSONAL DEDICADO A ACTIVIDADES DE I Y D		
		SCIENTISTS AND ENGINEERS PER MILLION POPULATION / SCIENTIFIQUES ET INGENIEURS PAR MILLION D'HABITANTS / CIENTIFICOS E INGENIEROS POR MILLON HABITANTES	TECHNICIANS PER MILLION POPULATION / TECHNICIENS PAR MILLION D'HABITANTS / TECNICOS POR MILLON HABITANTES	SCIENTISTS AND ENGINEERS (FTE) PER MILLION POPULATION / SCIENTIFIQUES ET INGENIEURS (FTE) PAR MILLION D'HABITANTS / CIENTIFICOS E INGENIEROS (FTE) POR MILLON HABITANTES	TECHNICIANS PER MILLION POPULATION / TECHNICIENS PAR MILLION D'HABITANTS / TECNICOS POR MILLON HABITANTES	NUMBER OF TECHNICIANS PER SCIENTIST AND ENGINEER / NOMBRE DE TECHNICIENS PAR SCIENTIFIQUE ET INGENIEUR / NUMERO DE TECNICOS POR CIENTIFICO E INGENIERO
		(1)	(2)	(3)	(4)	(5)
SAMOA ‡	1978	2 288	1 072	909	597	0.7
SOLOMON ISLANDS	1971	777	4 608	...	...	...
U.S.S.R.						
U.S.S.R. ‡	1978	40 694	56 544	5 024	...	...
BYELORUSSIAN S.S.R.‡	1977	41 023	55 651	3 649	...	...
UKRAINIAN S.S.R. ‡	1978	40 505	56 774	3 742	...	...

GENERAL NOTE / NOTE GENERALE / NOTA GENERAL:
E—> FOR FURTHER DETAILS CONCERNING THE COVERAGE
AND THE LIMITATIONS OF THE BASIC DATA USED FOR THE
INDICATORS, PLEASE REFER TO TABLES RELATING TO
SCIENTIFIC AND TECHNICAL MANPOWER (TABLES 5.1 AND
5.2) OR R&D EXPENDITURE (TABLE 5.6) AS APPROPRIATE.
IN THE ABSENCE OF R&D EXCHANGE RATES, THESE DATA
WHICH ARE IN THE NATIONAL CURRENCY, CAN BE COM-
PARED, ONE COUNTRY WITH ANOTHER, BY THE USE OF
OFFICIAL EXCHANGE RATES BETWEEN NATIONAL CURRENCIES
AND THE UNITED STATES DOLLAR GIVEN IN APPENDIX C.
IT SHOULD BE UNDERSTOOD, OF COURSE, THAT THESE
EXCHANGE RATES DO NOT ALWAYS REFLECT THE REAL COSTS
OF R&D ACTIVITIES.
FR—> POUR DES DETAILS PLUS COMPLETS EN CE QUI
CONCERNE LA PORTEE DES DONNEES DE BASE ET LES
ELEMENTS PRIS EN CONSIDERATION POUR LE CALCUL DES
INDICATEURS, SE REFERER SELON LE CAS, AUX TABLEAUX
5.1 ET 5.2 CONCERNANT LE PERSONNEL SCIENTIFIQUE ET
TECHNIQUE OU AU TABLEAU 5.6 CONCERNANT LES DEPENSES
AFFERENTES A LA R-D.
EN L'ABSENCE DE TAUX DE CHANGE APPLICABLES AUX
ACTIVITES DE R-D POUR COMPARER D'UN PAYS A L'AUTRE
LES DONNEES ETABLIES EN MONNAIE NATIONALE, IL
FAUDRA NECESSAIREMENT SE FONDER SUR LES TAUX DE
CHANGE OFFICIELS DE CONVERSION DES MONNAIES NATIO-
NALES EN DOLLARS DES ETATS-UNIS, TELS QU'IL FIGU-
RENT DANS L'ANNEXE C. IL VA SANS DIRE QUE CES
TAUX DE CHANGE NE REFLETENT PAS TOUJOURS LE COUT
REEL DES ACTIVITES DE R-D.
ESP> PARA UNA INFORMACION MAS COMPLETA EN LO QUE
SE REFIERE AL ALCANCE DE LOS DATOS DE BASE Y DE
LOS ELEMENTOS QUE SE TOMARON EN CONSIDERACION PARA
EL CALCULO DE LOS INDICADORES, SIRVANSE REFERIRSE,
SEGUN EL CASO, A LOS CUADROS 5.1 Y 5.2 RELATIVOS
AL PERSONAL CIENTIFICO Y TECNICO O AL CUADRO 5.6
SOBRE LOS GASTOS DEDICADOS A LA I Y D.
NO DISPONIENDO DE TIPOS DE CAMBIO APLICABLES A LAS
ACTIVIDADES DE I Y D PARA COMPARAR DE UN PAIS A
OTRO LOS DATOS ESTABLECIDOS EN MONEDA NACIONAL,
SERA NECESARIO BASARSE EN LOS TIPOS DE CAMBIO
OFICIALES DE CONVERSION DE LAS MONEDAS NACIONALES
EN DOLARES DE LOS ESTADOS UNIDOS, TAL Y COMO
FIGURAN EN EL ANEXO C. ES INUTIL SENALAR QUE ESOS
TIPOS DE CAMBIO NO SIEMPRE REFLEJAN EL COSTO REAL
DE LAS ACTIVIDADES DE I Y D.

ALGERIA:
E—> THE FIGURE IN COLUMN 7 REFERS TO EXPEN-
DITURE AS PERCENTAGE OF GROSS DOMESTIC PRODUCT.
FR-> LE CHIFFRE DE LA COLONNE 7 CONCERNE LES
DEPENSES EN POURCENTAGE DU PRODUIT INTERIEUR BRUT.
ESP> LA CIFRA DE LA COLUMNA 7 SE REFIERE A LOS
GASTOS EN PORCENTAJE DEL PRODUCTO INTERIOR BRUTO.

BOTSWANA:
E—> DATA SHOWN UNDER STOCK RELATE TO 1972.
FR-> LES DONNEES POUR L'EFFECTIF TOTAL SE
REFERENT A L'ANNEE 1972.
ESP> LOS DATOS RELATIVOS AL NUMERO TOTAL SE
REFIEREN A 1972.

CHAD:
E—> DATA FOR PERSONNEL ENGAGED IN R&D RELATE
TO 1971.
FR-> LES DONNEES RELATIVES AU PERSONNEL EMPLOYE
A DES TRAVAUX DE R-D SE REFERENT A L'ANNEE 1971.
ESP> LOS DATOS RELATIVOS AL PERSONAL EMPLEADO
EN TRABAJOS DE I Y D SE REFIEREN A 1971.

GABON:
E—> THE FIGURE IN COLUMN 7 REFERS TO EXPEN-
DITURE AS PERCENTAGE OF GROSS DOMESTIC PRODUCT.
FR-> LE CHIFFRE DE LA COLONNE 7 CONCERNE LES
DEPENSES EN POURCENTAGE DU PRODUIT INTERIEUR BRUT.
ESP> LA CIFRA DE LA COLUMNA 7 SE REFIERE A LOS
GASTOS EN PORCENTAJE DEL PRODUCTO INTERIOR BRUTO.

GHANA:
E—> DATA SHOWN IN COLUMNS 1, 2 AND 6 REFER TO
1970 AND EXPENDITURE FOR R&D RELATES TO 1971.
THE NUMBER OF TECHNICIANS USED TO CALCULATE
COLUMNS 4, 5 AND 6 INCLUDES AUXILIARY PERSONNEL.
FR-> LES DONNEES PRESENTEES DANS LES COLONNES
1, 2 ET 6 SE REFERENT A L'ANNEE 1970 ET LES
DEPENSES CONSACREES A LA R-D SE REFERENT A
L'ANNEE 1971. LE NOMBRE DE TECHNICIENS QUI
ENTRENT DANS LE CALCUL DES COLONNES 4, 5 ET 6
COMPREND LE PERSONNEL AUXILIAIRE.
ESP> LOS DATOS PRESENTADOS EN LAS COLUMNAS
1, 2 Y 6 SE REFIEREN A 1970 Y LOS GASTOS DEDI-
CADOS A LA I Y D A 1971. EL NUMERO DE TECNICOS
QUE SIRVIO PARA EL CALCULO DE LAS COLUMNAS 4, 5

Human and financial resources for R&D (indicators)   5.13
Ressources humaines et financières pour la R-D (indicateurs)
Recursos humanos y financieros para la I y D (indicadores)

| | EXPENDITURE FOR R&D
DEPENSES CONSACREES A R–D
GASTOS DEDICADOS A I Y D | | | |
SET IN R&D AS % OF TOTAL STOCK SET EN R–D EN % DE L'EFFECTIF TOTAL SET EN I Y D EN % DEL NUMERO TOTAL	AS PERCENTAGE OF GROSS NATIONAL PRODUCT (%) EN POURCENTAGE DU PRODUIT NATIONAL BRUT (%) EN PORCENTAJE DEL PRODUCTO NACIONAL BRUTO (%)	PER CAPITA (IN NATIONAL CURRENCY) PAR HABITANT (EN MONNAIE NATIONALE) POR PERSONA (EN MONEDA NACIONAL)	ANNUAL AVERAGE PER R&D SCIENTIST AND ENGINEER (IN NATIONAL CURRENCY) MOYENNE ANNUELLE PAR SCIENTIFIQUE ET INGENIEUR R–D (EN MONNAIE NATIONALE) PROMEDIO ANUAL POR CIENTIFICO E INGE– NIERO DE I Y D (EN MONEDA NACIONAL)	CURRENCY MONNAIE MONEDA
(6)	(7)	(8)	(9)	
40.0 ...	... ...	16.2 ...	17 860 ...	TALA
12.1 8.9 9.0	4.6	73.8 5.1 ...	14 700	ROUBLE ROUBLE

GHANA (CONT.):
Y 6 INCLUYE EL PERSONAL AUXILIAR.

KENYA:
 E—> EXPENDITURE FOR R&D RELATES TO 1971.
 FR-> LES DEPENSES CONSACREES A LA R–D SE
REFERENT A L'ANNEE 1971.
 ESP> LOS GASTOS DEDICADOS A LA I Y D SE
REFIEREN A 1971.

MADAGASCAR:
 E—> THE FIGURE IN COLUMN 7 REFERS TO EXPEN–
DITURE AS PERCENTAGE OF GROSS DOMESTIC PRODUCT.
 FR-> LE CHIFFRE DE LA COLONNE 7 CONCERNE LES
DEPENSES EN POURCENTAGE DU PRODUIT INTERIEUR BRUT.
 ESP> LA CIFRA DE LA COLUMNA 7 SE REFIERE A LOS
GASTOS EN PORCENTAJE DEL PRODUCTO INTERIOR BRUTO.

MAURITIUS:
 E—> DATA SHOWN IN COLUMNS 1, 2 AND 6 REFER TO
1972.
 FR-> LES DONNEES PRESENTEES DANS LES COLONNES
1, 2 ET 6 SE REFERENT A L'ANNEE 1972.
 ESP> LOS DATOS PRESENTADOS EN LAS COLUMNAS 1, 2
Y 6 SE REFIEREN A 1972.

NIGERIA:
 E—> THE FIGURE IN COLUMN 7 REFERS TO EXPEN–
DITURE AS PERCENTAGE OF GROSS DOMESTIC PRODUCT.
 FR-> LE CHIFFRE DE LA COLONNE 7 CONCERNE LES
DEPENSES EN POURCENTAGE DU PRODUIT INTERIEUR BRUT.
 ESP> LA CIFRA DE LA COLUMNA 7 SE REFIERE A LOS
GASTOS EN PORCENTAJE DEL PRODUCTO INTERIOR BRUTO.

SENEGAL:
 E—> THE FIGURE IN COLUMN 7 REFERS TO EXPEN–
DITURE AS PERCENTAGE OF GROSS DOMESTIC PRODUCT.
 FR-> LE CHIFFRE DE LA COLONNE 7 CONCERNE LES
DEPENSES EN POURCENTAGE DU PRODUIT INTERIEUR BRUT.
 ESP> LA CIFRA DE LA COLUMNA 7 SE REFIERE A LOS
GASTOS EN PORCENTAJE DEL PRODUCTO INTERIOR BRUTO.

SEYCHELLES:
 E—> THE FIGURE IN COLUMN 7 REFERS TO EXPEN–
DITURE AS PERCENTAGE OF GROSS DOMESTIC PRODUCT.

SEYCHELLES (CONT.):
 FR-> LE CHIFFRE DE LA COLONNE 7 CONCERNE LES
DEPENSES EN POURCENTAGE DU PRODUIT INTERIEUR BRUT.
 ESP> LA CIFRA DE LA COLUMNA 7 SE REFIERE A LOS
GASTOS EN PORCENTAJE DEL PRODUCTO INTERIOR BRUTO.

SUDAN:
 E—> DATA SHOWN IN COLUMNS 1, 2 AND 6 REFER TO
1971.
 FR-> LES DONNEES PRESENTEES DANS LES COLONNES
1, 2 ET 6 SE REFERENT A L'ANNEE 1971.
 ESP> LOS DATOS PRESENTADOS EN LAS COLUMNAS 1, 2
Y 6 SE REFIEREN A 1971.

TOGO:
 E—> DATA SHOWN IN COLUMNS 1, 2 AND 6 AS WELL AS
DATA FOR R&D EXPENDITURE REFER TO 1971.
 FR-> LES DONNEES PRESENTEES DANS LES COLONNES
1, 2 ET 6, AINSI QUE LES DEPENSES CONSACREES A LA
R–D, SE REFERENT A L'ANNEE 1971.
 ESP> LOS DATOS PRESENTADOS EN LAS COLUMNAS 1, 2
Y 6 Y LOS GASTOS DEDICADOS A LA I Y D SE REFIEREN
A 1971.

TUNISIA:
 E—> DATA FOR PERSONNEL ENGAGED IN R&D RELATE
TO 1972.
 FR-> LES DONNEES RELATIVES AU PERSONNEL EMPLOYE
A DES TRAVAUX DE R–D SE REFERENT A L'ANNEE 1972.
 ESP> LOS DATOS RELATIVOS AL PERSONAL EMPLEADO
EN TRABAJOS DE I Y D SE REFIEREN A 1972.

UNITED REPUBLIC OF CAMEROON:
 E—> THE FIGURE IN COLUMN 7 REFERS TO EXPEN–
DITURE AS PERCENTAGE OF GROSS DOMESTIC PRODUCT.
 FR-> LE CHIFFRE DE LA COLONNE 7 CONCERNE LES
DEPENSES EN POURCENTAGE DU PRODUIT INTERIEUR BRUT.
 ESP> LA CIFRA DE LA COLUMNA 7 SE REFIERE A LOS
GASTOS EN PORCENTAJE DEL PRODUCTO INTERIOR BRUTO.

ZAMBIA:
 E—> DATA SHOWN IN COLUMNS 1, 2 AND 6 REFER TO
1973 AND EXPENDITURE FOR R&D RELATES TO 1972.

5.13   Human and financial resources for R&D (indicators)
       Ressources humaines et financières pour la R-D (indicateurs)
       Recursos humanos y financieros para la I y D (indicadores)

ZAMBIA (CONT.):
   FR–> LES DONNEES PRESENTEES DANS LES COLONNES
1, 2 ET 6 SE REFERENT A L'ANNEE 1973 ET LES
DEPENSES CONSACREES A LA R–D SE REFERENT A
L'ANNEE 1972.
   ESP> LOS DATOS PRESENTADOS EN LAS COLUMNAS 1, 2
Y 6 SE REFIEREN A 1973 Y LOS GASTOS DEDICADOS A
LA I Y D A 1972.

CANADA:
   E—> DATA SHOWN IN COLUMNS 1, 2 AND 6 REFER TO
1971.
   FR–> LES DONNEES PRESENTEES DANS LES COLONNES
1, 2 ET 6 SE REFERENT A L'ANNEE 1971.
   ESP> LOS DATOS PRESENTADOS EN LAS COLUMNAS 1, 2
Y 6 SE REFIEREN A 1971.

CUBA:
   E—> DATA FOR STOCK AND PERSONNEL ENGAGED IN
R&D RELATE TO 1977.
   FR–> LES DONNEES POUR L'EFFECTIF TOTAL ET CELLES
RELATIVES AU PERSONNEL EMPLOYE A DES TRAVAUX DE
R–D SE REFERENT A L'ANNEE 1977.
   ESP> LOS DATOS RELATIVOS AL NUMERO TOTAL Y AL
PERSONAL EMPLEADO EN TRABAJOS DE I Y D SE REFIEREN
A 1977.

MEXICO:
   E—> DATA SHOWN IN COLUMNS 1, 2 AND 6 REFER TO
1969 AND EXPENDITURE FOR R&D RELATES TO 1973.
   FR–> LES DONNEES PRESENTEES DANS LES COLONNES
1, 2 ET 6 SE REFERENT A L'ANNEE 1969 ET LES
DEPENSES CONSACREES A LA R–D SE REFERENT A
L'ANNEE 1973.
   ESP> LOS DATOS PRESENTADOS EN LAS COLUMNAS
1, 2 Y 6 SE REFIEREN A 1969 Y LOS GASTOS DEDI-
CADOS A LA I Y D A 1973.

PANAMA:
   E—> DATA FOR PERSONNEL ENGAGED IN R&D RELATE
TO 1975 AND EXPENDITURE FOR R&D RELATES TO 1974.
   FR–> LES DONNEES RELATIVES AU PERSONNEL EMPLOYE
A DES TRAVAUX DE R–D SE REFERENT A L'ANNEE 1975
ET LES DEPENSES CONSACREES A LA R–D SE REFERENT A
L'ANNEE 1974.
   ESP> LOS DATOS RELATIVOS AL PERSONAL EMPLEADO
EN TRABAJOS DE I Y D SE REFIEREN A 1975 Y LOS
GASTOS DEDICADOS A LA I Y D A 1974.

TURKS AND CAICOS ISLANDS:
   E—> EXPENDITURE FOR R&D RELATES TO 1974.
   FR–> LES DEPENSES CONSACREES A LA R–D SE
REFERENT A L'ANNEE 1974.
   ESP> LOS GASTOS DEDICADOS A LA I Y D SE
REFIEREN A 1974.

UNITED STATES OF AMERICA:
   E—> DATA SHOWN IN COLUMNS 1, 2 AND 6 REFER TO
1976.
   FR–> LES DONNEES PRESENTEES DANS LES COLONNES
1, 2 ET 6 SE REFERENT A L'ANNEE 1976.
   ESP> LOS DATOS PRESENTADOS EN LAS COLUMNAS 1, 2
Y 6 SE REFIEREN A 1976.

ARGENTINA:
   E—> DATA SHOWN IN COLUMNS 1, 2 AND 6 REFER TO
1976.
   FR–> LES DONNEES PRESENTEES DANS LES COLONNES
1, 2 ET 6 SE REFERENT A L'ANNEE 1976.
   ESP> LOS DATOS PRESENTADOS EN LAS COLUMNAS 1, 2
Y 6 SE REFIEREN A 1976.

BRAZIL:
   E—> DATA SHOWN UNDER STOCK RELATE TO 1970.
   FR–> LES DONNEES POUR L'EFFECTIF TOTAL SE
REFERENT A L'ANNEE 1970.
   ESP> LOS DATOS RELATIVOS AL NUMERO TOTAL SE
REFIEREN A 1970.

CHILE:
   E—> DATA SHOWN UNDER STOCK RELATE TO 1970.
   FR–> LES DONNEES POUR L'EFFECTIF TOTAL SE
REFERENT A L'ANNEE 1970.
   ESP> LOS DATOS RELATIVOS AL NUMERO TOTAL SE
REFIEREN A 1970.

ECUADOR:
   E—> DATA SHOWN UNDER STOCK RELATE TO 1974.
   FR–> LES DONNEES POUR L'EFFECTIF TOTAL SE
REFERENT A L'ANNEE 1974.
   ESP> LOS DATOS RELATIVOS AL NUMERO TOTAL SE
REFIEREN A 1974.

PERU:
   E—> DATA SHOWN UNDER STOCK RELATE TO 1974 AND
DATA FOR PERSONNEL ENGAGED IN R&D RELATE TO 1975.
   FR–> LES DONNEES POUR L'EFFECTIF TOTAL SE
REFERENT A L'ANNEE 1974 ET LES DONNEES RELATIVES
AU PERSONNEL EMPLOYE A DES TRAVAUX DE R–D SE
REFERENT A L'ANNEE 1975.
   ESP> LOS DATOS RELATIVOS AL NUMERO TOTAL SE
REFIEREN A 1974 Y LOS DEL PERSONAL EMPLEADO EN
TRABAJOS DE I Y D A 1975.

URUGUAY:
   E—> DATA SHOWN UNDER STOCK RELATE TO 1970 AND
DATA FOR PERSONNEL ENGAGED IN R&D RELATE TO 1971.
   FR–> LES DONNEES POUR L'EFFECTIF TOTAL SE
REFERENT A L'ANNEE 1970 ET LES DONNEES RELATIVES
AU PERSONNEL EMPLOYE A DES TRAVAUX DE R–D SE
REFERENT A L'ANNEE 1971.
   ESP> LOS DATOS RELATIVOS AL NUMERO TOTAL SE
REFIEREN A 1970 Y LOS DEL PERSONAL EMPLEADO EN
TRABAJOS DE I Y D A 1971.

BANGLADESH:
   E—> DATA FOR STOCK AND PERSONNEL ENGAGED IN
R&D REFER TO 1973.
   FR–> LES DONNEES POUR L'EFFECTIF TOTAL ET CELLES
RELATIVES AU PERSONNEL EMPLOYE A DES TRAVAUX DE
R–D SE REFERENT A L'ANNEE 1973.
   ESP> LOS DATOS RELATIVOS AL NUMERO TOTAL Y AL
PERSONAL EMPLEADO EN TRABAJOS DE I Y D SE REFIEREN
A 1973.

BRUNEI:
   E—> DATA SHOWN IN COLUMNS 1, 2 AND 6 REFER TO
1971.
   FR–> LES DONNEES PRESENTEES DANS LES COLONNES
1, 2 ET 6 SE REFERENT A L'ANNEE 1971.
   ESP> LOS DATOS PRESENTADOS EN LAS COLUMNAS 1, 2
Y 6 SE REFIEREN A 1971.

BURMA:
   E—> EXPENDITURE FOR R&D RELATES TO 1973.
   FR–> LES DEPENSES CONSACREES A LA R–D SE
REFERENT A L'ANNEE 1973.
   ESP> LOS GASTOS DEDICADOS A LA I Y D SE
REFIEREN A 1973.

CYPRUS:
   E—> DATA SHOWN IN COLUMNS 1, 2 AND 6 REFER TO
1969.
   FR–> LES DONNEES PRESENTEES DANS LES COLONNES
1, 2 ET 6 SE REFERENT A L'ANNEE 1969.
   ESP> LOS DATOS PRESENTADOS EN LAS COLUMNAS 1, 2
Y 6 SE REFIEREN A 1969.

INDIA:
   E—> DATA FOR PERSONNEL ENGAGED IN R&D AND
EXPENDITURE FOR R&D RELATE TO 1976. DATA FOR
PERSONNEL ENGAGED IN R&D INCLUDE AUXILIARY
PERSONNEL.
   FR–> LES DONNEES RELATIVES AU PERSONNEL EMPLOYE
A DES TRAVAUX DE R–D, AINSI QUE LES DEPENSES
CONSACREES A LA R–D SE REFERENT A L'ANNEE 1976.
LES DONNEES POUR LE PERSONNEL EMPLOYE A DES

Human and financial resources for R&D (indicators)   5.13
Ressources humaines et financières pour la R-D (indicateurs)
Recursos humanos y financieros para la I y D (indicadores)

INDIA (CONT.):
TRAVAUX DE R—D COMPREND LE PERSONNEL AUXILIAIRE.
   ESP> LOS DATOS RELATIVOS AL PERSONAL EMPLEADO
EN TRABAJOS DE I Y D Y LOS GASTOS DEDICADOS A LA
I Y D SE REFIEREN A 1976.   EL PERSONAL EMPLEADO
EN TRABAJOS DE I Y D INCLUYE EL PERSONAL AUXILIAR.

INDONESIA:
   E—> DATA FOR PERSONNEL ENGAGED IN R&D AND
EXPENDITURE FOR R&D RELATE TO 1975.
   FR—> LES DONNEES RELATIVES AU PERSONNEL EMPLOYE
A DES TRAVAUX DE R—D, AINSI QUE LES DEPENSES
CONSACREES A LA R—D SE REFERENT A L'ANNEE 1975.
   ESP> LOS DATOS RELATIVOS AL PERSONAL EMPLEADO
EN TRABAJOS DE I Y D Y LOS GASTOS DEDICADOS A LA
I Y D SE REFIEREN A 1975.

IRAN:
   E—> DATA SHOWN IN COLUMNS 3 TO 9 REFER TO 1972.
THE FIGURE IN COLUMN 7 REFERS TO EXPENDITURE
AS PERCENTAGE OF GROSS DOMESTIC PRODUCT.
   FR—> LES DONNEES PRESENTEES DANS LES COLONNES
3 A 9 SE REFERENT A L'ANNEE 1972.   LE CHIFFRE DE
DE LA COLONNE 7 CONCERNE LES DEPENSES EN POUR—
CENTAGE DU PRODUIT INTERIEUR BRUT.
   ESP> LOS DATOS DE LAS COLUMNAS 3 A 9 SE REFIEREN
A 1972.   LA CIFRA DE LA COLUMNA 7 SE REFIERE A LOS
GASTOS EN PORCENTAJE DEL PRODUCTO INTERIOR BRUTO.

IRAK:
   E—> DATA SHOWN UNDER STOCK RELATE TO 1972.
   FR—> LES DONNEES POUR L'EFFECTIF TOTAL SE
REFERENT A L'ANNEE 1972.
   ESP> LOS DATOS RELATIVOS AL NUMERO TOTAL SE
REFIEREN A 1972.

ISRAEL:
   E—> DATA SHOWN IN COLUMNS 1, 2 AND 6 REFER TO
1974.
   FR—> LES DONNEES PRESENTEES DANS LES COLONNES
1, 2 ET 6 SE REFERENT A L'ANNEE 1974.
   ESP> LOS DATOS PRESENTADOS EN LAS COLUMNAS 1, 2
Y 6 SE REFIEREN A 1974.

JAPAN:
   E—> DATA SHOWN IN COLUMNS 1, 2 AND 6 REFER TO
1975 AND EXPENDITURE FOR R&D RELATES TO 1977.
   FR—> LES DONNEES PRESENTEES DANS LES COLONNES
1, 2 ET 6 SE REFERENT A L'ANNEE 1975 ET LES
DEPENSES CONSACREES A LA R—D SE REFERENT A
L'ANNEE 1977.
   ESP> LOS DATOS PRESENTADOS EN LAS COLUMNAS
1, 2 Y 6 SE REFIEREN A 1975 Y LOS GASTOS DEDI—
CADOS A LA I Y D A 1977.

JORDAN:
   E—> EXPENDITURE FOR R&D RELATES TO 1976.
   FR—> LES DEPENSES CONSACREES A LA R—D SE
REFERENT A L'ANNEE 1976.
   ESP> LOS GASTOS DEDICADOS A LA I Y D SE
REFIEREN A 1976.

KOREA, REPUBLIC OF:
   E—> DATA SHOWN IN COLUMNS 1, 2 AND 6 REFER TO
1977.
   FR—> LES DONNEES PRESENTEES DANS LES COLONNES
1, 2 ET 6 SE REFERENT A L'ANNEE 1977.
   ESP> LOS DATOS PRESENTADOS EN LAS COLUMNAS 1, 2
Y 6 SE REFIEREN A 1977.

KUWAIT:
   E—> DATA SHOWN UNDER STOCK RELATE TO 1975.
   FR—> LES DONNEES POUR L'EFFECTIF TOTAL SE
REFERENT A L'ANNEE 1975.
   ESP> LOS DATOS RELATIVOS AL NUMERO TOTAL SE
REFIEREN A 1975.

MONGOLIA:
   E—> DATA FOR PERSONNEL ENGAGED IN R&D AND
EXPENDITURE FOR R&D RELATE TO 1971.
   FR—> LES DONNEES RELATIVES AU PERSONNEL EMPLOYE
A DES TRAVAUX DE R—D, AINSI QUE LES DEPENSES
CONSACREES A LA R—D SE REFERENT A L'ANNEE 1971.
   ESP> LOS DATOS RELATIVOS AL PERSONAL EMPLEADO
EN TRABAJOS DE I Y D Y LOS GASTOS DEDICADOS A LA
I Y D SE REFIEREN A 1971.

PHILIPPINES:
   E—> DATA SHOWN UNDER STOCK RELATE TO 1970 AND
EXPENDITURE FOR R&D RELATES TO 1973.
   FR—> LES DONNEES POUR L'EFFECTIF TOTAL SE
REFERENT A L'ANNEE 1970 ET LES DEPENSES CONSACREES
A LA R—D SE REFERENT A L'ANNEE 1973.
   ESP> LOS DATOS RELATIVOS AL NUMERO TOTAL SE
REFIEREN A 1970 Y LOS GASTOS DEDICADOS A LA I Y D
A 1973.

SINGAPORE:
   E—> DATA SHOWN UNDER STOCK RELATE TO 1977.
   FR—> LES DONNEES POUR L'EFFECTIF TOTAL SE
REFERENT A L'ANNEE 1977.
   ESP> LOS DATOS RELATIVOS AL NUMERO TOTAL SE
REFIEREN A 1977.

SRI LANKA:
   E—> DATA SHOWN UNDER STOCK RELATE TO 1971 AND
DATA FOR PERSONNEL ENGAGED IN R&D RELATE TO 1972.
   FR—> LES DONNEES POUR L'EFFECTIF TOTAL SE
REFERENT A L'ANNEE 1971 ET LES DONNEES RELATIVES
AU PERSONNEL EMPLOYE A DES TRAVAUX DE R—D SE
REFERENT A L'ANNEE 1972.
   ESP> LOS DATOS RELATIVOS AL NUMERO TOTAL SE
REFIEREN A 1971 Y LOS DEL PERSONAL EMPLEADO EN
TRABAJOS DE I Y D A 1972.

THAILAND:
   E—> DATA FOR PERSONNEL ENGAGED IN R&D RELATE
TO 1974.
   FR—> LES DONNEES RELATIVES AU PERSONNEL EMPLOYE
A DES TRAVAUX DE R—D SE REFERENT A L'ANNEE 1974.
   ESP> LOS DATOS RELATIVOS AL PERSONAL EMPLEADO
EN TRABAJOS DE I Y D SE REFIEREN A 1974.

TURKEY:
   E—> DATA FOR PERSONNEL ENGAGED IN R&D RELATE
TO 1975.
   FR—> LES DONNEES RELATIVES AU PERSONNEL EMPLOYE
A DES TRAVAUX DE R—D SE REFERENT A L'ANNEE 1975.
   ESP> LOS DATOS RELATIVOS AL PERSONAL EMPLEADO
EN TRABAJOS DE I Y D SE REFIEREN A 1975.

VIET—NAM:
   E—> DATA FOR PERSONNEL ENGAGED IN R&D RELATE
TO 1978.
   FR—> LES DONNEES RELATIVES AU PERSONNEL EMPLOYE
A DES TRAVAUX DE R—D SE REFERENT A L'ANNEE 1978.
   ESP> LOS DATOS RELATIVOS AL PERSONAL EMPLEADO
EN TRABAJOS DE I Y D SE REFIEREN A 1978.

YEMEN:
   E—> THE FIGURE IN COLUMN 7 REFERS TO EXPEN—
DITURE AS PERCENTAGE OF GROSS DOMESTIC PRODUCT.
   FR—> LE CHIFFRE DE LA COLONNE 7 CONCERNE LES
DEPENSES EN POURCENTAGE DU PRODUIT INTERIEUR BRUT.
   ESP> LA CIFRA DE LA COLUMNA 7 SE REFIERE A LOS
GASTOS EN PORCENTAJE DEL PRODUCTO INTERIOR BRUTO.

AUSTRIA:
   E—> DATA SHOWN UNDER STOCK RELATE TO 1971.
   FR—> LES DONNEES POUR L'EFFECTIF TOTAL SE
REFERENT A L'ANNEE 1971.
   ESP> LOS DATOS RELATIVOS AL NUMERO TOTAL SE
REFIEREN A 1971.

5.13   Human and financial resources for R&D (indicators)
        Ressources humaines et financières pour la R-D (indicateurs)
        Recursos humanos y financieros para la I y D (indicadores)

BULGARIA:
   E—> DATA SHOWN IN COLUMNS 1, 2 AND 6 AS WELL AS
DATA FOR R&D EXPENDITURE REFER TO 1977. THE
FIGURE IN COLUMN 7 REFERS TO EXPENDITURE AS PER-
CENTAGE OF NET MATERIAL PRODUCT.
   FR—> LES DONNEES PRESENTEES DANS LES COLONNES
1, 2 ET 6, AINSI QUE LES DEPENSES CONSACREES A LA
R-D, SE REFERENT A L'ANNEE 1977. LE CHIFFRE DE
LA COLONNE 7 CONCERNE LES DEPENSES EN POURCENTAGE
DU PRODUIT MATERIEL NET.
   ESP> LOS DATOS PRESENTADOS EN LAS COLUMNAS 1, 2
Y 6 Y LOS GASTOS DEDICADOS A LA I Y D SE REFIEREN
A 1977. LA CIFRA DE LA COLUMNA 7 CORRESPONDE A
LOS GASTOS EN PORCENTAJE DEL PRODUCTO MATERIAL
NETO.

CZECHOSLOVAKIA:
   E—> DATA SHOWN IN COLUMNS 1 AND 6 REFER TO 1973.
THE FIGURE IN COLUMN 7 REFERS TO EXPENDITURE AS
PERCENTAGE OF NET MATERIAL PRODUCT.
   FR—> LES DONNEES PRESENTEES DANS LES COLONNES
1 ET 6 SE REFERENT A L'ANNEE 1973. LE CHIFFRE DE
LA COLONNE 7 CONCERNE LES DEPENSES EN POURCENTAGE
DU PRODUIT MATERIEL NET.
   ESP> LOS DATOS PRESENTADOS EN LAS COLUMNAS 1 Y 6
SE REFIEREN A 1973. LA CIFRA DE LA COLUMNA 7
CORRESPONDE A LOS GASTOS EN PORCENTAJE DEL PRODUCTO
MATERIAL NETO.

DENMARK:
   E—> THE FIGURE IN COLUMN 7 REFERS TO EXPEN-
DITURE AS PERCENTAGE OF GROSS DOMESTIC PRODUCT.
   FR—> LE CHIFFRE DE LA COLONNE 7 CONCERNE LES
DEPENSES EN POURCENTAGE DU PRODUIT INTERIEUR BRUT.
   ESP> LA CIFRA DE LA COLUMNA 7 SE REFIERE A LOS
GASTOS EN PORCENTAJE DEL PRODUCTO INTERIOR BRUTO.

FRANCE:
   E—> DATA SHOWN IN COLUMNS 1 AND 6 REFER TO
1975. THE NUMBER OF TECHNICIANS USED TO CALCULATE
COLUMNS 4, 5 AND 6 INCLUDES AUXILIARY PERSONNEL.
   FR—> LES DONNEES PRESENTEES DANS LES COLONNES
1 ET 6 SE REFERENT A L'ANNEE 1975. LE NOMBRE DE
TECHNICIENS QUI ENTRENT DANS LE CALCUL DES
COLONNES 4, 5 ET 6 COMPREND LE PERSONNEL
AUXILIAIRE.
   ESP> LOS DATOS PRESENTADOS EN LAS COLUMNAS 1 Y 6
SE REFIEREN A 1975. EL NUMERO DE TECNICOS QUE
SIRVIO PARA EL CALCULO DE LAS COLUMNAS 4, 5 Y 6
INCLUYE EL PERSONAL AUXILIAR.

GERMAN DEMOCRATIC REPUBLIC:
   E—> DATA SHOWN IN COLUMNS 3, 4, 5 AND 6 REFER TO
1975. THE NUMBER OF TECHNICIANS USED TO CALCULATE
COLUMNS 4, 5 AND 6 INCLUDES AUXILIARY PERSONNEL.
   FR—> LES DONNEES PRESENTEES DANS LES COLONNES
3, 4, 5 ET 6 SE REFERENT A L'ANNEE 1975. LE NOMBRE
DE TECHNICIENS QUI ENTRENT DANS LE CALCUL DES
COLONNES 4, 5 ET 6 COMPREND LE PERSONNEL
AUXILIAIRE.
   ESP> LOS DATOS PRESENTADOS EN LAS COLUMNAS 3, 4
5 Y 6 SE REFIEREN A 1975. EL NUMERO DE TECNICOS
QUE SIRVIO PARA EL CALCULO DE LAS COLUMNAS 4, 5 Y
6 INCLUYE EL PERSONAL AUXILIAR.

GERMANY, FEDERAL REPUBLIC OF:
   E—> DATA SHOWN IN COLUMNS 1, 2 AND 6 REFER TO
1970.
   FR—> LES DONNEES PRESENTEES DANS LES COLONNES
1, 2 ET 6 SE REFERENT A L'ANNEE 1970.
   ESP> LOS DATOS PRESENTADOS EN LAS COLUMNAS 1, 2
Y 6 SE REFIEREN A 1970.

GREECE:
   E—> DATA SHOWN UNDER STOCK RELATE TO 1971.
   FR—> LES DONNEES POUR L'EFFECTIF TOTAL SE
REFERENT A L'ANNEE 1971.

GREECE (CONT.):
   ESP> LOS DATOS RELATIVOS AL NUMERO TOTAL SE
REFIEREN A 1971.

HUNGARY:
   E—> DATA SHOWN IN COLUMNS 1, 2 AND 6 REFER TO
1973. THE FIGURE IN COLUMN 7 REFERS TO EXPENDI-
TURE AS PERCENTAGE OF NET MATERIAL PRODUCT.
   FR—> LES DONNEES PRESENTEES DANS LES COLONNES
1, 2 ET 6 SE REFERENT A L'ANNEE 1973. LE CHIFFRE
DE LA COLONNE 7 CONCERNE LES DEPENSES EN POURCEN-
TAGE DU PRODUIT MATERIEL NET.
   ESP> LOS DATOS PRESENTADOS EN LAS COLUMNAS 1, 2
Y 6 SE REFIEREN A 1973. LA CIFRA DE LA COLUMNA 7
CORRESPONDE A LOS GASTOS EN PORCENTAJE DEL PRODUCT
MATERIAL NETO.

ICELAND:
   E—> DATA SHOWN IN COLUMNS 1 AND 6 REFER TO
1970 AND EXPENDITURE FOR R&D RELATES TO 1973.
   FR—> LES DONNEES PRESENTEES DANS LES COLONNES
1 ET 6 SE REFERENT A L'ANNEE 1970 ET LES DEPENSES
CONSACREES A LA R-D SE REFERENT A L'ANNEE 1973.
   ESP> LOS DATOS PRESENTADOS EN LAS COLUMNAS
1 Y 6 SE REFIEREN A 1970 Y LOS GASTOS DEDICADOS
A LA I Y D A 1973.

IRELAND:
   E—> DATA SHOWN IN COLUMNS 1 AND 6 REFER TO 1971
   FR—> LES DONNEES PRESENTEES DANS LES COLONNES
1 ET 6 SE REFERENT A L'ANNEE 1971.
   ESP> LOS DATOS PRESENTADOS EN LAS COLUMNAS 1 Y 6
SE REFIEREN A 1971.

ITALY:
   E—> DATA SHOWN IN COLUMNS 1, 2 AND 6 REFER TO
1971.
   FR—> LES DONNEES PRESENTEES DANS LES COLONNES
1, 2 ET 6 SE REFERENT A L'ANNEE 1971.
   ESP> LOS DATOS PRESENTADOS EN LAS COLUMNAS 1, 2
Y 6 SE REFIEREN A 1971.

MALTA:
   E—> DATA SHOWN IN COLUMNS 1 AND 6 REFER TO 1969
   FR—> LES DONNEES PRESENTEES DANS LES COLONNES
1 ET 6 SE REFERENT A L'ANNEE 1969.
   ESP> LOS DATOS PRESENTADOS EN LAS COLUMNAS 1 Y 6
SE REFIEREN A 1969.

NETHERLANDS:
   E—> DATA SHOWN IN COLUMNS 1, 2 AND 6 REFER TO
1971. THE NUMBER OF TECHNICIANS USED TO CALCULATE
COLUMNS 4, 5 AND 6 INCLUDES AUXILIARY PERSONNEL.
   FR—> LES DONNEES PRESENTEES DANS LES COLONNES
1, 2 ET 6 SE REFERENT A L'ANNEE 1971. LE NOMBRE
DE TECHNICIENS QUI ENTRENT DANS LE CALCUL DES
COLONNES 4, 5 ET 6 COMPREND LE PERSONNEL
AUXILIAIRE.
   ESP> LOS DATOS PRESENTADOS EN LAS COLUMNAS 1, 2
Y 6 SE REFIEREN A 1971. EL NUMERO DE TECNICOS
QUE SIRVIO PARA EL CALCULO DE LAS COLUMNAS 4, 5 Y
6 INCLUYE EL PERSONAL AUXILIAR.

NORWAY:
   E—> DATA SHOWN IN COLUMNS 1 AND 6 AS WELL AS
DATA FOR R&D EXPENDITURE RELATES TO 1977. THE
THE NUMBER OF TECHNICIANS USED TO CALCULATE
COLUMNS 4, 5 AND 6 INCLUDES AUXILIARY PERSONNEL.
   FR—> LES DONNEES PRESENTEES DANS LES COLONNES
1 ET 6 AINSI QUE LES DEPENSES CONSACREES A LA
R-D SE REFERENT A L'ANNEE 1977. LE NOMBRE DE
TECHNICIENS QUI ENTRENT DANS LE CALCUL DES
COLONNES 4, 5 ET 6 COMPREND LE PERSONNEL
AUXILIAIRE.
   ESP> LOS DATOS PRESENTADOS EN LAS COLUMNAS 1 Y 6
Y LOS GASTOS DEDICADOS A LA I Y D SE REFIEREN A
1977. EL NUMERO DE TECNICOS QUE SIRVIO PARA EL
CALCULO DE LAS COLUMNAS 4, 5 Y 6 INCLUYE EL
PERSONAL AUXILIAR.

Human and financial resources for R&D (indicators)   5.13
Ressources humaines et financières pour la R-D (indicateurs)
Recursos humanos y financieros para la I y D (indicadores)

POLAND:
  E—> DATA SHOWN IN COLUMNS 1, 2 AND 6 REFER TO
1974.
  FR—> LES DONNEES PRESENTEES DANS LES COLONNES
1, 2 ET 6 SE REFERENT A L'ANNEE 1974.
  ESP> LOS DATOS PRESENTADOS EN LAS COLUMNAS 1, 2
Y 6 SE REFIEREN A 1974.

SWITZERLAND:
  E—> DATA SHOWN IN COLUMNS 1 AND 6 REFER TO
1975. THE NUMBER OF TECHNICIANS USED TO CALCULATE
COLUMNS 4, 5 AND 6 INCLUDES AUXILIARY PERSONNEL.
  FR—> LES DONNEES PRESENTEES DANS LES COLONNES
1 ET 6 SE REFERENT A L'ANNEE 1975. LE NOMBRE DE
TECHNICIENS QUI ENTRENT DANS LE CALCUL DES
COLONNES 4, 5 ET 6 COMPREND LE PERSONNEL
AUXILIAIRE.
  ESP> LOS DATOS PRESENTADOS EN LAS COLUMNAS 1 Y 6
SE REFIEREN A 1975. EL NUMERO DE TECNICOS QUE
SIRVIO PARA EL CALCULO DE LAS COLUMNAS 4, 5 Y 6
INCLUYE EL PERSONAL AUXILIAR.

YUGOSLAVIA:
  E—> DATA SHOWN IN COLUMNS 1, 2 AND 6 REFER TO
1976.
  FR—> LES DONNEES PRESENTEES DANS LES COLONNES
1, 2 ET 6 SE REFERENT A L'ANNEE 1976.
  ESP> LOS DATOS PRESENTADOS EN LAS COLUMNAS 1, 2
Y 6 SE REFIEREN A 1976.

AMERICAN SAMOA:
  E—> DATA FOR PERSONNEL ENGAGED IN R&D AND
EXPENDITURE FOR R&D RELATE TO 1971.
  FR—> LES DONNEES RELATIVES AU PERSONNEL EMPLOYE
A DES TRAVAUX DE R-D, AINSI QUE LES DEPENSES
CONSACREES A LA R-D SE REFERENT A L'ANNEE 1971.
  ESP> LOS DATOS RELATIVOS AL PERSONAL EMPLEADO
EN TRABAJOS DE I Y D Y LOS GASTOS DEDICADOS A LA
I Y D SE REFIEREN A 1971.

AUSTRALIA:
  E—> DATA SHOWN UNDER STOCK RELATE TO 1971.
  FR—> LES DONNEES POUR L'EFFECTIF TOTAL SE
REFERENT A L'ANNEE 1971.
  ESP> LOS DATOS RELATIVOS AL NUMERO TOTAL SE
REFIEREN A 1971.

COOK ISLANDS:
  E—> THE FIGURE IN COLUMN 7 REFERS TO EXPEN-
DITURE AS PERCENTAGE OF GROSS DOMESTIC PRODUCT.
  FR—> LE CHIFFRE DE LA COLONNE 7 CONCERNE LES
DEPENSES EN POURCENTAGE DU PRODUIT INTERIEUR BRUT.
  ESP> LA CIFRA DE LA COLUMNA 7 SE REFIERE A LOS
GASTOS EN PORCENTAJE DEL PRODUCTO INTERIOR BRUTO.

FRENCH POLYNESIA:
  E—> DATA SHOWN UNDER STOCK RELATE TO 1973.
  FR—> LES DONNEES POUR L'EFFECTIF TOTAL SE
REFERENT A L'ANNEE 1973.
  ESP> LOS DATOS RELATIVOS AL NUMERO TOTAL SE
REFIEREN A 1973.

GUAM:
  E—> DATA SHOWN UNDER STOCK RELATE TO 1977 AND
EXPENDITURE FOR R&D RELATES TO 1973.
  FR—> LES DONNEES POUR L'EFFECTIF TOTAL SE
REFERENT A L'ANNEE 1977 ET LES DEPENSES CONSACREES
A LA R-D SE REFERENT A L'ANNEE 1973.
  ESP> LOS DATOS RELATIVOS AL NUMERO TOTAL SE
REFIEREN A 1977 Y LOS GASTOS DEDICADOS A LA I Y D
A 1973.

NEW CALEDONIA:
  E—> DATA FOR PERSONNEL ENGAGED IN R&D AND
EXPENDITURE FOR R&D REFER TO 1971. THE FIGURE

NEW CALEDONIA (CONT.):
IN COLUMN 7 REFERS TO EXPENDITURE AS PERCENTAGE
OF GROSS DOMESTIC PRODUCT.
  FR—> LES DONNEES RELATIVES AU PERSONNEL EMPLOYE
A DES TRAVAUX DE R-D SE REFERENT A L'ANNEE 1971.
LE CHIFFRE DE LA COLONNE 7 CONCERNE LES DEPENSES
EN POURCENTAGE DU PRODUIT INTERIEUR BRUT.
  ESP> LOS DATOS RELATIVOS AL PERSONAL EMPLEADO
EN TRABAJOS DE I Y D Y LOS GASTOS DEDICADOS A LA
I Y D SE REFIEREN A 1971. LA CIFRA DE LA COLUMNA
7 SE REFIERE A LOS GASTOS EN PORCENTAJE DEL
PRODUCTO INTERIOR BRUTO.

NEW HEBRIDES:
  E—> DATA SHOWN IN COLUMNS 1, 2 AND 6 REFER TO
1972.
  FR—> LES DONNEES PRESENTEES DANS LES COLONNES
1, 2 ET 6 SE REFERENT A L'ANNEE 1972.
  ESP> LOS DATOS PRESENTADOS EN LAS COLUMNAS 1, 2
Y 6 SE REFIEREN A 1972.

NEW ZEALAND:
  E—> DATA SHOWN UNDER STOCK RELATE TO 1971.
  FR—> LES DONNEES POUR L'EFFECTIF TOTAL SE
REFERENT A L'ANNEE 1971.
  ESP> LOS DATOS RELATIVOS AL NUMERO TOTAL SE
REFIEREN A 1971.

NORFOLK ISLAND:
  E—> DATA FOR R&D RELATES TO 1973.
  FR—> LES DONNEES RELATIVES A LA R-D SE REFERENT
A L'ANNEE 1973.
  ESP> LOS DATOS RELATIVOS A LA I Y D SE REFIEREN
A 1973.

PACIFIC ISLANDS:
  E—> DATA SHOWN IN COLUMNS 1, 2 AND 6 REFER TO
1973.
  FR—> LES DONNEES PRESENTEES DANS LES COLONNES
1, 2 ET 6 SE REFERENT A L'ANNEE 1973.
  ESP> LOS DATOS PRESENTADOS EN LAS COLUMNAS 1, 2
Y 6 SE REFIEREN A 1973.

SAMOA:
  E—> DATA SHOWN IN COLUMNS 1, 2 AND 6 REFER TO
1977.
  FR—> LES DONNEES PRESENTEES DANS LES COLONNES
1, 2 ET 6 SE REFERENT A L'ANNEE 1977.
  ESP> LOS DATOS PRESENTADOS EN LAS COLUMNAS 1, 2
Y 6 SE REFIEREN A 1977.

U.S.S.R.:
  E—> DATA SHOWN IN COLUMNS 1, 2 AND 6 REFER TO
1977. THE FIGURE IN COLUMN 7 REFERS TO EXPEN-
DITURE AS PERCENTAGE OF NET MATERIAL PRODUCT.
  FR—> LES DONNEES PRESENTEES DANS LES COLONNES
1, 2 ET 6 SE REFERENT A L'ANNEE 1977. LE CHIFFRE
DE LA COLONNE 7 CONCERNE LES DEPENSES EN POURCEN-
TAGE DU PRODUIT MATERIEL NET.
  ESP> LOS DATOS PRESENTADOS EN LAS COLUMNAS 1, 2
Y 6 SE REFIEREN A 1977. LA CIFRA DE LA COLUMNA 7
CORRESPONDE A LOS GASTOS EN PORCENTAJE DEL PRODUCT
MATERIAL NETO.

BYELORUSSIAN S.S.R.:
  E—> EXPENDITURE FOR R&D RELATES TO 1970.
  FR—> LES DEPENSES CONSACREES A LA R-D SE
REFERENT A L'ANNEE 1970.
  ESP> LOS GASTOS DEDICADOS A LA I Y D SE
REFIEREN A 1970.

UKRAINIAN S.S.R.:
  E—> DATA SHOWN IN COLUMNS 1, 2 AND 6 REFER TO
1977.
  FR—> LES DONNEES PRESENTEES DANS LES COLONNES
1, 2 ET 6 SE REFERENT A L'ANNEE 1977.
  ESP> LOS DATOS PRESENTADOS EN LAS COLUMNAS 1, 2
Y 6 SE REFIEREN A 1977.

Summary tables for culture and communication 6
Tableaux récapitulatifs pour la culture et la communication
Cuadros recapitulativos para la cultura y la comunicación

6 Summary tables for culture and communication subjects by continents, major areas and groups of countries

Tableaux récapitulatifs pour la culture et la communication, par continents, grandes régions et groupes de pays

Cuadros recapitulativos para la cultura y la comunicación, por continentes, grandes regiones y grupos de países

This chapter provides a number of summary tables on some selected subjects of culture and communication. The statistics contained in these tables are distributed by continents, major areas and groups of countries the composition of which is given in footnote 1 to Table 1.2 of this Yearbook. The subjects dealt with are the following: book production, daily newspapers, cultural paper, cinemas, radio transmitters and receivers as well as television transmitters and receivers.

It has to be pointed out that due to the difficulties of assessing the reliability of the statistics available and the lack of information for many countries the calculated world and regional figures given in this chapter represent a very rough approximation of the existing situation.

Table 6.1
The object of this table is to show the evolution of book production (in number of titles) in the world from 1955 to 1978.

Table 6.2
This table gives world and regional estimates for daily newspapers in 1977. The statistics relate to the number of newspapers, their circulation and the circulation per 1,000 inhabitants.

Tables 6.3 and 6.4
On the basis of the statistics made available to Unesco by the Food and Agriculture Organization of the United Nations (FAO), world and regional estimates have been calculated for the production and consumption of 'cultural paper' (newsprint and printing and writing paper) for the years 1970, 1975, 1977 and 1978.

Table 6.5
This table shows the number of cinemas, their seating capacity and the seating capacity per 1,000 inhabitants for the years 1970 and 1977.

Table 6.6
This table gives the number of radio broadcasting transmitters for around 1965, 1970, 1975 and 1977.

Table 6.7
Total figures for radio receivers in the world for 1965, 1970, 1975 and 1977 respectively are shown in this table. It should be pointed out that many countries have reported the number of licences issued rather than the number of receivers in use. This has led to a certain under-enumeration of the number of receivers for those countries and regions where one licence covers the possession of several receivers.

Table 6.8
This table gives the number of television broadcasting transmitters for around 1965, 1970, 1975 and 1977. The figures which have been supplied to the Secretariat are sometimes incomplete due to the fact that not all countries include relay or re-broadcast transmitters in their statistics.

Table 6.9
Table 6.9 shows the number of television receivers for 1965, 1970, 1975 and 1977.

The following charts which deal with some aspects of radio and television broadcasting can be found in a special study on Statistics on Radio and Television 1960-1976 published by Unesco as No. 23 in the series *Statistical Reports and Studies*.

Ce chapitre présente une serie de tableaux récapitulatifs sur quelques sujets selectionnés relatifs à la culture et à la communication. Les statistiques qui figurent dans ces tableaux sont distribuées par continents, grandes régions et groupes de pays, dont la composition est indiquée dans la note 1 du tableau 1.2 de cet *Annuaire*. Les sujets considérés sont les suivants: édition de livres, journaux quotidiens, papier culturel, cinémas, émetteurs et récepteurs de radio ainsi que les émetteurs et récepteurs de télévision.

Il faut préciser que les difficultés qui existent pour déterminer la fiabilité des statistiques disponibles et les lacunes qui se manifestent dans les informations communiquées par plusieurs pays, font que les calculs sur les données mondiales et régionales qui figurent dans ce chapitre ne représentent tout au plus qu'une approximation très grossière de la situation réelle.

Tableau 6.1
Ce tableau a pour objet de présenter l'évolution de l'édition de livres (en

nombre de titres) dans le monde, entre 1955 et 1978.

Tableau 6.2
Ce tableau présente des estimations mondiales et régionales sur les journaux quotidiens en 1977. Les statistiques se refèrent au nombre de journaux, à leur tirage et au tirage pour 1.000 habitants.

Tableaux 6.3 et 6.4
Sur la base des statistiques disponibles, procurées à l'Unesco par l'Organisation des Nations Unies pour l'Agriculture et l'Alimentation (FAO), des estimations mondiales et régionales ont été effectuées sur la production et la consommation de 'papier culturel' (papier journal et papier d'impression et d'écriture) pour les années 1970, 1975, 1977 et 1978.

Tableau 6.5
Ce tableau présente le nombre de cinémas, le nombre de sièges, et le nombre de sièges pour 1.000 habitants pour les années 1970 et 1977.

6 Summary tables for culture and communication
Tableaux récapitulatifs pour la culture et la communication
Cuadros recapitulativos para la cultura y la comunicación

Tableau 6.6
Dans ce tableau figure le nombre d'émetteurs de radiodiffusion sonore autour de 1965, 1970, 1975 et 1977.

Tableau 6.7
Ce tableau présente le nombre total de récepteurs de radio dans le monde pour 1965, 1970, 1975 et 1977. Il faut préciser que plusieurs pays ont communiqué le nombre de licences délivrées plutôt que le nombre de récepteurs en service. Ceci explique qu'il y ait un certain sous dénombrement dans le nombre de récepteurs des pays et régions où une seule licence permet d'avoir plusieurs récepteurs.

Tableau 6.8
Ce tableau indique le nombre d'émetteurs de télévision autour de 1965, 1970, 1975 et 1977. Les chiffres communiqués au Secrétariat sont souvent incomplets, puisque tous les pays n'incluent pas dans leurs statistiques les réémetteurs.

Tableau 6.9
Le tableau 6.9 présente le nombre de récepteurs de télévision pour 1965, 1970, 1975 et 1977.

Les graphiques suivants présentent quelques aspects relatifs à la radio et à la télévision, qui figurent dans une étude spéciale portant sur les statistiques de la radio et de la télévision 1960-1976, publiée dans le numéro 23 de la collection *Rapports et études statistiques* de l'Unesco.

Este capítulo presenta una serie de cuadros recapitulativos sobre algunas materias seleccionadas relativas a la cultura y la comunicación. Las estadísticas que figuran en estos cuadros se distribuyen por continentes, grandes regiones y grupos de países cuya composición se indica en la nota 1 del cuadro 1.2. de este *Anuario*. Las materias consideradas son las siguientes: edición de libros, periódicos diarios, papel cultural, cines, transmisores y receptores de radio y transmisores y receptores de televisión.

Es necesario precisar que debido a las dificultades que existen para determinar la fiabilidad de las estadísticas disponibles y las lagunas que se manifiestan en la información proporcionada por varios países, los càlculos de los datos mundiales y regionales que figuran en este capítulo no constituyen a lo sumo·más que una aproximación muy relativa de la situación real.

Cuadro 6.1
El propósito de este cuadro es el de presentar la evolución de la edición de libros (en número de títulos) en el mundo entre 1955 y 1978.

Cuadro 6.2
Este cuadro presenta estimaciones mundiales y regionales sobre los periódicos diarios en 1977. Las estadísticas se refieren al número de periódicos, su tirada y la tirada por 1 000 habitantes.

Cuadros 6.3 y 6.4
Sobre la base de las estadísticas disponibles, proporcionadas a la Unesco por la Organización de las Naciones Unidas para la Agricultura y la Alimentación (FAO), se han efectuado estimaciones mundiales y regionales de la producción y el consumo de 'papel cultural' (papel de periódico y papel de imprenta y de escribir) para los años 1970, 1975, 1977 y 1978.

Cuadro 6.5
Este cuadro presenta el número de cines, el número de asientos y el número de asientos por 1 000 habitantes para los años 1970 y 1977.

Cuadro 6.6
En este cuadro figura el número de transmisores de radiodifusión sonora alrededor de 1965, 1970, 1975 y 1977.

Cuadro 6.7
El total de receptores de radio en el mundo para 1965, 1970, 1975 y 1977 figura en este cuadro. Es necesario precisar que varios países han comunicado el número de permisos concedidos más bien que el número de receptores en funcionamiento. Esto motiva que haya una cierta subenumeración en el número de receptores de los países y regiones donde un solo permiso autoriza a tener varios receptores.

Cuadro 6.8
Este cuadro indica el número de transmisores de televisión alrededor de 1965, 1970, 1975 y 1977. Las cifras que han sido communicadas al Secretariado son con frecuencia incompletas, ya que no todos los países incluyen en sus estadísticas los retransmisores.

Cuadro 6.9
El cuadro 6.9 presenta el número de receptores de televisión para 1965, 1970, 1975 y 1977.

Los gráficos siguientes presentan algunos aspectos relativos a la radio y la televisión, que figuran en un estudio especial sobre las estadísticas de la radio y la televisión 1960-1976, publicado en el número 23 de la colección *Informes y estudios estadísticos* de la Unesco.

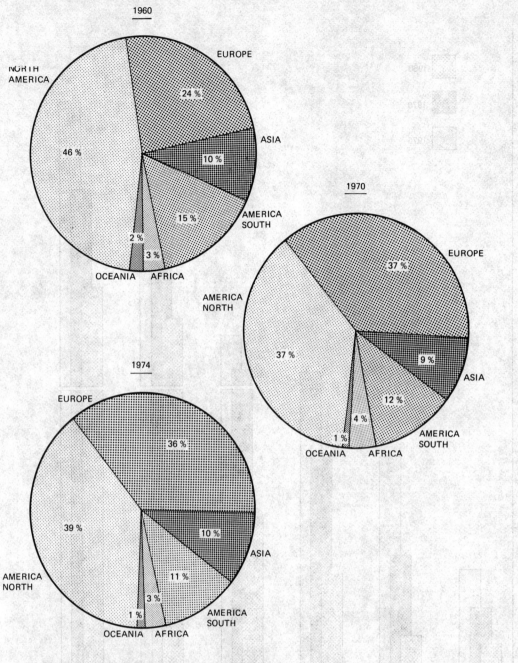

Figure 5 — Distribution of sound broadcasting transmitters by
continents (circa 1960, 1970, 1974).

Graphique 5 — Répartition des émetteurs de radio, par continents,
(autour de 1960, 1970, 1974).

Gráfico 5 — Distribución de los transmisores de radio, por
continentes (alrededor de 1960, 1970, 1974).

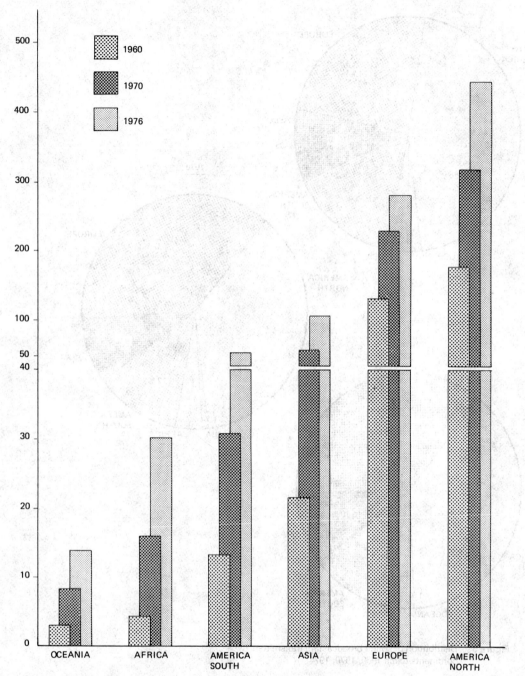

Figure 6 — Total number of radio receivers by continents:
1960, 1970 and 1976 (in millions).

Graphique 6 — Nombre total de récepteurs de radio, par continents:
1960, 1970 et 1976 (en millions).

Gráfico 6 — Número total de receptores de radio, por continentes:
1960, 1970 y 1976 (en millones).

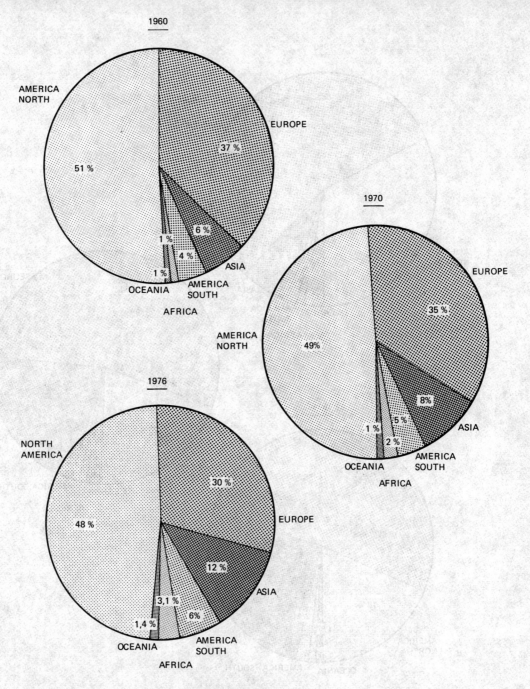

Figure 7 — Distribution of radio receivers by continents:
Estimated percentages 1960, 1970, 1976.

Graphique 7 — Répartition des récepteurs de radio, par continents:
Estimations en pourcentage pour 1960, 1970 et 1976.

Gráfico 7 — Distribución de los receptores de radio, por continentes:
Estimaciones en porcentaje para 1960, 1970 y 1976.

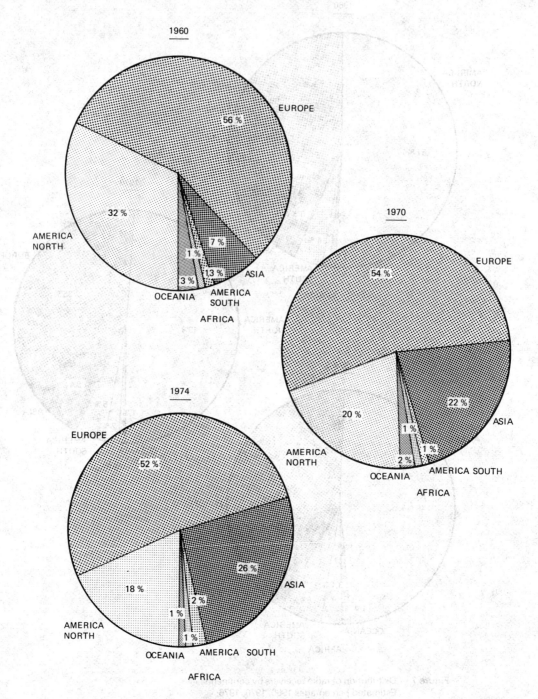

1960

EUROPE
56 %

AMERICA
NORTH
32 %

1 %

7 %

13 %

ASIA

3 %

OCEANIA

AMERICA
SOUTH

AFRICA

1970

EUROPE

54 %

AMERICA
NORTH
20 %

1 %

22 %

ASIA

1 %

2 %

OCEANIA

AMERICA SOUTH

AFRICA

1974

EUROPE
52 %

26 %

ASIA

AMERICA
NORTH
18 %

1 %

2 %

1 %

OCEANIA   AMERICA SOUTH

AFRICA

Figure 8 — Distribution of number of television broadcasting
transmitters by continents (circa 1960, 1970, 1974).

Graphique 8 — Répartition du nombre d'émetteurs de télévision, par
continents (autour de 1960, 1970, 1974).

Gráfico 8 — Distribución del número de transmisores de televisión,
por continentes (alrededor de 1960, 1970, 1974).

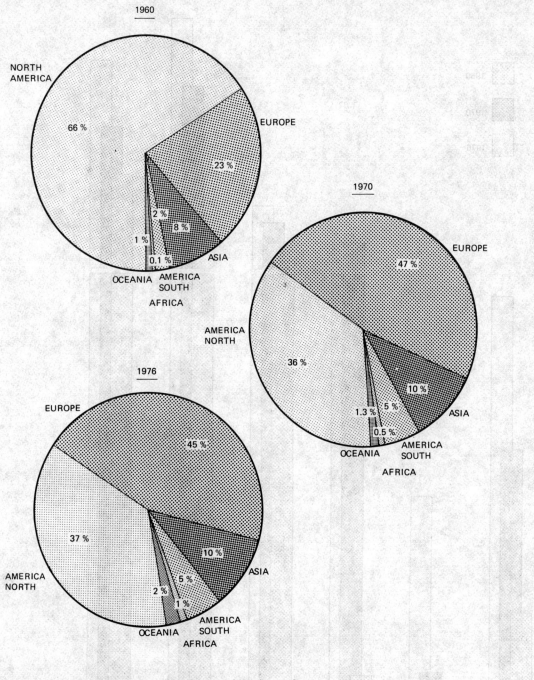

1960

NORTH
AMERICA

66 %

EUROPE

23 %

2 %

8 %

1 %

0.1 %

OCEANIA   AMERICA
           SOUTH

AFRICA

ASIA

1970

EUROPE

47 %

AMERICA
NORTH

36 %

10 %

1.3 %   5 %

0.5 %

OCEANIA   AMERICA
           SOUTH

AFRICA

ASIA

1976

EUROPE

45 %

37 %

AMERICA
NORTH

2 %

1 %

10 %

5 %

ASIA

OCEANIA   AMERICA
           SOUTH

AFRICA

Figure 9 — Total number of television receivers, by continents:
1960, 1970 and 1976 (in millions).

Graphique 9 — Nombre total de récepteurs de télévision, par continents:
1960, 1970 et 1976 (en millions).

Gráfico 9 — Número total de receptores de televisión, por continentes:
1960, 1970 y 1976 (en millones).

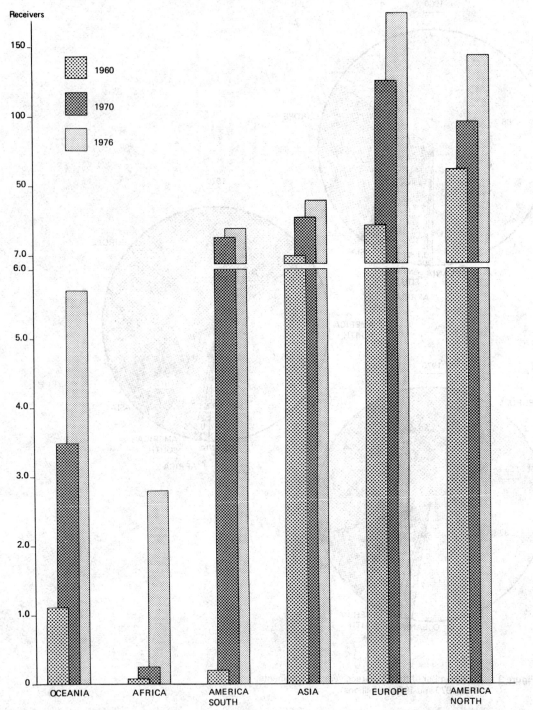

Figure 10 — Distribution of television receivers by continents:
Estimated percentages 1960, 1970 and 1976.

Graphique 10 — Répartition des récepteurs de télévision, par continents:
Estimations en pourcentage pour 1960, 1970 et 1976.

Gráfico 10 — Distributión de los receptores de televisión, por continentes:
Estimaciones en porcentaje para 1960, 1970 y 1976.

Number of book titles published 6.1
Nombre de titres de livres publiés
Número de títulos de libros publicados

6.1 Number of book titles published
Nombre de titres de livres publiés
Número de títulos de libros publicados

	1955	1960	1965	1970	1975	1978
BOOK PRODUCTION: NUMBER OF TITLES						
PRODUCTION DE LIVRES: NOMBRE DE TITRES						
PRODUCCION DE LIBROS: NUMERO DE TITULOS						
WORLD TOTAL ‡	269 000	332 000	426 000	521 000	568 000	642 000
AFRICA	3 000	5 000	7 000	8 000	11 000	11 000
AMERICA	25 000	35 000	77 000	105 000	121 000	130 000
ASIA ‡	54 000	51 000	61 000	75 000	88 000	121 000
EUROPE	131 000	163 000	200 000	247 000	264 000	288 000
OCEANIA	1 000	2 000	5 000	7 000	5 000	6 000
U.S.S.R.	55 000	76 000	76 000	79 000	79 000	86 000
DEVELOPED COUNTRIES	225 000	285 000	366 000	451 000	480 000	527 000
DEVELOPING COUNTRIES ‡	44 000	47 000	60 000	70 000	88 000	115 000
AFRICA (EXCLUDING						
ARAB STATES)	1 600	2 400	4 300	4 600	8 300	8 700
NORTHERN AMERICA	14 000	18 000	58 000	83 000	92 000	98 000
LATIN AMERICA	11 000	17 000	19 000	22 000	29 000	32 000
ASIA (EXCLUDING						
ARAB STATES) ‡	53 200	49 900	59 700	73 700	85 800	117 700
ARAB STATES	2 200	3 700	4 000	4 700	4 900	5 600
NUMBER OF TITLES PER MILLION INHABITANTS						
NOMBRE DE TITRES PAR MILLION D'HABITANTS						
NUMERO DE TITULOS POR MILLON DE HABITANTES						
WORLD TOTAL ‡	131	144	168	187	185	151
AFRICA	13	19	23	23	27	25
AMERICA	68	84	167	206	216	220
ASIA ‡	64	53	57	62	65	49
EUROPE	320	383	450	535	558	600
OCEANIA	68	121	286	361	235	259
U.S.S.R.	279	355	329	329	310	328
DEVELOPED COUNTRIES	249	296	357	420	424	450
DEVELOPING COUNTRIES ‡	38	35	40	41	45	37
AFRICA (EXCLUDING						
ARAB STATES)	10	12	18	17	27	26
NORTHERN AMERICA	77	91	271	367	389	405
LATIN AMERICA	60	79	77	78	89	91
ASIA (EXCLUDING						
ARAB STATES) ‡	65	53	58	63	65	49
ARAB STATES	27	40	38	38	35	38

6.1   Number of book titles published
Nombre de titres de livres publiés
Número de títulos de libros publicados

	1955	1960	1965	1970	1975	1978
PERCENTAGE DISTRIBUTION OF BOOK PRODUCTION						
REPARTITION DE LA PRODUCTION DE LIVRES EN POURCENTAGE						
DISTRIBUCION PORCENTUAL DE LA PRODUCCION DE LIBROS						
WORLD TOTAL ‡	100.0	100.0	100.0	100.0	100.0	100.0
AFRICA	1.1	1.5	1.6	1.5	1.9	1.7
AMERICA	9.3	10.5	18.1	20.2	21.3	20.3
ASIA ‡	20.1	15.4	14.3	14.4	15.5	18.9
EUROPE	48.7	49.1	46.9	47.4	46.5	44.9
OCEANIA	0.4	0.6	1.2	1.3	0.9	0.9
U.S.S.R.	20.4	22.9	17.8	15.2	13.9	13.4
DEVELOPED COUNTRIES	83.6	85.8	85.9	86.6	84.5	82.1
DEVELOPING COUNTRIES ‡	16.4	14.2	14.1	13.4	15.5	17.9
AFRICA (EXCLUDING						
ARAB STATES)	0.6	0.7	1.0	0.9	1.5	1.4
NORTHERN AMERICA	5.2	5.4	13.6	15.9	16.2	15.3
LATIN AMERICA	4.1	5.1	4.5	4.2	5.1	5.0
ASIA (EXCLUDING						
ARAB STATES) ‡	19.8	15.0	14.0	14.1	15.1	18.3
ARAB STATES	0.8	1.1	0.9	0.9	0.9	0.9
PERCENTAGE DISTRIBUTION OF POPULATION						
REPARTITION DE LA POPULATION EN POURCENTAGE						
DISTRIBUCION PORCENTUAL DE LA POBLACION						
WORLD TOTAL ‡	100.0	100.0	100.0	100.0	100.0	100.0
AFRICA	10.8	11.8	12.2	12.6	13.1	10.4
AMERICA	17.8	17.9	18.2	18.3	18.3	13.9
ASIA ‡	41.1	41.9	42.2	43.2	44.2	57.8
EUROPE	19.9	18.4	17.6	16.5	15.4	11.3
OCEANIA	0.7	0.7	0.7	0.7	0.7	0.5
U.S.S.R.	9.6	9.3	9.1	8.7	8.3	6.2
DEVELOPED COUNTRIES	44.0	41.6	40.5	38.5	36.9	27.5
DEVELOPING COUNTRIES ‡	56.0	58.4	59.5	61.5	63.1	72.5
AFRICA (EXCLUDING						
ARAB STATES)	8.0	9.0	9.3	9.5	9.9	8.0
NORTHERN AMERICA	8.8	8.6	8.4	8.1	7.7	5.7
LATIN AMERICA	9.0	9.3	9.8	10.2	10.6	8.2
ASIA (EXCLUDING						
ARAB STATES) ‡	40.0	40.7	40.9	41.9	42.8	56.7
ARAB STATES	4.0	4.1	4.2	4.4	4.6	3.5

WORLD TOTAL:
    E—> NOT INCLUDING CHINA AND THE DEMOCRATIC
PEOPLE'S REPUBLIC OF KOREA.
    FR—> NON COMPRIS LA CHINE ET LA REPUBLIQUE
POPULAIRE DEMOCRATIQUE DE COREE.
    ESP> EXCLUIDAS CHINA Y LA REPUBLICA POPULAR
DEMOCRATICA DE COREA.

ASIA:
    E—> NOT INCLUDING CHINA AND THE DEMOCRATIC
PEOPLE'S REPUBLIC OF KOREA.
    FR—> NON COMPRIS LA CHINE ET LA REPUBLIQUE
POPULAIRE DEMOCRATIQUE DE COREE.
    ESP> EXCLUIDAS CHINA Y LA REPUBLICA POPULAR
DEMOCRATICA DE COREA.

DEVELOPING COUNTRIES:
    E—> NOT INCLUDING CHINA AND THE DEMOCRATIC
PEOPLE'S REPUBLIC OF KOREA.
    FR—> NON COMPRIS LA CHINE ET LA REPUBLIQUE
POPULAIRE DEMOCRATIQUE DE COREE.
    ESP> EXCLUIDAS CHINA Y LA REPUBLICA POPULAR
DEMOCRATICA DE COREA.

ASIA (EXCLUDING ARAB STATES):
    E—> NOT INCLUDING CHINA AND THE DEMOCRATIC
PEOPLE'S REPUBLIC OF KOREA.
    FR—> NON COMPRIS LA CHINE ET LA REPUBLIQUE
POPULAIRE DEMOCRATIQUE DE COREE.
    ESP> EXCLUIDAS CHINA Y LA REPUBLICA POPULAR
DEMOCRATICA DE COREA.

Number and circulation of daily newspapers 6.2
Nombre et tirage des journaux quotidiens
Número y tirada de los periódicos diarios

6.2 Number and circulation of daily newspapers
Nombre et tirage des journaux quotidiens
Número y tirada de los periódicos diarios

CONTINENTS, MAJOR AREAS AND GROUPS OF COUNTRIES CONTINENTS, GRANDES REGIONS ET GROUPES DE PAYS CONTINENTES, GRANDES REGIONES Y GRUPOS DE PAISES	NUMBER OF DAILIES NOMBRE DE QUOTIDIENS NUMERO DE DIARIOS	ESTIMATED CIRCULATION TIRAGE (ESTIMATION) TIRADA (ESTIMACION)	
		TOTAL (MILLIONS) (MILLONES)	PER 1,000 INHABITANTS POUR 1 000 HABITANTS POR 1 000 HABITANTES
WORLD TOTAL ‡	8 210	443	136
AFRICA	180	9	21
AMERICA	3 110	92	158
ASIA ‡	2 380	107	72
EUROPE	1 740	127	264
OCEANIA	110	6	268
U.S.S.R.	690	102	394
DEVELOPED COUNTRIES	4 700	366	321
DEVELOPING COUNTRIES ‡	3 510	77	36
AFRICA (EXCLUDING ARAB STATES)	150	5	15
NORTHERN AMERICA	1 950	67	281
LATIN AMERICA	1 160	25	72
ASIA (EXCLUDING ARAB STATES) ‡	2 300	106	73
ARAB STATES	110	5	30

WORLD TOTAL:
   E—> NOT INCLUDING CHINA, THE DEMOCRATIC PEOPLE'S REPUBLIC OF KOREA AND THE SOCIALIST REPUBLIC OF VIET-NAM.
   FR-> NON COMPRIS LA CHINE, LA REPUBLIQUE POPULAIRE DEMOCRATIQUE DE COREE ET LA REPUBLIQUE SOCIALISTE DU VIET-NAM.
   ESP> NO INCLUYE CHINA, LA REPUBLICA POPULAR DEMOCRATICA DE COREA Y LA REPUBLICA SOCIALISTA DEL VIET-NAM.

ASIA:
   E—> NOT INCLUDING CHINA, THE DEMOCRATIC PEOPLE'S REPUBLIC OF KOREA AND THE SOCIALIST REPUBLIC OF VIET-NAM.
   FR-> NON COMPRIS LA CHINE, LA REPUBLIQUE POPULAIRE DEMOCRATIQUE DE COREE ET LA REPUBLIQUE SOCIALISTE DU VIET-NAM.
   ESP> NO INCLUYE CHINA, LA REPUBLICA POPULAR DEMOCRATICA DE COREA Y LA REPUBLICA SOCIALISTA DEL VIET-NAM.

DEVELOPING COUNTRIES:
   E—> NOT INCLUDING CHINA, THE DEMOCRATIC PEOPLE'S REPUBLIC OF KOREA AND THE SOCIALIST REPUBLIC OF VIET-NAM.
   FR-> NON COMPRIS LA CHINE, LA REPUBLIQUE POPULAIRE DEMOCRATIQUE DE COREE ET LA REPUBLIQUE SOCIALISTE DU VIET-NAM.
   ESP> NO INCLUYE CHINA, LA REPUBLICA POPULAR DEMOCRATICA DE COREA Y LA REPUBLICA SOCIALISTA DEL VIET-NAM.

ASIA (EXCLUDING ARAB STATES):
   E—> NOT INCLUDING CHINA, THE DEMOCRATIC PEOPLE'S REPUBLIC OF KOREA AND THE SOCIALIST REPUBLIC OF VIET-NAM.
   FR-> NON COMPRIS LA CHINE, LA REPUBLIQUE POPULAIRE DEMOCRATIQUE DE COREE ET LA REPUBLIQUE SOCIALISTE DU VIET-NAM.
   ESP> NO INCLUYE CHINA, LA REPUBLICA POPULAR DEMOCRATICA DE COREA Y LA REPUBLICA SOCIALISTA DEL VIET-NAM.

6.3 Newsprint production and consumption
Production et consommation de papier journal
Producción y consumo de papel de periódico

6.3 Newsprint production and consumption
Production et consommation de papier journal
Producción y consumo de papel de periódico

MT = MILLION METRIC TONS   MT = MILLIONS DE TONNES METRIQUES   MT = MILLONES DE TONELADAS METRICAS

CONTINENTS, MAJOR AREAS AND GROUPS OF COUNTRIES CONTINENTS, GRANDES REGIONS ET GROUPES DE PAYS CONTINENTES, GRANDES REGIONES Y GRUPOS DE PAISES	NEWSPRINT / PAPIER JOURNAL / PAPEL DE PERIODICO					
	PRODUCTION PRODUCTION PRODUCCION (MT) 1978	CONSUMPTION / CONSOMMATION / CONSUMO				
		TOTAL (MT) 1978	1970	PER INHABITANT (KG) PAR HABITANT (KG) POR HABITANTE (KG) 1976	1977	1978
WORLD TOTAL	24.1	24.5	5.9	5.6	5.7	5.8
AFRICA	0.2	0.3	0.9	0.7	0.7	0.6
AMERICA	12.4	11.9	21.1	19.2	19.4	20.4
ASIA	4.2	4.9	1.6	1.9	1.9	2.0
EUROPE	5.4	5.7	12.7	12.0	11.9	11.9
OCEANIA	0.5	0.5	28.7	24.7	28.0	24.9
U.S.S.R.	1.4	1.1	3.8	4.4	4.2	4.4
DEVELOPED COUNTRIES	22.0	20.9	17.8	17.6	17.4	18.2
DEVELOPING COUNTRIES	2.1	3.6	0.9	1.1	1.2	1.2
AFRICA (EXCLUDING ARAB STATES)	0.2	0.2	1.0	0.7	0.7	0.5
NORTHERN AMERICA	12.0	10.9	42.4	42.0	41.3	44.9
LATIN AMERICA	0.4	1.1	3.8	2.7	3.8	3.1
ASIA (EXCLUDING ARAB STATES)	4.2	4.8	1.6	1.9	2.0	2.0
ARAB STATES	–	0.1	0.5	0.8	0.9	0.9

Production and consumption of other cultural paper 6.4
Production et consommation des autres papiers culturels
Producción y consumo de otros papeles culturales

6.4 Production and consumption of other printing and writing paper

Production et consommation des autres papiers d'impression et papier d'écriture

Producción y consumo de otros papeles de imprenta y papel de escribir

MT = MILLION METRIC TONS MT = MILLIONS DE TONNES METRIQUES MT = MILLONES DE TONELADAS METRICAS

CONTINENTS, MAJOR AREAS AND GROUPS OF COUNTRIES CONTINENTS, GRANDES REGIONS ET GROUPES DE PAYS CONTINENTES, GRANDES REGIONES Y GRUPOS DE PAISES	OTHER PRINTING AND WRITING PAPER AUTRES PAPIERS D'IMPRESSION ET PAPIER D'ECRITURE OTROS PAPELES DE IMPRENTA Y PAPEL DE ESCRIBIR					
	PRODUCTION PRODUCTION PRODUCCION (MT) 1978	CONSUMPTION / CONSOMMATION / CONSUMO				
		TOTAL (MT) 1978	1970	PER INHABITANT (KG) PAR HABITANT (KG) POR HABITANTE (KG) 1976	1977	1978
WORLD TOTAL	38.6	38.2	7.4	8.2	8.5	9.1
AFRICA	0.3	0.5	1.1	1.0	1.0	1.1
AMERICA	16.1	16.6	23.1	25.1	26.5	28.2
ASIA	6.8	7.1	2.1	2.7	2.7	2.9
EUROPE	14.0	12.4	20.4	23.2	23.9	25.8
OCEANIA	0.2	0.3	14.7	11.0	15.4	15.4
U.S.S.R.	1.2	1.3	4.1	4.9	5.1	5.1
DEVELOPED COUNTRIES	33.7	32.5	22.2	25.2	26.3	28.4
DEVELOPING COUNTRIES	4.9	5.7	1.3	1.7	1.8	1.9
AFRICA (EXCLUDING ARAB STATES)	0.2	0.3	1.0	0.9	0.9	1.0
NORTHERN AMERICA	14.7	14.9	47.4	53.8	57.0	61.4
LATIN AMERICA	1.4	1.7	3.5	4.3	4.7	4.9
ASIA (EXCLUDING ARAB STATES)	6.8	7.0	2.1	2.7	2.7	2.9
ARAB STATES	0.1	0.2	1.3	1.3	1.6	1.6

6.5 Number and seating capacity of fixed cinemas
Nombre de cinémas fixes et de sièges
Número de cines fijos y de asientos

6.5 Number and seating capacity of fixed cinemas
Nombre de cinémas fixes et de sièges
Número de cines fijos y de asientos

CONTINENTS, MAJOR AREAS AND GROUPS OF COUNTRIES CONTINENTS, GRANDES REGIONS ET GROUPES DE PAYS CONTINENTES, GRANDES REGIONES Y GRUPOS DE PAISES	FIXED CINEMAS CINEMAS FIXES CINES FIJOS		SEATING CAPACITY NOMBRE DE SIEGES NUMERO DE ASIENTOS			
	NUMBER (THOUSANDS) NOMBRE (MILLIERS) NUMERO (MILES)		TOTAL (MILLIONS) TOTAL (MILLIONS) TOTAL (MILLONES)		PER 1,000 INHABITANTS POUR 1 000 HABITANTS POR 1 000 HABITANTES	
	1970	1977	1970	1977	1970	1977
WORLD TOTAL ‡	261	259	72	68	26	21
AFRICA	3.0	3.0	1.9	1.9	6	5
AMERICA	28	28	18	19	36	32
ASIA ‡	15	20	9.7	11	8	8
EUROPE	65	54	20	15	44	31
OCEANIA	1.5	1.3	0.8	0.5	41	23
U.S.S.R.	148	153	22	21	91	81
DEVELOPED COUNTRIES	235	229	56	51	48	45
DEVELOPING COUNTRIES ‡	26	30	16	17	9	8
AFRICA (EXCLUDING ARAB STATES)	1.8	2.1	1.2	1.2	5	4
NORTHERN AMERICA	16	18	11	13	50	53
LATIN AMERICA	12	10	7.1	6.2	25	18
ASIA (EXCLUDING ARAB STATES) ‡	14	19	9.4	11	8	8
ARAB STATES	1.6	1.6	0.9	1.1	7	8

WORLD TOTAL:
  E—> NOT INCLUDING CHINA AND THE DEMOCRATIC PEOPLE'S REPUBLIC OF KOREA.
  FR—> NON COMPRIS LA CHINE ET LA REPUBLIQUE POPULAIRE DEMOCRATIQUE DE COREE.
  ESP> NO INCLUYE CHINA Y LA REPUBLICA POPULAR DEMOCRATICA DE COREA.

ASIA:
  E—> NOT INCLUDING CHINA AND THE DEMOCRATIC PEOPLE'S REPUBLIC OF KOREA.
  FR—> NON COMPRIS LA CHINE ET LA REPUBLIQUE POPULAIRE DEMOCRATIQUE DE COREE.
  ESP> NO INCLUYE CHINA Y LA REPUBLICA POPULAR DEMOCRATICA DE COREA.

DEVELOPING COUNTRIES:
  E—> NOT INCLUDING CHINA AND THE DEMOCRATIC PEOPLE'S REPUBLIC OF KOREA.
  FR—> NON COMPRIS LA CHINE ET LA REPUBLIQUE POPULAIRE DEMOCRATIQUE DE COREE.
  ESP> NO INCLUYE CHINA Y LA REPUBLICA POPULAR DEMOCRATICA DE COREA.

ASIA (EXCLUDING ARAB STATES):
  E—> NOT INCLUDING CHINA AND THE DEMOCRATIC PEOPLE'S REPUBLIC OF KOREA.
  FR—> NON COMPRIS LA CHINE ET LA REPUBLIQUE POPULAIRE DEMOCRATIQUE DE COREE.
  ESP> NO INCLUYE CHINA Y LA REPUBLICA POPULAR DEMOCRATICA DE COREA.

Number of radio broadcasting transmitters 6.6
Nombre d'émetteurs de radio
Número de transmisores de radio

6.6 Number of radio broadcasting transmitters

Nombre d'émetteurs de radio

Número de transmisores de radio

CONTINENTS, MAJOR AREAS AND GROUPS OF COUNTRIES CONTINENTS, GRANDES REGIONS ET GROUPES DE PAYS CONTINENTES, GRANDES REGIONES Y GRUPOS DE PAISES	TOTAL NUMBER OF RADIO BROADCASTING TRANSMITTERS NOMBRE TOTAL DE POSTES EMETTEURS DE RADIODIFFUSION NUMERO TOTAL DE TRANSMISORES DE RADIODIFUSION			
	1965	1970	1975	1977
WORLD TOTAL ‡	16 400	22 100	25 800	28 000
AFRICA	500	680	730	790
AMERICA	9 640	10 910	12 730	13 400
ASIA ‡	1 390	1 930	2 730	3 740
EUROPE	4 170	5 240	5 980	6 190
OCEANIA	290	310	330	380
U.S.S.R.	410	3 030	3 300	3 500
DEVELOPED COUNTRIES	11 670	16 200	19 100	20 360
DEVELOPING COUNTRIES ‡	4 730	5 900	6 700	7 640
AFRICA (EXCLUDING ARAB STATES)	400	560	580	630
NORTHERN AMERICA	6 170	6 770	8 530	9 190
LATIN AMERICA	3 470	4 140	4 200	4 210
ASIA (EXCLUDING ARAB STATES) ‡	1 330	1 830	2 630	3 600
ARAB STATES	160	220	250	300

WORLD TOTAL:
  E—> NOT INCLUDING CHINA, THE DEMOCRATIC PEOPLE'S REPUBLIC OF KOREA AND THE SOCIALIST REPUBLIC OF VIET—NAM.
  FR-> NON COMPRIS LA CHINE, LA REPUBLIQUE POPULAIRE DEMOCRATIQUE DE COREE ET LA REPUBLIQUE SOCIALISTE DU VIET—NAM.
  ESP> NO INCLUYE CHINA, LA REPUBLICA POPULAR DEMOCRATICA DE COREA Y LA REPUBLICA SOCIALISTA DEL VIET—NAM.

ASIA:
  E—> NOT INCLUDING CHINA, THE DEMOCRATIC PEOPLE'S REPUBLIC OF KOREA AND THE SOCIALIST REPUBLIC OF VIET—NAM.
  FR-> NON COMPRIS LA CHINE, LA REPUBLIQUE POPULAIRE DEMOCRATIQUE DE COREE ET LA REPUBLIQUE SOCIALISTE DU VIET—NAM.
  ESP> NO INCLUYE CHINA, LA REPUBLICA POPULAR DEMOCRATICA DE COREA Y LA REPUBLICA SOCIALISTA DEL VIET—NAM.

DEVELOPING COUNTRIES:
  E—> NOT INCLUDING CHINA, THE DEMOCRATIC PEOPLE'S REPUBLIC OF KOREA AND THE SOCIALIST REPUBLIC OF VIET—NAM.
  FR-> NON COMPRIS LA CHINE, LA REPUBLIQUE POPULAIRE DEMOCRATIQUE DE COREE ET LA REPUBLIQUE SOCIALISTE DU VIET—NAM.
  ESP> NO INCLUYE CHINA, LA REPUBLICA POPULAR DEMOCRATICA DE COREA Y LA REPUBLICA SOCIALISTA DEL VIET—NAM.

ASIA (EXCLUDING ARAB STATES):
  E—> NOT INCLUDING CHINA, THE DEMOCRATIC PEOPLE'S REPUBLIC OF KOREA AND THE SOCIALIST REPUBLIC OF VIET—NAM.
  FR-> NON COMPRIS LA CHINE, LA REPUBLIQUE POPULAIRE DEMOCRATIQUE DE COREE ET LA REPUBLIQUE SOCIALISTE DU VIET—NAM.
  ESP> NO INCLUYE CHINA, LA REPUBLICA POPULAR DEMOCRATICA DE COREA Y LA REPUBLICA SOCIALISTA DEL VIET—NAM.

6.7 Number of radio receivers: total and per 1,000 inhabitants
Nombre de récepteurs de radio: total et pour 1 000 habitants
Número de receptores de radio: total y por 1 000 habitantes

6.7 Number of radio receivers and receivers per 1,000 inhabitants

Nombre de récepteurs de radio et de récepteurs pour 1 000 habitants

Número de receptores de radio y de receptores por 1 000 habitantes

CONTINENTS, MAJOR AREAS AND GROUPS OF COUNTRIES CONTINENTS, GRANDES REGIONS ET GROUPES DE PAYS CONTINENTES, GRANDES REGIONES Y GRUPOS DE PAISES	NUMBER OF RADIO RECEIVERS NOMBRE DE RECEPTEURS DE RADIO NUMERO DE RECEPTORES DE RADIO TOTAL (MILLIONS/MILLONES)				PER 1,000 INHABITANTS POUR 1 000 HABITANTS POR 1 000 HABITANTES			
	1965	1970	1975	1977	1965	1970	1975	1977
WORLD TOTAL ‡	524	672	931	1058	207	241	303	325
AFRICA	10	16	28	31	33	45	70	73
AMERICA	285	357	505	553	619	701	900	947
ASIA ‡	42	58	108	141	39	48	80	95
EUROPE	110	138	155	182	249	299	327	381
OCEANIA	3	8	13	17	189	428	606	773
U.S.S.R.	74	95	122	134	319	390	480	515
DEVELOPED COUNTRIES	460	572	770	869	449	533	687	762
DEVELOPING COUNTRIES ‡	64	100	161	189	42	58	83	89
AFRICA (EXCLUDING ARAB STATES)	6	8	17	20	24	31	55	62
NORTHERN AMERICA	251	306	424	466	1173	1353	1793	1942
LATIN AMERICA	34	51	81	87	138	180	249	252
ASIA (EXCLUDING ARAB STATES) ‡	40	56	102	133	39	48	77	92
ARAB STATES	6	10	17	19	59	83	120	130

WORLD TOTAL:
  E—> NOT INCLUDING CHINA, THE DEMOCRATIC PEOPLE'S REPUBLIC OF KOREA AND THE SOCIALIST REPUBLIC OF VIET—NAM.
  FR-> NON COMPRIS LA CHINE, LA REPUBLIQUE POPULAIRE DEMOCRATIQUE DE COREE ET LA REPUBLIQUE SOCIALISTE DU VIET—NAM.
  ESP> NO INCLUYE CHINA, LA REPUBLICA POPULAR DEMOCRATICA DE COREA Y LA REPUBLICA SOCIALISTA DEL VIET—NAM.

ASIA:
  E—> NOT INCLUDING CHINA, THE DEMOCRATIC PEOPLE'S REPUBLIC OF KOREA AND THE SOCIALIST REPUBLIC OF VIET—NAM.
  FR-> NON COMPRIS LA CHINE, LA REPUBLIQUE POPULAIRE DEMOCRATIQUE DE COREE ET LA REPUBLIQUE SOCIALISTE DU VIET—NAM.
  ESP> NO INCLUYE CHINA, LA REPUBLICA POPULAR DEMOCRATICA DE COREA Y LA REPUBLICA SOCIALISTA DEL VIET—NAM.

DEVELOPING COUNTRIES:
  E—> NOT INCLUDING CHINA, THE DEMOCRATIC PEOPLE'S REPUBLIC OF KOREA AND THE SOCIALIST REPUBLIC OF VIET—NAM.
  FR-> NON COMPRIS LA CHINE, LA REPUBLIQUE POPULAIRE DEMOCRATIQUE DE COREE ET LA REPUBLIQUE SOCIALISTE DU VIET—NAM.
  ESP> NO INCLUYE CHINA, LA REPUBLICA POPULAR DEMOCRATICA DE COREA Y LA REPUBLICA SOCIALISTA DEL VIET—NAM.

ASIA (EXCLUDING ARAB STATES):
  E—> NOT INCLUDING CHINA, THE DEMOCRATIC PEOPLE'S REPUBLIC OF KOREA AND THE SOCIALIST REPUBLIC OF VIET—NAM.
  FR-> NON COMPRIS LA CHINE, LA REPUBLIQUE POPULAIRE DEMOCRATIQUE DE COREE ET LA REPUBLIQUE SOCIALISTE DU VIET—NAM.
  ESP> NO INCLUYE CHINA, LA REPUBLICA POPULAR DEMOCRATICA DE COREA Y LA REPUBLICA SOCIALISTA DEL VIET—NAM.

Number of television transmitters 6.8
Nombre d'émetteurs de télévision
Número de transmisores de televisión

6.8 Number of television transmitters
Nombre d'émetteurs de télévision
Número de transmisores de televisión

CONTINENTS, MAJOR AREAS AND GROUPS OF COUNTRIES CONTINENTS, GRANDES REGIONS ET GROUPES DE PAYS CONTINENTES, GRANDES REGIONES Y GRUPOS DE PAISES	NUMBER OF REGULAR TELEVISION TRANSMITTERS NOMBRE D'EMETTEURS DE TELEVISION FONCTIONNANT REGULIEREMENT NUMERO DE TRANSMISORES DE TELEVISION QUE FUNCIONAN REGULARMENTE			
	1965	1970	1975	1977
WORLD TOTAL ‡	8 550	17 700	29 000	32 900
AFRICA	100	140	230	250
AMERICA	3 070	4 310	5 000	5 070
ASIA ‡	1 100	3 780	6 700	9 000
EUROPE	3 550	7 900	14 900	16 300
OCEANIA	80	230	370	440
U.S.S.R.	650	1 340	1 800	1 840
DEVELOPED COUNTRIES	8 100	16 900	27 580	31 250
DEVELOPING COUNTRIES ‡	450	800	1 420	1 650
AFRICA (EXCLUDING ARAB STATES)	55	70	120	130
NORTHERN AMERICA	2 820	3 850	4 360	4 420
LATIN AMERICA	250	460	640	650
ASIA (EXCLUDING ARAB STATES) ‡	1 070	3 730	6 630	8 930
ARAB STATES	75	120	180	190

WORLD TOTAL:
E—> NOT INCLUDING CHINA, THE DEMOCRATIC PEOPLE'S REPUBLIC OF KOREA AND THE SOCIALIST REPUBLIC OF VIET-NAM.
FR-> NON COMPRIS LA CHINE, LA REPUBLIQUE POPULAIRE DEMOCRATIQUE DE COREE ET LA REPUBLIQUE SOCIALISTE DU VIET-NAM.
ESP> NO INCLUYE CHINA, LA REPUBLICA POPULAR DEMOCRATICA DE COREA Y LA REPUBLICA SOCIALISTA DEL VIET-NAM.

ASIA:
E—> NOT INCLUDING CHINA, THE DEMOCRATIC PEOPLE'S REPUBLIC OF KOREA AND THE SOCIALIST REPUBLIC OF VIET-NAM.
FR-> NON COMPRIS LA CHINE, LA REPUBLIQUE POPULAIRE DEMOCRATIQUE DE COREE ET LA REPUBLIQUE SOCIALISTE DU VIET-NAM.
ESP> NO INCLUYE CHINA, LA REPUBLICA POPULAR DEMOCRATICA DE COREA Y LA REPUBLICA SOCIALISTA DEL VIET-NAM.

DEVELOPING COUNTRIES:
E—> NOT INCLUDING CHINA, THE DEMOCRATIC PEOPLE'S REPUBLIC OF KOREA AND THE SOCIALIST REPUBLIC OF VIET-NAM.
FR-> NON COMPRIS LA CHINE, LA REPUBLIQUE POPULAIRE DEMOCRATIQUE DE COREE ET LA REPUBLIQUE SOCIALISTE DU VIET-NAM.
ESP> NO INCLUYE CHINA, LA REPUBLICA POPULAR DEMOCRATICA DE COREA Y LA REPUBLICA SOCIALISTA DEL VIET-NAM.

ASIA (EXCLUDING ARAB STATES):
E—> NOT INCLUDING CHINA, THE DEMOCRATIC PEOPLE'S REPUBLIC OF KOREA AND THE SOCIALIST REPUBLIC OF VIET-NAM.
FR-> NON COMPRIS LA CHINE, LA REPUBLIQUE POPULAIRE DEMOCRATIQUE DE COREE ET LA REPUBLIQUE SOCIALISTE DU VIET-NAM.
ESP> NO INCLUYE CHINA, LA REPUBLICA POPULAR DEMOCRATICA DE COREA Y LA REPUBLICA SOCIALISTA DEL VIET-NAM.

6.9 Number of television receivers: total and per 1,000 inhabitants
Nombre de récepteurs de télévision: total et pour 1 000 habitants
Número de receptores de televisión: total y por 1 000 habitantes

6.9 Number of television receivers and receivers per 1,000 inhabitants

Nombre de récepteurs de télévision et de récepteurs pour 1 000 habitants

Número de receptores de televisión y de receptores por 1 000 habitantes

CONTINENTS, MAJOR AREAS AND GROUPS OF COUNTRIES CONTINENTS, GRANDES REGIONS ET GROUPES DE PAYS CONTINENTES, GRANDES REGIONES Y GRUPOS DE PAISES	NUMBER OF TELEVISION RECEIVERS NOMBRE DE RECEPTEURS DE TELEVISION NUMERO DE RECEPTORES DE TELEVISION TOTAL (MILLIONS/MILLONES)				PER 1,000 INHABITANTS POUR 1 000 HABITANTS POR 1 000 HABITANTES			
	1965	1970	1975	1977	1965	1970	1975	1977
WORLD TOTAL ‡	181	266	374	419	72	96	122	128
AFRICA	0.6	1.2	2.5	4.7	1.9	3.4	6.2	11
AMERICA	84	109	160	176	182	214	285	301
ASIA ‡	19.3	27.0	37.2	44.6	18	22	27	30
EUROPE	59	90	114	126	132	196	241	264
OCEANIA	2.4	3.5	5.5	5.9	137	200	258	268
U.S.S.R.	16	35	55	62	69	144	216	238
DEVELOPED COUNTRIES	170	244	334	368	166	227	298	322
DEVELOPING COUNTRIES ‡	11	22	40	51	7.3	13	21	24
AFRICA (EXCLUDING ARAB STATES)	0.1	0.3	0.6	2.1	0.4	1.1	2.0	6.5
NORTHERN AMERICA	76	92	133	145	355	407	562	604
LATIN AMERICA	8	17	27	31	32	60	83	90
ASIA (EXCLUDING ARAB STATES) ‡	18.8	26.0	35.7	42	18	22	27	29
ARAB STATES	0.9	1.9	3.4	5.2	8.4	15	24	36

WORLD TOTAL:
E—> NOT INCLUDING CHINA, THE DEMOCRATIC PEOPLE'S REPUBLIC OF KOREA AND THE SOCIALIST REPUBLIC OF VIET—NAM.
FR—> NON COMPRIS LA CHINE, LA REPUBLIQUE POPULAIRE DEMOCRATIQUE DE COREE ET LA REPUBLIQUE SOCIALISTE DU VIET—NAM.
ESP> NO INCLUYE CHINA, LA REPUBLICA POPULAR DEMOCRATICA DE COREA Y LA REPUBLICA SOCIALISTA DEL VIET—NAM.

ASIA:
E—> NOT INCLUDING CHINA, THE DEMOCRATIC PEOPLE'S REPUBLIC OF KOREA AND THE SOCIALIST REPUBLIC OF VIET—NAM.
FR—> NON COMPRIS LA CHINE, LA REPUBLIQUE POPULAIRE DEMOCRATIQUE DE COREE ET LA REPUBLIQUE SOCIALISTE DU VIET—NAM.
ESP> NO INCLUYE CHINA, LA REPUBLICA POPULAR DEMOCRATICA DE COREA Y LA REPUBLICA SOCIALISTA DEL VIET—NAM.

DEVELOPING COUNTRIES:
E—> NOT INCLUDING CHINA, THE DEMOCRATIC PEOPLE'S REPUBLIC OF KOREA AND THE SOCIALIST REPUBLIC OF VIET—NAM.
FR—> NON COMPRIS LA CHINE, LA REPUBLIQUE POPULAIRE DEMOCRATIQUE DE COREE ET LA REPUBLIQUE SOCIALISTE DU VIET—NAM.
ESP> NO INCLUYE CHINA, LA REPUBLICA POPULAR DEMOCRATICA DE COREA Y LA REPUBLICA SOCIALISTA DEL VIET—NAM.

ASIA (EXCLUDING ARAB STATES):
E—> NOT INCLUDING CHINA, THE DEMOCRATIC PEOPLE'S REPUBLIC OF KOREA AND THE SOCIALIST REPUBLIC OF VIET—NAM.
FR—> NON COMPRIS LA CHINE, LA REPUBLIQUE POPULAIRE DEMOCRATIQUE DE COREE ET LA REPUBLIQUE SOCIALISTE DU VIET—NAM.
ESP> NO INCLUYE CHINA, LA REPUBLICA POPULAR DEMOCRATICA DE COREA Y LA REPUBLICA SOCIALISTA DEL VIET—NAM.

7 Libraries
Bibliothèques
Bibliotecas

This chapter relates to national statistics on different types of libraries, their collections, acquisitions, lendings, expenditure, personnel, etc. Since 1950 Unesco has been collecting such statistics every other year. This periodicity was changed to three years following the Recommendation on the International Standardization of Library Statistics, adopted by the General Conference of Unesco at its sixteenth session in 1970. The three surveys which have been conducted since have requested data for 1971, 1974 and 1977 respectively. The figures reproduced in the tables of this chapter refer to the two latter years.

For the 1978 questionnaire, it was decided to revise the data collection programme slightly in order to better reflect library activities which are not covered by the Recommendation. This has led to the following changes in the content of the questionnaire: inclusion of audio-visual and other library materials in the questions on collections and annual additions, combining of the paragraphs on works loaned out to users and on inter-library lendings within the country and finally the counting of inter-library loan transactions in number of requests received (and satisfied) instead of in number of works loaned out. All these changes have been incorporated for information into the relevant parts of the Recommendation, extracts of which are shown below and are marked with an asterisk.

For the compilation of library statistics, the following definitions are given:

1. *Library*: irrespective of its title, any organized collection of printed books and periodicals or of any other graphic or audio-visual materials, with a staff to provide and facilitate the use of such materials as are required to meet the informational, research, educational or recreational needs of its users. Libraries should be counted in numbers of administrative units and of service points, as follows: (a) *administrative unit*, any independent library, or a group of libraries, under a single director or a single administration; (b) *service point*, any library serving users in premises of its own, whether the library itself be independent or one of a group of libraries forming an administrative unit. Independent libraries, central libraries and branch libraries (both static and mobile, library vans, ship libraries or train libraries) are considered to be service points provided there is direct service to users in them. The stops of library vans are not counted as service points.

Libraries thus defined are classified as follows:

2. *National libraries*: libraries which, irrespective of their title, are responsible for acquiring and conserving copies of all significant publications published in the country and functioning as 'deposit' libraries, either by law or under special agreements. Libraries described as 'national' but which do not conform to the above definition should not be placed in the 'national libraries' category.

3. *Libraries of institutions of higher education*: those primarily serving students and teachers in universities and other institutions of education at the third level. They can also be open to the general public. A distinction

should be made between:
(a) The main or central university library, or a group of libraries which may be in different places but is under one librarian.
(b) The libraries of university institutes or departments which are neither technically nor administratively under the main or central university library.
(c) Libraries attached to institutes of higher education which are not part of a university.

4. *Other major non-specialized libraries*: non-specialized libraries of a learned character which are neither libraries of institutions of higher education nor national libraries, though they may fulfil the functions of a national library for a specified geographical area.

5. *School libraries*: those attached to all types of schools below the level of education at the third level and serving primarily the pupils and teachers of such schools, even though they may also be open to the general public. Separate collections for the use of several classes in the same school should be regarded as a single library, which should be counted as an administrative unit and as a service point.

6. *Special libraries*: those maintained by an association, government service, parliament, research institution (excluding university institutes), learned society, professional association, museum, business firm, industrial enterprise, chamber of commerce, etc., or other organized group, the greater part of their collection being in a specific field or subject, e.g. natural sciences, social sciences, agriculture, chemistry, medicine, economics, engineering, law, history. A distinction should be made between:
(a) Libraries which provide materials and services to all members of the public who need them.
(b) Those libraries whose collections and services are for the most part designed to provide for the information needs of their primary users, even if in some cases they serve the information needs of specialists outside the group responsible for their maintenance.

7. *Public (or popular) libraries*: those which serve the population of a community or region free of charge or for a nominal fee; they may serve the general public or special categories of users such as children, members of the armed forces, hospital patients, prisoners, workers and employees. A distinction should be made between:
(a) Public libraries proper, i.e. those libraries receiving financial support, in whole or in large part from the public authorities (municipal or regional libraries).
(b) Libraries financed from private sources.

Each library should appear in one only of the foregoing categories, according to its primary function.

With respect to library holdings, acquisitions, lendings, expenditure, personnel etc., the following definitions and classifications are given:

8. *Collection*: all library materials provided by the library for its users.

Statistics relating to library collections should cover only the following documents available to users and including an allowance for material on loan: (a) books and (bound) periodicals, by metres of occupied shelves, volumes and titles*; (b) manuscripts, by metres of occupied shelves and volumes; (c) microforms of books, periodicals, manuscripts and other library materials* by number of physical units; (d) audio-visual documents* by number of physical units; (e) other library materials* by number of physical units.

9. *Annual additions*: all materials added to collections during the year whether by purchase, donation, exchange or any other method. Statistics relating to additions to collections should cover the following materials only (available to users): (a) books and (bound) periodicals* by titles, volumes and metres of shelves* added; (b) manuscripts, by number of units added and metres of shelves* added; (c) microforms of books, periodicals*, manuscripts and other library materials* by number of physical units added; (d) audio-visual materials*, by number of physical units added; (e) other library materials*, by number of physical units added.

10. *Printed*: this term covers all methods of reproduction whatever their nature, with the exception of microprinting.

11. *Periodicals*: publications constituting one issue in a continuous series under the same title published at regular or irregular intervals, over an indefinite period, individual issues in the series being numbered consecutively or each issue being dated. Newspapers as well as publications appearing annually or less frequently are included in the definition.

12. *Title*: the term used to describe a printed item which forms a separate whole, whether issued in one or several volumes.

13. *Volume*: a physical unit of any printed or manuscript work contained in one binding or portfolio.

14. *Audio-visual materials* : non-book, non-microform library materials which require the use of special equipment to be seen and/or heard. This includes materials such as records, tapes, cassettes, motion pictures, slides, transparencies, video recordings, etc.

15. *Other library materials* : all materials other than books, periodicals, manuscripts microforms and audio-visual materials. This includes materials such as maps, charts, art prints, photographs, dioramas etc.

16. *Library user*: any person utilizing the services of a library.

17. *Registered borrower*: any person registered with a library in order to borrow the materials of the collection for use outside the library. Only borrowers registered for the year under report should be counted.

18. *Ordinary expenditure*: expenditure incurred in the running of the library. Within this total the following only are shown separately:
  (a) *employees*: the total amount of money spent on salaries and wages, allowances and other related costs;
  (b) *acquisitions*: the cost of all items (printed, manuscript and audio-visual materials) added to the library.

19. *Trained librarians*: all persons employed in libraries who have received a general training in librarianship or information science. The training may be by formal methods or by means of an extended period of work in a library under supervision.

20. *Population served*: (a) by *public libraries*: the total number of inhabitants in the districts served by public libraries proper (libraries financed wholly or largely by the authorities); (b) by *school libraries*: the total number of pupils and teachers of primary and secondary schools served by school libraries; (c) by the *libraries of institutions of higher education*: the total number of students and teachers in institutions of higher education served by this category of library.

This chapter contains six statistical tables on libraries. Table 7.1 gives figures on the number of libraries, classified by categories, and the size of their stocks. The five following tables, 7.2 to 7.6 deal respectively with national libraries, libraries of institutions of higher education, school libraries, special libraries and public libraries as defined above. These tables contain information on collections, additions, borrowers, works loaned out, current expenditure, personnel and population served (where applicable).

Some items in the Unesco questionnaire do not figure in the tables for lack of answers. Even in this abridged form as compared with the programme of the Recommendation, tables 7.2 to 7.6 often show lacunae which in themselves are revelatory of the state of these statistics in the countries in question. The fact is that for a good many countries they leave much to be desired and caution is called for if comparisons between countries are made.

Countries and territories for which data were prior to 1974 have been omitted from the tables of this chapter. For these figures, the reader is referred to previous editions of the *Yearbook*.

Table 7.1

The number of libraries given in this table relate to *administrative units*. For the number of service points please refer to tables 7.2 to 7.6

Tables 7.2 - 7.6

These tables include only those countries whose statistics give more information than shown in Table 7.1. Unless otherwise indicated, the term 'volumes' designates only printed materials available to users.

Data referring to expenditure are expressed in national currency. The rates of exchange of national currency to the United States dollar are given in Appendix C.

Ce chapitre présente les statistiques nationales sur les différents types de bibliothèques, ses collections, acquisitions, prêts, dépenses, personnel, etc. Depuis 1950, l'Unesco rassemble ces statistiques tous les deux ans. Conformément à la Recommandation concernant la normalisation internationale des statistiques relatives aux bibliothèques, adoptée par la Conférence générale de l'Unesco à sa seizième session, en 1970, la périodicité a été portée à trois ans. Dans les trois enquêtes qui ont déjà été effectuées, les données demandées étaient pour 1971, 1974 et 1977 respectivement. Dans les tableaux de ce chapitre ne sont publiées que des données relatives aux deux dernières années.

Pour le questionnaire relatif à 1978, il avait été décidé de réviser légèrement le programme de collecte des données, afin qu'il reflète mieux certaines activités des bibliothèques qui ne sont pas couvertes par la Recommandation. En conséquence, les changements suivants ont été apportés au contenu du questionnaire: inclusion des matériels audio-visuels et autres matériels de bibliothèque dans les questions relatives aux collections et aux acquisitions annuelles, combinaison des paragraphes relatifs aux ouvrages prêtés aux usagers et aux bibliothèques du pays et finalement, procéder aux calculs des opérations de prêts entre bibliothèques en fonction du nombre de demandes reçues (et satisfaites) et non d'après le nombre d'ouvrages prêtés. Tous ces changements ont été ajoutés pour information dans les parties correspondantes des extraits de la Recommandation qui figurent ci-dessous et sont indiqués par un astérisque.

Pour le rassemblement des statistiques relatives aux bibliothèques les définitions sont les suivantes:

1. *Bibliothèque*: est considérée comme bibliothèque, quelle que soit sa dénomination, toute collection organisée de livres et de périodiques imprimés ou de tous autres documents, notamment graphiques et audio-visuels, ainsi que les services du personnel chargé de faciliter l'utilisation de ces documents par les usagers à des fins d'information, de recherche, d'éducation ou de récréation. Les bibliothèques sont comptées en nombre d'unités administratives et de points de desserte.

Est considérée comme: (a) *unité administrative*, toute bibliothèque indépendante ou un groupe de bibliothèques ayant un directeur ou une administration uniques; (b) *un point de desserte*, toute bibliothèque desservant les usagers dans un local séparé, qu'elle soit indépendante ou fasse partie d'un groupe de bibliothèques constituant une unité administrative. Sont considérées comme 'points de desserte' les bibliothèques indépendantes, les bibliothèques centrales, les succursales (qu'elles soient fixes ou mobiles, bibliobus, bibliothèques-navires, bibliothèques-trains), à condition que le service direct aux usagers y soit pratiqué. Les haltes de bibliobus ne sont pas des points de desserte.

Les bibliothèques ainsi définies sont classées comme suit:

2. *Bibliothèques nationales*: bibliothèques, quelle que soit leur appellation, qui sont responsables de l'acquisition et de la conservation d'exemplaires de toutes les publications éditées dans le pays et fonctionnant comme bibliothèques de 'dépôt', soit en vertu d'une loi, soit en vertu d'accords particuliers. Les bibliothèques appelées 'nationales' mais ne répondant pas à la définition ci-dessus ne devraient pas être classées dans la catégorie des bibliothèques nationales. 3. *Bibliothèques d'établissements d'enseignement supérieur*: bibliothèques qui sont, en premier lieu, au service des étudiants et du personnel enseignant des universités et autres établissements d'enseignement du troisième degré. Elles peuvent aussi être ouvertes au public. Une distinction devrait être faite entre:
  (a) La bibliothèque universitaire principale, ou centrale, ou encore un groupe de bibliothèques pouvant avoir des localisations distinctes, mais placées sous la responsabilité

d'un directeur unique;

(b) les bibliothèques d'instituts ou de départements universitaires qui ne sont ni dirigées ni administrées par la bibliothèque universitaire principale ou centrale;

(c) les bibliothèques d'établissements d'enseignement supérieur ne faisant pas partie d'une université.

4. *Autres bibliothèques importantes non spécialisées*: bibliothèques non spécialisées, de caractère savant qui ne sont ni des bibliothèques d'établissements d'enseignement supérieur ni des bibliothèques nationales, même si certaines remplissent les fonctions d'une bibliothèque nationale pour une aire géographique déterminée.

5. *Bibliothèques scolaires*: bibliothèques qui dépendent d'établissements d'enseignement de n'importe quel type au-dessous du niveau de l'enseignement du troisième degré et qui doivent avant tout être au service des élèves et des professeurs de ces établissements même si elles sont, par ailleurs, ouvertes au public. Les collections séparées des classes d'une même école devront être considérées comme constituant une seule bibliothèque, qui sera comptée comme une unité administrative et un point de desserte.

6. *Bibliothèques spécialisées*: bibliothèques qui relèvent d'une association, d'un service gouvernemental, d'un parlement, d'une institution de recherche (à l'exclusion des instituts d'université), d'une société savante, d'une association professionnelle, d'un musée, d'une entreprise commerciale ou industrielle, d'une chambre de commerce, etc., ou d'un autre organisme, la plus grande partie de leurs collections concernant une discipline ou un domaine particulier, par exemple: sciences naturelles, sciences sociales, agriculture, chimie, médecine, sciences économiques, sciences de l'ingénieur, droit, histoire. Une distinction devrait être faite entre:

(a) les bibliothèques qui fournissent documentation et services à toute personne faisant appel à elles;

(b) les bibliothèques dont les collections et les services sont essentiellement prévus pour répondre aux besoins d'information de leur clientèle particulière, même si, dans certains cas, elles sont utilisées par des spécialistes n'appartenant pas à l'organisme dont elles relèvent.

7. *Bibliothèques publiques (ou populaires)*: bibliothèques servant gratuitement ou contre une cotisation de principe une collectivité et, notamment, une collectivité locale ou régionale, et s'adressant soit à l'ensemble du public, soit à certaines catégories d'usagers, telles que les enfants, les membres des forces armées, les malades des hôpitaux, les prisonniers, les ouvriers et les employés. Une distinction devrait être faite entre:

(a) les bibliothèques publiques proprement dites, c'est-à-dire les bibliothèques financées en totalité ou en majeure partie par les pouvoirs publics (bibliothèques municipales ou régionales);

(b) Les bibliothèques financées par des fonds privés.

Chaque bibliothèque ne devra figurer que dans une seule des catégories précitées, compte tenu de sa fonction principale.

En ce qui concerne les collections, acquisitions, prêts, dépenses, personnel etc., les définitions et classifications sont les suivantes:

8. *Collection d'une bibliothèque*: l'ensemble des documents mis à la disposition des usagers.

Les statistiques concernant les collections des bibliothèques ne devraient porter que sur les documents suivants mis à la disposition des usagers y compris les documents prêtés au dehors: (a) livres et périodiques (reliés), comptés en mètres de rayonnages occupés, par volumes et par titres*; (b) manuscrits, comptés en mètres de rayonnages occupés et par volumes; (c) microcopies de livres, périodiques, manuscrits et autres matériels de bibliothèque*, comptés par nombre d'unités matérielles; (d) matériels audio-visuels*, comptés par nombre d'unités matérielles; (e) autres matériels de bibliothèque*, comptés par nombre d'unités matérielles.

9. *Acquisitions annuelles*: l'ensemble des documents qui sont venus enrichir les collections au cours de l'année, soit par voie d'achat, de don, d'échange ou de toute autre manière.

Les statistiques sur les acquisitions de collections ne devraient tenir compte que des documents suivants (mis à la disposition des usagers): (a) livres et périodiques (reliés), comptés par titres, par volumes et par mètres de rayonnages* ajoutés; (b) manuscrits, comptés par nombre d'unités acquises et par mètres de rayonnages* ajoutés; (c) microcopies de livres, périodiques*, manuscrits et autres matériels de bibliothèque*, comptés par nombre d'unités matérielles acquises; (d) matériels audio-visuels*, comptés par nombre d'unités matérielles acquises; autres matériels de bibliothèque*, comptés par nombre d'unités matérielles acquises.

10. *Imprimé*: ce terme recouvre tous les divers procédés d'impression quels qu'ils soient, à l'exception de la microcopie imprimée ('microprinting').

11. *Périodiques*: les publications qui paraissent en série continue sous un même titre, à intervalles réguliers ou irréguliers pendant une période indéterminée, les différents numéros de la série étant numérotés consécutivement ou chaque numéro étant daté. Sont compris dans cette définition les journaux ainsi que les publications annuelles ou à périodicité plus espacée.

12. *Titre*: terme utilisé pour désigner un document imprimé constituant un tout distinct, qu'il soit en un ou plusieurs volumes.

13. *Volume*: une unité matérielle de documents imprimés ou manuscrits contenus dans une reliure ou un carton.

14. *Matériels audio-visuels*: matériel de bibliothèque autre que les livres et les microcopies qui ont besoin d'un équipement spécial pour être vus et/ou entendus. Ceci comprend des matériels tels que disques, bandes, cassettes, films, diapositives, transparences, enregistrements video, etc.

15. *Autres matériels de bibliothèque*: tous les matériels de bibliothèque autre que les livres, périodiques, manuscrits, microcopies et matériels audio-visuels. Ceci comprend des matériels tels que cartes, graphiques, reproductions artistiques, photographies, diorama, etc.

16. *Usager de bibliothèque*: toute personne qui utilise les services de la bibliothèque.

17. *Emprunteur inscrit*: toute personne inscrite à une bibliothèque pour y emprunter des documents de la collection et en faire usage au dehors. Ne devraient être comptés que les emprunteurs dont l'inscription est valable pour l'année considérée.

18. *Dépenses ordinaires*: toutes dépenses qui résultent du fonctionnement de la bibliothèque. On distingue seulement à cet égard:

(a) *dépenses pour le personnel*: montant des dépenses pour les salaires, les indemnités et les charges diverses du même type;

(b) *dépenses pour les acquisitions*: montant des dépenses pour tous les documents (imprimés, manuscrits et audio-visuels) acquis par la bibliothèque.

19. *Bibliothécaire professionnel*: toute personne employée dans une bibliothèque ayant reçu une formation générale en bibliothéconomie ou en science de l'information. Cette formation peut consister en un enseignement théorique ou en un stage prolongé sous contrôle dans une bibliothèque.

20. *Population desservie*: (a) *par les bibliothèques publiques*: nombre total d'habitants des localités desservies par les bibliothèques publiques proprement dites (bibliothèques financées en totalité ou en majeure partie par les pouvoirs publics); (b) *par les bibliothèques scolaires*: nombre total d'élèves et de professeurs des écoles du premier et du second degré (écoles primaires et secondaires) desservis par les bibliothèques scolaires; (c) *par les bibliothèques des établissements d'enseignement supérieur*: nombre total d'étudiants et du personnel enseignant des établissements d'enseignement supérieur desservis par cette catégorie de bibliothèques.

Le présent chapitre comporte six tableaux sur les bibliothèques. Le tableau 7.1 donne des chiffres sur le nombre de bibliothèques, classées par catégories, et l'importance des collections qu'elles possèdent. Les cinq tableaux suivants, 7.2 à 7.6, sont consacrés respectivement aux bibliothèques nationales, aux bibliothèques d'établissements d'enseignement supérieur, aux bibliothèques scolaires, aux bibliothèques spécialisées et aux bibliothèques publiques, telles qu'elles sont définies plus haut. Ces tableaux contiennent des renseignements sur les collections, les acquisitions, les emprunteurs, les documents prêtés, les dépenses ordinaires, le personnel et la population desservie (dans les cas appropriés).

Toutefois, quelques questions figurant au questionnaire de l'Unesco ne se trouvent pas dans les tableaux, faute de réponses. Même ainsi réduits par rapport au programme de la Recommandation, les tableaux 7.2 à 7.6 comportent souvent des lacunes, qui, par elles-mêmes, illustrent l'état de ces statistiques dans les pays considérés. En effet, pour bon nombre de pays, elles laissent beaucoup à désirer et il importe de procéder avec prudence si l'on cherche à établir des comparaisons entre pays. Les pays et territoires dont l'ensemble des données étaient antérieures à 1974 ont été supprimés des tableaux de ce chapitre. Les lecteurs qui souhaiteraient prendre connaissance de ces chiffres doivent se référer aux précédentes éditions de l'*Annuaire*.

Tableaux 7.1

Le nombre de bibliothèques qui figurent dans ce tableau ne concerne que les *unités administratives*. Pour le nombre de points de desserte, il faut se reporter aux tableaux 7.2 à 7.6.

Tableaux 7.2 - 7.6
Ces tableaux ne comprennent que les pays dont les statistiques contiennent plus de données que celles qui figurent dans le tableaux 7.1. Sauf indication contraire, le terme 'volumes' désigne seulement les

documents imprimés mis à la disposition des usagers.
Les chiffres relatifs aux dépenses sont présentés en monnaie nationale. Les taux de change des monnaies nationales en dollars des Etats-Unis sont indiqués dans l'annexe C.

Este capítulo presenta las estadísticas nacionales sobre los diferentes tipos de bibliotecas, sus colecciones, adquisiciones, préstamos, gastos , personal, etc. Desde 1950, la Unesco ha compilado tales estadísticas cada dos años. De acuerdo con la Recomendación sobre la normalización internacional de las estadísticas relativas a las bibliotecas, aprobada por la Conferencia General de la Unesco, en 1970, la periodicidad ha sido fijada a tres años. En las tres encuestas que ya han sido efectuadas se han solicitado datos para 1971, 1974 y 1977 respectivamente. En los cuadros de este capítulo sólo se publican datos relativos a los dos últimos años.

En lo que se refiere al cuestionario relativo a 1978 se decidió una pequeña revisión del programa de recolección de datos, para que reflejara mejor ciertas de las actividades de las bibliotecas que no están cubiertas por la Recomendación. Por consiguiente, el contenido del cuestionario ha sufrido los cambios siguientes: inclusión de los materiales audiovisuales y otros materiales de biblioteca en las preguntas sobre las colecciones y las adquisiciones anuales, combinar los párrafos relativos a las obras prestadas a los usuarios y a las bibliotecas del país y finalmente, efectuar los cálculos de las operaciones de préstamo entre las bibliotecas de acuerdo con el número de peticiones recibidas (y atendidas) y no según el número de obras prestadas. Todos estos cambios se han añadido a título informativo en los apartados correspondientes de los extractos de la Recomendación que figuran a continuación y se señalan con un asterisco.

Para la recolección de las estadísticas relativas a las bibliotecas, deben tenerse en cuenta las siguientes definiciones:

1. *Biblioteca*: Se entenderá por biblioteca, sea cual fuere su denominación, toda colección organizada de libros y publicaciones periódicas impresas o de cualesquiera otros documentos, en especial gráficos y audiovisuales, así como los servicios del personal que facilite a los usuarios la utilización de estos documentos, con fines informativos, de investigación, de educación o recreativos. Las bibliotecas deberían contarse según el número de unidades administrativas y de puntos de servicio.

Se entenderá por: a) *unidad administrativa*, toda biblioteca independiente, o todo grupo de bibliotecas que tengan una misma dirección o una administración única; b) *punto de servicio*, toda biblioteca que preste servicio a los usuarios en un local aparte, tanto si es independiente, como si forma parte de un grupo de bibliotecas que constituyan una unidad administrativa.

Se considerarán 'puntos de servicio' las bibliotecas independientes, las bibliotecas centrales, las filiales (tanto fijas como móviles: bibliobuses, bibliotecas de buque, bibliotecas de tren) siempre que sirvan directamente a los usarios. No se considerarán puntos de servicio las paradas de los autobuses.

Las bibliotecas así definidas se clasifican como sigue:

2. *Bibliotecas nacionales*: · bibliotecas que cualquiera que sea su denominación, son responsables de la adquisición y conservación de ejemplares de todas las publicaciones impresas en el país y que funcionan como bibliotecas de 'depósito', en virtud de disposiciones sobre el depósito legal o de otras disposiciones. Las bibliotecas tituladas 'nacionales' que no correspondan a esta definición no deberían clasificarse en la categoría de bibliotecas nacionales.

3. *Bibliotecas de instituciones de enseñanza superior*: bibliotecas dedicadas primordialmente al servicio de los estudiantes y del personal docente de las universidades y demás instituciones de enseñanza superior. Pueden también estar abiertas al público . Conviene distinguir entre:
a) la biblioteca universitaria principal o central, o incluso un grupo de bibliotecas que pueden tener locales distintos pero que no dependen de un director único
b) Las bibliotecas de centros o de departamentos universitarios que no están dirigidas o administradas por la biblioteca universitaria principal o central;
c) las bibliotecas de instituciones de enseñanza superior que no formen parte de la universidad.

4. *Otras bibliotecas importantes no especializadas*: bibliotecas no especializadas, de carácter científico o erudito, que no son ni universitarias ni nacionales, aunque puedan ejercer funciones de biblioteca nacional en un área geográfica determinada.

5. *Bibliotecas escolares*: bibliotecas que dependen de instituciones de enseñanza de cualquier categoría inferior a la enseñanza superior y que,

ante todo, están al servicio de los alumnos y profesores de esos establecimientos, aunque estén abiertas al público. Los fondos particulares de las aulas de una misma escuela deberían considerarse como una sola biblioteca, que se contará como una unidad administritiva y un punto de servicio.

6. *Bibliotecas especializadas*: bibliotecas que dependen de una asociación, servicio oficial, parlamento, centro de investigación (excluidos los centros universitarios), sociedad erudita, asociación profesional, museo, empresa comercial o industrial, cámara de comercio, etc., o de cualquier otro organismo y cuyos fondos pertenezcan en su mayor parte a una disciplina o a una rama particular, por ejemplo: ciencias naturales, ciencias sociales, agricultura, química, medicina, ciencias económicas, derecho, historia. Conviene distinguir entre:
a) las bibliotecas que proporcionan documentación y servicios a todas las personas que lo pidan;
b) las bibliotecas cuyos fondos y servicios están esencialmente destinados a responder a las necesidades de información de su clientela particular, aunque en algunos casos las utilicen especialistas que no pertenecen al organismo del que ellas dependen.

7. *Bibliotecas públicas (o populares)*: bibliotecas que están, gratuitamente o por una módica suma, al servicio de una comunidad, especialmente de una comunidad local o regional, para atender al público en general o a cierta categoría de usuarios como niños, militares, enfermos de los hospitales y empleados. Conviene distinguir entre:
a) las bibliotecas públicas propiamente dichas, es decir, las bibliotecas financiadas totalmente o en su mayor parte por los poderes públicos (bibliotecas municipales o regionales);
b) las bibliotecas financiadas con fondos privados.

Cada biblioteca debe figurar en una sola de las mencionadas categorías, teniendo en cuenta su función principal.

En lo que se refiere a las colecciones, adquisiciones, préstamos, gastos, personal, etc., las definiciones y clasificaciones son las siguientes:

8. *Fondos de una biblioteca*: conjunto de documentos puestos a disposición de los usarios.

Los datos referentes a los fondos de las bibliotecas sólo deberían comprender los documentos siguientes puestos a disposición de los usarios, incluidos los préstamos: a) libros y publicaciones periódicas (encuadernadas) por metros de estantes ocupados, por número de volúmenes y por títulos*; b) manuscritos, por metros de estantes ocupados y número de volúmenes; c) microcopias de libros, publicaciones periódicas, manuscritos y otros materiales de biblioteca*, por número de unidades materiales; d) materiales audio-visuales*, por número de unidades materiales; e) otros materiales de biblioteca*, por número de unidades materiales.

9. *Adquisiciones anuales*: conjunto de documentos que han ido enriqueciendo el fondo durante el año, por compra, donación, intercambio o de cualquier otro modo.

Las estadísticas referentes a las adquisiciones sólo deberían tener en cuenta los documentos siguientes (puestos a disposición de los usarios): a) libros y publicaciones periódicas (encuadernadas), por número de títulos de volúmenes y por metros de estantes añadidos; b) manuscritos, por número de unidades adquiridas y por metros de estantes* añadidos; c) microcopias de libros, publicaciones periódicas*, manuscritos y otro materiales de biblioteca*, por número de unidades materiales adquiridas; d) materiales audio-visuales*, por número de unidades materiale adquiridas; e) otros materiales de biblioteca*, por número de unidade materiales adquiridas.

10. *Impresos*: este término abarca todos los procedimientos de impresió sean cuales fueren, excepto la microcopia (microprinting).

1l. *Publicaciones periódicas*: la publicación editada en serie continua co el mismo título, a intervalos regulares o irregulares, durante un períod indeterminado, estando numerados consecutivamente los números de l serie o fechado cada uno de ellos. Están comprendidos en esta definició los periódicos diarios, así como las publicaciones anuales o las o periodicidad más amplia.

12. *Título*: término utilizado para designar un documento impreso qu constituye un todo único, tanto si consta de uno como de vari volúmenes.

13. *Volumen*: la unidad material de documentos impresos o manuscritos contenidos en una encuadernación o carpeta.

14. *Materiales audio-visuales*: materiales de biblioteca otros que libros y microcopias que precisan de un equipo especial para ser vistas y/o oidas. Comprende materiales tales como discos, cintas, cassettes, películas, diapositivas, proyecciones por transparencia, grabaciones vidéo, etc.

15. *Otros materiales de biblioteca*: materiales de biblioteca otros que libros, publicaciones periódicas, manuscritos, microcopias y material audio-visual. Comprende materiales tales como mapas, gráficos, reproducciones artísticas, fotografías, diorama, etc.

16. *Usario de la biblioteca*: toda persona que utiliza los servicios de la biblioteca.

17. *Prestatario inscrito*: toda persona inscrita en una biblioteca con el fin de tomar en préstamo documentos para utilizarlos fuera de ella. Sólo deben tenerse en cuenta los prestatarios cuya inscripción es válida para el año de que se trata.

18. *Gastos ordinarios*: todos los gastos que ocasione el funcionamiento de la biblioteca. A este respecto, sólo se distingue entre:
    a) *Gastos de personal*: total de gastos por concepto de sueldos, subidios y otras atenciones de la misma índole;
    b) *Gastos de adquisiciones*: total de gastos para todos los documentos (impresos, manuscritos y audiovisuales) adquiridos por la biblioteca.

19. *Bibliotecario profesional*: toda persona empleada en una biblioteca que ha adquirido una formación general en biblioteconomía o en ciencia de la información. Esta formación puede haberla adquirido mediante una enseñanza teórica o trabajando durante un tiempo prolongado, bajo control, en una biblioteca.

20. *Poblacion servida*: a) *Por las bibliotecas públicas*: es decir, el número total de habitantes de las localidades servidas por las bibliotecas públicas propiamente dichas (bibliotecas financiadas totalmente o en su mayor parte por los poderes públicos); b) *por las bibliotecas escolares*: es decir, el número total de alumnos y el personal docente de las escuelas de primero y segundo grado (escuelas primarias y secundarias) provistas de servicios de bibliotecas escolares; c) *por las bibliotecas de instituciones de enseñanza superior*:

es decir, el número total de estudiantes y personal docente de las instituciones de enseñanza superior servidos por esta categoría de bibliotecas.

El presente capítulo comprende seis cuadros sobre las bibliotecas. El cuadro 7.1 indica el número de bibliotecas, clasificadas por categorías, y la importancia de los fondos que poseen. Los cinco cuadros siguientes, 7.2 a 7.6, se dedican respectivamente a las bibliotecas nacionales, las de instituciones de enseñanza superior, las escolares, las especializadas y las públicas, de acuerdo con las definiciones que figuran más arriba. Estos cuadros contienen información sobre las colecciones, las adquisiciones anuales, los prestatarios, los documentos prestados, los gastos ordinarios, el personal y la población servida (en los casos apropiados).

Sin embargo, algunas de las preguntas que figuran en el cuestionario de la Unesco no se ven reflejadas en ellos por no haberse recibido las respuestas esperadas. Aún en esta forma, reducida en relación con el programa de la Recomendación, los cuadros 7.2 a 7.6 tienen a menudo lagunas que por sí solas ponen de manifiesto el estado de dichas estadísticas en los países considerados. En efecto, en el caso de un buen número de ellos dejan mucho que desear, y será preciso proceder con prudencia si se desean establecer camparaciones entre países.

Se han omitido en los cuadros de este capítulo los países y territorios cuyos datos eran anteriores a 1974. Los lectores que deseen consultar dichas cifras pueden recurrir a las precedentes ediciones del *Anuario*.

Cuadro 7.1

El número de bibliotecas que figuran en este cuadro sólo se refiere a las *unidades administrativas*. Para el número de puntos de servicio hay que referirse a los cuadros 7.2 a 7.6.

Cuadros 7.2 - 7.6

En estos cuadros sólo se incluyen los países cuyas informaciones estadísticas contienen más datos que los que figuran en el cuadro 7.1. Salvo indicación contraria, el término 'volúmenes' se refiere solamente a los documentos impresos que están a disposición de los usuarios. Las cifras relativas a los gastos se indican en moneda nacional. Los tipos de conversión de las monedas nacionales en dólares de los Estados Unidos figuran en el Anexo C.

Libraries by category 7.1
Bibliothèques classées par catégories
Bibliotecas clasificadas por categorías

7.1 Libraries and their holdings by category of library

Bibliothèques classées par catégories, avec leurs collections

Bibliotecas, con sus colecciones, clasificadas por categorías

L = NUMBER OF LIBRARIES
V = NUMBER OF VOLUMES (THOUSANDS)
M = LENGTH OF SHELVING (IN METRES) OCCUPIED BY COLLECTIONS

L = NOMBRE DE BIBLIOTHÈQUES
V = NOMBRE DE VOLUMES (EN MILLIERS)
M = NOMBRE DE METRES DE RAYONNAGE OCCUPES PAR LES COLLECTIONS

L = NUMERO DE BIBLIOTECAS
V = NUMERO DE VOLUMENES (EN MILLARES)
M = NUMERO DE METROS DE ESTANTES OCCUPADOS POR LOS FONDOS

NUMBER OF COUNTRIES AND TERRITORIES PRESENTED IN THIS TABLE: 125

NOMBRE DE PAYS ET DE TERRITOIRES PRESENTES DANS CE TABLEAU: 125

NUMERO DE PAISES Y DE TERRITORIOS PRESENTADOS EN ESTE CUADRO: 125

COUNTRY	YEAR	TYPE OF DATA	CATEGORY OF LIBRARIES / CATEGORIES DE BIBLIOTHEQUES CATEGORIA DE BIBLIOTECAS					
			NATIONAL	HIGHER EDUCATION	SCHOOL	SPECIAL	PUBLIC	NON-SPECIALIZED
PAYS	ANNEE	CODE	NATIONALES	ENSEIGNEMENT SUPERIEUR	SCOLAIRES	SPECIALISEES	PUBLIQUES	NON-SPECIALISEES
PAIS	AÑO	TIPO DE DATOS	NACIONALES	ENSEÑANZA SUPERIOR	ESCOLARES	ESPECIALIZADAS	PUBLICAS	NO ESPECIALIZADAS
			(1)	(2)	(3)	(4)	(5)	(6)
AFRICA								
ALGERIA	1977	L	1	3	...	...	...	...
		V	900	734	...	...	...	...
		M		7 305				
BENIN	1977	L	1	...	...	...	...	...
		V	32	...	...	...	...	...

7.1 Libraries by category
Bibliothèques classées par catégories
Bibliotecas clasificadas por categorías

CATEGORY OF LIBRARIES / CATEGORIES DE BIBLIOTHEQUES
CATEGORIA DE BIBLIOTECAS

COUNTRY / PAYS / PAIS	YEAR / ANNEE / AÑO	TYPE OF DATA CODE / TIPO DE DATOS	NATIONAL / NATIONALES / NACIONALES (1)	HIGHER EDUCATION / ENSEIGNEMENT SUPERIEUR / ENSEÑANZA SUPERIOR (2)	SCHOOL / SCOLAIRES / ESCOLARES (3)	SPECIAL / SPECIALISEES / ESPECIALIZADAS (4)	PUBLIC / PUBLIQUES / PUBLICAS (5)	NON-SPECIALIZED / NON-SPECIALISEES / NO ESPECIALIZADAS (6)
BURUNDI	1978	L	...	4	...	...	...	...
		V	...	92				
		M	...	2 660				
COMORO	1975	L	—	1	2	—	2	...
		V	—		5	—	8	
DJIBOUTI	1975	L	—	—	3	—	1	...
		V	—	—	7	—	5	
		M			75			
EGYPT	1974	L	1	2	...	...	161	...
		V	1 118	760			980	
ETHIOPIA	1974	L	...	1	...	...	...	...
		V	...	325				
		M	...	8 668				
GAMBIA ‡	1978	L	...	3	129	17	2	...
		V	...	6		24	66	
		M	...	132	700	1 120	760	
GHANA ‡	1977	L	...	...	...	1	7	...
		V	...	...		38	929	
		M	...	...		330		
KENYA	1974	L	—	3	...	...	3	...
		V	—	230			150	
MADAGASCAR	1974	L	1	2	...	7	20	2
		V	138	172		30	134	80
		M	4 612	...		1 000	283	2 670
MALAWI	1977	L	1	1	74	...	1	...
		V	28	174	254		91	
MOROCCO	1974	L	2	30	5	81	...	...
		V	316	139	34	287		
NIGERIA	1977	L	2	...	...	60	31	4
		V	158			644	891	6
		M	1 368					
ST. HELENA	1974	L	—	1	12	...	1	...
		V	—	5	3		14	
		M		90	120		290	

Libraries by category   7.1
Bibliothèques classées par catégories
Bibliotecas clasificadas por categorías

Country	Year		(1)	(2)	(3)	(4)	(5)	(6)
SENEGAL	1975	L	...	...	...	1	1	...
		V	...	...	...	10	3	...
		M	...	...	...	...	10	...
SEYCHELLES	1974	L	—	—	4	1	1	...
		V	—	—	28	1	16	...
		M	...	...	642	16	408	...
SIERRA LEONE	1974	L	...	...	...	...	...	...
		V	...	...	...	...	...	...
TOGO	1978	L	1	...	...	...	392	...
		V	6	...	...	...	...	...
		M	201	...	...	...	...	...
TUNISIA	1977	L	1 000	...	...	...	694	...
		V	...	7	...	...	...	...
		M	12 000	445	...	...	...	...
UGANDA	1974	L	...	...	...	3	1	...
		V	...	...	...	17	90	...
ZAIRE	1977	L	1	...	...	...	8	...
		V	206	...	...	...	6	...
		M	...	...	...	...	119	...
ZAMBIA ‡	1977	L	...	...	...	8	4	...
		M	...	...	...	380	2 000	...
AMERICA, NORTH								
BAHAMAS ‡	1974	L	—	3	130	—	25	1
		V	—	33	65	—	95	1
		M	...	1 077	2 418	...	1 839	22
BARBADOS	1977	L	...	...	2	1	1	...
		V	...	...	29	100	...	...
		M	...	...	267	93	2 592	...
BELIZE	1974	L	1	—	1	...	1	...
		V	3	—	2	...	101	...
BERMUDA	1974	L	1	—	21	3	1	...
		V	122	—	166	21	...	...
		M	...	...	4 166	818	122	...
BRITISH VIRGIN ISLANDS ‡	1974	L	./.	—	1	5	1	...
		V	./.	—	...	...	21	...
		M	...	...	...	...	231	...
CANADA ‡	1977	L	...	255	8 692	...	754	...
		V	...	43 601	49 412	...	37 534	...
COSTA RICA	1977	L	1	...	...	...	...	...
		V	300	...	...	...	...	...
		M	4 755	...	...	...	...	...
EL SALVADOR	1978	L	1	...	...	...	...	...
		V	200	...	...	...	...	...

7.1 Libraries by category
Bibliothèques classées par catégories
Bibliotecas clasificadas por categorías

COUNTRY / PAYS / PAIS	YEAR / ANNEE / AÑO	TYPE OF DATA / CODE / TIPO DE DATOS	CATEGORY OF LIBRARIES / CATEGORIES DE BIBLIOTHEQUES / CATEGORIA DE BIBLIOTECAS					
			NATIONAL / NATIONALES / NACIONALES (1)	HIGHER EDUCATION / ENSEIGNEMENT SUPERIEUR / ENSEÑANZA SUPERIOR (2)	SCHOOL / SCOLAIRES / ESCOLARES (3)	SPECIAL / SPECIALISEES / ESPECIALIZADAS (4)	PUBLIC / PUBLIQUES / PUBLICAS (5)	NON-SPECIALIZED / NON-SPECIALISEES / NO ESPECIALIZADAS (6)
GREENLAND	1974	L	1	—	1	—	1	...
		V		—	72	—	93	...
GUATEMALA	1974	L	1	3	1	3	3	...
		V	361	24	4	73	54	...
		M	...	520	75	1 848	1 086	...
HONDURAS ‡	1977	L	...	1	...	3	...	...
		V	...	82	...	73	...	...
		M	...	...	...	1 848	...	...
MEXICO	1974	L	3	190	1 004	121	1 084	...
		V	963	1 511	2 132	882	2 777	...
		M	...	8 771	14 378	5 502	7 135	...
NETHERLANDS ANTILLES ‡	1974	L	—	4	...	...	1	...
		V	—	125	...	...	92	...
		M	—	...	...	...	...	...
PANAMA ‡	1977	L	...	2	54	1	1	...
		V	..	14	203	49	9	...
		M	...	2 050	1 610	568	60	...
FORMER CANAL ZONE	1977	L	—	1	..	..	..	...
		V	—	33	..	..	..	...
PUERTO RICO	1977	L	...	30	...	1	...	...
		V	...	1 948	...	4	...	...
		M	...	...	...	36	...	...
ST. LUCIA	1974	L	—	—	1	...	1	...
		V	—	—	14	...	46	...
		M	—	—	...	...	727	...
ST. PIERRE AND MIQUELON	1974	L	—	—	1	—	3	...
		V	—	—	2	—	15	...
		M	—	—	...	—	314	...
TRINIDAD AND TOBAGO ‡	1977	L	...	5	...	1	1	...
		V	...	182	...	5	68	...
		M	...	692	...	36	3 000	...
UNITED STATES OF AMERICA ‡	1977	L	3	3 021	74 625	1 143	8 337	...
		V	20 799	481 442	507 000	19 832	387 565	...

Libraries by category **7.1**
Bibliothèques classées par catégories
Bibliotecas clasificadas por categorías

	Year		(1)	(2)	(3)	(4)	(5)	(6)
U.S. VIRGIN ISLANDS	1977	L	—	1	...	...	—	...
		V	—	60	...	...	—	...
AMERICA, SOUTH								
ARGENTINA ‡	1977	L	1	29	...	...	1 528	...
		V	1 880	136	...	...	9 532	...
		M	24 310	43 805	...	...	317 723	...
BRAZIL	1974	L	1	613	...	572	2 332	...
		V	2 624	9 412	...	7 528	12 665	...
CHILE ‡	1977	L	1	182	296	...	130	...
		V	1 200	2 695	261	...	449	...
		M	17 500	...	...	1 024	...	...
COLOMBIA ‡	1974	L	1	...	...	191	...	...
		V	450	...	...	898	...	...
		M	37 073	...	...	1 586	...	...
PERU ‡	1977	L	1	1	81	...	...	...
		V	1	1	272	...	...	...
		M	15 569	10	...	...	...	...
SURINAME ‡	1978	L	—	2	3	27	2	7
		V	—	29	60	63	268	129
		M	—	1 027	1 425	1 586	3 070	71
URUGUAY	1974	L	1	...	...	...	...	...
		V	*554	...	...	...	...	...
		M	*16 000	...	...	...	...	...
VENEZUELA ‡	1978	L	1	...	46	35	1	...
		V	544	131	105	224	216	...
		M	2 722	...	...	...	1 081	...
ASIA								
BAHRAIN ‡	1974	L	—	...	...	12	1	9
		V	—	...	...	17	100	...
		M	...	...	...	700	2 000	...
BRUNEI ‡	1977	L	1	5	13	5	1	—
		V	53	38	59	6	76	—
		M	95	1 002	1 956	747	949	—
CYPRUS	1977	L	...	1	...	...	...	...
		V	...	21	...	...	...	...
		M	...	1 054	...	...	...	...
EAST TIMOR	1974	L	...	—	1	...	...	...
		V	...	—	2	...	...	...
HONG KONG ‡	1974	L	1	...	223	16	8	...
		V	650	10	948	237	230	...
		M	11 100	1 103	...	8 455	1 875	...
INDIA ‡	1977	L	1 608	93	...	...	...	...
		M	48 000	12 536	...	...	...	...

7.1 Libraries by category
Bibliothèques classées par catégories
Bibliotecas clasificadas por categorías

CATEGORY OF LIBRARIES / CATEGORIES DE BIBLIOTHEQUES / CATEGORIA DE BIBLIOTECAS

COUNTRY / PAYS / PAIS	YEAR / ANNEE / AÑO	TYPE OF DATA / CODE / TIPO DE DATOS	NATIONAL / NATIONALES / NACIONALES (1)	HIGHER EDUCATION / ENSEIGNEMENT SUPERIEUR / ENSEÑANZA SUPERIOR (2)	SCHOOL / SCOLAIRES / ESCOLARES (3)	SPECIAL / SPECIALISEES / ESPECIALIZADAS (4)	PUBLIC / PUBLIQUES / PUBLICAS (5)	NON-SPECIALIZED / NON-SPECIALISEES / NO ESPECIALIZADAS (6)
INDONESIA	1977	L	...	...	...	152	...	...
		V	...	...	...	1 327	...	...
IRAQ	1974	L	1	...	...	...	24	...
		V	68	...	...	...	195	...
		M	2 300	...	...	...	5 460	...
JAPAN ‡	1977	L	1	1 112	41 163	2 019	891	...
		V	3 248	106 414	200 792	31 164	58 786	...
JORDAN ‡	1974	L	...	15	954	18	11	...
		V	...	251	...	91	81	...
KOREA, REPUBLIC OF ‡	1977	L	2	159	3 954	153	110	...
		V	636	7 596	11 327	1 867	949	...
KUWAIT ‡	1977	L	...	6	1	...	1	...
		V	...	64	291	...	258	...
		M	...	...	24 826	...	5 238	...
MALAYSIA ‡	1977	L	1	30	...	119	16	...
		V	94	1 170	...	836	880	...
		M	1 875	23 400	...	16 729	17 240	...
PAKISTAN	1977	L	1	...	...	...	...	...
		V	80	...	...	...	...	...
		M	571	...	...	...	...	...
PHILIPPINES	1977	L	1	...	...	...	1 012	...
		V	182	...	...	...	...	...
		M	6 710	7 000	115 600	...	...	...
QATAR	1974	L	...	3	69	...	1	...
		V	...	9	154	...	53	...
		M	...	...	600	...	...	...
SAUDI ARABIA	1974	L	1	...	2 188	—	8	...
		V	23	...	5 436	—	...	...
		M	250	...	58 100	—	28 000	...
SINGAPORE ‡	1974	L	1	5	363	45	...	...
		V	800	975	2 244	440	...	...
		M	26 673	23 136	74 754	21 954	...	...

Libraries by category   **7.1**
Bibliothèques classées par catégories
Bibliotecas clasificadas por categorías

Country	Year		(1)	(2)	(3)	(4)	(5)	(6)
SRI LANKA ‡	1977	L	1	5	793	73	381	...
		V	13	540	1 972	528	727	...
		M	...	13 646	...	...	...	...
SYRIAN ARAB REPUBLIC	1974	L	...	14	...	3	...	...
		V	1 110	226	...	11	...	...
		M	2 600	29 184	...	97	...	...
THAILAND	1974	L	1	85	240	...	526	...
		V	882	1 297	153	...	586	...
		M	2 310	88 510	22 873	...	2 790	...
TURKEY	1978	L	1	...	...	...	...	...
		V	737	...	...	...	...	...
		M	...	...	...	...	...	...
UNITED ARAB EMIRATES	1977	L	...	4	...	...	...	...
		V	70	17	...	...	...	...
		M	...	4 343	...	...	...	...
VIET-NAM	1977	L	1	58	...	44	316	...
		V	818	2 922	...	1 070	4 879	...
		M	20 165	...	...	...	...	...
EUROPE								
AUSTRIA ‡	1977	L	1	742	5 600	512	426	5
		V	2 252	10 808	9 500	7 675	4 364	1 420
		M	53 928	...	...	...	142 454	47 300
BELGIUM	1977	L	*3 000	...	...	...	...	...
		V	*90 000	...	...	...	...	...
		M	...	...	...	...	...	...
BULGARIA	1977	L	1	25	3 700	10 290	5 902	27
		V	1 352	3 062	13 224	59 501	44 117	7 204
		M	...	...	...	...	...	...
CZECHOSLOVAKIA	1977	L	...	1 701	...	14	12 803	...
		V	...	11 887	...	14 996	45 425	...
		M	...	...	...	...	...	...
DENMARK ‡	1977	L	...	17	...	13	251	...
		V	2 300	6 104	...	1 324	32 713	...
		M	75 000	131 000	...	60 000	...	...
FAEROE ISLANDS	1974	L	1	...	...	—	14	...
		V	73	...	...	—	63	...
		M	2 085	...	...	...	1 796	...
FINLAND	1977	L	1	24	5 420	16	478	...
		V	1 875	5 661	7 500	1 865	19 221	...
		M	57 100	154 620	...	50 100	...	...

7.1 Libraries by category
Bibliothèques classées par catégories
Bibliotecas clasificadas por categorías

CATEGORY OF LIBRARIES / CATEGORIES DE BIBLIOTHEQUES / CATEGORIA DE BIBLIOTECAS

COUNTRY / PAYS / PAIS	YEAR ANNEE AÑO	TYPE OF DATA CODE TIPO DE DATOS	(1) NATIONAL NATIONALES NACIONALES	(2) HIGHER EDUCATION ENSEIGNEMENT SUPERIEUR ENSEÑANZA SUPERIOR	(3) SCHOOL SCOLAIRES ESCOLARES	(4) SPECIAL SPECIALISEES ESPECIALIZADAS	(5) PUBLIC PUBLIQUES PUBLICAS	(6) NON-SPECIALIZED NON-SPECIALISEES NO ESPECIALIZADAS
FRANCE ‡	1977	L	...	47	...	...	1 026	...
		V	...	14 400	...	...	48 661	...
		M	...	653 500	...	...	1 251 571	
GERMAN DEMOCRATIC REPUBLIC ‡	1977	L	2	532	...	...	9 418	2
		V	9 421	20 620	...	...	39 600	1 579
GERMANY, FEDERAL REPUBLIC OF	1977	L	3	...	...	...	...	27
		V	8 936	93 092	...	51 465	76 756	10 500
GIBRALTAR ‡	1978	L	—	1	10	—	3	...
		V	—	5	28	—	81	...
		M	—	66	913	—	2 203	...
HOLY SEE ‡	1977	L	—	12	—	1	—	1
		V	—	1 503	—	240	—	724
		M	—	126 887	—	6 000	—	21 202
HUNGARY ‡	1977	L	1	435	4 680	1 395	2 936	1
		V	2 073	9 463	14 912	12 359	33 649	1 019
ICELAND ‡	1974	L	1	2	...	4	251	...
		V	319	*91	...	*17	1 033	...
		M	7 093	*4 937	...	*900	...	...
IRELAND ‡	1974	L	1	6	...	7	31	...
		V	500	1 648	...	331	6 924	...
		M	15 500	*51 980	...	...	...	...
ITALY ‡	1977	L	8	...	...	...	...	...
		V	11 782	...	...	...	...	...
		M	272 547	...	...	...	...	...
LIECHTENSTEIN	1974	L	1	—	...	—	...	...
		M	45 000	—	...	—	...	...
LUXEMBOURG	1977	L	1	...	...	...	...	...
		V	580	...	...	...	...	...
		M	17 820	...	...	...	...	...
MALTA	1977	L	1	2	40	...	...	...
		V	347	197	45	...	...	...
		M	6 600	...	1 500	...	...	...

Libraries by category **7.1**
Bibliothèques classées par catégories
Bibliotecas clasificadas por categorías

Country	Year		(1)	(2)	(3)	(4)	(5)	(6)
MONACO	1977	L	—	—	1	...	...	...
		V	—	—	3	...	...	...
		M	...	...	55	...	...	...
NETHERLANDS ‡	1976	L	1	346	...	466	428	6
		V	1 065	10 039	...	9 660	22 253	1 136
		M	28 503	288 275	...	279 385	...	41 694
NORWAY ‡	1977	L	1	54	3 681	168	455	...
		V	3 775	7 475	5 105	2 752	12 001	...
		M	116 073	...	...	100 714	...	...
POLAND	1977	L	1	89	...	5 462	9 128	129
		V	1 714	30 484	...	19 118	81 870	11 678
PORTUGAL	1977	L	3	173	655	179	117	7
		V	3 138	1 998	1 554	2 256	5 893	40
ROMANIA ‡	1977	L	2	43	10 782	4 331	6 420	...
		V	12 521	17 301	41 382	18 532	55 559	...
SAN MARINO ‡	1974	L	1	—	3	—	1	...
		V	44	—	17	—	36	...
		M	800	...	75	...	...	...
SPAIN	1977	L	2	323	640	452	1 459	...
		V	4 855	6 687	2 190	8 092	11 135	...
		M	253 503	250 031	56 348	244 687	265 657	...
SWEDEN	1977	L	1	9	413	15	334	...
		V	56 498	235 379	27 919	101 695	34 615	...
		M	...	...	798 000	...	989 270	...
SWITZERLAND	1977	L	1	...	...	...	...	...
		V	1 182	...	...	...	...	...
		M	26 800	...	...	...	...	...
YUGOSLAVIA ‡	1977	L	8	425	8 411	1 072	1 922	11
		V	7 898	9 646	27 379	10 881	20 139	2 783
		M	132 386	177 972	...	200 488	331 447	48 801
OCEANIA								
AMERICAN SAMOA	1977	L	...	1	...	...	...	...
		V	...	12	...	...	...	...
AUSTRALIA	1977	L	1	92	...	...	...	...
		V	1 823	16 311	...	...	...	...
COOK ISLANDS	1974	L	...	2	—	—	1	...
		V	...	15	—	—	15	...
		M	...	414	...	...	570	...
FIJI ‡	1977	L	...	1	300	11	9	...
		V	...	*5 213	235	82	91	...
		M	...	...	5 800	6 625	...	...
FRENCH POLYNESIA ‡	1974	L	—	—	9	—	1	1
		V	—	—	16	—	18	14
		M	—	—	646	—	760	500

7.1 Libraries by category
Bibliothèques classées par catégories
Bibliotecas clasificadas por categorías

COUNTRY / PAYS / PAIS	YEAR / ANNEE / AÑO	TYPE OF DATA / CODE / TIPO DE DATOS	NATIONAL / NATIONALES / NACIONALES (1)	HIGHER EDUCATION / ENSEIGNEMENT SUPERIEUR / ENSEÑANZA SUPERIOR (2)	SCHOOL / SCOLAIRES / ESCOLARES (3)	SPECIAL / SPECIALISEES / ESPECIALIZADAS (4)	PUBLIC / PUBLIQUES / PUBLICAS (5)	NON-SPECIALIZED / NON-SPECIALISEES / NO ESPECIALIZADAS (6)
KIRIBATI	1974	L	—	3	5	4	1	...
		V	—	*10	*7	*1	*20	...
		M	—	230	...	38	...	...
NEW CALEDONIA	1974	L	—	—	...	...	1	...
		V	—	—	...	...	34	...
		M	—	—	...	...	1 034	...
NEW HEBRIDES ‡	1974	L	—	—	131	—	1	—
		V	—	—	26	—	12	—
		M	—	—	360	—	300	—
NEW ZEALAND	1974	L	1	34	1 067	98	191	
		V	4 245	2 743	4 829	1 165	4 902	
		M	103 678	124 039	177 744	26 986	231 218	
NIUE	1974	L	—	1	2	—	1	...
		V	—	1	20	—	6	...
		M	—	14	162	—	114	...
NORFOLK ISLAND ‡	1977	L	...	...	1	1	1	...
		V	...	...	6	...	4	...
		M	...	...	448	...	100	...
PACIFIC ISLANDS	1977	L	...	3	40	21		...
		V	...	15	92	...	16	...
SAMOA ‡	1978	L	—	1	...	...	1	...
		V	—	10	...	...	36	...
		M	—	300	...	...	...	...
SOLOMON ISLANDS	1974	L	1	2	6	6	2	...
		V	13	6	14	6	2	...
		M	336	158	345	179	334	...
TOKELAU ISLANDS	1974	L	—	—	3	—	—	...
TONGA	1978	L	—	2	10	2	...	—
		V	—	6	28	4	...	—
		M	—	...	81	18	...	—

Libraries by category 7.1
Bibliothèques classées par catégories
Bibliotecas clasificadas por categorías

U.S.S.R.			(1)	(2)	(3)	(4)	(5)	(6)
U.S.S.R.	1976	L	...	...	154 000	65 000	131 000	...
		V	...	...	602 000	1 959	1 608 000	...
BYELORUSSIAN S.S.R.	1977	L	...	...	...	...	7 028	...
		V	...	...	...	...	80 639	...
UKRAINIAN S.S.R. ‡	1974	L	2	67 141	25 700	3 531	26 593	5
		V	9 503	67 430	125 300	88 961	341 418	8 914

GAMBIA:
E—> DATA ON LIBRARIES OF INSTITUTIONS OF HIGHER EDUCATION REFER TO 1974.
FR—> LES DONNEES RELATIVES AUX BIBLIOTHEQUES D'ETABLISSEMENTS D'ENSEIGNEMENT SUPERIEUR SE REFERENT A 1974.
ESP> LOS DATOS RELATIVOS A LAS BIBLIOTECAS DE LOS ESTABLECIMIENTOS DE ENSEÑANZA SUPERIOR SE REFIEREN A 1974.

GHANA:
E—> DATA ON SPECIAL LIBRARIES REFER TO 1974.
FR—> LES DONNEES RELATIVES AUX BIBLIOTHEQUES SPECIALISEES SE REFERENT A 1974.
ESP> LOS DATOS RELATIVOS A LAS BIBLIOTECAS ESPECIALIZADAS SE REFIEREN A 1974.

ZAMBIA:
E—> DATA ON SPECIAL LIBRARIES REFER TO 1974.
FR—> LES DONNEES RELATIVES AUX BIBLIOTHEQUES SPECIALISEES SE REFERENT A 1974.
ESP> LOS DATOS RELATIVOS A LAS BIBLIOTECAS ESPECIALIZADAS SE REFIEREN A 1974.

BAHAMAS:
E—> DATA ON OTHER MAJOR NON-SPECIALIZED LIBRARIES REFER TO 1975.
FR—> LES DONNEES RELATIVES AUX AUTRES BIBLIOTHEQUES IMPORTANTES NON-SPECIALISEES SE REFERENT A 1975.
ESP> LOS DATOS RELATIVOS A LAS OTRAS BIBLIOTECAS IMPORTANTES ESPECIALIZADAS SE REFIEREN A 1975.

BRITISH VIRGIN ISLANDS:
E—> THE PUBLIC LIBRARY IS ALSO THE NATIONAL LIBRARY.
FR—> LA BIBLIOTHEQUE PUBLIQUE SERT AUSSI DE BIBLIOTHEQUE NATIONALE.
ESP> LA BIBLIOTECA PUBLICA DESEMPEÑA AL MISMO TIEMPO LA FUNCION DE BIBLIOTECA NACIONAL.

CANADA:
E—> THE NUMBER OF VOLUMES IN LIBRARIES OF INSTITUTIONS OF HIGHER EDUCATION INCLUDE PERIODICALS, NEWSPAPERS, GOVERNMENT DOCUMENTS AND TECHNICAL REPORTS. DATA ON PUBLIC LIBRARIES REFER TO 1976.

CANADA (CONT):
FR—> LE CHIFFRE QUI CONCERNE LE NOMBRE DE VOLUMES DES BIBLIOTHEQUES D'ETABLISSEMENTS D'ENSEIGNEMENT SUPERIEUR INCLUT LES PERIODIQUES, LES JOURNAUX, LES DOCUMENTS PUBLICS ET LES RAPPORTS TECHNIQUES. LES DONNEES RELATIVES AUX BIBLIOTHEQUES PUBLIQUES SE REFERENT A 1976.
ESP> LA CIFRA SOBRE EL NUMERO DE VOLUMENES DE LAS BIBLIOTECAS DE LOS ESTABLECIMIENTOS DE ENSEÑANZA SUPERIOR INCLUYE LOS PERIODICOS, LOS DIARIOS, LOS DOCUMENTOS PUBLICOS Y LOS INFORMES TECNICOS. LOS DATOS RELATIVOS A LAS BIBLIOTECAS PUBLICAS SE REFIEREN A 1976.

HONDURAS:
E—> DATA ON SPECIAL LIBRARIES REFER TO 1974.
FR—> LES DONNEES RELATIVES AUX BIBLIOTHEQUES SPECIALISEES SE REFERENT A 1974.
ESP> LOS DATOS RELATIVOS A LAS BIBLIOTECAS ESPECIALIZADAS SE REFIEREN A 1974.

NETHERLANDS ANTILLES:
E—> DATA ON PUBLIC LIBRARY REFER TO THE LIBRARY OF CURACAO ONLY.
FR—> LES DONNEES RELATIVES AUX BIBLIOTHEQUES PUBLIQUES CONCERNENT LA BIBLIOTHEQUE DE CURACAO SEULEMENT.
ESP> LOS DATOS RELATIVOS A LAS BIBLIOTECAS PUBLICAS SE REFIEREN A LA BIBLIOTECA DE CURACAO SOLAMENTE.

PANAMA:
E—> THE FIGURE CONCERNING THE NUMBER OF VOLUMES IN LIBRARIES OF INSTITUTIONS OF HIGHER EDUCATION REFER ONLY TO 1 LIBRARY.
FR—> LE CHIFFRE RELATIF AU NOMBRE DE VOLUMES DES BIBLIOTHEQUES D'ETABLISSEMENTS D'ENSEIGNEMENT SUPERIEUR NE CONCERNE QU'UNE BIBLIOTHEQUE.
ESP> LA CIFRA RELATIVA AL NUMERO DE VOLUMENES DE LAS BIBLIOTECAS DE LOS ESTABLECIMIENTOS DE ENSEÑANZA SUPERIOR, SE REFIERE A UNA SOLA BIBLIOTECA.

TRINIDAD AND TOBAGO:
E—> DATA ON SPECIAL LIBRARIES REFER TO 1974.
FR—> LES DONNEES RELATIVES AUX BIBLIOTHEQUES SPECIALISEES SE REFERENT A 1974.
ESP> LOS DATOS RELATIVOS A LAS BIBLIOTECAS ESPECIALIZADAS SE REFIEREN A 1974.

7.1 Libraries by category
Bibliothèques classées par catégories
Bibliotecas clasificadas por categorias

SURINAME (CONT):
ESP> LOS DATOS RELATIVOS A LAS "OTRAS
BIBLIOTECAS IMPORTANTES NO ESPECIALIZADAS" SE
REFIEREN A 1977.

VENEZUELA:
E—> DATA ON LIBRARIES OF INSTITUTIONS OF HIGHER
EDUCATION AND ON SPECIAL LIBRARIES REFER TO 1977.
FR—> LES DONNEES RELATIVES AUX BIBLIOTHEQUES
D'ETABLISSEMENTS D'ENSEIGNEMENT SUPERIEUR ET AUX
BIBLIOTHEQUES SPECIALISEES SE REFERENT A 1977.
ESP> LOS DATOS RELATIVOS A LAS BIBLIOTECAS
DE LOS ESTABLECIMIENTOS DE ENSEÑANZA SUPERIOR
Y A LAS BIBLIOTECAS ESPECIALIZADAS SE REFIEREN
A 1977.

BAHRAIN:
E—> THE FIGURES ON PUBLIC LIBRARIES DO NOT
INCLUDE LIBRARIES FINANCED FROM PRIVATE SOURCES.
FR—> LES CHIFFRES RELATIFS AUX BIBLIOTHEQUES
PUBLIQUES N'INCLUENT PAS LES BIBLIOTHEQUES
FINANCEES PAR DES FONDS PRIVES.
ESP> LAS CIFRAS RELATIVAS A LAS BIBLIOTECAS
PUBLICAS NO INCLUYEN LAS BIBLIOTECAS FINANCIADAS
CON FONDOS PRIVADOS.

BRUNEI:
E—> DATA ON THE NATIONAL LIBRARY REFER TO 1974.
FR—> LES DONNEES RELATIVES A LA BIBLIOTHEQUE
NATIONALE SE REFERENT A 1974.
ESP> LOS DATOS RELATIVOS A LA BIBLIOTECA
NACIONAL SE REFIEREN A 1974.

HONG KONG:
E—> THE NATIONAL LIBRARY SERVES ALSO AS A
PUBLIC LIBRARY.
FR> LA BIBLIOTHEQUE NATIONALE SERT AUSSI DE
BIBLIOTHEQUE PUBLIQUE.
ESP> LA BIBLIOTECA NACIONAL DESEMPEÑA AL MISMO
TIEMPO LA FUNCION DE BIBLIOTECA PUBLICA.

INDIA:
E—> DATA ON THE NATIONAL LIBRARY REFER TO 1978.
FR—> LES DONNEES RELATIVES A LA BIBLIOTHEQUE
NATIONALE SE REFERENT A 1978.
ESP> LOS DATOS RELATIVOS A LA BIBLIOTECA
NACIONAL SE REFIEREN A 1978.

JAPAN:
E—> DATA ON NATIONAL AND ON SPECIAL LIBRARIES
REFER TO 1978. THE FIGURE CONCERNING THE NUMBER
OF VOLUMES IN THE NATIONAL LIBRARY REPRESENT
ONLY BOOKS.
FR—> LES DONNEES RELATIVES AUX BIBLIOTHEQUES
NATIONALES ET SPECIALISEES SE REFERENT A 1978.
LE CHIFFRE QUI CONCERNE LE NOMBRE DE VOLUMES DE
LA BIBLIOTHEQUE NATIONALE INDIQUE LE NOMBRE DE
LIVRES SEULEMENT.
ESP> LOS DATOS RELATIVOS A LAS BIBLIOTECAS
NACIONALES Y ESPECIALIZADAS SE REFIEREN A 1978.
LA CIFRA SOBRE EL NUMERO DE VOLUMENES DE LA
BIBLIOTECA NACIONAL INDICA EL NUMERO DE LIBROS
SOLAMENTE.

UNITED STATES OF AMERICA:
E—> DATA ON NATIONAL LIBRARIES REFER TO 1978
AND THOSE ON SCHOOL AND PUBLIC LIBRARIES TO 1974.
ONLY FOR 1147 OUT OF 1366 SPECIAL LIBRARIES DATA
ARE AVAILABLE.
FR—> LES DONNEES RELATIVES AUX BIBLIOTHEQUES
NATIONALES SE REFERENT A 1978. CELLES DES
BIBLIOTHEQUES SCOLAIRES ET PUBLIQUES SE RAPPORTENT
A 1974. LES DONNEES RELATIVES AUX BIBLIOTHEQUES
SPECIALISEES NE TIENNENT COMPTE QUE DE 1147
BIBLIOTHEQUES SUR UN TOTAL DE 1366.
ESP> LOS DATOS RELATIVOS A LAS BIBLIOTECAS
NACIONALES SE REFIEREN A 1978; LOS DE LAS
BIBLIOTECAS ESCOLARES Y PUBLICAS A 1974. LOS
DATOS SOBRE LAS BIBLIOTECAS ESPECIALIZADAS SOLO
TOMAN EN CONSIDERACION 1147 BIBLIOTECAS, DE UN
TOTAL DE 1366.

ARGENTINA:
E—> DATA ON LIBRARIES OF INSTITUTIONS OF HIGHER
EDUCATION REFER TO 1974.
FR—> LES DONNEES RELATIVES AUX BIBLIOTHEQUES
D'ETABLISSEMENTS D'ENSEIGNEMENT SUPERIEUR SE
REFERENT A 1974.
ESP> LOS DATOS RELATIVOS A LAS BIBLIOTECAS DE
LOS ESTABLECIMIENTOS DE ENSEÑANZA SUPERIOR SE
REFIEREN A 1974.

CHILE:
E—> THE FIGURES ON SCHOOL LIBRARIES REFER TO
1976 AND THOSE ON PUBLIC LIBRARIES TO 1978.
FR—> LES CHIFFRES RELATIFS AUX BIBLIOTHEQUES
SCOLAIRES ET AUX BIBLIOTHEQUES PUBLIQUES SE
REFERENT RESPECTIVEMENT A 1976 ET A 1978.
ESP> LAS CIFRAS RELATIVAS A LAS BIBLIOTECAS
ESCOLARES Y A LAS BIBLIOTECAS PUBLICAS SE
REFIEREN RESPECTIVAMENTE A 1976 Y 1978.

COLOMBIA:
E—> THE FIGURES ON SPECIAL LIBRARIES REFER TO
1975.
FR—> LES CHIFFRES RELATIFS AUX BIBLIOTHEQUES
SPECIALISEES SE REFERENT A 1975.
ESP> LAS CIFRAS RELATIVAS A LAS BIBLIOTECAS
ESPECIALIZADAS SE REFIEREN A 1975.

PERU:
E—> DATA ON LIBRARIES OF INSTITUTIONS OF HIGHER
EDUCATION REFER TO 1974.
FR—> LES DONNEES RELATIVES AUX BIBLIOTHEQUES
D'ETABLISSEMENTS D'ENSEIGNEMENT SUPERIEUR SE
REFERENT A 1974.
ESP> LOS DATOS RELATIVOS A LAS BIBLIOTECAS DE
LOS ESTABLECIMIENTOS DE ENSEÑANZA SUPERIOR SE
REFIEREN A 1974.

SURINAME:
E—> DATA ON OTHER MAJOR NON-SPECIALIZED
LIBRARIES REFER TO 1977.
FR—> LES DONNEES RELATIVES AUX AUTRES
BIBLIOTHEQUES IMPORTANTES NON SPECIALISEES SE
REFERENT A 1977.

Libraries by category 7.1
Bibliothèques classées par catégories
Bibliotecas clasificadas por categorías

DENMARK:
E—> THE DATA ON LIBRARIES OF INSTITUTIONS OF HIGHER EDUCATION DO NOT INCLUDE 400 LIBRARIES ATTACHED TO INSTITUTES OR DEPARTMENTS AND 19 LIBRARIES FOR WHICH DATA ARE NOT AVAILABLE. IN ADDITION TO THE FIGURES SHOWN FOR SPECIAL LIBRARIES, THERE ARE 72 LIBRARIES FOR WHICH STATISTICS HAVE NOT BEEN COMMUNICATED. THE FIGURES ON PUBLIC LIBRARIES REFER TO 1974.
FR—> LES DONNEES RELATIVES AUX BIBLIOTHEQUES D'ETABLISSEMENTS D'ENSEIGNEMENT SUPERIEUR NE TIENNENT PAS COMPTE DE 400 BIBLIOTHEQUES RATTACHEES AUX INSTITUTS OU AUX DEPARTEMENTS UNIVERSITAIRES POUR LESQUELLES LES DONNEES NE SONT PAS DISPONIBLES. IL Y A, EN PLUS DES CHIFFRES INDIQUES, 72 BIBLIOTHEQUES SPECIALISEES, POUR LESQUELLES LES STATISTIQUES N'ONT PAS ETE COMMUNIQUEES. LES DONNEES CONCERNANT LES BIBLIOTHEQUES PUBLIQUES SE REFERENT A 1974.
ESP> LOS DATOS RELATIVOS A LAS BIBLIOTECAS DE LOS ESTABLECIMIENTOS DE ENSEÑANZA SUPERIOR NO TOMAN EN CONSIDERACION 400 BIBLIOTECAS DEPENDIENTES DE LOS INSTITUTOS O DEPARTAMENTOS UNIVERSITARIOS, PARA LAS QUE NO SE DISPONE DE DATOS. ADEMAS DE LAS CIFRAS INDICADAS, EXISTEN 72 BIBLIOTECAS ESPECIALIZADAS, CUYOS DATOS NO NOS HAN SIDO COMUNICADOS. LOS DATOS RELATIVOS A LAS BIBLIOTECAS PUBLICAS SE REFIEREN A 1974.

FRANCE:
E—> DATA ON LIBRARIES OF INSTITUTIONS OF HIGHER EDUCATION REFER TO 1976 AND DO NOT INCLUDE LIBRARIES ATTACHED TO INSTITUTES OR DEPARTMENTS.
FR—> LES DONNEES RELATIVES AUX BIBLIOTEQUES D' ETABLISSEMENTS D'ENSEIGNEMENT SUPERIEUR SE REFERENT A 1976 ET NE TIENNENT PAS COMPTE DES BIBLIOTHEQUES RATTACHEES AUX INSTITUTS OU DEPARTEMENTS UNIVERSITAIRES.
ESP> LOS DATOS RELATIVOS A LAS BIBLIOTECAS DE LOS ESTABLECIMIENTOS DE ENSEÑANZA SUPERIOR SE REFIEREN A 1976 Y NO TOMAN EN CONSIDERACION LAS BIBLIOTECAS DEPENDIENTES DE LOS INSTITUTOS O DEPARTAMENTOS UNIVERSITARIOS.

GERMAN DEMOCRATIC REPUBLIC:
E—> THE FIGURE CONCERNING THE NUMBER OF VOLUMES IN PUBLIC LIBRARIES INCLUDES MANUSCRIPTS AND MICROFORMS.
FR—> LE CHIFFRE QUI CONCERNE LE NOMBRE DE VOLUMES DES BIBLIOTHEQUES PUBLIQUES INCLUT LES MANUSCRITS ET LES MICROCOPIES.
ESP> LA CIFRA RELATIVA AL NUMERO DE VOLUMENES DE LAS BIBLIOTECAS PUBLICAS INCLUYE LOS MANUSCRITOS Y LAS MICROCOPIAS.

JORDAN:
E—> DATA REFER TO THE EAST BANK ONLY.
FR—> LES DONNEES SE REFERENT A LA RIVE ORIENTALE SEULEMENT.
ESP> LOS DATOS SE REFIEREN A LA ORILLA ORIENTAL SOLAMENTE.

KOREA, REPUBLIC OF:
E—> THE FIGURES ON SPECIAL LIBRARIES REFER TO 1974.
FR—> LES CHIFFRES RELATIFS AUX BIBLIOTHEQUES SPECIALISEES SE REFERENT A 1974.
ESP> LAS CIFRAS RELATIVAS A LAS BIBLIOTECAS ESPECIALIZADAS SE REFIEREN A 1974.

KUWAIT:
E—> DATA ON SCHOOL LIBRARIES REFER TO 1974.
FR—> LES DONNEES RELATIVES AUX BIBLIOTHEQUES SCOLAIRES SE REFERENT A 1974.
ESP> LOS DATOS RELATIVOS A LAS BIBLIOTECAS ESCOLARES SE REFIEREN A 1974.

MALAYSIA:
E—> DATA ON LIBRARIES OF INSTITUTIONS OF HIGHER EDUCATION REFER TO UNIVERSITY LIBRARIES ONLY.
FR—> LES DONNEES RELATIVES AUX BIBLIOTHEQUES D'ETABLISSEMENTS D'ENSEIGNEMENT SUPERIEUR NE CONCERNENT QUE LES BIBLIOTHEQUES UNIVERSITAIRES.
ESP> LOS DATOS RELATIVOS A LAS BIBLIOTECAS DE LOS ESTABLECIMIENTOS DE ENSEÑANZA SUPERIOR SE REFIEREN A LAS BIBLIOTECAS UNIVERSITARIAS SOLAMENTE.

SINGAPORE:
E—> THE NATIONAL LIBRARY SERVES ALSO AS A PUBLIC LIBRARY.
FR—> LA BIBLIOTHEQUE NATIONALE SERT AUSSI DE BIBLIOTHEQUE PUBLIQUE.
ESP> LA BIBLIOTECA NACIONAL DESEMPENA AL MISMO TIEMPO LA FUNCION DE BIBLIOTECA PUBLICA.

SRI LANKA:
E—> DATA ON LIBRARIES OF INSTITUTIONS OF HIGHER EDUCATION REFER TO UNIVERSITY LIBRARIES ONLY.
FR—> LES DONNEES RELATIVES AUX BIBLIOTHEQUES D'ETABLISSEMENTS D'ENSEIGNEMENT SUPERIEUR NE CONCERNENT QUE LES BIBLIOTHEQUES UNIVERSITAIRES.
ESP> LOS DATOS RELATIVOS A LAS BIBLIOTECAS DE LOS ESTABLECIMIENTOS DE ENSEÑANZA SUPERIOR SE REFIEREN A LAS BIBLIOTECAS UNIVERSITARIAS SOLAMENTE.

AUSTRIA:
E—> THE FIGURES ON PUBLIC LIBRARIES REFER TO 1974.
FR—> LES CHIFFRES RELATIFS AUX BIBLIOTHEQUES PUBLIQUES SE REFERENT A 1974.
ESP> LAS CIFRAS RELATIVAS A LAS BIBLIOTECAS PUBLICAS SE REFIEREN A 1974.

7.1 Libraries by category
Bibliothèques classées par catégories
Bibliotecas clasificadas por categorías

ITALY:
E—> THE FIGURE ON THE LENGTH OF SHELVING OCCUPIED BY BOOKS AND (BOUND) PERIODICALS INCLUDE MANUSCRIPTS.
FR—> LE CHIFFRE RELATIF AU NOMBRE DE METRES DE RAYONNAGE OCCUPES PAR LES LIVRES ET LES PERIODIQUES (RELIES) COMPREND AUSSI LES MANUSCRITS.
ESP> LA CIFRA RELATIVA AL NUMERO DE METROS DE ESTANTES OCUPADOS POR LOS LIBROS Y LOS PERIODICOS (ENCUADERNADOS) TAMBIEN COMPRENDE LOS MANUSCRITOS.

NETHERLANDS:
E—> DATA ON OTHER MAJOR NON-SPECIALIZED LIBRARIES REFER TO 1974.
FR—> LES DONNEES RELATIVES AUX AUTRES BIBLIOTHEQUES IMPORTANTES NON SPECIALISEES SE REFERENT A 1974.
ESP> LOS DATOS RELATIVOS A LOS OTRAS BIBLIOTECAS IMPORTANTES NO ESPECIALIZADAS SE REFIEREN A 1974.

NORWAY:
E—> DATA ON SCHOOL LIBRARIES INCLUDE ONLY LIBRARIES OF PRIMARY SCHOOLS.
FR—> LES DONNEES RELATIVES AUX BIBLIOTHEQUES SCOLAIRES NE COMPRENNENT QUE LES BIBLIOTHEQUES DES ECOLES PRIMAIRES.
ESP> LOS DATOS RELATIVOS A LAS BIBLIOTECAS ESCOLARES SOLO SE REFIEREN A LAS BIBLIOTECAS DE LAS ESCUELAS PRIMARIAS.

ROMANIA:
E—> DATA ON SPECIAL LIBRARIES REFER TO 1974.
FR—> LES DONNEES RELATIVES AUX BIBLIOTHEQUES SPECIALISEES SE REFERENT A 1974.
ESP> LOS DATOS RELATIVOS A LAS BIBLIOTECAS ESPECIALIZADAS SE REFIEREN A 1974.

SAN MARINO:
E—> THE FIGURE ON THE LENGTH OF SHELVING OCCUPIED BY COLLECTIONS IN THE SCHOOL LIBRARIES CONCERN ONLY 2 LIBRARIES WITH 2 SERVICE POINTS.
FR—> LE CHIFFRE RELATIF AU NOMBRE DE METRES DE RAYONNAGE OCCUPES PAR LES COLLECTIONS NE CONCERNE QUE 2 BIBLIOTHEQUES AVEC 2 POINTS DE DESSERTE.
ESP> LA CIFRA RELATIVA AL NUMERO DE METROS DE ESTANTES OCUPADOS POR LAS COLECCIONES SOLO SE REFIEREN A 2 BIBLIOTECAS CON 2 PUNTOS DE SERVICIO.

YUGOSLAVIA:
E—> DATA ON SCHOOL LIBRARIES REFER TO 1978.
FR—> LES DONNEES RELATIVES AUX BIBLIOTHEQUES SCOLAIRES SE REFERENT A 1978.
ESP> LOS DATOS RELATIVOS A LAS BIBLIOTECAS ESCOLARES SE REFIEREN A 1978.

GIBRALTAR:
E—> THE FIGURE CONCERNING THE NUMBER OF VOLUMES IN SCHOOL LIBRARIES INCLUDES 6 LIBRARIES ONLY. DATA ON PUBLIC LIBRARIES REFER TO 1974.
FR—> LE CHIFFRE QUI CONCERNE LE NOMBRE DE VOLUMES DES BIBLIOTHEQUES SCOLAIRES NE REPRESENTE QUE 6 BIBLIOTHEQUES. LES DONNEES RELATIVES AUX BIBLIOTHEQUES PUBLIQUES SE REFERENT A 1974.
ESP> LA CIFRA SOBRE EL NUMERO DE VOLUMENES DE LAS BIBLIOTECAS ESCOLARES SOLO SE REFIERE A 6 BIBLIOTECAS. LOS DATOS RELATIVOS A LAS BIBLIOTECAS PUBLICAS CORRESPONDEN A 1974.

HOLY SEE:
E—> THE FIGURE ON SPECIAL AND OTHER MAJOR NON-SPECIALIZED LIBRARIES REFER TO 1974. DATA ON SPECIAL LIBRARIES ARE INCOMPLETE.
FR—> LES DONNEES RELATIVES AUX BIBLIOTHEQUES SPECIALISEES SONT INCOMPLETES ET SE REFERENT AINSI QUE CELLES DES AUTRES BIBLIOTHEQUES IMPORTANTES NON SPECIALISEES A 1974.
ESP> LOS DATOS RELATIVOS A LAS BIBLIOTECAS ESPECIALIZADAS SON INCOMPLETOS Y SE REFIEREN COMO PARA LAS OTRAS BIBLIOTECAS IMPORTANTES NO ESPECIALIZADAS, A 1974.

HUNGARY:
E—> DATA ON THE NATIONAL AND ON THE OTHER MAJOR NON-SPECIALIZED LIBRARY REFER TO 1976 AND THOSE ON UNIVERSITY AND ON SPECIAL LIBRARIES TO 1974.
FR—> LES DONNEES RELATIVES A LA BIBLIOTHEQUE NATIONALE ET A L'AUTRE BIBLIOTHEQUE IMPORTANTE NON SPECIALISEE SE REFERENT A 1976, CELLES DES BIBLIOTHEQUES UNIVERSITAIRES ET SPECIALISEES CONCERNENT 1974.
ESP> LOS DATOS RELATIVOS A LA BIBLIOTECA NACIONAL Y A LA OTRA BIBLIOTECA IMPORTANTE NO ESPECIALIZADA SE REFIEREN A 1976; LOS DE LAS BIBLIOTECAS UNIVERSITARIAS Y ESPECIALES CORRESPONDEN A 1974.

ICELAND:
E—> DATA ON SPECIAL LIBRARIES REPRESENT ONLY 20% OF THE TOTAL LIBRARIES WHOSE ACTUAL NUMBER IS 20.
FR—> LES DONNEES RELATIVES AUX BIBLIOTHEQUES SPECIALISEES NE REPRESENTENT QUE 20% DU TOTAL QUI S'ELEVE A 20.
ESP> LOS DATOS RELATIVOS A LAS BIBLIOTECAS ESPECIALIZADAS SOLO REPRESENTAN EL 20% DEL TOTAL, QUE SE ELEVA A 20.

IRELAND:
E—> THE FIGURES ON PUBLIC LIBRARIES REFER TO 1977.
FR—> LES DONNEES RELATIVES AUX BIBLIOTHEQUES PUBLIQUES SE REFERENT A 1977.
ESP> LOS DATOS RELATIVOS A LAS BIBLIOTECAS PUBLICAS SE REFIEREN A 1977.

Libraries by category 7.1
Bibliothèques classées par catégories
Bibliotecas clasificadas por categorías

NORFOLK ISLAND:
E—> DATA ON THE SCHOOL AND THE SPECIAL LIBRARY REFER TO 1975.
FR—> LES DONNEES RELATIVES A LA BIBLIOTHEQUE SCOLAIRE ET A LA BIBLIOTHEQUE SPECIALISEE SE REFERENT A 1975.
ESP> LOS DATOS RELATIVOS A LA BIBLIOTECA ESCOLAR Y A LA BIBLIOTECA ESPECIALIZADA SE REFIEREN A 1975.

SAMOA:
E—> DATA ON THE PUBLIC LIBRARY REFER TO 1974.
FR—> LES DONNEES RELATIVES A LA BIBLIOTHEQUE PUBLIQUE SE REFERENT A 1974.
ESP> LOS DATOS RELATIVOS A LA BIBLIOTECA PUBLICA SE REFIEREN A 1974.

UKRAINIAN S.S.R.:
E—> DATA ON SCHOOL LIBRARIES REFER TO 1976 AND THOSE ON PUBLIC LIBRARIES TO 1977.
FR—> LES DONNEES RELATIVES AUX BIBLIOTHEQUES SCOLAIRES ET AUX BIBLIOTHEQUES PUBLIQUES SE REFERENT RESPECTIVEMENT A 1976 ET A 1977.
ESP> LOS DATOS RELATIVOS A LAS BIBLIOTECAS ESCOLARES Y A LAS BIBLIOTECAS PUBLICAS SE REFIEREN RESPECTIVAMENTE A 1976 Y 1977.

FIJI:
E—> DATA ON SPECIAL AND PUBLIC LIBRARIES REFER TO 1978.
FR—> LES DONNEES RELATIVES AUX BIBLIOTHEQUES PUBLIQUES ET SPECIALISEES SE REFERENT A 1978.
ESP> LOS DATOS RELATIVOS A LAS BIBLIOTECAS PUBLICAS Y ESPECIALIZADAS SE REFIEREN A 1978.

FRENCH POLYNESIA:
E—> DATA ON OTHER NON SPECIALIZED LIBRARIES REFER TO 1977
FR—> LES DONNEES RELATIVES AUX AUTRES BIBLIOTHEQUES IMPORTANTES NON SPECIALISEES SE REFERENT A 1977.
ESP> LOS DATOS RELATIVOS A LAS OTRAS BIBLIOTECAS IMPORTANTES NO ESPECIALIZADAS SE REFIEREN A 1977.

NEW HEBRIDES:
E—> DATA ON PUBLIC LIBRARIES REFER TO 1976.
FR—> LES DONNEES RELATIVES AUX BIBLIOTHEQUES PUBLIQUES SE REFERENT A 1976.
ESP> LOS DATOS RELATIVOS A LAS BIBLIOTECAS PUBLICAS SE REFIEREN A 1976.

7.2 National libraries: collections, borrowers, works loaned out, current expenditure, personnel

Bibliothèques nationales: collections, emprunteurs inscrits, documents prêtés au-dehors, dépenses ordinaires, personnel

Bibliotecas nacionales: colecciones, prestatarios inscritos, documentos prestados al exterior, gastos ordinarios, personal

NUMBER OF COUNTRIES AND TERRITORIES PRESENTED IN THIS TABLE: 70

NOMBRE DE PAYS ET DE TERRITOIRES PRESENTES DANS CE TABLEAU: 70

COUNTRY / PAYS / PAIS	YEAR / ANNEE / AÑO	ADMINIS-TRATIVE UNITS / UNITES ADMINIS-TRATIVES / UNIDADES ADMINIS-TRATIVAS	SERVICE POINTS / POINTS DE DESSERTE / PUNTOS DE SERVICIO	COLLECTIONS / COLLECTIONS / COLECCIONES				
				BOOKS/LIVRES/LIBROS		MICRO-FORMS / MICRO-COPIES / MICRO-COPIAS	AUDIO-VISUAL DOCUMENTS / MATERIELS AUDIO-VISUELS / MATERIALES AUDIO-VISUALES	OTHER LIBRARY MATERIALS / AUTRES MATERIELS DE BIBLIOTHEQUE / OTROS MATE-RIALES DE BIBLIOTECA
				METRES OF SHELVING / METRES DE RAYONNAGE / METROS DE ESTANTES	NUMBER OF VOLUMES / NOMBRE DE VOLUMES / NUMERO DE VOLUMENES (000)			
		(1)	(2)	(3)	(4)	(5)	(6)	(7)
AFRICA								
ALGERIA ‡	1977	1	...	...	900	...	4 850	7 12
BENIN ‡	1977	1	8	...	32	...	...	..
EGYPT	1974	1	12	...	1 118	...	...	..
MADAGASCAR	1974	1	1	4 612	138	...	...	..
MALAWI	1977	1	1	...	28	224	917	3 00
NIGERIA ‡	1977	2	3	...	158	4 214	...	28
TOGO	1978	1	...	201	6	–	–	
TUNISIA ‡	1977	1	...	12 000	1 000	...	...	
ZAIRE ‡	1977	1	1	206	...	...	...	..

NUMERO DE PAISES Y DE TERRITORIOS PRESENTADOS EN
ESTE CUADRO: 70

ANNUAL ADDITIONS ACQUISITIONS ANNUELLES ADQUISICIONES ANUALES			LOANS TO USERS	INTER- LIBRARY LOANS	CURRENT EXPENDITURE DEPENSES ORDINAIRES GASTOS ORDINARIOS		LIBRARY EMPLOYEES PERSONNEL DES BIBLIOTHEQUES PERSONAL DE LAS BIBLIOTECAS		
VOLUMES	OTHER MATERIALS	REGISTERED BORROWERS			TOTAL	STAFF	TOTAL	HOLDING A DIPLOMA	TRAINED ON THE JOB
VOLUMES	AUTRES MATERIELS	EM- PRUNTEURS INSCRITS	PRETS AUX USAGERS	PRETS ENTRE BIBLIO- THEQUES	TOTAL	PERSON- NEL	TOTAL	DIPLOME	FORME SUR LE TAS
VOLUMENES	OTROS MATERIALES	PRESTA- TARIOS INSCRITOS	PRESTAMOS A LOS USUARIOS	PRESTAMOS ENTRE BIBLIO- TECAS	TOTAL (000)	PER- SONAL (%)	TOTAL	DIPLO- MADO	FORMADO EN EJERCICIO
(8)	(9)	(10)	(11)	(12)	(13)	(14)	(15)	(16)	(17)
27 851	...	11 468	61 360	75	...	...	24	...	...
2 413	...	9 829	100 850	...	11 865	...	609	2	3
...	...			...	...	...		...	...
3 200	...	13 916	21 672	...	...	...	18	3	—
317	26	—	—	7	30	61	9	4	5
...	4 120	567	1 134	210	1 940	23	570	20	15
450	—	10	...	—	22 920	80	40	7	15
9 250	200	1 200	200	180	200	63	82	31	51
6 689	...	995	...	...	10	...	11	...	...

COUNTRY / PAYS / PAIS	YEAR / ANNEE / AÑO	ADMINIS- TRATIVE UNITS / UNITES ADMINIS- TRATIVES / UNIDADES ADMINIS- TRATIVAS	SERVICE POINTS / POINTS DE DESSERTE / PUNTOS DE SERVICIO	COLLECTIONS / COLLECTIONS / COLECCIONES				
				BOOKS/LIVRES/LIBROS		MICRO- FORMS / MICRO- COPIES / MICRO- COPIAS	AUDIO- VISUAL DOCUMENTS / MATERIELS AUDIO- VISUELS / MATERIALES AUDIO- VISUALES	OTHER LIBRARY MATERIALS / AUTRES MATERIELS DE BIBLIOTHEQUE / OTROS MATE- RIALES DE BIBLIOTECA
				METRES OF SHELVING / METRES DE RAYONNAGE / METROS DE ESTANTES	NUMBER OF VOLUMES / NOMBRE DE VOLUMES / NUMERO DE VOLUMENES (000)			
		(1)	(2)	(3)	(4)	(5)	(6)	(7)
AMERICA, NORTH								
BELIZE ‡	1974	1	7	...	3	...	...	...
BERMUDA	1974	1	4	...	122	...	...	...
COSTA RICA ‡	1977	1	1	4 755	300	...	239	...
EL SALVADOR	1978	1	1	...	200	...	...	...
GREENLAND ‡	1974	1	1	...	16	...	...	...
GUATEMALA	1974	1	54	...	361	...	...	...
MEXICO ‡	1975	2	2	...	1 116	...	...	...
UNITED STATES OF AMERICA	1978	3	...	...	20 799	3 448 150	9 599	50 162 930
AMERICA, SOUTH								
ARGENTINA	1977	1	1	24 310	1 880	120	8 000	–
BRAZIL	1974	1	1	...	2 624	...	...	...
CHILE	1974	1	44	85 000	2 000	...	...	...
COLOMBIA ‡	1974	1	...	37 073	*450	...	...	...
PERU ‡	1977	1	...	15 569	2 137	219	...	185 830
URUGUAY	1974	1	1	*16 000	*554	...	...	...
VENEZUELA	1978	1	5	2 722	544	1 109 251	113 426	–
ASIA								
BRUNEI	1974	1	9	95	53	...	...	...
HONG KONG ‡	1974	1	8	11 100	650	...	...	...
INDIA ‡	1978	1	3	48 000	1 608	...	...	72 201
IRAQ	1974	1	1	2 300	68	...	...	...
JAPAN ‡	1978	1	3	...	3 248	75 628	189 459	163 892
KOREA, REPUBLIC OF ‡	1977	2	2	...	636	...	...	...
MALAYSIA ‡	1977	1	1	1 875	94	1 196	180	913
PAKISTAN	1977	1	2	571	80	–	–	–
PHILIPPINES	1977	1	10	6 710	182	2 435	10	2 883
SAUDI ARABIA	1974	1	1	250	23	...	...	...
SINGAPORE ‡	1978	1	16	...	1 098	10 048	6 408	13 944
SRI LANKA	1977	1	3	...	13	...	...	...
THAILAND	1974	1	6	2 310	882	...	...	...
TURKEY ‡	1978	1	10	...	737	10 000	7 105	313 986
UNITED ARAB EMIRATES‡	1977	...	8	...	70	...	...	–
VIET–NAM	1977	1	1	20 165	818	...	2 490	2 990
EUROPE								
AUSTRIA ‡	1977	1	1	53 928	2 252	21 304	1 615 757	1 689 418
BELGIUM	1977	1	1	*90 000	*3 000	...	...	...
BULGARIA	1977	1	...	...	1 352	20 102	...	470 765
DENMARK	1977	1	3	75 000	2 300	49 669	3 935	3 101 587
FAEROE ISLANDS	1974	1	1	2 085	73	...	...	...

ANNUAL ADDITIONS ACQUISITIONS ANNUELLES ADQUISICIONES ANUALES		REGISTERED BORROWERS EMPRUNTEURS INSCRITS PRESTATARIOS INSCRITOS	LOANS TO USERS PRETS AUX USAGERS PRESTAMOS A LOS USUARIOS	INTER-LIBRARY LOANS PRETS ENTRE BIBLIOTHEQUES PRESTAMOS ENTRE BIBLIOTECAS	CURRENT EXPENDITURE DEPENSES ORDINAIRES GASTOS ORDINARIOS		LIBRARY EMPLOYEES PERSONNEL DES BIBLIOTHEQUES PERSONAL DE LAS BIBLIOTECAS		
VOLUMES VOLUMES VOLUMENES	OTHER MATERIALS AUTRES MATERIELS OTROS MATERIALES				TOTAL TOTAL TOTAL (000)	STAFF PERSONNEL PERSONAL (%)	TOTAL TOTAL TOTAL	HOLDING A DIPLOMA DIPLOME DIPLOMADO	TRAINED ON THE JOB FORME SUR LE TAS FORMADO EN EJERCICIO
(8)	(9)	(10)	(11)	(12)	(13)	(14)	(15)	(16)	(17)
75					66				
6 202	...	9 110	218 476	...	259	51	19	5	14
	...	722			5 506	73	98	10	12
2 201	...		372 573	...	470 493	92	61	1	34
1 764	...			...	2 143	37	17	5	...
2 251	...	...	316 382	...	85	70	90	–	9
153 341	...	354 929	...	...	3 189	...	203	...	...
359 656	451 732	...	2 290 260	300 738	185 111	52	5 194	...	...
7 080	–	...	115 000	6 180	37 116	100	116	8	–
	...	...	...	–	4 926	96	292	88	171
18 978	...	8 888	1 000 053	...	442 295	81	274	15	122
10 000	...	...	...	...	4 650	81	99	4	...
70 600	...	...	...	...	49 376	87	260	32	...
4 100	...	58	180 823	...	240 193	82	157	35	–
97 694	1 183 489	...	35 224	–	32 554	46	568	28	103
10 000	...	2 163	24 395	...	145	76	25	2	23
86 000	...	493 536	3 150 000	...	4 250	59	153	12	9
24 984	...	25 357	80 671	21	7 418	61	632	161	–
5 309	...	51 094	...	...	24	96	49	15	14
104 743	31 650	...	...	14 132	5 657 639	75	874	201	...
50 173	...	685 950	562 303	...	1 071 566	61	405	106	...
20 000	347	7 775	...	791	1 821	52	102	28	...
7 748	–	...	...	164	1 737	22	67	20	–
7 602	1 699	...	316 554	79	4 398 883	70	317	51	52
2 773	...	...	...	...	300	25	23	6	3
141 565	...	345 645	2 726 399	12	4 255	62	278	45	–
2 127	–	4 800	109	...	476	60	38	4	–
12 700		672 513	...	...	4 130	58	104	38	40
13 689	12 605	...	94 014	...	5 753	79	95	20	18
15 000	–	...	...	...	500	...	35	2	33
13 940	123	...	...	...	285	35	120	19	40
27 304	...	...	56 029'	10 276	35 729	...	243	114	...
12 642	...	*400	...	*30 900	341 222	56	280	32	9
42 980	30 404	30 547	578 127	...	1 322	46	217	181	36
133 617	37 213	...	70 010	41 768	46 790	73	329	122	...
2 827	...	...	3 026	...	836	61	8	3	–

COUNTRY / PAYS / PAIS	YEAR / ANNEE / AÑO	ADMINISTRATIVE UNITS / UNITES ADMINISTRATIVES / UNIDADES ADMINISTRATIVAS	SERVICE POINTS / POINTS DE DESSERTE / PUNTOS DE SERVICIO	COLLECTIONS / COLLECTIONS / COLECCIONES				
				BOOKS/LIVRES/LIBROS		MICRO-FORMS / MICRO-COPIES / MICRO-COPIAS	AUDIO-VISUAL DOCUMENTS / MATERIELS AUDIO-VISUELS / MATERIALES AUDIO-VISUALES	OTHER LIBRARY MATERIALS / AUTRES MATERIELS DE BIBLIOTHEQUE / OTROS MATERIALES DE BIBLIOTECA
				METRES OF SHELVING / METRES DE RAYONNAGE / METROS DE ESTANTES	NUMBER OF VOLUMES / NOMBRE DE VOLUMES / NUMERO DE VOLUMENES (000)			
		(1)	(2)	(3)	(4)	(5)	(6)	(7)
FINLAND ‡	1977	1	3	57 100	1 875	68 100	...	...
GERMAN DEMOCRATIC REPUBLIC ‡	1977	2	2	...	9 421	12 490	491 179	849 804
GERMANY, FEDERAL REPUBLIC OF	1977	3	4	...	8 936	331 750	3 145 228	972 205
HUNGARY ‡	1976	1	6		2 073	...	2 802 528	./.
ICELAND ‡	1974	1	1	7 093	319	...	...	...
IRELAND	1974	1	2	15 500	500	...		
ITALY ‡	1977	8	8	272 547	11 782	...	38 603	101 142
LIECHTENSTEIN	1974	1	–	45 000		...		...
LUXEMBOURG	1977	1	1	17 820	580	–	410	–
MALTA ‡	1977	1	1	6 600	347	–	–	–
NETHERLANDS ‡	1976	1	4	28 503	1 065	9 936	...	...
NORWAY ‡	1977	1	77	116 073	3 775	...	...	...
POLAND ‡	1977	1	–	...	1 714	104 000	6 000	1 536 000
PORTUGAL ‡	1977	3	...	3 138	...	...	...	...
ROMANIA	1974	2	...		12 071	...	...	...
SAN MARINO	1974	1	1	800	44	...	...	...
SPAIN ‡	1977	2	3	253 503	4 855	3 952	...	...
SWEDEN ‡	1977	1	1	56 498		44 400	...	...
SWITZERLAND	1977	1	–	26 800	1 182	142	8 370	228 000
UNITED KINGDOM ‡	1977	1	8	...	...	3 208 000	–	19 000 000
YUGOSLAVIA ‡	1977	8	8	132 386	7 898	581 094	114 977	1 119 949
OCEANIA								
AUSTRALIA ‡	1977	1	1	...	1 823	1 788 000	1 479 480	...
NEW ZEALAND	1974	1	7	103 678	4 245	...	...	...
SOLOMON ISLANDS	1974	1	1	336	13	...	...	...
U.S.S.R.								
UKRAINIAN S.S.R.	1974	2	2	...	9 503	...	...	...

ALGERIA:
E—> COLUMN 12 DOES NOT INCLUDE LIBRARY LOAN TRANSACTIONS ON THE NATIONAL LEVEL.
FR—> LA COLONNE 12 N'INCLUT PAS LES PRETS ENTRE BIBLIOTHEQUES AU NIVEAU NATIONAL.
ESP> LA COLUMNA 12 NO INCLUYE LOS PRESTAMOS ENTRE BIBLIOTECAS A NIVEL NACIONAL.

BENIN:
E—> THE FIGURE IN COLUMN 13 REFERS TO EXPENDITURE FOR EMPLOYEES ONLY. COLUMNS 15, 16 AND 17 DOES NOT INCLUDE PART-TIME STAFF ONLY.
FR—> LE CHIFFRE DE LA COLONNE 13 SE RAPPORTE AUX DEPENSES POUR LE PERSONNEL SEULEMENT. LES COLONNES 15, 16 ET 17 N'INCLUENT PAS LE PERSONNEL EMPLOYE A TEMPS PARTIEL.
ESP> LA CIFRA DE LA COLUMNA 13 SE REFIERE A LOS GASTOS DE PERSONAL SOLAMENTE. LAS COLUMNAS 15, 16 Y 17 NO INCLUYEN EL PERSONAL DE JORNADA PARCIAL.

NIGERIA:
E—> THE DATA ON ACQUISITIONS IN COLUMN 9 REFER ONLY TO MICROFORMS.
FR—> LES DONNEES CONCERNANT LES ACQUISITIONS, COLONNE 9, NE COMPRENNENT QUE LES MICROCOPIES.
ESP> LOS DATOS DE LA COLUMNA 9 RELATIVOS A LAS ADQUISICIONES, SOLO INCLUYEN LAS MICROCOPIAS.

TUNISIA:
E—> THE DATA ON ACQUISITIONS IN COLUMN 9 REFER ONLY TO MICROFORMS.
FR—> LES DONNEES CONCERNANT LES ACQUISITIONS, COLONNE 9, NE COMPRENNENT QUE LES MICROCOPIES.
ESP> LOS DATOS DE LA COLUMNA 9 RELATIVOS A LAS ADQUISICIONES, SOLO INCLUYEN LAS MICROCOPIAS.

ANNUAL ADDITIONS ACQUISITIONS ANNUELLES ADQUISICIONES ANUALES		REGISTERED BORROWERS	LOANS TO USERS	INTER— LIBRARY LOANS	CURRENT EXPENDITURE DEPENSES ORDINAIRES GASTOS ORDINARIOS		LIBRARY EMPLOYEES PERSONNEL DES BIBLIOTHEQUES PERSONAL DE LAS BIBLIOTECAS		
VOLUMES	OTHER MATERIALS			PRETS ENTRE BIBLIO— THEQUES	TOTAL	STAFF	TOTAL	HOLDING A DIPLOMA	TRAINED ON THE JOB
VOLUMES	AUTRES MATERIELS	EM— PRUNTEURS INSCRITS	PRETS AUX USAGERS		TOTAL	PERSON— NEL	TOTAL	DIPLOME	FORME SUR LE TAS
VOLUMENES	OTROS MATERIALES	PRESTA— TARIOS INSCRITOS	PRESTAMOS A LOS USUARIOS	PRESTAMOS ENTRE BIBLIO— TECAS	TOTAL (000)	PER— SONAL (%)	TOTAL	DIPLO— MADO	FORMADO EN EJERCICIO
(8)	(9)	(10)	(11)	(12)	(13)	(14)	(15)	(16)	(17)
40 380	14 830	...	292 550	11 110	8 976	76	171	69	—
173 008	12 936	54 560	1 187 324	8 832	...		999	459	—
368 843	75 391	46 520	320 598	113 966	73 080	62	1 097	473	463
48 472	119 913	13 266	...	7 479	15 024	...	840	231	131
5 982	...	276	25 798	...	24 482	74	22	6	7
				...	126	69	55	1	14
122 103	2 539	43 470	59 662	5 017	2 095 410	...	1 058	156	902
2 400		6 000	24 000	...	230	52	5	1	1
13 500	26	10 455	70 000	198	29 498	61	30	2	9
2 100	...	...	...	10	38	77	22		2
20 354	1 379	...	154 081		...	...	162	37	—
122 971		...		...	9 651	...	323	207	...
...	...	3 000	16 000	...	6 232	...	...	...	...
23 515	...	231 500	493 434	...	45 531	...	215	...	...
278 036	...	26 500	...	...	...	...	...	...	...
100	...	50	15	...	20 900	98	5	—	1
71 456	210	7 431	111 271	924	39 062	...	228	63	165
15 626			108 127	19 941	23 937	68	227	41	...
43 804	9 704	16 500	125 881	11 443	5 105	79	83	21	6
...	2 707 700	...	...	3 048 800	28 153	35	2 078	475	...
624 477	8 499	334 828	...	...	12 283 064	...	926	571	43
98 000	342 880	...	323 000	...	12 705	56	737	170	49
195 907	...	...	2 761 149	...	2 815	64	380	157	...
158	...	3 206	...	...	3	69	5	1	3
424 300	...	56 600	3 828 100	...	...	...	728	325	403

ZAIRE:
E—> THE FIGURE IN COLUMN 13 REFERS TO
EXPENDITURE FOR EMPLOYEES ONLY. COLUMN 16
DOES NOT INCLUDE PART—TIME STAFF ONLY.
FR—> LE CHIFFRE DE LA COLONNE 13 SE RAPPORTE
AUX DEPENSES POUR LE PERSONNEL SEULEMENT.
LA COLONNE 16 N'INCLUT PAS LE PERSONNEL
EMPLOYE A TEMPS PARTIEL.
ESP> LA CIFRA DE LA COLUMNA 13 SE REFIERE A LOS
GASTOS DE PERSONAL SOLAMENTE. LA COLUMNA 16 NO
INCLUYE EL PERSONAL DE JORNADA PARCIAL.

BELIZE:
E—> THE FIGURE IN COLUMN 13 INCLUDES
EXPENDITURE FOR PUBLIC LIBRARIES.
FR—> LE CHIFFRE DE LA COLONNE 13 INCLUT LES
DEPENSES RELATIVES AUX BIBLIOTHEQUES PUBLIQUES.
ESP> LA CIFRA DE LA COLUMNA 13 INCLUYE LOS
GASTOS RELATIVOS A LAS BIBLIOTECAS PUBLICAS.

COSTA RICA:
E—> COLUMNS 15, 16 AND 17 REFER TO FULL—TIME
STAFF ONLY.
FR—> LES COLONNES 15, 16 ET 17 SE REFERENT AU
PERSONNEL EMPLOYE A PLEIN TEMPS SEULEMENT.
ESP> LAS COLUMNAS 15, 16 Y 17 SE REFIEREN AL
PERSONAL DE JORNADA COMPLETA SOLAMENTE.

GREENLAND:
E—> THE DATA IN COLUMNS 13, 14, 15 AND 16
INCLUDE PUBLIC LIBRARIES.
FR—> LES DONNEES DES COLONNES 13, 14, 15 ET 16
INCLUENT LES BIBLIOTHEQUES PUBLIQUES.
ESP> LOS DATOS DE LAS COLUMNAS 13, 14, 15 Y 16
INCLUYEN LAS BIBLIOTECAS PUBLICAS.

MEXICO:
E—> COLUMN 10 REFER TO THE NUMBER OF READERS AND NOT TO THE NUMBER OF REGISTERED BORROWERS.
FR—> LA COLONNE 10 INDIQUE LE NOMBRE DE LECTEURS ET NON LE NOMBRE D'EMPRUNTEURS INSCRITS.
ESP> LA COLUMNA 10 INDICA EL NUMERO DE LECTORES Y NO EL DE PRESTATARIOS INSCRITOS.

COLOMBIA:
E—> THE FIGURES IN COLUMNS 15 AND 16 REFER TO FULL-TIME STAFF ONLY.
FR—> LES CHIFFRES DES COLONNES 15 ET 16 SE RAPPORTENT AU PERSONNEL EMPLOYE A PLEIN TEMPS SEULEMENT.
ESP> LAS CIFRAS DE LAS COLUMNAS 15 Y 16 SE REFIEREN AL PERSONAL DE JORNADA COMPLETA SOLAMENTE.

PERU:
E—> THE FIGURES IN COLUMNS 15 AND 16 REFER TO FULL-TIME STAFF ONLY.
FR—> LES CHIFFRES DES COLONNES 15 ET 16 SE RAPPORTENT AU PERSONNEL EMPLOYE A PLEIN TEMPS SEULEMENT.
ESP> LAS CIFRAS DE LAS COLUMNAS 15 Y 16 SE REFIEREN AL PERSONAL DE JORNADA COMPLETA SOLAMENTE.

HONG KONG:
E—> THE NATIONAL LIBRARY SERVES ALSO AS A PUBLIC LIBRARY.
FR—> LA BIBLIOTHEQUE NATIONALE SERT AUSSI DE BIBLIOTHEQUE PUBLIQUE.
ESP> LA BIBLIOTECA NACIONAL DESEMPENA AL MISMO TIEMPO LA FUNCION DE BIBLIOTECA PUBLICA.

INDIA:
E—> COLUMN 12 DOES NOT INCLUDE LIBRARY LOAN TRANSACTIONS ON THE NATIONAL LEVEL.
FR—> LA COLONNE 12 N'INCLUT PAS LES PRETS ENTRE BIBLIOTHEQUES AU NIVEAU NATIONAL.
ESP> LA COLUMNA 12 NO INCLUYE LOS PRESTAMOS ENTRE BIBLIOTECAS A NIVEL NACIONAL.

JAPAN:
E—> COLUMN 4 DOES NOT INCLUDE (BOUND) PERIODICALS; THE FIGURE IN COLUMN 6 REFER ONLY TO GRAMOPHONE RECORDS ONLY.
FR—> LA COLONNE 4 N'INCLUT PAS LES PERIODIQUES (RELIES); LE CHIFFRE DE LA COLONNE 6 SE RAPPORTE UNIQUEMENT AUX DISQUES.
ESP> LA COLUMNA 4 NO INCLUYE LOS PERIODICOS (ENCUADERNADOS); LA CIFRA DE LA COLUMNA 6 SE REFIERE UNICAMENTE A LOS DISCOS.

KOREA, REPUBLIC OF:
E—> THE FIGURE IN COLUMN 16 SHOWS FULL-TIME STAFF ONLY.
FR—> LE CHIFFRE DE LA COLONNE 16 NE TIENT COMPTE QUE DU PERSONNEL EMPLOYE A PLEIN TEMPS.
ESP> LA CIFRA DE LA COLUMNA 16 SOLO TOMA EN CONSIDERACION AL PERSONAL DE JORNADA COMPLETA.

MALAYSIA:
E—> THE FIGURES IN COLUMNS 15 AND 16 REFER TO FULL-TIME STAFF.
FR—> LES CHIFFRES DES COLONNES 15 ET 16 REPRESENTENT LE PERSONNEL EMPLOYE A PLEIN TEMPS SEULEMENT.
ESP> LAS CIFRAS DE LAS COLUMNAS 15 Y 16 REPRESENTAN EL PERSONAL DE JORNADA COMPLETA SOLAMENTE.

SINGAPORE:
E—> THE NATIONAL LIBRARY IS ALSO THE PUBLIC LIBRARY. COLUMN 12 DOES NOT INCLUDE LIBRARY LOAN TRANSACTIONS ON THE NATIONAL LEVEL.

SINGAPORE (CONT):
FR—> LA BIBLIOTHEQUE NATIONALE SERT AUSSI DE BIBLIOTHEQUE PUBLIQUE. LA COLONNE 12 N'INCLUT PAS LES PRETS ENTRE BIBLIOTHEQUES AU NIVEAU NATIONAL.
ESP> LA BIBLIOTECA NACIONAL TAMBIEN DESEMPENA LA FUNCION DE BIBLIOTECA PUBLICA. LA COLUMNA 12 NO INCLUYE LOS PRESTAMOS ENTRE BIBLIOTECAS A NIVEL NACIONAL.

TURKEY:
E—> COLUMN 11 REFERS ONLY TO WORKS USED IN READING-ROOMS.
FR—> LA COLONNE 11 SIGNALE LE NOMBRE D'OUVRAGES UTILISES DANS LES SALLES DE LECTURE SEULEMENT.
ESP> LA COLUMNA 11 INDICA EL NUMERO DE VOLUMENES UTILIZADOS EN LAS SALAS DE LECTURA.

UNITED ARAB EMIRATES:
E—> THE FIGURE IN COLUMN 13 REFERS ONLY TO EXPENDITURE FOR ACQUISITIONS.
FR—> LE CHIFFRE DE LA COLONNE 13 SE REFERE SEULEMENT AUX DEPENSES POUR LES ACQUISITIONS.
ESP> LA CIFRA DE LA COLUMNA 13 INCLUYE SOLAMENTE LOS GASTOS DESTINADOS A LAS ADQUISICIONES.

AUSTRIA:
E—> THE FIGURE IN COLUMN 13 INCLUDES ONLY EXPENDITURE FOR EMPLOYEES AND ACQUISITIONS.
FR—> LE CHIFFRE DE LA COLONNE 13 INCLUT SEULEMENT LES DEPENSES DESTINEES AU PERSONNEL ET AUX ACQUISITIONS.
ESP> LA CIFRA DE LA COLUMNA 13 INCLUYE SOLAMENTE LOS GASTOS DE PERSONAL Y DE ADQUISICIONES.

FINLAND:
E—> ACQUISITION DATA IN COLUMN 9 REFER TO MICROFILMS AND AUDIO-VISUAL DOCUMENTS ONLY.
FR—> LES DONNEES RELATIVES AUX ACQUISITIONS, DANS LA COLONNE 9 , NE CONCERNENT QUE LES MICROCOPIES ET LE MATERIEL AUDIOVISUEL.
ESP> LOS DATOS DE LA COLUMNA 9 RELATIVOS A LAS ADQUISICIONES SOLO SE REFIEREN A LAS MICROCOPIAS Y AL MATERIAL AUDIOVISUAL.

GERMAN DEMOCRATIC REPUBLIC:
E—> THE FIGURE IN COLUMN 11 INCLUDES BESIDES LOANS TO USERS, ITEMS COPIED TO TAKE THE PLACE OF ORIGINAL MATERIALS.
FR—> LE CHIFFRE DE LA COLONNE 11 COMPREND, EN PLUS DES LIVRES PRETES AUX USAGERS, LE NOMBRE D'UNITES COPIEES FOURNIES A LA PLACE DE DOCUMENTS ORIGINAUX.
ESP> LA CIFRA DE LA COLUMNA 11 COMPRENDE, ADEMAS DE LOS LIBROS PRESTADOS A LOS USUARIOS, EL NUMERO DE COPIAS FACILITADAS EN SUSTITUCION DE LOS DOCUMENTOS ORIGINALES.

HUNGARY:
E—> ACQUISITIONS IN COLUMN 9 DO NOT INCLUDE MICROFORMS. COLUMN 13 REFERS TO EXPENDITURE FOR ACQUISITIONS ONLY. ONLY FULL-TIME STAFF IS SHOWN IN COLUMNS 15, 16 AND 17.
FR—> LES DONNEES QUI PARAISSENT DANS LA COLONNE 9 N'INCLUENT PAS LES MICROCOPIES. LA COLONNE 13 SE RAPPORTE AUX DEPENSES POUR LES ACQUISITIONS SEULEMENT. LES COLONNES 15, 16 ET 17 CONCERNENT LE PERSONNEL EMPLOYE A PLEIN TEMPS SEULEMENT.
ESP> LOS DATOS QUE FIGURAN EN LA COLUMNA 9 NO INCLUYEN LAS MICROCOPIAS. LA COLUMNA 13 SOLO CONCIERNE LOS GASTOS RELATIVOS A LAS ADQUISICIONES. LAS COLUMNAS 15, 16 Y 17 SE REFIEREN AL PERSONAL DE JORNADA COMPLETA SOLAMENTE.

ICELAND:
E—> COLUMN 11 REFERS ONLY TO WORKS USED IN READING ROOMS.
FR—> LA COLONNE 11 SE REFERE SEULEMENT AUX

ICELAND (CONT):
OUVRAGES UTILISES DANS LES SALLES DE LECTURE.
  ESP> LA COLUMNA 11 SOLO SE REFIERE A LOS
VOLUMENES UTILIZADOS EN LAS SALAS DE LECTURA.

ITALY:
  E—> COLUMN 3 INCLUDES MANUSCRIPTS. THE FIGURE
IN COLUMN 6 REFERS TO AUDITORY MATERIALS ONLY,
THAT IN COLUMN 9 TO AUDITORY AND OTHER LIBRARY
MATERIALS ONLY. COLUMN 13 DOES NOT INCLUDE
EXPENDITURE FOR EMPLOYEES.
  FR—> LA COLONNE 3 COMPREND LES MANUSCRITS.
LE CHIFFRE DE LA COLONNE 6 SE RAPPORTE AUX
MATERIELS AUDITIFS, CELUI DE LA COLONNE 9 CONCERNE
LES MATERIELS AUDITIFS ET LES AUTRES MATERIELS DE
BIBLIOTHEQUE. LA COLONNE 13 N'INCLUT PAS LES
DEPENSES POUR LE PERSONNEL.
  ESP> LA COLUMNA 3 COMPRENDE LOS MANUSCRITOS.
LA CIFRA DE LA COLUMNA 6 SE REFIERE A LOS
MATERIALES AUDITIVOS, Y LA DE LA COLUMNA 9 A LOS
MATERIALES AUDITIVOS Y OTROS MATERIALES DE
BIBLIOTECA. LA COLUMNA 13 NO INCLUYE LOS GASTOS
DE PERSONAL.

MALTA:
  E—> COLUMN 8 SHOWS THE NUMBER OF TITLES AND NOT
THE NUMBER OF VOLUMES. THE FIGURES IN COLUMNS
15 AND 17 REFER TO FULL-TIME STAFF ONLY.
  FR—> LA COLONNE 8 INDIQUE LE NOMBRE DE TITRES
ET NON LE NOMBRE DE VOLUMES. LES CHIFFRES DES
COLONNES 15 ET 17 SE REFERENT AU PERSONNEL
EMPLOYE A PLEIN TEMPS SEULEMENT.
  ESP> LA COLUMNA 8 INDICA EL NUMERO DE TITULOS Y
NO EL DE VOLUMENES. LAS CIFRAS DE LAS COLUMNAS 15
Y 17 SE REFIEREN AL PERSONAL DE JORNADA COMPLETA
SOLAMENTE.

NETHERLANDS:
  E—> THE DATA ON ACQUISITIONS IN COLUMN 9 REFER
TO MICROFORMS ONLY. COLUMN 11 INCLUDES BESIDES
LOANS TO USERS, ITEMS COPIED TO TAKE THE PLACE
OF ORIGINAL MATERIALS.
  FR—> LES DONNEES DE LA COLONNE 9 SE RAPPORTENT
AUX MICROCOPIES SEULEMENT. LA COLONNE 11
COMPREND, EN PLUS DES LIVRES PRETES AUX USAGERS,
LE NOMBRE D'UNITES COPIEES FOURNIES A LA PLACE DE
DOCUMENTS ORIGINAUX.
  ESP> LOS DATOS DE LA COLUMNA 9 SE REFIEREN A LAS
MICROCOPIAS SOLAMENTE. LA COLUMNA 11 COMPRENDE,
ADEMAS DE LOS LIBROS PRESTADOS A LOS USUARIOS, EL
NUMERO DE COPIAS FACILITADAS EN SUSTITUCION DE LOS
DOCUMENTOS ORIGINALES.

NORWAY:
  E—> THE FIGURE IN COLUMN 13 DOES NOT INCLUDE
EXPENDITURE FOR EMPLOYEES.
  FR—> LE CHIFFRE DE LA COLONNE 13 N'INCLUT PAS
LES DEPENSES POUR LE PERSONNEL.
  ESP> LA CIFRA DE LA COLUMNA 13 NO INCLUYE LOS
GASTOS DE PERSONAL.

POLAND:
  E—> THE FIGURE IN COLUMN 13 DOES NOT INCLUDE
EXPENDITURE FOR EMPLOYEES.
  FR—> LE CHIFFRE DE LA COLONNE 13 N'INCLUT PAS
LES DEPENSES POUR LE PERSONNEL.
  ESP> LA CIFRA DE LA COLUMNA 13 NO INCLUYE LOS
GASTOS DE PERSONAL.

PORTUGAL:
  E—> COLUMN 11 REFERS ONLY TO WORKS USED IN
READING ROOMS. COLUMN 13 SHOWS ONLY EXPENDITURE
FOR EMPLOYEES AND ACQUISITIONS. COLUMN 15 DOES
NOT INCLUDE PART-TIME STAFF.
  FR—> LA COLONNE 11 SE REFERE SEULEMENT AUX
OUVRAGES UTILISEES DANS LES SALLES DE LECTURE.
LA COLONNE 13 MONTRE SEULEMENT LES DEPENSES POUR

PORTUGAL (CONT):
LE PERSONNEL ET LES ACQUISITIONS. LA COLONNE
15 N'INCLUT PAS LE PERSONNEL EMPLOYE A TEMPS
PARTIEL.
  ESP> LA COLUMNA 11 SE REFIERE SOLAMENTE A LOS
VOLUMENES UTILIZADOS EN LAS SALAS DE LECTURA.
LA COLUMNA 13 SOLO INCLUYE LOS GASTOS DE PERSONAL
Y DE ADQUISICIONES. LA COLUMNA 15 NO INCLUYE EL
PERSONAL DE JORNADA PARCIAL.

SPAIN:
  E—> THE FIGURES IN COLUMNS 9 AND 12 REFER TO
MICROFORMS ONLY. COLUMN 13 CONCERN FULL-TIME
STAFF ONLY.
  FR—> LES CHIFFRES DES COLONNES 9 ET 12 SE
RAPPORTENT AUX MICROCOPIES SEULEMENT. LA COLONNE
13 NE CONCERNE QUE LE PERSONNEL EMPLOYE A PLEIN
TEMPS.
  ESP> LAS CIFRAS DE LAS COLUMNAS 9 Y 12 SE
REFIEREN A LAS MICROCOPIAS SOLAMENTE. LA COLUMNA
13 SOLO CONCIERNE EL PERSONAL DE JORNADA COMPLETA.

SWEDEN:
  E—> COLUMN 8 SHOWS THE NUMBER OF METRES OF
OCCUPIED SHELVES AND NOT THE NUMBER OF VOLUMES.
THE FIGURES IN COLUMNS 15 AND 16 REFER TO FULL-
TIME STAFF ONLY.
  FR—> LA COLONNE 8 DONNE LE NOMBRE DE METRES
LINEAIRES DE RAYONNAGE OCCUPE, ET NON LE NOMBRE
DE VOLUMES. LES CHIFFRES DES COLONNES 15 ET 16
SE REFERENT SEULEMENT AU PERSONNEL EMPLOYE A
PLEIN TEMPS.
  ESP> LA COLUMNA 8 INDICA EL NUMERO DE METROS
LINEALES DE ESTANTES OCUPADOS Y NO EL NUMERO DE
VOLUMENES. LAS CIFRAS DE LAS COLUMNAS 15 Y 16 SE
REFIEREN SOLAMENTE AL PERSONAL DE JORNADA COMPLETA.

UNITED KINGDOM:
  E—> COLUMNS 15 AND 16 REFER TO FULL-TIME ONLY.
  FR—> LES COLONNES 15 ET 16 NE COMPRENNENT QUE
LE PERSONNEL EMPLOYE A PLEIN TEMPS.
  ESP> LAS COLUMNAS 15 Y 16 NO INCLUYEN EL
PERSONAL DE JORNADA COMPLETA.

YUGOSLAVIA:
  E—> THE FIGURE IN COLUMN 6 ONLY REFERS TO
AUDITORY MATERIALS. ACQUISITIONS IN COLUMN 9
REFER TO MICROFORMS ONLY. THE FIGURE IN COLUMN
13 SHOWS ONLY EXPENDITURE (IN MILLIONS) FOR
ACQUISITIONS. THE DATA IN COLUMNS 15, 16 AND 17
REFER TO FULL-TIME STAFF ONLY.
  FR—> LE CHIFFRE DE LA COLONNE 6 PREND EN
CONSIDERATION SEULEMENT LES MATERIELS AUDITIFS.
LES DONNEES DE LA COLONNE 9 SE RAPPORTENT AUX
MICROCOPIES SEULEMENT. LA COLONNE 13 NE TIENT
COMPTE QUE DES DEPENSES (EN MILLIONS) POUR LES
ACQUISITIONS. LES DONNEES DES COLONNES 15, 16 ET
17 SE REFERENT AU PERSONNEL EMPLOYE A PLEIN TEMPS
SEULEMENT.
  ESP> LA CIFRA DE LA COLUMNA 6 TOMA SOLAMENTE EN
CONSIDERACION LOS MATERIALES AUDITIVOS. LOS DATOS
DE LA COLUMNA 9 SOLO SE REFIEREN A LAS MICROCOPIAS.
LA COLUMNA 13 INCLUYE UNICAMENTE LOS GASTOS (EN
MILLONES) PARA LAS ADQUISICIONES. LOS DATOS DE
LAS COLUMNAS 15, 16 Y 17 SE REFIEREN AL PERSONAL
DE JORNADA COMPLETA SOLAMENTE.

AUSTRALIA:
  E—> THE DATA ON ACQUISITIONS IN COLUMN 9
CONCERN ONLY MICROFORMS AND AUDIO-VISUAL
DOCUMENTS.
  FR—> LES DONNEES RELATIVES AUX ACQUISITIONS
DANS LA COLONNE 9, NE CONCERNENT QUE LES
MICROCOPIES ET LES MATERIELS AUDIO-VISUELS.
  ESP> LOS DATOS DE LA COLUMNA 9 RELATIVOS A LAS
ADQUISICIONES, SOLO SE REFIEREN A LAS MICROCOPIAS
Y A LOS MATERIALES AUDIOVISUALES.

7.3 Libraries of institutions of higher education
Bibliothèques d'établissements d'enseignement supérieur
Bibliotecas de instituciones de enseñanza superior

7.3 Libraries of institutions of higher education: collections, borrowers, works loaned out, current expenditure, personnel

Bibliothèques d'établissements d'enseignement supérieur: collections, emprunteurs inscrits, documents prêtés au-dehors, dépenses ordinaires, personnel

Bibliotecas de instituciones de enseñanza superior: colecciones, prestatarios inscritos, documentos prestados al exterior, gastos ordinarios, personal

NUMBER OF COUNTRIES AND TERRITORIES PRESENTED IN THIS TABLE: 76

NOMBRE DE PAYS ET DE TERRITOIRES PRESENTES DANS CE TABLEAU: 76

COUNTRY / PAYS / PAIS	YEAR / ANNEE / AÑO	ADMINIS- TRATIVE UNITS / UNITES ADMINIS- TRATIVES / UNIDADES ADMINIS- TRATIVAS	SERVICE POINTS / POINTS DE DESSERTE / PUNTOS DE SERVICIO	COLLECTIONS / COLLECTIONS / COLECCIONES				
				BOOKS/LIVRES/LIBROS		MICRO- FORMS / MICRO- COPIES / MICRO- COPIAS	AUDIO- VISUAL DOCUMENTS / MATERIELS AUDIO- VISUELS / MATERIALES AUDIO- VISUALES	OTHER LIBRARY MATERIALS / AUTRES MATERIELS DE BIBLIOTHEQUE / OTROS MATE- RIALES DE BIBLIOTECA
				METRES OF SHELVING / METRES DE RAYONNAGE / METROS DE ESTANTES	NUMBER OF VOLUMES / NOMBRE DE VOLUMES / NUMERO DE VOLUMENES (000)			
		(1)	(2)	(3)	(4)	(5)	(6)	(7)
AFRICA								
ALGERIA	1975	3	20	7 305	734			
BURUNDI ‡	1978	4	6	2 660	92	100	3	4
COMORO ‡	1975	1	1	...	...	...	...	...
EGYPT ‡	1974	...	133	...	2 760	...	...	...
ETHIOPIA	1974	1	14	8 668	325	...	...	...
GAMBIA	1974	3	3	132	6			
KENYA	1974	3	8	...	230	...	...	...
MADAGASCAR ‡	1974	2	4	...	172			
MALAWI	1977	1	3	...	174	910	2 685	
NIGERIA	1977	...	44	...	1 368	136 416	...	1 553
ST. HELENA	1974	1	1	90	5	...	...	...
UGANDA	1974	7	9	...	445	...	...	...

Libraries of institutions of higher education   7.3
Bibliothèques d'établissements d'enseignement supérieur
Bibliotecas de instituciones de enseñanza superior

NUMERO DE PAISES Y DE TERRITORIOS PRESENTADOS EN
ESTE CUADRO: 76

ANNUAL ADDITIONS ACQUISITIONS ANNUELLES ADQUISICIONES ANUALES		REGISTERED BORROWERS EM— PRUNTEURS INSCRITS PRESTA— TARIOS INSCRITOS	LOANS TO USERS PRETS AUX USAGERS PRESTAMOS A LOS USUARIOS	INTER— LIBRARY LOANS PRETS ENTRE BIBLIO— THEQUES PRESTAMOS ENTRE BIBLIO— TECAS	CURRENT EXPENDITURE DEPENSES ORDINAIRES GASTOS ORDINARIOS		LIBRARY EMPLOYEES PERSONNEL DES BIBLIOTHEQUES PERSONAL DE LAS BIBLIOTECAS		
VOLUMES VOLUMES VOLUMENES	OTHER MATERIALS AUTRES MATERIELS OTROS MATERIALES				TOTAL TOTAL TOTAL (000)	STAFF PERSON— NEL PER— SONAL (%)	TOTAL TOTAL TOTAL	HOLDING A DIPLOMA DIPLOME DIPLO— MADO	TRAINED ON THE JOB FORME SUR LE TAS FORMADO EN EJERCICIO
(8)	(9)	(10)	(11)	(12)	(13)	(14)	(15)	(16)	(17)
17 280	...	34 836	3 210	...	1 393	...	135	6	32
4 000	4	1 890	45 360	118	92	...	36	7	...
20	...	20	...	...	...	...	1	...	...
	...	...	...	...	...	...	980	...	...
26 987	...	9 622	142 339	...	769	76	160	18	32
330	...	265	10 600		...	...	1	1	−
37 855	...	7 641	149 383	...	8 871	41	223	39	−
14 862	...	5 747	159	...	42 000	36	51	6	1
5 899	...	3 308	45 000	25	177	41	68	12	−
...	...	...	149 621	4 203	6 493	48	1 533	370	1122
	...	40	...	...	...	...	1	−	1
9 330	...	...	96 724	...	3 321	57	171	16	4

7.3 Libraries of institutions of higher education
Bibliothèques d'établissements d'enseignement supérieur
Bibliotecas de instituciones de enseñanza superior

COUNTRY	YEAR			COLLECTIONS / COLLECTIONS / COLECCIONES				
		ADMINIS-TRATIVE UNITS	SERVICE POINTS	BOOKS/LIVRES/LIBROS		MICRO-FORMS	AUDIO-VISUAL DOCUMENTS	OTHER LIBRARY MATERIALS
				METRES OF SHELVING	NUMBER OF VOLUMES			
PAYS	ANNEE	UNITES ADMINIS-TRATIVES	POINTS DE DESSERTE	METRES DE RAYONNAGE	NOMBRE DE VOLUMES	MICRO-COPIES	MATERIELS AUDIO-VISUELS	AUTRES MATERIELS DE BIBLIOTHEQUE
PAIS	AÑO	UNIDADES ADMINIS-TRATIVAS	PUNTOS DE SERVICIO	METROS DE ESTANTES	NUMERO DE VOLUMENES (000)	MICRO-COPIAS	MATERIALES AUDIO-VISUALES	OTROS MATE-RIALES DE BIBLIOTECA
		(1)	(2)	(3)	(4)	(5)	(6)	(7)
AMERICA, NORTH								
BAHAMAS	1974	3	3	1 077	33	...	...	...
CANADA ‡	1977	255	...	...	43 60118	481 209	3 128 912	...
GUATEMALA ‡	1978	1	1	...	160	...	...	...
HONDURAS	1977	1	6	...	82	46	–	–
MEXICO	1974	190	190	8 771	1 511	...	...	...
NETHERLANDS ANTILLES	1974	1	...	125	4	...	...	...
PANAMA	1977	2	2	2 050	14	...	...	–
FORMER CANAL ZONE	1977	1	...	...	33	3 633	19 728	
PUERTO RICO ‡	1977	30	...	...	1 948	136 870	69 083	——>
TRINIDAD AND TOBAGO	1977	5	5	692	182	4 364	1 346	424 317
UNITED STATES OF AMERICA	1977	3 021	...	...	481 442	210 291	88 904	——>
U.S. VIRGIN ISLANDS	1977	1	...	...	60	169 719	65	——>
AMERICA, SOUTH								
ARGENTINA	1974	*29	35	*43 805	2 136		101 598	
CHILE ‡	1977	182	...	...	2 695	–	101 598	
SURINAME ‡	1978	2	5	1 027	29	–	–	–
ASIA								
BRUNEI ‡	1977	5	3	1 002	38	...	...	...
CYPRUS ‡	1977	1	1	1 054	21	...	...	...
HONG KONG ‡	1974	10	20	...	1 103	...	...	...
INDIA	1977	93	...	...	12 536	...	...	...
JAPAN	1977	1 112	1 283	...	106 414	...	...	...
JORDAN ‡	1974	15	15	...	251	...	...	...
KOREA, REPUBLIC OF ‡	1977	159	185	...	7 596	...	...	...
KUWAIT	1977	6	...	...	64	...	...	...
MALAYSIA ‡	1977	30	40	23 400	1 170	193 000	19 500	14 000
QATAR	1974	3	3	7 000	9	...	...	...
SINGAPORE	1974	5	15	23 136	975	...	...	...
SRI LANKA ‡	1977	5	14	13 646	540	730	...	...
SYRIAN ARAB REPUBLIC	1974	14	15	29 184	226	...	...	...
THAILAND	1974	85	92	88 510	1 297	...	...	...
UNITED ARAB EMIRATES‡	1977	4	9	4 343	17	...	...	...
EUROPE								
BULGARIA ‡	1977	25	...	...	3 062	1 709	...	298 888
CZECHOSLOVAKIA	1977	1 701	1 701	...	11 887	...	...	...
DENMARK ‡	1977	17	27	131 000	6 104	683 238	527 980	21 955
FINLAND ‡	1977	24	164	154 620	5 661	435 615	...	...
FRANCE ‡	1976	47	177	653 500	14 400	107 000	...	366 000
GERMAN DEMOCRATIC REPUBLIC ‡	1977	532	532	...	20 620	69 145	47 805	279 459
GERMANY, FEDERAL REPUBLIC OF ‡	1977	...	3 355	...	93 092	...	...	...
GIBRALTAR ‡	1978	1	1	66	5	...	1 000	...
HOLY SEE ‡	1977	12	9	126 887	1 503	192 142	10	...
HUNGARY ‡	1974	435	435	...	9 463	...	2 568 830	——>

Libraries of institutions of higher education   7.3
Bibliothèques d'établissements d'enseignement supérieur
Bibliotecas de instituciones de enseñanza superior

ANNUAL ADDITIONS ACQUISITIONS ANNUELLES ADQUISICIONES ANUALES		REGISTERED BORROWERS	LOANS TO USERS	INTER-LIBRARY LOANS	CURRENT EXPENDITURE DEPENSES ORDINAIRES GASTOS ORDINARIOS		LIBRARY EMPLOYEES PERSONNEL DES BIBLIOTHEQUES PERSONAL DE LAS BIBLIOTECAS		
VOLUMES	OTHER MATERIALS	EM-PRUNTEURS INSCRITS	PRETS AUX USAGERS	PRETS ENTRE BIBLIO-THEQUES	TOTAL	STAFF PERSON-NEL	TOTAL	HOLDING A DIPLOMA	TRAINED ON THE JOB
VOLUMES	AUTRES MATERIELS	PRESTA-TARIOS INSCRITOS	PRESTAMOS A LOS USUARIOS	PRESTAMOS ENTRE BIBLIO-TECAS	TOTAL (000)	PER-SONAL (%)	TOTAL DIPLO-MADO	DIPLOME DIPLO-MADO	FORME SUR LE TAS FORMADO EN EJERCICIO
VOLUMENES	OTROS MATERIALES								
(8)	(9)	(10)	(11)	(12)	(13)	(14)	(15)	(16)	(17)
4 000	...	1 600	6 100	...	46	71	9	2	4
2 661 390	...	...	...	...	168 163	65	8 079	...	...
2 738	...	40 000	...	...	240	87	23	8	—
9 069	46	7 849	197 767	240	346	63	57	9	4
475 125	...	3 340 190	...	...	6 220	26	596	...	...
100	...	...	100	...	13	23		—	—
2 662	...	15 546	272 719	19	181	97	67	10	2
1 998	...	./.	...	...	41	73	...	...	...
137 301	...	...	1 552 671	2 348	8 038	74	...	...	...
11 118	26 281	4 895	52 190	62	2 204	60	90	21	—
22 366 931	21 562 234	...	198 719 411	2 802 492	1 251 296	61	...	...	...
5 071	...	...	28 480	6	220	48	...	...	...
*14 875	...	*212 892	841 284	...	...	...	454	103	151
...	...	...	...	...	...	...	1 090	451	...
1 720	...	...	4 579	...	...	...	11	8	3
1 063	22	457	...	...	62	50	7	...	2
962	...	...	...	...	5	92	2	1	1
49 098	...	*9 580	477 869	...	8 058	59	153	44	19
540 087	...	...	...	...	*45 714	...	3 714	1 157	2557
6 353 928	...	...	13 161 867	331 500	65 815 510	...	10 167	4 896	...
28 227	...	10 452	60 000	...	155	37	126	18	84
311 616	...	4 357 321	...	...	2 211 342	18	1 400	558	...
5 000	...	...	...	...	...	...	24	8	3
190 000	...	44 000	2 066 000	1 113	10 320	44	749	146	...
4 700	...	550	11 300	...	...	...	4	3	1
42 483	...	23 281	1 198 438	...	2 712	49	204	37	2
19 278	...	7 184	235 765	...	3 401	46	206	16	7
8 687	...	55 393	207 753	...	...	...	100	18	21
124 956	...	294 636	496 893	...	15 898	53	468	114	128
1 216	...	608	...	...	...	...	45	4	...
192 159	24 264	79 658	1 874 672	...	1 447	36	313	214	99
434 459	...	242 793	...	...	...	...	...	...	...
253 995	92 157	...	775 859	239 275	109 173	...	798	338	...
247 410	44 920	...	1 036 310	76 248	34 021	52	514	219	—
437 500	11 780	440 000	3 400 000	133 634	68 000	8	3 056	1 275	...
478 548	20 106	212 899	4 661 524	117 631	...	...	1 809	968	24
1 678 472	5 830	719 342	11 263 098	1 297 504	263 501	54	5 519	...	...
18	50	385	1 190	...	8	...	...	...	...
20 427	79	4 798	16 899	322	178 519	37	41	16	15
344 827	102 569	112 334	2 219 583	23 784	75 362	...	1 121	222	241

7.3 Libraries of institutions of higher education
Bibliothèques d'établissements d'enseignement supérieur
Bibliotecas de instituciones de enseñanza superior

COUNTRY / PAYS / PAIS	YEAR / ANNEE / AÑO	ADMINIS- TRATIVE UNITS / UNITES ADMINIS- TRATIVES / UNIDADES ADMINIS- TRATIVAS	SERVICE POINTS / POINTS DE DESSERTE / PUNTOS DE SERVICIO	COLLECTIONS / COLLECTIONS / COLECCIONES				
				BOOKS/LIVRES/LIBROS		MICRO- FORMS / MICRO- COPIES / MICRO- COPIAS	AUDIO- VISUAL DOCUMENTS / MATERIELS AUDIO- VISUELS / MATERIALES AUDIO- VISUALES	OTHER LIBRARY MATERIALS / AUTRES MATERIELS DE BIBLIOTHEQUE / OTROS MATE- RIALES DE BIBLIOTECA
				METRES OF SHELVING / METRES DE RAYONNAGE / METROS DE ESTANTES	NUMBER OF VOLUMES / NOMBRE DE VOLUMES / NUMERO DE VOLUMENES (000)			
		(1)	(2)	(3)	(4)	(5)	(6)	(7)
ICELAND ‡	1974	2	10	*4 937	*91	...	...	...
IRELAND	1974	6	14	*51 980	1 648	...	...	...
MALTA	1977	2	4	...	197	2 224	192	—
NETHERLANDS ‡	1976	346	553	288 275	10 039	600 017	...	...
NORWAY ‡	1977	54	...	...	7 475	...	...	...
POLAND ‡	1977	89	931	...	30 484	249 000	216 000	6 621 000
PORTUGAL ‡	1977	173	...	...	1 998	...	...	...
ROMANIA	1974	46	...	...	15 028	...	...	...
SPAIN	1977	323	721	250 031	6 687	6 462	25 714	—
SWEDEN ‡	1977	9	9	235 379	...	...	...	...
UNITED KINGDOM ‡	1976	...	...	1 345 651	47 961	...	...	...
YUGOSLAVIA ‡	1977	425	448	177 972	9 646	21 036	10 089	538 513
OCEANIA								
AMERICAN SAMOA ‡	1977	1	...	...	12	17 276	1 205	——>
AUSTRALIA ‡	1977	92	...	...	16 311	...	...	...
COOK ISLANDS	1974	2	2	414	15	...	...	...
FIJI	1977	1	1	*5 213	...	1 200	10	...
KIRIBATI	1974	3	3	230	10	...	...	...
NEW ZEALAND	1974	34	34	124 039	2 743	...	...	...
NIUE	1974	1	1	14	1	...	...	...
PACIFIC ISLANDS	1977	3	3	...	15	...	...	...
SAMOA	1978	1	1	300	10	10	3	4
SOLOMON ISLANDS	1974	2	2	158	6	...	...	...
TONGA	1978	2	—	...	6	—	—	—
U.S.S.R.								
UKRAINIAN S.S.R.	1974	141	190	...	67 430	...	...	...

BURUNDI:
E—> THE FIGURE IN COLUMN 13 REFERS TO EXPENDITURE FOR EMPLOYEES ONLY.
FR-> LE CHIFFRE DE LA COLONNE 13 SE RAPPORTE AUX DEPENSES POUR LE PERSONNEL SEULEMENT.
ESP> LA CIFRA DE LA COLUMNA 13 SE REFIERE A LOS GASTOS DE PERSONAL SOLAMENTE.

COMORO:
E—> COLUMN 15 DOES NOT INCLUDE FULL—TIME STAFF.
FR-> LA COLONNE 15 N'INCLUT PAS LE PERSONNEL EMPLOYE A PLEIN TEMPS.
ESP> LA COLUMNA 15 NO TOMA EN CONSIDERACION EL PERSONAL DE JORNADA COMPLETA.

EGYPT:
E—> COLUMN 15 REFERS TO FULL—TIME STAFF ONLY.
FR-> LA COLONNE 15 NE TIENT COMPTE QUE DU PERSONNEL EMPLOYE A PLEIN TEMPS.
ESP> LA COLUMNA 15 NO TOMA EN CONSIDERACION EL PERSONAL DE JORNADA COMPLETA.

MADAGASCAR:
E—> THE FIGURES IN COLUMNS 11 AND 13 REFER ONLY TO 1 LIBRARY WITH 3 SERVICE POINTS.
FR-> LES CHIFFRES DES COLONNES 11 ET 13 NE CONCERNENT QU'UNE BIBLIOTHEQUE AVEC 3 POINTS DE DESSERTE.
ESP> LAS CIFRAS DE LAS COLUMNAS 11 Y 13 SOLO SE REFIEREN A UNA BIBLIOTECA CON 3 PUNTOS DE SERVICIO.

CANADA:
E—> COLUMN 4 INCLUDES PERIODICALS, GOVERNMENT DOCUMENTS AND TECHNICAL REPORTS.
FR-> LA COLONNE 4 INCLUT LES PERIODIQUES, LES DOCUMENTS PUBLICS ET LES RAPPORTS TECHNIQUES.
ESP> LA COLUMNA 4 INCLUYE LOS PERIODICOS, LOS DOCUMENTOS OFICIALES Y LOS INFORMES TECNICOS.

Libraries of institutions of higher education 7.3
Bibliothèques d'établissements d'enseignement supérieur
Bibliotecas de instituciones de enseñanza superior

ANNUAL ADDITIONS / ACQUISITIONS ANNUELLES / ADQUISICIONES ANUALES		REGISTERED BORROWERS / EMPRUNTEURS INSCRITS / PRESTATARIOS INSCRITOS	LOANS TO USERS / PRETS AUX USAGERS / PRESTAMOS A LOS USUARIOS	INTERLIBRARY LOANS / PRETS ENTRE BIBLIOTHEQUES / PRESTAMOS ENTRE BIBLIOTECAS	CURRENT EXPENDITURE / DEPENSES ORDINAIRES / GASTOS ORDINARIOS		LIBRARY EMPLOYEES / PERSONNEL DES BIBLIOTHEQUES / PERSONAL DE LAS BIBLIOTECAS		
VOLUMES / VOLUMES / VOLUMENES	OTHER MATERIALS / AUTRES MATERIELS / OTROS MATERIALES				TOTAL / TOTAL / TOTAL (000)	STAFF / PERSONNEL / PERSONAL (%)	TOTAL / TOTAL / TOTAL	HOLDING A DIPLOMA / DIPLOME / DIPLOMADO	TRAINED ON THE JOB / FORME SUR LE TAS / FORMADO EN EJERCICIO
(8)	(9)	(10)	(11)	(12)	(13)	(14)	(15)	(16)	(17)
*5 233	...	*1 800	12 500	...	16	63	11	7	2
...	...	*6 901	...	...	*516	65	188	35	—
11 400	5	3 049	59 464	...	88	36	28	5	4
455 663	65 742	...	2 433 771	257 933	...	...	1 324	540	316
322 487	...	...	...	...	26 771	...	689	440	...
1 700	...	785 000	6 667 000	...	293 871	...	...	...	...
46 916	...	548 879	1 144 959	...	45 818	...	320	...	...
830 377	...	193 199	...	...	...	...	...	...	...
314 860	5 396	229 576	862 567	13 367	315 125	44	816	216	590
193 018	...	...	1 112 975	92 383	63 724	66	709	150	...
			...	...	28 147	...			
285 771	3 499	498 612	...	... 126	471 030	...	977	767	44
4 523	...	...	2 461	83	44	...	...	...	...
1 232 000	...	354 000	12 565 000	224 000	70 018	61	3 889	1 119	744
600	...	1 750	...	...	...	...	2	—	1
16 380	45	2 547	88 270	245	317	71	49	12	7
1 900	...	620	...	...	*4	—	3	—	3
209 279	...	115 916	1 538 140	...	4 094	56	819	220	...
52	...	...	...	...	...	...	...	1	1
...	...	...	...	...	...	...	6	2	4
4	80	150	350	...	...	...	...	...	...
70	...	786	...	...	...	...	2	—	—
...	...	250	...	...	...	...	2	1	—
4 196 000	...	968 800	83 670 700	...	...	...	4 095	2 809	1286

GUATEMALA:
E—> COLUMNS 4 AND 8 SHOW THE NUMBER OF TITLES AND NOT THE NUMBER OF VOLUMES; THE FIGURES IN COLUMNS 15 AND 16 REFER TO FULL—TIME STAFF ONLY.
FR—> LES COLONNES 4 ET 8 INDIQUENT LE NOMBRE DE TITRES ET NON LE NOMBRE DE VOLUMES; LES CHIFFRES DES COLONNES 15 ET 16 SE RAPPORTENT AU PERSONNEL EMPLOYE A PLEIN TEMPS SEULEMENT.
ESP> LAS COLUMNAS 4 Y 8 INDICAN EL NUMERO DE TITULOS Y NO EL NUMERO DE VOLUMENES. LAS CIFRAS DE LAS COLUMNAS 15 Y 16 SOLO SE REFIEREN AL PERSONAL DE JORNADA COMPLETA.

PANAMA:
E—> THE DATA IN COLUMN 4 CONCERN ONLY 1 LIBRARY.
FR—> LES DONNEES DE LA COLONNE 4 SE REFERENT A 1 BIBLIOTHEQUE SEULEMENT.
ESP> LOS DATOS DE LA COLUMNA 4 SE REFIEREN A 1 BIBLIOTECA SOLAMENTE.

PUERTO RICO:
E—> COLUMNS 11 AND 13 REFER TO 17 LIBRARIES AND COLUMN 12 TO 20 LIBRARIES ONLY.
FR—> LES COLONNES 11 ET 13 SE RAPPORTENT A 17 BIBLIOTHEQUES; LA COLONNE 12 A 20 BIBLIOTHEQUES.
ESP> LAS COLUMNAS 11 Y 13 SE REFIEREN A 17 BIBLIOTECAS; LA COLUMNA 12 A 20 BIBLIOTECAS.

CHILE:
E—> THE FIGURES IN COLUMNS 15 AND 16 REFER TO FULL—TIME STAFF ONLY.
FR—> LES CHIFFRES DES COLONNES 15 ET 16 NE TIENNENT COMPTE QUE DU PERSONNEL EMPLOYE A PLEIN TEMPS.
ESP> LAS CIFRAS DE LAS COLUMNAS 15 Y 16 SOLO TOMAN EN CONSIDERACION AL PERSONAL DE JORNADA COMPLETA.

7.3 Libraries of institutions of higher education
Bibliothèques d'établissements d'enseignement supérieur
Bibliotecas de instituciones de enseñanza superior

SURINAME:
 E—> THE FIGURES IN COLUMNS 15, 16 AND 17 REFER TO FULL-TIME STAFF ONLY.
 FR-> LES CHIFFRES DES COLONNES 15, 16 ET 17 NE TIENNENT COMPTE QUE DU PERSONNEL EMPLOYE A PLEIN TEMPS.
 ESP> LAS CIFRAS DE LAS COLUMNAS 15, 16 Y 17 SOLO TOMAN EN CONSIDERACION AL PERSONAL DE JORNADA COMPLETA.

BRUNEI:
 E—> THE FIGURES IN COLUMNS 15 AND 17 REFER TO FULL-TIME STAFF ONLY.
 FR-> LES CHIFFRES DES COLONNES 15 ET 17 SE REFERENT SEULEMENT AU PERSONNEL EMPLOYE A PLEIN TEMPS.
 ESP> LAS CIFRAS DE LAS COLUMNAS 15 Y 17 SE REFIEREN AL PERSONAL DE JORNADA COMPLETA SOLAMENTE.

CYPRUS:
 E—> THE FIGURES IN COLUMNS 15, 16 AND 17 REFER TO FULL-TIME STAFF ONLY.
 FR-> LES CHIFFRES DES COLONNES 15, 16 ET 17 SE REFERENT SEULEMENT AU PERSONNEL EMPLOYE A PLEIN TEMPS.
 ESP> LAS CIFRAS DE LAS COLUMNAS 15, 16 Y 17 SE REFIEREN AL PERSONAL DE JORNADA COMPLETA SOLAMENTE.

HONG KONG:
 E—> DATA IN COLUMN 13 REFER ONLY TO 3 LIBRAIRIES WITH 6 SERVICES POINTS.
 FR-> LES DONNEES DE LA COLONNE 13 SE RAPPORTENT SEULEMENT A 3 BIBLIOTHEQUES AVEC 6 POINTS DE DESSERTE.
 ESP> LOS DATOS DE LA COLUMNA 13 SOLO SE REFIEREN A 3 BIBLIOTECAS CON 6 PUNTOS DE SERVICIO.

JORDAN:
 E—> DATA REFER TO THE EAST BANK ONLY.
 FR-> LES DONNEES SE REFERENT A LA RIVE ORIENTALE SEULEMENT.
 ESP> LOS DATOS SE REFIEREN A LA ORILLA ORIENTAL SOLAMENTE.

KOREA, REPUBLIC OF:
 E—> DATA DO NOT INCLUDE LIBRARIES ATTACHED TO INSTITUTES OR DEPARTMENTS. THE FIGURES IN COLUMNS 13, 15 AND 16 REFER TO 157 LIBRARIES ONLY.
 FR-> LES DONNEES N'INCLUENT PAS LES BIBLIOTHEQUES RATTACHEES AUX INSTITUTS OU AUX DEPARTEMENTS. LES CHIFFRES DES COLONNES 13, 15 ET 16 CONCERNENT 157 BIBLIOTHEQUES SEULEMENT.
 ESP> LOS DATOS NO INCLUYEN LAS BIBLIOTECAS DEPENDIENTES DE LOS INSTITUTOS O DEPARTAMENTOS. LAS CIFRAS DE LAS COLUMNAS 13, 15 Y 16 SE REFIEREN A 157 BIBLIOTECAS SOLAMENTE.

MALAYSIA:
 E—> DATA REFER TO UNIVERSITY LIBRARIES ONLY. COLUMNS 15 AND 16 DO NOT INCLUDE PART-TIME STAFF.
 FR-> LES DONNEES NE SE REFERENT QU'AUX BIBLIOTHEQUES UNIVERSITAIRES. LES COLONNES 15 ET 16 N'INCLUENT PAS LE PERSONNEL EMPLOYE A TEMPS PARTIEL.
 ESP> LOS DATOS SOLO CONCIERNEN LAS BIBLIOTECAS UNIVERSITARIAS. LAS COLUMNAS 15 Y 16 NO INCLUYEN EL PERSONAL DE JORNADA PARCIAL.

SRI LANKA:
 E—> DATA REFER TO UNIVERSITY LIBRARIES ONLY.
 FR-> LES DONNEES SE REFERENT AUX BIBLIOTHEQUES UNIVERSITAIRES SEULEMENT.
 ESP> LOS DATOS SE REFIEREN A LAS BIBLIOTECAS UNIVERSITARIAS SOLAMENTE.

UNITED ARAB EMIRATES:
 E—> THE FIGURES IN COLUMNS 15 AND 16 REFER TO FULL-TIME ONLY.
 FR-> LES CHIFFRES DES COLONNES 15 ET 16 SE RAPPORTENT AU PERSONNEL EMPLOYE A PLEIN TEMPS SEULEMENT.
 ESP> LAS CIFRAS DE LAS COLUMNAS 15 Y 16 SE REFIEREN AL PERSONAL DE JORNADA COMPLETA SOLAMENTE.

BULGARIA:
 E—> THE FIGURE ON ACQUISITIONS IN COLUMN 9 DOES NOT INCLUDE AUDIO-VISUAL DOCUMENTS ONLY.
 FR-> LE CHIFFRE RELATIF AUX ACQUISITIONS, DANS LA COLONNE 9, N'INCLUT PAS LES MATERIELS AUDIO-VISUELS.
 ESP> LA CIFRA DE LA COLUMNA 9 RELATIVA A LAS ADQUISICIONES NO INCLUYE LOS MATERIALES AUDIO-VISUALES.

DENMARK:
 E—> THE DATA DO NOT INCLUDE 400 LIBRARIES ATTACHED TO INSTITUTES OR DEPARTMENTS AND 19 LIBRARIES FOR WHICH DATA ARE NOT AVAILABLE. THE FIGURE IN COLUMN 13 COMPRISES ONLY EXPENDITURE FOR EMPLOYEES AND FOR ACQUISITIONS.
 FR-> LES DONNEES N'INCLUENT PAS 400 BIBLIOTHEQUES RATTACHEES AUX INSTITUTS OU AUX DEPARTEMENTS ET 19 BIBLIOTHEQUES POUR LESQUELLES LES STATISTIQUES NE SONT PAS DISPONIBLES. LE CHIFFRE DE LA COLONNE 13 COMPREND SEULEMENT LES DEPENSES POUR LE PERSONNEL ET LES ACQUISITIONS.
 ESP> LOS DATOS NO INCLUYEN 400 BIBLIOTECAS DEPENDIENTES DE LOS INSTITUTOS O DEPARTAMENTOS Y 19 BIBLIOTECAS PARA LAS QUE NO SE DISPONE DE DATOS. LA CIFRA DE LA COLUMNA 13 INCLUYE SOLAMENTE LOS GASTOS PARA EL PERSONAL Y LAS ADQUISICIONES.

FINLAND:
 E—> THE DATA ON ACQUISITIONS IN COLUMN 9 REFER TO MICROFORMS ONLY.
 FR-> DANS LA COLONNE 9, LES DONNEES RELATIVES AUX ACQUISITIONS TIENNENT COMPTE DES MICROCOPIES SEULEMENT.
 ESP> EN LA COLUMNA 9, LOS DATOS RELATIVOS A LAS ADQUISICIONES SOLO SE REFIEREN A LAS MICROCOPIAS.

FRANCE:
 E—> DATA REFER TO UNIVERSITY LIBRARIES ONLY. THE FIGURES IN COLUMNS 15 AND 16 DO NOT INCLUDE PART-TIME STAFF.
 FR-> LES DONNEES SE RAPPORTENT AUX BIBLIOTHEQUES UNIVERSITAIRES SEULEMENT. LES CHIFFRES DES COLONNES 15 ET 16 N'INCLUENT PAS LE PERSONNEL EMPLOYE A TEMPS PARTIEL.
 ESP> LOS DATOS SE REFIEREN A LAS BIBLIOTECAS UNIVERSITARIAS SOLAMENTE. LAS CIFRAS DE LAS COLUMNAS 15 Y 16 NO INCLUYEN EL PERSONAL DE JORNADA PARCIAL.

GERMAN DEMOCRATIC REPUBLIC:
 E—> THE FIGURES IN COLUMNS 15, 16 AND 17 REFER TO FULL-TIME STAFF ONLY.
 FR-> LES CHIFFRES DES COLONNES 15, 16 ET 17 SE REFERENT AU PERSONNEL EMPLOYE A PLEIN TEMPS SEULEMENT.
 ESP> LAS CIFRAS DE LAS COLUMNAS 15, 16 Y 17 SE REFIEREN AL PERSONAL DE JORNADA COMPLETA SOLAMENTE.

Libraries of institutions of higher education   7.3
Bibliothèques d'établissements d'enseignement supérieur
Bibliotecas de instituciones de enseñanza superior

GERMANY, FEDERAL REPUBLIC OF:
   E—> DATA OTHER THAN THOSE ON THE NUMBER OF
SERVICE POINTS AND ON THE NUMBER OF VOLUMES
REFER TO UNIVERSITY LIBRARIES ONLY. THE DATA
ON ACQUISITIONS IN COLUMN 9 CONCERN AUDITORY
MATERIALS ONLY. COLUMN 12 DOES NOT INCLUDE
LIBRARY LOAN TRANSACTIONS ON THE INTERNATIONAL
LEVEL. THE FIGURE IN COLUMN 15 REFERS TO
FULL—TIME STAFF ONLY.
   FR—> A L'EXCEPTION DU NOMBRE DE POINTS DE
DESSERTE ET DU NOMBRE DE VOLUMES, LES DONNEES SE
REFERENT AUX BIBLIOTHEQUES UNIVERSITAIRES
SEULEMENT. COLONNE 9, LES DONNEES RELATIVES AUX
ACQUISITIONS CONCERNENT LES MATERIELS AUDITIFS
SEULEMENT. LA COLONNE 12 N'INCLUT PAS LES PRETS
ENTRE BIBLIOTHEQUES AU NIVEAU INTERNATIONAL.
LE CHIFFRE DE LA COLONNE 15 SE RAPPORTE AU
PERSONNEL EMPLOYE A PLEIN TEMPS SEULEMENT.
   ESP> SALVO EN LO QUE CONCIERNE EL NUMERO DE
PUNTOS DE SERVICIO Y EL NUMERO DE VOLUMENES,
LOS DATOS SE REFIEREN A LAS BIBLIOTECAS
UNIVERSITARIAS SOLAMENTE. EN LA COLUMNA 9, LOS
DATOS RELATIVOS A LAS ADQUISICIONES SOLO
COMPRENDEN LOS MATERIALES AUDITIVOS. LA COLUMNA
12 NO INCLUYE LOS PRESTAMOS ENTRE BIBLIOTECAS A
NIVEL INTERNACIONAL. LA CIFRA DE LA COLUMNA 15
SE REFIERE AL PERSONAL DE JORNADA COMPLETA
SOLAMENTE.

GIBRALTAR:
   E—> THE FIGURE IN COLUMN 13 REFERS ONLY TO
EXPENDITURE FOR ACQUISITIONS.
   FR—> LE CHIFFRE DE LA COLONNE 13 SE REFERE
SEULEMENT AUX DEPENSES POUR LES ACQUISITIONS.
   ESP> LA CIFRA DE LA COLUMNA 13 SE REFIERE A
LOS GASTOS RELATIVOS A LAS ADQUISICIONES
SOLAMENTE.

HOLY SEE:
   E—> THE DATA IN COLUMNS 5 AND 6 CONCERN 10
LIBRARIES ONLY. COLUMN 9 REFERS TO 7 LIBRARIES
AND COLUMN 11 TO 9 LIBRARIES ONLY.
   FR—> LES DONNEES DES COLONNES 5 ET 6 CONCERNENT
10 BIBLIOTHEQUES SEULEMENT, LA COLONNE 9 SE
REFERE A 7 BIBLIOTHEQUES ET LA COLONNE 11, A 9
SEULEMENT.
   ESP> LOS DATOS DE LAS COLUMNAS 5 Y 6 SE REFIEREN
A 10 BIBLIOTECAS SOLAMENTE, LOS DE LA COLUMNA 9 A
7 BIBLIOTECAS Y LOS DE LA COLUMNA 11 A 9
BIBLIOTECAS.

HUNGARY:
   E—> THE FIGURE ON ACQUISITIONS IN COLUMN 9 DOES
NOT INCLUDE MICROFORMS, COLUMN 13 REFERS TO
EXPENDITURE FOR ACQUISITIONS ONLY. COLUMNS 15, 16
AND 17 REFLECT ONLY FULL—TIME STAFF.
   FR—> DANS LA COLONNE 9, LES DONNEES RELATIVES
AUX ACQUISITIONS NE TIENNENT PAS COMPTE DES
MICROCOPIES. LA COLONNE 13 SE RAPPORTE AUX
DEPENSES POUR LES ACQUISITIONS SEULEMENT. LES
COLONNES 15, 16 ET 17 COMPRENNENT SEULEMENT LE
PERSONNEL EMPLOYE A PLEIN TEMPS.
   ESP> EN LA COLUMNA 9, LOS DATOS RELATIVOS A LAS
ADQUISICIONES NO COMPRENDEN LAS MICROCOPIAS. LA
COLUMNA 13 SOLO INCLUYE LOS GASTOS PARA LAS
ADQUISICIONES. LOS DATOS DE LAS COLUMNAS 15, 16
Y 17 SE REFIEREN AL PERSONAL DE JORNADA COMPLETA
SOLAMENTE.

ICELAND:
   E—> THE DATA IN COLUMN 12 CONCERN 1 LIBRARY
WITH 9 SERVICE POINTS.
   FR—> LES DONNEES DE LA COLONNE 12 CONCERNENT
1 BIBLIOTHEQUE AVEC 9 POINTS DE DESSERTE.
   ESP> LOS DATOS DE LA COLUMNA 12 SE REFIEREN A 1
BIBLIOTECA CON 9 PUNTOS DE SERVICIO.

NETHERLANDS:
   E—> ACQUISITIONS IN COLUMN 9 CONCERN ONLY
MICROFORMS. THE FIGURE IN COLUMN 11 INCLUDES
BESIDES LOANS TO USERS, ITEMS COPIED TO TAKE THE
PLACE OF ORIGINAL MATERIALS.
   FR—> LES DONNEES RELATIVES AUX ACQUISITIONS,
COLONNE 9, SE RAPPORTENT SEULEMENT AUX
MICROCOPIES. LE CHIFFRE DE LA COLONNE 11
COMPREND, EN PLUS DES LIVRES PRETES AUX USAGERS,
LE NOMBRE D'UNITES COPIEES FOURNIES A LA PLACE
DE DOCUMENTS ORIGINAUX.
   ESP> LOS DATOS DE LA COLUMNA 9 RELATIVOS A LAS
ADQUISICIONES SE REFIEREN SOLAMENTE A LAS
MICROCOPIAS. LA CIFRA DE LA COLUMNA 11 COMPRENDE,
ADEMAS DE LOS LIBROS PRESTADOS A LOS USUARIOS, EL
NUMERO DE COPIAS FACILITADAS EN SUSTITUCION DE LOS
DOCUMENTOS ORIGINALES.

NORWAY:
   E—> THE FIGURE IN COLUMN 13 DOES NOT INCLUDE
EXPENDITURE FOR EMPLOYEES.
   FR—> LE CHIFFRE DE LA COLONNE 13 N'INCLUT PAS
LES DEPENSES POUR LE PERSONNEL.
   ESP> LA CIFRA DE LA COLUMNA 13 NO COMPRENDE
LOS GASTOS DE PERSONAL.

POLAND:
   E—> THE FIGURE IN COLUMN 13 DOES NOT INCLUDE
EXPENDITURE FOR EMPLOYEES.
   FR—> LE CHIFFRE DE LA COLONNE 13 N'INCLUT PAS
LES DEPENSES POUR LE PERSONNEL.
   ESP> LA CIFRA DE LA COLUMNA 13 NO COMPRENDE
LOS GASTOS DE PERSONAL.

PORTUGAL:
   E—> COLUMN 11 REFERS TO WORKS USED IN READING
ROOMS ONLY. THE FIGURE IN COLUMN 13 COMPRISES
EXPENDITURE FOR EMPLOYEES AND FOR ACQUISITIONS.
COLUMN 15 DOES NOT INCLUDE PART—TIME STAFF.
   FR—> LA COLONNE 11 TIENT COMPTE SEULEMENT DES
OUVRAGES UTILISES DANS LES SALLES DE LECTURE. LE
CHIFFRE DE LA COLONNE 13 COMPREND LES DEPENSES
POUR LE PERSONNEL ET LES ACQUISITIONS. LA COLONNE
15 N'INCLUT PAS LE PERSONNEL EMPLOYE A TEMPS
PARTIEL.
   ESP> LA COLUMNA 11 TOMA SOLAMENTE EN
CONSIDERACION LAS OBRAS UTILIZADAS EN LAS SALAS DE
LECTURA. LA CIFRA DE LA COLUMNA 13 COMPRENDE LOS
GASTOS RELATIVOS AL PERSONAL Y A LAS ADQUISICIONES.
LA COLUMNA 15 NO INCLUYE EL PERSONAL DE JORNADA
PARCIAL.

SWEDEN:
   E—> THE FIGURES IN COLUMNS 15 AND 16 CONCERN
ONLY FULL—TIME STAFF.
   FR—> LES CHIFFRES DES COLONNES 15 ET 16
CONCERNENT SEULEMENT LE PERSONNEL EMPLOYE A PLEIN
TEMPS.
   ESP> LAS CIFRAS DE LAS COLUMNAS 15 Y 16 SOLO SE
REFIEREN AL PERSONAL DE JORNADA COMPLETA.

UNITED KINGDOM:
   E—> THE FIGURE IN COLUMN 13 REFERS TO
EXPENDITURE FOR EMPLOYEES ONLY.
   FR—> LE CHIFFRE DE LA COLONNE 13 SE REFERE AUX
DEPENSES POUR LE PERSONNEL SEULEMENT.
   ESP> LA CIFRA DE LA COLUMNA 13 SE REFIERE A LOS
GASTOS DE PERSONAL SOLAMENTE.

YUGOSLAVIA:
   E—> COLUMN 6 REFERS TO AUDITORY MATERIALS ONLY.
COLUMN 9 CONCERNS ONLY MICROFORMS. THE DATA IN
COLUMN 13 REFER TO EXPENDITURE FOR ACQUISITIONS
(IN MILLIONS). COLUMNS 15, 16 AND 17 DO NOT
INCLUDE PART—TIME STAFF.

7.3   **Libraries of institutions of higher education**
Bibliothèques d'établissements d'enseignement supérieur
Bibliotecas de instituciones de enseñanza superior

YUGOSLAVIA (CONT):
   FR—> LA COLONNE 6 SE RAPPORTE AUX MATERIELS
AUDITIFS SEULEMENT. LA COLONNE 9 NE TIENT COMPTE
QUE DES MICROCOPIES. LES DONNEES DE LA COLONNE
13 SE REFERENT AUX DEPENSES POUR LES ACQUISITIONS
(EN MILLIONS). LES COLONNES 15, 16 ET 17
N'INCLUENT PAS LE PERSONNEL EMPLOYE A TEMPS
PARTIEL.
   ESP> LOS DATOS DE LA COLUMNA 6 SE REFIEREN
SOLAMENTE A LOS MATERIALES AUDITIVOS. EN LA
COLUMNA 9 SOLO SE TOMAN EN CONSIDERACION LAS
MICROCOPIAS. LA CIFRA DE LA COLUMNA 13 SE REFIERE
A LOS GASTOS RELATIVOS A LAS ADQUISICIONES (EN
MILLONES). LAS COLUMNAS 15, 16 Y 17 NO INCLUYEN
EL PERSONAL DE JORNADA PARCIAL.

AMERICAN SAMOA:
   E—> NOT INCLUDED IN COLUMN 13 IS EXPENDITURE
FOR EMPLOYEES.
   FR—> LES DEPENSES POUR LE PERSONNEL NE SONT PAS
INCLUSES DANS LA COLONNE 13.
   ESP> LA COLUMNA 13 NO INCLUYE LOS GASTOS DE
PERSONAL.

AUSTRALIA:
   E—> ONLY FULL—TIME STAFF IS GIVEN IN COLUMNS
16 AND 17.
   FR—> LES COLONNES 16 ET 17 INDIQUENT SEULEMENT
LE PERSONNEL EMPLOYE A PLEIN TEMPS.
   ESP> LAS COLUMNAS 16 Y 17 SOLO COMPRENDEN EL
PERSONAL DE JORNADA COMPLETA.

7.4 School libraries: collections, borrowers, works loaned out, current expenditure, personnel

Bibliothèques scolaires: collections, emprunteurs inscrits, documents prêtès au-dehors, dépenses ordinaires, personnel

Bibliotecas escolares: colecciones, prestatarios inscritos, documentos prestados al exterior, gastos ordinarios, personal

NUMBER OF COUNTRIES AND TERRITORIES PRESENTED IN THIS TABLE: 56

NOMBRE DE PAYS ET DE TERRITOIRES PRESENTES DANS CE TABLEAU: 56

COUNTRY / PAYS / PAIS	YEAR / ANNEE / AÑO	ADMINIS-TRATIVE UNITS / UNITES ADMINIS-TRATIVES / UNIDADES ADMINIS-TRATIVAS	SERVICE POINTS / POINTS DE DESSERTE / PUNTOS DE SERVICIO	COLLECTIONS / COLLECTIONS / COLECCIONES				
				BOOKS/LIVRES/LIBROS		MICRO-FORMS / MICRO-COPIES / MICRO-COPIAS	AUDIO-VISUAL DOCUMENTS / MATERIELS AUDIO-VISUELS / MATERIALES AUDIO-VISUALES	OTHER LIBRARY MATERIALS / AUTRES MATERIELS DE BIBLIOTHEQUE / OTROS MATE-RIALES DE BIBLIOTECA
				METRES OF SHELVING / METRES DE RAYONNAGE / METROS DE ESTANTES	NUMBER OF VOLUMES / NOMBRE DE VOLUMES / NUMERO DE VOLUMENES (000)			
		(1)	(2)	(3)	(4)	(5)	(6)	(7)
AFRICA								
COMORO	1975	2	2	...	5			
DJIBOUTI	1975	3	3	75	7	...	...	...
GAMBIA ‡	1978	129	129	700		...	...	...
MALAWI ‡	1977	74	74	...	254	...	...	...
ST. HELENA ‡	1974	12	12	120	3	—	—	—
SEYCHELLES	1974	4	4	642	28	...	...	...
AMERICA, NORTH								
BAHAMAS	1974	130	130	2 418	65	...	...	...
BARBADOS	1977	2	2	267	29	...	...	...
BELIZE	1974	1	30		2	...	...	...
BERMUDA	1974	21	...	4 166	166	...	...	...
BRITISH VIRGIN ISLANDS	1974	1	10	...	...	...	...	...

NUMERO DE PAISES Y DE TERRITORIOS PRESENTADOS EN
ESTE CUADRO: 56

ANNUAL ADDITIONS ACQUISITIONS ANNUELLES ADQUISICIONES ANUALES		REGISTERED BORROWERS	LOANS TO USERS	CURRENT EXPENDITURE DEPENSES ORDINAIRES GASTOS ORDINARIOS		LIBRARY EMPLOYEES PERSONNEL DES BIBLIOTHEQUES PERSONAL DE LAS BIBLIOTECAS			POPULATION SERVED
VOLUMES	OTHER MATERIALS			TOTAL	STAFF	TOTAL	HOLDING A DIPLOMA	TRAINED ON THE JOB	POPULATION DESSERVIE
VOLUMES	AUTRES MATERIELS	EM— PRUNTEURS INSCRITS	PRETS AUX USAGERS	TOTAL	PERSON— NEL	TOTAL	DIPLOME	FORME SUR LE TAS	
VOLUMENES	OTROS MATERIALES	PRESTA— TARIOS INSCRITOS	PRESTAMOS A LOS USUARIOS	TOTAL (000)	PER— SONAL (%)	TOTAL	DIPLOMADO	FORMADO EN EJERCICIO	POBLACION SERVIDA (%)
(8)	(9)	(10)	(11)	(12)	(13)	(14)	(15)	(16)	(17)
		150	1 500	1 940	99	4	...	...	...
324	...	6 587	...	4 100	88	3	—	3	48
500	...	35 196	5 525	9	...	...	...	100	100
6 850	—	17 900	...	14	...	...	...	...	100
50	...	700	...	...	...	12	—	12	100
1 890	...	1 022	—	...	...	1	...	...	30
3 500	...	41 278	156 180	108	93	25	2	23	67
4 978	...	10 024	...	...	...	...	...	...	...
100	...	...	...	...	13	...	...	...	100
...	...	9 868	...	...	...	...	...	...	...
800	...	...	...	...	...	...	...	...	...

COUNTRY	YEAR	ADMINISTRATIVE UNITS	SERVICE POINTS	COLLECTIONS / COLLECTIONS / COLECCIONES				
				BOOKS/LIVRES/LIBROS		MICROFORMS	AUDIOVISUAL DOCUMENTS	OTHER LIBRARY MATERIALS
				METRES OF SHELVING	NUMBER OF VOLUMES			
PAYS	ANNEE	UNITES ADMINISTRATIVES	POINTS DE DESSERTE	METRES DE RAYONNAGE	NOMBRE DE VOLUMES	MICROCOPIES	MATERIELS AUDIOVISUELS	AUTRES MATERIELS DE BIBLIOTHEQUE
PAIS	AÑO	UNIDADES ADMINISTRATIVAS	PUNTOS DE SERVICIO	METROS DE ESTANTES	NUMERO DE VOLUMENES (000)	MICROCOPIAS	MATERIALES AUDIOVISUALES	OTROS MATERIALES DE BIBLIOTECA
		(1)	(2)	(3)	(4)	(5)	(6)	(7)
CANADA ‡	1977	8 692	8 692	...	49 412	75 042	6 892 830	2 813 381
GREENLAND	1974	1	24	...	72	...	...	...
GUATEMALA	1974	1	3	75	4	...	...	...
MEXICO	1974	1 004	1 004	14 378	2 132	...	...	...
PANAMA	1977	54	54	1 610	203	5 726	—	—
ST. LUCIA	1974	1	1	...	14			
ST. PIERRE AND MIQUELON ‡	1974	1	1	...	2	...	...	...
UNITED STATES OF AMERICA ‡	1974	74 625	...	...	507 000	...		...
AMERICA, SOUTH								
PERU ‡	1977	81	93	...	272	...	3 243	3
SURINAME	1978	3	49	1 425	60	—	—	—
VENEZUELA ‡	1978	46	...	...	105	...	144	1 820
ASIA								
BRUNEI ‡	1977	13	13	1 956	59	...	...	...
EAST TIMOR	1974	1	...	...	2	...	...	...
JAPAN ‡	1977	41 163	41 163	...	200 792	...	...	...
JORDAN ‡	1974	954	...	...	...	...	...	...
KOREA, REPUBLIC OF ‡	1977	3 954	3 954	...	11 327	...	...	...
KUWAIT	1977	...	326	...	1 610	...	...	...
MALAYSIA ‡	1977	...	...	...	5	...	...	...
QATAR	1974	69	...	115 600	154	...	...	...
SAUDI ARABIA ‡	1974	2 188	...	58 100	5 436	...	...	...
SINGAPORE	1974	363	...	74 754	2 244	...	...	...
SRI LANKA ‡	1974	595	595	31 015	1 319	...	...	...
THAILAND	1974	240	240	22 873	153	...	...	...
EUROPE								
BULGARIA ‡	1977	3 700	...	...	13 224	228	...	105 963
FINLAND ‡	1977	5 420	5 420	...	7 500	...	...	...
GIBRALTAR ‡	1978	10	12	913	28	...	—	...
HUNGARY ‡	1977	4 680	...	...	14 912	...	...	...
MALTA	1977	40	40	1 500	45	—	—	—
MONACO	1977	1	1	55	3	...	...	...
NORWAY ‡	1977	3 681	3 681	...	5 105	...	...	...
PORTUGAL	1977	655	...	...	1 554	...	...	...
ROMANIA	1974	10 689	...	...	36 644	...	...	...
SAN MARINO ‡	1974	3	...	75	17	...	...	...
SPAIN	1977	640	683	56 348	2 190	13 984	63 467	—
SWEDEN	1977	413	...	798 000	27 919	...	...	...
YUGOSLAVIA	1978	8 411	8 411	...	27 379	...	...	...

ANNUAL ADDITIONS ACQUISITIONS ANNUELLES ADQUISICIONES ANUALES		REGISTERED BORROWERS EM-PRUNTEURS INSCRITS PRESTA-TARIOS INSCRITOS	LOANS TO USERS PRETS AUX USAGERS PRESTAMOS A LOS USUARIOS	CURRENT EXPENDITURE DEPENSES ORDINAIRES GASTOS ORDINARIOS		LIBRARY EMPLOYEES PERSONNEL DES BIBLIOTHEQUES PERSONAL DE LAS BIBLIOTECAS			POPULATION SERVED POPULATION DESSERVIE POBLACION SERVIDA
VOLUMES VOLUMES VOLUMENES	OTHER MATERIALS AUTRES MATERIELS OTROS MATERIALES			TOTAL TOTAL TOTAL (000)	STAFF PERSON-NEL PER-SONAL (%)	TOTAL TOTAL TOTAL	HOLDING A DIPLOMA DIPLOME DIPLOMADO	TRAINED ON THE JOB FORME SUR LE TAS FORMADO EN EJERCICIO	(%)
(8)	(9)	(10)	(11)	(12)	(13)	(14)	(15)	(16)	(17)
10 688	...	...	191 100	...	...	5 405	539	...	85
	...	...	36 000	...	...	15	...	...	97
660	...					4			
576 090	...	6 176 348		8 960	27	1 618	...	...	46
16 655	...	41 346	136 075	60 791	61	76	12	64	...
1 500	...	1 185	13 191	24	58	6			
60	...	200		...	...	...	...	...	46
37 500 000	...		1 176	1 182 000	69	128 800	28 900	...	87
2 715	...		21 358	...	...	137	32	105	23
5 039	...	20 447	330 844	200	72	62	8	54	74
8 187	30	...		2 166	...	92	...	92	...
...	...	6 294		128	...	18	...	...	32
...	...	...	40	...	...	...	...	...	
11 661 467	...	...		13 192 569	...		...	...	97
1 051 672	...		601 957	657	92	...	1	26	...
1 046 333	...			1 049 198	...	4 477	36	...	...
142 522	...	160 000		...		573	80	307	89
	...			6 300	...	...	62	...	39
35 585	...	15 972	57 052	...	...	70	2	−	...
1 566 000	...	228 200	7 533 000	4 500	...	...	386		...
220 001	...	311 169	886 404	868	−	550	9	4	61
63 786	...	262 748	274 368	611	71	700	4	84	14
28 063	...	253 282	212 572	228	49	243	30	196	76
938 248	10 296	836 067	8 205 868	2 079	39	567	380	187	58
		5 000 000		...		...	...	...	
4 208	...	3 173	*64 580	5	...	6	1	5	...
1 245 082	...	848 034	6 045 229	34 997		...	...	...	80
7 000	−	...	*29 000	12	14	20	−	8	42
75	−	...		10	−	1	−	−	100
298 218	...		6 179 152	...		...	...	...	
		693 425				...	...	...	65
2 477 803	...	2 486 819		...		...	...	...	
150		3 000				6	−	6	100
124 076	5 243	216 090	279 934	53 478	31	437	36	401	...
			18 522 000	...	...	...	...	...	
1 536 880	...			...	...	...	...	...	

COUNTRY	YEAR	ADMINIS-TRATIVE UNITS	SERVICE POINTS	COLLECTIONS / COLLECTIONS / COLECCIONES		MICRO-FORMS	AUDIO-VISUAL DOCUMENTS	OTHER LIBRARY MATERIALS
				BOOKS/LIVRES/LIBROS				
				METRES OF SHELVING	NUMBER OF VOLUMES			
PAYS	ANNEE	UNITES ADMINIS-TRATIVES	POINTS DE DESSERTE	METRES DE RAYONNAGE	NOMBRE DE VOLUMES	MICRO-COPIES	MATERIELS AUDIO-VISUELS	AUTRES MATERIELS DE BIBLIOTHEQUE
PAIS	AÑO	UNIDADES ADMINIS-TRATIVAS	PUNTOS DE SERVICIO	METROS DE ESTANTES	NUMERO DE VOLUMENES (000)	MICRO-COPIAS	MATERIALES AUDIO-VISUALES	OTROS MATE-RIALES DE BIBLIOTECA
		(1)	(2)	(3)	(4)	(5)	(6)	(7)
OCEANIA								
FIJI ‡	1977	300	750	5 800	235	–	...	–
KIRIBATI	1974	5	5	...	*7	...	...	...
NEW ZEALAND ‡	1974	1 067	1 067	177 744	4 829	...	...	...
NIUE ‡	1974	2	8	162	20	...	...	...
NORFOLK ISLAND	1975	1	1	448	6	...	...	...
PACIFIC ISLANDS	1977	40	40	...	92	...	...	...
SOLOMON ISLANDS	1974	6	6	345	14	...	...	...
TONGA	1978	10	–	81	28	–	...	–
U.S.S.R.								
UKRAINIAN S.S.R.	1974	24 078	24 078	...	106 332	...	...	

GAMBIA:
    E—> THE FIGURE IN COLUMN 12 REPRESENTS ONLY
EXPENDITURE FOR ACQUISITIONS.
    FR—> LE CHIFFRE DE LA COLONNNE 12 REPRESENTE
SEULEMENT LES DEPENSES POUR LES ACQUISITIONS.
    ESP> LOS DATOS DE LA COLUMNA 12 SOLO REPRESENTAN
LOS GASTOS DESTINADOS A LAS ADQUISICIONES.

MALAWI:
    E—> THE FIGURE IN COLUMN 12 REFERS TO
EXPENDITURE FOR ACQUISITIONS ONLY.
    FR—> LE CHIFFRE DE LA COLONNE 12 SE REFERE
AUX DEPENSES POUR LES ACQUISITIONS SEULEMENT.
    ESP> LOS DATOS DE LA COLUMNA 12 SOLO SE
REFIEREN A LOS GASTOS RELATIVOS A LAS
ADQUISICIONES.

ST. HELENA:
    E—> COLUMN 8 SHOWS THE NUMBER OF TITLES AND
NOT THE NUMBER OF VOLUMES.
    FR—> LA COLONNE 8 INDIQUE LE NOMBRE DE TITRES
ET NON LE NOMBRE DE VOLUMES.
    ESP> EN LA COLUMNA 8 SE INDICA EL NUMERO DE
TITULOS Y NO EL DE VOLUMENES.

CANADA:
    E—> THE FIGURES IN COLUMNS 14 AND 15 REFER ONLY
TO FULL-TIME STAFF.
    FR—> LES CHIFFRES DES COLONNES 14 ET 15 SE
REFERENT AU PERSONNEL EMPLOYE A PLEIN TEMPS
SEULEMENT.
    ESP> LAS CIFRAS DE LAS COLUMNAS 14 Y 15 SE
REFIEREN AL PERSONAL DE JORNADA COMPLETA
SOLAMENTE.

ST. PIERRE AND MIQUELON:
    E—> COLUMN 8 SHOWS THE NUMBER OF TITLES AND
NOT THE NUMBER OF VOLUMES.
    FR—> LA COLONNE 8 INDIQUE LE NOMBRE DE TITRES
ET NON LE NOMBRE DE VOLUMES.

ST. PIERRE AND MIQUELON (CONT):
    ESP> EN LA COLUMNA 8 SE INDICA EL NUMERO DE
TITULOS Y NO EL DE VOLUMENES.

UNITED STATES OF AMERICA:
    E—> DATA IN COLUMN 11 ARE IN MILLIONS.
    FR—> LES DONNEES DE LA COLONNE 11 SONT
EXPRIMEES EN MILLIONS.
    ESP> LOS DATOS DE LA COLUMNA 11 SE EXPRESAN
EN MILLONES.

PERU:
    E—> THE FIGURE IN COLUMN 10 REFERS TO 20
LIBRARIES ONLY.
    FR—> LE CHIFFRE DE LA COLONNE 10 NE CONCERNE
QUE 20 BIBLIOTHEQUES.
    ESP> LA CIFRA DE LA COLUMNA 10 SE REFIERE
A 20 BIBLIOTECAS SOLAMENTE.

VENEZUELA:
    E—> THE FIGURES IN COLUMNS 14 AND 16 CONCERN
ONLY PART-TIME STAFF.
    FR—> LES CHIFFRES DES COLONNES 14 ET 16 SE
REFERENT AU PERSONNEL EMPLOYE A TEMPS PARTIEL
SEULEMENT.
    ESP> LAS CIFRAS DE LAS COLUMNAS 14 Y 16 SE
REFIEREN AL PERSONAL DE JORNADA PARCIAL SOLAMENTE.

BRUNEI:
    E—> COLUMN 12 DOES NOT INCLUDE EXPENDITURE FOR
ACQUISITIONS.
    FR—> LA COLONNE 12 N'INCLUT PAS LES DEPENSES
POUR LES ACQUISITIONS.
    ESP> LA COLUMNA 12 NO INCLUYE LOS GASTOS
RELATIVOS A LAS ADQUISICIONES.

ANNUAL ADDITIONS ACQUISITIONS ANNUELLES ADQUISICIONES ANUALES		REGISTERED BORROWERS EM-PRUNTEURS INSCRITS PRESTA-TARIOS INSCRITOS	LOANS TO USERS PRETS AUX USAGERS PRESTAMOS A LOS USUARIOS	CURRENT EXPENDITURE DEPENSES ORDINAIRES GASTOS ORDINARIOS		LIBRARY EMPLOYEES PERSONNEL DES BIBLIOTHEQUES PERSONAL DE LAS BIBLIOTECAS			POPULATION SERVED POPULATION DESSERVIE POBLACION SERVIDA
VOLUMES VOLUMES VOLUMENES	OTHER MATERIALS AUTRES MATERIELS OTROS MATERIALES			TOTAL TOTAL TOTAL (000)	STAFF PERSON-NEL PER-SONAL (%)	TOTAL TOTAL TOTAL	HOLDING A DIPLOMA DIPLOME DIPLOMADO	TRAINED ON THE JOB FORME SUR LE TAS FORMADO EN EJERCICIO	(%)
(8)	(9)	(10)	(11)	(12)	(13)	(14)	(15)	(16)	(17)
...	...	908	...	52	...	70	—	70	42
1 705				4					6
495 138	...	548 277	9 888 720	1 359	22	19 366	75	—	*76
2 526	...			*4	50	...	1	4	33
300	...	310	10 000	1	...	1			100
...	...	...			...	24		18	36
1 450	...	1 303	...			6		—	100
...	—	6 200	...		...	20	3	10	...
26 998 300		7 231 900	125 710 000	...					...

JAPAN:
E—> COLUMN 12 SHOWS EXPENDITURE FOR ACQUISITIONS ONLY.
FR—> LA COLONNE 12 PRESENTE SEULEMENT LES DEPENSES POUR LES ACQUISITIONS.
ESP> EN LA COLUMNA 12 SOLO FIGURAN LOS GASTOS RELATIVOS A LAS ADQUISICIONES.

JORDAN:
E—> DATA REFER TO THE EAST BANK ONLY. COLUMN 8 SHOWS THE NUMBER OF TITLES AND NOT THE NUMBER OF VOLUMES. THE FIGURES IN COLUMNS 15 AND 16 INCLUDE ONLY FULL-TIME STAFF.
FR—> LES DONNEES SE REFERENT A LA RIVE ORIENTALE SEULEMENT. LA COLONNE 8 INDIQUE LE NOMBRE DE TITRES ET NON LE NOMBRE DE VOLUMES. LES CHIFFRES DES COLONNES 15 ET 16 NE COMPRENNENT QUE LE PERSONNEL EMPLOYE A PLEIN TEMPS.
ESP> LOS DATOS SE REFIEREN A LA ORILLA ORIENTAL SOLAMENTE. EN LA COLUMNA 8 SE INDICA EL NUMERO DE TITULOS Y NO EL DE VOLUMENES. LAS CIFRAS DE LAS COLUMNAS 15 Y 16 SE REFIEREN AL PERSONAL DE JORNADA COMPLETA SOLAMENTE.

KOREA, REPUBLIC OF:
E—> THE FIGURE IN COLUMN 12 REFERS TO EXPENDITURE FOR EMPLOYEES. THE DATA IN COLUMNS 15 AND 16 DO NOT INCLUDE PART-TIME STAFF.
FR—> LE CHIFFRE DE LA COLONNE 12 SE RAPPORTE SEULEMENT AUX DEPENSES POUR LE PERSONNEL. LES DONNEES DES COLONNES 15 ET 16 N'INCLUENT PAS LE PERSONNEL EMPLOYE A TEMPS PARTIEL.
ESP> LA CIFRA DE LA COLUMNA 12 SOLO SE REFIERE A LOS GASTOS DE PERSONAL. LOS DATOS DE LAS COLUMNAS 15 Y 16 NO INCLUYEN EL PERSONAL DE JORNADA PARCIAL.

MALAYSIA:
E—> THE FIGURE IN COLUMN 12 REFERS ONLY TO EXPENDITURE FOR ACQUISITIONS. PART-TIME STAFF IS NOT INCLUDED IN COLUMN 15.
FR—> LE CHIFFRE DE LA COLONNE 12 SE REFERE AUX DEPENSES POUR LES ACQUISITIONS SEULEMENT. LE PERSONNEL EMPLOYE A TEMPS PARTIEL N'EST PAS COMPTE DANS LA COLONNE 15.
ESP> LA COLUMNA 12 SOLO INCLUYE LOS DATOS RELATIVOS A LAS ADQUISICIONES. EL PERSONAL DE JORNADA PARCIAL NO FIGURA INCLUIDO EN LA COLUMNA 15

SAUDI ARABIA:
E—> THE FIGURE IN COLUMN 15 REFER TO FULL-TIME STAFF ONLY.
FR—> LE CHIFFRE DE LA COLONNE 15 SE RAPPORTE AU PERSONNEL EMPLOYE A PLEIN TEMPS SEULEMENT.
ESP> LA CIFRA DE LA COLUMNA 15 SE REFIERE AL PERSONAL DE JORNADA COMPLETA SOLAMENTE.

SRI LANKA:
E—> THE FIGURES IN COLUMN 15 AND 16 REFERS TO FULL-TIME STAFF ONLY.
FR—> LES CHIFFRES DES COLONNES 15 ET 16 SE RAPPORTENT AU PERSONNEL EMPLOYE A PLEIN TEMPS SEULEMENT.
ESP> LAS CIFRAS DE LAS COLUMNAS 15 Y 16 SE REFIEREN AL PERSONAL DE JORNADA COMPLETA SOLAMENTE.

BULGARIA:
E—> THE ACQUISITION FIGURE IN COLUMN 9 DOES NOT INCLUDE AUDIO-VISUAL DOCUMENTS.
FR—> DANS LA COLONNE 9, LE CHIFFRE RELATIF AUX ACQUISITIONS N'INCLUT PAS LE MATERIEL AUDIO-VISUEL.

BULGARIA (CONT):
ESP> EN LA COLUMNA 9, LA CIFRA RELATIVA A LAS ADQUISICIONES NO INCLUYE EL MATERIAL AUDIOVISUAL.

FINLAND:
E—> THE FIGURES IN COLUMNS 14 AND 15 REFER ONLY TO FULL-TIME STAFF.
FR-> LES DONNEES DES COLONNES 14 ET 15 NE CONCERNENT QUE LE PERSONNEL EMPLOYE A PLEIN TEMPS.
ESP> LOS DATOS DE LAS COLUMNAS 14 Y 15 SOLO CONCIERNEN EL PERSONAL DE JORNADA COMPLETA.

GIBRALTAR:
E—> COLUMN 4 REFERS TO 6 LIBRARIES ONLY. THE FIGURE IN COLUMN 13 DOES NOT INCLUDE EXPENDITURE FOR EMPLOYEES.
FR-> LA COLONNE 4 SE RAPPORTE A 6 BIBLIOTHEQUES SEULEMENT. LE CHIFFRE DE LA COLONNE 13 N'INCLUT PAS LES DEPENSES POUR LE PERSONNEL.
ESP> LA COLUMNA 4 SE REFIERE A 6 BIBLIOTECAS SOLAMENTE. LA CIFRA DE LA COLUMNA 13 NO INCLUYE LOS GASTOS DE PERSONAL.

HUNGARY:
E—> THE FIGURE IN COLUMN 12 REFERS ONLY TO EXPENDITURE FOR ACQUISITIONS.
FR-> LE CHIFFRE DE LA COLONNE 12 NE SE REFERE QU'AUX DEPENSES POUR LES ACQUISITIONS.
ESP> EN LA COLUMNA 12 SOLO FIGURAN LOS DATOS RELATIVOS A LAS ADQUISICIONES.

NORWAY:
E—> DATA REFER TO LIBRARIES OF PRIMARY SCHOOLS ONLY.
FR-> LES DONNEES SE RAPPORTENT AUX BIBLIOTHEQUES DES ECOLES PRIMAIRES SEULEMENT.

NORWAY (CONT):
ESP> LOS DATOS SE REFIEREN A LAS BIBLIOTECAS DE LAS ESCUELAS PRIMARIAS SOLAMENTE.

SAN MARINO:
E—> DATA IN COLUMNS 3 AND 8 REFER ONLY TO 2 LIBRARIES.
FR-> LES DONNEES DES COLONNES 3 ET 8 NE SE RAPPORTENT QU'A 2 BIBLIOTHEQUES.
ESP> LOS DATOS DE LAS COLUMNAS 3 Y 8 SOLO SE REFIEREN A 2 BIBLIOTECAS.

FIJI:
E—> THE EXPENDITURE FIGURE IN COLUMN 12 REFERS ONLY TO ACQUISITIONS.
FR-> DANS LA COLONNE 12, LE CHIFFRE RELATIF AUX DEPENSES NE CONCERNE QUE LES ACQUISITIONS.
ESP> EN LA COLUMNA 12, LA CIFRA RELATIVA A LOS GASTOS SOLO SE REFIERE A LAS ADQUISICIONES.

NEW ZEALAND:
E—> COLUMN 8 SHOWS THE NUMBER OF TITLES AND NOT THE NUMBER OF VOLUMES.
FR-> LA COLONNE 8 INDIQUE LE NOMBRE DE TITRES ET NON LE NOMBRE DE VOLUMES.
ESP> EN LA COLUMNA 8 SE INDICA EL NUMERO DE TITULOS Y NO EL DE VOLUMENES.

NIUE:
E—> THE FIGURE IN COLUMN 15 REFERS TO FULL-TIME STAFF ONLY.
FR-> LE CHIFFRE DE LA COLONNE 15 SE RAPPORTE SEULEMENT AU PERSONNEL EMPLOYE A PLEIN TEMPS.
ESP> LA CIFRA DE LA COLUMNA 15 SE REFIERE AL PERSONAL DE JORNADA COMPLETA SOLAMENTE.

7.5 Special libraries: collections, borrowers, works loaned out, current expenditure, personnel

Bibliothèques spécialisées: collections, emprunteurs inscrits, documents prêtès au-dehors, dépenses ordinaires, personnel

Bibliotecas especializadas: colecciones, prestatarios inscritos, documentos prestados al exterior, gastos ordinarios, personal

NUMBER OF COUNTRIES AND TERRITORIES PRESENTED IN THIS TABLE: 53

NOMBRE DE PAYS ET DE TERRITOIRES PRESENTES DANS C[TABLEAU: 53

COUNTRY	YEAR	ADMINIS-TRATIVE UNITS	SERVICE POINTS	COLLECTIONS / COLLECTIONS / COLECCIONES				
				BOOKS/LIVRES/LIBROS		MICRO-FORMS	AUDIO-VISUAL DOCUMENTS	OTHE[LIBRAR[MATERIAL[
				METRES OF SHELVING	NUMBER OF VOLUMES			
PAYS	ANNEE	UNITES ADMINIS-TRATIVES	POINTS DE DESSERTE	METRES DE RAYONNAGE	NOMBRE DE VOLUMES	MICRO-COPIES	MATERIELS AUDIO-VISUELS	AUTRE[MATERIELS D[BIBLIOTHEQU[
PAIS	AÑO	UNIDADES ADMINIS-TRATIVAS	PUNTOS DE SERVICIO	METROS DE ESTANTES	NUMERO DE VOLUMENES (000)	MICRO-COPIAS	MATERIALES AUDIO-VISUALES	OTROS MATE[RIALES D[BIBLIOTEC[
		(1)	(2)	(3)	(4)	(5)	(6)	(7
AFRICA								
GAMBIA	1978	17	20	1 120	24	–	–	
GHANA	1974	1	5	330	38	...	...	.
MADAGASCAR	1974	7	10	1 000	30	...	...	.
NIGERIA ‡	1977	60	303	...	644	...	...	1 3[
SENEGAL ‡	1975	1	1	10		...	...	.
SEYCHELLES	1974	1	1	16	1	...	...	.
UGANDA	1974	3	6	...	17	...	...	.
ZAMBIA	1974	8	830	...	380	...	...	.

NUMERO DE PAISES Y DE TERRITORIOS PRESENTADOS EN
ESTE CUADRO: 53

ANNUAL ADDITIONS ACQUISITIONS ANNUELLES ADQUISICIONES ANUALES		REGISTERED BORROWERS	LOANS TO USERS	INTER— LIBRARY LOANS	CURRENT EXPENDITURE DEPENSES ORDINAIRES GASTOS ORDINARIOS		LIBRARY EMPLOYEES PERSONNEL DES BIBLIOTHEQUES PERSONAL DE LAS BIBLIOTECAS		
VOLUMES	OTHER MATERIALS				TOTAL	STAFF	TOTAL	HOLDING A DIPLOMA	TRAINED ON THE JOB
VOLUMES	AUTRES MATERIELS	EM— PRUNTEURS INSCRITS	PRETS AUX USAGERS	PRETS ENTRE BIBLIO— THEQUES	TOTAL	PERSON— NEL	TOTAL	DIPLOME	FORME SUR LE TAS
VOLUMENES	OTROS MATERIALES	PRESTA— TARIOS INSCRITOS	PRESTAMOS A LOS USUARIOS	PRESTAMOS ENTRE BIBLIO— TECAS	TOTAL (000)	PER— SONAL (%)	TOTAL	DIPLO— MADO	FORMADO EN EJERCICIO
(8)	(9)	(10)	(11)	(12)	(13)	(14)	(15)	(16)	(17)
500	—	...	...	...	...	...	16	—	16
67	...	...	2 707	...	25	37	7	1	—
320	...	...	...	...	...	...	9	—	—
...	...	11 285	...	1 515	734	51	593	72	368
...	...	...	10	...	...	...	1	...	...
100	...	...	500	...	50	54	3	—	—
1 000	...	...	3 100	...	...	...	14	5	2
30 000	...	...	152 098	...	95	...	60	14	2

COUNTRY	YEAR	ADMINIS-TRATIVE UNITS	SERVICE POINTS	COLLECTIONS / COLLECTIONS / COLECCIONES				
				BOOKS/LIVRES/LIBROS		MICRO-FORMS	AUDIO-VISUAL DOCUMENTS	OTHER LIBRARY MATERIALS
				METRES OF SHELVING	NUMBER OF VOLUMES			
PAYS	ANNEE	UNITES ADMINIS-TRATIVES	POINTS DE DESSERTE	METRES DE RAYONNAGE	NOMBRE DE VOLUMES	MICRO-COPIES	MATERIELS AUDIO-VISUELS	AUTRES MATERIELS DE BIBLIOTHEQUE
PAIS	AÑO	UNIDADES ADMINIS-TRATIVAS	PUNTOS DE SERVICIO	METROS DE ESTANTES	NUMERO DE VOLUMENES (000)	MICRO-COPIAS	MATERIALES AUDIO-VISUALES	OTROS MATE-RIALES DE BIBLIOTECA
		(1)	(2)	(3)	(4)	(5)	(6)	(7)
AMERICA, NORTH								
BARBADOS	1977	1	1	93	100	...	130	...
BERMUDA	1974	3	3	818	21	...	...	...
GUATEMALA	1974	3	57	1 848	73	...	...	...
MEXICO	1974	121	121	5 502	882	...	...	...
PANAMA	1977	1	1	568	49	–	–	–
PUERTO RICO	1977	1	1	36	4	...	426	...
TRINIDAD AND TOBAGO ‡	1974	1	1	36	5	...	...	...
UNITED STATES OF AMERICA ‡	1977	1 143	...	...	19 832	6 833 447	1 583 336	3 416 538
AMERICA, SOUTH								
CHILE ‡	1977	...	...	...	1 024	...	699 930	...
COLOMBIA ‡	1975	191	...	...	898	...	902	...
ECUADOR ‡	1978	1	1	...	5	...	...	...
SURINAME	1978	27	27	1 586	63	–	–	...
VENEZUELA	1977	35		...	224			
ASIA								
BAHRAIN ‡	1974	12	12	700	17	...	...	...
BRUNEI	1977	5	1	747	6	1	–	–
HONG KONG	1974	16	44	8 455	237	...	...	...
INDONESIA ‡	1977	152	...	...	1 327	64 584	...	271
JAPAN	1978	2 019	...	...	31 164	2 242 649	...	...
JORDAN ‡	1974	18	...	...	91	...		
KOREA, REPUBLIC OF	1974	153	153	...	1 867	...		
MALAYSIA ‡	1977	119	119	16 729	836	18 112	616 595	3 695
SINGAPORE	1974	45	–	21 954	440	...	...	...
SRI LANKA ‡	1977	73	...	...	528	...	...	...
SYRIAN ARAB REPUBLIC‡	1974	3	3	97	11		...	...
EUROPE								
BULGARIA ‡	1977	10 290	...	...	59 501	3 337 521	...	10 403 43
CZECHOSLOVAKIA ‡	1977	14	14	...	14 996	32 869	...	4 957 77
DENMARK ‡	1977	13	...	60 000	1 324	951 804	639	66 37
FINLAND ‡	1977	16	47	50 100	1 865	25 400	...	..
HUNGARY ‡	1974	1 395	...	...	12 359	...	10 879 059	—
IRELAND	1977	9	13	206 898	303	20 166	62	10 00
NETHERLANDS ‡	1976	466	662	279 385	9 660	3 100 320	...	..
NORWAY ‡	1977	168	168	100 714	2 752	...	...	
POLAND ‡	1977	5 462	...	...	19 118	20 413	37 073	36 82
PORTUGAL ‡	1977	179	...	...	2 256	...	...	
ROMANIA	1977	4 189	...	...	18 279	...		
SPAIN ‡	1977	452	571	244 687	8 092	9 270	437 522	..
SWEDEN	1977	15	20	101 695	...	...	...	
YUGOSLAVIA ‡	1977	1 072	1 073	200 488	10 881	49 946	23 064	340 59

ANNUAL ADDITIONS / ACQUISITIONS ANNUELLES / ADQUISICIONES ANUALES		REGISTERED BORROWERS / EMPRUNTEURS INSCRITS / PRESTATARIOS INSCRITOS	LOANS TO USERS / PRETS AUX USAGERS / PRESTAMOS A LOS USUARIOS	INTER-LIBRARY LOANS / PRETS ENTRE BIBLIOTHEQUES / PRESTAMOS ENTRE BIBLIOTECAS	CURRENT EXPENDITURE / DEPENSES ORDINAIRES / GASTOS ORDINARIOS		LIBRARY EMPLOYEES / PERSONNEL DES BIBLIOTHEQUES / PERSONAL DE LAS BIBLIOTECAS		
VOLUMES / VOLUMES / VOLUMENES	OTHER MATERIALS / AUTRES MATERIELS / OTROS MATERIALES				TOTAL (000)	STAFF / PERSONNEL / PERSONAL (%)	TOTAL	HOLDING A DIPLOMA / DIPLOME / DIPLOMADO	TRAINED ON THE JOB / FORME SUR LE TAS / FORMADO EN EJERCICIO
(8)	(9)	(10)	(11)	(12)	(13)	(14)	(15)	(16)	(17)
...	4	54	1 025	...	24	78	2	1	—
103	...	...	4 260	...	34	32	6	1	5
3 565	...	...	48 000	...	...	...	8	4	...
34 020	...	...	7 957	...	3 443	31	392	...	...
80	...	189	1 618	...	16 761	98	4	1	3
...	...	837	...	14	...	...	3	...	2
416	...	...	15 496	...	...	...	4	...	3
877 698	1 000 428	...	...	739 775	68 870	68	4 732	...	...
...	...	...	...	...	...	...	644	218	...
...	...	...	...	...	...	...	392	49	...
5	...	...	800	...	...	...	2	...	...
2 531	—	967	279	51	473	46	71	6	65
...	...	...	...	...	3 443	...	222	48	...
400	...	...	9 700	...	...	...	15	...	2
216	—	334	...	...	73	77	8	—	6
12 308	...	...	408 621	...	1 930	53	78	3	7
...	...	...	147 505	...	1 105 100	38	1 465	989	476
...	...	...	24 914 320	...	26 946 271	52	7 254	...	...
12 012	...	...	...	...	62	28	54	2	9
150 351	...	...	790 847	...	598 325	21	658	183	...
149 464	11 861	43 424	354 000	10	2 893	58	450	72	...
33 276	...	...	138 555	...	1 337	59	133	30	13
...	...	...	...	...	1 569	32	176	5	...
500	...	...	2 580	...	67	30	16	3	3
4 184 374	238 291	3 110 160	41 052 296	...	16 782	44	5 348	3 186	2162
421 000	752	208 212	5 376 000	165 611	138 926	...	2 090	1 301	789
43 295	122 708	...	153 622	39 917	17 103	...	160	59	...
43 100	7 290	...	105 660	35 740	11 481	71	194	85	—
579 337	706 461	218 520	3 839 130	50 642	185 609	...	2 320	360	576
6 289	2 151	6 641	168 899	11 322	326	59	55	21	13
276 882	188 666	...	2 092 233	264 568	...	...	1 515	658	430
93 135	...	...	...	...	...	...	392	309	43
...	...	1 072	7 420	...	1 510 266	...	...	...	...
38 649	...	123 325	243 780	...	76 597	...	493	...	...
...	...	...	5 297 000	...	...	...	...	...	...
256 270	64 941	144 208	358 269	126	395 301	54	1 132	310	822
124 867	...	...	730 452	221 238	7 376	...	356	90	...
...	...	313 831	...	...	86 366 616	...	1 351	923	85

COUNTRY	YEAR			COLLECTIONS / COLLECTIONS / COLECCIONES				
		ADMINIS- TRATIVE UNITS	SERVICE POINTS	BOOKS/LIVRES/LIBROS		MICRO- FORMS	AUDIO- VISUAL DOCUMENTS	OTHER LIBRARY MATERIALS
				METRES OF SHELVING	NUMBER OF VOLUMES			
PAYS	ANNEE		POINTS DE				MATERIELS	AUTRES
		UNITES ADMINIS- TRATIVES	DESSERTE	METRES DE RAYONNAGE	NOMBRE DE VOLUMES	MICRO- COPIES	AUDIO- VISUELS	MATERIELS DE BIBLIOTHEQUE
PAIS	AÑO	UNIDADES ADMINIS- TRATIVAS	PUNTOS DE SERVICIO	METROS DE ESTANTES	NUMERO DE VOLUMENES (000)	MICRO- COPIAS	MATERIALES AUDIO- VISUALES	OTROS MATE- RIALES DE BIBLIOTECA
		(1)	(2)	(3)	(4)	(5)	(6)	(7)
OCEANIA								
FIJI	1978	11	11	6 625	82	...	...	...
KIRIBATI	1974	4	4	38	*1	...	...	...
NEW ZEALAND	1974	98	98	26 986	1 165	...	...	...
NORFOLK ISLAND	1975	1	2	...	...	...	...	...
SOLOMON ISLANDS ‡	1974	6	25	179	6	...	...	...
TONGA	1978	2	...	18	4	...	...	...
U.S.S.R.								
UKRAINIAN S.S.R.	1974	3 531	13 799	...	88 961	...	...	...

NIGERIA:
E——> COLUMN 12 REFERS ONLY TO LIBRARY LOAN TRANSACTIONS ON THE NATIONAL LEVEL.
FR—> LA COLONNE 12 SE RAPPORTE SEULEMENT AUX PRETS ENTRE BIBLIOTHEQUES AU NIVEAU NATIONAL.
ESP> LA COLUMNA 12 SOLO SE REFIERE A LOS PRESTAMOS ENTRE BIBLIOTECAS A NIVEL NACIONAL.

SENEGAL:
E——> ONLY PART-TIME STAFF IS INCLUDED IN COLUMN 15.
FR—> LA COLONNE 15 NE CONCERNE QUE LE PERSONNEL EMPLOYE A TEMPS PARTIEL.
ESP> LA COLUMNA 15 SOLO CONCIERNE EL PERSONAL DE JORNADA PARCIAL.

TRINIDAD AND TOBAGO:
E——> COLUMN 17 REFERS TO FULL-TIME STAFF ONLY.
FR—> LA COLONNE 17 NE TIENT COMPTE QUE DU PERSONNEL A PLEIN TEMPS.
ESP> EN LA COLUMNA 17 SOLO SE TOMA EN CONSIDERACION AL PERSONAL DE JORNADA COMPLETA.

UNITED STATES OF AMERICA:
E——> THE DATA REPRESENT ONLY 84% OF THE SPECIAL LIBRARIES WHOSE TOTAL NUMBER IS 1366.
FR—> LES DONNEES NE REPRESENTENT QUE 84% DES BIBLIOTHEQUES SPECIALISEES DONT LE TOTAL S'ELEVE A 1366.
ESP> LOS DATOS REPRESENTAN EL 84% SOLAMENTE DE LAS BIBLIOTECAS ESPECIALIZADAS, CUYO TOTAL ASCIENDE A 1366.

CHILE:
E——> THE FIGURES IN COLUMNS 15 AND 16 REFER TO FULL-TIME STAFF ONLY.
FR—> LES CHIFFRES DES COLONNES 15 ET 16 SE RAPPORTENT AU PERSONNEL EMPLOYE A PLEIN TEMPS SEULEMENT.
ESP> LAS CIFRAS DE LAS COLUMNAS 15 Y 16 SE REFIEREN AL PERSONAL DE JORNADA COMPLETA SOLAMENTE.

COLOMBIA:
E——> THE FIGURES IN COLUMNS 15 AND 16 REFER TO FULL-TIME STAFF ONLY.
FR—> LES CHIFFRES DES COLONNES 15 ET 16 SE RAPPORTENT AU PERSONNEL EMPLOYE A PLEIN TEMPS SEULEMENT.
ESP> LAS CIFRAS DE LAS COLUMNAS 15 Y 16 SE REFIEREN AL PERSONAL DE JORNADA COMPLETA SOLAMENTE.

ECUADOR:
E——> THE FIGURE IN COLUMN 15 REFERS TO FULL-TIME STAFF ONLY.
FR—> LE CHIFFRE DE LA COLONNE 15 SE RAPPORTE AU PERSONNEL EMPLOYE A PLEIN TEMPS SEULEMENT.
ESP> LA CIFRA DE LA COLUMNA 15 SE REFIERE AL PERSONAL DE JORNADA COMPLETA SOLAMENTE.

BAHRAIN:
E——> THE FIGURES IN COLUMNS 15 AND 17 REFER TO FULL-TIME STAFF ONLY.
FR—> LES CHIFFRES DES COLONNES 15 ET 17 SE RAPPORTENT AU PERSONNEL EMPLOYE A PLEIN TEMPS SEULEMENT.
ESP> LAS CIFRAS DE LAS COLUMNAS 15 Y 17 SE REFIEREN AL PERSONAL DE JORNADA COMPLETA SOLAMENTE.

INDONESIA:
E——> THE FIGURES IN COLUMNS 15, 16 AND 17 REFER TO FULL-TIME STAFF ONLY.
FR—> LES CHIFFRES DES COLONNES 15, 16 ET 17 SE RAPPORTENT AU PERSONNEL EMPLOYE A PLEIN TEMPS SEULEMENT.
ESP> LAS CIFRAS DE LAS COLUMNAS 15, 16 Y 17 SE REFIEREN AL PERSONAL DE JORNADA COMPLETA SOLAMENTE.

JORDAN:
E——> DATA REFER TO THE EAST BANK ONLY. COLUMN 8 SHOWS THE NUMBER OF TITLES AND NOT THE NUMBER OF VOLUMES.

ANNUAL ADDITIONS ACQUISITIONS ANNUELLES ADQUISICIONES ANUALES		REGISTERED BORROWERS EM- PRUNTEURS INSCRITS PRESTA- TARIOS INSCRITOS	LOANS TO USERS PRETS AUX USAGERS PRESTAMOS A LOS USUARIOS	INTER- LIBRARY LOANS PRETS ENTRE BIBLIO- THEQUES PRESTAMOS ENTRE BIBLIO- TECAS	CURRENT EXPENDITURE DEPENSES ORDINAIRES GASTOS ORDINARIOS		LIBRARY EMPLOYEES PERSONNEL DES BIBLIOTHEQUES PERSONAL DE LAS BIBLIOTECAS		
VOLUMES VOLUMES VOLUMENES	OTHER MATERIALS AUTRES MATERIELS OTROS MATERIALES				TOTAL TOTAL TOTAL (000)	STAFF PERSON- NEL PER- SONAL (%)	TOTAL TOTAL TOTAL	HOLDING A DIPLOMA DIPLOME DIPLO- MADO	TRAINED ON THE JOB FORME SUR LE TAS FORMADO EN EJERCICIO
(8)	(9)	(10)	(11)	(12)	(13)	(14)	(15)	(16)	(17)
6 329	...	6 000	35 000	1 198	91	52	17	5	12
...	...								
68 035	...	...	170 729	...	769	50	254	63	...
455	...	...	...	...	2	...	1	...	...
							25	...	...
...	...	...	...	...	2	79	3	—	1
6 408 600	...	...	70 068 800	...	...	...	7 483	5 376	1376

JORDAN (CONT):
FR—> LES DONNEES SE REFERENT A LA RIVE ORIENTALE SEULEMENT. LA COLONNE 8 INDIQUE LE NOMBRE DE TITRES ET NON LE NOMBRE DE VOLUMES.
ESP> LOS DATOS SE REFIEREN A LA ORILLA ORIENTAL SOLAMENTE. EN LA COLUMNA 8 SE INDICA EL NUMERO DE TITULOS Y NO EL DE VOLUMENES.

MALAYSIA:
E—> COLUMNS 15 AND 16 CONCERN ONLY FULL-TIME STAFF.
FR—> LES COLONNES 15 ET 16 CONCERNENT SEULEMENT LE PERSONNEL EMPLOYE A PLEIN TEMPS.
ESP> LAS COLUMNAS 15 Y 16 SOLO SE REFIEREN AL PERSONAL DE JORNADA COMPLETA.

SRI LANKA:
E—> THE FIGURE IN COLUMN 13 REFERS TO 41 LIBRARIES ONLY. COLUMNS 15 AND 16 DO NOT INCLUDE PART-TIME STAFF.
FR—> LE CHIFFRE DE LA COLONNE 13 CONCERNE 41 BIBLIOTHEQUES SEULEMENT. LES COLONNES 15 ET 16 N'INCLUENT PAS LE PERSONNEL EMPLOYE A TEMPS PARTIEL.
ESP> LA CIFRA DE LA COLUMNA 13 SE REFIERE A 41 BIBLIOTECAS SOLAMENTE. LAS COLUMNAS 15 Y 16 NO INCLUYEN EL PERSONAL DE JORNADA PARCIAL.

SYRIAN ARAB REPUBLIC:
E—> THE FIGURE IN COLUMN 17 REFERS TO FULL-TIME STAFF ONLY.
FR—> LE CHIFFRE DE LA COLONNE 17 SE REFERE AU PERSONNEL EMPLOYE A PLEIN TEMPS SEULEMENT.
ESP> LA CIFRA DE LA COLUMNA 17 SE REFIERE AL PERSONAL DE JORNADA COMPLETA SOLAMENTE.

BULGARIA:
THE FIGURES IN COLUMNS 15, 16 AND 17 REFER TO FULL-TIME STAFF ONLY.
FR—> LES CHIFFRES DES COLONNES 15, 16 ET 17 NE SE RAPPORTENT QU'AU PERSONNEL EMPLOYE A PLEIN TEMPS.

BULGARIA (CONT):
ESP> LAS CIFRAS DE LAS COLUMNAS 15, 16 Y 17 SOLO SE REFIEREN AL PERSONAL DE JORNADA COMPLETA.

CZECHOSLOVAKIA:
E—> COLUMN 13 SHOWS ONLY EXPENDITURE FOR EMPLOYEES.
FR—> LA COLONNE 13 INDIQUE LES DEPENSES POUR LE PERSONNEL SEULEMENT.
ESP> EN LA COLUMNA 13 SOLO FIGURAN LOS GASTOS DE PERSONAL.

DENMARK:
E—> IN ADDITION TO THE FIGURES SHOWN HERE, THERE ARE 72 LIBRARIES FOR WHICH DATA ARE NOT AVAILABLE. THE DATA ON ACQUISITIONS IN COLUMN 9 COMPRISE ONLY MICROFORMS AND AUDIO-VISUAL DOCUMENTS. COLUMN 13 REFERS TO EXPENDITURE FOR EMPLOYEES AND ACQUISITIONS ONLY.
FR—> EN PLUS DES DONNEES PRESENTEES, IL Y A 72 BIBLIOTHEQUES POUR LESQUELLES LES STATISTIQUES NE SONT PAS DISPONIBLES. DANS LA COLONNE 9, LES CHIFFRES RELATIFS AUX ACQUISITIONS, COMPRENNENT SEULEMENT LES MICROCOPIES ET LE MATERIEL AUDIOVISUEL. LA COLONNE 13 SE RAPPORTE AUX DEPENSES POUR LE PERSONNEL ET LES ACQUISITIONS SEULEMENT.
ESP> ADEMAS DE LOS DATOS PRESENTADOS, EXISTEN 72 BIBLIOTECAS PARA LAS QUE NO SE DISPONE DE DATOS. EN LA COLUMNA 9, LAS CIFRAS RELATIVAS A LAS ADQUISICIONES SOLO COMPRENDEN LAS MICROCOPIAS Y EL MATERIAL AUDIOVISUAL. LA COLUMNA 13 SE REFIERE A LOS GASTOS DE PERSONAL Y DE ADQUISICIONES SOLAMENTE.

FINLAND:
E—> THE DATA ON ACQUISITIONS IN COLUMN 9 REFER ONLY TO MICROFORMS.
FR—> DANS LA COLONNE 9, LES DONNEES RELATIVES AUX ACQUISITIONS SE RAPPORTENT AUX MICROCOPIES SEULEMENT.

FINLAND (CONT):
   ESP> EN LA COLUMNA 9, LOS DATOS RELATIVOS A LAS ADQUISICIONES SE REFIEREN A LAS MICROCOPIAS SOLAMENTE.

HUNGARY:
   E—> THE DATA ON ACQUISITIONS IN COLUMN 9 DO NOT INCLUDE MICROFORMS. COLUMN 13 CONCERNS EXPENDITURE ON ACQUISITIONS ONLY.
   FR—> DANS LA COLONNE 9, LES DONNEES RELATIVES AUX ACQUISITIONS NE TIENNENT PAS COMPTE DES MICROCOPIES. LA COLONNE 13 NE CONCERNE QUE LES DEPENSES POUR LES ACQUISITIONS.
   ESP> EN LA COLUMNA 9, LOS DATOS RELATIVOS A LAS ADQUISICIONES NO TIENEN EN CUENTA LAS MICROCOPIAS. LA COLUMNA 13 SOLO CONCIERNE LOS GASTOS RELATIVOS A LAS ADQUISICIONES.

NETHERLANDS:
   E—> THE DATA ON ACQUISITIONS IN COLUMN 9 REFER TO MICROFORMS ONLY. THE FIGURE IN COLUMN 11 INCLUDES BESIDES LOANS TO USERS, ITEMS COPIED TO TAKE THE PLACE OF ORIGINAL MATERIALS.
   FR—> DANS LA COLONNE 9, LES DONNEES RELATIVES AUX ACQUISITIONS SE REFERENT AUX MICROCOPIES SEULEMENT. LE CHIFFRE DE LA COLONNE 11, COMPREND, EN PLUS DES LIVRES PRETES AUX USAGERS, LE NOMBRE D'UNITES COPIEES FOURNIES A LA PLACE DE DOCUMENTS ORIGINAUX.
   ESP> EN LA COLUMNA 9, LOS DATOS RELATIVOS A LAS ADQUISICIONES SE REFIEREN A LAS MICROCOPIAS SOLAMENTE. LA CIFRA DE LA COLUMNA 11 COMPRENDE, ADEMAS DE LOS LIBROS PRESTADOS A LOS USUARIOS, EL NUMERO DE COPIAS FACILITADAS EN SUSTITUCION DE LOS DOCUMENTOS ORIGINALES.

NORWAY:
   E—> COLUMN 17 REFERS TO FULL-TIME STAFF ONLY.
   FR—> LA COLONNE 17 SE RAPPORTE AU PERSONNEL EMPLOYE A PLEIN TEMPS SEULEMENT.
   ESP> LA COLUMNA 17 SE REFIERE AL PERSONAL DE JORNADA COMPLETA SOLAMENTE.

POLAND:
   E—> COLUMN 13 SHOWS ONLY EXPENDITURE FOR EMPLOYEES.
   FR—> LA COLONNE 13 INDIQUE SEULEMENT LES DEPENSES POUR LE PERSONNEL.
   ESP> LA COLUMNA 13 SE REFIERE A LOS GASTOS DE PERSONAL SOLAMENTE.

PORTUGAL:
   E—> COLUMN 11 REFERS ONLY TO WORKS USED IN READING ROOMS. ARE SHOWN IN COLUMN 13 ONLY EXPENDITURE FOR EMPLOYEES AND FOR ACQUISITIONS. COLUMN 15 REFERS TO FULL-TIME STAFF ONLY.
   FR—> LA COLONNE 11 SE RAPPORTE SEULEMENT AUX OUVRAGES UTILISES DANS LES SALLES DE LECTURE. LES CHIFFRES DE LA COLONNE 13 INDIQUENT LES DEPENSES POUR LE PERSONNEL ET LES ACQUISITIONS SEULEMENT. LA COLONNE 15 NE SE RAPPORTE QU'AU PERSONNEL EMPLOYE A PLEIN TEMPS.
   ESP> LA COLUMNA 11 SE REFIERE SOLAMENTE A LOS VOLUMENES UTILIZADOS EN LAS SALAS DE LECTURA. LA CIFRA DE LA COLUMNA 13 INDICA LOS GASTOS DE PERSONAL Y DE ADQUISICIONES SOLAMENTE. LA COLUMNA 15 SOLO SE REFIERE AL PERSONAL DE JORNADA COMPLETA.

SPAIN:
   E—> COLUMN 12 DOES NOT INCLUDE LIBRARY LOAN TRANSACTIONS ON THE NATIONAL LEVEL.
   FR—> LA COLONNE 12 NE TIENT PAS COMPTE DES PRETS ENTRE BIBLIOTHEQUES AU NIVEAU NATIONAL.
   ESP> LA COLUMNA 12 NO TOMA EN CONSIDERACION LOS PRESTAMOS ENTRE BIBLIOTECAS A NIVEL NACIONAL.

YUGOSLAVIA:
   E—> COLUMN 6 REFERS TO AUDITORY MATERIALS ONLY. THE FIGURE IN COLUMN 13 IS EXPRESSED IN MILLIONS.
   FR—> LE CHIFFRE DE LA COLONNE 6 SE RAPPORTE SEULEMENT AUX MATERIELS AUDITIFS. LE CHIFFRE DE LA COLONNE 13 EST EXPRIME EN MILLIONS.
   ESP> LA CIFRA DE LA COLUMNA 6 SE REFIERE SOLAMENTE AL MATERIAL AUDITIVO. LA CIFRA DE LA COLUMNA 13 SE EXPRESA EN MILLONES.

SOLOMON ISLANDS:
   E—> THE DATA ON ACQUISITIONS IN COLUMN 9 REFER TO NUMBER OF THE TITLES AND NOT TO THE NUMBER OF VOLUMES.
   FR—> LES DONNEES RELATIVES AUX ACQUISITIONS, DANS LA COLONNE 9, SE REFERENT AU NOMBRE DE TITRES ET NON AU NOMBRE DE VOLUMES.
   ESP> EN LA COLUMNA 9, LOS DATOS RELATIVOS A LAS ADQUISICIONES SE REFIEREN AL NUMERO DE TITULOS Y NO AL DE VOLUMENES.

7.6 Public libraries: collections, borrowers, works loaned out, current expenditure, personnel

Bibliothèques publiques: collections, emprunteurs inscrits, documents prêtès au-dehors, dépenses ordinaires, personnel

Bibliotecas públicas: colecciones, prestatarios inscritos, documentos prestados al exterior, gastos ordinarios, personal

NUMBER OF COUNTRIES AND TERRITORIES PRESENTED IN THIS TABLE: 86

NOMBRE DE PAYS ET DE TERRITOIRES PRESENTES DANS CE TABLEAU: 86

COUNTRY / PAYS / PAIS	YEAR / ANNEE / AÑO	ADMINIS-TRATIVE UNITS / UNITES ADMINIS-TRATIVES / UNIDADES ADMINIS-TRATIVAS	SERVICE POINTS / POINTS DE DESSERTE / PUNTOS DE SERVICIO	COLLECTIONS / COLLECTIONS / COLECCIONES				
				BOOKS/LIVRES/LIBROS		MICRO-FORMS / MICRO-COPIES / MICRO-COPIAS	AUDIO-VISUAL DOCUMENTS / MATERIELS AUDIO-VISUELS / MATERIALES AUDIO-VISUALES	OTHER LIBRARY MATERIALS / AUTRES MATERIELS DE BIBLIOTHEQUE / OTROS MATE-RIALES DE BIBLIOTECA
				METRES OF SHELVING / METRES DE RAYONNAGE / METROS DE ESTANTES	NUMBER OF VOLUMES / NOMBRE DE VOLUMES / NUMERO DE VOLUMENES (000)			
		(1)	(2)	(3)	(4)	(5)	(6)	(7)
AFRICA								
COMORO ‡	1975	2	2	...	8	...	...	...
DJIBOUTI	1975	1	5	...	5	...	...	...
GAMBIA ‡	1978	2	5	760	66	...	...	...
GHANA ‡	1977	7	40	...	929	...	...	...
KENYA	1974	3	3	...	150	...	...	
MADAGASCAR	1974	20	20	283	134	...	...	...
MALAWI	1974	2	96	...	122	...	...	...
NIGERIA ‡	1977	31	56	...	891	...	–	1 60
ST. HELENA	1974	1	6	290	14	...	...	...
SENEGAL	1975	1	1	10	3	...	...	...

NUMERO DE PAISES Y DE TERRITORIOS PRESENTADOS EN
ESTE CUADRO: 86

ANNUAL ADDITIONS ACQUISITIONS ANNUELLES ADQUISICIONES ANUALES		REGISTERED BORROWERS	LOANS TO USERS	CURRENT EXPENDITURE DEPENSES ORDINAIRES GASTOS ORDINARIOS		LIBRARY EMPLOYEES PERSONNEL DES BIBLIOTHEQUES PERSONAL DE LAS BIBLIOTECAS			POPULATION SERVED
VOLUMES	OTHER MATERIALS			TOTAL	STAFF	TOTAL	HOLDING A DIPLOMA	TRAINED ON THE JOB	POPULATION DESSERVIE
VOLUMES	AUTRES MATERIELS	EM— PRUNTEURS INSCRITS	PRETS AUX USAGERS	TOTAL	PERSON— NEL	TOTAL	DIPLOME	FORME SUR LE TAS	
VOLUMENES	OTROS MATERIALES	PRESTA— TARIOS INSCRITOS	PRESTAMOS A LOS USUARIOS	TOTAL (000)	PER— SONAL (%)	TOTAL	DIPLOMADO	FORMADO EN EJERCICIO	POBLACION SERVIDA (%)
(8)	(9)	(10)	(11)	(12)	(13)	(14)	(15)	(16)	(17)
280	...	370	...	410	32	4	...	...	....
500	...	430	2 500	2 400	83	5	—	5	...
5 300	...	16 975	30 434	85	67	15	3	10	10
44 000	...	70 000	822 553	1 825	50	520	50	65	30
8 000	...	25 000	22 200	69	58	45	11	—	77
4 820	...	...	135 328	...	...	40	4	4	
13 551	...	24 445	363 481	75	44	40	3	7	25
235 328	...	54 363	128 525	2 752	75	1 117	...	...	*50
600	...	100	...	1	73	8	—	8	
100	...	3	6	...	...	...	...	...	

COUNTRY	YEAR	ADMINIS-TRATIVE UNITS	SERVICE POINTS	COLLECTIONS / COLLECTIONS / COLECCIONES				
				BOOKS/LIVRES/LIBROS		MICRO-FORMS	AUDIO-VISUAL DOCUMENTS	OTHER LIBRARY MATERIALS
				METRES OF SHELVING	NUMBER OF VOLUMES			
PAYS	ANNEE	UNITES ADMINIS-TRATIVES	POINTS DE DESSERTE	METRES DE RAYONNAGE	NOMBRE DE VOLUMES	MICRO-COPIES	MATERIELS AUDIO-VISUELS	AUTRES MATERIELS DE BIBLIOTHEQUE
PAIS	AÑO	UNIDADES ADMINIS-TRATIVAS	PUNTOS DE SERVICIO	METROS DE ESTANTES	NUMERO DE VOLUMENES (000)	MICRO-COPIAS	MATERIALES AUDIO-VISUALES	OTROS MATE-RIALES DE BIBLIOTECA
		(1)	(2)	(3)	(4)	(5)	(6)	(7)
SEYCHELLES	1974	1	1	408	16	...	...	...
SIERRA LEONE	1974	1	11	...	392	...	...	...
TUNISIA ‡	1977	...	206	...	694	...	...	...
UGANDA	1974	1	19	...	90	...	...	...
ZAIRE ‡	1977	8	31	119	6	...	...	...
ZAMBIA	1977	4	56	2 000	...	10	14	
AMERICA, NORTH								
BAHAMAS	1974	25	25	1 839	95			
BARBADOS	1977	1	18	2 592	...	415	1 001	—
BELIZE ‡	1974	1	77	...	101	...	...	...
BERMUDA	1974	1	4	...	122	...	...	...
BRITISH VIRGIN ISLANDS ‡	1974	1	6	231	21	...	...	...
CANADA ‡	1976	754	2 664	...	37 534	...	...	...
COSTA RICA ‡	1977	18	18	...	...	...	...	...
GREENLAND ‡	1974	1	74	...	93	...	...	...
GUATEMALA ‡	1977	1	36	2 000	27	...	...	...
MEXICO	1974	1 084	1 084	7 135	2 777	...	...	...
NETHERLANDS ANTILLES‡	1974	1	3	...	92	...	...	...
ST. LUCIA	1974	1	9	727	46	...	...	...
ST. PIERRE AND MIQUELON	1974	3	3	314	15	...	...	...
TRINIDAD AND TOBAGO	1977	1	4	3 000	68	...	...	...
UNITED STATES OF AMERICA	1974	8 337	80 805	...	387 565	...	...	...
AMERICA, SOUTH								
ARGENTINA	1977	1 528	1 528	317 723	9 532	...	...	...
CHILE ‡	1978	130	...	...	449	...	800	...
SURINAME ‡	1978	2	68	3 070	268	—	—	—
VENEZUELA	1978	1	18	1 081	216	—	2 402	—
ASIA								
BAHRAIN ‡	1974	1	9	2 000	100	...	...	...
BRUNEI ‡	1977	1	29	949	76	...	...	...
HONG KONG	1974	8	10	1 875	230	...	...	...
IRAQ	1974	24	26	5 460	195	...	...	...
JAPAN ‡	1977	891	1 609	...	58 786	...	...	...
JORDAN ‡	1974	11	11	...	81	...	...	...
KOREA, REPUBLIC OF ‡	1977	110	110	...	949	...	...	...
KUWAIT	1974	1	19	7 614	178	...	...	...
MALAYSIA ‡	1977	16	188	17 240	880	...	272	128
PHILIPPINES ‡	1977	...	449	...	1 012	...	...	...
QATAR	1974	1	1	...	53	...	...	...
SAUDI ARABIA	1974	8	8	28 000	...	...	...	...
SRI LANKA ‡	1977	381	...	...	727	...	...	...
THAILAND	1974	526	527	2 790	586	...	...	...
TURKEY	1977	...	423	...	4 139	...	2 610	—

ANNUAL ADDITIONS / ACQUISITIONS ANNUELLES / ADQUISICIONES ANUALES		REGISTERED BORROWERS / EMPRUNTEURS INSCRITS / PRESTATARIOS INSCRITOS	LOANS TO USERS / PRETS AUX USAGERS / PRESTAMOS A LOS USUARIOS	CURRENT EXPENDITURE / DEPENSES ORDINAIRES / GASTOS ORDINARIOS		LIBRARY EMPLOYEES / PERSONNEL DES BIBLIOTHEQUES / PERSONAL DE LAS BIBLIOTECAS			POPULATION SERVED / DESSERVIE / SERVIDA
VOLUMES / VOLUMES / VOLUMENES	OTHER MATERIALS / AUTRES MATERIELS / OTROS MATERIALES			TOTAL / TOTAL / TOTAL (000)	STAFF / PERSONNEL / PERSONAL (%)	TOTAL / TOTAL / TOTAL	HOLDING A DIPLOMA / DIPLOME / DIPLOMADO	TRAINED ON THE JOB / FORME SUR LE TAS / FORMADO EN EJERCICIO	(%)
(8)	(9)	(10)	(11)	(12)	(13)	(14)	(15)	(16)	(17)
2 240	...	3 000	62 000	37	84	4	1	–	89
6 155	...	86 898	139 167	98	47	61	8	27	...
103 603	...	44 396	...	...	...	145	30	50	60
4 500	...	38 009	107 583	...	...	80	13	35	*30
470	...	9 238	16 555	54	...	45	...	5	5
7 936	250	17 593	143 329	170	59	48	5	12	...
8 746	...	7 585	128 841	143	74	36	4	11	67
13 566	...	66 567	605 321	623	77	66	8	15	...
9 000	...	21 000	121 000	66	78	26	3	–	70
6 202	...	9 110	218 476	259	51	19	5	14	100
1 349	...	4 609	20 815	27	68	5	1	1	42
...	...	...	112 240 346	156 635	62	6 516	1 607	...	...
...	162	...		...	...	46	2	1	...
19 093	...	...	116 071	2 143	37	8	5	–	*96
3 600	...	...	...	...	...	10	2	...	345
545 190	...	4 618 871	...	1 697	38	1 445	...	...	8
10 068	...	6 456	165 828	560	71	36	8	–	7
2 951	...	9 570	67 120	120	55	27	1	5	36
2 000	...	3 700	...	81	62	3	...	...	51
4 920	...	1 300	136 632	674	76	49	3	–	35
27 579 240	...	...	892 854 268	770 573	76	44 949	9 097	...	100
...	...	4 201 244	9 552 909	...	...	...	...	...	...
60 986	...	...	2 250 140	...	...	301	38	1	...
2 100	...	53 637	769 000	376	66	52	18	34	77
28 988	2 402	8 541	822 241	411 930	98	129	9	120	624
4 000	...	19 000	30 000	99	85	63	...	9	...
5 832	...	4 970	39 347	496	62	50	2	24	21
17 557	...	27 792	475 501	949	84	72	3	9	...
...	...	550 829	...	...	...	222	38	87	...
5 338 000	...	6 521 000	114 160 000	1 493 317	...	♀ 289	4 076	...	69
...	...	...	...	39	47	48	1	21	...
66 467	...	3 124 981	...	1 564 795	58	944	211	...	9
27 441	...	7 617	19 285	...	...	112	2	25	55
...	...	173 843	...	2 585	...	302	25	...	2
443 800	...	468 566	459 530	...	...	816	20	...	...
5 905	...	583	5 739	...	...	14	3	4	...
...	...	...	...	250	...	...	...	3	...
...	...	177 638	...	4 396	...	602	4	...	...
7 518	...	165 399	...	502	50	356	137	30	2
232 325	...	331 288	1 774 064	125 840	92	1 262	62	1 200	...

COUNTRY / PAYS / PAIS	YEAR / ANNEE / AÑO	ADMINISTRATIVE UNITS / UNITES ADMINISTRATIVES / UNIDADES ADMINISTRATIVAS	SERVICE POINTS / POINTS DE DESSERTE / PUNTOS DE SERVICIO	COLLECTIONS / COLLECTIONS / COLECCIONES				
				BOOKS/LIVRES/LIBROS		MICRO-FORMS / MICRO-COPIES / MICRO-COPIAS	AUDIO-VISUAL DOCUMENTS / MATERIELS AUDIO-VISUELS / MATERIALES AUDIO-VISUALES	OTHER LIBRARY MATERIALS / AUTRES MATERIELS DE BIBLIOTHEQUE / OTROS MATERIALES DE BIBLIOTECA
				METRES OF SHELVING / METRES DE RAYONNAGE / METROS DE ESTANTES	NUMBER OF VOLUMES / NOMBRE DE VOLUMES / NUMERO DE VOLUMENES (000)			
		(1)	(2)	(3)	(4)	(5)	(6)	(7)
EUROPE								
AUSTRIA	1974	426	2 318	142 454	4 364	...	...	...
BULGARIA ‡	1977	5 902	...	...	44 117	22 446	...	921 105
CZECHOSLOVAKIA ‡	1977	12 803	12 803	...	45 425	—	201 675	1 902 340
DENMARK	1974	251	1 351	...	32 713	...	...	...
FAEROE ISLANDS	1974	14	14	1 796	63	...	...	...
FINLAND	1977	478	...	...	19 221	*1 000	*50 000	...
FRANCE ‡	1977	1 026	1 816	1 251 571	48 661	...	592 128	...
GERMAN DEMOCRATIC REPUBLIC ‡	1977	9 418	17 760	...	39 600	——>	1 343 484	
GERMANY, FEDERAL REPUBLIC OF ‡	1977	...	13 763	...	76 756	...	...	...
GIBRALTAR	1974	3	3	2 203	81	...	...	...
HUNGARY ‡	1977	2 936	9 837	...	33 649	...	1 283 255	——>
ICELAND	1974	251	273	...	1 033	...	...	...
IRELAND ‡	1977	31	2 168	...	6 924	...	...	...
NETHERLANDS ‡	1976	428	989	...	22 253	...	449 635	191 081
NORWAY	1977	455	1 429	...	12 001	...	...	...
POLAND ‡	1977	9 128	27 539	...	81 870	...	280 000	473 000
PORTUGAL ‡	1977	117	...	...	5 893	...	...	...
ROMANIA	1974	6 575	...	...	52 882	...	...	...
SAN MARINO	1974	1	1	36	1	...	...	...
SPAIN	1977	1 459	1 820	265 657	11 135	2 783	10 645	—
SWEDEN ‡	1977	334	2 295	989 270	34 615	105 000	704 206	—
UNITED KINGDOM ‡	1975	...	13 596	...	122 824	738 806	2 562 817	...
YUGOSLAVIA ‡	1977	1 922	2 880	331 447	20 139	656	18 368	145 204
OCEANIA								
COOK ISLANDS	1974	1	3	570	15	...	...	...
FIJI	1978	9	9	...	91	...	...	...
FRENCH POLYNESIA	1974	1	2	760	18	...	...	...
KIRIBATI	1974	1	26	...	*20	...	...	...
NEW CALEDONIA	1974	1	1	1 034	34	...	...	...
NEW HEBRIDES ‡	1976	1	1	300	12	...	...	...
NEW ZEALAND	1974	191	278	231 218	4 902	...	...	...
NIUE	1974	1	1	114	6	...	...	...
NORFOLK ISLAND	1977	1	1	100	4	—	—	...
PACIFIC ISLANDS	1977	...	5	...	16	...	...	...
SAMOA	1974	1	3	...	36	...	...	...
SOLOMON ISLANDS	1974	2	2	334	2	...	...	...
U.S.S.R.								
UKRAINIAN S.S.R. ‡	1974	21 666	47 050	...	258 060	...	...	...

ANNUAL ADDITIONS ACQUISITIONS ANNUELLES ADQUISICIONES ANUALES		REGISTERED BORROWERS EMPRUNTEURS INSCRITS PRESTATARIOS INSCRITOS	LOANS TO USERS PRETS AUX USAGERS PRESTAMOS A LOS USUARIOS	CURRENT EXPENDITURE DEPENSES ORDINAIRES GASTOS ORDINARIOS		LIBRARY EMPLOYEES PERSONNEL DES BIBLIOTHEQUES PERSONAL DE LAS BIBLIOTECAS			POPULATION SERVED POPULATION DESSERVIE POBLACION SERVIDA
VOLUMES VOLUMES VOLUMENES	OTHER MATERIALS AUTRES MATERIELS OTROS MATERIALES			TOTAL (000)	STAFF PERSONNEL PERSONAL (%)	TOTAL TOTAL TOTAL	HOLDING A DIPLOMA DIPLOME DIPLOMADO	TRAINED ON THE JOB FORME SUR LE TAS FORMADO EN EJERCICIO	(%)
(8)	(9)	(10)	(11)	(12)	(13)	(14)	(15)	(16)	(17)
...	...	635 344	9 979 062	106 656	...	1 159	631	...	...
3 002 840	...	2 319 871	34 184 380	13 140	49	4 521	2 806	1 715	26
1 776 000	116 898	2 419 348	76 754 000	262 436	...	9 623	2 934	6 689	100
3 966 719	...		83 673 128	603 942	49	4 218	1 520	—	75
6 878	...	5 017	70 853	935	...	19	5	—	
*1 000 000	*10 300	1 729 315	66 368 484	165 000	61	*3 400	*1 600	...	85
2 976 394	132 363	3 635 564	79 889 067	523 493	55	6 910	2 252	—	89
...	...	4 778 138	86 298 100	99 246	39	6 640	2 220	4 420	100
...	...	...	*140 000 000	*400 000	*60	...	...	...	...
...	...	5 950	...	13	63	10	...	...	100
2 099 693	...	2 225 526	55 243 417	90 938	...	3 911	419	1 233	100
52 820	...	50 000	1 605 170	117 506	...	289	8	9	...
	...	922 768	25 376 042	5 917	46	979	200	...	...
2 339 326	88 608	3 370 643	126 845 597	162 944	60	5 375	...	...	100
747 331	...	860 381	15 956 915	189 738	57	...	...	...	...
4 200 000	88 000	7 252 000	144 127 000	262 145	...	...	...	...	21
231 011	...	2 249 675	8 504 722	90 219	...	322	...	...	...
3 209 300	...	3 918 411		...	...	...	...	...	...
500	...	100	500	1 000	—	1	—	1	...
529 572	1 364	1 005 676	6 128 566	572 314	59	1 821	362	1 459	68
2 213 000	70 000	...	76 694 000	666 511	53	4 836	1 840	——>	100
13 381 575	453 062	...	589 286	161 417	52	26 487	8 057	...	100
1 104 294	667	3 630 223	...	4 702 332	...	3 752	2 502	403	...
*200	...	2 898	...	6	93	2	1	1	...
10 469	...	33 044	313 698	...	...	36	3	6	26
250	...	3 040	88 797	148	95	4	—	4	33
1 380	...	...	...	3	24	3	—	3	68
900	...	1 660	72 786	7 467	71	7	1	—	45
1 000	...	650	...	15	55	2	...	...	20
405 581	...	1 040 651	23 120 926	5 814	62	1 860	353	...	*80
...	...	474	...	...	...	2	—	2	100
320	—	424	13 822	5	64	1	—	—	25
...	...	...	...	...	...	8	—	8	43
2 050	...	8 000	34 000	21	68	14	1	11	...
370	...	55	...	...	...	3	1	1	*27
24 506 000	...	22 775 300	471 082 700	...	...	33 874	23 133	10 741	...

COMORO:
  E—> THE FIGURE IN COLUMN 14 REFERS TO PART-TIME
STAFF ONLY.
  FR-> LE CHIFFRE DE LA COLONNE 14 SE REFERE AU
PERSONNEL EMPLOYE A TEMPS PARTIEL SEULEMENT.
  ESP> LA CIFRA DE LA COLUMNA 14 SE REFIERE AL
PERSONAL DE JORNADA PARCIAL SOLAMENTE.

GAMBIA:
  E—> THE DATA IN COLUMNS 12 AND 13 CONCERN 1
LIBRARY WITH 4 SERVICE POINTS FINANCED BY PUBLIC
AUTHORITIES.
  FR-> LES DONNEES DES COLONNES 12 ET 13
CONCERNENT 1 BIBLIOTHEQUE AVEC 4 POINTS DE
DESSERTE, FINANCEE PAR LES POUVOIRS PUBLICS.
  ESP> LOS DATOS DE LAS COLUMNAS 12 Y 13 SE
REFIEREN A 1 BIBLIOTECA CON 4 PUNTOS DE SERVICIO,
FINANCIADA POR LOS PODERES PUBLICOS.

GHANA:
  E—> THE FIGURES IN COLUMNS 15 AND 16 REFER TO
FULL-TIME STAFF ONLY.
  FR-> LES CHIFFRES DES COLONNES 15 ET 16 SE
RAPPORTENT AU PERSONNEL EMPLOYE A PLEIN TEMPS
SEULEMENT.
  ESP> LAS CIFRAS DE LAS COLUMNAS 15 Y 16 SE
REFIEREN AL PERSONAL DE JORNADA COMPLETA
SOLAMENTE.

NIGERIA:
  E—> COLUMN 10 REFERS TO 26 LIBRARIES WITH 43
SERVICE POINTS. COLUMNS 12 AND 13 REFER TO 27
LIBRARIES WITH 45 SERVICE POINTS.
  FR-> LA COLONNE 10 NE TIENT COMPTE QUE DE 26
BIBLIOTHEQUES AVEC 43 POINTS DE DESSERTE. LES
COLONNES 12 ET 13 SE RAPPORTENT A 27 BIBLIOTHEQUES
AVEC 45 POINTS DE DESSERTE.
  ESP> LA COLUMNA 10 SOLO TOMA EN CONSIDERACION
26 BIBLIOTECAS CON 43 PUNTOS DE SERVICIO. LAS
COLUMNAS 12 Y 13 SE REFIEREN A 27 BIBLIOTECAS
CON 45 PUNTOS DE SERVICIO.

TUNISIA:
  E—> THE FIGURES IN COLUMNS 14, 15 AND 16 REFER
TO FULL-TIME STAFF ONLY.
  FR-> LES CHIFFRES DES COLONNES 14, 15 ET 16 SE
REFERENT AU PERSONNEL EMPLOYE A PLEIN TEMPS
SEULEMENT.
  ESP> LAS CIFRAS DE LAS COLUMNAS 14, 15 Y 16 SE
REFIEREN AL PERSONAL DE JORNADA COMPLETA
SOLAMENTE.

ZAIRE:
  E—> THE FIGURE IN COLUMN 12 REFERS TO
EXPENDITURE FOR EMPLOYEES ONLY. THE DATA IN
COLUMNS 14 AND 16 DO NOT INCLUDE PART-TIME STAFF.
  FR-> LE CHIFFRE DE LA COLONNE 12 SE REFERE AUX
DEPENSES POUR LE PERSONNEL SEULEMENT. LES DONNEES
DES COLONNES 14 ET 16 N'INCLUENT PAS LE PERSONNEL
EMPLOYE A TEMPS PARTIEL.
  ESP> LA CIFRA DE LA COLUMNA 12 SE REFIERE A LOS
GASTOS DE PERSONAL SOLAMENTE. LOS DATOS DE LAS
COLUMNAS 14 Y 16 NO INCLUYEN EL PERSONAL DE
JORNADA PARCIAL.

BELIZE:
  E—> THE FIGURE IN COLUMN 12 INCLUDES
EXPENDITURE FOR THE NATIONAL LIBRARY.
  FR-> LE CHIFFRE DE LA COLONNE 12 INCLUT LES
DEPENSES RELATIVES A LA BIBLIOTHEQUE NATIONALE.
  ESP> LA CIFRA DE LA COLUMNA 12 INCLUYE LOS
GASTOS RELATIVOS A LA BIBLIOTECA NACIONAL.

BRITISH VIRGIN ISLANDS:
  E—> THE PUBLIC LIBRARY IS ALSO THE NATIONAL
LIBRARY.

BRITISH VIRGIN ISLANDS (CONT):
  FR-> LA BIBLIOTHEQUE PUBLIQUE SERT AUSSI DE
BIBLIOTHEQUE NATIONALE.
  ESP> LA BIBLIOTECA PUBLICA DESEMPENA AL MISMO
TIEMPO LA FUNCION DE BIBLIOTECA NACIONAL.

CANADA:
  E—> THE FIGURES IN COLUMNS 14 AND 15 REFER TO
FULL-TIME STAFF ONLY.
  FR-> LES CHIFFRES DES COLONNES 14 ET 15 SE
RAPPORTENT AU PERSONNEL EMPLOYE A PLEIN TEMPS
SEULEMENT.
  ESP> LAS CIFRAS DE LAS COLUMNAS 14 Y 15 SE
REFIEREN AL PERSONAL DE JORNADA COMPLETA
SOLAMENTE.

COSTA RICA:
  E—> THE FIGURES IN COLUMNS 14, 15 AND 16 REFER
TO FULL-TIME STAFF ONLY.
  FR-> LES CHIFFRES DES COLONNES 14, 15 ET 16 SE
REFERENT AU PERSONNEL EMPLOYE A PLEIN TEMPS
SEULEMENT.
  ESP> LAS CIFRAS DE LAS COLUMNAS 14, 15 Y 16 SE
REFIEREN AL PERSONAL DE JORNADA COMPLETA
SOLAMENTE.

GREENLAND:
  E—> COLUMNS 12, 13, 14 AND 15 INCLUDE DATA FOR
THE NATIONAL LIBRARY. THE FIGURE IN COLUMN 14
REFERS TO FULL-TIME STAFF ONLY.
  FR-> LES COLONNES 12, 13, 14 ET 15 INCLUENT LES
DONNEES RELATIVES A LA BIBLIOTHEQUE NATIONALE.
LE CHIFFRE DE LA COLONNE 14 SE REFERE AU
PERSONNEL EMPLOYE A PLEIN TEMPS SEULEMENT.
  ESP> LAS COLUMNAS 12, 13, 14 Y 15 INCLUYEN LOS
DATOS RELATIVOS A LA BIBLIOTECA NACIONAL. LA
CIFRA DE LA COLUMNA 14 SE REFIERE AL PERSONAL
DE JORNADA COMPLETA SOLAMENTE.

GUATEMALA:
  E—> THE FIGURES IN COLUMNS 14 AND 15 REFER TO
FULL-TIME STAFF ONLY.
  FR-> LES CHIFFRES DES COLONNES 14 ET 15 SE
REFERENT AU PERSONNEL EMPLOYE A PLEIN TEMPS
SEULEMENT.
  ESP> LAS CIFRAS DE LAS COLUMNAS 14 Y 15 SE
REFIEREN AL PERSONAL DE JORNADA COMPLETA
SOLAMENTE.

NETHERLANDS ANTILLES:
  E—> DATA REFER TO THE PUBLIC LIBRARY OF
CURACAO ONLY.
  FR-> LES DONNEES SE RAPPORTENT A LA BIBLIOTHEQUE
PUBLIQUE DE CURACAO SEULEMENT.
  ESP> LOS DATOS SE REFIEREN A LA BIBLIOTECA
PUBLICA DE CURACAO SOLAMENTE.

CHILE:
  E—> THE FIGURES IN COLUMNS 14, 15 AND 16 REFER
TO FULL-TIME STAFF ONLY.
  FR-> LES CHIFFRES DES COLONNES 14, 15 ET 16 SE
REFERENT AU PERSONNEL EMPLOYE A PLEIN TEMPS
SEULEMENT.
  ESP> LAS CIFRAS DE LAS COLUMNAS 14, 15 Y 16 SE
REFIEREN AL PERSONAL DE JORNADA COMPLETA
SOLAMENTE.

SURINAME:
  E—> THE FIGURES IN COLUMNS 14, 15 AND 16 REFER
TO FULL-TIME STAFF ONLY.
  FR-> LES CHIFFRES DES COLONNES 14, 15 ET 16 SE
REFERENT AU PERSONNEL EMPLOYE A PLEIN TEMPS
SEULEMENT.
  ESP> LAS CIFRAS DE LAS COLUMNAS 14, 15, Y 16 SE
REFIEREN AL PERSONAL DE JORNADA COMPLETA
SOLAMENTE.

BAHRAIN:
E—> DATA DO NOT INCLUDE LIBRARIES FINANCED FROM PRIVATE SOURCES. THE FIGURE IN COLUMN 16 REFERS TO FULL—TIME STAFF ONLY.
FR—> LES DONNEES N'INCLUENT PAS LES BIBLIOTHEQUES FINANCEES PAR DES FONDS PRIVES. LE CHIFFRE DE LA COLONNE 16 CONCERNE SEULEMENT LE PERSONNEL EMPLOYE A PLEIN TEMPS.
ESP> LOS DATOS NO INCLUYEN LAS BIBLIOTECAS FINANCIADAS CON FONDOS PRIVADOS. LA CIFRA DE LA COLUMNA 16 SE REFIERE AL PERSONAL DE JORNADA COMPLETA SOLAMENTE.

BRUNEI:
E—> THE FIGURES IN COLUMNS 14, 15 AND 16 REFER TO FULL—TIME STAFF ONLY.
FR—> LES CHIFFRES DES COLONNES 14, 15 ET 16 SE REFERENT AU PERSONNEL EMPLOYE A PLEIN TEMPS SEULEMENT.
ESP> LAS CIFRAS DE LAS COLUMNAS 14, 15 Y 16 SE REFIEREN AL PERSONAL DE JORNADA COMPLETA SOLAMENTE.

JAPAN:
E—> THE FIGURE IN COLUMN 12 DOES NOT INCLUDE EXPENDITURE FOR THE EMPLOYEES, THAT IN COLUMN 15 REFERS TO FULL—TIME STAFF ONLY.
FR—> LE CHIFFRE DE LA COLONNE 12 N'INCLUT PAS LES DEPENSES POUR LE PERSONNEL, CELUI DE LA COLONNE 15 SE RAPPORTE AU PERSONNEL EMPLOYE A PLEIN TEMPS SEULEMENT.
ESP> LA CIFRA DE LA COLUMNA 12 NO INCLUYE LOS GASTOS DE PERSONAL; LA DE LA COLUMNA 15 SE REFIERE AL PERSONAL DE JORNADA COMPLETA.

JORDAN:
E—> DATA REFER TO THE EAST BANK ONLY.
FR—> LES DONNEES SE REFERENT A LA RIVE ORIENTALE SEULEMENT.
ESP> LOS DATOS SE REFIEREN A LA ORILLA ORIENTAL SOLAMENTE.

KOREA, REPUBLIC OF:
E—> THE FIGURES IN COLUMNS 14 AND 15 DO NOT INCLUDE PART—TIME STAFF.
FR—> LES CHIFFRES DES COLONNES 14 ET 15 N'INCLUENT PAS LE PERSONNEL EMPLOYE A TEMPS PARTIEL.
ESP> LAS CIFRAS DE LAS COLUMNAS 14 Y 15 NO INCLUYEN EL PERSONAL DE JORNADA PARCIAL.

MALAYSIA:
E—> THE FIGURE IN COLUMN 15 REFERS TO FULL—TIME STAFF ONLY.
FR—> LE CHIFFRE DE LA COLONNE 15 CONCERNE LE PERSONNEL EMPLOYE A PLEIN TEMPS SEULEMENT.
ESP> LA CIFRA DE LA COLUMNA 15 SE REFIERE AL PERSONAL DE JORNADA COMPLETA SOLAMENTE.

PHILIPPINES:
E—> THE FIGURES IN COLUMNS 14 AND 15 REFER TO FULL—TIME STAFF ONLY.
FR—> LES CHIFFRES DES COLONNES 14 ET 15 CONCERNENT SEULEMENT LE PERSONNEL EMPLOYE A PLEIN TEMPS.
ESP> LAS CIFRAS DE LAS COLUMNAS 14 Y 15 SE REFIEREN AL PERSONAL DE JORNADA COMPLETA SOLAMENTE.

SRI LANKA:
E—> THE FIGURE IN COLUMN 12 COMPRISES ONLY EXPENDITURE FOR EMPLOYEES AND FOR ACQUISITIONS. DATA IN COLUMNS 14 AND 15 REFER TO FULL—TIME STAFF ONLY.

SRI LANKA (CONT):
FR—> LE CHIFFRE DE LA COLONNE 12 COMPREND SEULEMENT LES DEPENSES POUR LE PERSONNEL ET LES ACQUISITIONS. LES DONNEES DES COLONNES 14 ET 15 SE RAPPORTENT AU PERSONNEL EMPLOYE A PLEIN TEMPS SEULEMENT.
ESP> LA CIFRA DE LA COLUMNA 12 COMPRENDE UNICAMENTE LOS GASTOS DE PERSONAL Y DE ADQUISICIONES. LOS DATOS DE LAS COLUMNAS 14 Y 15 SE REFIEREN AL PERSONAL DE JORNADA COMPLETA SOLAMENTE.

BULGARIA:
E—> THE FIGURES IN COLUMNS 14, 15 AND 16 DO NOT INCLUDE PART—TIME STAFF.
FR—> LES CHIFFRES DES COLONNES 14, 15 ET 16 N'INCLUENT PAS LE PERSONNEL EMPLOYE A TEMPS PARTIEL.
ESP> LAS CIFRAS DE LAS COLUMNAS 14, 15 Y 16 NO INCLUYEN EL PERSONAL DE JORNADA PARCIAL.

CZECHOSLOVAKIA:
E—> THE DATA IN COLUMN 12 REFER TO EXPENDITURE FOR THE EMPLOYEES ONLY.
FR—> LES DONNEES DE LA COLONNE 12 NE TIENNENT COMPTE QUE DES DEPENSES POUR LE PERSONNEL
ESP> LOS DATOS DE LA COLUMNA 12 SOLO SE REFIEREN A LOS GASTOS DE PERSONAL.

FRANCE:
E—> DATA INCLUDE PUBLIC LIBRARIES IN OVERSEAS DEPARTMENTS. THE FIGURES IN COLUMNS 6 AND 9 CONCERN ONLY AUDITORY MATERIALS. COLUMN 15 DOES NOT INCLUDE PART—TIME STAFF.
FR—> LES DONNEES COMPRENNENT LES BIBLIOTHEQUES PUBLIQUES DES DEPARTEMENTS D'OUTRE—MER. LES CHIFFRES DES COLONNES 6 ET 9 NE CONCERNENT QUE LES MATERIELS AUDITIFS, CEUX DE LA COLONNE 15 N'INCLUENT PAS LE PERSONNEL EMPLOYE A TEMPS PARTIEL.
ESP> LOS DATOS INCLUYEN LAS BIBLIOTECAS PUBLICAS DE LOS DEPARTAMENTOS DE ULTRAMAR. LAS CIFRAS DE LAS COLUMNAS 6 Y 9 SOLO SE REFIEREN AL MATERIAL AUDITIVO, LAS DE LA COLUMNA 15 NO INCLUYEN EL PERSONAL DE JORNADA PARCIAL.

GERMAN DEMOCRATIC REPUBLIC:
E—> THE DATA IN COLUMN 4 INCLUDE MANUSCRIPTS AND MICROFORMS. THE FIGURES IN COLUMNS 14, 15 AND 16 INCLUDE PART—TIME STAFF BUT NOT IN FULL—TIME EQUIVALENT.
FR—> LES DONNEES DE LA COLONNE 4 INCLUENT LES MANUSCRITS ET LES MICROCOPIES. LES CHIFFRES DES COLONNES 14, 15 ET 16 INCLUENT LE PERSONNEL EMPLOYE A TEMPS PARTIEL NON CALCULE EN EQUIVALENT PLEIN TEMPS.
ESP> LOS DATOS DE LA COLUMNA 4 SE REFIEREN A LOS MANUSCRITOS Y MICROCOPIAS. LAS CIFRAS DE LAS COLUMNAS 14, 15 Y 16 INCLUYEN EL PERSONAL DE JORNADA PARCIAL, QUE NO SE HA CALCULADO EN EQUIVALENTE DE JORNADA COMPLETA.

GERMANY, FEDERAL REPUBLIC:
E—> THE FIGURES IN COLUMNS 12 AND 13 DO NOT INCLUDE EXPENDITURE FOR LIBRARIES FINANCED FROM PRIVATE SOURCES.
FR—> LES CHIFFRES DES COLONNES 12 ET 13 NE COMPRENNENT PAS LES BIBLIOTHEQUES FINANCEES PAR DES FONDS PRIVES
ESP> LAS CIFRAS DE LAS COLUMNAS 12 Y 13 NO COMPRENDEN LAS BIBLIOTECAS FINANCIADAS CON FONDOS PRIVADOS.

HUNGARY:
E—> THE DATA IN COLUMNS 6 AND 8 REFER TO
LIBRARIES FINANCED BY PUBLIC AUTHORITIES ONLY.
COLUMN 6 INCLUDES MANUSCRIPTS.   COLUMN 12 CONCERNS
EXPENDITURE FOR ACQUISITIONS ONLY.
FR—> LES DONNEES DES COLONNES 6 ET 8 SE
RAPPORTENT AUX BIBLIOTHEQUES FINANCEES PAR LES
POUVOIRS PUBLICS SEULEMENT.   LA COLONNE 6 INCLUT
LES MANUSCRITS.   LA COLONNE 12 N'INDIQUE QUE LES
DEPENSES POUR LES ACQUISITIONS.
ESP> LOS DATOS DE LAS COLUMNAS 6 Y 8 SE REFIEREN
A LAS BIBLIOTECAS FINANCIADAS POR LOS PODERES
PUBLICOS SOLAMENTE.   LA COLUMNA 6 INCLUYE LOS
MANUSCRITOS.   LA COLUMNA 12 SOLO SE REFIERE A LOS
GASTOS DE ADQUISICIONES.

IRELAND:
E—> THE FIGURE IN COLUMN 15 DOES NOT INCLUDE
PART-TIME STAFF.
FR—> LE CHIFFRE DE LA COLONNE 15 N'INCLUT PAS
LE PERSONNEL EMPLOYE A TEMPS PARTIEL.
ESP> LA CIFRA DE LA COLUMNA 15 NO INCLUYE EL
PERSONAL DE JORNADA PARCIAL.

NETHERLANDS:
E—> THE DATA ON ACQUISITIONS IN COLUMN 9 REFER
TO AUDIO-VISUAL DOCUMENTS ONLY.
FR—> DANS LA COLONNE 9, LES DONNEES RELATIVES
AUX ACQUISITIONS SE REFERENT AUX MATERIELS AUDIO-
VISUELS SEULEMENT.
ESP> EN LA COLUMNA 9, LOS DATOS RELATIVOS A LAS
ADQUISICIONES SE REFIEREN AL MATERIAL AUDIOVISUAL
SOLAMENTE.

POLAND:
E—> THE DATA ON ACQUISITIONS IN COLUMN 9 DO NOT
INCLUDE MICROFORMS.   THE FIGURE IN COLUMN 12 DOES
NOT INCLUDE EXPENDITURE FOR EMPLOYEES.
FR—> LES DONNEES RELATIVES AUX ACQUISITIONS,
COLONNE 9, N'INCLUENT PAS LES MICROCOPIES. LE
CHIFFRE DE LA COLONNE 12 NE COMPREND PAS LES
DEPENSES POUR LE PERSONNEL.
ESP> EN LA COLUMNA 9, LOS DATOS RELATIVOS A LAS
ADQUISICIONES NO INCLUYEN LAS MICROCOPIAS.   LA
CIFRA DE LA COLUMNA 12 NO COMPRENDE LOS GASTOS
DE PERSONAL.

PORTUGAL:
E—> THE FIGURE IN COLUMN 11 INCLUDES WORKS
USED IN READING ROOM.   DATA IN COLUMN 12 REFER TO
EXPENDITURE FOR EMPLOYEES AND ACQUISITIONS.
COLUMN 14 CONCERNS FULL-TIME STAFF ONLY.
FR—> LE CHIFFRE DE LA COLONNE 11 INCLUT LES
OUVRAGES UTILISES DANS LES SALLES DE LECTURE.
LES DONNEES DE LA COLONNE 12 SE RAPPORTENT AUX
DEPENSES POUR LE PERSONNEL ET LES ACQUISITIONS.
LA COLONNE 14 CONCERNE LE PERSONNEL EMPLOYE A
PLEIN TEMPS SEULEMENT.

PORTUGAL (CONT):
ESP> LA CIFRA DE LA COLUMNA 11 INCLUYE LOS
VOLUMENES UTILIZADOS EN LAS SALAS DE LECTURA.
LOS DATOS DE LA COLUMNA 12 SE REFIEREN A LOS
GASTOS DE PERSONAL Y DE ADQUISICIONES.   LA COLUMNA
14 SE REFIERE AL PERSONAL DE JORNADA COMPLETA
SOLAMENTE.

SWEDEN:
E—> THE DATA ON ACQUISITIONS IN COLUMN 9 REFER
TO AUDITORY MATERIALS ONLY.
FR—> DANS LA COLONNE 9, LES DONNEES RELATIVES
AUX ACQUISITIONS SE RAPPORTENT AUX MATERIELS
AUDITIFS SEULEMENT.
ESP> EN LA COLUMNA 9, LOS DATOS RELATIVOS A LAS
ADQUISICIONES SE REFIEREN AL MATERIAL AUDITIVO
SOLAMENTE.

UNITED KINGDOM:
E—> THE FIGURE IN COLUMN 6 REFERS TO AUDITORY
MATERIALS ONLY.
FR—> LE CHIFFRE DE LA COLONNE 6 SE RAPPORTE AUX
MATERIELS AUDITIFS SEULEMENT.
ESP> LA CIFRA DE LA COLUMNA 6 SE REFIERE AL
MATERIAL AUDITIVO SOLAMENTE

YUGOSLAVIA:
E—> THE FIGURE IN COLUMN 6 REFERS TO AUDITORY
MATERIALS ONLY.   THE DATA ON ACQUISITIONS IN
COLUMN 9 CONCERNS ONLY MICROFORMS.   COLUMN 12
REFERS TO EXPENDITURE (IN MILLIONS) FOR
ACQUISITIONS ONLY.
FR—> LE CHIFFRE DE LA COLONNE 6 SE RAPPORTE AUX
MATERIELS AUDITIFS SEULEMENT.   DANS LA COLONNE 9,
LES DONNEES RELATIVES AUX ACQUISITIONS CONCERNENT
SEULEMENT LES MICROCOPIES.   LA COLONNE 12 SE
REFERE AUX DEPENSES (EN MILLIONS) POUR LES
ACQUISITIONS SEULEMENT.
ESP> LA CIFRA DE LA COLUMNA 6 SE REFIERE AL
MATERIAL AUDITIVO SOLAMENTE.   EN LA COLUMNA 9,
LOS DATOS RELATIVOS A LAS ADQUISICIONES SOLO
CONCIERNEN LAS MICROCOPIAS.   LA COLUMNA 12 SE
REFIERE A LOS GASTOS (EN MILLONES) DE
ADQUISICIONES SOLAMENTE.

NEW HEBRIDES:
E—> THE FIGURE IN COLUMN 14 REFERS TO FULL-TIME
STAFF ONLY.
FR—> LE CHIFFRE DE LA COLONNE 14 SE RAPPORTE AU
PERSONNEL EMPLOYE A PLEIN TEMPS SEULEMENT.
ESP> LA CIFRA DE LA COLUMNA 14 SE REFIERE AL
PERSONAL DE JORNADA COMPLETA SOLAMENTE.

UKRAINIAN S.S.R.
E—> DATA IN COLUMN 12 DO NOT INCLUDE
MAINTENANCE STAFF.
FR—> LES DONNEES DE LA COLONNE 12 N'INCLUENT PAS
LE PERSONNEL DE MAINTENANCE.
ESP> LOS DATOS DE LA COLUMNA 12 NO INCLUYEN EL
PERSONAL DE MANTENENCIA.

8 Printed material

Imprimés

Impresos

This chapter is divided into three sections. Section 1, (Tables 8.1 to 8.13), deals with statistics on book production, including translations. The second section is concerned with statistics on newspapers and other periodical publications (Tables 8.14 to 8.16), while the last section, consisting of a single table, presents data on the production, importation, exportation, and consumption of newsprint and of other printing and writing paper.

The following text is divided into three sections in accordance with the different subject matters indicated above.

Section 1

In general, national book production statistics should be drawn up in accordance with the definitions and classifications set forth in the Recommendation concerning the International Standardization of Statistics relating to Book Production and Periodicals adopted in 1964 by the General Conference of Unesco.

In line with this Recommendation, book production statistics should cover printed non-periodical publications which are published in a particular country and made available to the public and which, in general, should be included in the national bibliographies of the various countries, with the exception of the following categories:

a) *Publications issued for advertising purposes*, provided that the literary or scientific text is subsidiary and that the publications are distributed free of charge (trade catalogues, prospectuses and other types of commercial, industrial and tourist advertising; publications describing activities or technical progress in some branch of industry or commerce and drawing attention to the products or services supplied by the publisher).

b) *Publications belonging to the following categories, when they are considered to be of a transitory character*: time-tables, price lists, telephone directories, etc.; programmes of entertainments, exhibitions, fairs, etc.; regulations and reports of business firms, company directives, circulars, etc.; calendars, almanacs, etc.

c) *Publications belonging to the following categories in which the text is not the most important part*: musical works (scores or music books), provided that the music is more important than the words; maps and charts, with the exception of atlases.

The following types of publication, inter alia, should be included in book production statistics:

1. *Government publications*, i.e. publications issued by public administrations or their subsidiary bodies, except for those which are confidential or designed for internal distribution only.

2. *School textbooks*, i.e. books prescribed for pupils receiving education at the first and second levels.

3. *University theses.*

4. *Offprints*, i.e. reprints of a part of a book or a periodical already published, provided that they have a title and a separate pagination and that they constitute a distinct work.

5. *Publications which form part of a series*, but which constitute separate bibliographical units.

6. *Illustrated works*: collections of prints, reproductions of works of art, drawings, etc., when such collections form complete paginated volumes and when the illustrations are accompanied by an explanatory text, however short, referring to these works or to the artists themselves; albums, illustrated books and pamphlets written in the form of continuous narratives, with pictures illustrating certain episodes; albums and picture books for children.

In compiling these statistics, the following definitions should be used:

a) A publication is considered to be *non-periodical* if it is published at one time or, at intervals, by volumes, the number of which is generally determined in advance.

b) The term *printed* includes reproduction by any method of mechanical impression, whatever it may be.

c) A publication is considered to be *published in a particular country* if the publisher has his registered office in the country where the statistics are compiled, the place of printing or place of circulation here being irrelevant. When a publication is issued by one or more publishers who have registered offices in two or more countries, it is considered as having been published in the country or countries where it is issued.

d) A publication is considered as being *made available to the public* when it is obtainable either by purchase or by distribution free of charge. Publications intended for a restricted readership, such as certain government publications, those of learned societies, political or professional organizations, etc., are also considered as being available to the public.

e) A *book* is a non-periodical printed publication of at least 49 pages, exclusive of the cover pages, published in the country and made available to the public.

f) A *pamphlet* is a non-periodical printed publication of at least 5 but not more than 48 pages, exclusive of the cover pages, published in a particular country and made available to the public.

g) A *first edition* is the first publication of an original or translated manuscript.

h) A *re-edition* is a publication distinguished from previous editions by change made in the contents (revised edition) or layout (new edition).

i) A *reprint* is unchanged in contents and layout, apart from correction of typographical errors in the previous edition. A reprint by any publisher other than the original publisher is regarded as a re-edition.

j) A *translation* is a publication which reproduces a work in a language other than the original language.

k) A *title* is a term used to designate a printed publication which forms a separate whole, whether issued in one or several volumes.

This section comprises thirteen tables, the first nine of which cover production as a whole, while the remaining four tables are limited exclusively to translation reproduction.

Tables 8.1 to 8.9 present data collected each year by questionnaires sent to Member States. Unless otherwise indicated it may be assumed that these data cover books and pamphlets, of original works or of translations. However, certain categories of publications which, according to the Recommendation, should be included in the book production statistics (e.g. government publications, school textbooks, university theses, offprints, illustrated works), or excluded from such statistics (e.g. publications issued for advertising purposes, publications of a transitory nature, publications in which the text is not the most important part) are classified differently, for statistical purposes, in different countries. In the absence of complete and precise information, it has not been possible to indicate certain differences of this kind ·between the various national statistics and the Recommendation.

Only those countries are included in tables 8.3, 8.4, 8.6 and 8.7 which were able to present statistics in accordance with the classification by subject set forth in the Recommendation. This classification is based upon the Universal Decimal Classification (UDC), details of which are given in a footnote to Table 8.3.

Whenever an indicated total does not correspond to the sum of its component items, the difference either represents the number of works not distributed among the nine main branches of the Universal Decimal Classification (Tables 8.1 and 8.5) or is explained by the rounding of figures (Tables 8.3 8.4, 8.6 and 8.7). These tables present for each country figures on books (A), pamphlets (B), and the total of the two groups (A+B). The figures received sometimes refer to the two groups separately or to the total of these or only to one group or the other. The tables show the different cases.

Table 8.1

Table 8.1 presents data for the years 1976 to 1978. This table includes only those countries for which Unesco can produce statistics relating to at least one of the three years under review. Unless otherwise stated, the data in this table refer to both *first editions* and *re-editions* of original works or of translations.

This table indicates that the ten countries with the largest book production (in terms of titles) in 1978 were the following: United States of America (85,126), Federal Republic of Germany (50,950), Japan (43,973), Republic of Korea (16,364), Netherlands (13,393), Canada (13,190), India (12,932), Poland (11,849), Italy (10,679), and Yugoslavia (10,509). Unfortunately, no 1978 data are available for the U.S.S.R., United Kingdom, France and Spain. For 1977 the number of titles published in these countries was: U.S.S.R. (85,395), United Kingdom (36,196), France (31,673) and Spain (24,896). The corresponding figure for Brazil in 1976 was 20,025.

Table 8.2

Unless otherwise stated, the data in this table refer to both *first editions* and *re-editions* of original works or of translations.

Tables 8.3 and 8.4

The figures given in Table 8.3 refer to both *first editions* and *re-editions* and those in Table 8.4 refer to *first editions* only.

Table 8.5

Unless otherwise stated, the data in Table 8.5 refer to *first editions*, *re-editions* and *reprints* of original works or of translations.

Tables 8.6 and 8.7

The figures given in Table 8.6 refer to *first editions*, *re-editions* and *reprints* and those in Table 8.7 to *first editions* only.

Table 8.8

The figures in this table refer to both *first editions* and *re-editions* of school textbooks which, in the Recommendation, are defined as books prescribed for pupils receiving education at the first and second levels.

Table 8.9

The figures in Table 8.9 refer to both *first editions* and *re-editions* of children's books.

Tables 8.10 to 8.13

Tables 8.10 to 8.12 give information on translations published in 1973, 1974 and 1975, while Table 8.13 contains information on the authors most translated during the period 1961-1975. These statistics are based on the information contained in the *Index Translationum*, the international bibliography of translations published by Unesco.

Section 2

The statistics in Tables 8.14 to 8.16 cover daily as well as non-daily newspapers of general interest and other periodicals.

In general, national statistics on newspapers and other periodicals should be drawn up in accordance with the definitions and classifications set forth in the Recommendation concerning the International Standardization of Statistics relating to Book Production and Periodicals adopted by the General Conference of Unesco in 1964. According to this Recommendation, national statistics on the press should cover printed periodical publications which are published in a particular country and made available to the public, with the exception of publications issued for advertising purposes, those of a transitory character, and those in which the text is not the most important part. However, the following types of publications, inter alia, should be included in statistics of periodicals: government periodicals, academic and scientific journals, periodicals of professional, trade union, political or sports organizations, etc., publications appearing annually or less frequently, parish magazines, school magazines and school newspapers, 'house organs'.

In compiling these statistics, the following definitions should be used:

1. A publication is considered to be a *periodical* if it constitutes one issue in a continuous series under the same title, published at regular or irregular intervals, over an indefinite period, individual issues in the series being numbered consecutively or each issue being dated.

2. Periodical publications are subdivided into two categories:

a) *General-interest newspapers* are periodicals intended for the general public and mainly designed to be a primary source of written information on current events connected with public affairs, international questions, politics, etc. A newspaper thus defined, issued at least four times a week, is considered to be a daily newspaper; those appearing three times a week or less frequently are considered as non-daily newspapers.

b) *Other periodicals* are those which are either concerned with subjects of very general interest or else mainly publish studies and factual information on such specialized subjects as legislation, finance, trade, medicine, fashion, sports, etc. This category covers specialized journals, reviews, magazines and all other periodicals apart from general-interest newspapers.

3. *Circulation* figures should show the average daily circulation, or the average circulation per issue in the case of non-daily publications. These figures should include the number of copies sold, either directly or by subscription, plus the number of free copies regularly distributed, both inside the country and abroad, except unsold copies. When circulation data are not available, the number of copies printed should be indicated. In interpreting data in the following tables, it should be borne in mind that in some cases, methods of enumeration, definitions and classifications applied by the different countries do not entirely conform to the standards recommended by Unesco. For example, circulation data refer either to the circulation itself as defined above or to the number of printed copies, and the corresponding figures are only estimates, usually official, of varying degrees of accuracy.

Table 8.14

Table 8.14 presents data on the number, total circulation and circulation per 1,000 inhabitants of daily general-interest newspapers for the years 1965, 1970, 1976 and 1977.

For the purpose of this table, a 'daily general-interest newspaper' is defined as a publication devoted primarily to recording news of current events in public affairs, international affairs, politics, etc., and which is published at least four times a week.

When the estimated circulation figures do not correspond to the total number of daily newspapers (this is indicated by a footnote) the number of copies per 1,000 inhabitants is not shown.

Table 8.15

This table gives for the latest year available, data on the number, total circulation and circulation per 1,000 inhabitants of non-daily newspapers of general-interest, as well as of other periodicals.

For the purpose of this table, a 'non-daily general-interest newspaper' is defined as a publication devoted primarily to recording news of current events in public affairs, international affairs, politics, etc., and which is published three times or less a week. Under the category of 'other periodicals' are included publications of periodical issue, other than newspapers containing information of general or of a specialized nature.

Table 8.16

Table 8.16 presents data concerning the number and circulation of periodicals other than general-interest newspapers, classified by subject groups. This classification is embodied in the above Recommendation. The data in this table refer to a given year in the period 1973-77.

For the purpose of this table, the category of 'other periodicals' includes publications of periodical issue, other than newspapers of general interest, containing information of a general or specialized nature.

The reader's attention is drawn to the fact that the addition of the two partial totals shown in this table should be identical to the total shown for 'other periodicals' in Table 8.15. This is not always the case, probably because data originate from different sources, or that it is not yet possible for certain countries to apply the international standardization. However, it has been considered preferable to publish data for as many countries as possible rather than to restrict their number to those for which statistics are complete and consistent. For this reason a clear warning is necessary so that the information provided in this table is interpreted and used with caution not forgetting that in many cases the figures represent at the most a very rough approximation of the existing situation.

Section 3

The data given in Table 8.17 relate to the consumption, production, export and import of 'cultural paper', i.e. newsprint as well as printing paper (other than newsprint) and writing paper. As in the preceding years, these data have been furnished by the *Food and Agriculture Organization of the United Nations* (FAO). Readers needing additional information should refer to the *Yearbook of Forest Products* published by FAO.

The term *newsprint* (item 641.1 of the Standard International Trade Classification, Revised) designates the bleached, unsized or slack-sized printing paper, without coating, of the type usually used for newspapers. Newsprint weighs from 45 to 60 grammes per square metre, at least 70 per cent of the weight of fibrous material usually being derived from mechanical pulp.

The expression *other printing and writing paper* (item 641.2 of the Standard International Trade Classification, Revised) covers paper other than newsprint in rolls or sheets, and which is suitable for use in printing and writing. It does not cover articles manufactured from printing and writing paper, such as stationery, exercise books, registers, etc.

For countries where no separate information for the two above-mentioned categories of paper is available, the totals are shown under the category 'newsprint'.

Ce Chapitre est divisé en trois sections. La section 1 se réfère aux statistiques sur l'édition de livres, y compris les traductions (tableaux 8.1 à 8.13). La section 2 concerne les statistiques relatives aux journaux et autres périodiques (tableaux 8.14 à 8.16); la dernière section présente des données sur la production, l'importation, l'exportation et la consommation de papier journal et autre papier d'impression et d'écriture.

Le texte suivant se compose donc de trois sections, en accord avec les différentes matières indiquées ci-dessus.

Section 1

D'une manière générale, les statistiques nationales de l'édition de livres devraient être établies conformément aux définitions et aux classifications figurant dans la Recommandation concernant la normalisation internationale des statistiques de l'édition de livres et de périodiques adoptée en 1964 par la Conférence Générale de l'Unesco.

Aux termes de la Recommandation, les statistiques de l'édition de livres devraient porter sur les publications non périodiques imprimées qui sont éditées dans le pays et offertes au public et qui devraient, en général, figurer dans les bibliographies nationales des différents pays, à l'exception des catégories suivantes:

a) *Publications éditées à des fins publicitaires*, à condition que le texte littéraire ou scientifique ne prédomine pas et que ces publications soient distribuées gratuitement (catalogues, prospectus et autres publications de propagande commerciale, industrielle et touristique; publications traitant de l'activité ou de l'évolution technique d'une branche de l'industrie ou du commerce en attirant l'attention sur les produits ou les services fournis par l'éditeur).

b) *Publications appartenant aux catégories suivantes, lorsqu'elles sont jugées comme ayant un caractère éphémère*: horaires, tarifs, annuaires téléphoniques, etc.; programmes de spectacles, d'expositions, de foires, etc.; statuts et bilans de sociétés, directives des entreprises, circulaires, etc.; calendriers, almanachs, etc.;

c) *Publications appartenant aux catégories suivantes dont le contenu prédominant n'est pas le texte*: les oeuvres musicales (partitions, cahiers de musique), à condition que la notation musicale soit plus importante que le texte; la production cartographique, excepté les atlas.

Les catégories suivantes de publications, notamment, devraient être comptées dans les statistiques de l'édition de livres:

1. *Publications officielles*, c'est-à-dire ouvrages publiés par les administrations publiques ou les organismes qui en dépendent, à l'exception de ceux qui sont confidentiels ou réservés à la distribution intérieure;

2. *Livres de classe* (manuels scolaires), c'est-à-dire ouvrages prescrits aux élèves de l'enseignement du premier degré et du second degré;

3. *Thèses universitaires*;

4) *Tirages à part* (c'est-à-dire réimpressions d'une partie d'un livre ou d'une publication périodique déjà parus), à condition qu'ils aient un titre et une pagination distincts et qu'ils constituent un ouvrage distinct;

5. *Publications faisant partie d'une série*, mais dont chacune constitue une unité bibliographique;

6. *Ouvrages illustrés*: recueils de gravures, de reproductions d'oeuvres d'art, de dessins, etc., pour autant que ces collections constituent des ouvrages complets et paginés et que les illustrations soient accompagnées d'un texte explicatif, même sommaire, se rapportant à ces oeuvres ou à leurs auteurs; albums, livres et brochures illustrés, rédigés sous la forme d'une narration continue et ornés d'images illustrant certains épisodes; albums et livres d'images pour les enfants.

Pour l'établissement de ces statistiques, les définitions ci-après devraient être utilisées:

a) Une publication est considérée comme *non périodique* si elle est publiée en une seule fois ou, à intervalles, par volumes dont le nombre est généralement déterminé d'avance;

b) Le terme *imprimé* recouvre tous les divers procédés d'impression, quels qu'ils soient;

c) Est considérée comme *éditée dans le pays* toute publication dont l'éditeur a son siège social dans le pays établissant les statistiques, sans qu'il soit tenu compte ni du lieu d'impression ni du lieu de distribution. Lorsqu'une publication est faite par un ou des éditeurs ayant leur siège social dans deux ou plusieurs pays, elle est considérée comme étant éditée dans celui ou ceux de ces pays où elle est distribuée;

d) Une publication est considérée comme *offerte au public* lorsqu'il peut se la procurer soit en la payant, soit gratuitement. Sont considérées comme offertes au public également les publications destinées à un nombre restreint de personnes, telles que certaines publications officielles, de sociétés savantes, d'organisations politiques ou professionnelles, etc.;

e) Un *livre* est une publication non périodique imprimée comptant au moins 49 pages (pages de couverture non comprises), éditée dans le pays et offerte au public;

f) Une *brochure* est une publication non périodique imprimée comptant au moins 5, mais pas plus de 48 pages (pages de couverture non comprises), éditée dans le pays et offerte au public;

g) Une *première édition* est la première publication d'un manuscrit original ou traduit;

h) Une *réédition* est une édition qui se distingue des éditions antérieures par des modifications apportées au contenu ou à la présentation;

i) Une *réimpression* ne comporte pas de modifications de contenu ou de présentation autres que des corrections typographiques par rapport à l'édition antérieure. Une réimpression faite par un éditeur autre que l'éditeur précédent est considérée comme une réédition;

j) Une *traduction* est une publication qui reproduit un ouvrage dans une langue autre que la langue originale;

k) Un *titre* est un terme utilisé pour désigner une publication imprimée, constituant un tout distinct, qu'elle soit en un ou en plusieurs volumes.

Le présent chapitre comprend treize tableaux, dont les neuf premiers se rapportent à la totalité de l'édition, tandis que les quatre derniers se réfèrent exclusivement à l'édition de traductions.

Les données présentées dans les tableaux 8.1 à 8.9 sont rassemblées chaque année au moyen de questionnaires adressés aux Etats membres. Sauf indication contraire, elles sont censées englober les livres et les brochures d'ouvrages originaux ou de traductions. Toutefois, certaines catégories de publications qui, selon la Recommandation, devraient être soit comprises dans les statistiques de l'édition de livres - par exemple les publications officielles, les livres de classe (manuels scolaires), les thèses universitaires, les tirages à part, les ouvrages illustrés - soit exclues de ces statistiques (telles que les publications éditées à des fins publicitaires, les publications de caractère éphémère et celles dont le contenu prédominant n'est pas le texte) sont traitées différemment, suivant les pays, lorsqu'il s'agit d'établir les statistiques. Faute de renseignements complets et précis, il n'a pas été possible d'indiquer dans quelle mesure les différentes statistiques nationales s'écartent, à cet égard, des normes formulées dans la Recommandation.

Seuls figurent dans les tableaux 8.3, 8.4, 8.6 et 8.7 les pays qui ont été en mesure de présenter des statistiques établies selon la classification par catégories de sujets préconisée dans la Recommandation. Cette classification est fondée sur la Classification Décimale Universelle (CDU) dont les détails sont donnés dans une note du tableau 8.3.

La différence éventuelle entre les totaux et la somme des chiffres correspondant aux neuf catégories de la Classification Décimale Universelle représente le nombre d'ouvrages qui n'ont pas été classés dans ces catégories (tableaux 8.1 et 8.5) ou s'explique du fait que les chiffres ont été arrondis (tableau 8.3, 8.4, 8.6 et 8.7). Ces tableaux sont conçus pour donner pour chaque pays les chiffres sur les livres (A), les brochures (B), et le total des deux groupes (A+B). Les chiffres reçus se réfèrent souvent aux deux groupes séparément et quelquefois au total des deux groupes ou à l'un ou l'autre groupe seulement. Les tableaux reflètent les différents cas.

Tableau 8.1

Dans le tableau 8.1 les données sont présentées pour les années 1976 à 1978 et ne se réfèrent qu'aux pays pour lesquels l'Unesco dispose de statistiques concernant au moins l'une des trois années considérées.

Sauf indication contraire, les données de ce tableau comprennent les *premières éditions* et les *rééditions* d'ouvrages originaux ou de traductions.

Il ressort de ce tableau que les dix pays qui sont les plus grands producteurs de livres (d'après le nombre de titres) en 1978 sont les suivants: Etats-Unis d'Amérique (85 126), République Fédérale d'Allemagne (50 950), Japon (43 973), République de Corée (16 364), Pays-Bas (13 393), Canada (13 190), Inde (12 932), Pologne (11 849), Italie (10 679) et Yougoslavie (10 509). Malheureusement, pour 1978 il n'y a pas de données disponibles pour l'U.R.S.S., le Royaume-Uni, la France et l'Espagne. En 1977, ces pays avaient publié le nombre de titres suivants: U.R.S.S. (85 395), Royaume-Uni (36 196), France (31 673) et Espagne (24 896). En 1976, le Brésil avait produit 20 025 titres.

Tableau 8.2

Sauf indication contraire, les données de ce tableau comprennent les *premières éditions* et les *rééditions* d'ouvrages originaux ou de traductions.

Tableaux 8.3 et 8.4

Les chiffres du tableau 8.3 se rapportent aux *premières éditions* et aux *rééditions* et ceux du tableau 8.4 aux *premières éditions* seulement.

Tableau 8.5

Sauf indication contraire, les données du tableau 8.5 se réfèrent aux *premières éditions*, *rééditions* et *réimpressions* d'ouvrages originaux ou de traductions.

Tableaux 8.6 et 8.7

Les chiffres du tableau 8.6 se rapportent aux *premières éditions*, aux *rééditions* et aux *réimpressions*, et ceux du tableau 8.7 aux *premières éditions* seulement.

Tableau 8.8

Les données de ce tableau se réfèrent aux *premières éditions* et aux *rééditions* des manuels scolaires qui, dans la Recommandation, sont définis comme ouvrages prescrits aux élèves de l'enseignement du premier degré et du second degré.

Tableau 8.9

Les données du tableau 8.9 se réfèrent aux *premières éditions* et aux *rééditions* des livres pour enfants.

Tableau 8.10 à 8.13

Les tableaux 8.10 à 8.12 présentent des données concernant les traductions publiées en 1973, 1974 et 1975, tandis que le tableau

8.13 contient des renseignements sur les auteurs les plus traduits durant la période 1961-1975. Ces statistiques ont été établies sur la base des renseignements publiés dans l'*Index Translationum*, bibliographie internationale des traductions publiée par l'Unesco.

Section 2

Les tableaux 8.14 à 8.16 contiennent des données relatives aux journaux quotidiens et non quotidiens d'information générale, ainsi qu'aux autres périodiques.

D'une manière générale, les statistiques nationales des journaux et des autres périodiques devraient être établies conformément aux définitions et aux classifications figurant dans la Recommandation concernant la normalisation internationale des statistiques de l'édition de livres et de périodiques adoptée par la Conférence Générale de l'Unesco en 1964. Aux termes de cette Recommandation, les statistiques nationales sur la presse devraient porter sur les publications périodiques imprimées qui sont éditées dans les pays et offertes au public, à l'exception des publications éditées à des fins publicitaires, celles de caractère éphémère et celles dont le contenu prédominant n'est pas le texte. Par contre, les catégories de publications ci-après, notamment, devraient être comptées dans les statistiques des périodiques: périodiques officiels, périodiques académiques et scientifiques, périodiques des organisations professionnelles, syndicales, politiques, sportives, etc., publications annuelles ou à périodicité plus espacée, bulletins paroissiaux, bulletins des écoles, journaux d'entreprise.

Pour l'établissement de ces statistiques, les définitions ci-après devraient être utilisées:

1. Une publication est considérée comme *périodique* si elle est publiée en série continue sous un même titre à intervalles réguliers ou irréguliers pendant une période indéterminée, les différents numéros de la série étant numérotés consécutivement ou chaque numéro étant daté.
2. Les publications périodiques sont subdivisés en deux catégories:
) Les *journaux d'information générale* sont des publications périodiques destinées au grand public, qui ont essentiellement pour objet de constituer une source originale d'information par écrit sur les événements d'actualité intéressant les affaires publiques, les questions internationales, la politique, etc. Un journal répondant à cette définition qui paraît au moins quatre fois par semaine est considéré comme un quotidien, un journal paraissant trois fois par semaine ou moins fréquemment est classé dans la catégorie des journaux non quotidiens;
b) Les *autres périodiques* sont ceux qui traitent des sujets d'intérêt général ou qui sont spécialement consacrés à des études et informations documentaires sur des questions particulières: législation, finances, commerce, médecine, mode, sports, etc. Cette catégorie englobe des journaux spécialisés, les revues, les magazines et tous les périodiques autres que les journaux d'information générale.
3. Les chiffres concernant la *diffusion* devraient représenter la diffusion moyenne par numéro. Ces chiffres devraient comprendre le nombre d'exemplaires vendus soit directement, soit par abonnement, plus le nombre d'exemplaires faisant l'objet d'un service gratuit régulier dans le pays et à l'étranger à l'exclusion des invendus. A défaut de données sur la diffusion le nombre d'exemplaires imprimés devrait être indiqué. En interprétant les données des tableaux ci-après, il ne faut pas perdre de vue que dans certains cas les méthodes de recensement, les définitions et les classifications utilisées par les pays ne s'ajustent pas entièrement aux normes préconisées par l'Unesco. Ainsi, par exemple, les tirages mentionnés se réfèrent soit à la diffusion, soit au nombre d'exemplaires imprimés et les chiffres correspondants ne représentent que des estimations, généralement officielles, mais d'exactitude variable.

Tableau 8.14

On trouvera dans le tableau 8.14 des données sur le nombre, le tirage total et le tirage pour 1.000 habitants des journaux quotidiens d'information générale en 1965, 1970, 1976 et 1977.

Dans ce tableau, on entend par 'journal quotidien d'information générale' toute publication qui a essentiellement pour objet de rendre compte des événements d'actualité dans les domaines des affaires publiques, des questions internationales, de la politique, etc., et qui paraît au moins quatre fois par semaine.

Lorsque le tirage ne correspond pas au total des journaux quotidiens (ce qui est indiqué par une note), le nombre d'exemplaires par 1,000 habitants ne figure pas sur le tableau.

Tableau 8.15

Ce tableau indique le nombre, le tirage total et le tirage pour 1.000 habitants des journaux non quotidiens d'information générale ainsi que le nombre et le tirage total des autres périodiques au cours de la dernière année pour laquelle on possède des chiffres.

Dans ce tableau, on entend par 'journal non quotidien d'information générale' toute publication qui a essentiellement pour objet de rendre compte des événements d'actualité dans les domaines des affaires publiques, des questions internationales, de la politique, etc., et qui paraît trois fois par semaine ou moins fréquemment. La catégorie 'autres périodiques' comprend les publications périodiques - autres que les journaux - contenant des informations de caractère général ou spécialisé.

Tableau 8.16

Le tableau 8.16 présente des données relatives aux périodiques autres que les journaux d'information générale, classées par groupes de sujets. Cette classification est indiquée dans la Recommandation ci-dessus. Les données de ce tableau se réfèrent à une des années de la période 1973-77.

Dans ce tableau, on entend par 'autres périodiques' les publications périodiques autres que les journaux d'information générale, contenant des informations de caractère général ou spécialisé.

Il faut souligner à l'attention des lecteurs que la somme des deux totaux partiels qui figurent dans ce tableau doit correspondre au total indiqué sous la rubrique 'autres périodiques' du tableau 8.15. On constatera que ce n'est pas toujours le cas, probablement parce que les sources nationales utilisées sont différentes ou qu'il n'a pas encore été possible pour certains pays d'appliquer les normes internationales. Néanmoins, il a été jugé préférable d'inclure dans ce tableau le plus grand nombre de pays possible, plutôt que

de limiter leur nombre aux seuls pays pour lesquels nous possédons des statistiques complètes et conséquentes. Pour cette raison, il est évident que les données publiées doivent être utilisées et interprétées avec circonspection, sans oublier que souvent les chiffres ne représentent tout au plus qu'une approximation très grossière de la situation réelle.

Section 3

Les données qui figurent dans le tableau 8.17 se rapportent à la consommation, à la production, à l'exportation et à l'importation de 'papier culturel', c'est-à-dire, de papier journal, ainsi que de papier d'impression (autre que le papier journal) et de papier d'écriture. Comme pour les années précédentes, ces données nous ont été fournies par l'*Organisation des Nations Unies pour l'Agriculture et l'Alimentation* (FAO). Les lecteurs qui souhaiteraient obtenir des renseignements complémentaires doivent se référer à l'*Annuaire des Produits Forestiers* publié par la FAO.

Le terme *papier journal* (sous-groupe 641.1 de la Classification Type pour le Commerce International, révisée) désigne le papier d'impression blanchi, non collé ou peu encollé, non couché, du type utilisé d'ordinaire pour les journaux. Le papier journal a un poids de 45 à 60 grammes au mètre carré et contient en général au moins 70 pour cent en poids de matière fibreuse tirée de la pâte mécanique.

L'expression *autres papiers d'impression et papier d'écriture* (sous-groupe 641.2 de la Classification Type pour le Commerce International, révisée) désigne les différents types de papiers (en feuilles ou en rouleaux) autres que le papier journal qui sont destinés à l'impression ainsi qu'à l'écriture. N'entrent pas dans cette catégorie les produits manufacturés tels que fournitures de bureau, cahiers, registres, etc.

Pour les pays sur lesquels on ne dispose pas de données séparées pour les deux catégories de papier définies ci-dessus, les chiffres globaux sont présentés sous la rubrique 'papier journal'.

Este Capítulo se divide en tres secciones. La sección 1 se refiere a las estadísticas de la edición de libros, incluidas las traducciones (cuadros 8.1 a 8.13). La sección 2 concierne las estadísticas relativas a los periódicos diarios y otras publicaciones periódicas (cuadros 8.14 a 8.16); la última sección presenta datos sobre la producción, la importación, la exportación y el consumo de papel de periódico y otro papel de imprenta y de escribir.

El texto que figura a continuación consta por consiguiente de tres secciones, de acuerdo con las diferentes materias más arriba indicadas.

Sección 1

En general, las estadísticas nacionales de edición de libros deberían establecerse con arreglo a las definiciones y clasificaciones que figuran en la Recomendación sobre la normalización internacional de las estadísticas relativas a la edición de libros y publicaciones periódicas aprobada en 1964 por la Conferencia General de la Unesco.

De acuerdo con la Recomendación, las estadísticas de edición de libros deberían referirse a las publicaciones no periódicas impresas, editadas en el país y puestas a la disposición del público, y que, en general, son publicaciones que deberían figurar en las bibliotecas nacionales de los diferentes países, con excepción de las siguientes categorías:

a) *Publicaciones editadas con fines publicitarios*, siempre que no predomine en ellas el texto literario o científico, y que su distribución sea gratuita (catálogos, prospectos y otras publicaciones de propaganda comercial, industrial y turística; publicaciones sobre la actividad o evolución técnica de una rama de la industria o del comercio y en las que se señalen a la atención de los lectores los productos o servicios suministrados por su editor).

b) *Publicaciones pertenecientes a las siguientes categorías, siempre que sean consideradas de carácter efímero*: horarios, tarifas, guías telefónicas, etc.; programas de espectáculos, exposiciones, ferias, etc.; estatutos y balances de sociedades, instrucciones formuladas por empresas, circulares, etc; calendarios, almanaques, etc.

c) *Publicaciones pertenecientes a las siguientes categorías, cuya parte más importante no es el texto*: las obras musicales (partituras, cuadernos de música) siempre que la música sea más importante que el texto; la producción cartográfica, excepto los atlas.

En las estadísticas relativas a la edición de libros, no deberían omitirse las siguientes categorías de publicaciones:

1. *Publicaciones oficiales*: es decir, las obras editadas por las

administraciones públicas o los organismos que de ellas dependen, excepto las que tengan carácter confidencial o sean distribuidas únicamente en el servicio interesado;

2. *Libros de texto*: es decir, obras prescritas a los alumnos que reciben enseñanza de primero o de segundo grado;

3. *Tesis universitarias*;

4. *Separatas*: es decir, las reimpresiones de partes de un libro o de una publicación periódica ya editados, siempre que tengan título y paginación propios y que constituyan una obra independiente;

5. *Publicaciones que forman parte de una serie* pero que constituyen una unidad bibliográfica diferente;

6. *Obras ilustradas*: colecciones de grabados, reproducciones de obras de arte, dibujos, etc., siempre que tales colecciones constituyan obras completas y paginadas, y que los grabados vayan acompañados de un texto explicativo, por breve que sea, referente a esas obras o a sus autores; albúmenes, libros y folletos ilustrados cuyo texto se presente como narración continua acompañada de imágenes para ilustrar determinados episodios; albúmenes y libros de imágenes para niños.

Al compilar las estadísticas deberían utilizarse las siguientes definiciones:

a) Se entiende por publicación *no periódica* la obra editada, de una sola vez o a intervalos en varios volúmenes, cuyo número se determina generalmente con antelación;

b) el término *impreso* comprende los diversos procedimientos de impresión que se puedan utilizar;

c) Se considera como *editada en el país* cualquier publicación cuyo editor tenga su domicilio social en el país en que se compilan las estadísticas; no se toman en consideración el lugar de impresión ni el de distribución. Las publicaciones hechas por uno o varios editores con domicilio social en dos o más países se considerarán como editadas en el país o países donde se distribuyan;

d) Se considerarán como *puestas a disposición del público* las publicaciones que éste pueda obtener pagando o gratuitamente. Se considerarán también como puestas a disposición del público las publicaciones destinadas a un número restringido de personas, por ejemplo, ciertas publicaciones oficiales de sociedades eruditas, de organizaciones políticas o profesionales, etc.;

e) Se entiende por *libro* una publicación impresa no periódica que consta como mínimo de 49 páginas sin contar las de cubierta, editada en el país y puesta a disposición del público;

f) Se entiende por *folleto* la publicación impresa no periódica que consta de 5 a 48 páginas sin las de cubierta, impresa, editada en el país y puesta a disposición del público;

g) Se entiende por *primera edición* la primera publicación de un manuscrito original o traducido;

h) Se entiende por *reedición* una edición que se distingue de las ediciones anteriores por algunas modificaciones introducidas en el contenido o en la presentación;

i) Una *reimpresión* no contiene otras modificaciones de contenido o de presentación sino las correcciones tipográficas realizadas en el texto de la edición anterior. Toda reimpresión hecha por un editor diferente al editor anterior se considera como una reedición;

j) Se entiende por *traducción* la publicación en que se reproduce una obra en un idioma distinto del original;

k) Un *título* es un término utilizado para designar una publicación impresa que constituye un todo único, tanto si consta de uno como de varios volúmenes.

Esta sección comprende 13 cuadros, de los cuales, los 9 primeros se refieren a la edición de libros en su totalidad, y los 4 últimos a las traducciones exclusivamente.

En los cuadros 8.1 a 8.9 figuran los datos que se compilan todos los años mediante los cuestionarios que se envían a los Estados Miembros. Salvo indicación contraria, cabe suponer que esos datos abarcan a la vez libros y folletos de obras originales o de traducciones. Ahora bien, ciertas categorías de publicaciones que, según la Recomendación, deberían quedar comprendidas en las estadísticas de edición de libros (por ejemplo, las publicaciones oficiales, los libros de texto, las tesis universitarias, las separatas, las obras ilustradas) o excluidas de esas estadísticas (por ejemplo, las publicaciones editadas con fines publicitarios, las de carácter efímero y aquellas otras cuyo contenido predomina en un texto escrito) reciben un trato distinto según los países, cuando se trata de preparar las estadísticas. Al no disponerse de datos completos y precisos, no ha sido posible indicar en qué medida las diferentes estadísticas nacionales se apartan a este respecto de las normas formuladas en la Recomendación.

Sólo figuran en los cuadros 8.3, 8.4, 8.6 y 8.7 los países que han podido proporcionarnos estadísticas establecidas de acuerdo con la clasificación por categorías de materias preconizada en la Recomendación. Esta clasificación se basa en la Clasificación Decimal Universal (CDU), indicándose en una nota del cuadro 8.3 los detalles correspondientes.

Las posibles diferencias entre los totales y la suma de las cifras correspondientes a las nueve categorías de la Clasificación Decimal Universal equivalen al número de obras que no han quedado clasificadas en esas categorías (cuadros 8.1 y 8.5) o se explican debido a que las cifras han sido redondeadas (cuadros 8.3, 8.4, 8.6 y 8.7). Estos cuadros se prepararon con vistas a ofrecer para cada país las cifras relativas a los libros (A), los folletos (B), y el total de los dos grupos (A+B). Las cifras recibidas se refieren frecuentemente a los dos grupos por separado y algunas veces al total de los dos grupos o a uno u otro grupo solamente. Los diferentes casos quedan reflejados en los cuadros.

Cuadro 8.1

El cuadro 8.1 presenta los datos relativos a los años 1976 a 1978 y sólo incluye los países con respecto a los cuales la Unesco dispone de estadísticas relativas por lo menos a uno de esos tres años.

Cuando no se indica otra cosa, los datos de este cuadro comprenden las *primeras ediciones* y las *reediciones* de obras originales y de traducciones.

De este cuadro se desprende igualmente que los diez países más importantes como productores de libros (según el número de títulos) en 1978, son los siguientes: Estados Unidos de América (85 126), República Federal de Alemania (50 950), Japón (43 973), República de Corea (16 364), Países-Bajos (13 393), Canadá (13 190), India (12 932), Polonia (11 849), Italia (10 679) y Yugoslavia (10 509). Desgraciadamente, para 1978 no se dispone de datos para la U.R.S.S., el Reino-Unido, Francia y España. En 1977, el número de títulos publicados por estos países fue el siguiente: U.R.S.S. (85 395), Reino-Unido (36 196), Francia (31 673) y España (24 896). En 1976, el Brasil había publicado 20 025 títulos.

Cuadro 8.2

Cuando no se indica otra cosa, los datos de este cuadro comprenden las *primeras ediciones* y las *reediciones* de obras originales.

Cuadros 8.3 y 8.4
Las cifras del cuadro 8.3 se refieren a las *primeras ediciones* y a las *reediciones* y las del cuadro 8.4 a las *primeras ediciones* solamente.

Cuadro 8.5

Salvo indicación contraria, los datos del cuadro 8.5 se refieren a las *primeras ediciones*, *reediciones* y *reimpresiones* de obras originales y de traducciones.

Cuadros 8.6 y 8.7
Las cifras del cuadro 8.6 se refieren a las *primeras ediciones*, a las *reediciones* y a las *reimpresiones* y las del cuadro 8.7 a las *primeras ediciones* solamente.

Cuadro 8.8
Los datos de este cuadro se refieren a las *primeras ediciones* y a las *reediciones* de los libros de texto escolares que, en la Recomendación, se definen como obras prescritas a los alumnos que reciben enseñanza de primero o de segundo grado.

Cuadro 8.9
Los datos del cuadro 8.9 se refieren a las *primeras ediciones* y a las *reediciones* de libros para niños.

Cuadro 8.10 a 8.13
Los cuadros 8.10 a 8.12 presentan datos referentes a las traducciones publicadas en 1973, 1974 y 1975, y el cuadro 8.13 proporciona información sobre los autores más traducidos de 1961 a 1975. Estas estadísticas se basan en los datos publicados en el *Index Translationum*, bibliografía internacional de las traducciones, que publica la Unesco.

Sección 2
Los cuadros 8.14 a 8.16 contienen datos relativos a los periódicos diarios y no diarios de información general, así como a las otras publicaciones periódicas.

En general, las estadísticas nacionales de los diarios y otras publicaciones periódicas deberían establecerse de conformidad con las definiciones y las clasificaciones que figuran en la Recomendación sobre la normalización internacional de las estadísticas relativas a la edición de libros y publicaciones periódicas, aprobada por la Conferencia General de la Unesco en 1964. De acuerdo con esta Recomendación, las estadísticas nacionales relativas a la prensa deberían referirse a las publicaciones periódicas impresas en el país y ofrecidas al público, a excepción de las publicaciones editadas con fines publicitarios de carácter efímero y de aquéllas cuyo contenido predominante no es el texto. En cambio, las categorías de publicaciones siguientes, entre otras, no deberían omitirse en las estadísticas de publicaciones periódicas: publicaciones periódicas oficiales, publicaciones periódicas académicas y científicas, publicaciones periódicas de entidades profesionales, sindicales, políticas, deportivas, etc., publicaciones anuales o de menor frecuencia de aparición, boletines parroquiales, boletines escolares, periódicos de empresa.

Para compilar esas estadísticas, deberían utilizarse las definiciones siguientes:

1. Se entiende por publicación *periódica* la editada en serie continua con el mismo título, a intervalos regulares e irregulares durante un período indeterminado de forma que los números de la serie lleven una numeración consecutiva o cada número esté fechado.

2. Las publicaciones periódicas se subdividen en dos categorías:

a) *Periódicos de información general*: son las publicaciones periódicas destinadas al gran público y que tengan esencialmente por objeto constituir una fuente de información escrita sobre los acontecimientos de actualidad relacionados con asuntos públicos, cuestiones internacionales, políticas, etc. Un periódico que responda a esa definición y que se publique al menos cuatro veces por semana se considerará como un diario; un periódico que aparezca tres veces por semana o con menor frecuencia, se clasificará en la categoría de los periódicos no diarios.

b) *Otras publicaciones periódicas*: son las que tratan de temas muy amplios o las dedicadas especialmente a estudios e informaciones documentales sobre determinadas cuestiones: legislación, hacienda, comercio, medicina, modas, deportes, etc. Esta definición abarca los periódicos especializados, las revistas ilustradas y todas las demás publicaciones periódicas que no sean de información general.

3. Las cifras concernientes a la *difusión* deberían expresar el promedio de difusión cotidiana y comprender el número de ejemplares vendidos, tanto directamente como por suscripción, sumado al número de ejemplares distribuidos regularmente en forma gratuita, en el país y en el extranjero, con exclusión de los ejemplares no vendidos. En caso de que no sea posible proporcionar los datos correspondientes al promedio de la difusión, debería indicarse el número total de ejemplares tirados.

Al interpretar los datos de los cuadros que figuran a continuación, no hay que perder de vista que en ciertos casos los métodos de compilación, y las definiciones y clasificaciones que aplican los países no se ajustan enteramente a las normas preconizadas por la Unesco. Por ejemplo, las tiradas que se mencionan se refieren ora a la difusión, ora al número de ejemplares impresos, y las cifras correspondientes no representan sino estimaciones, generalmente oficiales, pero de exactitud variable.

Cuadro 8.14

En el cuadro 8.14 figuran datos sobre el número, la tirada total y la tirada por 1.000 habitantes de los periódicos diarios de información general en 1965, 1970, 1976 y 1977.

En este cuadro, se entiende por 'periódico diario de información general' toda publicación que tenga esencialmente por objeto dar cuenta de acontecimientos de actualidad relacionados con asuntos públicos, cuestiones internacionales, política, etc. y que aparezca cuatro veces por semana como mínimo.

Cuando la tirada no corresponde al total de los periódicos diarios (circunstancia que se indica en una nota) el número de ejemplares por 1.000 habitantes no figura en el cuadro.

Cuadro 8.15

Este cuadro indica el número, la tirada total y la tirado por 1.000 habitantes de los periódicos no diarios de información general, así como el número y la tirada total de las otras publicaciones periódicas durante el último año para el cual se poseen cifras.

En este cuadro se entiende por 'periódico no diario de información general' toda publicación que tenga esencialmente por objeto dar cuenta de acontecimientos de actualidad relacionados con asuntos públicos, cuestiones internacionales, política, y que aparezca tres veces por semana o con menor frecuencia. La categoría 'otras publicaciones periódicas' comprende las publicaciones periódicas - que no sean los diarios - que contienen información de carácter general o especializada.

Cuadro 8.16

El cuadro 8.16 presenta datos relativos a las publicaciones periódicas distintas de los diarios de información general, clasificadas por grupos de materias. Esta clasificación se indica en la Recomendación arriba mencionada. Los datos de ese cuadro se refieren a uno de los años del periodo 1973-77.

En este cuadro se entiende por 'otras publicaciones periódicas' las publicaciones periódicas distintas de los diarios de información general, que contienen información de carácter general o especializada.

Hay que señalar a la atención de los lectores que la suma de los dos totales parciales que figuran en ese cuadro debe corresponder al total indicado bajo el epígrafe 'Otras publicaciones periódicas' del cuadro 8.15. Se observará que no es ese siempre el caso, probablemente porque las fuentes nacionales utilizadas son diferentes o porque en algunos países no ha sido todavía posible aplicar las normas internacionales. No obstante, se ha estimado preferible incluir en ese cuadro el mayor número posible de países, en lugar de limitarlo únicamente a los países cuyas estadísticas son completas y seguras. Por esta razón, es evidente que los datos publicados deberán utilizarse e interpretarse con circunspección, sin olvidar que, con frecuencia, las cifras no constituyen a lo sumo más que una aproximación muy relativa de la situación real.

Sección 3

Los datos que figuran en el Cuadro 8.17 se refieren al consumo, a la producción, a la exportación y a la importación de 'papel cultural', es decir, de papel de periódico, de papel de imprenta (distinto al papel de periódico) y de papel de escribir. Como para los años anteriores, estos datos nos han sido procurados por la *Organización de las Naciones Unidas para la Agricultura y la Alimentación* (FAO). Los lectores deseosos de obtener información complementaria deben referirse al *Anuario de Productos Forestales* publicado por la FAO.

El término *papel de periódico* (subgrupo 641.1 de la Clasificación Tipo para el Comercio Internacional, revisada) se refiere al papel de imprenta blanqueado, no encolado o poco encolado, no cuché, del tipo utilizado corrientemente para los periódicos. El papel de periódico tiene un peso de 45 a 60 gramos por metro cuadrado y contiene, en general, al menos un 70% en peso de materia fibrosa extraída de la pasta mecánica.

La expresión *otros papeles de imprenta y papel de escribir* (subgrupo 641.2 de la Clasificación Tipo para el Comercio Internacional, revisada) designa las diferentes clases de papel (en hojas o en rollo) que no sean el papel de periódico y que se destinan a la impresión y a la escritura. No se incluyen en esa categoría los productos manufacturados tales como material de oficina, cuadernos, libros de registro, etc.

Para los países sobre los cuales no se dispone de datos separados relativos a las dos categorías de papel arriba definidas, las cifras globales se presentan bajo la rúbrica 'papel de periódico'.

Equivalent en francais des groupes de sujets figurant dans les tableaux 8.3, 8.4, 8.6 et 8.7.

Total

1. Generalites (0)
2. Philosophie, psychologie (1)
3. Religion, theologie (2)
4. Sociologie, statistique (30-31)
5. Sciences politiques ... (32-33)
6. Droit, administration publique ... (34, 351-354, 36)
7. Art et science militaire (355-359)
8. Education, loisirs (37)
9. Commerce, transport ... (38)
10. Ethnographie, folklore ... (39)

11. Mathematiques (51)
12. Sciences naturelles (52-59)
13. Sciences medicales ... (61)
14. Art de l'ingenieur, metiers ... (62, 66-69)
15. Agriculture ... (63)
16. Economie domestique (64)
17. Gestion, administration ... (65)
18. Amenagement du territoire, architecture ... (70-72)
19. Arts graphiques et plastiques ... (73-77)
20. Arts du spectacle ... (78, 791-792)
21. Jeux et sports (793-799)
22. Linguistique, philologie ... (80-81)
23. Litterature (82)
    a) Histoire et critique litteraires
    b) Textes litteraires
24. Geographie (91)
25. Histoire, biographie (92-99)

- -

Equivalente en espanol de los grupos tematicos que figuran en los cuadros 8.3, 8.4, 8.6 y 8.7.

Total

1. Generalidades (0)
2. Filosofia, psicologia (1)
3. Religion, teologia (2)
4. Sociologia, estadistica (30-31)
5. Ciencias politicas ... (32-33)
6. Derecho, administracion publica (34, 351-354, 36)
7. Arte y ciencia militar (355-359)
8. Educacion, distracciones (37)
9. Comercio, transportes ... (38)
10. Etnografia, folklore ... (39)

11. Matematicas (51)
12. Ciencias naturales (52-59)
13. Ciencias medicas ... (61)
14. Ingenieria, oficios ... (62, 66-69)
15. Agricultura ... (63)
16. Economia domestica (64)
17. Gestion, administracion ... (65)
18. Acondicionamiento del territorio, arquitectura (70-72)
19. Artes plasticas y graficas ... (73-77)
20. Artes del espectaculo ... (78, 791-792)
21. Juegos y deportes (793-799)
22. Linguistica, filologia (80-81)
23. Literatura (82)
    a) Historia y critica literarias
    b) Textos literarios
24. Geografia (91)
25. Historia, biografia (92-99)

Equivalent en francais des groupes de sujets
figurant dans le tableau 8.16.

Total A + B

A. Total

1. Generalites (0)
2. Philosophie, psychologie (1)
3. Religion, theologie (2)
4. Sociologie, statistique (30–31)
5. Sciences politiques ... (32–33)
6. Droit ... (34, 351–354, 36)
7. Art militaire ... (355–359)
8. Enseignement, education (37)
9. Commerce, transport ... (38)
10. Ethnographie, folklore ... (39)
11. Linguistique, philologie (4)
12. Mathematiques (51)

13. Sciences naturelles (52–59)
14. Sciences medicales ... (61)
15. Industries ... (62, 66–69)
16. Agriculture ... (63)
17. Economie domestique (64)
18. Organisation du commerce ... (65)
19. Beaux–arts ... (70–78, 791–792)
20. Jeux, sports ... (790, 793–799)
21. Litterature (8)
22. Geographie, voyages (91)
23. Histoire, biographie (92–99)

B. Total

1. Periodiques pour enfants et adolescents
2. Periodiques humoristiques et bandes
    dessinees
3. Bulletins paroissiaux
4. Bulletins des ecoles
5. Journaux d'entreprise

Equivalente en espanol de los grupos tematicos
que figuran en el cuadro 8.16.

Total A + B

A. Total

1. Generalidades (0)
2. Filosofia, psycologia (1)
3. Religion, teologia (2)
4. Sociologia, estadistica (30–31)
5. Ciencias politicas ... (32–33)
6. Derecho ... (34, 351–354, 36)
7. Arte y ciencia militar ... (355–359)
8. Ensenanza, educacion (37)
9. Comercio, comunicaciones, transportes (38)
10. Etnografia, usos y costumbres, folklore (39)
11. Linguistica, filologia (4)
12. Matematicas (51)
13. Ciencias naturales (52–59)

14. Ciencias medicas ... (61)
15. Industrias ... (62, 66–69)
16. Agricultura ... (63)
17. Economia domestica (64)
18. Organizacion, administracion y tecnica del
    comercio ... (65)
19. Artes plasticas ... (70–78, 791–792)
20. Juegos, deportes ... (790, 793–799)
21. Literatura (8)
22. Geografia, viajes (91)
23. Historia, biografia (92–99)

B. Total

1. Periodicos para ninos y jovenes
2. Periodicos humoristicos, historietas
    ilustradas
3. Boletines parroquiales
4. Boletines escolares
5. Periodicos de empresa

Number of titles by UDC classes 8.1
Nombre de titres classés d'après la CDU
Número de títulos clasificados por materias (CDU)

8.1 Book production: number of titles by UDC classes

Edition de livres: nombre de titres classés d'après la CDU

Edición de libros: número de títulos clasificados por materias según la CDU

NUMBER OF COUNTRIES AND TERRITORIES PRESENTED IN THIS TABLE: 112
NOMBRE DE PAYS ET DE TERRITOIRES PRESENTES DANS CE TABLEAU: 112
NÚMERO DE PAISES Y DE TERRITORIOS PRESENTADOS EN ESTE CUADRO: 112

COUNTRY / PAYS / PAIS	YEAR / ANNEE / AÑO	TOTAL / TOTAL / TOTAL	GENER-ALITIES / GENERA-LITES / GENERA-LIDADES	PHILOS-OPHY / PHILO-SOPHIE / FILO-SOFIA	RELIGION / RELIGION / RELIGION	SOCIAL SCIENCES / SCIENCES SOCIALES / CIENCIAS SOCIALES	PURE SCIENCES / SCIENCES PURES / CIENCIAS PURAS	APPLIED SCIENCES / SCIENCES APPL. / CIENCIAS APLICADAS	ARTS / BEAUX-ARTS / ARTES PLASTICAS	LITERA-TURE / LITTERA-TURE / LITERA-TURA	GEOGR./HISTORY / GEOGR./HISTOIRE / GEOGR./HISTORIA
		(1)	(2)	(3)	(4)	(5)	(6)	(7)	(8)	(9)	(10)
AFRICA											
BENIN	1978	13	–	–	1	–	5	–	–	6	1
BOTSWANA	1976	79	7	–	1	50	6	12	–	–	3
	1977	71	5	–	2	47	1	10	3	–	3
	1978	103	5	–	1	82	2	8	4	–	1
CONGO ‡	1977	127	–	–	–	24	33	3	7	36	24
EGYPT ‡	1976	1 486	74	21	251	300	91	223	36	389	101
	1977	1 472	58	40	263	274	68	276	44	365	84
ETHIOPIA ‡	1978	353	2	1	49	74	9	28	2	23	44
GAMBIA ‡	1977	113	8	–	–	45	13	16	13	7	11
	1978	81	8	–	–	29	9	12	10	2	11
GHANA	1976	237	11	3	32	96	7	33	1	39	15
	1977	135	36	–	52	27	3	5	4	8	8
	1978	251	6	7	54	81	10	24	7	53	9
IVORY COAST	1976	395	48	–	39	147	59	58	18	17	9
	1977	125	10	–	23	38	13	26	9	4	2
KENYA	1976	183	4	–	59	65	13	7	3	19	13
MADAGASCAR	1976	228	3	5	41	73	11	18	5	60	12
	1977	211	7	5	38	56	13	24	5	53	10
	1978	219	5	6	55	60	10	17	10	44	12
MALAWI	1977	133	4	–	24	36	5	28	1	30	5

8.1 Number of titles by UDC classes
Nombre de titres classés d'après la CDU
Número de títulos clasificados por materias (CDU)

COUNTRY / PAYS / PAIS	YEAR / ANNEE / AÑO	TOTAL / TOTAL / TOTAL (1)	GENER-ALITIES / GENERA-LITES / GENERA-LIDADES (2)	PHILOS-OPHY / PHILO-SOPHIE / FILO-SOFIA (3)	RELIGION / RELIGION / RELIGION (4)	SOCIAL SCIENCES / SCIENCES SOCIALES / CIENCIAS SOCIALES (5)	PURE SCIENCES / SCIENCES PURES / CIENCIAS PURAS (6)	APPLIED SCIENCES / SCIENCES APPL. / CIENCIAS APLICADAS (7)	ARTS / BEAUX-ARTS / ARTES PLASTICAS (8)	LITERA-TURE / LITTERA-TURE / LITERA-TURA (9)	GEOGR./ HISTORY / GEOGR./ HISTOIRE / GEOGR./ HISTORIA (10)
MAURITANIA	1976	71	–	–	–	12	36	1	–	15	7
	1977	40	–	–	–	2	12	–	–	20	6
MAURITIUS ‡	1976	54	–	–	4	22	4	2	4	14	4
	1977	40	–	1	6	14	2	1	1	11	5
	1978	20	–	1	4	5	–	2	1	3	4
NIGER	1976	78	11	–	–	32	–	7	1	9	18
NIGERIA	1978	1 175	46	13	115	462	133	106	25	139	136
SENEGAL ‡	1976	47	13	–	–	10	1	2	3	18	13
	1977	48	–	–	2	22	–	1	1	6	3
SEYCHELLES ‡	1977	11	–	1	–	8	–	–	–	–	2
SIERRA LEONE ‡	1977	61	3	–	–	49	–	4	–	–	5
SUDAN ‡	1976	158	6	3	5	43	8	14	5	49	25
	1977	104	–	–	8	–	25	18	–	33	20
TUNISIA ‡	1976	48	1	2	2	3	1	4	1	13	7
	1977	85	2	3	4	11	17	6	–	32	10
	1978	85	–	2	4	5	26	6	2	26	14
UNITED REPUBLIC OF CAMEROON ‡	1978	54	–	–	–	13	6	–	1	31	3
UNITED REPUBLIC OF TANZANIA	1976	399	54	–	66	158	15	36	13	43	14
ZAIRE	1977	154	4	6	44	37	7	25	6	15	10
	1978	109	4	5	43	38	1	7	4	6	1
ZAMBIA ‡	1976	165	9	1	34	75	14	28	–	1	3
	1978	123	–	–	–	35	8	6	–	37	4
AMERICA, NORTH											
BARBADOS ‡	1976	199	8	–	9	108	3	57	8	3	3
	1977	173	8	–	10	91	2	49	9	1	3
	1978	216	13	–	7	107	3	69	9	2	6
CANADA ‡	1976	6 241	343	115	260	1 703	390	717	825	1 298	590
	1977	7 878	468	163	245	2 453	450	936	1 054	1 386	723
	1978	13 190	506	632	371	3 462	1 623	2 087	1 280	2 227	1 002
COSTA RICA	1976	60	–	4	–	3	2	–	–	48	7
	1977	78	–	–	1	9	2	5	2	52	4
	1978	24	2	–	1	12	–	–	2	4	3

Number of titles by UDC classes   **8.1**
Nombre de titres classés d'après la CDU
Número de títulos clasificados por materias (CDU)

		(1)	(2)	(3)	(4)	(5)	(6)	(7)	(8)	(9)	(10)
CUBA	1976	726	38	11	–	256	28	99	8	245	41
	1977	1 039	49	35	1	267	111	151	13	372	40
DOMINICAN REPUBLIC ‡	1976	48	4	–	1	12	1	8	1	15	6
EL SALVADOR	1978	144	–	1	1	25	4	64	5	37	7
JAMAICA ‡	1977	13	3	–	–	3	4	–	–	3	–
	1978	143	7	–	3	46	12	10	27	29	9
MEXICO	1976	4 851	43	85	35	498	297	2 882	166	583	262
NETHERLANDS ANTILLES	1977	52	3	–	3	18	4	4	–	14	6
PANAMA ‡	1976	106	2	3	–	29	17	7	3	35	10
	1977	84	10	3	–	35	–	11	2	20	3
	1978	126	7	1	–	51	7	20	2	26	12
TRINIDAD AND TOBAGO ‡	1976	18	–	–	–	3	7	8	–	–	–
UNITED STATES OF AMERICA ‡	1976	84 542	1 066	1 223	1 926	7 786	2 241	5 619	1 491	6 493	2 847
	1978	85 126	1 345	1 387	2 398	8 867	2 752	7 360	1 347	7 488	2 828
AMERICA, SOUTH											
ARGENTINA ‡	1976	6 719	2 324	651	../.	1 041	178	443	541	1 400	141
	1977	5 285	330	628	../.	945	213	615	649	1 727	178
	1978	4 627	309	592	../.	958	98	577	775	1 226	92
BRAZIL	1976	20 025	2 408	672	1 242	5 119	2 481	1 882	887	4 516	818
CHILE	1976	529	5	20	71	134	24	61	25	161	28
	1977	387	–	7	51	135	25	37	13	86	33
	1978	432	7	32	47	93	42	36	12	120	43
GUYANA	1976	213	4	1	8	72	8	48	10	50	12
	1977	107	9	1	4	62	–	13	3	7	8
	1978	97	5	–	4	50	6	9	6	14	3
PERU	1976	925	14	20	22	378	28	104	43	234	82
	1977	910	26	30	31	354	25	130	40	205	69
	1978	968	30	22	34	354	47	143	28	201	109
VENEZUELA	1977	257	6	4	6	82	16	66	9	44	24
ASIA											
AFGHANISTAN	1976	64	–	–	5	–	27	–	–	16	16
	1977	232	20	4	25	71	20	8	2	48	34
BANGLADESH	1978	1 229	31	17	113	399	197	124	49	211	88
BRUNEI	1977	94	25	–	–	32	14	–	–	22	1
	1978	32	5	–	9	2	13	–	–	1	2
CHINA ‡	1978	12 493	../.	1 736	../.	4 393	../.	../.	../.	1 750	../.
CYPRUS	1976	455	12	7	19	145	33	66	15	118	40
	1977	570	13	5	32	185	24	97	53	121	40

8.1 Number of titles by UDC classes
Nombre de titres classés d'après la CDU
Número de títulos clasificados por materias (CDU)

COUNTRY / PAYS / PAIS	YEAR / ANNEE / AÑO	TOTAL / TOTAL / TOTAL (1)	GENERALITIES / GENERALITES / GENERALIDADES (2)	PHILOSOPHY / PHILOSOPHIE / FILOSOFIA (3)	RELIGION / RELIGION / RELIGION (4)	SOCIAL SCIENCES / SCIENCES SOCIALES / CIENCIAS SOCIALES (5)	PURE SCIENCES / SCIENCES PURES / CIENCIAS PURAS (6)	APPLIED SCIENCES / SCIENCES APPL. / CIENCIAS APLICADAS (7)	ARTS / BEAUX-ARTS / ARTES PLASTICAS (8)	LITERATURE / LITTERATURE / LITERATURA (9)	GEOGR./HISTORY / GEOGR./HISTOIRE / GEOGR./HISTORIA (10)
HONG KONG	1976	1 494	52	6	53	494	98	103	91	511	86
	1977	1 735	61	9	35	631	86	152	100	517	144
INDIA	1976	15 802	262	419	1 462	4 277	753	2 139	326	5 062	1 102
	1977	12 885	208	370	922	3 649	785	1 228	278	4 458	987
	1978	12 932	256	421	964	3 518	648	911	262	4 796	1 156
INDONESIA	1976	2 667	392	56	256	847	131	473	117	184	211
	1977	2 265	311	48	200	700	125	354	95	297	135
IRAN	1977	3 027	110	122	648	386	129	264	92	941	335
IRAQ	1976	1 588	117	21	163	664	27	104	44	241	207
	1977	1 758	50	23	160	548	204	273	57	339	104
	1978	1 618	121	42	94	414	134	380	66	286	81
ISRAEL ‡	1977	2 214	16	45	361	308	65	178	43	564	206
JAPAN	1976	36 066	1 130	646	739	9 890	1 646	8 422	2 654	7 890	3 049
	1977	40 905	959	749	879	11 161	1 893	10 141	3 147	8 640	3 336
	1978	43 973	1 061	806	952	12 158	1 452	11 340	3 330	9 340	3 534
JORDAN ‡	1976	392	3	1	35	110	51	59	2	79	52
KOREA, REPUBLIC OF ‡	1976	13 334	607	702	742	1 478	587	1 629	1 093	5 566	930
	1977	13 081	643	930	829	1 362	737	1 594	418	5 673	895
	1978	16 364	733	872	1 391	2 058	1 108	1 320	1 325	5 947	983
KUWAIT	1976	118	44	2	2	35	-	5	7	18	5
	1977	67	18	-	3	23	-	3	5	14	1
	1978	50	8	-	-	20	-	1	3	17	1
LAO PEOPLE'S DEMO- CRATIC REPUBLIC ‡	1976	31	2	6	1	7	-	3	1	10	1
MALAYSIA	1976	1 302	46	28	62	355	127	120	24	428	112
	1977	1 341	151	13	67	380	121	147	24	347	91
	1978	1 328	46	18	132	449	100	205	19	289	70
MALDIVES ‡	1976	*8	1	-	-	5	-	-	1	-	-
	1977	3	1	1	-	1	-	-	-	-	1
PAKISTAN	1976	1 081	48	12	258	199	27	58	20	229	230
	1977	1 331	40	28	330	250	20	68	6	383	206
	1978	1 317	29	4	277	157	8	96	16	535	195
PHILIPPINES ‡	1976	1 616	17	26	73	588	116	506	129	118	43
	1977	1 753	65	29	161	540	102	524	91	198	43
QATAR	1978	159	9	3	56	21	22	-	-	36	12

Number of titles by UDC classes   8.1
Nombre de titres classés d'après la CDU
Número de títulos clasificados por materias (CDU)

		(1)	(2)	(3)	(4)	(5)	(6)	(7)	(8)	(9)	(10)
SINGAPORE ‡	1976	1 203	38	11	22	493	179	104	43	257	56
	1977	1 207	17	10	24	397	116	81	30	459	73
	1978	1 306	18	2	23	611	109	85	63	336	59
SRI LANKA	1976	1 140	5	26	186	333	47	149	107	196	91
	1977	1 201	26	20	211	403	45	111	113	184	88
	1978	1 405	11	29	314	341	60	133	120	299	98
SYRIAN ARAB REPUBLIC ‡	1976	200	4	3	3	43	47	60	4	27	9
	1978	230	1	3	3	38	35	78	6	35	19
THAILAND	1976	2 578	324	72	303	1 103	101	267	72	167	169
	1977	3 390	326	67	232	1 495	145	464	116	293	252
TURKEY	1976	6 320	510	147	337	1 977	400	956	316	1 191	486
	1977	6 830	689	196	327	2 158	502	1 013	346	1 116	483
UNITED ARAB EMIRATES‡	1977	15	6	–	–	7	–	–	1	1	–
VIET-NAM	1977	1 504	–	22	–	235	339	225	50	530	103
EUROPE											
AUSTRIA	1976	6 336	157	217	182	1 533	733	1 164	552	1 162	636
	1977	6 800	197	234	182	1 626	840	1 281	655	1 135	650
	1978	6 439	134	206	189	1 715	603	1 409	522	1 047	614
BELGIUM ‡	1976	6 414	144	169	253	1 230	542	765	627	2 091	593
	1977	5 964	115	163	189	1 119	465	781	595	1 880	657
	1978	9 012	233	198	329	1 659	663	1 081	876	3 214	759
BULGARIA	1976	3 813	119	39	6	998	238	1 039	211	915	248
	1977	4 088	171	62	11	1 045	244	1 080	262	985	228
	1978	4 234	161	59	7	1 105	240	1 106	246	1 019	291
CZECHOSLOVAKIA	1976	9 457	648	119	50	2 145	1 067	2 426	491	2 069	442
	1977	9 568	511	104	48	1 977	919	2 574	551	2 500	384
	1978	9 588	529	141	54	1 897	975	2 573	586	2 337	486
DENMARK	1976	6 783	214	143	193	1 360	522	476	503	1 688	684
	1977	8 021	240	170	214	1 625	640	704	512	2 140	776
	1978	9 415	241	264	305	1 826	783	2 038	678	2 434	846
FINLAND	1976	4 589	111	86	197	833	470	797	327	1 468	300
	1977	3 679	81	100	216	601	341	524	165	1 340	311
	1978	3 367	117	106	194	629	358	674	141	963	185
FRANCE ‡	1976	29 371	696	1 130	721	5 475	2 419	4 206	2 346	8 705	3 673
	1977	31 673	750	1 218	777	5 901	2 607	4 533	2 529	9 399	3 959
	1978	21 225	436	996	672	2 499	1 203	2 626	2 008	7 421	3 364
GERMAN DEMOCRATIC REPUBLIC ‡	1976	5 792	60	151	271	821	417	911	438	1 545	256
	1977	5 844	72	131	267	841	414	909	441	1 589	262
	1978	5 680	56	129	284	791	436	876	408	1 529	233
GERMANY, FEDERAL REPUBLIC OF	1976	44 477	3 607	1 275	2 136	12 372	2 547	4 835	2 722	11 665	3 318
	1977	48 736	3 745	1 289	2 438	13 312	2 478	5 298	3 556	11 497	5 123
	1978	50 950	3 492	1 283	2 464	13 702	2 681	5 899	4 091	13 947	3 391

8.1 Number of titles by UDC classes
Nombre de titres classés d'après la CDU
Número de títulos clasificados por materias (CDU)

COUNTRY / PAYS / PAIS	YEAR / ANNEE / AÑO	TOTAL / TOTAL / TOTAL	GENERALITIES / GENERALITES / GENERALIDADES	PHILOSOPHY / PHILOSOPHIE / FILOSOFIA	RELIGION / RELIGION / RELIGION	SOCIAL SCIENCES / SCIENCES SOCIALES / CIENCIAS SOCIALES	PURE SCIENCES / SCIENCES PURES / CIENCIAS PURAS	APPLIED SCIENCES / SCIENCES APPL. / CIENCIAS APLICADAS	ARTS / BEAUX-ARTS / ARTES PLASTICAS	LITERATURE / LITTERATURE / LITERATURA	GEOGR./HISTORY / GEOGR./HISTOIRE / GEOGR./HISTORIA
		(1)	(2)	(3)	(4)	(5)	(6)	(7)	(8)	(9)	(10)
GREECE	1976	3 935	46	142	326	839	172	356	171	1 526	357
	1977	4 981	66	216	343	1 059	209	392	181	1 880	635
HOLY SEE	1976	114	11	18	62	18	–	–	–	4	1
	1977	200	28	24	115	19	–	–	2	8	4
	1978	180	8	23	112	17	–	–	1	11	8
HUNGARY	1976	9 393	286	109	70	2 338	873	2 980	698	1 595	444
	1977	9 048	284	98	77	2 193	856	2 735	695	1 608	502
	1978	9 579	271	105	73	2 387	881	2 839	770	1 762	491
ICELAND ‡	1976	730	17	11	28	153	42	105	31	274	69
	1977	801	17	14	15	183	36	116	52	296	72
IRELAND	1976	633	18	5	45	170	43	51	85	124	92
	1977	500	8	3	40	117	34	75	49	103	71
	1978	632	28	5	33	143	22	67	68	158	108
ITALY	1976	9 463	320	473	502	2 293	602	1 232	688	2 662	691
	1977	10 116	500	486	677	2 295	464	1 443	889	2 513	849
	1978	10 679	310	589	704	2 573	613	1 207	1 135	2 613	935
LUXEMBOURG	1976	297	13	5	1	159	1	22	50	19	27
	1977	250	7	2	2	116	5	13	59	27	19
MALTA	1976	126	3	–	17	24	3	3	10	54	12
	1977	120	4	–	20	23	2	3	8	41	19
	1978	154	5	–	31	35	–	2	5	52	24
MONACO	1977	86	5	5	11	16	11	15	12	6	5
NETHERLANDS ‡	1976	12 557	159	455	502	1 861	1 240	1 271	653	5 212	1 204
	1977	13 111	192	492	477	1 987	1 225	1 304	748	5 498	1 188
	1978	13 393	134	556	535	2 079	1 153	1 399	748	5 605	1 184
NORWAY ‡	1976	5 723	152	96	250	1 592	500	912	347	1 442	432
	1977	4 823	123	79	228	1 168	463	693	229	1 499	341
	1978	4 407	121	70	271	956	278	578	235	1 546	352
POLAND	1976	11 418	223	121	168	2 397	1 030	3 957	703	2 146	673
	1977	11 552	230	159	172	2 347	1 038	4 078	685	2 130	713
	1978	11 849	287	151	172	2 474	1 052	4 263	666	2 149	635
PORTUGAL	1976	5 668	197	144	211	1 612	274	824	806	1 225	375
	1977	6 122	407	169	202	1 490	362	1 006	792	1 228	466
	1978	6 274	148	214	233	1 434	363	1 266	705	1 469	442
ROMANIA	1976	6 556	74	117	28	955	817	2 053	395	1 766	351
	1977	7 218	112	134	56	1 072	860	2 103	462	1 972	447
	1978	7 562	120	132	126	1 015	1 032	2 184	521	1 993	439

Number of titles by UDC classes   8.1
Nombre de titres classés d'après la CDU
Número de títulos clasificados por materias (CDU)

		(1)	(2)	(3)	(4)	(5)	(6)	(7)	(8)	(9)	(10)
SAN MARINO ‡	1978	15	–	–	–	4	–	2	4	2	3
SPAIN	1976	24 584	2 990	1 303	1 374	4 357	1 682	2 281	1 402	7 105	2 090
	1977	24 896	2 714	1 338	1 501	3 927	1 918	2 499	1 589	7 356	2 054
SWEDEN ‡	1976	7 988	158	170	205	1 211	559	1 821	340	2 985	539
	1977	6 009	159	123	213	831	323	977	323	1 959	451
	1978	5 256	119	122	159	807	366	836	231	1 758	393
SWITZERLAND ‡	1976	9 989	121	273	646	2 100	914	2 048	932	1 593	866
	1977	9 894	123	251	619	2 142	880	1 880	878	1 655	909
	1978	9 453	133	298	628	1 960	875	2 170	990	1 499	900
UNITED KINGDOM	1976	34 340	806	980	1 229	6 651	3 317	5 923	3 380	8 681	3 373
	1977	36 196	1 054	1 230	1 396	6 877	3 259	5 996	3 510	9 301	3 573
YUGOSLAVIA ‡	1976	9 054	144	129	306	3 709	309	1 304	950	1 909	294
	1977	10 418	187	121	197	3 765	343	1 740	1 243	2 473	349
	1978	10 509	166	98	187	4 073	352	1 661	1 416	2 236	320
OCEANIA											
AMERICAN SAMOA ‡	1978	86	7	–	–	18	1	1	–	12	1
AUSTRALIA ‡	1976	2 325	89	13	90	878	168	379	174	370	164
	1977	3 077	105	27	97	1 034	242	534	249	468	321
FIJI ‡	1976	139	–	–	–	50	47	24	2	16	–
FRENCH POLYNESIA	1977	12	–	–	–	7	–	3	–	2	–
GUAM ‡	1978	31	–	–	–	–	9	22	–	–	–
NEW ZEALAND	1976	1 835	48	10	61	632	147	381	168	190	198
	1977	1 939	62	11	55	613	204	438	222	153	181
	1978	2 079	84	15	51	648	193	469	223	194	202
NORFOLK ISLAND	1977	1	–	–	–	1	–	–	–	–	–
PACIFIC ISLANDS ‡	1978	41	–	–	–	41	–	–	–	–	–
SAMOA	1976	125	25	–	20	26	17	17	5	–	15
	1977	240	46	7	30	73	25	27	17	–	15
TONGA	1976	379	–	–	22	328	3	23	–	–	3
	1977	546	–	–	40	450	6	46	–	1	3
	1978	210	–	–	60	105	–	30	–	–	15
U.S.S.R.											
U.S.S.R.	1976	84 304	2 569	1 298	220	18 913	9 306	35 453	2 342	11 969	2 234
	1977	85 395	2 191	1 255	237	19 243	9 413	35 904	2 592	12 190	2 370
BYELORUSSIAN S.S.R.	1976	2 489	91	44	8	584	237	981	95	382	67
	1977	2 330	97	39	7	567	197	926	49	379	69
	1978	2 618	124	57	8	751	196	945	54	406	77
UKRAINIAN S.S.R.	1976	9 110	312	127	31	2 370	1 093	3 532	200	1 211	234
	1977	8 430	308	124	32	2 123	994	3 201	231	1 188	229

8.1 Number of titles by UDC classes
Nombre de titres classés d'après la CDU
Número de títulos clasificados por materias (CDU)

SIERRA LEONE (CONT.)
ESP> TODAS LAS OBRAS CONSIDERADAS SON PRIMERAS EDICIONES.

SUDAN:
E—> DATA FOR 1977 REFER TO SCHOOL TEXTBOOKS ONLY.
FR—> POUR 1977, LES DONNEES SE REFERENT AUX MANUELS SCOLAIRES SEULEMENT.
ESP> EN 1977, LOS DATOS SE REFIEREN A LOS MANUALES ESCOLARES SOLAMENTE.

TUNISIA:
E—> IN 1976 SCHOOL TEXTBOOKS (5) AND CHILDREN'S BOOKS (9) ARE INCLUDED IN THE TOTAL BUT NOT IDENTIFIED IN THE 9 GROUPS.
FR—> POUR 1976, LES MANUELS SCOLAIRES (5) ET LES LIVRES POUR ENFANTS (9) SONT COMPRIS DANS LE TOTAL MAIS NE SONT PAS REPARTIS ENTRE LES 9 GROUPES.
ESP> EN 1976, LOS MANUALES ESCOLARES (5) Y LOS LIBROS PARA NIÑOS (9) QUEDAN COMPRENDIDOS EN EL TOTAL PERO NO ESTAN REPARTIDOS ENTRE LOS 9 GRUPOS.

UNITED REPUBLIC OF CAMEROON:
E—> THE DATA REFER TO FIRST EDITIONS OF SCHOOL TEXTBOOKS ONLY.
FR—> LES DONNEES SE RAPPORTENT AUX PREMIERES EDITIONS DE MANUELS SCOLAIRES SEULEMENT.
ESP> LOS DATOS SE REFIEREN A LAS PRIMERAS EDICIONES DE LOS MANUALES ESCOLARES SOLAMENTE.

ZAMBIA:
E—> FOR 1978 SCHOOL TEXTBOOKS (31) AND CHILDREN'S BOOKS (2) ARE INCLUDED IN THE TOTAL BUT NOT DISTRIBUTED IN THE 9 GROUPS.
FR—> POUR 1978, LES MANUELS SCOLAIRES (31) ET LES LIVRES POUR ENFANTS (2) SONT COMPRIS DANS LE TOTAL MAIS NE SONT PAS REPARTIS ENTRE LES 9 GROUPES.
ESP> EN 1978, LOS MANUALES ESCOLARES (31) Y LOS LIBROS PARA NIÑOS (2) QUEDAN COMPRENDIDOS EN EL TOTAL PERO NO ESTAN REPARTIDOS ENTRE LOS 9 GRUPOS.

BARBADOS:
E—> THE FIGURES FOR 1977 SHOW ONLY FIRST EDITIONS.
FR—> POUR 1977, LES CHIFFRES SE REFERENT SEULEMENT AUX PREMIERES EDITIONS.
ESP> EN 1977, LAS CIFRAS SE REFIEREN SOLAMENTE A LAS PRIMERAS EDICIONES.

CANADA:
E—> THE DATA DO NOT INCLUDE GOVERNMENT PUBLICATIONS. DATA FOR 1978 INCLUDE UNIVERSITY THESES (4,369) WHICH ACCOUNT IN PART FOR THE INCREASE IN THE NUMBER OF TITLES COMPARED WITH PREVIOUS YEARS.
FR—> LES DONNEES N'INCLUENT PAS LES PUBLICATIONS OFFICIELLES. POUR 1978, LES CHIFFRES COMPRENNENT LES THESES UNIVERSITAIRES (4,369), CE QUI EXPLIQUE, EN PARTIE, L'AUGMENTATION DU

CONGO:
E—> ALL FIRST EDITIONS.
FR—> TOUS LES OUVRAGES RECENSES SONT DES PREMIERES EDITIONS.
ESP> TODAS LAS OBRAS CONSIDERADAS SON PRIMERAS EDICIONES.

EGYPT:
E—> THE FIGURES FOR 1977 ARE PRELIMINARY.
FR—> LES CHIFFRES RELATIFS A 1977 SONT PROVISOIRES.
ESP> LAS CIFRAS RELATIVAS A 1977 SON PROVISIONALES.

ETHIOPIA:
E—> THE DATA REFER TO FIRST EDITIONS ONLY. SCHOOL TEXTBOOKS (119) AND CHILDREN'S BOOKS (2) ARE INCLUDED IN THE TOTAL BUT NOT IDENTIFIED IN THE 9 GROUPS.
FR—> LES DONNEES SE REFERENT AUX PREMIERES EDITIONS SEULEMENT. LES MANUELS SCOLAIRES (119) ET LES LIVRES POUR ENFANTS (2) SONT COMPRIS DANS LE TOTAL MAIS NE SONT PAS REPARTIS ENTRE LES 9 GROUPES.
ESP> LOS DATOS SE REFIEREN A LAS PRIMERAS EDICIONES SOLAMENTE. LOS MANUALES ESCOLARES (119) Y LOS LIBROS PARA NIÑOS (2) QUEDAN COMPRENDIDOS EN EL TOTAL PERO NO ESTAN REPARTIDOS ENTRE LOS 9 GRUPOS.

GAMBIA:
E—> ALL FIRST EDITIONS.
FR—> TOUS LES OUVRAGES RECENSES SONT DES PREMIERES EDITIONS.
ESP> TODAS LAS OBRAS CONSIDERADAS SON PRIMERAS EDICIONES.

MAURITIUS:
E—> THE FIGURES FOR 1978 SHOW ONLY FIRST EDITIONS.
FR—> POUR 1978, LES CHIFFRES NE CONCERNENT QUE LES PREMIERES EDITIONS.
ESP> EN 1978, LAS CIFRAS SOLO SE REFIEREN A LAS PRIMERAS EDICIONES.

SENEGAL:
E—> ALL FIRST EDITIONS.
FR—> TOUS LES OUVRAGES RECENSES SONT DES PREMIERES EDITIONS.
ESP> TODAS LAS OBRAS CONSIDERADAS SON PRIMERAS EDICIONES.

SEYCHELLES:
E—> ALL FIRST EDITIONS.
FR—> TOUS LES OUVRAGES RECENSES SONT DES PREMIERES EDITIONS.
ESP> TODAS LAS OBRAS CONSIDERADAS SON PRIMERAS EDICIONES.

SIERRA LEONE:
E—> ALL FIRST EDITIONS.
FR—> TOUS LES OUVRAGES RECENSES SONT DES PREMIERES EDITIONS.

Number of titles by UDC classes 8.1
Nombre de titres classés d'après la CDU
Número de títulos clasificados por materias (CDU)

...STATES OF AMERICA (CONT.)
POUR LES JEUNES (EN 1976, 2 210; EN 1978, 2 911)
POUR LESQUELS LA REPARTITION PAR SUJETS N'EST PAS
DISPONIBLE.
ESP> LAS ESTADISTICAS SOLO SE REFIEREN A LOS
LIBROS PUBLICADOS CON FINES COMERCIALES (ES DECIR,
DESTINADOS A LA VENTA AL PUBLICO EN GENERAL)
Y OMITEN UNA GRAN PARTE DE LA PRODUCCION TOTAL
DE LIBROS (PUBLICACIONES DE LOS GOBIERNOS DE LOS
ESTADOS Y DE LAS AUTORIDADES LOCALES, DE LAS
UNIVERSIDADES, DE LAS ORGANIZACIONES RELIGIOSAS Y
DE OTRAS INSTITUCIONES, MANUALES ESCOLARES, ASI
COMO LA MAYORIA DE LOS INFORMES Y ACTAS, MANUALES
Y GUIAS DE LABORATORIO). COMPRENDEN SIN EMBARGO
LAS PUBLICACIONES DEL GOBIERNO FEDERAL (EN 1976,
16 931; EN 1978, 14 814), LAS TESIS UNIVERSITARIAS
(EN 1976, 34 709; EN 1978, 31 629) Y LOS TITULOS
DE NOVELAS PARA NIÑOS Y ADOLESCENTES (EN 1976,
2 210; EN 1978, 2 911), CUYA DISTRIBUCION POR
TEMAS NO SE CONOCE.

ARGENTINA:
E—> WORKS OF COLUMN 4 ARE INCLUDED WITH
THOSE OF COLUMN 3.
FR—> LES OUVRAGES DE LA COLONNE 4 SONT INCLUS
AVEC CEUX DE LA COLONNE 3.
ESP> LAS OBRAS DE LA COLUMNA 4 QUEDAN INCLUIDAS
CON LAS DE LA COLUMNA 3.

CHINA:
E—> FOR THE SUBJECT BREAKDOWN PLEASE REFER TO
THE CORRESPONDING FOOTNOTE TO TABLE 8.3. SCHOOL
TEXTBOOKS AND CHILDREN'S BOOKS (4,614) ARE
INCLUDED IN THE TOTAL BUT ARE NOT DISTRIBUTED
IN THE 9 GROUPS.
FR—> POUR LA REPARTITION PAR SUJETS, VEUILLEZ
VOUS REPORTER A LA NOTE CORRESPONDANTE DU TABLEAU
8.3. LES MANUELS SCOLAIRES ET LES LIVRES POUR
ENFANTS (4 614) SONT COMPRIS DANS LE TOTAL MAIS
NE SONT PAS REPARTIS ENTRE LES 9 GROUPES.
ESP> PARA LA REPARTICION POR MATERIAS, VEASE
LA NOTA CORRESPONDIENTE DEL CUADRO 8.3. LOS
MANUALES ESCOLARES Y LOS LIBROS PARA NIÑOS
(4 614 EN TOTAL) QUEDAN COMPRENDIDOS EN EL
TOTAL PERO NO ESTAN REPARTIDOS ENTRE LOS
9 GRUPOS.

ISRAEL:
E—> DATA DO NOT INCLUDE UNIVERSITY THESES.
SCHOOL TEXTBOOKS (197) AND CHILDREN'S BOOKS
(231) ARE INCLUDED IN THE TOTAL BUT NOT DISTRI-
BUTED IN THE 9 GROUPS.
FR—> LES DONNEES N'INCLUENT PAS LES THESES
UNIVERSITAIRES. LES MANUELS SCOLAIRES (197) ET
LES LIVRES POUR ENFANTS (231) SONT INCLUS DANS LE
TOTAL MAIS NE SONT PAS REPARTIS ENTRE LES 9
GROUPES.
ESP> LOS DATOS NO INCLUYEN LAS TESIS UNIVERSI-
TARIAS. LOS MANUALES ESCOLARES (197) Y LOS
LIBROS PARA NIÑOS (231) QUEDAN COMPRENDIDOS EN
EL TOTAL PERO NO ESTAN REPARTIDOS ENTRE LOS
9 GRUPOS.

NOMBRE DE TITRES PAR RAPPORT AUX ANNEES PRECE-
DENTES.
ESP> LOS DATOS NO INCLUYEN LAS PUBLICACIONES
OFICIALES. EN 1978, LAS CIFRAS COMPRENDEN LAS
TESIS UNIVERSITARIAS (4,369), LO QUE EXPLICA,
EN PARTE, EL AUMENTO DEL NUMERO DE TITULOS EN
RELACION CON LOS AÑOS ANTERIORES.

DOMINICAN REPUBLIC:
E—> ALL FIRST EDITIONS.
FR—> TOUS LES OUVRAGES RECENSES SONT DES
PREMIERES EDITIONS.
ESP> TODAS LAS OBRAS CONSIDERADAS SON
PRIMERAS EDICIONES.

JAMAICA:
E—> IN 1977 ALL FIRST EDITIONS.
FR—> POUR 1977, TOUS LES OUVRAGES RECENSES SONT
DES PREMIERES EDITIONS.
ESP> EN 1977, TODAS LAS OBRAS CONSIDERADAS SON
PRIMERAS EDICIONES.

PANAMA:
E—> THE FIGURES FOR 1976 DO NOT INCLUDE
UNIVERSITY THESES.
FR—> POUR 1976, LES DONNEES N'INCLUENT PAS LES
THESES UNIVERSITAIRES.
ESP> EN 1976, LOS DATOS NO INCLUYEN LAS TESIS
UNIVERSITARIAS.

TRINIDAD AND TOBAGO:
E—> UNIVERSITY THESES ONLY.
FR—> THESES UNIVERSITAIRES SEULEMENT.
ESP> TESIS UNIVERSITARIAS SOLAMENTE.

UNITED STATES OF AMERICA:
E—> THE STATISTICS COVER ONLY THE COMMERCIAL
BOOK PRODUCTION (I.E. THE PRODUCTION OF BOOKS
INTENDED FOR SALE TO THE GENERAL PUBLIC) AND
OMIT A LARGE PART OF THE TOTAL BOOK PRODUCTION
(I.E. PUBLICATIONS OF STATE GOVERNMENTS AND
LOCAL AUTHORITIES, UNIVERSITIES, CHURCHES AND
OTHER ORGANIZATIONS, SCHOOL TEXTBOOKS AS WELL AS
MOST REPORTS AND ACCOUNTS OF PROCEEDINGS, LABORA-
TORY MANUALS AND WORK BOOKS) INCLUDED IN THE
STATISTICS ARE PUBLICATIONS OF THE FEDERAL
GOVERNMENT (1976: 16,931; 1978: 14,814), THE
UNIVERSITY THESES (1976: 34,709; 1978: 31,629)
AND JUVENILE TITLES (1976: 2,210; 1978: 2,911)
WHOSE SUBJECT BREAKDOWN IS NOT AVAILABLE.
FR—> LES STATISTIQUES NE CONCERNENT QUE LES
LIVRES COMMERCIAUX (C'EST-A-DIRE, DESTINES A ETRE
VENDUS AU GRAND PUBLIC) ET FONT ABSTRACTION
D'UNE GRANDE PARTIE DE LA PRODUCTION DE LIVRES
(PUBLICATIONS DES GOUVERNEMENTS DES ETATS ET
AUTORITES LOCALES, DES UNIVERSITES, DES EGLISES
ET AUTRES INSTITUTIONS, MANUELS SCOLAIRES AINSI
QUE LA PLUPART DES RAPPORTS ET PROCES-VERBAUX,
MANUELS ET GUIDES DE LABORATOIRE). LES STATISTI-
QUES COMPRENNENT CEPENDANT LES PUBLICATIONS DU
GOUVERNEMENT FEDERAL (EN 1976, 16,931; EN 1978,
14,814), LES THESES UNIVERSITAIRES (EN 1976,
34,709; EN 1978, 31,629) ET LES TITRES DE ROMANS

8.1   Number of titles by UDC classes
Nombre de titres classés d'après la CDU
Número de títulos clasificados por materias (CDU)

UNITED ARAB EMIRATES:
E—> ALL FIRST EDITIONS.
FR—> TOUS LES OUVRAGES RECENSES SONT DES PREMIERES EDITIONS.
ESP> TODAS LAS OBRAS CONSIDERADAS SON PRIMERAS EDICIONES.

BELGIUM:
E—> THE DATA REFER ONLY TO TITLES INDEXED IN THE "BIBLIOGRAPHIE DE BELGIQUE".
FR—> LES DONNEES NE CONCERNENT QUE LES TITRES REPERTORIES DANS LA BIBLIOGRAPHIE DE BELGIQUE.
ESP> LOS DATOS SOLO SE REFIEREN A LOS LIBROS INSCRITOS EN EL REPERTORIO DE LA "BIBLIOGRAPHIE DE BELGIQUE".

FRANCE:
E—> DATA FOR 1978 DO NOT INCLUDE PAMPHLETS WHICH IN 1977 ACCOUNTED FOR 6,906 TITLES.
FR—> LES DONNEES POUR 1978 NE COMPRENNENT PAS LES BROCHURES DONT LE NOMBRE DE TITRES S'ELEVAIT A 6 906 EN 1977.
ESP> EN 1978, LOS DATOS NO INCLUYEN LOS FOLLETOS QUE EN 1977 ASCENDIERON A 6 906 TITULOS.

GERMAN DEMOCRATIC REPUBLIC:
E—> SCHOOL TEXTBOOKS (1976: 249; 1977: 237; 1978: 231) AND CHILDREN'S BOOKS (1976: 673; 1977: 681; 1978: 707) ARE INCLUDED IN THE TOTAL BUT NOT IDENTIFIED IN THE 9 GROUPS.
FR—> LES MANUELS SCOLAIRES (EN 1976, 249; EN 1977, 237; EN 1978, 231) ET LES LIVRES POUR EN-FANTS (EN 1976, 673; EN 1977, 681; EN 1978, 707) SONT COMPRIS DANS LE TOTAL MAIS NE SONT PAS REPARTIS ENTRE LES 9 GROUPES.
ESP> LOS MANUALES ESCOLARES (EN 1976, 249; EN 1977, 237; EN 1978, 231) Y LOS LIBROS PARA NIÑOS (EN 1976, 673; EN 1977, 681; EN 1978, 707) QUEDAN COMPRENDIDOS EN EL TOTAL PERO NO ESTAN REPARTIDOS ENTRE LOS 9 GRUPOS.

ICELAND:
E—> ALL FIRST EDITIONS.
FR—> TOUS LES OUVRAGES RECENSES SONT DES PRE-MIERES EDITIONS.
ESP> TODAS LAS OBRAS CONSIDERADAS SON PRIMERAS EDICIONES.

NETHERLANDS:
E—> DATA DO NOT INCLUDE PAMPHLETS.
FR—> LES DONNEES N'INCLUENT PAS LES BROCHURES.
ESP> LOS DATOS NO INCLUYEN LOS FOLLETOS.

NORWAY:
E—> STATISTICS ON PAMPHLETS ARE INCOMPLETE.
FR—> LES STATISTIQUES RELATIVES AUX BROCHURES SONT INCOMPLETES.
ESP> LAS ESTADISTICAS RELATIVAS A LOS FOLLETOS SON INCOMPLETAS.

SAN MARINO:
E—> ALL FIRST EDITIONS.
FR—> TOUS LES OUVRAGES RECENSES SONT DES PREMIERES EDITIONS.

JORDAN:
E—> THE DATA REFER TO THE EAST BANK ONLY. ALL FIRST EDITIONS.
FR—> LES DONNEES SE REFERENT A LA RIVE ORIENTALE SEULEMENT. TOUS LES OUVRAGES RECENSES SONT DES PREMIERES EDITIONS.
ESP> LOS DATOS SE REFIEREN A LA ORILLA ORIENTAL SOLAMENTE. TODAS LAS OBRAS CONSIDERADAS SON PRIMERAS EDICIONES.

KOREA, REPUBLIC OF:
E—> FOR 1978 SCHOOL TEXTBOOKS (687) AND CHILDREN'S BOOKS (1,028) ARE INCLUDED IN THE TOTAL BUT ARE NOT IDENTIFIED IN THE 9 GROUPS.
FR—> POUR 1978, LES MANUELS SCOLAIRES (687) ET LES LIVRES POUR ENFANTS (1 028) SONT COMPRIS DANS LE TOTAL MAIS NE SONT PAS REPARTIS ENTRE LES 9 GROUPES.
ESP> EN 1978, LOS MANUALES ESCOLARES (687) Y LOS LIBROS PARA NIÑOS (1 028) QUEDAN COMPRENDIDOS EN EL TOTAL PERO NO ESTAN REPARTIDOS ENTRE LOS 9 GRUPOS.

LAO, PEOPLE'S DEMOCRATIC REPUBLIC:
E—> ALL FIRST EDITIONS.
FR—> TOUS LES OUVRAGES RECENSES SONT DES PREMIERES EDITIONS.
ESP> TODAS LAS OBRAS CONSIDERADAS SON PRIMERAS EDICIONES.

MALDIVES:
E—> ALL FIRST EDITIONS.
FR—> TOUS LES OUVRAGES RECENSES SONT DES PREMIERES EDITIONS.
ESP> TODAS LAS OBRAS CONSIDERADAS SON PRIMERAS EDICIONES.

PHILIPPINES:
E—> THE FIGURES REPRESENT ONLY THOSE BOOKS WHICH HAVE BEEN RECEIVED IN THE NATIONAL LIBRARY.
FR—> LES CHIFFRES REPRESENTENT SEULEMENT LES LIVRES ENREGISTRES A LA BIBLIOTHEQUE NATIONALE.
ESP> LAS CIFRAS REPRESENTAN SOLAMENTE LOS LIBROS REGISTRADOS EN LA BIBLIOTECA NACIONAL.

SINGAPORE:
E—> THE DATA DO NOT INCLUDE GOVERNMENT PUBLI-CATIONS.
FR—> LES DONNEES N'INCLUENT PAS LES PUBLICATIONS OFFICIELLES.
ESP> LOS DATOS NO INCLUYEN LAS PUBLICACIONES OFICIALES.

SYRIAN ARAB REPUBLIC:
E—> FOR 1978 SCHOOL TEXTBOOKS (1) AND CHILDREN'S BOOKS (11) ARE INCLUDED IN THE TOTAL BUT ARE NOT IDENTIFIED IN THE 9 GROUPS.
FR—> POUR 1978, LES MANUELS SCOLAIRES (1) ET LES LIVRES POUR ENFANTS (11) SONT COMPRIS DANS LES 9 GROUPES. MAIS NE SONT PAS REPARTIS DANS LES 9 GROUPES.
E> EN 1978, LOS MANUALES ESCOLARES (1) Y LOS LIBROS PARA NIÑOS (11) QUEDAN COMPRENDIDOS EN EL TOTAL PERO NO ESTAN REPARTIDOS ENTRE LOS 9 GRUPOS.

Number of titles by UDC classes 8.1
Nombre de titres classés d'après la CDU
Número de títulos clasificados por materias (CDU)

ESP> TODAS LAS OBRAS CONSIDERADAS SON PRIMERAS EDICIONES.

SWEDEN:
E—> CHILDREN'S BOOKS (1976: 684; 1977: 650; 1978: 465) ARE INCLUDED IN THE TOTAL BUT NOT DISTRIBUTED IN THE 9 GROUPS.
FR—> LES LIVRES POUR ENFANTS (EN 1976, 684; EN 1977, 650, EN 1978, 465) SONT COMPRIS DANS LE TOTAL MAIS NE SONT PAS REPARTIS ENTRE LES NEUF GROUPES.
ESP> LOS LIBROS PARA NIÑOS (EN 1976, 684; EN 1977, 650; EN 1978, 465) QUEDAN COMPRENDIDOS EN EL TOTAL PERO NO ESTAN REPARTIDOS ENTRE LOS 9 GRUPOS.

SWITZERLAND:
E—> SCHOOL TEXTBOOKS (1976: 144; 1977: 122; 1978: 177) AND CHILDREN'S BOOKS (1976: 352; 1977: 435; 1978: 416) ARE INCLUDED IN THE TOTAL BUT ARE NOT DISTRIBUTED IN THE 9 GROUPS.
FR—> LES MANUELS SCOLAIRES (EN 1976, 144; EN 1977, 122; EN 1978, 177)ET LES LIVRES POUR ENFANTS (EN 1976, 352; EN 1977, 435; EN 1978, 416) SONT COMPRIS DANS LE TOTAL MAIS NE SONT PAS REPARTIS ENTRE LES 9 GROUPES.
ESP> LOS MANUALES ESCOLARES (EN 1976, 144; EN 1977, 122; EN 1978, 177) Y LOS LIBROS PARA NIÑOS (EN 1976, 352; EN 1977, 435; EN 1978, 416) QUEDAN COMPRENDIDOS EN EL TOTAL PERO NO ESTAN REPARTIDOS ENTRE LOS 9 GRUPOS.

YUGOSLAVIA:
E—> DATA FOR 1976 DO NOT INCLUDE UNIVERSITY BOOKS.
FR—> POUR 1976 LES DONNEES N'INCLUENT PAS LES LIVRES UTILISES DANS LES UNIVERSITES.
ESP> EN 1976, LOS DATOS NO INCLUYEN LOS LIBROS UTILIZADOS EN LAS UNIVERSIDADES.

E—> SCHOOL TEXTBOOKS (8) AND CHILDREN'S BOOKS (38) ARE INCLUDED IN THE TOTAL BUT NOT IDENTIFIED IN THE 9 GROUPS.
FR—> LES MANUELS SCOLAIRES (8) ET LES LIVRES POUR ENFANTS (38) SONT COMPRIS DANS LE TOTAL MAIS NE SONT PAS REPARTIS ENTRE LES 9 GROUPES.
ESP> LOS MANUALES ESCOLARES (8) Y LOS LIBROS PARA NIÑOS (38) QUEDAN COMPRENDIDOS EN EL TOTAL PERO NO ESTAN REPARTIDOS ENTRE LOS 9 GRUPOS.

AUSTRALIA:
E—> THE FIGURES FOR 1977 ARE PRELIMINARY.
FR—> LES CHIFFRES RELATIFS A 1977 SONT PROVISOIRES.
ESP> LAS CIFRAS RELATIVAS A 1977 SON PROVISIONALES.

FIJI:
E—> DATA REFER TO SCHOOL TEXTBOOKS ONLY.
FR—> LES DONNEES NE SE REFERENT QU'AUX MANUELS SCOLAIRES.
ESP> LOS DATOS SOLO SE REFIEREN A LOS MANUALES ESCOLARES.

GUAM:
E—> ALL FIRST EDITIONS.
FR—> TOUS LES OUVRAGES RECENSES SONT DES PREMIERES EDITIONS.
ESP> TODAS LAS OBRAS CONSIDERADAS SON PRIMERAS EDICIONES.

PACIFIC ISLANDS:
E—> ALL FIRST EDITIONS.
FR—> TOUS LES OUVRAGES RECENSES SONT DES PREMIERES EDITIONS.
ESP> TODAS LAS OBRAS CONSIDERADAS SON PRIMERAS EDICIONES.

8.2 Book production: number of titles by language of publication
Edition de livres: nombre de titres classés d'après la langue de publication

Edición de libros: número de obras clasificadas según la lengua en que se publican

8.2 Number of titles by language of publication
Nombre de titres classés d'après la langue de publication
Número de obras clasificadas según la lengua en que se publican

NUMBER OF COUNTRIES AND TERRITORIES PRESENTED IN THIS TABLE: 92
NOMBRE DE PAYS ET DE TERRITOIRES PRESENTES DANS CE TABLEAU: 92
NUMERO DE PAISES Y DE TERRITORIOS PRESENTADOS EN ESTE CUADRO: 92

COUNTRY / PAYS / PAIS	YEAR / ANNEE / AÑO	TOTAL	NATIONAL LANGUAGE LANGUE NATIONALE LENGUA NACIONAL	FOREIGN LANGUAGES / LANGUES ETRANGERES / LENGUAS EXTRANJERAS						TWO OR MORE LANGUAGES DEUX LANGUES OU PLUS DOS O MAS LENGUAS
				ENGLISH ANGLAIS INGLES	FRENCH FRANCAIS FRANCES	GERMAN ALLEMAND ALEMAN	SPANISH ESPAGNOL ESPAÑOL	RUSSIAN RUSSE RUSO	OTHERS AUTRES LANGUES OTRAS LENGUAS	
		(1)	(2)	(3)	(4)	(5)	(6)	(7)	(8)	(9)
AFRICA										
BOTSWANA	1978	103	103	./.	—	—	—	—	—	—
BENIN	1978	13	13	—	./.	—	—	—	—	—
CONGO ‡	1977	127	107	—	—	—	—	—	—	20
EGYPT ‡	1977	1 472	1 360	68	41	—	—	—	3	—
ETHIOPIA	1978	353	243	90	—	—	—	—	20	—
GAMBIA	1978	81	81	./.	—	—	—	—	—	—
GHANA ‡	1978	251	247	./.	1	—	—	—	2	1
KENYA ‡	1976	183	167	./.	3	—	—	—	13	—
MADAGASCAR ‡	1978	219	216	2	1	—	—	—	—	—
MAURITANIA ‡	1976	71	71	—	./.	—	—	—	—	—
MAURITIUS ‡	1978	20	18	./.	./.	—	—	—	—	2
NIGER ‡	1976	78	70	8	./.	—	—	—	—	—

Number of titles by language of publication 8.2
Nombre de titres classés d'après la langue de publication
Número de obras clasificadas según la lengua en que se publican

		(1)	(2)	(3)	(4)	(5)	(6)	(7)	(8)	(9)
SENEGAL ‡	1977	48	48	—	./.	—	—	—	—	—
SEYCHELLES ‡	1977	11	11	./.	—	—	—	—	—	—
SIERRA LEONE ‡	1977	61	61	./.	./.	—	—	—	—	—
SUDAN ‡	1976	151	151	./.	—	—	—	—	—	—
TUNISIA	1978	85	43	7	35	—	—	—	—	—
UNITED REPUBLIC OF CAMEROON ‡	1978	54	54	./.	./.	—	—	—	—	—
UNITED REPUBLIC OF TANZANIA	1976	399	213	181	1	—	—	—	4	—
ZAIRE	1977	154	154	—	—	—	—	—	—	—
ZAMBIA	1977	32	12	./.	./.	—	—	—	20	—
AMERICA, NORTH										
CANADA ‡	1977	7 878	7 780	./.	./.	6	—	—	70	21
COSTA RICA ‡	1978	24	24	—	—	—	—	—	—	—
DOMINICAN REPUBLIC ‡	1976	48	48	./.	—	—	1	—	—	—
JAMAICA ‡	1978	143	143	—	—	—	—	—	—	—
MEXICO	1976	4 851	4 825	6	2	—	—	—	10	8
NETHERLANDS ANTILLES ‡	1977	52	49	./.	—	—	—	—	—	—
PANAMA	1978	68	68	—	—	—	—	—	—	—
TRINIDAD AND TOBAGO ‡	1976	18	18	./.	—	—	1	1	—	2
AMERICA, SOUTH										
ARGENTINA	1978	4 627	4 623	2	65	1	—	—	1	—
BRAZIL	1977	20 025	18 659	266		3	1 015	—	5	12
CHILE	1978	432	429	1	—	—	—	—	1	1
GUYANA	1978	97	97	—	—	—	—	—	—	—
PERU ‡	1978	947	928	6	—	—	—	1	5	7
ASIA										
AFGHANISTAN	1977	232	232	—	—	—	—	—	—	—
BRUNEI ‡	1978	32	32	./.	36	—	—	—	—	—
CYPRUS	1977	570	373	102	—	32	—	16	11	—
HONG KONG ‡	1977	1 735	1 641	./.	—	—	—	—	12	—
INDIA ‡	1978	12 932	6 572	./.	—	—	—	—	6 360	82
IRAQ ‡	1976	1 588	1 521	63	4	—	—	—	—	—
ISRAEL ‡	1977	2 214	1 919	152	3	2	—	—	65	78
JAPAN	1978	43 973	43 254	711	1	—	—	2	1	—
JORDAN ‡	1976	392	357	35	—	—	—	—	—	—
KOREA, REPUBLIC OF	1978	15 737	15 241	436	4	6	—	—	—	50
KUWAIT	1978	50	50	—	—	—	—	—	—	—
LAO PEOPLE'S DEMOCRATIC REPUBLIC	1976	31	31	—	—	—	—	—	—	—
MALAYSIA	1978	1 328	624	467	2	—	—	—	102	133
MALDIVES	1976	8	8	—	—	—	—	—	—	—
PAKISTAN ‡	1978	1 317	1 151	./.	—	—	—	—	—	—
QATAR	1978	159	159	—	—	—	—	—	45	121

8.2 Number of titles by language of publication
Nombre de titres classés d'après la langue de publication
Número de obras clasificadas según la lengua en que se publican

COUNTRY / PAYS / PAIS	YEAR / ANNEE / AÑO	TOTAL (1)	NATIONAL LANGUAGE / LANGUE NATIONALE / LENGUA NACIONAL (2)	FOREIGN LANGUAGES / LANGUES ETRANGERES / LENGUAS EXTRANJERAS ENGLISH / ANGLAIS / INGLES (3)	FRENCH / FRANCAIS / FRANCES (4)	GERMAN / ALLEMAND / ALEMAN (5)	SPANISH / ESPAGNOL / ESPAÑOL (6)	RUSSIAN / RUSSE / RUSO (7)	OTHERS / AUTRES LANGUES / OTRAS LENGUAS (8)	TWO OR MORE LANGUAGES / DEUX LANGUES OU PLUS / DOS O MAS LENGUAS (9)
PHILIPPINES ‡	1977	1 753	756	./.	...	...	...	-	979	18
SINGAPORE ‡	1978	1 306	1 254	./.	-	-	-	-	-	52
SRI LANKA ‡	1978	1 406	1 015	302	./.	-	-	-	2	87
SYRIAN ARAB REPUBLIC	1978	230	226	./.	-	-	-	-	-	-
THAILAND	1977	3 390	3 209	181	-	-	-	-	-	-
UNITED ARAB EMIRATES ‡	1977	15	8	3	2	1	.	.	-	1
VIET-NAM ‡	1977	1 504	1 449	8	10	.	4	3	6	24
EUROPE										
AUSTRIA	1978	6 439	6 138	194	48	./.	3	1	55	-
BELGIUM ‡	1978	9 012	8 450	245	./.	./.	5	3	70	239
BULGARIA	1978	4 234	3 671	88	83	58	40	134	47	113
CZECHOSLOVAKIA ‡	1978	9 588	8 792	137	43	113	20	93	329	59
DENMARK	1978	9 415	8 091	783	69	92	8	17	113	242
FINLAND ‡	1978	3 367	2 845	369	2	18	-	1	4	128
GREECE	1977	4 981	4 432	272	219	35	17	-	23	-
HOLY SEE ‡	1978	179	3	41	13	8	16	-	91	6
HUNGARY ‡	1978	9 579	8 679	318	41	151	-	91	68	215
ICELAND	1977	801	801	-	-	-	-	-	-	-
IRELAND ‡	1978	632	628	./.	2	-	-	-	2	-
ITALY	1977	10 679	10 006	167	74	66	6	-	62	298
LUXEMBOURG ‡	1977	250	195	4	./.	./.	-	-	-	51
MALTA ‡	1978	154	141	./.	2	-	-	-	11	-
MONACO	1977	86	86	./.	./.	-	-	-	-	-
NETHERLANDS	1978	13 393	11 123	1 170	149	247	1	-	60	643
NORWAY ‡	1978	3 361	2 174	756	35	54	9	-	342	-
POLAND ‡	1978	11 849	10 900	372	99	131	9	187	151	-
ROMANIA	1978	7 562	6 274	154	83	251	-	-	686	114
SPAIN	1977	24 896	22 076	437	433	143	./.	-	1 358	449
SAN MARINO	1978	15	15	-	-	-	-	-	-	-
SWEDEN	1978	5 256	4 461	727	12	18	1	1	33	3
SWITZERLAND ‡	1978	9 785	8 491	905	./.	./.	1	-	./.	389
YUGOSLAVIA ‡	1978	10 509	9 420	103	33	42	-	25	638	248
OCEANIA										
GUAM ‡	1978	31	31	./.	-	-	-	-	-	-
FRENCH POLYNESIA ‡	1977	12	11	./.	./.	-	1	-	-	-
NEW ZEALAND ‡	1978	2 079	2 065	./.	./.	-	-	-	14	-
NORFOLK ISLAND	1977	1	1	./.	-	-	-	-	-	-
PACIFIC ISLANDS ‡	1978	41	40	./.	-	-	-	-	1	./
SAMOA ‡	1977	240	221	./.	-	-	-	-	19	-

Number of titles by language of publication   **8.2**
Nombre de titres classés d'après la langue de publication
Número de obras clasificadas según la lengua en que se publican

U.S.S.R.

		(1)	(2)	(3)	(4)	(5)	(6)	(7)	(8)	(9)
U.S.S.R. ‡	1977	85 395	80 862	1 987	592	409	300	./.	1 072	173
BYELORUSSIAN S.S.R. ‡	1978	2 618	2 553	–	–	33	–	./.	–	65
UKRAINIAN S.S.R. ‡	1977	8 430	8 093	110	23	33	5	./.	92	74

GENERAL NOTE – NOTE GENERALE – NOTA GENERAL:
E—> THE SYMBOL ./. INDICATES THAT DATA ARE
INCLUDED IN COLUMN 2 (NATIONAL LANGUAGE).
FR—> LE SIGNE ./. INDIQUE QUE LES CHIFFRES
SONT INCLUS DANS LA COLONNE 2 (LANGUE NATIONALE).
ESP> EL SIGNO ./. INDICA QUE LOS DATOS FIGURAN
EN LA COLUMNA 2 (LENGUA NACIONAL).

CONGO:
E—> FIRST EDITIONS OF BOOKS AND PAMPHLETS ONLY.
FR—> PREMIERES EDITIONS DE LIVRES ET BROCHURES
SEULEMENT.
ESP> PRIMERAS EDICIONES DE LIBROS Y FOLLETOS
SOLAMENTE.

EGYPT:
E—> PRELIMINARY FIGURES.
FR—> CHIFFRES PROVISOIRES.
ESP> CIFRAS PROVISIONALES.

GHANA:
E—> THE TITLES IN COLUMN 2 HAVE BEEN PUBLISHED
IN THE FOLLOWING LANGUAGES: ENGLISH (218) AND
OTHER NATIONAL LANGUAGES (29).
FR—> LES TITRES DE LA COLONNE 2 ONT ETE PUBLIES
DANS LES LANGUES SUIVANTES: ANGLAIS (218) ET
AUTRES LANGUES NATIONALES (29).
ESP> LOS TITULOS DE LA COLUMNA 2 HAN SIDO
PUBLICADOS EN LAS LENGUAS SIGUIENTES: INGLES (218)
Y OTRAS LENGUAS NACIONALES (29).

KENYA:
E—> THE TITLES IN COLUMN 2 HAVE BEEN PUBLISHED
IN THE FOLLOWING LANGUAGES: ENGLISH (121) AND
SWAHILI (46).
FR—> LES TITRES DE LA COLONNE 2 ONT ETE PUBLIES
DANS LES LANGUES SUIVANTES: ANGLAIS (121) ET
SWAHILI (46).
ESP> LOS TITULOS DE LA COLUMNA 2 HAN SIDO
PUBLICADOS EN LAS LENGUAS SIGUIENTES: INGLES (121)
Y SWAHILI (46).

MADAGASCAR:
E—> THE TITLES IN COLUMN 2 HAVE BEEN PUBLISHED
IN THE FOLLOWING LANGUAGES: MALAGASY (164) AND
FRENCH (52).
FR—> LES TITRES DE LA COLONNE 2 ONT ETE PUBLIES
DANS LES LANGUES SUIVANTES: MALGACHE (164) ET
FRANCAIS (52).

MADAGASCAR (CONT.):
ESP> LOS TITULOS DE LA COLUMNA 2 HAN SIDO
PUBLICADOS EN LAS LENGUAS SIGUIENTES: MALGACHE
(164) Y FRANCES (52).

MAURITANIA:
E—> THE TITLES IN COLUMN 2 HAVE BEEN PUBLISHED
IN THE FOLLOWING LANGUAGES: ARABIC (36), FRENCH
(31), ARABIC AND FRENCH (4).
FR—> LES TITRES DE LA COLONNE 2 ONT ETE PUBLIES
DANS LES LANGUES SUIVANTES: ARABE (36), FRANCAIS
(31) ARABE ET FRANCAIS (4).
ESP> LOS TITULOS DE LA COLUMNA 2 HAN SIDO
PUBLICADOS EN LAS LENGUAS SIGUIENTES: ARABE (36),
FRANCES (31), ARABE Y FRANCES (4).

MAURITIUS:
E—> THE TITLES IN COLUMN 2 HAVE BEEN PUBLISHED
IN THE FOLLOWING LANGUAGES: ENGLISH (6), FRENCH
(9), CREOLE (1) AND HINDI (2).
FR—> LES TITRES DE LA COLONNE 2 ONT ETE PUBLIES
DANS LES LANGUES SUIVANTES: ANGLAIS (6), FRANCAIS
(9), CREOLE (1) ET HINDI (2).
ESP> LOS TITULOS DE LA COLUMNA 2 HAN SIDO
PUBLICADOS EN LAS LENGUAS SIGUIENTES: INGLES (6),
FRANCES (9), CRIOLLA (1) Y HINDI (2).

NIGERIA:
E—> THE TITLES IN COLUMN 2 HAVE BEEN PUBLISHED
IN THE FOLLOWING LANGUAGES: ENGLISH (889) AND
OTHER NATIONAL LANGUAGES (286).
FR—> LES TITRES DE LA COLONNE 2 ONT ETE PUBLIES
DANS LES LANGUES SUIVANTES: ANGLAIS (889) ET
AUTRES LANGUES NATIONALES (286).
ESP> LOS TITULOS DE LA COLUMNA 2 HAN SIDO
PUBLICADOS EN LAS LENGUAS SIGUIENTES: INGLES (889)
Y OTRAS LENGUAS NACIONALES (286).

SENEGAL:
E—> FIRST EDITIONS OF BOOKS AND PAMPHLETS ONLY.
FR—> PREMIERES EDITIONS DE LIVRES ET BROCHURES
SEULEMENT.
ESP> PRIMERAS EDICIONES DE LIBROS Y FOLLETOS
SOLAMENTE.

SEYCHELLES:
E—> FIRST EDITIONS OF BOOKS AND PAMPHLETS ONLY.
FR—> PREMIERES EDITIONS DE LIVRES ET BROCHURES
SEULEMENT.

8.2 Number of titles by language of publication
Nombre de titres classés d'après la langue de publication
Número de obras clasificadas según la lengua en que se publican

JAMAICA:
E--> FIRST EDITIONS OF BOOKS AND PAMPHLETS ONLY.
FR--> PREMIERES EDITIONS DE LIVRES ET BROCHURES SEULEMENT.
ESP> PRIMERAS EDICIONES DE LIBROS Y FOLLETOS SOLAMENTE.

NETHERLANDS ANTILLES:
E--> THE TITLES IN COLUMN 2 HAVE BEEN PUBLISHED IN THE FOLLOWING LANGUAGES: PAPIAMENTU (19), ENGLISH (9) AND DUTCH (21).
FR--> LES TITRES DE LA COLONNE 2 ONT ETE PUBLIES DANS LES LANGUES SUIVANTES: PAPIAMENTU (19), ANGLAIS (9) ET NEERLANDAIS (21).
ESP> LOS TITULOS DE LA COLUMNA 2 HAN SIDO PUBLICADOS EN LAS LENGUAS SIGUIENTES: PAPIAMENTU (19), INGLES (9) Y NEERLANDES (21).

TRINIDAD AND TOBAGO:
E--> UNIVERSITY THESES ONLY.
FR--> THESES UNIVERSITAIRES SEULEMENT.
ESP> TESIS UNIVERSITARIAS SOLAMENTE.

PERU:
E--> THE TITLES IN COLUMN 2 HAVE BEEN PUBLISHED IN THE FOLLOWING LANGUAGES: SPANISH (927) AND QUECHUA (1).
FR--> LES TITRES DE LA COLONNE 2 ONT ETE PUBLIES DANS LES LANGUES SUIVANTES: ESPAGNOL (927) ET QUECHUA (1).
ESP> LOS TITULOS DE LA COLUMNA 2 HAN SIDO PUBLICADOS EN LAS LENGUAS SIGUIENTES: ESPAÑOL (927) Y QUECHUA (1).

BRUNEI:
E--> THE TITLES IN COLUMN 2 HAVE BEEN PUBLISHED IN THE FOLLOWING LANGUAGES: MALAY (28) AND ENGLISH (4).
FR--> LES TITRES DE LA COLONNE 2 ONT ETE PUBLIES DANS LES LANGUES SUIVANTES: MALAIS (28) ET ANGLAIS (4).
ESP> LOS TITULOS DE LA COLUMNA 2 HAN SIDO PUBLICADOS EN LAS LENGUAS SIGUIENTES: MALAYO (28) Y INGLES (4).

CYPRUS:
E--> THE TITLES IN COLUMN 2 HAVE BEEN PUBLISHED IN THE FOLLOWING LANGUAGES: GREEK (356) AND TURKISH (17).
FR--> LES TITRES DE LA COLONNE 2 ONT ETE PUBLIES DANS LES LANGUES SUIVANTES: GREC (356) ET TURC (17).
ESP> LOS TITULOS DE LA COLUMNA 2 HAN SIDO PUBLICADOS EN LAS LENGUAS SIGUIENTES: GRIEGO (356) Y TURCO (17).

HONG KONG:
E--> THE TITLES IN COLUMN 2 HAVE BEEN PUBLISHED IN THE FOLLOWING LANGUAGES: ENGLISH (617) AND CHINESE (1,024).
FR--> LES TITRES DE LA COLONNE 2 ONT ETE PUBLIES DANS LES LANGUES SUIVANTES: ANGLAIS (617) ET

SEYCHELLES (CONT.)
ESP> PRIMERAS EDICIONES DE LIBROS Y FOLLETOS SOLAMENTE.

SIERRA LEONE:
E--> FIRST EDITIONS OF BOOKS AND PAMPHLETS ONLY.
FR--> PREMIERES EDITIONS DE LIVRES ET BROCHURES SEULEMENT.
ESP> PRIMERAS EDICIONES DE LIBROS Y FOLLETOS SOLAMENTE.

SUDAN:
E--> FIRST EDITIONS OF BOOKS ONLY. THE TITLES IN COLUMN 2 HAVE BEEN PUBLISHED IN THE FOLLOWING LANGUAGES: ARABIC (94), ENGLISH (55), ARABIC AND ENGLISH (2).
FR--> PREMIERES EDITIONS DE LIVRES SEULEMENT. LES TITRES DE LA COLONNE 2 ONT ETE PUBLIES DANS LES LANGUES SUIVANTES: ARABE (94), ANGLAIS (55), ARABE ET ANGLAIS (2).
ESP> PRIMERAS EDICIONES DE LIBROS SOLAMENTE. LOS TITULOS DE LA COLUMNA 2 HAN SIDO PUBLICADOS EN LAS LENGUAS SIGUIENTES: ARABE (94), INGLES (55), ARABE Y INGLES (2).

UNITED REPUBLIC OF CAMEROON:
E--> THE TITLES IN COLUMN 2 HAVE BEEN PUBLISHED IN THE FOLLOWING LANGUAGES: FRENCH (40) AND ENGLISH (14).
FR--> LES TITRES DE LA COLONNE 2 ONT ETE PUBLIES DANS LES LANGUES SUIVANTES: FRANCAIS (40) ET ANGLAIS (14).
ESP> LOS TITULOS DE LA COLUMNA 2 HAN SIDO PUBLICADOS EN LAS LENGUAS SIGUIENTES: FRANCES (40) Y INGLES (14).

CANADA:
E--> NOT INCLUDING GOVERNMENT PUBLICATIONS. THE TITLES IN COLUMN 2 HAVE BEEN PUBLISHED IN THE FOLLOWING LANGUAGES: ENGLISH (4,825), FRENCH (2,651), ENGLISH AND FRENCH (304).
FR--> NON COMPRIS LES PUBLICATIONS OFFICIELLES. LES TITRES DE LA COLONNE 2 ONT ETE PUBLIES DANS LES LANGUES SUIVANTES: ANGLAIS (4 825), FRANCAIS (2 651) ANGLAIS ET FRANCAIS (304).
ESP> EXCLUIDAS LAS PUBLICACIONES OFICIALES. LOS TITULOS DE LA COLUMNA 2 HAN SIDO PUBLICADOS EN LAS LENGUAS SIGUIENTES: INGLES (4 825), FRANCES (2 651), INGLES Y FRANCES (304).

COSTA RICA:
E--> BOOKS ONLY.
FR--> LIVRES SEULEMENT.
ESP> LIBROS SOLAMENTE.

DOMINICAN REPUBLIC:
E--> FIRST EDITIONS OF BOOKS AND PAMPHLETS ONLY.
FR--> PREMIERES EDITIONS DE LIVRES ET BROCHURES SEULEMENT.
ESP> PRIMERAS EDICIONES DE LIBROS Y FOLLETOS SOLAMENTE.

Number of titles by language of publication 8.2
Nombre de titres classés d'après la langue de publication
Número de obras clasificadas según la lengua en que se publican

HONG KONG (CONT.)
CHINOIS (1 024).
ESP> LOS TITULOS DE LA COLUMNA 2 HAN SIDO
PUBLICADOS EN LAS LENGUAS SIGUIENTES: INGLES (617)
Y CHINO (1 024).

INDIA:
E—> THE TITLES IN COLUMN 2 HAVE BEEN PUBLISHED
IN THE FOLLOWING LANGUAGES: ENGLISH (4,393) AND
HINDI (2,179).
FR—> LES TITRES DE LA COLONNE 2 ONT ETE PUBLIES
DANS LES LANGUES SUIVANTES: ANGLAIS (4 393) ET
HINDI (2 179).
ESP> LOS TITULOS DE LA COLUMNA 2 HAN SIDO
PUBLICADOS EN LAS LENGUAS SIGUIENTES: INGLES
(4 393) Y HINDI (2 179).

IRAQ:
E—> THE TITLES IN COLUMN 2 HAVE BEEN PUBLISHED
IN THE FOLLOWING LANGUAGES: ARABIC (1,442), KUR-
DISH (70) AND TURKOMAN (9).
FR—> LES TITRES DE LA COLONNE 2 ONT ETE PUBLIES
DANS LES LANGUES SUIVANTES: ARABE (1 442), KURDE
(70) ET TURKMENE (9).
ESP> LOS TITULOS DE LA COLUMNA 2 HAN SIDO
PUBLICADOS EN LAS LENGUAS SIGUIENTES: ARABE
(1 442), KURDO (70) Y TURCOMANO (9).

ISRAEL:
E—> NOT INCLUDING UNIVERSITY THESES.
FR—> NON COMPRIS LES THESES UNIVERSITAIRES.
ESP> EXCLUIDAS LAS TESIS UNIVERSITARIAS.

JORDAN:
E—> FIRST EDITIONS OF BOOKS AND PAMPHLETS ONLY.
DATA REFER TO THE EAST BANK ONLY.
FR—> PREMIERES EDITIONS DE LIVRES ET BROCHURES
SEULEMENT. LES DONNEES SE REFERENT A LA RIVE
ORIENTALE SEULEMENT.
ESP> PRIMERAS EDICIONES DE LIBROS Y FOLLETOS
SOLAMENTE. LOS DATOS SE REFIEREN A LA ORILLA
ORIENTAL SOLAMENTE.

PAKISTAN:
E—> THE TITLES IN COLUMN 2 HAVE BEEN PUBLISHED
IN THE FOLLOWING LANGUAGES: ENGLISH (308) AND
URDU (843).
FR—> LES TITRES DE LA COLONNE 2 ONT ETE PUBLIES
DANS LES LANGUES SUIVANTES: ANGLAIS (308) ET
OURDOU (843).
ESP> LOS TITULOS DE LA COLUMNA 2 HAN SIDO
PUBLICADOS EN LAS LENGUAS SIGUIENTES: INGLES (308)
Y URDU (843).

SINGAPORE:
E—> NOT INCLUDING GOVERNMENT PUBLICATIONS.
THE TITLES IN COLUMN 2 HAVE BEEN PUBLISHED IN THE
FOLLOWING LANGUAGES: ENGLISH (645), CHINESE (510),
MALAY (89) AND TAMIL (10).
FR—> NON COMPRIS LES PUBLICATIONS OFFICIELLES.
LES TITRES DE LA COLONNE 2 ONT ETE PUBLIES DANS
LES LANGUES SUIVANTES: ANGLAIS (645), CHINOIS
(510), MALAIS (89) ET TAMOUL (10).

SINGAPORE (CONT.)
ESP> EXCLUIDAS LAS PUBLICACIONES OFICIALES.
LOS TITULOS DE LA COLUMNA 2 HAN SIDO PUBLICADOS
EN LAS LENGUAS SIGUIENTES: INGLES (645), CHINO
(510), MALAYO (89) Y TAMUL (10).

SRI LANKA:
E—> BOOKS ONLY. THE TITLES IN COLUMN 2 HAVE
BEEN PUBLISHED IN THE FOLLOWING LANGUAGES:
SINHALA (784) AND TAMIL (231).
FR—> LIVRES SEULEMENT. LES TITRES DE LA COLONNE
2 ONT ETE PUBLIES DANS LES LANGUES SUIVANTES:
SINHALA (784) ET TAMOUL (231).
ESP> LIBROS SOLAMENTE. LOS TITULOS DE LA COLUM-
NA 2 HAN SIDO PUBLICADOS EN LAS LENGUAS SIGUIEN-
TES: SINHALA (784) Y TAMUL (231).

UNITED ARAB EMIRATES:
E—> FIRST EDITIONS OF BOOKS AND PAMPHLETS ONLY.
FR—> PREMIERES EDITIONS DE LIVRES ET BROCHURES
SEULEMENT.
ESP> PRIMERAS EDICIONES DE LIBROS Y FOLLETOS
SOLAMENTE.

BELGIUM:
E—> DATA REFER ONLY TO TITLES INDEXED IN THE
"BIBLIOGRAPHIE DE BELGIQUE". THE TITLES IN COLUMN
2 HAVE BEEN PUBLISHED IN THE FOLLOWING LANGUAGES:
DUTCH (5,009), FRENCH (3,383) AND GERMAN (58).
FR—> LES DONNEES SE RAPPORTENT SEULEMENT AUX
TITRES REPERTORIES DANS LA BIBLIOGRAPHIE DE
BELGIQUE. LES TITRES DE LA COLONNE 2 ONT ETE
PUBLIES DANS LES LANGUES SUIVANTES: NEERLANDAIS
(5 009), FRANCAIS (3 383) ET ALLEMAND (58).
ESP> LOS DATOS SOLO SE REFIEREN A LOS LIBROS
INSCRITOS EN EL REPERTORIO DE LA "BIBLIOGRAPHIE
DE BELGIQUE". LOS TITULOS DE LA COLUMNA 2 HAN
SIDO PUBLICADOS EN LAS LENGUAS SIGUENTES:
NEERLANDES (5 009), FRANCES (3 383) Y ALEMAN
(58).

CZECHOSLOVAKIA:
E—> THE TITLES IN COLUMN 2 HAVE BEEN PUBLISHED
IN THE FOLLOWING LANGUAGES: CZECH (6.042), SLOVAK
(2,739), CZECH AND SLOVAK (11).
FR—> LES TITRES DE LA COLONNE 2 ONT ETE PUBLIES
DANS LES LANGUES SUIVANTES: TCHEQUE (6 042),
SLOVAQUE (2 739), TCHEQUE ET SLOVAQUE (11).
ESP> LOS TITULOS DE LA COLUMNA 2 HAN SIDO
PUBLICADOS EN LAS LENGUAS SIGUIENTES: CHECO
(6 042), ESLOVACO (2 739), CHECO Y ESLOVACO (11).

FINLAND:
E—> THE TITLES IN COLUMN 2 HAVE BEEN PUBLISHED
IN THE FOLLOWING LANGUAGES: FINNISH (2,702) AND
SWEDISH (143).
FR—> LES TITRES DE LA COLONNE 2 ONT ETE PUBLIES
DANS LES LANGUES SUIVANTES: FINNOIS (2 702) ET
SUEDOIS (143).
ESP> LOS TITULOS DE LA COLUMNA 2 HAN SIDO
PUBLICADOS EN LAS LENGUAS SIGUIENTES: FINLANDES
(2 702) Y SUECO (143).

8.2 Number of titles by language of publication
Nombre de titres classés d'après la langue de publication
Número de obras clasificadas según la lengua en que se publican

SWITZERLAND:
E—> FIRST EDITIONS OF BOOKS AND PAMPHLETS ONLY. THE TITLES IN COLUMN 2 HAVE BEEN PUBLISHED IN THE FOLLOWING LANGUAGES: GERMAN (5,934), FRENCH (2,336), ITALIAN (182) AND ROMANSH (39). THE DATA IN COLUMN 9 INCLUDE OTHER LANGUAGES.
FR—> PREMIERES EDITIONS DE LIVRES ET BROCHURES SEULEMENT LES TITRES DE LA COLONNE 2 ONT ETE PUBLIES DANS LES LANGUES SUIVANTES: ALLEMAND (5 934), FRANCAIS (2 336), ITALIEN (182) ET ROMANCHE (39). LES DONNEES DE LA COLONNE 9 COMPRENNENT LES AUTRES LANGUES.
ESP> PRIMERAS EDICIONES DE LIBROS Y FOLLETOS SOLAMENTE. LOS TITULOS DE LA COLUMNA 2 HAN SIDO PUBLICADOS EN LAS LENGUAS SIGUIENTES: ALEMAN (5 934), FRANCES (2 336), ITALIANO (182) Y ROMANCHE (39). LOS DATOS DE LA COLUMNA 9 INCLUYEN LAS OTRAS LENGUAS.

YUGOSLAVIA:
E—> THE TITLES IN COLUMN 2 HAVE BEEN PUBLISHED IN THE FOLLOWING LANGUAGES: SERBO-CROAT (7,102), SLOVENIAN (1,838) AND MACEDONIAN (480).
FR—> LES TITRES DE LA COLONNE 2 ONT ETE PUBLIES DANS LES LANGUES SUIVANTES: SERBO-CROATE (7 102), SLOVENE (1 838) ET MACEDONIEN (480).
ESP> LOS TITULOS DE LA COLUMNA 2 HAN SIDO PUBLICADOS EN LAS LENGUAS SIGUIENTES: SERBOCROATA (7 102), ESLOVENO (1 838) Y MACEDONIO (480).

GUAM:
E—> FIRST EDITIONS OF BOOKS AND PAMPHLETS ONLY.
FR—> PREMIERES EDITIONS DE LIVRES ET BROCHURES SEULEMENT.
ESP> PRIMERAS EDICIONES DE LIBROS Y FOLLETOS SOLAMENTE.

FRENCH POLYNESIA:
E—> THE TITLES IN COLUMN 2 HAVE BEEN PUBLISHED IN THE FOLLOWING LANGUAGES: FRENCH (7), FRENCH AND TAHITIAN (4).
FR—> LES TITRES DE LA COLONNE 2 ONT ETE PUBLIES DANS LES LANGUES SUIVANTES: FRANCAIS (7), FRANCAIS ET TAHITIEN (4).
ESP> LOS TITULOS DE LA COLUMNA 2 HAN SIDO PUBLICADOS EN LAS LENGUAS SIGUIENTES: FRANCES (7), FRANCES Y TAHITIANO (4).

NEW ZEALAND:
E—> THE TITLES IN COLUMN 2 HAVE BEEN PUBLISHED IN THE FOLLOWING LANGUAGES: ENGLISH (2,061) AND MAORI (4).
FR—> LES TITRES DE LA COLONNE 2 ONT ETE PUBLIES DANS LES LANGUES SUIVANTES: ANGLAIS (2 061) ET MAORI (4).
ESP> LOS TITULOS DE LA COLUMNA 2 HAN SIDO PUBLICADOS EN LAS LENGUAS SIGUIENTES: INGLES (2 061) Y MAORI (4).

PACIFIC ISLANDS:
E—> THE TITLES IN COLUMN 2 HAVE BEEN PUBLISHED IN THE FOLLOWING LANGUAGES: ENGLISH (27), PALAVAN (7), ENGLISH AND PALAVAN (6).

HOLY SEE:
E—> PARTIAL DATA.
FR—> DONNEES PARTIELLES.
ESP> DATOS PARCIALES.

HUNGARY:
E—> THE TITLES IN COLUMN 7 HAVE BEEN PUBLISHED IN RUSSIAN AND OTHER LANGUAGES OF THE U.S.S.R.
FR—> LES TITRES ET AUTRES LANGUES DE L'U.R.S.S.
ESP> LOS TITULOS DE LA COLUMNA 7 HAN SIDO PUBLICADOS EN RUSO Y EN OTRAS LENGUAS DE LA U.R.S.S.

IRELAND:
E—> FIRST EDITIONS OF BOOKS AND PAMPHLETS ONLY. THE TITLES IN COLUMN 2 HAVE BEEN PUBLISHED IN THE FOLLOWING LANGUAGES: ENGLISH (548) AND IRISH (80).
FR—> PREMIERES EDITIONS DE LIVRES ET BROCHURES SEULEMENT. LES TITRES DE LA COLONNE 2 ONT ETE PUBLIES DANS LES LANGUES SUIVANTES: ANGLAIS (548) ET IRLANDAIS (80).
ESP> PRIMERAS EDICIONES DE LIBROS Y FOLLETOS SOLAMENTE. LOS TITULOS DE LA COLUMNA 2 HAN SIDO PUBLICADOS EN LAS LENGUAS SIGUIENTES: INGLES (548) Y IRLANDES (80).

LUXEMBOURG:
E—> THE TITLES IN COLUMN 2 HAVE BEEN PUBLISHED IN THE FOLLOWING LANGUAGES: FRENCH (131), GERMAN (52) AND LUXEMBURGISH (12).
FR—> LES TITRES DE LA COLONNE 2 ONT ETE PUBLIES DANS LES LANGUES SUIVANTES: FRANCAIS (131), ALLEMAND (52) ET LUXEMBOURGEOIS (12).
ESP> LOS TITULOS DE LA COLUMNA 2 HAN SIDO PUBLICADOS EN LAS LENGUAS SIGUIENTES: FRANCES (131), ALEMAN (52) Y LUXEMBURGUES (12).

MALTA:
E—> THE TITLES IN COLUMN 2 HAVE BEEN PUBLISHED IN THE FOLLOWING LANGUAGES: MALTESE (93) AND ENGLISH (48).
FR—> LES TITRES DE LA COLONNE 2 ONT ETE PUBLIES DANS LES LANGUES SUIVANTES: MALTAIS (93) ET ANGLAIS (48).
ESP> LOS TITULOS DE LA COLUMNA 2 HAN SIDO PUBLICADOS EN LAS LENGUAS SIGUIENTES: MALTES (93) E INGLES (48).

NORWAY:
E—> BOOKS ONLY.
FR—> LIVRES SEULEMENT.
ESP> LIBROS SOLAMENTE.

POLAND:
E—> THE TITLES IN COLUMN 7 HAVE BEEN PUBLISHED IN RUSSIAN AND OTHER LANGUAGES OF THE U.S.S.R.
FR—> LES TITRES ET AUTRES LANGUES DE L'U.R.S.S.
ESP> LOS TITULOS DE LA COLUMNA 7 HAN SIDO PUBLICADOS EN RUSO Y EN OTRAS LENGUAS DE LA U.R.S.S.

Number of titles by language of publication 8.2
Nombre de titres classés d'après la langue de publication
Número de obras clasificadas según la lengua en que se publican

PACIFIC ISLANDS (CONT.)
FR-> LES TITRES DE LA COLONNE 2 ONT ETE PUBLIES
DANS LES LANGUES SUIVANTES: ANGLAIS (27), PALAVAN
(7), ANGLAIS ET PALAVAN (6).
ESP> LOS TITULOS DE LA COLUMNA 2 HAN SIDO
PUBLICADOS EN LAS LENGUAS SIGUIENTES: INGLES (27),
PALAVAN (7), INGLES Y PALAVAN (6).

SAMOA:
E-> THE TITLES IN COLUMN 2 HAVE BEEN PUBLISHED
IN THE FOLLOWING LANGUAGES: ENGLISH (91), SAMOAN
(62), ENGLISH AND SAMOAN (68).
FR-> LES TITRES DE LA COLONNE 2 ONT ETE PUBLIES
DANS LES LANGUES SUIVANTES: ANGLAIS (91), SAMOA
(62), ANGLAIS ET SAMOA (68).
ESP> LOS TITULOS DE LA COLUMNA 2 HAN SIDO
PUBLICADOS EN LAS LENGUAS SIGUIENTES: INGLES (91),
SAMOANO (62), INGLES Y SAMOANO (68).

TONGA:
E-> THE TITLES IN COLUMN 2 HAVE BEEN PUBLISHED
IN THE FOLLOWING LANGUAGES: TONGAN (68), TONGAN
AND ENGLISH (478).
FR-> LES TITRES DE LA COLONNE 2 ONT ETE PUBLIES
DANS LES LANGUES SUIVANTES: TONGAN (68), TONGAN
ET ANGLAIS (478).
ESP> LOS TITULOS DE LA COLUMNA 2 HAN SIDO
PUBLICADOS EN LAS LENGUAS SIGUIENTES: TONGAN (68),
TONGAN Y INGLES (478).

U.S.S.R.:
E-> THE TITLES IN COLUMN 2 HAVE BEEN PUBLISHED
IN THE FOLLOWING LANGUAGES: RUSSIAN (66,180),
UKRAINIAN (2,370), GEORGIAN (1,183), ESTONIAN
(1,462), LITHUANIAN (1,175), LATVIAN (1,175),
UZBEK (959), AZERBAIJAN (826), KAZAKH (767),
ARMENIAN (765), MOLDAVIAN (563), KIRGHIZ (467),
BIELORUSSIAN (395), TADZHIK (346), TURKMEN (248)
AND OTHER LANGUAGES OF THE U.S.S.R. (1,578).

U.S.S.R. (CONT.)
FR-> LES TITRES DE LA COLONNE 2 ONT ETE PUBLIES
DANS LES LANGUES SUIVANTES: RUSSE (66,180),
UKRAINIEN (2,370), GEORGIEN (1,578), ESTONIEN
(1,462), LITUANIEN (1,183), LETTON (1,175),
OUZBEK (959), AZERBAIDJANAIS (826), KAZAKH (767),
ARMENIEN (765), MOLDAVE (563), KIRGHIZ (467),
BIELORUSSIEN (395), TADJIK (346), TURKMENE (248)
ET AUTRES LANGUES DE L'U.R.S.S. (1 578).
ESP> LOS TITULOS DE LA COLUMNA 2 HAN SIDO
PUBLICADOS EN LAS LENGUAS SIGUIENTES: RUSO
(66 180), UCRANIO (2 370), GEORGIANO (1 578), ES-
TONIO (1 462), LITUANO (1 183), LETON (1 175), UZ-
BEK (959), AZERBAIJANES (826), KAZAK (767), ARMEN-
IO (765), MOLDAVO (563), KIRIGUIZ (467), BIELO-
RRUSO (395), TAKJIK (346), TURCOMANO (248), Y
OTRAS LENGUAS DE LA U.R.S.S. (1 578).

BYELORUSSIAN S.S.R.:
E-> THE TITLES IN COLUMN 2 HAVE BEEN PUBLISHED
IN THE FOLLOWING LANGUAGES: RUSSIAN (2,156) AND
BYELORUSSIAN (397).
FR-> LES TITRES DE LA COLONNE 2 ONT ETE PUBLIES
DANS LES LANGUES SUIVANTES: RUSSE (2 156) ET
BIELORUSSIEN (393).
ESP> LOS TITULOS DE LA COLUMNA 2 HAN SIDO
PUBLICADOS EN LAS LENGUAS SIGUIENTES: RUSO (2 156)
Y BIELORRUSO (397).

UKRAINIAN S.S.R.:
E-> THE TITLES IN COLUMN 2 HAVE BEEN PUBLISHED
IN THE FOLLOWING LANGUAGES: RUSSIAN (5,726) AND
UKRAINIAN (2,367).
FR-> LES TITRES DE LA COLONNE 2 ONT ETE PUBLIES
DANS LES LANGUES SUIVANTES: RUSSE (5 726) ET
UKRAINIEN (2 367).
ESP> LOS TITULOS DE LA COLUMNA 2 HAN SIDO
PUBLICADOS EN LAS LENGUAS SIGUIENTES: RUSO
(5 726) Y UCRANIO (2 367).

8.3 Number of titles by subject group
Nombre de titres par groupes de sujets
Número de obras por categorías de temas

8.3 Book production: number of titles by subject group

Edition de livres: nombre de titres par groupes de sujets

Edición de libros: número de obras por categorías de temas

A = BOOKS

B = PAMPHLETS

A = LIVRES

B = BROCHURES

A = LIBROS

B = FOLLETOS

NUMBER OF COUNTRIES AND
TERRITORIES PRESENTED IN
THIS TABLE: 112

NOMBRE DE PAYS ET DE
TERRITOIRES PRESENTES DANS
CE TABLEAU: 112

NUMERO DE PAISES Y DE
TERRITORIOS PRESENTADOS
EN ESTE CUADRO: 112

SUBJECT GROUP / GROUPE DE SUJETS / GRUPO TEMATICO AFRICA	BENIN (1978)			BOTSWANA (1978)		
	A	B	A+B	A	B	A+B
TOTAL	13	–	13	39	64	103
1. GENERALITIES	–	–	–	3	2	5
2. PHILOSOPHY, PSYCHOLOGY	–	–	–	–	–	–
3. RELIGION, THEOLOGY	1	–	1	–	1	1
4. SOCIOLOGY, STATISTICS	–	–	–	4	8	12
5. POLITICAL SCIENCE	–	–	–	18	14	32
6. LAW, PUBLIC ADMIN.	–	–	–	8	16	24
7. MILITARY ART	–	–	–	–	–	–
8. EDUCATION, LEISURE	–	–	–	1	12	13
9. TRADE, TRANSPORT	–	–	–	–	–	–
10. ETHNOGRAPHY, FOLKLORE	–	–	–	–	1	1
11. MATHEMATICS	1	–	1	–	–	–
12. NATURAL SCIENCES	4	–	4	2	–	2
13. MEDICAL SCIENCES	–	–	–	–	3	3
14. ENGINEERING, CRAFTS	–	–	–	–	–	–
15. AGRICULTURE	–	–	–	3	2	5
16. DOMESTIC SCIENCE	–	–	–	–	–	–
17. MANAGEMENT, ADMIN.	–	–	–	–	–	–
18. PLANNING, ARCHITECTURE	–	–	–	–	1	1
19. PLASTIC ARTS	–	–	–	–	–	–
20. PERFORMING ARTS	–	–	–	–	–	–
21. GAMES, SPORTS	–	–	–	–	3	3
22. LINGUISTICS, PHILOLOGY	4	–	4	–	–	–
23. LITERATURE						
(A) HISTORY AND CRITICISM	–	–	–	–	–	–
(B) LITERARY TEXTS	2	–	2	–	–	–
24. GEOGRAPHY, TRAVEL	1	–	1	–	–	–
25. HISTORY, BIOGRAPHY	–	–	–	–	1	1

Number of titles by subject group 8.3
Nombre de titres par groupes de sujets
Número de obras por categorías de temas

SUBJECT GROUP / GROUPE DE SUJETS / GRUPO TEMATICO	CONGO ‡ (1977)			EGYPT ‡ (1977)			ETHIOPIA ‡ (1978)		
	A	B	A+B	A	B	A+B	A	B	A+B
TOTAL	9	118	127	1 360	112	1 472	331	22	353
1. GENERALITIES	–	–	–	55	3	58	1	1	2
2. PHILOSOPHY, PSYCHOLOGY	–	–	–	40	–	40	1	–	1
3. RELIGION, THEOLOGY	–	–	–	228	35	263	48	1	49
4. SOCIOLOGY, STATISTICS	–	–	–	260	14	274	73	1	74
5. POLITICAL SCIENCE	2	14	16	./.	./.	./.	./.	./.	./.
6. LAW, PUBLIC ADMIN.	–	–	–	./.	./.	./.	./.	./.	./.
7. MILITARY ART	–	–	–	./.	./.	./.	./.	./.	./.
8. EDUCATION, LEISURE	–	8	8	./.	./.	./.	./.	./.	./.
9. TRADE, TRANSPORT	–	–	–	./.	./.	./.	./.	./.	./.
10. ETHNOGRAPHY, FOLKLORE	–	–	–	./.	./.	./.	./.	./.	./.
11. MATHEMATICS	–	6	6	65	3	68	9	–	9
12. NATURAL SCIENCES	–	27	27	./.	./.	./.	./.	./.	./.
13. MEDICAL SCIENCES	–	1	1	261	15	276	28	–	28
14. ENGINEERING, CRAFTS	–	–	–	./.	./.	./.	./.	./.	./.
15. AGRICULTURE	–	–	–	./.	./.	./.	./.	./.	./.
16. DOMESTIC SCIENCE	–	2	2	./.	./.	./.	./.	./.	./.
17. MANAGEMENT, ADMIN.	–	–	–	./.	./.	./.	./.	./.	./.
18. PLANNING, ARCHITECTURE	–	–	–	43	1	44	2	–	2
19. PLASTIC ARTS	–	–	–	./.	./.	./.	./.	./.	./.
20. PERFORMING ARTS	–	7	7	./.	./.	./.	./.	./.	./.
21. GAMES, SPORTS	–	–	–	./.	./.	./.	./.	./.	./.
22. LINGUISTICS, PHILOLOGY	–	20	20	158	14	172	13	–	13
23. LITERATURE									
(A) HISTORY AND CRITICISM	6	10	16	170	23	193	10	–	10
(B) LITERARY TEXTS	./.	./.	./.	./.	./.	./.	./.	–	./.
24. GEOGRAPHY, TRAVEL	1	17	18	80	4	84	27	17	44
25. HISTORY, BIOGRAPHY	–	6	6	./.	./.	./.	./.	./.	./.

SUBJECT GROUP / GROUPE DE SUJETS / GRUPO TEMATICO	GAMBIA ‡ (1978)			GHANA ‡ (1978)			IVORY COAST ‡ (1977)		
	A	B	A+B	A	B	A+B	A	B	A+B
TOTAL	21	60	81	158	93	251	62	63	125
1. GENERALITIES	1	7	8	3	3	6	–	10	10
2. PHILOSOPHY, PSYCHOLOGY	–	–	–	5	2	7	–	–	–
3. RELIGION, THEOLOGY	–	–	–	33	21	54	9	14	23
4. SOCIOLOGY, STATISTICS	1	4	5	3	3	6	7	2	9
5. POLITICAL SCIENCE	1	7	8	15	18	33	–	2	2
6. LAW, PUBLIC ADMIN.	–	7	7	10	3	13	4	–	4
7. MILITARY ART	–	–	–	–	1	1	–	–	–
8. EDUCATION, LEISURE	–	8	8	14	8	22	8	13	21
9. TRADE, TRANSPORT	–	1	1	4	1	5	1	–	1
10. ETHNOGRAPHY, FOLKLORE	–	–	–	–	1	1	1	–	1
11. MATHEMATICS	1	–	1	3	1	4	5	–	5
12. NATURAL SCIENCES	2	6	8	5	1	6	3	5	8
13. MEDICAL SCIENCES	4	2	6	5	1	6	2	3	5
14. ENGINEERING, CRAFTS	1	1	2	8	5	13	8	10	18
15. AGRICULTURE	2	1	3	1	1	2	–	–	–
16. DOMESTIC SCIENCE	–	1	1	1	–	1	–	–	–
17. MANAGEMENT, ADMIN.	–	–	–	2	–	2	2	–	2
18. PLANNING, ARCHITECTURE	3	7	10	–	1	1	6	–	6
19. PLASTIC ARTS	–	–	–	–	–	–	–	–	–
20. PERFORMING ARTS	–	–	–	2	–	2	1	2	3
21. GAMES, SPORTS	–	–	–	1	3	4	–	–	–
22. LINGUISTICS, PHILOLOGY	–	1	1	7	4	11	4	–	4
23. LITERATURE									
(A) HISTORY AND CRITICISM	–	–	–	1	–	1	–	–	–
(B) LITERARY TEXTS	–	1	1	31	10	41	2	–	2
24. GEOGRAPHY, TRAVEL	2	5	7	3	1	4	–	–	–
25. HISTORY, BIOGRAPHY	3	1	4	1	4	5	–	–	–

8.3 Number of titles by subject group
Nombre de titres par groupes de sujets
Número de obras por categorías de temas

SUBJECT GROUP / GROUPE DE SUJETS / GRUPO TEMATICO	KENYA (1976) A	B	A+B	MADAGASCAR ‡ (1978) A	B	A+B	MALAWI (1977) A	B	A+B
TOTAL	114	69	183	118	101	219	45	88	133
1. GENERALITIES	2	2	4	2	3	5	–	4	4
2. PHILOSOPHY, PSYCHOLOGY	–	–	–	2	4	6	–	–	–
3. RELIGION, THEOLOGY	34	25	59	40	15	55	15	9	24
4. SOCIOLOGY, STATISTICS	3	–	3	1	2	3	1	–	1
5. POLITICAL SCIENCE	4	1	5	7	5	12	8	13	21
6. LAW, PUBLIC ADMIN.	1	–	1	4	5	9	3	1	4
7. MILITARY ART	–	–	–	–	1	1	–	2	2
8. EDUCATION, LEISURE	29	23	52	18	5	23	3	–	3
9. TRADE, TRANSPORT	–	–	–	2	1	3	–	4	4
10. ETHNOGRAPHY, FOLKLORE	3	1	4	3	6	9	1	–	1
11. MATHEMATICS	3	–	3	–	4	4	1	–	1
12. NATURAL SCIENCES	7	3	10	4	2	6	1	3	4
13. MEDICAL SCIENCES	–	2	2	–	–	–	–	–	–
14. ENGINEERING, CRAFTS	2	1	3	–	3	3	–	4	4
15. AGRICULTURE	2	–	2	4	3	7	4	16	20
16. DOMESTIC SCIENCE	–	–	–	4	1	5	1	–	1
17. MANAGEMENT, ADMIN.	–	–	–	–	2	2	–	3	3
18. PLANNING, ARCHITECTURE	–	–	–	1	–	1	–	1	1
19. PLASTIC ARTS	–	–	–	–	–	–	–	–	–
20. PERFORMING ARTS	1	2	3	1	3	4	–	–	–
21. GAMES, SPORTS	–	–	–	1	4	5	–	–	–
22. LINGUISTICS, PHILOLOGY	2	3	5	4	–	4	1	1	2
23. LITERATURE									
(A) HISTORY AND CRITICISM	10	4	14	14	26	40	1	13	14
(B) LITERARY TEXTS	–	–	–	./.	./.	./.	1	13	14
24. GEOGRAPHY, TRAVEL	3	1	4	4	–	4	1	1	2
25. HISTORY, BIOGRAPHY	8	1	9	2	6	8	3	–	3

SUBJECT GROUP / GROUPE DE SUJETS / GRUPO TEMATICO	MAURITANIA (1977) A	B	A+B	MAURITIUS ‡ (1978) A	B	A+B	NIGER ‡ (1976) A+B
TOTAL	20	20	40	10	10	20	78
1. GENERALITIES	–	–	–	–	–	–	11
2. PHILOSOPHY, PSYCHOLOGY	–	–	–	1	–	1	–
3. RELIGION, THEOLOGY	–	–	–	2	2	4	–
4. SOCIOLOGY, STATISTICS	–	2	2	–	–	–	9
5. POLITICAL SCIENCE	–	–	–	2	2	4	6
6. LAW, PUBLIC ADMIN.	–	–	–	–	–	–	3
7. MILITARY ART	–	–	–	–	–	–	–
8. EDUCATION, LEISURE	–	–	–	–	–	–	11
9. TRADE, TRANSPORT	–	–	–	1	–	1	1
10. ETHNOGRAPHY, FOLKLORE	–	–	–	–	–	–	2
11. MATHEMATICS	1	4	5	–	–	–	–
12. NATURAL SCIENCES	5	2	7	–	–	–	–
13. MEDICAL SCIENCES	–	–	–	2	–	2	2
14. ENGINEERING, CRAFTS	–	–	–	–	–	–	–
15. AGRICULTURE	–	–	–	–	–	–	5
16. DOMESTIC SCIENCE	–	–	–	–	–	–	–
17. MANAGEMENT, ADMIN.	–	–	–	–	–	–	–
18. PLANNING, ARCHITECTURE	–	–	–	–	–	–	–
19. PLASTIC ARTS	–	–	–	–	–	–	1
20. PERFORMING ARTS	–	–	–	–	1	1	–
21. GAMES, SPORTS	–	–	–	–	–	–	–
22. LINGUISTICS, PHILOLOGY	10	10	20	–	–	–	5
23. LITERATURE							
(A) HISTORY AND CRITICISM	–	–	–	–	–	–	4
(B) LITERARY TEXTS	–	–	–	–	3	3	./.
24. GEOGRAPHY, TRAVEL	3	–	3	–	–	–	4
25. HISTORY, BIOGRAPHY	1	2	3	2	2	4	14

Number of titles by subject group 8.3
Nombre de titres par groupes de sujets
Número de obras por categorías de temas

SUBJECT GROUP / GROUPE DE SUJETS / GRUPO TEMATICO	NIGERIA (1978)			SENEGAL ‡ (1977)			SEYCHELLES ‡ (1977)		
	A	B	A+B	A	B	A+B	A	B	A+B
TOTAL	738	437	1 175	48	–	48	10	1	11
1. GENERALITIES	15	31	46	13	–	13	–	–	–
2. PHILOSOPHY, PSYCHOLOGY	8	5	13	–	–	–	1	–	1
3. RELIGION, THEOLOGY	72	43	115	2	–	2	–	1	1
4. SOCIOLOGY, STATISTICS	15	20	35	1	–	1	–	–	–
5. POLITICAL SCIENCE	51	82	133	1	–	1	4	–	4
6. LAW, PUBLIC ADMIN.	52	61	113	3	–	3	3	–	3
7. MILITARY ART	–	–	–	–	–	–	–	–	–
8. EDUCATION, LEISURE	99	30	129	17	–	17	–	–	–
9. TRADE, TRANSPORT	5	12	17	–	–	–	–	–	–
10. ETHNOGRAPHY, FOLKLORE	18	17	35	–	–	–	–	–	–
11. MATHEMATICS	130	–	130	–	–	–	–	–	–
12. NATURAL SCIENCES	3	–	3	–	–	–	–	–	–
13. MEDICAL SCIENCES	10	12	22	–	–	–	–	–	–
14. ENGINEERING, CRAFTS	9	7	16	–	–	–	–	–	–
15. AGRICULTURE	21	21	42	1	–	1	–	–	–
16. DOMESTIC SCIENCE	–	–	–	–	–	–	–	–	–
17. MANAGEMENT, ADMIN.	14	12	26	–	–	–	–	–	–
18. PLANNING, ARCHITECTURE	–	–	–	–	–	–	–	–	–
19. PLASTIC ARTS	–	3	3	–	–	–	–	–	–
20. PERFORMING ARTS	15	7	22	1	–	1	–	–	–
21. GAMES, SPORTS	–	–	–	–	–	–	–	–	–
22. LINGUISTICS, PHILOLOGY	62	8	70	1	–	1	–	–	–
23. LITERATURE									
(A) HISTORY AND CRITICISM	7	3	10	1	–	1	–	–	–
(B) LITERARY TEXTS	52	7	59	4	–	4	–	–	–
24. GEOGRAPHY, TRAVEL	7	13	20	1	–	1	2	–	2
25. HISTORY, BIOGRAPHY	73	43	116	2	–	2	–	–	–

SUBJECT GROUP / GROUPE DE SUJETS / GRUPO TEMATICO	SIERRA LEONE ‡ (1977)			SUDAN ‡ (1977)			TUNISIA (1978)		
	A	B	A+B	A	B	A+B	A	B	A+B
TOTAL	17	44	61	104	–	104	85	–	85
1. GENERALITIES	–	3	3	–	–	–	–	–	–
2. PHILOSOPHY, PSYCHOLOGY	–	–	–	–	–	–	2	–	2
3. RELIGION, THEOLOGY	–	–	–	8	–	8	4	–	4
4. SOCIOLOGY, STATISTICS	1	3	4	–	–	–	–	–	–
5. POLITICAL SCIENCE	5	19	24	–	–	–	1	–	1
6. LAW, PUBLIC ADMIN.	3	2	5	–	–	–	1	–	1
7. MILITARY ART	–	–	–	–	–	–	–	–	–
8. EDUCATION, LEISURE	3	12	15	–	–	–	3	–	3
9. TRADE, TRANSPORT	–	1	1	–	–	–	–	–	–
10. ETHNOGRAPHY, FOLKLORE	–	–	–	–	–	–	–	–	–
11. MATHEMATICS	–	–	–	13	–	13	23	–	23
12. NATURAL SCIENCES	–	–	–	12	–	12	3	–	3
13. MEDICAL SCIENCES	1	1	2	–	–	–	–	–	–
14. ENGINEERING, CRAFTS	–	–	–	13	–	13	3	–	3
15. AGRICULTURE	–	1	1	5	–	5	–	–	–
16. DOMESTIC SCIENCE	–	–	–	–	–	–	–	–	–
17. MANAGEMENT, ADMIN.	1	–	1	–	–	–	3	–	3
18. PLANNING, ARCHITECTURE	–	–	–	–	–	–	1	–	1
19. PLASTIC ARTS	–	–	–	–	–	–	–	–	–
20. PERFORMING ARTS	–	–	–	–	–	–	1	–	1
21. GAMES, SPORTS	–	–	–	–	–	–	–	–	–
22. LINGUISTICS, PHILOLOGY	–	–	–	24	–	24	17	–	17
23. LITERATURE									
(A) HISTORY AND CRITICISM	–	–	–	9	–	9	–	–	–
(B) LITERARY TEXTS	–	–	–	–	–	–	9	–	9
24. GEOGRAPHY, TRAVEL	3	–	3	12	–	12	5	–	5
25. HISTORY, BIOGRAPHY	–	2	2	8	–	8	9	–	9

8.3 Number of titles by subject group
Nombre de titres par groupes de sujets
Número de obras por categorías de temas

SUBJECT GROUP GROUPE DE SUJETS GRUPO TEMATICO	UNITED REP. OF CAMEROON ‡ (1978) A+B	UNITED REP. OF TANZANIA ‡ (1976) A	B	A+B	ZAIRE ‡ (1978) A	B	A+B
TOTAL	54	204	195	399	109	–	109
1. GENERALITIES	–	17	37	54	4	–	4
2. PHILOSOPHY, PSYCHOLOGY	–	–	–	–	5	–	5
3. RELIGION, THEOLOGY	–	41	25	66	43	–	43
4. SOCIOLOGY, STATISTICS	–	6	9	15	38	–	38
5. POLITICAL SCIENCE	5	36	27	63	./.	–	./.
6. LAW, PUBLIC ADMIN.	3	24	14	38	./.	–	./.
7. MILITARY ART	–	–	1	1	./.	–	./.
8. EDUCATION, LEISURE	5	15	15	30	./.	–	./.
9. TRADE, TRANSPORT	–	1	8	9	./.	–	./.
10. ETHNOGRAPHY, FOLKLORE	–	–	2	2	./.	–	./.
11. MATHEMATICS	4	15	–	15	1	–	1
12. NATURAL SCIENCES	2	–	–	–	./.	–	./.
13. MEDICAL SCIENCES	–	5	5	10	7	–	7
14. ENGINEERING, CRAFTS	–	1	1	2	./.	–	./.
15. AGRICULTURE	–	2	14	16	./.	–	./.
16. DOMESTIC SCIENCE	–	1	1	2	./.	–	./.
17. MANAGEMENT, ADMIN.	–	1	5	6	./.	–	./.
18. PLANNING, ARCHITECTURE	–	1	5	6	4	–	4
19. PLASTIC ARTS	–	–	–	–	./.	–	./.
20. PERFORMING ARTS	1	3	–	3	./.	–	./.
21. GAMES, SPORTS	–	3	1	4	./.	–	./.
22. LINGUISTICS, PHILOLOGY	17	14	13	27	./.	–	./.
23. LITERATURE							
(A) HISTORY AND CRITICISM	–	13	3	16	6	–	6
(B) LITERARY TEXTS	14	./.	./.	./.	./.	–	./.
24. GEOGRAPHY, TRAVEL	1	–	4	4	1	–	1
25. HISTORY, BIOGRAPHY	2	5	5	10	./.	–	./.

SUBJECT GROUP GROUPE DE SUJETS GRUPO TEMATICO	ZAMBIA ‡ (1978) A	B	A+B	AMERICA, NORTH	BARBADOS ‡ A	B	A+B
TOTAL	123	–	123		38	178	216
1. GENERALITIES	–	–	–		3	10	13
2. PHILOSOPHY, PSYCHOLOGY	–	–	–		–	–	–
3. RELIGION, THEOLOGY	–	–	–		2	5	7
4. SOCIOLOGY, STATISTICS	2	–	2		–	1	1
5. POLITICAL SCIENCE	1	–	1		5	28	33
6. LAW, PUBLIC ADMIN.	–	–	–		5	27	32
7. MILITARY ART	–	–	–		–	–	–
8. EDUCATION, LEISURE	–	–	–		2	23	25
9. TRADE, TRANSPORT	–	–	–		6	9	15
10. ETHNOGRAPHY, FOLKLORE	32	–	32		–	1	1
11. MATHEMATICS	8	–	8		–	–	–
12. NATURAL SCIENCES	–	–	–		1	2	3
13. MEDICAL SCIENCES	–	–	–		–	16	16
14. ENGINEERING, CRAFTS	–	–	–		–	18	18
15. AGRICULTURE	3	–	3		2	25	27
16. DOMESTIC SCIENCE	3	–	3		1	1	2
17. MANAGEMENT, ADMIN.	–	–	–		4	2	6
18. PLANNING, ARCHITECTURE	–	–	–		–	3	3
19. PLASTIC ARTS	–	–	–		–	1	1
20. PERFORMING ARTS	–	–	–		–	2	2
21. GAMES, SPORTS	–	–	–		3	–	3
22. LINGUISTICS, PHILOLOGY	6	–	6		1	–	1
23. LITERATURE							
(A) HISTORY AND CRITICISM	1	–	1		–	1	1
(B) LITERARY TEXTS	30	–	30		–	./.	./.
24. GEOGRAPHY, TRAVEL	–	–	–		1	3	4
25. HISTORY, BIOGRAPHY	4	–	4		2	–	2

Number of titles by subject group 8.3
Nombre de titres par groupes de sujets
Número de obras por categorías de temas

SUBJECT GROUP / GROUPE DE SUJETS / GRUPO TEMATICO	CANADA ‡ (1978) A	B	A+B	COSTA RICA (1978) A	B	A+B	CUBA (1977) A	B	A+B
TOTAL	12 557	633	13 190	24	–	24	939	100	1 039
1. GENERALITIES	473	33	506	2	–	2	43	6	49
2. PHILOSOPHY, PSYCHOLOGY	625	7	632	–	–	–	34	1	35
3. RELIGION, THEOLOGY	336	35	371	1	–	1	1	–	1
4. SOCIOLOGY, STATISTICS	493	18	511	2	–	2	20	2	22
5. POLITICAL SCIENCE	939	72	1 011	3	–	3	79	6	85
6. LAW, PUBLIC ADMIN.	856	81	937	1	–	1	10	5	15
7. MILITARY ART	18	–	18	–	–	–	4	2	6
8. EDUCATION, LEISURE	641	38	679	2	–	2	116	22	138
9. TRADE, TRANSPORT	262	3	265	–	–	–	1	–	1
10. ETHNOGRAPHY, FOLKLORE	41	–	41	4	–	4	–	–	–
11. MATHEMATICS	367	–	367	–	–	–	32	4	36
12. NATURAL SCIENCES	1 246	10	1 256	–	–	–	66	9	75
13. MEDICAL SCIENCES	465	74	539	–	–	–	39	6	45
14. ENGINEERING, CRAFTS	791	28	819	–	–	–	64	3	67
15. AGRICULTURE	230	14	244	–	–	–	24	13	37
16. DOMESTIC SCIENCE	206	33	239	–	–	–	–	–	–
17. MANAGEMENT, ADMIN.	233	13	246	–	–	–	2	–	2
18. PLANNING, ARCHITECTURE	862	139	1 001	–	–	–	–	–	–
19. PLASTIC ARTS	./.	./.	./.	–	–	–	–	–	–
20. PERFORMING ARTS	./.	./.	./.	2	–	2	5	1	6
21. GAMES, SPORTS	279	–	279	–	–	–	4	3	7
22. LINGUISTICS, PHILOLOGY	483	3	486	–	–	–	32	6	38
23. LITERATURE									
(A) HISTORY AND CRITICISM	597	3	600	1	–	1	24	–	24
(B) LITERARY TEXTS	1 141	–	1 141	3	–	3	310	–	310
24. GEOGRAPHY, TRAVEL	164	–	164	–	–	–	6	3	9
25. HISTORY, BIOGRAPHY	809	29	838	3	–	3	23	8	31

SUBJECT GROUP / GROUPE DE SUJETS / GRUPO TEMATICO	DOMINICAN REPUBLIC ‡ (1976) A	B	A+B	EL SALVADOR (1978) A	B	A+B	JAMAICA ‡ (1978) A	B	A+B
TOTAL	40	8	48	59	85	144	81	62	143
1. GENERALITIES	3	1	4	–	–	–	1	6	7
2. PHILOSOPHY, PSYCHOLOGY	–	–	–	1	–	1	–	3	3
3. RELIGION, THEOLOGY	1	–	1	–	1	1	–	3	3
4. SOCIOLOGY, STATISTICS	3	1	4	1	1	2	22	14	36
5. POLITICAL SCIENCE	3	2	5	4	6	10	–	2	2
6. LAW, PUBLIC ADMIN.	–	–	–	1	–	1	1	1	2
7. MILITARY ART	1	–	1	1	2	3	1	4	5
8. EDUCATION, LEISURE	1	1	2	1	2	3	1	4	5
9. TRADE, TRANSPORT	–	–	–	–	2	2	–	–	–
10. ETHNOGRAPHY, FOLKLORE	–	–	–	–	7	7	1	–	1
11. MATHEMATICS	1	–	1	1	–	1	3	6	9
12. NATURAL SCIENCES	–	–	–	3	–	3	5	4	9
13. MEDICAL SCIENCES	3	–	3	–	8	8	–	2	2
14. ENGINEERING, CRAFTS	–	–	–	1	–	1	–	2	2
15. AGRICULTURE	–	–	–	2	51	53	1	3	4
16. DOMESTIC SCIENCE	3	–	3	–	–	–	1	1	2
17. MANAGEMENT, ADMIN.	2	–	2	–	2	2	–	–	–
18. PLANNING, ARCHITECTURE	–	–	–	1	1	2	–	1	1
19. PLASTIC ARTS	–	–	–	–	1	1	–	–	–
20. PERFORMING ARTS	1	–	1	–	1	1	8	13	21
21. GAMES, SPORTS	–	–	–	–	1	1	1	4	5
22. LINGUISTICS, PHILOLOGY	–	–	–	6	–	6	22	–	22
23. LITERATURE									
(A) HISTORY AND CRITICISM	13	2	15	4	–	4	7	–	7
(B) LITERARY TEXTS	./.	./.	./.	26	1	27	./.	–	./.
24. GEOGRAPHY, TRAVEL	1	–	1	–	–	–	1	–	1
25. HISTORY, BIOGRAPHY	4	1	5	7	–	7	6	2	8

8.3 Number of titles by subject group
Nombre de titres par groupes de sujets
Número de obras por categorías de temas

SUBJECT GROUP / GROUPE DE SUJETS / GRUPO TEMATICO	MEXICO (1976) A	B	A+B	NETHERLANDS ANTILLES ‡ (1977) A	B	A+B	PANAMA (1978) A	B	A+B
TOTAL	4 218	633	4 851	*28	*24	*52	66	60	126
1. GENERALITIES	43	–	43	2	1	3	1	6	7
2. PHILOSOPHY, PSYCHOLOGY	85	–	85	–	–	–	1	–	1
3. RELIGION, THEOLOGY	33	2	35	3	–	3	–	–	–
4. SOCIOLOGY, STATISTICS	65	1	66	–	–	–	3	4	7
5. POLITICAL SCIENCE	85	1	86	–	4	4	2	6	8
6. LAW, PUBLIC ADMIN.	193	4	197	4	2	6	15	5	20
7. MILITARY ART	–	–	–	–	–	–	–	–	–
8. EDUCATION, LEISURE	115	3	118	1	–	1	1	4	5
9. TRADE, TRANSPORT	3	–	3	2	3	5	–	8	8
10. ETHNOGRAPHY, FOLKLORE	27	1	28	1	1	2	2	1	3
11. MATHEMATICS	63	–	63	–	–	–	3	–	3
12. NATURAL SCIENCES	209	25	234	3	1	4	4	–	4
13. MEDICAL SCIENCES	898	154	1 052	1	1	2	7	2	9
14. ENGINEERING, CRAFTS	911	207	1 118	–	–	–	–	6	6
15. AGRICULTURE	88	21	109	1	1	2	1	3	4
16. DOMESTIC SCIENCE	9	1	10	–	–	–	1	–	1
17. MANAGEMENT, ADMIN.	488	105	593	–	–	–	–	–	–
18. PLANNING, ARCHITECTURE	116	11	127	–	–	–	–	–	–
19. PLASTIC ARTS	–	–	–	–	–	–	–	–	–
20. PERFORMING ARTS	–	–	–	–	–	–	1	–	1
21. GAMES, SPORTS	19	20	39	–	–	–	–	1	1
22. LINGUISTICS, PHILOLOGY	149	28	177	–	2	2	2	–	2
23. LITERATURE									
(A) HISTORY AND CRITICISM	12	–	12	4	8	12	1	–	1
(B) LITERARY TEXTS	368	26	394	./.	./.	./.	10	13	23
24. GEOGRAPHY, TRAVEL	14	–	14	1	–	1	2	–	2
25. HISTORY, BIOGRAPHY	225	23	248	5	–	5	9	1	10

SUBJECT GROUP / GROUPE DE SUJETS / GRUPO TEMATICO	TRINIDAD AND TOBAGO ‡ (1976) A	B	A+B	UNITED STATES OF AMERICA ‡ (1978) A	B	A+B	AMERICA, SOUTH / ARGENTINA ‡ (1978) A+B
TOTAL	18	–	18	77 906	7 220	85 126	4 627
1. GENERALITIES	–	–	–	1 345			309
2. PHILOSOPHY, PSYCHOLOGY	–	–	–	1 387			592
3. RELIGION, THEOLOGY	–	–	–	2 398			./.
4. SOCIOLOGY, STATISTICS	–	–	–	2 029			378
5. POLITICAL SCIENCE	–	–	–	2 822			./.
6. LAW, PUBLIC ADMIN.	3	–	3	2 236			205
7. MILITARY ART	–	–	–	153			–
8. EDUCATION, LEISURE	–	–	–	1 078			375
9. TRADE, TRANSPORT	–	–	–	393			–
10. ETHNOGRAPHY, FOLKLORE	–	–	–	156			–
11. MATHEMATICS	1	–	1	690			74
12. NATURAL SCIENCES	6	–	6	2 062			24
13. MEDICAL SCIENCES	–	–	–	2 827			199
14. ENGINEERING, CRAFTS	2	–	2	1 872			291
15. AGRICULTURE	6	–	6	542			87
16. DOMESTIC SCIENCE	–	–	–	860			–
17. MANAGEMENT, ADMIN.	–	–	–	1 259			–
18. PLANNING, ARCHITECTURE	–	–	–	–			712
19. PLASTIC ARTS	–	–	–	–			./.
20. PERFORMING ARTS	–	–	–	492			./.
21. GAMES, SPORTS	–	–	–	855			63
22. LINGUISTICS, PHILOLOGY	–	–	–	426			./.
23. LITERATURE							
(A) HISTORY AND CRITICISM	–	–	–	7 062			./.
(B) LITERARY TEXTS	–	–	–	./.			1 226
24. GEOGRAPHY, TRAVEL	–	–	–	457			33
25. HISTORY, BIOGRAPHY	–	–	–	2 371			59

Number of titles by subject group 8.3
Nombre de titres par groupes de sujets
Número de obras por categorías de temas

SUBJECT GROUP GROUPE DE SUJETS GRUPO TEMATICO	BRAZIL ‡ (1976)			CHILE (1978)			GUYANA ‡ (1978)		
	A	B	A+B	A	B	A+B	A	B	A+B
TOTAL	11 539	8 486	20 025	373	59	432	33	64	97
1. GENERALITIES	644	1 764	2 408	6	1	7	1	4	5
2. PHILOSOPHY, PSYCHOLOGY	521	151	672	27	5	32	—	—	—
3. RELIGION, THEOLOGY	959	283	1 242	35	12	47	1	3	4
4. SOCIOLOGY, STATISTICS	244	273	517	7	1	8	—	2	2
5. POLITICAL SCIENCE	323	147	470	17	4	21	10	17	27
6. LAW, PUBLIC ADMIN.	840	265	1 105	37	4	41	1	8	9
7. MILITARY ART	4	29	33	3	—	3	—	2	2
8. EDUCATION, LEISURE	1 308	555	1 863	12	2	14	4	3	7
9. TRADE, TRANSPORT	69	101	170	5	—	5	—	—	—
10. ETHNOGRAPHY, FOLKLORE	66	895	961	1	—	1	—	3	3
11. MATHEMATICS	405	1 055	1 460	22	—	22	1	—	1
12. NATURAL SCIENCES	391	630	1 021	17	3	20	3	2	5
13. MEDICAL SCIENCES	206	48	254	14	—	14	1	1	2
14. ENGINEERING, CRAFTS	163	894	1 057	10	3	13	1	—	1
15. AGRICULTURE	100	248	348	4	2	6	3	—	3
16. DOMESTIC SCIENCE	40	1	41	—	—	—	—	3	3
17. MANAGEMENT, ADMIN.	169	13	182	3	—	3	—	—	—
18. PLANNING, ARCHITECTURE	29	1	30	3	1	4	—	—	—
19. PLASTIC ARTS	—	—	—	4	—	4	1	—	1
20. PERFORMING ARTS	357	39	396	3	—	3	—	3	3
21. GAMES, SPORTS	123	338	461	1	—	1	—	2	2
22. LINGUISTICS, PHILOLOGY	588	187	775	22	4	26	—	—	—
23. LITERATURE									
(A) HISTORY AND CRITICISM	3 542	199	3 741	16	1	17	6	8	14
(B) LITERARY TEXTS	./.	./.	./.	71	6	77	./.	./.	./.
24. GEOGRAPHY, TRAVEL	136	126	262	8	—	8	—	2	2
25. HISTORY, BIOGRAPHY	312	244	556	25	10	35	—	1	1

SUBJECT GROUP GROUPE DE SUJETS GRUPO TEMATICO	PERU ‡ (1978)			VENEZUELA ‡ (1977)		
	A	B	A+B	A	B	A+B
TOTAL	635	333	968	243	14	257
1. GENERALITIES	22	8	30	6	—	6
2. PHILOSOPHY, PSYCHOLOGY	20	2	22	4	—	4
3. RELIGION, THEOLOGY	20	14	34	6	—	6
4. SOCIOLOGY, STATISTICS	20	11	31	6	—	6
5. POLITICAL SCIENCE	95	55	150	20	—	20
6. LAW, PUBLIC ADMIN.	64	22	86	22	—	22
7. MILITARY ART	1	—	1	1	—	1
8. EDUCATION, LEISURE	33	26	59	19	5	24
9. TRADE, TRANSPORT	13	4	17	4	2	6
10. ETHNOGRAPHY, FOLKLORE	6	4	10	3	—	3
11. MATHEMATICS	24	4	28	8	—	8
12. NATURAL SCIENCES	12	7	19	8	—	8
13. MEDICAL SCIENCES	15	11	26	29	—	29
14. ENGINEERING, CRAFTS	18	25	43	16	—	16
15. AGRICULTURE	23	22	45	13	—	13
16. DOMESTIC SCIENCE	8	2	10	1	—	1
17. MANAGEMENT, ADMIN.	11	8	19	6	1	7
18. PLANNING, ARCHITECTURE	4	1	5	5	—	5
19. PLASTIC ARTS	3	3	6	3	—	3
20. PERFORMING ARTS	—	11	11	1	—	1
21. GAMES, SPORTS	4	2	6	—	—	—
22. LINGUISTICS, PHILOLOGY	7	3	10	1	—	1
23. LITERATURE						
(A) HISTORY AND CRITICISM	114	77	191	40	3	43
(B) LITERARY TEXTS	./.	./.	./.	./.	./.	./.
24. GEOGRAPHY, TRAVEL	3	2	5	2	1	3
25. HISTORY, BIOGRAPHY	95	9	104	19	2	21

8.3 Number of titles by subject group
Nombre de titres par groupes de sujets
Número de obras por categorías de temas

SUBJECT GROUP GROUPE DE SUJETS ASIA GRUPO TEMATICO	AFGHANISTAN ‡ (1977)			BANGLADESH (1978)			BRUNEI (1978)		
	A	B	A+B	A	B	A+B	A	B	A+B
TOTAL	199	33	232	1 063	166	1 229	21	11	32
1. GENERALITIES	12	8	20	21	10	31	5	—	5
2. PHILOSOPHY, PSYCHOLOGY	4	—	4	17	—	17	—	—	—
3. RELIGION, THEOLOGY	25	—	25	111	2	113	7	2	9
4. SOCIOLOGY, STATISTICS	8	4	12	50	9	59	—	—	—
5. POLITICAL SCIENCE	12	5	17	54	13	67	—	—	—
6. LAW, PUBLIC ADMIN.	5	—	5	28	5	33	—	—	—
7. MILITARY ART	—	—	—	—	—	—	—	—	—
8. EDUCATION, LEISURE	22	12	34	130	51	181	1	—	1
9. TRADE, TRANSPORT	1	—	1	5	4	9	—	—	—
10. ETHNOGRAPHY, FOLKLORE	1	1	2	49	1	50	1	—	1
11. MATHEMATICS	10	—	10	99	—	99	2	2	4
12. NATURAL SCIENCES	10	—	10	89	9	98	2	7	9
13. MEDICAL SCIENCES	3	—	3	16	1	17	—	—	—
14. ENGINEERING, CRAFTS	2	—	2	3	2	5	—	—	—
15. AGRICULTURE	—	2	2	51	31	82	—	—	—
16. DOMESTIC SCIENCE	—	—	—	7	—	7	—	—	—
17. MANAGEMENT, ADMIN.	—	1	1	11	2	13	—	—	—
18. PLANNING, ARCHITECTURE	—	—	—	8	—	8	—	—	—
19. PLASTIC ARTS	1	—	1	2	—	2	—	—	—
20. PERFORMING ARTS	1	—	1	32	2	34	—	—	—
21. GAMES, SPORTS	—	—	—	2	3	5	—	—	—
22. LINGUISTICS, PHILOLOGY	28	—	28	1	1	2	—	—	—
23. LITERATURE									
(A) HISTORY AND CRITICISM	20	—	20	9	3	12	—	—	—
(B) LITERARY TEXTS	./.	—	./.	183	14	197	1	—	1
24. GEOGRAPHY, TRAVEL	12	—	12	15	—	15	1	—	1
25. HISTORY, BIOGRAPHY	22	—	22	70	3	73	1	—	1

SUBJECT GROUP GROUPE DE SUJETS GRUPO TEMATICO	CHINA ‡ (1978)	CYPRUS (1977)			HONG KONG (1977)		
	A+B	A	B	A+B	A	B	A+B
TOTAL	12 493	150	420	570	940	795	1 735
1. GENERALITIES	./.	4	9	13	18	43	61
2. PHILOSOPHY, PSYCHOLOGY	1 736	2	3	5	8	1	9
3. RELIGION, THEOLOGY	./.	5	27	32	19	16	35
4. SOCIOLOGY, STATISTICS	./.	4	17	21	15	37	52
5. POLITICAL SCIENCE	./.	7	28	35	35	10	45
6. LAW, PUBLIC ADMIN.	./.	6	13	19	18	251	269
7. MILITARY ART	./.	—	18	18	8	6	14
8. EDUCATION, LEISURE	919	17	45	62	17	82	99
9. TRADE, TRANSPORT	3 474	3	14	17	19	16	35
10. ETHNOGRAPHY, FOLKLORE	./.	2	11	13	62	55	117
11. MATHEMATICS	./.	1	12	13	24	3	27
12. NATURAL SCIENCES	./.	5	6	11	46	13	59
13. MEDICAL SCIENCES	./.	2	17	19	41	17	58
14. ENGINEERING, CRAFTS	./.	5	12	17	44	7	51
15. AGRICULTURE	./.	4	25	29	3	—	3
16. DOMESTIC SCIENCE	./.	4	12	16	18	1	19
17. MANAGEMENT, ADMIN.	./.	2	14	16	5	16	21
18. PLANNING, ARCHITECTURE	./.	1	8	9	2	4	6
19. PLASTIC ARTS	./.	—	5	5	31	15	46
20. PERFORMING ARTS	./.	2	17	19	17	16	33
21. GAMES, SPORTS	./.	2	18	20	12	3	15
22. LINGUISTICS, PHILOLOGY	./.	3	16	19	79	32	111
23. LITERATURE							
(A) HISTORY AND CRITICISM	1 750	4	2	6	17	2	19
(B) LITERARY TEXTS	./.	60	36	96	279	108	387
24. GEOGRAPHY, TRAVEL	./.	2	14	16	23	11	34
25. HISTORY, BIOGRAPHY	./.	3	21	24	80	30	110

Number of titles by subject group 8.3
Nombre de titres par groupes de sujets
Número de obras por categorías de temas

SUBJECT GROUP / GROUPE DE SUJETS / GRUPO TEMATICO	INDIA ‡ (1978) A	B	A+B	INDONESIA (1977) A	B	A+B	IRAN (1977) A	B	A+B
TOTAL	12 638	294	12 932	1 446	819	2 265	3 027	—	3 027
1. GENERALITIES	247	9	256	153	158	311	110	—	110
2. PHILOSOPHY, PSYCHOLOGY	408	13	421	41	7	48	122	—	122
3. RELIGION, THEOLOGY	933	31	964	139	61	200	648	—	648
4. SOCIOLOGY, STATISTICS	402	13	415	113	65	178	128	—	128
5. POLITICAL SCIENCE	1 910	16	1 926	135	92	227	115	—	115
6. LAW, PUBLIC ADMIN.	632	46	678	78	26	104	58	—	58
7. MILITARY ART	11	—	11	10	7	17	—	—	—
8. EDUCATION, LEISURE	218	16	234	58	52	110	45	—	45
9. TRADE, TRANSPORT	164	16	180	24	19	43	—	—	—
10. ETHNOGRAPHY, FOLKLORE	67	7	74	16	5	21	40	—	40
11. MATHEMATICS	146	10	156	25	3	28	31	—	31
12. NATURAL SCIENCES	484	8	492	36	61	97	98	—	98
13. MEDICAL SCIENCES	174	4	178	32	29	61	104	—	104
14. ENGINEERING, CRAFTS	339	70	409	47	41	88	68	—	68
15. AGRICULTURE	152	3	155	37	75	112	45	—	45
16. DOMESTIC SCIENCE	55	—	55	14	3	17	9	—	9
17. MANAGEMENT, ADMIN.	106	8	114	53	23	76	38	—	38
18. PLANNING, ARCHITECTURE	64	5	69	29	25	54	16	—	16
19. PLASTIC ARTS	43	—	43	8	2	10	—	—	—
20. PERFORMING ARTS	66	—	66	11	7	18	64	—	64
21. GAMES, SPORTS	84	—	84	12	1	13	12	—	12
22. LINGUISTICS, PHILOLOGY	196	—	196	20	4	24	45	—	45
23. LITERATURE (A) HISTORY AND CRITICISM	4 588	12	4 600	9	3	12	83	—	83
(B) LITERARY TEXTS	./.	./.	./.	251	10	261	813	—	813
24. GEOGRAPHY, TRAVEL	280	—	280	15	6	21	38	—	38
25. HISTORY, BIOGRAPHY	869	7	876	80	34	114	297	—	297

SUBJECT GROUP / GROUPE DE SUJETS / GRUPO TEMATICO	IRAQ ‡ (1978) A	B	A+B	ISRAEL ‡ (1977) A	B	A+B	JAPAN (1978) A	B	A+B
TOTAL	1 417	201	1 618	1 788	426	2 214	40 866	3 107	43 973
1. GENERALITIES	101	20	121	13	3	16	858	203	1 061
2. PHILOSOPHY, PSYCHOLOGY	35	7	42	40	5	45	804	2	806
3. RELIGION, THEOLOGY	73	21	94	327	34	361	926	26	952
4. SOCIOLOGY, STATISTICS	32	3	35	37	93	130	1 332	148	1 480
5. POLITICAL SCIENCE	112	32	144	52	40	92	3 024	340	3 364
6. LAW, PUBLIC ADMIN.	129	20	149	20	2	22	2 389	153	2 542
7. MILITARY ART	2	—	2	2	—	2	86	11	97
8. EDUCATION, LEISURE	32	11	43	34	13	47	2 122	237	2 359
9. TRADE, TRANSPORT	6	3	9	5	9	14	1 573	139	1 712
10. ETHNOGRAPHY, FOLKLORE	24	8	32	—	1	1	575	29	604
11. MATHEMATICS	13	2	15	5	—	5	283	—	283
12. NATURAL SCIENCES	117	2	119	45	15	60	1 153	16	1 169
13. MEDICAL SCIENCES	68	5	73	19	5	24	1 783	114	1 897
14. ENGINEERING, CRAFTS	146	6	152	18	8	26	5 117	313	5 430
15. AGRICULTURE	92	13	105	22	34	56	2 255	346	2 601
16. DOMESTIC SCIENCE	—	—	—	31	4	35	591	8	599
17. MANAGEMENT, ADMIN.	44	6	50	26	11	37	789	24	813
18. PLANNING, ARCHITECTURE	29	4	33	6	—	6	414	21	435
19. PLASTIC ARTS	4	4	8	4	—	4	1 443	115	1 558
20. PERFORMING ARTS	9	3	12	6	11	17	534	22	556
21. GAMES, SPORTS	10	3	13	15	1	16	773	8	781
22. LINGUISTICS, PHILOLOGY	66	3	69	38	1	39	682	21	703
23. LITERATURE (A) HISTORY AND CRITICISM	195	22	217	./.	./.	./.	569	8	577
(B) LITERARY TEXTS	./.	./.	./.	489	36	525	7 502	558	8 060
24. GEOGRAPHY, TRAVEL	14	—	14	36	7	43	965	53	1 018
25. HISTORY, BIOGRAPHY	64	3	67	151	12	163	2 324	192	2 516

8.3 Number of titles by subject group
Nombre de titres par groupes de sujets
Número de obras por categorías de temas

SUBJECT GROUP / GROUPE DE SUJETS / GRUPO TEMATICO	JORDAN ‡ (1976)			KOREA, REPUBLIC OF ‡ (1978)			KUWAIT (1978)		
	A	B	A+B	A	B	A+B	A	B	A+B
TOTAL	379	13	392	15 836	588	16 364	34	16	50
1. GENERALITIES	3	—	3	568	165	733	1	7	8
2. PHILOSOPHY, PSYCHOLOGY	1	—	1	871	1	872	—	—	—
3. RELIGION, THEOLOGY	35	—	35	1 332	59	1 391	—	—	—
4. SOCIOLOGY, STATISTICS	17	—	17	339	2	341	1	1	2
5. POLITICAL SCIENCE	24	8	32	280	8	288	2	1	3
6. LAW, PUBLIC ADMIN.	6	—	6	420	8	428	7	2	9
7. MILITARY ART	—	—	—	38	—	38	2	2	4
8. EDUCATION, LEISURE	50	2	52	324	58	382	—	1	1
9. TRADE, TRANSPORT	—	—	—	531	8	539	—	1	1
10. ETHNOGRAPHY, FOLKLORE	3	—	3	42	—	42	—	—	—
11. MATHEMATICS	31	—	31	164	6	170	—	—	—
12. NATURAL SCIENCES	20	—	20	932	6	938	—	—	—
13. MEDICAL SCIENCES	10	—	10	144	1	145	—	—	—
14. ENGINEERING, CRAFTS	44	3	47	900	3	903	1	—	1
15. AGRICULTURE	2	—	2	129	1	130	—	—	—
16. DOMESTIC SCIENCE	—	—	—	62	2	64	—	—	—
17. MANAGEMENT, ADMIN.	—	—	—	76	2	78	—	—	—
18. PLANNING, ARCHITECTURE	2	—	2	109	—	109	1	—	1
19. PLASTIC ARTS	—	—	—	208	28	236	1	—	1
20. PERFORMING ARTS	—	—	—	855	40	895	—	1	1
21. GAMES, SPORTS	—	—	—	82	3	85	—	—	—
22. LINGUISTICS, PHILOLOGY	54	—	54	1 203	15	1 218	1	—	1
23. LITERATURE									
(A) HISTORY AND CRITICISM	25	—	25	259	—	259	2	—	2
(B) LITERARY TEXTS	./.	—	./.	4 306	164	4 470	14	—	14
24. GEOGRAPHY, TRAVEL	23	—	23	68	1	69	—	—	—
25. HISTORY, BIOGRAPHY	29	—	29	907	7	914	1	—	1

SUBJECT GROUP / GROUPE DE SUJETS / GRUPO TEMATICO	LAO PEOPLE'S DEMOCRATIC REPUBLIC ‡ (1976)			MALAYSIA ‡ (1978)			MALDIVES ‡ (1977)		
	A	B	A+B	A	B	A+B	A	B	A+B
TOTAL	—	31	31	837	491	1 328	3	—	3
1. GENERALITIES	—	2	2	27	19	46	1	—	1
2. PHILOSOPHY, PSYCHOLOGY	—	6	6	10	8	18	1	—	1
3. RELIGION, THEOLOGY	—	1	1	81	51	132	—	—	—
4. SOCIOLOGY, STATISTICS	—	—	—	52	10	62	—	—	—
5. POLITICAL SCIENCE	—	7	7	63	125	188	—	—	—
6. LAW, PUBLIC ADMIN.	—	—	—	28	22	50	—	—	—
7. MILITARY ART	—	—	—	—	—	—	—	—	—
8. EDUCATION, LEISURE	—	—	—	25	24	49	1	—	1
9. TRADE, TRANSPORT	—	—	—	7	12	19	—	—	—
10. ETHNOGRAPHY, FOLKLORE	—	—	—	16	65	81	—	—	—
11. MATHEMATICS	—	—	—	23	1	24	—	—	—
12. NATURAL SCIENCES	—	—	—	68	8	76	—	—	—
13. MEDICAL SCIENCES	—	3	3	14	11	25	—	—	—
14. ENGINEERING, CRAFTS	—	—	—	33	37	70	—	—	—
15. AGRICULTURE	—	—	—	43	20	63	—	—	—
16. DOMESTIC SCIENCE	—	—	—	2	3	5	—	—	—
17. MANAGEMENT, ADMIN.	—	—	—	30	12	42	—	—	—
18. PLANNING, ARCHITECTURE	—	—	—	3	2	5	—	—	—
19. PLASTIC ARTS	—	—	—	3	3	6	—	—	—
20. PERFORMING ARTS	—	1	1	4	1	5	—	—	—
21. GAMES, SPORTS	—	—	—	3	—	3	—	—	—
22. LINGUISTICS, PHILOLOGY	—	—	—	125	30	155	—	—	—
23. LITERATURE									
(A) HISTORY AND CRITICISM	—	1	1	118	16	134	—	—	—
(B) LITERARY TEXTS	—	9	9	./.	./.	./.	—	—	—
24. GEOGRAPHY, TRAVEL	—	1	1	15	2	17	—	—	—
25. HISTORY, BIOGRAPHY	—	—	—	44	9	53	—	—	—

Number of titles by subject group 8.3
Nombre de titres par groupes de sujets
Número de obras por categorías de temas

SUBJECT GROUP / GROUPE DE SUJETS / GRUPO TEMATICO	PAKISTAN ‡ (1978)			PHILIPPINES ‡ (1977)			QATAR (1978)		
	A	B	A+B	A	B	A+B	A	B	A+B
TOTAL	1 317	—	1 317	1 336	417	1 753	127	32	159
1. GENERALITIES	29	—	29	39	26	65	5	4	9
2. PHILOSOPHY, PSYCHOLOGY	4	—	4	28	1	29	3	—	3
3. RELIGION, THEOLOGY	277	—	277	127	34	161	38	18	56
4. SOCIOLOGY, STATISTICS	12	—	12	70	23	93	6	—	6
5. POLITICAL SCIENCE	65	—	65	96	32	128	—	—	—
6. LAW, PUBLIC ADMIN.	61	—	61	88	49	137	2	10	12
7. MILITARY ART	1	—	1	16	11	27	—	—	—
8. EDUCATION, LEISURE	8	—	8	104	18	122	3	—	3
9. TRADE, TRANSPORT	1	—	1	14	7	21	—	—	—
10. ETHNOGRAPHY, FOLKLORE	9	—	9	8	4	12	—	—	—
11. MATHEMATICS	1	—	1	12	—	12	9	—	9
12. NATURAL SCIENCES	7	—	7	81	9	90	13	—	13
13. MEDICAL SCIENCES	18	—	18	98	11	109	—	—	—
14. ENGINEERING, CRAFTS	71	—	71	66	17	83	—	—	—
15. AGRICULTURE	4	—	4	124	62	186	—	—	—
16. DOMESTIC SCIENCE	2	—	2	39	3	42	—	—	—
17. MANAGEMENT, ADMIN.	1	—	1	89	15	104	—	—	—
18. PLANNING, ARCHITECTURE	1	—	1	5	1	6	—	—	—
19. PLASTIC ARTS	7	—	7	5	1	6	—	—	—
20. PERFORMING ARTS	7	—	7	16	54	70	—	—	—
21. GAMES, SPORTS	1	—	1	7	2	9	—	—	—
22. LINGUISTICS, PHILOLOGY	266	—	266	105	19	124	30	—	30
23. LITERATURE									
(A) HISTORY AND CRITICISM	269	—	269	5	—	5	3	—	3
(B) LITERARY TEXTS	./.	—	./.	60	9	69	3	—	3
24. GEOGRAPHY, TRAVEL	16	—	16	10	—	10	3	—	3
25. HISTORY, BIOGRAPHY	179	—	179	24	9	33	9	—	9

SUBJECT GROUP / GROUPE DE SUJETS / GRUPO TEMATICO	SINGAPORE ‡ (1978)			SRI LANKA ‡ (1978)			SYRIAN ARAB REPUBLIC ‡ (1978)		
	A	B	A+B	A	B	A+B	A	B	A+B
TOTAL	888	418	1 306	626	779	1 405	225	5	230
1. GENERALITIES	11	7	18	9	2	11	1	—	1
2. PHILOSOPHY, PSYCHOLOGY	2	—	2	19	10	29	3	—	3
3. RELIGION, THEOLOGY	16	7	23	121	193	314	3	—	3
4. SOCIOLOGY, STATISTICS	12	14	26	36	16	52	2	—	2
5. POLITICAL SCIENCE	26	20	46	54	99	153	20	—	20
6. LAW, PUBLIC ADMIN.	18	5	23	24	31	55	7	—	7
7. MILITARY ART	—	—	—	—	2	2	—	—	—
8. EDUCATION, LEISURE	283	210	493	22	40	62	2	—	2
9. TRADE, TRANSPORT	8	7	15	6	10	16	7	—	7
10. ETHNOGRAPHY, FOLKLORE	6	2	8	—	1	1	—	—	—
11. MATHEMATICS	39	15	54	17	12	29	10	—	10
12. NATURAL SCIENCES	37	18	55	21	10	31	25	—	25
13. MEDICAL SCIENCES	14	7	21	19	22	41	23	—	23
14. ENGINEERING, CRAFTS	10	3	13	7	25	32	35	—	35
15. AGRICULTURE	2	3	5	15	13	28	20	—	20
16. DOMESTIC SCIENCE	6	1	7	2	—	2	—	—	—
17. MANAGEMENT, ADMIN.	15	24	39	12	18	30	—	—	—
18. PLANNING, ARCHITECTURE	2	1	3	16	79	95	—	—	—
19. PLASTIC ARTS	4	2	6	./.	./.	./.	3	—	3
20. PERFORMING ARTS	18	8	26	./.	./.	./.	3	—	3
21. GAMES, SPORTS	20	8	28	4	21	25	—	—	—
22. LINGUISTICS, PHILOLOGY	97	25	122	35	20	55	2	—	2
23. LITERATURE									
(A) HISTORY AND CRITICISM	12	12	24	24	21	45	5	—	5
(B) LITERARY TEXTS	179	11	190	108	91	199	28	—	28
24. GEOGRAPHY, TRAVEL	21	—	21	9	8	17	5	—	5
25. HISTORY, BIOGRAPHY	30	8	38	46	35	81	9	5	14

8.3 Number of titles by subject group
Nombre de titres par groupes de sujets
Número de obras por categorías de temas

SUBJECT GROUP GROUPE DE SUJETS GRUPO TEMATICO	THAILAND ‡ (1977) A	 B	 A+B	TURKEY ‡ (1977) A+B	UNITED ARAB EMIRATES (1977) A	 B	 A+B
TOTAL	3 062	328	3 390	6 830	13	2	15
1. GENERALITIES	295	31	326	689	6	–	6
2. PHILOSOPHY, PSYCHOLOGY	61	6	67	196	–	–	–
3. RELIGION, THEOLOGY	197	35	232	327	–	–	–
4. SOCIOLOGY, STATISTICS	88	5	93	2 158	–	–	–
5. POLITICAL SCIENCE	247	56	303	./.	–	–	–
6. LAW, PUBLIC ADMIN.	232	23	255	./.	1	–	1
7. MILITARY ART	23	3	26	./.	–	–	–
8. EDUCATION, LEISURE	724	29	753	./.	–	–	–
9. TRADE, TRANSPORT	19	3	22	./.	4	2	6
10. ETHNOGRAPHY, FOLKLORE	37	6	43	./.	–	–	–
11. MATHEMATICS	47	–	47	502	–	–	–
12. NATURAL SCIENCES	91	7	98	./.	–	–	–
13. MEDICAL SCIENCES	53	29	82	1 013	–	–	–
14. ENGINEERING, CRAFTS	180	48	228	./.	–	–	–
15. AGRICULTURE	58	6	64	./.	–	–	–
16. DOMESTIC SCIENCE	36	2	38	./.	–	–	–
17. MANAGEMENT, ADMIN.	47	5	52	./.	–	–	–
18. PLANNING, ARCHITECTURE	15	5	20	346	–	–	–
19. PLASTIC ARTS	20	2	22	./.	1	–	1
20. PERFORMING ARTS	26	–	26	./.	–	–	–
21. GAMES, SPORTS	47	1	48	./.	–	–	–
22. LINGUISTICS, PHILOLOGY	269	11	280	166	–	–	–
23. LITERATURE							
(A) HISTORY AND CRITICISM	13	–	13	950	–	–	–
(B) LITERARY TEXTS	./.	–	./.	./.	1	–	1
24. GEOGRAPHY, TRAVEL	60	6	66	483	–	–	–
25. HISTORY, BIOGRAPHY	177	9	186	./.	–	–	–

SUBJECT GROUP GROUPE DE SUJETS GRUPO TEMATICO	VIET NAM (1977) A	 B	 A+B	EUROPE	AUSTRIA (1978) A	 B	 A+B	BELGIUM ‡ (1978) A+B
TOTAL	1 446	58	1 504		5 175	1 264	6 439	9 012
1. GENERALITIES	–	–	–		92	42	134	233
2. PHILOSOPHY, PSYCHOLOGY	22	–	22		196	10	206	198
3. RELIGION, THEOLOGY	–	–	–		147	42	189	329
4. SOCIOLOGY, STATISTICS	5	–	5		193	45	238	109
5. POLITICAL SCIENCE	116	11	127		336	119	455	571
6. LAW, PUBLIC ADMIN.	14	5	19		281	72	353	459
7. MILITARY ART	14	–	14		3	5	8	84
8. EDUCATION, LEISURE	59	1	60		321	166	487	274
9. TRADE, TRANSPORT	6	–	6		54	16	70	117
10. ETHNOGRAPHY, FOLKLORE	4	–	4		81	23	104	45
11. MATHEMATICS	160	–	160		130	16	146	233
12. NATURAL SCIENCES	179	–	179		421	36	457	430
13. MEDICAL SCIENCES	58	6	64		125	63	188	315
14. ENGINEERING, CRAFTS	60	–	60		320	111	431	329
15. AGRICULTURE	69	6	75		100	12	112	150
16. DOMESTIC SCIENCE	3	–	3		39	3	42	180
17. MANAGEMENT, ADMIN.	23	–	23		584	52	636	107
18. PLANNING, ARCHITECTURE	2	–	2		22	18	40	666
19. PLASTIC ARTS	3	–	3		154	99	253	./.
20. PERFORMING ARTS	21	–	21		108	30	138	./.
21. GAMES, SPORTS	23	1	24		54	37	91	210
22. LINGUISTICS, PHILOLOGY	203	1	204		186	25	211	472
23. LITERATURE								
(A) HISTORY AND CRITICISM	27	–	27		107	8	115	111
(B) LITERARY TEXTS	274	25	299		615	106	721	2 631
24. GEOGRAPHY, TRAVEL	38	–	38		148	24	172	250
25. HISTORY, BIOGRAPHY	63	2	65		358	84	442	509

Number of titles by subject group   8.3
Nombre de titres par groupes de sujets
Número de obras por categorías de temas

SUBJECT GROUP GROUPE DE SUJETS GRUPO TEMATICO	BULGARIA ‡ (1978)			CZECHOSLOVAKIA ‡ (1978)			DENMARK (1978)		
	A	B	A+B	A	B	A+B	A	B	A+B
TOTAL	3 513	721	4 234	8 280	1 308	9 588	6 359	3 056	9 415
1. GENERALITIES	73	88	161	318	211	529	164	77	241
2. PHILOSOPHY, PSYCHOLOGY	53	6	59	139	2	141	193	71	264
3. RELIGION, THEOLOGY	6	1	7	54	–	54	198	107	305
4. SOCIOLOGY, STATISTICS	70	27	97	59	1	60	134	61	195
5. POLITICAL SCIENCE	510	132	642	675	140	815	410	226	636
6. LAW, PUBLIC ADMIN.	78	14	92	154	24	178	297	177	474
7. MILITARY ART	26	3	29	78	39	117	29	19	48
8. EDUCATION, LEISURE	155	40	195	542	83	625	278	110	388
9. TRADE, TRANSPORT	31	8	39	84	12	96	–	–	–
10. ETHNOGRAPHY, FOLKLORE	10	1	11	5	1	6	49	36	85
11. MATHEMATICS	46	1	47	278	9	287	112	78	190
12. NATURAL SCIENCES	181	12	193	660	28	688	332	261	593
13. MEDICAL SCIENCES	213	60	273	337	76	413	309	135	444
14. ENGINEERING, CRAFTS	408	67	475	1 453	126	1 579	566	352	918
15. AGRICULTURE	190	36	226	422	58	480	183	107	290
16. DOMESTIC SCIENCE	9	2	11	32	6	38	93	46	139
17. MANAGEMENT, ADMIN.	104	17	121	61	2	63	160	87	247
18. PLANNING, ARCHITECTURE	133	41	174	351	85	436	131	51	182
19. PLASTIC ARTS	./.	./.	./.	./.	./.	./.	143	63	206
20. PERFORMING ARTS	./.	./.	./.	./.	./.	./.	68	43	111
21. GAMES, SPORTS	68	4	72	136	24	160	130	49	179
22. LINGUISTICS, PHILOLOGY	134	1	135	386	10	396	197	143	340
23. LITERATURE									
(A) HISTORY AND CRITICISM	785	99	884	135	36	171	52	9	61
(B) LITERARY TEXTS	./.	./.	./.	1 498	272	1 770	1 489	544	2 033
24. GEOGRAPHY, TRAVEL	44	11	55	168	16	184	180	87	267
25. HISTORY, BIOGRAPHY	186	50	236	255	47	302	462	117	579

SUBJECT GROUP GROUPE DE SUJETS GRUPO TEMATICO	FINLAND (1978)			FRANCE ‡ (1978)	GERMAN DEMOCRATIC REP. ‡ (1978)		
	A	B	A+B	A+B	A	B	A+B
TOTAL	2 725	642	3 367	21 225	5 015	665	5 680
1. GENERALITIES	97	20	117	436	56	–	56
2. PHILOSOPHY, PSYCHOLOGY	98	8	106	996	126	3	129
3. RELIGION, THEOLOGY	169	25	194	672	214	70	284
4. SOCIOLOGY, STATISTICS	56	15	71	196	125	9	134
5. POLITICAL SCIENCE	137	34	171	1 098	136	11	147
6. LAW, PUBLIC ADMIN.	160	22	182	663	108	9	117
7. MILITARY ART	20	3	23	23	68	6	74
8. EDUCATION, LEISURE	95	22	117	324	192	31	223
9. TRADE, TRANSPORT	9	2	11	–	68	5	73
10. ETHNOGRAPHY, FOLKLORE	51	3	54	195	22	1	23
11. MATHEMATICS	32	21	53	362	119	–	119
12. NATURAL SCIENCES	150	155	305	841	294	23	317
13. MEDICAL SCIENCES	144	37	181	982	196	5	201
14. ENGINEERING, CRAFTS	145	70	215	788	503	32	535
15. AGRICULTURE	70	51	121	293	112	3	115
16. DOMESTIC SCIENCE	42	7	49	161	16	–	16
17. MANAGEMENT, ADMIN.	91	17	108	402	8	1	9
18. PLANNING, ARCHITECTURE	28	3	31	1 606	145	29	174
19. PLASTIC ARTS	31	14	45	./.	4	7	11
20. PERFORMING ARTS	29	1	30	./.	103	4	107
21. GAMES, SPORTS	34	1	35	402	112	4	116
22. LINGUISTICS, PHILOLOGY	130	16	146	423	252	8	260
23. LITERATURE							
(A) HISTORY AND CRITICISM	17	4	21	475	1 215	54	1 269
(B) LITERARY TEXTS	718	78	796	6 523	./.	./.	./.
24. GEOGRAPHY, TRAVEL	55	6	61	615	105	–	105
25. HISTORY, BIOGRAPHY	117	7	124	2 749	116	12	128

8.3 Number of titles by subject group
Nombre de titres par groupes de sujets
Número de obras por categorías de temas

SUBJECT GROUP GROUPE DE SUJETS GRUPO TEMATICO	GERMANY, FEDERAL REP. OF ‡ (1978)			GREECE (1977)			HOLY SEE (1978)		
	A	B	A+B	A	B	A+B	A	B	A+B
TOTAL	43 164	7 786	50 950	4 294	687	4 981	180	—	180
1. GENERALITIES	2 437	1 055	3 492	62	4	66	8	—	8
2. PHILOSOPHY, PSYCHOLOGY	1 199	84	1 283	195	21	216	23	—	23
3. RELIGION, THEOLOGY	2 073	391	2 464	305	38	343	112	—	112
4. SOCIOLOGY, STATISTICS	1 565	411	1 976	74	7	81	7	—	7
5. POLITICAL SCIENCE	1 880	585	2 465	110	20	130	—	—	—
6. LAW, PUBLIC ADMIN.	2 443	578	3 021	180	23	203	9	—	9
7. MILITARY ART	955	249	1 204	20	1	21	—	—	—
8. EDUCATION, LEISURE	3 651	858	4 509	353	83	436	1	—	1
9. TRADE, TRANSPORT	381	146	527	65	17	82	—	—	—
10. ETHNOGRAPHY, FOLKLORE	./.	./.	./.	98	8	106	—	—	—
11. MATHEMATICS	594	108	702	95	16	111	—	—	—
12. NATURAL SCIENCES	1 623	356	1 979	86	12	98	—	—	—
13. MEDICAL SCIENCES	1 879	384	2 263	86	26	112	—	—	—
14. ENGINEERING, CRAFTS	1 761	574	2 335	74	17	91	—	—	—
15. AGRICULTURE	1 101	200	1 301	59	10	69	—	—	—
16. DOMESTIC SCIENCE	./.	./.	./.	24	8	32	—	—	—
17. MANAGEMENT, ADMIN.	./.	./.	./.	84	4	88	—	—	—
18. PLANNING, ARCHITECTURE	./.	./.	./.	40	6	46	—	—	—
19. PLASTIC ARTS	1 843	826	2 669	63	14	77	—	—	—
20. PERFORMING ARTS	685	111	796	26	16	42	1	—	1
21. GAMES, SPORTS	533	93	626	14	2	16	—	—	—
22. LINGUISTICS, PHILOLOGY	1 644	139	1 783	121	28	149	11	—	11
23. LITERATURE									
(A) HISTORY AND CRITICISM	./.	./.	./.	199	56	255	—	—	—
(B) LITERARY TEXTS	11 860	304	12 164	1 320	156	1 476	—	—	—
24. GEOGRAPHY, TRAVEL	1 053	105	1 158	92	21	113	—	—	—
25. HISTORY, BIOGRAPHY	2 004	229	2 233	449	73	522	8	—	8

SUBJECT GROUP GROUPE DE SUJETS GRUPO TEMATICO	HUNGARY (1978)			ICELAND ‡ (1977)			IRELAND ‡ (1978)		
	A	B	A+B	A	B	A+B	A	B	A+B
TOTAL	8 556	1 023	9 579	575	226	801	440	192	632
1. GENERALITIES	254	17	271	12	5	17	18	10	28
2. PHILOSOPHY, PSYCHOLOGY	99	6	105	11	3	14	4	1	5
3. RELIGION, THEOLOGY	67	6	73	11	4	15	22	11	33
4. SOCIOLOGY, STATISTICS	159	3	162	9	1	10	16	7	23
5. POLITICAL SCIENCE	615	96	711	33	24	57	20	8	28
6. LAW, PUBLIC ADMIN.	269	54	323	16	12	28	27	15	42
7. MILITARY ART	28	3	31	—	—	—	—	—	—
8. EDUCATION, LEISURE	807	180	987	40	18	58	12	5	17
9. TRADE, TRANSPORT	93	3	96	11	5	16	10	6	16
10. ETHNOGRAPHY, FOLKLORE	68	9	77	11	3	14	15	2	17
11. MATHEMATICS	229	32	261	2	2	4	4	—	4
12. NATURAL SCIENCES	528	92	620	20	12	32	12	6	18
13. MEDICAL SCIENCES	251	19	270	7	6	13	6	3	9
14. ENGINEERING, CRAFTS	1 336	104	1 440	27	30	57	17	12	29
15. AGRICULTURE	349	59	408	11	20	31	12	8	20
16. DOMESTIC SCIENCE	71	5	76	3	4	7	3	—	3
17. MANAGEMENT, ADMIN.	594	51	645	6	2	8	4	2	6
18. PLANNING, ARCHITECTURE	79	4	83	17	6	23	6	2	8
19. PLASTIC ARTS	209	113	322	./.	./.	./.	10	8	18
20. PERFORMING ARTS	203	37	240	./.	./.	./.	14	7	21
21. GAMES, SPORTS	113	12	125	22	7	29	16	5	21
22. LINGUISTICS, PHILOLOGY	329	20	349	9	4	13	14	6	20
23. LITERATURE									
(A) HISTORY AND CRITICISM	221	6	227	8	—	8	9	2	11
(B) LITERARY TEXTS	1 135	51	1 186	226	49	275	90	37	127
24. GEOGRAPHY, TRAVEL	151	27	178	12	3	15	27	15	42
25. HISTORY, BIOGRAPHY	299	14	313	51	6	57	52	14	66

Number of titles by subject group 8.3
Nombre de titres par groupes de sujets
Número de obras por categorías de temas

SUBJECT GROUP / GROUPE DE SUJETS / GRUPO TEMATICO	ITALY (1978) A	B	A+B	LUXEMBOURG (1977) A	B	A+B	MALTA (1978) A	B	A+B
TOTAL	9 554	1 125	10 679	167	83	250	120	34	154
1. GENERALITIES	255	55	310	7	—	7	3	2	5
2. PHILOSOPHY, PSYCHOLOGY	581	8	589	2	—	2	—	—	—
3. RELIGION, THEOLOGY	532	172	704	1	1	2	25	6	31
4. SOCIOLOGY, STATISTICS	312	11	323	8	—	8	3	1	4
5. POLITICAL SCIENCE	643	21	664	19	11	30	4	5	9
6. LAW, PUBLIC ADMIN.	827	100	927	25	16	41	7	2	9
7. MILITARY ART	15	4	19	1	—	1	—	—	—
8. EDUCATION, LEISURE	385	95	480	14	13	27	5	1	6
9. TRADE, TRANSPORT	32	—	32	2	4	6	3	2	5
10. ETHNOGRAPHY, FOLKLORE	124	4	128	3	—	3	1	1	2
11. MATHEMATICS	149	8	157	2	1	3	—	—	—
12. NATURAL SCIENCES	337	119	456	1	1	2	—	—	—
13. MEDICAL SCIENCES	389	26	415	1	2	3	—	1	1
14. ENGINEERING, CRAFTS	398	79	477	5	3	8	—	—	—
15. AGRICULTURE	92	20	112	1	1	2	—	—	—
16. DOMESTIC SCIENCE	64	2	66	—	—	—	1	—	1
17. MANAGEMENT, ADMIN.	133	4	137	—	—	—	—	—	—
18. PLANNING, ARCHITECTURE	245	12	257	3	—	3	1	1	2
19. PLASTIC ARTS	242	25	267	8	2	10	—	—	—
20. PERFORMING ARTS	234	49	283	17	5	22	2	1	3
21. GAMES, SPORTS	238	90	328	11	13	24	—	—	—
22. LINGUISTICS, PHILOLOGY	266	4	270	2	—	2	4	—	4
23. LITERATURE									
(A) HISTORY AND CRITICISM	316	7	323	3	1	4	—	—	—
(B) LITERARY TEXTS	1 849	171	2 020	13	8	21	41	7	48
24. GEOGRAPHY, TRAVEL	214	19	233	—	—	—	9	3	12
25. HISTORY, BIOGRAPHY	682	20	702	18	1	19	11	1	12

SUBJECT GROUP / GROUPE DE SUJETS / GRUPO TEMATICO	MONACO (1977) A+B	NETHERLANDS ‡ (1978) A+B	NORWAY ‡ (1978) A	B	A+B	POLAND ‡ (1978) A	B	A+B	PORTUGAL ‡ (1978) A+B
TOTAL	86	13 393	3 361	1 046	4 407	9 179	2 670	11 849	6 274
1. GENERALITIES	5	134	74	47	121	175	112	287	148
2. PHILOSOPHY, PSYCHOLOGY	5	556	58	12	70	143	8	151	214
3. RELIGION, THEOLOGY	11	535	168	103	271	166	6	172	233
4. SOCIOLOGY, STATISTICS	—	1 786	137	31	168	173	18	191	1 434
5. POLITICAL SCIENCE	15	./.	202	96	298	648	264	912	./.
6. LAW, PUBLIC ADMIN.	—	./.	128	64	192	251	30	281	./.
7. MILITARY ART	—	9	10	4	14	141	27	168	./.
8. EDUCATION, LEISURE	1	284	121	64	185	533	208	741	./.
9. TRADE, TRANSPORT	—	./.	46	32	78	107	40	147	./.
10. ETHNOGRAPHY, FOLKLORE	—	./.	20	1	21	25	9	34	./.
11. MATHEMATICS	—	1 153	30	11	41	176	20	196	363
12. NATURAL SCIENCES	11	./.	125	112	237	690	166	856	./.
13. MEDICAL SCIENCES	1	499	124	33	157	407	60	467	1 266
14. ENGINEERING, CRAFTS	9	442	135	59	194	1 710	683	2 393	./.
15. AGRICULTURE	—	69	82	51	133	452	229	681	./.
16. DOMESTIC SCIENCE	—	389	31	4	35	78	2	80	./.
17. MANAGEMENT, ADMIN.	5	./.	45	14	59	431	211	642	./.
18. PLANNING, ARCHITECTURE	9	—	35	18	53	387	132	519	705
19. PLASTIC ARTS	—	615	58	15	73	./.	./.	./.	./.
20. PERFORMING ARTS	—	./.	35	9	44	./.	./.	./.	./.
21. GAMES, SPORTS	3	133	54	11	65	118	29	147	./.
22. LINGUISTICS, PHILOLOGY	—	1 703	74	16	90	443	60	503	./.
23. LITERATURE									
(A) HISTORY AND CRITICISM	2	./.	47	2	49	220	30	250	1 469
(B) LITERARY TEXTS	4	3 902	1 243	164	1 407	1 203	193	1 396	./.
24. GEOGRAPHY, TRAVEL	2	360	132	30	162	132	92	224	442
25. HISTORY, BIOGRAPHY	3	824	147	43	190	370	41	411	./.

8.3 Number of titles by subject group
Nombre de titres par groupes de sujets
Número de obras por categorías de temas

SUBJECT GROUP / GROUPE DE SUJETS / GRUPO TEMATICO	ROMANIA (1978)			SAN MARINO ‡ (1978)			SPAIN ‡ (1977)		
	A	B	A+B	A	B	A+B	A	B	A+B
TOTAL	5 648	1 914	7 562	14	1	15	20 646	4 250	24 896
1. GENERALITIES	91	29	120	–	–	–	1 555	1 159	2 714
2. PHILOSOPHY, PSYCHOLOGY	95	37	132	–	–	–	1 205	133	1 338
3. RELIGION, THEOLOGY	59	67	126	–	–	–	1 236	265	1 501
4. SOCIOLOGY, STATISTICS	91	115	206	–	–	–	475	67	542
5. POLITICAL SCIENCE	225	144	369	–	–	–	1 312	191	1 503
6. LAW, PUBLIC ADMIN.	95	34	129	–	–	–	711	135	846
7. MILITARY ART	37	2	39	–	–	–	54	5	59
8. EDUCATION, LEISURE	161	31	192	2	–	2	447	242	689
9. TRADE, TRANSPORT	37	11	48	2	–	2	60	6	66
10. ETHNOGRAPHY, FOLKLORE	16	16	32	–	–	–	184	38	222
11. MATHEMATICS	250	57	307	–	–	–	533	70	603
12. NATURAL SCIENCES	420	305	725	–	–	–	960	355	1 315
13. MEDICAL SCIENCES	406	196	602	1	–	1	725	147	872
14. ENGINEERING, CRAFTS	783	153	936	–	–	–	684	104	788
15. AGRICULTURE	301	175	476	–	–	–	170	153	323
16. DOMESTIC SCIENCE	22	1	23	–	–	–	202	29	231
17. MANAGEMENT, ADMIN.	138	9	147	1	–	1	254	31	285
18. PLANNING, ARCHITECTURE	50	21	71	2	1	3	877	443	1 320
19. PLASTIC ARTS	116	35	151	–	–	–	./.	./.	./.
20. PERFORMING ARTS	84	81	165	1	–	1	./.	./.	./.
21. GAMES, SPORTS	87	47	134	–	–	–	224	45	269
22. LINGUISTICS, PHILOLOGY	387	63	450	–	–	–	1 363	167	1 530
23. LITERATURE									
(A) HISTORY AND CRITICISM	174	51	225	–	–	–	5 543	283	5 826
(B) LITERARY TEXTS	1 222	96	1 318	2	–	2	./.	./.	./.
24. GEOGRAPHY, TRAVEL	135	68	203	–	–	–	212	39	251
25. HISTORY, BIOGRAPHY	166	70	236	3	–	3	1 660	143	1 803

SUBJECT GROUP / GROUPE DE SUJETS / GRUPO TEMATICO	SWEDEN ‡ (1978)	SWITZERLAND ‡ (1978)	UNITED KINGDOM ‡ (1977)			YUGOSLAVIA (1978)		
	A+B	A+B	A	B	A+B	A	B	A+B
TOTAL	5 256	9 453	33 276	2 920	36 196	8 013	2 496	10 509
1. GENERALITIES	119	133	940	114	1 054	131	35	166
2. PHILOSOPHY, PSYCHOLOGY	122	298	1 186	44	1 230	93	5	98
3. RELIGION, THEOLOGY	159	628	1 205	191	1 396	160	27	187
4. SOCIOLOGY, STATISTICS	65	322	983	29	1 012	124	21	145
5. POLITICAL SCIENCE	174	550	2 648	232	2 880	1 197	282	1 479
6. LAW, PUBLIC ADMIN.	276	443	1 092	109	1 201	463	145	608
7. MILITARY ART	18	27	136	17	153	23	3	26
8. EDUCATION, LEISURE	158	248	833	77	910	1 593	201	1 794
9. TRADE, TRANSPORT	95	114	426	86	512	–	–	–
10. ETHNOGRAPHY, FOLKLORE	21	256	181	28	209	15	6	21
11. MATHEMATICS	24	105	612	51	663	112	15	127
12. NATURAL SCIENCES	342	770	2 419	177	2 596	202	23	225
13. MEDICAL SCIENCES	361	1 419	1 913	71	1 984	255	36	291
14. ENGINEERING, CRAFTS	232	428	1 825	141	1 966	334	62	396
15. AGRICULTURE	103	120	598	67	665	121	34	155
16. DOMESTIC SCIENCE	65	61	588	72	660	33	13	46
17. MANAGEMENT, ADMIN.	75	142	681	40	721	448	325	773
18. PLANNING, ARCHITECTURE	56	198	2 467	198	2 665	45	30	75
19. PLASTIC ARTS	71	519	./.	./.	./.	158	411	569
20. PERFORMING ARTS	49	136	./.	./.	./.	155	467	622
21. GAMES, SPORTS	55	137	802	43	845	116	34	150
22. LINGUISTICS, PHILOLOGY	95	199	615	139	754	128	11	139
23. LITERATURE								
(A) HISTORY AND CRITICISM	98	200	764	40	804	123	15	138
(B) LITERARY TEXTS	1 565	1 100	7 085	658	7 743	1 720	239	1 959
24. GEOGRAPHY, TRAVEL	175	387	798	126	924	88	28	116
25. HISTORY, BIOGRAPHY	218	513	2 479	170	2 649	176	28	204

Number of titles by subject group   **8.3**
Nombre de titres par groupes de sujets
Número de obras por categorías de temas

SUBJECT GROUP GROUPE DE SUJETS OCEANIA GRUPO TEMATICO	AMERICAN SAMOA ‡ (1978)			AUSTRALIA ‡ (1977)			FIJI ‡ (1976)		
	A	B	A+B	A	B	A+B	A	B	A+B
TOTAL	86	—	86	2 286	791	3 077	73	66	139
1. GENERALITIES	7	—	7	69	36	105	—	—	—
2. PHILOSOPHY, PSYCHOLOGY	—	—	—	21	6	27	—	—	—
3. RELIGION, THEOLOGY	—	—	—	64	33	97	—	—	—
4. SOCIOLOGY, STATISTICS	—	—	—	152	36	188	2	2	4
5. POLITICAL SCIENCE	—	—	—	116	90	206	—	—	—
6. LAW, PUBLIC ADMIN.	—	—	—	176	57	233	—	—	—
7. MILITARY ART	6	—	6	8	4	12	—	—	—
8. EDUCATION, LEISURE	12	—	12	197	119	316	21	21	42
9. TRADE, TRANSPORT	—	—	—	33	29	62	2	—	2
10. ETHNOGRAPHY, FOLKLORE	—	—	—	15	2	17	—	2	2
11. MATHEMATICS	1	—	1	20	1	21	10	7	17
12. NATURAL SCIENCES	—	—	—	166	55	221	22	8	30
13. MEDICAL SCIENCES	—	—	—	56	24	80	—	2	2
14. ENGINEERING, CRAFTS	—	—	—	125	49	174	—	12	12
15. AGRICULTURE	—	—	—	49	32	81	4	1	5
16. DOMESTIC SCIENCE	1	—	1	108	9	117	2	—	2
17. MANAGEMENT, ADMIN.	—	—	—	73	9	82	2	1	3
18. PLANNING, ARCHITECTURE	—	—	—	52	26	78	—	—	—
19. PLASTIC ARTS	—	—	—	49	13	62	—	2	2
20. PERFORMING ARTS	—	—	—	39	8	47	—	—	—
21. GAMES, SPORTS	—	—	—	59	3	62	—	—	—
22. LINGUISTICS, PHILOLOGY	—	—	—	132	73	205	8	8	16
23. LITERATURE									
(A) HISTORY AND CRITICISM	12	—	12	216	41	257	—	—	—
(B) LITERARY TEXTS	—	—	—	5	1	6	—	—	—
24. GEOGRAPHY, TRAVEL	—	—	—	112	23	135	—	—	—
25. HISTORY, BIOGRAPHY	1	—	1	174	12	186	—	—	—

SUBJECT GROUP GROUPE DE SUJETS GRUPO TEMATICO	FRENCH POLYNESIA (1977)			GUAM ‡ (1978)			NEW ZEALAND (1978)		
	A	B	A+B	A	B	A+B	A	B	A+B
TOTAL	4	8	12	12	19	31	978	1 101	2 079
1. GENERALITIES	—	—	—	—	—	—	45	39	84
2. PHILOSOPHY, PSYCHOLOGY	—	—	—	—	—	—	12	3	15
3. RELIGION, THEOLOGY	—	—	—	—	—	—	24	27	51
4. SOCIOLOGY, STATISTICS	1	3	4	—	—	—	38	33	71
5. POLITICAL SCIENCE	—	—	—	—	—	—	99	129	228
6. LAW, PUBLIC ADMIN.	—	—	—	—	—	—	84	83	167
7. MILITARY ART	—	—	—	—	—	—	3	—	3
8. EDUCATION, LEISURE	—	—	—	—	—	—	59	60	119
9. TRADE, TRANSPORT	—	3	3	—	—	—	22	32	54
10. ETHNOGRAPHY, FOLKLORE	—	—	—	—	—	—	4	2	6
11. MATHEMATICS	—	—	—	—	—	—	8	20	28
12. NATURAL SCIENCES	—	—	—	9	—	9	61	104	165
13. MEDICAL SCIENCES	—	—	—	—	—	—	26	27	53
14. ENGINEERING, CRAFTS	—	—	—	—	—	—	86	96	182
15. AGRICULTURE	2	—	2	3	19	22	63	58	121
16. DOMESTIC SCIENCE	—	—	—	—	—	—	30	9	39
17. MANAGEMENT, ADMIN.	—	1	1	—	—	—	33	41	74
18. PLANNING, ARCHITECTURE	—	—	—	—	—	—	28	48	76
19. PLASTIC ARTS	—	—	—	—	—	—	19	17	36
20. PERFORMING ARTS	—	—	—	—	—	—	13	38	51
21. GAMES, SPORTS	—	—	—	—	—	—	41	19	60
22. LINGUISTICS, PHILOLOGY	—	1	1	—	—	—	3	2	5
23. LITERATURE									
(A) HISTORY AND CRITICISM	—	—	—	—	—	—	6	5	11
(B) LITERARY TEXTS	1	—	1	—	—	—	56	122	178
24. GEOGRAPHY, TRAVEL	—	—	—	—	—	—	34	44	78
25. HISTORY, BIOGRAPHY	—	—	—	—	—	—	81	43	124

8.3 Number of titles by subject group
Nombre de titres par groupes de sujets
Número de obras por categorías de temas

SUBJECT GROUP / GROUPE DE SUJETS / GRUPO TEMATICO	NORFOLK ISLAND (1977)			PACIFIC ISLANDS ‡ (1978)			SAMOA (1977)		
	A	B	A+B	A	B	A+B	A	B	A+B
TOTAL	—	1	1	21	20	41	95	145	240
1. GENERALITIES	—	—	—	—	—	—	21	25	46
2. PHILOSOPHY, PSYCHOLOGY	—	—	—	—	—	—	2	5	7
3. RELIGION, THEOLOGY	—	—	—	—	—	—	10	20	30
4. SOCIOLOGY, STATISTICS	—	—	—	1	—	1	5	—	5
5. POLITICAL SCIENCE	—	—	—	2	6	8	—	—	—
6. LAW, PUBLIC ADMIN.	—	—	—	13	2	15	—	—	—
7. MILITARY ART	—	—	—	—	—	—	10	—	10
8. EDUCATION, LEISURE	—	—	—	3	12	15	15	10	25
9. TRADE, TRANSPORT	—	1	1	1	—	1	3	20	23
10. ETHNOGRAPHY, FOLKLORE	—	—	—	1	—	1	—	10	10
11. MATHEMATICS	—	—	—	—	—	—	5	—	5
12. NATURAL SCIENCES	—	—	—	—	—	—	5	15	20
13. MEDICAL SCIENCES	—	—	—	—	—	—	2	6	8
14. ENGINEERING, CRAFTS	—	—	—	—	—	—	—	—	—
15. AGRICULTURE	—	—	—	—	—	—	4	10	14
16. DOMESTIC SCIENCE	—	—	—	—	—	—	1	4	5
17. MANAGEMENT, ADMIN.	—	—	—	—	—	—	—	—	—
18. PLANNING, ARCHITECTURE	—	—	—	—	—	—	—	—	—
19. PLASTIC ARTS	—	—	—	—	—	—	5	—	5
20. PERFORMING ARTS	—	—	—	—	—	—	—	—	—
21. GAMES, SPORTS	—	—	—	—	—	—	2	10	12
22. LINGUISTICS, PHILOLOGY	—	—	—	—	—	—	—	—	—
23. LITERATURE (A) HISTORY AND CRITICISM	—	—	—	—	—	—	—	—	—
(B) LITERARY TEXTS	—	—	—	—	—	—	—	—	—
24. GEOGRAPHY, TRAVEL	—	—	—	—	—	—	—	—	—
25. HISTORY, BIOGRAPHY	—	—	—	—	—	—	5	10	15

SUBJECT GROUP / GROUPE DE SUJETS / GRUPO TEMATICO	TONGA (1978)			U.S.S.R.	U.S.S.R. ‡ (1977)		
	A	B	A+B		A	B	A+B
TOTAL	20	190	210		54 693	30 702	85 395
1. GENERALITIES	—	—	—		1 144	1 047	2 191
2. PHILOSOPHY, PSYCHOLOGY	—	—	—		975	280	1 255
3. RELIGION, THEOLOGY	—	60	60		152	85	237
4. SOCIOLOGY, STATISTICS	—	40	40		551	181	732
5. POLITICAL SCIENCE	—	20	20		6 357	3 657	10 014
6. LAW, PUBLIC ADMIN.	—	—	—		1 164	737	1 901
7. MILITARY ART	—	—	—		1 647	276	1 923
8. EDUCATION, LEISURE	5	20	25		2 609	1 514	4 123
9. TRADE, TRANSPORT	—	10	10		342	208	550
10. ETHNOGRAPHY, FOLKLORE	—	10	10		—	—	—
11. MATHEMATICS	—	—	—		1 116	178	1 294
12. NATURAL SCIENCES	—	—	—		5 533	2 586	8 119
13. MEDICAL SCIENCES	—	20	20		2 491	1 421	3 912
14. ENGINEERING, CRAFTS	—	—	—		10 127	11 566	21 693
15. AGRICULTURE	—	—	—		3 149	1 656	4 805
16. DOMESTIC SCIENCE	—	10	10		168	192	360
17. MANAGEMENT, ADMIN.	—	—	—		3 327	1 807	5 134
18. PLANNING, ARCHITECTURE	—	—	—		1 121	717	1 838
19. PLASTIC ARTS	—	—	—		./.	./.	./.
20. PERFORMING ARTS	—	—	—		./.	./.	./.
21. GAMES, SPORTS	—	—	—		464	290	754
22. LINGUISTICS, PHILOLOGY	—	—	—		2 164	196	2 360
23. LITERATURE (A) HISTORY AND CRITICISM	—	—	—		1 354	128	1 482
(B) LITERARY TEXTS	—	—	—		6 680	1 668	8 348
24. GEOGRAPHY, TRAVEL	5	—	5		538	94	632
25. HISTORY, BIOGRAPHY	10	—	10		1 520	218	1 738

Number of titles by subject group 8.3
Nombre de titres par groupes de sujets
Número de obras por categorías de temas

SUBJECT GROUP GROUPE DE SUJETS GRUPO TEMATICO	BYELORUSSIAN S.S.R. (1978)			UKRAINIAN S.S.R. ‡ (1977)		
	A	B	A+B	A	B	A+B
TOTAL	1 665	953	2 618	5 045	3 385	8 430
1. GENERALITIES	62	62	124	126	182	308
2. PHILOSOPHY, PSYCHOLOGY	40	17	57	58	66	124
3. RELIGION, THEOLOGY	8	–	8	13	19	32
4. SOCIOLOGY, STATISTICS	20	15	35	69	53	122
5. POLITICAL SCIENCE	208	170	378	699	555	1 254
6. LAW, PUBLIC ADMIN.	61	17	78	84	100	184
7. MILITARY ART	4	8	12	17	26	43
8. EDUCATION, LEISURE	136	88	224	211	229	440
9. TRADE, TRANSPORT	12	12	24	35	45	80
10. ETHNOGRAPHY, FOLKLORE	–	–	–	–	–	–
11. MATHEMATICS	30	8	38	119	74	193
12. NATURAL SCIENCES	131	27	158	466	335	801
13. MEDICAL SCIENCES	58	57	115	272	205	477
14. ENGINEERING, CRAFTS	205	160	365	962	780	1 742
15. AGRICULTURE	150	107	257	285	185	470
16. DOMESTIC SCIENCE	22	24	46	16	16	32
17. MANAGEMENT, ADMIN.	79	83	162	295	185	480
18. PLANNING, ARCHITECTURE	3	–	3	79	98	177
19. PLASTIC ARTS	7	9	16	./.	./.	./.
20. PERFORMING ARTS	12	7	19	./.	./.	./.
21. GAMES, SPORTS	13	3	16	40	14	54
22. LINGUISTICS, PHILOLOGY	86	17	103	195	31	226
23. LITERATURE						
(A) HISTORY AND CRITICISM	40	7	47	111	25	136
(B) LITERARY TEXTS	214	42	256	703	123	826
24. GEOGRAPHY, TRAVEL	16	1	17	50	5	55
25. HISTORY, BIOGRAPHY	48	12	60	140	34	174

GENERAL NOTE/NOTE GENERALE/NOTA GENERAL:
E—> DATA SHOWN IN THIS TABLE REFER TO FIRST
EDITIONS AND RE–EDITIONS.
THE CLASSIFICATION GIVEN BELOW, WHICH IS BASED
UPON THE UNIVERSAL DECIMAL CLASSIFICATION (UDC)
IS TAKEN FROM THE RECOMMENDATION CONCERNING THE
INTERNATIONAL STANDARDIZATION OF STATISTICS RELA-
TING TO BOOK PRODUCTION AND PERIODICALS (THE COR-
RESPONDING UDC HEADINGS ARE SHOWN IN PARENTHESES):
1. GENERALITIES (0)
2. PHILOSOPHY, PSYCHOLOGY (1)
3. RELIGION, THEOLOGY (2)
4. SOCIOLOGY, STATISTICS (30–31)
5. POLITICS, ECONOMICS (32–33)
6. LAW, PUBLIC ADMINISTRATION, SOCIAL RELIEF
AND WELFARE, INSURANCE (34, 351–354, 36)
7. MILITARY ART AND SCIENCE (335–359)
8. EDUCATION, TEACHING, TRAINING,
LEISURE (37)
9. TRADE, COMMUNICATION, TRANSPORT,
TOURISM (38)
10. ETHNOGRAPHY, CULTURAL ANTHROPOLOGY,
(CUSTOMS, FOLKLORE, MORES, TRADITION (39)
11. MATHEMATICS (51)
12. NATURAL SCIENCE (52–59)
13. MEDICAL SCIENCES, PUBLIC HEALTH (61)
14. ENGINEERING, TECHNOLOGY,, INDUSTRIES,
TRADES AND CRAFTS (62, 66–69)
15. AGRICULTURE, FORESTRY, STOCKBREEDING,
HUNTING AND FISHERIES (63)
16. DOMESTIC SCIENCE (64)
17. MANAGEMENT, ADMINISTRATION AND ORGANIZA-
TION (65)
18. PHYSICAL PLANNING, TOWN AND COUNTRY
PLANNING, ARCHITECTURE (70–72)
19. PLASTIC AND GRAPHIC ARTS, PHOTOGRAPHY,
(73–77)
20. MUSIC, PERFORMING ART, THEATRE, FILM
AND CINEMA (78, 791–792)
21. GAMES AND SPORT (793–799)

22. LANGUAGES, LINGUISTICS, PHILOLOGY (80–81)
23. LITERATURE (82)
(A) HISTORY OF LITERATURE AND LITERARY
CRITICISM
(B) LITERARY TEXTS
24. GEOGRAPHY (91)
25. HISTORY, BIOGRAPHY (92–99)
FR–> LES DONNEES PRESENTEES DANS CE TABLEAU SE
REFERENT AUX PREMIERES EDITIONS ET AUX REEDITIONS.
LA CLASSIFICATION CI–APRES, FONDEE SUR LA CLASSI-
FICATION DECIMALE UNIVERSELLE (CDU) EST EXTRAITE
DE LA RECOMMANDATION CONCERNANT LA NORMALISATION
INTERNATIONALE DES STATISTIQUES DE L'EDITION DE
LIVRES ET DE PERIODIQUES (ENTRE PARENTHESES:
INDICES CORRESPONDANTS DE LA CDU):
1. GENERALITES (0)
2. PHILOSOPHIE, PSYCHOLOGIE (1)
3. RELIGION, THEOLOGIE (2)
4. SOCIOLOGIE, STATISTIQUE (30–31)
5. SCIENCES POLITIQUES, SCIENCES
ECONOMIQUES (32–33)
6. DROIT, ADMINISTRATION PUBLIQUE,
PREVOYANCE ET AIDE SOCIALE, ASSURANCE
(34, 351–354, 36)
7. ART ET SCIENCE MILITAIRE (355–359)
8. EDUCATION, ENSEIGNEMENT, FORMATION,
LOISIRS (37)
9. COMMERCE, COMMUNICATION, TRANSPORT,
TOURISME (38)
10. ETHNOGRAPHIE, ANTHROPOLOGIE CULTURELLE
(COUTUMES, FOLKLORE, MOEURS,
TRADITION) (39)
11. MATHEMATIQUES (51)
12. SCIENCES NATURELLES (52–59)
13. SCIENCES MEDICALES, SANTE PUBLIQUE (61)
14. ART DE L'INGENIEUR, TECHNOLOGIE,
INDUSTRIES, METIERS (62, 66–69)
15. AGRICULTURE, SYLVICULTURE, ELEVAGE,
CHASSE ET PECHE (63)
16. SCIENCE MENAGERE (64)

8.3   Number of titles by subject group
       Nombre de titres par groupes de sujets
       Número de obras por categorías de temas

GENERAL NOTE/NOTE GENERALE/NOTA GENERAL (CONT.):
  17. GESTION, ADMINISTRATION ET
      ORGANISATION (65)
  18. AMENAGEMENT DU TERRITOIRE, URBANISME,
      ARCHITECTURE (70–72)
  19. ARTS GRAPHIQUES ET PLASTIQUES,
      PHOTOGRAPHIE (73–77)
  20. MUSIQUE, ARTS DU SPECTACLE, THEATRE,
      FILM ET CINEMA (78, 791–792)
  21. JEUX ET SPORTS (793–799)
  22. LANGUES, LINGUISTIQUE, PHILOLOGIE (80–81)
  23. LITTERATURE (82)
      (A) HISTOIRE ET CRITIQUE LITTERAIRES
      (B) TEXTES LITTERAIRES
  24. GEOGRAPHIE (91)
  25. HISTOIRE, BIOGRAPHIE (92–99)

ESP> LOS DATOS PRESENTADOS EN ESTE CUADRO SE
REFIEREN A LAS PRIMERAS EDICIONES Y REEDICIONES.
LA SIGUIENTE CLASIFICACION, BASADA EN LA CLASIFI-
CACION DECIMAL UNIVERSAL (CDU), ESTA TOMADA DE
LA RECOMENDACION SOBRE LA NORMALIZACION INTERNA-
CIONAL DE LAS ESTADISTICAS RELATIVAS A LA EDICION
DE LIBROS Y PUBLICACIONES PERIODICAS (SE INDICAN
ENTRE PARENTESIS LOS INDICES CORRESPONDIENTES DE
LA CDU):
  1. GENERALIDADES (0)
  2. FILOSOFIA, PSICOLOGIA (1)
  3. RELIGION, TEOLOGIA (2)
  4. SOCIOLOGIA, ESTADISTICA (30–31)
  5. CIENCIAS POLITICAS, CIENCIAS
     ECONOMICAS (32–33)
  6. DERECHO, ADMINISTRACION PUBLICA,
     PREVISION Y ASISTENCIA SOCIAL, SEGUROS
     (34, 351–354, 36)
  7. ARTE Y CIENCIA MILITAR (355–359)
  8. EDUCACION, ENSEÑANZA, FORMACION,
     DISTRACCIONES (37)
  9. COMERCIO, COMUNICACIONES, TRANSPORTES,
     TURISMO (38)
  10. ETNOGRAFIA, ANTROPOLOGIA CULTURAL
      (COSTUMBRES, FOLKLORE, HABITOS,
      TRADICION) (39)
  11. MATEMATICAS (51)
  12. CIENCIAS NATURALES (52–59)
  13. CIENCIAS MEDICAS, SANIDAD (61)
  14. INGENIERIA, TECNOLOGIA, INDUSTRIAS,
      OFICIOS (62, 66–69)
  15. AGRICULTURA, SILVICULTURA, GANADERIA,
      CAZA Y PESCA (63)
  16. CIENCIA DOMESTICA (64)
  17. GESTION, ADMINISTRACION Y ORGANIZACION
      (65)
  18. ACONDICIONAMIENTO DEL TERRITORIO,
      URBANISMO, ARQUITECTURA (70–72)
  19. ARTES PLASTICAS Y GRAFICAS, FOTOGRAFIA
      (73–77)
  20. MUSICA, ARTES DEL ESPECTACULO, TEATRO,
      PELICULAS Y CINE (78, 791–792)
  21. JUEGOS Y DEPORTES (793–799)
  22. IDIOMAS, LINGUISTICA, FILOLOGIA (80–81)
  23. LITERATURA (82)
      (A) HISTORIA Y CRITICA LITERARIAS
      (B) TEXTOS LITERARIOS
  24. GEOGRAFIA (91)
  25. HISTORIA, BIOGRAFIA (92–99)

CONGO:
  E—> ALL FIRST EDITIONS. WORKS OF GROUP 23A
INCLUDE THOSE OF GROUP 23B.
  FR—> TOUS LES OUVRAGES RECENSES SONT DES PRE-
MIERES EDITIONS. LES OUVRAGES DU GROUPE 23A
INCLUENT CEUX DU GROUPE 23B.
  ESP> TODAS LAS OBRAS CONSIDERADAS SON PRIMERAS
EDICIONES. LAS OBRAS DEL GRUPO 23A QUEDAN INCLUI-
DAS EN EL GRUPO 23B.

EGYPT:
  E—> FIGURES ARE PRELIMINARY. WORKS OF GROUPS
5 TO 10 ARE INCLUDED IN GROUP 4; 12 IN GROUP 11;
14 TO 17 IN GROUP 13; 19 TO 21 IN GROUP 18; 23B
IN GROUP 23A; 25 IN GROUP 24.
  FR—> LES CHIFFRES SONT PROVISOIRES. LES OUVRA-
GES DES GROUPES 5 A 10 SONT INCLUS DANS LE GROUPE
4; LE GROUPE 12 DANS LE GROUPE 11; 14 A 17 DANS
LE GROUPE 13; 19 A 21 DANS LE GROUPE 18; 23B DANS
LE GROUPE 23A; 25 DANS LE GROUPE 24.
  ESP> DATOS PRELIMINARES. LAS OBRAS DE LOS GRU-
POS 5 A 10 QUEDAN INCLUIDAS EN EL GRUPO 4; LAS
DEL GRUPO 12 EN EL GRUPO 11; LAS DE LOS GRUPOS 14
A 17 EN EL GRUPO 13; LAS DE LOS GRUPOS 19 A 21 EN
EL GRUPO 18; LAS DEL GRUPO 23B EN EL GRUPO 23A;
LAS DEL GRUPO 25 EN EL GRUPO 24.

ETHIOPIA:
  E—> ALL FIRST EDITIONS. SCHOOL TEXTBOOKS (119)
AND CHILDREN'S BOOKS (2) ARE INCLUDED IN THE
TOTAL BUT NOT IDENTIFIED IN THE 25 GROUPS. WORKS
OF GROUPS 5 TO 10 ARE INCLUDED IN GROUP 4; 12 IN
GROUP 11; 14 TO 17 IN GROUP 13; 19 TO 21 IN GROUP
18; 25 IN GROUP 24; 23B IN 23A.
  FR—> TOUS LES OUVRAGES RECENSES SONT DES PRE-
MIERES EDITIONS. LES MANUELS SCOLAIRES (119) ET
LES LIVRES POUR ENFANTS (2) SONT COMPRIS DANS LE
TOTAL MAIS NE SONT PAS REPARTIS ENTRE LES 25
GROUPES. LES OUVRAGES DES GROUPES 5 A 10 SONT
INCLUS DANS LE GROUPE 4; 12 DANS LE GROUPE 11;
14 A 17 DANS LE GROUPE 13; 19 A 21 DANS LE GROUPE
18; 25 DANS LE GROUPE 24; 23B DANS LE GROUPE 23A.
  ESP> TODAS LAS OBRAS CONSIDERADAS SON PRIMERAS
EDICIONES. LOS MANUALES ESCOLARES (119) Y LOS
LIBROS PARA NIÑOS (2) QUEDAN COMPRENDIDOS EN EL
TOTAL PERO NO SE DESGLOSAN ENTRE LOS 25 GRUPOS.
LAS OBRAS DE LOS GRUPOS 5 A 10 QUEDAN INCLUIDAS
EN EL GRUPO 4; LAS DEL GRUPO 12 EN EL GRUPO 11;
LAS DE LOS GRUPOS 14 A 17 EN EL GRUPO 13; LAS DE
LOS GRUPOS 19 A 21 EN EL GRUPO 18; LAS DEL GRUPO
25 EN EL GRUPO 24; LAS DEL GRUPO 23B EN EL GRUPO
23A.

GAMBIA:
  E—> ALL FIRST EDITIONS.
  FR—> TOUS LES OUVRAGES RECENSES SONT DES PRE-
MIERES EDITIONS.
  ESP> TODAS LAS OBRAS CONSIDERADAS SON PRIMERAS
EDICIONES.

MADAGASCAR:
  E—> WORKS OF GROUP 23B ARE INCLUDED IN GROUP
23A.
  FR—> LES OUVRAGES DU GROUPE 23B SONT INCLUS
DANS LE GROUPE 23A.
  ESP> LAS OBRAS DEL GRUPO 23B QUEDAN INCLUIDAS
EN EL GRUPO 23A.

MAURITIUS:
  E—> ALL FIRST EDITIONS.
  FR—> TOUS LES OUVRAGES RECENSES SONT DES PRE-
MIERES EDITIONS.
  ESP> TODAS LAS OBRAS CONSIDERADAS SON PRIMERAS
EDICIONES.

NIGER:
  E—> WORKS OF GROUP 23B ARE INCLUDED IN GROUP
23A.
  FR—> LES OUVRAGES DU GROUPE 23B SONT INCLUS
DANS LE GROUPE 23A.
  ESP> LAS OBRAS DEL GRUPO 23B QUEDAN INCLUIDAS
EN EL GRUPO 23A.

Number of titles by subject group   8.3
Nombre de titres par groupes de sujets
Número de obras por categorías de temas

SENEGAL:
  E—> ALL FIRST EDITIONS.
  FR—> TOUS LES OUVRAGES RECENSES SONT DES PRE-
MIERES EDITIONS.
  ESP> TODAS LAS OBRAS CONSIDERADAS SON PRIMERAS
EDICIONES.

SEYCHELLES:
  E—> ALL FIRST EDITIONS.
  FR—> TOUS LES OUVRAGES RECENSES SONT DES PRE-
MIERES EDITIONS.
  ESP> TODAS LAS OBRAS CONSIDERADAS SON PRIMERAS
EDICIONES.

SIERRA LEONE:
  E—> ALL FIRST EDITIONS.
  FR—> TOUS LES OUVRAGES RECENSES SONT DES PRE-
MIERES EDITIONS.
  ESP> TODAS LAS OBRAS CONSIDERADAS SON PRIMERAS
EDICIONES.

SUDAN:
  E—> DATA REFER TO SCHOOL TEXTBOOKS ONLY.
  FR—> LES DONNEES NE TIENNENT COMPTE QUE DES
MANUELS SCOLAIRES.
  ESP> LOS DATOS SE REFIEREN A LOS MANUALES ESCO-
LARES SOLAMENTE.

UNITED REPUBLIC OF CAMEROON:
  E—> THE DATA REFER TO FIRST EDITIONS OF SCHOOL
TEXTBOOKS ONLY.
  FR—> LES DONNEES SE RAPPORTENT AUX PREMIERES
EDITIONS DES MANUELS SCOLAIRES SEULEMENT.
  ESP> LOS DATOS SE REFIEREN A LAS PRIMERAS EDI-
CIONES DE LOS MANUALES ESCOLARES SOLAMENTE.

UNITED REPUBLIC OF TANZANIA:
  E—> WORKS OF GROUP 23B ARE INCLUDED IN GROUP
23A.
  FR—> LES OUVRAGES DU GROUPE 23B SONT INCLUS
DANS LE GROUPE 23A.
  ESP> LAS OBRAS DEL GRUPO 23B QUEDAN INCLUIDAS
EN EL GRUPO 23A.

ZAIRE:
  E—> WORKS OF GROUPS 5 TO 10 ARE INCLUDED IN
GROUP 4; 12 IN GROUP 11; 14 TO 17 IN GROUP 13;
19 TO 21 IN GROUP 18; 22 AND 23B IN GROUP 23A;
25 IN GROUP 24.
  FR—> LES OUVRAGES DES GROUPES 5 A 10 SONT IN-
CLUS DANS LE GROUPE 4; 12 DANS LE GROUPE 11;
14 A 17 DANS LE GROUPE 13; 19 A 21 DANS LE GROUPE
18; 22 ET 23B DANS LE GROUPE 23A; 25 DANS LE
GROUPE 24.
  ESP> LAS OBRAS DE LOS GRUPOS 5 A 10 QUEDAN
INCLUIDAS EN EL GRUPO 4; 12 EN EL GRUPO 11; 14 A
17 EN EL GRUPO 13; 19 A 21 EN EL GRUPO 18; 22 Y
23B EN EL GRUPO 23A; 25 EN EL GRUPO 24.

ZAMBIA:
  E—> SCHOOL TEXTBOOKS (31) AND CHILDREN'S
BOOKS (2) ARE INCLUDED IN THE TOTAL BUT NOT
IDENTIFIED IN THE 25 GROUPS.
  FR—> LES MANUELS SCOLAIRES (31) ET LES LIVRES
POUR ENFANTS (2) SONT COMPRIS DANS LE TOTAL MAIS
NE SONT PAS REPARTIS ENTRE LES 25 GROUPES.
ESP> LOS MANUALES ESCOLARES (31) Y LOS LIBROS
PARA NIÑOS (2) QUEDAN COMPRENDIDOS EN EL TOTAL
PERO NO SE DESGLOSAN ENTRE LOS 25 GRUPOS.

BARBADOS:
  E—> ALL FIRST EDITIONS. WORKS OF GROUP 23B ARE
INCLUDED IN GROUP 23A.
  FR—> TOUS LES OUVRAGES RECENSES SONT DES PRE-
MIERES EDITIONS. LES OUVRAGES DU GROUPE 23B SONT
INCLUS DANS LE GROUPE 23A.

BARBADOS (CONT.)
  ESP> TODAS LAS OBRAS CONSIDERADAS SON PRIMERAS
EDICIONES. LAS OBRAS DEL GRUPO 23B QUEDAN INCLUI-
DAS EN EL GRUPO 23A.

CANADA:
  E—> DATA DO NOT INCLUDE GOVERNMENT PUBLI-
CATIONS, BUT INCLUDE FOR THE FIRST TIME, UNIVER-
SITY THESES (4,369). WORKS OF GROUP 19 AND 20 ARE
INCLUDED IN GROUP 18.
  FR—> LES DONNEES NE TIENNENT PAS COMPTE DES
PUBLICATIONS OFFICIELLES, MAIS INCLUENT POUR LA
PREMIERE FOIS LES THESES UNIVERSITAIRES (4 369).
LES OUVRAGES DES GROUPES 19 ET 20 SONT INCLUS
DANS LE GROUPE 18.
  ESP—> LOS DATOS EXCLUYEN LAS PUBLICACIONES
OFICIALES, PERO INCLUYEN POR PRIMERA VEZ, LAS
TESIS UNIVERSITARIAS (4 369). LAS OBRAS DE LOS
GRUPOS 19 Y 20 QUEDAN INCLUIDAS EN EL GRUPO 18.

DOMINICAN REPUBLIC:
  E—> ALL FIRST EDITIONS. WORKS OF GROUP 23B
ARE INCLUDED IN GROUP 23A.
  FR—> TOUS LES OUVRAGES RECENSES SONT DES PRE-
MIERES EDITIONS. LES OUVRAGES DU GROUPE 23B SONT
INCLUS DANS LE GROUPE 23A.
  ESP> TODAS LAS OBRAS CONSIDERADAS SON PRIMERAS
EDICIONES. LAS OBRAS DEL GRUPO 23B QUEDAN INCLUI-
DAS EN EL GRUPO 23A.

JAMAICA:
  E—> ALL FIRST EDITIONS. WORKS OF GROUP 23B ARE
INCLUDED IN GROUP 23A.
  FR—> TOUS LES OUVRAGES RECENSES SONT DES PRE-
MIERES EDITIONS. LES OUVRAGES DU GROUPE 23B SONT
INCLUS DANS LE GROUPE 23A.
  ESP> TODAS LAS OBRAS CONSIDERADAS SON PRIMERAS
EDICIONES. LAS OBRAS DEL GRUPO 23B QUEDAN INCLUI-
DAS EN EL GRUPO 23A.

NETHERLANDS ANTILLES:
  E—> WORKS OF GROUP 23B ARE INCLUDED IN THE
GROUP 23A.
  FR—> LES OUVRAGES DU GROUPE 23B SONT INCLUS
DANS LE GROUPE 23A.
  ESP—> LAS OBRAS DEL GRUPO 23B QUEDAN INCLUIDAS
EN EL GRUPO 23A.

TRINIDAD AND TOBAGO:
  E—> UNIVERSITY THESES ONLY.
  FR—> THESES UNIVERSITAIRES SEULEMENT.
  ESP> TESIS UNIVERSITARIAS SOLAMENTE.

UNITED STATES OF AMERICA:
  E—> DATA INCLUDE FEDERAL GOVERNMENT PUBLI-
CATIONS (14,814 , OF WHICH 7,220 PAMPHLETS), UNI-
VERSITY THESES (31,629) AND 2,911 JUVENILE TITLES
FOR WHICH THE SUBJECT BREAKDOWN IS NOT AVAILABLE.
WORKS OF GROUP 23B ARE INCLUDED IN GROUP 23A.
  FR—> LES DONNEES COMPRENNENT LES PUBLICATIONS
DU GOUVERNEMENT FEDERAL (14 814, DONT 7 220 BRO-
CHURES), LES THESES UNIVERSITAIRES (31 629) ET
2 911 TITRES DE ROMANS POUR LES JEUNES POUR LES-
QUELS LA REPARTITION PAR SUJET N'EST PAS DISPO-
NIBLE. LES OUVRAGES DU GROUPE 23B SONT INCLUS
DANS LE GROUPE 23A.
  ESP> LOS DATOS INCLUYEN LAS PUBLICACIONES DEL
GOBIERNO FEDERAL (14 814, DE LAS CUALES 7 220
FOLLETOS), LAS TESIS UNIVERSITARIAS (31 629) Y
2 911 TITULOS DE NOVELAS PARA NIÑOS Y ADOLESCEN-
TES CUYA DISTRIBUCION POR TEMAS NO SE CONOCE.
LAS OBRAS DEL GRUPO 23B QUEDAN INCLUIDAS EN EL
GRUPO 23A.

8.3 **Number of titles by subject group**
Nombre de titres par groupes de sujets
Número de obras por categorías de temas

ARGENTINA:
  E—> WORKS OF GROUPS 19 AND 20 ARE INCLUDED
IN GROUP 18; 3 IN GROUP 2; 5 IN GROUP 4; 22 AND
23A IN 23B.
  FR—> LES OUVRAGES DES GROUPES 19 ET 20 SONT
INCLUS DANS LE GROUPE 18; 3 DANS LE GROUPE 2;
5 DANS LE GROUPE 4; 22 ET 23A DANS LE GROUPE 23B.
  ESP> LAS OBRAS DE LOS GRUPOS 19 Y 20 QUEDAN
INCLUIDAS EN EL GRUPO 18; LAS DEL GRUPO 3 EN EL
GRUPO 2; LAS DEL GRUPO 5 EN EL GRUPO 4; LAS DE LOS
GRUPOS 22 Y 23A EN EL GRUPO 23B.

BRAZIL:
  E—> WORKS OF GROUP 23B ARE INCLUDED IN GROUP
23A.
  FR—> LES OUVRAGES DU GROUPE 23B SONT INCLUS DANS
LE GROUPE 23A.
  ESP> LAS OBRAS DEL GRUPO 23B QUEDAN INCLUIDAS
EN EL GRUPO 23A.

GUYANA:
  E—> WORKS OF GROUP 23B ARE INCLUDED IN GROUP
23A.
  FR—> LES OUVRAGES DU GROUPE 23B SONT INCLUS DANS
LE GROUPE 23A.
  ESP> LAS OBRAS DEL GRUPO 23B QUEDAN INCLUIDAS
EN EL GRUPO 23A.

PERU:
  E—> WORKS OF GROUP 23B ARE INCLUDED IN GROUP
23A.
  FR—> LES OUVRAGES DU GROUPE 23B SONT INCLUS DANS
LE GROUPE 23A.
  ESP> LAS OBRAS DEL GRUPO 23B QUEDAN INCLUIDAS
EN EL GRUPO 23A.

VENEZUELA:
  E—> WORKS OF GROUP 23B ARE INCLUDED IN GROUP
23A.
  FR—> LES OUVRAGES DU GROUPE 23B SONT INCLUS DANS
LE GROUPE 23A.
  ESP> LAS OBRAS DEL GRUPO 23B QUEDAN INCLUIDAS
EN EL GRUPO 23A.

AFGHANISTAN:
  E—> WORKS OF GROUP 23B ARE INCLUDED IN GROUP
23A.
  FR—> LES OUVRAGES DU GROUPE 23B SONT INCLUS DANS
LE GROUPE 23A.
  ESP> LAS OBRAS DEL GRUPO 23B QUEDAN INCLUIDAS
EN EL GRUPO 23A.

CHINA:
  E—> WORKS OF GROUPS 1, 3 TO 7, 17 AND 25 ARE
INCLUDED IN GROUP 2; 21 AND 24 IN GROUP 8; 18 TO
20 AND 22 IN GROUP 23; 11 TO 16 IN GROUP 9. SCHOOL
TEXTBOOKS AND CHILDREN'S BOOKS (4,614) ARE INCLU-
DED IN THE TOTAL BUT ARE NOT IDENTIFIED IN THE 25
GROUPS.
  FR—> LES OUVRAGES DU GROUPE 1, DES GROUPES 3 A 7
ET 17 A 25 SONT INCLUS DANS LE GROUPE 2; 21 ET 24
DANS LE GROUPE 8; 18 A 20 ET LE GROUPE 22 DANS LE
GROUPE 23; 11 A 16 DANS LE GROUPE 9. LES MANUELS
SCOLAIRES ET LES LIVRES POUR ENFANTS (4 614) SONT
COMPRIS DANS LE TOTAL MAIS NE SONT PAS REPARTIS
ENTRE LES 25 GROUPES.
ESP> LAS OBRAS DE LOS GRUPOS 1, 3 A 7 Y 17 A 25
QUEDAN INCLUIDAS EN EL GRUPO 2; LAS DE LOS GRUPOS
21 Y 24 EN EL GRUPO 8; LAS DE LOS GRUPOS 18 A 20
Y EL GRUPO 22 EN EL GRUPO 23; LAS DE LOS GRUPOS
11 A 16 EN EL GRUPO 9. LOS MANUALES ESCOLARES Y
LOS LIBROS PARA NIÑOS (4 614) QUEDAN COMPRENDIDOS
EN EL TOTAL PERO NO SE DESGLOSAN ENTRE LOS 25
GRUPOS.

INDIA:
  E—> WORKS OF GROUP 23B ARE INCLUDED IN GROUP
23A.

INDIA (CONT.):
  FR—> LES OUVRAGES DU GROUPE 23B SONT INCLUS
DANS LE GROUPE 23A.
  ESP> LAS OBRAS DEL GRUPO 23B QUEDAN INCLUIDAS
EN EL GRUPO 23A.

IRAQ:
  E—> WORKS OF GROUP 23B ARE INCLUDED IN GROUP
23A.
  FR—> LES OUVRAGES DU GROUPE 23B SONT INCLUS
DANS LE GROUPE 23A.
  ESP> LAS OBRAS DEL GRUPO 23B QUEDAN INCLUIDAS
EN EL GRUPO 23A.

ISRAEL:
  E—> DATA DO NOT INCLUDE UNIVERSITY THESES.
SCHOOL TEXTBOOKS (197) AND CHILDREN'S BOOKS (231)
ARE INCLUDED IN THE TOTAL BUT NOT IDENTIFIED IN
THE 25 GROUPS. WORKS OF GROUP 23A ARE INCLUDED
IN GROUP 23B.
  FR—> LES DONNEES N'INCLUENT PAS LES THESES
UNIVERSITAIRES. LES MANUELS SCOLAIRES (197) ET
LES LIVRES POUR ENFANTS (231) SONT INCLUS DANS LE
TOTAL MAIS NE SONT PAS REPARTIS ENTRE LES 25
GROUPES.LES OUVRAGES DU GROUPE 23A SONT INCLUS
DANS LE GROUPE 23B.
  ESP> LOS DATOS EXCLUYEN LAS TESIS UNIVERSITA-
RIAS. LOS MANUALES ESCOLARES (197) Y LOS LIBROS
PARA NIÑOS (231) QUEDAN INCLUIDOS EN EL TOTAL
PERO NO SE DESGLOSAN ENTRE LOS 25 GRUPOS.LAS
OBRAS DEL GRUPO 23A QUEDAN INCLUIDAS EN EL GRUPO
23B.

JORDAN:
  E—> THE DATA ARE ALL FIRST EDITIONS AND REFER
TO THE EAST BANK ONLY. WORKS OF GROUP 23B ARE
INCLUDED IN GROUP 23A.
  FR—> LES DONNEES SE REFERENT A LA RIVE ORIEN-
TALE SEULEMENT. TOUS LES OUVRAGES RECENSES SONT
DES PREMIERES EDITIONS. LES OUVRAGES DU GROUPE
23B SONT INCLUS DANS LE GROUPE 23A.
  ESP> LAS DATOS SE REFIEREN A LA ORILLA ORIENTAL
SOLAMENTE. TODAS LAS OBRAS CONSIDERADAS SON PRI-
MERAS EDICIONES. LAS OBRAS DEL GRUPO 23B QUEDAN
INCLUIDAS EN EL GRUPO 23A.

KOREA, REPUBLIC OF:
  E—> SCHOOL TEXTBOOKS (687) AND CHILDREN'S
BOOKS (1,028) ARE INCLUDED IN THE TOTAL BUT NOT
IDENTIFIED IN THE 25 GROUPS.
  FR—> LES MANUELS SCOLAIRES (687) ET LES LIVRES
POUR ENFANTS (1 028) SONT INCLUS DANS LE TOTAL
MAIS NE SONT PAS REPARTIS ENTRE LES 25 GROUPES.
  ESP> LOS MANUALES ESCOLARES (687) Y LOS LIBROS
PARA NINOS(1 028) QUEDAN INCLUIDOS EN EL TOTAL
PERO NO SE DESGLOSAN ENTRE LOS 25 GRUPOS.

LAO PEOPLE'S DEMOCRATIC REPUBLIC:
  E—> ALL FIRST EDITIONS.
  FR—> TOUS LES OUVRAGES RECENSES SONT DES PRE-
MIERES EDITIONS.
  ESP> TODAS LAS OBRAS CONSIDERADAS SON PRIME-
RAS EDICIONES.

MALAYSIA:
  E—> WORKS OF GROUP 23B ARE INCLUDED IN GROUP
23A.
  FR—> LES OUVRAGES DU GROUPE 23B SONT INCLUS
DANS LE GROUPE 23A.
  ESP> LAS OBRAS DEL GRUPO 23B QUEDAN INCLUI-
DAS EN EL GRUPO 23A.

MALDIVES:
  E—> ALL FIRST EDITIONS.
  FR—> TOUS LES OUVRAGES RECENSES SONT DES PRE-
MIERES EDITIONS.
  ESP> TODAS LAS OBRAS CONSIDERADAS SON PRIME-
RAS EDICIONES.

Number of titles by subject group   8.3
Nombre de titres par groupes de sujets
Número de obras por categorías de temas

PAKISTAN:
E—> WORKS OF GROUP 23B ARE INCLUDED IN GROUP 23A.
FR—> LES OUVRAGES DU GROUPE 23B SONT COMPRIS
DANS LE GROUPE 23A.
ESP> LAS OBRAS DEL GRUPO 23B QUEDAN INCLUIDAS
EN EL GRUPO 23A.

PHILIPPINES:
E—> THE FIGURES REPRESENT ONLY THOSE BOOKS
WHICH HAVE BEEN RECEIVED IN THE NATIONAL LIBRARY.
FR—> LES CHIFFRES REPRESENTENT SEULEMENT LES
LIVRES ENREGISTRES A LA BIBLIOTHEQUE NATIONALE.
ESP> LOS DATOS SOLO SE REFIEREN A LAS OBRAS
INSCRITAS EN EL REPERTORIO DE LA BIBLIOTECA
NACIONAL.

SINGAPORE:
E—> THE DATA DO NOT INCLUDE GOVERNMENT PUBLI-
CATIONS.
FR—> LES DONNEES NE TIENNENT PAS COMPTE DES
PUBLICATIONS OFFICIELLES.
ESP> LOS DATOS EXCLUYEN LAS PUBLICACIONES
OFICIALES.

SRI LANKA:
E—> WORKS OF GROUPS 19 AND 20 ARE INCLUDED
IN GROUP 18.
FR—> LES OUVRAGES DES GROUPES 19 ET 20 SONT
INCLUS DANS LE GROUPE 18.
ESP> LAS OBRAS DE LOS GRUPOS 19 Y 20 QUEDAN
INCLUIDAS EN EL GRUPO 18.

SYRIAN ARAB REPUBLIC:
E—> SCHOOL TEXTBOOKS (1) AND CHILDREN'S
BOOKS (11) ARE INCLUDED IN THE TOTAL BUT ARE NOT
IDENTIFIED IN THE 25 GROUPS.
FR—> LES MANUELS SCOLAIRES (1) ET LES LIVRES
POUR ENFANTS (11) SONT COMPRIS DANS LE TOTAL MAIS
NE SONT PAS REPARTIS ENTRE LES 25 GROUPES.
ESP> LAS MANUALES ESCOLARES (1) Y LOS LIBROS
PARA NIÑOS (11) QUEDAN INCLUIDOS EN EL TOTAL
PERO NO SE DESGLOSAN ENTRE LOS 25 GRUPOS.

THAILAND:
E—> WORKS OF GROUP 23B ARE INCLUDED IN GROUP
23A.
FR—: LES OUVRAGES DU GROUPE 23B SONT INCLUS
DANS LE GROUPE 23A.
ESP> LAS OBRAS DEL GRUPO 23B QUEDAN INCLUIDAS
EN EL GRUPO 23A.

TURKEY:
E—> WORKS OF GROUPS 5 TO 10 ARE INCLUDED IN
GROUP 4; 12 IN GROUP 11; 14 TO 17 IN GROUP 13; 19
TO 21 IN GROUP 18; 25 IN GROUP 24; 23B IN
GROUP 23A.
FR—> LES OUVRAGES DES GROUPES 5 A 10 SONT
INCLUS DANS LE GROUPE 4; 12 DANS LE GROUPE 11;
14 ET 17 DANS LE GROUPE 13; 19 A 21 DANS LE
GROUPE 18; 25 DANS LE GROUPE 24; 23B DANS LE
GROUPE 23A.
ESP> LAS OBRAS DE LOS GRUPOS 5 A 10 QUEDAN
INCLUIDAS EN EL GRUPO 4; LAS DEL GRUPO 12 EN EL
GRUPO 11; LAS DE LOS GRUPOS 14 A 17 EN EL GRUPO
13; LAS DE LOS GRUPOS 19 A 21 EN EL GRUPO 18;
LAS DEL GRUPO 25 EN EL GRUPO 24; LAS DEL GRUPO
23B EN EL GRUPO 23A.

UNITED ARAB EMIRATES:
E—> ALL FIRST EDITIONS.
FR—> TOUS LES OUVRAGES RECENSES SONT DES PRE-
MIERES EDITIONS.
ESP> TODAS LAS OBRAS CONSIDERADAS SON PRIMERAS
EDICIONES.

BELGIUM:
E—> DATA REFER ONLY TO TITLES INDEXED IN THE
"BIBLIOGRAPHIE DE BELGIQUE". WORKS OF GROUPS
19 AND 20 ARE INCLUDED IN GROUP 18.
FR—> LES DONNEES NE CONCERNENT QUE LES TITRES
REPERTORIES DANS LA BIBLIOGRAPHIE DE BELGIQUE.
LES OUVRAGES DES GROUPES 19 ET 20 SONT INCLUS
DANS LE GROUPE 18.
ESP> LOS DATOS SOLO SE REFIEREN A LOS LIBROS
INSCRITOS EN EL REPERTORIO DE LA "BIBLIOGRAPHIE
DE BELGIQUE". LAS OBRAS DE LOS GRUPOS 19 Y 20
QUEDAN INCLUIDAS EN EL GRUPO 18.

BULGARIA:
E—> WORKS OF GROUPS 19 AND 20 ARE INCLUDED IN
GROUP 18; 23B IN GROUP 23A.
FR—> LES OUVRAGES DES GROUPES 19 ET 20 SONT
INCLUS DANS LE GROUPE 18; 23B DANS LE GROUPE 23A.
ESP> LAS OBRAS DE LOS GRUPOS 19 Y 20 QUEDAN
INCLUIDAS EN EL GRUPO 18; LAS DEL GRUPO 23B EN EL
GRUPO 23A.

CZECHOSLOVAKIA:
E—> WORKS OF GROUPS 19 AND 20 ARE INCLUDED IN
GROUP 18.
FR—> LES OUVRAGES DES GROUPES 19 ET 20 SONT
INCLUS DANS LE GROUPE 18.
ESP> LAS OBRAS DE LOS GRUPOS 19 Y 20 QUEDAN
INCLUIDAS EN EL GRUPO 18.

FRANCE:
E—> DATA DO NOT INCLUDE PAMPHLETS WHICH, IN
1977, ACCOUNTED FOR 6,906 TITLES. WORKS OF GROUPS
19 AND 20 ARE INCLUDED IN GROUP 18; 9 IN GROUP
17.
FR—> LES DONNEES N'INCLUENT PAS LES BROCHURES
QUI COMPTAIENT 6 906 TITRES EN 1977. LES OUVRAGES
DES GROUPES 19 ET 20 SONT INCLUS DANS LE GROUPE
18; 9 DANS LE GROUPE 17.
ESP> LOS DATOS EXCLUYEN LOS FOLLETOS QUE EN
1977 SE ELEVARON A 6 906 TITULOS. LAS OBRAS DE
LOS GRUPOS 19 Y 20 QUEDAN INCLUIDAS EN EL GRUPO
18; LAS DEL GRUPO 9 EN EL GRUPO 17.

GERMAN DEMOCRATIC REPUBLIC:
E—> SCHOOL TEXTBOOKS (231) AND CHILDREN'S
BOOKS (707) ARE INCLUDED IN THE TOTAL BUT NOT
IDENTIFIED IN THE 25 GROUPS. WORKS OF GROUP 23B
ARE INCLUDED IN GROUP 23A. DATA INCLUDE ONLY
SERIES A OF THE GERMAN NATIONAL BIBLIOGRAPHY
(PUBLICATIONS ON THE BOOK MARKET) WHEREAS THOSE
OF THE SERIES B AND C (PUBLICATIONS OUTSIDE THE
BOOK MARKET AS WELL AS BOOKS PUBLISHED BY THE
UNIVERSITIES) ARE EXCLUDED.
FR—> LES MANUELS SCOLAIRES (231) ET LES LIVRES
POUR ENFANTS (707) SONT INCLUS DANS LE TOTAL
MAIS NE SONT PAS REPARTIS ENTRE LES 25 GROUPES.
LES OUVRAGES DU GROUPE 23B SONT INCLUS DANS LE
GROUPE 23A. LES DONNEES SE REFERENT SEULEMENT
A LA SERIE A DE LA BIBLIOGRAPHIE NATIONALE ALLE-
MANDE (PUBLICATIONS VENDUES DANS LE COMMERCE).
LES DONNEES RELATIVES AUX SERIES B ET C (PUBLICA-
TIONS NON VENDUES DANS LE COMMERCE ET LIVRES
PUBLIES PAR LES UNIVERSITES) NE SONT PAS PRISES
EN COMPTE.
ESP—> LOS MANUALES ESCOLARES (231) Y LOS LIBROS
PARA NINOS(707) QUEDAN INCLUIDOS EN EL TOTAL
PERO NO SE DESGLOSAN ENTRE LOS 25 GRUPOS. LAS
OBRAS DEL GRUPO 23B QUEDAN INCLUIDAS EN EL GRUPO
23A. LOS DATOS SOLO SE REFIEREN A LA SERIE A DE
LA BIBLIOGRAFIA NACIONAL ALEMANA (PUBLICACIONES
VENDIDAS EN EL COMERCIO). NO SE TOMAN EN CONSIDE-
RACION LOS DATOS RELATIVOS A LAS SERIES B Y C
(PUBLICACIONES QUE NO SE VENDEN EN EL COMERCIO Y
LIBROS PUBLICADOS POR LOS UNIVERSIDADES).

8.3 **Number of titles by subject group**
Nombre de titres par groupes de sujets
Número de obras por categorías de temas

GERMANY, FEDERAL REPUBLIC OF:
E—> WORKS OF GROUPS 17 AND 18 ARE INCLUDED IN
GROUP 14; 16 IN GROUP 15; 10 IN GROUP 25; 23A IN
GROUP 22.
FR—> LES OUVRAGES DES GROUPES 17 ET 18 SONT
INCLUS DANS LE GROUPE 14; 16 DANS LE GROUPE 15;
10 DANS LE GROUPE 25; 23A DANS LE GROUPE 22.
ESP> LAS OBRAS DE LOS GRUPOS 17 Y 18 QUEDAN
INCLUIDAS EN EL GRUPO 14; LAS DEL GRUPO 16 EN
EL GRUPO 15; LAS DEL GRUPO 10 EN EL GRUPO 25;
LAS DEL GRUPO 23A EN EL GRUPO 22.

ICELAND:
E—> WORKS OF GROUPS 19 AND 20 ARE INCLUDED IN
GROUP 18.
FR—> LES OUVRAGES DES GROUPES 19 ET 20 SONT
INCLUS DANS LE GROUPE 18.
ESP> LAS OBRAS DE LOS GRUPOS 19 Y 20 QUEDAN
INCLUIDAS EN EL GRUPO 18.

IRELAND:
E—> ALL FIRST EDITIONS.
FR—> TOUS LES OUVRAGES RECENSES SONT DES PRE-
MIERES EDITIONS.
ESP> TODAS LAS OBRAS CONSIDERADAS SON PRIME-
RAS EDICIONES.

NETHERLANDS:
E—> DATA DO NOT INCLUDE PAMPHLETS. WORKS OF
GROUPS 5, 6, 9 AND 17 ARE INCLUDED IN GROUP 4;
10 IN GROUP 24; 19 IN GROUP 20; 23A IN GROUP 22.
FR—> LES DONNEES N'INCLUENT PAS LES BROCHURES.
LES OUVRAGES DES GROUPES 5, 6, 9 ET 17 SONT
COMPRIS DANS LE GROUPE 4; 10 DANS LE GROUPE 24;
19 DANS LE GROUPE 20; 23A DANS LE GROUPE 22.
ESP> LOS DATOS EXCLUYEN LOS FOLLETOS. LAS
OBRAS DE LOS GRUPOS 5, 6, 9 Y 17 QUEDAN INCLUI-
DAS EN EL GRUPO 4; LAS DEL GRUPO 10 EN EL GRUPO
24; LAS DEL GRUPO 19 EN EL GRUPO 20; LAS DEL
GRUPO 23A EN EL GRUPO 22.

NORWAY:
E—> STATISTICS ON PAMPHLETS ARE INCOMPLETE.
FR—> LES STATISTIQUES CONCERNANT LES BROCHURES
SONT INCOMPLETES.
ESP> LAS ESTADISTICAS DE LOS FOLLETOS SON INCOM-
PLETAS.

POLAND:
E—> WORKS OF GROUPS 19 AND 20 ARE INCLUDED IN
GROUP 18.
FR—> LES OUVRAGES DES GROUPES 19 ET 20 SONT
INCLUS DANS LE GROUPE 18.
ESP> LAS OBRAS DE LOS GRUPOS 19 Y 20 QUEDAN
INCLUIDAS EN EL GRUPO 18.

PORTUGAL:
E—> WORKS OF GROUPS 5 TO 10 ARE INCLUDED IN
GROUP 4; 12 IN GROUP 11; 14 TO 17 IN GROUP 13;
19 TO 21 IN GROUP 18; 22 AND 23B IN GROUP 23A;
25 IN GROUP 24.
FR—> LES OUVRAGES DES GROUPES 5 A 10 SONT IN-
CLUS DANS LE GROUPE 4; 12 DANS LE GROUPE 11;
14 A 17 DANS LE GROUPE 13; 19 A 21 DANS LE GROUPE
18; 22 ET 23B DANS LE GROUPE 23A; 25 DANS LE
GROUPE 24.
ESP> LAS OBRAS DE LOS GRUPOS 5 A 10 QUEDAN
INCLUIDAS EN EL GRUPO 4; 12 EN EL GRUPO 11; 14 A
17 EN EL GRUPO 13; 19 A 21 EN EL GRUPO 18; 22 Y
23B EN EL GRUPO 23A; 25 EN EL GRUPO 24.

SAN MARINO:
E—> ALL FIRST EDITIONS.
FR—> TOUS LES OUVRAGES RECENSES SONT DES PRE-
MIERES EDITIONS.
ESP> TODAS LAS OBRAS CONSIDERADAS SON PRIME-
RAS EDICIONES.

SPAIN:
E—> WORKS OF GROUPS 19 AND 20 ARE INCLUDED IN
GROUP 18. WORKS OF GROUP 23B ARE INCLUDED IN
GROUP 23A.
FR—> LES OUVRAGES DES GROUPES 19 ET 20 SONT
INCLUS DANS LE GROUPE 18, CEUX DU GROUPE 23B
DANS LE GROUPE 23A.
ESP> LAS OBRAS DE LOS GRUPOS 19 Y 20 QUEDAN
INCLUIDAS EN EL GRUPO 18 Y LAS DEL GRUPO 23B
EN EL GRUPO 23A.

SWEDEN:
E—> CHILDREN'S BOOKS (465) ARE INCLUDED IN
THE TOTAL BUT NOT IDENTIFIED IN THE 25 GROUPS.
FR—> LES LIVRES POUR ENFANTS (465) SONT
COMPRIS DANS LE TOTAL MAIS NE SONT PAS REPARTIS
ENTRE LES 25 GROUPES.
ESP> LOS LIBROS PARA NIÑOS (465) QUEDAN
COMPRENDIDOS EN EL TOTAL PERO NO SE DESGLOSAN
ENTRE LOS 25 GRUPOS.

SWITZERLAND:
E—> SCHOOL TEXTBOOKS (177) AND CHILDREN'S
BOOKS (416) ARE INCLUDED IN THE TOTAL BUT NOT
IDENTIFIED IN THE 25 GROUPS.
FR—> LES MANUELS SCOLAIRES (177) ET LES LIVRES
POUR ENFANTS (416) SONT COMPRIS DANS LE TOTAL
MAIS NE SONT PAS REPARTIS ENTRE LES 25 GROUPES.
ESP> LOS MANUALES ESCOLARES (177) Y LOS LIBROS
PARA NIÑOS (416) QUEDAN COMPRENDIDOS EN EL TOTAL
PERO NO SE DESGLOSAN ENTRE LOS 25 GRUPOS.

UNITED KINGDOM:
E—> WORKS OF GROUPS 19 AND 20 ARE INCLUDED IN
GROUP 18.
FR—> LES OUVRAGES DES GROUPES 19 ET 20 SONT
INCLUS DANS LE GROUPE 18.
ESP> LAS OBRAS DE LOS GRUPOS 19 Y 20 QUEDAN
COMPRENDIDAS EN EL GRUPO 18.

AMERICAN SAMOA:
E—> SCHOOL TEXTBOOKS (8) AND CHILDREN'S
BOOKS (38) ARE INCLUDED IN THE TOTAL BUT NOT
IDENTIFIED IN THE 25 GROUPS.
FR—> LES MANUELS SCOLAIRES (8) ET LES LIVRES
POUR ENFANTS (38) SONT COMPRIS DANS LE TOTAL
MAIS NE SONT PAS REPARTIS ENTRE LES 25 GROUPES.
ESP> LOS MANUALES ESCOLARES (8) Y LOS LIBROS
PARA NIÑOS (38) QUEDAN COMPRENDIDOS EN EL TOTAL
PERO NO SE DESGLOSAN ENTRE LOS 25 GRUPOS.

AUSTRALIA:
E—> PRELIMINARY FIGURES.
FR—> DONNEES PROVISOIRES.
ESP> DATOS PRELIMINARES.

FIJI:
E—> DATA REFER TO SCHOOL TEXTBOOKS ONLY.
FR—> LES DONNEES CONCERNENT SEULEMENT LES
MANUELS SCOLAIRES.
ESP> LOS DATOS SE REFIEREN A LOS MANUALES ESCO-
LARES SOLAMENTE.

GUAM:
E—> ALL FIRST EDITIONS.
FR—> TOUS LES OUVRAGES RECENSES SONT DES PRE-
MIERES EDITIONS.
ESP> TODAS LAS OBRAS CONSIDERADAS SON PRIMERAS
EDICIONES.

PACIFIC ISLANDS:
E—> ALL FIRST EDITIONS.
FR—> TOUS LES OUVRAGES RECENSES SONT DES PRE-
MIERES EDITIONS.
ESP> TODAS LAS OBRAS CONSIDERADAS SON PRIMERAS
EDICIONES.

Number of titles by subject group   8.3
Nombre de titres par groupes de sujets
Número de obras por categorías de temas

U.S.S.R.:
   E—> WORKS OF GROUPS 19 AND 20 ARE INCLUDED
IN GROUP 18.
   FR-> LES OUVRAGES DES GROUPES 19 ET 20 SONT
INCLUS DANS LE GROUPE 18.
   ESP> LAS OBRAS DE LOS GRUPOS 19 Y 20 QUEDAN
COMPRENDIDAS EN EL GRUPO 18.

UKRAINIAN S.S.R.:
   E—> WORKS OF GROUPS 19 AND 20 ARE INCLUDED IN
GROUP 18.
   FR-> LES OUVRAGES DES GROUPES 19 ET 20 SONT
INCLUS DANS LE GROUPE 18.
   ESP> LAS OBRAS DE LOS GRUPOS 19 Y 20 QUEDAN
COMPRENDIDAS EN EL GRUPO 18.

8.4 Number of titles (first editions) by subject group
Nombre de titres (premières éditions) par groupes de sujets
Número de obras (primeras ediciones) por categoría de temas

8.4 Book production: number of titles (first editions only) by subject group

Edition de livres: nombre de titres (premières éditions seulement) par groupes de sujets

Edición de libros: número de obras (primeras ediciones solamente) por categoría de temas

A = BOOKS
B = PAMPHLETS

A = LIVRES
B = BROCHURES

A = LIBROS
B = FOLLETOS

NUMBER OF COUNTRIES AND
TERRITORIES PRESENTED IN
THIS TABLE: 93

NOMBRE DE PAYS ET DE
TERRITOIRES PRESENTES DANS
CE TABLEAU: 93

NUMERO DE PAISES Y DE
TERRITORIOS PRESENTADOS
EN ESTE CUADRO: 93

SUBJECT GROUP GROUPE DE SUJETS GRUPO TEMATICO	AFRICA	BOTSWANA (1978)			CONGO ‡ (1977)		
		A	B	A+B	A	B	A+B
TOTAL		29	36	65	9	118	127
1. GENERALITIES		2	–	2	–	–	–
2. PHILOSOPHY, PSYCHOLOGY		–	–	–	–	–	–
3. RELIGION, THEOLOGY		–	–	–	–	–	–
4. SOCIOLOGY, STATISTICS		4	8	12	–	–	–
5. POLITICAL SCIENCE		17	13	30	2	14	16
6. LAW, PUBLIC ADMIN.		2	2	4	–	–	–
7. MILITARY ART		–	–	–	–	–	–
8. EDUCATION, LEISURE		1	7	8	–	8	8
9. TRADE, TRANSPORT		–	–	–	–	–	–
10. ETHNOGRAPHY, FOLKLORE		–	1	1	–	–	–
11. MATHEMATICS		–	–	–	–	6	6
12. NATURAL SCIENCES		2	–	2	–	27	27
13. MEDICAL SCIENCES		–	1	1	–	1	1
14. ENGINEERING, CRAFTS		–	–	–	–	–	–
15. AGRICULTURE		1	–	1	–	–	–
16. DOMESTIC SCIENCE		–	–	–	–	2	2
17. MANAGEMENT, ADMIN.		–	–	–	–	–	–
18. PLANNING, ARCHITECTURE		–	1	1	–	–	–
19. PLASTIC ARTS		–	–	–	–	–	–
20. PERFORMING ARTS		–	–	–	–	7	7
21. GAMES, SPORTS		–	2	2	–	–	–
22. LINGUISTICS, PHILOLOGY		–	–	–	–	20	20
23. LITERATURE							
(A) HISTORY AND CRITICISM		–	–	–	6	10	16
(B) LITERARY TEXTS		–	–	–	./.	./.	./.
24. GEOGRAPHY, TRAVEL		–	–	–	1	17	18
25. HISTORY, BIOGRAPHY		–	1	1	–	6	6

Number of titles (first editions) by subject group   **8.4**
Nombre de titres (premières éditions) par groupes de sujets
Número de obras (primeras ediciones) por categoría de temas

SUBJECT GROUP / GROUPE DE SUJETS / GRUPO TEMATICO	EGYPT ‡ (1977)			ETHIOPIA ‡ (1978)			GAMBIA (1978)		
	A	B	A+B	A	B	A+B	A	B	A+B
TOTAL	1 294	111	1 405	331	22	353	20	53	73
1. GENERALITIES	55	3	58	1	1	2	1	7	8
2. PHILOSOPHY, PSYCHOLOGY	34	–	34	1	–	1	–	–	–
3. RELIGION, THEOLOGY	224	35	259	48	1	49	1	4	5
4. SOCIOLOGY, STATISTICS	254	14	268	73	1	74	1	7	8
5. POLITICAL SCIENCE	./.	./.	./.	./.	./.	./.	1	7	7
6. LAW, PUBLIC ADMIN.	./.	./.	./.	./.	./.	./.	–		
7. MILITARY ART	./.	./.	./.	./.	./.	./.	–		
8. EDUCATION, LEISURE	./.	./.	./.	./.	./.	./.	–	1	1
9. TRADE, TRANSPORT	./.	./.	./.	./.	./.	./.	–	1	1
10. ETHNOGRAPHY, FOLKLORE	./.	./.	./.	./.	./.	./.	–		
11. MATHEMATICS	63	3	66	9	–	9			
12. NATURAL SCIENCES	./.	./.	./.	./.		./.	2	6	8
13. MEDICAL SCIENCES	251	14	265	28	–	28	4	2	6
14. ENGINEERING, CRAFTS	./.	./.	./.	./.	–	./.	1	1	2
15. AGRICULTURE	./.	./.	./.	./.	–	./.	2	1	3
16. DOMESTIC SCIENCE	./.	./.	./.	./.		./.	–	1	1
17. MANAGEMENT, ADMIN.	./.	./.	./.	./.		./.	–		
18. PLANNING, ARCHITECTURE	40	1	41	2	–	2	3	7	10
19. PLASTIC ARTS	./.	./.	./.	./.	–	./.	–		
20. PERFORMING ARTS	./.	./.	./.	./.	–	./.	–		
21. GAMES, SPORTS	./.	./.	./.	./.	–	./.	–		
22. LINGUISTICS, PHILOLOGY	137	14	151	13	–	13	–	1	1
23. LITERATURE									
(A) HISTORY AND CRITICISM	157	23	180	10	–	10			
(B) LITERARY TEXTS	./.	./.	./.	./.	–	./.	–	1	1
24. GEOGRAPHY, TRAVEL	79	4	83	27	17	44	2	5	7
25. HISTORY, BIOGRAPHY	./.	./.	./.	./.	./.	./.	3	1	4

SUBJECT GROUP / GROUPE DE SUJETS / GRUPO TEMATICO	GHANA (1978)			IVORY COAST (1977)			MADAGASCAR ‡ (1978)		
	A	B	A+B	A	B	A+B	A	B	A+B
TOTAL	145	90	235	59	63	122	94	95	189
1. GENERALITIES	3	3	6	–	10	10	2	3	5
2. PHILOSOPHY, PSYCHOLOGY	3	2	5	–	–	–	2	4	6
3. RELIGION, THEOLOGY	32	21	53	9	14	23	19	15	34
4. SOCIOLOGY, STATISTICS	3	3	6	7	2	9	1	2	3
5. POLITICAL SCIENCE	15	18	33	–	2	2	7	5	12
6. LAW, PUBLIC ADMIN.	10	3	13	4	–	4	4	5	9
7. MILITARY ART	–	1	1	–	–	–	–	1	1
8. EDUCATION, LEISURE	14	8	22	8	13	21	18	5	23
9. TRADE, TRANSPORT	4	1	5	–	1	1	2	1	3
10. ETHNOGRAPHY, FOLKLORE	–	–	–	1	–	1	3	6	9
11. MATHEMATICS	3	1	4	5	–	5	4	–	4
12. NATURAL SCIENCES	4	1	5	3	5	8	4	2	6
13. MEDICAL SCIENCES	4	1	5	–	1	1	–	–	–
14. ENGINEERING, CRAFTS	8	5	13	2	3	5	4	3	7
15. AGRICULTURE	1	1	2	8	10	18	3	1	4
16. DOMESTIC SCIENCE	1	–	1	–	–	–	–	2	2
17. MANAGEMENT, ADMIN.	1	–	1	1	–	1	–	2	2
18. PLANNING, ARCHITECTURE	–	1	1	4	–	4	1	–	1
19. PLASTIC ARTS	–	–	–	–	–	–	–		
20. PERFORMING ARTS	2	–	2	1	2	3	1	3	4
21. GAMES, SPORTS	1	3	4	–	–	–	1	4	5
22. LINGUISTICS, PHILOLOGY	7	3	10	4	–	4	–	3	3
23. LITERATURE									
(A) HISTORY AND CRITICISM	1	–	1	–	–	–	10	24	34
(B) LITERARY TEXTS	26	9	35	–	–	–	./.	./.	./.
24. GEOGRAPHY, TRAVEL	1	1	2	2	–	2	3	–	3
25. HISTORY, BIOGRAPHY	1	4	5	–	–	–	2	6	8

8.4 Number of titles (first editions) by subject group
Nombre de titres (premières éditions) par groupes de sujets
Número de obras (primeras ediciones) por categoría de temas

SUBJECT GROUP GROUPE DE SUJETS GRUPO TEMATICO	MALAWI (1977)			MAURITANIA (1977)			MAURITIUS (1978)		
	A	B	A+B	A	B	A+B	A	B	A+B
TOTAL	24	50	74	20	12	32	10	10	20
1. GENERALITIES	–	–	–	–	–	–	–	–	–
2. PHILOSOPHY, PSYCHOLOGY	–	–	–	–	–	–	1	–	1
3. RELIGION, THEOLOGY	12	8	20	–	–	–	2	2	4
4. SOCIOLOGY, STATISTICS	–	–	–	–	2	2	–	–	–
5. POLITICAL SCIENCE	2	1	3	–	–	–	2	2	4
6. LAW, PUBLIC ADMIN.	2	1	3	–	–	–	–	–	–
7. MILITARY ART	–	–	–	–	–	–	–	–	–
8. EDUCATION, LEISURE	–	–	–	–	–	–	–	–	–
9. TRADE, TRANSPORT	–	1	1	–	–	–	1	–	1
10. ETHNOGRAPHY, FOLKLORE	1	–	1	–	–	–	–	–	–
11. MATHEMATICS	–	–	–	1	3	4	–	–	–
12. NATURAL SCIENCES	1	2	3	5	1	6	–	–	–
13. MEDICAL SCIENCES	–	–	–	–	–	–	2	–	2
14. ENGINEERING, CRAFTS	–	–	–	–	–	–	–	–	–
15. AGRICULTURE	3	11	14	–	–	–	–	–	–
16. DOMESTIC SCIENCE	–	–	–	–	–	–	–	–	–
17. MANAGEMENT, ADMIN.	–	–	–	–	–	–	–	–	–
18. PLANNING, ARCHITECTURE	–	–	–	–	–	–	–	–	–
19. PLASTIC ARTS	–	–	–	–	–	–	–	–	–
20. PERFORMING ARTS	–	–	–	–	–	–	–	1	1
21. GAMES, SPORTS	–	–	–	–	–	–	–	–	–
22. LINGUISTICS, PHILOLOGY	–	–	–	10	4	14	–	–	–
23. LITERATURE									
(A) HISTORY AND CRITICISM	–	13	13	–	–	–	–	–	–
(B) LITERARY TEXTS	–	13	13	–	–	–	–	3	3
24. GEOGRAPHY, TRAVEL	–	–	–	3	–	3	–	–	–
25. HISTORY, BIOGRAPHY	3	–	3	1	2	3	2	2	4

SUBJECT GROUP GROUPE DE SUJETS GRUPO TEMATICO	SENEGAL (1977)			SEYCHELLES (1977)			SIERRA LEONE (1977)		
	A	B	A+B	A	B	A+B	A	B	A+B
TOTAL	48	–	48	10	1	11	17	44	61
1. GENERALITIES	13	–	13	–	–	–	–	3	3
2. PHILOSOPHY, PSYCHOLOGY	–	–	–	1	–	1	–	–	–
3. RELIGION, THEOLOGY	2	–	2	–	–	–	–	–	–
4. SOCIOLOGY, STATISTICS	1	–	1	–	1	1	1	3	4
5. POLITICAL SCIENCE	1	–	1	4	–	4	5	19	24
6. LAW, PUBLIC ADMIN.	3	–	3	3	–	3	3	2	5
7. MILITARY ART	–	–	–	–	–	–	–	–	–
8. EDUCATION, LEISURE	17	–	17	–	–	–	3	12	15
9. TRADE, TRANSPORT	–	–	–	–	–	–	–	1	1
10. ETHNOGRAPHY, FOLKLORE	–	–	–	–	–	–	–	–	–
11. MATHEMATICS	–	–	–	–	–	–	–	–	–
12. NATURAL SCIENCES	–	–	–	–	–	–	–	–	–
13. MEDICAL SCIENCES	–	–	–	–	–	–	1	1	2
14. ENGINEERING, CRAFTS	–	–	–	–	–	–	–	–	–
15. AGRICULTURE	1	–	1	–	–	–	–	1	1
16. DOMESTIC SCIENCE	–	–	–	–	–	–	–	–	–
17. MANAGEMENT, ADMIN.	–	–	–	–	–	–	1	–	1
18. PLANNING, ARCHITECTURE	–	–	–	–	–	–	–	–	–
19. PLASTIC ARTS	–	–	–	–	–	–	–	–	–
20. PERFORMING ARTS	1	–	1	–	–	–	–	–	–
21. GAMES, SPORTS	–	–	–	–	–	–	–	–	–
22. LINGUISTICS, PHILOLOGY	1	–	1	–	–	–	–	–	–
23. LITERATURE									
(A) HISTORY AND CRITICISM	1	–	1	–	–	–	–	–	–
(B) LITERARY TEXTS	4	–	4	–	–	–	–	–	–
24. GEOGRAPHY, TRAVEL	1	–	1	2	–	2	3	–	3
25. HISTORY, BIOGRAPHY	2	–	2	–	–	–	–	2	2

Number of titles (first editions) by subject group **8.4**
Nombre de titres (premières éditions) par groupes de sujets
Número de obras (primeras ediciones) por categoría de temas

SUBJECT GROUP / GROUPE DE SUJETS / GRUPO TEMATICO	SUDAN ‡ (1977)			UNITED REP. OF CAMEROON ‡ (1978)	UNITED REP. OF TANZANIA ‡ (1976)		
	A	B	A+B	A+B	A	B	A+B
TOTAL	39	—	39	54	180	159	339
1. GENERALITIES	—	—	—	—	6	6	12
2. PHILOSOPHY, PSYCHOLOGY	—	—	—	—	—	—	—
3. RELIGION, THEOLOGY	2	—	2	—	37	24	61
4. SOCIOLOGY, STATISTICS	—	—	—	—	6	9	15
5. POLITICAL SCIENCE	—	—	—	5	33	24	57
6. LAW, PUBLIC ADMIN.	—	—	—	3	24	14	38
7. MILITARY ART	—	—	—	—	—	1	1
8. EDUCATION, LEISURE	—	—	—	5	15	15	30
9. TRADE, TRANSPORT	—	—	—	—	1	8	9
10. ETHNOGRAPHY, FOLKLORE	—	—	—	—	—	2	2
11. MATHEMATICS	4	—	4	4	13	—	13
12. NATURAL SCIENCES	6	—	6	2	—	—	—
13. MEDICAL SCIENCES	—	—	—	—	4	4	8
14. ENGINEERING, CRAFTS	13	—	13	—	1	1	2
15. AGRICULTURE	5	—	5	—	2	14	16
16. DOMESTIC SCIENCE	—	—	—	—	1	1	2
17. MANAGEMENT, ADMIN.	—	—	—	—	1	5	6
18. PLANNING, ARCHITECTURE	—	—	—	—	1	5	6
19. PLASTIC ARTS	—	—	—	—	—	—	—
20. PERFORMING ARTS	—	—	—	1	3	—	3
21. GAMES, SPORTS	—	—	—	—	3	1	4
22. LINGUISTICS, PHILOLOGY	2	—	2	17	13	13	26
23. LITERATURE							
(A) HISTORY AND CRITICISM	1	—	1	—	13	3	16
(B) LITERARY TEXTS	—	—	—	14	./.	./.	./.
24. GEOGRAPHY, TRAVEL	5	—	5	1	—	4	4
25. HISTORY, BIOGRAPHY	1	—	1	2	3	5	8

SUBJECT GROUP / GROUPE DE SUJETS / GRUPO TEMATICO	ZAMBIA ‡ (1978)			AMERICA, NORTH	BARBADOS ‡ (1978)		
	A	B	A+B		A	B	A+B
TOTAL	16	—	16		37	178	215
1. GENERALITIES	—	—	—		3	10	13
2. PHILOSOPHY, PSYCHOLOGY	—	—	—		—	—	—
3. RELIGION, THEOLOGY	—	—	—		2	5	7
4. SOCIOLOGY, STATISTICS	—	—	—		—	1	1
5. POLITICAL SCIENCE	1	—	1		5	28	33
6. LAW, PUBLIC ADMIN.	—	—	—		5	27	32
7. MILITARY ART	—	—	—		—	—	—
8. EDUCATION, LEISURE	—	—	—		2	23	25
9. TRADE, TRANSPORT	—	—	—		6	9	15
10. ETHNOGRAPHY, FOLKLORE	1	—	1		—	1	1
11. MATHEMATICS	3	—	3		—	—	—
12. NATURAL SCIENCES	—	—	—		1	2	3
13. MEDICAL SCIENCES	—	—	—		—	16	16
14. ENGINEERING, CRAFTS	—	—	—		—	18	18
15. AGRICULTURE	3	—	3		2	25	27
16. DOMESTIC SCIENCE	—	—	—		—	1	1
17. MANAGEMENT, ADMIN.	—	—	—		4	2	6
18. PLANNING, ARCHITECTURE	—	—	—		—	3	3
19. PLASTIC ARTS	—	—	—		—	1	1
20. PERFORMING ARTS	—	—	—		—	2	2
21. GAMES, SPORTS	—	—	—		3	—	3
22. LINGUISTICS, PHILOLOGY	3	—	3		1	—	1
23. LITERATURE							
(A) HISTORY AND CRITICISM	—	—	—		—	1	1
(B) LITERARY TEXTS	—	—	—		—	./.	./.
24. GEOGRAPHY, TRAVEL	—	—	—		1	3	4
25. HISTORY, BIOGRAPHY	1	—	1		2	—	2

8.4 Number of titles (first editions) by subject group
Nombre de titres (premières éditions) par groupes de sujets
Número de obras (primeras ediciones) por categoría de temas

SUBJECT GROUP / GROUPE DE SUJETS / GRUPO TEMATICO	CANADA ‡ (1978) A	B	A+B	COSTA RICA (1978) A	B	A+B	CUBA (1977) A+B
TOTAL	12 366	514	12 880	20	—	20	693
1. GENERALITIES	464	20	484	1	—	1	33
2. PHILOSOPHY, PSYCHOLOGY	620	5	625	—	—	—	17
3. RELIGION, THEOLOGY	330	33	363	—	—	—	1
4. SOCIOLOGY, STATISTICS	493	14	507	2	—	2	13
5. POLITICAL SCIENCE	927	60	987	2	—	2	63
6. LAW, PUBLIC ADMIN.	849	58	907	1	—	1	12
7. MILITARY ART	18	—	18	—	—	—	6
8. EDUCATION, LEISURE	639	30	669	2	—	2	107
9. TRADE, TRANSPORT	262	3	265	—	—	—	1
10. ETHNOGRAPHY, FOLKLORE	38	—	38	3	—	3	—
11. MATHEMATICS	364	—	364	—	—	—	14
12. NATURAL SCIENCES	1 242	8	1 250	—	—	—	33
13. MEDICAL SCIENCES	459	59	518	—	—	—	23
14. ENGINEERING, CRAFTS	783	25	808	—	—	—	16
15. AGRICULTURE	229	11	240	—	—	—	19
16. DOMESTIC SCIENCE	201	26	227	—	—	—	—
17. MANAGEMENT, ADMIN.	227	12	239	—	—	—	1
18. PLANNING, ARCHITECTURE	839	127	966	—	—	—	—
19. PLASTIC ARTS	./.	./.	./.	—	—	—	—
20. PERFORMING ARTS	./.	./.	./.	2	—	2	6
21. GAMES, SPORTS	273	—	273	—	—	—	7
22. LINGUISTICS, PHILOLOGY	477	1	478	—	—	—	13
23. LITERATURE							
(A) HISTORY AND CRITICISM	591	2	593	1	—	1	14
(B) LITERARY TEXTS	1 087	—	1 087	3	—	3	266
24. GEOGRAPHY, TRAVEL	158	—	158	—	—	—	6
25. HISTORY, BIOGRAPHY	796	20	816	3	—	3	22

SUBJECT GROUP / GROUPE DE SUJETS / GRUPO TEMATICO	DOMINICAN REPUBLIC (1976) A	B	A+B	EL SALVADOR (1978) A	B	A+B	JAMAICA ‡ (1978) A	B	A+B
TOTAL	40	8	48	39	83	122	79	62	141
1. GENERALITIES	3	1	4	—	—	—	1	6	7
2. PHILOSOPHY, PSYCHOLOGY	—	—	—	1	—	1	—	—	—
3. RELIGION, THEOLOGY	1	—	1	—	1	1	—	3	3
4. SOCIOLOGY, STATISTICS	3	1	4	1	1	2	22	14	36
5. POLITICAL SCIENCE	3	2	5	4	6	10	—	2	2
6. LAW, PUBLIC ADMIN.	—	—	—	—	—	—	1	1	2
7. MILITARY ART	1	—	1	—	—	—	—	—	—
8. EDUCATION, LEISURE	1	1	2	—	2	2	1	4	5
9. TRADE, TRANSPORT	—	—	—	—	2	2	—	—	—
10. ETHNOGRAPHY, FOLKLORE	—	—	—	—	7	7	1	—	1
11. MATHEMATICS	1	—	1	—	—	—	3	—	3
12. NATURAL SCIENCES	—	—	—	—	—	—	5	4	9
13. MEDICAL SCIENCES	3	—	3	—	8	8	2	—	2
14. ENGINEERING, CRAFTS	—	—	—	—	—	—	2	—	2
15. AGRICULTURE	—	—	—	—	51	51	1	3	4
16. DOMESTIC SCIENCE	3	—	3	—	—	—	2	—	2
17. MANAGEMENT, ADMIN.	2	—	2	—	2	2	—	—	—
18. PLANNING, ARCHITECTURE	—	—	—	—	1	1	—	1	1
19. PLASTIC ARTS	—	—	—	—	—	—	—	—	—
20. PERFORMING ARTS	1	—	1	—	1	1	8	13	21
21. GAMES, SPORTS	—	—	—	—	1	1	1	4	5
22. LINGUISTICS, PHILOLOGY	—	—	—	6	—	6	21	—	21
23. LITERATURE									
(A) HISTORY AND CRITICISM	13	2	15	4	—	4	7	—	7
(B) LITERARY TEXTS	./.	./.	./.	16	—	16	./.	./.	./.
24. GEOGRAPHY, TRAVEL	1	—	1	—	—	—	—	—	—
25. HISTORY, BIOGRAPHY	4	1	5	7	—	7	6	2	8

Number of titles (first editions) by subject group   8.4
Nombre de titres (premières éditions) par groupes de sujets
Número de obras (primeras ediciones) por categoría de temas

SUBJECT GROUP GROUPE DE SUJETS GRUPO TEMATICO	MEXICO (1976)			NETHERLANDS ANTILLES ‡ (1977)			PANAMA (1978)		
	A	B	A+B	A	B	A+B	A	B	A+B
TOTAL	1 898	367	2 265	*26	*24	*50	50	18	68
1. GENERALITIES	35	–	35	2	1	3	1	–	1
2. PHILOSOPHY, PSYCHOLOGY	59	–	59	–	–	–	–	–	–
3. RELIGION, THEOLOGY	25	2	27	2	–	2	–	–	–
4. SOCIOLOGY, STATISTICS	46	1	47	–	–	–	3	2	5
5. POLITICAL SCIENCE	58	1	59	–	4	4	2	1	3
6. LAW, PUBLIC ADMIN.	63	4	67	4	2	6	10	1	11
7. MILITARY ART	–	–	–	–	–	–	–	–	–
8. EDUCATION, LEISURE	83	1	84	1	–	1	–	–	–
9. TRADE, TRANSPORT	2	–	2	2	3	5	–	1	1
10. ETHNOGRAPHY, FOLKLORE	21	1	22	–	1	1	2	1	3
11. MATHEMATICS	45	–	45	–	–	–	3	–	3
12. NATURAL SCIENCES	111	10	121	3	1	4	3	–	3
13. MEDICAL SCIENCES	369	134	503	1	1	2	2	2	4
14. ENGINEERING, CRAFTS	207	107	314	–	–	–	1	–	1
15. AGRICULTURE	23	6	29	1	1	2	1	–	1
16. DOMESTIC SCIENCE	3	1	4	–	–	–	1	–	1
17. MANAGEMENT, ADMIN.	223	55	278	–	–	–	–	–	–
18. PLANNING, ARCHITECTURE	38	6	44	–	–	–	–	–	–
19. PLASTIC ARTS	–	–	–	–	–	–	1	–	1
20. PERFORMING ARTS	–	–	–	–	–	–	–	1	1
21. GAMES, SPORTS	9	–	9	–	–	–	–	–	–
22. LINGUISTICS, PHILOLOGY	49	7	56	–	2	2	2	–	2
23. LITERATURE									
(A) HISTORY AND CRITICISM	5	–	5	4	8	12	1	–	1
(B) LITERARY TEXTS	302	26	328	./.	./.	./.	7	8	15
24. GEOGRAPHY, TRAVEL	5	–	5	1	–	1	2	–	2
25. HISTORY, BIOGRAPHY	117	5	122	5	–	5	9	1	10

SUBJECT GROUP GROUPE DE SUJETS GRUPO TEMATICO	UNITED STATES OF AMERICA ‡ (1978)			AMERICA SOUTH	BRAZIL ‡ (1976)		
	A	B	A+B		A	B	A+B
TOTAL	69 156	7 220	76 376		7 620	3 790	11 410
1. GENERALITIES	1 073				428	442	870
2. PHILOSOPHY, PSYCHOLOGY	1 061				291	106	397
3. RELIGION, THEOLOGY	1 932				501	255	756
4. SOCIOLOGY, STATISTICS	1 655				152	143	295
5. POLITICAL SCIENCE	2 284				225	126	351
6. LAW, PUBLIC ADMIN.	1 776				613	229	842
7. MILITARY ART	125				3	28	31
8. EDUCATION, LEISURE	885				755	421	1 176
9. TRADE, TRANSPORT	327				45	69	114
10. ETHNOGRAPHY, FOLKLORE	97				41	119	160
11. MATHEMATICS	523				267	362	629
12. NATURAL SCIENCES	1 529				274	562	836
13. MEDICAL SCIENCES	2 209				142	43	185
14. ENGINEERING, CRAFTS	1 504				117	111	228
15. AGRICULTURE	402				82	13	95
16. DOMESTIC SCIENCE	727				15	1	16
17. MANAGEMENT, ADMIN.	934				74	13	87
18. PLANNING, ARCHITECTURE	–				14	1	15
19. PLASTIC ARTS	–				–	–	–
20. PERFORMING ARTS	380				305	33	338
21. GAMES, SPORTS	722				61	102	163
22. LINGUISTICS, PHILOLOGY	306				306	144	450
23. LITERATURE							
(A) HISTORY AND CRITICISM	4 859				2 619	152	2 771
(B) LITERARY TEXTS	./.				./.	./.	./.
24. GEOGRAPHY, TRAVEL	347				88	99	187
25. HISTORY, BIOGRAPHY	1 653				202	216	418

8.4 Number of titles (first editions) by subject group
Nombre de titres (premières éditions) par groupes de sujets
Número de obras (primeras ediciones) por categoría de temas

SUBJECT GROUP / GROUPE DE SUJETS / GRUPO TEMATICO	CHILE (1978)			GUYANA ‡ (1978)			PERU ‡ (1978)		
	A	B	A+B	A	B	A+B	A	B	A+B
TOTAL	330	59	389	32	62	94	620	327	947
1. GENERALITIES	5	1	6	1	4	5	21	8	29
2. PHILOSOPHY, PSYCHOLOGY	25	5	30	—	—	—	20	2	22
3. RELIGION, THEOLOGY	32	12	44	1	3	4	20	12	32
4. SOCIOLOGY, STATISTICS	7	1	8	—	2	2	20	11	31
5. POLITICAL SCIENCE	17	4	21	9	17	26	92	51	143
6. LAW, PUBLIC ADMIN.	27	4	31	1	8	9	64	22	86
7. MILITARY ART	3	—	3	—	2	2	1	—	1
8. EDUCATION, LEISURE	8	2	10	4	2	6	31	26	57
9. TRADE, TRANSPORT	5	—	5	—	—	—	13	4	17
10. ETHNOGRAPHY, FOLKLORE	1	—	1	—	3	3	6	4	10
11. MATHEMATICS	21	—	21	1	—	1	24	4	28
12. NATURAL SCIENCES	14	3	17	3	2	5	12	7	19
13. MEDICAL SCIENCES	10	—	10	1	1	2	15	11	26
14. ENGINEERING, CRAFTS	10	3	13	1	—	1	18	25	43
15. AGRICULTURE	4	2	6	3	—	3	22	22	44
16. DOMESTIC SCIENCE	—	—	—	—	2	2	8	2	10
17. MANAGEMENT, ADMIN.	3	—	3	—	—	—	11	8	19
18. PLANNING, ARCHITECTURE	3	1	4	—	—	—	4	1	5
19. PLASTIC ARTS	4	—	4	1	—	1	3	3	6
20. PERFORMING ARTS	2	—	2	—	3	3	—	11	11
21. GAMES, SPORTS	1	—	1	—	2	2	4	2	6
22. LINGUISTICS, PHILOLOGY	19	4	23	—	—	—	7	3	10
23. LITERATURE									
(A) HISTORY AND CRITICISM	14	1	15	6	8	14	110	77	187
(B) LITERARY TEXTS	66	6	72	./.	./.	./.	./.	./.	./.
24. GEOGRAPHY, TRAVEL	8	—	8	—	2	2	3	2	5
25. HISTORY, BIOGRAPHY	21	10	31	—	1	1	91	9	100

SUBJECT GROUP / GROUPE DE SUJETS ASIA / GRUPO TEMATICO	BANGLADESH (1978)			BRUNEI (1978)			CHINA ‡ (1978)
	A	B	A+B	A	B	A+B	A+B
TOTAL	932	39	971	19	10	29	9 803
1. GENERALITIES	21	6	27	5	—	5	./.
2. PHILOSOPHY, PSYCHOLOGY	15	—	15	—	—	—	1 503
3. RELIGION, THEOLOGY	106	—	106	7	2	9	./.
4. SOCIOLOGY, STATISTICS	44	—	44	—	—	—	./.
5. POLITICAL SCIENCE	54	4	58	—	—	—	./.
6. LAW, PUBLIC ADMIN.	13	—	13	—	—	—	./.
7. MILITARY ART	—	—	—	—	—	—	./.
8. EDUCATION, LEISURE	140	—	140	—	—	—	669
9. TRADE, TRANSPORT	5	4	9	—	—	—	2 999
10. ETHNOGRAPHY, FOLKLORE	44	—	44	—	—	—	./.
11. MATHEMATICS	59	—	59	2	1	3	./.
12. NATURAL SCIENCES	58	—	58	2	7	9	./.
13. MEDICAL SCIENCES	13	—	13	—	—	—	./.
14. ENGINEERING, CRAFTS	3	—	3	—	—	—	./.
15. AGRICULTURE	51	25	76	—	—	—	./.
16. DOMESTIC SCIENCE	7	—	7	—	—	—	./.
17. MANAGEMENT, ADMIN.	11	—	11	—	—	—	./.
18. PLANNING, ARCHITECTURE	8	—	8	—	—	—	./.
19. PLASTIC ARTS	2	—	2	—	—	—	./.
20. PERFORMING ARTS	3	—	3	—	—	—	./.
21. GAMES, SPORTS	2	—	2	—	—	—	./.
22. LINGUISTICS, PHILOLOGY	1	—	1	—	—	—	./.
23. LITERATURE							
(A) HISTORY AND CRITICISM	9	—	9	—	—	—	1 750
(B) LITERARY TEXTS	181	—	181	1	—	1	./.
24. GEOGRAPHY, TRAVEL	14	—	14	1	—	1	./.
25. HISTORY, BIOGRAPHY	68	—	68	1	—	1	./.

Number of titles (first editions) by subject group   **8.4**
Nombre de titres (premières éditions) par groupes de sujets
Número de obras (primeras ediciones) por categoría de temas

SUBJECT GROUP GROUPE DE SUJETS GRUPO TEMATICO	CYPRUS (1977)			HONG KONG (1977)			INDIA ‡ (1978)		
	A	B	A+B	A	B	A+B	A	B	A+B
TOTAL	144	412	556	884	790	1 674	11 868	294	12 162
1. GENERALITIES	4	9	13	18	43	61	220	9	229
2. PHILOSOPHY, PSYCHOLOGY	2	3	5	8	1	9	360	13	373
3. RELIGION, THEOLOGY	5	27	32	17	16	33	894	31	925
4. SOCIOLOGY, STATISTICS	4	17	21	14	37	51	387	13	400
5. POLITICAL SCIENCE	7	28	35	27	10	37	1 859	16	1 875
6. LAW, PUBLIC ADMIN.	6	13	19	17	251	268	591	46	637
7. MILITARY ART	–	18	18	8	6	14	11	–	11
8. EDUCATION, LEISURE	17	45	62	17	82	99	191	16	207
9. TRADE, TRANSPORT	3	14	17	19	16	35	160	16	176
10. ETHNOGRAPHY, FOLKLORE	2	11	13	61	55	116	66	7	73
11. MATHEMATICS	1	12	13	21	2	23	135	10	145
12. NATURAL SCIENCES	5	6	11	40	13	53	462	8	470
13. MEDICAL SCIENCES	2	17	19	41	17	58	162	4	166
14. ENGINEERING, CRAFTS	5	12	17	42	7	49	297	70	367
15. AGRICULTURE	4	25	29	2	–	2	142	3	145
16. DOMESTIC SCIENCE	4	12	16	17	–	17	49	–	49
17. MANAGEMENT, ADMIN.	2	14	16	5	16	21	94	8	102
18. PLANNING, ARCHITECTURE	1	8	9	2	4	6	53	5	58
19. PLASTIC ARTS	–	5	5	31	15	46	41	–	41
20. PERFORMING ARTS	2	17	19	14	15	29	66	–	66
21. GAMES, SPORTS	2	18	20	11	3	14	77	–	77
22. LINGUISTICS, PHILOLOGY	3	12	15	73	32	105	172	–	172
23. LITERATURE									
(A) HISTORY AND CRITICISM	4	2	6	17	2	19	4 309	12	4 321
(B) LITERARY TEXTS	54	36	90	268	106	374	./.	./.	./.
24. GEOGRAPHY, TRAVEL	2	13	15	19	11	30	256	–	256
25. HISTORY, BIOGRAPHY	3	18	21	75	30	105	814	7	821

SUBJECT GROUP GROUPE DE SUJETS GRUPO TEMATICO	INDONESIA (1977)			IRAN (1977)			IRAQ ‡ (1978)		
	A	B	A+B	A	B	A+B	A	B	A+B
TOTAL	1 221	787	2 008	2 289	–	2 289	1 555	191	1 556
1. GENERALITIES	137	156	293	93	–	93	92	20	112
2. PHILOSOPHY, PSYCHOLOGY	31	7	38	80	–	80	34	7	41
3. RELIGION, THEOLOGY	91	49	140	572	–	572	64	20	84
4. SOCIOLOGY, STATISTICS	105	64	169	106	–	106	32	3	35
5. POLITICAL SCIENCE	119	91	210	89	–	89	107	32	139
6. LAW, PUBLIC ADMIN.	57	26	83	45	–	45	124	20	144
7. MILITARY ART	10	7	17	–	–	–	2	–	2
8. EDUCATION, LEISURE	57	51	108	41	–	41	31	10	41
9. TRADE, TRANSPORT	20	19	39	–	–	–	6	3	9
10. ETHNOGRAPHY, FOLKLORE	12	5	17	34	–	34	24	8	32
11. MATHEMATICS	20	3	23	23	–	23	13	1	14
12. NATURAL SCIENCES	31	56	87	76	–	76	115	1	116
13. MEDICAL SCIENCES	28	29	57	85	–	85	66	4	70
14. ENGINEERING, CRAFTS	42	40	82	53	–	53	145	5	150
15. AGRICULTURE	34	70	104	39	–	39	92	12	104
16. DOMESTIC SCIENCE	7	3	10	4	–	4	–	–	–
17. MANAGEMENT, ADMIN.	34	23	57	36	–	36	42	6	48
18. PLANNING, ARCHITECTURE	29	25	54	14	–	14	28	4	32
19. PLASTIC ARTS	8	2	10	–	–	–	4	4	8
20. PERFORMING ARTS	11	6	17	53	–	53	8	3	11
21. GAMES, SPORTS	11	1	12	11	–	11	9	3	12
22. LINGUISTICS, PHILOLOGY	14	4	18	32	–	32	61	3	64
23. LITERATURE									
(A) HISTORY AND CRITICISM	5	3	8	48	–	48	190	20	210
(B) LITERARY TEXTS	233	10	243	522	–	522	./.	./.	./.
24. GEOGRAPHY, TRAVEL	13	6	19	25	–	25	13	–	13
25. HISTORY, BIOGRAPHY	62	31	93	208	–	208	63	2	65

8.4 Number of titles (first editions) by subject group
Nombre de titres (premières éditions) par groupes de sujets
Número de obras (primeras ediciones) por categoría de temas

SUBJECT GROUP / GROUPE DE SUJETS / GRUPO TEMATICO	ISRAEL ‡ (1977)			JAPAN ‡ (1978)			JORDAN ‡ (1976)		
	A	B	A+B	A	B	A+B	A	B	A+B
TOTAL	1 513	414	1 927	40 282	3 096	43 378	379	13	392
1. GENERALITIES	10	3	13	840	203	1 043	3	–	3
2. PHILOSOPHY, PSYCHOLOGY	29	5	34	795	2	797	1	–	1
3. RELIGION, THEOLOGY	266	33	299	833	26	859	35	–	35
4. SOCIOLOGY, STATISTICS	34	91	125	1 321	148	1 469	17	–	17
5. POLITICAL SCIENCE	49	40	89	3 015	338	3 353	24	8	32
6. LAW, PUBLIC ADMIN.	19	2	21	2 338	153	2 491	6	–	6
7. MILITARY ART	–	–	–	84	11	95	–	–	–
8. EDUCATION, LEISURE	31	13	44	2 117	237	2 354	50	2	52
9. TRADE, TRANSPORT	4	8	12	1 560	139	1 699	–	–	–
10. ETHNOGRAPHY, FOLKLORE	–	1	1	545	28	573	3	–	3
11. MATHEMATICS	4	–	4	277	–	277	31	–	31
12. NATURAL SCIENCES	41	15	56	1 145	16	1 161	20	–	20
13. MEDICAL SCIENCES	16	5	21	1 770	114	1 884	10	–	10
14. ENGINEERING, CRAFTS	18	8	26	5 097	310	5 407	44	3	47
15. AGRICULTURE	22	34	56	2 240	346	2 586	2	–	2
16. DOMESTIC SCIENCE	24	4	28	591	8	599	–	–	–
17. MANAGEMENT, ADMIN.	15	11	26	778	24	802	–	–	–
18. PLANNING, ARCHITECTURE	5	–	5	411	21	432	2	–	2
19. PLASTIC ARTS	3	–	3	1 425	115	1 540	–	–	–
20. PERFORMING ARTS	6	11	17	530	22	552	–	–	–
21. GAMES, SPORTS	13	1	14	770	8	778	–	–	–
22. LINGUISTICS, PHILOLOGY	35	1	36	654	21	675	54	–	54
23. LITERATURE									
(A) HISTORY AND CRITICISM	./.	./.	./.	564	7	571	25	–	25
(B) LITERARY TEXTS	423	30	453	7 403	556	7 959	./.	–	./.
24. GEOGRAPHY, TRAVEL	32	7	39	913	52	965	23	–	23
25. HISTORY, BIOGRAPHY	132	12	144	2 266	191	2 457	29	–	29

SUBJECT GROUP / GROUPE DE SUJETS / GRUPO TEMATICO	KOREA, REPUBLIC OF (1978)			LAO PEOPLE'S DEMOCRATIC REPUBLIC (1976)			MALAYSIA ‡ (1978)		
	A	B	A+B	A	B	A+B	A	B	A+B
TOTAL	10 500	427	10 927	–	31	31	787	480	1 267
1. GENERALITIES	482	145	627	–	2	2	25	19	44
2. PHILOSOPHY, PSYCHOLOGY	516	–	516	–	6	6	8	8	16
3. RELIGION, THEOLOGY	795	27	822	–	1	1	75	51	126
4. SOCIOLOGY, STATISTICS	233	–	233	–	–	–	50	8	58
5. POLITICAL SCIENCE	182	–	182	–	7	7	57	121	178
6. LAW, PUBLIC ADMIN.	141	–	141	–	–	–	26	22	48
7. MILITARY ART	21	–	21	–	–	–	–	–	–
8. EDUCATION, LEISURE	274	34	308	–	–	–	23	23	46
9. TRADE, TRANSPORT	218	8	226	–	–	–	7	11	18
10. ETHNOGRAPHY, FOLKLORE	22	–	22	–	–	–	12	63	75
11. MATHEMATICS	139	6	145	–	–	–	23	1	24
12. NATURAL SCIENCES	801	6	807	–	–	–	63	8	71
13. MEDICAL SCIENCES	114	1	115	–	3	3	14	11	25
14. ENGINEERING, CRAFTS	729	3	732	–	–	–	31	37	68
15. AGRICULTURE	112	1	113	–	–	–	43	20	63
16. DOMESTIC SCIENCE	56	2	58	–	–	–	2	3	5
17. MANAGEMENT, ADMIN.	55	–	55	–	–	–	28	12	40
18. PLANNING, ARCHITECTURE	67	–	67	–	–	–	3	2	5
19. PLASTIC ARTS	146	27	173	–	–	–	3	3	6
20. PERFORMING ARTS	493	2	495	–	1	1	4	1	5
21. GAMES, SPORTS	61	2	63	–	–	–	3	–	3
22. LINGUISTICS, PHILOLOGY	905	14	919	–	–	–	118	29	147
23. LITERATURE									
(A) HISTORY AND CRITICISM	250	–	250	–	1	1	114	16	130
(B) LITERARY TEXTS	2 320	141	2 461	–	9	9	./.	./.	./.
24. GEOGRAPHY, TRAVEL	36	1	37	–	1	1	15	2	17
25. HISTORY, BIOGRAPHY	645	7	652	–	–	–	40	9	49

Number of titles (first editions) by subject group 8.4
Nombre de titres (premières éditions) par groupes de sujets
Número de obras (primeras ediciones) por categoría de temas

SUBJECT GROUP GROUPE DE SUJETS GRUPO TEMATICO	MALDIVES (1977)			PHILIPPINES ‡ (1977)			QATAR (1978)		
	A	B	A+B	A	B	A+B	A	B	A+B
TOTAL	3	–	3	523	155	678	45	32	77
1. GENERALITIES	1	–	1	18	18	36	5	4	9
2. PHILOSOPHY, PSYCHOLOGY	1	–	1	14	–	14	–	–	–
3. RELIGION, THEOLOGY	–	–	–	43	17	60	13	18	31
4. SOCIOLOGY, STATISTICS	–	–	–	19	3	22	–	–	–
5. POLITICAL SCIENCE	–	–	–	25	8	33	–	–	–
6. LAW, PUBLIC ADMIN.	–	–	–	33	9	42	2	10	12
7. MILITARY ART	–	–	–	9	–	9	–	–	–
8. EDUCATION, LEISURE	1	–	1	77	3	80	3	–	3
9. TRADE, TRANSPORT	–	–	–	2	3	5	–	–	–
10. ETHNOGRAPHY, FOLKLORE	–	–	–	1	3	4	–	–	–
11. MATHEMATICS	–	–	–	8	–	8	9	–	9
12. NATURAL SCIENCES	–	–	–	34	3	37	13	–	13
13. MEDICAL SCIENCES	–	–	–	8	4	12	–	–	–
14. ENGINEERING, CRAFTS	–	–	–	8	–	8	–	–	–
15. AGRICULTURE	–	–	–	83	6	89	–	–	–
16. DOMESTIC SCIENCE	–	–	–	19	–	19	–	–	–
17. MANAGEMENT, ADMIN.	–	–	–	30	10	40	–	–	–
18. PLANNING, ARCHITECTURE	–	–	–	–	–	–	–	–	–
19. PLASTIC ARTS	–	–	–	1	1	2	–	–	–
20. PERFORMING ARTS	–	–	–	13	47	60	–	–	–
21. GAMES, SPORTS	–	–	–	3	2	5	–	–	–
22. LINGUISTICS, PHILOLOGY	–	–	–	40	6	46	–	–	–
23. LITERATURE									
(A) HISTORY AND CRITICISM	–	–	–	–	–	–	–	–	–
(B) LITERARY TEXTS	–	–	–	24	4	28	–	–	–
24. GEOGRAPHY, TRAVEL	–	–	–	–	–	–	–	–	–
25. HISTORY, BIOGRAPHY	–	–	–	11	8	19	–	–	–

SUBJECT GROUP GROUPE DE SUJETS GRUPO TEMATICO	SINGAPORE ‡ (1978)			SRI LANKA ‡ (1978)			SYRIAN ARAB REPUBLIC ‡ (1978)		
	A	B	A+B	A	B	A+B	A	B	A+B
TOTAL	620	266	886	489	677	1 166	152	5	157
1. GENERALITIES	1	3	4	8	2	10	1	–	1
2. PHILOSOPHY, PSYCHOLOGY	–	–	–	14	10	24	3	–	3
3. RELIGION, THEOLOGY	12	4	16	95	165	260	1	–	1
4. SOCIOLOGY, STATISTICS	7	2	9	28	12	40	2	–	2
5. POLITICAL SCIENCE	21	6	27	50	94	144	20	–	20
6. LAW, PUBLIC ADMIN.	11	–	11	23	30	53	2	–	2
7. MILITARY ART	–	–	–	–	2	2	–	–	–
8. EDUCATION, LEISURE	190	202	392	17	39	56	1	–	1
9. TRADE, TRANSPORT	4	1	5	5	9	14	7	–	7
10. ETHNOGRAPHY, FOLKLORE	5	–	5	–	1	1	7	–	7
11. MATHEMATICS	32	–	32	7	8	15	18	–	18
12. NATURAL SCIENCES	37	1	38	15	8	23	7	–	7
13. MEDICAL SCIENCES	14	3	17	13	21	34	7	–	7
14. ENGINEERING, CRAFTS	7	1	8	7	16	23	9	–	9
15. AGRICULTURE	–	–	–	15	13	28	–	–	–
16. DOMESTIC SCIENCE	2	–	2	2	–	2	–	–	–
17. MANAGEMENT, ADMIN.	12	17	29	10	18	28	–	–	–
18. PLANNING, ARCHITECTURE	1	–	1	15	79	94	–	–	–
19. PLASTIC ARTS	1	–	1	./.	./.	./.	3	–	3
20. PERFORMING ARTS	5	–	5	./.	./.	./.	3	–	3
21. GAMES, SPORTS	8	–	8	4	21	25	–	–	–
22. LINGUISTICS, PHILOLOGY	64	9	73	11	13	24	2	–	2
23. LITERATURE									
(A) HISTORY AND CRITICISM	10	8	18	18	15	33	5	–	5
(B) LITERARY TEXTS	145	9	154	90	62	152	28	–	28
24. GEOGRAPHY, TRAVEL	10	–	10	5	6	11	5	–	5
25. HISTORY, BIOGRAPHY	21	–	21	37	33	70	9	5	14

8.4 Number of titles (first editions) by subject group
Nombre de titres (premières éditions) par groupes de sujets
Número de obras (primeras ediciones) por categoría de temas

SUBJECT GROUP / GROUPE DE SUJETS / GRUPO TEMATICO	THAILAND ‡ (1977)			UNITED ARAB EMIRATES (1977)			VIET NAM (1977)		
	A	B	A+B	A	B	A+B	A	B	A+B
TOTAL	2 530	302	2 832	13	2	15	765	41	806
1. GENERALITIES	278	27	305	6	–	6	–	–	–
2. PHILOSOPHY, PSYCHOLOGY	54	6	60	–	–	–	–	–	–
3. RELIGION, THEOLOGY	167	34	201	–	–	–	3	–	3
4. SOCIOLOGY, STATISTICS	86	5	91	–	–	–	4	–	4
5. POLITICAL SCIENCE	242	51	293	–	–	–	86	7	93
6. LAW, PUBLIC ADMIN.	208	22	230	1	–	1	10	5	15
7. MILITARY ART	21	3	24	–	–	–	11	–	11
8. EDUCATION, LEISURE	438	17	455	–	–	–	29	–	29
9. TRADE, TRANSPORT	18	3	21	4	2	6	4	–	4
10. ETHNOGRAPHY, FOLKLORE	33	5	38	–	–	–	3	–	3
11. MATHEMATICS	32	–	32	–	–	–	32	–	32
12. NATURAL SCIENCES	71	7	78	–	–	–	70	–	70
13. MEDICAL SCIENCES	48	29	77	–	–	–	40	2	42
14. ENGINEERING, CRAFTS	166	48	214	–	–	–	53	–	53
15. AGRICULTURE	54	6	60	–	–	–	53	3	56
16. DOMESTIC SCIENCE	33	1	34	–	–	–	1	–	1
17. MANAGEMENT, ADMIN.	38	5	43	–	–	–	22	–	22
18. PLANNING, ARCHITECTURE	14	5	19	–	–	–	1	–	1
19. PLASTIC ARTS	19	2	21	1	–	1	3	–	3
20. PERFORMING ARTS	23	–	23	–	–	–	19	–	19
21. GAMES, SPORTS	33	1	34	–	–	–	20	1	21
22. LINGUISTICS, PHILOLOGY	236	10	246	–	–	–	37	–	37
23. LITERATURE									
(A) HISTORY AND CRITICISM	9	–	9	–	–	–	18	–	18
(B) LITERARY TEXTS	./.	–	./.	1	–	1	210	22	232
24. GEOGRAPHY, TRAVEL	47	6	53	–	–	–	14	–	14
25. HISTORY, BIOGRAPHY	162	9	171	–	–	–	22	1	23

SUBJECT GROUP / GROUPE DE SUJETS / GRUPO TEMATICO — EUROPE	AUSTRIA (1978)			BELGIUM ‡ (1978)	BULGARIA ‡ (1978)		
	A	B	A+B	A+B	A	B	A+B
TOTAL	4 265	1 115	5 380	7 570	3 070	712	3 782
1. GENERALITIES	81	41	122	215	72	88	160
2. PHILOSOPHY, PSYCHOLOGY	186	5	191	173	46	6	52
3. RELIGION, THEOLOGY	129	41	170	280	6	1	7
4. SOCIOLOGY, STATISTICS	184	42	226	100	69	27	96
5. POLITICAL SCIENCE	308	114	422	516	485	132	617
6. LAW, PUBLIC ADMIN.	219	49	268	390	76	14	90
7. MILITARY ART	2	5	7	69	26	3	29
8. EDUCATION, LEISURE	286	148	434	231	143	40	183
9. TRADE, TRANSPORT	50	12	62	96	31	8	39
10. ETHNOGRAPHY, FOLKLORE	72	23	95	44	9	1	10
11. MATHEMATICS	88	15	103	127	31	1	32
12. NATURAL SCIENCES	383	33	416	340	151	12	163
13. MEDICAL SCIENCES	107	61	168	270	169	60	229
14. ENGINEERING, CRAFTS	299	108	407	279	350	66	416
15. AGRICULTURE	98	12	110	137	171	35	206
16. DOMESTIC SCIENCE	16	2	18	145	7	2	9
17. MANAGEMENT, ADMIN.	541	45	586	93	96	17	113
18. PLANNING, ARCHITECTURE	13	17	30	624	115	41	156
19. PLASTIC ARTS	140	99	239	./.	./.	./.	./.
20. PERFORMING ARTS	91	27	118	./.	./.	./.	./.
21. GAMES, SPORTS	43	36	79	180	65	4	69
22. LINGUISTICS, PHILOLOGY	91	19	110	260	84	1	85
23. LITERATURE							
(A) HISTORY AND CRITICISM	106	5	111	101	668	95	763
(B) LITERARY TEXTS	350	72	422	2 270	./.	./.	./.
24. GEOGRAPHY, TRAVEL	101	24	125	187	40	9	49
25. HISTORY, BIOGRAPHY	281	60	341	443	160	49	209

Number of titles (first editions) by subject group 8.4
Nombre de titres (premières éditions) par groupes de sujets
Número de obras (primeras ediciones) por categoría de temas

SUBJECT GROUP / GROUPE DE SUJETS / GRUPO TEMATICO	CZECHOSLOVAKIA ‡ (1978)			DENMARK (1978)			FINLAND (1978)		
	A	B	A+B	A	B	A+B	A	B	A+B
TOTAL	5 953	1 033	6 986	5 236	2 750	7 986	2 166	602	2 768
1. GENERALITIES	246	199	445	126	66	192	79	19	98
2. PHILOSOPHY, PSYCHOLOGY	114	1	115	154	64	218	80	7	87
3. RELIGION, THEOLOGY	37	—	37	158	96	254	127	22	149
4. SOCIOLOGY, STATISTICS	34	1	35	117	60	177	47	14	61
5. POLITICAL SCIENCE	497	91	588	348	205	553	131	34	165
6. LAW, PUBLIC ADMIN.	114	21	135	196	135	331	148	19	167
7. MILITARY ART	72	35	107	24	17	41	14	3	17
8. EDUCATION, LEISURE	369	40	409	255	100	355	82	21	103
9. TRADE, TRANSPORT	77	10	87	—	—	—	9	2	11
10. ETHNOGRAPHY, FOLKLORE	5	—	5	39	34	73	41	2	43
11. MATHEMATICS	132	3	135	90	73	163	12	21	33
12. NATURAL SCIENCES	437	24	461	303	248	551	119	153	272
13. MEDICAL SCIENCES	192	57	249	265	121	386	125	37	162
14. ENGINEERING, CRAFTS	986	108	1 094	472	319	791	126	69	195
15. AGRICULTURE	336	53	389	153	102	255	64	51	115
16. DOMESTIC SCIENCE	18	6	24	78	26	104	27	6	33
17. MANAGEMENT, ADMIN.	46	1	47	134	76	210	69	17	86
18. PLANNING, ARCHITECTURE	294	65	359	125	47	172	27	3	30
19. PLASTIC ARTS	./.	./.	./.	114	62	176	27	11	38
20. PERFORMING ARTS	./.	./.	./.	54	43	97	22	1	23
21. GAMES, SPORTS	115	22	137	106	43	149	31	1	32
22. LINGUISTICS, PHILOLOGY	191	5	196	147	122	269	72	12	84
23. LITERATURE									
(A) HISTORY AND CRITICISM	95	22	117	51	9	60	14	3	17
(B) LITERARY TEXTS	1 272	217	1 489	1 175	496	1 671	533	62	595
24. GEOGRAPHY, TRAVEL	100	11	111	144	75	219	42	5	47
25. HISTORY, BIOGRAPHY	174	41	215	408	111	519	98	7	105

SUBJECT GROUP / GROUPE DE SUJETS / GRUPO TEMATICO	GERMAN DEMOCRATIC REPUBLIC ‡ (1978)			GERMANY, FEDERAL REPUBLIC OF ‡ (1978)			GREECE (1977)		
	A	B	A+B	A	B	A+B	A	B	A+B
TOTAL	2 618	382	3 000	34 896	6 756	41 652	1 928	227	2 155
1. GENERALITIES	50	—	50	1 806	886	2 692	20	2	22
2. PHILOSOPHY, PSYCHOLOGY	95	3	98	891	74	965	95	3	98
3. RELIGION, THEOLOGY	135	48	183	1 530	314	1 844	118	14	132
4. SOCIOLOGY, STATISTICS	82	6	88	1 374	376	1 750	33	1	34
5. POLITICAL SCIENCE	70	8	78	1 640	539	2 179	53	7	60
6. LAW, PUBLIC ADMIN.	72	4	76	1 648	423	2 071	91	6	97
7. MILITARY ART	39	4	43	822	231	1 053	10	—	10
8. EDUCATION, LEISURE	84	12	96	2 710	734	3 444	134	41	175
9. TRADE, TRANSPORT	44	4	48	331	132	463	29	2	31
10. ETHNOGRAPHY, FOLKLORE	15	1	16	./.	./.	./.	42	3	45
11. MATHEMATICS	66	—	66	510	106	616	51	3	54
12. NATURAL SCIENCES	170	20	190	1 369	350	1 719	35	6	41
13. MEDICAL SCIENCES	120	2	122	1 484	271	1 755	33	17	50
14. ENGINEERING, CRAFTS	225	19	244	1 436	559	1 995	29	11	40
15. AGRICULTURE	56	3	59	893	172	1 065	25	3	28
16. DOMESTIC SCIENCE	3	—	3	./.	./.	./.	10	4	14
17. MANAGEMENT, ADMIN.	3	1	4	./.	./.	./.	39	1	40
18. PLANNING, ARCHITECTURE	69	14	83	./.	./.	./.	20	3	23
19. PLASTIC ARTS	2	5	7	1 577	682	2 259	28	7	35
20. PERFORMING ARTS	64	3	67	580	109	689	10	4	14
21. GAMES, SPORTS	45	3	48	398	88	486	7	1	8
22. LINGUISTICS, PHILOLOGY	113	3	116	1 303	112	1 415	48	14	62
23. LITERATURE									
(A) HISTORY AND CRITICISM	651	52	703	./.	./.	./.	92	19	111
(B) LITERARY TEXTS	./.	./.	./.	10 032	282	10 314	618	21	639
24. GEOGRAPHY, TRAVEL	52	—	52	834	98	932	42	3	45
25. HISTORY, BIOGRAPHY	81	10	91	1 728	218	1 946	216	31	247

8.4 Number of titles (first editions) by subject group
Nombre de titres (premières éditions) par groupes de sujets
Número de obras (primeras ediciones) por categoría de temas

SUBJECT GROUP GROUPE DE SUJETS GRUPO TEMATICO	HOLY SEE (1978)			HUNGARY (1978)			ICELAND ‡ (1977)		
	A	B	A+B	A	B	A+B	A	B	A+B
TOTAL	129	—	129	6 620	909	7 529	469	200	669
1. GENERALITIES	2	—	2	216	12	228	12	5	17
2. PHILOSOPHY, PSYCHOLOGY	15	—	15	74	5	79	9	3	12
3. RELIGION, THEOLOGY	78	—	78	47	5	52	7	3	10
4. SOCIOLOGY, STATISTICS	7	—	7	140	3	143	9	1	10
5. POLITICAL SCIENCE	—	—	—	555	95	650	29	20	49
6. LAW, PUBLIC ADMIN.	9	—	9	237	40	277	13	12	25
7. MILITARY ART	—	—	—	27	2	29	—	—	—
8. EDUCATION, LEISURE	1	—	1	738	165	903	23	13	36
9. TRADE, TRANSPORT	—	—	—	89	3	92	9	3	12
10. ETHNOGRAPHY, FOLKLORE	—	—	—	58	9	67	10	2	12
11. MATHEMATICS	—	—	—	130	27	157	2	2	4
12. NATURAL SCIENCES	—	—	—	384	92	476	16	11	27
13. MEDICAL SCIENCES	—	—	—	196	18	214	6	5	11
14. ENGINEERING, CRAFTS	—	—	—	1 036	90	1 126	25	28	53
15. AGRICULTURE	—	—	—	281	59	340	10	20	30
16. DOMESTIC SCIENCE	—	—	—	45	4	49	2	3	5
17. MANAGEMENT, ADMIN.	—	—	—	484	38	522	2	2	4
18. PLANNING, ARCHITECTURE	—	—	—	66	4	70	17	6	23
19. PLASTIC ARTS	—	—	—	177	113	290	./.	./.	./.
20. PERFORMING ARTS	1	—	1	131	29	160	./.	./.	./.
21. GAMES, SPORTS	—	—	—	90	8	98	22	7	29
22. LINGUISTICS, PHILOLOGY	8	—	8	141	12	153	4	3	7
23. LITERATURE									
(A) HISTORY AND CRITICISM	—	—	—	170	6	176	6	—	6
(B) LITERARY TEXTS	—	—	—	790	47	837	185	44	229
24. GEOGRAPHY, TRAVEL	—	—	—	78	13	91	8	2	10
25. HISTORY, BIOGRAPHY	8	—	8	240	10	250	43	5	48

SUBJECT GROUP GROUPE DE SUJETS GRUPO TEMATICO	IRELAND (1978)			ITALY (1978)			LUXEMBOURG (1977)		
	A	B	A+B	A	B	A+B	A	B	A+B
TOTAL	422	192	614	8 140	1 515	9 209	157	82	239
1. GENERALITIES	18	10	28	195	46	241	6	—	6
2. PHILOSOPHY, PSYCHOLOGY	4	1	5	508	7	515	2	—	2
3. RELIGION, THEOLOGY	19	11	30	477	164	641	1	1	2
4. SOCIOLOGY, STATISTICS	15	7	22	277	11	288	8	—	8
5. POLITICAL SCIENCE	20	8	28	572	19	591	19	11	30
6. LAW, PUBLIC ADMIN.	26	15	41	692	98	790	23	15	38
7. MILITARY ART	—	—	—	14	4	18	1	—	1
8. EDUCATION, LEISURE	12	5	17	345	94	439	14	13	27
9. TRADE, TRANSPORT	10	6	16	23	—	23	2	4	6
10. ETHNOGRAPHY, FOLKLORE	11	2	13	112	3	115	2	—	2
11. MATHEMATICS	4	—	4	92	8	100	2	1	3
12. NATURAL SCIENCES	12	6	18	283	118	401	1	1	2
13. MEDICAL SCIENCES	6	3	9	343	26	369	1	2	3
14. ENGINEERING, CRAFTS	16	12	28	255	78	333	5	3	8
15. AGRICULTURE	12	8	20	71	15	86	1	1	2
16. DOMESTIC SCIENCE	3	—	3	60	2	62	—	—	—
17. MANAGEMENT, ADMIN.	4	2	6	47	4	51	—	—	—
18. PLANNING, ARCHITECTURE	6	2	8	229	12	241	3	—	3
19. PLASTIC ARTS	10	8	18	216	24	240	8	2	10
20. PERFORMING ARTS	13	7	20	210	48	258	16	5	21
21. GAMES, SPORTS	16	5	21	218	89	307	11	13	24
22. LINGUISTICS, PHILOLOGY	14	6	20	169	2	171	2	—	2
23. LITERATURE									
(A) HISTORY AND CRITICISM	8	2	10	277	6	283	3	1	4
(B) LITERARY TEXTS	85	37	122	1 665	157	1 822	11	8	19
24. GEOGRAPHY, TRAVEL	27	15	42	161	17	178	—	—	—
25. HISTORY, BIOGRAPHY	51	14	65	629	17	646	15	1	16

Number of titles (first editions) by subject group 8.4
Nombre de titres (premières éditions) par groupes de sujets
Número de obras (primeras ediciones) por categoría de temas

SUBJECT GROUP / GROUPE DE SUJETS / GRUPO TEMATICO	MALTA (1978)			NETHERLANDS ‡ (1978)	NORWAY (1978)		
	A	B	A+B	A+B	A	B	A+B
TOTAL	114	33	147	7 911	3 142	1 005	4 147
1. GENERALITIES	3	2	5	118	68	47	115
2. PHILOSOPHY, PSYCHOLOGY	—	—	—	343	52	12	64
3. RELIGION, THEOLOGY	24	6	30	362	160	99	259
4. SOCIOLOGY, STATISTICS	3	—	3	1 400	130	20	150
5. POLITICAL SCIENCE	4	5	9	./.	187	94	281
6. LAW, PUBLIC ADMIN.	7	2	9	./.	117	60	177
7. MILITARY ART	—	—	—	8	10	4	14
8. EDUCATION, LEISURE	5	1	6	182	98	60	158
9. TRADE, TRANSPORT	3	2	5	./.	45	32	77
10. ETHNOGRAPHY, FOLKLORE	1	1	2	./.	17	1	18
11. MATHEMATICS	—	—	—	663	24	9	33
12. NATURAL SCIENCES	—	—	—	./.	110	111	221
13. MEDICAL SCIENCES	—	1	1	365	110	29	139
14. ENGINEERING, CRAFTS	—	—	—	280	122	59	181
15. AGRICULTURE	—	—	—	48	73	48	121
16. DOMESTIC SCIENCE	1	—	1	209	27	3	30
17. MANAGEMENT, ADMIN.	—	—	—	./.	39	14	53
18. PLANNING, ARCHITECTURE	1	1	2	—	35	16	51
19. PLASTIC ARTS	—	—	—	364	51	15	66
20. PERFORMING ARTS	2	1	3	./.	32	9	41
21. GAMES, SPORTS	—	—	—	88	50	11	61
22. LINGUISTICS, PHILOLOGY	4	—	4	546	59	16	75
23. LITERATURE							
(A) HISTORY AND CRITICISM	—	—	—	./.	43	2	45
(B) LITERARY TEXTS	39	7	46	2 228	1 217	162	1 379
24. GEOGRAPHY, TRAVEL	6	3	9	160	121	29	150
25. HISTORY, BIOGRAPHY	11	1	12	547	145	43	188

SUBJECT GROUP / GROUPE DE SUJETS / GRUPO TEMATICO	POLAND ‡ (1978)			PORTUGAL ‡ (1978)	ROMANIA (1978)		
	A	B	A+B	A+B	A	B	A+B
TOTAL	6 893	2 479	9 372	5 165	5 496	1 914	7 410
1. GENERALITIES	165	98	263	86	90	29	119
2. PHILOSOPHY, PSYCHOLOGY	102	7	109	158	93	37	130
3. RELIGION, THEOLOGY	131	6	137	208	50	67	117
4. SOCIOLOGY, STATISTICS	154	17	171	1 094	88	115	203
5. POLITICAL SCIENCE	567	250	817	./.	209	144	353
6. LAW, PUBLIC ADMIN.	202	28	230	./.	88	34	122
7. MILITARY ART	114	27	141	./.	37	2	39
8. EDUCATION, LEISURE	476	201	677	./.	159	31	190
9. TRADE, TRANSPORT	99	38	137	./.	35	11	46
10. ETHNOGRAPHY, FOLKLORE	20	9	29	./.	16	16	32
11. MATHEMATICS	86	20	106	213	245	57	302
12. NATURAL SCIENCES	495	163	658	./.	414	305	719
13. MEDICAL SCIENCES	294	49	343	1 191	387	196	583
14. ENGINEERING, CRAFTS	1 352	650	2 002	./.	776	153	929
15. AGRICULTURE	338	221	559	./.	284	175	459
16. DOMESTIC SCIENCE	48	2	50	./.	22	1	23
17. MANAGEMENT, ADMIN.	340	204	544	./.	137	9	146
18. PLANNING, ARCHITECTURE	318	128	446	685	50	21	71
19. PLASTIC ARTS	./.	./.	./.	./.	114	35	149
20. PERFORMING ARTS	./.	./.	./.	./.	81	81	162
21. GAMES, SPORTS	97	28	125	./.	87	47	134
22. LINGUISTICS, PHILOLOGY	233	50	283	./.	376	63	439
23. LITERATURE							
(A) HISTORY AND CRITICISM	169	23	192	1 156	169	51	220
(B) LITERARY TEXTS	716	137	853	./.	1 193	96	1 289
24. GEOGRAPHY, TRAVEL	84	84	168	374	133	68	201
25. HISTORY, BIOGRAPHY	293	39	332	./.	163	70	233

8.4 Number of titles (first editions) by subject group
Nombre de titres (premières éditions) par groupes de sujets
Número de obras (primeras ediciones) por categoría de temas

SUBJECT GROUP / GROUPE DE SUJETS / GRUPO TEMATICO	SAN MARINO (1978)			SPAIN ‡ (1977)			SWITZERLAND (1978)
	A	B	A+B	A	B	A+B	A+B
TOTAL	14	1	15	16 714	4 116	20 830	9 192
1. GENERALITIES	–	–	–	1 214	1 101	2 315	132
2. PHILOSOPHY, PSYCHOLOGY	–	–	–	982	129	1 111	278
3. RELIGION, THEOLOGY	–	–	–	953	249	1 202	589
4. SOCIOLOGY, STATISTICS	–	–	–	418	67	485	319
5. POLITICAL SCIENCE	–	–	–	1 166	189	1 355	544
6. LAW, PUBLIC ADMIN.	–	–	–	605	135	740	428
7. MILITARY ART	–	–	–	51	5	56	26
8. EDUCATION, LEISURE	2	–	2	373	237	610	242
9. TRADE, TRANSPORT	2	–	2	55	6	61	112
10. ETHNOGRAPHY, FOLKLORE	–	–	–	167	38	205	253
11. MATHEMATICS	–	–	–	447	68	515	99
12. NATURAL SCIENCES	–	–	–	790	353	1 143	757
13. MEDICAL SCIENCES	1	–	1	614	147	761	1 402
14. ENGINEERING, CRAFTS	–	–	–	521	102	623	415
15. AGRICULTURE	–	–	–	138	152	290	117
16. DOMESTIC SCIENCE	–	–	–	161	28	189	58
17. MANAGEMENT, ADMIN.	1	–	1	193	31	224	141
18. PLANNING, ARCHITECTURE	2	1	3	766	431	1 197	168
19. PLASTIC ARTS	–	–	–	./.	./.	./.	505
20. PERFORMING ARTS	1	–	1	./.	./.	./.	130
21. GAMES, SPORTS	–	–	–	175	45	220	134
22. LINGUISTICS, PHILOLOGY	–	–	–	1 140	163	1 303	192
23. LITERATURE							
(A) HISTORY AND CRITICISM	–	–	–	4 214	264	4 478	198
(B) LITERARY TEXTS	2	–	2	./.	./.	./.	1 074
24. GEOGRAPHY, TRAVEL	–	–	–	159	38	197	372
25. HISTORY, BIOGRAPHY	3	–	3	1 412	138	1 550	507

SUBJECT GROUP / GROUPE DE SUJETS / GRUPO TEMATICO	UNITED KINGDOM ‡ (1977)			YUGOSLAVIA (1978)		
	A	B	A+B	A	B	A+B
TOTAL	25 108	2 500	27 608	6 480	2 354	8 834
1. GENERALITIES	778	91	869	125	35	160
2. PHILOSOPHY, PSYCHOLOGY	910	40	950	67	5	72
3. RELIGION, THEOLOGY	924	152	1 076	139	25	164
4. SOCIOLOGY, STATISTICS	806	23	829	113	21	134
5. POLITICAL SCIENCE	2 124	211	2 335	1 115	278	1 393
6. LAW, PUBLIC ADMIN.	798	93	891	421	144	565
7. MILITARY ART	96	16	112	21	3	24
8. EDUCATION, LEISURE	667	61	728	814	131	945
9. TRADE, TRANSPORT	327	69	396	–	–	–
10. ETHNOGRAPHY, FOLKLORE	138	23	161	15	6	21
11. MATHEMATICS	497	50	547	79	15	94
12. NATURAL SCIENCES	1 994	164	2 158	148	23	171
13. MEDICAL SCIENCES	1 523	59	1 582	208	34	242
14. ENGINEERING, CRAFTS	1 437	116	1 553	278	62	340
15. AGRICULTURE	479	60	539	110	34	144
16. DOMESTIC SCIENCE	470	64	534	26	13	39
17. MANAGEMENT, ADMIN.	495	36	531	406	323	729
18. PLANNING, ARCHITECTURE	1 886	168	2 054	33	29	62
19. PLASTIC ARTS	./.	./.	./.	151	409	560
20. PERFORMING ARTS	./.	./.	./.	143	432	575
21. GAMES, SPORTS	646	40	686	106	30	136
22. LINGUISTICS, PHILOLOGY	472	128	600	90	10	100
23. LITERATURE						
(A) HISTORY AND CRITICISM	629	35	664	115	15	130
(B) LITERARY TEXTS	4 689	564	5 253	1 510	225	1 735
24. GEOGRAPHY, TRAVEL	541	87	628	81	27	108
25. HISTORY, BIOGRAPHY	1 782	150	1 932	166	25	191

Number of titles (first editions) by subject group 8.4
Nombre de titres (premières éditions) par groupes de sujets
Número de obras (primeras ediciones) por categoría de temas

SUBJECT GROUP / GROUPE DE SUJETS OCEANIA / GRUPO TEMATICO	FIJI ‡ (1976)			FRENCH POLYNESIA (1977)			GUAM (1978)		
	A	B	A+B	A	B	A+B	A	B	A+B
TOTAL	70	66	136	4	1	5	12	19	31
1. GENERALITIES	–	–	–	–	–	–	–	–	–
2. PHILOSOPHY, PSYCHOLOGY	–	–	–	–	–	–	–	–	–
3. RELIGION, THEOLOGY	–	–	–	–	–	–	–	–	–
4. SOCIOLOGY, STATISTICS	2	2	4	1	–	1	–	–	–
5. POLITICAL SCIENCE	–	–	–	–	–	–	–	–	–
6. LAW, PUBLIC ADMIN.	–	–	–	–	–	–	–	–	–
7. MILITARY ART	–	–	–	–	–	–	–	–	–
8. EDUCATION, LEISURE	21	21	42	–	–	–	–	–	–
9. TRADE, TRANSPORT	2	–	2	–	–	–	–	–	–
10. ETHNOGRAPHY, FOLKLORE	–	2	2	–	–	–	–	–	–
11. MATHEMATICS	10	7	17	–	–	–	–	–	–
12. NATURAL SCIENCES	19	8	27	–	–	–	9	–	9
13. MEDICAL SCIENCES	–	2	2	–	–	–	–	–	–
14. ENGINEERING, CRAFTS	–	12	12	–	–	–	–	–	–
15. AGRICULTURE	4	1	5	2	–	2	3	19	22
16. DOMESTIC SCIENCE	2	–	2	–	–	–	–	–	–
17. MANAGEMENT, ADMIN.	2	1	3	–	–	–	–	–	–
18. PLANNING, ARCHITECTURE	–	–	–	–	–	–	–	–	–
19. PLASTIC ARTS	–	2	2	–	–	–	–	–	–
20. PERFORMING ARTS	–	–	–	–	–	–	–	–	–
21. GAMES, SPORTS	–	–	–	–	–	–	–	–	–
22. LINGUISTICS, PHILOLOGY	8	8	16	–	1	1	–	–	–
23. LITERATURE									
(A) HISTORY AND CRITICISM	–	–	–	–	–	–	–	–	–
(B) LITERARY TEXTS	–	–	–	1	–	1	–	–	–
24. GEOGRAPHY, TRAVEL	–	–	–	–	–	–	–	–	–
25. HISTORY, BIOGRAPHY	–	–	–	–	–	–	–	–	–

SUBJECT GROUP / GROUPE DE SUJETS / GRUPO TEMATICO	NEW ZEALAND (1978)			PACIFIC ISLANDS (1978)			SAMOA (1977)		
	A	B	A+B	A	B	A+B	A	B	A+B
TOTAL	844	1 028	1 872	21	20	41	45	35	80
1. GENERALITIES	32	33	65	–	–	–	10	6	16
2. PHILOSOPHY, PSYCHOLOGY	11	3	14	–	–	–	–	–	–
3. RELIGION, THEOLOGY	23	29	52	–	–	–	6	6	12
4. SOCIOLOGY, STATISTICS	35	32	67	1	–	1	5	–	5
5. POLITICAL SCIENCE	91	123	214	2	6	8	–	–	–
6. LAW, PUBLIC ADMIN.	69	78	147	13	2	15	–	–	–
7. MILITARY ART	3	–	3	–	–	–	–	–	–
8. EDUCATION, LEISURE	57	56	113	3	12	15	5	–	5
9. TRADE, TRANSPORT	19	27	46	1	–	1	–	–	–
10. ETHNOGRAPHY, FOLKLORE	3	2	5	1	–	1	–	2	2
11. MATHEMATICS	7	20	27	–	–	–	5	–	5
12. NATURAL SCIENCES	53	102	155	–	–	–	2	6	8
13. MEDICAL SCIENCES	21	25	46	–	–	–	–	3	3
14. ENGINEERING, CRAFTS	79	88	167	–	–	–	–	–	–
15. AGRICULTURE	55	54	109	–	–	–	1	2	3
16. DOMESTIC SCIENCE	23	8	31	–	–	–	1	4	5
17. MANAGEMENT, ADMIN.	20	40	60	–	–	–	–	–	–
18. PLANNING, ARCHITECTURE	28	41	69	–	–	–	–	–	–
19. PLASTIC ARTS	17	17	34	–	–	–	5	–	5
20. PERFORMING ARTS	11	36	47	–	–	–	–	–	–
21. GAMES, SPORTS	34	18	52	–	–	–	–	–	–
22. LINGUISTICS, PHILOLOGY	3	1	4	–	–	–	–	–	–
23. LITERATURE									
(A) HISTORY AND CRITICISM	6	5	11	–	–	–	–	–	–
(B) LITERARY TEXTS	51	110	161	–	–	–	–	–	–
24. GEOGRAPHY, TRAVEL	25	39	64	–	–	–	–	–	–
25. HISTORY, BIOGRAPHY	68	41	109	–	–	–	5	6	11

8.4   Number of titles (first editions) by subject group
      Nombre de titres (premières éditions) par groupes de sujets
      Número de obras (primeras ediciones) por categoría de temas

SUBJECT GROUP GROUPE DE SUJETS GRUPO TEMATICO	TONGA (1978)			U.S.S.R.	U.S.S.R. ‡ (1977)		
	A	B	A+B		A	B	A+B
TOTAL	13	92	105		49 910	29 998	79 908
1. GENERALITIES	–	–	–		1 127	1 039	2 166
2. PHILOSOPHY, PSYCHOLOGY	–	–	–		924	277	1 201
3. RELIGION, THEOLOGY	–	20	20		147	84	231
4. SOCIOLOGY, STATISTICS	–	40	40		532	174	706
5. POLITICAL SCIENCE	–	10	10		5 947	3 598	9 545
6. LAW, PUBLIC ADMIN.	–	–	–		1 088	608	1 696
7. MILITARY ART	–	–	–		1 615	269	1 884
8. EDUCATION, LEISURE	–	2	2		2 441	1 478	3 919
9. TRADE, TRANSPORT	–	10	10		327	208	535
10. ETHNOGRAPHY, FOLKLORE	–	5	5		–	–	–
11. MATHEMATICS	–	–	–		816	176	992
12. NATURAL SCIENCES	–	–	–		5 120	2 569	7 689
13. MEDICAL SCIENCES	–	–	–		2 375	1 404	3 779
14. ENGINEERING, CRAFTS	–	–	–		9 717	11 476	21 193
15. AGRICULTURE	–	–	–		3 026	1 643	4 669
16. DOMESTIC SCIENCE	–	5	5		158	192	350
17. MANAGEMENT, ADMIN.	–	–	–		3 123	1 787	4 910
18. PLANNING, ARCHITECTURE	–	–	–		1 030	711	1 741
19. PLASTIC ARTS	–	–	–		./.	./.	./.
20. PERFORMING ARTS	–	–	–		./.	./.	./.
21. GAMES, SPORTS	–	–	–		442	285	727
22. LINGUISTICS, PHILOLOGY	–	–	–		1 411	170	1 581
23. LITERATURE							
(A) HISTORY AND CRITICISM	–	–	–		1 010	121	1 131
(B) LITERARY TEXTS	–	–	–		5 825	1 427	7 252
24. GEOGRAPHY, TRAVEL	3	–	3		434	92	526
25. HISTORY, BIOGRAPHY	100	–	10		1 275	210	1 485

SUBJECT GROUP GROUPE DE SUJETS GRUPO TEMATICO	BYELORUSSIAN S.S.R. (1978)			UKRAINIAN S.S.R. ‡ (1977)		
	A	B	A+B	A	B	A+B
TOTAL	1 539	949	2 488	4 513	3 246	7 759
1. GENERALITIES	62	62	124	125	181	306
2. PHILOSOPHY, PSYCHOLOGY	38	17	55	54	66	120
3. RELIGION, THEOLOGY	8	–	8	11	19	30
4. SOCIOLOGY, STATISTICS	20	15	35	68	52	120
5. POLITICAL SCIENCE	204	169	373	643	547	1 190
6. LAW, PUBLIC ADMIN.	59	17	76	74	86	160
7. MILITARY ART	4	8	12	13	22	35
8. EDUCATION, LEISURE	131	88	219	198	223	421
9. TRADE, TRANSPORT	12	12	24	35	45	80
10. ETHNOGRAPHY, FOLKLORE	–	–	–	–	–	–
11. MATHEMATICS	19	8	27	98	74	172
12. NATURAL SCIENCES	111	27	138	440	331	771
13. MEDICAL SCIENCES	56	57	113	252	202	454
14. ENGINEERING, CRAFTS	197	160	357	927	732	1 659
15. AGRICULTURE	146	107	253	252	184	436
16. DOMESTIC SCIENCE	22	24	46	15	16	31
17. MANAGEMENT, ADMIN.	74	82	156	270	177	447
18. PLANNING, ARCHITECTURE	3	–	3	73	95	168
19. PLASTIC ARTS	7	8	15	./.	./.	./.
20. PERFORMING ARTS	6	8	14	./.	./.	./.
21. GAMES, SPORTS	13	3	16	37	14	51
22. LINGUISTICS, PHILOLOGY	65	16	81	112	28	140
23. LITERATURE						
(A) HISTORY AND CRITICISM	38	7	45	92	24	116
(B) LITERARY TEXTS	201	41	242	572	91	663
24. GEOGRAPHY, TRAVEL	10	1	11	39	4	43
25. HISTORY, BIOGRAPHY	33	12	45	113	33	146

Number of titles (first editions) by subject group   **8.4**
Nombre de titres (premières éditions) par groupes de sujets
Número de obras (primeras ediciones) por categoría de temas

GENERAL NOTE — NOTE GENERALE — NOTA GENERAL:
E—> FOR THE CLASSIFICATION BASED UPON THE
UNIVERSAL DECIMAL CLASSIFICATION (UDC) SEE
GENERAL NOTE TO TABLE 8.3.
FR—> POUR LA CLASSIFICATION, FONDEE SUR LA
CLASSIFICATION DECIMALE UNIVERSELLE (CDU), VOIR
LA NOTE GENERALE DU TABLEAU 8.3.
ESP> PARA LA CLASIFICACION, BASADA EN LA
CLASIFICACION DECIMAL UNIVERSAL (CDU), VEASE LA
NOTA GENERAL DEL CUADRO 8.3.

CONGO:
E—> WORKS OF GROUP 23B ARE INCLUDED IN GROUP
23A.
FR—> LES OUVRAGES DU GROUPE 23B SONT COMPRIS
DANS LE GROUPE 23A.
ESP> LAS OBRAS DEL GRUPO 23B QUEDAN INCLUIDAS
EN EL GRUPO 23A.

EGYPT:
E—> PRELIMINARY FIGURES. WORKS OF GROUPS 5 TO
10 ARE INCLUDED IN GROUP 4; 12 IN GROUP 11; 14 TO
17 IN GROUP 13; 19 TO 21 IN GROUP 18; 23B IN GROUP
23A; 25 IN GROUP 24.
FR—> DONNEES PROVISOIRES. LES OUVRAGES DES GROU—
PES 5 A 10 SONT COMPRIS DANS LE GROUPE 4; 12 DANS
LE GROUPE 11; 14 A 17 DANS LE GROUPE 13; 19 A 21
DANS LE GROUPE 18; 23B DANS 23A; 25 DANS LE GROU—
PE 24.
ESP> DATOS PRELIMINARES. LAS OBRAS DE LOS GRU—
POS 5 A 10 QUEDAN INCLUIDAS EN EL GRUPO 4; LAS DEL
GRUPO 12 EN EL GRUPO 11; LAS DE LOS GRUPOS 14 A 17
EN EL GRUPO 13; LAS DE LOS GRUPOS 19 A 21 EN EL
GRUPO 18; LAS DEL GRUPO 23B EN EL GRUPO 23A; LAS
DEL GRUPO 25 EN EL GRUPO 24.

ETHIOPIA:
E—> SCHOOLTEXTBOOKS (119) AND CHILDREN' BOOKS
(2) ARE INCLUDED IN THE TOTAL BUT NOT IDENTIFIED
IN THE 25 GROUPS. WORKS OF GROUP 5 TO 10 ARE IN—
CLUDED IN GROUP 4; 12 IN GROUP 11; 14 TO 17 IN
GROUP 13; 19 TO 21 IN GROUP 18; 23B IN GROUP 23A;
25 IN GROUP 24.
FR—> LES MANUELS SCOLAIRES (119) ET LES LIVRES
POUR ENFANTS (2) SONT COMPRIS DANS LE TOTAL MAIS
NE SONT PAS REPARTIS ENTRE LES 25 GROUPES. LES
OUVRAGES DES GROUPES 5 A 10 SONT COMPRIS DANS LE
GROUPE 4; 12 DANS LE GROUPE 11; 14 A 17 DANS LE
GROUPE 13; 19 A 21 DANS LE GROUPE 18; 23B DANS
LE GROUPE 23A; 25 DANS LE GROUPE 24.
ESP> LOS MANUALES ESCOLARES (119) Y LOS LIBROS
PARA NIÑOS (2) QUEDAN COMPRENDIDOS EN EL TOTAL
PERO NO SE DESGLOSAN ENTRE LOS 25 GRUPOS. LAS
OBRAS DE LOS GRUPOS 5 A 10 QUEDAN INCLUIDAS EN
EL GRUPO 4; LAS DEL GRUPO 12 EN EL GRUPO 11; LAS
DE LOS GRUPOS 14 A 17 EN EL GRUPO 13; LAS DE LOS
GRUPOS 19 A 21 EN EL GRUPO 18; LAS DEL GRUPO 23B
EN EL GRUPO 23A; LAS DEL GRUPO 25 EN EL GRUPO 24.

MADAGASCAR:
E—> WORKS OF GROUP 23B ARE INCLUDED IN GROUP
23A.
FR—> LES OUVRAGES DU GROUPE 23B SONT COMPRIS
DANS LE GROUPE 23A.
ESP> LAS OBRAS DEL GRUPO 23B QUEDAN INCLUIDAS
EN EL GRUPO 23A.

SUDAN:
E—> DATA REFER TO SCHOOLTEXT BOOKS ONLY.
FR—> LES DONNEES NE TIENNENT COMPTE QUE DES
MANUELS SCOLAIRES.
ESP> LOS DATOS SE REFIEREN A LOS MANUALES
ESCOLARES SOLAMENTE.

UNITED REPUBLIC OF CAMEROON:
E—> DATA REFER TO SCHOOLTEXT BOOKS ONLY.
FR—> LES DONNEES NE TIENNENT COMPTE QUE DES
MANUELS SCOLAIRES.

UNITED REPUBLIC OF CAMEROON (CONT.):
ESP> LOS DATOS SE REFIEREN A LOS MANUALES
ESCOLARES SOLAMENTE.

UNITED REPUBLIC OF TANZANIA:
E—> WORKS OF GROUP 23B ARE INCLUDED IN GROUP
23A.
FR—> LES OUVRAGES DU GROUPE 23B SONT COMPRIS
DANS LE GROUPE 23A.
ESP> LAS OBRAS DEL GRUPO 23B QUEDAN INCLUIDAS
EN EL GRUPO 23A.

ZAMBIA:
E—> SCHOOL TEXTBOOKS (3) AND CHILDREN'S BOOKS
(1) ARE INCLUDED IN THE TOTAL BUT NOT IDENTIFIED
IN THE 25 GROUPS.
FR—> LES MANUELS SCOLAIRES (3) ET LES LIVRES
POUR ENFANTS (1) SONT COMPRIS DANS LE TOTAL MAIS
NE SONT PAS REPARTIS ENTRE LES 25 GROUPES.
ESP> LOS MANUALES ESCOLARES (3) Y LOS LIBROS
PARA NIÑOS (1) QUEDAN COMPRENDIDOS EN EL TOTAL
PERO NO SE DESGLOSAN ENTRE LOS 25 GRUPOS.

BARBADOS:
E—> WORKS OF GROUP 23B ARE INCLUDED IN GROUP
23A.
FR—> LES OUVRAGES DU GROUPE 23B SONT COMPRIS
DANS LE GROUPE 23A.
ESP> LAS OBRAS DEL GRUPO 23B QUEDAN INCLUIDAS
EN EL GRUPO 23A.

CANADA:
E—> THE DATA DO NOT INCLUDE GOVERNMENTAL PUBLI—
CATIONS. WORKS OF GROUPS 19 AND 20 ARE INCLUDED
IN GROUP 18. DATA INCLUDE FOR THE FIRST TIME
UNIVERSITY THESES.
FR—> LES DONNEES N'INCLUENT PAS LES PUBLICATIONS
OFFICIELLES. POUR LA PREMIERE FOIS, LES THESES
UNIVERSITAIRES SONT PRISES EN CONSIDERATION. LES
OUVRAGES DES GROUPES 19 ET 20 SONT COMPRIS DANS LE
GROUPE 18.
ESP> LOS DATOS EXCLUYEN LAS PUBLICACIONES OFICIA—
LES. LAS TESIS UNIVERSITARIAS SE TOMAN EN CONSIDE—
RACION POR PRIMERA VEZ. LAS OBRAS DE LOS GRUPOS
19 Y 20 QUEDAN COMPRENDIDAS EN EL GRUPO 18.

DOMINICAN REPUBLIC:
E—> WORKS OF GROUP 23B ARE INCLUDED IN GROUP
23A.
FR—> LES OUVRAGES DU GROUPE 23B SONT COMPRIS
DANS LE GROUPE 23A.
ESP> LAS OBRAS DEL GRUPO 23B QUEDAN INCLUIDAS
EN EL GRUPO 23A.

JAMAICA:
E—> WORKS OF GROUP 23B ARE INCLUDED IN GROUP
23A.
FR—> LES OUVRAGES DU GROUPE 23B SONT COMPRIS
DANS LE GROUPE 23A.
ESP> LAS OBRAS DEL GRUPO 23B QUEDAN INCLUIDAS
EN EL GRUPO 23A.

NETHERLANDS ANTILLES:
E—> WORKS OF GROUP 23B ARE INCLUDED IN GROUP
23A.
FR—> LES OUVRAGES DU GROUPE 23B SONT COMPRIS
DANS LE GROUPE 23A.
ESP> LAS OBRAS DEL GRUPO 23B QUEDAN INCLUIDAS
EN EL GRUPO 23A.

UNITED STATES OF AMERICA:
E—>DATA INCLUDE FEDERAL GOVERNMENT PUBLICATIONS
(14,814, OF WHICH 7,220 PAMPHLETS), UNIVERSITY
THESIS (31,629) AND 2,911 JUVENILE TITLES FOR
WHICH THE SUBJECT BREAKDOWN IS NOT AVAILABLE.
WORKS OF GROUP 23B ARE INCLUDED IN GROUP 23A.

8.4 Number of titles (first editions) by subject group
Nombre de titres (premières éditions) par groupes de sujets
Número de obras (primeras ediciones) por categoría de temas

UNITED STATES OF AMERICA (CONT.):
FR─> LES DONNEES COMPRENNENT LES PUBLICATIONS DU
GOUVERNEMENT FEDERAL (14 814, DONT 7 220 BROCHURES),
LES THESES UNIVERSITAIRES (31 629) ET 2 911 TITRES
DE ROMANS POUR JEUNES POUR LESQUELS LA REPARTITION
PAR SUJETS N'EST PAS DISPONIBLE. LES OUVRAGES DU
GROUPE 23B SONT COMPRIS DANS LE GROUPE 23A.
ESP> LOS DATOS COMPRENDEN LAS PUBLICACIONES DEL
GOBIERNO FEDERAL (14 814, DE LAS CUALES 7 220
FOLLETOS), LAS TESIS UNIVERSITARIAS (31 629) Y
2 911 TITULOS DE NOVELAS PARA NIÑOS Y ADOLESCENTES
CUYA DISTRIBUCION POR TEMAS NO SE CONOCE. LAS
OBRAS DEL GRUPO 23B QUEDAN INCLUIDAS EN EL GRUPO
23A.

BRAZIL:
E─> WORKS OF GROUP 23B ARE INCLUDED IN GROUP
23A.
FR─> LES OUVRAGES DU GROUPE 23B SONT COMPRIS
DANS LE GROUPE 23A.
ESP> LAS OBRAS DEL GRUPO 23B QUEDAN INCLUIDAS
EN EL GRUPO 23A.

GUYANA:
E─> WORKS OF GROUP 23B ARE INCLUDED IN GROUP
23A.
FR─> LES OUVRAGES DU GROUPE 23B SONT COMPRIS
DANS LE GROUPE 23A.
ESP> LAS OBRAS DEL GRUPO 23B QUEDAN INCLUIDAS EN
EL GRUPO 23A.

PERU:
E─> WORKS OF GROUP 23B ARE INCLUDED IN GROUP
23A.
FR─> LES OUVRAGES DU GROUPE 23B SONT COMPRIS
DANS LE GROUPE 23A.
ESP> LAS OBRAS DEL GRUPO 23B QUEDAN INCLUIDAS
EN EL GRUPO 23A.

CHINA:
E─> WORKS OF GROUP 1 AND GROUPS 3 TO 7, 17 AND
25 ARE INCLUDED IN GROUP 2; 21 AND 24 IN GROUP 8;
18 TO 20 AND 22 IN GROUP 23; 11 TO 16 IN GROUP 9.
SCHOOL TEXTBOOKS AND CHILDREN'S BOOKS (3,167)
ARE INCLUDED IN THE TOTAL BUT ARE NOT IDENTIFIED
IN THE 25 GROUPS.
FR─> LES OUVRAGES DU GROUPE 1, DES GROUPES 3 A 7
ET 17 A 25 SONT COMPRIS DANS LE GROUPE 2; 21 ET 24
DANS LE GROUPE 8; 18 A 20 ET 22 DANS LE GROUPE 23;
11 A 16 DANS LE GROUPE 9. LES MANUELS SCOLAIRES
ET LES LIVRES POUR ENFANTS (3 167) SONT COMPRIS
DANS LE TOTAL MAIS NE SONT PAS REPARTIS ENTRE LES
25 GROUPES.
ESP> LAS OBRAS DEL GRUPO 1, LAS DE LOS GRUPOS 3
A 7 Y 17 A 25 QUEDAN INCLUIDAS EN EL GRUPO 2; LAS
DE LOS GRUPOS 21 Y 24 EN EL GRUPO 8; LAS DE LOS
GRUPOS 18 A 20 Y 22 EN EL GRUPO 23; LAS DE LOS
GRUPOS 11 A 16 EN EL GRUPO 9. LOS MANUALES ESCO-
LARES Y LOS LIBROS PARA NIÑOS (3 167) QUEDAN
COMPRENDIDOS EN EL TOTAL PERO NO SE DESGLOSAN
ENTRE LOS 25 GRUPOS.

INDIA:
E─> WORKS OF GROUP 23B ARE INCLUDED IN GROUP
23A.
FR─> LES OUVRAGES DU GROUPE 23B SONT COMPRIS
DANS LE GROUPE 23A.
ESP> LAS OBRAS DEL GRUPO 23B QUEDAN INCLUIDAS EN
EL GRUPO 23A.

IRAQ:
E─> WORKS OF GROUP 23B ARE INCLUDED IN GROUP
23A.
FR─> LES OUVRAGES DU GROUPE 23B SONT COMPRIS
DANS LE GROUPE 23A.
ESP> LAS OBRAS DEL GRUPO 23B QUEDAN INCLUIDAS
EN EL GRUPO 23A.

ISRAEL:
E─> DATA DO NOT INCLUDE UNIVERSITY THESES.
SCHOOL TEXTBOOKS (172) AND CHILDREN'S BOOKS (189)
ARE INCLUDED IN THE TOTAL BUT NOT DISTRIBUTED IN
THE 25 GROUPS. WORKS OF GROUP 23A ARE INCLUDED
IN GROUP 23B.
FR─> LES DONNEES N'INCLUENT PAS LES THESES
UNIVERSITAIRES. LES MANUELS SCOLAIRES (172) ET
LES LIVRES POUR ENFANTS (189) SONT COMPRIS DANS
LE TOTAL MAIS NE SONT PAS REPARTIS ENTRE LES 25
GROUPES. LES OUVRAGES DU GROUPE 23A SONT COMPRIS
DANS LE GROUPE 23B.
ESP> LOS DATOS EXCLUYEN LAS TESIS UNIVERSITARIAS.
LOS MANUALES ESCOLARES (172) Y LOS LIBROS PARA
NIÑOS (189) QUEDAN COMPRENDIDOS EN EL TOTAL PERO
NO SE DEGLOSAN ENTRE LOS 25 GRUPOS. LAS OBRAS DEL
GRUPO 23A QUEDAN INCLUIDAS EN EL GRUPO 23B.

JORDAN:
E─> DATA REFER TO THE EAST BANK ONLY. WORKS OF
GROUP 23B ARE INCLUDED IN GROUP 23A.
FR─> LES DONNEES SE REFERENT A LA RIVE ORIENTALE
SEULEMENT. LES OUVRAGES DU GROUPE 23B SONT COM-
PRIS DANS LE GROUPE 23A.
ESP> LOS DATOS SE REFIEREN A LA ORILLA ORIENTAL
SOLAMENTE. LAS OBRAS DEL GRUPO 23B QUEDAN IN-
CLUIDAS EN EL GRUPO 23A.

KOREA, REPUBLIC OF:
E─> SCHOOL TEXTBOOKS (687) AND CHILDREN'S BOOKS
(877) ARE INCLUDED IN THE TOTAL BUT ARE NOT IDEN-
TIFIED IN THE 25 GROUPS.
FR─> LES MANUELS SCOLAIRES (687) ET LES LIVRES
POUR ENFANTS (877) SONT COMPRIS DANS LE TOTAL MAIS
NE SONT PAS REPARTIS ENTRE LES 25 GROUPES.
ESP> LOS MANUALES ESCOLARES (687) Y LOS LIBROS
PARA NIÑOS (877) QUEDAN COMPRENDIDOS EN EL TOTAL
PERO NO SE DESGLOSAN ENTRE LOS 25 GRUPOS.

MALAYSIA:
E─> WORKS OF GROUP 23B ARE INCLUDED IN GROUP
23A.
FR─> LES OUVRAGES DU GROUPE 23B SONT COMPRIS
DANS LE GROUPE 23A.
ESP> LAS OBRAS DEL GRUPO 23B QUEDAN INCLUIDAS
EN EL GRUPO 23A.

PHILIPPINES:
E─> THE FIGURES REPRESENT ONLY THOSE BOOKS
WHICH HAVE BEEN RECEIVED IN THE NATIONAL LIBRARY.
FR─> LES CHIFFRES CONCERNENT SEULEMENT LE NOMBRE
DE TITRES ENREGISTRES A LA BIBLIOTHEQUE NATIONALE.
ESP> LOS DATOS SOLO COMPRENDEN EL NUMERO DE
OBRAS REGISTRADAS EN LA BIBLIOTECA NACIONAL.

SINGAPORE:
E─> DATA DO NOT INCLUDE GOVERNMENT PUBLICATIONS
FR─> LES DONNEES N'INCLUENT PAS LES PUBLICATIONS
OFFICIELLES.
ESP> LOS DATOS EXCLUYEN LAS PUBLICACIONES
OFICIALES.

SRI LANKA:
E─> WORKS OF GROUPS 19 AND 20 ARE INCLUDED IN
GROUP 18.
FR─> LES OUVRAGES DES GROUPES 19 ET 20 SONT
COMPRIS DANS LE GROUPE 18.
ESP> LAS OBRAS DE LOS GRUPOS 19 Y 20 QUEDAN
INCLUIDAS EN EL GRUPO 18.

SYRIAN ARAB REPUBLIC:
E─> SCHOOL TEXTBOOKS (1) AND CHILDREN'S BOOKS
(11) ARE INCLUDED IN THE TOTAL BUT NOT IDENTIFIED
IN THE 25 GROUPS.
FR─> LES MANUELS SCOLAIRES (1) ET LES LIVRES
POUR ENFANTS (11) SONT COMPRIS DANS LE TOTAL MAIS
NE SONT PAS REPARTIS ENTRE LES 25 GROUPES.

Number of titles (first editions) by subject group   8.4
Nombre de titres (premières éditions) par groupes de sujets
Número de obras (primeras ediciones) por categoría de temas

SYRIAN ARAB REPUBLIC (CONT.):
   ESP> LOS MANUALES ESCOLARES (1) Y LOS LIBROS
PARA NIÑOS (11) QUEDAN COMPRENDIDOS EN EL TOTAL
PERO NO SE DESGLOSAN ENTRE LOS 25 GRUPOS.

THAILAND:
   E—> WORKS OF GROUP 23B ARE INCLUDED IN GROUP
23A.
   FR-> LES OUVRAGES DU GROUPE 23B SONT COMPRIS
DANS LE GROUPE 23A.
   ESP> LAS OBRAS DEL GRUPO 23B QUEDAN INCLUIDAS
EN EL GRUPO 23A.

BELGIUM:
   E—> THE DATA REFER ONLY TO TITLES INDEXED IN
THE "BIBLIOGRAPHIE DE BELGIQUE". WORKS OF GROUPS
19 AND 20 ARE INCLUDED IN GROUP 18.
   FR-> LES DONNEES NE CONCERNENT QUE LES TITRES
REPERTORIES DANS LA BIBLIOGRAPHIE DE BELGIQUE.
LES OUVRAGES DES GROUPES 19 ET 20 SONT COMPRIS
DANS LE GROUPE 18.
   ESP> LOS DATOS SOLO SE REFIEREN A LOS LIBROS
INSCRITOS EN EL REPERTORIO DE LA "BIBLIOGRAPHIE
DE BELGIQUE". LAS OBRAS DE LOS GRUPOS 19 Y 20
QUEDAN INCLUIDAS EN EL GRUPO 18.

BULGARIA:
   E—> WORKS OF GROUPS 19 AND 20 ARE INCLUDED IN
GROUP 18; 23B IN GROUP 23A.
   FR-> LES OUVRAGES DES GROUPES 19 ET 20 SONT
COMPRIS DANS LE GROUPE 18; CEUX DU GROUPE 23B
DANS LE GROUPE 23A.
   ESP> LAS OBRAS DE LOS GRUPOS 19 Y 20 QUEDAN
INCLUIDAS EN EL GRUPO 18; LAS DEL GRUPO 23B EN
EL GRUPO 23A.

CZECHOSLOVAKIA:
   E—> WORKS OF GROUPS 19 AND 20 ARE INCLUDED IN
GROUP 18.
   FR-> LES OUVRAGES DES GROUPES 19 ET 20 SONT
COMPRIS DANS LE GROUPE 18.
   ESP> LAS OBRAS DE LOS GRUPOS 19 Y 20 QUEDAN
INCLUIDAS EN EL GRUPO 18.

GERMAN DEMOCRATIC REPUBLIC:
   E—> SCHOOL TEXTBOOKS (46) AND CHILDREN'S BOOKS
(323) ARE INCLUDED IN THE TOTAL BUT NOT IDENTIFIED
IN THE 25 GROUPS. WORKS OF GROUP 23B ARE INCLUDED
IN GROUP 23A. DATA INCLUDE ONLY SERIES A OF THE
GERMAN NATIONAL BIBLIOGRAPHY (PUBLICATIONS OF THE
BOOK MARKET) WHEREAS THOSE OF THE SERIES B AND C
(PUBLICATIONS OUTSIDE THE BOOK MARKET AS WELL AS
BOOKS PUBLISHED BY THE UNIVERSITIES) ARE EXCLUDED.
   FR-> LES MANUELS SCOLAIRES (46) ET LES LIVRES
POUR ENFANTS (323) SONT COMPRIS DANS LE TOTAL MAIS
NE SONT PAS REPARTIS ENTRE LES 25 GROUPES. LES
OUVRAGES DU GROUPE 23B SONT COMPRIS DANS LE GROUPE
23A. LES DONNEES SE REFERENT SEULEMENT A LA SERIE
A DE LA BIBLIOGRAPHIE NATIONALE ALLEMANDE (PUBLI-
CATIONS VENDUES DANS LE COMMERCE). LES DONNEES
RELATIVES AUX SERIES B ET C (PUBLICATIONS NON
VENDUES DANS LE COMMERCE ET LIVRES PUBLIES PAR LES
UNIVERSITES) NE SONT PAS PRISES EN COMPTE.
   ESP> LOS MANUALES ESCOLARES (46) Y LOS LIBROS
PARA NIÑOS (323) QUEDAN COMPRENDIDOS EN EL TOTAL
PERO NO SE DESGLOSAN ENTRE LOS 25 GRUPOS. LAS
OBRAS DEL GRUPO 23B QUEDAN INCLUIDAS EN EL GRUPO
23A. LOS DATOS SOLO SE REFIEREN A LA SERIE A DE
LA BIBLIOGRAFIA NACIONAL ALEMANA (PUBLICACIONES
VENDIDAS EN EL COMERCIO). NO SE TOMAN EN CONSIDE-
RACION LOS DATOS RELATIVOS A LAS SERIES B Y C
(PUBLICACIONES QUE NO SE VENDEN EN EL COMERCIO Y
LIBROS PUBLICADOS POR LAS UNIVERSIDADES).

GERMANY FEDERAL REPUBLIC OF:
   E—> WORKS OF GROUPS 17 AND 18 ARE INCLUDED IN
GROUP 14; 16 IN GROUP 15; 10 IN GROUP 25; 23A IN
GROUP 22.

GERMANY, FEDERAL REPUBLIC OF (CONT.):
   FR-> LES OUVRAGES DES GROUPES 17 ET 18 SONT
COMPRIS DANS LE GROUPE 14; 16 DANS LE GROUPE 15;
10 DANS LE GROUPE 25; 23A DANS LE GROUPE 22.
   ESP> LAS OBRAS DE LOS GRUPOS 17 Y 18 QUEDAN
INCLUIDAS EN EL GRUPO 14; LAS DEL GRUPO 16 EN EL
GRUPO 15; LAS DEL GRUPO 10 EN EL GRUPO 25; LAS DEL
GRUPO 23A EN EL GRUPO 22.

ICELAND:
   E—> WORKS OF GROUPS 19 AND 20 ARE INCLUDED IN
GROUP 18.
   FR-> LES OUVRAGES DES GROUPES 19 ET 20 SONT
COMPRIS DANS LE GROUPE 18.
   ESP> LAS OBRAS DE LOS GRUPOS 19 Y 20 QUEDAN
INCLUIDAS EN EL GRUPO 18.

NETHERLANDS:
   E—> DATA DO NOT INCLUDE PAMPHLETS. WORKS OF
GROUPS 5,6,9 AND 17 ARE INCLUDED IN GROUP 4; 10
IN GROUP 24; 19 IN GROUP 20; 23A IN GROUP 22.
   FR-> LES DONNEES N'INCLUENT PAS LES BROCHURES.
LES OUVRAGES DES GROUPES 5,6,9 ET 17 SONT COMPRIS
DANS LE GROUPE 4; 10 DANS LE GROUPE 24; 19 DANS
LE GROUPE 20; 23A DANS LE GROUPE 22.
   ESP> LOS DATOS EXCLUYEN LOS FOLLETOS. LAS OBRAS
DE LOS GRUPOS 5,6,9 Y 17 QUEDAN INCLUIDAS EN EL
GRUPO 4; LAS DEL GRUPO 10 EN EL GRUPO 24; LAS DEL
GRUPO 19 EN EL GRUPO 20; LAS DEL GRUPO 23B EN EL
GRUPO 22.

POLAND:
   E—> WORKS OF GROUPS 19 AND 20 ARE INCLUDED IN
GROUP 18.
   FR-> LES OUVRAGES DES GROUPES 19 ET 20 SONT
COMPRIS DANS LE GROUPE 18.
   ESP> LAS OBRAS DE LOS GRUPOS 19 Y 20 QUEDAN
INCLUIDAS EN EL GRUPO 18.

PORTUGAL:
   E—> WORKS OF GROUPS 5 TO 10 ARE INCLUDED IN
GROUP 4; 12 IN GROUP 11; 14 TO 17 IN GROUP 13;
19 TO 21 IN GROUP 18; 22 AND 23B IN GROUP 23A;
25 IN GROUP 24.
   FR-> LES OUVRAGES DES GROUPES 5 ET 10 SONT COM—
PRIS DANS LE GROUPE 4; 12 DANS LE GROUPE 11; 14
A 17 DANS LE GROUPE 13; 19 A 21 DANS LE GROUPE 18;
22 ET 23B DANS LE GROUPE 23A; 25 DANS LE GROUPE 24.
   ESP> LAS OBRAS DE LOS GRUPOS 5 A 10 QUEDAN
INCLUIDAS EN EL GRUPO 4; LAS DEL GRUPO 12 EN EL
GRUPO 11; LAS DE LOS GRUPOS 14 A 17 EN EL GRUPO 13;
LAS DE LOS GRUPOS 19 A 21 EN EL GRUPO 18; LAS DE
LOS GRUPOS 22 Y 23B EN EL GRUPO 23A; LAS DEL
GRUPO 25 EN EL GRUPO 24.

SPAIN:
   E—> WORKS OF GROUP 23B ARE INCLUDED IN GROUP
23A. 19 AND 20 IN GROUP 18.
   FR-> LES OUVRAGES DU GROUPE 23B SONT COMPRIS
DANS LE GROUPE 23A. 19 ET 20 DANS LE GROUPE 18.
   ESP> LAS OBRAS DEL GRUPO 23B QUEDAN INCLUIDAS
EN EL GRUPO 23A. LAS DE LOS GRUPOS 19 Y 20 EN EL
GRUPO 18.

UNITED KINGDOM:
   E—> WORKS OF GROUPS 19 AND 20 ARE INCLUDED IN
GROUP 18.
   FR-> LES OUVRAGES DES GROUPES 19 ET 20 SONT
COMPRIS DANS LE GROUPE 18.
   ESP> LAS OBRAS DE LOS GRUPOS 19 Y 20 QUEDAN
INCLUIDAS EN EL GRUPO 18.

FIJI:
   E—> DATA REFER TO SCHOOL TEXTBOOKS ONLY.
   FR-> LES DONNEES SE RAPPORTENT AUX MANUELS
SCOLAIRES SEULEMENT.
   ESP> LOS DATOS SE REFIEREN A LOS MANUALES
ESCOLARES SOLAMENTE.

8.4 Number of titles (first editions) by subject group
Nombre de titres (premières éditions) par groupes de sujets
Número de obras (primeras ediciones) por categoría de temas

U.S.S.R:
 E—> WORKS OF GROUPS 19 AND 20 ARE INCLUDED IN
GROUP 18.
 FR—> LES OUVRAGES DES GROUPES 19 ET 20 SONT
COMPRIS DANS LE GROUPE 18.
 ESP> LAS OBRAS DE LOS GRUPOS 19 Y 20 QUEDAN
INCLUIDAS EN EL GRUPO 18.

UKRAINIAN S.S.R:
 E—> WORKS OF GROUPS 19 AND 20 ARE INCLUDED IN
GROUP 18.
 FR—> LES OUVRAGES DES GROUPES 19 ET 20 SONT
COMPRIS DANS LE GROUPE 18.
 ESP> LAS OBRAS DE LOS GRUPOS 19 Y 20 QUEDAN
INCLUIDAS EN EL GRUPO 18.

Number of copies by UDC classes 8.5
Nombre d'exemplaires classés d'après la CDU
Número de ejemplares clasificados por materias (CDU)

please note correction inside front cover.

8.5 Book production: number of copies by UDC classes

Edition de livres: nombre d'exemplaires classés d'après la CDU

Edición de libros: número de ejemplares clasificados por materias (CDU)

NUMBER OF COUNTRIES AND TERRITORIES PRESENTED IN THIS TABLE: 67
NOMBRE DE PAYS ET DE TERRITOIRES PRESENTES DANS CE TABLEAU: 67
NUMERO DE PAISES Y DE TERRITORIOS PRESENTADOS EN ESTE CUADRO: 67

COUNTRY / PAYS / PAIS	YEAR / ANNEE / AÑO	TOTAL / TOTAL / TOTAL	GENER-ALITIES / GENERA-LITES / GENERA-LIDADES	PHILOS-OPHY / PHILO-SOPHIE / FILO-SOFIA	RELIGION / RELIGION / RELIGION	SOCIAL SCIENCES / SCIENCES SOCIALES / CIENCIAS SOCIALES	PURE SCIENCES / SCIENCES PURES / CIENCIAS PURAS	APPLIED SCIENCES / SCIENCES APPL. / CIENCIAS APLICADAS	ARTS / BEAUX-ARTS / ARTES PLASTICAS	LITERA-TURE / LITTERA-TURE / LITERA-TURA	GEOGR./ HISTORY / GEOGR./ HISTOIRE / GEOGR./ HISTORIA
		(1)	(2)	(3)	(4)	(5)	(6)	(7)	(8)	(9)	(10)
AFRICA											
BENIN	1978	18	–	–	5	–	5	–	–	7	1
BOTSWANA	1978	68	2	–	–	61	3	2	–	–	–
CONGO ‡	1977	1 756	–	–	–	21	21	420	984	255	55
EGYPT ‡	1976	31 667	832	207	4 919	2 247	3 688	4 178	107	13 487	2 002
	1977	35 758	455	344	5 041	2 694	3 112	7 079	184	11 584	5 265
ETHIOPIA ‡	1978	1 059	6	3	147	222	27	84	6	69	132
GAMBIA ‡	1977	7.4	0.3	–	–	2.5	0.8	1.7	0.5	0.6	1.0
	1978	8.8	0.5	–	–	2.7	1.2	1.8	0.6	0.8	1.3
GHANA	1977	1 114	131	–	716	134	30	11	24	68	–
KENYA	1976	2 039	26	–	249	1 191	252	55	10	162	94
MADAGASCAR ‡	1976	800	1	11	193	345	41	49	11	133	16
	1977	727	5	10	116	310	27	117	7	119	16
MAURITANIA	1976	63	–	–	–	5	29	2	–	13	14
MAURITIUS ‡	1976	210	–	–	21	38	19	8	7	114	3
	1977	85	–	–	12	54	3	2	1	9	7
	1978	30	–	1	16	7	–	1	2	1	4
SENEGAL ‡	1976	299	59	–	–	59	15	2	8	75	140
	1977	246		–	8	153	–	3	3	12	8

8.5 Number of copies by UDC classes
Nombre d'exemplaires classés d'après la CDU
Número de ejemplares clasificados por materias (CDU)

COUNTRY / PAYS / PAIS	YEAR / ANNEE / AÑO	TOTAL / TOTAL / TOTAL (1)	GENER-ALITIES / GENERA-LITES / GENERA-LIDADES (2)	PHILOS-OPHY / PHILO-SOPHIE / FILO-SOFIA (3)	RELIGION / RELIGION / RELIGION (4)	SOCIAL SCIENCES / SCIENCES SOCIALES / CIENCIAS SOCIALES (5)	PURE SCIENCES / SCIENCES PURES / CIENCIAS PURAS (6)	APPLIED SCIENCES / SCIENCES APPL. / CIENCIAS APLICADAS (7)	ARTS / BEAUX-ARTS / ARTES PLASTICAS (8)	LITERA-TURE / LITTERA-TURE / LITERA-TURA (9)	GEOGR./HISTORY / GEOGR./HISTOIRE / GEOGR./HISTORIA (10)
SEYCHELLES ‡	1977	5.9	-	0.2	-	5.4	-	-	-	-	0.3
SIERRA LEONE ‡	1977	21.3	0.4	-	-	10.8	-	1.4	-	-	8.7
SUDAN ‡	1977	10 476	-	-	900	-	2 940	90	-	3 915	2 631
TUNISIA ‡	1976	344	10	10	10	8	5	25	3	68	45
	1977	1 462	3	87	53	123	300	28	-	373	495
	1978	4 619	-	42	328	19	1 178	19	6	1 990	1 037
UNITED REPUBLIC OF CAMEROON ‡	1978	493	-	-	-	40	70	-	4	367	12
ZAIRE	1977	924	24	36	264	222	42	150	36	90	60
	1978	654	24	30	258	228	6	42	24	36	6
ZAMBIA ‡	1978	1 243	-	-	-	107	155	24	-	129	14
AMERICA, NORTH											
COSTA RICA	1976	240	-	-	-	12	8	-	-	213	7
	1977	272	9	20	-	67	8	9	3	155	10
	1978	121	9	-	10	53	-	9	10	22	17
CUBA	1976	34 528	913	84	-	20 701	116	525	96	11 396	697
	1977	32 243	1 924	617	2	12 456	3 317	639	326	11 245	1 717
JAMAICA ‡	1977	72	20	-	-	27	14	-	-	11	-
PANAMA	1976	375	2	3	-	102	196	21	3	28	19
	1977	97	10	3	-	41	-	18	2	20	3
	1978	351	8	1	-	144	36	59	5	60	43
AMERICA, SOUTH											
ARGENTINA ‡	1976	31 527	10 988	2 281	./.	4 721	425	1 989	1 535	8 800	788
	1977	22 298	3 349	2 205	./.	4 689	498	1 082	1 084	8 749	642
	1978	21 095	3 672	2 083	-	5 067	233	1 066	662	7 930	382
BRAZIL	1976	222 306	35 359	4 937	25 789	51 757	21 228	6 264	15 805	55 031	6 136
CHILE	1976	7 935	75	300	1 065	2 010	360	915	375	2 415	420
	1977	5 805	-	105	765	2 025	375	555	195	1 290	495
	1978	6 480	105	480	705	1 395	630	540	180	1 800	645
ASIA											
AFGHANISTAN	1976	3 072	-	-	135	-	1 290	-	-	1 098	549
BRUNEI	1977	383	200	-	-	44	59	-	-	75	5
	1978	146	4	-	43	4	75	-	-	5	15

Please note corrections inside front cover

Number of copies by UDC classes 8.5
Nombre d'exemplaires classés d'après la CDU
Número de ejemplares clasificados por materias (CDU)

		(1)	(2)	(3)	(4)	(5)	(6)	(7)	(8)	(9)	(10)
CHINA ‡	1978	3 566 160	./.	299 610	./.	528 270	./.	./.	./.	131 390	./.
CYPRUS	1976	971	9	5	53	429	61	50	17	265	82
	1977	2 127	10	3	86	1 078	73	253	90	379	155
HONG KONG	1976	10 558	156	8	357	5 948	595	400	374	2 289	431
	1977	9 219	311	21	141	4 433	435	473	686	1 922	797
ISRAEL ‡	1977	11 668	197	178	1 533	334	249	405	96	2 525	886
JORDAN ‡	1976	2 673	6	2	249	930	514	148	6	457	361
KOREA, REPUBLIC OF ‡	1976	39 305	2 142	1 951	2 051	2 487	5 154	4 133	2 454	17 081	1 852
	1977	38 788	4 423	2 193	2 099	3 513	5 714	2 309	729	16 139	1 669
	1978	81 264	10 705	2 427	4 866	11 976	5 842	2 099	4 395	17 086	3 956
KUWAIT	1976	887	114	29	24	209	—	4	26	175	306
	1977	599	47	—	207	170	—	31	8	70	66
	1978	232	68	—	—	56	—	12	8	884	10
LAO PEOPLE'S DEMOCRATIC REPUBLIC ‡	1976	268	55	37	5	88	—	8	7	61	7
MALAYSIA	1976	4 068	21	91	126	1 254	500	241	66	1 474	295
	1977	4 135	22	151	149	890	576	308	41	1 443	555
	1978	6 081	29	171	981	1 736	646	338	22	1 373	785
PHILIPPINES ‡	1977	3 118	110	44	320	731	136	1 155	293	252	77
QATAR	1978	371	22	6	216	33	22	—	—	—	12
SINGAPORE ‡	1976	5 334	63	52	77	1 995	1 087	357	205	1 118	380
	1977	4 931	35	22	94	1 369	623	271	76	2 072	369
	1978	6 948	61	3	94	4 023	575	220	331	1 264	377
SRI LANKA	1976	6 133	5	87	1 009	1 815	540	226	149	2 057	245
	1977	6 050	17	46	1 279	2 043	347	330	173	1 597	218
	1978	6 448	26	93	1 600	1 268	427	293	405	2 168	168
SYRIAN ARAB REPUBLIC‡	1976	428	11	9	3	98	73	74	10	134	16
	1978	565	3	9	15	163	59	127	13	92	44
UNITED ARAB EMIRATES‡	1977	82	46	—	—	29	—	—	3	4	—
VIET-NAM	1977	64 807	—	688	—	9 351	19 159	2 407	505	26 444	6 253
EUROPE											
BULGARIA	1976	53 672	207	287	55	7 838	4 656	5 429	2 099	30 447	2 654
	1977	51 286	392	360	41	6 632	5 779	5 287	2 012	27 545	3 238
	1978	50 228	275	358	17	7 473	4 983	5 532	1 936	26 474	3 180
CZECHOSLOVAKIA	1976	77 048	3 265	718	697	18 908	3 438	11 095	3 161	32 475	3 291
	1977	81 748	1 450	584	100	20 857	2 823	9 215	6 182	36 845	3 692
	1978	81 233	1 565	868	214	22 015	3 833	8 402	3 975	36 256	4 105
GERMAN DEMOCRATIC REPUBLIC ‡	1976	137 579	1 183	2 429	3 827	20 819	2 379	9 511	6 185	28 920	14 809
	1977	129 954	1 253	1 485	3 658	21 357	2 237	9 351	6 078	29 136	7 823
	1978	129 231	1 562	2 594	3 755	18 267	2 439	10 642	5 654	29 949	5 791

8.5 Number of copies by UDC classes
Nombre d'exemplaires classés d'après la CDU
Número de ejemplares clasificados por materias (CDU)

COUNTRY / PAYS / PAIS	YEAR / ANNEE / AÑO	TOTAL / TOTAL / TOTAL (1)	GENERALITIES / GENERALITES / GENERALIDADES (2)	PHILOSOPHY / PHILOSOPHIE / FILOSOFIA (3)	RELIGION / RELIGION / RELIGION (4)	SOCIAL SCIENCES / SCIENCES SOCIALES / CIENCIAS SOCIALES (5)	PURE SCIENCES / SCIENCES PURES / CIENCIAS PURAS (6)	APPLIED SCIENCES / SCIENCES APPL. / CIENCIAS APLICADAS (7)	ARTS / BEAUX-ARTS / ARTES PLASTICAS (8)	LITERATURE / LITTERATURE / LITERATURA (9)	GEOGR./HISTORY / GEOGR./HISTOIRE / GEOGR./HISTORIA (10)
HOLY SEE	1977	147	29	26	65	17	–	–	2	4	4
	1978	145	7	30	82	11	–	–	1	7	7
HUNGARY	1976	100 846	6 017	827	596	14 364	10 257	12 320	5 667	42 837	7 961
	1977	97 447	6 194	663	705	14 034	9 399	10 553	7 405	40 102	8 392
	1978	104 580	5 706	831	1 011	14 533	10 720	11 377	8 710	42 712	8 980
ITALY	1976	153 678	7 380	3 036	4 867	27 315	9 880	20 274	11 283	57 911	11 732
	1977	132 639	7 156	3 330	7 608	25 217	7 919	13 427	12 068	42 912	13 002
	1978	141 721	6 554	3 101	10 011	25 467	8 697	10 518	13 254	49 895	14 224
MONACO	1977	443	7	23	238	36	6	51	18	34	30
POLAND	1976	159 533	1 765	922	1 957	25 869	16 530	22 926	6 586	69 639	13 339
	1977	149 360	1 156	1 306	1 557	16 031	14 304	24 083	6 977	72 109	11 837
	1978	143 674	675	1 210	1 479	17 496	12 836	24 363	9 010	65 092	11 513
PORTUGAL	1976	35 213	1 304	511	1 001	14 671	1 652	2 509	5 559	6 387	1 619
ROMANIA	1976	88 969	2 841	947	435	9 832	16 086	12 262	3 590	36 482	6 494
	1977	94 304	2 890	1 425	172	11 271	14 252	12 304	5 018	39 679	7 293
	1978	97 349	2 533	1 550	564	12 133	15 537	13 079	5 991	38 568	7 394
SPAIN	1976	189 153	31 358	9 020	9 369	27 192	14 003	11 227	8 242	64 479	14 263
	1977	204 840	33 208	9 286	11 598	26 961	18 048	13 994	10 925	67 489	13 331
YUGOSLAVIA ‡	1976	52 552	232	433	1 675	32 072	649	4 020	2 850	9 473	1 148
	1977	60 544	442	588	988	35 562	856	5 121	3 004	12 469	1 514
	1978	56 660	401	297	1 039	31 747	890	4 630	4 525	11 516	1 615
OCEANIA											
AMERICAN SAMOA	1978	35	3	–	–	10	1	1	–	4	4
FIJI	1976	220	–	–	–	21	112	46	6	35	–
FRENCH POLYNESIA	1977	14.8	–	–	–	7.7	–	6.4	–	0.7	–
GUAM ‡	1978	1.9	–	–	–	–	1.3	0.6	–	–	–
NORFOLK ISLAND	1977	1	–	–	–	1	–	–	–	–	–
PACIFIC ISLANDS ‡	1978	17	–	–	–	17	–	–	–	–	–
SAMOA	1977	115.6	15.0	2.0	34.0	33.6	22.0	6.4	0.8	–	1.8
TONGA ‡	1976	59	–	–	4	8	8	5	–	–	7
	1977	50	–	–	7	16	10	6	–	1	10

Number of copies by UDC classes 8.5
Nombre d'exemplaires classés d'après la CDU
Número de ejemplares clasificados por materias (CDU)

		(1)	(2)	(3)	(4)	(5)	(6)	(7)	(8)	(9)	(10)
U.S.S.R.	1976	1 744 515	12 152	24 079	5 712	320 763	170 105	240 449	37 065	852 892	81 298
	1977	1 801 677	11 491	24 467	6 858	329 044	162 832	249 675	40 540	897 770	79 000
BYELORUSSIAN S.S.R.	1976	34 769	366	279	23	7 149	3 479	4 848	1 285	15 123	2 217
	1977	35 076	261	240	9	8 186	2 390	4 611	736	16 725	1 918
	1978	33 682	158	160	35	5 329	2 518	5 860	1 233	16 490	1 899
UKRAINIAN S.S.R.	1976	159 368	588	1 833	956	25 808	15 026	22 814	3 238	78 831	10 274
	1977	160 630	854	1 585	1 299	26 957	11 839	26 176	3 186	80 038	8 696

CONGO:
E—> ALL FIRST EDITIONS.
FR—> TOUS LES OUVRAGES RECENSES SONT DES PRE-
MIERES EDITIONS.
ESP> TODAS LAS OBRAS CONSIDERADAS SON PRIMERAS
EDICIONES.

EGYPT:
E—> THE FIGURES FOR 1977 ARE PRELIMINARY.
FR—> POUR 1977, LES CHIFFRES SONT PROVISOIRES.
ESP> LAS CIFRAS RELATIVAS A 1977 SON PRO-
VISIONALES.

ETHIOPIA:
E—> DATA REFER TO FIRST EDITIONS ONLY.
SCHOOL TEXTBOOKS (357,000) AND CHILDREN'S BOOKS
(6,000) ARE INCLUDED IN THE TOTAL BUT NOT IDENTI-
FIED IN THE 9 GROUPS.
FR—> LES DONNEES SE REFERENT AUX PREMIERES
EDITIONS SEULEMENT. LES MANUELS SCOLAIRES
(357 000) ET LES LIVRES POUR ENFANTS (6 000)
SONT COMPRIS DANS LE TOTAL MAIS NE SONT PAS
REPARTIS ENTRE LES 9 GROUPES.
ESP> LOS DATOS SE REFIEREN A LAS PRIMERAS
EDICIONES SOLAMENTE. LOS MANUALES ESCOLARES
(357 000) Y LOS LIBROS PARA NIÑOS (6 000) QUEDAN
COMPRENDIDOS EN EL TOTAL PERO NO ESTAN REPARTIDOS
ENTRE LOS 9 GRUPOS.

GAMBIA:
E—> ALL FIRST EDITIONS.
FR—> TOUT LES OUVRAGES RECENSES SONT DES PRE-
MIERES EDITIONS.
ESP> TODAS LAS OBRAS CONSIDERADAS SON PRIMERAS
EDICIONES.

MADAGASCAR:
E—> DATA FOR 1976 ARE PARTIAL
FR—> POUR 1976, LES DONNEES SONT INCOMPLETES.
ESP> EN 1976, DATOS INCOMPLETOS.

MAURITIUS:
E—> THE FIGURES FOR 1978 SHOW ONLY FIRST
EDITIONS.

MAURITIUS (CONT.):
FR—> POUR 1978, LES CHIFFRES CONCERNENT LES
PREMIERES EDITIONS SEULEMENT.
ESP> EN 1978, LAS CIFRAS SE REFIEREN A LAS
PRIMERAS EDICIONES SOLAMENTE.

SENEGAL:
E—> ALL FIRST EDITIONS.
FR—> TOUS LES OUVRAGES RECENSES SONT DES PRE-
MIERES EDITIONS.
ESP> TODAS LAS OBRAS CONSIDERADAS SON PRIMERAS
EDICIONES.

SEYCHELLES:
E—> ALL FIRST EDITIONS.
FR—> TOUS LES OUVRAGES RECENSES SONT DES PRE-
MIERES EDITIONS.
ESP> TODAS LAS OBRAS CONSIDERADAS SON PRIMERAS
EDICIONES.

SIERRA LEONE:
E—> ALL FIRST EDITIONS.
FR—> TOUS LES OUVRAGES RECENSES SONT DES PRE-
MIERES EDITIONS.
ESP> TODAS LAS OBRAS CONSIDERADAS SON PRIMERAS
EDICIONES.

SUDAN:
E—> DATA FOR 1977 REFER TO SCHOOL TEXTBOOKS
ONLY.
FR—> POUR 1977, LES DONNEES NE SE RAPPORTENT
QU'AUX MANUELS SCOLAIRES.
ESP> EN 1977, LOS DATOS SOLO SE REFIEREN A LOS
MANUALES ESCOLARES.

TUNISIA:
E—> IN 1976 SCHOOL TEXTBOOKS (75,000) AND
CHILDREN'S BOOKS (85,000) ARE INCLUDED IN THE
TOTAL BUT NOT IDENTIFIED IN THE 9 GROUPS.
FR—> POUR 1976, LES MANUELS SCOLAIRES (75 000)
ET LES LIVRES POUR ENFANTS (85 000) SONT COMPRIS
DANS LE TOTAL MAIS NE SONT PAS REPARTIS ENTRE
LES 9 GROUPES.

8.5 **Number of copies by UDC classes**
Nombre d'exemplaires classés d'après la CDU
Número de ejemplares clasificados por materias (CDU)

ISRAEL (CONT.):
FR—> LES DONNEES N'INCLUENT PAS LES THESES UNIVERSITAIRES. LES MANUELS SCOLAIRES (2 827 000) ET LES LIVRES POUR ENFANTS (2 438 000) SONT COMPRIS DANS LE TOTAL MAIS NE SONT PAR REPARTIS ENTRE LES 9 GROUPES.
ESP> LOS DATOS NO INCLUYEN LAS TESIS UNIVERSITARIAS. LOS MANUALES ESCOLARES (2 827 000) Y LOS LIBROS PARA NIÑOS (2 438 000) QUEDAN COMPRENDIDOS EN EL TOTAL PERO NO ESTAN REPARTIDOS ENTRE LOS 9 GRUPOS.

JORDAN:
E—> DATA SHOW ONLY FIRST EDITIONS AND REFER TO THE EAST BANK ONLY.
FR—> LES DONNEES SE REFERENT A LA RIVE ORIENTALE SEULEMENT. TOUS LES OUVRAGES RECENSES SONT DES PREMIERES EDITIONS.
ESP> LOS DATOS SE REFIEREN A LA ORILLA ORIENTAL SOLAMENTE. TODAS LAS OBRAS CONSIDERADAS SON PRIMERAS EDICIONES.

KOREA, REPUBLIC OF:
E—>, FOR 1978 SCHOOL TEXTBOOKS (13,780,000) AND CHILDREN'S BOOKS (4,132,000) ARE INCLUDED IN THE TOTAL BUT ARE NOT IDENTIFIED IN THE 9 GROUPS.
FR—> POUR 1978, LES MANUELS SCOLAIRES (13 780 000) ET LES LIVRES POUR ENFANTS (4 132 000) SONT COMPRIS DANS LE TOTAL MAIS NE SONT PAS REPARTIS ENTRE LES 9 GROUPES.
ESP> EN 1978, LOS MANUALES ESCOLARES (13 780 000) Y LOS LIBROS PARA NIÑOS (4 132 000) QUEDAN COMPRENDIDOS EN EL TOTAL PERO NO ESTAN REPARTIDOS ENTRE LOS 9 GRUPOS.

LAO, PEOPLE'S DEMOCRATIC REPUBLIC:
E—> ALL FIRST EDITIONS.
FR—> TOUS LES OUVRAGES RECENSES SONT DES PREMIERES EDITIONS.
ESP> TODAS LAS OBRAS CONSIDERADAS SON PRIMERAS EDICIONES.

PHILIPPINES:
E—> THE FIGURES REPRESENT ONLY THOSE COPIES OF WHICH TITLES HAVE BEEN RECEIVED IN THE NATIONAL LIBRARY.
FR—> LES DONNEES REPRESENTENT SEULEMENT LES EXEMPLAIRES DONT LES TITRES ONT ETE ENREGISTRES A LA BIBLIOTHEQUE NATIONALE.
ESP> LOS DATOS SOLO SE REFIEREN A LOS EJEMPLARES DE LOS TITULOS QUE HAN SIDO REGISTRADOS EN LA BIBLIOTECA NACIONAL.

SINGAPORE:
E—> DATA DO NOT INCLUDE GOVERNMENT PUBLICATIONS.
FR—> LES DONNEES N'INCLUENT PAS LES PUBLICATIONS OFFICIELLES.
ESP> LOS DATOS NO INCLUYEN LAS PUBLICACIONES OFICIALES.

TUNISIA (CONT.):
ESP> EN 1976, LOS MANUALES ESCOLARES (75 000) Y LOS LIBROS PARA NIÑOS (85 000) QUEDAN COMPRENDIDOS EN EL TOTAL PERO NO ESTAN REPARTIDOS ENTRE LOS 9 GRUPOS.

UNITED REPUBLIC OF CAMEROON:
E—> DATA REFER TO FIRST EDITIONS OF SCHOOL TEXTBOOKS ONLY.
FR—> TOUS LES OUVRAGES RECENSES SONT DES PREMIERES EDITIONS DE MANUELS SCOLAIRES SEULEMENT.
ESP> TODAS LAS OBRAS CONSIDERADAS SON PRIMERAS EDICIONES DE LOS MANUALES ESCOLARES SOLAMENTE.

ZAMBIA:
E—> FOR 1978 SCHOOL TEXTBOOKS (808,000) AND CHILDREN'S BOOKS (6,000) ARE INCLUDED IN THE TOTAL BUT NOT IDENTIFIED IN THE 9 GROUPS.
FR—> POUR 1978, LES MANUELS SCOLAIRES (808 000) ET LES LIVRES POUR ENFANTS (6 000) SONT COMPRIS DANS LE TOTAL MAIS NE SONT PAS REPARTIS ENTRE LES 9 GROUPES.
ESP> EN 1978, LOS MANUALES ESCOLARES (808 000) Y LOS LIBROS PARA NIÑOS (6 000) QUEDAN COMPRENDIDOS EN EL TOTAL PERO NO ESTAN REPARTIDOS ENTRE LOS 9 GRUPOS.

JAMAICA:
E—> IN 1977 ALL FIRST EDITIONS.
FR—> POUR 1977, TOUS LES OUVRAGES RECENSES SONT DES PREMIERES EDITIONS.
ESP> EN 1977, TODAS LAS OBRAS CONSIDERADAS SON PRIMERAS EDICIONES.

ARGENTINA:
E—> WORKS OF COLUMN 4 ARE INCLUDED WITH THOSE OF COLUMN 3.
FR—> LES OUVRAGES DE LA COLONNE 4 SONT COMPTES AVEC CEUX DE LA COLONNE 3.
ESP> LAS OBRAS DE LA COLUMNA 4 QUEDAN INCLUIDAS EN LA COLUMNA 3.

CHINA:
E—> FOR THE SUBJECT BREAKDOWN PLEASE REFER TO THE CORRESPONDING FOOTNOTE TO TABLE 8.6. SCHOOL TEXTBOOKS AND CHILDREN'S BOOKS (2,606,890,000) ARE INCLUDED IN THE TOTAL BUT ARE NOT IDENTIFIED IN THE 9 GROUPS.
FR—> POUR LA REPARTITION PAR SUJETS, VEUILLEZ VOUS REPORTER A LA NOTE CORRESPONDANTE DU TABLEAU 8.6. LES MANUELS SCOLAIRES ET LES LIVRES POUR ENFANTS (2 606 890 000) SONT COMPRIS DANS LE TOTAL MAIS NE SONT PAS REPARTIS ENTRE LES 9 GROUPES.
ESP> PARA LA REPARTICION POR MATERIAS, VEASE LA NOTA CORRESPONDIENTE DEL CUADRO 8.6. LOS MANUALES ESCOLARES Y LOS LIBROS PARA NIÑOS (2 606 890 000) QUEDAN COMPRENDIDOS EN EL TOTAL PERO NO ESTAN REPARTIDOS ENTRE LOS 9 GRUPOS.

ISRAEL:
E—> DATA DO NOT INCLUDE UNIVERSITY THESES. SCHOOL TEXTBOOKS (2,827,000) AND CHILDREN'S BOOKS (2,438,000) ARE INCLUDED IN THE TOTAL BUT NOT IDENTIFIED IN THE 9 GROUPS.

Please note corrections inside front cover

Number of copies by UDC classes 8.5
Nombre d'exemplaires classés d'après la CDU
Número de ejemplares clasificados por materias (CDU)

SYRIAN ARAB REPUBLIC:
E—> FOR 1978 SCHOOL TEXTBOOKS (2,000) AND CHILDREN'S BOOKS (37,500) ARE INCLUDED IN THE TOTAL BUT ARE NOT IDENTIFIED IN THE 9 GROUPS.
FR—> POUR 1978, LES MANUELS SCOLAIRES (2 000) ET LES LIVRES POUR ENFANTS (37 500) SONT COMPRIS DANS LE TOTAL MAIS NE SONT PAS REPARTIS ENTRE LES 9 GROUPES.
ESP> EN 1978, LOS MANUALES ESCOLARES (2 000) Y LOS LIBROS PARA NIÑOS (37 500) QUEDAN COMPRENDIDOS EN EL TOTAL PERO NO ESTAN REPARTIDOS ENTRE LOS 9 GRUPOS.

UNITED ARAB EMIRATES:
E—> ALL FIRST EDITIONS.
FR—> TOUS LES OUVRAGES RECENSES SONT DES PREMIERES EDITIONS.
ESP> TODAS LAS OBRAS CONSIDERADAS SON PRIMERAS EDICIONES.

GERMAN DEMOCRATIC REPUBLIC:
E—> SCHOOL TEXTBOOKS (1976: 30,200,000; 1977: 30,902,000; 1978: 30,957,000) AND CHILDREN'S BOOKS (1976: 16,560,000; 1977: 17,376,000; 1978: 17,676,000) ARE INCLUDED IN THE TOTAL BUT ARE NOT IDENTIFIED IN THE 9 GROUPS.
FR—> LES MANUELS SCOLAIRES (EN 1976: 30 957 000; EN 1977: 30 200 000; EN 1978: 30 902 000) ET LES LIVRES POUR ENFANTS (EN 1976: 16 560 000; EN 1977: 17 376 000; EN 1978: 17 676 000) SONT COMPRIS DANS LE TOTAL MAIS NE SONT PAS REPARTIS ENTRES LES 9 GROUPES.
ESP> LOS MANUALES ESCOLARES (EN 1976: 30 957 000; EN 1977: 30 200 000; EN 1978: 30 902 000) Y LOS LIBROS PARA NIÑOS (EN 1976: 16 560 000; EN 1977: 17 376 000; EN 1978: 17 676 000) QUEDAN COMPRENDIDOS EN EL TOTAL PERO NO ESTAN REPARTIDOS ENTRE LOS 9 GRUPOS.

YUGOSLAVIA:
E—> DATA FOR 1976 DO NOT INCLUDE 381,000 COPIES OF UNIVERSITY BOOKS.
FR—> POUR 1976, LES DONNEES NE TIENNENT PAS COMPTE DE 381 000 EXEMPLAIRES DE LIVRES UTILISES DANS LES UNIVERSITES.
ESP> EN 1976, LOS DATOS NO TOMAN EN CONSIDERACION 381 000 EJEMPLARES DE LIBROS DE ENSEÑANZA UNIVERSITARIA.

GUAM:
E—> ALL FIRST EDITIONS.
FR—> TOUS LES OUVRAGES RECENSES SONT DES PREMIERES EDITIONS.
ESP> TODAS LAS OBRAS CONSIDERADAS SON PRIMERAS EDICIONES.

PACIFIC ISLANDS:
E—> ALL FIRST EDITIONS.
FR—> TOUS LES OUVRAGES RECENSES SONT DES PREMIERES EDITIONS.
ESP> TODAS LAS OBRAS CONSIDERADAS SON PRIMERAS EDICIONES.

TONGA:
E—> FOR 1976 SCHOOL TEXTBOOKS (15,000) AND CHILDREN'S BOOKS (12,000) ARE INCLUDED IN THE TOTAL BUT ARE NOT IDENTIFIED IN THE 9 GROUPS.
FR—> POUR 1976, LES MANUELS SCOLAIRES (15 000) ET LES LIVRES POUR ENFANTS (12 000) SONT COMPRIS DANS LE TOTAL MAIS NE SONT PAS REPARTIS ENTRE LES 9 GROUPES.
ESP> EN 1976, LOS MANUALES ESCOLARES (15 000) Y LOS LIBROS PARA NIÑOS (12 000) QUEDAN COMPRENDIDOS EN EL TOTAL PERO NO ESTAN REPARTIDOS ENTRE LOS 9 GRUPOS.

8.6　Number of copies by subject group
Nombre d'exemplaires par groupes de sujets
Número de ejemplares por categorías de temas

8.6　Book production: number of copies by subject group

Edition de livres: nombre d'exemplaires par groupes de sujets

Edición de libros: número de ejemplares por categorías de temas

A = BOOKS
B = PAMPHLETS

DATA ARE PRESENTED
IN THOUSANDS

NUMBER OF COUNTRIES AND
TERRITORIES PRESENTED IN
THIS TABLE:　66

A = LIVRES
B = BROCHURES

LES DONNEES SONT PRE-
SENTEES EN MILLIERS

NOMBRE DE PAYS ET DE
TERRITOIRES PRESENTES DANS
CE TABLEAU:　66

A = LIBROS
B = FOLLETOS

LOS DATOS SE PRESENTAN
EN MILLARES

NUMERO DE PAISES Y DE
TERRITORIOS PRESENTADOS
EN ESTE CUADRO:　66

SUBJECT GROUP / GROUPE DE SUJETS / GRUPO TEMATICO	AFRICA	BENIN (1978)			BOTSWANA (1978)		
		A	B	A+B	A	B	A+B
TOTAL		18	—	18	35	33	68
1. GENERALITIES		—	—	—	2.2	0.2	2.4
2. PHILOSOPHY, PSYCHOLOGY		—	—	—	—	—	—
3. RELIGION, THEOLOGY		5	—	5	—	0.1	0.1
4. SOCIOLOGY, STATISTICS		—	—	—	1.1	4.8	5.9
5. POLITICAL SCIENCE		—	—	—	20	10	30
6. LAW, PUBLIC ADMIN.		—	—	—	5.9	9.2	15.1
7. MILITARY ART		—	—	—	—	—	—
8. EDUCATION, LEISURE		—	—	—	2	7.2	9.2
9. TRADE, TRANSPORT		—	—	—	—	—	—
10. ETHNOGRAPHY, FOLKLORE		—	—	—	—	0.4	0.4
11. MATHEMATICS		1	—	1	—	—	—
12. NATURAL SCIENCES		4	—	4	2.6	—	2.6
13. MEDICAL SCIENCES		—	—	—	—	0.8	0.8
14. ENGINEERING, CRAFTS		—	—	—	—	—	—
15. AGRICULTURE		—	—	—	1.2	0.1	1.3
16. DOMESTIC SCIENCE		—	—	—	—	—	—
17. MANAGEMENT, ADMIN.		—	—	—	—	—	—
18. PLANNING, ARCHITECTURE		—	—	—	—	0.1	0.1
19. PLASTIC ARTS		—	—	—	—	—	—
20. PERFORMING ARTS		—	—	—	—	—	—
21. GAMES, SPORTS		—	—	—	—	0.1	0.1
22. LINGUISTICS, PHILOLOGY		5	—	5	—	—	—
23. LITERATURE							
(A) HISTORY AND CRITICISM		—	—	—	—	—	—
(B) LITERARY TEXTS		2	—	2	—	—	—
24. GEOGRAPHY, TRAVEL		1	—	1	—	—	—
25. HISTORY, BIOGRAPHY		—	—	—	—	0.1	0.1

Number of copies by subject group 8.6
Nombre d'exemplaires par groupes de sujets
Número de ejemplares por categorías de temas

SUBJECT GROUP GROUPE DE SUJETS GRUPO TEMATICO	CONGO ‡ (1977)			EGYPT ‡ (1977)			ETHIOPIA ‡ (1978)		
	A	B	A+B	A	B	A+B	A	B	A+B
TOTAL	285	1 471	1 756	31 997	3 761	35 758	993	66	1 059
1. GENERALITIES	–	–	–	363	92	455	3	3	6
2. PHILOSOPHY, PSYCHOLOGY	–	–	–	344	–	344	3	–	3
3. RELIGION, THEOLOGY	–	–	–	4 000	1 041	5 041	144	3	147
4. SOCIOLOGY, STATISTICS	–	–	–	2 514	180	2 694	219	3	222
5. POLITICAL SCIENCE	5	14	19	./.	./.	./.	./.	./.	./.
6. LAW, PUBLIC ADMIN.	–	–	–	./.	./.	./.	./.	./.	./.
7. MILITARY ART	–	–	–	./.	./.	./.	./.	./.	./.
8. EDUCATION, LEISURE	–	2	2	./.	./.	./.	./.	./.	./.
9. TRADE, TRANSPORT	–	–	–	./.	./.	./.	./.	./.	./.
10. ETHNOGRAPHY, FOLKLORE	–	–	–	./.	./.	./.	./.	./.	./.
11. MATHEMATICS	–	5	5	3 043	69	3 112	27	–	27
12. NATURAL SCIENCES	–	16	16	./.	./.	./.	./.	–	./.
13. MEDICAL SCIENCES	–	140	140	6 745	334	7 079	84	–	84
14. ENGINEERING, CRAFTS	–	–	–	./.	./.	./.	./.	–	./.
15. AGRICULTURE	–	–	–	./.	./.	./.	./.	–	./.
16. DOMESTIC SCIENCE	–	280	280	./.	./.	./.	./.	–	./.
17. MANAGEMENT, ADMIN.	–	–	–	./.	./.	./.	./.	–	./.
18. PLANNING, ARCHITECTURE	–	–	–	181	3	184	6	–	6
19. PLASTIC ARTS	–	–	–	./.	./.	./.	./.	–	./.
20. PERFORMING ARTS	–	984	984	./.	./.	./.	./.	–	./.
21. GAMES, SPORTS	–	–	–	./.	./.	./.	./.	–	./.
22. LINGUISTICS, PHILOLOGY	–	7	7	6 433	1 077	7 510	39	–	39
23. LITERATURE									
(A) HISTORY AND CRITICISM	240	8	248	3 126	948	4 074	30	–	30
(B) LITERARY TEXTS	./.	./.	./.	./.	./.	./.	./.	./.	./.
24. GEOGRAPHY, TRAVEL	40	10	50	5 248	17	5 265	81	51	132
25. HISTORY, BIOGRAPHY	–	5	5	./.	./.	./.	./.	./.	./.

SUBJECT GROUP GROUPE DE SUJETS GRUPO TEMATICO	GAMBIA ‡ (1978)	GHANA ‡ (1977)			KENYA (1976)		
	A+B	A	B	A+B	A	B	A+B
TOTAL	*8.8	372	742	1 114	1 028	1 011	2 039
1. GENERALITIES	*0.5	18	113	131	6	20	26
2. PHILOSOPHY, PSYCHOLOGY	–	–	–	–	–	–	–
3. RELIGION, THEOLOGY	–	149	567	716	100	149	249
4. SOCIOLOGY, STATISTICS	*0.4	3	–	3	1	–	1
5. POLITICAL SCIENCE	*0.6	11	5	16	16	5	21
6. LAW, PUBLIC ADMIN.	*0.6	16	1	17	3	–	3
7. MILITARY ART	–	–	1	1	–	–	–
8. EDUCATION, LEISURE	*0.4	5	7	12	524	612	1 136
9. TRADE, TRANSPORT	*0.7	2	5	7	–	–	–
10. ETHNOGRAPHY, FOLKLORE	–	48	30	78	10	20	30
11. MATHEMATICS	*0.6	0	–	0	170	–	170
12. NATURAL SCIENCES	*0.5	30	–	30	56	26	82
13. MEDICAL SCIENCES	*0.5	–	–	–	–	13	13
14. ENGINEERING, CRAFTS	*0.4	–	1	1	15	10	25
15. AGRICULTURE	*0.6	3	–	3	17	–	17
16. DOMESTIC SCIENCE	*0.3	–	–	–	–	–	–
17. MANAGEMENT, ADMIN.	–	7	–	7	–	–	–
18. PLANNING, ARCHITECTURE	*0.6	–	5	5	–	–	–
19. PLASTIC ARTS	–	–	–	–	–	–	–
20. PERFORMING ARTS	–	14	5	19	5	5	10
21. GAMES, SPORTS	–	–	–	–	–	–	–
22. LINGUISTICS, PHILOLOGY	*0.5	–	–	–	8	70	78
23. LITERATURE							
(A) HISTORY AND CRITICISM	–	66	2	68	55	29	84
(B) LITERARY TEXTS	*0.3	./.	./.	./.	–	–	–
24. GEOGRAPHY, TRAVEL	*0.6	–	–	–	20	50	70
25. HISTORY, BIOGRAPHY	*0.7	–	–	–	22	2	24

8.6 Number of copies by subject group
Nombre d'exemplaires par groupes de sujets
Número de ejemplares por categorías de temas

SUBJECT GROUP GROUPE DE SUJETS GRUPO TEMATICO	MADAGASCAR (1977)			MAURITANIA (1976)			MAURITIUS ‡ (1978)		
	A	B	A+B	A	B	A+B	A	B	A+B
TOTAL	425	302	727	33	30	63	11	19	30
1. GENERALITIES	2	3	5	–	–	–	–	–	–
2. PHILOSOPHY, PSYCHOLOGY	1	9	10	–	–	–	1	–	1
3. RELIGION, THEOLOGY	77	39	116	–	–	–	4	12	16
4. SOCIOLOGY, STATISTICS	10	–	10	1	–	1	–	–	–
5. POLITICAL SCIENCE	31	14	45	–	–	–	2	4	6
6. LAW, PUBLIC ADMIN.	1	50	51	–	–	–	–	–	–
7. MILITARY ART	–	1	1	–	–	–	–	–	–
8. EDUCATION, LEISURE	179	17	196	2	2	4	–	–	–
9. TRADE, TRANSPORT	–	–	–	–	–	–	1	–	1
10. ETHNOGRAPHY, FOLKLORE	–	7	7	–	–	–	–	–	–
11. MATHEMATICS	10	–	10	11	11	22	–	–	–
12. NATURAL SCIENCES	16	1	17	3	4	7	–	–	–
13. MEDICAL SCIENCES	8	93	101	–	–	–	1	–	1
14. ENGINEERING, CRAFTS	5	1	6	–	2	2	–	–	–
15. AGRICULTURE	–	3	3	–	–	–	–	–	–
16. DOMESTIC SCIENCE	–	–	–	–	–	–	–	–	–
17. MANAGEMENT, ADMIN.	6	1	7	–	–	–	–	–	–
18. PLANNING, ARCHITECTURE	–	2	2	–	–	–	–	–	–
19. PLASTIC ARTS	–	1	1	–	–	–	–	–	–
20. PERFORMING ARTS	–	1	1	–	–	–	–	0.2	0.2
21. GAMES, SPORTS	–	3	3	–	–	–	–	–	–
22. LINGUISTICS, PHILOLOGY	18	1	19	7	6	13	–	–	–
23. LITERATURE									
(A) HISTORY AND CRITICISM	2	–	2	–	–	–	–	–	–
(B) LITERARY TEXTS	53	45	98	–	–	–	–	1	1
24. GEOGRAPHY, TRAVEL	4	1	5	5	3	8	–	–	–
25. HISTORY, BIOGRAPHY	2	9	11	4	2	6	2	2	4

SUBJECT GROUP GROUPE DE SUJETS GRUPO TEMATICO	SENEGAL ‡ (1977)			SEYCHELLES ‡ (1977)			SIERRA LEONE ‡ (1977)		
	A	B	A+B	A	B	A+B	A	B	A+B
TOTAL	246	–	246	5.8	0.1	5.9	9.1	12.2	21.3
1. GENERALITIES	59	–	59	–	–	–	–	0.4	0.4
2. PHILOSOPHY, PSYCHOLOGY	–	–	–	0.2	–	0.2	–	–	–
3. RELIGION, THEOLOGY	8	–	8	–	–	–	–	–	–
4. SOCIOLOGY, STATISTICS	3	–	3	–	0.1	0.1	0.3	0.3	0.6
5. POLITICAL SCIENCE	10	–	10	5.2	–	5.2	1.3	5.4	6.7
6. LAW, PUBLIC ADMIN.	20	–	20	0.1	–	0.1	0	0	0
7. MILITARY ART	–	–	–	–	–	–	–	–	–
8. EDUCATION, LEISURE	120	–	120	–	–	–	2	1.4	3.4
9. TRADE, TRANSPORT	–	–	–	–	–	–	–	0.1	0.1
10. ETHNOGRAPHY, FOLKLORE	–	–	–	–	–	–	–	–	–
11. MATHEMATICS	–	–	–	–	–	–	–	–	–
12. NATURAL SCIENCES	–	–	–	–	–	–	–	–	–
13. MEDICAL SCIENCES	–	–	–	–	–	–	0.3	0.3	0.6
14. ENGINEERING, CRAFTS	–	–	–	–	–	–	–	–	–
15. AGRICULTURE	3	–	3	–	–	–	–	0.3	0.3
16. DOMESTIC SCIENCE	–	–	–	–	–	–	–	–	–
17. MANAGEMENT, ADMIN.	–	–	–	–	–	–	0.5	–	0.5
18. PLANNING, ARCHITECTURE	–	–	–	–	–	–	–	–	–
19. PLASTIC ARTS	–	–	–	–	–	–	–	–	–
20. PERFORMING ARTS	3	–	3	–	–	–	–	–	–
21. GAMES, SPORTS	–	–	–	–	–	–	–	–	–
22. LINGUISTICS, PHILOLOGY	3	–	3	–	–	–	–	–	–
23. LITERATURE									
(A) HISTORY AND CRITICISM	3	–	3	–	–	–	–	–	–
(B) LITERARY TEXTS	6	–	6	–	–	–	–	–	–
24. GEOGRAPHY, TRAVEL	2	–	2	0.3	–	0.3	4.7	–	4.7
25. HISTORY, BIOGRAPHY	6	–	6	–	–	–	–	4.0	4.0

Number of copies by subject group 8.6
Nombre d'exemplaires par groupes de sujets
Número de ejemplares por categorías de temas

SUBJECT GROUP GROUPE DE SUJETS GRUPO TEMATICO	SUDAN ‡ (1977)			TUNISIA (1978)			UNITED REP. OF CAMEROON ‡ (1978)
	A	B	A+B	A	B	A+B	A+B
TOTAL	10 476	–	10 476	4 619	–	4 619	493
1. GENERALITIES	–	–	–	–	–	–	–
2. PHILOSOPHY, PSYCHOLOGY	–	–	–	42	–	42	–
3. RELIGION, THEOLOGY	900	–	900	328	–	328	–
4. SOCIOLOGY, STATISTICS	–	–	–	–	–	–	–
5. POLITICAL SCIENCE	–	–	–	3	–	3	31
6. LAW, PUBLIC ADMIN.	–	–	–	5	–	5	6
7. MILITARY ART	–	–	–	–	–	–	–
8. EDUCATION, LEISURE	–	–	–	11	–	11	3
9. TRADE, TRANSPORT	–	–	–	–	–	–	–
10. ETHNOGRAPHY, FOLKLORE	–	–	–	–	–	–	–
11. MATHEMATICS	1 890	–	1 890	899	–	899	60
12. NATURAL SCIENCES	1 050	–	1 050	279	–	279	10
13. MEDICAL SCIENCES	–	–	–	–	–	–	–
14. ENGINEERING, CRAFTS	65	–	65	8	–	8	–
15. AGRICULTURE	25	–	25	–	–	–	–
16. DOMESTIC SCIENCE	–	–	–	–	–	–	–
17. MANAGEMENT, ADMIN.	–	–	–	11	–	11	–
18. PLANNING, ARCHITECTURE	–	–	–	3	–	3	–
19. PLASTIC ARTS	–	–	–	–	–	–	–
20. PERFORMING ARTS	–	–	–	3	–	3	4
21. GAMES, SPORTS	–	–	–	–	–	–	–
22. LINGUISTICS, PHILOLOGY	2 925	–	2 925	639	–	639	297
23. LITERATURE							
(A) HISTORY AND CRITICISM	990	–	990	–	–	–	–
(B) LITERARY TEXTS	–	–	–	1 351	–	1 351	70
24. GEOGRAPHY, TRAVEL	1 695	–	1 695	424	–	424	3
25. HISTORY, BIOGRAPHY	936	–	936	613	–	613	9

SUBJECT GROUP GROUPE DE SUJETS GRUPO TEMATICO	ZAIRE ‡ (1978)			ZAMBIA ‡ (1978)		
	A	B	A+B	A	B	A+B
TOTAL	654	–	654	1 243	–	1 243
1. GENERALITIES	24	–	24	–	–	–
2. PHILOSOPHY, PSYCHOLOGY	30	–	30	–	–	–
3. RELIGION, THEOLOGY	258	–	258	–	–	–
4. SOCIOLOGY, STATISTICS	228	–	228	6	–	6
5. POLITICAL SCIENCE	./.	–	./.	5	–	5
6. LAW, PUBLIC ADMIN.	./.	–	./.	–	–	–
7. MILITARY ART	./.	–	./.	–	–	–
8. EDUCATION, LEISURE	./.	–	./.	–	–	–
9. TRADE, TRANSPORT	./.	–	./.	–	–	–
10. ETHNOGRAPHY, FOLKLORE	./.	–	./.	96	–	96
11. MATHEMATICS	6	–	6	155	–	155
12. NATURAL SCIENCES	./.	–	./.	–	–	–
13. MEDICAL SCIENCES	42	–	42	–	–	–
14. ENGINEERING, CRAFTS	./.	–	./.	–	–	–
15. AGRICULTURE	./.	–	./.	15	–	15
16. DOMESTIC SCIENCE	./.	–	./.	9	–	9
17. MANAGEMENT, ADMIN.	./.	–	./.	–	–	–
18. PLANNING, ARCHITECTURE	24	–	24	–	–	–
19. PLASTIC ARTS	./.	–	./.	–	–	–
20. PERFORMING ARTS	./.	–	./.	–	–	–
21. GAMES, SPORTS	./.	–	./.	–	–	–
22. LINGUISTICS, PHILOLOGY	./.	–	./.	23	–	23
23. LITERATURE						
(A) HISTORY AND CRITICISM	36	–	36	8	–	8
(B) LITERARY TEXTS	./.	–	./.	98	–	98
24. GEOGRAPHY, TRAVEL	6	–	6	–	–	–
25. HISTORY, BIOGRAPHY	./.	–	./.	14	–	14

8.6 Number of copies by subject group
Nombre d'exemplaires par groupes de sujets
Número de ejemplares por categorías de temas

SUBJECT GROUP GROUPE DE SUJETS AMERICA, NORTH GRUPO TEMATICO	COSTA RICA (1978)			CUBA (1977)			JAMAICA ‡ (1977)		
	A	B	A+B	A	B	A+B	A	B	A+B
TOTAL	121	–	121	28 745	3 498	32 243	72	–	72
1. GENERALITIES	9	–	9	1 451	473	1 924	20	–	20
2. PHILOSOPHY, PSYCHOLOGY	–	–	–	615	2	617	–	–	–
3. RELIGION, THEOLOGY	10	–	10	2	–	2	–	–	–
4. SOCIOLOGY, STATISTICS	5	–	5	208	9	217	–	–	–
5. POLITICAL SCIENCE	9	–	9	1 641	15	1 656	25	–	25
6. LAW, PUBLIC ADMIN.	3	–	3	46	44	90	–	–	–
7. MILITARY ART	–	–	–	16	4	20	–	–	–
8. EDUCATION, LEISURE	9	–	9	8 712	1 760	10 472	2	–	2
9. TRADE, TRANSPORT	–	–	–	1	–	1	–	–	–
10. ETHNOGRAPHY, FOLKLORE	27	–	27	–	–	–	–	–	–
11. MATHEMATICS	–	–	–	1 300	397	1 697	11	–	11
12. NATURAL SCIENCES	–	–	–	1 393	227	1 620	3	–	3
13. MEDICAL SCIENCES	–	–	–	129	21	150	–	–	–
14. ENGINEERING, CRAFTS	–	–	–	325	55	380	–	–	–
15. AGRICULTURE	–	–	–	75	26	101	–	–	–
16. DOMESTIC SCIENCE	–	–	–	–	–	–	–	–	–
17. MANAGEMENT, ADMIN.	–	–	–	8	–	8	–	–	–
18. PLANNING, ARCHITECTURE	–	–	–	–	–	–	–	–	–
19. PLASTIC ARTS	–	–	–	–	–	–	–	–	–
20. PERFORMING ARTS	10	–	10	6	58	64	–	–	–
21. GAMES, SPORTS	–	–	–	248	14	262	–	–	–
22. LINGUISTICS, PHILOLOGY	–	–	–	432	381	812	11	–	11
23. LITERATURE									
(A) HISTORY AND CRITICISM	7	–	7	953	–	953	–	–	–
(B) LITERARY TEXTS	15	–	15	9 479	–	9 479	–	–	–
24. GEOGRAPHY, TRAVEL	–	–	–	60	2	62	–	–	–
25. HISTORY, BIOGRAPHY	17	–	17	1 645	10	1 655	–	–	–

SUBJECT GROUP GROUPE DE SUJETS GRUPO TEMATICO	PANAMA ‡ (1978)			AMERICA, SOUTH	ARGENTINA ‡ (1978)	BRAZIL ‡ (1976)		
	A	B	A+B	A+B	A	B	A+B	
TOTAL	268	83	351	21 095	147 240	75 066	222 306	
1. GENERALITIES	1	7	8	3 672	8 780	26 579	35 359	
2. PHILOSOPHY, PSYCHOLOGY	1	–	1	2 083	3 043	1 894	4 937	
3. RELIGION, THEOLOGY	–	–	–	./.	9 787	16 002	25 789	
4. SOCIOLOGY, STATISTICS	2	1	3	1 748	835	6 340	7 175	
5. POLITICAL SCIENCE	1	6	7	./.	3 689	385	4 074	
6. LAW, PUBLIC ADMIN.	78	4	82	465	5 300	5 683	10 983	
7. MILITARY ART	–	–	–	–	16	18	34	
8. EDUCATION, LEISURE	10	28	38	2 854	20 114	3 825	23 939	
9. TRADE, TRANSPORT	–	8	8	–	1 524	348	1 872	
10. ETHNOGRAPHY, FOLKLORE	5	1	6	–	192	3 488	3 680	
11. MATHEMATICS	3	–	3	185	11 016	631	11 647	
12. NATURAL SCIENCES	33	–	33	48	8 994	587	9 581	
13. MEDICAL SCIENCES	23	2	25	576	1 136	262	1 398	
14. ENGINEERING, CRAFTS	–	9	9	329	2 063	570	2 633	
15. AGRICULTURE	15	9	24	161	290	285	575	
16. DOMESTIC SCIENCE	1	–	1	–	786	12	798	
17. MANAGEMENT, ADMIN.	–	–	–	–	779	81	860	
18. PLANNING, ARCHITECTURE	–	–	–	450	194	. 2	196	
19. PLASTIC ARTS	–	–	–	./.	–	–	–	
20. PERFORMING ARTS	0.3	–	0.3	./.	7 684	253	7 937	
21. GAMES, SPORTS	–	0.2	0.2	212	1 849	5 823	7 672	
22. LINGUISTICS, PHILOLOGY	30	–	30	./.	21 720	850	22 570	
23. LITERATURE								
(A) HISTORY AND CRITICISM	./.	–	./.	./.	31 772	689	32 461	
(B) LITERARY TEXTS	23	7	30	7 930	./.	./.	./.	
24. GEOGRAPHY, TRAVEL	30	–	30	92	2 404	150	2 554	
25. HISTORY, BIOGRAPHY	12	1	13	290	3 273	309	3 582	

Number of copies by subject group 8.6
Nombre d'exemplaires par groupes de sujets
Número de ejemplares por categorías de temas

SUBJECT GROUP / GROUPE DE SUJETS / GRUPO TEMATICO	CHILE (1978) A	B	A+B	ASIA	BRUNEI (1978) A	B	A+B	CHINA ‡ A+B
TOTAL	5 595	885	6 480		103	43	146	3 566 160
1. GENERALITIES	90	15	105		4	—	4	./.
2. PHILOSOPHY, PSYCHOLOGY	405	75	480		—	—	—	299 610
3. RELIGION, THEOLOGY	525	180	705		39	4	43	./.
4. SOCIOLOGY, STATISTICS	105	15	120		—	—	—	./.
5. POLITICAL SCIENCE	255	60	315		—	—	—	./.
6. LAW, PUBLIC ADMIN.	555	60	615		—	—	—	./.
7. MILITARY ART	45	—	45		—	—	—	./.
8. EDUCATION, LEISURE	180	30	210		1	—	1	275 030
9. TRADE, TRANSPORT	75	—	75		—	—	—	253 240
10. ETHNOGRAPHY, FOLKLORE	15	—	15		3	—	3	./.
11. MATHEMATICS	330	—	330		20	4	24	./.
12. NATURAL SCIENCES	255	45	300		16	35	51	./.
13. MEDICAL SCIENCES	210	—	210		—	—	—	./.
14. ENGINEERING, CRAFTS	150	45	195		—	—	—	./.
15. AGRICULTURE	60	30	90		—	—	—	./.
16. DOMESTIC SCIENCE	—	—	—		—	—	—	./.
17. MANAGEMENT, ADMIN.	45	—	45		—	—	—	./.
18. PLANNING, ARCHITECTURE	45	15	60		—	—	—	./.
19. PLASTIC ARTS	60	—	60		—	—	—	./.
20. PERFORMING ARTS	45	—	45		—	—	—	./.
21. GAMES, SPORTS	15	—	15		—	—	—	./.
22. LINGUISTICS, PHILOLOGY	330	60	390		—	—	—	./.
23. LITERATURE								
(A) HISTORY AND CRITICISM	240	15	255		—	—	—	...
(B) LITERARY TEXTS	1 065	90	1 155		5	—	5	...
24. GEOGRAPHY, TRAVEL	120	—	120		5	—	5	./.
25. HISTORY, BIOGRAPHY	375	150	525		10	—	10	./.

SUBJECT GROUP / GROUPE DE SUJETS / GRUPO TEMATICO	CYPRUS (1977) A	B	A+B	HONG KONG (1977) A	B	A+B	ISRAEL ‡ (1977) A+B
TOTAL	353	1 774	2 127	3 609	5 610	9 219	11 668
1. GENERALITIES	4	6	10	102	209	311	197
2. PHILOSOPHY, PSYCHOLOGY	2	1	3	15	6	21	178
3. RELIGION, THEOLOGY	5	81	86	63	78	141	1 533
4. SOCIOLOGY, STATISTICS	3	9	12	59	54	113	132
5. POLITICAL SCIENCE	7	140	147	135	20	155	101
6. LAW, PUBLIC ADMIN.	6	13	19	13	133	146	32
7. MILITARY ART	—	180	180	20	29	49	4
8. EDUCATION, LEISURE	92	450	542	38	2 954	2 992	42
9. TRADE, TRANSPORT	3	140	143	134	124	258	19
10. ETHNOGRAPHY, FOLKLORE	2	33	35	393	327	720	4
11. MATHEMATICS	3	50	53	101	81	182	15
12. NATURAL SCIENCES	5	15	20	221	32	253	234
13. MEDICAL SCIENCES	2	68	70	71	61	132	75
14. ENGINEERING, CRAFTS	5	72	77	135	52	187	49
15. AGRICULTURE	4	18	22	6	—	6	4
16. DOMESTIC SCIENCE	8	60	68	63	55	118	246
17. MANAGEMENT, ADMIN.	2	14	16	9	21	30	31
18. PLANNING, ARCHITECTURE	1	8	9	1	14	15	16
19. PLASTIC ARTS	—	3	3	49	25	74	14
20. PERFORMING ARTS	2	34	36	65	183	248	18
21. GAMES, SPORTS	2	40	42	318	31	349	48
22. LINGUISTICS, PHILOLOGY	3	80	83	244	170	414	260
23. LITERATURE							
(A) HISTORY AND CRITICISM	4	2	6	28	14	42	./.
(B) LITERARY TEXTS	166	124	290	820	646	1 466	2 265
24. GEOGRAPHY, TRAVEL	6	45	51	148	37	185	335
25. HISTORY, BIOGRAPHY	16	88	104	358	254	612	551

8.6 Number of copies by subject group
Nombre d'exemplaires par groupes de sujets
Número de ejemplares por categorías de temas

SUBJECT GROUP / GROUPE DE SUJETS / GRUPO TEMATICO	JORDAN ‡ (1976)			KOREA, REPUBLIC OF ‡ (1978)			KUWAIT (1978)		
	A	B	A+B	A	B	A+B	A	B	A+B
TOTAL	2 671	2	2 673	76 368	4 896	81 264	137	95	232
1. GENERALITIES	6	–	6	8 051	2 654	10 705	10	58	68
2. PHILOSOPHY, PSYCHOLOGY	2	–	2	2 425	2	2 427	–	–	–
3. RELIGION, THEOLOGY	249	–	249	4 816	50	4 866	–	–	–
4. SOCIOLOGY, STATISTICS	19	–	19	1 782	11	1 793	4	3	7
5. POLITICAL SCIENCE	52	1	53	650	11	661	10	1	11
6. LAW, PUBLIC ADMIN.	14	–	14	768	10	778	7	6	13
7. MILITARY ART	–	–	–	68	–	68	1	3	4
8. EDUCATION, LEISURE	838	–	838	6 627	1 177	7 804	–	16	16
9. TRADE, TRANSPORT	–	–	–	776	21	797	–	5	5
10. ETHNOGRAPHY, FOLKLORE	6	–	6	75	–	75	–	–	–
11. MATHEMATICS	315	–	315	1 838	18	1 856	–	–	–
12. NATURAL SCIENCES	199	–	199	3 892	94	3 986	–	–	–
13. MEDICAL SCIENCES	80	–	80	178	1	179	–	–	–
14. ENGINEERING, CRAFTS	7	1	8	1 176	12	1 188	1.2	–	1.2
15. AGRICULTURE	11	–	11	354	7	361	–	–	–
16. DOMESTIC SCIENCE	–	–	–	293	10	303	–	–	–
17. MANAGEMENT, ADMIN.	49	–	49	67	1	68	–	–	–
18. PLANNING, ARCHITECTURE	6	–	6	131	–	131	3	–	3
19. PLASTIC ARTS	–	–	–	452	73	525	2	–	2
20. PERFORMING ARTS	–	–	–	3 510	19	3 529	–	3	3
21. GAMES, SPORTS	–	–	–	207	3	210	–	–	–
22. LINGUISTICS, PHILOLOGY	108	–	108	4 930	30	4 960	4.4	–	4.4
23. LITERATURE									
(A) HISTORY AND CRITICISM	349	–	349	518	–	518	15	–	15
(B) LITERARY TEXTS	./.	–	./.	11 031	577	11 608	69	–	69
24. GEOGRAPHY, TRAVEL	177	–	177	334	1	335	–	–	–
25. HISTORY, BIOGRAPHY	184	–	184	3 587	34	3 621	10	–	10

SUBJECT GROUP / GROUPE DE SUJETS / GRUPO TEMATICO	LAO PEOPLE'S DEMOCRATIC REPUBLIC ‡ (1976)			MALAYSIA ‡ (1978)			PHILIPPINES ‡ (1977)		
	A	B	A+B	A	B	A+B	A	B	A+B
TOTAL	–	268	268	3 680	2 401	6 081	2 087	1 031	3 118
1. GENERALITIES	–	55	55	23	6	29	62	48	110
2. PHILOSOPHY, PSYCHOLOGY	–	37	37	170	1	171	43	1	44
3. RELIGION, THEOLOGY	–	5	5	210	771	981	264	56	320
4. SOCIOLOGY, STATISTICS	–	–	–	61	41	102	75	106	181
5. POLITICAL SCIENCE	–	88	88	121	580	701	96	58	154
6. LAW, PUBLIC ADMIN.	–	–	–	44	83	127	128	67	195
7. MILITARY ART	–	–	–	–	–	–	7	11	18
8. EDUCATION, LEISURE	–	–	–	60	85	145	99	20	119
9. TRADE, TRANSPORT	–	–	–	41	255	296	26	23	49
10. ETHNOGRAPHY, FOLKLORE	–	–	–	77	288	365	2	13	15
11. MATHEMATICS	–	–	–	170	20	190	22	–	22
12. NATURAL SCIENCES	–	–	–	436	20	456	100	14	114
13. MEDICAL SCIENCES	–	8	8	36	5	41	170	19	189
14. ENGINEERING, CRAFTS	–	–	–	31	31	62	117	15	132
15. AGRICULTURE	–	–	–	118	44	162	215	277	492
16. DOMESTIC SCIENCE	–	–	–	11	1	12	128	12	140
17. MANAGEMENT, ADMIN.	–	–	–	56	5	61	168	34	202
18. PLANNING, ARCHITECTURE	–	–	–	2	1	3	12	3	15
19. PLASTIC ARTS	–	–	–	3	1	4	31	94	125
20. PERFORMING ARTS	–	7	7	6	0	6	31	106	137
21. GAMES, SPORTS	–	–	–	9	–	9	12	4	16
22. LINGUISTICS, PHILOLOGY	–	–	–	839	108	947	116	22	138
23. LITERATURE									
(A) HISTORY AND CRITICISM	–	5	5	404	22	426	./.	–	./.
(B) LITERARY TEXTS	–	56	56	./.	./.	./.	104	10	114
24. GEOGRAPHY, TRAVEL	–	7	7	112	3	115	16	–	17
25. HISTORY, BIOGRAPHY	–	–	–	640	30	670	43	18	60

Number of copies by subject group   8.6
Nombre d'exemplaires par groupes de sujets
Número de ejemplares por categorías de temas

SUBJECT GROUP GROUPE DE SUJETS GRUPO TEMATICO	QATAR (1978)			SINGAPORE ‡ (1978)			SRI LANKA ‡ (1978)		
	A	B	A+B	A	B	A+B	A	B	A+B
TOTAL	313	58	371	4 124	2 824	6 948	3 399	3 049	6 448
1. GENERALITIES	10	12	22	29	32	61	20	6	26
2. PHILOSOPHY, PSYCHOLOGY	6	–	6	3	–	3	76	17	93
3. RELIGION, THEOLOGY	180	36	216	66	28	94	686	914	1 600
4. SOCIOLOGY, STATISTICS	18	–	18	17	22	39	100	11	111
5. POLITICAL SCIENCE	–	–	–	87	28	115	124	596	720
6. LAW, PUBLIC ADMIN.	2	10	12	27	1	28	63	89	152
7. MILITARY ART	–	–	–	–	–	–	–	1	1
8. EDUCATION, LEISURE	–	–	–	1 471	2 330	3 801	80	188	268
9. TRADE, TRANSPORT	3	–	3	12	10	22	6	10	16
10. ETHNOGRAPHY, FOLKLORE	–	–	–	12	6	18	–	0.2	0.2
11. MATHEMATICS	9	–	9	55	52	107	292	40	332
12. NATURAL SCIENCES	13	–	13	462	6	468	82	13	95
13. MEDICAL SCIENCES	–	–	–	46	29	75	37	71	108
14. ENGINEERING, CRAFTS	–	–	–	30	5	35	15	38	53
15. AGRICULTURE	–	–	–	8	14	22	32	25	57
16. DOMESTIC SCIENCE	–	–	–	35	5	40	10	–	10
17. MANAGEMENT, ADMIN.	–	–	–	33	15	48	22	43	65
18. PLANNING, ARCHITECTURE	–	–	–	1	.01	1	37	359	396
19. PLASTIC ARTS	–	–	–	12	7	19	./.	./.	./.
20. PERFORMING ARTS	–	–	–	168	4	172	./.	./.	./.
21. GAMES, SPORTS	–	–	–	104	35	139	2	7	9
22. LINGUISTICS, PHILOLOGY	60	–	60	532	136	668	1 263	252	1 515
23. LITERATURE									
(A) HISTORY AND CRITICISM	3	–	3	23	3	26	74	31	105
(B) LITERARY TEXTS	3	–	3	530	40	570	259	289	548
24. GEOGRAPHY, TRAVEL	3	–	3	95	–	95	28	11	39
25. HISTORY, BIOGRAPHY	9	–	9	266	16	282	90	39	129

SUBJECT GROUP GROUPE DE SUJETS GRUPO TEMATICO	SYRIAN ARAB REPUBLIC ‡ (1978)			UNITED ARAB EMIRATES ‡ (1977)			VIET NAM (1977)		
	A	B	A+B	A	B	A+B	A	B	A+B
TOTAL	554	11	565	72	10	82	62 090	2 717	64 807
1. GENERALITIES	3	–	3	46	–	46	–	–	–
2. PHILOSOPHY, PSYCHOLOGY	9	–	9	–	–	–	688	–	688
3. RELIGION, THEOLOGY	15	–	15	–	–	–	–	–	–
4. SOCIOLOGY, STATISTICS	4	–	4	–	–	–	67	–	67
5. POLITICAL SCIENCE	57	–	57	–	–	–	6 291	226	6 517
6. LAW, PUBLIC ADMIN.	39	–	39	3	–	3	255	152	407
7. MILITARY ART	–	–	–	–	–	–	220	–	220
8. EDUCATION, LEISURE	–	–	–	–	–	–	1 924	80	2 004
9. TRADE, TRANSPORT	8	–	8	16	10	26	60	–	60
10. ETHNOGRAPHY, FOLKLORE	55	–	55	–	–	–	76	–	76
11. MATHEMATICS	18	–	18	–	–	–	11 071	–	11 071
12. NATURAL SCIENCES	41	–	41	–	–	–	8 088	–	8 088
13. MEDICAL SCIENCES	46	–	46	–	–	–	554	128	682
14. ENGINEERING, CRAFTS	40	–	40	–	–	–	637	–	637
15. AGRICULTURE	41	–	41	–	–	–	723	44	767
16. DOMESTIC SCIENCE	–	–	–	–	–	–	98	–	98
17. MANAGEMENT, ADMIN.	–	–	–	–	–	–	223	–	223
18. PLANNING, ARCHITECTURE	–	–	–	–	–	–	14	–	14
19. PLASTIC ARTS	8	–	8	3	–	3	20	–	20
20. PERFORMING ARTS	5	–	5	–	–	–	226	–	226
21. GAMES, SPORTS	–	–	–	–	–	–	240	5	245
22. LINGUISTICS, PHILOLOGY	3	–	3	–	–	–	17 365	35	17 400
23. LITERATURE									
(A) HISTORY AND CRITICISM	27	–	27	–	–	–	320	–	320
(B) LITERARY TEXTS	62	–	62	4	–	4	6 878	1 846	8 724
24. GEOGRAPHY, TRAVEL	13	–	13	–	–	–	2 234	–	2 234
25. HISTORY, BIOGRAPHY	20	11	31	–	–	–	3 818	201	4 019

8.6 Number of copies by subject group
Nombre d'exemplaires par groupes de sujets
Número de ejemplares por categorías de temas

SUBJECT GROUP / GROUPE DE SUJETS EUROPE / GRUPO TEMATICO	BULGARIA ‡ (1978)			CZECHOSLOVAKIA ‡ (1978)		
	A	B	A+B	A	B	A+B
TOTAL	42 851	7 377	50 228	63 731	17 502	81 233
1. GENERALITIES	170	105	275	1 030	535	1 565
2. PHILOSOPHY, PSYCHOLOGY	346	12	358	862	6	868
3. RELIGION, THEOLOGY	14	3	17	214	–	214
4. SOCIOLOGY, STATISTICS	326	805	1 131	116	5	121
5. POLITICAL SCIENCE	3 438	861	4 299	4 255	2 963	7 218
6. LAW, PUBLIC ADMIN.	358	133	491	1 039	377	1 416
7. MILITARY ART	144	6	150	892	783	1 675
8. EDUCATION, LEISURE	1 125	107	1 232	9 083	1 932	11 015
9. TRADE, TRANSPORT	32	19	51	544	18	562
10. ETHNOGRAPHY, FOLKLORE	115	4	119	8	0.3	8.3
11. MATHEMATICS	2 442	0	2 442	1 602	26	1 628
12. NATURAL SCIENCES	2 432	109	2 541	2 095	110	2 205
13. MEDICAL SCIENCES	1 307	782	2 089	980	1 003	1 983
14. ENGINEERING, CRAFTS	1 687	139	1 826	3 481	403	3 884
15. AGRICULTURE	498	96	594	1 194	177	1 371
16. DOMESTIC SCIENCE	469	2	471	548	415	963
17. MANAGEMENT, ADMIN.	509	43	552	185	16	201
18. PLANNING, ARCHITECTURE	1 504	135	1 639	2 063	745	2 808
19. PLASTIC ARTS	./.	./.	./.	./.	./.	./.
20. PERFORMING ARTS	./.	./.	./.	./.	./.	./.
21. GAMES, SPORTS	281	16	297	1 059	108	1 167
22. LINGUISTICS, PHILOLOGY	3 499	2	3 501	1 908	5	1 913
23. LITERATURE						
(A) HISTORY AND CRITICISM	19 207	3 766	22 973	560	126	686
(B) LITERARY TEXTS	./.	./.	./.	26 212	7 445	33 657
24. GEOGRAPHY, TRAVEL	831	75	906	1 902	145	2 047
25. HISTORY, BIOGRAPHY	2 117	157	2 274	1 899	159	2 058

SUBJECT GROUP / GROUPE DE SUJETS / GRUPO TEMATICO	GERMAN DEMOCRATIC REPUBLIC ‡ (1978)			HOLY SEE (1978)			HUNGARY (1978)		
	A	B	A+B	A	B	A+B	A	B	A+B
TOTAL	104 785	24 446	129 231	145	–	145	93 265	11 315	104 580
1. GENERALITIES	1 562	–	1 562	7	–	7	5 617	89	5 706
2. PHILOSOPHY, PSYCHOLOGY	2 493	101	2 594	30	–	30	817	14	831
3. RELIGION, THEOLOGY	1 814	1 941	3 755	82	–	82	970	41	1 011
4. SOCIOLOGY, STATISTICS	2 184	184	2 368	4	–	4	513	1	514
5. POLITICAL SCIENCE	3 279	400	3 679	–	–	–	5 960	2 193	8 153
6. LAW, PUBLIC ADMIN.	6 331	558	6 889	6	–	6	1 209	421	1 630
7. MILITARY ART	944	277	1 221	–	–	–	441	106	547
8. EDUCATION, LEISURE	2 058	548	2 606	1	–	1	2 645	281	2 926
9. TRADE, TRANSPORT	1 176	99	1 275	–	–	–	166	99	265
10. ETHNOGRAPHY, FOLKLORE	209	20	229	–	–	–	492	6	498
11. MATHEMATICS	532	–	532	–	–	–	4 875	220	5 095
12. NATURAL SCIENCES	1 820	87	1 907	–	–	–	5 436	189	5 625
13. MEDICAL SCIENCES	2 133	213	2 346	–	–	–	1 530	775	2 305
14. ENGINEERING, CRAFTS	4 776	350	5 126	–	–	–	3 882	175	4 057
15. AGRICULTURE	1 699	31	1 730	–	–	–	1 378	83	1 461
16. DOMESTIC SCIENCE	1 320	–	1 320	–	–	–	1 336	44	1 380
17. MANAGEMENT, ADMIN.	45	75	120	–	–	–	1 712	462	2 174
18. PLANNING, ARCHITECTURE	1 591	439	2 030	–	–	–	478	26	504
19. PLASTIC ARTS	42	105	147	–	–	–	1 266	339	1 605
20. PERFORMING ARTS	1 062	251	1 313	1	–	1	2 459	642	3 101
21. GAMES, SPORTS	2 084	80	2 164	–	–	–	1 976	1 524	3 500
22. LINGUISTICS, PHILOLOGY	2 350	11	2 361	7	–	7	7 193	816	8 009
23. LITERATURE									
(A) HISTORY AND CRITICISM	23 267	4 321	27 588	–	–	–	2 637	86	2 723
(B) LITERARY TEXTS	./.	./.	./.	–	–	–	30 181	1 799	31 980
24. GEOGRAPHY, TRAVEL	1 982	–	1 982	–	–	–	4 616	382	4 998
25. HISTORY, BIOGRAPHY	3 270	539	3 809	7	–	7	3 480	502	3 982

Number of copies by subject group   8.6
Nombre d'exemplaires par groupes de sujets
Número de ejemplares por categorías de temas

SUBJECT GROUP GROUPE DE SUJETS GRUPO TEMATICO	ITALY (1978)			MONACO (1977)	POLAND ‡ (1978)			PORTUGAL ‡ (1976)
	A	B	A+B	A+B	A	B	A+B	A+B
TOTAL	127 590	14 131	141 721	443	114 070	29 604	143 674	35 213
1. GENERALITIES	6 438	116	6 554	7	518	157	675	1 304
2. PHILOSOPHY, PSYCHOLOGY	3 085	16	3 101	23	1 138	72	1 210	511
3. RELIGION, THEOLOGY	4 818	5 193	10 011	238	1 466	13	1 479	1 001
4. SOCIOLOGY, STATISTICS	1 496	52	1 548	—	1 871	157	2 028	14 671
5. POLITICAL SCIENCE	3 096	65	3 161	25	4 681	891	5 572	./.
6. LAW, PUBLIC ADMIN.	3 335	334	3 669	—	1 866	263	2 129	./.
7. MILITARY ART	200	60	260	—	3 803	445	4 248	./.
8. EDUCATION, LEISURE	14 614	1 454	16 068	11	2 469	588	3 057	./.
9. TRADE, TRANSPORT	193	—	193	—	170	31	201	./.
10. ETHNOGRAPHY, FOLKLORE	563	5	568	—	207	54	261	./.
11. MATHEMATICS	2 465	38	2 503	—	6 633	12	6 645	1 652
12. NATURAL SCIENCES	5 709	485	6 194	6	5 867	324	6 191	./.
13. MEDICAL SCIENCES	2 480	45	2 525	4	3 463	2 007	5 470	2 509
14. ENGINEERING, CRAFTS	2 779	59	2 838	22	7 148	1 104	8 252	./.
15. AGRICULTURE	809	101	910	—	2 981	1 833	4 814	./.
16. DOMESTIC SCIENCE	3 537	25	3 562	—	2 794		2 794	./.
17. MANAGEMENT, ADMIN.	676	7	683	25	2 219	814	3 033	./.
18. PLANNING, ARCHITECTURE	2 428	18	2 446	15	4 924	1 180	6 104	5 559
19. PLASTIC ARTS	2 719	171	2 890	—	./.	./.	./.	./.
20. PERFORMING ARTS	2 469	241	2 710	—	./.	./.	./.	./.
21. GAMES, SPORTS	3 568	1 640	5 208	3	2 138	768	2 906	./.
22. LINGUISTICS, PHILOLOGY	5 480	50	5 530	—	10 090	1 067	11 157	./.
23. LITERATURE								
(A) HISTORY AND CRITICISM	3 731	69	3 800	20	3 906	43	3 949	6 387
(B) LITERARY TEXTS	38 026	2 539	40 565	14	35 005	14 981	49 986	./.
24. GEOGRAPHY, TRAVEL	4 697	1 277	5 974	25	3 906	2 651	6 557	1 619
25. HISTORY, BIOGRAPHY	8 179	71	8 250	5	4 807	149	4 956	./.

SUBJECT GROUP GROUPE DE SUJETS GRUPO TEMATICO	ROMANIA (1978)			SPAIN ‡ (1977)			YUGOSLAVIA (1978)		
	A	B	A+B	A	B	A+B	A	B	A+B
TOTAL	85 073	12 276	97 349	166 471	38 369	204 840	45 051	11 609	56 660
1. GENERALITIES	1 331	1 202	2 533	16 599	16 609	33 208	340	61	401
2. PHILOSOPHY, PSYCHOLOGY	1 480	70	1 550	8 302	984	9 286	292	5	297
3. RELIGION, THEOLOGY	427	137	564	9 582	2 016	11 598	819	220	1 039
4. SOCIOLOGY, STATISTICS	1 411	2 925	4 336	4 240	176	4 416	440	83	523
5. POLITICAL SCIENCE	2 129	873	3 002	6 110	2 525	8 635	4 892	876	5 768
6. LAW, PUBLIC ADMIN.	748	131	879	2 031	361	2 392	1 620	1 176	2 796
7. MILITARY ART	171	0	171	235	18	253	119	22	141
8. EDUCATION, LEISURE	2 467	762	3 229	4 905	4 527	9 432	19 521	2 958	22 479
9. TRADE, TRANSPORT	243	29	272	320	2	322	—	—	—
10. ETHNOGRAPHY, FOLKLORE	236	8	244	1 450	61	1 511	34	6	40
11. MATHEMATICS	6 954	341	7 295	7 532	247	7 779	278	14	292
12. NATURAL SCIENCES	7 881	361	8 242	9 491	778	10 269	537	61	598
13. MEDICAL SCIENCES	2 980	1 929	4 909	3 246	578	3 824	941	204	1 145
14. ENGINEERING, CRAFTS	4 397	186	4 583	2 357	280	2 637	673	128	801
15. AGRICULTURE	1 406	540	1 946	787	725	1 512	558	51	609
16. DOMESTIC SCIENCE	917	20	937	3 624	608	4 232	364	115	479
17. MANAGEMENT, ADMIN.	702	2	704	1 454	335	1 789	1 179	417	1 596
18. PLANNING, ARCHITECTURE	450	9	459	6 811	2 366	9 177	102	187	289
19. PLASTIC ARTS	1 988	29	2 017	./.	./.	./.	476	447	923
20. PERFORMING ARTS	2 344	89	2 433	./.	./.	./.	277	2 383	2 660
21. GAMES, SPORTS	597	485	1 082	1 303	445	1 748	563	90	653
22. LINGUISTICS, PHILOLOGY	10 450	37	10 487	18 853	2 350	21 203	522	13	535
23. LITERATURE									
(A) HISTORY AND CRITICISM	2 539	5	2 544	44 843	1 443	46 286	495	53	548
(B) LITERARY TEXTS	23 895	1 642	25 537	./.	./.	./.	9 040	1 393	10 433
24. GEOGRAPHY, TRAVEL	3 136	121	3 257	2 242	208	2 450	296	541	837
25. HISTORY, BIOGRAPHY	3 794	343	4 137	10 154	727	10 881	673	105	778

8.6 Number of copies by subject group
Nombre d'exemplaires par groupes de sujets
Número de ejemplares por categorías de temas

SUBJECT GROUP / GROUPE DE SUJETS OCEANIA / GRUPO TEMATICO	AMERICAN SAMOA ‡ (1978)			FIJI ‡ (1976)		
	A	B	A+B	A	B	A+B
TOTAL	35	–	35	179	41	220
1. GENERALITIES	3	–	3	–	–	–
2. PHILOSOPHY, PSYCHOLOGY	–	–	–	–	–	–
3. RELIGION, THEOLOGY	–	–	–	–	–	–
4. SOCIOLOGY, STATISTICS	–	–	–	4	1	5
5. POLITICAL SCIENCE	–	–	–	–	–	–
6. LAW, PUBLIC ADMIN.	–	–	–	–	–	–
7. MILITARY ART	3	–	3	–	–	–
8. EDUCATION, LEISURE	7	–	7	11	2	13
9. TRADE, TRANSPORT	–	–	–	2	–	2
10. ETHNOGRAPHY, FOLKLORE	–	–	–	–	1	1
11. MATHEMATICS	1	–	1	31	5	36
12. NATURAL SCIENCES	–	–	–	71	5	76
13. MEDICAL SCIENCES	–	–	–	–	2	2
14. ENGINEERING, CRAFTS	–	–	–	–	11	11
15. AGRICULTURE	–	–	–	9	1	10
16. DOMESTIC SCIENCE	1	–	1	16	–	16
17. MANAGEMENT, ADMIN.	–	–	–	5	2	7
18. PLANNING, ARCHITECTURE	–	–	–	–	–	–
19. PLASTIC ARTS	–	–	–	–	6	6
20. PERFORMING ARTS	–	–	–	–	–	–
21. GAMES, SPORTS	–	–	–	–	–	–
22. LINGUISTICS, PHILOLOGY	–	–	–	30	5	35
23. LITERATURE						
(A) HISTORY AND CRITICISM	4	–	4	–	–	–
(B) LITERARY TEXTS	–	–	–	–	–	–
24. GEOGRAPHY, TRAVEL	–	–	–	–	–	–
25. HISTORY, BIOGRAPHY	0.4	–	0.4	–	–	–

SUBJECT GROUP / GROUPE DE SUJETS / GRUPO TEMATICO	FRENCH POLYNESIA (1977)			GUAM ‡ (1978)			NORFOLK ISLAND (1977)		
	A	B	A+B	A	B	A+B	A	B	A+B
TOTAL	6.2	8.6	14.8	1.8	0.1	1.9	–	1	1
1. GENERALITIES	–	–	–	–	–	–	–	–	–
2. PHILOSOPHY, PSYCHOLOGY	–	–	–	–	–	–	–	–	–
3. RELIGION, THEOLOGY	–	–	–	–	–	–	–	–	–
4. SOCIOLOGY, STATISTICS	0.6	5.1	5.7	–	–	–	–	–	–
5. POLITICAL SCIENCE	–	–	–	–	–	–	–	–	–
6. LAW, PUBLIC ADMIN.	–	–	–	–	–	–	–	–	–
7. MILITARY ART	–	–	–	–	–	–	–	–	–
8. EDUCATION, LEISURE	–	–	–	–	–	–	–	–	–
9. TRADE, TRANSPORT	–	2	2	–	–	–	–	1	1
10. ETHNOGRAPHY, FOLKLORE	–	–	–	–	–	–	–	–	–
11. MATHEMATICS	–	–	–	–	–	–	–	–	–
12. NATURAL SCIENCES	–	–	–	1.3	–	1.3	–	–	–
13. MEDICAL SCIENCES	–	–	–	–	–	–	–	–	–
14. ENGINEERING, CRAFTS	–	–	–	–	–	–	–	–	–
15. AGRICULTURE	5	–	5	0.5	0.1	0.6	–	–	–
16. DOMESTIC SCIENCE	–	–	–	–	–	–	–	–	–
17. MANAGEMENT, ADMIN.	–	1.4	1.4	–	–	–	–	–	–
18. PLANNING, ARCHITECTURE	–	–	–	–	–	–	–	–	–
19. PLASTIC ARTS	–	–	–	–	–	–	–	–	–
20. PERFORMING ARTS	–	–	–	–	–	–	–	–	–
21. GAMES, SPORTS	–	–	–	–	–	–	–	–	–
22. LINGUISTICS, PHILOLOGY	–	0.1	0.1	–	–	–	–	–	–
23. LITERATURE									
(A) HISTORY AND CRITICISM	–	–	–	–	–	–	–	–	–
(B) LITERARY TEXTS	0.6	–	0.6	–	–	–	–	–	–
24. GEOGRAPHY, TRAVEL	–	–	–	–	–	–	–	–	–
25. HISTORY, BIOGRAPHY	–	–	–	–	–	–	–	–	–

Number of copies by subject group 8.6
Nombre d'exemplaires par groupes de sujets
Número de ejemplares por categorías de temas

SUBJECT GROUP GROUPE DE SUJETS GRUPO TEMATICO	PACIFIC ISLANDS ‡ (1978)			SAMOA (1977)			TONGA (1977)		
	A	B	A+B	A	B	A+B	A	B	A+B
TOTAL	11	6	17	73.1	42.5	115.6	20.5	29.5	50
1. GENERALITIES	–	–	–	10	5	15	–	–	–
2. PHILOSOPHY, PSYCHOLOGY	–	–	–	1	1	2	–	–	–
3. RELIGION, THEOLOGY	–	–	–	12	22	34	–	7	7
4. SOCIOLOGY, STATISTICS	1	–	1	5	–	5	–	1	1
5. POLITICAL SCIENCE	1	2	3	–	–	–	–	–	–
6. LAW, PUBLIC ADMIN.	5	1	6	–	–	–	–	9	9
7. MILITARY ART	–	–	–	10	–	10	–	–	–
8. EDUCATION, LEISURE	2	3	5	10	6	16	0.3	5	5.3
9. TRADE, TRANSPORT	1	–	1	0.6	1	1.6	–	0.7	0.7
10. ETHNOGRAPHY, FOLKLORE	1	–	1	–	1	1	–	–	–
11. MATHEMATICS	–	–	–	20	–	20	10	–	10
12. NATURAL SCIENCES	–	–	–	1	1	2	–	–	–
13. MEDICAL SCIENCES	–	–	–	0.5	2	2.5	–	1	1
14. ENGINEERING, CRAFTS	–	–	–	–	–	–	–	–	–
15. AGRICULTURE	–	–	–	1	2	3	0.2	4	4.2
16. DOMESTIC SCIENCE	–	–	–	0.5	0.4	0.9	–	0.8	0.8
17. MANAGEMENT, ADMIN.	–	–	–	–	–	–	–	–	–
18. PLANNING, ARCHITECTURE	–	–	–	–	–	–	–	–	–
19. PLASTIC ARTS	–	–	–	0.6	–	0.6	–	–	–
20. PERFORMING ARTS	–	–	–	–	–	–	–	–	–
21. GAMES, SPORTS	–	–	–	0.1	0.1	0.2	–	–	–
22. LINGUISTICS, PHILOLOGY	–	–	–	–	–	–	–	–	–
23. LITERATURE									
(A) HISTORY AND CRITICISM	–	–	–	–	–	–	–	–	–
(B) LITERARY TEXTS	–	–	–	–	–	–	–	1	1
24. GEOGRAPHY, TRAVEL	–	–	–	–	–	–	5	–	5
25. HISTORY, BIOGRAPHY	–	–	–	0.8	1	1.8	5	–	5

SUBJECT GROUP GROUPE DE SUJETS U.S.S.R. GRUPO TEMATICO	U.S.S.R. ‡ (1977)			BYELORUSSIAN S.S.R. (1978)		
	A	B	A+B	A	B	A+B
TOTAL	1 227 376	574 301	1 801 677	27 774	5 908	33 682
1. GENERALITIES	8 845	2 646	11 491	120	38	158
2. PHILOSOPHY, PSYCHOLOGY	18 967	5 500	24 467	143	17	160
3. RELIGION, THEOLOGY	5 208	1 650	6 858	35	–	35
4. SOCIOLOGY, STATISTICS	3 876	723	4 599	64	6	70
5. POLITICAL SCIENCE	125 873	57 128	183 001	927	235	1 162
6. LAW, PUBLIC ADMIN.	27 313	16 080	43 393	930	191	1 121
7. MILITARY ART	27 336	3 270	30 606	257	90	347
8. EDUCATION, LEISURE	53 468	9 782	63 250	2 195	397	2 592
9. TRADE, TRANSPORT	3 399	796	4 195	15	22	37
10. ETHNOGRAPHY, FOLKLORE	–	–	–	–	–	–
11. MATHEMATICS	67 255	1 188	68 443	785	5	790
12. NATURAL SCIENCES	88 140	6 249	94 389	1 708	20	1 728
13. MEDICAL SCIENCES	27 017	9 104	36 121	799	256	1 055
14. ENGINEERING, CRAFTS	62 466	55 638	118 104	1 057	525	1 582
15. AGRICULTURE	25 933	5 963	31 896	1 424	241	1 665
16. DOMESTIC SCIENCE	4 166	672	4 838	253	51	304
17. MANAGEMENT, ADMIN.	47 780	10 936	58 716	1 056	198	1 254
18. PLANNING, ARCHITECTURE	22 025	5 534	27 559	4	–	4
19. PLASTIC ARTS	./.	./.	./.	101	34	135
20. PERFORMING ARTS	./.	./.	./.	501	60	561
21. GAMES, SPORTS	10 935	2 046	12 981	503	30	533
22. LINGUISTICS, PHILOLOGY	99 698	2 901	102 599	1 659	62	1 721
23. LITERATURE						
(A) HISTORY AND CRITICISM	50 320	1 221	51 541	1 051	7	1 058
(B) LITERARY TEXTS	372 850	370 780	743 630	10 325	3 386	13 711
24. GEOGRAPHY, TRAVEL	20 948	2 377	23 325	867	1	868
25. HISTORY, BIOGRAPHY	53 558	2 117	55 675	995	36	1 031

8.6 Number of copies by subject group
Nombre d'exemplaires par groupes de sujets
Número de ejemplares por categorías de temas

SUBJECT GROUP GROUPE DE SUJETS GRUPO TEMATICO	UKRAINIAN S.S.R. ‡ (1977)		
	A	B	A+B
TOTAL	108 129	52 501	160 630
1. GENERALITIES	633	221	854
2. PHILOSOPHY, PSYCHOLOGY	755	830	1 585
3. RELIGION, THEOLOGY	574	725	1 299
4. SOCIOLOGY, STATISTICS	208	175	383
5. POLITICAL SCIENCE	8 835	3 271	12 106
6. LAW, PUBLIC ADMIN.	1 925	4 042	5 967
7. MILITARY ART	767	287	1 054
8. EDUCATION, LEISURE	4 966	2 222	7 188
9. TRADE, TRANSPORT	194	65	259
10. ETHNOGRAPHY, FOLKLORE	–	–	–
11. MATHEMATICS	5 630	26	5 656
12. NATURAL SCIENCES	5 799	384	6 183
13. MEDICAL SCIENCES	3 215	1 270	4 485
14. ENGINEERING, CRAFTS	4 429	6 264	10 694
15. AGRICULTURE	3 366	791	4 157
16. DOMESTIC SCIENCE	352	153	505
17. MANAGEMENT, ADMIN.	5 518	818	6 335
18. PLANNING, ARCHITECTURE	1 023	1 150	2 173
19. PLASTIC ARTS	./.	./.	./.
20. PERFORMING ARTS	./.	./.	./.
21. GAMES, SPORTS	897	116	1 013
22. LINGUISTICS, PHILOLOGY	13 025	24	13 049
23. LITERATURE			
(A) HISTORY AND CRITICISM	4 434	292	4 726
(B) LITERARY TEXTS	33 425	28 838	62 263
24. GEOGRAPHY, TRAVEL	2 257	99	2 356
25. HISTORY, BIOGRAPHY	5 902	438	6 340

GENERAL NOTE/NOTE GENERALE/NOTA GENERAL:
E—> SEE GENERAL NOTE TO TABLE 8.3.
FR—> VOIR LA NOTE GENERALE DU TABLEAU 8.3.
ESP> VEASE LA NOTA GENERAL DEL CUADRO 8.3.

CONGO:
E—> ALL FIRST EDITIONS. WORKS OF GROUP 23B
ARE INCLUDED IN GROUP 23A.
FR—> TOUS LES OUVRAGES RECENSES SONT DES PRE-
MIERES EDITIONS. LES OUVRAGES DU GROUPE 23B
SONT INCLUS DANS LE GROUPE 23A.
ESP> TODAS LAS OBRAS CONSIDERADAS SON PRIMERAS
EDICIONES. LAS OBRAS DEL GRUPO 23B QUEDAN IN-
CLUIDAS EN EL GRUPO 23A.

EGYPT:
E—> FIGURES ARE PRELIMINARY. WORKS OF GROUPS
5 TO 10 ARE INCLUDED IN GROUP 4; 12 IN GROUP
11; 14 TO 17 IN GROUP 13; 19 TO 21 IN GROUP 18;
23B IN GROUP 23A; 25 IN GROUP 24.
FR—> LES CHIFFRES SONT PROVISOIRES. LES OUVRA-
GES DES GROUPES 5 A 10 SONT INCLUS DANS LE GROUPE
4; LE GROUPE 12 DANS LE GROUPE 11; 14 A 17 DANS
LE GROUPE 13; 19 A 21 DANS LE GROUPE 18; 23B DANS
LE GROUPE 23A; 25 DANS LE GROUPE 24.
ESP> DATOS PRELIMINARES. LAS OBRAS DE LOS GRU-
POS 5 A 10 QUEDAN INCLUIDAS EN EL GRUPO 4; LAS DE
DEL GRUPO 12 EN EL GRUPO 11; LAS DE LOS GRUPOS
14 A 17 EN EL GRUPO 13; LAS DE LOS GRUPOS 19 A 21
EN EL GRUPO 18; LAS DEL GRUPO 23B EN EL GRUPO 23A;
LAS DEL GRUPO 25 EN EL GRUPO 24.

ETHIOPIA:
E—> ALL FIRST EDITIONS. SCHOOL TEXTBOOKS
(357,000) AND CHILDREN'S BOOKS (6,000) ARE
INCLUDED IN THE TOTAL BUT NOT IDENTIFIED IN THE
25 GROUPS. WORKS OF GROUPS 5 TO 10 ARE INCLUDED
IN GROUP 4; 12 IN GROUP 11; 14 TO 17 IN GROUP 13
19 TO 21 IN GROUP 18; 25 IN GROUP 24; 23B IN
GROUP 23A;
FR—> TOUS LES OUVRAGES RECENSES SONT DES PRE-
MIERES EDITIONS. LES MANUELS SCOLAIRES (357 000)
ET LES LIVRES POUR ENFANTS (6 000) SONT COMPRIS
DANS LE TOTAL MAIS NE SONT PAS REPARTIS ENTRE
LES 25 GROUPES. LES OUVRAGES DES GROUPES 5 A 10
SONT INCLUS DANS LE GROUPE 4; 12 DANS LE GROUPE
11; 14 A 17 DANS LE GROUPE 13; 19 A 21 DANS LE
GROUPE 18; 25 DANS LE GROUPE 24; 23B DANS LE
GROUPE 23A.
ESP> TODAS LAS OBRAS CONSIDERADAS SON PRIMERAS
EDICIONES. LOS MANUALES ESCOLARES (357 000) Y
LOS LIBROS PARA NIÑOS (6 000) QUEDAN COMPREN-
DIDOS EN EL TOTAL PERO NO SE DESGLOSAN ENTRE LOS
25 GRUPOS. LAS OBRAS DE LOS GRUPOS 5 A 10 QUE-
DAN INCLUIDAS EN EL GRUPO 4; LAS DEL GRUPO 12 EN
EL GRUPO 11; LAS DE LAS GRUPOS 14 A 17 EN EL
GRUPO 13; LAS DE LOS GRUPOS 19 A 21 EN EL GRUPO
18; LAS DEL GRUPO 25 EN EL GRUPO 24; LAS DEL
GRUPO 23B EN EL GRUPO 23A.

GAMBIA:
E—> ALL FIRST EDITIONS.
FR—> TOUS LES OUVRAGES RECENSES SONT DES PRE-
MIERES EDITIONS.
ESP> TODAS LAS OBRAS CONSIDERADAS SON PRIMERAS
EDICIONES.

Number of copies by subject group   8.6
Nombre d'exemplaires par groupes de sujets
Número de ejemplares por categorías de temas

GHANA:
    E—> WORKS OF GROUP 23B ARE INCLUDED IN GROUP
23A.
    FR—> LES OUVRAGES DU GROUPE 23B SONT INCLUS
DANS LE GROUPE 23A.
    ESP> LAS OBRAS DEL GRUPO 23B QUEDAN INCLUIDAS
EN EL GRUPO 23A.

MAURITIUS:
    E—> ALL FIRST EDITIONS.
    FR—> TOUS LES OUVRAGES RECENSES SONT DES PRE—
MIERES EDITIONS.
    ESP> TODAS LOS OBRAS CONSIDERADAS SON PRIMERAS
EDICIONES.

SENEGAL:
    E—> ALL FIRST EDITIONS.
    FR—> TOUS LES OUVRAGES RECENSES SONT DES PRE—
MIERES EDITIONS.
    ESP> TODAS LOS OBRAS CONSIDERADAS SON PRIMERAS
EDICIONES.

SEYCHELLES:
    E—> ALL FIRST EDITIONS.
    FR—> TOUS LES OUVRAGES RECENSES SONT DES PRE—
MIERES EDITIONS.
    ESP> TODAS LOS OBRAS CONSIDERADAS SON PRIMERAS
EDICIONES.

SIERRA LEONE:
    E—> ALL FIRST EDITIONS.
    FR—> TOUS LES OUVRAGES RECENSES SONT DES PRE—
MIERES EDITIONS.
    ESP> TODAS LOS OBRAS CONSIDERADAS SON PRIMERAS
EDICIONES.

SUDAN:
    E—> DATA REFER TO SCHOOL TEXTBOOKS ONLY.
    FR—> LES DONNEES NE TIENNENT COMPTE QUE DES
MANUELS SCOLAIRES.
    ESP> LOS DATOS SE REFIEREN A LOS MANUALES ESCO—
LARES SOLAMENTE.

UNITED REPUBLIC OF CAMEROON:
    E—> DATA REFER TO FIRST EDITIONS OF SCHOOL
TEXTBOOKS ONLY.
    FR—> LES DONNEES SE REFERENT AUX PREMIERES EDI—
TIONS DES MANUELS SCOLAIRES SEULEMENT.
    ESP> LOS DATOS SE REFIEREN A LAS PRIMERAS EDI—
CIONES DE LOS MANUALES ESCOLARES SOLAMENTE.

ZAIRE:
    E—> WORKS OF GROUPS 5 TO 10 ARE INCLUDED IN
GROUP 4; 12 IN GROUP 11; 14 TO 17 IN GROUP 13;
19 TO 21 IN GROUP 18; 22 AND 23B IN GROUP 23A;
25 IN GROUP 24.
    FR—> LES OUVRAGES DES GROUPES 5 A 10 SONT
INCLUS DANS LE GROUPE 4; 12 DANS LE GROUPE 11;
14 A 17 DANS LE GROUPE 13; 19 A 21 DANS LE GROUPE
18; 22 ET 23B DANS LE GROUPE 23A; 25 DANS LE GROU—
PE 24.
    ESP> LAS OBRAS DE LOS GRUPOS 5 A 10 QUEDAN
INCLUIDAS EN EL GRUPO 4; LAS DEL GRUPO 12 EN EL
GRUPO 11; LAS DE LOS GRUPOS 14 A 17 EN EL GRUPO
13; LAS DE LOS GRUPOS 19 A 21 EN EL GRUPO 18; LAS
DE LOS GRUPOS 22 Y 23B EN EL GRUPO 23A; LAS DEL
GRUPO 25 EN EL GRUPO 24.

ZAMBIA:
    E—> SCHOOL TEXTBOOKS (808,000) AND CHILDREN'S
BOOKS (6,000) ARE INCLUDED IN THE TOTAL BUT NOT
IDENTIFIED IN THE 25 GROUPS.
    FR—> LES MANUELS SCOLAIRES (808 000) ET LES
LIOVRES POURS ENFANTS (6 000) SONT COMPRIS DANS
LE TOTAL MAIS NE SONT PAS REPARTIS ENTRE LES 25
GROUPES.

ZAMBIA (CONT.):
    ESP> LOS MANUALES ESCOLARES (808 000) Y LOS
LIBROS PARA NIÑOS QUEDAN COMPRENDIDOS EN EL TOTAL
PERO NO SE DESGLOSAN ENTRE LOS 25 GRUPOS.

JAMAICA:
    E—> ALL FIRST EDITIONS.
    FR—> TOUS LES OUVRAGES RECENSES SONT DES PRE—
MIERES EDITIONS.
    ESP> TODAS LAS OBRAS CONSIDERADAS SON PRIMERAS
EDICIONES.

PANAMA:
    E—> WORKS OF GROUP 23A ARE INCLUDED IN GROUP
23B.
    FR—> LES OUVRAGES DU GROUPE 23A SONT INCLUS
DANS LE GROUPE 23B.
    ESP> LAS OBRAS DEL GRUPO 23A QUEDAN INCLUIDAS
EN EL GRUPO 23B.

ARGENTINA:
    E—> WORKS OF GROUPS 19 AND 20 ARE INCLUDED IN
GROUP 18; 3 IN GROUP 2; 5 IN GROUP 4; 22 AND 23A
IN GROUP 23B.
    FR—> LES OUVRAGES DES GROUPES 19 ET 20 SONT
INCLUS DANS LE GROUPE 18; 3 DANS LE GROUPE 2;
5 DANS LE GROUPE 4; 22 ET 23A DANS LE GROUPE 23B.
    ESP> LAS OBRAS DE LOS GRUPOS 19 Y 20 QUEDAN
INCLUIDAS EN EL GRUPO 18; LAS DEL GRUPO 3 EN
EL GRUPO 2; LAS DEL GRUPO 5 EN EL GRUPO 4;
LAS DE LOS GRUPOS 22 Y 23A EN EL GRUPO 23B.

BRAZIL:
    E—> WORKS OF GROUPS 23B ARE INCLUDED IN GROUP
23A.
    FR—> LES OUVRAGES DU GROUPE 23B SONT INCLUS
DANS LE GROUPE 23A.
    ESP> LAS OBRAS DEL GRUPO 23B QUEDAN INCLUIDAS
EN EL GRUPO 23A.

CHINA:
    E—> SCHOOL TEXTBOOKS AND CHILDREN'S BOOKS
(2,606,890,000) ARE INCLUDED IN THE TOTAL BUT
ARE NOT IDENTIFIED IN THE 25 GROUPS. WORKS OF
GROUPS 1, 3 TO 7, 17 AND 25 ARE INCLUDED IN
GROUP 2; 21 AND 24 IN GROUP 8; 18 TO 20 AND
22 IN GROUP 23; 11 TO 16 IN GROUP 9.
    FR—> LES MANUELS SCOLAIRES ET LES LIVRES POUR
ENFANTS (2 606 890 000) SONT COMPRIS DANS LE
TOTAL MAIS NE SONT PAS REPARTIS ENTRE LES 25
GROUPES. LES OUVRAGES DES GROUPES 1, 3 A 7, 17
ET 25 SONT INCLUS DANS LE GROUPE 2; 21 ET 24
DANS LE GROUPE 8; 18 A 20 ET 22 DANS LE GROUPE 23;
11 A 16 DANS LE GROUPE 9.
    ESP> LOS MANUALES ESCOLARES Y LOS LIBROS PARA
NIÑOS (2 606 890 000) QUEDAN COMPRENDIDOS EN EL
TOTAL PERO NO SE DESGLOSAN ENTRE LOS 25
GRUPOS. LAS OBRAS DE LOS GRUPOS 1, 3 A 7, 17 Y
25 QUEDAN INCLUIDAS EN EL GRUPO 2; LAS DE LOS GRU—
POS 21 Y 24 EN EL GRUPO 8; LAS DE LOS GRUPOS 18 A
20 Y DEL GRUPO 22 EN EL GRUPO 23; LAS DE LOS
GRUPOS 11 A 16 EN EL GRUPO 9.

ISRAEL:
    E—> DATA DO NOT INCLUDE UNIVERSITY THESES.
SCHOOL TEXTBOOKS (2,827,000) AND CHILDREN'S
BOOKS (2,438,000) ARE INCLUDED IN THE TOTAL BUT
ARE NOT IDENTIFIED IN THE 25 GROUPS. WORKS OF
GROUP 23A ARE INCLUDED IN GROUP 23B.
    FR—> LES DONNEES N'INCLUENT PAS LES THESES
UNIVERSITAIRES. LES MANUELS SCOLAIRES (2 827 000)
ET LES LIVRES POUR ENFANTS (2 438 000) SONT COMPRIS
DANS LE TOTAL MAIS NE SONT PAS REPARTIS ENTRE LES
25 GROUPES. LES OUVRAGES DU GROUPE 23A SONT INCLUS
DANS LE GROUPE 23B.

8.6 Number of copies by subject group
Nombre d'exemplaires par groupes de sujets
Número de ejemplares por categorías de temas

ISRAEL (CONT.):
ESP> LOS DATOS EXLUYEN LAS TESIS UNIVERSITARIAS.
LOS MANUALES ESCOLARES (2 827 000) Y LOS LIBROS
PARA NIÑOS (2 438 000) QUEDAN COMPRENDIDOS EN EL
TOTAL PERO NO SE DESGLOSAN ENTRE LOS 25 GRUPOS.
LAS OBRAS DEL GRUPO 23A QUEDAN INCLUIDAS EN EL
GRUPO 23B.

JORDAN:
E—> THE DATA ARE ALL FIRST EDITIONS AND REFER
TO THE EAST BANK ONLY. WORKS OF GROUP 23B ARE
INCLUDED IN GROUP 23A.
FR-> LES DONNEES SE REFERENT A LA RIVE ORIENTALE
SEULEMENT. TOUS LES OUVRAGES RECENSES SONT DES
PREMIERES EDITIONS. LES OUVRAGES DU GROUPE 23B
SONT INCLUS DANS LE GROUPE 23A.
ESP> LOS DATOS SE REFIEREN A LA ORILLA ORIENTAL
SOLAMENTE. TODAS LAS OBRAS CONSIDERADAS SON PRI-
MERAS EDICIONES. LAS OBRAS DEL GRUPO 23B QUEDAN
INCLUIDAS EN EL GRUPO 23A.

KOREA, REPUBLIC OF:
E—> SCHOOL TEXTBOOKS (13,780,000) AND CHILD-
REN'S BOOKS (4,132,000) ARE INCLUDED IN THE
TOTAL BUT ARE NOT IDENTIFIED IN THE 25 GROUPS.
FR-> LES MANUELS SCOLAIRES (13 780 000) ET LES
LIVRES POUR ENFANTS (4 132 000) SONT COMPRIS DANS
LE TOTAL MAIS NE SONT PAS REPARTIS ENTRE LES 25
GROUPES.
ESP> LOS MANUALES ESCOLARES (13 780 000) Y LOS
LIBROS PARA NIÑOS (4 132 000) QUEDAN COMPRENDIDOS
EN EL TOTAL PERO NO SE DESGLOSAN ENTRE LOS 25
GRUPOS.

LAO PEOPLE'S DEMOCRATIC REPUBLIC:
E—> ALL FIRST EDITIONS.
FR-> TOUS LES OUVRAGES RECENSES SONT DES PRE-
MIERES EDITIONS.
ESP> TODAS LAS OBRAS CONSIDERADAS SON PRIMERAS
EDICIONES.

MALAYSIA:
E—> WORKS OF GROUP 23B ARE INCLUDED IN GROUP
23A.
FR-> LES OUVRAGES DU GROUPE 23B SONT INCLUS
DANS LE GROUPE 23A.
ESP> LAS OBRAS DEL GRUPO 23B QUEDAN INCLUIDAS
EN EL GRUPO 23A.

PHILIPPINES:
E—> THE FIGURES REPRESENT ONLY THOSE BOOKS
WHICH HAVE BEEN RECEIVED IN THE NATIONAL LIBRARY.
WORKS OF GROUP 23A ARE INCLUDED IN GROUP 23B.
FR-> LES CHIFFRES CONCERNENT SEULEMENT LE NOM-
BRE DE LIVRES ENREGISTRES A LA BIBLIOTHEQUE NATIO-
NALE. LES OUVRAGES DU GROUPE 23A SONT INCLUS DANS
LE GROUPE 23B.
ESP> LOS DATOS SOLO SE REFIEREN A LAS OBRAS INS-
CRITAS EN EL REPERTORIO DE LA BIBLIOTHECA NATIO-
NAL. LAS OBRAS DEL GRUPO 23A QUEDAN INCLUIDOS EN EL
GRUPO 23B.

SINGAPORE:
E—> THE DATA DO NOT INCLUDE GOVERNMENT PUBLI-
CATIONS.
FR-> LES DONNEES N'INCLUENT PAS LES PUBLICATIONS
OFFICIELLES.
ESP> LOS DATOS EXCLUYEN LAS PUBLICACIONES OFI-
CIALES.

SRI LANKA:
E—> WORKS OF GROUPS 19 AND 20 ARE INCLUDED IN
GROUP 18.
FR—> LES OUVRAGES DES GROUPES 19 ET 20 SONT
INCLUS DANS LE GROUPE 18.
ESP> LAS OBRAS DE LOS GRUPOS 19 Y 20 QUEDAN
INCLUIDAS EN EL GRUPO 18.

SYRIAN ARAB REPUBLIC:
E—> SCHOOL TEXTBOOKS (2,000) AND CHILDREN'S
BOOKS (37,500) ARE INCLUDED IN THE TOTAL BUT ARE
NOT IDENTIFIED IN THE 25 GROUPS.
FR-> LES MANUELS SCOLAIRES (2 000) ET LES
LIVRES POUR ENFANTS (37 500) SONT COMPRIS DANS
LE TOITAL MAIS NE SONT PAS REPARTIS ENTRE LES 25
GROUPES.
ESP> LOS MANUALES ESCOLARES (2 000) Y LOS LIBROS
PARA NIÑOS (37 500) QUEDAN INCLUIDOS EN EL TOTAL
PERO NO SE DESGLOSAN ENTRE LOS 25 GRUPOS.

UNITED ARAB EMIRATES:
E—> ALL FIRST EDITIONS.
FR-> TOUS LES OUVRAGES RECENSES SONT DES PREMIE-
RES EDITIONS.
ESP> TODAS LAS OBRAS CONSIDERADAS SON PRIMERAS
EDICIONES.

BULGARIA:
E—> WORKS OF GROUPS 19 AND 20 ARE INCLUDED IN
GROUP 18 ; 23B IN GROUP 23A.
FR-> LES OUVRAGES DES GROUPES 19 ET 20 SONT
INCLUS DANS LE GROUPE 18; 23B DANS LE GROUPE 23A.
ESP> LAS ORAS DE LOS GRUPOS 19 Y 20 QUEDAN IN-
CLUIDAS EN EL GRUPO 18; LAS DEL GRUPO 23B EN EL
GRUPO 23A .

CZECHOSLOVAKIA:
E—> WORKS OF GROUPS 19 AND 20 ARE INCLUDED IN
GROUP 18.
FR-> LES OUVRAGES DES GROUPES 19 ET 20 SONT
INCLUS DANS LE GROUPE 18.
ESP> LAS OBRAS DE LOS GRUPOS 19 Y 20 QUEDAN
INCLUIDAS EN EL GRUPO 18.

GERMAN DEMOCRATIC REPUBLIC:
E—> SCHOOL TEXTBOOKS (30,902,000) AND CHILD-
REN'S BOOKS (17,676,000) ARE INCLUDED IN THE
TOTAL BUT NOT IDENTIFIED IN THE 25 GROUPS.
WORKS OF GROUP 23B ARE INCLUDED IN GROUP 23A.
DATA INCLUDE ONLY SERIES A OF THE GERMAN BIBLIO-
GRAPHY (PUBLICATIONS ON THE BOOK MARKET) WHEREAS
THOSE OF THE SERIES B AND C (PUBLICATIONS OUTSIDE
THE BOOK MARKET AS WELL AS BOOKS PUBLISHED BY
UNIVERSITIES) ARE EXCLUDED.
FR-> LES MANUELS SCOLAIRES(30 902 000) ET LES
LIVRES POURS ENFANTS (17 676 000) SONT COMPRIS
DANS LE TOTAL MAIS NE SONT PAS REPARTIS ENTRE LES
25 GROUPES. LES OUVRAGES DU GROUPE 23B SONT
INCLUS DANS LE GROUPE 23A. LES DONNEES SE REFE-
RENT SEULEMENT A LA SERIE A DE LA BIBLIOGRAPHIE
NATIONALE ALLEMANDE (PUBLICATIONS VENDUES DANS LE
COMMERCE). LES DONNEES RELATIVES AUX SERIES B ET C
(PUBLICATIONS NON VENDUES DANS LE COMMERCE ET
LIVRES PUBLIES PAR LES UNIVERSITES) NE SONT PAS
PRISES EN COMPTE.
ESP> LOS MANUALES ESCOLARES (30 902 000) Y LOS
LIBROS PARA NIÑOS (17 676 000) QUEDAN INCLUIDOS
EN EL TOTAL PERO NO SE DESGLOSAN ENTRE LOS 25
GRUPOS. LAS OBRAS DEL GRUPO 23B QUEDAN INCLUIDAS
EN EL GRUPO 23A. LOS DATOS SOLO SE REFIEREN A LA
SERIE A DE LA BIBLIOGRAFIA NACIONAL ALEMANA
(PUBLICACIONES VENDIDAS EN EL COMERCIO). NO SE
TOMAN EN CONSIDERACION LOS DATOS RELATIVOS A LAS
SERIES B Y C (PUBLICACIONES QUE NE SE VENDEN EN
EL COMERCIO Y LIBROS PUBLICADOS POR LAS UNIVERSI-
DADES).

POLAND:
E—> WORKS OF GROUPS 19 AND 20 ARE INCLUDED IN
GROUP 18.
FR-> LES OUVRAGES DES GROUPES 19 ET 20 SONT
INCLUS DANS LE GROUPE 18.
ESP> LAS OBRAS DE LOS GRUPOS 19 Y 20 QUEDAN
INCLUIDAS EN EL GRUPO 18.

Number of copies by subject group   8.6
Nombre d'exemplaires par groupes de sujets
Número de ejemplares por categorías de temas

PORTUGAL:
E—> WORKS OF GROUPS 5 TO 10 ARE INCLUDED IN
GROUP 4; 12 IN GROUP 11; 14 TO 17 IN GROUP 13; 19
TO 21 IN GROUP 18; 22 AND 23B IN GROUP 23A;25 IN
GROUP 24.
FR—> LES OUVRAGES DES GROUPES 5 A 10 SONT
INCLUS DANS LE GROUPE 4; 12 DANS LE GROUPE 11;
14 A 17 DANS LE GROUPE 13; 19 A 21 DANS LE GROUPE
18; 22 ET 23B DANS LE GROUPE 23A; 25 DANS LE
GROUPE 24.
ESP> LAS OBRAS DE LOS GRUPOS 5 A 10 QUEDAN
INCLUIDAS EN EL GRUPO 4; LAS DEL GRUPO 12 EN EL
GRUPO 11; LAS DE LOS GRUPOS 14 A 17 EN EL GRUPO
13; LAS DE LOS GRUPOS 19 Y 21 EN EL GRUPO 18;
LAS DE LOS GRUPOS 22 Y 23B EN EL GRUPO 23A; LAS
DEL GRUPO 25 EN EL GRUPO 24.

SPAIN:
E—> WORKS OF GROUPS 19 AND 20 ARE INCLUDED IN
GROUP 18; 23B IN GROUP 23A.
FR—> LES OUVRAGES DES GROUPES 19 ET 20 SONT
INCLUS DANS LE GROUPE 18; 23B DANS LE GROUPE 23A.
ESP> LAS OBRAS DE LOS GRUPOS 19 Y 20 QUEDAN
INCLUIDAS EN EL GRUPO 18; LAS DEL GRUPO 23B EN EL
GRUPO 23A.

AMERICAN SAMOA:
E—> SCHOOL TEXTBOOKS (6,500) AND CHILDREN'S
BOOKS (10,400) ARE INCLUDED IN THE TOTAL BUT ARE
NOT IDENTIFIED IN THE 25 GROUPS.
FR—> LES MANUELS SCOLAIRES (6 500) ET LES LI-
VRES POUR ENFANTS (10 400) SONT COMPRIS DANS LE
TOTAL MAIS NE SONT PAS REPARTIS ENTRE LES 25
GROUPES.
ESP> LOS MANUALES ESCOLARES (6 500) Y LOS LI-
BROS PARA NIÑOS (10 400) QUEDAN COMPRENDIDOS EN
EL TOTAL PERO NO SE DESGLOSAN ENTRE LOS 25
GRUPOS.

FIJI:
E—> DATA REFER TO SCHOOL TEXTBOOKS ONLY.
FR—> LES DONNEES SE RAPPORTENT AUX MANUELS
SCOLAIRES SEULEMENT.
ESP> LOS DATOS SE REFIEREN A LOS MANUALES ESCO-
LARES SOLAMENTE.

GUAM:
E—> ALL FIRST EDITIONS.
FR—> TOUS LES OUVRAGES RECENSES SONT DES PRE-
MIERES EDITIONS.
ESP> TODAS LAS OBRAS CONSIDERADAS SON PRIMERAS
EDICIONES.

PACIFIC ISLANDS:
E—> ALL FIRST EDITIONS.
FR—> TOUS LES OUVRAGES RECENSES SONT DES PRE-
MIERES EDITIONS.
ESP> TODAS LAS OBRAS CONSIDERADAS SON PRIMERAS
EDICIONES.

U.S.S.R.
E—> WORKS OF GROUPS 19 AND 20 ARE INCLUDED IN
GROUP 18.
FR—> LES OUVRAGES DES GROUPES 19 ET 20 SONT
INLUS DANS LE GROUPE 18.
ESP> LAS OBRAS DE LOS GRUPOS 19 Y 20 QUEDAN
INCLUIDAS EN EL GRUPO 18.

UKRAINIAN S.S.R.
E—> WORKS OF GROUPS 19 AND 20 ARE INCLUDED
IN GROUP 18.
FR—> LES OUVRAGES DES GROUPES 19 ET 20 SONT
INCLUS DANS LE GROUPE 18.
ESP> LAS OBRAS DE LOS GRUPOS 19 Y 20 QUEDAN
INCLUIDAS EN EL GRUPO 18.

8.7 Number of copies (first editions) by subject groups
Nombre d'exemplaires (premières éditions) par groupes de sujets
Número de ejemplares (primeras ediciones) por categorías de temas

8.7 Book production: number of copies (first editions only) by subject groups

Edition de livres: nombre d'exemplaires (premières éditions seulement) par groupes de sujets

Edición de libros: número de ejemplares (primeras ediciones solamente) por categorías de temas

A = BOOKS
B = PAMPHLETS

DATA ARE PRESENTED
IN THOUSANDS

NUMBER OF COUNTRIES AND
TERRITORIES PRESENTED IN
THIS TABLE: 56

A = LIVRES
B = BROCHURES

LES DONNEES SONT PRE-
SENTEES EN MILLIERS

NOMBRE DE PAYS ET DE
TERRITOIRES PRESENTES DANS
CE TABLEAU: 56

A = LIBROS
B = FOLLETOS

LOS DATOS SE PRESENTAN
EN MILLARES

NUMERO DE PAISES Y DE
TERRITORIOS PRESENTADOS
EN ESTE CUADRO: 56

SUBJECT GROUP / GROUPE DE SUJETS / GRUPO TEMATICO	AFRICA	BOTSWANA (1978)			CONGO ‡ (1977)		
		A	B	A+B	A	B	A+B
TOTAL		26	18	44	285	1 471	1 756
1. GENERALITIES		0.7	–	0.7	–	–	–
2. PHILOSOPHY, PSYCHOLOGY		–	–	–	–	–	–
3. RELIGION, THEOLOGY		–	–	–	–	–	–
4. SOCIOLOGY, STATISTICS		1.1	4.8	5.9	–	–	–
5. POLITICAL SCIENCE		19	8	27	5	14	19
6. LAW, PUBLIC ADMIN.		0.6	1.6	2.2	–	–	–
7. MILITARY ART		–	–	–	–	–	–
8. EDUCATION, LEISURE		2	2.7	4.7	–	2	2
9. TRADE, TRANSPORT		–	–	–	–	–	–
10. ETHNOGRAPHY, FOLKLORE		–	0.4	0.4	–	–	–
11. MATHEMATICS		–	–	–	–	5	5
12. NATURAL SCIENCES		2.6	–	2.6	–	16	16
13. MEDICAL SCIENCES		–	0.1	0.1	–	140	140
14. ENGINEERING, CRAFTS		–	–	–	–	–	–
15. AGRICULTURE		0.1	–	0.1	–	–	–
16. DOMESTIC SCIENCE		–	–	–	–	280	280
17. MANAGEMENT, ADMIN.		–	–	–	–	–	–
18. PLANNING, ARCHITECTURE		–	0.1	0.1	–	–	–
19. PLASTIC ARTS		–	–	–	–	–	–
20. PERFORMING ARTS		–	–	–	–	984	984
21. GAMES, SPORTS		–	0.1	0.1	–	–	–
22. LINGUISTICS, PHILOLOGY		–	–	–	–	7	7
23. LITERATURE							
(A) HISTORY AND CRITICISM		–	–	–	240	8	248
(B) LITERARY TEXTS		–	–	–	./.	./.	./.
24. GEOGRAPHY, TRAVEL		–	–	–	40	10	50
25. HISTORY, BIOGRAPHY		–	0.1	0.1	–	5	5

Number of copies (first editions) by subject groups 8.7
Nombre d'exemplaires (premières éditions) par groupes de sujets
Número de ejemplares (primeras ediciones) por categorías de temas

SUBJECT GROUP / GROUPE DE SUJETS / GRUPO TEMATICO	EGYPT ‡ (1977)			ETHIOPIA ‡ (1978)			GAMBIA (1978)
	A	B	A+B	A	B	A+B	A+B
TOTAL	31 369	3 759	35 128	331	22	353	*4.6
1. GENERALITIES	363	92	455	1	1	2	*0.3
2. PHILOSOPHY, PSYCHOLOGY	307	–	307	1	–	1	–
3. RELIGION, THEOLOGY	3 973	1 041	5 014	48	1	49	–
4. SOCIOLOGY, STATISTICS	2 495	180	2 675	73	1	74	*0.2
5. POLITICAL SCIENCE	./.	./.	./.	./.	./.	./.	*0.4
6. LAW, PUBLIC ADMIN.	./.	./.	./.	./.	./.	./.	*0.2
7. MILITARY ART	./.	./.	./.	./.	./.	./.	–
8. EDUCATION, LEISURE	./.	./.	./.	./.	./.	./.	*0.4
9. TRADE, TRANSPORT	./.	./.	./.	./.	./.	./.	*0.3
10. ETHNOGRAPHY, FOLKLORE	./.	./.	./.	./.	./.	./.	–
11. MATHEMATICS	3 032	69	3 101	9	–	9	*0.2
12. NATURAL SCIENCES	./.	./.	./.	./.	–	./.	*0.2
13. MEDICAL SCIENCES	6 662	332	6 994	28	–	28	*0.4
14. ENGINEERING, CRAFTS	./.	./.	./.	./.	–	./.	*0.1
15. AGRICULTURE	./.	./.	./.	./.	–	./.	*0.6
16. DOMESTIC SCIENCE	./.	./.	./.	./.	–	./.	*0.1
17. MANAGEMENT, ADMIN.	./.	./.	./.	./.	–	./.	–
18. PLANNING, ARCHITECTURE	152	3	155	2	–	2	*0.2
19. PLASTIC ARTS	./.	./.	./.	./.	–	./.	–
20. PERFORMING ARTS	./.	./.	./.	./.	–	./.	–
21. GAMES, SPORTS	./.	./.	./.	./.	–	./.	–
22. LINGUISTICS, PHILOLOGY	6 119	1 077	7 196	13	–	13	*0.3
23. LITERATURE							
(A) HISTORY AND CRITICISM	3 019	948	3 967	10	–	10	–
(B) LITERARY TEXTS	./.	./.	./.	./.	–	./.	*0.2
24. GEOGRAPHY, TRAVEL	5 247	17	5 264	27	17	44	*0.2
25. HISTORY, BIOGRAPHY	./.	./.	./.	./.	./.	./.	*0.4

SUBJECT GROUP / GROUPE DE SUJETS / GRUPO TEMATICO	GHANA ‡ (1977)			MADAGASCAR (1977)			MAURITANIA (1976)		
	A	B	A+B	A	B	A+B	A	B	A+B
TOTAL	208	76	284	261	275	536	29	30	59
1. GENERALITIES	7	–	7	2	3	5	–	–	–
2. PHILOSOPHY, PSYCHOLOGY	–	–	–	–	9	9	–	–	–
3. RELIGION, THEOLOGY	61	17	78	77	38	115	–	–	–
4. SOCIOLOGY, STATISTICS	–	–	–	10	–	10	1	–	1
5. POLITICAL SCIENCE	10	5	15	29	11	40	–	–	–
6. LAW, PUBLIC ADMIN.	15	–	15	1	50	51	–	–	–
7. MILITARY ART	–	1	1	–	1	1	–	–	–
8. EDUCATION, LEISURE	–	11	11	48	12	60	1		3
9. TRADE, TRANSPORT	2	–	2	–	–	–	–	–	–
10. ETHNOGRAPHY, FOLKLORE	32	42	74	–	7	7	–	–	–
11. MATHEMATICS	–	–	–	4	–	4	11	11	22
12. NATURAL SCIENCES	30	–	30	16	1	17	3	4	7
13. MEDICAL SCIENCES	–	–	–	8	92	100	–	–	–
14. ENGINEERING, CRAFTS	–	–	–	5	1	6	–	2	2
15. AGRICULTURE	0	–	0	–	3	3	–	–	–
16. DOMESTIC SCIENCE	–	–	–	–	–	–	–	–	–
17. MANAGEMENT, ADMIN.	11	–	11	6	1	7	–	–	–
18. PLANNING, ARCHITECTURE	–	–	–	–	2	2	–	–	–
19. PLASTIC ARTS	–	–	–	–	1	1	–	–	–
20. PERFORMING ARTS	–	–	–	–	1	1	–	–	–
21. GAMES, SPORTS	–	–	–	–	3	3	–	–	–
22. LINGUISTICS, PHILOLOGY	–	–	–	9	–	9	4	6	10
23. LITERATURE									
(A) HISTORY AND CRITICISM	40	–	40	2	–	2	–	–	–
(B) LITERARY TEXTS	./.	–	./.	38	31	69	–	–	–
24. GEOGRAPHY, TRAVEL	–	–	–	4	–	4	5	3	8
25. HISTORY, BIOGRAPHY	–	–	–	2	8	10	4	2	6

8.7 Number of copies (first editions) by subject groups
Nombre d'exemplaires (premières éditions) par groupes de sujets
Número de ejemplares (primeras ediciones) por categorías de temas

SUBJECT GROUP / GROUPE DE SUJETS / GRUPO TEMATICO	MAURITIUS (1978)			SENEGAL (1977)			SEYCHELLES (1977)		
	A	B	A+B	A	B	A+B	A	B	A+B
TOTAL	11	19	30	246	—	246	5.8	0.1	5.9
1. GENERALITIES	—	—	—	59	—	59	—	—	—
2. PHILOSOPHY, PSYCHOLOGY	1	—	1	—	—	—	0.2	—	0.2
3. RELIGION, THEOLOGY	4	12	16	8	—	8	—	—	—
4. SOCIOLOGY, STATISTICS	—	—	—	3	—	3	—	0.1	0.1
5. POLITICAL SCIENCE	2	4	6	10	—	10	5.2	—	5.2
6. LAW, PUBLIC ADMIN.	—	—	—	20	—	20	0.1	—	0.1
7. MILITARY ART	—	—	—	—	—	—	—	—	—
8. EDUCATION, LEISURE	—	—	—	120	—	120	—	—	—
9. TRADE, TRANSPORT	1	—	1	—	—	—	—	—	—
10. ETHNOGRAPHY, FOLKLORE	—	—	—	—	—	—	—	—	—
11. MATHEMATICS	—	—	—	—	—	—	—	—	—
12. NATURAL SCIENCES	—	—	—	—	—	—	—	—	—
13. MEDICAL SCIENCES	1	—	1	—	—	—	—	—	—
14. ENGINEERING, CRAFTS	—	—	—	—	—	—	—	—	—
15. AGRICULTURE	—	—	—	3	—	3	—	—	—
16. DOMESTIC SCIENCE	—	—	—	—	—	—	—	—	—
17. MANAGEMENT, ADMIN.	—	—	—	—	—	—	—	—	—
18. PLANNING, ARCHITECTURE	—	—	—	—	—	—	—	—	—
19. PLASTIC ARTS	—	—	—	—	—	—	—	—	—
20. PERFORMING ARTS	—	0.2	0.2	3	—	3	—	—	—
21. GAMES, SPORTS	—	—	—	—	—	—	—	—	—
22. LINGUISTICS, PHILOLOGY	—	—	—	3	—	3	—	—	—
23. LITERATURE									
(A) HISTORY AND CRITICISM	—	—	—	3	—	3	—	—	—
(B) LITERARY TEXTS	—	1	1	6	—	6	—	—	—
24. GEOGRAPHY, TRAVEL	—	—	—	2	—	2	0.3	—	0.3
25. HISTORY, BIOGRAPHY	2	2	4	6	—	6	—	—	—

SUBJECT GROUP / GROUPE DE SUJETS / GRUPO TEMATICO	SIERRA LEONE (1977)			SUDAN ‡ (1977)			UNITED REP. OF CAMEROON ‡ (1977)
	A	B	A+B	A	B	A+B	A+B
TOTAL	9.1	12.2	21.3	3 635	—	3 635	493
1. GENERALITIES	—	0.4	0.4	—	—	—	—
2. PHILOSOPHY, PSYCHOLOGY	—	—	—	—	—	—	—
3. RELIGION, THEOLOGY	—	—	—	125	—	125	—
4. SOCIOLOGY, STATISTICS	0.3	0.3	0.6	—	—	—	—
5. POLITICAL SCIENCE	1.3	5.4	6.7	—	—	—	31
6. LAW, PUBLIC ADMIN.	0	0	0	—	—	—	6
7. MILITARY ART	—	—	—	—	—	—	—
8. EDUCATION, LEISURE	2.0	1.4	3.4	—	—	—	3
9. TRADE, TRANSPORT	—	0.1	0.1	—	—	—	—
10. ETHNOGRAPHY, FOLKLORE	—	—	—	—	—	—	—
11. MATHEMATICS	—	—	—	800	—	800	60
12. NATURAL SCIENCES	—	—	—	890	—	890	10
13. MEDICAL SCIENCES	0.3	0.3	0.6	—	—	—	—
14. ENGINEERING, CRAFTS	—	—	—	65	—	65	—
15. AGRICULTURE	—	0.3	0.3	25	—	25	—
16. DOMESTIC SCIENCE	—	—	—	—	—	—	—
17. MANAGEMENT, ADMIN.	0.5	—	0.5	—	—	—	—
18. PLANNING, ARCHITECTURE	—	—	—	—	—	—	—
19. PLASTIC ARTS	—	—	—	—	—	—	—
20. PERFORMING ARTS	—	—	—	—	—	—	4
21. GAMES, SPORTS	—	—	—	—	—	—	—
22. LINGUISTICS, PHILOLOGY	—	—	—	510	—	510	297
23. LITERATURE							
(A) HISTORY AND CRITICISM	—	—	—	70	—	70	—
(B) LITERARY TEXTS	—	—	—	—	—	—	70
24. GEOGRAPHY, TRAVEL	4.7	—	4.7	1 080	—	1 080	3
25. HISTORY, BIOGRAPHY	—	4.0	4.0	70	—	70	9

Number of copies (first editions) by subject groups 8.7
Nombre d'exemplaires (premières éditions) par groupes de sujets
Número de ejemplares (primeras ediciones) por categorías de temas

SUBJECT GROUP / GROUPE DE SUJETS / GRUPO TEMATICO	ZAMBIA ‡ (1978)			AMERICA, NORTH	COSTA RICA (1978)			CUBA (1977)
	A	B	A+B		A	B	A+B	A+B
TOTAL	72	–	72		92	–	92	19 766
1. GENERALITIES	–	–	–		3	–	3	804
2. PHILOSOPHY, PSYCHOLOGY	–	–	–		–	–	–	241
3. RELIGION, THEOLOGY	–	–	–		–	–	–	2
4. SOCIOLOGY, STATISTICS	–	–	–		5	–	5	226
5. POLITICAL SCIENCE	5	–	5		6	–	6	1 182
6. LAW, PUBLIC ADMIN.	–	–	–		3	–	3	153
7. MILITARY ART	–	–	–		–	–	–	30
8. EDUCATION, LEISURE	–	–	–		9	–	9	5 581
9. TRADE, TRANSPORT	–	–	–		–	–	–	1
10. ETHNOGRAPHY, FOLKLORE	3	–	3		17	–	17	–
11. MATHEMATICS	15	–	15		–	–	–	695
12. NATURAL SCIENCES	–	–	–		–	–	–	574
13. MEDICAL SCIENCES	–	–	–		–	–	–	73
14. ENGINEERING, CRAFTS	–	–	–		–	–	–	144
15. AGRICULTURE	15	–	15		–	–	–	45
16. DOMESTIC SCIENCE	–	–	–		–	–	–	–
17. MANAGEMENT, ADMIN.	–	–	–		–	–	–	7
18. PLANNING, ARCHITECTURE	–	–	–		–	–	–	–
19. PLASTIC ARTS	–	–	–		–	–	–	–
20. PERFORMING ARTS	–	–	–		10	–	10	6
21. GAMES, SPORTS	–	–	–		–	–	–	262
22. LINGUISTICS, PHILOLOGY	11	–	11		–	–	–	797
23. LITERATURE								
(A) HISTORY AND CRITICISM	–	–	–		7	–	7	491
(B) LITERARY TEXTS	–	–	–		15	–	15	6 964
24. GEOGRAPHY, TRAVEL	–	–	–		–	–	–	62
25. HISTORY, BIOGRAPHY	5	–	5		17	–	17	1 426

SUBJECT GROUP / GROUPE DE SUJETS / GRUPO TEMATICO	JAMAICA (1977)			PANAMA ‡ (1978)		
	A	B	A+B	A	B	A+B
TOTAL	72	–	72	181	10	191
1. GENERALITIES	20	–	20	1	–	1
2. PHILOSOPHY, PSYCHOLOGY	–	–	–	–	–	–
3. RELIGION, THEOLOGY	–	–	–	–	–	–
4. SOCIOLOGY, STATISTICS	–	–	–	1	1	2
5. POLITICAL SCIENCE	25	–	25	1	0.2	1.3
6. LAW, PUBLIC ADMIN.	–	–	–	40	0.2	40.2
7. MILITARY ART	–	–	–	–	–	–
8. EDUCATION, LEISURE	2	–	2	–	–	–
9. TRADE, TRANSPORT	–	–	–	–	1	1
10. ETHNOGRAPHY, FOLKLORE	–	–	–	5	1	6
11. MATHEMATICS	11	–	11	3	–	3
12. NATURAL SCIENCES	3	–	3	15	–	15
13. MEDICAL SCIENCES	–	–	–	4	2	6
14. ENGINEERING, CRAFTS	–	–	–	–	–	–
15. AGRICULTURE	–	–	–	15	–	15
16. DOMESTIC SCIENCE	–	–	–	1	–	1
17. MANAGEMENT, ADMIN.	–	–	–	–	–	–
18. PLANNING, ARCHITECTURE	–	–	–	–	–	–
19. PLASTIC ARTS	–	–	–	–	–	–
20. PERFORMING ARTS	–	–	–	0.3	–	0.3
21. GAMES, SPORTS	–	–	–	–	0.2	0.2
22. LINGUISTICS, PHILOLOGY	11	–	11	30	–	30
23. LITERATURE						
(A) HISTORY AND CRITICISM	–	–	–	./.	–	./.
(B) LITERARY TEXTS	–	–	–	23	4	27
24. GEOGRAPHY, TRAVEL	–	–	–	30	–	30
25. HISTORY, BIOGRAPHY	–	–	–	12	1	13

8.7 Number of copies (first editions) by subject groups
Nombre d'exemplaires (premières éditions) par groupes de sujets
Número de ejemplares (primeras ediciones) por categorías de temas

SUBJECT GROUP / GROUPE DE SUJETS / GRUPO TEMATICO AMERICA, SOUTH	BRAZIL ‡ (1976) A	B	A+B	CHILE (1978) A	B	A+B
TOTAL	82 185	62 579	144 764	4 950	885	5 835
1. GENERALITIES	2 318	24 467	26 785	75	15	90
2. PHILOSOPHY, PSYCHOLOGY	1 624	1 769	3 393	375	75	450
3. RELIGION, THEOLOGY	4 790	15 563	20 353	480	180	660
4. SOCIOLOGY, STATISTICS	439	6 327	6 766	105	15	120
5. POLITICAL SCIENCE	2 088	304	2 392	255	60	315
6. LAW, PUBLIC ADMIN.	4 097	4 819	8 916	405	60	465
7. MILITARY ART	10	2	12	45	—	45
8. EDUCATION, LEISURE	7 975	1 886	9 861	120	30	150
9. TRADE, TRANSPORT	553	241	794	75	—	75
10. ETHNOGRAPHY, FOLKLORE	122	1 092	1 214	15	—	15
11. MATHEMATICS	6 156	222	6 378	315	—	315
12. NATURAL SCIENCES	5 468	452	5 920	210	45	255
13. MEDICAL SCIENCES	664	243	907	150	—	150
14. ENGINEERING, CRAFTS	1 473	491	1 964	150	45	195
15. AGRICULTURE	239	261	500	60	30	90
16. DOMESTIC SCIENCE	128	12	140	—	—	—
17. MANAGEMENT, ADMIN.	347	81	428	45	—	45
18. PLANNING, ARCHITECTURE	36	2	38	45	15	60
19. PLASTIC ARTS	—	—	—	60	—	60
20. PERFORMING ARTS	7 278	249	7 527	30	—	30
21. GAMES, SPORTS	1 217	3 291	4 508	15	—	15
22. LINGUISTICS, PHILOLOGY	10 206	190	10 396	285	60	345
23. LITERATURE						
(A) HISTORY AND CRITICISM	22 084	362	22 446	210	15	225
(B) LITERARY TEXTS	./.	./.	./.	990	90	1 080
24. GEOGRAPHY, TRAVEL	1 079	78	1 157	120	—	120
25. HISTORY, BIOGRAPHY	1 794	175	1 969	315	150	465

SUBJECT GROUP / GROUPE DE SUJETS / GRUPO TEMATICO ASIA	BRUNEI (1978) A	B	A+B	CYPRUS (1977) A	B	A+B	HONG KONG (1977) A	B	A+B
TOTAL	88	43	131	331	1 757	2 088	2 999	5 444	8 443
1. GENERALITIES	4	—	4	4	6	10	102	209	311
2. PHILOSOPHY, PSYCHOLOGY	—	—	—	2	1	3	15	6	21
3. RELIGION, THEOLOGY	39	4	43	5	81	86	59	78	137
4. SOCIOLOGY, STATISTICS	—	—	—	3	9	12	57	54	111
5. POLITICAL SCIENCE	—	—	—	7	140	147	83	20	103
6. LAW, PUBLIC ADMIN.	—	—	—	6	13	19	12	133	145
7. MILITARY ART	—	—	—	—	180	180	20	29	49
8. EDUCATION, LEISURE	—	—	—	92	450	542	38	2 954	2 992
9. TRADE, TRANSPORT	—	—	—	3	140	143	134	124	258
10. ETHNOGRAPHY, FOLKLORE	—	—	—	2	33	35	392	327	719
11. MATHEMATICS	20	4	24	3	50	53	90	11	101
12. NATURAL SCIENCES	5	35	40	5	15	20	148	32	180
13. MEDICAL SCIENCES	—	—	—	2	68	70	71	61	132
14. ENGINEERING, CRAFTS	—	—	—	5	72	77	129	52	181
15. AGRICULTURE	—	—	—	4	25	29	3	—	3
16. DOMESTIC SCIENCE	—	—	—	8	60	68	53	—	53
17. MANAGEMENT, ADMIN.	—	—	—	2	14	16	9	21	30
18. PLANNING, ARCHITECTURE	—	—	—	1	8	9	1	14	15
19. PLASTIC ARTS	—	—	—	—	3	3	49	25	74
20. PERFORMING ARTS	—	—	—	2	34	36	45	163	208
21. GAMES, SPORTS	—	—	—	2	40	42	43	31	74
22. LINGUISTICS, PHILOLOGY	—	—	—	3	68	71	223	170	393
23. LITERATURE									
(A) HISTORY AND CRITICISM	—	—	—	4	2	6	28	14	42
(B) LITERARY TEXTS	5	—	5	144	124	268	740	625	1 365
24. GEOGRAPHY, TRAVEL	5	—	5	6	42	48	109	37	146
25. HISTORY, BIOGRAPHY	10	—	10	16	79	95	346	254	600

Number of copies (first editions) by subject groups 8.7
Nombre d'exemplaires (premières éditions) par groupes de sujets
Número de ejemplares (primeras ediciones) por categorías de temas

SUBJECT GROUP / GROUPE DE SUJETS / GRUPO TEMATICO	ISRAEL ‡ (1977)	JORDAN ‡ (1976)			KOREA, REPUBLIC OF ‡ (1978)		
	A+B	A	B	A+B	A	B	A+B
TOTAL	5 367	2 671	2	2 673	64 874	4 612	69 486
1. GENERALITIES	63	6	–	6	7 898	2 499	10 397
2. PHILOSOPHY, PSYCHOLOGY	105	2	–	2	1 777	–	1 777
3. RELIGION, THEOLOGY	667	249	–	249	2 277	43	2 320
4. SOCIOLOGY, STATISTICS	82	19	–	19	1 716	–	1 716
5. POLITICAL SCIENCE	81	52	1	53	539	–	539
6. LAW, PUBLIC ADMIN.	16	14	–	14	461	–	461
7. MILITARY ART	–	–	–	–	50	–	50
8. EDUCATION, LEISURE	36	838	–	838	6 606	1 177	7 783
9. TRADE, TRANSPORT	9	–	–	–	179	21	200
10. ETHNOGRAPHY, FOLKLORE	2	6	–	6	11	–	11
11. MATHEMATICS	9	315	–	315	1 741	18	1 759
12. NATURAL SCIENCES	186	199	–	199	3 463	92	3 555
13. MEDICAL SCIENCES	39	80	–	80	155	1	156
14. ENGINEERING, CRAFTS	32	7	1	8	246	12	258
15. AGRICULTURE	2	11	–	11	332	7	339
16. DOMESTIC SCIENCE	119	–	–	–	279	10	289
17. MANAGEMENT, ADMIN.	30	49	–	49	54	–	54
18. PLANNING, ARCHITECTURE	10	6	–	6	103	–	103
19. PLASTIC ARTS	9	–	–	–	433	68	501
20. PERFORMING ARTS	10	–	–	–	2 356	6	2 362
21. GAMES, SPORTS	24	–	–	–	192	3	195
22. LINGUISTICS, PHILOLOGY	101	108	–	108	4 420	24	4 444
23. LITERATURE							
(A) HISTORY AND CRITICISM	./.	349	–	349	501	–	501
(B) LITERARY TEXTS	1 588	./.	–	./.	7 989	551	8 540
24. GEOGRAPHY, TRAVEL	141	177	–	177	248	1	249
25. HISTORY, BIOGRAPHY	388	184	–	184	3 287	19	3 306

SUBJECT GROUP / GROUPE DE SUJETS / GRUPO TEMATICO	LAO PEOPLE'S DEMOCRATIC REPUBLIC (1976)			MALAYSIA ‡ (1978)			PHILIPPINES ‡ (1977)		
	A	B	A+B	A	B	A+B	A	B	A+B
TOTAL	–	268	268	3 289	2 291	5 580	629	303	932
1. GENERALITIES	–	55	55	22	6	28	36	36	72
2. PHILOSOPHY, PSYCHOLOGY	–	37	37	140	1	141	28	–	28
3. RELIGION, THEOLOGY	–	5	5	196	771	967	92	33	125
4. SOCIOLOGY, STATISTICS	–	–	–	51	33	84	13	6	19
5. POLITICAL SCIENCE	–	88	88	87	515	602	51	16	67
6. LAW, PUBLIC ADMIN.	–	–	–	42	83	125	62	18	80
7. MILITARY ART	–	–	–	–	–	–	0.1	–	0.1
8. EDUCATION, LEISURE	–	–	–	54	84	138	7	6	13
9. TRADE, TRANSPORT	–	–	–	41	235	276	4	6	10
10. ETHNOGRAPHY, FOLKLORE	–	–	–	58	282	340	2	6	8
11. MATHEMATICS	–	–	–	170	20	190	16	–	16
12. NATURAL SCIENCES	–	–	–	376	20	396	41	6	47
13. MEDICAL SCIENCES	–	8	8	36	5	41	63	8	71
14. ENGINEERING, CRAFTS	–	–	–	22	31	53	16	–	16
15. AGRICULTURE	–	–	–	118	44	162	4	12	16
16. DOMESTIC SCIENCE	–	–	–	11	1	12	16	–	16
17. MANAGEMENT, ADMIN.	–	–	–	44	5	49	66	20	86
18. PLANNING, ARCHITECTURE	–	–	–	2	1	3	–	–	–
19. PLASTIC ARTS	–	–	–	3	1	4	2	2	4
20. PERFORMING ARTS	–	7	7	6	0	6	26	94	120
21. GAMES, SPORTS	–	–	–	9	–	9	8	6	14
22. LINGUISTICS, PHILOLOGY	–	–	–	656	98	754	6	4	10
23. LITERATURE									
(A) HISTORY AND CRITICISM	–	5	5	398	22	420	–	–	–
(B) LITERARY TEXTS	–	56	56	./.	./.	./.	48	8	56
24. GEOGRAPHY, TRAVEL	–	7	7	112	3	115	–	–	–
25. HISTORY, BIOGRAPHY	–	–	–	635	30	665	22	16	38

8.7 Number of copies (first editions) by subject groups
Nombre d'exemplaires (premières éditions) par groupes de sujets
Número de ejemplares (primeras ediciones) por categorías de temas

SUBJECT GROUP / GROUPE DE SUJETS / GRUPO TEMATICO	QATAR (1978)			SINGAPORE ‡ (1978)			SRI LANKA ‡ (1978)		
	A	B	A+B	A	B	A+B	A	B	A+B
TOTAL	102	58	160	3 441	2 171	5 612	1 331	2 548	3 879
1. GENERALITIES	10	12	22	1	4	5	12	6	18
2. PHILOSOPHY, PSYCHOLOGY	—	—	—	—	—	—	64	17	81
3. RELIGION, THEOLOGY	65	36	101	39	10	49	398	825	1 223
4. SOCIOLOGY, STATISTICS	—	—	—	14	1	15	58	6	64
5. POLITICAL SCIENCE	—	—	—	78	14	92	118	580	698
6. LAW, PUBLIC ADMIN.	2	10	12	16	—	16	62	87	149
7. MILITARY ART	—	—	—	—	—	—	—	1	1
8. EDUCATION, LEISURE	—	—	—	1 428	2 034	3 462	55	186	241
9. TRADE, TRANSPORT	3	—	3	4	0.3	4.3	4	10	14
10. ETHNOGRAPHY, FOLKLORE	—	—	—	12	—	12	—	0.2	0.2
11. MATHEMATICS	9	—	9	55	—	55	17	26	43
12. NATURAL SCIENCES	13	—	13	462	4	466	61	7	68
13. MEDICAL SCIENCES	—	—	—	22	15	37	18	68	86
14. ENGINEERING, CRAFTS	—	—	—	27	1	28	15	11	26
15. AGRICULTURE	—	—	—	—	—	—	32	25	57
16. DOMESTIC SCIENCE	—	—	—	26	—	26	7	—	7
17. MANAGEMENT, ADMIN.	—	—	—	31	6	37	15	43	58
18. PLANNING, ARCHITECTURE	—	—	—	0.3	—	0.3	27	359	386
19. PLASTIC ARTS	—	—	—	0.2	—	0.2	./.	./.	./.
20. PERFORMING ARTS	—	—	—	162	—	162	./.	./.	./.
21. GAMES, SPORTS	—	—	—	101	—	101	2	7	9
22. LINGUISTICS, PHILOLOGY	—	—	—	355	49	404	47	43	90
23. LITERATURE									
(A) HISTORY AND CRITICISM	—	—	—	23	2	25	69	23	92
(B) LITERARY TEXTS	—	—	—	430	31	461	182	176	358
24. GEOGRAPHY, TRAVEL	—	—	—	62	—	62	6	7	13
25. HISTORY, BIOGRAPHY	—	—	—	92	—	92	62	35	97

SUBJECT GROUP / GROUPE DE SUJETS / GRUPO TEMATICO	SYRIAN ARAB REPUBLIC ‡ (1978)			UNITED ARAB EMIRATES (1977)			VIET NAM (1977)		
	A	B	A+B	A	B	A+B	A	B	A+B
TOTAL	429	11	440	72	10	82	17 027	1 981	19 008
1. GENERALITIES	3	—	3	46	—	46	—	—	—
2. PHILOSOPHY, PSYCHOLOGY	9	—	9	—	—	—	122	—	122
3. RELIGION, THEOLOGY	5	—	5	—	—	—	—	—	—
4. SOCIOLOGY, STATISTICS	4	—	4	—	—	—	37	—	37
5. POLITICAL SCIENCE	57	—	57	—	—	—	5 342	161	5 503
6. LAW, PUBLIC ADMIN.	21	—	21	3	—	3	204	152	356
7. MILITARY ART	—	—	—	—	—	—	125	—	125
8. EDUCATION, LEISURE	—	—	—	—	—	—	847	—	847
9. TRADE, TRANSPORT	5	—	5	16	10	26	34	—	34
10. ETHNOGRAPHY, FOLKLORE	55	—	55	—	—	—	61	—	61
11. MATHEMATICS	14	—	14	—	—	—	281	—	281
12. NATURAL SCIENCES	38	—	38	—	—	—	503	—	503
13. MEDICAL SCIENCES	8	—	8	—	—	—	356	18	374
14. ENGINEERING, CRAFTS	7	—	7	—	—	—	444	—	444
15. AGRICULTURE	25	—	25	—	—	—	342	18	360
16. DOMESTIC SCIENCE	—	—	—	—	—	—	50	—	50
17. MANAGEMENT, ADMIN.	—	—	—	—	—	—	217	—	217
18. PLANNING, ARCHITECTURE	—	—	—	—	—	—	6	—	6
19. PLASTIC ARTS	8	—	8	3	—	3	20	—	20
20. PERFORMING ARTS	5	—	5	—	—	—	204	—	204
21. GAMES, SPORTS	—	—	—	—	—	—	184	5	189
22. LINGUISTICS, PHILOLOGY	3	—	3	—	—	—	1 215	—	1 215
23. LITERATURE									
(A) HISTORY AND CRITICISM	27	—	27	—	—	—	183	—	183
(B) LITERARY TEXTS	62	—	62	4	—	4	5 231	1 527	6 758
24. GEOGRAPHY, TRAVEL	13	—	13	—	—	—	134	—	134
25. HISTORY, BIOGRAPHY	20	11	31	—	—	—	885	100	985

Number of copies (first editions) by subject groups 8.7
Nombre d'exemplaires (premières éditions) par groupes de sujets
Número de ejemplares (primeras ediciones) por categorías de temas

SUBJECT GROUP / GROUPE DE SUJETS EUROPE / GRUPO TEMATICO	BULGARIA ‡ (1978)			CZECHOSLOVAKIA ‡ (1978)		
	A	B	A+B	A	B	A+B
TOTAL	28 170	7 186	35 356	47 593	11 430	59 023
1. GENERALITIES	169	105	274	614	532	1 146
2. PHILOSOPHY, PSYCHOLOGY	276	12	288	697	5	702
3. RELIGION, THEOLOGY	14	3	17	177	–	177
4. SOCIOLOGY, STATISTICS	292	805	1 097	91	5	96
5. POLITICAL SCIENCE	3 040	861	3 901	3 168	1 375	4 543
6. LAW, PUBLIC ADMIN.	268	133	401	675	225	900
7. MILITARY ART	144	6	150	837	357	1 194
8. EDUCATION, LEISURE	951	107	1 058	4 164	484	4 648
9. TRADE, TRANSPORT	32	19	51	294	18	312
10. ETHNOGRAPHY, FOLKLORE	100	4	104	8	–	8
11. MATHEMATICS	861	0	861	525	13	538
12. NATURAL SCIENCES	1 637	109	1 746	984	107	1 091
13. MEDICAL SCIENCES	803	782	1 585	489	611	1 100
14. ENGINEERING, CRAFTS	1 367	138	1 505	2 541	395	2 936
15. AGRICULTURE	302	94	396	9 130	175	9 305
16. DOMESTIC SCIENCE	303	3	306	256	415	671
17. MANAGEMENT, ADMIN.	481	43	524	122	1	123
18. PLANNING, ARCHITECTURE	972	135	1 107	1 311	357	1 668
19. PLASTIC ARTS	./.	./.	./.	./.	./.	./.
20. PERFORMING ARTS	./.	./.	./.	./.	./.	./.
21. GAMES, SPORTS	234	16	250	845	102	948
22. LINGUISTICS, PHILOLOGY	1 053	1	1 054	579	2	581
23. LITERATURE						
(A) HISTORY AND CRITICISM	12 772	3 605	16 377	309	65	374
(B) LITERARY TEXTS	./.	./.	./.	17 424	5 935	23 359
24. GEOGRAPHY, TRAVEL	737	53	790	1 152	145	1 296
25. HISTORY, BIOGRAPHY	1 362	152	1 514	1 201	106	1 307

SUBJECT GROUP / GROUPE DE SUJETS / GRUPO TEMATICO	GERMAN DEMOCRATIC REPUBLIC ‡ (1978)			HOLY SEE (1978)			HUNGARY (1978)		
	A	B	A+B	A	B	A+B	A	B	A+B
TOTAL	44 953	13 595	58 548	102	–	102	47 878	8 221	56 099
1. GENERALITIES	1 287	–	1 287	0	–	0	4 286	60	4 346
2. PHILOSOPHY, PSYCHOLOGY	1 822	101	1 923	14	–	14	471	14	485
3. RELIGION, THEOLOGY	1 086	1 701	2 787	63	–	63	651	31	682
4. SOCIOLOGY, STATISTICS	1 056	111	1 167	4	–	4	305	1	306
5. POLITICAL SCIENCE	2 179	366	2 545	–	–	–	5 203	2 182	7 385
6. LAW, PUBLIC ADMIN.	1 715	173	1 888	6	–	6	1 043	303	1 346
7. MILITARY ART	660	76	736	–	–	–	437	100	537
8. EDUCATION, LEISURE	834	144	978	1	–	1	2 211	275	2 486
9. TRADE, TRANSPORT	568	60	628	–	–	–	143	99	242
10. ETHNOGRAPHY, FOLKLORE	61	20	81	–	–	–	309	6	315
11. MATHEMATICS	209	–	209	–	–	–	1 054	9	1 063
12. NATURAL SCIENCES	587	16	603	–	–	–	1 891	188	2 079
13. MEDICAL SCIENCES	733	41	774	–	–	–	829	394	1 223
14. ENGINEERING, CRAFTS	2 131	195	2 326	–	–	–	2 648	153	2 801
15. AGRICULTURE	701	32	733	–	–	–	826	84	910
16. DOMESTIC SCIENCE	410	–	410	–	–	–	994	42	1 036
17. MANAGEMENT, ADMIN.	12	75	87	–	–	–	1 188	436	1 624
18. PLANNING, ARCHITECTURE	726	267	993	–	–	–	246	26	272
19. PLASTIC ARTS	22	65	87	–	–	–	856	339	1 195
20. PERFORMING ARTS	565	247	812	1	–	1	988	161	1 149
21. GAMES, SPORTS	851	60	911	–	–	–	1 260	991	2 251
22. LINGUISTICS, PHILOLOGY	479	4	483	6	–	6	993	44	1 037
23. LITERATURE									
(A) HISTORY AND CRITICISM	12 983	4 320	17 303	–	–	–	932	86	1 018
(B) LITERARY TEXTS	./.	./.	./.	–	–	–	14 787	1 654	16 441
24. GEOGRAPHY, TRAVEL	884	–	884	–	–	–	1 359	139	1 498
25. HISTORY, BIOGRAPHY	2 753	509	3 262	7	–	7	1 968	404	2 372

8.7 Number of copies (first editions) by subject groups
Nombre d'exemplaires (premières éditions) par groupes de sujets
Número de ejemplares (primeras ediciones) por categorías de temas

SUBJECT GROUP / GROUPE DE SUJETS / GRUPO TEMATICO	ITALY (1978)			POLAND ‡ (1978)			PORTUGAL ‡ (1976)
	A	B	A+B	A	B	A+B	A+B
TOTAL	62 116	11 104	73 220	52 211	16 222	68 433	33 454
1. GENERALITIES	3 031	77	3 108	462	143	605	1 204
2. PHILOSOPHY, PSYCHOLOGY	1 687	5	1 692	746	66	812	395
3. RELIGION, THEOLOGY	2 584	4 579	7 163	800	12	812	901
4. SOCIOLOGY, STATISTICS	1 030	43	1 073	1 570	157	1 727	14 224
5. POLITICAL SCIENCE	2 062	59	2 121	3 024	841	3 865	./.
6. LAW, PUBLIC ADMIN.	2 225	298	2 523	1 102	219	1 321	./.
7. MILITARY ART	175	60	235	2 131	445	2 576	./.
8. EDUCATION, LEISURE	5 598	1 074	6 672	1 766	564	2 330	./.
9. TRADE, TRANSPORT	50	–	50	143	28	171	./.
10. ETHNOGRAPHY, FOLKLORE	445	4	449	63	54	117	./.
11. MATHEMATICS	457	21	478	1 054	12	1 066	1 471
12. NATURAL SCIENCES	2 103	456	2 559	1 899	293	2 192	./.
13. MEDICAL SCIENCES	1 518	28	1 546	1 586	660	2 246	2 366
14. ENGINEERING, CRAFTS	789	47	836	3 696	928	4 624	./.
15. AGRICULTURE	407	59	466	1 475	1 561	3 036	./.
16. DOMESTIC SCIENCE	2 470	25	2 495	1 179	0	1 179	./.
17. MANAGEMENT, ADMIN.	78	7	85	1 158	807	1 965	./.
18. PLANNING, ARCHITECTURE	1 872	15	1 887	2 763	1 127	3 890	5 481
19. PLASTIC ARTS	1 056	107	1 163	./.	./.	./.	./.
20. PERFORMING ARTS	817	59	876	./.	./.	./.	./.
21. GAMES, SPORTS	2 406	1 080	3 486	1 750	202	1 952	./.
22. LINGUISTICS, PHILOLOGY	918	7	925	1 985	402	2 387	./.
23. LITERATURE							
(A) HISTORY AND CRITICISM	1 601	67	1 668	1 182	38	1 220	5 910
(B) LITERARY TEXTS	20 336	1 639	21 975	17 227	6 276	23 503	./.
24. GEOGRAPHY, TRAVEL	1 687	1 238	2 925	1 132	1 239	2 371	1 502
25. HISTORY, BIOGRAPHY	4 714	50	4 764	2 318	148	2 466	./.

SUBJECT GROUP / GROUPE DE SUJETS / GRUPO TEMATICO	ROMANIA (1978)			SPAIN ‡ (1977)			YUGOSLAVIA (1978)		
	A	B	A+B	A	B	A+B	A	B	A+B
TOTAL	81 675	12 276	93 951	136 240	36 788	173 028	27 531	9 029	36 560
1. GENERALITIES	1 256	1 202	2 458	14 116	15 960	30 076	268	61	329
2. PHILOSOPHY, PSYCHOLOGY	1 459	70	1 529	6 849	968	7 817	220	5	225
3. RELIGION, THEOLOGY	343	137	480	6 647	1 905	8 552	641	205	846
4. SOCIOLOGY, STATISTICS	1 407	2 925	4 332	3 511	176	3 687	376	83	459
5. POLITICAL SCIENCE	2 019	873	2 892	5 407	2 504	7 911	4 442	812	5 254
6. LAW, PUBLIC ADMIN.	715	131	846	1 640	361	2 001	1 476	1 171	2 647
7. MILITARY ART	171	0	171	217	18	235	81	22	103
8. EDUCATION, LEISURE	2 455	762	3 217	4 116	4 232	8 348	6 390	1 070	7 460
9. TRADE, TRANSPORT	231	29	260	292	2	294	–	–	
10. ETHNOGRAPHY, FOLKLORE	236	8	244	1 358	61	1 419	34	6	40
11. MATHEMATICS	6 875	341	7 216	6 660	240	6 900	147	14	161
12. NATURAL SCIENCES	7 847	361	8 208	8 020	774	8 794	324	61	385
13. MEDICAL SCIENCES	2 723	1 929	4 652	2 483	578	3 061	672	202	874
14. ENGINEERING, CRAFTS	4 154	186	4 340	1 680	276	1 956	510	128	638
15. AGRICULTURE	1 227	540	1 767	631	705	1 336	482	51	533
16. DOMESTIC SCIENCE	917	20	937	3 303	578	3 881	293	115	408
17. MANAGEMENT, ADMIN.	700	2	702	1 209	335	1 544	925	402	1 327
18. PLANNING, ARCHITECTURE	450	9	459	5 901	2 276	8 177	56	182	238
19. PLASTIC ARTS	1 954	29	1 983	./.	./.	./.	441	442	883
20. PERFORMING ARTS	2 280	89	2 369	./.	./.	./.	219	2 101	2 320
21. GAMES, SPORTS	597	485	1 082	1 046	445	1 491	500	74	574
22. LINGUISTICS, PHILOLOGY	10 098	37	10 135	16 194	2 333	18 527	257	10	267
23. LITERATURE									
(A) HISTORY AND CRITICISM	2 505	5	2 510	34 378	1 158	35 536	345	53	398
(B) LITERARY TEXTS	22 323	1 642	23 965	./.	./.	./.	7 526	1 141	8 667
24. GEOGRAPHY, TRAVEL	3 004	121	3 125	1 890	205	2 095	275	538	813
25. HISTORY, BIOGRAPHY	3 729	343	4 072	8 692	698	9 390	631	80	711

Number of copies (first editions) by subject groups   8.7
Nombre d'exemplaires (premières éditions) par groupes de sujets
Número de ejemplares (primeras ediciones) por categorías de temas

SUBJECT GROUP / GROUPE DE SUJETS OCEANIA / GRUPO TEMATICO	FIJI ‡ (1976)			FRENCH POLYNESIA (1977)		
	A	B	A+B	A	B	A+B
TOTAL	170	41	211	6.2	0.1	6.3
1. GENERALITIES	–	–	–	–	–	–
2. PHILOSOPHY, PSYCHOLOGY	–	–	–	–	–	–
3. RELIGION, THEOLOGY	–	–	–	–	–	–
4. SOCIOLOGY, STATISTICS	4	1	5	0.6	–	0.6
5. POLITICAL SCIENCE	–	–	–	–	–	–
6. LAW, PUBLIC ADMIN.	–	–	–	–	–	–
7. MILITARY ART	–	–	–	–	–	–
8. EDUCATION, LEISURE	11	2	13	–	–	–
9. TRADE, TRANSPORT	2	–	2	–	–	–
10. ETHNOGRAPHY, FOLKLORE	–	1	1	–	–	–
11. MATHEMATICS	31	5	36	–	–	–
12. NATURAL SCIENCES	62	5	67	–	–	–
13. MEDICAL SCIENCES	–	2	2	–	–	–
14. ENGINEERING, CRAFTS	–	11	11	–	–	–
15. AGRICULTURE	9	1	10	5	–	5
16. DOMESTIC SCIENCE	16	–	16	–	–	–
17. MANAGEMENT, ADMIN.	5	2	7	–	–	–
18. PLANNING, ARCHITECTURE	–	–	–	–	–	–
19. PLASTIC ARTS	–	6	6	–	–	–
20. PERFORMING ARTS	–	–	–	–	–	–
21. GAMES, SPORTS	–	–	–	–	–	–
22. LINGUISTICS, PHILOLOGY	30	5	35	–	0.1	0.1
23. LITERATURE						
(A) HISTORY AND CRITICISM	–	–	–	–	–	–
(B) LITERARY TEXTS	–	–	–	0.6	–	0.6
24. GEOGRAPHY, TRAVEL	–	–	–	–	–	–
25. HISTORY, BIOGRAPHY	–	–	–	–	–	–

SUBJECT GROUP / GROUPE DE SUJETS / GRUPO TEMATICO	GUAM (1978)			PACIFIC ISLANDS (1978)			SAMOA (1977)		
	A	B	A+B	A	B	A+B	A	B	A+B
TOTAL	1.8	0.1	1.9	11	6	17	42.2	12.8	55
1. GENERALITIES	–	–	–	–	–	–	5	6	11
2. PHILOSOPHY, PSYCHOLOGY	–	–	–	–	–	–	–	–	–
3. RELIGION, THEOLOGY	–	–	–	–	–	–	5	4	9
4. SOCIOLOGY, STATISTICS	–	–	–	1	–	1	5	–	5
5. POLITICAL SCIENCE	–	–	–	1	2	3	–	–	–
6. LAW, PUBLIC ADMIN.	–	–	–	5	1	6	–	–	–
7. MILITARY ART	–	–	–	–	–	–	–	–	–
8. EDUCATION, LEISURE	–	–	–	2	3	5	5	–	5
9. TRADE, TRANSPORT	–	–	–	1	–	1	–	–	–
10. ETHNOGRAPHY, FOLKLORE	–	–	–	1	–	1	–	0.2	0.2
11. MATHEMATICS	–	–	–	–	–	–	20	–	20
12. NATURAL SCIENCES	1.3	–	1.3	–	–	–	0.2	0.6	0.8
13. MEDICAL SCIENCES	–	–	–	–	–	–	–	0.4	0.4
14. ENGINEERING, CRAFTS	–	–	–	–	–	–	–	–	–
15. AGRICULTURE	0.5	0.1	0.6	–	–	–	0.1	0.4	0.5
16. DOMESTIC SCIENCE	–	–	–	–	–	–	0.5	0.4	0.9
17. MANAGEMENT, ADMIN.	–	–	–	–	–	–	–	–	–
18. PLANNING, ARCHITECTURE	–	–	–	–	–	–	–	–	–
19. PLASTIC ARTS	–	–	–	–	–	–	0.6	–	0.6
20. PERFORMING ARTS	–	–	–	–	–	–	–	–	–
21. GAMES, SPORTS	–	–	–	–	–	–	–	–	–
22. LINGUISTICS, PHILOLOGY	–	–	–	–	–	–	–	–	–
23. LITERATURE									
(A) HISTORY AND CRITICISM	–	–	–	–	–	–	–	–	–
(B) LITERARY TEXTS	–	–	–	–	–	–	–	–	–
24. GEOGRAPHY, TRAVEL	–	–	–	–	–	–	–	–	–
25. HISTORY, BIOGRAPHY	–	–	–	–	–	–	0.8	0.8	1.6

8.7   Number of copies (first editions) by subject groups
Nombre d'exemplaires (premières éditions) par groupes de sujets
Número de ejemplares (primeras ediciones) por categorías de temas

SUBJECT GROUP / GROUPE DE SUJETS / GRUPO TEMATICO	TONGA (1977) A	B	A+B	U.S.S.R.	U.S.S.R. ‡ (1977) A	B	A+B
TOTAL	0.3	19.9	20.2		740 241	392 866	1 133 107
1. GENERALITIES	–	–	–		6 374	2 634	9 008
2. PHILOSOPHY, PSYCHOLOGY	–	–	–		11 494	5 499	16 993
3. RELIGION, THEOLOGY	–	7	7		4 833	1 550	6 383
4. SOCIOLOGY, STATISTICS	–	1	1		3 497	716	4 213
5. POLITICAL SCIENCE	–	–	–		97 992	47 115	145 107
6. LAW, PUBLIC ADMIN.	–	0.5	0.5		22 076	11 648	33 724
7. MILITARY ART	–	–	–		23 187	2 859	26 046
8. EDUCATION, LEISURE	0.3	5	5.3		44 103	9 284	53 387
9. TRADE, TRANSPORT	–	0.7	0.7		3 070	796	3 866
10. ETHNOGRAPHY, FOLKLORE	–	–	–		–	–	–
11. MATHEMATICS	–	–	–		12 963	1 186	14 149
12. NATURAL SCIENCES	–	–	–		33 417	5 988	39 405
13. MEDICAL SCIENCES	–	1	1		19 795	7 697	27 492
14. ENGINEERING, CRAFTS	–	–	–		43 660	54 100	97 760
15. AGRICULTURE	–	3.5	3.5		20 981	5 935	26 916
16. DOMESTIC SCIENCE	–	0.2	0.2		1 364	672	2 036
17. MANAGEMENT, ADMIN.	–	–	–		34 709	10 629	45 338
18. PLANNING, ARCHITECTURE	–	–	–		18 243	4 864	23 107
19. PLASTIC ARTS	–	–	–		./.	./.	./.
20. PERFORMING ARTS	–	–	–		./.	./.	./.
21. GAMES, SPORTS	–	–	–		9 745	1 861	11 606
22. LINGUISTICS, PHILOLOGY	–	–	–		21 756	1 345	23 101
23. LITERATURE							
(A) HISTORY AND CRITICISM	–	–	–		14 031	1 077	15 108
(B) LITERARY TEXTS	–	1	1		266 519	211 226	477 745
24. GEOGRAPHY, TRAVEL	–	–	–		9 357	2 319	11 676
25. HISTORY, BIOGRAPHY	–	–	–		17 075	1 866	18 941

SUBJECT GROUP / GROUPE DE SUJETS / GRUPO TEMATICO	BYELORUSSIAN S.S.R. (1978) A	B	A+B	UKRAINIAN S.S.R. ‡ (1977) A	B	A+B
TOTAL	20 548	5 753	26 301	54 387	35 424	89 811
1. GENERALITIES	120	38	158	606	219	825
2. PHILOSOPHY, PSYCHOLOGY	118	17	135	271	830	1 101
3. RELIGION, THEOLOGY	35	–	35	420	725	1 145
4. SOCIOLOGY, STATISTICS	64	6	70	206	170	376
5. POLITICAL SCIENCE	811	230	1 041	5 817	2 910	8 727
6. LAW, PUBLIC ADMIN.	911	191	1 102	1 303	2 732	4 035
7. MILITARY ART	257	90	347	505	187	692
8. EDUCATION, LEISURE	1 997	397	2 394	4 457	2 110	6 567
9. TRADE, TRANSPORT	15	22	37	194	65	259
10. ETHNOGRAPHY, FOLKLORE	–	–	–	–	–	–
11. MATHEMATICS	185	5	190	648	26	674
12. NATURAL SCIENCES	573	20	593	1 760	383	2 143
13. MEDICAL SCIENCES	729	256	985	2 019	1 179	3 198
14. ENGINEERING, CRAFTS	553	525	1 078	3 133	5 562	8 695
15. AGRICULTURE	1 008	241	1 249	2 235	778	3 013
16. DOMESTIC SCIENCE	253	51	304	310	153	463
17. MANAGEMENT, ADMIN.	926	198	1 124	2 258	695	2 953
18. PLANNING, ARCHITECTURE	4	–	4	677	500	1 177
19. PLASTIC ARTS	101	31	132	./.	./.	./.
20. PERFORMING ARTS	103	63	166	./.	./.	./.
21. GAMES, SPORTS	504	30	534	702	116	818
22. LINGUISTICS, PHILOLOGY	669	12	681	1 568	20	1 588
23. LITERATURE						
(A) HISTORY AND CRITICISM	896	7	903	922	289	1 211
(B) LITERARY TEXTS	8 539	3 286	11 825	21 292	15 368	36 660
24. GEOGRAPHY, TRAVEL	657	1	658	1 115	69	1 184
25. HISTORY, BIOGRAPHY	520	36	556	1 969	338	2 307

Number of copies (first editions) by subject groups **8.7**
Nombre d'exemplaires (premières éditions) par groupes de sujets
Número de ejemplares (primeras ediciones) por categorías de temas

GENERAL NOTE/NOTE GENERALE/NOTA GENERAL:

E—> FOR THE CLASSIFICATION BASED UPON THE UNI-
VERSAL DECIMAL CLASSIFICATION (UDC), SEE GENERAL
NOTE TO TABLE 8.3.
FR-> POUR LA CLASSIFICATION, FONDEE SUR LA CLAS-
SIFICATION DECIMALE UNIVERSELLE (CDU), VOIR LA
NOTE GENERALE DU TABLEAU 8.3.
ESP> PARA LA CLASIFICACION, BASADA EN LA CLASI-
FICACION DECIMAL UNIVERSAL (CDU) VEASE LA NOTA
GENERAL DEL CUADRO 8.3.

CONGO:
E—> WORKS OF GROUP 23B ARE INCLUDED IN GROUP
23A.
FR-> LES OUVRAGES DU GROUPE 23B SONT INCLUS
DANS LE GROUPE 23A.
ESP> LAS OBRAS DEL GRUPO 23B QUEDAN INCLUIDAS
EN EL GRUPO 23A.

EGYPT:
E—> FIGURES ARE PRELIMINARY. WORKS OF GROUPS 5
TO 10 ARE INCLUDED IN GROUP 4; 12 IN GROUP 11; 14
TO 17 IN GROUP 13; 19 TO 21 IN GROUP 18; 23B IN
GROUP 23A; 25 IN GROUP 24.
FR-> LES CHIFFRES SONT PROVISOIRES; LES OUVRAGES
DES GROUPES 5 A 10 SONT INCLUS DANS LE GROUPE 4;
12 DANS LE GROUPE 11; 14 A 17 DANS LE GROUPE 13;
19 A 21 DANS LE GROUPE 18; 23B DANS LE GROUPE 23A;
25 DANS LE GROUPE 24.
ESP> DATOS PRELIMINARES. LAS OBRAS DE LOS GRU-
POS 5 A 10 QUEDAN INCLUIDAS EN EL GRUPO 4; LAS DEL
GRUPO 12 EN EL GRUPO 11; LAS DE LOS GRUPOS 14 A 17
EN EL GRUPO 13; LAS DE LOS GRUPOS 19 A 21 EN EL
GRUPO 18; LAS DEL GRUPO 23B EN EL GRUPO 23A; LAS
DEL GRUPO 25 EN EL GRUPO 24.

ETHIOPIA:
E—> SCHOOL TEXTBOOKS (357,000) AND CHILDREN'S
BOOKS (6,000) ARE INCLUDED IN THE TOTAL BUT NOT
IDENTIFIED IN THE 25 GROUPS. WORKS OF GROUPS 5 TO
10 ARE INCLUDED IN GROUP 4; 12 IN GROUP 11; 14 TO
17 IN GROUP 13; 19 TO 21 IN GROUP 18; 25 IN GROUP
24; 23B IN GROUP 23A.
FR-> LES MANUELS SCOLAIRES (357 000) ET LES
LIVRES POUR ENFANTS (6 000) SONT COMPRIS DANS LE
TOTAL MAIS NE SONT PAS REPARTIS ENTRE LES 25 GROU-
PES. LES OUVRAGES DES GROUPES 5 A 10 SONT INCLUS
DANS LE GROUPE 4; 12 DANS LE GROUPE 11; 14 A 17
DANS LE GROUPE 13; 19 A 21 DANS LE GROUPE 18; 25
DANS LE GROUPE 24; 23B DANS LE GROUPE 23A.
ESP> LOS MANUALES ESCOLARES (357 000) Y LOS LI-
BROS PARA NIÑOS (6 000) QUEDAN COMPRENDIDOS EN EL
TOTAL PERO NO SE DESGLOSAN ENTRE LOS 25 GRUPOS.
LAS OBRAS DE LOS GRUPOS 5 A 10 QUEDAN INCLUIDAS EN
EL GRUPO 4; LAS DEL GRUPO 12 EN EL GRUPO 11; LAS
DE LOS GRUPOS 14 A 17 EN EL GRUPO 13; LAS DE LOS
GRUPOS 19 A 21 EN EL GRUPO 18; LAS DEL GRUPO 25
EN EL GRUPO 24; LAS DEL GRUPO 23B EN EL GRUPO 23A.

GHANA:
E—> WORKS OF GROUP 23B ARE INCLUDED IN GROUP
23A.
FR-> LES OUVRAGES DU GROUPE 23B SONT INCLUS
DANS LE GROUPE 23A.
ESP> LAS OBRAS DEL GRUPO 23B QUEDAN INCLUIDAS
EN EL GRUPO 23A.

SUDAN:
E—> DATA REFER TO SCHOOL TEXTBOOKS ONLY.
FR-> LES DONNEES NE TIENNENT COMPTE QUE DES
MANUELS SCOLAIRES.
ESP> LOS DATOS SE REFIEREN A LOS MANUALES
ESCOLARES SOLAMENTE.

UNITED REPUBLIC OF CAMEROON:
E—> DATA REFER TO SCHOOL TEXTBOOKS ONLY.

UNITED REPUBLIC OF CAMEROON (CONT.):
FR-> LES DONNEES NE TIENNENT COMPTE QUE DES
MANUELS SCOLAIRES.
ESP> LOS DATOS SE REFIEREN A LOS MANUALES
ESCOLARES SOLAMENTE.

ZAMBIA:
E—> SCHOOL TEXTBOOKS (15,000) AND CHILDREN'S
BOOKS (3,000) ARE INCLUDED IN THE TOTAL BUT NOT
IDENTIFIED IN THE 25 GROUPS.
FR-> LES MANUELS SCOLAIRES (15 000) ET LES
LIVRES POUR ENFANTS (6 000) SONT COMPRIS DANS
LE TOTAL MAIS NE SONT PAS REPARTIS ENTRE LES 25
GROUPES.
ESP> LOS MANUALES ESCOLARES (15 000) Y LOS
LIBROS PARA NIÑOS (3 000) QUEDAN COMPRENDIDOS EN
EL TOTAL PERO NO SE DESGLOSAN ENTRE LOS 25 GRUPOS.

PANAMA:
E—> WORKS OF GROUP 23A ARE INCLUDED IN GROUP
23B.
FR-> LES OUVRAGES DU GROUPE 23A SONT INCLUS
DANS LE GROUPE 23B.
ESP> LAS OBRAS DEL GRUPO 23A QUEDAN INCLUIDAS
EN EL GRUPO 23B.

BRAZIL:
E—> WORKS OF GROUP 23B ARE INCLUDED IN GROUP
23A.
FR-> LES OUVRAGES DU GROUPE 23B SONT INCLUS
DANS LE GROUPE 23A.
ESP> LAS OBRAS DEL GRUPO 23B QUEDAN INCLUIDAS
EN EL GRUPO 23A.

ISRAEL:
E—> DATA DO NOT INCLUDE UNIVERSITY THESES.
SCHOOL TEXTBOOKS (510,000) AND CHILDREN'S BOOKS
(1,108,000) ARE INCLUDED IN THE TOTAL BUT NOT
IDENTIFIED IN THE 25 GROUPS. WORKS OF GROUP 23A
ARE INCLUDED IN GROUP 23B.
FR-> LES DONNEES N'INCLUENT PAS LES THESES UNI-
VERSITAIRES. LES MANUELS SCOLAIRES (510 000) ET
LES LIVRES POUR ENFANTS (1 108 000) SONT COMPRIS
DANS LE TOTAL MAIS NE SONT PAS REPARTIS ENTRE LES
25 GROUPES. LES OUVRAGES DU GROUPE 23A SONT IN-
CLUS DANS LE GROUPE 23B.
ESP> LOS DATOS EXCLUYEN LAS TESIS UNIVERSITARIAS.
LOS MANUALES ESCOLARES (510 000) Y LOS LIBROS PARA
NIÑOS (1 108 000) QUEDAN COMPRENDIDOS EN EL TOTAL
PERO NO SE DESGLOSAN ENTRE LOS 25 GRUPOS. LAS
OBRAS DEL GRUPO 23A QUEDAN INCLUIDAS EN EL GRUPO
23B.

JORDAN:
E—> DATA REFER TO THE EAST BANK ONLY. WORKS OF
GROUP 23B ARE INCLUDED IN GROUP 23A.
FR-> LES DONNEES SE REFERENT A LA RIVE ORIENTALE
SEULEMENT. LES OUVRAGES DU GROUPE 23B SONT INCLUS
DANS LE GROUPE 23A.
ESP> LOS DATOS SE REFIEREN A LA ORILLA ORIENTAL
SOLAMENTE. LAS OBRAS DEL GRUPO 23B QUEDAN INCLUI-
DAS EN EL GRUPO 23A.

KOREA, REPUBLIC OF:
E—> SCHOOL TEXTBOOKS (13,780,000) AND CHILD-
REN'S BOOKS (3,841,000) ARE INCLUDED IN THE TOTAL
BUT NOT IDENTIFIED IN THE 25 GROUPS.
FR-> LES MANUELS SCOLAIRES (13 780 000) ET LES
LIVRES POUR ENFANTS (3 841 000) SONT COMPRIS DANS
LE TOTAL MAIS NE SONT PAS REPARTIS ENTRE LES 25
GROUPES.
ESP> LOS MANUALES ESCOLARES (13 780 000) Y LOS
LIBROS PARA NIÑOS (3 841 000) QUEDAN COMPRENDIDOS
EN EL TOTAL PERO NO SE DESGLOSAN ENTRE LOS 25
GRUPOS.

8.7 Number of copies (first editions) by subject groups
Nombre d'exemplaires (premières éditions) par groupes de sujets
Número de ejemplares (primeras ediciones) por categorías de temas

MALAYSIA:
E—> WORKS OF GROUP 23B ARE INCLUDED IN GROUP
23A.
FR—> LES OUVRAGES DU GROUPE 23B SONT INCLUS
DANS LE GROUPE 23A.
ESP> LAS OBRAS DEL GRUPO 23B QUEDAN INCLUIDAS
EN EL GRUPO 23A.

PHILIPPINES:
E—> THE FIGURES REPRESENT ONLY THOSE BOOKS
WHICH HAVE BEEN RECEIVED IN THE NATIONAL LIBRARY.
FR—> LES CHIFFRES CONCERNENT SEULEMENT LE NOMBRE
DE TITRES ENREGISTRES A LA BIBLIOTHEQUE NATIONALE.
ESP> LOS DATOS SOLO SE REFIEREN A LAS OBRAS INS-
CRITAS EN EL REPERTORIO DE LA BIBLIOTECA NACIONAL.

SINGAPORE:
E—> DATA DO NOT INCLUDE GOVERNMENT PUBLICATIONS.
FR—> LES DONNEES N'INCLUENT PAS LES PUBLICATIONS
OFFICIELLES.
ESP> LOS DATOS EXCLUYEN LAS PUBLICACIONES
OFICIALES.

SRI LANKA:
E—> WORKS OF GROUPS 19 AND 20 ARE INCLUDED
IN GROUP 18.
FR—> LES OUVRAGES DES GROUPES 19 ET 20 SONT
INCLUS DANS LE GROUPE 18.
ESP> LAS OBRAS DE LOS GRUPOS 19 Y 20 QUEDAN
INCLUIDAS EN EL GRUPO 18.

SYRIAN ARAB REPUBLIC:
E—> SCHOOL TEXTBOOKS (2,000) AND CHILDREN'S
BOOKS (37,500) ARE INCLUDED IN THE TOTAL BUT NOT
IDENTIFIED IN THE 25 GROUPS.
FR—> LES MANUELS SCOLAIRES (2 000) ET LES LI-
VRES POUR ENFANTS (37 500) SONT COMPRIS DANS LE
TOTAL MAIS NE SONT PAS REPARTIS ENTRE LES 25
GROUPES.
ESP> LOS MANUALES ESCOLARES (2 000) Y LOS LI-
BROS PARA NIÑOS (37 500) QUEDAN COMPRENDIDOS EN
EL TOTAL PERO NO SE DESGLOSAN ENTRE LOS 25 GRUPOS.

BULGARIA:
E—> WORKS OF GROUPS 19 AND 20 ARE INCLUDED IN
GROUP 18; 23B IN GROUP 23A.
FR—> LES OUVRAGES DES GROUPES 19 ET 20 SONT IN-
CLUS DANS LE GROUPE 18; CEUX DU GROUPE 23B DANS
LE GROUPE 23A.
ESP> LAS OBRAS DE LOS GRUPOS 19 Y 20 QUEDAN IN-
CLUIDAS EN EL GRUPO 18; LAS DEL GRUPO 23B EN EL
GRUPO 23A.

CZECHOSLOVAKIA:
E—> WORKS OF GROUPS 19 AND 20 ARE INCLUDED IN
GROUP 18.
FR—> LES OUVRAGES DES GROUPES 19 ET 20 SONT
INCLUS DANS LE GROUPE 18.
ESP> LAS OBRAS DE LOS GRUPOS 19 Y 20 QUEDAN
INCLUIDAS EN EL GRUPO 18.

GERMAN DEMOCRATIC REPUBLIC:
E—> SCHOOL TEXTBOOKS (6,222,000) AND CHILDREN'S
BOOKS (8,429,000) ARE INCLUDED IN THE TOTAL BUT
NOT IDENTIFIED IN THE 25 GROUPS. WORKS OF GROUP
23B ARE INCLUDED IN GROUP 23A. DATA INCLUDE ONLY
SERIES A OF THE GERMAN BIBLIOGRAPHY (PUBLICATIONS
ON THE BOOK MARKET) WHEREAS THOSE OF THE SERIES B
AND C (PUBLICATIONS OUTSIDE THE BOOK MARKET AS
WELL AS BOOKS PUBLISHED BY THE UNIVERSITIES) ARE
EXCLUDED.
FR—> LES MANUELS SCOLAIRES (6 222 000) ET LES
LIVRES POUR ENFANTS (8 429 000) SONT COMPRIS DANS
LE TOTAL MAIS NE SONT PAS REPARTIS ENTRE LES 25
GROUPES. LES OUVRAGES DU GROUPE 23B SONT INCLUS
DANS LE GROUPE 23A. LES DONNEES SE REFERENT SEULE-

GERMAN DEMOCRATIC REPUBLIC (CONT.):
MENT A LA SERIE A DE LA BIBLIOGRAPHIE NATIONALE
ALLEMANDE (PUBLICATIONS VENDUES DANS LE COMMERCE).
LES DONNEES RELATIVES AUX SERIES B ET C (PUBLICA-
TIONS NON VENDUES DANS LE COMMERCE ET LIVRES
PUBLIES PAR LES UNIVERSITES) NE SONT PAS PRISES
EN COMPTE.
ESP> LOS MANUALES ESCOLARES (6 222 000) Y LOS
LIBROS PARA NIÑOS (8 429 000) QUEDAN COMPRENDIDOS
EN EL TOTAL PERO NO SE DESGLOSAN ENTRE LOS 25
GRUPOS. LAS OBRAS DEL GRUPO 23B QUEDAN INCLUIDAS
EN EL GRUPO 23A.LOS DATOS SOLO SE REFIEREN A LA
SERIE A DE LA BIBLIOGRAFIA NACIONAL ALEMANA (PU-
BLICACIONES VENDIDAS EN EL COMERCIO). NO SE TOMAN
EN CONSIDERACION LOS DATOS RELATIVOS A LAS SERIES
B Y C (PUBLICACIONES QUE NO SE VENDEN EN EL COMER-
CIO Y LIBROS PUBLICADOS POR LAS UNIVERSIDADES).

POLAND:
E—> WORKS OF GROUPS 19 AND 20 ARE INCLUDED
IN GROUP 18.
FR—> LES OUVRAGES DES GROUPES 19 ET 20 SONT
INCLUS DANS LE GROUPE 18.
ESP> LAS OBRAS DE LOS GRUPOS 19 Y 20 QUEDAN
INCLUIDAS EN EL GRUPO 18.

PORTUGAL:
E—> WORKS OF GROUPS 5 TO 10 ARE INCLUDED IN
GROUP 4; 12 IN GROUP 11; 14 TO 17 IN GROUP 13;
19 TO 21 IN GROUP 18; 22 AND 23B IN GROUP 23A;
25 IN GROUP 24.
FR—> LES OUVRAGES DES GROUPES 5 A 10 SONT INCLUS
DANS LE GROUPE 4; 12 DANS LE GROUPE 11; 14 A 17
DANS LE GROUPE 13; 19 A 21 DANS LE GROUPE 18; 22
ET 23B DANS LE GROUPE 23A; 25 DANS LE GROUPE 24.
ESP> LAS OBRAS DE LOS GRUPOS 5 A 10 QUEDAN
INCLUIDAS EN EL GRUPO 4; LAS DEL GRUPO 12 EN EL
GRUPO 11; LAS DE LOS GRUPOS 14 A 17 EN EL GRUPO
13; LAS DE LOS GRUPOS 19 A 21 EN EL GRUPO 18; LAS
DE LOS GRUPOS 22 Y 23B EN EL GRUPO 23A; LAS DEL
GRUPO 25 EN EL GRUPO 24.

SPAIN:
E—> WORKS OF GROUPS 19 AND 20 ARE INCLUDED IN
GROUP 18; 23B IN GROUP 23A.
FR—> LES OUVRAGES DES GROUPES 19 ET 20 SONT IN-
CLUS DANS LE GROUPE 18; CEUX DU GROUPE 23B DANS
LE GROUPE 23A.
ESP> LAS OBRAS DE LOS GRUPOS 19 Y 20 QUEDAN IN-
CLUIDAS EN EL GRUPO 18; LAS DEL GRUPO 23B EN EL
GRUPO 23A.

FIJI:
E—> DATA REFER TO SCHOOL TEXTBOOKS ONLY.
FR—> LES DONNEES SE RAPPORTENT AUX MANUELS
SCOLAIRES SEULEMENT.
ESP> LOS DATOS SE REFIEREN A LOS MANUALES
ESCOLARES SOLAMENTE.

U.S.S.R.:
E—> WORKS OF GROUPS 19 AND 20 ARE INCLUDED
IN GROUP 18.
FR—> LES OUVRAGES DES GROUPES 19 ET 20 SONT
INCLUS DANS LE GROUPE 18.
ESP> LAS OBRAS DE LOS GRUPOS 19 Y 20 QUEDAN
INCLUIDAS EN EL GRUPO 18.

UKRAINIAN S.S.R.:
E—> WORKS OF GROUPS 19 AND 20 ARE INCLUDED
IN GROUP 18.
FR—> LES OUVRAGES DES GROUPES 19 ET 20 SONT
INCLUS DANS LE GROUPE 18.
ESP> LAS OBRAS DE LOS GRUPOS 19 Y 20 QUEDAN
INCLUIDAS EN EL GRUPO 18.

School textbooks: number of titles and copies
Manuels scolaires: nombre de titres et d'exemplaires
Libros de texto escolares: número de obras y de ejemplares

8 Production of school textbooks: number of titles and copies

Edition de manuels scolaires: nombre de titres et d'exemplaires

Edición de libros de texto escolares: número de obras y de ejemplares

NUMBER OF COUNTRIES AND
TERRITORIES PRESENTED IN
THIS TABLE: 87

NOMBRE DE PAYS ET DE
TERRITOIRES PRESENTES DANS
CE TABLEAU: 87

NUMERO DE PAISES Y DE
TERRITORIOS PRESENTADOS
EN ESTE CUADRO: 87

COUNTRY / PAYS / PAIS	YEAR / ANNEE / AÑO	NUMBER OF TITLES / NOMBRE DE TITRES / NUMERO DE TITULOS			NUMBER OF COPIES / NOMBRE D'EXEMPLAIRES / NUMERO DE EJEMPLARES		
		BOOKS LIVRES LIBROS	PAMPHLETS BROCHURES FOLLETOS	TOTAL	BOOKS LIVRES LIBROS (000)	PAMPHLETS BROCHURES FOLLETOS (000)	TOTAL (000)
AFRICA							
EGYPT	1977	414	41	455	23 778	1 572	25 350
ETHIOPIA	1978	118	1	119	354	3	357
GAMBIE	1978	*20	—	*20	*3.9	—	*3.9
GHANA	1978	27	2	29	...	...	...
IVORY COAST ‡	1977	8	13	21	...	...	...
KENYA	1976	26	—	26	108	—	108
MADAGASCAR	1978	37	1	38	212	3	215
MALAWI	1977	2	—	2	...	...	...
MAURITANIA	1977	21	22	43	...	...	...
MAURITIUS ‡	1977	—	2	2	—	33	33
NIGERIA	1978	583	298	881	...	...	...
SENEGAL	1977	7	—	7	28	—	28
SIERRA LEONE ‡	1977	2	—	2	4	—	4
SUDAN	1977	88	—	88	10 386	—	10 386
TUNISIA ‡	1978	69	—	69	2 651	—	2 651
UNITED REPUBLIC OF CAMEROON ‡	1978	54	—	54	493		493
UNITED REPUBLIC OF TANZANIA	1976	52	19	71	...	...	...
ZAIRE	1977	15	—	15	90	—	90
ZAMBIA	1978	31	—	31	808	—	808
AMERICA, NORTH							
CANADA	1978	500	—	500	...	—	...
COSTA RICA	1978	6	—	6	32	—	32
CUBA	1977	489	45	534	16 116	2 761	18 877
EL SALVADOR ‡	1978	6	—	6	...	—	...
JAMAICA ‡	1978	38	13	51	67	24	91
MEXICO	1976	341	5	346	...	...	...
PANAMA	1978	22	4	26	157	21	178
UNITED STATES OF AMERICA	1978	...	...	...	151 400	...	...

8.8 School textbooks: number of titles and copies
Manuels scolaires: nombre de titres et d'exemplaires
Libros de texto escolares: número de obras y de ejemplares

COUNTRY PAYS PAIS	YEAR ANNEE AÑO	NUMBER OF TITLES NOMBRE DE TITRES NUMERO DE TITULOS			NUMBER OF COPIES NOMBRE D'EXEMPLAIRES NUMERO DE EJEMPLARES		
		BOOKS LIVRES LIBROS	PAMPHLETS BROCHURES FOLLETOS	TOTAL	BOOKS LIVRES LIBROS (000)	PAMPHLETS BROCHURES FOLLETOS (000)	TOTAL (000)
AMERICA, SOUTH							
ARGENTINA	1978	...	...	375	...	...	2 854
BRAZIL	1976	3 950	956	4 906	68 908	30 960	99 868
CHILE ‡	1978	117	11	128	1 755	165	1 920
GUYANA	1978	–	7	7	–		
PERU ‡	1978	25	1	26	...		
ASIA							
AFGHANISTAN	1977	50	–	50	...	–	...
BRUNEI	1978	8	5	13	57	19	76
CHINA	1978	...	...	4 614	...	...	2 606 890
CYPRUS	1977	16	44	60	128	220	348
HONG KONG	1977	107	93	200	828	2 937	3 765
INDIA ‡	1978	864	–	864	...	–	...
INDONESIA	1977	660	172	832	...	...	...
IRAN	1977	36	–	36	...	–	...
IRAQ	1978	143	5	148	...	...	...
ISRAEL	1977	181	16	197	...	...	2 827
JAPAN ‡	1978	613	18	631	...	...	...
JORDAN ‡	1977	...	–	...	3 175	–	3 175
KOREA, REPUBLIC OF ‡	1978	687	–	687	13 780	–	13 780
KUWAIT ‡	1977	4	–	4	173	–	173
MALAYSIA	1978	206	6	212	1 268	36	1 304
PAKISTAN	1977	50	–	50	...	–	...
PHILIPPINES ‡	1977	120	–	120	240	–	240
QATAR	1978	111	–	111	232	–	232
SINGAPORE	1978	204	115	319	2 150	905	3 055
SRI LANKA	1978	52	13	65	1 839	253	2 092
SYRIAN ARAB REPUBLIC‡	1978	1	–	1	2	–	2
THAILAND	1977	150	7	157	...	...	...
VIET–NAM	1977	730	2	732	46 726	115	46 841
EUROPE							
AUSTRIA	1978	483	84	567	...	...	...
BULGARIA	1978	822	32	854	13 217	45	13 262
CZECHOSLOVAKIA	1978	2 591	58	2 649	12 994	1 250	14 244
DENMARK	1978	...	...	1 059	...	...	...
FINLAND	1978	249	32	281	...	...	...
GERMAN DEMOCRATIC REPUBLIC	1978	188	43	231	24 303	6 599	30 902
GERMANY, FEDERAL REPUBLIC OF	1978	1 400	403	1 803	...	...	...
GREECE	1977	160	18	178	...	...	...
HUNGARY	1978	808	44	852	24 804	2 679	27 483
ICELAND	1977	64	23	87	...	...	...
IRELAND ‡	1978	29	30	59	...	...	...
ITALY	1978	1 131	72	1 203	35 510	966	36 476
LUXEMBOURG	1977	6	2	8	...	...	...
MALTA ‡	1978	10	–	10	...	–	...
NETHERLANDS	1978	2 921	...	...	...	...	...

School textbooks: number of titles and copies 8.8
Manuels scolaires: nombre de titres et d'exemplaires
Libros de texto escolares: número de obras y de ejemplares

COUNTRY PAYS PAIS	YEAR ANNEE AÑO	NUMBER OF TITLES NOMBRE DE TITRES NUMERO DE TITULOS			NUMBER OF COPIES NOMBRE D'EXEMPLAIRES NUMERO DE EJEMPLARES		
		BOOKS LIVRES LIBROS	PAMPHLETS BROCHURES FOLLETOS	TOTAL	BOOKS LIVRES LIBROS (000)	PAMPHLETS BROCHURES FOLLETOS (000)	TOTAL (000)
NORWAY	1978	204	57	261	...	...	...
POLAND	1978	666	22	688	30 717	2 806	33 523
ROMANIA	1978	1 090	–	1 090	32 622	–	32 622
SPAIN	1977	3 480	774	4 254	49 771	9 458	59 229
SWITZERLAND	1978	...	...	177	...		
UNITED KINGDOM	1977	1 160	419	1 579	...	...	
YUGOSLAVIA	1978	1 300	135	1 435	19 056	2 813	21 869
OCEANIA							
AMERICAN SAMOA ‡	1978	8	–	8	7	–	7
AUSTRALIA	1976	209	85	294	...	...	
FIJI	1976	73	66	139	179	41	220
NEW ZEALAND	1976	29	43	72	...	...	...
PACIFIC ISLANDS ‡	1978	1	12	13	...	3	...
SAMOA	1977	21	–	21	20	–	20
TONGA	1978	–	5	5	–	100	100
U.S.S.R.							
U.S.S.R.	1977	2 279	52	2 331	307 803	7 083	314 886
BYELORUSSIAN S.S.R.	1978	95	1	96	5 441	50	5 491
UKRAINIAN S.S.R.	1977	187	2	189	30 875	241	31 116

GENERAL NOTE/NOTE GENERALE/NOTA GENERAL:

E—> WITH THE EXCEPTION OF JORDAN, DATA FOR
COUNTRIES SHOWN WITH THE SYMBOL ‡ ARE FIRST
EDITIONS.
FR—> A L'EXCEPTION DE LA JORDANIE, TOUTES LES
DONNEES RELATIVES AUX PAYS ACCOMPAGNES D'UN
SYMBOLE ‡ SONT DES PREMIERES EDITIONS.
ESP> EXCEPTO PARA JORDANIA, TODOS LOS DATOS
RELATIVOS A LOS PAISES EN LOS QUE APARECE UN
SIMBOLO ‡ SON PRIMERAS EDICIONES.

JORDAN:
E—> DATA REFER TO THE EAST BANK ONLY.
FR—> LES DONNEES SE REFERENT A LA RIVE
ORIENTALE SEULEMENT.
ESP> LOS DATOS SE REFIEREN A LA ORILLA ORIENTAL
SOLAMENTE.

8.9 Children's books: number of titles and copies
Livres pour enfants: nombre de titres et d'exemplaires
Libros para niños: número de obras y de ejemplares

8.9 Production of children's books: number of titles and copies
Edition de livres pour enfants: nombre de titres et d'exemplaires
Edición de libros para niños: número de obras y de ejemplares

NUMBER OF COUNTRIES AND TERRITORIES PRESENTED IN THIS TABLE: 85	NOMBRE DE PAYS ET DE TERRITOIRES PRESENTES DANS CE TABLEAU: 85	NUMERO DE PAISES Y DE TERRITORIOS PRESENTADOS EN ESTE CUADRO: 85

COUNTRY PAYS PAIS	YEAR ANNEE AÑO	NUMBER OF TITLES NOMBRE DE TITRES NUMERO DE TITULOS			NUMBER OF COPIES NOMBRE D'EXEMPLAIRES NUMERO DE EJEMPLARES		
		BOOKS LIVRES LIBROS	PAMPHLETS BROCHURES FOLLETOS	TOTAL	BOOKS LIVRES LIBROS (000)	PAMPHLETS BROCHURES FOLLETOS (000)	TOTAL (000)
AFRICA							
CONGO ‡	1977	–	2	2	–	2	2
EGYPT	1976	28	28	56	1 279	2 722	4 001
ETHIOPIA	1978	1	1	2	3	3	6
GAMBIA	1978	*7	–	*7	*0.5	–	*0.5
GHANA ‡	1978	3	10	13			
IVORY COAST ‡	1977	8	13	21	...	...	...
KENYA	1976	11	–	11	32		32
MADAGASCAR	1978	2	3	5	11	23	34
MALAWI	1977	1	–	1	...		...
MAURITANIA	1977	13	15	28			
MAURITIUS ‡	1978	–	1	1	0		0
NIGERIA	1978	9	75	84	...	...	...
SENEGAL ‡	1977	10	–	10	93	–	93
SUDAN ‡	1977	15	–	15	150	–	150
TUNISIA ‡	1977	10	–	10	93	–	93
UNITED REPUBLIC OF TANZANIA	1976	15	1	16	...	...	...
ZAMBIA	1978	2	–	2	6	–	6
AMERICA, NORTH							
BARBADOS ‡	1977	1	–	1	...	–	...
CANADA	1978	267	–	267	...	–	...
COSTA RICA	1977	2	–	2	4	–	4
CUBA	1977	70	2	72	3 999	5	4 004
EL SALVADOR ‡	1978	10	–	10	...		...
JAMAICA ‡	1978	2	–	2	10	–	10
MEXICO	1976	15	20	35	...	...	...
NETHERLANDS ANTILLES ‡	1977	–	1	1	–	...	...
PANAMA	1978	4	7	11	3	3	6
UNITED STATES OF AMERICA	1978	2 911	–	2 911	105 700	–	105 700

Children's books: number of titles and copies 8.9
Livres pour enfants: nombre de titres et d'exemplaires
Libros para niños: número de obras y de ejemplares

COUNTRY PAYS PAIS	YEAR ANNEE AÑO	NUMBER OF TITLES NOMBRE DE TITRES NUMERO DE TITULOS			NUMBER OF COPIES NOMBRE D'EXEMPLAIRES NUMERO DE EJEMPLARES		
		BOOKS LIVRES LIBROS	PAMPHLETS BROCHURES FOLLETOS	TOTAL	BOOKS LIVRES LIBROS (000)	PAMPHLETS BROCHURES FOLLETOS (000)	TOTAL (000)
AMERICA, SOUTH							
ARGENTINA	1978	...	...	344	...	...	3 609
BRAZIL	1976	2 275	146	2 421	27 710	9 153	36 863
CHILE ‡	1978	9	2	11	135	30	165
GUYANA ‡	1978	1	3	4	...	...	...
PERU ‡	1978	4	—	4	...	—	...
ASIA							
BRUNEI	1977	1	—	1	...	—	...
CYPRUS	1977	7	35	42	21	24	45
HONG KONG	1977	70	85	155	190	502	692
INDIA ‡	1978	466	—	466	...	—	...
INDONESIA	1977	116	146	262	...	...	...
IRAN	1977	173	—	173	...	—	...
IRAQ ‡	1978	3	23	26	...	...	...
ISRAEL	1977	166	65	231	...	...	2 438
JAPAN ‡	1978	2 339	554	2 893	...	...	...
JORDAN ‡	1976	47	2	49	832	1	833
KOREA, REPUBLIC OF	1978	952	76	1 028	4 052	80	4 132
MALAYSIA	1978	47	105	152	166	420	586
MALDIVES	1976	5	—	5	...	—	...
PAKISTAN	1977	183	—	183	...	...	...
PHILIPPINES ‡	1977	20	—	20	40	—	40
SINGAPORE	1978	42	57	99	184	503	687
SRI LANKA	1978	3	48	51	23	290	313
SYRIAN ARAB REPUBLIC ‡	1978	11	—	11	38	—	38
THAILAND	1977	13	9	22	...	...	...
VIET—NAM	1977	52	24	76	3 385	1 797	5 182
EUROPE							
AUSTRIA	1978	142	68	210	...	...	...
BELGIUM	1978	...	...	1 345	6 237	3 805	10 042
BULGARIA	1978	170	66	236	6 237	3 805	10 042
CZECHOSLOVAKIA	1978	366	229	595	8 388	7 878	16 266
DENMARK	1978	...	...	1 041	...	...	...
FINLAND	1978	76	118	194	...	...	...
GERMAN DEMOCRATIC REPUBLIC	1978	412	295	707	10 459	7 217	17 676
GERMANY, FEDERAL REPUBLIC OF	1978	1 770	866	2 636	...	...	...
GREECE	1977	154	40	194	...	...	...
HUNGARY	1978	285	45	330	11 451	1 787	13 238
ICELAND	1977	66	46	112	...	...	...
IRELAND ‡	1978	...	...	20	...	...	...
ITALY	1978	364	214	578	12 125	3 386	15 511
LUXEMBOURG	1977	2	—	2	...	—	...
MALTA ‡	1978	2	—	2	...	—	...
NETHERLANDS	1978	1 760	...	...	...	...	...
NORWAY	1978	227	98	325	...	...	...
POLAND	1978	219	96	315	9 550	12 061	21 611
ROMANIA	1978	148	30	178	3 617	1 535	5 152
SPAIN	1977	763	1 038	1 801	8 717	16 436	25 153

8.9 Children's books: number of titles and copies
Livres pour enfants: nombre de titres et d'exemplaires
Libros para niños: número de obras y de ejemplares

COUNTRY	YEAR	NUMBER OF TITLES NOMBRE DE TITRES NUMERO DE TITULOS			NUMBER OF COPIES NOMBRE D'EXEMPLAIRES NUMERO DE EJEMPLARES		
PAYS	ANNEE	BOOKS LIVRES	PAMPHLETS BROCHURES		BOOKS LIVRES	PAMPHLETS BROCHURES	
PAIS	AÑO	LIBROS	FOLLETOS	TOTAL	LIBROS (000)	FOLLETOS (000)	TOTAL (000)
SWEDEN	1978	...	...	465	...	...	...
SWITZERLAND	1978	...	...	416	...	...	...
UNITED KINGDOM	1977	2 330	483	2 813	...	...	...
YUGOSLAVIA	1978	239	76	315	2 114	1 022	3 136
OCEANIA							
AMERICAN SAMOA	1978	38	—	38	10	—	10
AUSTRALIA	1977	75	36	111	...	...	...
NEW ZEALAND	1977	11	32	43	...	...	...
PACIFIC ISLANDS	1978	—	—	—	—	—	—
SAMOA	1977	18	5	23	15	10	25
TONGA	1978	—	—	—	—	—	—
U.S.S.R.							
U.S.S.R.	1977	1 833	1 416	3 249	148 313	367 879	516 192
BYELORUSSIAN S.S.R.	1978	67	48	115	5 377	3 676	9 053
UKRAINIAN S.S.R.	1977	208	108	316	16 826	29 337	46 163

GENERAL NOTE/NOTE GENERALE/NOTA GENERAL:

E—> WITH THE EXCEPTION OF JORDAN, DATA FOR
COUNTRIES SHOWN WITH THE SYMBOL ‡ ARE FIRST
EDITIONS.
FR-> A L'EXCEPTION DE LA JORDANIE, TOUTES LES
DONNEES RELATIVES AUX PAYS ACCOMPAGNES D'UN
SYMBOLE ‡ SONT DES PREMIERES EDITIONS.
ESP> EXCEPTO PARA JORDANIA, TODOS LOS DATOS
RELATIVOS A LOS PAISES EN LOS QUE APARECE UN
SIMBOLO ‡ SON PRIMERAS EDICIONES.

JORDAN:
E—> DATA REFER TO THE EAST BANK ONLY.
FR-> LES DONNEES SE REFERENT A LA RIVE
ORIENTALE SEULEMENT.
ESP> LOS DATOS SE REFIEREN A LA ORILLA ORIENTAL
SOLAMENTE.

Translations by country of publication 8.10
Traductions classées par pays de publication
Traducciones clasificadas según el país de publicación

8.10 Translations by country of publication
Traductions classées par pays de publication
Traducciones clasificadas según el país de publicación

NUMBER OF COUNTRIES AND TERRITORIES PRESENTED IN THIS TABLE: 77
NOMBRE DE PAYS ET DE TERRITOIRES PRÉSENTES DANS CE TABLEAU: 77
NUMERO DE PAISES Y DE TERRITORIOS PRESENTADOS EN ESTE CUADRO: 77

COUNTRY / PAYS / PAIS	YEAR / ANNEE / AÑO	TOTAL / TOTAL / TOTAL	GENERALITIES / GENERALITES / GENERALIDADES	PHILOSOPHY / PHILOSOPHIE / FILOSOFIA	RELIGION / RELIGION / RELIGION	SOCIAL SCIENCES / SCIENCES SOCIALES / CIENCIAS SOCIALES	PURE SCIENCES / SCIENCES PURES / CIENCIAS PURAS	APPLIED SCIENCES / SCIENCES APPL. / CIENCIAS APLICADAS	ARTS / BEAUXARTS / ARTES PLASTICAS	LITERATURE / LITTERATURE / LITERATURA	GEOGR./ HISTORY / GEOGR./ HISTOIRE / GEOGR./ HISTORIA
		(1)	(2)	(3)	(4)	(5)	(6)	(7)	(8)	(9)	(10)
WORLD TOTAL	1973	47 038	327	2 263	2 657	5 966	2 953	3 984	2 407	22 906	3 575
	1974	47 922	398	2 408	3 084	5 856	3 197	3 823	2 444	22 999	3 713
	1975	47 775	357	2 563	2 701	6 375	3 549	4 214	2 340	22 324	3 352
ALBANIA	1973	74	1	—	—	17	1	2	—	52	1
	1974	79	23	—	—	—	3	3	1	47	2
	1975	93	—	—	—	38	3	3	3	43	3
ARGENTINA	1973	196	—	46	6	30	14	45	10	40	5
	1974	262	2	42	25	103	1	13	13	62	1
	1975	514	4	150	82	44	2	6	42	178	6
AUSTRALIA	1973	67	—	—	46	2	2	—	7	6	4
	1974	44	—	—	20	2	3	—	1	18	—
	1975	27	—	1	19	1	1	1	1	3	1
AUSTRIA	1973	418	3	12	15	34	16	15	23	263	37
	1974	459	1	13	17	18	19	26	26	300	39
	1975	338	1	15	10	6	18	23	15	219	31
BANGLADESH	1974	34	—	1	12	9	1	—	—	7	4
BELGIUM	1973	837	5	46	38	52	61	96	54	432	53
	1974	472	4	22	11	36	25	48	40	245	41
BRAZIL	1973	1 684	15	82	48	132	36	82	9	1 241	39
	1974	1 311	16	143	253	—	203		19	586	91
	1975	1 676	24	181	62	238	83	164	21	789	114
BULGARIA	1973	406	6	5	—	76	35	56	21	180	27
	1974	372	4	10	—	54	31	50	16	179	28
	1975	513	1	27	4	73	49	66	15	229	49

8.10 Translations by country of publication
Traductions classées par pays de publication
Traducciones clasificadas según el país de publicación

COUNTRY / PAYS / PAIS	YEAR / ANNEE / AÑO	TOTAL	GENER-ALITIES / GENERA-LITES / GENERA-LIDADES	PHILOS-OPHY / PHILO-SOPHIE / FILO-SOFIA	RELIGION / RELIGION / RELIGION	SOCIAL SCIENCES / SCIENCES SOCIALES / CIENCIAS SOCIALES	PURE SCIENCES / SCIENCES PURES / CIENCIAS PURAS	APPLIED SCIENCES / SCIENCES APPL. / CIENCIAS APLICADAS	ARTS / BEAUX-ARTS / ARTES PLASTICAS	LITERA-TURE / LITTERA-TURE / LITERA-TURA	GEOGR./ HISTORY / GEOGR./ HISTOIRE / GEOGR./ HISTORIA
		(1)	(2)	(3)	(4)	(5)	(6)	(7)	(8)	(9)	(10)
BURMA	1973	38	–	2	1	1	–	–	1	30	3
	1974	76	–	–	–	2	–	–	3	60	11
CANADA	1973	146	3	13	24	23	3	29	27	17	7
	1975	291	3	18	29	40	29	61	27	48	36
CHILE	1973	24	–	–	1	5	3	1	–	14	–
	1974	3	–	–	–	3	–	–	–	–	–
	1975	28	–	–	4	8	–	2	–	12	2
COLOMBIA	1973	15	–	2	–	7	1	–	–	4	1
	1974	10	–	–	–	2	6	1	–	1	–
	1975	76	–	6	6	16	8	16	2	18	4
CUBA	1975	24	–	–	–	12	–	–	–	12	–
CYPRUS	1973	3	–	–	–	–	–	–	–	2	1
	1974	3	–	–	–	–	–	–	–	1	2
CZECHOSLOVAKIA	1973	1 437	27	45	4	195	104	141	46	764	111
	1974	1 499	7	35	154	118	71	170	39	788	117
	1975	1 384	20	45	4	214	101	127	39	741	93
DENMARK	1973	1 415	8	66	98	123	29	91	38	886	76
	1974	1 865	6	46	110	194	60	115	49	1 166	119
	1975	1 943	5	64	107	184	101	167	60	1 167	88
ECUADOR	1973	1	–	–	1	–	–	–	–	–	–
	1974	1	–	1	–	–	–	–	–	–	–
EGYPT	1973	183	1	13	32	27	12	14	14	52	18
	1974	141	1	15	20	26	13	9	4	43	10
	1975	284	–	28	62	40	18	14	8	90	24
ETHIOPIA	1975	7	–	–	–	4	–	–	–	–	3
FINLAND	1973	1 030	4	30	78	52	33	94	27	636	76
	1974	789	3	29	36	35	21	77	21	521	46
	1975	912	5	25	60	36	39	74	23	602	48
FRANCE	1973	1 934	14	115	121	203	81	143	121	924	212
	1974	2 483	15	110	165	229	158	171	181	1 222	232
	1975	2 251	12	121	99	218	120	177	163	1 125	216
GERMAN DEMOCRATIC REPUBLIC	1973	1 765	28	48	36	245	144	109	85	975	95
	1974	406	11	11	4	69	38	19	16	217	31
	1975	791	2	48	12	79	67	49	42	447	45

Translations by country of publication   8.10
Traductions classées par pays de publication
Traducciones clasificadas según el país de publicación

		(1)	(2)	(3)	(4)	(5)	(6)	(7)	(8)	(9)	(10)
GERMANY, FEDERAL REPUBLIC OF	1973	6 458	34	253	408	572	360	371	305	3 676	479
	1974	6 634	24	274	397	493	318	343	381	3 870	534
	1975	4 757	11	206	351	360	231	270	331	2 651	346
GREECE	1973	698	8	30	8	84	10	39	17	442	60
	1974	146	1	13	4	23	7	3	3	86	6
	1975	63	—	4	4	17	—	2	1	30	5
GUATEMALA	1973	58	—	—	12	8	4	6	—	22	6
	1974	9	—	—	7	1	—	—	—	—	1
	1975	2	—	—	—	—	2	—	—	—	—
HAITI	1975	2	—	—	2	—	—	—	—	—	—
HOLY SEE	1973	15	—	—	15	—	—	—	—	—	—
	1974	37	—	—	37	—	—	—	—	—	—
	1975	35	—	—	35	—	—	—	—	—	—
HONDURAS	1974	1	—	—	1	—	—	—	—	—	—
HUNGARY	1973	1 083	22	16	10	172	110	154	83	439	77
	1974	1 163	33	29	7	197	150	145	104	385	113
	1975	1 264	41	19	16	216	168	162	105	432	105
ICELAND	1973	171	1	5	13	9	1	11	2	122	7
	1974	126	1	5	9	2	3	4	—	91	11
	1975	186	1	5	15	10	10	8	2	115	20
INDIA	1973	676	6	45	90	61	42	51	9	278	94
	1974	550	6	28	94	66	36	27	9	221	63
	1975	769	11	44	137	83	51	35	16	295	97
INDONESIA	1974	184	—	10	33	62	11	22	2	26	18
	1975	124	5	5	20	18	7	23	1	31	14
IRAN	1973	200	3	19	6	32	14	15	7	73	31
	1974	194	5	21	3	36	12	24	11	63	19
IRAQ	1973	23	—	—	1	9	1	1	1	3	7
	1974	28	—	—	—	11	3	1	5	6	2
	1975	10	—	—	—	3	1	1	3	—	2
IRELAND	1973	5	—	—	2	—	—	—	1	2	1
	1974	5	—	—	2	—	—	—	5	1	2
ISRAEL	1975	232	1	4	19	29	13	12	6	108	40
ITALY	1973	2 095	10	241	261	341	104	152	94	637	255
	1974	1 908	6	215	169	299	102	184	82	645	206
	1975	1 831	21	160	149	246	78	175	114	681	207
JAMAICA	1974	1	—	—	1	—	—	—	—	—	—
JAPAN	1973	2 284	16	147	77	424	261	228	138	816	177
	1974	2 482	24	190	93	423	243	271	186	864	188
	1975	2 651	31	186	85	411	289	285	216	910	238
JORDAN ‡	1973	6	—	—	—	2	—	—	—	2	2
	1974	2	—	—	—	1	—	—	—	—	1
	1975	2	—	—	—	2	—	—	—	—	—

8.10 Translations by country of publication
Traductions classées par pays de publication
Traducciones clasificadas según el país de publicación

COUNTRY / PAYS / PAIS	YEAR / ANNEE / AÑO	TOTAL (1)	GENERALITIES / GENERALITES / GENERALIDADES (2)	PHILOSOPHY / PHILOSOPHIE / FILOSOFIA (3)	RELIGION (4)	SOCIAL SCIENCES / SCIENCES SOCIALES / CIENCIAS SOCIALES (5)	PURE SCIENCES / SCIENCES PURES / CIENCIAS PURAS (6)	APPLIED SCIENCES / SCIENCES APPL. / CIENCIAS APLICADAS (7)	ARTS / BEAUX-ARTS / ARTES PLASTICAS (8)	LITERATURE / LITTERATURE / LITERATURA (9)	GEOGR./HISTORY / GEOGR./HISTOIRE / GEOGR./HISTORIA (10)
KENYA	1973	15	-	-	7	-	-	-	-	-	8
KOREA, REPUBLIC OF	1973	207	5	46	36	27	7	8	4	59	15
	1974	269	-	38	62	35	8	9	11	87	19
	1975	214	2	21	47	35	7	11	7	65	19
KUWAIT	1974	10	-	-	-	-	-	-	-	10	-
	1975	13	-	-	-	1	-	-	-	12	-
MADAGASCAR	1974	4	-	-	1	1	-	1	-	-	1
	1975	9	-	-	1	3	-	2	-	3	-
MALAYSIA	1973	46	-	-	2	25	8	2	-	3	6
	1974	58	1	12	-	6	9	2	-	20	8
	1975	137	-	12	2	11	28	10	2	61	11
MALTA	1973	3	-	-	-	-	-	-	-	3	-
	1974	4	-	-	1	-	-	-	-	3	-
	1975	5	-	-	1	-	-	-	-	4	-
MAURITIUS	1975	1	-	-	1	-	-	-	-	-	-
MEXICO	1973	218	-	22	3	46	28	85	4	27	3
	1974	280	-	42	12	64	28	94	18	12	10
	1975	276	-	33	2	47	62	93	12	11	16
MONGOLIA	1975	17	-	-	-	1	-	-	-	16	-
NETHERLANDS	1973	1 816	12	93	80	135	114	164	65	1 015	138
	1974	1 850	7	123	130	141	107	205	95	923	119
	1975	2 057	12	122	120	93	128	252	88	1 085	157
NEW ZEALAND	1975	1	-	-	-	-	-	-	-	1	-
NIGER	1973	1	-	-	-	-	-	-	1	-	-
NIGERIA	1974	1	-	-	-	1	-	-	-	-	-
	1975	2	-	-	-	1	-	-	-	1	-
NORWAY	1973	1 004	2	16	51	54	34	47	39	710	51
	1974	1 168	4	24	51	52	30	81	36	848	42
	1975	912	-	7	22	20	22	57	27	718	39
PAKISTAN	1975	44	-	-	18	7	1	-	-	11	7
PAPUA NEW GUINEA	1975	144	-	1	48	30	8	18	4	6	29
PARAGUAY	1973	1	-	-	1	-	-	-	-	-	-
PERU	1973	32	-	1	17	4	-	-	-	6	4
	1974	20	-	-	5	6	-	3	-	3	3
	1975	43	-	-	22	6	-	2	-	10	3

Translations by country of publication 8.10
Traductions classées par pays de publication
Traducciones clasificadas según el país de publicación

		(1)	(2)	(3)	(4)	(5)	(6)	(7)	(8)	(9)	(10)
PHILIPPINES	1975	22	—	—	9	—	—	—	—	9	4
POLAND	1973	958	2	28	54	80	105	134	31	436	88
	1974	900	8	16	45	91	88	136	45	417	54
	1975	1 990	20	32	78	188	208	290	124	910	140
ROMANIA	1973	840	8	16	5	163	90	60	72	356	70
	1974	755	9	18	3	147	54	78	41	338	67
	1975	865	4	21	1	181	80	50	81	391	56
SIERRA LEONE	1975	15	—	—	2	6	2	1	—	2	2
SINGAPORE	1973	2	—	—	—	—	—	—	—	—	1
	1974	5	5	—	—	1	—	—	—	—	—
SPAIN	1973	4 489	19	276	386	542	312	660	326	1 602	366
	1974	3 780	28	245	281	488	263	534	257	1 318	366
	1975	3 868	35	252	262	498	226	419	202	1 974	—
SRI LANKA	1973	35	—	2	11	4	2	—	—	10	6
	1974	68	—	1	21	11	10	5	—	13	7
	1975	68	—	—	16	17	1	4	—	23	7
SWEDEN	1973	1 599	1	47	66	70	43	92	36	1 152	92
	1974	3 422	8	106	136	152	122	180	78	2 440	200
	1975	1 874	4	59	62	73	61	116	61	1 349	89
SWITZERLAND	1973	718	4	29	65	54	37	54	56	338	81
	1974	992	3	73	97	55	57	69	80	461	97
	1975	983	2	62	81	49	56	66	67	459	141
SYRIAN ARAB REPUBLIC	1973	51	—	1	—	22	7	1	—	18	2
	1974	17	—	2	—	4	3	1	1	6	—
	1975	68	—	12	—	—	6	5	2	39	4
THAILAND	1973	32	—	—	1	3	3	—	1	15	9
	1974	141	—	3	3	9	8	3	2	87	26
	1975	39	—	2	—	10	2	1	1	19	4
TURKEY	1973	991	1	23	57	77	29	91	17	668	28
	1974	1 262	9	31	96	144	43	101	18	757	63
	1975	1 031	6	38	54	232	28	80	18	512	63
UKRAINIAN S.S.R.	1975	6 667	30	317	17	1 406	953	545	123	2 775	501
U.S.S.R.	1973	4 402	19	228	13	1 004	365	356	96	2 173	148
	1974	4 271	25	234	9	1 016	345	328	75	2 097	142
UNITED KINGDOM	1973	682	3	30	54	60	71	77	88	191	108
	1974	1 469	70	—	128	199	125	137	205	445	160
	1975	1 368	27	47	153	309	—	106	150	409	167
UNITED STATES OF AMERICA	1973	1 968	13	91	238	252	162	128	233	536	315
	1974	1 864	10	125	241	209	311	—	182	490	296
	1975	1 039	10	141	263	253	166	127	79	—	—
URUGUAY	1974	7	—	1	—	2	1	—	1	2	—
VENEZUELA	1975	20	—	3	1	6	—	4	1	4	1

8.10 Translations by country of publication
Traductions classées par pays de publication
Traducciones clasificadas según el país de publicación

COUNTRY / PAYS / PAIS	YEAR / ANNEE / AÑO	TOTAL / TOTAL / TOTAL	GENERALITIES / GENERALITES / GENERALIDADES	PHILOSOPHY / PHILOSOPHIE / FILOSOFIA	RELIGION / RELIGION / RELIGION	SOCIAL SCIENCES / SCIENCES SOCIALES / CIENCIAS SOCIALES	PURE SCIENCES / SCIENCES PURES / CIENCIAS PURAS	APPLIED SCIENCES / SCIENCES APPL. / CIENCIAS APLICADAS	ARTS / BEAUX-ARTS / ARTES PLASTICAS	LITERATURE / LITTERATURE / LITERATURA	GEOGR./HISTORY / GEOGR./HISTOIRE / GEOGR./HISTORIA
		(1)	(2)	(3)	(4)	(5)	(6)	(7)	(8)	(9)	(10)
YUGOSLAVIA	1973	1 482	23	33	58	405	54	79	199	549	82
	1974	1 526	28	51	78	509	47	130	87	501	95
	1975	903	6	19	25	247	15	32	36	469	54

GENERAL NOTE / NOTE GENERALE / NOTA GENERAL:
E—> PHILOLOGY IS INCLUDED WITH LITERATURE.
FR—> LA PHILOLOGIE EST COMPRISE DANS LA
LITTERATURE.
ESP> LA FILOLOGIA QUEDA COMPRENDIDA EN LA
LITERATURA.

JORDAN:
E—> DATA REFER TO THE EAST BANK ONLY.
FR—> LES DONNEES SE REFERENT A LA RIVE
ORIENTALE SEULEMENT.
ESP> LOS DATOS SE REFIEREN A LA ORILLA ORIENTAL
SOLAMENTE.

Translations by original language 8.11
Traductions classées d'après la langue originale
Traducciones clasificadas según la lengua original

8.11 Translations by original language
Traductions classées d'après la langue originale
Traducciones clasificadas según la lengua original

LANGUAGES ARE ARRANGED IN DECREASING ORDER OF NUMBER OF TRANSLATIONS IN 1975.
LES LANGUES SONT CLASSEES DANS UN ORDRE CORRESPONDANT AU NOMBRE DECROISSANT DES TRADUCTIONS EN 1975.
LOS IDIOMAS QUEDAN CLASIFICADOS POR ORDEN DECRECIENTE DEL NUMERO DE TRADUCCIONES EN 1975.

ORIGINAL LANGUAGE / LANGUE ORIGINALE / IDIOMA ORIGINAL	YEAR / ANNEE / AÑO	TOTAL / TOTAL / TOTAL	GENER-ALITIES / GENERA-LITES / GENERA-LIDADES	PHILOS-OPHY / PHILO-SOPHIE / FILO-SOFIA	RELIGION / RELIGION / RELIGION	SOCIAL SCIENCES / SCIENCES SOCIALES / CIENCIAS SOCIALES	PURE SCIENCES / SCIENCES PURES / CIENCIAS PURAS	APPLIED SCIENCES / SCIENCES APPL. / CIENCIAS APLICADAS	ARTS / BEAUX-ARTS / ARTES PLASTICAS	LITERA-TURE / LITTERA-TURE / LITERA-TURA	GEOGR./ HISTORY / GEOGR./ HISTOIRE / GEOGR./ HISTORIA
		(1)	(2)	(3)	(4)	(5)	(6)	(7)	(8)	(9)	(10)
TOTAL	1973	47 038	327	2 263	2 657	5 966	2 953	3 984	2 407	22 906	3 575
TOTAL	1974	47 922	398	2 408	3 084	5 856	3 197	3 823	2 444	22 999	3 713
TOTAL	1975	47 775	357	2 563	2 701	6 375	3 549	4 214	2 340	22 324	3 352
ENGLISH ANGLAIS INGLES	1973	18 350	105	829	727	1 654	1 326	1 587	678	10 237	1 207
	1974	20 411	109	976	994	1 613	1 487	1 681	725	11 484	1 342
	1975	19 020	136	942	831	1 615	1 447	1 882	753	10 211	1 203
RUSSIAN RUSSE RUSO	1973	5 113	58	287	29	1 447	460	452	159	1 912	309
	1974	4 824	35	253	63	1 441	486	343	130	1 768	305
	1975	6 563	40	370	35	1 808	1 026	540	188	1 956	600
FRENCH FRANCAIS FRANCES	1973	5 993	37	406	463	713	277	433	439	2 603	622
	1974	5 785	73	419	422	720	271	347	459	2 432	642
	1975	5 298	37	430	370	679	213	357	387	2 439	386
GERMAN ALLEMAND ALEMAN	1973	4 277	46	383	386	547	282	497	408	1 272	456
	1974	4 753	66	408	406	649	341	562	424	1 418	479
	1975	4 338	48	431	337	685	296	566	338	1 305	332
ITALIAN ITALIEN ITALIANO	1973	1 136	12	29	81	117	66	109	219	405	98
	1974	1 182	23	23	91	118	90	70	215	440	112
	1975	1 045	8	41	62	122	52	85	174	439	62
SWEDISH SUEDOIS SUECO	1973	1 006	8	21	26	61	35	111	47	614	83
	1974	1 178	8	17	38	88	50	131	62	721	63
	1975	1 043	4	14	37	55	25	124	45	692	47
SPANISH ESPAGNOL ESPAÑOL	1973	1 368	2	7	54	81	18	18	25	1 080	83
	1974	768	6	17	64	73	23	9	28	480	68
	1975	935	2	16	35	89	16	19	31	662	65

8.11 Translations by original language
Traductions classées d'après la langue originale
Traducciones clasificadas según la lengua original

ORIGINAL LANGUAGE / LANGUE ORIGINALE / IDIOMA ORIGINAL	YEAR / ANNEE / AÑO	TOTAL / TOTAL / TOTAL (1)	GENERALITIES / GENERALITES / GENERALIDADES (2)	PHILOSOPHY / PHILOSOPHIE / FILOSOFIA (3)	RELIGION / RELIGION / RELIGION (4)	SOCIAL SCIENCES / SCIENCES SOCIALES / CIENCIAS SOCIALES (5)	PURE SCIENCES / SCIENCES PURES / CIENCIAS PURAS (6)	APPLIED SCIENCES / SCIENCES APPL. / CIENCIAS APLICADAS (7)	ARTS / BEAUX-ARTS / ARTES PLASTICAS (8)	LITERATURE / LITTERATURE / LITERATURA (9)	GEOGR./HISTORY / GEOGR./HISTOIRE / GEOGR./HISTORIA (10)
HUNGARIAN HONGROIS HUNGARO	1973	578	10	6	4	74	66	79	75	223	41
	1974	747	15	7	6	129	114	78	73	255	70
	1975	696	18	3	3	107	91	82	76	238	78
POLISH ‡ POLONAIS ‡ POLACO ‡	1973	626	1	12	4	74	66	53	41	300	75
	1974	349	3	10	3	39	16	33	23	198	24
	1975	676	13	14	5	107	49	74	73	297	44
CZECH ‡ TCHEQUE ‡ CHECO ‡	1973	598	6	4	3	77	100	1 08	40	207	53
	1974	657	5	4	82	62	92	115	29	215	53
	1975	515	6	1	6	84	92	106	22	171	27
DANISH DANOIS DANES	1973	604	—	14	13	21	22	87	49	371	27
	1974	656	3	22	12	28	44	87	36	395	29
	1975	512	—	25	4	36	24	38	31	325	29
ROMANIAN ‡ ROUMAIN ‡ RUMANO ‡	1973	492	4	5	3	144	65	45	36	139	51
	1974	115	—	2	3	9	9	9	5	70	8
	1975	480	4	2	—	148	65	32	26	175	28
CLASSICAL GREEK GREC CLASSIQUE GRIEGO CLASICO	1973	424	—	61	174	10	8	5	3	130	33
	1974	478	4	64	156	20	5	3	6	189	31
	1975	478	1	77	180	16	4	2	2	169	27
LATIN LATIN LATIN	1973	374	1	36	119	22	6	11	8	116	55
	1974	430	6	36	117	23	14	5	10	128	91
	1975	443	2	51	153	22	3	6	5	128	73
DUTCH NEERLANDAIS NEERLANDES	1973	383	3	11	76	30	13	58	17	157	18
	1974	439	2	17	56	47	25	69	42	143	38
	1975	329	1	10	42	25	19	65	40	104	23
SERBO-CROATIAN ‡ SERBO-CROATE ‡ SERBOCROATA ‡	1973	499	5	3	2	299	13	29	20	93	37
	1974	540	7	4	2	328	10	44	23	80	42
	1975	307	—	2	1	171	4	3	12	90	24
BULGARIAN ‡ BULGARE ‡ BULGARO ‡	1973	221	2	8	—	35	9	13	7	121	26
	1974	131	—	1	2	19	—	5	4	86	14
	1975	247	—	3	6	32	14	17	5	136	34
UKRAINIAN UKRAINIEN UCRANIO	1973	134	1	1	1	3	4	1	1	118	4
	1974	138	—	2	2	5	3	2	2	120	4
	1975	229	—	—	1	27	4	4	5	175	13
NORWEGIAN NORVEGIEN NORUEGO	1973	297	—	9	29	8	3	10	2	212	24
	1974	269	—	6	26	18	3	19	7	164	26
	1975	224	1	6	24	21	6	13	3	136	14
CHINESE CHINOIS CHINO	1973	184	—	16	11	52	2	9	2	72	20
	1974	188	2	20	11	51	3	7	7	66	21
	1975	209	1	18	11	66	4	19	3	65	22

Translations by original language   **8.11**
Traductions classées d'après la langue originale
Traducciones clasificadas según la lengua original

		(1)	(2)	(3)	(4)	(5)	(6)	(7)	(8)	(9)	(10)
SANSKRIT ‡	1973	136	—	16	57	6	—	8	3	46	—
SANSKRIT ‡	1974	124	—	14	56	6	1	4	1	41	1
SANSCRITO ‡	1975	193	—	30	110	4	—	5	—	44	—
ARABIC	1973	156	—	8	47	35	—	2	1	57	6
ARABE	1974	201	3	10	87	45	5	—	—	38	13
ARABE	1975	192	2	7	66	51	4	7	1	39	15
HEBREW ‡	1973	161	—	5	101	14	1	1	—	25	14
HEBREU ‡	1974	157	—	—	108	5	2	—	3	23	16
HEBREO ‡	1975	161	1	2	103	9	1	4	2	26	13
SLOVAK ‡	1973	187	11	3	—	40	9	12	14	85	13
SLOVAQUE ‡	1974	140	2	—	17	7	2	25	4	71	12
ESLOVACO ‡	1975	153	—	3	1	22	10	13	10	85	9
PORTUGUESE	1973	124	1	3	8	26	1	2	1	69	14
PORTUGAIS	1974	129	—	4	17	30	2	1	2	65	9
PORTUGUES	1975	130	—	15	10	30	1	3	4	64	4
JAPANESE	1973	176	1	4	8	8	7	8	27	104	9
JAPONAIS	1974	165	—	5	5	14	4	11	18	98	10
JAPONES	1975	111	1	1	4	15	4	12	13	54	7
LITHUANIAN	1973	70	1	—	1	7	—	2	1	53	5
LITUANIEN	1974	67	2	—	9	—	—	1	—	53	2
LITUANO	1975	105	—	—	14	—	2	1	4	77	7
GEORGIAN	1973	58	—	—	—	4	—	—	1	52	1
GEORGIEN	1974	59	—	—	—	1	—	—	—	58	—
GEORGIANO	1975	104	1	—	—	2	—	1	2	97	1
BENGALI ‡‡	1973	80	—	1	3	1	—	1	—	71	3
BENGALI ‡‡‡	1974	60	—	2	1	2	—	—	—	52	3
BENGALI ‡	1975	100	—	1	4	3	1	1	—	82	8
ESTONIAN	1973	56	—	—	—	8	—	4	2	39	3
ESTONIEN	1974	68	—	—	—	4	—	3	—	52	7
ESTONIO	1975	93	—	—	—	13	—	5	4	60	11
FINNISH ‡‡	1973	107	—	2	8	7	12	8	4	54	12
FINNOIS ‡‡	1974	94	—	1	4	8	9	2	4	53	13
FINLANDES ‡	1975	91	2	1	2	9	3	3	1	67	3
BYELORUSSIAN	1973	61	—	—	—	4	—	—	—	57	—
BIELORUSSIEN	1974	66	—	—	—	—	—	—	—	65	—
BIELORRUSO	1975	88	—	—	—	—	—	—	—	87	1
ARMENIAN	1973	47	—	—	—	1	—	—	—	44	2
ARMENIEN	1974	45	—	—	1	—	—	—	—	40	4
ARMENIO	1975	75	—	1	1	1	—	—	2	68	2
LATVIAN	1973	52	—	1	—	1	—	2	—	46	3
LETTON	1974	60	1	5	—	2	—	—	2	53	3
LETON	1975	72	3	2	—	7	—	3	1	52	6
PERSIAN	1973	51	—	1	6	3	—	—	—	32	9
PERSAN	1974	55	—	5	18	2	—	—	—	22	8
PERSA	1975	71	—	2	19	1	—	—	—	43	6

8.11 Translations by original language
Traductions classées d'après la langue originale
Traducciones clasificadas según la lengua original

ORIGINAL LANGUAGE / LANGUE ORIGINALE / IDIOMA ORIGINAL	YEAR / ANNEE / AÑO	TOTAL / TOTAL / TOTAL	GENER-ALITIES / GENERA-LITES / GENERA-LIDADES	PHILOS-OPHY / PHILO-SOPHIE / FILO-SOFIA	RELIGION / RELIGION / RELIGION	SOCIAL SCIENCES / SCIENCES SOCIALES / CIENCIAS SOCIALES	PURE SCIENCES / SCIENCES PURES / CIENCIAS PURAS	APPLIED SCIENCES / SCIENCES APPL. / CIENCIAS APLICADAS	ARTS / BEAUX-ARTS / ARTES PLASTICAS	LITERA-TURE / LITTERA-TURE / LITERA-TURA	GEOGR./HISTORY / GEOGR./HISTOIRE / GEOGR./HISTORIA
		(1)	(2)	(3)	(4)	(5)	(6)	(7)	(8)	(9)	(10)
KIRGHIZ / KIRGHIZ / KIRIGUIZ	1973	41	—	—	—	—	—	—	—	41	—
	1974	35	—	—	—	1	—	—	—	34	—
	1975	62	—	—	—	1	—	—	—	61	—
KOREAN / COREEN / COREANO	1973	./	./	./	./	./	./	./	./	./	./
	1974	36	—	—	5	13	—	—	—	11	7
	1975	61	—	—	5	26	1	—	2	19	8
UZBEK / OUZBEK / UZBEK	1973	50	—	—	—	—	—	—	—	50	—
	1974	47	—	—	—	1	—	—	1	46	—
	1975	57	—	1	—	1	1	1	1	56	—
ALBANIAN / ALBANAIS / ALBANES	1973	26	—	—	1	13	—	1	—	9	3
	1974	13	—	—	3	2	—	—	—	11	—
	1975	56	—	1	3	35	1	—	3	13	3
TURKISH / TURC / TURCO	1973	70	—	—	—	8	—	—	1	57	3
	1974	58	—	—	1	1	1	—	—	39	14
	1975	54	—	—	1	4	—	—	2	44	1
YIDDISH ‡ / YIDDISH ‡ / YIDDISH ‡	1973	38	—	1	—	—	—	—	—	33	4
	1974	42	—	—	—	—	—	—	—	35	7
	1975	49	—	1	1	—	—	—	—	41	7
SLOVENIAN ‡ / SLOVENE ‡ / ESLOVENO ‡	1973	95	—	1	1	5	3	6	3	71	3
	1974	64	—	—	1	13	1	4	—	36	9
	1975	46	—	—	—	2	—	—	1	41	2
MACEDONIAN / MACEDONIEN / MACEDONIO	1973	./	./	./	./	./	./	./	./	./	./
	1974	42	—	—	1	25	—	1	—	12	4
	1975	45	—	—	—	17	—	—	4	23	—
HINDUSTANI ‡ / HINDOUSTANI ‡ / HINDUSTANI ‡	1973	56	—	—	6	2	—	4	—	37	7
	1974	51	1	4	13	3	—	2	—	24	4
	1975	44	1	3	8	2	1	1	—	23	6
TATAR / TARTARE / TARTARO	1973	./	./	./	./	./	./	./	./	./	./
	1974	30	—	—	—	1	—	—	—	29	—
	1975	43	—	—	1	1	—	—	—	42	—
KAZAKH / KAZAKH / KAZAK	1973	17	—	—	—	2	—	—	—	15	—
	1974	28	—	—	—	—	—	—	—	27	1
	1975	40	—	—	—	2	—	—	—	35	3
AZERBAIJAN / AZERBAIDJANAIS / AZERBAIJANES	1973	42	—	—	—	2	—	—	—	40	—
	1974	27	—	—	—	—	—	1	1	25	1
	1975	35	—	—	—	2	—	—	—	30	2
URDU / OURDOU / URDU	1973	34	—	—	9	1	—	1	—	18	5
	1974	38	—	—	25	1	—	1	—	9	2
	1975	35	—	—	18	5	—	—	—	12	—

Translations by original language   8.11
Traductions classées d'après la langue originale
Traducciones clasificadas según la lengua original

	(1)	(2)	(3)	(4)	(5)	(6)	(7)	(8)	(9)	(10)
VIETNAMESE 1973	44	—	—	—	8	—	—	—	34	2
VIETNAMIEN 1974	28	—	—	—	6	—	—	—	17	5
VIETNAMITA 1975	35	—	—	—	6	—	—	—	26	3
MODERN GREEK 1973	98	—	3	1	6	—	—	3	80	5
GREC MODERNE 1974	58	—	6	2	2	—	—	3	43	8
GRIEGO MODERNO 1975	34	—	1	1	2	—	—	—	30	—
ICELANDIC 1973	./.	./.	./.	./.	./.	./.	./.	./.	./.	./.
ISLANDAIS 1974	22	—	—	2	—	—	—	—	20	—
ISLANDES 1975	27	—	1	—	—	—	—	—	22	4
TADZHIK 1973	./.	./.	./.	./.	./.	./.	./.	./.	./.	./.
TADJIK 1974	24	—	—	—	—	—	—	—	23	—
TADJIK 1975	24	—	1	—	1	1	—	—	22	1
MARATHI 1973	—	—	—	—	—	—	—	—	—	—
MAHRATTE 1974	10	—	1	1	1	—	—	—	7	—
MAHRATTE 1975	23	1	1	2	1	1	1	—	15	3
AVARSKIJ 1973	—	—	—	—	—	—	—	—	—	—
AVARSKI 1974	—	—	—	—	—	—	—	—	—	—
AVARSKI 1975	21	—	—	—	—	—	—	—	21	—
OTHER LANGUAGES 1973	748	1	9	24	103	3	5	4	553	46
AUTRES LANGUES 1974	520	83	6	38	31	10	13	8	392	19
OTROS IDIOMAS 1975	677	2	5	43	41	4	8	5	540	29
TWO OR + LANGUAGES 1973	667	8	23	96	99	56	74	23	259	39
DEUX LANGUES OU + 1974	556	14	28	83	96	44	49	30	176	36
DOS IDIOMAS O MAS 1975	667	16	27	86	110	50	75	52	215	36
UNKNOWN 1973	790	3	34	69	83	21	128	43	370	39
INCONNU 1974	651	6	22	32	53	31	86	55	333	33
DESCONOCIDO 1975	314	6	6	56	36	11	36	8	135	20

GENERAL NOTE/NOTE GENERALE/NOTA GENERAL:
E—> MOST OF THE WORKS ORIGINALLY WRITTEN IN LANGUAGES SPOKEN IN THE U.S.S.R. WERE TRANSLATED AND PUBLISHED IN THE COUNTRY ITSELF; THE FOLLOW-ING ARE THE FIGURES FOR SUCH WORKS:
IN 1973: 2,107 TITLES FROM RUSSIAN, 104 FROM UKRAINIAN, 55 FROM LITHUANIAN, 53 FROM BYELO-RUSSIAN, 50 FROM GEORGIAN, 48 FROM UZBEK, 46 FROM LATVIAN, 41 FROM AZERBAIJAN, 41 FROM ARMENIAN, 40 FROM ESTONIAN, 26 FROM KIRGHIZ AND 16 FROM KAZAKH.
IN 1974: 2,082 TITLES FROM RUSSIAN, 100 FROM UKRAINIAN, 58 FROM BYELORUSSIAN, 54 FROM LITHUAN-IAN, 53 FROM LATVIAN, 49 FROM GEORGIAN, 44 FROM UZBEK, 38 FROM ARMENIAN, 28 FROM KAZAKH, 27 FROM KIRGHIZ, 25 FROM AZERBAIJAN, 15 FROM ESTONIAN.
IN 1975: 3,689 TITLES FROM RUSSIAN, 179 FROM UKRAINIAN, 96 FROM GEORGIAN, 81 FROM LITHUANIAN, 79 FROM ESTONIAN, 67 FROM LATVIAN, 56 FROM KIRGHIZ, 54 FROM UZBEK, 36 FROM KAZAKH AND 35 FROM AZERBAIJAN.
FOR THE FOLLOWING LANGUAGES, TRANSLATIONS PUB-LISHED IN 1973 HAVE BEEN INCLUDED IN THE CATEGORY "OTHER LANGUAGES": KOREAN, ICELANDIC, MACEDONIAN, TADZHIK.

FR—> LES OEUVRES REDIGEES DANS LES LANGUES PAR-LEES EN U.R.S.S. ONT ETE, POUR LA PLUPART, TRA-DUITES ET PUBLIEES DANS CE PAYS; VOICI LE RELEVE DE CES TRADUCTIONS:
EN 1973: 2 107 TITRES TRADUITS DU RUSSE, 104 DE L'UKRAINIEN, 55 DU LITUANIEN, 53 DU BIELORUSSIEN, 50 DU GEORGIEN, 48 DE L'OUZBEK, 46 DU LETTON, 41 DE L'AZERBAIDJANAIS, 41 DE L'ARMENIEN, 40 DE L'ESTONIEN, 26 DU KIRGHIZ ET 16 DU KAZAKH.
EN 1974: 2 082 TITRES TRADUITS DU RUSSE, 100 DE L'UKRAINIEN, 58 DU BIELORUSSIEN, 54 DU LITUANIEN, 53 DU LETTON, 49 DU GEORGIEN, 44 DE L'OUZBEK, 38 DE L'ARMENIEN, 28 DU KAZAKH, 27 DU KIRGHIZ, 25 DE L'AZERBAIDJANAIS ET 15 DE L'ESTONIEN.
EN 1975: 3 689 TITRES TRADUITS DU RUSSE, 179 DE L'UKRAINIEN, 96 DU GEORGIEN, 81 DU LITUANIEN, 79 DE L'ESTONIEN, 67 DU LETTON, 56 DU KIRGHIZ, 54 DE L'OUZBEK, 36 DU KAZAKH ET 35 DE L'AZERBAIDJANAIS.
POUR LES LANGUES SUIVANTES, LES TRADUCTIONS PUBLIEES EN 1973, SONT INCLUSES DANS LA RUBRIQUE "AUTRES LANGUES": COREEN, ISLANDAIS, MACEDONIEN, TARTARE ET TADJIK.

ESP> LA MAYORIA DE LAS OBRAS ESCRITAS ORIGINAL-MENTE EN LOS IDIOMAS QUE SE HABLAN EN LA U.R.S.S.

8.11 Translations by original language
Traductions classées d'après la langue originale
Traducciones clasificadas según la lengua original

SANSKRIT/SANSKRIT/SANSCRITO:
E—> INCLUDING TITLES PUBLISHED IN INDIA:
1973, 87; 1974, 63; 1975, 113.
FR—> Y COMPRIS LES TRADUCTIONS PUBLIEES EN
INDE: 1973, 87; 1974, 63; 1975, 113.
ESP> INCLUIDAS LAS TRADUCCIONES PUBLICADAS EN
LA INDIA: 1973, 87; 1974, 63; 1975, 113.

HEBREW/HEBREU/HEBREO:
E—> INCLUDING TITLES PUBLISHED IN ISRAEL:
1975, 38.
FR—> Y COMPRIS LES TRADUCTIONS PUBLIEES EN
ISRAEL: 1975, 38.
ESP> INCLUIDAS LAS TRADUCCIONES PUBLICADAS EN
ISRAEL: 1975, 38.

SLOVAK/SLOVAQUE/ESLOVACO:
E—> INCLUDING TITLES PUBLISHED IN CZECHOSLO-
VAKIA: 1973, 115; 1974, 92; 1975, 80.
FR—> Y COMPRIS LES TRADUCTIONS PUBLIEES EN
TCHECOSLOVAQUIE: 1973, 115; 1974, 92; 1975, 80.
ESP> INCLUIDAS LAS TRADUCCIONES PUBLICADAS EN
CHECOSLOVAQUIA: 1973, 115; 1974, 92; 1975, 80.

BENGALI/BENGALI/BENGALI:
E—> INCLUDING TITLES PUBLISHED IN INDIA:
1973, 48; 1974, 38; 1975, 76.
FR—> Y COMPRIS LES TRADUCTIONS PUBLIEES EN
INDE: 1973, 48; 1974, 38; 1975, 76.
ESP> INCLUIDAS LAS TRADUCCIONES PUBLICADAS
EN LA INDIA: 1973, 48; 1974, 38; 1975, 76.

FINNISH/FINNOIS/FINLANDES:
E—> INCLUDING TITLES PUBLISHED IN FINLAND:
1973, 42; 1974, 25; 1975, 11.
FR—> Y COMPRIS LES TRADUCTIONS PUBLIEES EN
FINLANDE: 1973, 42; 1974, 25; 1975, 11.
ESP> INCLUIDAS LAS TRADUCCIONES PUBLICADAS EN
FINLANDIA: 1973, 42; 1974, 25; 1975, 11.

YIDDISH/YIDDISH/YIDDISH:
E—> INCLUDING TITLES PUBLISHED IN ISRAEL:
1975, 16.
FR—> Y COMPRIS LES TRADUCTIONS PUBLIEES EN
ISRAEL: 1975, 16.
ESP> INCLUIDAS LAS TRADUCCIONES PUBLICADAS EN
ISRAEL: 1975, 16.

SLOVENIAN/SLOVENE/ESLOVENO:
E—> INCLUDING TITLES PUBLISHED IN YUGOSLAVIA:
1973, 72; 1974, 56; 1975, 35.
FR—> Y COMPRIS LES TRADUCTIONS PUBLIEES EN
YOUGOSLAVIE: 1973, 72; 1974, 56; 1975, 35.
ESP> INCLUIDAS LAS TRADUCCIONES PUBLICADAS EN
YUGOSLAVIA: 1973, 72; 1974, 56; 1975, 35.

HINDUSTANI/HINDOUSTANI/HINDUSTANI:
E—> INCLUDING TITLES PUBLISHED IN INDIA:
1973, 39; 1974, 29; 1975, 29.
FR—> Y COMPRIS LES TRADUCTIONS PUBLIEES EN
INDE: 1973, 39; 1974, 29; 1975, 29.
ESP> INCLUIDAS LAS TRADUCCIONES PUBLICADAS EN
LA INDIA: 1973, 39; 1974, 29; 1975, 29.

GENERAL NOTE/NOTE GENERALE/NOTA GENERAL (CONT.):
FUERON TRADUCIDAS Y PUBLICADAS EN ESTE PAIS. A
CONTINUACION SE INDICAN LAS CIFRAS CORRESPONDIEN-
TES A ESAS TRADUCCIONES.
EN 1973: 2 107 TITULOS TRADUCIDOS DEL RUSO, 104
DEL UCRANIANO, 55 DEL LITUANO, 46 DEL LETON, 53
DEL BIELORRUSO, 50 DEL GEORGIANO, 48 DEL UZBEK,
41 DEL AZERBAIJANES, 41 DEL ARMENIO, 40 DEL
ESTONIO, 26 DEL KIRIGUIZ Y 18 DEL KAZAK.
EN 1974: 2 082 TITULOS TRADUCIDOS DEL RUSO, 100
DEL UCRANIO, 58 DEL BIELORRUSO, 54 DEL LITUANO,
53 DEL LETON, 49 DEL GEORGIANO, 44 DEL UZBEK, 38
DEL ARMENIO, 28 DEL KAZAK, 27 DEL KIRIGUIZ, 25 DEL
AZERBAIJANES Y 15 DEL ESTONIO.
EN 1975: 3 689 TITULOS TRADUCIDOS DEL RUSO, 179
DEL UCRANIO, 96 DEL GEORGIANO, 81 DEL LITUANO, 79
DEL ESTONIO, 67 DEL BIELORRUSO, 66 DEL ARMENIO,
62 DEL LETON, 56 DEL KIRIGUIZ, 54 DEL UZBEK, 36
DEL KAZAK Y 35 DEL AZERBAIJANES.
POR LOS IDIOMAS SIGUIENTES, LAS TRADUCCIONES
PUBLICADAS EN 1973 QUEDAN COMPRENDIDAS EN LA
RUBRICA "OTROS IDIOMAS": COREANO, ISLANDES,
MACEDONIO, TARTARO, TADJIK.

POLISH/POLONAIS/POLACO:
E—> INCLUDING TITLES PUBLISHED IN POLAND:
1973, 155; 1974, 3; 1975, 274.
FR—> Y COMPRIS LES TRADUCTIONS PUBLIEES
EN POLOGNE: 1973, 155; 1974, 3; 1975, 274.
ESP> INCLUIDAS LAS TRADUCCIONES PUBLICADAS EN
POLONIA: 1973, 155; 1974, 3; 1975, 274.

CZECH/TCHEQUE/CHECO:
E—> INCLUDING TITLES PUBLISHED IN CZECHOSLO-
VAKIA: 1973, 298; 1974, 371; 1975, 248.
FR—> Y COMPRIS LES TRADUCTIONS PUBLIEES EN
TCHECOSLOVAQUIE: 1973, 298; 1974, 371; 1975, 248.
ESP> INCLUIDAS LAS TRADUCCIONES PUBLICADAS EN
CHECOSLOVAQUIA: 1973, 298; 1974, 371; 1975, 248.

ROMANIAN/ROUMAIN/RUMANO:
E—> INCLUDING TITLES PUBLISHED IN ROMANIA:
1973, 390; 1974, 2; 1975, 360.
FR—> Y COMPRIS LES TRADUCTIONS PUBLIEES EN
ROUMANIE: 1973, 390; 1974, 2; 1975, 360.
ESP> INCLUIDAS LAS TRADUCCIONES PUBLICADAS EN
RUMANIA: 1973, 390; 1974, 2; 1975, 360.

SERBO-CROATIAN/SERBO-CROATE/SERBOCROATA:
E—> INCLUDING TITLES PUBLISHED IN YUGOSLAVIA:
1973, 421; 1974, 462; 1975, 235.
FR—> Y COMPRIS LES TRADUCTIONS PUBLIEES EN
YOUGOSLAVIE: 1973, 421; 1974, 462; 1975, 235.
ESP> INCLUIDAS LAS TRADUCCIONES PUBLICADAS EN
YUGOSLAVIA: 1973, 421; 1974, 462; 1975, 235.

BULGARIAN/BULGARE/BULGARO:
E—> INCLUDING TITLES PUBLISHED IN BULGARIA:
1973, 66; 1974, 3; 1975, 93.
FR—> Y COMPRIS LES TRADUCTIONS PUBLIEES EN
BULGARIE: 1973, 66; 1974, 3; 1975, 93.
ESP> INCLUIDAS LAS TRADUCCIONES PUBLICADAS EN
BULGARIA: 1973, 66; 1974, 3; 1975, 93.

8.12 Translations from languages most frequently translated
Traductions à partir des langues les plus traduites
Traducciones de las lenguas más traducidas

8.12 Translations from languages most frequently translated by country of publication

Traductions à partir des langues les plus traduites, classées par pays de publication

Traducciones de las lenguas más traducidas, clasificadas por país de publicación

NUMBER OF COUNTRIES AND TERRITORIES PRESENTED IN THIS TABLE: 77

NOMBRE DE PAYS ET DE TERRITOIRES PRESENTES DANS CE TABLEAU: 77

COUNTRY	YEAR	TOTAL	ENGLISH	FRENCH	GERMAN	RUSSIAN
PAYS	ANNEE	TOTAL	ANGLAIS	FRANCAIS	ALLEMAND	RUSSE
PAIS	AÑO	TOTAL	INGLES	FRANCES	ALEMAN	RUSO
WORLD TOTAL	1973	47 038	18 350	5 993	4 277	5 113
	1974	47 922	20 411	5 785	4 753	4 824
	1975	47 775	19 020	5 298	4 338	6 563
ALBANIA	1973	74	18	12	8	8
	1974	79	24	11	8	16
	1975	93	6	7	9	11
ARGENTINA	1973	196	99	40	29	–
	1974	262	167	48	27	–
	1975	514	326	62	54	4
AUSTRALIA	1973	67	10	1	–	2
	1974	44	10	–	3	2
	1975	27	–	–	1	3
AUSTRIA	1973	418	260	72	9	5
	1974	459	273	61	54	5
	1975	338	212	55	16	7
BANGLADESH	1974	34	13	1	–	–
BELGIUM	1973	837	470	145	117	8
	1974	472	274	72	54	3
BRAZIL	1973	1 684	434	166	36	8
	1974	1 311	742	191	76	7
	1975	1 676	899	206	82	7
BULGARIA	1973	406	30	21	28	182
	1974	372	34	28	29	217
	1975	513	31	26	31	240
BURMA	1973	38	29	–	–	4
	1974	76	72	1	–	1
CANADA	1973	146	88	19	10	3
	1975	291	161	72	11	7
CHILE	1973	24	7	4	4	5
	1974	3	2	1	–	–
	1975	28	14	8	–	2
COLOMBIA	1973	15	2	5	2	–
	1974	10	7	–	1	1
	1975	76	42	6	6	–

Translations from languages most frequently translated   8.12
Traductions à partir des langues les plus traduites
Traducciones de las lenguas más traducidas

NUMERO DE PAISES Y DE TERRITORIOS PRESENTADOS EN
ESTE CUADRO: 77

ITALIAN	SCANDINAVIAN LANGUAGES	SPANISH	CLASSICS	ARABIC	JAPANESE	CHINESE	OTHER LANGUAGES
ITALIEN	LANGUES SCANDINAVES	ESPAGNOL	LANGUES CLASSIQUES	ARABE	JAPONAIS	CHINOIS	AUTRES LANGUES
ITALIANO	LENGUAS ESCANDINAVAS	ESPAÑOL	LENGUAS CLASICAS	ARABE	JAPONES	CHINO	OTROS IDIOMAS
1 136	1 907	1 368	798	156	176	184	7 580
1 182	2 103	768	908	201	165	188	6 634
1 045	1 779	935	921	192	111	209	7 364
1	1	—	2	—	1	—	23
7	—	4	—	—	—	1	8
1	1	2	1	—	—	4	51
1	3	—	12	—	—		12
6	3	—	1	—	—	—	10
16	12	—	24	—	—	—	16
7	—	1	37	—	1	1	7
—	2	—	18	—	3	—	6
1	—	—	14	—	—	—	8
9	19	3	3	1	—	—	37
10	21	2	4	1	—	—	28
3	23	1	3	—	2	—	16
—	—	—	1	5	—	—	14
5	21	7	10	3	1	—	50
9	18	6	4	1	1	—	30
18	3	772	5	12	—	3	227
29	4	179	10	2	1	—	70
29	2	344	6	5	1	2	93
5	2	10	2	2	2	—	122
5	1	6	4	—	1	—	47
6	1	15	5	2	—	—	156
—	1	—	—	—	—	1	3
—	1	—	—	—	—	1	—
6	—	3	6	—	—	—	11
3	2	5	12	—	—	1	17
—	2	—	1	—	—	—	1
—	—	—	—	—	—	—	4
—	—	—	—	—	—	—	
2	—	1	1	—	—	—	2
—	—	2	1	—	—	—	
6	—	2	2	4	—	—	8

8.12 Translations from languages most frequently translated
Traductions à partir des langues les plus traduites
Traducciones de las lenguas más traducidas

COUNTRY PAYS PAIS	YEAR ANNEE AÑO	TOTAL TOTAL TOTAL	ENGLISH ANGLAIS INGLES	FRENCH FRANCAIS FRANCES	GERMAN ALLEMAND ALEMAN	RUSSIAN RUSSE RUSO
CUBA	1975	24	6	6	–	–
CYPRUS	1973	3	2	1	–	–
	1974	3	3	–	–	–
CZECHOSLOVAKIA	1973	1 437	176	102	132	349
	1974	1 499	164	92	146	350
	1975	1 384	146	73	127	394
DENMARK	1973	1 415	732	116	124	19
	1974	1 865	968	139	200	29
	1975	1 943	1 017	172	217	15
ECUADOR	1973	1	–	–	–	–
	1974	1	–	–	–	1
EGYPT	1973	183	109	13	6	9
	1974	141	95	9	11	8
	1975	284	148	20	12	18
ETHIOPIA	1975	7	7	–	–	–
FINLAND	1973	1 030	522	60	76	30
	1974	789	390	54	57	14
	1975	912	468	78	71	32
FRANCE	1973	1 934	1 132	39	267	73
	1974	2 483	1 473	46	338	114
	1975	2 251	1 442	29	302	79
GERMAN DEMOCRATIC REPUBLIC	1973	1 765	297	147	4	745
	1974	406	56	30	–	200
	1975	791	95	50	–	375
GERMANY, FEDERAL REPUBLIC OF	1973	6 458	3 937	783	188	252
	1974	6 634	4 096	817	210	235
	1975	4 757	2 947	613	129	183
GREECE	1973	698	397	151	64	27
	1974	146	92	24	12	5
	1975	63	27	16	6	3
GUATEMALA	1973	58	3	–	–	–
	1974	9	3	–	–	–
	1975	2	2	–	–	–
HAITI	1975	2	–	–	–	–
HOLY SEE	1973	15	–	–	–	–
	1974	37	4	5	3	–
	1975	35	–	–	–	–
HONDURAS	1974	1	–	–	–	–
HUNGARY	1973	1 083	118	76	94	120
	1974	1 163	128	70	130	155
	1975	1 264	130	71	100	142
ICELAND	1973	171	89	14	18	2
	1974	126	59	17	7	–
	1975	186	91	21	15	4
INDIA	1973	676	274	9	18	42
	1974	550	210	9	8	65
	1975	769	289	18	9	63

Translations from languages most frequently translated   **8.12**
Traductions à partir des langues les plus traduites
Traducciones de las lenguas más traducidas

ITALIAN	SCANDINAVIAN LANGUAGES	SPANISH	CLASSICS	ARABIC	JAPANESE	CHINESE	OTHER LANGUAGES
ITALIEN	LANGUES SCANDINAVES	ESPAGNOL	LANGUES CLASSIQUES	ARABE	JAPONAIS	CHINOIS	AUTRES LANGUES
ITALIANO	LENGUAS ESCANDINAVAS	ESPAÑOL	LENGUAS CLASICAS	ARABE	JAPONES	CHINO	OTROS IDIOMAS
-	-	10	-	-	-	-	2
-	-	-	-	-	-	-	-
-	-	-	-	-	-	-	-
16	19	16	12	2	3	3	607
21	24	19	24	2	1	2	654
22	21	18	19	5	3	-	556
11	279	6	8	4	11	51	54
16	367	17	17	1	8	29	74
13	391	16	19	1	1	16	65
-	-	-	1	-	-	-	-
-	-	-	-	-	-	-	-
2	1	1	3	-	-	-	39
2	-	-	6	-	-	-	10
-	-	-	8	-	-	-	78
-	-	-	-	-	-	-	-
3	254	9	4	4	2	2	64
9	205	5	3	1	1	-	50
8	214	4	1	1	-	5	30
110	28	55	49	7	6	12	156
159	33	50	75	3	17	7	168
115	29	57	41	3	7	12	135
35	47	36	56	5	4	4	385
8	10	8	8	1	1	2	82
20	19	15	20	2	2	4	189
189	295	51	128	6	18	21	190
209	296	51	187	11	7	20	495
187	166	50	118	11	9	20	324
21	1	7	3	1	1	1	24
3	-	3	1	-	1	-	5
3	1	1	-	-	-	-	6
-	-	33	7	-	-	-	15
-	-	-	5	-	-	-	1
-	-	-	-	-	-	-	-
-	-	-	-	-	-	-	2
9	-	-	6	-	-	-	-
14	-	3	2	-	-	-	6
5	-	-	30	-	-	-	-
-	-	-	1	-	-	-	-
13	8	12	16	3	-	-	623
12	1	13	18	3	-	1	632
11	6	11	19	10	3	1	760
1	33	1	2	-	-	-	11
2	27	-	1	-	1	-	12
1	38	2	1	-	-	-	13
3	-	2	6	10	1	3	308
3	5	-	5	3	2	2	238
1	1	5	5	5	-	5	368

8.12 Translations from languages most frequently translated
Traductions à partir des langues les plus traduites
Traducciones de las lenguas más traducidas

COUNTRY PAYS PAIS	YEAR ANNEE AÑO	TOTAL TOTAL TOTAL	ENGLISH ANGLAIS INGLES	FRENCH FRANCAIS FRANCES	GERMAN ALLEMAND ALEMAN	RUSSIAN RUSSE RUSO
INDONESIA	1974 1975	184 124	92 65	3 4	23 9	— 2
IRAN	1973 1974	200 194	111 113	48 38	15 14	12 14
IRAQ	1973 1974 1975	23 28 10	7 14 6	— 2 1	1 3 —	2 3 3
IRELAND	1973 1974	5 5	— 1	1 1	— —	— —
ISRAEL	1975	232	103	15	16	17
ITALY	1973 1974 1975	2 095 1 908 1 831	869 814 800	577 559 441	307 268 249	67 62 51
JAMAICA	1974	1	—	—	—	—
JAPAN	1973 1974 1975	2 284 2 482 2 651	1 411 1 467 1 592	312 348 378	273 317 271	150 121 134
JORDAN ‡	1973 1974 1975	6 2 2	5 2 1	— — —	— — —	— — —
KENYA	1973	15	15	—	—	—
KOREA, REPUBLIC OF	1973 1974 1975	207 269 214	147 185 132	17 20 25	34 43 39	2 3 3
KUWAIT	1974 1975	10 13	4 5	2 5	— 1	1 —
MADAGASCAR	1974 1975	4 9	2 4	— 4	— —	— —
MALAYSIA	1973 1974 1975	46 58 137	25 54 126	— — 2	— — 1	— — 1
MALTA	1973 1974 1975	3 4 5	3 3 1	— — —	— — —	— — —
MAURITIUS	1975	1	—	—	—	—
MEXICO	1973 1974 1975	218 280 276	171 208 239	22 30 17	8 11 8	7 3 1
MONGOLIA	1975	17	—	—	1	9
NETHERLANDS	1973 1974 1975	1 816 1 850 2 057	1 068 1 045 1 219	145 152 181	317 377 406	48 46 31
NEW ZEALAND	1975	1	—	—	—	—
NIGER	1973	1	—	1	—	—
NIGERIA	1974 1975	1 2	1 1	— 1	— —	— —

Translations from languages most frequently translated 8.12
Traductions à partir des langues les plus traduites
Traducciones de las lenguas más traducidas

ITALIAN / ITALIEN / ITALIANO	SCANDINAVIAN LANGUAGES / LANGUES SCANDINAVES / LENGUAS ESCANDINAVAS	SPANISH / ESPAGNOL / ESPAÑOL	CLASSICS / LANGUES CLASSIQUES / LENGUAS CLASICAS	ARABIC / ARABE / ARABE	JAPANESE / JAPONAIS / JAPONES	CHINESE / CHINOIS / CHINO	OTHER LANGUAGES / AUTRES LANGUES / OTROS IDIOMAS
2	3	1	–	14	–	–	46
–	4	–	–	8	2	–	30
2	3	–	–	1	–	–	8
3	4	3	–	1	–	–	4
–	–	1	–	2	–	–	13
–	–	–	–	–	–	–	3
–	–	1	2	–	–	–	1
–	–	2	–	–	–	–	1
3	–	1	2	–	–	2	73
18	23	66	75	1	4	6	82
4	17	46	58	1	2	5	72
1	21	56	119	1	3	7	82
–	–	–	1	–	–	–	–
29	21	17	21	–	–	–	50
39	28	17	30	5	–	25	85
47	28	23	28	2	1	49	98
1	–	–	–	–	–	–	–
–	1	–	–	–	–	–	–
–	–	–	–	–	–	–	–
1	3	–	1	1	–	–	1
1	4	–	1	–	12	–	1
1	1	–	2	–	11	–	–
–	–	2	1	–	–	–	–
1	1	–	–	–	–	–	–
–	–	–	–	–	–	–	2
–	1	–	–	–	–	–	–
–	–	–	–	–	–	3	21
–	–	–	–	1	–	–	–
–	–	–	–	1	–	–	6
–	–	1	–	–	–	–	–
1	–	–	2	–	–	–	1
–	–	–	–	–	–	–	1
3	–	–	1	–	–	–	6
–	–	2	3	–	–	–	23
3	–	1	2	–	–	–	5
–	–	–	1	–	–	–	6
27	76	14	27	3	7	1	83
21	79	17	24	3	3	4	79
28	79	12	30	5	1	5	60
–	–	–	–	–	–	–	1
–	–	–	–	–	–	–	–
–	–	–	–	–	–	–	–
–	–	–	–	–	–	–	–

8.12 Translations from languages most frequently translated
Traductions à partir des langues les plus traduites
Traducciones de las lenguas más traducidas

COUNTRY PAYS PAIS	YEAR ANNEE AÑO	TOTAL TOTAL TOTAL	ENGLISH ANGLAIS INGLES	FRENCH FRANCAIS FRANCES	GERMAN ALLEMAND ALEMAN	RUSSIAN RUSSE RUSO
NORWAY	1973 1974 1975	1 004 1 168 912	585 724 623	50 40 31	72 65 37	27 22 9
PAKISTAN	1975	44	9	–	3	–
PAPUA NEW GUINEA	1975	144	104	–	–	–
PARAGUAY	1973	1	–	–	–	–
PERU	1973 1974 1975	32 20 43	5 5 4	– 1 2	3 – –	– – –
PHILIPPINES	1975	22	8	–	1	–
POLAND	1973 1974 1975	958 900 1 990	226 269 538	88 113 198	95 123 218	160 173 378
ROMANIA	1973 1974 1975	840 755 865	85 126 95	94 140 100	48 112 55	53 88 44
SIERRA LEONE	1975	15	8	–	–	–
SINGAPORE	1973 1974	2 5	2 5	– –	– –	– –
SPAIN	1973 1974 1975	4 489 3 780 3 868	1 709 1 513 1 686	1 232 967 999	527 450 516	126 121 123
SRI LANKA	1973 1974 1975	35 68 68	22 36 43	– 1 2	1 2 1	3 5 7
SWEDEN	1973 1974 1975	1 599 3 422 1 874	1 068 2 424 1 279	106 182 115	127 244 153	19 84 22
SWITZERLAND	1973 1974 1975	718 992 983	350 507 556	130 171 160	102 115 119	25 42 23
SYRIAN ARAB REPUBLIC	1973 1974 1975	51 17 68	16 5 20	7 6 8	3 3 35	10 3 2
THAILAND	1973 1974 1975	32 141 39	23 109 21	2 21 4	2 – 2	– 2 4
TURKEY	1973 1974 1975	991 1 262 1 032	389 538 392	209 241 195	94 87 99	38 62 81
UKRAINIAN S.S.R.	1975	6 667	550	148	242	3 689
U.S.S.R.	1973 1974	4 402 4 271	471 416	152 121	181 183	2 107 2 082
UNITED KINGDOM	1973 1974 1975	682 1 469 1 368	3 82 88	218 358 357	234 322 287	19 113 86

Translations from languages most frequently translated 8.12
Traductions à partir des langues les plus traduites
Traducciones de las lenguas más traducidas

COUNTRY PAYS PAIS	YEAR ANNEE AÑO	TOTAL TOTAL TOTAL	ENGLISH ANGLAIS INGLES	FRENCH FRANCAIS FRANCES	GERMAN ALLEMAND ALEMAN	RUSSIAN RUSSE RUSO
UNITED STATES OF AMERICA	1973 1974 1975	1 968 1 864 1 039	21 33 14	444 398 213	425 403 271	239 202 153
URUGUAY	1974	7	1	3	3	—
VENEZUELA	1975	20	3	6	7	—
YUGOSLAVIA	1973 1974 1975	1 482 1 526 903	307 254 179	142 141 77	174 211 93	106 144 101

GENERAL NOTE/NOTE GENERALE/NOTA GENERAL:
  E—> SCANDINAVIAN LANGUAGES INCLUDE DANISH,
NORVEGIAN AND SWEDISH. CLASSICS INCLUDE CLASSICAL
GREEK AND LATIN. VALUES ARE GIVEN SEPARATELY FOR
THESE LANGUAGES IN TABLE 8.11.
  FR—> LES LANGUES SCANDINAVES COMPRENNENT LE
DANOIS, LE NORVEGIEN ET LE SUEDOIS. LES LANGUES
CLASSIQUES COMPRENNENT LE GREC CLASSIQUE ET LE
LATIN. CES LANGUES SONT MONTREES SEPAREMENT DANS
LE TABLEAU 8.11.
  ESP> LAS LENGUAS ESCANDINAVAS INCLUYEN EL DANES,
EL NORVEGO Y EL SUECO. LAS LENGUAS CLASICAS
INCLUYEN EL GRIEGO CLASICO Y EL LATIN. LAS
LENGUAS SE PRESENTAN SEPARADAMENTE EN EL CUADRO
8.11.

8.12 Translations from languages most frequently translate
Traductions à partir des langues les plus traduites
Traducciones de las lenguas más traducidas

ITALIAN	SCANDINAVIAN LANGUAGES	SPANISH	CLASSICS	ARABIC	JAPANESE	CHINESE	OTHER LANGUAGES
ITALIEN	LANGUES SCANDINAVES	ESPAGNOL	LANGUES CLASSIQUES	ARABE	JAPONAIS	CHINOIS	AUTRES LANGUES
ITALIANO	LENGUAS ESCANDINAVAS	ESPAÑOL	LENGUAS CLASICAS	ARABE	JAPONES	CHINO	OTROS IDIOMAS
1	210	6	4	1	–	1	47
7	276	4	4	1	2	–	23
5	185	6	–	–	–	1	15
1	–	–	–	13	–	–	18
–	–	–	21	–	–	–	19
–	–	–	1	–	–	–	–
1	–	8	11	–	–	–	4
–	–	9	4	–	–	1	–
–	–	18	15	–	–	–	4
–	–	5	8	–	–	–	–
15	39	17	29	1	4	1	283
16	25	19	19	3	3	–	137
20	46	66	40	4	2	–	480
19	4	17	16	2	2	3	497
21	7	20	11	2	3	4	221
25	5	18	21	1	1	5	495
–	–	–	–	2	–	1	4
–	–	–	–	–	–	–	–
–	–	–	–	–	–	–	–
313	61	1	79	9	6	4	422
217	50	2	79	11	5	11	354
253	61	1	70	19	10	8	122
–	–	–	3	–	–	–	6
1	–	1	3	1	–	1	17
1	–	–	5	3	1	–	5
12	190	7	6	1	1	8	54
16	328	22	4	–	2	–	116
13	199	10	7	3	1	3	69
27	20	12	8	2	3	1	38
40	21	10	36	1	2	2	45
36	25	7	9	–	1	3	44
–	–	–	–	–	1	2	12
–	–	–	–	–	–	–	–
–	–	–	–	1	–	–	2
1	–	–	–	1	1	–	–
1	–	–	3	2	–	–	3
–	–	1	3	–	–	–	4
10	15	3	7	40	4	2	180
20	8	15	14	69	4	5	199
9	3	8	16	39	1	1	177
29	35	56	27	15	15	8	1 853
26	31	34	9	16	21	13	1 341
31	32	36	18	19	15	8	1 310
40	62	19	14	3	2	5	63
105	113	49	71	7	22	13	214
52	106	44	77	16	18	8	229

Translations from languages most frequently translated   8.12
Traductions à partir des langues les plus traduites
Traducciones de las lenguas más traducidas

ITALIAN	SCANDINAVIAN LANGUAGES	SPANISH	CLASSICS	ARABIC	JAPANESE	CHINESE	OTHER LANGUAGES
ITALIEN	LANGUES SCANDINAVES	ESPAGNOL	LANGUES CLASSIQUES	ARABE	JAPONAIS	CHINOIS	AUTRES LANGUES
ITALIANO	LENGUAS ESCANDINAVAS	ESPAÑOL	LENGUAS CLASICAS	ARABE	JAPONES	CHINO	OTROS IDIOMAS
91	98	103	87	14	67	34	345
69	80	110	109	19	42	41	358
33	31	30	58	10	15	28	183
–	–	–	–	–	–	–	–
1	–	1	–	–	–	–	2
32	34	17	17	–	2	1	650
45	10	13	19	5	3	–	681
31	20	13	10	–	–	–	379

JORDAN:
  E—> DATA REFER TO THE EAST BANK ONLY.
  FR—> LES DONNEES SE REFERENT A LA RIVE ORIENTALE
SEULEMENT.
  ESP> LOS DATOS SE REFIEREN A LA ORILLA ORIENTAL
SOLAMENTE.

8.13 Authors most frequently translated
Auteurs les plus traduits
Autores más traducidos

8.13 Authors most frequently translated
Auteurs les plus traduits
Autores más traducidos

AUTHORS AUTEURS AUTORES	COUNTRY WITH WHICH THE AUTHOR'S WORKS ARE ASSOCIATED PAYS AUQUEL APPARTIENT L'OEUVRE LITTERAIRE DE L'AUTEUR PAIS AL QUE PERTENCE LA OBRA LITERARIA DEL AUTOR	NUMBER OF TRANSLATIONS NOMBRE DE TRADUCTIONS NUMERO DE TRADUCCIONES					NUMBER OF TRANS—LATING COUNTRIES IN 1975 NOMBRE DE PAYS TRADUCTEURS EN 1975 NUMERO DE PAISES TRADUCTORES EN 1975
		1975	1974	1970	1965	1961—65	
V.I. LENIN ‡	U.S.S.R.	485	401	486	200	910	19
A. CHRISTIE ‡	UNITED KINGDOM	191	136	95	97	492	19
W. DISNEY	UNITED STATES OF AMERICA	191	110	73	20	148	13
K. MARX	GERMANY	187	196	83	73	378	26
J. VERNE	FRANCE	171	164	129	101	504	24
E. BLYTON	UNITED KINGDOM	156	149	116	91	418	13
J. LONDON	UNITED STATES OF AMERICA	121	130	97	46	213	20
J.W. GRIMM	GERMANY	116	85	44	33	256	16
G. SIMENON	BELGIUM	113	88	109	102	423	15
L.I. BREZNEV ‡	U.S.S.R.	103	149	84	46	58	8
F.M. DOSTOEVSKIJ ‡	U.S.S.R.	100	86	91	81	397	26
M. GOR'KIJ ‡	U.S.S.R.	97	92	53	50	339	22
L.N. TOLSTOJ ‡	U.S.S.R.	95	74	86	98	570	25
P.S. BUCK	UNITED STATES OF AMERICA	92	90	65	38	307	14
A. MACLEAN	UNITED KINGDOM	92	85	65	37	152	17
W. SHAKESPEARE	UNITED KINGDOM	89	97	111	99	660	29
C. PERRAULT	FRANCE	71	27	16	17	79	10
B. CARTLAND	UNITED KINGDOM	68	50	8	3	16	8
F.W. DIXON ‡	UNITED STATES OF AMERICA	68	83	87	36	203	7
R.L. STEVENSON	UNITED KINGDOM	65	55	61	44	213	23
M. TWAIN ‡	UNITED STATES OF AMERICA	65	69	71	64	332	21
E. HEMINGWAY	UNITED STATES OF AMERICA	64	73	68	57	279	18
F. ENGELS	GERMANY	60	44	80	45	317	15
R. GOSCINNY	FRANCE	60	40	20	1	5	11
M. LAFUENTE	...	60	25	—	53	120	1
A. LINDGREN	SWEDEN	60	52	45	32	172	15
R. SCARRY	UNITED STATES OF AMERICA	58	24	14	3	8	11
A. SOLZENICYN	U.S.S.R.	55	88	35	6	49	20
G. GREENE	UNITED KINGDOM	54	37	47	44	262	17
A.N. KOLMOGOROV ‡	U.S.S.R.	51	1	1	—	3	4

Authors most frequently translated 8.13
Auteurs les plus traduits
Autores más traducidos

AUTHORS AUTEURS AUTORES	COUNTRY WITH WHICH THE AUTHOR'S WORKS ARE ASSOCIATED PAYS AUQUEL APPARTIENT L'OEUVRE LITTERAIRE DE L'AUTEUR PAIS AL QUE PERTENCE LA OBRA LITERARIA DEL AUTOR	NUMBER OF TRANSLATIONS NOMBRE DE TRADUCTIONS NUMERO DE TRADUCCIONES					NUMBER OF TRANS—LATING COUNTRIES IN 1975 NOMBRE DE PAYS TRADUCTEURS EN 1975 NUMERO DE PAISES TRADUCTORES EN 1975
		1975	1974	1970	1965	1961–65	
H. DE BALZAC	FRANCE	50	64	77	58	311	14
M. BRAND	UNITED STATES OF AMERICA	50	20	32	13	43	4
E. WALLACE	UNITED KINGDOM	50	62	19	27	107	5
A.P. CEHOV ‡	U.S.S.R.	49	58	50	50	257	20
T. MANN	GERMANY	48	18	21	26	113	17
A.S. PUSKIN ‡	U.S.S.R.	46	43	26	41	198	13
PAULUS VI, POPE	HOLY SEE	45	44	29	32	55	7
PLATO	GREECE	45	48	49	33	183	17
H. ROBBINS ‡	UNITED STATES OF AMERICA	45	34	27	17	43	15
C. DICKENS	UNITED KINGDOM	44	50	78	42	265	18
M.L. WEST	AUSTRALIA	44	29	21	34	101	12
M. GROVER	UNITED STATES OF AMERICA	43	48	63	40	144	3
H. HESSE	GERMANY	42	57	27	12	72	16
H.G. KONSALIK	GERMANY	41	46	16	10	55	8
C. BROWN ‡	UNITED STATES OF AMERICA	40	51	51	70	434	7
D. DEFOE	UNITED KINGDOM	40	42	29	32	145	15
A. DUMAS (PERE)	FRANCE	40	58	45	41	192	17
J. PIAGET	SWITZERLAND	40	32	29	8	25	11
G. WOLDE	SWEDEN	40	21	–	–	–	5
A.J. CRONIN	UNITED KINGDOM	39	47	60	41	209	16
E. HUNTER ‡	UNITED STATES OF AMERICA	39	26	21	11	83	11
F.G. SLAUGHTER	UNITED STATES OF AMERICA	39	49	37	28	128	10
I.S. TURGENEV ‡	U.S.S.R.	38	36	51	33	195	18
N.V. GOGOL ‡	U.S.S.R.	37	32	33	41	186	18
M. SJOWALL	SWEDEN	37	19	14	–	–	11
F. FORSYTH	UNITED KINGDOM	36	33	1	–	–	17
E. QUEEN	UNITED STATES OF AMERICA	36	43	40	40	194	8
J.Y. COUSTEAU	FRANCE	35	24	4	4	15	9
S. FREUD	AUSTRIA	35	57	45	17	81	12
L. MASTERSON	NORWAY	35	30	–	–	–	5
E.A. POE	UNITED STATES OF AMERICA	35	38	33	27	107	13
E. SALGARI	ITALY	35	17	3	1	42	2
M. SOLOHOV ‡	U.S.S.R.	35	28	17	38	189	9
E.R. BURROUGHS	UNITED STATES OF AMERICA	34	28	60	41	209	8
A. HITCHCOCK	UNITED STATES OF AMERICA	34	31	25	11	48	10
MAO TSE—TUNG	CHINA	34	30	16	8	53	12
P. NERUDA	CHILE	34	35	10	6	31	20
E. ZOLA	FRANCE	34	49	39	48	226	12
L.M. ALCOTT	UNITED STATES OF AMERICA	33	24	28	18	75	7
I. ASIMOV	UNITED STATES OF AMERICA	33	42	39	20	66	14
A.C. DOYLE	UNITED KINGDOM	33	28	32	41	160	16
E.S. GARDNER	UNITED STATES OF AMERICA	33	47	69	62	451	14
J. SLADE	...	32	26	10	–	–	3
J. BURNINGHAM	UNITED KINGDOM	31	6	1	–	1	8
D. DU MAURIER	UNITED KINGDOM	31	48	31	19	102	10
F.W. NIETZSCHE	GERMANY	31	15	29	16	57	8
J.P. SARTRE	FRANCE	31	32	41	77	259	14
J.E. STEINBECK	UNITED STATES OF AMERICA	31	42	61	70	327	16
H. BOLL	GERMANY	30	38	11	30	97	15
N. CARTER	UNITED STATES OF AMERICA	30	42	43	10	11	5

8.13 Authors most frequently translated
Auteurs les plus traduits
Autores más traducidos

AUTHORS AUTEURS AUTORES	COUNTRY WITH WHICH THE AUTHOR'S WORKS ARE ASSOCIATED PAYS AUQUEL APPARTIENT L'OEUVRE LITTERAIRE DE L'AUTEUR PAIS AL QUE PERTENCE LA OBRA LITERARIA DEL AUTOR	NUMBER OF TRANSLATIONS NOMBRE DE TRADUCTIONS NUMERO DE TRADUCCIONES					NUMBER OF TRANSLATING COUNTRIES IN 1975 NOMBRE DE PAYS TRADUCTEURS EN 1975 NUMERO DE PAISES TRADUCTORES EN 1975
		1975	1974	1970	1965	1961–65	
W. SCOTT	UNITED KINGDOM	30	25	27	25	130	13
K.M. SIMONOV ‡	U.S.S.R.	30	13	10	18	64	10
J.H. CHASE	UNITED KINGDOM	29	64	55	24	110	9
A. GREE	...	29	32	12	–	1	8
K.F. MAY	GERMANY	29	39	26	45	223	7
J.F. COOPER	UNITED STATES OF AMERICA	28	26	26	23	141	14
G. FLAUBERT	FRANCE	28	25	26	22	107	15
A. MORAVIA	ITALY	28	26	49	37	186	16
I. WALLACE	UNITED STATES OF AMERICA	28	11	15	9	30	6
R. ARTHUR	UNITED KINGDOM	27	18	5	–	–	7
L. CARROLL ‡	UNITED KINGDOM	27	17	17	11	65	15
F. FITZGERALD	UNITED STATES OF AMERICA	27	21	6	8	44	13
P. GALLICO	UNITED STATES OF AMERICA	27	28	23	–	4	8
G.G. GILMAN	UNITED KINGDOM	27	5	–	–	–	3
HOMER	GREECE	27	42	32	12	72	11
C. SCHULZ	UNITED STATES OF AMERICA	27	31	28	5	17	4
J. SWIFT	UNITED KINGDOM	27	15	23	17	99	11
V. HUGO	FRANCE	26	40	48	29	184	12
A. HUXLEY	UNITED KINGDOM	26	24	29	12	82	12
I. KIM	KOREA	26	9	5	–	–	9
B. RUSSELL	UNITED KINGDOM	26	25	46	26	132	12
L.D. TROCKIJ	U.S.S.R.	26	34	24	10	42	8
O. WILDE	UNITED KINGDOM	26	29	26	19	112	12
H.C. ANDERSEN	DENMARK	25	60	56	49	282	16
ARISTOTELES	GREECE	25	25	30	19	97	16
R. BRADBURY	UNITED STATES OF AMERICA	25	20	6	11	45	10
C. COLLODI ‡	ITALY	25	16	8	13	61	14
E. VON DANIKEN	SWITZERLAND	25	26	–	–	–	13
G. HEYER	UNITED KINGDOM	25	38	24	8	43	2
V. HOLT ‡	UNITED KINGDOM	25	43	17	9	43	12
J.W. GOETHE	GERMANY	25	35	37	35	180	13
R.E. GWYTHER–JONES	...	25	–	–	–	–	1
E. LOBSANG RAMPA	...	25	14	2	7	21	5
R. TAGORE ‡	INDIA	25	29	31	31	378	12
P.G. WODEHOUSE	UNITED KINGDOM	25	27	5	13	74	9
G.K. CHESTERTON	UNITED KINGDOM	24	14	7	3	70	12
J.O. CURWOOD	UNITED STATES OF AMERICA	24	17	10	4	43	4
Z. GREY	UNITED STATES OF AMERICA	24	21	42	25	146	5
E. HOXHA	ALBANIA	24	–	14	–	19	4
W.S. MAUGHAM	UNITED KINGDOM	24	52	50	43	213	9
H. MILLER	UNITED STATES OF AMERICA	24	31	21	25	112	9
MOLIERE	FRANCE	24	29	26	29	110	15
G. ORWELL	UNITED KINGDOM	24	21	13	5	27	12
STENDHAL	FRANCE	24	26	35	33	150	13
A.G. ARTEM'EVA ‡	U.S.S.R.	23	–	–	–	–	1
S. DE BEAUVOIR	FRANCE	23	27	12	25	85	7
C. BRONTE	UNITED KINGDOM	23	24	16	12	48	12
E. FROMM	UNITED STATES OF AMERICA	23	20	31	19	64	12
A. HAILEY	UNITED KINGDOM	23	23	14	2	19	16
G.W.F. HEGEL	GERMANY	23	15	14	15	48	9

Authors most frequently translated   8.13
Auteurs les plus traduits
Autores más traducidos

AUTHORS / AUTEURS / AUTORES	COUNTRY WITH WHICH THE AUTHOR'S WORKS ARE ASSOCIATED / PAYS AUQUEL APPARTIENT L'OEUVRE LITTERAIRE DE L'AUTEUR / PAIS AL QUE PERTENCE LA OBRA LITERARIA DEL AUTOR	NUMBER OF TRANSLATIONS / NOMBRE DE TRADUCTIONS / NUMERO DE TRADUCCIONES					NUMBER OF TRANS-LATING COUNTRIES IN 1975 / NOMBRE DE PAYS TRADUCTEURS EN 1975 / NUMERO DE PAISES TRADUCTORES EN 1975
		1975	1974	1970	1965	1961–65	
F. KAFKA	AUSTRIA	23	25	18	30	102	12
R. KIPLING	UNITED KINGDOM	23	22	22	21	123	13
H.H. KIRST	GERMANY	23	22	21	16	84	10
J. DE LA FONTAINE	FRANCE	23	7	16	9	48	8
A. DE SAINT-EXUPERY	FRANCE	23	18	21	17	87	16
J.M. SIMMEL	GERMAN	23	16	5	3	12	9
J. SPYRI	SWITZERLAND	23	15	21	11	83	9
A. CAMUS	FRANCE	22	34	37	47	155	13
K. CAPEK	CZECHOSLOVAKIA	22	14	12	12	74	13
J. COLE	UNITED STATES OF AMERICA	22	31	35	43	173	3
A. DANTE	ITALY	22	16	15	25	93	13
F. GARCIA LORCA	SPAIN	22	12	14	15	66	9
B. GRZIMEK	GERMANY	22	10	5	6	25	5
L. KENT	UNITED STATES OF AMERICA	22	26	32	35	140	3
F.P. KOROVKIN ‡	U.S.S.R.	22	—	—	—	1	1
D.H. LAWRENCE	UNITED KINGDOM	22	17	19	19	106	9
J.R. MACDONALD ‡	UNITED STATES OF AMERICA	22	18	12	8	44	15
R. ROLLAND	FRANCE	22	10	21	24	111	9
F. SAGAN	FRANCE	22	22	34	23	105	10
C. AJTMATOV ‡	U.S.S.R.	21	17	11	21	93	5
M. BOND	UNITED KINGDOM	21	20	4	4	18	8
A.C. CLARKE	UNITED KINGDOM	21	21	8	16	52	11
H. MELVILLE	UNITED STATES OF AMERICA	21	19	28	18	77	12
I. SHAW	UNITED STATES OF AMERICA	21	19	6	6	43	12
K. F. STROEV ‡	U.S.S.R.	21	—	—	—	—	1
M. DE CERVANTES	SPAIN	20	13	23	23	100	12
S. HASSEL ‡	DENMARK	20	21	13	11	34	8
HERGE ‡	BELGIUM	20	27	15	20	45	5
G. DE MAUPASSANT	FRANCE	20	39	46	43	216	13
F. PETRARCA	ITALY	20	4	6	3	13	12
K. ROBESON	...	20	34	5	—	—	5
M.N. SKATKIN ‡	U.S.S.R.	20	—	—	1	8	1
A.I. SOLOV'EV ‡	U.S.S.R.	20	2	—	—	—	1
J.R.R. TOLKIEN	UNITED KINGDOM	20	12	5	4	13	11

8.13 Authors most frequently translated
Auteurs les plus traduits
Autores más traducidos

GENERAL NOTE/NOTE GENERALE/NOTA GENERAL:
E—> IN ADDITION, IN 1975, THE BIBLE WAS
TRANSLATED 302 TIMES IN 26 COUNTRIES (IN 1974,
286 TIMES IN 26 COUNTRIES; TOTAL 1961–65: 1,122)
AND "ARABIAN NIGHTS" 37 TIMES IN 15 COUNTRIES
(IN 1974, 32 TIMES IN 14 COUNTRIES; TOTAL
1961–65: 134).
FOR RUSSIAN AUTHORS, THE SYSTEM OF TRANSLITE–
RATION OF CYRILLIC CHARACTERS ADOPTED BY THE
INTERNATIONAL ORGANIZATION FOR STANDARDIZATION
AND FOLLOWED BY "INDEX TRANSLATIONUM" HAS BEEN
USED. THE NUMBER OF TRANSLATIONS FOR THESE
AUTHORS, ALSO INCLUDES WORKS PUBLISHED IN THE
U.S.S.R. IN 1975, THESE FIGURES WERE: V.I.
LENIN, 293; L.I. BREZNEV, 92; F.M. DOSTOEVSKIJ,9;
M. GOR'KIJ, 30; L.N. TOLSTOJ,20; A.N. KOLMOGOROV,
48; C.P. CEHOV, 9; A.S. PUSKIN, 12; I.S.
TURGENEV, 8; N.V. GOGOL, 3; M. SOLOHOV, 19; K.M.
SIMONOV, 6; A.G. ARTEM'EVA, 23; F.P. KOROVKIN,
22; C. AJTMATOV, 13; K.F. STROEV, 21; M.N.
SKATKIN, 20; A.I. SOLOV'EV, 20.
FR—> EN OUTRE, IL EST PARU EN 1975, 302
TRADUCTIONS DE LA BIBLE DANS 26 PAYS (EN 1974,
286 DANS 26 PAYS; TOTAL 1961–65: 1,122); 37
TRADUCTIONS DES "MILLE ET UNE NUITS" DANS 15 PAYS
(EN 1974, 32 DANS 14 PAYS; TOTAL 1961–65: 134).
POUR LES AUTEURS RUSSES, ON A UTILISE LE SYSTEM
DE TRANSLITTERATION DES CARACTERES CYRILLIQUES
ETABLIS PAR L'ORGANISATION INTERNATIONALE DE
NORMALISATION ET ADOPTE PAR L'"INDEX
TRANSLATIONUM". LE NOMBRE DE TRADUCTIONS POUR CES
AUTEURS COMPREND EGALEMENT LES TRADUCTIONS PARUES
EN U.R.S.S. EN 1975 CES CHIFFRES ETAIENT LES
SUIVANTS: V.I. LENIN, 293; L.I. BREZNEV, 92; F.M.
DOSTOEVSKIJ, 9; M. GOR'KIJ, 30; L.N. TOLSTOJ, 20;
A.N. KOLMOGOROV, 48; C.P. CEHOV, 9; A.S. PUSKIN,
12; I.S. TURGENEV, 8; N.V. GOGOL, 3; M. SOLOHOV,
19; K.M. SIMONOV, 6; A.G. ARTEM'EVA, 23; F.P.
KOROVKIN, 22; C. AJTMATOV, 13; K.F. STROEV, 21;
M.N. SKATKIN, 20; A.I. SOLOV'EV, 20.
ESP> SE PUBLICARON ADEMAS, EN 1975, 302
TRADUCCIONES DE LA BIBLIA EN 26 PAISES (EN 1974,
286 EN 26 PAISES; DE 1961 A 1965 EN TOTAL:
1,122); 37 TRADUCCIONES DE "LAS MIL Y UNA NOCHES"
EN 15 PAISES (EN 1974, 32 EN 14 PAISES; DE 1961
A 1965 EN TOTAL: 134).
EN EL CASO DE LOS AUTORES RUSOS, SE HA UTILIZADO
EL SISTEMA DE TRANSCRIPCION DE LOS CARACTERES
CIRILICOS ESTABLECIDO POR LA ORGANIZACION INTER–
NACIONAL DE NORMALIZACION Y ADOPTADO POR EL
"INDEX TRANSLATIONUM". EL NUMERO DE TRADUC–
CIONES DE ESTOS AUTORES COMPRENDE TAMBIEN LAS
PUBLICADAS EN LA U.R.S.S. EN 1975, LAS CIFRAS
FUERON LAS SIGUIENTES: V.I. LENIN, 293; L.I.
BREZNEV, 92; F.M. DOSTOEVSKIJ, 9; M. GOR'KIJ, 30;
L.N. TOLSTOJ, 20; A.N. KOLMOGOROV, 48; C.P.
CEHOV, 9; A.S. PUSKIN, 12; I.S. TURGENEV, 8; N.V.
GOGOL, 3; M. SOLOHOV, 19; K.M. SIMONOV, 6; A.G.
ARTEM'EVA, 23; F.P. KOROVKIN, 22; C. AJTMATOV,
13; K.F. STROEV, 21; M.N. SKATKIN, 20; A.I.
SOLOV'EV, 20.

V.I. LENIN :
E—> SEE GENERAL NOTE.
FR—> VOIR LA NOTE GENERALE.
ESP> VEASE LA NOTA GENERAL.

A. CHRISTIE:
E—> INCLUDING 1 UNDER THE PEN–NAME OF M.
WESTMACOTT IN 1975.
FR—> DONT 1 SOUS LE PSEUDONYME DE M. WESTMACOTT
EN 1975.
ESP> DE LAS CUALES 1 CON EL SEUDONIMO DE M.
WESTMACOTT EN 1975.

L.I. BREZNEV:
E—> SEE GENERAL NOTE.
FR—> VOIR LA NOTE GENERALE.
ESP> VEASE LA NOTA GENERAL.

F.M. DOSTOEVSKIJ:
E—> SEE GENERAL NOTE.
FR—> VOIR LA NOTE GENERALE.
ESP> VEASE LA NOTA GENERAL.

M. GOR'KIJ:
E—> SEE GENERAL NOTE.
FR—> VOIR LA NOTE GENERALE.
ESP> VEASE LA NOTA GENERAL.

L.N. TOLSTOJ:
E—> SEE GENERAL NOTE.
FR—> VOIR LA NOTE GENERALE.
ESP> VEASE LA NOTA GENERAL.

F.W. DIXON:
E—> INCLUDING 37 UNDER THE PEN–NAME OF C.
KEENE IN 1975.
FR—> DONT 37 SOUS LE PSEUDONYME DE C. KEENE EN
1975.
ESP> DE LAS CUALES 37 CON EL SEUDONIMO DE C.
KEENE EN 1975.

M. TWAIN:
E—> INCLUDING 1 UNDER THE NAME OF S.L. CLEMENS
IN 1975.
FR—> DONT 1 SOUS LE NOM DE S.L. CLEMENS EN 1975
ESP> DE LAS CUALES 1 CON EL NOMBRE DE S.L.
CLEMENS EN 1975.

A.N. KOLMOGOROV:
E—> SEE GENERAL NOTE.
FR—> VOIR LA NOTE GENERALE.
ESP> VEASE LA NOTA GENERAL.

A.P. CEHOV:
E—> SEE GENERAL NOTE.
FR—> VOIR LA NOTE GENERALE.
ESP> VEASE LA NOTA GENERAL.

A.S. PUSKIN:
E—> SEE GENERAL NOTE.
FR—> VOIR LA NOTE GENERALE.
ESP> VEASE LA NOTA GENERAL.

H. ROBBINS:
E—> INCLUDING 10 UNDER THE PEN–NAME OF H.
RUBIN IN 1975.
FR—> DONT 10 SOUS LE PSEUDONYME DE H. RUBIN EN
1975.
ESP> DE LAS CUALES 10 CON EL SEUDONIMO DE H.
RUBIN EN 1975.

C. BROWN:
E—> INCLUDING 2 UNDER THE PEN–NAME OF A.G.
YATES IN 1975.
FR—> DONT 2 SOUS LE PSEUDONYME DE A.G. YATES
EN 1975.
ESP> DE LAS CUALES 2 CON EL SEUDONIMO DE A.G.
YATES EN 1975.

E. HUNTER:
E—> INCLUDING 18 UNDER THE PEN–NAME OF E.
MCBAIN IN 1975.
FR—> DONT 18 SOUS LE PSEUDONYME DE E. MCBAIN
EN 1975.
ESP> DE LAS CUALES 18 CON EL SEUDONIMO DE E.
MCBAIN EN 1975.

Authors most frequently translated 8.13
Auteurs les plus traduits
Autores más traducidos

I.S. TURGENEV:
  E—> SEE GENERAL NOTE.
  FR-> VOIR LA NOTE GENERALE.
  ESP> VEASE LA NOTA GENERAL.

N.V. GOGOL:
  E—> SEE GENERAL NOTE.
  FR-> VOIR LA NOTE GENERALE.
  ESP> VEASE LA NOTA GENERAL.

M. SOLOHOV:
  E—> SEE GENERAL NOTE.
  FR-> VOIR LA NOTE GENERALE.
  ESP> VEASE LA NOTA GENERAL.

K.M. SIMONOV:
  E—> SEE GENERAL NOTE.
  FR-> VOIR LA NOTE GENERALE.
  ESP> VEASE LA NOTA GENERAL.

L. CARROLL:
  E—> INCLUDING 5 UNDER THE PEN—NAME OF C.L.
DODGSON IN 1975.
  FR-> DONT 5 SOUS LE PSEUDONYME DE C.L. DODGSON
EN 1975.
  ESP> DE LAS CUALES 5 CON EL SEUDONIMO DE C.L.
DODGSON EN 1975.

C. COLLODI:
  E—> INCLUDING 3 UNDER THE PEN—NAME OF C.
LORENZINI IN 1975.
  FR-> DONT 3 SOUS LE PSEUDONYME DE C. LORENZINI
EN 1975.
  ESP> DE LAS CUALES 3 CON EL SEUDONIMO DE C.
LORENZINI EN 1975.

V. HOLT:
  E—> INCLUDING 7 UNDER THE FOLLOWING PEN—NAMES
IN 1975: P. CARR, 3; E HIBBERT, 3; J. PLAIDY, 1.
  FR-> DONT 7 SOUS LES PSEUDONYMES SUIVANTS EN
1975: P. CARR, 3; E. HIBBERT, 3; J. PLAIDY, 1.
  ESP> DE LAS CUALES 7 CON LOS SEUDONIMOS
SIGUIENTES EN 1975: P. CARR, 3; E. HIBBERT, 3;
J. PLAIDY, 1.

R. TAGORE:
  E—> THE NUMBER OF TRANSLATIONS ALSO INCLUDES 9
WORKS PUBLISHED IN INDIA IN 1975.
  FR-> LE NOMBRE DE TRADUCTIONS COMPREND EGALE-
MENT 9 TRADUCTIONS PARUES EN INDE EN 1975.
  ESP> EL NUMERO DE TRADUCCIONES COMPRENDE TAM-
BIEN LAS PUBLICADAS EN LA INDIA (9 EN 1975).

A.G. ARTEM'EVA:
  E—> SEE GENERAL NOTE.
  FR-> VOIR LA NOTE GENERALE.
  ESP> VEASE LA NOTA GENERAL.

F.P. KOROVKIN:
  E—> SEE GENERAL NOTE.
  FR-> VOIR LA NOTE GENERALE.
  ESP> VEASE LA NOTA GENERAL.

J.R. MACDONALD:
  E—> INCLUDING 2 UNDER THE PEN—NAME OF K.
MILLAR IN 1975.
  FR-> DONT 2 SOUS LE PSEUDONYME DE K. MILLAR EN
1975.
  ESP> DE LAS CUALES 2 CON EL SEUDONIMO DE K.
MILLAR EN 1975.

C. AJTMATOV:
  E—> SEE GENERAL NOTE.
  FR-> VOIR LA NOTE GENERALE.
  ESP> VEASE LA NOTA GENERAL.

K.F. STROEV:
  E—> SEE GENERAL NOTE.
  FR-> VOIR LA NOTE GENERALE.
  ESP> VEASE LA NOTA GENERAL.

S. HASSEL:
  E—> INCLUDING 1 UNDER THE PEN—NAME OF S. HAZEL
IN 1975.
  FR-> DONT 1 SOUS LE PSEUDONYME DE S. HAZEL EN
1975.
  ESP> DE LAS CUALES 1 CON EL SEUDONIMO DE S.
HAZEL EN 1975.

HERGE:
  E—> INCLUDING 10 UNDER THE PEN—NAME OF G. REMY
IN 1975.
  FR-> DONT 10 SOUS LE PSEUDONYME DE G. REMY EN
1975.
  ESP> DE LAS CUALES 10 CON EL SEUDONIMO DE G.
REMY EN 1975.

M.N. SKATKIN:
  E—> SEE GENERAL NOTE.
  FR-> VOIR LA NOTE GENERALE.
  ESP> VEASE LA NOTA GENERAL.

A.I. SOLOV'EV:
  E—> SEE GENERAL NOTE.
  FR-> VOIR LA NOTE GENERALE.
  ESP> VEASE LA NOTA GENERAL.

8.14 Daily general-interest newspapers: number and circulation (total and per 1,000 inhabitants)

Journaux quotidiens d'information générale: nombre et tirage (total et pour 1 000 habitants)

Periódicos diarios de información general: número y tirada (total y por 1 000 habitantes)

NUMBER OF COUNTRIES AND TERRITORIES PRESENTED IN THIS TABLE: 165
NOMBRE DE PAYS ET DE TERRITOIRES PRESENTES DANS CE TABLEAU: 165
NUMERO DE PAISES Y DE TERRITORIOS PRESENTADOS EN ESTE CUADRO: 165

COUNTRY PAYS PAIS	NUMBER NOMBRE NUMERO				TOTAL (IN THOUSANDS / EN MILLIERS) ESTIMATED CIRCULATION / TIRAGE (ESTIMATION) / TIRADA (ESTIMACION)				PER 1 000 INHABITANTS POUR 1 000 HABITANTS POR 1 000 HABITANTES			
	1965	1970	1976	1977	1965	1970	1976	1977	1965	1970	1976	1977
	(1)	(2)	(3)	(4)	(5)	(6)	(7)	(8)	(9)	(10)	(11)	(12)
AFRICA												
ALGERIA	5	4	4	4	170	275	222	236	14	19	13	13
ANGOLA	...	...	5	...	...	...	119	...	...	...	19	...
BENIN	...	2	1	...	...	2	1	...	...	0.7	0.3	...
BOTSWANA	...	2	2	2	...	13	17	17	...	22	25	24
BURUNDI	...	1	1	...	...	0.3	...	...	...	0.1	...	...
CHAD	1	...	4	...	1.5	...	...	...	0.5	...	...	...
CONGO	4	3	10	...	1.7	745	3 012	...	2	22	79	...
EGYPT	...	14	2	...	...	...	...	...	...	...	...	...
EQUATORIAL GUINEA	2	...	2	2	1.1	...	...	...	4	...	1	1
ETHIOPIA ‡	8	8	3	2	34	28	35	35	2	...	1	...
GABON	...	...	1	...	...	...	435	...	...	...	42	...
GHANA	3	1	4	...	225	...	10	...	29	...	2	...
GUINEA	1	1	1	...	...	5	6	...	...	1	11	...
GUINEA-BISSAU	...	1	1	...	...	...	63	...	...	...	13	...
IVORY COAST	2	3	3	...	35	44	...	...	9	10	13	...
KENYA	5	4	3	...	69	155	154	...	7	14	11	...
LESOTHO	...	...	3	...	...	7	1.3	...	...	5	1	...
LIBERIA ‡	...	2	3	...	...	...	8	...	...	...	1	...
LIBYAN ARAB JAMAHIRIYA	4	8	2	...	...	53	64	...	...	8	...	...
MADAGASCAR	...	13	...	12	...	...	...	...	...	...	26	...

	(1)	(2)	(3)	(4)	(5)	(6)	(7)	(8)	(9)	(10)	(11)	(12)
MALAWI	...	...	2	...	...	...	18	18	...	...	3	3
MALI	...	...	2	2	...	...	...	...	...	...	...	...
MAURITIUS	12	14	10	10	93	243	75	85	122	...	84	94
MOROCCO ‡	...	6	10	...	...	55	190	...	...	...	4	...
MOZAMBIQUE ‡	...	...	2	...	...	...	42	...	...	...	...	...
NAMIBIA	2	3	3	...	...	...	18	...	...	...	0.6	1
NIGER	1	...	1	1	...	...	3	3	...	...	...	...
NIGERIA ‡	22	21	19	...	391	319	527	...	8	...	81	90
REUNION ‡	2	...	3	3	23	...	42	44	58	...	...	...
RWANDA	...	...	1	1	...	...	0.2	0.2	...	...	0.1	0.1
SENEGAL	...	1	1	...	20	20	25	...	6	5	5	...
SEYCHELLES	1	2	2	1	...	2	3.5	4	...	38	59	65
SIERRA LEONE	...	5	2	...	...	45	...	...	...	18	...	...
SOMALIA	1	1	1	...	...	4.5	...	...	...	2	...	...
SOUTH AFRICA	21	22	24	...	...	...	1 728	...	...	...	66	...
SUDAN ‡	9	—	4	...	...	...	26	...	...	...	...	...
SWAZILAND	—	1	1	...	—	—	5	...	—	—	10	...
TOGO	1	...	1	...	81	...	7	...	18	...	3	...
TUNISIA ‡	5	7	5	5	63	83	232	...	7	...	...	...
UGANDA	5	...	2	...	...	...	35	...	...	8	3	...
UNITED REPUBLIC OF CAMEROON	...	2	3	...	...	17	30	...	...	3	5	...
UNITED REPUBLIC OF TANZANIA ‡	6	...	2	2	...	...	131	...	...	...	...	...
UPPER VOLTA	...	1	1	...	...	1.5	1.5	133	...	0.3	8	8
ZAIRE ‡	8	13	6	...	...	200	45	...	7	9	0.2	...
ZAMBIA	1	1	2	...	25	57	101	...	...	14	20	...
ZIMBABWE	4	4	2	...	63	83	78	...	14	16	12	...
AMERICA, NORTH												
ANTIGUA	...	1	2	...	...	...	10	...	...	...	137	...
BAHAMAS	2	3	3	...	16	28	25	...	114	162	118	...
BARBADOS	2	1	1	...	27	23	29	...	113	95	115	...
BELIZE	2	1	2	...	...	4	...	...	...	33	45	...
BERMUDA	...	...	2	2	16	11	24	25	333	198	428	442
CANADA ‡	115	...	123	122	4 271	...	5 066	5 150	217	...	219	221
COSTA RICA	...	8	6	...	...	177	210	...	...	102	104	...
CUBA	7	16	16	...	...	...	...	...	28	...	...	...
DOMINICAN REPUBLIC ‡	...	...	10	...	98	365	208	...	...	...	...	...
EL SALVADOR ‡	...	13	12	...	...	...	331	...	...	...	...	...
GRENADA ‡	1	2	1	...	...	2.6	...	...	12	...	...	...
GUADELOUPE	1	2	2	...	1.2	24	23	...	...	74	...	...
GUATEMALA ‡	...	8	9	...	...	...	214	...	...	...	63	...
HAITI	6	7	6	...	...	...	92	...	6	...	...	...
HONDURAS ‡	...	...	8	...	23	79	140	...	...	19	20	...
JAMAICA	2	...	3	3	...	...	124	101	...	...	60	49
MARTINIQUE	1	2	1	1	...	...	25	27	...	...	68	72
MEXICO ‡	220	200	268	352	4 763	33	3 994	...	115	147	...	...
NETHERLANDS ANTILLES	...	5	5	...	...	...	54	...	...	...	224	...
NICARAGUA	6	...	6	...	81	...	113	...	50	...	51	...

DAILY NEWSPAPERS / JOURNAUX QUOTIDIENS / PERIODICOS DIARIOS

COUNTRY / PAYS / PAIS	NUMBER / NOMBRE / NUMERO				ESTIMATED CIRCULATION / TIRAGE (ESTIMATION) / TIRADA (ESTIMACION) — TOTAL (IN THOUSANDS / EN MILLIERS / EN MILLARES)				PER 1 000 INHABITANTS / POUR 1 000 HABITANTS / POR 1 000 HABITANTES			
	1965 (1)	1970 (2)	1976 (3)	1977 (4)	1965 (5)	1970 (6)	1976 (7)	1977 (8)	1965 (9)	1970 (10)	1976 (11)	1977 (12)
PANAMA	10	7	6	...	101	130	136	...	82	91	79	...
PUERTO RICO	4	4	4	...	166	495	430	...	64	182	134	...
ST. KITTS - NEVIS - ANGUILLA	...	2	1	...	...	...	1.5	...	...	...	23	...
ST. LUCIA	...	...	1	...	...	...	4	...	...	...	36	...
TRINIDAD AND TOBAGO ‡	3	3	3	...	97	140	144	...	100	136	...	...
UNITED STATES OF AMERICA ‡	1 751	1 763	1 781	1 829	60 358	62 108	61 714	62 159	311	303	287	287
U.S. VIRGIN ISLANDS	4	3	4	...	9	14	18	...	180	237	192	...
AMERICA, SOUTH												
ARGENTINA ‡	171	179	142	...	3 312	4 247	2 682	...	149	...	...	...
BOLIVIA ‡	9	21	13	...	95	208	150	...	22	...	26	...
BRAZIL	...	...	299	318	...	...	4 895	5 083	...	...	45	45
CHILE ‡	...	...	48	42	...	...	...	...	...	...	...	...
COLOMBIA ‡	39	...	42	...	...	...	1 330	...	...	...	...	...
ECUADOR ‡	23	25	29	37	...	250	332	350	43	41	45	46
FRENCH GUIANA	1	1	1	1	1.5	1.5	1.5	...	...	29	24	...
GUYANA	...	3	2	...	...	44	50	...	...	61	63	...
PARAGUAY ‡	...	11	4	...	...	99	106	828	...	...	39	51
PERU ‡	69	85	36	30	...	1 660	896	...	...	...	56	...
SURINAME	5	5	...	7	17	20	...	33	52	54	...	74
URUGUAY	...	...	30	26	...	...	...	...	...	...	150	...
VENEZUELA	33	...	54	54	608	...	1 850	2 263	70	...	...	178
ASIA												
AFGHANISTAN ‡	17	18	15	17	94	101	71	77	6	6	...	4
BANGLADESH ‡	...	...	28	...	...	...	350	...	...	...	...	...
BURMA	...	10	7	...	...	...	329	...	...	...	11	...
CYPRUS ‡	10	16	13	...	129	68	72	...	217	107	...	...
DEMOCRATIC KAMPUCHEA	14	...	17	...	...	...	...	...	...	...	...	...
HONG KONG ‡	47	57	82	83	1 325	...	...	1 393	368	...	...	...
INDIA ‡	525	...	875	929	6 323	...	9 338	10 672	13	...	...	...
INDONESIA ‡	85	33	178	...	709	222	2 358	...	...	...	...	...
IRAN ‡	18	4	23	...	...	...	473	...	...	...	...	...
IRAQ ‡	...	...	7	...	...	...	202	...	...	...	...	...
ISRAEL ‡	26	24	24	27	480	600	801	...	...	206	231	...
JAPAN	185	178	176	177	44 480	53 304	60 782	62 221	450	511	539	546
JORDAN ‡	7	5	6	5	17	56	80	85	9	24	29	29
KOREA, DEMOCRATIC PEOPLE'S REPUB. OF ‡	...	...	11	...	...	...	1 000	...	...	...	...	...
KOREA, REPUBLIC OF	41	44	36	44	...	4 396	6 010	7 169	136	136	168	197

	(1)	(2)	(3)	(4)	(5)	(6)	(7)	(8)	(9)	(10)	(11)	(12)
KUWAIT	4	5	7	7		20	180	180		27	175	159
LAO PEOPLE'S DEMOCRATIC REPUBLIC									4			
LEBANON ‡	37		3		10		281		84			
MACAU ‡	6	6	6		180		28			75	75	
MALAYSIA ‡	33	37	37		30	783	1 834		107			
MALDIVES			1	1								
MONGOLIA		2	1			133	112					
NEPAL ‡	16	16	29		28	27	96					
PAKISTAN ‡	95		103				965		3			
PHILIPPINES ‡		17	17	108	1 839	502	919		37	106		
SAUDI ARABIA ‡	7	5	12		55	60	143		8	8		
SINGAPORE	12	12	10	10	440		477	497			209	215
SRI LANKA	13	24	29	22	398	612			39	49		
SYRIAN ARAB REPUBLIC ‡		5	7				65					
THAILAND	33	35	24	23		749			13	21		
TURKEY	375	437	498	493								
UNITED ARAB EMIRATES									8			
VIET-NAM			3	3			2					
YEMEN		6		5		56						8
YEMEN, DEMOCRATIC ‡			4				12	250		10	9	5
EUROPE												
ALBANIA ‡	2	3	2		79	105	115		42		45	
ANDORRA			6									
AUSTRIA	36	33	30	31	1 806		2 436	2 529	249		324	336
BELGIUM	54	49	30	27	2 701		2 340	2 369	285		238	241
BULGARIA	11	12	12	12	1 408	1 642	2 098	2 083	172	193	239	237
CZECHOSLOVAKIA	27	28	29	29	3 971	3 641	4 398	4 453	280	254	295	296
DENMARK	67	58	48	49	1 649	1 790	1 756	1 840	347	363	346	362
FINLAND	68	67	61	60			2 185	2 202			462	465
FRANCE	121	106	92	96	12 041	12 067	10 615	10 863	247	238	201	205
GERMAN DEMOCRATIC REPUBLIC	40		39	39	7 181		8 108	8 317	422		483	496
GERMANY, FEDERAL REPUBLIC OF ‡	1 115	1 093	413	412	19 264	19 701	25 170	25 968	326	325	409	423
GIBRALTAR		2	1	1		6	3	3		242	100	100
GREECE	112	110	108	112		705				80		
HOLY SEE	1	1	1			70	70					
HUNGARY	24	27	27	27	1 809	2 207	2 481	2 585	178	213	235	243
ICELAND	5	5	6	6		86	121	123		430	550	554
IRELAND	7	7	6	7	702	686	699	702	244	233	221	220
ITALY	92	73	75	72	5 811	7 700	6 137	5 491	112	143	109	97
LIECHTENSTEIN		1	2				12	11	476	260		
LUXEMBOURG ‡	7		7		158		150				527	
MALTA		6	6	5			11					
MONACO		3	3	3								
NETHERLANDS ‡	88	169	67		3 598	4 100	4 371		293	315	420	420
NORWAY ‡	84	81	81	82	1 431	1 487	1 705	1 740	384	383	423	430
POLAND	42	43	44	44	5 246	6 832	8 284	8 331	167	210	241	240

DAILY NEWSPAPERS / JOURNAUX QUOTIDIENS / PERIODICOS DIARIOS

COUNTRY / PAYS / PAIS	NUMBER / NOMBRE / NUMERO				TOTAL (IN THOUSANDS / EN MILLIERS) ESTIMATED CIRCULATION / TIRAGE (ESTIMATION) / TIRADA (ESTIMACION)				PER 1 000 INHABITANTS / POUR 1 000 HABITANTES / POR 1 000 HABITANTES			
	1965	1970	1976	1977	1965	1970	1976	1977	1965	1970	1976	1977
	(1)	(2)	(3)	(4)	(5)	(6)	(7)	(8)	(9)	(10)	(11)	(12)
PORTUGAL	29	33	30	28	622	743	609	527	68	86	63	54
ROMANIA	33	55	32	34	2 993	3 422	3 338	3 711	157	169	156	171
SAN MARINO	...	3	3	3	...	1.3	1.3	...	...	68	65	...
SPAIN	...	116	134	143	...	3 450	4 254	4 710	...	102	118	128
SWEDEN	119	114	112	112	3 909	4 324	4 428	4 358	505	537	539	528
SWITZERLAND	132	117	95	91	2 210	2 318	2 574	2 622	377	375	406	414
UNITED KINGDOM	110	...	...	...	26 100	...	...	22 900	482	...	...	410
YUGOSLAVIA	23	24	26	26	1 755	1 738	2 073	2 085	90	85	96	96
OCEANIA												
AMERICAN SAMOA	1	1	1	1	1	2.6	2	3.8	40	90	65	112
AUSTRALIA	61	58	65	60	4 236	4 028	5 093	4 365	372	322	366	310
COOK ISLANDS	1	1	1	...	0.6	...	1.2	...	29	...	67	...
FIJI	1	1	2	...	0.8	16	38	...	17	31	66	...
FRENCH POLYNESIA	...	4	4	4	...	10	13	13	...	93	98	98
GUAM	1	2	1	1	...	17	18	20	...	187	174	195
NEW CALEDONIA ‡	1	1	2	2	6	7	18	22	66	64	133	162
NEW ZEALAND ‡	...	40	39	...	...	1 058	848	...	...	376	...	...
PAPUA NEW GUINEA	...	1	1	1	...	...	20	25	...	...	7	9
U.S.S.R.												
U.S.S.R.	639	639	687	686	60 948	81 633	101 929	102 462	264	336	397	396
BYELORUSSIAN S.S.R.	...	24	27	27	...	1 765	2 315	2 368	...	195	247	251

GENERAL NOTE/NOTE GENERALE/NOTA GENERAL:

E—> IT IS KNOWN OR BELIEVED THAT NO DAILY GENERAL-INTEREST NEWSPAPERS ARE PRODUCED IN THE FOLLOWING 34 COUNTRIES AND TERRITORIES:
AFRICA: CAPE VERDE, COMORO, DJIBOUTI, GAMBIA, ST HELENA, SAO TOME AND PRINCIPE, WESTERN SAHARA.
NORTH AMERICA: BRITISH VIRGIN ISLANDS, CAYMAN ISLANDS, DOMINICA, GREENLAND, MONTSERRAT, PANAMA (FORMER CANAL ZONE), ST PIERRE AND MIQUELON, ST. VINCENT AND THE GRENADINES, TURKS AND CAICOS ISLANDS.
SOUTH AMERICA: FALKLAND ISLANDS (MALVINAS).
ASIA: BAHRAIN, BHUTAN, BRUNEI, EAST TIMOR, OMAN, QATAR.
OCEANIA: KIRIBATI, NAURU, NEW HEBRIDES, NIUE, NORFOLK ISLAND, PACIFIC ISLANDS, SAMOA, SOLOMON ISLANDS, TOKELAU ISLANDS, TONGA.

FR—> LES RENSEIGNEMENTS DISPONIBLES INDIQUENT OU PERMETTENT DE PENSER QU'IL NE PARAIT AUCUN JOURNAL QUOTIDIEN D'INFORMATION GENERALE DANS LES 34 PAYS OU TERRITOIRES DONT LA LISTE SUIT:
AFRIQUE: CAP VERT, COMORES, DJIBOUTI, GAMBIE, SAINTE HELENE, SAO TOME ET PRINCIPE, SAHARA OCCI-DENTAL.
AMERIQUE DU NORD: ILES VIERGES BRITANNIQUES, ILES CAIMANES, DOMINIQUE, GROENLAND, MONTSERRAT, PANAMA (ANCIENNE ZONE DU CANAL), SAINT-PIERRE-ET-MIQUELON, ST. VINCENT ET LES GRENADINES, ILES TURQUES ET CAIQUES.
AMERIQUE DU SUD: ILES FALKLAND (MALVINAS).
ASIE: BAHREIN, BHUTAN, BRUNEI, OMAN, QATAR. TIMOR ORIENTAL.
OCEANIE: KIRIBATI, NAURU, NOUVELLES HEBRIDES, NIOUE, ILE NORFOLK, ILES DU PACIFIQUE, ILES SALOMON, SAMOA, ILES TOKELAOU, TONGA.

SUDAN (CONT.):
FR—> POUR 1976, LE CHIFFRE RELATIF AU TIRAGE NE
SE REFERE QU'A 2 QUOTIDIENS.
ESP> EN 1976, LA CIFRA RELATIVA A LA TIRADA SE
REFIERE A 2 DIARIOS SOLAMENTE.

TUNISIA:
E—> DATA CONCERN MORNING DAILIES ONLY. IN
1976, THE CIRCULATION FIGURE REFERS ONLY TO 4
DAILIES.
FR—> LES DONNEES SE RAPPORTENT AUX QUOTIDIENS
DU MATIN SEULEMENT. POUR 1976, LE CHIFFRE RELATIF
AU TIRAGE NE SE REFERE QU'A 4 QUOTIDIENS.
ESP> LOS DATOS SE REFIEREN A LOS DIARIOS DE LA
MANANA SOLAMENTE. EN 1976, LA CIFRA RELATIVA A LA
TIRADA SOLO CONCIERNE 4 DIARIOS.

UNITED REPUBLIC OF TANZANIA:
E—> DATA CONCERN MORNING DAILIES ONLY.
FR—> LES DONNEES SE RAPPORTENT AUX QUOTIDIENS
DU MATIN SEULEMENT.
ESP> LOS DATOS SE REFIEREN A LOS DIARIOS DE LA
MANANA SOLAMENTE.

ZAIRE:
E—> FOR 1976, THE CIRCULATION FIGURE REFERS
TO 2 DAILIES ONLY.
FR—> POUR 1976, LE CHIFFRE RELATIF AU TIRAGE NE
SE REFERE QU'A 2 QUOTIDIENS.
ESP> EN 1976, LA CIFRA RELATIVA A LA TIRADA SE
REFIERE A 2 DIARIOS SOLAMENTE.

CANADA:
E—> ALL DATA CONCERNING 1965 REFER TO ENGLISH
AND FRENCH LANGUAGE DAILIES ONLY.
FR—> TOUTES LES DONNEES QUI CONCERNENT L'ANNEE
1965 SE REFERENT AUX QUOTIDIENS DE LANGUE ANGLAISE
ET FRANCAISE SEULEMENT.
ESP> LOS DATOS RELATIVOS AL AÑO 1965 SE REFIEREN
A LOS DIARIOS DE LENGUA INGLESA Y FRANCESA SOLA—
MENTE.

DOMINICAN REPUBLIC:
E—> FOR 1976, THE CIRCULATION FIGURE REFERS
TO 7 DAILIES ONLY.
FR—> POUR 1976, LE CHIFFRE RELATIF AU TIRAGE NE
SE REFERE QU'A 7 QUOTIDIENS.
ESP> EN 1976, LA CIFRA RELATIVA A LA TIRADA SE
REFIERE A 7 DIARIOS SOLAMENTE.

EL SALVADOR:
E—> DATA ON CIRCULATION REFER, IN 1970, TO
10 DAILIES, AND IN 1976 TO 9 DAILIES ONLY.
FR—> LES DONNEES RELATIVES AU TIRAGE CONCERNENT
10 QUOTIDIENS EN 1970 ET 9 QUOTIDIENS EN 1976.
ESP> LOS DATOS RELATIVOS A LA TIRADA SE REFIEREN
A 10 DIARIOS EN 1970 Y A 9 EN 1976.

GRENADA:
E—> FOR 1970, THE CIRCULATION FIGURE REFERS
TO 1 DAILY ONLY.
FR—> POUR 1970, LE CHIFFRE RELATIF AU TIRAGE NE
SE REFERE QU'A 1 QUOTIDIEN.
ESP> EN 1970, LA CIFRA RELATIVA A LA TIRADA SOLO
REFIERE A 1 DIARIO.

ESP> LA INFORMACION DISPONIBLE INDICA Ó PERMITE
PENSAR QUE NO SE PUBLICA NINGUN PERIODICO DIARIO
DE INFORMACION GENERAL EN LOS 34 PAISES Y TERRI—
TORIOS SIGUIENTES:
AFRICA: CABO VERDE, COMORES, YIBUTI, GAMBIA,
SANTA ELENA, SANTO TOME Y PRINCIPE, SAHARA
OCCIDENTAL.
AMERICA DEL NORTE: ISLAS VIRGENES BRITANNICAS,
ISLAS CAIMAN, DOMINICA GROENLANDIA, MONTSERRAT,
PANAMA (ANTIGUA ZONA DEL CANAL), SAN PEDRO Y
MIQUELON, SAN VINCENTE Y GRANADINAS, ISLAS TURCAS
Y CAICOS.
AMERICA DEL SUR: ISLAS FALKLAND (MALVINAS).
ASIA: BAHREIN, BUTAN, BRUNEI, TIMOR ORIENTAL,
OMAN Y QATAR.
OCEANIA: KIRIBATI, NAURU, NUEVAS HEBRIDAS,
NIUE, ISLAS NORFOLK, ISLAS DEL PACIFICO, SAMOA,
ISLAS SALOMON, ISLAS TOKELAU Y TONGA.

ETHIOPIA:
E—> FOR 1970, THE CIRCULATION FIGURE REFERS
TO 6 DAILIES ONLY.
FR—> POUR 1970, LE CHIFFRE RELATIF AU TIRAGE NE
SE REFERE QU'A 6 QUOTIDIENS.
ESP> EN 1970, LA CIFRA RELATIVA A LA TIRADA SE
REFIERE A 6 DIARIOS SOLAMENTE.

LIBERIA:
E—> FOR 1976, THE CIRCULATION FIGURE REFERS
TO 2 DAILIES ONLY.
FR—> POUR 1976, LE CHIFFRE RELATIF AU TIRAGE NE
SE REFERE QU'A 2 QUOTIDIENS.
ESP> EN 1976, LA CIFRA RELATIVA A LA TIRADA SE
REFIERE A 2 DIARIOS SOLAMENTE.

MOROCCO:
E—> DATA ON CIRCULATION REFER, IN 1970, TO
10 DAILIES, AND IN 1976 TO 7 DAILIES ONLY.
FR—> LES DONNEES RELATIVES AU TIRAGE CONCERNENT
10 QUOTIDIENS EN 1970 ET 7 QUOTIDIENS EN 1976.
ESP> LOS DATOS RELATIVOS A LA TIRADA SE REFIEREN
A 10 DIARIOS EN 1970 Y 7 EN 1976.

MOZAMBIQUE:
E—> FOR 1970, THE CIRCULATION FIGURE REFERS
TO 5 DAILIES ONLY.
FR—> POUR 1970, LE CHIFFRE RELATIF AU TIRAGE NE
SE REFERE QU'A 5 QUOTIDIENS.
ESP> EN 1970, LA CIFRA RELATIVA A LA TIRADA SE
REFIERE A 5 DIARIOS SOLAMENTE.

NIGERIA:
E—> DATA ON CIRCULATION REFER, IN 1970, TO
15 DAILIES, AND IN 1976 TO 8 DAILIES ONLY.
FR—> LES DONNEES RELATIVES AU TIRAGE CONCERNENT
15 QUOTIDIENS EN 1970 ET 8 QUOTIDIENS EN 1976.
ESP> LOS DATOS RELATIVOS A LA TIRADA SE REFIEREN
A 15 DIARIOS EN 1970 Y A 8 EN 1976.

SUDAN:
E—> FOR 1976, THE CIRCULATION FIGURE REFERS
TO 2 DAILIES ONLY.

COLOMBIA:
E—> FOR 1976, THE CIRCULATION FIGURE REFERS
TO 35 DAILIES ONLY.
FR—> POUR 1976, LE CHIFFRE RELATIF AU TIRAGE NE
SE REFERE QU'A 35 QUOTIDIENS.
ESP> EN 1976, LA CIFRA RELATIVA A LA TIRADA SE
REFIERE A 35 DIARIOS SOLAMENTE.

ECUADOR:
E—> DATA SHOWN FOR 1977 REFER TO 1978.
FR—> LES DONNEES INDIQUEES POUR 1977 CORRESPON-
DENT A 1978.
ESP> LOS DATOS INDICADOS EN 1977 CORRESPONDEN A
1978.

PARAGUAY:
E—> FOR 1970, THE CIRCULATION FIGURE REFERS
TO 5 DAILIES ONLY.
FR—> POUR 1970, LE CHIFFRE RELATIF AU TIRAGE NE
SE REFERE QU'A 5 QUOTIDIENS.
ESP> EN 1970, LA CIFRA RELATIVA A LA TIRADA SE
REFIERE A 5 DIARIOS SOLAMENTE.

PERU:
E—> FOR 1970, THE CIRCULATION FIGURE REFERS
TO 59 DAILIES ONLY.
FR—> POUR 1970, LE CHIFFRE RELATIF AU TIRAGE NE
SE REFERE QU'A 59 QUOTIDIENS.
ESP> EN 1970, LA CIFRA RELATIVA A LA TIRADA SE
REFIERE A 59 DIARIOS SOLAMENTE.

AFGHANISTAN:
E—> FOR 1976, THE CIRCULATION FIGURE REFERS
TO 10 DAILIES ONLY.
FR—> POUR 1976, LE CHIFFRE RELATIF AU TIRAGE NE
SE REFERE QU'A 10 QUOTIDIENS.
ESP> EN 1976, LA CIFRA RELATIVA A LA TIRADA SE
REFIERE A 10 DIARIOS SOLAMENTE.

BANGLADESH:
E—> FOR 1976, THE CIRCULATION FIGURE REFERS
TO 19 DAILIES ONLY.
FR—> POUR 1976, LE CHIFFRE RELATIF AU TIRAGE NE
SE REFERE QU'A 19 QUOTIDIENS.
ESP> EN 1976, LA CIFRA RELATIVA A LA TIRADA SE
REFIERE A 19 DIARIOS SOLAMENTE.

CYPRUS:
E—> FOR 1976, THE CIRCULATION FIGURE REFERS
TO 10 DAILIES ONLY.
FR—> POUR 1976, LE CHIFFRE RELATIF AU TIRAGE NE
SE REFERE QU'A 10 QUOTIDIENS.
ESP> EN 1976, LA CIFRA RELATIVA A LA TIRADA SE
REFIERE A 10 DIARIOS SOLAMENTE.

HONG KONG:
E—> FOR 1977, THE CIRCULATION FIGURE REFERS
TO 19 DAILIES ONLY.
FR—> POUR 1977, LE CHIFFRE RELATIF AU TIRAGE NE
SE REFERE QU'A 19 QUOTIDIENS.
ESP> EN 1977, LA CIFRA RELATIVA A LA TIRADA SE
REFIERE A 19 DIARIOS SOLAMENTE.

GUATEMALA:
E—> FOR 1976, THE CIRCULATION FIGURE REFERS
TO 5 DAILIES ONLY.
FR—> POUR 1976, LE CHIFFRE RELATIF AU TIRAGE NE
SE REFERE QU'A 5 QUOTIDIENS.
ESP> EN 1976, LA CIFRA RELATIVA A LA TIRADA SE
REFIERE A 5 DIARIOS SOLAMENTE.

HONDURAS:
E—> FOR 1976, THE CIRCULATION FIGURE REFERS
TO 5 DAILIES ONLY.
FR—> POUR 1976, LE CHIFFRE RELATIF AU TIRAGE NE
SE REFERE QU'A 5 QUOTIDIENS.
ESP> EN 1976, LA CIFRA RELATIVA A LA TIRADA SE
REFIERE A 5 DIARIOS SOLAMENTE.

MEXICO:
E—> FOR 1976, THE CIRCULATION FIGURE REFERS
TO 146 DAILIES ONLY.
FR—> POUR 1976, LE CHIFFRE RELATIF AU TIRAGE NE
SE REFERE QU'A 146 QUOTIDIENS.
ESP> EN 1976, LA CIFRA RELATIVA A LA TIRADA SE
REFIERE A 146 DIARIOS SOLAMENTE.

TRINIDAD AND TOBAGO:
E—> FOR 1976, THE CIRCULATION FIGURE REFERS
TO 2 DAILIES ONLY.
FR—> POUR 1976, LE CHIFFRE RELATIF AU TIRAGE NE
SE REFERE QU'A 2 QUOTIDIENS.
ESP> EN 1976, LA CIFRA RELATIVA A LA TIRADA SE
REFIERE A 2 DIARIOS SOLAMENTE.

UNITED STATES OF AMERICA:
E—> WITH THE EXCEPTION OF 1977, DATA REFER TO
ENGLISH LANGUAGE DAILIES ONLY.
FR—> A L'EXCEPTION DE L'ANNEE 1977, LES DONNEES
SE REFERENT AUX QUOTIDIENS DE LANGUE ANGLAISE
SEULEMENT.
ESP> SALVO PARA 1977, LOS DATOS SE REFIEREN A
LOS DIARIOS DE LENGUA INGLESA SOLAMENTE.

ARGENTINA:
E—> DATA ON CIRCULATION REFER, IN 1970, TO
154 DAILIES, AND IN 1976 TO 117 DAILIES ONLY.
FR—> LES DONNEES RELATIVES AU TIRAGE CONCERNENT
154 QUOTIDIENS EN 1970 ET 117 QUOTIDIENS EN 1976.
ESP> LOS DATOS RELATIVOS A LA TIRADA SE REFIEREN
A 154 DIARIOS EN 1970 Y A 117 EN 1976.

BOLIVIA:
E—> FOR 1970, THE CIRCULATION FIGURE REFERS
TO 13 DAILIES ONLY.
FR—> POUR 1970, LE CHIFFRE RELATIF AU TIRAGE NE
SE REFERE QU'A 13 QUOTIDIENS.
ESP> EN 1970, LA CIFRA RELATIVA A LA TIRADA SE
REFIERE A 13 DIARIOS SOLAMENTE.

CHILE:
E—> DATA CONCERN MORNING DAILIES ONLY.
FR—> LES DONNEES SE RAPPORTENT AUX QUOTIDIENS
DU MATIN SEULEMENT.
ESP> LOS DATOS SE REFIEREN A LOS DIARIOS DE LA
MANANA SOLAMENTE.

INDIA:
E—> DATA FOR CIRCULATION REFER, IN 1976, TO 602 DAILIES, AND IN 1977 TO 603 DAILIES ONLY.
FR—> LES DONNEES RELATIVES AU TIRAGE CONCERNENT 602 QUOTIDIENS EN 1976 ET 603 QUOTIDIENS EN 1977
ESP> LOS DATOS RELATIVOS A LA TIRADA SE REFIEREN A 602 DIARIOS EN 1976 Y A 603 EN 1977.

INDONESIA:
E—> FOR 1976, THE CIRCULATION FIGURE REFERS TO 50 DAILIES ONLY.
FR—> POUR 1976, LE CHIFFRE RELATIF AU TIRAGE NE SE REFERE QU'A 50 QUOTIDIENS.
ESP> EN 1976, LA CIFRA RELATIVA A LA TIRADA SE REFIERE A 50 DIARIOS SOLAMENTE.

IRAN:
E—> DATA FOR CIRCULATION REFER, IN 1970, TO 18 DAILIES, AND IN 1976 TO 20 DAILIES ONLY.
FR—> LES DONNEES RELATIVES AU TIRAGE CONCERNENT 18 QUOTIDIENS EN 1970 ET 20 QUOTIDIENS EN 1976.
ESP> LOS DATOS RELATIVOS A LA TIRADA SE REFIEREN A 18 DIARIOS EN 1970 Y A 20 EN 1976.

IRAQ:
E—> FOR 1976, THE CIRCULATION FIGURE REFERS TO 5 DAILIES ONLY.
FR—> POUR 1976, LE CHIFFRE RELATIF AU TIRAGE NE SE REFERE QU'A 5 QUOTIDIENS.
ESP> EN 1976, LA CIFRA RELATIVA A LA TIRADA SE REFIERE A 5 DIARIOS SOLAMENTE.

ISRAEL:
E—> THE NUMBER OF DAILIES SHOWN FOR 1977 REFERS TO 1978. THE FIGURE ON CIRCULATION REFERS, IN 1976, TO 20 DAILIES ONLY.
FR—> LE NOMBRE DE QUOTIDIENS INDIQUE POUR 1977 CORRESPOND A 1978. LE CHIFFRE RELATIF AU TIRAGE NE SE REFERE, POUR 1976, QU'A 20 QUOTIDIENS.
ESP> EL NUMERO DE DIARIOS INDICADO PARA 1977 CORRESPONDE A 1978. LA CIFRA RELATIVA A LA TIRADA SE REFIERE A 20 DIARIOS SOLAMENTE.

JORDAN:
E—> DATA REFER TO THE EAST BANK ONLY.
FR—> LES DONNEES SE REFERENT A LA RIVE ORIENTALE SEULEMENT.
ESP> LOS DATOS SE REFIEREN A LA ORILLA ORIENTAL SOLAMENTE.

KOREA DEMOCRATIC PEOPLE'S REPUBLIC OF:
E—> THE CIRCULATION FIGURE REFERS TO 1 DAILY ONLY.
FR—> LE CHIFFRE RELATIF AU TIRAGE NE SE REFERE QU'A 1 QUOTIDIEN.
ESP> LA CIFRA RELATIVA A LA TIRADA SOLO SE REFIERE A 1 DIARIO.

LEBANON:
E—> FOR 1976, THE CIRCULATION FIGURE REFERS TO 15 DAILIES ONLY.
FR—> POUR 1976, LE CHIFFRE RELATIF AU TIRAGE NE SE REFERE QU'A 15 QUOTIDIENS.

LEBANON (CONT.):
ESP> EN 1976, LA CIFRA RELATIVA A LA TIRADA SE REFIERE A 15 DIARIOS SOLAMENTE.

MACAU:
E—> FOR 1976, THE CIRCULATION FIGURE REFERS TO 2 DAILIES ONLY.
FR—> POUR 1976, LE CHIFFRE RELATIF AU TIRAGE NE SE REFERE QU'A 2 QUOTIDIENS.
ESP> EN 1976, LA CIFRA RELATIVA A LA TIRADA SE REFIERE A 2 DIARIOS SOLAMENTE.

MALAYSIA:
E—> FOR 1976, THE CIRCULATION FIGURE REFERS TO 35 DAILIES ONLY.
FR—> POUR 1976, LE CHIFFRE RELATIF AU TIRAGE NE SE REFERE QU'A 35 QUOTIDIENS.
ESP> EN 1976, LA CIFRA RELATIVA A LA TIRADA SE REFIERE A 35 DIARIOS SOLAMENTE.

NEPAL:
E—> DATA FOR CIRCULATION REFER, IN 1970, TO 11 DAILIES, AND IN 1976 TO 13 DAILIES ONLY.
FR—> LES DONNEES RELATIVES AU TIRAGE CONCERNENT 11 QUOTIDIENS EN 1970 ET 13 QUOTIDIENS EN 1976.
ESP> LOS DATOS RELATIVOS A LA TIRADA SE REFIEREN A 11 DIARIOS EN 1970 Y A 13 EN 1976.

PAKISTAN:
E—> FOR 1976, THE CIRCULATION FIGURE REFERS TO 21 DAILIES ONLY.
FR—> POUR 1976, LE CHIFFRE RELATIF AU TIRAGE NE SE REFERE QU'A 21 QUOTIDIENS.
ESP> EN 1976, LA CIFRA RELATIVA A LA TIRADA SE REFIERE A 21 DIARIOS SOLAMENTE.

PHILIPPINES:
E—> DATA FOR CIRCULATION REFER, IN 1970, TO 14 DAILIES, AND IN 1976 TO 16 DAILIES ONLY.
FR—> LES DONNEES RELATIVES AU TIRAGE CONCERNENT 14 QUOTIDIENS EN 1970 ET 16 QUOTIDIENS EN 1976.
ESP> LOS DATOS RELATIVOS A LA TIRADA SE REFIEREN A 14 DIARIOS EN 1970 Y A 16 EN 1976.

SAUDI ARABIA:
E—> FOR 1976, THE CIRCULATION FIGURE REFERS TO 6 DAILIES ONLY.
FR—> POUR 1976, LE CHIFFRE RELATIF AU TIRAGE NE SE REFERE QU'A 6 QUOTIDIENS.
ESP> EN 1976, LA CIFRA RELATIVA A LA TIRADA SE REFIERE A 6 DIARIOS SOLAMENTE.

SYRIAN ARAB REPUBLIC:
E—> FOR 1976, THE CIRCULATION FIGURE REFERS TO 5 DAILIES ONLY.
FR—> POUR 1976, LE CHIFFRE RELATIF AU TIRAGE NE SE REFERE QU'A 5 QUOTIDIENS.
ESP> EN 1976, LA CIFRA RELATIVA A LA TIRADA SE REFIERE A 5 DIARIOS SOLAMENTE.

YEMEN DEMOCRATIC:
E—> THE CIRCULATION FIGURE CONCERNS ONLY 2 DAILIES.

YEMEN, DEMOCRATIC (CONT.):
FR—> LE CHIFFRE RELATIF AU TIRAGE NE SE RAPPORTE
QU'A 2 QUOTIDIENS.
ESP> LA CIFRA RELATIVA A LA TIRADA SE REFIERE A
2 DIARIOS SOLAMENTE.

ALBANIA:
E—> FOR 1970, THE CIRCULATION FIGURE REFERS
TO 2 DAILIES ONLY.
FR—> POUR 1970, LE CHIFFRE RELATIF AU TIRAGE NE
SE REFERE QU'A 2 QUOTIDIENS.
ESP> EN 1970, LA CIFRA RELATIVA A LA TIRADA SE
REFIERE A 2 DIARIOS SOLAMENTE.

GERMANY, FEDERAL REPUBLIC OF:
E—> FOR 1965 AND 1970, THE NUMBER OF DAILIES
INCLUDES REGIONAL EDITIONS.
FR—> POUR 1965 ET 1970 LE NOMBRE DE QUOTIDIENS
INCLUT LES EDITIONS REGIONALES.
ESP> EN 1965 Y 1970 EL NUMERO DE DIARIOS INCLUYE
LAS EDICIONES REGIONALES.

LUXEMBOURG:
E—> FOR 1976, THE CIRCULATION FIGURE REFERS
TO 6 DAILIES ONLY.

LUXEMBOURG (CONT.):
FR—> POUR 1976, LE CHIFFRE RELATIF AU TIRAGE NE
SE REFERE QU'A 6 QUOTIDIENS.
ESP> EN 1976, LA CIFRA RELATIVA A LA TIRADA SE
REFIERE A 6 DIARIOS SOLAMENTE.

NETHERLANDS:
E—> FOR 1976, THE CIRCULATION FIGURE REFERS
TO 56 DAILIES ONLY.
FR—> POUR 1976, LE CHIFFRE RELATIF AU TIRAGE NE
SE REFERE QU'A 56 QUOTIDIENS.
ESP> EN 1976 LA CIFRA RELATIVA A LA TIRADA SE
REFIERE A 56 DIARIOS SOLAMENTE.

NEW CALEDONIA:
E—> DATA SHOWN FOR 1977 REFER TO 1978.
FR—> LES DONNEES INDIQUEES POUR 1977 CORRESPON-
DENT A 1978.
ESP> LOS DATOS INDICADOS PARA 1977 CORRESPONDEN
A 1978.

NEW ZEALAND:
E—> FOR 1976, THE CIRCULATION FIGURE REFERS
TO 37 DAILIES ONLY.
FR—> POUR 1976, LE CHIFFRE RELATIF AU TIRAGE NE
SE REFERE QU'A 37 QUOTIDIENS.
ESP> EN 1976 LA CIFRA RELATIVA A LA TIRADA SE
REFIERE A 37 DIARIOS SOLAMENTE.

Non-daily newspapers 8.15
Journaux non quotidiens
Periódicos que no son diarios

8.15 Non-daily general-interest newspapers and other periodicals: number and circulation (total and per 1,000 inhabitants)

Journaux non quotidiens d'information générale et autres périodiques: nombre et tirage (total et pour 1 000 habitants)

Periódicos de información general que no son diarios y otras publicaciones periódicas: número y tirada (total y por 1 000 habitantes)

NUMBER OF COUNTRIES AND TERRITORIES PRESENTED IN THIS TABLE: 134
NOMBRE DE PAYS ET DE TERRITOIRES PRESENTES DANS CE TABLEAU: 134
NUMERO DE PAISES Y DE TERRITORIOS PRESENTADOS EN ESTE CUADRO: 134

COUNTRY / PAYS / PAIS	YEAR / ANNEE / AÑO	NON-DAILY NEWSPAPERS / JOURNAUX NON QUOTIDIENS / PERIODICOS NO DIARIOS					OTHER PERIODICALS / AUTRES PERIODIQUES / OTRAS PUBLICACIONES PERIODICAS		
		NUMBER / NOMBRE / NUMERO			ESTIMATED CIRCULATION TIRAGE (ESTIMATION) TIRADA (ESTIMACION)		NUMBER NOMBRE NUMERO	ESTIMATED CIRCULATION TIRAGE (ESTIMATION) TIRADA (ESTIMACION)	
		TOTAL	ONCE TO THREE TIMES A WEEK UNE A TROIS FOIS PAR SEMAINE UNA A TRES VECES POR SEMANA	ISSUED LESS FREQUENTLY PARAISSANT MOINS FREQUEMMENT PUBLICADOS CON MENOR FRECUENCIA	TOTAL (000)	PER 1 000 INHABITANTS POUR 1 000 HABITANTS POR 1 000 HABITANTES		TOTAL (000)	PER 1 000 INHABITANTS POUR 1 000 HABITANTS POR 1 000 HABITANTES
		(1)	(2)	(3)	(4)	(5)	(6)	(7)	(8)
AFRICA									
ALGERIA	1977	3	3	–	107	6	39	413.6	23
BENIN ‡	1976	4	...	...	8.5	...	...	...	...
BURUNDI ‡	1975	3	2	1	55	15	3	...	1
CENTRAL AFRICAN REPUBLIC ‡	1977	1	...	...	*1	...	...	5	...
CONGO ‡	1977	5	3	2	*25	*17	...	...	...
DJIBOUTI	1975	1	1	1	3.5	33	2	1.3	12
EGYPT	1974	19	12	7	1 338	37	186	1182.9	32
ETHIOPIA ‡	1977	2	1	1	67	2	132	...	...
GAMBIA	1976	7	1	6	2	4	2	...	...
GHANA	1977	6	5	1	...	...	74	254.2	24

8.15 Non-daily newspapers
Journaux non quotidiens
Periódicos que no son diarios

COUNTRY / PAYS / PAIS	YEAR / ANNEE / AÑO	NON-DAILY NEWSPAPERS / JOURNAUX NON QUOTIDIENS / PERIODICOS NO DIARIOS					OTHER PERIODICALS / AUTRES PERIODIQUES / OTRAS PUBLICACIONES PERIODICAS		
		NUMBER / NOMBRE / NUMERO			ESTIMATED CIRCULATION / TIRAGE (ESTIMATION) / TIRADA (ESTIMACION)		NUMBER / NOMBRE / NUMERO	ESTIMATED CIRCULATION / TIRAGE (ESTIMATION) / TIRADA (ESTIMACION)	
		TOTAL	ONCE TO THREE TIMES A WEEK / UNE A TROIS FOIS PAR SEMAINE / UNA A TRES VECES POR SEMANA	ISSUED LESS FREQUENTLY / PARAISSANT MOINS FREQUEMMENT / PUBLICADOS CON MENOR FRECUENCIA	TOTAL (000)	PER 1 000 INHABITANTS / POUR 1 000 HABITANTS / POR 1 000 HABITANTES		TOTAL (000)	PER 1 000 INHABITANTS / POUR 1 000 HABITANTS / POR 1 000 HABITANTES
		(1)	(2)	(3)	(4)	(5)	(6)	(7)	(8)
GUINEA	1977	2	2	—	18.5	4	...	...	...
IVORY COAST ‡	1976	2	...	...	65	...	...	...	...
LIBYAN ARAB JAMAHIRIYA	1976	5	1	4	111	45	...	...	...
MADAGASCAR	1977	31	...	...	291.6	34	121	...	...
MALAWI	1977	7	2	5	101	18	...	...	...
MALI ‡	1976	1	...	...	*12.5	...	...	...	...
MAURITIUS	1977	7	7	—	71.5	79	63	145	8
MOROCCO ‡	1975	31	31	—	...	...	...	...	...
NIGER	1977	15	1	14	*15	*3	25	...	...
NIGERIA	1974	25	25	—	460	8	...	210	3
REUNION	1977	2	2	—	6.6	13	6	18.7	38
RWANDA ‡	1977	5	3	2	72	...	...	...	...
ST. HELENA	1974	—	—	—	...	...	7	...	...
SENEGAL	1974	...	...	...	...	—	37	...	...
SEYCHELLES	1977	3	1	2	5.7	92	22	10.3	166
SIERRA LEONE	1975	9	7	2	90	32	...	...	...
SUDAN	1977	2	1	1	30	2	...	...	...
SWAZILAND	1974	2	1	1	53	111	...	...	...
TUNISIA	1977	107	16	91	732	121	104	870	144
UNITED REPUBLIC OF CAMEROON	1975	17	13	4	...	...	41	...	...
UPPER VOLTA ‡	1976	3	...	...	5.2	...	...	...	...
ZAIRE	1974	6	6	...	21	1	43	61	3
ZAMBIA	1977	...	...	...	...	...	3	18	4
AMERICA, NORTH									
BARBADOS	1975	1	1	—	24.8	101	120	...	...
BELIZE	1974	4	4	—	11.5	85	4	10	...
BERMUDA	1974	4	3	1	34	618	5	...	74
BRITISH VIRGIN ISLANDS	1975	1	1	—	2	182	...	2.1	191
CANADA	1977	1 215	...	...	11 955	514	953	46 076	1 979
CAYMAN ISLANDS	1974	1	1	—	5	455	11	...	...
GUADELOUPE ‡	1977	24	3	21	62.4	171	1	120	329
GUATEMALA ‡	1975	18	18	—	32	5	127	...	...
JAMAICA	1974	10	10	—	381	190	...	...	...
MARTINIQUE	1977	5	4	1	40.7	109	8	14.5	39

Non-daily newspapers   8.15
Journaux non quotidiens
Periódicos que no son diarios

		(1)	(2)	(3)	(4)	(5)	(6)	(7)	(8)
MEXICO	1977	483	269	214	...	...	1 964	...	...
MONTSERRAT	1977	1	1	—	1.5	115	...	...	...
PANAMA (FORMER CANAL ZONE) ‡	1977	1	1	—	18	474	2	27	614
PUERTO RICO	1974	...	...	...	...	...	14	186	61
ST. VINCENT AND THE GRENADINES	1974	7	3	4	10	...	3	0.8	*8
TRINIDAD AND TOBAGO	1974	2	2	—	167.2	156	...	...	...
TURKS AND CAICOS ISLANDS ‡	1977	2	2	2	...	...	1	0.3	50
UNITED STATES OF AMERICA	1977	9 281	9 127	154	...	...	9 732	...	...
AMERICA, SOUTH									
BRAZIL	1977	959	685	274	*3 068	*27	1 632	...	...
CHILE	1977	28	27	1	...	...	1 034	...	...
COLOMBIA	1975	8	6	2	125	5	284	...	...
ECUADOR	1978	101	32	69	...	...	...	...	...
FALKLAND ISLANDS (MALVINAS)	1977	—	—	—	—	—	3	1.8	900
GUYANA	1974	8	8	...	236.2	305	23	100	129
PERU	1975	31	7	24	2 799	179	595	...	...
SURINAME	1977	7	6	1	15	33	21	90.7	202
URUGUAY	1977	48	36	13	...	...	335	...	...
VENEZUELA	1977	3	3	—	500	39	...	...	...
ASIA									
AFGHANISTAN ‡	1975	11	7	4	89	5	25	61.7	3
BAHRAIN	1974	5	5	—	25	103	17	55	226
BRUNEI ‡	1977	3	3	—	60.5	318	10	20	136
BURMA	1975	...	...	...	...	...	6	118	4
HONG KONG ‡	1977	38	15	23	...	...	267	257.5	...
INDIA ‡	1977	4 908	3 318	1 590	7 962	...	8 844	536	...
IRAN	1974	51	...	...	95.6	3	176	1 102	17
IRAQ	1974	6	6	...	...	...	179	...	102
ISRAEL	1978	96	31	...	...	...	583	...	...
JAPAN	1977	...	...	65	...	...	25 604	...	...
JORDAN ‡	1977	4	4	—	30	10	40	100	35
KOREA, REPUBLIC OF ‡	1977	117	85	32	2 294	63	1 146	...	...
KUWAIT ‡	1977	19	19	—	145	128	49	171	151
MALAYSIA ‡	1977	28	28	...	...	...	847	...	...
MALDIVES ‡	1977	3	2	1	...	...	60	...	...
NEPAL	1976	52	52	11	...	...	94	...	...
PHILIPPINES	1975	84	73	8	...	...	101	2 530	60
SAUDI ARABIA	1974	8	8	4	30	3	20	67	8
SINGAPORE	1977	4	4	...	...	...	1 521	...	...
SRI LANKA	1977	196	47	149	297.4	129	465	1459.6	104
SYRIAN ARAB REPUBLIC	1975	6	6	...	...	...	35	...	...
THAILAND	1975	71	42	29	...	...	986	...	...
TURKEY	1977	618	...	...	...	8	...	25	106
UNITED ARAB EMIRATES	1977	3	3	...	2	5	8	...	...
VIET-NAM	1977	15	12	3	257	...	173	323	7

8.15 Non-daily newspapers
Journaux non quotidiens
Periódicos que no son diarios

Country / Pays / País	Year / Année / Año	NON-DAILY NEWSPAPERS — Number (1) Total	(2) Once to three times a week	(3) Issued less frequently	Estimated circulation (4) Total (000)	(5) Per 1 000 inhabitants	OTHER PERIODICALS — (6) Number	Estimated circulation (7) Total (000)	(8) Per 1 000 inhabitants
EUROPE									
AUSTRIA	1977	132	132	—	...	...	2 206	...	...
BELGIUM	1977	2	2	—	30	..3	9 651	8 491	..964
BULGARIA	1977	36	33	3	949	108	1 470	21758.5	1 448
CZECHOSLOVAKIA ‡	1977	111	42	69	984.1	65	921	...	...
DENMARK ‡	1977	2	2	—	163	32	594	...	...
FAEROE ISLANDS	1974	7	6	1	27.1	675	44	88	2 200
FINLAND ‡	1977	245	245	...	...	...	2 113	...	...
FRANCE	1977	694	395	299	15 451	291	13 716	183 379	3 455
GERMAN DEMOCRATIC REPUBLIC	1977	32	32	—	8 913	532	1 162	20 524	1 224
GERMANY, FEDERAL REPUBLIC OF ‡	1977	49	49	—	2 139	...	867	85 305	1 378
GIBRALTAR	1977	3	3	...	9.0	300	...	...	...
GREECE	1977	745	239	506	...	...	748	...	...
HOLY SEE	1975	6	6	...	..45	...	1	..30	...
HUNGARY	1977	86	...	69	5820.4	547	898	13 276	1 247
ICELAND ‡	1977	6	...	...	...	...	302	...	...
IRELAND ‡	1977	54	54	—	1672.6	524	159	1677.8	...
ITALY	1977	122	...	...	...	...	7 390	...	...
LIECHTENSTEIN	1974	11	2	...	6.9	314	209	...	...
MALTA ‡	1977	...	9	2	...	...	...	...	...
NETHERLANDS	1974	152	149	3	902.9	67	3 855	30 436	...
NORWAY ‡	1977	76	76	...	337	83	2 446	...	877
POLAND	1977	38	32	6	1 971	57	901	...	...
PORTUGAL ‡	1975	307	138	169	*712.9	*33	553	7 524	..358
ROMANIA ‡	1978	24	24	...	...	...	...	...	...
SAN MARINO	1974	12	—	12	4.4	232	5	4.7	..247
SPAIN	1977	24	23	1	1 013	28	5 508	55 352	1 509
SWEDEN	1977	69	68	1	512	62	3 690	...	...
SWITZERLAND	1975	169	152	17	882.5	139	1 463	31 696	5 010
UNITED KINGDOM	1975	1 092	...	...	...	...	5 221	...	...
YUGOSLAVIA	1977	2 512	161	2 351	13 470	619	1 509	14 293	..657

Non-daily newspapers   **8.15**
Journaux non quotidiens
Periódicos que no son diarios

		(1)	(2)	(3)	(4)	(5)	(6)	(7)	(8)
OCEANIA									
AMERICAN SAMOA	1977	1	1	—	6	176	16	8.4	247
AUSTRALIA ‡	1977	507	487	20	*9 126	*648	3 585	...	...
FIJI	1976	4	4	3	46	79	...	...	...
FRENCH POLYNESIA ‡	1977	4	1	—	6.8	50	15	10.1	76
GUAM	1974	1	1	—	19	196	22	77	794
KIRIBATI	1974	3	1	2	5.8	91	21	11.9	186
NAURU	1977	1	—	1	...	...	...	...	...
NEW CALEDONIA	1978	...	...	...	...	...	19	40	328
NEW ZEALAND	1976	111	78	33	...	...	4 653	...	...
NIUE	1976	1	—	1	1.3	325	...	...	...
NORFOLK ISLAND	1977	3	2	1	3.2	1 600	5	1.1	550
PACIFIC ISLANDS	1977	5	4	1	14	111	5	14	117
PAPUA NEW GUINEA	1977	7	5	2	360.2	124	72	...	...
SAMOA	1977	5	3	2	21.1	138	...	...	...
SOLOMON ISLANDS	1977	2	2	—	5	24	2	4	19
TOKELAU ISLANDS	1976	1	—	1	1	500	—	—	—
U.S.S.R.									
U.S.S.R. ‡	1977	7 237	6 066	1 171	67 621	261	4 772	2 140	227
BYELORUSSIAN S.S.R. ‡	1977	159	159	—	2 379	252	153	...	...
UKRAINIAN S.S.R.	1975	...	...	...	...	...	518	...	...

ETHIOPIA:
E—> THE FIGURE FOR OTHER PERIODICALS REFERS TO 1975.
FR—> LE CHIFFRE RELATIF AUX AUTRES PERIODIQUES SE REFERE A 1975.
ESP> LA CIFRA RELATIVA A LAS OTRAS PUBLICA- CIONES PERIODICAS SE REFIERE A 1975.

IVORY COAST:
E—> DATA CONCERN RURAL NON-DAILY NEWSPAPERS ONLY.
FR—> LES DONNEES CONCERNENT SEULEMENT LES JOURNAUX NON-QUOTIDIENS DE LA ZONE RURALE.
ESP> LOS DATOS SE REFIEREN SOLAMENTE A LOS PERIODICOS NO DIARIOS DE LA ZONA RURAL.

MALI:
E—> DATA CONCERN RURAL NON-DAILY NEWSPAPERS ONLY.
FR—> LES DONNEES CONCERNENT SEULEMENT LES JOURNAUX NON-QUOTIDIENS DE LA ZONE RURALE.
ESP> LOS DATOS SE REFIEREN SOLAMENTE A LOS PERIODICOS NO DIARIOS DE LA ZONA RURAL.

BENIN:
E—> DATA CONCERN RURAL NON-DAILY NEWSPAPERS ONLY.
FR—> LES DONNEES CONCERNENT SEULEMENT LES JOURNAUX NON-QUOTIDIENS DE LA ZONE RURALE.
ESP> LOS DATOS SE REFIEREN SOLAMENTE A LOS PERIODICOS NO DIARIOS DE LA ZONA RURAL.

BURUNDI:
E—> THE FIGURES FOR OTHER PERIODICALS REFER TO 1974.
FR—> LES CHIFFRES RELATIFS AUX AUTRES PERIO- DIQUES SE REFERENT A 1974.
ESP> LAS CIFRAS RELATIVAS A LAS OTRAS PUBLICA- CIONES PERIODICAS SE REFIEREN A 1974.

CENTRAL AFRICAN REPUBLIC:
E—> DATA CONCERN RURAL NON-DAILY NEWSPAPERS ONLY.
FR—> LES DONNEES CONCERNENT SEULEMENT LES JOURNAUX NON-QUOTIDIENS DE LA ZONE RURALE.
ESP> LOS DATOS SE REFIEREN SOLAMENTE A LOS PERIODICOS NO DIARIOS DE LA ZONA RURAL.

8.15 Non-daily newspapers
Journaux non quotidiens
Periódicos que no son diarios

HONG KONG:
E—> THE FIGURE IN COLUMN 7 CONCERNS 252 NON-
DAILIES ONLY.
FR—> LE CHIFFRE DE LA COLONNE 7 NE CONCERNE QUE
252 NON-QUOTIDIENS.
ESP> LA CIFRA DE LA COLUMNA 7 SOLO SE REFIERE A
252 PERIODICOS NO DIARIOS.

INDIA:
E—> THE FIGURE IN COLUMN 4 CONCERNS 2,444 NON-
DAILIES ONLY: THAT IN COLUMN 6 REFERS TO 1975.
FR—> LE CHIFFRE DE LA COLONNE 4 NE CONCERNE QUE
2 444 NON-QUOTIDIENS; CELUI DE LA COLONNE 6 SE
REFERE A 1975.
ESP> LA CIFRA DE LA COLUMNA 4 SOLO SE REFIERE A
2 444 PERIODICOS NO DIARIOS. LA DE LA COLUMNA 6
SE REFIERE A 1975.

JORDAN:
E—> DATA REFER TO THE EAST BANK ONLY.
FR—> LES DONNEES SE REFERENT A LA RIVE ORIENTALE
SEULEMENT.
ESP> LOS DATOS SE REFIEREN A LA ORILLA ORIENTAL
SOLAMENTE.

KOREA, REPUBLIC OF:
E—> THE FIGURE FOR OTHER PERIODICALS REFERS TO
1976.
FR—> LE CHIFFRE RELATIF AUX AUTRES PERIODIQUES
SE REFERE A 1976.
ESP> LA CIFRA RELATIVA A LAS OTRAS PUBLICA-
CIONES PERIODICAS SE REFIERE A 1976.

KUWAIT:
E—> THE FIGURES FOR OTHER PERIODICALS REFER TO
1976.
FR—> LES CHIFFRES RELATIFS AUX AUTRES PERIO-
DIQUES SE REFERENT A 1976.
ESP> LAS CIFRAS RELATIVAS A LAS OTRAS PUBLICA-
CIONES PERIODICAS SE REFIEREN A 1976.

MALAYSIA:
E—> THE FIGURES FOR OTHER PERIODICALS REFER TO
1975.
FR—> LE CHIFFRE RELATIF AUX AUTRES PERIODIQUES
SE REFERE A 1975.
ESP> LA CIFRA RELATIVA A LAS OTRAS PUBLICA-
CIONES PERIODICAS SE REFIERE A 1975.

MALDIVES:
E—> THE FIGURE FOR OTHER PERIODICALS REFERS TO
1975.
FR—> LE CHIFFRE RELATIF AUX AUTRES PERIODIQUES
SE REFERE A 1975.
ESP> LA CIFRA RELATIVA A LAS OTRAS PUBLICA-
CIONES PERIODICAS SE REFIERE A 1975.

DENMARK:
E—> THE FIGURE FOR OTHER PERIODICALS REFERS TO
1974.
FR—> LE CHIFFRE RELATIF AUX AUTRES PERIODIQUES
SE REFERE A 1974.
ESP> LA CIFRA RELATIVA A LAS OTRAS PUBLICA-
CIONES PERIODICAS SE REFIERE A 1974.

MOROCCO:
E—> THE FIGURES FOR OTHER PERIODICALS REFER TO
1976.
FR—> LES CHIFFRES RELATIFS AUX AUTRES PERIO-
DIQUES SE REFERENT A 1976.
ESP> LAS CIFRAS RELATIVAS A LAS OTRAS PUBLICA-
CIONES PERIODICAS SE REFIEREN A 1976.

RWANDA:
E—> THE CIRCULATION FIGURE IN COLUMN 4 REFERS
TO 3 NON-DAILIES ONLY.
FR—> LE CHIFFRE RELATIF AU TIRAGE, COLONNE 4,
NE CONCERNE QUE 3 NON-QUOTIDIENS.
ESP> LA CIFRA SOBRE LA TIRADA, COLUMNA 4, SOLO
SE REFIERE A 3 PERIODICOS NO DIARIOS.

UPPER VOLTA:
E—> DATA CONCERN RURAL NON-DAILY NEWSPAPERS
ONLY.
FR—> LES DONNEES CONCERNENT SEULEMENT LES
JOURNAUX NON-QUOTIDIENS DE LA ZONE RURALE.
ESP> LOS DATOS SE REFIEREN SOLAMENTE A LOS
PERIODICOS NO DIARIOS DE LA ZONA RURAL.

GUADELOUPE:
E—> THE FIGURES FOR OTHER PERIODICALS REFER TO
1976.
FR—> LES CHIFFRES RELATIFS AUX AUTRES PERIO-
DIQUES SE REFERENT A 1976.
ESP> LAS CIFRAS RELATIVAS A LAS OTRAS PUBLICA-
CIONES PERIODICAS SE REFIEREN A 1976.

PANAMA (FORMER CANAL ZONE):
E—> THE FIGURES FOR OTHER PERIODICALS REFER TO
1976.
FR—> LES CHIFFRES RELATIFS AUX AUTRES PERIO-
DIQUES SE REFERENT A 1976.
ESP> LAS CIFRAS RELATIVAS A LAS OTRAS PUBLICA-
CIONES PERIODICAS SE REFIEREN A 1976.

TURKS AND CAICOS ISLANDS:
E—> THE FIGURES FOR OTHER PERIODICALS REFER TO
1974.
FR—> LES CHIFFRES RELATIFS AUX AUTRES PERIO-
DIQUES SE REFERENT A 1974.
ESP> LAS CIFRAS RELATIVAS A LAS OTRAS PUBLICA-
CIONES PERIODICAS SE REFIEREN A 1974.

AFGHANISTAN:
E—> THE FIGURES FOR OTHER PERIODICALS REFER TO
1977.
FR—> LES CHIFFRES RELATIFS AUX AUTRES PERIO-
DIQUES SE REFERENT A 1977.
ESP> LAS CIFRAS RELATIVAS A LAS OTRAS PUBLICA-
CIONES PERIODICAS SE REFIEREN A 1977.

BRUNEI:
E—> THE FIGURES FOR OTHER PERIODICALS REFER TO
1975.
FR—> LES CHIFFRES RELATIFS AUX AUTRES PERIO-
DIQUES SE REFERENT A 1975.
ESP> LAS CIFRAS RELATIVAS A LAS OTRAS PUBLICA-
CIONES PERIODICAS SE REFIEREN A 1975.

Non-daily newspapers   8.15
Journaux non quotidiens
Periódicos que no son diarios

FINLAND:
E—> THE FIGURE FOR OTHER PERIODICALS REFERS TO
1975.
   FR-> LE CHIFFRE RELATIF AUX AUTRES PERIODIQUES
SE REFERE A 1975.
   ESP> LA CIFRA RELATIVA A LAS OTRAS PUBLICA—
CIONES PERIODICAS SE REFIERE A 1975.

GERMANY, FEDERAL REPUBLIC OF:
   E—> DATA CONCERN WEEKLY NEWSPAPERS ONLY. THE
FIGURES FOR OTHER PERIODICALS REFER TO 1974.
   FR-> LES DONNEES NE CONCERNENT QUE LES JOURNAUX
HEBDOMADAIRES. LES CHIFFRES RELATIFS AUX AUTRES
PERIODIQUES SE REFERENT A 1974.
   ESP> LOS DATOS SE REFIEREN A LOS PERIODICOS
SEMANALES SOLAMENTE. LAS CIFRAS RELATIVAS A LAS
OTRAS PUBLICACIONES PERIODICAS SE REFIEREN A 1974.

ICELAND:
   E—> THE FIGURE FOR OTHER PERIODICALS REFERS TO
1975.
   FR-> LE CHIFFRE RELATIF AUX AUTRES PERIODIQUES
SE REFERE A 1975.
   ESP> LA CIFRA RELATIVA A LAS OTRAS PUBLICA—
CIONES PERIODICAS SE REFIERE A 1975.

IRELAND:
   E—> DATA IN COLUMN 7 REFER TO 152 PERIODICALS
ONLY.
   FR-> LES DONNEES DE LA COLONNE 7 NE CONCERNENT
QUE 152 PERIODIQUES.
   ESP> LOS DATOS DE LA COLUMNA 7 SOLO SE REFIEREN
A 152 PERIODICOS NO DIARIOS.

NORWAY:
   E—> THE FIGURE FOR OTHER PERIODICALS REFERS TO
1975.
   FR-> LE CHIFFRE RELATIF AUX AUTRES PERIODIQUES
SE REFERE A 1975.
   ESP> LA CIFRA RELATIVA A LAS OTRAS PUBLICA—
CIONES PERIODICAS SE REFIERE A 1975.

PORTUGAL:
   E—> THE FIGURE FOR OTHER PERIODICALS REFERS TO
1977.
   FR-> LE CHIFFRE RELATIF AUX AUTRES PERIODIQUES
SE REFERE A 1977.
   ESP> LA CIFRA RELATIVA A LAS OTRAS PUBLICA—
CIONES PERIODICAS SE REFIERE A 1977.

ROMANIA:
E—> THE FIGURE FOR OTHER PERIODICALS REFERS TO
1974.
   FR-> LE CHIFFRE RELATIF AUX AUTRES PERIODIQUES
SE REFERE A 1974.
   ESP> LA CIFRA RELATIVA A LAS OTRAS PUBLICA—
CIONES PERIODICAS SE REFIERE A 1974.

AUSTRALIA:
   E—> THE FIGURE FOR OTHER PERIODICALS REFERS TO
1976 AND DOES NOT INCLUDE COMICS, PARISH AND
SCHOOL MAGAZINES AND "HOUSE ORGANS".
   FR-> LE CHIFFRE RELATIF AUX AUTRES PERIODIQUES
SE REFERE A 1976 ET N'INCLUT PAS LES PERIODIQUES
HUMORISTIQUES, LES BULLETINS PAROISSIAUX, LES
BULLETINS DES ECOLES ET LES JOURNAUX D'ENTREPRISE.
   ESP> LA CIFRA RELATIVA A LAS OTRAS PUBLICA—
CIONES PERIODICAS SE REFIERE A 1976 Y NO INCLUYE
LOS PERIODICOS HUMORISTICOS, LOS BOLETINES PARRO—
QUIALES, LOS BOLETINES DE LAS ESCUELAS Y LOS
PERIODICOS DE EMPRESA.

FRENCH POLYNESIA:
   E—> THE FIGURES FOR OTHER PERIODICALS REFER TO
1975.
   FR-> LES CHIFFRES RELATIFS AUX AUTRES PERIO—
DIQUES SE REFERENT A 1975.
   ESP> LAS CIFRAS RELATIVAS A LAS OTRAS PUBLICA—
CIONES PERIODICAS SE REFIEREN A 1975.

U.S.S.R.:
   E—> THE FIGURE FOR OTHER PERIODICALS DOES NOT
INCLUDE PARISH AND SCHOOL MAGAZINES, AND "HOUSE
ORGANS".
   FR-> LE CHIFFRE RELATIF AUX AUTRES PERIODIQUES
N'INCLUT PAS LES BULLETINS PAROISSIAUX, LES
BULLETINS DES ECOLES ET LES JOURNAUX D'ENTREPRISE.
   ESP> LA CIFRA RELATIVA A LAS OTRAS PUBLICA—
CIONES PERIODICAS NO INCLUYE LOS BOLETINES PARRO—
QUIALES, LOS BOLETINES DE LAS ESCUELAS Y LOS
PERIODICOS DE EMPRESA.

BYELORUSSIAN S.S.R.:
   E—> THE FIGURES FOR OTHER PERIODICALS DO NOT
INCLUDE "HOUSE ORGANS".
   FR-> LES CHIFFRES RELATIFS AUX AUTRES PERIO—
DIQUES N'INCLUENT PAS LES JOURNAUX D'ENTREPRISE.
   ESP> LAS CIFRAS RELATIVAS A LAS OTRAS PUBLICA—
CIONES PERIODICAS NO INCLUYEN LOS PERIODICOS DE
EMPRESA.

8.16 Periodicals, other than general-interest newspapers: number and circulation by subject group

Périodiques autres que les journaux d'information générale classés par sujets: nombre et tirage

Publicaciones periódicas distintas de los diarios de información general: número y tirada clasificados por materias

NUMBER OF COUNTRIES AND TERRITORIES
PRESENTED IN THIS TABLE: 82

NOMBRE DE PAYS ET DE TERRITOIRES
PRESENTES DANS CE TABLEAU: 82

NUMERO DE PAISES Y DE TERRITORIOS
PRESENTADOS EN ESTE CUADRO: 82

AFRICA	ALGERIA (1977)		BURUNDI (1974)		DJIBOUTI (1975)		EGYPT ‡ (1974)	
SUBJECT GROUP / GROUPE DE SUJETS / GRUPOS DE MATERIAS	NUMBER NOMBRE NUMERO	ESTIMATED CIRCULATION TIRAGE (ESTIMATION) TIRADA (ESTIMACION) (000)	NUMBER NOMBRE NUMERO	ESTIMATED CIRCULATION TIRAGE (ESTIMATION) TIRADA (ESTIMACION) (000)	NUMBER NOMBRE NUMERO	ESTIMATED CIRCULATION TIRAGE (ESTIMATION) TIRADA (ESTIMACION) (000)	NUMBER NOMBRE NUMERO	ESTIMATED CIRCULATION TIRAGE (ESTIMATION) TIRADA (ESTIMACION) (000)
TOTAL A+B	39	413.6	3	5	2	1.3	186	1182.9
A. TOTAL	34	378.6	3	5	2	1.3	182	1018.2
1. GENERALITIES	7	111.5	-	-	-	-	20	211.9
2. PHILOSOPHY, PSYCHOLOGY	1	1.1	-	-	-	-	-	-
3. RELIGION, THEOLOGY	1	1.1	1	3	-	-	33	79.6
4. SOCIOLOGY, STATISTICS	2	0.4	1	-	-	-	64	177.9
5. POLITICAL SCIENCE ...			-	-	-	-	./.	./.
6. LAW ...	8	12.6	1	1	-	-	./.	./.
7. MILITARY ART ...	2	90	1	1	-	-	./.	./.
8. EDUCATION	2	4	-	-	1	1	./.	./.
9. TRADE, TRANSPORT	-	-	-	-	1	0.3	-	-
10. ETHNOGRAPHY, FOLKLORE ...	-	-	-	-	-	-	-	-
11. LINGUISTICS, PHILOLOGY	-	-	-	-	-	-	./.	./.
12. MATHEMATICS	-	-	-	-	-	-	2	33.6
13. NATURAL SCIENCES	2	1.1	-	-	-	-	45	277.0
14. MEDICAL SCIENCES ...	-	-	-	-	-	-	./.	./.
15. INDUSTRIES ...	-	-	-	-	-	-	./.	./.
16. AGRICULTURE	1	7	-	-	-	-	./.	./.
17. DOMESTIC SCIENCE	1	1	-	-	-	-	./.	./.
18. COMMERCIAL TECHNIQUES ...	2	60	-	-	-	-	12	182.5
19. ARTS	1	58	-	-	-	-	./.	./.
20. GAMES, SPORTS ...	-	-	-	-	-	-	./.	./.
21. LITERATURE	3	15.5	-	-	-	-	6	55.7
22. GEOGRAPHY, TRAVEL	1	0.5	-	-	-	-	-	-
23. HISTORY, BIOGRAPHY	1	0.2	-	-	-	-	-	-
B. TOTAL	5	35	-	-	-	-	4	164.7
1. CHILD. & ADOLESCENTS MAGS.	3	33	-	-	-	-	4	164.7
2. COMICS AND HUMOUR MAGAZINES	2	2	-	-	-	-	-	-
3. PARISH MAGAZINES	-	-	-	-	-	-	-	-
4. SCHOOL MAGS. & NEWSPAPERS	-	-	-	-	-	-	-	-
5. "HOUSE ORGANS"	-	-	-	-	-	-	-	-

SUBJECT GROUP / GROUPE DE SUJETS / GRUPOS DE MATERIAS	GHANA (1977)		MALAWI (1977)	MOROCCO (1976)		REUNION (1977)		SEYCHELLES (1977)	
	NUMBER / NOMBRE / NUMERO	ESTIMATED CIRCULATION (000)	NUMBER / NOMBRE / NUMERO	NUMBER / NOMBRE / NUMERO	ESTIMATED CIRCULATION (000)	NUMBER / NOMBRE / NUMERO	ESTIMATED CIRCULATION (000)	NUMBER / NOMBRE / NUMERO	ESTIMATED CIRCULATION (000)
TOTAL A+B	74	254.2	121	63	145	6	18.7	22	10.3
A. TOTAL	29	115.5	93	63	145	6	18.7	16	5.8
1. GENERALITIES	6	22	6	40	90	1	0.8	—	—
2. PHILOSOPHY, PSYCHOLOGY	4	31	—	5	10	—	—	—	—
3. RELIGION, THEOLOGY	1	0.5	22	—	—	—	—	—	—
4. SOCIOLOGY, STATISTICS	1	—	1	—	—	—	—	—	—
5. POLITICAL SCIENCE	—	—	—	—	—	—	—	—	—
6. LAW	3	2.7	6	—	—	—	—	12	4.1
7. MILITARY ART	—	—	—	—	—	—	—	—	—
8. EDUCATION	—	—	3	—	—	1	2	—	—
9. TRADE, TRANSPORT	—	—	1	—	—	1	3.4	—	—
10. ETHNOGRAPHY, FOLKLORE	1	1.5	2	11	17	—	—	3	1.5
11. LINGUISTICS, PHILOLOGY	—	—	1	—	—	—	—	—	—
12. MATHEMATICS	—	—	1	—	—	—	—	—	—
13. NATURAL SCIENCES	3	1.8	4	—	—	—	—	—	—
14. MEDICAL SCIENCES	3	2.5	2	—	—	—	—	—	—
15. INDUSTRIES	—	—	5	—	—	—	—	—	—
16. AGRICULTURE	1	0.3	23	5	25	1	5	1	0.2
17. DOMESTIC SCIENCE	1	0.8	—	—	—	—	—	—	—
18. COMMERCIAL TECHNIQUES	1	15	5	—	—	—	—	—	—
19. ARTS	2	34.6	1	2	3	1	6.5	—	—
20. GAMES, SPORTS	—	—	—	—	—	1	1	—	—
21. LITERATURE	1	0.8	4	—	—	—	—	—	—
22. GEOGRAPHY, TRAVEL	1	0.1	3	—	—	—	—	—	—
23. HISTORY, BIOGRAPHY	—	—	3	—	—	—	—	—	—
B. TOTAL	45	138.7	28	—	—	—	—	6	4.5
1. CHILD. & ADOLESCENTS MAGS.	1	1	1	—	—	—	—	2	1.5
2. COMICS AND HUMOUR MAGAZINES	—	—	—	—	—	—	—	—	—
3. PARISH MAGAZINES	—	—	1	—	—	—	—	—	—
4. SCHOOL MAGS. & NEWSPAPERS	—	—	21	—	—	—	—	3	1.5
5. "HOUSE ORGANS"	44	137.7	5	—	—	—	—	1	1.5

GROUPE DE SUJETS / GRUPOS DE MATERIAS	SIERRA LEONE (1975)		TUNISIA (1977)		UN. REP. OF CAMEROON (1975)		ZAIRE (1974)		ZAMBIA (1977)	
SUBJECT GROUP	NUMBER NOMBRE NUMERO	ESTIMATED CIRCULATION TIRAGE (ESTIMATION) TIRADA (ESTIMACION) (000)	NUMBER NOMBRE NUMERO	ESTIMATED CIRCULATION TIRAGE (ESTIMATION) TIRADA (ESTIMACION) (000)	NUMBER NOMBRE NUMERO	ESTIMATED CIRCULATION TIRAGE (ESTIMATION) TIRADA (ESTIMACION) (000)	NUMBER NOMBRE NUMERO	ESTIMATED CIRCULATION TIRAGE (ESTIMATION) TIRADA (ESTIMACION) (000)	NUMBER NOMBRE NUMERO	ESTIMATED CIRCULATION TIRAGE (ESTIMATION) TIRADA (ESTIMACION) (000)
TOTAL A+B	...	...	104	870	41	—	43	61	3	18
A. TOTAL	8	100	100	790	31	—	25	26.5	3	18
1. GENERALITIES	—	—	37	442	3	—	1	4.5	3	18
2. PHILOSOPHY, PSYCHOLOGY	—	—	—	—	2	—	2	2	—	—
3. RELIGION, THEOLOGY	—	—	5	25	2	—	2	3	—	—
4. SOCIOLOGY, STATISTICS	—	—	—	—	2	—	—	—	—	—
5. POLITICAL SCIENCE ...	—	—	—	—	—	—	4	23	—	—
6. LAW ...	—	—	8	30	2	—	2	1.5	—	—
7. MILITARY ART ...	—	—	1	5	2	—	—	—	—	—
8. EDUCATION	1	15	6	55	4	—	2	3	—	—
9. TRADE, TRANSPORT ...	1	15	8	15	1	—	1	3	—	—
10. ETHNOGRAPHY, FOLKLORE ...	—	—	—	—	1	—	1	3	—	—
11. LINGUISTICS, PHILOLOGY	—	—	—	—	—	—	—	—	—	—
12. MATHEMATICS	—	—	—	—	—	—	2	1	—	—
13. NATURAL SCIENCES	..	..	—	—	1	—	—	—	—	—
14. MEDICAL SCIENCES ...	..	..	4	25	—	—	1	2	—	—
15. INDUSTRIES ...	1	15	3	15	—	—	1	—	—	—
16. AGRICULTURE	1	10	4	35	3	—	2	1	—	—
17. DOMESTIC SCIENCE	1	5	9	55	—	—	—	—	—	—
18. COMMERCIAL TECHNIQUES ...	1	10	4	20	4	—	1	—	—	—
19. ARTS ...	..	..	5	40	—	—	—	0.9	—	—
20. GAMES, SPORTS ...	—	—	—	—	4	—	—	—	—	—
21. LITERATURE	1	20	5	25	—	—	3	1.3	—	—
22. GEOGRAPHY, TRAVEL	1	10	—	—	—	—	—	—	—	—
23. HISTORY, BIOGRAPHY	1	...	1	3	1	—	2	1.5	—	—
B. TOTAL	..	..	4	80	10	—	18	34.5	—	—
1. CHILD. & ADOLESCENTS MAGS.	..	..	4	80	1	—	2	21	—	—
2. COMICS AND HUMOUR MAGAZINES	..	..	—	—	1	—	—	—	—	—
3. PARISH MAGAZINES	..	..	—	—	—	—	1	—	—	—
4. SCHOOL MAGS. & NEWSPAPERS	..	..	—	—	—	—	4	2.5	—	—
5. "HOUSE ORGANS"	..	..	—	—	8	—	12	11	—	—

AMERICA, NORTH

SUBJECT GROUP / GROUPE DE SUJETS / GRUPOS DE MATERIAS	BARBADOS (1975) NUMBER NOMBRE NUMERO	BRITISH VIRGIN ISLANDS (1975) NUMBER NOMBRE NUMERO	ESTIMATED CIRCULATION TIRAGE (ESTIMATION) TIRADA (ESTIMACION) (000)	CANADA (1977) NUMBER NOMBRE NUMERO	ESTIMATED CIRCULATION TIRAGE (ESTIMATION) TIRADA (ESTIMACION) (000)	CAYMAN ISLANDS (1974) NUMBER NOMBRE NUMERO	ESTIMATED CIRCULATION TIRAGE (ESTIMATION) TIRADA (ESTIMACION) (000)
TOTAL A+B	120	2	2.1	953	46 076	11	85
A. TOTAL	118	2	2.1	916	40 710	11	85
1. GENERALITIES	8	1	2	11	5 936	3	24
2. PHILOSOPHY, PSYCHOLOGY	—	—	—	—	—	1	1.5
3. RELIGION, THEOLOGY	3	—	—	30	1 188	1	0.4
4. SOCIOLOGY, STATISTICS	5	—	—	3	33	—	—
5. POLITICAL SCIENCE ...	20	—	—	33	880	—	—
6. LAW	14	—	—	47	463	2	0.7
7. MILITARY ART ...	—	1	—	1	11	1	1
8. EDUCATION	9	—	—	30	700	1	7
9. TRADE TRANSPORT	5	1	0.1	42	320	1	—
10. ETHNOGRAPHY, FOLKLORE ...	—	—	—	17	2 537	—	—
11. LINGUISTICS, PHILOLOGY	1	—	—	1	—	—	—
12. MATHEMATICS	—	—	—	1	2	—	—
13. NATURAL SCIENCES	6	—	—	11	147	—	—
14. MEDICAL SCIENCES ...	5	—	—	62	855	—	—
15. INDUSTRIES ...	5	—	—	180	3 324	—	—
16. AGRICULTURE	21	—	—	104	2 423	—	—
17. DOMESTIC SCIENCE	5	—	—	31	4 424	—	—
18. COMMERCIAL TECHNIQUES ...	2	—	—	117	2 083	1	—
19. ARTS ...	6	—	—	44	943	—	—
20. GAMES, SPORTS ...	3	—	—	129	12 975	—	—
21. LITERATURE	4	—	—	3	49	—	—
22. GEOGRAPHY, TRAVEL	—	—	—	19	1 413	1	50
23. HISTORY, BIOGRAPHY	1	—	—	1	4	—	—
B. TOTAL	2	—	—	37	5 366	—	—
1. CHILD. & ADOLESCENTS MAGS.	—	—	—	...	...	—	—
2. COMICS AND HUMOUR MAGAZINES	—	—	—	...	...	—	—
3. PARISH MAGAZINES	—	—	—	...	...	—	—
4. SCHOOL MAGS. & NEWSPAPERS	2	—	—	...	...	—	—
5. "HOUSE ORGANS"	—	—	—	...	...	—	—

SUBJECT GROUP / GROUPE DE SUJETS / GRUPOS DE MATERIAS	GUADELOUPE (1976)		MARTINIQUE (1977)		MEXICO ‡ (1977)		PUERTO RICO (1974)		ST. VINCENT AND THE GRENADINES (1974)	
	NUMBER NOMBRE NUMERO	ESTIMATED CIRCULATION TIRAGE (ESTIMATION) TIRADA (ESTIMACION) (000)	NUMBER NOMBRE NUMERO	ESTIMATED CIRCULATION TIRAGE (ESTIMATION) TIRADA (ESTIMACION) (000)	NUMBER NOMBRE NUMERO	ESTIMATED CIRCULATION TIRAGE (ESTIMATION) TIRADA (ESTIMACION) (000)	NUMBER NOMBRE NUMERO	ESTIMATED CIRCULATION TIRAGE (ESTIMATION) TIRADA (ESTIMACION) (000)	NUMBER NOMBRE NUMERO	ESTIMATED CIRCULATION TIRAGE (ESTIMATION) TIRADA (ESTIMACION) (000)
TOTAL A+B	1	120	8	14.5	1 964	—	14	186	3	0.8
A. TOTAL	1	120	6	11	1 577	—	14	186	3	0.8
1. GENERALITIES	—	—	1	0.4	364	—	6	162	—	—
2. PHILOSOPHY, PSYCHOLOGY	—	—	—	—	—	—	—	—	—	—
3. RELIGION, THEOLOGY	1	120	—	—	215	—	—	—	1	0.3
4. SOCIOLOGY, STATISTICS	—	—	—	—	94	—	—	—	—	—
5. POLITICAL SCIENCE	—	—	1	6	7	—	1	1	—	—
6. LAW	—	—	—	—	169	—	1	3	—	—
7. MILITARY ART	—	—	1	3	—	—	—	—	—	—
8. EDUCATION	—	—	1	—	136	—	—	—	2	0.5
9. TRADE, TRANSPORT	—	—	—	—	—	—	—	—	—	—
10. ETHNOGRAPHY, FOLKLORE	—	—	—	0.4	—	—	—	—	—	—
11. LINGUISTICS, PHILOLOGY	—	—	—	—	—	—	—	—	—	—
12. MATHEMATICS	—	—	—	—	—	—	—	—	—	—
13. NATURAL SCIENCES	—	—	—	—	60	—	—	—	—	—
14. MEDICAL SCIENCES	—	—	—	—	76	—	—	—	—	—
15. INDUSTRIES	—	—	—	—	—	—	—	—	—	—
16. AGRICULTURE	—	—	1	1	63	—	—	—	—	—
17. DOMESTIC SCIENCE	—	—	—	—	78	—	—	—	—	—
18. COMMERCIAL TECHNIQUES	—	—	—	—	114	—	1	6	—	—
19. ARTS	—	—	1	0.2	88	—	—	—	—	—
20. GAMES, SPORTS	—	—	—	—	63	—	—	—	—	—
21. LITERATURE	—	—	—	—	63	—	4	12	—	—
22. GEOGRAPHY, TRAVEL	—	—	—	—	—	—	1	2	—	—
23. HISTORY, BIOGRAPHY	—	—	—	—	—	—	—	—	—	—
B. TOTAL	—	—	2	3.5	387	—	—	—	—	—
1. CHILD. & ADOLESCENTS MAGS.	—	—	—	—	—	—	—	—	—	—
2. COMICS AND HUMOUR MAGAZINES	—	—	1	0.5	387	—	—	—	—	—
3. PARISH MAGAZINES	—	—	—	—	—	—	—	—	—	—
4. SCHOOL MAGS. & NEWSPAPERS	—	—	1	3.0	—	—	—	—	—	—
5. "HOUSE ORGANS"	—	—	—	—	—	—	—	—	—	—

AMERICA, SOUTH

SUBJECT GROUP / GROUPE DE SUJETS / GRUPOS DE MATERIAS	BRAZIL (1977) NUMBER NOMBRE NUMERO	COLOMBIA (1976) NUMBER NOMBRE NUMERO	ECUADOR ‡ (1978) NUMBER NOMBRE NUMERO	FALKLAND ISLANDS (1977) NUMBER NOMBRE NUMERO	FALKLAND ISLANDS (1977) ESTIMATED CIRCULATION TIRAGE (ESTIMATION) TIRADA (ESTIMACION) (000)	PERU (1975) NUMBER NOMBRE NUMERO	SURINAME (1977) NUMBER NOMBRE NUMERO	SURINAME (1977) ESTIMATED CIRCULATION TIRAGE (ESTIMATION) TIRADA (ESTIMACION) (000)
TOTAL A+B	1 632	1 034	284	3	1.8	595	21	90.7
A. TOTAL	1 355	727	255	3	1.8	595	19	83.2
1. GENERALITIES	374	16	35	3	1.8	116	1	30
2. PHILOSOPHY, PSYCHOLOGY	18	8	—	—	—	1	—	—
3. RELIGION, THEOLOGY	139	24	7	—	—	25	10	5.9
4. SOCIOLOGY, STATISTICS	36	52	—	—	—	2	2	35.5
5. POLITICAL SCIENCE	65	81	—	—	—	37	—	—
6. LAW	148	58	—	—	—	77	1	0.4
7. MILITARY ART	2	6	—	—	—	19	—	—
8. EDUCATION	43	92	—	—	—	52	1	2
9. TRADE, TRANSPORT	60	57	—	—	—	46	1	2
10. ETHNOGRAPHY, FOLKLORE	—	6	—	—	—	1	—	—
11. LINGUISTICS, PHILOLOGY	4	8	—	—	—	3	—	—
12. MATHEMATICS	—	5	—	—	—	—	—	—
13. NATURAL SCIENCES	6	19	—	—	—	5	—	—
14. MEDICAL SCIENCES	68	63	—	—	—	22	—	—
15. INDUSTRIES	84	36	—	—	—	52	—	—
16. AGRICULTURE	58	79	—	—	—	24	2	1.4
17. DOMESTIC SCIENCE	38	4	—	—	—	2	—	—
18. COMMERCIAL TECHNIQUES	20	—	6	—	—	9	—	—
19. ARTS	46	41	10	—	—	10	2	8
20. GAMES, SPORTS	85	32	31	—	—	26	—	—
21. LITERATURE	19	8	—	—	—	17	—	—
22. GEOGRAPHY, TRAVEL	31	18	—	—	—	12	—	—
23. HISTORY, BIOGRAPHY	11	14	—	—	—	37	—	—
B. TOTAL	277	307	29	—	—	—	2	7.5
1. CHILD. & ADOLESCENTS MAGS.	33	2	1	—	—	—	2	7.5
2. COMICS AND HUMOUR MAGAZINES	147	12	—	—	—	—	—	—
3. PARISH MAGAZINES	27	29	—	—	—	—	—	—
4. SCHOOL MAGS. & NEWSPAPERS	4	35	—	—	—	—	—	—
5. "HOUSE ORGANS"	66	129	28	—	—	—	—	—

SUBJECT GROUP / GROUPE DE SUJETS / GRUPOS DE MATERIAS	URUGUAY (1977) NUMBER / NOMBRE / NUMERO	AFGHANISTAN (1977) NUMBER / NOMBRE / NUMERO	AFGHANISTAN (1977) ESTIMATED CIRCULATION / TIRAGE (ESTIMATION) / TIRADA (ESTIMACION) (000)	BAHRAIN (1974) NUMBER / NOMBRE / NUMERO	BAHRAIN (1974) ESTIMATED CIRCULATION / TIRAGE (ESTIMATION) / TIRADA (ESTIMACION) (000)	BURMA (1975) NUMBER / NOMBRE / NUMERO	BURMA (1975) ESTIMATED CIRCULATION / TIRAGE (ESTIMATION) / TIRADA (ESTIMACION) (000)
TOTAL A+B	335	25	61.7	17	55	6	118
A. TOTAL	276	23	54.2	14	53	3	33
1. GENERALITIES	19	1	4.2	10	43	3	33
2. PHILOSOPHY, PSYCHOLOGY	2	1	0.1	—	—	—	—
3. RELIGION, THEOLOGY	15	1	.1	2	3	—	—
4. SOCIOLOGY, STATISTICS	18	1	.6	—	—	—	—
5. POLITICAL SCIENCE	16	1	0.5	—	—	—	—
6. LAW	19	1	.5	—	—	—	—
7. MILITARY ART	2	1	3	—	—	—	—
8. EDUCATION	18	1	.5	2	7	—	—
9. TRADE, TRANSPORT	24	1	2.5	—	—	—	—
10. ETHNOGRAPHY, FOLKLORE	1	1	1.3	—	—	—	—
11. LINGUISTICS, PHILOLOGY	1	1	0.7	—	—	—	—
12. MATHEMATICS	—	1	0.1	—	—	—	—
13. NATURAL SCIENCES	5	1	0.3	—	—	—	—
14. MEDICAL SCIENCES	25	1	0.3	—	—	—	—
15. INDUSTRIES	22	1	4.5	—	—	—	—
16. AGRICULTURE	24	1	0.5	—	—	—	—
17. DOMESTIC SCIENCE	—	1	2.5	—	—	—	—
18. COMMERCIAL TECHNIQUES	9	1	1.5	—	—	—	—
19. ARTS	4	1	1.0	—	—	—	—
20. GAMES, SPORTS	14	1	.8	—	—	—	—
21. LITERATURE	3	1	0.3	—	—	—	—
22. GEOGRAPHY, TRAVEL	1	1	.2	—	—	—	—
23. HISTORY, BIOGRAPHY	18	1	3	—	—	—	—
B. TOTAL	75	2	7.5	3	85	3	85
1. CHILD. & ADOLESCENTS MAGS.	3	1	.6	—	—	—	—
2. COMICS AND HUMOUR MAGAZINES	—	—	—	—	—	—	—
3. PARISH MAGAZINES	7	—	—	3	85	3	85
4. SCHOOL MAGS. & NEWSPAPERS	1	—	—	—	—	—	—
5. "HOUSE ORGANS"	64	1	1.5	—	—	—	—

GRUPOS DE MATERIAS	HONG KONG ‡ (1977) NUMBER	HONG KONG ‡ (1977) ESTIMATED CIRCULATION (000)	INDIA (1975) NUMBER	IRAN (1974) NUMBER	ISRAEL ‡ (1978) NUMBER	JAPAN ‡ (1977) NUMBER	JAPAN ‡ (1977) ESTIMATED CIRCULATION (000)	JORDAN ‡ (1977) NUMBER	JORDAN ‡ (1977) ESTIMATED CIRCULATION (000)
TOTAL A+B	252	257.5	8 844	176	583	1 640	25 604	40	100
A. TOTAL	221	216.1	7 542	119	537	1 412	13 153	40	100
1. GENERALITIES	39	34.1	1 440	3	26	81	3 124	8	12
2. PHILOSOPHY, PSYCHOLOGY	1	.10	—	2	5	17	198	—	—
3. RELIGION, THEOLOGY	13	4.8	1 260	2	42	9	14	5	6
4. SOCIOLOGY, STATISTICS	—	—	—	—	49	35	27	—	—
5. POLITICAL SCIENCE	13	10.8	—	10	99	142	405	—	—
6. LAW	5	1.6	586	7	35	25	48	3	8
7. MILITARY ART	—	.5	—	1	8	—	8	6	20
8. EDUCATION	6	4.8	224	4	37	103	306	3	18
9. TRADE, TRANSPORT	18	10.2	89	3	18	44	120	—	7
10. ETHNOGRAPHY, FOLKLORE	—	—	—	1	3	—	—	—	—
11. LINGUISTICS, PHILOLOGY	—	—	—	1	4	35	269	—	—
12. MATHEMATICS	4	2.8	—	—	3	—	—	—	—
13. NATURAL SCIENCES	10	7.5	147	16	27	38	171	3	7
14. MEDICAL SCIENCES	23	8.6	688	6	25	90	182	3	6
15. INDUSTRIES	—	—	219	—	23	201	272	—	—
16. AGRICULTURE	19	21.2	270	10	22	27	56	2	5
17. DOMESTIC SCIENCE	5	7.9	459	—	./.	86	1 351	—	—
18. COMMERCIAL TECHNIQUES	11	10.7	342	3	21	—	—	—	—
19. ARTS	26	29.2	57	10	13	92	680	—	3
20. GAMES, SPORTS	—	—	—	3	—	306	5 600	2	3
21. LITERATURE	10	7.3	1 761	25	35	65	265	2	8
22. GEOGRAPHY, TRAVEL	12	33.8	—	1	6	16	65	—	—
23. HISTORY, BIOGRAPHY	5	5.8	—	6	36	./.	./.	—	—
B. TOTAL	31	41.4	1 302	57	46	228	12 451	—	—
1. CHILD. & ADOLESCENTS MAGS.	24	13.8	900	6	39	54	5 446	—	—
2. COMICS AND HUMOUR MAGAZINES	3	25.3	—	2	7	96	3 806	—	—
3. PARISH MAGAZINES	—	—	—	—	—	—	—	—	—
4. SCHOOL MAGS. & NEWSPAPERS	4	2.3	402	19	—	53	1 510	—	—
5. "HOUSE ORGANS"	—	—	—	30	—	25	1 689	—	—

SUBJECT GROUP / GROUPE DE SUJETS / GRUPOS DE MATERIAS	KOREA, REP. OF (1976) NUMBER	KUWAIT (1976) NUMBER	KUWAIT (1976) ESTIMATED CIRCULATION (000)	MALAYSIA (1975) NUMBER	MALAYSIA (1975) ESTIMATED CIRCULATION (000)	NEPAL (1976) NUMBER	PHILIPPINES (1975) NUMBER	PHILIPPINES (1975) ESTIMATED CIRCULATION (000)	SINGAPORE (1977) NUMBER
TOTAL A+B	1 146	49	471	847	–	94	101	2 530	1 521
A. TOTAL	814	46	447	611	–	88	59	548	1 148
1. GENERALITIES	77	12	264	206	–	11	–	–	90
2. PHILOSOPHY, PSYCHOLOGY	4	–	–	–	–	–	–	–	3
3. RELIGION, THEOLOGY	66	2	65	44	–	6	1	42	74
4. SOCIOLOGY, STATISTICS	58	2	8	36	–	–	–	–	36
5. POLITICAL SCIENCE	17	1	4	30	–	3	–	–	179
6. LAW	58	2	8	115	–	4	3	24	132
7. MILITARY ART	2	1	5	2	–	–	1	19	14
8. EDUCATION	19	1	–	14	–	3	3	62	146
9. TRADE TRANSPORT	57	–	–	21	–	–	–	–	81
10. ETHNOGRAPHY, FOLKLORE	2	–	–	–	–	–	–	–	1
11. LINGUISTICS, PHILOLOGY	2	–	–	1	–	1	–	–	7
12. MATHEMATICS	2	1	4	7	–	1	–	–	8
13. NATURAL SCIENCES	34	5	13	11	–	3	–	–	18
14. MEDICAL SCIENCES	80	6	26	16	–	10	–	–	69
15. INDUSTRIES	101	–	–	–	–	3	–	–	59
16. AGRICULTURE	31	–	–	47	–	–	3	98	8
17. DOMESTIC SCIENCE	20	3	13	11	–	–	5	70	5
18. COMMERCIAL TECHNIQUES	83	1	5	6	–	–	14	92	38
19. ARTS	32	3	13	26	–	5	6	46	41
20. GAMES, SPORTS	31	3	–	8	–	4	23	95	58
21. LITERATURE	28	3	19	5	–	32	–	–	23
22. GEOGRAPHY, TRAVEL	5	–	–	–	–	1	–	–	31
23. HISTORY, BIOGRAPHY	5	–	–	5	–	1	–	–	27
B. TOTAL	332	3	24	236	–	6	42	1 982	373
1. CHILD. & ADOLESCENTS MAGS.	36	1	15	12	–	1	3	10	14
2. COMICS AND HUMOUR MAGAZINES	16	–	–	6	–	1	34	1 303	–
3. PARISH MAGAZINES	16	–	–	15	–	–	2	54	35
4. SCHOOL MAGS. & NEWSPAPERS	162	1	4	97	–	4	3	615	107
5. "HOUSE ORGANS"	102	1	5	106	–	–	–	–	217

GROUPE DE SUJETS / GRUPOS DE MATERIAS	SRI LANKA (1977) NUMBER NOMBRE NUMERO	SRI LANKA (1977) ESTIMATED CIRCULATION TIRAGE (ESTIMATION) TIRADA (ESTIMACION) (000)	THAILAND (1975) NUMBER NOMBRE NUMERO	UNITED ARAB EMIRATES (1977) NUMBER NOMBRE NUMERO	UNITED ARAB EMIRATES (1977) ESTIMATED CIRCULATION (000)	VIET-NAM (1977) NUMBER NOMBRE NUMERO	VIET-NAM (1977) ESTIMATED CIRCULATION (000)	EUROPE	AUSTRIA ‡ (1977) NUMBER NOMBRE NUMERO
TOTAL A+B	465	1459.6	986	8	25	173	323		2 206
A. TOTAL	432	1411.2	930	8	25	173	323		2 072
1. GENERALITIES	9	8.7	54	8	25	51	20		
2. PHILOSOPHY, PSYCHOLOGY	4	7.5	14	—	—	1	6		
3. RELIGION, THEOLOGY	107	157.5	69	—	—	4	6		236
4. SOCIOLOGY, STATISTICS	4	2.9	14	—	—	5	2		
5. POLITICAL SCIENCE	74	457.2	38	—	—	22	60		169
6. LAW	32	31.7	68	—	—	14	5		242
7. MILITARY ART	—	—	44	—	—	15	55		20
8. EDUCATION	18	44.2	49	—	—	8	20		118
9. TRADE, TRANSPORT	12	56.3	37	—	—	3	16		42
10. ETHNOGRAPHY, FOLKLORE	—	—	14	—	—	2	2		70
11. LINGUISTICS, PHILOLOGY	19	23.3	27	—	—	1	3		37
12. MATHEMATICS	18	85.0	3	—	—	2	25		—
13. NATURAL SCIENCES	13	23.0	24	—	—	3	5		
14. MEDICAL SCIENCES	19	73.1	88	—	—	7	7		63
15. INDUSTRIES		—	56	—	—	11	4		341
16. AGRICULTURE	—	—	47	—	—	6	5		88
17. DOMESTIC SCIENCE	—	—	6	—	—	—	—		
18. COMMERCIAL TECHNIQUES	3	5.7	42	—	—	4	3		105
19. ARTS	17	316.6	68	—	—	10	25		140
20. GAMES, SPORTS	4	4.0	123	—	—	1	25		192
21. LITERATURE	66	91.5	19	—	—	1	25		47
22. GEOGRAPHY, TRAVEL	6	18.2	9	—	—	2	—		36
23. HISTORY, BIOGRAPHY	7	4.9	17	—	—	2	4		65
B. TOTAL	33	48.4	56	—	—	—	—		134
1. CHILD. & ADOLESCENTS MAGS.	5	9.8	20	—	—	—	—		53
2. COMICS AND HUMOUR MAGAZINES	1	11.2	4	—	—	—	—		23
3. PARISH MAGAZINES	3	1.1	3	—	—	—	—		58
4. SCHOOL MAGS. & NEWSPAPERS	21	20.2	29	—	—	—	—		—
5. "HOUSE ORGANS"	3	6.1	—	—	—	—	—		—

SUBJECT GROUP / GROUPE DE SUJETS / GRUPOS DE MATERIAS	BELGIUM (1977) NUMBER / NOMBRE / NUMERO	BULGARIA (1977) NUMBER / NOMBRE / NUMERO	BULGARIA (1977) ESTIMATED CIRCULATION TIRAGE (ESTIMATION) TIRADA (ESTIMACION) (000)	CZECHOSLOVAKIA (1977) NUMBER / NOMBRE / NUMERO	CZECHOSLOVAKIA (1977) ESTIMATED CIRCULATION TIRAGE (ESTIMATION) TIRADA (ESTIMACION) (000)	DENMARK ‡ (1974) NUMBER / NOMBRE / NUMERO	FAEROE ISLANDS (1974) NUMBER / NOMBRE / NUMERO	FAEROE ISLANDS (1974) ESTIMATED CIRCULATION TIRAGE (ESTIMATION) TIRADA (ESTIMACION) (000)
TOTAL A+B	9 651	1 470	8 491	921	21758.5	3 594	44	88
A. TOTAL	9 296	1 120	6 070	620	15345.3	3 418	36	66
1. GENERALITIES	1 525	195	275	42	2653.2	580	11	32
2. PHILOSOPHY, PSYCHOLOGY	69	4	5	7	22.9	64	6	13
3. RELIGION, THEOLOGY	479	—	13	26	369.1	210	—	—
4. SOCIOLOGY, STATISTICS	126	41	459	9	21.4	42	5	5
5. POLITICAL SCIENCE	1 198	155	998	27	754.9	343	—	—
6. LAW	908	26	165	53	929.8	198	4	3
7. MILITARY ART	118	10	78	15	573.3	86	—	—
8. EDUCATION	533	39	241	27	427.7	339	3	3
9. TRADE, TRANSPORT	259	41	173	12	474.5	./.	—	—
10. ETHNOGRAPHY, FOLKLORE	66	20	791	6	82.5	14	—	—
11. LINGUISTICS, PHILOLOGY	54	12	25	18	252.8	23	—	—
12. MATHEMATICS	20	6	64	6	97.2	7	—	—
13. NATURAL SCIENCES	185	62	196	57	933.3	103	—	—
14. MEDICAL SCIENCES	364	104	492	49	630.3	149	—	—
15. INDUSTRIES	987	143	465	53	922.4	295	—	—
16. AGRICULTURE	338	54	290	60	1015.6	197	2	2
17. DOMESTIC SCIENCE	117	3	43	16	805.9	54	—	—
18. COMMERCIAL TECHNIQUES	303	64	271	14	468.4	174	—	—
19. ARTS	562	46	190	33	1135.8	124	4	4
20. GAMES, SPORTS	509	26	442	45	1903.3	133	—	—
21. LITERATURE	255	29	185	19	426.8	24	1	4
22. GEOGRAPHY, TRAVEL	79	10	84	5	77.8	133	—	—
23. HISTORY, BIOGRAPHY	242	26	125	21	366.4	126	—	—
B. TOTAL	355	350	2 421	301	6413.2	176	8	22
1. CHILD. & ADOLESCENTS MAGS.	49	14	1 484	38	3795.8	176	6	15
2. COMICS AND HUMOUR MAGAZINES	50	1	280	3	1194.6	./.	2	7
3. PARISH MAGAZINES	17	111	233	30	102.2	—	—	—
4. SCHOOL MAGS. & NEWSPAPERS	110	23	23	—	—	—	—	—
5. "HOUSE ORGANS"	129	201	401	230	1320.6	—	—	—

SUBJECT GROUP / GROUPE DE SUJETS / GRUPOS DE MATERIAS	FRANCE ‡ (1977) NUMBER	FRANCE ‡ (1977) ESTIMATED CIRCULATION (000)	GERMAN DEMOCRATIC REP. ‡ (1977) NUMBER	GERMAN DEMOCRATIC REP. ‡ (1977) ESTIMATED CIRCULATION (000)	GREECE (1977) NUMBER	HUNGARY (1977) NUMBER	HUNGARY (1977) ESTIMATED CIRCULATION (000)	ICELAND (1975) NUMBER
TOTAL A+B	13 716	183 379	1 162	20 524	748	898	13 276	302
A. TOTAL	10 478	153 159	519	18 524	655	592	9 135	262
1. GENERALITIES	3 827	45 713	12	674	90	28	554	29
2. PHILOSOPHY, PSYCHOLOGY	82	277	15	328	9	3	14	7
3. RELIGION, THEOLOGY	695	6 981	31	349	68	14	163	29
4. SOCIOLOGY, STATISTICS	210	623		27	18	9	23	5
5. POLITICAL SCIENCE	361	4 742	24	1 097	21	39	805	20
6. LAW	754	16 109	17	632	65	58	401	31
7. MILITARY ART	94	1 017	4	111			—	
8. EDUCATION	534	6 951	55	5 466	31	30	441	8
9. TRADE, TRANSPORT	128	2 052	11	85	34	22	135	15
10. ETHNOGRAPHY, FOLKLORE	./.	./.	5	9	35	3	17	—
11. LINGUISTICS, PHILOLOGY	47	79	9	34	7	12	77	1
12. MATHEMATICS	263	462	6	38	18	9	17	13
13. NATURAL SCIENCES	398	2 700	58	245	7	31	80	19
14. MEDICAL SCIENCES	289	2 275	54	573	30	46	735	11
15. INDUSTRIES	./.	./.	81	1 005	57	112	780	
16. AGRICULTURE	629	7 302	29	214	42	37	403	25
17. DOMESTIC SCIENCE	143	16 413	15	3 751	12	3	631	8
18. COMMERCIAL TECHNIQUES	409	9 270	8	82	26	42	880	8
19. ARTS	515	14 042	30	756	25	25	388	4
20. GAMES, SPORTS	432	11 923	25	2 424		27	2 207	14
21. LITERATURE	316	1 359	13	126	18	32	367	6
22. GEOGRAPHY, TRAVEL	86	1 581	6	477	29	3	8	7
23. HISTORY, BIOGRAPHY	266	1 288	8	21	4	7	9	2
B. TOTAL	3 238	30 220	668	6 449	93	306	4 141	40
1. CHILD. & ADOLESCENTS MAGS.	308	14 765	16	3 616	28	16	1 142	4
2. COMICS AND HUMOUR MAGAZINES	44	1 546	1	820	25	4	1 674	
3. PARISH MAGAZINES	2 101	3 913	8	13			—	7
4. SCHOOL MAGS. & NEWSPAPERS	395	644		—	15	19	107	22
5. "HOUSE ORGANS"	390	9 352	643	2 000	25	267	1 218	7

SUBJECT GROUP / GROUPE DE SUJETS / GRUPOS DE MATERIAS	IRELAND ‡ (1977) NUMBER NOMBRE NUMERO	IRELAND ‡ (1977) ESTIMATED CIRCULATION TIRAGE (ESTIMATION) TIRADA (ESTIMACION) (000)	ITALY (1977) NUMBER NOMBRE NUMERO	MALTA (1977) NUMBER NOMBRE NUMERO	POLAND (1977) NUMBER NOMBRE NUMERO	POLAND (1977) ESTIMATED CIRCULATION TIRAGE (ESTIMATION) TIRADA (ESTIMACION) (000)	PORTUGAL ‡ (1977) NUMBER NOMBRE NUMERO	ROMANIA (1974) NUMBER NOMBRE NUMERO	ROMANIA (1974) ESTIMATED CIRCULATION TIRAGE (ESTIMATION) TIRADA (ESTIMACION) (000)
TOTAL A+B	159	1677.8	7 390	209	2 446	30 436	901	553	7 524
A. TOTAL	152	1636.8	6 247	150	2 205	25 371	715	500	6 142
1. GENERALITIES	15	183	592	11	231	7 915	284	50	1 793
2. PHILOSOPHY, PSYCHOLOGY	-	-	63	-	23	29	5	12	10
3. RELIGION, THEOLOGY	29	515.1	583	51	94	412	106	20	82
4. SOCIOLOGY, STATISTICS	3	5.1	182	-	84	436	67	14	14
5. POLITICAL SCIENCE	-	-	1 079	11	191	2 277	./.	23	523
6. LAW	1	1.0	577	5	114	1 314	./.	61	182
7. MILITARY ART	2	4.5	50	1	26	339	./.	-	-
8. EDUCATION	7	17.0	163	16	86	1 019	./.	50	381
9. TRADE TRANSPORT	27	248.3	330	1	47	612	./.	24	175
10. ETHNOGRAPHY, FOLKLORE	-	-	124	1	7	13	./.	2	3
11. LINGUISTICS, PHILOLOGY	-	-	51	1	28	123	3	13	12
12. MATHEMATICS	-	-	16	1	22	37	16	15	90
13. NATURAL SCIENCES	-	-	105	3	170	217	./.	16	63
14. MEDICAL SCIENCES	13	41.0	371	1	119	885	100	36	189
15. INDUSTRIES	9	19.8	489	3	445	1 326	./.	77	530
16. AGRICULTURE	6	102.8	312	2	155	2 560	./.	28	251
17. DOMESTIC SCIENCE	4	118.8	91	3	17	1 237	./.	-	-
18. COMMERCIAL TECHNIQUES	9	39.5	78	6	77	929	./.	2	48
19. ARTS	4	95.4	286	6	90	892	119	14	1 131
20. GAMES, SPORTS	15	86.5	345	17	46	1 645	./.	10	338
21. LITERATURE	6	159.0	122	5	50	904	7	23	107
22. GEOGRAPHY, TRAVEL	-	-	126	1	18	144	8	11	64
23. HISTORY, BIOGRAPHY	-	-	112	2	65	106	./.	11	156
B. TOTAL	9	41	1 143	59	241	5 065	186	53	1 382
1. CHILD. & ADOLESCENTS MAGS.	2	41	125	5	54	4 485	50	10	980
2. COMICS AND HUMOUR MAGAZINES	-	-	10	-	-	-	4	1	125
3. PARISH MAGAZINES	-	-	638	34	-	-	153	-	-
4. SCHOOL MAGS. & NEWSPAPERS	7	-	74	6	-	-	4	-	-
5. "HOUSE ORGANS"	-	./.	296	14	187	580	29	42	277

SUBJECT GROUP / GROUPE DE SUJETS / GRUPOS DE MATERIAS	SAN MARINO (1974) NUMBER / NOMBRE / NUMERO	SAN MARINO (1974) ESTIMATED CIRCULATION / TIRAGE (ESTIMATION) / TIRADA (ESTIMACION) (000)	SPAIN ‡ (1977) NUMBER / NOMBRE / NUMERO	SPAIN ‡ (1977) ESTIMATED CIRCULATION / TIRAGE (ESTIMATION) / TIRADA (ESTIMACION) (000)	SWEDEN (1977) NUMBER / NOMBRE / NUMERO	SWITZERLAND (1977) NUMBER / NOMBRE / NUMERO	SWITZERLAND (1977) ESTIMATED CIRCULATION / TIRAGE (ESTIMATION) / TIRADA (ESTIMACION) (000)	YUGOSLAVIA (1977) NUMBER / NOMBRE / NUMERO	YUGOSLAVIA (1977) ESTIMATED CIRCULATION / TIRAGE (ESTIMATION) / TIRADA (ESTIMACION) (000)
TOTAL A+B	5	4.7	5 508	55 352	3 690	1 463	31 696	1 509	14 293
A. TOTAL	5	4.7	5 508	55 352	1 866	1 365	18 730	1 314	7 392
1. GENERALITIES	—	—	1 313	15 969	275	7	24	170	294
2. PHILOSOPHY, PSYCHOLOGY	—	—	34	143	15	7	22	12	11
3. RELIGION, THEOLOGY	—	—	598	5 459	158	49	544	53	356
4. SOCIOLOGY, STATISTICS	1	0.2	147	1 442	11	6	17	51	1 808
5. POLITICAL SCIENCE	—	—	163	1 159	260	62	680	127	641
6. LAW	1	0.8	331	1 342	115	153	1 838	66	136
7. MILITARY ART	—	—	16	75	34	47	322	21	314
8. EDUCATION	—	—	200	1 274	110	55	723	91	247
9. TRADE, TRANSPORT	—	—	124	1 073	92	41	285	12	83
10. ETHNOGRAPHY, FOLKLORE	—	—	308	1 703	3	11	28	6	5
11. LINGUISTICS, PHILOLOGY	—	—	29	45	20	—	—	7	8
12. MATHEMATICS	—	—	3	2	2	7	8	21	78
13. NATURAL SCIENCES	—	—	52	200	60	25	75	56	81
14. MEDICAL SCIENCES	—	—	401	5 150	102	131	594	128	344
15. INDUSTRIES	—	—	344	1 502	135	213	1 710	102	439
16. AGRICULTURE	1	0.5	152	1 238	114	116	1 208	75	585
17. DOMESTIC SCIENCE	—	—	83	2 197	33	25	348	4	54
18. COMMERCIAL TECHNIQUES	1	2	223	2 390	6	61	479	59	174
19. ARTS	1	1.2	252	2 639	88	94	1 451	73	1 107
20. GAMES, SPORTS	—	—	621	9 484	98	231	7 897	42	387
21. LITERATURE	—	—	71	415	44	8	100	90	188
22. GEOGRAPHY, TRAVEL	—	—	14	163	38	9	365	13	12
23. HISTORY, BIOGRAPHY	—	—	29	288	53	7	12	35	40
B. TOTAL	—	—	737	8 350	1 824	98	12 966	195	6 901
1. CHILD. & ADOLESCENTS MAGS.	—	—	99	2 884	36	19	751	14	176
2. COMICS AND HUMOUR MAGAZINES	—	—	75	2 107	67	1	5	58	4 676
3. PARISH MAGAZINES	—	—	162	1 017	1 000	10	119	—	—
4. SCHOOL MAGS. & NEWSPAPERS	—	—	28	70	275	19	106	48	1 851
5. "HOUSE ORGANS"	—	—	373	2 272	446	49	11 985	75	198

OCEANIA

SUBJECT GROUP / GROUPE DE SUJETS / GRUPOS DE MATERIAS	AMERICAN SAMOA (1977)		AUSTRALIA ‡ (1976)	FRENCH POLYNESIA (1975)		GUAM (1974)	
	NUMBER / NOMBRE / NUMERO	ESTIMATED CIRCULATION / TIRAGE (ESTIMATION) / TIRADA (ESTIMACION) (000)	NUMBER / NOMBRE / NUMERO	NUMBER / NOMBRE / NUMERO	ESTIMATED CIRCULATION / TIRAGE (ESTIMATION) / TIRADA (ESTIMACION) (000)	NUMBER / NOMBRE / NUMERO	ESTIMATED CIRCULATION / TIRAGE (ESTIMATION) / TIRADA (ESTIMACION) (000)
TOTAL A+B	16	8.4	3 585	15	10.1	22	77
A. TOTAL	4	2.4	3 575	6	6	22	77
1. GENERALITIES	—	—	204	3	3	—	—
2. PHILOSOPHY, PSYCHOLOGY	—	—	23	—	—	—	—
3. RELIGION, THEOLOGY	—	—	193	—	—	1	10
4. SOCIOLOGY, STATISTICS	—	—	27	—	—	6	4.5
5. POLITICAL SCIENCE	—	—	262	—	—	2	3.5
6. LAW ...	4	2.4	248	1	1.5	5	11
7. MILITARY ART ...	—	—	49	—	—	—	—
8. EDUCATION	—	—	340	—	—	4	33
9. TRADE, TRANSPORT	—	—	225	1	1	—	—
10. ETHNOGRAPHY, FOLKLORE	—	—	43	—	—	—	—
11. LINGUISTICS, PHILOLOGY	—	—	25	—	—	—	—
12. MATHEMATICS	—	—	7	—	—	—	—
13. NATURAL SCIENCES	—	—	65	—	—	—	—
14. MEDICAL SCIENCES	—	—	152	—	—	—	—
15. INDUSTRIES	—	—	437	—	—	—	—
16. AGRICULTURE	—	—	324	1	0.5	1	2
17. DOMESTIC SCIENCE	—	—	52	—	—	—	—
18. COMMERCIAL TECHNIQUES	—	—	161	—	—	1	—
19. ARTS	—	—	191	—	—	1	2
20. GAMES, SPORTS	—	—	303	—	—	2	11
21. LITERATURE	—	—	49	—	—	—	—
22. GEOGRAPHY, TRAVEL	—	—	91	—	—	—	—
23. HISTORY, BIOGRAPHY	—	—	104	—	—	—	—
B. TOTAL	12	6	10	9	4.1	—	—
1. CHILD. & ADOLESCENTS MAGS.	—	—	10	1	0.5	—	—
2. COMICS AND HUMOUR MAGAZINES	—	—	...	—	—	—	—
3. PARISH MAGAZINES	—	—	...	4	0.6	—	—
4. SCHOOL MAGS. & NEWSPAPERS	12	6	...	4	0.3	—	—
5. "HOUSE ORGANS"	—	—	...	—	—	—	—

SUBJECT GROUP / GROUPE DE SUJETS / GRUPOS DE MATERIAS	KIRIBATI (1974) NUMBER / NOMBRE / NUMERO	KIRIBATI (1974) ESTIMATED CIRCULATION / TIRAGE (ESTIMATION) / TIRADA (ESTIMACION) (000)	NEW CALEDONIA (1978) NUMBER	NEW CALEDONIA (1978) ESTIMATED CIRCULATION (000)	NORFOLK ISLAND (1977) NUMBER	NORFOLK ISLAND (1977) ESTIMATED CIRCULATION (000)	PAPUA NEW GUINEA (1977) NUMBER	PAPUA NEW GUINEA (1977) ESTIMATED CIRCULATION (000)	SOLOMON ISLANDS (1977) NUMBER	SOLOMON ISLANDS (1977) ESTIMATED CIRCULATION (000)
TOTAL A+B	21	11.9	19	40	5	1.1	72	—	2	4
A. TOTAL	16	6.5	18	34.5	5	1.1	72	—	2	4
1. GENERALITIES	—	—	—	—	—	—	9	—	1	3
2. PHILOSOPHY, PSYCHOLOGY	—	—	—	—	1	0.1	4	—	—	—
3. RELIGION, THEOLOGY	—	—	1	1	—	—	4	—	—	—
4. SOCIOLOGY, STATISTICS	2	0.4	—	—	—	—	—	—	—	—
5. POLITICAL SCIENCE	—	—	9	15	—	—	—	—	—	—
6. LAW	9	1.6	—	—	1	0.3	12	—	—	—
7. MILITARY ART	—	—	—	—	—	—	—	—	—	—
8. EDUCATION	1	0.2	—	—	—	—	2	—	—	—
9. TRADE, TRANSPORT	2	4	1	2.5	—	—	13	—	—	—
10. ETHNOGRAPHY, FOLKLORE	—	—	1	./.	—	—	2	—	—	—
11. LINGUISTICS, PHILOLOGY	—	—	—	—	—	—	—	—	—	—
12. MATHEMATICS	—	—	—	—	—	—	—	—	—	—
13. NATURAL SCIENCES	—	—	1	3.5	—	—	—	—	—	—
14. MEDICAL SCIENCES	1	0.2	—	—	—	—	2	—	—	—
15. INDUSTRIES	—	—	—	—	—	—	7	—	—	—
16. AGRICULTURE	1	0.1	—	—	—	—	2	—	—	—
17. DOMESTIC SCIENCE	—	—	—	—	—	—	4	—	—	—
18. COMMERCIAL TECHNIQUES	—	—	—	—	—	—	8	—	1	1
19. ARTS	—	—	2	7	3	0.7	—	—	—	—
20. GAMES, SPORTS	—	—	1	2	—	—	—	—	—	—
21. LITERATURE	—	—	1	2.5	—	—	—	—	—	—
22. GEOGRAPHY, TRAVEL	—	—	—	—	—	—	2	—	—	—
23. HISTORY, BIOGRAPHY	—	—	1	—	—	—	1	—	—	—
B. TOTAL	5	5.4	1	5.5	—	—	—	—	—	—
1. CHILD. & ADOLESCENTS MAGS.	—	—	—	—	—	—	—	—	—	—
2. COMICS AND HUMOUR MAGAZINES	—	—	—	—	—	—	—	—	—	—
3. PARISH MAGAZINES	4	5.2	—	—	—	—	—	—	—	—
4. SCHOOL MAGS. & NEWSPAPERS	1	0.2	1	5.5	—	—	—	—	—	—
5. "HOUSE ORGANS"	—	—	—	—	—	—	—	—	—	—

SUBJECT GROUP / GROUPE DE SUJETS / GRUPOS DE MATERIAS	U.S.S.R.‡ (1977) NUMBER / NOMBRE / NUMERO	ESTIMATED CIRCULATION TIRAGE (ESTIMATION) TIRADA (ESTIMACION) (000)	BYELORUSSIAN S.S.R.‡ (1977) NUMBER / NOMBRE / NUMERO	ESTIMATED CIRCULATION TIRAGE (ESTIMATION) TIRADA (ESTIMACION) (000)
TOTAL A+B	4 772		153	2 140
A. TOTAL	4 669		149	1 748
1. GENERALITIES	70		29	18
2. PHILOSOPHY, PSYCHOLOGY	40		1	3
3. RELIGION, THEOLOGY	12		1	—
4. SOCIOLOGY, STATISTICS	49		1	—
5. POLITICAL SCIENCE	382		9	675
6. LAW	119		1	7
7. MILITARY ART	60		—	—
8. EDUCATION	159		5	78
9. TRADE, TRANSPORT	320		10	334
10. ETHNOGRAPHY, FOLKLORE	—		—	—
11. LINGUISTICS, PHILOLOGY	44		6	6
12. MATHEMATICS	38		1	2
13. NATURAL SCIENCES	414		16	13
14. MEDICAL SCIENCES	185		4	26
15. INDUSTRIES	1 175		24	39
16. AGRICULTURE	259		24	60
17. DOMESTIC SCIENCE	75		2	42
18. COMMERCIAL TECHNIQUES	811		4	6
19. ARTS	134		3	197
20. GAMES, SPORTS	56		1	1
21. LITERATURE	217		4	183
22. GEOGRAPHY, TRAVEL	20		1	45
23. HISTORY, BIOGRAPHY	30		3	13
B. TOTAL	103		4	392
1. CHILD. & ADOLESCENTS MAGS.	80		3	157
2. COMICS AND HUMOUR MAGAZINES	23		1	235
3. PARISH MAGAZINES	...		—	—
4. SCHOOL MAGS. & NEWSPAPERS	...		—	—
5. "HOUSE ORGANS"	...		...	...

GENERAL NOTE/NOTE GENERALE/NOTA GENERAL.
E—> FOR THE UNIVERSAL DECIMAL CLASSIFICATION
(U.D.C.) SEE GENERAL NOTE TO TABLE 8.3.
FR—> POUR LA CLASSIFICATION DECIMALE UNI-
VERSELLE (C.D.U.) VOIR LA NOTE GENERALE DU
TABLEAU 8.3.
ESP> PARA LA CLASIFICACION DECIMAL UNIVERSAL
(C.D.U.) VEASE LA NOTA GENERAL DEL CUADRO 8.3.

EGYPT:
E—> PERIODICALS OF GROUPS 5, 6, 7, 8, 9, 10
AND 12 ARE INCLUDED IN GROUP 4; 15, 16, 17, 18
IN GROUP 14; 20 IN GROUP 19 AND 23 IN GROUP 22.
FR—> LES PERIODIQUES DES GROUPES 5, 6, 7, 8,
9, 10 ET 12 SONT INCLUS DANS LE GROUPE 4; 15,
16, 17, 18 DANS LE GROUPE 14; 20 DANS LE GROUPE
19 ET 23 DANS LE GROUPE 22.
ESP> LAS PUBLICACIONES PERIODICAS DE LOS GRU-
POS 5, 6, 7, 8, 9, 10 Y 12 ESTAN INCLUIDOS EN
EL GRUPO 4; LAS DE LOS GRUPOS 15, 16, 17 Y 18 EN
EL GRUPO 14; LAS DEL GRUPO 20 EN EL GRUPO 19 Y
LAS DEL 23 EN EL GRUPO 22.

MEXICO:
E—> DATA INCLUDE 50 PERIODICALS NOT IDENTI-
FIED IN THE U.D.C. GROUPS.
FR—> LES DONNEES COMPRENNENT 50 PERIODIQUES QUI
N'ONT PU ETRE IDENTIFIES D'APRES LES GROUPES DE
LA C.D.U.
ESP> LOS DATOS INCLUYEN 50 PUBLICACIONES PERIO-
DICAS QUE NO PUDIERON SER IDENTIFICADAS SEGUN LOS
GRUPOS DE LA C.D.U.

ECUADOR:
E—> DATA INCLUDE 166 PERIODICALS NOT IDEN-
TIFIED IN THE U.D.C. GROUPS.
FR—> LES DONNEES COMPRENNENT 166 PERIODIQUES
QUI N'ONT PU ETRE IDENTIFIES D'APRES LES GROUPES
DE LA C.D.U.
ESP> LOS DATOS INCLUYEN 166 PUBLICACIONES PERIO-
DICAS QUE NO PUDIERON SER IDENTIFICADAS SEGUN LOS
GRUPOS DE LA C.D.U.

HONG KONG:
E—> DATA REFER ONLY TO PERIODICALS FOR WHICH
CIRCULATION IS KNOWN.
FR—> LES DONNEES SE RAPPORTENT SEULEMENT AUX
PERIODIQUES POUR LESQUELS LE TIRAGE EST CONNU.
ESP> LOS DATOS SOLO SE REFIEREN A LAS PUBLICA-
CIONES PERIODICAS PARA LAS QUE SE CONOCE LA
TIRADA.

ISRAEL:
E—> PERIODICALS OF GROUP 18 ARE INCLUDED IN
GROUP 9.
FR—> LES PERIODIQUES DU GROUPE 18 SONT INCLUS
DANS LE GROUPE 9.
ESP> LAS PUBLICACIONES PERIODICAS DEL GRUPO 18
ESTAN INCLUIDAS EN EL GRUPO 9.

JAPAN:
E—> PERIODICALS OF GROUPS 22 AND 23 ARE COUNTED
TOGETHER.
FR—> LES PERIODIQUES DES GROUPES 22 ET 23 SONT
COMPTES ENSEMBLE.
ESP> LAS PUBLICACIONES PERIODICAS DE LOS GRUPOS
22 Y 23 FIGURAN EN LA MISMA RUBRICA.

JORDAN:
E—> DATA REFER TO THE EAST BANK ONLY.
FR—> LES DONNEES SE REFERENT A LA RIVE ORIENTALE
SEULEMENT.
ESP> LOS DATOS SE REFIEREN A LA ORILLA ORIENTAL
SOLAMENTE.

AUSTRIA:
E—> DATA INCLUDE 61 PERIODICALS NOT IDENTIFIED
IN THE U.D.C. GROUPS.
FR—> LES DONNEES COMPRENNENT 61 PERIODIQUES QUI
N'ONT PU ETRE IDENTIFIES D'APRES LES GROUPES DE
LA C.D.U.
ESP> LOS DATOS INCLUYEN 61 PUBLICACIONES PERIO-
DICAS QUE NO PUDIERON SER IDENTIFICADAS SEGUN LOS
GRUPOS DE LA C.D.U.

DENMARK:
E—> PERIODICALS OF GROUP 9 ARE INCLUDED IN
GROUP 18. COMICS AND HUMOUR MAGAZINES ARE INCLUDED
WITH CHILDREN'S AND ADOLESCENTS' MAGAZINES.
FR—> LES PERIODIQUES DU GROUPE 9 SONT INCLUS
DANS LE GROUPE 18. LES PERIODIQUES HUMORISTIQUES
SONT INCLUS AVEC LES PERIODIQUES POUR ENFANTS ET
ADOLESCENTS.
ESP> LAS PUBLICACIONES PERIODICAS DEL GRUPO 9
ESTAN INCLUIDAS EN EL GRUPO 18. LOS PERIODICOS
HUMORISTICOS QUEDAN INCLUIDOS CON LOS PERIODICOS
PARA NIÑOS Y JOVENES.

FRANCE:
E—> GROUP 10 IS INCLUDED IN GROUP 5. GROUPS 12
AND 13 ARE COUNTED TOGETHER.
FR—> LE GROUPE 10 EST INCLUS DANS LE GROUPE 5.
LES GROUPES 12 ET 13 SONT COMPTES ENSEMBLE.
ESP> LOS DATOS DEL GRUPO 10 ESTAN INCLUIDOS EN
EL GRUPO 5; LOS GRUPOS 12 Y 13 FIGURAN EN LA
MISMA RUBRICA.

GERMAN DEMOCRATIC REPUBLIC:
E—> CHILDREN'S MAGAZINES, COMICS AND PARISH
MAGAZINES ARE ALSO INCLUDED IN THE 23 GROUPS.
FR—> LES PERIODIQUES POUR ENFANTS, LES PERIODI-
QUES HUMORISTIQUES ET LES BULLETINS PAROISSIAUX
SONT AUSSI COMPTES DANS LES 23 GROUPES.
ESP> LOS PERIODICOS PARA NIÑOS, LOS PERIODICOS
HUMORISTICOS Y LOS BOLETINES PARROQUIALES TAMBIEN
SE CUENTAN EN LOS 23 GRUPOS.

IRELAND:
E—> THE CIRCULATION FIGURE DOES NOT INCLUDE SCHOOL MAGAZINES.
FR—> LE CHIFFRE RELATIF AU TIRAGE NE COMPREND PAS LES BULLETINS DES ECOLES.
ESP> LOS DATOS RELATIVOS A LA TIRADA NO INCLUYEN LOS BOLETINOS DE LA ESCUELA.

PORTUGAL:
E—> PERIODICALS OF GROUPS 5, 6, 7, 8, 9 AND 10 ARE INCLUDED IN GROUP 4; GROUP 18 IN GROUP 12; GROUPS 15, 16, 17 AND 18 IN GROUP 14; GROUP 20 IN 19 AND GROUP 23 IN 24. CHILDREN'S MAGAZINES, COMICS AND GENERAL INTEREST NEWSPAPERS ISSUED LESS THAN ONCE A WEEK ARE INCLUDED IN THE 23 GROUPS.
FR—> LES PERIODIQUES DES GROUPES 5, 6, 7, 8, 9 ET 10 SONT INCLUS DANS LE GROUPE 4; LE GROUPE 18 DANS LE GROUPE 12; LES GROUPES 15, 16, 17 ET 18 DANS LE GROUPE 14; LE GROUPE 20 DANS LE GROUPE 19; LE GROUPE 23 DANS LE GROUPE 24. LES PERIODIQUES POUR ENFANTS, LES PERIODIQUES HUMORISTIQUES ET LES JOURNAUX D'INFORMATION GENERALE PARAISSANT MOINS D'UNE FOIS PAR SEMAINE SONT COMPTES DANS LES 23 GROUPES.
ESP> LAS PUBLICACIONES PERIODICAS DE LOS GRUPOS 5, 6, 7, 8, 9 Y 10 ESTAN INCLUIDOS EN EL GRUPO 4; LAS DEL GRUPO 13 EN EL 12; LAS DE LOS GRUPOS 15, 16, 17 Y 18 EN EL GRUPO 14; LAS DEL GRUPO 20 EN EL 19 Y LAS DEL GRUPO 23 EN EL GRUPO 24. LOS PERIODICOS PARA NINOS, LOS PERIODICOS HUMORISTICOS Y LOS PERIODICOS DE INFORMACION QUE APARECEN MENOS DE UNA VEZ POR SEMANA FIGURAN INCLUIDOS EN LOS 23 GRUPOS.

SPAIN:
E—> CHILDREN'S MAGAZINES, COMICS, PARISH AND SCHOOL MAGAZINES, AND "HOUSE ORGANS" ARE ALSO INCLUDED IN THE 23 GROUPS.
FR—> LES PERIODIQUES POUR ENFANTS, LES PERIODIQUES HUMORISTIQUES, LES BULLETINS PAROISSIAUX ET DES ECOLES ET LES JOURNAUX D'ENTREPRISE SONT AUSSI COMPTES DANS LES 23 GROUPES.
ESP> LOS PERIODICOS PARA NINOS, LOS PERIODICOS HUMORISTICOS, LOS BOLETINES PARROQUIALES Y DE LAS ESCUELAS, Y LOS PERIODICOS DE EMPRESA TAMBIEN FIGURAN INCLUIDOS EN LOS 23 GRUPOS.

AUSTRALIA:
E—> DATA DO NOT INCLUDE COMICS, PARISH AND SCHOOL MAGAZINES AND "HOUSE ORGANS".
FR—> LES DONNEES NE COMPRENNENT PAS LES PERIODIQUES HUMORISTIQUES, LES BULLETINS PAROISSIAUX ET DES ECOLES ET LES JOURNAUX D'ENTREPRISE.
ESP> LOS DATOS EXCLUYEN LOS PERIODICOS HUMORISTICOS, LOS BOLETINES PARROQUIALES Y DE LAS ESCUELAS Y LOS PERIODICOS DE EMPRESA.

U.S.S.R.:
E—> DATA DO NOT INCLUDE PARISH AND SCHOOL MAGAZINES AND "HOUSE ORGANS".
FR—> LES DONNEES NE COMPRENNENT PAS LES BULLETINS PAROISSIAUX ET DES ECOLES, NI LES JOURNAUX D'ENTREPRISE.
ESP> LOS DATOS EXCLUYEN LOS BOLETINES PARROQUIALES Y DE LAS ESCUELAS Y LOS PERIODICOS DE EMPRESA.

BYELORUSSIAN S.S.R.:
E—> DATA DO NOT INCLUDE "HOUSE ORGANS".
FR—> LES DONNEES NE COMPRENNENT PAS LES JOURNAUX D'ENTREPRISE.
ESP> LOS DATOS EXCLUYEN LOS PERIODICOS DE EMPRESA.

8.17 Newsprint, printing and writing paper: production, imports, exports and consumption (total and per 1,000 inhabitants)

Papier journal, papier d'impression et papier d'écriture: production, importations, exportations et consommation (total et pour 1 000 habitants)

Papel de periódico, papel de imprenta y papel de escribir: producción, importaciones, exportaciones y consumo (total y por 1 000 habitantes)

A = PRODUCTION (METRIC TONS)
B = IMPORTS (METRIC TONS)
C = EXPORTS (METRIC TONS)
D = CONSUMPTION (METRIC TONS)
E = CONSUMPTION PER 1 000 INHABITANTS (KILOGRAMS)

A = PRODUCTION (TONNES METRIQUES)
B = IMPORTATIONS (TONNES METRIQUES)
C = EXPORTATIONS (TONNES METRIQUES)
D = CONSOMMATION (TONNES METRIQUES)
E = CONSOMMATION POUR 1 000 HABITANTS (KILOGRAMMES)

A = PRODUCCION (TONELADAS METRICAS)
B = IMPORTACIONES (TONELADAS METRICAS)
C = EXPORTACIONES (TONELADAS METRICAS)
D = CONSUMO (TONELADAS METRICAS)
E = CONSUMO POR 1 000 HABITANTES (KILOGRAMOS)

NUMBER OF COUNTRIES AND TERRITORIES PRESENTED IN THIS TABLE: 142
NOMBRE DE PAYS ET DE TERRITOIRES PRESENTES DANS CE TABLEAU: 142
NUMERO DE PAISES Y DE TERRITORIOS PRESENTADOS EN ESTE CUADRO: 142

COUNTRY / PAYS / PAIS	DEFINITION OF DATA / CODE / TIPO DE DATOS	NEWSPRINT / PAPIER JOURNAL / PAPEL DE PERIODICO				PRINTING AND WRITING PAPER / PAPIER D'IMPRESSION ET D'ECRITURE / PAPEL DE IMPRENTA Y DE ESCRIBIR			
		1965	1970	1977	1978	1965	1970	1977	1978
		(2)	(3)	(4)	(5)	(6)	(7)	(8)	(9)
AFRICA									
ALGERIA	A					19 800	23 000	18 000	18 000
	B	2 100	6 200	9 700	9 700	6 100	19 000	3 400	3 400
	C					17 200			
	D	2 100	6 200	9 700	9 700	8 700	42 000	21 400	21 400
	E	176	466	577	553	730	3 158	1 274	1 221
ANGOLA ‡	A	1 400	600	1 000	1 000		1 500	3 000	3 000
	B		100				2 000	2 700	2 700
	C		200	300	300				
	D	1 400	500	700	700		3 500	5 700	5 700
	E	272	88	104	101		617	847	825

Newsprint, printing and writing paper 8.17
Papier journal, papier d'impression et papier d'écriture
Papel de periódico, papel de imprenta y papel de escribir

	(1)	(2)	(3)	(4)	(5)	(6)	(7)	(8)	(9)
BENIN	B			100	100			500	500
	D			100	100			500	500
	E			31	30			154	150
CENTRAL AFRICAN REPUBLIC	B					100	200		
	D					100	200		
	E					69	124		
CHAD	B							100	100
	D							100	100
	E							24	24
CONGO	B						200	200	200
	D						200	200	200
	E						168	141	138
DJIBOUTI	B	400							
	D	400							
	E	4 706							
EGYPT	A					27 200	40 000	38 000	45 000
	B	40 900	32 900	70 200	75 000	11 000	5 000	42 400	44 500
	C								
	D	40 900	32 900	70 200	75 000	38 200	45 100	80 400	89 500
	E	1 392	1 045	1 890	1 974	1 300	1 430	2 164	2 355
ETHIOPIA	A							3 500	3 500
	B	1 200	900	1 100	1 100	1 000	900	1 100	1 100
	D	1 200	900	1 100	1 100	1 000	900	4 600	4 600
	E	54	36	37	36	45	36	155	152
GABON	B					300	100	1 500	600
	D					300	100	1 500	600
	E					640	200	2 825	1 119
GHANA	B		3 600	7 300	7 300	4 600	7 600	6 700	6 700
	D		3 600	7 300	7 300	4 600	7 600	6 700	6 700
	E		417	698	677	594	881	640	622
GUINEA-BISSAU	B			100	100				
	D			100	100				
	E			184	181				
IVORY COAST	B	2 000	900	800	800			4 200	4 200
	D	2 000	900	800	800			4 200	4 200
	E	522	152	113	110			595	579
KENYA	A						6 900	17 000	17 000
	B	3 200	5 000	4 800	4 800	6 300	100	2 000	2 000
	C							2 900	2 900
	D	3 200	5 000	4 800	4 800	6 300	6 800	16 100	16 100
	E	336	445	339	327	661	605	1 136	1 098
LIBERIA	B						200	350	
	D						200	350	
	E						144	214	
LIBYAN ARAB JAMAHIRIYA	B	100	800	1 400	1 400	1 200	1 400	7 700	7 700
	D	100	800	1 400	1 400	1 200	1 400	7 700	7 700
	E	62	389	551	533	742	682	3 029	2 933

8.17 Newsprint, printing and writing paper
Papier journal, papier d'impression et papier d'écriture
Papel de periódico, papel de imprenta y papel de escribir

COUNTRY / PAYS / PAIS	CODE / TIPO DE DATOS (1)	NEWSPRINT — PAPIER JOURNAL — PAPEL DE PERIODICO 1965 (2)	1970 (3)	1977 (4)	1978 (5)	PRINTING AND WRITING PAPER — PAPIER D'IMPRESSION ET D'ECRITURE — PAPEL DE IMPRENTA Y DE ESCRIBIR 1965 (6)	1970 (7)	1977 (8)	1978 (9)
MADAGASCAR	A						3 900		
	B			3 500	3 500	4 300	1 300	800	800
	C								
	D		300	3 500	3 500	4 300	2 600		
	E			411	399	707	375		
MALAWI	B	100	200	100	100	700	2 500	13 300	13 300
	D	100	200	100	100	700	2 500	13 300	13 300
	E	26	46	19	19	180	573	2 576	2 511
MALI	B		200	100	100			360	360
	D		200	100	100			360	360
	E		40	17	16			60	59
MAURITIUS	B	700	600	1 000	1 400	400	800	1 600	1 600
	D	700	600	1 000	1 400	400	800	1 600	1 600
	E	920	728	1 078	1 486	526	971	1 724	1 699
MOROCCO	A					4 000	10 000	13 000	13 000
	B	2 000	3 100	5 200	5 600	1 300	2 000	1 100	1 100
	D	2 000	3 100	5 200	5 600	5 300	12 000	14 100	14 100
	E	152	205	280	292	403	793	812	736
MOZAMBIQUE	B	1 200	200	1 300	1 300				
	D	1 200	200	1 300	1 300				
	E	163	24	134	131				
NIGER	B			100	100			100	100
	D			100	100			100	100
	E			21	20			21	20
NIGERIA	A						2 000	2 000	2 000
	B	5 300	17 100	23 700	23 700	10 400	25 200	29 000	29 000
	D	5 300	17 100	23 700	23 700	10 400	27 200	31 000	31 000
	E	109	310	355	345	214	494	464	451
REUNION	B		400	500	500	400	300		
	D		400	500	500	400	300		
	E		895	960	943	1 018	671		
SENEGAL	B	300	500	3 000	5 000	2 600	3 300	1 500	600
	D	300	500	3 000	5 000	2 600	3 300	1 500	600
	E	86	113	573	932	745	745	286	112
SIERRA LEONE	B	200	200	150	150	300	200	500	500
	D	200	200	150	150	300	200	500	500
	E	84	81	51	50	127	81	149	145
SOMALIA	B	100	500	600	600	100	100		
	D	100	500	600	600	100	100		
	E	40	179	179	174	36	36		

DEFINITION OF DATA

Newsprint, printing and writing paper   8.17
Papier journal, papier d'impression et papier d'écriture
Papel de periódico, papel de imprenta y papel de escribir

Country	(1)	(2)	(3)	(4)	(5)	(6)	(7)	(8)	(9)
SOUTH AFRICA	A	54 000	160 000	254 000	212 000	46 000	70 000	118 000	161 000
	B	50 200	52 500	300	800	70 800	130 500	65 900	65 900
	C			105 800	105 800	3 100	3 600	10 000	10 000
	D	104 200	212 500	148 200	106 800	113 700	196 900	173 900	216 900
	E	5 682	9 884	5 673	3 947	6 201	9 158	6 657	8 062
SUDAN	B	1 300	2 700	500	1 800	2 200	3 700	9 300	7 200
	D	1 300	2 700	500	1 800	2 200	3 700	9 300	7 200
	E	96	207	31	108	162	284	575	431
TOGO	B	200							
	D	200							
	E	118							
TUNISIA	A							21 000	21 000
	B	400		5 000	5 000	1 300		3 800	3 800
	C							17 200	17 200
	D	400		5 000	5 000	1 300			
	E	87		827	805	281		2 843	2 768
UGANDA	B	900	1 000	200	200	1 700	2 600	500	500
	D	900	1 000	200	200	1 700	2 600	500	500
	E	105	102	17	16	198	265	41	40
UNITED REPUBLIC OF CAMEROON	B	600	100	500	500	2 600	1 300	4 000	4 000
	D	600	100	500	500	2 600	1 300	4 000	4 000
	E	52	17	75	73	226	223	596	584
UNITED REPUBLIC OF TANZANIA	B	500	500	1 900	1 900	2 600	5 100	5 000	5 000
	D	500	500	1 900	1 900	2 600	5 100	5 000	5 000
	E	27	23	116	113	139	384	305	296
ZAIRE	B	1 100	2 100	1 000	1 100	1 700	2 400	4 000	
	D	1 100	2 100	1 000	1 100	1 700	2 400	4 000	
	E	298	489	39	42	460	111	155	
ZAMBIA	B			2 100	2 100		5 300	3 600	3 600
	D			2 100	2 100		5 300	3 600	3 600
	E			394	381		1 234	675	654
ZIMBABWE	A	5 000	10 000	12 000	12 000	10 300	10 300	10 300	10 300
	B	1 300	1 300	1 100	1 100				
	C	1 500	1 500			100	100		
	D	4 800	9 800	13 100	13 100	10 200	10 200	10 300	10 300
	E	1 085	1 846	1 949	1 882	2 305	1 922	1 532	1 480
AMERICA, NORTH									
BAHAMAS	B		1 000	1 000	1 000	100	500	300	300
	D		1 000	1 000	1 000	100	500	300	300
	E		5 650	4 673	4 566	426	2 825	1 402	1 370
BARBADOS	B	700	900	500	500		500	800	800
	D	700	900	500	500		500	800	800
	E	2 979	3 766	2 016	2 008		2 092	3 226	3 213
BELIZE	B	100	200	200	200		100	100	100
	D	100	200	200	200		100	100	100
	E	943	1 667	1 342	1 307		833	671	654

8.17 Newsprint, printing and writing paper
Papier journal, papier d'impression et papier d'écriture
Papel de periódico, papel de imprenta y papel de escribir

COUNTRY / PAYS / PAIS	DEFINITION OF DATA / CODE / TIPO DE DATOS	NEWSPRINT — PAPIER JOURNAL — PAPEL DE PERIODICO				PRINTING AND WRITING PAPER — PAPIER D'IMPRESSION ET D'ECRITURE — PAPEL DE IMPRENTA Y DE ESCRIBIR			
	(1)	1965 (2)	1970 (3)	1977 (4)	1978 (5)	1965 (6)	1970 (7)	1977 (8)	1978 (9)
CANADA	A	7 003 300	7 996 000	8 154 000	8 811 000	484 600	821 000	1 110 000	1 316 000
	B	6 522 600	7 339 300	7 266 000	7 868 300	12 600	35 000	115 800	118 000
	C	480 700	656 700	888 000	942 900	118 500	300 100	416 300	524 300
	D					378 700	555 900	809 900	909 700
	E	24 471	30 802	38 079	40 132	19 278	26 074	34 713	38 727
COSTA RICA	B	6 100	11 100	11 200	11 200	3 100	4 000	6 000	6 000
	D	6 100	11 100	11 200	11 200	3 100	4 000	6 000	6 000
	E	4 080	6 427	5 408	5 271	2 074	2 316	2 897	2 824
CUBA	A	18 900	22 800	27 000	27 000	18 800	20 000	30 000	30 000
	B	18 900	22 800	27 000	27 000	3 700	6 500	22 000	22 000
	D					22 500	26 500	52 000	52 000
	E	2 422	2 662	2 730	2 673	884	3 094	5 258	5 149
DOMINICAN REPUBLIC	B	700	4 200	2 600	2 600	800	3 600	5 900	5 900
	D	700	4 200	2 600	2 600	800	3 600	5 900	5 900
	E	189	967	475	460	216	829	1 078	1 043
EL SALVADOR	B	8 800	13 000	14 200	14 200	2 200	2 100	9 800	9 800
	C							500	500
	D	8 800	13 000	14 100	14 200	2 200	2 100	9 300	9 300
	E	2 979	3 697	3 246	3 144	745	597	2 126	2 059
GUADELOUPE	B			600		200			
	D			600		200			
	E			1 775		664			
GUATEMALA	A			300	300	4 000	6 700	12 000	12 000
	B	5 500	8 300	6 700	6 700	1 600	1 100	13 100	13 100
	C						4 100	7 400	7 400
	D	5 500	8 300	7 000	7 000	5 600	3 700	17 700	17 700
	E	1 200	1 742	1 197	1 347	1 222	776	3 027	3 406
HAITI	B	400	700	700	700	100	300	300	300
	D	400	700	700	700	100	300	300	300
	E	101	165	149	146	25	71	64	63
HONDURAS	B	1 600	2 700	2 100	2 100	1 100	2 500	2 800	2 800
	C							200	200
	D	1 600	2 700	2 100	2 100	1 100	2 500	2 600	2 600
	E	724	1 156	706	682	498	1 070	874	844
JAMAICA	B	6 300	8 600	4 700	5 200	3 000	4 100	5 300	5 700
	D	6 300	8 600	4 700	5 200	3 000	4 100	5 300	5 700
	E	3 580	4 570	2 252	2 459	1 705	2 179	2 540	2 695
MARTINIQUE	B	400		800	800	200			
	D	400		800	800	200			
	E	1 303		2 367	2 332	651			

Newsprint, printing and writing paper 8.17
Papier journal, papier d'impression et papier d'écriture
Papel de periódico, papel de imprenta y papel de escribir

Country	(1)	(2)	(3)	(4)	(5)	(6)	(7)	(8)	(9)
MEXICO	A	21 700	40 000	90 000	84 000	122 900	122 200	304 000	350 000
	B	91 300	118 800	297 200	161 000		236 800	233 200	87 000
	D	113 000	158 800	387 200	245 000	122 900	358 800	537 200	437 000
	E	2 637	3 156	6 120	3 745	2 868	7 131	8 491	6 680
NETHERLANDS ANTILLES	B	400	600	500	500	1 500	600	600	600
	D	400	600	500	500	1 500	600	600	600
	E	1 923	2 703	1 984	1 946	882	2 703	2 381	2 335
NICARAGUA	B	2 900	3 700	2 700	2 700	2 300	2 500	3 200	3 200
	D	2 900	3 700	2 700	2 700	2 300	2 500	3 200	3 200
	E	1 705	1 878	1 090	1 055	1 824	1 269	1 292	1 250
PANAMA	A							3 000	3 000
	B	3 500	5 900	4 200	4 200		5 900	1 500	1 500
	D	3 500	5 900	4 200	4 200		5 900	4 500	4 500
	E	2 776	4 047	2 368	2 301		4 067	2 537	2 466
TRINIDAD AND TOBAGO	B	4 400	5 600	6 300	6 300	1 300	2 800	1 900	1 900
	C							100	
	D	4 400	5 600	6 300	6 300	1 300	2 800	1 900	1 900
	E	4 846	5 864	6 117	6 052	1 432	2 932	1 845	1 825
UNITED STATES OF AMERICA	A	1 977 700	3 035 000	3 198 000	3 207 000	8 292 700	10 046 000	12 702 000	13 374 000
	B	5 735 900	6 019 300	5 950 700	6 787 000	99 900	278 100	475 000	857 900
	C	76 400	130 300	116 700	74 800	48 900	162 100	302 900	280 200
	D	7 637 200	8 924 000	9 031 300	9 919 200	8 343 700	10 162 100	12 874 100	13 951 700
	E	39 306	43 557	41 653	45 430	42 942	49 600	59 377	63 899
AMERICA, SOUTH									
ARGENTINA	A	4 400	3 200	16 000	39 000	101 400	122 700	142 000	145 000
	B	220 100	274 100	160 600	160 600	9 600	4 200	11 600	11 600
	C							21 000	21 000
	D	224 500	277 400	175 400	198 400	111 000	122 700	132 600	135 600
	E	10 122	11 681	6 732	7 517	5 005	5 167	5 089	5 138
BOLIVIA	B	3 100	4 700	6 300	7 700	1 700	3 900	4 600	5 200
	D	3 100	4 700	6 300	7 700	1 700	3 900	4 600	5 200
	E	730	1 176	1 323	1 575	400	976	966	1 064
BRAZIL	A	117 000	102 900	107 000	116 000	151 600	254 400	557 000	633 000
	B	54 300	149 100	234 200	235 200	3 200	12 800	16 500	112 300
	C							31 700	
	D	171 300	251 800	341 200	273 200	154 600	266 300	541 800	745 000
	E	2 075	2 645	2 938	2 287	1 873	2 797	4 665	6 236
CHILE	A	97 100	124 400	132 000	132 000	23 200	28 200	44 000	56 000
	B	5 200					7 900	900	900
	C	61 400	78 300	87 000	76 700			12 200	13 300
	D	40 900	46 600	45 400	55 300	23 200	36 100	31 800	42 700
	E	4 806	4 974	4 232	5 106	2 726	3 853	2 991	3 943
COLOMBIA	A	45 300	59 200	44 400	44 400	21 000	43 800	61 000	65 000
	B					2 400	2 500	9 200	9 200
	C					1 400	3 400	900	900
	D	45 300	59 200	44 400	44 400	22 000	42 900	69 300	73 300
	E	2 424	2 930	1 760	1 707	1 177	2 123	2 747	2 819

8.17 Newsprint, printing and writing paper
Papier journal, papier d'impression et papier d'écriture
Papel de periódico, papel de imprenta y papel de escribir

COUNTRY / PAYS / PAIS	DEFINITION OF DATA / CODE / TIPO DE DATOS (1)	NEWSPRINT — PAPIER JOURNAL — PAPEL DE PERIODICO				PRINTING AND WRITING PAPER — PAPIER D'IMPRESSION ET D'ECRITURE — PAPEL DE IMPRENTA Y DE ESCRIBIR			
		1965 (2)	1970 (3)	1977 (4)	1978 (5)	1965 (6)	1970 (7)	1977 (8)	1978 (9)
ECUADOR	A							3 000	3 000
	B	13 400	13 900	10 800	10 800	300	5 900	7 300	7 300
	D	13 400	13 900	10 800	10 800	300	5 900	10 300	10 300
	E	2 630	2 305	1 430	1 385	59	978	1 363	1 321
GUYANA	B	1 000	1 200	1 800	1 800	400	1 200	2 000	2 000
	D	1 000	1 200	1 800	1 800	400	1 200	2 000	2 000
	E	1 580	1 693	2 177	2 130	632	1 693	2 418	2 367
PARAGUAY	B	1 400	4 100	6 500	6 500	400	500	2 300	2 300
	D	1 400	4 100	6 500	6 500	400	500	2 300	2 300
	E	694	1 782	2 317	2 251	198	217	820	796
PERU	A	40 400	49 400	55 600	41 300	10 000	22 000	41 000	36 000
	B					4 100	2 700	300	100
	C			4 800	4 800				
	D	40 400	49 400	50 800	36 500	14 100	24 700	41 300	36 100
	E	3 531	3 729	3 128	2 183	1 233	1 661	2 543	2 159
SURINAME	B	400	500	600	600	100		500	500
	D	400	500	600	600	100		500	500
	E	1 205	1 348	1 342	1 302	301		1 119	1 085
URUGUAY	A	17 900	20 800	12 100	12 100	12 600	14 500	11 300	11 300
	B						100	400	400
	C							3 500	3 500
	D	17 900	20 800	12 100	12 100	12 600	14 600	8 200	8 200
	E	6 388	7 814	4 238	4 201	4 497	5 485	2 872	2 847
VENEZUELA	A	43 600	84 300	107 000	107 000	11 400	26 200	68 000	68 000
	B					16 300	8 800	19 000	19 000
	D	43 600	84 300	107 000	107 000	27 700	35 000	87 000	87 000
	E	4 789	7 984	8 264	8 026	3 042	3 315	6 720	6 526
ASIA									
AFGHANISTAN	B	300		1 200	1 200	300	400	1 600	1 600
	D	300		1 200	1 200	300	400	1 600	1 600
	E	20		59	57	20	24	79	77
BAHRAIN	B						400	1 500	1 500
	D						400	1 500	1 500
	E						1 860	5 618	5 435
BANGLADESH	A	34 000	36 000	32 000	27 000	28 000	32 000	24 000	19 000
	C			7 700	7 700			300	300
	D	34 000	36 000	24 300	19 300	28 000	32 000	23 700	18 700
	E	578	532	313	242	476	473	305	234
BRUNEI	B		100	200	200	100	200	200	200
	D		100	200	200	100	200	200	200
	E		752	1 316	1 290	877	1 504	1 316	1 290

Newsprint, printing and writing paper 8.17
Papier journal, papier d'impression et papier d'écriture
Papel de periódico, papel de imprenta y papel de escribir

Country	(1)	(2)	(3)	(4)	(5)	(6)	(7)	(8)	(9)
BURMA	A						400	7 000	7 000
	B		15 900	11 900	11 900	31 200	11 700	8 400	8 400
	D		15 900	11 900	11 900	31 200	12 100	15 400	15 400
	E		573	363	355	1 260	436	470	459
CHINA	A	367 200	571 000	1 209 000	1 277 000	926 000	1 150 000	2 127 000	2 270 000
	B		13 600	40 500	40 500		2 100	800	800
	C	22 500	13 000	2 200	2 200	20 200	13 300	26 400	26 400
	D	344 700	571 600	1 247 300	1 315 300	905 800	1 138 800	2 101 400	2 244 400
	E	485	741	1 440	1 494	1 275	1 475	2 426	2 550
CYPRUS	B	1 500	1 700	1 800	2 100	700	4 100	2 500	3 500
	D	1 500	1 700	1 800	2 100	700	4 100	2 200	3 500
	E	2 525	2 686	2 609	3 009	1 178	6 477	3 623	5 014
DEMOCRATIC KAMPUCHEA	A	600							
	B	5 400	500			500	2 400		
	D	6 000	500			500	2 400		
	E	977	71			81	340		
EAST TIMOR	B			100	100				
	D			100	100				
	E			142	139				
HONG KONG	B	34 300	48 200	62 400	86 800	25 000	53 700	77 100	110 500
	C	100	3 000			800	4 300		
	D	34 200	45 000	62 400	86 800	24 200	49 400	77 100	110 500
	E	9 263	11 416	14 371	19 727	6 555	12 532	17 757	25 114
INDIA	A	30 500	37 300	55 500	49 000	333 500	444 700	552 000	540 000
	B	85 300	144 200	167 100	167 100	8 600	2 800	2 500	2 500
	C					200	14 200	2 000	2 000
	D	115 800	181 500	223 200	216 700	341 900	433 300	552 500	540 500
	E	240	334	346	328	709	797	857	818
INDONESIA	A	1 000	3 000			5 000	6 000	61 000	61 000
	B	16 200	40 600	56 100	90 200	10 300	44 000	19 000	34 700
	D	17 200	43 600	56 100	90 200	15 300	50 000	80 000	95 700
	E	164	365	391	613	146	419	558	651
IRAN	A						12 000	38 000	38 000
	B	9 400	10 900	25 500	25 500		99 800	12 300	12 300
	D	9 400	10 900	25 500	25 500		111 800	50 300	50 300
	E	381	409	775	751		4 199	1 529	1 482
IRAQ	A							9 000	9 000
	B	800	3 100	3 800	3 800	4 900	11 100	1 700	1 700
	D	800	3 100	3 800	3 800	4 900	11 100	10 700	10 700
	E	100	331	321	310	614	1 186	903	872
ISRAEL	A	8 300	9 400	12 000	12 000	18 800	31 800	41 000	41 000
	B	10 300	24 600	38 000	38 000	1 000	5 100	3 000	3 000
	C						1 500	1 400	1 400
	D	18 800	34 000	50 000	50 000	19 800	35 400	42 600	42 600
	E	7 335	11 417	13 736	13 405	7 725	11 887	11 710	11 421
JAPAN	A	1 184 200	1 917 000	2 370 000	2 482 000	1 211 400	2 410 000	3 103 000	3 416 000
	B	11 100	88 000	42 000	52 400	200	2 000	46 000	37 800
	C	6 000	32 000	94 500	89 100	109 100	191 000	182 000	108 400
	D	1 188 500	1 973 000	2 317 500	2 444 700	1 102 500	2 221 000	2 967 400	3 345 400
	E	12 019	18 908	20 354	21 290	11 150	21 285	26 062	29 134

8.17 Newsprint, printing and writing paper
Papier journal, papier d'impression et papier d'écriture
Papel de periódico, papel de imprenta y papel de escribir

COUNTRY / PAYS / PAIS	DEFINITION OF DATA / CODE / TIPO DE DATOS	NEWSPRINT — PAPIER JOURNAL — PAPEL DE PERIODICO				PRINTING AND WRITING PAPER — PAPIER D'IMPRESSION ET D'ECRITURE — PAPEL DE IMPRENTA Y PAPEL DE ESCRIBIR			
		1965 (2)	1970 (3)	1977 (4)	1978 (5)	1965 (6)	1970 (7)	1977 (8)	1978 (9)
JORDAN	B	600	600	1 300	2 700	1 900	500	1 500	1 200
	D	600	600	1 300	2 700	1 900	500	1 500	1 200
	E	307	360	624	1 252	972	300	719	557
KOREA, DEMOCRATIC PEOPLE'S REPUB. OF	B		1 300	1 300	1 300		2 100	2 100	2 100
	D		1 300	1 300	1 300		2 100	2 100	2 100
	E		94	78	76		151	126	123
KOREA, REPUBLIC OF	A	45 400	101 700	198 000	185 000	29 700	22 300	187 000	247 000
	B	2 100	6 600	4 200	3 800	200	400	100	1 100
	C					200		33 500	35 900
	D	47 500	108 300	193 800	181 300	29 700	22 700	153 600	212 200
	E	1 691	3 453	5 379	4 933	1 057	724	4 263	5 777
KUWAIT	B	3 300	3 700	11 300	11 300	1 400	6 700	23 200	23 200
	C			500	500		300	1 400	1 500
	D	3 300	3 700	10 800	10 000	1 400	6 400	21 800	21 700
	E	6 947	14 919	9 507	9 000	2 947	9 078	19 190	18 083
LAO PEOPLE'S DEMOCRATIC REPUBLIC	B	300	300	200	200	500	400	500	500
	D	300	300	200	200	500	400	500	500
	E	113	101	58	56	189	135	144	141
LEBANON	B	3 900	5 100	8 000	8 000	11 600	23 500	25 400	25 400
	C					100	100	100	100
	D	3 900	5 100	8 000	8 000	11 500	23 500	25 400	25 400
	E	1 813	2 066	2 620	2 538	5 346	9 518	8 320	8 058
MACAU	B	2 400	2 800	2 800	2 800	500	2 500	1 900	1 900
	C					100			
	D	2 400	2 800	2 800	2 800	400	2 500	1 900	1 900
	E	10 762		10 036	9 894	1 794	10 081	6 810	6 714
MALAYSIA	A							1 000	1 000
	B		38 400	60 800	69 500		20 600	42 100	60 500
	C		200	200	4 000		600	300	400
	D		38 200	60 600	65 500		19 900	42 800	61 100
	E		3 650	4 725	4 959		1 901	3 337	4 626
PENINSULAR MALAYSIA	A							1 000	
	B	12 100	36 700	42 100		12 700	19 500	39 800	
	C		200	100			600	900	
	D	12 100	36 500	42 000		12 700	18 900	39 900	
	E	1 572	4 141	3 930		1 650	2 144	3 733	
SABAH	B	500	700	900		400	500	1 300	
	D	500	700	900		400	500	1 300	
	E	919	1 077	1 068		735	769	1 542	

Newsprint, printing and writing paper 8.17
Papier journal, papier d'impression et papier d'écriture
Papel de periódico, papel de imprenta y papel de escribir

Country	(1)	(2)	(3)	(4)	(5)	(6)	(7)	(8)	(9)
SARAWAK	B	400	1 000	1 700		500	500	2 400	1 900
	D	400	1 000	1 700		500	500	2 400	1 900
	E	477	999	1 313		597	500	1 853	1 205
MONGOLIA	B		2 400	2 300	2 300			1 900	
	D		2 400	2 300	2 300			1 900	
	E		1 923	1 501	1 458			1 240	
PAKISTAN	A	51 000	500	5 200		6 000	6 300	19 000	25 000
	B	45 500				8 600	4 800	15 100	15 100
	C								
	D	96 500	500	5 200		14 500	10 700	34 100	40 100
	E	3 013	8	69		277	177	453	516
PHILIPPINES	A		30 000	78 000	80 000	9 000	30 000	40 000	43 000
	B		45 500	400	5 000	13 100	10 700	9 100	9 100
	C								
	D		75 500	78 400	85 000	22 100	40 700	49 100	52 100
	E		2 121	1 746	1 833	690	1 143	1 093	1 123
QATAR	B						600	1 400	1 400
	D						600	1 400	1 400
	E						595	14 286	13 861
SAUDI ARABIA	B		500	8 000	8 000		6 700	11 000	11 000
	D		500	8 000	8 000		6 700	11 000	11 000
	E		81	1 049	1 018		1 081	1 443	1 399
SINGAPORE	B	12 500	24 500	32 500	42 400	17 500	23 600	48 100	62 100
	C		900	3 000	3 800	2 400	3 300	12 000	12 400
	D	11 700	23 600	29 500	38 800	15 100	20 300	36 100	49 700
	E	6 223	11 373	12 710	16 448	8 032	783	15 554	21 068
SRI LANKA	A	12 400	18 300	9 600	9 600	4 500	8 900	10 000	10 000
	B					5 100	4 300	200	200
	D	12 400	18 300	9 600	9 600	9 600	13 200	10 200	10 200
	E	1 111	1 462	659	646	860	1 055	700	686
SYRIAN ARAB REPUBLIC	B	400	1 500	1 100	4 400	7 700	7 200	2 900	14 700
	D	400	1 500	1 100	4 400	7 700	7 200	2 900	14 700
	E	75	240	142	551	1 447	1 153	375	1 840
THAILAND	A	25 900	36 300	74 200	85 400	16 300	32 000	21 700	34 000
	B					6 500	12 500	14 000	16 300
	C								
	D	25 900	36 300	74 200	85 400	22 800	44 200	35 700	50 200
	E	845	1 016	1 652	1 840	744	1 237	786	1 082
TURKEY	A	20 300	10 700	88 000	77 000	23 600	42 400	72 000	62 000
	B	22 700	15 400	19 900	13 500	1 300	4 300	4 200	2 800
	D	43 000	26 100	107 900	90 500	24 900	46 700	76 200	64 800
	E	1 380	741	2 571	2 101	799	1 325	1 816	1 505
VIET-NAM	A	12 600	21 700	2 000	2 000	14 000	15 000	18 000	18 000
	B								
	D	12 600	21 700	2 000	2 000	14 000	15 100	18 000	18 000
	E	362	555	44	43	402	386	396	387
YEMEN, DEMOCRATIC	B			200	200	500	400	700	700
	D			200	200	500	400	700	700
	E			114	110	399	279	397	386

8.17 Newsprint, printing and writing paper
Papier journal, papier d'impression et papier d'écriture
Papel de periódico, papel de imprenta y papel de escribir

COUNTRY / PAYS / PAIS	CODE / TIPO DE DATOS (1)	NEWSPRINT — PAPIER JOURNAL — PAPEL DE PERIODICO				PRINTING AND WRITING PAPER — PAPIER D'IMPRESSION ET D'ÉCRITURE — PAPEL DE IMPRENTA Y DE ESCRIBIR			
		1965 (2)	1970 (3)	1977 (4)	1978 (5)	1965 (6)	1970 (7)	1977 (8)	1978 (9)
EUROPE									
AUSTRIA	A	121 000	170 000	171 000	161 000	282 000	394 000	594 000	598 000
	B		400	3 300	2 400	7 400	8 100	17 200	25 600
	C	60 200	67 000	29 500	22 500	193 300	288 000	527 100	526 400
	D	60 800	103 400	144 800	140 900	96 100	114 000	84 100	97 200
	E	8 380	13 924	19 255	18 719	13 246	15 351	11 184	12 914
BELGIUM	A	89 000	95 000	83 000	86 000	131 000	352 000	394 000	415 000
	B	76 800	110 300	129 100	128 100	134 400	208 300	248 700	296 300
	C	32 400	25 600	22 900	20 200	34 700	237 400	252 900	262 300
	D	133 400	179 700	189 200	193 900	230 700	322 900	389 800	449 000
	E	13 618	17 979	18 575	19 014	23 550	32 306	38 268	44 028
BULGARIA	A	22 900	35 400	43 500	49 000	22 900	41 000	49 000	49 000
	B	22 900	35 400	43 500	49 000	9 000	9 500	18 700	17 000
	D					31 900	50 500	67 700	66 000
	E	2 792	4 170	4 946	5 549	3 890	5 948	7 698	7 475
CZECHOSLOVAKIA	A	77 800	81 400	80 000	75 000	136 400	176 500	168 000	174 000
	B		9 000	8 000	8 000	700	26 000	30 000	30 000
	C	34 800	40 700	17 000	17 000	26 100	39 500	54 000	54 000
	D	43 000	49 700	71 000	66 000	111 000	163 500	144 000	150 000
	E	3 037	3 466	4 742	4 381	7 847	11 402	9 617	9 956
DENMARK	A					62 700	71 000	79 000	95 000
	B	116 200	149 200	134 100	169 900	56 300	84 800	118 800	133 700
	C					7 300	10 800	21 800	36 000
	D	116 400	149 000	133 700	169 400	112 100	144 800	176 100	192 700
	E	24 464	30 229	26 267	33 177	23 560	29 377	34 597	37 740
FINLAND	A	1 213 000	1 305 000	979 000	1 126 000	493 000	981 000	1 686 000	1 906 000
	B		900		100	500	1 600	3 590	2 600
	C	1 100 500	1 187 000	840 000	1 113 400	410 500	779 200	1 526 590	1 634 000
	D	112 500	118 900	139 000	12 700	83 400	203 400	163 590	274 600
	E	24 649	25 814	29 343	2 674	18 273	44 160	34 535	57 823
FRANCE	A	450 200	430 200	255 000	287 000	933 200	1 418 000	1 691 000	1 886 000
	B	96 800	177 000	327 100	326 300	87 700	242 100	361 600	361 600
	C	1 800	1 700	1 900	2 200	76 600	166 600	271 600	271 600
	D	545 000	605 500	580 200	611 100	944 300	1 493 500	1 781 000	1 976 000
	E	11 178	11 926	10 937	11 478	19 367	29 417	33 572	37 115
GERMAN DEMOCRATIC REPUBLIC	A	93 600	96 800	100 000	103 000	204 300	197 000	170 000	176 000
	B	9 000	36 900	46 000	38 000		1 100	36 000	34 000
	C	12 600	16 400	2 000	10 000	16 100	21 900	12 000	14 000
	D	90 000	117 300	144 000	131 000	188 200	176 200	194 000	196 000
	E	5 288	6 877	8 589	7 819	11 058	10 329	11 572	11 698

	(1)	(2)	(3)	(4)	(5)	(6)	(7)	(8)	(9)
GERMANY, FEDERAL REPUBLIC OF	A	216 000	408 000	544 000	521 000	1 085 000	1 889 000	2 355 000	2 525 000
	B	520 100	695 300	734 100	734 100	341 300	520 800	851 400	851 400
	C	3 600	26 000	88 800	88 800	80 500	287 200	538 500	538 500
	D	732 500	1 077 300	1 189 300	1 166 300	1 345 800	2 122 600	2 667 900	2 837 900
	E	12 413	17 745	19 370	19 039	22 806	34 963	43 451	46 325
GREECE	A	45 400	31 600	45 600	43 600	23 000	30 000	37 000	62 000
	B			100	1 000	2 100	5 700	30 700	30 100
	C								
	D	45 400	31 600	38 700	42 600	25 700	35 700	67 600	92 600
	E	5 240	3 594	4 170	4 544	2 966	4 060	7 284	9 877
HUNGARY	A	37 600	53 600	61 000	63 600	38 400	74 200	110 000	109 000
	B					26 100	35 400	50 400	57 600
	C			1 400	100		1 200	23 900	22 200
	D	37 600	53 600	59 600	63 500	64 500	108 400	136 400	144 400
	E	3 703	5 185	5 596	5 918	6 353	10 486	12 817	13 458
ICELAND	B	2 400	3 100	4 000	3 730	1 200	1 800	2 300	2 890
	D	2 400	3 100	4 000	3 730	1 200	1 800	2 300	2 890
	E	12 500	15 196	17 937	16 578	6 250	8 824	10 314	12 844
IRELAND	A	8 000	6 000	45 300	50 300	11 000	*10 000	19 000	19 000
	B	34 300	48 200	400	400	4 000	5 300	16 000	18 300
	C			400	700	200	1 000	4 600	8 600
	D	42 300	54 200	45 300	50 000	14 800	14 300	30 600	28 700
	E	14 708	18 435	14 161	15 470	5 146	4 864	9 565	8 880
ITALY	A	379 400	311 000	234 000	261 000	573 700	1 167 000	1 481 000	1 718 000
	B	13 200	13 800	18 900	23 000		24 100	49 900	68 000
	C	51 800	42 500	35 500	29 700	63 700	133 100	211 900	302 700
	D	340 800	282 300	217 000	254 300	510 000	1 058 100	1 319 000	1 483 300
	E	6 561	5 261	3 844	4 485	9 818	19 719	23 367	26 162
MALTA	B	500	300	434	428	600	2 900	4 200	5 000
	D	500	300	434	428	600	2 900	4 200	5 000
	E	563	920	1 307	1 285	1 875	8 896	12 651	15 015
NETHERLANDS	A	164 000	167 000	123 000	127 000	328 000	489 000	501 000	541 000
	B	103 500	247 300	280 000	305 700	126 200	213 000	364 700	342 300
	C	37 300	35 600	20 300	21 100	129 100	151 200	261 300	216 100
	D	230 200	378 700	382 700	411 600	325 100	550 800	604 400	667 200
	E	18 728	29 059	27 626	29 527	26 448	42 265	43 630	47 862
NORWAY	A	308 000	554 000	435 000	480 000	215 000	317 000	287 000	305 000
	B					2 700	4 900	29 500	36 700
	C	247 400	475 600	339 500	369 100	155 000	223 600	193 200	214 196
	D	60 600	78 400	95 500	110 900	62 700	98 300	123 300	127 504
	E	16 277	20 222	23 586	27 255	16 841	25 355	30 452	31 335
POLAND	A	78 700	87 900	84 000	89 000	174 100	188 100	233 000	214 000
	B		15 000	43 000	40 000		21 000	28 000	28 000
	C	17 000	15 000			1 000		3 000	3 000
	D	61 700	87 900	127 000	129 000	173 100	209 000	258 000	239 000
	E	1 959	2 707	3 660	3 685	5 496	6 436	7 436	6 827
PORTUGAL	A	10 100	700	30 500	30 500	26 400	43 200	72 000	89 000
	B	22 900	43 500			1 500	1 500	600	600
	C	800	200		500	200	300	2 100	2 100
	D	32 200	44 000	30 500	30 000	27 700	44 400	70 500	87 500
	E	3 487	5 100	3 393	3 379	2 999	5 146	7 973	9 856

8.17 Newsprint, printing and writing paper
Papier journal, papier d'impression et papier d'écriture
Papel de periódico, papel de imprenta y papel de escribir

COUNTRY / PAYS / PAIS	CODE (TIPO DE DATOS)	NEWSPRINT — PAPIER JOURNAL — PAPEL DE PERIODICO				PRINTING AND WRITING PAPER — PAPIER D'IMPRESSION ET D'ECRITURE — PAPEL DE IMPRENTA Y DE ESCRIBIR			
		1965	1970	1977	1978	1965	1970	1977	1978
		(2)	(3)	(4)	(5)	(6)	(7)	(8)	(9)
ROMANIA	A	52 000	53 000	98 000	103 000	60 000	123 000	144 000	127 000
	B	500	9 500	12 000	12 000				
	C	3 400	10 800	17 000	19 000	6 500	81 900	67 000	74 000
	D	49 100	51 700	93 000	96 400	53 500		77 000	53 000
	E	2 581	2 553	4 300	4 400	2 812	4 044	3 560	2 429
SPAIN	A	72 500	115 000	106 000	110 000	167 800	322 800	602 000	585 000
	B	53 800	78 800	65 900	47 100	7 300	11 300	62 600	60 100
	C					3 600	15 900	90 200	125 400
	D	126 300	193 800	171 900	157 600	171 500	318 200	574 600	519 700
	E	3 958	5 765	4 780	4 340	5 374	9 466	15 979	14 312
SWEDEN	A	679 000	1 030 000	1 111 000	1 258 000	370 000	537 000	766 000	907 000
	B					10 900	16 100	25 100	26 900
	C	429 800	686 600	847 100	1 031 800	171 300	283 800	401 600	468 500
	D	249 200	343 400	263 900	227 000	209 600	269 300	389 500	465 400
	E	32 221	42 696	31 969	27 422	27 101	33 483	47 184	56 221
SWITZERLAND	A	120 000	143 000	173 000	190 000	197 000	249 000	249 000	263 000
	B	1 400	24 600	2 200	3 300	23 100	77 300	124 200	140 400
	C			22 700	21 700	500	8 900	50 100	64 400
	D	121 400	167 500	152 500	171 600	219 600	317 400	323 100	339 000
	E	20 727	27 060	24 092	27 195	37 494	51 276	51 043	53 724
UNITED KINGDOM	A	780 300	756 900	326 000	319 000	1 009 900	1 145 300	979 000	1 034 000
	B	596 800	789 100	964 300	1 033 200	103 200	274 700	670 000	765 500
	C	2 800	1 800	12 200	21 200	44 800	69 000	86 800	100 800
	D	1 374 800	1 544 200	1 278 100	1 330 800	1 068 300	1 351 000	1 562 200	1 698 700
	E	25 142	27 774	22 807	23 763	19 537	24 299	27 876	30 332
YUGOSLAVIA	A	45 900	75 000	96 000	96 000	127 800	139 900	201 000	201 000
	B	17 700	23 500	100	100	1 800	14 800	23 600	23 600
	C	2 800	10 000	17 270	17 270	25 100	33 400	24 000	24 600
	D	60 800	88 500	78 830	78 830	104 500	121 300	200 600	200 600
	E	3 129	4 344	3 622	3 588	5 377	5 955	9 216	9 131
OCEANIA									
AUSTRALIA	A	94 600	173 300	207 000	208 000	102 800	126 300	169 000	179 000
	B	285 000	275 300	320 700	266 200	62 000	122 900	137 900	129 200
	C	900			2 700	14 500	17 100	9 100	10 600
	D	378 700	448 500	527 700	471 500	150 300	232 100	297 600	297 600
	E	33 257	35 851	37 653	33 030	13 199	18 553	21 249	20 848
FIJI	B	100	800	1 000	1 000	300	500	2 000	2 000
	D	100	800	1 000	1 000	300	500	2 000	2 000
	E	216	1 538	1 667	1 634	647	962	3 333	3 268
FRENCH POLYNESIA	B		400	100	100				
	D		400	100	100				
	E		3 670	735	709				

Newsprint, printing and writing paper   **8.17**
Papier journal, papier d'impression et papier d'écriture
Papel de periódico, papel de imprenta y papel de escribir

	(1)	(2)	(3)	(4)	(5)	(6)	(7)	(8)	(9)
NEW CALEDONIA	B			1 100					
	D			1 100					
	E			8 333					
NEW ZEALAND	A	198 700	213 900	276 000	277 000	16 500	29 700	23 000	22 000
	B	4 100	500	231	7 200	14 100	16 900	17 900	17 300
	C	111 300	118 600	190 000	209 000				
	D	91 500	95 800	86 231	75 200	30 400	46 200	40 200	38 600
	E	34 817	34 080	27 772	24 103	11 568	16 435	12 947	12 372
PAPUA NEW GUINEA	B	100	600			700	700		
	D	100	600			700	700		
	E	47	249			326	290		
SAMOA	B		200			100	300		
	D		200			100	300		
	E		1 613			813	2 419		
U.S.S.R.	A	744 400	1 101 000	1 388 000	1 432 000	832 800	883 000	1 187 000	1 205 000
	B	56 500	86 800	30 700	27 000		143 200	158 100	167 600
	C	138 700	259 600	316 600	312 000		24 800	31 100	34 100
	D	662 200	928 200	1 102 100	1 147 000	832 800	1 001 400	1 314 000	1 338 500
	E	2 867	3 823	4 256	4 391	3 606	4 125	5 075	5 124

ANGOLA: E—> THE DATA ON CONSUMPTION AND CONSUMPTION
PER 1,000 INHABITANTS OF NEWSPRINT FOR 1965
INCLUDE ALL KINDS OF PRINTING PAPER.
FR—> LES DONNEES CONCERNANT LA CONSOMMATION
ET LA CONSOMMATION POUR 1 000 HABITANTS DU
PAPIER JOURNAL EN 1965 SE REFERENT AU PAPIER
D'IMPRESSION (TOUTES CATEGORIES).
ESP> LOS DATOS SOBRE EL CONSUMO Y EL CONSUMO
POR 1 000 HABITANTES DE PAPEL DE PERIODICO
EN 1965 SE REFIEREN AL PAPEL DE IMPRENTA (TODAS
CATEGORIAS).

Film and cinema 9
Films et cinémas
Películas y cines

9 Film and cinema

Films et cinémas

Películas y cines

The statistics in this chapter relate to the production and importation of long films intended for commercial exhibition in cinemas as well as to the number, seating capacity and annual attendance of such cinemas. The minimum length for films classified as 'long films' varies considerably from country to country, ranging from less than 1,000 metres in some countries to more than 3,000 metres in others; a number of countries, however, have adopted standards close to 2,000 metres. Wherever possible, the minimum length of the films covered by the statistics is given. Where such information is lacking, data refer, without exact definition, to long or 'feature' films.

The criteria used to determine that a film has been 'produced' or 'imported' during the year of reference are shown in the texts of the tables on the production and importation of films.

Table 9.1

This table gives, for 1965, 1970, 1976 and 1977, the number of long films produced for commercial exhibition in cinemas. Films produced solely for television broadcasting are not included. Figures on international co-productions are usually included in the national figures of each of the countries concerned, but they are also shown separately, where available. The table shows for each country the minimum length for films considered as long films (feature films). The criterion used for characterizing films as 'produced' during the year of reference is one of the following:

A: Production completed in the year stated
B: Approved by censor for public showing in the year stated
C: Commercially shown for the first time in the year stated.

Table 9.2

The data in this table refer to the number of long films imported in 1976 and 1977 for commercial exhibition in cinemas and they are classified according to the principal countries of origin. Films imported solely for television broadcasting are not included in this table. The criterion used for characterizing films as 'imported' during the year of reference is one of the following:

A: Imported in the year stated
B: Approved by censor for public showing in the year stated
C: Commercially shown for the first time in the year stated.

Table 9.3

The figures in this table refer to all cinema establishments regularly used for commercial exhibition of films of 16 mm and over. They refer to the number of cinemas, to the seating capacity (total number and number per 1,000 of the population) and to the annual attendance at cinema performances (total attendance and attendance per inhabitant) for the latest available year.

Data on cinemas refer to fixed cinemas and mobile units. 'Fixed cinemas' are establishments possessing their own equipment and include indoor cinemas (those with a permanent fixed roof over most of the seating accommodation), outdoor cinemas and drive-ins (establishments designed to enable the audience to watch a film while seated in their automobile). 'Mobile units' are defined as projection units equipped and used to serve more than one site.

The capacity for fixed cinemas refers to the number of seats and to the number of automobiles multiplied by a factor of 4 in the case of drive-in cinemas.

Cinema attendance is calculated from the number of tickets sold during the year and, wherever possible, includes drive-ins and mobile units.

As a rule, figures refer only to commercial establishments but in the case of mobile units, it is possible that the figures for some countries may also include non-commercial units. Gross receipts are given in national currency.

Countries for which the data were prior to 1972 have been omitted from this table. For these figures the reader is referred to previous editions of the *Yearbook*.

Les statistiques de ce chapitre se rapportent à la production et à l'importation de films de long métrage destinés à la projection cinématographique commerciale, ainsi qu'au nombre de cinémas, au nombre de sièges et à la fréquentation annuelle des cinémas. En ce qui concerne la longueur minimale des films considérés commes des 'longs métrages', les définitions diffèrent considérablement selon les pays: elles peuvent varier entre moins de 1 000 à plus de 3 000 mètres; cependant, beaucoup de pays ont adopté un chiffre voisin de 2 000 mètres. Chaque fois que cela était possible, on a signalé la longueur minimale des films sur lesquels portent les statistiques. En l'absence de telles informations, les chiffres donnés correspondent grosso modo aux films de long métrage ou aux 'films vedettes' des programmes.

Les divers critères utilisés pour considérer qu'un film a été produit ou importé au cours de l'année de référence, sont indiqués dans les textes des tableaux relatifs à la production et à l'importation de films.

Tableau 9.1

Ce tableau présente pour 1965, 1970, 1976 et 1977 le nombre de films de long métrage produits pour la projection cinématographique commerciale. Les films produits uniquement pour les besoins de la télévision sont exclus. Les données sur les coproductions internationales sont généralement comprises dans les données nationales de chaque pays concerné, mais elles sont aussi présentées séparément lorsque les chiffres

9 Film and cinema
Films et cinémas
Películas y cines

sont disponibles. Le tableau donne pour chaque pays la longueur minimale des films considérés comme de long métrage (films vedettes). Les critères utilisés pour considérer qu'un film a été 'produit' au cours de l'année de référence est un des suivants:

A: Production terminée dans l'année indiquée
B: Approuvé par la censure pour sa projection en publique dans l'année indiquée
C: Mise en exploitation commerciale pour la première fois dans l'année indiquée.

Tableau 9.2

Les données de ce tableau se réfèrent aux films de long métrage importés en 1976 et 1977 pour la projection commerciale dans les cinémas et ont été classés d'après les principaux pays d'origine. Les films importés uniquement pour les besoins de la télévision sont exclus de ce tableau. Les critères utilisés pour considérer qu'un film a été 'importé' au cours de l'année de référence est un des suivants:

A: Importation effective du film dans l'année indiquée
B: Approuvé par la censure pour sa projection en public dans l'année indiquée
C: Mise en exploitation commerciale pour la première fois dans l'année indiquée.

Tableau 9.3

Les données de ce tableau concernent les établissements d'exploitation commerciale de films de 16 mm. et plus. Elles se rapportent au nombre de cinémas, au nombre de sièges (nombre total et nombre pour 1 000 habitants) et à la fréquentation annuelle des cinémas (fréquentation totale et par habitant) pour la dernière année disponible.

Les données ayant trait au nombre de cinémas se réfèrent aux établissements fixes et aux cinémas itinérants. Le terme 'établissement fixe' désigne tout établissement doté de son propre équipement; il englobe les salles fermées (c'est-à-dire celles où un toit fixe recouvre la plupart des places), les cinémas de plein air et les cinémas pour automobilistes ou 'drive-ins' (conçu pour permettre aux spectateurs d'assister à la projection sans quitter leur voiture). Les 'cinémas itinérants' sont définis comme groupes mobiles de projection équipés de manière à pouvoir être utilisés dans des lieux différents. La capacité des cinémas fixes se réfère au nombre de sièges et celle des cinémas pour automobilistes au nombre d'automobiles multiplié par le facteur 4.

La fréquentation des cinémas est calculée sur la base du nombre de billets vendus au cours de l'année et comprend, chaque fois que cela est possible, les cinémas pour automobilistes et les cinémas itinérants.

En général, les statistiques présentées ne concernent que les établissements commerciaux; toutefois, dans le cas des cinémas itinérants, il se peut que les données relatives à certains pays tiennent compte aussi des établissements non-commerciaux. Les recettes brutes sont indiquées en monnaie nationale.

Les pays dont les données étaient antérieures à 1972 ont été supprimées de ce tableau. Les données antérieures peuvent être obtenues en consultant les précédentes éditions de l'*Annuaire*.

Las estadísticas de este capítulo se refieren a la producción y a la importación de películas de largo metraje destinadas a la proyección cinematográfica comercial, al igual que al número de cines, al número de asientos y a la frecuentación anual de los cines. En lo que se refiere a la longitud mínima de las películas consideradas como 'largo metraje', las definiciones difieren considerablemente según los países. Pueden variar de menos de 1 000 a más de 3 000 metros, pero son muchos los países que han adoptado una cifra próxima de 2 000 metros. Cada vez que ello es posible, se ha señalado la longitud mínima de las películas a que se refieren las estadísticas. A falta de esas informaciones, las cifras dadas corresponden, grosso modo, a las películas de largo metraje o a las 'películas principales' de los programas.

Los diversos criterios utilizados para considerar que una película ha sido producida o importada durante el año de referencia, se indican en los textos de los cuadros relativos a la producción y a la importación de películas.

Cuadro 9.1

Este cuadro presenta para 1965, 1970, 1976 y 1977 el número de películas de largo metraje destinadas a la proyección cinematográfica comercial. Las películas producidas exclusivamente para las necesidades de la televisión quedan excluidas. Los datos sobre las coproducciones internacionales se incluyen generalmente en la producción de cada país interesado, pero también son presentados por separado cuando las cifras son disponibles. Este cuadro indica para cada país la longitud mínima de las películas consideradas de largo metraje (películas principales). El criterio utilizado para considerar que una película ha sido 'producida' durante el año de referencia, es uno de los siguientes:

A: Producción terminada en el año indicado
B: Aprobada por la censura para su presentación al público en el año indicado
C: Puesta en explotación comercial por primera vez en el año indicado.

Cuadro 9.2

Los datos de este cuadro se refieren a las películas de largo metraje importadas en 1976 y 1977 destinadas a la proyección cinematográfica comercial, que han sido clasificadas según los principales países de origen. Las películas importadas exclusivamente para las necesidades de la televisión quedan excluidas. El criterio utilizado para considerar que una película ha sido importada durante el año de referencia, es uno de los siguientes:

A: Película efectivamente importada en el año indicado
B: Aprobada por la censura para su presentación al público en el año indicado
C: Puesta en explotación comercial por primera vez en el año indicado.

Cuadro 9.3

Los datos de este cuadro se refieren a los cines de explotación comercial de películas de 16 mm. o más. Esos datos se refieren al número de cines, al número de asientos (número total y número por 1 000 habitantes) y a la frecuentación anual de los cines (frecuentación total y por habitante) para el último año de que se dispone de cifras.

Los datos sobre el número de cines se refieren a los establecimientos fijos y a los cines ambulantes. La expresión 'establecimiento fijo' designa todo establecimiento dotado de su propio equipo y se comprenden en ella las salas cerradas (es decir, aquellas en las que un techo fijo protege la mayor parte de los asientos), los cines al aire libre y los cines para automovilistas o 'drive-ins' (concebidos para que los espectadores puedan asistir a la proyección sin salir de su vehículo). Los 'cines ambulantes' se definen como grupos móviles de proyección equipados de modo que puedan utilizarse en lugares diferentes. La capacidad de los establecimientos fijos se refiere al número de asientos y la de los cines para automovilistas al número de automóviles multiplicado por el factor 4.

La frecuentación de los cines se calcula tomando como base el número de billetes vendidos en el curso del año y comprende, cada vez que ello es posible, los cines para automovilistas y los cines ambulantes.

En general, las estadísticas que se presentan sólo se refieren a los establecimientos comerciales. No obstante, en el caso de los cines ambulantes, es posible que los datos relativos a ciertos países tengan también en cuenta establecimientos no comerciales. La recaudación total se indica en moneda nacional.

Los países cuyos datos eran anteriores a 1972 se han omitido de este cuadro. Las cifras anteriores pueden ser obtenidas consultando las precedentes ediciones del *Anuario*.

Production of long films 9.1
Production de films de long métrage
Producción de películas de large metraje

9.1 Long films: number produced
Films de long métrage: nombre de films produits
Películas de large metraje: número de películas producidas

DEFINITION OF DATA:

C = APPROVED BY CENSOR IN THE YEAR STATED

P = PRODUCTION COMPLETED IN THE YEAR STATED

S = COMMERCIALLY SHOWN FOR THE FIRST TIME IN THE YEAR STATED

LENGTH = MINIMUM LENGTH (IN METRES) WHICH CATEGORIZES THE FILM AS A "LONG FILM".

CODE:

C = FILMS APPROUVES PAR LA CENSURE DANS L'ANNEE INDIQUEE

P = PRODUCTION TERMINEE DANS L'ANNEE INDIQUEE

S = MISE EN EXPLOITATION COMMERCIALE DANS L'ANNEE INDIQUEE

LONGUEUR = LONGUEUR MINIMALE (EN METRES) DES FILMS CONSIDERES COMME DE "LONG METRAGE".

TIPO DE DATOS:

C = PELICULAS APROBADAS POR LA CENSURA EN EL AÑO INDICADO

P = PRODUCCION TERMINADA EN EL AÑO INDICADO

S = PUESTA EN EXPLOCACION COMER- CIAL EN EL AÑO INDICADO

LONGITUD = LONGITUD MINIMA (EN METROS) DE LAS PELICULAS CON- SIDERADAS DE "LARGO METRAJE"

NUMBER OF COUNTRIES AND TERRITORIES PRESENTED IN THIS TABLE: 71

NOMBRE DE PAYS ET DE TERRITOIRES PRESENTES DANS CE TABLEAU: 71

NUMERO DE PAISES Y DE TERRITORIOS PRESENTADOS EN ESTE CUADRO: 71

COUNTRY / PAYS / PAIS		LENGTH / LONGUEUR / LONGITUD	DEFINI- TION OF DATA CODE / TIPO DE DATOS	NUMBER OF LONG FILMS / NOMBRE DE FILMS DE LONG METRAGE / NUMERO DE PELICULAS DE LARGO METRAJE				
				1965	1970	1975	1976	1977
		(1)	(2)	(3)	(4)	(5)	(6)	(7)
AFRICA								
ALGERIA	TOTAL	2 500	P	5	3	3	3	1
	(CO-PRODUCTIONS/COPRODUCTIONS/COPRODUCCIONES)			1	2	...	-	1
BENIN	TOTAL	...	...	-	-	-	1	...
EGYPT	TOTAL	2 000	...	47	47	...	49	...
	(CO-PRODUCTIONS/COPRODUCTIONS/COPRODUCCIONES)			5	1	...	-	...
GHANA	TOTAL	2 000	P	-	3	1	-	-
IVORY COAST	TOTAL	1 700	S	-	...	...	3	1
	(CO-PRODUCTIONS/COPRODUCTIONS/COPRODUCCIONES)			-	...	...	1	...

9.1 Production of long films
Production de films de long métrage
Producción de películas de large metraje

COUNTRY / PAYS / PAIS		LENGTH LONGUEUR LONGITUD (1)	DEFINI-TION OF DATA CODE TIPO DE DATOS (2)	NUMBER OF LONG FILMS NOMBRE DE FILMS DE LONG METRAGE NUMERO DE PELICULAS DE LARGO METRAJE				
				1965 (3)	1970 (4)	1975 (5)	1976 (6)	1977 (7)
LIBYAN ARAB JAMAHIRIYA	TOTAL	...	...			2	2	—
	(CO-PRODUCTIONS/COPRODUCTIONS/COPRODUCCIONES)					1	1	—
MAURITANIA	TOTAL	...	C	—	—	...	1	...
MAURITIUS	TOTAL	1 400	C			—	2	—
MOROCCO	TOTAL	2 400	P		2	—	—	4
SIERRA LEONE	TOTAL	2 000	P					...
TUNISIA	TOTAL	2 200	C		3		1	1
	(CO-PRODUCTIONS/COPRODUCTIONS/COPRODUCCIONES)						1	1
UNITED REPUBLIC OF CAMEROON	TOTAL	3 000	S			1	—	—
UNITED REPUBLIC OF TANZANIA	TOTAL	...	S	—	—	—	1	—
AMERICA, NORTH								
CANADA	TOTAL	2 000	P	4		41	17	...
	(CO-PRODUCTIONS/COPRODUCTIONS/COPRODUCCIONES)							
CUBA	TOTAL	2 000	P		1			1
GUATEMALA	TOTAL	3 000	S			1	1	1
HAITI	TOTAL	...	...	—	—		1	...
MEXICO	TOTAL	900	S		124	162	97	91
	(CO-PRODUCTIONS/COPRODUCTIONS/COPRODUCCIONES)				2			
UNITED STATES OF AMERICA	TOTAL	...	...	191				...
	(CO-PRODUCTIONS/COPRODUCTIONS/COPRODUCCIONES)							
AMERICA, SOUTH								
ARGENTINA	TOTAL	1 620	S	32	28	34	20	25
	(CO-PRODUCTIONS/COPRODUCTIONS/COPRODUCCIONES)			1		1	1	—
BRAZIL	TOTAL	1 650	S		72	90	87	73
	(CO-PRODUCTIONS/COPRODUCTIONS/COPRODUCCIONES)					1	—	—
COLOMBIA	TOTAL	2 400	...			2	1	3
	(CO-PRODUCTIONS/COPRODUCTIONS/COPRODUCCIONES)					—	—	1
GUYANA	TOTAL	3 230	S			4		...

Production of long films 9.1
Production de films de long métrage
Producción de películas de large metraje

		(1)	(2)	(3)	(4)	(5)	(6)	(7)
PERU	TOTAL	2 500	...	...	...	1	2	3
	(CO-PRODUCTIONS/COPRODUCTIONS/COPRODUCCIONES)					-	-	1
VENEZUELA	TOTAL	2 380	S	...	3	9	9	9
	(CO-PRODUCTIONS/COPRODUCTIONS/COPRODUCCIONES)				3	1	1	3
ASIA								
AFGHANISTAN	TOTAL	...	S	...	1	...	...	...
BRUNEI	TOTAL	2 300	P	...	6	...	...	...
BURMA	TOTAL	4 000	C	81	...	66	...	...
CYPRUS	TOTAL	1 500	C	...	...	...	...	2
HONG KONG	TOTAL	600	S	203	137	112	104	115
	(CO-PRODUCTIONS/COPRODUCTIONS/COPRODUCCIONES)			-	-	3	-	1
INDIA	TOTAL	2 000	C	325	396	475	507	557
INDONESIA	TOTAL	3 000	C	...	14	41	57	134
	(CO-PRODUCTIONS/COPRODUCTIONS/COPRODUCCIONES)					3	-	-
IRAN	TOTAL	2 400	C	...	...	68	...	...
ISRAEL	TOTAL	2 000	S	6	8	8	13	14
	(CO-PRODUCTIONS/COPRODUCTIONS/COPRODUCCIONES)			2	8		4	2
JAPAN	TOTAL	1 370	S	490	423	333	356	337
	(CO-PRODUCTIONS/COPRODUCTIONS/COPRODUCCIONES)			3			-	-
KOREA, REPUBLIC OF	TOTAL	2 466	C	193	224	99	135	102
	(CO-PRODUCTIONS/COPRODUCTIONS/COPRODUCCIONES)			-	6	7	20	13
LEBANON	TOTAL	2 000	...	15	6	...	...	...
MALAYSIA	TOTAL	3 000	P	...	4	5	5	3
	(CO-PRODUCTIONS/COPRODUCTIONS/COPRODUCCIONES)				-	2	-	1
PAKISTAN	TOTAL	3 700	S	89	141	120	...	...
	(CO-PRODUCTIONS/COPRODUCTIONS/COPRODUCCIONES)				1			
PHILIPPINES	TOTAL	2 400	...	208	...	143	...	...
	(CO-PRODUCTIONS/COPRODUCTIONS/COPRODUCCIONES)							
QATAR	TOTAL	...	P	...	...	1	...	...
SINGAPORE	TOTAL	2 500	P	11	...	4	3	1
	(CO-PRODUCTIONS/COPRODUCTIONS/COPRODUCCIONES)					1	-	-
SRI LANKA	TOTAL	3 000	S	24	25	31	28	31
	(CO-PRODUCTIONS/COPRODUCTIONS/COPRODUCCIONES)			-	-	1	1	1
THAILAND	TOTAL	...	C	...	...	55	...	...
TURKEY	TOTAL	...	C	...	...	160	208	111
VIET-NAM	TOTAL	...	...	...	...	7	14	21

9.1 Production of long films
Production de films de long métrage
Producción de películas de large metraje

COUNTRY / PAYS / PAIS		LENGTH LONGUEUR LONGITUD (1)	DEFINITION OF DATA CODE TIPO DE DATOS (2)	NUMBER OF LONG FILMS / NOMBRE DE FILMS DE LONG METRAGE / NUMERO DE PELICULAS DE LARGO METRAJE				
				1965 (3)	1970 (4)	1975 (5)	1976 (6)	1977 (7)
EUROPE								
AUSTRIA	TOTAL	2 000	S	21	7	6	7	9
	(CO-PRODUCTIONS/COPRODUCTIONS/COPRODUCCIONES)			5	4	2	4	5
BELGIUM	TOTAL	1 600	C	1	13	7	11	3
	(CO-PRODUCTIONS/COPRODUCTIONS/COPRODUCCIONES)			1	7	...	6	3
BULGARIA	TOTAL	1 200	P	12	16	25	28	21
	(CO-PRODUCTIONS/COPRODUCTIONS/COPRODUCCIONES)			1	2	3	2	2
CZECHOSLOVAKIA	TOTAL	1 800	S	45	54	62	68	63
	(CO-PRODUCTIONS/COPRODUCTIONS/COPRODUCCIONES)			3	2	8	3	2
DENMARK	TOTAL	2 000	S	18	18	18	20	21
	(CO-PRODUCTIONS/COPRODUCTIONS/COPRODUCCIONES)			...	...	2	—	—
FINLAND	TOTAL	1 000	C	9	13	5	9	7
	(CO-PRODUCTIONS/COPRODUCTIONS/COPRODUCCIONES)			...	8	...	1	1
FRANCE	TOTAL	1 600	P	142	138	222	214	222
	(CO-PRODUCTIONS/COPRODUCTIONS/COPRODUCCIONES)			108	72	62	44	32
GERMAN DEMOCRATIC REPUBLIC	TOTAL	2 000	P	15	...	16	18	16
	(CO-PRODUCTIONS/COPRODUCTIONS/COPRODUCCIONES)			...	...	1	1	—
GERMANY, FEDERAL REPUBLIC OF	TOTAL	1 600	S	72	129	81	63	58
	(CO-PRODUCTIONS/COPRODUCTIONS/COPRODUCCIONES)			47	27	26	18	14
GREECE	TOTAL	2 000	C	112	112	70	42	27
	(CO-PRODUCTIONS/COPRODUCTIONS/COPRODUCCIONES)			...	...	...	2	—
HUNGARY	TOTAL	2 000	P	23	23	19	19	25
	(CO-PRODUCTIONS/COPRODUCTIONS/COPRODUCCIONES)			—	2	—	—	1
IRELAND	TOTAL	610	C	1	5	2	...	...
ITALY	TOTAL	1 600	S	188	240	203	237	165
	(CO-PRODUCTIONS/COPRODUCTIONS/COPRODUCCIONES)			126	135	43	34	23
NETHERLANDS	TOTAL	1 600	C	1	3	16	10	9
	(CO-PRODUCTIONS/COPRODUCTIONS/COPRODUCCIONES)			—	—	—	2	2
NORWAY	TOTAL	1 000	C	11	9	14	12	8
	(CO-PRODUCTIONS/COPRODUCTIONS/COPRODUCCIONES)			1	2	1	—	—
POLAND	TOTAL	2 000	P	26	28	36	37	28
PORTUGAL	TOTAL	1 800	P	6	4	...	8	78

Production of long films 9.1
Production de films de long métrage
Producción de películas de large metraje

		(1)	(2)	(3)	(4)	(5)	(6)	(7)
ROMANIA	TOTAL	1 800	C	15	11	23	22	23
	(CO-PRODUCTIONS/COPRODUCTIONS/COPRODUCCIONES)			1	2	–	3	–
SPAIN	TOTAL	1 800	C	135	105	105	108	102
	(CO-PRODUCTIONS/COPRODUCTIONS/COPRODUCCIONES)			73	63	21	18	19
SWEDEN	TOTAL	2 000	S	21	20	14	16	20
	(CO-PRODUCTIONS/COPRODUCTIONS/COPRODUCCIONES)			...	7	–	2	2
SWITZERLAND	TOTAL	1 600	S	10	5	30	20	20
	(CO-PRODUCTIONS/COPRODUCTIONS/COPRODUCCIONES)			...	...	2	1	4
UNITED KINGDOM	TOTAL	2 000	...	69	85	70	64	42
	(CO-PRODUCTIONS/COPRODUCTIONS/COPRODUCCIONES)			...	2	4	4	2
YUGOSLAVIA	TOTAL	2 000	C	19	29	21	16	21
	(CO-PRODUCTIONS/COPRODUCTIONS/COPRODUCCIONES)			6	5	3	1	–
OCEANIA								
AUSTRALIA	TOTAL	456	C	...	11	43	29	37
	(CO-PRODUCTIONS/COPRODUCTIONS/COPRODUCCIONES)			...	...	...	–	–
U.S.S.R.	TOTAL	1 800	P	167	218	184	156	148
U.S.S.R.	(CO-PRODUCTIONS/COPRODUCTIONS/COPRODUCCIONES)			...	3	8	6	2

CZECHOSLOVAKIA:
E—> INCLUDING FILMS PRODUCED FOR TELEVISION
BROADCASTING.
FR—> Y COMPRIS LES FILMS PRODUITS POUR LA
TELEVISION.
ESP> INCLUIDAS LAS PELICULAS PRODUCIDAS PARA
LA TELEVISION.

9.2 Importation of long films
Importation de films de long métrage
Importación de películas de largo metraje

9.2 Long films: number of long films imported by country of origin
Films de long métrage: nombre de films importés, par pays d'origine
Películas de largo metraje: número de películas importadas, por país de origen

DEFINITION OF DATA:

C = APPROVED BY CENSOR IN THE YEAR STATED

I = IMPORTED IN THE YEAR STATED

S = COMMERCIALLY SHOWN FOR THE FIRST TIME IN THE YEAR STATED

CODE:

C = FILMS APPROUVES PAR LA CENSURE DANS L'ANNEE INDIQUEE

I = IMPORTATION EFFECTIVE DANS L'ANNEE INDIQUEE

S = MISE EN EXPLOITATION COMMERCIALE DANS L'ANNEE INDIQUEE

TIPO DE DATOS:

C = PELICULAS APROBADAS POR LA CENSURA EN EL AÑO INDICADO

I = EFECTIVAMENTE IMPORTADA EN EL AÑO INDICADO

S = PUESTA EN EXPLOCACION COMER- CIAL EN EL AÑO INDICADO

NUMBER OF COUNTRIES AND TERRITORIES PRESENTED IN THIS TABLE: 87
NOMBRE DE PAYS ET DE TERRITOIRES PRESENTES DANS CE TABLEAU: 87
NUMERO DE PAISES Y DE TERRITORIOS PRESENTADOS EN ESTE CUADRO: 87

PRINCIPAL COUNTRIES OF ORIGIN / PRINCIPAUX PAYS D'ORIGINE / PRINCIPALES PAISES DE ORIGEN

COUNTRY / PAYS / PAIS	YEAR ANNEE AÑO	DEFI- NITION OF DATA CODE CODE TIPO DE DATOS	TOTAL	UNITED STATES OF AMERICA %	FRANCE %	ITALY %	INDIA %	USSR %	UNITED KINGDOM %	FEDERAL REPUB- LIC OF GERMANY %	JAPAN %	HONG- KONG %	OTHERS AUTRES OTROS %
			(1)	(2)	(3)	(4)	(5)	(6)	(7)	(8)	(9)	(10)	(11)
AFRICA													
ALGERIA	1975	C	210	28.6	23.3	9.5	...	...	...	...	...	...	38.6
	1976	C	254	31.5	22.8	15.7	8.7	...	5.1	...	...	...	16.1
CHAD	1976	S	692	18.4	26.3	23.3	14.6	...	2.5	...	...	...	15.0
	1977	S	732	19.4	25.8	24.2	9.0	...	3.4	...	...	...	18.2
EGYPT	1974	I	241	36.1	5.8	34.9	0.8	7.9	5.8	...	1.7	0.8	6.2
EQUATORIAL GUINEA	1976	...	48	—	—	—	—	87.5	—	—	—	—	12.5
	1977	...	57	—	—	—	—	73.7	—	—	—	—	26.3
GHANA	1976	S	29	58.6	—	—	—	—	13.8	—	—	27.6	—
	1977	S	24	58.3	—	—	—	—	—	—	—	41.7	—
IVORY COAST	1976	I	372	16.1	32.8	10.2	17.2	...	...	...	...	...	23.7
	1977	T	401	25.2	34.4	10.7	...	...	...	...	...	...	29.7

Importation of long films   9.2
Importation de films de long métrage
Importación de películas de largo metraje

Country	Year		(1)	(2)	(3)	(4)	(5)	(6)	(7)	(8)	(9)	(10)	(11)
KENYA	1976	I	219	40.6	...	8.7	26.9	...	1.4	...	4.1	17.8	0.5
	1977	I	142	28.9	...	2.1	51.4	...	4.2	...	...	9.9	3.5
LIBYAN ARAB JAMAHIRIYA	1976	...	213	28.2	0.9	3.8	10.8	-	2.8	-	-	-	53.5
	1977	...	347	33.4	0.3	5.5	6.9	-	8.9	-	-	-	45.0
MAURITANIA	1976	I	1 400	28.6	57.1	3.6	...	...	3.6	...	...	...	7.1
	1977	I	1 500	26.7	60.0	3.3	...	...	3.3	...	...	...	6.7
MAURITIUS	1976	C	431	-	67.1	-	20.9	-	-	-	...	12.1	-
	1977	C	429	-	75.5	-	15.6	-	-	-	...	8.9	-
MOROCCO	1976	C	473	20.9	28.5	9.5	11.0	0.6	2.3			...	27.1
	1977	C	586	11.3	28.5	8.4	25.6	0.7	1.5	0.5		...	23.0
SENEGAL	1976	I	248	38.7	17.3	20.6	8.9	2.0	4.4	1.6	0.5	...	6.5
SUDAN	1976	C	235	61.3	1.3	11.5	10.6	-	2.6	-	-	-	12.8
	1977	C	310	56.8	1.3	10.6	12.9	-	2.3	-	-	-	16.1
UGANDA	1976	C	936	33.3	-	16.7	-	-	-	-	-	50.0	-
	1977	C	936	35.0	-	15.2	-	-	-	-	-	49.8	-
UNITED REPUBLIC OF TANZANIA	1976	S	160	20.0	2.5	15.6	32.5	2.5	6.3	1.3	1.3	16.9	1.3
	1977	S	179	24.6	1.1	20.1	29.1	3.4	8.4	1.7	3.4	8.4	
TUNISIA	1976	C	230	31.7	28.3	4.8	...	...	0.4	...	...	...	34.8
	1977	C	261	29.5	22.6	5.7	...	...	0.8	...	...	...	41.4
AMERICA, NORTH													
BARBADOS	1975	...	1 083	57.4	0.8	11.6	0.1	-	6.4	0.4	0.4	22.5	0.4
BERMUDA	1976	C	136	89.7	-	-	-	-	4.4	-	-	5.9	-
	1977	C	150	88.7	-	-	-	-	10.7	-	-	0.7	-
CANADA	1975	S	715	44.1	17.3	11.0		...	7.3	2.7	...	...	14.5
	1976	S	650	58.5	16.8	4.9	3.1	...	6.6	...	...	...	13.2
COSTA RICA	1976	...	39	-	59.0	-	-	-	-	23.1	...	-	17.9
	1977	...	20	-	40.0	-	-	-	-	10.0	...	-	50.0
CUBA	1974	C	141	11.3	9.9	7.8		20.6	5.0	-	0.7	-	44.7
GUATEMALA	1976	...	314	47.8	15.9	22.3	-	-	6.4	-	-	-	7.6
	1977	...	418	38.3	12.4	22.7	-	-	5.5	-	-	-	21.1
HAITI	1977	...	349	-	100.0	-	-	-	13.3	-	-	-	-
JAMAICA	1974	C	150	66.7	-	10.0		-	-	-	-	10.0	-
MEXICO	1976	C	497	39.4	9.3	22.7	-	...	6.2		2.6	3.6	16.1
	1977	C	529	42.3	3.6	23.4	-	...	6.6	2.1	1.5	4.3	16.1
PANAMA FORMER CANAL ZONE	1975	...	642	90.0	...	...	...	...	...	...	...	...	10.0
TRINIDAD AND TOBAGO	1976	I	...	44.8	1.9	4.1	16.4	1.8	17.0	0.8	...	5.4	7.9
	1977	I	...	34.1	0.6	1.7	29.9	2.0	13.7	0.3	...	14.3	3.4

9.2 Importation of long films
Importation de films de long métrage
Importación de películas de largo metraje

PRINCIPAL COUNTRIES OF ORIGIN / PRINCIPAUX PAYS D'ORIGINE / PRINCIPALES PAISES DE ORIGEN

COUNTRY / PAYS / PAIS	YEAR ANNEE AÑO	DEFINITION OF DATA / CODE / TIPO DE DATOS	(1) TOTAL	(2) UNITED STATES OF AMERICA %	(3) FRANCE %	(4) ITALY %	(5) INDIA %	(6) USSR %	(7) UNITED KINGDOM %	(8) FEDERAL REPUBLIC OF GERMANY %	(9) JAPAN %	(10) HONG-KONG %	(11) OTHERS AUTRES OTROS %
TURKS AND CAICOS ISLANDS	1976	...	300	100.0	—	—	—	—	—	—	—	—	—
	1977	...	300	100.0	—	—	—	—	—	—	—	—	—
AMERICA, SOUTH													
ARGENTINA	1976	I	208	30.3	11.1	17.8	...	3.4	8.7	3.4	1.9	...	23.6
	1977	I	277	45.8	12.3	16.2	...	4.7	5.1	...	0.7	...	15.2
BRAZIL	1976	C	463	32.0	9.3	31.7	—	—	6.3	0.9	5.6	—	14.3
	1977	C	421	26.6	9.5	35.9	—	—	8.8	1.7	3.3	—	14.3
COLOMBIA	1976	C	320	57.2	8.8	34.1	—	—	—	—	—	—	—
	1977	C	205	60.0	9.3	30.7	—	—	—	—	—	—	—
ECUADOR	1974	...	2 184	30.0	...	16.0	—	—	—	—	...	...	54.0
GUYANA	1976	C	294	51.0	0.	1.0	22.4	3.1	5.8	...	1.0	...	15.6
	1977	C	268	52.6	0.4	3.0	22.0	2.2	3.4	...	1.9	...	14.6
PERU	1976	C	449	34.1	6.2	12.9	4.9	6.0	3.6	2.2	...	...	30.1
	1977	C	405	38.0	5.4	19.3	5.2	4.4	2.7	1.5	...	...	23.5
VENEZUELA	1976	S	782	43.6	6.5	16.9	...	...	4.3	...	...	...	28.6
	1977	S	652	48.2	5.8	15.3	...	...	4.3	...	...	...	26.4
ASIA													
BAHRAIN	1974	...	384	39.6	0.5	12.0	...	—	4.2	—	—	1.0	42.7
BRUNEI	1976	...	402	22.6	0.7	6.0	13.7	...	10.0	...	1.2	30.6	15.2
	1977	...	534	24.5	—	5.4	11.8	...	8.2	...	1.7	37.1	11.2
BURMA	1975	...	81				19.8	7.4				...	72.8
	1976	...	57	31.6	1.8	17.5	3.5	12.3	1.8	7.0	12.3	...	12.3
CYPRUS	1976	...	276	25.0	5.4	16.7	—	...	23.9	5.8	2.2	—	21.0
	1977	...	265	45.3	4.9	14.7	—	...	20.8	7.2	2.3	—	4.9
HONG KONG	1976	C	596	25.0	14.1	13.9	9.6	...	6.0	5.5	3.9	...	22.0
	1977	C	610	25.7	12.1	13.1	12.0	...	5.4	6.2	5.7	...	19.7
INDIA	1976	C	235	39.1	8.1	0.9	...	6.4	32.8	1.3	0.9	0.4	10.2
	1977	C	161	49.7	1.9	1.2	...	9.3	28.0	8.7	—	—	1.2
INDONESIA	1976	C	148	27.0	2.0	8.8	10.8	...	4.7	...	3.4	32.4	10.8
	1977	C	139	28.8	3.6	18.0	8.6	...	2.9	...	7.9	20.1	10.1
IRAN	1974	...	563	25.4	5.9	12.6	4.8	1.1	29.7	...	...	10.1	10.5
	1975	C	400	28.3	7.0	24.0	8.0	3.3	6.8	4.0	...	3.3	15.5

Importation of long films 9.2
Importation de films de long métrage
Importación de películas de largo metraje

			(1)	(2)	(3)	(4)	(5)	(6)	(7)	(8)	(9)	(10)	(11)
IRAQ	..	1974	523	0.4	15.3	28.3	8.2	—	10.5	—	0.2	—	37.1
	I	1975	129	10.9	10.1	15.5	3.9	—	10.1	—	0.8	—	48.8
ISRAEL	C	1976	438	30.6	11.2	16.9	./	—	14.6	2.5	—	./	24.2
	C	1977	413	29.5	11.4	10.2	7.3	—	14.3	3.4	—	6.1	17.9
JAPAN	S	1976	245	59.2	13.9	9.8	0.8	1.2	6.9	2.4	...	1.6	4.1
	S	1977	221	63.8	11.8	6.8	...	5.0	5.4	1.4	...	1.4	4.5
JORDAN	C	1976	738	20.3	4.1	8.1	—	1.4	7.9	—	2.7	—	55.6
	C	1977	737	18.3	1.1	3.1	—	—	14.9	—	2.7	27.1	32.7
KOREA, REPUBLIC OF	I	1976	43	58.1	9.3	16.3	...	...	4.7	2.3	...	4.7	4.7
	I	1977	42	54.8	4.8	19.0	...	...	9.5	2.4	...	4.8	4.8
KUWAIT	I	1975	314	31.2	7.6	11.1	19.4	1.0	1.6	—	—	—	28.0
MALAYSIA	..	1976	1 679	23.0	0.4	—	8.4	0.1	7.6	—	0.5	54.1	6.0
	..	1977	1 762	19.9	1.9	—	13.3	0.1	6.5	0.2	0.2	52.6	5.2
PHILIPPINES	..	1974	589	34.8	7.0	13.8	0.2	—	7.5	1.4	0.8	26.5	8.1
SINGAPORE	C	1976	730	21.5	2.6	6.7	15.6	...	6.6	...	...	29.2	17.7
	C	1977	841	25.6	2.5	5.1	12.5	...	4.9	...	...	30.9	18.5
SRI LANKA	I	1976	74	10.8	...	...	44.6	...	37.8	...	4.1	...	2.7
	I	1977	71	35.2	—	...	33.8	...	31.0	...	—	...	—
TURKEY	C	1976	198	19.2	8.6	33.8	...	2.5	8.6	7.6	3.0	3.5	13.1
	C	1977	91	18.7	15.4	26.4	...	4.4	17.6	2.2	3.3	6.6	5.5
UNITED ARAB EMIRATES	S	1976	*950	*52.1	*.5	*10.5	*17.4	—	*3.7	—	—	—	*15.8
	S	1977	*950	*53.2	*.5	*10.5	*17.4	—	*3.7	—	—	—	*14.7
VIET-NAM	..	1976	185	—	—	—	—	—	—	—	—	—	100.0
	..	1977	246	—	—	—	—	—	—	—	—	—	100.0
EUROPE													
AUSTRIA	S	1976	326	32.2	10.4	14.1	...	...	8.9	12.9	1.5	7.1	12.9
	S	1977	336	35.4	11.6	11.6	...	...	6.8	14.9	1.5	7.7	10.4
BULGARIA	I	1976	165	5.5	1.8	4.2	...	33.3	3.6	...	...	...	51.5
	I	1977	166	6.0	1.8	3.6	...	28.9	3.0	...	...	...	56.6
CZECHOSLOVAKIA	..	1976	185	16.2	7.0	6.5	...	19.5	5.4	...	...	—	45.4
	..	1977	199	4.5	4.0	12.6	...	26.1	2.5	...	...	—	50.3
DENMARK	S	1976	275	38.2	4.4	5.8	...	...	10.9	5.8	...	...	34.9
	S	1977	281	38.4	10.0	8.9	...	...	7.8	3.6	...	...	31.3
FINLAND	S	1976	191	36.6	9.4	6.3	...	7.3	9.9	3.7	...	...	26.7
	S	1977	189	34.9	7.9	7.4	...	5.8	7.9	3.7	...	...	32.3
FRANCE	C	1974	505	26.5		18.6			4.4	9.1		13.1	28.3
GERMAN DEMOCRATIC REPUBLIC	I	1976	138	5.8	9.4	3.6	...	23.2	0.7	...	...	...	57.2
	I	1977	142	7.0	9.2	4.2	...	25.4	...	...	...	...	54.2

9.2 Importation of long films
Importation de films de long métrage
Importación de películas de largo metraje

COUNTRY PAYS PAIS	YEAR ANNEE AÑO	DEFINITION OF DATA CODE TIPO DE DATOS	PRINCIPAL COUNTRIES OF ORIGIN / PRINCIPAUX PAYS D'ORIGINE / PRINCIPALES PAISES DE ORIGEN										
			TOTAL	UNITED STATES OF AMERICA %	FRANCE %	ITALY %	INDIA %	USSR %	UNITED KINGDOM %	FEDERAL REPUBLIC OF GERMANY %	JAPAN %	HONG-KONG %	OTHERS AUTRES OTROS %
			(1)	(2)	(3)	(4)	(5)	(6)	(7)	(8)	(9)	(10)	(11)
GERMANY, FEDERAL REPUBLIC OF	1976	C	261	36.0	11.5	11.5	...	...	12.3	.	1.5	14.6	12.6
	1977	C	259	38.6	9.6	14.7	...	...	8.9	.	2.7	11.2	14.3
GIBRALTAR	1976	C	415	81.9	-	1.2	-	...	./.	2.9	-	-	14.0
	1977	C	397	87.4	-	0.8	-	-	./.	4.8	-	-	7.1
GREECE	1976	C	713	43.9	13.0	14.3	...	...	7.9	8.4	...	...	12.5
	1977	C	629	39.1	16.9	14.3	...	...	6.0	4.8	...	...	18.9
HUNGARY	1976	I	210	2.4	10.0	5.2	...	25.2	5.2	2.9	...	...	49.0
	1977	I	156	9.6	7.7	9.0	...	22.4	1.3	7.1	...	...	42.9
IRELAND	1976	C	307	52.1	4.9	8.1	...	-	20.2	2.6	...	0.7	11.4
	1977	C	340	58.8	6.5	7.4	-	-	17.9	0.6	-	1.5	7.4
ITALY	1976	S	349	41.3	16.0	.	...	0.9	7.4	6.3	...	3.7	24.4
	1977	S	335	41.8	17.3	.	...	1.5	6.9	6.9	...	1.5	24.2
NETHERLANDS	1976	S	293	32.4	16.4	10.9	...	...	10.6	9.2	2.7	6.1	11.6
	1977	S	322	43.8	12.7	5.3	...	...	9.9	9.3	2.2	7.5	9.3
NORWAY	1976	C	251	41.8	11.6	7.2	...	4.0	14.7	3.2	...	...	17.5
	1977	C	309	49.8	6.5	9.1	...	2.3	10.4	4.2	...	...	17.8
POLAND	1976	S	231	10.8	10.8	7.8	...	20.8	4.8	...	...	...	45.0
	1977	S	254	8.7	12.2	5.5	...	24.0	3.5	...	...	...	46.1
PORTUGAL	1976	I	380	21.6	20.5	24.7	...	...	6.3	4.7	...	...	22.1
	1977	I	473	26.8	15.0	15.4	...	...	11.4	6.8	...	...	24.5
ROMANIA	1976	S	162	21.0	4.3	7.4	...	17.9	5.6	...	2.5	...	41.4
	1977	S	168	17.3	3.6	6.5	...	19.0	6.5	...	...	...	47.0
SAN MARINO	1975	S	429	30.8	11.4	39.2	...	...	13.5	...	...	...	5.1
	1976	S	379	30.3	12.4	39.8	...	...	8.4	...	...	...	9.0
SPAIN	1976	C	363	39.1	15.7	14.9	...	...	13.5	5.2	1.7	...	9.9
	1977	C	357	28.3	17.4	28.9	-	-	11.2	8.1	2.0	-	4.2
SWEDEN	1976	S	217	49.3	12.4	9.2	...	...	11.5	6.5	...	...	11.1
	1977	S	254	50.0	16.1	8.3	...	...	8.3	4.7	...	...	12.6
SWITZERLAND	1976	I	407	39.3	22.1	11.1	...	...	5.4	10.3	...	...	12.0
	1977	I	645	28.5	19.4	13.2	...	...	6.0	8.4	...	...	24.5
UNITED KINGDOM	1976	...	274	46.4	1.1	0.7	...	...	...	...	1.5	3.3	47.1
	1977	...	276	46.0	1.8	1.1	...	...	...	...	2.5	...	48.6

Importation of long films 9.2
Importation de films de long métrage
Importación de películas de largo metraje

			(1)	(2)	(3)	(4)	(5)	(6)	(7)	(8)	(9)	(10)	(11)
YUGOSLAVIA	1976	C	197	30.5	7.1	13.2	2.0	13.7	5.6	0.5	2.5	0.5	24.4
	1977	C	208	30.3	13.0	11.1	1.4	7.2	2.9	1.4	1.4	2.4	28.8
OCEANIA													
AUSTRALIA	1976	I	840	29.0	8.7	11.3	1.3	...	8.5	4.2	1.5	10.4	25.1
	1977	I	890	32.1	6.6	13.8	3.0	...	6.1	4.2	3.5	11.0	19.7
FRENCH POLYNESIA	1974	...	433	25.2	50.5	5.1	5.1	—	11.3	...	...	16.9	36.5
	1975	...	624	17.3	...	21.6	—	...	0.5	9.5	—	—	0.6
NEW CALEDONIA	1974	I	223	17.9	53.4	17.0	...	...	4.5	3.6	...	...	3.6
	1975	I	121	18.2	55.4	17.4	...	...	2.5	2.5	...	1.7	2.5
NEW ZEALAND	1976	C	586	54.3	7.5	5.8	...	...	14.3	4.8	1.4	2.9	9.1
	1977	C	465	45.6	12.3	4.7	...	...	12.7	5.0	2.6	2.4	14.8
PAPUA NEW GUINEA	1976	C	366	86.6	...	...	...	...	...	...	...	10.9	2.5
	1977	C	225	72.4	...	...	...	...	...	...	...	20.4	7.1
U.S.S.R.													
U.S.S.R.	1976	...	134	6.7	1.5	9.7	...	...	0.7	...	...	...	81.3
	1977	...	147	10.2	8.2	4.1	...	...	2.7	...	...	...	74.8
UKRAINIAN S.S.R.	1976	...	118	7.6	3.4	8.5	...	—	—	10.2	3.4	...	66.9
	1977	...	129	10.9	9.3	3.9	...	—	2.3	11.6	3.9	...	58.1

GIBRALTAR:
E—> DATA ON FILMS IMPORTED FROM THE UNITED
KINGDOM AND THE UNITED STATES OF AMERICA
ARE COUNTED TOGETHER.
FR—> LES DONNEES RELATIVES AUX FILMS IMPORTES
DU ROYAUME-UNI ET DES ETATS-UNIS D'AMERIQUE
SONT COMPTEES ENSEMBLE.
ESP> LOS DATOS RELATIVOS A LAS PELICULAS
IMPORTADAS DEL REINO UNIDO Y DE LOS ESTADOS
UNIDOS DE AMERICA SE CUENTA CONJUNTAMENTE.

JORDAN:
E—> DATA REFER TO THE EAST BANK ONLY.
FR—> LES DONNEES SE REFERENT A LA RIVE ORIENTALE
SEULEMENT.
ESP> LOS DATOS SE REFIEREN A LA ORILLA ORIENTAL
SOLAMENTE.

VIET-NAM:
E—> ALL FILMS IMPORTED ORIGINATE FROM THE
SOCIALIST COUNTRIES.
FR—> TOUS LES FILMS IMPORTES PROVIENNENT DE
PAYS SOCIALISTES.
ESP> TODAS LAS PELICULAS IMPORTADAS PROCEDEN DE
PAISES SOCIALISTAS.

9.3 Cinemas: number, seating capacity and annual attendance

Cinémas: nombre d'établissements, nombre de sièges et fréquentation annuelle

Cines: número de establecimientos, número de asientos y frecuentación anual

NUMBER OF COUNTRIES AND TERRITORIES PRESENTED IN THIS TABLE: 131

NOMBRE DE PAYS ET DE TERRITOIRES PRESENTES DANS CE TABLEAU: 131

COUNTRY	YEAR	FIXED CINEMAS ETABLISSEMENTS FIXES ESTABLECIMIENTOS FIJOS				MOBILE UNITS CINEMAS ITINERANTS UNIDADES MOVILES	
		NUMBER 35 MM AND OVER	NUMBER 16 MM	SEATING CAPACITY	ANNUAL ATTENDANCE	NUMBER 35 MM & 16 MM	ANNUAL ATTENDANCE
PAYS	ANNEE	NOMBRE 35 MM ET PLUS	NOMBRE 16 MM	NOMBRE DE SIEGES	FREQUEN- TATION ANNUELLE	NOMBRE 35 MM & 16 MM	FREQUEN- TATION ANNUELLE
PAIS	AÑO	NUMERO 35 MM Y MAS	NUMERO 16 MM	NUMERO DE ASIENTOS (000)	FRECUENTA- CION ANUAL (000 000)	NUMERO 35 MM & 16 MM	FRECUENTA- CION ANUAL (000 000)
AFRICA							
ALGERIA	1977	330	—	...	41.5	22	./.
BENIN	1976	4	...	4.4	0.8	1	0.3
BOTSWANA	1975	1	...	0.8	0.1	—	—
BURUNDI	1977	—	12	...	0.1	—	—
CHAD	1977	13	—	12.4	24.2	3	1.2
DJIBOUTI	1975	4	—	5.8	0.5	3	0.1
EGYPT	1974	239	—	211.0	70.0	—	—
EQUATORIAL GUINEA	1977	10	—	4.5	0.5	—	—
ETHIOPIA	1974	31	—	25.6	...	...	...
GABON	1974	6	—	4.1	1.1	—	—
GHANA	1977	8	—	13.2	1.0	—	—
IVORY COAST	1977	25	35	41.0	9.0	6	0.5
KENYA	1977	40	—	19.5	6.0	8	2.6
LIBERIA	1977	16	3	11.9	1.9	3	0.2
LIBYAN ARAB JAMAHIRIYA	1977	52	—	31.0	15.5	—	—
MADAGASCAR	1974	25	6	12.4	2.9	...	...
MALAWI	1975	3	1	2.3	0.2	13	1.0
MAURITANIA	1977	12	—	8.8	0.4	...	...
MAURITIUS	1977	48	—	48.0	17.5	...	...
MOROCCO	1977	227	—	146.8	35.8	...	...
RWANDA	1975	2	1	1.0	0.1	...	...
ST. HELENA	1976	1	1	1.2	0.0	1	0.0
SENEGAL	1976	60	...	...	3.8	...	...
SEYCHELLES	1975	2	—	0.8	0.5	4	0.1
SUDAN	1975	58	—	112.0	11.0	43	1.0

NUMERO DE PAISES Y DE TERRITORIOS PRESENTADOS EN
ESTE CUADRO: 131

DRIVE—IN CINEMAS CINEMAS POUR AUTOMOBILISTES CINES PARA AUTOMOVILISTAS			ALL CINEMAS TOUS LES CINEMAS TODOS LOS CINES			COUNTRY
NUMBER	CAPACITY	ANNUAL ATTENDANCE	SEATS PER 1,000 INHABITANTS	ANNUAL AT-TENDANCE PER INHABITANT	GROSS OFFICE RECEIPTS	
NOMBRE	CAPACITE	FREQUEN-TATION ANNUELLE	SIEGES POUR 1 000 HABITANTS	FREQUENTATION ANNUELLE PAR HABITANT	RECETTES BRUTES	PAYS
NUMERO	CAPACIDAD (000)	FRECUENTA-CION ANUAL (000 000)	ASIENTOS POR 1 000 HABITANTES	FRECUENTACION ANUAL POR HABITANTE	RECAUDACION TOTAL DE TAQUILLA (000 000)	PAIS
						AFRICA
—	—	—	...	2.3	112.1	ALGERIA
—	—	—	1.4	0.3	80.0	BENIN
—	—	—	1.2	0.2	...	BOTSWANA
—	—	—	...	0.0	7.5	BURUNDI
—	—	—	2.9	6.0	2537.2	CHAD
—	—	—	54.7	5.2	...	DJIBOUTI
—	—	—	5.8	1.9	21.0	EGYPT
—	—	—	14.0	1.6	...	EQUATORIAL GUINEA
—	—	—	0.9	...	...	ETHIOPIA
—	—	—	7.9	2.2	...	GABON
—	—	—	1.3	0.1	9.4	GHANA
—	—	—	8.0	1.8	1650.0	IVORY COAST
3	7.0	0.6	1.8	0.6	9.2	KENYA
—	—	—	6.6	1.2	...	LIBERIA
—	—	—	11.9	6.0	...	LIBYAN ARAB JAMAHIRIYA
—	—	—	1.6	0.4	...	MADAGASCAR
2	2.4	0.2	0.9	0.3	...	MALAWI
—	—	—	5.4	*0.3	12.8	MAURITANIA
—	—	—	52.8	19.3	30.0	MAURITIUS
—	—	—	8.0	2.0	72.5	MOROCCO
—	—	—	0.2	0.0	...	RWANDA
—	—	—	240.0	8.8	...	ST. HELENA
—	—	—	...	0.7	...	SENEGAL
—	—	—	13.8	9.3	...	SEYCHELLES
—	—	—	7.1	0.8	...	SUDAN

COUNTRY	YEAR	FIXED CINEMAS ETABLISSEMENTS FIXES ESTABLECIMIENTOS FIJOS				MOBILE UNITS CINEMAS ITINERANTS UNIDADES MOVILES	
		NUMBER 35 MM AND OVER	NUMBER 16 MM	SEATING CAPACITY	ANNUAL ATTENDANCE	NUMBER 35 MM & 16 MM	ANNUAL ATTENDANCE
PAYS	ANNEE	NOMBRE 35 MM ET PLUS	NOMBRE 16 MM	NOMBRE DE SIEGES	FREQUEN- TATION ANNUELLE	NOMBRE 35 MM & 16 MM	FREQUEN- TATION ANNUELLE
PAIS	AÑO	NUMERO 35 MM Y MAS	NUMERO 16 MM	NUMERO DE ASIENTOS (000)	FRECUENTA- CION ANUAL (000 000)	NUMERO 35 MM & 16 MM	FRECUENTA- CION ANUAL (000 000)
SWAZILAND	1975	2	2	1.3	0.1	...	...
TUNISIA	1977	80	2	41.0	8.8	–	–
UGANDA	1977	17	...	10.0	1.6	...	...
UNITED REPUBLIC OF CAMEROON	1977	45	./.	25.0	...	17	...
UNITED REPUBLIC OF TANZANIA	1977	34	–	13.4	*3.0	20	0.2
ZAIRE	1974	18	73	23.4	1.6	–	–
ZAMBIA	1976	12	–	4.1	1.6	–	–
AMERICA, NORTH							
BARBADOS	1975	6	–	4.9	1.1	2	0.0
BERMUDA	1977	4	–	2.0	0.3	–	–
BRITISH VIRGIN ISLANDS	1977	1	–	0.4	0.0	–	–
CANADA	1976	1107	22	652.5	82.3	...	...
CAYMAN ISLANDS	1974	1	2	1.1	0.2	–	–
CUBA	1976	458	–	...	...	637	33.7
DOMINICAN REPUBLIC	1975	83	...	46.5	6.8	...	...
EL SALVADOR	1974	72	–	...	14.1	–	–
GREENLAND	1975	–	73	...	...	–	–
GRENADA	1975	6	–	4.0	1.0	3	0.1
GUATEMALA	1976	104	./.	...	7.2	22	...
HAITI	1977	19	...	2.8	5.7	...	...
JAMAICA	1974	44	–	45.0	...	–	–
MEXICO	1977	2343	183	1833.0	262.4	138	...
PANAMA FORMER CANAL ZONE	1974	6	1	3.8	0.3	–	–
PUERTO RICO	1974	105	./.	...	6.8	...	...
ST. VINCENT AND THE GRENADINES	1974	3	–	2.4	0.0	1	0.0
TRINIDAD AND TOBAGO	1977	71	–	...	...	...	...
TURKS AND CAICOS ISLANDS	1977	–	3	1.0	0.5	–	–
UNITED STATES OF AMERICA	1977	12990	–	...	*1565	...	...
AMERICA, SOUTH							
ARGENTINA	1977	1356	–	750.0	65.6	3	0.0
BRAZIL	1977	2967	189	1732.8	208.3	22	0.0
CHILE	1977	239	–	164.0	19.4	...	...
COLOMBIA	1975	700	150	...	96.0	...	...
ECUADOR	1974	185	–	114.6	38.7	70	...
FALKLAND ISLANDS (MALVINAS)	1977	–	2	0.5	0.0	–	–
GUYANA	1977	50	–	40.0	10.2	9	0.0
PERU	1977	338	40	253.4	...	–	–
VENEZUELA	1977	563	./.	256.0	33.0	...	...

DRIVE—IN CINEMAS CINEMAS POUR AUTOMOBILISTES CINES PARA AUTOMOVILISTAS			ALL CINEMAS TOUS LES CINEMAS TODOS LOS CINES			COUNTRY
NUMBER	CAPACITY	ANNUAL ATTENDANCE	SEATS PER 1,000 INHABITANTS	ANNUAL AT-TENDANCE PER INHABITANT	GROSS OFFICE RECEIPTS	
NOMBRE	CAPACITE	FREQUEN-TATION ANNUELLE	SIEGES POUR 1 000 HABITANTS	FREQUENTATION ANNUELLE PAR HABITANT	RECETTES BRUTES	PAYS
NUMERO	CAPACIDAD (000)	FRECUENTA-CION ANUAL (000 000)	ASIENTOS POR 1 000 HABITANTES	FRECUENTACION ANUAL POR HABITANTE	RECAUDACION TOTAL DE TAQUILLA (000 000)	PAIS
1	2.4	0.0	7.5	0.2	...	SWAZILAND
—	—	—	6.8	1.5	2.1	TUNISIA
1	3.4	0.3	1.1	0.2	33.3	UGANDA
—	—	—	3.2	...	...	UNITED REPUBLIC OF CAMEROON
1	2.4	0.2	0.8	0.2	15.0	UNITED REPUBLIC OF TANZANIA
1	2.0	0.1	1.0	0.1	...	ZAIRE
1	1.2	0.1	0.8	0.3	...	ZAMBIA
						AMERICA, NORTH
2	2.3	0.1	29.4	5.2	1.3	BARBADOS
—	—	—	35.1	4.6	0.7	BERMUDA
—	—	—	29.2	3.3	...	BRITISH VIRGIN ISLANDS
309	581.8	13.0	53.3	4.1	224.0	CANADA
1	0.7	0.1	163.6	19.5	0.3	CAYMAN ISLANDS
...	...	...	...	...	...	CUBA
2	2.8	0.2	10.5	1.5	4.5	DOMINICAN REPUBLIC
—	—	—	...	3.6	9.5	EL SALVADOR
—	—	—	...	...	...	GREENLAND
1	0.6	0.1	47.9	12.1	1.5	GRENADA
...	...	...	...	...	3.1	GUATEMALA
4	...	0.5	0.6	1.3	...	HAITI
1	1.6	0.4	22.4	...	...	JAMAICA
8	16.0	3.1	28.6	4.1	3002.1	MEXICO
—	—	—	86.3	6.5	0.2	PANAMA FORMER CANAL ZONE
...	...	...	...	23	...	PUERTO RICO
1	1.0	0.0	34.0	0.6	...	ST. VINCENT AND THE GRENADINES
3	...	...	...	...	2.7	TRINIDAD AND TOBAGO
—	—	—	166.7	83.3	...	TURKS AND CAICOS ISLANDS
3564	...	./.	...	7.2	3490.0	UNITED STATES OF AMERICA
						AMERICA, SOUTH
9	16.0	1.4	29.4	2.6	16953.5	ARGENTINA
17	26.0	0.9	15.7	1.9	1873.5	BRAZIL
—	—	—	15.4	1.8	...	CHILE
—	—	—	...	4.1	...	COLOMBIA
—	—	—	16.5	5.6	464.8	ECUADOR
—	—	—	250.0	9.5	...	FALKLAND ISLANDS (MALVINAS)
1	1.5	0.2	51.2	12.9	9.1	GUYANA
—	—	—	15.5	...	...	PERU
25	26.0	./.	22.1	2.6	...	VENEZUELA

COUNTRY	YEAR	FIXED CINEMAS ETABLISSEMENTS FIXES ESTABLECIMIENTOS FIJOS				MOBILE UNITS CINEMAS ITINERANTS UNIDADES MOVILES	
		NUMBER 35 MM AND OVER	NUMBER 16 MM	SEATING CAPACITY	ANNUAL ATTENDANCE	NUMBER 35 MM & 16 MM	ANNUAL ATTENDANCE
PAYS	ANNEE	NOMBRE 35 MM ET PLUS	NOMBRE 16 MM	NOMBRE DE SIEGES	FREQUEN- TATION ANNUELLE	NOMBRE 35 MM & 16 MM	FREQUEN- TATION ANNUELLE
PAIS	AÑO	NUMERO 35 MM Y MAS	NUMERO 16 MM	NUMERO DE ASIENTOS (000)	FRECUENTA- CION ANUAL (000 000)	NUMERO 35 MM & 16 MM	FRECUENTA- CION ANUAL (000 000)
ASIA							
AFGHANISTAN	1975	33	1	20.0	10.0	...	...
BAHRAIN	1974	10	—	10.5	2.0	2	0.0
BANGLADESH	1976	194	...	103.0	...	...	...
BRUNEI	1977	9	—	8.3	2.6	8	0.2
BURMA	1976	175	...	135.6	...	...	...
HONG KONG	1977	78	—	97.2	60.2	—	—
INDIA	1975	5650	—	5638.0	2260.0	3585	...
INDONESIA	1977	1039	./.	642.2	111.3	315	...
IRAN	1975	448	—	297.3	25.0	...	...
ISRAEL	1977	227	./.	158.0	22.0	—	—
JAPAN	1977	2420	—	960.0	165.2	...	...
JORDAN ‡	1977	43	—	...	14.0	2	4.0
KOREA, REPUBLIC OF	1977	560	—	346.3	65.0	74	...
KUWAIT	1975	9	—	12.9	4.5	...	...
MALAYSIA	1977	425	—	...	34.0	350	./.
OMAN	1976	12	—	0.8	0.8	—	—
PAKISTAN	1975	650	—	...	...	220	...
PHILIPPINES	1975	716	—	569.8	318.0	84	...
QATAR	1975	3	—	3.0	...	—	—
SINGAPORE	1977	73	—	67.4	44.8	—	—
SRI LANKA	1977	352	—	185.5	65.5	...	...
SYRIAN ARAB REPUBLIC	1975	100	—	58.0	42.0	—	—
THAILAND	1977	376	...	267.2	...	—	—
UNITED ARAB EMIRATES	1977	21	53	29	6.9	9	0.0
VIET—NAM	1977	199	—	100.0	288.2	...	...
YEMEN	1975	14	—	16.9	...	...	...
YEMEN, DEMOCRATIC	1977	21	—	20.9	5.6	...	...
EUROPE							
AUSTRIA	1977	533	—	169.0	17.8	8	...
BELGIUM	1977	546	4	232.4	23.3	—	—
BULGARIA	1977	2995	530	726.1	112.5	50	0.9
CZECHOSLOVAKIA	1977	2152	1114	920.0	86.4	11	...
DENMARK	1977	420	—	122.0	16.9	3	0.2
FINLAND	1977	316	—	90.3	9.0	8	...
FRANCE	1977	4448	938	1601.4	171.1	./.	./.
GERMAN DEMOCRATIC REPUBLIC	1977	2057	—	350.0	71.0	4157	13.1
GERMANY, FEDERAL REPUBLIC OF	1977	3072	—	1016.0	124.2	37	./.
GIBRALTAR	1977	4	—	2.2	0.2	—	—
HUNGARY	1977	1126	2407	563.0	76.0	83	./.
ICELAND	1976	43	—	9.4	2.5	...	...
IRELAND	1977	177	—	...	...	—	—
ITALY	1977	8096	./.	...	372.3	250	1.6
MALTA	1977	38	—	29.0	3.1	—	—

DRIVE—IN CINEMAS CINEMAS POUR AUTOMOBILISTES CINES PARA AUTOMOVILISTAS			ALL CINEMAS TOUS LES CINEMAS TODOS LOS CINES			COUNTRY
NUMBER	CAPACITY	ANNUAL ATTENDANCE	SEATS PER 1,000 INHABITANTS	ANNUAL AT— TENDANCE PER INHABITANT	GROSS OFFICE RECEIPTS	
NOMBRE	CAPACITE	FREQUEN— TATION ANNUELLE	SIEGES POUR 1 000 HABITANTS	FREQUENTATION ANNUELLE PAR HABITANT	RECETTES BRUTES	PAYS
NUMERO	CAPACIDAD (000)	FRECUENTA— CION ANUAL (000 000)	ASIENTOS POR 1 000 HABITANTES	FRECUENTACION ANUAL POR HABITANTE	RECAUDACION TOTAL DE TAQUILLA (000 000)	PAIS
						ASIA
—	—	—	1.2	0.6	...	AFGHANISTAN
—	—	—	43.2	8.4	...	BAHRAIN
...	...	...	1.3	...	...	BANGLADESH
—	—	—	43.5	14.7	...	BRUNEI
...	...	...	4.4	...	...	BURMA
—	—	—	21.5	13.3	...	HONG KONG
...	...	...	9.4	3.8	...	INDIA
...	...	...	4.5	0.8	27658.3	INDONESIA
...	...	...	9.0	0.8	...	IRAN
1	...	...	43.8	6.1	...	ISRAEL
—	—	—	8.4	1.5	152.4	JAPAN
—	—	—	...	...	...	JORDAN ‡
—	—	—	9.5	1.8	...	KOREA, REPUBLIC OF
1	1.2	0.2	13.0	4.7	...	KUWAIT
—	—	—	...	2.7	...	MALAYSIA
—	—	—	1.0	1.1	...	OMAN
1	0.4	...	...	...	...	PAKISTAN
...	...	...	13.4	7.5	275.8	PHILIPPINES
—	—	—	1.8	...	...	QATAR
1	3.6	./.	30.8	19.4	...	SINGAPORE
—	—	—	13.3	4.7	82.4	SRI LANKA
—	—	—	7.9	5.7	35.0	SYRIAN ARAB REPUBLIC
—	—	—	6.1	...	...	THAILAND
—	—	—	122.9	29.1	...	UNITED ARAB EMIRATES
—	—	—	2.1	6.0	...	VIET—NAM
—	—	—	3.2	...	...	YEMEN
—	—	—	11.6	3.1	...	YEMEN, DEMOCRATIC
						EUROPE
2	4.0	0.3	22.5	2.4	640.0	AUSTRIA
—	—	—	23.6	2.3	...	BELGIUM
—	—	—	82.5	12.9	25.7	BULGARIA
—	—	—	61.2	5.7	322.3	CZECHOSLOVAKIA
—	—	—	24.0	3.4	221.4	DENMARK
—	—	—	19.1	1.9	90.7	FINLAND
...	...	...	30.2	3.2	1843.9	FRANCE
—	—	—	20.9	5.0	...	GERMAN DEMOCRATIC REPUBLIC
20	75.2	./.	17.8	2.0	652.4	GERMANY, FEDERAL REPUBLIC OF
—	—	—	73.3	8.1	...	GIBRALTAR
—	—	—	52.9	7.1	431.5	HUNGARY
...	...	...	42.7	11.4	...	ICELAND
—	—	—	...	...	...	IRELAND
1	3.9	0.1	...	6.6	342830.3	ITALY
—	—	—	87.3	9.3	...	MALTA

COUNTRY	YEAR	FIXED CINEMAS ETABLISSEMENTS FIXES ESTABLECIMIENTOS FIJOS				MOBILE UNITS CINEMAS ITINERANTS UNIDADES MOVILES	
		NUMBER 35 MM AND OVER	NUMBER 16 MM	SEATING CAPACITY	ANNUAL ATTENDANCE	NUMBER 35 MM & 16 MM	ANNUAL ATTENDANCE
PAYS	ANNEE	NOMBRE 35 MM ET PLUS	NOMBRE 16 MM	NOMBRE DE SIEGES	FREQUENTATION ANNUELLE	NOMBRE 35 MM & 16 MM	FREQUENTATION ANNUELLE
PAIS	AÑO	NUMERO 35 MM Y MAS	NUMERO 16 MM	NUMERO DE ASIENTOS (000)	FRECUENTACION ANUAL (000 000)	NUMERO 35 MM & 16 MM	FRECUENTACION ANUAL (000 000)
MONACO	1977	4	–	1.4	0.1	–	–
NETHERLANDS	1977	451	–	163.0	23.8	13	2.5
NORWAY	1977	430	–	140.3	16.4	22	0.4
POLAND	1977	1850	217	542.1	118.8	385	12.8
PORTUGAL	1977	474	./.	259.7	39.1	...	...
ROMANIA	1977	583	5217	231.0	178.6	76	4.9
SAN MARINO	1977	6	...	2.6	0.2	–	–
SPAIN	1977	4755	–	3140.0	211.9	–	–
SWEDEN	1977	1198	...	...	23.5	–	–
SWITZERLAND	1977	494	–	176.8	...	–	–
UNITED KINGDOM	1977	1510	–	763.8	103.5	–	–
YUGOSLAVIA	1977	1257	10	450.0	73.6	118	2.2
OCEANIA							
AMERICAN SAMOA	1975	5	–	2.3	0.2	6	0.0
AUSTRALIA	1977	591	...	...	...	–	–
FIJI	1976	50	–	40	0.3	–	–
FRENCH POLYNESIA	1975	6	–	3.2	0.4	6	0.0
GUAM	1974	7	–	5.2	1.0	–	–
KIRIBATI	1974	–	6	2.3	0.4	4	0.1
NEW CALEDONIA	1976	17	–	3.7	0.6	2	0.2
NEW HEBRIDES ‡	1976	3	–	1.3	0.1	–	–
NEW ZEALAND	1977	199	./.	113.4	...	–	–
NORFOLK ISLAND	1977	–	1	...	0.0	–	–
SAMOA	1975	2	6	4.2	0.3		...
SOLOMON ISLANDS	1977	2	–	0.8	0.0	...	...
TONGA	1975	4	3	7.5	0.1	8	0.1
U.S.S.R.							
U.S.S.R.	1977	152900	./.	...	4080.0	8400	./.
BYELORUSSIAN S.S.R.	1977	6189	./.	828.0	127.0	529	./.
UKRAINIAN S.S.R.	1977	25024	2000	5553.4	...	624	...

JORDAN:
  E—> DATA REFER TO THE EAST BANK ONLY.
  FR-> LES DONNEES SE REFERENT A LA RIVE ORIENTALE
SEULEMENT.
  ESP> LOS DATOS SE REFIEREN A LA ORILLA ORIENTAL
SOLAMENTE.

NEW HEBRIDES:
  E—> DATA REFER TO BRITISH ADMINISTRATION ONLY.
  FR-> LES DONNEES SE REFERENT A L'ADMINISTRATION
BRITANNIQUE SEULEMENT.
  ESP> LOS DATOS SE REFIEREN A LA ADMINISTRACION
BRITANICA SOLAMENTE.

DRIVE—IN CINEMAS CINEMAS POUR AUTOMOBILISTES CINES PARA AUTOMOVILISTAS			ALL CINEMAS TOUS LES CINEMAS TODOS LOS CINES			COUNTRY
NUMBER	CAPACITY	ANNUAL ATTENDANCE	SEATS PER 1,000 INHABITANTS	ANNUAL AT— TENDANCE PER INHABITANT	GROSS OFFICE RECEIPTS	
NOMBRE	CAPACITE	FREQUEN— TATION ANNUELLE	SIEGES POUR 1 000 HABITANTS	FREQUENTATION ANNUELLE PAR HABITANT	RECETTES BRUTES	PAYS
NUMERO	CAPACIDAD (000)	FRECUENTA— CION ANUAL (000 000)	ASIENTOS POR 1 000 HABITANTES	FRECUENTACION ANUAL POR HABITANTE	RECAUDACION TOTAL DE TAQUILLA (000 000)	PAIS
–	–	–	56.0	4.0	...	MONACO
1	...	./.	11.8	1.9	165.0	NETHERLANDS
–	–	–	34.7	4.2	162.7	NORWAY
–	–	–	15.6	4.0	1429.6	POLAND
–	–	–	26.7	4.0	992.6	PORTUGAL
–	–	–	10.7	8.5	...	ROMANIA
–	–	–	130.0	7.9	68.0	SAN MARINO
–	–	–	85.6	5.8	15934.9	SPAIN
–	–	–	...	2.8	359.0	SWEDEN
–	–	–	27.9	...	129.1	SWITZERLAND
–	–	–	13.7	1.9	...	UNITED KINGDOM
–	–	–	20.7	3.5	772.9	YUGOSLAVIA
						OCEANIA
–	–	–	79.3	6.7	0.1	AMERICAN SAMOA
288	...	...	...	...	...	AUSTRALIA
–	–	–	69.0	0.5	...	FIJI
2	4.0	0.1	25.0	4.0	60.8	FRENCH POLYNESIA
–	–	–	53.6	10.1	3.7	GUAM
–	–	–	35.9	7.3	0.1	KIRIBATI
3	6.8	0.2	77.8	6.9	172.7	NEW CALEDONIA
–	–	–	...	...	0.1	NEW HEBRIDES ‡
–	–	–	36.5	...	...	NEW ZEALAND
–	–	–	...	4.5	0.0	NORFOLK ISLAND
–	–	–	27.6	2.2	0.1	SAMOA
...	...	...	3.9	0.3	...	SOLOMON ISLANDS
–	–	–	73.5	1.2	0.0	TONGA
						U.S.S.R.
–	–	–	...	15.8	...	U.S.S.R.
–	–	–	87.7	13.5	...	BYELORUSSIAN S.S.R.
–	–	–	112.4	...	...	UKRAINIAN S.S.R.

10 Broadcasting
Radiodiffusion
Radiodifusión

This chapter provides statistical information on radio and television transmitters and receivers. Most of the figures for 1976 and 1977 have been obtained from a statistical survey carried out in 1978 using a new questionnaire, and based upon definitions and classifications contained in the Recommendation adopted by the General Conference in 1976 concerning the international standardization of statistics on radio and television.

Except for European countries, results of the survey, as regards data on constitutional status of the broadcasting institutions, revenue and expenditure, personnel and programmes have been disappointing. For this reason, only four tables are included in this chapter, since to present data here on those aspects noted above would have revealed a very incomplete picture and would not have served the purpose of international comparability. It is expected that with better application by all countries of the provisions laid down in the Recommendation, the survey to be held in 1980 will allow the publication of more comprehensive and reliable broadcasting statistics.

As concerns television broadcasting, the information available permits the assumption that in the following 51 countries and territories no television service has been introduced:

Africa: Angola, Botswana, Burundi, Cape Verde, Chad, Comoro, Gambia, Guinea, Guinea-Bissau, Lesotho, Malawi, Mali, Mauritania, Niger, Rwanda, St. Helena, Sao Tome and Principe, Seychelles, Somalia, Swaziland, United Republic of Cameroon.

America, North: Belize, Cayman Islands, Dominica, Grenada, Montserrat, St. Kitts - Nevis Anguilla, Turks and Caicos Islands.

America, South: Falkland Islands (Malvinas), Guyana.

Asia: Afghanistan, Bhutan, Burma, East Timor, Lao People's Democratic Republic, Macau, Maldives, Nepal, Sri Lanka.

Europe: Faeroe Islands.

Oceania: Cook Islands, Fiji, Kiribati, Nauru, New Hebrides, Niue, Norfolk Island, Papua New Guinea, Samoa, Solomon Islands, Tonga.

Table 10.1

This table gives the latest data available on the number of radio transmitters and their total transmitting power for the period 1974-1977. The figures relate in principle to transmitters in service used for domestic broadcasting to the general public, not including transmitters primarily used for external broadcasting. The table also gives data separately according to the type of agency responsible for the transmitters (government, public service, or commercial). Where only the total is given, this indicates that a breakdown by type of organization operating the transmitter has not been communicated. With regard to transmitters operating in the VHF and SHF bands the transmitting power is given in ERP (Effective Radiated Power).

Table 10.2

This table gives information on the number of radio receivers and/or licences for the years 1965, 1970, 1976 and 1977. Generally, data refer to the end of the year stated. The figures on receivers relate to all types of receivers for radio broadcasts to the general public, including those connected to a cable distribution system (wired receivers). The data include such individual private receivers as car radios, portable radio sets and private sets installed in public places as well as communal receivers. Data on receivers are estimates of the number of receivers in use. Such data vary widely in reliability from country to country and should be treated with caution. The number of radio licences as given in this table is composed of the number of licences for radio receivers only as well as the number of combined radio/television licenses, where applicable.

Table 10.3

This table gives the latest data available on the number of television transmitters and their transmitting power (in ERP) for the period 1974-1977. The figures relate to transmitters operating on a regular basis and used for broadcasting to the general public, regardless of whether the responsibility for them lies with broadcasting institutions or with other bodies such as Posts and Telegraphs. Unless otherwise stated the data on transmitters relate to both main and relay transmitters. As is the case for radio transmitters, this table also provides information on the agency responsible for the transmitters. Information is also given on the number of television transmitters which broadcast programmes in colour.

Table 10.4

This table gives statistics on the number of television receivers and/or licences for 138 countries and territories out of the 206 represented in the *Yearbook*.

On the basis of the available data the number of television receivers/licences per thousand inhabitants has been calculated for the years 1965, 1970, 1976 and 1977.

As is the case for radio, data relating to television receivers represent the estimated total number of receivers in use.

Ce chapitre donne des renseignements statistiques sur les émetteurs et les postes récepteurs de radio et de télévision. La plupart des chiffres pour 1976 et 1977 ont été obtenus grâce à une enquête statistique effectuée en 1978 avec un nouveau questionnaire préparé sur la base des définitions et classifications qui figurent dans la Recommandation concernant la normalisation internationale des statistiques relatives à la radio et à la télévision, adoptée par la Conférence générale en 1976.

A l'exception des pays européens, les résultats de l'enquête en ce qui concerne le statut des organismes de radiodiffusion sonore, l'origine des ressources et les dépenses, le personnel et les programmes, ont été décevants. C'est la raison pour laquelle ce chapitre ne contient que quatre tableaux, puisque les données dont nous disposons actuellement sur les sujets mentionnés ci-dessus sont très incomplètes et inutilisables à des fins de comparabilité internationale. Il faut espérer qu'avec une meilleure application par tous les pays des dispositions qui figurent dans la Recommandation, l'enquête qui sera effectuée en 1980 permettra la publication de statistiques plus complètes et plus sûres sur la radiodiffusion.

En ce qui concerne la télévision, les renseignements disponibles permettent de conclure que dans les 51 pays et territoires suivants, il n'existe pas encore un service de télévision:

Afrique: Angola, Botswana, Burundi, Cap-Vert, Tchad, Comores, Gambie, Guinée, Guinée-Bissau, Lesotho, Malawi, Mali, Mauritanie, Niger, Rwanda, Sainte Hélène, Sao Tome et Principe, Seychelles, Somalie, Swaziland, République unie du Cameroun.

Amérique du Nord: Belize, Iles Caïmanes, Dominique, Grenade, Montserrat, Saint-Christophe-Nieves et Anguilla, Iles Turques et Caïques.

Amérique du Sud: Iles Falkland (Malvinas), Guyane.

Asie: Afghanistan, Bhoutan, Birmanie, Timor oriental, République populaire démocratique Lao, Macao, Maldives, Népal, Sri Lanka.

Europe: Iles Féroé.

Océanie: Iles cook, Fidji, Kiribati, Nauru, Nouvelles-Hébrides, Nioué, Ile Norfolk, Papouasie Nouvelle Guinée, Samoa, Iles Salomon, Tonga.

Tableau 10.1

Ce tableau présente les dernières données disponibles pour la période 1974-1977 sur le nombre de postes émetteurs de radio et leur puissance totale. Les données se réfèrent en principe aux émetteurs en service qui diffusent des programmes destinés au public qui réside dans le pays et ne comprend pas les émetteurs réservés principalement aux émissions vers l'étranger. Le tableau présente également des données séparées sur le type d'institution responsable des émetteurs (gouvernemental, service public, ou commercial). Lorsque seul le total est présenté, il faut considérer que la répartition par type d'institution responsable des émetteurs n'a pas été communiquée. En ce qui concerne les émetteurs qui diffusent en ondes métriques et centimétriques, la puissance totale d'émission est exprimée en PAR maximale (puissance apparente rayonnée maximale).

Tableau 10.2

Ce tableau présente des renseignements sur le nombre de récepteurs de radio et/ou sur le total de licences délivrées, pour les années 1965, 1970, 1976 et 1977. En général, les données se réfèrent à la fin de l'année indiquée. Les statistiques portent sur tous les genres de postes récepteurs destinés à capter les programmes radiodiffusés à l'intention du grand public, y compris les postes récepteurs reliés à un réseau de distribution par câble. Les données se réfèrent à tous postes individuels privés, comme les récepteurs pour automobiles, les postes portatifs et les postes privés installés dans des lieux publics destinés à l'écoute collective. Les données sur les récepteurs sont des estimations du nombre de récepteurs en service. Ces données varient sensiblement d'un pays à l'autre et doivent être considérées avec prudence. Le nombre de récepteurs de radio présenté dans ce tableau concerne le nombre de licences délivrées pour les récepteurs de radio seulement, ainsi que le nombre de licences combinées de radio et de télévision, lorsque c'est applicable.

Tableau 10.3

Ce tableau présente les dernières données disponibles sur le nombre d'émetteurs de télévision et leur puissance d'émission (en PAR maximale) pour la période 1974-1977. Les données se réfèrent aux émetteurs qui fonctionnent régulièrement et qui diffusent des programmes destinés au grand public, sans considérer si la responsabilité appartient à une institution de radiodiffusion ou à d'autres organismes, comme par exemple les Postes et Télécommunications. Sauf indication contraire, les données sur les émetteurs comprennent les émetteurs principaux et les auxiliaires. Comme dans le cas des émetteurs de radio, ce tableau présente également des renseignements sur l'autorité responsable des émetteurs. Des renseignements sont procurés également sur le nombre des émetteurs de télévision qui diffusent des programmes en couleur.

Tableau 10.4

Le tableau 10.4 présente des statistiques sur le nombre de récepteurs de télévision et/ou les licences délivrées pour 138 pays et territoires, sur les 206 qui figurent dans cet Annuaire.

Sur la base des données disponibles, on a calculé le nombre de récepteurs/licences de télévision pour 1.000 habitants, pour les années 1965, 1970, 1976 et 1977.

Commme pour la radio, les données relatives aux récepteurs de télévision représentent une estimation du nombre total des récepteurs en service.

Este capítulo proporciona información sobre los transmisores y los receptores de radio y de televisión. La mayor parte de los datos para 1976 y 1977 han sido obtenidos por medio de la encuesta estadística efectuada en 1978 con un nuevo cuestionario basado en las definiciones y clasificaciones contenidas en la Recomendación sobre la normalización internacional de las estadísticas relativas a la radio y la televisión, adoptada por la Conferencia General en 1976.

Excepto para los países europeos, los resultados de la encuesta, en lo que concierne la situación constitucional de las instituciones de radiodifusión sonora, las fuentes de ingreso y los gastos, el personal y los programas, han sido desalentadores. Es por ello que este capítulo se limita solamente a cuatro cuadros, ya que los datos de que actualmente disponemos sobre dichos aspectos son muy incompletos y no son útiles para fines de comparabilidad internacional. Es de esperar que con una mejor aplicación por parte de todos los países de las disposiciones que figuran en la Recomendación, la encuesta que se efectuará en 1980 permitirá la publicación de estadísticas más completas y más fiables sobre la radiodifusión.

En lo que se refiere a la televisión, de la información disponible se desprende que en los 51 países y territorios siguientes no existe todavía un servicio de televisión:

Africa: Angola, Botswana, Burundi, Cabo Verde, Chad, Comores, Gambia, Guinea, Guinea-Bissau, Lesotho, Malawi, Mali, Mauritania, Niger, Rwanda, Santa Elena, Santo Tomé y Príncipe, Seychelles, Somalia, Swazilandia, República Unida de Camerún.

América del Norte: Belize, Islas Caimán, Dominica, Granada, Montserrat, San Cristóbal-Nieves-Anguilla, Islas Turcas y Caicos.

América del Sud: Islas Falkland (Malvinas), Guyana.

Asia: Afganistán, Bután, Birmania, Timor oriental, República Democrática Popular Lao, Macao, Maldivas, Nepal, Sri Lanka.

Europa: Islas Feroé.

Oceanía: Islas Cook, Viti, Kiribati, Nauru, Nuevas Hébridas, Niue, Islas Norfolk, Papua Nueva Guinea, Samoa, Islas Salomón, Tonga.

Cuadro 10.1

Este cuadro presenta los últimos datos disponibles sobre el número de transmisores de radio y su potencia total, para el periodo 1974-1977. En principio, los datos se refieren a los transmisores en funcionamiento que emiten programas destinados al público que reside en el país y no incluyen los transmisores reservados principalmente a las emisiones destinadas al extranjero. El cuadro también presenta datos sobre el tipo de institución responsable de los transmisores (gubernamental, servicio público, o comercial). Cuando sólo se presenta el total, debe considerarse que la distribución por tipo de institución responsable de los transmisores no ha sido comunicada. En lo que se refiere a los transmisores que emiten en VHF y SHF, la potencia total de emisión se expresa en ERP máxima (potencia efectiva radiada máxima).

Cuadro 10.2

Este cuadro procura información sobre el número de receptores de radio y/o los permisos existentes para 1965, 1970, 1976 y 1977. En general, los datos se refieren al final del año indicado. Las estadísticas se refieren a todos los tipos de receptores destinados a captar los programas emitidos para el público en general, incluidos los que están conectados por cable a una red de distribución. Los datos abarcan todos los receptores individuales privados, como los de los automóviles, los portátiles y los receptores privados instalados en locales públicos destinados a una escucha colectiva. Los datos sobre los receptores son estimaciones del número de receptores en uso. Estos datos varían sensiblemente de un país a otro y deben ser considerados con prudencia. El número de receptores de radio que figura en este cuadro se refiere al número de permisos concedidos para los receptores de radio solamente, además del número de permisos combinados de radio y de televisión, cuando ello es aplicable.

Cuadro 10.3

Este cuadro presenta los últimos datos disponibles sobre el número de transmisores de televisión y su potencia de emisión (en ERP máxima) para el periodo 1974-1977. Los datos se refieren a los transmisores que funcionan con carácter regular y que emiten programas destinados al público en general, sin considerar si la responsabilidad reside en una institución de radiofusión o en otros organismos, como por ejemplo correos y telégrafos. Salvo indicación contraria, los datos relativos a los transmisores comprenden los transmisores principales y los auxiliares. Igual que para los transmisores de radio, este cuadro también proporciona información sobre la autoridad responsable de los transmisores. Se presenta igualmente información con respecto al número de transmisores de televisión que emiten programas en color.

Cuadro 10.4

Este cuadro presenta estadísticas sobre el número de receptores de televisión y/o permisos concedidos para 138 países y territorios, sobre los 206 que figuran en este *Anuario*.

Sobre la base de los datos disponibles, se ha calculado el número de receptores/permisos de televisión por 1.000 habitantes para los años 1965, 1970, 1976 y 1977.

Como para la radio, los datos relativos a los receptores de televisión representan una estimación del número total de los receptores en uso.

10.1 Radio broadcasting: number of transmitters and transmitting power by frequency band

Radiodiffusion: nombre d'émetteurs et puissance d'émission par bande de fréquence

Radiodifusión: número de transmisores y potencia de emisión por banda de frecuencia

P = PUBLIC
C = COMMERCIAL

P = PUBLIC
C = COMMERCIAL

P = PUBLICA
C = COMERCIAL

FIGURES RELATE TO TRANSMITTERS IN SERVICE USED FOR DOMESTIC RADIO BROADCASTS TO THE GENERAL PUBLIC

LES DONNEES SE RAPPORTENT AUX EMETTEURS EN SERVICE QUI DIFFUSENT DES PROGRAMMES DESTINES AU PUBLIC QUI RESIDE DANS LE PAYS

LOS DATOS SE REFIEREN A LOS TRANSMISORES EN FUNCIONAMIENTO QUE EMITEN PROGRAMAS DESTINADOS AL PUBLICO QUE RESIDE EN EL PAIS

NUMBER OF COUNTRIES AND TERRITORIES PRESENTED IN THIS TABLE: 184

NOMBRE DE PAYS ET DE TERRITOIRES PRESENTES DANS CE TABLEAU: 184

NUMERO DE PAISES Y DE TERRITORIOS PRESENTADOS EN ESTE CUADRO: 184

FREQUENCY / ONDES / FRECUENCIA

COUNTRY / PAYS / PAIS	YEAR / ANNEE / AÑO	OWNER-SHIP / PRO-PRIETE / PRO-PIEDAD	TOTAL NUMBER OF TRANS-MITTERS / NOMBRE D'-EMETTEURS / NUMERO DE TRANS-MISORES	TOTAL TRANS-MITTING POWER / PUISSANCE D'EMISSION / POTENCIA DE EMISION	LOW & MEDIUM KILO- & HECTOMETRIQUES BAJA Y MEDIA NUMBER OF TRANS-MITTERS / NOMBRE D'-EMETTEURS / NUMERO DE TRANS-MISORES	LOW & MEDIUM TRANS-MITTING POWER / PUISSANCE D'EMISSION / POTENCIA DE EMISION	HIGH DECIMETRIQUES ALTA NUMBER OF TRANS-MITTERS / NOMBRE D'-EMETTEURS / NUMERO DE TRANS-MISORES	HIGH TRANS-MITTING POWER / PUISSANCE D'EMISSION / POTENCIA DE EMISION	VERY HIGH & SUPER HIGH METRIQUES & CENTIMETR. MUY ALTA Y SUPER ALTA NUMBER OF TRANS-MITTERS / NOMBRE D'-EMETTEURS / NUMERO DE TRANS-MISORES	VERY HIGH & SUPER HIGH TRANS-MITTING POWER / PUISSANCE D'EMISSION / POTENCIA DE EMISION
			(1)	(2)	(3)	(4)	(5)	(6)	(7)	(8)
AFRICA										
ALGERIA	1976	G	–	–	13	3 467	17	1 400	–	–
ANGOLA	1976	G	–	–	17	150	15	279	11	1
BENIN	1976	G	–	–	3	50	–	–	2	0
BOTSWANA	1976	G	–	–	1	50	4	40	1	0

FREQUENCY / ONDES / FRECUENCIA

COUNTRY / PAYS / PAIS	YEAR / ANNEE / AÑO	OWNERSHIP / PROPRIETE / PROPIEDAD	TOTAL		LOW & MEDIUM / KILO- & HECTOMETRIQUES / BAJA Y MEDIA		HIGH / DECIMETRIQUES / ALTA		VERY HIGH & SUPER HIGH / METRIQUES & CENTIMETR. / MUY ALTA Y SUPER ALTA	
			NUMBER OF TRANSMITTERS (1)	TRANSMITTING POWER (2)	NUMBER OF TRANSMITTERS (3)	TRANSMITTING POWER (4)	NUMBER OF TRANSMITTERS (5)	TRANSMITTING POWER (6)	NUMBER OF TRANSMITTERS (7)	TRANSMITTING POWER (8)
BURUNDI	1975	T	–	–	2	1	4	28	–	–
		G	–	–	1	1	2	25	–	–
		P	–	–	1	0	2	3	–	–
CAPE VERDE	1976	T	–	–	–	–	5	27	1	0
		G	–	–	–	–	1	1	–	–
		C	–	–	–	–	4	26	1	0
CENTRAL AFRICAN REPUBLIC	1976	G	–	–	1	1	2	200	1	..
CHAD	1976	G	–	–	1	20	2	200	–	–
COMORO	1976	G	–	–	1	40	1	4	1	0
CONGO	1976	G	–	–	2	80	9	308	1	..
DJIBOUTI	1976	P	–	–	2	8	1	4	–	–
EGYPT	1976	G	–	–	24	2 895	2	100	1	–
EQUATORIAL GUINEA	1976	T	–	–	–	–	2	15	–	–
		G	–	–	–	–	1	10	–	–
		C	–	–	–	–	1	5	–	–
ETHIOPIA	1976	T	–	–	4	251	4	400	–	–
		G	–	–	3	250	2	200	–	–
		P	–	–	1	1	2	200	–	–
GABON	1976	G	–	–	5	62	7	284	1	–
GAMBIA	1976	T	–	–	3	27	–	–	1	0
		G	–	–	2	22	–	–	1	0
		C	–	–	1	5	–	–	–	–
GHANA	1977	G	–	–	–	–	13	550	3	28
GUINEA	1976	G	–	–	1	100	5	254	–	–
GUINEA-BISSAU	1976	G	–	–	1	100	1	10	–	–

Country	Year		(1)	(2)	(3)	(4)	(5)	(6)	(7)	(8)
IVORY COAST	1977	G	—	—	3	26	5	170	18	360
KENYA	1976	G	—	—	9	281	5	310	2	2
LESOTHO	1976	G	—	—	1	10	1	10	1	10
LIBERIA ‡	1978	T	—	—	2	60	5	130	2	..
		G	—	—	1	50	1	10	1	..
		P	—	—	1	10	4	120	1	0
LIBYAN ARAB JAMAHIRIYA	1976	G	—	800	12	2 020	3	700	—	—
MADAGASCAR	1977	G	—	—	13	36	6	159	—	—
MALAWI	1976	P	—	—	6	64	3	220	4	2
MALI	1976	G	—	—	2	64	7	222	—	—
MAURITANIA	1976	G	—	—	2	30	3	230	—	—
MAURITIUS	1976	P	—	—	2	10	1	10	—	—
MOROCCO	1977	G	1	—	25	1 892	3	200	4	12
MOZAMBIQUE	1976	G	—	—	13	146	30	875	2	5
NAMIBIA	1976	G	—	—	—	—	—	—	—	—
NIGER	1976	G	—	—	8	2	6	43	7	7
NIGERIA	1978	T	—	—	60	2 550	36	1 070	15	86
		G	—	—	12	1 050	10	510	—	—
		P	—	—	48	1 500	26	560	15	86
REUNION	1976	P	—	—	2	12	2	55	2	3
RWANDA	1976	G	—	—	—	—	2	—	—	—
ST. HELENA	1977	G	—	—	2	1	—	—	1	0
SAO TOME AND PRINCIPE	1976	G	—	—	2	25	1	10	1	0
SENEGAL	1976	G	—	—	9	221	7	262	1	1
SEYCHELLES	1976	T	—	—	1	10	4	183	—	..
		G	—	—	1	10	—	—	—	..
		P	—	—	1	—	4	183	—	..
SIERRA LEONE	1977	G	—	—	1	10	2	260	—	—
SOMALIA	1976	G	—	—	2	160	3	105	—	—
SUDAN	1977	G	—	—	3	1 700	6	380	—	—
SWAZILAND	1977	G	—	—	3	31	4	210	2	0

FREQUENCY / ONDES / FRECUENCIA

COUNTRY / PAYS / PAIS	YEAR / ANNEE / AÑO	OWNER-SHIP / PRO-PRIETE / PRO-PIEDAD	TOTAL — NUMBER OF TRANS-MITTERS (1)	TOTAL — TRANS-MITTING POWER (2)	LOW & MEDIUM KILO- & HECTOMETRIQUES BAJA Y MEDIA — NUMBER OF TRANS-MITTERS (3)	LOW & MEDIUM — TRANS-MITTING POWER (4)	HIGH DECIMETRIQUES ALTA — NUMBER OF TRANS-MITTERS (5)	HIGH — TRANS-MITTING POWER (6)	VERY HIGH & SUPER HIGH METRIQUES & CENTIMETR. MUY ALTA Y SUPER ALTA — NUMBER OF TRANS-MITTERS (7)	VERY HIGH & SUPER HIGH — TRANS-MITTING POWER (8)
TOGO	1976	G	—	—	2	30	4	260	—	—
TUNISIA	1976	G	—	—	6	1 160	5	850	1	—
UGANDA	1976	G	—	—	7	552	5	38	—	—
UNITED REPUBLIC OF CAMEROON	1976	G	—	—	4	22	6	106	—	—
UNITED REPUBLIC OF TANZANIA	1976	G	—	—	8	256	10	304	2	0
UPPER VOLTA	1978	G	—	—	5	161	2	24	1	1
ZAIRE	1977	G	—	—	6	713	15	330	1	—
ZAMBIA	1977	G	—	—	2	426	2	253	1	4
AMERICA, NORTH										
ANTIGUA	1976	T	—	—	2	15	—	—	1	...
		G	—	—	1	5	—	—	—	...
		C	—	—	1	10	—	—	1	—
BAHAMAS	1976	T	—	—	3	22	—	—	2	—
BARBADOS	1977	C	—	—	1	10	—	—	—	—
BELIZE	1976	G	—	—	5	24	1	1	1	—
BERMUDA	1976	C	—	—	3	3	—	—	—	—
BRITISH VIRGIN ISLANDS	1977	C	—	—	1	10	—	—	—	—
CANADA	1974	T	365	...	101	...	9	...	—	...
		P	151	...	18	...	3	...	—	...
		C	214	...	83	...	6	...	—	...
CAYMAN ISLANDS	1977	G	—	—	2	11	—	—	1	0

	Year		(1)	(2)	(3)	(4)	(5)	(6)	(7)	(8)
COSTA RICA	1976	C	—	—	47	216	8	6	—	—
CUBA	1976	G	—	—	104	865	14	950	1	0
DOMINICA	1976	T	—	—	2	60	—	—	—	—
		G	—	—	1	10	—	—	—	—
		C	—	—	1	50	—	—	—	—
DOMINICAN REPUBLIC	1976	C	—	—	108	318	26	176	—	—
EL SALVADOR	1976	T	—	—	68	257	3	15	—	—
		G	—	—	2	15	—	—	—	—
		C	—	—	66	242	3	15	—	—
GREENLAND	1976	G	—	—	3	50	3	12	7	0
GRENADA	1976	G	—	—	1	1	3	15	—	—
GUADELOUPE	1976	P	—	—	2	24	—	—	—	—
GUATEMALA	1976	C	—	—	89	284	15	59	—	—
HAITI	1976	C	—	—	27	108	10	9	—	—
HONDURAS	1976	T	—	—	102	279	19	46	—	—
JAMAICA	1976	C	—	—	8	40	—	—	17	18
MARTINIQUE	1976	P	—	—	2	54	—	—	1	0
MEXICO	1977	T	...	...	597	...	26	...	118	...
		G	...	...	3	...	3	...	2	...
		P	...	...	14	...	8	...	3	...
		C	...	...	580	...	15	...	113	...
MONTSERRAT	1976	T	—	—	3	226	—	—	—	—
		G	—	—	1	1	—	—	—	—
		C	—	—	2	225	—	—	—	—
NETHERLANDS ANTILLES	1976	T	—	—	13	521	—	—	1	—
NICARAGUA	1976	T	—	—	66	430	8	154	—	—
PANAMA	1977	T	—	—	65	165	—	—	28	15
		G	—	—	6	15	—	—	4	3
		C	—	—	59	150	—	—	24	12
FORMER CANAL ZONE	1977	G	—	—	2	11	—	—	2	2
PUERTO RICO	1977	T	—	—	56	178	—	—	34	1 010
		G	—	—	1	10	—	—	1	125
		P	—	—	1	1	—	—	—	—
		C	—	—	54	167	—	—	33	≠885
ST. KITTS – NEVIS – ANGUILLA	1976	C	—	—	2	70	—	—	—	—

COUNTRY / PAYS / PAIS	YEAR / ANNEE / AÑO	OWNERSHIP / PROPRIETE / PROPIEDAD	TOTAL		FREQUENCY / ONDES / FRECUENCIA					
					LOW & MEDIUM / KILO- & HECTOMETRIQUES / BAJA Y MEDIA		HIGH / DECIMETRIQUES / ALTA		VERY HIGH & SUPER HIGH / METRIQUES & CENTIMETR. / MUY ALTA Y SUPER ALTA	
			NUMBER OF TRANSMITTERS / NOMBRE D'EMETTEURS / NUMERO DE TRANSMISORES	TRANSMITTING POWER / PUISSANCE D'EMISSION / POTENCIA DE EMISION	NUMBER OF TRANSMITTERS / NOMBRE D'EMETTEURS / NUMERO DE TRANSMISORES	TRANSMITTING POWER / PUISSANCE D'EMISSION / POTENCIA DE EMISION	NUMBER OF TRANSMITTERS / NOMBRE D'EMETTEURS / NUMERO DE TRANSMISORES	TRANSMITTING POWER / PUISSANCE D'EMISSION / POTENCIA DE EMISION	NUMBER OF TRANSMITTERS / NOMBRE D'EMETTEURS / NUMERO DE TRANSMISORES	TRANSMITTING POWER / PUISSANCE D'EMISSION / POTENCIA DE EMISION
			(1)	(2)	(3)	(4)	(5)	(6)	(7)	(8)
ST. LUCIA	1976	T	–	–	2	30	–	–	–	–
		P	–	–	1	20	–	–	–	–
		C	–	–	1	10	–	–	–	–
ST. PIERRE AND MIQUELON	1977	P	–	–	1	4	–	–	1	0
ST. VINCENT AND THE GRENADINES	1976	G	–	–	1	10	–	–	–	–
TRINIDAD AND TOBAGO	1976	T	–	–	2	30	–	–	2	4
		G	–	–	1	10	–	–	1	3
		C	–	–	1	20	–	–	1	1
TURKS AND CAICOS ISLANDS	1977	P	–	–	1	0	–	–	–	–
UNITED STATES OF AMERICA	1977	T	–	–	4 476	...	–	–	3 883	...
		G	–	–	–	...	–	–	414	...
		P	–	–	25	...	–	–	506	...
		C	–	–	4 451	...	–	–	2 963	...
U.S. VIRGIN ISLANDS	1977	C	–	–	4	7	–	–	3	61
ARGENTINA, SOUTH AMERICA	1976	T	–	–	149	2 250	14	418	–	–
		G	–	–	23	685	5	310	–	–
		P	–	–	13	191	–	–	–	–
		C	–	–	113	1 374	9	108	–	–
BOLIVIA	1976	T	–	–	73	130	63	118	–	–
		G	–	–	...	...	1	10	–	–
		C	–	–	...	...	62	108	–	–
BRAZIL	1977	T	789	2 524	113	683	30	688	30	93
		G	29	611	17	326	9	548	2	14
		C	760	1 913	96	357	21	140	28	79
CHILE	1976	T	193	–	143	716	24	263	–	–
ECUADOR	1974	T	–	...	...	...	62	...	14	9

	Year		(1)	(2)	(3)	(4)	(5)	(6)	(7)	(8)
FALKLAND ISLANDS (MALVINAS)	1977	G	—	—	1	5	1	5	—	—
FRENCH GUIANA	1976	P	—	—	2	4	3	9	2	...
GUYANA	1976	T	—	—	2	20	4	24	1	0
		G	—	—	1	10	2	20	1	0
		C	—	—	1	10	2	4	—	—
PARAGUAY	1976	T	—	—	26	284	10	237	—	—
		G	—	—	1	100	4	220	—	—
		C	—	—	25	184	6	17	—	—
PERU	1977	T	—	—	181	520	—	—	8	117
		G	—	—	35	156	—	—	—	—
		C	—	—	146	364	—	—	8	117
SURINAME	1976	C	—	—	6	77	—	—	1	0
URUGUAY	1976	T	—	—	83	525	22	118	—	—
		G	—	—	3	37	3	3	—	—
		C	—	—	80	488	19	115	—	—
VENEZUELA	1977	T	154	1 986	9	32	46	170	1	10
		G	8	171	1	10	2	20	—	—
		P	2	2	—	—	—	—	1	10
		C	144	1 813	8	22	44	150	—	—
ASIA										
AFGHANISTAN	1977	T	—	—	5	155	3	160	—	—
BAHRAIN	1977	G	—	—	3	21	—	—	1	8
BANGLADESH	1976	G	—	—	8	1 150	7	153	1	0
BHUTAN	1976	T	—	—	—	—	1	0	—	—
BRUNEI	1977	G	—	—	5	321	2	20	6	20
BURMA	1976	G	—	—	1	50	4	200	1	0
CYPRUS	1977	P	—	—	4	43	—	—	2	60
DEMOCRATIC KAMPUCHEA	1976	G	—	—	2	...	3	...	—	—
HONG KONG	1977	T	—	—	11	86	—	—	4	100
		G	—	—	2	40	—	—	4	100
		C	—	—	9	46	—	—	—	—
INDIA	1977	G	—	—	124	4 788	32	1 522	1	15
INDONESIA	1977	T	—	—	39	...	151	...	—	—
IRAN	1976	T	—	—	60	9 618	9	1 550	7	43
IRAQ	1977	G	—	—	10	3 740	16	2 300	—	—
ISRAEL	1976	T	—	—	14	1 898	16	1 920	18	...

FREQUENCY / ONDES / FRECUENCIA

COUNTRY / PAYS / PAIS	YEAR / ANNEE / AÑO	OWNERSHIP / PROPRIETE / PROPIEDAD	TOTAL — NUMBER OF TRANSMITTERS (1)	TOTAL — TRANSMITTING POWER (2)	LOW & MEDIUM KILO- & HECTOMETRIQUES BAJA Y MEDIA — NUMBER (3)	LOW & MEDIUM — POWER (4)	HIGH DECIMETRIQUES ALTA — NUMBER (5)	HIGH — POWER (6)	VERY HIGH & SUPER HIGH METRIQUES & CENTIMETR. MUY ALTA Y SUPER ALTA — NUMBER (7)	VERY HIGH & SUPER HIGH — POWER (8)
JAPAN	1977	T	—	—	493	3 730	7	190	476	154
		P	—	—	314	2 660	7	—	469	121
		C	—	—	179	1 070	7	190	7	33
JORDAN ‡	1976	G	—	—	3	810	4	305	1	...
KOREA, REPUBLIC OF	1977	T	—	—	107	3 661	7	619	4	4
		P	—	—	69	2 889	4	600	—	—
		C	—	—	38	772	3	19	4	4
KUWAIT	1976	G	—	—	4	2 450	12	2 800	—	—
LAO PEOPLE'S DEMOCRATIC REPUBLIC ‡	1978	G	...	...	3	30	1	25	...	...
LEBANON	1976	T	—	—	3	111	4	301	3	34
		G	—	—	1	100	3	300	1	10
		C	—	—	2	11	1	1	2	24
MACAU	1976	T	—	—	3	20	—	—	2	1
		G	—	—	2	10	—	—	1	1
		C	—	—	1	10	—	—	1	0
MALAYSIA	1977	G	—	—	58	2 300	29	1 090	2	200
MALDIVES	1977	G	1	2	1	2	5	13	2	0
NEPAL	1977	G	—	—	3	11	4	210	—	—
OMAN	1976	G	—	—	3	220	3	110	—	—
PAKISTAN	1977	P	—	—	13	1 990	15	1 060	—	—
PHILIPPINES	1977	T	—	—	241	724	25	1 296	—	—
		G	—	—	17	106	6	129	—	—
		P	—	—	32	258	19	1 167	—	—
		C	—	—	192	260			—	—
QATAR	1977	T	1	100	2	150	—	—	1	10
SAUDI ARABIA	1976	T	—	—	10	1 502	18	2 100	3	83
		G	—	—	10	1 502	18	2 100	3	83
		C	—	—	—	—	—	—	—	—

			(1)	(2)	(3)	(4)	(5)	(6)	(7)	(8)
SINGAPORE	1977	G	-	-	9	830	7	350	4	60
SRI LANKA	1977	G	-	-	11	265	18	460	-	-
SYRIAN ARAB REPUBLIC	1976	G	-	-	9	1 250	5	190	-	-
THAILAND	1977	G	3	1 520	132	2 931	9	197	76	83
TURKEY	1977	G	-	-	13	2 664	2	350	8	300
UNITED ARAB EMIRATES	1977	G	-	-	7	1 560	1	120	7	0
VIET-NAM	1976	G	-	-	10	...	32	...	1	...
YEMEN	1976	G	-	-	3	80	3	200	-	-
YEMEN, DEMOCRATIC	1976	G	-	-	1	50	4	308	-	-
EUROPE										
ALBANIA	1976	G	-	-	4	...	32	...	-	...
ANDORRA	1976	C	-	-	2	1 200	1	25	1	
AUSTRIA	1977	P	-	-	92	1 079	5	410	315	2 520
BELGIUM	1977	T	-	-	11	672	2	350	42	770
		G	-	-	-	-	-	-	26	522
		P	-	-	11	672	2	350	16	248
BULGARIA	1976	G	3	80	24	2 827	-	-	10	...
CZECHOSLOVAKIA	1977	G	1	150	45	4 168	-	-	41	1 700
DENMARK	1977	G	2	251	3	140	-	-	40	1 241
FINLAND	1977	P	1	2 100	10	267	3	380	85	489
FRANCE	1977	T	1	750	40	4 172	-	-	322	6 800
GERMAN DEMOCRATIC REPUBLIC	1977	G	1	250	27	2 125	10	1 110	44	2 645
GERMANY, FEDERAL REPUBLIC OF	1977	P	1	150	49	9 036	34	7 660	301	8 054
GIBRALTAR	1977	P	-	-	1	2	-	-	-	-
GREECE	1977	P	-	-	11	382	7	590	37	244
HOLY SEE	1975	T	-	-	3	455	12	645	2	5
HUNGARY	1977	G	2	-	12	2 515	8	765	25	173
ICELAND	1977	G	-	-	9	10	-	-	15	3
IRELAND	1977	P	-	-	6	...	-	-	8	...
ITALY	1977	P	1	1	128	2 700	-	-	1 833	1 500
LUXEMBOURG	1977	C	1	2 000	1	1 200	2	550	3	250

10.1 Radio broadcasting: transmitters
Radiodiffusion: émetteurs
Radiodifusión: transmisores

COUNTRY / PAYS / PAIS	YEAR ANNEE AÑO	OWNER-SHIP PROPRIETE PROPIEDAD	TOTAL — Number of transmitters (1)	TOTAL — Transmitting power (2)	LOW & MEDIUM — Number (3)	LOW & MEDIUM — Transmitting power (4)	HIGH — Number (5)	HIGH — Transmitting power (6)	VERY HIGH & SUPER HIGH — Number (7)	VERY HIGH & SUPER HIGH — Transmitting power (8)
MALTA	1977	C	–	–	2	15	–	–	1	1
MONACO	1977	P	1	2 000	2	1 400	–	–	2	1 120
NETHERLANDS	1977	P	'	–	7	274	–	–	9	456
NORWAY	1977	P	2	210	16	276	–	–	443	1 757
PORTUGAL	1977	T	–	–	39	820	10	770	54	393
		P	–	–	31	805	10	770	37	280
		C	–	–	8	15	–	–	17	113
ROMANIA	1976	G	1	1 200	22	3 748	36	4 320	17	112
SPAIN	1977	T	–	–	180	2 064	–	–	262	644
		G	–	–	63	1 693	–	–	116	500
		P	–	–	63	246	–	–	72	63
		C	–	–	54	125	–	–	74	81
SWEDEN ‡	1977	P	./.	./.	8	890	2	700	94	2 028
SWITZERLAND	1977	P	–	–	5	...	12	...	198	...
UNITED KINGDOM	1977	P	1	400	107	1 844	–	–	278	4 730
YUGOSLAVIA	1977	P	–	–	334	5 943	8	290	237	2 933
OCEANIA										
AMERICAN SAMOA	1977	C	–	–	1	10	1	–	–	–
AUSTRALIA	1977	T	–	–	220	1 348	7	102	13	176
		G	–	–	91	1 010	7	102	4	160
		P	–	–	7	2	–	–	9	16
		C	–	–	122	336	–	–	–	–
COOK ISLANDS	1977	C	–	–	1	10	1	1	–	–
FIJI	1977	P	10	55	–	–	–	–	2	1
GUAM	1977	C	–	–	3	25	–	–	2	7
KIRIBATI	1976	T	–	–	1	10	–	–	–	–

			(1)	(2)	(3)	(4)	(5)	(6)	(7)	(8)
NAURU	1976	G	—	—	1	0	—	—	—	—
NEW CALEDONIA	1976	T	—	—	1	20	4	48	—	—
NEW HEBRIDES	1976	G	—	—	1	1	3	4	—	—
NEW ZEALAND	1976	T	—	—	61	482	2	15	—	—
		P	—	—	53	459	2	15	—	—
		C	—	—	8	23	—	—	—	—
NIUE	1977	G	—	—	1	0	—	—	—	—
NORFOLK ISLAND	1977	G	—	—	1	1	—	—	—	—
PACIFIC ISLANDS	1977	T	—	—	8	48	—	—	2	0
		G	—	—	6	28	—	—	—	—
		P	—	—	1	10	—	—	—	—
		C	—	—	1	10	—	—	2	0
PAPUA NEW GUINEA	1977	P	—	—	6	12	20	104	—	—
SAMOA	1977	G	—	—	2	13	—	—	2	0
SOLOMON ISLANDS	1977	P	—	—	1	5	2	10	—	—
TONGA	1976	P	—	—	1	10	—	—	—	—

LIBERIA:
E—> DATA ON HIGH FREQUENCY TRANSMITTERS DO NOT
INCLUDE 8 TRANSMITTERS OF THE VOICE OF AMERICA.
FR—> LES DONNEES RELATIVES AUX EMETTEURS D'ONDES
DECAMETRIQUES N'INCLUENT PAS 8 EMETTEURS DE LA
"VOIX DE L'AMERIQUE".
ESP> LOS DATOS RELATIVOS A LOS TRANSMISORES DE
ALTA FRECUENCIA NO INCLUYEN 8 TRANSMISORES DE LA
"VOZ DE AMERICA".

JORDAN:
E—> DATA REFER TO THE EAST BANK ONLY.
FR—> LES DONNEES SE REFERENT A LA RIVE ORIENTALE
SEULEMENT.
ESP> LOS DATOS SE REFIEREN A LA ORILLA ORIENTAL
SOLAMENTE.

LAO PEOPLE'S DEMOCRATIC REPUBLIC:
E—> NOT INCLUDING 7 REGIONAL STATIONS.
FR—> NON COMPRIS 7 STATIONS REGIONALES.
ESP> NO INCLUYE 7 ESTACIONES REGIONALES.

SWEDEN:
E—> MEDIUM FREQUENCY AND LOW FREQUENCY
TRANSMITTERS ARE COUNTED TOGETHER.
FR—> LES EMETTEURS D'ONDES HECTOMETRIQUES
ET D'ONDES KILOMETRIQUES SONT COMPTES ENSEMBLE.
ESP> LOS TRANSMISORES DE ONDAS DE BAJA FRE-
CUENCIA Y DE MEDIA FRECUENCIA SE CUENTA
CONJUNTAMENTE.

10.2 Radio broadcasting: number of receivers and receivers per 1,000 inhabitants
Radiodiffusion: nombre total de récepteurs et de récepteurs pour 1 000 habitants
Radiodifusión: número de receptores y de receptores por 1 000 habitantes

L = NUMBER OF LICENCES ISSUED OR SETS DECLARED
L = NOMBRE DE LICENCES DELIVREES OU DE POSTES DECLARES
L = NUMERO DE PERMISOS CONCEDIDOS O DE RECEPTORES DECLARADOS

R = ESTIMATED NUMBER OF RECEIVERS IN USE
R = ESTIMATION DU NOMBRE DE RECEPTEURS EN SERVICE
R = ESTIMACION DE RECEPTORES EN FUNCIONAMIENTO

NUMBER OF COUNTRIES AND TERRITORIES PRESENTED IN THIS TABLE: 191
NOMBRE DE PAYS ET DE TERRITOIRES PRESENTES DANS CE TABLEAU: 191
NUMERO DE PAISES Y DE TERRITORIOS PRESENTADOS EN ESTE CUADRO: 191

COUNTRY / PAYS / PAIS	DEFINITION OF DATA / CODE / TIPO DE DATOS	NUMBER OF RECEIVERS IN USE AND/OR LICENCES ISSUED (THOUSANDS)				NUMBER OF RECEIVERS IN USE AND/OR LICENCES ISSUED PER 1 000 INHABITANTS			
		1965	1970	1976	1977	1965	1970	1976	1977
	(1)	(2)	(3)	(4)	(5)	(6)	(7)	(8)	(9)
AFRICA									
ALGERIA	R	480	870	3 000	...	40	61	173	...
	L				–				–
ANGOLA	R	79	95	116	118	15	17	18	18
BENIN	R	35	85	150	150	15	32	47	46
BOTSWANA	R	4	20	60	63	8	34	87	89
	L	...	9	...	...	...	15	...	...
BURUNDI	R	...	65	105	107	...	18	27	27
CAPE VERDE	R	4	5	36	40	16	17	119	131
CENTRAL AFRICAN REPUBLIC	R	30	46	75	80	...	...	...	...

	(1)	(2)	(3)	(4)	(5)	(6)	(7)	(8)	(9)
CHAD	R	25	60	76	80	8	16	18	19
COMORO	R	5	24	36	...	21	89	115	...
CONGO	R	47	65	83	88	44	55	60	61
DJIBOUTI	R	8	7	15	16	89	74	139	140
EGYPT	R	2 700	4 400	5 250	5 275	92	132	138	136
EQUATORIAL GUINEA	R	...	8	80	82	...	26	253	254
ETHIOPIA	R	...	160	210	215	...	6	7	7
GABON	R	36	62	93	95	78	124	175	178
GAMBIA	R	44	50	61	63	133	109	113	113
GHANA	R	555	703	1 080	1 095	72	81	105	105
GUINEA	R	75	91	120	120	21	23	26	26
GUINEA-BISSAU	R	3.3	4.0	11	15	7	8	21	28
IVORY COAST	R	60	75	600	800	16	17	120	155
KENYA	R	350	...	514	525	37	...	37	37
LESOTHO	L	5	...	23	25	6	...	19	20
LIBERIA	R	150	155	265	274	109	102	151	152
LIBYAN ARAB JAMAHIRIYA	R	50	85	110	125	31	43	44	48
MADAGASCAR	R	...	541	820	1 020	...	78	99	120
MALAWI	R	80	106	130	...	20	24	25	...
MALI	R	20	60	82	...	4	12	14	...
MAURITANIA	R	...	55	95	...	...	47	64	...
MAURITIUS	L	62	85	200	...	82	102	223	...
MOROCCO	R	700	935	1 500	1 600	53	60	84	88
MOZAMBIQUE	L	60	90	225	230	9	11	24	24
NIGER	R	45	145	...	...	13	36	...	...
NIGERIA	R	...	1 275	5 100	5 250	...	23	79	79
REUNION	R	46	79	95	100	116	177	186	204
RWANDA	R	...	30	70	80	...	8	16	18
ST. HELENA	R	...	.7	.9	1.0	...	140	180	200
SAO TOME AND PRINCIPE	R	1.9	6	20	21	31	89	247	256

COUNTRY / PAYS / PAIS	CODE / TIPO DE DATOS (1)	NUMBER OF RECEIVERS IN USE AND/OR LICENCES ISSUED (THOUSANDS)				NUMBER OF RECEIVERS IN USE AND/OR LICENCES ISSUED PER 1 000 INHABITANTS			
		1965 (2)	1970 (3)	1976 (4)	1977 (5)	1965 (6)	1970 (7)	1976 (8)	1977 (9)
SENEGAL	R	230	268	290	295	66	68	57	56
SEYCHELLES	R	6	7	17	18	128	135	288	289
SIERRA LEONE	R	27	40	305	315	11	16	98	91
SOMALIA	R	35	50	69	75	14	18	21	22
SOUTH AFRICA	R	1 500	2 000	2 500	2 500	76	89	96	93
SUDAN	R	...	...	...	1 400	...	...	...	83
SWAZILAND	R	8	30	60	70	22	71	121	138
TOGO	R	30	40	405	450	18	20	177	192
TUNISIA	R	...	388	810	866	...	76	141	143
UGANDA	R	200	...	250	250	23	...	21	20
UNITED REPUBLIC OF CAMEROON	R	115	212	...	240	22	36	...	30
UNITED REPUBLIC OF TANZANIA	R	115	150	300	310	10	11	19	19
UPPER VOLTA	R	50	87	105	110	10	16	17	17
WESTERN SAHARA	R	...	14	...	...	...	175	...	...
ZAIRE	R	...	63	108	125	...	2.9	4.3	4.9
ZAMBIA	R	43	75	110	115	12	18	21	22
ZIMBABWE		...	145	255	270	...	27	39	40
AMERICA, NORTH									
ANTIGUA	R	...	...	16	16	...	...	225	226
BAHAMAS	R	40	80	96	97	286	471	455	441
BARBADOS	R	40	89	96	100	167	371	389	394
BELIZE	R	30	57	70	85	280	475	486	570
BERMUDA	R	...	38	51	51	...	704	895	895
BRITISH VIRGIN ISLANDS	R	...	9	...	...	...	850	...	...

	(1)	(2)	(3)	(4)	(5)	(6)	(7)	(8)	(9)
CANADA	R	...	15 890	23 400	24 270	...	745	1011	1043
CAYMAN ISLANDS	R	2	...	6	7	150	...	545	636
COSTA RICA	R	...	130	150	156	...	75	74	75
CUBA	R	...	1 330	1 865	1 895	...	156	197	197
DOMINICA	R	...	...	...	18	...	...	...	225
DOMINICAN REPUBLIC	R	...	164	200	210	...	40	41	42
EL SALVADOR	R	396	405	1 400	1 415	135	115	340	333
GREENLAND	R	...	7	13	13	...	151	250	250
GRENADA	R	10	15	22	30	103	167	229	309
GUADELOUPE	R	...	26	...	...	...	80	...	...
GUATEMALA	R	...	220	265	275	...	42	42	43
HAITI	R	63	83	95	98	16	20	20	21
HONDURAS	R	135	147	161	163	60	56	50	49
JAMAICA	R	350	500	555	...	199	267	270	...
MARTINIQUE	R	...	32	35	40	...	95	95	107
MEXICO	R	8 593	14 005	...	...	208	276	...	385
MONTSERRAT	R	...	...	...	5	...	...	...	...
NETHERLANDS ANTILLES	R	100	115	150	175	481	518	622	694
NICARAGUA	R	100	109	600	600	62	60	...	260
PANAMA	R	...	230	270	275	...	161	157	157
PUERTO RICO	R	...	1 625	1 765	...	...	597	549	...
ST. KITTS – NEVIS ANGUILLA	R	...	...	...	60	...	...	...	909
ST. LUCIA	R	...	...	82	84	...	...	745	750
ST. PIERRE AND MIQUELON	R	...	...	2.2	2.6	...	...	440	442
TRINIDAD AND TOBAGO	R	165	...	270	275	169	217	245	246
TURKS AND CAICOS ISLANDS	R	...	1.3	3.0	...	...	217	500	...
UNITED STATES OF AMERICA	R	240 000	290 000	425 300	444 000	1235	1415	1977	2048
U.S. VIRGIN ISLANDS	R	...	33	76	80	...	559	792	...

COUNTRY / PAYS / PAIS	DEFINITION OF DATA / CODE / TIPO DE DATOS	NUMBER OF RECEIVERS IN USE AND/OR LICENCES ISSUED (THOUSANDS) — NOMBRE DE POSTES RECEPTEURS EN SERVICE ET/OU DE LICENCES DELIVREES (MILLIERS) — NUMERO DE RECEPTORES EN FUNCIONAMIENTO Y/O DE PERMISOS EXISTENTES (EN MILES)				NUMBER OF RECEIVERS IN USE AND/OR LICENCES ISSUED PER 1 000 INHABITANTS — NOMBRE DE POSTES RECEPTEURS EN SERVICE ET/OU DE LICENCES DELIVRES POUR 1 000 HABITANTS — NUMERO DE RECEPTORES EN FUNCIONAMIENTO Y/O DE PERMISOS EXISTENTES POR 1 000 HABITANTES			
		1965 (2)	1970 (3)	1976 (4)	1977 (5)	1965 (6)	1970 (7)	1976 (8)	1977 (9)
AMERICA, SOUTH									
ARGENTINA	R	6 600	9 000	...	10 000	298	379	...	384
BOLIVIA	R	...	402	430	440	...	82	74	74
BRAZIL	R	...	11 800	...	...	...	128	...	...
CHILE	R	...	1 400	1 800	2 000	...	149	172	188
COLOMBIA	R	...	2 217	2 850	2 930	...	108	117	117
ECUADOR	R	540	1 700	...	...	105	279	...	...
FALKLAND ISLANDS (MALVINAS)	R	1.0	1.1	...	...	500	550	...	...
FRENCH GUIANA	R	2.5	2.7	...	...	71	53	...	...
GUYANA	R	80	80	275	300	121	113	348	370
PARAGUAY	R	...	169	180	187	...	71	66	67
PERU	R	...	1 819	2 068	2 200	...	134	129	134
SURINAME	R	...	92	112	182	...	249	257	406
URUGUAY	R	900	1 000	1 600	1 625	331	347	565	571
VENEZUELA	R	...	...	5 034	5 273	...	...	407	414
ASIA									
AFGHANISTAN	R	...	...	...	823	...	...	...	40
BAHRAIN	R	...	56	...	100	...	260	...	375
BANGLADESH	R	...	...	...	500	...	...	...	6
BHUTAN	L	2	...	10	...	2	...	8	...
BRUNEI	R	10	15	26	30	99	115	147	157
BURMA	R	335	400	665	693	14	15	21	22
CYPRUS	R	130	167	200	212	219	264	313	331
	L	...	...	96	106	...	...	151	165
DEMOCRATIC KAMPUCHEA	R	97	103	...	...	16	15	...	...

	(1)	(2)	(3)	(4)	(5)	(6)	(7)	(8)	(9)
EAST TIMOR	L	1	3	...	...	3	4	...	...
HONG KONG	R	529	694	2 508	2 510	147	175	572	556
INDIA	L	5 401	11 747	17 839	20 503	11	22	29	33
INDONESIA	R	...	2 550	5 100	5 250	...	21	37	37
IRAN	R	...	1 800	2 100	2 125	...	63	62	62
IRAQ	R	...	...	...	2 000	...	...	...	168
ISRAEL	R	...	477	655	750	207	164	189	208
JAPAN	R	20 425	...	61 320	64 979	...	...	544	571
JORDAN ‡	R	...	370	531	532	...	161	191	184
KOREA, REPUBLIC OF	R	1 961	4 012	14 460	14 574	69	124	403	400
KUWAIT	R	...	105	502	550	...	140	487	487
LAO PEOPLE'S DEMOCRATIC REPUBLIC	R	...	50	200	200	...	17	59	58
LEBANON	R	...	600	1 600	...	...	243	540	...
MACAU	R	5	9	...	70	19	36	...	251
MALAYSIA	R	421	...	1 450	1 500	45	...	118	119
	L	...	...	368	354	...	...	30	28
MALDIVES	R	...	1.3	2.8	2.9	...	12	23	20
MONGOLIA	R	...	...	115	125	...	...	77	82
NEPAL	R	...	55	150	200	...	5	12	15
PAKISTAN	R	972	...	4 500	5 000	19	...	62	66
	L	...	...	1 400	1 470	...	...	19	20
PHILIPPINES	R	...	1 500	1 875	1 936	...	41	43	43
QATAR	R	...	25	...	...	...	316	...	...
SAUDI ARABIA	R	...	85	260	275	...	11	28	29
SINGAPORE	L	...	274	369	387	...	132	162	168
SRI LANKA	R	438	500	800	1 000	39	40	58	72
	L	...	...	548	550	...	...	40	39
SYRIAN ARAB REPUBLIC	R	...	1 367	...	...	...	218	...	...
THAILAND	R	...	2 775	...	5 700	...	77	...	129
TURKEY	L	2 443	3 096	4 228	4 261	78	89	105	101
UNITED ARAB EMIRATES	R	...	...	55	...	...	...	240	...
YEMEN	R	...	...	90	100	...	...	13	14

COUNTRY / PAYS / PAIS	DEFINITION OF DATA — CODE — TIPO DE DATOS	NUMBER OF RECEIVERS IN USE AND/OR LICENCES ISSUED (THOUSANDS)				NUMBER OF RECEIVERS IN USE AND/OR LICENCES ISSUED PER 1 000 INHABITANTS			
(1)	(1)	1965 (2)	1970 (3)	1976 (4)	1977 (5)	1965 (6)	1970 (7)	1976 (8)	1977 (9)
YEMEN, DEMOCRATIC	R	...	...	100	102	...	...	57	57
EUROPE									
ALBANIA	R	130	161	180	200	70	75	71	76
ANDORRA	R	4.6	...	7	7	418	...	228	279
AUSTRIA	L	...	2 012	2 054	2 068	...	271	273	275
BELGIUM	L	3 026	3 383	4 044	4 077	320	350	412	415
BULGARIA ‡	L	2 055	2 291	1 353	1 299	251	270	154	148
CZECHOSLOVAKIA ‡	L	3 727	3 858	3 928	3 721	263	269	263	248
DENMARK	R	1 587	1 597	3 975	4 200	334	324	784	825
	L			1 829	1 868			360	367
FAEROE ISLANDS	L	12	15	...	...	311	395	...	...
FINLAND	L	1 541	1 789	2 200	1 886	338	388	465	398
FRANCE	L	15 336	16 160	17 441	...	315	318	330	...
GERMAN DEMOCRATIC REPUBLIC	R				15 000				895
	L	5 743	5 985	6 205	6 261	337	351	370	373
GERMANY, FEDERAL REPUBLIC OF	L	...	19 622	21 850	22 198	...	323	355	362
GIBRALTAR	R	...	...	30	30	...	...	1000	1000
	L	...	10	...	...	...	381	...	...
GREECE	R	893	990	2 750	2 750	104	113	300	296
HUNGARY	L	2 484	2 530	2 559	2 577	245	245	242	242
ICELAND	L	...	60	...	65	...	300	...	293
IRELAND	R	610	...	949	...	212	...	300	...
ITALY	L	10 724	11 702	13 024	13 316	206	218	232	236
LIECHTENSTEIN	L	4	...	8	...	221	...	364	...
LUXEMBOURG	R	121	157	180	180	364	463	503	506

(1)		(2)	(3)	(4)	(5)	(6)	(7)	(8)	(9)
MALTA	R	...	...	...	85	...	...	...	256
	L	...	...	63	...	...	...	192	...
MONACO	R	6	7	8	8	274	275	300	320
NETHERLANDS	R	3 093	3 716	3 997	8 500	252	285	290	614
	L	1 089	1 191	1 302	4 105				296
NORWAY	L				1 318	293	307	323	326
POLAND	L	5 646	5 658	8 228	8 348	179	174	239	241
PORTUGAL	R	1 173	1 368	1 600	...	128	158	164	...
	L			-	-			-	-
ROMANIA	L	2 790	3 075	3 104	3 090	147	152	145	143
SAN MARINO	L	3.0	3.7	6	...	176	195	300	...
SPAIN	R	4 550	7 700	9 300	...	142	228	259	...
SWEDEN	R				8 300				1005
	L	2 954	2 847	3 204	3 265	382	354	390	395
SWITZERLAND	R			5 000	5 000			788	790
	L	1 654	1 864	2 108	2 134	282	301	332	337
UNITED KINGDOM	R	13 516	34 706	39 500	40 000		626	706	716
	L		16 309	18 271	18 409	249	294	327	330
YUGOSLAVIA	L	2 783	3 380	4 526	4 548	143	166	210	209
OCEANIA									
AMERICAN SAMOA	R	.8	4.0	...	28	32	138	...	824
AUSTRALIA	R	...	7 250	14 300	14 600	...	580	1027	1037
COOK ISLANDS	R	2	2	7	7	105	92	389	394
FIJI	R	...	...	300	308	...	...	517	517
FRENCH POLYNESIA	R	30	...	...	...	326	...	...	...
KIRIBATI	R	2	...	8	8	29	...	121	121
GUAM	R	...	90	87	89	...	1000	853	853
NAURU	R	...	...	3.6	3.6	...	...	450	450
NEW CALEDONIA	R	14	25	60	64	154	227	444	471
NEW HEBRIDES	R	...	10	15	16	...	119	155	162
NEW ZEALAND	R	...	...	2 715	2 725	60	...	879	878
NIUE	R	.3	.5	.8	.8	60	...	200	117
NORFOLK ISLAND	R	.4	.5	1.2	1.3	400	500	600	640
PACIFIC ISLANDS	R	6	60	...	...	67	588	...	...

COUNTRY / PAYS / PAIS	DEFINITION OF DATA / CODE / TIPO DE DATOS	NUMBER OF RECEIVERS IN USE AND/OR LICENCES ISSUED (THOUSANDS) NOMBRE DE POSTES RECEPTEURS EN SERVICE ET/OU DE LICENCES DELIVREES (MILLIERS) NUMERO DE RECEPTORES EN FUNCIONAMIENTO Y/O DE PERMISOS EXISTENTES (EN MILES)				NUMBER OF RECEIVERS IN USE AND/OR LICENCES ISSUED PER 1 000 INHABITANTS NOMBRE DE POSTES RECEPTEURS EN SERVICE ET/OU DE LICENCES DELIVREES POUR 1 000 HABITANTS NUMERO DE RECEPTORES EN FUNCIONAMIENTO Y/O DE PERMISOS EXISTENTES POR 1 000 HABITANTES			
		1965	1970	1976	1977	1965	1970	1976	1977
	(1)	(2)	(3)	(4)	(5)	(6)	(7)	(8)	(9)
PAPUA NEW GUINEA	R	...	...	...	125	...	...	...	43
SAMOA	R	14	32	...	...	110	224	...	...
SOLOMON ISLANDS	R	...	8	10	10	...	52	50	48
U.S.S.R.	R	73 800	94 600	...	...	320	390	...	...
BYELORUSSIAN S.S.R.	R	...	1 390	...	...	...	154	...	...
UKRAINIAN S.S.R.	R	14 927	18 424	24 661	25 780	329	389	502	522

GENERAL NOTE/NOTE GENERALE/NOTA GENERAL:
E—> FOR THE COUNTRIES LISTED BELOW, ONLY THE
ESTIMATED NUMBER OF RECEIVERS IN USE, BUT NOT THE
NUMBER OF LICENCES HAS BEEN COMMUNICATED, ALTHOUGH
IT IS KNOWN OR BELIEVED THAT A LICENCE SYSTEM IS
IN FORCE:
FR—> POUR LES PAYS CI-DESSOUS, SEULE UNE ESTI-
MATION DU NOMBRE DE RECEPTEURS EN SERVICE A ETE
COMMUNIQUEE, BIEN QUE CERTAINS RENSEIGNEMENTS
INDIQUENT OU PERMETTENT DE PENSER QU'UN SYSTEME
DE REDEVANCES EST EN VIGUEUR, LE NOMBRE DE
LICENCES DELIVREES N'A PAS ETE FOURNI:
ESP> PARA LOS PAISES QUE FIGURAN A CONTINUA-
CION, SOLO SE HA COMUNICADO UNA ESTIMACION DE LOS
RECEPTORES EN SERVICIO, AUNQUE CIERTAS INFOR-
MACIONES INDIQUEN O PERMITAN PENSAR QUE ESTA EN
VIGOR UN SISTEMA DE PERMISOS, EL NUMERO DE
PERMISOS CONCEDIDOS NO NOS HA SIDO FACILITADO:

AFRICA/AFRIQUE/AFRICA:
ANGOLA
BENIN
BURUNDI
CAPE VERDE/CAP-VERT/CABO VERDE
CENTRAL AFRICAN REPUBLIC/REPUBLIQUE CENTRAFRICAINE
REPUBLICA CENTROAFRICANA
COMORO/COMORES
CONGO
DJIBOUTI/YIBUTI
GHANA

AFRICA (CONT):
GUINEA-BISSAU
MAURITANIA/MAURITANIE
MOROCCO/MAROC/MARRUECOS
NIGERIA
REUNION
ST. HELENA/SAINTE-HELENE/SANTA ELENA
SAO TOME AND PRINCIPE/SAINT-THOMAS ET ILE DU
PRINCE/SANTO TOME Y PRINCIPE
SIERRA LEONE
SOUTH AFRICA/AFRIQUE DU SUD/SUDAFRICA
SWAZILAND/SWAZILANDIA
TUNISIA/TUNISIE/TUNEZ
UPPER VOLTA/HAUTE-VOLTA/ALTO VOLTA
WESTERN SAHARA/SAHARA OCCIDENTAL
ZIMBABWE

AMERICA, NORTH/AMERIQUE DU NORD/AMERICA
DEL NORTE
ANTIGUA
BAHAMAS
BERMUDA/BERMUDES/BERMUDAS
BRITISH VIRGIN ISLANDS/ILES VIERGES BRITANNIQUES/
ISLAS VIRGENES BRITANICAS
CANADA
DOMINICA/DOMINIQUE
GREENLAND/GROENLAND/GROENLANDIA
GRENADA/GRENADE/GRANADA
GUADELOUPE/GUADALUPE
MARTINIQUE/MARTINICA

MONTSERRAT
ST.KITTS-NEVIS AND ANGUILLA/SAINT CHRISTOPHE-
NIEVES ET ANGUILLA/SAN CRISTOBAL-NIEVES-
ANGUILA
ST. LUCIA/SAINTE LUCIE/SANTA LUCIA
ST. PIERRE AND MIQUELON/SAINT PIERRE ET MIQUELON/
SAN PEDRO Y MIQUELON
TURKS AND CAICOS ISLANDS/ILES TURQUES ET CAIQUES/
ISLAS TURCAS Y CAICOS
AMERICA, SOUTH/AMERIQUE DU SUD/AMERICA DEL SUR
FALKLAND ISLANDS/ILES FALKLAND/ISLAS FALKLAND
FRENCH GUIANA/GUYANE FRANCAISE/GUYANA FRANCESA
GUYANA/GUYANE
ASIA/ASIE
BAHRAIN/BAHREIN
BANGLADESH
BURMA/BIRMANIE/BIRMANIA
HONG KONG
INDONESIA/INDONESIE
ISRAEL
LAO PEOPLE'S DEMOCRATIC REPUBLIC/REPUBLIQUE POPU-
LAIRE DEMOCRATIQUE LAO/REPUBLICA POPULAR DEMO-
CRATICA LAO
MACAU/MACAO
MALDIVES/MALDIVAS
MONGOLIA/MONGOLIE
NEPAL
SYRIAN ARAB REPUBLIC/REPUBLIQUE ARABE SYRIENNE/
REPUBLICA ARABE SIRIA
UNITED ARAB EMIRATES/EMIRATS ARABES UNIS/EMIRATOS
ARABES UNIDOS

EUROPE/EUROPA
ALBANIA/ALBANIE
ANDORRA/ANDORRE
MONACO

OCEANIA/OCEANIE
COOK ISLANDS/ILES COOK/ISLAS COOK
FRENCH POLYNESIA/POLYNESIE FRANCAISE/POLINESIA
FRANCESA
KIRIBATI

OCEANIA (CONT):
NAURU
NEW CALEDONIA/NOUVELLE CALEDONIE/NUEVA CALEDONIA
NEW HEBRIDES/NOUVELLES HEBRIDES/NUEVAS HEBRIDAS
NEW ZEALAND/NOUVELLE ZELANDE/NUEVA ZELANDIA
PACIFIC ISLANDS/ILES DU PACIFIQUE/ISLAS DEL
PACIFICO

U.S.S.R./U.R.S.S.
BYELORUSSIAN S.S.R./RSS DE BIELORUSSIE/RSS DE
BIELORRUSIA
UKRAINIAN S.S.R./RSS D'UKRAINE/RSS DE UCRANIA

JORDAN:
E.—> DATA REFER TO THE EAST BANK ONLY.
FR-> LES DONNEES SE REFERENT A LA RIVE ORIENTALE
SEULEMENT.
ESP> LOS DATOS SE REFIEREN A LA ORILLA ORIENTAL
SOLAMENTE.

BULGARIA:
E.—> DATA FOR 1976 AND 1977 DO NOT INCLUDE
LICENCES FOR RECEIVERS CONNECTED BY WIRE TO A
REDISTRIBUTION SYSTEM.
FR-> LES DONNEES RELATIVES A 1976 ET 1977
N'INCLUENT PAS LES LICENCES DELIVREES POUR LES
RECEPTEURS RELIES PAR FIL A UN RESEAU DE
"REDISTRIBUTION".
ESP> LOS DATOS PARA 1976 Y 1977 NO INCLUYEN
LOS PERMISOS CONCEDIDOS A LOS RECEPTORES
CONECTADOS POR CABLE A UNA RED DE DISTRIBUCION.

CZECHOSLOVAKIA:
E.—> DATA FOR 1977 DO NOT INCLUDE LICENSES FOR
RECEIVERS CONNECTED BY WIRE TO A REDISTRIBUTION
SYSTEM.
FR-> LES DONNEES RELATIVES A 1977 N'INCLUENT
PAS LES LICENCES DELIVREES POUR LES RECEPTEURS
RELIES PAR FIL A UN RESEAU DE "REDISTRIBUTION".
ESP> LOS DATOS PARA 1977 NO INCLUYEN LOS
PERMISOS CONCEDIDOS A LOS RECEPTORES CONECTADOS
POR CABLE A UNA RED DE DISTRIBUCION.

10.3 Television broadcasting: number of transmitters
Télévision: nombre d'émetteurs
Televisión: número de transmisores

T = TOTAL	T = TOTAL
G = GOVERNMENTAL	G = GOUVERNEMENTAL
P = PUBLIC	P = PUBLIC
C = COMMERCIAL	C = COMMERCIAL

| T = TOTAL |
| G = GUBERNAMENTAL |
| P = PUBLICA |
| C = COMERCIAL |

FIGURES RELATE TO TRANSMITTERS
OPERATING ON A REGULAR BASIS
AND USED FOR BROADCASTING TO THE
GENERAL PUBLIC

LES DONNEES SE RAPPORTENT AUX
EMETTEURS QUI FONCTIONNENT DE
FACON REGULIERE ET QUI DIFFUSENT
DES EMISSIONS DESTINEES AU
GRAND PUBLIC

LOS DATOS SE REFIEREN A LOS
TRANSMISORES QUE FUNCIONAN CON
CARACTER REGULAR Y QUE EMITEN
PROGRAMAS DESTINADOS AL PUBLICO
EN GENERAL

NUMBER OF COUNTRIES AND TERRITORIES
PRESENTED IN THIS TABLE: 128

NOMBRE DE PAYS ET DE TERRITOIRES
PRESENTES DANS CE TABLEAU: 128

NUMERO DE PAISES Y DE TERRITORIOS
PRESENTADOS EN ESTE CUADRO: 128

COUNTRY / PAYS / PAIS	YEAR / ANNEE / AÑO	OWNERSHIP / PROPRIETE / PROPIEDAD	TOTAL		VERY HIGH FREQUENCY ONDES METRIQUES MUY ALTA FRECUENCIA		ULTRA HIGH FREQUENCY ONDES DECIMETRIQUES ULTRA ALTA FRECUENCIA	
			NUMBER OF TRANS-MITTERS / NOMBRE D'-EMETTEURS / NUMERO DE TRANS-MISORES	TRANS-MITTING POWER / PUISSANCE D'EMISSION / POTENCIA DE EMISION	NUMBER OF TRANS-MITTERS / NOMBRE D'-EMETTEURS / NUMERO DE TRANS-MISORES	TRANS-MITTING POWER / PUISSANCE D'EMISSION / POTENCIA DE EMISION	NUMBER OF TRANS-MITTERS / NOMBRE D'-EMETTEURS / NUMERO DE TRANS-MISORES	TRANS-MITTING POWER / PUISSANCE D'EMISSION / POTENCIA DE EMISION	NUMBER OF COLOR TRANSMITTERS / NOMBRE D'-EMETTEURS COULEUR / NUMERO DE TRANSMISORES EN COLOR
			(1)	(2)	(3)	(4)	(5)	(6)	(7)
AFRICA									
ALGERIA	1977	G	40	740	40	740	—	—	...
CONGO	1976	G	1	2	1	2	—	—	...
DJIBOUTI	1976	G	1	0	1	0	—	—	...
EGYPT	1977	G	27	2 848	27	2 848	—	—	...
ETHIOPIA	1976	G	8	3	...	...	—	—	...
GABON	1976	G	8	4	8	4	—	—	...

			(1)	(2)	(3)	(4)	(5)	(6)	(7)
GHANA	1977	G	6	126	6	126	–	–	–
IVORY COAST	1977	G	12	120	12	120	–	–	12
KENYA	1976	G	4	45	4	45	–	–	...
LIBERIA	1976	G	3	23	3	23	–	–	...
LIBYAN ARAB JAMAHIRIYA	1977	G	13	97	13	97	–	–	...
MADAGASCAR	1977	G	8	12	8	12	–	–	8
MAURITIUS	1976	P	4	16	4	16	–	–	...
MOROCCO	1977	G	24	954	24	954	–	–	...
NIGERIA	1978	G	28	...	28	...	–	–	12
REUNION ‡	1976	P	1	0	1	0	–	–	...
SENEGAL	1976	G	1	0	1	0	–	–	...
SIERRA LEONE	1977	G	2	11	2	11	–	–	2
SOUTH AFRICA ‡	1976	P	34	...	...	...	...	...	...
SUDAN	1977	G	4	22	4	22	–	–	4
TOGO	1977	G	3	900	3	900	–	–	3
TUNISIA	1977	G	10	1 821	10	1 821	–	–	...
UGANDA	1976	G	6	330	6	330	–	–	...
UPPER VOLTA	1977	G	1	0	1	0	–	–	...
ZAIRE	1976	G	3	14	3	42	–	–	...
ZAMBIA	1976	G	3	42	3	42	–	–	...
ZIMBABWE	1976	C	5	69	5	69	–	–	...
AMERICA, NORTH									
ANTIGUA	1976	G	2	6	2	6	–	–	...
BARBADOS	1977	P	2	5	2	5	–	–	2
BERMUDA	1976	C	2	50	2	50	–	–	...
CANADA	1976	T	626	...	...	...	...	...	...
		P	423	...	...	...	...	...	...
		C	203	...	...	...	...	...	...
COSTA RICA	1976	C	11	620	11	620	–	–	...
DOMINICAN REPUBLIC	1976	C	13	75	13	75	–	–	...
EL SALVADOR	1976	T	4	...	4	...	–	–	...
		G	1	...	1	...	–	–	...
		C	3	...	3	...	–	–	...

COUNTRY / PAYS / PAIS	YEAR ANNEE AÑO	OWNERSHIP PROPRIETE PROPIEDAD	TOTAL		VERY HIGH FREQUENCY ONDES METRIQUES MUY ALTA FRECUENCIA		ULTRA HIGH FREQUENCY ONDES DECIMETRIQUES ULTRA ALTA FRECUENCIA		NUMBER OF COLOR TRANSMITTERS NOMBRE D'EMETTEURS COULEUR NUMERO DE TRANSMISORES EN COLOR
			NUMBER OF TRANSMITTERS NOMBRE D'EMETTEURS NUMERO DE TRANSMISORES	TRANSMITTING POWER PUISSANCE D'EMISSION POTENCIA DE EMISION	NUMBER OF TRANSMITTERS NOMBRE D'EMETTEURS NUMERO DE TRANSMISORES	TRANSMITTING POWER PUISSANCE D'EMISSION POTENCIA DE EMISION	NUMBER OF TRANSMITTERS NOMBRE D'EMETTEURS NUMERO DE TRANSMISORES	TRANSMITTING POWER PUISSANCE D'EMISSION POTENCIA DE EMISION	
			(1)	(2)	(3)	(4)	(5)	(6)	(7)
GUADELOUPE	1976	P	3	1	3	1	–	–	..
GUATEMALA	1975	C	12	39	..	..	..	..	..
HAITI	1976	C	1	..	1	..	–	–	..
HONDURAS ‡	1976	C	3	31	3	31	–	–	..
JAMAICA	1976	C	9	87	9	87	–	–	..
MARTINIQUE	1976	P	5	1	5	1	–	–	..
MEXICO	1977	T	83	..	81	..	2	..	..
		G	1	..	1	..	–	..	..
		P	2	..	2	..	–	..	..
		C	80	..	78	..	2	..	..
NETHERLANDS ANTILLES	1976	T	2	5	2	5	–	–	..
		P	1	2	1	2	–	–	..
		C	1	3	1	3	–	–	..
NICARAGUA	1976	C	5	108	5	108	–	–	..
PANAMA	1977	C	10	1 679	10	1 679	–	–	..
FORMER CANAL ZONE	1977	G	2	10	2	10	–	–	..
PUERTO RICO	1977	T	10	1 728	9	733	1	995	2
		G	2	89	2	89	–	–	..
		C	8	1 639	7	644	1	995	..
ST. KITTS – NEVIS ANGUILLA	1976	G	5	220	5	220	–	–	..
ST. PIERRE AND MIQUELON	1976	P	1	0	1	0	–	–	..
ST. VINCENT AND THE GRENADINES	1974	G	2	0	..	..	..	..	..
TRINIDAD AND TOBAGO	1976	C	3	33	3	33	–	–	..

Country	Year		(1)	(2)	(3)	(4)	(5)	(6)	(7)
UNITED STATES OF AMERICA ‡	1974	T	972	...	607	...	365	...	972
		G	184	...	72	...	112	...	184
		P	71	...	28	...	43	...	71
		C	717	...	507	...	210	...	717
U.S. VIRGIN ISLANDS	1977	T	3	85	3	85	—	—	—
		P	2	17	1	17	—	—	—
		C	1	68	2	68	—	—	—
AMERICA, SOUTH									
ARGENTINA	1977	T	75	2 358	75	2 358	—	—	...
		G	8	483	8	483	—	—	...
		P	2	285	2	285	—	—	...
		C	65	1 590	65	1 590	—	—	—
BOLIVIA	1976	G	2	6	2	6	—	—	—
BRAZIL	1976	C	68	...	67	1 267	1	—	—
CHILE ‡	1976	T	31	329	31	329	—	—	—
		G	23	236	23	236	—	—	—
		P	8	93	8	93	—	—	—
COLOMBIA	1977	P	71	92	71	92	—	—	—
ECUADOR ‡	1976	C	16	...	16	...	—	—	—
FRENCH GUIANA	1976	P	2	0	2	0	—	—	—
PARAGUAY	1976	C	1	60	1	60	—	—	—
PERU ‡	1976	T	13	297	13	297	—	—	...
		G	1	150	1	150	—	—	...
		C	12	147	12	147	—	—	...
SURINAME	1976	G	4	8	4	8	—	—	—
URUGUAY	1976	G	19	...	19	...	—	—	—
VENEZUELA	1977	T	42	2 772	39	2 691	3	81	...
		G	19	1 380	16	1 299	3	81	...
		C	23	1 392	23	1 392	—	—	...
ASIA									
BAHRAIN	1977	G	1	75	1	75	—	—	1
BANGLADESH	1978	G	6	70	6	70	—	—	...
BRUNEI	1978	G	2	30	2	30	—	—	2
CYPRUS	1977	P	5	111	2	40	3	71	...
DEMOCRATIC KAMPUCHEA	1976	G	2	41	2	41	—	—	—
HONG KONG ‡	1977	C	5	50	—	—	5	50	5
INDIA	1977	G	14	671	14	671	—	—	...
INDONESIA	1978	G	97	...	97	671	—	—	...

COUNTRY / PAYS / PAIS	YEAR / ANNEE / AÑO	OWNERSHIP / PROPRIETE / PROPIEDAD	TOTAL		VERY HIGH FREQUENCY ONDES METRIQUES MUY ALTA FRECUENCIA		ULTRA HIGH FREQUENCY ONDES DECIMETRIQUES ULTRA ALTA FRECUENCIA		NUMBER OF COLOR TRANSMITTERS / NOMBRE D'EMETTEURS COULEUR / NUMERO DE TRANSMISORES EN COLOR
			NUMBER OF TRANSMITTERS / NOMBRE D'EMETTEURS / NUMERO DE TRANSMISORES	TRANSMITTING POWER / PUISSANCE D'EMISSION / POTENCIA DE EMISION	NUMBER OF TRANSMITTERS / NOMBRE D'EMETTEURS / NUMERO DE TRANSMISORES	TRANSMITTING POWER / PUISSANCE D'EMISSION / POTENCIA DE EMISION	NUMBER OF TRANSMITTERS / NOMBRE D'EMETTEURS / NUMERO DE TRANSMISORES	TRANSMITTING POWER / PUISSANCE D'EMISSION / POTENCIA DE EMISION	
			(1)	(2)	(3)	(4)	(5)	(6)	(7)
IRAN ‡	1976	P	17	210	17	210	–	–	...
IRAQ	1977	G	13	2 592	13	2 592	–	–	13
ISRAEL	1977	P	40	613	31	412	9	201	...
JAPAN	1977	T	8 205	1 904	1 502	955	6 703	949	8 205
		P	5 344	545	1 027	421	4 317	124	5 344
		C	2 861	1 359	475	534	2 386	825	2 861
JORDAN ‡	1977	G	5	200	5	200	...	...	...
KOREA, REPUBLIC OF	1977	T	126	195	125	194	1	1	–
		P	105	150	104	149	1	1	–
		C	21	45	21	45	–	–	–
KUWAIT	1976	G	4	52	...	...	...	...	...
LEBANON	1977	G	5	72	5	72	–	–	...
MALAYSIA	1977	G	51	2 806	51	2 806	–	–	51
MALDIVES	1977	G	2	1	2	1	–	–	...
OMAN ‡	1976	G	2	420	2	420	–	–	...
PAKISTAN	1977	P	13	1 452	13	1 452	–	–	13
PHILIPPINES	1977	T	24	209	24	209	–	–	..
		G	2	25	2	25	–	–	2
		P	1	5	1	5	–	–	..
		C	21	179	21	179	–	–	..
QATAR	1977	G	2	200	2	200	–	–	2
SAUDI ARABIA	1977	G	6	9	5	8	1	1	6
SINGAPORE	1977	G	2	240	2	240	–	–	2
SYRIAN ARAB REPUBLIC	1976	G	7	840	7	840	–	–	...
THAILAND	1976	G	8	139	8	139	–	–	...
TURKEY	1977	G	61	1 435	61	1 435	–	–	...

			(1)	(2)	(3)	(4)	(5)	(6)	(7)
UNITED ARAB EMIRATES	1977	T	10	5 134	8	3 134	2	2 000	10
		G	6	2 229	6	2 229	—	2 000	6
		P	3	2 900	1	900	2	—	3
		C	1	5	1	5	—	—	1
YEMEN, DEMOCRATIC ‡	1976	G	3	1	3	1	—	—	...
EUROPE									
ALBANIA	1977	G	1	0	1	0	—	—	...
AUSTRIA	1977	P	644	8 394	247	850	397	7 544	644
BELGIUM	1977	P	31	6 671	15	410	16	6 261	30
BULGARIA ‡	1977	G	16	245	...	...	—	—	...
CZECHOSLOVAKIA ‡	1977	G	59	11 014	31	1 423	28	9 591	53
DENMARK	1977	G	30	1 515	30	1 515	—	—	30
FINLAND	1977	G	105	9 464	85	1 243	20	8 221	...
FRANCE	1977	P	2 821	71 690	1 168	...	1 653	...	2 821
GERMAN DEMOCRATIC REPUBLIC	1977	G	505	9 340	381	920	124	8 420	505
GERMANY, FEDERAL REPUBLIC OF	1977	P	4 789	...	1 024	...	3 765	...	4 789
GIBRALTAR	1977	P	3	0	2	0	1	0	...
GREECE ‡	1977	P	84	356	84	356	—	—	...
HUNGARY	1977	G	42	1 575	35	620	7	955	...
ICELAND	1977	G	83	1 324	83	1 324	—	—	...
IRELAND	1977	P	21	710	21	710	—	—	16
ITALY	1977	G	1 379	12 000	855	2 000	524	10 000	1 379
LUXEMBOURG	1977	C	3	2 100	1	100	2	2 000	3
MALTA	1977	C	6	11	1	8	5	3	...
MONACO	1977	C	3	650	1	50	2	600	3
NETHERLANDS	1977	P	26	4 592	4	220	22	4 372	26
NORWAY	1977	P	917	1 772	915	1 770	2	2	917
POLAND	1977	G	163	7 872	145	2 764	18	5 108	163
PORTUGAL	1977	C	52	2 914	46	394	6	2 520	...
ROMANIA	1977	G	195	1 125	195	1 125	—	—	...
SPAIN ‡	1978	G	60	8 559	32	2 097	28	6 462	60
SWEDEN	1977	P	438	50 020	217	3 270	221	46 750	438

COUNTRY / PAYS / PAIS	YEAR / ANNEE / AÑO	OWNERSHIP / PROPRIETE / PROPIEDAD	TOTAL		VERY HIGH FREQUENCY ONDES METRIQUES MUY ALTA FRECUENCIA		ULTRA HIGH FREQUENCY ONDES DECIMETRIQUES ULTRA ALTA FRECUENCIA		NUMBER OF COLOR TRANSMITTERS NOMBRE D'EMETTEURS COULEUR NUMERO DE TRANSMISORES EN COLOR
			NUMBER OF TRANSMITTERS / NOMBRE D'EMETTEURS / NUMERO DE TRANSMISORES	TRANSMITTING POWER / PUISSANCE D'EMISSION / POTENCIA DE EMISION	NUMBER OF TRANSMITTERS / NOMBRE D'EMETTEURS / NUMERO DE TRANSMISORES	TRANSMITTING POWER / PUISSANCE D'EMISSION / POTENCIA DE EMISION	NUMBER OF TRANSMITTERS / NOMBRE D'EMETTEURS / NUMERO DE TRANSMISORES	TRANSMITTING POWER / PUISSANCE D'EMISSION / POTENCIA DE EMISION	
			(1)	(2)	(3)	(4)	(5)	(6)	(7)
SWITZERLAND	1977	P	825	4 792	290	583	535	4 209	825
UNITED KINGDOM	1977	P	1 098	35 024	157	4 962	941	30 062	...
YUGOSLAVIA	1977	P	643	17 010	...	...	...	...	...
OCEANIA									
AMERICAN SAMOA	1977	T G P	3 2 1	120 80 40	3 2 1	120 80 40	— — —	— — —	... ...
AUSTRALIA	1977	T G C	271 155 116	8 067 3 719 4 348	271 155 116	8 067 3 719 4 348	— — —	— — —	271 155 116
GUAM	1977	T P C	2 1 1	52 27 25	2 1 1	52 27 25	— — —	— — —	... ...
NEW CALEDONIA ‡	1976	P	2	1	...	...	...	...	...
NEW ZEALAND ‡	1975	T	144	761	...	...	...	...	...
PACIFIC ISLANDS	1977	C	5	5	5	5	—	—	—
U.S.S.R.	1974	G	1 749	...	...	...	.	.	...

REUNION:
  E—> NOT INCLUDING RELAY TRANSMITTERS.
  FR—> NON COMPRIS LES REEMETTEURS.
  ESP> EXCLUIDOS LOS RETRANSMISORES.
SOUTH AFRICA:
  E—> NOT INCLUDING RELAY TRANSMITTERS.
  FR—> NON COMPRIS LES REEMETTEURS.
  ESP> EXCLUIDOS LOS RETRANSMISORES.
HONDURAS:
  E—> NOT INCLUDING RELAY TRANSMITTERS.
  FR—> NON COMPRIS LES REEMETTEURS.
  ESP> EXCLUIDOS LOS RETRANSMISORES.
UNITED STATES OF AMERICA:
  E—> NOT INCLUDING RELAY TRANSMITTERS.
  FR—> NON COMPRIS LES REEMETTEURS.
  ESP> EXCLUIDOS LOS RETRANSMISORES.
CHILE:
  E—> NOT INCLUDING RELAY TRANSMITTERS.
  FR—> NON COMPRIS LES REEMETTEURS.
  ESP> EXCLUIDOS LOS RETRANSMISORES.
ECUADOR:
  E—> NOT INCLUDING RELAY TRANSMITTERS.
  FR—> NON COMPRIS LES REEMETTEURS.
  ESP> EXCLUIDOS LOS RETRANSMISORES.
PERU:
  E—> NOT INCLUDING RELAY TRANSMITTERS.
  FR—> NON COMPRIS LES REEMETTEURS.
  ESP> EXCLUIDOS LOS RETRANSMISORES.
HONG KONG:
  E—> NOT INCLUDING RELAY TRANSMITTERS.
  FR—> NON COMPRIS LES REEMETTEURS.
  ESP> EXCLUIDOS LOS RETRANSMISORES.
IRAN:
  E—> NOT INCLUDING RELAY TRANSMITTERS.
  FR—> NON COMPRIS LES REEMETTEURS.
  ESP> EXCLUIDOS LOS RETRANSMISORES.
JORDAN:
  E—> DATA REFER TO THE EAST BANK ONLY.
  FR—> LES DONNEES SE REFERENT A LA RIVE ORIENTALE SEULEMENT.
  ESP> LOS DATOS SE REFIEREN A LA ORILLA ORIENTAL SOLAMENTE.

OMAN:
  E—> NOT INCLUDING RELAY TRANSMITTERS.
  FR—> NON COMPRIS LES REEMETTEURS.
  ESP> EXCLUIDOS LOS RETRANSMISORES.
YEMEN, DEMOCRATIC:
  E—> NOT INCLUDING RELAY TRANSMITTERS.
  FR—> NON COMPRIS LES REEMETTEURS.
  ESP> EXCLUIDOS LOS RETRANSMISORES.
BULGARIA:
  E—> NOT INCLUDING RELAY TRANSMITTERS.
  FR—> NON COMPRIS LES REEMETTEURS.
  ESP> EXCLUIDOS LOS RETRANSMISORES.
CZECHOSLOVAKIA:
  E—> NOT INCLUDING RELAY TRANSMITTERS.
  FR—> NON COMPRIS LES REEMETTEURS.
  ESP> EXCLUIDOS LOS RETRANSMISORES.
GREECE:
  E—> NOT INCLUDING TRANSMITTERS OF THE GREEK ARMED FORCES.
  FR—> NON COMPRIS LES EMETTEURS DES FORCES ARMEES GRECQUES.
  ESP> EXCLUIDOS LOS TRANSMISORES DE LAS FUERZAS ARMADAS GRIEGAS.
SPAIN:
  E—> DATA ON TRANSMITTERS OPERATED BY COMMER-CIAL BROADCASTING ORGANIZATIONS HAVE NOT BEEN COMMUNICATED.
  FR—> LES DONNEES RELATIVES AUX EMETTEURS DEPEN-DANT D'ORGANISMES COMMERCIAUX N'ONT PAS ETE COMMUNIQUEES.
  ESP> LOS DATOS RELATIVOS A LOS TRANSMISORES QUE DEPENDEN DE ORGANISMOS COMERCIALES NO HAN SIDO COMUNICADOS.
NEW CALEDONIA:
  E—> NOT INCLUDING RELAY TRANSMITTERS.
  FR—> NON COMPRIS LES REEMETTEURS.
  ESP> EXCLUIDOS LOS RETRANSMISORES.
NEW ZEALAND:
  E—> TYPE OF ORGANIZATION OPERATING THE TRANS-MITTERS HAS NOT BEEN COMMUNICATED.
  FR—> LE TYPE D'ORGANISME DONT DEPENDENT LES EMETTEURS N'A PAS ETE COMMUNIQUE.
  ESP> EL TIPO DE ORGANISMO DE QUE DEPENDEN LOS TRANSMISORES NO HA SIDO COMUNICADO.

10.4 Television broadcasting: number of receivers and receivers per 1,000 inhabitants

Télévision: nombre total de récepteurs et de récepteurs pour 1 000 habitants

Televisión: número total de receptores y de receptores por 1 000 habitantes

L = NUMBER OF LICENCES ISSUED OR SETS DECLARED
R = ESTIMATED NUMBER OF RECEIVERS IN USE
NUMBER OF COUNTRIES AND TERRITORIES PRESENTED IN THIS TABLE: 138

L = NOMBRE DE LICENCES DELIVREES OU DE POSTES DECLARES
R = ESTIMATION DU NOMBRE DE RECEPTEURS EN SERVICE
NOMBRE DE PAYS ET DE TERRITOIRES PRESENTES DANS CE TABLEAU: 138

L = NUMERO DE PERMISOS CONCEDIDOS O DE RECEPTORES DECLARADOS
R = ESTIMACION DE RECEPTORES EN FUNCIONAMIENTO
NUMERO DE PAISES Y DE TERRITORIOS PRESENTADOS EN ESTE CUADRO: 138

COUNTRY / PAYS / PAIS	CODE / TIPO DE DATOS	NUMBER OF RECEIVERS IN USE AND/OR LICENCES ISSUED (THOUSANDS)				NUMBER OF RECEIVERS IN USE AND/OR LICENCES ISSUED PER 1 000 INHABITANTS			
		1965	1970	1976	1977	1965	1970	1976	1977
(1)		(2)	(3)	(4)	(5)	(6)	(7)	(8)	(9)
AFRICA									
ALGERIA	R	..	..	525	560	..	..	30	31
	L	72	110	—	—	6	8	—	—
BENIN	R	—	—	—	0.3	—	—	—	0.1
	L	—	—	—	—	—	—	—	—
CENTRAL AFRICAN REPUBLIC	R	—	—	0.1	0.1	—	—	...	...
CONGO	R	...	1.8	3.3	3.5	...	1.9	2.4	2.4
DJIBOUTI	R	...	1.0	3.5	3.5	...	11	32	32
EGYPT	R	323	529	...	1 000	11	16	...	26
EQUATORIAL GUINEA	R	—	—	—	1.0	—	—	—	3

	(1)	(2)	(3)	(4)	(5)	(6)	(7)	(8)	(9)
ETHIOPIA	R	2.5	8	21	25	0.1	0.3	1	1
GABON	R	...	1.2	9	9	...	2.4	16	17
GHANA	R	.9	16	35	40	0.1	1.8	3.4	3.8
IVORY COAST	R	6	...	250	300	1.6	...	50	58
KENYA	R	10	16	50	60	1.1	1.5	3.6	4.2
LIBERIA	R	2.7	7	9	10	2.0	4.3	5	6
LIBYAN ARAB JAMAHIRIYA	R	-	1.0	...	...	-	0.5	...	...
MADAGASCAR	R	-	3.5	10	12	-	0.5	1.0	1.4
MAURITIUS	L	3.6	19	41	...	5	23	46	...
MOROCCO	L	33	174	522	597	2.5	11	29	33
MOZAMBIQUE	R	-	-	1.2	1.2	-	-	0.1	0.1
NIGERIA	R	30	75	105	450	0.7	1.4	1.6	7
REUNION	R	2.7	21	37	39	7	47	73	80
SENEGAL	R	-	1.4	2.0	2.0	-	0.4	0.4	0.4
SIERRA LEONE	R	1.1	3.0	11	15	0.5	1.2	3.5	4.3
SUDAN	R	10	45	100	100	0.7	2.9	6	6
TOGO	R	-	-	1.5	7	-	-	0.7	3.0
TUNISIA	R	6	51	208	213	1.1	10	36	36
UGANDA	R	6	...	71	81	0.8	...	6	7
UNITED REPUBLIC OF TANZANIA	R	...	...	4.5	5.0	0.1	...	0.3	0.3
UPPER VOLTA	R	.3	6	...	...	...	1.0	...	...
WESTERN SAHARA	R	...	1.5	...	...	...	19	...	...
ZAIRE	R	...	7	7	8	...	0.3	0.3	0.3
ZAMBIA	L	9	17	-	-	2.3	4.1	-	-
ZIMBABWE	R	43	50	72	80	10	9	11	12
AMERICA, NORTH									
ANTIGUA	R	1.5	...	15	15	26	...	211	211
BARBADOS	R	6	16	48	50	25	67	194	197
BERMUDA	R	...	17	21	21	...	315	368	368
BRITISH VIRGIN ISLANDS	R	...	...	...	1.0	...	...	...	83

10.4 Television broadcasting: receivers
Télévision: récepteurs
Televisión: receptores

COUNTRY / PAYS / PAIS	DEFINITION OF DATA / CODE / TIPO DE DATOS	NUMBER OF RECEIVERS IN USE AND/OR LICENCES ISSUED (THOUSANDS) NOMBRE DE POSTES RECEPTEURS EN SERVICE ET/OU DE LICENCES DELIVREES (MILLIERS) NUMERO DE RECEPTORES EN FUNCIONAMIENTO Y/O DE PERMISOS EXISTENTES (EN MILES)				NUMBER OF RECEIVERS IN USE AND/OR LICENCES ISSUED PER 1 000 INHABITANTS NOMBRE DE POSTES RECEPTEURS EN SERVICE ET/OU DE LICENCES DELIVREES POUR 1 000 HABITANTS NUMERO DE RECEPTORES EN FUNCIONAMIENTO Y/O DE PERMISOS EXISTENTES POR 1 000 HABITANTES			
	(1)	1965 (2)	1970 (3)	1976 (4)	1977 (5)	1965 (6)	1970 (7)	1976 (8)	1977 (9)
CANADA	R	5 310	7 100	9 895	10 000	270	333	428	430
COSTA RICA	R	50	100	155	160	35	57	77	77
CUBA	R	...	...	635	800	...	...	67	83
DOMINICAN REPUBLIC	R	50	100	160	...	14	25	33	...
EL SALVADOR	R	35	92	136	148	12	26	33	35
GUADELOUPE	R	.7	...	...	20	2.3	...	...	5.5
GUATEMALA	R	55	72	120	150	12	14	19	23
HAITI	R	...	11	14	14	...	2.6	2.8	3.0
HONDURAS	R	2.2	22	48	48	1.0	8	15	14
JAMAICA	R	25	70	111	120	14	37	54	58
MARTINIQUE	R	1.5	10	20	20	5	28	54	54
MEXICO	R	1 218	2 993	...	5 480	30	59	...	84
NETHERLANDS ANTILLES	R	25	32	36	38	120	144	149	151
NICARAGUA	R	16	55	90	100	10	30	40	43
PANAMA	R	70	...	186	206	57	...	108	116
PUERTO RICO	R	...	410	...	535	...	151	...	162
ST. LUCIA	R	...	1.5	1.7	...	...	15	15	...
ST. PIERRE AND MIQUELON	R	...	1.3	1.7	2.0	...	260	340	340
TRINIDAD AND TOBAGO	R	20	60	110	125	21	58	100	112
UNITED STATES OF AMERICA	R	70 350	84 600	129 400	135 000	362	413	602	623
U.S. VIRGIN ISLANDS	R	...	9	30	32	...	159	313	...
AMERICA, SOUTH									
ARGENTINA	R	1 600	3 500	4 500	4 600	72	147	175	177
BOLIVIA	R	...	...	48	49	...	...	8	8

	(1)	(2)	(3)	(4)	(5)	(6)	(7)	(8)	(9)
BRAZIL	R	...	6 100	10 525	11 000	...	66	96	98
CHILE	R	...	500	710	...	...	53	68	...
COLOMBIA	R	350	810	1 700	1 850	19	39	70	74
ECUADOR	R	42	150	300	340	8	25	41	45
FRENCH GUIANA	R	...	1.9	5	...	...	37	81	...
PARAGUAY	R	...	...	55	55	...	...	20	20
PERU	R	210	395	718	825	18	29	45	50
SURINAME	R	7	28	38	39	21	76	87	87
URUGUAY	R	200	...	355	360	74	...	125	126
VENEZUELA	R	650	...	1 431	1 530	75	...	116	120
ASIA									
BAHRAIN	R	...	13	...	62	...	60	...	232
BANGLADESH	R	...	...	27	36	...	...	0.0	0.0
	L	...	...	23	31	...	...	0.0	0.0
BRUNEI	R	...	25	20	26	24	77	113	137
CYPRUS	L	14	49	57	68	24	77	90	105
DEMOCRATIC KAMPUCHEA	R	7	...	35	35	1.1	...	4.2	4.1
HONG KONG	R	50	444	839	871	14	112	191	193
INDIA	L	8	25	479	627	0.0	0.1	0.8	1.0
INDONESIA	R	45	90	...	1 000	0.4	0.7	...	7
	L	...	...	...	828	...	...	...	6
IRAN	R	...	533	1 720	1 900	...	19	51	55
IRAQ	R	171	350	425	475	21	37	37	40
ISRAEL	L	14	356	475	...	5	122	137	...
JAPAN	L	18 080	22 883	26 827	27 595	183	219	238	242
JORDAN ‡	R	–	46	125	165	–	20	45	57
KOREA, REPUBLIC OF	L	45	418	2 627	3 505	1.8	13	73	96
KUWAIT	R	...	100	...	540	63	133	...	478
LEBANON	R	135	260	425	450	63	105	144	147
MALAYSIA	R	53	130	555	665	6	13	45	53
	L	...	...	549	658	...	...	45	52
MONGOLIA	R	...	1.0	3.6	3.6	...	0.8	2.4	2.4

10.4 Television broadcasting: receivers
Télévision: récepteurs
Televisión: receptores

COUNTRY / PAYS / PAIS	DEFINITION OF DATA / CODE / TIPO DE DATOS	NUMBER OF RECEIVERS IN USE AND/OR LICENCES ISSUED (THOUSANDS) — NOMBRE DE POSTES RECEPTEURS EN SERVICE ET/OU DE LICENCES DELIVREES (MILLIERS) — NUMERO DE RECEPTORES EN FUNCIONAMIENTO Y/O DE PERMISOS EXISTENTES (EN MILES)				NUMBER OF RECEIVERS IN USE AND/OR LICENCES ISSUED PER 1 000 INHABITANTS — NOMBRE DE POSTES RECEPTEURS EN SERVICE ET/OU DE LICENCES DELIVREES POUR 1 000 HABITANTS — NUMERO DE RECEPTORES EN FUNCIONAMIENTO Y/O DE PERMISOS EXISTENTES POR 1 000 HABITANTES			
	(1)	1965 (2)	1970 (3)	1976 (4)	1977 (5)	1965 (6)	1970 (7)	1976 (8)	1977 (9)
PAKISTAN	R	10	99	553	625	0.1	1.6	8	8
	L	...	...	415	469	...	...	6	6
PHILIPPINES	R	120	400	800	850	3.8	11	18	19
QATAR	R	...	...	40	200	...	...	421	2041
SAUDI ARABIA	R	...	...	130	300	...	...	14	32
SINGAPORE	R	63	157	464	658	33	76	204	285
	L	...	...	309	329	...	...	136	143
SYRIAN ARAB REPUBLIC	R	65	116	230	250	12	19	30	32
THAILAND	R	200	...	761	765	6	...	18	17
TURKEY	L	1.6	...	1 769	2 272	0.1	...	44	54
UNITED ARAB EMIRATES	R	–				–	–	...	339
YEMEN, DEMOCRATIC	R	13	21	32	32	10	15	18	18
EUROPE									
ALBANIA	R	1.0	2.1	4.5	4.5	0.5	1.0	1.8	1.7
ANDORRA	R	.7	...	...	3.0	50	...	...	125
AUSTRIA	L	...	1 420	1 969	...	...	191	262	...
BELGIUM	L	1 543	2 100	2 646	2 811	163	217	269	286
BULGARIA	L	185	1 028	1 546	1 584	23	121	176	180
CZECHOSLOVAKIA	R	2 113	3 091	5 300	5 452	149	216	355	363
	L	...	...	3 793	3 903	...	...	254	260
DENMARK	R	1 084	1 330	2 250	2 395	228	270	444	471
	L	...	...	1 721	1 771	...	...	339	348
FINLAND	R	778	1 059	1 893	...	171	230	400	...
	L	...	...	1 779	1 886	...	...	376	398
FRANCE	L	6 489	11 008	14 693	...	133	217	278	...
GERMAN DEMOCRATIC REPUBLIC	L	3 216	4 499	5 351	5 451	189	264	319	325
GERMANY, FEDERAL REPUBLIC OF	L	...	16 675	19 930	20 169	...	275	324	328

Country	(1)	(2)	(3)	(4)	(5)	(6)	(7)	(8)	(9)
GIBRALTAR	R	...	...	7	8	...	...	220	250
	L	...	...	6	6	...	...	211	211
GREECE	L	—	170	1 070	...	—	19	117	...
HUNGARY	L	831	1 769	2 477	2 557	82	171	235	240
ICELAND	L	...	41	53	56	...	205	241	252
IRELAND	R	329	447	655	685	114	152	207	215
	L	...	...	549	581	...	...	174	182
ITALY	L	6 045	9 717	12 377	12 705	116	181	220	225
LUXEMBOURG	R	31	71	88	88	93	207	244	247
MALTA	R	26	...	178	...	...	...	539	...
	L	...	47	63	...	82	144	191	...
MONACO	R	...	...	16	16	...	...	640	640
NETHERLANDS	R	...	...	...	4 500	...	...	...	325
	L	2 113	3 086	3 754	3 878	172	237	273	280
NORWAY	L	488	854	1 079	1 111	131	220	268	275
POLAND	L	2 078	4 215	6 820	7 170	66	130	198	207
PORTUGAL	L	180	389	914	1 137	20	45	94	...
ROMANIA	L	501	1 484	2 963	3 161	26	73	138	146
SAN MARINO	L	1.5	2.4	4.0	...	88	126	200	...
SPAIN	R	...	4 115	7 425	...	...	122	206	...
SWEDEN	L	...	2 513	2 988	3 051	...	312	363	370
SWITZERLAND	R	621	1 281	2 100	2 200	106	207	331	348
	L	...	...	1 809	1 846	...	...	285	292
UNITED KINGDOM	R	13 516	16 309	21 100	21 800	249	294	377	390
	L	...	...	18 271	18 409	...	...	327	330
YUGOSLAVIA	L	577	1 798	3 463	3 701	30	88	161	170
OCEANIA									
AMERICAN SAMOA	R	...	2.1	6	6	...	72	184	184
AUSTRALIA	R	1 954	2 758	4 785	5 020	172	220	344	357
FRENCH POLYNESIA	R	.5	8	...	15	5	73	...	110
GUAM	R	28	40	55	57	364	444	539	545
NEW CALEDONIA	R	.4	8	15	20	4.4	73	111	147
NEW ZEALAND	R	413	661	813	817	157	235	263	263
PACIFIC ISLANDS	R	—	1.2	...	3.1	—	12	...	25

COUNTRY PAYS PAIS	DEFINITION OF DATA CODE TIPO DE DATOS	NUMBER OF RECEIVERS IN USE AND/OR LICENCES ISSUED (THOUSANDS) NOMBRE DE POSTES RECEPTEURS EN SERVICE ET/OU DE LICENCES DELIVREES (MILLIERS) NUMERO DE RECEPTORES EN FUNCIONAMIENTO Y/O DE PERMISOS EXISTENTES (EN MILES)				NUMBER OF RECEIVERS IN USE AND/OR LICENCES ISSUED PER 1 000 INHABITANTS NOMBRE DE POSTES RECEPTEURS EN SERVICE ET/OU DE LICENCES DELIVREES POUR 1 000 HABITANTS NUMERO DE RECEPTORES EN FUNCIONAMIENTO Y/O DE PERMISOS EXISTENTES POR 1 000 HABITANTES			
		1965	1970	1976	1977	1965	1970	1976	1977
(1)		(2)	(3)	(4)	(5)	(6)	(7)	(8)	(9)
U.S.S.R.									
U.S.S.R.	R	15 700	34 800	...	...	68	143	...	...
BYELORUSSIAN S.S.R.	R	...	1 111	...	...	...	123	...	...
UKRAINIAN S.S.R.	R L	2 797	7 167	11 404	11 754	62	151	232	238

GENERAL NOTE/NOTE GENERALE/NOTA GENERAL:
E—> FOR THE COUNTRIES LISTED BELOW, ONLY THE ESTIMATED NUMBER OF RECEIVERS IN USE, BUT NOT THE NUMBER OF LICENCES HAS BEEN COMMUNICATED, ALTHOUGH IT IS KNOWN OR BELIEVED THAT A LICENCE SYSTEM IS IN FORCE:

FR—> POUR LES PAYS CI-DESSOUS, SEULE UNE ESTI- MATION DU NOMBRE DE RECEPTEURS EN SERVICE A ETE COMMUNIQUEE. BIEN QUE CERTAINS RENSEIGNEMENTS INDIQUENT OU PERMETTENT DE PENSER QU'UN SYSTEME DE REDEVANCES EST EN VIGUEUR, LE NOMBRE DE LICENCES DELIVREES N'A PAS ETE FOURNI:

ESP> PARA LOS PAISES QUE FIGURAN A CONTINUA- CION, SOLO SE HA COMUNICADO UNA ESTIMACION DE LOS RECEPTORES EN SERVICIO. AUNQUE CIERTAS INFOR- MACIONES INDIQUEN O PERMITAN PENSAR QUE ESTA EN VIGOR UN SISTEMA DE PERMISOS, EL NUMERO DE PERMISOS CONCEDIDOS NO NOS HA SIDO FACILITADO:

AFRICA/AFRIQUE/AFRICA:

CONGO
DJIBOUTI/YIBUTI
EGYPT/EGYPTE/EGIPTO
ETHIOPIA/ETHIOPIE/ETIOPIA
GHANA
KENYA/KENIA
MADAGASCAR
NIGERIA
REUNION
SIERRA LEONE/SIERRA LEONA
TUNISIA/TUNISIE/TUNEZ
UGANDA/OUGANDA
UNITED REPUBLIC OF TANZANIA/REPUBLIQUE-UNIE DE TANZANIE/REPUBLICA UNIDA DE TANZANIA
UPPER VOLTA/HAUTE-VOLTA/ALTO VOLTA
WESTERN SAHARA/SAHARA OCCIDENTAL
ZIMBABWE

AMERICA, NORTH/AMERIQUE DU NORD/AMERICA DEL NORTE
ANTIGUA
BARBADOS/BARBADE
BERMUDA/BERMUDES/BERMUDAS
BRITISH VIRGIN ISLANDS/ILES VIERGES BRITANNIQUES/ ISLAS VIRGENES BRITANICAS
CANADA
COSTA RICA
GUADELOUPE/GUADALUPE
MARTINIQUE/MARTINICA
ST. LUCIA/SAINTE LUCIE/SANTA LUCIA
ST. PIERRE AND MIQUELON/SAINT PIERRE ET MIQUELON/ SAN PEDRO Y MIQUELON

AMERICA, SOUTH/AMERIQUE DU SUD/AMERICA DEL SUR
FRENCH GUIANA/GUYANE FRANCAISE/GUYANA FRANCESA

ASIA/ASIE
BAHRAIN/BAHREIN
DEMOCRATIC KAMPUCHEA/KAMPUCHEA DEMOCRATIQUE/ KAMPUCHEA DEMOCRATICA
JORDAN/JORDANIE/JORDANIA
KUWAIT/KOWEIT/KUWEIT
MONGOLIA/MONGOLIE
QATAR
SYRIAN ARAB REPUBLIC/REPUBLIQUE ARABE SYRIENNE/ REPUBLICA ARABE SIRIA

EUROPE/EUROPA
ALBANIA/ALBANIE
ANDORRA/ANDORRE
MONACO

OCEANIA/OCEANIE
AMERICAN SAMOA/SAMOA AMERICAINES/SAMOA AMERICANAS
FRENCH POLYNESIA/POLYNESIE FRANCAISE/POLINESIA
FRANCESA
NEW CALEDONIA/NOUVELLE-CALEDONIE/NUEVA CALEDONIA
NEW ZEALAND/NOUVELLE ZELANDE/NUEVA ZELANDIA
PACIFIC ISLANDS/ILES DU PACIFIQUE/ISLAS DEL
PACIFICO

U.S.S.R./U.R.S.S.
U.S.S.R./U.R.S.S.
BYELORUSSIAN S.S.R./RSS DE BIELORUSSIE/RSS DE
BIELORRUSIA
UKRAINIAN S.S.R./RSS D'UKRAINE/RSS DE UCRANIA

JORDAN:
E—> : DATA REFER TO THE EAST BANK ONLY.
FR—> LES DONNEES SE REFERENT A LA RIVE ORIENTALE
SEULEMENT.
ESP> LOS DATOS SE REFIEREN A LA ORILLA ORIENTAL
SOLAMENTE.

A Member States and Associate Members of Unesco
Etats membres et Membres associés de l'Unesco
Estados Miembros y Miembros Asociados de la Unesco

MEMBER STATE ETAT MEMBRE ESTADO MIEMBRO	DATE OF ENTRY DATE D'ADHESION FECHA DE INGRESO	SCALE OF CONTRIBUTIONS BAREME DES CONTRIBUTIONS ESCALA DE CONTRIBUCIONES %	TOTAL CONTRIBUTIONS 1979–80 MONTANT DES CONTRIBUTIONS 1979–80 TOTAL DE LAS CONTRIBUCIONES 1979–80 £
WORLD TOTAL		100.00	290 400 000
AFGHANISTAN	4.V.1948	0.01	29 040
ALBANIA	16.X.1958	0.01	29 040
ALGERIA	15.X.1962	0.10	290 400
ANGOLA	22.III.1977	0.02	58 080
ARGENTINA	15.IX.1948	0.83	2 410 320
AUSTRALIA	11.VI.1946	1.52	4 414 080
AUSTRIA	13.VIII.1948	0.63	1 829 520
BAHRAIN	19.I.1972	0.01	29 040
BANGLADESH	28.X.1972	0.04	116 160
BARBADOS	28.X.1968	0.01	29 040
BELGIUM	29.XI.1946	1.07	3 107 280
BENIN	19.X.1960	0.01	29 040
BOLIVIA	13.XI.1946	0.01	29 040
BRAZIL	14.X.1946	1.03	2 991 120
BULGARIA	17.V.1956	0.14	406 560
BURMA	27.VI.1949	0.01	29 040
BURUNDI	16.XI.1962	0.01	29 040
BYELORUSSIAN S.S.R.	12.V.1954	0.40	1 161 600
CANADA	6.IX.1946	3.01	8 741 040
CAPE VERDE	15.II.1978	0.01	29 040
CENTRAL AFRICAN REPUBLIC	12.XI.1960	0.01	29 040
CHAD	23.XII.1960	0.01	29 040
CHILE	7.VII.1953	0.09	261 360
CHINA	13.IX.1946	5.45	15 826 800
COLOMBIA	31.X.1947	0.11	319 440
COMORO	22.III.1977	0.01	29 040
CONGO	24.X.1960	0.01	29 040
COSTA RICA	19.V.1950	0.02	58 080
CUBA	29.VIII.1947	0.11	319 440
CYPRUS	9.II.1961	0.01	29 040
CZECHOSLOVAKIA	5.X.1946	0.83	2 410 320
DEMOCRATIC KAMPUCHEA	3.VII.1951	0.01	29 040
DENMARK	20.IX.1946	0.63	1 829 520
DOMINICAN REPUBLIC	2.VII.1946	0.02	58 080
ECUADOR	22.I.1947	0.02	58 080
EGYPT	16.VII.1946	0.08	232 320
EL SALVADOR	28.IV.1948	0.01	29 040
ETHIOPIA	1.VII.1955	0.01	29 040
FINLAND	10.X.1956	0.43	1 248 720

A Member States and Associate Members
Etats membres et Membres associés
Estados Miembros y Miembros Asociados

MEMBER STATE	DATE OF ENTRY	SCALE OF CONTRIBUTIONS	TOTAL CONTRIBUTIONS 1979-80
ETAT MEMBRE	DATE D'ADHESION	BAREME DES CONTRIBUTIONS	MONTANT DES CONTRIBUTIONS 1979-80
ESTADO MIEMBRO	FECHA DE INGRESO	ESCALA DE CONTRIBUCIONES %	TOTAL DE LAS CONTRIBUCIONES 1979-80 £
FRANCE	29.VI.1946	5.71	16 756 080
GABON	17.XI.1960	0.01	29 040
GAMBIA	1.VIII.1973	0.01	29 040
GERMAN DEMOCRATIC REPUBLIC	24.XI.1972	1.32	3 833 280
GERMANY, FEDERAL REPUBLIC OF	11.VII.1951	7.63	22 157 520
GHANA	11.IV.1958	0.02	58 080
GREECE	4.XI.1946	0.35	1 016 400
GRENADA	17.II.1975	0.01	29 040
GUATEMALA	2.7.1950	0.02	58 080
GUINEA	4.II.1960	0.01	29 040
GUINEA-BISSAU	1.XI.1974	0.01	29 040
GUYANA	21.III.1967	0.01	29 040
HAITI	18.XI.1946	0.01	29 040
HONDURAS	16.XII.1947	0.01	29 040
HUNGARY	14.IX.1948	0.33	958 320
ICELAND	8.VI.1964	0.02	58 080
INDIA	12.VI.1946	0.67	1 945 680
INDONESIA	27.V.1950	0.14	406 560
IRAN	6.IX.1948	0.40	1 161 600
IRAQ	21.X.1948	0.08	232 320
IRELAND	3.X.1961	0.15	435 600
ISRAEL	16.IX.1949	0.23	667 920
ITALY	27.I.1948	3.35	9 728 400
IVORY COAST	28.X.1960	0.02	58 080
JAMAICA	7.XI.1962	0.02	58 080
JAPAN	2.VII.1951	8.56	24 858 240
JORDAN	14.VI.1950	0.01	29 040
KENYA	7.IV.1964	0.01	29 040
KOREA, DEMOCRATIC PEOPLE'S REPUB. OF	18.X.1974	0.05	145 200
KOREA, REPUBLIC OF	14.VI.1950	0.13	377 520
KUWAIT	19.XI.1960	0.15	435 600
LAO PEOPLE'S DEMOCRATIC REPUBLIC	9.VII.1951	0.01	29 040
LEBANON	28.X.1946	0.03	87 120
LESOTHO	2.X.1967	0.01	29 040
LIBERIA	6.III.1947	0.01	29 040
LIBYAN ARAB JAMAHIRIYA	27.VI.1953	0.16	464 640
LUXEMBOURG	27.X.1947	0.04	116 160
MADAGASCAR	12.XI.1960	0.01	29 040
MALAWI	28.X.1964	0.01	29 040
MALAYSIA	16.VI.1958	0.09	261 360
MALI	8.XI.1960	0.01	29 040
MALTA	11.II.1965	0.01	29 040
MAURITANIA	11.I.1962	0.01	29 040
MAURITIUS	25.X.1968	0.01	29 040
MEXICO	12.VI.1946	0.78	2 265 120
MONACO	6.VII.1949	0.01	29 040
MONGOLIA	1.XI.1962	0.01	29 040
MOROCCO	7.XI.1956	0.05	145 200
MOZAMBIQUE	11.X.1976	0.02	58 080
NEPAL	1.V.1953	0.01	29 040

MEMBER STATE ETAT MEMBRE ESTADO MIEMBRO	DATE OF ENTRY DATE D'ADHESION FECHA DE INGRESO	SCALE OF CONTRIBUTIONS BAREME DES CONTRIBUTIONS ESCALA DE CONTRIBUCIONES %	TOTAL CONTRIBUTIONS 1979—80 MONTANT DES CONTRIBUTIONS 1979—80 TOTAL DE LAS CONTRIBUCIONES 1979—80 £
NETHERLANDS	1.I.1947	1.41	4 094 640
NEW ZEALAND	6.III.1946	0.25	726 000
NICARAGUA	22.II.1952	0.01	29 040
NIGER	10.XI.1960	0.01	29 040
NIGERIA	14.XI.1960	0.13	377 520
NORWAY	8.VIII.1946	0.44	1 277 760
OMAN	11.II.1972	0.01	29 040
PAKISTAN	14.IX.1949	0.07	203 280
PANAMA	10.I.1950	0.02	58 080
PAPUA NEW GUINEA	4.X.1976	0.01	29 040
PARAGUAY	20.VI.1955	0.01	29 040
PERU	21.XI.1946	0.06	174 240
PHILIPPINES	21.XI.1946	0.10	290 400
POLAND	6.XI.1946	1.38	4 007 520
PORTUGAL	11.IX.1974	0.19	551 760
QATAR	28.I.1972	0.02	58 080
ROMANIA	27.VII.1956	0.24	696 960
RWANDA	7.XI.1962	0.01	29 040
SAN MARINO	13.XI.1974	0.01	29 040
SAUDI ARABIA	30.IV.1946	0.23	667 920
SENEGAL	12.XI.1960	0.01	29 040
SEYCHELLES	18.X.1976	0.01	29 040
SIERRA LEONE	28.III.1962	0.01	29 040
SINGAPORE	28.X.1965	0.08	232 320
SOMALIA	15.XI.1960	0.01	29 040
SPAIN	30.I.1953	1.51	4 385 040
SRI LANKA	14.XI.1949	0.02	58 080
SUDAN	26.XI.1956	0.01	29 040
SURINAME	16.VII.1976	0.01	29 040
SWAZILAND	25.I.1978	0.01	29 040
SWEDEN	23.I.1950	1.23	3 571 920
SWITZERLAND	28.I.1949	0.95	2 758 800
SYRIAN ARAB REPUBLIC	16.XI.1946	0.02	58 080
THAILAND	1.I.1949	0.10	290 400
TOGO	18.XI.1960	0.01	29 040
TRINIDAD AND TOBAGO	2.XI.1962	0.03	87 120
TUNISIA	7.XI.1956	0.02	58 080
TURKEY	6.VII.1956	0.30	871 200
UGANDA	9.XI.1962	0.01	29 040
UKRAINIAN S.S.R.	12.V.1954	1.51	4 385 040
U.S.S.R.	21.IV.1954	11.49	33 366 960
UNITED ARAB EMIRATES	21.IV.1972	0.07	203 280
UNITED KINGDOM	20.II.1946	4.48	13 009 920
UNITED REPUBLIC OF CAMEROON	12.XI.1960	0.01	29 040
UNITED REPUBLIC OF TANZANIA	7.III.1962	0.01	29 040
UNITED STATES OF AMERICA	30.IX.1946	25.00	72 600 000
UPPER VOLTA	14.XI.1960	0.01	29 040
URUGUAY	8.XI.1947	0.04	116 160
VENEZUELA	25.XI.1946	0.39	1 132 560
VIET—NAM	6.VII.1951	0.03	87 120

A Member States and Associate Members
Etats membres et Membres associés
Estados Miembros y Miembros Asociados

MEMBER STATE	DATE OF ENTRY	SCALE OF CONTRIBUTIONS	TOTAL CONTRIBUTIONS 1979-80
ETAT MEMBRE	DATE D'ADHESION	BAREME DES CONTRIBUTIONS	MONTANT DES CONTRIBUTIONS 1979-80
ESTADO MIEMBRO	FECHA DE INGRESO	ESCALA DE CONTRIBUCIONES	TOTAL DE LAS CONTRIBUCIONES 1979-80
		%	£
YEMEN	2.IV.1962	0.01	29 040
YEMEN, DEMOCRATIC	16.X.1968	0.01	29 040
YUGOSLAVIA	31.III.1950	0.39	1 132 560
ZAIRE	26.XI.1960	0.02	58 080
ZAMBIA	10.XI.1964	0.02	58 080

GENERAL NOTE/NOTE GENERALE/NOTA GENERAL:

E—> THE SCALE OF CONTRIBUTIONS IS BASED UPON THE SCALE OF CONTRIBUTIONS OF THE UNITED NATIONS, aDJUSTED TO TAKE INTO ACCOUNT THE DIFFERENCE IN THE MEMBERSHIP OF THE TWO ORGANIZATIONS. THE TOTAL CONTRIBUTIONS 1979-80 DOES NOT INCLUDE ADVANCES TO THE WORKING CAPITAL FUND.

FR—> LE BAREME DES CONTRIBUTIONS EST ETABLI SUR LA BASE DU BAREME DE L'ORGANISATION DES NATIONS UNIES, AJUSTE DE FACON A TENIR COMPTE DE LA COMPOSITION DIFFERENTE DES DEUX ORGANISA-TIONS. LE MONTANT DES CONTRIBUTIONS 1979-80 NE TIENT PAS COMPTE DES AVANCES AU FONDS DE ROULEMENT.

ESP> LA ESCALA DE CONTRIBUCIONES SE BASA EN EN LA ESCALA DE CONTRIBUCIONES DE LAS NACIONES UNIDAS, REAJUSTADA TENIENDO EN CUENTA LA DISTINTA COMPOSICION DE LAS DOS ORGANIZACIONES. EL TOTAL DE LAS CONTRIBUCIONES 1979-80 NO INCLUYE LOS ANTICIPOS AL FONDO DE OPERACIONES.

ASSOCIATE MEMBERS AND THEIR DATE OF ENTRY	MEMBRES ASSOCIES ET DATE D'ADHESION	MIEMBROS ASOCIADOS Y FECHA DE INGRESO
ASOCIATE MEMBER	DATE OF ENTRY	CONTRIBUTION
MEMBRE ASSOCIE	DATE D'ADHESION	CONTRIBUTION
MIEMBRO ASOCIADO	FECHA DE INGRESO	CONTRIBUCION

BRITISH EASTERN CARIBBEAN
  GROUP   21.X.1964   THE CONTRIBUTIONS OF ASSOCIATE MEMBERS ARE ASSESSED AT 60 % OF THE MINIMUM PERCENTAGE ASSESSMENT OF MEMBER STATES.

NAMIBIA   21.X.1974   LES CONTRIBUTIONS DES MEMBRES ASSOCIES SONT FIXEES A 60 % DE LA CONTRIBUTION MINIMALE DES ETATS MEMBRES.

LA CONTRIBUCION DE LOS MIEMBROS ASOCIADOS SE FIJA EN UN 60 % DE LA CONTRIBUCION MINIMA DE LOS ESTADOS MIEMBROS.

School and financial years **B**
Année scolaire et année de financement
Año escolar y ejercicio económico

B School and financial years

Année scolaire et année de financement

Año escolar y ejercicio económico

IN THE FOLLOWING TABLE, THE MONTHS ARE REPRESENTED BY ROMAN NUMERALS:	DANS LE TABLEAU SUIVANT, LES MOIS SONT REPRESENTES PAR DES CHIFFRES ROMAINS:	EN EL CUADRO SIGUIENTE, LOS MESES ESTAN REPRE- SENTADOS POR CIFRAS ROMANAS:
JANUARY = I	JANVIER = I	ENERO = I
FEBRUARY = II	FEVRIER = II	FEBRERO = II
MARCH = III	MARS = III	MARZO = III
APRIL = IV	AVRIL = IV	ABRIL = IV
MAY = V	MAI = V	MAYO = V
JUNE = VI	JUIN = VI	JUNIO = VI
JULY = VII	JUILLET = VII	JULIO = VII
AUGUST = VIII	AOUT = VIII	AGOSTO = VIII
SEPTEMBER = IX	SEPTEMBRE = IX	SEPTIEMBRE = IX
OCTOBER = X	OCTOBRE = X	OCTUBRE = X
NOVEMBER = XI	NOVEMBRE = XI	NOVIEMBRE = XI
DECEMBER = XII	DECEMBRE = XII	DICIEMBRE = XII

COUNTRY / PAYS / PAIS	SCHOOL YEAR / ANNEE SCOLAIRE / AÑO ESCOLAR		START OF FINANCIAL YEAR / DEBUT DE L'EXERCICE FINANCIER / COMIENZO DEL EJERCICIO ECONOMICO
	START DEBUT COMIENZO	END FIN FIN	
AFRICA			
ALGERIA	IX	VII	I
ANGOLA	IX	VII	I
BENIN	II	XII	I
BOTSWANA	I	XII	IV
BURUNDI	IX	VII	I
CAPE VERDE	X	VII	I
CENTRAL AFRICAN REPUBLIC	X	VI	I
CHAD	IX	VI	I
COMORO	X	VI	I
CONGO	X	VI	I
EGYPT	X	VI	I
EQUATORIAL GUINEA	IX	VI	I
ETHIOPIA	IX	VI	VII
DJIBOUTI	IX	VI	I
GABON	X	VI	I
GAMBIA	IX	VII	VII
GHANA	IX	VII	VII
GUINEA	X	IX	X
GUINEA-BISSAU	X	VII	I
IVORY COAST	IX	VI	I

COUNTRY / PAYS / PAIS	SCHOOL YEAR / ANNEE SCOLAIRE / AÑO ESCOLAR		START OF FINANCIAL YEAR / DEBUT DE L'EXERCICE FINANCIER / COMIENZO DEL EJERCICIO ECONOMICO
	START DEBUT COMIENZO	END FIN FIN	
KENYA	I	XII	VII
LESOTHO	I	XII	IV
LIBERIA	III	XII	I
LIBYAN ARAB JAMAHIRIYA	X	VI	I
MADAGASCAR	II	X	I
MALAWI	X	VIII	IV
MALI	X	VII	I
MAURITANIA	X	VII	I
MAURITIUS	I	XII	VII
MOROCCO	IX	VI	I
MOZAMBIQUE	IX	VIII	I
NAMIBIA	II		IV
NIGER	X	VI	X
NIGERIA	IX	VI	IV
REUNION	IX	VIII	I
RWANDA	IX	VII	I
ST. HELENA	IX	VIII	IV
SAO TOME AND PRINCIPE	IV	XII	I
SENEGAL	X	VI	VII
SEYCHELLES	I	XII	I
SIERRA LEONE	IX	VII	VII
SOMALIA	XI	VII	I
SOUTH AFRICA	II	...	IV
SUDAN	VII	III	VII
SWAZILAND	I	XII	IV

B School and financial years
Année scolaire et année de financement
Año escolar y ejercicio económico

COUNTRY / PAYS / PAIS	SCHOOL YEAR / ANNEE SCOLAIRE / AÑO ESCOLAR START DEBUT COMIENZO	END FIN FIN	START OF FINANCIAL YEAR DEBUT DE L'EXERCICE FINANCIER COMIENZO DEL EJERCICIO ECONOMICO
TOGO	IX	VI	X
TUNISIA	IX	VI	I
UGANDA	I	XII	VII
UNITED REPUBLIC OF CAMEROON			VII
	IX	VI	
	X	VI	
UNITED REPUBLIC OF TANZANIA	XI	IX	VII
UPPER VOLTA	X	VII	I
WESTERN SAHARA	IX	VIII	I
ZAIRE	IX	VII	I
ZAMBIA	I	XII	I
ZIMBABWE	I	...	VII
AMERICA, NORTH			
ANTIGUA	IX	VII	I
BAHAMAS	IX	VI	I
BARBADOS	IX	VIII	IV
BELIZE	VIII	VII	I
BERMUDA	IX	VII	IV
BRITISH VIRGIN ISLANDS	IX	VII	I
CANADA	IX	VI	IV
CAYMAN ISLANDS	IX	VII	I
COSTA RICA	III	XI	I
CUBA	IX	VI	I
DOMINICA	IX	VII	I
DOMINICAN REPUBLIC	IX	VI	I
EL SALVADOR	I	X	I
GREENLAND	IX	VI	I
GRENADA	IX	VIII	I
GUADELOUPE	IX	VII	I
GUATEMALA	I	X	I
HAITI	X	VI	X
HONDURAS	II	XI	I
JAMAICA	IX	VII	IV
MARTINIQUE	X	VII	I
MEXICO	IX	VI	I
MONTSERRAT	IX	VII	I
NETHERLANDS ANTILLES	IX	VII	I
NICARAGUA	II	XI	I
PANAMA	IV	XII	I
FORMER CANAL ZONE	IX	VI	VII
PUERTO RICO	IX	VI	VII
ST. KITTS – NEVIS ANGUILLA	IX	VII	I
ST. LUCIA	IX	VII	I
ST. PIERRE AND MIQUELON	IX	VI	I
ST. VINCENT AND THE GRENADINES	IX	VII	I
TRINIDAD AND TOBAGO	IX	VII	I
TURKS AND CAICOS ISLANDS	IX	VII	I
UNITED STATES OF AMERICA	IX	VI	VII
U.S. VIRGIN ISLANDS	IX	VI	VII
AMERICA, SOUTH			
ARGENTINA	III	XII	I
	IX	V	
BOLIVIA	II	XI	I
BRAZIL	III	XII	I
CHILE	III	XII	I
COLOMBIA	II	XI	I
ECUADOR			I
	X	VII	I
	IV	XII	
FALKLAND ISLANDS (MALVINAS)	II	XII	VII
FRENCH GUIANA	X	VII	I
GUYANA	IX	VIII	I
PARAGUAY	II	XI	I
PERU	IV	XII	I
SURINAME	X	VIII	I
URUGUAY	III	XII	I
VENEZUELA	X	VII	I
ASIA			
AFGHANISTAN	III	XI	III
	IX	VI	
BAHRAIN	X	VI	I
BANGLADESH	I	XII	VII
BHUTAN	III	XII	IV
BRUNEI	I	XII	I
BURMA	V	III	X
CHINA	X	...	...
CYPRUS	IX	VI	I
DEMOCRATIC KAMPUCHEA	X	VI	I
EAST TIMOR	X	VII	I
HONG KONG	IX	VII	IV
INDIA	IV	III	IV
INDONESIA	I	XII	IV
IRAN	IX	VI	III
IRAQ	IX	V	I
ISRAEL	IX	VI	IV
JAPAN	IV	III	IV
JORDAN	IX	VI	I
KOREA, REPUBLIC OF	III	II	I

School and financial years
Année scolaire et année de financement
Año escolar y ejercicio económico

B

COUNTRY PAYS PAIS	SCHOOL YEAR ANNEE SCOLAIRE AÑO ESCOLAR		START OF FINANCIAL YEAR DEBUT DE L'EXERCICE FINANCIER COMIENZO DEL EJERCICIO ECONOMICO
	START DEBUT COMIENZO	END FIN FIN	
KOREA, DEMOCRATIC PEOPLE'S REPUB. OF	IX	VIII	...
KUWAIT	IX	VI	VII
LAO PEOPLE'S DEMOCRATIC REPUBLIC	IX	VI	VII
LEBANON	X	VI	I
MACAU	X	VII	I
MALAYSIA			
PENINSULAR MALAYSIA	I	XI	I
SABAH	I	XI	I
SARAWAK	I	XI	I
MALDIVES	II	XII	I
MONGOLIA	IX	V	I
NEPAL	II	XII	VII
OMAN	IX	V	I
PAKISTAN	IV	III	VII
	VII	VI	
PHILIPPINES	VI	III	I
QATAR	IX	VI	XII
SAUDI ARABIA	IX	V	VII
SINGAPORE	I	XII	IV
SRI LANKA	I	XII	I
SYRIAN ARAB REPUBLIC	IX	VI	I
THAILAND	VI	III	X
TURKEY	IX	VI	III
UNITED ARAB EMIRATES	X	VI	I
VIET—NAM	IX	V	...
YEMEN	IX	VI	IV
YEMEN, DEMOCRATIC	IX	VI	I
EUROPE			
ALBANIA	IX	V/VI	I
ANDORRA			I
	IX	VI	I
	IX	VI	
AUSTRIA	IX	VI	I
BELGIUM	IX	VI	I
BULGARIA	IX	VI	I
CZECHOSLOVAKIA	IX	VI	I
DENMARK	VIII	VI	IV
FAEROE ISLANDS	VIII	VII	IV
FINLAND	VIII	V	I
FRANCE	IX	VI	I
GERMAN DEMOCRATIC REPUBLIC	IX	VI	I
GERMANY, FEDERAL REPUBLIC OF	VIII/IX	VI/VII	I
GIBRALTAR	IX	VII	IV
GREECE	IX	VI	I
HUNGARY	IX	VI	I
ICELAND	IX	V	I
IRELAND	VII	VI	I
ITALY	IX	VI	I

COUNTRY PAYS PAIS	SCHOOL YEAR ANNEE SCOLAIRE AÑO ESCOLAR		START OF FINANCIAL YEAR DEBUT DE L'EXERCICE FINANCIER COMIENZO DEL EJERCICIO ECONOMICO
	START DEBUT COMIENZO	END FIN FIN	
LIECHTENSTEIN	IV	III	I
LUXEMBOURG	IX	VII	I
MALTA	IX	VII	IV
MONACO	IX	VI	I
NETHERLANDS	VIII	VI/VII	I
NORWAY	VIII	VI	I
POLAND	VIII	VI	I
PORTUGAL	X	VII	I
ROMANIA	IX	VI	I
SAN MARINO	IX	VI	I
SPAIN	X	IX	I
SWEDEN	VIII	VI	VII
SWITZERLAND	IV	III	I
	VIII—IX	VII	
UNITED KINGDOM	VIII	VI	IV
YUGOSLAVIA	IX	VI	I
OCEANIA			
AMERICAN SAMOA	IX	VI	VII
AUSTRALIA	I/II	XII	VII
SOLOMON ISLANDS	I	XII	I
COOK ISLANDS	II	XII	IV
FIJI	II	XII	I
FRENCH POLYNESIA	IX	VI	I
GUAM	IX	VI	VII
KIRIBATI	I	XII	I
NAURU	II	XII	VII
NEW CALEDONIA	III	XII	I
NEW HEBRIDES	III	XII	I
	II	XI	IV
NEW ZEALAND	II	XII	IV
NIUE	II	XII	IV
NORFOLK ISLAND	II	XII	VII
PACIFIC ISLANDS	IX	VI	X
PAPUA NEW GUINEA	II	XII	VII
SAMOA	I	XII	I
TOKELAU ISLANDS	II	XII	IV
TONGA	II	XII	VII
U.S.S.R.			
U.S.S.R.	IX	V	I
BYELORUSSIAN S.S.R.	IX	V	I
UKRAINIAN S.S.R.	IX	V	I

B   School and financial years
Année scolaire et année de financement
Año escolar y ejercicio económico

GENERAL NOTE/NOTE GENERALE/NOTA GENERAL:
   E—> FOR THE FOLLOWING COUNTRIES, 2 LINES ARE
SHOWN INSTEAD OF 1 AS CONCERNS THE START AND THE
END OF THE SCHOOL YEAR. THE AREAS OR TYPES OF
SCHOOLS TO WHICH THESE LINES REFER ARE INDICATED
BELOW:
   FR-> POUR LES PAYS SUIVANTS, LES DONNEES RELA-
TIVES AU DEBUT ET A LA FIN DE L'ANNEE SCOLAIRE
SONT PRESENTEES EN DEUX LIGNES A LA PLACE D'UNE.
LES REGIONS OU LES TYPES D'ECOLES CONCERNES PAR
CES LIGNES SONT INDIQUES CI—DESSOUS:
   ESP> PARA LOS PAISES SIGUIENTES, LOS DATOS
RELATIVOS AL COMIENZO Y AL FINAL DEL AÑO ESCOLAR
SE PRESENTAN EN DOS LINEAS EN VEZ DE UNA. LAS
REGIONES O LOS TIPOS DE ESCUELAS A QUE SE RE-
FIEREN DICHAS LINEAS, SE INDICAN A CONTINUACION:

COUNTRY	LINE	REGION OR TYPES OF SCHOOLS
PAYS	LIGNE	REGION OU TYPES D'ECOLES
PAIS	LINEA	REGION O TIPOS DE ESCUELAS
UNITED REPUBLIC OF CAMEROON	1	WESTERN / OCCIDENTAL
	2	EASTERN / ORIENTAL
ARGENTINA	2	COLD REGIONS / REGIONS FROIDES / REGIONES FRIAS
ECUADOR	1	SIERRA
	2	COASTAL REGION / REGION COTIERE / REGION COSTERA
AFGHANISTAN	2	WARM REGIONS / REGIONS CHAUDES / REGIONES CALIDAS
PAKISTAN	2	KARACHI REGION / REGION DE KARACHI
ANDORRA	1	SPANISH SCHOOLS / ECOLES ESPAGNOLES / ESCUELAS ESPAÑOLAS
	2	FRENCH SCHOOLS / ECOLES FRANCAISES / ESCUELAS FRANCESAS
NEW HEBRIDES	1	FRENCH SCHOOLS / ECOLES FRANCAISES / ESCUELAS FRANCESAS
	2	ENGLISH SCHOOLS / ECOLES ANGLAISES / ESCUELAS INGLESAS

School and financial years   **B**
Année scolaire et année de financement
Año escolar y ejercicio económico

SUMMARY OF THE START OF THE
SCHOOL YEAR, 1978

SOMMAIRE RELATIF A L'ANNEE
SCOLAIRE, 1978

RESUMEN RELATIVO AL AÑO ESCOLAR,
1978

NUMBER OF COUNTRIES IN WHICH SCHOOL YEARS BEGINS IN
NOMBRE DE PAYS DONT L'ANNEE SCOLAIRE COMMENCE EN
NUMERO DE PAISES EN LOS QUE EL AÑO ESCOLAR EMPIEZA EN

CONTINENTS CONTINENTS CONTINENTES	JANUARY FEBRUARY JANVIER FEVRIER ENERO FEBRERO	MARCH APRIL MARS AVRIL MARZO ABRIL	MAY JUNE MAI JUIN MAYO JUNIO	JULY AUGUST JUILLET AOUT JULIO AGOSTO	SEPTEMBER OCTOBER SEPTEMBRE OCTOBRE SEPTIEMBRE OCTUBRE	NOVEMBER DECEMBER NOVEMBRE DECEMBRE NOVIEMBRE DICIEMBRE	MIXED OR NOT SPECIFIED MIXTE OU NON SPECIFIE MIXTO O SIN ESPECIFICAR	TOTAL
AFRICA	13	2	0	1	36	2	1	55
AMERICA, NORTH	4	2	0	1	29	0	0	36
AMERICA, SOUTH	4	4	0	0	4	0	2	14
ASIA	10	4	3	1	24	0	2	44
EUROPE AND U.S.S.R	0	1	0	10	23	0	4	38
OCEANIA	12	1	0	0	4	0	2	19
ARAB STATES	(0)	(0)	(0)	(1)	(17)	(0)	(0)	(18)
TOTAL	43	14	3	13	120	2	11	206

SUMMARY OF THE START OF THE
FINANCIAL YEAR, 1978

SOMMAIRE RELATIF A L'EXERCICE
FINANCIER, 1978

RESUMEN RELATIVO AL EJERCICIO
ECONOMICO, 1978

NUMBER OF COUNTRIES IN WHICH FINANCIAL YEAR BEGINS IN
NOMBRE DE PAYS DONT L'EXERCICE FINANCIER COMMENCE EN
NUMERO DE PAISES EN LOS QUE EL EJERCICIO ECONOMICO EMPIEZA EN

CONTINENTS CONTINENTS CONTINENTES	JANUARY FEBRUARY JANVIER FEVRIER ENERO FEBRERO	MARCH APRIL MARS AVRIL MARZO ABRIL	MAY JUNE MAI JUIN MAYO JUNIO	JULY AUGUST JUILLET AOUT JULIO AGOSTO	SEPTEMBER OCTOBER SEPTEMBRE OCTOBRE SEPTIEMBRE OCTUBRE	NOVEMBER DECEMBER NOVEMBRE DECEMBRE NOVIEMBRE DICIEMBRE	MIXED OR NOT SPECIFIED MIXTE OU NON SPECIFIE MIXTO O SIN ESPECIFICAR	TOTAL
AFRICA	32	8	0	12	3	0	0	55
AMERICA, NORTH	27	4	0	4	1	0	0	36
AMERICA, SOUTH	13	0	0	1	0	0	0	14
ASIA	21	11	0	6	2	1	3	44
EUROPE AND U.S.S.R	30	7	0	0	1	0	0	38
OCEANIA	6	3	0	8	1	0	1	19
ARAB STATES	(10)	(5)	(0)	(3)	(0)	(0)	(0)	(18)
TOTAL	129	33	0	31	8	1	4	206

Exchange rates
Taux de change
Tipos de cambio

C

Exchange rates

Taux de change

Tipos de cambio

The following table lists rates of exchange to the United States dollar for the figures on expenditure expressed in national currencies which appear in Tables 4.1 to 4.4, 5.6 to 5.10, 5.12, 5.13 and 7.2 to 7.6.

These rates are given in order to help the reader to interpret different currencies shown in the above-mentioned tables. It should be noted that the rates listed do not normally represent comparative purchasing power. They have been established according to the criteria considered by the International Monetary Fund as most suitable for conversion purposes (par values, central rates, monthly average of mid-point of buying and selling rates, selling rates, buying rates, official rates, etc.).

Where an external change in relation to the United States dollar

occurred in the course of a calendar year, the conversion rate presented in Appendix C has been computed according to a weighted average of the number of months the new and old rates were in force.

The data were supplied by the International Monetary Fund, and the reader can consult their monthly bulletin, *International Financial Statistics* for more details on the methodology used for calculating the conversion rates. Additional information has been extracted from the *United Nations Monthly Bulletin of Statistics*.

Following the Spanish text will be found a table covering countries in the Rouble/Yuan zone which gives the non-commercial exchange rates applied to tourism and to the conversion of remittances received from other countries outside the Rouble/Yuan zone.

Le tableau ci-après présente les taux de conversion en dollars des Etats-Unis, applicable aux données relatives aux dépenses, qui sont exprimées en monnaie nationale dans les tableaux 4.1 à 4.4, 5.6 à 5.10, 5.12, 5.13 et 7.2 à 7.6.

Ces taux de conversion sont publiés pour aider le lecteur à interpréter les différentes monnaies qui figurent dans les tableaux ci-dessus mentionnés. Il faut toutefois signaler que les taux indiqués ne représentent pas une base de comparaison de pouvoirs d'achat. Ils ont été établis d'après les critères considérés par le Fonds Monétaire International comme étant les plus valables aux fins de conversion (parité, cours central, moyenne mensuelle des cours d'achat et de vente, cours de vente, cours d'achat, cours officiels, etc.).

Quand un changement d'un taux de conversion d'une monnaie par rapport au dollar des Etats-Unis s'est produit dans le courant de l'année

civile, le taux de change présenté dans l'annexe C a été calculé d'après la moyenne pondérée, qui tient compte du nombre de mois pendant lesquels le nouveau et l'ancien taux ont été en vigueur.

Les données nous ont été procurées par le Fonds Monétaire International, dont le bulletin mensuel *International Financial Statistics* peut e+tre consulté par le lecteur s'il souhaite avoir d'autres détails sur la méthodologie qui a été appliquée pour le calcul des taux de conversion. Des renseignements supplémentaires ont été tirés du *Bulletin Mensuel de Statistique des Nations Unies*.

Après le texte espagnol, vous trouverez un tableau qui se refère aux pays de la zone Rouble/Yuan et qui donne le taux de change non-commercial appliqué au tourisme et aux envois de fonds provenant des pays autres que ceux de la zone Rouble/Yuan.

En el cuadro que figura a continuación se indican, en dólares de los Estados Unidos, los tipos de cambio que deben aplicarse a los datos relativos a los gastos expresados en moneda nacional en los cuadros 4.1 a 4.4, 5.6 a 5.10, 5.12, 5.13 y 7.2 a 7.6.

Esos tipos de cambio se publican para ayudar al lector a interpretar al valor de las diferentes monedas que figuran en los cuadros anteriormente mencionados. Cabe señalar, sin embargo, que los tipos de cambio indicados no representan una base de comparación del poder adquisitivo. Los tipos de cambio han sido establecidos en función de los criterios que el Fondo Monetario Internacional ha considerado más adecuados para las conversiones (paridad, curso central, media mensual de los cursos de compra y venta, cursos de venta, cursos de compra, cursos oficiales, etc.).

Cuando una modificación del tipo de cambio de una moneda con

respecto al dólar de los Estados Unidos se ha producido en el curso del año civil, el tipo de cambio que figura en el Anexo C se ha calculado de acuerdo con la media ponderada, que tiene en cuenta los meses durante los cuales estuvieron en vigor el nuevo y el antiguo tipo de cambio.

Los datos nos han sido proporcionados por el Fondo Monetario Internacional, cuyo boletín *International Financial Statistics* puede ser consultado por el lector si desea conocer otros detalles relativos a la metodología que ha sido aplicada para el cálculo de los tipos de cambio. Ciertos datos suplementarios han sido tomados del *United Nations Monthly Bulletin of Statistics*.

A continuación figura un cuadro que se refiere a los países de la zona Rubio/Yuan y que presenta el tipo de cambio no comercial que se aplica al turismo y a los envíos de fondos procedentes de países otros que los de la zona Rublo/Yuan.

ROUBLE/YUAN ZONE				ZONE ROUBLE/YUAN				ZONA RUBLO/YUAN			
COUNTRY/PAYS/PAIS	1969	1970	1971	1972	1973	1974	1975	1976	1977	1978	1979
ALBANIA					0.244	0.244	0.244	0.244	0.244	0.132	0.143
BULGARIA	0.50	0.50	0.54	0.54	0.61	0.83	0.83	1.031	1.031	1.136	1.136
CHINA				0.446	0.495	0.544	0.508	0.532	0.526	0.625	0.662
CZECHOSLOVAKIA	0.0617	0.0617	0.0670	0.0668	0.0747	0.0994	0.0985	0.0873	0.0898	0.094	0.096
GERMAN DEMOCRATIC REPUBLIC	0.273	0.273	0.306	0.313	0.370	0.417	0.382	0.417	0.465	0.526	0.575
HUNGARY	0.0333	0.0362	0.0362	0.0362	0.0428	0.0428	0.0489	0.0484	0.0493	0.0562	0.0492
MONGOLIA	0.167	0.167	0.181	0.181	0.314	0.298	0.296	0.300	0.307	0.333	0.345
POLAND	0.0417	0.0417	0.0453	0.0453	0.0502	0.0502	0.0502	0.0502	0.0502	0.0301	0.0301
U.S.S.R.				1.220	1.326	1.319	1.319	1.337	1.340	1.515	1.538

C   Exchange rates
    Taux de change
    Tipos de cambio

COUNTRY PAYS PAIS	NATIONAL CURRENCY MONNAIE NATIONALE MONEDA NACIONAL	EXCHANGE RATES IN UNITED STATES DOLLARS TAUX DE CHANGE EN DOLLARS DES ETATS—UNIS TIPOS DE CAMBIO EN DOLARES DE LOS ESTADOS UNIDOS				
		1960	1965	1967	1968	1969
AFRICA						
ALGERIA	DINAR	0.20255	0.20255	0.20255	0.20255	0.20255
ANGOLA	KWANZA	0.03478	0.03478	0.03478	0.03478	0.03478
BENIN	FRANC C.F.A.	0.00405	0.00405	0.00405	0.00405	0.00386
BOTSWANA	PULA	1.4000	1.4000	1.4000	1.4000	1.4000
BURUNDI	FRANC	0.02000	0.01214	0.01143	0.01143	0.01143
CAPE VERDE	ESCUDO	0.03478	0.03478	0.03478	0.03478	0.03478
CENTRAL AFRICAN EMPIRE	FRANC C.F.A.	0.00405	0.00405	0.00405	0.00405	0.00386
CHAD	FRANC C.F.A.	0.00405	0.00405	0.00405	0.00405	0.00386
COMORO	FRANC	0.00405	0.00405	0.00405	0.00405	0.00386
CONGO	FRANC C.F.A.	0.00405	0.00405	0.00405	0.00405	0.00386
DJIBOUTI	FRANC	0.00466	0.00466	0.00466	0.00466	0.00466
EGYPT	POUND	2.8716	2.3000	2.3000	2.3000	2.3000
EQUATORIAL GUINEA	EKUELE	0.01667	0.01667	0.01627	0.01429	0.01429
ETHIOPIA	BIRR	0.40250	0.40000	0.40000	0.40000	0.40000
GABON	FRANC C.F.A.	0.00405	0.00405	0.00405	0.00405	0.00386
GAMBIA	DALASI	0.56000	0.56000	0.54667	0.48000	0.48000
GHANA	CEDI	1.4000	1.4000	1.1900	0.9800	0.9800
GUINEA	SYLI	0.04051	0.04051	0.04051	0.04051	0.04051
GUINEA—BISSAU	ESCUDO	0.03478	0.03478	0.03478	0.03478	0.03478
IVORY COAST	FRANC C.F.A.	0.00405	0.00405	0.00405	0.00405	0.00386
KENYA	SHILLING	0.14000	0.14000	0.14000	0.14000	0.14000
LESOTHO	RAND	1.4000	1.4000	1.4000	1.4000	1.4000
LIBERIA	DOLLAR	1.0000	1.0000	1.0000	1.0000	1.0000
LIBYAN ARAB JAMAHIRIYA	DINAR	2.8000	2.8000	2.8000	2.8000	2.8000
MADAGASCAR	FRANC	0.00405	0.00405	0.00405	0.00405	0.00386
MALAWI	KWACHA	1.4000	1.4000	1.3833	1.2000	1.2000
MALI	FRANC	0.00203	0.00203	0.00203	0.00203	0.00193
MAURITANIA	OUGUIYA	0.02026	0.02026	0.02026	0.02026	0.01932
MAURITIUS	RUPEE	0.21000	0.21000	0.20750	0.18000	0.18000
MOROCCO	DIRHAM	0.19761	0.19761	0.19761	0.19761	0.19761
MOZAMBIQUE	ESCUDO	0.03478	0.03478	0.03478	0.03478	0.03478
NAMIBIA	SOUTH AFRICAN RAND	1.4000	1.4000	1.4000	1.4000	1.4000
NIGER	FRANC C.F.A.	0.00405	0.00405	0.00405	0.00405	0.00386
NIGERIA	NAIRA	1.4000	1.4000	1.4000	1.4000	1.4000
REUNION	FRANC C.F.A.	0.00405	0.00405	0.00405	0.00405	0.00386
RWANDA	FRANC	0.02000	0.02000	0.01000	0.01000	0.01000
ST. HELENA	POUND STERLING	2.8000	2.8000	2.7667	2.4000	2.4000
SAO TOME AND PRINCIPE	DOBRA	0.03478	0.03478	0.03478	0.03478	0.03478
SENEGAL	FRANC C.F.A.	0.00405	0.00405	0.00405	0.00405	0.00386
SEYCHELLES	RUPEE	0.21000	0.21000	0.20750	0.18000	0.18000
SIERRA LEONE	LEONE	1.4000	1.4000	1.3833	1.2000	1.2000
SOMALIA	SHILLING	0.14000	0.14000	0.14000	0.14000	0.14000
SOUTH AFRICA	RAND	1.4000	1.4000	1.4000	1.4000	1.4000
SUDAN	POUND	2.8716	2.8716	2.8716	2.8716	2.8716
SWAZILAND	LILANGENI	1.4000	1.4000	1.4000	1.4000	1.4000
TOGO	FRANC C.F.A.	0.00405	0.00405	0.00405	0.00405	0.00386
TUNISIA	DINAR	2.3810	1.9048	1.9048	1.9048	1.9048
UGANDA	SHILLING	0.14000	0.14000	0.14000	0.14000	0.14000
UNITED REPUBLIC OF CAMEROON	FRANC C.F.A.	0.00405	0.00405	0.00405	0.00405	0.00386

Exchange rates   C
Taux de change
Tipos de cambio

EXCHANGE RATES IN UNITED STATES DOLLARS
TAUX DE CHANGE EN DOLLARS DES ETATS UNIS
TIPOS DE CAMBIO EN DOLARES DE LOS ESTADOS UNIDOS

1970	1971	1972	1973	1974	1975	1976	1977	1978
0.20255	0.20362	0.22304	0.25347	0.23927	0.25352	0.24017	0.24116	0.25223
0.03478	0.03532	0.03702	0.04068	0.03938	0.03922	0.03309	0.02612	0.02173
0.00360	0.00361	0.00397	0.00451	0.00416	0.00467	0.00419	0.00407	0.00444
1.4000	1.3982	1.3018	1.4441	1.4722	1.3663	1.1500	1.1883	1.2027
0.01143	0.01143	0.01143	0.01259	0.01270	0.01270	0.01164	0.01111	0.01111
0.03478	0.03532	0.03702	0.04068	0.03938	0.03922	0.03326	0.02612	0.02173
0.00360	0.00361	0.00397	0.00451	0.00416	0.00467	0.00419	0.00407	0.00444
0.00360	0.00361	0.00397	0.00451	0.00416	0.00467	0.00419	0.00407	0.00444
0.00360	0.00361	0.00397	0.00451	0.00416	0.00467	0.00419	0.00407	0.00444
0.00360	0.00361	0.00397	0.00451	0.00416	0.00467	0.00419	0.00407	0.00444
0.00466	0.00468	0.00514	0.00584	0.00538	0.00605	0.00542	0.00527	0.00527
2.3000	2.3000	2.3000	2.5266	2.5556	2.5556	2.5556	2.5556	2.5556
0.01429	0.01438	0.01556	0.01718	0.01733	0.01740	0.01497	0.01329	0.01308
0.40000	0.40259	0.43105	0.47546	0.47950	0.48309	0.48309	0.48309	0.48309
0.00360	0.00361	0.00397	0.00451	0.00416	0.00467	0.00419	0.00407	0.00444
0.48000	0.48146	0.50053	0.59312	0.58476	0.55545	0.45155	0.43638	0.47988
0.9800	0.9722	0.7620	0.8622	0.8696	0.8696	0.8696	0.8696	0.6602
0.04051	0.04063	0.04398	0.04832	0.04865	0.04822	0.04677	0.04737	0.05097
0.03478	0.03532	0.03702	0.04068	0.03938	0.03922	0.03317	0.02972	0.02858
0.00360	0.00361	0.00397	0.00451	0.00416	0.00467	0.00419	0.00407	0.00444
0.14000	0.14000	0.14000	0.14246	0.13998	0.13659	0.11952	0.12084	0.12950
1.4000	1.3982	1.3018	1.4441	1.4722	1.3663	1.1500	1.1500	1.1500
1.0000	1.0000	1.0000	1.0000	1.0000	1.0000	1.0000	1.0000	1.1500
2.8000	2.8200	3.0400	3.3497	3.3778	3.3778	3.3778	3.3778	3.3778
0.00360	0.00361	0.00397	0.00451	0.00416	0.00467	0.00419	0.00407	0.00444
1.2000	1.2036	1.2420	1.2258	1.1908	1.1588	1.0954	1.1077	1.1860
0.00180	0.00181	0.00198	0.00225	0.00208	0.00234	0.00210	0.00204	0.00222
0.01800	0.01805	0.01983	0.02253	0.02214	0.02319	0.02225	0.02190	0.02167
0.18000	0.18079	0.18764	0.18392	0.17543	0.16664	0.14965	0.15155	0.16299
0.19761	0.19523	0.18064	0.24405	0.22892	0.24695	0.22641	0.22208	0.24032
0.03478	0.03532	0.03702	0.04068	0.03938	0.03922	0.03317	0.02628	0.02283
1.4000	1.3982	1.3018	1.4441	1.4722	1.3663	1.1500	1.1500	1.1500
0.00360	0.00361	0.00397	0.00451	0.00416	0.00467	0.00419	0.00407	0.00444
1.4000	1.4043	1.5200	1.5227	1.5881	1.6248	1.5959	1.5514	1.5745
0.00360	0.00361	0.00397	0.00451	0.00416	0.00467	0.00419	0.00407	0.00444
0.01000	0.01003	0.01086	0.01193	0.01077	0.01077	0.01077	0.01077	0.01077
2.4000	2.4344	2.5018	2.4522	2.3390	2.2218	1.8062	1.7455	1.9195
0.03478	0.03534	0.03684	0.04068	0.03938	0.03922	0.03317	0.02657	0.02781
0.00360	0.00361	0.00397	0.00451	0.00416	0.00467	0.00419	0.00407	0.00444
0.18000	0.18079	0.18757	0.18382	0.17545	0.16661	0.13547	0.13091	0.14396
1.2000	1.2053	1.2509	1.2261	1.1695	1.1109	0.9031	0.8728	0.9523
0.14000	0.14029	0.14329	0.15937	0.15886	0.15886	0.15886	0.15886	0.15886
1.4000	1.3982	1.3018	1.4441	1.4722	1.3663	1.1500	1.1500	1.1500
2.8716	2.8716	2.8716	2.8716	2.8716	2.8716	2.8716	2.8716	2.6619
1.4000	1.3982	1.3018	1.4441	1.4722	1.3663	1.1500	1.1500	1.1500
0.00360	0.00361	0.00397	0.00451	0.00416	0.00467	0.00419	0.00407	0.00444
1.9048	1.9194	2.0954	2.3887	2.2933	2.4897	2.3325	2.3319	2.4032
0.14000	0.14000	0.14000	0.14246	0.13998	0.13541	0.11951	0.12101	0.13012
0.00360	0.00361	0.00397	0.00451	0.00416	0.00467	0.00419	0.00407	0.00444

C Exchange rates
Taux de change
Tipos de cambio

COUNTRY PAYS PAIS	NATIONAL CURRENCY MONNAIE NATIONALE MONEDA NACIONAL	EXCHANGE RATES IN UNITED STATES DOLLARS TAUX DE CHANGE EN DOLLARS DES ETATS—UNIS TIPOS DE CAMBIO EN DOLARES DE LOS ESTADOS UNIDOS				
		1960	1965	1967	1968	1969
UNITED REPUBLIC OF						
TANZANIA	SHILLING	0.14000	0.14000	0.14000	0.14000	0.14000
UPPER VOLTA	FRANC C.F.A.	0.00405	0.00405	0.00405	0.00405	0.00386
WESTERN SAHARA	PESETA	0.01667	0.01667	0.01647	0.01429	0.01429
ZAIRE	ZAIRE	20.000	6.061	4.030	2.000	2.000
ZAMBIA	KWACHA	1.4000	1.4000	1.4000	1.4000	1.4000
ZIMBABWE	DOLLAR	1.4000	1.4000	1.4000	1.4000	1.4000
AMERICA, NORTH						
ANTIGUA	E. CARIBBEAN DOLLAR	0.58333	0.58333	0.56944	0.50000	0.50000
BAHAMAS	DOLLAR	0.9800	0.9800	0.9800	0.9800	0.9800
BARBADOS	DOLLAR	0.58333	0.58333	0.57639	0.50000	0.50000
BELIZE	DOLLAR	0.7000	0.7000	0.6917	0.6000	0.6000
BERMUDA	DOLLAR	1.1667	1.1667	1.1528	1.0000	1.0000
BRITISH VIRGIN						
ISLANDS	UNITED STATES DOLLAR	1.0000	1.0000	1.0000	1.0000	1.0000
CANADA	DOLLAR	1.0316	0.9250	0.9250	0.9250	0.9250
CAYMAN ISLANDS	JAMAICAN DOLLAR	1.4000	1.4000	1.3833	1.2000	1.2000
COSTA RICA	COLON	0.17809	0.15094	0.15094	0.15094	0.15094
CUBA	PESO	1.00	1.00	1.00	1.00	1.00
DOMINICA	DOLLAR	0.58333	0.58333	0.57639	0.50000	0.50000
DOMINICAN REPUBLIC	PESO	1.0000	1.0000	1.0000	1.0000	1.0000
EL SALVADOR	COLON	0.40000	0.40000	0.40000	0.40000	0.40000
GRENADA	DOLLAR	0.58333	0.58333	0.56944	0.50000	0.50000
GUADELOUPE	FRANC	0.20255	0.20255	0.20255	0.20255	0.19317
GUATEMALA	QUETZAL	1.0000	1.0000	1.0000	1.0000	1.0000
HAITI	GOURDE	0.20000	0.20000	0.20000	0.20000	0.20000
HONDURAS	LEMPIRA	0.50000	0.50000	0.50000	0.50000	0.50000
JAMAICA	DOLLAR	1.4000	1.4000	1.3833	1.2000	1.2000
MARTINIQUE	FRANC	0.20255	0.20255	0.20255	0.20255	0.19317
MEXICO	PESO	0.08000	0.08000	0.08000	0.08000	0.08000
MONTSERRAT	E. CARIBBEAN DOLLAR	0.58333	0.58333	0.57639	0.50000	0.50000
NETHERLANDS ANTILLES	GUILDER	0.53026	0.53027	0.53027	0.53027	0.53027
NICARAGUA	CORDOBA	0.14286	0.14286	0.14286	0.14286	0.14286
PANAMA	BALBOA	1.0000	1.0000	1.0000	1.0000	1.0000
FORMER CANAL ZONE	UNITED STATES DOLLAR	1.0000	1.0000	1.0000	1.0000	1.0000
PUERTO RICO	UNITED STATES DOLLAR	1.0000	1.0000	1.0000	1.0000	1.0000
ST. KITTS — NEVIS						
ANGUILLA	E. CARIBBEAN DOLLAR	0.58333	0.58333	0.57639	0.50000	0.50000
ST. LUCIA	E. CARIBBEAN DOLLAR	0.58333	0.58333	0.57639	0.50000	0.50000
ST. PIERRE AND						
MIQUELON	FRANC C.F.A.	0.00405	0.00405	0.00405	0.00405	0.00386
ST. VINCENT AND						
THE GRENADINES	E. CARIBBEAN DOLLAR	0.58333	0.58333	0.57639	0.50000	0.50000
TRINIDAD AND TOBAGO	DOLLAR	0.58333	0.58333	0.57639	0.50000	0.50000
TURKS AND CAICOS						
ISLANDS	DOLLAR	1.4000	1.4000	1.3833	1.2000	1.2000
UNITED STATES OF						
AMERICA	DOLLAR	1.00000	1.00000	1.00000	1.00000	1.00000
U.S. VIRGIN ISLANDS	UNITED STATES DOLLAR	1.0000	1.0000	1.0000	1.0000	1.0000
AMERICA, SOUTH						
ARGENTINA	PESO	1.206	0.597	0.307	0.286	0.286
BOLIVIA	PESO	0.084	0.084	0.084	0.084	0.084
BRAZIL	CRUZEIRO	7.34	0.57	0.39	0.32	0.25
CHILE	PESO	992.00000	320.00000	199.00000	146.00000	117.00000
COLOMBIA	PESO	0.15540	0.10303	0.07112	0.06254	0.05808

Exchange rates C
Taux de change
Tipos de cambio

EXCHANGE RATES IN UNITED STATES DOLLARS
TAUX DE CHANGE EN DOLLARS DES ETATS UNIS
TIPOS DE CAMBIO EN DOLARES DE LOS ESTADOS UNIDOS

1970	1971	1972	1973	1974	1975	1976	1977	1978
0.14000	0.14000	0.14000	0.14246	0.13998	0.13540	0.11935	0.12088	0.13016
0.00360	0.00361	0.00397	0.00451	0.00416	0.00467	0.00419	0.00407	0.00444
0.01429	0.01438	0.01556	0.01718	0.01733	0.01740	...	...	...
2.000	2.000	2.000	2.000	2.000	2.000	1.292	1.167	1.204
1.4000	1.4000	1.3999	1.5411	1.5541	1.5541	1.4019	1.2675	1.2307
1.4000	1.4043	1.5200	1.7202	1.7760	...	...	...	...
0.50000	0.50650	0.52138	0.51087	0.48730	0.46288	0.40663	0.37037	0.37037
0.9983	1.0000	1.0000	1.0000	1.0000	1.0000	1.0000	1.0000	1.0000
0.50000	0.50650	0.52138	0.51087	0.48730	0.49516	0.49905	0.49830	0.49720
0.6000	0.6086	0.6255	0.6130	0.5848	0.5555	0.4493	0.4361	...
1.0000	1.0000	1.0000	1.0000	1.0000	1.0000	1.0000	1.0000	1.0000
1.0000	1.0000	1.0000	1.0000	1.0000	1.0000	1.0000	1.0000	1.0000
0.9554	0.9903	1.0094	0.9998	1.0226	0.9833	1.0144	0.9410	0.8771
1.2000	1.2173	1.2504	1.1000	1.1000	1.1000	1.1000	1.1000	0.7274
0.15094	0.15092	0.15072	0.15045	0.12792	0.11669	0.11669	0.11669	0.11669
1.00	1.09	1.09	1.21	1.21	1.21	1.21	1.21	1.35
0.50000	0.50717	0.52122	0.51087	0.48730	0.46288	0.40663	0.37037	0.37037
1.0000	1.0000	1.0000	1.0000	1.0000	1.0000	1.0000	1.0000	1.0000
0.40000	0.40000	0.40000	0.40000	0.40000	0.40000	0.40000	0.40000	0.40000
0.50000	0.50650	0.52138	0.51087	0.48730	0.46288	0.40663	0.37037	0.37037
0.18004	0.18050	0.19826	0.22531	0.20781	0.23362	0.20956	0.20356	0.22200
1.0000	1.0000	1.0000	1.0000	1.0000	1.0000	1.0000	1.0000	1.0000
0.20000	0.20000	0.20000	0.20000	0.20000	0.20000	0.20000	0.20000	0.20000
0.50000	0.50000	0.50000	0.50000	0.50000	0.50000	0.50000	0.50000	0.50000
1.2000	1.2173	1.2504	1.1000	1.1000	1.1000	1.1000	1.1000	0.72743
0.18004	0.18050	0.19826	0.22531	0.20781	0.23362	0.20956	0.20356	0.22200
0.08000	0.08000	0.08000	0.08000	0.08000	0.08002	0.06910	0.04433	0.04392
0.50000	0.50717	0.52122	0.51087	0.48730	0.46288	0.40663	0.37037	0.37037
0.53027	0.53096	0.55550	0.55550	0.55550	0.55551	0.55556	0.55556	...
0.14286	0.14286	0.14286	0.14286	0.14259	0.14232	0.14232	0.14232	0.14232
1.0000	1.0000	1.0000	1.0000	1.0000	1.0000	1.0000	1.0000	1.0000
1.0000	1.0000	1.0000	1.0000	1.0000	1.0000	1.0000	1.0000	1.0000
1.0000	1.0000	1.0000	1.0000	1.0000	1.0000	1.0000	1.0000	1.0000
0.50000	0.50717	0.52122	0.51087	0.48730	0.46288	0.40663	0.37037	0.37037
0.50000	0.50717	0.52122	0.51087	0.48730	0.46288	0.40663	0.37037	0.37037
0.00360	0.00361	0.00397	0.00451	0.00416	0.00467	0.00419	0.00407	0.00444
0.50000	0.50717	0.52122	0.51087	0.48730	0.46288	0.40663	0.37037	0.37037
0.50000	0.50650	0.52138	0.51087	0.48730	0.46288	0.41074	0.41667	0.41667
1.2000	1.2173	1.2504	1.1000	1.1000	1.1000	1.1000	1.1000	...
1.00000	1.00000	1.00000	1.00000	1.00000	1.00000	1.00000	1.00000	1.00000
1.0000	1.0000	1.0000	1.0000	1.0000	1.0000	1.0000	1.0000	1.00000
0.266	0.221	0.124	0.107	0.113	0.0459	0.0076	0.0026	0.0013
0.084	0.084	0.079	0.050	0.050	0.050	0.050	0.050	0.050
0.22	0.19	0.17	0.16	0.15	0.123	0.094	0.071	0.056
89.00000	82.00000	52.00000	24.00000	2.00000	0.20362	0.07660	0.04645	0.03159
0.05454	0.04984	0.04544	0.04202	0.03694	0.03210	0.02861	0.02703	0.02544

C   Exchange rates
    Taux de change
    Tipos de cambio

COUNTRY PAYS PAIS	NATIONAL CURRENCY MONNAIE NATIONALE MONEDA NACIONAL	EXCHANGE RATES IN UNITED STATES DOLLARS TAUX DE CHANGE EN DOLLARS DES ETATS—UNIS TIPOS DE CAMBIO EN DOLARES DE LOS ESTADOS UNIDOS				
		1960	1965	1967	1968	1969
ECUADOR	SUCRE	0.06667	0.05556	0.05556	0.05556	0.05556
FALKLAND ISLANDS						
(MALVINAS)	POUND	2.8000	2.8000	2.7667	2.4000	2.4000
FRENCH GUIANA	FRANC	0.20255	0.20255	0.20255	0.20255	0.19317
GUYANA	DOLLAR	0.58333	0.58333	0.57639	0.50000	0.50000
PARAGUAY	GUARANI	0.00863	0.00794	0.00794	0.00794	0.00794
PERU	SOL	0.03701	0.03729	0.03350	0.02584	0.02584
SURINAME	GUILDER	0.53026	0.53027	0.53027	0.53027	0.53027
URUGUAY	PESO	88.72	21.57	9.57	4.25	4.00
VENEZUELA	BOLIVAR	0.29851	0.22222	0.22222	0.22222	0.22222
ASIA						
AFGHANISTAN	AFGHANI	0.05000	0.02222	0.02222	0.02222	0.02222
BAHRAIN	DINAR			2.1000	2.1000	2.1000
BANGLADESH	TAKA					
BHUTAN	INDIAN RUPEE	0.21000	0.21000	0.13333	0.13333	0.13333
BRUNEI	DOLLAR	0.32667	0.32667	0.32667	0.32667	0.32667
BURMA	KYAT	0.21000	0.21000	0.21000	0.21000	0.21000
CHINA	YUAN		0.4065	0.4065	0.4065	0.4065
CYPRUS	POUND	2.8000	2.8000	2.7667	2.4000	2.4000
DEMOCRATIC KAMPUCHEA	RIEL	0.02857	0.02857	0.02857	0.02857	0.02417
EAST TIMOR	PORTUGUESE ESCUDO	0.03478	0.03478	0.03478	0.03478	0.03478
HONG KONG	DOLLAR	0.17500	0.17500	0.17417	0.16500	0.16500
INDIA	RUPEE	0.21000	0.21000	0.13333	0.13333	0.13333
INDONESIA	RUPIAH			0.00099	0.00224	0.00307
IRAN	RIAL	0.01320	0.01320	0.01320	0.01320	0.01320
IRAQ	DINAR	2.8000	2.8000	2.8000	2.8000	2.8000
ISRAEL	POUND	0.5556	0.3333	0.3294	0.2857	0.2857
JAPAN	YEN	0.00278	0.00278	0.00278	0.00278	0.00278
JORDAN	DINAR	2.8000	2.8000	2.8000	2.8000	2.8000
KOREA, REPUBLIC OF	WON	0.0158	0.0038	0.0037	0.0036	0.0035
KUWAIT	DINAR	2.8000	2.8000	2.8000	2.8000	2.8000
LAO PEOPLE'S						
DEMOCRATIC REPUBLIC	KIP	0.01250	0.00417	0.00417	0.00417	0.00417
LEBANON	POUND	0.31553	0.32554	0.31208	0.31678	0.30728
MACAU	PATACA	0.03478	0.03478	0.03478	0.03478	0.03478
MALAYSIA	RINGGIT	0.32667	0.32667	0.32667	0.32667	0.32667
PENINSULAR MALAYSIA	RINGGIT	0.32667	0.32667	0.32667	0.32667	0.32667
SABAH	RINGGIT	0.32667	0.32667	0.32667	0.32667	0.32667
SARAWAK	RINGGIT	0.32667	0.32667	0.32667	0.32667	0.32667
MALDIVES	RUPEE	0.21000	0.21000	0.20650	0.16800	0.16800
MONGOLIA	TUGRIK		0.2500	0.2500	0.2500	0.2500
NEPAL	RUPEE	0.13344	0.13125	0.12588	0.09877	0.09877
OMAN	RIAL	2.8000	2.8000	2.7667	2.4000	2.4000
PAKISTAN	RUPEE	0.21000	0.21000	0.21000	0.21000	0.21000
PHILIPPINES	PESO	0.49933	0.25773	0.25641	0.25641	0.25641
QATAR	RIYAL			0.21000	0.21000	0.21000
SAUDI ARABIA	RIYAL	0.22222	0.22222	0.22222	0.22222	0.22222
SINGAPORE	DOLLAR	0.32667	0.32667	0.32667	0.32667	0.32667
SRI LANKA	RUPEE	0.21000	0.21000	0.20650	0.16800	0.16800
SYRIAN ARAB REPUBLIC	POUND	0.27933	0.26178	0.26178	0.26178	0.26178
THAILAND	BAHT	0.04738	0.04808	0.04808	0.04808	0.04808
TURKEY	LIRA	0.27513	0.11111	0.11111	0.11111	0.11111
UNITED ARAB EMIRATES	DIRHAM			0.2100	0.2100	0.2100
VIET—NAM,						
(FORMER SOUTH)	PIASTRE	0.02857	0.01667	0.00848	0.00848	0.00848
YEMEN	RIAL				0.35800	0.22533
YEMEN, DEMOCRATIC	DINAR	2.8000	2.8000	2.7667	2.4000	2.4000

Exchange rates C
Taux de change
Tipos de cambio

EXCHANGE RATES IN UNITED STATES DOLLARS
TAUX DE CHANGE EN DOLLARS DES ETATS UNIS
TIPOS DE CAMBIO EN DOLARES DE LOS ESTADOS UNIDOS

1970	1971	1972	1973	1974	1975	1976	1977	1978
0.04907	0.04000	0.04000	0.04000	0.04000	0.04000	0.04000	0.04000	0.04000
2.4000	2.4344	2.5018	2.4522	2.3390	2.2218	1.8062	1.7455	1.9195
0.18004	0.18050	0.19826	0.22531	0.20781	0.23362	0.20956	0.20356	0.22200
0.50000	0.50498	0.47990	0.47054	0.44883	0.42639	0.39216	0.39216	0.39216
0.00794	0.00794	0.00794	0.00794	0.00794	0.00794	0.00794	0.00794	0.00794
0.02584	0.02584	0.02584	0.02584	0.02584	0.02463	0.01806	0.01223	0.00654
0.53027	0.53116	0.55905	0.55736	0.55964	0.56022	0.56022	0.56022	0.56022
4.00	3.89	1.85	1.15	0.85	0.440	0.299	0.212	0.165
0.22222	0.22222	0.22727	0.23236	0.23337	0.23337	0.23311	0.23296	0.23296
0.02222	0.02222	0.02222	0.02222	0.02222	0.02222	0.02222	0.02222	0.02222
2.1000	2.1064	2.2800	2.5046	2.5333	2.5284	2.5278	2.5275	2.5797
	0.12885	0.13190	0.12928	0.12332	0.08948	0.06581	0.06511	0.06666
0.13333	0.13332	0.13190	0.12928	0.12349	0.11976	0.11161	0.11446	0.12212
0.32667	0.32766	0.35467	0.41078	0.41558	0.41778	0.39346	0.40629	...
0.21000	0.20774	0.18336	0.20396	0.20586	0.15507	0.14773	0.14036	0.14578
0.4065	0.4093	0.4405	0.4861	0.5110	0.02632	0.02632	0.02632	0.02705
2.4000	2.4355	2.6071	2.8612	2.7426	2.7162	2.4371	2.4510	2.6797
0.01801	0.01534	0.00632	0.00411	0.00193	...	...	...	...
0.03478	0.03532	0.03702	0.04068	0.03938	0.03922	0.03317	0.02628	0.02283
0.16500	0.16736	0.17784	0.19443	0.19851	0.20252	0.20486	0.21470	...
0.13333	0.13332	0.13190	0.12928	0.12349	0.11976	0.11161	0.11446	0.12212
0.00275	0.00255	0.00241	0.00241	0.00241	0.00241	0.00241	0.00241	0.00231
0.01320	0.01320	0.01320	0.01453	0.01479	0.01479	0.01424	0.01416	0.01419
2.8000	2.8200	3.0400	3.3497	3.3778	3.3862	3.3862	3.3862	3.3862
0.2857	0.2698	0.2381	0.2381	0.2262	0.1573	0.1258	0.0989	0.0575
0.00278	0.00286	0.00325	0.00368	0.00343	0.00337	0.00337	0.00374	0.00480
2.8000	2.8000	2.8000	3.0550	3.1198	3.1305	3.0115	3.0373	3.2620
0.0032	0.0029	0.0025	0.0025	0.0025	0.0021	0.0021	0.0021	0.0021
2.8000	2.8085	3.0400	3.3898	3.4104	3.4483	3.4203	3.4898	3.6362
0.00417	0.00417	0.00229	0.00167	0.00167	...	...	0.00500	...
0.30591	0.30988	0.32789	0.38466	0.42998	0.43339	0.34826	0.32589	0.33841
0.03478	0.03534	0.03684	0.04096	0.03959	0.03900	...	...	...
0.32667	0.32766	0.35467	0.41078	0.41558	0.41775	0.39350	0.40642	0.43221
0.32667	0.32766	0.35467	0.41078	0.41558	0.41775	0.39350	0.40642	0.43221
0.32667	0.32766	0.35467	0.41078	0.41558	0.41775	0.39350	0.40642	0.43221
0.32667	0.32766	0.35467	0.41078	0.41558	0.41775	0.39350	0.40642	0.43221
0.16800	0.16851	0.16791	0.15629	0.15047	0.17134	0.11840	0.11360	...
0.2500	0.2717	0.2717	0.3012	0.3012	0.3012	0.3012	0.3012	0.3333
0.09877	0.09877	0.09877	0.09504	0.09470	0.09102	0.08000	0.08000	0.08278
2.4000	2.4073	2.6057	2.8711	2.8952	2.8981	2.8952	2.8952	2.8952
0.21000	0.21000	0.13044	0.09986	0.10070	0.10069	0.10069	0.10069	0.10069
0.17734	0.15688	0.15001	0.14812	0.14716	0.13761	0.13428	0.13500	0.13547
0.21000	0.21064	0.22800	0.25046	0.25333	0.25441	0.25238	0.25259	0.25795
0.22222	0.22290	0.24127	0.27071	0.28169	0.28430	0.28329	0.28368	0.29426
0.32667	0.32818	0.35602	0.41033	0.41054	0.42250	0.40473	0.41002	0.44007
0.16800	0.16851	0.16791	0.15629	0.15047	0.14251	0.11849	0.11770	0.06408
0.26178	0.26178	0.26178	0.26173	0.26869	0.27027	0.25744	0.25317	0.25317
0.04808	0.04808	0.04808	0.04851	0.04908	0.04907	0.04902	0.04902	0.04918
0.09259	0.06706	0.07067	0.07067	0.07183	0.06931	0.06236	0.05570	0.04158
0.2100	0.2106	0.2280	0.2505	0.2526	0.2524	0.2532	0.2556	0.2583
0.00848	0.00848	0.00290	0.00200	0.00159	...			
0.18182	0.18444	0.21322	0.21678	0.21858	0.21903	0.21918	0.21918	0.21918
2.4000	2.4073	2.6057	2.8624	2.8952	2.8952	2.8952	2.8952	2.8952

C Exchange rates
Taux de change
Tipos de cambio

COUNTRY	NATIONAL CURRENCY	EXCHANGE RATES IN UNITED STATES DOLLARS TAUX DE CHANGE EN DOLLARS DES ETATS-UNIS TIPOS DE CAMBIO EN DOLARES DE LOS ESTADOS UNIDOS				
PAYS	MONNAIE NATIONALE					
PAIS	MONEDA NACIONAL	1960	1965	1967	1968	1969
EUROPE						
ALBANIA	LEK	0.020	0.200	0.200	0.200	0.200
ANDORRA	FRANC FRANCAIS	0.20255	0.20255	0.20255	0.20255	0.19317
ANDORRA	PESETA	0.01667	0.01667	0.01647	0.01429	0.01429
AUSTRIA	SCHILLING	0.03846	0.03846	0.03846	0.03846	0.03846
BELGIUM	FRANC	0.02000	0.02000	0.02000	0.02000	0.02000
BULGARIA	LEV	0.855	0.855	0.855	0.855	0.855
CZECHOSLOVAKIA	KORUNA	0.1389	0.1389	0.1389	0.1389	0.1389
DENMARK	KRONE	0.14478	0.14478	0.14382	0.13333	0.13333
FINLAND	MARKKA	0.31250	0.31250	0.29390	0.23810	0.23810
FRANCE	FRANC	0.20255	0.20255	0.20255	0.20255	0.19317
GERMAN DEMOCRATIC REPUBLIC	DDR MARK	0.238	0.238	0.451	0.451	0.451
GERMANY, FEDERAL REPUBLIC OF	DEUTSCHE MARK	0.23810	0.25000	0.25000	0.25000	0.25387
GIBRALTAR	POUND	2.8000	2.8000	2.7667	2.4000	2.4000
GREECE	DRACHMA	0.03333	0.03333	0.03333	0.03333	0.03333
HUNGARY	FORINT	0.085	0.085	0.085	0.085	0.085
ICELAND	KRONA	0.03216	0.02326	0.02278	0.01651	0.01136
IRELAND	POUND	2.8000	2.8000	2.7667	2.4000	2.4000
ITALY	LIRA	0.00160	0.00160	0.00160	0.00160	0.00160
LIECHTENSTEIN	FRANC SUISSE	0.22868	0.22868	0.22868	0.22868	0.22868
LUXEMBOURG	FRANC	0.02000	0.02000	0.02000	0.02000	0.02000
MALTA	POUND	2.8000	2.8000	2.7667	2.4000	2.4000
MONACO	FRANC FRANCAIS	0.20255	0.20255	0.20255	0.20255	0.19317
NETHERLANDS	GUILDER	0.26316	0.27624	0.27624	0.27624	0.27624
NORWAY	KRONE	0.14000	0.14000	0.14000	0.14000	0.14000
POLAND	ZLOTY	0.250	0.250	0.250	0.250	0.250
PORTUGAL	ESCUDO	0.03478	0.03478	0.03478	0.03478	0.03478
ROMANIA	LEU	0.167	0.167	0.167	0.167	0.167
SAN MARINO	LIRA	0.00160	0.00160	0.00160	0.00160	0.00160
SPAIN	PESETA	0.01667	0.01667	0.01647	0.01429	0.01429
SWEDEN	KRONA	0.19330	0.19330	0.19330	0.19330	0.19330
SWITZERLAND	FRANC	0.22868	0.22868	0.22868	0.22868	0.22868
UNITED KINGDOM	POUND STERLING	2.8000	2.8000	2.7667	2.4000	2.4000
YUGOSLAVIA	DINAR	0.3333	0.2067	0.0800	0.0800	0.0800
OCEANIA						
AMERICAN SAMOA	UNITED STATES DOLLAR	1.00000	1.00000	1.00000	1.00000	1.00000
AUSTRALIA	DOLLAR	1.1200	1.1200	1.1200	1.1200	1.1200
COOK ISLANDS	NEW ZEALAND DOLLAR	1.4000	1.3905	1.3679	1.1200	1.1200
FIJI	DOLLAR	1.2613	1.2613	1.2519	1.1483	1.1483
FRENCH POLYNESIA	FRANC C.F.P.	0.01114	0.01114	0.01114	0.01114	0.01062
GUAM	UNITED STATES DOLLAR	1.00000	1.00000	1.00000	1.00000	1.00000
KIRIBATI	AUSTRALIAN DOLLAR	1.1200	1.1200	1.1200	1.1200	1.1200
NAURU	AUSTRALIAN DOLLAR	1.1200	1.1200	1.1200	1.1200	1.1200
NEW CALEDONIA	FRANC C.F.P.	0.01114	0.01114	0.01114	0.01114	0.01062
NEW HEBRIDES	AUSTRALIAN DOLLAR	1.1200	1.1200	1.1200	1.1200	1.1200
NEW HEBRIDES	FRANC C.F.P.	0.01114	0.01114	0.01114	0.01114	0.01062
NEW ZEALAND	DOLLAR	1.4000	1.3905	1.3679	1.1200	1.1200
NIUE ISLAND	NEW ZEALAND DOLLAR	1.4000	1.3905	1.3679	1.1200	1.1200
NORFOLK ISLAND	AUSTRALIAN DOLLAR	1.1200	1.1200	1.1200	1.1200	1.1200
PACIFIC ISLANDS	UNITED STATES DOLLAR	1.00000	1.00000	1.00000	1.00000	1.00000

Exchange rates C
Taux de change
Tipos de cambio

EXCHANGE RATES IN UNITED STATES DOLLARS
TAUX DE CHANGE EN DOLLARS DES ETATS UNIS
TIPOS DE CAMBIO EN DOLARES DE LOS ESTADOS UNIDOS

1970	1971	1972	1973	1974	1975	1976	1977	1978
0.200	0.204	0.217	0.240	0.242	0.242	0.244	0.244	0.244
0.18004	0.18050	0.19826	0.22531	0.20781	0.23362	0.20956	0.20356	0.22200
0.01429	0.01438	0.01556	0.01718	0.01733	0.01740	0.01497	0.01329	0.01308
0.03846	0.04010	0.04326	0.05145	0.05361	0.05754	0.05579	0.06056	0.06897
0.02000	0.02049	0.02272	0.02575	0.02572	0.02727	0.02592	0.02792	0.03181
0.855	0.855	0.926	1.022	1.031	1.031	1.031	1.031	1.136
0.1389	0.1389	0.1508	0.1661	0.1675	0.1675	0.1675	0.1675	...
0.13333	0.13486	0.14337	0.16592	0.16434	0.17443	0.16549	0.16663	0.18161
0.23810	0.23805	0.24022	0.26165	0.26622	0.27231	0.25878	0.24845	0.24313
0.18004	0.18050	0.19826	0.22531	0.20781	0.23362	0.20956	0.20356	0.22200
0.451	0.454	0.488	0.539	0.543	0.543	0.543	0.529	0.488
0.27322	0.28694	0.31359	0.37748	0.38665	0.40745	0.39746	0.43106	0.49889
2.4000	2.4344	2.5018	2.4522	2.3391	2.2218	1.8062	1.7455	1.9195
0.03333	0.03333	0.03333	0.03377	0.03333	0.03113	0.02735	0.02715	0.02729
0.085	0.088	0.093	0.108	0.109	0.118	0.118	...	...
0.01136	0.01136	0.01133	0.01113	0.01018	0.00657	0.00550	0.00504	0.00374
2.4000	2.4342	2.5018	2.4530	2.3391	2.2215	1.8061	1.7448	1.9190
0.00160	0.00161	0.00172	0.00172	0.00153	0.00153	0.00121	0.00113	0.00118
0.22868	0.24232	0.26186	0.31732	0.33691	0.38780	0.40006	0.41606	0.61728
0.02000	0.02049	0.02272	0.02575	0.02572	0.02727	0.02592	0.02792	0.03181
2.4000	2.4569	2.6095	2.7232	2.5947	2.6202	2.3534	2.3688	2.5974
0.18004	0.18050	0.19826	0.22531	0.20781	0.23362	0.20956	0.20356	0.22200
0.27624	0.28572	0.31159	0.35956	0.37247	0.39635	0.37860	0.40762	0.46308
0.14000	0.14207	0.15180	0.17406	0.18100	0.19185	0.18336	0.18791	0.19096
0.250	0.257	0.272	0.299	0.301	0.301	0.301	0.301	0.333
0.03478	0.03532	0.03702	0.04068	0.03938	0.03922	0.03317	0.02628	0.02283
0.167	0.167	0.181	0.199	0.201	0.201	0.201	0.201	0.220
0.00160	0.00161	0.00172	0.00172	0.00153	0.00153	0.00121	0.00113	0.00118
0.01429	0.01438	0.01556	0.01718	0.01733	0.01740	0.01497	0.01329	0.01308
0.19330	0.19549	0.20999	0.22947	0.22558	0.24146	0.22968	0.22377	0.22151
0.22868	0.24232	0.26186	0.31732	0.33691	0.38780	0.40006	0.41606	0.61728
2.4000	2.4344	2.5018	2.4522	2.3390	2.2218	1.8062	1.7455	1.9195
0.0800	0.0671	0.0588	0.0619	0.0630	0.0576	0.0550	0.0547	0.0536
1.00000	1.00000	1.00000	1.00000	1.00000	1.00000	1.00000	1.00000	1.00000
1.1200	1.1342	1.1923	1.4227	1.4408	1.3102	1.2252	1.1090	1.1447
1.1200	1.1361	1.1950	1.3630	1.4011	1.2146	0.9964	0.9708	1.0378
1.1483	1.1648	1.2128	1.2599	1.2444	1.2149	1.1101	1.0904	1.1812
0.00990	0.00995	0.01091	0.01239	0.01144	0.01285	0.01151	0.01119	...
1.00000	1.00000	1.00000	1.00000	1.00000	1.00000	1.00000	1.00000	1.00000
1.1200	1.1342	1.1980	1.4227	1.4396	1.3102	1.2252	1.1090	1.1447
1.1200	1.1342	1.1980	1.4227	1.4396	1.3102	1.2252	1.1090	1.1447
0.00990	0.00993	0.01091	0.01239	0.01144	0.01285	0.01151	0.01119	...
1.1200	1.1342	1.1923	1.4227	1.4408	1.3102	1.2252	1.1090	1.1447
0.00990	0.00993	0.01091	0.01239	0.01144	0.01285	0.01151	0.01119	...
1.1200	1.1361	1.1950	1.3630	1.4011	1.2146	0.9964	0.9708	1.0378
1.1200	1.1361	1.1950	1.3630	1.4011	1.2146	0.9964	0.9708	1.0378
1.1200	1.1342	1.1923	1.4227	1.4408	1.3102	1.2252	1.1090	1.1447
1.00000	1.00000	1.00000	1.00000	1.00000	1.00000	1.00000	1.00000	1.00000

C Exchange rates
Taux de change
Tipos de cambio

COUNTRY	NATIONAL CURRENCY	EXCHANGE RATES IN UNITED STATES DOLLARS TAUX DE CHANGE EN DOLLARS DES ETATS—UNIS TIPOS DE CAMBIO EN DOLARES DE LOS ESTADOS UNIDOS				
PAYS	MONNAIE NATIONALE					
PAIS	MONEDA NACIONAL	1960	1965	1967	1968	1969
PAPUA NEW GUINEA	KINA	1.1200	1.1200	1.1200	1.1200	1.1200
SAMOA	TALA	1.4000	1.3905	1.3899	1.3868	1.3868
SOLOMON ISLANDS	AUSTRALIAN DOLLAR	1.1200	1.1200	1.1200	1.1200	1.1200
TOKELAU ISLANDS	NEW ZEALAND DOLLAR	1.4000	1.3905	1.3679	1.1200	1.1200
TONGA	DOLLAR	1.1200	1.1200	1.1200	1.1200	1.1200
U.S.S.R.						
U.S.S.R.	ROUBLE	1.111	1.111	1.111	1.111	1.111
BYELORUSSIAN S.S.R.	ROUBLE	1.111	1.111	1.111	1.111	1.111
UKRAINIAN S.S.R.	ROUBLE	1.111	1.111	1.111	1.111	1.111

Exchange rates   C
Taux de change
Tipos de cambio

EXCHANGE RATES IN UNITED STATES DOLLARS
TAUX DE CHANGE EN DOLLARS DES ETATS UNIS
TIPOS DE CAMBIO EN DOLARES DE LOS ESTADOS UNIDOS

1970	1971	1972	1973	1974	1975	1976	1977	1978
1.1200	1.1384	1.1980	1.4227	1.4409	1.3102	1.2620	1.2640	1.4117
1.3868	1.3944	1.4807	1.6349	1.6486	1.5853	1.2547	1.2706	1.3584
1.1200	1.1342	1.1923	1.4227	1.4408	1.3102	1.2252	1.1090	1.1447
1.1200	1.1361	1.1950	1.3630	1.4011	1.2146	0.9964	0.9708	1.0378
1.1200	1.1342	1.1980	1.4227	1.4396	1.3102	1.2219	1.1089	...
1.111	1.111	1.215	1.350	1.322	1.340	1.340	1.340	...
1.111	1.111	1.215	1.350	1.322	1.340	1.340	1.340	...
1.111	1.111	1.215	1.350	1.322	1.340	1.340	1.340	...

D   Selected list of Unesco statistcal publications
     Liste sélective d'ouvrages statistiques publiés par l'Unesco
     Lista selectiva de obras de estadística publicadas por la Unesco

D   Selected list of Unesco statistical publications

Liste sélective d'ouvrages statistiques publiés par l'Unesco

Lista selectiva de obras de estadísticas publicadas por la Unesco

THIS APPENDIX IS IN THREE SECTIONS PRESENTING RESPECTIVELY SELECTIVE LISTS OF STATISTICAL PUBLICATIONS IN ENGLISH, FRENCH AND SPANISH. THUS, THOSE PUBLICATIONS IN THE THREE LANGUAGES ARE SHOWN IN EACH LIST WHILST WORKS AVAILABLE IN ONLY A SPECIFIC LANGUAGE ARE SHOWN IN THE RELEVANT SECTION. THOSE PUBLISHED IN A BILINGUAL, TRILINGUAL OR MULTILINGUAL VERSION ARE INDICATED ACCORDINGLY IN THE APPROPRIATE LISTS. WORKS PUBLISHED IN ARABIC OR RUSSIAN ARE ALSO LISTED, APPROPRIATELY INDICATED.

_ _

CETTE ANNEXE EST PRESENTEE EN TROIS PARTIES (PUBLICATIONS EN ANGLAIS, EN FRANCAIS ET EN ESPAGNOL) OU SONT INDIQUES LES OUVRAGES STATISTIQUES PUBLIES DANS LA LANGUE CORRESPONDANTE. LES PUBLICATIONS PARUES EN ANGLAIS, FRANCAIS ET ESPAGNOL FIGURENT PAR CONSEQUENT DANS LES TROIS PARTIES. CELLES QUI NE SONT PAS PUBLIEES DANS LES TROIS LANGUES, SE TROUVENT SEULEMENT DANS LES PARTIES CONCERNEES. SI UNE PUBLICATION EST EN VERSION BILINGUE, TRILINGUE OU POLYGLOTTE, LE FAIT EST INDIQUE DANS LES LANGUES APPROPRIEES. LES OUVRAGES PARUS EN RUSSE ET EN ARABE SONT EGALEMENT MENTIONNES.

_ _

ESTE ANEXO SE PRESENTA EN TRES PARTES (PUBLICACIONES EN INGLES, EN FRANCES Y EN ESPANOL) EN LAS QUE SE INDICAN LAS OBRAS ESTADISTICAS PUBLICADAS EN EL IDIOMA CORRESPONDIENTE. LAS PUBLICACIONES APARECIDAS EN INGLES, FRANCES Y ESPAÑOL FIGURAN POR CONSIGUIENTE EN LAS TRES PARTES; LAS QUE NO SE PUBLICAN EN LAS TRES LENGUAS SOLO SE ENCUENTRAN EN LAS PARTES QUE LAS ATAÑEN. CUANDO UNA PUBLICACION ES BILINGUE, TRILINGUE O PLURILINGUE, SE DA LA DEBIDA INDICACION EN LAS LENGUAS APROPIADAS. TAMBIEN SE SEÑALAN LAS OBRAS APARECIDAS EN RUSO Y EN ARABE.

Selected list of Unesco statistcal publications D
Liste sélective d'ouvrages statistiques publiés par l'Unesco
Lista selectiva de obras de estadística publicadas por la Unesco

IDENTIFICATION	TITLE	PUBLISHED IN	AVAILABILITY/ PRICE
ISBN 92–3–001800–7	UNESCO STATISTICAL YEARBOOK, 1978–79 TRILINGUAL: ENGLISH/FRENCH/SPANISH – PUBLISHED ANNUALLY FROM 1963 TO 1980	1980	FF 230

STATISTICAL REPORTS AND STUDIES

NO. 1	FILM AND CINEMA STATISTICS		OUT OF PRINT
NO. 2	BOOK PRODUCTION 1937–1954 AND TRANSLATIONS 1950–1954	1957	OUT OF PRINT
NO. 3	STATISTICS ON LIBRARIES	1959	OUT OF PRINT
NO. 4	STATISTICS ON NEWSPAPERS AND OTHER PERIODICALS	1959	OUT OF PRINT
NO. 5	STATISTICS ON SPECIAL EDUCATION	1960	OUT OF PRINT
NO. 6	REQUIREMENTS AND RESOURCES OF SCIENTIFIC AND TECHNICAL PERSONNEL IN TEN ASIAN COUNTRIES	1960	OUT OF PRINT
NO. 7	PRE–SCHOOL EDUCATION	1963	OUT OF PRINT
NO. 8	STATISTICS ON RADIO AND TELEVISION, 1950–1960	1963	OUT OF PRINT
NO. 9	METHODS OF ESTIMATING THE DEMAND FOR SPECIALISTS AND OF PLANNING SPECIALIZED TRAINING WITHIN THE U.S.S.R.	1964	FF 6
NO. 10	ESTIMATING FUTURE SCHOOL ENROLMENT IN DEVELOPING COUNTRIES. A MANUAL OF METHODOLOGY	1966	FF 10
NO. 11	METHODS OF ANALYSING EDUCATIONAL OUTLAY (AVAILABLE IN FRENCH ONLY)	1966	OUT OF PRINT
NO. 12	METHODS OF LONG–TERM PROJECTION OF REQUIREMENTS FOR AND SUPPLY OF QUALIFIED MANPOWER (AVAILABLE IN FRENCH ONLY)	1967	OUT OF PRINT
NO. 13	STATISTICS ON EDUCATION IN DEVELOPING COUNTRIES. AN INTRODUCTION TO THEIR COLLECTION AND PRESENTATION	1968	OUT OF PRINT
NO. 14	INTERNATIONAL DEVELOPMENTS OF EDUCATIONAL EXPENDITURE, 1950–1965 (ALSO PUBLISHED IN FRENCH)	1969	FF 10
NO. 15	THE MEASUREMENT OF SCIENTIFIC AND TECHNOLOGICAL ACTIVITIES. PROPOSALS FOR THE COLLECTION OF STATISTICS ON SCIENCE AND TECHNOLOGY ON AN INTERNATIONALLY UNIFORM BASIS (ALSO PUBLISHED IN FRENCH)	1969	FF 8
NO. 16	MEASUREMENT OF OUTPUT OF RESEARCH AND EXPERI- MENTAL DEVELOPMENT. A REVIEW PAPER (ALSO PUBLISHED IN FRENCH)	1969	FF 6
NO. 17	WORLD SUMMARY OF STATISTICS ON SCIENCE AND TECHNOLOGY. BILINGUAL: ENGLISH/FRENCH	1970	FF 8
NO. 18	STATISTICS OF STUDENTS ABROAD: 1962–1968. WHERE THEY GO. WHERE THEY COME FROM. WHAT THEY STUDY BILINGUAL: ENGLISH/FRENCH	1972	FF 26
NO. 19	HIGHER EDUCATION: INTERNATIONAL TRENDS, 1960–1970 (ALSO PUBLISHED IN FRENCH)	1975	FF 26

D   Selected list of Unesco statistcal publications
Liste sélective d'ouvrages statistiques publiés par l'Unesco
Lista selectiva de obras de estadística publicadas por la Unesco

IDENTIFICATION	TITLE	PUBLISHED IN	AVAILABILITY/ PRICE
NO. 20	STATISTICS ON SCIENCE AND TECHNOLOGY IN LATIN AMERICA. EXPERIENCE WITH UNESCO PILOT PROJECTS, 1972–1974 (ALSO PUBLISHED IN FRENCH AND SPANISH)	1976	FF 10
NO. 21	STATISTICS OF STUDENTS ABROAD, 1969–1973 BILINGUAL: ENGLISH/FRENCH	1976	FF 32
NO. 22	STATISTICS OF EDUCATIONAL ATTAINMENT AND ILLITERACY 1945–1974 TRILINGUAL: ENGLISH/FRENCH/SPANISH	1977	FF 26
NO. 23	STATISTICS ON RADIO AND TELEVISION, 1960–1976	1979	FF 14
NO. 24	ANALYZING AND PROJECTING SCHOOL ENROLMENT IN DEVELOPING COUNTRIES — A MANUAL OF METHODOLOGY (ALSO TO BE PUBLISHED IN FRENCH AND SPANISH) FORESEEN FOR 1980		
	CURRENT SURVEYS AND RESEARCH IN STATISTICS (CSR)		
CSR–S–1	THE MEASUREMENT OF SCIENTIFIC ACTIVITES IN THE SOCIAL SCIENCES AND THE HUMANITIES (ALSO PUBLISHED IN FRENCH AND RUSSIAN)	1971	ON REQUEST
CSR–S–2	THE QUANTITATIVE MEASUREMENT OF SCIENTIFIC AND TECHNOLOGICAL ACTIVITES RELATED TO RESEARCH AND EXPERIMENTAL DEVELOPMENT (ALSO PUBLISHED IN FRENCH AND SPANISH)	1975	ON REQUEST
CSR–S–3	R&D ACTIVITIES IN INTERNATIONAL ORGANIZATIONS (ALSO PUBLISHED IN FRENCH AND SPANISH)	1977	ON REQUEST
CSR–S–4	THE STATISTICAL MEASUREMENT OF SCIENTIFIC AND TECHNOLOGICAL ACTIVITIES RELATED TO RESEARCH AND EXPERIMENTAL DEVELOPMENT: A FEASIBILITY STUDY (ALSO PUBLISHED IN FRENCH AND SPANISH)	1977	ON REQUEST
CSR–S–5	DEVELOPMENT IN HUMAN AND FINANCIAL RESOURCES FOR SCIENCE AND TECHNOLOGY. BASIC TABLES SHOWING THE EARLIEST AND LATEST YEARS FOR WHICH DATA ARE AVAILABLE (ALSO PUBLISHED IN FRENCH AND SPANISH)	1978	ON REQUEST
CSR–S–6	STATISTICS ON RESEARCH AND EXPERIMENTAL DEVELOPMENT IN THE EUROPEAN AND NORTH AMERICAN REGION (IN ENGLISH ONLY)	1979	ON REQUEST
CSR–S–7	ESTIMATION OF HUMAN AND FINANCIAL RESOURCES DEVOTED TO R&D AT THE WORLD AND REGIONAL LEVEL (ALSO PUBLISHED IN FRENCH)	1979	ON REQUEST
CSR–S–8	STATISTICS ON SCIENCE AND TECHNOLOGY — LATEST AVAILABLE DATA TRILINGUAL: ENGLISH/FRENCH/SPANISH	1980	ON REQUEST
CSR–E–1	COSTING EDUCATIONAL WASTAGE: A PILOT SIMU– LATION STUDY. MAY 1970 (ALSO PUBLISHED IN FRENCH)	1971	ON REQUEST
CSR–E–3	FURTHER STUDIES ON THE EVALUATION OF INTERNAL EFFICIENCY OF EDUCATIONAL SYSTEMS: A SYMPOSIUM (ALSO PUBLISHED IN FRENCH)	1973	ON REQUEST
CSR–E–4	A SURVEY OF STATISTICS TEACHING IN DEVELOPING COUNTRIES TRILINGUAL: ENGLISH/FRENCH/SPANISH	1974	ON REQUEST
CSR–E–5	EDUCATIONAL GROWTH AND EDUCATIONAL DISPARITY (ALSO PUBLISHED IN FRENCH)	1974	ON REQUEST

Selected list of Unesco statistcal publications   D
Liste sélective d'ouvrages statistiques publiés par l'Unesco
Lista selectiva de obras de estadística publicadas por la Unesco

IDENTIFICATION	TITLE	PUBLISHED IN	AVAILABILITY/ PRICE
CSR—E—6	THE STATISTICAL DIMENSION OF OUT—OF—SCHOOL YOUTH IN ASIA (ALSO PUBLISHED IN FRENCH)	1974	ON REQUEST
CSR—E—7	FOREIGN STUDENTS IN MEDICAL SCHOOLS	1974	OUT OF PRINT
CSR—E—8	SPECIAL EDUCATION STATISTICS BILINGUAL: ENGLISH/FRENCH	1974	ON REQUEST
CSR—E—9	POPULATION AND SCHOOL ENROLMENT: A STATISTICAL ANALYSIS (ALSO PUBLISHED IN FRENCH)	1975	ON REQUEST
CSR—E—10	PROJECTIONS OF TEACHER REQUIREMENTS IN 1985: A WORLD AND CONTINENTAL STATISTICAL ANALYSIS (ALSO PUBLISHED IN FRENCH)	1975	ON REQUEST
CSR—E—11	WASTAGE IN PRIMARY EDUCATION IN AFRICA: A STATISTICAL STUDY BILINGUAL: ENGLISH/FRENCH	1975	ON REQUEST
CSR—E—12	ISCED HANDBOOK: UNITED KINGDOM (ENGLAND AND WALES) (IN ENGLISH ONLY)	1975	ON REQUEST
CSR—E—14	ISCED HANDBOOK: EGYPT (AND OTHER ARAB STATES) (IN ARABIC ONLY)	1976	ON REQUEST
CSR—E—15	MANUAL FOR THE COLLECTION OF ADULT EDUCATION STATISTICS (ALSO PUBLISHED IN ARABIC, FRENCH, RUSSIAN AND SPANISH)	1975	ON REQUEST
CSR—E—16	THE DIMENSIONS OF SCHOOL ENROLMENT. A STUDY OF ENROLMENT RATIOS IN THE WORLD (ALSO PUBLISHED IN FRENCH)	1975	ON REQUEST
CSR—E—17	STATISTICAL TABLES: AFRICA BILINGUAL: ENGLISH/FRENCH	1975	ON REQUEST
CSR—E—19	METHODS OF PROJECTING SCHOOL ENROLMENT IN DEVELOPING COUNTRIES (ALSO PUBLISHED IN FRENCH)	1976	ON REQUEST
CSR—E—21	TRENDS AND PROJECTIONS OF ENROLMENT BY LEVEL OF EDUCATION AND BY AGE (ALSO PUBLISHED IN FRENCH)	1977	ON REQUEST
CSR—E—23	SURVEY OF TEACHERS' QUALIFICATIONS BILINGUAL: ENGLISH/FRENCH	1977	ON REQUEST
CSR—E—25	ISCED HANDBOOK: DEMOCRATIC REPUBLIC OF THE SUDAN (IN ENGLISH ONLY)	1977	ON REQUEST
CSR—E—28	TOWARDS A METHODOLOGY FOR PROJECTING RATES OF LITERACY AND EDUCATIONAL ATTAINMENT (ALSO PUBLISHED IN FRENCH)	1978	ON REQUEST
CSR—E—29	ESTIMATES AND PROJECTIONS OF ILLITERACY (IN ENGLISH ONLY)	1978	ON REQUEST
CSR—E—30	EDUCATION STATISTICS — LATEST YEAR AVAILABLE TRILIGUAL: ENGLISH/FRENCH/SPANISH	1979	ON REQUEST
CSR—E—31	ISCED HANDBOOK: MAURITIUS (IN ENGLISH ONLY)	1979	ON REQUEST
CSR—E—32	PRE—PRIMARY EDUCATION IN THE WORLD — REGIONAL STUDY, 1960—1975. TRILINGUAL: ENGLISH/FRENCH/ SPANISH	1979	ON REQUEST
CSR—E—33	EDUCATION IN LATIN AMERICA AND THE CARRIBEAN, ENROLMENT AND ENROLMENT RATIOS, 1960—1976. TRILINGUAL: ENGLISH/FRENCH/SPANISH	1979	ON REQUEST

D   Selected list of Unesco statistcal publications
Liste sélective d'ouvrages statistiques publiés par l'Unesco
Lista selectiva de obras de estadistica publicadas por la Unesco

.

IDENTIFICATION	TITLE	PUBLISHED IN	AVAILABILITY/ PRICE
CSR—E—34	GUIDELINES FOR THE COLLECTION OF STATISTICS ON LITERACY PROGRAMMES (PRELIMINARY MANUAL) (ALSO PUBLISHED IN FRENCH AND SPANISH)	1979	ON REQUEST
CSR—E—35	THE ALLOCATION OF RESOURCES TO EDUCATION THROUGHOUT THE WORLD (ALSO PUBLISHED IN FRENCH AND SPANISH)	1980	ON REQUEST
CSR—E—36	COMPARATIVE ANALYSIS OF MALE AND FEMALE SCHOOL ENROLMENT AND ILLITERACY (ALSO PUBLISHED IN FRENCH AND SPANISH)	1980	ON REQUEST
CSR—E—37	WASTAGE IN PRIMARY AND GENERAL SECONDARY EDUCATION: A STATISTICAL STUDY OF TRENDS AND PATTERNS IN REPETITION AND DROPOUT (ALSO PUBLISHED IN FRENCH)	1980	ON REQUEST
CSR—C—1	CULTURAL PAPER: CONSUMPTION, PRODUCTION AND SELF—SUFFICIENCY FOR THE WORLD REGIONS (IN ENGLISH ONLY)	1978	ON REQUEST

ANNOTATED ACCESSIONS LISTS OF STUDIES AND
REPORTS IN THE FIELD OF SCIENCE STATISTICS

NO. 1	ST/R/22, AUGUST 1966	1966	ON REQUEST
NO. 2	COM/MD/1, SEPTEMBER 1967 (ALSO PUBLISHED IN FRENCH)	1967	ON REQUEST
NO. 3	COM/MD/5, OCTOBER 1968 (ALSO PUBLISHED IN FRENCH)	1968	ON REQUEST
NO. 4	COM/MD/9, SEPTEMBER 1969 (ALSO PUBLISHED IN FRENCH AND SPANISH)	1969	ON REQUEST
NO. 5	COM/MD/17, SEPTEMBER 1970 (ALSO PUBLISHED IN FRENCH AND SPANISH)	1970	ON REQUEST
NO. 6	COM/WS/189, AUGUST 1971 (ALSO PUBLISHED IN FRENCH)	1971	ON REQUEST
NO. 7	COM/WS/287, SEPTEMBER 1972 (ALSO PUBLISHED IN FRENCH)	1972	ON REQUEST
NO. 8	COM/WS/345, SEPTEMBER 1973 (ALSO PUBLISHED IN FRENCH AND SPANISH)	1973	ON REQUEST
NO. 9	COM. 74/WS/17, SEPTEMBER 1974 (ALSO PUBLISHED IN FRENCH AND SPANISH)	1974	ON REQUEST
NO. 10	COM. 75/WS/19, OCTOBER 1975 (ALSO PUBLISHED IN FRENCH AND SPANISH)	1975	ON REQUEST
NO. 11	ST. 76/WS/4, 1976 (ALSO PUBLISHED IN FRENCH AND SPANISH)	1976	ON REQUEST
NO. 12	ST.77/WS/11, SEPTEMBER 1977 (ALSO PUBLISHED IN FRENCH AND SPANISH)	1977	ON REQUEST
NO. 13	ST.78/WS/16, SEPTEMBER 1978 (ALSO PUBLISHED IN FRENCH AND SPANISH)	1978	ON REQUEST
NO. 14	ST.79/WS/11, SEPTEMBER 1979 (ALSO PUBLISHED IN FRENCH AND SPANISH)	1979	ON REQUEST

IDENTIFICATION	TITLE	PUBLISHED IN	AVAILABILITY/ PRICE

RECOMMENDATIONS FOR INTERNATIONAL STANDARDIZATIONS

	RECOMMENDATION CONCERNING THE INTERNATIONAL STANDARDIZATION OF STATISTICS RELATING TO BOOK PRODUCTION AND PERIODICALS ADOPTED BY THE GENERAL CONFERENCE AT ITS THIRTEENTH SESSION, PARIS, 19 NOVEMBER 1964 MULTILINGUAL: ENGLISH/FRENCH/SPANISH/RUSSIAN	1964	ON REQUEST
	RECOMMENDATION CONCERNING THE INTERNATIONAL STANDARDIZATION OF LIBRARY STATISTICS ADOPTED BY THE GENERAL CONFERENCE AT ITS SIXTEENTH SESSION, PARIS, 13 NOVEMBER 1970 MULTILINGUAL: ENGLISH/FRENCH/SPANISH/RUSSIAN	1970	ON REQUEST
	RECOMMENDATION CONCERNING THE INTERNATIONAL STANDARDIZATION OF STATISTICS ON RADIO AND TELEVISION ADOPTED BY THE GENERAL CONFERENCE AT ITS NINETEENTH SESSION, NAIROBI, 22 NOVEMBER 1976 MULTILINGUAL: ARABIC/ENGLISH/FRENCH/ SPANISH/RUSSIAN	1976	ON REQUEST
	REVISED RECOMMENDATION CONCERNING THE INTERNATIONAL STANDARDIZATION OF EDUCATIONAL STATISTICS, ADOPTED BY THE GENERAL CONFERENCE AT ITS TWENTIETH SESSION, PARIS, 27 NOVEMBER 1978 MULTILINGUAL: ARABIC/ ENGLISH/FRENCH/SPANISH/RUSSIAN	1978	ON REQUEST
	RECOMMENDATION CONCERNING THE INTERNATIONAL STANDARDIZATION OF STATISTICS ON SCIENCE AND TECHNOLOGY, ADOPTED BY THE GENERAL CONFERENCE OF UNESCO AT ITS TWENTIETH SESSION, PARIS, 27 NOVEMBER 1978 MULTILINGUAL: ARABIC/ ENGLISH/FRENCH/SPANISH/RUSSIAN	1978	ON REQUEST
	MANUAL OF EDUCATIONAL STATISTICS, SECOND PRINTING	1961	OUT OF PRINT
ST/WS/4	GUIDE TO THE COLLECTION OF STATISTICS ON SCIENCE AND TECHNOLOGY (ALSO PUBLISHED IN FRENCH AND SPANISH)	1977	ON REQUEST
ST.77/WS/10	PRELIMINARY STUDY ON THE SCOPE AND COVERAGE OF A SYSTEM OF CULTURAL STATISTICS (IN ENGLISH ONLY)	1977	ON REQUEST
ST.77/WS/15	DRAFT CLASSIFICATION OF R&D ACTIVITIES BY OBJECTIVES (ALSO PUBLISHED IN FRENCH, SPANISH, RUSSIAN AND ARABIC)	1978	ON REQUEST
ST.80/WS/8	MANUAL FOR STATISTICS ON SCIENTIFIC AND TECHNOLOGICAL ACTIVITIES (PROVISIONAL) (ALSO PUBLISHED IN FRENCH, SPANISH, RUSSIAN AND ARABIC)	1980	ON REQUEST
ST.78/WS/211	CONSUMPTION OF CULTURAL PAPER IN THE WORLD REGIONS: PAST AND FUTURE TRENDS (IN ENGLISH ONLY)	1978	ON REQUEST
	COMPARATIVE STATISTICAL DATA ON EDUCATION IN THE ARAB STATES, 1961–1967/68 (ALSO PUBLISHED IN ARABIC)	1969	OUT OF PRINT
	DEVELOPMENT AND TRENDS IN THE EXPANSION OF EDUCATION IN LATIN AMERICA AND THE CARIBBEAN: STATISTICAL DATA TRILINGUAL: ENGLISH/FRENCH/SPANISH	1971	ON REQUEST

D   Selected list of Unesco statistcal publications
Liste sélective d'ouvrages statistiques publiés par l'Unesco
Lista selectiva de obras de estadística publicadas por la Unesco

IDENTIFICATION	TITLE	PUBLISHED IN	AVAILABILITY/ PRICE
	THE STATISTICAL MEASUREMENT OF EDUCATIONAL WASTAGE, INTERNATIONAL CONFERENCE ON EDUCATION	1970	OUT OF PRINT
ED/BIE/CONFIN-TED 36/REF 2	DEVELOPMENT OF SCHOOL ENROLMENT, WORLD AND REGIONAL STATISTICAL TRENDS AND PROJECTIONS, 1960–2000, INTERNATIONAL CONFERENCE ON EDUCATION, AUGUST/SEPTEMBER 1977 (ALSO PUBLISHED IN ARABIC, FRENCH, RUSSIAN AND SPANISH)	1977	ON REQUEST
ED/BIE/CONFIN-TED 37/ REF 1	A SUMMARY STATISTICAL REVIEW OF EDUCATION IN THE WORLD, 1960–1976. INTERNATIONAL CONFERENCE ON EDUCATION, 37TH SESSION, JULY 1979 (IN ENGLISH ONLY)	1979	ON REQUEST
ED/BIE/CONFIN-TED 37/ REF 2	WASTAGE IN PRIMARY EDUCATION: A STATISTICAL STUDY OF TRENDS AND PATTERNS IN REPETITION AND DROUPOUT. INTERNATIONAL CONFERENCE ON EDUCATION, 37TH SESSION, JULY 1979 (IN ENGLISH ONLY)	1979	ON REQUEST
UNESCO:CES/ AC.23/20	A SYSTEM OF STATISTICS ON EDUCATION (ALSO PUBLISHED IN FRENCH AND RUSSIAN)	1975	ON REQUEST
UNESCO:CES/ AC.23/21	CURRENT SOCIAL INDICATORS IN THE FIELD OF EDUCATION (ALSO PUBLISHED IN FRENCH AND RUSSIAN	1976	ON REQUEST
ED–76/MINED– AF REF. 1	EDUCATIONAL DEVELOPMENT IN AFRICA: TRENDS AND PROJECTIONS UNTIL 1985 (ALSO PUBLISHED IN FRENCH)	1976	ON REQUEST
ED–76/MINED– AF REF. 6	EDUCATION IN AFRICA SINCE 1960: A STATISTICAL REVIEW (ALSO PUBLISHED IN FRENCH)	1976	ON REQUEST
ED–77/MINED– ARAB REF. 3	RECENT QUANTITATIVE TRENDS AND PROJECTIONS CONCERNING ENROLMENT IN EDUCATION IN THE ARAB COUNTRIES (ALSO PUBLISHED IN ARABIC AND FRENCH)	1977	ON REQUEST
ED–78/MINED– ASO REF. 2	DEVELOPMENT OF EDUCATION IN ASIA AND OCEANIA STATISTICAL TRENDS AND PROJECTIONS 1965–1985 (ALSO PUBLISHED IN FRENCH)	1978	ON REQUEST
ED–80/MINED– EUROPE/REF. 2	DEVELOPMENT OF EDUCATION IN EUROPE: A STATISTICAL REVIEW (ALSO PUBLISHED IN FRENCH, SPANISH AND RUSSIAN)	1980	ON REQUEST
UNESCO/MINES– POL II/6	STATISTICS ON RESEARCH AND EXPERIMENTAL DEVELOPMENT IN THE EUROPEAN AND NORTH AMERICAN REGION (ALSO PUBLISHED IN FRENCH)	1978	ON REQUEST
COM/ST/ISCED	INTERNATIONAL STANDARD CLASSIFICATION OF EDUCATION (ISCED) (ALSO PUBLISHED IN FRENCH, RUSSIAN AND SPANISH)	1976	ON REQUEST
ED/BIE/CONFIN-TED 35/REF. 8	ABRIDGED VERSION OF ISCED (ALSO PUBLISHED IN ARABIC, FRENCH, RUSSIAN AND SPANISH)	1975	ON REQUEST
ED.75/CONFIN-TED 601/REF. 1	NATIONAL DIRECTORY OF ADULT EDUCATION PRO-GRAMMES IN THE LIBYAN ARAB JAMAHIRIYA, 1973 (ALSO PUBLISHED IN ARABIC BY THE DEPARTMENT OF PLANNING AND FOLLOW-UP, MINISTRY OF EDUCATION, TRIPOLI, LIBYAN ARAB JAMAHIRIYA)	1974	ON REQUEST

Selected list of Unesco statistcal publications   **D**
Liste sélective d'ouvrages statistiques publiés par l'Unesco
Lista selectiva de obras de estadística publicadas por la Unesco

IDENTIFICATION	TITLE	PUBLISHED IN	AVAILABILITY/ PRICE
COM/74/ISCED REF. 2	STATISTICS ON FORMAL PROGRAMMES OF ADULT EDUCATION IN THE LIBYAN ARAB JAMAHIRIYA, 1973, CLASSIFIED BY ISCED (ALSO PUBLISHED IN ARABIC BY THE DEPARTMENT OF PLANNING AND FOLLOW—UP, MINISTRY OF EDUCATION, TRIPOLI, LIBYAN ARAB JAMAHIRIYA)	1974	ON REQUEST

WORLD SURVEY OF EDUCATION
───────────────────────

VOL. I : HANDBOOK OF EDUCATIONAL ORGANIZA— TION AND STATISTICS, 3RD IMP.		1965	OUT OF PRINT
VOL. II : PRIMARY EDUCATION		1959	OUT OF PRINT
VOL. III : SECONDARY EDUCATION (AVAILABLE IN FRENCH ONLY)		1962	OUT OF PRINT
VOL. IV : HIGHER EDUCATION		1966	OUT OF PRINT
VOL. V : EDUCATIONAL POLICY, LEGISLATION AND ADMINISTRATION (ALSO PUBLISHED IN FRENCH)		1971	FF 180 (PAPER) FF 240 (CLOTH)

WORLD COMMUNICATIONS. PRESS, FILM, RADIO AND TELEVISION (CO—EDITION: GOWER PRESS/UNIPUB/ UNESCO)	1975	OUT OF PRINT
STUDY ABROAD. INTERNATIONAL SCHOLARSHIPS AND COURSES (PUBLISHED BIENNIALLY) TRILINGUAL: ENGLISH/FRENCH/SPANISH (VOL. XXII, 1979—1980, 1980—1981)	1978	FF 36
INTERNATIONAL YEARBOOK OF EDUCATION PUBLISHED JOINTLY BY UNESCO AND THE INTER— NATIONAL BUREAU OF EDUCATION LATEST EDITION: VOL XXXI (ALSO PUBLISHED IN FRENCH)	1969	OUT OF PRINT
A STATISTICAL STUDY OF WASTAGE AT SCHOOL — STUDY PREPARED FOR THE INTERNATIONAL BUREAU OF EDUCATION BY THE UNESCO OFFICE OF STATISTICS (UNESCO: IBE, STUDIES AND SURVEYS IN COMPARATIVE EDUCATION) (ALSO PUBLISHED IN FRENCH)	1972	FF 18 (PAPER)
EDUCATIONAL STATISTICS: NATIONAL AND INTER— NATIONAL SOURCES AND SERVICES, EDUCATIONAL DOCUMENTATION AND INFORMATION, BULLETIN OF THE INTERNATIONAL BUREAU OF EDUCATION NO. 202 (ALSO PUBLISHED IN FRENCH)	1977	ON REQUEST
INDEX TRANSLATIONUM. INTERNATIONAL BIBLIOGRAPHY OF TRANSLATIONS TRILINGUAL INTRODUCTION: ENGLISH/FRENCH/SPANISH (VOL. 28 — 1975)	1979	FF 250
AN ASIAN MODEL OF EDUCATIONAL DEVELOPMENT FOR 1965—1980 (ALSO PUBLISHED IN FRENCH)	1966	OUT OF PRINT

- -

D   Selected list of Unesco statistcal publications
Liste sélective d'ouvrages statistiques publiés par l'Unesco
Lista selectiva de obras de estadística publicadas por la Unesco

IDENTIFICATION	TITRE	PUBLIES EN	DISPONIBILITE/ PRIX
ISBN 92-3-001800-7	ANNUAIRE STATISTIQUE DE L'UNESCO, 1978-79 TRILINGUE: ANGLAIS/FRANCAIS/ESPAGNOL — PUBLIE CHAQUE ANNEE DE 1963 A 1980	1980	FF 230

RAPPORTS ET ETUDES STATISTIQUES

NO. 1	FILM AND CINEMA STATISTICS (RESUME EN FRANCAIS)		OUVRAGE EPUISE
NO. 2	PRODUCTION DE LIVRES 1937-1954 ET TRADUCTIONS 1950-1954	1957	OUVRAGE EPUISE
NO. 3	STATISTIQUES SUR LES BIBLIOTHEQUES	1959	OUVRAGE EPUISE
NO. 4	STATISTIQUES SUR LES JOURNAUX ET AUTRES PERIODIQUES	1959	OUVRAGE EPUISE
NO. 5	RAPPORT STATISTIQUE SUR L'ENSEIGNEMENT SPECIAL	1960	OUVRAGE EPUISE
NO. 6	BESOINS ET RESSOURCES DE DIX PAYS D'ASIE EN PERSONNEL SCIENTIFIQUE ET TECHNIQUE	1960	OUVRAGE EPUISE
NO. 7	L'EDUCATION PRESCOLAIRE	1963	OUVRAGE EPUISE
NO. 8	STATISTIQUES DE LA RADIODIFFUSION ET DE LA TELEVISION, 1950-1960	1963	OUVRAGE EPUISE
NO. 9	METHODES D'EVALUATION DES BESOINS EN SPECIA- LISTES ET DE PLANIFICATION DE LA FORMATION SPECIALISEE EN U.R.S.S.	1964	FF 6
NO. 10	ESTIMATION DES EFFECTIFS SCOLAIRES FUTURS DANS LES PAYS EN VOIE DE DEVELOPPEMENT. MANUEL DE METHODOLOGIE (DISPONIBLE EN ANGLAIS SEULEMENT)	1967	OUVRAGE EPUISE
NO. 11	METHODES D'ANALYSE DES DEPENSES D'ENSEIGNEMENT	1967	FF 6
NO. 12	METHODES DE PROJECTION A LONG TERME DE L'OFFRE ET DE LA DEMANDE DE MAIN-D'OEUVRE QUALIFIEE	1967	FF 6
NO. 13	STATISTIQUES DE L'EDUCATION DANS LES PAYS EN VOIE DE DEVELOPPEMENT. COMMENT LES RASSEMBLER ET LES PRESENTER	1968	OUVRAGE EPUISE
NO. 14	L'EVOLUTION INTERNATIONALE DES DEPENSES D'EDU- CATION ENTRE 1950 ET 1965 (PUBLIE AUSSI EN ANGLAIS)	1969	FF 10
NO. 15	LA MESURE DES ACTIVITES SCIENTIFIQUES ET TECH- NIQUES. PROPOSITIONS VISANT A LA NORMALISATION DES STATISTIQUES RELATIVES A LA SCIENCE ET A LA TECHNOLOGIE (PUBLIE AUSSI EN ANGLAIS)	1969	FF 8
NO. 16	MESURE DE L'OUTPUT DE LA RECHERCHE ET DU DEVE- LOPPEMENT EXPERIMENTAL. RAPPORT-INVENTAIRE (PUBLIE AUSSI EN ANGLAIS)	1970	FF 6
NO. 17	STATISTIQUES DE LA SCIENCE ET DE LA TECHNOLO- GIE; APERCU MONDIAL. BILINGUE: ANGLAIS/ FRANCAIS	1970	FF 8
NO. 18	STATISTIQUES DES ETUDIANTS A L'ETRANGER: 1962- 1968. OU VONT-ILS? D'OU VIENNENT-ILS? QU'ETU- DIENT-ILS? BILINGUE: ANGLAIS/FRANCAIS	1972	FF 26
NO. 19	ENSEIGNEMENT SUPERIEUR: TENDANCES INTERNATIO- NALES, 1960-1970 (PUBLIE AUSSI EN ANGLAIS)	1975	FF 26

Selected list of Unesco statistcal publications   D
Liste sélective d'ouvrages statistiques publiés par l'Unesco
Lista selectiva de obras de estadística publicadas por la Unesco

IDENTIFICATION	TITRE	PUBLIES EN	DISPONIBILITE/ PRIX
NO. 20	LES STATISTIQUES DE LA SCIENCE ET DE LA TECHNO— GIE EN AMERIQUE LATINE. L'EXPERIENCE DES PROJETS—PILOTES DE L'UNESCO, 1972—1974 (PUBLIE AUSSI EN ANGLAIS ET EN ESPAGNOL)	1976	FF 10
NO. 21	STATISTIQUES DES ETUDIANTS A L'ETRANGER, 1969— 1973 BILINGUE: ANGLAIS/FRANCAIS	1976	FF 32
NO. 22	STATISTIQUES SUR LE NIVEAU D'INSTRUCTION ET L'ANALPHABETISME 1945—1974 TRILINGUE: ANGLAIS/FRANCAIS/ESPAGNOL	1977	FF 26
NO. 24	ANALYSER ET PROJETER LES EFFECTIFS SCOLAIRES DANS LES PAYS EN DEVELOPPEMENT — UN MANUEL DE METHODOLOGIE (EGALEMENT PUBLIE EN ANGLAIS ET EN ESPAGNOL) PUBLICATION PREVUE POUR 1980		

ENQUETES ET RECHERCHES STATISTIQUES

TRAVAUX EN COURS (CSR)

CSR—S—1	LA MESURE DES ACTIVITES SCIENTIFIQUES DANS LES SCIENCES SOCIALES ET HUMAINES (PUBLIE AUSSI EN ANGLAIS ET EN RUSSE)	1971	SUR DEMANDE
CSR—S—2	LA MESURE QUANTITATIVE DES ACTIVITES SCIENTIFIQUES ET TECHNIQUES CONNEXES A LA RECHERCHE ET AU DEVELOPPEMENT EXPERIMENTAL (PUBLIE AUSSI EN ANGLAIS ET EN ESPAGNOL)	1975	SUR DEMANDE
CSR—S—3	ACTIVITES DE LA R—D DANS LES ORGANISATIONS INTERNATIONALES (PUBLIE AUSSI EN ANGLAIS ET EN ESPAGNOL)	1976	SUR DEMANDE
CSR—S—4	LA MESURE STATISTIQUE DES ACTIVITES SCIENTIFIQUES ET TECHNIQUES CONNEXES A LA RECHERCHE ET AU DEVELOPPEMENT EXPERIMENTAL: ETUDE DE FAISABILITE (PUBLIE AUSSI EN ANGLAIS ET EN ESPAGNOL)	1977	SUR DEMANDE
CSR—S—5	LE DEVELOPPEMENT DES RESSOURCES FINANCIERES ET HUMAINES POUR LA SCIENCE ET LA TECHNOLOGIE. TABLEAUX STATISTIQUES PRESENTANT DES DONNEES DE BASE POUR LES PREMIERES ET DERNIERES ANNEES DISPONIBLES (PUBLIE AUSSI EN ANGLAIS ET EN ESPAGNOL)	1978	SUR DEMANDE
CSR—S—7	ESTIMATION DES RESSOURCES HUMAINES ET FINAN— CIERES CONSACREES A LA R—D AU NIVEAU MONDIAL ET REGIONAL (PUBLIE AUSSI EN ANGLAIS)	1979	SUR DEMANDE
CSR—S—8	STATISTIQUES RELATIVES A LA SCIENCE ET A LA TECHNOLOGIE — DERNIERES DONNEES DISPONIBLES TRILINGUE: ANGLAIS/FRANCAIS/ESPAGNOL	1980	SUR DEMANDE
CSR—E—1	COMMENT EVALUER LE COUT DE LA DEPERDITION SCOLAIRE; ETUDE PILOTE PAR SIMULATION, MAI 1970 (PUBLIE AUSSI EN ANGLAIS)	1971	SUR DEMANDE
CSR—E—3	NOUVELLES ETUDES CONCERNANT L'EVALUATION DE L'EFFICACITE INTERNE DES SYSTEMES D'ENSEIGNE— MENT: COLLOQUE (PUBLIE AUSSI EN ANGLAIS)	1973	SUR DEMANDE
CSR—E—4	UNE ENQUETE SUR L'ENSEIGNEMENT DE LA STATIS— TIQUE DANS LES PAYS EN VOIE DE DEVELOPPEMENT TRILINGUE: ANGLAIS/FRANCAIS/ESPAGNOL	1974	SUR DEMANDE
CSR—E—5	CROISSANCE ET DISPARITES DANS LE DOMAINE DE L'EDUCATION (PUBLIE AUSSI EN ANGLAIS)	1974	SUR DEMANDE

D   Selected list of Unesco statistcal publications
    Liste sélective d'ouvrages statistiques publiés par l'Unesco
    Lista selectiva de obras de estadística publicadas por la Unesco

IDENTIFICATION	TITRE	PUBLIES EN	DISPONIBILITE/ PRIX
CSR-E-6	L'IMPORTANCE STATISTIQUE DE LA JEUNESSE NON SCOLARISEE D'ASIE (PUBLIE AUSSI EN ANGLAIS)	1974	SUR DEMANDE
CSR-E-7	LES ETUDIANTS ETRANGERS DANS LES ECOLES DE MEDECINE	1974	OUVRAGE EPUISE
CSR-E-8	STATISTIQUES DE L'EDUCATION SPECIALE BILINGUE: ANGLAIS/FRANCAIS	1974	SUR DEMANDE
CSR-E-9	POPULATION ET SCOLARISATION: UNE ANALYSE STATISTIQUE (PUBLIE AUSSI EN ANGLAIS)	1975	SUR DEMANDE
CSR-E-10	PROJECTIONS DES BESOINS EN PERSONNEL ENSEI-GNANT EN 1985: ANALYSE STATISTIQUE MONDIALE ET PAR CONTINENT (PUBLIE AUSSI EN ANGLAIS)	1975	SUR DEMANDE
CSR-E-11	LES DEPERDITIONS SCOLAIRES DANS L'ENSEIGNEMENT PRIMAIRE EN AFRIQUE. ETUDE STATISTIQUE. BILINGUE: ANGLAIS/FRANCAIS	1975	SUR DEMANDE
CSR-E-13	GUIDE DE LA CLASSIFICATION INTERNATIONALE TYPE DE L'EDUCATION: FRANCE (EN FRANCAIS SEULEMENT)	1976	SUR DEMANDE
CSR-E-14	GUIDE DE LA CLASSIFICATION INTERNATIONALE TYPE DE L'EDUCATION: EGYPTE (ET AUTRES ETATS ARABES) (EN ARABE SEULEMENT)	1976	SUR DEMANDE
CSR-E-15	MANUEL POUR LA COLLECTE DES STATISTIQUES DE L'EDUCATION DES ADULTES (PUBLIE AUSSI EN ANGLAIS, ARABE, ESPAGNOL ET RUSSE)	1975	SUR DEMANDE
CSR-E-16	LES DIMENSIONS DE LA SCOLARITE. ETUDE DES TAUX DE SCOLARISATION DANS LE MONDE. (PUBLIE AUSSI EN ANGLAIS)	1975	SUR DEMANDE
CSR-E-17	TABLEAUX STATISTIQUES: AFRIQUE BILINGUE: ANGLAIS/FRANCAIS	1975	SUR DEMANDE
CSR-E-19	METHODES DE PROJECTION DES EFFECTIFS SCOLAIRES DANS LES PAYS EN VOIE DE DEVELOPPEMENT (PUBLIE AUSSI EN ANGLAIS)	1976	SUR DEMANDE
CSR-E-21	TENDANCES ET PROJECTIONS DES EFFECTIFS SCOLAIRES PAR NIVEAU D'INSTRUCTION ET PAR AGE (PUBLIE AUSSI EN ANGLAIS)	1977	SUR DEMANDE
CSR-E-23	ENQUETE SUR LA QUALIFICATION DES ENSEIGNANTS BILINGUE: ANGLAIS/FRANCAIS	1977	SUR DEMANDE
CSR-E-27	LA VALEUR DES INVESTISSEMENTS DANS L'ENSEI-GNEMENT SUPERIEUR: ENQUETE DANS SIX PAYS AFRICAINS (EN FRANCAIS SEULEMENT)	1978	SUR DEMANDE
CSR-E-28	VERS UNE METHODE DE PROJECTION DES TAUX D'ALPHABETISME ET DES NIVEAUX D'INSTRUCTION (PUBLIE AUSSI EN ANGLAIS)	1978	SUR DEMANDE
CSR-E-30	STATISTIQUES SCOLAIRES — DERNIERE ANNEE DISPONIBLE. TRILINGUE: ANGLAIS/FRANCAIS/ ESPAGNOL	1979	SUR DEMANDE
CSR-E-32	L'ENSEIGNEMENT PRE-PRIMAIRE DANS LE MONDE — ETUDE REGIONALE, 1960-1975. TRILINGUE: ANGLAIS/FRANCAIS/ESPAGNOL	1979	SUR DEMANDE
CSR-E-33	L'ENSEIGNEMENT EN AMERIQUE LATINE ET AUX CARAIBES, EFFECTIFS SCOLAIRES ET TAUX D'INSCRIPTION, 1960-1976. TRILINGUE: ANGLAIS/FRANCAIS/ESPAGNOL	1979	SUR DEMANDE

IDENTIFICATION	TITRE	PUBLIES EN	DISPONIBILITE/ PRIX
CSR—E—34	GUIDE POUR LA COLLECTE DE STATISTIQUES SUR LES PROGRAMMES D'ALPHABETISATION (MANUEL PROVISOIRE) (PUBLIE AUSSI EN ANGLAIS ET ESPAGNOL)	1979	SUR DEMANDE
CSR—E—35	L'ALLOCATION DES RESSOURCES A L'EDUCATION DANS LE MONDE (PUBLIE AUSSI EN ANGLAIS ET ESPAGNOL)	1979	SUR DEMANDE
CSR—E—36	ANALYSE COMPARATIVE DE LA SCOLARISATION ET DE L'ANALPHABETISME FEMININS ET MASCULINS (PUBLIE AUSSI EN ANGLAIS ET ESPAGNOL)	1980	SUR DEMANDE
CSR—E—37	LA DEPERDITION DANS LES ENSEIGNEMENTS DU 1ER DEGRE ET DU 2ND DEGRE GENERAL: UNE ANALYSE STATISTIQUE DES TENDANCES ET CARACTERISTIQUES DU REDOUBLEMENT ET DE L'ABANDON (PUBLIE AUSSI EN ANGLAIS)	1980	SUR DEMANDE

LISTES ANNOTEES DES ACQUISITIONS NOUVELLES

ETUDES ET RAPPORTS CONCERNANT LES STATISTIQUES

RELATIVES AUX SCIENCES

NO. 2	COM/MD/1, SEPTEMBRE 1967 (PUBLIE AUSSI EN ANGLAIS)	1967	SUR DEMANDE
NO. 3	COM/MD/5, OCTOBRE 1968 (PUBLIE AUSSI EN ANGLAIS)	1968	SUR DEMANDE
NO. 4	COM/MD/9, SEPTEMBRE 1969 (PUBLIE AUSSI EN ANGLAIS ET EN ESPAGNOL)	1969	SUR DEMANDE
NO. 5	COM/MD/17, SEPTEMBRE 1970 (PUBLIE AUSSI EN ANGLAIS ET EN ESPAGNOL)	1970	SUR DEMANDE
NO. 6	COM/WS/189, AOUT 1971 (PUBLIE AUSSI EN ANGLAIS)	1971	SUR DEMANDE
NO. 7	COM/WS/287, SEPTEMBRE 1972 (PUBLIE AUSSI EN ANGLAIS)	1972	SUR DEMANDE
NO. 8	COM/WS/345, SEPTEMBRE 1973 (PUBLIE AUSSI EN ANGLAIS ET EN ESPAGNOL)	1973	SUR DEMANDE
NO. 9	COM.74/WS/17, SEPTEMBRE 1974 (PUBLIE AUSSI EN ANGLAIS ET EN ESPAGNOL)	1974	SUR DEMANDE
NO. 10	COM.75/WS/19, OCTOBRE 1975 (PUBLIE AUSSI EN ANGLAIS ET EN ESPAGNOL)	1975	SUR DEMANDE
NO. 11	ST.76/WS/4, 1976 (PUBLIE AUSSI EN ANGLAIS ET EN ESPAGNOL)	1976	SUR DEMANDE
NO. 12	ST.77/WS/11, OCTOBRE 1977 (PUBLIE AUSSI EN ANGLAIS ET EN ESPAGNOL)	1977	SUR DEMANDE
NO. 13	ST.78/WS/16, SEPTEMBRE 1978 (PUBLIE AUSSI EN ANGLAIS ET EN ESPAGNOL)	1978	SUR DEMANDE
NO. 14	ST.79/WS/11, SEPTEMBRE 1979 (PUBLIE AUSSI EN ANGLAIS ET EN ESPAGNOL)	1979	SUR DEMANDE

D   Selected list of Unesco statistcal publications
    Liste sélective d'ouvrages statistiques publiés par l'Unesco
    Lista selectiva de obras de estadística publicadas por la Unesco

IDENTIFICATION	TITRE	PUBLIES EN	DISPONIBILITE/ PRIX

RECOMMANDATIONS POUR LES NORMALISATIONS

INTERNATIONALES

IDENTIFICATION	TITRE	PUBLIES EN	DISPONIBILITE/ PRIX
	RECOMMANDATION CONCERNANT LA NORMALISATION INTERNATIONALE DES STATISTIQUES DE L'EDITION DE LIVRES ET DE PERIODIQUES ADOPTEE PAR LA CONFERENCE GENERALE A SA TREIZIEME SESSION, PARIS, 19 NOVEMBRE 1964 POLYGLOTTE: ANGLAIS/FRANCAIS/ESPAGNOL/RUSSE	1964	SUR DEMANDE
	RECOMMANDATION CONCERNANT LA NORMALISATION INTERNATIONALE DES STATISTIQUES RELATIVES AUX BIBLIOTHEQUES ADOPTEE PAR LA CONFERENCE GENE- RALE A SA SEIZIEME SESSION, PARIS, LE 13 NOVEMBRE 1970 POLYGLOTTE: ANGLAIS/FRANCAIS/ESPAGNOL/RUSSE	1970	SUR DEMANDE
	RECOMMANDATION CONCERNANT LA NORMALISATION INTERNATIONALE DES STATISTIQUES RELATIVES A LA RADIO ET A LA TELEVISION, ADOPTEE PAR LA CONFERENCE GENERALE A SA DIX—NEUVIEME SESSION, NAIROBI, 22 NOVEMBRE 1976 POLYGLOTTE: ANGLAIS/ARABE/FRANCAIS/ESPAGNOL/ RUSSE	1976	SUR DEMANDE
	RECOMMANDATION REVISEE CONCERNANT LA NORMALISA- TION INTERNATIONALE DES STATISTIQUES DE L'EDU- CATION, ADOPTEE PAR LA CONFERENCE GENERALE A SA VINGTIEME SESSION, PARIS, 27 NOVEMBRE 1978 POLYGLOTTE: ANGLAIS/ARABE/FRANCAIS/ESPAGNOL/ RUSSE	1978	SUR DEMANDE
	RECOMMANDATION CONCERNANT LA NORMALISATION INTERNATIONALE DES STATISTIQUES RELATIVES A LA SCIENCE ET A LA TECHNOLOGIE, ADOPTEE PAR LA CONFERENCE GENERALE A SA VINGTIEME SESSION, PARIS, 27 NOVEMBRE 1978 POLYGLOTTE: ANGLAIS/ARABE/ESPAGNOL/FRANCAIS/ RUSSE	1978	SUR DEMANDE
	MANUEL DES STATISTIQUES DE L'EDUCATION	1961	OUVRAGE EPUISE
ST/WS/4	GUIDE POUR LA COLLECTE DES DONNEES STATISTIQUES RELATIVES A LA SCIENCE ET LA TECHNOLOGIE (PUBLIE AUSSI EN ANGLAIS ET EN ESPAGNOL)	1977	SUR DEMANDE
ST.77/WS/15	PROJET DE CLASSIFICATION DES ACTIVITES DE R—D PAR OBJECTIFS (PUBLIE AUSSI EN ANGLAIS, ARABE, ESPAGNOL ET RUSSE)	1978	SUR DEMANDE
ST.80/WS/8	MANUEL POUR LES STATISTIQUES RELATIVES AUX ACTIVITES SCIENTIFIQUES ET TECHNIQUES (PROVISOIRE). (PUBLIE AUSSI EN ANGLAIS, ARABE, ESPAGNOL ET RUSSE)	1980	SUR DEMANDE
	STATISTIQUES DE L'EDUCATION DANS LES ETATS ARABES. ANALYSE COMPARATIVE: 1960/61 — 1967/68 (PUBLIE AUSSI EN ARABE)	1969	SUR DEMANDE
	EVOLUTION ET TENDANCES DU DEVELOPPEMENT DE L'EDUCATION EN AMERIQUE LATINE ET DANS LA REGION DES CARAIBES: DONNEES STATISTIQUES TRILINGUE: ANGLAIS/FRANCAIS/ESPAGNOL	1971	SUR DEMANDE
	MESURE STATISTIQUE DE LA DEPERDITION SCOLAIRE CONFERENCE INTERNATIONALE DE L'EDUCATION, JUILLET 1970	1970	OUVRAGE EPUISE

Selected list of Unesco statistcal publications **D**
Liste sélective d'ouvrages statistiques publiés par l'Unesco
Lista selectiva de obras de estadística publicadas por la Unesco

IDENTIFICATION	TITRE	PUBLIES EN	DISPONIBILITE/ PRIX
ED/BIE/CONFINTED 36/REF. 2	EVOLUTION DES EFFECTIFS SCOLAIRES: TENDANCES ET PROJECTIONS STATISTIQUES MONDIALES ET REGIONALES, 1960–2000. CONFERENCE INTERNATIONALE DE L'EDUCATION, AOUT–SEPTEMBRE 1977 (PUBLIE AUSSI EN ANGLAIS, ARABE, ESPAGNOL ET RUSSE)	1977	SUR DEMANDE
	PROJECTION DES NIVEAUX D'EDUCATION JUSQU'EN 1985: METHODOLOGIE, EXEMPLES (EN FRANCAIS SEULEMENT)	1976	SUR DEMANDE
UNESCO:CES/AC. 23/20	SYSTEME DE STATISTIQUES DE L'EDUCATION (PUBLIE AUSSI EN ANGLAIS ET RUSSE)	1975	SUR DEMANDE
UNESCO:CES/AC. 23/21	INDICATEURS SOCIAUX D'USAGE COURANT DANS LE DOMAINE DE L'EDUCATION (PUBLIE AUSSI EN ANGLAIS ET RUSSE)	1976	SUR DEMANDE
ED–76/MINEDAF REF. 1	LA CROISSANCE DES EFFECTIFS SCOLARISES EN AFRIQUE: TENDANCES ET PROJECTIONS JUSQU'EN 1985 (PUBLIE AUSSI EN ANGLAIS)	1976	SUR DEMANDE
ED–76/MINEDAF REF. 6	L'EDUCATION EN AFRIQUE DEPUIS 1960: ETUDE STATISTIQUE (PUBLIE AUSSI EN ANGLAIS)	1976	SUR DEMANDE
ED–77/MINEDARAB REF. 3	TENDANCES QUANTITATIVES RECENTES ET PROJECTIONS DE LA SCOLARISATION DANS LES PAYS ARABES (PUBLIE AUSSI EN ANGLAIS ET ARABE)	1977	SUR DEMANDE
ED–78/MINEDASO REF. 2	DEVELOPPEMENT DE L'EDUCATION EN ASIE ET EN OCEANIE, TENDANCES STATISTIQUES ET PROJECTIONS POUR 1965–1985 (PUBLIE AUSSI EN ANGLAIS)	1978	SUR DEMANDE
ED–80/MINEDEUROPE/REF. 2	DEVELOPPEMENT DE L'EDUCATION EN EUROPE: ANALYSE STATISTIQUE (PUBLIE AUSSI EN ANGLAIS, ESPAGNOL ET RUSSE)	1980	SUR DEMANDE
UNESCO/MINESPOL II/6	STATISTIQUES SUR LA RECHERCHE ET LE DEVELOPPEMENT EXPERIMENTAL DANS LA REGION D'EUROPE ET D'AMERIQUE DU NORD (PUBLIE AUSSI EN ANGLAIS)	1978	OUVRAGE EPUISE
COM/ST/ISCED	CLASSIFICATION INTERNATIONALE TYPE DE L'EDUCATION (CITE) (PUBLIE AUSSI EN ANGLAIS, ESPAGNOL ET RUSSE)	1976	SUR DEMANDE
ED/BIE/CONFINTED 35/ REF.8	VERSION ABREGEE DE LA CITE (PUBLIE AUSSI EN ANGLAIS,ARABE, ESPAGNOL, ET RUSSE)	1975	SUR DEMANDE
	L'EDUCATION DANS LE MONDE		
	VOL. I : ORGANISATION ET STATISTIQUES	1955	OUVRAGE EPUISE
	VOL. II : L'ENSEIGNEMENT DU PREMIER DEGRE. EN FRANCE SEULEMENT, COEDITION UNESCO/BOURRELIER	1960	OUVRAGE EPUISE
	VOL. III : L'ENSEIGNEMENT DU SECOND DEGRE	1963	FF 150 (RELIE)
	VOL. IV : L'ENSEIGNEMENT SUPERIEUR	1967	OUVRAGE EPUISE
	VOL. V : POLITIQUE, LEGISLATION ET ADMINISTRATION DE L'EDUCATION (PUBLIE AUSSI EN ANGLAIS)	1972	FF 180 (BROCHE)
	L'INFORMATION A TRAVERS LE MONDE – PRESSE, FILM, RADIO, TELEVISION (4EME EDITION)	1966	OUVRAGE EPUISE

D   Selected list of Unesco statistcal publications
Liste sélective d'ouvrages statistiques publiés par l'Unesco
Lista selectiva de obras de estadística publicadas por la Unesco

IDENTIFICATION	TITRE	PUBLIES EN	DISPONIBILITE/ PRIX
	ETUDES A L'ETRANGER. BOURSES ET COURS INTERNATIONAUX. PARAIT TOUS LES DEUX ANS. TRILINGUE: ANGLAIS/FRANCAIS/ESPAGNOL VOL. XXII, 1979–1980 / 1980 – 1981	1978	FF 36
	ANNUAIRE INTERNATIONAL DE L'EDUCATION CONJOINTEMENT AVEC LE BUREAU INTERNATIONAL DE L'EDUCATION. DERNIERE EDITION : VOL XXXI (PUBLIE AUSSI EN ANGLAIS)	1969	FF 26
	ETUDE STATISTIQUE SUR LES DEPERDITIONS SCOLAIRES (ETUDE PREPAREE POUR LE BUREAU INTERNATIONAL DE L'EDUCATION PAR L'OFFICE DES STATISTIQUES DE L'UNESCO) UNESCO:BIE, ETUDES ET ENQUETES D'EDUCATION COMPARATIVE (PUBLIE AUSSI EN ANGLAIS)	1972	FF 18 (BROCHE)
	STATISTIQUES RELATIVES A L'EDUCATION: SOURCES ET SERVICES NATIONAUX ET INTERNATIONAUX. DOCUMENTATION ET INFORMATION PEDAGOGIQUES, BULLETIN DU BUREAU INTERNATIONAL D'EDUCATION NO. 202 (PUBLIE AUSSI EN ANGLAIS)	1977	SUR DEMANDE
	INDEX TRANSLATIONUM REPERTOIRE INTERNATIONAL DES TRADUCTIONS INTRODUCTION TRILINGUE: ANGLAIS/FRANCAIS/ ESPAGNOL VOL. 28 (1975)	1979	FF 250 (RELIE)
	MODELE DE DEVELOPPEMENT DE L'EDUCATION PERSPECTIVES POUR L'ASIE, 1965–1980 (PUBLIE AUSSI EN ANGLAIS)	1967	FF 7

Selected list of Unesco statistcal publications   D
Liste sélective d'ouvrages statistiques publiés par l'Unesco
Lista selectiva de obras de estadística publicadas por la Unesco

IDENTIFICACION	TITULO	PUBLICADO EN	DISPONIBILIDAD/ PRECIO
ISBN 92–3 001800–7	ANUARIO ESTADISTICO DE LA UNESCO 1978–79 TRILINGUE: INGLES/FRANCES/ESPANOL PUBLICADO ANUALMENTE DE 1963 A 1980 (FOLLETO CON LA TRADUCCION DE LOS TEXTOS, TITULOS, ENCABEZAMIENTOS, ETC.) DISPONIBLE EN ESPAÑOL PARA LAS EDICIONES 1973 Y 1974	1980 1975/76	FF 230 A PETICION

INFORMES Y ESTUDIOS ESTADISTICOS
_____

NO. 20	LAS ESTADISTICAS DE LA CIENCIA Y LA TECNOLOGIA EN AMERICA LATINA. LA EXPERIENCIA DE LOS PROYECTOS PILOTO DE LA UNESCO 1972–1974 (PUBLICADO IGUALMENTE EN INGLES Y EN FRANCES)	1976	AGOTADA
NO. 22	ESTADISTICAS SOBRE EL NIVEL DE INSTRUCCION Y EL ANALFABETISMO 1945–1974 TRILINGUE: INGLES/FRANCES/ESPANOL	1977	FF 26
NO. 24	ANALISIS Y PROYECCION DE LA MATRICULA ESCOLAR EN LOS PAISES EN DESARROLLO – MANUAL METODO– LOGICO (PUBLICADO IGUALMENTE EN INGLES Y EN FRANCES) PUBLICACION PREVISTA PARA 1980.		

ENCUESTAS E INVESTIGACIONES ESTADISTICAS:
_____

TRABAJOS EN CURSO (CSR):
_____

CSR–S–2	MEDICION CUANTITATIVA DE LAS ACTIVIDADES CIENTIFICAS Y TECNICAS CONEXAS DE LA INVESTI– GACION Y EL DESARROLLO EXPERIMENTAL (PUBLICADO IGUALMENTE EN INGLES Y EN FRANCES)	1975	A PETICION
CSR–S–3	ACTIVIDADES DE I Y D EN LAS ORGANIZACIONES INTERNACIONALES (PUBLICADO IGUALMENTE EN INGLES Y FRANCES)	1976	A PETICION
CSR–S–4	MEDICION ESTADISTICA DE LAS ACTIVIDADES CIENTIFICAS Y TECNICAS CONEXAS DE LA INVESTI– GACION Y EL DESARROLLO EXPERIMENTAL. ESTUDIO DE VIABILIDAD. (PUBLICADO IGUALMENTE EN INGLES Y EN FRANCES)	1977	A PETICION
CSR–S–5	DESARROLLO DE LOS RECURSOS HUMANOS Y FINAN– CIEROS DE CIENCIA Y TECNOLOGIA. CUADROS ESTADISTICOS BASICOS CON INDICACION DEL PRI– MERO Y DEL ULTIMO AÑO PARA LOS QUE EXISTEN ESTADISTICAS (PUBLICADO IGUALMENTE EN INGLES Y EN FRANCES)	1978	A PETICION
CSR–S–8	ESTADISTICAS RELATIVAS A LA CIENCIA Y A LA TECNOLOGIA – ULTIMOS DATOS DISPONIBLES TRILINGUE: INGLES/FRANCES/ESPANOL	1980	A PETICION
CSR–E–2	LAS ESTADISTICAS DE LA EDUCACION EN LOS PAISES EN VIAS DE DESARROLLO; COMO REUNIRLAS Y PRESEN– TARLAS (EN ESPAÑOL SOLAMENTE)	1972	A PETICION
CSR–E–4	ENCUESTA SOBRE LA ENSEÑANZA DE LA ESTADISTICA EN LOS PAISES EN VIAS DE DESARROLLO TRILINGUE: INGLES/FRANCES/ESPANOL	1974	A PETICION
CSR–E–14	GUIA DE LA CLASIFICACION INTERNACIONAL NORMALI– ZADA DE LA EDUCACION: EGIPTO (Y OTROS ESTADOS ARABES) EN ARABE SOLAMENTE	1976	A PETICION

D   Selected list of Unesco statistcal publications
Liste sélective d'ouvrages statistiques publiés par l'Unesco
Lista selectiva de obras de estadística publicadas por la Unesco

IDENTIFICACION	TITULO	PUBLICADO EN	DISPONIBILIDAD/ PRECIO
CSR—E—15	MANUAL PARA EL ACOPIO DE ESTADISTICAS SOBRE LA EDUCACION DE ADULTOS (PUBLICADO IGUALMENTE EN ARABE, FRANCES, INGLES Y RUSO)	1975	A PETICION
CSR—E—24	GUIA DE LA CLASIFICACION INTERNACIONAL NORMALI- ZADA DE LA EDUCACION: PERU (EN ESPAÑOL SOLAMENTE)	1977	A PETICION
CSR—E—30	ESTADISTICAS DE EDUCACION — ULTIMO AÑO DISPONIBLE TRILINGUE: INGLES/FRANCES/ESPANOL	1979	A PETICION
CSR—E—32	LA EDUCACION PRE—PRIMARIA EN EL MUNDO — ESTUDIO REGIONAL, 1960—1975. TRILINGUE: INGLES/FRANCES/ESPANOL	1979	A PETICION
CSR—E—33	LA ENSEÑANZA EN AMERICA LATINA Y EL CARIBE — MATRICULA Y TASAS DE ESCOLARIZACION, 1960— 1976. TRILINGUE: INGLES/FRANCES/ESPANOL	1979	A PETICION
CSR—E—34	GUIA PARA EL ACOPIO DE ESTADISTICAS SOBRE PROGRAMAS DE ALFABETIZACION (MANUAL PROVI- SIONAL) (PUBLICADO IGUALMENTE EN INGLES Y EN FRANCES)	1980	A PETICION
CSR—E—35	LA ASIGNACION DE RECURSOS PARA LA EDUCACION EN EL MUNDO (PUBLICADO IGUALMENTE EN INGLES Y EN FRANCES)	1980	A PETICION
CSR—E—36	ANALISIS COMPARADO DE LA ESCOLARIZACION Y DEL ANALFABETISMO FEMENINOS Y MASCULINOS (PUBLICADO IGUALMENTE EN INGLES Y EN FRANCES)	1980	A PETICION

LISTAS ANOTADAS DE LAS NUEVAS ADQUISICIONES

ESTUDIOS E INFORMES SOBRE LAS ESTADISTICAS

RELATIVAS A LAS CIENCIAS

NO. 4	COM/MD/9, SEPTIEMBRE 1969 (PUBLICADA IGUALMENTE EN INGLES Y EN FRANCES)	1969	A PETICION
NO. 5	COM/MD/17, SEPTIEMBRE 1970 (PUBLICADA IGUALMENTE EN INGLES Y EN FRANCES)	1970	A PETICION
NO. 8	COM/WS/345, SEPTIEMBRE 1973 (PUBLICADA IGUALMENTE EN INGLES Y EN FRANCES)	1973	A PETICION
NO. 9	COM.74/WS/17, SEPTIEMBRE 1974 (PUBLICADA IGUALMENTE EN INGLES Y EN FRANCES)	1974	A PETICION
NO. 10	COM.75/WS/19, OCTUBRE 1975 (PUBLICADA IGUALMENTE EN INGLES Y EN FRANCES)	1975	A PETICION
NO. 11	ST.76/WS/4, 1976 (PUBLICADA IGUALMENTE EN INGLES Y EN FRANCES)	1976	A PETICION
NO. 12	ST.77/WS/11, OCTUBRE 1977 (PUBLICADA IGUALMENTE EN INGLES Y EN FRANCES)	1977	A PETICION
NO. 13	ST.78/WS/16, SEPTIEMBRE 1978 (PUBLICADA IGUALMENTE EN INGLES Y EN FRANCES)	1978	A PETICION
NO. 14	ST.79/WS/11, SEPTIEMBRE 1979 (PUBLICADA IGUALMENTE EN INGLES Y EN FRANCES)	1979	A PETICION

Selected list of Unesco statistcal publications D
Liste sélective d'ouvrages statistiques publiés par l'Unesco
Lista selectiva de obras de estadística publicadas por la Unesco

IDENTIFICACION	TITULO	PUBLICADO EN	DISPONIBILIDAD/ PRECIO
	RECOMENDACIONES PARA LAS NORMALIZACIONES		
	INTERNACIONALES		
	RECOMENDACION SOBRE LA NORMALIZACION INTERNA-CIONAL DE LAS ESTADISTICAS RELATIVAS A LA EDICION DE LIBROS Y PUBLICACIONES PERIODICAS, APROBADA POR LA CONFERENCIA GENERAL EN SU DECIMOTERCERA REUNION, PARIS, 19 DE NOVIEMBRE DE 1964. PLURILINGUE: INGLES/FRANCES/ESPANOL/RUSO	1964	A PETICION
	RECOMENDACION SOBRE LA NORMALIZACION INTERNA-CIONAL DE LAS ESTADISTICAS RELATIVAS A LAS BIBLIOTECAS, APROBADA POR LA CONFERENCIA GENERAL EN SU DECIMOSEXTA REUNION, PARIS, 13 DE NOVIEMBRE DE 1970. PLURILINGUE: INGLES/FRANCES/ESPANOL/RUSO	1970	A PETICION
	RECOMENDACION SOBRE LA NORMALIZACION INTERNA-CIONAL DE LAS ESTADISTICAS RELATIVAS A LA RADIO Y LA TELEVISION, APROBADA POR LA CONFERENCIA GENERAL EN SU DECIMONOVENA REUNION, NAIROBI, 22 DE NOVIEMBRE DE 1976. PLURILINGUE: INGLES/FRANCES/ESPANOL/RUSO/ARABE	1976	A PETICION
	RECOMENDACION REVISADA SOBRE LA NORMALIZACION INTERNACIONAL DE LAS ESTADISTICAS RELATIVAS A LA EDUCACION, APROBADA POR LA CONFERENCIA GENERAL EN SU VIGESIMA REUNION, PARIS, 27 DE NOVIEMBRE DE 1978. PLURILINGUE: ARABE/INGLES/FRANCES/ESPANOL/RUSO	1978	A PETICION
	RECOMENDACION SOBRE LA NORMALIZACION INTER-NACIONAL DE LAS ESTADISTICAS RELATIVAS A LA CIENCIA Y LA TECNOLOGIA APROBADA POR LA CONFERENCIA GENERAL EN SU VIGESIMA REUNION, PARIS, 27 DE NOVIEMBRE DE 1978. PLURILINGUE: ARABE/INGLES/ESPANOL/FRANCES/RUSO	1978	A PETICION
	MANUAL UNESCO DE ESTADISTICAS DE LA EDUCACION	1965	AGOTADA
ST/WS/4	GUIA PARA LA COMPILACION DE ESTADISTICAS RE-LATIVAS A LA CIENCIA Y LA TECNOLOGIA (PUBLICADA IGUALMENTE EN INGLES Y EN FRANCES)	1977	A PETICION
ST.77/WS/15	PROYECTO DE CLASIFICACION POR OBJETIVOS DE LAS ACTIVIDADES DE I Y D (PUBLICADO IGUALMENTE EN INGLES, FRANCES, RUSO Y ARABE)	1978	A PETICION
ST.80/WS/8	MANUAL PARA LAS ESTADISTICAS RELATIVAS A LAS ACTIVIDADES CIENTIFICAS Y TECNOLOGICAS (PROVISIONAL) (PUBLICADO IGUALMENTE EN ARABE, FRANCES, INGLES Y RUSO)	1980	A PETICION
	EVOLUCION Y TENDENCIAS DEL CRECIMIENTO DE LA EDUCACION EN AMERICA LATINA Y EL CARIBE. DATOS ESTADISTICOS. TRILINGUE: INGLES/FRANCES/ESPANOL	1971	A PETICION
ED/BIE/CONFIN-TED 36/REF. 2	EVOLUCION DE LA MATRICULA ESCOLAR: TENDENCIAS Y PROYECCIONES ESTADISTICAS, REGIONALES Y MUNDIALES 1960–2000. CONFERENCIA INTERNACIONAL DE EDUCACION, AGOSTO–SEPTIEMBRE 1977 (PUBLICADO IGUALMENTE EN ARABE, FRANCES, INGLES Y RUSO)	1977	A PETICION

D   Selected list of Unesco statistcal publications
Liste sélective d'ouvrages statistiques publiés par l'Unesco
Lista selectiva de obras de estadística publicadas por la Unesco

IDENTIFICACION	TITULO	PUBLICADO EN	DISPONIBILIDAD/ PRECIO
COM/ST/ISCED	CLASIFICACION INTERNACIONAL NORMALIZADA DE LA EDUCACION (CINE) (PUBLICADA IGUALMENTE EN FRANCES, INGLES Y RUSO)	1976	A PETICION
ED/BIE/CONFIN- TED 35/REF. 8	EDICION ABREVIADA DE LA "CINE" (PUBLICADA IGUALMENTE EN ARABE, FRANCES, INGLES Y RUSO)	1975	A PETICION
ED—79/MINED— LAC REF. 2	EVOLUCION CUANTITATIVA Y PROYECCIONES DE MATRICULA DE LOS SISTEMAS EDUCATIVOS DE AMERICA LATINA Y EL CARIBE — ANALISIS ESTADISTICO (EN ESPAÑOL SOLAMENTE)	1979	A PETICION
ED—80/MINED— EUROPE/ REF. 2	DESARROLLO DE LA EDUCACION EN EUROPA: UNA REVISION ESTADISTICA (PUBLICADO IGUALMENTE EN INGLES, FRANCES Y RUSO)	1980	A PETICION
	ESTUDIOS EN EL EXTRANJERO, BECAS Y CURSOS INTERNACIONALES SE PUBLICA CADA DOS AÑOS TRILINGUE: INGLES/FRANCES/ESPANOL (VOL. XXII, 1979—1980, 1980—1981)	1978	FF 36

E Tables omitted

Tableaux supprimés

Cuadros suprimidos

THE LAST EDITION IN WHICH THE TABLES APPEARED IS SHOWN IN PARENTHESES FOR EACH TABLE.

LA DERNIERE EDITION DANS LAQUELLE LES TABLEAUX ONT ETE PUBLIES EST INDIQUEE DANS CHAQUE CAS ENTRE PARENTHESES.

LA ULTIMA EDICION EN LA QUE LOS CUADROS FUERON PUBLICADOS SE INDICA EN CADA CASO ENTRE PARENTESIS.

LITERACY

ESTIMATED ADULT POPULATION AND LITERACY BY CONTINENTS, MAJOR AREAS AND GROUPS OF COUNTRIES (1972 EDITION)

LITERACY COURSES (1972 EDITION)

SUMMARY TABLES FOR ALL LEVELS OF EDUCATION

ENROLMENT RATIOS BY AGE–GROUPS AND SEX (1978–79 EDITION)

EDUCATION AT THE FIRST LEVEL

SCHOOLS ACCORDING TO THE NUMBER OF GRADES PROVIDED (1972 EDITION)

SPECIAL EDUCATION

SPECIAL EDUCATION: TEACHERS AND PUPILS (1974 EDITION)

EDUCATION AT THE THIRD LEVEL

PERCENTAGE DISTRIBUTION OF STUDENTS BY BROAD FIELDS OF STUDY (1969 EDITION)

PERCENTAGE DISTRIBUTION OF STUDENTS GRADUATING BY BROAD FIELDS OF STUDY (1969 EDITION)

FOREIGN STUDENTS BY FIELDS OF STUDY (1972 EDITION)

EDUCATIONAL EXPENDITURE

PUBLIC CURRENT EXPENDITURE PER PUPIL (FIRST LEVEL) IN UNITED STATES DOLLARS AND INDEX NUMBERS OF EXPENDITURE PER PUPIL, BY LEVEL OF EDUCATION (1976 EDITION)

PUBLIC CAPITAL EXPENDITURE ON EDUCATION: DISTRIBUTION BY LEVEL OF EDUCATION (1978–79 EDITION)

STATISTICS ON SCIENCE AND TECHNOLOGY

GENERAL INDICATORS FOR CURRENT RESOURCES AND FUTURE SUPPLY OF SCIENTIFIC AND TECHNICAL MANPOWER FOR RESEARCH AND EXPERIMENTAL DEVELOPMENT (1975 EDITION)

NUMBER OF ORGANIZATIONS IN THE PRODUCTIVE AND GENERAL SERVICE SECTORS BY SIZE ACCORDING TO NUMBER OF SCIENTISTS AND ENGINEERS ENGAGED IN RESEARCH AND EXPERIMENTAL DEVELOPMENT (1978–79 EDITION)

CULTURE

PUBLIC EXPENDITURE ON CULTURE (1971 EDITION)

MUSEUMS AND RELATED INSTITUTIONS

NUMBER OF MUSEUMS (BY OWNERSHIP), VISITORS AND PERSONNEL (1978–79 EDITION)

NUMBER OF MUSEUMS (BY SUBJECT OF COLLECTION), VISITORS AND PERSONNEL (1978–79 EDITION)

THEATRE AND OTHER DRAMATIC ARTS

NUMBER OF PERFORMANCES, ANNUAL ATTENDANCE, VISITS FROM AND TO ABROAD (1978–79 EDITION)

NUMBER OF THEATRES, PROFESSIONAL COMPANIES AND AMATEUR TROUPES (1978–79 EDITION)

RADIO BROADCASTING

RADIO BROADCASTING: PROGRAMMES BY TYPE (1976 EDITION)

TELEVISION

TELEVISION BROADCASTING: PROGRAMMES BY TYPE (1976 EDITION)

EDUCACION ESPECIAL: PERSONAL DOCENTE Y
ALUMNOS (EDICION 1974)

ENSEÑANZA DE TERCER GRADO

DISTRIBUCION DE LOS ESTUDIANTES (EN POR-
CENTAJE) POR GRUPOS DE RAMAS DE ESTUDIO
(EDICION 1969)

DISTRIBUCION EN PORCENTAJE DE LOS ESTUDIANTES
QUE OBTUVIERON UN DIPLOMA, POR GRUPOS DE RAMAS
DE ESTUDIO (EDICION 1969)

ESTUDIANTES EXTRANJEROS POR RAMAS DE ESTUDIO
(EDICION 1972)

GASTOS DE LA EDUCACION

GASTOS PUBLICOS ORDINARIOS POR ALUMNO (PRIMER
GRADO) EN DOLARES DE LOS ESTADOS UNIDOS E
INDICES DE LOS GASTOS POR ALUMNO, POR GRADOS DE
ENSEÑANZA (EDICION 1976)

GASTOS PUBLICOS DE CAPITAL DESTINADOS A LA
EDUCACION: DISTRIBUCION POR GRADOS DE ENSEÑANZA
(EDICION 1978-79)

ESTADISTICAS RELATIVAS A LA CIENCIA Y LA
TECNOLOGIA

INDICADORES DE LOS EFECTIVOS ACTUALES Y DE LAS
DISPONIBILIDADES FUTURAS EN PERSONAL CIENTIFICO
Y TECNICO PARA LA INVESTIGACION Y EL DESARROLLO
EXPERIMENTAL (EDICION 1975)

NUMERO DE ORGANIZACIONES EN LOS SECTORES PRO-
DUCTIVO Y DE SERVICIO GENERAL, CLASIFICADAS DE
ACUERDO CON EL NUMERO DE CIENTIFICOS E INGENIEROS
EMPLEADOS EN TRABAJOS DE INVESTIGACION Y DE
DESARROLLO EXPERIMENTAL (EDICION 1978-79)

CULTURA

GASTOS PUBLICOS DESTINADOS A LA CULTURA
(EDICION 1971)

MUSEOS E INSTITUCIONES SIMILARES

NUMERO DE MUSEOS (SEGUN SU PROPIEDAD),
VISITANTES Y PERSONAL (EDICION 1978-79)

NUMERO DE MUSEOS (SEGUN LA NATURALEZA DE SUS
COLECCIONES), VISITANTES Y PERSONAL
(EDICION 1978-79)

TEATRO Y ESPECTACULO

NUMERO DE REPRESENTACIONES, FRECUENTACION
ANUAL, VISITAS DEL Y AL EXTRANJERO
(EDICION 1978-79)

NUMERO DE TEATROS, COMPANIAS DE PROFESIONALES
Y GRUPOS DE AFICIONADOS (EDICION 1978-79)

RADIODIFUSION SONORA

RADIODIFUSION: PROGRAMAS POR TIPO (EDICION 1976)

TELEVISION

TELEVISION: PROGRAMAS POR TIPO (EDICION 1976)